THE OXFORD COMPAN
TO
POPULAR MUSIC

Gammond, Peter (*b* Northwich, Cheshire, 30 Sept. 1925). British author and critic. After service in Europe and the Far East 1942–7, he studied at Wadham College, Oxford, 1947–50. Failing to write a West End musical, he became literary editor (popular) with the Decca Record Company in 1951 in the pioneering days of the LP. He left in order to freelance in 1960 and was appointed editor of *Gramophone Record Review* in 1964, remaining music editor until 1980 after its amalgamation with *Hi-Fi News*.

Peter Gammond is author or editor of a number of books in the field of popular music, including: *The Decca Book of Jazz* (ed.) (London, 1958); *Duke Ellington: his Life and Music* (ed.) (London, 1958; repr. New York, 1977); *A Guide to Popular Music* (with Peter Clayton; London, 1960); *Jazz on Record* (with Charles Fox, Alun Morgan, and Alexis Korner; London, 1960; repr. New York, 1978); *Know About Jazz* (with Peter Clayton; London, 1963); *14 Miles on a Clear Night* [Jazz] (with Peter Clayton; London, 1966; repr. New York, 1978); *Your Own, Your Very Own* [music-hall] (Shepperton, 1971); *Scott Joplin and the Ragtime Era* (London, 1975); *Music Hall Songbook* (ed.) (Newton Abbot, 1975); *The Music Goes Round and Round* (edited with Raymond Horricks; London, 1980); *Music on Record: Brass Bands* (edited with Horricks; Cambridge, 1980); *The Good Old Days Songbook* (ed.) (London, 1980); *Offenbach: his Life and Times* (Tunbridge Wells, 1980; repr. London, 1986); *Music on Record: Big Bands* (edited with Horricks; Cambridge, 1981); *The Guinness Jazz A–Z* (with Peter Clayton; London, 1986); *Duke Ellington* (London, 1987); *Bluff Your Way in Jazz* (with Clayton; London, 1987); *Bluff Your Way in Music* (London, 1966; repr. 1985); and *Bluff Your Way in Opera* (1989). He is also the author of various books on classical composers, music, and recordings, and was a contributor to *The New Oxford Companion to Music* (1983).

THE OXFORD COMPANION TO POPULAR MUSIC

Peter Gammond

Oxford New York
OXFORD UNIVERSITY PRESS
1993

Oxford University Press, Walton Street, Oxford OX2 6DP
Oxford New York Toronto
Delhi Bombay Calcutta Madras Karachi
Kuala Lumpur Singapore Hong Kong Tokyo
Nairobi Dar es Salaam Cape Town
Melbourne Auckland Madrid
and associated companies in
Berlin Ibadan

Oxford is a trade mark of Oxford University Press

First published 1991
First issued (with corrections) as an Oxford University Press paperback 1993

British Library Cataloguing in Publication Data
Data available

Library of Congress Cataloging in Publication Data
The Oxford companion to popular music / Peter Gammond.
Includes bibliographical references and index.
1. Popular music—Dictionaries. 2. Popular music—Bio—bibliography. I. Title.
ML102.P66G35 1991 781.64'03—dc20 90-14209
ISBN 0-19-280004-3

Printed in Great Britain
on acid-free paper by
Bookcraft Ltd.,
Midsomer Norton, Avon

INTRODUCTION

WHILE this present volume follows the precept of the compiler of the first *Oxford Companion* in wishing to 'provide a useful companion to ordinary everyday readers' it also attempts to provide a substantial reference book that will be of value to the student and the professional user. A limited reference work of the nature of these well-established *Companions* must necessarily be harshly selective, particularly in such a diverse and crowded field of interest as popular music. It is inevitable that omissions will be criticized, as will the personal choice of entries, but every effort has been made to take a balanced view, to include every name and topic of obvious importance, to include a few interesting sidelines, and at least to mention all reasonably well-known names even if only under some collective heading. The object of the book is to steer those interested enough to take the ride through a vast, intriguing, and increasingly important subject and direct them towards further sources of specialized information. In this last respect this volume offers selective basic bibliographical listings, confined to the most recommendable and reasonably available printed books.

Many of the established *Companions* (like Percy Scholes's long-admired and well-loved volume on music, which enjoyed a freedom of expression and personal bias that is no longer permissible) have now found themselves in the enjoyable position of being re-edited and up-dated. The present volume comes along at a time when its subject-matter has only comparatively recently been accepted as respectably academic. Its primary purpose is, of course, to offer reliable and sensibly selected information; but an almost equally important concern has been to make a meaningful whole of the many divisions of popular music. Compared to 1960, when the compiler first attempted *A Guide to Popular Music*, the sources of reference have multiplied many times over, but most of them are concerned with one aspect of the field. The prime intention of this present work is to be a linking volume that investigates as widely as possible, yet ends up by dealing with one cohesive subject—popular music.

There is no need to explain or justify the term 'popular' at this point, as it is done at greater length in the appropriate entries in the book. It is perhaps only necessary to say that within 'popular' we embrace all music that would not normally be found in a reference book on 'classical' or 'serious' music (though most of them today feel compelled to give token coverage to the popular world); and to cover the essential elements and personalities concerned with popular song of all periods. Its divisions include the musical theatre, starting with operetta and including such specialized fields as music-hall, cabaret, and revue; folk-music (in the traditional sense), to a degree where it has impinged on commercial popular music; jazz and all its sources and offshoots; the massively growing world of pop music that has emerged from the developments of the last two centuries or so of lowbrow endeavour; and the miscellaneous world of light music that lies on the frontiers of our subject. The coverage accorded to different subjects is also bound to be controversial. We have felt it necessary to make the history of popular song of every period and style and of the popular musical theatre the central threads of the book, with all other fields of music-making having to suffer in varying degrees from our enforced selectivity. In defence let it be pleaded that no compiler could ever be totally free from personal bias or have sufficient width of knowledge to be omniscient on every branch of the art.

Historically we have gone as far back as we sensibly can. In fact a factual treatment of *published* popular music does not need to go back very often beyond the early years of the 19th century. The bulk of commercial popular musical developments have taken place since *c.*1850, when lower- and middle-class spending power began to assert its rights to choose its enjoyed branches of entertainment, and the necessary commercial set-up (including printing, publishing, and promotion) was organized to deal with these demands.

Geographically, we are essentially concerned with the English-speaking world, with the USA obviously taking prime place as the modern home of popular music but with the pioneering but comparatively neglected (in terms of literary coverage) British claims given a fair balance in order to assess their proper place. Further coverage of European music is made on the basis of its universal impact and no claims as to the adequacy of the treatment of such countries as Austria, Germany, France, and Spain are made; still less of places outside western Europe. Areas beyond, such as Eastern or African music, are excluded; these areas need *Companions* of their own.

Much of the book inevitably deals with the living, and we are greatly aware of the inherent dangers, particularly in the current haste for commercial recognition, of passing judgement on what is still a raw product. A breathing space of some five or so years is therefore allowed, although ongoing activities are followed to a logical conclusion wherever possible. People are given entries and graded in importance according to their apparent impact on the area of music they inhabit. The world of popular music has spawned at least as much worthless rubbish as its classical counterpart, possibly more. Countless items have been published (and praised) that could have been written by anyone with the most basic musical knowledge and not an ounce of wit or sensitivity. Thousands of names never even merited inclusion and hundreds more, which we would like to have included for some nostalgic reason or other, had to be discarded during the final editing, though many that would have been lost have been given a token inclusion in more general entries. It can only be hoped that this newly exploring *Companion* will justify a further edition in the not too distant future when any imbalances can be adjusted in the useful light of hindsight.

Such a work must inevitably be indebted to an enormous number of people who have researched the various branches of popular music and many who have given help and advice. Any work of this nature must inevitably draw much of its information from other published sources, the gaps filled in by more detailed articles and personal contact. Over the years, in fact ever since the publication of the now wholly inadequate *A Guide to Popular Music*, which owed its existence to the late John Baker and his Phoenix House publishing activities, work has been done on a prospective complete reference guide to popular music, much of it in continued collaboration with the co-author of the original book, Peter Clayton, whose friendship and continual help I must acknowledge first of all. The limits of the present work have precluded the use of much detailed work done by the late W. A. Chislett in the brass and military band areas, but some of it remains and I have benefited greatly from years of close work with him; also from the help given by such hardy colleagues as Fred Dellar and Stephen Gammond (who led me into the pop world), Nigel Hunter, Arthur Jackson, Ralph Harvey, and others who have helped over the years. I should like to add a list of people who have helped either knowingly or unknowingly through their own published researches, otherwise broadcast efforts, and personal knowledge, including (alphabetically): Gerald Bordman, Roy Busby, Ian Carr, Digby Fairweather, and Brian Priestley, authors of *Jazz: the Essential Companion*, John Chilton, James Lincoln Collier, Chris Ellis, Leonard Feather, James J. Fuld, Kurt Gänzl, Stanley Green, Phil Hardy and Dave Laing, Clive Hirschhorn, Raymond Horricks, Diana Howard, the late Burnett James, Peter Kemp, Michael Kennedy, Roger D. Kinkle, Andrew Lamb, Mark Lubbock, Paul Oliver, Brian Rust, Nat Shapiro, Nicolas Slominsky, Irving Stambler, Paul Taylor, Richard Traubner; others who have sadly left the battlefield, and many others whose works have been regularly consulted or brains otherwise picked. Full acknowledgement, particularly in specialized fields, is further made by way of the bibliographical listings.

Inevitably a compiler's dreams and ambitions must conflict with the publisher's practical and economic outlook. While frustrated by the unwillingness of the Oxford University Press to allow this volume to be five times as extensive as it is, I would like to acknowledge the courteous and interested help of their editors, notably David Blackwell, and the well-informed and experienced advice of Sheldon Meyer of the Oxford University Press in New York. The ultimate wisdom of their considered judgements has greatly eased the pain of the loss of many pages. I would especially like to thank my copy-editor Betty Palmer, who made the final adjustments in a painlessly expert way and added a great deal from her own knowledge of certain areas.

Shepperton 1990 PETER GAMMOND

NOTE TO THE READER

Entries are in simple letter-by-letter alphabetical order, with spaces and hyphens ignored; definite and indefinite articles, in all languages, are also ignored where they fall at the beginning of a title. Names beginning with Mc are ordered as though they were spelled Mac, and St as Saint.

An asterisk indicates that a separate entry will be found for the name or word that immediately follows.

Abbreviations

b	born
d	died
fl.	floruit
c.	*circa*
m	music by
w	words by
p	performances
rev.	revised
repr.	reprinted

CONTENTS

AACM [Association for the Advancement of Creative Musicians). Chicago jazz collective formed in May 1965 to encourage self-employment of progressive black musicians. It grew out of the Experimental Band of 1961 led by the eventual founder and director of AACM, Muhal Richard Abrams (*b* 1930). The Association runs a music school, produces records, and organizes concerts: a sort of present-day *Clef Club.

Aaronson, Irving (*b* New York, 7 Feb. 1895; *d* Hollywood, 10 May 1963). American bandleader, pianist, and composer. At the age of 11 he was playing in silent film cinemas. He formed a group called the Versatile Sextette, but first became well-known with an orchestra (originally the Crusaders) billed as 'Irving Aaronson and his Commanders', which visited London in 1926, appeared in the musical *Paris* (1928), and toured Europe in the 1930s. Later, he was musical adviser to MGM films. His compositions included 'The song angels sing', used in the film *Because You're Mine* (1952), and 'The loveliest night of the year' (based on Rosa's 'Over the waves') from *The Great Caruso* (1951).

Abarbanell, Lina (*b* Berlin, 3 Feb. 1880; *d* New York, 6 Jan. 1963). German singer and actress. She started her musical career in Europe, appearing mainly in operetta; then, in 1905, went to the USA to play the role of Hansel in Humperdinck's *Hänsel und Gretel* at the Metropolitan Opera in New York. Afterwards she appeared in many musical shows, including *The *Merry Widow* (1907); **Madame Sherry* (1910); *Miss Princess* (1912); *The *Geisha* (1913); *Flora Bella* (1916); *Happy Go Lucky* (1926); and *The Silver Swan* (1929).

Abba. Swedish vocal pop group formed in 1973. Its founder members, who were already well established in their own right, were Agnetha Fältskog (*b* 1950) (vocal), Anni-Frid Lyngstad-Fredriksson (*b* 1945) (vocal), Bjorn Ulvaeus (*b* 1946) (guitar and vocal) who led, produced, and wrote for the group, and Benny Andersson (*b* 1945) (keyboard, synthesizer, and vocal), co-writer. Working in a popularized style, with an appeal that reached beyond the teenage rock market, they set their sights on winning the *Eurovision Song Contest, failing in 1973 (when they first called themselves Abba, a title based on the initial letters of their first names) with 'Ring ring', but winning in 1974 with 'Waterloo'. The song became the No. 1 hit throughout Europe and No. 6 in America, making the group one of Sweden's biggest export earners. Their clean image and neat singing, with bright harmonies and clever ideas, made them slightly suspect in the rock market, but they consolidated their success with several No. 1 hits including 'Mamma mia' (1975); 'Fernando' (1976); 'Dancing queen' (USA and UK, 1976); 'Knowing me knowing you' (1977); 'The name of the game' (1977); 'Take a chance on me' (1978); 'The winner takes it all' (1980); and 'Super trouper' (1980). After 13 successful LP albums, with *Arrival* a world top-seller of 1977, the group broke up in 1983.

Ulvaeus and Andersson's music was the basis of a stage show, *Abbacadabra*, at the Lyric, Hammersmith, 8 Dec. 1983, also seen earlier in France. They also wrote the score of **Chess* (1986).

M. Lindvall: *ABBA: the Ultimate Pop Group* (London, 1977). H. Edgington and P. Himmelstrand: *ABBA* (London, 1978). J. Tobler: *Abba for the Record* (Knutsford, 1980). R. York (ed.): *Abba in Their Own Words* (London, 1982).

Music: B. Ulvaeus and B. Andersson: *ABBA: a Lyrical Collection 1972–1982* (Iver, 1982).

Abbott, George (*b* Forestville, NY, 25 June 1887). American librettist, director, and producer. After education at Rochester and Harvard, he started his stage career as an actor, first appearing on the stage in 1913 and having his greatest success in *Dulcy* (1921) by George S. *Kaufman. He started directing in 1919, specializing in comedy, and began to write plays in 1925, among them being *Broadway* and *Three Men on a Horse*. He moved into writing for the musical theatre by collaborating with *Rodgers and *Hart on the book of **On Your Toes* (1936; filmed 1939), having, in 1935, directed *Jumbo* by the same team. He directed several of their musicals and was part-writer of *The *Boys from Syracuse* (1938; filmed 1940). He directed or produced **Best Foot Forward* (1941); **On the Town* (1944); *Billion Dollar Baby* (1945); *Barefoot Boy with Cheek* (1947); **High Button Shoes* (1947); *Look Ma, I'm Dancing* (1948); *Touch and Go* (1949); **Call Me Madam* (1950); **Wonderful Town* (1953); **Me and Juliet* (1953); *On Your Toes* (1954 and 1984 revivals); *Once Upon a Mattress* (1959); *A *Funny Thing Happened on the Way to the Forum* (1963); *Fade Out—Fade In* (1964); *How Now, Dow Jones* (1967); *The Education of H*y*m*a*n K*a*p*l*a*n* (1968); and *The Fig Leaves are Falling* (1969).

He also both directed or produced, and wrote the librettos, for many shows, including *Beat the Band* (1942); **Where's Charley?* (1948); *A Tree Grows in Brooklyn* (1951); *The *Pajama Game* (1954, 1973 revival; filmed 1957); **Damn Yankees* (1955; filmed 1958); *New Girl in Town* (1957); **Fiorello!* (1959);

Tenderloin (1960); *Flora the Red Menace* (1965); and *Anya* (1965). Abbott was the creator of a whole new approach to the staging of musicals, calling for fast-moving changes, overlapping, 'seguing in' (to use a TV term)—techniques he was applying to farces from the 1920s and to musicals from around 1936.

G. Abbott: *Mr Abbott* (New York, 1963).

'Abide with me'. Well-known English hymn with words by the Revd Henry Francis Lyte (1793–1847) and music by William Henry Monk (1823–89). Lyte was curate and vicar of Charlton, Lower Brixham, Devon, for 25 years, and also a poet and hymn-writer. He was an ailing man when he wrote 'Abide with me' at Berry Head, Brixham, in the summer of 1847, and it was sung for the first time a few months later at his funeral. Monk was a prolific composer and edited *Hymns Ancient and Modern* (1861), where 'Abide with me' (to his tune 'Eventide') first appeared in print. With its plangent harmonies it has become the hymn for big emotional occasions and public gatherings.

H. J. Garland: *Henry Francis Lyte and the Story of 'Abide With Me'* (Manchester, n.d.).

Abrahám, Paul (*b* Apatin, 2 Nov. 1892; *d* Hamburg, 6 May 1960). Hungarian composer. After studying in Budapest 1910–16, he started his composing career writing mainly chamber and instrumental music. His first operetta *Der Gatte des Fräuleins* was performed in 1928 while he was conductor of the Budapest Hauptstadtischen Operettentheater; and his first great success came with **Viktoria und ihr Husar* in 1930. He led an orchestra in Berlin from 1931 to 1933 and during this time wrote a considerable amount of film music. In 1933 his work was banned by the Nazis and he left Berlin for Vienna, later moving to Paris for a time and then to the USA. His music found very little favour there as it was written in a style that was rapidly becoming old-fashioned. The failure and the consequent struggle for survival brought on mental illness and he was confined to hospital for many years. In 1956 the West Germans became aware of his plight and he was brought back to Hamburg to be cared for, dying in an asylum there in 1960.

Belonging to the last generation of true operetta composers in the old Viennese tradition, his main works such as *Viktoria und ihr Husar* (Vienna, 1930)—'Mausi', 'Pardon, Madame'; *Die Blume von Hawaii* (Leipzig, 1931)—'My golden baby'; and *Ball im Savoy* (Vienna, 1933; London, as *Ball at the Savoy*, 1933) are interesting for their curious mingling of traditional Austro-Hungarian operetta strains with a stylized German version of the pseudo-ragtime-cum-Dixieland innovations of the 1920s and 1930s, as typified in the vivaciously hysterical hit 'Mausi' (Eng. 'Mousie'). The jazz element always remains an added ingredient rather than a naturally integrated part, as it was in American equivalents of the time. Abrahám's music is a link between the Strauss–Lehár operetta era and the modern jazz-oriented musical. He also wrote *Zenebona* (Budapest, 1928); *Märchen im Grand-Hotel* (Vienna, 1934); *Dschainah, das Mädchen aus dem Teehaus* (Vienna, 1935); and *Roxy und ihr Wunderteam* (Vienna, 1937). One of his best-known songs—'Ich bin ja heut' so glücklich' (known in English as 'Today I feel so happy') was written for the film *Die Privatsekretärin* in 1931.

Abrahams, Maurice [Abrams, Maurie] (*b* Russia, 18 Mar. 1883; *d* New York, 13 Apr. 1931). Russian-born American composer. He became the manager of various New York publishing firms before starting his own in 1923, and was a writer of specialist material for vaudeville artistes, including Belle *Baker, whom he married. He wrote in the white, *Tin Pan Alley, *ragtime idiom of the early 1900s that also led Irving *Berlin to fame. His songs included: 'Hitchy-koo' (with Lewis F. *Muir, 1912; *w* L. Wolfe *Gilbert); 'Ragtime Cowboy Joe' (with Muir, 1912; *w* Grant *Clarke); 'Pullman porters on parade' (1913, *w* Berlin)—used in the London revue *Not Likely* (1914); 'He'd have to get under, get out and get under' (1913, *w* Clarke and Edgar Leslie)—used in *The Pleasure Seekers* (1913; 'The 20th Century rag' (1914, *w* Clarke and Leslie); and 'Take me to that midnight cakewalk ball' (1916, *w* Eddie Cox and Arthur Jackson).

Academy of Motion Picture Arts and Sciences. American society which offers annual awards for works judged to be of outstanding merit in the cinema world. They are given in the shape of gold-plated statuettes popularly known as Oscars, which are highly regarded in the film business. They were first presented in 1929 for the year 1927–8. Special awards for the best film song and the best film score were introduced in 1934. The Best Film Song Award (which has since continued to be a useful reflection of changing tastes over the years) first went to 'The Continental' (*m* Con *Conrad, *w* Herb Magidson) from *The Gay Divorcée*. The first Award for Best Film Score went in 1934 to *One Night of Love* (*m* Louis *Silvers). In 1938 this Award was further divided (except for 1957) between Best Film Score and Best Musical Film Score with the new award going in 1938 to *Alexander's Ragtime Band* (*m* Alfred *Newman).

P. Michael: *The Academy Awards: a Pictorial History* (New York, 1968). N. Fredriks: *Hollywood and the Academy Awards* (Hollywood, 1972). R. Shale (ed.): *The Academy Awards* (New York, 1978).

Accordion. Piano Accordion. Portable instrument supported in front of the body by a shoulder strap, sounded by free reeds blown by bellows, which has a treble keyboard for the right hand and on the left a series of buttons which operate chords (hence the name of the instrument). One of the earliest forms was the *Handäoline* which was made in Berlin in 1822 by Friedrich Buschmann. The actual name *Akkordion* or *Accordion* was first given to an improved version of this instrument introduced in Vienna by an Armenian, Cyrill Demian, in 1829. It was a primitive instrument, though now basically similar to the modern instrument, with models of various sizes having from 5 to 50 metal keys or studs which opened valves to admit air from the bellows to motivate metal reeds. Each key operated two notes, one while the bellows were compressed and one while they were being recharged; the instrument being more or less a mechanized mouth organ or *harmonica. There were usually only two keys on the left-hand or bass-side of the instrument which, by admitting air to a selected group of reeds, could supply a simple tonic–dominant underlying harmony. This instrument could only be played in one key, which limited its professional use.

In 1829 an Englishman, Charles Wheatstone, patented a similar instrument with a distinctive octagonal shape which was developed by others as the *concertina. Two main types of accordion now developed in answer to a practical demand for them. There was the *Melodeon* or German accordion which was a single-action instrument on the lines described above, with a single row of melody buttons giving a diatonic scale, usually in C (but also G, D, or A). On the bass side were sited two large keys, one giving a bass note and the other a chord either in the tonic or the dominant according to the direction of movement of the bellows. This instrument, which became popular in European folk-music, was improved over the years by the addition of more rows of melodic buttons, taking the instrument into more keys with alternative fingering. Large models with four or five rows of buttons, known as Helicon bass accordions, were popular in mid-European countries and were also imported into the USA.

The very rhythmical nature of these instruments made them ideal as an accompaniment to dancing. What has become known as the British chromatic accordion offered a second row of buttons tuned a semitone higher than the first, allowing more dexterity, though the continuing reliance on the direction of movement of the bellows to produce certain notes remained a technical difficulty. The ultimate in this model was one with three rows, each a semitone apart, which was developed around 1946 and has been used extensively in Scottish dance music, notably in the hands of such experts as Jimmy *Shand. Similar instruments with technical variations that offer different fingerings and facilities were developed in France (where it is known as the *musette*) and in the USSR. The necessity for a double-action valve mechanism which produced a constant note whichever way the bellows were moving was a result of the separate development of the piano accordion, clearly distinguished by having a piano-type keyboard for the right hand and anything from 8 to 120 buttons for the left, laid out in up to six rows giving a full range of bass chords. The first piano-type keyboard was experimented with as early as 1852 by the French maker Busson, what he produced being more or less an adaptation of the organ that was played on the lap with the bellows sounding the reeds only on the compression movement, the whole working on the harmonium principle. The first modern-style piano accordion came in around 1911, made in Italy, and by the 1920s the instrument had become widely popular now that it was completely flexible and produced a stable scale irrespective of bellows movement.

While the melodeon-type instruments flourished in Scottish, Irish, and other European folk-music areas, the piano accordion now became widely used on the variety stage in the 1920s and 1930s, with such performers as Thoralf Tollefson, Erik Frank, and William Starr becoming well-known. The accordion band became a popular phenomenon in the same period, one of the best-known being the London Piano Accordion Band led by George *Scott-Wood from 1934 to 1940. Now almost entirely absent from the modern commercial pop scene, the accordion continues to thrive in folk-music, becoming a main feature of *Cajun music, and in various country dance circles. There is also a keen interest amongst amateur players, with the usual associated competitions and a monthly magazine, *Accordion Times*, devoted to its promotion. Germany is the main manufacturer of the instruments today.

Acid rock. Loosely used term for the highly amplified, electronic rock that was favoured by the drug-oriented cult. At its height during the hippie period of the mid-1960s and typified by the music played by the San Francisco Bay bands such as *Jefferson Airplane and The *Grateful Dead. It connected rock with the concept of the mind-expansion associated with LSD usage, its desired extra insight and inspiration supplemented by electronic fuzz and feedback and bemusing visual effects; the music generally had a disorganized and improvised nature. The associated psychedelic rock was of a gentler and more art-oriented character.

Acuff, Roy Claxton (*b* Maynardsville, Tenn., 15 Sept. 1903; *d* Nashville, Tenn., 23 Nov. 1992). American Country and Western singer, fiddler, songwriter, and bandleader. He wanted to be a baseball player but, inspired by his father's interest in the fiddle and fiddle-tunes, he moved towards a musical career and started professionally around the age of 25. He began to build a reputation on radio and joined the Nashville **Grand Ole Opry* show in 1938, becoming as popular as its other star performer, 'Uncle' Dave *Macon, and soon considered one of America's leading singers of country music. He was foremost in developing the traditional style rather than following or leading the more pop-oriented trends of modern Country and Western. He also introduced a strong line of comedy into his act.

With his Smoky Mountain Boys and/or the *Nitty Gritty Dirt Band he recorded such country classics as 'Tennessee waltz', 'Mule skinner's blues', 'Night train', 'Will the circle be unbroken', 'Precious jewel', 'Wreck on the highway', 'I saw the light', 'Freight train blues' (on which Bob *Dylan based his version), 'Wabash Cannonball', 'Carry me back to the mountains', and his first popular hit, 'Great speckled bird'. In 1943 he formed an influential country-music publishing company with songwriter Fred *Rose. He appeared in several films in the 1940s and travelled abroad to entertain US troops. Often appearing on TV, he remained active into the 1960s still adhering to the old-time sound of fiddle and steel guitar, 'Southern rurality evoked through railroad and religion'. After a motor accident in 1965 he worked mainly in publishing and recording, being part-owner of Hickory Records. He was elected to the *Country Music Hall of Fame in 1962.

A. C. Dunklebberger: *King of Country Music* (Nashville, 1971). E. Schlappi: *Roy Acuff: the Smoky Mountain Boy* (Gretna, La., 1978).

Adam, Adolphe (*b* Paris, 24 July 1803; *d* Paris, 3 May 1856). French composer. Even if his works are judged to be those of a talented minor composer, he remains an important figure in the move towards the popular musical theatre forms of the mid-19th century. After studies at the Paris Conservatoire, and some practical experience in theatre orchestras, his writing first received attention when Adrien Boïeldieu (1775–1834) asked him, in 1825, to assist with the orchestration of *La Dame blanche*. His own *Pierre et Catherine* was produced at the Paris Opéra-Comique in 1829. Berlioz later described Adam's music as 'stylish, fluent, undistinguished, and full of catchy little tunes that one can whistle on the way home'. His adoption of a light vaudeville style is first detected in *Le Châlet* (1834) which has been pinpointed by some historians as the first true French operetta; though he still lacked the truly popular touch that *Offenbach, who was greatly influenced by Adam, was soon to achieve.

Most of his works are now neglected, apart from the sturdy *Le Postillon de Longjumeau* (1836), which contains a clear operetta element, some of his charming overtures, and the ballet *Giselle* (1841). Other works that remain known, at least by repute, are *Le Fidèle Berger* (1838); *Le Roi d'Yvetot* (1842); *Le Toréador* (1849); *Giralda* (1850); *La Poupée de Nuremberg* (1852); and *Si j'étais roi* (1852). He wrote 24 operas altogether and several ballets. In 1847 he founded the Théâtre National and in 1849 became Professor of Composition at the Paris Conservatoire. He wrote *Souvenirs d'un musicien* (Paris, 1857) and *Derniers Souvenirs d'un musicien* (Paris, 1859).

J. Halèvy: *Souvenirs et Portraits* (Paris, 1861), ch. 'Adam'. A. Pougin: *Adolphe Adam: sa vie, sa carrière, ses mémoires artistiques* (Paris, 1877).

Adamo, Salvatore (*b* Cosimo, Sicily, 1943). Italian-born composer, lyricist, and singer. In 1947 he moved with his family to Belgium where his father was a miner. After singing at local concerts and dances, he turned professional and soon got engagements in various European cities, eventually making an appearance at the famous *Olympia music-hall in Paris where his song 'Vous permettez, Monsieur?' was a great hit. His rather harsh and unusual voice gained him a popular following, particularly among the younger audiences, and he became a very successful recording artist. His other songs include 'Les filles du bord de mer' (1965), 'Mes mains sur tes hanches', 'La nuit', 'A vot' bon coeur', 'Le néon', 'Tombe la neige', 'Inch'Allah', 'A demain sur la lune', 'Ah, les belles dames', 'Pauvre Verlaine' and 'Les grattes-ciel'.

Adams, Cliff (*b* Southwark, London, 21 Aug. 1923). British conductor and arranger. He was a boy chorister at St Mary-le-Bow, Cheapside, studied piano and organ, and started a career as a dance-band pianist before joining the RAF in the Second World War. After the war he worked as a pianist and arranger for Ted *Heath, Cyril Stapleton, *Ambrose, Eric *Winstone, and Stanley *Black. In 1949 he formed the Stargazers which became one of the best-known vocal groups of the 1950s, and then, in 1954, formed the Cliff Adams Singers to work with the BBC Show Band and on such programmes as the *Val Doonican Show*. They had their own radio programme, *Sing Something Simple,* from 1959. Adams has been a prolific writer for TV commercials and composed a musical, *Liza of Lambeth* (1976).

Adams, Lee [Richard] (*b* Mansfield, Ohio, 14 Aug. 1924). American librettist and lyricist. He studied journalism at Ohio State University, then joined forces in 1955 with the composer Charles *Strouse to write material for revues. Ben *Bagley used their material in his popular *Shoestring* revues and *The Littlest Revue* (1956). Thereafter the team became well-known for their variously successful shows: **Bye Bye Birdie* (1960); *All American* (1962); **Golden Boy* (1964); *It's a Bird, It's a Plane, It's Superman* (1966); **Applause* (1970); *I and Albert* (1972); *A Broadway Musical* (1978); and *Bring Back Birdie* (1980).

Adams, Pepper [Park] (*b* Highland, Mich., 8 Oct. 1930; *d* New York, 10 Sept. 1986). American baritone-saxophonist, composer, and arranger. He was educated at Wayne State University and after service in Korea went to New York in 1956 to pursue a jazz career. In 1957 he joined Stan *Kenton and began to attract critical attention. Later he played and toured with John *Coltrane, Dizzy *Gillespie, and Benny *Goodman, and he had a long association with the Thad *Jones–Mel Lewis band. His early playing was intense, full of notes and often ferocious. Later he disciplined his sound without losing any of the passion. Coming after the Harry *Carney-inspired baritone-saxophone era, he became the influential voice on that instrument in post-war bop, translating its resonant tones and its swing era image into terms best suited to modern jazz. He suffered from cancer in his last two years but managed to play to within two months of his death.

Adams, Stephen [pen-name of Michael Maybrick] (*b* Liverpool, 31 Jan. 1884; *d* Buxton, 25 Aug. 1913). English composer and singer, performing under his own name but mainly writing as Adams. He was organist at St Peter's Church, Liverpool, from 1858, then studied music at Leipzig Conservatory 1866–8 and singing in Milan. He made his first appearance in London at the New Philharmonic Concerts in 1870, after which he became a popular performer at ballad concerts and in opera and toured the USA and Canada in 1884. He wrote a large number of songs of the *drawing-room ballad type (which had a certain robust quality whether they were of a religious nature (as many were) or secular. Some of them were tremendously successful, particularly those that were written to lyrics by the barrister/poet Fred E. *Weatherly, who deserves much of the credit for his memorable words. Naturally Michael Maybrick featured many Stephen Adams songs in his concerts; and they have been well used by robust singers of the Peter *Dawson and Frederick Harvey kind ever since. Among his best-known are 'Nancy Lee' (1876); 'They all loved Jack' (1880); 'The midshipmite' (1885); 'Star of Bethlehem' (1890); 'The Holy City' (1905); 'Roses' (1905); 'Thorns' (1905); all with words by Weatherly. At the height of its popularity 'The Holy City' regularly sold some 50,000 copies a year.

Adamson, Harold (*b* Greenville, NJ, 10 Dec. 1906; *d* Beverly Hills, Calif., 17 Aug. 1980). American lyricist. On leaving Harvard, he became a professional songwriter in New York in the late 1920s, becoming involved in such Broadway shows as *Smiles* (1930); **Earl Carroll's Vanities* (1931); *The Third Little Show* (1931); *Keep Off the Grass* (1940); *Banjo Eyes* (1942); **As the Girls Go* (1948); and writing for such Hollywood films as *Dancing Lady* (1933); *Kid Millions* (1934); *Bottoms Up* (1934); *Reckless* (1935); *The Great Ziegfeld* (1936); *Suzy* (1936); *You're a Sweetheart* (1937); *That Certain Age* (1938); *Nob Hill* (1945); *If You Knew Susie* (1948); *Gentlemen Prefer Blondes* (1952); *An Affair to Remember* (1957); and many more. He worked mainly with Jimmy *McHugh; also with Hoagy *Carmichael, Louis *Alter, Peter *De Rose, Walter *Donaldson, Vernon *Duke, Duke *Ellington, Burton *Lane, Vincent *Youmans, and Victor *Young.

Some of his best-known songs include: 'Time on my hands', 'Have a heart', 'Everything I have is yours', 'There's no two ways about it', 'You're a sweetheart', 'You're as pretty as a picture', 'Ferry-boat serenade', 'The woodpecker song', 'Manhattan serenade', 'A lovely way to spend an evening', 'I couldn't sleep a wink last night', 'It's a most unusual day', 'Around the world', 'My resistance is low', and 'An Affair to remember'.

Adderley, 'Cannonball' [Julian Edwin] (*b* Tampa, Fla., 15 Sept. 1928; *d* Gary, Ind., 8 Aug. 1975). American jazz alto-saxophonist. He started his professional career at a Greenwich Village club and in 1956 formed his own Quintet with his cornet-playing brother Nat Adderley (*b* Tampa, 25 Nov. 1931). He became known through his recordings, having a great success with 'Africa waltz' in 1961, followed by 'Dis here', 'Sermonette', 'Work song', 'Jive samba', 'Mercy, mercy, mercy', and 'Walk tall'. Continuing in the bop field, he worked successfully with Miles *Davis for two years and with John *Coltrane 1957–9. He owed much of his success to an engaging personality and his humorous presentation (which gave him a wide following) and was admired for his inspired improvisations. He died of a stroke during a concert.

Addinsell, Richard Stewart (*b* Oxford, 13 Jan. 1904; *d* London, 14 Nov. 1977). British composer. He read law at Hertford College, Oxford, but became increasingly interested in music, especially in connection with the theatre. He studied briefly at the Royal College of Music and had further musical training in Berlin and Vienna, 1929–32. His first music for the theatre was contributed to *The Charlot Show of 1926*. During a visit to the USA in 1933 he began to write for films and during the next few years he was mainly occupied in this field and in writing incidental music for plays. His most famous composition was to be the 'Warsaw Concerto' which, originally an integral part of the score of the film *Dangerous Moonlight* (1941), played on the sound-track by Louis Kentner, caught the public's fancy and became immensely popular in its own right. His *Times* obituary described his work as showing 'a gift for seemingly artless, delicately romantic melodies supported by subtle harmony and an ability to set words naturally'. He worked with distinction for British films in the pre-war and wartime eras.

He contributed to many stage revues, notably with Joyce *Grenfell as his collaborator, including *Jumbles* (1927); *The Lyric Revue* (1951); **Penny Plain* (1951); *The Globe Revue* (1952); **Airs on a Shoestring* (1953); *Joyce Grenfell Requests the Pleasure* (1954); *Living for Pleasure* (1956); *Joyce Grenfell—a Miscellany* (1957); and further Grenfell shows in 1962 and 1965. He wrote music for *Adam's Opera* by Clemence Dane (Old Vic, 1928); *The Good Companions* by J. B. Priestley (His Majesty's, 1931); *Alice in Wonderland* (1932); *Come of Age* by Clemence Dane (1933); *Moonlight is Silver* (Dane, 1934); *The Happy Hypocrite* (Dane, based on Beerbohm; His Majesty's, 1936); *The Taming of the Shrew* (New, 1937); *Alice in Wonderland and Through the Looking Glass* (1943); and *Ring Round the Moon* trans. Christopher Fry (Globe, 1950).

His film scores included: *The Amateur Gentleman* (1936); *Dark Journey* (1937); *Farewell Again* (1937); *South Riding* (1938); *Fire Over England* (1937); *Vessel of Wrath* (1938); *Goodbye, Mr Chips* (1939); *The Lion Has Wings* (1939); *Contraband* (1940); *Men of the Lightships* (1940); *Gaslight* (1940); *Dangerous Moonlight* (1940); *Love on the Dole* (1941); *The Siege of Tobruk* (1942); *Blithe Spirit* (1945); *Diary for Timothy* (1946); *The Black Rose* (1950); *Scrooge* (1951); *Tom Brown's Schooldays*

(1951); *Beau Brummell* (1954); *The Prince and the Showgirl* (1957); *The Admirable Crichton* (1957); *A Tale of Two Cities* (1958); *Loss of Innocence* (1961); *The Greengage Summer* (1961); *The Waltz of the Toreadors* (1962); and *The Roman Spring of Mrs Stone* (1962).

Addison, John Mervin (*b* Cobham, Surrey, 16 Mar. 1920). British composer. He originally intended to take up a military career, but then studied at the Royal College of Music 1938–9, continuing, after wartime military service 1947–8, with Gordon Jacob for composition; piano with Herbert Fryer; oboe and clarinet with Leon Goossens and Frederick Thurston. He was appointed Professor of Composition at the RCM, 1950–7. His compositions include a trumpet concerto, chamber music, and the ballet *Carte Blanche* (1953). In 1949 he was appointed musical director to Boulting Bros. His light and sophisticated touch brought him a considerable success with the revue *Cranks* (1955). Later musical scores included *Keep Your Hair On* (1958); *The Amazons* (1971); and *Popkiss* (with David *Heneker, 1972).

His music for films includes: *The Guinea Pig* (1949); *Seven Days to Noon* (1950); *The Man Between* (1953); *Private's Progress* (1955); *Reach for the Sky* (1956); *Lucky Jim* (1957); *I was Monty's Double* (1958); *Look Back in Anger* (1959); *The Entertainer* (1960); *A Taste of Honey* (1961); *The Loneliness of the Long Distance Runner* (1962); *Tom Jones* (1963); *Guns at Batasi* (1964); *The Amorous Adventures of Moll Flanders* (1965); *Torn Curtain* (1966); *A Fine Madness* (1966); *The Honey Pot* (1967); *Smashing Time* (1967); *The Charge of the Light Brigade* (1968); *Country Dance* (1970); *Mr Forbush and the Penguins* (1971); *Sleuth* (1972); *Dead Cert* (1974); *A Bridge Too Far* (1977); *The Seven Per Cent Solution* (1977); *Strange Invaders* (1983).

Ade, George (*b* Kentland, Ind., 9 Feb. 1866; *d* Brook, Ind., 16 May 1944). American humorist and librettist mainly admired for his *Fables in Slang*. His first writing for the theatre was the libretto for *The Night of the Fourth* (1901) which was a failure. This was followed by *The Sultan of Sulu* (1902, *m* Alfred G. Wathall) which started a fashion for stories in which Americans were transported to various unexpected places. His subsequent musicals included: *Peggy from Paris* (1903); *The Sho-gun* (1904); *The Fair Co-Ed* (1909); and *The Old Town* (1910). His liking for slang, on which he was an authority, colours his librettos which therefore now seem dated.

'Adeste fideles'. A hymn with words and music by John Francis Wade (1710–86), a plainchant copyist at the Catholic Douai College in France, written *c.*1740–3. The words were first printed in London in 1760, translated as 'Draw near ye faithful Christians', the music in *An Essay on the Church Plain Chant* in London in 1782. The more familiar translation was made by Fr Frederick Oakley (1802–80) in 1841, with the now famous opening line 'O come all ye faithful' an amendment by James R. Murray in 1852. It is sometimes called, for reason unknown, the 'Portuguese hymn'.

Adler, Larry [Lawrence Cecil] (*b* Baltimore, 10 Feb. 1914). American harmonica player and composer. He won a harmonica contest at 13 and went on to become the world's most famous practitioner of the once humble 'mouth organ', a name he has always preferred. He has appeared in many musical shows and revues, including *Smiles* (1931); *Flying Colors* (1932); *Streamline* (London, 1934); and in films such as *Many Happy Returns* (1934) (with Duke *Ellington); *Operator 13* (1934); *The Big Broadcast of 1937* (1936); *The Singing Marine* (1937)—'Night over Shanghai'; *St Martin's Lane* (1938); *Music for Millions* (1945); *Three Daring Daughters* (1948). He wrote the popular theme and background music for the British film *Genevieve* (1954); also music for *The Hellions* (1961); *The Hook* (1963); *King and Country* (1963); and *High Wind in Jamaica* (1964). He had the experience of playing *'Rhapsody in blue' with Gershwin and premièred a specially written 'Romance' by Vaughan Williams in 1952. Attacked for alleged communist leanings in 1948, he moved to England but later returned to the USA.

Adler, Richard (*b* New York, 3 Aug. 1921). American composer and lyricist. He was the son of a professional pianist, had no musical training himself, but studied playwriting at the University of North Carolina. After wartime service in the US Navy, he started writing songs as a hobby. Meeting Jerry *Ross, a singer with a similar ambition to write, in 1950 they began to work as a team, producing words and music together, until Ross died in 1955. To begin with they wrote material for various singers, acts, and radio programmes, and were contracted by publisher/composer *Frank Loesser. Their first hit was 'Rags to riches' in 1953, which sold a million copies and reached the Hit Parade. Following a few more moderate successes and the contribution of four items to *John Murray Anderson's Almanac* in 1953, they were commissioned by George *Abbott to write the score of *The *Pajama Game* which proved to be a great success in 1954 (filmed 1957), as was **Damn Yankees* in 1955, described by Stanley Green as 'the most successful musical ever to deal with a sport [baseball] subject'. This was filmed in 1958 and shown in the UK as *Whatever Lola Wants*. After Ross's death, Adler wrote *Kwamina* (1961)—'Nothing more to look forward to', 'What's wrong with me?', 'Another time, another place'—which starred his wife, Sally Ann *Howes, and proved a failure. After that he mainly worked in TV advertising, writing jingles and producing, and was active in many administrative positions in the arts.

Adonis. American burlesque extravaganza with music by Edward E. *Rice produced at the New York Bijou Opera House 4 Sept. 1884. It was notable both for being the show which established the reputation of its part-composer and director Henry E. *Dixey, a talented singer, dancer, and comic actor; and as the first Broadway musical to surpass the mark of 500 consecutive performances, eventually achieving the then astonishing total of 603. Subsequently the show toured the USA, had 105 performances at the *Gaiety Theatre in London, and was revived in New York in 1893.

Adrian, Max [Bor, Max] (*b* Ireland, 1 Nov. 1903; *d* London, 19 Jan. 1973). Irish actor with a witty, biting Restoration style and voice, who had a distinguished dramatic career. He was outstandingly effective in intimate revue, featuring in such productions as *Light and Shade* (1942); *Tuppence Coloured* (1947); *Oranges and Lemons* (1948); **Penny Plain* (1951); **Airs on a Shoestring* (1953); *From Here and There* (1955); *Fresh Airs* (1956); and also in the first production of **Candide* (1956). He starred in the film version of *The *Boy Friend* (1972); and played a most effective lead in Ken Russell's TV film about the dying Frederick Delius.

Afro-American music. The major revolution in popular music in the 20th century has come about through the supplanting of the long-established European musical tradition by the Afro-American: that is, the kind of music with the enhanced rhythmic and associated verbal impact that is found in jazz and other forms of music stemming from black cultures. The beginnings of this revolution began to be felt in the USA at the end of the 19th century in the emerging spheres of *spirituals, *minstrel shows, the *cakewalk, *ragtime, and the early forms of *jazz that developed in the Southern 'slave' states of the country. The newly *syncopated music began to take over most spheres of popular music by the 1920s, leaving only a small section of the *musical theatre and various traditional and revivalist areas of music-making (e.g. *brass and *military bands, white *folk-music, and *light music) still using the European mode.

The spread of Afro culture in the USA began with the arrival of slaves from West Africa. For generations the potential African influence was limited by the social restrictions imposed on black people. The white population of America first became aware of a different flavour in the music they heard by way of spiritual concerts and minstrel shows. The music, by then, was no longer purely African but had grafted itself on to white American musical forms and styles and, at this time, the Afro element was far from dominant. It was only with the fuller manifestation of the colloquial African style and spirit in the more genuine forms of black jazz, such as the *blues, that the full force of Afro music, so long confined, really made itself felt. Given strength by the added musical flavours that had come to the USA by way of South America and the Caribbean, and given the commercial opportunity that had been denied to black musicians until the abolition of slavery in 1865, Afro music gradually crept into and took over popular music. Even in the early jazz days of the 20th century, the music still came over in a modified form. It was not until the second quarter of the century that it was appreciated by the few early jazz lovers who enjoyed the blues and *gospel music mainly disseminated through *race recordings and limited early releases of unadulterated jazz.

The Afro idiom was taken over in the 1950s by *rhythm 'n' blues and *rock artists who were excited by the primitive power and persuasion of the style. With remarkable speed the European tradition was thrown overboard by *Tin Pan Alley and the world moved into the rock age. Under the umbrella name of *pop, the Afro-American tradition not only changed the face of popular music throughout the world but also the social outlook and attitudes of the younger generations, who were strongly affected by the music.

The prefix Afro- is now appended to any music which has strongly black or African overtones; as in the admixture of two cultures found in Afro-Cuban music, a style evolving from the mingling of jazz and certain Latin American characteristics as exploited by Dizzy *Gillespie in the 1940s, Stan *Kenton in the 1950s, and in Cuba itself. Now that jazz is no longer a peculiarly black phenomenon, the term Afro-jazz is generally applied to the reverse process of Euro-American jazz styles being imposed on African folk styles, as in the urbanized kwela music of the 1940s. Afro-rock is a brand of rock music with strong African characteristics, much of it developed in London in the 1970s, under such names as high life and juju music, by Nigerian musicians. See also under BLACK AMERICAN MUSIC.

O. M. Walton; *Music: black, white and blue; a sociological survey of the use and misuse of Afro-American music* (New York, 1972).

'After the ball'. Song, with music and words by Charles K. *Harris, written in 1892 for an amateur minstrel show in Milwaukee. On its first airing the singer forgot his words and the song made little impression; but Harris had faith in it and published it himself. Taken up by J. Aldrich Libby, who sang it in the touring production of the extravaganza *A *Trip to Chinatown* (1892), it began to catch on, particularly when *Sousa and his band played it daily at the Chicago World's Fair. In England it was promoted by George *Lashwood. It became wildly popular and was the first song to sell more than five million copies. Jerome *Kern made effective use of it in **Show Boat* (1927).

Ager, Milton (*b* Chicago, 6 Oct. 1893; *d* Los Angeles, 6 Apr. 1979). American composer. A self-taught pianist, he went straight into the songwriting world from school, starting as a song-plugger with a Chicago music-publisher. He moved to the publisher's New York office in 1913 and had his first big success in 1918 with 'Everything is peaches down in Georgia' which was taken up by Al *Jolson. He worked as arranger for Waterson, Berlin & Snyder and, after military service in the First World War, for George M. *Cohan. In 1920 he was commissioned to write the score for *What's in a Name* which brought him into partnership with Jack *Yellen, with whom he was to write many successful shows and songs. From around 1929 they wrote songs for Hollywood films including: *Honky Tonk* (1929)—'I'm the last of the red hot mommas'; *The Glad Rag Doll* (1929)—'Glad rag doll'; *Chasing Rainbows* (1930)—'Happy days are here again'—used as the campaign song for Roosevelt's New Deal; *They Learned about Women* (1930); and *King of Jazz* (1930)—'A bench in the park', 'The song of the dawn', and 'Music hath charms'. Other songs by the duo included: 'Louisville Lou' (1923); 'Bagdad' (1924); 'Ain't that a grand and glorious feeling' (1927); 'Crazy words, crazy tune' (1927); and 'Ain't she sweet?' (1927); all typical hits of the 1920s.

Ahlert, Fred E. (*b* New York, 19 Sep. 1892; *d* New York, 20 Oct. 1953). American composer. Like many popular composers, he intended to practise law and to keep his interest in music (he was gifted with perfect pitch) as a hobby. But after working during college vacations as a café entertainer, he became even more interested in music and show-business and got a job with the New York publishers Waterson, Berlin & Snyder. He also worked as an arranger for Fred *Waring. His first song was published in 1914 and his first big success came in 1920 with the amply titled 'I'd love to fall asleep and wake up in my mammy's arms'. Other main successes were 'I'll get by' (1928); 'Mean to me' (1929); 'Walkin' my baby back home' (1930); 'Where the blue of the night meets the gold of the day' (1931); 'I'm gonna sit right down and write myself a letter' (1935), notably recorded by Fats *Waller, Bing *Crosby, and, a hit in 1957, by Billy Williams (1916–72); and 'Life is a song, let's sing it together' (1935). His most fruitful collaboration was with Roy Turk; others included Sam *Lewis, Joe *Young, and Edgar *Leslie.

Ain't Misbehavin'. Revue in two acts, produced at the Longacre Theatre on 9 May 1978. It was one of several successful attempts to put back the clock in the entertainment world by way of a certain vintage of popular music. Here, as the title suggests, the music was by Thomas 'Fats' *Waller, some of it written for shows and revues (including the famous title-song, originally written by Waller and Andy *Razaf for the revue **Hot Chocolates* produced at Connie's Inn in 1929). It had a run of 1604 performances, and was seen in London (Her Majesty's) 22 Mar. 1979.

Airmen's Songs. Airmen's songs do not go back so far nor do they have such a glorious history as the comparable literature that can be claimed by the navy or the army. Nevertheless there has now been a long enough period from the year 1912, when the Royal Flying Corps was formed from the Balloon Section of the Royal Engineers, for some history and material to accumulate. The oldest airman's song of all, according to C. H. Ward-Jackson (see below) is 'The bold aviator' or 'The dying airman' which arose from those days and was sung in messes in the First and Second World Wars. A parody of 'The tarpaulin jacket' and sung to that well-known and lugubrious tune, it will be familiar to many who never served with the RAF:

> Take the cylinders out of my kidneys,
> The connecting rod out of my brain (my brain)
> From the small of my back take the crankshaft
> And assemble the engine again.

Most RAF songs, as with their army equivalents, are plaintive, complaining, non-patriotic, blasphemous, and obscene—and not entirely for public consumption. The majority of them take old familiar tunes and add parodied words; e.g. 'We are Fred Karno's Air Corps' based on 'We are Fred Karno's Army' itself a crude use of the hymn 'The Church's one foundation'. One song which the Royal Naval Air Service made its own was 'Bless 'em all' written by a then serving member, Fred *Godfrey, in 1916—in a version not intended for publication. With cleaned-up words and music by Jimmy Hughes and Frank Lake, it became another universal favourite and has since been used as the unofficial Trooping Song of the RAF. Such parodies continue into the Second World War, as typified by 'He had to go and prang 'er in the hangar' written by two officers of 609 Squadron to the tune of 'She had to go and lose it at the Astor'; and the grim humour of 'We are McIndoe's Army, we are his guinea pigs'—Archibald McIndoe being the famous consulting plastic-surgeon to the RAF.

C. H. Ward-Jackson: *Airman's Song Book* (London, 1945).

Airs on a Shoestring. British revue. The intimate review had a remarkable revival in England during the 1950s. Perhaps it was a favourable sort of investment for those austerity years. Perhaps the mood of gentle cynicism was just right. Following the remarkable success of the *Lyric Revue* in 1951 and its predecessors and successors, some of the same team worked for the Royal Court Theatre (22 Apr. 1953) to notch up another success with the aptly named *Airs on a Shoestring*. A cast of future stars included Max *Adrian, Moyra Fraser (*b* 1923), Betty Marsden (*b* 1919), Denis Quilley (*b* 1933), and others who made the most of material supplied by up-and-coming writers like *Flanders and *Swann, John Pritchett, Richard *Addinsell, and Joyce *Grenfell, achieving a run of 772 performances.

Akst, Harry (*b* New York, 15 Aug. 1894; *d* Hollywood, 31 Mar. 1963). American composer. He was the son of a professional musician, Maurice Akst, who taught him to play the piano when he was five, and he was playing in public at the age of ten. It was intended that he should study music in Germany and in order to finance this he worked as a song-plugger in a music store. As he became fully involved in the music business, the trip to Germany never materialized. He worked first as a band agent, then as accompanist to Nora *Bayes and others. While serving in the army during the First World War, he started to write songs and had an early hit with 'Laddie boy' in 1918. During his service years he met Irving *Berlin whom he worked for after his return to civilian life. He wrote music for some Broadway revues and later for Hollywood films. His best-known songs were: 'Home again blues' (1920); 'Dinah' (1925); 'Baby face' (1926)—used in *Ziegfeld's *Glorifying the American Girl* (1930); 'Am I blue?' (1929)—sung by Ethel *Waters in *On With the Show*; and 'Stand up and cheer' (1934). During the Second World War he toured as an accompanist, entertaining the troops, and went with Al *Jolson to Korea in 1950. Akst made a few recordings as a pianist in the 1920s.

Albam, Manny [Emmanuel] (*b* Samana, Dominican Republic, 24 June 1922). Composer and arranger. He was a saxophonist with Bob Chester, Georgie Auld, and Boyd *Raeburn in the 1940s. Gaining experience as an arranger, he wrote for the Charlie *Spivak band for several years before military service 1945–6. Then he worked for Charlie *Barnet and Charlie Ventura (1916–92), and for Jerry Wald from 1949. In 1951 he became a full-time freelance arranger and writer, with his compositions used by Woody *Herman, Count *Basie, Stan *Kenton, and others. In the 1950s and 1960s he organized various recorded jazz sessions and wrote some extended jazz compositions, including 'Drum suite' for Terry Gibbs (*b* 1924).

Albany, Joe [Albani, Joseph] (*b* Atlantic City, 24 Jan. 1924; *d* New York, 11 Jan. 1988). American jazz pianist. He was playing jazz in California, inspired by Art *Tatum and Teddy *Wilson, at the age of 17; then toured with Benny *Carter and George Auld. He went to New York to work with Charlie *Parker and Stan Levey as a trio at the Door. Differences of opinion with Parker led to a split though each retained an admiration for the other. A recording session with Lester *Young in 1946 of semi-bop material for the Aladdin label impressed many with his talent and the clear, commanding tone of his playing. He worked with Stan *Getz in 1947. Thereafter his career was to be erratic and frequently interrupted by drug addiction, though he was with Charles *Mingus during the 1960s and appeared as a soloist in the 1970s. He spent most of his final years in Europe and London, occasionally playing and recording.

Albert, Eddie [Heimberger, Edward Albert] (*b* Rock Island, Ill., 22 Apr. 1908). American actor and singer. He played memorably in one or two Broadway musicals such as *The *Boys from Syracuse* (1938) and **Miss Liberty* (1949), and replaced Robert *Preston in *The *Music Man* in 1960.

Alda, Robert [d'Abruzzo, Alphonso Roberto] (*b* New York, 26 Feb. 1914). American stage and screen actor. He was mainly a straight actor in films, but is remembered for a successful portrayal of George *Gershwin in the 1945 film biography **Rhapsody in Blue*; also in *Cinderella Jones* (1946); *The Man I Love* (1947); and *April Showers* (1948). He made his mark in Broadway musicals by starring in **Guys and Dolls* (1950) and **What Makes Sammy Run?* (1964).

Aldrich, Ronnie [Ronald] (*b* Erith, Kent, 15 Feb. 1916). British conductor, arranger, saxophonist, and pianist. He studied at the Guildhall School of Music and his first musical job was playing in the Folkestone Municipal Orchestra. During the Second World War he joined the RAF and became pianist and arranger for the RAF dance orchestra, then directed by Sgt Jimmy Miller. It was later known as the Squadronaires and became one of the finest swing bands of the day: Aldrich took over the leadership after the war and led it until the 1950s, later conducting radio orchestras and recording and broadcasting with his own band. Latterly he worked as a freelance conductor, arranger, and pianist.

'Alexander's Ragtime Band'. Song with music and words by Irving *Berlin written in 1911. It was his first really big hit and established him as one of the most successful songwriters of modern times. The end of the chorus, 'if you want to hear that Swanee River played in ragtime', quotes from Stephen *Foster's 'Old folks at home'; otherwise the melody is in the ebullient pseudo-ragtime style (which descended from the early ragtime songs, rather than the classical rags) soon to be all the rage in *Tin Pan Alley. It has an excellent verse as well as an unforgettable chorus. The song was introduced by the composer in the 1911 annual Friar's Club show, and first performed publicly by the female baritone Emma Carus. It was immediately taken up by Al *Jolson, then with Lew *Dockstader's Minstrels, and used in vaudeville by Eddie Miller and Helen Vincent. It became immensely popular and sparked off a fruitful succession of such songs, many by Berlin himself.

Alford, Harry [Harold L.] (*b* Blissfield, Mich., 1883; *d* Chicago, 4 Mar. 1939). American composer. He became one of the best-known and most popular composers of marches since *Sousa; as a result, he and the English march composer Kenneth *Alford are often confused. Early in his career he was a church organist, later working in the musical theatre. He founded a bureau for the arranging of music for vaudeville acts which became much in demand. The University of Illinois commissioned him to write some of the first of the great football band extravaganzas, such as 'My hero' and 'The world is waiting for the sunrise', and he took a big part in the development of a flourishing area of school band activities. His two best-known marches are 'Purple carnival' and 'Glory of the gridiron'. Others include: 'Imp', 'Law and order', 'March of the Jackies', 'March of the Illini', 'Skyliner', 'Call of the Elk', and 'Hustler'.

Alford, Kenneth J. [pen-name adopted by Major Frederick Joseph Ricketts] (*b* London, 25 Feb. 1881; *d* Reigate, 15 May 1945). British composer and bandmaster. He joined the Royal Irish Regiment as a band boy at the age of 15, and was sent to the Royal Military School of Music at Kneller Hall in 1904. He was appointed Organist and Assistant Director there from 1906 to 1908, then became Bandmaster of the 2nd Battalion, the Argyll and Sutherland Highlanders (93rd). One of his first marches, 'The Thin Red Line' (1909), commemorates a nickname of which the regiment is particularly proud. The idea for his most famous march, 'Colonel Bogey', came in 1913. The composer is said to have been walking across the golf-course at St George's Hill in Weybridge, Surrey, and, not being a golfer, did not understand the significance of the cry of 'Fore!' The player whom he was holding up attracted his attention by whistling the two notes C and A. These stuck in the composer's mind and, that evening, became the opening notes of a new march, which years later took on a new lease of life as part of the score of the film *The Bridge on the River Kwai* (1957).

Marches of the First World War years included 'Cavalry of the Clouds', a tribute to the Royal Flying Corps; 'The Great Little Army' (1916), a reply to the Kaiser's reference to the British Expeditionary Force as 'a contemptible little army'; 'The Mad Major', a reference to a courageous officer in his regiment; and 'The Vanished Army', dedicated to all who died in the war. The band spent several weeks in New Zealand in 1926 and 'Old Panama' was inspired by their passage through the Canal on the way home. In 1928, Ricketts was commissioned as Director of Music of the Deal Division of the Royal Marines, and was transferred to the Plymouth Division two years later. He was promoted to the rank of Major just before the Second World War. The march 'HM Jollies' is dedicated to the Marines. He remained with the band during the early years of the war but ill-health forced his retirement in 1944.

During the war he wrote 'Eagle Squadron' in tribute to the Americans who volunteered to join the RAF, and 'The Army of the Nile' to commemorate Wavell's 1940–1 campaign in Egypt and Libya. Other marches include: 'The Middy', 'The voice of the guns', 'On the quarterdeck', 'By land and sea', and 'The Standard of St George'. While at Kneller Hall he would write marches for less gifted students to submit as exercises and one of these, the still popular 'Namur', he published under the pseudonym of W. V. Richards.

Alhambra Theatre. London theatre opened in Leicester Square on 18 Mar. 1854 and originally known as the Royal Panopticon of Science and Art (1854–8), then as the Alhambra Palace (1858). It existed in that burgeoning period when the popular musical theatre was still finding its bearings, entering the history of ballet, opera, musical comedy, and music-hall. It was built in Moorish style at a cost of £100,000. Under the management of Mr E. T. Smith, once manager of the *Vauxhall Gardens, its first seasons were given over to circus. Then a proper stage was built and it was first used as a music-hall in 1860. William Wilde was manager 1861–4 and Léotard, the famous acrobat, made his first British appearance there in 1861—'the man on the flying trapeze'. The name changed to the Royal Alhambra Palace in 1863. After rebuilding in 1864, it became a legitimate theatre in April 1871 (a music-hall and dancing licence having been refused in 1870) with its first production the operetta *Le Roi Carotte* by *Offenbach in 1872; followed by *The *Black Crook* imported from America. The next few years included: *La *Belle Hélène* (1873); *Whittington* (1874); **Chilpéric* (1875); *Die *Fledermaus* (1876); *Indigo* (1877); **Orphée aux Enfers* (1877); *La *Fille de Madame Angot* (1877); *La *Grande-Duchesse de Gérolstein* (1878); **Geneviève de Brabant* (1878); and *La *Périchole* (1878).

After it was destroyed by a fire in 1882, the Alhambra was rebuilt and re-opened in 1883, and there was a season of music-hall in 1884, but thereafter its stage was dominated by a succession of spectacular shows, ballets, and occasional operettas. The greatest period for British musicals came between 1912 and 1918, ending with the three Nat D. *Ayer shows—*The *Bing Boys Are Here* (1916); *The Bing Girls Are There* (1917); and *The Bing Boys on Broadway* (1918)—starring George *Robey and Violet *Loraine. While such large theatres as the Alhambra, seating 2208 and supporting a large orchestra and a permanent ballet troupe, still flourished, the English musical theatre was in a very healthy state. The Alhambra helped to speed its own end by being one of the first theatres to show a newsreel film: in 1896 they proudly advertised a film of the Derby run the day before. The theatre closed in 1936, was demolished in 1937, and an Odeon cinema was built on the site.

M. W. Disher: *The Personality of the Alhambra* (London, 1937).

Allegro. Musical play in two acts, with music by Richard *Rodgers, book and lyrics by Oscar *Hammerstein II. Produced at the Majestic Theater, New York, 10 Oct. 1947, directed by Agnes De Mille, with John Battles, Roberta Jonay, and Lisa Kirk, it was, coming after such massive hits as **Oklahoma!* and **Carousel,* considered a commercial failure, managing only 315 performances. It was an experimental piece, the action told by a chorus on-stage; after which Rodgers and Hammerstein returned to more conventional successes. The score, orchestrated by Robert Russell *Bennett, included: 'A fellow needs a girl', 'So far', 'You are never away', 'To have and to hold', 'Yatata, yatata, yatata', 'The gentleman is a dope', 'Allegro', and 'No other love'; but no special hit. The show never came to London; but it was revived occasionally in the USA.

Allen, Fred [Sullivan, John Florence] (*b* Cambridge, Mass., 31 May 1894; *d* New York, 17 Mar. 1956). American actor, comedian, and singer. He appeared in *vaudeville for many years becoming well-known as a revue artist. He was to become even better known as a radio star, appearing with his wife Portland Hoffa in the 1930s and 1940s. He was in *The *Passing Show* (1922); *The *Little Show* (1929); and *Three's a Crowd* (1930); and his films included: *Thanks a Million* (1935); *Sally, Irene and Mary* (1938); *Buck Benny Rides Again* (1940); and *Love Thy Neighbour* (1940).

F. Allen: *Much Ado About Me* (Boston, 1956).

Allen, Henry 'Red' (*b* Algiers, La., 7 Jan. 1908; *d* New York, 17 April 1967). American jazz trumpeter, vocalist, and composer. Son of a famous New Orleans brass band trumpeter, Henry Allen (1877–1952), he came from an entirely musical family. After playing in his father's band, he joined the Excelsior Band in 1924. He was with King *Oliver in St Louis in 1927, then worked on the riverboats with Fate *Marable, 1928–9. He went to New York to record with his own band before joining Luis *Russell 1929–32; and was with Fletcher *Henderson 1932–4, Mills Blue Rhythm Band 1934–7, and Louis *Armstrong 1937–40. He earned a high reputation as player, often considered to be a close rival to Armstrong, playing in a hard-hitting, somewhat frenetic manner. Allen frequently led and recorded with his own bands and appeared as a star soloist, visiting Europe for the first time in 1959 and touring Britain in 1963, 1964, and 1966. He played at Ryan's in New York in 1966 and was taken ill at the end of the year. After an operation, he toured Britain in 1967, returned to New York, and died of cancer.

Allison, Mose (*b* Tippo, Miss., 11 Nov. 1927). American pianist and vocalist. He became known locally before his first visit to New York in 1951, where he played for a year with Stan *Getz 1956–7, with Gerry *Mulligan 1958, then led his own trio. He visited Europe in 1959. A modern player with a traditional, blues flavouring, he had a big vogue in the 1960s as a pianist/singer, having a considerable hit with his recordings of 'Back Country suite' (1957) and 'Parchman Farm' (1958).

Allman Brothers Band. American Southern rock group formed in 1969 with the original line-up of Duane Allman (1946–71) (guitar), Gregg Allman (*b* 1947) (guitar, vocal, and keyboard), Richard 'Dickie' Betts (*b* 1943) (guitar), Berry Oakley (1948–72) (bass), Jai Johanny Johanson (*b* 1944) (drums), and Butch Trucks (drums). The Allmans first ran a group called Hour Glass in the 1960s which broke up in 1967. While working with Butch Trucks's band they joined up with other future members and the Allman Brothers Band was officially formed early in 1969. Playing a hard-hitting mixture of progressive rock and rhythm 'n' blues, the band attracted immediate attention on making its first LP for Phil Walden's Capricorn label in 1969. Its reputation grew rapidly and 10 more albums were to be made for Capricorn up to 1980. Duane Allman also played with various other groups. But in 1971 he was killed in a motor-cycle accident in Atlanta, aged only 24. The band decided to continue, only to have Berry Oakley killed in a similar accident in 1972. With new players recruited, they now moved towards a country-rock sound. Various internal wrangles almost split the group from time to time but it has kept going under the leadership of Gregg Allman and Dickie Betts.

T. Nolan: *The Allman Brothers Band* (New York, 1976).

Allyson, June [Geisman, Ella] (*b* Bronx, NY, 7 Oct. 1917). American singer and actress. She became known for her attractively husky singing voice in various musical films of the 1940s. After appearing in the Broadway musicals *Sing Out the News* (1938); **Very Warm for May* (1939); *Higher and Higher* (1940); **Panama Hattie* (1940); and **Best Foot Forward* (1941), she went to Hollywood to star in the film version of *Best Foot Forward* (1943) and thereafter appeared in such films as **Girl Crazy* (1943); *Thousands Cheer* (1943); *Meet the People* (1944); *Two Girls and a Sailor* (1944); *Music for Millions* (1945); *The Sailor Takes a Wife* (1946); *Two Sisters from Boston* (1946); *Till the Clouds Roll By* (1946); **Good News* (1947); *Words and Music* (1948); one of her most memorable successes being in *The Glenn Miller Story* (1954) with James Stewart. She appeared on TV with her husband (1945–63) Dick *Powell in the 1950s and 1960s and made a brief return to the stage in the 1970s.

J. Allyson & F. S. Leighton: *June Allyson* (New York, 1982).

Almanac Singers. Historic folk-music group formed in late 1940 by Pete *Seeger, Lee Hays, and Millard Lampell. After recording two albums of peace and union songs in 1941 for Folkways, they were joined by Woody *Guthrie. The group travelled throughout the USA singing such songs as 'Union maid', 'Talking Union', 'Which side are you on?' and 'The ballad of Harry Bridges'. During the early years of the war they did much to try to encourage America's participation with songs like Guthrie's 'Reuben James' and 'Round and round Hitler's grave'. At various times the group also included Sis Cunningham, Butch Hawes, Cisco Houston, Bess Lomax, and Arthur Stern. They were responsible for popularizing the word *hootenanny, which was much used in the 1960s. They disbanded in 1942, each pursuing a distinguished career in the folk-music world.

Almeida, Laurindo (*b* São Paulo, 2 Sept. 1917). Brazilian guitarist. He went to the USA in 1947 and soon made a considerable reputation with the Stan *Kenton band. Later he worked in Hollywood with his own trio, playing an unamplified guitar, proving himself a great and individual virtuoso, notably in the *bossa nova style. He wrote music for various films including *Viva Zapata!* (1952); *The Old Man and the Sea* (1958); and *Maracaibo* (1958).

'Aloha Oe' (Farewell to thee). Song with music and words by Liliuokalani (1838–1917), Princess Regent of Honolulu. During a Republican period of government the princess was imprisoned at Maunawili, Hawaii; she wrote the song during her captivity in 1878. She became Queen of Hawaii in 1891 and was deposed in 1893. The song was published in San Francisco in 1884 and later printed in Hawaii in *Songs of Hawaii* edited by A. R. Cunha (1902).

'Alouette'. Song of obscure origins, said, by Dr Marius Barbeau, in *Jongleur Songs of Old Quebec* (1962), to be of French origin. The first known printing, however, seems to have been in Canada in *A Pocket Song Book for the Use of Students and Graduates of McGill College* (Montreal, 1879), the first printing in France being in a periodical in 1893. It is possibly a French-Canadian worksong to be sung while plucking chickens.

Alpert, Herb (*b* Los Angeles, 31 Mar. 1937). American bandleader, trumpeter, vocalist, and composer. Having played the trumpet from the age of eight, he started in the music business as a songwriter working in collaboration with Lou Adler writing 'Wonderful world', which was made into a hit by Sam *Cooke. He first recorded, without success, under the name of Dore Alpert. While watching a bull fight in Tijuana, Mexico, he conceived the idea of a commercial version of the typical Tijuana brass band sound complete with spectator noises. He adapted one of his early pieces under the name of 'The lonely bull' which became his first best-seller in America in 1962. The Alpert 'Tijuana' sound was a mixture of basic rock, jazz, and traditional Mexican music, the unique timbre achieved by multi-recording the trumpet with a backing of such instruments as mandolin, tambourine, and maracas. Such items as 'Spanish flea' (1965), 'Taste of honey' (1965), and 'Zorba the Greek' (1966) became very popular in the USA and Europe. Alpert had No. 1 hits with 'This guy's in love with you' (1968) and 'Rise' (1979); and a number of best-selling LP albums, mainly on the A & M label which he founded with Jerry Moss in 1962, setting it on its way with 'The lonely bull'.

Alter, Louis (*b* Haverhill, Mass., 18 June 1902; *d* New York, 3 Nov. 1980). American composer. His first connection with the world of professional music came in the days of the silent film when he worked as a cinema pianist. Then he acted as stage accompanist (to Beatrice *Lillie among others), in his time off doing arrangements for a New York publisher. Through these various contacts he got his songs into various Broadway revues including *Earl Carroll's Vanities* (1925 and 1928); *A La Carte* (1927); *Americana* (1928); *Sweet and Low* (1930); and *Hold Your Horses* (1933). In 1929 he made a return to the cinema, now moving into the talkie era, and started writing music for films. His best-known songs included 'Love ain' nothin' but the blues' from *Lord Byron of Broadway* (1929); 'Isn't love the grandest thing', 'I've got sand in my shoes', and 'You turned the tables on me' in *Sing, Baby, Sing* (1936); 'Twilight on the trail' and 'Melody from the sky' in *Trail of the Lonesome Pine* (1936); 'Rainbow on the river' (1936), in the film of the same name; and 'Dolores' in *Las Vegas Nights* (1941). His instrumental numbers included 'Manhattan serenade', 'Manhattan moonlight', and 'Manhattan masquerade'.

Alwyn, William (*b* Northampton, 7 Nov. 1905; *d* Southwold, 11 Sept. 1985). English composer. He studied at the Royal Academy of Music 1920–3, leaving for a while to work as an orchestral musician and returning there in 1926 to take up a teaching post which he held for 28 years. He wrote a piano concerto in 1930 and scores for some 60 films between 1936 and 1963. These included: *They Flew Alone* (1942); *Squadron Leader X* (1942); *Escape to Danger* (1943); *Desert Victory* (1943); *The Way Ahead* (1944); *The Rake's Progress* (1945); *Odd Man Out* (1947); *Fallen Idol* (1948); *The Golden Salamander* (1950); *The Magic Box* (1951); *The Card* (1952); *The Silent Enemy* (1958); *Swiss Family Robinson* (1960); *The Naked Edge* (1961); and *The Running Man* (1963). He wrote an opera, *Miss Julie*, in 1977.

Ambrose, Bert (*b* London, 1897; *d* Leeds, 12 June 1971). British bandleader and violinist. After studying music in London he went to America for further study and played in theatre and symphony orchestras. In 1947 he became musical director at the Club de Vingt and led a band at the Palais Royal. He returned to London in 1920 to lead the band at the Embassy Club, going to New York again in 1922 but returning to the Embassy Club at the end of the year. He began his prolific recording career during this period. He left the Embassy in 1927 to form a band at the Mayfair Hotel, which included both British and American musicians, which was considered to be probably the best British dance band of the period, playing dance music with a strong Ellington-inspired jazz flavour, coming out in the arrangements written by Sid *Phillips and Bert Barnes. The band included many future bandleaders such as Ted *Heath, Lew *Stone, Stanley *Black, George *Melachrino, and George *Shearing in its ranks; and the vocalists Vera *Lynn, Sam Browne, Elsie Carlisle (1902–77), and Evelyn Dall. Ambrose continued to lead the band in the 1940s and 1950s before moving into musical and theatrical management; they appeared in the film *Soft Lights and Sweet Music* in 1935.

B. Amstell: *Don't Fuss, Mr Ambrose* (Tunbridge Wells, 1986).

Ameche, Don [Amici, Dominic Felix] (*b* Kenosha, Win., 31 May 1908). American film actor who featured in a number of musical films. He began his career on radio in 1930 and made his first noteworthy film, *Sins of Man*, in 1936. His first singing part was in *One in a Million* (1936) in which Sonja Henie (1910–69) made her film debut, followed by *Ramona* (1936); *You Can't Have Everything* (1937); *In Old Chicago* (1938); *Alexander's Ragtime Band* (1938); *The Three Musketeers* (1939); and a portrayal of Stephen *Foster in *Swanee River* (1939). He co-starred with Alice *Faye and Betty *Grable in the 1940s and later with Frances *Langford, with whom he shared a TV show in 1951. He appeared in the Broadway musicals **Silk Stockings* (1955); *Goldilocks* (1958); and *Henry, Sweet Henry* (1967).

America. American pop group formed in 1971 with Dewey Bunnell (*b* 1952), Gerry Beckley (*b* 1952), and Dan Peek (*b* 1950), guitarists and vocalists. They had first met while serving in the US Air Force in Britain; and they achieved a No. 1 hit in 1972 with 'A horse with no name'. Peek left in 1977, but after his return in 1982 the group regained some of their popularity and have since produced many worthy albums.

'America (My country! 'Tis of thee)'. National American song, music based on *'God save the King', words by Samuel Francis Smith (1808–95), written in 1831. It is now a national song ranking next only to 'The *Star-spangled Banner', The melody was first published in the USA *c.* 1761 and had various texts attached before Smith, a clergyman and professor of languages, made his version after a commission from music editor and publisher Lowell Mason (1792–1872), the organist at Park Street Church, Boston, where the song was first performed on 4 July 1831. It was first published in the hymn collection *The Choir* (Boston, 1832), appearing soon after as 'My country! 'Tis of thee'.

Americana. Revue with music by Con *Conrad and others. New York (Belmont Theatre) 26 July 1926 [224p]. The then unknown Helen *Morgan was seen in this revue by Jerome *Kern and as a result was asked to play the part of Julie in **Show Boat*, a part which established her name. A second edition was seen in New York (Lew Fields' Theatre) 30 Oct. 1928 [12p], and a third edition was staged in 1932.

American Bandstand. Influential USA rock music TV outlet. The equivalent of the UK *Top of the Pops*, it presents the latest discs and their performers to a live, dancing studio audience. Hosted by Dick Clark (*b* 1929), it began as a local Philadelphia TV show, but in 1957 became a daily late afternoon feature shown on the national ABC network, a showcase for what was happening in the pop world and its fickle charts; and, through its amateur audience, frequently establishing the latest dance crazes overnight. Clark also ran his own show, and was involved in the 'payola' scandal of 1960.

M. Shore and D. Clarke: *The History of American Bandstand* (New York, 1985).

'American in Paris, An'. Jazz-based tone poem by George *Gershwin first heard in New York in 1928. By this time Gershwin was an assured orchestrator, with a clear personal approach and the whole work is less self-conscious than *'Rhapsody in blue' (1924). It catches the spirit of the 1920s and the sounds of Paris at a time when creative Americans habitually went there to recharge their creative batteries as part of a complete artistic education.

American in Paris, An. MGM film of 1951 produced by Arthur *Freed and directed by Vincente *Minnelli with choreography by Gene *Kelly.

Based on the programmatic notion of Gershwin's work of the same name, it tells the story of an expatriate American painter (Gene Kelly) who falls in love with a charming young French girl (Leslie Caron, *b* 1931) who is already promised to an older man (Georges Guétary, *b* 1915) who saved her life during the Resistance. With the help of a mutual friend (Oscar *Levant) matters are sorted out and Kelly wins the day.

Ira Gershwin allowed the title to be used provided that all the music for the film was by his brother George, to its great benefit, of course, because it is full of Gershwin masterpieces including the title-piece used for a ballet with scenes done in the style of various famous French painters. The economics of film-making dictated that it was all filmed in America. It won five Academy Awards.

D. Knox: *The Magic Factory: How MGM Made An American in Paris* (New York, 1973).

'America the Beautiful'. Song with music by Samuel Augustus Ward (1847–1903) (tune 'Materna') and words by Katherine Lee Bates (1859–1929). The tune was first used for the words 'O Mother dear, Jerusalem' in *The Parish Choir*, Boston 12 July 1895, and words and music were first printed together in Boston in 1913. Katherine Bates was inspired to write the words after a visit to the summit of Pikes Peak in Colorado.

Amfitheatrof, Daniele [or Amfiteatrov]. (*b* St Petersburg, 29 Oct. 1901; *d* Rome, 7 June 1983). Russian composer and conductor. Of mixed Russian and Italian extraction, he studied music in St Petersburg and Prague and privately with Respighi in Rome. For many years he worked in Italy, becoming conductor and manager for Radio Turin. He visited the USA as a guest conductor and settled there in 1937, becoming associate conductor of the Minneapolis Symphony Orchestra. He moved to Hollywood in 1939, adopting American citizenship in 1944, and became a specialist writer of film background music with more than 80 scores to his credit.

These include: *Lassie Come Home* (1943); *I'll Be Seeing You* (1943); *An Act of Murder* (1948); *Another Part of the Forest* (1948); *Letter from an Unknown Woman* (1948); *The Lost Moment* (1948); *House of Strangers* (1949); *The Fan* (1949); *Storm Warning* (1951); *Rommel, Desert Fox* (1951); *Salome* (1953); *The Naked Jungle* (1954); *The Trial* (1955); *The Last Hunt* (1956); *The Mountain* (1956); *From Hell to Texas* (1958); *The Spanish Affair* (1958); *Edge of Eternity* (1959); *That Kind of Woman* (1959); *Heller in Pink Tights* (1960); *Major Dundee* (1965). The influence of Respighi shows throughout his music.

Ammons, Albert C. (*b* Chicago, 23 Sept. 1907; *d* Chicago, 2 Dec. 1949). American pianist. He has been credited with being one of the founder figures of *boogie-woogie, but he was a versatile pianist in other styles as well. He mainly played in Chicago with various bands, leading his own group at the Club DeLisa and elsewhere, 1934–8. He made his first recordings with his Rhythm Kings (for Decca) in January 1936, exhibiting a powerful, driving style full of blues feeling that did much to popularize boogie-woogie in the 1930s and 1940s, particularly in some pounding duets he recorded for Victor in 1941 in partnership with Pete *Johnson ('Cuttin' the boogie', 'Barrelhouse boogie', etc.). They occasionally worked as a trio with Meade Lux *Lewis . In 1938 he went to New York to appear at Carnegie Hall and was regularly heard at Café Society. He continued to work and record in Hollywood and Chicago until just before his final illness in the late 1940s. His son Gene Ammons (1925–74) was a well-known jazz tenor-saxophonist.

Ancliffe, Charles (*b* Kildare, 1880; *d* London, 20 Dec. 1952). Irish composer and conductor. Son of John Ancliffe, who was bandmaster of the 2nd Battalion the Somerset Light Infantry, 1894–1908, he joined his father's regiment in 1896. In 1900 he was appointed bandmaster of the 1st Battalion the South Wales Borderers and remained with them until he retired from the army in 1918. As a civilian he conducted the Scarborough Military Band and various light orchestras. He was a prolific composer of light music and is best remembered for his waltz 'Nights of gladness' which was written on Christmas Eve, 1912. Next in popularity was the intermezzo 'Secrets'. He wrote many waltzes, intermezzos, entr'actes, suites, and marches, including 'Castles in Spain', 'The Liberator', a tango, 'El Salute', and songs including 'Someday in somebody's eyes' (1924, *w*. Percy Edgar).

Andersen, Lale (*b* Bremerhaven, 23 Mar. 1910; *d* Vienna, 29 Aug. 1972). Danish singer. She came to international prominence in 1940 after her 1939 recording of the song *'Lili Marlene', composed in 1938 by Norbert Schultze. The first issue sold only 700 copies but it caught on later in the year when it was used as a signing-off tune for the German forces network in Yugoslavia. Later it was to become equally popular among the Allied armies. It made the husky-voiced singer a well-known star and was the first German recording to sell more than a million copies. Her career faltered a little after the war but in 1960 she recorded 'Never on Sunday' in German and achieved another best-seller. She won the *Song for Europe* contest in 1961 and an LP of her best-known recordings was issued in 1962. A film by Rainer Werner Fassbinder, *Lili Marleen* (1980), was based on her life.

Anderson, Cat [William Alonzo] (*b* Greenville, SC, 12 Sept. 1916; *d* California, 29 Apr. 1981). American jazz trumpeter. He played in local groups, then with Claude *Hopkins, Lucky *Millinder, Erskine *Hawkins, and Lionel *Hampton before he joined the Duke *Ellington band in 1944. He was to remain with it on and off until 1971, his high-register squealing relished by Ellington as an extra effect in his more advanced compositions of the 1950s and 1960s ('Madness in great ones' from *Such Sweet Thunder* is a typical example). He could also play in a driving, *Armstrong-inspired style. He went to Hollywood in 1971 and appeared in the film *Lady Sings the Blues*.

Anderson, Eddie (Edward] (*b* Oakland, 18 Sept. 1905; *d* Los Angeles, 28 Feb. 1977). American actor and singer. Short, agile comedian with a gravelly Louis *Armstrong-type voice who became immortal as Jack Benny's impertinent valet, Rochester. He was with Benny from 1937 to 1964 and appeared with him in the films *Man about Town* (1939); *Buck Benny Rides Again* (1940); *Love Thy Neighbour* (1940); and *What's Buzzin' Cousin?* (1943). Playing similar roles in his highly individual style, his first appearance was as Little Joe Jackson in the all-black *Cabin in the Sky* (1943). Other films included: *Show Boat* (1936); *The Music Goes Round* (1936); *Melody for Two* (1937); *Gold Diggers in Paris* (1938);; *Thanks for the Memory* (1938); *Going Places* (1938); *Honolulu* (1939); *Birth of the Blues* (1941); *Kiss the Boys Goodbye* (1941); *Star Spangled Rhythm* (1943); *Broadway Rhythm* (1944); *I Love a Bandleader* (1945).

Anderson, Ivie Marie (*b* Gilroy, Calif., 10 July 1905; *d* Los Angeles, 28 Dec. 1949). American jazz singer. She first began to be noticed in *Cotton Club revues, including the *Sissle and *Blake **Shuffle Along* (1921), and sang with various bands before joining Duke *Ellington at a Paramount Theatre engagement in New York in February 1931. Most critics agree that she was the most successful and appropriate vocalist that Ellington ever had and just as influential as soloists like *Carney, *Hodges, and *Nanton. She fitted well into the band's warm, swinging style of the 1930s and introduced such classics as 'It don't mean a thing' (1932). Greatly loved and admired by musicians within and without the band, she left in 1942 to open a restaurant in Los Angeles.

Anderson, John Murray (*b* St John's, Newfoundland, 20 Sept. 1886; *d* New York, 30 Jan. 1954). American impresario, director, producer, author, and lyricist. He made his Broadway reputation with the historic **Greenwich Village Follies* revues, 1919–24, many of which he wrote and which rivalled in lavishness the famous *Ziegfeld productions. He directed, produced, or wrote some 29 Broadway revues and 5 in London, including: *The League of Notions* (1921); *Music Box Revue* (1924); *Dearest Enemy* (1925); *John Murray Anderson's Almanac* (1929 and 1953); *Bow Bells* (1932); *Ziegfeld Follies* (1934, 1936, and 1943); *Life Begins at 8:40* (1934); and *Jumbo* (1935). He also directed the film *King of Jazz* (1930) and was director of Billy *Rose's Diamond Horseshoe club 1938-50. Among his numerous song lyrics 'A young man's fancy', written for *What's in a Name* (1920), remains the best-known.

J. M. Anderson: *Out Without my Rubbers* (New York, 1954).

Anderson, Leroy (*b* Cambridge, Mass., 29 June 1908; *d* Woodbury, Conn., 18 May 1975). American composer and conductor of Swedish ancestry. He studied at the New England Conservatory and Harvard, reading Scandinavian languages and music. He became organist and choirmaster, 1929–35, and orchestra director, 1929–30 and 1932–5, at Harvard. In 1935 he became a freelance composer and arranger, mainly working for the Boston 'Pops' Orchestra and Arthur Fiedler, with whom he was frequently a guest conductor. He served in the army 1942–6, and only started to make an international reputation thereafter when many of his light and often humorous compositions were widely recorded, many with himself as conductor.

Among his best-known compositions were: 'Jazz pizzicato' (1939); 'Jazz legato' (1944); 'Fiddle-faddle' (1947); 'Promenade' (1947); 'The syncopated clock' (1950); 'Sleigh ride' (1950, *add. w* Mitchell Parish); 'Blue tango' (1951, *w* Parish, 1952)—it reached the top of the Hit Parade in 1952; 'Belle of the ball' (1952); 'The typewriter' (1953)—used in the film *But Not For Me* (1959); 'The bugler's holiday' (1954); 'Plink-plank-plunk' (1954); 'Sandpaper ballet' (1955); and 'Forgotten dreams' (1955), which became his signature tune. He wrote the score of the highly melodic musical pantomime *Goldilocks* in 1958.

Anderson, Marian (*b* South Philadelphia, 17 Feb. 1902; *d* Portland, Oregon, 8 Apr. 1993). American singer. Born into a poor family, she sang in a local Baptist choir and went on to win prizes for singing in Philadelphia (1923) and New York (1925). She soon won renown, giving a Carnegie Hall concert in 1929 and appearing in London in 1930. She was particularly acclaimed for her singing of spirituals, doing much to promote their popularity, and was a great campaigner for black equality, earning many honours for her work in this respect, culminating in a US Congressional Medal on the occasion of her 75th birthday.

M. Anderson: *My Lord, What a Morning* (New York, 1956). J. Stevenson: *Marian Anderson: Singing for the World* (Chicago, 1963). S. P. Newman: *Marian Anderson: Lady from Philadelphia* (Philadelphia, 1965).

Anderson, Maxwell (*b* Atlantic, Pa., 15 Dec. 1888; *d* Stamford, Conn., 28 Feb. 1959). American playwright and lyricist. His best-known stage works include *What Price Glory?*, *Winterset*, and *Key Largo*. He wrote the librettos for two musicals with scores by Kurt *Weill: **Knickerbocker Holiday* (1938), which included 'September song' and 'It never was you'; and **Lost in the Stars* (1949); also songs in the films *Never Steal Anything Small* (1959) and *Midnight Lace* (1960).

Anderson, Moira (*b* Kirkintilloch, 5 June 1938). Scottish singer. She studied at the Royal Scottish Academy of Music, taking singing, piano, and clarinet, taught music in schools for two years, then auditioned for the BBC and made her first broadcast in 1959. She became known through her appearances in the TV *White Heather Club* in 1960 and soon had her own TV programme. She had her own show at the London Palladium in 1970. An accomplished singer, she naturally specialized in Scottish songs.

André Charlot's London Revue of 1924. The first of the series under *Charlot's name introduced New York to a remarkable new range of British talent. The music was supplied by Noël *Coward ('Parisian pierrot', 'There's life in the old girl yet'), Philip *Braham ('Limehouse blues'), and Ivor *Novello ('March with me', 'Night may have its sadness'), with additional numbers such as 'You were meant for me' (*Sissle and *Blake). Lyrics were by Coward, Ronald Jeans (1887–1973), Dion Titheradge (1889–1934), Douglas Furber (1885–1961), and others. Much of the material had been gathered from previous revues produced by Charlot. It opened at the Times Square Theatre, New York, on 9 Jan. 1924, with Beatrice *Lillie, Gertrude *Lawrence, Jack *Buchanan (later replaced by Nelson *Keys), Fred *Leslie, Douglas Furber, and Jessie *Matthews among the cast, and had 298 performances. Its main success was to come back in London (Prince of Wales Theatre, 1925) where, first billed as *Charlot's Revue* and somewhat amended but with a similar cast, it had a run of 513 performances.

Andrews, Julie [Wells, Julia Elizabeth] (*b* Walton-on-Thames, Surrey, 1 Oct. 1935). English singer and actress. The daughter and stepdaughter of stage performers, she first made her mark as a singing child prodigy on radio and in the revue *Starlight Roof* in 1947. The role of Polly in *The *Boy Friend* took her to New York in 1954 and thereafter her career was mainly in the USA. The important role of Eliza Doolittle in *My Fair Lady* (NY, 1956; London, 1958) sealed her reputation for playing parts of 'patrician innocence' and her fine, wide-ranging voice and impeccable diction led to many similar roles: **Camelot* (1960) and then mainly films and TV—**Mary Poppins* (1964); *The *Sound of Music* (1965); **Thoroughly Modern Millie* (1967); *Star!* (1968), in which she played the part of Gertrude *Lawrence; and *Darling Lili* (1969)—'Whistling away the dark'; also non-musical films.

J. Cottrell: *Julie Andrews* (London, 1968). R. Windeler: *Julie Andrews* (New York–London, 1970). L. Spindle: *Julie Andrews: a Bio-bibliography (Westport, Conn., 1989).*

Andrews Sisters. (Laverne, *b* Minneapolis, 6 July 1915; *d* 8 May 1967; Maxine, *b* Minneapolis, 3 Jan. 1918; Patti [Patricia], *b* Minneapolis, 16 Feb. 1920). American vocal trio who did much to create the 1940s vogue for their kind of rhythmic close-harmony singing. They started their career with Leon Belasco's Orchestra in New York. Their first major record hit, and subsequent signature tune, was 'Bei mir bist du schön' in 1937; thereafter they recorded prolifically, often in the company of other stars such as Bing *Crosby with whom they had many hits. They were the first singers of many well-known film songs such as 'Boogie woogie bugle boy' and 'Pennsylvania polka'. Their films, in which they always played themselves, included: *Argentine Nights* (1940); *Buck Privates* (1941)—'Boogie woogie bugle boy', 'You're a lucky fellow, Mr Smith'; *In the Navy* (1941); *Hold That Ghost* (1941); *What's Cookin'* (1942); *Private Buckaroos* (1942); *Give Out, Sisters* (1942)—'Pennsylvaania polka'; *How's About It?* (1943); *Always a Bridesmaid* (1943); *Follow the Boys* (1944); *Moonlight and Cactus* (1944); *Swingtime Johnny* (1944); *Hollywood Canteen* (1944)—'Don't fence me in' (*Porter); *Road to Rio* (1947); and the sound-tracks for *Make Mine Music* (1946) and *Melody Time* (1948). Patti Andrews had her own best-seller with 'I can dream, can't I?' (1949).

And So to Bed. Comedy with music that augured reviving success for the post-war British musical. The score by Vivian *Ellis was largely a pastiche of Restoration styles; the book by J. B. Fagan, its action set on a June evening in London during the year 1669—soon after the last entry in Samuel Pepys's diary—was mainly concerned with the diarist's bedtime romps. Opening at the New Theatre, London, on 17 Oct. 1951, it achieved 323 performances. The director was Wendy Toye (*b* 1917), Pepys was played by the frog-faced comedian Leslie *Henson, with Denis Quilley (*b* 1933), the American actress Jessie Royce Landis (1904–72), and Keith Michell (*b* 1928) in the cast; and musical direction was by *Mantovani.

Animals, The. British group formed in 1960 (as the Alan Price Combo) with the original personnel of Alan *Price (keyboard), Hilton Valentine (guitar), Charles Chandler (bass), and John Steel (drums); joined by Eric *Burdon (vocal) in 1962. One of the most important groups in the booming British rhythm 'n' blues scene of the 1960s, it started out in the Newcastle area and arrived in London in 1964. Here they achieved their first big hit (No. 1 in USA and UK) with the traditional 'House of the Rising Sun' (1964) inspired by Bob *Dylan's rendition. They had many hits under the guidance of producer Mickie Most without repeating the major success of this one, but nevertheless continued as a connoisseur's group with the major talents of Eric Burdon and Alan Price attracting a solid following. The group split up in 1966, Price forming his own group and Burdon moving to Los Angeles, where he formed New Animals, worked with Jimi *Hendrix, and then formed War, a highly successful *funk band. Price became a respectable TV figure with a wider following. There were reunions for recording and tours in 1976 and 1983.

Anka, Paul (*b* Ottawa, 30 July 1941). Canadian singer and composer. He made his first public appearance at the age of 10. By 1957 he had written 'Diana' which topped the American best-selling record charts for 13 weeks, and he became part of the high-school rock craze along with such figures as Tommy Sands (*b* 1937), Frankie *Avalon, and Fabian (*b* 1943). At 18 he embarked on his first world tour and one year later could claim to be a millionaire. He had written more than 200 songs by the age of 21, the list later including 'I love you baby' (1957); 'I lost my love last night' (1957); 'You are my destiny' (1957); 'Crazy love' (1958); 'Lonely boy' (1959); 'Put you hand on my shoulder' (1959); 'It doesn't matter any more' (1959)—Buddy *Holly's big hit; 'It's time to cry' (1959); 'Puppy love' (1960), 'My home town' (1960); 'Love me warm and tender' (1962); 'Can't get you out of my mind' (1968); 'She's a lady' (1970); 'We made it happen' (1971); 'Do I love you?' (1971); 'Jubilation' (1972); 'Let me try again' (1973); 'I'm not anyone' (1973); 'Anytime' (1975); and 'I don't like to sleep alone' (1975).

Annie. Highly successful Broadway musical based on Harold Gray's sentimental comic strip *Little Orphan Annie*. The show was conceived by its lyric-writer and director Martin Charnin, the book was written by Thomas Meehan and the score by Charles *Strouse.

Three characters from the strip, Annie, Daddy Warbucks, and Sandy, were put into an original story set in the depression years with little Annie longing to be rescued from the orphanage and a billionaire sugar daddy coming along in the shape of Oliver Warbucks. Wanting to adopt her, he overcomes the many obstacles in his way with the help of his pal, President Roosevelt, and all ends happily.

Tried out in Connecticut, the show reached the new Alvin Theatre on Broadway on 21 Apr. 1977 and became the third longest running musical of the 1970s with 2377 performances. One of the few hits to emerge from a Broadway musical in the 1970s was the song 'Tomorrow'. It was a great triumph for its first Annie, Andrea McArdle, and others who took on the various roles during the long run. It was staged in London (Victoria Palace) 2 May 1978, and a film version, directed by John Huston, with Albert Finney (*b* 1936), Ann Reinking (*b* 1949), and Carol Burnett (*b* 1933) was released in 1982.

Annie Get Your Gun. Record-breaking American musical comedy which, along with **Oklahoma!*, helped to establish a new tradition in the 1940s for original, realistic American-based stories and characterization, as well as a truly American musical style. A fictionalized story about a real Western gun-toting lady called Annie Oakley (1860–1926), the score was originally commissioned from Jerome *Kern, but he died in 1945 before he could make a start on it. It is open to surmise as to whether his contribution would have had the same effect as the punchy, melodic, homespun score that Irving *Berlin composed.

With Ethel *Merman a raucously ideal Annie, the show achieved 1147 performances in New York (Imperial Theatre) from 16 May 1946; and, with Dolores *Gray in the lead, 1304 in London (Coliseum) from 7 June 1947. It has been frequently revived and was filmed in 1950 with Betty *Hutton and Howard *Keel. A classic of the musical theatre, its wholly memorable score includes such lasting items as: 'Doin' what comes naturally', 'The girl that I marry', 'You can't get a man with a gun', 'There's no business like show business', 'They say it's wonderful', 'My defenses are down', 'I got the sun in the mornin'', and 'Anything you can do'.

'Annie Laurie'. Scottish song first published anonymously in vol. 3 of a 'new edition' of *Vocal Melodies of Scotland* arranged by Finlay Dun and John Thomson and published in Edinburgh in 1838. It was published separately soon after. Alicia Ann Spottiswood (1810–1900), later Lady John Douglas Scott, claimed to have written the tune, adapting an air she had originally written to an old ballad, 'Kempye Kaye', probably drawing on a traditional air. The story of the song is based on a real Annie Laurie, youngest daughter of Sir Robert Laurie of Maxwelton, who died in 1764 at the age of 83. She rejected her lover, a soldier-poet William Douglas of Fingland, who wrote two verses of the poem which (according to Robert Ford) first appeared in an Edinburgh paper and 'created quite a sensation'. This publication has not been traced, the first known available printing being in a *Ballad Book* published in 1823. When Lady Scott edited the song and set it to music she left Douglas's first verse intact, altered the second, and added a third.

'Annie Lisle'. Song with words by H. S. Thompson, published in 1858. It seems to have been very popular in the American college world, as the melody was later used for Cornell University's 'Alma Mater'—'Far above Cayuga's Waters', words by Archibald C. Weeks (1850–1927) and Wilmot M. Smith (1852–1906)—and utilized by several other colleges. Its original composer has not been traced.

Ansell, John (*b* London, 26 Mar. 1874; *d* Marlow-on-Thames, 14 Dec. 1948). British composer and conductor. He studied at the Guildhall School of Music under Hamish MacCunn, and was a violinist in various London orchestras before being appointed musical director of the Playhouse, 1907–13, composing the incidental music to all the plays produced there during that period. He was musical director of the *Alhambra from Nov. 1913 to 1920; musical director of *The Little Whopper* at the Shaftesbury Theatre (1920) and *The Naughty Princess* at the Adelphi (1920); later musical director of the Winter Garden Theatre. He composed incidental music to the successful *The Young Visiters* (Court, 1920) and his musical scores included: *The Toymaker of Nuremburg* (1910); *Rip Van Winkle* (1911); *The King's Bride* (1911); *Eastward Ho!* (1919). His popular light musical pieces included: 'Aubade', 'Three Irish pictures', 'Three Irish dances', 'Plymouth Hoe', 'A children's suite', and a ballet, 'The Shoe'.

Anthony, Ray (*b* Cleveland, 22 Jan. 1922). American trumpet-player, bandleader, and composer. He played with the bands of Al Donahue, Jimmy *Dorsey, and Glenn *Miller before navy service in the Second World War. After the war he led his own band and recorded prolifically for Capitol in the early 1950s. He based his orchestral style on Glenn Miller, but his own trumpet sound gave the band a blend of sweetness and swing which pleased a large public. In the 1960s economics reduced the band to a sextet which became a popular club and TV attraction. He appeared with his band in the films *Daddy Long Legs* (1955); *The Girl Can't Help It* (1957); *This Could Be the Night* (1957); *Girls' Town* (1959); *The Beat Generation* (1959); and acted in *Night of the Quarter Moon* (1959) and *Five Pennies* (1959). In collaboration with George Williams he wrote such pieces as 'Skycoach', 'Trumpet boogie', 'Thunderbird', 'Cook's tour', 'The fox', and 'Rollin' home'.

Anything Goes. American musical comedy, notable as the source of many popular classics including the title-song. With a sparkling score by Cole *Porter and book by Guy *Bolton and P. G. *Wodehouse, it achieved a then excellent run of 420 performances at New York's Alvin Theatre, 21 Nov. 1934. The cast included Ethel *Merman (lastingly connected with some of its hits), William *Gaxton, Victor *Moore, and Bettina Hall (*b* 1906), and the producer was Howard *Lindsay. In London it opened at the Palace Theatre 14 June 1935, with Sydney Howard (1886–1960), Peter Haddon (1898–1962), Jack *Whiting, Adele Dixon

(1908–92), and Jeanne Aubert, and ran for 261 performances.

The show was the idea of Vinton *Freedley who, following an Alvin Theatre failure with *Pardon my English* in 1933, thought up his ideal musical comedy to be produced by this team and played by this cast. It started out as *Bon Voyage*, then became *Hard to Get*, but the title was changed and the shipwreck story scrapped when a real-life shipwreck tragedy was inopportunely in the news. Re-written by Howard Lindsay and Russell *Crouse, it now became a comedy of doubtful characters on board a ship with its new title chosen as a whimsical reflection of the circumstances of its creation. Ethel Merman (later replaced by Benay Venuta) was involved in three hits which she made her own—'I get a kick out of you', 'Blow, Gabriel, blow', and the duet 'You're the top' which she sang with William Gaxton. Other songs were 'There'll always be a lady fair', 'All through the night', 'Anything goes', and 'The gypsy in me'. A definitive recording of 'You're the top' was made in England by Jack Whiting and Jeanne Aubert.

It was filmed in 1936 with Ethel Merman supported by Bing *Crosby and Charles Ruggles (1886–1970); and again in 1956, in a much adulterated version that had little to do with the original, again starring Crosby with Mitzi Gaynor (*b* 1930), Donald *O'Connor, and Zizi Jeanmaire (*b* 1924), with additional songs by Jimmy *Van Heusen and Sammy *Cahn. The show was revived off-Broadway in 1962 with more Porter songs interpolated and ran for 239 performances; another revival, with Marian Montgomery, was seen in London (Saville) 18 Nov. 1969; and a 1987 Lincoln Center revival, starring Patty Lupone, ran for two years and went to London.

Apache dance. A popular cabaret feature in a pseudo-sadistic vein with a lightly clad lady being thrown around and whipped by a macho male. She clearly loved it, as did the sensation-seeking audience. It was first introduced by *Mistinguett and Max Dearly at the Moulin Rouge in Paris in 1908. The unlikely choice of music was the 'Valse de rayons' from *Offenbach's ballet *Le Papillon*, first produced at the Opéra in Nov. 1860. In La Revue de Moulin Rouge it was billed as 'Valse Chaloupée' (the Apache's Dance); becoming 'La Danse des Apaches' when it was seen in London in the Empire Ballet *A Day in Paris* (1908) danced by Beatrice Collier and Fred Farren.

Apollo Theatre. Famous theatre in Harlem, New York, situated at 253 West 125th Street between Seventh and Eighth Avenues, originally known as Hurtig and Seamon's Music Hall. It became the Apollo in 1934 and soon became the major outlet for black entertainers, singers, dancers, comedians, and famous jazz and swing bands. A regular Wednesday amateur night marked the beginnings of a career for many later famous names. Among the professional entertainers (the best in their field) were to be heard such stars as Duke *Ellington, Billie *Holiday, Count *Basie, Ella *Fitzgerald, Bill 'Bojangles' *Robinson, and the Nicholas Brothers. It was a hotbed for the rhythm 'n' blues revolution of the 1950s and in the 1970s featured such stars as Dionne *Warwick and Smokey *Robinson. It closed in 1975 after a shooting incident, re-opening later, and closing again in 1983. It is now used as a cable TV centre.

J. Schiffman: *Uptown: the Story of Harlem's Apollo Theater* (New York, 1971). T. Fox: *Showtime at the Apollo* (New York–London, 1983).

Applause. Musical with score by Charles *Strouse, lyrics by Lee *Adams, and book by Betty *Comden and Adolph *Green based on the 1950 film *All About Eve* and a story by Mary Orr. After tryouts in Baltimore and Detroit, it opened at the Palace in New York, 30 Mar. 1970, becoming a personal stage triumph for the film star Lauren Bacall (*b* 1924) as the actress Margo Channing, who befriends a fan, Eve Harrington, who then proceeds to scheme against her benefactor both in the theatre and in real life. Eve was originally played by Penny Fuller, later replaced in the long run of 896 performances by Anne Baxter (*b* 1923), who had played the role in the original film, and Arlene Dahl (*b* 1924). Lauren Bacall was also in the London production at Her Majesty's Theatre 16 Nov. 1972.

Apple Sauce. Popular London wartime revue written by George Black (1890–1945) and others with music by Michael *Carr and Jack *Strachey. It opened at the Holborn Empire on 27 Aug. 1940 and ran for 462 performances, transferring to the London Palladium on 5 Mar. 1941 when its run was interrupted by the blitz and the destruction of the Holborn Empire. The star was the Cockney comedian Max Miller (1895–1963) supported by Doris Hare (*b* 1905) and the new 'Forces' Sweetheart' Vera *Lynn. At the Palladium, Florence *Desmond replaced Doris Hare.

Apple Tree, The. An entertainment made up of three one-act musicals, initially intended to have a linking 'Garden of Eden' theme; but they ended up with nothing much in common. The books by Sheldon *Harnick and Jerry *Ross were based on (1) Mark Twain's story *The Diary of Adam and Eve*; (2) Frank R. Stockton's *The Lady or the Tiger?* (the subject of a musical as far back as 1888) in which a man's fate is decided by the door he enters; and (3) Jules Feiffer's *Passionella*, a story of a chimney sweep who becomes a movie star. This mixture, linked by the music of Jerry *Bock (orch. Eddie *Sauter), proved intriguing enough to run for 463 performances, opening at the Shubert Theatre on 18 Oct. 1966. The cast included Barbara Harris, Larry Blyden, and Alan Alda and the musical director was Elliott *Lawrence.

Arcadians, The. Highly successful, tuneful, and long-lasting musical play with a score by Lionel *Monckton and Howard *Talbot, book by Mark

Ambient (1860–1937) and Alexander M. Thompson, lyrics by Arthur *Wimperis. It opened at the Shaftesbury Theatre, London, on 28 Apr. 1909 where it was to run for 809 performances. It has since been frequently revived and is a great favourite with amateur societies.

A caterer-cum-aviator, James Smith, crash-lands in Arcady and becomes an Arcadian himself renamed Simplicitas. The plot that ensues is both absurd and complicated but is made highly palatable by a score rich in good songs including 'The pipes of Pan', sung by the Arcadian girl Sombra, 'The girl with a brogue', sung with great success by Phyllis *Dare in the role of Eileen, the catchy 'Charming weather' and 'Half-past two', and the optimistic 'My motter' sung with deep pessimism by gloom specialist Alfred Lester (1875–1925) as a jockey called Peter Doody; and many more. Also in the cast were Dan Rolyat (1882–1927), Harry *Welchman, Nelson *Keys, Akerman May (1867–1933), Florence Smithson (1884–1936), Ada Blanche (1862–1953), and Cicely *Courtneidge. It never had the same success in America, achieving only 193 performances at the Liberty Theatre from 17 Jan. 1910.

Archer, Harry [Auracher, Harry] (*b* Creston, Iowa, 21 Feb. 1888; *d* New York, 23 Apr. 1960). American composer and musical director. He was an early member of the Paul *Whiteman orchestra and an accomplished player of most brass instruments; and he had led his own orchestra before joining Whiteman. One of his musical scores, *Little Jesse James* (1923), enjoyed success owing to the popularity of the song 'I love you' which became one of the top hits of the 1920s. He also wrote the scores of *The Pearl Maiden* (1912); *Love for Sale* (1915); *Frivolities of 1920* (1920); *Peek-a-boo* (1922); *Paradise Alley* (1924); *My Girl* (1924); *Merry, Merry* (1924); *Twinkle, Twinkle* (1926); and *Lucky Break* (1934).

Arlen, Harold [Arluck, Hyman] (*b* Buffalo, 15 Feb. 1905; *d* New York, 23 Apr. 1986). American composer. His father was a cantor in the local synagogue and Arlen's first musical experience was in the synagogue choir. Most of his musical knowledge was gained from his mother. Leaving school as a teenager, he began to earn a living as a pianist on lake steamers and in nightclubs and he formed his own three-piece band, the Buffalodians, with whom he recorded in 1926. In New York he worked as a jazz band singer, pianist, and arranger and led his own group in a Broadway café. Until then he had mainly thought of himself as a vocalist with, it is said, a *Sinatra-like approach to ballads. He was noticed by the composer Vincent *Youmans who gave him a part in *Great Day* (1929). At a rehearsal he wrote a song, in collaboration with lyric-writer Ted *Koehler, called 'Get happy', which convinced the show's backers that he had great potential as a songwriter. It was used in *9:15 Revue* and was made into a hit by the singer Ruth *Etting. He worked for a time with the publishers J. H. Remick and, in the 1930s, recorded as a singer with Red *Nichols, Benny *Goodman, Joe *Venuti, and Eddie *Duchin.

During the 1930s he wrote many songs, often in collaboration with Koehler, for revues at the *Cotton Club, which are now classics—'Between the devil and the deep blue sea', 'Stormy weather', etc.—many of them introduced by Duke *Ellington and his vocalist Ivie *Anderson. His theatre scores included **Earl Carroll's Vanities* (1930 and 1932)—'I gotta right to sing the blues'; *You Said It* (1931); *Life Begins at 8:40* (1934); *The Show is On* (1936); *Hooray for What?* (1937); he contributed to the revue *Star and Garter* (1942)—'Blues in the night'; followed by his most successful scores like **Bloomer Girl* (1944)—'Right as the rain', 'When the boys come home'; **St Louis Woman* (1946)—'Legalize my name', 'Any place I hang my hat is home', 'Come rain or come shine'; **House of Flowers* (1954); *Jamaica* (1957); *Saratoga* (1959); and *Free and Easy* (1959). He was a prolific writer for films which included *The Big Broadcast* (1932); *Manhattan Parade* (1932); *Take a Chance* (1933)—'It's only a paper moon'; *Let's Fall In Love* (1934); *Strike Me Pink* (1936); *The Singing Kid* (1936)—'You're the cure for what ails me'; *Stage Struck* (1936); **Gold Diggers of 1937* (1936); **Artists and Models* (1937); *Love Affair* (1939); **Babes in Arms* (1939); *At the Circus* (1939)—'Two blind loves'; *Blues in the Night* (1941)—'Blues in the night', 'This time the dream's on me'; *Road to Zanzibar* (1941); *Captains of the Clouds* (1942); **Rio Rita* (1942); *Star-Spangled Rhythm* (1942)—'That old black magic' memorably danced to by Vera Zorina (*b* 1917); **Cabin in the Sky* (1943)—'Happiness is a thing called Joe'; *The Sky's the Limit* (1943)—'One for my baby'; *They Got Me Covered* (1943); *Up in Arms* (1944)—'Now I know'; **Kismet* (1944); *Here Come the Waves* (1944)—'Ac-cent-tchu-ate the positive' (*w* Johnny *Mercer), sung by Bing *Crosby and Sonny Tufts (1911–70), 'Tess's torch song'; *Out of this World* (1945); *Casbah* (1948); *My Blue Heaven* (1950); *Summer Stock* (1950); *The Petty Girl* (1950)—'Fancy free'; *Mr Imperium* (1951); *The Farmer Takes a Wife* (1953)—'Today I love ev'rybody'; *Down among the Sheltering Palms* (1953); *A *Star is Born* (1954)—'The man that got away'; and *The Country Girl* (1954)—'The search is through'.

His biggest film success was *The *Wizard of Oz* in 1939 with Judy *Garland and such songs (words by E. Y. *Harburg) as 'If I only had a heart', 'We're off to see the Wizard', 'Follow the yellow brick road', and 'Somewhere over the rainbow'. This last song became, as one writer said, 'an anthem of hope for a generation of children groping its way out of the Depression'. Judy Garland said: 'It's kind of sacred. I don't want anybody anywhere to lose the thing they have about that song.' But it was not typical of Arlen. His best-known songs have a bluesy, jazz-tinged character (as much as or more than those of his friend George *Gershwin) that made them particularly attractive to black artists and bands such as Duke Ellington's; and it was those that were written in the rich Cotton Club years (mainly with Ted Koehler, E. Y. Harburg, or Johnny Mercer) that have been his most lasting contributions to the popular song repertoire—'Get happy' (1930); 'Between the devil and the deep blue sea' (1931); 'Kickin' the gong around' (1931); 'I've got the world on a string' (1932); 'Minnie the Moocher's wedding day' (1932); 'It's only a paper moon' (1932); 'Stormy weather' (1932); 'Raisin' the rent' (1933); 'As long as I live' (1934); and so on. Some effective instrumental works include: 'Minor gaff' (1926); 'Buffalo rhythm' (1927); 'Rhythmic moments' (1928); 'Mood in six minutes' (1935); and 'American minuet' (1939).

E. Jablonski: *Harold Arlen: Happy With the Blues* (New York, 1961). See also A. Wilder: *American Popular Song* (New York, 1972).

Armatrading, Joan (*b* St Kitts, 9 Dec. 1950). British singer, guitarist, and composer. She came to England with her family in 1958 and settled in Birmingham where she was in amateur theatricals and sang locally. She began to write songs in collaboration with another West Indian immigrant, Pam Nester, and they went to London in 1971 where disagreements over the Cube album, *Whatever's For Us*, led to the breakup of the partnership. After two quiet years she began to record for A & M, now writing her own lyrics, and producing the album *Back to the Night* (1975). She had a hit in 1976 with 'Love and affection' and gradually achieved a large following. Since 1978 she has been a popular entertainer all over Europe.

S. Mayes: *Joan Armatrading* (London, 1990).

Armstrong, Harry [Henry W.] (*b* Somerville, Mass., 22 July 1879; *d* New York, 28 Feb. 1951). American composer and singer. After an early career as a boxer, he became a pianist at Coney Island and worked for a New York publisher. Later he was a booking agent and producer. On the strength of his immortal hit 'Sweet Adeline' (*w* Richard Husch Gerard), originally written in 1896 as 'Down home in old New England', published under the new title in 1903, and popularized by the Qua ker City Quartette, he became a vaudeville entertainer. His other songs included: 'Shore acres' (1900, *w* Vincent P. Bryan); 'Nellie dear' (1906, *w* Billy Clarke); 'I love my wife, but oh, you kid' (1909, *w* Clarke).

Armstrong, Lil [Hardin, Lillian] (*b* Memphis, 3 Feb. 1898; *d* Chicago, 27 Aug. 1971). American pianist, bandleader, and composer. A pioneer jazz pianist, she played in King *Oliver's band in Chicago from 1921 and there met Louis *Armstrong, whom she married in 1924. The marriage lasted until 1938. She played in the classic Hot Five and Hot Seven recordings of 1925–7 and continued a career as a jazz pianist until her death in 1971 at a concert given as a memorial tribute to Louis Armstrong. She wrote a number of standard jazz tunes, including: 'Jazz lips' (1926); 'Papa dip' (1926); 'Perdido Street blues' (1926); 'Skit-dat-de-dat' (1926); 'Too tight blues' (1926); and 'Struttin' with some barbecue' (with Louis Armstrong, 1927).

Armstrong, [Daniel] **Louis 'Satchmo'** (*b* New Orleans, 4 Aug. 1901; *d* New York, 6 July 1971). American jazz trumpeter, singer, bandleader, actor, and composer. Considered to be one of the greatest of all jazz musicians and one of the world's finest trumpet players, the possessor of a phenomenal natural technique and an inherent jazz sense, he learned to play the cornet in a waifs' home in New Orleans where he had been sent for firing his stepfather's gun in the street during a New Year's Eve celebration. He worked at various manual jobs before taking up a musical career, playing mainly in the Storyville district of New Orleans. In 1919 he joined Kid *Ory's band, replacing King *Oliver. Later in 1919 he was playing on the Mississippi riverboats and in various New Orleans clubs. In 1922 he was asked by Oliver to join his famous Creole Jazz Band in Chicago as second cornet. He recorded with them for the Gennett label, producing a series of performances of items such as 'Dippermouth blues' and 'Canal Street blues' that have become some of the most famous and influential of any early jazz recordings. In 1924 he married pianist Lil Hardin and left Oliver to play at the Dreamland Ballroom in Chicago, later that year joining Fletcher *Henderson in New York.

Returning to Chicago in 1925, he started making his famous Hot Five recordings with such players as Johnny *Dodds, Kid Ory, Lil *Armstrong, and Johnny St Cyr (1890–1966), and played at the Dreamland and with Erskine Tate's Vendome Theater band. In 1926 he was with the Carroll Dickerson band which he took over and led at the Savoy Ballroom. His exceptional solos, with their vocalized line and inherent vibrato, rapidly became a model for all advanced jazz musicians, including players on other instruments such as saxophonist Coleman *Hawkins and pianist Earl *Hines. Now established on the trumpet, he recorded such influential numbers as 'Savoy blues', 'Potato head blues', 'Willie the Weeper', 'Weary blues', and 'Ory's Creole trombone'; later the classic 'West End blues', 'Skip the gutter', and 'Weather bird rag'. He went to New York to play at Connie's Inn and in 1932 visited England and played at the Palladium. He came again in 1934 and toured Europe. His scat and trumpet-phrased singing became as influential as his playing and he began to appear in various jazz-oriented films. Many deplored his hokum and an apparent 'Uncle Tom' attitude, but Armstrong was a dedicated promoter of his race. His playing remained magnificent until the end; although some of the later All Star groups he led from *c.* 1947 onwards lacked the integrated flavour that some of his followers expected. They included, at times, such eminent musicians as Edmond Hall (1901–67) 1955–8, Trummy *Young, Jack *Teagarden, Billy Kyle (1914–66) 1953–66, Earl *Hines, and Barney *Bigard. He toured Europe in 1949, 1952, and 1956 and visited Africa like a king in 1957.

Thereafter he mainly worked in films, TV, and radio, with occasional starring appearances in concerts. His recording of 'Hello Dolly' became a best-seller in 1964, as did 'What a wonderful world' in 1970, and he remained a unique performer until his last years. His film appearances included: *Pennies from Heaven* (1936); **Cabin in the Sky* (1943); *New Orleans* (1947); *Glory Alley* (1951); *The Glenn Miller Story* (1954); **High Society* (1956); *Satchmo the Great* (1957); *The Five Pennies* (1959); *Paris Blues* (1961); *A Man Called Adam* (1966); and **Hello, Dolly!* (1969). Armstrong composed or had a hand in various items that have become jazz standards such as: 'I wish I could shimmy like my Sister Kate' (with Clarence *Williams, 1919); 'Dippermouth blues' (with King Oliver, 1923, later re-arranged as 'Sugar foot stomp'); 'Coal cart blues' (with Lil Hardin, 1925); 'Gut bucket blues' (1925); 'Drop that sack' (1926); 'Cornet chop suey' (1926); 'Wild man blues' (with Jelly Roll *Morton, 1927); 'Potato head blues' (1927); 'Struttin' with some barbecue' (with Lil Armstrong, 1927); 'Beau Koo Jack' (with Alex *Hill, 1928); 'Muggles' (with Earl Hines, 1929); 'Knockin' a jug' (with Eddie *Condon, 1929); 'In the barrel' (1929); 'Hear me talkin' to ya' (with Don *Redman, 1929); 'Ol' man Mose' (with Zilmer Randolph, 1938); and 'Back o' town blues' (with Luis *Russell, 1945).

Armstrong emerged as the first inspirational genius of jazz in the 1920s, astonishing all who heard him with the effortlessly imaginative and lyrical quality of his improvisations. These were not necessarily of a complex nature, frequently keeping close to the thematic material, but showed a flexibility of tone and phrasing, an inherent sense of beat which could bring life to any ensemble he played in, and a general sense of freedom and self-expression that first revealed the potential of jazz and the importance of the individual soloist. So great was Armstrong's first leap into the unknown that he never needed to, or could, change or surpass his own early creations which still sound as fresh and un-dated today, while his later work sounded uniquely effective in almost any new context. He was an immediate influence on musicians who worked with him, not only the long succession of trumpet players who were clearly indebted to his example, but everyone else who was capable of transforming his ideas to their own instruments, once he had revealed the possibilities. There was no predecessor in jazz of anything like the same stature. Although his natural musical flair must have absorbed hints of the music's possibilities from players like *Bolden and Oliver, he wove these threads into his own prophetic thinking, thus releasing jazz from the bondage of its limited early styles and making it into a showcase for the inspirational soloist.

L. Armstrong: *Swing That Music* (New York–London, 1936). R. Goffin: *Louis Armstrong: Roi du Jazz* (Paris, 1947; as *Horn of Plenty*, New York, 1947; repr. 1977). H. Panassié: *Louis Armstrong* (Paris, 1947; New York, 1971). L. Armstrong: *Satchmo: my Life in New Orleans* (New York, 1953; London, 1955). A. McCarthy: *Louis Armstrong* (London, 1960; New York, 1961). M. Jones and J. Chilton: *Louis: the Louis Armstrong Story* (London, 1971; Boston, 1972). J. L. Collier: *Louis Armstrong, an American Genius* (New York, 1983; London, 1984).

Arndt, Felix (*b* New York, 20 May 1889; *d* Harmon-on-Hudson, NY, 16 Oct. 1918). American composer and pianist. He studied at the New York Conservatory and became organist at Trinity Church, New York, before working as a pianist with various music publishers and leading his own orchestra. He made more than 3000 piano rolls of light and popular classics. His wife Nola Arndt (1889–1977), after whom his most famous piece was named, was also a composer and well-known as a singer and teacher. 'Nola' (written in 1915 with words added in 1924 by James F. Burns) was his chief claim to fame; though he wrote many more pieces, such as 'Polly' (1916), in similar vein.

Arnheim, Gus (*b* Philadelphia, 11 Sept. 1897; *d* Los Angeles, 19 Jan. 1955). American bandleader. Most of his career was on the West Coast of the USA, though he first worked as a pianist in Chicago. With Abe *Lyman he formed the Syncopated Five, then became accompanist to Sophie *Tucker. He formed his own band in 1928 and toured Europe and America before becoming resident bandleader at the Cocoanut Grove in Los Angeles. He worked with Bing *Crosby on and off in the 1930s, was active throughout the 1940s, then retired, making a brief comeback in 1954. He composed popular songs including: 'I cried for you' (1923); 'Mandalay' (1924); 'It must be true' (1930); 'Sweet and lovely' (1931); 'I'm gonna get you' (1931); 'After all is said and done' (1932). With his band he appeared in the films *Broadway Street Girl* (1929); *Puttin' on the Ritz* (1930); *Cuban Love Song* (1931); *Flying High* (1931); *Trocadero* (1944). The Arnheim band had a distinctive, closely-knit, light and swinging quality, with early arrangements by Jimmy Grier. Russ *Columbo and Donald Novis were among the featured vocalists; Woody *Herman, Joe Dixon (*b* 1917), and Irving Fazola were members of the band. In 1936 the band reached its peak of smooth, swinging excellence when Budd *Johnson was the principal arranger, and Stan *Kenton added his talents in 1937.

Arnold, Eddy [Richard Edward] (*b* Henderson, Tenn., 15 May 1918). American Country and Western performer. He was billed, early in his long and worthy career, as the Tennessee Ploughboy. After some years of obscurity, he became better-known when he joined Pee Wee King (1940–3) and became a regular on the **Grand Ole Opry* programme in Nashville. In 1946 he had a big hit with 'That's how much I love you', followed by 'Bouquet of roses' and 'Anytime'. He had a daily radio show in 1947 and a TV programme in 1950 but was not heard from much in the period 1955–63. He then came back with a new commercialized urban country style with well-arranged backings, and had top hits in the 1960s with 'What's he doing with my world', 'Make the world go away', 'Misty blue', 'Turn the world around', 'Here comes heaven', etc. In 1966 he was the first Country and Western artist to lead a Carnegie Hall concert and was elected to the Country Music Hall of Fame. He remained active on TV, stage, and record into the 1970s. He was part-composer of many songs, including: 'Just a little lovin'', 'I'll hold you in my heart', 'Easy on the eye', 'One kiss too many', and 'You don't know me'.

E. Arnold: *It's a Long Way from Chester County* (Nashville, 1969).

Arnold, Malcolm (*b* Northampton, 21 Oct. 1921). British composer. He started his career as an orchestral trumpet player and was with the London Philharmonic Orchestra from 1941. After war service he joined the BBC Symphony Orchestra in 1945 and was with the LPO again in 1946. He became a full-time composer in 1954 and achieved a high reputation in the symphonic field; but he has also been an active and effective writer of memorable film scores, including: *The Sound Barrier* (1952); *The Captain's Paradise* (1953); *I Am a Camera* (1955); *Trapeze* (1956); *Island in the Sun* (1957); *The Bridge on the River Kwai* (1957); *The Inn of the Sixth Happiness* (1958); *The Key* (1958); *The Roots of Heaven* (1958); *Tunes of Glory* (1960); *The Angry Silence* (1960); *The Inspector* (1961); *Whistle Down the Wind* (1961); *The Lion* (1962); *The Chalk Garden* (1963); *Nine Hours to Rama* (1963); and *The Thin Red Line* (1964). He has taken a special interest in the brass band and his works in this field include 'Fantasy for Brass Band'—the 1974 National Championship test-piece, 'Fantasy for Tuba', 'Fantasy for Trombone', 'Little Suites, Nos 1 & 2', 'Quintet for Brass' (1961), 'Song of Freedom' (1972), and the well-known march 'The Padstow Lifeboat'.

A. Poulton: *Malcolm Arnold: a Catalogue of his Music* (London, 1983).

Art Ensemble of Chicago. American modern jazz group formed in 1968 by saxophonist Roscoe Mitchell (*b* 1940) and trumpeter Lester Bowie (*b* 1941) along with such progressive black jazz players as Joseph Jarman (*b* 1937) (sax), Malachi Favors (*b* 1937) (bass), and Don Moye (*b* 1946) (drums). The group spent their initial period in Paris, then a particularly fruitful location for black musicians, and during an 18-month stay there recorded 12 LPs of their experimental jazz which drew its elements from many styles ranging from New Orleans to free jazz with an overriding Afro flavouring. They returned to America in 1971 where their theatrical stage presentations won them a large following. Dressed and made-up in traditional African guise, the stage full of African instruments, their performance was described as 'running the gamut from the traditional to the absurd and the surreal'. They toured the world from 1971 with regular success and have recorded for several major companies including Atlantic, winning many awards.

Artists and Models. A series of revues staged by the *Shubert brothers in 1923, 1924, 1925, 1927, and 1930. They evolved from an intimate show produced in Greenwich Village by the Illustrators Society of New York, and achieved their renown by being the first revues to introduce nude females to the Broadway stage. They aimed at a fairly low-brow audience and although composers of the calibre of Jean *Schwartz, J. Fred *Coots, Sigmund *Romberg, Alfred *Goodman, Maurice Rubens, Harry *Akst, and Harry *Warren were employed in various editions, they did not produce much of lasting musical value.

Artist's Model, An. One of the many successful musical comedies of the 1890s, staged by George *Edwardes at London's *Daly's Theatre which helped to establish its golden age. With music by Sidney *Jones, book by Owen *Hall, and lyrics by Harry Greenbank (1865–99), it opened on 2 Feb. 1895 and achieved 392 performances, a considerable run for those days. The leading lady was the talented Marie *Tempest and the leading man the handsome Hayden *Coffin. A light and frothy score contained such items as 'The gay tom-tit' and 'Little Daisy with a dimple', padded out by a few additional numbers by Leslie *Stuart including 'Soldiers of the Queen' and 'The military model'.

Art of Maryland, The. The first of the famous extravaganzas featuring the popular partnership of Joe *Weber and Lew *Fields. It opened at the Weber & Fields Music Hall, New York, on 2 Sept. 1896 with a score by John *Stromberg and book by Joseph Herbert (1866–1923). This show set the pattern by featuring a burlesque (in this instance based on *The Heart of Maryland*) supported by a revue-type entertainment with such regulars as Lottie Gilson, Sam *Bernard, and John T. Kelly.

Art rock. A somewhat pretentious pop jargon term applied with maximum indiscretion to those rock artists deemed to have carried their art beyond the realms of mere commerce to an inspirational level. Early and obvious figures to be thus classified beyond question were the *Beatles and Bob *Dylan, but later application of the accolade has often been more open to dissent. Latterly the term has been applied to the more avant-garde, and often pretentious, exponents of rock whose aims are deemed to be artistic rather than self-promotional.

ASCAP [American Society of Composers, Authors and Publishers. Address: 1 Lincoln Plaza, New York, NY 10023.] The idea for a protective society for the music writing and publishing world came from publisher George Maxwell and copyright lawyer Nathan Burkan. At a first meeting at Luchow's Restaurant in New York in Oct. 1913, nine people attended: Maxwell, Burkan, composers Victor *Herbert (who had been recruited as one of the most powerful men in music at the time), Silvio Hein, Raymond *Hubbell, Louis A. *Hirsch, Gustave *Kerker, lyricist Glen MacDonough, and publisher Jay Witmark. The Society was formed on 13 Feb. 1914 at the Hotel Claridge at 44th Street and Broadway, when 170 composers and writers and 22 publishers attended the meeting and George Maxwell became the Society's first President (1914–24). As a first test-case Victor Herbert went to the courts over the unpaid use of his composition 'Sweethearts' in a New York restaurant. Many such lawsuits had to be fought and it was not until 1921 that the first financial benefits were markedly felt. The royalties that the Society now obtains, which first topped the $20 million mark in the 1920s, are shared among composers, writers, and publishers; and ASCAP is now established as the leading American songwriters' trade union. Editions of *The ASCAP Biographical Dictionary of Composers, Authors and Publishers* have been published in 1948, 1952, 1966, and 1980.

Asche, Oscar [Heiss, John Strange] (*b* Geelong, Australia, 16 Jan. 1871; *d* London, 23 Mar. 1936). Actor, singer, librettist, lyric-writer, director, and producer. He began his London stage career acting in Shakespeare. As a writer, he collaborated with Frederick *Norton, Grace Torrens, and Percy *Fletcher. His biggest success was **Chu Chin Chow*, for which he wrote the book, starring in it with his wife Lily Brayton (1876–1953). Other librettos he wrote included: *Eastward Ho!* (1919); *Mecca* (1920); *Cairo* (1921); *The Good Old Days* (1925); *Marjolaine* (1928); and *El Dorado* (1930). He appeared in and directed many of these and also directed *The *Maid of the Mountains* (1917); *A Southern Maid* (1920); *Frasquita* (1925); *Cleopatra* (1925); and *The White Camellia* (1929).

O. Asche: *Oscar Asche: his Life by Himself* (London, 1929).

Ascher, Leo (*b* Vienna, 17 Aug. 1880; *d* New York, 25 Feb. 1942). Austrian composer. He studied law (which he also practised) and music at Vienna University. He decided to devote his time to composing in 1905 and was to write some 50 works for the stage, including many operettas, and a considerable amount of film music. His first successful operetta was *Vergeltsgott* which was produced at the Theater an der Wien 14 Oct. 1905 and enjoyed 69 performances; his greatest success was to be *Hoheit tanzt Walzer*, produced at the Raimundtheater 24 Feb. 1912 and achieving more than 2500 performances in its first 10 years. Other works included: *Die arme Lori* (1909); *Die keusche Susanne* (1910); *Eine fidele Nacht* (1911); *Die goldene Hanna* (1913); *Der Soldat der Marie* (1917); *Ein Jahr ohne Liebe* (1923); *Frühling im Wienerwald* (1930); *Sonja* (1925); and *Bravo Peggy* (1932). He left Austria in 1938 and settled in New York.

Ascherberg, Hopwood & Crew. London music-publishers, an amalgamation of several companies effected by the music-publishing and piano-making company of E. Ascherberg & Co in 1906. In 1904 they had purchased the Thomas Blockley publishing business and now merged with Hopwood & Crew (regular publishers of music-hall material) to form the new company with Eugene Ascherberg as its managing director. Other interests acquired along the way were the catalogues of Duncan Davison & Co., Osborne & Tuckwood, and Howard & Co. The company published many operettas, including: *La Poupée*; *The *Geisha*; *The *Belle of New York*; *A *Chinese Honeymoon*; *The *Maid of the Mountains*; *A Southern Maid*; *The Lady of the Rose*; and *The Last Waltz*. They published the waltzes of Emil *Waldteufel and works by Archibald *Joyce, Charles *Ancliffe, and Sir Edward Elgar. In 1969 the firm was taken over by *Chappell & Co.

Askey, Arthur [Bowden, Arthur] (*b* Liverpool, 6 June 1900; *d* London, 16 Nov. 1982). British comedian and singer of diminutive stature and cheery demeanour. He remained an amateur until 1924 when he joined the Song Salad concert party in Colchester and later appeared in London with them. He became nationally known when he appeared in the radio show *Band Waggon*, a pioneering situation comedy series, first heard in Jan. 1938, in partnership with Richard Murdoch (1907–90). Thereafter he starred in various radio and TV shows; made a number of films; regularly appeared in pantomime, including *Aladdin and his Wonderful Lamp* (1964); and was in the musicals *The Love Racket* (1943), *Follow the Girls* (1945), and *Bet Your Life* (1952). He popularized the use of the catchphrase, his best-known being 'Hello, playmates'; and his signature tune was 'Big-hearted Arthur'. He wrote and performed a number of humorous songs about such creatures as 'The bee' and 'The seagull'.

A. Askey: *Before Your Very Eyes* (London, 1975).

Asmussen, Svend (*b* Copenhagen, 28 Feb. 1916). Danish violinist. He played in the Danish Rhythm Clubs Orchestra led by Vilfred Kjaer, then in 1933 formed a jazz quartet on the same lines as the Joe *Venuti Blue Four, first recording with it in 1935. He became very popular in Scandinavia through frequent broadcasts from Kalundborg and Copenhagen. Also a singer and playing other instruments, and adding comedy to his act, he veered towards a vaudeville career and many of his later recordings were in a lighter popular style. Nevertheless he retained a high reputation as one of Europe's finest exponents of the jazz violin.

Aspects of Love. Musical show with music and book (based on the novel by David Garnett) by Andrew *Lloyd Webber, lyrics by Don Black (*b* 1900) and Charles Hart (*b* 1961). Produced London (Prince of Wales) Apr. 1989, with Ann Crumb as the actress, Rose Vibert, and Michael Ball as a young Englishman, Alex Dillingham, in a story where the realities of true-life love become confused with love portrayed in the theatre. It proved to be one of Lloyd Webber's most gentle and sensitive scores. Its hit song 'Love changes everything' was rivalled by 'Seeing is believing', 'There is more to love', 'Anything but lonely', and the delightful Thirties pastiche of 'The first man you remember'.

Association Française: Musique Recreative [AFMR]. An organization founded in Paris in 1951 by the writer and broadcaster Pierre-Marcel Onder for the promotion of light (non-vocal) music in the broadest sense. A bulletin, 'Musiques Pittoresques', published 10 times a year, maintains contact between members, announcing meetings in Paris and elsewhere, detailing radio broadcasts made in conjunction with the association, reviewing new books and recordings, and containing articles of light musical interest. The Association sponsors the Académie de Musique de Divertissement which, since 1969, has given awards (Cithares) to the three best light music recordings of the year.

Astaire, Adele [Austerlitz, Adele] (*b* Omaha, 10 Sept. 1898; *d* Phoenix, 25 Jan. 1981). American actress, dancer, and singer. She appeared in vaudeville from 1916 as a dancing and singing partner of her brother Fred *Astaire before they appeared on Broadway in 1917 and had their first real hit with *For Goodness Sake* (1922), which also had a great success in London as *Stop Flirting* (1923). They were particularly associated with such *Gershwin shows as **Lady, Be Good* (1924) and **Funny Face* (1924). After *The *Band Wagon* in 1932, Adele Astaire retired to marry Lord Charles Cavendish and Fred continued his career with other illustrious partners. But none, as many believe, was more delightful or graceful than the boyish Adele. Her stage appearances also included: *Over the Top* (1917); *The *Passing Show* (1918); *Apple Blossoms* (1919); *The Love Letter* (1921); *The Bunch and Judy* (1922); and *Smiles* (1930). Writing about *The Love Letter*, Noël *Coward said: 'I hadn't realized before that such rhythm and taste in dancing were possible.'

Astaire, Fred [Austerlitz, Frederick] (*b* Omaha, 10 May 1899; *d* Los Angeles, 22 June 1987). American dancer, singer, actor, and composer. He made his professional debut as an entertainer at the age of five. From 1916 to 1932 he had a dancing and singing partnership with his sister Adele and they co-starred in many shows (see above), notably in several *Gershwin productions. He appeared with Claire Luce (*b* 1903) in **Gay Divorce* in 1932, but after his sister's retirement from the stage in favour of married life, worked on his own for some time and turned his attention to Hollywood, first making a brief appearance with Joan Crawford (1906–77) as his dancing partner in *Dancing Lady* (1933). In the same year he performed some dance numbers with a relatively unknown dancer, Ginger *Rogers, in *Flying Down to Rio*, creating such an immediate stir that the partnership went on to make another eight films that have become classics of the musical and dancing screen: *The Gay Divorcée* (1934); **Roberta* (1934); **Top Hat* (1935); **Follow the Fleet* (1936); **Swing Time* (1936); **Shall We Dance* (1937); *Carefree* (1938); and *The Story of Vernon and Irene Castle* (1939). In 1937 his partner in *A *Damsel in Distress* was Joan Fontaine (*b* 1917). After his partnership with Ginger Rogers broke up in 1939, he appeared with a variety of partners, in **Broadway Melody of 1940*, with BEleanor *Powell; *Second Chorus* (1940), with Paulette Goddard (1911–90); *You'll Never Get Rich* (1941), with Rita Hayworth (1918–87); *Holiday Inn* (1942); *You Were Never Lovelier* (1942), with Rita Hayworth; *The Sky's the Limit* (1943), with Joan *Leslie; *Ziegfeld Follies* (1944)—'The babbit and the bromide' with Gene *Kelly; *Yolanda and the Thief* (1945), with Lucille Bremer (*b* 1923); *Blue Skies* (1946); **Easter Parade* (1948), with Judy *Garland'; *The Barkleys of Broadway* (1949), with Ginger Rogers; *Three Little Words* (1950), with Vera-Ellen (b 1920); *Let's Dance* (1950), with Betty *Hutton; *Royal Wedding* (1951; *Wedding Bells* in UK), with Jane *Powell; *The *Belle of New York* (1952), with Vera-Ellen; *The Band Wagon* (1953), with Cyd Charisse (*b* 1921); *Daddy Long Legs* (1955), with Leslie Caron (*b* 1931); **Funny Face* (1956), with Audrey Hepburn (1929–93); **Silk Stockings* (1957), with Cyd Charisse; **Finian's Rainbow* (1968), with Petula *Clark. He later turned to more serious acting roles in non-musical films. He made many TV appearances in his own shows and in various dramas, and notably introduced two compilations of extracts from MGM musicals *That's Entertainment* (1974 and 1975).

Astaire's contribution to the history of popular music may lie most obviously in his exploitation of the possibilities of the dance. The perfect partnership with Ginger Rogers will always be treasured for its evocation of the 1930s musical and for the wonderful timing and imagination involved in the dance routines, many of which took weeks to perfect. But in musical terms he will also be seriously considered as the singer who gave perfect form and lasting life to many classic songs by *Kern, *Gershwin, *Porter, *Berlin, and others, most of whom said, at one time or another, that they would sooner have Astaire sing their songs than anyone else. He was not a trained singer and yet he contrived to be the perfect popular songster in the 1930s style, giving more meaning and strength to the songs than many with more impressive vocal chords could ever achieve. He helped to make the musical film an art form and raised many a slight story into a classic production. His acting ability was achieved through perfect timing and telling understatement. Astaire would most like to have been a songwriter himself and his achievement in this field was far from negligible, his writings including 'Blue without you' (1930); 'Not my girl' (1935); 'I'm building up to an awful let down' (1935, *w* Johnny *Mercer); 'I'll never let you go'

(1936); 'Tappin' the time (1936); 'Just one more dance with you, madame' (1936); 'Rise and shine' (1936); 'Just like taking candy from a baby' (1940, *w* Gladys Shelley); 'Sweet sorrow' (1940); 'If swing goes, I go too' (1944); 'Oh, my achin' back' (1945); 'There's no time like the present' (1952); 'Hello, baby' (1956); 'Lovely melody' (1956); 'Calypso hooray' (1957); 'The afterbeat' (1959); 'I love everybody but you' (1962); 'Girls like you' (1962).

F. Astaire: *Steps in Time* (New York, 1959; London, 1960). A. Hackl: *Fred Astaire and his Work* (Vienna, 1970). A. Croce: *The Fred Astaire and Ginger Rogers Book* (New York–London, 1972). S. Green and B. Goldblatt: *Starring Fred Astaire* (New York, 1973; London, 1974). M. Friedland: *Fred Astaire* (London, 1976). S. Topper: *Astaire and Rogers* (New York, 1976). B. Green: *Fred Astaire* (London, 1979). B. Thomas: *Astaire : the Man, the Dancer* (New York, 1984).

As the Girls Go. American musical comedy that ran for 420 performances at the Winter Garden, New York, from 13 Nov. 1946, transferring to the Broadway Theatre 14 Sep. 1949 for a further 141 performances. It had a bright score by Jimmy *McHugh which included 'As the girls go', 'You say the nicest things, baby', 'Nobody's heart but mine', 'I got lucky in the rain'; the lyrics, as usual, were by Harold *Adamson.

The book imagined, in a light-hearted burlesque sort of way, what would happen when the first woman was elected President of the United States. President Lucille Thompson Wellington was played by Irene Rich; her husband Waldo, who had most of the funny bits and a show-stopping song, 'It takes a woman to take a man', and amused himself with the girls, by Bobby *Clark. The show was unfortunate in that it ran into an ASCAP strike when no recordings could be made. Having cost $340,000, it failed to make a profit in spite of its healthy run.

As Thousands Cheer. A musical revue that had the clever and novel idea of basing each of its items on a newspaper headline, e.g. HEAT WAVE HITS NEW YORK resulting in the song 'Heat wave' sung with great success by Ethel *Waters. The sketches were written by Moss *Hart and the excellent songs (music and lyrics) were by Irving *Berlin. The first act finale made use of the well-known 'Easter parade' and other numbers included 'Harlem on my mind', 'Supper time', 'Our wedding day', 'Not for all the rice in China', and 'Lonely heart'. The scenario allowed for plenty of satirical impersonation of prominent people excellently done by a cast that also included Marilyn *Miller, Helen *Broderick, and Clifton *Webb. Opening at Berlin's Music Box Theatre on 30 Sept. 1933, it ran for 400 performances and, directed by Hassard Short (1877–1956), set a new fashion for thought-provoking, intelligent revues. It was presented in London, at the Adelphi 21 Feb. 1935, under the title *Stop Press*, but was not as successful with British audiences.

'As time goes by'. Song with music and words by Herman *Hupfeld first used as an additional number in the musical comedy *Everybody's Welcome* (13 Oct. 1931) having been published in New York in July of that year. It had quite a success at the time and became a standard number. The song was given a new and lasting lease of life when it was sung by Dooley Wilson (1894–1953) in the film *Casablanca* (1942), starring Humphrey Bogart (1899–1957) and Ingrid Bergman (1915–82), in response to the request: 'Play that song, Sam'.

As You Were. Revue produced at the London Pavilion 3 Aug. 1918 which cashed in on wartime memories and ran for 434 performances. The book was by Arthur *Wimperis, and the score by Herman *Darewski and Edouard Mathé included such items as 'The aeroplane walk', 'A blighty one', 'Helen of Troy', 'If you could care', and 'What ho, Mr Watteau'. The cast included Alice *Delysia, John Humphries (1864–1927), and Hayden *Coffin. The show was adapted for the USA with a mainly new score by E. Ray Goetz and book by Glen McDonough, opening at the Central Theatre 7 Jan. 1920. In spite of an impressive cast including Sam *Bernard, Irene *Bordoni, and Clifton *Webb, it failed to attain the same success as it had in London.

Atkins, Chet [Chester Burton] (*b* Luttrell, Tenn., 20 June 1924). American Country and Western guitarist and entertainer. He achieved renown from around 1941 through his appearances on the **Grand Ole Opry* programme from Nashville and elsewhere. In 1957 he became an executive with RCA, managing the Nashville recording studio where he was influential in evolving the country pop or Nashville sound utilizing electronic instruments. Among the artists he helped on their way were the young Elvis *Presley, the *Everly Brothers, Jim *Reeves, Charley *Pride, and many more. He continued to play in the Merle *Travis tradition in country music and also in the jazz field, made tours of Europe, the Far East, and Africa, and was elected to the Country Music Hall of Fame in 1973.

C. Atkins: *Country Gentleman* (Chicago, 1974).

At the Drop of a Hat. Highly successful two-man show described as 'an after-dinner farrago' which highlighted the writing and singing talents of composer-pianist Donald *Swann and actor-writer Michael *Flanders. They had previously worked on revue material together and embarked on their show at the New Lindsey Theatre, London, on 31 Dec. 1956. It was immediately a hit and transferred to the Fortune Theatre 24 Jan. 1957, where it completed a run of 808 performances. In 1959 the show was seen at the John Golden Theatre in New York. In addition to the friendly and intimate atmosphere that Flanders and Swann achieved, their material was of quite exceptional quality by revue standards, both well-written and memorable. Individual songs included such classics as 'A transport of delight', 'Song of reproduction', 'Greensleeves', 'A gnu', 'A song of the weather', 'The reluctant cannibal', 'Misalliance', 'Have some madeira, m'dear', and the perennial 'Hippopotamus song', to which were added Sydney Carter's 'The youth of the heart' and many other memorable items. Its success demanded a second edition, *At the Drop of Another Hat*, which was seen at the Haymarket and Globe theatres from 2 Oct. 1963 and in New York in 1966, adding to the catalogue such items as 'The gas-man cometh', 'Sounding brass', 'A song of patriotic prejudice', and the touching 'Armadillo idyll'.

Atwell, Winifred [Levisohn, Winifred] (*b* Tuna-Puna, Port of Spain, 27 Apr. 1914; *d* Sydney, 12 Feb. 1983). Trinidadian pianist. She trained to be a pharmacist, but decided on a pianistic career instead. In London, finding the concert world hard to break into, she played ragtime and boogie-woogie in variety shows. Her success in a Coliseum charity concert led to a recording session in which she played George *Botsford's 'Black and white rag' on an old upright piano which had been bought in a Battersea junk shop for £2.50. It proved a profitable gimmick and Winifred Atwell and her 'other' piano became a popular variety and recording turn, pounding out souped-up ragtime and boogie with infectious exuberance and joviality. Her vogue waned in the 1950s and she emigrated to Australia in the 1960s, becoming naturalized in 1981. She wrote much of her own material, including the popular 'Jubilee rag' (1952).

Audran, Edmond (*b* Lyons, 12 Apr. 1842; *d* Tierceville, 17 Aug. 1901). French composer. He studied at the Ecole Niedermeyer in Paris and in 1861 became organist at the Church of St Joseph in Marseilles. It was there that he produced his first operetta, *L'Ours et le pacha* in 1862, followed by *La Chercheuse d'esprit* in 1864. His first big theatrical success was *Le Grand Mogol* originally performed in Marseilles in 1877, then seen in New York in 1882 starring Lillian *Russell, in Paris in 1884, and in London as *The Grand Mogul* in 1884 and 1886. *Les Noces d'Olivette* (1879) brought him further renown and international fame followed in 1880 with *La *Mascotte* which had achieved more than 1700 performances in Paris by 1897 and thousands more worldwide. He wrote prolifically, producing almost one operetta a year, among the better-known being *Gillette de Narbonne* (1882); *La Cigale et la fourmi* (1886); *Miss Hélyett* (1890); *L'Oncle Celestin* (1891); *Sainte-Freya* (1892); *Madame Suzette* (1893); *Mon Prince* (1893); *L'Enlèvement de la Toledad* (1894); *La Duchesse de Ferrare* (1895); *La Poupée* (1896)—almost as big a success as *La Mascotte*; *Monsieur Lohengrin* (1896); and *Les Petites Femmes* (1897).

Aufderheide, May Francis (*b* Indianapolis, 21 May 1888; *d* Pasadena, Calif., 1 Sept. 1972). American composer and pianist. She was one of the earliest published white ragtime composers and one of the first women in the field. Her father, a financier, went into music-publishing especially to publish the work of his daughter and of another Indianapolis composer Paul Pratt (1890–1948). Her works included: 'Dusty rag' (1908); 'Richmond rag' (1908); 'The thriller' (1909); 'Buzzer rag' (1909); 'Blue ribbon rag' (1910); 'A totally different rag' (1910); 'I want a real lovin' man' (1911, *w* Pratt); 'Novelty rag' (1911); and 'Dusty rag song' (1912, *w* J. Will Callahan).

'Auld lang syne'. Scottish song internationally used as the concluding anthem of any convivial evening, especially on New Year's Eve, usually sung with the singers in a circle with arms crossed and hands held; a moment of great sentiment. 'Auld lang syne' (literally 'old long since'), with its emotional lyric 'should auld acquaintance be forgot and never brought to mind' is loosely credited to Robert Burns (1759–96), but he himself refers to an old tune 'which has never been in print nor even in manuscript until I took it down from an old man's singing' and elsewhere speaks of 'the heaven-inspired poet who composed this glorious fragment'. Here he refers to the oft-used first verse which it is generally agreed was not by Burns, nor probably were the fourth and fifth verses, though the rest of the 10 verses printed in his collected poems are presumed to be his additions. Words in similar vein can be found in the Bannatyne MS of 1586 titled 'Auld kyndness forgot'; and in James Watson's *Scots Poems*, printed in 1711, there in a poem called 'Old long syne' attributed to either Sir Robert Aytoun or Francis Semphill. Another version by Allan Ramsay (1686–1758) appeared in vol. 1 of James Johnson's *The Scots Musical Museum*, while Burns's version first appeared in vol. 5 of the same work in 1799, three years after the poet's death.

The melody used in most of these instances is not the one we now know. A number of tunes akin to the modern 'Auld lang syne' were printed under various titles between 1687 and 1793, one appearing in the overture to William *Shield's *Rosina* (1783). The well-known melody, previously attached to a song called 'I fee'd a lass at Martinmas', was finally trimmed to its present shape and first printed with Burns's words in *A Select Collection of Original Scottish Airs* (3rd set) printed in London in 1798 and edited by George Thomson. 'Auld lang syne' has been heard in many unexpected places since, including an arrangement by Beethoven and an appearance at the 1964 Olympic Games in Tokyo.

'Aura Lea'. Song with music by George R. Poulton (1828–67) and words by William Whiteman Fosdick (1825–62) published in Cincinnati in 1861. Intended as a minstrel song, it became popular in the Civil War with both armies, and, with words by L. W. Becklaw, was published as 'Army blue' or 'Song of the Class of 1865'. A new version of the song under the title 'Love me tender' (*w* Elvis *Presley and Vera Matson) was published in 1956 and used in the film of the same name. George Poulton was born in England and went to America with his parents when he was seven, settling in Lansingburgh, NY. He became known as a violinist, pianist, singer, and conductor and began to compose in the 1840s, publishing around 22 songs and piano pieces. He led a dissolute life and died at the age of 39.

Auric, Georges (*b* Lofdève, Hérault, 15 Feb. 1899; *d* Paris, 23 July 1983). French composer. Influenced by Ravel and Satie, he became one of the group of composers, including Honegger, Milhaud, and Poulenc, known as 'Les Six'. One of his most prominent activites was the writing of scores for films, his French products including *Le Sang d'un poète* (1930); *A nous le liberté* (1932); *Le Lac aux dames* (1934); *Les Mystères de Paris* (1936); *L'Alibi* (1937); *Gribouille* (1937); *Orage* (1938); *Entrée des artistes* (1938); *Maceo, l'enfer du jeu* (1938); *L'Assassin a peur de la nuit* (1942); *L'Éternel Retour* (1943); *La Belle Aventure* (1944); *La Belle et la bête* (1946); *La Symphonie pastorale* (1946); *Les Jeux sont faits* (1947); *L'Aigle à deux têtes* (1948); *Les Parents terribles* (1948); *Orphée* (1949); *Belles de nuit* (1952); *La Salaire de la peur* (1953); *Rififi* (1955); *Lola Montès* (1955); *Le Mystère Picasso* (1956); *Gervaise* (1956); *Les Sorcières de Salem* (1956); *Celui qui doit mourir* (1957); *Aimez-vous Brahms?* (1961); and *Le Rendez-vous de minuit* (1962).

For the English speaking cinema his scores included: *Dead of Night* (1945); *Caesar and Cleopatra* (1945); *Hue and Cry* (1946); *It Always Rains on Sundays* (1947); *Another Shore* (1948); *Corridor of Mirrors* (1948); *Silent Dust* (1948); *The Queen of Spades* (1949); *Passport to Pimlico* (1949); *The Spider and the Fly* (1949); *Cage of Gold* (1950); *The Galloping Major* (1950); *The Lavender Hill Mob* (1951); *Moulin Rouge* (1952)—with the popular 'But where is your heart' theme song; *Roman Holiday* (1953); *Father Brown* (1954); *Bonjour tristesse* (1957); *Heaven Knows, Mr Allison* (1957); and *The Innocents* (1961).

Austin, Gene [Lucas, Eugene] (*b* Gainsville, Texas, 24 June 1900; *d* Palm Springs, Calif., 24 Jan. 1972). American singer, pianist, composer, and lyric-writer. He left home at 15 to join a circus, served with the American forces in Mexico and Europe during the First World War as a bugler, and returned to Baltimore University in 1919 where he formed a band. In 1923 he became a professional singer in vaudeville, teaming up in a double-act with Roy Bergere with whom he wrote a hit song of 1924 'How come you do me like you do?' He became a solo entertainer in 1924, singing in a relaxed, soft voice (a pioneer *crooner) and playing a gentle piano style which made him well-known in the 1920s billed as 'The Voice of the Southland'. He made numerous recordings between 1924 and 1942, selling altogether some 86 million discs, his big hit being 'My blue heaven' in 1927 which sold five million copies (and became his signature tune); followed by 'Ramona' in 1928. His record of sales was only surpassed when Bing *Crosby came along.

Although his reputation began to fade in the 1930s he appeared in several films—*Broadway Rhapsody* (1933); *The Gift of Gab* (1934); *Sadie McKee* (1934); *Klondike Annie* (1935)—for which he wrote 'I'm an occidental woman in an oriental mood' for the film's star Mae *West; and *Going Places* (1935). In the 1940s he ran his own club in California. He visited London in 1958 and was seen on TV, where he made his last public appearance in 1971 in the USA. He wrote a number of lasting songs including 'When my sugar walks down the street' (1924); 'The lonesome road' (1928; *m* Nathaniel Shilkret, 1895–1982) which was used in the film of *Show Boat* (1929); and 'Ridin' around in the rain' (1934).

Autry, Gene [Orvon] (*b* Tioga Springs, Texas, 29 Sept. 1907). American actor and vocalist, pioneer singing cowboy of Hollywood films, radio and recording star. One of the founding figures of modern Country and Western music, he worked on his father's ranch in Oklahoma before he began singing on the radio, first becoming known from Tulsa 1929–30. He went to Chicago and during 1930–4 was heard on the WLS National Barn Dance programme. He went to Hollywood in 1934 and appeared in his first film, *In Old Santa Fe*. His first starring role was in *Tumbling Tumbleweeds* (1939); others included *Carolina Moon* (1940); *Back in the Saddle* (1941); *Sunset in Wyoming* (1942); *Range War* (1946); *Guns and Saddles* (1949); *Goldtown Ghost Riders* (1953)—more than 100 altogether. He had his own radio show in the 1940s and 1950s, and made many hit records for children such as 'Here comes Santa Claus' (1947), 'Rudolph the red-nosed reindeer' (1949), and 'Frosty the Snowman' (1950). In the 1950s he made numerous TV films.

He was composer or part-composer of a large number of songs, including many used in his films, such as: 'Ridin' down the canyon' (1931); 'That silver-haired daddy of mine' (with Jimmy Long, 1932)—by 1939, his first million-seller; 'You're the only star in my blue heaven' (1938); 'Be honest with me' (with Fred Rose, 1940)—used in *Ridin' on a Rainbow* (1941); 'Back in the saddle again' (with Ray Whitley, 1940)—his theme song; 'Goodbye, little darling, goodbye' (with Johnny Marvin, 1940); 'Tears on my pillow' (with Rose, 1941); 'Have I told you lately that I love you?' (1942). He was elected to the Country Music Hall of Fame in 1969.

Avalon, Frankie [Avallone, Francis Thomas] (*b* Philadelphia, 18 Sept. 1940). American singer, a teenage idol of the late 1950s. He began as a child prodigy trumpeter, but the novelty of this act soon wore off. In 1957 he joined a local group known as Rocco and his Saints and began recording for the Chancellor label in 1956. He became widely known through the **American Bandstand* TV programme, and achieved a hit in 1958 with 'DeDe Dinah', a No. 7 million-seller, followed by 'Ginger Bread' (1958); 'I'll wait for you' (1958); 'Venus' (1959)—a No. 1 hit; 'From bobby sox to stockings' (1959);

'A boy without a girl' (1959); 'Just ask your heart' (1959); and a No. 1 hit 'Why' (1960). He appeared in the films *Jamboree* (1957); *The Alamo* (1960); *Voyage to the Bottom of the Sea* (1962); *Beach Party* (1963); *The Carpetbaggers* (1964); *Muscle Beach Party* (1964); *Bikini Beach* (1964); *Jet Set* (1965); *Fireball 500* (1966); and others; projecting a clean Beach Boy image and performing with a polished style and pleasant voice. In the 1970s he appeared in TV dramas and in the 1978 musical **Grease*, in which he parodied himself.

Average White Band, The. Group formed in 1972 by six Scottish musicians, Hamish Stuart (vocal), Alan Gorrie (vocal and bass), Onnie McIntyre (guitar), Robbie McIntosh (drums), Roger Ball (saxophones), and Malcolm 'Molly' Duncan (saxes), while they were working in America. They performed with Eric *Clapton in 1973. Successful recordings with Atlantic from 1974 resulted in a No. 1 hit, 'Pick up the pieces' in 1975. When Robbie McIntosh died of a heroin overdose in 1974 he was replaced by Brighton-born drummer Steve Ferrone. The Band settled in Los Angeles and became a leading group in the soul/funk style, making albums for Atlantic 1974–8 and for RCA from 1979.

Avon Comedy Four. American comedy singing group, formed just before the First World War by Max Hart, which remained a popular vaudeville turn for many years and appeared on Broadway in *The *Passing Show of 1919*. The principal and most lasting members were Joe Smith and Charlie Dale. The original group also included John Coleman and Will Lester, later replaced. When they finally broke up Smith and Dale continued as a comedy team, specializing in a famous Dr Kronkeit-and-patient act.

Ayer, Nat D. [Nathaniel Davis] (*b* Boston, 30 Sept. 1887; *d* Bath, 19 Sept. 1952). American-born composer and pianist. After an obscure early career in the USA as a pianist and entertainer, he came to England in 1911 with the American Ragtime Octette and stayed to make a lucrative and successful career writing for the London musical theatre. His scores included the vastly popular *The *Bing Boys Are Here* (1916), followed by *Look Who's Here* (1916); *Houp-La* (1916); *Pell-Mell* (1916); *The Bing Girls Are There* (1917); *Yes, Uncle!* (1917); *The Bing Boys on Broadway* (1918); *Baby Bunting* (1919)—'If you love me as I love you'; *Snap* (1922); *The Smith Family* (1922); *Stop . . . Go* (1935); *Somewhere in England* (1939). Some of his best songs, such as 'Oh, you beautiful doll' (1911) and 'If you were the only girl in the world' from *The Bing Boys Are Here*, have the quality of the best music-hall songs, very professionally written with strong melodies and apt harmonies that have kept them very much alive and sung.

Other songs include: 'Moving day in Jungle Town' (1909, *w* A. Seymour Brown); 'If you talk in your sleep, don't mention my name (1911, *w* Brown); 'You great big wonderful baby' (1912); 'Someday I'll make you love me' (1914, *w* Clifford *Grey); 'She was wonderful' (1919, *w* Grey); 'Linger a little longer with me' (1912, *w* Ralph Stanley); 'Shufflin' along' (1922, *w* Stanley); 'Oh, how I've waited for you' (1925, *w* Harry Carlton).

Ayler, Albert (*b* Cleveland, 13 July 1936; *d* New York, 25 Nov. 1970). American jazz saxophonist. He began playing the alto in his father's band, switched to tenor and became a leading avant-garde jazz musician in New York. He also toured in Europe. At a time when he was still building a high reputation as an interesting experimenter, his body was found in the East River; a verdict of accidental death was returned.

Aylward, Florence (*b* Brede, East Sussex, 10 Mar. 1862; *d* St Leonard's-on-Sea, 14 Oct. 1950). English composer. She began to write songs when she was 12, and her first published song, 'Daydawn', was issued by Boosey in 1888 after she had made enquiries as to the cost of having 100 copies printed. Later, on the advice of William Boosey, she studied music at the Guildhall School. Her most popular song was 'Beloved, it is morn' (1896, *w* Emily Hickey), almost matched by 'Love's coronation' (1899) and 'How dear you are' (1908, *w* Gwendolin Paget). *A Florence Aylward Album* was published by Chappell in 'The Portrait Series' in 1906.

Aznavour, Charles [Aznavourian, Varenagh] (*b* Saint-Germain-des-Près, Paris, 22 May 1924). French-born Armenian singer, actor, and composer. The child of Armenian immigrants who helped to run a family restaurant and earned a living as singers and actors, Aznavour himself was on the stage at the age of 11 playing child roles at the famous Théâtre Marigny. An ambition to write songs was first realized in 1941 when he wrote the lyric of 'J'ai bu' to music by Pierre Roche (*b* 1919). Sung by Georges Ulmer (*b* 1919), it won a 1947 Grand Prix du Disque. The talents of Roche and Aznavour were noted by Edith *Piaf who took them, along with Les Compagnons de la Chanson, on an American tour. He regularly wrote songs for Piaf, including 'Il pleut' (1949) and 'Il y avait' (1950) as well as for other singers like Juliette *Gréco ('Je hais les dimanches', 1950) and Gilbert *Bécaud ('Viens' and 'Donne-moi', 1952). Piaf encouraged his talents as a singer, but his first appearances were harshly criticized: 'To put oneself before the public with such a voice and such a physique', said one critic, 'is pure folly!' The deserved success came in 1955 with the song 'Sur ma vie'. By 1965 he had achieved a one-man show at the Olympia Theatre singing 30 of his own songs.

Aznavour does not depend on glamour.There is something of a *Chaplin in him, the haunted eyes of *Leno, the defiant art of Piaf. Cocteau said that before Aznavour despair was unpopular. Aznavour's reply was to quote an old French saying: 'Happy people have nothing to tell'. His attractive French-flavoured singing and his lived-in looks have made him an international star, equally well-known as an actor. His best role was in the 1960 film *Tirez sur le pianiste (Shoot the pianist)*. In the 1982 *Edith et Marcel* (based on Piaf's romance with a boxer) he played himself as a struggling composer. His songs include: 'Père Noël est Swing' (1942), 'Il faut savoir' (1949), 'Viens pleurer aux creux de mon épaule' (1953), 'Je t'attends (1961), 'La mamma' (1964), 'Esperanza', 'Bon anniversaire', 'For me—formidable', 'La Bohème', 'Paris au mois d'août', 'On ne sait jamais', 'Comme des étrangers', 'Ce jour tant attendu', and 'Sarah'. He wrote an operetta, *Monsieur Carnaval*, which was produced in Paris in 1965.

Y. Salgues: *Charles Aznavour* (Paris, 1964). C. Aznavour: *Aznavour on Aznavour* (Paris, 1970). C. Aznavour: *Yesterday When I Was Young* (London, 1979).

B

Babes in Arms. Musical comedy with book and lyrics by Lorenz* Hart and music by Richard *Rodgers (who also contributed to the book), produced at the Shubert Theatre on 14 Apr. 1937 [298p]. The delightful score, written at the peak of the Rodgers–Hart collaboration, included such evergreen songs as 'Babes in arms', 'I wish I were in love again', 'Johnny One Note', 'The lady is a tramp', 'My funny Valentine', and 'Where or when'. The story, concerning some children who try to stage their own revue, was notable as a vehicle for introducing many still unknown performers such as Alfred *Drake, Mitzi Green (1920–69)—then only 16, Robert Rounseville (1914–74), and, in the chorus, Dan Dailey (1914–78). The cast also included Wynn Murray, who sang 'Johnny One Note', and there was a ballet arranged by George Balanchine (1964–83). 'Where or when' was interesting in having probably the first lyric to dwell on the psychic experience of 'déjà vu'. Filmed in 1939 with Judy *Garland, Mickey *Rooney, and Charles *Winninger, it was the first MGM picture to be directed by Busby Berkeley (1895–1976).

Babes in Toyland. Historic musical extravaganza with score by Victor *Herbert, which found a more lasting niche in musical stage history than its original run of 192 performances suggests. It was commissioned by the producers Fred R. Hamlin and Julian Mitchell as a successor to the highly successful childhood fantasy *The *Wizard of Oz,* which had occupied the Majestic Theatre, New York, from the beginning of 1903. *Babes in Toyland,* with a similar tale of a journey through forests and storms to the happy goal of Toyland, was written by Glen McDonough (1870–1924) and opened at the Majestic Theatre on 13 Oct. 1903 with a cast that included William Norris and Mabel Barrison as the babes, George Denham, and Bessie Wynn. Its songs included 'I can't do the sum', 'Go to sleep, slumber deep', 'Song of the poet', 'March of the toys', and 'Toyland'; and it turned out to be the best Herbert–McDonough collaboration. It was filmed in 1934 with Laurel and Hardy, and in 1961 with Ray *Bolger, Ed *Wynn, and Tommy Sands (*b* 1937).

Bacharach, Burt (*b* Kansas City, Mo., 12 May 1928). American composer and conductor. The son of a journalist, he was at first an unwilling student of the piano and wanted to be a footballer. While at high school in the 1940s his interest in music grew, particularly in the area of bebop, and he appeared in shows with Dizzy *Gillespie and Charlie *Parker. He ran his own band for a while, then studied music at McGraw University. Later he attended courses given by Darius Milhaud, Bohuslav Martinu, and Henry Cowell at the New School for Social Research in New York, and won a scholarship to the Music Academy of the West in Santa Barbara. After service in the army, 1950–2, he worked as conductor and arranger for various record companies and acted as accompanist to Vic *Damone, Polly Bergen, Steve *Lawrence, and the Ames Brothers. During 1958–61 he was accompanist and arranger for Marlene *Dietrich, conducting the orchestra on the recordings she made on her return to Germany and Berlin in 1960.

His own songs began to gather notice, some of them in the country rock idiom written for Gene *Pitney. 'The story of my life' was made into a hit by Marty *Robbins and 'Magic moments' (1957) by Perry *Como. He had found an ideal lyricist in Hal David with whom he continued to collaborate on such songs as 'Wives and lovers', 'Walk on by', 'What the world needs now is love', 'Reach out for me', 'Trains and boats and planes', 'Make it easy on yourself', 'Blue on blue', 'Always something there to remind me', 'The look of love', 'I'll never fall in love again', 'Our little secret', and 'Do you know the way to San José'. He wrote title-songs and music for the films *Wonderful to be Young* (1962); *What's New, Pussycat?* (1965)—the title-song helped to make a star of Tom *Jones; *After the Fox* (1966); *Promise her Anything* (1966); *Alfie* (1966); *Casino Royal* (1967); *Butch Cassidy and the Sundance Kid* (1969)—'Raindrops keep falling on my head' (Academy Award); and *The April Fools* (1969). His songs 'Alfie' (1966), 'The look of love' (1968), 'I'll say a little prayer' (1968), 'This girl's in love with you' (1969), and many others, were made into hits by Dionne *Warwick. He made many recordings under his own name in the 1970s. He was highly praised for the successful musical **Promises, Promises* (1968; lyrics by Hal David and book by Neil *Simon, based on the film *The Apartment*); and was involved in two film musicals, *Lost Horizon* (1972) and *Together?* (1980).

Bachman-Turner Overdrive. Canadian group formed in 1972 with the line-up of Randy Bachman (guitar and vocal), Fred Turner (bass and vocal), Robbie Bachman (drums), and Tim Bachman (guitar). Randy Bachman had previously had a promising career with a group called the Guess Who in the 1960s. The new group played in a *heavy metal style but kept a melodic content, having a No. 1

hit with 'You ain't seen nothing yet' in 1974. Robbie Bachman left the band in 1977 but it was re-formed in 1983 with a new drummer, Gary Peterson, and has continued a successful recording career with many popular albums.

M. Melhuish: *Bachman-Turner Overdrive: the Authorized Biography* (New York, 1976).

Baddeley, Hermione (*b* Shropshire, 13 Nov. 1906; *d* Los Angeles, 19 Aug. 1986). British actress and singer. A distinguished career in the theatre included many appearances in intimate revue where she showed a rich and versatile vein of comedy in such shows as *The Punch Bowl* (1924) *The *Co-Optimists* (1924); **On With the Dance* (1925): *Cochran's Revue* (1926); *Queen High* (1926); *The Five o'Clock Girl* (1929); *After Dinner* (1932); *Ballyhoo* (1932); *The Floodlight* (1937); **Nine Sharp* (1938); *The *Little Revue* (1940); *Rise Above It* (1941); *The Gaieties* (1945); *A la Carte* (1948); and *At the Lyric* (1953); frequently in hilarious partnership with Hermione *Gingold. She appeared in such films as *The *Unsinkable Molly Brown* (1960) and **Mary Poppins* (1964).

H. Baddeley: *The Unsinkable Hermione Baddeley* (London–New York, 1984).

Baer, Abel (*b* Baltimore, 16 Mar. 1893; *d* New York, 5 Oct. 1976). American composer. He originally intended to make a career in dentistry but, after a chance to conduct an orchestra in Boston 1918–20, decided to try to make a living writing music. He was encouraged by George *Gershwin and Milton *Ager and had some of his numbers used by Paul *Whiteman. His most successful songs included: 'All that I need is you' (*w* Lester Santly), 'Lucky Lindy' (*w* L. Wolfe *Gilbert)—written to celebrate Lindbergh's solo crossing of the Atlantic in 1927, 'I ain't got nobody' (1928, *w* Sam *Lewis). He wrote a musical comedy, *Lady Do*, in 1927 which ran for 56 nights at the Liberty Theatre in New York.

Baez, Joan (*b* Staten Island, NY, 9 Jan. 1941). American folk-singer and songwriter who has had a great impact on the modern folk scene in the dual fields of music and nonviolent social activism. She sang in her school choir and learned the guitar while developing an interest in folk-music, becoming active in the folk revival of the early 1960s when she moved with her family to Boston. She had a voice of remarkable purity, clarity, and flexibility for a folk-singer that was to bring popularity far beyond her special field. Her professional debut was at the Newport Folk Festival in 1959 and she began to record with Vanguard in 1960, her first solo albums being a vital part of the 1960s folk revival. She appeared at Carnegie Hall in 1962 and began a close association with Bob *Dylan at that time, introducing him at concerts and using many of his songs ('Don't think twice, it's all right', etc.) in her performances and recordings; one album, *Any Day Now* (1968), was entirely Dylan material. She made her political feelings public by refusing to pay war taxes in 1964 and was jailed for civil disobedience after an anti-Vietnam War demonstration in 1967. She has produced numerous LP albums and engaged in many world tours, writing much of her own material. Her sister Mimi, also well-known as a folk-singer, was married to the ill-fated Richard Farina (1937–66) who was killed in a motorcycle accident.

J. Baez: *Daybreak: an Intimate Journal* (New York–London, 1966). J. Baez: *And a Voice to Sing With* (New York–London, 1987). J. Swanekamp: *Diamonds and Rust: a bibliography & discography on Joan Baez* (Ann Arbor, Mich. 1979).

Music: The Joan Baez Song Book (New York–London, 1975).

Bagley, Ben [Benjamin James] (*b* Hardwick, Vt., 18 Oct. 1933). American producer. He was particularly active in the revue field where his triumphs included *The Shoestring Revue* (1955), *The Littlest Revue* (1956), *Shoestring '57* (1957), where writers like Charles *Strouse, Lee *Adams, Sheldon *Harnick, Harvey *Schmidt, and Tom Jones found their first opportunities; a witty series that utilized such artists as Chita *Rivera, Beatrice Arthur, Joel *Grey, and Dorothy Greener. Later he moved into recording and, founding the Painted Smiles label, started a worthy 'Revisited' series dedicated to reviving the lesser-known songs of various notable show composers of the past. These were always tastefully and stylishly done and provided valuable documentation as well as pleasant entertainment. He had a great success with the revue *The Decline and Fall of the Entire World as Seen Through the Eyes of Cole Porter* (1965) which included Ronald Graham and Kay Ballard (*b* 1926).

Bagley, Edwin E. (*b* 1857; *d* 1922). American composer and bandmaster, member and bandmaster of several bands that flourished in New Hampshire. His brother Ezra M. Bagley was also a famous cornettist in the *Gilmore band. Edwin had a lasting hit with the march 'National Emblem' in 1906, so-called because of a brief quote from 'The Star-spangled Banner'. The irreverent words 'And the monkey wrapped its tail around the flagpole' are frequently sung to the melody. Other marches included: 'Ambassador', 'America Victorious', 'Bagley's Imperial', 'Father of his country', 'Front section', 'Imperial', and 'Knight Templar'.

Bailey, Mildred [Rinker, Mildred] (*b* Tekoa, Wash., 27 Feb. 1907; *d* Poughkeepsie, NY, 12 Dec. 1951). American jazz and blues singer, sister of Al Rinker (*b* 1907). Both of them worked with Paul *Whiteman, Mildred from 1929 to 1933. She married the xylophonist Red *Norvo in 1933 and was divorced in 1945. She sang with the bands of Ben *Bernie, Willard Robison, Red Norvo, and Benny *Goodman, pursuing a mainly solo career in New York clubs from 1940. From 1949 she suffered from diabetes and heart trouble and worked only intermittently. She made many recordings under her own name and had a pleasantly mellifluous, high-pitched, and clearly articulated style that worked well with small jazz groups such as her own Alley Cats and with jazz sophisticates like Norvo, Teddy *Wilson, and John *Kirby. She is remembered in jazz history as one of the first female band vocalists and one of the first white singers to earn a jazz reputation.

Bailey, Pearl [Mae] (*b* Newport News, Va., 29 Mar. 1918; *d* Philadelphia, 17 Aug. 1990). American singer. She started her career in various nightclubs in Washington DC, Baltimore, and New York (where she won a singing contest at Harlem's *Apollo Theatre), then sang with the bands of Noble *Sissle, Edgar Hayes, Cootie *Williams, and Cab *Calloway. She continued her career as a solo singer and starred in many Broadway productions including **St Louis Woman* (1946); *Arms and the Girl* (1950); *Bless You All* (1950); **House of Flowers* (1954); and the all-black version of **Hello, Dolly!* (1967)—her greatest success. She also appeared in films, including: *Variety Girl* (1947); *Isn't It Romantic* (1948); **Carmen Jones* (1954); **St Louis Blues* (1958); and **Porgy and Bess* (1959). She had her own TV show 1970–1 and, in spite of ill-health, continued working into the 1980s.

P. Bailey: *The Raw Pearl* (New York, 1968). P. Bailey: *Talking to Myself* (New York, 1971).

Baker, Belle [Becker, Bella] (*b* New York, 1895; *d* Los Angeles, 28 Apr. 1957). American-Jewish vaudeville entertainer, singer, and character comedienne. She made her Broadway debut in a minor role in *Vera Violetta* (1911) and starred in *Betsy* (1926) in which she sang 'Blue skies' by Irving *Berlin. But she mainly worked in vaudeville singing such songs as 'My Yiddische mama', 'All of me', 'Put it on, take it off, wrap it up and take it home', and 'Cohen owes me $97'. She first recorded in 1919, appeared in London in cabaret and music-hall 1934–5, and made occasional films. She was married to the songwriter Maurice *Abrahams who wrote much of her material.

Baker, Chet [Chesney H.] (*b* Yale, Okla., 23 Dec. 1929; *d* Amsterdam, 13 May 1988). American trumpet player and singer. After service as an army musician, he studied theory and harmony, and first came into jazz by way of West Coast engagements with Charlie *Parker and Gerry *Mulligan. He formed his own band in 1953 and toured Europe 1955–6. He played modern jazz in a light, clear way, reminiscent of Miles *Davis, and was very popular in the 1950s. His drug addiction complicated his career, a facet dwelt on in the biographical film *Let's Get Lost* (1989). While it was being made, Baker died falling from a hotel window.

Baker, George (*b* Birkenhead, 10 Feb. 1885; *d* Pontrilas, Hereford, 8 Jan. 1976). British baritone, particularly known as a pioneering recording artist whose clear voice and articulation were well-suited to early techniques. He was already an active musician in 1901 and first recorded in 1909. After early performances in ballad concerts and opera, he became a regular recording artist and worked under many pseudonyms. He was particularly active in a light, popular vein; e.g. Leslie *Stuart songs, and *Fraser-Simson's settings of *The Hums of Pooh* and Lewis Carroll; but he was especially remembered for his *Gilbert and Sullivan. He was never a member of the D'Oyly *Carte company but was an important contributor to various complete recordings, notably the six with Sir Malcolm Sargent in the late 1950s. He was then in his mid-seventies, and he broadcast from the Albert Hall in *Trial by Jury* in 1966 at the age of 81. His first wife died in 1933 and he married the singer Olive Groves who died in 1974. In later years he was active as a musical and charitable administrator.

G. Baker: *This Singing Business* (London, 1947).

Baker, Josephine (*b* St Louis, Mo., 3 June 1906; *d* Paris, 12 Apr. 1975). American singer and dancer. The daughter of a black American mother and a Jewish father, she was educated in Philadelphia, then went to New York to train as a dancer and had an early dancing career in Harlem nightclubs. She toured in the *Sissle and *Blake all-black revue **Shuffle Along* (1921) and appeared 'as a sort of black Fanny *Brice' in their subsequent musical *The Chocolate Dandies*. But her early reputation was mainly built in Paris when, after touring Britain and Europe with Lew *Leslie's **Blackbirds*, it was presented as *Revue Nègre* at the Champs-Elysées Music Hall in 1925. She made tremendous impact on Paris, was a fashionable rage for many weeks, and a key influence in France's growing obsession with black entertainment. She subsequently appeared in variety, revues, operetta—in *Offenbach's *La Belle Créole* (originally *La Créole*)—and in films. She was booked by Paul Derval at the Folies-Bergère in 1927 for a revue, *Un Vent du folie*, where she appeared with two cheetahs and dressed only in a girdle of imitation bananas. She sang in her uniquely seductive manner such numbers as 'La petite Tonkinoise' and 'J'ai deux amours'. When she returned to New York to appear in the **Ziegfeld Follies of 1936*, New York was not so impressed, and she was soon back in Paris where she appeared with Maurice *Chevalier in 1939.

In contrast to her somewhat scandalous stage image, she led a distinguished life outside the theatre. At the outbreak of war she joined the French Women's Air Force and, after the fall of France in 1940, joined the French Resistance movement, earning the Croix de Guerre with Palm, the Legion of Honour, and the Rosette of the Resistance. Back in the USA in the 1940s she was a tireless campaigner for Civil Rights. In 1948 she bought a château in the Dordogne and ran a multi-racial orphanage with her third husband, the conductor Jo Bouillon, whom she married in 1947. It was primarily to raise funds for her 'children' that she returned to the stage at the Olympia Theatre in Paris in 1959, in *Paris mes amours*; and continued to make appearances, including a show in New York in 1964; the French production of *Hello, Dolly!* in 1968; in the Leeds *Good Old Days* TV show in 1973; at the London Palladium in 1974; and a final gala show to celebrate 50 years in entertainment, *Josephine*, at the Bobino Music Hall (1975) just five days before she died. Her magnificently athletic body had been a major asset at the Folies-Bergère, but she also had a very personal way with a song, spontaneous and fickle, and a stage personality that was both magnetic and relaxed. A documentary film of her life, *Chasing a Rainbow*, was made in 1986.

J. Baker & J. Bouillon: *Josephine: an Autobiography* (Paris, 1978). L. Hanley: *Naked at the Feast: a Biography* (London–New York, 1981). B. Hammond & P. O'Connor: *Josephine Baker* (London, 1988). P. Rose: *Jazz Cleopatra: the Story of Josephine Baker* (London, 1990).

Baker, Kenny [Kenneth Lawrence] (*b* Monrovia, Calif., 30 Sept. 1912; *d* 1985). American tenor and actor. He had intended to be a violinist but, after winning a talent contest at the Cocoanut Grove in Los Angeles and a contract to appear with Eddie *Duchin and his Orchestra, he started on a singing career. He joined the Jack Benny radio show in 1935; was on the Texaco Star Theatre show 1939–40; worked with Fred *Allen; and had his own show from 1944. He had a long and successful career in films beginning with the operatic satire *Metropolitan* (1935), with Lawrence Tibbett, and *King of Burlesque* (1936). He continued with *Turn off the Moon* (1936); *A Day at the Races* (1937); *The King and the Chorus Girl* (1937); *Goldwyn Follies* (1938); *Radio City Revels* (1938); *The Mikado* (1939); *A Day at the Circus* (1939); *Hit Parade of 1941* (1940): *Doughboys in Ireland* (1943); his last being *The Harvey Girls* (1946). He appeared on Broadway in **One Touch of Venus* with Mary *Martin in 1943.

Baker, Kenny (*b* Withernsea, York., 1 Mar. 1921). British trumpet player, bandleader, and composer. He played in brass bands, and began his professional career with Lew *Stone in 1939, later with Maurice *Winnick, Jack *Hylton, and *Ambrose. He made his first record (a public jam session) in 1941 and thereafter was at the top of the British musical journal popularity polls throughout his career. Some of his best recordings were made with Harry Hayes and Buddy Featherstonaugh in 1944–5. He was lead trumpeter with *Ted Heath 1946–8, recording such hits as 'Bakerloo non-stop'. In the 1950s he led his own Baker's Dozen and recorded prolifically with them and others, writing many original numbers. In the 1950s, 1960s, and 1970s he was in much demand for films—he recorded the Kay Kendall trumpet solo in *Genevieve* (1954)—and studio work; and regularly played in jazz clubs. With Don Lusher (*b* 1923) and Betty Smith (*b* 1929), he formed the touring show *The Best of British Jazz* in 1976 and has continued to be one of Britain's finest jazz trumpeters.

Baker, LaVern (*b* Chicago, 11 Nov. 1928). American singer. She first sang in gospel choirs and moved to the rhythm 'n' blues field in her teens, her career shadowing that of Ruth *Brown in the 1950s. After Brown had pioneered R & B on the Atlantic label, Baker was signed up in 1953 and became one of their top stars in 1955 with 'That's all I need' and 'Tweedle dee'. If she never outshone such singers as Diana *Ross or Dionne *Warwick in the 1960s, she was highly rated by connoisseurs and demonstrated her jazz and blues abilities with such fine albums as *LaVern Baker Sings Bessie Smith*. She toured Europe in the late 1950s and had hits with 'I can't love you long enough' (1956), 'Still' (1956), 'Jim Dandy' (1957), 'I waited too long' (1959), and her biggest success 'I cried a tear' (1959).

Baker, Phil (*b* Philadelphia, 24 Aug. 1896; *d* Copenhagen, 30 Nov. 1963). American author, comedian, actor, singer, accordionist, and MC. He first appeared in amateur shows in Boston, then teamed up with violinist Ed Janis in a violin/accordion act that became well known in vaudeville. Later he did a similar act with Ben *Bernie, with whom he made his first recording in 1918. After service in the First World War, he resumed his vaudeville career, being one of the first American comedians to employ a stooge. He made his first Broadway appearance in **Greenwich Village Follies of 1920* and was later seen in **Music Box Revue* (1923); **Artists and Models* (1925 and 1930); *A Night in Spain* (1927); *Pleasure Bound* (1929); *Billy Rose's Crazy Quilt* (1931); **Americana* (1932); *Calling All Stars* (1934); and *Priorities* (1942). He had his own radio quiz show from 1933–4, 1934–5, and 1937 through the war years; and appeared in films in the 1930s and 1940s. His best-known composition was 'Strange interlude' (with Ben Bernie and Walter Hirsch, 1932); others included: 'Did you mean it?', 'Love and kisses', 'Look at those eyes', and 'Pretty little baby'.

Baker Street. Probably one of the best attempts to put Sherlock Holmes into a musical comedy, this show, with music and lyrics by Marian Grudeff and Raymond Jessel, and book by Jerome Coopersmith, based on the Arthur Conan Doyle stories, was staged at New York's Broadway Theatre on 16 Feb. 1965 [313p]. The score did not contain any lasting hits and the show, in spite of its subject, never reached London.

Balalaika. British musical play that has been remembered for an excellent score by Bernard *Grun and George *Posford. A re-working of an earlier musical, *The Gay Hussar* (1933), it was produced at the Adelphi Theatre on 22 Dec. 1936 and had an outstanding run of 570 performances. The book was by the distinguished author and BBC executive Eric *Maschwitz and the cast included Clifford Mollison (1897–1986) and Betty Warren (1907–90), with the orchestra leader Walford Hayden as musical director. The songs, still frequently heard, included 'At the balalaika', 'If the world were mine', and 'Ballerina, sad and lonely'. There was an MGM film version in 1939 with Ilona Massey (1912–74) and Nelson *Eddy, with added music by Sigmund *Romberg.

Ball, Eric Walter John (*b* Kingswood, Glos., 31 Oct. 1903; *d* Bournemouth, 1 Oct. 1989). British composer, arranger, and conductor. One of the most prolific writers and influential figures in the brass band and choral world which he was associated with all his life, having been born into a Salvation Army family. After the First World War he wanted to become an organist, but at 18 joined the Music Editorial department of the Salvation Army and started writing music. In 1926 he became an officer of the Army and started the Salvationist Publishing and Supplies Band. He conducted the International Staff Band for a time in 1942 but left to tour abroad entertaining the troops. John Henry Iles of *The British Bandsman* asked him to write a test-piece for the 1946 Belle Vue contest, which he did, calling it 'Salute to Freedom'. He became editor of *The British Bandsman* and seriously started on a conducting career, his first appointment being with the Brighouse & Rastrick Band with whom he won the National Championship in 1946. Later he conducted the CWS (Manchester) Band, Ransome & Marles, and the City of Coventry Band.

Well-known as a lecturer and adjudicator, his other notable test-piece compositions include 'Resurgam' (1950); 'The Conquerors' (1951); 'Tournament for Brass' (1954); 'A Sunset Rhapsody' (1958); 'Festival Music' (1956); 'The Undaunted' (1959); 'Main Street' (1961); 'Journey into Freedom' (1967); 'High Peak' (1969); 'A Kensington Concerto' (1972); and 'Sinfonietta for Brass—The Wayfarer' (1976). In 1972 he wrote 'A Christchurch Cantata' for New Zealand and in 1973 'For All Mankind', a cantata for chorus and band. His long list of brass-band compositions also includes such oft-recorded items as 'Akhnaton', 'Cornish Festival Overture', 'Devon Fantasy', 'Prelude to a Comedy', 'Prelude to Pageantry', 'Quid pro quo', 'Rhapsody on Negro Spirituals' (Nos 1, 2, and 3), 'Rosslyn', 'September Fantasy', 'Sure and Steadfast' and 'Torch of Freedom'; some 30 well-used arrangements of classical pieces (including Bliss's 1978 test-piece 'Checkmate'); and some 80 items composed for Salvation Army use.

Ball, Ernest R. (*b* Cleveland, Ohio, 21 July 1878; *d* Santa Ana, Calif., 3 May 1927). American composer. He studied at the Cleveland Conservatory and wrote his first piece, a march, at 15. His first musical employment was as a relief pianist in vaudeville, playing in various American towns until 1905. He became staff composer to the publishing-house of Witmark & Co., 1907–27. He is remembered for a number of sham Irish (but unforgettable) songs mainly contributed to various musical plays in the pre-war years. From *Barry of Ballymore* (1910) came 'Mother Machree' (with Chauncey *Olcott; *w* Rida Johnson *Young) and others in similar vein; from *Isle of Dreams* (1913) came 'When Irish eyes are smiling' and 'Kathleen Aroon' both with Olcott; *w* George Graff, 1887–1973); from *The Heart of Paddy Whack* (1915) came 'A little bit of heaven' (*w* J. Keirn Brennan, 1873–1948); and many more.

His first song success had come with 'Will you love me in December as you do in May?' (with words by the future Mayor of New York, James J. Walker) in 1905; and other remembered songs included: 'Love me and the world is mine' (1906, *w* Dave Reed); 'In the garden of my heart' (1908, *w* Caro Roma); 'Till the sands of the desert grow cold' (1911, *w* Graff); with words by Brennan: 'Turn back the universe and give me yesterday' (1916), 'Dear little boy of mine' (1918), 'Molly Aroon' (1918), 'Let the rest of the world go by' (1919)—later used in his film biography, *When Irish Eyes Are Smiling* (1944), in which the composer was played by Dick *Haymes; and 'Down the winding road of dreams (1922, *w* Margaret Cantrell). Many of these were sung by such famous artists as John McCormack and became standard party songs. Ball was a founder-member of *ASCAP.

Ball, Kenny [Kenneth] (*b* Ilford, Essex, 22 May 1930). British jazz trumpeter, bandleader, and vocalist. He played in bands led by Sid *Phillips and Eric Delaney before forming his own group in 1958. Since then he has led a good quality *Dixieland band that has become well-known through its appearances on TV and in clubs and concerts. They backed Louis *Armstrong in 1968 and in 1985 toured USSR. An excellent trumpeter, Ball maintains a good standard of popularly slanted traditional jazz fare.

Ball, Lucille Desirée (*b* Jamestown, NY, 6 Aug. 1911; *d* Los Angeles, 26 Apr. 1989). American actress, comedienne, and singer. She went to drama school at the age of 15 but decided she was not a serious actress and took up dancing. She became a model and got a few small parts in films, 1933–5, gradually making a mark in such titles as **Roberta* (1935); **Top Hat* (1935); **Follow the Fleet* (1936); *Having Wonderful Time* (1938); *Too Many Girls* (1940); and *Seven Days' Leave* (1942). Her big break came when she took over the Ethel *Merman role in the film version of **DuBarry Was a Lady* (1943); followed by **Best Foot Forward* (1943); *Thousands Cheer* (1943); *Meet the People* (1944); *Without Love* (1945); but she never became a really big film star. It was through TV that she rose to worldwide popularity in the *I Love Lucy* series. In these she worked with her real-life husband, bandleader Desi Arnaz (1917–86), whom she had married in 1940 and divorced in 1960. By 1955 they owned RKO pictures and established a TV company called Desilu. She played on Broadway in *Wildcat* (1960); and, beyond her peak, in the film version of **Mame* (1970).

E. Harris: *The Real Story of Lucille Ball* (New York, 1954). J. Morella & E. Z. Epstein: *Lucy: the Bittersweet Life of Lucille Ball* (Secaucus, NJ, 1973). J. Gregory: *The Lucille Ball Story* (New York, 1974). B. Andrews & T. J. Watson: *Loving Lucy* (New York, 1980).

Ballad. The term has been attached to many kinds of song, and with various qualifying adjectives has suggested a varied assortment of musical activities. Originally, in the Middle Ages, a ballad, from the Italian *ballare*, was a song to which one danced, hence of a light and rhythmic nature. By the 16th century the word was loosely used to describe almost any solo song that was of a light and folky character, as opposed to the art song. By the 18th century the scholars had changed its import, as in their categorization of Traditional ballad to mean a dramatic (though sometimes humorous) song which was usually an objective telling of a story of some folk-hero or historical event, generally passed down in unwritten form. Famous folk-ballads included 'Sir Patrick Spens', 'Earl Brand', 'The outlandish knight', 'Twa corbies', 'The two sisters', and 'The cruel brother'. A basic collection of folk-ballads that cemented this meaning was Professor James Francis Child's *English and Scottish Popular Ballads*, published in 1898 and containing 305 items which form the basis of British folk-ballad literature. The street ballad, or *broadsheet, was a tradition begun towards the end of the Middle Ages, when crudely printed ballads, sometimes with music, were sold in the streets, acting as a sort of predecessor of the newspaper. They were generally about current events and considerations and flourished in the pre-professional ages of the 16th to 19th centuries. They often parodied known poems and were frequently styled on the rhythms of well-known folk-tunes, whether the music was printed or not, so that the singing of them by ballad-mongers in the streets was also an early form of song-plugging. Alongside these public activities the literary ballad, itself an extension of the traditional ballad, a poem telling a story, flourished in Germany in the 17th and 18th centuries; in England through poets like Scott, Burns, Wordsworth (the *Lyrical Ballads*), and Coleridge (*The Rime of the Ancient Mariner*); in the USA with Longfellow and his contemporaries.

In its next phase the ballad had become a sort of popularized operatic extract, watered down, but blatantly sentimental and succulent and generally referred to as the *Drawing-room ballad, as it was much favoured by the middle-class Victorians who possessed pianos and liked to entertain themselves at home with amateur music-making. These polite forerunners of the popular song were written largely by a growing race of professional songwriters, often female. The songs often still told a story in the old ballad tradition, but were now more frequently simply high-flown songs expressing romantic or religious sentiments. These songs, created alongside the music-hall and minstrel show songs, saw the first manifestations of modern song-plugging in the ballad concerts that were regularly mounted by certain publishers, where their wares were demonstrated by professional performers in order to persuade the amateur to purchase the sheet music and other musical appurtenances. The ballad of 20th-century *Tin Pan Alley times was not so very different. The term had now settled into meaning some sort of love song, generally slow, moody, and sentimental. One sub-division of the category was found in the torch song of the 1930s, which invariably dealt with unrequited love. Even into the rock era the concept of the ballad has persisted. Slow numbers are still referred to as ballads and still have much the same intent as their Victorian predecessors.

F. E. A. Bryant: *A History of English Balladry* (Boston, 1913). F. J. Childs: *The English and Scottish Popular Ballads* (London, 1882–9); repr. New York, 1957). F. Kidson: *Traditional Tunes: a Collection of Ballad Airs* (Oxford, 1891; repr. Wakefield, 1972). T. F. Henderson: *The Ballad in Literature* (Cambridge, 1912). G. H. Gerould: *The Ballad of Tradition* (London, 1923). S. B. Hustvedt: *Ballad Books and Ballad Men* (Harvard, 1930). S. Northcote: *The Ballad in Music* (Oxford, 1942). R. Nettel: *Sing a Song of England* (London, 1954). See also under: BROADSIDE BALLADS; DRAWING-ROOM BALLADS.

Ballad Opera. A theatrical entertainment formulated in England in the early 18th century which consisted of a play interspersed at appropriate places with songs, a degenerate form of the opera which it usually burlesqued. It was an important step in the emancipation of both the musical stage and the popular song. The musical items generally took their tunes from traditional sources, sometimes from opera and other musical forms. *The *Beggar's Opera*, conceived by the poet John Gay with music arranged by Dr Johann Christian Pepusch, produced in 1728, is generally credited with being the first fully formed ballad opera. Its very great success immediately inspired the hopeful production of many similar stage pieces, whose writers saw the attraction of being able to cull a musical score of ready-made hit tunes from the various volumes of folk-song and dance which were then beginning to appear. Several of the leading actors in *The Beggar's Opera*, pleasantly surprised by their 'overnight' success, saw no reason why they should not do as well as Gay in this sort of enterprise. One was Thomas Walker, who had played Macheath and become something of an alcoholic on the strength of his new-found fame and fortune. He managed nevertheless to find time, and the talent, to write several plays and to compile several ballad operas including *The Quaker's Opera* and *Robin Hood*, which both enjoyed some popularity after productions in 1728 and 1730 at Lee and Harper's booth at Bartholomew Fair. Harper was one of the leading comedians of the day and was later one of the company who set themselves up at the Little Theatre in the Haymarket in defiance of Drury Lane's monopoly of popular entertainment. *The Beggar's Opera* also established some star actors and actresses, notably Lavinia Fenton who was a great success as Polly, in spite of her youth and inexperience. She was to become a prototype 'musical comedy' star, a glamorous leading lady and an 18th-century sex symbol; also turning out a most talented and versatile actress, singer, and producer. She also helped to establish another theatrical tradition by marrying into the aristocracy and becoming the Duchess of Bolton.

Gay himself made the mistake of trying to write a sequel to *The Beggar's Opera* called *Polly* which proved to be inferior. It was not seen on the stage until 1777, partly through the machinations of the prime minister, Robert Walpole, who had not enjoyed the satire on himself in its predecessor as much as he had publicly pretended, and had it 'suppress'. In the meantime Gay contrived to get *Polly* printed and did well out of its sales.

Gay's most eminent successor in the ballad opera field was Colley Cibber (1671–1757), who had originally turned down the task of producing *The Beggar's Opera*. He was a skilled playwright and was much involved in the beginnings of pantomime at Drury Lane. It was also thought that he had a hand in the suppression of *Polly*, so when he put on his ballad opera *Love in a Riddle* at Drury Lane in 1729, Gay's supporters turned up in force to howl it down. Cibber managed to restore enough order to have his piece heard but had to promise to withdraw it the following night. This he duly did, but he then produced another ballad opera shortly after called *Damon and Philida* which won warm public approval. Cibber had the last laugh because the piece turned out to be simply *Love in a Riddle* re-named. This production fostered another notable leading lady called Kitty Clive who became a popular figure in the London theatre after her beginnings in ballad opera.

Another prolific creator of ballad operas was the Irishman Charles Coffey (*d* 1745) who had a notable string of successes starting with *Southwark Fair, or The Sheep-Shearing*, which was seen at Southwark Fair in 1729. His best-known work was *The Beggar's Wedding* (neatly cashing in on Gay's title) which was staged in 1729 at Smock Alley in Dublin, at the Haymarket in London, and, in a shortened version entitled *Phoebe*, at Drury Lane. These were followed by *The Devil upon Two Sticks* (1729); *Philida* (1729); *The Female Parson* (1730); *The Devil to Pay* (1731); *The Boarding-School* (1733); and *The Merry Cobbler* (1735). Another famous name in ballad opera was Henry Fielding (1707–54) who wrote *The Welsh Opera*, which became better known, in an extended version, as *The Grub Street Opera* in 1731; *The Mock Doctor* (1732); *The Lottery* (1732); *The Intriguing Chambermaid* (1734); *An Old Man Taught Wisdom* (1735); and *Miss Lucy in Town* (1742).

The heyday of ballad operas was from 1728 to *c.* 1750, after which they began to pall. The public had enjoyed them for their tunes and many writers found it a convenient way of presenting new plays, for the genre remained essentially a straight play with interpolated songs (a form that would be later taken up by *musical comedy) rather than developing into integrated opera. The ballad operas produced in these halcyon years (a comprehensive list will be found in Gagey: *Ballad Opera*) used more than 1000 melodies between them. The supply of good tunes was limited and it was as much a drying-up of this source that brought the era to an end as anything else. By the time the public had heard 'Lillibullero' and 'Tweedside' (two of the great favourites) used countless times, the effect was wearing thin. Another source was opera itself; but it was becoming obvious that there was now a call for original scores to be written.

There was a brief but significant revival of ballad opera in 1762 with Thomas Arne's *Love in a Village* (based on *The Villlage Opera* of 1729) which showed much less dependence on traditional tunes and was now mainly new music—albeit written in the ballad style. In this case the overture and 10 songs were written by Arne, some were borrowed from such composers as Agus, Boyce, Howard, and Weldon, while just three were based on traditional melodies, with the finale a medley of such material. With a libretto by Isaac Bickerstaffe, it had a great success at Covent Garden in December 1762 and had been heard in Philadelphia, USA, by 1767, where it was to have a strong influence. A work of similar nature was Dibdin's *Lionel and Clarissa* of 1768 (Philadelphia, 1772). These now led to a flourishing period of British *light opera.

Ballad opera was categorized in *Grove* (5th edn) as 'a species of stage production peculiar to England'. Its influence spread abroad, however, mainly due to the universal popularity of Coffey's *The Devil to Pay* which was produced in Germany in 1743 as *Der Teufel ist los* and helped to establish the German Singspiel tradition; a genre of German vernacular opera that was to flourish as a defiant native rival to the all-pervading Italian opera. In England, and subsequently in the USA, the ballad opera fostered the establishment of a popular musical theatre that continued to grow, in answer to a public demand throughout the 19th century.

F. Kidson: *The Beggar's Opera, its Predecessors and Successors* (Cambridge, 1922). E. M. Gagey: *Ballad Opera* (New York, 1937; rev. 1965). R. Fiske: *English Theatre Music in the Eighteenth Century* (London, 1973).

Ball im Savoy. Operetta in three acts with music by Paul *Abrahám and words by Alfred Grünwald and Fritz Löhner-Beda, first heard in Berlin at the Grosses-Schauspielhaus 23 Dec. 1932 and then in Vienna at the Johann Strausstheater 25 Dec. 1933. As *Ball at the Savoy* it was staged at the Drury Lane Theatre in London 8 Sept. 1922 with English book by Oscar *Hammerstein II, and has been performed all over the world. It has the usual Paul Abrahám mixture of Viennese schmaltz and 1920s pseudo-jazz, though more inclined to the former than some of his works. It has some lasting songs including (in English) 'I always keep my girl out late', 'Oh why, oh why, oh why', 'I think I'm in love with my wife', 'A girl like Nina', and 'I live for love'.

'Ballin' the jack'. The exact meaning of the name of the dance step or movement called 'Ballin' the jack' is somewhat obscure. It has been suggested that it came from railroad slang, a 'jack' being a locomotive and 'balling' meaning to get on the move. Perry *Bradford remembered seeing the steps performed around 1909, but it was probably well-established by then. The dance was standardized by the *Savoy Ballroom professionals and given a musical form in 1913 by Chris *Smith and Roy Burris, the lyric mentioning other steps such as the Eagle rock. It became a popular success when heard and seen in the **Ziegfeld Follies* of 1913, although the dance was always considered somewhat rough and low-down until it was more politely presented by Danny *Kaye in the film *On the Riviera* (1951) when it found a new popularity. There had already been revivals in the 1920s, 1930s, and 1940s in various hands.

Ballroom dancing. In the modern sense of the term, ballroom dancing really started with the *waltz, the first dance in which the couples remained together throughout and elaborated on natural walking steps, in contrast to the more balletic steps of earlier dances like the gavotte, the *polka, and the *quadrille, though all these were being performed when the public ballroom was already an established venue. Although Vienna was the earliest outlet for the composition of ballroom music, it was to be superseded by the USA in the later jazz age. But most of the 20th-century formalization of standard ballroom dances was to take place in the British Isles.

The waltz craze began to supplant the polka around 1812 when the waltz was introduced at Almack's Ballroom in London. It was to remain the principal and most popular ballroom dance for more or less a century. As late as 1910 it was common to find two-thirds of a ballroom evening taken up by waltzes, though by the beginning of the 20th century its nature had changed, the old rotating waltz being replaced by the less dizzying *Boston which first appeared around 1903. About 1910 the *tango heralded an introduction of Latin American rhythms to the American and European ballroom, but such dances never became universally popular as the steps were beyond most amateurs. The *barn dance and *galop had a brief vogue before 1914. The *veleta and the *military two-step were keenly promoted from 1900, the latter surviving in a number of new forms. During the First World War the *foxtrot, popularized by Vernon and Irene *Castle, became the new craze and the waltz suddenly went out of fashion, though it was to survive and soon made a come-back as one of the standard dances. Jazz rhythms brought in new syncopated dances like the *quickstep, a simplified version of the *Charleston, which has remained the most popular dance of modern times. Numerous novelty dances have had their brief vogues, while the modern jazz dances like the *jitterbug or *jive and the dances of the rock age like the *twist now find their way into most dance evenings, even those of a traditional kind. As in the sporting field, there is a great divide between the stumbling amateur, who prefers to confine his embarrassment to attempts at the quickstep and waltz, and the dedicated enthusiast or professional who performs Latin American and other intricate dances with such enviable agility and grace. See also DANCE.

I. & V. Castle: *Modern Dancing* (New York, 1914). T. & M. W. Kinney: *Social Dancing of Today* (New York, 1914). P. J. S. Richardson & V. Silvester: *The Art of the Ballroom* (London, 1938). A. H. Franks: *The Ballroom Dancer's Handbook* (London, 1940). P. J. S. Richardson: *A History of English Ballroom Dancing (1910–1945)* (London, 1948). A. H. Franks: *Social Dance: a Short History* (London, 1963). V. Silvester: *Modern Ballroom Dancing* (London, n.d.; repr. 1977). P. Buckman: *Let's Dance* (New York–London, 1978).

Band. A group of musicians, usually half a dozen or more. A term of interestingly variable use, generally interchanging with other group words like orchestra. The use of the word 'band' seems to imply a moving, or at least moveable, unit, a potential marching ensemble. It is used in this spirit in *brass band and *military band, for although both of these kinds of bands might well be seated in performance, their original purpose was to lead in processions and to play in march-time. In a similar spirit it has come to be the general unitary term in *jazz, the jazz band not originally intended as a concert unit but as a marching band for festive occasions. In general terms, therefore, the word 'band' suggests a mobile and generally (but not always) smaller group with portable instruments; the word 'orchestra' suggesting an ensemble using non-portable instruments (strings) and probably larger. As with all such general terms the usage has become blurred, particularly in jazz where, although 'orchestra' still implies a larger unit, the word 'band' is used with less discrimination. There is a certain amount of class distinction involved; 'orchestra' sounding rather more high-class, as do classically-based descriptions such as quartet (*Modern Jazz Quartet), quintet (*Quintet of the Hot Club of France), or the term 'ensemble' (*Art Ensemble of Chicago). 'Band' tends to be confined to traditional jazz. In the field of light music, the word 'orchestra' is favoured as in Palm Court Orchestra, essentially a sedentary ensemble. Rock music, on the other hand, has taken to the word 'group'.

Band, The. A mainly Canadian *rhythm 'n' blues group formed around 1965 to accompany Bob *Dylan. The original members, who had all played together in the late 1950s as the Hawks, a backing group of the Toronto rock-and-roller Ronnie Hawkins, were Levon Helm (drums), from Arkansas, Jaime Robbie Robertson (1943–86) (guitar), Garth Hudson (organ), Richard Manuel (piano), and Rick Danko (bass), all Canadians. Leaving Hawkins they played with the white blues singer John Hammond Jr. and he introduced them to Dylan who was just then moving into electric music.

The first record made with Dylan was 'Can you please crawl out of your window' (1965); the group were at their creative best in the rock concert tours of 1965–6 and in numbers such as 'Just like Tom Thumb's blues'. They played at the Albert Hall in London and, after Dylan's motorcycle accident in July 1966, settled in Woodstock to work with him. The Band took on some of the Dylan poetry and style and Dylan became more bluesy, as was heard on the *John Wesley Harding* album. They started to record without Dylan, Robertson creating such numbers as 'The night they drove old Dixie down', 'King Harvest', and 'Up on Cripple Creek' all in the second *The Band* album. The Band toured as a powerful unit promulgating the hard-core spirit of rhythm 'n' blues combined with the surge of rock and roll. They backed Dylan once more on two albums in the 1970s; and finally broke up in 1976 with a triumphal farewell concert and a final LP, *Islands*, issued in 1977.

Bandmaster [Fr. *chef de musique*; Ger. *Kapellmeister*]. The conductor of a brass or military band. The 18th century had other titles such as Music Master, Music Major, Master Musician, and Leader of the Band. Very often the bandmaster of a military band would be a civilian. In 1803 the War Office made it an official post carrying the rank of sergeant, but each bandmaster was to be paid from a band fund provided by the officers, except in the Royal Artillery and certain colleges and schools. In 1856 the Royal Military School of Music was founded at *Kneller Hall in Twickenham, Middlesex, where bandsmen could be properly trained. An advanced course takes qualified bandsmen on to the rank of Bandmaster, with a further chance of becoming a commissioned Director of Music, qualifying them to use p.s.m. ('passed school of music') after their name. In 1881 bandmasters were promoted to the rank of warrant officer (1st class). In 1887 the Grenadier Guards bandmaster Daniel *Godfrey was given an honorary commission and in 1898, by royal command, the bandmasters of the Royal Horse Guards, Royal Artillery, and Royal Marines were similarly honoured. Since then a higher post of Director of Music has been created which carries full commissioned rank and promotion as for any other officer.

Band Wagon, The. A well-remembered New York revue which opened at the Amsterdam Theatre on 3 June 1931 and had 260 performances. It was a worthy successor to *Three's a Crowd* (1930) with the same creative team behind it—music by Arthur *Schwartz, lyrics by Howard *Dietz, book by Dietz and George S. *Kaufman, but a different cast that included Helen *Broderick, Fred *Astaire, and Adele *Astaire in her last Broadway show. It was stylish, intelligent, witty, and done with good taste. The songs included: 'It better be good', 'Sweet music', 'High and low', 'I love Louisa', 'Where can he be', 'White heat', and the imperishable 'Dancing in the dark'. The MD was Al *Goodman. The MGM film version of 1953 starring Astaire, Cyd Charisse, and Jack *Buchanan, and directed by Vincente *Minelli, added the song 'That's entertainment'.

Banjo. Finger-played, fretted, stringed instrument, once widely used in popular music for rhythmic accompaniment, but now largely supplanted by the guitar in this respect. It seems likely that the banjo derived from a similar African instrument, variously called the banja, banjar, bania, bandja, or banza, that is still in use today. Primitive stringed instruments of a similar nature were made by the black slaves in America using for a soundbox a halved gourd or a shaped piece of wood with sheepskin or parchment fastened over it. In his *A Voyage to the Islands Madere, Barbados, Jamaica* (1707), Sir Hans Sloane described instruments he had seen during his travels in 1688: 'in imitation of lutes made of small gourds fitted with necks, strung with horsehair or the peeled stalks of climbing plants' or 'sometimes made of hollowed timber covered with parchment or other skin'. In 1781 the black musicians in America were described by the future President Jefferson as using the 'banjar which they brought from Africa', also known as the banger (with a soft g) and in England as the banga (similarly pronounced). It was thus seen, by the beginning of the 19th century, as the typical Negro instrument. In the pantomime *Obi, or Three-fingered Jack* put on in 1800 at the Theatre Royal in the Haymarket, London, one of the characters sings a song that has the line 'Go dance to the Banga just like mad'; while Charles *Dibdin, a distant but frequent delineator of Negro life, wrote a 'Bonja song' in 1802.

It is not easy to pinpoint exactly when the first commercial banjos were made in the USA or who decided on the modern name. By 1840 the musical instrument firm of Elias Howe in Boston was advertising a wide range of professional instruments. It is said that the first banjos had a plain unfretted fingerboard, the frets being added to aid the amateur performer around 1830. It was the *minstrel show craze in the 1840s that made the banjo a popular instrument among both professionals and amateurs, and its status was helped by the composition of 'The banjo' (1854–5) by Louis Moreaux *Gottschalk.

The banjo most favoured in the USA has been the five-stringed instrument, hence widely referred to as the 'American' banjo. This is the favourite solo instrument played in what is called 'finger-style'. It is tuned to middle C, G, B, and D with the fifth string a high G. The four-string plectrum banjo, usually an accompanying instrument, discards this top string.

The body of the modern banjo is a metal or wooden hoop over which the head or 'vellum' of calf skin (more recently plastic) is fastened by bracket hooks. A circular resonator, slightly larger in diameter than the rim, is generally fixed over the back. In England in the early days of banjo history *c.* 1800 or even earlier, instruments with 6, 7, 8, or 9 strings were in use and the English makers favoured an instrument with a very long neck. The neck of the commonly used instruments is generally made of walnut or mahogany with a fingerboard, as with the violin, of ebony or rosewood. Metal frets were inserted at an early stage of its history as an aid to finding the position of the notes.

By the mid-19th century, by which time the banjo orchestra (probably with mandolins and guitars added) was common, a variety of instruments was available. The most popular instrument for solo work was the one known as the zither-banjo (sometimes referred to, after the name of its inventor, as a Dobson), in which the rim and vellum are suspended inside a round, box-like body which becomes a surrounding resonator with the sound passing through the space between the rim and the outer case, thus giving a clear and sharp sound. There was also the banjorine, with a shorter neck tuned to a higher pitch; the tenor banjo with violin tuning; the four-stringed banjolin; the banjo-mandolin which was made like a zither-banjo but had mandolin-style double strings; and rarer high and low pitched instruments like the piccolo-banjo or, below, the bass and contrabass models.

In the banjo and minstrel bands of the mid-19th century, thimble-style playing was popular to give the instrument more impact. This involved the use of a small thimble-like implement on the first finger of the strumming hand which gave a more plangent tone. The folk-music users favoured the finger-style, as still heard in the *bluegrass music of Virginia and the Blue Ridge Mountain states. It was the impact of the banjo's sound that made it the most popular recording instrument in the early days of the phonograph; a sound that the primitive techniques could most easily capture. A large percentage of early recordings were banjo solos or duets by such players as Burt Earle, Harry Clark, Vess L. Ossman in the USA, Olly Oakley, Sydney Turner, John Pidoux in Britain, and Will Blanche from South Africa. It is easy to see why the emerging black music of the 20th century, which first entered the mainstream as ragtime in the 1890s, should have a strong banjo characteristic. The very nature of early minstrel songs and ragtime piano pieces seems to have been dictated by the strumming, syncopated banjo rhythms.

The coincidental emergence of jazz and the phonograph had the effect of forcing a number of jazz guitarists to use the banjo in order to provide an audible rhythmic basis through the mush of early recordings and the hubbub of collective improvisation. As soon as recording could cope with the softer-toned but more flexible guitar, favoured by the blues singers, it came back into jazz. Around 1930 the banjo generally went out of favour, retaining its place in popular music in certain areas such as revival jazz and minstrelsy and marching bands; or simply among those who enjoy the nostalgic flavour of its sound and repertoire.

A British Federation of Banjoists, Mandolinists, and Guitarists was formed in 1929 and there is still a substantial amateur following that compares with the barber-shop movement.

Barber, Chris (*b* Welwyn Garden City, Herts., 17 Apr. 1930). British trombonist, bassist, bandleader, arranger, and composer. He led his first band in 1950. In 1953 he joined forces with Ken *Colyer but there was internal disagreement and in 1954 Colyer left and Barber assumed leadership with Pat Halcox (*b* 1930) on trumpet, Monty Sunshine (*b* 1928) on clarinet, singer/banjoist Lonnie *Donegan, and blues singer Ottilie Patterson (*b* 1932)—one of the few convincing British blues singers—whom he married. When Donegan left to pursue a solo career after the success of 'Rock Island Line', he was replaced by Eddie Smith. The Barber band produced a crisp, professional, semi-commercial sound, individualized by its pianoless policy and Barber's incisive trombone style. They took many jazz numbers such as 'Whistling Rufus', 'Bobby Shafto', and 'Petite fleur' into the hit parade and were influential in the British traditional jazz boom of the 1950s. In 1959 they appeared on the Ed Sullivan show in the USA, the first British band to do so, and in the film *Look Back in Anger*. Sunshine left to form his own band in 1960 with which he built a big reputation in Europe. The trad boom over and the pop boom beginning, Barber adopted a rock-cum-jazz style, with electronic backing, and produced the remarkable album *Battersea Rain Dance* using pieces by himself, Joe Harriot, Paul *McCartney, Charles *Mingus, Duke *Ellington, Randy *Newman, and others. The band maintained a fresh outlook and sound and toured extensively, working with many American musicians. In the 1980s Barber organized a stage presentation *Take Me Back to New Orleans*. An important British jazz individualist, he has kept abreast of changes of taste without losing a healthily traditionalist flavour and always maintaining high musical standards.

Barber shop ballads/music. The singing of barber shop music has become a popular phenomenon in recent years, with countless groups ranging from quartets to sizeable choirs flourishing in the USA and Great Britain, and other European countries, with regular international competitions and conventions. Remarkable standards are achieved, with material ranging from the basic classics of the genre like 'Nellie Dean', 'Sweet Genevieve', and 'Heart of my heart' (William Jerome, 1865–1932, and Andrew Mack, 1863–1931); 'Sweet Adeline' (1903); and 'Down by the old mill stream' (1910), to more recent ingenuities; the perpetuated ingredients being a strong melody and close, succulent chromatic harmonies.

The connection with the barber's shop seems to have started in England in Shakespeare's time and was strongly revived in the American West in gold-rush days. It was common practice to have a lute (later a guitar) on hand and for male quartets to pass the time in convivial harmonizing while waiting for the barber's services. The material originally used may have partly come from, may even have added to, the vast repertoire of glees which were once a peculiarly British phenomenon. A Society for the Preservation and Encouragement of Barber-Shop Singing was formed in America in 1938, with impressive results.

Barbieri, Francisco Asenjo (*b* Madrid, 3 Aug. 1823; *d* Madrid, 19 Feb. 1894). Spanish composer. From 1837 he studied clarinet, voice, and composition (the latter under Pedro Albéniz) at the Madrid Conservatory. While he was trying to make his mark as a composer he spent many years playing the clarinet in military bands and theatre orchestras, and the piano in cafés, working as music copyist, chorus-master, and producer of *zarzuelas, and as a singer. Family connections with the opera led him in that direction and he finally broke into theatre composition with *Gloria y peluca*, produced in Madrid, 9 Mar. 1850; followed by an acclaimed success with *Jugar con fuego*, 6 Oct. 1851, a work with a strongly Italian flavour. He was one of the first to discover a genuinely Spanish style, and became a leading, though always modest, figure in the developing world of Spanish zarzuela, his music now full of traditional themes and colours.

His personal style is most satisfyingly represented by *Pan y Toros* (22 Dec. 1864) and *El Barberillo de Lavapiés* (18 Dec. 1874) whose overture is a quintessential piece of Spanish entertainment music. He founded the Sociedad de Conciertos de Madrid in 1866 and did much to widen Spanish tastes for European music, as well as editing the important collection *Cancionero musical do los siglos XV y XVI* and publishing many essays on Spanish music. The tunefulness and exuberance of his zarzuelas, of which he wrote almost 80, has earned many of them a lasting place as classics of the golden era of the genre. Others included: *Tramoya* (1850); *La Hechicera* (1852); *Los diamantes de la corona* (1854); *El Diablo en el poder* (1856); *El pan de la boda* (1868); *El proceso del Can-can* (1873); *El Diabolo cojuelo* (1878); *La Guerra Santa* (1879).

J. Subirá: *Manuscritos de Barbieri, existentes en la Biblioteca Nacional* (Madrid, 1936). A. Martínez Olmedilla: *El maestro Barbieri y su tiempo* (Madrid, 1950).

Bard, Wilkie [Smith, William Augustus] (*b* Manchester, 19 Mar. 1874; *d* London, 5 Mar. 1944). British comedian and singer. While working as a clerk in the cotton industry he made many amateur appearances, and eventually decided to become a professional entertainer, making his first appearance in Feb. 1895 under the name of Will Gibbard. By the time he made his London debut at Collins Music Hall, Islington, later in 1895, he was calling himself Wilkie Bard and performed in Cockney coster tradition. Soon after he developed a highly individual style, often eccentrically made up with a domed bald head and black spots above each eyebrow. He specialized in character studies, most effectively in female guise singing such pseudo-highbrow items as 'I want to sing in opera'. Other songs he made famous, many written by Frank Leo, included the anti-suffragette 'Put me on an island where the girls are few', a policeman number, 'I'm here if you want me', and 'O, O, capital O'. He regularly appeared as a pantomime dame, twice at Drury Lane where he introduced 'She sells sea shells on the seashore'; and he was the originator of the interrupted monologue. Bard toured America and was in *The Bing Girls Are There* at the *Alhambra in 1917. He continued to perform up to the year he died.

Barker, Danny [Daniel] (*b* New Orleans, 13 Jan. 1909). American banjoist, guitarist, and composer. He worked in various groups in New Orleans, Chicago, and New York, before becoming known in the ranks of bands led by Benny *Carter, Lucky *Millinder, and Cab *Calloway from 1939 to 1946. He accompanied his singer wife Blue Lu and from 1965 increasingly based himself in New Orleans, becoming a prominent figure in the jazz revival there. He was still leading his French Market Jazz Band in Tradition Hall in the late 1970s. A tireless jazz researcher, he was for many years assistant curator of the New Orleans Jazz Museum, and regularly appeared in this role on radio and TV. He wrote a searching study of New Orleans music, *Bourbon Street Black* (in collaboration with Jack Buerkle; New York, 1973); and his autobiography, *A Life in Jazz* (London, 1988).

Barker, George Arthur (*b* London, 15 Apr. 1812; *d* Aylestone, Leics., 2 Mar. 1876). British composer and singer. He became well-known as an opera singer and recitalist in the English provinces and Scotland; and as a prolific writer of ballads and songs, including 'The Irish emigrant' (1846, *w* Lady Dufferin), 'Scottish blue bells', 'Mary Blane' (1846), 'White squall' (1847), 'My skiff is on the shore', 'Dublin Bay', 'Ellen Astore', 'A dream of life', 'I cannot smile, dear Mother', 'The old sailor's daughter', 'The pride of the village', 'Breathe not that name', 'Excelsior', 'Gallant men of old', and 'Roses of youth'. Many of these were issued in his 'Song Albums'—12 vols. published from 1853—and 'Songs of the Army and Navy'—an early partwork (1855). He also wrote many waltzes and piano pieces.

Barnard, Charlotte [*née* Alington] (*b* Louth, 23 Dec. 1830; *d* Dover, 30 Jan. 1869). British songwriter who generally wrote under the name of 'Claribel'. She studied under the pianist and composer William Henry Holmes (1812–85). She married Charles C. Barnard in 1854 and was able to pursue her composing career on an amateur and pseudonymous basis, but did achieve some best-sellers such as 'Come back to Erin' (1866) which Sigmund *Spaeth described in the 20th century as 'still heard with honest pleasure and often regarded as an Irish folksong'. Others that became favourites included: 'Janet's choice' (1860), 'Won't you tell me why, Robin?' (1861), 'Five o'clock in the morning' (1863), 'Take back the heart thou gavest' (1864), 'Oh Mother, take the wheel away' (1865), to mention but a few from a very lengthy list.

P. Smith: *The Story of Claribel [Charlotte Alington Barnard]* (Lincoln, 1965).

Barn dance. A dance originally known as the military schottisch, acquiring its more familiar title from being danced to a tune called 'Dancing in the barn'. It became popular in England around 1888, though known in the USA some years earlier, where there was a custom of holding a dance to celebrate the building of a new barn. Similar to any ordinary *schottisch, it was danced by couples, with the standard waltz turn. The actual originator is not known. It was frequently danced in its heyday to the 'Pas de quatre' by Meyer *Lutz from the Gaiety burlesque *Faust-up-to-Date* and therefore often referred to as a pas de quatre. By the 1920s it had become a 'progressive' dance, with a change of partners among the movements, and is still in use at old-time dances.

Barnes, Fred [Frederick Jester] (*b* Birmingham, 31 May 1885; *d* Southend, 23 Oct. 1938). British light comedian and singer. He made his first stage appearance at the Gaiety Theatre, Birmingham, Dec. 1907, and appeared in London at the Empress Theatre, Brixton, in 1908. Immaculately dressed in tails, he was a very professional artist with a good baritone voice and was heard at all the best variety theatres. He also toured Australia, South Africa, and the USA. His featured songs included: 'Ragtime violin', 'The black sheep of the family', 'What you never have you never miss', 'Give me a million beautiful girls', 'Sally, the sunshine of our alley', 'Give me the moonlight' (also sung by Elsie *Janis and later revived by Frankie *Vaughan), and 'On Mother Kelly's doorstep', later taken up with great success by Randolph Sutton (1888–1970). He was a heavy drinker and a homosexual and after public revelations about him, and contracting TB, he committed suicide.

T. Barker: 'Fred Barnes' in *Music-Hall*, No. 30 (London, Mar. 1984).

Barnet, Charlie [Charles Daly] (*b* New York, 26 Oct. 1913; *d* San Diego, 4 Sept. 1991). American bandleader, saxophonist, and composer. He came from a wealthy family. Deciding on jazz as a career, he joined the Frank Winegar band at the age of 16. After working with Red *Norvo, Adrian *Rollini, and Barney *Bigard, he led a small band at the Paramount Theatre in 1932, then formed his first big band in 1933. The success of his recording of 'Cherokee' in 1939 established him as a swing era favourite, and he recorded prolifically for RCA and Decca. With the decline of the big band world he semi-retired but made a brief come-back in 1967. He was strongly influenced by Duke *Ellington but contrived a personal style and was an outstanding alto and tenor soloist. He composed 'The right idea' (with Skip Martin, 1939); 'The wrong idea' (with Billy *May, 1939); 'Count's idea' (with May, 1939); 'Duke's idea' (with May, 1939); 'Redskin rumba' (1940); 'Dark Avenue' (with Haven Johnson, 1940); 'Murder at Peyton Hall' (1941); and his biggest hit 'Skyliner' (1944). He appeared both with and without his band in numerous films in the 1940s and 1950s, including *The Fabulous Dorseys* (1947) and *A Song is Born* (1948).

C. Barnet & S. Dance: *Those Swinging Years: the Autobiography of Charlie Barnet* (New York, 1984).

Barnum. Musical based on the life of the showman Phineas Taylor Barnum (1810–91), basically a colourful evocation of 'The Greatest Show on Earth' with a mere thread of story supplied by the constant desire of Barnum's wife Chairy to lead a normal life. The stage was mainly filled with such varied characters as General Tom Thumb, George Washington's 160-year-old nurse, Jumbo the elephant, and Jenny Lind. The score by Cy *Coleman included 'There's a sucker born ev'ry minute', 'One brick at a time', 'Bigger isn't better', and 'The Prince of Humbug'; with lyrics by Michael Stewart and book by Mark Bramble. The British actor Jim Dale (*b* 1939) had a great success in the title role, showing he could perform all the circus tricks as well as sing; Glenn Close played his wife. Opening at the St James Theatre, New York, 30 Apr. 1980, it had 854 performances. In the London Palladium production of 11 June 1981, Michael *Crawford provided a similarly athletic lead; as in the TV film version (1986).

Barrelhouse. An American drinking dive serving (often bootleg) beer from the barrel and home-made liquor; generally a gambling shop as well. In such places the entertainment was usually a pianist operating on a knocked-out instrument which had to be played forcefully to impress itself on the noisy clientele. The pounding style that evolved became known as barrelhouse piano and included some types of *boogie-woogie, alternatively referred to as *honky-tonk music.

Barrel-organ. A pipe-organ activated by a revolving barrel or cylinder in which pins are set to operate small levers which open the valve of the requisite organ pipe. The term 'barrel-organ' has often been wrongly applied to the *street piano which is not an organ at all. It is correctly used of a mechanical organ, usually implying one of the smaller hand-operated variety; the larger ones operated by steam or electricity are more usually referred to as a *mechanical organ, *street organ, *fairground organ, or orchestrion.

The earliest barrel-organs were made in the 18th century and were small instruments in a wooden box with no more than 10 pipes, sometimes called 'canary' organs or 'serinetjes', which played a single-line melody and were used to coax canaries and other cage birds into singing. The first portable street organs came early in the 19th century, ranging from the familiar organ-grinder's instrument on a supporting leg to the larger piano-like instruments. Before the arrival of the gramophone they were an important means of disseminating popular ditties among the population, selections from the operas or operettas of the day, polkas and marches, and music-hall songs being among the favoured repertoire.

Barri, Odoardo [Slater, Edward] (*b* 1884; *d* London, 23 Jan. 1920). British composer remembered for one stirring song 'The old brigade' (words by Fred E. *Weatherly) written in typically patriotic British style in 1886. He wrote many others, including 'Saved from the storm' (*w* Weatherly), 'Patchwork' (*w* D'Arcy Jaxone), 'The child and the flowers' (*w* Mary Mark-Lemon), 'A happy day' (Weatherly), 'Alone for ever' (*w* Mme Foli), 'A shadow' (*w* Adelaide Anne Proctor), 'At peace but still on guard' (Weatherly); but he never repeated the success. He also wrote *M.D.*, a 'musical absurdity', which was produced at the Garrick Theatre in 1879.

Barrington, Rutland [Fleet, George Rutland] (*b* Penge, 15 Jan. 1853; *d* London, 31 May 1922). British actor and singer particularly remembered for his pioneering roles in the *Gilbert and Sullivan operas. After joining Mrs Howard Paul in her 'entertainment' in 1875, he became a member of the D'Oyly *Carte Company, then operating from the Opéra-Comique theatre, and created the part of Dr Daly in *The *Sorcerer* (1877). He went with the company to the *Savoy where he played leading parts in **HMS Pinafore* (1878); *The *Pirates of Penzance* (1880); **Patience* (1881); **Iolanthe* (1882); **Princess Ida* (1884); *The *Mikado* (1885); and **Ruddigore* (1887). He appeared in several revivals but left the D'Oyly Carte in 1888 to manage the St James's Theatre, though he returned in 1889 for *The *Gondoliers*. He made further musical appearances in *The Nautch Girl* (1892); *The *Geisha* (1896); *A Greek Slave* (1898); **San Toy* (1899); *A *Country Girl* (1902); *The *Cingalee* (1904); and *Amasis* (1906). He was also an author and journalist, and a regular contributor to *Punch*.

R. Barrington: *Rutland Barrington* (London, 1908).
R. Barrington: *More Rutland Barrington* (London, 1911).

Barris, Harry (*b* New York, 24 Nov. 1905; *d* Burbank, Calif., 13 Dec. 1962). American singer, pianist, composer, and author. He started out as a professional pianist but became known as one of the original Rhythm Boys (the others being Bing *Crosby and Al Rinker) who were featured with the Paul *Whiteman orchestra. After many years with Whiteman, he became a solo entertainer. He wrote many songs, including: 'Mississippi mud' (with James Cavanagh, 1927); 'From Monday on' (with Bing Crosby, 1928); 'So the bluebirds and the blackbirds got together' (1929, *w* Billy Moll); 'At your command' (1921, *w* Harry Tobias and Crosby); 'I surrender, dear' (1931, *w* Gordon Clifford); and 'Wrap your troubles in dreams' (with Ted *Koehler and Moll, 1931).

Barry, John [Prendergast, John Barry] (*b* York, 3 Nov. 1933). British composer. He acquired an early interest in and knowledge of films while working in his teens as a projectionist in his father's cinemas. At 19 he was a trumpeter in an army band, afterwards studying music with Dr Francis Jackson at York Minster and in correspondence with Bill *Russo. He worked as an arranger for several bands before forming the John Barry Seven in 1957, which was the accompanying group for Adam *Faith for five years, participated in various pop shows, made many recordings, and first broadcast in 1959. He wrote the theme for TV's *Juke Box Jury* and radio's *Easy Beat*. Since 1959 he has been a prolific composer for films, has written music for many TV shows and commercials, and has been musical director and arranger for EMI.

His film scores include: *Beat Girl* (1959); *Never Let Go* (1960); *Mix Me a Person* (1962); *The L-Shaped Room* (1962); *The Amorous Prawn* (1962); *Dr No* (1962); *The Party's Over* (1963); *From Russia With Love* (1963); *Zulu* (1963); *Goldfinger* (1964); *Man in the Middle* (1964); *The Ipcress File* (1965); *King Rat* (1965); *Thunderball* (1965); *The Quiller Memorandum* (1966); *Born Free* (1966); *The Chase* (1966); *The Wrong Box* (1966); *The Whisperers* (1967); *You Only Live Twice* (1967); *The Lion in Winter* (1968; Academy Award); *Midnight Cowboy* (1969); *The Appointment* (1969); *The Last Valley* (1971); *Walkabout* (1971); *Murphy's War* (1971); *The Persuaders* (1971); *Alice's Adventures in Wonderland* (1972); *Mary Queen of Scots* (1972); *Diamonds Are Forever* (1972); *The Tamarind Seed* (1973); *The Man With the Golden Gun* (1974); *King Kong* (1976); *The Deep* (1977); *The White Buffalo* (1977); *The Betsy* (1978); *Moonraker* (1979); *The Black Hole* (1979); *Raise the Titanic* (1980); *Somewhere in Time* (1980); *Superman 2* (1980); *Body Heat* (1981); *Hammett* (1982); *Francis* (1982); and *Octopussy* (1983). For the theatre he wrote the scores of *Passion Flower Hotel* (with Trevor Peacock; Prince of Wales Theatre, 24 Aug. 1964) and **Billy* (1974).

Barsotti, Roger (*b* London, 17 Sept. 1901). British composer. He was taught by his father who was a professor at the Milan Conservatory. He first performed as flautist with the Hastings Municipal Orchestra at the age of 14 and in 1916 enlisted as a band boy in the East Kent Regiment (The Buffs) becoming band sergeant in 1923. He studied at *Kneller Hall and became bandmaster of the 2nd Battalion, The Queen's Royal Regiment in 1930, retiring from this position and the army in 1945. In 1946 he became Director of Music of the Metropolitan Police Band, holding this position until 1968. A prolific composer, his more than 100 published works include: 'Three Women', 'Carnaval du Bal', 'Neapolitan Suite', 'Fantasia on British Airs'; the marches 'Banner of Victory', 'The Capitol', 'Colonel and Commodore', 'The Commissioner', 'Silver Pageantry', and 'State Trumpeters'; also 'Bell bird polka', 'In the Cloisters', 'Sundown'; many of them have been recorded by leading bands.

Bart, Lionel [Begleiter, Lionel] (*b* London, 1 Aug. 1930). British composer and lyricist. He was brought up in the East End of London, a childhood he partly shared with Georgia *Brown, for whom he was later to write the part of Nancy in *Oliver!* He won a scholarship to the St Martin's School of Art and began a career in commercial art, then became interested in the theatre and wrote for and acted in amateur productions. In 1956 he joined a *skiffle group called the Cavemen playing in a small café, The Cave, in Waterloo Bridge Road. A fellow-member was Tommy *Steele who sang the songs written by Bart and Mike Pratt; those which he eventually made famous included 'Rock with the Cavemen', 'Handful of songs', and 'Butterfingers'. They also supplied the score for Steele's early films *The Tommy Steele Story* and *Tommy the Toreador*, and wrote 'Living doll' (1959) for Cliff *Richard. After meeting Joan Littlewood, Bart became associated with the Theatre Workshop group at the Theatre Royal, Stratford, and wrote the music and lyrics for a play by ex-gaolbird Frank Norman, **Fings Ain't Wot They Used T'Be* (1959). The English musical, again in the doldrums since the unexpected success of *The *Boy Friend*, came to life once more with Bart's **Oliver!* (based on Dickens's *Oliver Twist*) which enjoyed one of the longest runs of the London theatre (second only to *The Mousetrap*) when it opened in 1960, eventually achieving 2618 performances and setting a new record for a musical. He formed his own music publishing company, Apollo Music, in 1961 under the management of Les *Paul. Other shows such as **Lock Up Your Daughters* (1959), *Blitz!* (1962), and **Maggie May* (1964) were all substantial successes and allowed Bart to live in millionaire style with homes in Chelsea, Jamaica, and Morocco. Bart was able to turn down a $2 million Hollywood offer for *Oliver!*, which was later filmed at Shepperton.

In 1965 he put on a show called *Twang!!* (based on the Robin Hood stories) backing it himself (against the advice of Noël *Coward) and ending with an expensive failure on his hands. Although it was not such a financial disaster as it was made out to be, it had the effect of virtually ending Bart's career in the theatre. He had many new ideas for shows which never materialized. At his peak Bart had given the London theatre shows with a genuine London character—Cockney situations and humour backed up by robust music-hall type songs that people could sing; although they were on occasion criticized as being somewhat derivative. *Oliver!* survives in stage and film revival as an entirely viable musical recreation of a literary classic—something which has rarely been achieved.

T. Staveacre: 'Lionel Bart' in *The Songwriters* (London, 1980).

Basie, 'Count' [William] (*b* Red Bank, NJ, 21 Aug. 1904; *d* Hollywood, Fla., 26 Apr. 1984). American pianist, bandleader, and composer. He studied piano with his mother and was helped in his early jazz days by Fats *Waller and Willie 'The Lion' *Smith. He worked in New York, accompanying blues singers; then in Kansas City where, in 1929, he joined Walter Page's Blue Devils. He was pianist with Bennie *Moten until 1935 when he took over the band on Moten's death. It was heard by the promoter John *Hammond, who booked them into New York's Famous Door Club where the band achieved international fame. Its early style was based on head arrangements and the exploitation of the uniquely economic solo playing of Basie himself, the work of inspired soloists such as Lester *Young (tenor-saxophone), Buck *Clayton and Joe Newman (1922–92) (trumpets), backed by one of the finest rhythm sections in big band jazz including Walter Page (1900–57) (bass), Freddie Green (1911–87) (guitar), and Jo *Jones (drums). The band's performances were enlivened by the ebullient blues-shouting of Jimmy *Rushing. In the mid-1950s, Basie adopted a new style based on dynamic ensemble playing and achieving real and lasting success, at a time when the big band was supposed to be on its way out, with scores by Henry 'Buster' Smith (1904–91), Neal *Hefti, Ernie Wilkins, and Quincy *Jones. He made regular tours (tenor-saxophone), Buck *Clayton and Joe Newman of Europe and recorded with singers like Frank *Sinatra, Bing *Crosby, and Tony *Bennett, Basie himself retaining his old, sparse, bluesy style until the end. He had led a big band from 1935–50 and from 1951 until his death in 1984.

R. Horricks: *Count Basie and his Orchestra* (London, 1957). S. Dance: *The World of Count Basie* (New York–London, 1980). C. Basie and A. Murray: *Good Morning Blues: Autobiography* (New York, 1985). C. Sheridan: *Count Basie: a Bio-Discography* (Westport, 1986).

Bassey, Shirley (*b* Cardiff, 8 Jan. 1937). British singer. Daughter of a West Indian seaman, she was discovered by Jack *Hylton who heard and admired her and put her in the Al Read revue *Such Is Life*. She had her first hit record with an authentic version of 'Banana boat song' in 1957. An unexpected chance to appear at the London Palladium in 1958 led to a demand for her recording of 'As I love you' (1959); followed by 'Kiss me honey, honey, kiss me (1959); 'As long as he needs me' (1960); 'You'll never know' (1961); 'Reach for the stars' (1961); 'What now my love?' (1962); 'I (who have nothing)' (1963); 'Goldfinger (1964); 'Big spender' (1967); 'Something' (1970); and the theme-song from *Diamonds Are Forever* (1972). One of the few soloists to withstand the dominance of the pop group, she remained a much admired singer in the cabaret field and on TV, theatrical in appearance and talent, making many successful LP albums, her vibrant voice and strong personality taking her more into show-business. She went to live in Switzerland in 1969 and, although not so much in the hit parade in the 1970s continued to be a popular attraction and name into the 1990s.

Bath, Hubert (*b* Barnstaple, 6 Nov. 1883; *d* Harefield, 24 Apr. 1945). British composer and conductor. He studied at the Royal Academy of Music, and began his musical career by conducting for a touring opera company. For many years he was musical adviser to the London County Council, his duties including the organizing of band concerts in the

London parks. He collaborated with G. H. *Clutsam and Basil *Hood on the light opera *Young England* (1916) and wrote other stage works and incidental music. But he is chiefly remembered for his film music, of which 'Cornish rhapsody' from *Love Story* (1944) is the best known by virtue of its many performances and recordings. In 1929 he had written the music for the first full-length British talking film, Alfred Hitchcock's *Blackmail*. He died while working on the score of *The Wicked Lady*. Two light orchestral suites, 'Woodland scenes' and 'Pierrette by the stream', achieved some popularity, as did his 'Summer night waltz' written in 1919.

His film scores also included: *Kitty* (1929); *Under the Greenwood Tree* (1929); *Wings over Everest* (1932); *Chu Chin Chow* (1932); *His Lordship* (1932); *Waltzes from Vienna* (1934); *Evensong* (1934); *The Thirty-Nine Steps* (1935); *The Tunnel* (1935); *Tudor Rose* (1936); *Rhodes of Africa* (1936)—the 'Empire Builders' march; *The Passing of the Third Floor Back* (1936); *Doctor Syn* (1937); *A Yank at Oxford* (1938); *Dear Octopus* (1939); *Millions Like Us* (1943); and *A Place of One's Own* (1943).

'Battle hymn of the Republic'. The patriotic American song as now known and sung was first printed in Boston, with words by Mrs Howe (1819–1910), a well-known reformer, sociological writer, and poet, in April 1862; 'adapted to the favorite Melody of "Glory Hallelujah".' Mrs Howe, better known as Julia Ward Howe, had written the poem on 19 Nov. 1861 without the 'Glory Hallelujah' chorus or any indication that she had the tune in mind. The poem was published in the *New York Daily Tribune* on 14 Jan. 1862, having been taken from an advance proof of the February issue of the *Atlantic Monthly* (Boston) where its first appearance is generally credited.

The history of the music is long, and still fundamentally unsettled. To state the basic facts, without any of the complicated side-issues, it seems to have started its public career as a Methodist hymn, 'Brothers will you meet us', in 1858, but it has never been ascertained who wrote the original melody, sometimes said to have derived from a Swedish song. In the fervour of the Civil War a version using its 'Glory, glory, Hallelujah' refrain and the familiar opening verse of 'John Brown's body lies a-moulding in the grave' had been copyrighted in broadside form, and as 'John Brown's body' it was played for the first time at a flag-raising ceremony at Fort Warren and sung by the Northern troops as they marched in Boston in July 1861. The John Brown thus immortalized was an army sergeant at Fort Warren. It was, however, the famous anti-slavery John Brown who became associated with it and who was in mind when the parody 'John Brown's baby has a cold upon his chest' was devised.

Baxter, Les [Leslie] (*b* Mexia, Texas, 14 Mar. 1922). American conductor, composer, singer, and pianist. He intended to be a concert pianist, but at 23 took the opportunity to become a singer as one of Mel *Tormé's Meltones working with the Artie *Shaw band. This led to work on radio as an arranger and later as conductor of the Bob Hope Show, Halls of Ivy, and the Abbot and Costello Show. He went to Capitol Records in 1950 as conductor-arranger-producer of vocal artists ranging from Nat 'King' *Cole to Yma *Sumac. Later he produced many LPs of his own, often exotic compositions under such collective titles as *Le Sacré du Sauvage* (1951); *Festival of the Gnomes* (1953); *Tamboo* (1955); *Ports of Pleasure* (1958); *Love is a Fabulous Thing* (1959); *Teen Drums* (1960); *Miracles* (1972). He wrote music for the films *The Pit and the Pendulum* (1961), *The Raven* (1963), and *Frogs* (1972).

Baxter, Phil (*b* Navarro County, Texas, 5 Sept. 1896; *d* Dallas, 2 Nov. 1972). American bandleader and composer. He was a member of Paul *Whiteman's band during the First World War at Mare Island Navy Yard. Then he organized his own band which he called Phil Baxter's Texas Tommies. He led various orchestras and wrote songs, many recorded by Guy *Lombardo, including: 'I'm a ding dong daddy from Dumas' (1928); 'Piccolo Pete' (1929); 'A faded summer love' (1931); and 'Have a little dream on me' (with John Murray and Billy *Rose, 1934).

Bay City Rollers. British vocal and instrumental group formed in 1970, considered by some rock connoisseurs to be the rightful successors to the *Beatles and the *Rolling Stones. They lacked the originality of these groups, used more outside material and session musicians, and never moved into the art rock category; nevertheless they built up a besotted and demonstrative following among the 'teenyboppers' of the 1970s. The original personnel was Leslie McKeown, Stuart 'Woody' Wood, Eric Faulkner, Alan Longmuir, and Derek Longmuir. They achieved an initial hit with 'Keep on dancing' in 1971. Building a 'bovver-boy' image, they reached the top of the charts with 'Bye bye baby' and 'Give a little love' in 1975, and on a triumphant tour of the USA made 'Saturday night' a No. 1 hit there. The group had split up by the 1980s.

E. Allen: *The Bay City Rollers* (St Alban's, 1975). T. Paton: *The Bay City Rollers* (London, 1975).

Bayes, Nora [Goldberg, Dora] (*b* Joliet, Ill., 1880; *d* Brooklyn, NY, 19 Mar. 1928). American singer with a deep voice and a dynamic style who became a popular entertainer in vaudeville and on Broadway. She had a particularly successful show partnership with her second husband (she had five marriages) Jack *Norworth, with whom she wrote the lasting 'Shine on harvest moon' in 1908, which they introduced together in the **Ziegfeld Follies*. Among her other hits were the British songs 'Anybody here seen Kelly' and 'Come along, my Mandy', which she sang in *The Jolly Bachelors* (1910). In the

Orpheum Theatre in Brooklyn she had another big hit (aided and abetted by its composer Harry *Von Tilzer) in 'Down where the Wurzburger flows'—which failed in London but led, in a roundabout way, to *'Down at the old Bull and Bush'. In 1917 she was exploiting George M. *Cohan's 'Over there', and in 1920 a song called 'Japanese sandman'. She made many appearances in Lew *Fields' Music Hall (later the 44th Street Theatre), was very popular in London during her appearances there in the 1920s, and recorded prolifically from 1910 to 1927. She appeared in *The Rogers Brothers in Washington* (1901); *Ziegfeld Follies* (1907, 1908, and 1909); *The Jolly Bachelors* (1910); *Little Miss Fix-It* (1911); *Roly Poly* (1912); *The Merry-go-Round* (1914); *Maid in America* (1915); *The Cohan Revue* (1917); *Ladies First* (1918); *Her Family Tree* (1920); and *Queen o' Hearts* (1922). In the film story of her life, *Shine on Harvest Moon* (1944), she was portrayed by Ann Sheridan (1915–67).

Bayly, Thomas Haynes (*b* Bath, 13 Oct. 1797; *d* London, 22 Apr. 1839). British composer, poet, and author. He was most active and effective as a lyricist for other composers such as Sir Henry Bishop (1786–1855) and J. P. Knight (1812–87). He wrote the words and music of 'Long, long ago!' (*c.* 1835) which was rewritten as 'Don't sit under the apple tree' by Lew *Brown, Charles *Tobias, and Sammy *Stept in 1942; also 'The bower', 'The deserter', 'The carrier dove', 'I cannot dance tonight', 'The old bachelor', 'Oh, come to me', 'She wore a wreath of roses', and 'Fly away, pretty moth'.

Beach Boys, The. Vocal and instrumental group formed in 1961 by five South Californian high-school boys who combined an interest in pop music with a love of surfing. They were three Wilson brothers, Brian (*b* Hawthorne, Calif., 20 June 1942), Dennis (4 Dec. 1944), and Carl (21 Dec. 1946), their cousin Mike Love (*b* Los Angeles, 15 Mar. 1941), and a friend Alan Jardine (*b* Lima, Ohio, 3 Sep. 1942). In the 1960s the Beach Boys were matched in inventiveness only by the English team of *Lennon and *McCartney. In Brian Wilson they possessed a songwriter and producer of an ingenuity and ability rivalling that of either of the two Beatles, achieving almost a cross between the melodic genius of McCartney and the production flair of Phil *Spector. At first they simply played for fun, the idea of forming a professional rock band coming in 1961 along with a song, 'Surfin'', composed on the beach one day by Brian Wilson and Mike Love. This was issued on the small Candix label and gradually received national coverage, thanks to its combination of a simple lyric with a sound reminiscent of the *Four Freshmen. Their first public appearance was on New Year's Eve 1961, and in 1962 they made their first national tour and issued their first recording on the Capitol label, 'Surfin' safari'. This was followed by a number of titles on the surfing theme, motorcycles, and motor racing, or anything connected with the interests of teenage high-school Americans. Thus was the 'surfing beat' launched, and it seemed, at the time, that it might be America's answer to the invading *Beatles and *Rolling Stones. The Beach Boys consolidated the success of their first single with more surfing numbers: 'Surfer girl' and 'Surfin' USA'—their biggest early single, for which Wilson openly borrowed the tune and rhythm of Chuck *Berry's 'Sweet little sixteen'.

In the years 1964 to 1966 the group produced a run of vocal classics: 'Fun, fun, fun' (1964); 'Don't worry, baby (1964); 'I get around' (1964); 'Help me Rhonda' (1965)—these last two both No. 1 hits—and 'California girls' (1965). The culmination of this period was the *Pet Sounds* album, which saw Wilson experimenting with melody and instrumentation, heavily influenced by the techniques of Phil Spector. Unfortunately this album was overshadowed by the Beatles' *Revolver* and then by *Sergeant Pepper*; which led Wilson to scrap the intended follow-up, *Smile*, which was eventually edited and released as *Smiley Smile*. This period also saw the release of what is generally considered the Beach Boys' classic single 'Good vibrations' (1966), their first million-seller, which took Wilson's interest in the effects of over-dubbing and innovative arrangements to its logical conclusion.

In 1966 they displaced the Beatles as the most popular group in England in the *Melody Maker* polls. The group continued to produce hit singles: 'Wild honey' (1967); 'Darlin'' (1967); 'Do it again' (1968); 'I can hear music' (1969); and 'Break away' (1969); but never managed to recapture the brilliance of their peak 1960s period, mainly due to the virtual retirement of their leading light, Brian Wilson, who was replaced first by Glen Campbell and then by Bruce Johnson. Their work through the 1970s was patchy and mainly unimpressive. The group still surfed on into the 1980s, though by 1985 their albums were beginning to be mostly nostalgic and retrospective issues. It seemed a symbolic end when Dennis Wilson was drowned at Marina Del Rey in California on 26 Dec. 1983. The secret of the Beach Boys' success had lain in Brian Wilson's ability to isolate memorable phrases and surround them with a layer of harmony over a simple rhythm. The relatively emotionless quality of the vocals was more than compensated for by the beauty and excitement of the whole.

K. Barnes: *The Beach Boys: a Biography in Words and Pictures* (New York, 1976). B. Golden: *The Beach Boys: a Southern Californian Pastoral* (Hollywood, 1976). J. Tobler: *The Beach Boys* (London, 1977). D. Leaf: *The Beach Boys and the Californian Myth* (New York, 1978). B. Preiss: *The Beach Boys* (New York), 1979. B. Elliott: *Surfs Up: the Beach Boys on Record* (Ann Arbor, 1982).

Beat. Regularly accented pulse in a bar of music, spoken of as so many beats to the bar—three = 3/4, two = 2/4, and so on. In jazz and subsequent popular music the word has an added meaning. Because the basic character of jazz depends upon a regular and impelling disposition of the beats and, in the melodic line, phrasing which variously anticipates or moves away from the beat, to say that a group has a good beat is synonymous with saying, in jazz terms, that it *swings. The beat is also the insistent foundation of every type of rock music, all embraced by the name 'beat music'. This usage has become intertwined with the hipster connotation, the 'beat generation' who regard pop music as a necessary adjunct to life.

Beatles, The. British rock group. Any history or sociological survey of Britain in the 1960s would have to include a section on the phenomenon of the Beatles. Clearly the most important group in the history of pop music, their influence is incalculable. They were to the British pop music industry what Elvis *Presley and Bob *Dylan were to America in the 1950s and 1960s respectively. They created the pop boom in Britain, simultaneously overcoming the half-century dominance of American popular music, moving the focus of the English music scene away from London, with its glib songwriting professionals and bland performers. The Beatles instigated a British sound, despite the fact that they freely acknowledged their debt to the American rock-and-rollers and *rhythm 'n' blues artists. The British *beat boom of the 1960s recaptured the energy and exuberance of *rock and roll and for the first time since the early 1900s British popular music was leading the way instead of being a pale reflection of what was happening in the USA.

The Beatles came along at the right time, when the young had become relatively affluent and the new heroes were working-class—Jimmy Porter and Arthur Seaton in literature, now the Beatles in music. Originally in their dress and style they were archetypal teddy-boy rebels. Their band format was the same as that developed by Buddy *Holly: drums, bass, and rhythm guitars. The crucial period in their development was during their four tours in Hamburg, the only place where they could find regular work, when they achieved their simple, economical, distinctive style, soon to be dubbed the 'Liverpool' sound. Intermittently, during this time, they played in the now famous Cavern in Liverpool where they came to the attention of Brian Epstein, who became their manager. His drive and push eventually secured them a contract with EMI's Parlophone label, where they were lucky in their producer George *Martin. By now the group was a settled unit. An early member, bassist Stuart Sutcliffe (1940–62), had left them in Hamburg to work as an artist and died of a brain tumour. Pete Best, a drummer of modest ability, was replaced by Ringo *Starr, who with Paul *McCartney, John *Lennon, and George *Harrison, all natives of Liverpool, formed the classic Beatles group.

Their early vocal style was a combination of the gospel call-and-response of the *Drifters and the early Motown groups and the frantic rock and roll of the Specialty label singers *Little Richard and Larry *Williams. It was a new sound to British ears and accounted for the original appeal of the band. Their first single, 'Love me do', made the Top 20 in Dec. 1962; and 'Please please me' was No. 1 in early 1963. This marked the beginning of Beatlemania. 'From me to you' (1963) and 'She loves you' (1963) followed to the top. The Beatles' popularity resembled that achieved by Elvis Presley, but with a new intensity: screaming teenage fans, continual press coverage, and every record company looking for a saleable equivalent. The Beatles' arrangements were simple, their sound immediate. As personalities they were endearing, arrogant, witty, cynical by turns; interesting and articulate, but out to have a good time; with a self-deprecating honesty that cut through the publicity hype. After the success of their first album and their fifth single, 'I want to hold your hand' (1963), the Beatles were established in Britain. America capitulated soon after—thanks to Brian Epstein's efforts, £20,000-worth of publicity from Capitol Records, and top billing on the Ed Sullivan show. Their Englishness helped greatly in the USA; added to the fact that their work showed a direct line from the genius of Buddy Holly and the 1950s songwriters to the inventions of Lennon and McCartney. Like the best songwriters they caught the imagination and memory with simple and instinctively right lines and images. Even in the early songs there is a hint of the tension between the repetitive directness of Lennon and the catchy melodiousness of McCartney which at this stage simply resulted in freshness and spontaneity, just as their vocal styles complemented each other.

By mid-1964 the Beatles were touring incessantly, but they managed to produce *A Hard Day's Night*, an original and inventive film directed by Dick Lester, depicting life on the road with a combination of realism and surrealism, and winning much critical acclaim. A turning-point in their career came with the albums *Rubber Soul* and, especially, *Revolver*. They had been improving as musicians; but sometimes there was a loss of intensity, a certain glibness, a move towards being a little too practised and slick, especially in the work of McCartney, though Lennon maintained his sensitivity. On these albums the group moved away from simplicity, experimenting with electronic effects and added instruments in the studio, moving in all kinds of stylistic directions. The culmination of this thinking-man's pop (so-called *art rock) came in 1967 with what many consider to be among the finest singles and albums ever released: 'Strawberry fields forever'/'Penny Lane', 'Hello goodbye'/'I am the walrus', and, in the summer, *Sergeant Pepper's Lonely Hearts Club Band*—a mixture of surrealism, mysticism, vaudeville, and rock that took pop music to new levels of inventiveness. It may now seem inconsistent and patchy, but it was undoubtedly the summit of the Beatles' creativity and, at the time, of pop music.

The next LP, *Magical Mystery Tour* (1967), saw the Beatles trying too hard to repeat the formula; but it also contained some superb tracks. They were to return, almost with relief, to their rhythm 'n' blues roots with 'Lady Madonna' and 'Get back'

(1969). From *Revolver* on, the paths of Lennon and McCartney had been diverging. The sprawling *The Beatles (The White Album)* (1968), was almost a showcase for their separate talents, and Harrison had also, by this time, developed as a songwriter. The rift in the group is clearly seen in the film *Let It Be*, which simply highlights their work as solo artists. The album *Abbey Road* only delayed the end. The group split up in 1970. Their recordings have already taken on the patina of nostalgia, while posterity will be interested in the songwriting ability of Lennon and McCartney, having already put them alongside the Gershwins and Kerns, as a true reflection of the spirit of the 1960s.

A compilation show, *Beatlemania*, was staged in London (Astoria) 18 Oct. 1979, and later went to New York.

M. Braun: *Love Me Do: the Beatles' Progress* (London, 1964). B. Epstein: *A Cellarful of Noise* (London, 1964). H. Davies: *The Beatles* (London, 1968). A. Scaduto: *The Beatles* (New York, 1968). R. DiLello: *The Longest Cocktail Party* (London, 1972). P. McCabe & R. Schonfeld: *Apple to the Core: the Un-Making of the Beatles* (London, 1972). The Beatles: *The Fabulous Story of John, Paul, George and Ringo* (London, 1975). R. Carr & T. Tyler: *The Beatles: an Illustrated Record* (London, 1975). H. Castleman & W. J. Podrazik: *All Together Now: the First Complete Beatles Discography, 1961–75* (Ann Arbor, 1976). W. Mellers: *Twilight of the Gods* (London, 1976). J. P. Di Franco (ed.): *The Beatles: a Hard Day's Night* (London, 1977). P. Marchbank, J. Coke, & C. A. Sansom (eds): *Pocket Beatles Complete* (London–New York, 1979). P. Norman: *Shout! The True Story of the Beatles* (London, 1981). B. Harry: *The Beatles Who's Who* (London–New York, 1982). J. Rossell: *The Beatles Album File and Complete Discography* (London, 1982). N. Stannard: *The Beatles: a History of the Beatles on Record* (2 vols) (London, 1982/3). P. Brown & S. Gaines: *The Love You Make: an Insider's Story of the Beatles* (London–New York, 1983). C. Bedford: *Waiting for the Beatles* (London, 1984). M. Lewisohn: *The Beatles: a Chronology 1962–87* (New York, 1987). T. Riley: *Tell Me Why: a Beatles Commentary* (London, 1988). W. McKeen: *The Beatles: a Bio-Bibliography* (Westport, Conn., 1989).

Beat music. A fortunate coincidence of name and achievement led to the successors of the *Beatles *c.* 1960 specifically appropriating the categorical label of beat music or *Merseybeat. It thus became applied to the Beatles-style music that invaded the USA in the shape of *Gerry and the Pacemakers, the Dave Clark Five, the *Searchers, and the *Hollies.

R. Ellis: *The Big Beat Scene* (London, 1961). C. May: *British Beat* (London, 1974).

Beaver, Jack (*b* Clapham, London, 1900; *d* London, 10 Sept. 1963. British composer. He was educated at the Royal Academy of Music and became known for the background music he wrote for films and documentaries, beginning in the silent cinema era. His first talking picture score was the RKO production *Baroud* (1932). He worked with Louis Levy at Shepherds Bush on such films as *The Thirty-Nine Steps* (1935) and was resident composer with Gaumont British from 1934 and conductor from 1939. From 1936 to 1941 he was responsible for many radio adaptations of film material and in 1946 was MD of the series *Picture Parade*. He wrote 'Sovereign Heritage' for the National brass band championship in 1954 (used at the Open in Belle-Vue, Manchester, in 1972).

Bebop/Bop. Popular name given to the early modern jazz developments of *c.* 1940; an alliterative word possibly derived from the cry of 'arriba' heard in the Latin American bands of the period. It may have been merely coincidental that the scat vocalization of jazz musicians like Lionel *Hampton and Dizzy *Gillespie evolved along 'hey-baba-rebop' lines. Bebop was a deliberate attempt by serious black jazz musicians to move jazz away from the simple harmonies and basic rhythms of the earlier styles: they were looking for something more interesting and demanding to play, which would also keep out the white musicians who were holding all the most lucrative jobs and frequently stole their ideas. Employing extended chordal harmonies and broken rhythms, bop changed the face of jazz as the 12-tone innovations had in classical music. Foremost in the move were such musicians as Charlie *Parker, Dizzy Gillespie, and Thelonious *Monk, following in the steps of the pioneering guitarist Charlie *Christian. The name fell out of usage as the more self-conscious elements of bop were relinquished in the general broadening and loosening of modern jazz of subsequent decades.

L. Feather: *Inside Be-Bop* (New York, 1949; repr. 1959). A. B. Spellman: *Four Lives in the Be-bop Business* (London, 1966).

Bécaud, Gilbert [Silly, François] (*b* Toulon, 24 Oct. 1927). French composer and singer. He studied music in Nice and began to write songs at the age of 19. On tour in the USA as accompanist to Jacques Pills he found models for his own singing style in artists such as Frankie *Laine and Johnny *Ray. He composed songs for André Claveau and Edith *Piaf, appeared in cabaret in 1946, and first set some of Pierre Delanoë's lyrics to music. In 1952, Piaf (whom he accompanied on various American tours) persuaded him to work with Louis Amade, who was to remain his principal collaborator. He made his stage debut at Versailles in 1952 and had a major success at the *Olympia Music Hall in Paris in 1954. Now billed as 'Monsieur 100,000 volts' he embarked on a lucrative career as singer/pianist, rivalling Charles *Trenet in national popularity.

His first big hit song was 'Quand tu danses (1953) and later favourites included: 'Couventine', 'Le jour où la pluie viendra', 'Je t'ai dans le peau', 'Heureusement, y'a les copains', 'Viens danser', 'Dimanche à Orly', 'L'important, c'est la rose', 'Ah! si j'avais des sous', 'Plein soleil', 'L'orange', 'Cornélius', 'Tu le regretteras', 'Le pianiste de Varsovie', and 'La rivière', a varied output in romantic, sophisticated, simple, jazz-flavoured, modernistic, patriotic, and political modes.

P-X. Giannoli: *Bécaud* (Paris, 1970).

Bechet, Sidney (*b* New Orleans, 14 May 1897; *d* Paris, 14 May 1959). American jazz soprano-saxophonist, clarinettist, and composer. He learned the clarinet with George Baquet (1883–1949); and, by 1912, had played with Freddie *Keppard, Buddy Petit, the Eagle Band, and other pioneer jazz groups. He toured with Clarence *Williams, in 1916 with King *Oliver, and in 1919 with Will Marion *Cook, touring Europe (including England), coming to the enthusiastic notice of conductor Ernest Ansermet, and becoming one of jazz's first important soloists. He worked in Paris for two years, then returned to New York and made his first recordings in the early 1920s with Clarence Williams's Blue Five. In 1928 he joined the Noble *Sissle Band in Paris and toured with them until 1938 when he left music to run a tailoring business.

Bechet came back to jazz in 1940, making many fine recordings for RCA Victor with his Feetwarmers, on which his warm, forceful but lyrical, and entirely unmistakable soprano-saxophone playing established him as the leading voice on that instrument, copied by many but never excelled; and he made some worthy recordings with Louis *Armstrong. From the late 1940s he made his home in Paris, from 1951 playing in theatres, his style permeating and influencing most of the traditional French jazz scene, and occasionally returning to USA to record. He wrote many attractive jazz themes, often Creole-flavoured, such as 'Les oignons' (1949) and 'Petite fleur' (1952), which became best-sellers. In 1956 he collaborated with James Toliver on the ballet *La Nuit est une sorcière*.

R. Mouly: *Sidney Bechet: Notre Ami* (Paris, 1959). S. Bechet: *Treat it Gentle* (New York, 1960). J. Chilton: *Sidney Bechet: the Wizard of Jazz* (London–New York, 1987).

Bedford, Harry (*b* Pimlico, London, 1873; *d* London, 17 Oct. 1939). British comedian and vocalist who made his first stage appearance, in Battersea, at the age of seven. He gave up a boat-building apprenticeship to become a professional entertainer in 1888, first appearing in minstrel shows and pantomime, then on the variety stage in Portsmouth in 1889. In 1895 he was at the Middlesex Music Hall in London and thereafter continued a successful solo career with an act that was considered pleasantly risqué for those times. His principal hit song was 'A little bit off the top' which he managed to load with innuendo. Others were 'Cock of the North', 'When I get some money', and 'One of the shabby genteel'.

Bee Gees, The. British pop group formed in the 1950s, the nucleus being Barry Gibb (*b* 1946) and his twin brothers Robin and Maurice (*b* 1949). The original trio had used the group name (based on Barry Gibb's initials) from their earliest days in Manchester. The family emigrated to Australia in 1958 where the brothers began to establish themselves, returning to England in 1967 with Colin Petersen added on drums and a guitarist, Vince Melouney, recruited in London. They had their first British hit with 'New York Mining Disaster 1941' in 1967, and No. 1 hits with 'Massachusetts' (1967) and 'I've gotta get a message to you' (1968). The group split up in 1969 to reunite in 1970. They achieved two million-selling discs in the USA with 'Lonely days' and 'How can you mend a broken heart'.

The Bee Gees had worked on somewhat introspective and gloomy ballads but in 1975 moved to a more outward-looking soul/disco style which produced top hits in 'Jive talkin'' (1975), 'You should be dancing' (1976), 'Too much heaven' (1978), 'Tragedy' (1979), and 'Love you inside and out' (1979). They were in the forefront of the *disco boom, achieving maximum effect with their score for the disco movie *Saturday Night Fever* (1976), which had world sales of over 30 million and included three No. 1 hits in 'How deep is your love', 'Stayin' alive', and 'Night fever'. By the late 1970s they were among the leading pop groups, having moved to the USA and based themselves in Miami, where they run their own recording studio. The brothers have written well over 1000 published songs between them, while Barry Gibb has written material for other singers, including Barbra *Streisand in 1980.

K. Stevens: *The Bee Gees* (New York–London, 1978). K. Barnes: *The Bee Gees: an Authorized Biography* (London, 1979). D. Leaf (ed.): *The Illustrated Bee Gees* (New York, 1979). L. Pryce: *The Bee Gees* (St Albans, 1979).

Beggar's Opera, The. Historically important *ballad opera that started a great vogue for the genre and set the musical theatre on its way to finding truly popular forms of opera that would suit the tastes of the increasingly affluent middle and working classes of the 19th century. John Gay (1685–1732), its creator, was not a composer but he had a strong, almost obsessive, interest in common song and other evocations of the folk tradition that were around him, as yet mainly undocumented. Much of his inspiration was drawn from his observation of the lives of the poor and humble. His eventual concept of a ballad opera, that drew for its music on folk dances and songs that were current at the time, was revolutionary enough for him to be considered a true innovator, although he was not the first to utilize folk melodies, nor was he the first to rebel against the artificialities of Italian opera. Thomas *D'Urfey could well be considered the father of ballad opera, for he had done something of the kind in *Wonders of the Sun* (1706), and his bawdy verse collection *Wit and Mirth, or Pills to Purge Melancholy* was a major source for Gay's inspiration, as it was for many other ballad opera compilers; while one of Gay's main musical sources was John *Playford's *The *Dancing Master*. Much encouragement came from literary friends like Jonathan Swift who was the one to suggest a 'Newgate Pastoral' and to set Gay to work. We know from Gay's letters that *The Beggar's Opera* was completed by October 1727. At one stage he had written out his verses but had not thought of having a musical accompaniment. The producer John Rich and the Duchess of Queensbury urged him to have musical arrangements made of the songs upon which his script was based and Dr Johann Christoph Pepusch (1667–1752), musical director at Lincoln's Inn Fields, was called in to supply the necessary orchestration and an overture.

Gay succeeded admirably, frequently elevating the combination of words and music to the level of totally conceived masterpieces as in 'Were I laid on Greenland's coast', the exquisite 'Over the hills and far away', and 'Oh what pain it is to part'. Some of Gay's inspiration may have come from Allan Ramsay (1686–1758), poet, collector, and bookseller, who was taking similar notice of the native songs and rhymes of Scotland. His *Tea-Table Miscellany* (1724–40) was an early source of Scottish lyrics and ballads. In 1725 he published a pastoral play, *The Gentle Shepherd*, not originally intended for the stage, that turned the raw Scots vernacular into polite English, the songs set to Scottish tunes. In revised form it was presented in Edinburgh at the Taylor's Hall in 1729, having already achieved great popularity in its verse form. If such considerations temper Dr Johnson's assertion that Gay invented the ballad opera, we may still grant that it was Gay who gave it a complete conception, style, and genius.

Gay daringly set his tale in London's criminal underworld. The Peachums' daughter Polly is secretly married to the highwayman Captain Macheath, and they decide to turn this situation to good account by turning him over to the law and thus make Polly a rich widow. She overhears their plot and warns Macheath. He is planning his next escapade when Peachum and the law arrive and arrest him. It now transpires that Lucy, the daughter of the prison gaoler Lockitt, is pregnant by Macheath and she tries to make him marry her. Lucy and Polly have a fierce argument over this unexpected situation. Macheath escapes from gaol and Peachum and Lockitt join forces and bribe Polly to give him away. Macheath, recaptured, is now faced with Polly and Lucy, not to mention several other ladies with marital claims. He decides that perhaps hanging is the best way out, but he is reprieved and is left trying to sort out his problems.

The audience on the first night of *The Beggar's Opera* on 29 Jan. 1728 at Lincoln's Inn Fields were at first slightly puzzled by it. Composed of 'a prodigious concourse of Nobility and Gentry' and many famous literary figures of the day, they took some time to adapt to its roistering nature and low-life setting; but were applauding with unbounded enthusiasm by the end. Much of its satire was taken to be aimed at the prime minister Robert Walpole, who, on that first night, was quick-witted enough to take credit with a show of apparent good humour. The opera had an initial run of 62 performances before it travelled all over England, Ireland, Scotland, and Wales—and even to Minorca. Gay and his manager Rich made a fortune out of it; hence the apt lines that 'it made Gay rich and Rich gay', and it established its leading lady, Lavinia Fenton (1717–60). It inspired a spate of ballad operas in the next 30 years or so, until the taste for such things soon suffered a decline in the face of the new fashions in the musical theatre and the gradual emergence of the lighter forms of opera. *The Beggar's Opera*, on sheer merit, proved to be the exception and survived, frequently revived in the 18th and 19th centuries; it was first seen at Covent Garden in 1732, with the last successful production of the period at the Avenue Theatre in 1886, starring Sims Reeves (1818–1900). It had first been staged in New York in 1750 and exerted a comparable influence in the USA; also in Europe where it gave impetus to similar works of a ballad opera nature.

With the appearance of a new version by Frederic Austin, produced by Nigel Playfair at the Lyric Theatre, Hammersmith, on 5 June 1920, *The Beggar's Opera*, after running continuously until the end of 1923, became established as a classic of the musical theatre and is now included in all the annals of English opera. Further editions included those made by Edward J. Dent in the 1930s, Benjamin Britten in 1948 (which virtually made it into a new Britten opera), and a film version by Sir Arthur Bliss in 1952, notable as Laurence Olivier's first musical film and the first film directed by Peter Brook. There were outstanding London revivals at the Haymarket 5 Mar. 1940 and at the Apollo 12 Sept. 1968. The work has also inspired new pieces, with only the loosest of connections and original music, such as *Brecht and *Weill's *Die *Dreigroschenoper* (1936) and Duke *Ellington's *Beggar's Holiday* (1946).

C. E. Pearce: *Polly Peachum: the Story of 'Polly' and 'The Beggar's Opera'* (London, 1912). F. Kidson: *The Beggar's Opera, its Predecessors and Successors* (Cambridge, 1922). W. E. Schultz: *Gay's 'Beggar's Opera': its Content, History and Influence* (New Haven–London, 1923). E. M. Gagey: *Ballad-Opera* (New York, 1937; repr. 1965). Y. Noble (ed.); *Twentieth Century Interpretations of The Beggar's Opera: a Collection of Critical Essays* (Englewood Cliffs, NJ, 1975).

Beguine/Biguine. (The second spelling is the one generally used in its native haunts, the first being a later American/European adaptation.) A national dance from Martinique in the West Indies, as integral there as the *rumba was in Cuba. It is in 2/4 time, rather like a slow polka with a dotted rhythm, generally supplied by claves, *maracas, *bongos, and *congas playing variations on the basic pattern. The dance is performed on one spot with undulating movements of the body, the partners not touching. There was an attempt to introduce it as a ballroom dance in Paris in 1932, but it never caught on. Its public recognition was almost entirely based on the success of Cole *Porter's famous song 'Begin the beguine', first heard in *Jubilee* (1935), established by an Artie *Shaw recording in 1938, and memorably parodied by Noël Coward in 'Nina' (1945).

Beiderbecke, Leon **Bix** (*b* Davenport, Iowa, 10 Mar. 1903; *d* New York, 7 Aug. 1931). American jazz cornet player, pianist, and composer. His early death added a romantic flavour to his jazz career and he became a legendary figure with a reputation that could have exceeded his actual achievement. There is no doubt, however, about the brilliance of his playing, the unique and unmistakable quality of his tone, which was of almost bell-like clarity, and his advanced musical ideas. He shone out in the few recordings he made, many, unfortunately, with rather undistinguished bands. One real achievement was in providing early proof that a white musician could add something individual and special to jazz, and his playing was both a source of inspiration to many subsequent white trumpeters and much admired by many leading black musicians.

He joined the famous Wolverines orchestra in Ohio in 1923; two years later he went to Chicago and then to St Louis with the Frankie *Trumbauer orchestra, recordings with them producing such classics as 'Singin' the blues' and 'I'm coming, Virginia'; and he joined Paul *Whiteman in 1927. The demanding jazz life and an addiction to alcohol weakened his health and he died of pneumonia in 1931, leaving the legacy of one of the most exciting sounds ever heard from a cornet (the instrument he always favoured). He was also a searchingly experimental pianist and composer, his compositions including 'Davenport blues', which he recorded with his Rhythm Jugglers in 1925, and 'In a mist', which he recorded as a piano solo in 1927. A novel, *Young Man with a Horn* (1938), by Dorothy Baker, was loosely based on his life, as was the subsequent film (1950).

C. H. Wareing & G. Garlick: *Bugles for Beiderbecke* (London, 1958). B. James: *Bix Beiderbecke* (London, 1959). R. Berton: *Remembering Bix* (New York, 1974). R. M. Sudhalter, P. R. Evans, & W. Dean-Myatt: *Bix: Man and Legend* (New Rochelle, 1974).

Belafonte, Harry [Harold George] (*b* New York, 1 Mar. 1927). American folk-singer very popular in the 1950s and 1960s, thereafter continuing as a performer though with less prominence. He lived with his parents for many years in Jamaica, then returned to New York and served in the navy in the Second World War. He studied acting and singing and appeared in clubs in the 1940s. Discouraged by his lack of progress, he opened a restaurant in Greenwich Village in 1951. There he began to specialize in his early interest, the music of the West Indies, especially *calypso; and had a great success with recordings of such songs as 'Jamaica farewell' (1956), 'Day-O (The banana boat song)' (1957), 'Brown-skin girl', and 'Matilda', helping the surge of interest in calypso music that was at its height around 1956–7. He had a top hit with 'Mary's Boy Child' (1957). He appeared in *John Murray Anderson's Almanac* (1953) and *Three for Tonight* (1954) and starred in a number of movies from 1953 to 1972 including **Carmen Jones* (1954) and *Island in the Sun* (1957). His later activities were largely confined to his own publishing firm and film company.

A. J. Shaw: *Belafonte* (New York, 1961).

Bell, Thom (*b* Philadelphia, 1941). American composer, arranger, and producer. He studied classical piano, making his first moves into the pop field in 1959, but not making his mark as a producer/arranger until 1968 with some recordings made with a vocal group the Delfonics—'La la means I love you' and 'Break your promise'. Bell's style was a fusion of soft vocals with classical orchestral backing that was to become classified as *doo-wop in the 1950s, a broadening of the pop sound into a more commercialized idiom. He teamed up with lyric-writer Linda Creed to produce a series of songs for the Stylistics—'Stop, look and listen' (1970), 'You are everything' (1970), 'Betcha by golly, wow', and 'Stone in love with you' (1972). He continued to produce similar material for such as Johnny *Mathis and the *Spinners—'I'll be around' (1972) and 'Games people play' (1975). He managed to create an artistic product, in spite of the mood music quality of his lush orchestrations, that still had some credence in the pop world.

Belle Hélène, La. Opéra-bouffe in three acts with music by Jacques *Offenbach and words by his most effective collaborators Henri Meilhac (1831–97) and Ludovic *Halévy, produced at the Théâtre des Variétés in Paris 17 Dec. 1864. It was the more polished and lyrical successor to his *Orphée aux Enfers*, treading the same classical ground with irreverent step and a saucy score, and a perfect feature for the emerging Hortense Schneider who was to be the key figure in several Offenbach productions. Its composer being by now an international celebrity, *La Belle Hélène* soon found its way to Vienna (1865), where it marked the debut of Marie *Geistinger, London (1866), and New York (1867). It was very popular in London and had frequent productions there, a notable modern one being as *Helen* (words by A. P. Herbert and the score arranged by Erich *Korngold) at the Adelphi Theatre in 1932 with George *Robey, W. H. *Berry, and Evelyn *Laye in the cast. Its excellent score is remembered by such items as 'Amours divins', 'Au Mont Ida', 'On me nomme Hélène la blonde', 'Dis-moi, Vénus', and 'Oui, c'est un rêve'.

Belle of Mayfair, The. Musical comedy in two acts with score by Leslie *Stuart, book by Charles H. E. Brookfield and Cosmo Hamilton, and lyrics by George Arthurs, produced at the Vaudeville Theatre, London, 11 Apr. 1906. The cast included Farren Soutar and Edna *May (replaced by Phyllis *Dare, and later by Billie Burke); the songs included 'Where you go, will I go'; and it achieved a run of 416 performances. In New York at *Daly's it was less well received and ran for 140 performances. There its most lasting hit was the added 'Why do they call me a Gibson girl?' (*w* Leslie Stiles), sung by Camille Clifford; but the score did not match Stuart's masterpiece **Florodora*.

Belle of New York, The. Musical comedy in two acts with score by Gustave *Kerker and book by C. M. S. McLellan (1865–1916), who wrote as Hugh

Morton. Curiously, although it had a very modest initial run of 56 performances at the New York Casino from 28 Sept. 1897, it had a staggering success in London where it was something of a theatrical landmark in being one of the first American musicals to reverse the trend of British dominance and, up to then, the regular east to west traffic. With Edna *May and Harry Davenport in the lead, it opened at the Shaftesbury Theatre on 12 Apr. 1898 and ran for 697 performances. New Yorkers realized they had missed out and it subsequently became a comparable success there. It was revived in the USA in 1921 as *The Whirl of New York* [124p]. The score is a pleasant if not particularly distinguished one with such items as 'They all follow me', 'Teach me how to kiss', 'The Anti-Cigarette Society', and a memorable waltz, 'She is the belle of New York'. It was frequently revived in London into the 1940s and was made into an only remotely connected MGM film in 1952 starring Fred *Astaire and Vera-Ellen.

Bells Are Ringing. Delightful musical comedy, with score by Jule *Styne and book by Betty *Comden and Adolph *Green, staged at New York's Shubert Theatre 29 Nov. 1956 [270p]. It had a sophisticated and amusing story about a talkative telephone operator who gets so involved with one caller, a failed playwright, that she arranges to meet and help him—with the inevitable result. The leading part was specially written for Judy *Holliday who handled it to perfection, with Sydney Chaplin as the writer; and she repeated her triumph with no less impact in the 1960 film version with Dean *Martin as partner. There were some very effective songs such as 'It's a perfect relationship', 'Long before I knew you', 'Just in time', and 'The party's over'; and it was one of the most fruitful of the Styne/Comden/Green collaborations. It was produced in London (Coliseum, 14 Nov. 1957) with Janet Blair and George Gaynes [292p].

Bellson, Louis [Balassoni, Louis] (*b* Rock Falls, Ill., 16 July 1924). American jazz drummer and bandleader. A showy soloist who started his career by winning the Gene *Krupa national drum contest, he played with Ted *Fiorito (1942) and joined Benny *Goodman later the same year. After military service he rejoined Goodman in 1946; and was with Tommy *Dorsey 1947–9; Terry Gibbs 1949–50; Tommy Dorsey and Harry *James 1950; and Duke *Ellington 1951–3; subsequently freelancing or leading his own groups. He married the singer Pearl *Bailey, often working with her, including her 1971 TV show, having been with Ellington again in 1965, and with Doc Severinson in 1972. He composed some well-used jazz numbers such as 'The Hawk talks', 'Skin deep', 'Ting-a-ling', and 'You gotta dance'.

Benatzky, Ralph [Rudolf Josef Frantisek] (*b* Maravaské-Budejovice, 5 June 1884; *d* Zurich, 16 Oct. 1957). Czech composer and author, a prolific producer of operettas, Singspiele, musical comedy, vaudeville, revue, ballet, film music, and numerous songs, as well as being a novelist and librettist. The son of a headmaster, he studied music in Prague and Munich, became a doctor of philosophy at Vienna University, and later lived mostly in Vienna or Berlin. In 1910 he was conductor of the Kleines Theater in Munich where he wrote his first one-act operetta *Der Walzer von heute Nacht*. He directed cabaret in Nuremberg and married the singer Josma Selim (1898–1929). His first success came with cabaret songs such as 'Draussen im Schönbrunner Parke', 'Ich muss wieder einmal in Grinzing sein', 'Einmal kommt der Tag', and 'Ich weiss auf der Wieden ein kleines Hotel'. He wrote many operettas before experiencing a lasting triumph with **Im Weissen Rossl* (*White Horse Inn*), Berlin 1930, a spectacular 'revue-operette' cum 'Singspiel' (on which he worked with Robert *Stolz) which was tremendously popular in England and America as well as in Germany and Austria. This led to a series of lavish shows which departed in style from his early operettas but remained elegantly melodic and well-written. Altogether it is estimated that he wrote some 92 theatre shows, over 250 film scores, and around 5000 songs.

His other stage works included: *Laridon* (1912); *Der lachende Dreibond* (1913); *Prinzchens Frühlingserwachen* (1914); *Das Scheckbuch des Teufels* (1914); *Fräulein Don Juan* (1915); *Liebe im Schnee* (1916); *Die tanzende Maske* (1918); *Die Verliebten* (1919); *Graf Chevreux* (1920); *Apachen* (1920); *Pipsi* (1921); *Yuschi Tanzt (1920); Ein Marchen aus Florenz* (1923); *An Alle* (1924); *Adieu Mimi* (1926); *Casanova* (1928); *Die drei Musketier* (1929); *Mein Schwester und Ich* (1930); *Zur goldenen Liebe* (1931); *Zirkus Aimé* (1932); *Bezauberndes Fräulein* (1933); *Das kleine Café* (1934); *Der König mit dem Regenschirm* (1935); *Axel an der Himmelstür* (1936); *Herzen im Schnee* (1937); *Majestät–Privat* (1937); *Kleinstadtzauber* (1947); *Ein Liebestraum* (1951); *Don Juans Wiederkehr* (1953). He left Austria for the USA as the Nazis invaded in 1938, settling after the war in Switzerland. Many of his works were translated into English and produced in England, the USA, and elsewhere.

Beneke, Tex [Gordon] (*b* Forth Worth, Texas, 12 Feb. 1914). American saxophonist, vocalist, and bandleader. He was with the Ben Young band in Texas 1939–42, before joining Glenn *Miller and becoming one of the leading lights of the famous band with his warm and dextrous solos, and occasional distinctive vocals. He was heard and seen in the two Miller films, *Sun Valley Serenade* (1941) and *Orchestra Wives* (1942). He continued in Miller's army band; then, after Miller's untimely death, he led from 1946 a band to perpetuate the Miller name and sound. From 1950 he led a band under his own name that still had Miller overtones, and continued making concert tours into the 1970s.

Benjamin, Bennie [Claude] (*b* St Croix, Virgin Islands, 4 Nov. 1907). West Indian composer. He went to New York in 1927 and studied banjo and guitar with Hy Smith. He was to spend several years in various orchestras before becoming staff composer to a music-publisher. He wrote music and theme tunes for the films *Fun and Fancy Free* (1947) and *Melody Time* (1948); and many others. Among his popular song hits were: 'I don't want to set the world on fire' (with Sol Marcus and Ed Durham, 1941); 'Strictly instrumental' (1941) and 'When the lights go on again all over the world' (1942), both with Marcus; *w* Ed Seiler; 'Oh what it seemed to be' (1945), 'Surrender (1946), 'When tonight is just a memory' (1947), 'I don't see me in your eyes any more' (1949), 'I'll keep the lovelight burning' (1949), and 'Wheel of fortune' (1952), all with words by George Weiss.

Bennard, Revd George (*b* Youngstown, Ohio, 4 Feb. 1873; *d* Reed City, Mich., 10 Oct. 1958). American composer. He was an officer of the Salvation Army from 1892 and an interdenominational evangelist in the USA and Canada from 1907. The compiler of many books of religious songs, his most lasting creation was 'The old rugged cross', written in 1913.

Bennett, Richard Rodney (*b* Broadstairs, 29 Mar. 1936). British composer and pianist. He studied at the Royal Academy of Music (1953–7) with Lennox Berkeley and Howard Ferguson; and in Paris (1957–9) with Pierre Boulez. His music shows the influence of Bartók and his more serious works use serial techniques. He is an accomplished pianist in both classical and jazz idioms, which has led him to write a ballet 'Jazz Calendar' (1963–4) and pieces for jazz ensemble such as 'Soliloquy' (1966) and 'Jazz pastoral' (1969). He had an early admiration for the pianist Billy *Mayerl (whose music he has recorded), and has made many arrangements of American and English popular songs (usually 1920–50 vintage), including transcriptions of *Gershwin (for the King's Singers), *Rodgers, *Porter, and *Weill. He has written arrangements for Eartha *Kitt (for whom he was accompanist for a while) and a *Coward anthology for the 1970 Edinburgh Festival.

His film scores include: *The World Assured* (1956); *Interpol* (1957); *Indiscreet* (1958); *Only Two Can Play* (1961); *Billy Liar* (1963); *One Way Pendulum* (1964); *The Nanny* (1965); *Far From the Madding Crowd* (1967); *Billion Dollar Brain* (1967); *Secret Ceremony* (1968); *Figures in a Landscape* (1969); *Nicholas and Alexandra* (1971); *Lady Caroline Lamb* (1972); *Voices* (1973); *Murder on the Orient Express* (1974); *Equus* (1977); *Yanks* (1979); *The Brinks Job* (1979); and *The Return of the Soldier* (1982).

Bennett, Robert Russell (*b* Kansas City, 15 June 1894; *d* New York, 17 Aug. 1981). American composer, arranger, and orchestrator. After varied music studies he went to New York in 1916 and earned a living as a copyist with the music publishers G. Schirmer & Co. He served in the army in the First World War and on his return in 1919 began a career as an orchestrator of musical comedy scores. He took time off to study in Paris in 1926 with Nadia Boulanger and held a Guggenheim Fellowship 1927–8, living in Paris, Berlin, and London. His own pleasant and approachable works were frequently played in the USA, and he won awards in 1930 for his symphonic 'Abraham Lincoln' and 'Sights and Sounds'. He wrote an opera, *Maria Malibran* (1935), and his many works using the popular or jazz idiom include 'Charleston rhapsody' (1926); 'March for two pianos and orchestra' (1930); 'Concerto grosso for jazz band and orchestra' (1932); 'Variations on a theme of Jerome Kern' (1933); 'A symphonic picture of Gershwin's *Porgy and Bess*' (1937); and many more. His skill at theatrical orchestration was unmatched and he arranged for *Kern, *Gershwin, most of *Rodgers's musicals and his 'Victory at Sea' (1952). Among the shows were *Oklahoma!*; *Show Boat*; *South Pacific*; *The King and I*; *My Fair Lady*; and *The Sound of Music*. He conducted on radio from 1941 and wrote music for TV's *The Real West* (1960) and *The Valiant Years* (1961).

Bennett, Tony [Benedetto, Anthony Dominick] (*b* Queens, NY, 13 Aug. 1926). American singer. Early club engagements led to gradual recognition and his Columbia recording of 'Boulevard of broken dreams' led to a further recording contract that produced 'Because of you', 'Cold, cold heart', and 'Rags to riches'. His sophisticated, jazz-coloured way with a song was appreciated by those who still favoured the older, articulate way of singing. In the 1960s he found a new surge of popularity coinciding with TV appearances, a Carnegie Hall concert, and his association with pianist/conductor Ralph Sharon. He recorded such hits as 'I left my heart in San Francisco' and 'I wanna be around'; and continued in the 1970s singing with many leading big bands.

T. Jasper: *Tony Bennett* (London, 1984).

Berigan, Bunny [Roland Bernard] (*b* Hilbert, Wis., 2 Nov. 1908; *d* New York, 2 June 1942). American trumpeter and bandleader. He developed a distinctive, husky, wide-ranging style of trumpet playing that became well-known through his recording of 'I can't get started', widely copied in the jazz world. He started out by playing in local Wisconsin bands, moving to Philadelphia and New York. His first important engagement was with Hal Kemp with whom he toured in Europe. He worked with the *Dorsey Brothers band and was with Paul *Whiteman 1932–3, Abe *Lyman 1934, Benny *Goodman 1935, and Tommy *Dorsey 1937, with whom he recorded 'Marie' and 'Song of India'. He led his own first big band 1937–40, recording extensively and often heard on radio; and was with Tommy Dorsey again in 1940. In 1941 he worked in Hollywood; and he had just formed a new big band in 1942 when he collapsed and died, as so many early jazz men did, of overwork and drink.

Berle, Milton [Berlinger, Milton] (*b* New York, 12 July 1908). American comedian, singer, and songwriter. He began performing at the age of five and was in vaudeville in his early years. In 1931 he was acting as MC at the Palace Hotel and this led to nightclub and theatre appearances. He was in **Earl Carroll's Vanities* (1932); *Saluta* (1934); **Ziegfeld Follies* (1943). From around 1948 he became one of the first big comic stars of the TV age, and was involved in many popular series. He specialized in toothy, offbeat character parts and in his vaudeville act went in for rapid-fire patter. He appeared in many films, including *New Faces of 1937* (1937); *Radio City Revels* (1937); *Sun Valley Serenade* (1941); *Rise and Shine* (1941); *Tall, Dark and Handsome* (1941); *The Dolly Sisters* (1945); *Always Leave Them Laughing* (1949); and *Let's Make Love* (1960); and he starred in a popular TV variety show, *Texaco Star Theater*. He was the composer or lyric-writer of many of the songs used in his films, such as 'Always leave 'em laughing'; and he had a long list to his credit including 'I'd give a million tomorrows' and 'Sam, you made the pants too long'.

M. Berle & H. Frankel: *Milton Berle: an Autobiography* (New York, 1974).

Berlin, Irving [Baline, Israel] (*b* Temun, Siberia, 11 May 1888; *d* New York, 22 Sept. 1989). American composer and lyricist. His family left Russia when he was four and his father became a cantor in a New York synagogue, working in his spare time in a kosher slaughterhouse. The family lived in extreme poverty, their situation worsening when the father died in 1896, forcing Israel, at the age of eight, to find work. He started selling newspapers and led a blind busker known as 'Blind Sol' through the streets of the Bowery. He began busking himself, singing the popular songs of the day from street to street. At the age of 16 he got his first regular job as a singing waiter in Jimmy Kelly's restaurant in Union Square. When the premises were closed he would work out tunes of his own on the piano. While working in Nigger Mike Salter's saloon, his first published work appeared—the lyrics to 'Marie from sunny Italy' (1907) with music by the saloon's pianist Nick Nicholson. By this time he was calling himself (as the result of a printer's error) Irving Berlin, and in 1909 he became staff lyric-writer in the music-publishing business of Ted *Snyder with whom he frequently collaborated. In 1909 he published more than 20 songs including several humorous items which were to be his first substantial successes, some of them like 'Sadie Salome, go home' (*w* Edgar *Leslie) and 'My wife's gone to the country' (with Snyder; *w* George Whiting, 1884–1943) selling as many as 300,000 copies. On the strength of this Snyder took him into partnership. In 1910 he appeared as a singer in a vaudeville show *Up Stage and Down* and had two songs sung by Fanny *Brice in the **Ziegfeld Follies* show of that year.

Around 1896 a pianist called Ben *Harney had arrived in New York with some songs that he had written, including 'Mister Johnson, turn me loose' and 'You've been a good old wagon', which were in a novel syncopated style, and demonstrated an intriguing new piano technique which he called 'ragging'. In his stage act he would 'rag' any tune the audience requested, popular or classical, one of his own favourites being Mendelssohn's 'Spring song'. In 1897 he wrote a *Rag-Time Instructor* which helped to bolster his claim to be the man who introduced ragtime to New York. It was by no means the best or even the genuine ragtime—that was being written by black composers like Scott *Joplin in towns like St Louis—but his effect was considerable. By the early 1900s, ragtime, ersatz or real, was a national craze. Probably Irving Berlin was among the many who went to see Ben Harney at Tony *Pastor's vaudeville theatre, for his first ragtime song, written in 1909, was 'That mesmerizing Mendelssohn tune' based on 'Spring song'. Among the sentimental and comic songs in older vein, Berlin now began to write some of the best (and most influential) commercial ragtime songs ever to come from *Tin Pan Alley. He gave them catchy tunes, simple but satirical lyrics with amusingly contrived rhymes (such as having an 'itch again to go back to Michigan') and easy, flowing Charleston rhythms that had more immediate appeal to popular taste than the rather sedate rhythms of classical ragtime. In 1911 he set the popular song world alight by creating what has become one of the best-known of all 'rag' songs. Adding a simple bugle call to a quote from 'Swanee River' to create a lightly syncopated melody and an off-white lyric that brought in a bit of the 'oh, ma honey' stuff, he swept the public off its feet with *'Alexander's Ragtime Band'. He followed up this success in the same year with 'Everybody's doin' it now' which was used in a London revue of the same name in 1912 and thus spread the new gospel to Britain. 'At the Devil's ball' was a ragtime-flavoured hit in 1912, 'That international rag' appeared in 1913, and the dancers enjoyed 'I want to go back to Michigan' in 1914.

By this time Berlin was setting his sights on Broadway and wrote his first complete Broadway score, **Watch Your Step*, in 1914; it was followed the next year by *Stop, Look and Listen*, which appeared at the Empire Theatre in London as *Follow the Crowd*. He contributed to the American war effort with his show *Yip, Yip, Yaphank* which gave the harassed soldier 'Oh, how I hate to get up in the morning'. In 1919 he founded his own music-publishing company and contributed to the fabulous **Ziegfeld Follies*, the main hit being 'A pretty girl is like a melody' which became the series theme-song, and the audience also enjoyed the rather naughty 'You'd be surprised' sung by Eddie *Cantor. Berlin contributed to subsequent editions and was the first composer, in 1927, to be asked to write a complete score for the *Follies*. In the meantime, in 1921, in association with Sam H. Harris, he had built the Music Box Theatre where, for several years, he wrote his own **Music Box Revue*, which rivalled the Ziegfeld productions in splendour and gimmicks and were full of good music and first-class comedy. People were prepared to pay higher prices than usual to see these polished shows in the new theatre especially built for them. The 1923 edition had among its hits the charming 'What'll I do' and the wistful 'All alone' came in 1924. Both of these are good examples of the effective simplicity that gave Berlin's songs such wide appeal. In 1925 he married the heiress Ellin Mackay (1903–88), in spite of strong opposition from her father, and was inspired to write one of his tenderest songs, 'Always'.

The years of depression which now hit America and the world were not conducive to writing light revues and, after the *Follies* of 1927 there was quite a lengthy silence on Broadway where Berlin was concerned. He dabbled in various business enterprises, most of which collapsed in the slump of 1929. He was now having to rely on song-writing for a living after many years of treating it as more or less a sideline. It was a period that produced a number of potboilers that were not up to his best standards, apart from which he began to contribute to such early talkies as *Hallelujah* (1929), *Mammy* (1930), and *Puttin' on the Ritz* (1930). He often feared at this time that his talent might desert him or he would lose public favour, but these fears proved groundless and most of his best work was still to come. When he did return to the theatre in 1932 it was with a daring show called **Face the Music* which was set in the depression and dealt with police and political corruption as well as guying other stage shows. One of its hits was the cheerfully cynical 'Let's have another cup of coffee'. The same year Rudy Vallee made a hit of 'Say it isn't so' and in 1933 came **As Thousands Cheer* with its briskly romantic 'Easter parade'. Some of the best of all Berlin songs, perhaps the ones that came closest to the more sophisticated vein of Gershwin and Rodgers, were the ones he wrote for the *Astaire–Rogers films from 1935 and other films into the war years. For this war he wrote an all-soldier revue, *This is the Army*, in which he sang his old First World War hit 'Oh, how I hate to get up in the morning' and where songs like 'This is the Army, Mr Jones' almost convinced the Americans that it really was their war. Berlin himself recorded the latter song and 'My British buddy' in London in 1943. His biggest single hit had come in 1942 with 'White Christmas', which was an all-time best-selling recording and became as firm a fixture in the Christmas festivities as 'Good King Wenceslas' or 'Silent night'. His most memorable score of all came in 1946 with the folky and tune-packed **Annie Get Your Gun*; followed in 1950 by the lightly satirical **Call Me Madam*.

The flavour and style of a typical Irving Berlin song is, with few exceptions, quite different from the sophisticated material that Rodgers and Hart, Jerome Kern with Bolton and Wodehouse, Cole Porter, and the Gershwins contributed to the Broadway stage and Hollywood films. A Berlin tune and lyric are closer to the natural American song of the *'Dixie' kind, and both his tunes and his humour are more blatant. They have a naturalness that makes them easily memorable. Berlin is much more of a Tin Pan Alley composer than those mentioned above: a writer with a common touch, but indubitably the best that Tin Pan Alley has produced. And only Berlin would come up with such a cheeky rhyme as 'My Uncle Al in Texas | Can't even write his name. | He signs his cheques with Xes. | But they cash them just the same'. At the age of 75 or thereabouts he had grown tired of the pressures of show and song creation and retired to apply his sharp judgement to his business interests. His 80th and 90th birthdays were celebrated with special TV shows and Presidential messages. Berlin remained a recluse in his East Side mansion and passed his 100th birthday out of sight of a warmly remembering world, but a recognized national monument.

The early shows to which he contributed included: *The Boys and Betty* (1908); *The Girl and the Wizard* (1909); *Ziegfeld Follies* (1910)—'Doing the grizzly bear', 'Good-bye Becky Cohen'; *He Came From Milwaukee* (1910); *The Jolly Bachelors* (1910)—'If the managers only thought the same as Mother'; *Up and down Broadway* (1910); *Temptations* (1911); *Ziegfeld Follies* (1911); *Everybody's Doing It* (London, 1912)—'Everybody's doing it' (1911); *The Whirls of Society* (1912)—'That society bear'; *The Sun Dodgers* (1913)—'At the picture show'; *All Aboard* (1913)—'Somebody's coming to my house'; before producing the complete score (or most of it) for such shows as: **Watch Your Step* (1914); *Stop! Look! Listen!* (1915)—'I love a piano', 'The girl on the magazine cover'; *The Century Girl* (with Victor *Herbert, 1916); *Cohan Revue of 1918* (with George M. *Cohan, 1917); *Dance and Grow Thin* (1918); *Yip, Yip, Yaphank* (1918)—'Oh, how I hate to get up in the morning'; *Ziegfeld Follies* (1919)—'Mandy', 'A pretty girl is like a melody', 'You'd be surprised'; (1920)—'Tell me, little gypsy'; *The Music Box Revue* (1921)—'Say it with music'; (1922)—'Lady of the evening'; (1923)—'What'll I do' (added later); (1924); 'All alone' (added later), 'Tell her in the Springtime'; *The *Cocoanuts* (1925); *Ziegfeld Follies* (1927)—'Shaking the blues away'; *Face the Music* (1932)—'Let's have another cup of coffee', 'Soft lights and sweet music'; *As Thousands Cheer* (1933)—'Easter parade', 'Heat wave', 'Not for all the rice in China', 'Harlem on my mind'; **Louisiana Purchase* (1940); *This is the Army* (1942)—'This is the Army, Mr Jones', 'I left my heart at the Stage Door Canteen'; *Annie Get Your Gun* (1946) [see entry]; *Miss Liberty* (1949)—'Give me your tired, your poor', 'I love you', 'Let's take an old-fashioned walk'; *Call Me Madam* (1950) [see entry]; *Mr President* (1962)—'Let's go back to the waltz'.

Berlin's main contributions to films were: *Hallelujah* (1929)—'Waiting at the end of the road' 'Swanee shuffle'; *Puttin' on the Ritz* (1929)—'Puttin' on the Ritz'; *Mammy* (1929)—'Let me sing—and I'm happy'; *Reaching for the Moon* (1931); **Top Hat* (1935)—'Cheek to cheek', 'Isn't this a lovely day', 'No strings', 'The Piccolino', 'Top hat, white tie and tails'; **Follow the Fleet* (1936)—'I'd rather lead a band', 'I'm putting all my eggs in one basket', 'But where are you', 'Let's face the music and dance', 'Let yourself go', 'We saw the sea'; **On the Avenue* (1937)—'I've got my love to keep me warm', 'You're laughing at me', 'This year's kisses', 'He ain't got rhythm', 'Slumming on Park Avenue'; *Carefree* (1938)—'Change partners', 'The yam'; *Alexander's Ragtime Band* (1938)—the first film with a score made up of past hits of one composer: 'Now it can be told', etc.; *Second Fiddle* (1939)—'I'm sorry for myself', 'I poured my heart into a song', 'Back to back'; *Holiday Inn* (1942)—'Abraham', 'Be careful, it's my heart', 'You're easy to dance with', 'Easter parade', and the best-selling 'White Christmas'; *Blue Skies* (1946)—many old hits and 'A couple of song and dance men', 'You keep coming back like a song'; **Easter Parade* (1948)—many old hits and 'Better luck next time', 'A couple of swells', 'It only happens when I dance with you', 'Steppin' out with my baby'; **White Christmas* (1954); and *There's No Business Like Show Business* (1954). *Annie Get Your Gun* and *Call Me Madam* were filmed in 1950 and 1953. Other Berlin songs include: 'Piano man' (1910); 'Play a simple melody' (1914); 'When I leave the world behind' (1915); 'You forgot to remember' (1925); 'Blue skies' (1926); 'Because I love you' (1926); 'Russian lullaby' (1927); 'The song is ended' (1927); 'Marie' (1928); 'Coquette' (1928); 'Say it isn't so' (1932); 'How deep is the ocean' (1932); 'I never had a chance' (1934); and 'God bless America' (1938); notably promoted by Kate *Smith.

A. Woollcott: *The Story of Irving Berlin* (New York, 1925; repr. 1938). D. Ewen: *The Story of Irving Berlin* (New York, 1950). D. Jay: *The Irving Berlin Songography 1907–1966 [New Rochelle, NY, 1969)*. M. Freedland: *Irving Berlin* (London–New York, 1974). I. Whitcomb: *Irving Berlin and Ragtime America* (London, 1987). L. Bergreen: *As Thousands Cheer: the Life of Irving Berlin* (New York–London, 1990).

Bernard, Felix (*b* Brooklyn, NY, 28 Apr. 1897; *d* Hollywood, 20 Oct. 1944). American composer and pianist. He learned his music from his father who was a professional violinist. At an early age he became a professional himself, playing the piano as a song-plugger and in various orchestras. He became a vaudeville entertainer, piano-playing and tap-dancing. In 1919 he wrote 'Dardanella' with Johnny Black and lyrics by Fred *Fisher which was recorded that year by Ben Selvin and his orchestra and became the first record of dance music to sell more than a million copies. Including all the other versions recorded it was to sell more than 6,500,000 copies in the 1920s. Although it did not match this first effort, he had another seller in 1934 with 'Winter wonderland' (*w* Dick Smith).

Bernard, Sam [Barnett, Samuel] (*b* London, 1863; *d* New York, 1927). English-born comedian who was taken to America as a child. He appeared in New York in vaudeville, touring during the years 1885–96, including a return visit to England. He became type-cast as a Jewish character actor before being spotted by the famous burlesque team of *Weber and Fields who signed him on in their newly formed Music Hall company. He appeared in several of their classic pieces such as *The Geezer* (1896); *The Glad Hand* (1897); and *Pousse-Café* (1897). He left Weber and Fields (except for a reunion in *Hoity Toity* (1901)) to star in a long series of musical shows that included: *A Dangerous Maid* (1898); *The Man in the Moon* (1899); *The Casino Girl* (1900); *The Belle of Bohemia* (1900); *The Silver Slipper* (1902); *The Girl from Kay's* (1903)—in which he created his famous character of Mr Hoggenheimer; *The Rollicking Girl* (1905); *The Rich Mr Hoggenheimer* (1906); *The Girl and the Wizard* (1909); *He Came from Milwaukee* (1910); *All for the Ladies* (1912); *The Modiste Shop* (1913); *The Belle of Bond Street* (1914); *The Century Girl* (1916); *As You Were* (1920). He moved into the revue world in **Music Box Revue* (1921–2) and starred in and mainly wrote *Nifties of 1923*.

Bernie, Ben [Anzelovitz, Benjamin Woodruff] (*b* Bayonne, NJ, 30 May 1891; *d* Beverly Hills, Calif., 20 Oct. 1943). American bandleader. He studied both music and mining but chose the former, going into vaudeville as reciter and violinist, and, for a while, in partnership with Phil *Baker. He formed his first dance band in 1922 and soon became known on radio and records for his mellifluous and humorous introductions, and for his catch-phrase 'Yowsah!' The band played in the sweet style, but with a hot element provided by such players as Jack Pettis, Dick Stabile, and Bill Moore, with arrangements by pianist Al Goering, ably led by 'The Old Maestro'—as he styled himself. He went to London in 1929 to play at the Kit-Kat Club and the Palladium. Two of the band's biggest hits were the opening and closing numbers, 'It's a lonesome old town' and 'Au revoir, pleasant dreams'. He appeared in the films *Shoot the Works* (1934); *Stolen Harmony* (1935); *Wake Up and Live* (1937); *Love and Hisses* (1937); and in various radio shows. He was co-writer of 'Sweet Georgia Brown' (1925); 'Who's your little who-zis?' (1931); 'I can't believe it's true' (1932); and 'Strange interlude' (1932).

Bernstein, Elmer (*b* New York, 4 Apr. 1922). American composer and conductor. After studies at the Juilliard School with Aaron Copland, Stefan Wolpe, and Roger Sessions, he wrote scores for Army Air Force and United Nations shows (1949–51) which led to his being asked by Columbia to write music for films. He made a notable success of using the jazz idiom in all kinds of compositions including his very successful TV and film scores which have been extensively recorded. They include: *Saturday's Hero* (1951); *Sudden Fear* (1952); *Cat Women of the Moon* (1953); *Make Haste to Live* (1954); *The Eternal Sea*

(1955); *The Man With the Golden Arm* (1956); *The Ten Commandments* (1956); *The Tin Star* (1957); *The Sweet Smell of Success* (1957); *Desire Under the Elms* (1958); *God's Little Acre* (1958); *The Buccaneer* (1959); *Anna Lucasta* (1959); *The Magnificent Seven* (1960); *By Love Possessed* (1961); *A Walk on the Wild Side* (1962); *Bird Man of Alcatraz* (1962); *To Kill a Mockingbird* (1962); *The Caretakers* (1963); *Love With the Proper Stranger* (1964); *The Carpetbaggers* (1964); *Baby, the Rain Must Fall* (1965); *The Sons of Katie Elder* (1965); *The Reward* (1965); *Cast a Giant Shadow* (1966); *The Return of the Seven* (1966); *Thoroughly Modern Millie* (1967); *The Scalp Hunters* (1968); *The Midas Run* (1969); *True Grit* (1970); *A Cannon for Cordoba* (1970); *Blind Terror* (1971); *The Shootist* (1976); *Zulu Dawn* (1979); *Airplane* (1980); *An American Werewolf in London* (1981); *Honky Tonk Freeway* (1981); *Five Days One Summer* (1982); *Class 82* (1982); and *Trading Places* (1983).

Bernstein, Leonard (*b* Lawrence, Mass., 25 Aug. 1918; *d* New York, 14 Oct. 1990). American composer author, pianist, and conductor. His training was entirely academic and he showed startling promise even as a student. His teachers included Walter Piston. He graduated from Harvard in 1939 and entered Curtis Institute to study conducting under Fritz Reiner, coming into prominence as a conductor by deputizing at short notice for Bruno Walter. After that he conducted every principal orchestra over the world and made innumerable classical recordings, many as a pianist. A man of furious energy, he conducted, composed, lectured, and broadcast, almost without pause. His compositions on the classical side were broad-based but are often tinged with the flavours of Yiddish music, as in the popular 'Chichester Psalms' which also uses a Hebrew text. On the other hand he had a strongly American popular bent which came out with great force and effect in his jazz-oriented scores for **On the Town* (1944); **Wonderful Town* (1953), and one of the finest musicals of all time, **West Side Story* (1957). After becoming conductor of the New York Philharmonic in 1958 he devoted less time to composition than his admirers would have wished, and he resigned in 1969 in order to compose; but unfortunately another *West Side Story* did not materialize. The delightful **Candide* (1956), later revised, always gave hopes of further operettas but *1600 Pennsylvania Avenue* (1976) was a comparative failure. His score for *On the Waterfront* (1954) showed his untapped potential as a film composer. Latterly he returned mainly to conducting and recording.

J. Gruen: *The Private World of Leonard Bernstein* (New York, 1968). J. Peyser: *Leonard Bernstein* (New York, 1987).

Berry, Chuck [Anderson, Charles Edward] (*b* San Jose, Calif., 18 Oct. 1926). American singer and songwriter. It has been argued that if Chuck Berry had been white he would have been as big a star as Elvis *Presley. However, he never had quite the same emotional impact. He was more concerned than Presley with the articulate and witty delivery of his lyrics, skilfully written and immensely influential, which took as their subject the America of the 1950s. He cast the eye of a satirist on the consumer society, especially the preoccupations of the teenager searching for excitement, which he expressed with vivid humour and imagery. His expert melding of words and melody was a model for other such innovators as Bob *Dylan and the *Beach Boys. His records were instantly recognizable, with their wailing guitar introductions and chiming lead guitar figures. He has been seen as the link between the rock-and-rollers of the 1950s and the pop bands of the 1970s, and between black and white cultures. His music is a marriage between his black heritage, drawn from such musicians as Muddy *Waters, and his debt to such diverse influences as Frank *Sinatra, Charlie *Christian, Louis *Jordan, and Nat 'King' *Cole.

With the help of the disc jockey Alan *Freed, who sat in on the sessions, Chuck Berry had his first record hit with his first recording, 'Maybelline', made in May 1955 for Chess Records of Chicago. It was a carefully formulated song, tailored to meet the demand created by the Western Swing style of Bill *Haley and the rockabilly music then being developed by Sun's country-rooted artists in Memphis. Berry's clear enunciation was already noteworthy. Concentrating on the rock-and-roll elements, his next success came with 'Roll over Beethoven' (1955), a dig at highbrow culture, which paved the way for such commercially viable singles as 'School days' and 'Rock and roll music' (1957); 'Sweet little sixteen' and 'Johnny B. Goode' (1958). He was a prolific and consistent writer but found such classics as 'Sweet little rock 'n' roller' (1958), 'Little Queenie' and 'Back in the USA' (1959), 'Too pooped to pop' and 'Let it rock' (1960) only attaining the lower reaches of the charts.

His career was interrupted in 1959 when he faced long court proceedings for transporting a juvenile across a state line, reputedly for immoral purposes, a charge he has always denied. The racial bias of the first trial had its verdict overthrown, but he was convicted at a second trial and was in prison 1962–3. He resumed his recording career in 1964 with 'Nadine' and 'No particular place to go'. In Britain, thanks to artists like the *Beatles and the *Rolling Stones, Berry had become a cult hero. They recorded his songs and John *Lennon was clearly influenced by Berry in his own songwriting. The Rolling Stones used Berry material for much of their repertoire, their version of his 'Around and around' being one of their early classics. Other copyists included the *Kinks, the *Beach Boys, and Bob Dylan whose 'Subterranean homesick blues' was a re-working of 'Too much monkey business'.

In 1972, Berry had an unexpected hit with a lewd novelty song, 'My ding-a-ling', which gave him his first No. 1 hit in both Britain and America. His career from the beginning of the 1970s was mixed, with mannered stage performances and often poor back-up bands, but his songs have continued to flourish. His stage act had once been good with his impish, slightly satanic looks underlining his natural flair for comedy. He will be remembered as the most consistently witty and expressive of the rock-and-rollers; as a distinctive guitar stylist; and for his fine songs.

H. A. Dewitt: *Chuck Berry: rock 'n' roll music* (Fremont, Calif., 1981). C. Berry: *The Autobiography* (New York, 1988).

Berry, W. H. [William Henry] (*b* London, 23 Mar. 1872; *d* London, 2 May 1951). British actor, comedian, and singer. He originally had a commercial career in the City of London, but eventually deserted this for the field of entertainment. He spent some 12 years in summer seaside shows interspersed with off-season appearances on the concert stage. His first theatre appearance, at the London Pavilion in 1905, earned him a contract with the impresario George *Edwardes, which led to parts in such musicals as *The Little Cherub* (1906); *Les Merveilleuses* (1907); *The *Merry Widow* (1908); *Havana* (1908); *The *Dollar Princess* (1909); *A *Waltz Dream* (1911); *The *Count of Luxembourg* (1911); *Gypsy Love* (1912); *A *Country Girl* (1914); *Betty* (1915); *Tina* (1915); *High Jinks* (1916); *The Boy* (1917); *Who's Hooper?* (1919); *Poppy* (1924); *The Blue Kitten* (1925); and **Lilac Time* (1927); among many. He first appeared in films in 1934.

W. H. Berry: *Forty Years in the Limelight* (London, 1939).

Berté, Heinrich (*b* Galgócz, 8 May 1858; *d* Vienna, 25 Aug. 1924). Hungarian composer. He wrote a number of operettas in his own right, but is chiefly remembered for his construction of the score of *Das Dreimädlerhaus* (1916), based on the music of Franz Schubert. He undertook this task somewhat reluctantly; but the show achieved more than 7000 performances in its first five years, only a few less than *The *Merry Widow*; and its popularity continued in the English adaptation **Lilac Time*. He wrote several ballets and his other operettas included: *Die Schneeflocke* (1896); *Der neue Bürgmeister* (1904); *Die Millionenbraut* (1904); *Der kleine Chevalier* (1907); *Der schöne Gardist* (1908); *Der Glücksnarr* (1908); *Kreolenblut* (1911); *Der Marchenprinz* (1914); *Musik im Mai* (1927); and *Das Kaiserliebchen* (1930).

Besoyan, Rick [Richard] (*b* Reedley, Calif., 2 July 1924; *d* Sayville, Long Island, 13 Mar. 1970). American composer. After going to the Trinity College of Music, London, on a scholarship, he returned to New York to start a career as singer and actor. He toured with the Savoy Light Opera Company and during this time started to write **Little Mary Sunshine*, which took three years to complete. A shortened version was used in a revue but it was a struggle to find the backing to stage it in full. Called 'a new musical about an old operetta', it poked fun at *Herbert, *Friml, *Romberg, and the rest, and it eventually had a great vogue. His later musicals, *The Student Gypsy* (1963) and *Babes in the Wood* (1964), were failures. He died while writing the lyrics of *Mrs 'Arris Goes to Paris*.

Besses o' th' Barn. British brass band, possibly the oldest to have remained a leading band throughout its career and one of the best-known in the field. It was famous as a brass and reed band long before it became an all-brass band in 1851. Besses o' th' Barn is a village in Lancashire, situated on the turnpike road about five miles from Manchester. The band has toured the world twice and is entitled to the accolade 'Royal' granted by King Edward VII. It has won all the most coveted awards in the brass band world, being National Champions in 1903 and British Open Champions in 1892, 1894, 1920, 1925, 1931, 1937, and 1959, mainly under the direction of Alex Owen (1851–1920).

Best Foot Forward. American musical produced by George *Abbott, music and lyrics by Hugh *Martin and Ralph *Blane, book by John Cecil Holm. It was staged at the Ethel Barrymore Theatre, 1 Oct. 1941, gave first major roles to Nancy *Walker and June *Allyson, was choreographed by Gene *Kelly, and ran for 326 performances. It was revived off-Broadway in 1963 with Liza *Minnelli getting her first big part. The setting is a prep school in Winsocki, Penn., where, as a publicity stunt, a Hollywood starlet arrives to attend the annual dance. This causes all sorts of jealousies and complications of a pleasantly trivial kind, padded out with a few catchy songs like 'Buckle down, Winsocki' and 'What do you think I am?' It was filmed in 1943 with Lucille *Ball, Nancy Walker, and June Allyson.

Best Little Whorehouse in Texas, The. American musical set in the Chicken Ranch, a brothel in Texas where the customers paid in poultry, active from the 1840s to 1973 when it was forced to close. It was originally an off-Broadway production at the Entermedia Theatre from 17 Apr. 1978, where it had 85 performances, but proved popular enough to move to the 46th Street Theatre on 19 June 1978 where it completed a run of 1703 performances. Music and lyrics were by Carol Hall and the book by Larry L. King and Peter Masterton. It was staged in London (Drury Lane) 26 Feb. 1981; and filmed in 1982 with Dolly *Parton and Burt Reynolds.

Bettelstudent, Der (The Beggar Student). Operetta with score by Karl *Millöcker and book by F. Zell (Camillo Walzell) and Richard *Genée, first produced on 6 Dec. 1882 at the Theater an der Wien in Vienna with Karolin Finaly as Laura, Felix Schweighofer as Colonel Ollendorf, and Alexander Girardi as Symon. It was first seen in London at the Alhambra Theatre, 12 Apr. 1884. The somewhat involved story of the poor student who is dressed up as a prince to further a Cracowian intrigue is hard going, but it has a romantically tuneful score whose arias have remained perennially popular with operetta tenors and sopranos, notably 'Ach ich hab' sie ja nur auf Schulter geküsst' ('Once I gave her a kiss'), 'Ich knüpfte manche zarte Bande an', 'Ich setz' den Fall', and 'Ich hab' kein Geld, bin vogelfrei'.

Better 'Ole, The. Categorized as 'a fragment from France', this musical was based on the very popular First World War cartoons by artist Bruce Bairnsfather (1888–1959); the title comes from the one with the caption 'If you know of a better 'ole, go to it' spoken by one of two gloomy soldiers sitting in a shell crater. Bairnsfather and Arthur Eliot wrote the book, James Hurd the lyrics, and the score by Herman *Darewski contained such popular items as 'What do you want to make those eyes at me for', 'When you look in the heart of a rose', 'Tommy', 'She's my gal', and 'From someone in France to someone in Somerset'. Opening at the Oxford Theatre 4 Aug. 1917, with Arthur Bouchier as Old Bill, it attracted a home-on-leave audience to the tune of 811 performances; with another 353 in New York when it opened there at the Greenwich Village Theatre 19 Oct. 1918.

Beyond the Fringe. The British intimate revue had enjoyed a brilliant revival after the Second World War, the 1950s enjoying such productions as *The *Lyric Revue* and **Airs on a Shoestring* with the work of people like Alan *Melville, Peter Myers, Michael *Flanders, and Donald *Swann presented in a polished, witty, and musical way, following in the steps of Nöel *Coward, and with all the actors still using public-school accents. Then in 1960 came *Beyond the Fringe*, a 'revue' involving four young Cambridge graduates not purveying song and dance but shafted satire aimed at the morals and outlook of the day, a trendsetting show that sparked off the satire boom. Starting out as a 'fringe' entertainment at the 1960 Edinburgh Festival in August, the show came into London's West End at the small Fortune Theatre on 10 May 1961. It was to stay there for 1184 performances, with a second edition opening at the Mayfair Theatre 15 Apr. 1964 for a further run of 1016. London acclaimed the talented team of Alan Bennett, Jonathan Miller, Peter Cook, and Dudley *Moore (who also wrote the music), and their popularity has not diminished with the years. *Beyond the Fringe* went to New York in the meantime, opening at the John Golden Theatre 27 Oct. 1962 for 673 performances.

Big Apple. One of the many party dances that were created during the dance craze years of the 1920s and 1930s. It first appeared in New York in 1935 and had a vogue in England 1937–8. Its name derived from the Big Apple Club in Columbia, South Carolina, where it originated. Described as a 'swing square dance' it was performed in a circle by a number of couples, led by a caller, with one couple improvising a truckin' *Charleston-like dance in the centre; the whole deriving from an earlier black dance called the Shout. Big Apple has long been a widely used nickname for the city of New York, 'apple' being American slang for any big town.

Bigard, Barney [Leon Albany] (*b* New Orleans, 3 Mar. 1906; *d* Culver City, Calif. 27 June 1980). American jazz clarinettist, saxophonist, and composer. He studied the clarinet with Lorenzo Tio Jr. (1884–1933), and first played professionally, doubling on tenor-saxophone, in 1921. He formed a light-hearted duo with clarinettist Albert Nicholas in 1922, and joined King *Oliver at the Plantation Club in Chicago in 1925, working intermittently with Charlie Elgar, Albert Wynn (1907–75), and Luis *Russell. The most important part of his career was with the Duke *Ellington band which he joined in 1928 and left in 1942, during this time becoming recognized as one of jazz's leading clarinettists. He was involved in the composition of several of the band's popular numbers such as 'East St Louis toodle-oo' (1925); 'Saturday night function' (1928); 'Saratoga swing' (1929); 'Beggar blues (1929); 'Sloppy Joe' (1929); *'Mood indigo' (1930); and 'C-jam blues' (1942). Some of his most notable solos with the band included 'Clarinet lament' (1936) and 'Jack the Bear' (1940). In 1943 he settled in California playing with Freddie *Slack, leading his own band, and working with Kid *Ory.

From 1946 he was with the Louis *Armstrong All-Stars for five years, leaving for a period to play with Ben *Pollack and Cozy *Cole, rejoining in 1960–1. He freelanced thereafter, giving up full-time playing in 1965 but continuing to make many notable appearances and recordings. Long before Benny *Goodman became king of the clarinet, Bigard had helped to establish it as a widely known jazz instrument.

B. Bigard (ed. Martun): *With Louis and the Duke* (New York–London, 1985).

Big band jazz. Descriptive phrase that has become synonymous with the *swing or *dance band unit of the mid-1930s and thereafter. It was first used, sometimes in a slightly derogatory way by the purists, of any band that had expanded beyond the New Orleans grouping of single instruments and used more than one of each instrument. The term became specifically attached to such bands as those led by Fletcher *Henderson and Duke *Ellington, which were not really 'big' by anything but jazz standards, and was understood to imply arranged jazz with a preponderance of section work. As the big bands became bigger and more formalized the term lost any precise meaning, while the smaller 'bands within bands' became a greater focus of interest. In days when such large units are not generally commercially viable, the big band is becoming a threatened species. The music, styling, etc. is discussed more fully under SWING.

G. T. Simon: *The Big Bands* (New York–London, 1967; rev. 1971). A. McCarthy: *Big Band Jazz* (London, 1974). A. Jackson: *The World of Big Bands* (Newton Abbot, 1977). P. Gammond & R. Horricks: *The Big Bands* (Cambridge, 1981).

Bilk, Acker [Bernard Stanley] (*b* Pensford, Somerset, 28 Jan. 1929). British clarinettist, vocalist, and bandleader. He began his jazz career in the 1950s working with Ken *Colyer. He formed his own band in the mid-1950s and began a highly successful career in the *traditional boom years playing a polished sort of *Dixieland shuffle-beat jazz featuring his skilful and individual clarinet playing. The recording of Bilk's own 'Stranger on the shore' became an international hit and was later used as a TV theme tune. Keeping in the *mainstream area of traditional jazz, he led excellent bands with changing personnel throughout the 1960s, 1970s, and 1980s.

P. Leslie & P. Gwynn-Jones: *The Book of Bilk* (London, 1961).

'Bill Bailey, won't you please come home'. A standard song of lasting popularity with music and words by Hughie Cannon (1877–1912), published in 1902 and widely used in the late music-hall era; latterly in jazzed-up guise. Some interesting background history came to light in 1973 when the real Mrs Bill Bailey (by then Mrs Sarah Bailey Williams) revealed, while celebrating her 100th birthday in Jackson, Michigan, that 'that darned song broke our marriage'. Her first husband, the original Bill Bailey, a music teacher when she married him in 1893, was a convivial man who liked to linger on at the Whistler Bar in Jackson, frequently getting a hot reception from his wife when he returned late. He confided this to the pianist in the bar, Hughie Cannon, who was inspired to create the immortal ditty in a couple of hours with Bill Bailey right there at his side. It drew unwelcome attention to his domestic life when it became a nationwide hit, so irritating Mrs Bailey that she divorced her husband; a mistake, she said, as she still loved him in spite of his dilatory ways. She married a farmer; Bill Bailey died in 1954.

Cannon, who sold his song outright for £170, had no other comparable successes. Born in Detroit in 1877, he had a varied career as entertainer and pianist, took to drink and drugs, was in Wayne County workhouse from 1910, and died in Toledo in 1912.

***Billboard*.** Prominent USA music trade weekly established in 1894, largely an advertising outlet but providing practical guidance and advice for professional musicians and of burning interest also to those outside the trade by virtue of its reviews and its popular music and record rating charts.

***Billy*.** British musical which opened in London (Drury Lane) 1 May 1974 [904p]. It was made popular by the personable performance of Michael *Crawford as the highly imaginative, day-dreaming Billy Fisher, a sort of British Walter Mitty, who, among other fantasies which he dreams up in his Yorkshire birthplace, sees himself as President, Commander-in-Chief, and captain of the World Cup football team in the land of Ambrosia. The music was by John *Barry, lyrics by Don Black, with book by Dick Clement and Ian La Fresnais, based on the play and novel *Billy Liar* by Keith Waterhouse.

***Bing Boys Are Here, The*.** The first of a series of very popular wartime revues, described as 'a picture of London life in seven panels', devised by George *Grossmith Jr. and Fred *Thompson, lyrics by Clifford *Grey, and score by Nat D. *Ayer with some assistance from Eustace Ponsonby, Philip *Braham, and Ivor *Novello. Opening at the *Alhambra, London, on 19 Apr. 1916, it enjoyed a run of 378 performances, a Mecca, along with **Chu Chin Chow*, for the boys home on leave. The stars were Violet *Loraine (a great singer of recruiting songs in those days) and the famous comedian George *Robey. They achieved a lasting hit with 'If you were the only girl in the world'. Also in the cast were Maidie Andrews, Gillie Potter, Alfred *Lester, and Phyllis Monkman, with John *Ansell as MD. A rich score also included: 'Another little drink', 'Dear old Shepherd's Bush', 'I stopped, I looked and I listened' (a Robey feature), 'The Kipling walk', 'Ragging the dog', and 'The whistler'.

The successor to this show was *The Bing Girls Are There* (Alhambra, 24 Feb. 1917) without Robey, but with Wilkie *Bard, Joseph *Coyne, and Laddie *Cliff joining Violet Loraine—'Let the great big world keep turning'; followed by *The Bing Boys on Broadway* (Alhambra, 16 Feb. 1918) [562p] with Violet Loraine and George Robey—'First love, last love, best love' etc.

Binge, Ronald (*b* Derby, 15 July 1910; *d* Ringwood, 6 Sept. 1979). British composer, arranger, pianist, and conductor. Mainly self-taught, he started out as an organist in silent film theatres meanwhile trying his hand at composing for a local orchestra. He went to London in 1930 and played in all manner of ensembles and places, doing some arranging and composing including, from 1934, work for *Mantovani which was recorded and broadcast. He gave up playing just before the war to concentrate on writing, his first hit coming with 'Spitfire'. After serving in the RAF, 1941–6, he became responsible for the re-organization of the Mantovani orchestra and for the creation of its new echoing strings effect, with such arrangements as 'Charmaine' widely acclaimed. Maintaining a strong link with Mantovani, he became a freelance and was greatly helped by the success of his 'Elizabethan serenade' in 1952 which became known worldwide and was a top seller in Germany. He had his own broadcast series *String Song*, 1955–63. Among his later works was a 'Festival Te Deum', a symphony, and many songs. He wrote much music for brass and military band such as: 'Flash Harry' (1950), 'Old London' (1958), 'Cornet carillon' (1961)—probably one of the most popular brass pieces ever written, 'Duel for Conductors' (1968), and 'Trumpet spectacular' (1972).

Birdland. New York nightclub with strong jazz affiliations, situated at 1678 Broadway, named in honour of alto-saxophonist Charlie *Parker who played there after its opening in 1948.

Bitter-Sweet. Operetta by Noël *Coward produced at His Majesty's Theatre, London 12 July 1929, with the American actress Peggy *Wood in the lead and with Ivy *St Helier, George Metaxa (1899–1950), Robert Newton (1905–56), Betty Huntley-Wright (*b* 1911), and Billy Milton (1905–89) in the cast.

An elderly marchioness is asked to help her niece to decide whether to marry for love or riches. She tells the story of her own past romance in Vienna with an impoverished singer, later killed in a duel; and how she became a famous opera singer and then married a marquis.

The excellent score, in Viennese vein with a strong dash of Coward, included the lasting 'I'll see you again' as well as 'Tokay', 'If love were all', 'Zigeuner', and 'Dear little café', ensuring a good run of 697 performances and a lasting place in British musical annals. It was produced in New York at the Ziegfeld Theatre on 5 Nov. 1929 with the British acress Evelyn *Laye in the leading role [159p]; she also starred in a 1931 London revival. It was filmed in 1933 with Anna *Neagle; and again in 1941 with Jeanette *MacDonald and Nelson *Eddy. There was a revival at Sadler's Wells, London, 23 Feb. 1988.

Black, Cilla [White, Priscilla Maria Veronica] (*b* Liverpool, 27 May 1943). British singer. While working as a secretary, she sang with then unkown groups including the *Beatles and *Gerry and the Pacemakers in the famous Cavern and elsewhere. Deputizing for a group in a Beatles show in 1963, she was persuaded by Brian Epstein to become a full-time professional. She made her radio debuts on Radio Luxembourg's *Friday Spectacular* and BBC's *Easy Beat* and appeared on British TV in *Ready, Steady, Go* before the end of that year. In 1964 she had a No. 1 hit with the Burt *Bacharach song 'Anyone who had a heart' which sold more than 800,000 copies in a month. This was followed by 'You're my world' which became No. 1 and sold 1½ million copies. She has remained a popular singer and entertainer, in recent years presenting her own TV shows.

Black, Stanley (*b* London, 14 June 1913). British composer, arranger, pianist, and conductor. He studied at the Tobias Mathay School of Music, and then, from 1928, became pianist and arranger with various dance orchestras led by *Ambrose, Harry *Roy, Maurice *Winnick, including a notable period with the Lew *Stone band in the 1930s. After serving with the RAF, 1939–44, he became house conductor and arranger for the Decca Record Company. In 1944 he was appointed conductor of the BBC Dance Orchestra, a post which he held until 1952. He appeared in numerous radio shows such as *Hi Gang*, *Much Binding in the Marsh*, and *Black Magic* and made thousands of broadcasts with the band, appearing in the Royal Command performance in 1951 and several times thereafter. He has composed for BBC documentaries and wrote the theme tunes for *The Goons* and *Double Top*. He is an authority on Latin American music, which he recorded extensively on LP. He married the singer Edna Kaye in 1947. He has written around 200 film scores, including: *Rhythm Racketeers* (1936); *Mrs Fitzherbert* (1947); *Laughter in Paradise* (1950); *The Young Ones* (1961); *Summer Holiday* (1963); *City Under the Sea* (1965); and *Crossplot* (1969).

Black American Music. In the whole of musical history, let alone popular musical history, there has never been quite such a revolutionary and drastic change of emphasis and style as that brought about by the implantation of the emerging Afro-American idiom on the existing white American strains. The first effects were apparent in the mid-19th century with the emergence of spirituals and minstrelsy, but really began to make a fundamental difference in the jazz development years from *c.* 1890 to 1920. These effects intensified in the 1940s; with the black idiom taking over popular music in the 1950s and thereafter. It is now a rarity to hear any popular music played in anything but a jazz idiom, and black styling predominates. The revolution that occurred might well appear to have been a sudden one; but, in fact, it was simmering for centuries. The emergence of black music was of a volcanic nature. The pressures had been building up for some 300 years before the eruption came. The same problems occur in the study of black music in those formative years as occur in the study of any folk-music, arising from a complete lack of documentation. Much of what scanty knowledge there is depends on the casual observations of people not primarily concerned with music.

The first mention of black slaves arriving in America goes back to 1619, a year before the Pilgrim Fathers arrived, in Captain John Smith's *Generall Historie of Virginia*. A Dutch ship landed and sold 20 Africans, the beginning of a long and unworthy trade. Those who visited Africa in this pursuit probably found its music much as it was 300 years later. As early as 1623, Richard Jobson, an English captain, wrote 'no people on earth are more naturally affected to the sound of music' than the Africans he met and observed.

It is an obvious assumption that the deported Africans, now slaves in America, would continue to follow their old musical traditions for their own amusement and solace, much as the early settlers in the USA utilized European folk-songs. It is also logical to assume that the music would gradually lose much of the primitive and emotional ferocity of the original in these subdued circumstances and gradually blend with the surrounding European traditions of white American folk-song and popular music. Because there was no way of looking further back, the histories of jazz tended to see it as something which emerged in a formulated shape in the early 1900s; but there is some logic in speculating that something closely related to New Orleans jazz, though played on African instruments, might have been heard at any time during those obscure and dark decades of the 17th, 18th, and 19th centuries. Gradually the music was transferred to the fiddle, the flute, and the banjo, with percussion accompaniment, eventually to emerge as *ragtime and *jazz. It is interesting to read in George Foster's *New York by Gaslight* (1850) a description of a dance hall frequented by black people which he visited in 1842. There he heard a band consisting of a fiddler, a trumpeter, and a drummer. He described the trumpeter as producing 'red-hot knitting needles of sound'; the drummer 'sweats and deals his blows in all violation of the laws of rhythm' (as Foster knew them). Was he perhaps listening to a band playing jazz in 1842? Even the association of the word 'hot' with the music is of prophetic interest.

A considerable literature has attempted to discover black music in those dark centuries. Three dominating characteristics emerge: a melodic line which is a clear ancestor of ragtime (perhaps based on primitive banjo phrases); a strong rhythmic accent; and songs which alternate improvised lines, shouts, and cries, with repeated choruses.

The white traditions of 17th-century America which the black musicians would also draw upon were firmly based on two primary sources: the psalms and hymns brought over by European immigrants; and the folk-songs and dances similarly imported. White Americans spent the same three centuries absorbing European influences. What was to be the distinctive racy and syncopated American idiom may well have rubbed off, to some extent, from the music their slaves were making. America did not produce its truly individual composers until they had, to some degree, absorbed and exploited black music. American music became the dominating influence in the world only after it was thoroughly black.

As the musical historian Eileen Southern has observed, comments on early black music could only come from mainly white sources. For example, great value was placed upon the musical accomplishments of slaves offered for sale during the 18th century. Southern collects a number of such references in sale posters: 'plays on the French horn', 'a fiddler', 'plays remarkably well on violin', 'beats the drum tolerably well', 'a remarkable whistler and plays on the violin', 'plays on the fife and German flute', 'a mighty singer'—and so on. These suggest that the white masters considered musicality a considerable asset. Had they in mind the thought that such musicians would keep their fellow-slaves peacefully entertained; or was it because they would be useful as musicians at white social gatherings? These mid-18th-century advertisements suggest that the white population of the South were well acquainted with black music, even if only in a politer form than the slaves used themselves.

If the development of black instrumental music was to be delayed for some time before the options and the facilities became available, there could be no confinement of their vocal music. In the cotton fields, on the riverside wharfs and elsewhere, the slaves improvised their worksongs in the traditions of African music, a leader intoning the verses and the others responding with a repeated chorus. The rhythmic chant helped to sustain the effort for their laborious and tedious toil. The white overseers accepted the singing as an aid to productivity; though it was also used as a means of secret communication. In church the same improvisational traditions were used and developed. Many white observers were shocked at the rhythmic abandon of this joyful approach to religious music; but the black congregations could not be prevented from expressing themselves in their own way. But their most intimate music was the *blues; the last kind of black music to emerge into general public spheres and hence most obscure in its history. In common with most folk-music, the element of protest was strong in the blues and this, in itself, delayed its use in wider entertainment fields.

Toward the end of the 18th century the situation of the black population began to improve. In 1775, alongside the American revolution, came the Dunmore Proclamation that offered freedom to slaves who joined the British army; and the first anti-slavery society was formed by the Quakers in Philadelphia. With the Declaration of Independence in 1776 came the establishment of the Negro Baptist Church. In Aird's *A Selection of Scotch, English, Irish and Foreign Airs* (1782) the first Negro Jig was printed—alongside *'Yankee Doodle'. Massachusetts abolished slavery in 1783 and in 1784 the first black preachers were officially ordained. By 1787, Negro freemasonry was established and slavery was prohibited in the Northwest Territory. In the first Negro census taken in 1790, of a total of 750,000 black people, 59,000 were listed as free citizens. The first black hymnal was published in 1801, two years before the Louisiana Purchase. Military bands had been officially allowed in America since 1792; the first all-black band was formed in 1820. The slave trade was officially abolished by a Congressional Act in 1808, but there was still a need for an Anti-Slavery Society which was formed on a national basis in Philadelphia in 1833. Slavery itself was not totally abolished until the Thirteenth Amendment of 1865 finally forbade it throughout the United States. *Uncle Tom's Cabin* had been published in 1856. The first Negro College was established in Wilberforce, Ohio, in 1856. The 1860 census now found the Negro population risen to an astonishing 4,880,009 with 488,000 now ranked as free citizens. The Civil War of 1861–5 came as the final act of a long period of inhuman suppression. But the only public outlet for the spirit of black music was in Congo Square, New Orleans, where slaves were allowed to dance, play, and sing on Sundays, a privilege permitted under strict laws from the late 17th century. It was these activities and sounds that first influenced the composer Louis Moreau *Gottschalk.

From 1865 onward, though mainly around the 1890s, *Afro-American music began to emerge in such areas as the *minstrel show, *spirituals, *blues, *ragtime, and finally *jazz. As white audiences began to have an understanding and appreciation of the fundamental black styles, they also began to take over the whole of popular music, emerging as *rhythm 'n' blues, *rock and roll, *soul music, and all the other ramifications of the *pop scene. (The developments in these areas are discussed further under those headings.) The definitive history of black music is far from resolved, but its general outlines are now reasonably well established. There is now a considerable literature devoted to it, the emphasis varying according to the colour and sympathies of its authors.

M. Cuney-Hare: *Negro Musicians and their Music* (Washington DC, 1936; repr. New York, 1974). R. D. Abrahams: *Positively Black* (Englewood Cliffs, NJ, 1970). D-R De Lerma: *Black Music in Our Culture* (Kent, Ohio, 1970). H. Roach: *Black Music in America* (Springfield, Va., 1970; repr. 1973). E. Southern: *The Music of Black Americans* (New York, 1971). S. A. Floyd & M. J. Reiser: *Black Music in the United States: an Annotated Bibliography* (New York, 1983).

Black and White Minstrel Show. Long-lasting and immensely popular British TV show which began in 1960 and ran for many years, reviving the old blackfaced minstrel show and the Kentucky Minstrels tradition at a time when such entertainment was generally thought to be a thing of the past. Devised by George Inns and with George Mitchell as MD, its nucleus was the George Mitchell Choir which had been popular on radio and TV from the Glee Club days of 1949–50 into 1956. The remarkable and unexpected popularity of the Minstrels on TV, and the wide sales of their LPs, led to a stage version which opened at the Victoria Palace, London, 25 May 1962 and ran for many years in various shapes and guises. The show made household names of singers Tony Mercer, Dai Francis, John Boulter, Ted Darling, Les Rawlings, and others and introduced many to the comic talents of the much-acclaimed jazz trombonist George *Chisholm.

Blackbirds. Famous revues, devised by Lew *Leslie, that did much to implant the talents of black artists and musicians on the London scene. The first *Blackbirds* revue was staged at the London Pavilion on 11 Sept. 1926 and notably introduced the talents of the brilliant but short-lived Florence *Mills singing 'Arabella's wedding day' and 'Silver rose'. The music was supplied by the Plantation Orchestra and greatly influenced British musicians who heard it. It featured the novel 'wa-wa' mute playing of trumpeter Johnny Dunn, who also danced while he played. In New York, *Blackbirds of 1928* was even more successful and was to achieve a long unmatched run of 518 performances with white *Cotton Club composer Jimmy *McHugh, in partnership with Dorothy *Fields, supplying such excellent songs as 'I can't give you anything but love, baby', 'Dida-diga-doo', 'I must have that man', 'Porgy', 'Doin' the new low-down', 'Bandanna babies', and 'Magnolia's wedding day', which all greatly impressed the New York audience, as did the talents of Bill *Robinson, Adelaide *Hall, and a brilliantly talented cast.

In 1929 one of the first top-class all-black bands led by Noble *Sissle visited England; and in 1933 the Duke *Ellington band furthered the cause of jazz in the British Isles. *Blackbirds of 1934* (Coliseum, 25 Aug. 1934) was a natural follow-up. By now, if the novelty had gone, the quality continued. One of the rare features of this edition was the girl trumpet player and singer Valaida *Snow. There was a further London edition (Gaiety, 9 July 1936) in which the main attraction was the dancing Nicholas Brothers. The New York editions of *Blackbirds* in 1930 and 1933 were comparatively short-lived affairs and a revival attempt by the originating producer Lew Leslie in 1939 was a total failure.

Black Bottom, The. A jazz dance of the *shimmy variety which originated in the late 19th or early 20th century among southern black dancers probably in Atlanta, Georgia. Musically it was put into concrete form when Perry *Bradford published 'The original Black bottom dance' in 1919, the melody based on one of his earlier compositions 'Jacksonville rounder's dance' of 1907; new words replaced the disliked epithet 'rounder', which meant a pimp. It had been well-known as a dance, using a variety of tunes, for many decades but found its first popularity amongst black dancers in pre-1915 vaudeville and minstrel shows, becoming a national craze in the 1920s after its appearance in a black show, *Dinah*, in 1924.

The dance became known to white audiences when Ann *Pennington introduced it in George *White's *Scandals of 1926* with a new song, 'Black Bottom', written by Ray *Henderson, Buddy *DeSylva, and Lew *Brown. This became the best-known version. It managed to retain much of the original *ragtime flavour of the *Charleston, which it both replaced in popular favour and somewhat resembled, with its alternating block chords and flowing melodic line. Jelly Roll *Morton wrote his 'Black Bottom stomp' in 1926, translating its characteristics into jazz terms.

It has been tastefully explained that the 'black bottom' referred to is the muddy bottom of a river, rather than any part of the human anatomy, and that the name came from the black waterfront area of Black Bottom in Nashville, Tennessee. Notwithstanding, one of the original movements in the dance involved what was considered by some to be an indecorous slapping of the buttocks.

Black Crook, The. A musical extravaganza with music (original and adapted) by Guiseppe Operti, words by Charles M. Barras. Generally spoken of as America's first true musical comedy, it was the joint conception of theatre manager William Wheatley, producers Henry C. Jarrett and Harry Palmer, and actor/writer Charles M. Barras. A stage 'spectacular' it was reviewed at the time as 'an indecent and demoralizing exhibition' (which, of course, helped its success enormously), though the only really daring thing about it was a chorus of padded beauties in short costumes and tights. It was a mixture of melodrama (the 'Black Crook' being an evil sorcerer called Hertzog) and ballet (featuring such later famous names as Maria Bonfanti and Rita Sangalli) with a sprinkling of songs.

After the first successful presentation at *Niblo's Gardens, New York, on 12 Sept. 1866, where it achieved 475 performances, it was revived there in 1870 [122p], 1872 [120p], and elsewhere in 1929 and 1936. The musical material used was continually changed. The most popular items were 'You naughty, naughty men'—a song in Sullivanesque vein composed for and sung by Millie Cavendish (an English singer making her American debut who died in 1867) in the original show; and 'Amazon's March' by Operti, then musical director of Niblo's Gardens. A version was first produced in London at the Alhambra 23 Dec. 1872. A later show, *The Girl in Pink Tights* (1984), told the story of *The Black Crook*'s origins.

J. Whitton: *The Naked Truth* (Philadelphia, 1897).

Black Dyke Mills Band. One of the oldest brass bands still flourishing in the British Isles, its early history traceable to 1815 in the town of Queensbury near Bradford. At this time it was described as 'a good reed band' and was known as Peter Wharton's Band after its leader. A member of the band was a mill-owner, John Foster, and when the band was in danger of disbanding in 1855 it was taken over by the mill and became known as the Black Dike Mills Band (the spelling 'Dyke' being adopted later). Its members were employed at the mill, uniforms and instruments were provided, and Samuel Longbottom was engaged as musical director and instructor. The band won its first prize at a contest in Hull in 1856. It won the top honours at the first Crystal Palace contest in 1860 and two years later in Belle Vue, Manchester. A distinguished roll of bandmasters and conductors has established the band as one of the most prestigious in the country, winning the National Championship no less than 13 times and the World Championship in 1970. It has made countless broadcasts and recordings and has frequently toured in Europe.

Black Velvet. Revue staged at the London Hippodrome 14 Nov. 1939 that did much to help carry Londoners through the early stages of the war. With a score by the rising composer Harry *Parr-Davies, and book by George Black (*b* 1911), Mary Dunn, and Douglas Furber, it was to run for 620 performances and confirm the talents of pantomime principal boy Pat Kirkwood. Also in the cast were Vic Oliver (1898–1964), xylophonist Teddy *Brown, and Max and Harry *Nesbitt. The score contained such topical items as 'Crash! bang! I want to go home'; but Pat Kirkwood mainly shone in two imported Cole *Porter numbers, from *Leave it to Me* (1938), 'Most gentlemen don't like love' and 'My heart belongs to daddy'.

Blackwell, Otis (*b* Brooklyn, NY, 1931). American composer, singer, and pianist. His own achievements as a performer have generally been put into the shade by the effective use that other rock artists have made of his compositions. After winning a talent contest at the *Apollo Theatre, he worked with Doc *Pomus who encouraged his writing talents. His 'Daddy Rollin' Stone', which he recorded in 1953, was later made popular by The *Who; 'Don't be cruel' and 'All shook up' were made into No. 1 hits by Elvis *Presley, followed by 'Return to sender' and 'One broken heart for sale'; 'Fever' was recorded by Peggy *Lee; 'Great balls of fire' and 'Breathless' by Jerry Lee *Lewis. He continued to record himself with moderate success. Acknowledged as the writer of more than 900 songs, he was only given full credit for his compositional achievements in the 1970s: an LP, *These Are My Songs*, appeared in 1977.

Blake, Eubie [James Hubert] (*b* Baltimore, 7 Feb. 1883; *d* Brooklyn, NY, 12 Feb. 1983). American jazz pianist, dancer, and composer. The son of former slaves, he grew up in the heady days of the emergence of ragtime, had a few piano lessons from a local organist, then, at 15, got a job as pianist in a 'sporting-house'. His brilliant playing was soon recognized and, having won a national piano-playing contest, he toured in vaudeville for many years. In 1899 he wrote his first successful piano piece, 'Charleston rag'; and in 1900 he first felt an ambition to write for the theatre, inspired by hearing Leslie *Stuart's **Florodora*. In 1907 he became assistant conductor to Jim *Europe, whose famous band did much to put early jazz and the work of black composers before the general public. During the First World War the band became the 369th Infantry Band and was led by Blake after Europe's death in 1919.

In 1915 he had also joined forces with singer Noble *Sissle and they appeared as a double-act in vaudeville billed as the Dixie Duo. They produced the pioneering all-black musical **Shuffle Along* in 1927, the score of which contained Blake's greatest hit of all—'I'm just wild about Harry' which was later aptly used as a campaign song for Harry S. Truman in 1948. Blake wrote songs for a musical, *Elsie* (1923); for the revue *Chocolate Dandies* (1924); for **Blackbirds of 1930*, including the long-lasting 'Memories of you'; *Folies Bergère* (1930); *Shuffle Along of 1933*; *Swing It* (1937); and *Shuffle Along of 1952*. His ragtime compositions included 'Tricky fingers' (1908); 'Troublesome ivories' (1911); 'Chevy chase' (1914); 'Fizz water' (1914); 'Black keys on parade' (1935); and 'Dicty's on Seventh Avenue' (1952).

The ragtime revival brought Blake out of retirement in his eighties. In 1969 he recorded an album, *The Eighty-Six Years of Eubie Blake*, and in 1972 he formed his own record company and recorded several more LPs. In tribute to his 75 years in show-business a Broadway musical, *Eubie!*, featuring his many compositions was staged in 1978; it was also seen in London and televised. He was awarded the Presidential Medal of Honour in 1981 and made his last public appearance at the Lincoln Center in New York on 19 June 1982, at the age of 99. Interviewed on his 100th birthday, he made the classic remark, having confessed that he drank, smoked, and liked women: 'If I'd known I was going to live so long, I'd have taken better care of myself.'

W. Bolcom & R. Kimball: *Reminiscing with Sissle and Blake* (New York, 1973). A. Rose: *Eubie Blake* (New York, 1979).

Blakey, Art (*b* Pittsburgh, 11 Oct. 1919; *d* New York, 16. Oct. 1990). American jazz drummer. He studied piano before becoming a drummer, then played with Fletcher *Henderson 1939–40, Mary Lou *Williams 1941, Billy *Eckstine 1944–7, and Buddy De Franco 1952–3. In 1955 he formed the modern jazz group known as the Jazz Messengers whose original line-up was Horace Silver (*b* 1928) (director and pianist), Kenny Dorham (1924–72) (trumpet), Hank Mobley (1930–86) (saxophone), and Doug Watkins (1934–62) (bass); a group that was re-formed many times, to include musicians like Donald Byrd (*b* 1932) and Keith Jarrett (*b* 1945), and became a leading influence in the hard bop school. Blakey's advanced styling made him a pioneer in the early days of the *bebop movement and its transition into the modern jazz period; he continued to hold a leading position in the jazz world with his exciting cross-rhythm drumming and his ability to drive an ensemble.

Bland, Bobby [Robert Calvin] (*b* Rosemark, Tenn., 27 Jan. 1930). American blues singer. In the 1940s he joined the Beale Streeters, a package of young talents that also included B. B. *King, and established his swinging, articulate blues style. He was signed up by Duke Records in 1954 and had his first rhythm 'n' blues success with 'It's my life, baby' in 1955; followed by 'I smell trouble', 'Little boy blue', and 'Farther up the road'. He appeared at the *Apollo Theatre and similar venues accompanied by a band led by his long-serving musical director and arranger Joe Scott, who helped him further establish a driving, bluesy style and wrote many of his main successes in the 1960s such as 'Cry, cry, cry', 'I pity the fool', 'Call on me', and 'Two steps from the blues'. He moved into the modern soul field under the guidance of producer Andre Williams in the 1970s.

Bland, James A. (*b* Flushing, NY, 22 Oct. 1854; *d* Philadelphia, 5 May 1911). American composer. He spent most of his youth in Washington DC and studied law at Howard University. Involvement in amateur entertainments led him to make a career in music. He learned the banjo and joined the Original Creole Minstrels. He often improvised songs in the spiritual style and began to compose, having a lasting success with 'Carry me back to old Virginny' in 1878 (in 1940 it was adopted as the official song of the State of Virginia), and becoming one of America's first successful black composers. From 1881 to 1901 he lived in England, performing in the music-hall and minstrel shows and giving a command performance before Queen Victoria.

During this period he wrote many songs for which he received little credit and even less money as they were frequently pirated, as Stephen *Foster's songs had been. What money he had managed to save was soon dissipated and when he died in America, penniless and forgotten, he was buried in an unmarked grave. It has remained difficult to ascertain his total output; but some of his known songs were 'In the evening by the moonlight' (1879); 'Oh, dem golden slippers' (1879); 'Dancing on the kitchen floor' (1880); 'Hand me down my walking cane' (1880); 'Way up yonder' (1880); and 'Come along, sister Mary' (1885).

C. Haywood (ed.): *The James A. Bland Album of Outstanding Songs* (New York, 1946). J. J. Daly: *With a Song in his Heart: the Life and Times of James A. Bland* (Philadelphia, 1951).

Blane, Ralph [Hunsecker, Ralph Uriah] *b* Broken Arrow, Okla., 26 July 1914). American composer, author, singer, and actor. He appeared in **New Faces of 1936* and *Hooray for What?* (1937); and sang in and arranged for *Too Many Girls* (1939); **Dubarry Was a Lady* (1939); **Louisiana Purchase* (1940); and *The Lady Comes Across* (1942). He formed a song-writing partnership with Hugh *Martin and together they organized a mixed quartet, the Four Martins. From 1943 he mainly worked in Hollywood. For Broadway they wrote **Best Foot Forward* (1941) and *Four Wishes for Jamie* (1952); and for the screen *Meet Me in St Louis* (1941) which gave Judy *Garland such hits as 'The trolley song', 'The boy next door', and 'Have yourself a merry little Christmas' (there was a stage version in 1989 with new songs); **Ziegfeld Follies* (1946), in which Lena *Horne sang 'Love'; *Athena* (1954); and *The Girl Most Likely* (1958).

Blanton, Jimmy [James] (*b* Chattanooga, Oct. 1918; *d* Monrovia, Calif., 30 July 1942). American bass-player, a crucial figure in the emancipation of the bass from an accompanying instrument to a leading voice in jazz. Following in the steps of players like John *Kirby, Walter Page, and Milt Hinton, he employed a more mobile walking bass line, adding his own melodic flair, an exciting rhythmic sense, and a richly rounded tone. Having worked with Fate *Marable 1936–7 and the Jeter-Pillars band in St Louis 1937–9, he joined Duke *Ellington in October 1939. It was a fortunate conjunction of talents. Ellington realized the potential and fully exploited this new voice, even arranging unique piano-bass recording sessions and making Blanton the foundation of some of his most exciting and lasting orchestral creations of the next two years. It was an unfortunately brief flowering of talent, as Blanton died of tuberculosis at the age of 23.

Bledsoe, Jules (*b* Waco, Texas, 29 Dec. 1898; *d* Hollywood, 14 July 1943). American singer and composer. He studied at the Chicago Musical College and in Europe; then had a distinguished career in musical comedy and opera, including the leading roles in **Show Boat* (1927), where he was the first to sing 'Ol' Man River', and in Gruenberg's opera *The Emperor Jones* (1932). He composed an 'African Suite' and wrote many songs in spiritual style.

Blesh, Rudi [Rudolph Pickett] (*b* Guthrie, Okla., 21 Jan. 1899; *d* Gilmarton, NH, 25 Aug. 1985). American critic and author. After graduating from the University of California in 1925, he followed a career in interior and industrial design and was also a painter. An interest in jazz which began in 1917 led to him writing a valuable, if somewhat traditionally biased, history of jazz, *Shining Trumpets* (1946). This was followed by what remains the basic history of its subject, *They All Played Ragtime* (1950), written in collaboration with Harriet Janis. With Janis, he ran Circle Records 1946–52, supervising many sessions of veteran New Orleans musicians, and helping to rediscover many neglected artists. On radio he presented the 'This is Jazz' series; and he organized many jazz concerts. He lectured on jazz at Queen's College, NYC, and was also a student of all kinds of music.

Bless the Bride British musical produced at the Adelphi Theatre, London, 26 Apr. 1947. Vivian *Ellis, the composer of the score, who had previously written mainly (though not always) in a lightly sophisticated vein, came up with a substantial work in the older British musical comedy tradition, warmly romantic and memorably tuneful. Songs like 'I was never kissed before', 'Ma belle Marguerite', and 'This is my lovely day' became immediately popular; and the show was destined to become a favourite choice for amateur production, an indicator of solid worth and tunefulness. The book was provided by Ellis's old collaborator A. P. Herbert. It enjoyed an initial run of 886 performances with the French film star Georges Guétary (*b* 1915) well cast in the romantic lead, Lizbeth Webb, Anona Winn, Betty Paul, and Brian Reece (1913–62). It was revived at Sadler's Wells (1987).

Blewitt, Jonathan (*b* London, 1782; *d* London, 4 Sept. 1853). British composer, conductor, organist, and teacher. He was the son of Jonas Blewitt (1750–1805), a well-known organist. He studied with his father and under Battishill, and became, successively, organist in Haverhill, Brecon, Sheffield, and Dublin. After acting as composer and conductor to the Theatre Royal, Dublin, from 1811, he returned to London in 1826 to become musical director at Bermondsey Spa 1827–8 and at Sadler's Wells 1828–9. He wrote incidental music for many plays, orchestral and organ works, and was the composer of numerous popular, mainly comic, songs. Many were written in collaboration with the well-known poet and humorist Thomas Hood, including 'Ben Battle', 'Lieutenant Luff', 'Mary's ghost', 'Tim Turpin', and 'Young Ben he was a nice young man'.

With other writers, including Thomas *Hudson and Thomas Dibdin, he wrote 'The monkey and the nuts', 'Oh dear, nobody pops the question', 'Paddy from Cork', 'When a man's a little bit poorly', 'The handsome man', and 'Why don't the men propose, mamma'; many of them (there were some 2000 in all) much used in the early music-hall and similar venues. His greatest hit, a favourite in the song-and-supper rooms, was 'The little merry fat gray man' for which he wrote both words and music. J. L. *Hatton, in the preface to his *Humorous Songs* (1875), in which many of Blewitt's songs appeared, called him 'the best composer of comic songs in the days immediately preceding our own', adding 'no one sang Blewitt's songs like Blewitt himself'.

Blitzstein, Marc (*b* Philadelphia, 2 Mar. 1905; *d* Fort-de-France, Martinique, 22 Jan. 1964). American composer. He had an academic musical training with Nadia Boulanger and Arnold Schoenberg. His first compositions tended to be obscurely intellectual, but during the depression years he switched direction, becoming politically left-wing and moved to write popular music with a message, following in the steps of *Brecht and *Weill.

His best-known work, *The *Cradle Will Rock* (1937), was banned because of its left-wing views just before the curtain went up in a government-backed theatre in Washington. A hasty search, while the audience was kept happy, was made for an empty theatre, to which the cast and audience moved. The show was then put on without costume or scenery, Blitzstein playing the piano and explaining the action, thereby transforming what was intended to be a fairly straightforward musical into a successful piece of experimental theatre. It was to run in similar form, once it had found a backer, for several months. In similar popular vein was his TV musical *I've Got the Tune* (1941). A musical revue, *Regina* (1949), based on Lillian Hellman's *The Little Foxes* was expanded into full operatic form. Blitzstein received much praise for his adaptation of Kurt Weill's *The *Threepenny Opera* in 1954.

E. Gordon: *Mark the Music: The Life and Work of Marc Blitzstein* (New York, 1989).

Blockley, John (*b* London, 1800; *d* London, 24 Dec. 1882). British composer, author, and music-publisher. He ran a publishing business in London, firstly in partnership, then on his own, issuing many popular ballads of the day. He composed a number of songs himself, many of them settings of words by the Hon. Mrs Norton, including: 'The Arab's farewell to his steed', 'I remember thy voice', 'We have been friends together', and 'The absent one'. Others were: 'Love on' (*w* Eliza Cook), 'Jessie's dream' (*w* Grace Carpenter), 'The arrow and the song' (Longfellow), 'Many happy returns of the day' (Cook), 'The charge of the Light Brigade' (Tennyson), and 'Excelsior' (Longfellow).

Blood, Sweat and Tears. American rock group formed in 1967, the idea of organist/pianist/singer Al Kooper (*b* 1944) and guitarist/singer Steve Katz (*b* 1945), both ex-members of the 1966 Blues Project, with Bobby Colomby (*b* 1944). Its music was a fusion of jazz and rock, using trumpet, flugelhorn, and trombone in the line-up; its music raw, powerful, and hard-hitting at first but, in such things as 'My days are numbered', becoming more organized and orchestral in sound. In 1969 they achieved three million-sellers, all No. 2 hits in America, 'You've made me so very happy', 'Spinning wheel', and 'And when I die'. Kopper left in 1968 to become a producer.

Bloomer Girl. American musical with score by Harold *Arlen and book by Sig Herzig and Fred Saidy, based on a play by Dan and Lillith James; lyrics by E. Y. *Harburg. It was produced at the Shubert Theatre, New York, 5 Oct. 1944, running for 654 performances, and had a brief revival in 1947.

Set in Cicero Falls, New York, in the Civil War year 1861, it is a story of the rebellion of Evelina Applegate against her domineering father, a manufacturer of ladies' clothing, who has ordered her to marry one of his salesmen. She is so angered that she joins her aunt, the famous Amelia Bloomer, in her campaigns for civil rights, the women's reform movement, and the wearing of such practical clothing as the controversial bloomers. It had a lot to say but said it entertainingly, with some pleasing songs: 'The Eagle and me', 'Evelina', 'It was good enough for grandma', the romantic 'Right as the rain', 'Sunday in Cicero Falls', and 'I got a song'; managing well without any outstanding hits.

The show was notable for making a star of Celeste Holm, who played Evelina, and for an effective 'Civil War ballet' choreographed by Agnes de Mille. It was the most successful of the musicals set in the Civil War years.

Blossom, Henry (*b* St Louis, Mo., 6 May 1866; *d* New York, 23 Mar. 1919). American author, playwright, and librettist. He left his father's insurance business to become a writer, producing several novels and turning one into a successful play. For the stage he produced the librettos of various musicals, frequently in collaboration with Victor *Herbert. These notably included: *The Yankee Consul* (1904, *m* Alfred Robyn, 1860–1935); **Mlle Modiste* (1905); *The *Red Mill* (1906); *Prima Donna* (1908)—all with music by Herbert; *The Candy Shop* (1909, *m* John Golden, 1874–1955); *The Slim Princess* (1911, *m* Leslie *Stuart); *The Man From Cook's* (1912, *m* Raymond *Hubbell); *All For the Ladies* (1912, *m* Robyn); *The Only Girl* (1914); *The Princess Pat* (1915); *The Century Girl* (1916); *Eileen* (1917); and *The Velvet Lady* (1919)—all with music by Herbert. His light and airy librettos were very much of their period.

Blossom Time. The American version of the operetta *Das Dreimädlerhaus* (based on the life and music of Franz Schubert), first produced at the Ambassador Theatre, New York, 29 Sept. 1921. Like the original and the English version, **Lilac Time*, the charms of Schubert's music, here heavily arranged by Sigmund *Romberg, mitigated the over-romanticized story, adapted by Dorothy Donnelly; it enjoyed an initial run of 592 performances and was produced all over America up to the Second World War. It was not always ideally mounted and 'a road company of *Blossom Time*' became something of a jokey catchphrase. Nevertheless the show was to inspire a growing number of equally fictionalized musicals and musical films on composers' lives.

Bluebell in Fairyland. Musical dream play which became a stock Christmas production in London after its initial showing at the Vaudeville Theatre 18 Dec. 1901. It was revived in 1905, 1916, 1917, 1919, 1923, 1925, 1927, 1935, 1936, 1937, finally to be killed off by the war. It was a profitable vehicle for its original stars, Seymour *Hicks and Ellaline *Terriss, and many people made early appearances in it including Phyllis *Dare and, in the 1917 edition, Jessie *Matthews in her first stage role. The basic score was by Walter *Slaughter but it was lavishly padded out with songs suitable for Miss Terriss's girlish charms—Yvette *Guilbert's 'I want yer, ma honey', Leslie *Stuart's 'Louisiana Lou', Lionel *Monckton's 'Simple little string', Caryll and Monckton's 'The boy guessed right'; and an American import, 'The honeysuckle and the bee'.

Blue blowing. Polite euphemism for the playing of such homely instruments as the *kazoo or the even homelier paper-and-comb or jug. One of the best known exponents of the art was William 'Red' *McKenzie who was associated with a group called The Mound City Blue Blowers, introducing the term to the world from around 1924 when its members were McKenzie (paper-and-comb), Dick Slevin (kazoo), and Jack Bland (banjo).

'Blue Danube, The'. Probably the world's best-known waltz, it is positively idiolized in Vienna where it is played in public, live or recorded, innumerable times a day. The familiar German title 'An der schönen, blauen Donau' ('On the beautiful, blue Danube') was not part of the original conception of its composer, the younger and more famous Johann *Strauss.

Early in 1865, Strauss had been asked by the Wiener Männergesang-Verein to compose a choral work for their special use. Interested in the challenge of writing his first choral waltz, he got around to sketching out some themes in 1866 and eventually sent along a four-part unaccompanied piece to which he added a hastily-written piano accompaniment a few days later. It was made up of an introduction, four waltz strains, and a coda, to which the choir's poet, Josef Weyl, added words. Strauss decided to add a fifth waltz and Weyl adjusted his lyrics accordingly. Just before its first performance on 15 Feb. 1867 in the Dianabad-Saal, Strauss quickly orchestrated the work; it was announced baldly as a 'waltz for chorus and orchestra' and dedicated to the choir. It is not known who added the name 'An der schönen, blauen Donau' (a quotation from a poem by Karl Isidor Beck), these words not actually appearing in Weyl's text which was mildly satirical, urging rich and poor alike to join in the carnival festivities. This was not altogether approved of and muted Vienna's initial reception of the work. The first performance, as Strauss was engaged elsewhere with his own orchestra that night, was conducted by the chorus-master. The music of the waltz was warmly acclaimed in the next day's reviews, but Strauss seems to have been slightly annoyed that it only had one encore.

It first burst on the world in general, soon to become an international favourite, when Strauss himself conducted it in Paris later that year. The choral version, often amended and with the appropriate words inserted into an 1890 edition, was only used on special occasions thereafter. But the waltz, first heard for orchestra alone on 10 Mar. 1867 in the Volksgarten, became, as the critic Hanslick wrote some seven years later, 'another national anthem which sings of our land and people'.

V. Keldorfer: *An der schönen, blauen Donau: ein Gedenkblatt* (Vienna, 1917). See also books listed under STRAUSS.

Blue For A Boy. British musical comedy with score by Harry *Parr-Davies, book by Austin Melford, and lyrics by Harold Purcell which opened at His Majesty's Theatre 30 Nov. 1950. It was a typical British comedy thriller (sub-titled 'What shall we do with the body?'), and it ran for 664 performances. In the cast were those worthy comics Fred Emney and Richard Hearne with Eve Lister, Bertha Belmore, and Austin Melford, and its title-song 'Blue for a boy' achieved some popularity.

Bluegrass. A name generally adopted in the mid-1940s to distinguish a brand of American country music that was a descendant of what used to be called *hillbilly music, the old-style, rural 'corn-shucking' banjo and fiddle music allied to the typical balladry of the southern mountains. Early recorded examples were those made by the Mountain Ramblers in the Blue Ridge Mountains. The style became recognizably formalized and widely popular through the work of Bill *Monroe and his original Bluegrass Boys (who gave the music its name) during the years 1945–8; with Monroe on mandolin, Lester *Flatt on guitar, Earl *Scruggs on banjo, Howard Watts on bass, and Chubby Wise on fiddle. The name Bluegrass was chosen to mark their origins in the Bluegrass State (as it was known) of Kentucky where this type of string band music had long flourished. In essence their style was a sort of *Chicago jazz in country music terms, with such instruments as the *banjo, guitar, *dobro, and fiddle soloing against a rhythmic background. Perhaps the most exciting effect is when the lead is taken on the bright-voiced mandolin: Bill Monroe had done much to popularize the modern Orville Gibson mandolin in the 1930s. Another essential flavour of bluegrass music comes from the melodic, three-finger style of picking the banjo evolved by Earl Scruggs, making it a prominent solo instrument.

The overall style of banjo and guitar picking, which reaches a peak of virtuosity in the bluegrass bands, is the result of a long process of interbreeding between the minstrel styles that evolved from the primitive African banjo playing and various localized white instrumental styles. The vocal element is well integrated with the instrumental playing and close harmony singing is extensively used. The dobro became a feature of the Flatt and Scruggs Foggy Mountain Boys Band around 1955 and later bluegrass groups have varied their sound by the use of such instruments as drums, autoharp, *jew's harp, *accordion, and piano. The genuine bluegrass band tended not to use electrically amplified instruments, but they have been employed quite frequently in recording studios. Others who helped to establish the mid-1940s revival were the brothers Ralph and Carter Stanley (Stanley Brothers Band and the Clinch Mountain Boys), Don Reno, Mac Wiseman, Doc Watson, and Mike Seegers, to name but a few. Much of the music used is traditional; some items, such as 'Ground hog' by Hammond Williamson, were written in the pre-revival days; and much new material has been added in recent years.

D. Cyporyn (ed.): *The Bluegrass Songbook* (New York–London, 1972). B. Artis: *Bluegrass* (New York, 1975). S. D. Price: *Old As The Hills: the Story of Bluegrass Music* (New York, 1975).

Blues (1). The blues is the folk-song of black music, stemming from origins so obscured by years of anonymity that a logical history is virtually impossible. The blues, unlike ragtime or jazz, can only be defined as a form in its more superficial aspect. The wider implication of the blues lies in its spirit, a spirit which is the basic ingredient of all true jazz. Paul Oliver, in *The Story of the Blues* (1969), wrote: 'the blues is both a state of mind and the music which gives voice to it . . . the personal emotion of the individual finding through music a vehicle for self-expression.' While this also applies to other music-making, it is especially applicable to the more emotional styles founded on the blues, ranging from the intuitive work of the primitive blues singer to the current world of rhythm 'n' blues and rock. It is essentially a sombre music, reflecting on the sadder side of life, its tragedies, frustrations, and bitterness; ranging from the personal lament to the generalized song of protest. Its early history can only be pieced together through the annals and memories of obscure folk-singers; there are no accounts of its beginning or development.

When jazz first emerged, mainly through recordings, there was a danger that blues would be thought of only as the comparatively controlled styling of the vaudeville blues singers like Ma *Rainey, Bessie *Smith, Sippie Wallace (1898–1986), Lizzie Miles (1895–1963), Victoria *Spivey, and, later, Willie Mae 'Big Mama' Thornton (1926–84), or the Europeanized compositions of W. C. *Handy. These were all genuine later manifestations of the blues, formalized as a 12-bar form, and deprived of some of the natural folk element through contact with white conventions. Scholarly research came just in time, as it did in the wider folk-music field, to capture on record the work of the natural, primitive singers. In the early writings on jazz the blues were treated as a minor element of the music—simply a primitive ancestor. Hindsight and insight have since altered this perspective and acknowledged the blues as the essence of all truly committed black music, the basis of the art of such varied players as Louis *Armstrong, Sidney *Bechet, Count *Basie, and Charlie *Parker, and of the popular music that developed in the 1950s. In modern times it is the white element in jazz and popular music which has become the minority survivor.

The perceptive blues researcher attempted to seek out the oldest propagators of the tradition; often going back to find its roots in African music. Some of these singers like Blind *Lemon Jefferson were sufficiently recorded in the early gramophone age to become universally recognized figures. The singing of the great 'classic' blues singers like Bessie Smith could then be seen, in comparison, as the work of skilled entertainers.

The blues as a musical form became recognizable through a standard (though not exclusively) 12-bar pattern with a fixed chord sequence (basically 4 bars on the tonic chord modulating in the last half-bar to 2 on the sub-dominant, 2 bars tonic, 2 dominant 7th and 2 tonic, but subject to much variation) that had grown up as a musical package that fitted its repetitious three-line stanza vocal form. This formalization owed much to the work of W. C. Handy, who put many traditional blues songs into printed form. As the one easily recognizable distinguishing trait, it led to a tendency to call anything in 12-bar form a blues, even if its spirit was totally out of keeping. *Boogie-woogie used the same form for often different though equally valid ends. On the other hand many Tin Pan Alley products were designated blues simply because somebody was experiencing an emotional hangover in them.

In the early jazz days the volcanic force of the blues simmered underground waiting its moment to erupt. Even the classic blues of Rainey and Smith were only deeply appreciated by a minority audience; while the more ethnic blues were confined to obscure performances and *race records. By the 1940s the truer folk blues were beginning to find a wider audience and in the 1950s finally found a widely acceptable form in the rhythm 'n' blues explosion; eventually to become the unstoppable flood of emotive, protesting, cavorting music that has become the substance of the exploding pop scene of the present.

A reactionary mind could justifiably see the blues as an unmelodic and harmonically unadventurous antithesis of classically derived music such as the Gershwins and Kerns created in the 1930s; simply an anarchic spirit let loose to create either freedom or disruption—whichever way one sees it. It was certainly the key to the kind of popular music that the young and unfettered were waiting for.

The blues remains, however, a hazily poetical concept that still cannot ultimately be expressed more accurately than in the words of an old slave woman, quoted in the mid-19th century, who described it as music that could only be created with 'a full heart and a troubled spirit'. In spite of this, the literary coverage of the blues has become immense, the mystique of the subject clearly having a magnetic attraction. Many of the earlier books are now made inadequate because the wider sociological and musical implications and effects recognized today were not then apparent. Most early general histories only dealt with the 'classic' blues singers. Iain Lang's *Background to the Blues* (1941) was an understanding look at the background to jazz and was wisely re-titled *Jazz in Perspective* in 1947. W. C. Handy had already made good use of blues material in producing his own commercialized versions suitable for pale ears and published *Blues: an Anthology* as early as 1926. It was not until the 1960s that the more dedicated and perceptive books on the blues began to appear such as the pioneering *The Country Blues* by Samuel Charters in 1959, counter-balanced by Charles Keil's *Urban Blues* in 1966. In England, Paul Oliver established himself as the leading authority, backing his insights on the subject with extensive research in America and Africa. From the black viewpoint, the blues was a manifestation of protest discussed in books by LeRoi Jones and others. The subsequent link between the blues and rock has been the subject of many more books, one of the most scholarly being *Pop Music and the Blues* by Richard Middleton.

W. C. Handy: *Blues: an Anthology* (New York, 1926; rev. 1970). J. E. Berendt: *Blues* (Munich, 1957). S. Charters: *The Country Blues* (New Orleans, 1959; repr. New York, 1970). P. Oliver: *Blues Fell this Morning: the Meaning of the Blues* (London, 1960; New York, 1963). S. Charters (ed.): *The Poetry of the Blues* (New York, 1963). L. Jones: *Blues People* (New York, 1963). P. Oliver: *Conversation with the Blues* (London, 1965). C. Keil: *Urban Blues* (Chicago, 1966). S. Charters: *The Bluesmen* (New York, 1967). M. Leadbitter & N. Slaven: *Blues Records 1943–1966* (London, 1968; rev. 1987). P. Oliver: *Screening the Blues* (London, 1968). P. Oliver: *The Story of the Blues* (London, 1968; Philadelphia, 1969). R. W. Dixon & J. Godrich: *Recording the Blues* [race records] (London, 1970). W. Ferris Jr.: *Blues from the Delta* [Mississippi Delta blues] (London, 1970). P. Oliver: *Savannah Syncopators: African Retention in the Blues* (London, 1970). T. Russell: *Blacks, Whites and Blues* (London, 1970). D. Stewart-Baxter: *Ma Rainey and the Classic Blues Singers* (London, 1970). B. Bastin: *Crying for the Carolines* [Piedmont blues style] (London, 1971).

F. Boom: *Laughing to Keep from Crying* [satire in the blues] (London, 1971). K. Boegart: *Blues Lexicon* (Antwerp, 1972). R. Middleton: *Pop Music and the Blues* (London, 1972). B. Cook: *Listen to the Blues* (London, 1973). E. Sackheim: *The Blues Line: a Collection of Blues Lyrics* (New York, 1973). S. Charters: *The Legacy of the Blues* (London, 1975). G. Oakley: *The Devil's Music: a History of the Blues* (London, 1976). S. Harris: *Blues Who's Who* (New Rochelle, NY, 1979). S. Charters: *The Roots of the Blues* (London, 1980). P. Oliver: *Blues Off the Record* (Tunbridge Wells, 1984). P. Oliver, M. Harrison, & W. Bolcom: *The New Grove Gospel, Blues and Jazz* (London, 1986). M. L. Hart: *The Blues: a Bibliographical Guide* (New York, 1988).

Blues (2). A ballroom dance which developed in America in the early 1920s and reached Britain about 1923. It came in with the jazz vogue and was danced to a very slow rhythm that supposedly approximated to the authentic blues. Requiring a degree of control and balance, it never became really popular and was modified and speeded up to become the *foxtrot, which then became the basis of most ballroom dancing.

Blues shouting. A declamatory style of blues singing that developed in the swing era, much associated with Kansas City; usually a blues-styled performance in a forceful manner with *big-band backing. With such as Jimmy *Rushing, Big Joe *Turner, and Jimmy *Witherspoon among the principal exponents, it came as an interim link between the more introspective early blues style and the rhythm 'n' blues era.

Bock, Jerry [Jerrold Lewis] (*b* New Haven, Conn., 23 Nov. 1928). American composer. He studied at the University of Wisconsin, where he wrote for student productions. Afterwards he settled in New York and wrote material for the Sid Caesar and Imogene Coca TV shows and for revues. With Larry Holofcener as collaborator, he wrote songs for the Broadway revue *Catch a Star* (1955) followed by the score for **Mr Wonderful* (1956) which spotlighted the talents of Sammy *Davis Jr. He then teamed up with lyricist Sheldon *Harnick to write *The Body Beautiful* (1958); *Fiorello!* (1959), which won a Pulitzer Prize; *Tenderloin* (1960); **She Loves Me* (1963); and then the long-running musical hit **Fiddler on the Roof* (1964) whose songs 'Matchmaker, matchmaker', 'If I were a rich man', and 'Sunrise, sunset' carried it to a 3242 run in New York, followed by 2030 in London. After this came *The *Apple Tree* (1966) and *The Rothschilds* (1970). Bock's scores, while not always replete with obvious hits, are excellently tailored for the matter in hand and he has a gift for supplying the correctly dramatic music at the right moment.

Bolan, Marc [Feld, Mark] (*b* London, 30 July 1947; *d* London 16 Sept. 1977). British singer, guitarist, and composer. After a brief career as a model, Mark Feld changed his name to Bolan and recorded 'The wizard' for Decca in 1966. He played with short-lived groups, then worked with Steve Peregrine-Took (1949–80) in a folk-rock duo as Tyrannosaurus Rex, promoting the cause of love and peace. Took was replaced by Mickey Finn in 1970 and Bolan switched from acoustic to electric guitar. They now operated in abbreviated form as T. Rex, and changed from the somewhat pretentious folk style into a rock unit. With the change Bolan became a teenage pop idol and had No. 1 hits in 'Hot love' (1971); 'Get it on' (1971); 'Telegram Sam' (1972); and 'Metal guru' (1972). A film about T. Rex directed by Ringo *Starr in 1973 was not a success and fortunes waned. Producing less profitable material in the mid-1970s, Bolan abandoned the pop scene and went to live as a tax exile in Los Angeles. He made a comeback in 1976 with a new T. Rex group playing in the new wave style and had a TV show in 1977. He died in an automobile accident on Barnes Common.

G. Tremlett: *The Marc Bolan Story* (London, 1975). T. Dicks & P. Platz: *Marc Bolan: a Tribute* (London, 1978).

Bolcom, William [Elden] (*b* Seattle, 26 May 1938). American pianist and composer. He studied at the University of Washington, Mills College, Oakland, Stanford University, and the Paris Conservatoire. He had several university teaching posts, before joining the musical faculty of the University of Michigan in 1973 and being appointed Professor in 1983. While his studies and his serious works were in a modern experimental idiom, he also cultivated an understanding interest in popular music of the past and with his wife, the singer Joan Morris, gave recitals and made recordings of turn-of-the-century American songs as well as playing and recording ragtime with considerable flair. He has written many pieces in the ragtime vein himself. He produced his own adaptation of *The *Beggar's Opera* (1973); and collaborated with Robert Kimball on the book *Reminiscing with Sissle and Blake* (1973).

Bolden, Charles 'Buddy' (*b* New Orleans, 6 Sept. 1877; *d* Jackson, La., 4 Nov. 1931). Almost legendary American cornet player and bandleader. He has always been a somewhat shadowy figure with many questionable 'facts' surrounding his life, e.g. that he was a barber, ran a newspaper, and could be heard playing his trumpet at a distance of 14 miles—all of which have now been proved unlikely. He was, however, an important jazz pioneer, helping to shape the New Orleans jazz idiom and influencing many great players who heard him. Jelly Roll *Morton described him as 'the most powerful trumpet player I ever heard'. He was admitted to the Insane Asylum of Louisiana at Jackson (for the second time) in 1907, categorized as an alcoholic, an affliction which had brought on his insanity. He spent 24 years in the hospital and died there, aged 54.

D. M. Marquis: *In Search of Buddy Bolden* (Baton Rouge, 1978).

Boles, John (*b* Greenville, Tex., 27 Oct. 1900; *d* San Angelo, Tex., 27 Feb. 1969). American actor, film star, and singer. Handsome heart-throb of the early sound film era, he was the son of a banker, and studied at the University of Texas intending to become a doctor. He served in France in the First World War, remained there to study singing, and completed his training in New York, but found it difficult to make a career. He appeared in the musical play *Little Jesse James* (1923); sang in operetta with Geraldine Farrar; and was in *Kitty's Kisses* (1926). This led to roles in silent films, but he became well-known only in the talkies era when he appeared in a singing part with Bebe Daniels in **Rio Rita* (1929). Boles was also in *The *Desert Song* (1929); *King of Jazz* (1930); **Music in the Air* (1935); *Rose of the Rancho* (1936); in various films with Shirley *Temple; and in many non-musical roles. He made a return to Broadway in **One Touch of Venus* (1943) and appeared in touring versions of **Show Boat* (1940) and **Gentlemen Prefer Blondes* (1950). His last film was *Babes in Baghdad* (1952) with Paulette Goddard (1911–90), after which he went into the oil business.

Bolger, Ray [Raymond Wallace] (*b* Dorchester, Mass., 10 Jan. 1904; *d* 1987). American actor, singer, comedian, and eccentric dancer. His first professional work was with a stock musical company in Boston. After many years touring and in vaudeville, he appeared on Broadway in *The Merry World* (1926) followed by *A Night in Paris* and the touring company of *The *Passing Show of 1926*. He appeared in *Heads Up* (1929); **George White's Scandals of 1931* (where he made his name as a dancer); starred in *Life Begins at 8:40* (1934); **On Your Toes* (1936); *Keep Off the Grass* (1940); **By Jupiter* (1942); *Three to Make Ready* (1946); *All Americain* (1962). His most successful part was in **Where's Charley?* (1948) where he had a great hit with 'Once in love with Amy' which henceforth became his theme song. However, most people remember him as the Scarecrow in the film of *The *Wizard of Oz* (1939).

Bolton, Guy [Reginald] (*b* Broxbourne, Herts, 23 Nov. 1884; *d* 6 Sept. 1979). Librettist, born in England of American parents. He trained as an architect and practised this profession in New York. He first wrote for the stage in 1912, when he collaborated with Douglas J. Wood on *The Drone*; followed by *The Rule of Three* (1914); *The Fallen Idol* (1915) and *Hit-the-Trail Holliday* (1915). The turning-point in his career came in 1915 when he met Jerome *Kern and began to collaborate with him on the famous series of *Princess Theatre shows, the first being *90 in the Shade* (1915). The series continued with *Nobody Home* (1915) and **Very Good, Eddie* (1915); and in 1916 he provided the book for a *Kálmán score, *Miss Springtime*.

Bolton liked collaborating on his librettos and now found an ideal partner in the British author and humorist P. G. *Wodehouse, with whom he wrote the books for *Have A Heart* (1917); **Oh Boy!* (1917); **Leave it to Jane* (1917), all with music by Kern; *The Riviera Girl* (1917, *m* Kálmán); *Miss 1917* (1917, *m* Kern and Victor *Herbert); **Oh, Lady! Lady!* (1918, Kern); *The Girl Behind the Gun* (1918, *m* Ivan *Caryll); *Oh, My Dear!* (1918, *m* Louis *Hirsch); and *The Rose of China* (1919, *m* Armand *Vecsey). He wrote the book of *Sally* (1920, Kern), which enjoyed a run of 570 performances in New York and 387 in London; *Tangerine* (1921, *m* Alma M. Sanders); *The Hotel Mouse* (1922, Vecsey); *Daffy Dilly* (1922, *m* Herbert *Stothart); and collaborated with Wodehouse on *Sitting Pretty* (1924, Kern). For London he wrote **Primrose* (1924, *m* George *Gershwin); and collaborated with Fred *Thompson on **Lady, Be Good* (1924, Gershwin).

A London show *The Bamboula* (1925, *m* Albert *Sirmay) followed; then Thompson was his partner again on **Tip-Toes* (1925, Gershwin). After *The Ramblers* (1926, *m* Harry *Ruby), he again worked with Wodehouse on **Oh, Kay!* (1926, Gershwin) and *The Nightingale* (1927, Vecsey); with Thompson on **Rio Rita* (1927, *m* Harry *Tierney) and *The Five o'Clock Girl* (1927, Ruby). He wrote *She's my Baby* (1927, *m* Richard *Rodgers); **Rosalie* (1928, *m* Sigmund *Romberg); *Blue Eyes* (1928, Kern); *Polly* (1929, *m* Phil *Charig); *Top Speed* (1929, Ruby); *Simple Simon* (1930, Rodgers), with Ed *Wynn; **Girl Crazy* (1930, Gershwin); worked with Thompson on *Song of the Drum* (1931, *m* Vivian *Ellis and Herman *Finck); and the London show *Give me a Ring* (1933, *m* Martin *Broones). His last collaboration with Wodehouse was on **Anything Goes* (1934, *m* Cole *Porter). With Fred Thompson he wrote *Seeing Stars* (1935, Broones) and a series of London shows: *Swing Along* (1936, Broones); *This'll Make you Whistle* (1936, *m* Sigler, *Goodhart, and *Hoffman); *Going Places* (1936, Ellis); *Going Greek* (1937, *m* Hoffman and Goodhart); *Hide and Seek* (1937, Ellis); *The *Fleet's Lit Up* (1938, Ellis); a solo effort, *Running Riot* (1938, Ellis); and, again with Thompson, *Bobby Get Your Gun* (1938, *m* *Waller and *Tunbridge) and *Magyar Melody* (1939, *m* *Posford and *Grun).

Back in New York he wrote *Walk With Music* (1940, *m* Hoagy *Carmichael); *Hold on to Your Hats* (1940, *m* Burton *Lane); *Jackpot* (1944, *m* Vernon *Duke); and (with Thompson); **Follow the Girls* (1944, Charig). He wrote the English book for a revival of Oscar Straus's *The Chocolate Soldier* (1947). He collaborated on *Ankles Aweigh* (1955), and his final Broadway production was *Anya* (1965, *m* *Wright and *Forrest). He also wrote the book of the film based on Jerome Kern's life—*Till the Clouds Roll By* (1946); various plays; and two novels. His collaboration with Wodehouse is amusingly chronicled in the book they wrote together, *Bring on the Girls* (New York, 1953). Gerald Bordman wrote: 'His main claim to fame may well be the literate, witty and cohesive librettos he created for the Princess Theatre shows between 1915 and 1918 . . . they helped move an adolescent genre to maturity.'

Bond, Carrie Jacobs (*b* Janesville, Wis., 11 Aug. 1862; *d* Glendale, Calif., 28 Dec. 1946). American songwriter. She became known as the composer of rather sentimental but highly successful songs, mainly written in order to keep herself and her family alive. Her husband was a doctor whose practice was not flourishing so they moved to Chicago and it was here that she decided to make use of her natural gifts for music and painting. Her first published song was 'Is my dolly dead?' When her husband died she was left with a small son and the need to make a living from her writing. With the help and encouragement of the singer Jessie Bartlet she had privately published a book of seven songs. Two of them became so successful that she set her self up in business as a publisher (The Bond Shop) and separately issued 'Just a-wearyin' for you' (1901, *w* Frank Stanton) and 'I love you truly' (with her own words) in 1906. She went to New York but had no success there and returned to Chicago. She became ill, but in 1910, helped by her friend Walter Gale, produced her greatest hit 'A perfect day' which at last brought her fame and fortune. She sang her songs in vaudeville and entertained the troops in the First World War. Her other songs included: 'God remembers when the world forgets' and 'Life's garden'. She also published a book of poems, *The End of the Road*, and her autobiography.

C. J. Bond: *The Roads of Melody* (New York, 1927).

Bond, Jessie (*b* Camden Town, London, 10 Jan. 1853; *d* Worthing, 17 June 1942). British actress and singer. It was intended that she should be a professional pianist and, when the family moved to Liverpool, she gave her first concert there at the age of eight. At 17 she was in the Royal Liverpool Choral Society and studied at the Royal Academy of Music. She was heard by Richard D'Oyly *Carte at a St George's Hall concert and he asked her to join his company. In the next operetta to be staged, **HMS Pinafore*, she was given the role of Phoebe; and thus she began an association with the *Gilbert and Sullivan operas that lasted until 1891. Her favourite role during that period was Mad Margaret in **Ruddigore*. 'The Savoy is not the same without you', wrote Gilbert, after her departure. She returned for a few revivals and appeared in musical comedy.

J. Bond & E. MacGeorge: *The Life and Reminiscences of Jessie Bond: the Old Savoyard* (London, 1930).

Bongos. Small joined twin tunable drums, each a different size to give two distinct pitches, which are held between the knees and played with the fingers; widely used in Latin American-styled music.

Boogie-woogie (1). A style of jazz piano playing whose basis is almost inevitably a series of formal (rather than melodic) improvisations on a 12-bar blues basis in the right hand played over a repetitive bass figure in the left. This manner of playing, said to have come from the Lower Mississippi area and based on the guitar blues, was developed in Texas and later introduced to the jazz cities such as Chicago where it was originally designated *barrel-house music. Those in the know as to its origins also referred to it as 'fast Western style'. Among the pioneers of boogie style were 'Cow Cow' *Davenport, Wesley Wallace, 'Cripple' Clarence Lofton, and 'Blind' Leroy Garnett. One of those responsible for introducing the music to Chicago *c.* 1927 was Clarence 'Pine Top' *Smith, credited with being the first to use 'boogie-woogie' as a commercial title—in his 'Pine Top's boogie-woogie' recorded in 1928. Some pianists, such as Jimmy Blythe (1901–31), had designated similar pieces as 'stomps'; others, such as Meade 'Lux' *Lewis simply called them 'blues', as in his 1927 'Honky-tonk train blues' whose pounding bass made a startling contrast with the delicate habañera-type bass of the bluesman Jimmy *Yancey. Even if boogie is limited in form, there has still been an immense variety of approach. The style had a great vogue in the 1930s, made popular by the duets of Albert *Ammons and Pete *Johnson; and in many big swing band arrangements. A peak of popularity was reached in 1938 when a Carnegie Hall concert featured many of the masters of the art.

P. Silvester: *A Left Hand Like God: a Study of Boogie-Woogie* (London, 1989).

Boogie-woogie (2). An early name for the dance that was later called the *jitterbug or *jive; taking its names from the piano music (1) above, and having a parallel peak of popularity *c.* 1938.

Booker T and the MGs [Memphis Group]. American soul band formed in 1960, originally to act as house rhythm group for Stax Records. On this basis they made some classic 1960s soul recordings with various artists such as Otis *Redding and on their own. They produced an instantly recognizable funky sound that took 'Green onions' to third place in the American hit list in 1962. It set the pattern for many of their subsequent recordings, based on simple *riffs with a solid rhythmical backing. In 1968 they created and performed the sound-track for the film *Uptight* and were partly responsible for its success, with 'Time is tight' becoming a best-seller. The band outlived its fashion and split up in 1972. Its moving spirit, keyboard player Booker T. Jones, went to California and made recordings under his own name. The MGs' recordings are still looked upon as models of cohesive and exciting soul backing.

'Boomps-a-daisy'. A dance of the wartime knees-up genre, written by Annette Mills and introduced by her at a tango competition at Dorchester House, London, in 1939. The music was a simple, corny tune in 3/4 time and the words exhorted the dancers to use 'hands, knees, and boomps-a-daisy' the last accompanying a polite collision of the partners' posteriors. It was just right for wartime hops and the enforced camaraderie of the times, and survived throughout the war years.

Boone, Pat [Charles Eugene] (*b* Jacksonville, Fla., 1 June 1934). American singer, for a time second only in popularity to Elvis *Presley, with a string of hit recordings beginning in 1955 through to the early 1960s. He had a clean, decent American boy image and translated the mean and moody Presley sound into a palatable commodity for the middle class. He first came to light as a Country and Western singer in Nashville and was signed up in 1955 by Randy Wood of Dot Records, who used him to record cover versions of songs like 'Ain't that a shame', 'Tutti frutti', and 'Long tall Sally'. These were so successful that he was able to record in his own image, between 1956 and 1962, songs like 'I'll be home' (1956); 'Friendly persuasion' (1956); 'Remember you're mine (1956); 'I almost lost my mind' (1956); 'Love letters in the sand' (1957); 'Don't forbid me' (1957); 'Why, baby, why' (1957); 'April love' (1958); 'If dreams come true' (1958); and 'Sugar moon' (1958). This was rock greatly watered down with a touch of *Crosby. Two rather more gutsy performances came with 'Moody river' (1961) and 'Speedy Gonzales' (1962), which both became No. 1 hits. Still a student in the early days of his singing career, and retaining the high-school image throughout, he purveyed the clean character in films such as *Bernadine* and *April Love*. Later he devoted his energies and music to evangelical causes. His third daughter, Debbie Boone (*b* 1955) began singing with the family act in 1960 and had huge solo successes in the late 1970s, but is mainly known in the USA.

P. Boone: *A New Song* (New York, 1970). P. Boone: *Together* (Nashville, 1979).

Booth, Webster (*b* Lincoln, 21 Jan. 1902; *d* Llandudno, 22 June 1984). British singer. He attended Lincoln Choir School, and later studied to be an accountant, but then decided on a singing career. He joined the D'Oyly Carte Company in *The *Yeomen of the Guard* in 1924 and spent three years with them. He appeared in *The Three Musketeers* at Drury Lane in 1930 and sang at Covent Garden. The deciding factor in his career was his marriage (his second) to Anne Ziegler (*b* 1910), whom he met while they were filming *Faust* in 1938. His warm tenor voice and her bright soprano proved to be ideally matched and they embarked on a career as duettists, mainly in the field of light operetta and ballads. Their frequent broadcasts and recordings earned them great popularity throughout the war years and after. By the mid-1950s there was less demand for their kind of music and in 1956 they emigrated to South Africa where they lived and worked for 22 years. They returned to Britain in 1978 and settled in north Wales, teaching and occasionally singing.

A. Ziegler & W. Booth: *Duet* (London, 1951).

Bordoni, Irene (*b* Corsica, 16 Jan. 1895; *d* New York, 19 Mar. 1953). Singer, dancer, and comedienne. Described as 'eye-rolling, coquettish', in the Anna *Held tradition, she first appeared on the stage of the famous Variétés in Paris 1907–9, and thereafter generally played the role of the flirtatious French girl in many musicals. Her New York debut was in the *The First Affair* in Nov. 1912 (where she both sang and danced), then in *Broadway to Paris* (1912), and she made her London debut in *L'Impresario* at the Palace Theatre (1914). She appeared in *Miss Information* (1915); *Hitchy-Koo* (1917 and 1918); *As You Were* (1920); *The French Doll* (1922); *Little Miss Bluebeard* (1923; London, Wyndham's, 1925); *Paris* (1928)—singing 'Let's do it' (also in film version); *Great Lady* (1938); **Louisiana Purchase* (1940); and the American tour of **South Pacific* (1951). She was in the film *Paris in Spring* (1935). At one time she was married to the producer E. Ray Goetz, who produced some of her shows and whom she later divorced.

Borel-Clerc, Charles (*b* Pau, 22 Sept. 1879; *d* Cannes, 9 Apr. 1959). French composer. His original name was simply Charles Clerc, but for writing purposes he added his mother's maiden name. He studied music at the Toulouse and Paris Conservatoires and became an oboist in various Paris orchestras. He wrote operettas, revues, and a variety of songs. His biggest early success was 'La Matchiche' in 1903 which he wrote for the publisher Ricordi in response for a request for a dance on Spanish themes. The accompanying dance was created by M. Eugenio, maître of the Alcazar d'Eté Ballet and both song and dance were popularized by Felix Mayol (1872–1941), becoming a vogue in France. Mayol also launched 'Amour de Trottin'; while the popular singer Bérard included 'Le moulin de Maître Jean', 'Le train fatal', and 'Lison-Lisette' in his repertoire. Borel-Clerc was then commissioned to write for the revues at the Casino de Paris. In 1918 he collaborated with Lucien Boyer (1876–1942) on another great hit song, 'Madelon de la Victoire', which was popularized by Maurice *Chevalier.

He wrote many items that were taken up and popularized by such artists as *Mistinguett, Chevalier, Tino *Rossi, Lucienne *Boyer, Alibert, and others; another special success being 'Le petit vin blanc' which he wrote with Jean Dréjac. His other songs included 'C'est jeune et ça n'sait pas', 'Une femme qui passe', 'Monte là-d'ssus', 'Ma pomme', 'Ah, si vous connaissez ma poule', 'Vous n'êtes pas venue dimanche', 'Un amour comme le notre', and 'Tout le pays l'a su'.

Bossa nova. Translated literally, the name means 'new bump'. Music of Brazilian ancestry interbred with jazz, it became a fashionable rage in North America when Bud Shank, a Californian saxophonist and Laurindo *Almeida, the Brazilian guitarist, returned from a late 1950s tour of Brazil bringing with them some jazz-tinged sambas. The new name did not evolve until Stan *Getz and Charlie *Byrd later returned from a tour of Brazil with some of the work of Antonio Carlos *Jobim ('Desafinado'), Joāo Gilberto, and others; many of them in bossa nova style. An early bossa nova hit in the USA was 'The girl from Ipanema'. The rhythm is a hybrid combination of the *samba and the Brazilian baiao.

Bostic, Earl (*b* Tulsa, Okla., 25 Apr. 1913; *d* Rochester, NY, 28 Oct. 1965). Alto-saxophonist, singer, arranger, and composer. He studied at Xavier University in New Orleans where he was already active as a musician. In the years 1934–7 he worked with Joe Robicheaux, Ernie Fields, Charlie Creath, Fate *Marable, and other New Orleans bandleaders. He went to New York in 1938 and played with Don *Redman and Edgar Hayes, then led his own band 1938–42, mainly playing at Small's Paradise in Harlem. In the 1940s he began to arrange for various leading bands including those of Louis *Prima, Hot Lips *Page, Lionel *Hampton, Jack *Teagarden, and Paul *Whiteman. In 1945 he formed his own band again and started recording with Majestic Records, moving from modern jazz to something more commercially oriented in a jump style that included biting, punchy but melodic saxophone playing by the leader, resulting in hit records with such items as 'Flamingo' (a million-seller), 'Cherokee', and 'Moonglow'. Owing to recurring heart trouble, he had to leave music in the 1950s but resumed playing in 1959. During a residence at the Midtown Tower Hotel in Rochester he had a heart-attack and died soon after. His own writings included: 'The major and the minor', 'Scotch jam', 'Let me off Uptown', and 'Brooklyn boogie'.

Boston. A social dance that came into vogue around 1903, which was originally a modified version of the *waltz with the simplified walking steps that were about to revolutionize and popularize ballroom dancing for the amateur. The *foxtrot and the *two-step were to become the main movers in this along with the Bostonized waltz. The term 'Boston' became synonymous with this new styling and became more of a generic term, as in 'Boston two-step'. This had no connection with the black slang use of the word implying an inspired moment in jazz, as in the title 'B sharp Boston'.

Boswell, Connee [Connie] (*b* New Orleans, 3 Dec. 1907; *d* New York, 11 Oct. 1976). American singer. She was the best-known of the vocal and instrumental trio the *Boswell Sisters, who started out in 1924 and had great success in the 1930s. She also sang as a soloist and, when all three sisters married (Connie to the trio's manager Harold Leedy in 1935; he died in 1975) she changed her name to Connee and embarked in that year on her own singing career. A victim of polio in childhood, her condition later aggravated by a fall, she carried out most of her engagements in a wheelchair. She sang and recorded with Bing *Crosby, Bob *Crosby, Victor *Young, and Ben *Pollack and made successful recordings of 'Stormy weather' and 'Sand in my shoes', continuing to add to a prolific list of recordings until 1956.

One of the earliest white jazz singers and a pioneer of microphone technique, she influenced many who followed, notably Ella *Fitzgerald, but adopted a rather more commercial style in later years. She also played cello, saxophone, trombone, and piano. She appeared in many films, including: *Artists and Models* (1937); *Kiss the Boys Goodbye* (1941); *Syncopation* (1942); *Swing Parade* (1946); *Senior Prom* (1959); and took the leading role in the 1950s TV series *Pete Kelly's Blues* with Jack Webb. She was also a gifted arranger, writing most of the Boswell Sisters' neat yet interesting and very individual arrangements.

Boswell Sisters, The. Highly successful vocal trio formed *c.* 1924. As well as singing they also played instruments: Martha (1908–58), piano; Helvetia [known as Vet] (1909–88), violin, guitar, and banjo; and Connie (see above), cello, saxophone, trombone, and piano. All born in New Orleans, they came from a comfortable home and acquired their interest in jazz from their servants. They started their career in local stage shows and on radio and then toured in vaudeville. Winning a radio contest, they went to California, filming, recording, and broadcasting in 1930 on the Los Angeles station KFWB, where they evolved their very individual and then novel close harmony style which was to be the model for many groups that followed, such as the *Andrews Sisters. They went to New York in 1931 and, after a sensational appearance at the Paramount Theatre, began a recording career with Brunswick Records that led to worldwide fame.

They worked in a natural jazz idiom, using many top jazzmen in their backing groups, including Joe *Venuti, the *Dorsey brothers, Mannie *Klein, Eddie *Lang, Bunny *Berigan, and Benny *Goodman. They made regular appearances on the Chesterfield Show (1932) and the Bing *Crosby Show (1934–5). They visited London in 1933 and 1935 and recorded with *Ambrose; and went on to Holland to record with the Ramblers. They appeared in the films *The Big Broadcast of 1932* (1932); *Moulin Rouge* (1934); and *Transatlantic Merry-go-round* (1934). The group broke up in 1935 when all three sisters married and Connie (now calling herself Connee) embarked on a solo career. There were brief reunions in 1937 and on other occasions.

Botsford, George (*b* Sioux Falls, S. Dak., 24 Feb. 1874; *d* New York, 11 Feb. 1949). American composer, writer of many popular ragtime numbers, some with words added. He ran his own publishing business 1914–15 and for several years was a busy director of musical shows. His compositions included: 'The Katy Flier' (1899); 'Black and white rag' (1908), later popularized by Winifred *Atwell; 'Klondike rag' (1908); 'Pianophiends rag' (1909); 'Texas steer rag' (1909); 'The big jubilee' (1909); 'Old crow rag' (1909); 'Wiggle rag' (1909); 'Fat men on parade' (1909); 'Chatterbox rag' (1910); 'Grizzly bear rag' (1910)—as 'Doin' the grizzly bear' (*w* Irving *Berlin) it was sung by Fanny *Brice in *Ziegfeld Follies of 1910* and in the film *Wharf Angel* (1934); 'Lovey-dovey rag' (1910); 'Hyacinth rag' (1910); 'Honeysuckle rag' (1911); 'Royal flush rag' (1911); 'Eskimo rag' (1912, *w* Jean C. Havez); 'Buckeye rag' (1913); 'Incandescent rag' (1913); 'Rag, baby mine' (1913); 'Universal rag' (1913); 'Sailing down the Chesapeake Bay' (*w* Havez); 'Boomerang rag' (1916); and 'When Big Profundo sang low C' (1921, *w* Marion T. Bohannon).

Bouffes-Parisiens, Les. Tiny theatre opened by Jacques *Offenbach in the Champs-Elysées, Paris, in 1855, after he had become thoroughly frustrated in attempts to get his works played elsewhere. With a seating capacity of 50, it was nicknamed 'Le Bonbonnière'. The Great Exhibition of 1855 brought in hordes of visitors, and it was soon doing good business in spite of harsh licensing laws that only allowed three speaking characters on the stage at a time. Later in 1855 the theatre moved to new but only slightly larger premises in the Passage Choiseul, its greatest success coming in 1858 with **Orphée aux Enfers*, whose scandalous satire drew in the fashionable and wealthy. Offenbach went on to greater things and no longer required his own theatre, but he kept an interest in it, under various managers; and the theatre is still extant.

H. Buguet: *Bouffes-Parisiens* (Paris, 1873).

Bowie, David [Jones, David Robert] (*b* London, 8 Jan. 1947). British singer, composer, actor, and producer. He had a brief career as a commercial artist before entering the pop business and appeared with various now forgotten rhythm 'n' blues groups. It was the success of the *Monkees at this time that caused him to change his name to Bowie, so that he would not be confused with that group's David Jones. He began to record, singing in an Anthony *Newley vein, but still had no real success. He left music for a while and joined a mime group, coming back in 1969 to record the flower-power hit 'Space oddity' in 1969. This launched him on some ambitious albums that involved the world of machines, frustration, loneliness, and extra-terrestrial vision—a weirdly compelling amalgam of oddity that came out in a cult-forming album, *The Man Who Sold the World* (1971), sparking off a new category of rock known as glitter rock.

He went on to create a superstar character destroyed by his own fantasies and produced two even weirder conceptual albums, *Hunky Dory* (1971) and *The Rise and Fall of Ziggy Stardust and the Spiders from Mars* (1973; the basis of a 1983 film), which made him one of the leading rock figures of the 1970s with a somewhat unhealthy image, typified by such songs as 'Rock-'n'-roll suicide'. Hits of the early 1970s included 'The jean genie' (1972); 'Drive in Saturday' (1973); and 'Sorrow' (1973); with 'Space oddity' coming back to a No. 1 position in 1975. The Ziggy Stardust image was continued in a film, *The Man Who Fell to Earth* (1976); and a move towards more conventional rock styling began to make his work less eccentric. The soul/R & B-styled 'Fame' (1975) was a top hit in the USA.

Having been one of the most important figures in British rock in the 1970s, he fortified his image in the 1980s by demonstrating his capacity as a leading actor in such films as *Just a Gigolo* (1978); *The Hunger* (1983); *Merry Christmas, Mr Lawrence* (1983); *Into the Night* (1984); and *Absolute Beginners* (1986); on the Broadway stage in *The Elephant Man* (1980); and on TV in *Baal* (1981). His recordings successfully continued with 'Ashes to ashes' (1980) and 'Let's dance' (1983). There was even an album with Bing *Crosby, *Peace on Earth* (1982); and the excellent *Dancing in the Street* with Mick Jagger in 1985.

A. Bowie: *Free Spirit* (London, 1981). R. Carr: *David Bowie: an Illustrated Record* (London, 1981). G. Tremlett: *The David Bowie Story* (London, 1981). D. Bowie: *Bowie in His Own Words* (London, 1982). K. Juby: *David Bowie* (Tunbridge Wells, 1982). K. Cann: *David Bowie: a Chronology* (London, 1983).

Bowlly, Al [Albert Alick] (*b* Maputo, Mozambique, 7 Jan. 1899; *d* London, 17 Apr. 1941). South African singer who became one of the most popular band vocalists in Great Britain in the 1930s. He was brought up in Johannesburg where he was apprenticed as a barber in his uncle's hairdressing saloon; learning to play piano, banjo, guitar, and ukulele, he sang to entertain the customers. He joined the band of Edgar Adeler in 1923 and toured South Africa and the Far East mainly as a guitarist, leaving Adeler after a disagreement and going to Calcutta to join a band led by an American, Jimmy Lequime. He left, along with the pianist Monia Liter, and went to work in Berlin where he made his first vocal recordings with Arthur Briggs and his Savoy Syncopators and orchestras led by Fred Bird and George Carhart. He was invited to London by Fred *Elizalde to join his band as vocalist at the Savoy Hotel. The band broke up in 1929 and he joined Roy *Fox in 1930 to sing with his new band at the Monseigneur Restaurant.

Bowlly became a prolific recording artist, notably with Ray *Noble with whom he toured the USA 1934–6. By now a well-known name to millions, he sang at various times with Lew *Stone, *Geraldo, Oscar Rabin, and Ken 'Snakehips' Johnson, and appeared regularly on radio and in several films. After considerable success in America, he returned to London in 1937 and from 1939 spent much of his time entertaining British troops. He was killed when a land-mine fell near his flat in Jermyn Street. He had a rich, smooth, dark voice, which he used with feeling and intelligence, matching the dark, handsomely masculine looks that so affected his female admirers. He has become something of a cult figure among those who follow dance music of the 1930s and many of his recordings have now been re-issued. Rust's *Entertainment Discography* (1973) lists 37 pages of his recordings.

C. M. Harvey & B. Rust: *The Al Bowlly Discography* (London, 1965). S. Colin & T. Staveacre: *Al Bowlly* (London,

1979). R. Pallett: *Goodnight Sweetheart: Life and Times of Al Bowlly* (Tunbridge Wells, 1986).

Bowman, Euday L[ouis] (*b* Fort Worth, Texas, 9 Nov. 1887; *d* New York, 26 May 1949). American composer, arranger, and author. He arranged for many orchestras of the 1920s and 1930s and wrote one or two popular numbers including 'Twelfth Street rag' (1914). A song version was used in the film *Close Harmony* (1929; *w* Spencer *Williams), and the rag became a best-seller in a recording made by Pee Wee *Hunt in 1948.

Boy, The. British musical comedy which opened at the Adelphi Theatre, London, 14 Sept. 1917 and ran for 801 performances. The score was by Lionel *Monckton and Howard *Talbot, book by Fred *Thompson, based on Pinero's farce *The Magistrate*, and lyrics by Adrian Ross and Percy *Greenbank. The cast included W. H. *Berry, Peter Gawthorne, and Maisie Gay.

Boyer, Lucienne (*b* Paris, 1903; *d* Paris, 6 Dec. 1983). French cabaret singer. A 'lissom, sensual brunette' who had been in cabaret from the age of 16, she soon became well-known in Paris, dominating the Montparnasse and Montmartre cabaret world of the 1930s with her intimate and sultry style of entertainment. It was a recording of 'Parlez-moi d'amour' in 1930 that brought her world fame; followed, though not quite matched, by 'Un amour comme le nôtre' and her wartime 'Mon p'tit Kaki' from among the many records she made. She appeared in several films, notably in *La Belle Saison* (1937), and made successful appearances in New York in the late 1930s.

Boy Friend, The. British musical comedy that came along at a reassuring time to prove that the British could still produce something that would fill a theatre, even if it was quite a small one. It was a landmark in theatrical history and made a number of reputations as well as breaking all existing records with a run of 2084 performances.

The story is set on the Riviera in 1926 where Polly, an heiress pupil at Mme Dubonnet's finishing school, meets Tony, a lad of noble birth, disguised as a messenger boy. Farcical complications ensue, but all is sorted out at a carnival ball. The score by ex-Oxford revue writer Sandy *Wilson (who also wrote the words) was a neat pastiche of 1920s society music, with one or two memorable songs such as 'The boy friend', 'Won't you Charleston with me', 'I could be happy with you', 'Sur le plage', 'A room in Bloomsbury', 'The Riviera', and 'It's never too late to fall in love'.

The show first attracted attention as a Players' Theatre production on 14 Apr. 1953 and was revived there 13 Oct. It was then considered worthy of a further airing at the small Embassy Theatre in Swiss Cottage in December. By now it had created such a demand that it was put on in London's West End at Wyndham's Theatre 14 Jan. 1954 and there went on to make its record-breaking run with the lead played by the original Polly, Anne *Rogers, whose reputation had been established in the part. In New York, at the Royale Theatre, 30 Sept. 1954, it started another young star on the road to substantial fame when Julie *Andrews went there to take on the role. It achieved 485 performances; and another 763 when it was revived at the off-Broadway Downtown Theatre in 1958. There was a notable revival [365p] at London's Comedy Theatre in 1967, and it was seen again in New York in 1970 with Judy Carne in the lead. For something so typically English and undergraduate in character (matched in similar vein by the comparably successful **Salad Days*), it was a remarkable phenomenon. There was more success to come in the shape of a lavish Ken Russell film version made in 1972 with Twiggy (*b* 1946) in the leading role, ably abetted by the veteran Max *Adrian.

S. Wilson: *I Could Be Happy* (London, 1975).

Boy George [O'Dowd, George Alan] (*b* London, 14 June 1961). British singer, songwriter, and band leader. After various early careers, he became known with the group Culture Club in the early 1980s and achieved big hits with songs in the albums *Kissing to Be Clever* (1982) and *Colour by Numbers* (1983), including the No. 1 hit 'Karma chameleon'. His appearance in drag with pretty dresses and heavy makeup was derided at first, but was later taken in the spirit of fun intended and did not lessen the appeal of his widely-liked performances. He continued to produce goodish albums like *From Luxury to Heartache* (1986), but blurred his image by occasional undrag appearances and revelations of drug addiction. Although this may have temporarily diminished his popularity, he proved himself capable of producing more mature work.

Boys from Syracuse, The. The first Broadway musical to be based on a Shakespeare play, in this case *The Comedy of Errors*. The hilarious story, set in Ephesus in Asia Minor, is about two boys from Syracuse who set out to find their long-lost twins. Much confusion is created by the fact that both sets of twins have the same names so that even their wives get muddled. The score by Richard *Rodgers, with book by George *Abbott and lyrics by Lorenz *Hart, had such delightful numbers as 'Falling in love with love', 'The shortest day of the year', 'This can't be love', 'He and she', and 'Sing for your supper'.

It opened at the Alvin Theatre, New York, 23 Nov. 1938, with Teddy Hart, Jimmy Savo (1895–1960), Eddie *Albert, Ronald Graham, and Muriel Angelus (*b* 1909), and had 235 performances. It was filmed in 1940 with Allan *Jones, Joe Penner (1904–41), and Martha Raye (*b* 1916). The show did not come to London, owing to the war, but three of the songs were lifted for the London revue *Up and Doin'* in 1948. It had to wait for its first London production until 1963, after a remarkable 502-

performance off-Broadway revival, and even then it ran for less than three months.

Bradford, Perry 'Mule' [John Henry] (*b* Montgomery, Ala., 14 Feb. 1893; *d* New York, 20 Apr. 1970). American composer and pianist. An influential figure in pioneering jazz days, he was one of those who travelled around in show-business in the early years of the 20th century, bringing the newly developing jazz from the South up to the northern cities, and providing some of its early published examples. He settled in New York *c.* 1920. At this time he was acting as manager for the blues singer Mamie *Smith and it was her recording of Bradford's songs 'That thing called love' and 'You can't keep a good man down' (issued on the Okeh label in July 1920) that marked the real beginnings of black recording. The company had, in fact, wanted to use Sophie *Tucker, but Bradford persuaded them to use his client and thus put black music on the recording map. The record sold well and Mamie Smith continued to record. But it was one side from a session held on 10 Aug. 1920 which sparked off the boom in *race records; Bradford's 'Crazy blues' backed by 'It's right here for you', which sold in unprecedented numbers. From there on, every record company hastened to add some black singers to its catalogue. 'Crazy blues' not only launched race recordings, but helped to popularize the *blues and bring the jazz idiom to the attention of the wider world.

Bradford continued to tour with various singers, working at the same time as a record talent scout and plugging songs, which he also published, spending a brief time in gaol for infringing the copyright laws. He led a pioneering jazz group in the 1920s, generally billed as Perry Bradford's Jazz Phools, which included such prestigious names as Louis *Armstrong, Don *Redman, and James P. *Johnson.

P. Bradford: *Born With the Blues: Perry Bradford's Own Story* (New York, 1965).

Bradley, Will [Schwichtenberg, Wilbur] (*b* Newton, NJ, 12 July 1912). American bandleader, trombonist, and composer. A staff musician with CBS in the 1930s, he joined the Ray *Noble band during its American period in 1933, Playing in the trombone section alongside Glenn *Miller. He played in a number of bands and then, in 1939, formed his own group in partnership with drummer Ray *McKinley. They played in the bouncing big-band idiom of the period, featuring many *boogie-woogie based numbers, his own trombone playing much admired for its fluency and lyricism, and they made a number of best-selling LPs. He folded the band in 1942 and continued a career as a studio musician.

Bradshaw, Tiny [Myron] (*b* Youngstown, Ohio, 23 Sept. 1905; *d* Cincinnati, 26 Nov. 1958). American pianist, singer, and bandleader. He sang with New York bands before forming his own big band in 1934. At the end of the 1940s he moved into the *rhythm 'n' blues field and was to lead the most popular R & B bands of the 1950s, recording with the King label as leader, accompanist to Roy *Brown and others, and piano soloist. He achieved a number of best-selling records in the *jump idiom, including 'Soft' (1953), influencing such major artists as Buddy *Holly; and toured all over America. A stroke ended his musical career in 1958.

Braham, David [Anthony Cannon] (*b* London, 1838; *d* New York, 11 Apr. 1905). British composer who went to America in 1853 to pursue a career as a professional musician. He studied the harp but found the violin a better prospect and got his first job with it in the pit orchestra of the Pony Moore Minstrels. Later he played in many theatre orchestras and conducted a military band, becoming Tony *Pastor's musical director. By the 1870s he had written various songs in an English music-hall style, such as 'The bootblack', 'Sailing on the lake', and 'Over the hill to the poorhouse', with moderate acclaim.

His real fame was to come as the writer of songs for the various popular *burlesque shows put on in the 1870s and 1880s by *Harrington and Hart, starting with *The Mulligan Guards' Picnic* (1878)—'The Mulligan Guard'; and followed by *The *Mulligan Guards' Ball* (1879)—'The Skidmore fancy ball', 'The babies on our block'; *The Mulligan Guards' Chowder* (1879); *The Mulligan Guards' Christmas* (1879); *The Skidmore Fancy Ball* (1879); *The Mulligan Guards' Surprise* (1880)—which contained his biggest hit 'Whist, the bogie man'; *The Mulligan Guards' Nominee* (1880); *The Mulligans' Silver Wedding* (1881); *The Major* (1881); *Squatter Sovereignty* (1882)—'Paddy Duffy's cart', 'The widow Nolan's goat', and 'The forlorn old maid'; *The Blackbird* (1882); *Mordecai Lyons* (1882); *McSorley's Inflation* (1882); *The Muddy Day* (1883); *Cordelia's Aspirations* (1883); *Dan's Tribulations* (1884); *Investigation* (1885); *McAllister's Legacy* (1885); *Old Lavender* (1885)—'When poverty's tears ebb and flow'; *The Grip* (1885); *The Leather Patch* (1886); *The O'Reagans* (1886); *McNooney's Visit* (1887); *Waddy Googan* (1888); *The Lorgaire* (1889); *Reilly and the Four Hundred* (1890)—'Maggie Murphy's home'; *The Last of the Hogans* (1891); *The Woollen Stocking* (1893); and *The Merry Malone* (1896). After the initial success of the Harrigan & Hart shows, Braham rarely wrote for anyone else until the partnership broke up in 1885. His daughter married Harrigan.

Braham, John [Abraham, John] (*b* London, 20 Mar. 1774; *d* London, 17 Feb. 1856). English composer and singer. Born of Jewish parents, he was left an orphan and lived in poverty for many years, selling pencils in the street and doing odd jobs in order to keep alive. The well-known Jewish singer Leoni took him under his care and trained him, and he first appeared in public at Covent Garden in 1787 singing 'The soldier tir'd of war's alarms' and 'Ma chère amie' at a benefit concert for his benefactor. He sang regularly at the Royalty Theatre and earned such praises as 'he promises fair to attain perfection; possessing every requisite necessary to form a capital singer'. He developed a remarkably expressive tenor voice of great range and power. His first adult appearances were at Bath in 1794 and later at Drury Lane in Storace's opera *Mahmoud*. He also became a teacher of singing and piano.

Although Braham had a triumphal career as a singer, his main ambition was to be a composer. According to the custom then, he began to contribute his own songs to the productions he appeared in including *The Cabinet* (1802); *The English Fleet in 1342* (1803)—'All's well'; *Thirty Thousand* (1804); *Out of Place* (1805); *False Alarms* (1807); *Kais* (1808); and *The Americans* (1811)—'The Death of Nelson'. In 1831 he went into theatrical promotion, buying the Colosseum in Regent's Park for £40,000 in 1836 and building the St James's Theatre at a cost of £26,000. Neither prospered and he lost all his money. He had to recoup by further work as an opera singer, visiting the USA in 1836 and creating quite a sensation there. His last public appearance was in 1852, after which he took orders in the Anglican Church and was appointed to a post in Canterbury, changing his name to Meadows. Such songs as 'The death of Nelson', 'All's well', and 'Aileen Aroon' achieved true popular success, also becoming best-sellers in the USA.

J. M. Levien: *The Singing of John Braham* (London, 1945).
J. M. Levien: 'Braham' in *Six Sovereigns of Song* (London, n.d.).

Braham, Leonora (*b* 1853; *d* London, 23 Nov. 1931). British actress and singer. She made her first stage appearance in W. S. *Gilbert's *Ages Ago* (music by Frederic *Clay) at the Royal Gallery of Illustration in 1869. She eventually joined the D'Oyly *Carte company and was the originator of Patience, Phyllis in **Iolanthe*, Princess Ida, Yum-Yum in *The *Mikado*, and Rose Maybud in **Ruddigore*. The fact that all three of the leading ladies of that time—Braham, Jessie *Bond, and Sybil Grey—were petite, is said to have inspired Gilbert to write 'Three little maids'.

Braham, Philip (*b* London, 1882; *d* London, 2 May 1934). British composer and conductor. He was musical director at Wembley Studios in the early days of the talking film and a prolific writer of music for the theatre, his scores including *Blighty* (1916); *Bubbly* (1917); *Tails Up* (1918); *The Officer's Mess* (1918); *Bran Pie* (1919); *Jumble Sale* (1920); *Battling Butler* (1922); *Rats* (1923); *Boodle* (1925); **On With the Dance* (1925); and *Up With the Lark* (1927). No song of his achieved more lasting popularity than 'Limehouse blues' (*w* Douglas Furber) which was first heard, as an added number, in the revue *A to Z* (1921) where it was sung by Teddie Gerrard (1890–1942). It was then used in *Charlot's Revue* (1924), and became a great hit when Gertrude *Lawrence (who had also been in *A to Z*) took it over in the 1925 New York edition, recorded it, and was lastingly associated with the song.

Brandram, Rosina [Moult, Rosina] (*b* 1846; *d* London, 28 Feb. 1907). British actress and contralto singer. It was to be her lot to sing all the 'unattractive old thing' parts in every original production of the *Gilbert and Sullivan operas at the Savoy, a list of forbidding ladies and *grandes dames* like Katisha, Dame Hannah, Dame Carruthers, the Duchess of Plaza-Toro, Lady Sophy, and Little Buttercup. Gilbert described her as 'Rosina of the golden voice' but complained that she never managed to look more than 28 in roles demanding a lady of 65. When the Savoy company was inactive for a few years, she appeared in *Little Hans Andersen* (1903) and **Veronique* (1904). Richard D'Oyly *Carte left her a legacy of £1000 in gratitude for her services to the company.

Brass band. A band made up of brass instruments, with or without percussion. In Britain and most European countries this differentiates it from the wind band or the *military band which includes woodwind as well as brass, the kind most commonly found in the USA.

In Britain, where the competitive festival has become the *raison d'être* of the brass band movement, the bands must be constituted in accordance with strict rules. For many years they were not allowed percussion instruments, though many used them for concert purposes. The first relaxation of the rule came only in 1969 when percussion was permitted both in the new championship contest promoted by the tobacco firm of W. D. & H. O. Wills, and then in the old-established British Open Championship at Belle Vue, Manchester. Another innovation from that year was that the judges of the contest sat in the open where they could see as well as hear. Previously, to avoid any prejudice, they had been incarcerated in boxes or tents where they could hear perfectly well but not see, and the bands were not identified. The instrumentation for contests has long been strictly organized and limited to 25 wind instruments. Outside the contests the bands take on a more flexible format.

What is commonly called the Brass Band Movement started in the early 19th century. Some of the mounted bands of cavalry regiments adopted the all-brass format at this time; and amateurs found this the easiest combination to deal with, the similarity of fingering (trombones apart) facilitating the interchange of players and instruments and the writing of parts. The date of the formation of the first brass band has never been firmly established, but there was certainly one in York and one in Monmouthshire in the early 1830s, the latter being formed in connection with some iron works in Blaina (Blaenau). Others quickly followed, many of them sponsored and supported by industry, others by temperance societies, mechanics' institutes, religious bodies, and other organizations. Of the bands still flourishing the oldest are *Besses o' th'

Barn and *Black Dyke Mills which became all-brass bands in 1853 and 1855 respectively, both existing previously as brass and woodwind combinations.

The brass band movement has thrived on its contests for many years, the competition being a constant urge to maintain and improve standards. The principal contests today are the British Open held at Belle Vue, Manchester, and the National Brass Championship in London. The former started in September 1853, when the two test pieces were of the bands' own choice (the winner was the Mossley Temperance Band), and they have continued without interruption ever since. The first Crystal Palace contest was in 1860, founded through the enterprise of Enderby Jackson. Others followed at intervals, but it was not until 1900 that a National Championship was established on a regular footing in London and this was due to the enthusiasm and effort of John Henry Iles (1871–1951). His earlier interests had been choral but he was so excited by a visit to Belle Vue in 1898 that he contacted Samuel Cope (1856–1947), founder of *The British Bandsman* magazine, and before the end of the year he had become the owner, with Cope still editor. On 20 Jan. 1900, to support the *Daily Mail* Kipling Fund in aid of those fighting in the Boer War, he organized a large concert in the Albert Hall at which 11 of the best brass bands in the country appeared. Sir Arthur *Sullivan conducted, the programme including his setting of Kipling's 'The absent-minded beggar'. This was followed up by the first National Contest at the Crystal Palace, for which 29 bands entered, the test-piece being a selection of 'Gems from Sullivan's Operas' arranged by James Ord *Hume. The winner was the Denton Original Band with Black Dyke Mills second and Wingate's Temperance Band third. This contest has continued ever since except for the war years.

A big landmark was the commissioning of specially written test-pieces for the Championship section at the Crystal Palace in 1913. The first was 'Labour and Love' by Percy *Fletcher and the composer was one of the judges. Since then most test-pieces have been original compositions. The next noteworthy change was in 1922. Up to then the contest bands had played standing in a square formation with the conductor in the middle; this year they played in concert platform manner, seated with the conductor in front.

The first band from abroad to compete was the Newcastle Steel Works Band from Australia in 1924 and they finished third. In the 1930s the *Fodens Motor Works Band, then conducted by Fred *Mortimer, was pre-eminent and won seven years out of nine. (Bands which won for three years in succession were barred for one year by the rules.) In 1936 the Crystal Palace was destroyed by fire and a temporary home was found at the Alexandra Palace for the 1937 and 1938 contests. After the wartime break in 1945, John Henry Iles, then over 70, obtained the support of the *Daily Herald* for a renewed championship at the Royal Albert Hall. Fodens were still barred under the three-year rule, and the first post-war winner was the *Fairey Aviation Works band. In 1961 the *Daily Herald* felt it could no longer shoulder the responsibility and the *People* stepped in with Edwin Vaughan Morris (*b* 1901) the guiding hand. He introduced a National Youth Championship in 1965 and in 1966 managed to promote the National Contest on an independent basis. As interest grew a World Championship was inaugurated in 1968. Traditionally European bands have been differently constituted, but many now adopted the British style and the movement spread throughout Europe. Bands had long flourished in Australia and New Zealand and now Canada, South Africa, and the United States began to appreciate the merits of the British band. The brass band world flourishes and many new composers are being encouraged to write music for bands and new test-pieces. Some of the composers who have supplied excellent works in the field have been Malcolm Arnold, Eric *Ball, Sir Granville Bantock (1868–1946), Hubert *Bath, Jack *Beaver, Ronald *Binge, Sir Arthur Bliss (1891–1975), Derek Bourgeois (*b* 1941), Sir Edward Elgar (1857–1934), Percy *Fletcher, Henry *Geehl, Henry Charles Goffin (1883–1973), John Dean Goffin (*b* 1909), Edward Gregson (*b* 1945), George W. Hespe (*b* 1900), Joseph Holbrooke (1878–1958), Gustav Holst (1872–1934), Herbert Howells (1892–1983), John Ireland (1879–1962), Gordon Jacob (1895–1984), J. Ord Hume, Cyril Jenkins (1889–1978), Maurice Johnstone (*b* 1900), Haydn Morris (*d* 1965), R. Maldwyn Price (*d* 1952), Edmund Rubbra (1901–86), Edrich Siebert (*b* 1903), Robert Simpson (*b* 1921), Gilbert *Vinter, Ralph Vaughan Williams (1872–1958), and Denis Wright (1895–1967).

Some of the principal bands of Britain (with their foundation dates) were: Besses o' th' Barn (1853), Black Dyke Mills (1855), Brighouse and Rastrick (1881), Carlton Main Frickley Colliery (1890), City of Coventry (1939), The Cory Band (1884), Creswell Colliery (1899), CWS (Manchester) (1900), Desford Colliery (1898), Dobcross (1875), Ever Ready (GB) (1926), Fairey Aviation (1937), Fodens Motor Works (1902), Grimethorpe Colliery (1917), GUS (Footwear) [previously Munn & Felton] (1933), Hammonds Sauce Works (1946), Mirrlees Works (1949), Morris Motors (1924), Parc and Dare (1894), Rochdale (1952), Salvation Army International Staff (1891), Scottish CWS (1918), Tredegar Town (1876), Wingates Temperance (1873), and Yorkshire Imperial Metals (1936).

H. C. Hind: *The Brass Band* (London, 1934; repr. 1952). J. F. Russell & J. H. Elliot: *The Brass Band Movement* (London, 1936). K. Cook: *The Bandsman's Everything Within* (London, 1950). K. Cook (ed.): *Oh! Listen to the Band* (London, 1950). F. Wright (ed.): *Brass Today* (London, 1957). D. Wright: *The Complete Bandmaster* (Oxford, 1963). D. Wright: *Scoring for Brass Band* (4th edn, London, 1967). H. Livings: *That the Medals and the Baton be Put on View: the Story of a Village Band,*

1875–1975 [Dobcross] (Newton Abbot, 1973). T. R. Cooper: *Brass Bands of Yorkshire* (York, 1974). V. & G. Brand: *Brass Bands in the 20th Century* (Letchworth, 1979). A. R. Taylor: *Brass Bands* (London, 1979). P. Gammond & R. Horricks: *Music on Record 1: Brass Bands* (Cambridge, 1980). C. Weir: *Village and Town Bands* (Princes Risborough, 1981).

Brassens, Georges (*b* Sète, 22 Oct. 1921; *d* Sète, 30 Oct. 1981). French singer and songwriter. He sang in a number of small Paris clubs in the 1940s before he was discovered by the cabaret singer Patachou in 1952. His simple melodies and traditionally French style, earthy and Rabelaisian, a combination of Parisian know-how and his native Midi humour, and his satirical jibes at the clergy, police, and politicians, brought him a growing following. Over his active years, interspersed with many periods of illness, he sold more than 20 million records. His guitar playing and his music earned him the Grand Prix du Disque of the Académie Charles-Gros in 1964; and for his equally admired lyrics the Grand Prix de Poésie of the Académie Française in 1967. The kidney complaint that killed him had kept him away from performing for some years, but he was planning a return when he died.

Bratton, John W. (*b* Wilmington, Del., 21 Jan. 1867; *d* Brooklyn, NY, 7 Feb. 1947). American composer and producer. After study at the Philadelphia College he started a career as a baritone singer. He organized amateur operettas and from those beginnings became a professional actor and producer of musical comedies, founding the firm of Leffler & Bratton. He began to compose for the stage in 1900 with *Hodge, Podge & Co*; followed by *Star and Garter* (1900); *The Liberty Belles* (1901); *The Man from China* (1904); *The Pearl and the Pumpkin* (1905); *Buster Brown* (1908); and *The Newlyweds and their Baby* (1909).

His songs included: 'Only me' (1894); 'The sunshine of Paradise Alley' (1895); 'I love you in the same old way, darling Sue' (1896); 'Beneath the evening star' (1900); 'My sunflower Sue' (1900); 'You never can tell what a kiss will do' (1900); 'My sunbeam from the South' (1900); 'In a cozy corner' (1901); 'I'm on the water wagon now' (1903); 'In a garden of faded flowers' (1903); 'Make believe' (1904); 'You'll always be just sweet sixteen to me' (1907); 'The Teddy Bears' picnic' (1907); 'I'll be your honey' (1908); 'Loving time' (1909).

Break. Part of a performance (particularly in jazz) where one or more instruments play a linking phrase without the support of the rhythm section or the band. It may even be taken by a member of the rhythm section but with the main movement of the rhythm suspended. In some pieces, e.g. 'Tiger rag', 'Bugle call rag', 'Snag it', the break is written into the composition; but in many cases it is improvised.

Brecht, Bertolt (*b* Augsburg, Bavaria, 10 Feb. 1898; *d* Berlin, 14 Aug. 1956). German writer. Educated at Munich University, followed by short war service, he won the Kleist Prize with his second play *Drums in the Night* in 1922 and soon became known as a writer. He moved to Berlin in 1924 where he published his first book of poems and had an international success with *Die *Dreigroschenoper*. From 1929 he was a committed member of the Communist Party and became increasingly involved in politics as the Nazis came to power. As a poet Brecht wrote with spoken or sung performances in mind and, from the beginning, he would sing his words to guitar accompaniment with his own or borrowed tunes, touring the music-halls and cabarets and singing in a rough but well-articulated way. He emigrated to Denmark in 1933, lived in various Scandinavian countries 1939–41, and finally arrived in the USA in 1941. His plays *Mother Courage*, *The Caucasian Chalk Circle*, and others had music by Paul Dessau (1894–1979).

It was Brecht's association with Kurt *Weill that made the most lasting impression on the music scene, starting with the original *Mahagonny* in 1927 and typified by the immediately successful and long-lasting *Threepenny Opera*. Their styles seemed made for each other and each gained an identity from the association. Even music written by other composers such as Hanns Eisler (1898–1962) seemed to have the same characteristic, either dictated by Brecht's dominating personality or reflecting the association with Weill: certainly Weill's music changed and took on its strong identity after meeting and working with Brecht in 1927, and it was an association of ideas that Weill found it difficult to break away from. Brecht's similar association with Eisler continued until the poet's death in 1956.

Brel, Jacques (*b* Brussels, 8 Apr. 1929; *d* Bobigny, Paris, 9 Oct. 1978). Belgian singer, composer, and author. Son of an industrialist, Brel started performing locally at an early age, eventually going to Paris and singing at the Trois Baudets where his career was taken in hand by Jacques Canetti. He began to record for Philips and Barclay backed by the orchestras of André Grassi, Michel *Legrand, André Popp, and François Rauber; but, later, mainly working with Gérard Jouannest who wrote the music for some of his songs. His reputation as an original and inspired writer with a biting, critical, satirical wit balanced by idealism and a message of hope for the world, made him into a cult figure—so much so that a cabaret-revue with the commentary and songs entirely by Brel opened at the Village Gate in New York 22 Jan. 1968 under the title *Jacques Brel is Alive and Well and Living in Paris*. It was partly adapted by Mort Shuman who was one of the performers, with Ellie Stone outstanding in it, and ran for 1847 performances.

Among his best-known songs were 'La parlotte', 'Les vieux', 'Il nous faut regarder', 'Quand on n'a que l'amour', 'Les biches', 'Le moribond', 'A mon dernier repas', 'Les bourgeois', 'Les bigottes', 'Les dames patronesses', 'La, la, la', 'L'air de la bêtise', 'Mathilde', 'Jackie', 'Amsterdam', 'Next', 'Funeral tango', 'My death', 'Sons of', 'You're not alone', 'If you go away', and 'I'm not afraid'. Many of them were taken up by such artists as Judy *Collins, Joan *Baez, Dusty *Springfield, Ray *Charles, Neil *Diamond, Rod *McKuen, and Frank *Sinatra. He appeared in films and in the Paris production of *Man of La Mancha*. An original and evocative performer of his own work, it was ironic, in view of the revue title above, that he had to give up public appearances in 1967 and cancer forced him to abandon his career in 1974, though he did record a final album, *Brel*, in Paris in 1977 which sold more than two million copies.

J. Clouzet: *Jacques Brel* (Paris, 1965).

Bretón y Hernández, Tomás (*b* Salamanca, 29 Dec. 1850; *d* Madrid, 2 Dec. 1923). Spanish composer, conductor, and violinist. Coming from a poor family, he had to earn his living as a musician from the age of 10. At 15 he went to Madrid to play in cafés and theatres and was, for a time, assistant conductor to the well-known writer of waltzes Olivier Metra. He won a scholarship to the Madrid Conservatory where he studied under the zarzuela composer Emilio Arrieta. Later he won grants that enabled him to study in Rome, Paris, and Vienna. He became conductor of the Unión-Artistico-Musical Orchestra and in 1891 was taken to London by Isaac Albéniz, where he conducted two concerts at St James's Hall. The programme included some of his own works and it was afterwards suggested to him that he ought to concentrate on furthering the cause of Spanish music. By 1889 he had had some success with his second full-length opera *Los Amantes de Teruel*, produced in Madrid, and he increasingly turned to the popular musical theatre.

He had already written several short zarzuelas but now achieved real fame with *La verbena de la Paloma*, produced at the Apolo Theatre in Madrid 19 Feb. 1894, which provided the genre with one of its best-loved classics, a deeply Spanish work dealing in a picturesque way with the typical life of Madrid. Its famous jota, in its directness and simplicity, is quintessentially Spanish in flavour. The one-act piece was written to a libretto originally intended for Ruperto *Chapí, but the directors of the Apolo had quarrelled with Chapí and asked Bretón to take it on. Written in 19 days, it is arguably the most popular zarzuela of them all. It was influential in establishing the new school of Spanish operetta and proved as popular in South America as it was in Spain. It was followed by the almost equally successful *La Dolores* in 1895, a three-act opera which had worldwide acclaim. Frequently writing his own libretti and a lifelong campaigner for Spanish national music, he never quite matched these two great successes with any subsequent works, which included: *Las nieves* (1895); *El Guardia de Corps* (1897); *El Puente del Diablo* (1898); *El reloj de Cuco* (1898); *La Cariñosa* (1899); and *El caballo del señorito* (1902).

A. S. Salcedo: *Tomás Bretón: su vida y sus obras* (Madrid, 1924).

Brewer, Teresa (*b* Toledo, 7 May 1931). American singer. She started her singing career at the age of two and continued throughout her childhood and teens, becoming widely known in 1950 with the hit 'Music! Music! Music!' followed by 'Choo'n gum' (1950); 'Longing for you' (1951); 'Till I waltz again with you' (1952); 'Ricochet' (1953); 'Bell bottom blues' (1954); 'Jilted' (1954); 'I gotta go get my baby' (1955); 'Silver dollar' (1955); 'A sweet old-fashioned girl' (1956); 'A tear fell' (1956); and many more of the punchy, unsophisticated kind on the borders of country music and leading towards the rock scene. She recorded some rhythm 'n' blues numbers like 'Bo weevil' (1956) and 'You send me' (1957). In 1972 she married the producer Bob Thiele, who featured her in rather more sophisticated and interesting albums with such artists as Count *Basie, Duke *Ellington, Stéphane *Grappelli, Bobby *Hackett, Svend *Asmussen, and Earl *Hines. She has continued to appear in various unpredictable settings and guises.

Brian, Donald (*b* St John's, Newfoundland, 17 Feb. 1877; *d* Great Neck, NY, 22 Dec. 1948). Canadian singer. He went to New York in 1899 and made his debut there in the play *On the Wabash*. His first singing part was in a touring company of *The Chaperones* and small parts in *The Supper Club*, **Florodora*, and *The Belle of Broadway* followed. In 1904 he joined George M. *Cohan's company and appeared in **Little Johnny Jones* (1904) and **Forty-Five Minutes from Broadway* (1906). His stardom came with the role of Danilo in *The *Merry Widow* (1907), leading to roles in such successful musicals as *The *Dollar Princess* (1909); *The Marriage Market* (1913); *The *Girl from Utah* (1914); **Sybil* (1916); *Her Regiment* (1917); *The Girl Behind the Gun* (1918); *The *Chocolate Soldier* (1921 revival); *Up She Goes* (1922); **No, No, Nanette* (1926 tour); *The Merry Widow* (1932 revival); *Music in the Air* (1933). His last Broadway appearance was in *Very Warm for May* (1939).

Bric-a-Brac. Described as a 'musical piece', it was simply a glorified revue. In the cast were Arthur Playfair, Nelson *Keys, Teddie Gerrard, Gwendoline Brogden, Lauri Wylie, and, its leading glory, the effervescent Gertie *Millar: 'the most famous of our musical comedy stars ... there's an air of real cockney sauciness in the bus-route song delivered in her most fetching manner'—as the Gramophone Co. copywriter wrote of her rendering of 'Chalk Farm to Camberwell Green', one of the most delightful numbers that her husband Lionel *Monckton ever created for her. Monckton and Herman *Finck provided a good score (Finck was also MD), with additional items by Nat D. *Ayer, while Arthur *Wimperis and Basil *Hood provided the words. It opened at the Palace Theatre, London, 18 Sept. 1915 and ran for 385 performances.

Brice, Fanny [Borach, Fannie] (*b* New York, 29 Oct. 1891; *d* Hollywood, 29 May 1951). American actress, comedienne, and singer. She made her first appearance at Keeney's Theatre, Brooklyn, in 1903. It was a strongly Jewish performance of Irving *Berlin's 'Sadie Salome' in 1905 that earned her her first show part in the burlesque *College Girls*. While touring with this she was seen by Florenz *Ziegfeld who put her into his *Ziegfeld Follies of 1910* in which she had a success with another Berlin song, 'Goodbye, Becky Cohen', and with 'Lovey Joe' (a song taken up in 1911 by the singer/actress Elizabeth Brice, who was not related). She became a fixture in the *Follies* productions, appearing in the 1911, 1916, 1917, 1920, 1921, and 1923 editions, and in two later versions produced by the Shuberts in 1934 and 1936. In 1913 she was in *Honeymoon Express* and appeared in London at the Coliseum and the London Hippodrome, introducing London to her Baby Snooks act; followed by *Nobody Home* (1915); *The *Music Box Revue* (1924/5); *Fioretta* (1929); **Sweet and Low* (1930); and *Crazy Quilt* (1931) which was produced by her third husband Billy *Rose. She appeared in a number of films starting with *My Man* in 1928.

Her act varied between being the strident Jewish comedienne singing songs like 'Second-hand rose', 'I'm an Indian', and 'Old wicked willage of Wenice'; and the heart-rending singer of torch ballads—'My man', 'Rose of Washington Square', 'I found a million dollar baby in a ten-cent store', and 'Overnight'. She had a radio career 1939–51 portraying the immortal brat Baby Snooks. She was an exceptional satirist and portrayer of comic characters, yet able to give great depth and poignancy to a role. Her own life was something of a burlesque. At one time she was married to gangster Nicky Arnstein, a period of her life that was splendidly portrayed by Barbra *Streisand in **Funny Girl* (1964; filmed 1968) and in the sequel *Funny Lady* (1975).

N. Katkov: *The Fabulous Fanny: the Story of Fanny Brice* (New York, 1953).

Bricusse, Leslie (*b* London, 29 Jan. 1931). British composer and librettist. While at Cambridge University he wrote and directed a revue, *Out of the Blue*, which was transferred to the West End; followed by an appearance, using his own material, in *An Evening with Beatrice Lillie*. His first stage musical (for which he wrote the lyrics) was *Lady at the Wheel* (1958)—'Love Is'; followed by his collaborations with Anthony *Newley on **Stop the World—I Want to Get Off* (1961; filmed 1965)—'What kind of fool am I?', 'Gonna build a mountain', 'Once in a lifetime'; *The Roar of the Greasepaint—the Smell of the Crowd* (1965; première in New York)—'A wonderful day like today', 'Who can I turn to?', 'Nothing can stop me now'; and *The Good Old Bad Old Days* (1972)—'The people tree'. He wrote the lyrics for **Pickwick* (1963)—'If I ruled the world'; *Peter Pan* (TV show with Newley, 1976); *The Travelling Music Show* (1978); *Beyond the Rainbow* (1978); and both words and music for the heavily panned *Kings and Clowns* (1978) which, being based on the love life of King Henry VIII, was originally going to be called *Great Harry*.

Writings for films include such varied items as *Charley Moon* (1956); *Doctor Doolittle* (1967)—Academy Award for 'Talk to the animals'; *Goodbye, Mr Chips* (1969); *Scrooge* (1970)—'I hate people', 'I like life', 'Thank you very much'; *Willie Wonka and the Chocolate Factory* (1970)—'Candy man'; with John *Barry: *Goldfinger* (1964); *Thunderball* (1965); *The Knack* (1965); *The Ipcress File* (1965); and *You Only Live Twice* (1967); with Jerry *Goldsmith: *The Sand Pebbles* (1966); *In Like Flint* (1967); with John *Williams: *How to Steal a Million* (1966); *Superman* (1978); with Henry *Mancini: *The Return of the Pink Panther* (1975) and *House Calls* (1978). His other songs include 'A good idea, son' (1956), for Max *Bygraves, 'My kind of girl (1960), for the *Eurovision Song Contest, and 'Summertime in Rome'.

Bridge. The third section of either four or (usually) eight bars of the typical popular song following the pattern a-a-b-a, main theme repeated twice, bridge, theme. Often it is a weaker link than the rest, but composers like Jerome *Kern and Richard *Rodgers were adept at making an interesting feature of the bridge (as in Kern's 'Smoke gets in your eyes' with an enharmonic shift of which he was particularly fond). Also referred to as the middle eight, the release, the channel, or linking passage.

Bridgewater, Leslie (*b* Halesowen, Worcs., 31 Aug. 1893; *d* Hong Kong, 19 Mar. 1975). British composer and conductor. He studied at Birmingham with Granville Bantock, C. H. Kitson, and York Bowen. He began a conducting career as MD for the touring version of *Going Up* (1919); his first London production was *The Circle of Chalk* (1929). He became musical director at the Globe Theatre in 1929, was musical adviser to H. M. Tennent Ltd 1933–74, and consultant in light music for the BBC from 1935. He was conductor of the BBC Salon Orchestra 1939–42; the BBC Chorus 1943–8; and made more than 1500 wartime broadcasts with the Leslie Bridgewater Quintet. As director of music for the Shakespeare Memorial Theatre, Stratford-upon-Avon, from 1948 he composed incidental music (including 19 Shakespeare plays) for that and other theatres. He also wrote for films. His theatre and film scores included: *Delilah* (1930); *Hamlet* (1930); *The Venetian* (1931); *Punchinello* (1932); *Escape Me Never* (1933); *Immortal Garden* (1933); *Pageant of Parliament* (with Roger Quilter, 1933); *Dear Octopus* (1938); *The Relapse* (1947); and *The Way of the World* (1953).

Brigadoon. Musical play with score by Frederick *Loewe and book and lyrics by Alan Jay *Lerner, produced at the Ziegfeld Theatre, New York, 13 Mar. 1947 where it had 581 performances. In London, at His Majesty's Theatre, it ran for 685 performances. It was revived in New York at the City Center 1950 and 1957, had a Broadway revival in 1980, and was filmed in 1954 starring Gene *Kelly, Cyd Charisse, and Van Johnson.

Set in Scotland, it tells of two travellers who come across a strange village of the past. Finding it a ghost place that only comes back for a day once a century, they flee. But one of them has fallen in love with a girl there and returns. The village reappears just long enough for him to become a part of it. Much of the show was sensitively written but it has never satisfied all critics. The songs include 'I'll go home with bonnie Jean', 'The heather on the hill', 'Come to me, bend to me', and 'Almost like being in love'; and the Agnes De Mille ballets were very effective.

Brisson, Carl [Pedersen, Carl] (*b* Copenhagen, 24 Dec. 1895; *d* Copenhagen, 26 Sept. 1958). Danish actor, singer, and dancer who first gained fame as a boxer and sportsman under his original name. He made his stage debut in 1916 as a dancer and came to London in 1921 to appear in vaudeville. He starred in *The Apache* (1927) and had a success in *Wonder Bar* at the Savoy Theatre in 1930, making his New York stage debut in *Forbidden Melody* (1936). His reputation rests with his film appearances, including *The Ring* (1928); *Song of Soho* (1929); *All the King's Horses* (1935). He was a prolific recording artist, singing in both English and Swedish in a cornily romantic manner.

'Britannia, the pride of the ocean' or 'The red, white and blue'. Song of much debated origin. It is most probably an American song, first published in Philadelphia in 1843 under the title 'Columbia, the land of the brave' with music and words attributed to David T. Shaw. A new edition in 1844 changed the title to 'Columbia, the gem of the ocean' with Thomas A'Beckett, an English musician and writer, claiming to be sole author of the song. The first English edition, 'Britannia, the gem of the ocean', was published in London in July 1852; a second edition in December changed the title to 'The pride of the ocean' and says that the song was 'collected by Mr Davenport abroad'. This refers to the actor C. L. Davenport who sang it in the drama *Black-Eyed Susan*, first staged in 1829, but revived by Davenport in 1853.

Confusion was added by its publication in 1855 as 'The red, white and blue', and again in the USA in 1861 under the same title (equally apt for both flags), suggesting a bit of reverse pirating. It was published many times in London, eventually established as 'Britannia, the pride of the ocean (The red, white and blue)', with Mr Davenport credited with its promotion and having written the last verse. At some later stage it was claimed that its true authors were Thomas E. Williams (music) and Stephen J. Meany (words), neither of whom had hitherto been mentioned. Williams was the composer of 'The larboard watch' and other popular 19th-century songs and may have become involved as an arranger.

Britt, Elton (*b* Marshall, Ark., 7 July 1917; *d* Pennsylvania, 23 June 1972). American country singer and yodeller. Discovered at the age of 15 by talent scouts, he embarked on a busy radio career which included shows on Hollywood and New York networks, on the **Grand Ole Opry* from Nashville, and in his own 'Elton Britt Show'. He recorded for 22 years for Victor, Decca, and other labels, appeared in Western films, and wrote many of his own songs. He had a great success with his recording of 'There's a star-spangled banner waving somewhere' (by Paul Roberts, Shelby Darnell, and Bob Miller) in 1942; it cashed in opportunely on the war years to become the best-selling sheet music and a million-seller record by 1944, receiving the first gold disc awarded to a country music recording. Other hits were 'Chime bells' (1948), which he wrote, 'Candy kisses' (1949), and 'Quicksilver' (1950).

Broadside ballads. In the days before any extensive popular music-publishing, when the printing of music was prohibitively expensive, the main outlet for popular lyrics and, to a lesser extent, music were the cheaply printed and priced broadside ballads. The production of broadsides started some time after 1500. The first newspapers were not to appear for another hundred years or so and the broadside became a popular means of spreading news and opinion. It was a single sheet of paper printed on one side, in the earliest issues generally of folio size but later, in the 1700s, becoming of a longer and thinner shape and often referred to as a slip-ballad. The name 'broadsheet' applied to a similar item with the printing on both side. Once established the broadsides grew in size and scope and were often folded into several sheets, eventually becoming small pamphlets or booklets. Collections of broadside ballads, songs, stories, jokes, and almanacs were thus cheaply printed and became the first 'cheap-books' (later 'chapbooks'), the paperbacks of the 16th to 19th centuries. Another common name for such a collection was 'garland', a name that survived in the title of many collections of versified ballads.

Although the broadsides occasionally printed traditional 'rural' ballads, the bulk of them were of urban origin, written by the journalistic hacks of the day to cover such news as a robbery or a hanging, to moralize, or simply to offer entertainment. In their diversity they covered all the duties of the modern newspaper. The use of crude verse or doggerel was common, as this was thought to heighten the dramatic impact. The verses themselves would be based on the rhythms of various traditional airs that were in common circulation, sometimes credited, occasionally with the melody line printed. This gave the verses shape and substance and helped to make them memorable. A widely known tune like 'Greensleeves' was frequently used in this way; and the more popular items were employed *ad nauseam*.

An astronomical number of broadsides and broadsheets was issued, with a centre of activity in the Seven Dials district of London. During the peak period, from the time of Elizabeth to around 1700, they were printed in a distinctive 'black letter' type, with crude woodcuts added by way of illustration and attraction. If any music was printed it would generally be only a few lines. Whole tunes rarely appeared until the later broadside period, coinciding with the increased use of contemporary song on the stage, when their circulation was good publicity for the play and might guarantee some financial sponsorship.

The broadside may have done little to foster the commercial progress of popular music (in some ways it was more of a parasite on it), but it was an important fringe activity that kept folk tunes in circulation and created some awareness of the popular songs prior to the 19th century and the era of cheap music-publishing.

W. Ashton: *Modern Street Ballads* (London, n.d.). W. Ashton: *A History of Chapbooks of the 18th Century* (London, 1852). C. Hindley (ed.): *Curiosities of Street Literature* [2 vols] (London, 1871; repr. 1966). W. A. Barrett: *Fifty-Four Folk Airs to Broadside Ballads* (London, 1882). G. M. Laws: *American Balladry from British Broadsides* (Philadelphia, 1937; repr. 1957). L. Shepard: *The Broadside Ballad: a Study in Origins and Meanings* (London, 1962). C. M. Simpson: *The British Broadside Ballad and its Music* (New Brunswick, 1966). L. Shepard: *The History of Street Literature* (Newton Abbot, 1973).

Broadway Melody, The. A series of revue-styled musical films put out by MGM, the first appearing in 1929. They were a rewarding outlet for songwriter Nacio Herb *Brown and the source of many of his standard hits. The 1929 edition, starring Charles King (1899–1957) and Bessie Love (*b* 1898), score by Brown, included such stalwart items as 'Broadway melody', 'The wedding of the painted doll', 'You were meant for me', 'The boy friend', and, additionally, George M. *Cohan's 'Give my regards to Broadway'. It won an Academy Award and was the model for many Hollywood musicals of the 1930s that had backstage plots and stage performances.

The Broadway Melody of 1936 (1935) had Eleanor *Powell, Robert Taylor (1911–69), Buddy Ebsen (*b* 1908), Frances *Langford, Jack Benny, and Sid *Silvers. Brown provided 'You are my lucky star', 'I've got a feelin' you're foolin'', and 'Broadway rhythm'. *The Broadway Melody of 1938* (1937) starred Eleanor *Powell, George Murphy (1902–92), Sophie *Tucker, Judy *Garland, Buddy Ebsen, Robert Taylor, and Sid *Silvers. The Nacio Herb Brown songs were 'I'm feeling like a million', 'Yours and mine', 'Everybody sing'; and the McCarthy/*Monaco 'You made me love you' was revived. For *The Broadway Melody of 1940* (1939), Cole *Porter was called in for the songs and provided a magnificent feast including 'I've got my eyes on you', 'I concentrate on you', 'Begin the beguine', 'Between you and me', and 'Please don't monkey with Broadway'. The stars were Eleanor Powell, Fred *Astaire, and George Murphy, and the director Norman Taurog (1899–1981).

Broderick, Helen (*b* Philadelphia, 1891; *d* Beverly Hills, Calif., 25 Sept. 1959). American actress with a deadpan but biting style who made her debut in the chorus of the **Ziegfeld Follies* in 1907 and went on to star in several Broadway musicals such as *Oh, Please!* (1926); **Fifty Million Frenchmen* (1929); *The *Band Wagon* (1931); **As Thousands Cheer* (1933). She mainly appeared in vaudeville in partnership with her husband Lester Crawford; towards the end of her career she made several films including **Top Hat* (1935) and **Swing Time* (1936).

Brodszky, Nicholas (*b* Odessa, 1905; *d* London, 24 Dec. 1958). Russian-born composer. He studied music in Russia and finished his studies in Rome, Vienna, and Budapest. He mainly specialized in film music, writing his first score in Vienna for a film starring Richard *Tauber and Gitta Alpar. He went to England in the 1930s, and in 1936 was commissioned to write music for the *Cochran revue *Home and Beauty*. Many film scores followed in England and in Hollywood, sometimes written in collaboration with others like Charles *Williams.

His film scores included: *French Without Tears* (1939); *Spy For a Day* (1940); *Quiet Wedding* (1940); *Freedom Radio* (1941); *Unpublished Copy* (1942); *Tomorrow We Live* (1943); *The Demi-Paradise* (1944); *English Without Tears* (1944); *The Way to the Stars* (1945); *Carnival* (1946); *Beware of Pity* (1946); *While the Sun Shines* (1946); *A Man About the House* (1947); *The Turners of Prospect Road* (1947); *The Toast of New Orleans* (1950)—'Be my love' sung by Mario *Lanza; *Rich, Young and Pretty* (1951)—'Wonder why'; *Because You're Mine* (1952); *Small Town Girl* (1953); *Latin Lovers* (1953); *The Flame and the Flesh* (1954); *Love Me or Leave Me* (1955)—'I'll never stop loving you'; *Serenade* (1956); and *The Opposite Sex* (1956).

Brooks, Shelton (*b* Amesburg, Ontario, 4 May 1886; *d* San Fernando Valley, Calif., 6 Sept. 1975). American composer, lyric-writer, and entertainer. He went to Detroit with his family at an early age, where his interest in music was encouraged by his parents and he taught himself to play on an old harmonium. He played ragtime-style piano in Detroit cafés, then went into vaudeville where he specialized in imitations of Bert *Williams, the famous black entertainer. In 1910 he wrote 'Some of these days' which took the fancy of the up-and-coming Sophie *Tucker; she and the song rose to fame together. He also wrote material for Nora *Bayes and Al *Jolson. He appeared in various all-black shows like *Plantation Revue* (1922), toured Europe with Lew *Leslie's **Blackbirds* in 1923, and took part in that year's Royal Command Performance in London. He was also in *Dixie to Broadway* (1924) and *Ken Murray's Blackouts* (1949). He retired from the stage in the 1950s.

His other great hit was 'The Darktown strutters' ball' which appeared in 1917. He made recordings of this and his other songs which included 'Honey gal' (1909); 'You ain't talking to me' (1910); 'There'll come a time' (1911); 'Jean' (1911, *w* Benny Davis); 'All night long' (1912); 'You ain't no place but down South' (1912); 'I wonder where my easy rider's gone' (1913); 'Rufus Johnson's ragtime harmony band' (with Maurice *Abrahams, 1914); 'Walkin' the dog' (1916).

Broones, Martin (*b* New York, 10 June 1892; *d* Beverly Hills, Calif., 10 Aug. 1971). American composer. Educated in New York and at Columbia University, he started his composing career by contributing songs to *The Blue Pearl* at the Longacre Theatre in 1918; his first complete score, *Park Theatre Revue*, was written in the same year. He worked as co-producer and manager with May Tully; contributed to *The Goldfish* (1922); *Hassard Short's Ritz Revue* (1924); *The Odd Spot* (1924); and wrote the score of *Rufus Le Maire's Affairs* (1927). During 1928–32 he was with the MGM studios in Culver City, California, as organizer, and eventually chief executive, of their music department, selecting and supervising for all films. He became an associate producer and was involved in some 160 MGM productions. He was married to the actress Charlotte Greenwood (1890–1978). Returning to the theatre, he contributed to *The Alarm Clock* (1934) and wrote several London shows including *Give Me a Ring* (1933); *Gay Deceivers* (1935); *Seeing Stars* (1935); and *Swing Along* (1936).

Broonzy, 'Big Bill' [William Lee Conley] (*b* Scott, Miss., 26 June 1893; *d* Chicago, 15 Aug. 1958). American blues singer, one of the finest of the black traditional blues singers with powerful delivery and driving rhythmic sense. He grew up in Arkansas and did military service after the First World War 1919–20. He played the violin in Little Rock and worked on the railroad in Chicago in the early 1920s, returning to music in 1924, by now playing the guitar and singing. He worked with leading jazz musicians and started to make many recordings as 'Big Bill'. In the 1930s he played in Chicago, but went through many periods of enforced non-musical activity. He was helped by John *Hammond in the 1930s but really only became widely recognized in the jazz and folk revival of the late 1940s, when he became an international figure after touring Europe in 1951, 1955, and 1957. In later years he recorded a number of LPs that showed his talents undiminished.

B. Broonzy & Y. Bruynoghe: *Big Bill Blues* (London, 1955; New York, 1964).

Brown, Georgia [Klot, Lillie] (*b* London, 21 Oct. 1933; *d* London, 5 July 1992). British actress and singer. She made her first appearance on the stage at the Royal Court Theatre in London as Lucy in *The *Threepenny Opera* in 1956, playing the part in New York in 1957, and became well-known as Nancy in Lionel *Bart's **Oliver!* (1960), leaving the London production to play the part in America in 1962. As well as taking over the part of Maggie in **Maggie May* (1971), she pursued a career in cabaret and variety in Britain and the USA and as a jazz singer.

Brown, James (*b* Barnwell, SC, 3 May 1928). American gospel/soul singer. He formed a group called the Famous Flames and in 1956 had a hit with the song 'Please, please, please'; followed up by 'Try me', 'Prisoner of love', 'It's a man's man's man's world', 'Out of sight', and 'Papa's got a brand new bag'. He formed the James Brown Revue to produce stage shows. His songs became increasingly militant in tone—'Black is beautiful', 'Say it loud, I'm black and I'm proud'; and he boldly proclaimed the fascinations of sex—'Hot pants', 'Body heat', and 'Sex machine'. Hailed at his peak by such titles as 'Soul Brother Number One', 'Godfather of Soul', and 'King of Soul', he has been a very influential figure in black pop music, a leader in the *funk world, advanced enough to influence jazz musicians as well; and otherwise admired for his independence and his political convictions. At the time of Martin Luther King's murder, he became a new figurehead of the black movement. When he was imprisoned for six years on a drugs charge in 1988, this naturally aroused a great storm of protest and a vehement 'Free James Brown' campaign.

J. Brown & B. Tucker: *James Brown: the Godfather of Soul* (New York, 1987).

Brown Les [Lester Raymond] (*b* Reinertown, Pa., 14 Mar. 1912). American bandleader, arranger, and saxophonist/clarinettist. As a student at Duke University, 1932–5, he led the Duke Blue Devils Band, which continued its activities until 1937. He went to New York to work as an arranger for Isham *Jones, Jimmy *Dorsey, Red *Nichols, and Larry *Clinton. In 1938 he formed his own big band to play at the Hotel Edison in New York, started to record for Bluebird, and made frequent broadcasts. He had a hit with 'Joltin' Joe DiMaggio' in 1941 and his top success with 'Sentimental journey' in 1944.

The band had a clean, popular sound which he modernized in the late 1940s, using the arrangements of Frank Comstock. Billed in 1947 as Les Brown and his Band of Renown, he began an association with Bob *Hope that lasted into the 1970s, working on the Hope TV show, based in California. In 1948 he had a hit with 'I've got my love to keep me warm' arranged by Skip Martin. The band became an American institution with its well-known theme 'Leap frog'. Brown himself wrote such items as 'Dance of the Blue Devils', 'Duckfoot waddle', 'My number one dream came true', 'We wish you the merriest', and the hit 'Sentimental journey' (1944).

Brown, Lew [Brownstein, Louis] (*b* Odessa, 10 Dec. 1893; *d* New York, 5 Feb. 1958). American lyricist, producer, and publisher. He was taken to America at the age of five and settled in New York. While working as a lifeguard at Rockaway Beach, he began writing parodies of popular songs and finally got into the songwriting business. His first success was with a lyric for Albert *Von Tilzer's 'I'm the lonesomest gal in town' (1912). In 1922 he formed a partnership with the composer Ray *Henderson and, when they were joined by Buddy *DeSylva in 1925, a long association was formed and they went into the publishing business together. The business was sold at the end of the 1930s and Brown went to Hollywood to write for films. Later he returned to publishing in New York and continued his career as a songwriter.

He wrote the book and/or lyrics for *Linger Longer, Letty* (1919); **Greenwich Village Follies* (1922); **Hold Everything* (1928); **George White's Scandals* (1928 and 1931); **Follow Thru* (1929); *Flying High* (1930); *Strike Me Pink* (1933). His scripts for films included: *Sunny Side Up* (1929); *Tarnished Angels* (1933); *Carolina* (1934); *Stand Up and Cheer* (1934); *The Music Goes Round and Round* (1936); *Vogues* (1938). Other than with Ray Henderson, he wrote lyrics for Harry *Akst, Louis *Alter, Harold *Arlen, Sidney Clare, Con *Conrad, Sammy *Fain, Cliff *Friend, Jay *Gorney, Charles *Tobias, and Harry *Warren; and his song-hits included: 'I may be gone a long, long time', 'It all depends on you', 'Dapper Dan', 'Give me the moonlight, give me the girl', 'My sin', 'That old feeling', 'Beer barrel polka', 'Life is just a bowl of cherries', 'The birth of the blues', 'Sonny boy', 'Oh, by jingo', 'The thrill is gone', and 'Let's call it a day'.

Brown, Nacio Herb (*b* Deming, New Mexico, 22 Feb. 1896; *d* Beverly Hills, Calif., 28 Sept. 1964). American composer. At the age of eight he moved with his family to Los Angeles. After school he worked for a time as a vaudeville pianist but then went into merchant tailoring and, in 1920, the booming real estate business. Writing songs in his spare time, he came up with such things as 'Coral sea' (1920) and 'When Buddha smiles' (1921). He looked on songwriting as a sideline until 1928 when he was asked to write the score for MGM's first musical picture *The Broadway Melody*, for which he composed the hits 'The wedding of the painted doll' and 'You were meant for me'. He went to New York and wrote for various revues but was soon back with MGM, producing and writing, usually collaborating with Arthur *Freed; and he continued to write film hits until the 1950s, proving to be one of the important composers for films of those early years, also working with Buddy *De Sylva, Gus *Kahn, and Leo Robin, among many. His only Broadway show was **Take a Chance* in 1932.

His film scores included: *The Broadway Melody* (1929); *Marianne* (1929)—'Blondy'; *Hollywood Revue* (1929)—'Singin' in the rain' (*w* Freed), later used in *Little Nelly Kelly* (1940) and Gene *Kelly's *Singin' in the Rain* (1952); *Untamed* (1929)—'Chant of the jungle'; *The Pagan* (1929)—'Pagan love song'; *Lord Byron of Broadway* (1930); *Montana Moon* (1930)—'The moon is low'; *Whoopee* (1930); *A Woman Commands* (1932); *The Barbarian* (1933); *Going Hollywood* (1933)—'After sundown', 'Temptation', 'We'll make hay while the sun shines'; *Hold Your Man* (1933); *Peg o' my Heart* (1933); *Riptide* (1933); *Stage Mother* (1933); *Take a Chance* (1934); *Sadie McKee* (1934)—'All I do is dream of you'; *Hollywood Party* (1934); *Student Tour* (1934)—'From now on'; *Hideout* (1934); *The Broadway Melody of 1936* (1935)—'You are my lucky star', 'I've got a feelin' you're foolin'', 'Broadway rhythm'; *A Night at the Opera* (1935)—'Alone'; *China Seas* (1935); *The Devil is a Sissy* (1936); *San Francisco* (1936); *After the Thin Man* (1936); *Broadway Melody of 1938* (1937)—'Yours and mine', 'I'm feeling like a million', 'Everybody sing'; *Thoroughbreds Don't Cry* (1937); **Babes in Arms* (1939)—'Good morning'; *Two Girls on Broadway* (1940); *Ziegfeld Girl* (1941)—'You stepped out of a dream'; *Wintertime* (1943); *Greenwich Village* (1944); *On an Island With You* (1948); *The Kissing Bandit* (1948)—'Love is where you find it'; and **Singin' in the Rain* (1952)—'Make 'em laugh'.

Brown, Roy James (*b* New Orleans, 10 Sept. 1925; *d* Pacoima, Calif., 25 May 1981). American singer and composer. He began singing in gospel groups as a child and learned the piano at home. Moving to Los Angeles in 1942, he worked for a while as a boxer, then gradually became known as a blues singer. His first recording session in New Orleans in 1947 produced a lasting hit with his own 'Good rockin' tonight' which later became a rock and roll standard when Elvis *Presley recorded it in 1954. This was followed by 'Hard luck blues' (1950), 'Boogie at midnight', and 'Love don't love nobody'. He faded from the scene in the 1950s as the new rock singers took over but his warm, driving rhythm 'n' blues style was a lasting influence on people like Joe *Turner and *Little Richard. 'Let the four winds blow' (1957) was a late success, but he left the music business for many years until the end of the 1960s when he re-emerged to tour with Johnny *Otis, and had a new hit with 'Love for sale'. He visited Britain in 1978.

Brown, Ruth [*née* Weston] (*b* Portsmouth, Va., 30 Jan. 1928). American singer. She was the daughter of a Methodist preacher who installed her in his choir and forbade any contact with jazz and blues. She left home in her mid-teens and was singing in Norfolk, Va., when she met her husband, trumpet player Jimmy Brown. She began to tour more extensively and in Detroit was hired by Lucky *Millinder but fired after a few weeks. She then worked with Blanche Calloway and was heard and signed up by Ahmet Ertegun of Atlantic Records. At first she recorded blues ballads in the fashion of Dinah *Washington and Billie *Holiday but decided she had not the right approach for jazz singing. After one minor rhythm 'n' blues hit it became increasingly clear that this was her forte; a decision that was to make her the most popular female R & B singer of the 1950s.

She recorded a string of hits with Atlantic from 1949 to 1961, earning herself the title of 'Miss Rhythm', her warm and very personal tone with its falsetto touches bringing her material from the best writers, beginning with 'Teardrops from my eyes (1950) by Rudolph Toombs and also his '5-10-15 hours' (1952) and 'Daddy daddy' (1952). At this time she was the only female singer among the top ten R & B performers. She moved into the mambo field which was then all the rage with 'Mama, he treats your daughter mean' which was Atlantic's best-selling record of the year. She made her TV debut in 1955 on the Steve Allen show, had two No. 1 hits with 'Mambo baby' and 'What a dream', and the same year received a gold disc for a total of 5,000,000 record sales. As rock and roll took over she gradually lost her top position but made occasional chart appearances, the last in 1960 with 'Don't deceive me' by Chuck Willis. Her classic R & B recordings remain among the best in this genre.

Brown, Teddy [Himmebrand, Abraham] (*b* 1900; *d* Birmingham, 12 Apr. 1946). American xylophonist, saxophonist, and drummer. He first played with the New York Philharmonic Orchestra but then moved into the dance-band world. He went to London in 1926 to lead his own orchestra at the Café de Paris; and was at the Kit Kat Club, the Silver Slipper, and the Café de Paris in 1927. In 1928 he went to Paris for a while but was back in London in 1929 to play at Circo's Club and back at the Kit Kat again in 1931. From 1931 his virtuoso xylophone playing (coupled with his vast girth) made him a popular radio and variety act, and he appeared in the Royal Variety Performance of that year. He continued a busy career on stage and in films until 1946 when he died while on tour with the *Road to Laughter* show.

Browne, Jackson (*b* Heidelberg, Germany, 9 Oct. 1948). American folk-rock singer, guitarist, and composer. He was taken to California as a child, where he sang in *hootenannies, then joined the *Nitty Gritty Dirt Band. He starred in a popular chat show with Linda *Ronstadt in Hollywood. In 1971 he joined with David Lindley to produce the hit 'Doctor, my eyes'; continuing with 'Jamaica' and 'Say you will'. His LPs were regular best-sellers. He is a dedicated campaigner for nuclear disarmament, on behalf of which he financed the film *Nukes* in 1979 and served a brief jail sentence in 1981.

Bruant, Aristide (*b* Courtenay, Loiret, 1851; *d* Courtenay, 1925). French composer and singer. Having to leave school early through family misfortunes, he worked at various jobs, served in the Franco-Prussian war (1870–1), then worked on the railway. Among his first songs to become known was 'Les gens de Courtenay' (1873). He began to make appearances in cabarets such as the *Chat Noir and *café-concerts singing his satirical and humorous songs like 'L'enterrement de belle-maman' and 'Mad'moiselle écoutez-moi donc' (1881) which were mostly written in collaboration with Jules Jouy. During his army service he had written 'Marche du 113e de ligne' which was a great success at the Chat Noir when introduced by Jules Jouy and Marcel-Legay in 1883. He opened his own cabaret, La Mirliton, in 1885 where he purveyed his radical and satirical songs until he retired to Courtenay in 1924, becoming a pivotal figure in the Parisian cabaret world; he was frequently portrayed by artists like Toulouse-Lautrec. His songs have in them all the vigour of Parisian life—'A Saint-Lazare', 'A la chapelle'; some folky—'La route de Louviers'; many political—'Les canuts', 'Le peuple', 'Sur la route', 'L'impôt sur la rente'; and many deeply poetical—'Dans la rue', 'Rose blanche', so that he was acclaimed the new Villon.

Brubeck, Dave [David Warren] (*b* Concord, Calif., 6 Dec. 1920). American pianist and composer. He played jazz piano as a boy before studying with Milhaud and Schoenberg and was in an army band in Europe during the Second World War. He organized his famous jazz quartet in 1951, playing avant-garde music that had classical contrapuntal elements mingling with modern jazz styling, creating fugal improvisations with his alto-sax playing partner Paul *Desmond; the music was always tasteful but exciting and captured the attention of a wide public. The Dave Brubeck Quartet became one of the leading jazz groups of the 1950s. Desmond left the group on and off during the 1960s when Brubeck worked with other soloists such as Gerry *Mulligan and Bill Smith. He kept up a very active schedule of concerts, recordings, lecturing, and composing, producing an oratorio *Truth Has Fallen* in 1971. In the 1970s he moved towards the rock field, working with his three rock-musician sons, Darius, Chris, and Danny.

Bruce, Carol (*b* Great Neck, NY, 15 Nov. 1919). American singer. She started a singing career in Canada, returning to New York to join *George White's Scandals of* 1939; followed by an impressive performance in **Louisiana Purchase* (1940). She appeared in the films *This Woman is Mine* (1941); *Keep 'Em Flying* (1941); *Behind the Eight Ball* (1942); in various radio shows; and in *New Priorities of 1943*. She was in the successful revival of **Show Boat* in 1946; *Along Fifth Avenue* (1949); **Pal Joey* (1961 revival); **Do I Hear a Waltz?* (1965); and *Henry, Sweet Henry* (1967).

Bryan, Dora [Broadbent, Dora] (*b* Southport, Lancs., 7 Feb. 1924). British actress and singer. She made her first stage appearance in pantomime in Manchester in 1935, her first London appearance in 1947. Keeping her Lancashire accent and a wide-eyed look, she had a notable early career in the 1950s intimate revue revival in *The *Lyric Revue* (1951); *The Globe Revue* (1952); *At the Lyric* (1954); *Going to Town* (1954). She appeared in *The Water Gipsies* (1955); *Living for Pleasure* (1958); **Gentlemen Prefer Blondes* (1962); and had a notable success in **Hello, Dolly!* when she took over the London lead in 1966. She started a career in films in 1948 in *The Fallen Idol.*

Bryant, Boudleaux (*b* Shellman, Ga., 13 Feb. 1920; *d* Gatlinburg, Tenn., 30 June 1987) and **Felice** [*née* Scaduto] (*b* Milwaukee, Wis., 7 Aug. 1925). American songwriting duo (married 1945) who wrote many of the *Everly Brothers' hits of the 1950s. Boudleaux earned a living as a violinist and started writing songs, with his wife Felice, in 1948. Their first hit was with 'Country boy', originally recorded by the hillbilly singer Little Jimmy Dickens (*b* 1925). They continued with such country hits as 'It's a lovely, lovely world' (1952), 'Our honeymoon' (1952), 'Just wait till I get you alone' (1953), and 'This orchid means goodbye' (1953). 'Have a good time' (1953) was recorded by Tony *Bennett, 'Hey Joe!' (1953) by Frankie *Laine, and 'Willie can' (1954) by Alma Cogan in England.

The Bryants settled in *Nashville in 1950 and in 1957 and there met the Everly Brothers for whom they wrote the best-selling 'Bye bye love' (1957); to be followed, by demand, with 'Wake up, little Susie' (1957), 'Problems' (1958), 'Bird dog' (1958), 'All I have to do is dream' (1958), and 'Poor Jenny' (1959), all of which reached the magical million. They also wrote 'Raining in my heart' (1958) for Buddy *Holly; Blue boy' (1958) for Jim *Reeves; 'Let's think about living' (1960) for Bob Luman; 'Baltimore' (1961) for Sonny James; and, in the 1970s, 'We could' for Charlie *Pride and 'Raining in my heart' for Leo *Sayer; and they were still producing good songs into the 1980s. They issued their own LP, *Surfin' on a New Wave* (1980), while working with their own publishing house and running a motel in Gatlinburg.

Bryant, Willie [William Stevens] (*b* New Orleans, 30 Aug. 1908). American bandleader. He organized an influential swing band 1933–9 and 1946–8 which had in its ranks, at times, such musicians as Benny *Carter, Cozy *Cole, Ben *Webster, and Teddy *Wilson. Bryant sang with the band and wrote its theme song 'It's over because we're through'. In later years he pursued a career as a disc jockey and as a master of ceremonies, notably at the *Apollo Theatre in Harlem.

Brymn, James Tim (*b* Kinston, NC, 5 Oct. 1881; *d* New York, 3 Oct. 1946). American bandleader and composer. He studied music in New York and became well-known as a bandmaster during the First World War, leading the 75-piece 350th Field Artillery Band which, after the war, became known as the Black Devils and toured under that name. Before the war he had written a number of popular songs, working mostly with Richard C. McPherson (1883–1944), another black songwriter who also worked under the name of Cecil Mack, including 'Nobody sees us but the man in the moon' (1900); 'Good-morning, Carrie' (1901); 'Josephine, my jo' (1901); 'Please go 'way and let me sleep' (1902)—a very popular number often attributed to Harry *Von Tilzer who published it; 'By wireless telephone' (1902); 'Those tantalizing eyes' (1902); 'I take things easy' (1903); and 'Zongo, my Congo queen' (1904). He was active in the popular music business in New York: as well as being musical director of the *Clef Club he was an early dance band organizer, supplying units in such places as Reisenweber's, the Jardin de Dance, and Ziegfeld's Roof. Later he wrote, with Chris *Smith, a dance number called 'The camel walk' (1925) which had a temporary vogue.

Brynner, Yul [Bryner, Youl] (*b* Sakhalin, 11 July 1915; *d* 10 Oct. 1985). Actor. Born of Swiss and Mongolian parents in Russia, he spent his childhood in Peking, was brought up in Paris, and went to the USA in 1941. He joined a touring theatre company in Connecticut, afterwards becoming a radio commentator with Voice of America. Returning to the theatre in 1945, he played opposite Mary *Martin in *Lute Song.* Following a musical failure in London called *Dark Eyes*, he acted and directed on CBS TV and began to appear in films. At Mary Martin's suggestion he was offered the eventual award-winning part of the King of Siam in *The *King and I* (1951), a role he was to play 4625 times in New York and London, and in the 1956 film version. After this he mainly starred in films, including *The Magnificent Seven* (1960), with one more musical role in *Home Sweet Homer* (1975).

Bubblegum. A genre of pop music aimed at the preteenage listener. The association with bubblegum came about through the rock-based jingles that were produced for the product in the USA. A similarly slanted kind of rock was put out by the Buddah record label in the 1960s, under the guidance of its manager Neil Bogart, who saw that there was a special market for a watered-down and sweetened-up product for children, producing items like 'Yummy, yummy, yummy' by the Ohio Express. In fact, the more melodic type of music that ensued attracted a much wider audience, and was approached at various points by such groups as the *Beatles—'Yellow submarine', the *Monkees, the *Jackson Five, the *Osmonds, the Wombles, the clean *Eurovision Song Contest groups, and artists like Bobby Sherman.

Buchanan, Jack (*b* Helensburgh, Scotland, 2 Apr. 1891; *d* London, 20 Oct. 1957). British singer, dancer, actor, and director. The English approximation to Fred *Astaire; a usually dapper, immaculately top-hatted and tailed figure, with an aristocratic accent and a throaty singing voice; presenting the unusual apparition of a British gentleman who could sing and dance to perfection. He appeared in several London shows from 1912 on, but first made a real impression in *Bubbly* in 1917. His popularity continued to grow in such shows as *Round the Map* (1917); *Tails Up* (1918); *Bran Pie* (1920); *A to Z* (1921)—in which he sang 'And her Mother came too'; and *Battling Butler* (1922)—'Dancing honeymoon.

He had visited the USA in a touring company of *Tonight's the Night* (1915) but made his first substantial Broadway appearance in *André Charlot's London Revue of 1924*. His starry career continued in *Toni* (1924); *Boodle* (1925); *The Charlot Revue of 1926* (NY); **Sunny* (1926); *That's a Good Girl* (1928)—'Fancy our meeting; **Wake Up and Dream* (NY, 1929); *Stand up and Sing* (1931); **Mr Whittington* (1934); *The Flying Trapeze* (1935); *This'll Make You Whistle* (1936)—'I'm, in a dancing mood', 'This'll make you whistle'; *Between the Devil* (NY, 1937)—'By myself'; *It's Time to Dance* (1943); and *Fine Feathers* (1945). He also appeared in the films *Paris* (1929); *Monte Carlo* (1930); *This'll Make You Whistle* (1936); and made a memorable appearance in partnership with Fred Astaire in the American *The *Band Wagon* (1953) in which they sang 'I guess I'll have to change my plan'. A frequent partner throughout his career was the actress Elsie *Randolph. In later years he was increasingly active as a director.

M. Marshall: *Top Hat & Tails: the Story of Jack Buchanan* (London, 1978).

Buck, Gene [Edward Eugene] (*b* Detroit, 8 Aug. 1885; *d* Great Neck, NY, 25 Feb. 1957). American lyricist, writer, and director. After starting a career as a bank messenger, he became a highly successful designer of colourful covers for sheet-music. Working at first for a printer, he was eventually commissioned to design all the covers for Remick, one of the largest New York publishers, and is said to have produced more than 5000. His sight began to fail and he had to give up this work so, inspired by his long contact with popular music, he tried his hand at writing song-lyrics. In 1911 his first efforts, 'Daddy has a sweetheart and Mother is her name' and 'Some boy' (both with music by Dave *Stamper), were both taken up by the vaudeville artist Lillian *Lorraine; both sold more than a million copies.

*Ziegfeld inserted 'Daddy has a sweetheart' into the 1912 edition of his *Follies* and this started Gene Buck's long association with these shows. He wrote songs and sketches for 20 editions of the *Follies* and also for 16 editions of Ziegfeld's *Midnight Frolics* at the Amsterdam Theatre. Among his best-known efforts were: 'Hello, Frisco, hello' (1915, *m* Louis A. *Hirsch); 'Garden of my dreams' (1918, Hirsch); 'Tulip time' (1919, Stamper); ''Neath the Southern moon' (1922, Hirsch and Stamper); and 'Lovely little melody' (1924, Stamper). He became personal assistant to Ziegfeld and helped build the *Follies* into a national institution, in between times producing his own shows—*Yours Truly* (1927); *Take the Air* (1927); and *No Foolin'* (1926), which he wrote with Rudolf *Friml and James F. *Hanley. He also worked with Raymond *Hubbell, Jerome *Kern, and Irving *Berlin. He was President of *ASCAP 1924–41.

Buck and Bubbles. American song and dance team of Ford Lee 'Buck' Washington (*b* Louisville, Ky., 16 Oct. 1903; *d* New York, 31 Jan. 1955), also a pianist and trumpeter; and **William 'Bubbles' Sublett** (*b* Louisville, 19 Feb. 1902; *d* New York, 18 May 1986), an expert tapdancer. They began their partnership as children, became known in vaudeville and were the first black act to appear at the *Radio City Music Hall. They toured Europe in 1931 and 1936 and appeared in the films *A *Star is Born* (1937) and **Cabin in the Sky* (1943). Each had his own solo achievements, Buck Washington recording with Louis *Armstrong, Bessie *Smith, Coleman *Hawkins, and Billie *Holiday; and Bubbles appearing as Sportin' Life in the first production of **Porgy and Bess*. The partnership broke up in 1953.

Buckley's Serenaders. Pioneer blackface minstrel group formed in 1853. Sometimes more fully known as Buckley's New Orleans Serenaders, they were led by George Swayne Buckley and his brothers Frederick and R. Bishop Buckley who had all previously been with the New Orleans Operatic Serenaders. It was one of the first minstrel troupes to tour the USA and it became a great rival to the Christy outfits. George Buckley was known as one of the finest minstrels, a multi-instrumentalist and singer, whose favourite number was 'The laughing song'. The troupe disbanded some time during the Civil War.

Buckner, Milt (*b* St Louis, Mo., 10 July 1915; *d* Chicago, 27 July 1977). American pianist and organist, noted for his block-chord or locked-hands style of playing (in which the left hand doubles the top note of the right, in Glenn *Miller sax style) later made popular by George *Shearing. In Detroit in the 1930s, he mainly worked as an arranger. He made his name with Lionel *Hampton 1941–8 as pianist and main arranger, responsible for such standards as 'Flying home' and 'Hamp's boogie woogie'. He led his own bands from 1948, was with Hampton again 1950–2, and was active until the 1970s.

Bullock, Chick [Charles] (*b* Butte, Mont., 16 Sept. 1908; *d* California, 15 Sept. 1981). Little seems to be known about this prolific recording artist who sang with numerous bands 1930–42 making more than 500 titles with such people as Bunny *Berigan, Duke *Ellington, Dick McDonough, Miff *Mole, Russ *Morgan, Ben *Pollack, Adrian *Rollini, Nathaniel Shilkret, Fred *Waring, and many others; as well as under his own leadership. He avoided all personal publicity and often recorded under other names, also being heard on radio. He had a distinctive, husky voice and a swinging style. In the mid-1940s he moved to the West Coast and went into real estate, emerging once in the 1950s for a radio 'Tribute to Bunny Berigan'.

Bunn, Teddy [Theodore Leroy] (*b* Freeport, NY, 1909; *d* Lancaster, Calif., 20 July 1978). American jazz and blues guitarist and vocalist. A musician with a very distinctive and fluent style, and a fine blues player, he made his first recordings with Spencer *Williams and with Duke *Ellington in 1929. He was with the Washboard Serenaders in the early 1930s and then became known for his work with the Spirits of Rhythm who worked at many famous clubs in New York and Chicago and recorded frequently. He left them in 1937 to work with John *Kirby, rejoining in 1939. The group formed and re-formed several times in the 1940s, Bunn meantime freelancing and leading small groups. Whenever he recorded he made a notable contribution, as with the Mezzrow–Ladnier sides in 1938. He played less often in the 1960s because of illness, and retired from jazz in the 1970s.

Burdon, Eric (*b* Newcastle upon Tyne, 11 May 1941). British singer, bandleader, and composer. He became interested in rock as a boy and was inspired to start singing by hearing recordings of Fats *Domino and Bill Doggett. He studied commercial art and then, in 1960, turned a hobby into his profession and formed a group, the *Animals. They were well-known by 1963, had achieved a No. 1 hit by 1964, and, after a visit to the USA, disbanded in 1966. Burdon moved to Los Angeles, taking time off to work on writing and musical projects and, it was rumoured, to sort out drug problems. In 1969 he was persuaded to form a *funk band which he called War, a mainly black group, and had a hit with 'Spill the wine' in 1970. He worked with Jimmy *Witherspoon in the early 1970s and returned to the English rock scene in 1973, having an up-and-down period in the 1970s, engrossed in personal problems, until the original Animals temporarily re-formed in 1983.

Burke, Joe [Joseph A.] (*b* Philadelphia, 18 Mar. 1884; *d* Upper Darby, Pa., 9 June 1950). American composer. He began his career as an arranger for a Philadelphia music-publisher and achieved a hit with his first song, 'Down Honolulu way', in 1916. He wrote his first Hollywood score in 1929 for *Gold Diggers of Broadway* which contained the Edwardian-flavoured 'Tip-toe through the tulips'. Most of his successful songs were written with one of three lyricists, Benny Davis, Al *Dubin (mainly on film work), or Edgar *Leslie. With Dubin he wrote 'Dancing with tears in my eyes' for a 1930 film. It was rejected, but sold well when it was eventually published separately. He returned to New York, and during the mid-1930s wrote such hits as 'It looks like rain in Cherry Blossom Lane'. He wrote less in the 1940s but produced his last number, 'Rambling rose', in 1948.

His film scores included: **Gold Diggers of Broadway* (1929)—'Tip-toe through the tulips', 'Painting the clouds with sunshine'; *In the Headlines* (1929)—'Love will find a way'; **Sally* (1929); *Dancing Sweeties* (1930); *She Couldn't Say No* (1930); *Hold Everything* (1930); *Top Speed* (1930); *Big Boy* (1930)—'What would I do without you'; *Blessed Event* (1932); *The Crooner* (1932). Other songs included: 'Oh, how I miss you tonight' (1924, *w* Davis and Fisher); 'Carolina moon' (1928, Davis); 'Pagan moon' (1931, Dubin and Bryan); 'If you should ever need me' (1931, Dubin); 'On Treasure Island' (1935, Leslie); 'A little bit independent' (1935, Leslie); 'In a little gypsy tea room' (1935, Leslie); 'Moon over Miami' (1936, Leslie); 'Diana' (1944, Dubin).

Burke, Johnny (*b* Antioch, Calif., 3 Oct. 1908; *d* New York, 25 Feb. 1964). American lyric-writer, author, and publisher. He worked with publishers in Chicago and New York, then became a staff composer in Hollywood. For the theatre he wrote the book of *Nelly Bly* (1946) and *Donnybrook* (1961). Film work included *Pennies from Heaven* (1936) from which came 'Pennies from heaven' and 'One, two, buckle my shoe'. Other songs were: 'On the sentimental side' (1938), 'My heart is taking lessons' (1938), 'I've got a pocketful of dreams (1938), 'Sing a song of sunbeams' (1939), all with music by James V. *Monaco; 'Scatterbrain' (1939); 'Polka dots and moonbeams' (1940), 'Moonlight becomes you' (1942), 'Sunday, Monday, or always' (1943), and 'Swinging on a star' (1944), all with music by Jimmy *Van Heusen.

Burkhard, Paul (*b* Zurich, 21 Dec. 1911; *d* Zell, Tüsstal, nr. Zurich, 6 Sept. 1977). Swiss composer. Educated in Zurich, he studied at the Conservatory there, and became repetiteur at the State Theatre, Berne, in 1932 and musical director 1933–5. He wrote light music and songs, and had his first operetta, *Hopsa*, commissioned by the Zurich State Theatre in 1935. A series of tuneful operettas in Viennese vein followed, the most successful being *Der schwarze Hecht* (1939), although its full success did not come until it was revived in Munich in 1950, as *Feuerwerk*, and later, in English, as *Oh! my Papa*. He wrote many of his own librettos. In 1938–45 he was musical director of the Zurich Opera, from 1942 musical director of Swiss Radio, and conductor of the Studio Orchestra of Landessender Beromünster 1945–57. Other operettas included: *Dreimal Georges* (1936); *Paradies der Frauen* (1938); *Tic-Tac* (1944); *Casanova in der Schweiz* (1944); *Die kleine Niederdorfoper* (1952); *Spiegel, das Kätzchen der Brille* (1962); *Bunbury* (1965). The song 'O, mein papa' (from the similarly named operetta), became very popular in 1953, with English words by Geoffrey Parsons and John Turner, and was made into a recorded hit by trumpeter Eddie *Calvert.

Burlesque. Between the heyday of the *ballad opera and the beginnings of *operetta, most European countries and the USA enjoyed a musical entertainment known as 'burlesque', in which a satirical text was interspersed with songs and other musical items; a tentative step towards the true operetta. Burlesque, as the name suggests, was a parody or skit on serious opera (with a special love of ridiculing the Italian conventions) or on drama (in its non-musical form). Its spirit clearly lived on in the works of *Offenbach and *Gilbert and Sullivan.

The flourishing period for burlesque was most of the 19th century up until the 1890s. One of the first important authors of burlesque was J. R. Planché (1796–1880), his first being *Olympic Revels* produced at Drury Lane in 1818 by Madame Vestris. The great years of burlesque centred on the impresario John Hollingshead (1827–1904), whose *Gaiety burlesques such as *Aladdin* and *Carmen-up-to-date*, to his last, *Jack Sheppard*, in 1886, made stars of such actors as J. L. Toole (1830–1906), Edward Terry (1844–1912), Nellie Farren (1845–1904), Fred *Leslie, Arthur *Roberts, Letty Lind (1862–1923), E. J. Lonnen (1860–1901), Phyllis Broughton (1862–1926), and Willie Warde (1857–1943). The music continued the ballad opera tradition in a Victorian style, being mainly arranged from various sources; but gradually composers such as Meyer *Lutz began to contribute original scores. With George *Edwardes's later Gaiety productions, such as *Monte Cristo*, *Miss Esmeralda* (a skit on Hugo's *Notre Dame*), and *Ruy Blas and the Blasé Roué*, burlesque moved ever nearer to the *musical comedy that was to succeed it. Other prominent authors who specialized in burlesque were Francis Cowley Burnand (1838–1917) and W. S. *Gilbert, who learned his skill as a librettist in this field. The general style of entertainment that burlesque featured was siphoned off into the 'spectacular' *revue field from the early 1900s.

The American burlesque tradition was equally strong, flourishing in straight dramatic form, as it did in Britain in the 18th century, with some of the Gaiety burlesque shows imported and the native versions copied from these: e.g. *Pocahontas* (1855) which, with borrowed music, burlesqued the Red Indian stage story tradition, and *Evangeline* (1874). The tradition was carried on in the *Weber & Fields shows of the 1890s and after. These were generally made up of a short musical comedy in one half and a burlesque of a current Broadway success in the other. The definition of 'burlesque' in its theatrical application has never been entirely clear-cut, as reference books tend to admit by default. In some ways, much of operetta and its successors is a burlesque of the grand opera style; so that there was never, anywhere, a clear line of demarcation between what was a comic imitation and what was meant to be burlesque with an intended satirical edge. The confusion was either cleared or furthered in the USA by burlesque's becoming something entirely different; whereas in England it simply disappeared as a theatrical term. Following in the tradition of *The *Black Crook*, burlesque (or 'burley-cue', as the Americans called it) came to mean a sort of variety show or spectacular revue, with lightly clad ladies an obligatory feature. The momentum towards this genre was given by Lydia Thompson (1836–1908) and a troupe known as her 'British Blondes' who arrived in New York in 1868 and burlesqued their way through whole shows such as *Ixion* and *The Forty Thieves*, with ladies playing the male roles as well as their own and their satire much softened by female allure. By the date of Miss Thompson's last product, *The Crust of Society* in 1894, several other developments had confusingly entwined the burlesque tradition with the purely comical tradition; such as the end of the true *minstrel show and the growing sophistication of *vaudeville in the hands of such as Tony *Pastor; so that the whole field of such miscellaneous entertainment became generally referred to as burlesque, long after the true burlesquing element had gone. What was now considered as typifying burlesque were the shows at Minksy's and the art of Gypsy Rose Lee (1913–70), a mixture of striptease and low comedy such as pervaded the remaining music-hall theatres of London, where no one thought of calling it burlesque. The police moved in on the American burlesque theatres in the 1930s and closed many venues, a gloriously confused scene recalled in the Broadway musical **Sugar Babies* in 1979.

W. D. Adams: *A Book of Burlesque* (London, 1891). B. Sobell: *Burleycue: an Underground History of Burlesque Days* (New York, 1931). V. C. Clinton-Baddeley: *The Burlesque Tradition in the English Theatre after 1660* (London, 1952). B. Sobell: *A Pictorial History of Burlesque* (New York, 1956). I. Zeidman: *The American Burlesque Show* (New York, 1967). A. Corie & J. DiMona: *This was Burlesque* (New York, 1968).

Chapters in: W. R. Titterton: *From Theatre to Music Hall* (London, 1912). E. Short & A. Compton-Rickett: *Ring Up the Curtain* (London, 1938). E. Short: *Fifty Years of Vaudeville* (London, 1946). W. Macqueen-Pope: *Nights of Gladness* (London, 1956).

Burnette, Johnny (*b* Memphis, Tenn., 25 Mar. 1934; *d* 1 Aug. 1964). American singer, guitarist, and composer. He formed a rock-and-roll trio called the Texans in Memphis in 1956 and gained some local renown. On a visit to New York he won an amateur talent contest and this led to a contract with Coral records, but the releases failed to make their hoped-for mark. He decided to embark on a solo career as a country singer, coming to the fore when he joined Liberty records in 1960 and achieved a series of hits: 'Dreamin'' (1960); 'You're sixteen' (1960); 'Little boy sad' (1961); and 'God, country and my baby' (1961). He enjoyed two years as a teenage idol but by 1963 his career was on the slide. Burnette was typical of the *Presley-inspired rock-and-roll singers, and suffered from being too much like the star. In retrospect, the rejected Coral records are now looked upon as classics of country rock—noisy, aggressive, and with an urgent guitar style. Around 1957 he also wrote songs, with his brother Dorsey (1932–79), for such singers as Ricky *Nelson—'Waitin' in school' (1957); 'Believe what you say' (1958); and 'Just a little too much' (1959)—and Roy *Brown. He died in a boating accident on a fishing holiday, never having realized his full potential.

Burns, David (*b* New York, 22 June 1902; *d* Philadelphia, 12 Mar. 1971). American actor who generally played the less popular roles in Broadway musicals, the fall guy, ranging from the incompetent, like Ali Hakim in *Oklahoma! (1943), to the pompous, like Horace Vandergelder in *Hello, Dolly! (1964), one of his most effective roles. He usually found a way to make his mark in such shows (including several in London in the 1930s) as *Face the Music (1932); *Nymph Errant (1933); Laughter Over London (1936); Big Business (1937); Hide and Seek (1937); Bobby Get Your Gun (1938); *Pal Joey (1941); *Make Mine Manhattan (1948); *South Pacific (1951); Two's Company (1952); The *Music Man (1957); *Do Re Mi (1960); and A *Funny Thing Happened on the Way to the Forum (1962).

Burrows, Abe [Borowitz, Abram Solman] (*b* New York, 18 Dec. 1910; *d* New York, 19 May 1985). American librettist and director. He intended to be a doctor but became an accountant instead, switching to being a salesman before he started appearing on the stage in humorous roles. He began writing for radio in 1938, working for *Duffy's Tavern* and other top programmes. He worked in Hollywood for a time writing smart revue-type songs with titles like 'I looked under a rock and I found you'. He recorded two albums of these and published the *Abe Burrows Song Book*. Later he collaborated on various Broadway musicals such as *Guys and Dolls* (1950); *Make a Wish* (1951); *Three Wishes for Jaimie* (1952); *Can-Can* (1953); *Silk Stockings* (1955); *Say Darling* (1958); and won a Pulitzer Prize for *How to Succeed in Business Without Really Trying* (1964). He directed many of the above as well as *Two on the Aisle* (1951); *Happy Hunting* (1956); and *What Makes Sammy Run?* (1964). He was active as 'doctor' (re-writer) on many Broadway shows, especially musicals.

A. Burrows: *Honest Abe* (Boston, 1980).

Bush, Kate [Catherine] (*b* Plumstead, Surrey, 30 July 1958). British singer and composer. She achieved an early recording contract with EMI, and produced a No. 1 hit with her first record, 'Wuthering Heights' (1978), an ingenious three-minute reduction of Emily Brontë's novel. Her highly individual style was affirmed in the album *The Kick Inside* (1978), and in the singles 'Man with the child in his eyes' and 'Wow' (1979). Her on-stage work has also been highly professional and exciting, in contrast to a quiet personal image. She tackled difficult material in her album *The Dreaming* (1982); and has continued in a worthily experimental vein, occasionally working with Peter Gabriel (*b* 1950). She contributed songs to the films *Castaway* (1987) and *She's Having a Baby* (1988).

F. & J. Vermorel: *Kate Bush* (London, 1980). K. Bush: *Leaving my Tracks* (London, 1982).

Busse, Henry (*b* Magdeburg, Germany, 19 May 1894; *d* Memphis, Tenn., 23 Apr. 1955). Trumpeter, bandleader, and composer. He went to the USA in 1912. In 1918–28 he was trumpet soloist in Paul *Whiteman's orchestra, where his distinctive tone and muted work on numbers like 'Wang wang blues' (1920) and 'Hot lips' (1922), both of which he wrote, 'When day is done' (1927), and 'Haunting blues' made him widely popular. He formed his own orchestra in 1930, which had a big following on radio and in films with its sweet but swinging shuffle rhythm arrangements, and had a big hit with 'Have you forgotten' in 1931. Ideal for dancing, the band attracted attention during its important engagement at the Chez Paree in Chicago in the mid-1930s, then toured the USA and Europe, and had a further hit with 'Stomping room only' (1941). He continued leading the band until he died just before an appearance at the Peabody Hotel in Memphis.

Butterfield, Billy [Charles William] (*b* Middleton, Ohio, 14 Jan. 1917; *d* Fort Lauderdale, Fla., 18 Mar. 1988). American jazz trumpeter. He first came to attention with the Bob *Crosby orchestra, 1937–40, through his impeccable full-toned playing. He was with Artie *Shaw in 1940, Benny *Goodman in 1941, and Les *Brown in 1942. He led his own band 1945–7, but found it less demanding to work as a freelance in the 1950s. He was heard to good effect backing Louis *Armstrong in his recording of 'Blueberry Hill'. In the 1960s he was part of the World's Greatest Jazz Band, a group of veteran players (several from the old Bob Crosby band), which he left in 1972. He worked with Flip Phillips in the 1970s and was in the revived Gramercy Five with Johnny *Guarnieri in 1974.

Butterworth, Arthur (*b* Manchester, 4 Aug. 1923). British composer, trumpet player, and conductor. He was a member of the *Besses o' th' Barn band 1939–42. After the war, in 1949, he joined the Scottish National Orchestra; he was with the Hallé Orchestra 1955–61; then devoted his time to composing and conducting with the Huddersfield Philharmonic. He has added some valuable works to the brass band repertoire including: 'A Dales Suite', 'Three Impressions for Brass', 'Heroic Overture', 'Blenheim'; and has also written many pieces for light orchestra.

Buzz-Buzz. Successful London revue which had 612 performances at the Vaudeville Theatre from 20 Dec. 1918. It showcased many rising talents such as Nelson *Keys and Gertrude *Lawrence. The words were by Arthur *Wimperis and Ronald Jeans and the music by Herman *Darewski. The score was bright and topical, with items like 'Coupons for kisses' and 'Percy with the one pip up'. Other songs were 'Everything is buzz-buzz now', 'I've been waiting for someone like you', 'Live and let live', 'There are so many girls', and, a popular additional number, 'K-K-K-Katy' (*w* Geoffrey O'Hara).

Bye Bye, Birdie. The first musical to dwell on the world of rock and roll. Its singing idol, Conrad

Birdie, loosely based on Elvis *Presley and played by Dick Gautier, has a great effect on the lives of the middle-class teenagers of Sweet Apple, Ohio. His manager, played by Dick *Van Dyke, with Chita *Rivera as his secretary, plan a publicity stunt that shows Kim (Susan Watson) kissing Birdie on a TV show. This greatly upsets her boyfriend and causes all sorts of family problems.

The show started off the careers of composer Charles *Strouse, lyric-writer Lee *Adams, and librettist Michael Stewart and was the first musical production by Gower Champion. A bright and vivacious score included 'The telephone hour', 'Put on a happy face', 'A lot of livin' to do', 'One last kiss', 'Baby, talk to me', and 'Rosie'. Opening at the Martin Beck Theatre 14 Apr. 1960, it ran for 607 performances. In London at Her Majesty's Theatre, with Angela Baddeley, Chita Rivera, Peter Marshall, Sidney James, and Marty Wilde as the pop star, it managed 268. It was filmed in 1963 with Dick Van Dyke and Ann-Margret. There was also a less successful 1981 sequel, *Bring Back Birdie*.

Bygraves, Max [Walter] (*b* London, 16 Oct. 1922). British singer and comedian. He was influenced as a boy by seeing such performers as Max Miller (from whom he took his stage name) and Billy Bennett. Meanwhile he worked at various menial jobs, served for five years in the RAF, and got his first experience in wartime shows. In 1946 he made his first broadcast and had a worthwhile appearance at the Sheffield Empire. His first real success came with the radio show *Educating Archie*. He developed a homely, friendly, pleasantly corny personality and act, performing family songs such as 'Cowpuncher's cantata' (his first hit in 1952), 'Gilly Gilly Ossenfeffer Katzenellen Bogen by the Sea', 'Heart of my heart', and 'You need hands' (which he wrote and which won a Novello Award in 1958). His string of recorded hits carried on into the the 1970s with 'Back in my childhood days' and 'Deck of cards'. He continued in the 'Family Favourite' world of entertainment with undiminished success and many big-selling 'Singalong' albums, with Cyril Stapleton (1914–74), has appeared in a number of films, and in 18 Royal Command Performances.

M. Bygraves: *I Wanna Tell You a Story* (London, 1976).

By Jupiter. A Richard *Rodgers–Lorenz *Hart musical set in the days of ancient Greece (as was the preceding *The *Boys from Syracuse*, 1938). Based on the war between the Greeks and the Amazons, it centres on the attempts of the wily Hercules to steal the strength-giving girdle of the even wilier Diana. It is love, however, that wins the day. This was the last Rodgers and Hart collaboration and their longest Broadway run (427), at the Shubert Theatre from 3 June 1942. The original cast included Ray *Bolger and Constance Moore, later replaced by Nanette Fabray (*b* 1920). The songs, not the team's most notable, included 'Nobody's heart', 'Ev'rything I got', and 'Wait till you see her' (which was taken out of the show after a month). There was an off-Broadway revival in 1967.

Byng, Douglas (*b* Nottingham, 17 Mar. 1893; *d* Brighton, 24 Aug. 1987). British actor and singer. He started out as a costume designer, but soon moved into acting, appearing in concert parties, musical comedy, and cabaret where he performed his own songs. In 1921 he appeared in his first pantomime, *Aladdin*, at the Palladium and thenceforth was a regular and highly popular Dame. From 1925 to 1930 he appeared in a series of *Cochran revues, here also playing female roles with dignified comedy. He regularly appeared at the Café de Paris and the Monseigneur with his sophisticated cabaret act. The BBC found it a little outrageous and banned him on several occasions; but forgave him enough to offer a 90th birthday tribute.

His stage shows included: *Theodore & Co* (1917); *Yes, Uncle!* (1917); *A Night Out* (1920); **On With the Dance* (1925); **Cochran's Revue of 1926* (1926); **One Dam Thing After Another* (1927); **This Year of Grace* (1928); **Wake Up and Dream!* (1929); **Cochran's 1930 Revue* (1930); *How D'You Do?* (1933); *Hi-Diddle-Diddle* (1934); *Stop—Go* (1935); *Maritza* (1938); *Strike Up the Music* (1941); *Fine and Dandy* (1942); **Flying Colours* (1943); *The Shephard Show* (1946); *Sauce Piquant* (1950); *The Bells of St Martin's* (1952); *The Love Doctor* (1959); *House of Cards* (1963).

D. Byng: *As You Were: Reminiscences* (London, 1970).

Byrd, Charlie [Charles L.] (*b* Suffolk, Va., 16 Sept. 1925). American jazz and classical guitarist. He toured with Joe Marsala 1947–9, studied guitar (with Andrés Segovia amongst others), and settled in Washington. He played with Woody *Herman 1958–9, touring Europe with the band. After a South American tour, he became keenly interested in Latin American popular music, and was to be a key figure in the *bossa nova innovations of the 1960s, recording with Stan *Getz in 1962. He generally plays an unamplified finger-style guitar.

Byrds, The. American rock group formed in 1964. It started as a trio—Jim (later Roger) McGuinn (*b* 1942) (guitar and vocal), David Crosby (*b* 1941) (guitar), Gene Clark (1944–91) (vocal)—calling itself the Jet Set, and became the Byrds with the addition of Chris Hillman (*b* 1942) (bass) and Michael Clarke (*b* 1943) (drums). Recording for Columbia Records, they made the million-selling No. 1 hit 'Mr Tambourine man' in 1965 and were hailed as America's answer to the *Beatles, thanks to the lyrical and melodic flair that this and other recordings showed. They used material written by Gene Clark and many Bob *Dylan numbers, achieving another top hit with 'Turn! Turn! Turn!' (1965). Gene Clark left the group and in 1966 there were signs that they might disband. But 1967 brought the album *Younger than Yesterday* which showed that, in Crosby and Hillman, the group had writers capable of replacing Clark. There were many inner conflicts and Crosby left in 1967. By 1968 their style had moved towards the country idiom, gradually being completely restructured as various members left, until Roger McGuinn, now leader of the group, was the only original; they disbanded in 1972. They are remembered as a pioneering group in such styles as folk rock, raga rock, and space rock; afterwards heading the country rock boom of the 1970s.

B. Scoppa: *The Byrds* (New York, 1971). J. Rogan: *Timeless Flight* (London, 1981).

Byrne, David (*b* Dumbarton, Scotland, 14 May 1952). American rock musician and composer. He studied at the Rhode Island School of Design, became lead singer and guitarist with the new-wave rock group *Talking Heads, and wrote the modern dance score 'The Catherine Wheel' (1980) for Twyla Tharp. Byrne utilizes African music in his compositions and is renowned for the strange quality of his songs.

C

Caballero, Manuel Fernández (*b* Murcia, 14 Mar. 1835; *d* Madrid, 20 Feb. 1906). Spanish composer. He studied harmony and composition at the Madrid Conservatory. He started his musical career as leader of the orchestra at the Teatro Real in Madrid, becoming musical director of the Teatro de Variedades in 1853; and subsequently conducted at the Teatro Lope de Vega, the Teatro Lírico, and the Teatro Español, for which he wrote numerous overtures and much incidental music. He toured Cuba with an operetta company and, on his return to Madrid in 1871, became increasingly occupied with composition, eventually writing about 220 *zarzuelas, many of which have remained in the repertoire. He went blind in 1893 and dictated his works thereafter to his son. He was elected a member of the Academy of Fine Arts, Madrid, in 1902.

His works included: *La Marsellesa* (1876); *El lucero del Alba* (1879); *Los aparecidos* (1892); *El dúo de la Africana* (1893); *Los dineros del sacristán* (1894); *Campañero y sacristán* (1894); *Los Africanistas* (1894); *El cabo primero* (1895); *El padrino del Nene* (1896); *La rueda de la Fortuna* (1896); *La viejecita* (1897); *Gigantes y cabezudos* (1898); *El señor Joaquín* (1898); *Los sobrinos del Capitán Grant* (1899); *El traje de luces* (1899); and *Los estudiantes* (1900).

Cabaret. A hybrid form of entertainment that combines aspects of *music-hall and *revue, adding to these popular genres an element of serious artistic and satirical intent. The setting for cabaret is usually a small stage in the intimate atmosphere of the nightclub, and it is therefore a display of the art of an individual performer or a small group. The music is often provided by a piano or a small ensemble.

Cabaret, at its best, has been an intellectual as well as an entertainment outlet, a vehicle for social and political comment and satire. It originated in Paris in the 1870s, the name deriving from the French wine cellar or tavern where entertainment was generally provided. The custom was transferred to the cafés and bistros where the *chanson thrived and developed; becoming the modern French equivalent of the British *broadside. As the entertainment expanded beyond the single singer it became known as *café-concert, a kind of French song-and-supper-room entertainment, the progenitor of the music-hall. It was the more intellectual form of café-concert and the radical chanson that diverged from music-hall to become cabaret.

Entertainment of this nature was the aim of a literary society called the Hydropathes who gathered in Paris in the 1870s. Some of its members saw the artistic (and commercial) possibilities of such gatherings and opened the Chat Noir cabaret in Montmartre in 1881, making Montmartre the cultural entertainment centre of Paris. It was a natural habitat for the talents of political satirists such as Aristide *Bruant, who opened his own cabaret, Le Mirliton, in 1885. The Chat Noir closed in 1897, its inaugural duty done, and cabaret was launched as a 20th-century form and style of entertainment.

Berlin took to the cabaret around 1900 followed by Munich, then considered the artistic centre of Germany. Vienna was another flourishing outlet. The sinister element, as portrayed in the show **Cabaret*, the *Weill–*Brecht products, and the film *The Blue Angel*, was a Germanic ingredient, an expression of the underlying political currents of the time. In the 1920s, in the cynical aftermath of war, intellectual and political cabaret thrived; in Paris its headquarters was now to be Le Bœuf sur le toit which opened in 1922; in Berlin it was the boiling pot of much that was to shatter the world later.

Cabaret, at its most effective, was the seed from which the satirical revue of the 1950s grew. On the other hand cabaret often degenerated into meaning any seedy striptease or speakeasy; or, as in London and New York, simply an intimate sort of variety show.

L. Appignanesi: *The Cabaret* (New York–London, 1975). H. B. Segel: *Turn-of-the-Century Cabaret* (New York, 1987).

Cabaret. Evocative and powerful musical play with score by John *Kander, lyrics by Fred *Ebb, and book by Joe Masteroff, based on the play *I Am a Camera* by John Van Druten and *Berlin Stories* by Christopher Isherwood. It opened at the Broadhurst Theatre, New York, on 20 Nov. 1966 and was to run for 1166 performances.

Set in a sleazy Berlin nightclub, the Kit Kat Klub, the cabaret run by the sinister MC, superbly played by Joel *Grey, is the background to the decadent prewar world of Germany and the sordid love affairs of singer Sally Bowles (Jill Haworth) and Fräulein Schneider (Lotte *Lenya). The Kander score successfully caught the tones of Kurt *Weill and Berlin cabaret of the 1930s with songs like 'Willkommen', 'Don't tell mama', 'Perfectly marvellous', 'Two ladies', 'It couldn't please me more', 'The money song', 'If you could see her', and 'Cabaret'.

It ran for 326 performances at the Palace Theatre, London, from 28 Feb. 1968 with Judi Dench and Peter Sallis; and was a success at the Theater an der Wien in Vienna in 1970. A powerful film, directed by

Bob *Fosse, emerged from it in 1972, altering the story, but still a very effective and evocative creation in which Liza *Minnelli was impressive; and with Joel Grey still as the MC. It added two songs: 'Mein Herr' and 'Maybe this time' which had been cut from *Flora the Red Menace*.

Cabin in the Sky. American musical with score by Vernon *Duke, lyrics by John *Latouche, and book by Lynn Root. It was the first major musical to be staged at the Martin Beck Theatre on 45th Street, New York, running for 156 performances, and its all-black cast included Ethel *Waters, Todd *Duncan, Dooley Wilson, Katherine Dunham, Rex Ingram, and J. Rosamond *Johnson.

The story is the old one, much favoured in American musicals and plays, of the Lord, represented by his General (Todd Duncan), in a contest with Lucifer Jr. (Rex Ingram) for possession of the soul of one Little Joe Jackson (Dooley Wilson), a hopeless layabout and gambler. The prayers of his wife Petunia (Ethel Waters) give him a six-month chance to make amends for his shiftless life and earn a ticket for heaven—which he manages in spite of the temptations offered by Georgia Brown (Katherine Dunham).

It was a cosily Uncle Tom-ish sentimental comedy which made an equally whimsical film in 1943 with Ethel Waters again in the lead, Eddie 'Rochester' *Anderson as Joe, and Lena *Horne (in her first acting role) as the temptress; with the added attractions of Louis *Armstrong, as the Devil's trumpeter, many popular black stars, and the Duke *Ellington Orchestra. It was redeemed by such fine songs as 'Taking a chance on love' (*w* Ted Fetter), which Ethel Waters made into a hit; 'Cabin in the sky'; 'Love turned out the light'; 'Honey in the honeycomb'; 'My old Virginia home'; and 'Do what you wanna do'; the film adding 'Happiness is a thing called Joe' by Harold *Arlen and E. Y. *Harburg; and Ellington playing 'Things ain't what they used to be'.

Caesar, Irving [Isidor] (*b* New York, 4 July 1895). American lyric-writer and librettist. He worked with Henry Ford during the First World War. After the war, he renewed a friendship with George *Gershwin, with whom he had been at school, and became interested in song-writing. He was organizer and first president of the Songwriters' Protective Association. He wrote for stage, screen, and radio, including the words for *Kissing Time* (1919); various **Greenwich Village Follies* (1922–5); *Mercenary Mary* (1925); **No, No, Nanette* (1925); **Hit the Deck!* (1926); *No Foolin'* (1926); *Yes, Yes, Yvette* (1927); *Here's Howe* (1928); various **Ziegfeld Follies* and **George White's Scandals* (1929–31); *Nina Rosa* (1930); *The Wonder Bar* (1931); *White Horse Inn* (1936); *Transatlantic Rhythm* (1936); and *My Dear Public* (1943).

Songs (from the above shows and elsewhere) include: 'Swanee' (1919, *m* Gershwin)—which he claims they wrote in ten minutes; 'Sixty seconds every minute' (1922, *m* Louis A. *Hirsch); 'I love her, she loves me' (with Eddie *Cantor, 1922); 'I want to be happy' (1924, *m* Vincent *Youmans); 'Tea for two' (1924, Youmans); 'Sometimes I'm happy' (1926, Youmans); 'Crazy rhythm' (1928, *m* Joseph *Meyer and Roger Wolfe); 'Just a gigolo' (1930, *m* Leonello Casucci); 'Is it true what they say about Dixie' (1936, *m* Sammy Lerner and Gerald Marks).

Café-concerts, café-chantants. The French equivalent of the English song-and-supper room, though flourishing in Paris and other cities somewhat earlier, from the 1770s. Places where the clients could enjoy a song while they partook of food and drink, they were the home and breeding-ground of the *chanson and its entertainers; and the begetters of intimate revue, *cabaret, and *music-hall.

Romi: *Petite histoire des cafés-concerts Parisiens* (Paris, 1950). F. Caradec & A. Weill: *Le café-concert* (Paris, 1980).

Cage aux Folles, La. Musical with score by Jerry *Herman (his first big hit since **Mame* in 1966) and book by Harvey Fierstein, first produced at the Palace Theatre, New York, 21 Aug. 1983. Based on the novel by Jean Poiret, it was the first musical with a homosexual theme to come to Broadway.

The story concerns the relationship between the owner of a drag-queen nightclub and his main star Albin, known on the stage as Zaza, who, in order to add a note of respectability to their set-up when there is to be a conventional marriage in the family, pretends to be the owner's wife. Apart from its homosexual setting, it was very much the big spectacular musical with a glamorous chorus line composed mainly of men in drag. The songs had titles like 'A little more mascara', 'I am what I am', and 'Masculinity'. It was produced in London (Palladium), 7 May 1986.

Cagney, James [Francis] (*b* New York, 17 July 1899; *d* New York, 30 Mar. 1986). American actor. His highly successful career as a film tough guy, starting with Warner Brothers' *Sinner's Holiday* (1930) and blossoming with *The Public Enemy* (1931), tended to overshadow his musical talents. He began his career in vaudeville, cabaret, and Broadway shows as female impersonator, chorus boy, singer, and dancer. After his first starring role in *Blonde Crazy* (1931), he was to make several appearances in musical films, including: *Footlight Parade* (1933); *Something to Sing About* (1937); *Yankee Doodle Dandy* (1942), his own favourite film, in which he memorably sang, danced, and played the part of George M. *Cohan; *West Point Story* (1950); *Starlift* (1951, guest appearance); *Love Me or Leave Me* (1955), with Doris *Day; *The Seven Little Foys* (1955)—again playing the part of Cohan; and *Never Steal Anything Small* (1959).

H. Dickens: *Films of James Cagney* (New York, 1972). J. Cagney: *Cagney by Cagney* (New York, 1976). P. McGilligan: *Cagney: the Actor as Auteur* (New York, 1980).

Cahill, Marie [Mrs Daniel V. Arthur] (*b* Brooklyn, NY, 7 Feb. 1870; *d* New York, 23 Aug. 1933). American actress, comedienne, and singer, described by Stanley Green as 'plump and pugnacious'. She made her Broadway debut in *C.O.D.* at Poole's Eighth Street Theatre on 1 July 1889; thereafter she was with Charles Hoyt in *A Tin Soldier* (1889). She spent several seasons in Paris and London, appearing at the Shaftesbury Theatre, London, in *Morocco Bound* (1896). Back in New York she was in *The Gold Bug* (1896); *Sporting Life* (1897); *A *Runaway Girl* (1897); *Monte Carlo* (1898); and had her first starring role in *The Wild Rose* (1902). Her best-known song was 'Under the bamboo tree' which she sang in *Sally in Our Alley* (1902). She was in *Nancy Brown* (1903); *It Happened in Nordland* (1904); *Moonshine* (1905); *Marrying Mary* (1906); *The Boys and Betty* (1908); *Judy Forgot* (1910); *The Opera Ball* (1912); and *Ninety in the Shade* (1915). She was then in vaudeville for many years but reappeared on Broadway in *Merry-go-Round* (1927) and *The New Yorkers* (1930).

Cahn, Sammy [Cohen, Samuel] (*b* New York, 18 June 1913; *d* Los Angeles, 15 Jan. 1993). American lyricist and librettist. His earliest songs included 'Bei mir bist du schön', popularized by the *Andrews Sisters, and 'Joseph! Joseph!' both in 1938. He ran a dance band with Saul *Chaplin and their signature tune 'Rhythm is our business' was recorded by Jimmie *Lunceford. In 1942 he went to Hollywood and teamed up in a long-lasting partnership with Jule *Styne. Their first joint effort, 'I've heard that song before' (1942), was used in the film *Youth on Parade* (1942), and their first Broadway success was **High Button Shoes* (1947). He also wrote many songs with Johnny *Burke and Jimmy *Van Heusen. He won Academy Awards for his contributions to the films *Three Coins in the Fountain* (1954); *All the Way* (1957); *High Hopes* (1959); and *Call Me Irresponsible* (1963); and an Emmy for 'Love and marriage' from the TV version of Thornton Wilder's *Our Town*. He returned to Broadway with *Skyscraper* (1966), *Walking Happy* (1967), and *Look to the Lilies* (1970). With the growing interest in the history and achievement of popular song he used an ebullient personality to become a raconteur/entertainer on radio, TV, and stage, with his own show, *Words and Music* (entirely devoted to his lyrics), on Broadway in 1974 and in London, as *The Sammy Cahn Songbook*.

He made an LP of his own songs, many of which had been introduced by Frank Sinatra. These include, in addition to those mentioned above: 'Shoe shine boy' (1936), 'Until the real thing comes along' (1936), 'Please be kind' (1938), all with music by Chaplin; 'Victory polka' (1943), 'I'll walk alone' (1944), 'Saturday night is the loneliest night of the week' (1944), 'There goes that song again' (1944), 'Let it snow, let it snow, let it snow' (1945), all with music by Styne; 'I should care' (1945, *m* Axel Stordhal and Paul *Weston); 'The tender trap' (1955), 'Style' (1964), 'My kind of town' (1964), 'I like to lead when I dance' (1964)—the last three from the film *Robin and the 7 Hoods*, and 'Thoroughly modern Millie' (1965), all with music by Van Heusen.

S. Cahn: *I Should Care: the Sammy Cahn Story* (New York, 1974; London, 1975).

Cajun music. Cajun is the name given to a French-speaking native of the state of Louisiana; otherwise the Acadians, the French-Canadians of Acadia, who settled in south-west Louisiana in the late 18th century, after the English had invaded their country in 1713 and renamed it Nova Scotia. Refusing to swear allegiance to the King of England or renounce their Catholic faith, they left to wander through America and finally settled along the Mississippi River. Cajun country is an area of 22 parishes, with Lafayette and Baton Rouge its main centres. The Cajun language has remained almost pure old French and has bred a distinctive style of folk-song, with concertina or accordion prominent in the accompaniment, that has some affinity with *Creole music. Its typical tunes have been tellingly exploited by Virgil Thomson (in the film *Louisiana Story*) and other modern American composers. Cajun music, as might be expected in such pockets of isolated culture, is in a mode that might have flourished and been heard more than a century ago; old-style fiddle playing, the violin sometimes used, solo or in pairs, as the only accompaniment to singing or dancing. Otherwise the Cajun accordion (a simplified version of the standard instrument with two bass keys and ten treble which still works on the *harmonica principle and is confined to the tonic and dominant of two keys only) is the overriding sound; with the triangle (locally known as the 'tit fer', or *petit fer*) and the guitar added as rhythm.

Among the groups of more recent times that have preserved and developed Cajun music are the Balfa Frères and the Louisiana Aces, and an important figure was Amadée Ardoin (*c* 1900–36). The composer Doug Kershaw has highlighted Cajun fiddling in such songs as 'Louisiana man', 'Diggy diggy lo', and 'Sweet jole blon' (i.e. 'jolie blonde') recorded in the 1920s and revived in 1947 by the fiddler Harry Choates. The film *Dedans le sud de la Louisiane* helped to revive interest in Cajun music, featuring such artists as Dewey Balfa (1927–92) and the Balfa Brothers, Nathan Abshire (1913–81), Dennis McGee, and Sady Courville. The black rock music that developed from the same roots is known as *zydeco.

G. W. Cable: *Creoles and Cajuns* (New York, 1959).

Cakewalk. A dance performed to a formally syncopated music that was first a forerunner of, then part of, the emerging *ragtime era; made popular through black minstrel shows of the late 19th century. The name derives from plantation dancing competitions for which the prize was traditionally a large cake. It was basically a strutting kind of walk, a sort of syncopated goosestep, which had its ancestry in similar African dances and came to Florida, and thence to the southern states of

America, via the Caribbean. It has also been suggested that it was influenced by traditional dances of the Seminole Indians.

The music was of a brisk, marching nature with elements of the *two-step and the *polka, usually, like the classic ragtime compositions, in several contrasting sections in imitation of the ballroom dances and marches of the period. A late classic cakewalk was Kerry *Mills's 'Whistling Rufus', written in 1899, where the overlapping affinity with ragtime is clearly noticeable, the two terms often being used without discrimination. The early cakewalk involved, according to one authority, 'wild and hilarious jumping and gyrating steps alternating with slow processions in which the dancers walk solemnly in couples', a plantation knees-up to the music of banjo and fiddle. There was some element of burlesque in it, the black dancers dressing up in finery and strutting in emulation of their masters. It was introduced to the white public by dancing waiters, and was first brought into the theatre in an 1877 *Harrigan and Hart show to the strains of 'Walkin' for dat cake' written by David *Braham. It became a national craze in America in the 1880s, arrived in Europe soon after, and was very popular in the north of England where there was a strong clog-dancing tradition. The dates of the origin of the cakewalk are difficult to pinpoint but the phrase 'to take the cake' was in common use by 1840.

Caldwell, Anne (*b* Boston, 30 Aug. 1867; *d* Hollywood, 22 Oct. 1936). American librettist, lyricist, singer, and actress. She first appeared with a juvenile opera company and followed a stage career for many years, occasionally trying her hand as a composer and having songs interpolated into *The Social Whirl* (1906). She was first involved as a writer in *Top o' the World* (1907) and became known through Victor *Herbert's *The Lady of the Slipper* (1912). She wrote librettos and/or lyrics for *When Claudia Smiles* (1914); *Chin-Chin* (1914); *Pom-Pom* (1916); and many Fred *Stone shows like *Jack o'Lantern* (1917)—'Wait till the cows come home'. She became much in demand in her field and collaborated with Raymond *Hubbell, Jerome *Kern, Vincent *Youmans, and others on such shows as: *She's a Good Fellow* (1919); *Tip Top* (1920); *The Night Boat* (1920); *The Sweetheart Shop* (1920); *Hitchy-Koo* (1920); **Good Morning, Dearie* (1921); *The Bunch and Judy* (1922); *Stepping Stones* (1923); *The City Chap* (1925); *Oh, Please!* (1926)—'I know that you know'; *Take the Air* (1927); *Three Cheers* (1928).

California Ramblers, The. Influential white band playing in the formative *big band style, partly arranged but still with plenty of freedom for improvised jazz solos in a rather corny *Charleston style. Formed in 1920 by its long-time manager Ed W. T. Kirkeby (1891–1978), later Fats *Waller's manager, it became one of the most popular bands of the 1920s, its jazz content kept alive by such players as Red *Nichols, Tommy and Jimmy *Dorsey, and Adrian *Rollini. They played for many years in their own roadhouse, the Ramblers' Inn, near New York and made countless recordings 1921–8 under various names.

Calliope. A mechanical organ with its pipes activated by steam. It is popularly connected with its use on the old Mississippi steamboats, but like the conventional fair organ (sometimes referred to as steam organ because of the steam engines used as generators, but activated by air) it existed in various guises, sometimes small and portable as used by street musicians, at other times large and elaborate as used on the boats, at fairs, and in dance halls. A well-known exponent of the calliope was Fate *Marable, entertainment manager and bandleader on the Streckfus Line steamboats.

Call Me Madam. Musical comedy with book by Howard *Lindsay and Russel *Crouse and music and lyrics by Irving *Berlin, his last big Broadway success. Produced at the Imperial Theatre, New York, 12 Oct. 1950, it ran for 644 performances.

The leading character Sally Adams, ambassador to Lichtenburg (forcefully played by Ethel *Merman) was based on the Washington society leader Perle Mesta, appointed as an ambassador by Harry S. Truman, 'The hostess with the mostess' as the song has it. She has an affair with the Prime Minister (Paul Lukas), while her assistant Kenneth (Russell Nype) falls in love with the Princess (Galina Talva). Sally and Kenneth console one another with the famous contrapuntal duet 'You're just in love' and all works out right in the the end.

Other musical numbers were 'Washington square dance', 'Marrying for love', 'The ocarina', 'It's a lovely day today', 'The best thing for you would be me', and 'Something to dance about'. It was an exuberant show and score, and was memorably filmed in 1953 with Ethel Merman, George Sanders (1906–72), Donald *O'Connor, and Carole Richards. In London it was seen at the Coliseum [486p], with Billie Worth, Robert Henderson, Anton Walbrook, Shani Wallis, and Arthur Lowe.

Call Me Mister. Long-running revue [734p], a sort of sequel to *This is the Army*, with a cast of ex-GI actors now back in civilian clothes and taking a wry look at the army and their new life. It opened at the National Theatre (later re-named the Nederlander) on 18 Apr. 1946. The score, by Harold *Rome, included 'Along with me', 'The face on the dime', and 'South America, take it away'. A cohesive story line was added when the show was filmed in 1951 with Betty Grable (1916–73) and Dan Dailey (1914–78).

Calloway, Cab [Cabell] (*b* Rochester, NY, 25 Dec. 1907). American bandleader, vocalist, and composer. He began as a part-time singer in Baltimore clubs while he studied law, then turned professional under the name of Marion Hardy. In 1927 he joined a male quartet in the show *Plantation Days*, leaving it in Chicago to work as singer and drummer in the Dreamland and Sunset Cafés there. In 1929 he became leader of a band called the Alabamians which finally broke up in New York. Calloway then moved into the *Connie's Hot Chocolates* company leaving in 1930 to lead the Missourians, a touring band that was to become the nucleus of his future orchestras. Working at the *Savoy he developed a line in eccentric showmanship and *scat singing, and next moved into the *Cotton Club as relief band for *Ellington's. When Ellington left, Calloway took over and continued to develop his zany act and to purvey a frenetic sort of big-band jazz that made a hit of their theme song 'Minnie the Moocher' in 1931. After the Cotton Club residency the band became a touring unit, recording such hits as 'The lady with the fan', 'Zah-zuh-zah', and their only million-seller, 'Jumpin' jive' (1939), reaching a peak in the 1940s when he employed such sidemen as Milt Hinton (*b* 1910), Hilton Jefferson (1903–68), Chu Berry (1910–41), and Jonah Jones (*b* 1909). He gave up leading a big band in 1948.

Calloway appeared as Sporting Life in the 1952–4 revival of *Gershwin's **Porgy and Bess* and toured with it for many years. He worked as an entertainer with the Harlem Globetrotters, appeared in the all-black production of **Hello, Dolly!* in 1974 and in *Bubbling Brown Sugar* (1975), and in the film *The Blues Brothers* (1980). He was consultant for and appeared in the Coppola film *The Cotton Club* (1985) and visited London at the time for TV promotions. In spite of his antics, his reputation as a bandleader remains high. He wrote and collaborated on a number of songs and instrumentals including: 'Minnie the Moocher' (1931), 'Scat song' (1932), 'The lady with the fan' (1933), 'Zah zuh zah' (1933), 'Good sauce from the gravy bowl' (1935), 'Rustle of swing' (1938), 'Boog-it' (1940), 'Are you hep to the jive' (1940), and 'Are you all reet' (1941).

C. Calloway: *Of Minnie the Moocher and Me* (New York, 1976).

Calvert, Eddie (*b* Preston, Lancs., 15 Mar. 1922; *d* Johannesburg, 7 Aug. 1978). British trumpet player. He played in northern brass bands before working with Billy *Ternent and *Geraldo in the 1940s. In the 1950s he worked as a variety soloist and had hits with 'Oh, my Papa' (1954) and 'Cherry pink and apple blossom white' (1955), becoming known as 'The Man with the Golden Trumpet'. He played on film sound-tracks and produced several more hit recordings before moving to South Africa in 1968.

Calypso. Folk-song of the West Indies—Jamaica, Barbados, Granada, Antigua, and Trinidad, with the last-named considered to be its focal point. It is thought to have originated with the slaves on the plantations who, being forbidden to talk, chanted to tom-tom rhythms as they worked, passing on their news and views in melodic patois. This developed into the modern calypso where the singer or calypsonian tells of events, scandal, sporting achievements, and politics in racy, humorous language. Against the calypso rhythm in 4/4 time on the guitar, tom-tom, and other rhythm instruments, or perhaps a steel band, the words are sung in a lilting manner derived from the French patois of the early calypsos; with endless subtle variations of the length and shape of the melodic line in order to fit in as many words and syllables as the singer fancies. A great time for calypso singing is at the Carnival in Trinidad on the two days preceding Ash Wednesday. It had a great period of international popularity just after the Second World War; its style and spirit have continued in dances like the cadence and as an obvious ingredient of modern *reggae music.

Camelot. Musical loosely based on the Arthurian legends, by way of T. H. White's sequence of novels *The Once and Future King*, adapted by Alan Jay *Lerner. Guinevere (Julie *Andrews), married to King Arthur (Richard Burton, 1925–84), falls in love with Lancelot (Robert Goulet) and is betrayed by Mordred (Roddy McDowell). The show opened at New York's Majestic Theatre 3 Dec. 1960 in spite of Lerner having a serious illness and producer Moss *Hart suffering a heart-attack which killed him a year later.

With lyrics by Lerner and score by Frederick *Loewe, it followed in the wake of the sensationally successful **My Fair Lady*, and the critics found it wanting by comparison. Despite this it had the right sort of sentimental appeal for the big public, had record advance sales, and achieved a run of 873 performances. The songs included: 'I wonder what the King is doing tonight', 'Camelot', 'Follow me', 'C'est moi', 'How to handle a woman', 'If ever I would leave you', and 'What do the simple folk do'. It was successfully revived in 1980 with Richard Burton again as Arthur, succeeded later by Richard Harris (*b* 1932). Burton was also in the 1967 film version with Vanessa Redgrave (*b* 1937). In London, at Drury Lane, Laurence Harvey (1928–73) was Arthur [518p].

Campbell, Glen [Travis] (*b* Delight, Ark., 22 Apr. 1936). American country singer and guitarist. He started out as a studio musician on the West Coast, afterwards moving to Nashville where he embarked on a solo career in country music; also working in backing groups with the *Monkees, the *Mamas and the Papas, and the *Beach Boys. He had his first recording success with 'Turn around look at me' in 1961 and important hits in 1967 with 'Gentle on my mind' (by John Hartford) and 'By the time I get to Phoenix'. His gentle crooning style has promoted the work of many writers, further hits coming with Jim *Webb's 'Wichita lineman', 'Galveston', and others like 'Houston' and 'Southern nights'. He continued his popularity in the 1970s with a big-selling disc in 1975, 'Rhinestone cowboy', which some thought rather blandly commercial in view of his more powerful capabilities.

F. Kramer: *The Glen Campbell Story* (New York, 1970).

Can-can. This fast, furious, and athletic dance, usually performed by a troupe of glamorous dancing girls, whose high kicks reveal immodest frills and upper thighs with saucy abandon, became internationally appreciated in various operettas by Jacques *Offenbach, notably in *Orphée aux Enfers* (1858), the can-can finale of which has become the quintessential music of the dance. Before this it had evolved in the French cabaret world of the early 1800s, possibly originally imported from Algiers where such a high-kicking dance was part of fertility rites. Even then it was regarded as somewhat disreputable; hence the name—the word 'can-can' meaning tittle-tattle or gossip, particularly of a scandalous nature. It was regarded with the same righteous horror as most new dances, often of only marginally scandalous nature, and various societies worked for its suppression.

P. Mariel & J. Trocher: *Paris Cancan* (Paris–London, 1961).

Can-Can. American musical with music and lyrics by Cole *Porter and book by its director Abe *Burrows, first produced at the Shubert Theatre 7 May 1953.

The story, set in 1893, is of the lady proprietor of the cabaret Bal du Paradis, where the immoral *can-can is the main attraction both to its public and the societies trying to suppress it. She sets out to seduce the judge who is heading an investigation into her activities, they fall in love, and he takes over the defence role. The proprietor Pistache (a part originally intended for Carol *Channing) was played by the French actress Lilo, but the show was also a major success for the dancer and actress Gwen *Verdon, on her first Broadway appearance, who shone in an *Apache dance and the ballet 'Garden of Eden'. The songs included: 'Never give anything away', 'C'est magnifique', 'Come along with me', 'Live and let live', and the hit 'I love Paris'.

The American production ran for 892 performances and the London production at the Coliseum, 14 Oct. 1954, for 394. The 1960 film, with a much changed story, starred Frank *Sinatra, Shirley *MacLaine, Maurice *Chevalier, and Louis *Jordan. There were New York revivals in 1959, 1962, and in 1981 with Zizi Jeanmaire.

Candide. Musical with score by Leonard *Bernstein and book by Lillian Hellman based on the Voltaire classic. The hero has been taught that this is 'The best of all possible worlds' (as one of thé songs proclaims), but comes to realize that there are several flaws in it. The production was highly praised, but being perhaps nearer, musically, to an opera it never achieved wide popularity; though its superb overture has remained a modern classic. A modest run of 73 performances was achieved at the Martin Beck Theatre from 1 Dec. 1956; the cast including Max *Adrian, Robert Rounseville (1914–74), and Barbara *Cook; directed by Tyrone Guthrie. A revised version in 1973 had a libretto by Hugh Wheeler and additional lyrics by Stephen *Sondheim. In 1982 it found its home in the repertoire of the New York City Opera, and a further expanded version was seen in New York and London in 1988.

Canned Heat. American country blues group formed in 1966 by blues experts Bob Hite (1945–81) (harmonica and vocal) and Al Wilson (1943–70) (guitar, harmonica, and vocal), with Henry Vestine (*b* 1944) (guitar), Larry Taylor (*b* 1942) (bass), and Bob Cook (drums). They made their first album for Liberty in 1967 and became nationally known at that year's Monterey Festival. The group suffered many changes and Wilson died in 1970. Featuring electric guitars but maintaining a traditional feel to their work, they cut many albums (including one with John Lee *Hooker) and had a world hit with Wilbert Harrison's 'Let's work together' in 1970. Numerous changes left the band without its old appeal and it broke up in 1976.

Canova, Judy (*b* Jacksonville, Fla., 20 Nov. 1916; *d* 1983). American singer, yodeller, and comedienne. She studied to be an opera singer but gave it up to go to New York with her sister Annie and brother Zeke to form a vaudeville team. After being spotted in a Greenwich Village club she was given a part in the musical *Calling All Stars* (1934). She appeared in the **Ziegfeld Follies* of 1936, and in several films in the 1930s, but mainly made her reputation on radio with Paul *Whiteman in 1936 and in the *Rippling Rhythm Revue* (1937). In 1939 the Canovas were the first hillbilly act to appear on television. She starred in *Yokel Boy* (1939) and appeared in many films in the 1940s and 1950s including **Louisiana Hayride* (1944) and *Huckleberry Finn* (1960). Her own radio show ran 1943–53, introduced by the song 'Go to sleep, little baby' of which she was part-composer.

Canterbury Tales. It was the playwright and producer Martin Starkie (*b* 1925) who first had the fruitful idea of making a stage play out of Nevill Coghill's prestigious modern version of *The Canterbury Tales*. He directed it himself at the Oxford Playhouse as part of the 650th anniversary celebrations of Exeter College. The Oxford production was so successful that Starkie and Coghill wrote a more commercially slanted version. In the meantime, and quite independently, two young composers, Richard Hill and John Hawkins, had been writing a musical suite based on the Canterbury pilgrimage. For a recording of this Starkie was asked to add excerpts from the Coghill translation and the idea evolved of turning it all into a musical. It was presented at the Phoenix Theatre, London, 21 Mar. 1968, where it was highly acclaimed, running for 2038 performances and was seen in New York in 1969. The original cast included Nicky Henson, Kenneth J. Warren, Wilfrid Brambell, and Jessie Evans. There was a revival in London in 1979 and in New York in 1980.

Cantor, Eddie [Itzkowitz, Isidore] (*b* New York, 31 Jan. 1892; *d* Hollywood, 10 Oct. 1964). American comedian, singer, and dancer. Known as 'Banjo Eyes' because of his large and expressive optics. The child of Russian immigrants, he was orphaned at an early age and raised by his grandmother. As a youth he joined the Gus *Edwards troupe and worked in vaudeville, appearing at the Clinton Music Hall in New York in 1907. He became well-known on the vaudeville stage, usually doing a blackface routine. He went to London in 1914 to appear in the revue *Not Likely*, returning on the outbreak of war to appear with Lila Lee in the act Cantor and Lee. As a solo artist he appeared in the **Ziegfeld Follies* of 1917, 1918, and 1919 (later in the 1923 and 1927 versions) and this made him a star. He took the lead in *Kid Boots* (1923) and **Whoopee* (1928), his last Broadway show being *Banjo Eyes* (1941). He lost his fortune in the Wall Street crash of 1929 but recovered by way of show-business successes.

Cantor was a unique and stylish singer of such songs as 'Margie', 'Yes sir, that's my baby', 'Dinah', 'Ida', 'Makin' whoopee', 'Now's the time to fall in love', 'Josephine', 'If you knew Susie', and similar Twenties-style hits. He began a fruitful film career in 1930, appearing in *Whoopee* (1930); *Glorifying the American Girl* (1930); *Palmy Days* (1931); *The Kid from Spain* (1932); *Roman Scandals* (1933); *Kid Millions* (1934); *Strike me Pink* (1936); *Ali Baba Goes to Town* (1937); *Forty Little Mothers* (1940); *Show Business* (1940); *Hollywood Canteen* (1940); *Thank Your Lucky Stars* (1943); *If You Knew Susie* (1948); and *The Story of Will Rogers* (1952). A film of his life, *The Eddie Cantor Story*, was made in 1953 with Cantor providing the voice, Keefe Brasselle the face. He had his own radio shows from the 1930s into the 1960s but heart trouble forced his retirement. He wrote the lyrics of many songs and several books.

E. Cantor: *My Life is in Your Hands* (New York, 1928). E. Cantor & J. K. Ardmore: *Take My Life* (Garden City, NY, 1957). E. Cantor (ed. P. Rosenteur): *The Way I See It* (Englewood Cliffs, NJ, 1959). E. Cantor: *As I Remember Them* (New York, 1963).

Captain Beefheart [Van Vliet, Don] (*b* Glendale, Calif., 15 Jan. 1941). American blues/rock singer who appeared as Captain Beefheart and his Magic Band in 1964, recording the hectic 'Diddy wah diddy' and 'Frying pan'. He had a deep, gruff voice and the potential to be a fine white singer of the blues, but moved away from legitimate performance with show-business antics, surrealistic, punning lyrics, and commercial ideas which laced the basic Delta blues style with modernistic extravagances. His best work was in the album *Trout Mask Replica* (1969) and his most bluesy in *Unconditionally Guaranteed* (1974). In 1975 he briefly joined Frank *Zappa in the Mothers of Invention.

Careless Rapture. Musical play with words and music by Ivor *Novello, lyrics by Christopher Hassall, presented at London's Drury Lane Theatre 11 Sept. 1936, with Dorothy *Dickson, Ivor *Novello, Peter Graves, Zena *Dare, and Olive Gilbert in the cast, running for 296 performances. One of Novello's Viennese-style, big romantic efforts, it introduced such lasting songs as 'Music in May', 'Why is there ever goodbye', 'Wait for me', and 'There are times'.

Carle, Frankie [Carlone, Francis Nunzio] (*b* Providence, RI, 25 Mar. 1903). American pianist, bandleader, and composer. A professional musician by the age of 18, he played with the Mal Hallett band for four years in the mid-1930s, led his own band for a while, then joined Horace Heidt; here his lightly swinging style of playing first became recognized, with the band billed as the Heidt–Carle Orchestra. He organized a big band in 1944 which remained popular throughout the 1950s, with the piano its prominent feature and its theme song 'Sunrise serenade' (1939), Carle's best-known composition, becoming a popular standard. He also wrote 'Dispossessed by you' (1937); 'Georgianna' (1937); 'Falling leaves' (1940); 'Lover's lullaby' (1940); 'Passing fancy' (1944); 'Dream lullaby' (1945); and 'Roses in the rain' (1947). He was in a number of musical films.

Carlisle, Kitty (*b* New Orleans, 3 Sept. 1914). American singer who first became known in **Rio Rita* (1932), followed by *Champagne Sec* (1933). She appeared in the film *Murder at the Vanities* (1934). Her popularity grew after two Bing *Crosby movies, *She Loves Me Not* (1934) and *Here Is My Heart* (1935), and with the Marx Brothers in *A Night at the Opera* (1935). Her last film was *Hollywood Canteen* (1944). She made various stage musical appearances and was popular on radio. After her singing career was over she was known as a TV quiz-show panellist for many years. She was married to Moss *Hart.

Carmen Jones. Interesting and successful adaptation of Bizet's opera *Carmen*, using the original music with a new libretto by Oscar *Hammerstein II and produced with an all-black cast. The toreador becomes a boxer and the well-known songs appear as 'Dat's love', 'Dere's a café on the corner', 'Dis flower', 'My Joe', 'Stan' up and fight', 'Beat out dat rhythm on a drum', etc. Staged at New York's Broadway Theatre 2 Dec. 1943, it ran for 502 performances; and has since been revived several times. The film version in 1954 starred Dorothy Dandridge (sung by Marilyn Horne), Harry *Belafonte (LaVern Hutcherson), and Pearl *Bailey.

Carmichael, Hoagy [Hoagland Howard] (*b* Bloomington, Ind., 22 Nov. 1899; *d* Palm Springs, Calif., 27 Dec. 1981). American composer, pianist, singer, and actor. He was taught to play the piano by his mother who was a pianist in the local cinema in silent film days. When he was 16 the family moved to Indianapolis where he studied further with a black ragtime pianist, Reggie Duval. He left school early, but later returned in order to study law and eventually graduated at Indiana University. During this time he did a great deal of part-time playing and got to know a number of jazzmen. In 1926 he offered one of his early compositions, 'Riverboat shuffle', to the publisher Irving Mills who accepted it; and it was taken up by various bands, including the Wolverines and their cornettist Bix *Beiderbecke. Mills offered him a job, but Carmichael decided to pursue his law career and moved to Florida, intending to practise there. A further success with 'Washboard blues' finally persuaded him that his career was destined to be music rather than the law. In 1927 he wrote a number called 'Barnyard shuffle' which, with considerable changes of mood and tempo, was later to become his greatest song-hit, 'Stardust', when, in 1929, it was given lyrics by Mitchell Parish. It was frequently recorded, notably in 1940 by Artie *Shaw, a version which sold two million copies. In the late 1920s Carmichael played and recorded with a number of well-known jazzmen, notably Beiderbecke, the *Dorsey brothers, King *Oliver, and Louis *Armstrong and he made a number of records under his own name.

While 'Stardust' was becoming one of the most popular songs in the world, Carmichael was writing others including: 'One night in Havana' (1929, *w* Parish), 'Georgia on my mind' (1930, *w* Stuart Gorrell), 'Rockin' chair' (1930), 'Lazy river' (with Sidney Arodin, 1931), 'New Orleans' (1932), 'In the still of the night' (1932, *w* Trent), 'Lazybones' (with Johnny *Mercer, 1933), 'Snowball' (1933), 'Moonburn' (1935, *w* Edward Heyman), 'Little old lady' (1936, *w* Stanley Adams), 'Small fry' (1938), 'Two sleepy people' (1938, *w* Frank *Loesser), 'I get along without you very well' (1939), 'The nearness of you' (1938, *w* Ned *Washington), 'Baltimore oriole' (1942, *w* Paul Francis Webster), 'The lamplighter's serenade' (1942, Webster), 'Skylark' (1942, Mercer), 'Ole buttermilk sky' (with Jack Brooks, 1946)—from the film *Canyon Passage*, 'Follow the swallow' (1949, Webster), 'In the cool, cool, cool of the evening' (1951, Mercer), and 'My resistance is low' (1951, *w* Harold *Adamson). Many of these were written for or used in films and many were performed by Carmichael himself, who had a very individual piano style and singing voice, particularly effective in such off-beat humorous items as 'Hong Kong blues' (1939) and 'The old music master' (1943), from the film *True to Life*. He appeared in many films as singer/pianist and was also a successful character actor. He wrote one musical comedy, *Walk With Music*, which had 55 performances at the Ethel Barrymore Theatre, New York, 4 June 1940.

H. Carmichael: *The Stardust Road* (New York, 1946).
H. Carmichael & S. Longstreet: *Sometimes I Wonder* (New York, 1965).

Carmichael, Ian (*b* Hull, 18 June 1920). British actor and singer. He studied at the Royal Academy of Dramatic Art and made his first stage appearance at the People's Palace, Mile End, in 1939. Best-known as a comedy actor taking upper-class roles in British films and plays, and ideally suited to such TV parts as Lord Peter Wimsey and Bertie Wooster in the *Jeeves* series, he was also a talented revue and musical comedy artist in the Jack *Buchanan style. He appeared with great aplomb in *Nine Sharp* (1940 tour); *What Goes On?* (1948); *The Lilac Domino* (1949 tour); *Wild Violets* (1951 revival); *The *Lyric Revue* (1951); *The Globe Revue* (1952); *High Spirits* (1953); *At the Lyric* (1953); *Going to Town* (1954); *The Love Doctor* (1959); and *I Do! I Do!* (1968).

I. Carmichael: *Will the Real Ian Carmichael* (London, 1979).

Carney, Harry [Howell] (*b* Boston, 1 Apr. 1910; *d* New York, 8 Oct. 1974). American jazz saxophonist. At only 16 he was heard by Duke *Ellington, who enlisted him into his newly-formed orchestra. He was with Ellington throughout his career from 1926 to 1974 until Ellington died; and Carney soon followed. He was not only the pivot of the band throughout these years but, by the 1940s, recognized as the first great jazz exponent of the baritone-saxophone, unequalled until the arrival of Gerry *Mulligan.

Carney, Kate (*b* London, 1869; *d* London, 1 Jan. 1950). British singer and comedienne. Famous in the heyday of the *music-hall for her coster songs and characterizations, she first appeared at the Albert Music Hall in Canning Town in Feb. 1890 as a singer of Irish ballads. She made her reputation with her heartfelt renditions, in Cockney vein, of such numbers as 'A donkey cart built for two', 'Sarah', and 'Three pots a shilling'. Her act was a mixture of humour and pathos as typified in her most famous song 'Are we to part like this, Bill?' She ran her own supporting company and continued to perform until just before her death at the age of 80, having appeared in the Royal Variety Performance in 1935.

T. Barker: 'Kate Carney' in *Music-Hall Records*, No. 4 (London, Dec. 1978).

Carnival. American musical produced at the Imperial Theatre, New York, on 13 Apr. 1961, which followed an old tradition of musicals based on circuses and travelling shows. Joining the unsuccessful carnival troupe portrayed here, the young girl hopeful at first falls for the boastful magician but ends up in love with the sad puppeteer in a tear-jerking story which was based on the film *Lili* (1952). The music by Bob *Merrill included a fantasy ballet, 'Grand Imperial Cirque de Paris', and a catchy theme-song 'Love makes the world go round'. Merrill also wrote the lyrics and Michael Stewart the book, and the director was Gower Champion. It ran for 719 performances with Anna Maria Alberghetti (*b* 1936) originally taking the leading role, and Jerry Orbach (*b* 1935). It was seen at London's Lyric Theatre, 8 Feb. 1963.

Carousel. American musical which further confirmed the phenomenal success of the Richard *Rodgers/Oscar *Hammerstein II partnership after the triumph of *Oklahoma!* in 1943. The two shows were playing opposite one another on Broadway for two years, *Carousel*, opening at the Majestic Theatre, 19 Apr. 1945, eventually running for 890 performances.

It was based on the play by Benjamin F. Glazer, which was an adaptation of Ferenc Molnár's *Liliom* transposed in time and place to New England in the period 1870–80. A big-headed carnival man and a local girl, Julie Jordan, fall in love but he, desperate for money, is killed in an attempted robbery. He is allowed to return to earth to perform one good deed. The lead parts in the original were taken by John *Raitt and Jan Clayton (*b* 1917). It had a fine score including the haunting 'Carousel waltz' and the songs 'You're a queer one, Julie Jordan', 'Mr Snow', 'If I loved you', 'Blow high, blow low', 'June is bustin' out all over', 'When the children are asleep', 'Soliloquy', and 'You'll never walk alone'.

There was a run of 566 performances at the Drury Lane Theatre, London, 7 June 1950; a filmed version in 1956 with Gordon *MacRae and Shirley Jones (*b* 1934); and a Lincoln Center revival in 1965 with John Raitt playing his original part.

Carpenter, Karen (*b* New Haven, Conn., 2 Mar. 1950; *d* Downey, Calif., 4 Feb. 1983) and **Richard** (*b* New Haven, 15 Oct. 1946). American pop singers. They began to play with various pop groups, Karen on drums, Richard on keyboards, and eventually made their name as a singing duo, the Carpenters, purveying a gentle and melodic style of pop music that became known as 'soft rock', later promoted by such groups as *Abba. It was highly successful and they sold more than 60 million records on Herb *Alpert's A & M label. They chose good songs and presented them well including such items as Burt *Bacharach's 'Close to you' (1970). Other hits included: 'We've only just begun' (1970); 'For all we know' (1971); 'Rainy days and Mondays' (1971); 'Superstar' (1971); 'Hurting each other' (1972); 'Top of the World' (1973); 'Yesterday once more' (1973); 'Please, Mr Postman' (1975); and 'Only yesterday' (1975). They won two Grammy Awards in 1970 and another for the album *The Carpenters* in 1971. Karen died of heart failure brought on by anorexia nervosa.

Carr, Frank Osmond (*b* Bradford, 23 Apr. 1858; *d* Uxbridge, Middx., 29 Aug. 1916). British composer and conductor. After studying music at both Oxford and Cambridge, he composed a number of popular *burlesques, *light operas, and pioneering *musical comedies that included: *Joan of Arc* (1891); *Blue-Eyed Susan* (1892); *In Town* (1892); *Morocco Bound* (1893); *Go Bang* (1894); *His Excellency* (1894, *w* W. S. *Gilbert); *Biarritz* (1896); *Lord Tom Noddy* (1896); *My Girl* (1896); *The Maid of Athens* (1897); *The Rose of the Riviera* (1899); and a ballet, *Roger de Coverley* (1907).

Carr, Leroy (*b* Nashville, 27 Mar. 1905; *d* Indianapolis, 29 Apr. 1935). American pianist and blues singer. He teamed up with Francis Hillman 'Scrapper' Blackwell (*b* NC, 21 Feb. 1903; *d* Indianapolis, 7 Oct. 1962), blues singer, pianist, and guitarist, in 1928; they toured together and produced some notable recordings and songs like 'How long blues' and 'In the evening when the sun goes down' which had a great influence on future urban blues developments and rhythm 'n' blues. Blackwell also worked on his own and with Chippie *Hill and Thomas A. Dorsey (*b* 1899), but retired from the music scene after Carr died of alcoholism, returning to make some new recordings 1959–61. He died of gunshot wounds.

Carr, Michael [Cohen, Maurice] (*b* Leeds, 1904; *d* London, 16 Sept. 1968). British songwriter. Son of a boxer, 'Cockney' Cohen, who later kept a restaurant in Dublin, he ran away to sea and had seen most of the world by the time he was 18. He went to America to work as a journalist and later appeared in several Hollywood films. He wrote the shows *London Rhapsody* (1937) and **Apple Sauce* (1941); and music for the *Crazy Gang film *O-Kay for Sound* (1937). His cornily successful songs, many written with Jimmy *Kennedy, and many in the pseudo-*hillbilly style of the 1930s, included 'Ole faithful' (with Kennedy, 1934); 'Dinner for one please, James' (1935); 'Orchids to my lady' (1935); 'The girl with the dreamy eyes' (with Eddie Pola, 1935); 'The wheel of the wagon is broken' (with Harold Box and Desmond Cox, 1935); 'Why did she fall for the leader of the band' (with Kennedy, 1935); 'Did your Mother come from Ireland?' (with Kennedy, 1936); 'Misty islands of the Highlands' (with Kennedy, 1936); 'The sunset trail' (with Kennedy, 1936); 'Cinderella, stay in my arms' (with Kennedy, 1938); 'The little boy that Santa Claus forgot' (with Tommy Connor and Jimmy Leach, 1938); 'Merrily we roll along' (with Raymond Wallace, 1938); 'On Linger Longer Island' (with Kennedy, 1938); 'On the outside looking in' (1939); 'South of the border' (with Kennedy, 1939); 'We're gonna hang out the washing on the Siegfried Line' (with Kennedy, 1939); 'A pair of silver wings' (1941, *w* Eric *Maschwitz); 'In old Mexico' (with Jack Popplewell, 1943); and the orchestral 'Lonely ballerina' (with *Mantovani, 1954).

Carr, Vikki [Cardona, Florencia Bisenta de Casillas Martinez] (*b* El Paso, Texas, 19 July 1942). American singer. She began her career with the Pepe Callahan Mexican-Irish Band in Los Angeles, then pursued a successful solo career in nightclubs, later as an actress. Her most popular songs include 'It must be him', 'With pen in hand', and 'Can't take my eyes off you'.

Carroll, Earl (*b* Pittsburgh, 16 Sept. 1893; *d* Mt Carmel, Pa., 17 June 1948). American producer, director, composer, and lyricist. He began his theatrical career at 10 as a programme-seller. At 16 he worked his way round the world, ending up penniless in New York where he was staff songwriter in Feist's music-publishing house 1912–17. Working mainly with composers Alfred Robyn and Alfred Francis, he produced his first full music score in 1916, *So Long, Letty*, followed by *Canary Cottage* in 1917. He was a pilot in the US Army during the First World War; then, in 1919, he became a theatrical manager and produced several shows before opening his own Earl Carroll Theatre in New York in 1922. There he produced a famous series of revues, **Earl Carroll's Vanities*, which ran for 10 editions between 1923 and 1932, revived in 1940; plus the *Earl Carroll Sketchbook*, 1929 and 1935. These were a strong rival to the famous **Ziegfeld Follies*, lavishly produced with nudes and near-the-knuckle humour; the stars included Sophie *Tucker, Jessie *Matthews, Jack Benny, Milton *Berle, and Helen *Broderick. He built a second theatre in 1931 and opened the Earl Carroll Restaurant in Hollywood in 1939. He also worked on films and became an authority on theatre construction. He was part-writer of *Murder at the Vanities* (1933) and producer of more than 60 plays. He was killed in a plane crash when flying from Los Angeles to New York.

Carroll, Harry (*b* Atlantic City, NJ, 28 Nov. 1892; *d* Santa Barbara, Calif., 26 Dec. 1962). American composer, arranger, pianist, and singer. As a boy he became a silent cinema pianist, continuing his career as an arranger and club entertainer. He was contracted by the Shuberts to write revue scores and contributed to the **Passing Show* series (1912) and the famous **Ziegfeld Follies* (1920–1). He also became well-known as a vaudeville artiste. He wrote scores for *The Whirl of Society* (1912); *Dancing Around* (1914); *The Belle of Bond Street* (1914); *Maid in America* (1915); *Oh, Look!* (1918); *The Little Blue Devil* (1919); and *Ziegfeld's 9 o'Clock Frolic* (1921). His song hits included 'The trail of the lonesome pine' (1913, *w* Ballard MacDonald), 'By the beautiful sea' (1914, *w* Harold *Atteridge), and 'Down in Bom-Bom Bay' (1915, *w* MacDonald).

Carson, John (*b* Fannin County, Ga., 23 Mar. 1868; *d* Atlanta, 11 Dec. 1949). American singer and fiddler. As a teenager he was a jockey, later working in a cotton mill for 20 years, then becoming a decorator. In his spare time he played on a fiddle that had been brought to America from Ireland by his grandfather, and he earned great renown for his country-style playing. Between 1913 and 1922 he was seven times the winner of the Georgia Old-Time Fiddlers' Association championship. On 9 Sept. 1922 he broadcast on WSB Radio from Atlanta to become one of the first country musicians to be heard on radio. In 1923 he was one of the first hillbilly artists to record, with 'The old hen cackled and the rooster's going to crow' and 'The little old log cabin in the lane' issued on the Okeh label; 'Old Joe Clark' and his own 'You will never miss your mother until she's gone' became best-sellers. Other country singers had just preceded him but Carson was the first to spark off commercial interest in country music and set it on its revival road to popularity. As 'Fiddlin'' John Carson he recorded some 150 sides for Okeh between 1923 and 1931, often with a group known as the Virginia Reelers, and 24 sides were made for Victor in 1934. He wrote most of his own repertoire. His last years were spent as an elevator operator.

Carte, Richard D'Oyly (*b* London, 3 May 1844; *d* London 3 Apr. 1901). British impresario. After studying at London University, he wrote an opera and some songs but, achieving nothing of great merit, turned to theatrical management. He became particularly interested in operetta and staged productions of *Lecocq's *Giroflé-Girofla* and *Offenbach's *La *Périchole*. It was as a filler to the latter that he commissioned **Trial by Jury* in 1875. This led to the formation of a syndicate to stage further works of *Gilbert and *Sullivan and the promotion of a very famous partnership, beginning at the *Opéra-Comique Theatre then moving to the *Savoy Theatre which he built in 1881. He ran the theatre and the D'Oyly Carte Opera Company until his death. In 1887 he attempted to put English opera on its feet by building the Royal English Opera House, now known as the Palace Theatre, producing Sullivan's *Ivanhoe* there in 1891 and commissioning work from other composers.

F. Cellier & C. Bridgeman: *Gilbert, Sullivan and D'Oyly Carte* (London, 1914). C. Bettany (ed.): *100 Years of D'Oyly Carte and Gilbert and Sullivan* (London, 1975).

Carter, Benny [Bennett Lester] (*b* New York, 8 Aug. 1907). American jazz saxophonist, trumpeter, composer, arranger, and bandleader. He studied the piano as a boy, but later took to the alto-saxophone and in 1924 played with June Clark, Lois Deppe, and Earl *Hines. He was then with Fletcher *Henderson for a while; with Charlie *Johnson 1927–8; led his own band 1928–9; with Fletcher Henderson 1930–1 (during which time he established himself as an accomplished arranger); Chick *Webb 1931; *McKinney's Cotton Pickers 1931–2; his own band 1932–4; the Fletcher Henderson and Willie *Bryant bands 1934–5. He went to Europe in 1935, working with Willie Lewis in Paris; 1936–8 he was in London as staff arranger to the BBC Dance Orchestra then led by Henry *Hall, and at this time he organized several historic recordings with British musicians. He led his own band from 1939 until the 1940s, but never became a star bandleader; rather a jazz musician who was universally admired by the aficionados. he was a prolific arranger and composer in the 1930s, supplying material for the Cotton Pickers, Duke *Ellington, Fletcher Henderson, Teddy *Hill, and Benny *Goodman, and remained an active arranger into the 1970s and a regular player, leading pickup bands and making recordings (including many classic ones under the name of the Chocolate Dandies). Basically he was a *mainstream musician, but modernized his approach over the years. He must be reckoned one of the most versatile jazz musicians of his time. He appeared in the films *Thousands Cheer* (1943), *The Snows of Kilimanjaro* (1952), and *The View from Pompey's Head* (1955). He settled in Los Angeles to write for such films as *An *American in Paris* (1951); *A Man Called Adam* (1966); *Red Sky at Morning* (1970); and *Buck and the Preacher* (1972).

His songs included: 'Blues in my heart' (1931, *w* Irving *Mills); 'Lonesome nights' (1934, *w* Mills); 'Blue interlude' (1934, *w* Mills and Manny Kurtz); 'I gotta go' (1936, *w* Spencer *Williams); 'When lights are low' (1936, *w* Williams); 'Just a mood' (1937, *w* Williams); and 'Cow Cow boogie' (1941, *w* Don *Raye and Gene *De Paul). His numerous instrumentals included: 'Goodbye blues' (1930); 'Dee blues' (1930); 'Hot toddy' (1931); 'Jazz cocktail' (1932); 'Krazy kapers' (1933); 'Swing it' (1934); 'Shoot the works' (1934); 'Symphony in riffs' (1935); 'Accent on swing' (1936); 'Back Bay boogie' (1940); and many more.

M. Berger, E. Berger, & J. Patrick: *Benny Carter: a Life in American Music* (Metuchen, NJ, 1982).

Carter Family, The. A remarkable family folk group who did much to revive interest in American folk and country music in the 1920s, re-establishing the repertoire and setting the patterns of performance with what became known as the 'Carter Family' style. The moving spirit of the group was Maybelle Addington Carter (*b* Copper Creek, Va., 10 May 1909; *d* Nashville, 23 Oct. 1978). She was a member of the highly musical Addington family, one of ten children who all played and sang. The equally musical and highly religious Carter family lived in Poor Valley over the Clinch Mountain. Alvin Pleasant [generally known as A. P.] Carter (*b* Maces Springs, Va., 15 Dec. 1891; *d* Maces Springs, 7 Nov. 1960) was the eldest of eight Carter children, a dedicated collector of Irish and English folk-songs. In 1915 he married Maybelle Addington's cousin Sara Dougherty (*b* Wise County, Va., 21 July 1889; *d* Lodi, Calif., 8 Jan. 1979); ten years later Ezra J. Carter, his younger brother, married Maybelle, thus uniting a whole dynasty of musicians.

In 1926, Maybelle, by then adept on banjo, guitar, autoharp, fiddle, and lute, organized the Carter Family trio (Alvin, Sara, and herself), and soon they were performing in schools, churches, and social gatherings in Virginia, Tennessee, and North Carolina. They made their first recordings in 1927, then, discovered by Ralph Peer of Victor, they made a dozen sides in Camden in 1928, among them 'Wildwood flower' which eventually sold more than a million copies. As their popularity grew, and they travelled more widely, they moved in 1938 to Del Rio in Texas, where they were sponsored by the Consolidated Drug Company. In 1942 they went to Charlotte, North Carolina, to work for WBT Radio. A. P. and Sara had separated in 1933 and Sara re-married, but continued to work with the family group. The original Carter Family trio did their last broadcast together in 1942; thereafter Maybelle continued with her daughters Anita, Helen, and June as Mother Maybelle Carter and the Carter Sisters working from Richmond, Virginia. Later she appeared as a solo artist.

The original trio recorded more than 300 songs, preserving much that might have been lost and creating their own material which itself became traditional material for many younger country folk-singers. The tradition was carried on by Maybelle's daughters, June especially becoming a well-known artist in her own right and marrying Johnny *Cash in 1968; and by other members of the family who joined the group like Joe and Janette Carter, children of A. P. and Sara. The songs the Carter Family have passed on include 'Wildwood flower', 'Little Moses', 'Engine 143', 'Little darling, pal of mine', and 'Gospel ship' (all later recorded by Joan *Baez); 'Will the circle be unbroken', 'Wabash Cannonball', 'Keep on the sunny side' (their radio theme song), 'This land is your land', 'The good Reuben James', 'The big Grand Coulee dam' (all recorded by Woody *Guthrie); My Clinch Mountain home', 'Foggy mountain top', 'Will you miss me when I'm gone', 'It takes a worried man to sing a worried song', 'Amazing grace'; and countless more. Maybelle Carter, long dubbed 'The Queen of Country Music', appeared in the 1950s on the **Grand Ole Opry* in Nashville (where she settled) and continued singing into the 1970s, often with her son-in-law Johnny Cash. The Carter Family were elected to the Country Music Hall of Fame in 1970.

J. Atkins: *The Carter Family* (London, 1973). R. K. Krishef: *The Carter Family* (Minneapolis, 1978).

Caryll, Ivan [Tilken, Félix] (*b* Liège, Belgium, 1860; *d* New York, 29 Nov. 1921). Composer and conductor. He studied at the Conservatory in Liège and then in Paris where his teachers included Ysaÿe and Saint-Saëns. He wrote the operas *The Lily of Léoville* (1886) and *La Marraine de Charley* (1894) in Paris. Amongst his early theatrical activities was the adaptation of Chabrier's *L'Étoile* which was staged in the USA in 1890 as *The Merry Monarch* and in London in 1899 as *The Lucky Star*. By the time he had completed his 'adaptation' most of the score was his original music with only one Chabrier number remaining intact. This was followed by an arrangement of *Audran's *La Cigale* produced in London in 1890 and in New York in 1891; and of Lacôme's *Ma Mie Rosette* (1892). He settled in London in 1891 and became musical director at the *Gaiety Theatre in 1894 where he was both immensely popular and a figure of great influence in the developing years of British musical comedy.

He wrote a number of very successful works for the Gaiety and elsewhere including: *Love's Trickery*

(1889); *Love and Law* (1890); *The Sentry* (1890); *Little Christopher Columbus* (1893); *The *Shop Girl* (1894); *Dandy Dick Whittington* (1895); *The Gay Parisienne* (1896); *The Circus Girl* (1896); *The Girl from Paris* (1896); *A *Runaway Girl* (1898); *The Messenger Boy* (1900); *The Ladies' Paradise* (NY, 1901); *The *Toreador* (1901); *The Girl from Kay's* (1902); *The Duchess of Dantzic* (1903); *The *Orchid* (1903); *The *Earl and the Girl* (1903); *The Cherry Girl* (1903); *The Spring Chicken* (1905); *The New Aladdin* (1906); *The Little Cherub* (1906); *Nelly Neil* (1907); *The Girls of Gottenberg* (1907); *Son Altesse Royale* (1908); **Our Miss Gibbs* (1909); *The Satyr* (1910); several of these in collaboration with other composers. In 1911 he went to America with a tremendous reputation behind him and had a further run of successes there with *Marriage à la Carte* (1911); *The *Pink Lady* (1911)—a popular show that made pink a fashionable colour for women's clothes; *Oh! Oh! Delphine!* (1912); *The Belle of Bond Street* (1914); *Papa's Darling* (1914); *The Little Café* (1914); *Chin-Chin* (1914); *Jack O'Lantern* (1917); *The Girl Behind the Gun* (1918); *The Canary* (1918); *The Kiss Call* (1919); *Kissing Time* (1920); *Tip Tip* (1920); and *The Hotel Mouse* (1922). Working for most of his life in English-speaking spheres, his music always retained the light, sophisticated touch of French operetta.

Casa Loma Orchestra. American jazz orchestra. It began life as the Orange Blossoms, part of the Jean *Goldkette organization in Detroit. The augmented group was engaged to appear at a Canadian roadhouse, the Casa Loma, which never opened; but the band kept the name, working on a co-operative basis under the leadership of Glen Gray (1906–63) with Gene *Gifford as President and arranger. It was a pioneer group of the emerging swing era, making its first recordings in New York in 1929 and enjoying peak popularity 1932–5. Although precise and expert in its musicianship, it now seems to lack the relaxation and easy swing of the black bands it tried to emulate, and after Gifford left in 1935 it became just another dance band.

Casanova. Revue-operetta with music by Johann *Strauss II, selected and arranged by Ralph *Benatzky from the scores of some of Strauss's lesser-known works (such as *Indigo* and *Die Blindekuh*), and book by Hans Müller. The libretto follows the love affairs of the principal characters through the capitals of 18th-century Europe and the score includes several colourful ballets. The 'Nuns' chorus' ('O Madonna, auf uns sieh'), with its effective organ obbligato, has become a lastingly popular item. It was first produced in Berlin in 1928 with a cast that included Michael Bohmen, Anni Frind, Anny Ahlers, Paul Morgan, Emmy Sturm, and Siegfried Arno. With English book by Harry Graham, it was staged at the London Coliseum, 24 May 1932, where it followed the highly successful **White Horse Inn*. The cast included Arthur Fear as Casanova, Dorothy *Dickson, and Marie Löhr and it had 429 performances. There was a popular production in Vienna in 1935.

Cash, Johnny (*b* Kingsland, Ark., 26 Feb. 1932). American singer. Born in a railroad shack, the son of a poor cotton farmer, he was of part Indian descent. As a boy he sang in his local church, and at 17 won an amateur talent contest. He served in the US Air Force during the Korean War, 1950–4, during which time he learned the guitar. In 1955 he began to broadcast and to appear in Country and Western concerts, mostly singing his own compositions. Without the benefit of a musical education, his songs had an earthy quality and mainly dealt with poverty and repression. He recorded for Sun Records in his early days, later becoming a Columbia/CBS artist. One of his most popular songs was inspired by a brief spell in prison on a smuggling charge—'Folsom Prison blues'. He had a hit in 1956 with the rather gloomy 'I walk the line' which took him outside the C & W area; and had his greatest success with 'A boy named Sue' in 1969. Coming through a difficult period of drugs and divorce, he turned to the religious background of his childhood and moved into gospel music in the 1970s. He is a stylish and highly individual performer and showed himself an accomplished actor in several films.

J. L. Smith: *Johnny Cash Discography and Recording History* (Los Angeles, 1969). C. S. Wren: *Winners Got Scars Too: the Life and Legend of Johnny Cash* (New York, 1971). J. Cash: *Man in Black* (Grand Rapids, 1975).

Cass, Ronald (*b* Llanelli, Wales, 21 Apr. 1923). British composer and lyricist. Educated at the University College of Wales, he worked as a teacher while contributing to revues and became fully occupied with music from 1950, composing for TV and, from 1961, for films. His revue work included *10:15* (1951); *The Irving Revue* (1952); *Just Lately* (1952); *Intimacy at Eight* (1952); *High Spirits* (1953); **Intimacy at 8:30* (1954); *For Amusement Only* (1956); *Harmony Close* (1957); *For Adults Only* (1958); and *The Lord Chamberlain Regrets* (1961). His film scores include: *The Young Ones* (1961); *Go To Blazes* (1962); *Summer Holiday* (1963); *French Dressing* (1964); and *The Gypsy* (1970). He has written songs for Tom *Jones, Cliff *Richard, the *Seekers, Petula *Clark, and others.

Castle, Irene [née Foote] (*b* New Rochelle, NY, 7 Apr. 1893; *d* Eureka Springs, Kan., 25 Jan. 1969) and **Vernon** Blyth (*b* Norwich, 2 May 1887; *d* Houston, 15 Feb. 1918). Actors and dancers, the world's leading exponents of ballroom dancing. Vernon went to America in 1906 and started a stage career as a stooge to Lew *Fields, appearing with him in seven Broadway shows. He also appeared in *About Town* (1906); *The Girl Behind the Counter* (1907); *The Mimic World* (1908); *The Midnight Sons* (1909); and *Old Dutch* (1909). He married Irene in 1911, and they both appeared in *The Summer Widowers* (1910); *The Hen-Pecks* (1911);

The Sunshine Girl (1913); and *Watch Your Step* (1914).

They worked out a polished dancing act and started American crazes for such things as the Castle Walk and the Hesitation Waltz. Their first international mark was made as a dancing team in Paris in 1912, where they performed the Texas Tommy and the Grizzly Bear. They had a tremendous influence on the modern ballroom scene, introducing such dances as the Turkey Trot and the *maxixe, and formulating the popular version of the *tango. In 1914 they wrote the best-selling *Modern Dancing*, which became a standard work on the subject. Vernon joined the Royal Canadian Flying Corps in 1914 and was killed in an aeroplane crash in 1918. Irene retired from the stage and dancing, devoting much of her life to running a dogs' home and marrying three more times. In 1939, Ginger *Rogers and Fred *Astaire starred in a film on their lives, *The Story of Vernon and Irene Castle*.

I. Castle: *Castles in the Air* (New York, 1958; repr. 1980).

Cat and the Fiddle, The. Musical comedy with music by Jerome *Kern and book by Otto *Harbach, produced at the Globe Theatre, New York, 15 Oct. 1931, with Odette Myrtil (1898–1978), Georges Metaxa (1899–1950), Bettina Hall (*b* 1906), Eddie *Foy Jr., and Lawrence Grossmith (1877–1944), where it had 395 performances. Its operetta-style story of an earnest-minded composer of Romanian origins (Metaxa) at odds with a lady composer of jazzy inclinations who tries to pep up his score (Hall), who naturally get over their difficulties with the help of Cupid in the end, was ephemeral; but its magnificent songs have lasted—'The night was made for love', 'Try to forget', 'She didn't say 'yes'', among them. In a way it echoed Kern's own beginnings when he was often called upon to add a little modern spice to rusty scores—as in *The *Catch of the Season*. It had 219 performances, from 4 Mar. 1932 at the Palace Theatre, London, with Muriel Barron, Alice *Delysia, Peggy *Wood, Francis Lederer (*b* 1906), and Henri Leoni. It was filmed in 1934 with the leading roles taken by Jeanette *MacDonald and Ramon Novarro (1899–1968).

Catch of the Season, The. Successful British musical play which had 621 performances at the Vaudeville Theatre, London, 9 Sept. 1904, with Zena *Dare as its leading lady. The book was by Seymour *Hicks and Cosmo Hamilton, the score by Herbert E. Haines and Evelyn Baker containing a few popular hits such as 'The church parade' and 'Cigarette'. But it was not considered strong enough for the New York production, at Daly's Theatre 28 Aug. 1905, starring Edna *May. The score was heavily revised with the young Jerome *Kern, among others, providing new material, but it still only managed 106 performances.

Catlett, Sidney (*b* Evansville, Ind., 17 Jan. 1910; *d* Chicago, 24 Mar. 1951). American jazz drummer, popularly known throughout his career as 'Big Sid'. He played in the bands of Fletcher *Henderson, 1936, Don *Redman 1936–8, and Louis *Armstrong 1938–42, among many. He led his own group from 1944 to 1947 and was with the Louis Armstrong All-Stars 1947–9. He was a drummer with a strong propulsive beat and a show-business streak.

Catlett, Walter (*b* San Francisco, 4 Feb. 1889; *d* Los Angeles, 4 Nov. 1960). American actor and singer. He became known in American musical productions including *The Prince of Pilsen* (1910); *So Long, Letty* (1916); **Ziegfeld Follies* (1917); *Follow the Girl* (1918); *Baby Bunting* (1919); **Sally* (1920); *Lady, Be Good* (1924)—in which he sang 'Oh, lady be good'; *Lucky* (1922); and **Rio Rita* (1922); often playing the elderly buffoon. He appeared in films from 1929.

Cats. A remarkable musical show best described as a feline fantasy. The composer Andrew *Lloyd Webber (already with many successes behind him) had set some of T. S. Eliot's poems from *Old Possum's Book of Practical Cats* in 1977, and, with the help of director Trevor Nunn, reworked them into the unlikely stage production that opened at the New London Theatre in Drury Lane on 11 May 1981 and by 1990 had created the impression that it would go on for ever. The original cast included Elaine *Paige, Wayne Sleep, Bonnie Langford, Sarah Brightman, and Brian Blessed. The audience found themselves revolving round a circular garbage dump which became alive with cats of all kinds, as conceived by Eliot, and a stunningly athletic display of dancing that became the main focus of the entertainment based on the familiar poems and the imaginative staging. The score neatly fulfilled its purpose in a modern idiom with one hit song, 'Memory'. A similarly remarkable production took New York by storm at the Winter Garden Theatre, 7 Oct. 1982, and there was a touring company in America from 1983. Even the historic Theater an der Wien in Vienna succumbed to its feline allure from 24 Sept. 1983.

Cavalcade. Musical spectacle devised by Noël *Coward who wrote both words and music. The show presented various moments of recent British history in a jingoistic display of historical pride and patriotism, using the huge Drury Lane stage and its hydraulic wonders to the full with scenes that included the sinking of the *Titanic* and scenes from the First World War. There were also some good dramatic moments which the critics tended to overlook. Beside his own music, Coward utilized such period items as Ivor *Novello's 'Keep the home fires burning'. Opening on 13 Oct. 1931, it had 405 performances. It was filmed in 1933 with Clive Brook, Diana Wynyard, and Irene Brown. Coward's own music included 'Twentieth century blues', 'Lover of my dreams', and 'The Mirabelle waltz'.

Cavallaro, Carmen (*b* New York, 6 May 1913; *d* 1990). American pianist and bandleader. He was trained as a classical pianist but gradually drifted into the dance-band world, playing with the Alk Kavelin band 1933–7. He worked with Rudy *Vallee for a year, then, from 1939, led his own five-piece band in St Louis. After a stint in Detroit he went to New York in the late 1940s and mainly worked there and in Chicago at various top hotels, popularizing his brand of sweet, swinging dance music and his own decorative style of playing. He appeared in several films, including *Hollywood Canteen* (1944); *Out of this World* (1945); *Diamond Horseshoe* (1945); *The Time, the Place and the Girl* (1946); and playing on the sound-track in *The Eddy Duchin Story* in 1956.

Cawthorn, Joseph (*b* New York, 29 Mar. 1867; *d* Beverly Hills, Calif., 21 Jan. 1949). American actor, comedian, and singer, specializing in German dialect roles. He began his career in minstrel shows and appeared in the British music-hall. His name became established in several musicals 1913–18 in which he starred with Julia *Sanderson. He appeared in *Nature* (1897); *Miss Philadelphia* (1897); *The *Fortune Teller* (1898); *The Rounders* (1899); *Fritz in Tammany Hall* (1905); *The Free Lance* (1906); *The Hoyden* (1907); *Little Nemo* (1908); *The Slim Princess* (1911); *The Sunshine Girl* (1913); *The *Girl from Utah* (1914); *Sybil* (1916); *The Rambler Rose* (1917); *The Canary* (1918); *The Half Moon* (1920); *Tangerine* (1921); *The Blue Kitten* (1922); and **Sunny* (1925). From 1928 he transferred his activities to the film world and appeared in such things as *The *Cat and the Fiddle* (1934); *Twenty Million Sweethearts* (1934); **Gold Diggers of 1935* (1935); **Music in the Air* (1935); **Naughty Marietta* (1935); *The Great Ziegfeld* (1936); and *Lillian Russell* (1940).

Celestin, 'Papa' [Oscar Phillip] (*b* Napoleonville, La., 1 Jan. 1884; *d* New Orleans, 15 Dec. 1954). American jazz trumpeter, vocalist, and bandleader. He went to New Orleans in 1906 and played in the Algiers Brass Band, later with the Olympia Band, before leading his own band at the Tuxedo Hall 1910–17. He founded the Tuxedo Brass Band in 1911 and from 1917 to 1925 he led the Original Tuxedo Jazz Orchestra. A pioneering figure in jazz history, he left jazz during the war years to work in a shipyard and was injured in a motor accident in 1944. He came back to jazz in the rediscovery years *c.* 1946, made some recordings in 1947, and led a band at the Paddock in New Orleans.

Cellier, Alfred (*b* London, 1 Dec. 1844; *d* London, 28 Dec. 1891). British composer and conductor. He was trained in church music and was a member of the Chapel Royal 1855–60. After being organist in several churches 1862–8, he conducted in Belfast; at the Prince's Theatre, Manchester, 1873–7; and at the *Opéra-Comique, London, 1877–9. His future career as a writer of operettas continued to coincide with the career of his contemporary Arthur *Sullivan, who had been in the Chapel Royal choir at the same time. Cellier wrote many works for German *Reed at the Gallery of Illustration, the most popular being *Charity Begins at Home* in 1870; and he had some success with *The Sultan of Mocha* in 1874.

In 1877, Cellier was among the composers approached by Richard D'Oyly *Carte to write 'native' opera for the Opéra-Comique, but the first commission went to Gilbert and Sullivan who produced *The *Sorcerer*. Cellier was the conductor of **HMS Pinafore* at the time of the disgraceful fracas between rival backers, and produced the first amateur performance in Kingston in 1879. He helped Sullivan from time to time with orchestrations and overtures and was resident conductor to the D'Oyly Carte company until 1878 when his brother François (below) took over. Cellier now wrote *After All* (1878) and *In the Sulks* (1880); and in 1886 he became a rival to Sullivan with his very successful musical **Dorothy* which was to achieve 931 performances, thus outstripping all the G & S operas including the contemporary *The *Mikado*. This made Sullivan inclined to retire from the arena; Gilbert and Carte were equally determined that Cellier should be beaten. But it was Cellier who had a further success with his sequel *Doris* (1889) and in 1892, after the breakup of the Savoy team, Cellier found himself collaborating with Gilbert on *The Mountebanks*, which used a plot about a magic lozenge which Sullivan had spurned, ran for 229 performances, and proved to some extent that Gilbert could work without Sullivan. The opera has not stood the test of time though it contains one of Cellier's best tunes, the waltz 'An hour, 'twill rapidly pass'.

Cellier, François (*b* London, 1849; *d* London, 5 Jan. 1914). British conductor and composer. Brother of Alfred *Cellier, whom he succeeded as musical director at the Savoy in 1878, remaining there until 1914 when he was succeeded by Walter Hann. His own works included *Captain Billy* (1891); *Old Sarah* (1897); and, with his brother, *Mrs Jarramie's Genie* (1888). He was co-author in 1914 of a book on the Savoy collaborators.

Cha cha cha. A Cuban dance that became universally popular and had a great vogue around 1958–60, remaining a favourite ballroom item. A descendant of the danzón it has become, outside Cuba, a slow, rocking *mambo with double-tempo interludes in normal mambo time.

Chacksfield, Frank (*b* Battle, Sussex, 9 May 1914). British conductor and composer. He started his working life in a solicitor's office, but had formed his first band at the age of 15 and decided to make music his career. He joined the Royal Army Service Corps in 1939 and became staff arranger for 'Stars in Battledress'. He first broadcast regularly with the wartime *Charlie Chester Show* and continued as an arranger and conductor after the war, gaining international prominence with his light orchestral recordings made for Decca, and achieving top sellers with 'Limelight' and 'Ebb tide'. He continued to record, broadcast, and compose into the 1970s, with a long list of works to his credit.

Châlet, Le. One-act operetta with music by Adolphe *Adam produced at the Opéra-Comique, Paris, 25 Sept. 1834, and often pinpointed by historians as the first genuine French operetta. It was popular and influential in England being performed in London in 1837, 1845, and 1871, and it was heard in Vienna in 1858.

Champion, Harry [Crump, William Henry] (*b* Shoreditch, London, 23 Mar. 1866; *d* London, 14 Jan. 1942). British comedian and singer. He first appeared on the halls in 1882 at the age of 15, sometimes as a blackface artist, turning to his more natural role as a Cockney comedian around 1888. Up to then he had been billed as Will Conray, but with a new name provided by his agent and such songs as 'Any old iron', 'Boiled beef and carrots', 'I'm Henery the Eighth I am', 'The end of my old cigar', and 'Ginger, you're barmy', all delivered at breakneck speed, he now became one of music-hall's most successful artists. His repertoire included a large proportion of songs praising food and drink. His immense vitality kept him on the halls into his seventies, with a first appearance in the Royal Variety Show in 1935 and an appearance with the *Crazy Gang at the London Palladium in 1937, 'Any old iron' was put to good use to encourage the salvage of metal in the Second World War. He broadcast frequently and was a prolific recording artist.

T. Barker: 'Harry Champion' in *Music-Hall*, No. 26 (London, Aug. 1982). Discography in No. 25 (Jun. 1982).

Channing, Carol [Elaine] (*b* Seattle, 31 Jan. 1921). American actress and singer. Wide-eyed, blonde, and scatty, with a distinctive husky voice she first made her name in **Gentlemen Prefer Blondes* in 1949, singing such songs as 'Diamonds are a girl's best friend'. The image stayed with her both in her nightclub work and in her most notable leading role in **Hello, Dolly!* in 1964. She was also in *Lend an Ear* (1948); **Wonderful Town* (1954); *The Vamp* (1955); *Show Girl* (1961); *Lorelei* (1974), a remake of *Gentlemen Prefer Blondes*; and in the films *Thoroughly Modern Millie* (1967) and *Skidoo* (1968).

Chanson. The word 'chanson' has a wider and deeper meaning to the French than is conveyed by the translation 'song'. The 'chanson' is part of the French way of life and its singers and writers have continued the troubadour tradition far more than in other countries. They may frequently attack the establishment in their songs, but they are a fixed part of it. The chanson is equally a medium for social comment, politics, and the joys and sorrows of nature and love. It was a vital part of French literature as far back as the Middle Ages, and in the golden years between 1400 and 1520 more than 125 collections of chansons appeared. One of the most influential was *Chansons nouvelles* published by Pierre Attaignant 1527/8. In 1538, Attaignant became Printer of the King's Music and much of his work consisted of the promotion of the chanson through some 100 or so collections that became known throughout Europe. The 17th and 18th centuries saw chanson flourishing in court circles and in the theatre, becoming increasingly a political weapon in the years that led to the revolution of 1789. In the 19th century the French became more fully aware of their very special cultural heritage of song, and literature on the subject rapidly increased. In 1953 a national collection of 'La chanson du pays' was inaugurated.

The *café-concerts of the 1770s and thereafter were a natural home for the chanson, which now flourished more than ever and was to continue to do so into the radio and television eras. The chanson has always been a mirror of the times; sometimes strongly patriotic, as in revolutionary and war periods; romantic during the 'belle époque'; in post-war times often cynical and pessimistic. The changes wrought by the jazz age did not alter the essential commentary nature of the chanson.

The chanson was at its most distinctively French in the literary and satirical guise popular in the cabarets of Montmartre, such as the famous *Chat Noir, where Aristide *Bruant and others founded the 'chanson réaliste', a vein which is still strong; alongside the more romantic vein which has thrived from the days of *Guilbert and *Mistinguett, through *Chevalier, *Trenet, *Rossi, *Sablon, and *Piaf, to modern troubadours such as *Aznavour, *Brassens, *Brel, Moustaki; and many more.

P. Anjou: *Histoire de la chanson française au temps du 'Chat Noir'* (Paris, 1943). A. Adelmann: *Chansons à vendre* (Paris, 1967). G. Erisman: *Histoire de la chanson* (Paris, 1967). M. Herbert: *La chanson à Montmartre* (Paris, 1967). C. Brunschwig, L-J. Calvet, & J-C. Klein: *100 Ans de chanson française* (Paris, 1972).

Chapí y Lorente, Ruperto (*b* Villena, 27 Mar. 1851; *d* Madrid, 25 Mar. 1909). Spanish composer. The son of a barber, he became interested in music at the age of 5 and at 16 went to complete his studies at the Madrid Conservatory. While a student he supported himself by playing the cornet in theatre orchestras and wrote his first *zarzuela. In 1872 he became a bandmaster in the Spanish artillery and the following year won an award from the Academía de Bellas Artes which enabled him to continue his studies in Rome during 1874. He tried his hand at grand opera in *La hija de Jefté* (1876), and continued to do so, but he found that his true talent lay in the lighter field of operetta. After a prolonged struggle against poverty he had his first real success as a writer for the theatre with the zarzuela *La Tempestad* (1882) which clearly showed his capacity for graceful melody and tasteful orchestration.

He produced 161 stage works in all, including 155 zarzuelas, which eventually brought him much fame and wealth and made him one of the best-known composers for the Spanish theatre. His most celebrated work was *La Revoltosa* (1897) of which Saint-Saëns said that Bizet would have been proud to have written it. Elsewhere he was described as 'the Spanish Massenet'.

In 1893 he founded the Sociedád de Autores, Compositores y Editores de Musica, the Spanish equivalent of ASCAP or the Performing Right Society.

His other zarzuelas included: *La bruja* (1887); *Las hijas del Zebedeo* (1889); *El rey que rabió* (1891); *La Czarina* (1892); *El tambor de Granaderos* (1894); *Mujer y reina* (1895); *Las bravias* (1896); *Los golfos* (1896); *La chavala* (1898); *La cara di Dios* (1899); *El barquillero* (1900); *La cortijera* (1900); *El puñao de rosas* (1902); *Don Juan de Austria* (1902); *La venta de Don Quijote* (1902); *La patria chica* (1907) and, his last, *Margarita la Tornera* (1909), produced just before he died.

A. S. Salcedo: *Ruperto Chapí, su vida y sus obras* (Madrid, 1929). J. A. Gómez: *Ruperto Chapí y su obra lírica* (Alicante, 1973). A. Sagardía: *Ruperto Chapí* (Madrid, 1979).

Chapin, Harry (*b* New York, 7 Dec. 1942; *d* New York, 16 July 1981). American songwriter and singer. Before entering the world of pop music he was a pilot, pool-player, film director, and composer. For a while he was a member of the Brothers and Sisters, before establishing himself as a popular folk-rock singer performing his own songs which had a strong sociological context particularly concerned with poverty. He continued to devote much of his time to these matters beyond the musical world and in 1979 was appointed to the Presidential Council on World Hunger by President Carter. He appeared in *The Night That Made America Famous*, an experimental revue for which he wrote some of the songs. He had a No. 1 hit in America with 'Cat's in the cradle' in 1974 and his albums included such songs as 'Sniper', 'I still remember you', 'You're the only song', 'All my life's a circle', and 'Taxi'; but his fame had barely begun to spread beyond the USA when he was killed in a car crash.

Chaplin, Charlie [Charles Spencer] (*b* London, 16 Apr. 1889; *d* Vaud, Vevey, Switzerland, 25 Dec. 1977). British actor, author, composer, and film director. He started his career in the British music-hall as part of Fred Karno's troupe, going to Hollywood with them in 1914, and remaining there to become the most famous of all silent film comedians. His career, often made difficult in the USA because of his left-wing sympathies, continued with less success into the era of the talkies, but his reputation was already established. His major films included *Easy Street* (1917); *The Immigrant* (1917); *The Kid* (1921); *The Gold Rush* (1925); *City Lights* (1931); *Modern Times* (1936); *The Great Dictator* (1940); *Monsieur Verdoux* (1947); and *Limelight* (1952). He wrote the music for most of his films, sometimes in collaboration (e.g. with David *Raksin and Edward Powell on *Modern Times*). This facet of his talent was brought to public attention by the popular success of the theme from *Limelight*. His son Sydney (*b* 1926) was an actor and singer who appeared in *Limelight* and such musicals as **Bells Are Ringing* (1956); *Subways Are For Sleeping* (1961); and **Funny Girl* (1964).

C. Chaplin: *My Autobiography* (New York–London, 1964).

Chaplin, Saul [Kaplan, Saul] (*b* Brooklyn, NY, 19 Feb. 1912). American composer and pianist. At one time he ran an orchestra with Sammy *Cahn. He was the composer of the *Lunceford theme tune 'Rhythm is our business' and writer for various orchestras and for films, working in Hollywood from 1941. He wrote a musical, *Bonanza Bound* (1948), and his songs include 'Until the real thing comes along' (1936, *w* Cahn and Freeman), 'Shoeshine boy' (1936), 'If it's the last thing I do' (1937), 'Please be kind' (1938), 'You're a lucky guy' (1939), all with lyrics by Cahn; and 'The anniversary song' (with Al *Jolson, 1946). His film scores include *Cover Girl* (1944); *The Jolson Story* (1946); **On the Town* (1949); *Summer Stock* (1950); *An *American in Paris* (1951); **Kiss Me Kate* (1953); **Seven Brides for Seven Brothers* (1954); **High Society* (1956); *The Teahouse of the August Moon* (1956); *Merry Andrew* (1958); **West Side Story* (1961); and *Star!* (1968) which was one of the many movies he produced or directed from 1957.

Chappell & Co. British music publishers founded in 1810 by Samuel Chappell, J. B. Cramer, and F. T. Latour. When the last of these partners, Samuel Chappell, died in 1834 the business was taken over by his son William Chappell (1809–88) who expanded it in many directions and showed a strong interest in popular music by editing *A Collection of National English Airs* (2 vols) in 1838/9, which was expanded into *Popular Music of the Olden Time* (2 vols) (1855/9) since reissued in revised editions. The firm did a valuable service to the drawing-room ballad by promoting Ballad Concerts, the 'Monday and Saturday Pops' referred to by W. S. Gilbert. When William Boosey became managing director the firm moved into the operetta field and was to publish most of the Gilbert and Sullivan scores. Its interest in the musical comedy world was widened when the firm was bought up by Louis Dreyfus in 1929. The American branch, under Max Dreyfus, published such composers as Richard *Rodgers, Jerome *Kern, Cole *Porter, and Harold *Arlen. A disastrous fire in the firm's Bond Street premises in 1965 destroyed much valuable documentary material.

C. Mair: *The Chappell Story, 1811–1961* (London, 1961).

Charig, Phil [Philip] (*b* New York, 31 Aug. 1902; *d* New York, 21 July 1960). American composer. He wrote many musical shows, having his greatest Broadway hit with **Follow the Girls* in 1944. Others included: *Yes, Yes, Yvette* (1927); *Just Fancy* (1927); *Allez-Oop* (1927); *Lady Mary* (1928); *Lucky Girl* (1928); *Polly* (1929); and for London *That's a Good Girl* (1928) and *Stand Up and Sing* (1931) both starring Jack *Buchanan. He contributed to the revue *Artists and Models* (1943). His best-known song was 'Sunny disposish' (*w* Ira *Gershwin) used in **Americana* (1926). He collaborated on several occasions with the composer Joseph *Meyer.

Charles, Ray [Robinson, Ray Charles] (*b* Albany, Ga., 23 Sept. 1930). American pianist and singer. He had already started to learn the piano when he became totally blind at the age of six, but he continued with a musical career and became a band pianist. He soon formed his own group and began to write songs in the rhythm 'n' blues style of the 1950s, later delving into *jazz, *soul, and *country music for his varied inspiration. He achieved R & B hits with 'It should have been me' (1954) and 'Hallelujah! I love her so' (1956). Up to then his work had been greatly influenced by Nat 'King' *Cole but he now moved away from this style and broke into the pop market with 'What'd I say' in 1959. His biggest success came with the No. 1 hit 'Georgia on my mind' (1960); to be followed, among many, with 'Hit the road Jack' (1961), 'I can't stop loving you' (1962), and 'Busted' (1963). Having recorded with the Atlantic and ABC-Paramount labels, he formed his own record company, Crossover, in 1973 which was later marketed by Atlantic.

R. Charles & D. Ritz: *Brother Ray: Ray Charles' Own Story* (New York, 1978).

Charleston. A popular dance that probably had African, possibly Ashanti, origins, before it emerged in its earliest form in the Southern states of America. A dance of the *shimmy variety, it was essentially feminine in the first place but became more masculine in its later commercial forms. It was well-known among Southern black people around the turn of the century and Noble *Sissle recalled being taught to dance it in 1903. It became more widely known when introduced into black musicals such as *Liza* (1922) and *How Come* (1923), achieving some popularity to the accompaniment of a tune called 'Charleston, South Carolina' written by James P. *Johnson in 1923 which fixed its intriguing stop-time rhythms in the public's mind. Johnson improved on this with the number simply called 'Charleston' which was introduced in *Runnin' Wild*, a popular black revue touring the USA in 1923.

The dance was introduced to white audiences by Ned Wayburn, in the **Ziegfeld Follies of 1923* at the Amsterdam Theatre in New York, and he claimed the invention of the widely popular steps that now invaded the dance halls. During the next two or three years the Charleston became a world-wide craze. Ginger *Rogers started her career as 'Queen of the Charleston' and Joan Crawford came to fame with it in the film *Our Dancing Daughters*. It became a regular dance-band item by 1925 and was introduced to London in a revue early that year at the Hotel Metropole. In July 1925 a special demonstration was given by Annette Mills and Robert Sielle which helped to promote its popularity in English dancing circles. Some newspapers condemned its wild cavortings, but it went on to a peak of popularity with a Charleston Ball arranged by C. B. *Cochran at the Royal Albert Hall on 15 Dec. 1926, a mammoth competition with Josephine Bradley, Fred *Astaire, Lew *Leslie, and Jack *Hylton among the judges. The Charleston was pushed out of top favour by the craze for the *Black Bottom in 1927, and its eccentric sidekicks and exhilarating syncopations were merged into a less agile dance more suited to the general public, the *quick-step. Since then the Charleston has had many revivals and remains the dance which typifies the gay and turbulent 1920s.

Charlie Girl. British musical which had 2202 performances at the Adelphi Theatre, London, from 15 Dec. 1965, then the sixth longest run in London. The score by David *Heneker and John Taylor, which included such numbers as 'Charlie girl', 'Let's do a deal', 'My favourite occupation', 'I was young', and 'The party of a lifetime', was not especially distinguished. The story, by Hugh and Margaret Williams, was a farcical one set in a stately home, with Lady Charlotte chasing a rich American playboy but finally settling for a nice local lad. It brought Anna *Neagle back to the musical stage after a 12-year absence (later succeeded by Evelyn *Laye) and the cast also included pop singer Joe Brown (*b* 1941), Hy Hazell (1922–70), and Derek Nimmo (*b* 1931). There was a revised version at the Victoria Palace, 19 June 1986, with Cyd Charisse (*b* 1921) in the lead.

Charlot, André (*b* Paris, 26 July 1882; *d* Woodland, Calif., 20 May 1956). French producer and director. He is chiefly remembered for the sophisticated intimate revues that bore his name in 1924/25/26/28/30/35/37 (see also under ANDRÉ CHARLOT'S LONDON REVUE OF 1924); and which introduced Beatrice *Lillie, Gertrude *Lawrence, and Jack *Buchanan to the New York stage. But before and after that he had a long string of musical successes in London including *Kill That Fly!* (1912); *Eightpence a Mile* (1913); *Keep Smiling* (1913); *Not Likely!* (1914); *5064 Gerard* (1915); *Now's the Time!* (1915); *Samples* (1915); *Some* (1916); *This and That* (1916); *See-Saw* (1916); *Three Cheers* (1916); *Cheep* (1917); *Bubbly* (1917); *Flora* (1918); *Tabs* (1918); **Very Good, Eddie* (1918); *Tails Up* (1918); *The Officer's Mess* (1918); **Buzz-Buzz* (1918); *Bran Pie* (1919); *Just Fancy* (1920); *Jumble Sale* (1920); *Puss-Puss* (1921); *Now and Then* (1921); *A to Z* (1921); *Pot Luck* (1921); *Snap* (1922); *Dé-Dé* (1922); *Rats* (1923); *London Calling!* (1923); *Yes!* (1923); *Puppets* (1924); *The Wonder Bar* (1930); *How D'You Do?* (1933); *Please* (1933); *Hi-Diddle-Diddle* (1934); *Dancing City* (1935); *Shall We Reverse?* (1935); *Stop . . . Go!* (1935); *The Town Talks* (1936); and *Red, Bright and Blue* (1937). In 1937 he went to Hollywood to work in the film world.

Charts. The baldly practical name by which the record rating lists have been known in recent years. The charts showing the current rating of various record issues, singles and albums, and nowadays in various categories, are usually compiled from information gathered from a selected number of substantial record dealers. While the method of collecting the information is reasonably fair and accurate the statistics, as is their wont, can easily give a distorted and seller-biased view of the situation. A record becomes a No. 1 hit when it has sold more than any other, while the fact that it is a No. 1 hit is what makes it sell; a classic egg-and-chicken situation. Elevation to the charts is also dependent on radio and TV coverage and the whims of reviewers and *disc jockeys. They help to create top hits in the first place by continual playing of discs. Such a position of influence is likely, in view of human nature, to involve a certain amount of bribery and corruption, but this is generally kept within acceptable bounds. There was a notorious 'payola' scandal in the USA in the late 1950s and, in the UK, a period of discontented rumblings in the 1970s when the main chart supplied by the British Market Research Bureau was accused of being fixed and manipulated, a matter closely pursued by the upright British press. It was the compilers of the charts themselves who had originally expressed unease. In the end little criminal evidence came to light and with the promised help of the record companies the charts were considered to have been regularized. It remains a potentially explosive area with so much prestige and money at stake.

Charts have a fairly long history and go back to the times when the record was not the be-all and end-all of the popular music world. The American **Billboard* had printed lists of published songs from 1913; and from 1938 the long-established American show-business magazine **Variety* started printing lists, in its *Variety Radio Directory*, of the important songs published during the year. This was simply a random listing and the magazine, through its editor Abel Green, was one of the first to condemn the 'Top 40' evil which created the payola scandal of the 1960s when it was revealed how much some of the top 'deejays' were being paid to push records over the air. The first definitive rating of songs came in with a radio programme called *Your Lucky Strike Hit Parade* which started 20 Apr. 1935 in the USA and ran until 29 Apr. 1959, by which time the phrase 'hit parade' had become one of the most over-used in the English language. The programme featured the 15 most popular songs of the week. The first No. 1 was Irving *Berlin's 'Cheek to cheek'. The first printed listing in the USA was John G. Peatman's *Weekly Survey* which started on 3 Jun. 1942. In England, **Melody Maker* began to print a similar list in 1946.

The first record chart appeared in the American magazine *Billboard* on 20 Jul. 1940; but Britain lagged well behind with the *New Musical Express* lists, based on record retailers' returns, not appearing until 14 Nov. 1952. The two main chart sources in the UK became the British Market Reearch Bureau compilation published in *Music Week*, on which the BBC's *Top of the Pops* bases its choices; and the one published in the trade paper, *Record Business*.

A related activity was the practice of awarding *Golden Discs; something that developed within the record industry to mark the achievement of selling a million copies of a recording.

J. Edwards: *Top 10's and Trivia of Rock & Roll and Rhythm & Blues* (St Louis, 1974; etc.). T. Jasper: *British Record Charts 1955–1982* (London, 1975; etc.). C. Miron: *Rock Gold: all the Hit Charts from 1955–76* (New York, 1977; etc.). J. Rice, T. Rice, P. Gambaccini, & M. Read: *The Guinness Book of British Hit Singles* (Enfield, 1977; etc.). S. Goldstein: *Oldies but Goodies* (New York, 1978). J. Rice, T. Rice, P. Gambaccini, & M. Read: *The Guinness Book of British Hit Albums* (Enfield, 1983; etc). K. Albert & F. Hoffmann: *Cash Box Album Charts 1955–1974* (Metuchen, 1988).

Chat Noir. Famous café-chantant in Paris which became the home of the new **chanson réaliste* and the birthplace of the modern cabaret and satirical *revue. Named after a stray black cat that made its home there after being found on the building site, it was founded by Rudolphe Salis in 1881 in the Boulevard Rochechouart, near the Place Blanche in Montmartre, which had, by then, become the bohemian centre of Paris. It was originally a private club and home of a literary society known as the Hydropathes: Salis used them and other bohemian intellectuals to get his enterprise off the ground. He rightly sensed that such an establishment would prove a great attraction in such a quarter and, with a licensed bar and decorated in the Louis XIII style (rather like an old English pub full of brass and pewter), the Chat Noir quickly became a popular haunt of the intellectual and the fashionable. The purveyors of the satirical *chanson réaliste*, bohemian, anti-bourgeois and anti-establishment, rebellious and seditious—Jules Jouy, Xavier Privas, and the greatest chansonnier of all Aristide *Bruant—flourished under the chairmanship of Salis. Another great attraction was a shadow theatre, conceived by Jouy, who used puppet silhouettes to illustrate his songs, the whole thing growing more elaborate until it was like an early cartoon film. The Chat Noir soon moved to larger premises in the nearby Rue Victor Massé, while Bruant took over the old premises to found his own club, the Mirliton. The Chat Noir closed in 1897.

R. de Casteras: *Avant le Chat Noir—Les Hydropathes* (Paris, 1945).

Chattaway, Thurland (*b* Springfield, Mass., 8 Apr. 1872; *d* Milford, Conn., 12 Nov. 1947. American composer and lyricist. He started his career as a boy soprano, then went to New York in 1896 to work for a musical magazine edited by Paul *Dresser. A talented pianist and performer, he eventually devoted most of his time to song-writing, achieving such hits as 'Mandy Lee' (1899); 'When the blue sky turns to gold' (1901); 'My honey Lou' (1904);

and the best-selling 'Red Wing' (1905, *m* Kerry *Mills).

Chauve Souris. A Russian song-and-dance revue presented by a troupe from the Bat Theatre of Moscow, which had a notable success in America when it was presented at the 46th Street Theatre 3 Feb. 1922 and ran for 544 performances. Few of the cast spoke English so it was mainly song and mime, the whole introduced in attractively broken English by its director/compère Nikita Balieff. It was one of the new-styled intimate revues that helped to swing fashion away from the lavish Ziegfeld-type productions. Its songs naturally included Russian items such as 'Anuska' and 'Dark eyes', but one of its lasting attractions was a perky march number by the German composer Leon *Jessel—'Parade of the wooden soldiers'. There were less successful later editions and revivals.

Chauvin, Louis (*b* St Louis, Mo., 13 Mar. 1881; *d* Chicago, 26 Mar. 1908). American pianist, entertainer, and composer of Spanish-Indian-Negro descent. He toured America in a dancing/singing partnership with Sam Patterson and had a fair success with such songs as 'The moon is shining in the skies' (1903) and 'Babe, it's too long off' (1906). Mortally ill and destitute in 1907, he was helped by the composer Scott *Joplin who took some of Chauvin's attractive themes, added some of his own, and published them as the exquisite 'Heliotrope bouquet' (1907).

Checker, Chubby [Evans, Ernest] (*b* Philadelphia, 3 Oct. 1941). American singer. He was originally encouraged by the Philadelphia record label Parkway which signed him up in 1959 and achieved a minor hit with his first record, 'The class'. His performing name was given to him because he looked like a young Fats *Domino. He was to make pop history with his recording of 'The twist' in 1960. The song and its accompanying *twist dance was conceived by Hank Ballard (*b* 1936) in 1958, and he made a recording of it with the Midnighters in 1959 without attracting much attention. It was recorded by Checker to accompany his appearance on **American Bandstand*, and his rocking version became a No. 1 hit in 1960, selling more than three million copies and starting the long-lasting and universal dance craze on its way. He cashed in on this success with a series of similarly styled dance songs such as 'Pony time', 'Let's twist again', and 'The fly', regularly appearing on TV and films to demonstrate. After a decline in popularity, he made some reappearances and now rates as a historic figure who features in revival shows.

Chess. Musical with book by Tim *Rice and music by Bjorn Ulvaeus and Benny Anderson (see under ABBA), produced at the Prince Edward Theatre, London, 14 May 1986. Based on the increasingly newsworthy and somewhat conspiratorial world of championship chess, it had Tommy Korberg as the USSR champion, Anatoly Sergeievsky, and Murray Head as the USA champion, Frederick Trumper. A revised version, with book by Richard Nelson, was staged at the Imperial Theatre, New York, 28 Apr. 1988.

Chevalier, Albert Onesime Britannicus Gwathevеoyd Louis (*b* Notting Hill, London, 21 Mar. 1862; *d* London, 11 July 1923). British comedian, actor, singer, author, and composer. He started his career as a straight actor, appearing in a farce at the Prince of Wales Theatre in 1877, working from 1878 to 1887 with the Kendals, George Alexander, and others. He became a solo entertainer, doing his own sketches and songs, and, finding that other people were using his material in the music-halls, decided reluctantly to appear in *music-hall himself. He first did so at the new London Pavilion on 5 Feb. 1891, followed by appearances at the Tivoli and the Metropolitan.

As a result of the growing popularity of his Cockney songs, he became known as 'The Coster's Laureate', even rating the description of 'the Kipling of the music-hall'. He wrote most of his own words, and sometimes the music, but this was often supplied by his brother Auguste Chevalier (1863–1940), who wrote under the name of 'Charles Ingle' and acted as his manager, by his pianist Alfred H. West, or his music director John *Crook. The song 'Wot cher!' or 'Knocked 'em in the Old Kent Road' was inspired by a tune his brother improvised and wrote one Sunday morning; 'My old dutch' (his most successful song) was thought up between engagements and first sung at the Alhambra, Brighton in 1892. It was later the basis of a play, *My Old Dutch*, which he wrote with Arthur Shirley in 1919 and which was also filmed. He ran his own touring company for many years and his lasting success on the stage allowed him to acquire considerable capital, much of which he lost in theatrical ventures, including trying to run the Trocadero Music Hall, but he still left £7000 on his death, a considerable sum for those days.

He made several recordings and published numerous songs that were collected in *Albert Chevalier's Song Album*—'The future Mrs 'Awkins', 'Wot cher!', etc; *Albert Chevalier's 2nd Song Album*—'Our little nipper', 'Wot's the good of hanyfink', etc.; *Songs for Smokers*—'I shouldn't do it if I were you', 'Not a bit of good'; *Albert Chevalier's 4th Song Album*—'My old dutch', 'Jerusalem's dead', etc.; *Albert Chevalier's 5th Song Album*—'A fallen star', 'I've got 'er 'at', etc.; *Chevalier Recital Album*—'Vot vur do 'ee love oi', 'Hif not, why not', etc.; all published by Reynolds Music. Words and melody line of some were reprinted in *Best Music Hall and Variety Songs* (London, 1972).

A. Chevalier & B. Daly: *Albert Chevalier: a Record by Himself* (London, 1896). A. Chevalier: *Before I Forget: the Autobiography of a Chevalier d'Industrie* (London, 1901).

Chevalier, Maurice [Auguste] (*b* Menilmontant, nr. Paris, 12 Sept. 1888; *d* Paris, 1 Jan. 1972).

French comedian, singer, actor, songwriter, and author. He made his debut on the French music-hall stage in 1906 and became a popular figure at the *Folies-Bergère, in company with *Mistinguett, 1909–13. He joined the army in 1914, was taken prisoner and released in 1918, and went back to the Folies-Bergère and other Parisian revues. In London he co-starred with Ethel *Levey in *Hullo, America!* in 1919. From 1919 to 1921 he appeared in a song-and-dance act with Yvonne Vallée (whom he married, and later divorced) appearing with her in *White Birds* in London in 1927. He went to the USA in 1919, appearing at Ziegfeld's Amsterdam Roof Garden in a programme of the songs now intimately connected with his name such as his signature tune 'Louise', 'Valentine', and 'Ma pomme'. He was in the London revue *Stop Press* in 1935.

He appeared in many films including 12 silent films made in New York 1908–24; *Bonjour, New York* (1928); *Innocents of Paris* (1929)—'Louise'; *The Love Parade* (1929)—'Mon cocktail d'amour'; *Paramount on Parade* (1930)—'All I want is just one girl'; *The Big Pond* (1930); *Playboy of Paris* (1930); *The Smiling Lieutenant* (1931); *One Hour With You* (1932); *Love Me Tonight* (1932)—'Mimi'; *Bedtime Story* (1933); *The Way to Love* (1933); *The *Merry Widow* (1934); *Folies Bergère* (1935); *The Beloved Vagabond* (1936); *Break the News* (1938); *Love in the Afternoon* (1957); **Gigi* (1958); *Count Your Blessings* (1959); **Can-Can* (1960); *Pepe* (1960); **Fanny* (1961); *Jessica* (1962); *In Search of the Castaways* (1962); *I'd Rather Be Rich* (1964); and many made in France. He became a universal star, epitomizing the roguish, amorous, handsome Frenchman, and wrote several volumes of memoirs.

A. Rivollet: *Maurice Chevalier: de Ménilmontant au Casino de Paris* (Paris, 1927). W. Boyer: *The Romantic Life of Maurice Chevalier* (London, 1937). A. Willemetz: *Maurice Chevalier* (Geneva, 1954). M. Chevalier: *C'est l'amour* (Paris, 1960; Boston, as *With Love*, 1960). M. Chevalier: *Bravo, Maurice!: a Compilation from the Autobiographical Writings* (Paris, 1968; London, 1973). M. Chevalier: *Môme à cheveux blancs* (Paris, 1969; London, 1971, as *I Remember It Well*). G. Ringold & D. Bodeen: *Chevalier: the Films and Career of Maurice Chevalier* (Secaucus, NJ, 1973). M. Freedland: *Maurice Chevalier* (New York–London, 1981). J. Harding: *Maurice Chevalier: his Life 1888–1972* (London, 1983).

Chicago. American musical with score by John *Kander and book by Fred *Ebb and Bob *Fosse, opening at the 46th Street Theatre on 3 June 1975. Based on a 1916 play by Maurine Dallas Watkins, it tells the story of a married chorus girl who kills her faithless lover, is saved by a clever lawyer, and ends up a star; a cynical, decadent tale, it has something of the flavour of **Cabaret*, being staged as a vaudeville entertainment with an MC introducing each number. The stars were Gwen *Verdon (replaced for a while by Liza *Minnelli), Jerry *Orbach, and Chita *Rivera; and it ran for 898 performances.

Chicago blues. A genre of the rhythm 'n' blues scene of the late 1940s and early 1950s, the beginnings of the heavily amplified, driving rock blues as played by the Muddy *Waters band. It had its strongest hold around 1954–5 when such singers and musicians as Sonny Boy Williamson (1914–48), Little Walter (1930–68), Otis Spann (1930–70), and Jimmy Reed (1925–76) pounded the style home. A strain of the Chicago blues has flourished throughout rock history in such singers as *Howlin' Wolf and Bo *Diddley; among its most successful British exponents are the *Rolling Stones.

Chicago Jazz. Many kinds of jazz have been played in Chicago over the years since King *Oliver and his Creole Jazz Band were there in the early 1920s. But the kind of jazz to which the name of Chicago has been especially linked was that which was played by the young white imitators of the New Orleans style, who formalized their performances into a series of individual solos for each instrument with the rest providing a backing, starting and rounding off with an all-out ensemble. The only real advance was in the development of the jazz solo. Its chief exponents were those who played with the *McKenzie and *Condon Chicagoans, including its leaders and Jimmy *McPartland (trumpet), Frank *Teschemacher (clarinet), Bud *Freeman (saxophone), Joe *Sullivan (piano), with cornettist Bix *Beiderbecke hovering on the fringes.

Chilpéric. Opéra-bouffe in three acts with music by *Hervé produced at the Théâtre des Folies-Dramatiques, Paris, 24 Oct. 1868. It had a great vogue in England, being produced at the Lyceum in 1870, at the Globe in 1872, and revived at the Empire in 1884. It was seen in Vienna in 1869, New York in 1874, and Berlin in 1895.

Chinese Honeymoon, A. Musical comedy with music by Howard *Talbot and book by George Dance (1858–1932) which had a great success at the Royal Strand Theatre, London, 5 Oct. 1901, running for 1075 performances and starring Louie Freear (1873–1939). It neatly cashed in on the vogue for Eastern subjects started off by *The *Mikado*, followed by *The *Geisha*, and pursued by **Chu Chin Chow*. Its lightly tuneful score included 'A paper fan', 'The twiddly bits', 'I want to be a lidy', and 'Daisy with the dimple'. In New York, at the Casino 2 June 1902, with additional music by Gustave *Kerker, starring Adele Ritchie (1874–1930), and Thomas Q. Seabrooke (1860–1913), it had 404 performances. There was a revival in London at the Prince of Wales Theatre in 1915.

Chinn and Chapman. Song-writing team of Nicky [Nicholas] Chinn (*b* London, 16 May 1945) and Mike [Michael] Chapman (*b* Queensland, Australia, 15 Apr. 1947). They met in London in 1970 and had their first minor success with 'Funny, funny' which was recorded by the Sweet in 1971. Working with producer Mickie Most (*b* 1938), they had a series of major hits with such items as 'Blockbuster'

(Sweet, 1972); 'Tiger feet', 'Lonely this Christmas', and 'Oh, boy' (Mud, 1974–5); 'Can the can', 'Devil Gate drive', 'Daytona demon', '48 crash', and 'The wild one' (Suzi Quatro (*b* 1950), 1973–5). They found their tuneful efforts less in demand as the *punk rock movement developed, and they went to the USA to provide material for Blondie ('Heart of glass', 1978), the Knack ('My Sharona', 1979), Patti Smith, and others.

Chirgwin, G. H. [George] (*b* London, 13 Dec. 1854; *d* London, 14 Nov. 1922). British comedian and singer. He was born and raised in the notorious Seven Dials area of London, the youngest of four children; his father had been a circus clown. Chirgwin first appeared with his brothers and sister in the Chirgwin Family troupe in 1861, doing a blackface minstrel show in imitation of the Ethiopian and Buckley Serenaders, then just starting the minstrel vogue in England, and by 1863 they had graduated to the Middlesex Music Hall. They toured until 1868 when Chirgwin made his first solo appearance in Margate, singing 'Come home, Father' with such feeling that he was given a summer engagement. He worked for a while as a busker and a travelling musical instrument salesman during which time he achieved his mastery of a number of instruments—violin, cello, bagpipes, piano, banjo, and one-string fiddle—which were all used in his act later. He toured the halls with his brother Tom as the Brothers Chirgwin. Due to appear at the Gaiety in Liverpool, they had a quarrel, so he appeared on his own as Bros Chirgwin, explaining that his mother had expected twins but, disappointed, had christened him Bros. He was engaged at the Oxford Music Hall on Easter Monday 1877.

By then he had adopted his strange make-up, blackened up except for a white diamond-shaped patch round one eye and dressed in black tights, a long coat, and a very high top hat—and billed as 'The White-Eyed Kaffir'. Sometimes he would reverse the colour scheme, black on white. The initials G. H. were borrowed from G. H. *McDermott. He would ad-lib with the audience, having a great rapport with his own working class, and always ended singing 'The blind boy' or 'My fiddle is my sweetheart'—often both. He became one of the most popular music-hall performers of the day, and also appeared with great success in pantomime. In 1896 he visited Australia. He retired in 1919 and in 1921 became the landlord of the Anchor Hotel in Shepperton, Middlesex.

G. H. Chirgwin: *Chirgwin's Chirrup* (London, 1912). T. Barker: 'G. H. Chirgwin' in *Music-Hall Records*, No. 2 (London, Aug. 1978). B. Anthony: 'Chirgwin Continued' in *Music-Hall*, No. 20 (London, Aug. 1981).

Chisholm, George (*b* Glasgow, 29 Mar. 1915). British jazz trombonist and comedian; also plays euphonium, baritone, piano, vibraphone, and xylophone. He was mainly self-taught, and at the age of 14 was playing the piano in a Glasgow cinema. He played in several dance bands in Glasgow, before moving to London in 1936 where he worked at the Nest Club. He took the opportunity to sit in with visiting black American jazz musicians and so impressed Benny *Carter that he was asked to play on some recordings Carter was making in Holland. He was trombonist with Lew *Stone, Harry *Roy, and Jack Harris, and joined the *Ambrose band in 1937. In 1939 he joined the RAF and was a member of the *Squadronaires dance band 1939–50. He recorded with Fats *Waller in 1939. He was with the BBC Show Band 1950–5. By this time he was recognized as the finest jazz trombonist that Britain had produced and was able to play with the best musicians, including Louis *Armstrong in 1958. A talent as a comedian developed during his work with various BBC radio shows and he became widely known to audiences outside jazz with his TV appearances on the **Black and White Minstrel Show*, but he continued to play jazz with his own Gentlemen of Jazz, and other groups.

Chocolate Soldier, The see **Tapfere Soldat, Der*.

Chorus Line, A. Spectacularly successful American musical first seen at the Public Theatre, New York, 15 Apr. 1975. The show, conceived by director and choreographer Michael Bennett (*b* 1943) had music by Marvin *Hamlisch, lyrics by Edward Kleban (1939–87), and book by James Kirkwood (1924–89) and Nicholas Dante. Dealing with the hopes and frustrations of a particular chorus auditioning for a musical production it was based on taped interviews with 24 dancers made in 1974. Very much an experimental idea to give a little credit to the unsung heroes of the chorus line, it was not so much a story as a series of vignettes and character studies of 18 dancers of varied character and ambition; and very much a corporate production rather than a star vehicle. It ran at the downtown theatre for 101 performances and then switched to Broadway and the Shubert Theatre 25 July 1975, running until 28 Apr. 1990. It opened in London at the Theatre Royal, Drury Lane, 22 July 1976; won a *Pulitzer Prize in 1976; and was filmed in 1985.

Christian, Charlie [Charles] (*b* Bonham, Tex., 29 July 1916; *d* New York, 2 Mar. 1942). American guitarist and blues singer. He came from a very musical family and played in the family band as a child. He took up the guitar and by 1934 was a professional musician playing in the Oklahoma City area with various local bands. By 1937 he was specializing in the electric guitar and was heard by John *Hammond who introduced him to Benny *Goodman. Goodman was unimpressed, but Christian was smuggled along with his amplifier on stage at the Victor Hugo Hotel in Beverley Hills where his extended improvisations on 'Rose room' persuaded Goodman into hiring him as a member of his sextet. He played with Goodman from 1939 to 1941, in his time off becoming a regular at *Minton's Playhouse where he did much to help the guitar become a solo voice in modern jazz. Towards the end of 1940 TB had been diagnosed and he was admitted to Bellevue Hospital. In 1942 well-meaning friends smuggled him out of a sanatorium to a party, where he caught pneumonia from which he died. His extension of the vocabulary of the electric guitar made him a key figure in the emergence of modern jazz and many later players remained indebted to him; perhaps they would have been even more so if drugs, drink, women, and all the excesses of after-hours life had not taken their toll so early.

R. Blash: Chap. in *Combo: USA* (Philadelphia, 1971).

Christiné, Henri Marius (*b* Geneva, 27 Dec. 1867; *d* Paris, 12 Nov. 1941). Swiss/French composer. Son of a French Savoyard who had taken Swiss nationality, he found the possibilities of a musical or theatrical career limited in Switzerland, so he went to Paris at the age of 23 and worked as an entertainer at café-concerts and began to write songs. Early attempts to write and sell an operetta (e.g. *Service d'Amour* in 1903) proved difficult, but success came at last with the gay and tuneful **Phi-Phi* in 1918, followed by *Dédé* (1921); *Madame* (1923); *La Poule* (1936); *Temps du Merveilleuse* (1937); and *Yana* (1937). He was a prolific writer of cabaret songs, the best-known being 'Valentine' (*w* Albert Willemetz, 1887–1964), which was first sung by Maurice *Chevalier in *Paris qui chant* (1925); also 'La petite Tonkinoise' (written for Harry *Fragson and later revived by Josphine *Baker) and 'L'homme du dancing' (1923, *w* Willemetz), which became better-known as 'Do I love you' (1925, *w* E. Ray Goetz).

Christy, June [Luster, Shirley] (*b* Springfield, Ill., 20 Nov. 1925; *d* Sherman Oaks, Calif., 21 June 1990). American singer. She developed a jazz-inflected style with Boyd *Raeburn and became known through her work with the Stan *Kenton band which she joined in 1945 as a replacement for Anita *O'Day. She recorded such items as 'Tampico', 'It's been a long, long time', 'Just a-sittin' and a-rockin'', and 'Lonely woman' and married saxophonist Bob Cooper. She left Kenton in 1948 to pursue a solo career. She worked with Ted *Heath in the 1950s, and gradually retired from the musical scene in the 1960s after a number of LPs, including *Something Cool*, made for Capitol records.

Chu Chin Chow. Famous British spectacular musical which was one of the treats for the soldiers on leave during the First World War. It was conceived by the actor/writer Oscar *Asche, who had a special line in Eastern spectaculars, and it was provided with an excellent score by the largely unheralded Frederic *Norton—'Here be oysters stewed in honey', 'I am Chu Chin Chow', 'The robbers' chorus', 'Any time's kissing time', and the immortal 'Cobbler's song' so beloved of bass-baritones. It opened at His Majesty's Theatre 31 Aug. 1916 and was to break all London theatre records of the time with a run of 2238 performances, not exceeded until the 1950s. In the cast were Oscar Asche, Courtice Pounds (1862–1927), Lily Brayton (Mrs Oscar Asche), Aileen d'Orme (1875–1939), and Sydney Fairbrother (1872–1941), and the musical director was Percy *Fletcher. It opened in New York at the Manhattan Opera House 22 Oct. 1917, with Tyrone Power (1869–1931), Florence Reed (1883–1967), and Henry E. *Dixey, but New York was not so impressed and it only had 158 performances. There was a London revival in 1941; and it was filmed in 1932 with George *Robey, Anna May Wong (1907–61), and Malcolm McEachern (1885–1945).

Chueca, Federico (*b* Madrid, 5 May 1846; *d* Madrid, 20 June 1908). Spanish composer. It was intended that he should become a doctor and he began to study medicine in Madrid, but he became increasingly interested in music and, during the vacations, he and his friends organized a street band. He was given an opportunity to conduct theatre orchestras, and when a set of his waltzes, *Lamento de un preso*, was performed under *Barbieri by the Sociedád de Conciertos to great acclaim he decided that music must be his career. He began to compose for the stage in collaboration with Joaquín *Valverde who helped with the harmony and orchestration. Chueca had no academic training but he had a remarkable gift for writing tuneful and memorable music with popular appeal; a sort of Spanish Irving *Berlin. Active at a time when the zarzuela was having a popular revival, his own contribution was a series of delightful one-act pieces full of catchy tunes that took the Spanish audiences by storm and a charm and lightness of touch that put him in the *Offenbach or *Sullivan class. With Valverde, writing as Chueca y Valverde, he achieved some lively results, notably with the 'Madrid revue' *La Gran Vía* (2 July 1886), an immediate success and fodder for all the barrel-organs in Spain. It was performed more than 1000 times in Madrid alone and also became popular in South America. In the USA and London it was staged as *Castles in Spain*, with some loss of Spanish flavour.

Chueca's own *Agua, azucarillos y aguardiente* (1897) was equally popular, as were *Cádiz* (1886), which contained a march that was the Spanish national anthem for a time and is still a regular military band item; *Caramelo* (1884); *El año pasado por agua* (with Valverde, 1889), remembered for its lively dances; *El chaleco blanco* (1890); and *El último chulo* (1889). Chueca (and Valverde) found much of their inspiration in the folk-songs and street songs of Spain, *La alegría de la huerta* (1900) with Murcian flavour and *La Caza del Oso* (1891) utilizing melodies from the Asturias. As with Offenbach, much of their humour and satire was local in nature; *La Gran Vía* was full of references to the municipal affairs of Madrid, and Chueca himself became a powerful political propagandist. But it was his melodies that carried all before them; even though the insidious and easy charms of the famous 'Jota de los ratas' in *La Gran Vía* led Nietzsche to remark scornfully that 'the nation that has produced this music is beyond salvation'. Chueca is regarded as one of the founding creators of the 'género chico' of the *zarzuela.

Churchill, Frank (*b* Rumford, Me., 20 Oct. 1901; *d* Castaic, Calif., 14 May 1942). American composer. He studied for a medical career, but gave it up to become a cinema pianist. From 1930 until his death he was under contract as composer to the Walt Disney studios, where he wrote the music for many famous full-length cartoons and won an Academy Award for his music to *Dumbo* (1941). He is best remembered, though, for his 1937 **Snow White* score with such lasting titles (lyrics by Larry Morey) as 'Someday my Prince will come', 'With a smile and a song', 'I'm wishing', 'Heigh-ho', 'One song', 'Whistle while you work', and 'Silly song'. *Bambi* (1942) won an Academy Award for 'Love is a song', while earlier *The Three Little Pigs* (1933) had introduced 'Who's afraid of the big bad wolf?'.

Cigarette cards. The earliest cigarette cards were issued in the USA in the 1880s. Making practical use of the card (or 'stiffener' as it was known in the trade) which was inserted in the packet to help protect the cigarettes, it was first used as extra advertising space and then to carry an attractive numbered set of pictures which, it was rightly surmised, might turn the human urge to collect into a sales asset. The very first card is thought to have been a one-off portrait of the Marquis of Lorne (a handsome English nobleman, eldest son of the Duke of Argyle, who was then Governor General of Canada) which was included in 1879 in a brand of cigarettes bearing his name.

The first cards to be issued in Britain were a series of famous personalities and celebrities put out by Allen & Ginter (makers of Richmond Gem, a brand frequently advertised in theatre programmes of the time), an American firm operating in England. Favourite hobbies of the Victorians included collecting postcards and compiling scrapbooks, so these enthusiasms were easily diversified to the new and attractive miniatures. The issuing and collecting of cigarette cards very quickly became popular. In America, by the turn of the century, some 500 different series had already been issued.

Well established by the heyday of the music-hall, an obvious series was one featuring the popular stars of the day, especially alluring to the heavily smoking working class. The first music-hall series seems to have come from Hignett Bros & Co. in 1898, a set of 20 cards called 'Music Hall Artistes'. A set of these is now hard to find and they are priced at over £20 a card. The next series came from Gallagher in 1899, a set of 85 'Stage & Variety Celebrities', also rare items and fetching over £30 a card. In 1901 the Richmond Cavendish Co. issued a series of 20 'Music Hall Artistes', now worth over £250 a set; and in 1902 Salmon & Gluckstein, who issued exotic-looking packages under the brand name of 'Snake Charmer', came out with a set of 30 'Music Hall Celebrities'. These were eye-catching cards, slightly larger than the norm, with colourful drawings of the artistes in costume reflecting the art of Concanen and the *music covers of the time. Lambert & Butler issued a set in 1906 and Ogden's overseas brands such as 'Polo' and 'Tabs' issued identical photographic sets of 50 'Music Hall Celebrities' in 1911. The Wills 'Scissors' set of the same year were also similar. Cope's series of 50 'Music Hall Artistes' in 1913 went back to delicately coloured artwork in the musical comedy music cover style of the day. By 1930 the artwork on such sets as R. & J. Hill's 'Music Hall Celebrities' (now available in both the smaller 10-cigarette size and the larger 20 format) had settled on a heavily screened newsprint type of colour reproduction which lacks the charm of earlier issues. There were also interesting sets which featured the songs and catchphrases of singers of the time, two attractive sets coming from Adkin & Sons in 1901 and 1902 (12 in each), 'A Living Picture' and 'Character Sketches'. Fairly scarce and fetching between £3 and £10 a card nowadays are the 10 series (25 cards each) of 'Songs' issued by the American Tobacco Company in 1900, with the words of the songs printed on the backs of the cards—often of rare gems like 'Mother says I mustn't' and 'It's naughty but it's nice'.

The 1930s boom in smoking (when the non-smoker was usually the odd one out) brought a proliferation of cards that might interest the theatre, film, and music enthusiast. There were numerous series of Cinema Stars and Film Favourites, Stars of the Stage and Screen, and later, Radio Celebrities. The field also covered Musical Celebrities and Musical Instruments. Of special note were Faulkner's 'Street Cries' (1902); Player's 'Cries of London' (1912 and 1914); and two 'Gilbert & Sullivan' series (1925 and 1927).

Cinema Organ. The super-cinemas of the 1930s were no longer content with a piano or even a small orchestra. It was the period of the mighty Wurlitzer, and even the provincial cinema would have its organ which appeared from the depths with its popular organist ensconced before the glittering monster. Oddly, the organ came into prominence after the films themselves had been equipped with sound; their role was not to provide background music but to offer extra entertainment as overture and entr'acte, with short recitals of popular music of the day given before the start of the film programme proper or between films. The cinema organ was a complete pipe organ plus as many novelty effects as money could buy (most had drums, some had a complete set of piano strings, masses of comic percussion and built-in tremolo effects, train noises, etc.). It was played from an electric console usually with three or four manuals and an ostentatiously large array of stops. It fostered a race of well-loved cinema organists—in Britain names like Reginald Foort, Reginald Porter-Brown, Dudley Savage, Reginald New, Henry Croudson, Ena Baga, Harold Ramsay, Charles Smart, Harold Smart, and Robin Richmond. Concurrently the instrument was played at the Tower Ballroom, Blackpool, for dancing, making Reginald *Dixon a household name; while the BBC had Sandy McPherson (1897–1975) as resident organist 1938–63. The two most famous makes of instrument were Wurlitzer and Compton.

Cingalee, The. One of the long-running series of musical plays staged at *Daly's Theatre, London, in the early 1900s; with score by Lionel *Monckton, book by James T. Tanner, lyrics by Adrian *Ross and Percy *Greenbank; and additional music by Paul *Rubens and Howard *Talbot. It opened 5 Mar. 1904, with Sybil Arundale, Hayden *Coffin, and Rutland *Barrington in an illustrious cast, and ran for 365 performances. It had a brief run in New York later in 1904.

Circus Girl, The. Musical comedy which opened at the *Gaiety Theatre, London, 5 Dec. 1896 with Ellaline *Terris and Seymour *Hicks as its stars, running for 497 performances. Ivan *Caryll was composer and conductor, with additional music by Lionel *Monckton, book by James T. Tanner and Walter Pallant, and lyrics by Adrian *Ross and Harry *Greenbank. It had a run of 171 performances at *Daly's in New York from 23 Apr. 1897; and was twice staged in Vienna in 1902.

Circus Music. The circus was a popular feature of Roman life, heavily featuring, as it still does, displays of equestrian skill. The circus in England became popular in the mid-18th century when Philip Astley (1742–1814) started giving exhibitions of trick-riding and in 1770 opened a circus in Lambeth. His drum-and-fife accompaniment was the first English circus band. Other famous names that followed were Ducrow, Hengler, and Sanger. The younger of two Sanger brothers took to himself the title of Lord George Sanger as a riposte to 'The Hon.' William Cody, better known as 'Buffalo Bill', who was touring England with his Wild West show. Later names included those of Bertram Mills and the Chipperfield family.

The circus pre-eminently flourished in the USA. It was introduced there around 1792 by John Ricketts, an Englishman, who founded an Astley-type circus in Philadelphia. Countless circuses have toured America since then, ever growing in size and culminating in 1919 with the amalgamation of the Ringling Brothers and Barnum & Bailey (founded in 1884 and 1871 respectively). The Quick and Mead Circus performed to a hurdy-gurdy and drum in 1826; while the first sizeable band we read about was when the Purdy, Welch, Macomber cavalcade arrived in Albany, New York, led by a band of 15 musicians, some riding the horses and elephants. By 1884 the Sells Brothers 'Monster 50 Cage Menagerie and Great 4 Ring Circus' had a military-style band of 29 (including the conductor)—piccolo, one E♭ and six B♭ clarinets, two E♭ and five B♭ cornets, four altos (presumably keyed-bugles or fluegelhorns), one bass and three tenor trombones, two tubas, and three percussion.

Many bandmasters achieved fame with circus bands, but the greatest name of all was that of Merle Evans. Born in 1892, he joined a travelling circus in 1909 and 10 years later was conducting the combined bands of the Ringling and Barnum & Bailey shows, which he did until 1969 when he retired after 50 years' service; and there was Frederick Jewell (1875–1936) who was also with Ringling and Barnum & Bailey.

The circus band sets the atmosphere and mood for the various acts, and must be always on its toes to respond to what is going on, designed or accidental. Much music has been composed or adopted for circus performance, the best-known being Fucik's 'Entry of the Gladiators' which was in circus use shortly after it was written for military band in 1897.

The circus has been the inspiration of a great deal of art, literature, and music and there are many musical shows with a circus background, including: Piccini's *Jocko* (1825); Cogniard's *L'Ile de la Folée* (1838); Smetana's *The Bartered Bride* (1866); Pessard's *Le Capitaine Fracasse* (1878); Camondo's *Le Clown* (1906); *Caryll's *The *Circus Girl* (1896); *Ganne's *Les Saltimbanques* (1899); *Kálmán's *Die Zirkusprinzessin* (1925); Merrill's **Carnival* (1961); and Coleman's **Barnum* (1980).

City Center Light Opera Company. Established in the New York City Center in 1954 to stage short-run revivals of classic musicals. William Hammerstein was its director 1954–6 and Jean Dalrymple 1957–68, after which the enterprise ceased. In its time 30 different musicals were staged including **Brigadoon*, **South Pacific*, *The *King and I*, **Carousel*, **Finian's Rainbow*, **Guys and Dolls*, **Oklahoma!*, and **Wonderful Town*.

Clancy Brothers, The. A family of Irish-American folk-singers and musicians born in Carrick-on-Suir in Ireland. Patrick [Paddy], Tom, and Liam became interested in folk-song through the recordings of Burl *Ives and others, which led them to a search for the authentic originals and their performance. They went to the USA, where Paddy started Tradition Records in New York in 1956, and they ran the Cherry Lane Theatre which staged Irish plays. They continued their pursuit of the Irish-American connection in folk-music, discovering songs with Irish origins in Virginia and Carolina. In 1957, they were joined by the Irish singer and songwriter Tommy Makem (*b* 1932), who worked with them until 1969, and together they recorded many influential collections of folk material. Regularly billed as the Clancy Brothers and Tommy Makem, an extended appearance on the Ed Sullivan show established their American reputation. Since then they have pursued individual and collective careers in the theatre and the recording world.

Clapton, Eric (*b* Ripley, Surrey, 30 Mar. 1945). British guitarist. Inspired by recordings of Big Bill *Broonzy, Muddy *Waters, and Chuck *Berry, he learned to play the a guitar when he was 17 while he was studying at Kingston College of Art. In 1963 he formed a rhythm 'n' blues band called the Roosters; then he joined the Metropolis Blues Quartet, which later changed its name to the Yardbirds. Finding the group too commercial for his tastes, he left in 1965 to join John *Mayall's Bluesbreakers, where he began to win a reputation as Britain's leading blues guitarist. A year later he formed his own *Cream, a revolutionary group in the *heavy rock field with its lengthy improvisations and experimental harmonies. Clapton, always looking for a further challenge to his virtuosity, disbanded Cream in 1968 to organize a short-lived group with expert rockers Ginger Baker, Stevie Winwood, and Rick Grech, under the name of Blind Faith. He made his first solo album in 1970, moving somewhat away from his blues roots, as Derek and the Dominoes. A drug problem kept him out of the limelight for several years but he came back in 1974, rebluesified and somewhat countrified with a No. 1 hit 'I shot the sheriff', a *reggae-influenced number introduced by Bob *Marley. Thereafter, not inclined to chase the pop-star image, he pursued a quiet career, catering for the connoisseur and singing and playing his own gently pessimistic material in songs like 'E.C. was here', 'There's one in every crowd', and 'No reason to cry'. He found another hit in 1978 with 'Lay down Sally'. He has been as influential a figure in British R & B circles as Broonzy and the others had been to him.

E. Clapton: *461 Ocean Boulevard* (New York, 1975). J. Pidgeon: *Eric Clapton* (London, 1976). S. Turner: *Conversations with Eric Clapton* (London, 1976).

Clark, Bobby [Robert Edwin] (*b* Springfield, Ohio, 16 June 1888; *d* New York, 12 Feb. 1960). American comedian and singer. A clownish comic with painted-on glasses, a short cane, and a cigar, who played likeable scoundrels. He teamed up with Paul McCullough (1883–1936), another native of Springfield, in 1905. They worked together, until McCullough died, in minstrel shows, circuses, and vaudeville, before becoming widely known through their appearances in Irving *Berlin's **Music Box Revue* (1922 and 1924). After this they were in *The Ramblers* (1926); **Strike Up the Band* (1930); *Cochran's 1931 Revue* (London, 1931); *Here Goes the Bride* (1931); *Walk a Little Faster* (1932); and *Thumbs Up!* (1934). After McCullough's death, Clark appeared in **Ziegfeld Follies* (1936); *The Streets of Paris* (1939); *Star and Garter* (1942); **Mexican Hayride* (1944); *Sweethearts* (1947 revival); and **As the Girls Go* (1948); his last Broadway appearance. He directed *Michael Todd's Peep Show* (1956); and toured with **Damn Yankees* in 1956. One critic observed that he was 'funny just standing still'.

Clark, Buddy [Goldberg, Samuel] (*b* Dorchester, Mass., 26 July 1912; *d* Los Angeles, 1 Oct. 1949). American singer. He started his singing career in 1932, coming to attention 1934–5 with Benny *Goodman on the historic *Let's Dance* radio series. He had his own show in 1935, was a regular singer on *Hit Parade* 1936–8, and was with Ben *Bernie 1938, and Wayne *King 1940–1. He became a household name in the 1940s with his radio show *Here's to Romance* and in 1945 with *The Contented Hour*, making many recordings in this period for Columbia. He was in the film *I Wonder Who's Kissing Her Now* (1947); and on the sound-tracks of *Melody Time* (1948) and *Song of Surrender* (1949). Just as he was becoming widely known, he was killed when a light plane, in which he was returning from a football game, crashed in the middle of Los Angeles.

Clark, Petula [Owen, Sally] (*b* Ewell, Surrey, 15 Nov. 1932). British singer and actress. A Welsh mother led her towards singing in a choir and local concerts; she first broadcast at the age of 9 and was seen in the films *London Town* (1946) and *Dance Hall* (1950). Put under contract by the J. Arthur Rank organization, she appeared in several more films including *The Card* (1952) with Alec Guinness. She began to make hit records in the 1950s and soon became a star name, reaching No. 1 in America with 'Downtown' in 1965. She tended to achieve better results in the USA than in Britain and spent a considerable time there, appearing on various prestigious radio shows. This led to her starring role opposite Fred *Astaire in **Finian's Rainbow* (1968); and with Peter O'Toole in *Goodbye Mr Chips* (1969) singing 'Walk through the day'. From then on she was an international figure, making frequent world tours and appearing in the revival of *The *Sound of Music* in 1981. Making her home in Switzerland, she has continued to use her talents well in a variety of roles and has moved with the fashions.

A. Kon: *This is my Song: a Biography of Petula Clark* (London, 1983).

Clarke, Grant (*b* Akron, Ohio, 14 May 1891; *d* California, 16 May 1931). American lyricist. He started out as an actor but turned to songwriting, at first working with a New York publisher but eventually forming his own business. He was one of the first writers to work permanently in Hollywood in the pioneering years of the cinema, writing for *Dixie to Broadway* in 1924 and thereafter contributing to many films. He wrote special material for such stars as Bert *Williams, Fanny *Brice, Eva *Tanguay, Nora *Bayes, and Al *Jolson. His songs, written in collaboration with such composers as Milton *Ager, Harry *Akst, Fred *Fisher, James *Hanley, James V. *Monaco, and Harry *Warren, include such early classics as 'Ragtime cowboy Joe' (1912); 'He'd have to get under' (1913); 'Everything is peaches down in Georgia' (1918); 'In the land of beginning again' (1918); 'My little bimbo down on the Bamboo Isle' (1920); 'Second-hand rose' (1921); 'Mandy, make up your mind' (1924); 'I'm a little blackbird looking for a bluebird' (1924); and 'Am I blue?' (1929).

Clarke, Kenny [Kenneth Spearman] (*b* Pittsburgh, 9 Jan. 1914; *d* Paris, 25 Jan. 1985). American jazz drummer. He began his professional career in the early 1930s with the Leroy Bradley Band and joined Roy *Eldridge in 1935, Edgar Hayes 1937–8, Claude *Hopkins 1938, and Teddy *Hill 1939–40. It was the association with Hill, who managed and played at the historic *Minton's Playhouse club in Harlem, that led to his place as the key drummer in the *bebop developments of the 1940s. Playing with Charlie *Parker, Dizzy *Gillespie, Thelonious *Monk, and others, he pioneered the new style of drumming, breaking away from the steady-four-beat rhythms of early jazz with off-beat accents, sudden explosions, and immensely varied rhythms; generally giving the drums a more organic role in the jazz group and raising the musical status of drumming. Later he played with Benny *Carter and Red *Allen and led his own bop groups. He worked with Gillespie in the 1940s, making many tours of Europe, and 1952–5 played as founding member of the *Modern Jazz Quartet. He mainly worked in France from 1956, playing at the Blue Note 1961–7 and forming the Clarke–Boland big band in 1960 in partnership with the Belgian pianist Francy Boland (*b* 1929). It survived until 1973, after which he played with various small groups in Europe with occasional visits to the USA. Generally known by his nickname 'Klook', he always played with great discretion and taste.

Classical adaptations. Never lacking any melodic inspiration, the world of popular music has nevertheless pilfered profitably from the more serious world of music-making. Many of the great composers' melodies have been adapted to modern lyrics and found their place in the Hit Parade. With due acknowledgement made, it is perhaps not quite as sinful an activity as many critics have tried to make out; though it has certainly led to much legal wrangling. One of the first successful borrowings was 'I'm always chasing rainbows' (1918) for which Harry *Carroll and Joseph McCarthy used the main theme from Chopin's Fantaisie Impromptu, Op. 66. The famous music critic Ernest Newman protested most vigorously. Others of that period were 'Avalon' by Vincent *Rose and Al *Jolson which borrowed rather more slyly from an aria in Puccini's *Tosca*, resulting in a legal action which awarded Puccini and his publishers £25,000; 'In an 18th-century drawing-room' by Raymond *Scott drew on Mozart's Piano Sonata in C, K525; 'On the Isle of May' by Mack David and André *Kostelanetz took a theme from Tchaikovsky's String Quartet; 'Concerto for two' by Jack *Lawrence and Robert C. Haring filched from Tchaikovsky's Piano Concerto in B♭ minor; 'Till the end of time' by Buddy Kaye and Ted Mossman came from Chopin's Polonaise in A♭; the best-selling 'Red Wing' by *Chattaway and *Mills took, not for the first time, Schumann's piano piece 'The merry peasant'; 'My reverie' (Larry *Clinton) was really Debussy's 'Rêverie' demoted; 'The lamp is low' by Paris, *De Rose, and Shefter came from Ravel's 'Pavane pour une infante défunte'; 'So deep is the night' came from Chopin's Étude No. 3 in E; 'The story of a starry night' by Jerry *Livingston from Tchaikovsky's 6th Symphony; 'Moon love' by Kostelanetz from the 5th. There was also the wholesale jazzing up of tunes such as Liszt's 'Liebesträume', Rimsky-Korsakov's 'Song of India', and Rubinstein's 'Melody' in F; with even such unlikely material as Rossini's 'Stabat Mater' coming in handy for Woody *Herman's 'Blues on parade'; while Glenn *Miller made good use of Verdi's 'Anvil chorus'. The wholesale lifting of the works of composers for stage musicals involved Schubert (*Blossom Time*, *Das *Dreimädelhaus*, and **Lilac Time*); while Borodin (**Kismet*) and Grieg (**Song of Norway*) were among the victims of the famous body-snatchers *Forrest and *Wright.

Clay, Frédéric (*b* Paris, 3 Aug. 1838; *d* Great Marlow, 24 Nov. 1889). British composer. The son of James Clay, MP for Hull, he studied music in Paris and Leipzig. His earliest musical activities were as an amateur with such writings as the operettas *The Pirate's Isle* (1859), *Out of Sight* (1860), and *Court and Cottage* (1861) which was produced at Covent Garden; as was *Constance* (1865). He had an early success, *Ages Ago* (1869), in partnership with W. S. *Gilbert but made the mistake of introducing his collaborator to Arthur *Sullivan. Other works included *The Gentleman in Black* (1870); *The Bold Recruit* (1870); parts of *The *Black Crook* (1872) and *Babil and Bijou* (1872); *Happy Arcadia* (1872), *Cattarina* (1874), *Princess Toto* (1876)—these last three with Gilbert; *Don Quixote* (1876); *The Merry Duchess* (1883); and *The Golden Ring* (1883). His music was of a rather sentimental Victorian nature with not enough vitality to last, except in one or two songs such as 'I'll sing thee songs of Araby' (1877), 'The sands of Dee' (1879, *w* Kingsley), and 'She wandered down the mountainside' (1881).

Clayton, Buck [Wilbur Dorsey] (*b* Parsons, Kans., 12 Nov. 1911; *d* New York, 8 Dec. 1991). American jazz trumpeter and arranger. He played with various bands on the West Coast in the early 1930s, led his own band in Los Angeles, travelling with it to Shanghai 1934–6, and eventually came to prominence in the Count *Basie band 1936–43, where his clean-cut, swinging, inventive playing and effective use of mutes made him stand out in a star line-up. After military service he arranged for Basie, *Goodman, and others. He joined Jazz at the Philharmonic in 1946, played with various leading jazz groups, and led his own band in Europe 1949–50. He was with Jimmy *Rushing in the early 1950s and joined Benny Goodman on the sound-track of *The Benny Goodman Story* (1956). He later worked with Goodman, *Condon, and *Bechet, touring into the 1970s.

B. Clayton: *Buck Clayton's Jazz World* (New York, 1987).

Clef Club. A club-cum-union for black American musicians founded by James Reese *Europe in 1910. It was not a club in the usual sense but an organization which ran its own Clef Club Orchestra to give employment and raise funds, its inaugural concert being at the Manhattan Casino in 1910. Not predominantly jazz-flavoured, the orchestra reached vast, amorphous proportions by 1914 when it performed at Carnegie Hall, featuring 30 pianists on 10 pianos. While the Clef Club acted as an agency for musicians in the popular fields of music, the New Amsterdam Musical Association of New York, formed in 1906, was doing similar work in the classical field.

'Clementine'. The words, to a different tune from the now familiar one, were first printed under the title 'Down by the river lived a maiden' in 1863. The well-known tune was first printed in Boston in 1884 with words and music credited to Percy Montrose—of whom nothing seems to be known. An 1885 edition credited the equally obscure Barker Bradford. Almost certainly it started as a song of the American *gold-rush period; but the tune may have had Irish origins.

Cliff, Laddie [Perry, Clifford Albyn] (*b* Bristol, 3 Sept. 1891; *d* Montana, Switzerland, 8 Dec. 1937). British actor, producer, and director. He went to the USA and started his career in vaudeville there 1907–17. He appeared in New York in *Folies Bergère* (1911); then returned to London to appear in *The Bing Girls Are There* (1917). He was to appear in numerous London musicals and revues up to 1937, including three editions of the *Co-Optimists (1921/24/29), which he latterly directed, and **Tip-Toes* (1926). An active producer, he worked with Stanley *Lupino on five musicals 1928–35.

Clifton, Harry [Henry Robert] (*b* Hoddesdon, Herts., 1832; *d* Shepherd's Bush, London, 15 July 1872). British author, composer, singer, and entertainer. Educated in Cheshunt, he was left an orphan at the age of three and eventually earned his living as a singer. He became well-known in the song-and-supper rooms and early music-halls, purveying his own 'motto' songs with such titles as 'Paddle your own canoe', 'Pulling hard against the stream', 'There's nothing succeeds like success', 'A motto for every man', 'Never look behind', 'It's better to laugh than to cry', 'Wait for the turn of the tide', and 'Work, boys, work and be contented!'

He is best-remembered for the folky 'Polly Perkins of Paddington Green', one of the most charming songs of the early halls and a lasting favourite; with, in similar style the delightful 'Shelling green peas' and 'The weepin' willer'. He also wrote and performed many comic songs that were prototypes for the music-hall years to come: 'The agreeable young man', 'Jemima Brown', 'On board of the "Kangaroo"', 'Shabby genteel', 'The convivial man', and many drawing-room duets. He toured with his own Cosmopolitan Concert Company from 1866 and for many years lived in and worked from Glasgow. One of the great pioneers of music-hall song, Clifton was one of those active in a period when such popular musical efforts were scantily chronicled; and much less is known about him than his legacy deserves. Two or three collections of his songs were published in his short lifetime.

Cline, Patsy [Hensley, Virginia Petterson] (*b* Winchester, Va., 8 Sept. 1932; *d* Camden, Tenn., 5 Mar. 1963). American country singer. She was discovered on Arthur Godfrey's TV *Talent Scouts* programme in 1957 when she sang 'Walkin' after midnight', and had later hits with 'Heartaches' and 'Sweet dreams of you'. Just as she was becoming well-known she was killed in an aeroplane crash. She was elected to the *Country Music Hall of Fame, 1973.

E. Nassour: *Patsy Cline* (New York, 1981).

Clinton, Larry (*b* Brooklyn, NY, 17 Aug. 1909; *d* Tucson, Arizona, 2 May 1987). American bandleader, arranger, composer, trumpeter, and lyricist. In the early 1930s he became an arranger for the Dorsey Brothers Orchestra and the *Casa Loma Orchestra and wrote many of his early compositions for these bands. In 1937 he was arranger for Tommy *Dorsey, who helped him to form and finance his own band. They recorded prolifically for RCA Victor but remained mainly known in the USA. He joined the US Air Force in 1941, leading a band again after the war but never regaining his pre-war popularity. In the 1950s he set up publishing and recording businesses as well as working as an A & R man for Kapp Records. His compositions included: 'Dipsy doodle' (1937)—his band theme song, 'Satan takes a holiday' (1937), 'My reverie' (1938), 'Our love' (1939), and many orchestral items. A speciality of his was the adaptation of classical material.

Cloches de Corneville, Les. Opéra-comique with score by Robert *Planquette, words by 'Clairville' [Louis Nicolaie] (1811–79) and Charles Gabet. This very popular and successful work, which was played all over the world until into the 1930s, was first produced at the Folies-Dramatiques, Paris, 19 Apr. 1877 and ran there for 408 performances. It was seen at the Folly Theatre in London 28 Feb. 1878 with English words by H. B. *Farnie; and at the Theater an der Wien in September in the same year. It is still kept in the recorded repertoire and still played in France, with its 'Digue, digue, digue' ('The legend of the bells') remembered as the most obvious item of an excellent score.

Clooney, Rosemary (*b* Maysville, Ky., 23 May 1928). American singer. Her clear, melodic style earned her great popularity in the 1950s. She had a radio show with her sister in the mid-1940s while still at high school and they worked as vocalists with Tony Pastor, Rosemary first working on her own in 1949. She was seen on TV's *Songs for Sale* and began recording for Columbia, her first big hit being 'Come on-a my house' in 1951, followed by 'Tenderly', 'This ole house', by Hollywood westerns actor Stuart Hamblen (1908–89), and 'Hey there'.

She appeared in the films *The Stars are Singing* (1953); *Here Come the Girls* (1953); *Red Garters* (1954); **White Christmas* (1954); and *Deep in my Heart* (1955). She sang regularly into the 1960s, since making occasional appearances.

R. Clooney: *This For Remembrance: Autobiography* (New York, 1977).

Clutsam, George H. (*b* Sydney, 26 Sept. 1866; *d* London, 17 Nov. 1951). Australian composer, arranger, pianist, and music critic. He began a successful career as a pianist in Australia and New Zealand. Following tours of Asia and Europe, he settled in London in 1889 and became well-known as an accompanist, working with Nellie Melba among others. From 1908 to 1918 he was music critic of the *Observer*; and he wrote for various musical journals. He made a reputation as a composer, writing the operetta *The Queen's Jester* (1905) and having a modest success with a one-act opera *A Summer Night* which was produced by Sir Thomas Beecham at His Majesty's Theatre 23 July 1910. After two more operas, he turned to operetta, collaborating with Hubert *Bath on *Young England* (1916) followed by *Gabrielle*; *Lavender*; and *The Little Duchess*—all in 1922. His greatest and most lasting success came with his English adaptation of the Viennese production *Das Dreimädelhaus* which used Schubert's melodies, arranged by Heinrich *Berté. Clutsam made considerable changes and added more popular items for his version, **Lilac Time*, which was produced at the Lyric Theatre on 22 Dec. 1922, ran for 626 performances, and is still a popular amateur show. Less success attended his utilization of Chopin in *The Damask Rose* (1929).

Among many popular songs he wrote 'Ma curly headed babby' (1926) and several song cycles. In spite of a predilection for writing pseudo-Negro ballads, he was a fierce opponent of jazz, writing to that effect in **Melody Maker* and elsewhere and making the inaccurate forecast in 1925: 'I think the present phase will pass. The public will not continue indefinitely its admiration of the hectic, unsatisfying fare known popularly as jazz. The ear cannot permanently be tickled by infectious combinations of trite tunes (seldom the composer's), hurting harmonies, and rhythmical vulgarities. The plague will inevitably die out, and its victims return to sanity.'

Coasters, The. American vocal group. The best and most famous of the *doo-wop groups, they released a succession of classic comic hits in the 1950s. All superb singers, the group, formed by Bobby Nunn (1925–86), owed much of their success to the songwriting talents of *Leiber and Stoller, combining humour and social comment in a balanced mixture. They used good session musicians, including guitarist Mickey Baker and saxophonist King Curtis (1934–71). The arrangements were conventional but exploited the contrasted voices well. Originally billed as the Robins, they achieved (with the help of Leiber and Stoller) several local hits such as 'Riot in Cell Block No. 9', 'Double crossing blues', 'Framed', and 'Smokey Joe's Café'. In Oct. 1955 they changed their name to the Coasters; their hits as the Robins remained in their repertoire.

They signed up with Atlantic in 1956 and a series of hits followed: 'Down in Mexico' (1956); 'One kiss leads to another' (1956); 'Searchin'', 'Young blood' (1957); 'Yakety yak' (1958—a No. 1 in the USA); 'Charlie Brown' (1959); 'Along came Jones' (1959); 'Poison ivy' (1959); and 'Little Egypt' (1961). Fashions changed and their fame dwindled, to be revived in 1964 with ''Tain't nothin' to me', recorded live at the *Apollo Theatre. They signed with Columbia in 1967. Groups under the same name, but with changed personnel, have continued into the 1980s. They had a considerable influence on others groups while proving that comedy could still come into the serious business of rock and roll.

B. Millar: *The Coasters* (London, 1975).

Coates, Eric (*b* Hucknall, Notts., 27 Aug. 1886; *d* Chichester, 21 Dec. 1957). British composer, conductor, and violist. He studied at the Royal Academy of Music, taking viola with Lionel Tertis and composition with Frederick Corder. He played in various theatre orchestras (including the pit orchestra for the London production of *The *Merry Widow*) and in Sir Thomas Beecham's opera orchestra; then joined the Queen's Hall Orchestra under Henry Wood in 1910 and became lead viola in 1912. This gave him the opportunity to play under the baton of such composers as Elgar, *German, Delius, Holst, Walford Davies, Bantock, Richard Strauss, Debussy. Ethel Smyth, Harty, Stanford, Bridge, Schoenberg, and Vaughan Williams. He wrote a successful 'Miniature Suite' in 1911 which was conducted by Wood in the Proms. Its 'Scène de bal' movement became very popular when performed at a *Chappell Ballad Concert under Alick Maclean in 1915. He left the orchestra in 1919 to concentrate on composing and conducting, experiencing some difficult years before he had further success with the 'Merrymakers' overture in 1922.

An idyllic but impecunious sojourn in Sussex preceded a return to London and a flat in Baker Street where he and his wife stayed until the war; there Coates wrote 'By the sleepy lagoon' (1930) and many more saleable items, including the ever-popular 'London' (1932) and 'London Again' (1936) suites. The use of 'Knightsbridge march' from the former as the signature tune of the BBC's *In Town Tonight* programme established Coates as London's own composer. The war inspired 'Calling All Workers' which was first broadcast by the BBC Theatre Orchestra under Stanford Robinson from Cheltenham in 1940. Requisition of the London flat forced the composer back to the country near the Malvern Hills where he wrote the 'Three Elizabeths' suite in 1944. Coates returned to London at the end of the war, writing and conducting his own works and taking over from Edward German as England's most esteemed composer of light music. Among many excellent songs were 'Stonecracker John'

(1909), 'A dinder courtship' (1912), and 'The green hills o' Somerset' (1916), all with words by Fred E. *Weatherly; 'I pitch my lonely caravan' (1921, *w* Annette Horey); 'Thinkin' of you' (1922, *w* Dorothy Dickson); and 'Bird songs at eventide' (1926, *w* Royden Barrie).

E. Coates: *Suite in Four Movements: an Autobiography* (London, 1953).

Cobb, George L. (*b* Mexico, NY, 31 Aug. 1886; *d* Brookline, Mass., 25 Dec. 1942). American composer, arranger, and lyric-writer. He studied music at Syracuse University, then worked in a publishing-house in Boston for many years. He wrote 'All aboard for Dixie Land' (1913) and 'Alabama Jubilee' (1915), both with Jack *Yellen, and the instrumentals 'Aggravatin' rag' (1910) and 'Russian rag' (1918).

Cobb, Will D. (*b* Philadelphia, 6 July 1876; *d* New York, 20 Jan. 1930). American lyricist. He started out as a sales clerk in a department store, but gradually became a full-time songwriter. His songs included: 'I can't tell why I love you but I do' (1900, *m* Gus *Edwards); 'Goodbye, Dolly Gray' (with Paul Barnes, 1900); 'Goodbye, little girl, goodbye' (1904, *m* Edwards); 'Waltz me around again, Willie' (1906, *m* Ren *Shields); 'Sunbonnet Sue' (1908, *m* Edwards); 'I just can't make my eyes behave' (1906, *m* Edwards); and 'Yip-i-addy-i-ay' (1908, *m* John H. Flynn).

Coborn, Charles [McCallum, Colin Whitton] (*b* Mile End, London, 4 Aug. 1852; *d* London, 23 Nov. 1945). British music-hall comedian and singer. He made his first music-hall appearance in 1872 at the Alhambra in Greenwich and took his stage name from Coborn Road in Bow. By 1879 he was being billed at the *Oxford Music Hall in London as 'The Comic of the Day'. His two most popular hits were his own 'Two lovely black eyes', which he first sang at the Paragon Music Hall, Mile End, in 1886; and 'The man who broke the bank at Monte Carlo', which he bought from Fred *Gilbert after almost turning it down (it had already been refused by Albert *Chevalier), and first sang in 1891. It took time to catch on but ever after was his main party piece. He also wrote 'He's all right when you know him'. He appeared at Pastor's Music Hall in New York in 1900, in Brooklyn, and in Toronto. From 1901 he toured with his own concert party and he continued to make appearances until he was in his nineties.

C. Coborn: *The Man who Broke the Bank* (London, 1930).

Cochran, C. B. [Charles Blake] (*b* Lindfield, Sussex, 25 Sept. 1872; *d* London, 31 Jan. 1951). British impresario and producer. In his day he was Britain's leading showman, responsible for a large proportion of the plays, musicals, and revues of the 1920s and 1930s (as well as other entertainment spectacles) including five musicals by Noël *Coward. A typical Cochran revue was lavishly staged in the *Ziegfeld tradition and was similarly famed for its chorus girls, popularly known as 'Mr Cochran's Young Ladies', from the ranks of whom came many future British stars.

Some of the important shows for which he was responsible were: *The *Better 'Ole* (1917); **As You Were* (1918); *Afgar* (1919); *League of Notions* (1921); **Phi-Phi* (1922); **Music Box Revue* (1923); **On With the Dance* (1925); **Cochran's Revue of 1926*; **Blackbirds* (1926); **One Dam Thing After Another* (1927); **This Year of Grace* (1928); **Wake Up And Dream* (1929); **Bitter Sweet* (1929); **Cochran's 1930 Revue*; **Ever Green* (1930); *Cochran's 1931 Revue*; *Helen* (1932); *The *Cat and the Fiddle* (1932); *Words and Music* (1932); **Music in the Air* (1933); **Nymph Errant* (1933); **Conversation Piece* (1934); **Anything Goes* (1935); **Blackbirds of 1936*; *Home and Beauty* (1937); *Paganini* (1937); *Lights Up* (1940); *Big Ben* (1946); **Bless the Bride* (1947); and *Tough at the Top* (1949). He edited *CBC's Review of Revues* (London, 1930).

C. B. Cochran: *The Secrets of a Showman* (London, 1925). C. B. Cochran: *I Had Almost Forgotten* (London, 1932). J. Cleugh: *Charles B. Cochran* (London, 1937). C. B. Cochran: *Cock-a-Doodle-Doo* (London, 1941). C. B. Cochran: *Showman Looks On* (London, 1949). C. Graves: *The Cochran Story* (London, 1952). S. Heppner: *Cookie: an Authoritative Life of C. B. Cochran—Master Showman* (London, 1969).

Cochran, Eddie [Cochrane] (*b* Oklahoma City, 3 Oct. 1938; *d* Bristol, 17 Apr. 1960). American rock singer. He started as one of a duo billed as the Cochran Brothers (with Hank Cochran—who was not related) and made his first solo recording in the *hillbilly style. His eventual association with Liberty Records produced his best efforts. Perhaps recordings never fully revealed his explosive stage style, but he soon became a pop idol because of his extensive touring, being especially popular in Britain, which he first visited, along with Gene *Vincent, early in 1960, proving a strong influence on British guitarists, who liked his sound and method.

Along with Chuck *Berry and Buddy *Holly, he was one of the great singer/songwriters of rock and roll—a chronicler of teenage rebellion, excitement, and frustration. His three greatest records—'Summertime blues' (1958), 'C'mon everybody' (1959), and 'Somethin' else' (1959)—are among the best youth anthems ever released summing up the trauma of American teenage life in the late 1950s. His vocal style here was near to Elvis *Presley's, moody and rough, in keeping with the material. Like Holly he was a fine guitarist and a pioneer of multi-recording techniques. His first Liberty release was 'Sittin' in the balcony' (1957); other classics included 'Twenty flight rock', which he performed in the film *The Girl Can't Help It* (1957), 'Cut across Shorty' (1959), 'Three steps to heaven', which was No. 1 in the UK in 1960, and 'Weekend' (1961). He interrupted a UK tour, intending to make a brief visit to Los Angeles, but on the way to the airport received fatal injuries in a car crash. His death is remembered as one of rock and roll's greatest losses.

Cochran Revue. The first of C. B. *Cochran's historic revues was produced at the London Pavilion on 19 Apr. 1926, the cast including Hermione *Baddeley; it ran for 149 performances. It was the next version at the same theatre 27 Mar. 1930 that really made its mark through lavish variety and the famous Young Ladies of the chorus. Running for 245 performances, the cast included Roy Royston, Douglas *Byng, Serge Lifar, Maisie Gay, Richard Murdoch, and Leslie *Hutchinson (Hutch). The score, mainly by Vivian *Ellis, was bolstered by *Rodgers and *Hart's 'With a song in my heart'. The 1931 edition was entirely the work of Noël *Coward, who provided such classic revue numbers as 'Any little fish' and 'Half-caste woman'. It opened at the Apollo Theatre 1 Nov. 1931, with the American duo *Clark and McCullough, John Mills, Ada May, and Queenie Leonard [716p]; and there was a revival in 1944 with John Clements, Kay Hammond, and Raymond Huntley.

Cocker, Joe [John Robert] (*b* Sheffield, 20 May 1944). British singer and composer. As a youth he felt the influence of Ray *Charles on whom he modelled his vocal style. The future exponent of 'blue-eyed soul' was given leave from his employment with the Gas Board to form his first band, Big Blues, which toured as a supporting act with the *Rolling Stones, *Manfred Mann, and the *Hollies. Achieving no individual success, he went back to the gas works. He formed the Grease Band and had a moderate hit with his own song 'Marjorine'; but the break came when he managed a No. 1 hit with the *Lennon/McCartney song 'With a little help from my friends' in 1968.

Now with an international reputation, he visited the USA, appeared at the 1969 *Woodstock Festival, and followed up with 'Delta lady' (1969). He toured with a 40-strong package called Mad Dogs and Englishmen but had a breakdown and had to retire for a while. He came back in 1972 and toured the USA. He overcame drug problems to achieve a hit in 1974 with 'You are so beautiful', written by Billy Preston. A strong revival in the 1980s produced a fine mixed soul and rock album, *Sheffield Steel*, and the composition of the sound-track for *An Officer and a Gentleman* (1982), which included his first No. 1 hit in America, 'Up where we belong', which he recorded with Jennifer Warnes in 1983.

Cocoanuts, The. The second of three Marx Brothers stage musicals, a loosely constructed musical comedy with a typical Marx Brothers story about a hotel (run by Groucho) in which jewel thefts from a rich dowager (Margaret Dumont), and her daughter's love affair, were reduced to chaotic confusion by the lunacy of Chico, Harpo, and Zeppo. It opened at the Lyric Theatre, New York, 8 Dec. 1925 for 276 performances. The book was by George S. *Kaufman and Morrie Ryskind, the music by Irving *Berlin. It became the basis of the Marx Brothers' first full-length film in 1929.

Coffin, C. Hayden (*b* Manchester, 22 Apr. 1862; *d* London, 8 Dec. 1935). British actor and singer. A handsome leading man, he first made a musical hit singing 'Queen of my heart' in **Dorothy* at the *Gaiety Theatre in 1886. He subsequently appeared in *Doris* (1889); *The Red Hussar* (1889); *Marjorie* (1889); *Maid Marian* (1890); *Miss Decima* (1891); with Lillian *Russell's Opera Company in the USA, 1892; *A *Gaiety Girl* (1893); *An Artist's Model* (1895); *The *Geisha* (1896); *A *Greek Slave* (1898); **San Toy* (1899); *A *Country Girl* (1901); *The *Cingalee* (1930); **Véronique* (1904); and *The Girl Behind the Counter* (1906).

H. Coffin: *Hayden Coffin's Book* (London, 1930).

Cogan, Alma (*b* Worthing, 19 May 1932; *d* London, 26 Oct. 1966). British singer. She started her entertainment career in the chorus of **High Button Shoes* in 1948, and made her first record in 1952. Becoming known for her bright and breezy style, she had recorded hits with 'Bell bottom blues' (1954), 'I can't tell a waltz from a tango' (1954), 'Dreamboat' (1955), 'You, me and us' (1956), and 'Just couldn't resist her with her pocket transistor' (1960). She became the first female vocalist to have her own TV series in Britain, 1959–61.

Cohan, George M[ichael] (*b* Providence, RI, 3 July 1878; *d* New York, 5 Nov. 1942). American actor, composer, writer, director, and producer. He first appeared on the stage in *Daniel Boone* in 1888; then he was in a vaudeville act known as the Four Cohans along with his parents Jerry and Nellie and his sister Josie. But his typical American vigour, virtuosity, brashness, and patriotic naïveté, which typified both his acting and his writing, were destined to make him a one-man band of talents and he was soon writing and starring in his own shows which he packed with prototype American songs like 'The Yankee Doodle boy' and 'Give my regards to Broadway' (both from *Little Johnny Jones*). From 1904 to 1920 he was also the producer, at the beginning in partnership with Sam H. Harris.

His shows were mainly fast, corny, and ostentatiously American; mainly designed as a framework for his tireless gifts as an actor, singer, and dancer. They included: *The Governor's Son* (1901); *Running For Office* (1903); **Little Johnny Jones* (1904; filmed 1930); **Forty-Five Minutes from Broadway* (1906)—'Mary's a grand old name', 'So long, Mary', 'Forty-five minutes from Broadway'; *George Washington Jr.* (1906)—'You're a grand old flag', 'I was born in Virginia'; *The Honeymooners* (1907); *The Talk of New York* (1907); *Fifty Miles from Boston* (1908)—'Harrigan'; *The Yankee Prince* (1908); *The American Idea* (1908); *The Man Who Owns Broadway* (1909)—'The man who owns Broadway'; *The Little Millionaire* (1910); *Hello, Broadway* (1914); *The Cohan Revue of 1916*; *The Cohan Revue of 1918*; *The Voice of McConnell* (1918); *The Royal Vagabond* (1919); *Little Nellie Kelly* (1922; filmed 1940)—'Nelly Kelly, I love you'; *The Rise of Rosie O'Reilly* (1923); *The Merry Malones* (1927); *Billie* (1928).

He also wrote twenty plays and appeared in two shows which he did not write, including the musical *I'd Rather Be Right* (1937) in which he played Franklin D. Roosevelt. His first wife, whom he married in 1899, was the singer Ethel *Levey. **George M!*, produced in 1968, was a musical based on his life, as was the film *Yankee Doodle Dandy* (1942), made under his supervision, in which James *Cagney brilliantly played and danced Cohan. He appeared in several films but only one of them musical; and wrote and appeared in *The Phantom President* (1932). Other songs which made their mark were 'When the girl you love is miles away' (1893), 'I guess I'll have to telegraph my baby' (1898), 'Always leave them laughing when you say goodbye' (1903), 'I want to hear a Yankee Doodle tune' (1903), 'Over there' (1917); 'This is our side of the ocean' (1940).

G. M. Cohan: *Twenty Years on Broadway* (New York, 1925). W. Morehouse: *George M. Cohan: Prince of the American Theatre* (New York, 1943; repr. 1972). J. McCabe: *George M. Cohan: the Man Who Owned Broadway* (New York, 1973; repr. 1980).

Cohen, Leonard (*b* Montreal, 21 Sept. 1934). Canadian-Jewish pop-folk singer. After studying at McGill University, he began a literary career and became known as a poet and novelist. He started to set his poems to music, but with little success until Judy *Collins recorded his 'Suzanne' in 1966 and put him on the pop road. He signed with Columbia records in 1968 and recorded an album of his doom-laden songs, which he puts over in a flat, droning style that adds to their depressive effect. His second album, *Songs from a Room*, led to extensive singing tours. He has recorded sparsely, like *Dylan and other fashionable artists taking time off every now and then for meditation and re-assessment. Some of his later work, on albums such as *I'm Your Man* (1988), even surprised his critics by exhibiting a sense of humour, albeit of a black and cynical kind. Among his most lasting songs are: 'So long, Marianne', 'Stranger song', 'Hey, that's no way to say goodbye', and 'Sisters of Mercy'.

Cole, Cozy [William Randolph] (*b* East Orange, NJ, 17 Oct. 1909; *d* Columbus, Ohio, 29 Jan. 1981). American jazz drummer. He started drumming as a boy and became a professional in 1928, playing with such luminaries as Jelly Roll *Morton and Stuff *Smith before joining Benny *Carter, 1933–4, and Cab *Calloway, 1938–42. A widely varied jazz career included appearances in the musical **Carmen Jones* (1943), where he featured in 'Beat out dat rhythm on a drum'; in *The Seven Lively Arts* (1945) with the Benny *Goodman Quintet; and in *The Glenn Miller Story* (1954). A crisp, attacking and inventive drummer, long considered one of the finest exponents of the swing era, he also became involved in the bop scene, recording with Dizzy *Gillespie and Charlie *Parker on the 'Groovin' high' session, and played with the Louis *Armstrong All Stars for four years from 1949. He formed his own band, producing a hit record, 'Topsy', in 1958, and toured Africa with it in 1962. He was with the Jonah Jones Quintet 1969–76. A student at the Juilliard School at one time, he also showed a scholarly interest in jazz, writing a series of instruction books, running a percussion school in partnership with Gene *Krupa, and latterly teaching at Capital University in Columbus, Ohio.

Cole, Nat 'King' [Nathaniel Adams] (*b* Montgomery, Ala., 17 Mar. 1917; *d* Santa Monica, Calif., 15 Feb. 1965). American singer, pianist, and actor. He grew up in Chicago where he was leading his own band by 1934. He toured with **Shuffle Along* and settled in California, playing the piano in various clubs. He formed the King Cole Trio (with Oscar Moore and Wesley Prince) in 1939 and, playing neat cocktail jazz based on the Earl Hines style, he occasionally broke into song. The singing gradually became his most important activity and he had hits with 'Straighten up' and 'Fly right' (1944) (which he wrote), and 'It's only a paper moon' (1945). He continued with a changed trio and made many recordings with string accompaniment, having a big hit with 'Nature boy' in 1948 with Frank DeVol's orchestra and 'Little girl' with the trio. He finally cast aside the trio in 1951, continued to make such hits as 'Mona Lisa' (1950); 'Too young' (1951); 'Answer me, my love' (1954); 'A blossom fell' (1955); and 'Ramblin' rose' (1962); and had his own TV show 1956–7.

During his career he appeared in many films, including: *Here Comes Elmer* (1943); *Pistol Packin' Mama* (1943); *Pin-Up Girl* (1944); *Swing in the Saddle* (1944); *Stars on Parade* (1944); *See My Lawyer* (1945); *Breakfast in Hollywood* (1946); *Make Believe Ballroom* (1949); *Blue Gardenia* (1953); *Small Town Girl* (1953); *Istanbul* (1957); *China Gate* (1957); *St Louis Blues* (1958)—his favourite film in which he portrayed W. C. *Handy, his only acting role; *Night of the Quarter Moon* (1959); and *Cat Ballou* (1956). His daughter Natalie (*b* 1950) has also had a career as a singer.

M. Cole & L. Robinson: *Nat 'King' Cole* (New York, 1971). J. Haskins: *Nat 'King' Cole* (London, 1986).

Coleman, Cy [Kaufman, Seymour] (*b* New York, 14 June 1929). American composer and pianist. He showed a precocious musical talent and was giving piano recitals at the age of six. He studied at the New York College of Music, gradually moved into the popular music field, and formed a trio which played in nightclubs. From 1950 to 1953 he was writing for the TV show *Date in Manhattan* and in 1953 contributed to *John Murray Anderson's Almanac*, and began to write popular songs. He worked with the Kate *Smith TV show 1955–6 and became musical director. With Joseph McCarthy he wrote 'Why try to change me now' (1952) and 'I'm gonna laugh you out of my life' (1955).

He met Carolyn *Leigh in 1957 and found her an ideal lyricist who helped him to achieve a number of hit songs such as 'Witchcraft' (1957)—which was made into a hit by Frank *Sinatra; 'I walk a little faster' (1957); 'A doodlin' song' (1958); 'You fascinate me so' (1958); 'Firefly' (1958); 'It amazes me' (1958); 'The best is yet to come' (1959); and the 'Playboy' theme (1960). He wrote his first Broadway score, *Wildcat*, in 1960 and then **Little Me* (1962); **Sweet Charity* (1966); *Seesaw* (1973); *I Love My Wife* (1977); **On the Twentieth Century* (1978); and **Barnum* (1980). He wrote for films: *Father Goose* (1964)—'Pass me by' (*w* Leigh); *The Troublemaker* (1964); and *The Art of Love* (1965).

Coleman, Ornette (*b* Fort Worth, Texas, 19 Mar. 1930). American jazz saxophonist, trumpeter, violinist, and composer. Largely self-taught, he was helped by a local tenor-saxophonist who introduced him to the recordings of Charlie *Parker. He worked in local bands and rhythm 'n' blues groups, eventually forming his own backing group which worked with Big Joe *Turner. His unorthodox jazz ideas made headway difficult, but he eventually gathered together some similarly progressive spirits like Don Cherry and Charlie Haden and formed the Ornette Coleman Quartet. They first recorded in 1958 with Contemporary Records and found encouragers in Nat Hentoff, John *Lewis, and Gunther *Schuller.

In 1959 he took his Quartet into the Five Spot Club in New York and there established the cult of free jazz, appearing to the jazz world as a newly fully-fledged talent. His music had no harmony or chordal structure, and no form, but it still swung and the blues influence remained strong. He played along with John *Coltrane at this time, each advancing the other's ideas. From 1963 to 1964 he studied trumpet and violin and re-emerged on the jazz scene in 1965 with a new trio, with David Izenzon on bass and Charles Moffett on drums, with which he toured Europe. In the late 1960s he led a quartet which included Dewey Redman on tenor, but by now he was turning more to composition than playing. In 1972 his quartet, backed by a symphony orchestra, played his 'Skies of America' at the Newport Festival. From 1975 he was using rock rhythms and electric instruments in his Prime Time Band. The Hartford Festival of 1985 centred on his works, three of his chamber pieces being performed there. Some, including John Lewis and Leonard *Bernstein, have seen him as the way ahead; others see him as a man with no talent to hide; but he unquestionably stirs controversy and interest.

B. McRae: *Ornette Coleman* (London, 1988).

Collette, Buddy [William Marcel] (*b* Los Angeles, 6 Aug. 1921). American jazz saxophonist, clarinettist, and flautist. He worked in Los Angeles before leading a US Navy band 1942–5; then worked with Britt Woodman and Charles *Mingus, freelanced, and joined a West Coast studio band 1951–5, the first black musician to do so. He made his first notable recordings with the quintet led by Chico Hamilton (*b* 1921). A sensitive saxophonist, it is nevertheless his flute playing which has gained attention because of the comparative rarity of its jazz exponents. He has played flute notably with the Henry *Mancini, Quincy *Jones, and Benny *Carter bands; and at the San Remo Festival in 1962 and at Monterey 1964–6. An adherent of the West Coast cool jazz style, he composed the jazz standard 'Blue sands'.

Collier, Graham James (*b* Tynemouth, Durham, 21 Feb. 1937). British jazz composer, director, and keyboard player. Having played trumpet in local bands, he joined the army at 16 as a bandsman and spent 6 years in this capacity, also playing in army dance and jazz groups. In 1961 he won a *Down Beat* scholarship to the Berklee School of Music and became the school's first British graduate. He has led his own band in the UK since 1964 under the title of Graham Collier Music, using many leading British and European players. In 1967 he was the first jazz composer to win an Arts Council grant and wrote 'Workpoints' for a 12-piece band. He formed his own record company Mosaic records in 1976, and has composed for major festivals, TV commercials, films, and the theatre. A busy teacher, he has written several books, including *Inside Jazz* (London, 1973) and *Jazz—a Student's and Teacher's Guide* (Cambridge, 1975).

Collins, José (*b* London, 23 May 1887; *d* London, 6 Dec. 1958). British actress and singer. The daughter of Lottie *Collins, her first appearance was as a child on the music-hall stage with Harry *Lauder, posing as the bluebell mentioned in his song 'I love a lassie'. In 1904 she toured in *A *Chinese Honeymoon*; then she was in *Aladdin* with Lauder in Glasgow in 1905. She appeared as a singer at the Holborn Empire, the *Oxford, and the London Pavilion. She went to America in 1911 and appeared in various musicals, including *Vera Violetta* (1911); *The Whirl of Society* (1912); *The Merry Countess* (1912); **Ziegfeld Follies* (1913); *The *Passing Show* (1914); *Suzi* (1914); and *Alone at Last* (1915). Returning to London in 1916, she was seen in *The Happy Day* (1916); then in her best-remembered role as Theresa in *The *Maid of the Mountains* (1917). Her subsequent musical appearances were in *The Southern Maid* (1920); *Sybil* (1921); *The Last Waltz* (1922); *Catherine* (1923); *Our Nell* (1924); *Frasquita* (1925); and *Whitebirds* (1927).

J. Collins: *The Maid of the Mountains* (London, 1912).

Collins, Judy [Judith Marjorie] (*b* Denver, Col., 1 May 1939). American folk-singer. She studied the piano with the intention of becoming a concert pianist, but became discouraged and took to folk-singing, beginning her career in this field after university studies in 1959. Learning the guitar, she sang in Denver clubs and, using a wide knowledge of music, was immediately the complete professional with an interesting repertoire ranging from European folk-songs to *Brecht. She recorded for Elektra in the early 1960s and gained her reputation with 'Maid of constant sorrow' and

'Golden apples of the sun'. A popular favourite was her 'Hey Nelly, Nelly', but she was to become a particularly influential figure in the way she was able to give a boost to up-and-coming young writers like Tom *Paxton, Richard Farina, Bob *Dylan, Eric Anderson, Phil *Ochs, and Gordon Lightfoot by using their songs; and she also introduced the work of Leonard *Cohen and Jacques *Brel. She was very involved politically in the 1960s in black and feminist causes. In 1967 she made a hit of Joni *Mitchell's 'Both sides now' and recorded some of her own compositions—'Sky fell' and 'Albatross'—all contained in the album *Wildflowers*, which sold more than a million copies. Her biggest hit of all was 'Amazing grace' in 1970, a best-seller on both sides of the Atlantic. She has continued with undimmed vigour her political and folk-song career, publishing *The Judy Collins Songbook* and other writings.

V. Claire: *Judy Collins* (New York, 1977).

Collins, Lottie [Tate, Charlotte Louise] (*b* London, 1866; *d* London, 2 May 1910). British music-hall comedienne and singer. The daughter of a blackface minstrel, she first appeared on the halls as a speciality dancer in 1877. She worked with her sisters as the Three Sisters Collins, appearing at the *Oxford and in three Pavilion pantomimes, then went solo in 1881 singing and whistling minstrel songs such as 'The whistling coon'. She appeared in the burlesque *Monte Cristo Jr.* (1886), but swept to national stardom by her performance of one rather inane song of American origin, 'Ta-ra-ra-boom-de-ay', with English words by Richard Morton. She first presented it at the Tivoli Music Hall in 1891 and thereafter could never appear without singing it. She added a ferocious *can-can kind of dance which caused a sensation with its bravado and abandon. She was engaged to perform the song in the George *Edwardes burlesque *Cinder-Ellen Up-to-Date* at the *Gaiety (1891), and the song became something of a symbol of the naughty Nineties. Its constant performance was said to have exhausted her and caused her early death. She toured the halls in England and the USA with various sketches but still had to produce 'Ta-ra-ra-boom-de-ay' with regularity. Her third husband was James W. *Tate, composer and partner of Clarice *Mayne.

Collins, Phil [Philip David Charles] (*b* London, 31 Jan. 1951). British singer, drummer, and composer. He appeared as a child actor as the Artful Dodger in **Oliver!* (1964). After a time with Flaming Youth, he joined *Genesis as drummer, turning vocalist on their 1976 album *A Trick of the Tail*. He also played drums with the jazz-rock group Brand X. He issued his first solo album in 1981 and had a No. 2 hit with 'In the air tonight' (1981); following up with the No. 1 USA and UK hits 'You can't hurry love' (1982); 'Against all odds' (1984); 'One more night' (1985); and 'Separate lives' (with Marilyn Martin, 1985). On balance, he has been more successful in the USA, where he toured for the first time in 1983.

Collins, Sam [Vagg, Samuel Thomas Collins] (*b* London, 1826; *d* Islington, 25 May 1865). British music-hall artist and proprietor. A chimney-sweep by trade, he had a genial nature and a winning way which made him a great favourite in the song-and-supper rooms and early *music-halls of London, dancing and singing such songs as 'Paddy's wedding', 'Limerick races', and 'The rocky road to Dublin', earning him, in spite of his London origins, the name of 'The Singing Irishman'. He is still regarded as the prototype stage Irish comic. In 1855 he appeared at Weston's and became proprietor of the Rose of Normandy tavern in the Edgware Road, turning it into the Marylebone Music Hall. He sold out in 1861 and resumed his career on the stage. Later that year he took over the Lansdowne Arms in Islington and converted the music room there into a theatre which opened as *Collins Music Hall in 1863.

Collins Music Hall. Built in Islington, London, on part of the site of the Lansdowne Arms (where there had been a music room since 1840), by London-born 'Irish' comic Sam *Collins, the music-hall (to be known to all as 'The Chapel on the Green') opened on 4 Nov. 1863. Collins died in 1865 but his hall continued, rebuilt and enlarged in 1897 with part of the old Lansdowne Arms incorporated as the bar. The theatre was destroyed by fire in 1958 but the bar, with its ephemera-covered walls, remained until it made way for an office development in 1962.

Coltrane, John William (*b* Hamlet, NC, 23 Sept. 1926; *d* New York, 17 July 1967). American jazz saxophonist. After playing with a US Navy band 1945–7, he worked with various rhythm 'n' blues bands before joining Dizzy *Gillespie in 1949. Work with Earl *Bostic, Johnny *Hodges, and more R & B bands preceded the first really significant part of his career when he joined the Miles *Davis Quintet in 1955. Coltrane's fluid style and big tone made an interesting contrast to Davis's introspective trumpet-playing. He left Davis in 1956, was with Thelonious *Monk in the summer of 1957, recorded his own *Blue Train* album, and returned to the Davis fold in late 1957, to remain there until 1960. He was on the Davis LP *Kind of Blue*, which adapted modal techniques to jazz. A cult hero for young black musicians, Coltrane then formed his own quartet, of which the most celebrated line-up comprised McCoy Tyner (piano), Jimmy Garrison (bass), and Elvin Jones (drums). He recorded 'My Favourite Things' on soprano-saxophone, and then had a remarkable success with *A Love Supreme*, which sold around a quarter of a million copies. He moved into the area of free jazz before the quartet disbanded in 1966. Coltrane, a long-time drug addict, succumbed to cancer of the liver and died with much still to offer. His work was complex and often undisciplined but it had a great influence on many musicians who followed.

B. Cole: *John Coltrane* (New York, 1976). H. Swoboda: *The John Coltrane Discography 1949–67* (Stuttgart, 1968).

Columbo, Russ [Ruggiero de Rudolpho] (*b* Philadelphia, 14 Jan. 1908; *d* Hollywood, 2 Sept. 1934). American singer, actor, composer, author, violinist, and bandleader. He began his professional career as a violinist, joining Gus *Arnheim's band at the Cocoanut Grove in Hollywood when he was 21. The band's vocalist at that time was Bing *Crosby, so Columbo remained strictly a violinist until Crosby had departed; thereafter took over the vocals and became an attraction with his silky high baritone and romantic good looks, and he appeared with the band in such films as *Street Girl* (1929). He left Arnheim after two years and in 1931 formed his own band which played at New York's Park Central Hotel and made frequent broadcasts. He was co-writer of its theme song, 'You call it madness' (1931), and such songs as 'Prisoner of love' (1931), 'Let's pretend there's a moon' (1934), and 'Too beautiful for words' (1934). His singing remained the main attraction and he starred in the films *Broadway Through a Keyhole* (1933); *Moulin Rouge* (1934); *Wake Up and Dream* (1934). Surpassed in popularity in his day only by Crosby and Rudy *Vallee, his career ended prematurely when he was killed at a friend's house while handling a duelling pistol which was assumed to be unloaded.

Colyer, Ken (*b* Great Yarmouth, Norfolk, 18 Apr. 1928; *d* South of France, 11 Mar. 1988). British jazz trumpeter and bandleader. A father-figure of the British traditional jazz revival for many years, he was one of the few to maintain an undeviating loyalty to the collectively improvised New Orleans style. A visit to the jazz city in his early days, when he was a seaman, led to his formation of the Crane River Jazz Band in 1949. He worked as a seaman again in order to revisit New Orleans and while there in 1953 was able to record with some of the local musicians. Returning from the USA he took over the leadership of a band which included Chris *Barber, Monty Sunshine, and Lonnie *Donegan; and began the *skiffle revival that was to make a star of Donegan. He and the band parted through stylistic differences, Chris Barber becoming its leader. Colyer continued to adhere to his musical beliefs and in 1967 played with the New Orleans veteran George *Lewis when he toured Britain; and he still played and survived in clubs after the traditional jazz boom years were over. Stomach cancer forced him to retire in the 1970s, but he overcame his illness and returned to spread the gospel into the 1980s, by now something of a cult figure.

Comden, Betty (*b* New York, 3 May 1917). American librettist and lyricist, mostly working in partnership throughout her career with Adolph *Green. After attending New York University, Betty Comden appeared in cabaret at the Village Vanguard in the late 1930s with Green and Judy *Holliday, later at the Rainbow Room and the Blue Angel. The first Comden/Green book was for Bernstein's **On the Town* (1944); followed by *Billion Dollar Baby* (1945); *Bonanza Bound* (1947); **High Button Shoes* (1947); *Two on the Aisle* (1951); **Wonderful Town* (1953); *Peter Pan* (1954); **Bells Are Ringing* (1956); *Say, Darling* (1958); **Do Re Mi* (1960); *Subways Are For Sleeping* (1961); *Fade Out—Fade In* (1964); *Hallelujah, Baby!* (1967); **Applause* (1970). In Hollywood they wrote scripts and songs for various Arthur *Freed MGM musicals including *Greenwich Village* (1944); **Good News* (1947); *Take Me Out to the Ball Game* (1949); *The Barkleys of Broadway* (1949); *On the Town* (1949); **Singin' in the Rain* (1953); *The *Band Wagon* (1953); *It's Always Fair Weather* (1955); *Bells Are Ringing* (1960); *What a Way to Go* (1964). The partners appeared on Broadway in *A Party With Betty Comden and Adolph Green* (1958), and a revised revival in 1977.

Comedy (Comedian) Harmonists. German quintet of close-harmony novelty vocalists who were immensely popular in their home country and on the Continent in the late 1920s and 1930s; their fame spreading to England and the USA where they were a strong influence on the similar groups that became popular at the time such as the *Mills Brothers. The group was formed by German vocalist and comedian Harry Frohman in early 1928. He advertised the formation of such a quartet and got hundreds of applicants, the one discovery being Robert Biberti, the son of an opera singer, who became their *basso profundo*. The rest of an international group were eventually recruited from the State Academy of Music in Berlin and from the Erik Charell company, including tenors Ari Lechnikoff, a Bulgarian, and Erich Collin, high-voiced Erwin Bootz, and baritone Roman Cycowski, with Emil Gerhardt as accompanist.

Calling themselves Die Comedian Harmonists they appeared with enormous success in the Charell spectacular *Casanova*, which led to variety, revue, and cabaret appearances in Berlin, Paris, Brussels, Amsterdam, Copenhagen, and Vienna. They appeared in films and made many broadcasts and recordings. Their material ranged from 'instrumentals' such as *The Barber of Seville* overture and Strauss's 'Perpetuum mobile' to German songs such as 'Veronika', 'Gitarren spielt auf', 'Mein kleiner grüner Kaktus', and 'Das ist die Liebe der Matrosen', to arrangements of popular American pieces from 'Night and day' to 'Creole love call'. Their arrangers included Gerhardt, Paul Kuhn, Fried Walter, and Daryl Runswick. Their career was a short one. The Nazis disapproved of their Americanized material and the Jewish origins of several of their members, and the original group disbanded in 1935.

Como, Perry [Pierino] (*b* Canonsburg, Pa., 18 May 1912). American singer. He started a career as a barber and owned his own shop in his home town. Adept in barber-shop singing, he gave up the business in 1933 to tour as vocalist with a local band. In 1936 he joined Ted *Weems, and his warm, friendly *Crosby-like voice soon became known. He broadcast with the band and was with it until it broke up in 1942. Thereafter he pursued a solo career in clubs and theatres and appeared in the films *Something for the Boys* (1944), *Doll Face* (1945), *If I'm Lucky* (1946), all with Vivian Blaine; and *Words and Music* (1948). His relaxed voice and style brought him many hit records starting in 1945 with 'Till the end of time' (1945), 'If I loved you' (1945), 'Temptation' (1945), and 'Prisoner of love' (1946); followed by 'Because', 'When you were sweet sixteen' (1947), 'Magic moments' (1958), and his theme song 'Dream along with me'. He had his own popular TV show from 1955 to 1963 and made occasional appearances thereafter including the 1973 TV presentation *Cole Porter in Paris*.

Company. First of a series of prestigious musicals written by composer Stephen *Sondheim with director Harold Prince. Based on five one-act plays by George Furth, the musical has as its central character Robert, a bachelor, interacting with five married friends who all lead turbulent matrimonial lives. It opened at the Alvin Theatre, 26 Apr. 1970, and ran for 706 performances. The original Robert, Dean Jones, had to leave after a month because of illness and was replaced by Larry Kert; and the impressive Elaine Stritch (*b* 1925) was followed by Jane Russell (*b* 1921) and Vivian Blaine.

Notably choreographed by Michael Bennett (*b* 1943), it was a typically way-out Sondheim production with the songs used as dramatic commentary rather than spot numbers, including: 'Company', 'The little things you do together', 'The ladies who lunch', 'Another hundred people', and 'Being alive'. The show came to London at Her Majesty's Theatre, 18 Jan. 1972.

Concert party. An entertainment that had its origins in the minstrel show and was otherwise known as the pierrot show. It flourished widely in the years up to the Second World War, being a favourite seaside spectacle. Usually a small company, with a pianist, sang and performed sketches and comedy routines in a sort of popularized revue format. Several professional groups were elevated to the London theatre, e.g. the *Follies and the *Co-Optimists.

C. Rose: *Beside the Seaside* (London, 1960). G. J. Mellor: *Pom-Poms and Ruffles: the Story of Northern Seaside Entertainment* (Clapham, Yorks., 1966). B. Pertwee: *Pertwee's Promenades and Pierrots: One Hundred Years of Seaside Entertainment* (Newton Abbot, 1979).

Concertina. A type of small *accordion, patented by Charles Wheatstone in 1829, recognizable by the hexagonal shape of its two ends, popular in the minstrel world, as a portable accompaniment for singing or dancing, and in the *morris dance world. The buttons at either end produce single notes and the chords have to be formed by the player. The German version, introduced by Carl Friedrich Uhlig in Chemnitz in 1834 had rectangular, later square, ends. A similar instrument with different fingering was the bandonion (*bandonéon*), developed in 1846 by Heinrich Band, which was taken to Argentina and became a popular instrument there. The German type of concertina was the one that also flourished in the USA. A heavier and fuller-sounding version known as the duet concertina was patented in 1884 and became a popular Salvation Army instrument. A hybrid hexagonal instrument with German fingering became known as the Anglo-German concertina and is the model favoured in folk-song and dance circles.

Condon, Eddie [Albert Edwin] (*b* Goodland, Ind., 16 Nov. 1905; *d* New York, 4 Aug. 1973). American guitarist, banjoist, jazz promoter, and bandleader. He started his playing career in Chicago in the mid-1920s and was involved in a number of historic Chicago bands and recording sessions alongside such musicians as Bud *Freeman, Gene *Krupa, Jimmy *McPartland, Dave Tough (1908–48), Floyd O'Brien (1904–68), and Red *McKenzie. Although not a notable soloist, he was an excellent rhythm guitarist and was continually in demand in the *Dixieland world. He worked in New York in the 1930s and was a frequenter of Nick's in Greenwich Village, where from 1944 he maintained a close partnership with pianist Gene Schroeder (1915–75). In 1942 he moved into jazz promotion with concerts at the Town Hall; and in 1945 he opened his own jazz club in Greenwich Village, moving to the upper East Side of New York in 1958 and active until 1967. Although afflicted by cancer in his final years, he played on and off until the end, making his last appearance at the New York–Newport Festival in 1973.

E. Condon & T. Sugrue: *We Called It Music: a Generation of Jazz* (New York, 1947). E. Condon: *Eddie Condon's Treasury of Jazz* (New York, 1956). E. Condon: *The Eddie Condon Scrapbook of Jazz* (New York, 1973).

Confrey, Zez [Edward Elzear] (*b* Peru, Ill., 3 Apr. 1895; *d* Lakewood, NJ, 22 Nov. 1971). American composer, pianist, and bandleader. He studied at the Chicago Musical College before becoming a drummer in a theatre orchestra and beginning to compose piano pieces. He made countless piano rolls of his own and other people's music, and toured in vaudeville with his own orchestra which he led throughout the 1920s. Later he was a solo act in nightclubs and on the radio. He wrote many popular compositions that worked equally well as orchestral or piano pieces, the best-known being 'Kitten on the keys' (1921), 'Stumbling' (1922), and 'Dizzy fingers' (1923); but there were many more.

Conga (1). A drum originating in Cuba, the equivalent of the African tom-tom. A large instrument which, in its primitive state, is made from a hollowed-out tree-trunk with parchment stretched over one end. It has a very powerful sound and was used, as the tom-tom is, as a message-sending device in the South American jungle until the Cuban government banned its use. The modern conga is more scientifically made but maintains a decorative appearance. It is played with the hands. Smaller versions are the enkomo and the *bongos.

Conga (2). Cuban carnival dance performed by revellers in a single line through the streets behind the comparsa bands. The choreography is 'one-two-three-kick' and this lively processional dance, each performer holding on to the one in front, has become a popular end-of-function feature all over the world. Its rhythm is 2/4 and its melodic phrases are short. Probably of African origin, it is a cross between a *rumba and a *paso doble. It had a considerable vogue as a ballroom dance around 1934.

Connecticut Yankee, A. American musical comedy with score by Richard *Rodgers, book by Herbert *Fields, based on Mark Twain's *A Connecticut Yankee in King Arthur's Court*, and lyrics by Lorenz *Hart. At the Vanderbilt Theatre, New York, 3 Nov. 1927, directed by Alexander Leftwich (1884–1947), with William *Gaxton and Constance Carpenter (1906–92) heading the cast, it had 418 performances. With some Rodgers and Hart classics in its score—'My heart stood still', 'Thou swell' among them—it was revived at the Martin Beck Theatre 17 Nov. 1943 for 135 performances, starring Vivienne *Segal. There was a London production 17 Nov. 1929 at *Daly's Theatre under the title *A Yankee at the Court of King Arthur*. It was filmed under the original Mark Twain title in 1949 with Bing *Crosby and William Bendix and a film score by Victor *Young.

Connelly, Reg (*b* Buckhurst Hill, Essex, 1895; *d* Bournemouth, Hants., 23 Sept. 1963). British composer, lyricist, and publisher. He worked in collaboration as both writer and publisher, with Jimmy Campbell. It was the success of the song 'Show me the way to go home' which they published in 1925 that allowed them to start up business in a single room in the Charing Cross Road in London. Within a year the song had sold two million copies and they were firmly established. Campbell, Connelly & Co. became one of the leading British popular music publishers and when Connelly died in 1963 he left £207,840.

The songs they wrote together included: 'The more we are together' (1926); 'The two of us' (1926); 'In a street of Chinese lanterns' (1927); 'If I had you' (1928); 'Goodnight, sweetheart' (with Ray *Noble, 1932); 'Underneath the arches' (1932); 'Try a little tenderness' (1932); and 'Just an echo in the valley' (1933).

Conniff, Ray (*b* Attleboro, Mass., 6 Nov. 1916). American trombonist, arranger, and conductor. He started playing professionally in a society band in Boston. His talents were soon recognized and he graduated to the brass sections of the bands of Bunny *Berigan 1938–9, Bob *Crosby 1939–40, Vaughn *Monroe 1941, Artie *Shaw 1941–2, making many arrangements for all of these. He served in the US Army, working in the musical division with Meredith *Willson and Walter Schumann, and played in Shaw's US Navy Band. In the late 1940s he joined Harry *James as composer-arranger, and was later with Jerry Wald, Sonny Burke, and Frank DeVol. In 1953 he became musical director for Columbia Records, writing and conducting backings for their leading singers. By 1956 he was experimenting with voices as an integral part of the orchestra and made many LPs that developed the old swing era formula he had used with Shaw and James and others, starting a trend that was widely copied. He continued with somewhat diminished impact into the 1970s and toured England in 1973.

Conrad, Con [Dober, Conrad K.] (*b* New York, 18 June 1891; *d* Van Nuys, Calif., 28 Sept. 1938). American composer. By the age of 16 he was working as pianist in a New York theatre and formed a double-act with Jay Whidden. He appeared in revue in London, and in 1913 produced *The Honeymoon Express* starring Al *Jolson. In 1920 he became a partner in a music-publishing business. He wrote the scores of *Bombo* (1921); **Greenwich Village Follies* (1923); *Betty Lee* (1924); *Moonlight* (1924); *Mercenary Mary* (1925); *The Comic Supplement* (1925); *Kitty's Kisses* (1926); **Americana* (1926); and, for Hollywood films: *Fox Movietone Follies* (1929); *Happy Days* (1930)—'Crazy feet'; *Palmy Days* (1931); *The Gift of Gab* (1934); *I Like It That Way* (1934); *The Gay Divorcée* (1934)—'The continental' (*w* Herb Magidson, *b* 1906), 'Looking for a needle in a haystack'; *Here's to Romance* (1935)—'Midnight in Paris'; *Reckless* (1935); *King Solomon of Broadway* (1935); *I'd Give My Life* (1936); and *The Story of Vernon and Irene Castle* (1939). His best-known songs were: 'Singin' the blues' (1920); 'Margie' (1920); 'Palesteena' (1920); 'Ma, he's making eyes at me' (1921); 'Barney Google' (1922); 'You gotta see mama every night' (1922); 'She's everybody's sweetheart but nobody's gal' (1924); 'Prisoner of love' (1931); 'You call it madness but I call it love' (1931); 'The champagne waltz' (1934).

Conversation Piece. Romantic comedy with music and words by Noël *Coward, produced at His Majesty's Theatre, London, 16 Feb. 1934. Coward's second 'operetta' (**Bitter Sweet* was the first in 1929), it was written to suit the talents of its leading lady Yvonne *Printemps; and was set in Regency England, where a poverty-stricken French nobleman (played by Coward) takes his ward Melanie to Brighton to find her a rich husband, but falls in love with her himself. It contained such Coward classics as 'I'll follow my secret heart', 'Regency rakes', 'Charming, charming', and 'There's always something fishy about the French'; and initially ran for 177 performances. It was seen in New York at the 44th Street Theatre, 23 Oct. 1934, with Pierre Fresnay (1897–1975) taking Coward's role.

Conway, Russ [Stanford, Trevor Herbert] (*b* Bristol, 2 Sept. 1927). British pianist and composer. He made his first musical appearance at the age of 10 with an accordion band. He spent his early years, from the age of 15, in the Merchant and Royal Navy, and was awarded the DSM during the Second World War. Discharged in 1955, he became a club pianist in London and was accompanist to Gracie *Fields, Joan Regan, Lita Roza, and others. His first solo stage appearance was at the Metropolitan Music Hall in London in 1957 and he made his first record that year, adopting the name of Russ Conway. He became a very popular pianist/entertainer on radio and TV, frequently playing his own compositions, and having his first big hit with 'Side saddle' (1959), followed by 'Roulette' (1959) and 'China tea' (1959). By 1961 he had sold 250,000 LPs. He wrote the score of a musical comedy, *Mister Venus* (1958); and has remained active, working mainly in clubs.

Cook, Barbara (*b* Atlanta, Ga., 25 Oct. 1927). American actress and singer with an excellent soprano voice and vivacious personality. She was seen in *Flahooley* (1951); the touring company of **Oklahoma!* (1953); **Plain and Fancy* (1955); **Candide* (1956); *The *Music Man* (1957); *The Gay Life* (1961); **She Loves Me* (1963); *Something More* (1964); and *The Grass Harp* (1971). *Barbara Cook at Carnegie Hall* was recorded by CBS in 1975. She worked in London clubs in the late 1970s and recorded *Carousel* in 1987.

Cook, Will Marion (*b* Washington DC, 27 Jan. 1869; *d* New York, 19 July 1944). American composer, conductor, and violinist. He studied in Europe under Joachim and when illness forced his return to the USA, he continued his studies at the National Conservatory under Dvořák. He started composing for shows starring the dancer-comedians Walker and *Williams (Bert); and continued to write regularly for the theatre; including *Clorindy* or *The Origin of the Cakewalk* (1898) with which he visited London in 1899 and gave a Command Performance for Edward VII.

He also wrote *The Wild Rose* (1902); **In Dahomey* (1903); *The Southerners* (1904); *Abyssinia* (1906); *Bandana Land* (1908); and a number of songs that were in vogue in the early 1900s such as 'Down de lover's lane', used in *The Casino Girl* (1900); and 'Dat's all', used in *The New Yorkers* (1901); 'Bon bon buddy' (1907); 'Lovey Joe' (1910); and 'I'm coming, Virginia' (1927). In 1919 he organized an all-black Syncopated Orchestra which toured America and Europe.

Cooke, Sam [Cook] (*b* Chicago, 22 Jan. 1935; *d* Los Angeles, 11 Dec. 1964). American singer and composer. An important performer and writer whose songs have long outlived his brief career; and promoter of a gentle style of singing that had its roots in the Negro *spirituals. He was originally in a gospel group, the Soul Stirrers, and continued to write many songs in a religious vein, moving into more secular areas in the late 1950s. His first big song hit was 'You send me' (1957) which became No. 1 in the USA; followed by 'For sentimental reasons' (1958); 'I'll come running back to you' (1958); 'Only sixteen' (1959); 'Wonderful world' (1960); 'Chain gang' (1960); 'Cupid' (1961); 'Twistin' the night away' (1962); 'Having a party' (1962); 'Bring it on home to me' (1963); and many more. He started his own record company in 1960 and remained a leading performer until his death in 1964 when he accidentally entered the wrong room at a motel and was shot by its female occupant. He has remained one of the most admired soul singers, and his songs have been recorded by Aretha *Franklin, Otis *Redding, Rod *Stewart, and many others.

Cool. Applied to modern forms of jazz which tend to be intellectual and introspective in instrumental tone, phrasing, and overall feeling; in contrast to the *hot leanings of traditional jazz which aimed at emotional excitement and rhythmic drive to create its effect. The term was first used in West Coast jazz circles and quickly became a vogue word of the 1950s.

Cooley, Spade [Donnell Clyde] (*b* Pack Saddle Creek, Okla., 17 Dec. 1910; *d* Oakland, Calif., 23 Nov. 1969). Part Cherokee Indian, he played the violin for square dances before joining various *Country and Western groups. In the mid-1930s he became a Hollywood extra and musician and achieved several small roles in Roy Rogers films. He earned his name 'Spade' through several fluke wins at poker. He sang with the Riders of the Purple Sage group; but by 1942 he was leading his own band and from 1946 leased and worked at the Santa Monica Ballroom and had his own radio show. His band became well-known in the 1950s, playing anything from C & W to jazz and ballads and he became known as the 'King of Western Swing'. He wrote 'Shame on you' (1944). In 1961 he was imprisoned for murdering his wife; he died while on parole.

Coon–Sanders Orchestra. Popular dance band of the 1920s and 1930s formed and jointly led by drummer Carlton Coon (*b* Rochester, Minn., 5 Feb. 1894; *d* Chicago, 3 May 1932) and pianist Joe Sanders (1896–1965). Both had grown up in Missouri and they met in Kansas City, where they formed the band in 1920. Broadcasts from the Muehlbach Hotel made it known in the Midwest, where its late-night shows earned it the nickname of the Kansas City Night Hawks. The orchestra worked in Chicago from 1924, notably at the Blackhawk Restaurant in 1926, but remained based in Kansas City. They had their own show on NBC and recorded such hits as 'Here comes my ball and chain' and 'Slue foot', continuing a successful and stable career until, while playing at the College Inn in Chicago, Coon died suddenly from an abscessed tooth. Without its singing duo leadership the band broke up a year later; though Joe Sanders continued to lead his own band. Theirs was one of the best of the jazz-oriented dance bands that helped to steer the music towards the boom swing years of the 1930s.

Cooper, Alice. Name assumed by the vocalist and composer Vincent Furnier (*b* Detroit, 4 Feb. 1948) who formed the group known collectively as Alice Cooper. They were signed by Straight Records in 1969, and were the instigators of frantic stage activities to smudge over a band's artistic limitations. But they had successes with such numbers as 'School's out' (1972) and, after wholesale changes of personnel, 'I never cry' (1976) and 'You and me' (1977). Drink problems and the arrival of even more bizarre groups kept the band out of the news until Cooper returned with a new band in 1982 playing in a revivalist rock idiom.

Co-Optimists, The. Pierrot-style concert-party which contained a number of famous names in its ranks. The idea for the company was conceived in Leslie *Henson's dressing-room at the Winter Garden Theatre in May 1921. The cast of the show *A Night Out*, then playing there, included Henson, Davy Burnaby (1881–1949), Phyllis *Monkman, Stanley *Holloway, and Elsa MacFarlane, who were to form the nucleus of the Co-Optimists. Davy Burnaby, who had long nurtured the ambition for such a group, was the leading spirit; while the business partners in the background were Laddie *Cliff, Archie de Bear, and Clifford Whitely.

The first edition, at the Royalty Theatre 27 June 1921, in spite of a heat-wave and strikes, had a notable success and a run of 500 performances. The group continued to appear in various London theatres until 1931 and toured the British Isles. Burnaby remained the inspirational leader throughout while Henson, though never actually able to appear in the show, always gave considerable help and encouragement. The accompaniment and much of the musical material was supplied by Melville Gideon. Others who joined the show were Gilbert Childs, H. B. Hedley, Betty Chester, Austin Melford, Mary Leigh, and, after a temporary break-up in 1927, Herbert Mundin, Elsie *Randolph, Mimi Crawford, Wolseley Charles, and Cyril *Ritchard. The producer was Greatrex Newman (1892–1984), who contributed much material. An 83-minute film of a stage performance was made in 1927.

A. Sterne & A. de Bear: *The Comic History of the Co-Optimists* (London, 1926).

Coots, J. Fred [John Frederick] (*b* Brooklyn, 2 May 1897). American composer. In his early days he worked as a song-plugger, then as a pianist in vaudeville and clubs. He wrote scores for the Broadway shows *Sally, Irene and Mary* (1922); **Artists and Models* (1925); *June Days* (1925); *Gay Paree* (1925); *A Night in Paris* (1926); *The Merry World* (1926); *White Lights* (1927); *Sons o' Guns* (1929); and for three editions of the *Cotton Club revue in the 1930s. His songs, many of them written for films, included: 'Mister Ford, you've got the right idea' (1917); 'Time will tell' (1922); 'A precious little thing called love' (1929); 'Love letters in the sand' (1931); 'Santa Claus is coming to town' (1934); 'A beautiful lady in blue' (1935); 'Alabama barbecue' (1936); 'You go to my head' (1938); and 'There's honey on the moon tonight' (1938).

Copper Family. English folk-singing family who trace their origins in Rottingdean back to the 1500s. A long tradition of unaccompanied singing was revived by Bob [Robert James] Copper (*b* 1915), his daughter, Jill Susan (*b* 1945), his son, John James (*b* 1949), and other relatives, following in a long unbroken line of performers. Their revelations of the traditions of harmonic part-singing has had a wide influence on others in the English folk revival, and their material has been sung and recorded by many. Bob Copper has published three books on the family—*A Song for Every Season* (1971); *Songs and Southern Breezes* (1973); and *Early to Rise* (1975). They recorded several albums in the 1970s.

Cornet. The valved cornet, or *cornet à pistons*, was introduced in Paris in the 1860s and was to become a major instrument in light and popular music. Taken up by *military and *brass bands throughout the world, and favoured over the trumpet for its warm and mellifluous tone, it became the instrument of many virtuoso players such as Koenig with the *Jullien band, and it was soon a popular instrument in amateur circles. It was also to be the leading instrument of jazz in pioneer days, for the practical reason that there were many of them cheaply available after the American Civil War when many military units disbanded. Virtuoso jazz players mainly switched to the trumpet later for its more brilliant and incisive tone, but there has always been a core of cornet adherents in both traditional and modern jazz such as Bix *Beiderbecke, Muggsy *Spanier, Rex *Stewart, Wild Bill *Davison, Ken *Colyer, Ruby Braff, Nat Adderley, Thad *Jones, and Marc Charig.

Coslow, Sam (*b* New York, 27 Dec. 1902; *d* 1982). American composer and lyricist. He began writing soon after leaving school and, doing well at it, formed the publishing firm of Spier & Coslow in 1928, which he and Larry Spier later sold to Paramount Pictures. He had an early part-time career as a band vocalist and was to make recordings as a singer into the 1930s. He went to Hollywood in 1929 to work for Paramount, writing for many Bing *Crosby films, an association that continued until 1938. In 1940, in partnership with Col. James Rossevelt, he introduced Soundies (short sound films that operated in *juke-box-type machines). He left music for the financial world before retiring to Florida.

The films he contributed to included: *The Dance of Life* (1929); *Honey* (1930)—'Sing you sinners'; *Paramount on Parade* (1930); *The *Vagabond King* (1930); *Hello, Everybody* (1933); *College Humour* (1933)—'Moonstruck', 'Down the old ox road', 'Learn to croon'; *Too Much Harmony* (1933); *Belle of the Nineties* (1934); *Murder at the Vanities* (1934)—'Cocktails for two'; *All the King's Horses* (1935); *Coronado* (1935); *Goin' to Town* (1935); *Rhythm on the Range* (1936); *It's Love Again* (1936); *Make Way for Tomorrow* (1937); *Double or Nothing* (1937); *Swing High, Swing Low* (1937); *A Hundred Men and a Girl* (1937); *Thrill of a Lifetime* (1938); *St Louis Blues* (1938); *Copacabana* (1947); *Summer Stock* (1950); *Affair With a Stranger* (1953). Other songs included: 'Was it a dream?', 'Just one more chance', 'Thanks', 'Moon song', 'My old flame'.

S. Coslow: *Cocktails for Two* (New Rochelle, NJ, 1977).

Costello, Elvis [McManus, Declan Patrick] (*b* London, 25 Aug. 1955). British rock singer and guitarist. After a slow start, he was signed by Stiff Records in 1976, changed his name, and had a modest success with his first LP. In 1977 he formed his permanent backing group the Attractions and had his first hit single, 'Watching the detectives'. 'Oliver's army' (1979) reached No. 2 in the charts and was closely rivalled by 'I can't stand up for falling down' (1980) and 'Good year for the roses' (1982). His abrasive, doom-laden, introspective style has led to comparisons with Bob *Dylan and general critical acclaim and, although his output is still limited, he seems to be on the way to becoming a cult figure.

Costello, Tom [Costellow, Thomas] (*b* Birmingham, 30 Apr. 1863; *d* London, 8 Nov. 1943). British music-hall comedian and singer. He worked as an engraver until he was 20 and then decided to try the stage, first appearing in pantomime in Wolverhampton. His first London appearance was in *Robinson Crusoe* at the Surrey Theatre in 1885; and his first appearance in a London music-hall was in 1886 when he performed at the South London Palace, the Middlesex, and the Bedford in Camden Town. One of his earliest songs was 'My Nellie's blue eyes' which was the subject parodied in Charles *Coborn's 'Two lovely black eyes' in 1886. He specialized in black humour on the one hand, and sentimental and patriotic ballads on the other, having a strong and expressive singing voice. The songs he became especially associated with were 'At Trinity Church I met my doom', 'The ship I love', and Felix *McGlennon's soul-stirring 'Comrades', which he was invariably asked to sing. He continued his career in pantomime and was with the 'Veterans of Variety' company in 1923, later touring with a similar unit of his own. He recorded a medley of his famous songs in 1933, with surviving vigour, and lived to an unusually grand old age for a music-hall star.

T. Barker: 'Tom Costello' in *Music-Hall Records*, No. 8 (London, 1979).

Cotton, Billy [William Edward] (*b* London, 6 May 1899; *d* Wembley, 25 Mar. 1969). British bandleader. He started his musical career as a drummer in the army, although he thought of becoming a racing driver and pursued the activity as an amateur for many years. He moved into the dance band world in the early 1920s and formed his first band in 1926. He played for many years at such prestigious spots as the Astoria and Ciro's, and presented his first stage show at the *Alhambra in 1936. This became very popular on radio, and later TV, fronted by Cotton with vulgar, brash good humour and his piercing battle-cry of 'Wakey, Wakey!' The popular comic approach never hid the fact that he led a first-rate band full of good musicians and excellent vocalists such as Alan Breeze (*b* 1909) who was with him for several decades. Despite the economic difficulties of maintaining a dance band in modern times, the band and his attendant show kept going until he died. His son Bill Cotton Jr. has pursued an executive career in the BBC.

B. Cotton: *I Did It My Way* (London, 1970).

Cotton Club, The. Renowned New York nightclub at 644 Lenox Avenue on the corner of 142nd Street in Harlem. The premises first became a club in 1920, then known as the Club Deluxe, but it was taken over in 1922 by a syndicate of bootleggers headed by Owney Madden, and renamed the Cotton Club. The use of such a name and the policy of providing black entertainment for a whites-only audience has besmirched its reputation; but none the less some high-quality entertainment evolved there following its grand opening in 1923. It survived various closures for its flouting of the Prohibition laws. The resident bands were led by Andy Preer 1923–7, Duke *Ellington 1927–30, 1937, and 1938, his *jungle music doing much to establish the nature of Cotton Club entertainment, Cab *Calloway 1930–4 and 1936–7, Jimmie *Lunceford 1934–6; the shows featured such notable entertainers as Ethel *Waters and Bill 'Bojangles' *Robinson and an especially fine tradition of dancers. There was a period of decline in the early 1930s; the Harlem premises closed in 1936 and the Club moved to Broadway and 48th Street, finally closing in 1940. Several Cotton Club revues were staged at other places in subsequent years and its glorious but tainted history has been immortalized in the show *Bubbling Brown Sugar* (1976) and the film *Cotton Club* (1985).

J. Haskins: *The Cotton Club* (New York, 1977).

Cottrau, Teodoro (*b* Naples, 27 Nov. 1827; *d* Naples, 30 Mar. 1879). Italian composer. He was the writer of numerous songs that have become classics of the *Neapolitan song repertoire, notably 'Santa Lucia' (1850) and 'Addio a Napoli' (1868). He was the manager of a music-publishing business in Naples. His father, Guglielmo Louis Cottrau (1797–1847), and his brother Giulio (1831–1916) were also composers of Neapolitan songs.

Count of Luxembourg, The see **Gráf von Luxemburg, Der*.

Country dancing. General term synonymous with folk-dancing. It came into use during the period when Cecil *Sharp was discovering (or, more precisely, rediscovering) English rural dances, in particular those which came under the heading of *morris dances. For a while he was mainly concerned with the educational use of these and took some of his figures and instructions from John *Playford's various editions of *The *Dancing Master*. As his researches continued, however, it became plain that even Playford had already popularized: the real folk-dances of the British Isles were less elaborate but more vigorous, and their origins lay in ritual. Hence the grotesque figures, such as the hobby-horse or the dragon, that occasionally feature in dances performed at certain places at special times of the year. The *square dance, generally credited as an import from the USA, was only new in its use of a caller; many of the dances and the tunes were found to have their counterparts still lingering in English rural counties.

C. Sharp: *The Country Dance Book* (6 vols) (London, 1909–22; and reprints).

'Country gardens'. Dance tune first published in London in 1728 in *The Quaker's Opera*; also known as 'The Vicar of Bray' and clearly a close variant of the song. It became commonly used as a handkerchief dance, slightly amended, and was printed by Cecil *Sharp and Herbert C. MacIlwaine in *Morris Dance Tunes*, Set 1 (1907). It was the subject of a well-known arrangement by Percy Grainger (1852–1961) in 1919, which established its popularity.

Country Girl, A. British 'musical play' with score mainly by Lionel *Monckton, book by James T. Tanner (1859–1956), and lyrics by Adrian *Ross and Percy *Greenbank. Produced at London's *Daly's Theatre, 18 Jan. 1902 with Evie Greene (1878–1917), Hayden *Coffin, Huntley Wright (1869–1943), and Willie Warde (1857–1943) among the cast, it had a highly successful run of 729 performances. Much of its success was due to a tuneful score which provided such popular bandstand material of the day as 'Yo ho, little girls, yo ho', 'Boy and girl', 'Molly the Marchioness', 'Under the deodar'; and numbers such as 'Two little chicks' added by Paul *Rubens. It was produced at *Daly's Theatre, New York, 22 Sept. 1902 [112p]; and revived at the London branch in 1914 [173p] and 1931.

Country Music, Country and Western. All-embracing term for the musical culture and forms that evolved in the USA as it absorbed folk-music of the British Isles, Europe, and elsewhere in the early days of national growth. The 'country' in question is generally pinpointed as lying in such Southern rural areas as the Appalachian mountains, where folklorists have found many of the earliest surviving strains. It emerged in the folk revival of this century under such names as *hillbilly, mountain or hill-country music, old-time, and *bluegrass, and, until it gained nationwide status, maintained regional forms and styles. The Western element of 'Country and Western' came in with the addition of the cowboy themes that had developed in such areas as railroad and gold-rush songs, a particularly identifiable American strain that emerged in commercial form through the efforts of such singers as Jimmie *Rodgers whose songs were founded on many intermingling styles. Country music began to establish itself commercially as a special genre when old-time fiddlers like John *Carson first recorded around 1923. Okeh records issued its first special country catalogue in 1924 and the blind singer Riley Puckett (1884–1946) became one of the first country singers to record in that year, establishing the popular yodelling style and many of the traits of country guitar playing. Rodgers and the *Carter Family were getting on to record around 1927. As soon as the radio started using country music for commercials that asked for a rural slant, the wider public was quickly attracted to the music and whole programmes were soon devoted to country dance music, including the WSM *Barn Dance* programme of 1925 which was to develop into the **Grand Ole Opry*.

Typical American country music, with infinite variation, is built on an infectious rhythmic basis of guitar, banjo, or mandolin with a style of fiddle lead that clearly has its roots in Scottish and Irish fiddle music. Lyrics, when added, tend to be of a rustically amorous, humorous, and sometimes narrative kind.

Some country music activities moved towards the commercialized areas of hillbilly or Country and Western style; the singing cowboys of the screen like Gene *Autry and Roy Rogers popularized the Tin Pan Alley brand of Western music. On the other hand there were the purists like the famous Carter family who worked to keep the old regional rural traditions intact. It was perhaps after the retirement of the Carters in 1941 that the commercial strains won the upper hand and professional country music took over, with its mecca in *Nashville, Tennessee (the subject of a vivid film, *Nashville*, 1975), and its main outlet the *Grand Ole Opry* radio series. Nashville survived as the strongest challenger for country supremacy, outliving other pioneering efforts like the *Louisiana Hayride* programme from Shreveport.

A whole cult of music and singers grew and built a huge following, not only in the USA but in Europe as well. Names like Willie *Nelson, Patsy *Cline, Tammy *Wynette, Red *Foley, Eddie *Arnold, Hank *Williams, Roy *Acuff, and Johnny *Cash became known internationally, The music lost its straw-sucking hillbilly image and became brashly *honky-tonk and westernized, moving into the pop field in the hands of polished artists like Roger *Miller and the entertainers like Dolly *Parton.

The authentic performing of such as the Carter family clearly laid down a repertoire of genuine country music. In specific fields like *bluegrass music the pioneering work of Bill Monroe and others established in the public mind what real, traditional country music sounded like. By the 1950s there was a clear divide between the authentic school, with its often scholarly adherents, and, as in the wider folk-music field, the country music which became a part of the commercial world of pop/country fusion, with singers like Kitty *Wells and Hank *Snow often passing from one sphere to the other.

L. Gentry: *A History and Encyclopedia of Country, Western and Gospel Music* (Nashville, 1961). R. Shelton: *The Country Music Story* (Indianapolis, 1966). B. C. Malone: *Country Music USA* (Austin–London, 1968). T. Moore: *Pictorial History of Country Music*, 2 vols (Denver, 1969). I. Stambler & G. Landon: *Encyclopedia of Folk, Country and Western Music* (New York, 1969). J. Grissom: *Country Music: White Man's Blues* (New York, 1970). L. Brown & G. Friedrich: *The Encyclopedia of Country and Western Music* (New York, 1971). S. D. Price: *Country and Western Music* (New York, 1973). D. B. Green: *Country Roots* (New York, 1976). F. Dellar, R. Thompson, & D. B. Green: *The Illustrated Encyclopedia of Country Music* (London, 1977). M. Shestack: *The Country Music Encyclopedia* (London–New York–Sydney, 1977). F. Gaillard: *Watermelon Wine: the Spirit of Country Music* (New York, 1978). T. Byworth: *The History of Country & Western Music* (London, 1984). C. T. Brown: *Music USA: America's Country and Western Tradition* (Englewood Cliffs, NJ, 1986).

Country Music Hall of Fame. An offshoot of the commercialized country music scene has been the Country Music Hall of Fame, a part of the museum at the Country Music Foundation (founded in 1964) in *Nashville, Tennessee. As a reward for services to *country music, members are selected by a nominating committee and finally chosen by a 250-strong electorate, from the music industry and associated activities, and their names are inscribed on bronze plaques for posterity. The Hall of Fame does not maintain the distinction that some people would like to draw between genuine folk country and its commercial counterpart; nevertheless, membership reflects sustained and genuine achievement in the field. The first choices, made in 1961, were Fred *Rose (composer and publisher), Jimmie *Rodgers, and Hank *Williams; among the names added in subsequent years were Roy *Acuff (1962), Tex *Ritter (1964), Ernest *Tubb (1965), Eddy *Arnold (1966), Dave *Macon (1966), Jim *Reeves (1967), Red *Foley (1967), Gene *Autry (1969), the *Carter Family (1970), Bill *Monroe (1970), Jimmy *Davis (1972), Patsy *Cline (1973), and Chet *Atkins (1973).

Country rock. Commercialized amalgam of rock and contemporary country styles that developed in the late 1960s in California. A leading figure in its development was Gram Parsons, and it was given some impetus by Bob *Dylan in his *Nashville Skyline* album and by his work with Johnny *Cash and Hank *Williams. Leading country rock bands include the Flying Burrito Brothers, Poco, the Eagles, Hearts and Flowers, and Dillard and Clark.

Courtneidge, Cicely [Esmeralda] (*b* Sydney, 1 Apr. 1893; *d* London, 26 Apr. 1980). British actress and singer. Daughter of actor and producer/manager Robert Courtneidge (1859–1939), she was born while he was on tour in Australia and first appeared on the stage under his management in Manchester in 1901. She returned to Australia until 1907; then appeared in the musicals *The *Arcadians* (1909), *The Mousmé* (1911), and *Princess Caprice* (1912). She played opposite Jack *Hulbert in *The Pearl Girl* in 1913; they were married in 1916. She performed on the music-hall stage in cameo sketches, but both she and her husband built their reputation appearing, often together, in numerous London revues and musicals. They became a thoroughly integrated team until 1923, appeared almost exclusively as a duo for many years, then tended to go their separate ways again from 1931, though with frequent renewals of the partnership right to the end of their careers when they toured in a reminiscent revue of their roles.

The productions she appeared in included: *The Cinema Star* (1914); *The Arcadians* (1915 revival); *The Light Blues* (1916); *Ring Up* (1921); *The *Little Revue Starts at 9* (1923); *By the Way* (1925); *Lido Lady* (1926); *Clowns in Clover* (1927); *The House that Jack Built* (1929); *Folly to be Wise* (1931)—in which she sang 'The King's horses'; *Hide and Seek* (1937); *Under Your Hat* (1938; filmed 1940); *Full Swing* (1942); *Something in the Air* (1943)—'Home'; *Under the Counter* (1945); *Her Excellency* (1949); **Gay's the Word* (1951)—'Vitality'; *Over the Moon* (1953); *High Spirits* (1964). She appeared in several films in the 1930s, including: *The Ghost Train* (1932); *Jack's the Boy* (1932); *Soldiers of the King* (1933)—'The moment I saw you'; and *Aunt Sally* (1934)—'We'll all go riding on a rainbow'.

C. Courtneidge: *Cicely* (London, 1953). J. Hulbert: *The Little Woman's Always Right* (London, 1975).

Cover version. Recording of a song already made into a hit by a popular artist, who today would probably also be its composer, by someone of lesser fame, often to provide a cheap label version or for promotional reasons. Earlier, in the sheet music era, the term had been more loosely used of any general exploitation of songs in a specified field; but in the early *rhythm 'n' blues years the activity became especially associated with lesser-known, often British, artists making versions of hit songs already made famous by top American artists (i.e. until the *Beatles reversed the process); and there have been occasions when the cover version has superseded the original.

Coward, Noël [Pierce] (*b* Teddington, Middx., 16 Dec. 1899; *d* Port Maria, Jamaica, 26 Mar. 1973). British composer, librettist, playwright, actor, and director, one of the best-known figures in the 20th-century English theatre. He received no formal musical education but had the fortune to be born into a naturally musical family: Dr Coward, a great-uncle, had been organist at the Crystal Palace, and his mother and father, who first met as members of the choir of St Alban's church in Teddington, were amateur operatic singers of considerable ability; his father worked for a firm of piano manufacturers.

Coward developed his interest in music at an early age, exhibiting a tendency to dance in church whenever the organ voluntaries or hymns struck him as being more lively than usual. At the age of 10 he won a prize for singing at a seaside concert and he was regularly composing by the time he was 15. By the age of 18 his output showed a distinct *revue flavour and was moving towards the style he was to bring to perfection in the late 1920s and early 1930s. He worked rapidly and often found the happy knack of arriving at the tune and words simultaneously. Sometimes they came out of the blue. 'I'll see you again' materialized in a New York taxi; 'Matelot' turned up as a few bars of melody while he was dressing one morning.

Although a rival to his friend Ivor *Novello in writing the romantic operetta score, as in **Bitter Sweet* and **Conversation Piece*, he is probably remembered first for witty, satirical songs, that made him the rightful successor to W. S. Gilbert, rather than his sentimental ones. For all its popularity, 'Some day I'll find you' must yield in rating to 'Mad dogs and Englishmen' and 'The stately homes of England'. Although he continued to write after the Second World War, the best of Coward's output was firmly based in the 1930s, and his fruitful stage partnerships with such fellow spirits as Gertrude *Lawrence, Beatrice *Lillie, and Jack *Buchanan. The world after 1945 lacked the blasé spirit and atmosphere in which his ripely whimsical humour thrived. He tried to work in the more meanly satirical post-war world ('Don't let's be beastly to the Germans'), but the tone was different. As Ellington's music seems to lose much without the flavour of the Ellington band; so does most of Coward's inimitable output lose impact without the wryly precise voice that was the basis of its style. His art is a curious mixture of artifice and naturalness to his own self. He mocked the manner of the 1930s in his songs and then, in the 1950s, was able to mock himself. Coward suffered very much from changes of fashion and critical taste and went through a period of unpopularity in the war years. He came back, not by dint of new creativity but through the classic perfection of his best work. He was tardily knighted in 1972; and in 1973 a revue, *Cowardy Custard*, using his classic songs and sketches, was produced at the Mermaid Theatre. His final years were spent mainly in either Switzerland or Jamaica.

His principal scores were: *London Calling* (1923)—'There's life in the old girl yet'; *André Charlot's London Revue of 1924*—'Parisian pierrot', 'Poor little rich girl'; **On With The Dance* (1925); **This Year of Grace* (1928)—'A room with a view', 'Dance, little lady', 'World weary'; **Bitter Sweet* (1929)—'I'll see you again', 'Zigeuner', 'If love were all', 'Tokay'; a play with music, *Private Lives* (1930)—'Someday I'll find you'; **Cochran's Revue* (1931); **Cavalcade* (1931)—'Twentieth century blues'; *Words and Music* (1932)—'Mad about the boy', 'Mad dogs and Englishmen', 'The party's over', 'Let's live dangerously'; **Conversation Piece* (1934)—'I'll follow my secret heart', 'Nevermore', 'Regency rakes'; **Tonight at Eight-Thirty* (1936: 9 one-act plays; 3 musical)—'Has anybody seen our ship?', 'You were there'; *Operette* (1938)—'Dearest love'; *Set to Music* (NY, 1939)—'I'm so weary of it all', 'I've been to a marvellous party', 'The stately homes of England'; *Sigh No More* (1945)—'Sigh no more', 'Matelot', 'This is the end of the news', 'I wonder what happened to him', 'Nina'; *Pacific 1860* (1946); *Ace of Clubs* (1950); *After the Ball* (1954); *Sail Away* (1961)—'Later than Spring'; and *The Girl Who Came To Supper* (1963)—'I'll remember her'.

His films were: *Cavalcade* (1933); *In Which We Serve* (1942); *This Happy Breed* (1944). He wrote a ballet, *London Morning* (1959); and his best-remembered songs, apart from those already mentioned, include: 'Forbidden fruits' (1916); 'The bar on the Piccola Marina' (1933); 'Alice is at it again' (1934); 'Don't put your daughter on the stage, Mrs Worthington' (1935); 'Imagine the Duchess's feelings' (1941); 'London pride' (1941). To other revues he contributed 'Mad dogs and Englishmen' (*The Third *Little Show*, 1931); 'Half caste woman' (**Ziegfeld Follies*, 1931); 'Don't make fun of the fair' (**Lyric Revue*, 1951); 'There are bad times just around the corner' (*Globe Revue*, 1952). He wrote a number of straight plays, novels, and short stories, as well as the volumes of autobiography listed below.

P. Braybrooke: *The Amazing Mr Noël Coward* (London, 1933; repr. 1975). N. Coward: *Present Indicative* (London, 1937; repr. 1980, 1988). N. Coward: *Australia Visited, 1940* (London, 1941). N. Coward: *Middle East Diary* (London, 1944). R. Greacan: *The Art of Noël Coward* (Aldington, 1953). N. Coward: *Future Indefinite* (London, 1954; repr. 1980, 1988). R. Mander & J. Mitchenson: *Theatrical Companion to Coward* (London, 1957). M. Levin: *Noël Coward* (Boston, 1958). S. Morley: *A Talent to Amuse* (London, 1969; rev. 1974; repr. 1985). C. Castle: *Noël* (London, 1972). J. Hadfield (ed.): *Cowardy Custard: the World of Noël Coward* (London, 1973). C. Lesley: *The Life of Noël Coward* (London, 1976). C. Lesley, G. Payn, & S. Morley: *Noël Coward and His Friends* (London, 1979).

Music and lyrics: *The Noël Coward Songbook* (London, 1953). *The Lyrics of Noël Coward* (London, 1965).

Cowell, Sam [Samuel] (*b* London, 5 Apr. 1820; *d* Blandford, 11 Mar. 1864). British music-hall performer. Son of an actor, he went on tour with his family in America in 1821 and while there established his own reputation as a comic actor, making his first stage appearance at the age of nine. He returned to England in 1840 and continued his acting career. Gradually he made a separate reputation as a singer, appearing at the Cremorne Gardens in 1846 and at *Vauxhall in 1847. By 1850 he was making a good living as a singer at the song-and-supper rooms—the Coal Hole, the Cyder Cellars, and *Evans's—his speciality being comedy character songs such as *'Vilikens and his Dinah' and 'The ratcatcher's daughter'. He appeared at the Grecian in burlesque sketches and was starring at the Canterbury Music Hall in 1851; and he ran his own touring company. In 1859 he went to the USA and spent an arduous 20 months touring there and in Canada, his wife's recorded account of these days giving a fascinating insight into pre-Civil War America. He returned to London and was at the *Oxford Music Hall in 1861; but consumption, alcohol, and overwork soon took their toll and he died early.

Mrs S. Cowell (ed. Disher): *The Cowells in America* (London, 1934).

Cox, Desmond (*b* London, 1903; *d* London, 14 Nov. 1966). British composer, lyricist, and publisher. Director of the music-publishing firm of Box & Cox Ltd. His compositions were mainly written in collaboration with his business partner Harold Box, including: 'We all went up, up, up the mountain' (1933); 'The wheel of the wagon is broken' (1935); 'Horsey, horsey' (1937); 'In the quartermaster's store' (1940); 'I've got sixpence' (1941); 'When you know you're not forgotten' (1942); and 'Just a little fond affection' (1944).

Cox, Ida [Prather, Ida] (*b* Toccoa, Ga., 25 Feb. 1896; *d* Knoxville, Tenn., 10 Nov. 1967). American blues singer and composer. She began her career at the age of 14 singing in minstrel shows, then worked in vaudeville in the early 1920s. She had a special line in somewhat sombre blues which were none the less popular—'Monkey man blues', 'Death letter blues', 'Black crepe blues', 'Coffin blues', and 'Graveyard bound blues' among them. She started recording for Paramount in 1923, often with Lovie Austin and her Blues Serenaders. Her second husband was pianist Jesse Crump (*b* 1906) with whom she also worked and recorded. In 1925 she recorded with Fletcher *Henderson, and she toured the USA with her own package show in the 1930s. She stopped performing for a few years in the mid-1930s, but was talked out of retirement in 1939 by Hot Lips *Page who brought her to New York for a Café Society broadcast, to record with him, and to appear at a Carnegie Hall concert. She had a stroke in 1944 and retired to Knoxville, briefly emerging in 1961 to make some recordings for Riverside with Coleman *Hawkins, Roy *Eldridge, and Sammy Price (1908–92). Her own compositions included: 'Bone orchard blues', 'Midnight hour blues', 'Mojo hand blues', 'Fore day creep', and 'Western Union blues', all from around 1928.

Cox and Box. Arthur *Sullivan's first venture into the field of operetta, a modest three-character piece described as a 'musical triumviretta'. It was inspired by *Offenbach's *Les Deux Aveugles* (first performed in London in 1857) which Sullivan and the burlesque writer Francis C. Burnand had heard performed at Moray Lodge, the house of Arthur Lewis, a London store director and amateur music-lover, at Campden Hill. Deciding to do something similar in English, they hit on the idea of adapting a popular farce of the day, John Maddison Morton's *Box and Cox* (1847), an ideal task for Burnand and an enjoyable outlet for Sullivan. It was given a try-out at Burnand's house in November 1866, followed by its first performance by the 'Moray Minstrels' at Moray Lodge on 27 Apr. 1867, with Harold Power as Cox, George du Maurier as Box, John Forster as Bouncer, and Sullivan at the piano.

The first public performance was at the Adelphi Theatre, 11 May 1867 (along with *Les Deux Aveugles* and other items), with Quintin Twiss as Cox, George du Maurier as Box, Arthur Blunt as Bouncer, and Sullivan conducting the now orchestrated piece. Sullivan added an overture for a repeat benefit performance at the Theatre Royal, Manchester, 29 July 1867 with the same cast. The work then disappeared until after Sullivan had made his second venture into operetta with *The Contrabandista* written for the German *Reed company at St George's Hall at the end of 1867. The German Reeds staged *Cox and Box* at the small Royal Gallery of Illustration (at first without an orchestra) on 29 Mar. 1869, with Arthur Cecil, J. Seymour, and Thomas German Reed in the cast; it caught on with the public and was given 300 performances. It was revived at the *Alhambra Theatre in 1871. It was first seen in New York on 13 Aug. 1875, and revived at the Standard Theatre 14 Apr. 1879. Its amusing libretto and pleasant score gives a modest foretaste of the riches to come when Sullivan really got into his stride with W. S. *Gilbert in *Trial by Jury* in 1875. A film version was made in 1982.

Coyne, Joseph (*b* New York, 27 Mar. 1867; *d* Virginia Water, Surrey, 17 Feb. 1941). American actor, singer, and dancer. A good romantic lead with a sense of comedy and a moderate singing voice put to effective use in a semi-spoken style, he appeared in New York in *The Good Mr Best* (1897); *The Girl in the Barracks* (1899); *Star and Garter* (1900); *The Night of the 4th* (1901); *The Girl From Up There* (1901); *The *Toreador* (1902); *The Rogers Brothers in London* (1903); *In Newport* (1904); *The Rollicking Girl* (1905); *The Social Whirl* (1906); *My Lady's Maid* (1906). His reputation was made as a surprise choice for the role of Prince Danilo, opposite Lily *Elsie, in the London production of *The *Merry Widow*—a tremendous success and trend-setter. He settled in London in 1907 and was seen in *The *Dollar Princess* (1909); *The *Quaker Girl* (1910); *The Dancing Mistress* (1912); *The *Girl From Utah* (1913); **Watch Your Step* (1915); *Follow the Crowd* (1916); *The Bing Girls Are There* (1917); *Arlette* (1917); *Going Up* (1918); *Dé-Dé* (1922); *Katinka* (1923); **No, No, Nanette* (1925); *Queen High* (1926); and *My Sister and I* (1931).

Cradle Will Rock, The. Historic musical drama with music and words by Marc *Blitzstein. It was to be his making and memorial, but it had a precarious beginning. Originally sponsored by the WPA Federal Theatre, with Orson Welles (1915–85) as director, its left-wing views and story dealing with union struggles attracted right-wing political pressures and the production scheduled for the Maxine Elliott Theatre on 16 Jun. 1937 was cancelled at the last minute. But Welles was not to be thwarted and managed to find a venue the same night at the Venice Theatre on 59th Street where the actors, forbidden by their own union to go on stage, performed from seats in the auditorium while Blitzstein played the piano. It was given 19 performances in this manner.

It was then performed on stage, but with no scenery and the composer as accompanist and commentator, at the Windsor Theatre 3 Jan. 1938, with Howard DaSilva as the union man and Will Geer as the capitalist Mr Mister [108p]. Its witty score draws upon all kinds of popular musical idioms in such items as 'Croon-spoon', 'Honolulu', and 'The freedom of the press'; and there have been revivals in 1947, 1964, and 1983.

Craven, Gemma (*b* Dublin, 1 June 1950). Irish actress and singer. A vivacious success in various musical roles, she made her first stage appearance as a maid in *Let's Get a Divorce* at Westcliff-on-Sea, and appeared in provincial theatres before coming to London in a minor part in **Fiddler on the Roof*. She worked with the Bristol Old Vic and appeared in London in *Trelawny* (1972); *Dandy Dick* (1973); *Songbook* (1979); *They're Playing Our Song* (1980); *Song and Dance* (1983); and *Loot* (1984). Confirmed as a talented singer and dancer, she starred in the TV series *Pennies From Heaven* (1978); in the film *Wagner* (1984); and has won many awards. She was in the London revival of **South Pacific* (1987).

Crawford, Jesse (*b* Woodland, Calif., 2 Dec. 1895; *d* Sherman Oaks, Calif., 28 May, 1962). American organist, immensely popular in the 1920s and 1930s, particularly around 1928–31 when he made such hit recordings as 'At dawning' and 'Roses of Picardy' for Victor and was frequently heard on the radio. He began his musical career *c.* 1908 as a dance-band pianist, first playing the organ at the Gem Theatre in Spokane in 1911. He was soloist at the famous Grauman's Theatre in Los Angeles in 1918 and then worked in Chicago. As organist at the Paramount Theatre in New York 1926–33, he often worked with his organist wife Helen. He made a theatre tour of England in the late 1930s, and led a dance orchestra 1937–8 with a duo on two electric organs. He wrote various popular compositions for the organ and was active into the 1950s.

Crawford, Michael (*b* London, 19 Jan. 1942). British actor and singer. He has built a dual reputation, coming to public recognition through his hilarious portrayal of the disaster-prone hero of the TV series *Some Mothers Do 'Ave 'Em*; but simultaneously successful, by virtue of his athleticism, robust voice, and excellent character-playing, in such musical spectacles as **Billy* (1974); **Barnum* (1980); and **Phantom of the Opera* (1986).

Crazy Gang, The. The coincidental appearance of the comedy teams *Flanagan and Allen (Bud Flanagan and Chesney Allen), Nervo and Knox (Jimmy Nervo and Teddy Knox), and Naughton and Gold (Charlie Naughton and Jimmy Gold) in the George Black revue *Crazy Month* at the London Palladium in 1932 led to the formation of the lunatic outfit known as the Crazy Gang. They were to remain together until 1960, appearing in such revues as *Life Begins at Oxford Circus* (1935); *Round About Regent Street* (1935); *All Alight at Oxford Circus* (1936); *Okay for Sound* (1936); *London Rhapsody* (1937); *These Foolish Things* (1938); and *The Little Dog Laughed* (1940). The war years broke up the team, which was re-formed by Jack *Hylton in 1947 to appear in a series of shows at the Victoria Palace—*Together Again* (1947) [1566p]; *Knights of Madness* (1950) [1361p]; *Ring Out the Bells* (1952) [987p]; *Jokers Wild* (1954) [911p]; *These Foolish Kings* (1956) [882p]; *Clown Jewels* (1959) [803p]; and *Young in Heart* (1960).

M. Owen: *The Crazy Gang* (London, 1986).

Cream. Short-lived but reputable British rock blues group formed in 1966 by Eric *Clapton (guitar), Jack Bruce (vocals), and Ginger Baker (drums) which immediately made its mark at the 1966 Windsor Festival. The blues influence was strong in their first album, *Fresh Cream* (1966), and succeeding albums all sold more than a million copies with such songs as 'I feel free' (1966), 'Strange brew' (1967), 'Sunshine of your love' (1968), 'White room' (1968), and 'Badge' (1969) becoming hit singles. Their influential partnership came to an end with a farewell concert at the Albert Hall in 1968.

Creamer, Henry (*b* Richmond, Va., 21 June 1879; *d* New York, 14 Oct. 1930). American lyricist, author, actor, producer, and dancer. One of the original founders of the *Clef Club and an early associate of Gotham-Attucks Music Publishing Company. As a vaudeville entertainer, he toured the USA and Europe in the partnership Creamer and Layton with pianist Turner *Layton, with whom he wrote most of his songs. He wrote books for musical shows including *Three Showers* (1920), *Strut, Miss Lizzie* (1922), and *Keep Shufflin'* (1928); and the lyrics for such classics as 'That's a-plenty' (1909), 'After you've gone' (1918), 'Dear old Southland' (1921), 'Way down yonder in New Orleans' (1922), 'If I could be with you one hour tonight' (1930), and many more.

Creedence Clearwater Revival. American rock group formed in 1967 with John Fogerty (*b* 1945) (vocal and guitar), Tom Fogerty (1941–90) (guitar), Stu Cook (*b* 1945) (bass), and Doug Clifford (*b* 1945) (drums); a high-school group who first played under other names before choosing the above in 1968 and making an album under that title for Fantasy Records. Their first hit single was Dale Hawkins's 'Suzie Q' (1968), followed by many songs that have become rock standards such as 'Proud Mary' (1969), 'Bad moon rising' (1969)—a No. 1 hit in the UK, 'Green River' (1969), 'Up around the bend' (1970), 'Lookin' out my back door' (1970), and 'Sweet hitchhiker' (1971), mainly written or arranged by John Fogerty. They produced a tight, together, rocking sound that now seems essentially a Sixties flavour, long outmoded by electronic pop. The increasing dominance of Fogerty led to the group's breaking-up in 1972 and he went on to pursue a notable career, as did the rest of the team.

J. Hallowell: *Inside Creedence* (New York, 1971).

Creole Music. While there has always been a degree of confusion as to exactly what a Creole is, it is accepted that Creole music is that which developed in New Orleans and the adjacent South, having some affinity with the *Cajun music of French-speaking Louisiana. Creole music descends from French folk, gaining its special flavour from the Creole patois which was a kind of simplified French used to communicate with the blacks; and musically from Spanish and calypso-style rhythms imported via New Orleans from the West Indies. It is thus a gently lilting, syncopated music with a French flavour, and hence a distinctive type of Creole jazz that employed such rhythms and patois lyrics, a typical item being 'Mo pas lemmé cas', the equivalent of the French for 'you don't love me'. The term Creole became loosely used in connection with New Orleans, as in the famous Creole Jazz Band led by King *Oliver which was notably light on both Creole personnel and style.

C. G. Peterson (ed.): *Creole Songs from New Orleans* (New Orleans, 1909). I. T. Whitfield (ed.): *Louisiana French Folk Songs* (Baton Rouge, La., 1939; new edn, New York, 1969). G. W. Cable: *Creoles and Cajuns* (New York, 1959).

Croce, Jim (*b* Philadelphia, 10 Jan. 1943; *d* Natchitoches, La., 20 Sept. 1973). American singer, guitarist, and composer. He played in bands while still attending university and later survived by working in cafés and driving trucks. Eventually he broke through with songs such as 'You don't mess around with Jim' and 'Operator' (1972) which were part of a Cashman and West album produced in 1971. The partnership thrived on Croce's well-written songs with their intelligent lyrics, strong melodies, and interesting harmonies; and 'Bad bad Leroy Brown' and 'Time in a bottle' became No. 1 hits in 1972 and 1973. He was clearly heading for the top of the rock world, but in 1973 he was killed when his light plane crashed.

Crook, John (*b* Manchester, 1852; *d* London, 10 Nov. 1922). British composer and conductor. Early in his career he worked mainly in Manchester as conductor at the Theatre Royal. He was brought to London by H. B. *Farnie to act as musical director for his productions and was then engaged by Augustus Harris at Drury Lane. Later he was musical director at the Adelphi, the Vaudeville, and the Duke of York's theatres. He wrote the scores of *Venus* (1879); *Sage and Onions* (1880); *The King's Dragoons* (1880); *Quits* (1884); *Robinson Crusoe* (1887); *Lancelot the Lovely* (1889); *The Young Recruit* (1892); *The Lady Slavey* (1893); *A Modern Don Quixote* (1893); *Jaunty Jane Shore* (1894); *Claude Du-Val* (1894); *King Kodak* (1894); *The New Barmaid* (1895); *The Transferred Ghost* (1896); and incidental music for J. M. Barrie's *Peter Pan* (1904) and other plays. He wrote many songs including 'The coster's serenade' (1890); 'Yours, etc.' (1893); and 'Jerusalem's dead' (1895) with Albert *Chevalier.

Croon, Crooning. A type of popular singing introduced by such singers as Rudy *Vallee, 'Whispering' Jack *Smith, and Bing *Crosby; a style which deviated from preceding straight singing by a modified jazz intonation and phrasing and the employment of a deep, sensual, ululating tone from deep in the throat; sliding up to notes rather than hitting them instantly. It came in along with the regular use of the microphone which may have had something to do with its evolution. The term was coined in the 1930s when the need to label such jazz-derived forms was keenly felt, and probably comes from a black slang word meaning to sing in a soft and mellow way, as in a lullaby, which would indicate some early awareness of the black influence on popular song. The *Concise Oxford Dictionary* says it derives from the Middle Low German word for groaning or lamenting, *krönen*, which may have been taken to the USA. The last great exponent of old-style crooning was Bing Crosby, since whose demise it has become a lost art.

Crosby, Bing [Harry Lillis] (*b* Spokane, 2 May 1903; *d* Madrid, 14 Oct. 1977). American singer and actor. He read law at Gonzaga University, where he formed a band with fellow-student Al Rinker (*b* 1907). When they decided to give up law in favour of music they were helped by Rinker's sister Mildred *Bailey and joined the Paul *Whiteman band in 1926 as a singing duo. Later, with the addition of Harry *Barris, they became known as the Rhythm Boys, becoming a popular feature of Whiteman's programmes, appearing with him in the film *The King of Jazz* in 1930, and making many recordings with the orchestra. The trio joined Gus *Arnheim in 1930, but Crosby's individual talent soon led him to a solo career and by early 1931 he was a regular broadcaster, already introducing his programmes with his everlasting theme song 'Where the blue of the night'.

He began a prodigious and sustained recording career, firstly with Brunswick, later and thereafter with the American Decca label. Late in 1931 he started making a series of short films for Mack Sennett and others and had a weekly radio series with CBS. He had taken small parts in the films *Check and Double Check* (1930) and *Reaching for the Moon* (1931) and his appearance in *The Big Broadcast of 1932*, coinciding with his new radio popularity, led to a contract with Paramount Pictures for whom he worked without a break for 24 years. His films of the 1930s introduced many songs that were for ever to be associated with his fine performances of them; and in the 1940s the series of 'Road' films with his friendly rival Bob *Hope and Dorothy *Lamour, plus an Academy Award-winning role in *Going My Way* (1944), made him the world's top box-office attraction for a time. In addition his records were invariably top sellers (his first million-seller, out of 22, was 'Sweet Leilani' in 1937) and he was long credited with having sold more records than any other performer in popular music. Eventually he relaxed his activities in both media and formed his own television production company.

It is impossible to overrate Bing Crosby's influence. He took popular song out of the realm of the vaudeville singers and paved the way for the many who copied (but never outshone) his relaxed phrasing, impeccable diction, warmth of approach, and the rich baritone quality that made the most banal song into a work of art. When the thinking singers likes *Sinatra came along, many considered the Crosby art to be outmoded but it never seemed to be in any way diminished by the comparison. His unique and innate sense of rhythm qualified him to be called a jazz singer, as was proved by the records he made with Duke *Ellington, Louis *Armstrong, and other jazz musicians. He never sang authentic jazz material but he brought a jazzman's phrasing and sense of improvisation to everything he did and this has given his work its lasting quality. A relaxed, and therefore excellent, golfer, he died, as he might have wished, of a heart-attack after a pleasant round of golf in Spain.

His best-remembered recordings, many backed from the 1930s by the tasteful work of John Scott Trotter (1908–75), who worked with him for 15 years, include many classics such as the perennial 'White Christmas' (1942) by Irving *Berlin, which was long the world's best-selling single. Other hits included 'San Antonio rose' (1940), 'Silent night' (1942), 'Jingle bells' (1943); 'Pistol packin' mama' (1943), and 'Don't fence me in' (1944), with the *Andrews Sisters; 'Wait till the sun shines, Nellie', with Mary *Martin, and 'The waiter and the porter', with Jack *Teagarden and Mary Martin; 'Now is the hour'; 'Swinging on a star' (1944); 'Dear hearts and gentle people' (1949); 'The Spaniard that blighted my life' (1947), with Al *Jolson; and his humorous duets with Louis Armstrong. The songs that he was the first to introduce included: 'Temptation', 'Love is just around the corner', 'It's easy to remember', 'I'm an old cowhand', 'Pennies from heaven', 'Small fry', 'Moonlight becomes you', 'Swinging on a star', and 'White Christmas'. He had a hand as composer and/or lyricist in such songs as 'From Monday on' (1928); 'At your command' (1931), 'Where the blue of the night' (1931), 'Waltzing in a dream' (1931), and 'A ghost of a chance' (1933).

His films included: *King of Jazz* (1930); *Check and Double Check* (1930); *Reaching for the Moon* (1931); *I Surrender, Dear* (1931); *The Big Broadcast* (1932); *College Humour* (1933); *Going Hollywood* (1933); *We're Not Dressing* (1934); *She Loves Me Not* (1934); *Mississippi* (1935); *The Big Broadcast of 1936* (1936); *Anything Goes* (1936); *Rhythm on the Range* (1936); *Pennies From Heaven* (1936); *Waikiki Wedding* (1937); *Double or Nothing* (1937); *Doctor Rhythm* (1938); *Sing You Sinners* (1938); *Paris Honeymoon* (1939); *Road to Singapore* (1940); *If I Had My Way* (1940); *Rhythm on the River* (1940); *Road to Zanzibar* (1941); *Birth of the Blues* (1941); *Holiday Inn* (1942); *Angels of Mercy* (1942); *Road to Morocco* (1942); *Star-Spangled Rhythm* (1942); *My Favourite Blonde* (1942); *Dixie* (1943); *Going My Way* (1944); *The Princess and the Pirate* (1944); *Here Come the Waves* (1944); *Out of this World* (1945); *Duffy's Tavern* (1945); *The Bells of St Mary's* (1945); *Road to Utopia* (1946); *Road to Hollywood* (1946); *Blue Skies* (1946); *Variety Girl* (1947); *My Favourite Brunette* (1947); *Welcome Stranger* (1947); *Road to Rio* (1947); *The Emperor Waltz* (1948); *A Connecticut Yankee in King Arthur's Court* (1948); *Top o' the Morning* (1949); *The Adventures of Ichabod and Mr Toad* (1949); *Down Memory Lane* (1949); *Ridin' High* (1950); *Mr Music* (1950); *Here Comes the Groom* (1951); *The Greatest Show on Earth* (1952); *Son of Paleface* (1952); *Just For You* (1952); *Road to Bali* (1952); *Little Boy Lost* (1953); *White Christmas* (1954); *The Country Girl* (1954); *Anything Goes* (1956); **High Society* (1956); *Man On Fire* (1957); *Showdown at Ulcer Gulch* (1958); *Say One For Me* (1959); *Alias Jesse James* (1959); *Let's Make Love* (1960); *Pepe* (1960); *High Time* (1960); *Road to Hong Kong* (1962); *The Sound of Laughter* (1963); *Robin and the Seven Hoods* (1964); and *Stagecoach* (1966).

E. J. Crosby: *The Story of Bing Crosby* (Cleveland, 1946). B. Ulanov: *The Incredible Crosby* (New York, 1948). B. Crosby & P. Martin: *Call Me Lucky!* (New York, 1953). C. Thompson: *Bing: the Authorised Biography* (London, 1975; revised as *The Complete Crosby*, 1978). R. Bookbinder: *The Films of Bing Crosby* (Secaucus, NJ, 1977). B. Thomas: *The One and Only Bing* (New York, 1977). L. J. Zwisohn: *Bing Crosby: a Lifetime of Music* (Los Angeles, 1978). K. Barnes: *The Crosby Years* (London, 1979). D. Shepherd & R. F. Slatzer: *Bing Crosby: the Hollow Man* (New York, 1981). K. Crosby: *My Life With Bing* (Wheeling, Ill., 1983). T. A. Morgareth: *Bing Crosby: Discography, Radio Programme List and Filmography* (Jefferson, NC, 1988).

Crosby, Bob [George Robert] (*b* Spokane, 25 Aug. 1913; *d* La Jolla, Calif., 9 Mar. 1993). American bandleader, singer, actor, and composer. Although he never achieved the eminence of his brother Bing, Bob Crosby had a pleasant vocal style and achieved prominence as the front man of one of the best swing bands of the 1930s.

He started out as a vocalist with Anson Weeks's Orchestra; then was invited to front musicians from Ben *Pollack's band who functioned under the management of Gil Rodin (1906–74). Their big-band arrangements of Dixieland music were excellently done and a small group, the Bobcats, drawn from within the band, made good jazz records, with the sterling rhythm section of 'Nappy' Lamare (1907–88) (guitar), Bob Haggart (*b* 1914) (bass), and Ray Bauduc (1906–88) (drums); and featuring such fine players as Yank Lawson (*b* 1911) (trumpet), Irving Fazola (1912–49) (clarinet), Eddie Miller (1911–91) (saxophone), and Bob Zurke (1912–44) (piano).

In the 1940s, before and after the war, the band becamed increasingly commercial and Crosby eventually worked again as a solo singer, as MC on radio and TV, and in clubs. He appeared in films such as *Let's Make Music* (1940); *Rookies on Parade* (1941); *Presenting Lily Mars* (1942); *Thousands Cheer* (1943); *Pardon My Rhythm* (1944); *When You're Smiling* (1950); *Two Tickets to Broadway* (1951); *Road to Bali* (1952); and *The Five Pennies* (1959).

W. F. Van Eyle: *Discography of Bob Crosby* (Zandaam, 1966). J. Chilton: *Stomp Off! Let's Go!—the Story of Bob Crosby's Bobcats and Big Band* (London, 1983).

Crosby, Stills, Nash [and Young]. American vocal and instrumental group formed in 1968 by David Crosby (*b* 1941), ex-*Byrds (guitar and vocal), Stephen Stills (*b* 1945), ex-Buffalo Springfield (guitar, piano, and vocal), and Graham Nash (*b* 1942), ex-*Hollies (vocal). Having all felt limited in their former groups, they gelled together perfectly to produce their first trio album, *Crosby, Stills and Nash* (1969) with their daring harmonies, good tunes, and outspoken ideas revealed on such items as 'Suite: Judy Blue Eyes' and 'Wooden ships'. With Neil Young (*b* 1945) (guitar and piano) added, their second album, *Déjà Vu* (1970), became even more adventurous and interesting, while the high spirits of their stage act came out in *Four Way Street* (1971). They parted to follow solo careers in 1971, Crosby and Nash working together for a while, with a quartet reunion in 1974, and the original trio coming more firmly together in 1977 and working together, on and off, into the 1980s. A varied but often compatible mixture of talents produced some remarkable, yet also commercially viable, work throughout their chaotic career.

D. Zimmer: *Crosby, Stills & Nash: the Authorized Biography* (New York, 1984).

Crouse, Russel (*b* Findlay, Ohio, 20 Feb. 1893; *d* New York, 3 Apr. 1966). American librettist and manager. Early in his career he was a journalist with the *New York Globe*, *New York Evening Mail*, and *New York Evening Post*, writing for the latter a humorous column, 'Left at the Post', from 1924 to 1929. He made his first stage appearance in 1928 and became press representative of the Theatre Guild. He started writing librettos in 1931, mainly working in collaboration with Howard *Lindsay, four of them for shows starring Ethel *Merman. These included: *The Gang's All Here* (1931); *Hold Your Horses* (1933); **Anything Goes* (1934); **Red, Hot and Blue* (1936); *Hooray For What!* (1937); **Call Me Madam* (1950); *Happy Hunting* (1956); *The *Sound of Music* (1959); and *Mr President* (1962).

Crumit, Frank (*b* Jackson, Ohio, 26 Sept. 1889; *d* Longmeadow, Mass., 7 Sept. 1943). American composer, author, actor, and entertainer. He studied at Jackson High School and for three years at the Culver Military Academy in Indiana. He matriculated at the University of Ohio, where he was renowned for his prowess at baseball and football, started an engineering career, but gave it up in 1913 to follow a stage career and to sing *c.* 1920–1 with Paul Biese. He became a successful vaudeville entertainer and was a hit in the 1919 and 1920 **Greenwich Village Follies*. He appeared in various musicals with Julia *Sanderson (whom he married in 1927) including their major success *Tangerine* (1921) for which he wrote several of the songs. He was in *Nifties of 1923*; *Moonlight* (1924); and touring companies of **No, No, Nanette* (1925), *Oh, Kay!* (1927), and *Queen High* (1927). His fame was spread by a prolific recording career from 1919 on; he became especially popular in the 1930s with his lively and humorous renderings of songs, many of his own creation or adapted from folk-songs. Curiously, he seems to be better remembered and held in even greater affection in Britain than in the USA. After quitting the stage, Crumit and his wife became a popular radio team 1929–43, running a pioneering radio quiz called 'Battle of the Sexes' and appearing in numerous programmes. He was President (Shepherd) of the New York theatrical club and charity known as The Lambs from 1935 for four years.

A pleasant, good-humoured nature came through on his recordings where his friendly voice and lively accompaniments to catchy tunes have given a lasting quality to a number of them. His songs included: 'The prune song' (1928); 'The gay caballero' (1929); 'There is no-one with endurance like the man who sells insurance' (1930); 'Donald the Dub' (1930); 'Down by the railroad track' (1930); and he arranged 'Abdul Abulbul Amir' (after Percy *French, 1927); 'Frankie and Johnny' (1927); 'Get away, old man, get away' (1927); 'Little brown jug'. Among his top recording hits were 'The prune song', 'Granny's old armchair', 'The pig got up and slowly walked away' (*m* Frederick V. Bowers, 1874–1961; *w* Benjamin Hapgood Burt); and versions of popular songs ranging from 'Kingdom coming' to 'Mountain greenery' and 'Ukulele lady'.

Csárdásfürstin, Die. Three-act operetta with music by Emmerich *Kálmán and book by Leo Stein and Belá Jenbach, first heard at the Johann Strauss Theater, Vienna, 13 Nov. 1915, with Mitzi *Günther in the star role. It was staged in New York at the Amsterdam Theatre 24 Sept. 1917, as *The Riviera Girl*, with the book adapted by Guy *Bolton and P. G. *Wodehouse, additional music by Jerome

*Kern, and Wilda Bennett in the lead; and in London (Prince of Wales) 20 May 1921, as *The Gypsy Princess* with Sari Petras.

Cugat, Xavier [Cugat de Bru y Deulofeo, Francisco de Asis Javier] (*b* Gerona, nr. Barcelona, 1 Jan. 1900; *d* Barcelona, 27 Oct. 1990). Spanish-American violinist, bandleader, cartoonist, and composer. Brought up in Havana from 1904, he was a child prodigy and became a violinist in the National Theatre Symphony Orchestra of Havana at the age of 12. He was taken to the USA, gave two unsuccessful concerts at the Carnegie Hall, and played at concerts with Caruso. Deciding to try the popular music world, he joined the Vincent *Lopez orchestra. Later he went to Los Angeles and worked as a cartoonist for the *Los Angeles Times*, as film producer, and as sound mixer for Charlie *Chaplin. In 1928 he formed his own orchestra, specializing in Latin American music, which played at the Cocoanut Grove. In 1933 he was engaged as bandleader at the Waldorf-Astoria Hotel in New York; and thereafter had a successfully varied career in hotels and nightclubs and on radio.

His clever arrangements of traditional Latin American material did much to popularize the music in the USA and internationally, his richly melodic and colourfully costumed orchestra featuring in many musical films—notably MGM's wartime escapist movies such as *You Were Never Lovelier* (1942); *Stage Door Canteen* (1943); *Two Girls and a Sailor* (1944); *Weekend at the Waldorf* (1945); *This Time for Keeps* (1946); *On an Island with You* (1947); *Date with Judy* (1948); and *Neptune's Daughter* (1949).

X. Cugat: *The Rumba is My Life* (New York, 1948).

Curzon, Frederic Ernest (*b* London, 1899; *d* Bournemouth, 6 Dec. 1973). British composer, conductor, pianist, and organist. He was musical director in many London theatres 1920–38, then chiefly involved in broadcasting 1938–58. He wrote music for theatre, documentary films, and radio and was editor for Boosey & Hawkes. He was best-known for his many light orchestral compositions such as 'The boulevardier', 'Dance of an ostracized imp', 'Pulchinello' overture, 'Robin Hood' suite, 'Charm of youth' suite, and 'Saltarello' for piano and orchestra.

Cuvillier, Charles (*b* Paris, 24 Apr. 1877; *d* Paris, 14 Feb. 1955). French composer. He studied privately with Fauré and *Messager and with Massenet at the Paris Opéra. His musical interests centred mostly on the theatre. His first operetta *Avant-hier matin* was produced in Paris in 1905. This was followed by *Son p'tit frère* (1907); *Afgar* (1909), which had an international success, especially at the London Pavilion in 1919 with Alice *Delysia and Harry *Welchman [300p]; *La Fausse Ingénue* or *Les Muscadines* (1910); *Sapho* (1912); his greatest French success, *La Reine s'amuse* (1912), later revised as *La Reine joyeuse* (1918), long remembered by its very popular waltz 'O! la troublante volupté de la première étreinte', and produced in London as *The Naughty Princess* (1920); *Rêve de valse* (1915); *Flora Bella* (1916); *Annabella* (1924); *Bob et Moi* (1924); *Nonnette* (1927); *Boufard et ses filles* (1929). For the London and American stage he wrote or adapted (some from German productions) the popular **Lilac Domino* (1914); *Florabella* (NY, 1916); a revue, *Johnny Jones* (1920); *Wild Geese* (1920); and *Sunshine of the World* (1920). For many years he was music director at the Odéon in Paris.

Czibulka, Alphons (*b* Szepes-Várallya, 14 May 1842; *d* Vienna, 27 Oct. 1894). Hungarian bandmaster and composer. He started his musical career as a pianist, then became Kapellmeister at the Karl Theater, Vienna, in 1865. He was Bandmaster of the 17th Regiment in Vienna and later of the 25th Regiment in Prague. He settled in Vienna and wrote the operettas *Pfingsten in Florenz* (1884); *Der Jagdjunker der Kaiserin* (1886); *Der Glücksritter* (1887); *Gil Blas* (1889); *Der Bajazzo* (1892); *Signor Annibale* (1893). He wrote a large quantity of dance music, light orchestral pieces, piano compositions, and works for military band; but is now mainly remembered for the Victorian drawing-room favourite 'Stephanie-gavotte' (1880) and a waltz 'Love's dream after the ball' (1885).

D

Dabney, Ford T. (*b* Washington DC, 15 Mar. 1883; *d* New York, 21 June 1958). American composer, pianist, and conductor. He became a professional pianist in 1904, and in 1913 he organized the Tempo Club in New York, an agency for black entertainers. He was long associated with Irene and Vernon *Castle and created many dance numbers for them. He was director of the Ziegfeld Midnight Frolics orchestra for eight years; and wrote the song 'That's why they call me Shine' in 1910, (*w* Cecil Mack, 1883–1944)—republished in 1924 as 'S-H-I-N-E' (with Lew *Brown).

Dacre, Harry [Decker, Henry] (*b* London, 1860; *d* London, 1922). British composer who emigrated to America and had considerable success there with his vaudeville songs, many of which filtered back to England and became hits of the music-hall era. The best-known of them all, and perhaps one of the best-known of all music-hall songs, was 'Daisy Bell' or 'A bicycle built for two' (1892), which was heard in America by the singer Katie Lawrence, who brought it back to England and helped it to world-wide renown. Dacre returned to England to found the Frank Dean publishing company and wrote and published a vast number of songs including: 'Playmates' (1889); 'Katie O'Connor' (1891, *w* Pat Rafferty); 'Elsie from Chelsea' (1896); 'I can't think of nuthin' else but you, Lulu' (1896); 'I'll be your sweetheart' (1899); 'Oh! Flo! (The great motor-car song)' (1901); 'Mary from Maryland' (1903); and 'Jolly little Polly on her gee-gee-gee' (1905).

D'Albert, Charles Louis Napoléon (*b* Nienstetten, Hamburg, 25 Feb. 1809; *d* London, 26 May 1886). German composer and dancing master. He was the son of a cavalry captain in the French Army who died in 1816. He studied piano and composition at the Paris Conservatoire and came to England to learn dancing at the King's Theatre, where he became ballet master; later he was also at Covent Garden. He eventually gave up these posts to run his own dancing school and compose. He was a prolific writer of dance music which had wide sales in the 1850s and 1860s, for several years issuing lavishly produced annual albums of his pieces that adorned many Victorian parlours, published by Chappell of New Bond Street, London. He settled for a while in Newcastle upon Tyne and was living in Glasgow when his even more famous son Eugène (the composer of the opera *Tiefland* and a celebrated pianist) was born. He was the author of *Ballroom Etiquette* (1835), and spent his later years in London where he continued with a substantial output of polkas, waltzes, and quadrilles; one of his most popular pieces being 'The bridal polka' (1845).

Daltrey, Roger (*b* London, 1 Mar. 1944). British singer and actor. At 15 he formed his own band, the Detours, in which he played the guitar for two years before becoming lead singer with the group which was now renamed the *Who. His first important solo album, *Daltrey*, was issued in 1973, featuring songs by Leo *Sayer and Dave Courtney and including the hit song 'Giving it all away'. He was the soloist in many Peter Townshend songs written for the Who; and in 1975 he appeared in the title role of the film *Tommy* featuring the group and directed by Ken Russell, from which the song 'I'm free' became widely popular. He worked again with Russell, portraying Liszt as a 19th-century pop star in the film *Lisztomania*. Further film appearances have included *The Legacy* (1978) and *McVicar* (1980) and he was in Jonathan Miller's TV version of **The Beggar's Opera*. Besides his work with the Who he has made a number of interesting solo LP albums.

Daly's Theatre, London. Famous theatre, situated in Leicester Square, the venue for many long-running musical comedies of the early 1900s, built by George *Edwardes who also built the *Empire and *Gaiety theatres. The original purpose was to provide an outlet for the Augustin Daly company (hence the name) and its star Agnes Huntingdon, but the arrangement fell through before the theatre was completed and Edwardes decided to run one of his own companies there.

The productions at Daly's tended to be a notch higher in taste than those concurrently staged at the Gaiety: *The *Merry Widow* was one of those considered more suited to its ambience. The theatre opened in 1893 with a performance of *The Taming of the Shrew*, but after that its productions were predominantly musical and included *An *Artist's Model* (1894); *The *Geisha* (1896); *A Greek Slave* (1898); *A *Gaiety Girl* (1899); **San Toy* (1899); *A *Country Girl* (1902); *The *Cingalee* (1904); *The Little Michus* (1905); *The Merry Widow* (1907); *The Dollar Princess* (1909); *A *Waltz Dream* (1911); *The *Count of Luxembourg* (1911); **Gypsy Love* (1912); *A Country Girl* (1914); *The *Maid of the Mountains* (1917); *A Southern Maid* (1920); **Sybil* (1921); **Madame Pompadour* (1923); *Katja the Dancer* (1925); **Lilac Time* (1927); and many revivals of these and other musical shows. Daly's closed on 25 Sept. 1937 and was transformed into a cinema.

D. Forbes-Winslow: *Daly's: the Biography of a Theatre* (London, 1944).

Daly's Theatre, New York. Theatre founded by the renowned producer, director, and playwright Augustin Daly (1838–99) in 1879. In 1869 he had leased the Fifth Avenue Theatre to create there what he hoped would be the finest drama company in the USA. It was burned down in 1873, so, after a temporary retirement, he restored an old theatre and called it Daly's. Here he moulded a fine new company with Ada Rehan as its star. It was originally intended that new American operettas and musical comedies would be the main feature there, but this plan was abandoned in favour of importing ready-made London shows.

F. J. Daly: *The Life of Augustin Daly* (New York, 1917).

Dameron, Tadd [Tadley Ewing Peake] (*b* Cleveland, 21 Feb. 1917; *d* New York, 8 Mar. 1965). American jazz pianist and arranger. He worked as pianist with various bands from the mid-1930s to the early 1940s and then began contributing arrangements for Jimmie *Lunceford, Georgie Auld, Billy *Eckstine, Count *Basie ('Good Bait', etc.), and, while working with Dizzy *Gillespie, and Charlie *Parker, recorded 'Hot house' in 1945. He played and recorded with his own groups as well as with Babs Gonzales, Fats *Navarro, and Miles *Davis. Some of his arrangements were written for the British band of Ted *Heath; and for Artie *Shaw, Max *Roach–Clifford Brown, and Carmen *McRae. Dameron was always admired by fellow musicians, his work being a link between the *swing band era and the *bebop of the 1940s onward, with many of his arrangements and compositions becoming modern standards and a source of inspiration to many who followed. His career was bedevilled by an addiction to drugs which led to three years' imprisonment in the late 1950s. He was inactive in his final years owing to cancer.

Dames at Sea. American musical with score by Jim Wise and book by George Haimsohn and Robin Miller which owed its successful 575 performances to its joyful take-off of Hollywood musicals of the 1930s. It was produced at the Bouwerie Lane Theatre, New York, 20 Dec. 1968 with Bernadette Peters, David Christmas, Steve Elmore, and Tamara Long and was revived in 1985.

Damn Yankees. American musical with score and lyrics by Richard *Adler and Jerry *Ross, book by George *Abbott, Douglas Wallop, and Richard Bissell, which followed on the success of *The *Pajama Game* (1954) by the same team. It was produced at the 46th Street Theatre, New York, on 5 May 1955, directed by George Abbott, and was to achieve the satisfactory run of 1019 performances.

Based on Wallop's novel *The Year the Yankees Lost the Pennant*, it was the first musical to tackle convincingly the popular American subject of baseball, adding to this sporting background the old Faustian plot of the man who sells his soul to the Devil to buy success, in this case a devoted fan of the team. Transformed into a young man who becomes its star player, he is seduced by a lady called Lola (a role which made Gwen *Verdon into a known name). Stephen Douglass was the baseball hero and Ray Walston an excellently smooth Devil.

It was produced at the London Coliseum with less success in 1957, so that when the 1958 film, with Gwen Verdon, Ray Walston (*b* 1917), and Tab Hunter (*b* 1931) was seen in England it was retitled *What Lola Wants* to circumvent the English lack of enthusiasm for baseball.

Damned The. British *punk rock group formed in 1976 with Rat Scabies (drums), Captain Sensible (bass), Dave Vanian (vocal), and Brian James (guitar). Following the *Sex Pistols' assault on the established canons of rock, the group caught the juvenile imagination with an album called *Damned, Damned, Damned* in 1977; their biggest single hit was with 'Eloise' in 1986. The handsome Captain Sensible also branched out as a solo artist and achieved a No. 1 hit with 'Happy talk' in 1982.

Damone, Vic [Farinola, Vito Rocco] (*b* Brooklyn, NY, 12 June. 1928). American singer in the *Sinatra mould. He became known in clubs, theatres, and on radio in the 1940s with his own radio show for CBS 1947–8. He appeared in a number of films in the 1950s and 1960s, notably *An Affair to Remember* (1957) in which he sang the title song, and continued as a popular recording star.

Damsel in Distress, A. Musical film produced by RKO in 1937 which was notable for a number of memorable songs by George *Gershwin, including 'A foggy day', 'I can't be bothered now', 'Nice work if you can get it', 'The jolly tar and the milkmaid', and 'Things are looking up'; with a worthy cast of Fred *Astaire, Joan Fontaine (*b* 1917), George Burns (*b* 1896) and Gracie Allen (1902–64), Reginald Gardiner (1903–80), and Ray *Noble and his orchestra.

Dance. The greater part of popular musical history is concerned with song, the emphasis on vocal music brought about by an obsessive interest in the performers, particularly since the cult of singers that began in the mid-1800s. Nevertheless, many advances in popular music have been brought about through the demands of social dancing and its regular changes of fashion. One of the most influential early publications was John *Playford's *The *Dancing Master* (1651) brought out in response to a demand for instruction in the collective art of dancing. This helped to draw attention to the wealth of folk-dance music and to the gradual collection and collation of this material in published form.

The cult of social dancing began at private balls held by the rich and noble in the 16th century, each new dance fashion such as the pavane and galliard, succeeded by the gavotte, minuet, courante, cotillion, and allemande, spawning music to fit its requirements and generally supplied by the eminent academic composers of the day in their more commercial moments. *Ballroom dancing did not go public until the early 19th century, when ballrooms opened in many European cities, and the popularization of the *waltz and the *polka opened the way for the professional popular composers of such material, such as Josef *Lanner and the *Strauss family in Vienna. The early formation dances like the *lancers and *quadrilles made their appearance at this time and helped to create a prolific performing and publishing industry. Into the 20th century and the new jazz age, the demands of the dancer tended to shape the course of ragtime and jazz rather than the obverse being the order of the day, and this status has continued into the rock age.

An important aspect of 20th-century dance has been the increasingly sensitive and imaginative use of it in films (with *Astaire and *Kelly most notable); and the introduction of ballet to the Broadway stage by such dance directors as George Balanchine (1903–83), Agnes De Mille (*b* 1905), Jerome *Robbins, and others who followed.

T. & M. W. Kinney: *The Dance: its Place in Art and Life* (New York, 1935). P. D. Magriel: *A Bibliography of Dancing* (New York, 1936, 1966). E. Porter: *Music through the Dance* (London, 1937). K. Sachs: *World History of the Dance* (New York, 1937; London, 1938). L. Kirstein: *The Book of the Dance* (New York, 1942). P. J. S. Richardson: *The Social Dances of the 19th Century* (London, 1960). A. De Mille: *The Book of the Dance* (London–New York, 1963). A. H. Franks: *Social Dance: a Short History* (London, 1963). J. Martin: *The Dance* (New York, 1963). F. Rust: *Dance in Society* (London, 1969). B. Quirey, S. Bradshaw & R. Smedley: *May I have the Pleasure: the Story of Popular Dancing* (London, 1976). P. Buckman: *Let's Dance: Social, Ballroom & Folk Dancing* (London, 1978).

Dance bands, dance music. Although the dance developments outlined above and elsewhere would have required dance orchestras long before the advent of the jazz age, it is the period from *c.*1910 onwards that is most likely to be under discussion when the phrases 'dance band' and 'dance music' are used. The term 'dance band' is often used of many bands and orchestras of the swing era that come under the *big band label; and rather than try to organize several overlapping and confusing categories it is best to think of them all as part of the activity of producing music for dancing in whatever vein is demanded.

Among the earliest dance bands, in the modern sense of the word, were those of Wilbur C. *Sweatman, Erskine Tate, and Art Hickman, all of which were flourishing around Chicago 1911–12. British dance history tends to follow on in imitation of the American equivalent with a time-lapse of a year or so. American visitors to Britain around the First World War period included Murray Pilcer with his Sherbo Sextette, who settled into the Lyons Corner House in Oxford Street; the *Original Dixieland Jazz Band, who eventually found a home at the Hammersmith Palais; Will Marion *Cook's Southern Syncopated Orchestra at the Philharmonic Hall; and Joe Wilbur's Savoy Quartet at the Savoy Hotel.

During the period 1920–1, pianist Jack *Hylton left the Queen's Hall Dance Orchestra to form his own band and Bert Ralton (1900–27) formed the first of many resident orchestras in the *Savoy—a name always associated with the history of modern British dance music. The Savoy Havana Band was led by Ralton, then by Reg Batten and Cyril Newton; while 1923 saw the first formation of the *Savoy Orpheans, started by Debroy Somers (1890–1952), continued by Ramon Newton, and finally led, until his death in 1954, by the American Carroll *Gibbons.

Some of the most famous American dance bands came into being immediately after the war: Paul Specht (1895–1954), the first dance band to broadcast, in 1920; Paul *Whiteman; Vincent *Lopez; Ted *Lewis; Jan Garber (1897–1977); George *Olsen; the Benson Orchestra of Chicago; and the *Coon–Sanders Nighthawks were some of those who commenced activities 1919–20. Dance music had not yet reached any degree of sophistication, as is borne out by recordings of the time, but it was an interesting period of development with the full effect of jazz yet to come. The introduction of the professional arranger was to bring a musical maturity to dance-band music. Some of the earliest to use full-scale arrangements were Paul Whiteman, Fletcher *Henderson, Duke *Ellington, Isham *Jones, and the *Casa Loma Orchestra. Their recordings influenced their counterparts in Britain and Europe. Thus Jack Hylton followed the Whiteman ideal by building a show band whose reputation as a stage attraction was second to none in Britain. The slick arrangements of the Casa Loma Orchestra formed a basis for Lew *Stone's style, one of the finest sounds in Britain in the early 1930s. Guy *Lombardo's saxophone style was echoed by Maurice *Winnick, while Harry *Roy's antics were based on the Cab *Calloway showmanship.

Much of the popularity of dance music was due to the various flourishing radio stations in America and the BBC in England. The first British broadcast of dance music (by an uncredited group) was on 23 Dec. 1922, the first name band being heard two months later when Marius B. Winter broadcast from Marconi House. The BBC's dance-band programmes at regular peak times established unbreakable listening habits that boosted an interest in the music, and the corporation had its own BBC Dance Orchestra, led by Jack *Payne 1928–32, by Henry *Hall until 1937, then by Billy *Ternent until the outbreak of war, later by Stanley *Black. In the 1950s a part of the Northern Variety Orchestra operated as a dance unit under Alyn Ainsworth, later becoming the BBC Northern Dance Orchestra directed by Bernard *Herrmann. In the late 1920s–1930s there were regular tea-time broadcasts by resident bands at London hotels and restaurants and also late-night sessions—Roy *Fox at the Kit Kat Club, Lew Stone at the Monseigneur Restaurant, *Ambrose at the Mayfair, Jack *Jackson at the

Dorchester, Sidney *Lipton at Grosvenor House, and Harry Roy at the Café Anglais, all of them popular broadcasters. Some played programmes of straightforward dance music, but some presented their orchestras as self-contained entertainment units—Jack Hylton and Jack Payne particularly—while Harry Roy and Billy *Cotton also became variety-hall favourites with their polished comedy routines. There were also the primarily comic outfits like Syd Seymour and his Mad Hatters, Sid Millward and the Nitwits, and Dr Crock and his Crackpots.

Until the beginning of the *swing era American bands also worked mostly in hotels and on radio providing commercially pleasant rather than imaginative music. Their popularity mainly grew as the result of what the Americans termed 'remotes'—late-night broadcasts made on location.

Guy Lombardo led the field among hotel bands and the so-called 'society' orchestras included those led by Freddy *Martin, Ted *Fiorito, Russ *Morgan, Ted *Weems, Carmen *Cavallaro, Eddie *Duchin, Ozzie Nelson (1906–75), Jan Garber (1897–1977), Roger Wolfe Kahn (1907–62) and Hal Kemp (1905–40). A number of 'Mickey Mouse' bands traded on some corny musical gimmick suggested by their names—Shep Fields and his Rippling Rhythm, Gray Gordon's Tic-Toc Rhythm, Art Kassel and his Kassels in the Air, Horace Heidt and his Musical Knights, Lawrence *Welk's Champagne Music, Kay *Kyser and his Kollege of Musical Knowledge, Swing and Sway with Sammy Kaye (1910–87), and Enoch Light (1907–78) and the Light Brigade.

Many of these bands retained their own public during the swing era but from 1935 the big bands took over and dance music increasingly showed its jazz influence as sidemen from bands like Ben *Pollack's and Red *Nichols's went out on their own as bandleaders creating famous bands such as those led by Jimmy and Tommy *Dorsey, Harry *James, Benny *Goodman, Count *Basie, Charlie *Barnet, Jimmie *Lunceford, Bob *Crosby, Chick *Webb, Gene *Krupa, Stan *Kenton, and Woody *Herman (see SWING). The greatest attraction of all, in person and on records, was Glenn *Miller who, more than any other bandleader, epitomized modern dance music of his period. He led a band for only four years but after his death in 1944 his style was kept alive by other leaders from the ranks of the band.

The recording ban of 1943 signalled the end of the great dance-band era, their popularity then usurped by singers who were allowed to go on recording. Another cause was to be found in the increasing complexity of band arrangements and the jazz flavouring which made them less suitable for dancing.

British dance music of the 1930s remained in the hands of the top radio bandleaders mentioned above, with the notable addition of Ray *Noble who, as musical director for HMV records, made some of the finest dance music recordings of all time featuring his own advanced scores and the singing of Al *Bowlly. Noble went to America and British dancing continued along conventional lines until the Second World War, when the influence of the big band boom in the USA began to be felt and the new jive dances came into vogue. Big, swinging bands became the norm. Former Gaucho Tango Orchestra leader *Geraldo was engaged by the BBC to front a big band heard on the air virtually every day of the war; while Billy *Ternent and the BBC Dance Orchestra were a utility band providing music for variety shows as well as dancing in a nostalgic 'sweet rhythm' style. Eric *Winstone, Oscar Rabin (1899–1958), Frank Weir (1911–81), Joe *Loss, Ivy Benson (1914–93; ladies' band), Lou Preager, *Mantovani, Harry Bidgood (better known as Primo Scala, 1898–1955), Sydney Kyte (1896–1981), Maurice Winnick, and others became household names, somehow overcoming the shortage of musicians caused by the war.

On both sides of the Atlantic the conscription of musicians into the armed forces fortuitously gave rise to some particularly fine orchestras which were not constricted by commercial considerations. There were the three AEF Orchestras, the American led by Major Glenn Miller, the Canadian led by Captain Robert *Farnon, and the British led by RSM George *Melachrino, all achieving fine standards of performance, as did the RAF *Squadronaires and Skyrockets, led by Jimmy Miller and Paul Fenhoulet respectively, and the RAOC Blue Rockets led by Eric Robinson. America also specialized in fine navy bands led by Artie *Shaw, Sam *Donahue, and Claude *Thornhill. With the end of the war, dance music seemed to pass its peak in America but Britain's best period was still to come with trombonist Ted *Heath starting his own modern swing band in 1944, followed by Vic *Lewis, Tommy Sampson, George Evans, Jack Parnell, Johnny *Dankworth, Teddy Foster, Ken Mackintosh, Eric Delaney, and others who kept the ballrooms and palais de danse venues open until the coming of rock and roll in the mid-1950 when the pop groups and discotheques began their takeover.

Ballroom dancing has become a more specialized activity, with its basis the professional and amateur competitive world. Victor *Silvester's Ballroom Orchestra, created in the 1930s, continued to make strict tempo records until the leader's death; while bands led by Syd *Lawrence, Tony Evans, Ray McVay, Bob Miller, Ken Mackintosh, and Joe Loss remained in great demand. Old-time dancing was supported by Sydney Thompson, Sidney Bowman, and Harry Davidson who had started the revival craze for it in the 1940s. Then there was the special field of Latin American dance music and dancing catered for by Edmundo *Ros in Britain, following in the steps of Xavier *Cugat and his Waldorf-Astoria orchestra, the *Lecuona Cuban Rhythm Boys, Noro *Morales, Perez *Prado, who sparked off a transient mambo craze in the 1950s, and Machito.

There is an enormous nostalgic interest in the

dance music of the pre-war era and there has been a steady re-issue of dance band recordings.

A. P. Graham: *Strike Up the Band: Bandleaders of Today* (New York, 1949, rev. 1964). J. Vedey: *Band Leaders* (London, 1950). L. Walker: *The Wonderful Era of the Great Dance Bands* (Berkeley, Calif., 1964). G. Fernett: *A Thousand Golden Horns: the Exciting Age of America's Greatest Dance Bands* (Midland, Mich., 1966). G. T. Simon: *The Big Bands* (New York–London, 1967). G. Fernett: *Swing Out; Great Negro Dance Bands* (Midland, Mich., 1970). A. McCarthy: *The Dance Band Era* (London, 1971; New York, 1972). B. Rust: *The Dance Bands* (Shepperton, Middx., 1972). B. Rust: *American Dance Band Discography 1917–1942* (New Rochelle, 1973). S. Colin: *And the Bands Played On: an Informal History of British Dance Bands* (London, 1977). E. Towler: *British Dance Bands (1920–1949) on 12-inch Long Playing Records* (London, 1985; supplement, 1987). B. Rust & S. Forbes: *British Dance Bands on Record 1911–1945* (London, 1987).

Dance organs. The larger kind of mechanical organ, similar to the *street organ, installed in continental dance-halls from the end of the 19th century up to the Second World War era. The firm of Ateliers Theöfil Mortier was one of the last of the well-known makers. One of their typical instruments, made in Antwerp in 1938, had 112 keys operating 561 pipes and a piano-accordion, and multiple effects to produce the sounds of a dance orchestra of the time. Various instruments have been recorded on British and Dutch labels.

Dancing Master, The. A volume of community country dances as danced in the mid-17th century first edited and published by John *Playford from his shop in the Inner Temple, London, in 1650 (originally printed as 1651 but available earlier, the year then beginning on 25 March). Playford collected the dances with the help of several friends, and details of the dance steps were given thus offering a valuable indication of the fashions in dancing at the time. A suggestion that such dancing, for long an outdoor fair-weather activity, was becoming an indoor winter pursuit comes from most of them being done 'longways' i.e. with the couples facing each other in a long line as would be best suited to the average hall. The work soon became a best-seller and went into several editions in spite of appearing in the middle of the Protectorate period with its puritanical outlook on such frivolities. The notation changed over the years, much of it being written originally in the French violin clef, later adapted to the treble clef with various melodic changes as fashion dictated a move from the modal to the newer diatonic forms. The book preserved much material that might otherwise have vanished and was a rich source for writers of *ballad operas such as John *Gay who drew on it for *The *Beggar's Opera*. The first modern reprint appeared in 1933 under the editorship of Hugh Mellor and Leslie *Bridgewater.

Dancing Years, The. British musical play with words and music by Ivor *Novello and lyrics by Christopher Hassall (1912–63), first performed at the Drury Lane Theatre on 23 Mar. 1939. The cast included Mary *Ellis, Ivor Novello, Roma Beaumont (*b* 1914), Peter Graves *b* 1911), and Olive Gilbert (*d* 1981). It was one of the last of the great British shows to dominate the large stage of Drury Lane, many of them by Novello, and became one of his most popular works. Audiences gradually became thinner as the outbreak of war loomed and it had to close on 1 Sept. after 187 performances, thus ending Novello's reign at the great theatre. It was to open again at the Palace Theatre, Manchester, in 1942 after a triumphal tour and was back in London 14 Mar. 1942 at the Adelphi Theatre, this time going on to 969 performances. There was a film version in 1947 with Dennis Price (1915–73) and Patricia Dainton (*b* 1930); and a notable stage revival at the Saville Theatre in 1968.

The play was an affectionate tribute to the great days of musical comedy at Daly's and the Gaiety where Novello himself had contributed to *Theodore and Co.* in 1916. The composer played the part of Rudi Kleber, a struggling musician and composer, portraying him from the days of youth when, in a play within a play, he took over from the MD and conducted his own opera, to weary old age when he was a political prisoner. Its songs included 'I can give you the starlight', 'The leap year waltz', 'Lorelei', 'My dearest dear', and 'Waltz of my heart'.

Dandridge, Dorothy (*b* Cleveland, 9 Nov. 1920; *d* Hollywood, 8 Sept. 1965). American actress and singer. She first appeared in films as a child, and later notable movies included *A Day at the Races* (1937); *Sun Valley Serenade* (1941); *Hit Parade of 1943* (1943); *Atlantic City* (1944); **Carmen Jones* (1954); and **Porgy and Bess* (1959); these last two being her greatest successes, though with the singing voice dubbed in by others. She appeared in cabaret in her latter years.

D. Dandridge & X. Carol: *Everything and Nothing: the Dorothy Dandridge Tragedy* (New York, 1970).

Daniels, Bebe [Virginia] (*b* Dallas, 14 Jan. 1901; *d* London, 16 Mar. 1971). American actress and singer. She started a career in films at the age of 5, starring in Harold Lloyd comedies from the age of 13, notably in *Just Nuts* in 1917. She became a Mack Sennett bathing beauty and a glamorous star of silent days and early musicals, singing in **Rio Rita* (1929); *Dixiana* (1930); *Reaching for the Moon* (1931); **42nd Street* (1933); and *The Song You Gave Me* (1933). She married Ben Lyon and they worked as a team, becoming very popular in England, and settling there in the mid-1930s to become national favourites on radio during the war years, notably in the *Hi Gang!* series with Vic Oliver (1898–1964) from 1939. She starred in *Gangway* at the London Palladium (1942) and in **Panama Hattie* (1944), followed by the radio series *Life With the Lyons*. She retired in 1963 after a stroke and concentrated on writing.

J. Allgood: *Bebe & Ben* (London, 1975).

Daniels, Billy (*b* Jacksonville, Fla., 12 Sept. 1915; *d* Los Angeles, 7 Oct. 1988). American singer noted for his energetic style and reputation founded on a robust rendering of 'That old black magic', which became his theme song. He appeared in clubs and on radio, becoming well-known by the 1940s. He was in a number of films in both singing and non-singing roles and continued into the 1950s with Benny Payne as his regular accompanist and partner. In 1964 he was in the musical **Golden Boy* with Sammy *Davis Jr.

Daniels, Charles Neil (*b* Leavenworth, Kansas, 12 Apr. 1878; *d* Los Angeles, 23 Jan. 1943). American composer. He began to write songs around the age of 17 and at 18 wrote the prize-winning 'Margery' which was featured by the *Sousa band. He had a tremendous hit with 'Hiawatha' which appeared as a piano piece in 1901 and a song in 1903, and which he sold for $10,000. He went into song-publishing in 1904, becoming an executive of Remicks before forming his own company in 1915. He generally wrote under the pseudonym of Neil Moret.

Hist best-known works included: 'The poster girl' (1899); 'Moonlight' (1905); 'Silver heels' (1905); 'I had a dream, dear' (1908, *w* Seymour A. Rice and Al H. Brown); 'On Mobile Bay' (1910, *w* Earle C. Jones); 'That banjo rag' (1912); 'Moonlight and roses' (with Ben Black, 1925)—based on Edwin H. Lemare's 'Andantino'; 'Chloe' (1927, *w* Gus *Kahn); 'She's funny that way' (1928 *w* Richard A. *Whiting); 'You tell me your dreams, I'll tell you mine' (1928, *w* Kahn); 'Put your little arms around me' (with Gus *Arnheim and Harry Tobias, 1931).

Daniels, Charlie (*b* Wilmington, NC, 28 Oct. 1937). American country music violinist. He played in the Jaguar Band before making his reputation with units led by Earl *Scruggs and Marty *Robbins. He formed his own band in 1971 which became one of America's most popular Country and Western groups and won a Grammy Award in 1980.

Dankworth, John Philip William (*b* Walthamstow, London, 20 Sept. 1927). British saxophonist, bandleader, composer, and arranger. He started his jazz career playing in ships' bands on the Atlantic run and was greatly influenced by Charlie *Parker and other American jazz musicians whom he heard in New York. He worked with Tito Burns, then formed his own septet in 1950. He started a big band in 1953 and has remained one of the few British bandleaders to maintain a large group since then, winning many awards in the 1950s as musician, composer, and arranger, and regularly heading the popularity polls. In 1958 he married the singer Cleo *Laine and they have since continued a fruitful show-business partnership, and run a music workshop at their home.

A consistently fine soloist with Carter/Parker influences, he has become increasingly well-known as an ambitious jazz composer, with such works as 'Improvisations' (1959); 'Escapade' (1967); 'Tom Sawyer's Saturday' (1967); 'String Quintet' (1971); 'Piano concerto' (1972); and he has written the scores of many films, including: *Saturday Night and Sunday Morning* (1960); *The Servant* (1964); *Accident* (1967); and *Ten Rillington Place* (1970).

Dare, Phyllis [Dones, Phyllis] (*b* London 15 Aug. 1890; *d* Brighton, 27 Apr. 1975). English actress and singer, younger sister of Zena *Dare, a popular postcard favourite of the early 1900s and still popular in the 1940s. She appeared in **Bluebell in Fairyland* (1901, as a child actress); *The *Catch of the Season* (1904); *The *Belle of Mayfair* (1906); *The *Arcadians* (1909); *The Girl in the Train* (1910); *Peggy* (1911); *The Sunshine Girl* (1912); *The Dancing Mistress* (1913); *The *Girl from Utah* (1913); **Miss Hook of Holland* (1914); *Tina* (1915); *Hanky-Panky* (1917); *Kissing Time* (1919); *The Lady of the Rose* (1922); *The Street Singer* (1924); **Lido Lady* (1926); *The Yellow Mask* (1928); *Words and Music* (1932); **Music in the Air* (1934); **King's Rhapsody* (1949).

P. Dare: *From School to Stage* (London, 1907). P. Dare: *Phyllis Dare: by Herself* (London, 1921).

Dare, Zena [Dones, Zena] (*b* London, 4 Feb. 1887; *d* London, Mar. 1975). English actress, elder sister of Phyllis *Dare, more involved than her sister as a straight actress, but also making many notable appearances in musicals, including: *An English Daisy* (1902); *Sergeant Brue* (1904); *The *Catch of the Season* (1904); *Lady Madcap* (1905); *The Little Cherub* (1906); *The Beauty of Bath* (1906); *The Gay Gordons* (1907). Married in 1910, she retired from the stage to make a return in many straight plays, but returned to the musical in **Careless Rapture* (1936); **Perchance to Dream* (1945); **King's Rhapsody* (1949); and **My Fair Lady* (1958).

Darewski, Herman (*b* Minsk, 17 Apr. 1883; *d* London, 21 June 1947). British composer, conductor, and publisher. Born in Russia, he was educated in London, and studied in Vienna. Returning to England, he became a prolific composer of marches and songs, having his first success with 'Au revoir, little hyacinth' which he contributed to *The Beauty of Bath* in 1906. He joined the publishers *Francis, Day & Hunter in 1904 but left to form his own publishing business in 1916, which prospered, especially when it acquired the extensive catalogue of Charles Sheard & Co. in 1918. The aftermath of war brought difficulties and the firm was acquired by Bert *Feldman, thence eventually coming to the F D & H fold. Darewski was musical director at the Spa Royal Hall, Bridlington, 1923–6; and the Winter Gardens, Blackpool, 1927–30 and 1933–9. He led his own orchestra in 1927 which played in variety theatres and was a pioneer in making recordings of show music.

He wrote numerous scores (mainly revues) for the London theatre, including: *Happy Days* (1914);

On Duty (1914); *Business as Usual* (1914); *Rosy Rapture* (1915); *Push and Go* (1915); *Shell Out* (1915); *Keep to the Right* (1915); *Fads and Fancies* (1915); *All Scotch* (1915); *Joyland* (1915); *Razzle-Dazzle* (1916); *Three Cheers* (1916); *Topsy Turvy* (1917); *The *Better 'Ole* (1917); *Any Old Thing* (1917); *Jolly Jack Tar* (1918); *Buzz-Buzz* (1918); **As You Were* (1918); *Laughing Eyes* (1919); *The Eclipse* (1919); *Just Fancy* (1920); *Oh, Julie* (1920); *Dover Street to Dixie* (1923); also contributing to *The Gay Gordons* (1907); *The *Shop Girl* (1920 revival); *Saucy Sue* (1925). His songs included 'In the twi-twi-twilight' (1908, *w* Charles Wilmot); 'Sue, Sue, Sue' (1908, *w* Lester Barrett); 'I used to sigh for the silvery moon' (1909, *w* Barrett); 'Hello! Susie Green (1911, *w* Barrett); 'Sister Susie's sewing shirts for soldiers' (1914, *w* R. P. *Weston); 'Plum and apple' (with Arthur Eliot and J. P. Harrington, 1917); 'If you could only care' (1918, *w* Arthur *Wimperis); 'The Army, the Navy and the Air Force' (1938, *w* Edward Lockton).

H. Darewski: *Musical Memories* (London, 1937).

Darewski, Max (*b* Manchester, 3 Nov. 1894; *d* London, 26 Sept. 1929). British composer and conductor, brother of Herman *Darewski. Mainly known during his brief life as a *brass band conductor, he also wrote scores for *Now's the Time* (1915); *Hanky Panky* (1917); *Suzette* (1917); *Hammerstein's Nine o'Clock Revue* (1923); *Hearts and Diamonds* (1926). He was married to the actress Ruby Miller.

Darin, Bobby [Cassoto, Walden Robert] (*b* New York, 14 May 1936; *d* Los Angeles, 20 Dec. 1973). American singer and composer. He was described in Hardy and Laing's *Encyclopedia of Rock* as 'a series of identities, a collection of counterfeits, Melville's Confidence Man returning as the rock'n'roll trickster'; in other words, something of a chameleon, performing in a number of fashionable styles. With Decca he recorded 'Rock Island Line' (after Lonnie *Donegan) and 'Blue-eyed mermaid', moving to Atco and the rock field in 1956 and producing such popular hits as 'Splish splash', 'Queen of the hop', and 'Plain Jane'. He wrote a top hit in 1960, 'Dream lover', then switched to the *Sinatra image and recorded 'Mack the Knife'; followed by a Ray *Charles imitation in 'You're the reason I'm living' in 1962. He appeared in films, and recorded 'If I were a carpenter' by Tim Hardin (1941–80) in 1966. He suffered from ill-health as the result of childhood rheumatic fever, had heart surgery in 1971, and died of a heart-attack two years later.

A. DiOrio: *Borrowed Time: 37 Years of Bobby Darin* (Philadelphia, 1981).

Davenport, 'Cow-Cow' [Charles Edward] (*b* Anniston, Ala., 23 Apr. 1894; *d* Cleveland, 3 Dec. 1955). American composer and pianist. He studied theology but was asked to leave the college because of his predilection for ragtime, and so decided on music as a career. He was a pianist in vaudeville for many years and was part of a double-act, then worked as a talent scout for Vocalion Records in the 1920s. He settled in Cleveland, where he ran a music and record shop for time. A stroke in 1938 forced him to work more as a vocalist. Mainly in Cleveland during the latter part of his life, he recorded many of his own compositions such as 'Cow-Cow blues' (1928) which Freddie Slack and Ella Mae *Morse both made into a record hit as 'Cow-Cow boogie' in 1942. He also wrote 'State Street jive' (1928), 'Mama don't allow' (1929), and 'I'll be glad when you're dead, you rascal, you' (1931).

Davis, Eddie 'Lockjaw' (*b* New York, 2 Mar. 1921; *d* Las Vegas, 3 Nov. 1986). American jazz saxophonist, an aggressive big-toned player also capable of a more sensitive style for which he was less credited. Self-taught, he began his career playing in a Harlem club. He worked with Cootie *Williams and Louis *Armstrong in the 1940s and formed his own band in 1945, regularly playing at *Minton's until 1952 when he joined the Count *Basie band. In 1955 he formed a trio and toured Britain and France with Basie, afterwards playing at the Basie Club in New York and acting as Basie's road manager. He toured England again in 1960 and 1970.

Davis, Jimmie [James Houston] (*b* Beech Springs, Quitman, La., 11 Sept. 1902). American singer and composer. He had a varied and distinguished career during which he was a professor of history and social science at Dodd College, a professional entertainer, police commissioner of Shreveport, acted in films and had one—*Louisiana* (1947)—made about him, and was twice elected governor of Lousiana 1944–8 and 1960–4. He achieved great popularity as a country-style singer and is remembered by such compositions as 'Nobody's darling but mine' (1935); 'When it's roundup time in Heaven' (1936); 'It makes no difference now' (1937); 'Let's be sweethearts again' (1938); 'Worried mind' (1942); 'Sweethearts or strangers' (1942); 'Columbus Stockade blues' (1943); 'There's a new moon over my shoulder' (1944); but particularly 'You are my sunshine' (1940), which he used as a campaign song. In between his two terms of office he also diverted his activities to the field of gospel music, continuing in the 1970s with such items as 'At the crossing', 'I still believe', 'Amazing grace', and 'Christ is sunshine'. In his earlier field he had a hit with 'Where the old Red River flows' (1962). In his country vein, he performed in a simple style reminiscent of Jimmie *Rodgers. He was elected to the *Country Music Hall of Fame in 1972.

Davis, Mac [Morris] (*b* Lubbock, Texas, 21 Jan. 1942). American singer and songwriter. He started writing songs when he was five or six years old and took up the guitar in his teens. He went to Emory University in Atlanta where he organized his own rock group. His songs gained a wide circulation by being sung by more than 150 popular artists including Nancy Sinatra, Kenny *Rogers, Glen

*Campbell, and particularly Elvis *Presley, who really made Davis's songs known. Although often working in the rock field, he thinks of himself primarily as a country artist and his best songs have usually inclined to that vein. His own records are in country style and he had a great hit with his own 'Baby, don't get hooked on me' in 1972. His most popular songs include 'Something burning' (recorded by Kenny Rogers), 'I'm in the ghetto' (Presley), 'Don't cry, daddy' ($1\frac{1}{2}$ million recordings of the Presley version sold), 'I believe in music', and 'Stop and smell the roses'.

Davis, Miles Dewey (*b* Alton, Ill., 26 May 1926; *d* Santa Monica, Calif., 28 Sept. 1991). American jazz trumpeter. He was in at the blossom time of *bebop, playing with Sonny Stitt and Clark *Terry in an early group, later with Charlie *Parker, Coleman *Hawkins, Benny *Carter, and Billy *Eckstine. A prophet of the 'cool' school from 1948, he showed the way in such numbers as 'Boplicity'. It was the Davis recordings of 1948–9 (later re-issued under the title *The Birth of the Cool*) that launched the movement and such musicians as Gerry *Mulligan, Lee Konitz, and John *Lewis. Later he recorded three influential albums of Gil *Evans arrangements—*Miles Ahead* (1957), *Porgy and Bess* (1958), and *Sketches of Spain* (1960), using musicians like John *Coltrane and Philly Joe *Jones. In his own writings he favoured modal settings (*Kind of Blue*, 1959), experimenting particularly with the Lydian scale. By 1958 he was moving somewhat beyond the borders of even cool bop and produced such exercises in mysticism as 'Nefertiti' and 'Sorcerer'. He experimented with electronic instruments and a fusion with hard rock, boosting his inspiration with drugs but achieving spectacular record sales; he displayed a hint of musical megalomania with a 1981 album entitled *We Want Miles*.

M. James: *Miles Davis* (London, 1961). B. Cole: *Miles Davis: a Musical Biography* (New York, 1974). I. Carr: *Miles Davis* (New York, 1982). M. Davis & Q. Troupe: *Miles: the Autobiography* (New York, 1990).

Davis, Sammy, Jr. (*b* New York, 8 Dec. 1925; *d* Los Angeles, 16 May 1990). American singer, actor, and dancer. His father, Sammy Davis Sr. (1900–88) was a vaudeville dancer and his mother a chorus girl and he travelled with them as a child, first appearing on stage at the age of 18 months, and had his first film part at the age of 8. He became aversatile and fashionable entertainer in nightclubs (for a time with his father in the Will Mastin Trio) and on TV consorting with the cream of American show-business society (notably associated and filming with Frank *Sinatra) and making many recordings. He appeared in the Broadway shows **Mr Wonderful* (1956) and **Golden Boy* (1964), both written as a showcase for his talents, and starred in the film *Taps* (1980). He was a popular figure in Britain where he made many stage appearances.

S. Davis & J. & B. Boyar: *Yes I Can: the Story of Sammy Davis Jr.* (New York, 1965). S. Davis: *Hollywood in a Suitcase* (New York, 1980).

Davis, Skeeter [Penick, Mary Frances] (*b* Dry Ridge, Ken., 20 Dec 1931). American country singer. She began her career in 1953 in a duo known as the Davis Sisters with a recording of 'I forgot more than you'll ever know'. After a motor accident in which her partner Betty Jack Davis was killed she retired from entertainment for a time but emerged in the 1950s, recording 'Set him free' (1959); 'I'm falling too' (1960); and 'The end of the world' (1962). She has made occasional excursions into rock, working with Buddy *Holly and the *Rolling Stones, but has always kept her first allegiance to country music and the **Grand Ole Opry* which she joined in 1959. She was suspended from this for a time for criticizing the Nashville Police Department in a 1973 broadcast. Other best-selling recordings include: I'm saving my love' (1963); 'Gonna get along without you now' (1964); 'What does it take?' (1967); 'I'm a lover—not a fighter' (1969).

Davison, 'Wild Bill' [William Edward] (*b* Defiance, Ohio, 5 Jan. 1906; *d* Santa Barbara, Calif., 14 Nov. 1989). American jazz cornettist, valve trombonist, singer, and bandleader; a leading light of the *Dixieland world for some 50 years, playing in a forceful, gutsy manner that earned him his nickname. He began playing in the 1920s in Ohio, leading a band called the Ohio Lucky Seven, eventually becoming a major figure in the world of Chicago jazz. He worked with the clarinettist Frank *Teschemacher and was driving the car in which Teschemacher was killed in 1932. In the 1940s revival period he led bands in Boston and New York, and in 1945 began a long association with Eddie *Condon and the Condon Club, first touring England with Condon in 1957. He was featured at the Newport Festival in 1978 and was active into the 1980s.

Dawson, Peter (*b* Adelaide, 31 Jan. 1882; *d* Sydney, 26 Sept. 1961). Australian singer and composer. The son of a successful industrialist, he was intended for the family business, but after winning a singing competition he decided, despite parental opposition, to make music his career. He went to England and studied with Charles Santley (1834–1922), toured the West of England with Santley and Mme Albani, and made his London debut in 1904. He made his first records that year, as Leonard Dawson, for the Edison-Bell company—the first title being 'To my first love'. He started to record under his own name for G&T (later HMV) beginning with 'Navajo', issued in October 1904; though he made many stage and concert hall appearances, he was always pre-eminently thought of as a gramophone artist and continued to be associated with the HMV label until he retired in 1956. He made more than 3000 recordings and sold more than 25 million, his recording career extending from cylinder days to 1955 and stereo LPs. The most popular was of Katie Moss's 'Floral dance' which he first recorded in 1912, and several more times.

He served in the Australian Army in the First World War, but being too old in 1939, returned to

Australia to work in the family metal factory. After the war he made several recordings with the D'Oyly *Carte company. He not only recorded under his own name but as 'Frank Danby' in light songs, as 'Will Strong' in music-hall songs, and as 'Hector Grant' for an extended series of Harry *Lauder material. According to Fred Gaisberg's *Music on Record* (1947), Lauder never forgave Dawson for these, resenting the perfect mimicry as well as his own loss of sales. Dawson also wrote Scottish songs under this name and appeared as Hector Grant, with side-whiskers and kilt, in London and provincial halls. Elsewhere he used such pseudonyms as 'Peter Allison', 'Evelyn Byrd', 'Denton Thomas', 'Charles Webber', 'Arnold Flint', 'Gilbert Mundy', 'Geoffrey Baxter', and 'Alison Miller'; but the most favoured was 'J. P. McColl', under which name he wrote his most popular song, 'Boots', to words by Rudyard Kipling. Other songs in a prolific output included 'Route marching' and 'Cells', both with words by Kipling.

P. Dawson: *Fifty Years of Song* (London, 1952).

Day, Dennis [McNulty, Eugene Patrick] (*b* New York, 21 May 1917; *d* Brentwood, Calif., 22 May 1988). American singer of Irish parentage. He planned to study law but a natural talent for singing led him to send a recording of his work to Mary Livingston, the wife of Jack Benny. It earned him an audition and a first appearance, as Dennis Day, on the Jack Benny show on 8 Oct. 1939. He was to remain a foil and straight man to the comedian on radio and TV for more than 25 years, with his catchphrase 'Oh Mr Benny' driving Benny to such desperation that he would cry 'Oh, for heaven's sake sing, Dennis!' Amongst his most popular items and recordings were 'Danny Boy', 'McNamara's Band', 'Clancy lowered the boom', 'Peg o' my heart', and 'That's an Irish lullaby'. After leaving the Benny show in 1955 he had his own show and worked with Milton *Berle. He appeared in eight films.

Day, Doris [Von Kappelhoff, Doris Mary Anne] (*b* Cincinnati, 3 Apr. 1922). American actress and singer. She started her singing career with the Les *Brown band in the early 1940s, and is heard on the popular 'Sentimental journey' recording. A vivacious blonde with freckles, she became known for her clear singing and clean-living image in a number of Hollywood musicals. She worked mainly for Warner Brothers 1948–54, often in partnership with Gordon *McRae, and later with MGM, starting with the acclaimed *Love Me or Leave Me* (1955). Her films included: *Romance on the High Seas* (1948); *It's a Great Feeling* (1949); *My Dream is Yours* (1949); *Young Man With a Horn* (1950); *Tea for Two* (1950); *West Point Story* (1950); *Lullaby of Broadway* (1951); *On Moonlight Bay* (1951); *Starlift* (1951); *I'll See You in My Dreams* (1951); *April in Paris* (1952); *By the Light of the Silvery Moon* (1953); *Calamity Jane* (1953); *Lucky Me* (1954); *Young at Heart* (1954); *The *Pajama Game* (1957); and *Jumbo* (1962). Later she appeared mainly in straight comedies and had her own TV show. Her biggest recorded hits were 'Secret love' (1954) and 'Que será, será' ('Whatever will be, will be') (1956).

D. Day & A. E. Hotchner: *Doris Day: Her Own Story* (New York, 1975). C. Young: *Films of Doris Day* (Secaucus, NJ, 1977). G. Morris: *Doris Day* (New York, 1976: Munich, 1983).

Day, Edith (*b* Minneapolis, 10 Apr. 1896; *d* London, 2 May 1971). American actress, singer, and dancer. She made her first New York stage appearance in *Pom-Pom* in 1916 and first attracted attention in *Going Up* in 1917. Her biggest hit came with **Irene* in 1919, which ran for 670 performances. She left the New York cast to take the lead in London in 1920, and became a popular favourite there with her rendering of 'Alice blue gown' and 'Irene O'Dare'. She returned to the USA, appearing in *Orange Blossoms* (1922), but in 1925 went back to London to reign supreme at Drury Lane in such big-scale shows as **Rose Marie* (1925; revival, 1929); *The *Desert Song* (1927; revival, 1936); **Show Boat* (1928), with Paul *Robeson and Marie Burke; **Rio Rita* (1930); *Sunny River* (1943); and *Sail Away* (1962). She also appeared in variety and made many broadcasts.

Day, Frances [Schenck, Frances Victoria] (*b* East Orange, NJ, 16 Dec. 1908). American actress and singer. She started her career in New York nightclubs in New York and London before appearing in various London musical comedies such as *Out of the Bottle* (1932); *How D'You Do?* (1933); **Jill Darling* (1934)—the show which made her name; *Floodlight* (1937); *The Fleet's Lit Up* (1938); *Black and Blue* (1939); *Black Vanities* (1941); **DuBarry Was a Lady* (1942); *Evangeline* (1946); and *Latin Quarter* (1949). Singing in a sexy voice with a fascinating squeak, she made many delightful recordings that included Cole *Porter's 'It's d'lovely' and, from the film *Public Nuisance No. 1*, 'Me and my dog'. She appeared in a number of films.

Deep Purple. British pop group formed in Germany in 1968 with Rod Evans (vocal—later replaced by Ian Gillan and then David Coverdale), Ritchie Blackmore (guitar), Jon Lord (keyboard), Nick Simper (bass—later replaced by Roger Glover), and Ian Paice (drums) and immediately finding favour in the USA with a recording of 'Hush' (1968). Success in England came with 'Black night' (1970). Developing in the heavy metal rock style, they became one of the most influential bands of the early 1970s, purveying their high-decibel music around the world. Quieter fashions ensued before the group folded in 1976. They re-formed with comparable success in 1984.

C. Charlesworth: *Deep Purple: the Illustrated Biography* (London, 1983).

De Koven, Reginald (*b* Middletown, Conn., 3 Apr. 1859; *d* Chicago, 16 Jan. 1920). American composer, a pioneer figure of the American operetta scene. He left the USA for Europe when he was 13 and subsequently studied at St John's College, Oxford, graduating in 1879. He then went to study music in Stuttgart and Frankfurt, with *Genée, with *Suppé in Vienna, and with Delibes in Paris. He returned to the USA in 1882 and went into banking, married a rich woman, made a fortune in real estate, and then returned to music. With Harry B. *Smith he wrote *The Begum* (1888) and *Don Quixote* (1889), both failures, then had a great hit with **Robin Hood* in 1890. Though his operas are hardly ever performed now, he had a strong following in his lifetime. He was also music critic of the *Chicago Evening Post* (1889–90), *New York World* (1891–7), and *New York Journal* (1898–1906). His works included: *The Knickerbockers* (1892); *The Algerian* (1893); *Rob Roy* (1894); *The Mandarin* (1896); *The Highwayman* (1897); *Papa's Wife* (1899); *Foxy Quiller in Corsica* (1900); *The Little Duchess* (1901); *Maid Marian* (1902); *The Beauty Spot* (1909).

De Koven (Mrs): *A Musician and his Wife* (New York, 1926).

Del Riego, Teresa (*b* London, 1876; *d* London, 23 Jan. 1968). British composer. She was educated at the Convent of the Sacred Heart in Highgate, and studied composition, violin, and singing privately before going to the West Central College of Music. She composed from the age of 12, but her first published work was the song 'Speak on, sweet voices' in 1898. During the First World War she took part in and organized many concerts for wounded soldiers and in aid of war charities; her husband was killed in France in 1917. One of her most popular songs was 'O dry those tears' (1901) which sold 23,000 copies in the first six weeks of publication and 60,000 in its first year. 'Homing' (1917) was equally successful in the war years, and her song 'The unknown warrior' was a feature of the British Armistice Day commemoration for many years.

Delysia, Alice [Lapize, Alice] (*b* Paris, 3 Mar. 1889; *d* South of France, 10 Feb. 1979). French singer and actress. She began her working life as a midinette, and was to earn a reputation for her chic appearance, becoming a 'naughty' sex symbol of her day with a penchant for low-cut dresses, but also sang in a fine voice with impressive high notes. Her first stage appearance was in 1903 at the Moulin Rouge in the chorus of *The *Belle of New York*. In the USA she appeared in *The *Catch of the Season*, returning to Paris to appear in revue. She was becoming famous in Paris when C. B. *Cochran engaged her for the London revue *Odds and Ends* (1914). She became a great favourite with London audiences and appeared in *More* (1915); *Pell-Mell* (1916); *Carminetta* (1917)—in which she sang 'Cliquot'; **As You Were* (1918)—'If you could care', 'Helen of Troy'; *Afgar* (1919; NY, 1920)—'Dardanella', 'Night was made for love', 'You'd be surprised'; *Mayfair and Montmartre* (1922); *On With the Dance* (1925)—'Poor little rich girl', 'Remember'; *Princess Charming* (1926)—'Babying you'; *The *Cat and the Fiddle* (1932); and *Mother of Pearl* (1933)—'Every woman thinks she wants to wander'. Rejecting offers from the London theatre, she worked for ENSA 1941–3, and retired to the South of France after the war with her husband, a French diplomat.

Dennis, Matt (*b* Seattle, 11 Feb. 1914). American composer, arranger, singer, and pianist. His parents, who were part of a vaudeville act called the Five Musical Lovelands, taught him music and he started playing and arranging while still at high school. In the mid-1920s he was engaged by Tommy *Dorsey as arranger and composer of special material for the band, which at that time employed Frank *Sinatra, Jo *Stafford, and Connie Haines who introduced many of his songs. In the US Army Air Force during the war, he worked with the radio production unit and for a short spell was with the Glenn *Miller Army Air Force Band. He worked as a solo act after the war, his songs-at-the-piano becoming popular with sophisticated nightclub audiences and on TV, and he had his own NBC TV show before acting in the *Johnny Ringo* series. He did not become widely popular but was very much a musician's musician, his songs polished and skilfully written. His own singing and piano playing complemented his songs to perfection and his interpretations were unique.

He wrote: 'Love turns winter to spring' (1939); 'Relax' (1939); 'Who's Yehoodi?' (1940); 'Everything happens to me' (1940), 'Let's get away from it all' (1941), 'Let's just pretend' (1941), 'The night we called it a day' (1941), 'Violets for your furs' (1941); 'Free for all' (1941), 'Will you still be mine' (1941), all with Tom Adair, 'Little man with a candy cigar' (1941, *w* Frank Kilduff), 'Skunk song' (1941, *w* Bill Seckler), 'I tried' (1941), 'You'd never know the old place now' (1941, *w* Marve Fisher); 'Show me the way to get out of this world' (1950, *w* Les Clark); 'Compared to you' (1952); 'It's over, it's over, it's over' (1952); 'We belong together' (1952); and 'Angel eyes' (1953), used in the film *Jennifer*.

Denver, John [Deutschendorf, Henry John] (*b* Roswell, New Mexico, 31 Dec. 1943). American singer and actor. The son of a distinguished air force pilot, he had similar ambitions until lured into music by the sounds of Elvis *Presley and a growing interest in rock and roll and country music. He studied architecture but learned the guitar in the meantime and opted for a career in entertainment, playing in clubs and joining the Mitchell Trio. He sang in various styles but mainly with a country flavour and wrote such popular hits as 'Leaving on a jet plane', 'Country roads', 'Rocky Mountain high', and 'Thank God I'm a country boy'. Since 1968 he has had a highly successful career as a solo artist, with a clean-cut all-American image, and has appeared in films.

D. Dachs: *John Denver* (New York, 1976). L. Fleischer: *John Denver* (New York–London, 1976). J. Martin: *Rocky Mountain Wonderboy* (London, 1977).

Denza, Luigi (*b* Castellamare di Stabia, Campania, 24 Feb. 1846; *d* London, 26 Jan. 1922). Italian composer and teacher. He studied composition at the Naples Conservatory. His opera *Wallenstein* (1876) was produced without much success in Naples; thereafter he devoted his efforts to writing some 600 songs, many of which were to attain great popularity. He settled in London in 1879 and became Professor of Singing at the Royal Academy of Music in 1898. His best-known song was 'Funiculi-funicula' (1880), which soon sold more than half-a-million copies and was quoted by Richard Strauss in his 'Aus Italien' under the impression that it was a genuine folk-song. Other songs particularly favoured by Italian tenors were 'Se, occhi Turchini', 'Occhi di fata', 'Luna fedel', 'Non t'amo più'; in French, 'Si vous l'aviez compris'; and his English songs included 'A May morning' (1894, *w* Fred E. *Weatherley), 'No more' (1899, *w* Weatherly), 'Marguerite', 'Come to me', 'My song for you', 'The dawn of love', 'Call me back', and 'Love's own land'.

De Paul, Gene Vincent (*b* New York, 17 June 1919; *d* Los Angeles, 1988). American composer and pianist. He played with various orchestras and recorded as a pianist, before settling in Hollywood to write for such films as *Seven Brides for Seven Brothers* (1954)—'Spring, Spring, Spring', 'When you're in love' (winning an Academy Award for his score), and *You Can't Run Away From It* (1956). He worked for the Walt Disney studios and wrote the score for *Alice in Wonderland* (1951). Other songs included: 'I'll remember April' (1941); 'Mr Five by Five' (1942); 'He's my guy (1943); 'Star eyes' (1943); 'Teach me tonight' (1953); and he wrote the Broadway score **L'il Abner* in 1950.

De Rose, Peter (*b* New York, 10 Mar. 1900; *d* New York, 23 Apr. 1953). American composer and writer. After working in the music-publishing house of Ricordi, he became a professional pianist and songwriter. He had a radio series with his wife, Singhi Breen, 1923–9 called *Sweethearts of the Air*. He contributed to various revues and his songs included: 'Muddy water' (with Harry *Richman, 1926; *w* Jo Trent); 'When your hair has turned to silver' (1931, *w* Charles *Tobias); 'Wagon wheels' (1931, *w* Billy *Hill)—used in the **Ziegfeld Follies* of 1934; 'Somebody loves you' (1932, Tobias); 'Have you ever been lonely?' (1933, *w* George Brown); 'Deep purple' (1933)—song version (1939, *w* Mitchell Parish); 'The lamp is low' (with Bert Shefter, 1939, *w* Parish); 'Lilacs in the rain' (1939, Parish); and many more, continuing to write until the end of his life.

Desert Song, The. Operetta with music by Sigmund *Romberg and book by Otto *Harbach, Oscar *Hammerstein II, and Frank Mandel, staged at the New York Casino Theatre 30 Nov. 1926. By this time, with the jazz age sweeping in, it was almost an archaic survivor of the romantic era of Viennese-style operetta. But its big tunes and melodramatic tale of the Sahara (inspired by the Riff uprisings in Morocco, the exploits of Lawrence of Arabia, and the Valentino image) and the mysterious Red Shadow (played by Robert Halliday), who turns out to be an ordinary sort of chap beneath the guise, and Vivienne *Segal in the female lead, made it eventually one of the most popular operettas of all time. It had 471 performances in New York and came to London's Drury Lane Theatre 7 Apr. 1927 where the Red Shadow was played by Harry *Welchman and the heroine by Edith *Day, running for 432 performances.

It has since been revived many times and in England became a star role for the singer John *Hanson, who first appeared in it in London in 1954 and toured with it for many years. It was filmed in 1929 with John *Boles and Carlotta King; in 1943 with Dennis Morgan (*b* 1910) and Irene Manning (*b* 1917); and in 1953 with Gordon *McRae and Kathryn *Grayson. It became a great favourite with amateur performers. Its well-remembered songs included: 'Riff song', 'Romance', 'The desert song', 'Let love go', 'The sabre song', and 'One alone'.

Deslys, Gaby (*b* Marseilles, 1883; *d* Paris, 11 Feb. 1920). French actress and singer who became popular in America in such Broadway shows as *Vera Violetta* (1911), in which she and her American partner Harry Pilcer popularized a dance called 'The Gaby glide'; *The Whirl of Society* (1912); *The Honeymoon Express* (1913)—all with Al *Jolson; *The Belle of Bond Street* (1914); and *Stop! Look! Listen!* (1915).

J. Gardner: *Gaby Deslys: a Fatal Attraction* (London, 1987).

Desmond, Florence [Dawson] (*b* London, 31 May 1905; *d* Guildford, 16 Jan. 1993). British actress, singer, dancer, and impressionist. She began her career in pantomine as a dancer, was one of *Cochran's Young Ladies and became well-known in various London revues and shows, including: **On With the Dance* (1925); **Cochran's Revue of 1926*; **This Year of Grace* (1928); *Charlot's Masquerade* (1930); *Savoy Follies* (1932); *Why Not Tonight?* (1934); *Streamline* (1934); *Seeing Stars* (1935); *Let's Raise the Curtain* (1936); *Wonderful World* (1937); *Funny Side Up* (1940); **Apple Sauce* (1940); *Hi-De-Hi* (1943); and *Under the Counter* (1946). She was a popular entertainer in variety and on radio.

F. Desmond: *Florence Desmond: by Herself* (London, 1953).

Desmond, Johnny (De Simone, Giovanni Alfredo] (*b* Detroit, 14 Nov. 1920; *d* Los Angeles, 6 Sept. 1985). American singer and actor. He began his career with the Bob *Crosby band and the Bob-O-Links, then was with the Gene *Krupa orchestra. Joining the US Army, he was with the Glenn *Miller

Army Air Force Band in England and Europe, becoming known as the 'GI Sinatra' and a famed member of that now legendary set-up. After the war he had his own radio show and worked on the Chicago radio feature *Breakfast Club*. He made a number of hit records in the 1950s and appeared in the Broadway shows *Say Darling* (1958) and **Funny Girl* (1964); and in several films. One of his last appearances was in a TV tribute to the Glenn Miller band with Tex *Beneke and others.

Desmond, Paul [Breitenfeld, Paul Emil] (*b* San Francisco, 25 Nov. 1924; *d* San Francisco, 30 May 1977). American jazz alto-saxophonist. He quickly became known when he joined the Dave *Brubeck Quartet in 1951, staying with it until it disbanded in 1967, and winning the *Playboy* Jazz Poll Award from 1957 to 1960. He toured Britain in 1958 and 1959, and Europe and the Middle East. He was an elegant stylist and also wrote many pieces for the quartet, among them its signature tune 'Take five', a piece in 5/4 time which became popular.

Destry Rides Again. Musical comedy with music and lyrics by Harold *Rome and book by Leonard Gersche based on a story by Max Brand. It was seen at the Imperial Theatre, New York, 23 Apr. 1959 with Andy Griffiths as Destry Jr. and Dolores *Gray as Frenchy, directed by Michael Kidd (*b* 1919). It ran for 473 performances. The stage show was permitted a happy ending with Frenchy, an entertainer of easy virtue, reformed and in the good guy's arms. It drew much reflected strength from the classic film of 1939 (one of three filmed versions) starring James Stewart as the sheriff who refused to tote a gun and Marlene *Dietrich with her memorable rendering of 'See what the boys in the backroom will have'.

DeSylva, 'Buddy' or **B.G.** [George Gard] (*b* New York, 27 Jan. 1895; *d* Los Angeles, 11 July 1950). American lyricist and producer. He began writing lyrics while at college, 1915–16, and went to New York to work with Al *Jolson who introduced his first song 'N'everything' (written with Gus *Kahn and Jolson, 1918). His first Broadway assignment was with *La, La, Lucille* in 1919. In a famous partnership with Lew *Brown and Ray *Henderson he wrote the successful shows **Good News* (1927); **Hold Everything* (1928); **Follow Thru* (1929); *Three Cheers* (1929); *Flying High* (1930); and regularly wrote for **George White's Scandals*. He produced his own shows and had his own publishing house, which he sold in 1929 when he went to Hollywood to write and produce several Shirley *Temple films. He was the head of Paramount Pictures for many years and later an executive of Capitol Records.

Working with many leading composers he produced a good crop of lasting song-hits that included: 'April showers' (1921, Louis *Silvers); 'A kiss in the dark' (1922, Victor *Herbert); 'Do it again' (1922, George *Gershwin); 'I'll build a stairway to Paradise' (1922, Gershwin); 'California, here I come' (1924, Jolson and Joseph *Meyer); 'Somebody loves me' (1924, Gershwin); 'If you knew Susie' (1925); 'When day is done' (1926, Robert Katscher); and, with the Brown and Henderson team, 'Black bottom' (1926); 'You're the cream in my coffee' (1928); 'It all depends on you' (1928); 'Together' (1928); and 'Button up your overcoat' (1929).

Diamond, Neil [Leslie] (*b* New York, 24 Jan. 1941). American singer and songwriter. Brought up in a tough part of Brooklyn, he bought his first guitar in 1957 and began writing poems and setting them to music. His first recordings were made on the obscure Shell label, later moving to Bang Records for whom he recorded several hits under his own name. He played in nightclubs where his subtly sexual songs were much appreciated. Success was assured when the *Monkees recorded his 'I'm a believer' in 1966 and sold six million copies. They later recorded his 'A little bit me, a little bit you' (1966) and 'Pleasant Valley Sunday' (1967) while *Lulu was doing the same for 'The boat that I row' (1966) in Britain. Other hits, which he recorded himself, were 'Cherry, cherry', 'I got the feeling' (1966); 'Girl, you'll be a woman soon', 'You got to me', 'I thank the Lord for the night time' (1967); 'Shilo' (1968); 'Sweet Caroline', 'Holly, holy' (1969); 'Cracklin' Rosie', 'He ain't heavy—he's my brother' (1970); 'I am, I said' (1971); the No. hit 'Song sung blue', 'Play me', and 'Walk on water' (1972).

His work steadily matured and he wrote the important 'African trilogy', a 22-minute folk ballet (1971). In 1973 he moved to CBS with a million-dollar advance, his early clean-cut image now replaced by that of the long-haired introspective poet, which only increased his popular appeal. The hits continued—'Longfellow serenade' (1974); 'If you know what I mean', 'Beautiful noise' (1976); 'Desiree' (1978); 'Forever in blue jeans', 'September morn' (1979); 'Love on the rocks' (1980); 'Hello again', 'America', 'Yesterday's song' (1981); and 'Heartlight' (1982). He teamed up with Barbra *Streisand in 1978 for the triumphant *You Don't Bring Me Flowers* album; and in 1980 showed his talent as an actor when he co-starred with Laurence Olivier in a re-make of *The *Jazz Singer*. He has matured as a distinctive and immensely creative writer of some of the more aesthetic products of the 1980s scene as typified by the fine 'Love on the rocks'.

Dibdin, Charles (*b* Southampton, 4 Mar. 1745; *d* London, 25 July 1814). British composer, dramatist, author, and entertainer. He was one of the first noteworthy popular British composers, writing genuinely popular songs in the folk-song tradition. The 18th child of a respectable middle-class family, his father a parish clerk, he was sent to school in Winchester with the Church in mind as a prospective career. He was a chorister at Winchester Cathedral, 1756–9, where his musical talents were encouraged by the organist. He showed considerable talent as a singer and was taken to London by his brother Tom, captain of an East Indiaman, later drowned and commemorated in Dibdin's finest song 'Tom Bowling'. He worked for a time in a music warehouse, started to write songs, and was taken on by the famous Mr Rich at Covent Garden as a member of the chorus. After Rich's death, his son-in-law Beard took over and encouraged Dibdin to try his hand at light opera. His early inspiration in this field came from attending a rehearsal of Arne's *Thomas and Sally* when he was 16. He was 19 when *The Shepherd's Artifice* was produced in 1764, a work containing a song which he had written some three years before—'In every fertile valley' which, with its occasional advanced harmony, immediately became popular. The Italian influence evident here was soon to be replaced, as Dibdin took in the products of the ballad opera boom, with something nearer to British folk-song, a mark of the genuine Dibdin style as heard by 1775 in such songs as 'The lads of the village' from his best-known opera *The Quaker*.

He was fortunate to have the redoubtable Isaac Bickerstaff as his librettist in such works as *Lionel and Clarissa* (1768) and his first great success, *The Padlock*, in the same year. The freshness and grace of the melodies gave it lasting popularity. Bickerstaff kept the rights to the libretto and sold 28,000 copies, making a considerable profit, for those days, of £1700. Dibdin who had appeared in the opera himself in the black role of Mungo, received only £45, a reflection of the difficulties of printing and marketing music at that time. After several more works with Bickerstaff and others in the Arne vein he resolved his ultimate style by writing his own words as well as the music, with marked success in *The Waterman* of 1774 and *The Quaker* of 1775. These were to hold the British stage for the next 70 years or so with songs such as 'The lads of the village' gradually replacing the public's accustomed stock of earlier folk-songs. But Dibdin was still only managing an income of £200 a year and tried to supplement this by going into theatre management. Two failures made him decide to follow in his brother's steps and try to make a fortune in India, but he only got as far as Torbay where his ship was obliged to take refuge from severe storms. It was here that he conceived the idea of a one-man musical entertainment, a sort of early revue. Supplying his own words and music he gave such shows in an auction room in King Street, Covent Garden, and the formula was immediately successful. His second production, *The Oddities*, was performed for 79 nights, and he began to make a good income from selling the librettos and songs. 'The Greenwich pensioner' from *The Oddities* sold 10,750 copies from which he made a profit of £400. He can now be seen as a pioneer in the British theatrical and musical business which was to evolve over the next few decades. By 1791 he was running his own little theatre in the Strand, the Sans Souci, where his private theatricals inspired some wit to write:

> What more conviction need there be
> That Dibdin's plan will do,
> Since now we find him *Sans Souci*
> Who late was *sans six-sous*?

Dibdin was able to open a second theatre in Leicester Square and in October 1804 offered the public a series of 18 lectures on music and, as a sideline, sold a sort of tutor called *The Harmonic Preceptor*. Rather a superficial work, it never received much academic credence; nor did his other books in similar vein, but he toured England, Scotland, and Ireland to general acclaim. He was a handsome man and an easy narrator of his own words. Singing with a sweet and mellow baritone voice, he accompanied himself on an instrument of his own devising which was a cross between a piano and an organ with bells, side drum, and tambourine for rhythm accompaniment.

Dibdin was a forward-looking pioneer in every way. He was particularly known for his sea-songs, a typically British commodity, personally inspired by his beloved brother's career, culminating with the finely wrought 'Tom Bowling' which stands comparison with any popular song in the world of its own time or since.

In 1805 he retired and sold all his stocks and the copyright of 360 songs to Messrs Bland & Weller of Oxford Street for £1800 with a promise of a forthcoming £100 for anything he might produce. This was supplemented by a government pension, awarded in 1803, of £200 a year, which was later withdrawn, forcing his return to the theatre in 1808. He opened a music-shop, but this resulted in bankruptcy. Friends came to his aid and a benefit dinner was arranged at the City of London Tavern, with all the popular performers of the day participating, which raised £400. He then retired to a house in Arlington Street, Camden Town, where he resided until his death. His last stage piece, *The Round Robin*, was performed at the Haymarket Theatre in 1811 but with little success; and he wrote twelve songs for the popular cultural publication *La Belle Assembleé* for which he received £60. In 1813 he suffered a stroke and he died in 1814, aged 69. He was buried in St Martin's burial ground in Camden Town with the words of his finest song engraved on the headstone:

> His form was of the manliest beauty;
> His heart was kind and soft;
> Faithful below he did his duty,
> But now he's gone aloft.

Dibdin's words were often superior to his music, straightforward and natural, the language simple but vigorous—'gay and playful as well as sweet and tender' in the words of George Hogarth, who edited his collected songs with a memoir in 1842. His music was less technically accomplished except in those moments of inspiration like 'Tom Bowling'. Spanning the years between the heyday of *ballad opera and the start of the 19th century, which was to see the rapid spread of popular culture made possible by cheaper methods of printing and paper production and improved transport and communications, Dibdin now appears as a vital link between the misty era of folklore and the new entertainment industry. His songs led the way to the early music-hall songs; he was the progenitor of the one-man entertainment to be perpetuated by such men as Henry *Russell and George *Grossmith; the founder of a tradition of British sea-songs; and in a facet of his industry that might well escape attention, a pioneer of the popular 'negro' act in what was to become a favourite entertainment of the middle classes, the blackfaced minstrel show. Nor was the influence of Dibdin confined to England. Sonneck's *Bibliography of Early Secular American Music* indicates that well over 50 of his songs, not including a collected edition of them, were published in the USA before 1800, as well as the librettos of at least six of his stage works.

C. Dibdin: *The Musical Tour of Mr Dibdin* (Sheffield, 1788). C Dibdin: *Observations on a Tour Through Almost the Whole of England and a Considerable Part of Scotland* (2 vols) (London, 1801/2). C. Dibdin: *The Professional Life of Mr Dibdin* (London, 1803). C. Dibdin: *The Public Undeceived (on the Question of his Pension)* (London, 1807). G. Hogarth (ed.): *The Songs of Charles Dibdin, Chronologically Arranged with Notes, Historical, Biographical and Critical* (with a Memoir) (2 vols) (London, 1842). W. Kitchener: *A Brief Memoir of Charles Dibdin* (London, 1884). H. G. Thorn: *Charles Dibdin, one of Southampton's Sons* (London, 1888). E. R. Dibdin: *A Charles Dibdin Bibliography* (Liverpool, 1937). E. Holmes: *Charles Dibdin* (Southampton, 1974).

Di Capua, Edoardo (*b* Naples, 1864; *d* Naples, 1917). Italian composer. He earned a living by singing and playing his Neapolitan songs in cafés and smaller theatres in and around Naples, and also gave piano lessons. His most famous song, still known all over the world, was 'O sole mio!' (*w* Giovanni Capurro, 1859–1920) which he wrote in 1898. Most of his songs, in the current fashion, he sold outright for miserable sums to publishers and so gained little reward and died in poverty. Others included 'Maria Mari' (1899); 'Torna maggio' (1900); and 'Canzona bella' (1903).

Dickenson, Vic [Victor] (*b* Xenia, Ohio, 6 Aug. 1906; *d* New York, 16 Nov. 1984). American jazz trombonist. He began his working career as a plasterer but, after an accident, turned to the trombone which he had played at school. He worked with the bands of Blanche Calloway 1933–6, Benny *Moten 1937, Claude *Hopkins 1938, Benny *Carter 1939, Count *Basie 1940–1, Sidney *Bechet 1941; and in 1943 joined a popular sextet run by Eddie *Heywood. In 1949 he formed a band of his own, but thereafter mainly played in Dixieland units with people like Red *Allen, Edmond Hall, Wild Bill *Davison, Bobby *Hackett; and he was a regular at the Eddie *Condon Club in New York. He could play ballads with a soft, singing tone but was mostly appreciated as a boisterously sardonic soloist with a rasping tone.

Dickson, Barbara (*b* Dunfermline, Scotland, 27 Sept. 1947). British actress, pianist, and singer. She began singing in folk clubs and made her first stage appearance in Liverpool in 1973 in a musical about the *Beatles, *John, Paul, George, Ringo and Bert* which later went to London. She had a hit record with 'Answer me' in 1974. She appeared on TV, worked at the Ronnie *Scott Club, and really made her mark in **Evita* (1976). She had a one-woman show at the Royal Albert Hall in 1980 and appeared in the musical *Blood Brothers* (1983).

Dickson, Dorothy (*b* Kansas City, Mo., 26 July 1896). American actress and singer who made her first appearances as a dancer in such Broadway shows as **Oh Boy!* (1917) and **Ziegfeld Follies* (1917), moving to acting roles in *Girl o' Mine* (1918); *Rock-a-bye Baby* (1918); *Ziegfeld Follies* (1918); *The Royal Vagabond* (1919); *Lassie* (1920). She settled in London in 1921 and became a favourite of the musical stage there in such prestigious shows as **Sally* (1921); *The Cabaret Girl* (1922); *The Beauty Prize* (1923); *Patricia* (1924); *Charlot's Revue* (1925); **Tip-Toes* (1926); **Peggy-Ann* (1927); **Hold Everything* (1929); *The Wonder Bar* (1930); **Casanova* (1931); *Stop Press* (1935); *Spread it Abroad* (1936)—in which she sang 'These foolish things'; **Careless Rapture* (1936); *Crest of the Wave* (1937); and *Fine and Dandy* (1942).

Diddley, Bo [McDaniel, Ellas] (*b* McComb, Miss., 30 Dec. 1928). American rock singer. Famous for the bump-and-grind shuffle tempo of his records, a beat which became known as 'shave-and-a-haircut, six bits', a phrase which echoes the metre of the songs and their African drum beat rhythm which has haunted rock music ever since. This hypnotic repetition was the basis of his most successful recordings 'Hey Bo Diddley', 'Mona', 'Pretty thing', and 'Who do you love'. He also worked in a more orthodox blues manner with an exuberant, impassioned, and raw style and utilized a slightly incongruous strait-laced appearance by featuring several unexpectedly comic numbers in his shows. He was a pioneer in exploring the potential of a punchy electric guitar sound and its distortions. He made his professional debut in 1951 and in 1955 recorded for Checker his first and most famous hit 'Hey Bo Diddley'. The British rhythm 'n' blues boom brought his name to the fore, his numbers being heavily featured by the *Rolling Stones and others, 'Diddley Daddy', 'Cops and robbers', 'Say man', 'Road runner', 'Nursery rhyme', 'Mona' among them. Every R & B band must have at one time used a Bo Diddley classic or at least borrowed his famous African sound.

Dietrich, Marlene [Maria Magdalena] (*b* Berlin, 27 Dec. 1901; *d* Paris, 6 May 1992). German actress and singer. She studied music and intended to follow a career as a violinist, but was soon diverted to the theatre and started a film career in 1923. The film that confirmed the seductive but fallible Dietrich image for most people was *Der blaue Engel (The Blue Angel*, 1930) in which she sang the song that was forever to be associated with her, 'Falling in love again'. The Austrian director Josef von Sternberg helped to perpetuate the image until 1935. Another famous Dietrich number was heard in the 1939 film *Destry Rides Again*, 'See what the boys in the backroom will have'. Such songs as 'Ich bin die fesche Lola', 'Mein blondes Baby', 'Peter', and 'Wer wird denn weinen', many written by Friedrich *Holländer, were ideally suited to her husky, drawling interpretation and others that were later drawn into her repertoire were the wartime *'Lili Marlene' and, during her 1960s excursions into cabaret, Pete *Seeger's 'Where have all the flowers gone'. Of the 20 or so films she made, none could be termed a musical nor did she ever work on the musical comedy stage; in spite of which she is remembered as an inimitable singer of songs.

L. Frewin: *Dietrich: the Story of a Star* (London, 1967). H. Dickens: *The Films of Marlene Dietrich* (New York, 1968). J. Kobal: *Marlene Dietrich* (London, 1968). S. Morley: *Marlene Dietrich* (London, 1976). C. Higham: *Marlene* (New York, 1977). D. Spoto: *Falling in Love Again* (Boston, 1985); as *Dietrich* (London, 1992). M. Dietrich: *My Life* (London, 1989). P. O'Connor: *The Amazing Blonde Woman: Dietrich's Own Style* (London, 1991).

Dietz, Howard (*b* New York, 8 Sept. 1896; *d* New York, 30 July 1983). American lyric-writer and librettist. One of the great lyric-writers, his contributions mainly came in collaboration with the composer Arthur *Schwartz, with whom he worked throughout his career until incapacitated by Parkinson's disease around 1965. Many of his best efforts were for the revue stage and were heard in such shows as *Dear Sir* (1924); *Merry-go-round* (1927); *The *Little Show* (1929); *Here Comes the Bride* (1930); *The Second Little Show* (1930); *Three's a Crowd* (1930); *The *Band Wagon* (1931); *Flying Colors* (1932); *Revenge With Music* (1933); *At Home Abroad* (1935); *Follow the Sun* (1936); *Between the Devil* (1937); *Dancing in the Streets* (1943); *Jackpot* (1944); *Sadie Thompson* (1944); *Inside USA* (1948); *The Gay Life* (1961); and *Jennie* (1963).

Among the songs he wrote with Schwartz were 'I guess I'll have to change my plan', 'Something to remember you by', 'Dancing in the dark', 'I love Louisa', 'Louisiana hayride', 'You and the night and the music', 'Love is a dancing thing', 'Alone together'; while he also wrote other songs with Jerome *Kern, Jay *Gorney, Ralph *Rainger ('Moanin' low'), and Vernon *Duke. Alan Jay *Lerner said 'his lyrics were distinguished for their wit, their grace, their imaginative rhyming and, above all, for their charm'. He was also a vice-president in charge of publicity for MGM and was responsible for their lion trademark. In spite of his illness, his memoirs were as witty and sparkling as anything he had written.

H. Dietz: *Dancing in the Dark* (New York, 1974).

Disc jockey. A now familiar and influential occupation; one who plays and introduces records over the radio and whose preferences thus have a potent influence on the all-pervading charts and record sales. The occupation arrived with the concurrent blossoming of broadcasting and popular recording. One of Britain's first recognized disc jockeys (though not then thus described) was Christopher Stone (1882–1965) who started his record programme in 1927 and was followed by others such as Doris Arnold (*b* 1904) with *These You Have Loved* in 1938. The disc jockey came into his own with the pop era and one of the first in Britain to be so-called was Alan Freeman (*b* 1928). Such programmes as *Juke Box Jury*, followed later by *Top of the Pops* (1964), gave further prominence to the power of persuasion and established such names as David Jacobs (*b* 1926) and Pete Murray (*b* 1928).

In the USA the first important disc jockey was Martin Block who conducted *The Make Believe Ballroom* programme on New York radio station WNEW from the mid-1930s. Notable successors were Gene Nobles, who began exploiting race records from Nashville in 1946, followed by John Richbourg with *Randy's Record Mart Show* and Bill 'Hoss' Allen. America's top disc jockey from 1951 was Alan *Freed, who started his *Moondog Show* that year. As the power of DJs to influence record sales increased, a degree of corruption was perhaps bound to creep into the business and there were 'payola' scandals in both Britain and the USA in the ensuing years. Disc jockeys may sometimes seem to fill the spaces in between the records with an inane babble of sweet nothings, but they serve a purpose, as do insects, and the profession is graced by an occasional intelligent member such as John *Peel who actually rebels against the status figures of the *charts.

Disco (from the French, *discothèque*). Modern substitute for the dance hall and the almost extinct dance orchestra, a gathering where pop records are played at a high dynamic level and introduced by a disc-jockeying MC, for the benefit of youthful but prematurely deaf dancers; probably semi-blind, too, as the décor is invariably dominated by banks of flashing coloured lights. Discos had become widely popular by the 1970s, having been first introduced in the USA in the mid-1960s with music provided by the popular *juke box. The kind of music used was mainly black in origin, such as played by Sly and the Family Stone. The record companies conscientiously produced special disco records with the beats per minute indicated for the help of DJs. For some time the disco remained a limited cult, but it became a widely accepted activity promoted by the film *Saturday Night Fever* (1977). Even pop enthusiasts tend to agree that the music associated with discos, with the most essential element a thumping regular bass and the other elements mainly ignored, has tended to produce a somewhat debased form of pop music.

Discography. The gramophone world's equivalent to bibliography; the listing, documentation, and description of recordings for the benefit of collectors. Pioneer work in discography mainly developed in jazz circles where knowledge of who played what and when was considered a necessary adjunct to listening in the 1930s, and it started in various periodicals. The first published jazz discography to establish itself was Charles Delauney's *Hot Discography* printed in Paris in 1936 and, as *New Hot Discography*, in the USA in 1948. In England, *Rhythm on Record* by Hilton R. Schleman had also appeared in 1936 but failed to propagate owing to its failure to offer systematic information. The first American magazine to concentrate its efforts on jazz discography was *Rag*, first published by the Hot Record Society in 1938. A discography is now considered as necessary an appendix to a musical biography or reference work as a bibliography, and the activity has now extended into all areas of popular music-making.

Distel, Sacha (*b* Paris, 29 Jan. 1933). French singer, guitarist, and composer. A nephew of the French bandleader Ray *Ventura, Distel took up the guitar at the age of 14 and joined his college jazz band at the Lycée Claud Bernard in Paris. Three years later he won an amateur contest and a few years after that was voted France's top guitarist for five years in succession. He played with many visiting American jazz musicians and recorded with John *Lewis and the *Modern Jazz Quartet. After war service he began to play and sing his own compositions, achieving his first minor hit in 1959; his biggest hit of all came in 1970 with his version of 'Raindrops keep falling on my head'.

His songs include: 'Scoubidou', 'Les Cariocas', 'Oui et non', 'Dites à l'orchestre', and 'Oh yeah-yeah-yeah' (all with Maurice Teze and *c.*1959); 'Calin Calinette', 'Sacha's theme' (1960); 'The good life' (1963); 'Now is now', 'That Italian summer', 'Sacha's tune' (1970); 'Most things are possible', 'More and more' (1971); 'How could I settle for less', 'Baby, I love you', and 'My first guitar' (1972).

Distin. A family of musicians who organized a famous virtuoso *brass band that had a great influence in its day, touring the British Isles and Europe. Many a *galop or *quadrille of the mid-1800s bore the inscription 'played by the Famous Distin Band'. The head of the family was John Henry Distin (1793–1863) who helped to develop the popular keyed bugle (forerunner of the cornet and trumpet) when he was a musician in the Grenadier Guards. He was the inventor of the 'ballad horn' (also known as the 'amateur voice horn' and 'vocal horn'), a non-transposing horn intended for amateur use, easy to play and with a mellow tone that gave 'a good imitation of a male voice'. The most celebrated member of the family after John Henry was Theodore Distin (1823–93) who studied with his father and played french horn in the band 1836–44. He gave this up to study singing and became a well-known operatic baritone and teacher. A family business, Distin & Sons, was opened in Cranbourn Street, off Leicester Square, in 1845, and was taken over by one of the sons, Henry, in 1849, to become one of the leading manufacturers of brass instruments. The firm, known as Henry Distin & Co., from 1849, was purchased by Boosey & Co. in 1868, but continued under the old name until 1874.

Dixey, Henry E. (*b* Boston, 6 Jan. 1859; *d* Atlantic City, 25 Feb. 1943). American actor and singer. He began his stage career in Boston 1875–9, becoming known on Broadway in **Adonis* (1884) which he wrote with the composer Edward *Rice. He also appeared in **Evangeline* (1877); *Babes in the Wood* (1879); *Fatinitza* (1880); *Billee Taylor* (1880); *The Merry Duchess* (1883); *Gayest Manhattan* (1897); **Erminie* (1898); *The Burgomaster* (1900); **Chu Chin Chow* (1917); and *The Merry Malones* (1928).

'Dixie'. Song first mentioned in the programme of Bryant's Minstrels as 'Mr Dan Emmett's original Plantation Song and Dance, *Dixie's Land*' in 1859; the words were first published that year and the music in New Orleans in 1860, crediting various composers and authors. It soon became a favourite of all minstrels as an inevitable finale number and became even more widely known when used in the show *Pocahontas* in 1860. Several broadside versions appeared during the Civil War years from *c.* 1861 and it became popular with both sides involved in the conflict. The first edition to credit its real creator, Daniel Decatur *Emmett, appeared in New York in 1860 when it was printed as 'I wish I was in Dixie's Land'. Although there have been many unresolved arguments as to where the name Dixie came from, it seems certain that the use of Dixie or Dixieland as a general name for the Southern states (and later the music that came from it) only started after the popularization of the word through the song.

H. Nathan: *Dan Emmett and the Rise of Early Negro Minstrelsy* (Norman, Okla., 1962).

Dixieland jazz. Name given to the brash, marching style of jazz that emerged in New Orleans around the turn of the century. Essentially a black jazz, a confusion arose through the association of the term with white groups such as the *Original Dixieland Jazz Band, and hence the term was often applied to such groups playing in the revivalist tradition.

Dixon, Reginald (*b* Sheffield, 1905; *d* Blackpool 9 May 1985). British organist. At 13 he was playing the organ in a local Methodist church and a few years later found employment as the organist in a silent cinema. In 1930 he was offered a job in the Tower Ballroom in Blackpool on a trial basis, for both him and the organ. He was to stay there, apart from a period during the war when he served in the RAF, until he retired in 1970; one of the best-known figures of the cinema organ heyday, a frequent broadcaster, and instantly recognizable from his apt signature tune 'I do like to be beside the seaside' and his bright and breezy style.

Dobro. A modified kind of guitar with raised strings and an inbuilt metal resonator in the front of the belly designed to produce an acoustically amplified sound. The name was derived from the first letters of Dopyera Brothers, i.e. John, Ed, and Randy Dopyera who originated the instrument in California in 1925. A feature of country music, it was most effectively employed by Roy *Acuff; while some of the principal users in country music today are Josh Graves, Bashful Brother Oswald, Mike Auldridge, and Tut Taylor.

Dockstader, Lew [Clapp, George Alfred] (*b* 1856; *d* 26 Oct. 1924). American minstrel. One of the great names of the American blackface minstrel scene, he became a professional in 1873 with Bloodgood's Comic Alliance and later the Emmett and Wilde Minstrels. In 1876 he organized a troupe with Charles Dockstader which was known as the Dockstader Brothers. Dockstader retired in 1883 but George Clapp (as he was then) retained the name both for himself and his troupe. He opened his own theatre on Broadway in 1886 and turned to vaudeville in 1890, toured in a minstrel duo with George Primrose from 1898–1913, and continued to perform until 1923. He did much to improve the status of the minstrel show by giving it a much more satirical edge.

Dodds, Johnny [John M.] (*b* Waverly, La., 12 Apr. 1892; *d* Chicago, 8 Aug. 1940). American jazz clarinettist. A pioneer jazz stylist with a forceful, invigorating but far from crude style which proved to be an ideal complement to the cornet of Louis *Armstrong in many early groups. He studied with Lorenzo Tio (1885–1933) and worked with Kid *Ory, King *Oliver, and Freddie *Keppard. Dodds was on the classic Hot Five recordings with Armstrong, worked with Jelly Roll *Morton, and made some recordings under his own name just as the jazz revival was beginning; but he died before he might have reaped the rewards. His brother Warren 'Baby' Dodds (*b* New Orleans, 24 Dec. 1898; *d* Chicago, 14 Feb. 1959), the youngest of six children, was equally well-known; a pioneer jazz drummer, his career followed much the same pattern. He suffered much ill-health from 1949 but played on and off until 1957.

G. E. Lambert: *Johnny Dodds* (London, 1961).

Dolan, Robert Emmett (*b* Hartford, Conn., 3 Aug. 1906; *d* California, 26 Sept. 1972). American conductor, composer, and arranger. He was very active on American radio in the 1930s as a conductor and was musical director for such Broadway shows as **Good News*, **Follow Thru*, *Flying Colors*, *Hooray for What?*, *Very Warm for May*, and **Louisiana Purchase*. In the 1940s he worked mainly in the film world and composed or arranged scores for *Star-Spangled Rhythm* (1943); **Lady in the Dark* (1944); *The Bells of St Mary's* (1945); *Salty O'Rourke* (1945); *Murder, He Says* (1945); *Incendiary Blonde* (1945); *Blue Skies* (1946); and *Road to Rio* (1946). He wrote the scores for the musicals *Texas, Li'l Darlin'* (1949) and *Foxy* (1964). His songs included: 'At last I'm in love', 'Little by little', 'Red hot rhythm', 'Out of the past', 'You', 'Here is my heart', and 'It's great to be alive'.

Dollarprinzessin, Die. Musical play in three acts with music by Leo *Fall, book by A. M. Willner and Fritz Grunbäum, based on a comedy by Gatti-Trotha. It was an immediate success when staged at the Carl Theater, Vienna, 2 Nov. 1907, with a scintillating score and a cast that included Mizzi Guenther, Luise Kartousch, and Louis Treuman. It was to pursue a successful career as *The Dollar Princess* all over the world, in Manchester (Princes Theatre) 24 Dec. 1908, with English book by Basil *Hood and Adrian *Ross; New York (Knickerbocker Theatre) 6 Sept. 1909, with added music by Jerome *Kern and Edmund *Eysler; in London (*Daly's Theatre) 25 Sept. 1909, with a fine cast that included Joseph *Coyne, Lily *Elsie, Robert Michaelis, W. H. *Berry, and Gladys Cooper, conducted by Ivan *Caryll, running for 428 performances. There was a London revival in 1925 with Evelyn *Laye and Carl *Brisson. The work is frequently played in Austria and Germany and its songs are often recorded.

Dolly Sisters. Popular act in American vaudeville and revues, beautiful and glamorous sisters who were born in Hungary and raised in New York: Jennie [Janszieka Deutsch] (*b* 1902; *d* 1 June 1941) and Rosie [Roszicka Deutsch] (*b* 25 Oct. 1892; *d* 1970). Their speciality was dancing, but they also sang and acted well and were a great hit in such Broadway musicals as *The Echo* (1910); **Ziegfeld Follies* (1911); *A Winsome Widow* (1912); *Oh, Look!* (1918); and **Greenwich Village Follies* (1924). They also appeared in straight plays and in Paris revues in the 1920s, and in London in the revue *The League of Notions* (1921). A film of their lives, *The Dolly Sisters*, was made in 1945 with Betty *Grable as Jennie and June Haver (*b* 1926) as Rosie reviving their songs and dances.

Dolphy, Eric Allan (*b* Los Angeles, 20 June 1928; *d* Berlin, 29 June 1964). American jazz alto-saxophonist, flautist, and clarinettist. He started playing clarinet at school and first worked with various West Coast groups and with army bands 1950–2. He joined the Chico Hamilton quintet in 1958; and first went to New York in 1959 to work with Charlie *Mingus. He was with John *Coltrane 1961–2, rejoined Mingus in 1964, then freelanced in the short period before his untimely death from diabetes. In the six years that he was playing in top-class company, Dolphy had an influence on the jazz scene that has been likened to that of *Beiderbecke, *Blanton, or Charlie *Christian, particularly in finding a role in modern jazz for such instruments as the bass-clarinet and flute; showing how effective they could be in such masterly hands as his; and leading the way towards free and unfettered jazz.

V. Simosko & B. Tepperman: *Eric Dolphy: a Musical Biography and Discography* (New York, 1971). U. Reichardt: *Like a Human Voice: the Eric Dolphy Discography* (Schnitten, 1986). R. Horricks: *The Importance of Being Eric Dolphy* (Tunbridge Wells, 1989).

Domino, Fats [Antoine] (*b* New Orleans, 26 Feb. 1928). American rock pianist and bandleader. He badly injured his hands as a youth but persevered with his playing and overcame the difficulties. His playing represents much that is best in the spirit of rock and roll; humorous, warm, seemingly spontaneous and effortless. His style is clearly New Orleans-based, showing discernible influence of pianists like Albert *Ammons with his full-chorded boogie flavour and trilling right hand. He uses the characteristic devices of New Orleans jazz and gospel music to build up a kind of dance-hall atmosphere in his performances. He was one of the first black artists to get into the best-selling charts with a string of hits in the 1950s, beginning with his first release 'The fat man' (1950) which sold more than a million copies; and such classics as 'Ain't that a shame' (1955); 'Blueberry Hill' (1956), and 'Blue Monday' (1957). On his early records he sang with a high-pitched fervour that became slightly less rough in his later recordings.

As he moved further into rock and roll and away from rhythm 'n' blues his voice deepened and his playing became more disciplined, much helped by the guidance of his partner, arranger, and record supervisor, former jazz trumpeter Dave Bartholomew. He was in top form in the mid-1950s through to the early 1960s and in 'Walkin' to New Orleans' (1960). At this time he was rivalling Elvis *Presley as one of the world's top-selling rock artists. He may not have surpassed this peak but remained happy to revive his old hits with the same relaxed charm, his music communicating a sense of happiness with apparent effortlessness.

Donahue, Jack (*b* Charleston, Mass., 1892; *d* New York, 1 Oct. 1930). American actor, singer, dancer, and librettist. He played in vaudeville with a 'shadow dance' routine and a light and loose-limbed style, later developing as a singer and a comic actor. He was in *Angel Face* (1919); **Ziegfeld Follies* (1920); *Molly Darling* (1922); *Be Yourself* (1924); becoming widely known through his partnership with Marilyn *Miller in **Sunny* (1925) and **Rosalie* (1928); and as the star of *Sons o' Guns* (1929).

J. Donahue: *Letters of a Hoofer to his Ma* (New York, 1930/1).

Donahue, Sam [Koontz, Samuel] (*b* Detroit, 18 Mar. 1918; *d* Reno, Nevada, 22 Mar. 1974). American bandleader and saxophonist. He led his first band in Detroit in the 1930s and it was taken over by Sonny Burke when Donahue joined the Gene *Krupa band in 1938. He was with Harry *James and Benny *Goodman in 1940, before taking over his original band again in 1942. During military serice he led Artie *Shaw's Navy Band. In 1946 he formed his finest band, a swinging outfit playing excellent arrangements. He joined Tommy *Dorsey in 1951, leaving in 1953 to form yet another band, and in 1954 he took over the Billy *May band. He was with Stan *Kenton 1960–1; then took over the Tommy Dorsey orchestra in 1961 which later became a backing unit for Frank *Sinatra. He was music director of the Playboy Club in New York. From 1969 he led a band in Reno until he contracted cancer.

Donaldson, Walter (*b* Brooklyn, NY, 15 Feb. 1893; *d* Santa Monica, Calif., 15 July 1947). American composer. He worked for a New York broker before entering music-publishing as a songplugger/pianist. He entertained the troops during the First World War, then joined Irving *Berlin's publishing company. By 1928 he had formed his own company. He wrote scores for the Broadway productions *Sweetheart Time* (1926) and **Whoopee* (1928).

He went to Hollywood in the 1930s to join the swelling army of film composers and his scores included: *Glorifying the American Girl* (1929); *Kansas City Kitty* (1929); *Hot for Paris* (1929); *The Prize Fighter and the Lady* (1933); *Kid Millions* (1934); *Let's Talk It Over* (1934); *Million Dollar Ransom* (1934); *Hollywood Party* (1934); *Reckless* (1935); *Here Comes the Band* (1935); *Piccadilly Jim* (1936); *Suzy* (1936); *The Great Ziegfeld* (1936); *Sinner Take All* (1937); *That's Right—You're Wrong* (1939); *Broadway Serenade* (1940); *Two Girls on Broadway* (1941); **Panama Hattie* (1942); *Give Out Sister* (1942); and *Follow the Boys* (1944).

Among his prodigious output of songs he is remembered for: 'Aba daba honeymoon' (1914); 'Back home in Tennessee' (1915); 'The daughter of Rosie O'Grady' (1918); 'How you gonna keep 'em down on the farm' (1919); 'Tired of me' (1920); 'My mammy' (1921); 'Carolina in the morning' (1922); 'Georgia' (1922); 'Beside a babbling brook' (1923); 'My best girls' (1924); 'Let it rain, let it pour' (1925); 'That certain party' (1925); 'Yes sir, that's my baby' (1925); 'Where'd you get those eyes' (1926); 'After I say I'm sorry' (1926); 'At sundown' (1927); 'My blue heaven' (1927, *w* George Whiting, 1884–1943); 'Makin' whoopee' (1928); 'Love me or leave me' (1928); 'Tain't no sin' (1930); 'Little white lies' (1930); 'My baby just cares for me' (1930), among many others.

Donegan, Lonnie [Anthony] (*b* Glasgow, 29 Apr. 1931). British singer and guitarist. His first interest was in folk-music, but he took up the guitar at 17 and began to play jazz. After playing in a jazz group in the army he joined the Ken *Colyer band and began to play *skiffle. In 1951 he formed his own group and changed his name to Lonnie after working with the fine guitarist and singer Lonnie Johnson. He joined the Chris *Barber band in 1953 and in 1954 recorded 'Rock Island Line' which caught on in 1956 and sparked off a skiffle craze and an unparalleled sale of guitars and washboards. He started a solo career in 1956 and continued to record a series of similarly styled hits such as 'Lost John' (1956); 'Cumberland Gap' (1957); 'My Dixie darling' (1957); 'Putting on the style' (1957); 'Don't you rock me, daddy-o' (1957); 'Battle of New Orleans' (1959); 'My old man's a dustman' (1960); and 'Pick a bale of cotton' (1962). He moved into show-business and worked in a comedy vein. The onset of heavy rock in the 1960s put his kind of music out of the top fashion bracket, but he continued as a popular entertainer in cabaret.

Donovan [Leitch, Donovan] (*b* Glasgow, 10 May 1946). British singer and guitarist. He first came to notice on TV in 1965 hailed as a potential British answer to Bob *Dylan and continued the pastiche with similar clothing, props, and material as in his first recorded hit 'Catch the wind' (1965). He found his own personal folk-pop style in 1966 and recorded 'Sunshine superman' (1966) and 'Mellow yellow' (1967). The drug culture intruded into his work in 1968—superseded by Eastern mysticism and songs like 'Barabajagal' in 1969. In 1972 he wrote the score for and appeared in the film *The Pied Piper* and in 1973 in *Brother Sun, Sister Moon*. The decline of flower-power culture saw the decline and virtual retirement of Donovan in the 1970s though he occasionally emerged thereafter.

Donovan, Dan (*b* Cardiff, 1901; *d* S. Wales, 6 Dec. 1986). British singer who first became known as an early 'crooning' star in the Rudy *Vallee image in the 1920s and the pioneering days of radio. He sang with the bands of Bert *Ambrose, Harry *Roy, Roy *Fox, Lew *Stone, Nat *Gonella, and Charlie *Kunz, becoming especially popular in his period with Henry *Hall. He made more than 8000 broadcasts and recorded such hits as 'Red sails in the sunset' and 'When day is done' which became his signature tune when he toured as a solo act in the 1930s. He became a publican in Wales after retirement from the music world.

Don't Bother Me, I Can't Cope. Musical produced at the Playhouse Theatre, New York, 19 Apr. 1972 which took a pleasantly tongue-in-cheek though none the less pointed look at some of the social problems of black people in America. Starting as a small theatre production, it was seen in various towns before opening on Broadway and justifying itself with a run of 1065 performances. The score, a mixture of gospel, rock, calypso, and folk-music, was by Micki Grant and the show was conceived and directed by Vinnette Carroll.

Doonican, Val (*b* Waterford, 3 Feb. 1928). Irish singer and entertainer. After many amateur ventures, he first began a professional career in 1947 playing guitar in a small dance band. After long service as a band guitarist and drummer he joined a vocal group, the Four Ramblers, and came to London with them in 1952 to broadcast. While doing his song-and-guitar act in a cabaret, he was given a regular TV spot, followed by a successful radio series that led to his own TV programme which ran for 120 weeks. He now quickly moved into the big time in cabaret and variety and really made his mark in an appearance in *Sunday Night at the London Palladium*. He achieved his first hit record with 'Walk tall' in 1964 and thereafter became a favourite with his 'live' TV series.

V. Doonican: *The Special Years* (London, 1980).

Doors, The. American psychedelic rock group formed in 1965 with the original personnel of Jim Morrison (vocal), Ray Manzarek (*b* 1935) (keyboard), Robby Krieger (*b* 1946) (bass), and John Densmore (*b* 1945) (drums). The group's activities revolved around the bizarre personality and talents of Jim Morrison (James Douglas Morrison, the son of a rear-admiral, *b* Melbourne, Fla., 8 Dec. 1943; *d* Paris, 3 July 1971). Soon after the group's beginnings they were banned from the famous Whiskey-a-Go-Go Club in Los Angeles for a performance of 'The end', in which a young man murders his parents. Mixed with other appurtenances of drug-culture and psychedelia, 'The end' was included in their sensation-seeking first album, *Doors*, in 1967. The group continued with its commercial exploitation of anarchy, sex, and drug-taking, producing such hits as 'Light my fire' (1967), 'People are strange' (1967), 'Hello, I love you' (1968), 'Touch me' (1969), 'Love her madly' (1971), and 'Riders on the storm' (1971), Morrison being regularly arrested for various transgressions; they reached a disturbing apex with their album *La Woman* in 1971. Worn out by a life of sex, drugs, drink, and rock, Morrison left the group that year to live in Paris where he was reputed to have died of a heart attack in his bath. Some claim he still lives. The survivors continued their joint activities into the early 1980s.

Doo-wop. Descriptive term applied to the style of singing used by rhythm 'n' blues groups of the 1950s, an imitation of the sort of backing phrases frequently employed. It had its beginnings in the sort of vocal work that such groups as the *Ink Spots made popular in the 1940s. Doo-woppery and R & B in general became a craze around 1953–4, starting with a group called the Orioles and 'Crying in the chapel' and leading to the great commercial success of groups like the *Platters, *Coasters, *Drifters, and Cleftones (1955). It was a simple and effective vocal development of the jazz riff and remained a popular device into the 1960s after the original black concept had been almost done to death by its white imitators, banded in innumerable groups with fanciful names. Doo-wop belonged to an era when a certain politeness and sweetness still lingered in pop performance.

Do-Re-Mi. American musical comedy with score by Jule *Styne, book by Garson Kanin, lyrics by Betty *Comden and Adolph *Green, opening at the St James Theatre, New York, 26 Dec. 1960. The cast included Phil Silvers (1912–85) and Nancy Walker (*b* 1921) and it ran for 400 performances. The London production at the Prince of Wales Theatre 12 Oct. 1961 starred Maggie Fitzgibbon and Max *Bygraves. The show was a satire on the juke-box industry, with Phil Silvers in his habitual wide-boy role employing three mobsters to make a litle loot from the racket. The songs included 'It's legitimate', 'I know about love', 'Cry like the wind', 'What's new at the Zoo?', and 'Make someone happy'.

Dorothy. A now neglected comic opera (originally staged as *Nell Gwynne* in 1876) which has its place in history as the show which outran its contemporary *The *Mikado* when staged at the *Gaiety Theatre, London, on 25 Sept. 1886. Its composer, Alfred *Cellier, had been the conductor at the *Savoy until he left with the intention of rivalling the Savoyards and did so, much to the annoyance of both *Sullivan and *Gilbert. *Dorothy* ran (after being transferred to the Prince of Wales Theatre, 20 Dec. 1886, and the Lyric Theatre, 17 Dec. 1888) for 931 performances on the strength of a pleasant score with such numbers as 'Be wise in time, O Phyllis mine' and a later addition 'Queen of my heart'. Marion Hood (1853–1912), later replaced by Marie *Tempest, and Hayden *Coffin were its stars and it had revivals in 1892 and 1908. It was also produced in New York at the Standard Theatre, 5 Nov. 1887, with Lillian *Russell in the lead, conducted by Ivan *Caryll [48p].

Dorsey, Jimmy [James Francis] (*b* Shenandoah, Penn., 29 Feb. 1904; *d* New York, 12 June 1957). American bandleader, saxophonist, and composer. He was taught (along with his younger brother Tommy) by their bandmaster father. They formed their own band while still teenagers, but this failed and they joined a band known as the Scranton Sirens. Sometimes with his brother, Jimmy played with various bands, including those of Paul *Whiteman and Jean *Goldkette and with the *California Ramblers as well as numerous studio orchestras and recording groups. A Dorsey band had existed on and off for some time on an *ad hoc* basis, but the two formed the famous Dorsey Brothers Orchestra as a permanent unit in April 1934. One of their frequent disagreements resulted in Tommy leaving to form his own band in 1935 and the start of a cooling in their relationship that was to last for some 10 years. Jimmy was an easy-going sort of person while Tommy was full of ruthless drive, so they never got on easily.

Jimmy continued to lead the old orchestra with Bobby Byrne as a replacement for his brother on trombone. The Jimmy Dorsey band had a highly successful run in the 1930s swing era with good arrangements that ideally highlighted the vocal talents of Bob Eberly, Kay Weber, and June Richmond (1915–62). The arrangers he used included Larry *Clinton, Bobby Van Eps, Skeets Herfurt, Fud Livingston, and Toots Camarata. The band's theme song was Jimmy's own 'Contrasts' and they had early hits with his 'John Silver' and 'Dusk in Upper Sandusky'. Helen O'Donnell joined the band to team with Eberly in 1939 and the band had its most successful period in the early 1940s, cashing in on the Latin American craze with 'Green eyes', 'Yours', 'Maria Elena' and 'Amapola' (best-sellers of 1941), and other swing items such as 'Blue champagne', 'Time was', 'Embraceable you', 'Tangerine', and with Joe Lippman, Hal Mooney, and Don *Redman added to the list of arrangers. The band featured in films: **Lady Be Good* (1941); *The *Fleet's In* (1942); *I Dood It* (1943); *Lost in a Harem* (1944); *Four Jills in a Jeep* (1944); *Hollywood Canteen* (1944); *Music Man* (1948); *Make Believe Ballroom* (1949).

A biographical film, *The Fabulous Dorseys* (1947), brought the brothers together again and they formed another joint band in 1953 which survived until Tommy's death in 1956. Jimmy continued until ill-health forced him to retire in 1957. While never at the very top of the swing world, Jimmy led a quality band with an individual sound based on his own playing. He wrote such songs as 'Just lately' (1937), 'It's the dreamer in me' (1938), 'So many times' (1939), and 'I'm glad there is you' (1941), as well as numerous instrumental pieces played by the orchestra.

D. Sanford: *Tommy and Jimmy; the Dorsey Years* (New York, 1970).

Dorsey, Lee (*b* Portland, Or., 24 Dec. 1924; *d* New Orleans, 1 Dec. 1986). American rhythm 'n' blues singer. He sang for many years before becoming popular in the 1950s with songs like 'Ya ya' and 'Do re mi'. He performed in an energetic manner with a raw but attractive voice and had hits with 'Working in the coal mine' and 'Ride your pony', reaching his peak in the 1960s with much of his material from the pen of the gifted New Orleans composer Allan *Toussaint. Often a gimmicky singer, Dorsey was well able to handle more subtle material such as Toussaint's deeply felt civil rights ballad 'Freedom for the stallion'.

Dorsey, Thomas A[ndrew] (*b* Villa Rica, Ga., 1 July 1899; *d* Chicago, 23 Jan. 1993). American singer, pianist, guitarist, and composer. Brought up in a Baptist family, his father a minister, he started to write music as a boy and studied it in Chicago around 1916. He worked as a club pianist and as accompanist to Ma *Rainey, arranged for Chicago publishers, and began to record, often under the name of Georgia Tom, producing such items as 'Beedle um bum' and 'Sellin' that stuff' in 1928. He moved into the area of gospel music, being credited with the coining of the term 'gospel song'. Cheaply printed gospel song sheets which he sold were known as 'Dorseys' for many years. He wrote and accompanied gospel music and formed vocal groups, one of his first popular items in this field being 'If you see my Saviour' (1930). That year he formed a publishing business, worked with Sallie Martin (*b* 1896), who wrote 'Nearer my God to Thee', and discovered Clara Ward and Mahalia *Jackson. He toured with the Gospel Choral Union, 1932–44, and formed an association of gospel choirs. He established gospel music on a national basis and wrote more than 1000 songs, including 'Peace in the Valley', 'Take my hand, precious Lord', and 'Sweet bye and bye'.

Dorsey, Tommy [Thomas Francis] (*b* Shenandoah, Penn., 19 Nov. 1905; *d* Greenwich, Conn., 26 Nov. 1956). American bandleader, trombonist, and composer. After leaving the 1934 Dorsey Brothers Orchestra in 1935 (see DORSEY, JIMMY, above), Tommy took over the Joe Haymes band at the McAlpin Hotel in New York and with Paul *Weston and Axel Stordhal as arrangers set about creating his own very individual style, an expert blend of sweet music and swing. With 'I'm getting sentimental over you' (1932, *m* George Bassman, *b* 1914; *w* Ned *Washington) as his theme tune, he soon became known as 'The Sentimental Gentleman of Swing', his own solos played in a remarkably smooth and gentle legato manner that hardly anyone had thought possible on the trombone until then. It became widely imitated and even a model for the singers he used, such as Frank *Sinatra, who was his star vocalist 1940–2, Connie Haines, Jo *Stafford, Dick *Haymes, and the Pied Pipers. Sy *Oliver became his most important arranger in 1939 and others who contributed were Deane Kincaide (*b* 1911) and Bill *Finegan, leading to such big hits as 'Who?', 'Blue moon', 'Marie' (1937), 'Song of India', adapted by Dorsey from Rimsky-Korsakov's 'Chanson d'Hindou', 'Boogie woogie' (1938); later 'Once in a while', 'Music, maestro, please', Sy Oliver's arrangements—'On the sunny side of the street', 'Opus 1', and 'Well, git it'; and 'Trombonology' (Dorsey, 1947). A string section was added in 1942.

During the 1940s the band appeared in several films: *Las Vegas Nights* (1941); *Ship Ahoy* (1942); *Presenting Lily Mars* (1942); **Dubarry Was a Lady* (1943); **Girl Crazy* (1943); *Broadway Rhythm* (1944); *Thrill of a Romance* (1945); *A Song is Born* (1948); *Disc Jockey* (1951); while both the Dorseys appeared together again in *The Fabulous Dorseys* (1947). They rejoined in 1953 to form another Dorsey Brothers Band, Tommy dying in 1956 when he choked to death in his sleep after a heavy meal. The Tommy Dorsey band was one of the finest and most influential units of the swing era, constantly exploring new ground and pioneering the sweet and swinging sound that so many others were to use in the 1940s and 1950s.

D. Sanford: *Tommy and Jimmy: The Dorsey Years* (New York, 1970).

Dostal, Nico (*b* Korneuburg, 27 Nov. 1895; *d* Vienna, 27 Oct. 1981). Austrian composer. He was the nephew of Hermann Dostal (1874–1930), a well-known composer of military band music, and his grandfather had also been a bandmaster. Coming from such a musical family, he was soon involved in musical activities; he was organist at his local church while still at school and wrote a mass in 1913. In 1914 he went to Vienna to study law, but switched to the Academy of Church Music in Klosterneuberg until he joined the army in 1915 and served with the infantry in Russia and Italy. In 1919 he played in the orchestra of the Stadttheater in Innsbruck, worked in Romania for a while, and by 1923 was in Salzburg. His first operetta, *Lagunenzauber*, was produced in Graz in 1923, but made no mark, and from 1925 to 1933 he worked mainly in Berlin as an arranger (including Kollo's *Drei arme kleine Mädel* and *Stolz's *Zwei Herzen in Dreivierteltakt*) and held various posts as a theatre conductor. He wrote a great deal of light orchestral and dance music and in 1932 started writing for films. In Berlin in 1933 he at last had success as an operetta composer with *Clivia* (starring Lillie Claus) which was then followed by a regular output of stage works until around 1963. These included: *Die Vielgeliebte* (1934); *Prinzessin Nofretete* (1935); *Extrablätter* (1937); *Monika* (1937); *Die Flucht ins Glück* (1940); *Manina* (1942); *Zirkusblut* (1951); *Dr Eisenbart* (1952); *Rhapsodie der Liebe* (1963); his biggest and most lasting success being *Die ungarische Hochzeit*, first produced in Stuttgart 4 Feb. 1939. He married Lillie Claus in 1942 and thereafter lived mainly in Salzburg, being active as a teacher from 1959.

Dostal's music has all the lively traditional elements of Viennese and Hungarian operetta, with the usual emphasis on the waltz and a natural affinity with the march. Into a generally sentimental vein he also successfully integrated a modern jazz touch and thus helped to keep the operetta spirit alive and kicking into the 1960s. His film scores included: *Kaiserwalzer* (1932); *Fiakerlied* (1936); *Dreizehn Stühle* (1938); *Mordsache Holm* (1938); *Das Lied der Wüste* (1939); *Die Geierwally* (1940); *Glück bei Frauen* (1944). His best-known light orchestral pieces are 'Spanische Skizzen' (1930); 'In meinen Bergen' (1944); 'Lyrische Szenen' (1955); and 'Orientalische Skizzen' (1958).

Dowling, Eddie [Goucher, Joseph Nelson] (*b* Woonsocket, RI, 11 Dec. 1895; *d* 1976). American composer, lyricist, playwright, actor, and producer. He started out as a boy soprano and sang on a world tour with the St Paul's, Providence, cathedral choir, then went into repertory. He married the British entertainer Ray Dooley and they toured the vaudeville circuit 1911–19. He appeared in **Ziegfeld Follies* (1918 and 1920); *The Velvet Lady* (1919); and *The Girl in the Spotlight* (1920); then had a considerable success in *Sally, Irene and Mary* (1922) and *Honeymoon Lane* (1926), also writing the book and lyrics and producing the latter, as he did for *Sidewalks of New York* (1927) in which his wife also appeared. He played in and produced *Thumbs Up* (1934). He appeared in the film *The Rainbow Man* (1929) and, with his wife, in the 1931 film version of *Honeymoon Lane*. In 1936 he worked with the Benny *Goodman band on the Elgin radio show.

Most of his subsequent career was spent as a producer of Broadway plays, being awarded a Pulitzer Prize for *The Time of Your Life* in 1940 and the Drama Critic's Award for three other productions. He retired from show-business in the 1950s. In collaboration with such composers as James F. *Hanley, Victor *Herbert, J. Fred *Coots, and others he wrote or composed such songs as 'The little white house', 'Sally, Irene and Mary', 'Honeymoon Lane', 'Little log cabin of dreams', 'High up on a housetop', 'Time will tell', and 'Sidewalks of New York'.

'Down at the Old Bull and Bush'. Latter-day music-hall song which has traditionally been used as a favourite final chorus in *Good Old Days*-type revivals such as were regularly televised from Leeds and flourished at the Player's Theatre in London. Although sounding eminently British, it is of American origin and was first popularized in Britain by Florrie *Forde. On tour in the USA she heard a Harry *Von Tilzer song that was being made into a great hit in 1902 by Nora *Bayes, 'Down where the Wurzburger flows'. Forde brought the song back to England and found herself sharply criticized for singing songs about foreign rivers, so she seized upon another Von Tilzer hit, an equally blatant melody with words by Andrew B. *Sterling, 'Under the Anheuser Bush' (1903), and had the words adapted by Messrs Sterling, Russell Hunting, and Percy Krone into their now very familiar form 'Down at the Old Bull and Bush'. It was an immediate hit; and just shows that nothing can be taken at its face value in *Tin Pan Alley.

Down Beat. American bi-weekly magazine founded and edited by Jack Maher in 1934. Intended initially for the professional dance band and jazz musician, it continues to have interest for a wider readership of enthusiasts by virtue of its good jazz coverage and its yearly awards. A series of *Down Beat* yearbooks was published from 1954.

'Down by the old mill stream'. American song with music and words by Tell Taylor, published in Chicago in 1910. An original credit to Earl Smith as co-author was not perpetuated in later editions. Taylor was a songwriter who was born in Vanlue, near Findlay, Ohio, in 1876 and died in Chicago in 1937. His song became immensely popular, particularly in *barber-shop circles, and sold four million copies in its first year of publication.

Dragon, Carmen (*b* Antioch, Calif., 28 July 1914; *d* Santa Monica, Calif., 28 Mar. 1984). American conductor, composer, and arranger. He learned to play a number of instruments, studied at San Jose State College, then started his musical career as a nightclub pianist in San Francisco. He went to Hollywood to work as an arranger, winning an Academy Award for his work, with Morris Stolof, on Jerome *Kern's score for *Cover Girl* in 1944. He began conducting for radio shows; and he won great popularity for his concerts of light music and his association, over a number of years, with the Hollywood Bowl orchestra. He wrote the patriotic song 'I'm an American'.

Drake, Alfred [Capurro, Alfred] (*b* New York, 7 Oct. 1914; *d* New York, 25 July 1992). American singer. He made his stage debut in 1933 in the chorus of *Gilbert and Sullivan operettas, moving from the chorus as an understudy in **White Horse Inn* (1936). He had a small part in **Babes in Arms* (1937); then appeared in *Two Bouquets* (1938); *One For the Money* (1939); and *Straw Hat Revue* (1939). His rich baritone voice found its métier in the hit show **Oklahoma!* (1943) which was followed by *Sing Out, Sweet Land* (1944) and *Beggar's Holiday* (1947), before his long-running appearances in **Kiss Me, Kate* (1949) and **Kismet* (1953). After this he acted in Shakespeare, appeared in various TV productions, and starred in the musical *Kean* in 1961.

Drawing-room ballads. Songs which had little connection with the traditional *ballad apart from occasionally telling a story. They were mainly songs of the strophic kind (a number of verses to an identical melody, and probably with repeated chorus), often of a romantic or sentimental nature and of a polite character that made them suitable, as the name suggests, for the Victorian family drawing-room. There were also the more robust male songs of the 'open road', 'roaring main', or patriotic variety.

The drawing-room ballad flourished throughout the 19th century and into the early years of the 20th, beginning around 1800 when cheaper music-printing methods were being discovered. The origins of the genre are to be found in the kind of songs that were to be heard in the London pleasure gardens, some written by eminent composers like J. C. Bach and Handel, deriving from the fashionable Italian opera but with simplified melodies and accompaniments that were technically within the capacity of the amateur performer. Another factor that helped to promote the drawing-room culture was the development of the parlour piano. Broadwood and other pioneers, having abandoned the harpsichord, were considerably expanding the piano market by the early 1800s, turning out hundreds of models each year. By 1830 the makers of cheaper models like D'Almain were advertising them at around 7 to 12 guineas. London was becoming the centre of the piano boom; and by 1851 visitors to the Great Exhibition could see a wide range of instruments—some 66 models from English makers, 45 from France, and 26 from Germany, where both the Bechstein and Blüthner businesses were set up in 1853 as was the Steinway business in New York. This all had a direct link with the publisher's ability to market drawing-room music.

It is not easy to pinpoint the first genuine 'drawing-room' ballad. Many folk-song arrangements or folk-style songs might be accepted into the category; but the slightly 'higher-class' ballad, with a distinctively operatic nature and typical arpeggio accompaniment, became established in such songs as those written by William *Shield—'The Arethusa', 'The wolf'—and isolated items drawn from the popular British operas of the period. The tradition flourished with the professional composers like Sir Henry Bishop providing such basic classics as *'Home, sweet home' and 'My pretty Jane', on to Michael William Balfe (1808–70) and his *Bohemian Girl* (1843) arias, and 'Come into the garden, Maud' (1856). Other popular early items were 'Kathleen Mavourneen' (1839) by Frederick William Crouch (1808–96), 'When the swallows homeward fly' (1846) by Franz Abt (1819–85), 'Mary of Argyle' (1860) by Sidney Nelson (1800–62), and 'Alice, where art thou' (1861) by Joseph Ascher (1828–69) and Wellington Guernsey (1817–55). After these professional initiatives the drawing-room song became very much a field for the dilettante composer—especially musically talented young ladies of the Victorian household, with nothing much else to do, setting the words of sentimental poetasters and popular lyrics from English literary sources. Many of them became professional simply because commerce grabbed their delicate works and made them into best-sellers. If the goodness and purity of the songs that these respectable ladies produced has given rise to much mirth in our present cynical times, they must still be judged on their musical craftsmanship which was often first-class.

By the 1860s such publishers as Chappell and many others were finding the ballad market a most profitable line, with a middle-class clientele to rival the growing lower-class audience for the *music-hall, the two spheres occasionally overlapping. In 1859, Chappell had begun the serious promotion of their ballad sales with their Popular Concerts, soon better-known, as they became more and more devoted to song, as Ballad Concerts. The original series of 'Monday Pops' started at the new St James's Hall in 1859 became exclusively ballad concerts under John Boosey and his son William, moving to the Queen's Hall in 1905 when St James's Hall was demolished. Chappell took a lease of the hall and the Boosey and Chappell Ballad Concerts were given there on alternate Saturdays. The performers included such respected names as Antoinette Sterling, Sainton-Dolby, Sims Reeves, Edward Lloyd, Sir Charles Santley, Foli, Maybrick (*Adams), Clara Novello, Liza *Lehmann, and many others whose names were boldly printed on the published sheets; 'sung by ***** to great applause'. The ballad business flourished throughout the 19th century, the final decline only being brought about in the gramophone and radio age of the 20th century when the new jazz influence swept the old styles away.

The nature of many drawing-room ballads made it a sphere where the lady composer flourished with Liza *Lehmann, Frances Allitsen, Florence Aylward, Teresa *Del Riego, Guy D'*Hardelot, Isidore de Lara (1858–1935), Ellen Dickson (1819–78), and Amy *Woodforde-Finden among the better-known names. The men took over in the latter part of the century as the songs tended to become more robust—with names like William Michael Watson (1840–89)—'Anchored'; Milton Wellings (1850–1929)—'At the ferry', 'Turnham Toll'; Théophile Marzials (1850–1920)—'Twickenham Ferry'; Frank L. Moir (1852–1904)—'Down the vale'; Ernest Newton (1860–1929)—'Going to Kildare'; the most successful and prominent being J. L. *Molloy, Stephen *Adams, and Wilfred *Sanderson. The tradition was then carried to its end by such as Eric *Coates and Haydn *Wood, who brought the drawing-room ballad to the cultural fringes of the art song. The true drawing-room ballad period came to end, as did other Victorian hangovers like the *music-hall and *musical comedy, with the First World War. Its last manifestations were in songs like 'Somewhere a voice is calling' by Arthur F. Tate (1870–1950), 'I'll walk beside you' by Alan Murray (1890–1952), and 'The floral dance' by Katie Moss (1887–1947).

British ballads were heavily imported to the USA from the early 19th century on but, as in other spheres of musical activity, the Americans soon came up with a strong tradition; with a background of pleasure gardens, booming publishing business and ballad concerts of their own and academics like Ethelbert *Nevin and Edward MacDowell vying, as in Britain, with the specialist balladeers like Oley *Speaks, and a host of amateurs.

Similar traditions flourished in Europe, notably in France, Germany, and Italy in appropriate but parallel styles and at roughly the same time.

H. Simpson: *A Century of Ballads 1810–1910: their Composers and Singers* (London, 1910). W. Boosey: *Fifty Years of Music* (London, 1931). C. Pulling: *They Were Singing: and What They Sang About* (London, 1952). M. W. Disher: *Victorian Song: from Dive to Drawing-Room* (London, 1955). M. R. Turner (ed.): *The Parlour Song Book: a Casquet of Vocal Gems* (London, 1972). J. S. Bratton: *The Victorian Popular Ballad* (London, 1975). M. R. Turner (ed.): *Just a Song at Twilight: the Second Parlour Song Book* (London, 1975). M. R. Turner (ed.): *The Edwardian Song Book* (London, 1982).

***Dreigroschenoper, Die* (The Threepenny Opera).** Singspiel in three acts with music by Kurt *Weill and book by Bertolt *Brecht, an updated version of John *Gay's *The *Beggar's Opera*. It was first produced at the Theatre am Schiffbauerdam in Berlin 31 Aug. 1928, with Lotte *Lenya, Erika Helmke, Kurt Gerron, Erich Ponto, and Willy Trenke-Trebitsch in the cast and Theo Mackeben as musical director. Its cynical, tongue-in-cheek, satirical nature had an influence in Germany as profound as, and more disturbing than, *The Beggar's Opera* had in England 200 years earlier; although the hopeful morality that Brecht preached throughout his works could not hope to influence the political course of events in Germany. The work had something like 4000 performances in its first year. Its songs, especially 'Mack the Knife', have become classics; but its flavour, perhaps because of Weill's inimitability, has remained more or less unique, except where the style of Brecht brushed off on to other composers such as Eisler and Dessau. It was performed in Vienna in 1929 and made a fleeting appearance in New York in 1933.

In the aftermath of the war the impact of the work was, if anything, sharpened by its nostalgic edge and it came to typify the sinister undertones of German history and morality. The later successful performances in English have largely been in the revised version by Marc *Blitzstein, as in New York at the De Lys Theatre 10 Mar. 1953. That production had to be curtailed, but when the show returned by demand on 20 Sept. 1955 it ran for 2611 performances. There were notable productions in London in 1956 and 1965 and it was filmed in 1930.

Dresser, Paul [Dreiser] (*b* Terre Haute, Ind., 21 Apr. 1857; *d* New York, 30 Jan. 1906). American composer. One of 13 children of a family of German descent; a younger brother was Theodore Dreiser who became a well-known novelist. He left home at 20 to join a travelling medicine show as a singing attraction, and joined the Buckingham Theatre stock company as 'Paul Dresser, the Sensational Comic'. In his spare time he wrote songs and published the *Paul Dresser Song Book*. In 1885 he joined the Billy Rice Minstrels and wrote his first real hit song 'The letter that never came'. He started his own publishing business which became the firm of Howley, Haviland & Dresser. For the next five or six years he turned out a succession of hits that included 'On the banks of the Wabash' (1899) up to 1905 when he wrote his best song, 'My gal Sal'. Over-generous to others, he was never financially successful so that he could not afford to publish it and died of heart disease, never having seen 'My gal Sal' in print. Other songs, from a long list, include: 'The pardon came too late' (1891); 'Just tell them that you saw me' (1895); 'In good old New York town' (1899); 'I wonder where she is tonight' (1899); 'Where are the friends of other days' (1903); most of them were of either a patriotic or sentimental nature. In the film biography *My Gal Sal* (1942, Dresser was portrayed by Victor Mature.

Dressler, Marie [Koerber, Leila Marie] (*b* Coburg, Canada, 9 Nov. 1869; *d* Santa Barbara, Calif., 28 July 1934). American actress and singer. Large, boot-faced lady who was an excellent foil and comedienne in both stage and film productions. In the theatre she appeared in *The Robber of the Nile* (1892); *Princess Nicotine* (1893); *Giroflé-Girofla* (1894); *Madeleine* (1895); *A Stag Party* (1895); *The Lady Slavey* (1896); *Hotel Topsy-Turvy* (1898); *The Man in the Moon* (1899); *Miss Prinnt* (1900); *The King's Carnival* (1901); *The Hall of Fame* (1902); *King Highball* (1902); *Higgledy Piggledy* (1904); *Twiddle Twaddle* (1906); *The Boy and the Girl* (1909); *Tillie's Nightmare* (1910)—in which she sang 'Heaven will protect the working girl'; *Roly Poly* (1912); *The Century Girl* (1916); **The Passing Show* (1920); *The Dancing Girl* (1923). She started her career in films in 1914, appearing in the filmed version of *Tillie's Nightmare*, and worked with many of the leading film comedians.

M. Dressler: *Life Story of an Ugly Duckling* (New York, 1925). M Dressler: *My Own Story* (New York, 1934).

Dreyer, Dave (*b* Brooklyn, 22 Sept. 1894; *d* New York). American composer and pianist. After working in music-publishing, he became accompanist to Al *Jolson, Sophie *Tucker, Belle *Baker, and Frank Fay. He returned to publishing in 1923, wrote for films 1929–40, and opened his own publishing business in 1947. His songs included: 'My country, I hear you calling me' (1916); 'Does your mother know you're out, Cecilia' (1925); 'Me and my shadow' (1927); 'There's a rainbow 'round my shoulder' (1928)—used in *The Singing Fool* (1929); 'Back in your own backyard' (1929); 'Wabash moon' (1931); and 'I'll never let you go' (1936).

Drifters, The. Group formed in 1953 with their original lead singer the gospel-inspired Clyde McPhatter and masterminded and managed by George Treadwell (then the husband of Sarah *Vaughan), with Bill Pinkney (*b* 1923) and Gerhard and Andrew Thrasher. They were aptly named, as the group went through a remarkable number of personnel permutations; but throughout they kept to the simple formation of a soaring lead vocal backed by gospel and 'bird-group' harmonizing; a formula which succeeds when the lead singers, producers, and writers are of such a high standard. Their first hits in the rhythm 'n' blues idiom were 'Money honey' and 'Such a night'.

When McPhatter left in 1955, they languished for a while with various lead singers and disbanded in 1958. Treadwell re-formed the group in 1958 with Ben E. King (*b* 1938) as its new star. Now mainly using the songs of *Leiber and Stoller, their next recording, 'There goes my baby' (1959), was both an enormous hit and their most innovative sound so far, combining a loose non-rhyming lyric, Latin American rhythm, and string and timpani backing. They followed this with 'Dance with me' (1959); 'This magic moment' (1960), and their most famous and popular recording 'Save the last dance for me' (1960) which became a No. 1 hit. King eventually left for a solo career to be replaced by Rudy Lewis (of the Clara Ward Singers) who led on 'On Broadway' (1963) and 'Up on the roof' (1963). A notable female back-up quartet of Dionne *Warwick, Dee Dee Warwick, Doris Troy, and Cissy Houston, and material by Phil *Spector, Burt *Bacharach, and Carole *King, all helped towards future successes. Lewis died just as the group was about to record 'Under the boardwalk' and Johnnie Moore, who was to be their most consistent member, took over the post.

The group lost some of its popularity in the late 1960s in spite of good material such as 'Saturday night at the movies' (1964), but was kept alive with re-issues of their old material. In 1972 the Roger Cook/Roger Greenaway team of British writers came in, having studied the Drifters' formula, and wrote a number of made-to-measure hits—'Like sister and brother' (1973); 'Kissing in the back row of the movies' (1974); and 'Down on the beach tonight' (1974). Although they never recaptured the effortless brilliance of some of their 1960s material, the newly assembled combination of Ben E. King, Johnnie Moore, Clyde Brown, and Joe Blunt continued in the same spirit from 1984.

B. Millar: *The Drifters: the Rise and Fall of the Black Vocal Group* (New York, 1971).

Dryden, Leo [Wheeler, George Dryden] (*b* London, 6 June 1863; *d* London, 21 Apr. 1939). British music-hall singer. He first appeared on the stage in 1881 and continued his career in an act based on Charles *Godfrey's. On the recommendation of the comedienne Jenny *Hill, he appeared at the *Oxford Music Hall in 1889 and quickly became a star on the strength of his rendering of 'The miner's dream of home', which greatly appealed to an audience concerned by the Boer War (1899–1902). Dressed for the part, he continued his career with a repertoire of similar jingoistic items such as 'India's reply', 'What Britishers are made of', 'The great white Mother', 'The gallant Gordon Highlanders', and 'Bravo Dublin Fusiliers'. He appeared in the Veterans of Variety show in the 1930s, still singing 'The miner's dream of home' to great applause, and was, for a time, chairman at *Collins Music Hall.

B. Anthony: 'Leo Dryden' in *Music-Hall* No. 33 (London, 1986).

Du Barry Was a Lady. American musical comedy, long-running for its time, with music and lyrics by Cole *Porter, book by B. G. *DeSylva and Herbert *Fields, produced at the 46th Street Theatre, New York, 6 Dec. 1939, with a cast that included Ethel *Merman, Bert *Lahr, Ronald Graham, Betty *Grable, and Benny Baker, running for 408 performances. In London, at His Majesty's Theatre, 22 Oct. 1942, it starred Arthur Riscoe, Jackie Hunter, Bruce Trent, Frances *Day, Inga Anderson, and Bud *Flanagan [178p].

The story of a washroom attendant who dreams he is Louis XV, its highspot was a noisy avowal of faithfulness in the duet 'Friendship' sung by Lahr and Merman. Another attraction was the glamorous Grable, who went to Hollywood on the strength of her appearance here. A high-spirited score also contained 'When love beckoned', 'Well, did you evah?', 'But in the morning, no', 'Do I love you?', 'Give him the oo-la-la', and 'Katie went to Haiti'. It was filmed in 1943 with Lucille *Ball, Gene *Kelly, and Red Skelton.

Dubin, Al [Albert] (*b* Zurich, Switzerland, 10 June 1891; *d* New York, 11 Feb. 1945). American lyricist. He went to the USA in 1893 and later worked in song-publishing. He was in at the beginning of the talking film era in Hollywood, mainly working with the composer Harry *Warren, but also with Jimmy *McHugh, Joe *Burke, and others, supplying the words for such songs as 'A cup of coffee, a sandwich and you', 'Dancing with tears in my eyes', 'Lullaby of Broadway', 'Tip-toe through the tulips', 'Shuffle off to Buffalo', 'Painting the clouds with sunshine', 'Indian summer', 'Along the Santa Fé trail', '42nd Street', 'You're getting to be a habit with me', 'I'll string along with you', 'I only have eyes for you', 'She's a Latin from Manhattan', 'The anniversary waltz', 'Lulu's back in town', and 'September in the rain'.

P. D. McGuire: *Lullaby of Broadway: a Biography of Al Dubin* (Secaucus, NJ, 1983).

Duchin, Eddy [Edward] (*b* Cambridge, Mass., 1 Apr. 1910; *d* New York, 9 Feb. 1951). American pianist, bandleader, and composer. He studied for a career in pharmacy, but turned to music around 1929, working with the Leo Reisman band and soon becoming recognized for his good looks and light and fanciful piano style. He formed his own band in 1931 with which he developed his individual style and notable piano intros which became very much a trademark. He broadcast with many prestigious shows—Ed *Wynn 1934–5, Burns and Allen 1936, La Salle 1937–9; appeared in several films; and made a large number of recordings. His peak years were 1934–6. He was with Eddie *Foy 1947, and had his own radio show in 1949. He died from leukaemia. A biographical film, *The Eddy Duchin Story* (1956), had Tyrone Power playing Duchin and Carmen *Cavallaro imitating his piano style. His son Peter Duchin follows in the same tradition.

Duke, Vernon [Dukelsky, Vladimir] (*b* Parfianovka, 10 Oct. 1903; *d* Santa Monica, Calif., 16 Jan. 1969). Russian-born American composer. He was born in the station of Parfianovka while his mother was on a journey to Pskov. He studied at the Kiev Conservatory but his family, who were White Russians, left Russia in 1920 and went to Constantinople, eventually arriving in the USA in 1921. He lived in Paris and London for a while but eventually settled in New York in 1929 and was naturalized in 1936. Apart from a stay in Paris 1947–8, he spent the rest of his life in New York and Hollywood. Introduced to Diaghilev, he began to compose at an early age and was a writer of serious music throughout his life, with numerous performances of his works in America. Unable to make a living out of this, he turned to popular music, playing the piano in burlesque shows and writing music for vaudeville acts. He made the acquaintance of George *Gershwin, who helped him develop his abilities as a songwriter and suggested the use of the name Vernon Duke in connection with his lighter activities. In 1955 he dropped the name of Dukelsky altogether.

While in London in the 1920s he wrote the scores

of *Yvonne* (1926) and *The Yellow Mask* (1927), for which Edgar Wallace supplied the words. In 1929 he worked in the Hollywood film studios and first wrote as Vernon Duke in 1930. His first published popular song in America was 'I'm only human after all' which was used in *The *Garrick Gaieties* (1930). He wrote music for *Three's a Crowd* (1930); *Shoot the Works* (1931); **Americana* (1932); *Walk a Little Faster* (1932); **Ziegfeld Follies* (1934 and 1936); **Cabin in the Sky* (1940); *Banjo Eyes* (1941); *The Lady Comes Across* (1942); *Dancing in the Street* (1943); *Jackpot* (1944); *Sadie Thompson* (1944); *Sweet Bye and Bye* (1946); *Two's Company* (1952)—'Roundabout'; *The Littlest Revue* (1956); working with such writers as John *Latouche, E. Y. *Harburg, Ira *Gershwin, Ogden Nash, and Howard *Dietz. He also wrote for the film *The Goldwyn Follies* (1938). Among his best-known songs were 'April in Paris' (1932); 'Where have we met before?' (1932); 'I like the likes of you' (1934); 'What is there to say?' (1934); 'Autumn in New York' (1935); 'I can't get started' (1936); 'That moment of moments' (1936); 'Taking a chance on love' (1940); 'Cabin in the sky' (1940); 'Honey in the honeycomb' (1940); 'Double or nothing ' (1940); 'Long ago' (1940); 'Not a care in the world' (1942); 'We're having a baby' (1944). A stylish composer of well-constructed and harmonically interesting songs, as might be expected from a classically-trained musician, he was almost in the George Gershwin class in being able to combine technique with tuneful memorability.

V. Duke: *Passport to Paris* (New York, 1955).

Dunayevsky, Isaak Osipovitch (*b* Lokhvitza, nr. Poltava, Ukraine, 30 Jan. 1900; *d* Moscow, 25 July 1955). Russian composer. From a working-class family, he picked up an interest in music at school and started composing. He learned the piano and went to the Kharkov Conservatory, where he studied the violin with Joseph Achron. After the October revolution of 1917, he became a lecturer and official conductor for government-sponsored musical activities. His theatre career started in 1919 when he wrote music for several plays at the Charkov Theatre. An early operetta, *Die Freier* (1924), was produced in Moscow. From 1936 to 1948 he was musical director of the Central Song and Dance Ensemble in Moscow. Having accepted the dictum that music should be subservient to the needs of the state, he produced a series of 12 very tuneful operettas between 1937 and 1955 and 28 film scores of which the best-known is *Circus* (1936); its 'Circus march' continues to be one of the most popular pieces in the USSR today, matched by 'The song of the Fatherland', which has almost attained the status of a national anthem, and 'Song of youth'. Among his film scores (translated) are *Merry Boys* (1934); *Three Friends* (1935); *The Children of Captain Grant* (1936); *The Wealthy Bride* (1937); *Wolga, Wolga* (1938); *The Bright Way* (1940); *Spring* (1947); *Coassacks* (1950); *Goalman* (1952).

L. Danilevitch: *Isaak Dunayevsky* (Moscow, 1947). A. Tchernov: *Isaak Dunayevsky* (Moscow, 1961).

Duncan, Rosetta Florence (*b* Los Angeles, 23 Nov. 1900; *d* Chicago 4 Dec. 1959) and **Vivian** (*b* Los Angeles, 17 Jun. 1902; *d* 1986). Composers, lyric-writers, actresses, singers, and publishers. Popular as the Duncan Sisters in the 1920s and 1930s on both stage and screen. They wrote and performed (with Gus *Edwards) in their famous show *Topsy and Eva* (1924), which included their well-known Topsy and Eva routine and which they brought to London in 1928. The song 'Rememb'ring' became quite a hit at the time. They also appeared in *Doing Our Bit* (1917); *She's a Good Fellow* (1919); *Tip Top* (1920); and in London in *Pins and Needles* (1921) and *Clowns in Clover* (1928); in New York in the revue **New Faces* (1936); and they starred in the film *It's a Great Life* (1930). They were active in vaudeville and appeared in cabaret in London. In the final stages of their career they became music publishers. Rosetta Duncan was killed in a car crash.

Duncan, Todd [Robert] (*b* Danville, Ky., 12 Feb. 1900). American actor well remembered for his leading role in **Porgy and Bess* (1935 and revivals) where he was the first to sing such numbers as 'I got plenty o' nuttin'' and 'Bess, you is my woman now'. He also appeared in *The Sun Never Sets* (London, 1938); **Cabin in the Sky* (1940); and **Lost in the Stars* (1949).

Duncan, Trevor [Trebilco, Leonard] (*b* Cornwall, 27 Feb. 1924). British composer. He had a natural gift for music but no formal training, although working as a sound engineer with the BBC gave him a feeling for good, balanced scoring. In 1954 he was promoted to music producer. His first work to be published was a light orchestral piece, 'High heels', in 1949. Similar works followed and he retired from the BBC in 1956 to devote himself to composition. He became best-known by his 'Little Suite' the march from which was adopted as the signature tune of the television series *Dr Finlay's Casebook*. Other works include: 'The girl from Corsica', 'Enchanted April', 'The wine harvest', and 'Children in the park'. He has also written for films and contrived a good deal of pastiche mood music.

Dunn, [Sir] Francis Vivian (*b* London, 24 Dec. 1908). British conductor and composer. Son of a Director of Music of the Royal Horse Guards, he studied music in Cologne, 1922–4, and at the Royal Academy of Music under Sir Henry Wood, 1925–9. He played the violin in the Queen's Hall, Royal Philharmonic, and London Symphony orchestras and was an original member of the BBC Symphony Orchestra 1930–1. Appointed Director of Music of the Royal Marines, Portsmouth, in 1931, he went to the Royal Marines School of Music on becoming Principal Director of Music. He retired in 1968 and was knighted in 1969. He continued to conduct light orchestral concerts and to make recordings of British music. He composed in many forms but is chiefly known for such marches as 'Cockleshell heroes', 'The Captain General', 'Passing by', 'Soldiers of the Sea', 'Commando patrol', 'Royal Vanguard', and 'Salute to Amethyst'.

Dunne, Irene [Marie] (*b* Louisville, Ky., 20 Dec. 1898; *d* Los Angeles, 4 Sept. 1990). American actress and singer. Her trained soprano voice was heard to good effect in such Broadway shows as **Irene* (1920); *The Clinging Vine* (1922); *Lollipop* (1924); *The City Chap* (1925); *Sweetheart Time* (1926); *Yours Truly* (1927); *She's My Baby* (1928); *Luckee Girl* (1928); and in the touring company of **Show Boat* (1929). She made her film debut in *Present Arms* in 1930; other musical films were *Leathernecking* (1930); *Sweet Adeline* (1935); **Roberta* (1935); **Show Boat* (1936); *High, Wide and Handsome* (1937); *Joy of Living* (1938); *Love Affair* (1939); *Never a Dull Moment* (1950); and she appeared as a straight actress in many films between 1930 and 1948, with a total of 40 film parts.

Dunville, T. E. [Wallen, Thomas Edward] (*b* Coventry, 26 July 1868; *d* Reading, 23 Mar. 1924). British comedian and singer. He started out in a blackface minstrel act called the Three Spires then, in partnership with Robert Martell, played in pantomine and toured the USA. His first solo music-hall appearance was in 1889 in Bolton, and he appeared in London in 1890. His eccentric act gradually evolved with fanciful clown costumes and the singing of nonsense songs, often with short-lined lyrics that he delivered in a staccato manner. He was as popular in variety and pantomine for some 30 years, but found himself out of fashion after the war and, having heard someone refer to him as a 'fallen star', he drowned himself in the River Thames.

T. E. Dunville: *The Autobiography of an Eccentric Comedian* (London, 1912). T. Barker: 'The Tragic Death of T. E. Dunville' in *Music-Hall Records* No. 4 (London, Dec. 1978) and 'T. E. Dunville' in *Music-Hall Records* No. 8, (London, Aug. 1979).

Dupree, 'Champion' Jack [William Thomas] (*b* New Orleans, 4 July 1910; *d* Hanover, 21 Jan. 1992). American pianist. He got his nickname from his activities as a boxer during the depression years. He became known when he started recording for Okeh in 1940, proving himself a superb *barrelhouse pianist and exponent of the blues. In 1944 he moved to New York, recorded for several labels, moved into the rhythm 'n' blues Top 10 with 'Walking the blues', and produced a fine album for Atlantic called *Blues from the Gutter*—an inspiration for later pianists such as Fats *Domino.

Duran Duran. British pop group formed in Birmingham in 1978 with the line-up of Simon Le Bon (vocal), Andy Taylor (guitar), Nick Rhodes (synthesizer), John Taylor (bass), and Roger Taylor (drums). They began to record for EMI and achieved a consistent output of hit records—reaching No. 1 with 'Is there something I should know' (1983); 'The reflex' (1984); and 'Wild boys' (1984)—and equally successful albums. With the advantage of being seemly to look at and musically well-equipped they became one of the most widely followed groups in Britain and almost equally popular in the USA.

Durante, Jimmy [James Francis] (*b* New York, 10 Feb. 1893; *d* Santa Monica, Calif., 29 Jan. 1980). American actor, comedian, composer, singer, and pianist. His parents were Italian and the whole family was musical. By the age of 14 his pianistic prowess had earned him the title of Ragtime Jimmy and he became a professional, for a time acting as accompanist to Eddie *Cantor. After a period as a soloist, he formed the Durante Original Jazz Novelty Band which lasted from 1917 to 1923, a pioneering jazz group who recorded for the historic Gennett label. Ragtime expert Rudi *Blesh expressed the opinion that 'Jimmy Durante was the best white ragtime pianist who ever lived'. He opened the Club Durant where he became increasingly known for his comedy routines with Lou Clayton and Eddie Jackson. The trio moved into Broadway in Ziegfeld's *Show Girl* (1929) and made their first film, *Roadhouse Nights*, in the same year. His amusing personality, raucous voice, and prominent nose, which earned him the nickname of 'Schnozzola' (or 'Schnozzle'), destined him for individual stardom and after an appearance in *The New Yorkers* (1930) the trio broke up and Durante went on his own triumphant way, mainly to be remembered for his rasping, choppy delivery of songs, many of which he wrote himself.

He starred in the Broadway musicals *Strike Me Pink* (1933); *Jumbo* (1935); *Red Hot and Blue* (1936); *Stars in Your Eyes* (1939); *Keep Off the Grass* (1940); and he appeared in clubs and on radio and TV, but his reputation was mainly founded on a number of films. Those with a musical content include: *Cuban Love Song* (1931); *Blondie of the Follies* (1931); *The Phantom President* (1931); *Broadway to Hollywood* (1932); *Palooka* (1932); *George White's Scandals* (1932); *Hollywood Party* (1932); *Strictly Dynamite* (1932); *Start Cheering* (1938); *Sally, Irene and Mary* (1938); *Little Miss Broadway* (1938); *Melody Ranch* (1940); *Two Girls and a Sailor* (1944); *Music for Millions* (1944); *Two Sisters from Boston* (1945); **It Happened in Brooklyn* (1947); *This Time for Keeps* (1947); and *On an Island with You* (1948). He appeared at the London Palladium in 1952. The songs he wrote or composed included 'I've got my habits on' (1921); 'Everybody wants to get into the act' (1926); 'Broadway's a phoney' (1926); 'Jimmy, the well-dressed man' (1928); 'I can do without Broadway (but can Broadway do without me?)' (1928); 'Who will be with you when I'm far away' (1929); 'I ups to him and he ups to me' (1929); 'Inka dinka doo' (1934); 'Umbriago' (1944); 'Start off each day with a song' (1944); and 'I'm the guy who found the lost chord';

most of them are remembered from his own inimitable (but much imitated) performances. He suffered a stroke in 1974 and spent the rest of his life in a wheelchair.

G. Fowler: *Schnozzola: the Story of Jimmy Durante* (Garden City, NY, 1953). W. Cahn: *Goodnight, Mrs Calabash: the Secret of Jimmy Durante* (New York, 1963). S. Green: 'Jimmy Durante', in *The Great Clowns of Broadway* (New York, 1984).

Durbin, Deanna [Edna May] (*b* Winnipeg, 4 Dec. 1921). Canadian actress and singer. Discovered by Joe Pasternak (1901–91) (who was to direct nine of her films), after a successful appearance on the Eddie *Cantor show, she starred in a series of nice but precocious teenager roles, moving to the lightly romantic format later, always admired for her clear, classically-trained voice. She first appeared in a short film with Judy *Garland, *Every Sunday*, in 1935; and became a star after her first full-length feature *Three Smart Girls* (1936); followed by *One Hundred Men and a Girl* (1937); *Mad About Music* (1938); *That Certain Age* (1938); *Three Smart Girls Grow Up* (1939); *First Love* (1939); *It's a Date* (1940); *Spring Parade* (1940); *Nice Girl?* (1941); *It Started With Eve* (1941); *The Amazing Mrs Holiday* (1943); *Hers to Hold* (1943); *His Butler's Sister* (1943); *Can't Help Singing* (1944); *Lady on a Train* (1945); *Because of Him* (1946); *I'll Be Yours* (1947); *Something in the Wind* (1947); *Up in Central Park* (1948); and *For the Love of Mary* (1948). She married a French film director in 1950 and retired to live in France.

D'Urfey, Thomas (*b* Exeter, 1653; *d* London, 26 Feb. 1723). British author, lyricist, composer, and singer. His French parents came to England in 1628. Intended for the law, he took to writing for the stage and earned a reputation as a singer of his own songs in 'the licentious and joyous circles which moved round Charles II', while a constant occupation was 'the making of songs and odes to the hardest and most taking of tunes'. When Henry Playford, son of the famous John, gave up publishing the many editions of the collection *Wit and Mirth: or Pills to Purge Melancoly* in 1707 it was taken over by other editors, notably in 1719 by D'Urfey. His reputation as a entertainer of royalty 'to happy and commendable approbation' probably greatly enhanced the possibilities of the publication. Addison, in *The Guardian* of 1713, recalls seeing 'King Charles the Second leaning on Tom D'Urfey's shoulder and humming over a song with him'. D'Urfey was the possessor of a large nose and a loud bass voice, and a stutter which he could only control when singing. He had a lively, vulgar nature and a high opinion of himself, with no doubts as to his qualifications as an editor—'scarce any other man could have performed the like, my double Genius for Poetry and Musick giving me still that ability which others perhaps might want'. This opinion was not entirely shared by others. Pope saw his work as 'the lowest manifestation of current literature' and Addison described his output as 'trivial'.

Could we be more certain of what he actually conceived and what he simply edited from earlier sources, there might be grounds for accepting D'Urfey as one of the first true popular songwriters. He was responsible for the words of more than 500 songs, frequently adding them to existing tunes as was then customary. As a composer he was responsible for some neat additions and for some tunes in the same vein as those he edited. He drew on Playford's *The *Dancing Master* and earlier editions of *Wit and Mirth* and others of the 150 or so songbooks published between 1660 and 1700 after the lifting of earlier Puritan restrictions.

C. L. Day: *The Songs of Thomas D'Urfey* (Cambridge, Mass., 1933). S. A. J. Bradley (ed.): *Sixty Ribald Songs from 'Pills to Purge Melancholy'* (London, 1968).

Durham, Eddie [Edward] (*b* San Marcos, Tex., 19 Aug. 1906; *d* New York, 6 Mar. 1987). American guitarist, trombonist, and arranger. One of several musical brothers who formed a local Durham Brothers orchestra, he was active in Kansas City in the late 1920s. He worked with Bennie *Moten 1929–33, Willie *Bryant 1934, Jimmie *Lunceford 1935–7; as trombonist and arranger, Count *Basie 1937–8, Ina Ray Hutton 1938–9; later he arranged for Glenn *Miller, Artie *Shaw, and Jan *Savitt and he led his own bands on and off from 1940 into the 1970s. He devised a non-electrical method of amplifying the guitar which made him prominent in the Moten recordings of *c.* 1929. His best-known arrangements include 'Moten swing'; for Lunceford: 'Pigeon walk', 'Lunceford special', 'Hittin' the bottle'; for Basie: 'Sent for you yesterday and here you come today', 'Topsy', 'Out the window', 'Time out'; for Miller: 'In the mood', 'Slip horn jive'; and countless more.

Dury, Ian (*b* Upminster, Essex, 12 May 1942). British singer, composer, and bandleader. He studied at the Royal College of Art and became a teacher, but his interest in music gradually outgrew his interest in art and he formed his own rock band which played in London pubs and achieved an LP, *Watabunch*, in 1977. His early writings like 'Billericay Dickie', 'Plaistow Patricia', 'Sweet Gene Vincent' (from the acclaimed album *New Boots and Panties* (1977)), 'Rough kids', and 'Upminster kid' showed a blackly humorous lyrical talent and a nicely balanced view of pop requirements. He became widely known in 1978 with items like 'England's glory' (recorded by Max Wall), 'What a waste', 'Hit me with your rhythm stick', 'Sink my boats', 'This is what we find', 'Reasons to be cheeful', and the album *Do It Yourself* (1979). He continued with *Laughter* (1980); and his first solo album, *Lord Upminster* (1981), included some excellent items like 'The body song' and 'Spasticus autisticus' (he was himself moderately handicapped by childhood polio), which was banned by the BBC. He continued as one of the pop scene's most intelligent contributors, with *Juke Box Dury* (1981), the theme for TV's *The Secret Diary of Adrian Mole* (1985)—'Profoundly in love with Pandora', appeared in films 1985–6, and was with Bob *Dylan in *Hearts of Fire* (1987).

Dylan, Bob [Zimmerman, Robert Allen] (*b* Duluth, Minn., 24 May 1941). American singer and songwriter. He adopted the name of Dylan in homage to the poet Dylan Thomas whom he much admired. He spent a wandering youth, riding freight trains across America, playing guitar and singing in coffee-houses, improvising his own songs and lyrics. He was to become the representative voice of a generation, the guru of radical causes and pop music's leading poet. As important as the *Beatles or Elvis *Presley, Dylan clung to the old ethnic forms, notably the semi-spoken protest song, adding modern themes. On the way he changed the popular conception of what a song lyric should be and went a long way towards shaping the future of the pop song.

He was always determined to become a famous folk-singer. On his arrival in New York in 1960 he visited the dying Woody *Guthrie. He played in Greenwich Village clubs and, in 1961, signed up with Columbia Records under the veteran producer John *Hammond; his debut album was rich in folk tradition with Dylan singing in the Guthrie manner. Lonnie Johnson was another strong influence at this time. Dylan's second album, *The Freewheelin' Bob Dylan* (1963), established him as a leader of the civil rights and anti-war movements with now classic protest songs such as 'A hard rain's a gonna fall' and 'Blowin' in the wind'. He was not merely didactic, however; his songs combined indictment with wit and frequent warmth as in 'Girl from the North country'. His tunes were always simple but he handled the different and complex lyrics with skill and ingenuity.

His third album, *The Times They Are A-Changin'* (1964) continued in the vein of the first two but became a commercial success after he appeared in a New York Town Hall concert and at the Newport Folk Festival. In the same year, *Peter, Paul and Mary brought him to the attention of a wider audience with their popularized version of 'Blowin' in the wind' which became a national hit. Dylan has always been unpredictable. As soon as he was accepted as the nation's radical prophet, his next album, *Another Side of Bob Dylan*, expressed his irritation with the role. *Bringing it all Back Home* (1965), which included the popular 'Mr Tambourine Man', outraged his now vast and fanatical following even more. Dylan had gone electric, inspired by the *Animals' rendering of the traditional 'House of the Rising Sun'. This was, however, only a preview of his finest work which came on *Highway 61 Revisited* (1965) and *Blonde on Blonde* (1966). By this time he had lost some of his purist followers by appearing at the 1965 Newport Festival backed by the Butterfield Blues Band and, on a later tour, by the *Band. The indignation died down, overcome by the quality of such songs as 'Like a rolling stone', 'Just like Tom Thumb's blues', 'Just like a woman', 'I want you', and 'Sad-eyed lady of the lowlands'.

On 29 July 1966, Dylan broke his neck in a motorcycle accident. It was perhaps not as serious as it sounded, but he was able to use it as a useful excuse for retiring from show-business for the best part of two years; Columbia used the recording gap to issue a retrospective, *Bob Dylan's Greatest Hits* (1967). His work done in that period has since been released on *The Basement Tapes* (1975) which includes some of his most honest and personal songs. He reappeared, unheralded, before the public at the 1968 Woody Guthrie Memorial Concert and his next new release, *John Wesley Harding* (1968), saw him returning to the simplicity of his early albums with an almost English folk feel of understatement. *Nashville Skyline* (1969) was equally unsophisticated, delving back into his country influences with the superb 'Lay lady lay' and 'Tonight I'll be staying here with you'. It inspired other artists to make their way to Nashville.

His subsequent albums received mixed reviews. For many *New Morning* was Dylan's re-awakening but some found it patchy and contrived. *Self Portrait* (1970), an amalgam of other people's songs, was universally disliked; while *Planet Waves* (1974), perhaps underrated, was thought too conventional. The sound-track for the film *Pat Garrett and Billy the Kid* (1973) had contained some classic songs, notably 'Knocking on Heaven's door'. His best album of the 1970s was *Blood on the Tracks* (1975), standing beside his finest work; it used a mixture of styles with its best songs 'Tangled up in blue', 'Simple twist of fate', the economical 'Lily, Rosemary and the Jack of Hearts', and the beautifully simple 'If you see her, say hello'.

His work since has continued to vary in standard. *Desire* (1976) saw his re-introduction of the protest song; *Hard Rain* (1976) was of high quality; *Street-Legal* (1978) moved into gospel song. Almost inevitably, Dylan, tired of things of this world, turned to religion—again alienating some of his followers. It is debatable whether the new mysticism affected the quality of his work, but most of his albums since then—*Slow Train Coming* (1979); *Saved* (1980); *Infidels* (1983); *Real Live* (1984); *Empire Burlesque* (1985)—have been received with less than enthusiasm.

Dylan has often been hailed as a marvellous lyricist, but as a vocalist and performer he is often underrated. On virtually every album he has introduced a new vocal style. Singing protest songs, his voice was rough and searing in the blues tradition; in country songs he is smoother; elsewhere he can be raw and coarse. He uses his voices like an instrument to create atmosphere and effect. More than any other artist Dylan has moulded the thoughts and preoccupations of young people and opened up new avenues of musical and lyrical exploration. In 1970 he was awarded an honorary doctorate at Princeton University, the first to be given to a pop singer. In New York a group of militants called themselves 'Weathermen' after the line 'You don't need a weatherman to know which way the wind blows' in 'Subterranean homesick blues' and planted several bombs in the city during 1969 and 1970. The effect of Dylan has been far-reaching and deep-rooted. He wrote and published *Tarantula* (New York, 1971); *Writings and Drawings by Bob Dylan* (New York, 1973); *The Songs of Bob Dylan from 1966 through 1975* (1976); *Lyrics, 1962–1985* (1986). His songs have been collected in the *Bob Dylan Songbook* (1965) and *Bob Dylan* (1974); while individual songbooks were published with each record album.

D. Kramer: *Bob Dylan* (New York, 1967). A. Scaduto: *Bob Dylan: an Intimate Biography* (New York, 1971; rev. 1979). T. Thompson: *Positively Main Street: an Unorthodox View of Bob Dylan* (New York, 1971). M. Gray: *Song and Dance Man; the Art of Bob Dylan* (London, 1972). M. Gross: *Bob Dylan: an Illustrated History* (New York, 1978). P. Marchbank (ed.): *Bob Dylan: in his own Words* (London, 1978). L. Sloman: *On the Road with Bob Dylan* (New York, 1978). T. Dowley & B. Dunnage: *Bob Dylan: From a Hard Rain to a Slow Train* (Tunbridge Wells, 1982). R. Shelton: *No Direction Home: the Life and Music of Bob Dylan* (New York–London, 1986). M. Gray & J. Bauldie: *All Across the Telegraph: a Bob Dylan Handbook* (London, 1988). B. Spitz: *Bob Dylan: a Biography* (New York–London, 1989).

E

Eagles, The. American West Coast group formed in 1971 by Don Henley (*b* 1946) (drums) and Glenn Frey (*b* 1946) (guitar), with Bernie Leadon (*b* 1947) (guitar) and Randy Meisner (*b* 1946) (bass). They first played in a country rock style as heard in their first album, *The Eagles* (1972), recorded in London. Their first single success was with 'Take it easy' (1972), and their first No. 1 hit 'Best of my love' (1974), followed by 'One of these nights' (1975) and 'Lyin' eyes' (1975). Leadon left after this to be replaced by guitarist Joe Walsh (*b* 1945). Their polished playing and effective harmonies made them the top band in the USA, although they were sometimes criticized for being too slickly commercial. Their album *Hotel California* (1976) sold 11 million copies, with songs from it like the title song, 'New kid in town', and 'Life in the fast lane', becoming top hits. *The Long Run* (1979) included their last No. 1 hit, 'Heartache tonight'. The group broke up in 1981.

Earl and the Girl, The. Musical comedy with score by Ivan *Caryll, book by Seymour *Hicks, and lyrics by Percy *Greenbank. Produced at the Adelphi Theatre, London, 10 Dec. 1903, transferring to the Lyric Theatre 12 Sept. 1904, and running for a total of 371 performances, the cast included Louis Pounds, Phyllis Broughton, Henry A. *Lytton, and Robert Evett. It was one of the typical turn-of-the century romantic trifles that succeeded without having musical distinction. Before it made its inevitable way to New York, it was updated by the up-and-coming Jerome *Kern who added the song 'How'd you like to spoon with me' to bolster its New York opening at the Casino Theatre 4 Nov. 1905. A London revival with Ellaline *Terriss at the Aldwych, 4 Nov. 1914, also found the bland Caryll score wanting and its needs were supplemented by such songs as 'My cosy corner girl' (John W. *Bratton), 'In Zanzibar' (Gus *Edwards and Will D. *Cobb), 'A bit of string' (Lionel *Monckton), and 'I want to go back to Michigan' (Irving *Berlin).

Earl Carroll's Vanities. A series of New York revues (running to 10 editions) staged by producer Earl *Carroll from 1923 (at his own Earl Carroll Theatre until 1929). A rival in the spectacular revue field to the famous *Ziegfeld productions, and initially choreographed by Sammy Lee (1890–1968), they featured lavishly undressed ladies and risqué humour and were thus a fashionable entertainment. The earlier productions survived on these bare essentials. Sophie *Tucker was in the 1924 edition, the musical and theatrical quality improved over the years with composers like Harold *Arlen contributing to the editions of 1930 (staged at the New Amsterdam Theatre 1 July 1930) and 1932, and Burton *Lane in 1931. Concurrently the similarly designed *Earl Carroll Sketch Book* was produced at the Earl Carroll Theatre (1929) and the *Winter Garden Theatre (1935). Lillian Roth (*b* 1911) appeared in the 1928, 1931, and 1932 editions. The fashion for intimate revue gradually outmoded the spectaculars. There was an attempted revival of the *Vanities* in 1940 but it was clearly a last fling and only survived for 25 performances. Many stars graced the *Vanities*, but the shows were not notable for producing memorable music apart from the occasional Arlen songs in the peak 1930 production—'Hittin' the bottle', 'Out of a clear blue sky'—and 'I've got a right to sing the blues' in 1932.

Early to Bed. Musical comedy with music by Fats *Waller and book by George Marion Jr., staged at the Broadhurst Theatre, New York, 17 June 1943, the first non-black show to be composed by a black musician. The cast (which was originally intended to include Waller) included Mary Small, Muriel Angelus, Richard Kollmar, George Zivich and it ran for 382 performances. The songs had typically sly Waller titles—'The ladies who sing with a band', 'There's a man in my life', 'This is so nice', 'Slightly less than wonderful', and 'Hi de hi ho in Harlem' among them. The book was strictly 'for adults only' and it achieved its moderate success in spite of a musicians' union dispute that prevented any recordings.

Easter Parade. Notable MGM musical film of 1948 that featured the songs of Irving *Berlin, the score partly made up of older numbers but with much excellent material specially written such as 'Better luck next time', 'A couple of swells', 'A fella with an umbrella', and 'Steppin' out with my baby', all superbly put over by a star cast of Fred *Astaire, Judy *Garland, Peter Lawford (1923–84), and Ann Miller (*b* 1919). The story is mediocre, but it remains a classic for its musical content.

Ebb, Fred (*b* New York, 8 Apr. 1932). American librettist and lyric-writer. He studied in New York and at Columbia University and made his first Broadway contributions to the revue *From A to Z* (1960). He worked on other revues, wrote the book for *Morning Sun* (1963), and contributed to the TV show *That Was the Week That Was*. In 1965 he teamed up with composer John *Kander and wrote well-tailored lyrics for *Flora, the Red Menace* (1965); **Cabaret* (1966; filmed 1972); *The Happy Time* (1968); *70, Girls, 70* (1971, also book); *Liza* (1974); **Chicago* (1975, book); and **Woman of the Year* (1981). Their films included: *Funny Lady* (1975); *A Matter of Time* (1976); and *New York, New York* (1977)—its title song sung by Liza *Minnelli and made into a classic by Frank *Sinatra.

Eckstine, Billy [Eckstein, William Clarence] (*b* Pittsburgh, 8 July 1914; *d* Pittsburgh, 8 Mar. 1993). American singer, trumpeter, and bandleader. After attending Washington University, he became a club singer in Washington, Buffalo, Detroit, and Chicago. He first won attention as vocalist with the Earl *Hines band 1939–43, where he also began to play the trumpet. With Budd Johnson he formed a band in 1944 which was to be one of the pioneering units in the *bebop revolution with Dizzy *Gillespie as player, arranger, and leader and such players as Charlie *Parker, Gene Ammons (1925–74), Lucky Thompson (*b* 1924), Dexter *Gordon (1923–90), Art *Blakey, Fats Navarro (1923–50), and Miles *Davis in its ranks from time to time. Sarah *Vaughan was the vocalist for a while alongside Eckstine himself and the arrangements were by Gillespie, Tadd *Dameron, and Budd Johnson (1910–84). Having earned a niche in jazz history, the band broke up in 1947. Eckstine continued as a solo entertainer and made many recordings in the 1950s. He moved from the jazz limelight in the 1960s but continued as a cabaret entertainer into the 1970s.

Eddy, Duane (*b* Corning, NY, 26 Apr. 1938). American guitarist. He started playing at the age of five and, after gigging at local dances, joined up with guitarist Al Casey (*b* 1915) in 1955. He recorded with Casey and the Rebels and began to promote a new 'twangy' guitar sound achieved by echo effects and a bass-line melody which made a best-seller of 'Rebel-rouser' in 1958. 'Cannonball' and 'Peter Gunn' followed; by 1960 Eddy's popularity was at a peak in Britain, where he was continually among the top hits. He had further hits in 1962, with 'Deep in the heart of Texas' and the 'The ballad of Palladin', and in 1963, with 'Dance with the guitar man' and 'Boss guitar'. He moved out of the top ratings after this and worked as a producer for MCA Records in Hollywood, making a temporary comeback in 1975 with 'Play me like you play your guitar'.

Eddy, Nelson (*b* Providence, RI, 29 June 1901; *d* Miami Beach, 6 Mar. 1967). American actor and singer. He was with the Philadelphia Opera for four years, but was to be remembered as the prototype operetta singer in film musicals of an old-fashioned romantic Viennese vein. He made eight films in a famous partnership with Jeanette *MacDonald at the MGM studios in screen versions of musicals by Victor *Herbert, Rudolf *Friml, Sigmund *Romberg, and Noël *Coward. He was also active as a concert recitalist and a recording star.

His films (those with MacDonald marked †) included: *Broadway to Hollywood* (1933); *Dancing Lady* (1933); *Student Tour* (1934); **Naughty Marietta* (1935); **Rose-Marie*† (1936); **Maytime*† (1937); *Rosalie* (1937); **The Girl of the Golden West*† (1938); **Sweethearts*† (1938); *Let Freedom Ring* (1939); **Balalaika* (1939); **New Moon*† (1940); **Bitter Sweet*† (1940); *The *Chocolate Soldier* (1941); **I Married an Angel*† (1942); **Phantom of the Opera* (1943); **Knickerbocker Holiday* (1944); *Make Mine Music* (1946); *Northwest Outpost* (1947).

E. Knowles: *The Films of Jeanette MacDonald and Nelson Eddy* (New York, 1975).

Edison, Harry 'Sweets' (*b* Columbus, Ohio, 10 Oct. 1915). American jazz trumpeter. He played with a warm tone that survived into fringe modernism later in his career. From 1933 to 1936 he was mainly in St Louis and working with the Jeter–Pillars band; with Lucky *Millinder and the Blue Rhythm Band 1937; with Count *Basie 1938–50. He toured with Jimmy *Rushing and Jazz at the Philharmonic, worked with Buddy *Rich, and accompanied Josephine *Baker. He led a group featuring Joe Williams (*b* 1918) and worked with Basie again in the 1960s and 1970s. He collaborated in the writing of 'Jive at five', 'Beaver Junction', 'Shorty George', and many other Basie features.

Edwardes, George [orig. Edwards] (*b* Clee, Lincs., 14 Oct. 1855; *d* London 4 Oct. 1915). British producer; in his heyday the best-known and most influential London impresario who presided over the golden age of British *musical comedy, beginning with such shows as *In Town* and *A *Gaiety Girl*. Taking over the *Gaiety Theatre from John *Hollingshead in 1885, he then built *Daly's Theatre in 1893 and the two venues almost dominated London's musical theatre activities during the Edwardian period. Abandoning the burlesque he promoted a new world of musical comedy, ranging from *In Town* in 1892 to *After the Girl* and *Adele* in 1914. He used and built up such stars as Gertie *Millar, Lily *Elsie, Ellaline *Terriss, Edna *May, Joseph *Coyne, George *Grossmith Jr., and Seymour *Hicks; while his team of composers included Ivan *Caryll, Sidney *Jones, Lionel *Monckton, Paul *Rubens, and Howard *Talbot.

U. Bloom: *Curtain Call for the Guv'nor* (London, 1954).

Edwards, Cliff [Clifton A.] (*b* Hannibal, Mo., 14 June 1895; *d* Hollywood, 18 July 1972). American singer and entertainer. He left school at 14 and went to St Louis where he sang in saloons, making his theatre debut there in 1900. He then went to Chicago where he teamed up with drummer Joe Frisco in a vaudeville act and worked with composer Bob Carleton on 'Ja da'. It was here that a waiter gave him the name of 'Ukulele Ike' under which he often worked and recorded. He appeared in the Broadway musicals **Lady Be Good* (1924); **Sunny* (1925); **Ziegfeld Follies* (1927); **George White's Scandals* (1935). He became popular in films, playing in more than 100 altogether, beginning with *Hollywood Revue of 1929* in which his high-pitched voice made 'Singing in the rain' popular. He was the voice of Jiminy Cricket in the Walt Disney cartoon film *Pinocchio* (1939), singing 'When you wish upon a star', and in *Fun and Fancy Free* (1946). His best film roles were in *Take a chance* (1933); *George White's Scandals* (1934 and 1935); *Girl of the Golden West* (1938). He recorded prolifically between 1919 and 1936.

Edwards, Gus [Simon, Gus] (*b* Hohensalza, Prussia, 18 Aug. 1879; *d* Hollywood, 7 Nov. 1945). American composer, entertainer, and producer. He emigrated with his parents as a child and settled in America in 1881. He became stage-struck at an early age, singing in saloons and on the ferry-boats of New York, spending his free time hanging around theatres, and got his first chance as a member of the Newsboy Quintet. The rest of his career was divided between singing in various shows, promoting and producing them, and writing songs. He ran his own troupes of young actors and was instrumental in discovering Eddie *Cantor, George Jessel, and Walter Winchell, among many who played in his companies. He retired early owing to ill-health.

He wrote the shows *When We Were Forty-One* (1905); *Hip-Hip-Hooray* (1907); *The Merry-Go-Round* (1908); *School Days* (1908); *Breaking Into Society* (1909); **Ziegfeld Follies of 1910*; *Sunbonnet Sue* (1923); *Broadway Sho-Window* (1936); and music for the films *Hollywood Revue of 1929* and *The Star Maker* (1939). His best-known songs included: 'All I want is my black baby back' (1898, *w* Tom Daly); 'I couldn't stand to see my baby lose' (1899, *w* Will D. *Cobb); 'The singer and the song' (1899, *w* Cobb); 'All for a man whose god was gold' (1900, *w* Cobb); 'I can't tell why I love you, but I do (1900, *w* Cobb); 'I don't want money, I just want you' (1901, *w* Cobb); 'Louisana Lou' (1902, *w* Andrew B. Sterling); 'Could you be true to eyes of blue if you looked into eyes of brown? (1902, *w* Cobb); 'Goodbye, little girl, goodbye' (1904, *w* Cobb); 'In Zanzibar' (1904, *w* Cobb); 'He's my pal' (1905, *w* Vincent Bryan, 1883–1937); 'If a girl like you loved a boy like me' (1905, *w* Cobb); 'In my merry Oldsmobile' (1905, *w* Bryan); 'I just can't make my eyes behave' (1906, *w* Cobb); 'I'd like to see a little more of you' (1906, *w* Bryan); 'Two dirty little hands' (1906, *w* Cobb); 'Sunbonnet Sue' (1908, *w* Cobb); 'By the light of the silv'ry moon' (1909, *w* Edward Madden, 1878–1952); 'Up, up, up in my aeroplane' (1909, *w* Madden); 'Jimmy Valentine' (1911, *w* Madden); 'I lost my heart in Honolulu' (1915, *w* Cobb); and 'Laddie boy' (1918, *w* Cobb).

Edwards, Julian (*b* Manchester, 11 Dec. 1855; *d* Yonkers, NY, 5 Sept. 1910). British composer. He wrote two operettas in Manchester and became well-known as a theatre conductor. From 1877 he was with the Royal English Opera Co., and at Covent Garden from 1883. He went to America in 1888 to concentrate on composition, writing what Isidore Witmark considered to be the only operettas of the time comparable with Victor *Herbert's. He was also an influential director associated with the Duff Opera Company and later directed most of his own productions. An amiable and pleasant-natured man, always anxious to please, he nevertheless wrote music full of verve and passion. He wrote a number of operas, and, in lighter vein for the Broadway stage: *Princess Chic* (1900); *Dolly Varden* (1902)—one of his biggest successes; *When Johnny Comes Marching Home* (1902); *Love's Lottery* (1904); *His Honor the Mayor* (1906); *The Girl and the Governor* (1907); *The Gay Musician* (1908); *The Motor Girl* (1909); *The Girl and the Wizard* (1909); and *Molly May* (1910)

Eldridge, Roy [David] (*b* Pittsburgh, Pa., 30 Jan. 1911; *d* New York, 26 Feb. 1989). American jazz trumpeter, drummer, and vocalist. He started out in 1927 leading a road show band and his first important job was with Fletcher *Henderson's Dixie Stompers in 1928. He was with various big swing bands in the early 1930s (during which time the nickname 'Little Jazz' was given to him by Elmer Snowden) and led his own band in Pittsburgh in 1933. He joined *McKinney's Cotton Pickers in 1934, was with Teddy *Hill in 1935, and Fletcher Henderson in 1936, where he first became known as a soloist. Around this time he recorded with Henderson, Mildred *Bailey, Billie *Holiday, and Benny *Goodman. He led his own band from the late 1930s to the early 1940s, frequently broadcasting from the Three Deuces in Chicago. He was with Gene *Krupa 1941–3; and with Artie *Shaw 1944–5; He led his own band again and toured Europe with *Benny Goodman in 1950, staying in Paris and prominent again as a soloist with Jazz at the Philharmonic. He worked with Ella *Fitzgerald 1963–5, toured abroad, and was at Ryan's in New York 1971–4, also toured Europe with Basie in 1972, and continued to lead a band at Ryan's until he had a stroke in 1980. He was an outstanding *mainstream trumpeter, taking on a degree of modernism in his later years, with a powerful and propulsive style that he skilfully moulded to various needs.

Elen, Gus [Ernest Augustus] (*b* London, 22 July 1862; *d* London, 17 Feb. 1940). British comedian and singer, acknowledged as the greatest of the coster comedians of the music-hall era. He started out in 1882 busking in the London streets and singing in public houses, and in 1883 was with a blackface minstrel troupe in Margate and Ramsgate. He made his first music-hall appearance as part of a minstrel duo at the Seabright Music Hall in Hackney in March 1884, and his first solo appearance was at Charles *Godfrey's Music Hall and Tavern in Camberwell billed as 'Gus Elen, the quaint comedian'. He toured the country and appeared in London again, deputizing for Dan

*Leno (who was ill) at the Middlesex and *Collins in 1887. He became widely known when he first introduced his Cockney songs at the Middlesex Music Hall in 1891 in imitation of Albert *Chevalier.

The first of these was 'Never introduce your donah to a pal' written by his cousin A. E. Durandeau; and he embarked on his coster comedian career with a succession of such songs which he sang with touching pathos in his croaking voice—'Down the Dials', 'E dunno where 'e are', 'Down the road' (by Fred *Gilbert), 'The 'ouses in between', 'It's a great big shame', 'The golden dustman', 'Don't stop my 'arf a pint of beer', and many others which kept Elen at the top of the bill with their mixture of irony and sentimentality. By 1898 he was able to buy a fine house in Balham and in 1907 he toured America. He retired during the First World War but returned to the halls for a while in 1931 and at this time made some recordings of his best songs. He appeared in a Royal Command Performance in 1935 and made a BBC broadcast in 1937.

T. Barker: 'Gus Elen' in *Music-Hall Records* No. 5 (London, Feb. 1979).

Elgart, Les (*b* New Haven, Conn., 3 Aug. 1918). American bandleader and trumpeter. In the early 1940s he played lead trumpet with Bunny *Berigan, Charlie *Spivak, Harry *James, Woody *Herman, and others; forming his first band, with his brother Larry (*b* 1922) on saxophone, 1945–6. He really came to the forefront of the dance-band world when he joined with arranger Charles Albertine to form the quickly acclaimed Les Elgart Band in 1953. It continued, with its distinctive ensemble style, into the 1960s.

Elizalde, Fred [Federico] (*b* Manila, Philippines, 12 Dec. 1908; *d* Manila, 16 Jan. 1969). Spanish composer and conductor. He studied at the Madrid Conservatory and read law at Stanford University in California. He went to England in 1925 to study at Cambridge where, in 1926, he organized a band for the annual *Footlights Revue*. Inspired by the influx of recordings by Duke *Ellington and other American jazz musicians, the band continued as Fred Elizalde's Varsity Band (and other titles), with future cricket star Maurice Allom on tenor-saxophone, and its success led Elizalde for a while to earn a living in the dance music field. He became a pioneering figure in the British jazz world, making some records with such players as Joe Crossman, Jack Miranda, and Max Bacon. To general professional surprise he was then asked to lead a hot band at the Savoy Hotel in London, a venue noted for rather more sedate kinds of dance music. He ensured the success of this venture by going to America and hiring such players as Chelsea Quealey, Adrian *Rollini, and Fud Livingston; their playing, and recordings made 1928–30, were a revelatory influence on the British dance-band world. Thereafter Elizalde returned to an international life of serious music-making and conducting.

Ellington, Duke [Edward Kennedy] (*b* Washington DC, 29 Apr. 1899; *d* New York, 24 May 1974). American jazz composer, bandleader, and pianist. Still the major 'composer' of jazz and an important creative figure in American music. After relinquishing a career in art, he started playing the piano with various groups around Washington, joined Elmer Snowden (1900–73) and in 1923, with some boyhood musician friends, formed his first band. There was a period of ups and downs but finally the band settled into the Kentucky Club in New York and here began to develop the highly individual Ellington sound. At a period when most bands and leaders, apart from Jelly Roll *Morton, were pursuing similar paths and sounds, Ellington, from his own individual imagination, and by utilizing the tonal colours of various skilled musicians, was creating a totally identifiable sound which came to full fruition when the band was engaged to play at the famous *Cotton Club in Harlem in 1927. Here, as a black band playing for a white clientele, they created what was then dubbed the 'jungle' sound that involved much use of mutes and growl techniques. Under the guiding hand of Irving Mills (1894–1985), the band became well-known through being heard on radio; playing for shows, such as *Ziegfeld's *Show Girl* (1929) with score by George *Gershwin; and the film *Check and Double Check* (1930) with Amos 'n' Andy. Ellington's early creations, with their contrasting sections, vivid colours, and endless variety, have remained classics of jazz and he never ceased to replay them, constantly up-dated according to his band resources: 'Black and tan fantasy' (1927); 'East St Louis toodle-oo' (1927); 'Creole love call' (1928); 'Hot and bothered' (1929); 'Mood indigo' (1930); and extended works beyond the normal one record-side length like 'Creole rhapsody' (1931). The band travelled to London in 1933, where Ellington grew to understand that jazz and his own music were taken very seriously by the dedicated jazz fans.

The important members of his bands up to then, whose individual sounds were the ingredients of his inspiration, were Bubber *Miley, Freddy Jenkins (1906–78), Arthur Whetsol (1905–40) and Cootie *Williams (trumpets), Joe *Nanton and Juan *Tizol (trombones), Johnny *Hodges (alto-saxophone), Otto Hardwicke (1904–70) (clarinet and saxophone), Harry *Carney (baritone-saxophone), Barney *Bigard (clarinet), Wellman Braud (1891–1966) (bass), Fred Guy (1897–1971) (guitar), and Sonny Greer (1895–1982) (drums); with Ellington's probing and imaginative piano a good deal more important and effective than some early critics allowed. The finest vocalist he ever had, Ivie *Anderson, was with the band from 1931 to 1942. Some of these musicians, like Hodges and Carney, were to be with him for most of his career and became essential to his identity as a composer. Lawrence Brown (1907–88) was added to the trombones from 1932. By 1940, Miley was long gone and the main trumpet lead came from Cootie Williams, with Rex *Stewart on cornet and Ray

*Nance (trumpet and violin) joining at the end of the year; Ben *Webster a short-term addition to the saxes; and a remarkably inventive and progressive young bass-player, Jimmy *Blanton, whose life was sadly short (1918–42) but who had a crucial effect on the Ellington band and on bass playing in general. The early 1940s saw what many considered to be the peak of Ellington's imaginative achievement in such compositions as 'Jack the Bear', 'Ko-Ko', 'Concerto for Cootie', 'Cotton tail', 'Bojangles', and 'Portrait of Bert Williams'; and there was a constant re-statement of his fine songs penned in the 1930s such as 'It don't mean a thing if it ain't got that swing' (1932); 'Sophisticated lady' (1933); and 'I let a song go out of my heart' (1938). In 1938, Billy *Strayhorn had joined the band as pianist, arranger, amenuensis, and the composer of many items including the band's theme tune 'Take the A train'. An important series of Carnegie Hall concerts began in 1943, in which *Black, Brown and Beige* was introduced.

The band moved into an impressionistic period in the late 1940s, to some extent with Strayhorn's younger outlook prevailing, to produce such things as the 'Liberian suite', and into the LP age with at last a chance to create more substantial works, usually in suite form. Al Hibbler (*b* 1915) was the main vocalist 1943–51; and important new voices in the band were now Harold Baker (1913–66), Taft Jordan (1915–81), Cat *Anderson (trumpets); Jimmy Hamilton (*b* 1917) and Russell Procope (1908–81) (clarinets); Quentin Jackson (1909–76) (trombone); and Oscar Pettiford (1922–60) (bass).

The influential voice of Paul Gonsalves (1920–74) (tenor-saxophone) was added in 1950 and Clark *Terry (trumpet) and Britt Woodman (*b* 1920) (trombone) joined in 1951. After a rather commercial period with Capitol records in 1953–4 and an excursion with Bethlehem 1956 which produced the finely resurgent *Historically Speaking* album, there was a notable extended success with the Shakespearian suite *Such Sweet Thunder* and an exciting new look at the major 1942 work *Black, Brown and Beige*. By this time jazz was well into its modern period and it left an uncertain course open for Ellington. As one whose inspiration had blossomed in the 1930s and who clearly liked the swinging band style, it would not have been true to his nature to move into the *be-bop idiom. He remained mainly true to himself, but the musicians he had available could not re-create exactly things that were perfect in their form and material when they first appeared.

Ellington and the band soldiered on, occasionally finding new inspiration as in the sincere tribute to Strayhorn *And his Mother Called him Bill* (1957) and the *New Orleans Suite* of 1970. There were some rather embarrassingly pretentious departures like the Sacred Concerts, but by now Ellington was an honoured legend and the tributes flowed. No one else in jazz has so far equalled his massive achievement nor over-topped his level of creative writing. The Ellington band was kept together until its creator died in 1974, all those years constantly playing dances and concerts, broadcasting, filming, recording, and tirelessly travelling the world, so that his output, in the face of all the problems and stresses, was astonishing. Like most jazz creators, Ellington's reputation was at the mercy of the gramophone which emphasizes the novel position of a composer of jazz whose works are not for recreation by others, as in the classical field, but must be heard performed by their creator to achieve their true effect. This in spite of the fact that their recordings only represent a very small part of their activities. But at least the records have saved the legacy of a great composer whose works were rarely committed to paper.

Sophisticated Ladies, a celebration of Ellington's music conceived by Donald McKayle and with a 21-piece orchestra conducted by the composer's son Mercer Ellington (*b* 1919) was seen at the Lunt-Fontanne Theatre, New York, 1 Mar. 1981 [767p].

B. Ulanov: *Duke Ellington* (New York, 1946). P. Gammond (ed.): *Duke Ellington: his Life and Music* (London, 1958; repr. New York, 1977). S. Dance: *The World of Duke Ellington* (New York, 1970). D. Ellington: *Music is my Mistress* (New York, 1973). D. Jewell: *Duke* (London, 1977). M. Ellington & S. Dance: *Duke Ellington in Person* (New York, 1978). H. Ruland: *Duke Ellington: sein Leben, seine Musik, seine Schallplatten* (Gauting-Buchendorf, 1985). J. L. Collier: *Duke Ellington* (New York, 1987). P. Gammond: *Duke Ellington* (London, 1987).

Elliott, G. H. [George Henry] (*b* Rochdale, Lancs., 3 Nov. 1884; *d* Brighton, 1 Nov. 1962). British singer. He was taken to the USA as a child and worked for a time with the Primrose West Minstrels. From his return to England in 1901, well trained in minstrelsy, he was to continue the blackface tradition into the 1940s, earning the music-hall title of the 'Chocolate Coloured Coon'. He appeared with the Harry Reynolds's Minstrels at Colwyn Bay, singing mainly American material and first appeared in the London halls in 1902. He was to become the successor to Eugene *Stratton, who died in 1918, reviving many of the Leslie *Stuart songs that Stratton sang and adding to a considerable repertoire with such items as 'I want to go to Idaho', 'Sue, Sue, Sue', 'Hello, Susie Green', 'I'se a waitin' for yer, Josie', 'Rastus Brown', and 'I used to sigh for the silv'ry moon'. He appeared at a Royal Variety Performance in 1925 and again in 1948 with the *Thanks for the Memory* company.

Elliott, 'Ramblin' Jack [Adnopoz, Elliott Charles] (*b* Brooklyn, NY, 1 Aug. 1931). American folk-singer and guitarist. The son of a doctor, he left home to become a wandering troubadour and lived out in the open, interpreting the songs of Woody *Guthrie (who was a special idol and one of the first he made a point of meeting), Jimmie *Rodgers, and the *Carter Family. He was adept at imitating their characteristics (Guthrie once said: 'Elliott sounds more like me than I do'), which he gradually absorbed into a distinct style of his own. He came to Europe in the 1950s and in London was welcomed as the prophet of the folk blues, with British musicians and singers eager to absorb all he could tell them. He appeared in clubs, on radio and TV, and recorded for Topic Records, working for a time with Derroll Adams, who had also come to Britain. He returned to California for a year but was back in Britain in 1959 and furthered his influence both on the music and the lifestyle of the new folk generation. He appeared at the Mariposa Folk Festival in 1971 and 1975; and the 'singing cowboy from Brooklyn' has continued to wander the world with his guitar, perpetuating his own and other people's legends.

Ellis, Don [Donald Johnson] (*b* Los Angeles, 25 July 1934; *d* Hollywood, 17 Dec. 1978). American jazz trumpeter. He became thoroughly versed in music after studying the trumpet with seven different teachers and studying composition at Boston University. From 1956 to 1960 he worked with various bands and groups including those of Maynard *Ferguson and George Russell, basing his trumpet style on that of players like *Gillespie, *Navarro, and *Terry. He went to Los Angeles in 1964 for further study and, discovering a special interest in Indian music, he formed the Hindustani Jazz Sextet.

From 1965 he led a series of big bands which pioneered the use of rock rhythms and electronic instruments and the general advancement of the jazz-rock movement of the 1970s. From 1966 he used a four-valve trumpet that could produce quarter-tones and equipped his trumpet section to do the same; also adding Indian elements to the sound, including the sitar. He made bold experiments with time-signatures with bars of anything from 9 to 19 beats and even up to 85. Anything so common as common time was not permitted on most of his recordings, and yet he contrived not to make the music sound too self-conscious. His creations included 'Turkish bath' (in 7/4 time) and 'Indian lady' (in 5/4). His most ambitious scores were 'Contrasts for Two Orchestras and Trumpet', written in 1965 and premièred by the Los Angeles Symphony Orchestra, and 'Reach', a cantata performed at the Berlin Jazz Festival. He was an articulate exponent of his theories, writing and lecturing from the 1960s. In spite of a heart-attack in 1975 he returned to playing, appearing at the Jazz Yatra in Bombay in 1978 some months before he died. He was an invigorating prophet of the more intellectual elements of jazz.

Ellis, Mary [Elsas, Mary] (*b* New York, 15 June 1900). American actress. She appeared on Broadway in **Rose-Marie* (1924). She settled in London in 1930 and was in *Kern's **Music in the Air* (1933); but was especially remembered as an Ivor *Novello leading lady, in **Glamorous Night* (1935); *The *Dancing Years* (1939); and *Arc de Triomphe* (1943). She was also in *Coward's *After the Ball* (1954). She played many non-musical roles and her appearances in films included *All the King's Horses* (1935).

M. Ellis: *Those Dancing Years* (London, 1982).

Ellis, Vivian (*b* Hampstead, London, 29 Oct. 1904). British composer and author, a grandson of the composer Julian Woolf. He studied piano with Myra Hess and started his musical career as a concert pianist. His first song was published when he was 15, and he soon became attracted by the theatre; starting by contributing to revues—*The Curate's Egg* (1922); *The Second Little Revue Starts at Nine* 1924); *Yoicks* (1924). He then embarked on a series of musical comedies in the light upper-crust British vein then dominating the British musical theatre: *By-the-Way* (1925); *Mercenary Mary* (1925)—which included the hit song 'Over my shoulder'; *Still Dancing* (1925); *Kid Boots* (1926); more revues—*Palladium Pleasures* (1926); *Cochran's Revue of 1926; Blue Skies* (1927); *Clowns in Clover* (1927); *Will o' the Whispers* (1928); *Charlot's Revue* (1928); musicals—*The Girl Friend* (1927); **Mr Cinders* (1929); *The House that Jack Built* (1929); *Follow a Star* (1930); *Little Tommy Tucker* (1930); *Blue Roses* (1931); *Stand Up and Sing* (1931); *The Song of the Drum* (1931); *Out of the Bottle* (1932); *Please* (1933); **Jill Darling* (1933); *Streamline* (1934); revues—*Folly to be Wise* (1931); *The Town Talks* (1936); *Going Places* (1936); *Floodlight* (1937); musicals—*Hide and Seek* (1937); *The Fleet's Lit Up* (1938); *Running Riot* (1938); *Under Your Hat* (1938). Most of these productions were in the Eton-accented musical-comedy style that made the British musical such a domestic affair; although many of them had considerable success in the London theatre as promoters of Ellis's politely memorable songs such as 'Spread a little happiness', 'The wind in the willows', and 'I'm on a see-saw'.

The intervention of war seemed to lower the Ellis tone a degree or two; or perhaps fashions changed after the new and robust American musicals like **Annie Get Your Gun* appeared. In the mid-1940s he seemed to switch quite clearly to a more substantial, almost operetta vein with *Big Ben* (1946) and his biggest and most lasting work **Bless the Bride* (1947). He continued with *Tough at the Top* (1949); **And So to Bed* (1951); *Over the Moon* (1953); *The Water Gypsies* (1955); *Half in Earnest* (1958). He also wrote for such typically British films as *Jack's the Boy* (1932)—'The flies crawled up the window', 'I want to cling to Ivy'; *Falling for You* (1933)—'Sweep'; *Public Nusiance No. 1* (1935)—'Me and my dog', 'Between you and me and the carpet', 'Give me a place in the sun'. Other creations ranged from 'The Yale blues' (*w* Collie Knox) which was used for a dance craze of the same name invented by Cecil H. Taylor and demonstrated at the Park Lane Hotel, London, in 1927, to 'Coronation Scot' (1948) a popular radio theme tune for the Paul Temple series. He was the author of novels and humorous books.

V. Ellis: *I'm on a See-Saw* (London, 1953; repr. 1974).
V. Ellis: *Good-bye, Dollie* (London, 1970).

Elman, Ziggy [Finkelman, Harold] (*b* Philadelphia, 26 May 1914; *d* Van Nuys, Calif., 26 June 1968). American trumpeter and bandleader. He played in local bands before joining Benny *Goodman in 1936, with whom he became well-known for his solo playing in such items as 'And the angels sing' (which he wrote), succeeding Harry *James as lead trumpeter when James left to form his own band in 1938. In 1939 he made a series of recordings under his own name mostly with contingents from the Goodman band which he left in 1940. He was with Tommy *Dorsey 1940–3 and 1946–7; led his own bands on the West Coast; toured with Goodman in 1953; and was active until the 1960s when illness prevented him from playing and he ran a music shop.

Elsie, Lily [Cotton, Lily Elsie] (*b* Wortley, Yorks. 8 Apr. 1886; *d* London, 16 Dec. 1962). British actress and singer; a star of musical comedy, with a light but attractive voice and lovely face, who was to capture the heart of the British public and set fashions in the British production of *The *Merry Widow* in 1907. She also appeared in: *A *Chinese Honeymoon* (1901); *Lady Madcap* (1904); *The *Cingalee* (1904); *The Little Michus* (1905); *The Little Cherub* (1906); *See-See* (1906); *The New Aladdin* (1906); *The *Dollar Princess* (1909); *A *Waltz Dream* (1911); *The *Count of Luxembourg* (1911); *Pamela* (1917); and *The Blue Train* (1927).

Emerald Isle, The, *or The Caves of Carrig-Cleena*. Comic opera noteworthy as the last to be worked on by Sir Arthur *Sullivan, who was writing the score to a book by Basil *Hood when he died in 1900; and the first by Edward *German, who was given the task of finishing the job. It was eventually produced at the Savoy Theatre 27 Apr. 1901 and achieved 205 performances; being seen in New York at the Herald Square Theatre 1 Sept. 1902. It had a brief vogue but is rarely heard today.

Emmett, Daniel Decatur (*b* Mt Vernon, Ohio, 29 Oct. 1815; *d* Mt Vernon, 28 June 1904). American minstrel and composer. He began his career as a military band drummer, then joined the Virginia Minstrels as singer and banjo player, and was later with the famous Bryant's Minstrels. In 1859 he added to musical history by writing the words and music of *'Dixie' or 'I wish I was in Dixie's Land', which became enormously popular in the Civil War years, particularly as a soldiers' song in the South—although Emmett himself was a Northerner and it was equally popular there. He also wrote 'Old Dan Tucker', 'The road to Richmond', and 'Walk along' which were almost as popular in their day.

C. B. Galbreath: *Daniel Decatur Emmett* (Columbus, Ohio, 1904). H. O. Wintermute: *Daniel Decatur Emmett* (Mt Vernon, Ohio, 1955). H. Nathan: *Dan Emmett and the Rise of Early Negro Minstrelsy* (Norman, Okla., 1962).

Empire Theatre. Celebrated London theatre which opened on 17 Apr. 1884 with a performance of *Chilpéric* by Hervé. It was built on the site of Saville House on the north side of Leicester Square which was burnt down in 1865. After many delays the grand new theatre, horseshoe-shaped, with a balcony and a famous promenade that was to become notorious, was opened with a total audience capacity of 3500. The venture was not, however, a total success. Burlesque, operettas, and ballets failed to draw large audiences and even a spectacular *Round the World in Eighty Days* failed. The theatre closed in 1886 to re-open in 1887 as the Empire Theatre of Varieties under the management of George *Edwardes and Augustus Harris. In addition to prestigious variety shows it became famous for its spectacular ballets and a new entrance and foyer were considered necessary in 1893. It was at this time that the promenade, which had become a well-known rendezvous for 'ladies of the town' and their gentlemen customers, came under the scrutiny of the famous reformer Mrs Ormiston Chant, and the LCC had to close the Empire, reopening it when the promenade had been partitioned off. This so outraged the male patrons they tore the partitions down and the promenade continued its career until 1916 when the theatre was no longer used as a music-hall. From 1898 it was known as the Empire Theatre.

In 1905 it staged its first revue, variety and ballet were ousted, and it mainly became a home for such musical shows as *The *Lilac Domino, *Irene, The Rebel Maid,* and Jack *Buchanan in *Boodle* (1925). The last musical was *Gershwin's **Lady Be Good* starring the *Astaires. The premises were bought by the MGM Film Corporation, the last stage performance was given on 22 Jan. 1927, and it was closed for demolition. A cinema was built on the site, opening on 8 Nov. 1928 and showing *Trelawny of the 'Wells'*. Even then its live performance days were not over as from Dec. 1949 to 1952 the stage was used for interposed revue presentations. The Empire Cinema closed in May 1961 and was redesigned as a combined smaller cinema and the Mecca dance-hall.

R. Mander & J. Mitchenson: 'The Empire Theatre' in *The Lost Theatres of London* (London, 1968).

Engel, Lehman (*b* Jackson, Miss., 14 Sept. 1910; *d* New York, 29 Aug. 1982). American composer, and author. He studied at the Cincinnati College of Music 1927–9 and at the Juilliard School of Music 1930–4, and started to write for the ballet and theatre while still a student. He conducted the premières of *Weill's *Der Jasager* in 1933 and *Johnny Johnson* in 1937. In 1935–9 he led the Madrigal Singers and later worked with the Mercury Theatre. After the war he wrote a considerable amount of incidental music, notably for *Murder in the Cathedral* and *A Streetcar Named Desire,* and worked with others on such musicals as **Fanny* and **Li'l Abner*. He conducted *The *Threepenny Opera; *Show Boat*; **Brigadoon*; **Annie Get Your Gun*; *Fanny*; **Guys and Dolls*; **Carousel*; *The Consul*; and works by *Gilbert and Sullivan. A teacher and lecturer, he wrote many important books on the American musical theatre including: *Planning and Producing the Musical Show* (1957); *The American Musical Theater: a Consideration* (1967); *The Musical Book* (1971); *Words and Music* (1972); *Their Words are Music: the Great Theatre Lyricists and their Lyrics* (1975); and *Getting the Show On* (1983).

L. Engel: *This Bright Day: an Autobiography* (New York, 1974).

Englander, Ludwig (*b* Vienna, 1859; *d* Far Rockaway, NY, 13 Sept. 1914). American composer. He studied music in Vienna and had some lessons with *Offenbach, moving to America in 1882 and becoming conductor at the Thalia Theatre under Heinrich Conried, where his first operetta, *The Prince Consort*, was produced. His reputation was made with his contributions to *The *Passing Show* (1894) and he became a prolific and successful writer, his best-known work being *The Casino Girl* in 1900. Towards the end of his career his melodic invention seemed to falter and his old-fashioned, Viennese-style scores required the addition of new material by younger composers like Jerome *Kern.

He wrote 35 musicals shows, none of which have shown any lasting qualities, including: *The Twentieth Century Girl* (1895); *The Little Corporal* (1898); *The Rounders* (1899); *The Belle of Bohemia* (1900); *The Strollers* (1901); *The New Yorkers* (1901); *The Wild Rose* (1902); *Sally in our Alley* (1902); *The Office Boy* (1903); *A Madcap Princess* (1904); *The Rich Mr Hoggenheimer* (1905); *The Gay White Way* (1907); and *Miss Innocence* (1908).

English Folk Dance and Song Society. A society formed by the amalgamation of the Folksong Society, founded in 1898, and the English Folk Dance Society, founded by Cecil *Sharp in 1911. Its object is the study and revival of British folk-music to which end it keeps a valuable archive, publishes books and journals, and holds concerts and festivals. The first director was Cecil Sharp and after his death it became the joint responsibility of Ralph Vaughan Williams (1872–1958), Maud Karpeles (1885–1976), and Douglas Kennedy.

Ennis, Skinnay [Robert] (*b* Salisbury, NC, 13 Aug. 1909; *d* Beverly Hills, Calif., 3 June 1963). American singer. He began to sing with the Hal Kemp band while still a student in 1927, both he and the band becoming professional in the late 1920s, and toured Europe in 1930. He became known for his intimate, breathless style and with such songs as 'Got a date with an angel' and 'Lamplight'. He left Kemp in 1938 to become a bandleader, taking over the Gil *Evans band, with Evans staying on as arranger and Claude *Thornhill joining its ranks. He appeared in many films in the 1940s, worked on the Bob Hope show and with Abbott and Costello 1946–7, and in the 1950s was playing in Los Angeles.

Erdman, Ernie (*b* Pittsburgh, 23 Oct. 1879; *d* Rockford, Ill., 1 Nov. 1946). American songwriter. A popular pianist in Chicago in his younger days, he was the house pianist at Schiller's restaurant and for a time played with the *Original Dixieland Jazz Band, becoming involved in a famous lawsuit over the tune 'Livery stable blues' of which he was part-creator. Later he joined a music-publishing business and wrote 'Toot, toot, tootsie, goodbye' (1922) and 'Nobody's sweetheart' (1924).

Erminie. Early operetta with score by Edward Jakobowski, first produced at the Comedy Theatre, London, 9 Nov. 1885, which had a notable success in the USA (for its time) running for 1256 performances at the New York Casino Theatre from 10 May 1886. Its American star was the handsome, acrobatic Francis Wilson (1854–1935), a prototype film star, who sang the role of Cadeaux some 1300 times altogether; the cast also included Kitty Cheatham (1864–1945). *Erminie* became a model for many romantic, picaresque operettas to come and its pink ballroom scene set an early fashion for the colour. 'Dear mother, in dreams I see her' became one of the most popular songs of the day. It became a part of American musical theatre history and was often revived there into the 1920s. There was a production at the Carltheater in Vienna, 7 Nov. 1890 as *Erminy*.

Essex, David [Cook, Albert David] (*b* London, 23 July 1947). British singer and actor. He began his career as a rock drummer who sang a bit, was given a chance to record, but made little progress in the musical world and went into repertory as an actor. He played in a *Flanders and Swann revue, *Ten Years Hard*, at the Mayfair Theatre in 1970, but became a known name when he was given the role of Jesus in the rock-musical **Godspell* in 1971 and was in the film *That'll be the Day*. His records now began to sell and 'Gonna make you a star' became a No. 1 hit. The song 'Stardust' became the title of a film he made with Adam *Faith and more hits followed—'Rolling stone', 'Hold me close', and 'If I could'. Another West End success came with the role of Che Guevara in **Evita* (1978). His subsequent career has been divided between acting and recording.

G. Tremlett: *The David Essex Story* (London, 1974).

Estes, 'Sleepy' John Adam (*b* Ripley, Tenn., 25 Jan. 1899; *d* Brownsville, Tenn., 5 June 1977). American blues singer, guitarist, and composer. One of 16 children of a tenant farmer, his family moved to Brownsville, which was to be the singer's lifelong home. Blinded in one eye as a boy, he gradually lost his sight completely. Learning from the singer 'Hambone' Willie Newbern, he built his guitar technique and formulated his own approach, writing many personalized blues such as 'Brownsville blues', 'Shelby County Workhouse blues', and 'Floating bridge'. He became a pioneer recording artist in Memphis before the depression years, first recording in 1929 in the company of other local bluesmen such as harmonica player Hammie

Nixon, James 'Yank' Rachel, and Son Bonds. He made some more records in 1934 then slipped into obscurity and poverty until the booming interest in jazz and folk-music brought him back to attention and a vital appearance at the Newport Folk Festival in 1964. He toured Europe in 1964 and 1968 and continued to appear at important festivals, touring Japan in 1974.

Etting, Ruth (*b* David City, Neb., 23 Nov. 1896; *d* Colorado Springs, 24 Sept. 1978). American actress and singer. She made her first appearance in the chorus of a Chicago revue in 1925 and first appeared in the **Ziegfeld Follies* in 1927 singing 'Shaking the blues away'. Slim, blonde, and dramatic, she was to be pre-eminently known as a torch singer and was particularly in her element as a nightclub entertainer. She made a mark with various songs of this genre—'Love me or leave me' in **Whoopee* (1928); 'Get happy' in *9:15 Revue* (1930); 'Ten cents a dance' in *Simple Simon* (1930); and 'Shine on harvest moon' in *Ziegfeld Follies* (1931). She was seen in London in *Transatlantic Rhythm* (1936). In Hollywood she appeared in such films as *Roman Scandals* (1933); *Mr Broadway* (1933); *Hips Hips Hooray* (1934); and *The Gift of Gab* (1934). She retired from the entertainment scene in 1938 except for brief radio appearances during the war; thus becoming a legendary figure deemed worthy of a film biography, *Love Me or Leave Me* (1955), in which she was played by Doris *Day and her gangster husband by James *Cagney.

Europe, James Reese (*b* Mobile, Ala., 22 Feb. 1881; *d* Boston, Mass., 9 May 1919). American pianist, violinist, and conductor. He went to New York in 1904 and became an important figure in black musical circles by organizing the Amsterdam Musical Association (1906) and forming the orchestra of the *Clef Club, both units concerned with the employment and payment of black musicians. He formed his own orchestra in 1910 which backed the dancers Vernon and Irene *Castle in **Watch Your Step* (1912) and introduced many of their dances. He joined the army in the First World War to become director of the famous 369th Light Infantry Band. During its triumphant peacetime tour of the USA in 1919 he was involved in an argument with a drummer who stabbed him to death.

Eurovision Song Contest. Glamorized contest run on Miss World lines, started by BBC Television in 1956. Although it appeals to a wide public and occasionally produces best-selling groups, it is treated with disdain by the rock connoisseur because it operates within a confined and inbred *Tin Pan Alley orbit and tends to favour bland, formulated music and performers of the clean, upstanding, family-oriented kind, only marginally related to the introspective world of art rock. Britain had its first notable success in 1967 with Sandie Shaw (*b* 1947) singing 'Puppet on a string' which was a prototype of the tuneful but rather trite songs which continued with Cliff *Richard's 'Congratulations' the following year. The contest brought success to the sort of performers that conformed to or courted its requirements, such groups as Dana, Brotherhood of Man, Bucks Fizz, and *Abba (winners in 1973).

Evangeline. Historic American *burlesque musical, one of the first to be conceived in the modern mould with its score and book written by one composer, Edward E. *Rice, and one author, J. Cheever Goodwin (1850–1912), also remembered for his book for *Wang* and the first American to make a career as a librettist. It made a short appearance for 16 performances at Niblo's Gardens 27 July 1874, went to Boston, and then toured before being seen at *Daly's Theatre, New York, 4 June 1877. After two months the show again went on tour but for 30 years was on and off the New York stage including 251 performances at the 14th Street Theatre in 1885. It was inspired by the success of *The *Black Crook* (1866) and the vogue for bare-legged dancers like the British troupe led by Lydia Thompson. A travesty of a poem by Longfellow, the story tells of the worldwide journeys of Evangeline in search of her true love and it had such quaint numbers as its 'Spinning-wheel song', 'Thinking, love, of thee', 'Sweet Evangeline', and a march that became a current favourite.

Evans, Bill [William John] (*b* Plainfield, NJ, 16 Aug. 1929; *d* New York, 15 Sept. 1980). American jazz pianist and composer, an influential musician who suddenly appeared on the scene in the 1950s, joining Tony Scott (*b* 1921) in 1956 and making a solo album that year. He had a productive eight months with the Miles *Davis Quintet in 1959, also recording with Charlie *Mingus and George Russell (*b* 1923), and led his own trio from 1959. He was a strong influence in the Davis band and in the two albums he recorded with it—*Jazz Track* and *Kind of Blue*—using impressionist-inspired harmonies (Debussy and Satie) and a modal base to foreshadow much of the cool jazz of the 1970s and 1980s in compositions like 'Peace piece'. His distinctive piano style, influenced by Lennie *Tristano, varied in touch and lyrically expressive, influenced the style of many groups that followed. Other compositions included 'Blue in green', 'Waltz for Debby', and 'Turn out the stars'. His life was sadly shortened by drug addiction.

Evans, George 'Honey Boy' (*b* Wales, 1870; *d* Baltimore, 1915). Composer and singer. He went to the USA at the age of seven and became a well-known minstrel and comedian, taking his stage name from his song success of 1894 'I'll be true to my honey boy'. His biggest hit was 'In the good old summer time' which was sung by Blanche *Ring in *The Defender* (1902) and he also wrote 'In the merry month of June' (1903); 'Come, take a trip in my airship' (1904); 'You'll have to wait till my ship comes in' (1906), and 'Come to the land of Bohemia' (1907)—all written in collaboration with Ren *Shields.

Evans, Gil [Green, Ian Ernest Gilmore] (*b* Toronto, 13 May 1912; *d* Mexico, 20 Mar. 1988). Canadian jazz pianist and composer of Australian parentage. Becoming interested in jazz through recordings by Louis *Armstrong and others, he taught himself to play the piano and studied arranging and composition. The family moved to Stockton, California, from where he led a band 1933–8. The band was then taken over by Skinnay *Ennis, Evans staying as arranger until he joined Claude *Thornhill in 1941, remaining with him until 1948. He became known for his varied and original arrangements that involved additional French horns and tuba. In 1947 he set out to achieve a full band sound with the nine-piece band led by Miles *Davis and including Gerry *Mulligan and John *Lewis (with French horn in the line-up); and arranged such pieces as 'Moondreams' and 'Boplicity' which were hailed as jazz masterpieces. After a quiet period in the 1950s, he re-emerged with a 19-piece band featuring Miles Davis (including horn, tuba, and woodwind) to produce three albums which have been reckoned as among some of the finest orchestral arrangements this century—*Miles Ahead* (1957); *Porgy and Bess* (1958); and *Sketches of Spain* (1959–60). Each took on the stature of a concerto for trumpet with orchestral colouring and sounds that were new to both jazz and orchestral music as a whole.

In 1961, Evans performed with Davis at Carnegie Hall, and he spent the 1960s in arranging for various artists, making rare appearances with his band at festivals and concerts. From 1970 into the 1980s he made regular appearances at the Village Vanguard in New York with leading jazz musicians, experimenting with various instruments, including augmented percussion, electronic instruments, and synthesizers, and using rock rhythms. He made extensive tours abroad in the 1970s, making his first appearance in Britain in 1978 and coming again in 1983 to lead an orchestra of British musicians. An extraordinary jazz and composing talent, not making his full impact as either writer or pianist until he was in his forties, he then became one of the most influential and original figures in the jazz world (Gerry Mulligan awarded him the anagrammatic name 'Svengali'); a natural successor to Duke *Ellington in the creation of compositional but living jazz. His writing for various instruments has always shown a deep understanding of their capabilities and inherent possibilities. He continued into the 1980s to produce music that became increasingly improvisational yet still inimitably his own—vital, probing, adventurous, and a source of inspiration to other jazz musicians.

R. Horricks: *Gil Evans* (London, 1984).

Evans, Tolchard [Sydney] (*b* London, 1901; *d* London, 12 Mar. 1978). British composer. He began his working life as office boy with publisher Lawrence Wright and was a cinema pianist for a while before moving back into the music-publishing business. He sold his first song when he was in his teens and during his songwriting career was to produce more than a thousand titles, most of them published. At one time four major London dance bands were using Tolchard Evans numbers as signature tunes; and he led his own band from 1925 into the 1950s. His first big song success came with 'Barcelona' in 1926; his biggest hit, 'Lady of Spain', in 1931. He continued in the 1930s (mainly in collaboration with Stanley J. Damerell and Robert Hargreaves) with 'Life's desire' (1931); 'Let's all sing like the birdies sing' (1932); 'If' (1934); 'Unless' (1934); 'Song of the trees' (1935);'There's a lovely lake in London' (1935); 'Dance, gypsy, dance' (1937); and 'Butterflies in the rain' (1940). In the 1950s he was winning awards with such songs as 'Everywhere' (1955) and 'My September love' (1956). Although the pop era found him outmoded, he continued to be a popular and influentially outspoken figure and won the Ivor Novello Award for Outstanding Services to British Music 1973–4.

Evans's Music and Supper Rooms. Historic venue in the development of music-hall history, a precursor of the halls where a chairman presided over the entertainment which had to win its way over the gastronomic and drinking activities of its customers. Situated at 43 King Street in Covent Garden, London, in fine premises built in the reign of Charles II, the house was used by various aristocratic families but started on a downward path in 1773 when it became a family hotel, one of its later managers being a Mr Joy who named it Joy's Hotel.

The next proprietor was a Mr W. C. Evans who now traded under the name of 'Evans's (late Joy's)'—the *'Late Joys' tag later providing an apt title for the music-hall revival activities that were promoted by the Players' Theatre group founded by Leonard Sachs (1909–90) and Peter Ridgeway in 1936. Evans turned the premises into a music-and-supper room (with flats above) which started its operations at midnight and provided a bawdy meeting-place for the men-about-town of the day.

Evans retired in 1844 and the new proprietor was Paddy Green who had the premises entirely rebuilt with a 72-foot-long music-hall, a stage, alternative seating accommodation for ladies, and a separate restaurant. The rest became the Covent Garden Hotel. Its total capacity was now 1000, with performances starting at eight o'clock, and it was here, and in similar establishments elsewhere in London, that music-hall took its first steps to becoming a popular art form. After the song-and-supper days were over the premises became the Grand Hotel in 1854, the Falstaff Club in 1880, and thereafter the National Sporting Club.

Even Dozen Jug Band. A short-lived group that made some impact in the urban folk revival period of the 1960s, playing 'for fun' a commercialized but earthy ragtime-cum-folk sort of bluesy *spasm band music with rock overtones. It was an uneasily poised effort, recording one album in 1964, and then disbanding. With a nucleus of some seven players, plus friends, it contained some remarkable talents that were to disperse into the musical scene in various ways—mandolist Dave Grisman, country and ragtime guitarist Stefan Grossman, ragtime revivalist Joshua *Rifkin, Steve Katz of *Blood, Sweat and Tears fame, John Sebastian of the *Lovin' Spoonful, and leading record man Peter Siegl.

Ever Green. Musical show written for London by composer Richard *Rodgers, with book by Benn W. Levy and lyrics by Lorenz *Hart. It opened at the Adelphi Theatre 3 Dec. 1930, and was to be a successful showcase for the talents of Sonnie *Hale and Jessie *Matthews, running for 254 performances. Its best-remembered item was the song 'Dancing on the ceiling' (originally written for *Simple Simon* but not used) which produced a memorable Jessie Matthews performance, especially as seen in the filmed version, *Evergreen* (1934), directed by Victor Saville (1896–1979).

Everly Brothers: Don (*b* Brownie, Ky., 1 Feb. 1937); **Phil** (*b* Brownie, 19 Jan. 1939). American singing duo. Don Everly made his first appearance on radio at the age of eight and both brothers toured the USA with their parents before moving to Nashville and adopting the new rock-cum-Country-and-Western-cum-rhythm-'n'-blues style that was to bring them joint fame. They had successful hits with such items as 'Bye bye love' (1957) and the No. 1 hits 'Wake up little Susie' (1957), 'All I have to do is dream' (1957), and 'Cathy's clown' (1960). Unlike their contemporaries, *Haley, *Presley, and *Holly, the Everlys were not directly influenced by black rhythm 'n' blues but were basically a fairly conventional hillbilly act singing in the typical close-harmony Country and Western style. Their songs, mainly written by the husband and wife team of Boudleaux and Felice *Bryant, were typically teenage-slanted numbers concentrating on the romantic problems of the 14–18 age group, nearer to the Ricky *Nelson style than to Presley. Nevertheless they had a substantial influence on many later singers and groups, including the *Beatles, *Beach Boys, *Hollies, *Lovin' Spoonful, *Byrds and, most clearly, *Simon and Garfunkel. Brotherly relations became strained and in 1973 they went their separate ways with only occasional contrived reunions.

'Ever of thee'. Song, with music by Foley Hall and words by George *Linley published in London in 1852, of unsurpassed sentimentality, which moved the Victorians to tears and became a remarkable best-seller. The playwright Arthur Wing Pinero recalls being thus moved when he heard it as a boy and later included a rendering in the farewell party scene of *Trelawny of the 'Wells'* (1898) where it was sung by Irene Vanbrugh. George Bernard Shaw, in his review of the play, drew attention to the song's plagiarisms from Henry *Russell's 'Cheer, boys, cheer'. It was still in use in the National Theatre production in the 1960s. Little is known of Foley Hall, who died *c.* 1866, though he did write and publish a number of similar songs.

Evita. Musical with score by Andrew *Lloyd Webber and book by Tim *Rice, first produced in London (Prince Edward Theatre) 21 June 1978. Almost operatic in form, with the plot related entirely through songs and dances, the work had originally been conceived as a recording project, but an imaginative production and the popularity of 'Don't cry for me, Argentina' made it an unassailable success that was to achieve a spectacular run.

The story was based on the life of Argentina's scheming Eva Perón who rose from being a model and minor actress to become the wife of General Juan Perón. When he was elected president she became No. 1 lady in the country and, though almost entirely self-seeking, was looked upon as a saint when she died of cancer at the age of 33. The part of Evita was first played by Elaine *Paige, Perón by Joss Ackland (*b* 1928), and the narrator and observing conscience of the events, Che Guevára, by David *Essex.

The show's success in London gave it sufficient impetus in the USA to survive some hostile reviews and with Patti LuPone as Eva (succeeded by six other leading ladies in turn), Bob Gunton as Perón, and Mandy Patinkin as Guevára, it ran at the Broadway Theatre from 25 Sept. 1979 for 1568 performances. It was staged at the Theater an der Wien, Vienna, 20 Jan. 1981.

Ewing, Montague (*b* London, 1890; *d* London, 4 Mar. 1957). British composer and pianist, writer of light orchestral works, piano pieces, and music for films, also working under the name of Sherman Myers. His compositions included 'The policeman's holiday' (1911); 'If ever you are dreaming' (1920, *w* Edward Lockton); 'Portrait of a toy soldier' (1934); 'Ev'rywhere' (1935, *w* Larry Kahn); 'Fairies in the moon' (1934); 'At the ladybird's ball' (1935); 'Butterflies in the rain' (1938); and 'My September love' (1955, *w* Richard Mullan).

Expresso Bongo. Musical satire with score by David *Heneker and Monty *Norman, book by Wolf Mankowitz and Julian More, produced in London at the Saville Theatre, 23 Apr. 1958. It had the distinguished cast of Paul Scofield (*b* 1922), James Kenney (*b* 1930), Hy Hazell (1920–70), and Millicent *Martin, and achieved 315 performances. It was filmed in 1959 with Laurence Harvey (1928–73), Sylvia Sims, Yolande Donlan, and Cliff *Richard.

Eysler, Edmund (*b* Vienna, 12 Mar. 1874; *d* Vienna, 4 Oct. 1949). Austrian composer. He studied at the Vienna Conservatory, and found his métier in the popular musical theatre, supplying it with tuneful, romantic, and often very attractive songs and well-written scores. He wrote 63 stage works including 40 full-length operettas, the first of these being *Das Gastmahl des Luculus* (1901) and the second, and most lastingly popular, *Bruder Straubinger* produced in Vienna 20 Feb. 1903 at the famous Theater an der Wien, with over 100 performances in its first year and a best-selling hit in 'Küssen ist keine Sünd'. He was in the USA for a time in 1909 to adapt *The *Dollar Princess* and had several shows produced there. Other popular works were *Pufferl* (1905); *Künstlerblut* (1906)—performed in New York as *The Love Cure* (1909); *Vera Violetta* (1907; NY, 1911); *Das Glückschweinchen* (1908); *Der unsterbliche Lumpe* (1910); *Das Zirkuskind* (1911); *Der Frauenfresser* (1911)—New York as *The Woman Haters* (1912); *Der lachende Ehemann* (1913)—New York as *The Laughing Husband* (1914); and many more mainly produced in Vienna; one of his last great successes being *Die goldene Meisterin*, produced in Vienna 13 Sept. 1927; his last work was aptly called *Wiener Musik* (1947). In the 1920s he spiced his predominantly romantic style with the spreading pseudo-jazz style that currently pleased the public.

R. Prosl: *Edmund Eysler* (Vienna, 1947).

F

Faces, The. British rock group formed in 1968 with three ex-members of the Small Faces—Ronnie Lane, Ian McLagan, and Kenny Jones, joining two ex-members of the Jeff Beck Group—Rod *Stewart and Ron Wood. Their first LP was issued under the name Small Faces. It took two years or so for the new group to establish itself; and then by virtue of their exciting live performances rather than the usual gramophone success. Their 'boozy and easy-going approach' and the parallel success of Rod Stewart as a solo artist, with such hits as 'Maggie May' (1971) to his credit, gave them a keen following. In the end, Stewart's dominance of the group led to others leaving for their own solo careers or with other groups (Wood into the *Rolling Stones, Jones eventually into the *Who) and they broke up in 1975.

Face the Music. Musical comedy with music and lyrics by Irving *Berlin, book by Moss *Hart, produced at the New Amsterdam Theatre, New York 17 Feb. 1932 for 165 performances, with a further 32 at the 44th Street Theatre 31 Jan. 1933. The cast was headed by Mary Boland. It was one of a number of shows of the period that took on a new cynically satirical tone in the wake of the depression years, its target the corruptible politicians and police and its story, a regular favourite, that of an over-rich person who tries to lose some wealth by backing an obviously bad show which, in due reflection of public taste, becomes a hit. *Face the Music* is remembered as the source of such Berlin classics as 'Let's have another cup of coffee', 'Soft lights and sweet music', and 'On a roof in Manhattan'.

Fagan, Barney (*fl.* 1890–1927). An Irishman who became one of the great buck-and-wing dancers of the American minstrel scene and responsible for introducing the *cakewalk to the American stage. He was a stage director for Primrose and West and also ran his own minstrel show. He wrote 'Decolette' (1893), 'My gal is a high born lady' (1896), and 'Give me the good old-fashioned girl' (1900), and appeared in the film *The *Jazz Singer* (1927).

Fain, Sammy [Feinberg, Samuel] (*b* New York, 17 June 1902; *d* Los Angeles, 6 Dec. 1989). American composer. A self-taught pianist, he began to write songs while he was still at school. The family left New York, but he returned to try his luck in *Tin Pan Alley. The music-publisher Jack Mills employed him as a staff pianist and he followed the routine career of accompanist and singer in vaudeville and on radio. He published his first song in 1925 and in 1927 met Irving Kahal, who was to be his main collaborator until Kahal's death in 1942. They wrote in a popularized jazz idiom and produced such period numbers as 'When I take my sugar to tea' (1931). He followed the trail to Hollywood in the 1930s and had his songs made popular by such stars as Maurice *Chevalier, Dick *Powell, Rudy *Vallee, Mae *West, Doris *Day, Howard *Keel, and Dean *Martin. He made some records himself in the 1930s billed as 'The Singing Composer'. His biggest stage and screen success was the zany revue **Hellzapoppin* (1938), his other Broadway shows being *Manhattan Mary* (1927); *Everybody's Welcome* (1931); *Right this Way* (1935)—'I'll be seeing you', 'I can dream, can't I'; **George White's Scandals* (1939)—'Are you having any fun?'; *Boys and Girls Together* (1940); *Sons o' Fun* (1941); *Topolitsky of Notre Dame* (1946); *Michael Todd's Peep Show* (1950); *Flahooley* (1951); *Ankles Aweigh* (1955)—'His and hers'; and *Christine* (1960).

The films he contributed to included *The Big Pond* (1930)—'You brought a new kind of love to me'; *Young Man of Manhattan* (1930); *The Crooner* (1932); *Footlight Parade* (1933)—'By a waterfall'; *College Coach* (1933); *Moonlight and Pretzels* (1933); *Fashion Follies of 1934*; *Easy to Love* (1934)—'Easy to love'; *Strictly Dynamite* (1934); *Harold Teen* (1934); *Mandalay* (1934); *Here Comes the Navy* (1934); *Dames* (1934); *Happiness Ahead* (1934); *Desirable* (1934); *Sweet Music* (1935); *Goin' to Town* (1935); *The Great Ziegfeld* (1936); *Vogues of 1938* (1937)—'That old feeling' (*w* Lew *Brown); **New Faces of 1937*; *Tarnished Angel* (1938); *Swing Fever* (1943); *I'll Be Seeing You* (1944)—'I'll be seeing you'; *Two Girls and a Sailor* (1944); *Lost in a Harem* (1944); *Maisie Goes to Reno* (1944); *Meet the People* (1944); *Weekend at the Waldorf* (1945); *Thrill of Romance* (1945); *George White's Scandals of 1945*; *Anchors Aweigh* (1945); *No Leave, No Love* (1945); *Two Sister from Boston* (1946); *Little Mr Jim* (1946); *This Time for Keeps* (1947); *The Unfinished Dance* (1947); *Three Daring Daughters* (1948); *Alice in Wonderland* (1951); *Call Me Mister* (1951); *The *Jazz Singer* (1953); *Peter Pan* (1953); *Three Sailors and a Girl* (1953); *Calamity Jane* (1953)—'Secret love' (*w* Paul Francis Webster, 1907–84); *Lucky Me* (1954); *Love is a Many-Splendored Thing* (1955)—'Love is a many-splendored thing' (*w* Webster); *Hollywood or Bust* (1956); *April Love* (1957)—'April love' (Webster); *A Certain Smile* (1958)—'A certain smile'

(Webster); *Mardi Gras* (1958); *A Diamond for Carla* (1959); *The Big Circus* (1959); *A New Kind of Love* (1963).

The Fain songs that stick in the memory (in addition to those mentioned above) are 'Let a smile be your umbrella' (1927); 'I left my sugar standing in the rain' (1927); 'Wedding bells (are breaking up that old gang of mine)' (1929); 'Was that the human thing to do' (1931); 'The secretary song' (1948); and 'Dear hearts and gentle people' (1949).

Fairey Aviation Band. Celebrated British brass band formed at the Fairey Aviation Works in Stockport, Cheshire, in 1937. Well-organized from the start, it had reached championship status by 1938 to take its place among the great bands in the history of the *brass band movement. By 1972 it had won the British Open Championship a dozen times, including a hat-trick of wins 1961–3. National Champions in 1945, 1952, 1954, 1956, and 1965, it became well-known on radio and TV. Latterly it was known as the Fairey (Engineering Works) Band.

Fairground Organs. Many kinds of organs have been used at fairs since the 1870s, including the various *barrel organs. After 1892, when the firm of Gavioli of Paris introduced the system of using books of perforated cards to activate the mechanism, the instruments gradually became larger and more elaborate. Half the attraction of the fairground organ lies in the splendidly decorated instruments with their nostalgic sounds once heard and seen at the centre of the merry-go-rounds; half in the splendid steam road locomotives that were used for both haulage and supplying power. The latter attract a large number of enthusiasts who regularly attend rallies and there are various museums at St Albans and elsewhere. The organs were manufactured by such famous firms as Gavioli, Marenghi, Limonaire, Mortier, and Becquart in France; Hooghuys and Van der Beeck in Belgium; Chiappa, Wright & Holmes, and Varetto in England. Many have been restored and are once again in regular use and there is a flourishing Fair Organ Preservation Society, which was formed in 1958. The organs are a valuable reflector and preserver of the tastes of their times and LPs of various surviving organs are a valuable source of popular musical material.

E. V. Cockayne: *The Fair Organ—How it Works* (Hyde, 1967). A. Beaumont: *Fair Organs* (Hemel Hempstead, 1968). E. V. Cockayne: *The Fairground Organ* (Newton Abbot, 1970).

Fairport Convention. British folk-rock group formed in 1967 with Simon Nichol (*b* 1950) (guitar and vocal), Richard Thompson (*b* 1949) (guitar and vocal), Ashley Hutchings (*b* 1945) (bass), Martin Lamble (1949–69) (drums), Judy Dyble (*b* 1948) (autoharp and vocal). The group folded in 1979, having changed its personnel some 14 times involving 20 members. They were acclaimed in the folk field as well as in the wider world of rock for a wide-ranging repertoire that took them into *rock and roll, *blues, *Country and Western, *Cajun, and *bluegrass music. They moved from their early folk-rock work into a more traditional folk-song idiom when Sandy Denny (1947–78) replaced Dyble in 1968. She left in 1969, returning in 1974 after a period as a solo artist, and leaving again in 1976; she died after a fall downstairs in 1978. Various accidents and events enforced the many changes, with an especially fluid period in 1972. From the ranks of the group spread the nucleus of such groups as Steeleye Span and the Albion Country Band. A total of 18 LP albums issued between 1968 and 1979 give a varied picture of the group's fluctuating but steadily maturing progress. The group re-formed in the 1980s.

P. Humphries: *Meet on the Ledge: a History of Fairport Convention* (London, 1982).

Faith, Adam [Nelhams, Terry] (*b* London, 23 June 1940). British singer, actor, and producer. After starting out as a messenger in a film studio, he began his musical career in a *skiffle group, the Worried Men, but was soon persuaded by TV producer Jack Good to go out on his own—and to change his name to Adam Faith. He appeared on the TV **Six-Five Special* show and recorded, but failed to make any mark and returned to the film business. After a successful and extended stay on the TV *Drumbeat* programme, which led to a film appearance in *Beat Girl* (1959), he gradually gained recognition. Two No. 1 hits, 'What do you want?' (1959) and 'Poor me' (1960), made him one of the biggest pop stars of the early 1960s, although his reputation was mainly in the UK. As his pop reputation faded he was increasingly involved in acting and became widely known in the TV series *Budgie*. He made a recording comeback in the 1970s with work which some considered even better than his early efforts, also working as a record producer; but latterly he has been more effective in his acting capacity.

A. Faith: *Poor Me* (London, 1961).

Faith, Percy (*b* Toronto, 7 Apr. 1908; *d* Encino, Calif., 9 Feb. 1976). Canadian composer, arranger, and conductor. He began his career as a silent film cinema pianist, before studying at Toronto Conservatory. After burning his hands in an accident, his budding career as a pianist was curtailed; he turned to arranging, and by 1931 was leading the radio orchestra of the Canadian Broadcasting Corporation. He went to the USA in 1940 to conduct for the NBC Carnation Contented Hour. During the war years he became known for his arranging and conducting work, at first very much in the *Kostelanetz mode but gradually finding his own original style, based on an adroit and effective blending of string voicings and a strong brass sound. It was one of the few big 'easy listening' string orchestras that contrived to swing effectively. Another successful area was in his exploitation of large-scale Latin

American arrangements that featured on several of his many LPs made for Columbia Records, for whom he was music director from 1950.

He wrote for such films as *Love Me or Leave Me* (1955); *I'd Rather Be Rich* (1964); *The Virginian* (1964); *The Love Goddess* (1965); *The Third Way* (1965); *The Oscar* (1966). His compositions included: 'Brazilian sleighbells' (1949); 'Swedish rhapsody' (adapted from Alfven, 1953); 'Music till midnight' (1954); 'Theme for young lovers' (1960); 'Mucho gusto' (1961); 'Blue is the night' (1961); and 'Kahlua' (1965).

Fall, Leo [Leopold] (*b* Olmütz, 2 Feb. 1873; *d* Vienna, 16 Sept. 1925). Austrian composer and conductor. Son of a military bandmaster, he began to study the violin at the age of five. He enrolled at the Vienna Conservatory at 14 and at 17 was playing in a military band alongside the young Franz *Lehár under bandmaster Lehár Sr. His professional career began as a conductor at theatres in Berlin, Hamburg, and Cologne. Thereafter he spent most of his working life in Vienna, writing operettas in the typical, lightly romantic, melodic Viennese vein. He was fairly unadventurous harmonically and melodically but had a fine sense of word setting and the dramatic use of the voice; his works were generally well constructed and unified. His first staged production was the one-act *Frau Denise*, staged in Berlin in 1902, followed by *Irrlicht* (Mannheim, 1904). *Der Rebell*, staged in Berlin and Vienna (Theater an der Wien) in 1905 was a failure at first, but became a popular hit when revised in Vienna as *Der liebe Augustin* in 1912.

He wrote more than 20 operettas, among which were *Der fidele Bauer* (Mannheim, 1907; Vienna, Theatre an der Wien, 1908), put on in London as *The Merry Peasant* in 1909; *Die *Dollarprinzessin* (Vienna, 2 Nov. 1907), which was to travel the world for many years as *The Dollar Princess*; *Die geschiedene Frau* (1908); *Brüderlein Fein* (1909); *Der Puppenmädel* (1910), put on in New York as *The Doll Girl* (1913); *Die schöne Risette* (1910); *Die Sirene* (1911); *The Eternal Waltz* (London, 1911); *Leute vom Stand* (1913); *Der Studenten Gräfin* (1913); *Der Nachtschnellzug* (1913); *Jung England* (1914); *Der künstliche Mensch* (1915); *Fürstenliebe* (1916), revised as *Die Kaiserin* (1935); *Die Rose von Stambul* (1916); *Der heilige Ambrosius* (1921); *Die Strassensängerin* (1922); **Madame Pompadour* (1923); *Der süsse Kavalier* (1924); *Die spanische Nachtigall* (1926); and *Rosen aus Florida* (1929).

W. Zimmerli: *Leo Fall* (Zurich, 1957).

Fame, Georgie [Powell, Clive] (*b* Leigh, Lancs., 26 June 1943). British singer, pianist, and composer. After working as pianist to Billy *Fury, he started a singing career as Georgie Fame with a backing band called the Blue Flames. During a stay at the Flamingo Club in London, they became a fashionable cult with their rhythm 'n' blues, jazz, soul, reggae mixture, working with such American stars as Mose *Allison (on whom Fame to some extent moulded his own style). Proving themselves an outstandingly musicianly group they achieved a No. 1 hit (which displaced the *Beatles from that position) with 'Yeh, yeh' (1964) and again with 'Get away' (1966). Fame left the small-group world to work with the big bands of Harry South and Count *Basie. He reached No. 1 again in 1967 with 'Bonnie and Clyde' but thereafter moved out of the pop world to gain a more eclectic audience and worked as a duo with Alan *Price. He returned in 1973 to the rhythm 'n' blues scene with newly formed Blue Flames but mainly worked in clubs.

***Fanny*.** American musical play with music and lyrics by Harold *Rome, book by S. N. Behrman (1893–1973) and Joshua *Logan; a condensed version of three plays by Marcel Pagnol, *Marius*, *César*, and *Fanny*, set on the Marseilles waterfront, which had already made up a classic film trilogy. Produced at the Majestic Theatre 4 Nov. 1954, with Ezio *Pinza, Walter Slezak (1902–83), William Tabbert (1921–74), and Florence Henderson (*b* 1934), it ran for 888 performances. At London's Drury Lane Theatre 15 Nov. 1956, with Ian Wallace (*b* 1919); Robert Morley (*b* 1908), Janet Pavek, and Kevin Scott, it achieved 333. The insubstantial yet pleasant score included 'Never too late for love', 'Restless heart', 'Why be afraid to dance?', 'Welcome home', 'I have to tell you', 'Fanny', 'Love is a very light thing', and 'I like you'. It was filmed in 1960 with Leslie Caron, Maurice *Chevalier, and Charles Boyer.

***Fantasticks, The*.** For a rather arty story based on Edmund Rostand's play *Les Romanesques* (first translated into English as *The Fantasticks*) this small-scale musical had a remarkable success. Composer Harvey *Schmidt and librettist Tom Jones had first written an elaborate musical which had to be reduced to an hour for a college presentation in 1959. It was seen by producer Lore Noto, who agreed to present it in an off-Broadway theatre if it was extended to a full evening's entertainment.

The story is of two young people, whose fathers oppose their marriage in order to encourage it, and who come together after many disillusioning experiences. In spite of mixed notices, which almost had it taken off after a week, it soon found an appreciative audience which kept coming to the small Sullivan Street Playhouse in Greenwich Village from 3 May 1960. It was still running at the end of 1989 having clocked up well over 12,000 performances. There have been more than 8000 other productions in the USA, with 15 touring companies, and it has been seen in 66 countries abroad, including a brief run at the Apollo Theatre in London in 1961. It returned to London in 1990 with Roy Hudd in the lead. Part of its success was due to a folky little song, 'Try to remember', first sung by Jerry *Orbach.

Farjeon, Herbert (*b* South Hempstead, Herts., 5 Mar. 1887; *d* London, 3 May 1945). British lyric-writer, librettist, dramatist, producer, and director. Of American theatrical ancestry, he had a noteworthy career in the London theatre as a writer, the creator and to some degree pioneer of the intimate revue of the 1930s. He was especially successful with *Nine Sharp* (1938) and *The *Little Revue* (1939), both with scores by Walter *Leigh. Other revues and miscellanies included *Many Happy Returns* (1928); *Yours Sincerely* (1934); *Why Not Tonight?* (1934); *Spread it Abroad* (1936); *The Two Bouquets* (1936); *An Elephant in Arcady* (1938); *In Town Again* (1940); *Big Top* (1942); and *Light and Shade* (1942).

Farnie, H. B. [Harold Bulwer] (*b* London, 1820; *d* London, 22 Sept. 1889). British playwright and librettist. He was an indefatigable translator of French operettas and plays, so that his name appears time and again on the English texts of many of the important productions seen in London in the latter half of the 19th century. His influence was great but little seems to have been recorded of his life.

Farnon, Robert Joseph (*b* Toronto, 24 July 1917). Canadian composer, arranger, and conductor. He played with the Toronto Juvenile Symphony Orchestra at 11 and was a multi-instrumentalist at 14. In 1932 he joined the Canadian Broadcasting Corporation orchestra and did most of the choral arrangements for Percy *Faith, then its director, while he was only 18. In 1936 he was with the *Happy Gang* radio show and wrote his Symphony No. 1 which was performed by Eugene Ormandy and the Philadelphia Orchestra. He joined the Canadian Army when war broke out and came to Europe as a captain and a leader of the Canadian Band of the AEF. After the war he stayed in Britain and worked as arranger with *Geraldo and Ted *Heath, also forming his own orchestra which had a regular BBC series and recorded prolifically for Decca. He wrote innumerable pieces for Chappell's Recorded Music Library and composed music for Wilcox–Neagle film productions such as *I Live in Grosvenor Square* (1946); *Spring in Park Lane* (1948); *Maytime in Mayfair* (1949); *Lilacs in the Spring* (1949); *Elizabeth of Ladymead* (1950); *Paper Orchid* (1950); *Circle of Danger* (1951); and *Captain Horatio Hornblower RN* (1951).

He continued as a writer of film music and also of much high-quality light music which has always been highly regarded for its workmanship and worth. From a long catalogue of achievement might be mentioned: 'Canadian caravan' (1944); 'Journey into melody' (1947); 'Jumping bean' (1948); 'Portrait of a flirt' (1949); 'Manhattan playboy' (1950); 'Peanut polka' (1951); 'White heather' (1951); 'Hall of fame' (1952); 'Poodle parade' (1954); 'A la clair fontaine' (1955); 'Westminster waltz' (1956); 'Piano playtime' (1957); 'On the seashore' (1961); 'Portrait of Lorraine' (1965); 'Winter jasmine' (1968); and 'Colditz march' (1972).

Faye, Alice [Leppert, Alice Jeanne] (*b* New York, 5 May 1912). American singer and actress. Blonde, snub-nosed, slim singing star of many Fox films of the 1930s and 1940s, whose dark voice introduced such songs as 'You say the sweetest things, baby', 'Wake up and live', and 'You'll never know'. Her films included: *She Learned about Sailors* (1934); *Every Night at Eight* (1935); *Poor Little Rich Girl* (1936); **On the Avenue* (1937); *Wake Up and Live* (1937); *You're a Sweetheart* (1937); *Sally, Irene and Mary* (1938); *In Old Chicago* (1938); *Alexander's Ragtime Band* (1938); *Rose of Washington Square* (1939)—in which she portrayed Fanny *Brice; *Lillian Russell* (1940); *Tin Pan Alley* (1940); *That Night in Rio* (1941); *The Great American Broadcast* (1941); *Weekend in Havana* (1941); *Hello, Frisco, Hello* (1943); *The Gang's All Here* (1943); *Four Jills in a Jeep* (1944); and **State Fair* (1962). She married Phil *Harris.

W. F. Moshier: *The Alice Faye Movie Book* (Harrisburg, Pa., 1974).

Feather, Leonard Geoffrey (*b* London, 13 Sept. 1914). British-born American author and jazz critic. He studied at St Paul's School in London and went to the USA in 1935. There he worked as an arranger, lyric-writer, broadcaster, and lecturer and compiled the standard jazz reference books *The Encyclopedia of Jazz* (New York, 1955); and supplementary volumes; *The Encyclopedia of Jazz in the Sixties* (New York, 1966); *The Encyclopedia of Jazz in the Seventies* (New York, 1976); also *Inside Bebop* (New York, 1949) and *Inside Jazz* (New York, 1957).

Feldman, Bert [Albert James] (*b* Hull, 29 Sept. 1874; *d* Blackpool, 25 Mar. 1945). British music-publisher. Son of a piano maker, he went to London in 1896 with a song he had bought from an old music-hall comedian, Charlie Deane, and £3 in cash, hired an office near Oxford Street, and set up in business. Hard-headed but generous to his writers, he thrived by taking up the English rights to such American songs as 'A bird in a gilded cage', 'Down at the old Bull and Bush', and 'Alexander's Ragtime Band', being one of the first to recognize the rising talents of Irving *Berlin. He had tremendous wartime sales with 'It's a long way to Tipperary'. Continuing to prosper, after the war he bought up the firm of Herman *Darewski which included the Charles Sheard catalogue. When he died he left a personal fortune of some £500,000. His executors sold the business to *Francis, Day & Hunter in 1953.

Feldman, Vic [Victor Stanley] (*b* London, 7 Apr. 1934; *d* Los Angeles, 12 May 1987). British jazz pianist, vibraphonist, and drummer. He played professionally from the age of seven and became a prominent modernist on the British jazz scene working with Ted *Heath and with Ronnie *Scott 1954–5. In 1955 he emigrated to the USA to join the Woody *Herman band and settled in Los Angeles in 1957. He played for periods with 'Cannonball' *Adderley 1960–1, but mainly worked as a session musician. He wrote 'Seven steps to Heaven' which was recorded by Miles *Davis.

Felix, Hugo (*b* Vienna, 19 Nov. 1866; *d* Hollywood, 24 Aug. 1934). Austrian composer. He started his operetta output with a work written in his teens called *Die kleine Katze* (1890). This was followed by *Das Kätzchen* (1902) and *Husarenblut* (1894), both staged in Vienna, then several productions in Berlin. His first big success came with **Madame Sherry* (Berlin, 1902) followed by *Les Merveilleuses* (Paris, 1903). Both of these were very popular in London and the composer settled there for several years, writing *Tantilizing Tommy* for the *Gaiety Theatre in 1904 and *The Pearl Girl* in collaboration with Howard *Talbot in 1913. *Madam Sherry* (revised by Karl *Hoschna) was a great success in New York, too, as were *Lassie* (1920) and *The Sweetheart Shop* (1920), so Felix went to the USA and eventually settled in Hollywood for the rest of his life. In spite of his origins, his music was not particularly Viennese in character. He adapted it well for his various countries of residence, but achieved little of a memorable quality.

Felix, Lennie (*b* London, 16 Aug. 1920; *d* London, 29 Dec. 1981). British jazz pianist. He started by playing in nightclubs before the war and after 1945 became known as a pianist and entertainer in the style of Fats *Waller whom he resembled in both looks and vocal style. He also found inspiration in the work of such pianists as Art *Tatum, Earl *Hines, and Teddy *Wilson, becoming a remarkably fluent and professional performer. He played briefly with the bands of Nat *Gonella, Freddie Randall, and Harry Gold in the 1950s, but preferred to work as a solo act or fronting his own trio which he did throughout the 1960s and 1970s, playing in clubs and travelling in Europe. He was becoming known to a wider public through radio when he was knocked down by a car as he was leaving the 606 Club in Fulham and died three months later.

Ferguson, Maynard (*b* Montreal, 4 May 1928). Canadian trumpeter and bandleader. He studied at the Montreal Conservatory and began his musical career in a band led by Stan Woods in Montreal. He then formed a band with his brother in 1944 which survived for three years. He went to the USA in 1949 and played in bands led by Boyd *Raeburn, Jimmy *Dorsey, and Charlie *Barnet, joining Stan *Kenton in 1950. It was here that he became known for his high-register playing. He left Kenton in 1953 to freelance, and formed a band in 1956 for New York's Birdland which was known as the Dream Band of Birdland. It disbanded in 1967 and he went to work in England in 1968. He worked for a while in India and took a British band to America in 1972.

Ferry, Bryan (*b* Washington, Co. Durham, 26 Sept. 1945). British singer. He graduated from Newcastle University and worked as a teacher, but decided on a career in music and in 1970 formed the group *Roxy Music; they made their first album, *Roxy Music*, in 1972. Having some success as a soloist, he disbanded the group in 1976 but failed to make much headway until an album entitled *The Bride Stripped Bare* (1978) caught on. He re-formed Roxy Music in 1978, its albums now very much a showcase for his own languid style of singing, which became a well-established feature of the British rock scene.

R. Balfour: *The Bryan Ferry Story* (London, 1976).

Fiddler on the Roof. American musical play with score by Jerry *Bock, book by Joseph Stein (*b* 1912), based on stories by Sholom Aleichem, lyrics by Sheldon *Harnick, brilliantly conceived and staged by Jerome *Robbins. At the Imperial Theatre, New York, 22 Sept. 1964, with Zero *Mostel, Marià Karnilova (*b* 1920), and Beatrice Arthur in the cast, it reached 3242 performances to become the longest-running musical on Broadway in the 1960s. It was produced in 20 countries, including Vienna (Theater an der Wien) 1968, East Berlin (Komische Oper) 1970, London (Her Majesty's) 16 Feb. 1967, where it ran for 2030 performances. The production in London cost £67,000 and by the time it closed on 2 Oct. 1971 it had taken more than £2,500,000 at the box-office.

The star of the London cast was the Israeli actor Topol and when he left the role was taken by various actors including Alfie Bass (1921–87). The excellent and memorable score included 'Matchmaker, matchmaker', 'If I were a rich man', 'Sabbath prayer', 'To life', 'Miracle of miracles', 'Sunrise, sunset', 'Now I have everything', 'Do you love me'; and its richly sentimental Jewish story of the poor but pious dairyman Tevye and his wife Golde, who hire a matchmaker to find husbands for their five daughters, was a real tear-jerker. It was filmed in 1971 with Topol.

Fields, Dorothy (*b* Allenhurst, NJ, 15 July 1904; *d* New York, 28 Mar. 1974). American lyric-writer and librettist. The daughter of comedian Lew *Fields and sister of Herbert and Joseph *Fields. She formed a notable song-writing partnership with Jimmy *McHugh, writing mainly for the *Cotton Club revues, one of their first great successes being 'I can't give you anything but love, baby' from *Blackbirds of 1928*. She had a sophisticated and individual humour and produced some very memorable lyrics with other composers including Harold *Arlen and Jerome *Kern. With her brother Herbert she wrote several film scenarios.

Shows she contributed to were *Hello, Daddy* (1928); *International Revue* (1930)—'Exactly like you', 'On the sunny side of the street' (*m* McHugh); *Stars in Your Eyes* (1939); **Let's Face It* (1941); *Something for the Boys* (1943); **Mexican Hayride* (1944); **Up in Central Park* (1945); **Annie Get Your Gun* (1946); *A *Tree Grows in Brooklyn* (1951); *By the Beautiful Sea* (1954); *Redhead* (1959); **Sweet*

Charity (1966)—'Big spender', 'If my friends could see me now' (*m* Cy *Coleman); *Seesaw* (1973). Other songs include: 'I must have that man', 'Go home and tell your mother', 'I'm in the mood for love' (all *m* McHugh), 'A fine romance', 'The way you look tonight', 'Lovely to look at', 'Waltz in swingtime' (*m* Kern), 'Close as pages in a book', and 'Don't blame me'.

C. Brahms & N. Sherrin: 'Dorothy Fields' in *Song By Song* (London, 1984).

Fields, Gracie [Stansfield, Grace] (*b* Rochdale, Lancs., 9 Jan. 1898; *d* Capri, 27 Sept. 1979). British singer, comedienne, and actress. She made her first stage appearance in 1908 in Rochdale and her first professional appearance there at the New Hippodrome in 1910. After working in the north of England in variety and concert parties, she made her first London appearance at the Middlesex Music Hall in 1915 in a revue, *Yes I Think So*. She next appeared in Archie Pitt's *Mr Tower of London* in 1917. The show was to run for 9½ years and during its run, in 1925, Gracie Fields and Archie Pitt were married. The show was booked into the London Alhambra in 1922 and took London by storm, making her a star. She now appeared as top of the bill at the Coliseum and other halls and in cabaret at the Café Royal and elsewhere. A combination of broad Lancashire humour and a flair for singing comic songs like 'Walter, lead me to the altar', 'In my little bottom drawer', 'Heaven will protect an honest girl', 'I took my harp to a party', and 'The biggest aspidistra in the world' in a croaking tone did not prepare the audience for an excellent soprano voice with clear, resounding high notes which she switched to to sing her other kind of song like 'Little old lady' and 'Now is the hour'. In 1928 she appeared in her first Royal Command performance.

While appearing at the Metropolitan, Edgware Road in 1931, she came across the song 'Sally' which was to become her signature tune and which was used in her first film *Sally in our Alley* (1931). This was followed by *Looking on the Bright Side* (1932) and *This Week of Grace* (1933). With films like *Sing As We Go* (1934), with its catchy title-song, she now became a popular film star, appearing in *Queen of Hearts* (1936); *The Show Goes On* (1937); *Keep Smiling* (1938); and coming into the war years with films like *Shipyard Sally* (1939), with its inspirational 'Wish me luck as you wave me goodbye'.

In 1940 her second marriage to Monty Banks [Mario Bianchi] led to a decline in her popularity. As he was of Italian origin he would have been interned, so the couple went to America and for a time she was regarded as a deserter. In fact she spent most of the subsequent war years with ENSA entertaining the troops; in between making the films *Holy Matrimony* (1943); *Molly and Me* (1945); and *Paris Underground* (1945; *Madame Pimpernel* in UK). It was not until after the war that she fully reinstated herself in England with a comeback at the London Palladium. She made no films after 1945, but made a series of radio appearances in 1947, topped the bill at the London Palladium in 1948, then, in the early 1950s, went into semi-retirement on the island of Capri, making only occasional TV appearances. Monty Banks died in 1950, and she married a Yugoslavian, Boris Alperovici, in 1952.

G. Fields: *Sing As We Go!—her Autobiography* (London, 1960). P. Hudson: *Gracie Fields: her Life in Pictures* (London, 1989).

Fields, Herbert (*b* New York, 26 July 1897; *d* New York, 24 Mar. 1958). American librettist. Son of Lew *Fields, brother of Dorothy and Joseph *Fields. He started a career as an actor, but an association with Richard *Rodgers and Lorenz *Hart led to writing librettos for *The Melody Man* (1924); *Dearest Enemy* (1925); *The Girl Friend* (1926); and *Peggy-Ann* (1926), considered among the wittiest and most literate of their time. His librettos with various distinguished composers included **Hit the Deck* (1927); *A *Connecticut Yankee* (1927); *Present Arms* (1928); *Chee-Chee* (1928); *Hello, Daddy* (1928); **Fifty Million Frenchmen* (1929); *The New Yorkers* (1930); *America's Sweetheart* (1931); *Pardon My English* (1933); **DuBarry Was a Lady* (1939); **Panama Hattie* (1940); in collaboration with Dorothy Fields: **Let's Face It* (1941); *Something for the Boys* (1943); **Mexican Hayride* (1944); **Up in Central Park* (1945); **Annie Get Your Gun* (1946); *Arms and the Girl* (1950); *By the Beautiful Sea* (1954); and *Redhead* (1959).

Fields, Joseph Albert (*b* New York, 21 Feb. 1885; *d* New York, 3 Mar. 1966). American librettist and playwright. Son of Lew *Fields, brother of Dorothy and Joseph *Fields. He attended New York University, intending to become a lawyer, but wrote sketches for First World War shows while serving in the navy, and decided to follow the rest of the family into the theatre. His main works were straight plays but he contributed the following to the musical theatre: **Gentlemen Prefer Blondes* (with Anita Loos, 1949); **Wonderful Town* (with Jerome Chodorov, 1953)—based on their play *My Sister Eileen*, both deriving from Ruth McKinney's *New Yorker* short stories; *The Girl in Pink Tights* (1954); **Flower Drum Song* (with Oscar *Hammerstein II, 1958). He also worked as a director.

Fields, Lew [Shanfield, Lewis Morris] (*b* New York, 1 Jan. 1867; *d* Beverly Hills, Calif., 20 July 1941). American actor, producer, and director. As a boy he joined an amateur vaudeville act, the Standard Four, pushing out Joe *Weber. When the rest dropped out Weber and Fields joined forces in 1877, becoming professionals in burlesque and developing a 'Dutch' routine that was to make them famous. They gained popularity as they toured in vaudeville and by 1887 they were running a substantial regular company. In 1896 they took over the small Broadway Music Hall, renaming it Weber & Fields'

Music Hall, and here staged a series of burlesque musicals that confirmed one of the most popular partnerships in American stage history, including: *The Art of Maryland* (1896); *The Geezer* (1896); *Under the Red Globe* (1897); *The Glad Hand* (1897); *Pousse-Café* (1897); *The Con-Curers* (1898); *Hurly Burly* (1898); *Cyranose de Bricabrac* (1898); *Helter Skelter* (1899); *Catherine* (1899); *Whirl-i-gig* (1899); *Fiddle-Dee-Dee* (1900)—'Ma blushin' Rosie'; *Hoity Toity* (1901); *Twirly Whirly* (1902); *Whoop-Dee-Doo* (1903); *An English Daisy* (1904).

The partners split up in 1904, Lew Fields continuing in *It Happened in Nordland* (1904); *About Town* (1906); *The Girl Behind the Counter* (1907); *Old Dutch* (1909); *The Summer Widowers* (1910); and *The Hen-Pecks* (1911), in which he first appeared on Broadway with his wife to be, Blossom *Seeley. Weber and Fields came together again in *Hokey Pokey* (1912) and *Roly Poly* (1912), but only occasionally thereafter. Fields was in *Step This Way* (1916); *Miss 1917* (1917); *A Lonely Romeo* (1919); *Blue Eyes* (1921); *Jack and Jill* (1923); *Hello, Daddy* (1929); but latterly was mainly active as a producer and was involved in six *Rodgers and Hart musicals between 1920 and 1928.

F. Isman: *Weber and Fields* (New York, 1924).

Fifty Million Frenchmen. Musical comedy with music and lyrics by Cole *Porter, book by Herbert *Fields, at the Lyric Theatre, New York, 27 Nov. 1929. Billed as a 'musical comedy tour of Paris', it was Cole Porter's first considerable success, running for 254 performances, and the first of many collaborations with Fields.

The hero, in love with an attractive girl, bets his friend that he will be engaged to her within a month. To keep in touch with her he becomes a guide and pursues her through all the well-known sights of Paris. The cast included William *Gaxton as the smitten Peter, Genevieve Tobin as his girlfriend, and Jack Thomson as his friend, with Helen *Broderick, Evelyn Hoey, Betty Compton, and Thurston Hall. The songs included 'You do something to me', 'Find me a primitive man', 'You've got that thing', 'Paree, what did you do to me?', and 'The tale of an oyster'. It was filmed in 1931 with Olsen and Johnson, William Gaxton, and Helen Broderick.

Fille de Madame Angot, La. Lastingly popular French operetta with score by Charles *Lecocq and words by Clairville, Siraudin, and König, first produced in Brussels at the Théâtre des Fantaisies Parisiennes (Alcazar Royal) 4 Dec. 1872. It was one of the works that was to challenge the supremacy of *Offenbach and bring in a new wave of composers like Lecocq. It ran in Paris at the Folies-Dramatiques 21 Feb. 1873 for 411 performances and was seen in London in French at the St James's Theatre in May 1873; and in English at the Philharmonic in Islington in October. There was a further successful run of 235 performances at the *Gaiety 25 Nov. 1874, with English book by H. B. *Farnie and Emily *Soldene in the leading role. It has remained one of the classics of the French operetta genre and its scintillating music arranged by Gordon Jacob, had a further lease of life as a ballet, *Mam'zelle Angot* produced by the American Ballet Theatre in 1943 and by the Sadler's Wells Ballet at Covent Garden 26 Nov. 1947.

Fillmore, Henry (*b* Cincinnati, 2 Dec. 1881; *d* Miami, Fla., 7 Dec. 1956). American composer, conductor, and trombonist. He was to be one of America's best-known band musicians for around half a century, having started on the trombone at the age of 11 and first played in various circus bands. From 1916 to 1938 he directed the Fillmore Concert Band, later known as the WLW Radio Band. He also directed the Syrian Temple Band and the Otto Kahn Grotto Band in Cincinnati. He founded and was president of the Fillmore Music House, and was awarded an honorary degree of Doctor of Music by Miami University in 1956. Under such names as Harold Bennett, Harry Hartley, Will Huff, Al Hayes, and Ray Hall, as well as his own, he wrote many well-known marches including 'Miami', 'Noble Men', 'Golden friendships', 'Americans we', 'The President's march', 'The footlifter', and 'His Honor'; a number of ragtime-flavoured trombone solos: 'Hot trombone', 'Slim trombone', 'Ham trombone', and 'Bull trombone'; and the brilliant clarinet piece ' Lightning fingers'.

P. E. Bierley: *The Music of Henry Fillmore and Will Huff* (Columbus, Ohio, 1982).

Film Music. Now seen as an important artistic adjunct to a film, the idea of having background music arose in the first place out of the practical need to cover the noise of the early projectors. In the silent film era pianists were engaged to provide a continuous accompaniment, more or less without regard to the story. Soon, more imaginative players began to improvise music that matched the action and helped to build the atmosphere of a scene. It then became the custom to supply a specially composed piano score along with the film and later, when orchestras had begun to replace pianists, complete scores were written and circulated. The first known film score is generally reckoned to be that for *L'Assassination du Duc de Guise* (1908) which was written by the French composer Camille Saint-Saëns. The earliest complete scores written for Hollywood films were by Victor *Schertzinger for *Civilization* and by Victor *Herbert for *The Fall of a Nation*, both in 1916.

With the coming of sound, the orchestras were dispensed with but the habit of background music was now ingrained and it became an integral part of the sound-track. Because it was regularly used to excess and indiscriminately, it became a fashionable gimmick occasionally to have films without any sound-track music at all. Meanwhile the art developed, with a more sophisticated sound system available and a new awareness of how effective a proper integration of dialogue, action, sound effects, and music could be. A new breed of specialist composers emerged with an experienced understanding of how suitably conceived music could lend artistic support to the story. Some of the earlier composers like Erich Wolfgang *Korngold and Max *Steiner were trained in the Viennese classical tradition. Some, like Alfred *Newman, came from the Broadway theatre or *Tin Pan Alley. By the 1930s film music was recognized as an important branch of music-making.

One of the first film scores to be acclaimed on purely musical criteria was written for *King Kong* (1933) by Max Steiner, who later won Academy Awards for *The Informer* (1935) and *Gone With the Wind* (1939). The status of film music grew in the hands of composer-conductors like Victor *Young, Franz *Waxman, Miklos *Rozsa, and Bronislaw *Kaper, and their names in the credit lists were soon considered an important attraction. The British film industry followed suit in a more modest way, finding an early film music landmark in the score written by Arthur Bliss (1891–1975) for the Korda production of H. G. Wells's *Things to Come* (1936), worthy music that is still performed separately and recorded.

There had been another precedent for the involvement of academic composers (Saint-Saëns apart) when Sergei Prokofiev (1891–1953) wrote complete scores for the Russian films *Alexander Nevsky* and *Lieutenant Kije* in 1933. This and Bliss's example later encouraged other leading composers to lend their talents to the craft, often with memorable results. William Walton (1902–83) began with *Major Barbara* (1941) and *The Foreman Went to France* (1942) before writing the prestigious scores for Olivier's *Henry V* (1945) and *Hamlet* (1948). Ralph Vaughan Williams (1872–1958) wrote the music for *The 49th Parallel* (1941), while his score for *Scott of the Antarctic* (1948) formed the basis of his *Sinfonia Antarctica*. William *Alwyn and Malcolm *Arnold both entered the film music world wholeheartedly, joining the hard core of British screen composers such as Richard *Addinsell, Charles *Williams, Hans *May, and Mischa *Spoliansky. In the USA leading composers like Aaron Copland (*b* 1900), with *The City* (1939); *Of Mice and Men* (1939); *Our Town* (1940); *North Star* (1943); *The Cummington Story* (1945); *The Red Pony* (1948); *The Heiress* (1948; Academy Award); and *Something Wild* (1948); and Virgil Thomson (1896–1989), with *The Plow that Broke the Plains* (1936); *Louisiana Story* (1948); *The Goddess* (1957); and *Power Among Men* (1958), were among those who contributed distinguished scores that did much to elevate the art.

The 1940s saw a phenomenon that began the close linkage between films, the concert platform, the recording industry, and Tin Pan Alley. This was the big orchestral theme which could be extracted from a film score for individual performance. A lasting precursor was Richard Addinsell's 'Warsaw Concerto' which was heard in the film *Dangerous Moonlight* (1942) as a concerto performed by Anton Walbrook (Louis Kentner did the actual playing). The piece has frequently been criticized as little more than imitation Rachmaninov, but it is only fair to point out that Addinsell's commission was to provide a concerto-style piece that would work within the context of the film, with no thought of its becoming a well-used concert item. It was followed by Hubert *Bath's 'Cornish Rhapsody' from *Love Story* (1944); the Charles Williams/Nicholas *Brodszky theme from *The Way to the Stars* (1944); Williams's own 'Dream of Olwen' from *While I Live* (1947); and Nino *Rota's theme from *The Glass Mountain* (1948). In this particular activity Britain led the way, but Hollywood had its own equivalent in the concerto which Miklos Rozsa supplied for *Spellbound* (1945), the first of many distinctive 'themes' that he was to contribute over the years.

The use of a brief but persistent theme as a continuing motif throughout a film was given notable prominence in Carol Reed's *The Third Man* (1949) in the shape of the 'Harry Lime' theme composed and played on the zither by Anton *Karas. It remained a simple but effective device either employing specially written pieces or already established music: the use of Scott *Joplin's 'The entertainer' in *The Sting* (1973), for example, which helped to bring about a revival of interest in the composer's work and ragtime in general. By the mid-1950s the *big band motif was in vogue, pioneered by Elmer *Bernstein in *The Man With the Golden Arm* (1955); a fashion pursued by Henry *Mancini with his music for TV drama *Peter Gunn* (1958–61) and numerous films. By the early 1970s, jazz-influenced scores by composers like Quincy *Jones, Lalo *Schifrin, Pete *Rugolo, and John *Dankworth had become a normal background for films with a modern theme. Many recording conductors proved adept at using their orchestral techniques for film music and the names of Phil Green, Stanley *Black, Robert *Farnon, Nelson *Riddle, Billy *May, Ron *Goodwin, and John *Barry were prominent among the credits for the products of Hollywood and the main British studios. When films became more international, names like Michel *Legrand, Ennio Morricone (*b* 1928) and Francis *Lai emerged from Europe.

If the sort of imitation concert music that many of these composers provided was so effective, then why not the real thing? The 1970s saw a great vogue for the use of so-called 'classical' themes, notably Richard Strauss's impressive 'Also sprach Zarathustra' opening for *2001: a Space Odyssey* (1968); Mahler's newly fashionable music for *Death in Venice* (1971); and the insistent use of a Mozart concerto for the Swedish film *Elvira Madigan* (1967).

As fashions changed and pop music took over the main slice of current music-making, rock and its offshoots became heavily used, either by loading the sound-track with as many potential hit records as possible, as in *The Graduate* (1967), *Easy Rider* (1969), and *Midnight Cowboy* (1969), or in a more integrated total background of music from the featured stars as in the *Beatles' *Sergeant Pepper*

(1978). This area is more fully discussed under ROCK ON FILM.

It was in the 1950s that film theme songs first became almost as important as the films themselves and often more lasting. The idea went back to silent film days. The first big film songs were Erno *Rapee and Lew *Pollack's 'Charmaine' and 'Diane' used in *What Price Glory* (1926) and *Seventh Heaven* (1927). The title-song of *Ramona* (1928) became an enormous hit, sung on promotional tours throughout the USA by the star Dolores del Rio. The earliest big hit from a talking picture was 'Pagan love song', sung by Ramon Navarro in *The Pagan* (1929) and written by Nacio Herb *Brown and Arthur *Freed, composers of many of the earliest talkie hits. Many songs, like 'All this and heaven too' and 'To each his own' were never actually featured in the associated films but were merely cashing in or written as promotional numbers: Johnny *Green's 'I cover the waterfront' (1933) was so successful in this last role that it had to be hurriedly added to the film's soundtrack.

Many of the film song hits of the 1930s and 1940s (apart from those in specifically *Musical films) were interpolated items like 'Falling in love again' and 'See what the boys in the back room will have' featured by Marlene *Dietrich in *The Blue Angel* (1930) and **Destry Rides Again* (1939) respectively; and 'Two sleepy people' sung by Bob *Hope and Shirley *Ross in *Thanks for the Memory* (1938). Two notable examples of older songs being given a new lease of life as film hits were 'As time goes by', written by Herman *Hupfield in 1931, when it was heard in *Casablanca* (1942); and 'Moonglow', which had been popular since 1934 and found renewed life in *Picnic* (1963). Many song hits came about when words were later added to strong themes embedded in important films such as the title theme from *Laura* (1945) by David *Raksin and virtually every outstanding theme by Max Steiner ranging from 'Tara's theme' from *Gone With the Wind* (1939) to *A Summer Place* (1960).

By the 1950s the film theme song was more or less mandatory, often heard in the first place sung behind the credits by a singing star who was not actually featured in the film—'Love is a many-splendored thing', 'Friendly persuasion', 'Three coins in the fountain', 'Around the world' (in 80 days), being among those riding to the top of the charts in this way, and continuing to do so. The film music business proliferated, with many film companies creating their own record labels to promote theme songs and sound-track LPs. It by no means reflected a purely commercial activity and outlook, even if money-making remained a prominent purpose, as, alongside the musical theatre, the screen was to become one of the main outlets for 'quality' songs and music. In many cases the film disappeared into limbo, with a famous associated title all that the general public remembered.

E. Lang & G. West: *Musical Accompaniment of Moving Pictures: Exposition of the Principles Underlying the Musical Interpretation of Moving Pictures* (London, 1920). E. Rapee: *Motion Picture Moods for Pianist and Organists: a Rapid-Reference Collection of Selected Pieces* (New York, 1925; repr. New York, 1970, as *Encyclopedia of Music for Films*). L. Sabaneer: *Music for the Films: a Handbook for Composers and Conductors* (London, 1935). K. London: *Film Music: a Summary of the Characteristic Features of its History, Aesthetics, Technique and Possible Developments* (London, 1936; repr. New York, 1970). G. Cockshott; *Incidental Music in the Sound Film* (London, 1947). H. Eisler: *Composing for the Films* (New York, 1947; Frankfurt, 1951). J. Huntley: *British Film Music* (London, 1947). L. Levy: *Music for the Movies* (London, 1948). C. McCarty: *Film Composers in America: a Checklist of their Works* (Glendale, Calif., 1953; repr. New York, 1972). J. Huntley & R. Manvell: *The Technique of Film Music* (London, 1957; new edn 1975). B. G. Biamonte: *Musica e film* (Rome, 1959). G. Hacquard: *La Musique et le cinéma* (Paris, 1959). H. A. Thomas: *Die deutsche Tonfilmmusik* (Berlin, 1962). H. Colphi: *Défense et illustration de la musique dans la film* (Lyons, 1963). Record Undertaker: *A Handbook of Film, Theater & Television Music on Record 1948–69* (New York, 1970). D. Meeker: *Jazz in the Movies* (London, 1971; new edn 1977). T. Thomas: *Music for the Movies* (New York–London, 1973). J. L. Limbacher: *Film Music from Violins to Video* (Metuchen, NJ, 1974). G. Evans: *Soundtrack: the Music of the Movies* (New York, 1975). P. Elley: *The Film Music Book: a Guide to Composers* (London, 1980).

General film references: L. Halliwell: *The Filmgoer's Companion* (London, 1965 and reprints). T. Cawkwell & J. M. Smith: *The World Encyclopedia of Film* (London, 1972). D. Gifford: *The British Film Catalogue 1895–1970* (Newton Abbot, 1973). L-A. Bawden: *The Oxford Companion to Film* (London–New York, 1976).

Finck, Herman [von der Finck, Hermann] (*b* London, 4 Nov. 1872; *d* London, 21 Apr. 1939). British composer and conductor. His father was a German who settled in England and was conductor at *Drury Lane and the *Gaiety Theatre. Herman Finck followed the family tradition by playing in the Princess Theatre orchestra when he was 14. He studied for a time at the Guildhall School of Music, then, aged 16, joined the Palace Theatre orchestra as pianist and violinist. He became assistant conductor under Alfred Plumpton and principal Conductor in 1900.

Finck wrote a considerable amount of theatre music and did much to raise the standard of theatre and music-hall orchestras. He composed many attractive orchestral pieces with 'In the shadows' (1910) becoming a perennial best-seller; and wrote scores for: **The Passing Show* (1914); *By Jingo—If We Do* (1914); **The Passing Show of* 1915; *My Lady Frayle* (1916); *Vanity Fair* (1916); *Round the Map* (1917); *Hullo America* (1918); *It's All Wrong* (1920); *Brighter London* (1923); *The Little Revue Starts at Nine* (1923); *Good Luck* (1923); *Leap Year* (1924); *Better Days* (1925); and *Merely Molly* (1926).

H. Finck: *My Melodious Memories* (London, 1937).

Finegan, Bill (William J.] (*b* Newark, NJ, 3 Apr. 1917). American composer, arranger, and conductor. He studied at the Paris Conservatoire and with various leading American teachers; and first achieved a reputation with his arrangements for Glenn *Miller, which included 'Little brown jug' and 'Jingle bells', and Horace Heidt. He then joined Tommy *Dorsey, for whom he arranged 'Lonesome road', staying with him until the formation of the Sauter–Finegan Orchestra in 1952. Both Ed *Sauter and Bill *Finegan wrote individual scores for this unit, but most of its popular original numbers were joint creations and remarkable for their unconventional instrumentation that included tuba, harp, oboes, and fifes, a new sound for the 1950s—'Doodletown fifers', 'Tweedle-dee and Tweedle-dum', 'Yankee Doodletown', 'Lazy mambo', and 'Doodletown races'.

Fings Ain't Wot They Used T'Be. Musical with score and lyrics by Lionel *Bart and book by Frank Norman, first presented by Joan Littlewood's Theatre Workshop at the Theatre Royal, Stratford, 17 Feb. 1959, subsequently at the Garrick Theatre, London, from 11 Feb. 1960. It was one of a new wave of British musicals depicting low-life London, Jewish-Cockney in flavour, with its story woven around the lives of prostitutes, pimps, and gamblers. It was Littlewood's suggestion that Norman's play should be turned into a musical and she set Bart on his composing path with the commission.

The 'hero', Fred Cochran, wins a fortune on the horses and makes his lowdown café into a smart restaurant, only to fall foul of the police who have not had their usual bribe. All turns out well for him in the end. Fred was played by Glynn Edwards, his girlfriend Lily by Miriam Karlin, and others in the improvising cast were James Booth, Wallas Eaton, Barbara Windsor, and Toni Palmer. The reminiscent theme song 'Fings ain't wot they used t'be' was the only lasting number.

Finian's Rainbow. American musical with score by Burton *Lane, book by E. Y. *Harburg and Fred Sady, produced at the 46th Street Theatre, New York, on 10 Jan. 1947.

The story is of a simple Irish immigrant, Finian McLonergan (Albert Sharpe), who thinks he might get rich, in emulation of Fort Knox, by burying a crock of gold which he has stolen from a leprechaun (David Wayne) in Rainbow Valley. He doesn't, of course, but is forced to the cosily moral conclusion that love, friendship, and trust are better than riches in the end. Finian's daughter Sharon (Ella *Logan) has a crush on union officer Woody (Donald Richards). The score contained such attractive numbers as 'How are things in Glocca Morra?', 'If this isn't love', 'Look to the rainbow', 'Old devil moon', 'Something sort of grandish', 'Necessity', 'When the idle poor become the idle rich', 'When I'm not near the girl I love', and 'The begat'.

It was seen at the Palace Theatre, London, 21 Oct. 1947, where, in contrast to its run of 725 performances in New York, it only lasted for 55. There was a City Center revival in 1960 and it was filmed in 1968 with Fred *Astaire, Petula *Clark, and Tommy *Steele.

Fiorello! American musical based on the life of the well-remembered and three-times-elected Mayor of New York from 1933 to 1945, Fiorello Henry LaGuardia (1882–1947). Its insights into the tangled ways of American politics earned a Pulitzer Prize for Drama, only the third musical to receive that honour. The music was by Jerry *Bock, lyrics by Sheldon *Harnick, book by Jerome Weidman and George *Abbott, who also directed. It was staged at the Broadhurst Theatre 23 Nov. 1959 and ran for 795 performances. Tom Bosley as LaGuardia made a successful first appearance on Broadway. The principal songs were 'Politics and poker', 'I love a cop', 'Till tomorrow', 'When did I fall in love?', and 'Little tin box'.

Fiorito, Ted (*b* Newark, NJ, 20 Dec. 1900; *d* Scottsdale, Ariz., 22 July 1971). American composer, pianist, and bandleader. He played piano in a nickelodeon before starting a career in music-publishing. In the 1920s he formed a band with Sam Russo, originally known as the Oriole Terrace Orchestra, which played at the Edgewater Beach Hotel in Chicago. Fiorito bought out Russo in the late 1920s and continued to lead the band also playing organ and piano, with 'Rio Rita' as his theme song. It was never one of the great dance-bands but a pleasant, sweet-sounding 'society' band with vocalists who included Muzzy Marcellino, Candy Candido, the young Betty *Grable around 1933, and June Haver in the early 1940s.

The band's peak of popularity was in the 1930s when it appeared in such films as *Sweetheart of Sigma Chi* (1933); *Twenty Million Sweethearts* (1934), and *Broadway Gondolier* (1935), both with Dick *Powell; *Every Night at Eight* (1935); *Rhythm Parade* (1942); *Silver Skates* (1943); *Melody Parade* (1943); *Out of this World* (1945); and in various radio shows. In the 1950s Fiorito led a band at the Chez Paree in Chicago, and in the 1960s was working in Scottsdale. Among his many successful songs were: 'I need some pettin'' (1922); 'Toot toot tootsie, goodbye' (1922); 'When lights are low' (1923); 'Sometime' (1924); 'When I dream of the last waltz with you' (1925); 'Drifting apart' (1926); 'Laugh, clown, laugh' (1928); 'Now that you're gone' (1931); 'Alone at a table for two' (1935); 'Roll along, prairie moon' (1935); and 'Then you've never been blue' (1935).

Firefly, The. Operetta with music by Rudolf *Friml and book by Otto *Harbach, first put on in Syracuse in 1912 and seen at the Lyric Theatre, New York, 2 Dec. 1912, starring Emma Trentini and Roy Atwell. It had a modest run of 120 performances and contained some pleasant songs—'Love is like a firefly', 'Something', 'Giannina mia', 'Sympathy', 'A woman's smile', and 'When a maid comes knocking at your door'. It was made into a very popular film, with Jeanette *MacDonald and Allan

*Jones in 1937, when the score was enlivened by the well-remembered 'Donkey serenade' (written by Herbert *Stothart, Robert *Wright, and Chet *Forrest) which was adapted from an instrumental piece by Friml.

Fisher, Doris (*b* New York, 2 May 1915). American composer, author, and singer; the daughter of songwriter Fred *Fisher with whom she collaborated on her first song hit 'Whispering grass' in 1940. She began her career as a nightclub singer and was soon heard on the radio, worked with the Eddy *Duchin band in 1943, and recorded with her own group under the name of Penny Wise and her Wise Guys. She spent some years producing floorshows, and then became a songwriter for Columbia Films, working with lyric-writer Allan Roberts (1905–66) on such numbers as 'Into each life a little rain must fall' (1944); 'You always hurt the one you love' (1944); and 'You can't see the sun when you're crying' (1946). She contributed songs to the films *A Small World* (1944); *Gilda* (1946)—'Amado mio', 'Put the blame on Mame'; *Dead Reckoning* (1946); *The Thrill of Brazil* (1946); *Singin' in the Corn* (1946); *Talk About a Lady* (1946); *Cigarette Girl* (1947); *Down to Earth* (1947); *Variety Girl* (1947); *The Lady from Shanghai* (1948); and many more.

Fisher, Eddie [Edwin Jack] (*b* Philadelphia, 10 Aug. 1928). American singer. He had a strong voice, ideal for show songs, and he often performed in imitation of Al *Jolson. He was with the Buddy Morrow and Charlie *Ventura bands in 1946. While singing in a New York Club, he was invited on to the Eddie *Cantor show in 1949 and made an immediate hit with the American public. He served in the army 1952–3 and became even more popular on his return in 1953–4 when he had his own show on TV. His publicity was helped by short eventful marriages to Debbie *Reynolds, Elizabeth Taylor, and Connie Stevens. He appeared in films and was still singing in the 1970s.

M. Greene: *The Eddie Fisher Story* (Middleburg, Vt., 1978). E. Fisher: *My Life, My Loves* (New York, 1981).

Fisher, Fred [Fischer, Frederic] (*b* Cologne, 30 Sept. 1875; *d* New York, 14 Jan. 1942). American composer. Born and educated in Germany, he served in the German Navy and the French Foreign Legion. He went to America and worked as a songwriter in Chicago, forming his own publishing business in 1905. He had his first big song hit in 1906 with 'If the man in the moon were a coon' which quickly sold a million copies. He continued with 'The meanest man in town' (1907, *w* Alfred Bryan); 'My brudda, Sylvest'' (1908, *w* Jesse Lasky and Sam Stern); 'In sunny Italy' (1909); 'Come Josephine, in my flying machine' (1910, *w* Bryan); 'Goodbye, Becky Cohn' (1910, *w* Harry Breen)—used in **Ziegfeld Follies* of 1910, 'When I get you alone tonight' (1912); 'Peg o' my heart' (1913, *w* Bryan); 'Who paid the rent for Mrs Rip Van Winkle when Rip Van Winkle went away?' (1914, *w* Bryan); 'When it's moonlight on the Alamo' (1914, *w* Bryan); 'There's a little bit of bad in every good little girl' (1916, *w* Grant *Clarke); 'When it's night time in little Italy' (1917, *w* Bryan); 'They go wild, simply wild, over me' (1917, *w* Joe McCarthy); 'Dardanella' (with Johnny Black and Felix Bernard, 1919); 'Chicago (that toddlin' town)' (1922). The recording of 'Dardanella' by Ben Selvin (1898–1980) in 1920 was the first commercial dance-band record to sell a million copies; by 1963 it had sold $6\frac{1}{2}$ million. He wrote for the films *Hollywood Revue of 1929*; *Wonder of Women* (1929); *So This is College* (1929); *Their own Desire* (1930); *Children of Pleasure* (1930). In 1940 he collaborated with his daughter Doris on 'Whispering grass', which was his last song. A film based on his life story was made in 1949 under the title *Oh, You Beautiful Doll* with Fisher played by S. Z. Sakall.

Fitzgerald, Ella (*b* Newport News, Va., 25 Apr. 1918). American singer and composer. Her parents both died while she was young and she was raised by an aunt in Harlem. She entered a talent contest at the Opera House as a dancer but, losing her nerve, sang a song instead and won first prize. It landed her a contract with bandleader Chick *Webb who was in the audience. Webb and his wife adopted the 16-year-old orphan and she sang with the band from 1934, becoming an integral part of it and a great favourite with the jazz fans. She came to the attention of the wider public in 1938 with their recording of 'A-tisket, a-tasket', which she wrote with Van Alexander and Al Feldman, and which became a best-selling hit. When Chick Webb died in 1939 she took over the band, with 'Let's get together' as a theme song.

In 1942 she embarked on a solo career and from 1946 to 1950 toured on and off with Jazz at the Philharmonic, first appearing in London at the Palladium in 1948. Her reputation was mainly built in the jazz field, where she has always been considered one of its pre-eminent singers and a tremendous influence on others, but she had a wider hit record with 'My happiness' in 1948, thereafter aiming more of her recordings at an audience which liked sophisticated standards and show tunes. This policy was emphasized by the impresario Norman *Granz, who signed her for his Clef and Verve labels and produced a number of 'Songbook' LPs in which she explored the music of *Gershwin, *Porter, *Rodgers and Hart, and *Ellington, and which are still steady sellers in various reissue forms. She appeared in the films *Ride 'em Cowboy* (1941); *Pete Kelly's Blues* (1955); *St Louis Blues* (1958); *Let No Man Write My Epitaph* (1960). An eye operation in 1972 put her career in the balance but she recovered and continued to sing.

Her polished virtuosity, with a wide-ranging voice, beautiful tone, and superb phrasing has made her the jazz ballad singer supreme; a *scat expert and equally at home in the swing and modern bop idioms. She wrote a number of songs, including 'You showed me the way' (with Chick Webb, 1937); 'Once is enough for me' (with Webb, 1939); 'Please tell me the truth' (with Edgar *Sampson, 1939); 'Rough ridin'' (with Hank Jones, 1952); and 'Shiny stockings' (with Frank *Loesser, 1957).

Flack, Roberta (*b* Asheville, Black Mountain, NC, 10 Feb. 1939). American singer. She studied music in Washington DC and graduated as a BA from Howard University in 1958, afterwards starting a teaching career and also giving singing lessons and working as an accompanist. In 1968 she switched to playing blues and rhythm 'n' blues music in nightclubs and revealed such a singing flair that she was soon signed up by Atlantic Records. Her first album, *First Take*, was issued in 1969 and included a sensitive version of Ewan *MacColl's 'The first time ever I saw your face'; but not until 1972, after it had been featured in the film *Play Misty for Me*, did it catch on with the public. It became a No. 1 hit and made her a well-known name. Two more LPs had appeared in the meantime and she had started working regularly with the brilliant singer Donny Hathaway. 'Killing me softly with his song' was another No. 1 hit in 1973 and 'Feel like makin' love' was a success in 1974. Hathaway's unfortunate death in 1979 ended a fruitful partnership. She recorded an album with Peabo Bryson in 1981 and had a further hit with 'Making love', which was used as the title song for a film in 1982. Her classical background combines with her blues, jazz, and soul interests to produce a highly individual and effective style.

Flamenco. Traditional Spanish music based on the folk-songs and dances of Andalusia. There is much controversy about its distant origins but it is not difficult to accept, on aural evidence, that some of the oriental qualities, particularly as reflected in its vocal melodic lines, could have come from the Moors of adjacent Africa who were a dominating force in Andalusia for around eight centuries. Other elements may have come from wandering gypsies who, as in so much European folk-music, gave it richly melancholic strains and much of the rhythmic excitement derived from their fiddle music and heel-clicking dances. But some of its character must have arisen from Andalusia itself, its hot, dry climate, and the passionate and dramatic nature of its people.

There are also many theories as to how the name arose; one being that when Archduke Charles V arrived from the Low Countries to be crowned Charles I of Spain, his followers were known as 'flamencos' (Flemish); and this was later applied to the gypsies who spread flamenco by way of a subtle gibe at any unwelcome foreigner. Another theory is that it derives from the Moorish workers who left their mark on Spanish music during their period of occupation—they were known as the *falah men eikum*.

Cante flamenco is roughly divided into two main kinds; the *cante jondo* (or *grande*) which is the more serious, traditionally inclined side, its songs dealing with the themes of love, sorrow, and death and involving such forms as the martinette, serrana, siguiruya, and soleares; and the *cante chico* (or *pequeño*), which covers the lighter, more commercialized songs and dances designed for entertainment, such as the alegria, buleria, fandango, and *habanera or *tango.

Well into the 19th century, Spain, like other European countries, had been much dominated by foreign musical strains, particularly those of Italy. A need was felt in the mid-19th century to assert nationality in the arts, so there came about a tremendous revival of flamenco music and it became the popular form of entertainment in the cafés and nightclubs. It was at this point that the guitar, by now a flourishing classical instrument, became an integral part of flamenco, first as an accompaniment to the singers and gradually adding its own rhythmic patterns and characteristics to the music. The guitarists began to assert themselves and to create their own flamenco idiom based on the various dance forms; eventually flamenco guitar playing became a specialized art in its own right. While flamenco was being revived, Spanish theatrical traditions were also reasserting their national character, especially in the Spanish operetta known as *zarzuela in which flamenco rhythms were adapted into the simplified forms that are the hallmark of Spanish music—the fandango, the habanera, and so on.

Moving beyond the purely folk-art stage as practised by the gypsies, the commercial entertainment value of flamenco was eventually realized and professional singers (*cantadores*) and dancers (*bailadores*) took the music in popular stylized forms to the night-haunts of the cities and towns. Troupes of dancers (*cuadro flamenco*) became a popular theatrical entertainment with their accompanying singers, guitarists, and players of the bandore and the pandore and the typical percussive heel-tapping and hand-clapping choruses (*jaleadores*). Such companies (*juerga flamenco*), like the one led by Antonio, travelled the world in the 1950s and the 1960s making flamenco a universally popular and much recorded music.

One of the pioneers of the flamenco guitar tradition was Ramón Montoya, who was one of the first to play it as solo guitar music. It was later popularized by such virtuosos as Carlos Montoya (*b* 1903) and Andrés Segovia (1893–1987). While it is essentially an improvised art, flamenco, like the ragas of India, works to strict rules. Each region has its own pattern of basic rhythms and chords (*rasgueado*) played in an established order. Everything the guitarist does is based on such a framework, which maintains the essential spirit and flavour, over which he improvises his own complex variations (*falseta*).

The traditional folk flamenco survives mainly in the vocal forms, in a world akin to that of the blues singer. The idiom is personal, inward-looking, and harsh and only for those on its special wavelength.

Flanagan and Allen. British singing and comedy duo: Bud Flanagan [Reuben Weintrop] (*b* Whitechapel, London, 14 Oct. 1896; *d* London, 20 Oct. 1968) and [William Ernest] Chesney Allen (*b* Brighton, 5 Apr. 1894; *d* London, 13 Nov. 1982).

Flanagan came from an impoverished Polish-Jewish immigrant family. He was working as a call-boy at the Cambridge Music Hall in Shoreditch when he was 10 and made his first stage appearance at the London Music Hall as a would-be conjuror in 1908. He took to singing and ran away to sea at 14, ending up in the USA where he did a Jewish comedy act in vaudeville and was later in a blackface duo with Dale Burgess. After returning to England to serve in the army 1915–19, he toured in variety with various partners until he met Allen in 1924 and adopted his guise of moth-eaten fur coat and tattered straw hat.

Allen came from a middle-class background and had an early career as a straight actor. He went into variety as the straight man in an act called Stanford and Allen, which joined the Florrie Forde company in the early 1920s, also acting as her business manager. Flanagan replaced Stanford in 1924 and the famous partnership was born. Allen was always the smartly dressed straight man to Flanagan's eccentric hobo, and their voices blended perfectly in such songs as 'Forget-me-not Lane' and 'We're just ordinary people'.

They left the Forde company to go into variety, making their debut with their popular 'Underneath the arches' act at the famous Argyle Theatre in Birkenhead at the beginning of 1931. A few weeks later they appeared at the Holborn Empire in London and proved so popular that they were booked for the London Palladium. They pursued a highly successful top-of-the-bill career in variety and recorded extensively for HMV. An appearance in a revue, *Crazy Month*, at the Palladium brought them into association with the comedy teams of Nervo and Knox, Naughton and Gold, and Caryll and Mundy; the first two pairs combining with Flanagan and Allen to form the nucleus of the highly successful and inseparable Crazy Gang featured in such shows as *Life Begins at Oxford Circus* (1935); *Round about Regent Street* (1935); *All Alight at Oxford Circus* (1936); *Okay for Sound* (1936); *London Rhapsody* (1937); *These Foolish Things* (1938); and *The Little Dog Laughed* (1940). The duo individually toured in variety and worked with ENSA during the war years, cheering the British with such basic classics as 'We're going to hang out the washing on the Siegfried Line', 'Run, rabbit, run', 'Umbrella man', and the imperishable 'Underneath the arches'. They appeared in the wartime revues *Top of the World* (1940); *Black Vanities* (1941); and *Hi De Hi* (1943). After ill-health forced Allen to retire in 1946, Bud Flanagan continued as a solo act but was soon back with the re-formed Crazy Gang starting with *Together Again* (1947), which had 1566 performances; *Knights of Madness* (1950); *Ring Out the Bells* (1952); *Jokers Wild* (1954); *These Foolish Kings* (1956); *Clown Jewels* (1959); and *Young In Heart* (1960).

Although he was the first to retire, because of persistent arthritis, Allen eventually survived all the other members of the Crazy Gang, making a nostalgic comeback in his eighties in a Royal Command Performance; starring in a reminiscent one-man TV show; and appearing in a musical about the Crazy Gang, *Underneath the Arches*, in 1981, with Roy Hudd (*b* 1933) as Flanagan and Christopher Timothy as Allen.

B. Flanagan: *My Crazy Life* (London, 1961).

Flanders, Michael (*b* London, 1 Mar. 1922; *d* Betws-y-Coed, Wales, 15 Apr. 1975). British actor and writer. After reading history at Christ Church, Oxford, he started an acting career at the Oxford Playhouse in 1941. He joined the navy and, after being torpedoed at sea, contracted polio which condemned him to life in a wheelchair. He turned to writing and started a professional collaboration with the composer Donald *Swann producing items for revues such as *Penny Plain* (1951); **Airs on a Shoestring* (1953); and *Fresh Airs* (1956). Hitting an inspired and very personal vein of literary and musical humour, they decided to perform their own material, first appearing on stage at the intimate New Lindsey Theatre in Noting Hill Gate on 31 Dec. 1956. Their 'after-dinner farrago' *At the Drop of a Hat* proved so successful that it was soon moved to the West End to enjoy a run of 759 performances. They appeared in New York in 1959, where Flanders married an American. A second version of the show, *At the Drop of Another Hat*, was a comparable success. Flanders wrote for and appeared on radio and TV and remained cheerfully active. His skilful and witty lyrics for such songs as 'The hippopotamus', 'The warthog', 'The armadillo idyll', and other animal songs, 'Misalliance', and other satirical items, have a memorable quality.

Flatt, Lester Raymond (*b* Overton County, Tenn., 28 June 1914; *d* Nashville, 11 May 1979). American country singer and guitarist. He spent his early life working in textile mills and playing his music at the weekends. Such was his obvious talent that he was urged to become a professional and did so in 1939. He became well-known on the **Grand Ole Opry* as a singer with Bill *Monroe's Blue Grass Boys whom he joined in 1944. In 1945 a young banjo player, Earl *Scruggs joined the group and the famous Flatt and Scruggs duo was formed. They parted from Monroe and formed their own band, the Foggy Mountain Boys, which became the most successful and popular *bluegrass unit in the USA, recording for Mercury and Columbia and mainly responsible for making America aware of its country music heritage. Flatt's trademark was his G run on the guitar; Scruggs's his distinctive three-finger banjo playing. They rejoined the *Grand Ole Opry* in 1955 and their Saturday night programme, together with their records, purveyed some of the most exciting bluegrass music ever to have been conceived, with a breathtaking virtuosity and a true folk quality, as heard in 'Foggy Mountain breakdown' (used as the theme of the film *Bonnie and Clyde*, 1967), 'Pike County breakdown', 'Earl's breakdown', 'Flint Hill special', and 'Randy Lynn rag'. They toured continuously, spreading the gospel with singers Everett Lilly and Curly Sechler, and became a national institution.

In 1955 the sound of the Foggy Mountain Boys changed a little when the mandolin was dropped from their line-up and the *dobro steel guitar, played by Buck Graves, was added. By the 1960s they had become more commercialized, playing with more precision but less fire than they had in the old days. The Flatt-Scruggs partnership ended in 1969, Flatt maintaining the band which became known as the Nashville Brass. Their best-remembered songs included 'Roll in my sweet baby's arms', 'Old salty dog blues', 'The ballad of Jed Clampett', and the classic 'Foggy Mountain breakdown'.

Fledermaus, Die. Generally proclaimed as the finest ever example of the Viennese operetta, being both prodigiously melodic and memorable and also a worthwhile challenge to the opera singer, so that it is constantly being performed all over the world and frequently recorded. It offers two excellent female roles which opera stars like Elisabeth Schwarzkopf and Kiri Te Kanawa have eagerly tackled. After several relatively unsuccessful attempts at operetta the composer Johann *Strauss at last met up with the libretto which inspired his melodic genius; written by Richard *Genée and Karl Haffner, based on the vaudeville *La Réveillon* by Henri Meilhac. The neatly farcical plot finds its pivot at a masked ball and it ends in a slapstick prison scene where the musical riches run somewhat thin and the finale depends on good comic acting, its only weakness.

It was presented at the famous Theater an der Wien in Vienna on 5 Apr. 1874 with Johann Strauss conducting at the first night (Karl *Millöcker thereafter) with Marie *Geistinger, Jani Szika, and Karoline Charles-Hirsch in the cast. Its allure spread rapidly through the world—Berlin in 1874, Paris in 1875, London in 1876, and New York in 1879—with constant revivals ever since. The fairly meaningless title, which has little to do with the main content of the play, has tempted many alternatives in English—such as *Night Birds*, *The Merry Countess*, *A Wonderful Night*, *Champagne Sec*, and, perhaps best remembered *Gay Rosalinda*, a 1945 production with Cyril *Ritchard. It is generally known in France as *La Chauve-souris*. Recent years have seen various TV presentations, notably under Carlos Kleiber, who has also made a fine recording.

Fleetwood Mac. In 1967 bassist John McVie (*b* London, 26 Nov. 1945), guitarist and vocalist Peter Green (*b* London, 29 Oct. 1946), and drummer Mick Fleetwood (*b* London, 24 June 1942) left John *Mayall's Bluesbreakers to form the group Fleetwood Mac, with Jeremy Spencer added as guitarist and vocalist. They made their debut at the Windsor Festival in August 1967, had a No. 1 hit with 'Albatross' in 1968, and two runners-up with 'Man of the world' and 'Oh well' in 1969. Their early blues-oriented albums have remained highly regarded. The group went through innumerable changes of personnel and by 1973 seemed to be disintegrating. John McVie married Christine Perfect (*b* Greenodd, Lancs., 26 May 1948) and she joined the group in 1970. It was during a visit to California that it took on its highly successful grouping of the McVies, Fleetwood, Lindsey Buckingham (*b* Palo Alto, Calif., 3 Oct. 1949) (guitar), and Stephanie ('Stevie') Nicks (*b* Phoenix, 26 May 1948) (vocal). A re-release of 'Albatross' in 1973 did as well as the first and their career flourished into the 1980s in spite of the rise to stardom of Stevie Nicks, and the break-up of the McVie marriage. By then the blues trend had given way to a more pop-oriented sound heard in numbers like 'Future games', 'Over my head', 'Say you love me', 'Go your own way', and 'You make loving fun'. Their overall success can be measured by the sales of their albums *Fleetwood Mac* and *Rumours*, which surpassed 14 million copies.

M. Fleetwood & S. Davis: *Fleetwood* (London, 1990).

Fletcher, Percy E. (*b* Derby, 12 Dec. 1879; *d* London, 10 Sept. 1932). British composer and conductor. He went to London in 1899 and most of his life was spent as a theatre conductor. He wrote the scores of *An Exile from Home* (1906); *Mecca* (1920), recast as *Cairo* (1921); and *The Good Old Days* (1925). He was a regular composer of light orchestral music, with the waltz 'Bal masqué' from Parisian sketches (1914) attaining considerable popularity, and 'Songe adoré' (1911), 'The march of the manikins' (1911), 'Woodland pictures', 'Sylvan scenes', 'Three Frivolities', and the overture 'Vanity Fair' often heard. Before the First World War he was a considerable figure in the brass band world, writing the first major test-piece 'Labour and love' for the National Championship in 1913. Later he wrote 'An Epic Symphony' for the 1926 contest (also used in 1938 and 1951). His march 'The Spirit of Pageantry' was a regular band favourite.

Florodora. British musical comedy with score by Leslie *Stuart, book by Owen *Hall, and lyrics by Ernest Boyd-Jones (1869–1904) and Paul *Rubens. It opened at the Lyric Theatre, London, 11 Nov. 1899, with Ada *Reeve, Willie Edouin (1841–1908), and Evie Greene (1878–1917) in the cast, and had a good run of 455 performances. Its revolutionary qualities were perhaps not fully appreciated in England. Stuart's music was taking a clear step towards the future in its now genteel but then racy cakewalk rhythms and near-jazz melodies, clearly inspired by the minstrel world (which he also exploited in his fine songs written for the blackface singer and dancer Eugene *Stratton). There were excellent songs like 'The shade of the palm', 'The Queen of the Philippine Islands', and 'I want to be a military man'; but the high spot was undoubtedly the ingenious ensemble 'Tell me, pretty maiden' sung by pairs of parasol-carrying ladies and straw-hatted men. When it went to the Casino Theatre in New York 12 Nov. 1900, it was this that really caught the imagination of the American musical world.

There seems to have been hardly any up-and-coming composer of the day who has not mentioned *Florodora* as a youthful influence—from *Kern, *Rodgers, and *Gershwin to Eubie *Blake; and its effect on the course of American musical comedy history was immense. There were American revivals in 1902, 1905, and 1920 and in London in 1915 and 1931. It was seen in Paris at the Théâtre des *Bouffes-Parisiens in 1903.

Flotsam and Jetsam. Popular variety, broadcasting, and recording duo that made its first appearance at the Victoria Palace in 1926 and continued until 1945. The attraction was the contrast of the deep booming voice of Jetsam, the Australian singer Malcolm McEachern (*b* Melbourne, 1884; *d* London, 17 Jan. 1945)—'I sing all the low notes'—and the reedy tones of Flotsam, B. C. *Hilliam—'you wonder how he gets 'em'—who played the piano and wrote most of the witty material. They appeared in the Royal Variety Performance of 1927, made many records for Columbia, and started broadcasting from Savoy Hill days, giving nightly news bulletins in verse and appearing in several radio programmes of their own.

Flower Drum Song. Richard *Rodgers–Oscar *Hammerstein II musical that followed *The *King and I*. The idea of turning Chin Y. Lee's novel into a musical came from co-librettist Joseph *Fields. The show, directed by Gene *Kelly, portrayed the conflict between the old traditional Chinese and their trendy Americanized children. It may not have matched its substantial predecessors but it earned 600 performances with its light charm and songs like 'You are beautiful', 'I enjoy being a girl', 'Don't marry me', and 'Sunday'. With a cosmopolitan cast it opened at the St James Theatre 1 Dec. 1958. It was staged in London at the Palace Theatre 24 Mar. 1960, and was filmed in 1961 with its original star Miyoshi Umeki, Nancy Kwan, and James Shigeta.

Fodens Motor Works Band. Illustrious British brass band having its origins in the Elworth Silver Band which was formed in 1900 in the year of the Relief of Mafeking. This survived only two years and when its instruments were sold in 1902 they were bought by Edwin Foden, the young head of an agricultural machinery firm in Sandbach, Cheshire, who decided it was time for his firm to run its own brass band. The band immediately plunged into the competitive world of brass; under the guidance of such pioneer figures as Samuel Charlesworth, Alfred Jackson, and William Rimmer it began to win prizes, including the British Open at Belle Vue in 1909 and, under William Halliwell (1865–1929), one of the most successful trainers and directors in brass band history, the Open and the National in 1910. It carried on as one of the country's leading bands, with Fred *Mortimer as bandmaster from 1924, winning the Open in 1926, 1927, and 1928. Mortimer took over as musical director when Halliwell died in 1929, and his illustrious son Harry *Mortimer became bandmaster. The band won the National Championship in 1930, 1932, 1933, 1934, 1936, 1937, and 1938, thus dominating the decade. After Fred Mortimer died in 1953, Harry and Rex Mortimer kept the family tradition going until 1974, when John Golland took over followed by James Scott in 1975.

F. O. Burgess: *By Royal Command: the Story of Fodens Motor Works Band* (Sandbach, 1977).

Foley, Red [Clyde Julian] (*b* Blue Lick, Ky., 17 June 1910; *d* Fort Wayne, Ind., 19 Sept. 1968). American country singer. He had his own *Renfro Valley Barn Dance* radio programme in 1937 and appeared frequently on the **Grand Ole Opry* programme from Nashville. He became one of the leading figures in the country music revival and recorded such classics as 'Chattanooga shoeshine boy', 'Peace in the valley', and 'Beyond the sunset'. He was elected to the *Country Music Hall of Fame in 1967.

Folies-Bergère. Famed revue theatre on the Rue Richer in Paris, first opened as a music-hall on 1 May 1869 and immortalized in the early days by Toulouse-Lautrec. The only reason for the name is its proximity to the Rue Bergère. With a small stage some 20 feet deep it founded its lavish effect on stairways, mirrors, flowing lace, and other materials which focused attention on the contrastingly undressed ladies. Its first actual revue, *Place aux jeunes*, was staged there in 1886, beginning the tradition of unclad beauties to soothe the souls of tired businessmen. Among those who appeared at the Folies were *Mistinguett, Maurice *Chevalier, Colette, Polaire, Harry Pilcer, Mayol, Josephine *Baker, Anna *Held (later the star of the **Ziegfeld Follies*), Fernandel, Yvette *Guilbert, Gaby *Deslys, Yvonne *Printemps, and Max Dearly; and, from abroad, Grock, Harry *Fragson, Little Tich, Charlie *Chaplin, and W. C. Fields. The 40-strong chorus has traditionally been well-stocked with British girls. The theatre was taken over by Paul Derval and his wife in 1923 and was rebuilt in 1926.

Hermite: *Vingt Ans chez les femmes nues* (*Les Dessous des Folies-Bergère*) (Paris, 1948). P. Derval: *Les Folies-Bergère* (Paris, 1954; London, 1955). C. Castle: *The Folies-Bergère* (London, 1982).

Folk-music, Folk-song. It could be said that all popular music is folk-music. It belongs to that part of a nation's culture that has accumulated from the experiences and needs of the people as a whole, rather than being created by and for an intellectual minority. Folk-music is certainly the ancestor and the moving spirit of all popular music-making. Maybe such an all-embracing definition could not satisfy the folk purist who feels that the folk element ceases to exist once a creation becomes commercially conceived and exploited. But much of that thinking arises from the anonymous past of folk-music; and it is a view less firmly held today as the boundaries become less well defined and 20th-century popular music, having passed through its most artificial period in the 1930s, has reverted to being far more folk-oriented and flavoured.

What is thought of as 'true' folk music, timeless and beyond documentation, is almost inevitably of no known authorship; and, as it is handed on in unwritten form from person to person, changes in detail and style occur as the result of inexact memory, or simply because the creation takes on a different personality in different hands and different environments. Thus the British ballad 'Barbara Allen' is undoubtedly older than derived American versions such as 'Bobby Allen', but has no real claim to be more correct or more authentic. Each has become folk-music of its own time and place. The folk performer draws upon the common stock of stories and ideas and converts it to his own ends; a process of adaptation rather than total creation. The impersonal flavour that results helps to define what is genuine folk-music and what is not.

The Hungarian composer Béla Bartók (1881–1945), an avid collector of folk material, defined folk-song as 'peasant song'; and the English collector Cecil *Sharp similarly saw it as music that sprang from the 'common people'. Although these definitions are basically true, they introduce an unfortunate suggestion of class distinction. There is no proven reason why the original creator of a folk-song should be either lower-class or uneducated, which is what Sharp went on to define as the circumstances of common people. A. L. *Lloyd, in his *Folk Song in England*, doubted if such a class, entirely cut off from the advances of civilization, had really existed since the Middle Ages.

Musicologists incessantly argue over the origins of folk-music, one school of thought implying that it arose spontaneously from 'the people' whose combined will, needs, and history brought it forth in some sort of mystic birth. The more pragmatic theorist suggests that any tune, any lyric, any combination of them, must have had a beginning in one author. In the case of early folk-music the author simply happened to be forgotten and had no means of staking a claim to his creation. The truth, as ever, is probably somewhere in between, with probably one moving spirit at source but the material almost immediately transformed to the public domain.

There can be no firm rules or definitions that clearly identify a genuine folk-song. Folk-music tends to be of a fairly simple musical structure to the point of being structureless, of the nature of an incantation. The spirit and the artlessness suggest that ballads like 'The Golden Vanity' or 'Pretty fair miss' are the real thing; a more contrived quality suggests that 'Davy Crockett' is not. A singer-composer like Ewan *MacColl, however, so immersed himself in industrial folk-song that he created folk-music which in form and content is indistinguishable from the real article. If such creations pass into the common stock of song, aligning themselves to any region, ethnic group, or trade, then they clearly become folk-songs, repeating the long-established process. In the past this public appropriation was often imposed by early 19th-century compilers of folk collections who frequently printed composed songs without attribution and with perhaps only the melody line, which were then taken as folk-songs. It was only modern scholarship that gave such assumed folk-songs as 'The Ploughboy' or 'Clementine' a firm composer credit. Considerations of this kind open up the question of whether some of these composer-written songs, from Stephen Foster to present-day 'folk' revivalists, old favourites among roisterers like 'Nellie Dean', or any of the universally familiar music-hall songs like 'Don't dilly dally', might not therefore creep into the category of folk-music. Since people nowadays do not spontaneously make up their own songs (if they ever did in the past), at least in the commercialized society that has produced all the credited material in this book, then the songs that they take to their hearts and which seep into their subconscious minds might be considered as their folk-music. Several people have been credited with the answer to an earnest question as to what was folk-music: that all music was folk-music because horses (and by implication all the rest of the earth's fauna) didn't have any music. But this is not proposed as a real answer to our queries.

The British composer Benjamin Britten, among many, arranged a number of folk-songs (or what he took to be folk-songs—'The ploughboy' among them). Taking one regional set of words and usually the most cultured version of, for instance, 'The foggy foggy dew' (which is known in innumerable variants, some of which are not in the least related to his version), he produced what, in spite of traditionally slanted words, is no longer a folk-song. It had become a created affair, an art song with a formal melody and a contrived accompaniment. One could rationalize that the piano is not an instrument for folk-music, nor is a trained singer's voice which inevitably destroys the folkiness of anything, even a popular song. There is no longer any sense of artlessness that we get from a version of the same song sung by Bill Cox, a Norfolk fisherman, in such ripe East Anglian as to be unintelligible to many, but clearly a folk performance. One can always sense the archness of a deliberate attempt to appear folky ('Lavender blue', for instance). A great deal of classical music has folk-melody as its source. The fascinating rub is that many of us, enchanted by the Pears-Britten 1946 recording of 'The foggy foggy dew', have been singing it in our own version of that particular source for 40 years; and it has therefore become a part of our personal folk tradition.

W. Chappell: *Popular Music of the Olden Times* (London, 1855/9; New York, 1961). C. Sharp: *English Folk Song: Some Conclusions* (Taunton, 1907; London, 1954). F. Howes: *Folk Music of Britain* (London, 1937; rev. as *Folk Music of Britain and Beyond*, 1969). D. K. Wilgus: *Anglo-American Folksong Scholarship Since 1898* (New Brunswick, NJ, 1959). S. Finkelstein: *Composer and Nation: the Folk Heritage of Music* (New York, 1960). B. Nettl: *An Introduction to Folk Music in the United States* (Detroit, 1962; repr. 1972). B. Nettl: *Folk and Traditional Music of Western Continents* (Englewood Cliffs, NJ, 1965). R. D. Abrahams & G. Foss: *Anglo-American Folksong Style* (Englewood Cliffs, NJ, 1968). M. Karpeles: *An Introduction to English Folk Song* (London, 1973). P. Kennedy: *Folk Songs of Britain and Ireland* (London, 1974).

Folk-song revival. Following the strong resurgence of public interest in folk-music since the Second World War, a whole genre of created folk-music has become an accepted and important part of the popular musical scene. The modern folk composer, author, and performer has slipped back into the skills of creating in a folk idiom that are clearly distinct from those previously dominant in the *Tin Pan Alley or 'commercialized' idiom. The fact that what is now defined as 'folk' music is just as 'commercialized' as the 'pop' variety no longer prevents it from being the genuine thing. It is simply that the position of folk musicians has changed. They are no longer anonymous and they are rewarded by a gratified society.

Interest in folk-music was fuelled by the research and books listed above, among many of a more specific national and regional nature, but especially those, like *English Folk Songs from the Southern Appalachians* (1932), which not only revived interest in the American genre but emphasized the universality of folk-music. The 1940s and 1950s saw the growth of widespread folk revival activities: books, periodicals, recordings, and the formation of folk clubs throughout the world.

One of the salient elements of the folk revival was a move away from the inbuilt notion that folk-music was essentially rural, a product of the country whose naturalness died in town and city. The whole trend of the folk revival was towards urbanization, its themes no longer mainly confined to agricultural areas but now focusing on the industrial and commercial life of urban communities. The key figure in the USA was Woody *Guthrie, who came from a poor rural community to bring the themes of poverty and politics into the realm of folk-song. His learned disciple Pete *Seeger was one of those who found their course halted by running into the political terrorizations of the McCarthy era. The flame was carried by those who made folk-music more of an entertainment, like Burl *Ives and Oscar Brand (*b* 1920), and the prolific *Carter Family who were among the first to blur the edges of the distinction between what was traditional and what was newly conceived. The Guthrie message was carried abroad by singers like Jack *Elliott who helped to set the English scene on its feet, so much so that when Seeger came to England later he found the writing activities there a source of return inspiration.

Those who followed, like Bob *Dylan and Phil *Ochs on the down-to-earth side and the Kingston Trio and Joan *Baez on the more polished entertainment wavelength, now found that it was accepted that folk-music was written as well as sung, and singers like Hank *Williams and Big Bill *Broonzy were hailed as the great creators of folk-songs. After them, in their various spheres of activity, came professionals like Tom *Paxton, Arlo *Guthrie, Buffy Saint-Marie, and all those in the Country and Western field, a specialized branch of folk revival. There were soon 'red-neck' and 'outlaw' movements objecting to the over-commercialization and demanding a back-to-the-roots approach, but by now it was often difficult to decide whether a performer like Bob Dylan was a folk-singer who had moved into the rock field or a rock singer with folk roots.

Beyond this there was, of course, the pure and simple revival of folk-song, as opposed to the folk revival. In the USA writers and collectors like John and Alan *Lomax, in the UK, A. L. *Lloyd and Ewan *MacColl, had provided the research for those who simply wanted to preserve old folk-singing traditions, like the Watersons and the Copper Family, Jake Thackeray, and the host of singers keenly aware of the strength of the folk tradition.

What has happened, no doubt to the eternal gratification of those pioneer folk revivers now in their graves, is that popular music has found and acknowledged its roots and, having gone through a tenuous period when all sorts of academic and social aspects were grafted on to it, has returned to a situation where many popular entertainers are simply folk musicians, the only difference being that they are no longer anonymous.

D. Laing, K. Dallas, R. Denselow, & R. Shelton: *The Electric Muse: the Story of Folk into Rock* (London, 1975). K. Baggelaar & D. Milton: *The Folk Music Encyclopedia* (New York, 1976; London, 1977). B. Pegg: *Folk: a Portrait of English Traditional Music, Musicians and Customs* (London, 1976). L. Sandberg & D. Weissman: *The Folk Music Source Book* (New York, 1976). J. Vassal: *Electric Children: Roots and Branches of Modern Folk Rock* (New York, 1976).

Follies. American musical with score by Stephen *Sondheim, book by James Goldman, produced at the Winter Gardens Theatre, New York, 4 Apr. 1971 and running for 522 performances. A typically intelligent and integrated Sondheim musical, it is set at a reunion of the Weismann Follies (on the Ziegfeld model) in which the unhappy lives of two of the couples, played by Alexis Smith, John McMartin, Dorothy Collins, and Gene Nelson, is contrasted with the surface happiness of their theatre roles. Flashbacks to younger days gave the composer opportunities for telling pastiches of musical comedy and earlier popular composers in such songs as 'Broadway baby', 'Losing my mind', 'Who's that woman?', 'Beautiful women', 'I'm still here', and

'Too many mornings'. The show was an important summation of the musical stage. There was a London version in 1987 with Diana Rigg (*b* 1938) and Julia McKenzie.

Follies, The. Pierrot-style entertainment that had a great success in the early 1900s in London, and inspired other groups of the same kind such as the later *Co-Optimists. It grew from an amateur ensemble known as the Baddeley Troupe (featuring the Baddeley Brothers) run by Sherrington Chinn. The troupe was taken over by H. G. *Pélissier in 1895. Under his leadership they appeared at Aberystwyth, Folkestone, and other seaside towns, where they popularized their special brand of burlesque skits which had rather more strength and purpose than the average pierrot shows of the day. They were booked to appear at the *Alhambra in 1900 and were at the Palace Theatre from 14 Oct. 1901 as part of a revue. They also appeared between 1901 and 1904 at the St George's Hall and the Tivoli Music Hall. At the Palace in 1904 they made a great impression with a skit on conventional pantomime, *Bill Bailey*, and in December of that year (by then under the management of Charles Morton) they played a royal command performance at Sandringham.

The group at this time consisted of Pélissier, Lewis Sydney, Dan Everard, Marjorie Napier, Ethel Allandale, and Gwennie Mars. In 1906 they deemed themselves capable of sustaining a complete theatrical programme and, after a trial run at the theatre attached to the Midland Hotel, Manchester, opened at the Royalty Theatre in London on 19 Mar. 1907, adding to the bill in April a much-praised 'potty play' entitled *Baffles: a Peter-Pan-tomime*, which was a combined satire on *Raffles* and *Peter Pan*. They became a popular London theatre attraction and staged a new edition at Terry's Theatre on 18 Sept. 1907. Touring engagements in Glasgow, Edinburgh, Dublin, Newcastle, Birmingham, and various seaside towns occupied the summer of 1908 and on 1 Dec. 1908 they opened at their first large London theatre, the Apollo, this edition running for 571 consecutive performances. The company was augmented so that a splinter group could fulfil a Christmas engagement in Manchester. A new edition at the Apollo, 30 Aug. 1910, ran for 521 performances and there was a third on 29 Oct. 1912. Most of the musical items were written by Pélissier.

F. Gardner: *Pure Folly: the Story of those Remarkable People 'The Follies'* (London, 1909).

Follies of 1907. American revue (no connection with the London show above) that was staged at the Jardin de Paris in New York on 8 July 1907. As suggested by Florenz Ziegfeld's wife Anna *Held, who had appeared at the *Folies-Bergère in Paris, it was based on the satirical French revues, intermingling topical sketches with lavish showgirl numbers featuring the 64 Anna Held Girls. With such luminaries in the cast as Grace *LaRue, Emma Carus, Helen *Broderick, and (later) Nora *Bayes, it was the beginning of the famous **Ziegfeld Follies* which were to run, on and off, until 1957.

Follow the Fleet. RKO-Radio film of 1936, with music and lyrics by Irving *Berlin and screenplay by Dwight Taylor and Allan Scott, based on Hugh Osborne's play *Shore Leave* (which was also the basis of **Hit the Deck*). Directed by Mark Sandrich, it proved to be one of the most musically memorable of the series of films starring Fred *Astaire and Ginger *Rogers, co-starring with Randolph Scott (1898–1987) and Harriet Hilliard (*b* 1914). Also in the cast were such up-and-coming names as Lucille *Ball, Betty *Grable, and Tony *Martin. It was perhaps not as impressively staged as some of the Astaire-Rogers films but there were great dancing moments, notably the Rogers interpretation of 'Let's face the music and dance'.

Although Berlin had already most successfully supplied the music for **Top Hat*, there were those at RKO who wanted the music of Harry *Warren (fresh from 'Lullaby of Broadway') for this film, but the producer insisted on Berlin. It proved to be one of his most fruitful scores, including 'We saw the sea', 'Let yourself go', 'I'd rather lead a band', 'But where are you?', 'I'm putting all my eggs in one basket', and 'Let's face the music and dance'.

Follow the Girls. American musical which was a great Broadway attraction during the Second World War, opening at the New Century Theatre (hitherto known as Jolson's 59th Street Theatre) 8 Apr. 1944 and enjoying a run of 882 performances. Its show-bizzy story about a burlesque queen is now forgotten and unlikely to be revived, but it brought to light the new talents of Gertrude Niesen (1910–75) who had a hit with the song 'I wanna get married', comedian Jackie *Gleason, and dancer Irina Baranova. It came to London, opening at His Majesty's Theatre 25 Oct. 1945, with Evelyn Dall, Arthur *Askey, and Wendy Toye in the equivalent roles and had 572 performances.

Follow Thru. American musical all about golf, as the name obliquely suggests. The book by B. G. *DeSylva and Laurence Schwab (1893–1951), with lyrics by DeSylva and Lew *Brown, followed a sporting tradition: their previous shows, *Good News!* (1927) and *Hold Everything!* (1928), had been about American football and boxing. It opened at the 46th Street Theatre, 9 Jan. 1929 and gave Jack Haley (1899–1979) his first big Broadway part, running for 403 performances. It is remembered now by some catchy Ray *Henderson tunes like 'Button up your overcoat' sung by Zelma O'Neal (*b* 1907), 'My lucky star', 'You wouldn't fool me, would you?', and 'I want to be bad'. In London, as *Follow Through*, at the Dominion Theatre 3 Oct. 1929, it had Leslie *Henson, Mark Lester, Elsie *Randolph, and Harry *Pélissier in the cast and ran for 148 performances. It was filmed in 1930 with Haley, Nancy

Carroll (1905–65), and Buddy Rogers (*b* 1904).

'For he's a jolly good fellow'. One of the most embarrassing jingles of all time possibly has its origins as far back as the age of the crusaders. Its original tune was probably used as a hunting song. Around 1709 the melody became associated with a song called 'Malbrouk' (or 'Malbourouck')—'Malbrouk s'en va t'en guerre' which was first published in 1762. It was next used with the words 'We won't go home till morning', first published in England in this form *c.*1841, credited to Charles Blondel; in America in 1842 arranged by William Clifton. The ''For he's a jolly good fellow' version, of English origin, was probably of a similar age but did not appear thus in print in London until 1901, and then only as a brief quotation in another song. The first complete printing was in America in 1905. An American lyric 'The bear went over the mountain' was first attached in 1920.

Ford, 'Tennessee' Ernie [Ernest Jennings] (*b* Bristol, Tenn., 13 Feb. 1919; *d* Reston. Va. 17 Oct. 1991). American country singer. He studied at the Cincinnati Conservatory of Music and was an announcer on local radio before serving in the American Air Force during the Second World War. After the war he spent a time as a disc jockey in California before auditioning for Capitol records and establishing a singing career with 'Mule train', 'Smokie Mountain boogie', and 'Shot gun boogie'. In the rock and roll field he had a hit with 'Sixteen tons' (written by Merle *Travis in 1947), recording it in 1955 when it became a No. 1 hit within four months of issue, followed by 'Give me your word' (1955). He thus combined a career as 'Mister Country Music' (with his catchphrase, 'Howdy, pea-pickers') with that of a popular recording star.

Forde, Florrie [Flanagan, Florence] (*b* Fitzroy, nr. Melbourne, 14 Aug. 1876; *d* Aberdeen, 18 Apr. 1940). Australian music-hall singer. She had an early career in the theatre and music-hall in Sydney and on tour, earning herself the title of 'The Australian Marie Lloyd'. She first appeared in England at the London Pavilion 2 Aug. 1897. Described as a 'fine buxom woman', she specialized in rousing choruses in which she drilled the audience and owed her success to an unerring choice of song material that included some of music-hall's most lasting hits—'Oh, oh, Antonio', 'She's a lassie from Lancashire', 'Hold your hand out, naughty boy', 'Swing me higher, Obadiah', 'A bird in a gilded cage', 'Has anyone seen a German band', and her best-remembered number *'Down at the old Bull and Bush'.

At her peak during the First World War, she lifted the nation's spirits with such deathless ditties as 'Pack up your troubles in your old kit bag', 'Take me back to dear old Blighty', and *'It's a long way to Tipperary'. She ran her own revue company 'Flo and Co', in which *Flanagan and Allen, among others, came to light; and was a great summer favourite in the Isle of Man with special songs to please the inhabitants like 'Flanagan' ('Take me to the Isle of Man again') and 'Has anybody here seen Kelly?' She appeared in the the first Royal Command Performance in 1912. She continued her career in variety and as an impressively proportioned principal boy in pantomime, particularly at the Lyceum Theatre. In the early days of the Second World War she was there to entertain again, but died suddenly in 1940. A public house in Hampstead, the Old Bull and Bush, keeps her memory alive and has a Florrie Forde bar.

Foresythe, Reginald (*b* London, 28 May 1907; *d* London, 28 Dec. 1958). British composer, arranger, and pianist. Son of a British barrister and a West Indian mother, he started playing the piano as a boy and after leaving school worked in Paris as an accompanist to the singer Zaidee Jackson, later touring Australia with Walter Richardson. He went to California, where he worked for United Artists and MGM films and made his first recordings with Paul Howard, then moved to Chicago where he wrote 'Deep forest', the signature tune of the Earl *Hines orchestra. He returned to London in 1933 and appeared at the Café de la Paix with a 10–piece orchestra, returning to the USA in 1934 to work with Paul *Whiteman. He was in London again in 1935 at the 400 Club and appeared in the film *Jimmy Boy*. He was a prolific composer in the 1930s with such numbers as 'Strange interlude', 'Landscape', 'Southern holiday', 'Dodging a divorce', 'Serenade for a wealthy widow', 'Garden of weeds', many in Ellingtonian vein and played by the leading dance bands. With Andy *Razaf he wrote 'Mississippi Basin' and 'He's a son of the South'. He was a prolific recording artist in both Britain and America.

Formby, George [Booth, James] (*b* Ashton-under-Lyne, 1877; *d* Newcastle upon Tyne, 8 Feb. 1921). British comedian and singer. At the age of 12 he was working in an iron foundry where fumes damaged his lungs and left him with lasting bronchial trouble. His mother was an alcoholic and he had to make his own way in life. After performing locally he was offered a booking at the Argyle Theatre in Birkenhead. He took his stage name, Formby, from the town of that name. In 1900 he settled in Wigan where he was a regular at the Empire and was credited with the popularization of Wigan Pier. With his croaking voice he became one of the first widely-known Lancashire comedians, appearing in the guise of the simple John Willie who featured in many of his songs like 'John Willie, come on', 'Send for John Willie', and 'John Willie's Ragtime Band'. Among his biggest hits were 'Playing the game in the West' (recorded in 1909); 'Standing at the corner of the street' (1910); 'I put on my coat and went home' (1910); 'I parted my hair in the middle' (1914); 'I had my hand in my pocket at the time' (1915); 'All of a sudden it struck me' (1915); 'Twice nightly' (1916); and 'We all went home in a cab' (1919); to mention but a few.

Becoming one of Britain's highest-paid comedians, appearing in pantomime and in the London revue *Razzle Dazzle* (1916), he made a comic feature of the painful cough which eventually killed him while he was appearing at the Empire Theatre in Newcastle.

Formby, George [Booth, George Hoy] (*b* Wigan, 26 May 1904; *d* Penwortham, 6 Mar. 1961). Apprenticed as a jockey from 1911, he won his first race in 1915, leaving racing in 1921 when his father George *Formby Sr, died, to carry on the family tradition on the stage as George Hoy. He began by re-creating his father's recorded songs in his old costumes, coached by his old accompanist, and perpetuating the old John Willie character. In 1926 he recorded such Formby Sr. numbers as 'The man was a stranger to me', 'John Willie, come on', and 'I parted my hair in the middle'. He gradually developed his own personality and started to use the name George Formby. In 1926 he was appearing in revues and pantomimes and in 1931–2 had his own variety show. He became as big a variety star as his father, with an extensive repertoire of songs which he recorded in his distinctive Lancashire manner accompanying himself on the ukulele-banjo. He was co-writer of many of these. Some of his earliest hits were 'Like the big pots do' (1929); 'The old kitchen kettle' (1932); 'Chinese laundry blues' (1932); 'Swimmin' with the wimmin' (1933); 'You can't keep a growing lad down' (1934); and 'With my little stick of Blackpool rock' (1937). Most of his hits were originally (or later) associated with his many films.

He started his highly successful film career in 1934 with *Boots, Boots*—'Why don't women like me?'; followed by *Off the Dole* (1935)—'With my little ukulele in my hand'; *No Limit* (1936)—'Riding in the T. T. Races'; *Keep Your Seats Please* (1936)—'When I'm cleaning windows'; *Feather Your Nest* (1937)—'Leaning on a lamp post'; *Keep Fit* (1937)—'Keep fit', 'I don't like it'; *I See Ice* (1938)—'In my little snapshot album'; *It's in the Air* (1938)—'It's in the air', 'Our Sergeant-Major', 'They can't fool me'; *Trouble Brewing* (1939)—'Hitting the highspots now', 'Fanlight Fanny'; *Come On George* (1939)—'I'm making headway now'; *Let George Do It* (1940)—'Grandad's flannelette nightshirt', 'Mr Wu's a window cleaner now', 'Oh, don't the wind blow cold'; *Spare a Copper* (1940)—'I'm shy'; *Turned Out Nice Again* (1941)—'Auntie Maggie's remedy'; *South American George* (1941)—'The barmaid at the Rose and Crown'; *Much Too Shy* (1942)—'Andy the handy man'; *Get Cracking* (1943)—'Under the blasted oak'; *Bell Bottom George* (1943)—'It serves you right'; *He Snoops to Conquer* (1944); *I Didn't Do It* (1945); *George in Civvy Street* (1946). As a favourite entertainer of King George VI, he appeared in the Royal Command Performance in 1937. He toured with ENSA during the war and toured Canada and the USA in 1949 and 1950. In 1951 he made his first musical comedy appearance in **Zip Goes a Million*, but in 1952 he suffered a coronary thrombosis and was replaced by Reg Dixon. He recovered and returned to appear in variety, in *The Fun of the Fair* at the London Palladium and on TV. He continued to make stage apearances until 1960 when he was in *The Time of Your Life* in Blackpool. The death of his wife and early stage partner Beryl at the end of 1960 brought on a further bout of illness. He was about to marry again when he died.

A. Randall: *George Formby: a Biography* (London, 1974).
A. Bailey & P. Foss (eds): *George Formby Complete* [songs] (London, n.d.).

Forrest, George 'Chet' [Chichester, George Forrest] (*b* Brooklyn, NY, 31 July 1915). American lyric-writer, composer, and director. With his partner Robert *Wright, he scored many Hollywood films and wrote a number of musical shows that mainly adapted the works of classical composers. Films include: *Maytime* (1937); *The Firefly* (1937); *Sweethearts* (1937); **Balalaika* (1939); *Music in my Heart* (1940). Their stage shows were **Song of Norway* (1940; Grieg); *Gypsy Lad* (1946; Victor *Herbert—a combination of *The *Fortune Teller* and *The Serenade*); *Magdalena* (1948; Villa-Lobos); **Kismet* (1953; Borodin); *The Love Doctor* (1959); *Kean* (1961); *Anya* (1965; Rachmaninov); and *The *Great Waltz* (1970; Johann *Strauss).

Fortune Teller, The. Operetta with music by Victor *Herbert and book by Harry B. *Smith, first produced in Toronto in 1898, then seen at New York's Wallack's Theatre 26 Sept. 1898. It was commissioned for the newly formed Alice Nielsen Opera Co. as a vehicle for Nielsen (1876–1943). It also had Richard Golden, Joseph *Cawthorn, and Eugene Cowles (1860–1948) in the cast. The story was of two look-alike Hungarian girls, one an heiress, the other a gypsy fortune-teller, and their romantic entanglements. It contained such Herbert classics as 'Always do as people say you should', 'Romany life', and 'Gypsy love song'. Mounted by a touring company, the show had only 40 Broadway performances. It was seen in London at the Shaftesbury Theatre 9 Apr. 1901.

Forty-Five Minutes from Broadway. A comedy with music, written by George M. *Cohan. The story pivots round a millionaire's missing will. The will is discovered by Kid Burns (Victor *Moore); it leaves everything to the housekeeper Mary (Fay *Templeton), who loves Kid; but he refuses to marry a rich woman, so Mary tears up the will. It ran for only 90 performances on Broadway—New Amsterdam Theatre 1 Jan. 1906—but it was a great hit all over America not least because of its five Cohan songs: 'Gentlemen of the press', 'I want to be a popular millionaire', 'Mary's a grand old name', 'So long, Mary', and 'Forty-five minutes from Broadway'. It was revived at the Cohan Theatre in 1912 with Cohan as Kid Burns and Sallie Fisher as Mary.

Forty-Second Street. Hollywood musical film of 1933 that did much to advance the genre into its liveliest and most rewarding years by revitalizing what was already becoming a rather static art. It presented a back-stage story that was, in the words of Clive Hirschborn, 'simultaneously hard-hitting and escapist', a tonic for the depression years, with the Busby Berkeley dance routines for such numbers as 'Young and healthy' and 'Shuffle off to Buffalo' really making their mark. It introduced the talents of Dick *Powell and Ruby *Keeler; Ginger *Rogers and Bebe *Daniels were also in the cast; and helped to build the reputation of Harry *Warren ('You're getting to be a habit with me', etc.) as Hollywood's leading composer. It became a New York stage musical at the Winter Garden Theatre, 25 Aug. 1980, and was seen in London at the Theatre Royal, Drury Lane, 8 Aug. 1984.

Fosse, Bob [Robert Louis] (*b* Chicago, 23 June 1927; *d* Washington, 23 Sept. 1987). American choreographer and director. He began dancing while at school and, after serving in the US Navy, joined a dance team in New York which left to go to Hollywood to appear in a minor MGM musical, *Give a Girl a Break* (1953). After this he appeared in the film version of **Kiss Me, Kate* (1953). Feeling that he was not destined to be on stage, he went to New York and was taken on as a choreographer by George *Abbott. The success of *The *Pajama Game* (1957) led to many Broadway assignments. His first venture as a director was with **Sweet Charity* (1969), which was not a total success and brought a temporary halt to his career. A new chance came with the film version of **Cabaret* (1972), which won him an Academy Award as director.

Fosse's up-and-down career was typified by the winning of two Tony Awards for his Broadway show **Pippin* (1973), balanced by the poor reception of his film *Lenny* (1974). He suffered a heart-attack, brought on by these setbacks and overwork, somewhat ghoulishly portrayed in the film *All That Jazz* (1979). Its main character, based on Fosse, died; but Fosse survived and directed the musical *Dancin'* (1978). His tendency to work in overdrive, drinking, smoking, three marriages and three divorces, led to his death at 60, just before a revival of *Sweet Charity*.

Foster, Stephen Collins (*b* Lawrenceville, Pa., 4 July 1826; *d* New York, 13 Jan. 1864). American composer. He learned music at home and published his first song, 'Open thy lattice, love', when he was 18. His father, a civil servant, opposed his musical ambitions and he was sent to Cincinnati to work for his brother, a wholesale grocer, as a book-keeper. While in this occupation he continued to write songs for amateur vocalist friends and managed to sell some of them to music-publishers. These songs, some of the first popular songs that were truly and naturally American, swept the country, sung by the enormously popular minstrel shows (then billed as Ethiopian Minstrels). But as Foster was both commercially naïve and somewhat thriftless by nature, he received scant financial reward for many of his acknowledged masterpieces. Furthermore, he deliberately withheld his name from the cover of his 'Old folks at home', allowing Edwin Christy of *Christy Minstrel fame to publish it in his name in return for a payment of $15, because he felt that such a song might spoil his chances with his 'serious' drawing-room ballad style compositions which he felt had greater merit.

It has always been said that Foster was poorly paid for his creations. Probably he failed to receive all that he was entitled to, or anything approaching what he would have earned today with the help of the copyright laws, but he made a fair income in his peak years. It has been estimated that between 1849 and 1860 he received about $15,000 in royalties. He did sell many of his early songs outright for a few dollars apiece, as was the custom in those days; but when he was established as a songwriter he was able to bargain for royalties and at this stage he left the grocery business and went to live in Pennsylvania, where he devoted his time to songwriting and composing dance music. He wrote prolifically (189 songs altogether) but was defeated by his spendthrift nature. In 1860, then in poor health, he signed a contract with a publisher that waived all royalties in favour of a regular $800 a year in return for a minimum of 12 new songs.

He had been married to Jane MacDowell in Pittsburgh in 1850, and they had a daughter. It was an unhappy union and when Foster became unable to support the family there were frequent separations. He went to New York, where he ran into further debt and began to drink heavily. His wife left him for good and he became more and more a hack, writing mediocre songs in return for drinking money. He was taken into hospital on 10 Jan. 1864, from a cheap Bowery hotel where he had fallen and gashed his throat, and he died in a coma three days later.

Many of Foster's drawing-room ballads are typical of the day, and most have some merit. But it is his minstrel songs, which are unquestionably classics of their kind and a part of the American heritage, which are best remembered—'Oh! Susanna' (1848); 'Old Uncle Ned' (1848); 'Nelly was a lady (1849); Camptown Races (1850); 'Nelly Bly' (1850); 'Way down in Ca-i-ro' (1850); 'Old folks at home' (or 'Swanee River') (1851); 'Ring de banjo' (1851); 'Massa's in de cold ground' (1852); 'My old Kentucky home' (1853); 'Some folks' (1855); 'Old black Joe' (1860); 'The Glendy Burk' (1860); and 'Don't bet your money on the Shanghai' (1861). Among the best of his other writings (including his Civil War songs) are: 'Open thy lattice, love' (1844); 'There's a good time coming' (1846); 'Ah! may the red rose live alway!' (1850); 'Wilt thou be gone, love?' (1851); 'Maggie by my side' (1852); 'Old dog Tray' (1853); 'Jeanie with the light brown hair' (1854); 'Come where my love lies dreaming' (1855); 'Hard times come again no more' (1855); 'The village maiden' (1855); 'Gentle Annie' (1856); 'Thou art the Queen of my song' (1859); 'Down among the cane-brakes' (1860);

'Better times are coming' (1862); 'Gentle Lena Clare' (1862); 'That's what's the matter' (1862); 'There are plenty of fish in the sea' (1862); 'We are coming, Father Abraham' (1862); 'My wife is a most knowing woman' (1863); 'Nothing but a plain old soldier' (1863); 'The song of all songs' (1863); 'When this dreadful war is ended' (1863); 'Willie has gone to the war' (1863); 'Beautiful dreamer' (1864); 'If you've only got a moustache' (1864); and 'The voices that are gone' (1865). The 40 songs listed above are the ones included in the *Stephen Foster Song Book* (ed. Jackson). He also wrote 12 instrumental pieces and made various arrangements for small salon orchestras for the collection *Foster's Social Orchestra* (New York, 1854).

M. Foster: *Biography, Songs and Musical Compositions of Stephen C. Foster* (Pittsburgh, 1896). W. R. Whittlesey & O. Sonneck: *Catalogue of First Editions of Stephen Foster* (Washington, 1915). J. T. Howard: *Stephen Foster, America's Troubadour* (New York, 1934). R. W. Walter: *Stephen Foster, Youth's Golden Dream* (Princeton, 1936). J. T. Howard (ed.): *A Treasury of Stephen Foster* (New York, 1946). J. J. Fuld: *A Pictorial Bibliography of the First Editions of Stephen C. Foster* (Philadelphia, 1957). R. Jackson (ed.): *Stephen Foster Song Book* (New York, 1974). C. Elliker: *Stephen Collins Foster: a Resource Manual* (New York, 1988).

Four Freshmen, The. American vocal and instrumental quartet who had a big influence on modern group singing with their innovative ideas. The group came together in 1948, the original line-up being Ross Barbour (*b* 31 Dec. 1928), Don Barbour (*b* 19 Apr. 1927), Bob Flanigan (*b* 22 Aug. 1926), and Hal Kratsch, who was replaced by Ken Errair (*b* 23 Jan. 1928) in 1953, all of them students of the Arthur Jordan Conservatory of Music in Indianapolis. Performing in the Midwest (at first known as the Toppers) they gradually became recognized and were signed up by Capitol Records. They sang with great variety, in quiet unison or full-throated harmony, using modern jazz harmonies and varied dynamics, a considerable advance on the typical close-harmony quartets that had preceded them. They appeared in the film *Rich, Young and Pretty* in 1951. The group continued into the 1970s with Ken Albers replacing Errair in 1956, Bill Comstock replacing Don Barbour in 1960, and Ray Brown replacing Comstock in 1973.

Four Seasons, The. American vocal pop group formed in 1956 as the Four Lovers, becoming the Four Seasons in 1962, considered by some at the time to be America's answer to the *Beatles. The original personnel was Frankie Valli [Francis Castellucio] (*b* Newark, NJ, 3 May 1937), whose falsetto lead vocals were a main attraction and set a long-lasting fashion for high-pitched youths; Tommy DeVito (*b* Belleville, NJ, 19 June 1936); Hank Majewski—soon replaced by Nick Massi (*b* 19 Sept. 1935), and Nick DeVito on guitar. They had their first hit in 1956 with 'You're the apple of my eye'. Bob Gaudio (*b* Bronx, NY, 17 Nov. 1942), a talented songwriter, replaced Tommy DeVito and helped the group move from their basic *doo-wop sound.

They were eventually to sell 80 million records, with 'Sherry' (1962), 'Big girls don't cry' (1962), 'Walk like a man' (1963), 'Rag doll' (1964), and 'Let's hang on' (1965) all becoming No. 1 hits in the USA. Their rise to fame neatly coincided with the Merseyside explosion during which only the Four Seasons and the *Beach Boys in the USA proved to be substantial rivals to the fabulous Beatles. When the trend for progressive and experimental rock/pop was set in motion by the Beatles' *Sergeant Pepper* LP, the Four Seasons responded with an album called *Genuine Imitation Life Gazette* (1969) which, in spite of being enormously expensive to produce, proved a commercial and artistic failure. The result was a recording silence for several years and a parting from their long-standing producer Bob Crewe, but thanks to the excellent writing of Bob Gaudio they remained an attraction in the USA. Valli left in 1977 to pursue an already thriving solo career, but the group proved its worth by long outlasting, with various changes of personnel, all their contemporary rivals.

Four Tops, The. American vocal group formed in Detroit as the Four Aims in 1953, becoming the Four Tops in 1954; originally Levi Stubbs, Renaldo Benson, Abdul 'Duke' Fakir, and Lawrence Payton, who became one of the star attractions of the Motown stable. Their first No. 1 hit came in 1965 with 'I can't help myself'. With a forceful lead in Levi Stubbs and backing close-harmony trio, the group followed conventional quartet styling but came up with a freshly rhythmic and hard-hitting recording in 'Reach out, I'll be there' in 1955 which helped to establish the Motown image by becoming an international No. 1. In the 1970s it looked as though the group might be ending its career, but in 1981 they marked a revival of spirit with the pop/soul album *Tonight* and continued to make their mark as a classic black pop group, maybe not particularly experimental but full of the true Motown spirit.

Fox, Roy (*b* Denver, 25 Oct. 1901; *d* London, 20 Mar. 1982). American bandleader. He started his career in Santa Monica, California, where he played with the Abe *Lyman band. At 19 he was leading his own group in Culver City and went on to front bands in Los Angeles, Miami, and New York, with a 15-month stay at the Cocoanut Grove in Hollywood. He supervised music for Fox Studios in the late 1920s. In 1929 he took a band to London to work at the Café de Paris, decided to remain in England, and became musical director for Decca Records. It was during a long stay at the Monseigneur Restaurant that he established a reputation as one of England's most popular bandleaders, heading a sweet but swinging group with Lew *Stone on piano, Nat *Gonella as lead trumpet, Al *Bowlly as its popular vocalist (later Denny Dennis, *b* 1913), and 'Whispering' as its theme song. Fox was taken ill in late 1932 and Lew Stone took over the band. He returned with his own band and was prominent until 1939 but continued ill-health took him to the better climate of Australia. During the Second World War he was back in California, but afterwards came back to England to try and pick up his career. He abandoned the band world in 1952 and became a theatre agent.

R. Fox: *Hollywood, Mayfair and All That Jazz: the Roy Fox Story* (London, 1975).

Foxtrot. A basic modern ballroom dance from which many of the popular modern dance steps derive. As it needed considerable space to perform its expansive movements properly, the tendency has been for the more economical and easier *quickstep to take over. Although a dance similar to the foxtrot was developing in America around 1912, the name does not seem to have become fixed until about 1914, when the first records bearing the name of the dance were issued. It has been claimed that the name derives from actor-singer Harry Fox (1882–1959), who introduced a few trotting steps into his routine in the **Ziegfeld Follies* in 1913 to a ragtime accompaniment. The early foxtrot included trotting steps but these soon disappeared in favour of the smoother, gliding steps that were its main attraction. Earlier variants of the foxtrot were the horse-trot and the fish-walk, both direct descendants of the *one-step and the *rag. By 1924 there was a distinction between the slow foxtrot and the simplified quick foxtrot, which soon became known as the quickstep. The standard foxtrot was then danced to music in common time with the 1st and 3rd beats accented at a tempo of 30 to 32 bars a minute. The foxtrot was first demonstrated in England by Stroud Haxton at the 400 Club in Bond Street. It was then featured in **Tonight's the Night* at the *Gaiety and in many revues, such as *Push and Go* at the Hippodrome and *Watch Your Step* at the Empire; all of these giving it a good initial boost. The trot part of the dance was soon discarded and a smoother movement named the saunter was established and remains the basis of the foxtrot as it is known today.

Foy, Eddie [Fitzgerald, Edwin] (*b* New York, 9 Mar. 1854; *d* Kansas City, 16 Feb. 1928). American dancer and comedian. He grew up in Chicago and started dancing as a boy. He toured in minstrel shows and vaudeville, made his first stage appearance in *Henderson's Extravaganzas* in 1884, and was in many Broadway musicals. His odd sibilant voice is remembered in a song called 'He goes to Church on Sunday' and his eccentric dancing was featured in such shows as *Hotel Topsy Turvy* (1898); *The Strollers* (1901); *The Wild Rose* (1902); *Mr Bluebeard* (1903); *Piff! Paff! Puff!* (1904); *The *Earl and the Girl* (1905); *The *Orchid* (1907); *Mr Hamlet of Broadway* (1908); *Up and Down Broadway* (1910); and *Over the River* (1912). At one time he led a vaudeville act, which included his children, billed as Eddie Foy and the Seven Little Foys. One of them, Eddie *Foy Jr., went on to become a dancer and film star in his own right. In 1955 the film *The Seven Little Foys* had Bob *Hope taking the part of Eddie Foy Sr.

E. Foy: *Clowning Through Life* (New York, 1928).

Foy, Eddie, Jr. [Fitzgerald, Edwin, Jr.] (*b* New Rochelle, NY, 4 Feb. 1905). American actor, singer, and dancer. Son of comedian Eddie *Foy, with whom he appeared in the vaudeville act Eddie Foy and the Seven Little Foys. Later he followed his father in similar style and similar career, appearing in Broadway shows and films, mainly in small comic character roles. He portrayed his father in two films *Lillian Russell* (1940) and *Yankee Doodle Dandy* (1942), and was the narrator of *The Seven Little Foys* (1955). His Broadway appearances included *The *Cat and the Fiddle* (1931), *At Home Abroad* (1935), and *Donnybrook!* (1961); his finest role was a leading one in *The *Pajama Game* (1954). He was in several film versions of musicals including *Yokel Boy* (1942); *The Pajama Game* (1957); and **Bells Are Ringing* (1960); and he had a good role in *Lucky Me* (1954). His own show, *Eddy Foy and the Music Hall* in 1947, also featured the Eddy *Duchin band, and he was active into the 1960s.

Fragson, Harry [Pott, Léon Philippe] (*b* London, 2 July 1869; *d* Paris, 30 Dec. 1913). Composer, pianist, and entertainer. Of mixed English and Belgian parentage, the son of a publican, he was completely bilingual and able to pursue equally successful stage careers in both countries. After building a reputation as an amateur he tried to get a music-hall engagement at the Middlesex in 1885, but found that his kind of songs-at-the-piano act was not yet in demand. He went to France in 1889 and had a brilliant cabaret season at the Quat-z-arts in Paris in 1891. Elegantly dressed, accompanying himself at the piano, he sang well and was an excellent mimic and comedian. In various cabarets and revues, including the famous *Folies-Bergère, he had a terrific success with a song called 'La boiteuse' (written by Lelièvre and Briollet). He did not return to England (except for a brief visit in 1896) until 1905, when he appeared in the pantomime *Cinderella* at Drury Lane in a part specially written for him by Francis Burnand and J. Hickory Wood. His humorous French-styled act was popular in England and his Englishness was popular in France.

Among the songs he sang were 'Elle est de Marseille', 'La petite dame du Métro', and 'Je connais une blonde'; his most popular number in France was 'Reviens!' which he wrote with Henri *Christiné in 1900. He composed a number of songs for the British music-hall and musical comedy stage (*Castles in Spain*, 1906), including the ever popular 'Hello! Hello! Who's your lady friend?' (1913) and 'Whispers of love' (1906), 'The music-hall Shakespeare' (1910), 'The other department please (1910), and 'All the girls are lovely by the seaside' (1913). At the height of his career he came to a violent end when, about to embark on a long tour and carrying on an affair with Christiné's widow, he arranged to have his father put in an old people's home. His father was so incensed at the idea that he shot his son with a revolver.

Frampton, Peter Kenneth (*b* Beckenham, Kent, 22 Apr. 1950). British rock singer and guitarist. As leader of the Herd, he became a teenage-idol when only 16 himself, seized upon by the press for his boyish good looks as much as for his talent. Not liking this assessment, he left the Herd to form a more aspiring group called Humble Pie, with which he toured the USA. He left in 1971 to foster his own talents as a tasteful guitarist and an intelligent singer, and worked with George *Harrison and Harry *Nilsson. His 1975 album *Frampton Comes Alive!* was a sensational success, selling more than 12 million copies, the best-selling live album of all time. He survived a near-fatal car crash in 1978 to re-emerge as a potent and effective pop entertainer.

M. Daly: *Peter Frampton* (New York, 1978). S. Katz: *Frampton! an Unauthorized Biography* (New York, 1978). I. Adler: *Peter Frampton* (New York, 1979).

Francis, Connie [Franconero, Concetta Rosa Maria] (*b* Newark, NJ, 12 Dec. 1938). American singer. She made her first mark in the entertainment world at the age of 11 as a singer and accordionist on the children's TV show *Startime*, became a featured vocalist on the show, and was signed up by MGM records in 1955. She had a hit record with Marvin Rainwater in 1957, 'Majesty of love', and her first solo million-seller coming with 'Who's sorry now?' (1958), followed by 'Stupid Cupid' (1958). In the 1950s and 1960s she was one of the most successful female singers on record and by 1967 had sold 35 million discs. She also played the piano and composed. Her film appearances included *Where the Boys Are* (1960); *Follow the Boys* (1963); *Looking for Love* (1964); *When the Boys Meet the Girls* (1965). She had a beautifully direct style, almost conversational and laced with humour, with immaculately clear diction.

C. Francis: *Who's Sorry Now?* (New York, 1984).

Francis, Day & Hunter. Well-known British publishers of popular music. Their formation came directly out of the blackface minstrel vogue of the 1860s. In 1867 the brothers James and William Francis were employed by the famous publishers *Chappell & Co. They were inspired by the Moore & Crocker Minstrels at St James's Hall to form their own troupe, which they called the Mohawk Minstrels and by 1873 the troupe were so successful that they left the publishing business. In 1874 they were joined by a talented young singer and composer, Harry Hunter, from a rival minstrel troupe. Soon their repertoire of songs written by Hunter and others was so large that they decided to go back into publishing on their own account and in 1877, in partnership with David Day who gave up a good position at Hopwood & Crew to join them, they set up the business as Francis Bros & Day at 351 Oxford Street. Besides publishing minstrel songs and books and the *Mohawk Minstrel* magazine, they soon moved into the music-hall field. When James Francis died, Harry Hunter, who had branched out into music-hall management, took his place and the firm became Francis, Day & Hunter, a title it kept even when Hunter sold out his interest in 1900. As one of the main music-hall publishers and vital to its flourishing history, the firm prospered. In 1897 they moved to 142 Charing Cross Road, thus helping to found London's Tin Pan Alley community around Denmark Street and in 1905 a branch was opened in New York. In 1882 the first *Comic Annuals* had been issued, and these continued until well after the Second World War. The firm absorbed the businesses of Bert Feldman in 1953 (which had itself acquired the Charles Sheard and Herman *Darewski catalogues) and Robbins Music in 1957, the group operating as Affiliated Music Publishers Ltd. In 1972 it was taken over by EMI Music Publishing which also had Keith Prowse music.

J. Abbott: *The Story of Francis, Day & Hunter* (London, 1952). P. Gammond: *Music Hall Songbook* (Newton Abbot, 1975).

'Frankie and Johnny'. A song, now best known in its 12-bar blues form, telling a poignant story on the theme 'he was her man—but he done her wrong'. A related traditional melody has been traced back to a Scottish folk-song, 'Tattie Jock'; in fact two closely related but distinct versions evolved by way of the folky 'Single girl' and the more bluesey 'Josie'. Specific versions on the lines of the modern song are pinpointed in 1863 and later, some based on the story of Frankie and Albert and some hinting at a homosexual slant to the story. The best-known version is said to be based on the true story of the shooting of her lover by one Frankie Baker on 15 Oct. 1899 in a St Louis lodging-house; but this is only one of many sources claimed.

The amalgamated story has slipped into folklore and has given rise, according to John *Lomax, to more than 300 variants. The folkier versions can be followed in the recording 'Frankie' (1928) made by blues singer Mississippi John Hurt (1893–1966). The more commercial version first appeared in print in 1904 as 'He done me wrong', the authorship claimed by Hughie Cannon (1877–1912), the writer of *'Bill Bailey, won't you please come home', which has related portions to some versions of 'Frankie and Johnny'. The song was first published under this modern title in 1912, the music and words now credited to the Leighton Brothers (who did much to popularize it) and Ren *Shields. It became known to a wider audience on record by way of recordings by Frank *Crumit in 1927 and Jimmie Rodgers in 1931; these were followed by a multitude of versions, including those by Fats *Waller (1939) and Duke *Ellington (1945).

Franklin, Aretha (*b* Memphis, 25 Mar. 1942). American soul singer. Daughter of the Revd C. L.

Franklin, a Baptist preacher well-known for his numerous recordings of sermons, she naturally grew up with gospel songs and evangelical choruses, and recorded some songs with a local record label. She went to New York in 1960 and began to build a national reputation. After a noteworthy appearance at the Newport Jazz Festival in 1963 she made some minority interest albums with Columbia. On signing up with Atlantic Records in 1967 her career took off: she had a No. 1 hit with 'Respect' (1967) and her first album, *I Never Loved a Man* (1967), was proclaimed a classic. Her albums continued to sell in millions and her early singles were always high in the ratings—'Baby, I love you' (1967); 'A natural woman' (1967); 'Chain of fools' (1968). She toured Europe in 1967 and shook the democratic Convention in Chicago in 1968 with a soul rendering of 'The Star-spangled Banner'. There was a trend towards commercial rock after this, but she returned firmly to her gospel roots in 1972 for the album *Amazing Grace*. She was acclaimed 'Lady Soul' in the 1970s, and although her supremacy has since been challenged she continues to maintain the highest standards and to perform with excitement and sincerity. In many recordings she was backed by her sisters Emma and Carolyn (1944–88), the latter writing such hits as 'In't no way' and 'Angel' (1973).

M. Bego: *Aretha Franklin: the Queen of Soul* (New York, 1990).

Fraser-Simson, Harold (*b* London, 15 Aug. 1878; *d* London, 19 Jan. 1944). British composer. Mainly educated in France, he then worked in the shipping business before turning to music professionally. He always seemed to be more like a businessman than a composer, with a retiring nature, and he continued to lead a very private life even after the great success of *The* **Maid of the Mountains* (1916). He also composed *Bonita* (1911); *A Southern Maid* (1917); *Our Peg* (1919); *Head over Heels* (1923); *Our Nell* (1924); *The Street Singer* (1924); *Betty in Mayfair* (1925); and *Vaudeville Vanities* (1926). Another successful venture was his settings of the 'Winnie the Pooh' poems of A. A. Milne in several volumes 1924–8 (recorded by George *Baker and later Robert Tear). He also wrote incidental music for Milne's *Toad of Toad Hall* (1929).

Freed, Alan (*b* Johnstown, Pa., 15 Dec. 1922; *d* Palm Springs, Calif., 20 Jan. 1965). American disc jockey. An influential figure in the early popularization of rock and roll and notable for his introduction of black music on programmes broadcast by hitherto white-biased American radio stations. He is actually credited with originating the term 'rock 'n' roll' in 1951; even if that claim does not stand up he certainly put it on everybody's lips. He began his broadcasting career in Cleveland, moving to New York in 1954 to work on the WINS station which became the main pioneering outlet of the burgeoning pop scene, and appeared in the famous film *Rock around the Clock* (1956). He ran into trouble with unruly audiences at his concerts in the late 1950s, and then ran into disaster when he was convicted of accepting bribes in the infamous 'payola' case of 1963, and of income tax evasion. He returned to California and oblivion before he died in 1965.

Freed, Arthur [Grossman, Arthur] (Charleston, SC, 9 Sept. 1894; *d* Hollywood, 12 Apr. 1973). American film producer and lyricist. He became associated with the Marx Brothers and Gus *Edwards, and appeared in vaudeville with Louis *Silvers as his partner. They started to write for revues and during the First World War wrote army shows. He settled in Seattle after the war, returned to vaudeville for a while, became a theatre manager in Los Angeles, and began producing his own shows. Having written lyrics for the first full-length musical film, **Broadway Melody* (1929), he settled in Hollywood in 1929 to work for MGM, becoming the most important and prolific producer of musical films, using the best talent, and helping to discover performers like Gene *Kelly.

He produced such classics as **Babes in Arms* (1939); *The* **Wizard of Oz* (1939); **Strike Up the Band* (1940); **Lady Be Good* (1941); **Cabin in the Sky* (1942); *For Me and My Gal* (1942); **Dubarry Was a Lady* (1943); **Girl Crazy* (1943); *Meet Me in St Louis* (1944); *The Harvey Girls* (1945); **Easter Parade* (1948); **Annie Get Your Gun* (1949); **On the Town* (1949); *An* **American in Paris* (1951); **Show Boat* (1951); *Tbe* **Belle of New York* (1952); **Singing in the Rain* (1952); **Brigadoon* (1955); **Silk Stockings* (1956); **Gigi* (1958); and **Bells Are Ringing* (1960). Mainly in partnership with Nacio Herb *Brown, he wrote many classic film songs heard in such films as *Broadway Melody*; *Hollywood Revue* (1929); *The Big Broadcast* (1932); *Babes in Arms*; *Strike Up the Band*; *Lady Be Good*; and *Singin' in the Rain*.

Freedley, Vinton (*b* Philadelphia, 5 Nov. 1891; *d* New York, 5 June 1969). American producer. He started out as an actor but then joined Alex A. Aarons (1891–1943) in 1923 to form a team that produced many of the historic musicals of the 1920s, seven of them by *Gershwin, and in 1928 built the Alvin Theatre in New York. From 1934, Freedley continued on his own with further shows, including four by Cole *Porter. He was co-producer or producer of *For Goodness Sake* (1922); *Elsie* (1923); **Lady, Be Good!* (1924); **Tip-Toes* (1925); **Oh, Kay!* (1926); **Funny Face* (1927); *Here's Howe* (1928); **Hold Everything!* (1928); *Treasure Girl* (1928); *Spring is Here* (1929); *Heads Up* (1929); **Girl Crazy* (1930); *Pardon My English* (1933); **Anything Goes* (1934); **Red, Hot and Blue* (1935); **Leave it to Me!* (1938); **Cabin in the Sky* (1940); **Let's Face It!* (1941); *Jackpot* (1944); *Memphis Bound* (1945); and *Great To Be Alive!* (1950).

Freeman, Bud [Lawrence] (*b* Chicago, 13 Apr. 1906; *d* Chicago, 15 Mar. 1991). American tenor-saxophonist. One of the few genuine Chicagoans to be associated with the rise of the original white Chicago-style jazz of the 1920s, early associated with the Austin High School Gang. He played in Europe in 1928 and remained a true cosmopolitan, playing traditional but cool-toned jazz, in a style that foresaw the work of Lester *Young. He worked with such jazz figures as Red *McKenzie, Gene *Krupa, Bunny *Berigan, Claude *Thornhill, Eddie *Condon, and Cozy *Cole, regularly leading his own groups, including the Summa Cum Laude Orchestra 1939–40. Amongst his best tracks was 'The eel', made with Condon in 1933, and the sessions with his Chicagoans and Jack *Teagarden (1940) have remained classics of the Chicago genre. After serving in the war, 1943–5 he remained a freelance musician, ever in demand for traditional and mainstream sessions, living in London from 1974, and returning to Chicago in 1984.

French, William Percy (*b* nr Castlebar, 1 May 1854; *d* Formby, Lancs., 24 Jan. 1920). Irish composer and author. He was sent to Trinity College, Dublin, intended for a career in mathematics; but he spent most of his time in writing songs, painting, and playing in amateur theatricals. He managed, however, to pass his exams and became employed on a government drainage scheme. When this came to an end he abandoned engineering and moved to Dublin, where he became involved in many kinds of artistic activities. In 1900 he went to London and became a professional entertainer, achieving success and making a number of overseas tours. He wrote librettos for the operas *The Knight of the Road* (1891), music by W. A. Houston Collison (1865–1920) and *Freda and the Fairies* (1900), music by Caroline Maude, both produced in Dublin. In 1920, during an engagement in Glasgow, he was taken ill, and, having contracted pneumonia, died soon after at his cousin's home in Formby.

Writing most of his own material, French turned out many excellent songs, mostly in humorous Irish vein, some of which have become almost folk classics, including 'Abdulla Bulbul Ameer' (1877), later published without credit to French, as in the *Scottish Students' Song Book*, arranged and popularized by Frank *Crumit, and only in recent years assigned to its true composer; 'Phil the Fluter's ball' (1889); 'Shlathery's Mounted Fut' (1889); 'The emigrant ship' (1890); 'The mountains of Mourne' (1896); 'When Erin wakes' (1900); 'Eileen Oge' (1903); 'The darlin' girl from Clare' (1906); 'Ballyjamesduff' (1912); 'Come back, Paddy Reilly' (1912). Many of them used traditional Irish airs arranged by either French or Houston Collison, his long-standing partner. His lyrics were especially noteworthy, lively, polished, often moving and poetic.

De B. Daly (ed.): *Chronicles and Poems of Percy French* (Dublin–London, 1922). J. N. Healy: *Percy French and his Songs* (Cork–London, 1966). P. O'Dowda: *The World of Percy French* (Dundonald, 1981). *Songs of Percy French*, 3 vols (London, n.d.).

Friedhofer, Hugo Wilhelm (*b* San Francisco, 3 May 1901; *d* Los Angeles, 17 May 1981). American composer. The son of a cellist, he left school at 16 to become an office boy, eventually working in lithograhic design and studying painting. At 18 he turned to music and in 1923 became a professional cellist, playing until 1925 with the People's Symphony Orchestra in San Francisco. In 1925 he joined the Granada Theatre Orchestra and in 1929 went to Hollywood to become an arranger for Fox films, transferring to Warner Bros in 1935 as orchestrator for Leo Forbstein. He remained with Warners for 11 years, during which time he worked with and learned from Erich Wolfgang *Korngold and Max *Steiner.

He wrote his first complete film score in 1938, *The Adventures of Marco Polo*, and in the following years composed music for some 70 films including: *A Wing and a Prayer* (1944); *Brewster's Millions* (1945); *The Best Years of Our Lives* (1946)—Academy Award; *A Song is Born* (1947); *Joan of Arc* (1948); *Bride of Vengeance* (1949); *The Sound of Fury* (1950); *Ace in the Hole* (1951); *Lydia Bailey* (1952); *Island in the Sky* (1953); *Vera Cruz* (1954); *Violent Saturday* (1955); *Between Heaven and Hell* (1956); *Boy on a Dolphin* (1957); *The Sun Also Rises* (1957); *An Affair to Remember* (1957); *The Young Lions* (1958); *This Earth is Mine* (1959); *One-Eyed Jacks* (1960); *Homicidal* (1961); and *Beauty and the Beast* (1962). The only native Californian composer working in the Hollywood studios at that time, among a host of famous Europeans, he won general esteem for his ability to maintain musical excellence while providing the right dramatic background.

Friend, Cliff (*b* Cincinnati, 1 Oct. 1893; *d* Las Vegas, 27 June 1974). American composer. His father was a theatre musician and he followed the rest of a musical family by learning the piano and studying at the Cincinnati Conservatory. In his teens he became part of a musical double act in vaudeville, later joined by Buddy *DeSylva. He became an accompanist, had a few moderate successes in songwriting, and toured the world as an entertainer. Back in the USA in the 1920s he found his style and began to turn out regular hits, weathering the depression and carrying on into the late 1940s.

He wrote the scores of *The *Passing Show of 1921* (1920); *Bombo* (1921); *The Midnight Rounders* (1921); *Piggy* (1927); **George White's Scandals* (1929); **Earl Carroll's Vanities* (1931); and for the films *The Crooner* (1933); *Cross My Heart* (1938); *Shine On, Harvest Moon* (1944)—which included 'Time waits for no-one' (with Charles *Tobias). His jazz-tinged, vaudeville-styled songs, many written for Al *Jolson, included: 'Blue Hoosier blues' (1923); 'Chili bom bom' (1923); 'Let me linger longer in your arms' (1924); 'Mama loves papa' (1924); 'There's yes, yes in your eyes' (1924); 'Big butter and egg man' (1924); 'Where the lazy daisies grow' (1924); 'Let it rain! Let it pour!' (1925); 'Give me a night in June' (1927); 'My blackbirds are bluebirds now' (1928); 'You're a real sweetheart' (1928); 'Just because you're you' (1932); 'South American Joe' (1934); 'When my dreamboat comes home' (1936); 'It's the gypsy in me' (1936); 'The merry-go-round broke down' (1937); 'I must see Annie tonight' (1939); 'Trade winds' (1940); mainly written in collaboration.

Friml, Rudolf (*b* Prague, 7 Dec. 1879; *d* Los Angeles, 12 Nov. 1972). Bohemian-American composer. Son of a baker whose hobby was music, he showed great promise as a child and at the age of 10 had a 'Barcarolle' for piano published. He was sent to the Prague Conservatory, at one time studying composition under Dvořák. On leaving the conservatory he was engaged by the violin virtuoso Jan Kubelik as his accompanist and during the next 10 years he toured the world in this capacity. He went to the USA in 1901 and again in 1906, this time deciding to stay in America to build his career as pianist and composer. He was a successful performer, giving many recitals both solo and with orchestra, and he played his own piano concerto with the New York Symphony Orchestra.

His introduction to the musical theatre came in 1912 when the singer Emma *Trentini had a quarrel with the composer Victor *Herbert and Friml was asked to take over the scoring of an operetta, *The *Firefly*, which Herbert was writing for her as a follow-up to **Naughty Marietta*. The producer Arthur Hammerstein was persuaded by the publisher Schirmer to try Friml and was rewarded with one of the freshest and most charming scores to appear for some time. It was to have a further success in 1937 as a film, at which time Friml added 'Donkey serenade', a song adapted from a piano piece called 'Chanson'. This had first been heard in 1924, in a jazz arrangement, in the same Paul *Whiteman concert in which *Gershwin's *'Rhapsody in Blue' first appeared. *The Firefly* immediately established Friml as an operetta composer. Alongside other immigrants from Europe, such as Victor *Herbert and Sigmund *Romberg, he helped to establish a strong school of Viennese-style operetta and musical comedy with works which were enormously popular in America and elsewhere (and have continued to be so on the professional and amateur stage alike) in the days before the jazz craze took a real hold. His two greatest successes were certainly **Rose Marie* (1924) and *The *Vagabond King* (1925). Although he continued to write for the rest of his life, his last real stage success was *The Three Musketeers* in 1928: he was never able to adapt to the new styles which then started to dominate the theatre.

In the 1930s he mainly wrote for Hollywood films such as *Lottery Bride* (1930); *Music for Madame* (1937); *The Firefly* (1937); and later *Northwest Outpost* (1947). He also wrote a considerable number of piano pieces in a light drawing-room style, but these too became outmoded in the 1930s. His other stage scores included: *High Jinks* (1913); *The Peasant Girl* (1915); *Katinka* (1915); *You're in Love* (1917); *Kitty Darlin'* (1917); *Sometime* (1918); *Glorianna* (1918); *Tumble Inn* (1919); *The Little Whopper* (1919); *June Love* (1921); **Ziegfeld Follies* (1921); *The Blue Kitten* (1922); *Cinders* (1923); *No Foolin'* (1926); *The Wild Rose* (1926); *The White Eagle* (1927); *Luana* (1930); *and Music Hath Charms* (1934).

Frohman, Charles (*b* Sandusky, Ohio, 17 June 1860; *d* 7 May 1915). American producer. He worked almost equally on Broadway and in London, where he built and managed the Aldwych and the Hicks Theatre on behalf of Seymour *Hicks and presented many important shows. He was involved in such productions (some in New York and London) as *His Excellency* (1895); *The *Shop Girl* (1895); *An *Artist's Model* (1895); *In Town* (1897); *Hotel Topsy-Turvy* (1898); **Bluebell in Fairyland* (1901); *Three Little Maids* (1902); *The School Girls* (1903); *The Girl From Kay's* (1903); *Madame Sherry* (1903); *My Lady Molly* (1903); *The *Catch of the Season* (1904); *The Beauty of Bath* (1906); *The Little Cherub* (1906); *The Rich Mr Hoggenheimer* (1906); *The Dairymaids* (1907); *The Gay Gordons* (1907); **Miss Hook of Holland* (1907); *A *Waltz Dream* (1908); *The Girls of Gottenberg* (1908); *Kitty Grey* (1909); *The *Dollar Princess* (1909); *The *Arcadians* (1910); **Our Miss Gibbs* (1910); *The *Pink Lady* (1912); *The Sunshine Girl* (1913); and *The *Girl From Utah* (1914). He died when the *Lusitania* was torpedoed.

Fuller, Jesse (*b* Jonesboro, Ga., 12 Mar. 1896; *d* Oakland, Calif., 29 Jan. 1976). American blues singer, guitarist, and composer. He became interested in music as a boy, and gained his nickname, 'Lone Cat', as a youth when he was moving around the South, working in jobs ranging from cow-herding to car-washing, and listening to music wherever he could. He moved to Cincinnati in 1920 and sang in the streets, going to California in 1922 where he got small parts in films. It was not until the late 1930s that he worked more regularly as a musician, becoming quite well-known in the San Francisco area, and he made his first recordings in the late 1940s. By the 1950s he had become known to folk and blues enthusiasts, singing in a nasal, instrumental manner and accompanying himself with his one-man band in which he played 12-string guitar, harmonica, kazoo, washboard, and fotdella. He appeared in festivals and toured Europe and Britain in the late 1950s and early 1960s. In 1954 he wrote his classic 'San Francisco Bay blues' which has been used by many other singers.

Funk. From 'funky', meaning bad-smelling, the word was gradually associated with music that was low-down, earthy, and crude. In modern jazz circles it was used to describe a kind of post-bop music that still retained some elements of the older swing and a degree of emotional feeling or 'soul'. It was associated with musicians like Milt *Jackson who wrote 'Opus de funk' (1954), Horace *Silver, and Herbie *Hancock. The term moved into the rhythm 'n' blues world, still associated with the more earthy songs that went back to the word's sources with items like James *Brown's 'It's too funky in here' (1979), and the rougher kinds of music-making.

Funny Face. Musical comedy of historic noteworthiness with score by George *Gershwin, book by Fred *Thompson and Paul Gerard Smith, lyrics by Ira *Gershwin, first seen in Philadelphia in Oct. 1927 under the name *Smarty* and coming to New York at the Alvin Theatre, 22 Nov. 1927. It was a worthy successor to the popular **Lady Be Good* (1924), with the same team of Fred and Adele *Astaire in the cast, songs by the Gershwins, produced by Aarons and *Freedley, with Victor *Moore, William Kent, Allen Kearns, Betty Compton, and piano-duettists Phil Ohman and Vic Arden.

The story was a farcical one involving the theft of a romantic secret diary and a valuable bracelet, and took place in various hotels. With many changes of cast and material at the teething stage with seven songs cut (including 'How long has this been going on') and five added, it eventually settled to a run of 244 performances. The combination of the Astaires and the novel music of Gershwin made it a fashionable success in London when it opened at the Prince's Theatre 8 Nov. 1928, with Leslie *Henson and Sydney Howard also in the cast, and had 263 performances. Musical numbers included 'Funny face', 'High hat', 'S'wonderful', 'Let's kiss and make up', 'He loves and she loves', 'My one and only', 'The babbitt and the bromide'.

It was filmed in 1957 with Fred Astaire, Audrey Hepburn (1929–93) and Kay Thompson (*b* 1913), choreographed by Eugene Loring (*b* 1914), the story completely different and 'How long has this been going on' restored.

Funny Girl. American musical based on the life of vaudeville star Fanny *Brice, recounting her stage triumphs and her stormy marriage to a gambler. The score by Jule *Styne was boisterously catchy, with such items as 'If a girl isn't pretty', 'His love makes me beautiful', 'You are woman', 'I'm the greatest star', 'Sadie, Sadie', 'People', and 'Don't rain on my parade'. The book was by Isobel Lennart and the lyrics by Bob *Merrill.

The show provided the perfect part for the up-and-coming Barbra *Streisand, who was established as a star in her first major role. Sydney Chaplin (*b* 1926) played her gambling husband. Opening in New York at the Winter Garden Theatre 26 Mar. 1964, it achieved 1348 performances. In London, at the Prince of Wales Theatre 13 Apr. 1966, it had a short run of 104 performances, curtailed because of Streisand's advanced pregnancy. She was in good shape again for the 1968 film version with Omar Sharif; and for the lively sequel, *Funny Lady* (1974).

Funny Thing Happened on the Way to the Forum, A. American musical comedy with music and lyrics by Stephen *Sondheim, book by Burt Shevelove (*b* 1915) and Larry Gelbart, loosely founded on Plautus. It opened at the Alvin Theatre, New York, 8 May 1962, with Zero *Mostel, Jack Gilford (1907–90), David Burns (1902–71), Raymond Walburn (1887–1969), and John Carradine (*b* 1906), and ran for 964 performances. At the Strand Theatre, London, from 3 Oct. 1963, with the slapstick cast of Frankie Howerd (1921–92), Kenneth Connor (*b* 1918), Jon Pertwee (*b* 1919), Robertson Hare (1891–1979), and Eddie Gray (1898–1969), it ran for 762 performances. It was filmed in 1966 with Zero Mostel, Phil Silvers (1912–1985), and Buster Keaton (1895–1966).

Fury, Billy [Wycherly, Ronald] (*b* Liverpool, 17 Apr. 1941; *d* London, 28 Jan. 1983). British rock singer. He was working on a tug when he made his first stage appearance in Birkenhead in 1958. Having inveigled his way into a supporting role in a Marty Wilde show, his first record 'Maybe tomorrow' reached the charts in 1959. He never reached No. 1, but was nearly there with 'Halfway to Paradise' (1961), 'Jealousy' (1961), 'Last night was made for love' (1962), 'Like I've never been gone' (1963), and 'When will you say I love you' (1963). His best work came in the album *The Sound of Fury* (1960), which was made up entirely of his own songs. He moved more into the big ballad field and after leaving the rock scene in the late 1960s worked in cabaret. He suffered from ill-health throughout his career and died of a heart-attack as he was trying to make a come-back. Greasy-haired, and sexy, he was the British poor girl's Elvis *Presley.

Fusion. A term variously used to designate an amalgamation of two styles of music, as in the fusion of classical and jazz, folk and rock, electronic and acoustic. First used in association with the classical–jazz experiments of Gunther *Schuller and John *Lewis, later known as *third stream, it has become most firmly attached to the sounds created by the fusion of jazz and rock music, which produced a somewhat superior kind of *art rock. The jazz–rock fusion came to fruition in the work of Miles *Davis in such LPs as *In a Silent Way* and *Bitches Brew* (1969), these beginnings followed up by John McLaughlin (*b* 1942) in England, Chick Corea (*b* 1941), and Joe Zawinul (*b* 1932), whose work with Wayne Shorter (*b* 1933) and *Weather Report, managed to overcome its pretensions and become commercially successful. Many rock groups have lifted their content by the addition of the well-proven element of jazz; and jazz groups, ranging from Chris *Barber's to *Loose Tubes have given their jazz a contemporary pep by the judicious use of rock elements. Beyond these, groups like *Talking Heads have contrived fusions of various rock/pop styles, while others have fused rock and folk into a viable entity. The 'in' term for such experiments is 'fuzak'.

J. Coryell: *Jazz–Rock Fusion: the People, the Music* (New York, 1978).

Fyffe, Will (*b* Dundee, 16 Feb. 1885; *d* St Andrews, 14 Dec. 1947). Scottish comedian, actor, and singer. He played juvenile roles in a repertory company run by his father and for years toured in potboiling productions. When some sketches he had written for Harry *Lauder were turned down, he decided to do them himself. He first appeared in music-hall at the Middlesex in London in 1916, but was not really widely known until around 1921 when he first made the London Palladium. His character studies included a railway guard, a shepherd, a poacher, and especially the tipsy Scottish working-man who sang 'I belong to Glasgow'. He made Royal Variety appearances in 1922, 1925, 1932, and 1937, and was in *Earl Carroll's Vanities* in New York in 1932. He also appeared in a number of British films.

G

Gaiety Girl, A. British musical comedy with score by Sidney *Jones, book by Owen *Hall, and lyrics by Harry Greenbank, which, in spite of its name, was staged at the Prince of Wales Theatre, 14 Oct. 1893. It was the first musical show in London to call itself specifically a 'musical comedy', thus initiating a golden era of the genre. The cast included Hayden *Coffin, Fred Kaye, W. Louis Bradfield, Leedham Bantock, Lawrance D'Orsay, Kate Cutler, Marie Studholme, and Louie Pounds, with Jones himself conducting, and it ran for 413 performances.

The Gaiety connection is in the story: four Gaiety girls go to a garden party and are persuaded to entertain the guests. One of them attracts a wealthy young man but is accused of theft. She is cleared of any guilt, and it all ends, as musical comedies should end, in romance. The show clearly should have been at the *Gaiety but it was kept out by other long-running bookings and transferred to *Daly's in 1894; it was also revived there in 1899. It was produced at the New York Daly's Theatre 17 Sept. 1894. Its success in London and on tour led to Edwardes's lasting faith in musical comedy.

F. G. Aflalo and G. Bantock: *Round the World with 'A Gaiety Girl'* (London, 1896).

Gaiety Theatre. Famous London theatre, originally in the Strand, built on the site of the old Strand Musick Hall and opened on 21 Dec. 1886 under the management of John *Hollingshead. It was to be the source of much burlesque and early musical comedy history, especially under the later management of George *Edwardes who took it over in 1885, making it his outlet for more popular musical shows, the slightly 'better-class' ones being staged at *Daly's. The original theatre was demolished in 1903, the last production being *The *Toreador*, a performance of Act 2 augmented on the last night with a gala performance by Gaiety stars of *The Linkman* or *Gaiety Memories*. A new theatre was built on the corner of Aldwych by the London County Council and opened on 4 Aug. 1903. It was due for demolition in 1938 to allow for the proposed road widening to accommodate the traffic from the new Waterloo Bridge, and *Running Riot* was the last show, closing on 25 Feb. 1938. The war intervened, demolition was delayed, and in 1949 there was talk of its being reopened by Lupino *Lane. But eventually it went and a large block of offices now stands on the site.

The old Gaiety staged a varied repertoire of burlesques and imported operettas by *Offenbach and his followers, the first big English success being Alfred *Cellier's **Dorothy*, which had 931 performances there from 1886, followed by such popular shows as *Frankenstein* (1887); *Faust-up-to-Date* (1888); *Ruy Blas* (1889); *Carmen-up-to-Data* (1890); *In Town* (1893); *The *Shop Girl* (1894); *The *Circus Girl* (1896); *A *Runaway Girl* (1898); *The Messenger Boy* (1900); and *The Toreador* (1901). The new Gaiety continued with *The Orchid* (1903); *The Spring Chicken* (1905); *The Girls of Gottenberg* (1907); *Havana* (1908); **Our Miss Gibbs* (1909); and *Peggy* (1911). It was closed when war broke out in 1914 but reopened in 1915 with **Tonight's the Night* (1915); *Theodore & Co.* (1916); *The Beauty Spot* (1917); and *Going Up* (1918); pursuing a mainly musical history until 1938.

J. Hollingshead: *Gaiety Chronicles* (London, 1898). J. Hollingshead: *Good Old Gaiety: an Historiette and Remembrance* (London, 1903). S. Naylor: *Gaiety and George Grossmith* (London, 1913). J. Jupp: *The Gaiety Stage Door* (London, 1949). W. Macqueen Pope: *Gaiety: Theatre of Enchantment* (London, 1949). U. Bloom: *Curtain Call for the Guv'nor: a Biography of George Edwardes* (London, 1954). S. Hyman: *The Gaiety Years* (London, 1975).

Gaillard, Slim [Bulee] (*b* Santa Clara, Cuba, 1 Jan. 1916; *d* London, 26 Feb. 1991). American singer, guitarist, pianist, and songwriter. He became known through the Slim and Slam partnership with bassist Leroy 'Slam' Stewart (1914–87), 1938–9, especially remembered for the Gaillard nonsense song 'Flat foot floogie' which became a great hit and was recorded by such stars as Fats *Waller, Benny *Goodman, Charlie *Parker, and the *Mills Brothers. He formed his own small group in 1939, served as a pilot during the war, then was active on the West Coast. In 1947 he went to New York and had further hits with 'Cement mixer' (1946) and 'Down by the station' (1949). He invented a hip jive language known as Vouty which was taken up by modern jazzmen, and recorded some samples of it with Parker, *Gillespie, and Jack McVea (*b* 1914) in 1945. Having settled in England he recorded with Buddy Tate (*b* 1913) and Jay McShann in 1982, and his appearances on TV included an eccentric autobiographical series seen in 1989.

S. Gaillard: *I Was There* (London, 1990)

Gallagher, Rory (*b* Ballyshannon, 2 Mar. 1949). Irish singer, guitarist, and composer. He worked in Ireland for some years before going to London in 1969, where he formed a trio with Richard McCracken (*b* 1948) and John Wilson (*b* 1947). From 1971 he recorded some fine solo rock albums for Polydor and gained a high reputation as a powerful guitarist and a skilful exponent of the blues idiom. He moved to Chrysalis from 1975, now more than ever dedicated to the blues, and recorded with Muddy *Waters, Jerry Lee *Lewis, Lonnie *Donegan, and Mike Batt. His peak of popularity was in the 1970s; his uncompromising approach saw him gradually fall out of fashion to remain a connoisseur's musician.

Gallagher and Shean. American comedy and singing duo, Ed Gallagher and Al Shean, who joined up as a vaudeville team in 1910, remaining together until 1925. Their reputation was largely founded on their question-and-answer song 'Mr Gallagher and Mr Shean' (the only thing they ever recorded) which they introduced in **Ziegfeld Follies* (1922) which ran for 541 performances at the New Amsterdam Theatre. Al Shean (*b* Dornum, Germany, May 1868; *d* 1949), who was an uncle of the Marx Brothers, also appeared in *The Rose Maid* (1912); *The Princess Pat* (1915); *Cinderella on Broadway* (1920); **Music in the Air* (1932); and was in several films.

Galop. Lively ballroom dance in 2/4 time which became very popular under this name in Paris in 1829, though it had been around previously as the *Hopser* or *Rutscher*, names which describe the kind of steps involved. Johann *Strauss I wrote several galops in the 1820s and his celebrated family followed the tradition. It became a popular dance in mid-Victorian times both in its own right and as part of the *quadrille.

Gamble, Kenny (*b* Philadelphia, 1941). American producer active in Philadelphia, working since the early 1960s with Phil Huff to develop the Philadelphia International record label and the Philadelphia ('Philly') sound, a sort of big-band dance beat with a black flavour. Gamble led a group, the Romeos, with Thom *Bell, a later rival composer-producer on keyboards and Phil Huff on piano. They built up such artists as Dusty *Springfield and Wilson *Pickett, their recordings later distributed by CBS. Gamble fell into payola trouble in the 1970s but they continued an influential joint career as producers and songwriters.

Ganne, Louis Gaston (*b* Buxières-les-Mines, Allier, 5 Apr. 1862; *d* Paris, 13 July 1923). French composer and conductor. A pupil of Dubois, Massenet, and Franck at the Paris Conservatoire, he began his composing career early with a ballet, *La Source du Nil*, which was staged at the *Folies-Bergère in 1882. Other stage works followed, including operettas, mostly produced at the Folies-Bergère or the Casino de Paris, including *Tout Paris* (1891); *L'Heureuse Rencontre* (1892); *Les Colles des femmes* (1893); *Merveilleuses et gigolettes* (1894); his best-known work *Les Saltimbanques* (1899), which dealt with circus life; *Cythère* (1900); *Miss Bouton d'Or* (1902); *Hans, le joueur de flûte* (1906); *Le Paradis de Mahomed* (1906; completion of a work by *Planquette); *Rhodope* (1910); *Cocorico* (1914); and *La Belle de Paris* (1922). Some of these were produced at Monte Carlo, where he conducted at the Casino. He was also conductor of the balls at the Opéra in Paris. He is perhaps remembered most of all by two famous marches, 'Marche Française' and 'Marche Lorraine' (1892). Both, with words set to them, have become national songs of France, the former as 'Le Père de la Victoire' (*w* Paulus).

Gardel, Carlos (*b* Tacuarembó, 11 Dec. 1887; *d* Medellín, Colombia, 24 June 1935). Uruguayan singer. Of mixed and obscure ancestry (some sources give him as being born in France in 1890), he emerged in Argentina as a popular carnival and café singer, earning himself the nicknames of 'La Voz Azul' and 'Zorzal' ('The Thrush'). In 1912 he joined with Francisco Martino and José Razzano in a vocal trio that revealed a wealth of South American folk-music, and they were largely responsible for bringing the *tango to public attention. Their first recording, 'Mi noche triste' (1917), was a pioneer in setting words to a tango tune. His most successful years were 1925–9; in Paris alone he sold 70,000 records in three months. He appeared in Paris, Madrid, and Barcelona and, immaculately styled, appeared in 10 films between 1931 and 1935 including the musicals *Tango on Broadway* (1934) and *Tango Bar* (1935). He died in an aeroplane accident on his way to Colombia and his funeral in Buenos Aires was the biggest that the city had ever seen.

F. G. Jiménez: *Vida de Carlos Gardel* (Buenos Aires, 1936).

Garland, Joe [Joseph Copeland] (*b* Norfolk, Va., 15 Aug. 1903; *d* 21 Apr. 1977). American composer, arranger, and saxophonist. After attending the Aeolian Conservatory in Baltimore, he played in brass and military bands before moving into the dance-band world with the Elmer Snowden and Joe Steele orchestras. Freelancing in New York in the 1920s, he worked with Jelly Roll *Morton for a time. He was with the Mills Blue Rhythm Band 1932–6, Edgar Hayes 1937–8, Don *Redman 1938, Louis *Armstrong 1939–42 and 1945–7, and Earl *Hines 1948–9. Throughout his jazz career he was a prolific arranger for most of these bands and composed a number of standard instrumentals such as 'In the mood' (which became a big hit when played by the Glenn *Miller band, and as a song with words by Andy *Razaf in 1939), 'Tar paper stomp', 'There's rhythm in Harlem', 'Hot and anxious', 'Jumpy nerves', and 'Leap frog' (which became Les *Brown's theme tune).

Garland, Judy [Gumm, Frances Ethel] (*b* Grand Rapids, 10 June 1922; *d* London, 22 June. 1969). American singer and actress. Coming from a show-business family, she made her first stage appearances with her sisters as a singing group, the Gumm Sisters. When she appeared with George Jessel in Chicago, it was he who suggested the change of name. She moved with the family to California and was signed by MGM, first appearing with Deanna *Durbin in a short film, *Every Sunday*, in 1936. She first made a telling impression in *Broadway Melody of 1938* (1937) where she sang 'You made me love you' to a photograph of Clark Gable. She teamed up with Mickey *Rooney and was with him in many of her earliest musicals. Her freshness and remarkably clear and intelligent jazz-phrased singing soon earned her a big following, with *The *Wizard of Oz* (1939) and 'Over the rainbow' (recorded 1939) making her an international star. Her remarkable talents were best seen in the 1940s in films such as *For Me and My Gal* (1942); *Meet Me in St Louis* (1944)—'The trolley song'; and *The Harvey Girls* (1946). She was married to Vincente *Minnelli, 1945–50.

There were many setbacks in her career owing to ill-health and alcoholism but, after a period of obscurity, she came back with exciting concerts in London and New York in the early 1950s, and a memorable role in the remade *A *Star is Born* (1954). Her eccentrically interesting stage personality was always part of her attraction, beyond her utterly convincing handling of words and melodies, but she was visibly declining in the 1960s through her drink and weight problems and continuing ill-health. She appeared at the London *Palladium in 1964 and, a horrifying shadow of the young charmer of *Wizard of Oz* days, she struggled on till 1967, but died two years later. Her daughter Liza *Minnelli was to become as big a star as she was.

Other films included *Pigskin Parade* (1936); *Thoroughbreds Don't Cry* (1937); *Everybody Sing* (1938); *Love Finds Andy Hardy* (1938); *Listen, Darling* (1938); **Babes in Arms* (1939); *Andy Hardy Meets a Debutante* (1940)—'I'm nobody's baby'; **Strike Up the Band* (1940)—'Nobody' (Roger Edens); *Little Nellie Kelly* (1940); *Ziegfeld Girl* (1941); *Life Begins for Andy Hardy* (1941); *Babes on Broadway* (1941); *Presenting Lily Mars* (1943); **Girl Crazy* (1943); *Thousands Cheer* (1943); *The Clock* (1945; *Under the Clock* in UK); **Ziegfeld Follies* (1946); *Till the Clouds Roll By* (1947); *The Pirate* (1948); **Easter Parade* (1948)—in which she notably appeared with Fred *Astaire; *Words and Music* (1948); *In the Good Old Summer Time* (1949); *Summer Stock* (1950; *If You Feel Like Singing* in UK); *Pepe* (1960); *Judgment at Nuremberg* (1961); *Gay Purr-ee* (1962); *A Child is Waiting* (1963); and *I Could Go On Singing* (1963).

J. Morella and E. Z. Epstein: *Judy: the Films and Career of Judy Garland* (Secaucus, NJ, 1969; Paris, 1977). M. Deans and A. Pinchot: *Weep No More My Lady* (London, 1972). A. DiOrio: *Little Girl Lost: the Life and Hard Times of Judy Garland* (New York, 1973). B. Baxter: *The Films of Judy Garland* (Bembridge, IOW, 1974). D. Dahl and B. Kehoe: *Young Judy* (New York, 1975). A. Edwards: *Judy Garland: a Mortgaged Life* (New York, 1975). C. Finch: *Rainbow: the Stormy Life of Judy Garland* (New York, 1975). G. Frank: *Judy* (New York, 1975). L. Smith: *Judy, with Love* (London, 1975). S. Glickmann: *Judy Garland* (Paris, 1981). J. Meyer: *Heartbreaker* (Garden City, NY, 1983). J. Spada and K. Swenson: *Judy and Liza* (Garden City, NY, 1983).

Garner, Erroll Louis (*b* Pittsburgh, 15 June 1923; *d* Los Angeles, 2 Jan. 1977). American jazz pianist and composer. Self-taught, he was playing on Pittsburgh radio at the age of seven with a group called the Candy Kids. In his teens he played on riverboats and in nightclubs and restaurants. He developed an immediately recognizable, individual, and unorthodox style, with heavy chords in the left hand and behind-the-beat phrasing in the right; modernish but still in touch with the Harlem school, foot-tapping and spirit-lifting. His performances were enhanced by an attractive personality (he was so small that he had to sit on a telephone directory) and a performance full of sly grunts and humour, so that he soon became popular on television. In 1944 he moved to New York to join the Slam Stewart trio; and formed his own trio in 1946. He went to Paris in 1948, made European tours in 1962, 1964, 1966, and 1969, and was labelled by the French press 'The Picasso of the Piano'. His lack of technical knowledge extended to his composing, which was usually of an extempore nature with someone else taking down the notes for him. By this method 'Misty' became a popular jazz standard and he wrote 200 or more songs, among them 'Dreamy', 'Solitaire', 'Blues Garni', and 'That's my kick'; and he also contrived music for the film *A New Kind of Love* (1963).

J. M. Doran: *Erroll Garner: The Most Happy Piano* (Metuchan, 1984).

Garrick Gaieties. American revue that marked the first Broadway success of the partnership of Richard *Rodgers (music) and Lorenz *Hart (lyrics), with sketches supplied by Benjamin Kaye, Arthur Sullivan, Morrie Ryskind, and others. It was presented by the Theatre Guild at the Garrick Theatre, New York, 8 June 1925 with a cast of young Theatre Guild actors that included Sterling Holloway, Romney Brent, Betty Starbuck, Philip Loeb, and Libby *Holman. It was a forerunner of many youthfully satirical revues. Intended to play for two Sundays only, it was properly staged by public demand and had 211 performances. Songs in the first edition included 'An old-fashioned girl', 'April fool', 'Manhattan', 'Do you love me?', and 'Sentimental me'. A second edition with similar forces opened 10 May 1926 for 174 performances, introducing the Rodgers and Hart classic 'Mountain greenery'; and there was a third version in 1930 [158p] with some of the young participants now seasoned veterans but much new blood, such as Imogene Coca (*b* 1908) added; and new material by such coming notables as Johnny *Mercer, Ira *Gershwin, E. Y. *Harburg, Vernon *Duke, and Marc *Blitzstein.

Gaskill, Clarence (*b* Philadelphia, 2 Feb. 1892; *d* Fort Hill, NY, 29 Apr. 1947). American composer and author. He started out as a pianist and entertained troops in the First World War, but went into music-publishing as a young man and had a steady but small output of personal song successes such as 'Sweet Adeline' (1919); 'Doo wacka doo' (1924); 'I can't believe that you're in love with me' (with Jimmy *McHugh, 1926) which was used in the revue *Gay Paree* (1927) and later in the film *The Caine Mutiny* (1945); 'I don't mind being all alone when I'm with you' (with McHugh and Irving Mills, 1926); 'Minnie the Moocher' (with Cab *Calloway and Mills, 1931); and 'Prisoner of love' (with Russ *Colombo and Leo Robin, 1931). He wrote songs for *Frank Fay's Fables* (1922) and **Earl Carroll's Vanities* (1925).

Gaxton, William [Gaxiola, Arturo Antonio] (*b* San Francisco, 2 Dec. 1893; *d* New York, 2 Feb. 1963). American actor and singer who became well-known as the neurotically aggressive foil to Victor *Moore in various Broadway musicals. He also happened to introduce some very well-known songs in many of them, including: **Music Box Revue* (1922); *A *Connecticut Yankee* (1927)—'My heart stood still', 'Thou swell'; **Fifty Million Frenchmen* (1929)—'You do something to me'; **Of Thee I Sing* (1931); *Let 'Em Eat Cake* (1933); **Anything Goes* (1934)—'You're the top', 'All through the night'; **White Horse Inn* (1936); **Leave It To Me!* (1938)—'From now on'; and **Lousiana Purchase* (1940). His films included: *Stage Door Canteen* (1943); **Best Foot Forward* (1943); *Something to Shout About* (1943); and *Diamond Horseshoe* (1945).

Gay, Noel [Armitage, Reginald Moxon] (*b* Wakefield, 15 July 1898; *d* London, 3 Mar. 1954). British composer and lyricist. Educated at Wakefield Cathedral School and Christ's College, Cambridge, he intended to follow a career in classical music, and became assistant organist to the Chapel Royal, St James's, London. At 18 he became organist and director of music at St Anne's, Soho. A special interest in the works of *Gilbert and Sullivan gave him the urge to write for the theatre himself. In 1925 he had some songs included in a revue, *Stop Press*, which were well received, and his reputation was further substantiated by his contributions to the *Charlot Show of* 1926 and the revue *Clowns in Clover* (1927). A penchant for writing simple and memorable tunes in a clearly English style made him one of the most popular of pre-war and wartime British songwriters, particularly successful in the 1930s with songs ranging from 'The King's horses' in 1930 to 'Run, rabbit, run' in 1939. His biggest success of all was 'The *Lambeth Walk' written for the score of **Me and My Girl* (1937) which, as a dance, reached craze proportions in 1937–8 when the vogue for sequence dances was at its height.

He also contributed to or wrote: *Merry Mexico* (1926); *Jumbles* (1927); *Hold my Hand* (1931); *She Couldn't Say No* (1932); *That's a Pretty Thing* (1933); *Jack o'Diamonds* (1935); *Love Laughs* (1935); *O-Kay for Sound* (1936)—'The fleet's in port again'; *Wild Oats* (1938); *The Little Dog Laughed* (1939); *Lights Up* (1940)—'You've done something to my heart', 'Let the people sing', 'Only a glass of champagne'; *Present Arms* (1940); *Susie* (1942); *La-Di-Da-Di-Da* (1943); *The *Love Racket* (1943); *Meet Me Victoria* (1944); *Sweetheart Mine* (1946); *Bob's Your Uncle* (1948); etc. He wrote songs for the films *White Cargo*—'Tondeleyo'; *Sleepless Nights* (1932), starring Stanley *Lupino—'I don't want to go to bed'; *Soldiers of the King* (1933), with Cicely *Courtneidge—'There's something about a soldier'; *Happy* (1934), with Lupino—'Happy'; *The Camels are Coming* (1934), with Jack *Hulbert—'Who's been polishing the sun?'; and *Sailors Three* (1940), with Tommy Trinder—'All over the place' (*w* Frank Eyton).

His other songs included: 'The King's horses (and the King's men)' (with Harry Graham, 1930); 'The sun has got his hat on' (with Ralph Butler, 1932), revived by Jonathan King in 1971; 'Round the Marble Arch' (with Butler, 1932); 'All for the love of a lady' (with Archie Gottler, 1932); 'I took my harp to a party' (1933, *w* Desmond Carter); 'The moment I saw you' (1933, *w* Clifford Grey); 'All for a shilling a day' (1935, *w* Grey), used in the film *Me and Marlborough*; 'Let's have a tiddley at the milk bar' (1936); 'Leaning on a lamp-post' (1937), sung by George *Formby in the film *Feather Your Nest*; 'Red, white and blue' (1937); 'Love makes the world go round' (1938), used in *These Foolish Things*; 'The moon remembered but you forgot' (with Frank Eyton, 1939); 'Run, rabbit, run' (1939); 'The girl who loves a soldier' (1939); 'The birthday of the little Princess' (1939); 'Are we downhearted—no!' (1941); 'Hey, little hen' (1941); 'Just a little fond affection' (1942, *w* Eyton), and many more. He founded the Noel Gay Publishing Company in 1938. His son, Richard Armitage (1928–86), was a well-known agent and impresario who took over his father's business in 1954 and successfully revived *Me and My Girl* in 1984.

Gay Divorce. Musical comedy with music and lyrics by Cole *Porter and book by Dwight Taylor, which opened at the Ethel Barrymore Theatre, New York, on 29 Nov. 1932, with Fred *Astaire, Luella Gear (1899–1980), Eric Blore (1887–1959), Claire Luce (*b* 1903), and Grace *Moore, and had 248 performances. Astaire and others of the American cast were in the London production at the Palace Theatre, 2 Nov. 1933. The distinguished score included such Porter classics as 'After you, who?', 'Night and day', and 'I've got you on my mind'.

The rather weak and aimless plot about a British novelist wooing an about-to-be-divorced lady was turned into a good Astaire/Ginger *Rogers RKO film, re-titled *The Gay Divorcée* (1934), which kept only 'Night and day' from the original score and added the *Conrad/Magidson 'The continental' and others. The cast also included Edward Everett Horton (1886–1970) and Betty *Grable.

Gaye, Marvin Pentz (*b* Washington DC, 2 Apr. 1939; *d* Los Angeles, 1 Apr. 1984). American singer, composer, pianist, and drummer. The son of a minister, he started his singing career in a church choir then, after air force service, sang in various *doo-wop groups and eventually with a black vocal group called the Rainbows. With other members of this he formed the Marquees in 1957 which became the backing group for Harvey Fuqua (*b* 1929). Gaye moved with Fuqua to Detroit where they eventually entered the Motown fold. Still waiting for the big break in his career, he worked as a drummer on Motown sessions. Recording in his own right, the hits began to come with 'Pride and joy' (1963), 'You're a wonderful one' (1964), 'Try it, baby' (1964), 'How sweet it is' (1964), 'I'll be doggone' (1965), and 'Ain't that peculiar' (1965); finally reaching No. 1 with 'I heard it through the grapevine' (1968). He was to become one of Motown's greatest craftsmen, a versatile producer, songwriter, and singer who recorded a number of standards in many styles, singing in a light tenor voice, gospel-inspired but adaptable. One of his specialities was romantic duets: he teamed successfully with Kim Weston, Tammi Terrell ('Ain't no mountain high enough', 'Ain't nothing like the real thing'), and Diana *Ross.

A period of retirement followed the death of Terrell in 1970, broken by the album *What's Going On?* which found him tackling social issues, introspective and philosophical. He returned to the romantic vein with the 1973 eroticism of *Let's Get It On*. Although his work after that was mixed, and his life troubled by drugs, divorce, and money problems, he remained one of pop music's foremost artists. His early material still sounds strong and 'I heard it through the grapevine' is generally reckoned to be one of the all-time pop classics. He was shot dead by his father during a quarrel.

Gayle, Crystal [Webb, Brenda Gail] (*b* Paintsville, Ky., 9 Jan. 1951). American country singer. The younger sister of Loretta *Lynn, they made several concert tours together. Later, on her own, she produced such country hits as 'I'll get over you' and 'Don't it make my brown eyes blue', which stylistically also had a foot in the pop market. Her popularity grew, reaching a peak in 1982 when she had 9 hits in the country Top 100, and 29 albums to her credit.

Gay's the Word. British musical play which was the final product of composer-writer Ivor *Novello before he died in 1951. Written to star Cicely *Courtneidge, and based on an idea by her husband Jack *Hulbert, it was a send-up of Novello's own romantic operettas.

Gay Daventry, an ageing operetta star, opens an acting school which fails because of her out-of-date ideas, but eventually she gets backing from the father of one of her pupils to appear in a modern musical which proves a success. The show opened at the Saville Theatre 16 Feb. 1951 with Cicely *Courtneidge, Lizbeth Webb, Thorley Walters, Maidie Andrews, and Elizabeth Seal and ran for 502 performances. Its sprightly score (with lyrics by Alan *Melville) included: 'It's bound to be right on the night', 'If only he'd look my way', 'On such a night as this', and the ebullient 'Vitality'.

Geehl, Henry Ernest (*b* London, 28 Sept. 1881; *d* Beaconsfield, Bucks., 14 Jan. 1961). British composer, conductor, and pianist. He toured as a theatre conductor 1902–8, joined the staff of the Trinity College of Music in 1918, and retired in 1960. He had a special interest in the *brass band movement and wrote and arranged various test-pieces: 'Oliver Cromwell' (used in 1923, 1941, and 1946), 'On the Cornish Coast' (1924 and 1948), 'Robin Hood' (1936 and 1941), and 'Scena sinfonica' (1952); also 'Festival Overture', 'In Tudor days', 'Normandy', 'Sinfonietta pastorale', 'A Happy Suite', 'James Hook', 'Threnody', and 'Thames Valley'. He also wrote many piano pieces and a number of songs, one of which, 'For you alone' (1909), is said to have been the first song that Caruso sang in English.

Geisha, The. British musical comedy with a memorably tuneful score by Sidney *Jones, book by Owen *Hall, and lyrics by Harry Greenbank, staged at *Daly's Theatre, London, 25 Apr. 1896, running for 760 performances. Its star was Marie *Tempest, with Hayden *Coffin, W. Louis Bradfield (1866–1919), and Huntley Wright (1869–1943). It confirmed the popularity of Far Eastern stories on the opera and musical comedy stage and has been fondly remembered for songs like 'The amorous goldfish', 'Chin Chin Chinaman', 'The interfering parrot', and 'Star of my soul'. It was staged at *Daly's Theatre, New York, 9 Sept. 1896 and in Vienna at the Carltheater in 1897 and at the Theater an der Wien in 1901.

Geistinger, Marie [Maria Charlotte Cäcilia] (*b* Graz, Styria, 26 July 1833; *d* Rastenfeld, 29 Sept. 1903). Polish singer. Of now legendary fame as a star of operetta, she spent most of her career in Vienna where she was the original Rosalinda in *Die *Fledermaus* (1874), and appeared in other Strauss productions. She sang in Prague, Leipzig, and Berlin and appeared in New York in 1897.

Geldof, Bob [Frederick Zenon] (*b* Dublin, 5 Oct. 1952). Irish singer and guitarist. In 1975 he formed the Boomtown Rats, an Irish punk rock band that had its first hit with 'Looking after No. 1' in 1977 and went to No. 1 in 1978 and 1979 with 'Rat trap' and 'I don't like Mondays'. Geldof became a public figure when, in 1984, he organized Band Aid which, by means of large benefit concerts and recordings and TV appearances which were keenly supported by the pop fraternity and the general public alike, raised more than £50 million to help the starving populations of Africa. This initiative sparked off other worldwide conscience-driven efforts on similar lines such as Live Aid (1985), Farm Aid (1985), and Comic Relief (1988).

B. Geldof: *Is That It?* (London, 1986).

Genée, Franz Friedrich **Richard** (*b* Danzig, 7 Feb. 1823; *d* Baden, 15 June 1895). Polish composer and conductor. The eldest son of the theatrical entrepreneur Friedrich Genée, he studied medicine before switching to music and pursuing a conducting career at, successively, the municipal theatres of Reval, Riga, Cologne, Aachen, Dusseldorf, Danzig, Mainz, Schwerin, Amsterdam, and Prague. He was conductor at the Theater an der Wien in Vienna 1868–78. He composed many operettas and also wrote librettos for other composers including *Czibulka, *Millöcker, Roth, Johann *Strauss II, *Suppé, and *Zeller. He made translations of W. S. Gilbert's librettos for German productions of *The *Mikado* (1888), *The *Pirates of Penzance* (1889), and *The *Gondoliers* (1890). After settling in Vienna in 1867, he retired to a villa in Pressbaum in 1879.

His operettas included: *Der Geiger aus Tirol* (1857); *Die Generalprobe* (1862); *Der Musikfeind* (1862); *Rosita* (1864); *Der schwarze Prinz* (1866); *Schwefeles der Höllenagent* (1869); *Der Seekadett* (1876); *Nanon* (1877); *Im Wunderlände der Pyramiden* (1877); *Die letzten Mohikaner* (1878); *Nisida* (1880); *Rosina* (1881); *Eine *Nacht in Venedig* (1883); *Die Zwillinge* (1885); and *Die Dreizehn* (1887).

Genesis. British progressive rock group formed in 1967; its original members—Anthony Phillips, Michael Rutherford (*b* 1950), Tony Banks (*b* 1950), and Peter Gabriel (*b* 1950)—were all at Charterhouse School at the time. There were several changes of personnel before the band began to make its mark around 1971 and developed an individual sound. They also became noted for their outrageous costumes, a trend followed by many other groups in the 1980s. The albums *Foxtrot* (1972) and *Genesis Live* (1973) put them in the forefront of progressive rock developments. When their popular vocalist Gabriel left in 1975 he was successfully replaced by Phil *Collins, then drummer with the group. It took until 1977 for the group to get in the Top 10, which they achieved in the USA with 'Follow me, follow you'. They continued as an energetic band of experimenters, disdaining the hunt for commercial success, and became a rock institution.

Geneviève de Brabant. Comic opera with music by Jacques *Offenbach and book by Hector Crémieux and Etienne Tréfue, produced at the *Bouffes-Parisiens in Paris 19 Nov. 1859. If not one of Offenbach's top-ranking operettas, it has nevertheless stayed in fond memory as the source of one of his best-known melodies—the 'Gendarmes' duet', which much pleased the audience at the Theater an de Wien in 1868 and made the work a popular success at the Philharmonic in Islington in 1871 with English words by H. B. *Farnie and with Emily *Soldene as its star. It became a fashionable show, visited on more than one occasion by the Prince of Wales, and its famous duet was almost certainly a source of inspiration for *Gilbert and Sullivan and many other skits on the police force that followed. It was produced in New York in 1868 and 1874. The tune was eventually lifted for use as the American 'Marine's hymn' copyrighted in 1919 with the words 'From the halls of Montezuma to the shores of Tripoli', variously attributed.

Gentlemen Prefer Blondes. American musical comedy based on the best-selling novel by Anita Loos, adapted by the author and Joseph *Fields, scored by Jule *Styne, with lyrics by Leo Robin (1900–85). It opened at the Ziegfeld Theatre 8 Dec. 1949, with Carol *Channing, who made her name in the role of Lorelei Lee, a gold-digging lady whose occupation is the hooking of rich gentlemen admirers, and whose best-known number was 'Diamonds are a girl's best friend'. Such sentiments went down well in New York and the show ran for 740 performances. In London, at the Prince's Theatre 20 Aug. 1962, Dora *Bryan took the part for 223 performances. It was filmed in 1953 with Marilyn Monroe and Jane Russell, when it was given a brand new score. Another good run of 320 performances was achieved by the revised and updated version, again with Carol Channing in 1974 at the Palace Theatre, New York (after a long preceding tour), under the title of *Lorelei*, subtitled 'Gentlemen Still Prefer Blondes'.

Gentry, Bobbie [Streeter, Roberta] (*b* Chickasaw County, Miss., 27 July 1944). American country singer and guitarist. She learned to play piano, banjo, and guitar before studying music at the University of California, then entered the country music scene and had her first hit with 'Ode to Billy Joe' in 1967. She has continued as a very popular artist, touring the USA and Europe, and had further hits with 'All I hope to do is dream' and 'I'll never fall in love again'.

George M! Musical comedy based on the life of George M. *Cohan, utilizing music and words taken from his various productions including such perennial hits as 'Give my regards to Broadway', 'Mary's a grand old name', 'You're a grand old flag', 'Harrigan', 'Forty-five minutes from Broadway', 'So long, Mary', and 'Yankee-Doodle dandy'—32 items in all. Joel *Grey took the part of Cohan in his first starring role. Opening at the Palace Theatre, New York, 10 Apr. 1968, it had 435 performances.

George White's Scandals. A series of New York spectacular revues, modelling themselves on the already celebrated **Ziegfeld Follies*, but younger in style, full of dancing, and less bitty. The scores and librettos were usually the work of one team, giving each show a greater sense of cohesion. The series started in 1919 and there were to be 11 editions in 13 years. The first production, with George *White, Ann *Pennington, and Lou Holtz, and a score by George A. Whiting, opened at the Liberty Theatre 2 June 1919 and ran for 128 performances. The 1920 edition introduced the music of George *Gershwin and, with Pennington again its star, opened at the Globe Theatre 7 Jun. 1920 [134p]. Gershwin was again the composer in 1921 with

'Drifting along with the tide' the main hit, at the Liberty Theatre 11 July 1921 [97p]. His 1922 score included 'I'll build a stairway to Paradise' and (for the first night only) proffered a one-act black opera *Blue Monday* (to be revived at Carnegie Hall in 1925 as *135th Street*). W. C. Fields was in the cast, supported by Paul *Whiteman's orchestra, at the Globe Theatre 28 Aug. 1922 [88p]. Gershwin's 1923 score was not one of his most distinguished, but the edition ran for 168 performances at the Globe, 18 June 1923; and at the Apollo 30 June 1924 [192p] there was 'Somebody loves me'. The team of *DeSylva, *Brown, and *Henderson took over in 1925 and the cast included Helen *Morgan, opening at the Apollo 22 June 1925.

By now the *Scandals* had become a fashionable attraction and the 1926 edition saw the series at its peak, with Pennington the star and Willie and Eugene *Howard, Harry *Richman, and Frances Williams making their first appearances. It opened at the Apollo Theatre on 14 Jun. 1926 and, although the seats were now very expensive, it was to run for 424 performances, part of the attraction being a DeSylva, Brown, and Henderson score that included 'Lucky day', *'Black Bottom', 'The birth of the blues', and 'The girl is you and the boy is me', with Gershwin's *'Rhapsody in blue' for dancing. Much the same cast and writers were used in the 1928 edition at the Apollo on 2 July 1928 [240p]. In 1929 the main composer was Cliff *Friend (Apollo 23 Sept. 1929) [161p]; while Henderson and Brown were back in 1931 (Apollo, 14 Sep.) with 'Life is just a bowl of cherries', 'This is the missus', 'My song', 'The thrill is gone', and 'That's why darkies were born'. The Howards shared the billing with Rudy *Vallee, Ethel *Merman, and Ray *Bolger to produce another vintage edition that had 202 performances. In 1932 there was a depression economy version billed as *George White's Music Hall Varieties* with Harry Richman, Bert *Lahr, and Eleanor *Powell. The 1935–6 edition became the *Scandals* again, moving to the New Amsterdam Theatre 25 Dec. 1925, with Lahr and Cliff *Edwards [110p]. The final edition, at the Alvin Theatre 28 Aug. 1939 [120p], had a score by Sammy *Fain—'Are you having any fun', after which the *Scandals* became outmoded.

There were three filmed versions (with a plot added): in 1934 with Rudy Vallee, Jimmy *Durante, and Alice *Faye; in 1935 with James Dunn, Alice Faye, and Eleanor Powell; and in 1945 with Jack Haley and Joan Davis.

Geraldo [Bright, Gerald] (*b* London, 10 Aug. 1904; *d* Vevey, Switzerland, 4 May 1974). British bandleader. After a youth spent in extensive travel, which gave him a comprehensively international view of music, Geraldo started his bandleading career with five years at the Hotel Majestic at St Anne's in Lancashire. He directed various orchestras in England and Europe before he appeared at the Savoy Hotel in London billed as Geraldo and his Gaucho Tango Orchestra, having become a devotee of the *tango and the rhythms of South America. In 1933 he moved into the dance-band world, now leading two bands at the Savoy, and became one of the popular leaders of the 1930s. His approach was always meticulous, suave, polished, and personal, he himself always immaculately dressed and presenting a smooth image to the world, whether it was his wealthy dance clients or the general public by way of radio. The bands appeared in numerous radio series with Al *Bowlly as their regular singer 1938–9, and Eve Boswell (*b* 1924) the leading vocalist 1949–51. During the Second World War the band did much entertaining of the troops, and after the war modernized its style, finally breaking up in the 1960s when Geraldo became an agent.

German, Edward [Jones, Edward German] (*b* Whitchurch, Salop, 17 Feb. 1862; *d* London, 11 Nov. 1936). British composer, conductor, and violinist. Reared in a musical family (his father was a local organist and choirmaster and Edward followed in his footsteps at an early age), he was given every opportunity to study music while receiving his normal education at Bridge House School in Chester. He was prepared for the Royal Academy of Music examinations by Walter Hay, conductor of the Whitchurch Choral Society, and was to study at the Academy for seven years, specializing in the violin and leaving in 1887.

He had already written a considerable amount of music, including his First Symphony (1886) and a two-act operetta, *The Two Poets* (published in 1900 as *The Rival Poets*), which was produced at the Academy in 1886; then, with a distinguished cast, at St George's Hall in 1901, directed by Randegger. It was Randegger who helped German to obtain the post of musical director at the Globe Theatre in 1888, where he was to make a tremendous effort to raise the current standards of theatre music. It gave him the opportunity to write incidental music for various productions, including many Shakespeare plays, and it was his music to Richard Mansfield's production of *Richard III* that first established his reputation as a composer. The overture was performed at the Crystal Palace in 1890 and his 'Gypsy Suite' was heard there in 1892. His work at the Globe led to other commissions, notably from Henry Irving who was producing *Henry VIII* at the Lyceum. The music for this and other plays occupied his attention for the next few years.

In 1900, Sullivan died and left the score of his final operetta, *The Emerald Isle*, uncompleted. The librettist Basil *Hood and the executors looked around for another composer and asked German to complete the score. He had the difficult task of completing 15 unfinished items in someone else's style; to which he added 11 of his own, including the popular 'Devonshire song'. He worked well with Hood, who had written *The Rose of Persia* for Sullivan and who subsequently presented German with the completed libretto of **Merrie England* (1902)—which might well have been another Sullivan score if fate had not dictated otherwise. Its popularity, after a modest start at the Savoy Theatre, could not have been greater than that which German's thoroughly English score achieved. He continued conducting and composing and filling academic posts, and had further operetta successes with *A Princess of Kensington* (1903) and *Tom Jones* (1907)—'For tonight' (waltz song), 'Dream o'day Jill'. In 1909, W. S. *Gilbert was his librettist for *Fallen Fairies*, which was fairly well received but had a disappointing run.

German became a much respected figure and was knighted in 1928. A number of his songs became popular, including 'Love, the pedlar' (1899, *w* Caryll Battersby); 'Love is meant to make us glad (1904, *w* Hood); 'Four jolly sailormen' (1904, *w* Hood); 'Glorious Devon' (1905, *w* Harold Boulton); 'Have you news of my boy Jack' (1914, *w* Rudyard Kipling); and he also set 12 of Kipling's 'Just-So' songs (1904). A considerable output of orchestral music included two symphonies, the 'Gypsy Suite' (1892), and a 'Welsh rhapsody', besides the incidental music to *Nell Gwynn* (1900) and many other plays.

He was the most popular and best-known composer of light music after Sullivan, certainly in the pre-First World War period when his works were regularly performed. Today his music seems very Edwardian, polite, and often blatantly nationalistic; but *Merrie England* survives as a favourite of amateur societies; the suites of his memorable incidental music are still performed by light orchestras and brass bands; even a few of his more serious works have been revived and recorded.

W. H. Scott: *Edward German: an Intimate Biography* (London, 1932). B. Rees: *A Musical Pacemaker: the Life and Work of Sir Edward German* (London, 1988).

Gerry and the Pacemakers. British Merseyside rock group formed in 1961 with Gerry Marsden (*b* 1942) (vocals and guitar), Freddie Marsden (*b* 1940) (drums), Leslie Maguire (*b* 1941) (piano), and Les Chadwick (*b* 1943) (bass). They were taken on by the *Beatles' manager Brian Epstein in 1962 and were the first group to achieve three No. 1 hits with their first three recordings—'How do you like it?', 'I like it', and the *Rogers and *Hammerstein song 'You'll never walk alone' (now a Liverpool football anthem), all in 1963. They performed in a lightly popular style, with Marsden's happy vocals prominent. Such dazzling success was not easily repeated but the band continued a successful career for some years before losing its popularity and breaking up in 1968, after Marsden went solo and appeared with Anna *Neagle in **Charlie Girl*. They re-formed for revival tours in 1975 and 1979; and Gerry Marsden remained a popular entertainer, retaining some of his rock background and recording 'You'll never walk alone' again in 1985, with friends, to raise money for the Bradford City Football Club fire disaster.

Gershwin, George [Gershvin, Jacob] (*b* Brooklyn, NY, 26 Sept. 1898; *d* Beverly Hills, Calif., 11 July 1937). American composer and pianist. He became interested in music around the age of 10 and taught himself the rudiments of harmony, soon putting together melodies of his own in imitation of the popular tunes of the day. His first important teacher, Charles Hambitzer, was not entirely sympathetic to his tastes, but he was impressed by his young pupil's earnest desire to make an artistic contribution to American popular song. Gershwin's first noteworthy published song, 'When you want 'em you can't get 'em', appeared when he was 18, and he had his first big hit with 'Swanee' when he was 20. Early piano pieces like 'Rialto ripples' (1917), written with Will Donaldson, are interesting in showing a composer building his own style on a ragtime basis. At 22 he was writing music for **George White's Scandals* and contributing occasional numbers to many Broadway productions. He soon showed a gift for distinctive melody that has hardly ever been equalled; and unlike the older Jerome *Kern, who had always kept one foot in the world of operetta, his music ideally given a 'straight' performance, Gershwin's songs were, as he affirmed in 'I got rhythm', full of rhythmic impulse. Some of his romantic numbers like 'The man I love', 'Somebody loves me', 'Someone to watch over me', and 'But not for me' used a *blues element with a restrained feeling that may not satisfy the blues purist but which gave them the subjective strength and emotional vitality that only a few popular songs had previously achieved. Gershwin's music was always a curious combination of conflicting elements—elegance and vivacity, forcefulness and charm, sincerity and wit—the latter quality being injected by the work of his most frequent collaborator, his brother Ira (below).

He was still only 25 when his most famous creation, *'Rhapsody in Blue', was played, along with a selection of other American light and popular music (and with much advance ballyhoo), at the Paul *Whiteman concert given at the Aeolian Hall, New York, on 12 Feb. 1924. The public had already been brainwashed into accepting Whiteman as 'The King of Jazz' and the 'Rhapsody' was acclaimed as a sort of missing link, the work that would reconcile the far from polite jazz with its more respectable musical relations. Even after more than 60 years it still occupies a curiously ambiguous position, not particularly liked by either highbrows or connoisseurs of jazz, but immensely popular and endlessly performed. In the hands of many over-serious or over-romantic interpreters it can seem a little hollow. It is best to go back to Gershwin's own wiry interpretation and the original small 'jazz band' orchestration to find that it has real muscular strength and remains one of the most successful pieces of jazz pastiche ever written.

Gershwin continued to write prolifically for the theatre, achieving his best music against shallow plots and forgettable stories, but with the help of inspired lyricists like brother Ira and ideal interpreters like the *Astaires. The rather pretentious **Of Thee I Sing* (1931) was the first musical comedy to win a *Pulitzer Prize. Meanwhile he was drawn towards the prestigious world of serious music and moved furthest in that direction with his Piano Concerto in F (1925) which is still the most frequently played American concerto. His concert pieces such as 'An *American in Paris' (1928) and 'Cuban Overture' are still regularly heard. But it was always the songs that remained his most potent and most admired products.

His biggest theatrical success was the folk-opera **Porgy and Bess*. First produced in New York on 30 Sept. 1935, it was unfavourably received and, like many operatic composers, Gershwin was only to see half of its success, never able to enjoy its acceptance by the modern opera world. Its place may well be argued for ever, but some of his loveliest and most affecting music is to be found in the score. After *Porgy and Bess* he went to Hollywood to work on two Fred Astaire films, **Shall We Dance* and *A *Damsel in Distress*, whose joyful songs showed him advancing toward a new high-water mark of popular music. Had he been able to continue, perhaps Gershwin would have found the ideal marriage of the two worlds of music. But he suddenly began to lose control of his brilliant playing and while working on the score of *Goldwyn Follies* he collapsed. At first the symptoms were put down to overwork, but a second collapse followed and it was discovered that he had a brain tumour. The operation came too late and he died at the age of 39.

He contributed to: *The *Passing Show* (1916); *Hitchy-Koo* (1918); *Ladies First* (1918)—'Some wonderful sort of someone'; *Half-Past Eight* (1918); *Good Morning, Judge* (1919)—'I was so young (you were so beautiful)'; *The Lady in Red* (1919); *The Capitol Revue* (1919)—'Swanee'; *Ed Wynn's Carnival* (1920); *The Sweetheart Song* (1920); *Broadway Brevities* (1920); *The Perfect Fool* (1921); *The French Doll* (1922)—'Do it again'; *Mayfair and Montmartre* (1922); *For Goodness Sake* (1922); *The Dancing Girl* (1923); *Little Miss Bluebeard* (1923)—'I won't say I will (but I won't say I won't)' *Nine-Fifteen Revue* (1930); *The Show is On* (1936)—'By Strauss'. His complete scores were: *La-La Lucille* (1919)—'Nobody but you' (added later); *Morris Gest's Midnight Whirl* (1919); **George White's Scandals* (1920, 1921, 1922, 1923, 1924)—'I'll build a stairway to Paradise' (1922), 'Somebody loves me' (1924); *A Dangerous Maid* (1921); *Our Nell* (with William Daly, 1922); *The Rainbow* (1923); *Sweet Little Devil* (1924); **Primrose* (1924); **Lady, Be Good* (1924)—'Oh, lady be good', 'Fascinating rhythm', 'So am I', 'The half-of-it, dearie, blues' ('The man I love' was dropped from the score before the New York opening); *Tell Me More* (1925); **Tip-Toes* (1925)—'Sweet and low-down', 'Looking for a boy', 'That certain feeling'; *Song of the Flame* (1925); **Oh, Kay!* (1926)—'Maybe', 'Clap yo' hands' 'Do, do, do', 'Someone to watch over me'; **Strike Up the Band* (1927)—'Strike up the band'; **Funny Face* (1927)—'High hat', 'He loves and she loves', 'S'wonderful', 'My one and only'; **Rosalie* (with Sigmund *Romberg, 1927)—'How long has this been going on?'; *Treasure Girl* (1928)—'Feeling I'm falling'; *Show Girl* (1929)—'Do what you do', 'Liza'; **Girl Crazy* (1930)—'Embraceable you', 'But not for me', 'Bidin' my time', 'I got rhythm'; *Of Thee I Sing* (1931)—'Of thee I sing', 'Love is sweeping the country', 'Who cares?'; *Pardon my English* (1932)—'The Lorelei', 'My cousin in Milwaukee'; *Let 'Em Eat Cake* (1933)—'Mine'; and *Porgy and Bess* (1935)—'Summertime', 'It ain't necessarily so', 'Bess, you is my woman now'.

His film scores included: *The Sunshine Trail* (1923)—theme song and orchestral interludes including 'Walking the dog', later published as 'Promenade'; *Delicious* (1931); **Shall We Dance* (1937)—'Let's call the whole thing off'. 'They can't take that away from me', 'They all laughed', 'I've got beginner's luck'; *A *Damsel In Distress* (1937)—'A foggy day', 'Nice work if you can get it', 'The jolly tar and the milkmaid', 'Things are looking up'; *Goldwyn Follies* (1938)—'Love walked in', 'Love is here to stay'.

A film based on the composer's life, **Rhapsody in Blue*, was made in 1945, with Robert *Alda as Gershwin, using all his best songs. Others utilizing his music have been *The Shocking Miss Pilgrim* (1947)—'Aren't you kind of glad we did?', 'Changing my tune', 'Back Bay polka'; *An *American in Paris* (1951); and *Kiss Me Stupid* (1964).

Among his best piano writings were the transcriptions of 18 songs collectively known as 'George Gershwin's Song Book' (1932) and the intricate 'I got rhythm variations' (1934). Gershwin once said that he had more tunes in his head than he could write down in a lifetime. The number he achieved during the short span that was allotted amply bore out this claim.

With the hindsight of what has since happened in the popular song world, Gershwin may now be categorized as the composer who came closest to bringing the popular and classical worlds of music together. A Gershwin song was (perhaps with the exception of some by *Jerome Kern) as near to an art song as the popular song ever needed, or wanted, to go. He used the jazz idiom (however modified) with greater success than perhaps anyone else before or since to produce a new kind of popular song. Jazz was totally integrated in his style, distinguishing him from composers like Ravel, who simply sprinkled a little jazz into their compositions o1here and there; like Stravinsky, who never grasped the idiom at all; and many of his contemporaries in *Tin Pan Alley, who simply took over the more superficial elements. Apart from his longer works (which are often criticized for a certain degree of artificiality), Gershwin's music, with its sophistication and polish, was saved from seeming pretentious by a fine sense of melody and its constant vitality. Proof of his lasting potential is to be seen in the number of Gershwin songs that became jazz standards by virtue of the melodic and harmonic interest they offered. After Gershwin and the 1940s, popular music was to move away from craft to folk-art, with the theatre proving to be the last bastion of the kind of music that Gershwin, Kern, Cole *Porter, and Richard *Rodgers created. A song of their period was something that could still be performed by anyone from the printed page; but concurrently the predominance of jazz was leading to popular music's being almost entirely what the performer made it and how it was interpreted on record.

I. Goldberg: *George Gershwin: a Study in American Music* (New York, 1931; repr. 1958, 1962). M. Armitage (ed.): *George Gershwin* (New York, 1938). R. Chalupt: *George Gershwin* (Paris, 1948). D. Ewen: *A Journey to Greatness* (New York, 1956; rev. 1970). M. Armitage: *George Gershwin: Man and Legend* (New York, 1958; repr. 1970). E. Jablonski and L. D. Stewart: *The Gershwin Years* (New York, 1958; rev. 1973). M. Pasi: *George Gershwin* (Parma, 1958). C. Longolius: *George Gershwin* (Berlin, 1959). E. Jablonski: *George Gershwin* (New York, 1962). R. Rushmore: *The Life of George Gershwin* (New York, 1966). A. Gauthier: *George Gershwin* (Paris, 1973). R. Kimball and A. Simon: *The Gershwins* (New York, 1973; London, 1974). C. Schwartz: *George Gershwin: a Selective Bibliography and Discography* (Detroit, 1973; repr. 1979). C. Schwartz: *Gershwin: his Life and Music* (Indianapolis, 1973). A. Kendall: *George Gershwin* (London, 1987). E. Jablonski: *Gershwin: a Biography* (New York, 1987; London, 1988).

Music: R. Sirmay (ed.): *The George and Ira Gershwin Songbook* (New York, 1960.

Gershwin, Ira [Gershvin, Israel] (*b* New York, 6 Dec. 1896; *d* Hollywood, 17 Aug. 1983). American lyric-writer and librettist, older brother of George *Gershwin. Educated Townsend Harris Hall 1910–14, City University of New York College 1914–16, Columbia University 1918. From 1918 he frequently collaborated with his brother, during 1924–6 writing under the name of Arthur Francis (a pseudonym derived from the names of his younger brother and sister). He used his own name professionally for the first time in writing the musical comedy *Be Yourself* (1924, *m* Lewis Gensler), after which he wrote the book and lyrics for most of the George Gershwin output. His writing was brightly aggressive like George's music and suited it perfectly, colloquial and full of verbal idiosyncrasies, the sentiment exposed in a tongue-in-cheek way.

He wrote the lyrics for *A Dangerous Maid* (1921); **Lady, Be Good* (1924); **Primrose* (1924); *Tell me More* (1925); **Tip-Toes* (1925); **Oh, Kay!* (1926); **Funny Face* (1927); **Rosalie* (1928); *Treasure Girl* (1928); *Show Girl* (1929); **Girl Crazy* (1930); **Strike Up the Band* (1930); **Of Thee I Sing* (1931); *Pardon my English* (1933); *Let 'Em Eat Cake* (1933); **Porgy and Bess* (1935); and for the films *Delicious* (1931); **Shall We Dance* (1937); *A *Damsel in Distress* (1937); *Goldwyn Follies* (1938)—all with George Gershwin. With other composers he wrote *Two Little Girls in Blue* (Vincent *Youmans, 1921); *For Goodness Sake* (1924, *m* Paul Lannin, William Daly, and two numbers by George Gershwin); **Americana* (1926, *m* Phil *Charig)—'Sunny disposish'; and *That's a Good Girl* (1928, *m* *Meyer and Charig). He contributed isolated numbers to many shows, including *Life Begins at 8:40* (1934); **Ziegfeld Follies* (1936)—'I can't get started' (*m* Vernon *Duke); *Lady in the Dark* (1941, *m* Kurt *Weill); *The Firebrand of Florence* (1945, Weill); *Park Avenue* (1946, *m* Arthur *Schwartz); and the films *Cover Girl* (1944, *m* Jerome *Kern)—'Long ago and far away'; and *Where Do We Go From Here?* (1945, Weill); *The Barkleys of Broadway* (1949, *m* Harry *Warren); *Give a Girl a Break* (1953, *m* Burton *Lane); *A *Star is Born* (1954, *m* Harold *Arlen); and *The Country Girl* (1954, Arlen).

I. Gershwin: *Lyrics on Several Occasions* (New York, 1959; repr. 1972, 1977). G. and I. Gershwin: *The George and Ira Gershwin Song Book* (New York, 1960). R. Kimball and A. Simon: *The Gershwins* (New York, 1973). See also books listed under GERSHWIN, GEORGE.

Getz, Stan [Gayetzsky, Stanley] (*b* Philadelphia, 2 Feb. 1927; *d* Los Angeles, 6 June 1991). American jazz tenor-saxophonist. He played in the Jack *Teagarden band in his teens; then with Stan *Kenton, Jimmy *Dorsey, Benny *Goodman, and Woody *Herman. One of the leaders of the cool school of jazz, he made important recordings with Gerry *Mulligan, Dizzy *Gillespie, and many others. He developed from being a Lester *Young disciple to a distinctive stylist of the 1960s with a sound that was both emotive and attacking. His most famous jazz solo was on 'Early Autumn' (1948) with Woody Herman, and his breathy tone was heard to good effect on the *bossa nova recordings of the 1960s with João Gilberto (*b* 1931) among which 'The Girl from Ipanema' (1963) was especially popular.

Gibbons, Carroll (*b* Clinton, Mass., 4 Jan. 1903; *d* London, 10 May 1954). American composer, pianist, and conductor. He had already made his debut as a pianist at the age of 10 before he went to study at the Boston Conservatory. Mainly to study further, he came to London with Rudy *Vallee in 1924 but instead joined the orchestra at the *Savoy Hotel in London. In 1927 he assumed the leadership of the Savoy Orpheans. They disbanded in 1928 and he was appointed musical director for HMV Records and also took over leadership of the New Mayfair Orchestra. He returned to America in 1930 to work for MGM, but was back in London a year later to lead the Savoy Hotel Orpheans, eventually becoming the hotel's director of entertainments, a post he held until his death in 1954. In the 1930s he wrote music for many British films, appearing in *The Common Touch* (1941), and for several West End shows. The Carroll Gibbons Orchestra was very popular on the radio in the 1930s and 1940s. While not outstanding musically and not contributing greatly to the jazz scene, his own fluent and melodic playing in the best standard songs was always pleasant and attractive.

Gibbs, Mike [Michael Clement Irving] (*b* Salisbury, Zimbabwe, 25 Sept. 1937). Rhodesian composer, arranger, trombonist, and pianist. He studied at the Berklee School of Music in Boston and at the Lennox School of Jazz, where he was a pupil of Gunther *Schuller. Later he won a scholarship to Tanglewood Summer School where he studied with leading modern composers such as Copland, Xenakis, Schuller, and Foss. After a brief return to Southern Rhodesia (as it then was), he went to England in 1965 where he played trombone with Graham *Collier, John *Dankworth, and Tubby Hayes and worked as a studio musician. By the late 1960s his composing and arranging abilities were widely recognized. Initially influenced by Gil *Evans and Messiaen, he found his own jazz-rock style and wrote 'Family joy', 'Oh boy!', 'Tanglewood '63', and 'On the third day'. He went to America in 1974 to become composer in residence at Berklee, but continued to tour the USA and Europe as a jazz musician. In 1983 he left Berklee to become an international composer, orchestrator, and record producer, settling in London again in 1985 where he wrote film music and ballet scores.

Gibson, Orville (*b* Chateaugay, NY, 1856; *d* Ogdensburg, NY, 19 Aug. 1918). American musician and instrument manufacturer. He settled in Kalamazoo, Michigan, in the 1870s, where he eventually opened his own musical instrument shop and became an important pioneer in the modern developments of the mandolin and the guitar. His hand-carved models included the A and F (or 'Artists') model mandolin, and he formed the Gibson Mandolin-Guitar Manufacturing Company in 1902 which produced mandolins, mandolas, mando-cellos and basses, harp guitars, and tenor guitars that have become the Strads of the modern instrumental world.

Gifford, Gene [H. Eugene] (*b* Americus, Ga., 31 May 1908; *d* Memphis, 12 Nov. 1970). American composer, arranger, bandleader, and guitarist. His name is mainly associated with the *Casa Loma Orchestra whose style he formulated in the years 1929–35, his progressive arrangements making it a popular radio and recording band. Both he and the band outlived their association, but neither was quite so distinctive or successful again. After he left in 1935, Gifford worked with CBS radio and various record companies. His compositions included 'Casa Loma stomp' (1930); 'White jazz' (1931); 'Black jazz' (1932); 'Rhythm man' (1933); 'Stompin' around' (1934), and 'Nothin' but the blues' (1935).

Gigi. American film made by MGM in 1958, directed by Vincente *Minnelli, with a script by Alan Jay *Lerner (based on a novel by Colette) and music by Frederick *Loewe. In the Parisian demi-monde, Gigi rebels against family traditions by marrying a decent man. It starred Leslie Caron (*b* 1931), Maurice *Chevalier, Louis Jourdan, Hermione *Gingold, and Isabel Jeans; and its memorable score included 'Gigi', 'Thank heaven for little girls', 'The night they invented champagne', 'I remember it well', 'Say a prayer for me tonight', 'She is not thinking of me', and 'I'm glad I'm not young anymore'. One of the great musical film classics, and the first Hollywood musical to be shot entirely in Paris, it followed the unusual pattern of becoming a stage musical later (and less successfully), produced at the Uris Theatre 13 Nov. 1973, with Alfred *Drake, Daniel Massey, Agnes Moorehead, and Maria Karnilova.

Gilbert, Fred [Frederick] (*b* London, 1849; *d* London, 12 Apr. 1903). British composer and singer. He started his professional career as a child actor at the Adelphi Theatre and later was in the choir at *Evans's Supper Rooms. He developed a prolific talent for writing songs and wrote many for the Great *MacDermott in a vein of topical political satire such as 'Charlie Dilke' (1885) when the prominent MP was involved in a divorce scandal. His biggest hit was 'The man who broke the bank at Monte Carlo', which he wrote in 1891 after seeing a headline to that effect on a billboard in the Strand hailing the good fortune of one Arthur deCourcey Bower. Having written the song, Gilbert had difficulty in selling it. It was rejected by Albert *Chevalier but eventually bought by Charles *Coborn who, having at first refused it, spent a sleepless night and hastened back in the morning to pay an outright fee of £20. It was to make him a small fortune. It also had a big success in the USA, where it was sung by William Hoey, and it was published there in 1892. Among Gilbert's other big hits were 'At Trinity Church I met my doom' (1894)—sung by Tom *Costello, 'Down the road' (1893)—sung by Gus *Elen, and 'Brighton' (with Percy Gaunt, 1892)—sung by R. G. *Knowles.

C. Coborn: *The Man who Broke the Bank* (London, 1930).

Gilbert, Jean [Winterfeld, Max] (*b* Hamburg, 11 Feb. 1879; *d* Buenos Aires, 20 Dec. 1942). German composer and conductor. After studies in Kiel, Sondershausen, and Berlin, he became conductor at the Stadttheater, Bremerhaven, in 1897 and the Carl-Schutze-Theater, Hamburg, from 1898. In 1890 his son Robert, later to be part-librettist of the famous *White Horse Inn*, was born. From 1900 he conducted at the Centralhallen-Theater in Berlin and from 1903 at the Apollo. He continued his conducting career and worked as an arranger until, from about 1910, he was able to make a livelihood as a composer.

A fast worker, he produced 57 stage works in the space of 15 years. His biggest successes were *Die keusche Susanne* (Magdeburg, 1910), which was seen in Vienna (1911), London (1912, as *The Girl in the Taxi*), and New York (1912, as *Modest Suzanne*); and *Die Kino-Königin* (Berlin 1913), which was seen in New York as *The Queen of the Movies* and in London as *The Cinema Star*. Both these were well written but many of his works were too hastily thrown together. Others that had a fair success were *Polnische Wirtschaft* (1910); *Autoliebchen* (1912); *Püppchen* (1912), from which the song 'Püppchen du bist mein Augenstern' became immensely popular; *Die Tangoprinzessin* (1912); *Fräulein Trallala* (1913); *Die Fährt ins Glück* (1916); *Die Frau im Hermelin* (1918); *Die Braut des Lucullus*

(1920); *Katja, die Tänzerin* (1922)—'Komm, Liebchen, wander'; *Das Weib im Purpur* (1923); *In der Johannisnacht* (1926); *Hotel Stadt Lemberg* (1929); *Das Mädel am Steuer*; and, in New York, *The Girl from Cook's* (1927); *The Red Robe* (1928); and *The Street Singer* (1928). He left Germany in 1930 when Hitler came to power and settled in South America.

Gilbert, L. Wolfe (*b* Odessa, Russia, 31 Aug. 1886; *d* Beverly Hills, Calif., 12 July 1970). American composer and lyric-writer. Taken by his family to the USA in 1887, he was educated in Philadelphia. At the age of 14 he went to New York and sang in cafés at Coney Island, in burlesque theatres, nightclubs, and vaudeville. He toured with the boxer John L. Sullivan's entertainment unit, and became a columnist of the *New York Clipper*. He started writing songs in collaboration with Lewis F. *Muir, their earliest big successes being 'Waiting for the Robert E. Lee' and 'Hitchy koo', both written in 1912 and introduced to Europe by the American Ragtime Octet. These were followed by 'Take me to that Swanee shore' (1912); 'Ragging the baby to sleep' (1912); 'Mammy Jinny's jubilee' (1913); 'I had a gal, I had a pal' (1913); 'Down yonder' (1921); 'Lucky Lindy' (1927—*m* Abel Blair), celebrating Lindbergh's Atlantic flight; 'Ramona' (1927, *m* Mabel *Wayne); 'Jeanine, I dream of lilac time' (1928, *m* Nathaniel Shilkret); 'Mama don't want no peas and rice and cocoanut oil' (*m* Charlie Lofthouse), and 'Peanut vendor' (1931). He continued to appear on the stage with various partners for many years, then settled in Hollywood in 1929 where he formed his own publishing company. He wrote more than 250 songs.

Gilbert, W. S. [William Schwenck] (*b* London, 18 Nov. 1836; *d* Harrow Weald, Middx., 29 May 1911). British dramatist and librettist. After studying the law and briefly practising it, he began a literary career in 1861 as a regular contributor to *Fun*. An excellent writer of comic verse, he became particularly known for his ballads which he wrote under the pseudonym of 'Bab', a first collected edition, *Bab Ballads*, being published in 1869. He wrote the burlesque *Dulcamara* (1886) and a number of very successful plays, including *The Palace of Truth* and *Pygmalion and Galatea* (1870). His collaboration with Arthur *Sullivan on a highly successful series of operettas (later to be known as the Savoy Operas) began tentatively with **Thespis* (1871) and developed into a fluent succession of creations beginning with **Trial by Jury* (1875) (see under GILBERT AND SULLIVAN).

Gilbert must be credited with the vital spark that inspired all these immortal works and for making Sullivan a first-rate writer of operettas rather than a second-rate academic composer. Gilbert's topsy-turvy humour has made the adjective 'Gilbertian' a synonym for paradoxical wit. Sullivan never had much success in this field without Gilbert, but Gilbert managed fairly successful collaborations with other composers on such pieces as *Ages Ago* (1869, with Frédéric *Clay); *Princess Toto* (1876, Clay); *The Mountebanks* (1892, Alfred *Cellier); *His Excellency* (1894, F. Osmond Carr); and *Fallen Fairies* (1909, Edward *German). A superb lyricist, he was hailed as a model by such modern successors as Lorenz *Hart and Ira *Gershwin. He was knighted in 1907. While attempting to rescue a young woman from drowning in a lake at his home, Grimsdyke, he died of a heart attack.

E. A. Browne: *W. S. Gilbert* (London, 1907). S. Dark and R. Grey: *William Schwenck Gilbert, his Life and Letters* (London, 1923). T. Searle: *Sir William Schwenck Gilbert, a Topsy Turvy Adventure* (London, 1931) [bibliography]. H. Pearson: *Gilbert, his Life and Strife* (London, 1957). R. Allen: *W. S. Gilbert: an Anniversary Survey* (Charlottesville, 1963). J. B. Jones (ed.): *W. S. Gilbert: a Century of Scholarship and Comment* (New York, 1970). M. K. Sutton: *W. S. Gilbert* (Boston, 1975). W. Cox-Ife: *W. S. Gilbert: Stage Director* (London, 1977).

Works: J. W. Stedman (ed.): *Gilbert Before Sullivan* (Chicago, 1967; London, 1969). G. Rowell (ed.): *Plays by W. S. Gilbert* (Cambridge, 1982). See also books listed under GILBERT AND SULLIVAN.

Gilbert and Sullivan. The collaboration between W. S. *Gilbert and Arthur *Sullivan on the famous Savoy Operas began in 1875 with **Trial by Jury*. They had first met in 1869 at a rehearsal of an operetta, *Ages Ago*. The composer, Frédéric *Clay, had asked Sullivan along to give him some practical criticism and he took the opportunity to introduce him to his librettist, Gilbert. The G & S history was set in motion by the enterprising and energetic impresario John *Hollingshead who had founded the *Gaiety Theatre and was busy setting it on its feet. It had opened with a play by Gilbert, *Robert the Devil*, the success of which was small but sufficient to convince Hollingshead of Gilbert's capabilities. He took a libretto of Gilbert's, **Thespis or The Gods Grown Old*, and persuaded Sullivan to set it to music. It was put together in three weeks, ran for 80 nights, and was then forgotten. Even the score was lost. The only remarkable thing was to see the name of Queen Victoria's favourite composer on the playbills of the Gaiety.

One man remembered this venture, however, and saw some possibilities for the future in it. This was Richard D'Oyly *Carte, manager of the Royalty Theatre in Dean Street. With a production of *Offenbach's *La *Périchole* on his hands and not doing too well, he decided that he needed a curtain-raiser to give more substance to the evening's entertainment. By divine chance, Gilbert happened to call as D'Oyly Carte was pondering the subject and, asked if he had anything to offer, brought out of his pocket a piece which he described as a mock trial which had been expanded from a ballad written some years before and which he was hoping to have set to music by Carl Rosa. D'Oyly Carte had a look at it, declared that Sullivan was the only man in England to stand alongside Offenbach, and asked Gilbert to take the manuscript to him. Gilbert read the piece to Sullivan, who was so amused by it that he set to work immediately and wrote the music in what was to be his customary three weeks. It opened at the Royalty Theatre on 25 Mar. 1875, was highly acclaimed by the critics, and ran for 128 performances. The event was hailed as the re-awakening of English comic opera.

By 1876, Sullivan had become the head of the newly founded National Training School of Music (now the Royal College), and had written the best-selling 'The lost chord'. He was now being told by his colleagues that he must lead the way in writing some serious British music. These considerations were to tug at his conscience throughout the years of working with Gilbert. The collaborators were two very different people: Sullivan, serious about music but enjoying a frivolous and gay society life; Gilbert, frivolous in his art but a stern figure in real life, spending his latter years as a highly respectable magistrate. Their collaboration was to be full of ups and downs, but their writings were a magical combination. In 1877 the collaboration began in earnest with *The *Sorcerer*, which was produced on 17 Nov. in a small warren of a theatre, the *Opera-Comique, which was approached from the Strand by a long burrow called Theatre Royal Tunnels. It was not up to their later best, but it introduced the comic character John Wellington Wells who was a prototype of many such characters to come.

By 1878 even Sullivan seems to have admitted to himself that such writing was his true métier. In order to write **HMS Pinafore*, he put aside an oratorio intended for the Leeds Festival. The first of the full-length classics, it opened on 25 May 1878 and was put on its feet by some unplanned publicity arising from a rival production put on by fellow-directors of Carte's who had decided to break away from his Comedy Opera company. At a performance on 31 July, a gang arrived to remove the scenery from the theatre and there was a free fight on stage. The invaders were repelled and the ensuing publicity brought in the audiences. Soon *Pinafore* was a current craze and the music shops were said to be selling 10,000 copies of the score in a day. The production had also been pirated in America, so Gilbert and Sullivan went there to launch the next work, *The *Pirates of Penzance* which opened in December 1879. The English copyright première was staged in Paignton and it was not seen in London until April 1880. The operas which followed confirmed the success of the G & S formula. **Patience*, a sharp satire on the aesthetic movement, came in 1881 and ran for an initial 578 performances; **Iolanthe* followed in 1882; and then the delightful but often neglected **Princess Ida*, breaking precedence with three acts.

At this point Gilbert came up with a favourite plot of his concerning a magic lozenge which Sullivan, in a dark mood, strongly objected to. Gilbert found his objections 'arbitrary and capricious'; the partnership almost ended at this point and for a moment came to a halt. Gilbert solved the impasse by producing his best libretto so far. Inspired by a Japanese sword on the wall of his home in Harrington Gardens, Kensington, he wrote *The *Mikado*. Sullivan had already relented and promised to set whatever came along; he was duly inspired to write one of his brightest scores. The Savoy first night was on 14 Mar. 1885 and the show ran for 672 performances, almost equalling *Pinafore*'s 700. But behind the scenes more quarrels were brewing, Gilbert in disagreement with Carte about the running of the company and annoyed with Sullivan because he would not be involved in the matter. **Ruddigore* was produced in 1887 with only a mildly successful run of 283; *The *Yeomen of the Guard* in 1888 fared only slightly better with 423. The success of *Cellier's **Dorothy*, which had run for 931 performances, depressed Sullivan, whose heart was now set upon writing a grand opera, *Ivanhoe*, which was a failure at the Royal English Opera House (now the Palace Theatre). Gilbert pressed on with *The *Gondoliers* which turned out, in spite of everything, to be one of their most light-hearted pieces, running for 544 performances. Nine months later there was the most violent quarrel so far. Gilbert was shocked to find that expenses of £4500 had been taken from their earnings, some spent on scenery, some on theatre improvements, but £500 of it on 'new carpets for the front of the house'. Once again Sullivan refused to back Gilbert in his arguments with Carte, and the partnership foundered. Carte was hurt, Gilbert contracted gout, and Sullivan went off to fight a long-standing liver complaint.

The truly productive years were over. The two last G & S operettas, *Utopia Limited* in 1893 and *The Grand Duke* in 1896 were far from their best efforts. Each turned to other partners with limited success. Sullivan finally succumbed to his old disease while trying to write *The *Emerald Isle* with Basil *Hood and died in 1900. Gilbert himself was ill when Sullivan died and always regretted not having had a chance to make peace with his old partner. Carte died soon after.

The Savoy operas have continued to delight the English-speaking world. The insularity of Gilbert's humour has not helped them to find a place in Europe, though one or two like *The Mikado* have travelled on the strength of Sullivan's music. The D'Oyly Carte company continued to stage them until 1982 when general hard times in the theatre caused the company to close down. By then the works were out of copyright and modern productions were a regular event—most of them proving very successful. The D'Oyly Carte company was re-formed in 1988 after receiving a £1 million legacy from Bridget D'Oyly Carte who had died in 1985.

See also under CARTE, GILBERT, SULLIVAN, and the various operetta titles.

P. Fitzgerald: *The Savoy Opera: and the Savoyards* (London, 1894). F. Cellier and C. Bridgman: *Gilbert, Sullivan and D'Oyly Carte* (London, 1914). H. M. Walbrook: *Gilbert and Sullivan Opera* (London, 1920). S. J. A. Fitz-Gerald: *The Story of the Savoy Operas* (London, 1924). A. H. Godwin: *The Story of the Savoy Operas* (New York, 1925). I. Goldberg: *The Story of Gilbert and Sullivan, or The Compleat Savoyard* (New York, 1928). H. Pearson: *Gilbert and Sullivan* (London, 1935). W. A. Darlington: *The*

World of Gilbert and Sullivan (New York, 1950). A. Jacobs: *Gilbert and Sullivan* (London, 1951). L. Bailey: *The Gilbert and Sullivan Book* (London, 1952). A. Williamson: *Gilbert and Sullivan Opera* (London, 1953). R. Mander and J. Mitchenson: *A Picture History of Gilbert and Sullivan* (London, 1962). F. L. Moore: *The Handbook of Gilbert and Sullivan* (New York, 1962). C. Rollins and R. J. Witts: *The D'Oyly Carte Company in Gilbert and Sullivan* (London, 1962, with supplements). L. Ayre: *The Gilbert and Sullivan Companion* (London, 1972). L. Baily: *Gilbert and Sullivan and their World* (London, 1973). C. Brahms: *Gilbert and Sullivan: Chords and Discords* (London, 1975). C. Hibbert: *Gilbert and Sullivan and their Victorian World* (New York, 1976). R. Wilson and F. Lloyd: *Gilbert & Sullivan: the D'Oyly Carte Years* (London, 1984). D. Eden: *Gilbert and Sullivan: the Creative Conflict* (London, 1986).

Music and words: W. S. Gilbert and A. Sullivan: *Songs of Two Savoyards* (London, 1892; various reprints). M. Green (ed.): *Martyn Green's Treasury of Gilbert & Sullivan* (New York, 1961; etc.).

Texts: R. Allen: *The First Night Gilbert and Sullivan* (New York, 1958; repr. 1976). I. Bradley (ed.): *The Annotated Gilbert and Sullivan* (London, 1982 and 1984).

Gillespie, 'Dizzy' [John Birks] (*b* Cheraw, SC, 21 Oct. 1917; *d* Englewood, NJ, 6 Jan. 1993). American jazz trumpeter, bandleader, composer, and arranger. Influenced by his father who was a part-time musician, he started to play music as a child; but it was not until he was 18, when the family moved to Philadelphia, that he joined his first band. Two years later he joined the Teddy *Hill band, with whom he first recorded and paid a visit to Britain. He played with Edgar Hayes, Benny *Carter, and Cab *Calloway; in the meantime spending his off-duty hours at *Minton's Playhouse in Harlem (which was to be the shrine of modern jazz) where he exchanged musical thoughts with such kindred spirits as Charlie *Parker and Thelonious *Monk. They experimented with the new harmonic ideas which emerged as *bebop. Generally credited with the introduction of the word, Gillespie disclaimed any intentional invention, the name arising from the sort of scat vocals that were improvised to the new musical phraseology. In the 1940s he was active as a composer-arranger, guesting with Boyd *Raeburn, Lionel *Hampton, Duke *Ellington, Earl *Hines, and others. He formed and directed the orchestra nominally led by singer Billy *Eckstine in 1944, where he first became generally known to jazz musicians and followers as bebop became the latest jazz cult. Leaving Eckstine in 1945 to lead a small jazz group at the famous Three Deuces, he soon expanded to a large band, meanwhile touring with an All-Star Quintet. He recorded the first notable bebop items such as 'Shaw 'nuff', 'Salt peanuts', and 'Hot house' (1941), where both his innovative ideas and sheer virtuosity made their impact, particularly in the introduction of important Afro-Cuban elements, with Candido (*b* 1921) as percussionist. He led his large band from 1946 to 1950.

During this period he was to play a major part in the jazz revolution, establishing the trends of modern jazz, extending the possibilities of the jazz trumpet and proving an inspiring master to those who were to follow. While he was an organizer and a thinker, he also remained a great entertainer and humorist. His compositions provided a basic library of bebop: 'Night in Tunisia' (1942); 'Woody'n you' (1942); 'Groovin' high' (1944); 'Blue 'n' boogie' (with Frank Paparelli, 1944); and many other modern standards. His speed of execution, security on long high notes, his daring deviations backed by a tremendous sense of swing, made him the father figure of modern jazz trumpet as *Armstrong had been to the earlier style. He used a special trumpet with its bell slanted upwards to achieve a soaring sound. During the 1950s he mainly led small groups and worked with the Norman *Granz Jazz at the Philharmonic units. In 1956 he led a large band on overseas tours on behalf of the US State Department. In the 1960s he garnered some new ideas from his pianist Lalo *Schifrin, and in the 1970s continued his worldwide touring with a notable 'Tribute to Dizzy Gillespie' concert at Avery Fisher Hall in New York in 1975, featuring him with various combinations and the players with whom he had been associated over the years. He survived the criticism of too much clowning (as Armstrong had done) to become one of the giants of jazz; and continued to play and record into the 1980s.

M. James: *Dizzy Gillespie* (London, 1959). D. Gillespie: *To Be or Not to Bop: Autobiography* (New York, 1979). R. Horricks: *Dizzy Gillespie* (Tunbridge Wells, 1984).

Gilmore, Patrick S[arsfield] (*b* Athlone, Ireland, 25 Dec. 1829; *d* St Louis, Mo., 24 Sept. 1892). Irish-American conductor and composer. He learned the cornet at the age of 16 and two years later joined the army and went to Canada. A year later he resigned and went to Boston where he worked in a music store. At 23 he was appointed bandmaster of the Boston Band, transferring to the Salem Band in 1855. In 1861 he and the entire Gilmore Band enlisted in the Massachusetts 24th Volunteer Regiment and served in the Civil War, until 1862 when all regimental bands were returned to safer duties. In Boston they played in their tattered service uniforms and in 1863 he gave massive concerts, often with some 500 musicians drawn from various military units. At this time he achieved immortality by writing 'When Johnny comes marching home' (1863), in anticipation of the end of the war, and it became immensely popular in both the South and the North. In 1867 he conceived the idea for a great Peace Jubilee which eventually came to fruition in Boston in June 1869 with an orchestra of 1000 and a chorus of 10,000, with such visiting attractions as Johann *Strauss II and a Viennese orchestra of 56 musicians, the Grenadier Guards Band from England under Daniel *Godfrey, the Garde Republicaine Band from France, and the Kaiser Franz Grenadier Band from Germany. In 1873 he became the director of the 22nd Regiment Band in New York which he continued to direct until his death. It came to be acknowledged as one of the world's finest bands, touring throughout the USA and visiting Europe in 1878. He wrote a number of marches and other works but is still remembered as a composer by his one immortal success. The Gilmore Band tradition has been continued by members of the family.

M. Darlington: *Irish Orpheus: the Life of Patrick S. Gilmore* (Philadelphia, 1950).

Giménez, Jerónimo (*b* Seville, 10 Oct. 1854; *d* Madrid, 19 Feb. 1923). Spanish composer. By the age of 12 he was working in a theatre orchestra in Cadiz. He won a scholarship to the Paris Conservatoire, where one of his teachers was Ambroise Thomas and a contemporary student was Claude Debussy. He returned to Spain to become conductor of the Sociedád de Conciertos in Madrid, becoming a popular figure and responsible over the years for introducing some 150 new works by Spanish composers. His own success as a composer lay in the *zarzuela field, particularly with two works based on the life of the famous Spanish dancer Luis Alonso. In the first, *El Baile de Luis Alonso*, first performed at the Teatro de la Zarzuela in Madrid on 27 Feb. 1896, he added music to an already popular play. Such was its success that a sequel was called for, and *La Boda de Luis Alonso*, this time an original zarzuela, was produced in Madrid on 27 Jan. 1897. Both these works did much to establish a growing interest in Andalusian music, introducing boleros, fandangos, and the like and popular folk melodies. Both had intermezzos that became national favourites, the one from *El Baile* a graceful scherzo, the one from *La Boda* in the repertoire of every Spanish orchestra. He wrote some 60 operettas altogether including: *La Torre del Oro* (1892); *La Tempranica* (1900); El Húsar de la Guardia (with *Vives, 1905); and *La Gatita Blanca* (1906).

Gingold, Hermione Ferdinanda (*b* London, 9 Dec. 1897; *d* New York, 24 May 1987). British actress and singer. She appeared in *Pinkie and the Fairies* at the age of 11, then in various classical plays, before making her debut, and finding her place, as one of the most individual and effective of all revue artists, achieving a major success (with the help of the wit of Herbert *Farjeon) in *Spread it Abroad* at the Saville in 1936. For 10 years from 1938 she appeared entirely in revues, many in the West End, but the most prestigious being the 'little' revues at the Ambassadors' in Notting Hill Gate—*The Gate Revue* (1938); *Swinging the Gate* (1940); **Sweet and Low* (1943); *Sweeter and Lower* (1944); *Sweetest and Lowest* (1945). A rivalry with the other Hermione (*Baddeley) developed nicely in *Slings and Arrows* (1948). She went to the USA in 1951 to appear in the musical *The *Music Man* (1957) and the film **Gigi* (1958), among others, returning to London in 1969 and appearing in *A *Little Night Music* (1975). Her husbands included the publisher Michael Joseph and Eric *Maschwitz. She is affectionately remembered for the famous extended drawl and the explosive consonants that underlined her immaculate timing and keen sense of the ridiculous.

H. Gingold: *The World is Square* (New York, 1958).
H. Gingold: *Sirens Should be Seen and Not Heard* (Philadelphia, 1963).

Girl Crazy. American musical comedy with score by George *Gershwin, book by Guy *Bolton and John McGowan, lyrics by Ira *Gershwin, first heard in Philadelphia then produced at the Alvin Theatre, New York, 14 Oct. 1930 where it had 272 performances. It marked a return from the satirical ambitions of **Strike Up the Band* (1930) to the simple world of musical comedy.

Set in Arizona, the plot concerned the amours of playboy Danny Churchill and was very forgettable; but it brought forth a clutch of mature Gershwin hits including 'Embraceable you', 'Sam and Delilah', 'I got rhythm', 'But not for me', 'Bidin' my time', 'Could you use me?', and 'Treat me rough', interpreted by a star cast that included Ginger *Rogers, Allen *Kearns, Ethel *Merman (her first major Broadway role), and Willie *Howard, supported by the Red *Nichols Orchestra with such notable jazzmen as Benny *Goodman, Glenn *Miller, Jimmy *Dorsey, Jack *Teagarden, and Gene *Krupa in its ranks. Merman stopped the show with 'I got rhythm' and Rogers was equally successful with 'But not for me'.

It was filmed in 1932 (with Wheeler and Woolsey among the attractions); in 1943 with Judy *Garland, Mickey *Rooney, June *Allyson, and the Tommy *Dorsey Orchestra, directed by Norman Taurog (1899–1981); and in 1965 (retitled *When the Boys Meet the Girls*) with such mixed forces as Connie *Francis, *Herman's Hermits, *Liberace, and Louis *Armstrong.

Girl from Utah, The. Musical play with score by Paul *Rubens and Sidney *Jones, book by James T. Tanner and Rubens, lyrics by Adrian *Ross and Percy *Greenbank, first seen at the Adelphi Theatre, London, 18 Oct. 1913 with Joseph *Coyne and Phyllis *Dare in the leading roles, running for 195 performances. It might have escaped historical notice if its somewhat undistinguished score had not been embellished for its New York debut by the up-and-coming Jerome *Kern (whose task it then was to undertake such modernizations) who contributed seven or eight numbers including his first big success 'They wouldn't believe me'. In spite of these enrichments it ran for only 120 performances at the Knickerbocker Theatre from 24 Aug. 1914, with Julia *Sanderson and Donald Brian; but it made its modest mark as the first American musical of the First World War; and a pointer towards the new American dominance in this field.

Gitana, Gertie (*b* Longport, 1888; *d* London, 5 Jan. 1957). British music-hall singer. She started her stage career as member of a gypsy children's group at the age of four and first appeared on the music-hall stage in Barrow-in-Furness in 1896 billed as 'Little Gitana'. As Gertie Gitana from *c.* 1900 she had a success at the Lyceum during its period as a music-hall 1905–6, appeared at the Holborn Empire, and was a top artist for the next 30 years or so. She had a sweet voice and a flighty manner which made her a cult artist whose name was often quoted as the epitome of femininity ('I've just had a banana with Gertie Gitana', as 'Burlington Bertie' sang), and had her principal hit with 'Nellie Dean' supported by such plaintive ditties as 'Silver bell', 'When the harvest moon is shining', and 'Never mind'. She retired in 1938 but returned to the stage with the *Thanks for the Memory* troupe and appeared in a Royal Variety Performance in 1948.

Glamorous Night. Musical play with words and music by Ivor *Novello, lyrics by Christopher Hassall (1912–63). Produced at the Theatre Royal, Drury Lane, 2 May 1935, with Mary *Ellis and Novello in the leading roles, it included such hits as 'Fold your wings', 'Glamorous night', 'Shine through my dreams', and 'When the gypsy played', and ran for 243 performances. One of the highly successful series of Viennese-style operettas that Novello produced, its romantic story of love and moonlight was suitably enfolded in a matching score. It was filmed in 1937 with Barry Mackay (*b* 1906) and Mary Ellis.

Gleason, Jackie [Herbert John] (*b* Brooklyn, NY, 26 Feb. 1916; *d* New York, 24 June 1987). American actor, comedian, composer, and conductor. He served a show-business apprenticeship in circuses, aquashows, and carnivals before making his rotund mark in such productions as *Keep Off the Grass* (1940); **Artists and Models* (1941); **Follow the Girls* (1944); *Along Fifth Avenue* (1949); and *Take me Along* (1959); and films *Navy Blues* (1941); *Orchestra Wives* (1942); and *Springtime in the Rockies* (1943). Essentially an American star and less appreciated abroad, he had a popular CBS TV show that led to his more serious successes in dramatic films, the best of which was probably *Gigot* in 1962, for which he also wrote the entire score. Another line to fame came with his LP productions such as *Music for Lovers Only* which in 1953 began a vogue for mood music and led to many other LPs under his name, often featuring the trumpeter Bobby *Hackett. He worked often as an ideas man for other arranger-conductors, favouring the large string section, and writing much material himself in the 1950s and 1960s, after which he retired.

J. Bishop: *The Golden Ham* (New York, 1956).

Glitter, Gary [Gadd, Paul] (*b* Banbury, Oxon, 8 May 1944). British pop singer. Under the name of Paul Raven he followed a prolific but not especially successful performing and recording career from the mid-1960s. He changed his stage name to Gary Glitter in 1971 and was rewarded with a No. 1 USA hit 'Rock & roll' (No. 2 in the UK) in 1972. Between 1972 and 1975 he achieved 11 UK Top 10 hits including the No. 1 'I'm the leader of the gang' (1973); 'I love you love me love' (1973); and 'Always yours' (1974). He retired briefly in 1976 but soon came back to continue an entertainment career that wavered between affluence and bankruptcy; but remained defiantly *Alive and Kicking*, as a 1985 album proclaimed.

Glover, Jimmy [James Mackay] (*b* Kingstown, Dublin, 18 June 1861; *d* Hastings, 8 Sept. 1931). British composer, arranger, conductor, manager, journalist, and author. Grandson of Prof. John William Glover (on his mother's side), his father was James Mackay; he assumed the name of Glover in 1880. He was director of music at Drury Lane from 1893 to 1923, arranging the music for most of the Drury Lane pantomimes during this period and becoming the friend and confidante of many stars of theatre and music-hall and a well-known and substantial figure in London musical life.

He wrote scores for *The Poet and the Puppets* (1892); *A Life of Pleasure* (1893); *The Little Genius* (1896); *The Telephone Girl* (1896); and *The Babes in the Wood* (1897), starring Dan *Leno; also incidental music to *The White Heather* (1897); and his songs included: 'Dearie, dearie' (1896); and 'Archibald, certainly not' (1909). He wrote three gossipy autobiographies: *Jimmy Glover—His Book* (London, 1911); *Jimmy Glover and his Friends* (London, 1913); and *Hims Ancient and Modern* (London, 1926).

Godfrey. Famous family of English military and brass band musicians whose work and influence extended over more than a century.

Charles Godfrey (*b* Kingston, Surrey, 22 Nov. 1790; *d* London, 12 Dec. 1863) joined the Coldstream Guards in 1813 and was appointed their bandmaster in 1825, a post he held until his death although in a civilian capacity for the last 40 years. From 1847 he was editor of *Jullien's Journal* (of military band music), which did much to standardize military band scoring in Britain. He had five sons, three of whom, Daniel, Adolphus, and Charles, followed in his footsteps.

Daniel Godfrey (*b* London, 4 Sept. 1831; *d* Beeston, Notts., 30 June 1903) entered the Royal Academy of Music in 1847 and became Professor of Military Music there. He was appointed bandmaster of the Grenadier Guards in 1856, holding this post until he formed his own band in 1896. He was the first bandmaster to be given commissioned rank (in 1887). In 1869 he took the Guards Band to Boston, USA, on the occasion of the Peace Festival (see under GILMORE), the first visit of a British army band to America since Independence. He wrote the military band waltzes 'Guards', 'Hilda', and 'Mabel' among many.

Adolphus Frederick Godfrey (*b* London, 1837; *d* London, 28 Aug. 1882) was also educated at the Royal College of Music. He joined the band of the Coldstream Guards in 1856 and in 1863 succeeded his father as bandmaster, retaining this appointment until he resigned in 1880. He became a famous arranger for the military band medium, and many of his arrangements are in regular use today.

Charles Godfrey (*b* London, 17 Jan. 1839; *d* London, 5 Apr. 1919) was also a student at the Royal Academy of Music and started his professional career playing with *Jullien's Orchestra. In 1859 he was appointed bandmaster of the Scots Fusilier Guards at the unusually early age of 20. In 1868 he became bandmaster of the Royal Horse Guards, an appointment he held until he retired in 1904; being promoted to commissioned rank in 1899. He was, at various times, professor at both the Royal College of Music and the Guildhall School of Music; and he founded the military band journal *Orpheus* in which he published many of his band arrangements. He was also closely connected with brass band music, adjudicating at Belle Vue for many years until 1914.

Charles George Godfrey (*b* London, 1 Dec. 1866; *d* London, 24 July 1935), son of the second Charles, was educated at St Paul's School and the Royal Academy of Music. He gained early experience in military music by occasionally acting as deputy for his father. In 1887 he was appointed bandmaster to the Corps of Commissionaires and from 1889 to 1897 he was conductor of the military band at the Crystal Palace, London. After two years at the Pavilion Gardens, Buxton, he was appointed musical director at the Spa in Scarborough, a post which he held for ten years. From 1911 to 1924 he conducted the Royal Parks Band, Hyde Park. Like his father and uncles he was better known for his arrangements for military band than for his original compositions.

Daniel Eyers Godfrey (*b* London, 20 June 1868; *d* Bournemouth, 20 July 1939), the son of Daniel, was to become the most widely known of the family, latterly as Sir Dan Godfrey Jr. He was educated at King's College School and the Royal Academy of Music and followed in the family tradition by being appointed conductor of the London Military Band (a civilian organization) from 1889 to 1891. After some operatic experience in South Africa, he took over the then small Winter Gardens orchestra in Bournemouth, where he was to live for the rest of his life. He established the Symphonic Concerts there in 1894 and conducted them till he retired in 1935, having raised the orchestra to full symphonic status. No one did more than he, in his time, to encourage the composition and performance of English orchestral music, for which he was knighted in 1922. He wrote his memoirs, *Memories and Musicians* (London, 1924).

Arthur Eugene Godfrey (*b* London, 28 Sept. 1868; *d* London, 23 Feb. 1939), another son of the second Charles, was a chorister at St Paul's Cathedral, 1877–83 and studied at the Royal Academy of Music 1883–9. He wrote music in many forms but, as both composer and conductor, he was mainly concerned with the theatre. His most successful piece was the musical comedy *Little Miss Nobody* which was produced at the Lyric Theatre in London in September 1898 and ran for six months. From 1921 to 1929 he was musical director at the Alhambra Theatre in Glasgow.

Dan Stuart Godfrey (*b* London, 21 May 1893; *d* Durban, S. Africa, 24 Apr. 1935) was the son of Sir Dan Godfrey. After leaving the Royal Academy of Music he enlisted in the Coldstream Guards, hoping to qualify for an army bandmastership. The First World War intervened, during which he served, attaining the rank of captain in the Dorsetshire Regiment. After the war he conducted the orchestras at Harrogate and St Leonards-on-Sea. He joined the BBC and in 1926 was appointed conductor of the London Wireless Orchestra. In 1928 he went to Durban as musical director of the municipal orchestra.

Godfrey, Charles [Lacey, Paul] (*b* London, 26 Apr. 1851; *d* Brierly Hill, Staffs., 28 Mar. 1900). British music-hall sketch artist and singer. His earliest experiences were in melodrama, his first music-hall appearance being at Day's in Birmingham in 1875. Soon after he was at the Royal Holborn in London, doing a 'lion-comique' act based on du Maurier's 'Postlethwaite' drawings in *Punch*, and singing such songs as 'The masher king' and 'Hi-tiddly-hi-ti'. He also continued in his old melodramatic line with items such as 'Across the bridge' and 'The lost daughter'. Later he specialized in patriotic sketches, correctly attired in uniforms to match the part, and was soon earning £5000 a year. Another song he favoured was 'After the ball'. Drink and overwork ruined his health when he was only 45. A tour of Australia aggravated his condition and he died after an engagement in Birmingham where his music-hall career had begun.

R. Morton (ed.): *Francis & Day's Album of Charles Godfrey's Popular Songs* [with a biographical sketch] (London, 1898).

Godfrey, Fred [Williams, Llewellyn] (*b* Swansea, 1880; *d* London, 1953). British composer of music-hall songs. He appeared in a music-hall act with Tom Finglas in the 1920s. A prolific composer, his songs included such music-hall classics as 'Now I have to call him Father' (with Charles Collins, 1911); 'Who were you with last night' (with Mark Sheridan, 1912); 'The kangaroo hop' (with Billy Williams, 1912); 'We're Irish and proud of it too' (with Mellor and Gifford, 1914); and 'Take me back to dear old Blighty' (with A. J. Mills and Bennett Scott, 1916). He published more than 250 songs, writing many of them for Billy Williams, others for Mark Sheridan, Dorothy Ward, Shaun Glenville, and Florrie *Forde.

Godfrey, Isidore (*b* London, 27 Sept. 1900; *d* Sussex, 12 Sept. 1977). English conductor. Educated at the Guildhall School of Music, he joined the D'Oyly *Carte opera company as conductor in 1925 and was their musical director from 1929 to 1968, when he retired.

'God save the King [Queen]'. The original authorship of the British national anthem has remained a matter for much controversy and many published words. The phrase 'God save the King' goes back as far as the Old Testament. The first appearance of the verses might well have been on a Jacobite drinking-glass around 1725. It was then printed in 1744 with the opening phrase 'God save our Lord the King' and again in 1745 as 'God save great George our King'. It is unlikely that the true authorship will ever be determined. There are many claims on behalf of various composers for the musical credit, but this also remains undetermined, with the name of John Bull a tempting proposition but no more provable than any other. The tune is also used by the Germans, and by the Americans as *'America (My country, 'tis of thee)' with words by Samuel Francis Smith written in 1831.

R. Clark: *An Account of the National Anthem entitled 'God Save the King'* (London, 1822). F. K. Harford: *Who Wrote 'God Save the King'?* (London, 1899). W. H. Cummings: *God Save the King: the Origin and History of the Music and Words of the National Anthem* (London, 1902). P. Scholes: *God Save the King: its History and Romance* (London, 1942). P. Scholes: *God Save the Queen: the History and Romance of the World's First National Anthem* (London, 1954).

Godspell. American rock musical with music and lyrics by Stephen *Schwartz and book by John-Michael Tebelak. Based on St Matthew's Gospel, it has been described as a 'whimsical retelling' of the story of the Seven Last Days in the life of Jesus Christ. It was first written as a non-musical piece, then turned into a musical which was first presented at the Cherry Lane Theatre in Greenwich Village on 17 May 1971; it then moved to the Promenade Theatre off-Broadway, finally to the Broadhurst on-Broadway, to achieve a total run of 2651 performances. At one time there were seven touring companies in the USA. It was seen in London at Wyndham's Theatre, 26 Jan. 1972; and was filmed in 1973 with Victor Garber and David Haskell. Its songs include: 'Day by day', 'All for the best', and 'All good gifts'.

Goffin, Gerry (*b* New York, 11 Feb. 1939). American lyricist and producer. One of the most successful specialist non-singing writers of the pop age, he studied to be a chemist at Queens College of the City of New York, where he met and married the composer Carole *King. They started a fruitful collaboration with 'Will you love me tomorrow' (1961) and their fame as songwriters was only eclipsed by the rise of the *Beatles team. Goffin supplied lyrics for 'Girls grow up faster than boys' (1963), working with such composers as Barry *Mann—'Who put the bomp' (1963), and supplying hits for the *Everly Brothers—'How can I meet her' (1963), the *Hollies—'Yes I will' (1965), and Aretha *Franklin—'A natural woman' (1967).

He was divorced from King in 1968 and his work after that seemed to take on a more gloomy aspect as in the politically slanted album *It Ain't Exactly Entertainment* (1969). Working with various composers, and more active as a producer, he continued with such songs as: 'I've got to use my imagination' (1973), sung by Gladys *Knight; 'It's not the spotlight' (1973), sung by Rod *Stewart; the 'Theme from Mahogany' (1975)—Diana *Ross; 'Tonight I celebrate my love' (1982)—Roberta *Flack; and 'Saving all my love for you' (1985)—Whitney *Houston. He still wrote at times with King but continued to be torn between the popular song and a desire to write more deeply personal lyrics.

Gold, Ernest (*b* Vienna, 13 July 1921). Austro-American composer. Coming from a musical family, he was able to study the piano with his grandfather and the violin with his father. He began writing music when he was five and later studied at the Vienna State Academy. Always having an ambition to write film music, he emigrated to the USA in 1938 and studied harmony in New York with Otto Cesana. He earned a living by working as an accompanist and began to write songs, having an early hit with 'Practice makes perfect' in 1940, followed by 'Accidentally on purpose' (1940). In the 1940s he wrote 'Pan American Symphony', a piano concerto (1945), a string quartet, and a piano sonata. In 1945 he settled in Hollywood to work as an arranger and was soon writing scores. He studied with George *Antheil, 1946–8.

His films include: *The Girl of the Limberlost* (1945); *The Falcon's Alibi* (1946); *Smooth as Silk* (1946); *GI War Brides* (1946); *Lighthouse* (1947); *Wyoming* (1947); *Exposed* (1947); *Old Los Angeles* (1948); *Unknown World* (1951); *Willie the Kid* (1952); *Jennifer* (1953); *Man Crazy* (1953); *Karamoja* (1954); *The Other Woman* (1954); *The Naked Street* (1955); *Unidentified Flying Objects* (1956); *Edge of Hell* (1956); *Running Target* (1956); *Affair in Havana* (1957); *Man on the Prowl* (1957); *Too Much, Too Soon* (1958); *Wink of an Eye* (1958); *The Defiant Ones* (1958); *The Screaming Skull* (1958); *The True Story of the Civil War* (1958); *The Young Philadelphians* (1959); *Battle of the Coral Sea* (1959); *On the Beach* (1959); *Inherit the Wind* (1960); *Exodus* (1960)—Academy Award for main theme; *A Fever in the Blood* (1961); *The Last Sunset* (1961); *Judgment at Nuremberg* (1961); *A Child is Waiting* (1962); *Pressure Point* (1962); *It's a Mad, Mad, Mad, Mad World* (1963); *Ship of Fools* (1965); and *The Secret of Santa Vittoria* (1969). He also wrote the musical *I'm Solomon* (New York, 23 Apr. 1968). Gold was the first screen composer to have his name on Hollywood's Walk of Fame.

Gold Diggers of Broadway. Several popular films were loosely founded on a 1919 play *The Gold Digger*; first a 1919 silent film and then *Gold Diggers of Broadway*, which came from Warner Brothers in 1929 with such vaudeville names as William Bakewell (*b* 1908), Winnie Lightner (1901–71), Ann *Pennington, and Lilyan Tashman (1899–1934). It is remembered for the Joe *Burke–Al *Dubin songs which included 'Tiptoe through the tulips' and 'Painting the clouds with sunshine', both sung by Nick Lucas. *Gold Diggers of 1933* was the first of a classic series which spun out a thin story of a rich man and a chorus girl mainly as an excuse for some good songs and lavish dance scenes directed by Busby Berkeley (1895–1976). It did, however, have some fairly serious comments on the depression years, poor housing, and the difficulties of the theatre in those barren days. Dick *Powell was the star throughout, aided in the first instalment by Joan Blondell (1909–79), Ruby *Keeler, and Ginger *Rogers. The songs by Harry *Warren and Al Dubin included 'Pettin' in the park', 'Remember my forgotten man', 'The shadow waltz', 'I've got to sing a torch song', and the cynical 'We're in the money'. *Gold Diggers of 1935* had Powell as a poor student chasing a wealthy Gloria Stuart (*b* 1909) and Russian Adolphe Menjou (1890–1963) after the fortune of Alice Brady (1892–1939). The Warren–Dubin songs were 'The words are in my heart', 'I'm going shopping with you', and the classic 'Lullaby of Broadway' which was sung by Winifred Shaw (*b* 1910). *Gold Diggers of 1937* (1936) saw Dick Powell as an insurance salesman and Joan Blondell back as his romance, with Victor *Moore and Glenda Farrell (1904–71). The songs were mainly by Harold *Arlen and E. Y. *Harburg, but Warren and Dubin were brought in to provide the best two: 'With plenty of money and you' and 'All's fair in love and war'. There was also *Gold Diggers in Paris* (1938) which Dick Powell refused, to be replaced by Rudy *Vallee, who sang Warren and Dubin's 'The Latin Quarter'.

A. Hove (ed.): *Gold Diggers of 1933* (New York, 1980).

Golden Apple, The. Effective and memorable, but initially short-lived Broadway musical, based on Homer's *Iliad* and relating the marital mix-ups of Paris, Menelaus, Helen, Ulysses, and Penelope. The book and lyrics were by John *Latouche, but there was little dialogue and the action was mainly carried on in the musical numbers by Jerome *Moross, of which 'Lazy afternoon', sung by Kay Ballard (*b* 1926), became popular. The show opened at the Phoenix Theatre 11 Mar. 1954; moving to the Alvin 20 Apr. 1954; but surprisingly, in view of its warm reception, it had a short run of only 173 performances. It was revived at the Playhouse in 1962 [112 p]; and since then has continually gained status, now being bracketed with *Porgy and Bess*, as an important contribution to American 'opera'.

Golden Boy. The story, based on Clifford Odet's 1937 play, was changed to make this Broadway musical a vehicle for the talents of Sammy *Davis Jr., who played a black boxer, Joe Wellington. The music was by Charles *Strouse, lyrics by Lee *Adams. Its highlights were the expertly choreographed training and fight scenes and the show had a successful run of 569 performances on the strength of Davis's talents, opening at the Majestic Theatre 20 Oct. 1964. Davis also starred in the London production, at the Palladium 4 June 1968.

Golden discs. As much is made in the record industry of the award of Golden Discs as of arrivals in the Top 10. The fact that they are awarded by the record companies to their own artists makes them less revelatory and exciting to the public, but they faithfully reflect high sales. The idea is said to go back to 1905 when Marie Hall, a violinist who became a popular recording artist, was presented with a bracelet with seven miniature gold records; but the first actual gold disc was probably presented by RCA in Feb. 1942 to the Glenn *Miller orchestra, during the Chesterfield Radio Broadcast, when 'Chattanooga choo choo' achieved sales of 1,200,000 on the Bluebird label. The first golden disc for a country recording was given to Elton *Britt for 'There's a star-spangled banner waving somewhere' in 1944; it now rests in the *Country Music Hall of Fame. The awards have been for one million copies sold of a single or one million dollars'-worth of sales for an album. The American award was confined to sales in the USA; but British awards also took into account worldwide sales; though discs are also awarded for British-only sales of 500,000 singles and 200,000 albums. Other countries have their own scales of assessment. America also has a platinum disc for the sale of two million singles or one million copies of an album. The highest number of Golden Discs won by one artist is Elvis *Presley (65), followed by the *Beatles (59).

J. Murrells: *The Book of Golden Discs* (London, 1974).

Golden Gate Quartet. American vocal group, pioneers in the performing and recording of close-harmony black spirituals, which they did with great jazz spirit and rhythmic verve. They originated in Norfolk, Virginia, singing with the Glee Club of the Booker T. Washington High School, and soon became known throughout the state. They first broadcast while still at school and, as favourites of Mrs Eleanor Roosevelt, made several appearances at the White House. They became a popular professional group and, at the height of their fame, toured England in 1956; at which time only Orlandus Wilson (bass) remained from the original quartet, the others being Clyde Riddick, Clyde Wright (tenors), J. Caleb Ginyard (baritone); with Emel Burgess at the piano.

Goldkette, Jean (*b* Valenciennes, 18 Mar. 1899; *d* Santa Barbara, Cal., 24 Mar. 1962. French-American pianist and bandleader. He lived in Greece and Russia before going to the USA in 1911 to work as a pianist in Chicago and Detroit. He settled in Detroit and bought the Greystone Ballroom, where he formed his own band in 1924 which recorded for Victor. He worked with Russ *Morgan in 1926 as arranger, and formed another band 1926–7 which included such players as Joe *Venuti, Bix *Beiderbecke, Frankie *Trumbauer, Eddie *Lang, and the *Dorsey brothers in its ranks, and made some historic recordings. As a band booker he also handled *McKinney's Cotton Pickers and the *Casa Loma Orchestra. He was leading a band in Detroit in 1944 and was active until the 1950s, settling in California in 1961.

Goldman, Edwin Franko (*b* Louisville, Ky., 1 Jan. 1878; *d* New York, 21 Feb. 1956). American conductor and composer. He moved, with his family, to New York in 1916 where he studied music at the National Conservatory under Dvořák. In 1895 he studied cornet with Jules Levy, and from 1895 to 1905 played the trumpet in the orchestra of the Metropolitan Opera in New York, under Toscanini and Mahler among others. In 1912 he formed the New York Military Band which became known as the Goldman Band in 1918 when it began giving outdoor concerts. From 1924 they gave regular concerts on the campus of Columbia University and on the Mall in Central Park, sponsored by the Guggenheims (they were later known as the Guggenheim Memorial Concerts). He directed the band until his death, wrote more than 100 compositions, mostly marches, the best known being 'On the Mall'; and several books.

His son Richard Franko Goldman (*b* New York, 7 Dec. 1910; *d* Baltimore, 19 Jan. 1980) became associate director of the band in 1937 and took it over in 1956, retiring in 1979 when the band was dissolved. He taught at Juilliard and, from 1968, was Director of the Peabody Conservatory of Music in Baltimore; and President 1969–77. He was the author of various books on military band and other music: *The Band's Music* (1938); *Landmarks of Early American Music* (ed.) (1943; repr. 1975); *The Concert Band* (1946); *The Wind Band* (1961; repr. 1974); and a composer.

Gold Rush songs. The first discovery of gold in America was on 24 Jan. 1848 by James Wilson Marshall at a sawmill on the American River near Coloma, California. President Polk gave out the news in his message to Congress in December, starting off the great Gold Rush of 1849. As more gold was discovered along the foothills of the Sierra Nevada, and people's imaginations and greed were inflamed by newspaper reports and books such as Bayard Taylor's *El Dorado* (1850), thousands of prospectors rushed to California, many perishing *en route*, the majority of them disappointed when they got there. The population of San Francisco rose from 500 in 1840 to 34,776 in 1850. The call for entertainment (somewhat akin to that in wartime) led to a special literature of 'gold rush' songs (of which 'Clementine' is a well-known example), very often the adaptation of traditional and existing songs to new words.

S. Sherwin (ed.): *Songs of the Goldminers* (New York, 1932). E. Black and S. Robertson (eds): *The Gold Rush Song Book* (San Francisco, 1940). R. A. Dwyer and R. E. Lingenfelter (eds): *The Songs of the Gold Rush* (New York, 1964).

Goldsmith, Jerry (*b* Los Angeles, 10 Feb. 1929). American composer. He studied music at the University of South Carolina and in 1950 joined the music department of CBS's West Coast headquarters in Los Angeles. He made a special study of film music with Miklos *Rozsa, and during the 1950s composed for TV, writing theme tunes for *Playhouse 90*, *The Twilight Zone*, *Gunsmoke*, *Climax*, *Thriller*, *The Man from U.N.C.L.E*, *Dr Kildare*, and others. He became staff composer with 20th Century Fox and started composing for films from 1957, his first notable score being for *Lonely Are the Brave* (1962).

His film scores include: *Black Patch* (1957); *City of Fear* (1959); *Face of a Fugitive* (1959); *Studs Lonigan* (1960); *The Spiral Road* (1962); *Freud* (1962); *The Stripper* (1963); *The List of Adrian Messenger* (1963); *A Gathering of Eagles* (1963); *Lilies of the Field* (1963); *The Prize* (1963); *Take Her, She's Mine* (1963); *Seven Days in May* (1964); *Shock Treatment* (1964); *Fate is the Hunter* (1964); *Rio Conchos* (1964); *The Satan Bug* (1965); *In Harm's Way* (1965); *Von Ryan's Express* (1965); *Morituri* (1965); *A Patch of Blue* (1965); *Our Man Flint* (1965); *To Trap a Spy* (1966); *The Trouble With Angels* (1966); *Stagecoach* (1966); *The Blue Max* (1966); *Seconds* (1966); *The Sand Pebbles* (1966); *Warning Shot* (1966); *In Like Flint* (1967); *The Flim-Flam Man* (1967); *Hour of the Gun* (1967); *Sebastian* (1967); *Planet of the Apes* (1968); *The Detective* (1968); *Bandolero!* (1968); *The Illustrated Man* (1969); *100 Rifles* (1969); *The Chairman* (1969); *Justine* (1969); *The Ballad of Cable Hogue* (1970); *Patton* (1970); *Tora! Tora! Tora!* (1970); *Rio Lobo* (1970); *The Mephisto Waltz* (1971); *Klute* (1971); and *Wild Rovers* (1971).

Gondoliers, The, or **The King of Barataria.** The eleventh of the major *Gilbert and Sullivan collaborations, written against a background of artistic disagreement, but one of their most sparkling scores. It was first produced at the *Savoy Theatre 7 Dec. 1889 and ran for 554 performances. The cast included Rutland *Barrington, Courtice Pounds, Jessie *Bond, and Rosina *Brandram; the MD was François *Cellier. From it came such gems as 'We're called gondolieri', 'From the sunny Spanish shore', 'In enterprise of martial kind', 'When a merry maiden marries', 'Take a pair of sparkling eyes', 'Dance a cachucha', 'There lived a King', 'In a contemplative fashion', 'Small titles and orders', and 'I am a courtier grave and serious'. It was produced in New York (New Park Theatre) 7 Jan. 1890 [103p]. There was a colourful film, made in 1982.

Gonella, Nat [Nathaniel Charles] (*b* London, 7 Mar. 1908). British trumpeter, bandleader, and vocalist. He started his music career in Archie Pitt's Busby Boys band, becoming interested in jazz through hearing records of Louis *Armstrong. He played with Bob Dryden in Margate from 1928, then joined the Billy *Cotton band, and was later with Roy *Fox, Lew *Stone (with whom he formed a band-within-a-band group, the Georgians, which later became his own band), and Ray *Noble. His trumpet and vocal style clearly based on Armstrong's (individualized by his own vocal peculiarities), he moved out of the jazz field as styles changed; although there was a brief flirtation with *bebop. He appeared on the halls for some time but came back into jazz in the 1960s for a while before the pop explosion. Afterwards he lived an obscure life in Lancashire, playing in clubs and occasionally recording, until the 1970s when he had success with a recording of one of his early numbers, 'Oh Monah'.

Goodhart, Al (*b* New York, 26 Jan. 1905; *d* New York, 30 Nov. 1955). American composer. After a period as a radio announcer, he appeared in vaudeville and started writing special material for various artists. He was a member of a two-piano team playing for New York musicals and ran his own theatrical agency. Having some success with 'I apologise' (written with his regular collaborator Al *Hoffman) in 1931, he turned to full-time songwriting. He spent several years in London writing for films and the theatre, returning to the USA in 1938. His songs included: 'Sooner or later' (1931); 'Auf wiedersehen, my dear' (1931); 'Fit as a fiddle' (1932); 'She shall have music' (1936); 'I'm in a dancing mood' (1936); and 'There isn't any limit to my love' (1936).

Goodman, Al [Alfred] (*b* Nikopol, Russia, 12 Aug. 1890; *d* New York, 10 Jan. 1972). American composer, conductor, pianist, and arranger. He studied at the Peabody Conservatory in Baltimore, and then played in vaudeville and was a pianist in movie houses. After working for Earl *Carroll in 1915 he was conductor for Al *Jolson for a while, then joined the Shubert organization, conducting many famous Broadway shows in the 1920s, including the **Ziegfeld Follies* and **George White's Scandals*. He wrote scores for *Linger Longer Letty* (1919); *Cinderella on Broadway* (1920); *The Whirl of New York* (1921); *The *Passing Show of 1922*; *Lady in Ermine* (1922); **Artists and Models* (1923); *Dew Drop Inn* (1923); and *Gay Paree* (1925); his best-known song being 'When hearts are young' (with Sigmund *Romberg, 1922). He conducted the orchestra for the first part-sound film, *The *Jazz Singer* (1927), and continued as a very active conductor on radio into the early 1950s; also as musical director for many famous name shows.

Goodman, Benny [Benjamin David] (*b* Chicago, 30 May 1909; *d* New York, 13 June 1986). American clarinettist and bandleader. An accomplished classical clarinettist, he developed a strong full-toned, extremely fluid and inventive style which can already be heard on his earliest recordings and hardly changed. He was playing professionally by the age of 12, joined the band of the Chicago drummer Ben *Pollack in Los Angeles in 1925, and continued with him until 1929. His first recordings as leader were made in 1926, and he had a prolific recording period 1928–33. He worked in Broadway theatre orchestras and with various radio bands led by Shilkret, *Kostelanetz, *Whiteman, and others. In the summer of 1932 he formed a band to accompany Russ *Columbo. Recording sessions with all-star bands organized by John *Hammond built his reputation in 1933–4; and in the summer of 1934 he formed his first big band to play at Billy Rose's Music Hall. Later that year he won the coveted *Let's Dance* radio show job and was influentially heard coast-to-coast at the peak time of late Saturday night, 1934–5. The popularity of the band was confirmed at the Palomar Ballroom in Los Angeles; and suddenly they were the most important band of the *swing-crazed era that started in 1936, when Goodman himself became labelled 'The King of Swing'.

During the next few years he led one of America's top bands, innovative in mixing black and white musicians. Harry *James joined the band in 1937 to lead the great 1937–8 trumpet section of James, Ziggy *Elman, and Chris Griffin (*b* 1915); the smoothly swinging saxophone section was led by Hymie Schertzer, Jess *Stacy played fine piano, and Gene *Krupa laid down a rocking beat on drums; Fletcher *Henderson wrote many ambitious arrangements. The chamber group trio, with Goodman, Teddy *Wilson on piano, and Krupa, first recorded in 1935; vibist *Lionel Hampton joining in 1936 to make it a quartet. The band played the first jazz concert at Carnegie Hall in Jan. 1938, with sensational results.

The Goodman band continued, with many changes of personnel until 1944. James, Elman, and Krupa had left to form their own bands, but their places were taken by other jazz stars. Vocalists with the band over the years included Helen Ward (*b* 1916) 1934–6, Martha Tilton (*b* 1918) 1937–9, Mildred *Bailey 1939, Helen Forrest (*b* 1918) 1940–1, Peggy *Lee 1941–3. The band re-emerged in 1945, but by the early 1950s Goodman was no longer leading a permanent group. He travelled the world (including a tour of the USSR in 1962) into the 1970s as featured soloist with various assembled units. Goodman and the band appeared in many films including *Hollywood Hotel* (1937); *The Powers Girl* (1942); *The Gang's All Here* (1943); *Stage Door Canteen* (1943); *Sweet and Lowdown* (1944); and *Make Mine Music* (1946, sound-track); and he appeared in *A Song is Born* (1948). In 1955 a film biography of his own life, *The Benny Goodman Story*, was made with Steve Allen (*b* 1921) as Goodman and Sammy *Davis Jr. as Henderson, with Goodman and an all-star band providing the sound-track. He was composer or part-composer of innumerable jazz standards, including: 'Clarinetitis' (1928); 'After awhile' (1929); 'Stompin' at the Savoy' (1936); 'Swingtime in the Rockies' (1936); 'Life goes to a party' (1937); 'Dizzy spells' (1938); 'Don't be that way' (1938); 'Lullaby in rhythm' (1938); 'Opus' (1939); 'Boy meets girl' (1940); and 'Air mail special' (1941).

B. Goodman and I. Kolodin: *The Kingdom of Swing* (New York, 1939). D. R. Connor and W. W. Hicks: *BG—on the Record: a Bio-Discography* (New York, 1970). S. Baron: *Benny: King of Swing* (New York, 1979). D. R. Connor: *The Record of a Legend* (New York, 1984). D. R. Connor: *Benny Goodman: Listen to his Legacy* (New York, 1988). J. L. Collier: *Benny Goodman and the Swing Era* (Oxford and New York, 1990).

Good Morning, Dearie. American musical comedy with score by Jerome *Kern and book by Anne *Caldwell, first seen at the Globe Theatre, New York, 1 Nov. 1921, with Louise Groody (1897–1961), Oscar Shaw (1889–1967), and William Kent; running for 347 performances. The Kern classics that it introduced included: 'Ka-lu-a', 'Blue Danube blues', 'Good morning, dearie', and 'Look for the silver lining'.

Good News. American musical by *DeSylva, *Brown, and *Henderson, produced at the 46th Street Theatre, New York, 6 Sept. 1927, running for 551 performances. It was the first of four lively musicals by the team to have a background of popular sport, in this instance football. The plot revolved around the question of whether hero Tom Marlowe would be allowed to represent the college in spite of his poor academic results. The numbers that added sparkle to this were 'Just imagine', 'The best things in life are free', 'The Varsity drag'—memorably sung by Zelma O'Neal (*b* 1907), and 'Lucky in love'. It was filmed in 1930 with Mary Lawlor and Stanley Smith; and in 1947 with June *Allyson and Peter Lawford (*b* 1923).

Goodwin, Ron (*b* Plymouth, 17 Feb. 1925). British composer, conductor, arranger, and trumpeter. He started his working career in an insurance office, but tired of this and, music calling, became a copyist with the music-publishers Campbell, Connelly, & Co. He studied arranging with Harry Stafford, and played trumpet with Harry Gold and his Pieces of Eight, meanwhile studying in his spare time at the Guildhall School of Music. He became staff arranger for Edward Kassner and arranged for Ted *Heath, *Geraldo, and Stanley *Black; also arranging for and backing singers such as Petula *Clark and Jimmy Young. He was contracted by EMI to provide a similar service. In 1951 he was regularly broadcasting with his Concert Orchestra and making recordings of his own arrangements.

He first scored two documentary films in 1958 and was to continue in this field with more than 60 film scores written in the next 25 years, including: *Trials of Oscar Wilde* (1960)—'Café Royal theme'; *Murder She Said* (1961)—'Miss Marples theme'; *633 Squadron* (1963); *Those Magnificent Men in their Flying Machines* (1965); *Where Eagles Dare* (1968); *Monte Carlo or Bust* (1968); *The Battle of Britain* (1969); *Frenzy* (1972); establishing himself as a craftsman in composing on the grand scale for prestige films, with a style that is individual and recognizable; a master of the light touch, avoiding pomposity or over-scoring. In the early 1970s he brought popular and film music to the concert platform via guest appearances with many of the principal symphony orchestras, also appearing in Canada with the Toronto Symphony, and as a regular conductor on BBC light music programmes.

Gordon, Dexter Keith (*b* Los Angeles, 27 Feb. 1923; *d* Philadelphia, 25 Apr. 1990). American jazz tenor- and soprano-saxophonist and actor. At first he studied the clarinet, harmony, and musical theory, but had turned to the saxophone by the age of 15. In 1940 he joined the Lionel *Hampton band where he first gained recognition as a jazz musician, basing his style on players like Lester *Young, Dick Wilson (1911–41), and Herschel Evans (1909–39) rather than the all-pervading Coleman *Hawkins and his disciples, and working alongside Illinois Jacquet (*b* 1922). He left Hampton in 1943, later in the year joining the Fletcher *Henderson orchestra, and in 1944 he was with the Louis *Armstrong big band for six months. Concurrently he led his own quintet in Los Angeles which included Harry Edison (*b* 1915) and Nat 'King' *Cole. He joined the Billy *Eckstine band in New York in 1944 where he came under the influence of Dizzy *Gillespie and other modernists and gradually built himself a niche as the tenor-saxophonist of the bop movement. In the Eckstine band he played alongside Gene Ammons (1925–74), recording 'Blowin' the blues away' and, with Wardell Gray (1921–55), 'The chase' (1947) which became a jazz best-seller. In 1945 he had also recorded the bebop classics, 'Groovin' high' and 'Blue 'n' boogie', with the Dizzy Gillespie Quintet and played at the Spotlite Club with Charlie *Parker, Miles *Davis, Bud *Powell, and Max *Roach.

He returned to Los Angeles in 1946 to enter a life of club playing and drug-taking, an indulgence that greatly curtailed his activities in the 1950s through prison sentences 1952–4 and 1956–60. While he was in prison he became interested in acting and had a small part in a film. In 1960 he was in *The Connection* by Jack Gelber, a play about drug addicts, and made some of his best recordings for the Blue Note label. Unable to get a permit to work in the USA, he moved to Europe and settled in Copenhagen where he was to work for 14 years with only occasional visits to the USA. He recorded with such jazz stars as Charlie *Mingus, Ben *Webster, and Stan *Getz and played in British jazz clubs. He was semi-retired from 1983, but made a startling come-back to the limelight when he played the leading part in the film *Round Midnight* (1986) and won an Academy Award.

Gordon, Mack [Gittler, Morris] (*b* Warsaw, 21 June 1904; *d* New York, 1 Mar. 1959). American lyric-writer. He went to the USA as a boy and sang in minstrel shows for many years. Then he became a comedian on the vaudeville circuit where he met and teamed up with composer Harry *Revel, with whom he was to work until 1939. During this period he wrote for the shows *Smiles* (1930)—'Time on my hands' (*m* Vincent *Youmans); **Ziegfeld Follies* (1931); *Everybody's Welcome* (1931); and for the films *Song of Love* (1929); *Pointed Heels* (1929); *Swing High* (1930); *Broadway through a Keyhole* (1933); *Shoot the Works* (1934)—'With my eyes wide open; *Sitting Pretty* (1934)—'Did you ever see a dream walking', 'You're such a comfort to me'; *We're Not Dressing* (1934); *The Gay Divorcée* (1934); *She Loves Me Not* (1934); *College Rhythm* (1934)—'Stay as sweet as you are' (*m* Ray *Noble); *Love in Bloom* (1935)—'Here comes cookie', 'My heart is an open book'; *Two for Tonight* (1935)—'Without a word of warning'; *Paris in Spring* (1935); *Collegiate* (1936); *Poor Little Rich Girl* (1936); *Stowaway* (1936); *Wake Up and Live* (1937); *Head Over Heels in Love* (1937); *You Can't Have Everything* (1937); *In Old Chicago* (1938); *Thanks for Everything* (1938); *Love Finds Andy Hardy* (1938); *My Lucky Star* (1938); *Sally, Irene and Mary* (1938); *Rebecca of Sunnybrook Farm* (1938); and *Rose of Washington Square* (1939).

With Harry *Warren he wrote songs for: *Down Argentine Way* (1940); *Tin Pan Alley* (1940); *That Night in Rio* (1941)—'Chica chica boom chic', 'I, yi, yi, yi, yi, I like you very much'; *The Great American Broadcast* (1941); *Weekend in Havana* (1941); *Sun Valley Serenade* (1941)—'Chattanooga choo choo'; *Orchestra Wives* (1942)—'Serenade in blue', 'I got a gal in Kalamazoo'; *Springtime in the Rockies* (1942); *Iceland* (1942); *Sweet Rosie O'Grady* (1943); *Hello, Frisco, Hello* (1943)—'You'll never know'; *Diamond Horseshoe* (1945); *Summer Stock* (1950); and many others with various composers.

Gordy, Berry, Jr. (*b* Detroit, 28 Nov. 1929). American record producer. A significant figure in the *rhythm 'n' blues and *soul scene, he was the inspirer of the Motown sound and the vital recordings that emanated from the motor town of Detroit. After service in the US Army he worked for a while in a car factory and began writing songs. He founded the Motown recording enterprise in 1959, making a start by introducing Stevie *Wonder who remained one of his major performers. Others he attracted were Smokey *Robinson (who later joined the board of directors), the Miracles, Mary Wells, the *Supremes, Gladys *Knight, Diana *Ross, Marvin *Gaye, and the *Jackson Five, to name but a few among the galaxy of black talent recorded by Motown. The impact and popularity of these artists finally integrated black music into the popular music scene. Gordy moved from Detroit in 1967 to operate from Los Angeles.

Gorney, Jay [Daniel Jason] (*b* Bialystok, Russia, 12 Dec. 1896; *d* New York, 14 June 1990). American composer, author, and producer. He went to the USA as a child in 1906 and showed early musical promise, studying music at the University of Michigan where he formed a student jazz band. He led a navy band during the First World War and afterwards took a law degree. In 1923 he had a song interpolated in the score of *The Dancing Girl* and continued to contribute to shows such as *Vogues of 1924*, *Top-Hole* (1924); **Greenwich Village Follies* (1924); *Sweetheart Time* (1926); *Merry-go-round* (1927); *Earl Carroll's Sketchbook* (1929); **Ziegfeld Follies* (1931); *Shoot the Works* (1931); and **Americana* (1932)—including his biggest hit, 'Brother, can you spare a dime?', which became a symbol of the depression years. He wrote the scores of *Meet the People* (1940) which set a number of people like June Haver (*b* 1926), Jan Clayton (*b* 1917), and Nanette Fabray (*b* 1920) on their way; *Heaven on Earth* (1948)—'Home is where the heart is'; and *Touch and Go* (1949).

He was head of music for Paramount's New York studios 1929–30, then went to Hollywood in 1933 to work for 20th Century Fox and had a hand in the discovery of Shirley *Temple; later he worked as a producer for Columbia. He wrote songs for numerous films between 1929 and 1938 with an occasional hit such as 'You're my thrill' in *Stand Up and Cheer* (1934), but failed to produce much of a durable character. After the Second World War he practised law in Detroit.

Gospel. The oppressive nature of the years of slavery led the black people of America to find their spiritual uplift and salvation in fundamental religious beliefs based on a literal interpretation of the Bible and the Gospels; especially where there was a promise of hope and escape from bondage. Building on the foundations provided by the Nonconformist hymns of Isaac Watts and other writers, brought over from England, a repertoire of gospel songs and *spirituals evolved. During the 19th century, when there was considerable movement of blacks from the slave-owning South to the more liberal North by furtive 'underground' means, such songs as 'Crossing the Jordan' and 'Going to the Promised Land' took on a double significance. Spirituals began to impinge on the outside world in the 1870s through the national, and subsequent international, tours of the Fisk *Jubilee Singers, who diluted such songs as 'Swing low, sweet chariot', 'Nobody knows the trouble I've seen' and 'Shout all over God's Heaven' for white ears, but still made a strong enough impact to help the spiritual to gain worldwide recognition. This was the tradition continued in the work of later respected professional singers such as Paul *Robeson and Marian *Anderson.

But the commercial spiritual was only a pale shadow of the fervent, jazz-flavoured singing that went on in the black churches and it was not until the time was properly ripe for the emergence of true gospel music in the 1930s that the world began to hear the real thing. Recordings made in black churches revealed the hot gospelling tones of the Revd J. M. Gates and his brethren and genuine gospel singers like Arizona Dranes and Blind Willie Johnson were recorded. The polished and infectiously rhythmic performances of the *Golden Gate Quartet and similar units led to an appreciation of the gospel song as entertainment and the emergence of such performers as Thomas A. *Dorsey (generally regarded as the Father of Gospel Music); Mahalia *Jackson (the Gospel Queen) and Sister Rosetta *Tharpe, who mingled the art of gospel and blues in recordings such as 'This train'; Marie Knight; Marian Williams; and Brother John Sellers (*b* 1924). The compositions of Thomas A. Dorsey (known secularly as Georgia Tom) were as influential in the 1930s as the hymns of Isaac Watts had been two centuries earlier.

Gospel music emerged at first as a relation of jazz and was mainly appreciated in jazz circles. But in the mid-1940s Gospel Song became an entertainment category in its own right, with new small record labels such as Apollo, King, and Specialty issuing gospel material, radio programmes devoted to it, and the rise of specialist groups like the Famous Ward Singers and Albertina Walker's Caravans. Inspired by Clara Ward (1924–73) and other pioneers, a new generation of pop gospel artists such as Aretha *Franklin emerged, most of them coming from a religious family background with early singing experience in church choirs. The unaccompanied singing groups like the Soul Stirrers with Sam Cooke led to the *Temptations and James *Brown. Gospel music became its recognizable self, the spiritual with a jazz rhythm and the spirit of the blues. Popular gospel performers are now as likely to be white as black. The commercialized strain of black gospel music that put Motown on the map is now labelled *soul.

R. M. W. Dixon and J. Godrich: *Blues and Gospel Records 1902–42* (London, 1942). J. Burt and D. Allen: *The History of Gospel Music* (Nashville, 1971). T. Heilbut: *The Gospel Sound* (New York, 1971). R. Anderson and G. North: *Gospel Music Encyclopedia* (New York, 1979).

Gottschalk, Louis Moreau (*b* New Orleans, 8 May 1829; *d* Rio de Janeiro, 18 Dec. 1869). American composer and pianist. An extraordinary figure in American music who uniquely, for his day, bridged the worlds of established classical music and the emerging strains of popular music. In the first instance he was a showman pianist in the Franz Liszt mould and when not writing in his very individual *Creole vein he would slip back (as *Foster and *Joplin did later) to the platitudes of the Victorian drawing-room in such pieces as 'The dying poet'; even here he was a distinctive melodist. A revealing chapter on Gottschalk in *Music and Musicians in Early America* (1964) by Irving Lowens is entitled 'Our First Matinee Idol'. Using his immense drawing power as such, Gottschalk could also write and perform his other forward-looking music whose character gives it an impression of being more recent than it actually was. Jazz was not to make its impression until the 20th century was under way; ragtime had its practical beginnings in the 1890s; and Latin American strains were creeping into North American music at about the same time. Yet in Gottschalk we find portents of all these styles some 50 years earlier. There is a strong Creole element, as might be expected from a native of New Orleans, mingling with West Indian, Cuban, and Spanish strains. They combine remarkably to produce an orchestral work like 'Night in the Tropics' that might well have been written by Copland or Gershwin, with decades of such music behind them. A clear ragtime element is to be found in the syncopated phrases of 'Bamboula', 'Le bananier', and 'The banjo'—all written between 1844 and 1854. It is possible that Joplin and other ragtime composers found some of the inspiration for their creations here. The powerful mixture that is found in 'Heliotrope bouquet' (partly by the Creole Louis *Chauvin, partly by *Joplin) is very close to Gottschalk in spirit.

Our fragmentary knowledge of the long incubatory history of Afro-American music perhaps makes Gottschalk seem more of a prophet than he actually was. Presumably he was using musical features and flavours that were current in unrecorded popular music of the time. We know that he was fascinated as a boy by the slave gatherings in Congo Square, New Orleans, where he came across the bamboula and other dances. To the happy accident of having been born in New Orleans, he added the experiences of music-making in Europe, including Spain, and visits to the West Indies, Cuba, and South America.

He died in Rio de Janeiro in 1869, at only 40, a spent force. But he lived long enough to create plenty of music that used popular ethnic elements in a way that was not yet open to their originators. His art confirms that elements of jazz and ragtime were around well before they fully emerged. His 'Bamboula' has been described as 'one of the remarkable piano pieces of the nineteenth century'. It is also remarkable that his Victorian public seemed to like its exotic flavours and clamoured for more. Audiences who would have been shocked to find a black performer before them were delighted by the sensuous rhythms and impertinent tunes that Gottschalk purveyed. Strains that they may have heard drifting through the warm air of a summer night from a distant plantation, or through their shutters from Congo Square, were acceptable when played at the piano by a white virtuoso in tails. Along with the *minstrel shows and Stephen Foster, Gottschalk prepared America for its musical revolution; meanwhile offering some fascinating music that itself has only recently been rediscovered in various collections of his piano music and recordings of his works.

O. Hensel: *Life and Letters of Louis Moreau Gottschalk* (Boston, 1870). C. Gottschalk (ed.): *Notes of a Pianist* (Philadelphia, 1881; repr. New York, 1964). V. Loggins: *Where the World Ends: the Life of Louis Moreau Gottschalk* (Baton Rouge, 1958).

Music: R. Jackson (ed.): *Piano Music of Louis Moreau Gottschalk* [26 pieces] (New York, 1974).

Gould, Morton (*b* Richmond Hill, NY, 10 Dec. 1913). American composer, arranger, pianist, and conductor of mixed Austrian and Russian parentage. He studied music at New York University, then played in jazz bands and was staff pianist at Radio City Music Hall 1931–2. He was director of the radio series 'Music for Today' 1934–42 and from 1943 musical director of the CBS 'Chrysler Hour'. He bridged the musical worlds with his 'American symphonette No. 1' (1933) and 'Chorale and fugue in jazz' (1934); and had a popular hit with his 'Pavane' from 'American symphonette No. 3' (1938). He continued to integrate popular music into extended forms in such works as 'Latin-American symphonette' (1940); 'Spirituals' (1941); 'A Lincoln legend' (1941); 'Cowboy rhapsody' (1943); 'Fall River Legend' (1945); to 'American Ballads' (1976). For the theatre he wrote *Billion Dollar Baby* (1945) and *Arms and the Girl* (1950); and he wrote many film scores, including: *Ring of Steel* (1941); *Delightfully Dangerous* (1945); *San Francisco Conference* (1946); *Windjammer* (1948); and *Cinerama Holiday* (1955).

Gow, Nathaniel (*b* Inver, nr. Dunkeld, 28 May 1763; *d* Edinburgh, 19 Jan. 1831). Scottish violinist, arranger, and music-publisher, the fourth son of Niel *Gow. He started playing the trumpet in various bands, but then changed to violin. After some academic training he became leader of the Edinburgh Concerts in 1791. He was a partner in a music-publishing business in Edinburgh 1796–1813, gave it up for a time, but returned to it in partnership with his son Niel Gow Jr. (see below) until 1827 when he went bankrupt. He published many of his father's works in *The Beauties of Niel Gow* (1819); also *The Vocal Melodies of Scotland* (1820) and numerous collections of dances. He led a society band for many years, and was the composer of 'Caller herrin'', 'Bothwell Castle', and many other songs.

Gow, Niel (*b* Strathband, Perthshire, 22 Mar. 1727; *d* Inver, 1 Mar. 1807). Scottish violinist and composer. He started to earn his living playing the violin at social gatherings in Edinburgh and London, becoming an expert at the Scottish reel and other dances. He married twice and had large families, starting a Gow dynasty that might be compared to the *Strauss dynasty of Vienna. He did much to establish many of the set dances and collected and arranged traditional tunes as well as writing many of his own strathspeys and reels. Collections were published under his name in 1784, 1788, 1792, 1800, 1809, and 1822. Mainly self-taught, his fame as a fiddler spread far abroad together with many legends concerning his eccentric behaviour. He also received the credit for many tunes that were not actually his own. Various members of his family continued his work in regularly published 'Repositories' of Scots strathspeys and reels.

Other descendants who became particularly well-known as fiddlers and musicians were William Gow (1751–91), Andrew Gow (1760–1803), Nathaniel *Gow, and John Gow (1764–1826), all composers of dances and songs. Nathaniel's son Niel Gow Jr. (1795–1823) partnered his father in the music business and was a renowned collector and editor. He is remembered for his songs 'Bonnie Prince Charlie' and 'Flora Macdonald's lament' and for his settings of various poems by James Hogg; but he died young before fulfilling his great promise.

G. S. Emmerson: *Rantin' Pipe and Tremblin' String: a History of Scottish Dance Music* (London, 1971).

Grable, Betty [Grasle, Ruth Elizabeth] (*b* St Louis, Mo., 18 Dec. 1918; *d* Santa Monica, Calif., 3 July 1973). American actress, singer, and dancer. She made her mark in the musical **DuBarry Was a Lady* (1939). She came into films as a successor to Alice *Faye, was famous for her lovely legs as well as her vivacious acting, and sang and danced her way through almost 50 musical films of very varying quality. From chorus and minor parts in the 1930s she emerged in such titles as **Follow the Fleet* (1936); *College Swing* (1938); *Down Argentine Way* (1940)—singing 'Down Argentina way'; *Tin Pan Alley* (1940); *Moon over Miami* (1941); *Song of the Islands* (1942); *Springtime in the Rockies* (1942); *Coney Island* (1943); *Sweet Rosie O'Grady* (1943)—'My heart tells me'; *Four Jills in a Jeep* (1944); *Pin-Up Girl* (1944); *Diamond Horseshoe* (1945); *The Dolly Sisters* (1945)—'I can't begin to tell you'; *The Shocking Miss Pilgrim* (1947)—'Changing my tune', 'For you, for me, for evermore'; *Mother Wore Tights* (1945)—'You do'; *That Lady in Ermine* (1948); *When My Baby Smiles at Me* (1948); *My Blue Heaven* (1950); *Call Me Mister* (1951); *The Farmer Takes a Wife* (1953); and *Three for the Show* (1955). She was married to Jackie Coogan and Harry *James.

D. Warren: *Betty Grable: the Reluctant Movie Queen* (New York, 1981).

Gräfin Dubarry. Operetta in three acts with score by Karl *Millöcker, book by F. Zell (Camillo Walzel) and Richard *Genée, produced in Vienna (Theater an der Wien) 31 Oct. 1879. It had a short run but was destined to find its way in a new version, *Die Dubarry*, with the music adapted and supplemented by Theo Mackeben, produced at the Admiralspalast Theater, Berlin, in 1931 with Gitta Alpar as the Countess. It was this version, with English words by Rowland Leigh and Desmond Carter, that came to His Majesty's Theatre, London, 14 Apr. 1932, with Anny Ahlers and Heddle Nash in the leading roles, achieving a run of 397 performances. It had less success in New York in 1932 with Grace *Moore and William Hain [87p].

The story is of a calculating little shop girl called Jeanne who becomes a singer, spurns an artist lover, and ends up as the Countess Dubarry.

Anny Ahlers (1906–33) was taken ill during the London production in Sept. 1932, returning to the cast at the end of the month to a great reception. In Feb. 1933 she was taken ill again and died in a nursing-home on 28 March. She was a great favourite in Vienna and had a personal triumph in *The Dubarry* in London.

Gräfin Mariza. Operetta in three acts with score by Emmerich *Kálmán, book by Julius Brammer and Alfred Grünwald, produced in Vienna (Theater an der Wien) 28 Feb. 1924, with Hubert Marischka and Betty Fischer, and running for 396 performances. It began its international career at the Shubert Theatre, New York, 18 Sept. 1926 as *Countess Maritza*, with English words by Harry B. *Smith; Yvonne D'Arle and Walter Woolf played the leading roles [321p]. It was not seen in London until it was produced at the Palace Theatre 6 July 1938, with Marie Lossef and John Garrick.

The story is of the turbulent love affair between the young heiress the Countess Maritza and her bailiff Bela Török (who, of course, is Count Tassilo Endrödy-Wittemberg in disguise). Avoiding the wily Baron Zsupan, she finds her true love in the end. Kálmán's Hungarian background comes out strongly in such songs as the ever-popular 'Komm' Zigány' ('Play, gypsy!'); with others in Viennese vein.

Gráf von Luxemburg, Der. Operetta in three acts with score by Franz *Lehár and book by A. M. Willner and Robert Bodanzky, produced in Vienna (Theater an der Wien) 12 Nov. 1909, with Otto Storm, Fräulein von Ligety, Louise Kartousch, and Max Pallenberg in the leading roles. It ran for an initial 299 performances in Vienna before slipping into the international operetta repertoire, a lesser manifestation of Lehár's art than *The *Merry Widow*, but full of good melodies—'Ich bin verliebt', 'Mädel klein, Mädel fein', and the waltz-song 'Bist du's, lachendes Glück' among them.

The story is of René, the young Count who has run through a fortune and is now a struggling artist, passing through his involved love affair with the famous Parisian singer Angèle Didier and his restoration to wealth and a happy marriage; as well as the affairs of other characters involved. It came to *Daly's Theatre, London (as *The Count of Luxembourg*), 20 May 1911, with English words by Basil *Hood and Adrian *Ross; Lily *Elsie, Bertram Wallis, Huntley Wright, Willie Warde, and W. H. *Berry were in the cast [340p]. It was seen in New York at the New Amsterdam Theatre, 16 Sept. 1912 [120p]. A new version by Wolf Völker was staged in Berlin in 1937.

Graham, Charles (*d* New York, 1899). American composer. Following the great success of Charles K. *Harris's 'After the ball', Graham followed almost identical lines to produce his great hit of 1893, 'Two little girls in blue', which was made popular by Lily Burnand. Previously he had written 'If the waters could speak as they flow' (1886); 'The bank has failed today' (1890); 'In friendship's name' (1891); and followed it with 'The picture that is turned to the wall' (1894) and 'My dad's the engineer' ('Daddy's on the engine') (1805). Few details are known about Graham's life, except that he made very little out of his songs and died a penniless alcoholic in Bellevue Hospital, New York, leaving behind a poverty-stricken family.

Grain, Corney [Corney, Richard] (*b* 1844; *d* London, 16 Mar. 1895). British entertainer, author, and composer. He read law 1863–5 and was called to the Bar in 1866; but became more interested in the theatre, having appeared in his first play in 1865. He soon became popular as a comic entertainer, mainly singing his own songs at the piano. Having deserted the law completely, he joined the Thomas German *Reed troupe in 1870 and was to spend the rest of his short career in their famous presentations at the Gallery of Illustration and St George's Hall. He was once acclaimed as the funniest man on the London stage. He wrote about 50 sketches for the German Reeds, and scores for *£100 Reward* (1879); *A Flying Visit* (1880); *All at Sea* (1881); *That Dreadful Boy* (1882); *A Terrible Fright* (1865); and his best musical piece, *Music à la Mode* (1895); and many songs to his own words and those of other writers such as Arthur Law, including 'The first cigar' (1893).

Thomas German Reed died in 1888 and the entertainments were continued by his son Alfred who became Grain's closest friend. The last presentation they appeared in together was *Melodramania* (1884) with music by Walter *Slaughter. Grain, a massive, lumbering man, appeared in hilarious guise as a jockey. On 10 Mar. 1895, Alfred German Reed died suddenly and the shock made Grain so ill that he became deaf and died on 16 March. Mrs German Reed (widow of Thomas) died on the 21st, thus bringing the history of these famous entertainments to an abrupt end.

C. Grain: *Corney Grain: by Himself* (London, 1883).
D. Williamson: *The German Reeds and Corney Grain: Records and Reminiscences* (London, 1895).

Grainer, Ron (*b* Atherton, Queensland, 11 Aug. 1922; *d* London, 1981). Australian composer. He studied music in Brisbane and Sydney, then went to England where he soon established a reputation as a writer of memorable theme tunes and songs for many famous TV series, including *Maigret*; *Dr Who*; *Steptoe and Son*; *The Flying Swan*; *Not So Much a Programme, More a Way of Life*; *The Old Curiosity Shop*; *That Was the Week That Was*; and *Songs for Europe*; all noted for their inventive orchestration. For the theatre he wrote the long-running **Robert and Elizabeth* (1964); *On the Level* (1966); and *Sing a Rude Song* (1970); and scores for many films, including: *Some People* (1962); *Station Six Sahara* (1962); *The Finest Hours* (1964); *The Moon Spinners* (1964); and *Nothing but the Best* (1964).

Grammy Awards. Awards inaugurated in the USA by the National Academy of Recording Arts and Sciences (founded 1957) in 1958, given for artistic achievement in writing, performing, musicianship, and engineering in the field of recording.

Gramophone, Phonograph. The discovery that sound creates vibrations and therefore vibrations create sound led to much early speculation as to how and when man would be able to record sound and what benefits would arise, before it was actually done by Thomas Alva Edison (1847–

1931). Choosing the immortal words 'Mary had a little lamb', on 15 Aug. 1877 he spoke into the horn of a hand-cranked phonograph (i.e. speaking machine) and cut wavy grooves into tinfoil wrapped round a cylinder, which he was then able to play back with recognizable results. Originally intended as a business aid, the phonograph was soon to revolutionize the spread of music and other aural entertainments. Edison patented his invention in 1878 and the wax cylinder was patented by Bell & Tainter in 1886. In 1888 the German inventor Emile Berliner (1851–1929) patented the flat disc which was to be the main means of reproduction until the tape was developed. Cylinders went completely out of use only in 1929, although the wax disc had been firmly estalished as the most practical medium by *c*.1899.

The refinements that followed each helped to make the gramophone a satisfying and effective means of sound communication. Clockwork-driven motors were introduced in 1896; the first unbreakable shellac disc was claimed in 1903 and the first 12-inch disc was issued that year; the speed of 78 revolutions per minute was established by *c*.1918; and the biggest advance in terms of sound quality came in 1925, when electrical recording replaced the old acoustic methods. The first long-playing record was made by Columbia records in 1948 and was universally established at $33\frac{1}{3}$ rpm by 1950, the year that Decca Records first issued them in Britain. The 45 rpm 7-inch disc was introduced in 1949 and the 45 rpm extended play (EP) in 1950 by EMI as a hoped-for rival to the LP. The first stereophonic recordings were sold in 1958 in the USA. The reel-to-reel tape recorder had been used by enthusiasts in the late 1940s but the first serious commercial rival to the disc came when Philips Records launched the musicassette at the Berlin Radio Show in 1965—since when, by virtue of its wide use in car radios and personal stereos, the cassette has become the biggest selling medium of all. Digital recording and the compact digital disc (CD) came along to upset the long-established analogue methods in the 1980s; and a disc which combined hi-fi sound and vision (CD/Video) was introduced in 1989.

Whereas, in pre-gramophone days, musical-hall and vaudeville artists would have to travel to theatres all over the country to be heard by their public (which at least permitted them to use the same material over and over again), the gramophone was soon to bring their voices right into the home. The first recordings by anyone of repute would have been made *c*.1888 and the first record catalogue was issued by the Columbia Record Company in 1891. By 1897 the record industry was becoming viably commercialized with Fred Gaisberg opening the first professional recording studio in Philadelphia, where the first retail record shop was also opened that year. In 1897 the first dance-band recordings were issued by the *Sousa band. The Hotel Cecil Orchestra made some dance records in 1898 and that year saw many pioneering efforts in the UK with the first male vocalist to record being Ted Hanley singing 'They've all gone in for them' and the first female vocalist Syria Lamont singing 'Comin' through the rye'. The first genuine musical-hall recording is credited to George Lashwood, while Scott Russell was the first to record excerpts from musical comedies.

After that things moved fast, though the limitations of the current recording techniques confined the scope of the entertainment provided. The celebrated Neapolitan tenor Enrico Caruso (1873–1921) made his first record for the Gramophone Company in Milan in 1901 and in 1903 made a version of 'Vesti la giubba' ('On with the motley') from *I Pagliacci* (Leoncavallo), which was to become the first million-selling disc. During his lifetime Caruso was to earn more than $3,500,000 in royalties on his recordings; and no one needed convincing any more that this was a business of the future. The first popular recording to achieve the same success was 'The preacher and the bear' recorded by Arthur Collins in 1905 which, up to 1925, had sold more than any other disc in that period. Other early million-sellers were 'Laughing song' recorded by Burt Shepard (1910); 'Ragging the baby to sleep' (Al *Jolson, 1912); 'The Spaniard that blighted my life' (Al Jolson, 1913); the first best-selling dialogue disc 'Cohen on the telephone' (Joe Hayman, 1914); 'Carry me back to old Virginny' (Alma Gluck, 1915); and 'Just a baby's prayer at twilight' (Henry Burr, 1918). It has been said that the three minutes or so duration of a performance imposed by the 78 rpm disc was something of a blessing and it is difficult to refute the argument in view of some of the over-extended performances that have been perpetrated on LP; particularly in the field of jazz.

The first jazz record issued was the RCA Victor recording of the *Original Dixieland Jazz Band's 'Livery stable blues'/'Original Dixieland one-step' in Feb. 1917. The first black artist to achieve hit status was Mamie *Smith with 'Crazy blues' in 1920, the true beginnings of the *race record boom and the first seeds of *rhythm 'n' blues leading to the pop music years. Although the record industry was to run into serious financial trouble in the depression years, it managed to survive and by the late 1930s was booming. A supreme example of an artist created by records (and publicized by the talkies) was Bing *Crosby who had sold 200,000,000 records by 1960, including what for many years was the best-selling record of all: 'White Christmas' (1942).

R. Gellatt: *The Fabulous Phonograph* (New York, 1955). O. Read and W. L. Welch: *From Tin Foil to Stereo: Evolution of the Phonograph* (Indianapolis, 1959). V. Chew: *Talking Machines (1887–1914)* (London, 1967). P. Gammond and R. Horricks (eds): *The Music Goes Round and Round: a Cool Look at the Record Industry* (London, 1980). R. and C. Dearling and B. Rust: *The Guinness Book of Recorded Sound* (Enfield, 1984).

Grande-Duchesse de Gérolstein, La. Opéra-bouffe in three acts with music by Jacques *Offenbach, first produced at Les Variétés, Paris, 12 Apr. 1867, with book by Henri Meilhac and Ludovic *Halévy, one of Offenbach's most sparkling and satirical scores. The star of the show was Hortense Schneider (1830–1920), who became so identified with the part that when she rode in her carriage through Paris she was everywhere deferred to as the 'Grande-Duchesse'.

The Duchess has a crush on the humble soldier Fritz whom she promotes in quick stages to the rank of Commander-in-Chief, to the frustration and anger of Baron Puck and General Boum. Fritz, however, still loves the beautiful Wanda. Equally rapid demotion follows this discovery, with the Duchess now betrothed to the noble Prince Paul, though her eye has already been seen to rove towards another handsome young soldier. The Duchess is well supplied with such songs as 'Ah! que j'aime les militaires', 'Voici le sabre de mon père', and 'Dites-lui qu'on l'a remarqué'. It was seen in Vienna (Theater an der Wien) in 1867 and in London (Covent Garden) in the same year. Lilian *Russell starred in it in New York and created a new vogue for French operetta; since when it has been repeatedly revived and occasionally recorded.

Grand Funk. American *heavy metal rock group formed in 1968 from ex-members of bands in the Michigan area, known for some time as Grand Funk Railroad. The original members were Mark Farmer (vocal and guitar), Mel Schacher (bass), and Don Brewer (drums), with Terry Knight (who had conceived the group) acting as business manager. They made their mark at the Atlanta Pop Festival in 1969 with their sense-numbingly loud and driving rock style and were signed up by Capitol Records. They had hits with their first album *On Time* (1970) and two singles that year—'Time machine' and 'Mr Limousine driver'. Their popularity continued among the lovers of volume and they were a great live attraction in such large venues as the Shea Stadium in New York. The band parted from Terry Knight in 1971 and tried to move towards a more artistic image, as heard in their No. 1 hits 'We're an American band' in 1973 and 'Locomotion' in 1974. An album produced by Frank *Zappa, *Good Singin' Good Playin'* (1976), marked their fall from favour and the group was disbanded in that year. They re-formed in 1981 to make the album *Grand Funk Lives*, but disbanded again in 1983.

Grand Ole Opry. Pioneer *hillbilly WSM radio programme originally broadcast from the Ryman Auditorium in Nashville, Tennessee, from 1925, founded by George Dewey Hay (1895–1968), one of the earliest 'barn dance' shows. It has continued to be the international showcase for Country and Western music and first made the world aware of such names as Dave *Macon, Minnie Pearl, Red *Foley, Hank *Williams, and Roy *Acuff, to mention but a few. The generally packed Grand Ole Opry House held 3500 and the show was syndicated to more than 30 million listeners every Saturday night. Although the financial rewards have always been minimal, every country artist needs the accolade of having been heard at the Grand Ole Opry. The old-fashioned Ryman Auditorium was abandoned in 1974 in favour of an auditorium in Opryland on the outskirts of Nashville.

J. Hurst: *Nashville's Grand 'Ole Opry* (New York, 1975).

Grand Street Follies, The. Pioneering series of American intimate revues which inspired such successors as the **Garrick Gaieties, The *Little Show*, and **Pins and Needles*. It started at the small Neighborhood Playhouse in 1922 with book written by Agnes Morgan, and Albert Carroll heading the cast. The 1926 version had contributions by the up-and-coming Arthur *Schwartz, his first efforts for the Broadway stage. A notable addition to the cast in 1928 and 1929 was the tap-dancer James *Cagney.

Granz, Norman (*b* Los Angeles, 6 Aug. 1918). American producer and impresario. Originally a film editor with MGM, just before serving in the army, 1941–4, he started to promote jazz concerts in Los Angeles. After the war he organized a concert at the Philharmonic Auditorium in Los Angeles, hence the now familiar name of Jazz at the Philharmonic, the series in which he proved to himself and the world that there was 'money to be made in good jazz'. He firmly pursued a non-racial policy and refused to present JATP before segregated audiences. His show toured in the USA in 1945 and he formed his own record label, Clef, in 1951 which had the rights to all the JATP performances and performers, followed by Verve, which was one of the leading jazz labels of the 1950s and 1960s. He specialized in recording *mainstream musicians, and is notably remembered for his recordings of Art *Tatum and the series of 'Songbooks' with Ella *Fitzgerald. But he also gave good coverage to Dizzy *Gillespie. European tours began in the late 1950s and first came to Britain in 1958. He founded the Pablo label in the early 1970s.

Grappelli, Stéphane [Grappelly] (*b* Paris, 26 Jan. 1908). French jazz violinist. He trained as a classical musician but turned to jazz and became known in 1934 as the co-leader, with gypsy guitarist Django *Reinhardt, of the Quintette du Hot Club de France. His inventive and dextrous improvisations in the 'hot jazz' style were recognized as the first contributions to jazz that were basically European and owed little to the American brand. He continued playing and recording into his eighties, including some recordings in partnership with the classical violinist Yehudi Menuhin.

G. Smith: *Stephane Grappelli* (London, 1967).

Grateful Dead. Influential American rock band that emerged from various groups on the San Francisco scene of the mid-1960s. It was formed in 1966 with Jerry Garcia (*b* 1942) (guitar), Phil Lesh (*b* 1940) (bass), Ron 'Pigpen' McKernan (1945–73) (keyboards), Bob Weir (*b* 1947) (guitar), Bill Kreutzmann (*b* 1946) (drums), with Robert Hunter as resident lyricist. It became a fairly large travelling unit, with impeccable sound equipment and a very personal style which was not fully exploited on their first albums, *Grateful Dead* (1967), *Anthem of the Sun* (1968), and *Aoxomoxoa* (1969), but was glimpsed on *Live Dead* (1970). In later recordings they became more aware of studio requirements and tightened up their presentation, still maintaining freedom of expression but now with more country-rock-style discipline, Hunter, at the same time, providing simpler and more coherent lyrics. This was all heard on the albums *Workingman's Dead* and *American Beauty* in 1970. The personnel changed for various reasons, including the sad death of 'Pigpen' in 1973 from a liver disease; but they have continued to be a leading voice in the San Franciscan rock scene and have constantly inspired others with their free-form jamming which veers between the aimless and the meaningful. They attracted a gang of 'groupies' who follow the band around.

H. Harrison: *The Dead Book: a Social History of the Grateful Dead* (New York, 1973; as *The Grateful Dead*, London, 1975). H. Harrison: *The Dead* (Millbrae, Calif., 1976).

Gray, Dolores (*b* Chicago, 7 June 1924). American actress and singer. In the early part of her career she was a dance-band vocalist. She was a lusty performer well suited to the part of Annie Oakley in Irving *Berlin's **Annie Get Your Gun* (1947), the major role in her career, which she sang in the London production. She was also in *Seven Lively Arts* (1944); *Are You With It?* (1945); *Sweet Bye and Bye* (1946); *Two on the Aisle* (1951); **Destry Rides Again* (1959); *Sherry!* (1967); the London productions of **Gypsy* (1973); and **Follies* (1987).

Gray, Jerry [Graziano, Jerry] (*b* East Boston, Mass., 3 July 1915; *d* Dallas, 10 Aug. 1976). American composer, arranger, bandleader, violinist, and accordionist. He took up music at an early age and appeared as soloist and leader with the Boston Junior Symphony Orchestra at 13. Later he became more interested in popular music and earned a reputation as one of the few jazz accordionists. He was the arranger for Artie *Shaw's first little band in 1936 and played in the string quartet which it featured. A year or two later he helped to formulate the style of the better-known Shaw band, his arrangement of 'Begin the beguine' helping to establish its identity.

Joining Glenn *Miller as full-time arranger, he contributed many of the band's most popular arrangements and compositions such as 'Pennsylvania 6-5000' (1940) and 'String of pearls' (1942). He continued with Miller in the Army Air Force Orchestra and assumed its leadership when Miller was killed in 1944. After the war he led his own radio orchestra and had his own radio show (1946–52), returning to the limelight when the Miller sound became popular again in the 1950s, reviving the old scores in the Miller style. Later he went to Hollywood to work for Warner Brothers and as MD of the Bob *Crosby radio show.

Grayson, Kathryn [Hedrick, Zelma Kathryn Elizabeth] (*b* Winson-Salem, NC, 9 Feb. 1922). American actress and singer. A fine and well-endowed singer with operatic potential, who came along as a successor to Jeanette *MacDonald in many MGM musicals. She appeared in **Rio Rita* (1942); *Seven Sweethearts* (1942); with Gene *Kelly in *Thousands Cheer* (1943) and *Anchors Aweigh* (1945); **Ziegfeld Follies* (1946); *Two Sisters from Boston* (1946); *Till the Clouds Roll By* (1946); with Frank *Sinatra in *It Happened in Brooklyn* (1947) and *The Kissing Bandit* (1948); with Mario *Lanza in *That Midnight Kiss* (1949), *The Toast of New Orleans* (1950)—'Be my love', and *Lovely to Look At* (1952); with Howard *Keel in **Show Boat* (1951) and **Kiss Me, Kate* (1953); *So This is Love* (1953), where she played the part of Grace *Moore; and *The *Vagabond King* (1956).

Grease. American rock musical with music, lyrics, and libretto by Jim Jacobs and Warren Casey, produced by Kenneth Waissman and Maxine Fox at the off-Broadway Eden Theatre, 14 Feb. 1972, directed by Tom Moore. Starting out as an amateur show in Chicago, it proved an unexpected hit and soon moved on to Broadway at the Broadhurst Theatre, where it was to run until April 1980 for 3388 performances, a record that was not surpassed until *A *Chorus Line* arrived in 1975.

It took a highly satirical view of the life-style and morals of the rock generation, set in a Chicago high school and centred on the love affair between greaser Danny Zuko and an unsullied schoolgirl, Sandy Dumbrowski, who soon falls from grace. It drew its audience mainly from teenagers who felt in tune with its message. The leading roles were originally taken by Carole Demas and Barry Bostwick, but there were many changes during the run; in London, at the New London Theatre 26 June 1973, Stacey Gregg and Richard Gere played the parts; while John Travolta and Olivia *Newton-John starred in the 1978 film—'You're the one that I want'.

Great Waltz, The. Spectacular musical stage show of the 1930s which was first seen at the 3822-seat Center Theatre in the Rockefeller Center, New York, 22 Sept. 1934. The music of Johann *Strauss Sr. and Jr. was arranged by G. H. *Clutsam, Herbert Griffiths, Erich Wolfgang *Korngold, and Julius Bittner; the book by Moss *Hart was an amalgam of many Strauss plots, with a linking story based on the life-story of the Strauss family. A huge cast of 23 actors and 77 singers, supported by 33 dancers and 53 musicians, told the story of the rivalry between father and son, to the familiar strains of 'The Blue Danube' and other Viennese favourites. It originally ran for 289 performances (with an additional 49 in 1935) and was filmed in 1938 with the book entirely revised by Oscar *Hammerstein II. Thereafter the work was been frequently re-staged and revised, notably by Korngold, *Wright, and

*Forrest'; and at London's Drury Lane Theatre in 1970. A new film version appeared in 1972.

Gréco, Juliette (*b* Montpelier, 1927). French actress and singer. Starting her career in the cafés of Saint-Germain-des-Prés, she made her first cabaret appearance at the Bœuf sur le Toit in 1949, made her mark at the *Olympia in 1954, then returned to the cabaret world. She built a reputation as a leader in the world of French *chanson, recording such songs as Prévert and *Kosma's 'Je suis comme je suis' and 'Les feuilles mortes', *Brel's 'Je suis bien', Ferré's 'Jolie môme', Béart's 'Il n'y a plus d'après', *Aznavour's 'Je hais les dimanches', and Escudero's 'Je t'attends à Charonne', a mistress of the art of the diseuse, a veritable 'chanteuse classique'. She appeared in such films as *Au Royaume des cieux* (1949); *The Green Glove* (1952); *The Sun also Rises* (1957); *Naked Earth* (1958); *Roots of Heaven* (1959); *Whirlpool* (1959); and *Crack in the Mirror* (1960).

Green, Adolph (*b* New York, 2 Dec. 1915). American lyricist and librettist. He has been inseparably linked as a writing team with Betty *Comden, with whom he attended New York University, played in amateur dramatics, and developed a nightclub act singing the songs they had written together. Their first notable stage writing came with **On the Town* (1944), with music by Leonard *Bernstein, followed by a series of shows that were usually set in New York, including *Billion Dollar Baby* (1945, Morton *Gould); *Two on the Aisle* (1951, Jule *Styne); **Wonderful Town* (1953, Bernstein); and then with Styne, *Peter Pan* (1954); **Bells are Ringing* (1956); *Say, Darling* (1958); **Do-Re-Mi* (1960); *Subways are for Sleeping* (1961); *Fade Out—Fade In* (1964); *Hallelujah, Baby!* (1967); **Applause!* (1970); **On the 20th Century* (1978); *A Doll's Life* (1982). He appeared in many shows, with Comden in *On the Town* and in their own revue *A Party with Betty Comden and Adolph Green* (1958, revised revival 1977).

Green, John [earlier **Johnny**] (*b* New York, 10 Oct. 1908; *d* Los Angeles, 15 May 1989). American composer, arranger, conductor, bandleader, and pianist. One of the great all-rounders of popular music, a leading songwriter who also conducted symphony orchestras, dance-band leader, accompanist, and TV producer. Son of a prominent banker, he left Harvard with a degree in economics and began to work on Wall Street; but he had gone into the music world by the time he was 19, starting as arranger for Guy *Lombardo. From 1930 he arranged, composed, and conducted scores for Paramount's New York studio, including *Murder at the Vanities* (1933)—'Weep no more'; **Top Hat* (1935); and **Shall We Dance* (1937). Concurrently he worked as accompanist to such stars as Gertrude *Lawrence and Ethel *Merman, frequently recording, with them and others, and wrote music for Paul *Whiteman to perform at Carnegie Hall. His first song hit was 'Coquette' in 1928 but he really made his name with 'Body and soul', which was sung by Libby *Holman in *Three's a Crowd* in 1930. In 1932 he worked as pianist and assistant director with the Buddy Rogers band, then led his own band from 1933 to 1941 with 'Body and soul' as its theme tune. He worked on radio, backing Ruth *Etting (1934), Ethel *Merman (1935), Jack Benny (1935–6), and Fred *Astaire (1936–7), and on the Philip Morris Show (1939–40).

In 1942 he settled in Hollywood and worked for MGM, conducting such musicals as *Broadway Rhythm* (1943); *Bathing Beauty* (1944); *Weekend at the Waldorf* (1945); *It Happened in Brooklyn* (1946); before being appointed General Musical Director in 1948. In this capacity he received Academy Awards for **Easter Parade* (1948) and *An *American in Paris* (1951). He supervised and conducted many of the best-known MGM musicals, including **Brigadoon* (1954); **High Society* (1956); **Oliver!* (1968), and, elsewhere, received another Oscar for **West Side Story* (1961). During the 1950s he had branched out as conductor at the Hollywood Bowl, with the Denver Symphony and the Philadelphia Orchestra, and at the Los Angeles Philharmonic Promenade Concerts (1959–63). It was at this stage that he abandoned his earlier billing as Johnny for the more respectable John. Later he regularly wrote for and appeared on TV, composing and as producer for Lucille *Ball's Desilu Productions.

Among his other song hits were 'I'm yours' (1930); 'Out of nowhere' (1931)—which was Bing *Crosby's first solo recording; 'I cover the waterfront' and 'You're mine, you' (1933); 'Easy come, easy go' (1934)—featured (with other songs of his) in the film about the dance marathons of the depression years, *They Shoot Horses, Don't They?* (1969); 'The song of Raintree County' (from the film, 1957); and many more. He had less success on Broadway with such shows as *Here Goes the Bride* (1931) and the revue *Beat the Band* (1942). The John Green Music Awards were founded in 1973 in his honour.

Green, Martyn [Martyn-Green, William] (*b* London, 22 Apr. 1899; *d* Hollywood, 10 Feb. 1975). British actor and singer. He studied at the Royal College of Music 1919–21 and in 1921 made his London debut in *Thirty Minutes of Melody* at the Palladium. His long association with *Gilbert and Sullivan and the D'Oyly *Carte Opera Company began in 1922 when he appeared in the minor role of Luiz in *The *Gondoliers*. In 1934 he began to take over the major comic roles as successor to Sir Henry *Lytton and played them until he retired from the company in 1951. He put real character into such parts as Bunthorne, the Major-General, Ko-Ko, and Jack Point and was noted for his clear and well-timed delivery. He recorded all his main roles in the early LP days. He then went to the USA and started a new career as a straight actor, though still often involved in G & S productions and recordings. In 1959 he lost a leg in a lift accident, but still managed to perform with an artificial leg and appeared in many stage productions and films. He edited *Martyn Green's Treasury of Gilbert & Sullivan* (New York, 1961); and wrote an autobiography, *Here's a How-De-Do: my Life in and Travelling with Gilbert and Sullivan* (London–New York, 1952).

Greenaway, Roger (*b* Southmead, nr. Bristol, 23 Aug. 1938). British composer, author, publisher, and producer. After army service, 1957–9, he joined a Bristol pop group, the Kestrels, where he also met fellow Bristolian Roger Cook (*b* Bristol, 19 Aug. 1941) who was to become his songwriting partner. They left the group to form a duo under the name of David and Jonathan, gained the support of producer George *Martin, and had a hit with 'Lovers of the world unite' (1966). They had already decided to concentrate on composition, having had a major success with 'You've got your troubles' in 1965 which had been recorded by several artists, including Neil *Diamond. However, they continued to perform together and separately and produced a list of best-selling songs including: 'I was Kaiser Bill's batman' (1967); 'Green grass' (1967); 'Something's gotten hold of my heart' (1967); 'My baby loves lovin'' (1970); 'I've got you on my mind' (1970); 'Home lovin' man' (1970); 'Melting pot' (1971); 'Banner man' (1971); 'Something tells me' (1971); 'Long cool woman in a black dress' (1971); 'Kissin' in the back row of the movies' (1971); 'I'd like to teach the world to sing' (1971)—which was No. 1 in the UK and sold more than five million copies in the New *Seekers recording; 'Doctor's orders' (1973); 'Hello summertime' (1974); 'It oughta sell a million' (1974); 'Jeans on' (1976); and many more. Greenaway has also worked with Barry Mason, Geoff Stephens, and Tony Macaulay.

Greenbank, Percy (*b* London, 24 Jan. 1878; *d* Rickmansworth, 19 Dec. 1968). British librettist and lyricist. He studied for the law, then began writing by contributing to *Punch* and other periodicals. He became a prolific provider of words for musical comedies, many of which enjoyed very long runs and were also heard in the USA. They included: **San Toy* (1899); *The Messenger Boy* (1900); *The *Toreador* (1901); *A *Country Girl* (1902); *The *Earl and the Girl* (1903); *The *Orchid* (1903); *The *Cingalee* (1904); *The Little Michus* (1905); *The Spring Chicken* (1905); *The Blue Moon* (1906); *My Lady's Maid* (1906); *The Belle of Brittany* (1908); **Our Miss Gibbs* (1909); *The *Quaker Girl* (1910); **Tonight's the Night* (1914); *Betty* (1916); *The Boy* (1917); *Good Morning, Judge* (1919); and *The Street Singer* (1924).

Greenwich, Ellie (*b* Brooklyn, 23 Oct. 1940). American composer and singer. After a period as a teacher she joined *Leiber and *Stoller's Trio Music Co., where she met the songwriter Jeff Barry whom she later married. Together they wrote material for Phil *Spector artists before moving on to the Red Bird record company where they worked with producer Shadow Morton. They also recorded under the name of the Raindrops. During 1966–8 they produced Neil *Diamond's records for Bang and then formed Tallyrand Music with Diamond. Greenwich divorced Barry and later worked with Mike Rashkon, producing a hit recording in 'I want you to be my baby'. She continued to write and record hits in the 1970s.

Her other songs include: 'Today I met the boy I'm gonna marry' (1963); 'Then he kissed me' (1963); 'Be my baby' (1963); 'Doo wah diddy diddy' (1964); 'I'll take you where the music's playing' (1965), 'River deep, mountain high' (1966); 'Baby, look what you've done to my heart' (1967); and 'I can hear music' (1969).

Greenwich Village Follies. Long-running series of American revues, modelled on but on a slightly less lavish scale than the famous *Follies* produced by Florenz *Ziegfeld (who threatened a lawsuit over the use of the word 'Follies' in the title). They were directed by John Murray *Anderson who made his debut with the 1919 production and was connected with six out of the total of eight editions. The 1919 production started out at the Greenwich Village Theatre but eventually moved uptown to the Nora Bayes Theatre, running for 232 performances from 15 July 1919. The music was by A. Baldwin *Sloane, Irving *Berlin, Bill Munro (who provided 'When my baby smiles at me'), and others. Harry Delf, Bessie McCoy Davis, and the Ted *Lewis Orchestra were among the attractions. The 1920 edition opened 30 Aug. 1920 [192p] and the cast included Frank *Crumit. The 1921 edition opened at the Shubert Theatre 31 Aug. 1921 [167p]; the songs included 'Three o'clock in the morning' by Julian Robledo and Dorothy Terriss [Theodora Morse], but most of the music was by Carey Morgan (1885–1960). The next edition, 12 Sept. 1922 [216p], was mainly composed by Louis A. *Hirsch. The 1923 edition was at the *Winter Garden Theatre 20 Sept. 1923 [140p], with Con *Conrad supplying much of the score. The next edition, at the Shubert Theatre 16 Sept. 1924 [127p], had music by Jay *Gorney and Cole *Porter ('Two little babes in the woods', 'I'm in love again'). The 1925 edition, at the 46th Street Theatre 24 Dec. 1925 [180p], was taken over by Hassard Short (whom Anderson had replaced in **Music Box Revue*); and the final edition, at the Winter Garden Theatre 9 Apr. 1928 [158p], with music by Maurie Rubens (1893–1948], was directed by J. C. Huffman. The musical content of the revues was not always great, their reputation mainly resting on a tradition of good comedy, first-rate female impersonations, and good dancing.

Gregg, Hubert (*b* London, 19 July 1914). British producer, writer, composer, and actor. He made his first professional stage appearance in *Martine* (1933) and thereafter appeared in many plays, films, and on radio and TV. For some years he was the presenter of a pleasantly nostalgic BBC record programme revolving around the musical theatre. He contributed to *Strike a New Note* (1943)—'I'm going to get lit up'; *The *Love Racket* (1944); **Sweet and Low* (1944); and *Strike It Again* (1945); and also wrote 'Maybe it's because I'm a Londoner' (1947).

Grenfell, Joyce [Phipps, Joyce Irene] (*b* London, 10 Feb. 1910; *d* 30 Nov. 1979). British actress, singer, and author. She specialized in portraying gauche and toothy females, mainly of the spinster or schoolteacher variety, and appeared in many revues, including *The Little Revue* (1939); *Light and Shade* (1942); *Sigh No More* (1945); *Tuppence Coloured* (1947); **Penny Plain* (1951); and in several of her own one-woman shows such as *Joyce Grenfell Requests the Pleasure* (1954). She appeared in many British films including some Ealing comedies and the St Trinian's series; and was often seen on TV. She wrote many songs in collaboration with Richard Addinsell, which she sang in a light and refined manner, and several books.

Grey, Clifford (*b* Birmingham, 5 Jan. 1887; *d* Ipswich, 25 Sept. 1941). British lyric-writer and librettist. He became an actor when he was 19, but soon left the stage in order to write for it, producing the librettos for many well-known revues and musical comedies produced in both New York and London, including the 'Bing Boys' shows, with music by Nat D. *Ayers, which produced his most lasting song 'If you were the only girl in the world'. From other London productions came items such as 'Spread a little happiness' and 'Got a date with an angel'; while in the USA his best work was done with Vincent *Youmans.

He wrote: *The *Bing Boys Are Here* (1916); *Pell-Mell* (1916); *Theodore & Co.* (1916); *The Bing Girls Are There* (1917); *The Other Bing Boys* (1917); *Arlette* (1917); *Yes, Uncle!* (1917); *The Bing Boys on Broadway* (1918); *Hullo, America!* (1918); *Who's Hooper?* (1919); *Johnny Jones* (1920); *A Night Out* (1920); **Sally* (1920); *The Hotel Mouse* (1922); **Phi-Phi* (1922); *The Smith Family* (1922); *Lady Butterfly* (1923); *The Rainbow* (1923); *Vogues of 1924*; *Marjorie* (1924); **Artists and Models* (1924 and 1925); *Annie Dear* (1924); *June Days* (1925); *Gay Paree* (1925); *Mayflowers* (1925); *A Night in Paris* (1926); *The Great Temptations* (1926); *The Merry World* (1926); **Hit the Deck* (1927); *The Three Musketeers* (1928); **Mr Cinders* (1929); *Smiles* (1930); *For the Love of Mike* (1931); *Out of the Bottle* (1932); *The One Girl* (1923); **Mr Whittington* (1934); *Jack o'Diamonds* (1935); *Love Laughs* (1935); and *Bobby Get Your Gun* (1938).

Grey, Joel [Katz, Joel] (*b* Cleveland, Ohio, 11 Apr. 1932). American actor, singer, and dancer, son of the comedian Mickey Katz. A slim, saturnine actor, he made a considerable impact as the Master of Ceremonies in **Cabaret* (1966; and film, 1972), afterwards starring as George M. *Cohan in **George M!* (1968).

Grofé, Ferde [von Grofé, Ferdinand Rudolph] (*b* New York, 27 Mar. 1892; *d* Santa Monica, Calif., 3 Apr. 1972). American composer, conductor, arranger, and pianist. He started his professional career as a violist in the Los Angeles Symphony Orchestra, at the same time working as a pianist in vaudeville and cabaret and conducting in theatres. He became a professional manager with a music-publisher before plunging wholly into the world of popular music and working as pianist with the Art Hickman orchestra. He also had a talent as a banjoist. A pioneer in the field of jazz arrangements for large orchestras, he joined the Paul *Whiteman band as a pianist in 1919 and was its principal arranger 1920–7. His scoring of George *Gershwin's *'Rhapsody in blue' won wide recognition in 1924. He toured abroad with Whiteman 1939–43, conducted radio orchestras, and taught at the Juilliard Summer School. He won an Academy Award for his score for *Minstrel Man* (1944); other film scores included *Time Out of Mind* (1947), which used his 'New England suite', and *Grand Canyon* (1959).

His orchestral works, mainly using jazz rhythms and folky melodies to produce a popular American style, included: 'Broadway at Night' (1924); 'Mississippi suite' (1925); 'Grand Canyon suite' (1931); a piano concerto (1932; rev. 1959); 'Tabloid suite' (1933); 'Symphony in steel' (1937); 'Hollywood suite' (1937); 'Hudson River suite' (1955); 'San Francisco suite' (1960); 'Niagara Falls suite' (1961); 'World's Fair suite' (1964); and 'Requiem for a ghost town' (1968).

Groody, Louise (*b* Waco, Texas, 26 Mar. 1897; *d* Canadensis, Pa., 16 Sept. 1961). American actress, singer, and dancer. After starting her career as a cabaret dancer she appeared in *Around the Map* (1915); *Good Morning, Dearie* (1921), and other shows. She made her name as Nanette in **No, No, Nanette* (1925), where she introduced 'I want to be happy' and 'Tea for two'; and in **Hit the Deck* (1927), where she sang 'Sometimes I'm happy'.

Groovy, in the groove. Introduced in the 1930s as a word/phrase descriptive of jazz or swing music that had settled into a steady swinging state of exhilaration; presumably deriving from gramophone sources. It has widened its meaning to cover a general feeling of empathy with the music: 'Groovy is real good' (S. Longstreet).

Grossmith, George (*b* London, 9 Dec. 1847; *d* Folkestone, 1 Mar. 1912). British entertainer, actor, singer, and composer. Starting out as a journalist, around 1864 he began to give amateur performances of his own songs and sketches at 'penny readings'. In 1870 he was professionally engaged by Henry Pepper to perform at the Polytechnic in Regent Street and similar engagements followed. In 1877 he was recruited by Richard D'Oyly *Carte for the role of John Wellington Wells in *Gilbert and *Sullivan's *The *Sorcerer*. He continued with the D'Oyly Carte company for 12 years, creating the roles of Sir Joseph Porter in **HMS Pinafore*, Major-

General Stanley in *The *Pirates of Penzance*, Bunthorne in **Patience*, the Lord Chancellor in **Iolanthe*, Ko-Ko in *The *Mikado*, and other celebrated comic parts.

During this time he continued with his humorous musical recitals, and he left the D'Oyly Carte company in 1889 to devote himself entirely to this form of entertainment, performing at private functions as well as in theatres and concert halls and becoming popular in the USA and Canada as well as Britain. His own writings and compositions were disginguished by sharp satire. Among his best-known songs were 'The Muddle Puddle porter', 'The happy Fatherland', 'He was a careful man', 'An awful little scrub', 'The first cigar', and 'See me dance the polka'. He wrote the curtain-raisers *Cups and Saucers* (1878); *Mr Guffin's Elopement* (1822); and (in collaboration with W. S. Gilbert) *Haste to the Wedding* (1892). He wrote two volumes of autobiographical reminiscences and was co-author, with his actor brother Weedon Grossmith (1852–1919), of *The Diary of a Nobody* (1894), which first appeared in serial form in *Punch*.

G. Grossmith: *A Society Clown: Reminiscences* (London–Bristol, 1888). G. Grossmith: *Piano and I: further Reminiscences* (London–Bristol, 1910). T. Joseph: *George Grossmith: Biography of a Savoyard* (Bristol, 1982).

Grossmith, George, Jr. (*b* London, 11 May 1874; *d* London, 6 June 1935). British actor, singer, librettist, lyricist, director, and producer. The son of the famous Savoyard George *Grossmith, he followed in his father's footsteps as a talented comic actor, generally playing the top-hatted and monocled silly-ass sort of character which the Victorians identified as a 'dude'. Starting typically as Lord Percy Pimpleton in the pioneer musical comedy *Morocco Bound* in 1893, he was to star in numerous celebrated shows and contributed to many from *c*.1900 as sketch writer or librettist, working on several occasions as lyricist to Jerome *Kern, in London productions which he also presented. He was an active producer, in association with Edward Laurillard 1914–21; and with J. A. E. Malone 1921–6.

He played in or †contributed to the following shows: *Go-Bang* (1894); *A *Gaiety Girl* (1894); *The *Shop Girl* (1894); *The Gay Pretenders* (1900); *The *Toreador* (1901); *The *Orchid* (1903); *The Spring Chicken* (1905); *The New Aladdin* (1906); *The Girls of Gottenberg* (1907); *A *Waltz Dream* (1908); **Our Miss Gibbs* (1909); *Peggy* (1911); *The Sunshine Girl* (1912); *The Girl on the Film* (1913); **Tonight's the Night* (1915); **Theodore & Co.* (1916); *Kissing Time* (1919); *The Naughty Princess* (1920); **Sally* (1921); *The Cabaret Girl* (1922); *The Beauty Prize* (1923); **No, No, Nanette* (1925); *Princess Charming* (1926); *Lady Mary* (1928); *The Five o'Clock Girl* (1929); *My Sister and I* (1931); and wrote or produced many more.

S. Naylor: *Gaiety and George Grossmith* (London, 1913). G. Grossmith: *GG* (London, 1933).

Grun, Bernard (*b* Arztsohn, Czechoslovakia, 11 Feb. 1901; *d* London, 28 Dec. 1972). Composer, author, and conductor. Educated in Vienna and Prague, he studied law and philosophy but took up a musical career and studied with Berg and Weingartner. He became musical director of the National Theatre, Prague, 1924–9; at the State Opera House, Karlsruhe, 1930–2; at the Theater an der Wien, Vienna, 1935–8; and at His Majesty's Theatre, London, 1942–4. Having settled in London he was musical adviser to the Jack *Hylton organization for many years.

He was composer or part-composer of many musical shows, including: *Uncle Perl* (1923); *The Great David* (1924); *Miss Chocolate* (1927); *Czech Musician* (1927); *Amelie* (1931); *Freut' euch des Lebens* (1932; based on the music of Johann and Josef *Strauss) (1932); *Musik um Susi* (1933); Fanny Ellsler (1934); *Gaby Deslys* (1935); *Wo die Liebe bluht* (1935); **Balalaika* (1936); *Madame Sans-Gene* (1937); *Paprika* (1938); *Magyar Melody* (1939); *Waltz without End* (1942; based on the music of Chopin); *Old Chelsea* (1943, with Richard *Tauber); *Pink Champagne* (1952, an adaptation of *Die *Fledermaus*). He wrote music for films in the 1940s and was the author of *Private Lives of the Great Composers* (London, 1953); *Prince of Vienna: the Life, Times and Melodies of Oscar Straus* (London, 1954); *Die leichte Muse: Kulturgeschichte der Operette* (Munich, 1961); *Gold and Silver: the Life and Times of Franz Lehár* (London, 1970); and several novels.

Guarnieri, Johnny (John Albert] (*b* New York, 23 Mar. 1917; *d* New York, 7 Jan. 1985). American jazz pianist, composer, and author. Descended from the famous violin-making family of Cremona, he first studied classical piano; but at the age of 20 he was making a living playing in dance bands and joined the Benny *Goodman band in 1939. He became known as a versatile and stylish performer with a talent for musical mimicry: his favourite adopted style was in the manner of Fats *Waller, whom he greatly admired. He worked with Artie *Shaw 1940–1, who sometimes featured him on the harpsichord, later with Jimmy *Dorsey, Raymond *Scott, and Cozy *Cole; and he toured Europe in the 1970s with Slam Stewart. He wrote a large number of piano compositions, including a piano concerto in 5/4 time which he performed in Los Angeles in 1970.

Guilbert, Yvette [Emma Laure Esther] (*b* Paris, 20 Jan. 1865; *d* Aix-en-Provence, 3 Feb. 1944). French diseuse and singer. She started out as an actress in 1885 but by 1890 had changed to a career as a folk-singer and cabaret entertainer, earning a great reputation in Paris and embarking on tours of Europe and the USA, which she first visited in 1896. She continued to think of herself as an actress, and later returned to the stage, but her highly personal and droll interpretations of folk-song and chanson made her primarily recognized in this field. She had a strangely angular figure, a plain but personable face, and a hypnotic personality (an earlier *Piaf) which soon made her the favourite of Montmartre.

Coming across a copy of *Chansons sans gêne* by Léon *Xanrof, she found there many items which she was destined to make famous like 'Le fiacre': songs which saw Paris through the eyes of students and the young and which, for their time, were considered daring, and thus went down well at the café-concerts and cabarets where she was a popular attraction. Favourites in her repertoire were 'Le fiacre', 'La complainte des 4 z'étudiants', and 'L'Hôtel de No. 3'—all by Xanrof; 'Je suis pocharde!' and 'Madame Arthur' were among those for which she wrote the words; 'Ma tête' and Aristide *Bruant's 'A la Villette'; 'L'idiot' and 'Le convoi funèbre' by Rollinat; 'Moi, j'casse les noisettes en m'asseyant dessus', 'Les vieux messieurs', 'Le petit cochon'; and her masterpiece 'La soûlarde' in which she portrayed a drunken woman. All of these she sang in a racy, sarcastic manner, always in a drawling, monotonous voice and without gesture, almost hypnotizing her audiences to accept lyrics which one writer described as 'songs of concentrated spiciness, designed to bring a blush to a monkey's cheek'.

From her beginnings in the back streets of Paris she became one of the most popular singers in Europe and America, immortalized by the artist Toulouse-Lautrec, admired by Shaw, Freud, Gounod, Zola, and Edward VII, a rival of Bernhardt and Melba. Her songs lived on in the hands of such singers as Jean *Sablon, Maurice *Chevalier, and Edith Piaf. Besides all this she was a talented writer and novelist.

G. Geffroy: *Yvette Guilbert* (Paris, 1894). Y. Guilbert and H. Simpson: *Yvette Guilbert: Struggles and Victories* (London, 1910). Y. Guilbert: *La Chanson de ma vie* (Paris, 1927). Y. Guilbert: *Autres temps, autres chants* (Paris, 1946). B. Knapp and M. Chipman: *That Was Yvette: the biography of a Great Diseuse* (New York, 1964).

Gungl, Josef (*b* Zsámbék, 1 Dec. 1810; *d* Weimar, 31 Jan. 1889). Hungarian composer, bandmaster, and oboist. He played in and was later bandmaster of the 4th Regiment of Artillery in the Austrian Army: his Op. 1 was a 'Hungarian march' written for the band. He left the army in 1843, having made many successful concert tours with the band, and formed his own band of 25 musicians in Berlin which played in most of the European capitals and toured the USA 1848–9. On his return to Europe he was appointed Musikdirektor to the King of Prussia and, in 1859, Kapellmeister to the Emperor of Austria. Living mainly in Munich and Frankfurt, he continued his activities as a prolific composer of more than 500 dances and marches—including 'Amorettentänze', 'Frühlingslieder', 'Jungherrentänze', 'Soldatenlieder', 'Casinotänze', 'Träume auf dem Ozean', 'Immortellen', and 'Die Hydropathen'—most of them of an ephemeral nature. His nephew Johann Gungl (1823–83) was also known in a similar field of music and composition.

Guthrie, Arlo (*b* New York, 10 July 1947). American folk-singer and guitarist. Son of Woody *Guthrie, he inherited similar talents and physical weaknesses, and the same dedication to unpopular causes. An appearance at the Newport Folk Festival in 1967 confirmed this hereditary ability and gained immediate popularity for his album *Alice's Restaurant* (1967), which was mainly taken up with the ironic ballad story of his avoidance of service in Vietnam, adapted for a film in 1969. He tried not to copy his father's musical and lifestyle too obviously, but had a keen interest in peace and environmental causes, colouring his work with a friendly humour that made him a popular entertainer. He often worked with Pete *Seeger, and also used his great talents as a guitarist to work with musicians such as Sonny *Terry and Brownie *McGhee. His best-known single is 'The City of New Orleans' (1972). Latterly he settled on a farm in Massachusetts, limiting his performances owing to ill-health.

Guthrie, Woody [Woodrow Wilson] (*b* Okemah, Okla., 14 July 1912; *d* New York, 3 Oct. 1967). American folk-singer. Son of a prizefighting guitarist, he was brought up in poverty and during the depression years took to the road, playing in saloons and at open-air meetings, particularly liking to visit hobo camps and picket lines and singing to children. Being himself a genuine refugee from the poverty of the Oklahoma Dust Bowl he was able to put over his songs of social significance with true feeling. During the Second World War he was a merchant seaman and his ship was torpedoed twice. A life-long left-winger and champion of the poor, he was to some extent reacting against his father, who had been a land speculator and an active racist. His was a background of violence—his mother murdered his 12-year-old sister and tried to kill her husband—and of a fight against Huntinton's chorea, a hereditary disease passed on from his mother's side. He was bedridden from 1957 and spent his last years in a Brooklyn hospital.

In his peak years he joined Pete *Seeger and others in the *Almanac Singers and wrote his classic book *Bound for Glory* (1943), which was used as the basis of an embarrassing film in 1976. But he is most famous for his 'Dust Bowl Ballads', describing the forced migration of families from the barren lands of Oklahoma to the extortions and greed of get-rich California. His heroes were hobos and bums; the victims he championed were the poor rural workers. He was a skilful and evocative lyricist (at times reminiscent of Walt Whitman or Carl Sandburg) and a clear influence on disciples like Bob *Dylan who adapted his songs and style for their personal use without always following through his radical ideas. He would probably have recoiled at the souped-up versions of his songs rendered by some of the more commercial folk groups and singers. In a broadcast he said to his working-class audience: 'I am out to sing the songs that will make you take pride in yourself and your work.' These included some of America's greatest folk ballads like 'This land is your land', 'Pastures of plenty', and 'Vigilante man'. He edited *American Folksong* (New York, 1947).

His uncompromising political stance, his forthright guitar and harmonica playing, his hobo lifestyle and his meaningful songs made Guthrie the leading source of inspiration for the 1960s folk revival in the USA and Europe. The timeless lines and images in his songs have survived long after his own tragic battle with life and he has become one of the genuine legends of popular music.

W. Guthrie: *Bound for Glory* (New York, 1943). W. Guthrie (ed. R. Shelton): *Born to Win* (New York, 1965). H. Yurchenko: *A Mighty Hard Road: the Woody Guthrie Story* (with 30 songs] (New York, 1970). J. Klein: *Woody Guthrie: a Life* (New York–London, 1981).

Guys and Dolls. American musical comedy with music and lyrics by Frank *Loesser, book by Abe *Burrows, based on stories by Damon Runyon (1884–1946). Staged at the 46th Street Theatre, New York, 24 Nov. 1950, with Robert *Alda, Vivian Blaine (*b* 1921), Sam Levene (1905–80), Isabel Bigley, Pat Rooney, and Stubby Kaye; achieving 1200 performances. The choreography of Michael Kidd (*b* 1919) came in for special acclaim. It was produced at the London Coliseum 28 May 1955, with many of the same cast but with Jerry Wayne replacing Alda as Sky Masterson and Lizbeth Webb replacing Bigley as Sarah Brown; it had 555 performances.

Originally planned as a serious romance, *Guys and Dolls* turned out to be one of the funniest musicals to come out of the USA, telling the story of an unlikely romance between a staid Salvation Army lass and a Broadway gambler; backed up by a hilarious cast of characters ranging from gambling promoter Nathan Detroit to nightclub performer Miss Adelaide. One of the best songs was sung by Nicely-Nicely Johnson (splendidly played by the corpulent Stubby Kaye), 'Sit down, you're rocking the boat', but there were plenty more gems like 'Adelaide's lament', 'A bushel and a peck', 'Fugue for tinhorns', 'If I were a bell', 'I've never been in love before', 'If luck were a lady', 'A woman in love', 'More I cannot wish you', sung by Pat Rooney (1880–1962), 'Take back your mink', and 'Sue me'.

It was one of the longest-running Broadway musicals to date, and has frequently been revived both on the professional and amateur stage. It was filmed in 1955 with Frank *Sinatra, Jean Simmons (*b* 1929), Marlon Brando (*b* 1924), and Vivian Blaine. The show successfully joined the repertoire of London's National Theatre in 1984.

Gypsy. American musical with score by Jule *Styne, lyrics by Stephen *Sondheim, and book by Arthur Laurents based on the memoirs of the famous dancer, actress, and striptease artist Gypsy Rose Lee (1914–70). It opened at the Broadway Theatre, New York, 21 May 1959, transferring to the Imperial 15 Aug. 1960 and running for 702 performances.

The show provided a starring role for Ethel *Merman as the ambitious mother who tries to build a stage career for her younger daughter June (Lane Bradbury), who elopes with a dancer. Her ambition is achieved with her less talented daughter Louise (Sandra Church), who does well under the guise of stripper Gypsy Rose Lee and soon no longer needs her support. It was Merman's last great stage role, enhanced by an excellent score full of dramatically cogent songs such as 'Some people', 'Small world', 'All I need is the girl', 'Everything's coming up roses', and 'Rose's turn'.

The London production, at the Piccadilly Theatre, 29 May 1973, starred Angela *Lansbury, Bonnie Langford, and Barrie Ingham [120p]. It was filmed in 1972 with Rosalind Russell (1912–76), Natalie Wood (1938–81), and Karl Malden (*b* 1913). There was an American stage revival at the end of 1989 with Tyne Daly (*b* 1947), star of the TV series *Cagney and Lacy*, as Mama Rose.

Gypsy Baron, The see *Zigeunerbaron, Der.*

Gypsy Love see *Zigeunerliebe.*

Gypsy Music. The composer and folk-music collector Béla Bartók, among others, suggested that there was perhaps no such thing as gypsy music; that it was simply the new Hungarian popular music. This is basically true, but ignores the differences between the gypsy-styled music exclusive to Hungary (*cigányzene*) and the true gypsy folk-music which is to be found, in varying form, wherever gypsies have wandered. However, it is the Hungarian-based gypsy music that is generally thought of under this name and the style that has become a distinct genre of entertainment music. It was reckoned in one book on the subject that some 8000 gypsy musicians would have been actively flourishing in Hungary by the late 1870s. These would be the true gypsies (*cigány*) referred to in France as *bohémiens*, elsewhere as *walachs*, and in English-speaking countries as *romanies*, as opposed to the many vagrants who describe themselves as such but are not true gypsies (*gadzos*). The Magyar gypsy musician does not generally play folk-music (though, as in any culture, there are a few who do) but rather the popular music of Hungary which, in fact, they created in much the same way as Jewish musicians created the popular music of America in the Tin Pan Alley days of the early 20th century. A dance such as the csárdás, which starts in a slow, romantic way and builds up to an exhilarating pace, is typical of gypsy music which features gypsy fiddling along with cimbalom and guitar accompaniment.

B. Sárosi: *Gypsy Music* (Budapest, 1971; trans. 1978).

H

Habanera. A dance developed in Cuba and from there imported into Spain and Europe. In 2/4 time, with the first quaver dotted, it is basically identical to the Argentine *tango. One of the earliest published habaneras was 'El arreglito' by Sebastian *Yradier (composer of the later famous 'La paloma') which appeared in 1840. This was the piece which inspired the habanera song that Bizet used to good effect in his opera *Carmen* in 1875. An Argentine musicologist, Carlos Vegas, suggested that the habanera was developed from an English country dance which was taken to Spain as the *contradanza*, thence fo Cuba where it was known as the *danza* or *danza Habanera* (i.e. 'from Havana')—finally returning to Spain.

Hackett, Bobby [Robert Leo] (*b* Providence, RI, 31 Jan. 1915; *d* West Chatham, Mass., 7 June 1976). American jazz trumpeter and guitarist. He started as a guitarist at the age of eight, changing to trumpet to earn a living in clubs in Boston and New York. Playing in a trio with Pee Wee *Russell in Boston in 1933, he began to be looked upon as a natural successor to Bix *Beiderbecke, with similar inventive ideas and bell-like trumpet tone. He became more generally known with Benny *Goodman in 1938 when he appeared in the famous Carnegie Hall concert. After leading his own band in New York he was with Glenn *Miller 1941–2 as guitarist and cornettist. In 1944 he was with the *Casa Loma Orchestra. He was plagued at this time by a drink problem which caused diabetes, but he overcame this sufficiently to work at the Eddie *Condon club and to play alongside Louis *Armstrong for many years.

From 1951 he worked with Jackie *Gleason to produce some very popular strings-backed mood albums for which he received inadequate reward. At the same time he had a productive partnership with Jack *Teagarden. From 1956 he led a band at the Henry Hudson Hotel which is fondly remembered by Dixieland enthusiasts. He worked with Benny Goodman again, 1962–3, with Ray *McKinley, and as a backing musician to singer Tony *Bennett. In the 1960s he was in a distinctive quintet with Vic *Dickenson and occasionally played with the World's Greatest Jazz Band. He toured Europe in 1974, but diabetes put an end to a career of tasteful trumpet-playing.

Hadjidakis, Manos (*b* Xanthi, Macedonia, 23 Oct. 1925). Greek composer. He studied music in Athens and began his composing career as a writer of modern piano music. From 1946 he found his *métier* in writing for films. A prolific output notably included such items as: *I Mayiki Polis* (1955); *Stella* (1955); *Drakos* (1956); *I Paranomi* (1957); *Pote tin Kyriaki* (1959); *To Potami* (1962); *Never on Sunday* (1960)—for which he received an Academy Award; *The Zoo Spartans* (1962); *America, America* (1963); *Topkapi* (1964); *Blue* (1968); and *The Invincible Six* (1970). He wrote a musical, *Ilya, Darling*, based on the film *Never on Sunday*, which was produced at the Mark Hellinger Theatre, New York, from 11 Apr. 1967 for 318 performances.

Haggard, Merle (*b* Bakersfield, Calif., 6 Apr. 1937). American Country and Western singer, fiddler, and guitarist. An impoverished childhood led to a life of crime; he escaped seven times from reform school and later from San Quentin prison. There he met the rapist Caryl Chessman who influenced the songs he began to write on such depressive subjects as poverty, crime, and the despairing state of mind that arose from a background such as his. He was pardoned and released in 1972 and quickly moved into a highly lucrative career as a singer and balladist, becoming a star of the Nashville C & W scene. His hits include 'Okie from Muskogee', 'Workin' man blues', 'Daddy Frank', and 'Hungry eyes'.

Hague, Albert (*b* Berlin, 13 Oct. 1920). American composer. He went to the USA where he completed his musical studies, served in the US Air Force, and after the war settled in New York. After an initial attempt at a musical, *Reluctant Lady*, produced in Cleveland in 1947, he reached Broadway with *Plain and Fancy* (1955) and *Redhead* (1959). *The Fig Leaves are Falling* (1969), starring Allan Sherman, was a failure.

Hahn, Reynaldo (*b* Caracas, 9 Aug. 1875; *d* Paris, 28 Jan. 1947). Venezuelan-French composer. His family moved to Paris when he was five, and he studied singing, conducting, and composition at the Paris Conservatoire, afterwards taking up a professional career as a conductor. Although Jewish on his father's side he managed to survive the war in France and in 1945 became director of the Paris Opéra. He was a brilliant wit and a fluent writer and journalist, and he had a gift for lightly melodious music, as his many songs show. He was a fine singer himself and made several recordings.

Having written operas he moved, with delightful results, into the world of operetta, including: *Miou-*

sic (1914); *Ciboulette* (1923); *Mozart* (1925), based on a play by Sacha Guitry and starring Guitry and Yvonne *Printemps; *Le Temps d'aimer* (1926); *Brummel* (1931); *O mon bel inconnu* (1933); and *Malvina* (1935). He also wrote for films.

D. Bendahan: *Reynaldo Hahn: su vida y su obra* (Caracas, 1973). B. Gavoty: *Reynaldo Hahn: le musicien de la belle époque* (Paris, 1976).

'Hail Columbia'. American patriotic song, the tune of which was first conceived as an instrumental composition by violinist Philip Phile (1734–93), originally titled 'The President's march', and published in 1793. Words were added in 1798 by Joseph Hopkinson (*b* 1770), son of America's first poet-composer Francis Hopkinson (1737–91). It was first performed in Philadelphia by Gilbert Fox and immediately became popular.

Hair. 'American Tribal Love-Rock Musical' with score by Galt *MacDermot and lyrics and book by Gerome Ragni (*b* 1942) and James Rado (*b* 1939), first seen at the New York Shakespeare Festival Public Theatre near Astor Place, New York, 29 Oct. 1967. After a month and a half there it transferred to a nightclub before reaching Broadway at the Biltmore Theatre 29 Apr. 1968, where it was to achieve 1750 performances.

An almost non-existent story concerned itself with the drug- and sex-obsessed scene of the Vietnam years, portraying the unconventional lifestyle of the hippies and flower people; the first act ended in a pioneering way, with the whole cast stark naked (though in semi-darkness). The song 'Aquarius' stood out and became something of a hippy anthem. In London, at the Shaftesbury Theatre from 27 Sept. 1968, it had 1998 performances; and there was a film version directed by Milos Forman (*b* 1932) in 1979.

L. Davis: *Letting Down My Hair* (New York, 1972).

Hale, Binnie [Hale-Monro, Beatrice Mary] (*b* Liverpool, 22 May 1899; *d* London, 10 Jan. 1984). British actress and singer. She made her stage debut in the revue *Follow the Crowd* (1916) and later that year was in *Cochran's musical comedy production *Houp-La!* Most of her career was to be in the musical theatre, initially in such pot-boilers as *We're All in It* (1916); *150 Pound Revue* (1917); *The Kiss Call* (1919); *Just Fancy* (1920); *Jumble Sale* (1920); *My Nieces* (1921); *Katinka* (1923); *Puppets* (1924); and *The Odd Spot* (1924); before she found a worthy part and made her reputation in **No, No, Nanette* (1925)—'I want to be happy', 'Tea for two', with George *Grossmith Jr. and Joseph *Coyne. Her career as a blonde, vivacious songster blossomed in such shows as **Sunny* (1926); **Mr Cinders* (1929), with Bobby *Howes, in which she sang 'Spread a little happiness'; *Nippy* (1930); *Bow Bells* (1932)—'You're blasé'; *The DuBarry* (1932); *Yes, Madam?* (1934); *Rise and Shine* (1936); the Cochran revue *Home and Beauty* (1937), in which she sang 'A nice cup of tea'; *Magyar Melody* (1939); and *Up and Doing* (1940)—'London pride'; after which her career tailed off in minor revues.

Hale, Sonnie [Hale-Munro, John Robert] (*b* London, 1 May 1902; *d* London 9 June 1959). British actor and singer. The son of actor Robert Hale and brother of Binnie *Hale, he played the bland English gent in many musicals. He was married to Evelyn *Laye, later to Jessie *Matthews, with whom he appeared in **One Dam Thing after Another* (1927); **This Year of Grace* (1928), in which he sang 'A room with a view' and 'Dance, little lady'; **Wake Up and Dream!* (1929); **Ever Green* (1930), in which he sang 'Dancing on the ceiling'; *Hold My Hand* (1931); and *Come Out to Play* (1940). He starred in a number of British films in the 1930s; then concentrated more on directing both stage shows and films.

Halévy, Ludovic (*b* Paris, 1 Jan. 1834; *d* Paris, 8 May 1908). French librettist, playwright, and novelist, the son of opera composer Fromental Halévy (1799–1862). He was the author, mostly in collaboration with Henri Meilhac (1831–97), of many operetta librettos, including **Orphée aux enfers* (1861); *La *Belle Hélène* (1864); *La *Vie Parisienne* (1866); *La *Grande Duchesse de Gérolstein* (1867); *La *Périchole* (1868); *Les Brigands* (1869); *Le Petit Duc* (1878); as well as that of Bizet's opera *Carmen* (1875).

Haley, Bill [William John Clifton] (*b* Highland Park, Mich., 6 July 1925; *d* Harlingen, Texas, 9 Feb. 1981). American singer, guitarist, and bandleader. At 15 he was touring with Country and Western bands and then formed his own group, the Saddlemen. Renamed the Comets in 1952, Haley and his band gave some hint of the *rock and roll era to come when they recorded Jackie Brenston's rhythm 'n' blues hit 'Rocket 88' in aggressive rockabilly style. The hillbilly element was dropped in a rocking version of Haley's own 'Crazy, man, crazy' (1953) and Joe *Turner's 'Shake, rattle and roll' (1954), in which elements of boogie-woogie and country music combined with spontaneous rhythmic zest.

The rock boom really started with the strident 'Rock around the clock' (1954) which became an international best-seller when it was used as background to the opening sequence of the film *The Blackboard Jungle* (1955). It became the anthem of the younger generation and sold 22 million copies. From then until March 1957 every Haley record released moved quickly into the Top 20—'See you later, alligator', 'R-O-C-K', etc., and 'Rock around the clock' had regular revivals. Haley's voice was distinctly white and his style was what has been described as 'western swing' with a basis of propulsive jazz rhythm, made cornier but more readily acceptable to white listeners and dancers by the emphasis on the second and fourth beats of the bar. Haley was never a sex symbol like Frankie *Laine or Elvis *Presley; his appeal was based on the exuberance and togetherness of his music, which had none of the menace and alienation that other rock stars imparted.

In 1957, Haley toured England and although his music was liked his personal image was disappointing—not at all the rock-superstar but rather sedate, conventional, and on the plump side. This perhaps marked the end of his stardom but he survived well for many years as a revival figure; remaining the same chubby, unageing nice guy, realizing his limitations, and still playing with high-spirited good humour.

J. Swenson: *Bill Haley* (London, 1982).

Half a Sixpence. British musical with music and lyrics by David *Heneker and book by Beverley Cross, based on the novel *Kipps* by H. G. Wells. Starring Tommy *Steele and Marti Webb, it opened at the Cambridge Theatre, London, 21 Mar. 1963 and ran for 678 performances.

The story of the orphan who goes into the drapery business, inherits a fortune, marries a working-class girl, loses his fortune, and ends up running a bookshop was pleasantly sentimental, full of good humour and Cockney-style songs, tailored for Steele's talents, such as 'Money to burn' and 'Flash, bang, wallop'. Steele starred again in New York at the Broadhurst Theatre, 25 Apr. 1965, for 512 performances, with Polly James as his lady love. It was filmed in 1967 with Steele, Julia Foster, and Cyril *Ritchard.

Hall, Adelaide Louise (*b* Brooklyn, NY, 20 Oct. 1909). American singer. She was spotted by Lew *Leslie, the producer of **Blackbirds*, when singing in a school concert. She appeared in the chorus of **Shuffle Along* (1921) and in *Runnin' Wild* (1923), then took over Florence *Mills's leading role in *Blackbirds*, when the star died in 1927, singing such songs as 'Diga diga doo', 'I can't give you anything but love', and 'I must have that man'. She was in *Brown Buddies* (1930) and went to London in 1931 to appear in revue. Returning to New York, she appeared in the *Cotton Club revues of the 1930s, singing with the Duke *Ellington band with whom she had earlier (1927) made her classic vocalise recording of 'Creole love call' and 'The blues I love to sing'. In the late 1930s she ran a nightclub, the Big Apple, in Paris. After a singing tour of Europe, she settled in London where she appeared in several films and in productions of **Kiss Me Kate* (1951) and **Love from Judy* (1952). She was with Lena *Horne in the New York production of *Jamaica* (1957).

Hall, Daryl [Hohl] (*b* Pottstown, Penn., 11 Oct. 1948) and **Oates, John** (*b* New York, 7 Apr. 1949). American rock singing duo. They first met in 1967 in *doo-wop groups around Philadelphia and formed their singing partnership in 1969, soon becoming one of the most successful duos in the business. They signed up with Atlantic Records in 1972 and recorded three albums, none of which was outstandingly profitable; they left Atlantic in 1974. They then signed with RCA and had their first hit single with 'Sara Smile'. The album *Bigger than Both of Us* (1976) contained their first No. 1 hit, 'Rich girl', the first of six in the USA, the others being 'Kiss on my list' (1981); 'Private eyes' (1981); 'I can't go for that' (1981); 'Maneater' (1982); and 'Out of touch' (1984). Having found their individual style they continued to be popular in the USA but never found the same acclaim in Britain, 'Maneater' proving to be their best-selling British disc. They have also worked separately and with others. In 1985 they appeared at the re-opening concert of the *Apollo Theater 'an ultimate accolade for two great exponents of "blue-eyed soul"' after 15 years of rewarding partnership.

Hall, Henry (*b* Peckham, London, 2 May 1898; *d* Eastbourne, 28 Oct. 1989). British bandleader, composer, and arranger. He learned the trumpet, later playing in the Salvation Army International Staff Band, and worked in the editorial department of the Salvation Army. He then studied at Trinity College of Music before serving in the army in the First World War. He tried a stage career, but ended up playing the piano in a cinema. He joined the band at the Midland Hotel, Manchester, as pianist; then became conductor at the Gleneagles Hotel in Perthshire, first broadcasting from there in 1924. He began to record for Columbia and became musical director for the hotels of the LMS (the old London, Midland, & Scottish Railway), controlling 32 bands.

At the beginning of 1932 he was asked to take over from Jack *Payne at the BBC and to form a new regular broadcasting band. The famous BBC Dance Orchestra made its first broadcast on 15 Mar. 1932, the first from the new Broadcasting House, and Henry Hall became one of the best-known names in England, starting his 'Guest Night', a popular weekly programme, in 1934. George Elrick (*b* 1910) was the band's vocalist 1935–7. Hall wrote many songs, including his own signing-off number 'Here's to the next time' (1932) and 'It's time to say goodnight' (1934). The band recruited many famous musicians, including the American Benny *Carter, and appeared in the film *Music Hath Charms* (1935), for which Hall wrote the score and title-song. He left the BBC in 1937 to tour the variety halls with his own orchestra, but returned to host a second series of 'Guest Night' in 1939. He continued his band activities until 1945 when he became an impresario, staging such shows as *Something in the Air*; *Buttons and Bows*; *Irma La Douce*; and **Annie Get Your Gun*. He made a come-back in the 1950s with a TV show, *Face the Music*, but finally gave up broadcasting in 1964.

H. Hall: *Here's to the Next Time* (London, 1955).

Hall, Owen. [Davis, James] (*b* Dublin, 1853; *d* Harrogate, 9 Apr. 1907). Irish librettist, author, and journalist. He studied at the University of London and practised law 1874–86. During this time he did much journalistic work, and he became a full-time journalist in 1888. He happened to meet George *Edwardes in a railway carriage and, in conversation, told him he thought he could write much better librettos than those then being used at the *Gaiety Theatre. The challenge was accepted, and so was *A *Gaiety Girl* which was produced in 1893. He followed this with *An *Artist's Model* (1895); *The *Geisha* (1896); *A Greek Slave* (1898); **Florodora* (1899); *The Silver Slipper* (1901); *The Girl From Kay's* (1902); *The Medal and the Maid* (1903); *Sergeant Brue* (1904); and *The Little Cherub* (1906).

Hall, Tom T. (*b* Olive Hill, Ky., 25 May 1936). American country singer and composer. He first worked in a band known as the Kentucky Travellers 1952–4, then served in the US Army. Afterwards he became a disc jockey and went to Nashville in 1962. Here he became known as the Nashville Storyteller, writing stories and songs about his own experiences that included such country classics as 'DJ for a day' (1963); 'Mad' (1964); 'What are we fighting for' (1964); and 'Back pocket money' (1964), which were sung by such stars as Jimmy C. Newman (*b* 1927), Dave Dudley (*b* 1928), and Burl *Ives. He recorded for Mercury Records from 1967, producing such hits as 'I washed my face in the morning dew' (1967); 'Harper Valley PTA' (1968)—made into a No. 1 country hit by Jennie C. Riley (*b* 1945); 'Ballad of forty dollars' (1968); 'A week in a country jail' (1969); and 'Uptight band' for *Flatt and *Scruggs. He recorded a number of albums in the 1970s and had hits with 'The old side of town' (1979) and 'Soldier of fortune' (1980). He wrote books on songwriting, had a best-seller with *The Story Teller's Nashville* (1979), and became a popular TV personality, continuing with a large output of recordings.

Hall, Wendell Woods (*b* St George, Kan., 23 Aug. 1896; *d* Fairhope, Ala., 2 Apr. 1969). American composer, writer, singer, and guitarist. He began in vaudeville as a singing xylophonist, and became well-known on radio as 'The Red-Headed Music Maker'. He made a world tour singing many of his own compositions, including the very popular 'It ain't gonna rain no mo'' (1923), which he based on an old country-dance tune. His own recording of it, accompanying himself on the *ukelele (an instrument he helped to popularize), sold more than two million copies in 1923 and went on to sell around five million. He also wrote 'Mellow moon', and was still composing in the 1960s.

Hamilton, Nancy (*b* Sewickley, Pa., 27 July 1908; *d* 1985). American author, singer, and actress. She started her career as an understudy for Katharine Hepburn in 1933, appearing in **New Faces* (1934) and in many straight plays. She wrote radio scripts for Beatrice *Lillie 1934–6 and for various radio shows, then wrote for MGM films 1941–2. Her librettos include: *One for the Money* (1939); *Two for the Show* (1940)—'How high the moon' (*m* Morgan *Lewis); *Three to Make Ready* (1946)—'If it's love', 'The old soft shoe' (*m* Lewis).

Hamlisch, Marvin (*b* New York, 2 June 1944). American composer, pianist, and conductor. He studied piano at the Juilliard School of Music and Queen's College. He had his first hit song at 16 when Jack Jones sang 'Sunshine, lollipops and rainbows'. He wrote Las Vegas cabaret material for Ann-Margret (*b* 1941) and Liza *Minnelli, toured as pianist for Groucho Marx, and spent four years as a television rehearsal pianist. His first real acclaim came in 1974 when he won Academy Awards for his scores for *The Way We Were*, with Barbra *Streisand and Robert Redford, and *The Sting*, which was mainly by Scott *Joplin and orchestrated by Gunther *Schuller. Among many other film scores were *The Swimmer* (1968); *April Fools* (1969); and *The Spy Who Loved Me* (1977)—'Nobody does it better'. He wrote the score for the long-lasting theatrical success *A *Chorus Line* (1975), which received a Tony Award for its music. This was followed by *They're Playing Our Song* (1979) and more film scores. He is a polished entertainer at the piano in the Sammy *Cahn mould.

Hammerstein, Oscar, II [Greeley Glendenning] (*b* New York, 12 July 1895; *d* Doylestown, Pa., 23 Aug. 1960). American librettist, lyric-writer, and producer. From a famous theatrical family, his grandfather Oscar Hammerstein (1847–1919) was a celebrated impresario who built several opera houses and theatres in the USA, and his father was a theatre manager. He studied law at Columbia University and graduated in 1917, but the family call was too great and, having acted in university shows, he abandoned the law and became stage manager for his uncle Arthur Hammerstein.

He began writing for the theatre, producing librettos for several minor shows 1920–2; then came *Wildflower* (1923); *Mary Jane McKane* (1923); *Gypsy Jim* (1924); *New Toys* (1924); **Rose-Marie* (1924); **Sunny* (1925); *Song of the Flame* (1925); *The Wild Rose* (1926); *The *Desert Song* (1926); *Golden Dawn* (1927); **Show Boat* (1927); *The *New Moon* (1927); *Good Boy* (1928); *Rainbow* (1928); *Madeleine* (1929); *Sweet Adeline* (1929); *The Gang's All Here* (1931); *Free for All* (1931); *East Wind* (1931); **Music in the Air* (1932); **Ball at the Savoy* (1933); *Three Sisters* (1934); *May Wine* (1935); *Gentlemen Unafraid* (1938); *Very Warm for May* (1939); and *Sunny River* (1941). He then began his notable collaborations with Richard *Rodgers on **Oklahoma!* (1943); **Carousel* (1945); **Allegro* (1947); **South Pacific* (1949); *The *King and I* (1950); *Me and Juliet* (1953); *Pipe Dream* (1955); *Cinderella* (1957); **Flower Drum Song* (1958); and *The *Sound of Music* (1959). He wrote the libretto of **Carmen Jones* (1943) to the music of Bizet. He won a *Pulitzer Prize for *Oklahoma!*, a Donaldson Award for *Carmen Jones* and *Carousel*, Academy Awards for 'The last time I saw Paris' (from *Lady Be Good*,

1941) and 'It might as well be Spring' (from *State Fair*, 1945). He also wrote for films with *Kern, *Korngold, *Romberg, and other composers.

The far more robust and sentimental (though still sophisticated) lyrics of Hammerstein, and the big-scale works that he produced with Rodgers, will always be compared with the brittle wittiness of the lyrics of his predecessor, Lorenz *Hart. Hammerstein's real talent was for the big theatrical gesture, first notably manifested in *Show Boat*, and the power of his writing was enough to change the character of Rodgers's music.

D. Taylor: *Some Enchanted Evening; the Story of Rodgers and Hammerstein I* (New York, 1953). S. Green: *The Rodgers and Hammerstein Story* (New York, 1963). H. Fordin: *Getting to Know Him: a Biography of Oscar Hammerstein II* (New York, 1977). F. Nolan: *The Sound of Their Music: the Story of Rodgers and Hammerstein* (New York–London, 1978).

Lyrics: O. Hammerstein: *Lyrics* (New York, 1949). *The Rodgers and Hammerstein Song Book* (New York, 1958).

Hammond, John Henry (*b* New York, 15 Dec. 1910; *d* New York, 10 July 1987). American record producer. Born into a rich family, he was able to indulge his interest in black culture, especially jazz, as a young man. He went to Yale but left in 1931 to work as a disc jockey and radio jazz producer. In 1933 he became recording director of the English branch of Columbia Records, where he used his own finances to subsidize jazz recordings; and also wrote on jazz and popular music for the *New York Times* and the British *Melody Maker*. He helped to discover and promote Billie *Holiday when she was an unknown force; brought Count *Basie from Kansas City to the lights of New York; discovered Charlie *Christian; and had the idea for the racially integrated Benny *Goodman Trio. He promoted the Carnegie Hall 'From Spirituals to Swing' concerts and was a tireless worker for civil rights. Latterly he brought Aretha *Franklin, Bob *Dylan, and Bruce *Springsteen into the Columbia fold.

J. Hammond: *John Hammond on Record* (New York, 1977).

Hammond Organ. One of the first widely promoted electronic organs that began to supplant the wind-blown pipe organ in the 1930s. It was invented by Laurens Hammond (1895–1973) in 1929 and was first put on the market in 1935. Working on the principle of synchronized motor impulses, the basic mechanism was a series of revolving discs with raised portions varying in number according to the note they served. As each is put into operation it revolves in front of its own magnetic coil in which a current is induced and an amplified note is produced: a disc with 440 raised portions passing the magnet each second produces concert A, and so on. Various combinations of sounds could produce varying tones and passable imitations of other instruments. An entirely mechanical instrument, the Aeolian-Hammond Player-Organ was produced in 1938. Hammond also patented the Novachord in 1939, the Solovox in 1940, and the chord organ in 1950. The Hammond organ had a great vogue in dance bands, its variety of tones useful for augmenting small groups. Specialist performers like Ethel Smith in the USA and Harry Farmer in Britain began to build its popularity as a solo instrument, followed by many eminent performers. An immense variety of electronic keyboard instruments has since evolved from Hammond's pioneering work.

Hampton, Lionel (*b* Louisville, Ky., 12 Apr. 1909). American jazz vibraphonist, pianist, drummer, and bandleader. Brought up in Alabama, Chicago, and Los Angeles, he intended to go to university but instead started as a drummer in Paul Howard's Quality Serenaders. He made his first recordings with the Les Hite band in the 1930 sessions with Louis *Amstrong, and he was featured in Armstrong's 'Skeleton in the closet' number in the film *Pennies from Heaven* (1936). In the early years he played xylophone but soon switched to vibraphone and was one of the first to exploit its possibilities in jazz. In 1936 he joined the Benny *Goodman band and became known for his sparklingly virtuosic work with the Goodman quartets and quintets 1936–40. He recorded many sides for RCA Victor with all-star personnel, before starting a bandleading career in earnest in 1941.

The Hampton big band of the 1940s was one of the most exciting around, with frenetic sound over propulsive riffs and driving rhythm, inspired by Hampton's own ever-swinging and dextrous vibraphone playing or occasionally by his two-finger piano-playing or lively drumming. It included such exciting soloists as Arnett Cobb (1918–89). On the vibes Hampton was equally capable of sensitive and imaginative work on slow ballads. The band continued its activities long after many had gone out of business, visiting Europe several times from 1956 on and moving into the rhythm 'n' blues orbit. He gave up the big band in 1965 and founded the Jazz Inner Circle sextet. He appeared in various films, including: *A Song is Born* (1948), *The Benny Goodman Story* (1955), and, with the band, in several rock films of the 1950s. He composed 'Vibraphone blues (1936); 'Blues in my flat' (1938); 'Opus ½' (1938); 'Flyin' home' (1939); 'Central Avenue breakdown' (1940); 'Hey-baba-re-bop' (1945); 'Hamp's boogie-woogie' (1945); 'Midnight sun' (1947); and many more items.

L. Hampton & J. Haskins: *Hamp: an Autobiography* (New York, 1990).

Hancock, Herbie [Herbert Jeffrey] (*b* Chicago, 12 Apr. 1940). American jazz pianist. He appeared with the Chicago Symphony Orchestra when he was 12, playing a Mozart piano concerto. After studying engineering and music 1956–60, he went to New York in 1961 to follow a jazz career, first working with Donald Byrd. He played with Phil Woods and Oliver Nelson and recorded an album under his own name, *Takin' Off*, which was described as an 'accomplished and stunning' debut. He was with Eric *Dolphy 1962–3, and with the Miles *Davis Quintet 1963–8, during which time he established an international reputation. In 1968 he started the Herbie Hancock Sextet, reducing it to a quartet in 1973, when he recorded the best-selling jazz album *Headhunters*, with 'Chameleon' becoming a hit single. This turned him into a semi-pop star and the music he produced with electronic instruments showed how the elements of rock and jazz could most tastefully and effectively combine. Thereafter he spent his time searching for new avenues in electronic music, working with the rock group Material and coming up with a new best-selling album *Future Shock* in 1983. He won an Academy Award for his score to *Round Midnight* (1986) starring Dexter *Gordon.

Handy, W. C. [William Christopher] (*b* Florence, Ala., 16 Nov. 1873; *d* New York, 28 Mar. 1958). American composer and conductor. He was the son and grandson of a pastor and his father was one for whom music, in the old Puritan tradition, was a branch of the devil's malign activities. He thought it some trick of the devil that he had been given a musical son and there were bitter quarrels between them as the boy grew up. Handy was refused permission to learn the guitar and he finally bought an old trumpet which he practised in secret. At one time he left home to join a touring minstrel show, but he settled down to study, graduated from the Teachers' Agricultural and Mechanical College in Huntsville, Alabama, and became a schoolteacher. Finding the pay insufficient, he worked in an iron foundry for a time, organizing a brass band in his spare time, and eventually went into music professionally as a freelance cornettist. He played at the Chicago World's Fair in 1893, then became leader of the band of the Mahara Minstrels, a post which he held on and off from 1896 to 1903. During all this time, playing on the fringes of the newly emerging ragtime and jazz, he was listening to the blues in their folk form as he travelled round the South. A small jazz band he heard in Cleveland, Mississippi, made a great impression on him and he tried to write pieces for his own band, which he led from 1903–21, that captured something of the spirit of what he heard. He digested his material well, and a piece written as a campaign song in 1909 for E. H. Crump, the prospective mayor of Memphis, where he had settled, was published as 'Memphis blues' in 1912 and became his first big success, in reputation if not money: he sold it to a New York publisher for $50. He followed this with others in similar vein. Unable to sell *'St Louis blues' (1914) he started a publishing-house in collaboration with Harry Pace and profitably marketed it himself. An immensely influential publication, it led popular music away from the artificialities of *ragtime to the blues-tinged ballad that was to become the next staple diet of Tin Pan Alley, as well as towards the world's understanding of jazz.

Among his most lasting compositions after these were: 'Yellow Dog blues' (1914); 'Joe Turner blues' (1915); 'The hesitating blues' (1915); the march 'Hail to the spirit of freedom' (1915); 'Beale Street blues' (1917); 'Long gone' (1920); 'Aunt Hagar's blues' (1920); 'Loveless love' (1921); 'John Henry blues' (1922); 'Harlem blues' (1923); 'Atlanta blues' (1924); 'Friendless blues' (1926); 'Chantez la bas' (1931), to mention but a few: and he made numerous arrangements of folk-songs and spirituals from 1920 on. He published *Blues: an Anthology* in 1926; rev. as *A Treasury of the Blues*, 1949 and 1972; *Negro Authors and Composers of the US* (New York, 1936); *Book of Negro Spirituals* (New York, 1938); *Negro Music and Musicians* (New York, 1944); and his autobiography.

He received the Award of the National Association of Negro Music in 1937. When he died in 1958 he had been blind for 15 years. A film based on his life story, *St Louis Blues* was made in 1958, with Nat 'King' *Cole, as Handy, and Eartha *Kitt.

The glib ways of the popular press led to Handy's being dubbed 'The Father of the Blues'. This he emphatically was not (any more than Paul *Whiteman was the 'King of Jazz'); but he might justifiably be called the father of jazz notation, for he was one of the first to collect and successfully transcribe blues melodies—and, considering the rigidity of musical notation and the endless flexibility of the blues, with great accuracy and purpose. Just how much of such tunes as 'St Louis blues' and 'Memphis blues' are Handy's work and how much his recollection and editing of snatches of heard black song is now impossible to say; their endless durability, in both the jazz and the popular music worlds, speaks for their authenticity of feeling. It was largely due to Handy's transcriptions of traditional blues that the twelve-bar blues form became the accepted pattern and proved itself capable of endless interesting variation; one of the great organic forms of music.

W. C. Handy: *Father of the Blues: an Autobiography* (New York, 1941; London, 1957).

Hanley, James F[rederick] (*b* Rensselaer, Ind., 17 Feb. 1892; *d* Douglaston, Long Island, 8 Feb. 1942). American composer and author. While serving in the US 82nd Division in the First World War he wrote an army show, *Toot Sweet*. After the war he became a vaudeville accompanist and started writing for Broadway productions and later for films. His theatre music included: *Robinson Crusoe Jr.* (1916); *Jim Jam Jems* (1920); *Pins and Needles* (1922); *Spice of 1922*; *Honeymoon Lane* (1926); *The Sidewalks of New York* (1927); and he contributed to editions of *Ziegfeld Follies*, *George White's Scandals*, and *The *Greenwich Village Follies*. His best-known songs were 'Back home again in Indiana' (1917); 'Rose of Washington Square' (1920); 'Second-hand rose' (1921); 'Little log cabin of dreams' (1927); and 'Zing went the strings of my heart' (1934).

Hanshaw, Annette (*b* New York, 18 Oct. 1910). American singer. Although as a child she was a natural singer, she never studied music and only took up singing professionally because she was heard at a party by a Pathé executive, Herman

Rose, whom she married in 1934. She was only 15 when she signed a recording contract and her first Pathé record was issued in 1926. She recorded prolifically until 1934 and appeared in various short films and on radio with her own show, billed as 'The Personality Girl', but she never enjoyed the pressures of show-business and retired from all such activities in 1936.

She was a greatly talented performer with an easy, rhythmic delivery and an ability to put character and meaning into a lyric, as well as a talented mimic—her favourite subject being the 'boop-boop-a-doop' girl, Helen Kane. On some of her recordings she also played piano or ukulele. Her natural jazz-inflected delivery was usually backed by a pickup group (often labelled the Sizzling Syncopators) that contained, from time to time, such players as James P. *Johnson, Clarence *Williams, Benny *Goodman, Joe *Venuti, Jimmy and Tommy *Dorsey, Phil Napoleon, and Muggsy *Spanier; and her recordings of the songs of the period have become treasured by jazz collectors.

Hanson, John [Watts, John Stanley] (*b* Oshawa, Ontario, 31 Aug. 1921). British singer and actor. He went to England with his English parents in 1925, soon moving to Scotland, and was educated at Dumfries. He worked in engineering, but sang in amateur shows and on the BBC, making his first professional appearance in Birmingham in 1946, and in 1947 appearing in a summer show at the Pavilion in Sandown. He appeared on radio in 1949 in *Songs from the Shows*, *Melody Time* with *Geraldo, and *Variety Bandbox*, gradually building a substantial reputation through regular radio and TV work. In 1954 he made his first tour as the Red Shadow in *The *Desert Song*, the part with which he was to become indelibly associated, and he appeared in *The *Student Prince* in 1959, *The *Vagabond King* in 1960, and a succession of revivals. He had his own radio shows, *The Hanson Hour* and *John Hanson Sings*; and he wrote the music for *Smilin' Through* (1966), utilizing the song by Arthur A. Penn (1875–1941), and his own theme song 'A song of romance'. He continued an active and varied career into the late 1980s.

J. Hanson: *Me and My Red Shadow* (London, 1980).

'Happy birthday to you'. One of the world's most used songs and possibly one of the most embarrassing. The music by Mildred J. Hill (1859–1916), organist, pianist, composer, and authority on Negro spirituals, was published as 'Good morning to all' in *Song Stories for the Kindergarten* in Chicago in 1893, later as a march re-titled 'Happy birthday', Chicago, 1934. It was published as the song 'Happy birthday to you', with words by Patty Smith Hill (1868–1916), in *Union School Chorus Music* in 1935. In England it gradually displaced 'Many happy returns of the day' with music by John *Blockley and words by Eliza Cook.

Harbach, Otto [Hauerbach, Otto Abels] (*b* Salt Lake City, 18 Aug. 1873; *d* New York, 24 Jan. 1963). American librettist and lyricist. He started life as an English teacher, became a reporter on the *New York News*, and first became known as a librettist in collaboration with Karl *Hoschna on *The Three Twins* (1908) and **Madame Sherry* (1910). He worked with Hoschna several more times in the next three years, then, after the composer's death in 1911, with Rudolf *Friml on *The *Firefly* (1912) and **Rose-Marie* (1924); with Louis *Hirsch on *Going Up* (1917) and *Mary* (1920); with Vincent *Youmans on **Wildflower* (1923) and **No, No, Nanette* (1925); with George *Gershwin on *A Song of the Flame* (1925); with Jerome *Kern on **Sunny* (1925), *Criss Cross* (1926), *The *Cat and the Fiddle* (1931), and **Roberta* (1933); and with Sigmund *Romberg on *The *Desert Song* (1926). In 1925 he had five shows running on Broadway at the same time. He was president of *ASCAP, 1950 and 1953.

Harburg, E. Y. [Edgar 'Yip'; orig. Hochberg, Isidore] (*b* New York, 8 Apr. 1898; *d* Los Angeles, 5 Mar. 1981). American lyricist, producer, and director. The electrical business which he part-owned was bankrupted in the depression, so in 1929 he went into songwriting.

He wrote for *Earl Carroll's Sketchbook* (1929); **Earl Carroll's Vanities* (1930)—'Knee deep in daisies'; **Garrick Gaieties* (1930)—'I'm only human after all'; *Shoot the Works* (1931); *Ballyhoo* (1932); **Americana* (1932)—'Brother, can you spare a dime?'; **Walk a Little Faster* (1932)—'April in Paris'; *Ziegfeld Follies* (1934)—'I like the likes of you', 'What is there to say?'; **Life Begins at 8:40* (1934)—'You're a builder upper', 'Let's take a walk around the block'; *Hooray for What?* (1937); *Hold On to Your Hats* (1940); *Bloomer Girl* (1944)—'Pretty as a picture'; **Finian's Rainbow* (1947; filmed 1968)—'How are things in Glocca Morra?', 'If this isn't love'; *Jamaica* (1957).

Films he wrote for include: **Rio Rita* (1929); **Applause* (1929); *Glorifying the American Girl* (1930); *Moonlight and Pretzels* (1933); *Take a Chance* (1933)—'It's only a paper moon'; *The Singing Kid* (1936); *Stage Struck* (1936); *Gold Diggers of 1937* (1937); *The *Wizard of Oz* (1939)—'Over the rainbow', etc.; *The Marx Brothers at the Circus* (1939); *Babes on Broadway* (1941); *Ship Ahoy* (1942); *Cairo* (1942); **Cabin in the Sky* (1943)—'Happiness is just a thing called Joe'; *Can't Help Singing* (1944)—'Can't help singing'; *Hollywood Canteen* (1944); **Kismet* (1944); *Meet the People* (1944); *Centennial Summer* (1946)—'Cinderella Sue'; *California* (1946); and *Gay Purr-ee* (1962).

C. Brahms & N. Sherrin: 'E. Y. Harburg' in *Song by Song* (London, 1984).

Lyrics: E. Y. Harburg: *Rhymes for the Irreverent* (New York, 1968); and *At this Point in Rhyme* (New York, 1976).

Hard Day's Night, A. British United Artists film, made in 1964, starring the *Beatles. The story was based on a day in the lives of the celebrated quartet, and although it was a low budget film, primarily intended as publicity for an LP, it became one of the few accepted classic films in the rock field. The personalities of *Lennon, *McCartney, *Harrison, and *Starr, and an amusing script, were additional assets to a score full of their best songs, including: 'A hard day's night', 'I should have known better', 'I want to be your man', 'All my loving', 'Can't buy me love', 'I'm happy just to dance with you', 'Tell me why', and 'She loves you'.

Hardelot, Guy d' [Guy, Helen] (*b* Château d'Hardelot, Boulogne-sur-Mer, 1858; *d* Shepperton, Middx., 7 Jan. 1936). French songwriter. She studied at the Paris Conservatoire, and travelled with the singer Emma Calvé in the USA in 1896. After marriage, she settled in England where she wrote widely popular songs under the pen-name of Guy d'Hardelot, notably 'Because' (1902, Edward Teschemacher); also 'I know a lovely garden' (1903, *w* Teschemacher); 'My message' (1911, *w* Julian Gade); 'Until one day' (1911, *w* Alfred H. Hyatt); 'Love's words' (1912, *w* Helen Lanyen); 'A summer song' (1913, *w* G. Hubi-Newcombe); and 'Wait' (1916, *w* A. L. Salmon).

Harline, Leigh (*b* Salt Lake City, 26 Mar. 1907; *d* Long Beach, Calif., 10 Dec. 1969). American composer and conductor. He studied composition, piano, and organ at the University of Utah, settled in Los Angeles in 1928, and worked with various radio stations. In 1931–2 he was arranger for the first transcontinental broadcasts from Los Angeles. He was with the Walt Disney studios as composer and arranger 1932–42, winning Academy Awards for *Pinocchio* and 'When you wish upon a star', then worked as a freelance film composer in Hollywood.

He wrote music for: *The Grasshopper and the Ant* (1934); **Snow White and the Seven Dwarfs* (1937); *Pinocchio* (1940)—'Give a little whistle'; *You Were Never Lovelier* (1942); *The Sky's the Limit* (1943); *Follow the Boys* (1944); *Road to Utopia* (1945); *Beat the Band* (1946); and *Mr Blandings Builds his Dream House* (1948); continuing into the 1960s.

Harmonica. Small mouth-blown instrument also known as the mouth-harmonica and mouth-organ. The basic diatonic instrument has a centre wooden or plastic block with ten square apertures. Riveted to brass plates on either side of this are twenty reeds, ten at the top fixed so that they only vibrate when air is blown into the aperture, ten at the bottom fixed so that they only vibrate when air is sucked out. A metal cover on each side acts as a sound amplifier. The basic instrument, known as a 'vamper', can provide a simple accompaniment or play basic melodies in the key of C or whatever key the instrument is tuned to. The harmonica is sometimes used on a frame which holds it near the mouth so that the hands may be left free to play the guitar or some other instrument, and is often thus used in folk-music. An outstanding exponent in this field of music-making was Sonny *Terry.

A more advanced instrument, the chromatic harmonica, has two rows of reeds on either side tuned a semitone apart, with a spring-loaded button which cuts off one or the other so that the chromatic scale can be achieved. This is the kind of instrument used by virtuoso players like Larry *Adler whose capabilities are boundless. A great variety of models is available, from miniatures to large bass instruments, in any key, and designed for different melodic and harmonic purposes, as used in the once popular harmonica bands such as the Harmonicats led by Jerry Murad in the USA in the 1940s and Borrah Minevitch and his Harmonica Rascals.

The invention of the harmonica is credited to Christian Friedrich L. Buschmann (1805–64); the most famous maker was Matthias Hohner (1833–1902), who started his business at Trossingen, Württemberg, in 1857. Hohner was responsible for introducing many variants working on the same principle, notably the Melodica, an instrument with its notes selected by a small piano-type keyboard working from a single wind source. This idea had previously been developed by the British inventor Wheatstone, who made a mouth-organ of this type around 1829. Similar principles were used in various toy instruments shaped like trumpets or saxophones. One sold under the name of the Goofus achieved a temporary place in the annals of jazz in the 1930s.

Harney, Ben [Benjamin Robertson] (*b* Middleboro, Ky., 1 Mar. 1871; *d* Philadelphia, 1 Mar. 1938). American composer and ragtime pianist. He was long accepted by such authorities as Rudi *Blesh as a white musician; but others who knew him, like Eubie *Blake and Willie 'The Lion' *Smith, affirm that he was a light-skinned black. Harney himself, for obvious reasons, was happy to exploit his ability to be taken for a white performer. He is generally credited with the introduction of ragtime to New York, playing it in what Blake described as a 'white style'. He arrived in New York in 1896 and made an immediate hit at Keith's Union Square Theatre. His ragtime songs 'You've been a good old wagon but you've done broke down' (1895) and 'Mister Johnson, turn me loose' (which May *Irwin sang in *Courted Into Court* (1986))' (1896) made him a pioneer in the field, being the first syncopated songs to be published in America, as did his *Ragtime Instructor* published in 1897.

Harney and his wife were experienced entertainers before they arrived in New York, but it was here that he made his name at Tony *Pastor's famous vaudeville theatre and elsewhere. His success sparked off a host of imitators, including Mike Bernard, the musical director at Pastor's, who at one time billed himself as 'King of Ragtime'. Harney's popularity set off a succession of ragtime contests, which he often participated in and frequently won, and it was not long before *Tin Pan Alley was cashing in on the craze. He wrote many songs in a comic minstrel vein such as 'I love my honey' (1897); 'You may go but this will bring you back' (1898); 'The cake-walk in the sky' (1899); and 'The only way to keep her is in a cage' (1901).

Harnick, Sheldon (*b* Chicago, 30 Apr. 1924). American composer and librettist. He contributed songs to **New Faces* (1952)—'Boston beguine'; *Two's Company* (1952); *John Murray Anderson's Almanac* (1953); *Shoestring Revue* (1955 and 1957); *The Littlest Revue* (1955); and *Shangri-la* (1956). As librettist, he teamed up with composer Jerry *Bock to write *The Body Beautiful* (1958); **Fiorello!* (1959); *Tenderloin* (1960); **She Loves Me* (1963); **Fiddler on the Roof* (1964); *The *Apple Tree* (1966); and *The Rothschilds* (1970). He also wrote *Smiling the Boy Fell Dead* (1961, *m* David Baker); *Captain Jinks of the Horse Marines* (1975, *m* Jack Beeson); *Rex* (1976, *m* Richard *Rodgers); and translated *The Umbrellas of Cherbourg* (1979, *m* Michel *Legrand).

C. Brahms & N. Sherrin: 'Sheldon Harnick' in *Song by Song* (London, 1984).

Harrigan and Hart. Famous partnership of Edward Harrigan (*b* New York, 26 Oct. 1844; *d* New York, 6 June 1911) and Tony Hart [Anthony J. Cannon] (*b* Worcester, Mass., 25 July 1855; *d* Worcester, 4 Nov. 1891), who worked as a comedy duo, occasionally separately, in a series of 'knockdown' farces with music mainly written by David *Braham, Harrigan directing and writing the librettos. These usually revolved around 'The Mulligan Guards' and pioneered much of the Irish, German, Italian, and Jewish humour that later became commonplace in the USA. Harrigan and Hart were the epitome of American burlesque.

Their productions included *The Mulligan Guards' Picnic* (1878); *The Mulligan Guards' Ball* (1879); *The Mulligan Guards' Chowder* (1879); *The Mulligan Guards' Christmas* (1879); *The Mulligan Guards' Surprise* (1880); *The Mulligan Guards' Nominee* (1880); *The Mulligans' Silver Wedding* (1881); *The Major* (1881); *Squatter Sovereignty* (1882); *Mordecai Lyons* (1882); *McSorley's Inflation* (1882); *The Muddy Day* (1883); *Cordelia's Aspirations* (1883); *Dan's Tribulations* (1884); *Investigation* (1884); *McAllister's Legacy* (1885). The partners then fell out and parted, with Harrigan continuing in his own busy career.

E. J. Kahn: *The Merry Partners* (New York, 1955).

Harrington, J. P. [John Patrick] (*b* London, 1 May 1865; *d* London, 19 Aug. 1939). British composer and lyricist. He worked as a journalist on *Funny Folk* and other magazines and collaborated with George *Le Brunn for 21 years until Le Brunn died in 1905. Harrington then became a partner of James W. *Tate in a theatrical agency and went into publishing in 1906. He was the author of numerous music-hall sketches and was involved in the creation of more than a thousand published songs, including: 'The seven ages of man' (1889); 'The pretty maid was young and fair' (1893); 'Looking for a coon like me' (1894); 'It's a jolly fine game played slow' (1895); 'Tricky little Trilby' (1895); 'The wrong girl' (1895); 'The idler' (1896); 'The smartest girl in town' (1896); 'Everything in the garden's lovely' (1898); 'The girl in the khaki dress' (1900); 'All the girls are love-er-ly-ov-er-ly' (1903); 'The directoire girl' (1908); 'Put on your slippers' (1912); many of them written for Marie *Lloyd.

Harris, Charles K[assell] (*b* Poughkeepsie, NY, 1 May 1867; *d* New York, 22 Dec. 1930). American composer and publisher. He had a varied career as a bellhop, pawnbroker, and banjoist. At 18 he was advertising 'Songs written to order', but it was not until 1891 that he achieved his first hit with 'Kiss and let's make up'. It was *'After the ball', written for an amateur minstrel show in Milwaukee in 1892, that really established him as well as making popular song history. It was sung to tremendous acclaim by J. Aldrich Libbey in *A *Trip to Chinatown* (1892) and then was taken up by the bandleader John Philip *Sousa who played it daily at the Chicago World's Fair and in his regular band concerts. It achieved the phenomenal sale, for those days, of five million copies and marked a turning-point in popular music-publishing history by making the publication of sheet music into big business.

Subsequently Harris founded his own music-publishing businesses in Milwaukee and New York, having notable publishing successes with such songs as 'Silver threads among the gold' (1873) by Hart Pease Danks (1834–1903) which sold more than two million copies in its year of publication. He passed on his experience in a book, *How to Write a Popular Song*. His other songs included: 'I'm trying so hard to forget' (1893); 'There'll come a time' (1895); 'Better than gold' (1896); 'Break the news to Mother' (1897); ''Mid the green fields of Virginia' (1898); 'For old time's sake' (1900); 'I've a longing in my heart for you, Louise' (1900); 'Hello Central, give me Heaven' (1901); 'For sale: a baby' (1903); 'Would you care?' (1905); and 'The best thing in life' (1907).

C. K. Harris: *After the Ball: Forty Years of Melody* (New York, 1926).

Harris, Emmylou (*b* Birmingham, Ala., 12 Apr. 1949). American country-rock singer. She spent her childhood in Washington DC and went to the University of North Carolina. A natural liking for singing folk and country music led her to clubs in Greenwich Village, New York, in the 1960s and she made some recordings for the Jubilee label. It was not until 1975 that her distinctive talents first emerged when her recording of 'If I could only win your love' reached the No. 1 position in the country music charts. This was followed by two albums, *Elite Hotel* (1975) and *Luxury Liner* (1976), which established her as a rock singer as well. In the country field *Blue Kentucky Girl* won a Grammy Award in 1979. She continued with a high reputation and good album sales into the 1980s.

Harris, Max (*b* Bournemouth, 15 Sept. 1918). British pianist, bandleader, arranger, and composer. His first job was as pianist at the Paramount

Dance Palais in London, and he made his first radio appearance on BBC's *Jazz Club* in 1950. He arranged for Ted *Heath and the BBC Show Band, led his own orchestra behind several top radio comedy shows, and wrote many TV theme tunes including those for *Doomwatch*; *Mickey Dunne*; *The Spies*; *Poldark*; *A Horseman Riding By*; *Porridge*; *Gurney Slade*; and many more. He arranged and led the violin-duo recordings made by Stéphane *Grappelli and Yehudi Menuhin.

Harris, Phil (*b* Linton, Ind., 16 Jan. 1904). American singer and bandleader. He grew up in *Nashville and played as a drummer in local bands, was with the Henry Halstead orchestra in Los Angeles 1924–7, toured the USA, and then co-led a group with Carol Lofner 1928–30. He led his own band at the St Francis Hotel in San Francisco 1931–2 and then at the Cocoanut Grove in Los Angeles. Becoming widely known for his showy presentations and novelty vocals, he began a film career in 1933 with a short feature called *So This is Harris*. In 1934 he had his own radio show, *Let's Listen to Harris*, and he continued to lead a good swinging band featuring vocalist Leah Ray, with 'Rose room' as his signature tune. He was with the Jack Benny show 1937–46, playing the role of a hard-drinking, wise-guy musician.

From 1937 on he made a number of very popular records in his distinctive, gravelly-voiced, semi-speaking manner, including 'Woodman, spare that tree' and 'That's what I like about the South'; later, in the same vein, 'The preacher and the bear'. 'The Darktown poker club', 'The thing', and many songs from the Bert *Williams repertoire. He married Alice *Faye in 1941 and co-starred with her in a radio show 1947–54. He appeared in the films *Melody Cruise* (1936); *Turn off the Moon* (1937); *Man about Town* (1939); *Buck Benny Rides Again* (1940); *Dreaming Out Loud* (1940); *I Love a Bandleader* (1945); *Wabash Avenue* (1950); *Starlift* (1951); *The Wild Blue Yonder* (1951); *The High and the Mighty* (1954); **Anything Goes* (1956); *Goodbye Lady* (1956); *The Wheeler Dealers* (1963); *The Patsy* (1964); *The Cool Ones* (1967); and *King Gun* (1969). He was still active in the 1970s and later often appeared on TV to make obituary tributes.

Harrison, George (*b* Liverpool, 25 Feb. 1943). British rock singer, guitarist, and composer. During his period as a member of the *Beatles he tended to be pushed into the background by the talents of John *Lennon and Paul *McCartney and the showmanship of Ringo *Starr, but it was his great interest in Eastern music that led the group's music into these cultural areas and his own songs took on many Indian themes and involved such instruments as the sitar. One of his most successful songs in the Beatles era was 'Something' (1969). After the demise of the Beatles in 1970 he was able to follow his own course and made a personal mark with such experimental albums as *All Things Must Pass* (1970) and *Living in the Material World* (1973). Phil *Spector guided him into creating his own sound, which came to fruition with the help of Eric *Clapton and Dave Mason, producing such compelling hits as 'My sweet Lord'. A firm believer in the humane message that rock music could spread, he was concerned with a Concert for Bangladesh in 1973 that involved Bob *Dylan and others. Another notable hit was 'Give me love' in 1973. After the first two solo albums Harrison seemed to lose impetus and subsequent albums did not prove particularly remarkable, since when he has given more of his personal attention to record and film production. In 1982 he published a lavishly bound, signed, and limited edition of his 'works', *I Me Mine*, which sold for £164.

R. Michaels: *George Harrison: Yesterday and Today* (New York, 1977; London, 1982). G. Guiliano: *Dark Horse: the Secret Life of George Harrison* (London, 1990).

Harrison, Rex [Reginald Carey] (*b* Huyton, 5 Mar. 1908; *d* New York, 2 June 1990). British actor. A notable straight and comedy actor on the London stage and in films, his name was fixed in the musical annals by an outstanding and unforgettable characterization of the role of Professor Higgins in the classic musical **My Fair Lady* (1956), a role he played in New York and London, and in the 1964 film version. His half-spoken delivery of the lyrics became much imitated by other vocally insecure actors. He also appeared in the film musical *Doctor Dolittle* (1967). He was knighted in 1989.

R. Harrison: *Rex an Autobiography* (London, 1974). A. Eyles: *Rex Harrison* (London, 1985).

Hart, Lorenz Milton (*b* New York, 2 May 1895; *d* New York, 22 Nov. 1943). American lyric-writer and librettist. He was educated at Columbia University where he met and first collaborated with Richard *Rodgers, the only composer he ever actually worked with, though he did write the lyrics for the film version of Lehár's *The *Merry Widow* (1934). Over the years they collaborated on 26 Broadway musicals, 3 London shows, and 20 film scores, taking the musical from its brittle 1920s era to the more sophisticated, message-bearing shows of the 1940s. Hart's wit, reflecting his own up-and-down melancholic character, and his increasing drink problem, was often cynical and bitter, but this aspect was usually offset by the sheer audacity of his rhythms and rhymes and what has been described as a 'peppery playfulness'. Following in the footsteps of W. S. *Gilbert, his only rival in lyrical dexterity in his heyday was probably Ira *Gershwin. Both produced the same period mixture of light romance and feathery wit.

The first Rodgers and Hart Broadway collaboration was *Poor Little Ritz Girl* in 1920, but they first really came to fame with their work in *The *Garrick Gaieties* (1925)—'Manhattan', 'Sentimental me'. This was followed by *Dearest Enemy* (1925)—'Here in my arms'; *The Girl Friend*

(1926)—'Blue room'; *The *Garrick Gaieties* (1926)—'Mountain greenery'; *Lido Lady* (London, 1926); **Peggy-Ann* (1926); *Betsy* (1926); **One Dam Thing after Another* (London, 1927); *A *Connecticut Yankee* (1927)—'My heart stood still', 'Thou swell'; *She's My Baby* (1928); *Present Arms* (1928)—'You took advantage of me'; *Chee-Chee* (1928); *Spring is Here* (1929)—'With a song in my heart'; *Heads Up* (1929)—'A ship without a sail'; *Simple Simon* (1930)—'Ten cents a dance'; **Ever Green* (London, 1930)—'Dancing on the ceiling'; *America's Sweetheart* (1931); *Jumbo* (1935)—'The most beautiful girl in the world', 'My romance', 'Little girl blue'; **On Your Toes* (1936)—'There's a small hotel'; **Babes in Arms* (1937)—'My funny Valentine', 'Johnny One Note', 'The lady is a tramp', 'Where or when'; **I'd Rather Be Right* (1937)—'Have you met Miss Jones?'; **I Married an Angel* (1938)—'I married an angel', 'Spring is here'; *The *Boys from Syracuse* (1938)—'Falling in love with love', 'This can't be love'; *Too Many Girls* (1939)—'I didn't know what time it was'; *Higher and Higher* (1940); **Pal Joey* (1940)—'Bewitched', 'I could write a book'; **By Jupiter* (1941)—'Wait till you see her'; *A Connecticut Yankee* (revised, 1943)—'To keep my love alive'.

The gap in the Rodgers and Hart musicals output 1930–5 was accounted for by a concentrated film effort, including: *Spring is Here* (1930); *Leathernecking* (1930); *Heads Up* (1930); *The Hot Heiress* (1931); *Love Me Tonight* (1932)—'Lover', 'Isn't it romantic'; *The Phantom President* (1932)—'Give her a kiss'; *Hallelujah, I'm a bum* (1933), in which Hart appeared—'You are too beautiful'; *Hollywood Party* (1934); *Evergreen* (1934); *Mississippi* (1935)—'Soon', 'It's easy to remember', 'Down by the river'; continuing with *Dancing Pirate* (1936); *Fool for Scandal* (1938); *Babes in Arms* (1939); *The Boys from Syracuse* (1940); *Too Many Girls* (1940); *They Met in Argentina* (1941); *I Married an Angel* (1942); *Words and Music* (1948); *Pal Joey* (1957); and *Jumbo* (1962)—12 of these being filmed versions of stage shows under the original or new names.

R. Rodgers: *Musical Stages* (New York, 1975). D. Hart: *Thou Swell, Thou Witty* (New York, 1976). S. Marx & J. Clayton: *Rodgers and Hart* (New York, 1976).

Lyrics: R. Rodgers & L. Hart: *The Rodgers and Hart Songbook* (New York, 1951). R. Kimball & D. Hart (eds.): *The Complete Lyrics of Lorenz Hart* (New York, 1987).

Hart, Moss (*b* New York, 24 Oct. 1904; *d* Palm Springs, 20 Dec. 1961). American librettist and director. He contributed sketches to the revue **As Thousands Cheer* (1932) and others, and was the librettist of: *Jonica* (1930); *The *Great Waltz* (1934); *Jubilee* (1935); **I'd Rather Be Right* (1937); *Sing Out the News* (1938); and **Lady in the Dark* (1941). He was equally well-known for his non-musical contributions to the theatre, including several collaborations with George S. *Kaufman, and later as the director of such musical classics as **My Fair Lady* (1956) and **Camelot* (1960).

M. Hart: *Act One: an Autobiography* (New York, 1959).

Hartley, Fred (*b* Dundee, 29 Dec. 1905). British composer, conductor, and pianist. He studied at the Royal Academy of Music. Mainly to be known throughout his career as a broadcaster, he was first heard on the radio as a piano soloist in 1924 and became a regular accompanist with the BBC in Dundee from 1927. He toured as a recitalist until 1931 and played with Jack *Hylton's Kit-Kat band. In 1931 he formed his own quintet, later extending it to a sextet and septet, was music supervisor for the BBC 1941–5, and worked for periods in Australia and South Africa. He had his own radio programme, *The Fred Hartley Hour* from 1935, writing his own theme tune, 'Life is nothing without music' (1933), and 'Angel on the loose' (1934).

Hatch, Tony (*b* Pinner, Middx., June 1939). British composer, author, pianist, arranger, and publisher. He was educated at the London Choir School and was head chorister at All Souls, Langham Place, London, for two years. He worked as tea-boy with a London music-publisher, and was with Rank Records before serving three years in the Coldstream Guards. Back in civilian life he published his first song 'Look for a star' in 1960 and had his first hit with 'Messing about on the river'. He worked as a producer with Pye Records and wrote a top hit for Petula *Clark, 'Downtown' (1964). That year he met singer Jackie Trent (*b* Newcastle-under-Lyme, Sept. 1940) who had been in theatre and cabaret since 1947 before she auditioned for Hatch. This began a personal relationship which led to marriage in 1967 and a song-writing partnership which resulted in a No. 1 hit, 'Where are you now', recorded by Trent in 1965.

A succession of collaborations included 'I know a place', 'Call me', 'My love', 'Don't sleep in the subway', 'Who am I?', 'The two of us', 'Colour my world', 'The other man's grass', and 'Joanna'. They concentrated on performing in the 1970s, with Jackie Trent taking the title role in *Nell* (1970) for which Tony Hatch was musical director. In 1973 they wrote the musical *The Card* and in 1975 *Rock Nativity*.

Hatton, John Liptrot (*b* Liverpool, 12 Oct. 1809; *d* Margate, 20 Sept. 1886). British composer and singer. He followed a theatrical career as an actor, comic singer, and pianist, and composed a number of songs that were very popular in their day such as 'Simon the cellarer' (1861), 'To Anthea', 'Goodbye, sweetheart, goodbye', 'I'm very fond of water', 'Kitty Carew', and 'The Lark now leaves his wat'ry nest', often writing under the pseudonym of Czapek. He settled in London in 1832, becoming pianist at Drury Lane, wrote an operetta, *The Queen of the Thames* (1843), and had an opera, *Pasqual Bruno*, performed in Vienna in 1844. He toured America as an entertainer 1848–50 and it was reported that, after giving the first Boston performance of Mendelssohn's Piano Concerto in D, he delighted the audience with a recital of popular songs. In 1853–9 he was musical director of the Princess's Theatre,

London, then managed by Charles Kean, and wrote music for many productions there. An opera, *Rose* (1864), was performed at Covent Garden. From 1866 he was accompanist and conductor at the St James's Hall ballad concerts.

He edited *Humorous Songs* (Boosey, 1875), which included his own 'Alexander of Kerry', 'The chair-mender', 'Don't come teasing me, sir', and 'The showman', with six new songs added in the third edition; three volumes of *Songs of England* (1886); and *Songs of Ireland* (with J. L. *Molloy, 1888). He provided many new lyrics for old English songs and ballads, some of which, like 'The Lincolnshire poacher', have now become the established texts.

Hawkins, Coleman Randolph (*b* St Joseph, Mo., 21 Nov. 1901; *d* New York, 19 May 1969). American jazz saxophonist. He played with the Jazz Hounds in Kansas City in 1921; toured with blues singer Mamie *Smith 1921–3; freelanced in New York 1923–4; and was with Fletcher *Henderson in New York 1923–34. It was while playing alongside Louis *Armstrong in the Henderson band that he absorbed some of Armstrong's phrasing and ideas into his own style, setting a new standard for imaginative and flexible playing which did much to establish the saxophone as an important jazz instrument; and he was to remain the leading player of the early 1930s.

He worked in Europe 1934–9 and on his return to the USA led his own band in New York 1939–41, during which time he made his famous recording of 'Body and Soul' (1939). This showed a new extempore daring that took jazz another step away from its traditional mould and provided some of the impetus for the move towards the new stream of modern jazz that developed in the 1940s. He kept, however, a full-bodied tone and heavy vibrato which contrasted with the lighter tones used by Lester *Young in the *Basie band. He consolidated his position as a leading light of the mainstream world of jazz until his playing roughened and deteriorated in his later years, when he played on the West Coast and opened the Billy Berg Club in Los Angeles in 1945. He visited Europe twice in the late 1940s and toured with Norman *Granz's Jazz at the Philharmonic in the 1950s, led various groups in the 1950s and 1960s, mainly in New York, and toured England in 1967. He was an active player until his death.

A. McCarthy: *Coleman Hawkins* (London, 1963). J. Chilton: *The Song of the Hawk: the Life and Recordings of Coleman Hawkins* (London, 1990).

Hawkins, Erskine Ramsey (*b* Birmingham, Ala., 26 July 1914). American jazz trumpeter and bandleader. An accomplished player at 13, he made his reputation in the South as an Armstrong impersonator. He formed his own band from a group based at the Alabama State Teacher's College and took it to New York in 1934 as the 'Bama State Collegians'. In 1939 the Erskine Hawkins band took over from Chick *Webb's as the unofficial house band of the *Savoy Ballroom in Harlem. He recorded regularly for the Bluebird label and rivalled the *Henderson and *Basie bands in popularity. He had a hit recording with 'Tuxedo Junction' (1939), of which he was part-composer, followed by 'Someone's rockin' my dreamboat' (1941) and 'Tippin'' (1945). The band survived the decline in big band popularity through the 1950s, but had to reduce its size in 1955. From 1960 he led a quartet at the Embers and worked into the 1970s, appearing at the Nice Jazz Festival in 1979.

Hayes, Isaac (*b* Covington, Tenn., 20 Aug. 1942). American rhythm 'n' blues singer, composer, and producer. He recorded for minor record labels in the 1960s, mainly working in the style of Brook Benton. He joined David Porter as a writer and producer for Stax Records and they produced the Sam and Dave records 'Hold on I'm coming' and 'Soul man' which were influential in the emergence of the Memphis sound. His own album *Hot Buttered Soul* led the way to a more sophisticated soul sound with added rhythm and large orchestral backing, which culminated in the album *Black Moses* and Hayes now an influential leader in the field. His finest work went into his score for the film *Shaft* in 1971. His later work was less effective and he left Stax in 1974 to join ABC in 1975. In the 1980s he mainly concentrated on writing, arranging, and producing. His songs include: 'B-A-B-Y', 'Soul man', 'Walk on by', and 'By the time I get to Phoenix'.

Haymes, Dick [Richard Benjamin] (*b* Buenos Aires, 13 Sept. 1916; *d* Los Angeles, Calif., 28 Mar. 1980). American singer with an English father and an Irish mother. He travelled in many countries with his family, his mother being a concert singer, finally settling in the USA, first in New York, later in California. At 16 he was vocalist with the Johnny Johnson band and he worked in Hollywood 1933–8 as a songwriter, film extra, and occasional actor and broadcaster. In 1940 he tried to sell some of his songs to Harry *James, who took him on as a singer. He became well known with the Benny *Goodman band in 1942, then with Tommy *Dorsey in 1943. That year he appeared in the film **Dubarry Was a Lady* and in 1944 was in *Two Jills and a Jeep*.

In the 1940s he was considered a strong rival to Bing *Crosby and Frank *Sinatra and appeared in many good film musicals in his peak years, including *Irish Eyes are Smiling* (1944); *Diamond Horseshoe* (1945); *State Fair* (1945); *Do You Love Me?* (1946); *The Shocking Miss Pilgrim* (1947); *Carnival in Costa Rica* (1947); **Up in Central Park* (1948); and **One Touch of Venus* (1948); introducing such songs as 'The more I see you', 'It's a grand night for singing', and 'For you, for me, for evermore'. His film career declined in the 1950s, and his troubles included finance, seven wives, and deportation. He worked in London, Ireland, and Spain in the 1960s, with a modest return to fame in the USA in the 1970s.

Hazelwood, Lee (*b* Mannford, Okla., 9 July 1929). American composer, author, singer, and producer. After service in Korea, he became a disc jockey in Phoenix, Arizona, specializing in Country and Western music. He sang and recorded occasionally, then in 1955 turned to song-writing. He became a record producer, having his first success with Sanford Clark's 'The Fool' on the Dot label in 1956. He formed the Jamie label with Lester Sill in Philadelphia and launched the career of Duane *Eddy, with whom he collaborated on 'Rebel rouser' (1959) and 'Guitar man' (1960). In 1961, Hazlewood and Sill formed the Gregmark label with Phil *Spector as producer. After a failure with the Eden label, Lee left the record business but returned to make further hits for the Reprise label, including Nancy Sinatra singing his own 'These boots are made for walkin''. He also wrote: 'Houston', 'How does that grab you darlin'?', 'Not the lovin' kind', 'So long, babe', and 'My baby cried the whole night long'.

Heath, Ted [Edward] (*b* Wandworth, London, 30 Mar. 1900; *d* Virginia Water, Surrey, 18 Nov. 1969). British bandleader, trombonist, and composer. He had early teaching from his father, who was conductor of the Wandsworth Borough Band, on tenor-horn and trombone. His first playing opportunity came wth Will Marion *Cook's Southern Syncopators, whom he joined on their European tour in the 1920s; but when the band was stranded in Vienna he returned to London. He was playing in a group of street buskers when he was heard by Jack *Hylton and offered a job with the band. Later he played with Bert Firman at the Metropole Hotel, with Hylton's touring band, with Al Starita at the Kit Kat Club, and with *Ambrose at the Mayfair Hotel, where he began to establish himself as a first-class band musician. He left Ambrose to work with Sydney *Lipton at Grosvenor House until war broke out, when he joined *Geraldo, the band most frequently heard on the radio during the war years.

The influx of American musicians playing with the Glenn *Miller and Sam *Donahue service bands inspired him to form a swing band that would try to raise British musicianship to their level. On the proceeds from his hit song 'That lovely weekend' (1942), he was able to make the Ted Heath Band a reality in 1944, writing his own theme song 'Listen to my music' (1944). The band was to remain in operation until his death in 1969, recording a large number of best-selling and highly regarded LPs for Decca, and such hits as 'Swinging shepherd blues' and 'Hot toddy' (1953). They regularly played at the Hammersmith Palais de Danse and gave important concerts at the London Palladium. The featured musicians included Kenny *Baker, Jack Parnell, Ronnie *Scott, John Keating, Don Lusher, Ronnie Verrall, and Johnny Hawksworth, and the singers included Dennis Lotis (*b* 1925), Beryl Davis and Lita Roza (*b* 1926). It was the only British big band to make successful tours of the USA, beginning in 1956, and it was accepted by American critics as being a swing band that rivalled the best in the USA.

T. Heath: *Listen to My Music* (London, 1957).

Heavy metal. A brand of rock music developed in the 1960s by blues-based groups like *Cream and those led by Jimi *Hendrix, using heavily amplified guitar and bass to produce an overwhelming output of sound. The term was established by Steppenwolf (1967–70), who utilized a William Burroughs phrase, 'heavy metal thunder', in their 1968 recording 'Born to be wild'. Others to qualify for heavy metal distinction were *Deep Purple, *Grand Funk, *Led Zeppelin, and Ted Nugent (*b* 1949), all dynamic practitioners. Bands of this kind come into their own at live concerts, and rock festivals, where their followers, known as headbangers, can enjoy the physical nature of the music, in their own macho way. The bands tend to produce the basic rock and roll that appeals to the unsophisticated follower of the music, which had a particularly strong vogue in the early 1980s.

B. Harrigan: *The HM A-Z* (London, 1981). T. Jasper: *The International Encyclopedia of Hard Rock & Heavy Metal* (London, 1984).

Hefti, Neal Paul (*b* Hastings, Nebr. 29 Oct. 1922). American composer, conductor, arranger, and trumpeter. He started arranging in his teens, making his first mark with work done for Earl *Hines in the early 1940s. He played with and arranged for Charlie *Barnet 1942; arranged for Alvino Rey; was with Woody *Herman's First Herd 1944–6, and made many recordings with the band and small groups drawn from it in the mid-1940s. He left to join Benny *Carter, wrote for Charlie *Ventura 1946, Georgie Auld 1946, Harry *James 1948–9, and Count *Basie 1950–62. Hefti formed his own short-lived big band in 1951 and began to make recordings under his own name; but he is best remembered for his excellent work for the Basie band and compositions such as 'Whirlybird' and 'Li'l darlin''.

Held, Anna (*b* Warsaw, 18 Mar. 1873; *d* New York, 13 Aug 1918). Actress with a legendary reputation in early musical comedy days. She was raised in Paris and became thought of as a typical French actress, wide-eyed, coquettish, and flaunting the fashionable hour-glass figure of the 1890s. Orphaned at an early age, she joined a travelling drama company and toured Europe, returning to Paris, aged 16, to appear in musical comedies. A growing reputation took her to London to sing in the music-halls. She appeared in cabaret in Paris and Berlin, and was brought by Florenz *Ziegfeld to New York in 1896 where she enraptured the Americans in such shows as *A Parlor Match* (1896); *La Poupée* (1897); *Papa's Wife* (1899); *The Little Duchess* (1901); *Mam'selle Napoleon* (1903); *Higgledy Piggledy* (1904); *A Parisian Model* (1906)—'It's delightful to be married'; and *Miss Innocence* (1908). Her best-known songs were 'I can't make my eyes behave' and 'Won't you come and play with me'.

Ziegfeld managed her and produced most of her shows; they were married in 1897 and divorced in 1913. It was her suggestion that he should stage a Parisian cabaret-revue type of performance in New York; and this led to the beginnings of the famous **Ziegfeld Follies* in 1907 with one of its main features the glamorous chorus of Anna Held Girls. She retired for a while after her divorce but later returned to the vaudeville stage.

Hello, Dolly! Long-running Broadway show with music and lyrics by Jerry *Herman and a book by Michael Stewart with an unusually long lineage. It was based on Thornton Wilder's play *The Matchmaker* (1955), a revised version of his *The Merchant of Yonkers* (1938). This in turn was based on a Viennese farce by Johann Nestroy, *Einen Jux will er sich machen* (1842), itself expanded from a one-act play by the English writer John Oxenford, *A Day Well Spent* (1835). The musical looked set for failure when first tried out on Broadway, but with some changes and four additional songs it went on, at the St James Theatre, 16 Jan. 1964, to complete a run of 2844 performances, a record eventually beaten by **Fiddler on the Roof*.

The story is of Dolly Gallagher Levi, a New York matrimonial agent of the 1890s, who manages to help three young couples to marital bliss and meanwhile snares a rich businessman for herself. Her big moment, and the one big song 'Hello, Dolly!', occur when she makes a grand reappearance at the Harmonia Gardens Restaurant, where her unfortunate beau finally has his wallet stolen and is unable to pay the bill.

A ripely comic part for any actress, it was originally written with Ethel *Merman in mind but she rejected the offer. It thus turned out to be a great triumph for Carol *Channing; and the part was later played by Martha Raye (*b* 1908), Betty *Grable, Pearl *Bailey with an all-black cast, Phyllis Diller, and, eventually, Ethel Merman. Mary *Martin starred in a touring company which played in 11 American cities and went to the Far East before opening in London at the Drury Lane Theatre, 2 Dec. 1965, for 794 performances under the musical direction of Alyn Ainsworth (*b* 1924). Dora *Bryan took over in 1966. There were two other touring companies in America. It was filmed with Barbra *Streisand, Walter Matthau, and Michael *Crawford in 1969.

Jerry Herman was sued by Mack David who claimed that the main theme of 'Hello, Dolly' was taken from his 1948 song 'Sunflower', the case being settled out of court. The outstanding hit recording of this turn-of-the-century pastiche song came not from one of its many glamorous Dollies but from jazz-singer Louis *Armstrong in 1969.

Hellzapoppin. Lunatic revue featuring the crazy act of *Olsen and Johnson, with music by Sammy *Fain and others, lyrics by Charles *Tobias and others, and sketches by Ole Olsen (1892–1963) and Chick Johnson (1891–1962). In what was virtually a Marx Brother-style vaudeville show, the plot was incidental to the running gags. It opened at the 46th Street Theatre, New York, 22 Sept. 1938, transferring to the Winter Garden Theatre two months later where it achieved 1404 performances, the longest run in Broadway history up to then, next topped by **Oklahoma!* It was filmed with Olsen and Johnson and Martha Raye (*b* 1908) and a new score, in 1941.

Henderson, Fletcher Hamilton (*b* Cuthbert, Ga., 18 Dec. 1897; *d* New York, 28 Dec. 1952). American bandleader, composer, arranger, and pianist. He studied to be a chemist but went with his younger brother Horace Henderson (*b* 22 Nov. 1904), also a pianist, arranger, and bandleader, to New York to explore the world of jazz and found a job with W. C. *Handy's orchestra, later becoming accompanist to Ethel *Waters. From 1921 he was recording manager with the Black Swan record company (see RACE RECORDS), where he became known for his firm handling of artists and clear-headed administration, allied to good musical judgement and the ability to create fine arrangements for singers like Bessie *Smith who recorded with them. An ambition to lead a band materialized in 1924 when he took over the orchestra at the Club Alabam. Later that year he took up residence at the famous Roseland Ballroom, forming an orchestra that was to establish many of the great names of jazz such as Louis *Armstrong, Coleman *Hawkins, Don *Redman, Tommy *Ladnier, Buster Bailey (1902–67), Benny *Carter and trombonist Jimmy Harrison (1900–31), at the same time becoming known for the ambitious and forward-looking arrangements that Henderson and others provided. The band recorded for many labels under assorted names and Henderson's fine piano-playing backed many blues artists active at the time. His band did not achieve the success with white audiences that others like Jimmie *Lunceford's and Chick *Webb's had, but it was admired by the true connoisseurs of jazz.

Henderson was involved in a serious car accident in 1928 which seemed to leave him with diminished energy and ambition. Many of his best arrangements were taken up by the Benny *Goodman band, together with some newly written ones, and by 1936 he was staff arranger to Goodman. When his own band folded in 1939, Henderson joined Goodman as pianist. He tried to re-form his band, without success, and spent the 1940s organizing various groups in New York. By 1950 he was leading a sextet in New York's Café Society, but later that year he suffered a stroke which ended his playing career. Latterly he survived on the benefits of his early association with Goodman. His own orchestral works included: 'Henderson stomp' (1926); 'Stampede' (1926); 'Hot mustard' (1926); 'Hot 'n' anxious (1931); 'Just blues' (1931); 'Big John's special' (1935); and 'Grand Terrace rhythm' (1936).

W. Allen: *Hendersonia* (New York, 1973). See also: R. Stewart: *Jazz Masters of the 30s* (New York, 1972; repr. 1982).

Henderson, Ray [Raymond Brost] (*b* Buffalo, NY, 1 Dec. 1896; *d* Greenwich, Conn., 31 Dec. 1970). American composer. He was educated at the University of South Carolina and Chicago Conservatory of Music, then became a pianist in dance bands and vaudeville and played the organ in churches in Buffalo, before joining a New York music-publisher as arranger and song-plugger. He began to write songs with lyricist Lew *Brown and others in 1922, contributing to the **Greenwich Village Follies* and having his first hit with 'Georgette' from that show. Other early successes were 'Annabelle' (1923); 'That old gang of mine' (1923); 'Follow the swallow' (1924); 'Alabamy bound' (1927, *w* Bud Green, *b* 1897); 'Five foot two, eyes of blue' (1925); 'Don't bring Lulu' (1925); 'I'm sitting on top of the world' (1925); and 'Bye bye, blackbird' (1926). Brown and Henderson were joined by Buddy *DeSylva in 1925 to form a famous team who contributed to *Big Boy* (1925)—'It all depends on you', and wrote the scores and lyrics for **George White's Scandals* (1925); (1926)—'Lucky day', 'Birth of the blues', *'Black bottom'; (1928)—'I'm on the crest of a wave'; **Good News* (1927)—'The best things in life are free', 'Varsity drag', 'Just imagine', 'Lucky in love'; *Manhattan Mary* (1927)—'The five-step', 'I'd like you to love me'; **Hold Everything* (1928)—'You're the cream in my coffee', 'My lucky star', 'Too good to be true'; *Three Cheers* (1928); **Follow Thru* (1929)—'Button up your overcoat', 'My lucky star'; *Flying High* (1930). They wrote for the films *The Singing Fool* (1928)—'It all depends on you', 'Sonny boy'; *Say it With Songs* (1929)—'Little pal', 'I'm in seventh heaven'; *Sunny Side Up* (1929)—'I'm a dreamer, aren't we all', 'Keep your sunny side up', sung by Janet Gaynor (*b* 1906), and 'If I had a talking picture of you', sung by Charles Farrell (*b* 1901); *In Old Arizona* (1929); *Just Imagine* (1930); *Indiscreet* (1931); and versions of various stage shows.

Buddy DeSylva left them in 1935 to go into film production, and the Brown and Henderson partnership continued with *George White's Scandals* (1931)—'The thrill is gone', 'That's why darkies were born', 'Life is just a bowl of cherries', 'This is the missus', 'My song'; *Hot-Cha* (1932); and *Strike Me Pink* (1933). Henderson continued to write with other partners: *Say When* (1934); *George White's Scandals* (1934)—'Nasty man', 'Anything can happen'; *Transatlantic Rhythm* (London, 1936), with Irving *Caesar, with whom he recorded a medley from the show that year; *Ziefgeld Follies* (1943); and contributed to the Shirley *Temple film *Curly Top* (1935)—'Animal crackers in my soup'. A film based on the life of DeSylva, Brown, and Henderson, *The Best Things in Life Are Free*, was made in 1956, Gordon *McRae, Ernest Borgnine (*b* 1915), and Dan Dailey (1914–78) in the principal roles, with Sheree North (*b* 1933).

Hendrix, Jimi [James Marshall] (*b* Seattle, 27 Nov. 1942; *d* London, 18 Sept. 1970). American rock singer and guitarist. Born in a poor family, he taught himself to play the guitar while at school by listening to the recorded work of Southern blues singers like Robert *Johnson and B. B. *King. After military service he played in groups backing King, Sam *Cooke, *Little Richard, and Ike and Tina *Turner. Moving to New York he played with the *Isley Brothers before becoming lead guitarist in the Curtis Knight (*b* 1945) band. With a reputation as a remarkable guitarist he went to London in 1966 and there formed the Jimi Hendrix Experience, a three-piece unit of powerful *heavy metal impact featuring Noel Redding (bass) and Mitch Mitchell (drums), which became a cult group and inspired many British musicians. He toured Europe and had record hits with 'Hey Joe' and 'Purple haze'. He had a personal triumph at the Monterey Festival, needlessly adding to his guitar virtuosity by eccentric stage antics, but by 1968 had given up these gimmicks and produced technically advanced and imaginatively exciting albums.

Hendrix found difficulty in reconciling his fundamental appeal to white audiences, who admired his technicalities, and his comparative failure with his own people, even when he fronted his black Band of Gypsies at Woodstock, Madison Square Gardens, and the Isle of Wight. At a time when he thought his powers might be declining, though there is no evidence on record to support this, he died of asphyxiation in his sleep. His probing experimental guitar style revolutionized the use of the instrument in rock music, leading to degrees of sound that had not been imagined hitherto.

C. Welch: *Hendrix: a Biography* (London, 1972; New York, 1975; repr. 1982). C. Knight: *Jimi: an Intimate Biography of Jimi Hendrix* (New York, 1974). J. Henderson: *Jimi Hendrix: Voodoo Child of the Aquarian Age* (New York, 1976; repr. 1981). T. Nolan: *Jimi Hendrix: a Biography in Words and Pictures* (New York, 1977). S. Tarshis: *Original Hendrix* (London, 1982). J. Hopkins: *Hit and Run: the Jimi Hendrix Story (New York, 1983).*

Heneker, David (*b* Southsea, 31 Mar. 1906). British composer and lyricist. The son of a general, he was educated at Wellington College and Sandhurst and was a regular army officer 1925–48. He turned to writing for the stage and had immediate hits in 1958 with **Expresso Bongo* and **Irma la Douce* (adaptation and lyrics); followed by *Make Me an Offer* (1959); *The Art of Living* (1960); **Half a Sixpence* (1963); **Charlie Girl* (1965); *Jorrocks* (1966); *Phil the Fluter* (1969), based on the music of Percy *French; *Popkiss* (1972); *The Biograph Girl* (1980); and *Peg* (1982). From 1968 he was chairman of the Songwriters Guild of Great Britain.

Henson, Leslie (*b* London, 3 Aug. 1891; *d* Harrow, 2 Dec. 1957). British actor, director, and producer. He first appeared on stage with the Tatlers Concert Party in Bath in 1910. The major part of his career was spent in London musicals, beginning in 1914 with *Tonight's the Night* in New York, and the following year in London. Pop-eyed, with a croaky upper-class voice to match his looks, he was an able successor to the singer-comedians who have been a major asset of the London musical stage. From 1914 to 1926 he worked with George *Grossmith Jr. on six musicals and from 1929 he was associated with producer Firth Shephard as either co-producer or director of the shows he appeared in, beginning with *Lady Luck* in 1927.

He was in *Theodore & Co.* (1916); *Yes, Uncle!* (1917); *Kissing Time* (1919); *A Night Out* (1920); **Sally* (1921); *The Cabaret Girl* (1923); *The Beauty Prize* (1923); **Primrose* (1924); *Tell Me More* (1925); *Kid Boots* (1926); *Lady Luck* (1927); *So This is Love* (1928); **Funny Face* (1928); **Follow Through* (1929); *Nice Goings On* (1933); *Lucky Break* (1934); *Seeing Stars* (1935); *Swing Along* (1936); *Going Greek* (1937); *Running Riot* (1938); *Up and Doing* (1940); *Fine and Dandy* (1942); *The Gaieties* (1945); *Bob's Your Uncle* (1948); and **And So To Bed* (1951).

L. Henson: *My Laugh Story* (London, 1926). L. Henson: *Yours Faithfully* (London, 1948).

Herbert, Victor (*b* Dublin, 1 Feb. 1859; *d* New York, 26 May 1924) Irish-American composer. He was to become the dominant and most influential composer for the musical theatre in America at that transitional stage when operetta in the Viennese tradition was giving way to musical comedy, first promoted in England and then finding its feet in the USA. Herbert's music was mainly in the operetta vein, but gradually became American in flavour, leading towards and existing alongside the work of Jerome *Kern. His father having died when he was three, he spent his childhood and early years with his maternal grandmother in Sevenoaks, Kent. His grandfather, Samuel Lover, a dilettante novelist and poet, surrounded himself with talented people and Herbert's early musical promise was strongly encouraged. His mother settled in Stuttgart in 1867 and he went with her to study at the Stuttgart High School. He chose to study the cello and became a professional cellist in various orchestras in Germany, France, Italy, and Switzerland, played in Eduard *Strauss's orchestra in Vienna, and eventually in the Court Orchestra in Stuttgart, where he also studied composition at the Conservatory. Here, in 1886, he met Therese Förster (1861–1927), a soprano with the Stuttgart Opera, married her, and accompanied her to America when she signed a contract with the Metropolitan Opera in New York. She made her New York debut in 1888 with her husband playing as cellist in the orchestra. Although his cello concerto had been performed with the New York Philharmonic in 1887, Herbert's early years in America were overshadowed by his wife's career.

They became naturalized Americans and Herbert began to identify himself with American music. The well-known bandleader Patrick S. *Gilmore died in 1892 and Herbert was asked to take over the remnants of his band in 1893; he led them until 1897. He became principal conductor of the Pittsburgh Symphony Orchestra 1898–1904, with whom he presented many of his own orchestral works.

His first operetta, *Prince Ananias*, written for the Boston Ideal Opera Company, appeared in 1894 and was well received. *The Wizard of the Nile* did even better in 1895. Herbert was a man who ate, drank, and worked on a grand scale and he continued his career with an enormous output of operettas. *The Gold Bug* in 1896 was followed by his first great success, *The Serenade* (1897). His subsequent works included: *The Idol's Eye* (1897); *The *Fortune Teller* (1898), for Alice Nielsen (1870–1943)—'Gypsy love song'; *Cyrano de Bergerac* (1899); *The Singing Girl* (1899); *The Ameer* (1899); *The Viceroy* (1900); **Babes in Toyland* (1903; filmed 1934 and 1961)—'March of the Toys', 'Toyland'; *Babette* (1903); **It Happened in Nordland* (1904)—'Absinthe frappé'; *Miss Dolly Dollars* (1905)—'A woman is only a woman but a good cigar is a smoke'; *Wonderland* (1905); *Mlle Modiste* (1905; filmed 1931 as *Kiss Me Again*)—'Kiss me again', 'I want what I want when I want it'; *The *Red Mill* (1906)—'When you're pretty and the world is fair', 'Moonbeams', 'Every day is ladies' day with me', 'The streets of New York'; *Dream City* and *The Magic Knight* (1906); *The Tattooed Man* (1907); *Algeria* (1908); *Little Nemo* (1908); *The Prima Donna* (1908); *Old Dutch* (1909); **Naughty Marietta* (1910; filmed 1935)—'Tramp! tramp! tramp!', 'Italian street song', 'Ah! sweet mystery of life', ''Neath the southern moon', 'I'm falling in love with someone'; *When Sweet Sixteen* (1911); *The Duchess* (1911); *The Enchantress* (1911); *The Lady of the Slipper* (1912); **Sweethearts* (1913; filmed 1938)—'Sweethearts', 'Every lover must meet his fate'; *The Madcap Duchess* (1913); *The Only Girl* (1914)—'When you're away'; *The Débutante* (1914); *The Princess Pat* (1915)—'Love is the best of all', sung with great effect by Eleanor Painter (1890–1947); *The Century Girl* (1916); *Eileen* (1917)—'Thine alone'; *Miss 1917* (1917); *Her Regiment* (1917); *The Velvet Lady* (1919); *Angel Face* (1919)—'I might be your once-in-a-while'; *My Golden Girl* (1920); *The Girl in the Spotlight* (1920); **Ziegfeld Follies* (1921 and 1923); *Orange Blossoms* (1922)—'A kiss in the dark'; and *The Dream Girl* (1924). He also wrote the operas *Natouma* (1911) and *Madeleine* (1914).

In 1916 he had broken interesting new ground by providing what is accounted the first musical score specifically designed to accompany a silent film in America—*The Fall of a Nation*; and he also wrote for *When Knighthood Was in Flower* (1922) and *Little Old New York* (1923). He provided songs for many other shows and was represented posthumously by 'Indian summer', originally a piano piece (1919) to which Al *Dubin added words in 1939. In 1946 an operetta, *Gypsy Lady*, was staged in New York with its songs drawn from various earlier operettas. At the time of his death in 1924 he was working on songs for the next version of *Ziegfeld Follies*. A film of his life, *The Great Victor Herbert*, was made in 1939 with Walter Connolly in the role of the composer.

J. Kaye: *Victor Herbert: the Biography of America's Greatest Composer of Romantic Music* (New York, 1931; repr. 1970). C. L. Purdy: *Victor Herbert: American Music-Master* (New York, 1944; repr. 1976). E. N. Waters: *Victor Herbert: a Life in Music* (New York, 1955).

Herman, Jerry [Gerald] (*b* New York, 10 July 1933). American composer. He studied drama at Miami University, then became a TV scriptwriter. He started to write musicals, for which he wrote both lyrics and music, with *I Feel Wonderful*, which was produced off-Broadway in 1954. After serving in the armed forces, he wrote revue and cabaret material for Garry Moore, Hermione *Gingold, Jane Froman, Tallulah Bankhead, and others. He wrote for an off-Broadway revue, *Nightcap* (1958), which ran for more than 400 performances; contributed 'Best gold' to *From A to Z* (1960); wrote and directed *Parade* (1960); and wrote *Milk and Honey* (1961) and *Madame Aphrodite* (1961); before having an outstanding success with **Hello, Dolly!* (1964; filmed 1969)—'Hello, Dolly!', 'Ribbons down my back'. The show received many awards and achieved the longest run in Broadway history up till then. He followed this with **Mame* (1966; filmed 1974); *Dear World* (1969); *Mack and Mabel* (1974)—'When Mabel comes in the room'; and *La *Cage aux Folles* (1983).

Herman, Woody [Woodrow Charles] (*b* Milwaukee, 16 May 1913; *d* Los Angeles, 28 Oct. 1987). American bandleader, clarinettist, saxophonist, and composer. He was one of the last of the great swing band leaders whose tastes were for fast and exciting music, hot brass ensembles, and progress. The son of show-business parents, he joined their act at the age of nine, billed as 'The Boy Wonder of the Clarinet', and also danced and sang. He became a professional musician with a roadhouse band and played with Tom Gerun at the Schroeder Hotel in Milwaukee, then worked with Harry Sosnick and Isham* Jones, with whom he was also featured as a singer. When Jones retired from bandleading in 1936, Herman took over the orchestra and billed it as 'The Band That Plays the Blues'. It took its place among the leading groups of the swing era when 'Woodchoppers' ball', which Herman wrote with Joe Bishop (1907–76), was recorded in 1939 and sold more than a million copies. This became Herman's theme tune which he was to play more times than he enjoyed. The band starred in the films *What's Cookin'* (1942); *Wintertime* (1943); *Sensations of 1945* (1944); *Earl Carroll's Vanities* (1945); *Hit Parade of 1947* (1946); and *New Orleans* (1947).

From 1939 the Herman band was known by the unofficial nickname of the Herd, first bestowed by the magazine *Metronome*. In the early 1940s the band's style changed from its original Dixieland manner to an ultra-modern approach based on arrangements by Neal *Hefti and Ralph Burns (*b* 1922) with, by 1943, a five-piece trumpet section, and the rock-steady beat of drummer Dave Tough (1908–48) 1944–5. What was to become officially known as the First Herd had recorded hits with 'Apple honey' and 'Caldonia'. In 1946, Igor Stravinsky wrote 'Ebony concerto' for the band. The Second Herd (1947–9) was even more advanced and was also known as 'The Four Brothers Band' after a tune of that name which created its identifying sound. Herman's lasting financial troubles, which made him toil on long after his health was gone, began when this band made a loss of $175,000. A Third Herd was formed in 1953 and Herman made his first European tour in 1954, but a clear identity was lost in a number of scratch bands that went under that title. In 1959, on a British tour, the band's American personnel was augmented by nine British musicians and thus became the Anglo-American Herd. A Fourth Herd was formed in 1962, after which people lost count, while the band dabbled in rock sounds and continually changed.

Herman was a considerable and very individual clarinettist with a sharp tone which he contrasted with a much mellower Johnny *Hodges kind of sound on saxophone. He composed many songs and instrumental pieces.

S. Voce: *Woody Herman* (London, 1986).

Herman's Hermits. British pop group formed in 1963 with the widely smiling and boyish Peter Noone (*b* London, 5 Nov. 1947) as their heartthrob leader and vocalist, Keith Hopwood (*b* 1946) (guitar), Derek Leckenby (*b* 1945) (guitar), Karl Green (*b* 1946) (bass), and Barry Whitwam (*b* 1946) (drums). Noone had been spotted acting in TV's *Coronation Street* by producer Mickie Most, who added him, with a change of name to Herman, to a group known as the Heartbeats. The group was initially mainly a front, recording with other musicians backing them, and started with a No. 1 hit in the UK in 'I'm into something good' (1964). Their next No. 1 hits were in the USA with 'Mrs Brown, you've got a lovely daughter' and 'I'm Henry the Eighth, I am' in 1965; they generally seemed to achieve a better response in the USA. Noone became a solo artist in 1970 and the Hermits settled in the USA to continue playing their essentially happy entertainment music. There was a reunion for a British tour in 1973. Noone formed a new band, the Tremblers, in 1979 and starred in a modernized **Pirates of Penzance* in 1983.

Herrmann, Bernard (*b* New York, 29 June 1911; *d* Los Angeles, 24 Dec. 1975). American composer and conductor. After studying music at New York University and the Juilliard School of Music he joined CBS in 1934 as a composer of radio music and conducted the CBS Symphony Orchestra 1940–55 in their summer radio series. He became associated with Orson Welles through various dramatic assignments, and the first of his accredited 61 film background scores (many of them for Alfred Hitchcock) was for *Citizen Kane* in 1940. This was followed by *The Devil and Daniel Webster* (or *All that Money can Buy*, 1941; Academy Award); *The Magnificent Ambersons* (1942); *Jane Eyre* (1942); *Hangover Square* (1943); *Anna and the King of Siam* (1946); *The Ghost and Mrs Muir* (1947); *The Day the Earth Stood Still* (1951); *On Dangerous Ground* (1951); *The Snows of Kilimanjaro* (1952); *Five Fingers* (1952); *White Witch Doctor* (1953); *Beneath the 12-Mile Reef* (1953); *King of the Khyber Rifles* (1953); *Garden of Evil* (1954); *The Egyptian* (with Alfred *Newman, 1954); *Prince of Players* (1955); *The Kentuckian* (1955); *The Trouble With Harry* (1955); *The Man in the Grey Flannel Suit* (1956); *The Man Who Knew Too Much* (1956, in which Herrmann appeared as the conductor in the Albert Hall scene); *The Wrong Man* (1956); *A Hatful of Rain* (1957); *The Williamsburg Story* (1957); *Vertigo* (1958); *The Naked and the Dead* (1958); *The 7th Voyage of Sinbad* (1958); *North by Northwest* (1959); *Blue Denim* (1959); *Journey to the Center of the Earth* (1959); *Psycho* (1960); *The Three Worlds of Gulliver* (1960); *Mysterious Island* (1961); *Cape Fear* (1961); *Tender is the Night* (1961); *Jason and the Argonauts* (1963); *The Birds* (1963); *Marnie* (1964); *Joy in the Morning* (1965); *Fahrenheit 451* (1966); *The Bride Wore Black* (1968); *Twisted Nerve* (1969); *Obsession* (1969); *The Battle of Neretva* (1970); *The Night Digger* (1971); *Sisters* (1973); *Taxi Driver* (1975). He also wrote TV scores for *Hitchcock Presents* and *The Virginians*. He lived in England for the last ten years of his life.

E. Johnson: *Bernard Herrmann* (Rickmansworth, 1977).

Herth, Milt (*b* Kenosha, Wis., date unknown; *d* New York, 18 June 1969). American organist. He had a varied career as an organist in the Mid-west and Hollywood before he became known through his own NBC radio shows from 1938 on. With pianist Willie 'The Lion' *Smith and drummer O'Neill Spencer, he formed the popular Milt Herth Trio. Guitarist Teddy *Bunn was added for a time in 1938 and later Frankie Froeba (1907–81), with Billy Kyle (1914–66) replacing Smith as pianist. Their theme tune was 'Church mouse on a spree' and their most popular record 'The dipsy doodle' (1937). The Trio continued into the 1950s.

Hervé [Rogé, Florimond] (*b* Houdain, nr. Arras, 30 June 1825; *d* Paris, 3 Nov. 1892). French composer, conductor, and actor. He started his musical career as a choirboy, studied music with Elwart and Auber and became organist at St Eustache for eight years. He wrote his first musical score, *L'Ours et le Pacha*, in 1842 and had his first truly successful production in 1848 with *Don Quichotte et Sancho Pansa* at the Opéra National in Paris, in which he appeared as a singer. In 1849 he became musical director at the Odéon, moving to the Palais-Royal in 1851.

From now on his career was to run parallel to that of Jacques *Offenbach. Both have been credited as the founder of French operetta and there was little to choose between the rival claims. They remained friendly rivals throughout their lives and staged each other's works. Hervé opened his own small theatre, the Folies-Concertantes in 1855, the same year that Offenbach opened his *Bouffes-Parisiens, with the intention of writing and producing there (as with Offenbach) light pieces, pantomimes, burlesques, small operettas (*saynètes*)—all limited by the current licensing laws to two characters. From these small beginnings grew the influential world of French operetta, the seed of the musical theatre of the 19th and 20th centuries. Hervé usually wrote both words and music and either conducted or appeared in most of his own works. He gave up personal management of his own theatre (variously known as the Folies-Nouvelles and Folies-Dramatiques) in 1856 so that he could find more time for composing and acting, working at various Paris theatres until 1869 with limitless energy, including a period 1859–62 as conductor at the Délassements-Comiques. When the Franco-Prussian War and the Commune brought a halt to Parisian theatre life he worked for a while in Marseilles and Montpellier, then, in 1871, went to London to conduct concerts of Strauss's music at Covent Garden and to appear in English productions of his operettas. For a while he was musical director at the Empire Theatre.

Hervé wrote some 120 stage works in all. The majority of them never achieved the lasting fame of Offenbach's: they were well contrived but lacked Offenbach's melodic genius. The only one to become a comparative success was *Mam'zelle Nitouche* (1883); though *L'Oeil crevé* (1867), **Chilpéric* (1868), and *Le Petit Faust* (1869) were all very popular in their day in Paris, London, and the USA.

L. Schneider: *Les Maîtres de l'opérette française: Hervé, Charles Lecocq* (Paris, 1924).

Heuberger, Richard [Franz Joseph] (*b* Graz, 28 June 1850; *d* Vienna, 27 Oct. 1914). Austrian composer and conductor. He studied and worked as a civil engineer before taking up music professionally in 1876. He became choirmaster of the Vienna Gesangverein, conductor of the Singakademie (1878), conductor of the Männergesangverein (1902–9), and was a professor at the Vienna Conservatory from 1902; also being music critic and editor of various musical journals. He wrote an opera, *Abenteuer einer Neujahrsnacht* (1886), followed by two others. His first operetta was *Mirjam* (1894), but his real triumph in this field came with the still remembered *Der *Opernball* (1898) with its lusciously romantic 'Im chambre separée'. Others, all produced in Vienna, were *Ihre Excellenz* (1899), later rewritten as *Eine entzückende Frau* (1899); *Der Sechsuhrzug* (1900); *Das Baby* (1902); *Der Fürst von Düsterstein* (1909); *Don Quixote* (1910); and *Barfussele* (1915). He also wrote a ballet based on *Struwwelpeter*, produced in Dresden in 1897. All his music was pleasantly tuneful in the Viennese style. An interesting sidelight to musical history was his rejection of a libretto that was given instead to

Franz *Lehár—and became known to the world as *The *Merry Widow*. He wrote a biography of Schubert in 1902.

Heywood, Eddie [Edward Jr.] (*b* Atlanta, Ga., 4 Dec. 1915; *d* New York, 2 Jan. 1989). American pianist, bandleader, composer, and arranger. He learned the piano from his father Eddie Heywood Sr. and played in his band. He worked in theatre orchestras and toured with various groups 1932–5, was with Clarence Love in the mid-1930s in Kansas City, led a band in Dallas 1937–9, and was with Benny *Carter 1939–40. In the 1940s he played with Zutty *Singleton and Georgie Auld at the Three Deuces. He became accompanist to Billie *Holiday and, with his own sextet (which included Doc Cheatham, *b* 1905, and Vic *Dickenson), recorded classic sides with her and with Ella *Fitzgerald, Bing *Crosby, and the *Andrews Sisters. He had a big hit with a recording of 'Begin the Beguine' in 1943, and again in 1944 with 'Near you'. From 1947 he suffered from arthritic hands and, even when he was partly cured in 1950, found playing difficult and turned to composition, encouraged by Cole *Porter. He had hits with 'Canadian sunset' (1956), 'Land of dreams', 'Soft summer breeze', and 'I'm saving myself for you'; and also wrote a 'Martha's Vineyard suite'. He was able to resume club playing and was still active in New York in the 1970s, appearing at the Newport Jazz Festival in 1974.

Hicks, Edward **Seymour** [Sir] (*b* St Helier, Jersey, 30 Jan. 1871; *d* London, 6 Apr. 1954). British actor, manager, and author. His reputation mainly lies with his work as a distinguished actor in the theatre and, after 1946, in films. But he was also a successful and adventurous manager who did much to encourage French drama in London for which he was made a Chevalier of the Legion of Honour. He married the star of plays and musicals Ellaline *Terriss, with whom he had a fruitful stage partnership.

He was important in the musical comedy field as writer or part-writer of the librettos of some very popular shows, many of which he managed and produced or played in. These include: *Under the Clock* (1893); *Little Jack Sheppard* (1894); *The *Shop Girl* (1894); *Papa's Wife* (1895); *The *Circus Girl* (1896); *The Yashmak* (1897); *A *Runaway Girl* (1898); **Bluebell in Fairyland* (1901); *The Cherry Girl* (1902); *The *Catch of the Season* (1904); *The Beauty of Bath* (1906); *The Gay Gordons* (1907); *The Dashing Little Duke* (1909); *Captain Kidd* (1910); *All the Winners* (1913); *The Happy Day* (1916); *Cash on Delivery* (1917); *Jolly Jack Tar* (1918); *A Little Dutch Girl* (1920); and *Head Over Heels* (1923). He wrote several autobiographical books including: *Seymour Hicks: Twenty-Four Years of an Actor's Life* (1910); *Me and my Missus* (1939); and *Vintage Years* (1943).

Higginbotham, J. C. [Jack] (*b* Social Circle, nr. Atlanta, 11 May 1906; *d* New York, 26 May 1973). American jazz trombonist. He worked in Cincinnati as a teenager, touring 1925–8; joined Luis *Russell 1928–30; had spells with Chick *Webb and with Fletcher *Henderson 1931–3; and was with Benny *Carter 1933, Mills Blue Rhythm Band 1934–6, Henderson 1937, Louis *Armstrong 1937–40, Red *Allen 1940–7. He mainly worked in New York, led his own groups from time to time, and was active until the 1970s. He had a splendidly full sound and natural trombone style that added great richness to any band he played in.

High Button Shoes. American musical, with music by Jule *Styne, lyrics by Sammy *Cahn, and book by George *Abbott and Phil Silvers, based on a novel by Stephen Longstreet, which opened at the New Century Theatre, New York, 9 Oct. 1947, and ran for 727 performances. The show provided an ideal first starring role for Phil Silvers (1912–85) who played Harrison Floy, a con man who helps a family to sell some property then absconds with the money to Atlantic City, only to have it stolen from him. Recovering it, he loses it in gambling. It was presented by Jack *Hylton at the London Hippodrome, 22 Dec. 1948 [291p] with Alma Cogan (1935–66). The songs included 'Can't you just see yourself', 'There's nothing like a Model T', 'You're my girl', and 'I still get jealous'. A high spot of the show was Jerome *Robbins's 'Mack Sennett Ballet'.

High Society. MGM film of 1956, directed and choreographed by Charles Walters (1911–82), Starring Bing *Crosby, Frank *Sinatra, Grace Kelly (1928–82), Celeste Holm (*b* 1919), and Louis *Armstrong and his All Stars. It had music and words by Cole *Porter and screenplay by John Patrick [John Patrick Goggan] (*b* 1905), based on Philip Barry's *The Philadelphia Story*. A rich score included: 'Who wants to be a millionaire', 'True love', 'You're sensational', 'I love you, Samantha', 'Now you has jazz', and (lifted from *Dubarry Was a Lady*) 'Well, did you evah'.

High, Wide and Handsome. Paramount film of 1937 starring Irene *Dunn, Randolph Scott (*b* 1903), Dorothy *Lamour, William Frawley (1887–1966), and Akim Tamiroff (1899–1972), with music by Jerome *Kern and words by Oscar *Hammerstein II, based on *The Black Gold Rush*. The Kern songs included: 'Can I forget you', 'The things I want', 'The folk who live on the hill', and the title-song.

Hildegarde [Sell, Hildegarde Loretta] (*b* Adell, Wis., 1906). American singer and pianist. Her elegant dresses and theme song 'Je vous aime beaucoup', written by her manager Anna Sosenko (*b* 1910) in 1935, left a lingering impression of some sultry French star. She was, however, raised in Milwaukee and started out as a pianist in a silent cinema. She toured in vaudeville and, as an accompanist, worked with Gus *Edwards and, at one time, sang Dutch songs. Gradually she evolved her elegant cabaret act and was in London 1933–6. She appeared on her own American radio show and with others in the 1940s when she was at her most popular. She toured Europe in 1948 and was recording for Decca until 1949; but was less heard of in the 1950s, though she did record 'Lili Marlene' on an RCA Victor LP in 1953.

Hill, Alex [Alexander] (*b* Little Rock, Ark., 19 Apr. 1906; *d* Little Rock, 1 Feb. 1936). American composer, arranger, and pianist. He organized his own orchestra in 1924 and toured with it in 1925. Afterwards he led a theatre orchestra and then went to Hollywood to act as pianist for such stars of the silent screen as Adolphe Menjou and Pola Negri. In 1927 he went to Chicago and worked with Jimmy Wade, Carroll Dickerson, Jimmie *Noone 1928–9, Sammy Stewart 1929–30, and Andy Kirk. He led his own groups for recording in the 1930s. As staff arranger for the Irving Mills organization he arranged for Fats *Waller, Claude *Hopkins, Paul *Whiteman, Duke *Ellington, Eddie *Condon, Willie *Bryant, and Benny *Carter. He had his own big band at the Savoy Ballroom in New York 1935 but had to disband through illness and died of TB. He wrote an unsuccessful musical, *Humming Sam* (1933); his other compositions include: 'Ain't that a shame', 'Baby Brown', 'I'm crazy 'bout my baby', 'Long about midnight', 'Beau Koo Jack', and 'Ain't it nice'.

Hill, Bertha 'Chippie' (*b* Charleston, SC, 15 Mar. 1905; *d* New York, 7 May 1950). American jazz singer. She began her career at 16 as a dancer at LeRoy's in Harlem, then toured with the Rabbit Foot Minstrels and Ma *Rainey. She became a solo act and settled in Chicago in 1925, to start a prolific recording career which included four sides made with Louis *Armstrong. She worked in Chicago clubs in 1930, then retired to raise a family of seven children. Rudi *Blesh rediscovered her working in a bakery, in 1946. She was then heard in the *This is Jazz* radio series, worked at Ryan's and the Blue Note Club, appeared at Carnegie Hall, and visited Paris in 1948. She was knocked down and killed by a car in Harlem.

Hill, Billy [William J.] (*b* Boston, 14 July 1899; *d* Boston, 24 Dec. 1940). American composer and lyricist. He studied music at the New England Conservatory and was a violinist in the Boston Symphony Orchestra when he was 16. At the age of 17 he decided to travel in the West, working as a cowboy and with prospectors and surveyors, picking up much of the folk material that he was later to incorporate into his Tin Pan Alley songs. He played violin and piano in various Western dance halls and for a while led what was probably the first dance band in Salt Lake City. He went to New York in 1930 and while working as a doorman wrote his first songs, many of which he sold outright for a few dollars. His first hit came with 'The last roundup' in 1933 which was included in the *Ziegfeld Follies* of 1934 and established his reputation, leading him to a rich career in the popular song business. He usually wrote his own words, and lyrics for others such as 'Wagon wheels' (1934, *m* Peter *DeRose) which was in the 1935 *Follies*.

Other songs were 'There's a cabin in the pines' (1933); 'The old spinning wheel' (1933); 'Alone at a table for two' (with Ted *Fiorito, 1935); 'The Oregon trail' (1935); 'Empty saddles' (*w* J. Keirn Brennan, 1875–1948), sung by Bing *Crosby in *Rhythm on the Range* (1936); 'The scene changes' (1936); 'In the chapel in the moonlight' (1936); 'The glory of love' (1936); 'All ashore' (1938); and 'Call of the canyon' (1940). His wife, Dedette Lee Hill (*b* Lynchburg, Va., 2 Nov. 1900), wrote the lyrics for 'Put on an old pair of shoes' (1935) and 'There's a little box of pine on the 7:29'.

Hill, Jenny [Woodley, Jane] (*b* London, 1848; *d* Brixton, London, 28 June 1896). British music-hall singer and dancer. She made her stage debut in pantomime at the age of seven. One of the earliest women in the halls, she made her first appearance at the Doctor Johnson Concert Room in Bolt Court off Fleet Street, was spotted by the agent Maurice de Frece, and was soon making her mark at the London Pavilion, the *Oxford, and the Canterbury. Affectionately known, because of her sharp wit, as 'The Vital Spark', she sang working-class character songs such as 'The coffee shop girl', 'Maggie Murphy's home', and 'I'm a woman of very few words' and had a special hit with 'The boy I love is up in the gallery' (also sung by Nelly Power, 1853–87). She was one of the first British music-hall artists to appear in the USA, at Tony *Pastor's in New York. She left the halls for a while to appear in pantomime, *Gaiety burlesques, and other plays, proving herself an able actress. Ill-health forced her to retire. In 1895 she accepted an invitation to South Africa but was too weak to sing, returning to England where a hard life and several unfortunate marriages extinguished the vital spark at the early age of 46.

Hill, Teddy [Theodore] (*b* Birmingham, Ala., 7 Dec. 1909; *d* Cleveland, 19 May 1978). American saxophonist and band leader. He toured in vaudeville bands and played at the Nest Club in New York before joining the Luis *Russell band 1928–9 of which he was also manager. He was in the pit band of the Lafayette Theatre 1931–2, and with James P. *Johnson 1932. He formed his own hard-swinging band in 1934 which played at the Lafayette, the Ubangi Club, the Roseland, but mainly at the famous *Savoy Ballroom in Harlem where it included such distinguished sidemen as Chu Berry (1910–41), Roy *Eldridge, Bill Coleman (1904–81), Dicky *Wells, and Dizzy *Gillespie. He toured England and France in 1937, played at the New York World's Fair in 1939, then gave up bandleading in 1940 to become manager of *Minton's club in Harlem, where modern jazz was born, until the late 1950s.

Hillbilly. Early name for American *country music in general use in its first commercialized period of the 1920s and 1930s when pioneers like 'Fiddlin'' John *Carson made some of the first recordings for Okeh in 1923. The very first to record was probably the Virginian mountain musician Henry Whitter. Another pioneer hillbilly recording artist was Vernon Dalhert [Marion Try Slaughter] (*b* Jefferson, Texas, 6 Apr. 1883; *d* 15 Sept. 1948), who achieved a best-selling disc with 'The prisoner's song'/'The wreck of the old 97' (1924, based on a previous recording by Whitter). His sales figures, recording under various names, were staggering, outselling all other artists (including Jimmie *Rodgers) with 'The prisoner's song' (which he recorded for nearly 30 labels) selling a total of 25 million discs. Others were Carson J. Robison and Frank Luther. From these promising beginnings hillbilly activities became a major concern of the recording companies in the 1920s, with Okeh in the lead, closely followed by the major companies like Columbia, Decca, Victor, and MGM, and with many field recordings as well as studio creations. The rediscovery of country and *bluegrass music as part of the 1940s folk-music revival, led to the promotion of many authentic artists in the field and the need for a less rural name than hillbilly.

Hilliam, B. C. [Bentley Collingwood] (*b* Scarborough, 6 Nov. 1890; *d* London, 19 Dec. 1968). British composer, author, pianist, and entertainer. He started in local productions under the name of Lloyd Holland, then went to Canada in 1905 where he formed the Canadian Follies concert party. He served in the Canadian Army in the First World War (and organized several army shows), then went to New York where he worked for six years, touring in vaudeville, appearing in the **Ziegfeld Follies* and having a great success with a musical comedy, *Buddies* (1919), which had a good run in Boston and played at the Selwyn Theatre, New York for two years. A second musical, *Princess Virtue* (1921), with Gitz Rice (1891–1947), fared less well. After more work in vaudeville, he returned to England early in 1926 and a month later met the Australian bass singer Malcolm McEachern (1884–1945). Their contrasting voices suggested a good basis for a double act and the team of *Flotsam and Jetsam (Hilliam being Flotsam) was soon launched with a first appearance at the Victoria Palace along with the Jack *Hylton orchestra.

They were immediately liked, were booked for the Coliseum and the Alhambra, and appeared in the Royal Variety Performance in 1927. Between variety tours they recorded extensively for Columbia and regularly broadcast, at one time doing a nightly newscast in verse. They had several radio programmes of their own and continued in partnership until McEachern's death in 1945. Hilliam wrote much of their material, including their theme song, 'The changing of the Guard' (1931), and 'Little Miss Bouncer' (1934). Later he formed his own summer show *Flotsam's Follies* for which he wrote the theme tune 'Valse de folies'.

B. C. Hilliam: *Flotsam's Follies* (London, 1948).

Hilliard, Bob [Robert] (*b* New York, 28 Jan. 1918; *d* Hollywood, 1 Feb. 1971). American lyricist. He was an active writer for Broadway and films in the 1940s and 1960s before having to retire owing to ill-health. He collaborated with the composers Carl Sigman, Jule *Styne, and Sammy *Fain, and wrote the shows *Angel in the Wings* (1947)—'Civilization', and *Hazel Flagg* (1953)—'Every street's a boulevard in old New York'. His songs included: 'The coffee song (There's an awful lot of coffee in Brazil' (1946); 'Careless hands' (1948); 'Dear hearts and gentle people' (1949); 'Dearie' (1950); 'Be my life's companion' (1951); 'Bouquet of roses' (1952);. He also wrote songs for the cartoon film *Alice in Wonderland* (1952) and the film *Living It Up* (1954, *m* Styne).

Hines, Earl Kenneth 'Fatha' (*b* Duquesne, Pittsburgh, 28 Dec. 1903; *d* Oakland, Calif., 22 Apr. 1983). American pianist, bandleader, and composer. From a very musical family, he studied the piano from the age of nine aspiring to a concert career. He worked in a trio in Pittsburgh and in a band led by the singer Lois Deppe, then went to Chicago in 1922 to play at the Entertainer's Club. He toured with the Carroll Dickerson band, then was in Chicago with Dickerson, Erskine Tate, Louis *Armstrong 1927, and Jimmie *Noone 1927–8 at the Sunset Café. He made some classic recordings with Armstrong in 1927 ('West End blues', 'Weather bird', etc.) and by then was recognized as one of the finest of all jazz pianists, never stereotyped, a great virtuoso, constantly inventive and swinging, and an ideal foil to the genius of Armstrong with his piano playing matching Louis's trumpet style. His unorthodox ideas and individual rhythmic patterns were to liberate jazz piano and were copied by many advanced pianists.

At the end of 1928 he formed his own band at the Grand Terrace, Chicago, where they played many residencies throughout the 1930s, Hines continuing to record with Armstrong and during this time acquiring the nickname of 'Fatha'. The band was to be the breeding ground for many modern pioneers like Dizzy *Gillespie, Charlie *Parker, Benny Green, and Billy *Eckstine. Hines disbanded for a while in 1940 to run his own club, re-formed his band to work with it in California until 1947, then joined the Armstrong All-Stars 1948–51. He led his own small group from 1951 and was at the Hangover Club in San Francisco 1955–7. He visited Europe in 1957 (with Jack *Teagarden), 1965, 1966 (including Russia), 1969, and 1970, in between times working in his own club in Oakland, California, and making freelance recordings for many labels. To the end he never ceased to amaze with his constant invention and pointful technique. He provided enthusiastically happy, swinging entertainment; and he was working the weekend before he died. He was a fertile composer of jazz numbers including 'Rosetta' (1928); 'My Monday date' (1928); 'Apex blues' (1928); 'You can depend on me' (1932); 'Deep forest' (with Reginald *Foresythe, 1933)—later his band theme; 'Blues in thirds' (1935); 'Piano man' (1942); 'Grand Terrace shuffle'; 'Boogie woogie on the St Louis blues'; 'Tantalizing a Cuban'; and 'Child of a disordered brain'.

S. Dance: *The World of Earl Hines* (New York, 1977).

Hip-hop. A term which loosely embraces the New York City pop scene and mainly black music of the 1980s (especially *rap), and the in things that go with it: DJs and their ways, break dancing and body popping, training shoes and track suits, electronic sounds, modern graffiti, and all things consumed and sniffed. The phenomenon inevitably invaded Britain along with its electro music and rap.

Hirsch, Louis A[chille] (*b* New York, 28 Nov. 1887; *d* New York, 13 May 1924). American composer. One of the most popular American theatre composers of the First World War period; at one time a dozen or so shows containing his music were runnng at the same time. A musical prodigy, he taught himself the piano, later going to Europe with his parents and studying for a while at the Berlin Stern Conservatory, with the intention of becoming a concert pianist. On his return to the USA in 1906 he gave up this ambition in favour of writing popular music. He became a staff pianist with a music-publisher and started composing songs and learning the art of arranging. He wrote for Lew *Dockstader's Minstrels and his work began to appear in revues and musicals: *The Gay White Way* (1907); *The Mimic World* (1908); *Miss Innocence* (1908)—'My post card girl'; and *The Girl and the Wizard* (1909)—'La belle Parisienne', 'Military Mary Ann'. In 1910 he became staff composer to the *Shubert Brothers, his first complete musical being *He Came from Milwaukee* (1910) and his first complete revue *The Revue of Revues* (1911), which introduced Gaby *Deslys to the American public. His first big success was *Vera Violetta* (1911); followed by *The Whirl of Society* (1912), starring Al *Jolson, and *The *Passing Show* (1912). He relinquished his post to Sigmund *Romberg and went to London to work on **Hullo, Ragtime!* (1912); *Come Over Here* (1913); *Hullo, Tango!* (1913); *Honeymoon Express* (1914); and *Dora's Doze* (1914).

When war broke out he returned to the USA and wrote for the **Ziegfeld Follies* (1915, 1916, 1918, 1922, and 1923); *My Home Town Girl* (1916); *The Grass Widow* (1917); *Going Up* (1917)—'The tickle toe'; *The Rainbow Girl* (1918); *Oh, My Dear!* (1918); *See-Saw* (1919); *Mary* (1920)—'The love nest'; *The O'Brien Girl* (1921); **Greenwich Village Follies* (1922 and 1923); *Yoicks* (1924); and *Betty Lee* (1924).

Hitchcock, Raymond (*b* Auburn, NY, 22 Oct. 1865; *d* Beverly Hills, Calif., 24 Nov. 1929). American actor and producer. A singing comic, he first appeared on the stage in 1890 and first starred in *The Yankee Consul* (1904), in which he sang 'Ain't it funny what a difference just a few hours make?' His other notable appearances were in *The Student King* (1906), *The Man Who Owns Broadway* (1909), and *The Beauty Shop* (1914). He is mainly remembered in connection with his revue productions under the title of *Hitchy-Koo* (1917–20) and others of the 1917–27 period. He was married to the actress and singer Flora Zabelle (1888–1968) who appeared in many of his shows.

Hit Parade, The. Radio programme started in the USA in 1935 which presented the top-selling tunes of the week, the forerunner of many such ratings and lists that have now become an accepted part of the popular music rat-race. The first programme on 20 Apr. 1935 awarded top position to Jerome *Kern's 'Lovely to look at', with the runners-up Kern's 'I won't dance', Harry *Warren's 'Lullaby of Broadway', and George *Gershwin's 'Soon'. Early stars of the show included Frank *Sinatra, replaced by Andy Russell (1919–92) in 1947. The tune which appeared most frequently in the lists in pre-pop days was Irving *Berlin's 'White Christmas', followed by Richard *Rodgers's 'People will say we're in love', Hugh Williams's 'Harbour lights', Sammy *Fain's 'I'll be seeing you', Warren's 'You'll never know'; with Sid Lippman's 'Too young' most frequently in the No. 1 position. The programme was a reflection of the growing power of radio, and later television, to make or break song hits, soon rendering the old *Tin Pan Alley song-plugging methods obsolete. The practice continued in various Top 10 *charts run by American and British journals such as *Billboard* and *New Musical Express*, with the American radio cashing in with **American Bandstand* and BBC TV with **Top of the Pops*.

Hit the Deck. American musical comedy with score by Vincent *Youmans, lyrics by Clifford *Grey and Leo Robin (1900–85), book by Herbert *Fields, based on Hubert Osborne's play *Shore Leave*. Directed by Alexander Leftwich (1884–1947), it was presented at the Belasco Theatre, New York, 25 Apr. 1927, with Louise *Groody and Charles King (1894–1944) in the leading roles, and ran for 352 performances. Its bright and happy score included 'Sometimes I'm happy' and 'Hallelujah'.

Loulou, who owns a coffee-house, falls in love with Bilge Smith, a sailor. She expresses her love by buying him a ship with her savings, but he is too proud to accept it. Involving a trip to China, the matter is eventually sorted out. It came to the London Hippodrome 3 Nov. 1927, with Ivy Tresman as Loulou and Stanley *Holloway as Bill, and had 277 performances. It was filmed by RKO in 1930, with Jack Oakie (1903–78) and Polly Walker (*b* 1908), and more notably in 1937 with Fred *Astaire, Ginger *Rogers, and Polly Walker, with a somewhat changed story and new songs added, and now called **Follow the Fleet*; and by MGM as *Hit the Deck*, starring Jane *Powell, Tony *Martin, Debby *Reynolds, and Russ Tamblyn (*b* 1934).

***HMS Pinafore* or The Lass That Loved a Sailor.** The third important *Gilbert and Sullivan/D'Oyly

*Carte collaboration, after *Trial by Jury* (1875) and *The *Sorcerer* (1877), first produced at the Opera-Comique Theatre, London, 25 May 1878, with George *Grossmith, Rutland *Barrington, and Jessie *Bond in the cast and Alfred *Cellier as musical director. The production began under the management of the Comedy-Opera Company but after 14 months there was a disagreement between Richard D'Oyly Carte and the directors of the company who tried unsuccessfully, on 31 July 1879, to carry away the scenery. There were fisticuffs between the rival employees. They then put on their own production at the Imperial Theatre from 1 Aug. 1879 which was transferred to the Royal Olympic, but was taken off after 91 performances through lack of support, From 4 Aug. 1879 the original company was known as Mr D'Oyly Carte's Opera Company and their production carried on to a triumphant 571 performances.

It is one of Sullivan's breeziest and brightest scores, with a lightly nonsensical story concerning Captain Corcoran's daughter Josephine who refuses to marry the kindly Sir Joseph Porter, First Lord of the Admiralty, because she is in love with Ralph Rackstraw, a humble and modest sailor. Corcoran himself loves a sweets-and-tobacco vendor called Buttercup. Matters are resolved in the usual Gilbertian way when Buttercup reveals that Corcoran and Ralph, both of whom she nursed, were mixed up as babies. Sir Joseph no longer desires the daughter of a common sailor and Corcoran now finds himself eminently suited.

The work was first performed in the USA in a pirated version at the Boston Museum, 25 Nov. 1878, and then at the Standard Theatre, New York, 15 Jan. 1879. Subsequently it was staged by some 150 unauthorized companies, before the first genuine D'Oyly Carte production, 'promoting the collaborators' own conception of the opera', was first seen at the Fifth Avenue Theatre, 1 Dec. 1879. A lively score included such classics as: 'I'm called little Buttercup', 'I am the Captain of the Pinafore', 'I am the monarch of the sea', 'When I was a lad', 'Sorry her lot', and 'Never mind the why and wherefore'. There were film versions in 1982 and 1986.

Hodeir, André (*b* Paris, 22 Jan. 1921). French jazz critic. He studied at the Paris Conservatoire, founded and led the Jazz Group of Paris 1954–60, and was editor of *Jazz Hot* 1947–50. The author of several penetrating books on jazz, he intrigued the jazz world with his fresh and controversial outlook in *Hommes et problèmes du jazz* (Paris, 1954), published in English as *Jazz, its Evolution and Essence* (1956). Other works were *Introduction à la musique de jazz* (1948); *Toward Jazz* (1963); and *Les Mondes du Jazz* (1970); as well as books on other fields of music.

Hodges, Johnny [John Cornelius] (*b* Cambridge, Mass., 25 July 1907; *d* New York, 11 May 1970). American jazz saxophonist. Virtuoso performer on the soprano- and alto-saxes, notably the latter which he gave an entirely individual personality and sound and a distinctive sweet-and-sour lyricism. After an early start as a drummer and pianist he studied the saxophone with Sidney *Bechet, whose influence remained obvious, then worked with Willie 'The Lion' *Smith, Bechet, and Chick *Webb. In 1928 he joined Duke *Ellington and was to become an essential part of the Ellington sound until 1951. He broke away to lead his own groups for several years, but neither he nor the Ellington band seemed quite the same without one another, and he rejoined Ellington in 1955 and remained with him until his death. His work was heard to best advantage in the many small-group recordings they made, including 'Daydream', 'Things ain't what they used to be', and 'Junior hop' in the 1940s.

Hoffman, Al (*b* Derevno, nr. Minsk, 25 Sept. 1902; *d* New York, 21 July 1960). American composer. Son of a cantor who emigrated to America, he sang as a boy soprano in a synagogue before entering the dance-band world and leading his own band in Seattle. He went to New York in 1928 and, having a hit with his song 'Heartaches' in 1930, gave up playing to concentrate on composing. He worked in England for several years in the 1930s, writing film music, musical comedies, and revues with Al *Goodhart and Maurice Sigler, and returning to the USA in 1937. He wrote scores for *Going Greek* (1937) and *Hide and Seek* (1937); and for films (several starring Jack *Buchanan) including: *Squibs* (1934); *Jack of All Trades* (1935); *First a Girl* (1935)—'Everything's in rhythm with my heart'; *She Shall Have Music* (1935)—'She shall have music'; *Come Out of the Pantry* (1935)—Everything stops for tea; *This'll Make You Whistle* (1936)—'I'm in a dancing mood', 'This'll make you whistle', 'There isn't any limit to my love'; *When Knights Were Bold* (1936); *Gangway* (1937). Other songs included: 'Auf wiedersehen, my dear' (1932); 'Come out, come out, wherever you are' (1933); 'I saw stars' (1934); 'Little man you've had a busy day' (1934); 'The story of a starry night' (1942); 'Goodnight, wherever you are' (1943); 'Mairzy doats' (1944); 'Promises' (1945); and 'Me and my imagination' (1950).

Hold Everything. American musical comedy with score by Ray *Henderson, lyrics by B. G. *DeSylva and Lew *Brown, which contained such lasting songs as 'You're the cream in my coffee', 'To know you is to love you', and 'When I love I love'. It opened at the Broadhurst Theatre 10 Oct. 1928 and had 413 performances.

It was the second of four DeSylva, Brown, and Henderson musicals with a sporting background, this one, in spite of the title, set in the boxing world and telling the story of a welterweight who defends his title and the honour of the girl he loves. The boxer, Sonny Jim Brooks, was played by Jack *Whiting. In London, at the Palace Theatre,

12 Jun. 1929, Owen Nares (1888–1943) took the part.

Holiday, Billie [Fagan, Eleanora] (*b* Baltimore, 7 Apr. 1915; *d* New York, 17 July 1959). American jazz singer. She began her career around the age of 15, singing in Harlem nightclubs where she was heard by record producer John *Hammond and Benny *Goodman with whose band she appeared in 1933. She started a rich recording career in 1935, working with musicians like Buck *Clayton, Teddy *Wilson, and saxophonist Lester *Young, with whom she had a special affinity. It was he who christened her 'Lady Day' and she named him 'Prez'. She toured with Count Basie in 1937 and with Artie Shaw in 1938, but she disliked the band world and became a solo act in 1939 at the Café Society club. She had a hit record in 1939 with 'Strange fruit', but the club life and her insecure personality led to a reliance on drink and drugs and to an early sense of strain in her work. Never a true blues-singer, in spite of her billing, she was a searching interpreter of the torch-song and the intelligent ballad, which she sang with a harshly grating voice. Earlier her wonderful timing and happy jazz phrasing had promised a fruitful career, but from the mid-1940s on it was a tale of sad decline, although she was still considered by many to be the greatest jazz singer of all time. She underwent cures and made many come-backs, notably in 1954, when she toured Europe and Britain, and in 1957, when she worked with Lester Young again on TV. She made frequent recordings for Norman *Granz in the 1950s. Her autobiography was published in 1956 and a film of her life was made in 1972, under the same title of *Lady Sings the Blues*, starring Diana *Ross.

B. Holiday & W. Dufty: *Lady Sings the Blues* (New York, 1956; pb. 1984). J. Chilton: *Billie's Blues* (London, 1975). B. James: *Billie Holiday* (Tunbridge Wells, 1984).

Holland, Dozier, and Holland. Song-writing team responsible for much of the material that came from the highly successful Motown label in the 1960s. The Detroit-born team was made up of Lamont Dozier (*b* 16 June 1941), Eddie Holland (*b* 30 Oct. 1939), and his brother Brian Holland (*b* 15 Feb. 1941). Dozier had a fitful career as a singer before meeting Berry *Gordy, the founder of Motown, and joining forces with producer Brian Holland in 1961 to write 'Please Mr Postman' for the Marvelettes. Eddie Holland had joined Motown as a demo singer and later recorded 'Jamie', which was a top hit in 1962. At this period the three joined forces and from 1962 onwards, turned out a steady stream of hit songs for the *Supremes (seven No. 1 hits 1964–9), the *Temptations, the *Four Tops, Marvin *Gaye, *Martha and the Vandellas, the *Isley Brothers, and many more. Friction with Gordy led to their leaving Motown in 1968 to form their own labels Invictus and Hot Wax. Brian Holland and Dozier recommenced their own recording career in 1971, but Dozier left the Hollands in 1973 to follow a solo career with Warner Brothers and Columbia and work as an independent producer.

Their main songs include 'Come and get these memories' (1962); 'Baby love' (1964); 'Where did our love go?' (1964); 'Stop! in the name of love' (1965); 'I hear a symphony' (1965); 'I can't help myself' (1965); 'Back in my arms again' (1965); 'Come see about me' (1965); 'You can't hurry love' (1965); 'Reach out, I'll be there' (1966); 'You keep me hanging on' (1966); 'This old heart of mine' (1966); 'Same old song' (1966); 'The happening' (1967); 'Reflections' (1967); 'In and out of love' (1967); 'Love is here and now you're gone' (1967); 'Forever came today' (1968); and 'Bernadette' (1969)

Hollander, Frederick [Holländer, Friedrich] (*b* London, 18 Oct. 1896; *d* Munich, 18 Jan. 1976). Composer. Son of the theatre composer Viktor Holländer (1886–1940), who was a musical director in London at the time of his birth, he was educated at the Berlin Conservatory and by the age of 18 was associate conductor at the Prague Opera House. During the First World War he directed an operetta company and was associated with Max Reinhardt in Berlin with whom he wrote the revue *Tingel Tangel*. He visited America and became interested in writing film music. On his return to Germany, he wrote the score for the film *Der Blaue Engel* (*The Blue Angel*, 1930), with the cynical 'Falling in love again' for ever associated with its star Marlene *Dietrich.

His other film scores included: *Der Andere* (1930); *Der Mann der Seinen Mörder sucht* (1931); *Stürme der Leidenschaft* (1932); *Ich und die Kaiserin* (1933); and in Hollywood *Desire* (1936); **Anything Goes* (1936)—'My heart and I'; *Jungle Princess* (1937)—'Moonlight and shadows'; *Angel* (1937); *The Thrill of a Lifetime* (1937); *True Confession* (1937); *100 Men and a Girl* (1937); *Zaza* (1938); **Destry Rides Again* (1939)—'See what the boys in the back room will have', 'You've got that look'; *Man about Town* (1939); *Invitation to Happiness* (1939); *Moon Over Burma* (1940); *Seven Sinners* (1940); *Typhoon* (1940); *Aloma of the South Seas* (1941); *The Man Who Came to Dinner* (1942); *Tornado* (1943); *Conflict* (1945); *A Foreign Affair* (1948); *That Lady in Ermine* (1948); *Born Yesterday* (1951); and *The Five Thousand Fingers of Dr T* (1953). He returned to Germany in 1956.

Holliday, Judy [Tuvin, Judith] (*b* New York, 21 June 1922; *d* New York, 7 June 1965). American actress and singer. She worked in the dumb blonde tradition, but with an attractive personality, hidden intelligence, comedy skills, and an intriguingly piping voice. She first became widely known in the Broadway play *Born Yesterday* (1946; filmed 1950). This led to a fitting role in **Bells Are Ringing* (1956) which was filmed in 1960. She was also in the musical *Hot Spot* (1963); and the films *It Should Happen to You* (1953) and *The Solid Gold Cadillac* (1956).

G. Carey: *Judy Holliday* (New York, 1982). W. Holtzmann: *Judy Holliday* (New York, 1982).

Hollies, The. British rock group formed in Manchester in 1962 with Allan Clarke (vocals), Graham Nash (guitar), Tony Hicks (*b* 1943) (guitar), Eric Haydock (*b* 1943) (bass), and Don Rathbone (*b* 1943) (drums). In action at the same time as the *Beatles, they were their strongest rivals in Britain in terms of chart successes. Lacking the show-business flair of the Liverpool group, they relied on good commercial songs and a very personal way of putting them over, based on the singing of Allan Clarke (*b* 15 Apr. 1942) and the guitar-playing of Graham Nash (b 2 Feb. 1942). They moved into the Top 10 with 'Searchin'' and 'Stay' in 1963, followed by 'Just one look' (1964), and 'Here I go again' (1964), and in 1965 had a No. 1 hit in 'I'm alive'. Relying until then on other people's material, they were writing their own songs by 1966 and had a peak period 1966–7, producing many singles that had both humour and charm. Curiously, they had much less success with their albums, which failed to cash in on the psychedelic boom of 1967 and after. Graham Nash left in 1968 to form *Crosby, Stills, and Nash. The group continued to work in cabaret and recorded in the 1970s, achieving a hit with 'The air I breathe' (1974) and proving to be one of the most stable of British groups.

Holloway, Stanley [Augustus] (*b* London, 1 Oct. 1890; *d* Littlehampton, 30 Jan. 1982). British actor and singer. He started his working life as an office boy in Billingsgate Market, and his acting career in seaside concert parties. His first London appearances were in *Kissing Time* (1919) and *A Night Out* (1920). He became an original member of the famous concert party group *The *Co-Optimists* (1921) and appeared in all their productions in London and elsewhere until they disbanded in 1927. Subsequently he appeared in **Hit the Deck* (1927); *Song of the Sea* (1928); *Coo-ee* (1929); revivals of *The Co-Optimists* (1929 and 1930); *The Savoy Follies* (1932); *Three Sisters* (1934); *All Wave* (1936); *London Rhapsody* (1938); *Up and Doing* (1940); and *Fine and Dandy* (1942).

His most lasting role of all came when he was 66, as Alfred P. Doolittle in **My Fair Lady* (NY, 1956), a part he also played in London in 1958 and in the 1964 film. He had a long career in British films, including some musicals like *Champagne Charlie* (1944), but mainly prominent in the famous series of post-war Ealing comedies. In Britain he was equally well known as the writer and speaker of a memorable series of monologues featuring Albert, Sam, and other Lancastrian characters, which he wrote, performed, and recorded in the 1930s.

S. Holloway: *Wiv a Little Bit o' Luck* (London, 1967).

Holly, Buddy [Holley, Charles Hardin] (*b* Lubbock, Texas, 7 Sept. 1936; *d* Clear Lake, Iowa, 3 Feb. 1959). American rock singer, guitarist, and composer. He started on local radio and in nearby towns, performing in a *hillbilly style. Following enthusiastic reports of his ability he was signed up by Decca Records in 1956 to make some records in Nashville. At least two worthy items came from these early sessions—'Midnight shift' and 'Rock around with Ollie Vee'—and the collaboration with musicians like Sonny Curtis and Jerry Allison, later in the Crickets, began. He moved to an independent label in 1957 and eventually to Coral, where the Cricket's recordings of 'That'll be the day', 'I'm, looking for someone to love', 'Oh boy', and 'Not fade away' were immediate successes. He had his first hits under his own name in 1957 with 'Peggy Sue', 'Listen to me', and 'Rave on', and toured Britain with the Crickets in 1958 before the group split up.

It is debatable what Holly would have achieved had he not been killed in a plane crash, after a concert at Clear Lake, at the age of 22. Although he had steady success with his recordings he had not, at the time, appeared to be outstanding, but his early death had the usual result of making him a legend. The first posthumous release of his work 'It doesn't matter anymore'/'Raining in my heart' was a huge hit worldwide, and his recordings continued to sell into the 1960s.

In retrospect he is seen as being as great an influence in shaping the pop scene as Elvis *Presley, and rather more talented. He is bracketed with Chuck *Berry as the greatest singer-songwriter and a pioneer in rock guitar styling and the use of the line-up of two guitars, bass, and drums. He was the first regularly to double-track his voice and the first to use strings. His work was simple and direct but also versatile, exhibiting a full range of moods. His best work is probably to be found in 'That'll be the day'. In 1977 a compiled album of his best songs sold a million copies in Britain alone; and a film based on his life, *The Buddy Holly Story*, was made in 1978.

D. Laing: *Buddy Holly* (London–New York, 1971). J. J. Goldrosen: *Buddy Holly: his Life and Music* (London, 1975). J. Tobler: *The Buddy Holly Story* (London, 1979).

Holman, Libby [Holtzman, Elizabeth] (*b* Cincinnati, 23 May 1906; *d* Stamford, Conn., 18 June 1971). American actress and singer. She is remembered as the prototype torch singer of the 1920s and 1930s as exemplified in her famous rendering of 'Moanin' low' in *The *Little Show* in 1929. Her other stage appearances were in **Garrick Gaieties* (1925); **Greenwich Village Follies* (1926); *Merry-go-round* (1927); *Rainbow* (1928); *Three's a Crowd* (1930)—'Body and soul', 'Something to remember you by'; *Revenge With Music* (1934)—'You and the night and the music'; and *You Never Know* (1938).

H. D. Perry: *Libby Holman, Body and Soul* (Boston, 1983).

Holzmann, Abe [Abraham] (*b* New York, 19 Aug. 1874; *d* East Orange, NJ, 16 Jan. 1939). American composer. He studied at the New York Conservatory before becoming staff composer and manager with a music publisher. Later he was advertising manager of the *International Musician*. His spirited

'Blaze away' (1901) has remained one of the world's most popular marches, well-known in the ballroom, too, as the music for the *military two-step. He also wrote the popular cakewalk 'Smokey mokes' (1899); 'Bunch o' blackberries' (1900); 'Hunky dory' (1900); 'Alagazam' (1902); 'Blaze of glory' (1910); and 'The spirit of independence' (1912).

'Home on the range'. Often thought of as a traditional cowboy song, the music was written by Daniel E. Kelly (1843–1905) and the words by Dr Brewster M. Higley (1823–1911) and it was conceived in Smith County, Kansas, *c.* 1872–3. The words were first published in the *Smith County Pioneer* in 1873 as 'Oh give me a home where the buffalo roam'. Music and words were first published together as 'An Arizona home', St Louis 1905, and reprinted in John A. *Lomax's *Cowboy Songs* in 1910. It has since been used as the official Kansas state song.

'Home, sweet home'. The music of this anthem of the British Victorian drawing-room first appeared in *Melodies of Various Nations* in 1821 under the title 'To the home of my childhood', with words by Thomas Bayly and the tune described as a Sicilian air. It was later revealed that a Sicilian air had been needed to fill a gap in the publication so this one was anonymously contributed by Henry M. Bishop (1786–1855). He was hoist by his own petard for, when he used the tune again in his opera *Clari* (1823), as 'Home, sweet home' with words by John Howard Payne (1791–1852), where it was an immediate success, he was accused of stealing a traditional air and calling it his own.

Honky-tonk. The name given in America to a low-class nightclub, usually a one-room affair with a piano or small jazz group, such as was generally frequented by less affluent black people in early jazz days. The beer was generally served direct from barrels, hence an alternative name of 'barrel house'. The name 'honky-tonk' or 'barrelhouse' was then applied to the kind of boisterous music that was generally played there, such as *boogie-woogie, necessary to cut through the noise. The name was rather curiously perpetuated in Meade Lux *Lewis's 'Honky tonk train blues' which he first recorded in 1928 and in many other tune titles.

Hood, Basil (*b* Yorkshire, 5 Apr. 1864; *d* London, 7 Aug. 1917). British dramatist, librettist, and lyric-writer. He served as an officer in the Yorkshire Regiment 1883–93, finally retiring as a captain in 1898. While still a serving officer he began to write for the stage, producing both straight plays and several influential musicals including: *The French Maid* (1897), *Dandy Dan* (1897), *Orlando Dando* (1898), *Her Royal Highness* (1898), all with Walter *Slaughter; *The Rose of Persia* (1899, *Sullivan); *The *Emerald Isle* (1901, Sullivan/*German); **Merrie England* (1902) and *A Princess of Kensington* (1903), both with German. He also wrote English librettos for *The Merveilleuses* (1906); *The Merry Widow* (1907); *A Waltz Dream* (1908); *The Dollar Princess.* (1909); *The Count of Luxembourg* (1911); *Gypsy Love* (1912); and *The Pearl Girl* (1913). His work, said *The Green Room Book*, always displayed 'exceptional taste and sentiment, while his humour was always playful and light, and never caustic'.

Hooker, John Lee (*b* Clarksdale, Miss., 22 Aug. 1917). American blues singer and guitarist. He moved to Memphis in his teens, but first made his mark in Detroit where he went in 1943. He first recorded in 1948, producing the best-selling 'Boogie chillen' which immediately made him famous. His distinctive Afro-American rhythms came out in 'Driftin'' and 'Hobo blues'. Centred on Chicago in the mid-1950s, he recorded under various pseudonyms, and produced such best-sellers as 'Maudie', 'Crawlin' King Snake', 'Tupelo', 'Birmingham blues', and 'I'm in the mood'. He was a key figure in the rhythm 'n' blues developments of the 1960s, when he recorded 'Boom boom', 'Dimples', 'I'm mad again', and 'Serve you right to suffer'.

Hootenanny. American slang word once used for almost anything; a replacement for a forgotten word or a word that was not respectable enough for polite usage—the equivalent of 'whatsit', 'thingumajig', or 'doo-da'. Sometimes abbreviated to 'hoot', it gradually evolved into meaning a spontaneous happening or get-together. In the folk-music world it was used of an improvised musical gathering, this usage being credited to Terry Pettus and put into general circulation by singers Pete *Seeger and Woody *Guthrie *c.* 1959. See the song collection *Hootenanny Tonight!* ed. Leisy (New York, 1964).

Hope, Bob [Townes, Leslie] (*b* Eltham, London, 26 May 1903). American actor, comedian, and singer. Now thought of primarily as the wise-cracking, golf-playing comedian of radio and TV, he rose to fame as a song-and-dance man, first in vaudeville and then in such Broadway shows as *The Ramblers* (1926), in the chorus; *The Sidewalks of New York* (1927); **Roberta* (1933), his first success; *Say When* (1934); **Ziegfeld Follies* (1936)—singing 'I can't get started'; and **Red, Hot and Blue* (1936)—'It's de-lovely'. Further song-and-dance, if not dramatic, ability was added to his sly humour in a long succession of musical films starting with *The Big Broadcast of 1938*—'Thanks for the memory', sung by Hope and Shirley *Ross, which became Hope's theme song; *Thanks for the Memory* (1938)—'Two sleepy people' (Hope and Ross); *Some Like it Hot* (1939)—'The lady's in love with you' (Hope and Ross); through a long series of 'Road' films with Bing *Crosby and Dorothy *Lamour—*Road to Singapore* (1940); *Road to Zanzibar* (1941); *Road to Morocco* (1942); *Road to Utopia* (1945); *Road to Rio* (1947); *Road to Bali* (1952); *Road to Hong Kong* (1962); as well as **Louisiana Purchase*

(1941); *Star-spangled Rhythm* (1942); *Let's Face It* (1943); *Duffy's Tavern* (1945); *The Paleface* (1948)—'Buttons and bows'; *Fancy Pants* (1950); *The Lemon Drop Kid* (1951)—'Silver bells' (Hope and Marilyn Maxwell, 1921–72); *Son of Paleface* (1952)—'Buttons and bows' (Roy Rogers, Jane Russell, and Hope); *Here Come the Girls* (1953); *The Seven Little Foys* (1955); *Beau James* (1957); and *The Five Pennies* (1959).

B. Hope: *Have Tux Will Travel* (New York, 1954). J. Morelli, E. Epstein, & E. Clarke: *The Amazing Careers of Bob Hope* (New York, 1973). B. Hope: *The Road to Hollywood* (New York, 1977).

Hopkins, Claude (*b* Alexandria, Va., 24 Aug. 1903; *d* Riverdale, NY, 19 Feb. 1984). American jazz pianist and bandleader. A graduate of Howard University, Washington DC, he went into music as co-leader of a band with Bernard Addison (*b* 1905), worked with Wilbur *Sweatman in the mid-1920s, then went to Paris as musical director for Josephine *Baker and led a band which featured Sidney *Bechet. Returning to the USA, he led a band at the Cocoanut Grove in Harlem and subsequently, in 1930s, at the *Savoy Ballroom, the Roseland Ballroom, and the *Cotton Club. He did most of his own arranging and wrote the band's theme 'I would do anything for you'. He was a regular broadcaster and led a West Coast band 1941–5, in the 1950s in New York and Boston. He was still active as a pianist into the 1970s.

Hopkins, Sam 'Lightnin'' (*b* Centerville, Texas, 15 Mar. 1912; *d* Houston, 30 Jan. 1982). American country-blues singer and guitarist. He spent most of his life in Houston, starting life as a farmworker, teaching himself the guitar (with a few tips from 'Blind Lemon' *Jefferson) and accompanying his cousin, blues singer Texas Alexander. He started singing professionally in 1946 when he first recorded in Houston, later in Los Angeles, New York, and Hollywood. He developed a very individual boogie-woogie-based guitar style, with deep bass and varied rhythms; unfortunately he seemed addicted, in his early recordings, to over-amplification. Remaining outside the showbiz orbit, he remained a natural performer and a perceptive commentator, through his blues, on black life and the activities of humanity in general, most of his songs only being effective in his own interpretations. Later he took to acoustic guitar and produced, around 1950–1, some of his best and most sensitive performances. He became a popular singer at the Village Gate in New York and worked with others such as Joan *Baez and Pete *Seeger. The blues historian Samuel Charters considered him to be the last of the great blues singers.

Hopper, William **De Wolf** (*b* New York, 30 Mar. 1858; *d* Kansas City, Mo., 23 Sept. 1935). American actor and bass-singer. He made his first stage appearance in 1878 and became an established feature of Wallack's Theatre in New York where he appeared in *The Black Hussar* (1885); *The Beggar Student* (1885); *The Begum* (1887); and other shows. He became well-known for his *Gilbert and Sullivan roles and appeared in a succession of musicals until 1928, including *Castles in the Air* (1890); *Wang* (1891); *Panjandrum* (1893); *El Capitan* (1899); and *The *Passing Show* (1917). Among his six wives were the petite singer and actress Edna Wallace Hopper (1864–1959), star of *El Capitan* and **Florodora*, and the writer Hedda Hopper.

De W. Hopper: *Once a Clown, Always a Clown* (Boston, 1927).

Horne, Lena [Calhoun, Lena] (*b* Brooklyn, NY, 30 June 1917). American singer and actress. She began her career as a dancer and chorus-girl at the *Cotton Club, was vocalist with Noble *Sissle 1935–6, worked as a solo club artist, then appeared on stage in Lew *Leslie's **Blackbirds* of 1939 and 1940. She was with the Charlie *Barnet band 1940–1. Her stunning good looks and elegance and her attractive husky voice soon made her a popular entertainer and she made a number of film appearances including: *The Duke is Tops* (1938); **Panama Hattie* (1942); **Cabin in the Sky* (1943); *Stormy Weather* (1943); *I Dood It* (1943); *Thousands Cheer* (1943); *Swing Fever* (1943); *Broadway Rhythm* (1944); *Two Girls and a Sailor* (1944); **Ziegfeld Follies* (1946); *Till the Clouds Roll By* (1946); *Words and Music* (1948); *The Duchess of Idaho* (1950); *Meet Me in Las Vegas* (1956); *Death of a Gunfighter* (1969); and *The Wiz* (1978). She married the pianist and bandleader Lennie Hayton (1908–71) in 1947 and he was also her musical director and accompanist until he died. Her main stage role was in *Jamaica* (1957). She made several European tours in the 1940s and 1950s and was frequently on television in the 1950s and 1960s.

L. Horne: *In Person—Lena Horne* (New York, 1950). L. Horne: *Lena* (New York, 1965). J. Haskins & K. Benson: *Lena: a Personal and Professional Biography of Lena Horne* (New York, 1984).

Hornpipe. Dance of British origin going back to the 13th century, so-called because the traditional accompaniment in early days was on a pipe made from an animal's horn. Early examples are in 3/2 time but by the end of the 18th century this had been changed to 2/4 time. It is strictly a solo dance. Although it has long been associated with sailors, there is no evidence of its having seafaring origins. It was probably danced on board ships because, with its solo nature and being a step-dance, it took up little space in performance.

Horovitz, Joseph (*b* Vienna, 26 May 1926). Austro-British composer. His family moved to England after the *Anschluss* of 1938 and he studied music at Oxford and with Nadia Boulanger in Paris. Writing in a melodic modern style with a great awareness of popular music idioms, he has produced popularly slanted works such as his children's choral work *Captain Noah and his Floating Zoo* (1970); light-hearted ballets—*Les femmes d'Alger* (1952) and *Alice in Wonderland* (1955); several tuneful stage works; many works for brass band or ensemble, including the pastiche—'Music Hall Suite' (1965), 'Sinfonietta for brass' and 'Concerto for Euphonium' (1972); and many jazz-flavoured works including 'Four dances for orchestra' (1952) and 'Jazz concerto for harpsichord' (1965).

Hoschna, Karl (*b* Kuschwarda, Bohemia, 16 Aug. 1877; *d* New York, 22 Dec. 1911). American composer. He went to the USA in 1896 after studying at the Vienna Conservatory, to become one of many immigrant composers on the American scene in the early 1900s. He played in Victor *Herbert's orchestra for two years as an oboist, then became an arranger and orchestrator for the publisher Witmark. He wrote three unsuccessful operettas, *Belle of the West* (1905), *The Girl from Broadway* (1906), and *Prince Humbug* (1908); and was then asked to collaborate with Otto *Harbach (then Hauerbach) on an adaptation of a play *Incog*. They renamed it *The Three Twins* and, in 1908, it proved to be one of Hoschna's main successes, closely rivalled by **Madame Sherry* (1910), another of the eight operettas he wrote with Harbach. His scores included: *Katy Did* (1910); *Bright Eyes* (1910); *Madame Sherry* (1910)—'Every little movement has a meaning of its own'; *Jumping Jupiter* (1911); *Dr De Luxe* (1911)—'For every boy that's lonely there's a girl that's lonely too'; *The Girl of My Dreams* (1911); *The Fascinating Widow* (1911)—'Put your arms around me'; and *The Wall Street Girl* (1912).

Hot. An adjective that crept into the musical world in the emergent years of jazz. When jazz was something of a novelty, its fervour and freneticism made the word 'hot' seem an appropriate description to contrast with the gentle warmth of the music that preceded it. The exact year of its adoption is hard to pinpoint, and it was likely that it was in use for some time before it became common currency. Written references to a trumpet's sound as being 'red-hot' can be found as far back as 1850. In the 1920s and 1930s 'hot music' became a synonym for jazz and Hot Clubs were formed in both the USA and Europe. Louis *Armstrong recorded with his Hot Fives and Sevens and Jelly Roll *Morton called his band the Red Hot Peppers. As jazz became established less emphasis was laid on the word until, in the 1940s, the word 'cool' came in to describe the new jazz that was the antithesis of hot. Thereafter 'hot' simply became a synonym for 'traditional'.

Hot Chocolates. Famous all-black revue staged at Connie's Inn in Harlem 20 June 1929 and transferred in 1930 to the Hudson Theatre. The performers included Jazzlips Richardson, Jimmy Baskette, Eddie Green, Baby Cox, Thelma and Paul Morres, Edith Wilson, Margaret Simms, Paul Bass (later replaced by Louis *Armstrong), and Russell Wooding's Jubilee Singers. With words by Andy *Razaf and music by Fats *Waller and Harry Brooks (1895–1970), it is remembered as the source of the Waller classics *'Ain't misbehavin'' and 'What did I do to be so black and blue'.

House of Flowers. American musical play with score by Harold *Arlen and book by the New Orleans novelist Truman Capote (1924–84), based on his own short story. It opened at the Alvin Theatre, New York, 30 Dec. 1954 and had 165 performances.

The story is set in a Haitian bordello run by Madame Fleur (played by Pearl *Bailey) which has a close competitor run by Madame Tango (Juanita Hall, 1901–68). An attractive new prospect, Ottilie (Diahann Carroll, *b* 1935), fails to live up to expectations when she decides to remain unsullied for her loved one. It had an attractively atmospheric and sensitive score with numbers like 'A sleepin' bee', 'House of flowers', and 'I never has seen snow'. There was an off-Broadway revival at the Theatre de Lys, 28 Jan. 1968.

Houston, Whitney (*b* Newark, NJ, 9 Aug 1963). American soul singer. She first sang in Baptist churches around the age of 11, then appeared in New York clubs in the early 1980s with her mother, singer Cissy Houston (*b* 1932). She had a great hit with her first album, *Whitney Houston*, recorded for Arista, which sold 14 million copies, won a Grammy Award, and included such ballads as 'Saving all my love for you', 'How will I know', and 'Greatest love', making her the first female singer to have an album go straight to No. 1 in the charts, an accolade repeated by *Whitney* in 1987. She had her 7th consecutive No. 1 hit single in 1988 with 'Where do broken hearts go?'

Howard, Eugene and Willie. Vaudeville and revue Yiddish comedy partnership, with actor Willie Howard [Wilhelm Levkowitz] (*b* Neustadt, Germany, 13 Apr. 1886; *d* New York, 12 Jan. 1949) the comic half, and his brother Eugene (1881–1965) the straight man. Willie first appeared as a boy soprano in *The Little Duchess* (1901), Eugene started in the chorus of *The *Belle of New York* (1899). After a period in vaudeville 1903–12, their partnership became staple fare in several well-known series of revues—*The *Passing Show* (1912, 1915, 1918, 1920, 1922); **George White's Scandals* (1926, 1928, 1929, 1931, 1935); and **Ziegfeld Follies* (1934). Willie Howard also appeared in *Sky High* (1925); **Girl Crazy* (1930); and other shows.

Howard, Joe [Joseph Edgar] (*b* New York, 12 Feb. 1878; *d* Chicago, 19 May 1961). American composer and singer. He ran away from home at the age of 8 and at 11 appeared in vaudeville as a boy soprano. When he was 19 he returned to New York to appear in vaudeville where he did a song-and-dance routine. He became a star of musical comedy and in the radio *Gay Nineties Revue* 1939–40. He had started writing songs in 1897 with 'On the boulevard', and he had a national success with 'Hello! my baby' (1899), one of the earliest telephone songs, which he performed with his wife, Ida Emerson, who wrote the words; 'Honey, will you miss me when I'm gone' (1902); 'On a Saturday night' (1902); 'Goodbye, my lady love' (1904); 'Central, give me back my dime' (1905); and 'I'm gonna leave you' (1906).

For the stage, mainly in collaboration with Frank R. Adams (1884–1963), who also produced, he wrote: *The Isle of Bong Bong* (1905)—'I'm lonesome for you'; '*The Umpire* (1905)—'I want a girl like you'; *His Highness, the Bey* (1905); *The District Leader* (1906). These were only seen in Chicago; the subsequent shows mostly started out in Chicago before going on to New York, including: *The Land of Nod* (1907); *The Time, the Place, and the Girl* (1907)—'I'm lonesome tonight'; *The Girl Question* (1907); *The Flower of the Ranch* (1908); *Honeymoon Trail* (1908); *Goddess of Liberty* (1909); *A Stubborn Cinderella* (1909); *The Golden Girl* (1909)—'Everybody wonders why they marry'; *The Prince of Tonight* (1909)—'I wonder who's kissing her now'; *Miss Nobody from Starland* (1910)—'It must be great to be a general (but I'd rather lead a band)'; *The Sweetest Girl in Paris* (1910)—'I want a man'; *The Flirting Princess* (1911)—'Tell her in the golden summer', 'Never choose a girl from her photograph'; *A Broadway Honeymoon* (1911)—'When the girl you love loves you'; *Love and Politics* (1911); *Lower Berth Thirteen* (1912); and *In and Out* (1915). A film of his life, *I Wonder Who's Kissing Her Now* (1947), had Mark Stevens playing the part of Howard.

Howes, Bobby [Robert William] (*b* London, 4 Aug. 1895; *d* London, 27 Apr. 1972). British actor, singer, and dancer. He began his career in music-hall, starting at the Battersea Palace and graduating to the Tivoli. He spent many years in concert parties and touring in variety. His first West End stage appearance was in *The Litle Revue Starts at 9* (1923), followed by *The Second Little Revue* (1924); *The Punch Bowl* (1925); *The Blue Kitten* (1925); and *Vaudeville Vanities* (1926). Generally playing the role of an upper-class nitwit with the compulsory refined accent of the period, he was the star of a long string of forgettable British musicals (recalled by the occasional song hit) including *The Blue Train* (1927); *The Yellow Mask* (1928); **Mr Cinders* (1929), his first with Binnie *Hale—'I'm a one-man girl', 'Every little moment'; *Sons o' Guns* (1930); *Song of the Drum* (1931); *For the Love of Mike* (1931)—'Got a date with an angel', 'Who do you love'; *Tell Her the Truth* (1932)—'Horrortorio'; *He Wanted Adventure* (1933); *Yes, Madam?* (1934); *Please, Teacher* (1935); *Big Business* (1937); *Hide and Seek* (1937)—'She's my lovely'; *Bobby Get Your Gun* (1938); and *All Clear* (1939). After further revue appearances he starred with his daughter, Sally Ann *Howes, in **Paint Your Wagon* (1953).

Howes, Sally Ann (*b* London, 20 July 1930). British actress and singer. The daughter of Bobby *Howes, she appeared in *Fancy Free* (1951); *Bet Your Life* (1952); **Paint Your Wagon* (1953), with her father; *Romance in Candlelight* (1955); *Summer Song* (1956); **My Fair Lady* (NY, 1958); *Kwamina* (1961); **What Makes Sammy Run?* (1964); and *The *King and I* (1973).

'How high the moon'. Song with music by Morgan *Lewis and words by Nancy *Hamilton, originally part of the revue *Two for the Show* (1940). It became notable because its interesting harmonic structure happened to 'strike a chord' with the ideas of the modern jazz experimenters of the 1940s. It was used so often by so many as a harmonic basis for improvisations and jazz compositions that it more or less gained itself the position of theme song of the modern jazz movement.

Howland, Jobyna (*b* Indianapolis, 31 Mar. 1880; *d* Los Angeles, 7 June 1936). American actress and singer. She was the glamorous leading lady of many Broadway plays and musicals. In the musical field she took part in *Miss Prinnt* (1900); *The Messenger Boy* (1901); *Winsome Winnie* (1903); and *The Ham Tree* (1905). By now a star, she took the leading part in *The *Passing Show* (1912); *Ruggles of Red Gap* (1916); and *Follow the Girl* (1918); and co-starred with Eddie *Cantor in *Kid Boots* (1924).

Howlin' Wolf [Burnett, Chester Arthur] (*b* West Point, Miss., 10 June 1910; *d* Hines, Ill., 10 Jan. 1976). American blues singer, composer, guitarist, and harmonica player. He started his working life as a farmer, learned the guitar with Charley *Patton in 1928, and became a travelling musician. By 1948 he was playing with his own band in Arkansas and was regularly broadcasting from Memphis. He was asked to record for Sun Records and had a top rhythm 'n' blues hit with 'How many more years' in 1952. His falsetto singing style earned him the name of Howlin' Wolf, which he adopted as a commercial name. He was to become one of the leading post-war blues musicians, and made a number of influential recordings of his own songs between 1954 and 1964 which became standard material, much used by other singers—'Smokestack lightning', 'Spoonful', 'Little red rooster', 'Back door man', 'Wang dang doodle', 'I ain't superstitious', 'Killin' floor', 'Evil', and 'Tail dragger' among the best known. He went to London in 1972 and recorded with Eric *Clapton, Ringo *Starr, and others. He recovered from several heart attacks, but was involved in a car accident in 1973 which curtailed his activities and eventually caused his death through kidney damage.

How to Succeed in Business Without Really Trying. American musical based on a play that was based on a real business manual by Shepherd Mead, book by Abe *Burrows with music and lyrics by Frank *Loesser. Opening on Broadway at the 46th

Street Theatre, 14 Oct. 1961, it ran for 1417 performances.

The young hero of the plot owes his astonishing rise from window-cleaner to company chairman to every back-stabbing and devious method that has ever been tried. Robert Morse (*b* 1931) was the climbing J. Pierpoint Finch and Rudy *Vallee was the company president. For its honest satire on big business and a well-integrated score it became the fourth musical to win a *Pulitzer Prize. It was seen in London at the Shaftesbury Theatre, 28 Mar. 1963, where it had 520 performances. The score is particularly strong in concerted numbers like 'Been a long day' and 'Brotherhood of man'; even the romantic numbers like 'I believe in you' are sharply satirical. A film version was made in 1967.

Hubbell, Raymond (*b* Urbana, Ohio, 1 June 1879; *d* Miami, 13 Dec. 1954). American composer. He had a musical education in Chicago where he led his own dance orchestra and worked as staff composer to the Charles K. *Harris publishing company. Moving to New York he wrote prolifically for the stage, including many large-scale extravaganzas and spectacular revues, and was able to retire to Florida in 1928. He was a founder member of *ASCAP.

His scores included: *The Runaways* (1903); *Fantana* (1905); *Mexicana* (1906); *Mam'selle Sallie* (1906); *About Town* (1906); *A Knight for a Day* (1907); *The Girl at the Helm* (1908); *The Midnight Sons* (1909); *The Air King* (1909); *The Jolly Bachelors* (1910); *The Bachelor Belles* (1910); *The Never Homes* (1911); *The Three Romeos* (1911); **Ziegfeld Follies* (1911, 1912, 1913, 1914, 1917, 1924, 1925); *The Man from Cook's* (1912); *A Winsome Widow* (1912); *Fads and Fancies* (1915); *Hip-Hip-Hooray* (1915); *The Big Show* (1916)—which had his biggest hit 'Poor butterfly' (*w* John L. Golden, 1874–1955); *Cheer Up* (with Golden, 1917); *Hitchy-Koo* (1918); *The Kiss Burglar* (1918); *Happy Days* (1919); *Miss Millions* (1919); *Good Times* (1920); *Sonny* (1921); *Better Times* (1922); *Yours Truly* (1927); *The Girl from Cook's* (1927); and *Three Cheers* (1928).

Hudson, Thomas (*b* London, Apr. 1791; *d* London, 26 June 1844). British singer and composer. One of the earliest stars of the developing music-hall and a talented vocalist who helped to make the song-and-supper rooms popular haunts for the fashionable and better-off. At first apprenticed to a grocer, he then started his own shop, but found his natural musical talents drawing him into a career in the entertainment world. At the time when *Moore's *Irish Melodies* and *Dibdin's sea-songs were popular, he started out by writing effective parodies of these before he found his own style.

Showing considerable literary talent, he wrote a number of songs that were well circulated in the early halls. One of his hits was 'Jack Robinson', whose final line 'Before you could say Jack Robinson' became a well-known catch-phrase. Others were 'The spider and the fly' (also performed by Henry *Russell), 'Walker, the tuppenny postman', 'The lively flea', 'The ghost of Kitty Maggs', 'Poor Robinson Crusoe', 'The dog's meat man'—songs, as their advertisements claimed, 'unstained by vulgarity and abounding in a rich and racy humour peculiar to their author'. He also cashed in on the great vogue for stagey Irish songs some of which were sung by Sam *Collins; and often worked in collaboration with Jonathan *Blewitt. He published collections of his songs yearly from 1818 to 1831 and for many years ran a theatrical tavern near Covent Garden.

Hudson, Will (*b* Barstow, Calif., 8 Mar. 1908). American composer and bandleader. He studied music in Detroit and became a professional arranger in 1929, writing for *McKinney's Cotton Pickers, Erskine Tate, and Cab *Calloway, who brought him to New York where he was to work with Irving Mills. He formed his own band in 1931 and arranged for Benny *Goodman, Andy Kirk, Earl *Hines, Fletcher *Henderson, Don *Redman, Louis *Armstrong, and Jimmie *Lunceford, for whom he wrote 'White heat' and 'Jazznocracy'. His clean, swinging arrangements were liked by all. In 1934 he wrote the classic 'Moonglow', and joined forces with Eddie De Lange to co-lead a greatly admired big band known as the Hudson–De Lange Orchestra which used their compositions and arrangements, including their theme-tune 'Sophisticated swing'. De Lange left in 1938 and Hudson continued to lead the orchestra until 1941. In the mid-1930s he was particularly active in arranging for the Goodman band. He arranged 'Cherokee' for Ray *Noble in 1938, wrote for Glenn *Miller in the 1940s, and later turned to more serious fields of composition. His other writings included: 'Don't kiss me again' (1935); 'Tormented' (1936); 'Organ grinder's swing' (1936); 'Sophisticated swing' (1936); 'With all my heart and soul' (1937); 'Midnight at the Onyx' (1937); and 'You're my desire' (1937).

Hughes, Spike [Patrick Cairns] (*b* London, 19 Oct. 1908; *d* London, 2 Feb. 1987). British composer, arranger, writer, bandleader, and bassist. Son of the Irish composer, folk-song collector, and critic Herbert Hughes (1882–1937), and mainly self-educated, he travelled widely with his father before settling to study composition in Vienna 1923–5. He then went to Cambridge, where he became interested in jazz. For many years he was jazz critic of **Melody Maker*. He formed his own dance orchestra in 1928 and recorded extensively for Decca (with the Decca-Dents) using many of his own clever arrangements and compositions. He toured in Holland with the band, worked as arranger and orchestrator for C. B. *Cochran, and was particularly involved in several Noël *Coward shows. His compositions at this time included 'A Harlem Symphony' and a jazz ballet, *High Yellow* (1932). He played bass with and arranged for Jack *Hylton; then, in 1933, he went to the USA where he made a series of recordings with the Benny *Carter band (with the addition of Henry 'Red' *Allen, Coleman *Hawkins, and Chu Berry) that got as close to rivalling the supreme jazz writing of his principal inspiration, Duke *Ellington, as any British jazz composer ever managed. The tracks, including 'Nocturne', 'Pastoral', 'Arabesque', 'Music at midnight', 'Air in D flat', 'Firebird', and 'Donegal cradle song', showed great originality and imagination and have remained classics of their kind. It was greatly to the loss of jazz and popular music that Spike Hughes turned to other fields to become a perceptive critic of opera and the historian of Glyndebourne, as well as a writer on wider non-musical interests.

S. Hughes: *Opening Bars* (London, 1946). S. Hughes: *Second Movement* (London, 1952).

Hulbert, Jack (*b* Ely, 24 Apr. 1892; *d* London, 25 Mar. 1978). British actor, singer, dancer, librettist, and director. While still studying at Cambridge he clearly saw the stage as his future and appeared in various undergraduate and professional concerts and revues. His final show there was *Cheer-oh! Cambridge* which moved to the Queen's Theatre, London, in 1913. He was engaged to appear in *The Pearl Girl* that same year by producer Robert Courtneidge, whose daughter Cicely was also in the show. They were married and worked together throughout their careers on stage (including 13 London musicals) and in films.

His jaunty dancing and singing and irrepressible good humour were heard and seen in: *The Cinema Star* (1914); *The *Arcadians* (1915); *The Light Blues* (1916); *See-Saw* (1916); *Bubbly* (1917); *Bran-Pie* (1919); *A Little Dutch Girl* (1920); *Ring Up* (1921); *Pot Luck* (1921); *The Little Revue Starts at* 9 (1923). From 1925 on Hulbert was also director of all the productions he appeared in: *By the Way* (1925); *Lido Lady* (1926); *Clowns in Clover* (1927); *The House that Jack Built* (1929); *Follow a Star* (1930); *Under Your Hat* (1938); *Full Swing* (1942); and *Something in the Air* (1943). He appeared in several bright and breezy British comedy films and recorded such airy items as 'The sun has got his hat on' and 'The flies crawled up the window'.

J. Hulbert: *The Little Woman's Always Right* (London, 1975).

Hullo, Ragtime. Historic London revue at the London Hippodrome, 23 Dec. 1912 which did much to push the new *ragtime song craze in England. The score was mainly supplied by the American composer Louis *Hirsch—'Miss Ragtime', 'The wedding guide', 'The Gaby glide', 'Bacchanale rag'—and was effectively supplemented by such numbers as 'Hitchy koo' (Lewis F. *Muir, Maurice *Abrahams, and L. Wolfe *Gilbert), 'Row! row! row!' and 'Ragtime soldier man' by Jimmy *Monaco. The American stars Shirley Kellogg and Ethel *Levey helped to add the right flavour and it enjoyed 451 performances. Its successor was *Hullo, Tango* (1913), with the same stars and such songs as 'Get out and get under'. The jazz age was ushered in a little later by *Hullo, America* (1918).

Human League, The. An early electronic-based pop group formed in Sheffield, Yorkshire, in 1977. It had some immediate success after which the original line-up was changed, leaving Phil Oakey and Adrian Wright to carry the torch with Ian Burden and Jo Callis (synthesizers) and Joanne Catherall and Suzanne Sulley (vocalists). Synthesizer expert Martin Rushent now produced their recordings and the years 1980–1 were rich in hits. Their melodic songs and polished presentation have given them an international following among a widely divergent audience.

P. Nash: *The Human League* (London, 1982). A. Ross: *The Story of a Band Called The Human League* (London–New York, 1982).

Hume, James Ord (*b* nr. Edinburgh, 14 Sept. 1864; *d* London, 27 Nov. 1932). British composer and conductor. An important figure in British *brass band history, he started as a boy cornettist in the band of the 3rd Battalion, The Royal Scots, and in 1881 he was solo cornettist with the Royal Scots Greys and had already started composing. He left the army to devote himself to the brass band movement. He arranged the test-piece 'Gems from Sullivan's Operas' for the first National Championship at the Crystal Palace in 1900 by which time he had already written his best-known march 'B. B. and C. F.', which won a competition run by the leading journal, *British Band and Contest Field*. He was military band editor of Boosey & Co. and served in many capacities as conductor and adjudicator.

As he wrote under many pseudonyms as well as his own name it is impossible to judge the extent of his writing, but it has been estimated that he composed or arranged more than 2000 items. He is mainly remembered for his lively marches—'Lynwood', 'Brilliant', 'The elephant', 'Roll away bet', besides 'B. B. and C. F.', all of them often recorded by leading bands; as well as his cornet solos and duets such as 'Tranquillity' (1924).

Humes, Helen (*b* Louisville, Ky., 23 June 1913; *d* Santa Monica, Calif., 9 Sept. 1981). American jazz and blues singer. She went to New York in her teens to work in theatres and clubs; and was also active in Chicago and other locales. She made her first records at the age of 15 with James P. *Johnson. She sang and recorded with Harry *James in 1938; then rose to fame with the Count *Basie band 1938–42 with such items as 'Sing for your supper' and 'Between the devil and the deep blue sea'. Subsequently she worked as a soloist, mainly on the West Coast in the 1940s, making some rhythm 'n' blues recordings and having a big hit with 'Be-baba-leba' in 1945. Thereafter her career declined. She settled in California and sang for a while with the Red *Norvo Trio, which whom she toured Australia and recorded. She retired in 1967 but re-emerged at the Newport Jazz Festival in 1973 in a 'Tribute to Count Basie'. This revived interest in her work and she made more European tours and visited the Ronnie *Scott Club in London in 1978.

Humperdinck, Englebert [Dorsey, Arnold George] (*b* Madras, 2 May 1936). British rock singer. His family moved to England, where he soon developed his boisterously sentimental manner of singing in pubs and clubs, and worked as a dance-band singer until 1967. Spotted by agent Gordon Mills, he chose a name at random from a musical dictionary and recorded 'Release me' (1967) which became an immediate hit, followed by 'The Last waltz' (1967) and 'Man without love'. Never in favour with the hard rockers, his moody presentation and good looks have kept him in demand as an international cabaret star.

Hunt, G. W. [George William] (*b* London, 1825; *d* London, 3 Mar. 1904). British composer and writer. He had a career as a comic vocalist before he concentrated on writing and was, at one time, manager of the Cambridge Music Hall. He became, with Alfred *Lee, one of the leading writers for the lion-comiques of the 1870s, especially for George *Leybourne. The idea for his greatest song success, 'We don't want to fight, but by jingo if we do' (1878), was coolly received by its future singer, the 'Great' *Macdermott, but was bought for a guinea and proved to be well timed to coincide with the Russo-Turkish War, setting off a whole cult of jingoism and adding a new word to the English language. It became almost a national anthem and afterwards the composer was always known as 'Jingo' Hunt. His other songs included: 'Awfully clever' (1870); 'Don't make a noise or else you'll wake the baby' (1876); 'The nautical swell' (1878); 'Up in a balloon, boys' (1879); 'My Sairey Ann'; 'Gold, gold, gold'; 'She does the fandango all over the place'; 'Under the sea'; 'On the sly'; and 'Run for the doctor'.

Hunt, Pee Wee [Walter] (*b* Mt Healthy, Ohio, 10 May 1907; *d* Plymouth, Mass., 22 June 1979). American trombonist, vocalist, and bandleader. He played the banjo in local bands, then joined the Jean *Goldkette band in Kansas City 1927–8. After working in Detroit he became a founder-member of the *Casa Loma Orchestra 1929–43, and was then a disc jockey in Hollywood before joining the US merchant navy in 1945. He formed his own Dixieland group in Los Angeles in 1946 and achieved a popular hit with his Capitol recording of 'Twelfth Street rag' in 1948 and other tongue-in-cheek items like 'Oh!' (1953).

Hunter, Alberta (*b* Memphis, 1 Apr. 1895; *d* New York, 17 Oct. 1984). American blues singer. She went to Chicago, and at the age of 15 was singing with such notable jazz musicians as Tony *Jackson, King *Oliver, Sidney *Bechet, and Louis *Armstrong. Her recording career began in 1921, sometimes under the name of Josephine Beatty. She went to London in 1927 to appear at the Palladium and to sing at the Green Park Hotel, the Florida Club, and the Argyle Rooms, giving British audiences an early taste of genuine blues. She appeared in **Show Boat* at Drury Lane. Later she was in cabaret in Paris, returning to America and establishing her reputation there. Further journeys abroad in the 1930s took her to Cairo, Alexandria, Edinburgh, and London, where she appeared at the Dorchester Hotel and recorded with Jack *Jackson. She retired from singing in 1957 and trained as a nurse. Then in 1977 she reappeared at the Cookery in New York, highly acclaimed as a remarkable survivor from the jazz age of Oliver and Bessie *Smith.

Hunter, Charles W. (*b* Columbia, Tenn., 16 May 1876; *d* St Louis, Mo., 23 Jan. 1906). American ragtime composer. Born almost totally blind, he worked with a piano manufacturer as a tuner, at the same time teaching himself to play and picking up melodies and harmonies by ear. He had his first rag, 'Tickled to death', published in Nashville in 1899. It became very popular and several piano rolls and cylinder recordings of it were made. In 1902 the piano company transferred him to St Louis where he was in demand in the saloons, sadly indulging in a life of too many women and too much liquor. He married in 1906 and tried to reform, but died six weeks later of TB. His compositions included: 'A Tennessee tantalizer' (1900); 'Possum and 'taters' (1900); 'Cotton bolls' (1901); 'Queen of love' (1901); 'Just ask me' (1902); 'Why we smile' (1903); 'Back to life' (1905); and 'Seraphine waltzes' (1905).

Hupfeld, Herman (*b* Montclair, NJ, 1 Feb. 1894; *d* Montclair, 8 June 1951). American composer, conductor, and pianist. He went to Germany at the age of nine to study the violin, returning to study in the USA. He sang and played his own songs in *Ziegfeld's Midnight Frolic* and continued a career as pianist and entertainer in America and Europe. He contributed to *A la Carte* (1927) and wrote 'Sing something simple' (1930)—used in *The Second Little Show*; 'When Yuba plays the rumba on the tuba' (1931, *Third Little Show*); *'As time goes by' (1931, used in the film *Everybody's Welcome*, and again in *Casablanca*, 1943); 'Let's put out the lights and go to sleep' (1932).

Hurdy-gurdy. A semi-mechanical instrument, dating from the Middle Ages and now virtually obsolete, looking something like a clumsily built mandolin. The strings, which are enclosed for most of their length, are sounded by a resined wheel which rubs against them when the player turns a handle. The player's left hand stops the strings by using a small set of keys, a little like those on a typewriter, which project from the side of the instrument. One string (or sometimes two) plays the melody and the others give a drone accompaniment at a fifth or an octave below. Like most of its kind it was primarily intended as a street instrument, though some concert music was written for it in the 18th century. Its sound is somewhat melancholy and insecure but not without charm, and surviving instruments have been used in recent times by a dwindling number of folk musicians in north-east Europe. The name is frequently misapplied to similar cranked instruments, particularly to the smaller varieties of *barrel-organ.

Hutchinson, Leslie 'Hutch' (*b* Grenada, West Indies, 1900; *d* London, 18 Aug. 1969). Singer, pianist, and entertainer. He went to study in New York at 19 but any serious intent was sidetracked by his interest in and flair for music. Forced to sing in cafés to earn a living, he became a protégé of Cole *Porter who liked the way the young man sang his songs. He went to Paris in 1926 to study piano and performed at Joselli's Bar in the Place Clichy. The British impresario C. B. *Cochran heard him there in 1927 and brought him to London to appear in the revue **One Dam Thing After Another* at the London Pavilion. He formed his own band and toured Europe and the Middle East. Back in London he appeared in *Cochran's 1930 Revue* and also in variety, becoming a popular entertainer at such high-class London haunts as the Café de Paris, the Café Anglais, and Quaglino's (where he was a feature for many years). During the Second World War he travelled extensively to entertain the troops, appeared on radio and stage in *Happidrome* (1942), toured India, and became well-known on radio and records. He was forced to retire to a warmer climate through illness and settled in Nairobi. His rich, resonant, 'milk chocolate' voice and sophisticated playing produced hit recordings of such songs as 'Begin the beguine' and 'A nightingale sang in Berkeley Square'.

Hutchinson Family. American singers, important in the history of popular song because they came along at a time when the USA was beginning to establish its own artistic identity rather than taking at second-hand what had been originated in Europe; and at a time when the arts were beginning to sound a note of political and social protest rather than simply providing entertainment.

Richard Hutchinson had emigrated from England in 1634 and settled in Salem, Massachusetts, with his wife Alice, where they raised four children. The family stayed in Salem unti 1799 when Elisha, born in 1751, moved to Milford, New Hampshire. Elisha's son Jesse, born in 1778, married Mary Leavitt (then aged 15) and they had 16 children, 13 surviving into adulthood. A strong musical streak flourished in the family and they all sang in the choir of Milford Baptist Church. Jesse, stern and hard-working, disapproved of time being wasted on music, so his sons Judson, John, and Asa, who all wanted to make music their career, had to practise in secret. On Thanksgiving Day in 1839 the children gave a concert at the Baptist church, drawing their repertoire from *The Social Choir* and the typical polite music in vogue at the time.

The next year John Hutchinson heard a concert given by the Rainer Family, a group who had come to America in 1839 and entertained as the Tyrolese Minstrels, performing their native songs with great success. Deciding that his family should do something similar, he coached his brothers Jesse, Joshua, Judson, and Asa and they gave their first concert in Lynn, Massachusetts. John, Judson, and Asa settled there and were joined by their sister Abby in a group which they called the Aeolian Vocalists. Judson was the most talented of the group, a violinist, singer, and composer, but John remained the leader. In 1842 they toured the eastern states, now billed as the Hutchinson Family, singing in a close-harmony style with Abby on the guitar, their repertoire including songs by Henry *Russell and contemporary American composers.

They had their first song published in 1843 and that year went to New York, sang for President Tyler at the White House, and performed with the Philadelphia Music Society, returning home in 1844 with a handsome profit. They now sang more of their own material, which their audiences liked, and in 1845 travelled to England with ex-slave Frederick Douglass, giving their first concert in Liverpool. Greatly moved by the poverty they saw, they began to sing at labour meetings and developed a friendship with Charles Dickens. Although this social concern harmed their popularity in some circles, their fame won them an invitation to sing at Covent Garden along with John *Braham, Henry *Russell, and other famous entertainers of the day.

The Hutchinsons returned to America committed to social reform. They had seen much drunkeness in their travels and promoted temperance, Jesse's song 'King Alcohol' (published in 1843) being prominent in the crusade. From 1843 they took up the anti-slavery cause, giving electrifying performances at conventions and meetings. Some of their more passionate songs like 'Get off the track' were refused by publishers and they faced occasional violence, but this only helped their cause. By 1846 they were opposing the war in Mexico. Abby married in 1849 and gave up singing and Jesse left to join the Alleghenians, who sang many of the Hutchinsons' songs, but younger members of the family replaced them. By 1851 they were campaigning on behalf of the suffragettes with Thomas Hood's 'Song of the shirt' added to their repertoire. The final tour of the founding group was made in 1855 when a new town called Hutchinson was founded in Minnesota.

Each of the brothers went on to found his own family group, setting the pattern for folk-singers ever since and helping to establish a radical tradition in America. Always their sincerity and simplicity appealed to all classes and intellects. Intensely patriotic, they did much to establish a truly American repertoire founded on the old New England traditions. William Lloyd Garrison wrote in 1874: 'Never before has the singing of ballads been made so directly subservient to the freedom, welfare, happiness, and moral elevation of the people.'

C. E. Mann (ed.): *Story of the Hutchinsons (Tribe of Jesse)* (2 vols) (Boston, 1896). P. D. Jordan: *Singin' Yankees: the Hutchinson Family* (Minneapolis, 1946). C. Brink: *Harps in the Wind: the Story of the Singing Hutchinsons* (New York, 1947).

Hutton, Betty [Thornburg, Elizabeth June] (*b* Battle Creek, Mich., 26 Feb. 1921). American actress and singer. She was vocalist with the Vincent *Lopez band 1936–8, before she became the exuberant star of musical films at a time when these were going through a post-war phase of escapism and determined optimism. She was usually cast as the ambitious girl-next-door type, in conflict with more subtle characters, but winning her man in the end; and introducing to the world such extrovert numbers as '"Murder" he says' and 'Doctor, lawyer, Indian Chief'.

She appeared in: *The Fleet's In* (1942); *Star-Spangled Rhythm* (1942); *Happy Go Lucky* (1943); *Let's Face It* (1943); *And the Angels Sing* (1944); *Here Come the Waves* (1944); *Incendiary Blonde* (1945); *Duffy's Tavern* (1945); *The Stork Club* (1945); *Cross My Heart* (1946); *The Perils of Pauline* (1947); *Dream Girl* (1948); *Red, Hot and Blue* (1949); **Annie Get Your Gun* (1950); *Let's Dance* (1950); *Sailor Beware* (1951); *The Greatest Show on Earth* (1952); and *Somebody Loves Me* (1952).

Hylton, Jack (*b* Great Lever, Lancs., 2 July 1892; *d* London, 29 Jan. 1965). British bandleader. He started his career as a cinema pianist in Stoke Newington and first led a band in the Queens Hall Roof ballroom in Langham Place, London, just after the First World War, later at the Piccadilly Hotel. He began to record for EMI in 1921. He was to make a speciality of stage shows with the band as centrepiece, in the *Whiteman mould, which led towards his later career as an agent, producer, and impresario. In the course of various European tours he played in Berlin in 1928, 1929, and 1930. His band became one of the most popular of all British bands of the 1930s with many famous future bandleaders like Billy *Ternent, Peter *Yorke, Ted *Heath, Jack *Jackson, and Woolf Phillips passing through its ranks. The American saxophonist Coleman *Hawkins played with the band 1934–5 and in 1939.

Hylton's was the first British dance band to broadcast to America where, not having been allowed to take his own band owing to current bans, he led a band of American musicians 1935–6, broadcasting frequently and playing at the Drake Hotel in Chicago. He continued throughout the 1930s, with vocalist Sam Browne (1913–73) featured, and at the outbreak of war in 1939 there were two Hylton bands, one with the BBC in Bristol, featuring in such shows as *ITMA*, and another touring with the stage version of *Band Waggon*. When many of his musicians were conscripted in 1940, Hylton gave up his band rather than lower his standards. Compared to some of the other British bands of the period, Hylton's was straight in flavour, playing smooth dance-music with strings and featuring light orchestral pieces. He conducted the orchestra in grand style, so that 'Jack's back' became a trademark of his presentations. His theme tune was 'She shall have music'. After 1940 he pursued a rewarding career in theatrical promotion.

Hyman, Dick [Richard Roven] (*b* New York, 8 Mar. 1927). American pianist, organist, clarinettist, and composer. After studying music, with some lessons from Teddy *Wilson, he played from 1948 at Wells' Club in Harlem. As staff musician for various radio and TV outlets in the 1950s, he became known through a series of 'History of Jazz' concerts which he created with the critic Leonard *Feather. In the 1960s he was variously involved in composing, free jazz, experimenting with synthesizers and jazz-rock; but after 1970 he became particularly interested in classic jazz, working with the New York Jazz Repertory Company in concerts and recordings of the music of Louis *Armstrong, James P. *Johnson, Jelly Roll *Morton, and Scott *Joplin, proving himself both a talented and exuberant musician and a scholarly researcher. In the 1970s he worked with his Perfect Jazz Quintet and played at the Cookery in Greenwich Village. He produced some programmes for the BBC in the 1980s.

I

I Do! I Do! American musical, unusual in having a cast of only two, a couple who tell in song the story of their wedding, married and family life, quarrels, and love. This *tour de force* was beautifully handled by Mary *Martin and Robert *Preston (succeeded by Carol Lawrence and Gordon *McRae) and was seen at the 46th Street Theatre, New York, 5 Dec. 1966, running for 560 performances. The book and lyrics were by Tom Jones, adapted from Jan de Hartog's play *The Fourposter*, and the neatly appropriate score by Harvey *Schmidt had such songs as 'I love my wife', 'Love isn't everything', 'Nobody's perfect', 'When the kids get married', and 'Someone needs me'.

I'd Rather Be Right. American musical, the only one starring George M. *Cohan that he did not write himself. It also marked his return to the musical stage after 10 years' absence to play the part of Franklin D. Roosevelt.

The story concerned two young lovers who cannot get married until he gets a rise, and he cannot get a rise until FDR gets the budget right. He dreams that he meets the President, who promises to help, and thence leads the story through some mild political satire. It ran at the Alvin Theatre, New York, for 290 performances from 2 Nov. 1937. The book was by George S. *Kaufman and Moss *Hart and the Richard *Rodgers/Lorenz *Hart songs included 'Have you met Miss Jones?' and 'I'd rather be right'.

Ifield, Frank (*b* Coventry, 30 Nov. 1937). British singer. He spent his childhood and youth in Australia, returning to England in 1959 with a high reputation as a singer made on Australian radio and TV. He made a number of Columbia records under the supervision of Norrie *Paramor who provided the musical arrangements for Ifield's lusty country-style singing and yodelling which, in 1962, made No. 1 hits of 'I remember you' (which sold more than two million copies), 'Lovesick blues', and 'The wayward wind'—making him the first singer to complete the hat-trick. Although his popularity quickly declined, and from 1964 he worked mainly in Europe and back in Australia, he regularly reappeared singing his style of country music as effectively as ever.

I Love My Wife. American musical, a modern morality drawn from the modern practice of spouse-swapping, an activity planned by two hitherto happily married couples as an experience, but abandoned at the last moment. The slight plot was the basis for various songs aimed at the moral decay of the times. The music was by Cy *Coleman, book and lyrics by Michael Stewart, and it was produced at the Ethel Barrymore Theatre, New York, 17 Apr. 1977, running for 872 performances.

I Married an Angel. Highly praised American musical fantasy with music, book, and lyrics by Richard *Rodgers and Lorenz *Hart which opened at the Shubert Theatre, New York, 11 May 1938, running for 338 performances.

Set in Budapest, it tells of a young banker (Dennis *King) who vows that he will only marry an angel, and succeeds. One critic aptly called it a '44th Street miracle' with its songs 'I married an angel', 'Spring is here', and a show-stopping diversion, 'At the Roxy Music Hall', which simply burlesqued vaudeville. It was the first of 14 musicals directed by Joshua *Logan and the Broadway debut of Vera Zorina who played the part of the angel. It was filmed in 1942 with Jeanette *MacDonald and Nelson *Eddy, Edward Everett Horton (1886–1970), and Binnie Barnes (1905–83).

Impressions, The. Vocal group formed in Chicago in 1957, originally as an anonymous backing group. They soon developed a distinctive style built round the expressive singing and musical guitar playing of founder-member Curtis *Mayfield, who left the group to make a distinguished solo career in 1970. Taking over the lead from Jerry Butler (*b* 1939), whom the group had originally backed, Mayfield, with Richard Brooks, Arthur Brooks, Sam Gooden (*b* 1939), and Fred Cash (*b* 1940), recorded several early Butler hits like 'Gypsy woman'. They had their first really big hit with 'It's all right' (1963), a gently rhythmic and melodious number typical of their style, followed up by 'Talking about my baby', 'You must believe me', 'I'm so proud', 'Keep on pushing' (all 1964), and 'People get ready' (1965). The group moved away from the Chicago style and came nearer to the Motown sound in the 1960s. When Mayfield left his place was taken briefly by Leroy Hutson and then by Reggie Torian and they had a further big hit with 'Finally got myself together', written by Ed Townsend, in 1974. They continued as a four-man group with Torian and Ralph Johnson as the lead voices.

Im Weissen Rössl. Very popular Singspiel, more widely known to the English-speaking world as *White Horse Inn*, which was produced at the Grosses

Schauspielhaus, Berlin, 8 Nov. 1930. The book, based on a farce of the same name, was by Hans Müller and Erik Charell with lyrics by Robert Gilbert. The score was basically by Ralph *Benatzky with additional items by Robert Gilbert (*b* 1899), Bruno Granichstädten (1879–1944), Hans Frankowski, and, most notably, Robert *Stolz. Even then, Eduard *Künneke was added to the list as orchestrator. Although the show stayed within the operetta tradition, with easy, catchy melodies of the Viennese kind, it was not an operetta in the formal sense—rather a pioneer of the spectacular musical, combining realism with romance. One critic wrote of it gloomily as 'a Weimar-Republic musical comedy, a morbid growth that dealt operetta a crippling blow'. It was also new in being the combined effort of so many writers. It was a great success in Berlin and the British spies for Sir Oswald Stoll reported that it would be an ideal production for filling the large stage of the London Coliseum.

As *White Horse Inn*, with English words by Harry Graham, it opened there on 8 Apr. 1931 with Clifford Mollison, Amy Augarde, and Lea Seidl in the cast. The British public were entranced by its Tyrolean yodellers, dancers, and general lavishness, as well as its melodies, several of which, like the popular 'Goodbye', were added to the production at this stage. (Listeners to recordings of the original version are sometimes disappointed to find some 'old favourites' missing.) It ran in London for 651 performances and there was a 268-performance revival at the Coliseum in 1940. It opened at the Mogador in Paris in 1932 as *L'Auberge du Cheval Blanc*, and in New York 1 Oct. 1936 for 211 performances at the Center Theatre. Set within and without the now famous White Horse Inn at St Wolfgang in the Salzkammergut, near Salzburg, it unwinds an involved romantic plot of the operetta type, and nowadays is almost looked upon, by virtue of its setting and Stolz's involvement, as an Austrian legacy.

Incredible String Band, The. British folk duo of Mike Heron (*b* 12 Dec. 1942) and Robin Williamson (*b* 24 Nov. 1943), both from Glasgow, who could play some 30 instruments between them. The impact of their early albums, *Incredible String Band* (1966, with Clive Palmer added) and *5000 Spirits, or The Layers of the Onion* (1967), with its childlike mysticism, has been spoken of as the folk world's equivalent of the effect that the *Beatles were having at that particular time (*Sergeant Pepper*). Their song 'First girl I love' was recorded by Judy *Collins and they made a successful appearance in 1967 at the Newport Folk Festival. They continued to produce similarly effective hits in 'A very cellular song' and the *Gilbert and Sullivan-like 'Minotaur's song', and their concerts were intensely spiritual gatherings. A tendency towards self-indulgence and preciousness, and an unsuccessful move toward electric rock, were mainly put aside in their exploratory albums of the 1970s. The duo split up in 1974 and each of them went on to produce first-rate solo work, Williamson, who made many albums in the 1970s and 1980s (*Winter's Turning*, 1987; *Songs for Children*, 1988), becoming a revered father figure of the folk movement.

In Dahomey. Pioneering American musical comedy, the first full-length show written and performed by black Americans to be presented at a major Broadway theatre. It proved an uncontentious first, stirring no resentments, and was in fact fairly unremarkable in musical terms. The best part of the Will Marion *Cook score was a *cakewalk competition, which was judged by the audience, while songs like 'Jonah man', 'On Emancipation Day', and 'I want to be a real lady' are remembered.

J. A. Shipp's libretto tells how a group of unscrupulous Americans plan to colonize Africa with the help of money conned out of an old miser. It was a good excuse for some impressive dancing and the acclaimed comedy acting of George Walker and Bert *Williams. Opening at the New York Theatre 18 Feb. 1903, it had only 53 performances but made a much greater impression on the cakewalk-hungry British public when Williams and Walker brought it to the Shaftesbury Theatre, London, 16 May 1903, where it had 251 performances, doing much to make Britain aware of the new musical stirrings in the USA.

Ink Spots, The. American vocal group which became very popular around 1939 and throughout the 1940s. The original line-up (all of them working as porters at the Paramount Theatre in New York) was Jerry Daniels, Orville Jones (1905–44), Ivory Watson, and Charlie Fuqua (who were also the guitarists). They began to perform in the conventional jazz or jive vein purveyed by earlier groups like the *Mills Brothers and appeared in England singing in this style with the Jack *Hylton band in the 1930s. It was a change to stylized slow-tempo numbers like 'If I didn't care' (which became a hit in 1939), 'Whispering grass', 'Do I worry', 'My prayer', and 'Maybe' which brought them popularity, though they still purveyed the occasional up-tempo number like 'Java jive' by Milton Drake (*b* 1916). The combination made a feature of the high falsetto lead of Bill Kenny (1915–78), who replaced Daniels in 1939, and the deep-voiced spoken interludes by Orville Jones. When Jones died in 1944 he was replaced by Herb Kenny (1914–92) and other changes have followed to the present when a totally different group keeps on the tradition. They became known through radio and recordings and appeared in the films *The Great American Broadcast* (1941) and *Pardon My Sarong* (1942). In the 1950s there was a legal tangle and some public confusion when Bill Kenny and Charlie Fuqua split and both were running groups which called themselves the Ink Spots. They became overshadowed by new trends in the 1950s but are now the subject of much nostalgic adulation.

D. Watson: *The Story of the Ink Spots* (New York, 1967).

Inside USA. Intimate revue which was the last to be produced by the partnership of Arthur *Schwartz and Howard *Dietz, seen at the New Century Theatre, New York, 30 Apr. 1948. The cast included Beatrice *Lillie and Jack Haley (1899–1979); its numbers included 'Inside USA', 'Rhode Island is famous for you', and 'Haunted heart'; and it had 399 performances.

'Internationale, L''. First official anthem of the Soviet Union 1917–44 and a hymn of the socialist movement. The words were written by Eugène Ediné Pottier (1816–87) in 1871 and were first sung to the tune by Pierre Chrétien Degeyter (1848–1932) (whose brother Adolphe also claimed the composership) in Lille in 1888. It was first published *c.*1894.

E. Tersen: *L'Internationale* (Paris, 1962).

Intimacy at 8:30. Intimate London revue which ran at the Criterion Theatre, 29 Apr. 1954, for 551 performances. The cast included such revue stalwarts as Pip Hinton, Hugh Paddick, Ron Moody, Joan Heal, and Joan Sims, and it caught the new public fancy for the mildly satirical with such items as 'The boy friend's girl friend', 'Surrey side up', and 'There's an awful lot of coffee in Hay Hill'. The music was by Ronald *Cass (who was also musical director) and John Pritchett, with words by Peter Myers (1923–78), Alec Grahame, and David Climie.

***Iolanthe* or The Peer and the Peri.** The sixth of the accredited *Gilbert and Sullivan/*D'Oyly Carte productions which opened at the Savoy Theatre, London, 25 Nov. 1882, with a cast that included George *Grossmith, Rutland *Barrington, Durward Lely, Richard *Temple, Sybil Grey, Leonora *Braham, and Jessie *Bond. This first production ran for 398 performances and it was first seen in New York at the Standard Theatre, 1 Dec. 1882.

The tale has much gentle fun at the expense of the House of Lords and the Lord Chancellor, who strongly opposes, as well he might, the marriage of his ward Phyllis to a fairy. He happens to be Strephon, the son of Iolanthe (exiled by the Fairy Queen, who herself has an amorous attraction towards one Private Willis, a great philosopher). It is all elaborately sorted out to such airs as 'Tripping hither, tripping thither', 'Welcome to our hearts again', 'When I went to the Bar', 'When all night long a chap remains', 'Oh, foolish fay', and 'The nightmare' song. It was filmed in 1982.

Irene. American musical comedy of 1919 which outran the previous record holder, *A *Trip to Chinatown*, to become the longest-running Broadway show for the next 18 years. With music by Harry *Tierney, lyrics by Joseph McCarthy (1885–1943), and book by James Montgomery, it opened at the Vanderbilt Theatre 18 Nov. 1919 and had 670 performances. It came to London, at the Empire Theatre, 7 Apr. 1920 [399p].

The plot was a modern variation of the Cinderella story with Edith *Day (for whom the show was written) an upholsterer who wins the heart of a rich socialite (Walter Regan) who gets his dressmaking friend to use her as a model. The show's one outstanding hit was 'Alice blue gown' which long outlived its showcase until *Irene* was revived in New York in 1973 (London, 1976), with the score now retaining only five original items (including the obvious one) and padded out by other songs of the show's original period. The heroine had now become a piano-tuner. It seemed surprising that such a weak story and patchy score should have been so successful in the first place. There was a film version in 1940 with Anna *Neagle and Ray Milland (*b* 1905).

'Irish emigrant, The'. Popular song of the late 19th century 'composed and sung by George *Barker, of the Theatre Royal, Drury Lane' with words by the Lady Dufferin (1807–67), published in London in 1867. Lady Dufferin was one of the famous Sheridan sisters, renowned beauties of the day, another being the Hon. Mrs Norton who also wrote popular ditties. The song was inspired by the activities of her husband, a notable diplomat who was rewarded with the title of Lord Dufferin and Ava in 1888 and wrote a book *Irish Emigration and the Tenure of Land in Ireland* in 1867. It tells of a poor Irishman whose wife has died and who is off to seek his fortune in the USA where 'there's bread and work for all'.

Irma La Douce. One of the first French musicals since the heyday of the operetta to become an international hit, it was originally seen at the Théâtre Gramont, Paris, 12 Nov. 1956, where it ran for four years. The music was by Marguerite *Monnot and the words by Alexandre Breffort. With an English book by Julian More, David *Heneker, and Monty *Norman, it opened at the Saville Theatre, London, 17 July 1958, with Elizabeth Seal (*b* 1933) as the prostitute with a heart of gold (the only female role in the show), Keith Michell (*b* 1928), and Clive Revill (*b* 1930); it had 1512 performances.

A poor student wants to have the sole services of Irma and disguises himself as an aged benefactor. Her lover grows jealous and, accused of murdering the student, is sent to prison. He escapes and proves his innocence and all turns out well. The same cast took the play to New York, Plymouth Theatre 29 Sept. 1960, where it had 524 performances. It was filmed in 1963 with Shirley *MacLaine and Jack Lemmon (*b* 1925) but without the music.

Irving, Ernest (*b* Godalming, Surrey, 6 Nov. 1877; *d* London, 24 Oct. 1953). British composer and conductor. He spent the years 1900–40 as musical director at various London theatres and also conducted in Paris and Madrid. In 1953 he became musical director of Ealing Studios and helped to raise the standards of British film music by commissioning scores from distinguished British and foreign composers. He wrote film music himself: *The Great Mr Handel* (1942); *Whisky Galore* (1949), etc.; incidental music for several Shakespeare plays at Stratford and others including *The Circle of Chalk* (1929); and musical scores which included *The Two Bouquets* (1936) and *An Elephant in Arcady* (1938). He was also a chess expert.

E. Irving: *Cue for Music* (London, 1959).

Irwin, May [Campbell, Ada] (*b* Whitby, Ontario, 27 June 1862; *d* New York, 22 Oct. 1938). Canadian actress and singer. She made her stage debut with her sister Flora in 1875 and became a regular at Tony *Pastor's vaudeville theatre in New York. She wrote 'Mamie' and sang it in *A Country Sport* (1893). Her speciality was adapting black folk-songs, her biggest successes in this line being 'The bully song', which she performed in *The Widow Jones* (1896), and 'The frog song', which became famous as 'May Irwin's frog song' (she recorded it in 1907). She sang similar items by such composers as the ragtimer Ben *Harney and Gus *Edwards. She appeared in some early films in 1896 and 1914.

Isley Brothers. Singing trio (earlier a quartet) of brothers, O'Kelly (1937–86), Rudolph (*b* 1939), and Ronald (*b* 1941), who were all raised in Cincinnati. Having developed a working stage act, they went to New York in 1957 where they recorded some insignificant *doo-wop and *rock and roll sides. In 1959 they moved into a more effective gospel style with 'Shout'. They worked with writer-producers *Leiber and Stoller on the Atlantic label 1961–2, and with Bert Berns 1962–4, 'Twist and shout' (1962) becoming their first Top 20 hit. Forming their own production company in 1964, they recorded 'Testify' and 'The last girl' with Jimi *Hendrix as guitarist. They joined the *Tamla label 1965–6, recording 'This old heart of mine' and 'I guess I'll always love you', then revived their own company and had a million-selling disc with 'It's your thing', moving into a heavier style of rock. In the 1970s they were using more searching material such as Bob *Dylan's 'Lay, lady, lay' and Hendrix's 'Machine gun' (1971). The group always contrived to move with the times and styles, in 1979 recording 'It's a disco night', and moving successfully into the 1980s with suitably fashioned material.

'It's a long way to Tipperary'. Perennially popular hit of the First World War which had words and music credited to Jack Judge (1878–1938) and Harry Williams (1858–1930). Judge claimed later that he wrote both words and music, the credit to Williams being in repayment for a loan. The song was actually conceived before the outbreak of war, being composed at the New Market Inn in Stalybridge at the beginning of 1912, sung by Judge at the Grand Theatre in Stalybridge that evening, and issued by the London publishers Bert *Feldman (1874–1945) in Oct. 1912 as No. 549 of their 'sixpenny' edition. It caught the public's attention when it was sung by Florrie *Forde in a pantomime in 1914.

Turning out to be an ideal marching song, and telling the story of an Irishman on a visit to London who longs to get back to his native greenery in spite of the legendary streets paved with gold, these sentiments, and such lines as 'Goodbye, Piccadilly; farewell, Leicester Square', were soon re-interpreted as the soldiers' longing for home. Wartime editions were quick to bear such legends as 'The Marching Anthem on the Battlefields of Europe', 'Sung by the Soldiers of the King', and a uniformed portrait of King George V. There were those, like F. T. Nettleingham in his *Tommy's Tunes* (1917), who suggested that 'Tipperary was never greatly sung by soldiers, its popularity mainly created by the music-halls at home.' Other songs credited to Judge and Williams never even began to match its surprising success.

Ives, Burl [Charles Icle Ivanhoe] (*b* Hunt Township, Ill., 14 June 1909). American folk-singer and actor. He left college to travel through the USA and Canada, doing odd jobs and boosting his income by playing the guitar and singing, in between playing some professional football. Already interested in folk-song, he picked up more material in his travels and, arriving in New York, became a popular performer in Greenwich Village clubs. He took some singing lessons and studied at the New York University School of Music for a while, then turned to acting and appeared in **I Married an Angel* (1938); *The *Boys from Syracuse* (1938); and *Heavenly Express* (1939). He sang at the Village Vanguard, then did some military service and appeared in Irving Berlin's *This Is the Army* (1942). He began to sing on radio in *The Wayfaring Stranger* and was in the Broadway show *Sing Out Sweet Land* (1944).

Gradually he became internationally known through his commercialized but straightforward recordings of folk-songs, which he arranged in such publications as *The Burl Ives Song Book* and *America's Musical Heritage*. He brought to a wide audience such songs as 'Blue tail fly', 'The foggy, foggy dew', 'It makes no difference now', mingled with contemporary creations such as 'Rodger Young' (*m* Frank *Loesser), 'Big Rock Candy Mountain' (*m* and *w* Harry Kirby McClintock, 1882–1957), and 'Hallelujah, I'm a bum' (McClintock). He recorded several LPs for Decca in a pleasantly relaxed and clear style, and showed his versatility on a United Artists recording of the songs of Irving *Berlin. He was in the 1954 revival of **Show Boat* and had a personal triumph in the play *Cat on a Hot Tin Roof* (1955)—also in the film version. He appeared in various TV serials and had his own series, and between 1946 and 1969 was in more than 25 films.

B. Ives: *Wayfaring Stranger* (New York, 1948).

Ivor Novello Awards. British awards for outstanding achievement in popular and light music established by the Songwriters' Guild of Great Britain in 1955. They were given for such varied categories as

(a) best-selling song of the year; (b) outstanding popular song; (c) best novelty or comedy song; (d) best ballad; (e) best jazz or beat item; (f) best light orchestral or instrumental item; (g) outstanding contribution to stage play, film, radio, or TV programme; (h) most effective musical play score; (i) outstanding service to popular music; with others added later to embrace more modern developments.

The 1955 awards were as follows: (a) 'Ev'rywhere' (Tolchard *Evans; Larry Kahn); (b) 'In love for the very first time' (Jack Woodman; Paddy Roberts); (c) 'Got'n idea' (Woodman; Roberts); (d) special award to Haydn *Wood; (e) 'Big City suite' (Ralph Dollimore); (f) 'The Dam Busters march' (Eric *Coates); (h) **Salad Days* (Julian *Slade; Dorothy Reynolds); (i) Jack *Payne.

J

Jackson, Jack (*b* Barnsley, Yorks., 20 Feb. 1906; *d* Rickmansworth, 14 Jan. 1978). British trumpeter, bandleader, and disc jockey. Having learned the cornet at the age of six, he played with a local brass band, in the Erith Town Orchestra, and in cinema orchestras, moving to semi-professional dance-band work in London before studying at the Royal Academy of Music. He joined Bert Railton's band in 1926 and toured with him in South Africa until Railton was killed in a hunting accident; returning in 1927 to join Jack *Hylton, with whom he recorded some of the best hot trumpet solos to be heard in England at the time. Later he played with Howard Jacobs, Percival Mackey, and Arthur Lally before joining Jack *Payne in 1931.

In 1932 he formed his own band, which began recording at the beginning of 1933 with Al *Bowlly, Sam Costa (1910–81), and Denny Dennis (*b* 1913) as featured vocalists; later in the year they became the resident band at the Dorchester Hotel, where Alberta *Hunter sang with them in 1934. Jackson toured, played in dance halls, and worked with the BBC on such programmes as *Band Call*, *Salute to Rhythm*, and *Band Parade* (which he compèred). A natural ability as a showman and humorist led to his abandonment of the declining dance-band scene in the late 1940s to become a disc jockey, responsible for such entertaining presentations as *Record Round-Up*, *Record Roundabout*, and *Jackson's Juke Box*, on BBC and Radio Luxemburg, which widened the entertainment aspect of record presentation and achieved a dedicated following.

Jackson, Mahalia (*b* New Orleans, 26 Oct. 1911; *d* Evergreen Park, Ill., 27 Jan. 1972). American gospel singer. Settling in Chicago, she eventually ran a beauty salon and owned a flower shop, in the meantime becoming known as a talented gospel singer in Baptist church choirs and conventions. She refused to mix religion with commerce and would never appear in a nightclub, but eventually made many triumphant concert tours in both America and Europe. She made a number of hit records for the Apollo label between 1946 and 1953, always done with simple taste and dignity, with Mildred Falls as her regular accompanist. The titles included 'Move on up a little higher' and 'Prayer changes things'. Moving to the Columbia label, she became even more widely known. She was a prominent worker in the civil rights movement with her rallying song of 'We shall overcome'.

L. Goreau: *Mahalia* (New York, 1976).

Jackson, Michael Joe (*b* Gary, Ind., 29 Aug. 1958). American rock singer and entertainer. He began his professional career as a rhythm 'n' blues performer before joining his four brothers as lead singer in the *Jackson Five, later known as the Jacksons. When their contract with Motown ended in 1976 they moved to the Epic label which also promoted Michael Jackson as a solo singer. Changing from the teeny-bop style of the Jacksons, he moved into the pop-soul genre and in 1979 recorded an album, *Off the Wall*, which was produced by Quincy *Jones. It had excellent songs by Rod Temperton and by Jackson himself who contributed 'Don't stop till you get enough', 'Working day and night', and (with Louis Johnson) 'Get on the floor'. This was followed by the best-selling pop album to date, *Thriller*, released in 1982. It had sold more than 24 million copies by the end of 1983 and soon went on to pass the 30 million mark and gain a place in *The Guinness Book of World Records*, with five of its songs top hits in their own right. It became the subject of a video, *The Making of Thriller*, in which Jackson turned into a werewolf. His natural talent as a dancer was tellingly exploited in the new video exploitation of records and the fashionable trend for planned action in presentation as well as sound. Becoming the greatest pop idol of all time, he continued to write good material for himself and other artists such as Diana *Ross. He made his own film debut with her in *The *Wiz* (1983), the black version of *The *Wizard of Oz*. He achieved a new record with eight Grammy awards in 1984 and his superstar career continued unabated. He has been described as 'a painfully shy, curiously childlike, private person who had paid a great deal for his success'. It is this hinted contrast that probably adds the special touch of mystery that makes a star, a contrast with his physical agility, sure singing technique in the solid gospel tradition, and apparent pleasure in appearing before an audience.

G. Brown: *Michael Jackson: Body and Soul: an Illustrated Biography* (London, 1984). N. George: *The Michael Jackson Story* (New York, 1984). D. Magee: *Michael Jackson* (London–New York, 1984). S. Regan: *Michael Jackson* (Guildford, 1984). T. Gold: *The Man in the Mirror* (London, 1989).

Jackson, Milt [Milton] (*b* Detroit, 1 Jan. 1923). American jazz pianist, vibraphonist, and guitarist. He began his jazz career with Dizzy *Gillespie in 1945, and worked with various groups before forming the Milt Jackson Quartet in 1951 with John *Lewis, Ray Brown, and Kenny *Clarke. In 1952 this became the *Modern Jazz Quartet which survived until 1974, purveying that mixture of the cool and the classical which was to become labelled third stream music.

Jackson, Tony [Anthony] (*b* New Orleans, 5 June 1876; *d* Chicago, 20 Apr. 1921). American jazz pianist, vocalist, and composer. He played in various jazz groups in the pioneering days before 1900 and worked as an entertainer in New Orleans. A life-long invalid and an alcoholic, he was nevertheless a skilled and persuasive performer who won the rare accolade of admiration from Jelly Roll *Morton, who rated him one of the greatest jazz pianists he had heard. Clarence *Williams also considered him the supreme New Orleans musician of his day, the one whom everyone tried to emulate. Jackson went to Chicago in 1912 where he played in various well-known haunts until his death. His reputation was achieved without the benefit of making a recording. He composed a number of piano solos and songs that were standard repertoire in the early 1900s including: 'The naked dance' (1902), used by Morton; 'Michigan Water' (1912); 'Pretty baby' (with Egbert *Van Alstyne, 1916; *w* Gus *Kahn), used in the revue *Houp-La*; 'Miss Samantha Johnson's wedding day' (1916); 'I've got 'em' (1916); 'Some sweet day' (with Abe *Olman and Ed Rose, 1917); and 'Pick-it boy' (1917).

Jackson Five, The. The Jacksons. American pop vocal and instrumental group formed around 1965, made up of five brothers all born in Gary, Indiana: Jackie [Sigmund Esco] (*b* 4 May 1951), Tito [Toriano Adryll] (*b* 15 Oct. 1953), Jermaine [Jermaine LaJaune] (*b* 11 Dec. 1954), Marlon [Marlon David] (*b* 12 Mar. 1957), and Michael [Michael Joe] (*b* 29 Aug. 1958). There were four other children who all made musical careers, following in the footsteps of musical parents. The quintet started out by winning talent contests before they recorded for Steeltown and were billed as the Jackson Five. They sang in support of various black acts, then moved to the Motown label and in 1969–70 achieved the unique distinction of their first four recorded singles ('I want you back', 'ABC', 'The love you save', and 'I'll be there') all becoming No. 1 hits. Michael *Jackson began his solo career in 1971, but also continued with the group, and they had 14 recordings in the best-selling lists 1969–75. On moving to the Epic label the name had to be changed to the Jacksons and they made many very successful albums up to 1986 when Michael left the group because his participation was making them too expensive.

S. Manning: *The Jacksons* (Indianapolis, 1977). L. Pitts: *Papa Joe's Boys: the Jacksons' Story* (Cresskill, NJ, 1983).

Jacquet, Illinois [Jean-Baptiste] (*b* Broussard, La., 31 Oct. 1922). American jazz tenor-saxophonist. He was brought up in Houston, Texas, where he first worked as a musician 1939–40. After joining the Lionel *Hampton band 1941–2, he was with Cab *Calloway 1943–4, Count *Basie 1945–6, and Norman *Granz's Jazz at the Philharmonic 1944, 1947, and 1955. He led his own band in 1945 and from 1947, was later in a trio with Milt Buckner 1966–74, and had various reunions with the Basie band. He toured Europe on several occasions from 1984 and led the Jazz Legends big band. He played with a strong *blues flavour in a *mainstream manner and did much to establish a modern style of tenor-saxophone playing.

Jam. The act of informal collective jazz improvisation. Hence a jam-session, when such music-making took place. Earlier the word was occasionally used as a slang synonym for all jazz.

Jam, The. British *new wave group playing from 1974 to 1982. They were led by Paul Weller (*b* 1958) (guitar and vocal), with Bruce Foxton (*b* 1955) (bass) and Rick Butler (*b* 1955) (drums), starting out by being influenced by such modern-sounding rock groups as Small Faces and the *Who. Their early work was aggressive and bright, lacking their later subtlety. Weller's own work was influenced by Wilson *Pickett and the *Kinks. Their first big hits came with 'All around the world', 'Strange town', 'When you're young', and the album *All Mod Cons* (1978), which included 'Down in the tube station at midnight'. Weller's ability visibly grew in 'Eton rifles', 'Little boy soldiers', and 'Saturday's kids', with 'Going underground' moving immediately to the No. 1 hit position. His best song is generally considered to be the bitter 'That's entertainment' (1982). The album *The Gift* of that year included similarly biting songs like 'Town called Malice' and 'The planner's dream gone wrong'. At this point they decided to break up while they were still at a peak of achievement; each continued a separate career, with Weller forming the group Style Council.

James, Elmore (*b* Richland, Miss., 27 Jan. 1918; *d* Chicago, 24 May 1963). American blues singer. He began his career on a part-time basis, occasionally performing with Sonny Boy Williamson and Robert *Johnson. His first recording was a version of Johnson's 'Dust my broom' made in Jackson in 1952, a best-seller in the rhythm 'n' blues market. He became famous for his intense and powerful delivery and heavily amplified guitar, based on Johnson's style. A distinctive reiterated riff, used on his first recording, became a feature of most of his later works and, by imitation, a standard feature of British blues of the 1960s as epitomized by *Fleetwood Mac and John *Mayall's Bluesbreakers. His best-known recordings included: 'The sun is shining', 'Shake your money maker', 'Rollin' and tumblin'', and, most notably, the superbly impassioned slow blues 'It hurts me too'. He died of a heart-attack just as he was becoming internationally recognized.

James, Harry Haag (*b* Albany, Ga., 15 Mar. 1916; *d* Las Vegas, 5 July 1983). American bandleader and trumpeter. His father was bandmaster of the Haag Circus, later with the Christy Brothers Circus, and Harry played in circus bands as a child, also performing as a contortionist. His first dance-band work was in Texas, then in 1935 he joined the Ben *Pollack band and made an immediate impression with his virtuosic, forthright and pugnacious playing. He recorded with Teddy *Wilson, Buster Bailey, and Johnny *Hodges, among others, making a feature of hard-hitting *boogie-woogie numbers. In 1937 he left Pollack to join Benny *Goodman, leading the brass section and making an international reputation before he left in 1939 to form his own band. This made its debut at the Benjamin Franklin Hotel in Philadelphia, moving to the Roseland Ballroom with Frank *Sinatra as vocalist.

The fierce power with which James distinguished the Goodman band was now developed in such trumpet virtuosity as 'Concerto for trumpet', 'Carnival of Venice', 'Flight of the bumble-bee', and 'Trumpet rhapsody' (recorded 1939–41). His vocalist was now Dick *Haymes and James recorded his first million-seller, 'One o'clock jump', in 1938, and had his biggest hit with a sweet version with strings of 'You made me love you' (1941). He compromised between the hot and sweet styles until the 1960s, when his latest band played big-band jazz somewhat in the *Basie idiom. He visited England in 1972. His much publicized second marriage to Betty *Grable in 1943 did much to enhance his image and lasted, to most people's surprise, until 1965. Technically one of the greatest jazz trumpeters, he was sometimes inclined to over-emphasize his technique in the big-band context and was at his best in his occasional small group recordings. He appeared in the films *Hollywood Hotel* (1937), with the Benny Goodman band; *Syncopation* (1942); **Best Foot Forward* (1942); *Springtime in the Rockies* (1942); *Two Girls and a Sailor* (1944); *Bathing Beauty* (1944); *Do You Love Me* (1946); and *The Benny Goodman Story* (1955), among others; and played the trumpet on the sound-track of *Young Man With a Horn* (1950).

Janis, Elsie [Bierbower, Elsie] (*b* Columbus, Ohio, 16 Mar. 1889; *d* Los Angeles, 26 Feb. 1956). American actress and singer. She started her stage career as a child in 1897, appearing in vaudeville as Little Elsie. Her first Broadway appearance was in *The Vanderbilt Cup* (1906); followed by *The Hoyden* (1907); *The Fair Co-Ed* (1909); *The Slim Princess* (1911); *The Lady of the Slipper* (1912); *Miss Information* (1915); and *The Century Girl* (1916). She appeared in London in 1914 in *The *Passing Show* and again in 1915, and entertained the American forces during the war, becoming known as the Sweetheart of the AEF. She appeared in films from 1917. She was in London in *Hullo, America!* (1918); in 1919 she produced her own show, *Elsie Janis and Her Gang*, in Baltimore, taking a revised version to New York in 1922 and to London in 1924. She managed the Queen's Theatre, London, from 1924; and starred in **Oh, Kay!* (1927) and *Clowns in Clover* (1928). She also wrote music and words for some of her shows, several books and plays, and many song lyrics, retiring from the stage in 1929 to write and direct films.

E. Janis: *The Big Show: my Six Months with the American Expeditionary Force* (New York, 1919). E. Janis: *So Far, So Good!: an Autobiography* (New York, 1932; London, 1933).

Jarre, Maurice (*b* Lyons, 13 Sept. 1924). French composer. He studied electrical engineering before switching to music and attending the Paris Conservatoire in 1944. He joined the orchestra of the Jean-Louis Barrault Theatre, along with Pierre Boulez, and wrote his first theatre score in 1951 for Jean Vilar's production of *Le Prince de Homburg* by Kleist. Vilar became director of the Théâtre National Populaire and appointed Jarre as musical director and composer; he wrote incidental music and a musical comedy *Loin de Rueil*.

He started writing for films in 1951 and his scores include: *Hôtel des Invalides* (1952); *Théâtre National Populaire* (1956); *Sur le pont d'Avignon* (1956); *Le Bel Indifférent* (1957); *La Tête contre les murs* (1958); *Les Yeux sans visage* (*Eyes Without a Face*, 1959); *Les Dragueurs* (1959); *Crack in the Mirror* (1960); *The Big Gamble* (1960); *Pleins feux sur l'assassin* (1961); *Les temps du ghetto* (1961); *La Bride sur le cou* (1961); *Lawrence of Arabia* (1962; Academy Award); *The Longest Day* (1962); *Cybèle* (1962); *Les Oliviers de la Justice* (1962); *Thérèse Desqueyroux* (1962); *Mourir à Madrid* (1963); *Judex* (1963) *Behold a Pale Horse* (1964); *The Collector* (1965); *Weekend at Dunkirk* (1965); *Doctor Zhivago* (1965; Academy Award); *The Train* (1965); *Grand Prix* (1966); *The Professionals* (1966); *The Night of the Generals* (1967); *The Extraordinary Seaman* (1967); *Isadora* (1968); *Villa Rides* (1968); *Five Card Stud* (1968); *The Fixer* (1968); *Topaz* (1969); *The Damned* (1969); *El Condor* (1970); *Ryan's Daughter* (1970); *Soleil Rouge* (1971); *Ash Wednesday* (1974); *The Last Tycoon* (1976); *Mohammed* (1976); *March or Die* (1977); *Winter Kills* (1979); *Resurrection* (1980); *The Black Marble* (1980); *Taps* (1981); *Lion of the Desert* (1981); *Young Doctors in Love* (1982); and *Firefox* (1982).

Jaubert, Maurice (*b* Nice, 3 Jan. 1900; *d* Azerailles, 19 June 1940). French composer. He studied music at the Nice Conservatory; but also studied law and practised as a lawyer for some years. He became director of music for Pathé 1930–5, and later worked for the GPO Film Unit in London. He was killed in action.

His film scores included: *Le Petit Chaperon* (1929): *Rouge* (1929); *L'Affaire est dans le sac* (1932); *La Vie d'un fleuve* (1933); *Zéro de conduite* (1933); *Le Quatorze Juillet* (1933)—'A Paris dans chaque Faubourg'; *Le Dernier Milliardaire* (1934); *L'Atalante* (1934); *Drôle de drame* (1936); *Un Carnet de bal* (1937), one of his greatest achievements; *Les Maisons de la misère* (1937); *Altitude 3,200* (1937);

We Live in Two Worlds (1937); *Quai des brumes* (1938); *Hôtel du Nord* (1938); *La Fin du jour* (1939); *Le Jour se lève* (1939); and *Air pur* (1939).

Jazz. A distinctive genre of music-making, recognized by its propulsively moving rhythms, syncopated melodic nature, and improvisational (to varying degrees) nature. It is generally assumed to be of black origin and first emerged in the USA in various modified strains at the end of the 19th century.

1 *Origins and developments*. The eventual emergence of jazz as a clearly definable kind of music came at the end of a long and obscure period of incubation and evolution that was hidden in the history of black people in America. It is unfortunate that their ghetto position as slaves led to an almost complete lack of historical documentation, so that the actual birth and early developments of jazz remain very much matters for conjecture. Although there is much division of opinion on the subject, it seems likely that its special rhythmic characteristics had some roots in the distant music of Africa, later mingling with traits drawn from native American music to produce jazz as the world knew it when it emerged after the emancipation of the slaves at the end of the 19th century. It is quite probable that music which the modern ear would recognize as having jazz characteristics was being played by black slaves many generations before its emergence as a common musical property, an accidental creation like most folk-music, the strength of its traditions ensuring its continuity even under suppressive and unremarked conditions.

Jazz only became a conscious creation after the black musician had achieved more freedom of movement and had come into contact with the mainstream of American popular music. Those ingredients which did not evolve in black folk-music (mainly rhythmical and some melodic characteristics) could well claim to have come from the folk-music that was taken to America by early white settlers—much of it from the British Isles, notably Scotland, some from other European countries. In the early days of American settlement, popular music had to fight a long battle against the strong Puritan element which saw all secular music as a tool of the Devil. Secretly at first, then more openly, a distinctive style of American folk-music evolved, with fiddle and banjo recreating the same sort of headlong impulse that is to be found in Scottish dance music. This, enhanced by American legend and speech, developed into the distinctive American folk style that eventually produced composers who wrote in a clearly American mode, typified by such songs of the 1800s as 'Arkansas traveller' and 'Turkey in the straw', leading to the more conspicuously composed songs like *'Dixie' and the works of Stephen *Foster.

The first powerful surge of black influence came with the minstrel show tradition which, ironically, was largely perpetrated by white performers disguised as blacks. The minstrel strains were spread abroad by the various troupes that went to Europe, or were founded there, and gave the world the first hint of something musically different from the European tradition; as did the spirituals taken abroad by the Fisk *Jubilee Singers and others which had an even larger black element in their make-up. Then in the 1890s came the first emergence of a music of black origin in the shape of *ragtime, where the minstrel-cum-Foster-cum-Sousa strains of current white American music were given the extra impetus of strong banjo rhythms and a new use of the effects of melodic syncopation.

The emergence of fully-fledged jazz was but a short step from there and it is not really surprising that initially it was exploited largely by white bands, who were just as capable of handling its ragtime-associated strains as black musicians, and had all the existing commercial advantages in their control. As the world absorbed the exciting new musical beverage that was served out by the *Original Dixieland Jazz Band, and other pioneers, it was unaware of the richer depths of the true black jazz that was still being created by the blacks for their own use and pleasure.

A brand of jazz that was perhaps too exclusively labelled *New Orleans was certainly finding as fruitful a soil there as could possibly be found—a cosmopolitan city, a seaport open to the Caribbean and further black influences from that direction, a city with a strong Creole tradition. New Orleans jazz was essentially a utility jazz which took the discarded military band instruments from the Civil War and added to the existing white marching band style the elements of free improvisation and the pulsive off-the-beat rhythms that had their distant ancestry in the music of Africa. Much of early New Orleans jazz was played by marching bands before it settled in the black dance halls and clubs and there joined up with the ragtime piano to produce that early, sometimes stilted jazz, founded on banjo rhythms, that traditionalists like to think of as the genuine article. In fact it was already a hybrid music, and this was how jazz was to develop and how popular music was to take inspiration from it through the 1930s and beyond; jazz and popular music still loosely linked with the old European tradition of music-making through its partial white ancestry.

Behind the scenes, as it were, the deeper and blacker strains of jazz, as typified in the looser, essentially improvised, chanting lines of the blues, were still a private music for black use only. It was listened to on specially issued 'race' records that only gradually became available to the general public. But fitfully the world learned to appreciate and accept jazz, whether it was being presented in its pure or adulterated forms, until eventually this potent new musical idiom was almost completely to overshadow the European styles of popular music-making, and spread to all corners of the world.

By now the only superficially black strains of minstrelsy, of ragtime, of early Dixieland jazz, and subsequent white styles developed in Chicago and elsewhere have been superseded, but not obliterated. They have taken their place in musical history alongside the *drawing-room ballad and the Viennese waltz, as enjoyably nostalgic modes of music-making that still have much to offer. Jazz itself has become intellectualized and the black and white divisions no longer have much validity; while the blues-based popular music has mainly gone back to the unrestrained freedoms of the African origins of jazz.

2 *The name and the genre*. The establishment of the name 'Jazz' has centred in many jazz histories on the activities of the *Original Dixieland Jazz Band, a white group who were the first to record a jazz session and who introduced the music to New York. It has been stated (see Brunn: *The Story of the Original Dixieland Jazz Band*) that it was during their engagement at Schiller's Café in Chicago in 1916 (then playing under the name of Johnny Stein) that the word 'jass' was first applied to this kind of music, when an inebriated 'retired vaudeville entertainer', excited by the music, leapt to his feet and yelled: 'Jass it up, boys!' 'Jass', in the black slang current in the Chicago underworld and emanating from the deep South, was a word with specific sexual connotations. Up to then it had not generally been associated with any musical activities, but it clearly struck all who heard it, thus applied to this syncopated music, as aptly descriptive. It is reported that this history-making customer was given a retainer to be there every night and utter his cry of 'Jass it up, boys'; and the band soon became known as Stein's Dixie Jass Band. Later, at Reisenweber's in New York, it became the Original Dixieland Jass Band, variously printed through error or in the spirit of experiment as 'jasz' and 'jaz', until it finally evolved as the punchy and enduring 'jazz' that history has accepted.

It is likely that the word, defined by Wentworth and Flexner in *Dictionary of American Slang* as 'copulation: the vagina; sex; a woman considered solely as a sexual object' had been used by Southern blacks long before 1900; and it had also long been broadened to mean anything that engendered excitement. It was a natural association of ideas (occurring in a similar way to the appending of the name 'ragtime' to any earlier modified form of jazz), but there is no evidence that the word 'jazz' was used to describe this new musical style until around the date given for its spontaneous emergence. The word was soon in general use as a noun and was widely used as a verb by 1920 in such phrases as 'jazz it', 'jazz it up', 'jazz that thing', etc.

Jazz clearly came upon the world as something of a cultural shock. The rhythmic impulse that 'jazzing' music induced was something totally new to the European tradition and was soon to revolutionize the whole world of popular music. Much that went on in the way of harmony and conflicting counterpoint was perhaps not quite so revolutionary in the light of what was happening to modern music; but jazz seemed harshly discordant to many ears accustomed to the polite rhythms and harmonies of the popular music of the 1890s and early 1900s. Ragtime had partly paved the way by its syncopated melodies, but it still had a degree of Edwardian dignity about it. It is difficult now to appreciate just how aggressive and foreign jazz sounded to many people; and the fact that no one had thought of creating music in this idiom before gives some further credence to the theory that it arose as the result of African musical culture being grafted on to American.

It is easy enough to ridicule the confusion of early writers and their frequent inability to distinguish between ragtime and jazz, or the commercial manifestations of both. The anti-jazz faction was to remain highly vocal throughout the 1930s, at which stage they gave up public protest in the realization that they were well and truly beaten. Many hopefully predicted that jazz could not last; others, however reluctantly, conceded that it was here to stay.

The rhythmic nature of jazz derived from its African ancestry and the heightened sense of rhythm that the black exponents brought to it through the exploitation of the banjo and improvised rhythm instruments. Jazz melody was partly an extension of the natural flavours of American popular song; partly the result of the shapes imposed upon it by the underlying rhythms and harmonies. Jazz harmony, at least in its early stages before the more advanced jazz musician was qualified to manipulate it, was probably mainly advanced, more than most jazz writers allow, by the composers from *Tin Pan Alley. If they were undoubtedly forced into new ways by the coming of ragtime and jazz, there was also a return trade in which they led jazz into new paths by the development of new harmonic ideas. Carl Engel wrote in *Atlantic Monthly* in August 1922: 'I have not given the subject sufficient study to say definitely at what point the course of popular American music took a new turn, but unless I am very much mistaken, "The magic melody" by Jerome Kern was the opening chorus of an epoch. It is not a composition of genius but it is very ingenious . . . its principal claim to immortality is that it introduces a modulation which, at the time it was first heard by the masses, seized their ears with the power of magic.'

This point was revived by Irving Schwerké in the *Chicago Tribune*, Paris, March 1926, when he wrote: 'Harmonic variety did not become a feature of American syncopated music until 1915 when "The magic melody" of Mr Jerome Kern was produced. "The magic melody" was the first introduction into popular music of the peculiar harmonies which now pass for jazz harmonies or blues.' Gerald Bordman, in *Jerome Kern: his Life and Music* (1980), identifies the modulation pinpointed in this now almost unobtainable *Kern item as 'the characteristic jazz change from a tonic to a chord based on its fourth tone and raised to a seventh: in this case a B♭ seventh chord succeeding an F'; but goes on to point out that Engel, in 'seeking the origins of commercialized jazz' took no note of even more dramatic jazz harmonies that Kern invented in 'They didn't believe me', written in 1914 and described by Alec Wilder in *American Popular Song* as 'a definite departure from all the songs which preceded it'. Certainly over the two decades after 1915 jazz developed by using the advanced compositions of writers like Kern and *Gershwin as a basis for improvisation as well as by the increasing complexity of improvisation in the hands of adventurous performers ranging from *Armstrong, through *Beiderbecke and *Hawkins, to the innovatory work of *Young and *Parker.

There has been perhaps too great a tendency to isolate jazz. Pure jazz is certainly a minority interest, its appeal partly limited by the fact that most of it is instrumental music while the wider public is more interested in songs and singers. Jazz singers have helped to bridge the gap by using Tin Pan Alley material and it is clearly evident that jazz and popular music from the 1920s on go hand in hand. The popular song is a commercialized form of jazz; and jazz is a folk version of popular song; but each is now dependent on the other.

3 *History*. If jazz became apparent to the world at large through the pioneering efforts of the white Original Dixieland Jass Band from *c*.1916, it had been emerging in a more circumscribed way in the black ghettos of New Orleans and elsewhere from possibly as far back as the mid-19th century. Jazz, in the hands of musicians who were too early to be recorded, like the legendary Buddy *Bolden, was very actively shaping its language and conventions in the 1890s. Possibly New Orleans has been too emphatically pinpointed as the birthplace of jazz. Although this is impossible to prove, as no one knows where the first definable jazz performance took place, New Orleans was ideally situated in every way to incubate jazz and there is everything to support the contention that this is where jazz grew and emerged; and its back streets gave birth to many of its most distinguished early exponents. The natural urge of the academic to put everything into categories and neat packages has similarly given rise to the over-indulgence of seeing jazz as a regional product—*New Orleans jazz, *Chicago jazz, *Kansas City jazz, and so on. Certain traits can be seen breeding in certain places; but jazz, like other music, like literature and art, has mainly been advanced by inspired individuals. Any attempt to rationalize jazz in area packages is soon halted by the weight of exceptions to the rule. Louis Armstrong, although a native of New Orleans, was the first powerful influence that took jazz away from the so-called New Orleans style; while Johnny *Dodds and Jimmie *Noone, two New Orleans-bred clarinettists of roughly the same vintage, were players of a totally different nature.

New Orleans spawned the marching band that utilized the clarinet, trumpet, and trombone frontline derived from ex-military band stock instruments, and instilled the basic rules of collective improvisation, with each instrument playing a role that supplemented and enhanced the others. The respect accorded to Bolden almost certainly arose because he, as much as anyone, devised many of the tricks and phrases of New Orleans jazz that were to become the crude basis of the jazz language. His unofficial 'pupils', like Joe 'King' *Oliver and Louis Armstrong, learned the basic New Orleans jazz, outgrew its conventions and went on their way to Chicago and New York to play on a new level of coherence. The rudimentary New Orleans style was a simple, fundamental, highly satisfying formula that was left to musicians of lesser skills to enlighten with their sincerity. Basically it comprised a trumpet or cornet playing a leading line which kept fairly near to the tune, with the clarinet playing rococo variations, mainly in the higher reaches, and the trombone underlaying both with bass harmonies and connecting passages. The banjo, the tuba, and the drummer provided the basic rhythmic foundation when the jazz group was acting as a marching band at various festive functions; with piano and double-bass used on more sedentary occasions. But there were no rules as to how New Orleans jazz was presented. The leader might be a clarinettist. The saxophone was commonly used (Bolden had one in his band). The guitar was only less favoured in early recordings because the banjo came through better. Some musicians, like clarinettist Dodds and trombonist Kid *Ory, passed their career playing in the earthy, simplistic style that is thought of as *echt* New Orleans; others moved on.

Many early writers and pundits laid great emphasis on the fact that jazz was an improvised music. It would perhaps be more accurate to say that it maintains an improvisatory nature and flavour. Most jazz is at least partly arranged, in that it makes use of fixed melodic and harmonic patterns and most soloists will be playing something of what they have previously worked out. Jazz totally played as written is almost impossible; jazz totally improvised is rarely attempted, or leads to something that is only of interest to the player. As it 'progressed', jazz tended to become less improvised, until the art was revived in modern free jazz.

The next step in jazz history usually leads the student on to Chicago, where many New Orleans musicians had arrived by the earliest possible riverboat, and the so-called Chicago style. The change of emphasis is towards more isolated solos and harder-driven rhythms, pointing towards the swing era when rhythm was nearly all. In fact, pure Chicago jazz was only played by a small number of white musicians who called themselves Chicagoans when they felt like it. Much of the music going on in Chicago at the same time was, as ever, dictated by the whims and inventions of talented musicians doing their own thing or, alternatively, playing a somewhat more polished kind of New Orleans jazz as fashioned by King Oliver's Creole Jazz Band of the early 1920s, which was not particularly Creole in flavour and would probably have been the same had it stayed in New Orleans or moved to St Louis.

Although jazz life was to be sustained in various large cities like New Orleans, Chicago, Kansas City,

Los Angeles, and San Francisco (and was there given some individuality by the musicians who happened to be around), the majority of jazz activities were bound to gravitate towards America's cosmopolitan trade and cultural centre, which happened to be New York. Jazz might be most realistically viewed as a series of developments that were shaped by various gifted musicians who just happened to be in various locations on their way to Harlem.

We can never fully know the part played by early leaders like cornettists Buddy Bolden and Freddie *Keppard, clarinettist Alphonse Picou (1878–1961), and other New Orleans pioneers without knowing what the music that they helped to shape was originally like. We can get a fairly clear idea of the sound of early New Orleans jazz from the revivalist work of such survivors as Bunk *Johnson (trumpet), George *Lewis (clarinet), Jim Robinson (1890–1976) (trombone), though there is no reason to suppose that all New Orleans jazz was as crude as they made it in their decline. From such samples and suppositions it can be seen that the art of Louis Armstrong is simply a case of advanced and positive ideas outgrowing one environment and moving on to look for another where his ideas are better supported. The magic that he achieved in the company of Johnny Dodds and Kid Ory is by no means diminished by the fact that he had to find a partner like Earl *Hines and competitors like Coleman *Hawkins before he could find a full outlet for his expression. Subsequently the full force of a larger band seemed necessary to support his powerful playing. At a certain point he had said all he had to say, and he spent the rest of his career repeating himself and enjoying a justified reputation while jazz moved on.

This is essentially the pattern of any artistic history. Some players and creators, like the other great New Orleans musician Jelly Roll *Morton, came on the scene too early for their advanced ideas to be appreciated and when they at last achieved their due recognition they were almost beyond their creative peak.

The folky jazz world of New Orleans was outpaced by the more commercial centres like Chicago and New York. In Chicago jazz simply took more account of its Armstrongs and allowed more prominance to the soloist, at the same time continuing the tidying up and controlling tendency that was considered progress by some and a retrograde step by others. Out of the Chicago environment, or passing through it, came the talents of white players like Bix Beiderbecke, the Texan Jack *Teagarden, saxophonist/leader Frankie *Trumbauer, who progressed harmonically and cooled jazz a degree or two, substituting exciting ideas for emotional heat.

Once jazz had moved inexorably to New York the need for regional labels diminishes. Certain styles that led to the swing era were developed in Kansas City, and later certain cool trends developed on the West Coast of America, but basically everyone played in New York at some time or another to create a universal style. It was now purely a matter of personalities. Coleman Hawkins had no sooner given the saxophone a warmly expressive and inventive style of its own that put it on a competitive level with the trumpet as a group leader, than the world was intrigued by the cooler, more sidelong approach of Lester Young in the ranks of the early Count *Basie band. He was left in the *mainstream world when the even cooler and more cerebral playing of Charlie Parker and the other modernists at *Minton's substantially changed the character of jazz. In unscientific terms it was a development that paralleled what was going on in the classical world. Instead of music being an outgoing art, aiming to please the customers who basked in its warmth and friendliness, it became introspective, with the customer expected to make the effort to find out what it was all about. The progressive music-lover has, perhaps rightly, always seen progress and novelty as the criteria of modern art; the reactionary still deems beauty and truth as all that matters.

The move towards *big band jazz started early. In basic terms, bigness, that is the employment of more than one of each instrument at a time—sections of three or four of any one voice—necessitated arrangement and the development of varying formulas. The big-band jazz that became *swing was specifically catering for the requirements of dancers and other commercial needs. But not all big-band jazz necessarily came into the swing category. The big band was variously used by leaders from Morton, via Duke *Ellington to Gil *Evans to create jazz on an orchestral basis, to achieve blends of tone colour and contrapuntal ideas that were beyond chamber jazz groups. A band like Ellington's passed through the swing era without ever becoming simply a swing band in the most functional sense.

At the other end of the scale the individual soloist was still the main focus of interest. The complex fantasies of virtuosos like Art *Tatum and Oscar *Peterson were not to be confined by other instrumentalists hogging the limelight; others were there simply to provide backing for the star. To some, such solo extravagances are the peak of jazz creation; others prefer the collective spirit. Possibly the greatest jazzmen have always been those who could do both things: shine as soloists and yet combine with others in collective creativity. Add to that the ability always to come up with fresh ideas rather than simply trot out old formulas and the ideal might be somebody like pianist Earl Hines or saxophonist Charlie Parker.

With 100 years of jazz now more or less upon us (though which year will be fixed on for the centenary celebrations will be difficult to decide) jazz has already become too big a subject, like classical music, to be summed up as one thing, or even an art that can be wholly appreciated by a person of average appreciative capacity. But while jazz can conveniently be parcelled into such broad categories as *traditional, mainstream, and *modern, or further divided into regional packages, a present critical dilemma is that the first two chapters happened too quickly: we have now been living with an art known as modern jazz for virtually half of jazz's entire history. Possibly the only critical solution is to see modern jazz as the start of a new art that ought to be given a new name. The earlier jazz periods could then be packaged into nostalgic units like ragtime, *music-hall, and baroque concertos, to be constantly dusted and polished but never radically changed or taken beyond the bounds of authenticity. Certain elements of modernity in jazz are as far beyond the appreciation of certain traditionalists as the twelve-tone school is ever likely to be to those whose ears are still attuned only to diatonic music.

The history of jazz is not all American, but 90 per cent of it is. It does not diminish the value of exponents of jazz in Britain and Europe to say that they have generally followed where the USA led. America had the irreplaceable asset of its black population, who at least must be given the credit for creating and incubating jazz and producing a great proportion of its creative geniuses—however skilled the white exponents of the art have since become. Jazz may now be a universal art but it started as an American idea and nothing can change its lineage. So far there have been no other national jazz styles that have not been copies of the American originals, and now that the language of jazz has become the language of virtually all popular music, the specialized art of true jazz has become even more of a minority taste.

General Histories: R. Blesh: *Shining Trumpets: a History of Jazz* (New York, 1946). B. Ulanov: *A History of Jazz in America* (New York, 1950). M. Stearns: *The Story of Jazz* (New York, 1956). J. L. Collier: *The Making of Jazz: a Comprehensive History* (New York, 1978). P. Oliver, M. Harrison, and W. Bolcom: *The New Grove Gospel, Blues and Jazz* (London–New York, 1986).

Encyclopedias and Dictionaries: L. Feather: *The Encyclopedia of Jazz* (New York, 1955; with new editions and supplements). J. Chilton: *Who's Who of Jazz* (London, 1972; rev. 1985). P. Clayton and P. Gammond: *The Guinness Jazz A–Z* (London, 1986). I. Carr, D. Fairweather, and B. Priestley: *Jazz: the Essential Companion* (London, 1987). B. Kernfeld (ed.): *The New Grove Dictionary of Jazz* (London, 1988).

Critical Studies and Essays: A. Hodeir: *Jazz: its Evolution and Essence* (New York, 1956). M. Williams (ed.): *The Art of Jazz* (New York, 1959). G. Schuller: *Early Jazz* (New York, 1968). C. Fox: *Jazz in Perspective* (London, 1969).

Regional: J. Godbolt: *A History of Jazz in Britain 1919–50* (London, 1984; rev. 1988). C. Goddard: *Jazz Away from Home* [Europe] (New York–London, 1979).

Bibliography: B. Hefele: *Jazz-Bibliography* (Munich, 1981).

See also books listed under BIG BAND JAZZ; BLUES; CHICAGO JAZZ; DISCOGRAPHY; KANSAS CITY; MAINSTREAM; MODERN JAZZ; NEW ORLEANS; NEW YORK; RAGTIME; SWING; etc.

Jazz Dance. The observer's view of jazz (largely built up from records and other mechanical presentations of the music) as something to be listened to, obscures the practicalities of its history and its everyday growth as a dance music. It was not so much the onset of jazz that dictated fashions in dancing as the demands of dancers that shaped the course of jazz. Most bands passed a greater percentage of their time on dance-hall bandstands than they ever did in the concert hall or the recording studio.

Jazz dances have always inclined towards an improvisational nature, a free expression of bodily excitement and mental elation rather than the formal expression of graceful deportment that seems to have been the prime object of the European ballroom styles. In this light they have a natural affinity with the folk-dances that had been modified and bowdlerized to create the ballroom dance.

Jazz dance, like jazz itself, goes back into the dark recesses of the history of the black population of the USA. That its character arose at least partly from African dance customs seems beyond question. The black dancer inherited the use of dance as a passionate outlet, a physical recreation, and an expression of suppressed vitality. Jazz dance is centred on the pelvic regions and can hardly help having sexual undertones which are induced by the essentially rhythmic nature of the musical accompaniment. While the slave population partly copied the white dance fashion, a natural independence ensured the survival of dances of African and West Indian origin such as were danced in Congo Square in New Orleans on permitted holidays—the bamboula, the calinda, and the juba among them.

The gradual emergence of black American music in the watered-down strains of minstrelsy came as an accompaniment to the comic dances of the mid-19th century that had some affinity with the European clog dance. The frequent imitation of animals also had its roots in folklore and many of the basic steps that evolved had names like the Buzzard Lope or the Eagle Rock. The jigging steps that evolved had a clear influence on ragtime when it emerged in the 1890s, developing alongside the high-kicking steps of the *cakewalk, whose music was almost indistinguishable from ragtime and occasionally identical with it. These partly Americanized social and entertainment dances developed in such popular crazes as the *Charleston; while the more emotionally physical side of jazz that had the *blues as its essence, saw the physical movements of the Grind and the Mooche leading jazz dance towards the physical explosions of *jive and *jitterbug that accompanied the *boogie-woogie and *swing crazes. Both sides met and compromised in ballroom modifications like the *Black Bottom.

All these physically demanding dances disappeared when the ritualized movements of the *twist and other *rock dances commercialized jazz dance by putting it within reach of the untalented. In the entertainment world jazz dance developed to a fine art, mainly under the heading of tap, in the hands of talented black dancers like Bert *Williams and Bill *Robinson and perpetuated eventually by the master imitator Fred *Astaire.

M. Stearns: *Jazz Dance: the Story of American Vernacular Dance* (New York, 1968).

Jazz–Rock Fusion. The whole phenomenon of rock (to use the most general term for the modern pop scene) evolved from Tin Pan Alley's absorption of the jazz and blues language. By the latter part of the 1960s rock had become the popular music of the day while jazz, desiccated by its new adherence to the intellectual tendencies of *bebop and modernism, was fast losing its commercial hold on the young. It was therefore a natural U-turn for jazz to try to reassert its hold by borrowing some of the superficial elements of rock in order to create a popular jazz idiom once again.

A move toward such an amalgamation of styles came within the Miles *Davis band from 1964 on, with the idea further exploited by such musicians as Don *Ellis, Herbie *Hancock, Keith Jarrett (*b* 1945), Tom Scott (*b* 1948), and Bob Moses (*b* 1948). The final impetus came from the Miles Davis albums *Filles de Kilimanjaro* (1968), *In a Silent Way* (1969), and *Bitches Brew* (1969), which excitingly utilized rock rhythms and electronic means to underline Davis's latest musings. Most of the musicians involved in these sessions then went their own ways to spread the gospel of jazz-rock which led to a much more natural amalgam of ethnic styles and jazz with a peak of activity in the years 1969–75. Unfortunately, in one light, the whole phenomenon then underwent the blighting process of intellectualization, with the emergence of units like the Mahavishnu Orchestra which specialized in playing mathematics rather than music and, although jazz maintained its new contact with electronics, most of the natural fusion had seen its best by 1980.

J. Coryell and L. Friedman: *Jazz-Rock Fusion: the People, the Music* (New York, 1978).

Jazz Singer, The. Generally given the credit of being the first sound film and by virtue of its nature, also the first musical film. It opened the new era of the talkies when its star, Al *Jolson, after singing 'Dirty hands, dirty face' electrified the audience by stepping forward and saying 'Wait a minute, wait a minute. You ain't heard nothin' yet' before introducing 'Toot, toot, tootsie, goodbye'. Elsewhere Jolson spoke more lengthily to his mother, telling her of all that he would do for her once he was a success. Other songs included were: 'My gal Sal', 'Waiting for the Robert E. Lee', 'Blue skies', 'Mother of mine', and 'Mammy'.

Experiments had been made with talking pictures as far back as 1900 and full-length films had appeared with an associated orchestral sound-track. But with *The Jazz Singer*, which adapted a play in which George Jessel (1898–1981) originally starred, Warner Brothers launched the first full-length feature; with songs and dialogue emerging from the story.

It was first presented at the Warners Theatre in New York on 6 Oct. 1927 and seen in London at the Piccadilly Theatre on 28 Sept. 1928; and, like all innovations, it was greeted with some dismay. The **Melody Maker* of Nov. 1927 spoke of musicians' worries about the future of their livelihood and tried to comfort them by reporting the inadequacies of the film, a sound-track which might as well have been provided by a number of poorly recorded gramophone records, and a generally disjointed production. However, these trial errors were soon eradicated and the sound film eventually produced a glut of employment for everyone in the business. *The Jazz Singer* made more than $3 million for its far-sighted producers and helped to change the whole future of the cinema. A new version of the story was made in 1953 with Danny Thomas (*b* 1914), Peggy *Lee, and Eduard Franz (1902–83); and a third in 1981 with Neil *Diamond and Laurence Olivier (1907–89).

R. L. Carringer (ed.): *The Jazz Singer* (New York, 1979).

Jefferson, Clarence 'Blind Lemon' (*b* Couchman, Texas, 11 July 1897; *d* Chicago, Dec. 1929). American blues-singer and composer. He was typical of the untutored raw blues-singing pioneers whose primitive, forceful style was not appreciated until the white public acquired a taste for these black styles in the 1950s. Born blind, he was forced to make a living as a youth by singing and begging on the streets, with an occasional engagement as an entertainer. He went to Dallas in 1917 and for a time made a living as a wrestler. Playing mostly his own songs, he became an expert guitarist and a leading blues-shouter, occasionally teaming up with Huddie Ledbetter (better known as *Leadbelly). He went to Chicago in 1925 and recorded quite prolifically until 1929, including such items as 'Cannon ball moan', D. B. blues', ''Lectric chair blues', 'Prison cell blues', and 'See that my grave is kept clean'. He died in a snowstorm.

Jefferson Airplane. American rock group formed in 1965 with the line-up of Marty Balin (*b* 1942) (vocal), Paul Kantner (*b* 1942) (guitar), Signe Anderson (vocal), Jorma Kaukonen (guitar), Jack Casady (bass), and Skip Spence (drums). They made their name around Washington DC with a newsy hippie image and a folk-rock sound that led to a contract with RCA Records in 1966 and their first LP, *Jefferson Airplane Takes Off*. By now Spencer Dryden had replaced Spence, and Grace Slick (*b* 1939), with a powerful voice and great songwriting talent, had replaced Anderson. The new line-up had hits with 'Somebody to love' and 'White rabbit' in 1967; and their album *Surrealistic Pillow* made them the West Coast's leading acid rock group. They had moved from their original folk-rock basis, to bring in elements of jazz and blues, often producing music of an exciting nature with unique guitar work, complex harmonies, and a drug-oriented and increasingly radical political vocabulary. But the group generally lacked a clear sense of direction and suffered from constant changes in personnel; its impetus faded along with the decline of hippie culture, its output became more idiosyncratic, and it gradually fell apart.

Slick and Kantner decided to re-form the band in 1974, with a change of name to Jefferson Starship, to keep up with the times. The band was now generally more successful and purposeful in such hits as 'Miracles' (1975), 'With Your Love' (1976), 'Runaway' (1978), 'Count on me' (1978), and 'Jane' (1979). Kantner and Slick parted, personally and musically, in 1984, to the accompaniment of several lawsuits. Kantner departed and a new group, now known simply as Starship, had a No. 1 hit with 'We built this city' in 1985. While the group's main success was in the USA, it goes down in rock history as one of the most creative units of the 1960s and 1970s.

R. J. Gleason: *The Jefferson Airplane and the San Francisco Sound* (New York, 1969).

Jenkins, Gordon (*b* Webster Groves, Mo., 12 May 1910; *d* Malibu, Calif., 24 Apr. 1984). American composer, lyricist, pianist, and conductor. He won a banjo-playing contest in St Louis when he was 15 and began a musical career under the sponsorship of 'Ukele Ike' Edwards. He played in jazz groups, then became staff musician and arranger on St Louis radio. He soon developed a distinctive style that ensured much of the success of the Isham *Jones orchestra; and did freelance work for Andre *Kostelanetz, Paul *Whiteman, and Benny *Goodman (including the band's closing theme 'Goodbye'). He went to Hollywood to conduct for NBC and became the first musical director of the newly formed Capital Records in 1942. For this company and for American Decca he made many records which featured his one-finger style of piano-playing or accompanied solo singers. He developed a sonorous choral-orchestral effect that showed a melodic richness and a liking for minor keys, and a style that worked well as a backing for such singers as Frank *Sinatra and Nat 'King' *Cole.

One of the first strictly popular composers to attempt more extended works as LP productions, he had a long-lasting, though initially much criticized, success with *Manhattan Tower* in 1945 which was revised 11 years later dramatized for stage and TV; followed by *California, the Golden State* (1945), *Seven Dreams* (1951), and others. For the stage he wrote *Along Fifth Avenue* (1949), and for TV *What It Was Was Love* (1969). His songs included: 'Blue prelude' (1933); 'When a woman loves a man' (1934); 'PS, I love you' (1934); 'Blue evening' (1939); 'San Fernando Valley' (1943).

Jennings, Waylon [Arnold] (*b* Littlefield, Texas, 15 June 1937). American singer, guitarist, and composer. He made a local reputation in his teens as a country singer and disc jockey, before joining the Buddy *Holly band as a bass-player in 1958–9. After a brief period with A & M Records he signed up with RCA in 1965, first making country albums but eventually pioneering a tougher kind of style which earned the label 'outlaw music' and was fully evident in his 1973 album *Honky Tonk Heroes*. His music was not too well received in *Nashville, although it appealed to a wider rock audience, but further hard-hitting albums such as *Outlaws* (1976) saw him accepted as a highly individual star of country music, alongside such fellow-outlaws as Willie *Nelson, Jessi Colter (*b* 1945), and Tompall Glaser (*b* 1933).

B. Allen: *Waylon and Willie* (New York, 1979).

Jerome, M. K. (*b* New York, 18 July 1893). American composer and pianist. He worked in vaudeville and cinemas before becoming staff pianist with the music-publishers Waterson, Berlin & Snyder. He went to Hollywood in 1929 to write for Warner Brothers films for the next 10 years and started his own publishing business in 1931. His hits included 'Just a baby's prayer at twilight' (1918), the hit record of the year, recorded by Henry Burr (1882–1941) and selling a million copies of the music; 'If I meet the guy who made this country dry' (1920); 'Bright eyes' (1920); 'Mary dear' (1922); 'Dream kisses' (1927); 'I idolize my baby's eyes' (1931); 'My little buckaroo', in the film *Cherokee Strip* (1937); 'You, you darlin'' (1940); 'Youth must have its fling', in *The Hard Way* (1942); 'Knock on wood', in *Casablanca* (1943); 'Hollywood Canteen', in *Hollywood Canteen* (1944); 'The wish that I wish tonight', in *Christmas in Connecticut* (1945); and 'Some Sunday morning', in *San Antonio* (1946).

Jessel, Léon (*b* Stettin, 22 Jan. 1871; *d* Berlin, 4 Jan. 1942). German composer and conductor. After completing his musical studies he held conducting posts in Gelsenkirchen, Mühlheim, Celle, where he wrote his first operetta *Die Brautwerbung* (1894), Freiberg, Paderborn, Stettin, Chemnitz, and Neustrelitz. From 1899 on he was mainly in Lübeck and Kiel and making a name as a composer of piano music, popular waltzes, gavottes, and marches.

He was to become best-known for two works—the operetta *Das Schwarzwaldmädel* (1917), which has remained firmly in the German musical repertoire; and an insidious little 'Charakterstuck' called 'Die Parade der Zinnsoldaten' ('The parade of the tin soldiers', 1911), which has since been published in numerous forms ranging from piano solo and duet to full orchestra. As 'Parade of the wooden soldiers' it was used in the touring revue **Chauve Souris* (1922) where it became immensely popular and achieved numerous recordings. A piece written in the same year, 'The wedding of the rose', also enjoyed a wide popularity. He wrote another 18 or so operettas between 1894 and 1937 without repeating the success of *Das Schwarzwaldmädel*. These included *Die beiden Husaren* (1913); *Verliebte Frauen* (1920); *Die Postmeisterin* (1921); *Schwalbenhochzeit* (1921); *Des Königs Wein* (1933); and *Die goldene Mühle* (1940). Of Jewish extraction, from 1933 Jessel found it hard to pursue a musical career and eventually died in a concentration camp.

Jesus Christ Superstar. British rock opera with music by Andrew *Lloyd Webber, book by Tom O'Horgan, and lyrics by Tim *Rice. It had the unusual genesis of arising from a song, 'Superstar', which was expanded into a record production whose popularity induced several concert tours of the show (the first Jesus being Kim Milford, 1951–88), before it finally became a stage show and was produced at the Mark Hellinger Theatre, New York, on 12 Oct. 1971, where it achieved 711 performances.

It told the tale, in its own terms, of the last days of the life of Jesus Christ, with Judas interestingly portrayed as a man of troubled mind, and was written in a fresh, literate, and natural style with an accessible use of pop music idioms. The elaborate New York production was more simply and effectively staged in London at the Palace Theatre 9 Aug. 1972 and had 3358 performances. Like many subsequent Lloyd Webber shows its overall impact and sense of theatre overcame a lack of hit tunes (apart from the insistent theme song) and star performers. It was filmed in 1973 with Ted Neeley and Carl Anderson.

Jethro Tull. British rock group formed in Blackpool in 1968 with the original line-up of Ian Anderson (*b* 1947) (vocal and flute), Glenn Cornick (*b* 1947) (bass), Mick Abrahams (*b* 1943) (guitar), and Clive Bunker (*b* 1946) (drums), and named after a 17th-century agriculturalist. Their eccentric stage presence and fancy dress, and Anderson's highly individual singing and flute-playing, gave them a standing as 'art-rock' exponents and they were pioneers in video presentation, concept albums, and ambitious products like the rock opera *Aqualung* (1971) which was immensely successful in the USA. This was followed by *Thick as a Brick* (1972) and *A Passion Play* (1973). These somewhat pretentious leanings proved rather too much for even their most loyal followers and the band returned to early comparative normality with *War Child* (1974). Thereafter their productions were unsettled in direction and although the group, with Ian Anderson the only survivor from the frenetic 1960s, continued through the 1980s it was resting on the laurels of past notable achievements.

Jew's harp. A primitive musical instrument more accurately, but less frequently, known as a jaw's harp. The instrument, possibly of prehistoric origin, has a simple horseshoe-shaped frame nowadays generally made of metal but formerly of wood. At the midpoint of the curve is fixed a steel tongue with its free end lying between the open ends of the curve. The player holds the ends between his teeth and twangs the steel tongue with his finger. The hollow formed by the mouth and cheeks makes a natural soundbox which can be varied to adjust the pitch and amplify the overtones. It is found all over the world in use as a folk instrument. At one time cheap mass-produced versions were sold for a few pence in every toyshop.

Jig. A vigorous rustic dance, the origin of which remains obscure: England, Ireland, and Scotland all lay claim to it. It was taken up by composers of other countries as a musical form after its appearance in English virginal and lute music in the late 16th century and became one of the regular items of the classical suite. The rhythm is usually three beats in a measure or some multiple of three.

In the late 16th and early 17th centuries the word was applied to a lively song and dance show, comic in nature, inserted in theatrical performances: a famous exponent was Richard Tarlton who died in 1588. These developed in time into something between a ballet and a ballad opera and it was suggested by Percy Scholes that some of these, taken by English artists to Europe, were the foundation of the old German style of opera, *Singspiel*, in which songs intermingled with spoken dialogue.

A further usage of the word appears in the USA where the jig song and dance appear to be early ancestors of the ragtime equivalent and possibly with jig simply an alternative form of the word rag. A certain minstrel-cum-cakewalk style of ragtime playing as performed by the St Louis pianist Tom *Turpin is specifically categorized as jig piano.

C. R. Baskerville: *The Elizabethan Jig: and Related Song Drama* (Chicago, 1929; repr. New York, 1965).

Jill Darling. Musical play with score by Vivian *Ellis, book by Marriott Edgar and Desmond Carter. It was first produced at the Alhambra Theatre, Glasgow, 24 Dec. 1933 under the title of *Jack and Jill*, but by the time it had reached London, at the Saville Theatre 19 Dec. 1934, it had been retitled. The cast included Arthur Riscoe (1896–1954), Frances *Day, Teddie St Denis (*b* 1909), and John *Mills, and the show had 242 performances. The lightly English score included 'I'm on a see-saw' which was recorded by Mills.

Jingle. Apt name now given to those insidious but fortunately brief musical interludes (usually vocal) which radio and television advertisers use to herald their wares. It became a profitable source of income to many well-known writers who generally prefer to perform the task anonymously; though there are also specialists in the field who were already earning up to £100 a week as far back as 1958. Among those who have confessed to jingleism are Steve Race and Jack Jordan (who wrote the BBC's *Have a Go* signature tune in the same spirit). Some of the pre-war jingles have now assumed an almost classical status and people fondly remember such gems as 'Hurrah for Beetox, what a delightful smell' and 'We are the Ovaltinies, little girls and boys'. Latterly there has been a tendency to replace the contrived jingle with appropriate (or inappropriate) excerpts from the works of the great composers, or the use of pop song. One jingle written for a Coca-Cola commercial, with slight modification, became the hit 'I'd like to teach the world to sing'.

Jitterbug. A freely improvised dance developed *c.*1938, during the *boogie-woogie craze of the

1930s. The tendency away from the politer ballroom dances of earlier days had come in with the *Charleston and earlier *jazz dances. Young dancers, with a few basic shuffles and twirls as foundation, copied the free-jointed black dancers in an athletic frenzy that might fairly be described as 'all-in' dancing. Somersaults, splits, and acrobatics of all kinds resulted in an exhausting but exhilarating art-form that has since sobered down a little under the re-introduced original name, *jive. It became very much a part of the *swing era scene, widely popularized in an exciting scene in the Marx Brothers film *A Day at the Races* (1937), although for a time it was not allowed in many dance-halls. It was reluctantly accepted, as the waltz and the tango had been before it, and was soon being carefully indulged in by elderly couples. The craze was given a great boost in Britain by the influx of US servicemen during the war. Among black dancers the most energetic form was known as the *Lindy or Lindy-hop. The name is derived, as is common in jazz-related terms, from a word denoting sexual stimulation.

Jive. A word used, before its almost synonymous use quoted above in relation to *jitterbug, to imply deception, fooling, kidding, as used in the Louis *Armstrong title of 1928—'Don't jive me' or the phrase 'Don't give me that jive'. In the *swing era *c.*1935–6 it became another name for jazz and hence a verb meaning to dance to that music, essentially in the *Lindy or jitterbug style. It has also become one of the many slang names for marijuana. After the excesses of the jitterbug craze, jive became the more acceptable name for the English style that was taught in established schools of dancing and is now a regular part of competition ballroom dancing; respectability was conferred on it by the high priest of strict tempo Victor *Silvester, who ran a Jive Band at one time.

Jobim, Antonio Carlos (*b* Rio de Janeiro, Brazil, 1927). South American composer, author, pianist, guitarist, and singer. He learned the piano as a child. Later he studied architecture, but his interest in Brazilian music gradually occupied his time and brought him an ever-increasing musical reputation in his own country. This became international when he and Luiz Bonfa wrote the score for the film *Orfeo Negro* (*Black Orpheus*, 1959) and songs such as 'A felicidade' and 'Desafinado' became the basis of the *bossa nova innovations in the early 1960s. The craze for this new music took him to the USA where he gave concerts and made many recordings.

His works have a haunting, evocative quality with great musical sophistication and subtle rhythms of which he, as a guitarist, is a natural master. They have proved durable beyond the initial bossa nova craze and include: 'Samba de una nota só' ('One-note samba', 1961); 'Desafinado' (song version, 1962); 'Chega de saudade' ('No more blues', 1962); 'Água de beber' ('Drinking water', 1962); 'Meditação' ('Meditation', 1963); 'Corcovado' ('Quiet nights of quiet stars', 1963–4); 'Garota de Ipanema' ('The girl from Ipanema', 1963–4); 'Insensataz' ('How insensitive', 1963–4); 'Se todos fossem iguais a você' ('Someone to light up my life', 1965); 'Por causa de você' (Don't ever go away', 1966); 'Bonita' (1967); 'Wave' (1969); 'Triste' (1970); and numerous instrumental and orchestral works. He wrote the sound-track for the film *Copacabana Palace* (1963).

Joel, Billy (*b* Hicksville, NY, 9 May 1949). American singer, pianist, and composer. He studied classical piano, but turned to the rock idiom and joined a group known as the Echoes which later became Lost Souls. He moved to a more aggressive group known as the Hassles, which recorded two tracks for United Artists, and then teamed up with drummer Jon Small as a duo under the name of Attila. With a group of his own he recorded an album, *Cold Spring Harbour* (1972), which made little impression. The next album for Columbia, *Piano Man* (1973), had a hit in the title-number and was eventually to earn a platinum award.

He moved into a succession of memorable melodies and narrative lyrics that caught the public's fancy in a big way and produced a steady string of hits such as 'Just the way you are' (1978); 'Movin' out' (1978); 'She's always a woman' (1978); 'My life' (1978); 'Big shot' (1979); 'You may be right' (1980); 'It's still rock and roll to me' (1980); 'Say goodbye to Hollywood' (1981); 'Pressure' (1982); 'Allentown' (1983); 'Tell her about it' (1983); 'Uptown girl' (1983); 'An innocent man' (1984); 'The longest time' (1984); 'Keeping the faith' (1985); and 'You're only human' (1985); with many successful albums including *The Stranger* (1977), which became Columbia's biggest-selling album in the USA. Joel had a serious motorcycle accident in 1982 which seemed to put him into a sober vein that emerged in *The Nylon Curtain* (1982). He continues to write widely appealing songs and ballads that keep their roots firmly in the rhythm 'n' blues and rock flavours of his struggling days.

P. Gambaccini: *Billy Joel: a Personal File* (New York, 1979).

John, Elton [Dwight, Reginald Kenneth] (*b* Pinner, Middx., 25 Mar. 1947). British rock singer, pianist, and composer. He began his musical career by playing the piano in the evenings at the Northwood Hills Hotel, then spent four years as organist with Bluesology, a soul backing group which worked with various visiting stars including Long John Baldry in 1967. John wrote their 'Come back, baby' in 1965. He left to join up with lyric-writer Bernie Taupin (*b* 1950), but they had little success with their songs until some acclaim in the USA helped their albums *Elton John* and *Tumbleweed Connection* to become best-sellers there in 1970. An album of a radio show, *Friends*, and *Madman Across the Water* in 1971 found him with four items in the Top 20 in America while still relatively unaccepted in Britain. Eventually his showmanship and his emotive style won through and by 1973 he was a highly successful artist on both sides of the Atlantic with such acclaimed albums as *Don't Shoot Me, I'm Only the Piano Player* and *Goodbye Yellow Brick Road*. By 1974 he was Britain's highest-earning pop artist of all time and his albums now sold everywhere. In 1976 he had a No. 1 hit in the USA and Britain duetting with Kiki Dee on 'Don't go breaking my heart'.

An interest in football, especially the Watford club, dominated his activities in 1976. His next albums were done with lyricist Gary Osbourne. He was the first British rock star, in 1979, to perform in Moscow, a visit that was documented in the film *From Elton with Love*. Otherwise a period of relative quiet was broken when he re-united with Bernie Taupin in 1980 and returned to the hit parade with 'Blue eyes', 'I guess that's why they call it the blues', and 'I'm still standing'; Watford also did well. Problems with his throat forced a retirement from singing in 1987. One of the most successful rock entertainers that Britain has produced, he remains difficult to categorize as he has adjusted his style so often. His pre-eminence is probably due to the fact that his talents as a writer and singer are enhanced by the somewhat old-fashioned merit of being a professional and larger-than-life entertainer.

P. Gambaccini: *A Conversation with Elton John and Bernie Taupin* (New York, 1975). G. Newman: *Elton John* (London, 1976). G. Shaw: *Elton John: a Biography in Words and Pictures* (New York, 1976). D. Tatham and T. Jasper: *Elton John* (London, 1976). B. Taupin: *Elton: It's a Little Bit Funny* (London, 1977).

Johnson, Buddy [Woodrow Wilson] (*b* Darlington, SC, 10 Jan. 1915; *d* New York, 9 Feb. 1977). American bandleader, pianist, singer, composer, and arranger. He toured Europe with the *Cotton Club Revue in the late 1930s. He then settled in New York in 1938 working with small groups that often featured his sister Ella Johnson (*b* 1923) as vocalist. A gifted pianist and arranger, he started recording for Decca and had a hit in 1939 with 'Stop pretending'. He formed a big band in 1944 which was immensely popular at the *Savoy Ballroom in Harlem and in the Southern states of the USA, where his powerful ensemble style and pounding beat particularly pleased the black dancing clientele.

He achieved top hits with 'They all say I'm the biggest fool' (1946); 'Because' (1950); and, with his sister as singer, 'Since I fell for you' (1948); 'I'm just your fool' (1954); 'Upside your head' (1955); and 'I don't want nobody' (1956). Arthur Prysock, a fine but greatly underrated jazz vocalist, also sang with the band 1944–52; and Johnson shared the arranging with Slide Hampton (*b* 1932) 1955–6. In the late 1950s he was equally effective in the rhythm 'n' blues field. By 1960 he had left music professionally and become a minister with his own parish in the Bronx, but still played occasionally with a small band.

Johnson, Bunk [William Geary] (*b* New Orleans, 27 Dec. 1889; *d* New Iberia, La., 7 July 1949). American jazz trumpeter. He began playing the cornet as a child and in the early 1900s played with early New Orleans bands including that led by Buddy *Bolden. He worked with minstrel troupes and on transatlantic liners, before settling down in New Orleans in 1910 to play in bands led by Frank Duson (1881–1936), Billy Marrero (1874–1935), and in cabaret. In 1915 he left New Orleans to tour with minstrel shows and circuses and continued to move around the Southern states, playing with many bands until around 1933 when he had to stop playing because of dental problems. He came back into the news in 1939, when he was interviewed by William Russell and Frederick Ramsey for their book *Jazzmen* (1940), for which he provided much misleading information—including the date of his birth, which he pushed back ten years. He taught music 1940–1 and, with new teeth, made some recordings in 1942, and returned to jazz to become a guru of the New Orleans revival, making the celebrated Decca and Victor recordings with George *Lewis and Jim Robinson (1892–1976) in 1945, which did much to awaken an interest in authentic jazz sounds. He worked at the Stuyvesant Casino in New York in 1946, in and around Chicago in 1947, and with New York Town Hall concerts in the autumn of that year. He made some final recordings in December before suffering a stroke and spending the rest of his life as an invalid.

Johnson, Charles L[eslie] (*b* Kansas City, 3 Dec. 1876; *d* Kansas City, 28 Dec. 1950). American composer and pianist. He worked as a pianist in Kansas City orchestras, hotels, and theatres for some 20 years. He had his own music-publishing business for a time but sold it to become staff composer and arranger for a larger concern. One of the leading white pioneers of ragtime, he wrote hundreds of pieces under several pseudonyms and was still composing and arranging in his seventies. His biggest song hit was 'Sweet and low' (1919) and he also wrote 'It takes a coon to do the ragtime dance' (1899); 'Iola' (1906); and 'I'm going, goodbye, I'm gone' (1912). His rags included: 'Scandalous Thompson' (1899); 'Doc Brown's cakewalk' (1899); 'A black smoke' (1902); 'Dill pickles rag' (1906); 'Fine and dandy' (1907); 'Porcupine rag' (1909); 'Apple jack' (1909); 'Tar babies (1911); 'Swanee rag' (1912); 'Snookums' (1918); and many written under the name of Raymond Birch.

Johnson, Charlie (*b* Philadelphia, 21 Nov. 1891; *d* New York, 13 Dec. 1959). American bandleader and pianist. He began as a trombonist in New York but, on moving to Atlantic City in 1918 to lead a band there, changed to piano. Bringing his band to Small's Paradise Club in Harlem, he was resident there from 1925 to the mid-1930s. He toured with the band until it broke up in 1938, after which he played with various groups until having to retire through ill-health in the 1950s. His band at its peak had a style similar to the Fletcher *Henderson orchestra and included such players as Jabbo Smith (*b* 1908), Sidney De Paris (1905–67), Jimmy Harrison (1900–31), Edgar *Sampson, Benny *Carter, Dicky *Wells, Roy *Eldridge, and Frankie Newton (1906–54).

Johnson, Dink [Oliver] (*b* Biloxi, Miss., 28 Oct. 1892; *d* Portland, Oreg., 29 Nov. 1954). American pianist, drummer, and clarinettist. He first worked as a drummer and was with the Original Creole Orchestra before the First World War. He moved to Los Angeles where he led his own Louisiana Six, then played, as a drummer, with his brother-in-law Jelly Roll *Morton. By 1920, when he joined Kid *Ory and played on his pioneering 1922 recording sessions, he had changed to clarinet. He worked in Los Angeles 1923 and in Chicago 1924, returned to California, and was now mainly active as a pianist. In the 1940s he retired from music to run a restaurant in Los Angeles, but still played occasionally and recorded some tracks in 1945 and 1947 for Bill Russell's American Music label. These remarkably atmospheric recordings, with Johnson singing and playing in an entirely relaxed and informal way, give a finer sense of the old *jig piano style of bygone days than almost anything put on record.

Johnson, James P[rice] (*b* New Brunswick, NJ, 1 Feb. 1894; *d* New York, 17 Nov. 1955). American composer and pianist. Pioneer of the Harlem style of jazz piano playing, teacher of Fats *Waller, and a model for many pianists of the 1920s and 1930s including Duke *Ellington. His own style was based on the playing of Luckey *Roberts. He became well-known outside jazz as a stage and screen entertainer and worked as accompanist for many famous singers such as Bessie *Smith, Trixie Smith (1895–1943), Mamie *Smith, and Ethel *Waters. He also performed as a concert pianist and was musical director for Dudley's *Black Sensations* and *Smart Set* revues. He went to England with the *Plantation Days* revue in 1923, then led his own band in New York in the 1920s and 1930s.

Johnson became renowned as the composer of the revue *Runnin' Wild* (1923) in which the comedians Miller and Lyles started his *'Charleston' off on its popular conquest of America and Europe. He followed this with an extended choral and orchestral piece 'Yamecraw' (1928); worked with Fats Waller in *Keep Shufflin'* (1928); was musical director for the Bessie Smith film *St Louis Blues* (1929); wrote further stage shows: *Messin' 'Round* (1929); *Change Your Luck* (1930); *Sugar Hill* (1931); and composed 'Symphony in Harlem' (1932). His songs included 'Stop it, Joe' (1917); 'If I could be with you one hour tonight' (1926); 'Slippery hips' (1926); and 'Ain'tcha got music' (1932); and his piano works included 'Caprice rag' (1914); 'Daintiness rag' (1916); 'Mama and papa blues' (1916); 'Harlem strut' (1917); 'After hours' (1923); 'Carolina shout' (1925); 'Keep off the grass' (1926); 'Snowy morning blues' (1927); 'You've got to be modernistic' (1930); 'Riffs' (1930); and 'Over the bars' (1936).

Johnson, James Weldon (*b* Jacksonville, Fla., 17 June 1871; *d* Wiscasset, Maine, 26 June 1938). American author and educationalist. Educated at Atlanta University, he became principal of Stanton School and editor of the *Daily American*, the first black daily paper in the USA. He studied law and was admitted to the Bar in Florida, and was appointed US Consul in several countries. A poem written for school use in 1900 in honour of Abraham Lincoln, 'Lift every voice and sing', was set to music by his brother J. Rosamond *Johnson and became known as 'the Negro National Anthem'.

The brothers continued to collaborate on songs, many of which were used in revues, and in 1902 formed a song-writing team with Bob Cole (1863–1911) to produce such hits as 'Under the bamboo tree' (1902); 'Congo love song' (1903); and (under the name of Will Handy) 'Oh, didn't he ramble' (1902). These and other songs earned them the title of 'the Ebony Offenbachs'. While Johnson was consul in Venezuela in 1906 and later in Nicaragua, he wrote *The Autobiography of an Ex-Colored Man* (Boston, 1912), a vivid portrait of musical life in New York in the early 1900s. He also edited *The Book of American Negro Spirituals* (New York, 1926; repr. 1977) and *The Second Book of Negro Spirituals* (New York, 1927) in collaboration with his brother, and wrote *Black Manhattan* (1930; repr. 1968), giving further insight into black musical activities. The James Weldon Johnson Memorial Collection of Negro Arts and Letters is held in the Beinecke Rare Books and Manuscripts Library at Yale University.

J. W. Johnson: *Along This Way: the Autobiography of James Weldon Johnson* (New York, 1931; repr. 1968).

Johnson, J[ames] **C.** (*b* Chicago, 14 Sept. 1896; *d* New York, 27 Feb. 1981). American composer and lyric-writer. He studied music in Chicago and for many years was a pianist and bandleader. He gave up performing to write for nightclub revues and musical shows, including *Change Your Luck* (1930); *Runnin' the Town* (1940); *A la Carte* (1948); and *The Jazz Train* (1955). His songs included: 'You can't do what my last man did' (1923); 'Dusky stevedore' (1928); 'Louisiana' (1928); 'Empty bed blues' (1928); 'Take your tomorrow (and give me today)' (1928); 'Jet black blues' (1929); 'My baby sure knows how to love' (1929); 'Believe it, beloved' (1933); 'Rhythm and romance' (1935), 'The joint is jumpin'' (with Fats *Waller, 1937); 'The spider and the fly' (with Waller, 1938); and 'I'm stepping out with Lulu' (1948).

Johnson, J. J. [James Louis] (*b* Indianapolis, 22 Jan. 1924). American jazz trombonist and composer. He took up the trombone under the influence of Jack *Teagarden and Tommy *Dorsey at the age of 14 and joined the Benny *Carter band in 1942. He was with Count *Basie 1945–7 and Illinois *Jacquet 1947–9; later with Woody *Herman and Dizzy *Gillespie. He left jazz for three years, returning to work with the Danish trombonist Kai Winding (1922–83) in an effective duo 1954–6 which made many recordings; after which he formed his own quintet and toured Europe. He was an influential figure in the modern jazz scene of the 1950s.

Johnson, J[ohn] **Rosamond** (*b* Jacksonville, Fla., 11 Aug. 1873: *d* New York, 11 Nov. 1954). American composer and singer. Brother of James Weldon *Johnson, he studied at Atlanta University and the New England Conservatory of Music. After writing 'Lift every voice and sing' (which became known as the black national anthem) with his brother, they joined up with Bob Cole (1863–1911) and the partnership wrote many songs that became popular in vaudeville and musicals. Their most successful song was 'Under the bamboo tree', the melody of which is an inversion of the Negro spiritual 'Nobody knows the trouble I've seen'. They composed it one night while walking through the streets of New York and immediately realized they had a hit, though Johnson was reluctant to exploit a tune thus contrived. The song was shown to Marie *Cahill, who was so taken with it that she insisted on putting it in the musical *Sally in Our Alley* (1902) where it became the hit of the show.

Johnson was musical director of Hammerstein's Opera House in London 1912–13. He toured the USA and Europe with programmes of Negro spirituals and compiled two volumes of spirituals with his brother in 1926 and 1927, as well as writing *Rolling Along in Song* (New York, 1937), a history of black music with 85 songs. He appeared in the early productions of Gershwin's **Porgy and Bess* and wrote the scores of *The Belle of Bridgeport* (1900); *In Newport* (1904); *Humpty Dumpty* (1904); *The Shoo-Fly Regiment* (1907); *The Red Moon* (1909); *Mr Lode of Koal* (1909); and *Hello Paris* (1911). His songs included: 'I hope these few lines will find you well' (1897); 'I must have been a-dreaming' (1900); 'My castle on the Nile' (1901); 'Tell me, dusky maiden' (1901); 'The old flag never touched the ground' (1902); 'Oh, didn't he ramble' (1902); 'Under the bamboo tree' (1902); 'Big Indian chief' (1903); 'Maid of Timbuctoo' (1903); 'Congo love song' (1903); 'Mandy, won't you let me be your beau' (1903); 'Moonlight on the Mississippi' (1904); 'Hottentot love song' (1905); 'I'll keep a warm spot in my heart for you' (1906); 'Since you went away' (1913); 'Three questions' (1917); 'An old banjo' (1934); 'Dry bones' (1938); 'Song of the heart' (1945); and many more, some written under the joint name of Will Handy. The J. Rosamond Johnson Archive is now in the Yale University Library.

Johnson, Laurie (*b* Hampstead, London, 7 Feb. 1927). British composer. Writer of film scores including *Frenchman's Creek* (1954); *Rue de la Paix* (1956); *Tiger Bay* (1959); *I Aim at the Stars* (1960); *Dr Strangelove* (1963); *The Beauty Jungle* (1964); *First Men in the Moon* (1964); *Hot Millions* (1968); *The Belstone Fox* (1973); and of music for TV productions including *The Avengers*, *Jason King*, *Shirley's World*, *The Adventurer*, *Thriller*, and many theme tunes. For the theatre he wrote for the revue *Pieces of Eight* (1959) and scores for *Little Old King Cole* (1961); **Lock Up Your Daughters* (1962); and *The Four Musketeers* (1967); also orchestral and military band pieces, and many songs.

Johnson, Pete (*b* Kansas City, 24 Mar. 1904; *d* Buffalo, NY, 23 Mar. 1967). American pianist. Early in his career he was a drummer in Kansas City, but, turning to the piano, worked there in nightclubs 1926–38, usually as a soloist but sometimes with blues-shouter Joe *Turner. They were both in the famous 'Spirituals to Swing' concert in Carnegie Hall in 1938 and frequently recorded together. He appeared with Benny *Goodman while working at Café Society in New York. He helped to foster the 1930s *boogie-woogie craze with his duet performances and recordings with Albert *Ammons and trios with Meade Lux *Lewis added. He worked with both during the 1940s, and later was in California. In 1958 he went to Europe with Jazz at the Philharmonic and Joe Turner. Illness in 1958 limited his subsequent activities. He wrote much of his own material, including 'Roll 'em Pete' and 'Death ray boogie'.

H. J. Maurerer: *The Pete Johnson Story* (Bremen, 1965).

Johnson, Robert (*b* Hazlehurst, Miss., 8 May 1911; *d* Greenwood, Miss., 16 Aug. 1938). American blues singer. Despite his early death and a recording tally of only some 29 songs, 16 recorded in San Antonio in 1936 and 13 in Dallas in 1937, he has become one of the most important of all pre-war blues artists, certainly in terms of his effect on the rhythm 'n' blues movement of the 1960s. The atmosphere of his recordings was tortured and oppressive, his light but intense and haunting singing complemented by his piercing bottleneck Delta guitar style. His songs included: 'I was standing at the crossroads', 'Love in vain', 'Walking blues', 'Hellbound on my trail', 'From four till late', 'Dust my blues', 'Rambling on my mind', 'Got no place to go', 'Come on, baby, take a walk with me'—many of them taken up and recorded by such artists as Eric *Clapton, the *Rolling Stones, *Cream, and John *Mayall in the 1960s. Very little is known about the background and life of the man hailed as 'King of the Delta Blues Singers', but he is said to have died as the result of being poisoned by his girlfriend.

B. Groom: *Robert Johnson* (London, 1969). S. Charters: *Robert Johnson* (New York, 1973).

Music: *Robert Johnson: King of the Delta Blues* [29 blues] (London, 1969).

Johnston, Arthur James (*b* New York, 10 Jan. 1898; *d* Corona del Mar, Calif., 1 May 1954). American composer, pianist, organist, and arranger. At 15 he was playing piano in silent cinemas and organ in the local church; and at 17 he became a vocal arranger in a New York publishing house. He was personal pianist and amanuensis to Irving *Berlin and the musical director of most of his early stage productions. In 1929 he went to Hollywood, scoring and composing for films, one of the first being *Chaplin's *City Lights* in 1931. He made four trips to England to write for revues and films, and wrote the score of *Dixie to Broadway* (1924), which included 'Mandy, make up your mind' and 'I'm a little blackbird looking for a bluebird'. In 1931 he wrote 'Just one more chance' which was used in the film *College Coach* (1932).

His other film scores included: *College Humour* (1933), one of many with Bing Crosby—'Learn to croon', 'Down the old Ox Road', 'Moonstruck'; *Her Bodyguard* (1933); *Too Much Harmony* (1933)—'Thanks'; *The Way to Love* (1933); *Hello Everybody* (1933)—'Twenty million people'; *Murder at the Vanities* (1934), with the Duke *Ellington Orchestra—'Cocktails for two', 'Live and love tonight'; *Belle of the Nineties* (1934)—'My old flame'; *Many Happy Returns* (1934); *Thanks a Million* (1935)—'Thanks a million', 'Sitting high on a hilltop', 'Sing, brother, sing'; *The Girl Friend* (1935); *The Gilded Lily* (1935); *Go West Young Man* (1936); *Pennies From Heaven* (1936)—'One, two, button your shoe', 'Pennies from Heaven', 'So do I'; *Double or Nothing* (1937)—'It's the natural thing to do', 'All you want to do is dance'; *Sailing Along* (1938); and *Song of the South* (1947)—'Song of the South'.

Jolson, Al [Yoelson, Asa] (*b* Srednik, Russia, 26 May 1886; *d* San Francisco, 23 Oct. 1950). American singer, actor, composer, and author. He was brought to the USA by his parents in 1893. His father was a cantor and Asa was intended to follow him into the synagogue, but he became enraptured by the vaudeville stage. After appearing as an extra in Israel Zangwill's play *Children of the Ghetto* in 1899, he changed his name to Al Jolson and toured with various stage shows before joining Lew *Dockstader's Minstrels. Realizing his future was as a solo performer, he branched out on his own and made his Broadway debut in *Vera Violetta* in 1911.

His stage reputation grew along with his many recordings of minstrel-style songs and in 1923 he started to make a silent film, *Mammy's Boy*, for D. W. Griffith. Seeing no point in a singer appearing in a silent film, he refused to finish it and was then persuaded by Lee De Forest to star in an early sound short. The sound technique was satisfactory and taken on by Warner Brothers who featured Jolson in a sequel, *April Showers*, in 1926. Feeling that the time was ripe to apply sound techniques to a feature film, Warners made screen history with Jolson the first to talk and sing in a full-length film—*The *Jazz Singer*. In 1928 he had his first big record hit with 'Sonny boy'/'There's a rainbow round my shoulder' (which was to sell more than 3 million copies). But Warners over-capitalized on Jolson and his stage reputation by bringing out a series of Jolson vehicles tailored to a formula of which audiences eventually grew tired. His reputation as a star declined, only reviving when Columbia Pictures produced *The Jolson Story* (1946), with Jolson dubbing the songs to the miming of actor Larry Parks. Once more a big record and radio star, his story was brought up to date in the sequel *Jolson Sings Again* (1949), also with Larry Parks. He had just returned from entertaining US troops abroad when he died.

In the light of later singing styles and performers, Jolson may seem corny and old-fashioned. His act was pure ham, but it was still such a genuine part of his strong personality and overpowering ego that he always managed to convey a real sense of enjoyment and even sincerity to his audience. As George Burns said: 'If you can fake *that*, you're made.' His pseudo-black 'Mammy' diction and phrasing did not completely obscure a basically good voice which gained in warmth and quality over the years. He had a hand in many of the songs he made famous, being lyricist or co-writer of such hits as 'Avalon' (1920); 'Yoo-hoo' (1921); 'Old-fashioned girl' (1922); 'Dirty hands, dirty face' (1923); 'California, here I come' (1924); 'Keep smiling at trouble' (1924); 'Me and my shadow' (1927); 'Back in your own backyard' (1928); 'There's a rainbow round my shoulder' (1928); 'Sonny boy' (1928); 'Evangeline' (1929); and 'Anniversary song' (1947); mostly written in collaboration with Vincent *Rose, B. G. *DeSylva, James V. *Monaco, and Billy *Rose.

Nowadays Jolson's film career often seems to overshadow his stage achievement. He was a great star on Broadway almost from the start. It was there that he introduced most of his best-known songs, a regular tenant of the *Winter Garden Theatre, where he had a runway down into the audience for closer contact. Everyone who saw and heard him described him as a magnetic performer.

His shows included: *La Belle Paree* (1911); *Vera Violetta* (1911); *The Whirl of Society* (1912); *Honeymoon Express* (1913); *Robinson Crusoe Jr.* (1916); *Sinbad* (1918); *Bombo* (1921)—'April showers'; *Wonder Bar* (1924); *Big Boy* (1925); and *Hold On to Your Hats* (1940); and his films: *The Jazz Singer* (1927); *The Singing Fool* (1928); *Say it With Songs* (1929); *Sonny Boy* (1929); *Mammy* (1930); *Big Boy* (1930); *Hallelujah, I'm a Bum* (1933); *Wonder Bar* (1934); *Go into Your Dance* (1935); *The Singing Kid* (1936); *Swanee River* (1939); *Rose of Washington Square* (1939); and *Rhapsody in Blue* (1945).

P. Sieben: *The Immortal Jolson: his Life and Times* (New York, 1962). M. Freedland: *Al Jolson* (New York–London, 1972; rev. 1984). B. Anderton: *Sonny Boy* (London, 1975). R. Oberfirst: *You Ain't Heard Nothin' Yet: Al Jolson* (San Diego, 1980; rev. 1984). L. F. Kiner: *The Al Jolson Discography* (Westport, Conn., 1983). H. G. Goldman: *Jolson* (New York, Oxford, 1990)

Jonas, Emile (*b* Paris, 5 Mar. 1827; *d* Saint-Germain-en-Laye, 22 May 1905). French composer. He studied at the Paris Conservatoire and subsequently taught singing there 1847–66 and military band harmony 1859–70. Among later posts he held was that of bandmaster of the Garde Nationale and director of music at the Portuguese Synagogue in Paris, for which he edited and published *Recueil de chants hébraïques* in 1854. In 1867 he organized the military bands at the Paris Exhibition. His first operetta, *Le Duel de Benjamin*, was produced at the *Bouffes-Parisiens in 1855 and his later works included *La Parade* (1856); *Le Roi boit* (1857); *Les Petits Prodiges* (1857); *Job et son chien* (1863); *Le Manoir de la Renardière* (1864); *Avant la noce* (1865); *Les Deux Arlequins* (1865; London, 1868, as *The Two Harlequins*)—his best-known work; *Le Canard à trois becs* (1869); *Désiré, sire de Champigny* (1869); *Cinderella the Younger* (London, 1871; Paris, 1871 as *Javotte*); *Japanesin* (Vienna, 1874); *Die Goldchignon* (Vienna, 1874); and others.

Jones, Allan (*b* Old Forge, Pa., 14 Oct. 1908; *d* New York, 27 June 1992). American singer. After singing in touring operettas and other shows, he achieved a minor Broadway role in **Roberta* (1933). This led to a larger part in **Bitter Sweet* (1934), but he became known mainly through his film appearances in the Marx Brothers' *A Night at the Opera* (1935)—'Alone', Cosi-cosa'; then in **Rose Marie* (1936); **Show Boat* (1936); and *A Day at the Races* (1937); before starring with Jeanette *MacDonald in *The Firefly* (1937) in which he sang 'Donkey serenade'. Other prominent roles were in *The Great Victor Herbert* (1939); and *The *Boys from Syracuse* (1940). He continued in films until *Stage to Thunder Rock* in 1964 and was in a Broadway musical, *Jackpot*, in 1944. He was less prominent in the 1950s but continued to work in clubs, radio, and TV. His son Jack Jones (*b* 1938) had a successful career in the 1960s, singing in the Frank *Sinatra style.

Jones, Isham (*b* Coalton, Ohio, 31 Jan. 1894; *d* Florida, 19 Oct. 1956). American composer, bandleader, pianist, and saxophonist. He was leading his own band in Saginaw and Bay City by the time he was 19, then went to Chicago to study the saxophone in 1921. He led small groups in Chicago and on the Streckfus Line steamers, and later led big bands at the Green Mill, the Rainbow Gardens, and the Sherman Hotel. He had a big hit in 1921 with his recording of 'Wabash blues'. His reputation grew and he took the band to New York and, in 1924, to London. By the early 1930s his orchestra was rated as the best 'sweet music' outfit in America, his sound given distinction by the arrangements of Gordon *Jenkins and Joe Bishop.

During his bandleading days he became one of the most prolific songwriters of the 1920s and 1930s writing (with Gus *Kahn) 'Broken-hearted melody' (1922); 'On the Alamo' (1922); 'Swinging down the lane' (1923); 'I'll see you in my dreams' (1924); 'It had to be you' (1924); 'The one I love (belongs to somebody else)' (1924); 'Spain' (1925); and many more with other lyricists including his theme song 'You're just a dream come true' (1931); 'I'll never have to dream again' (1932); 'You've got me crying again' (1933); and 'No greater love' (1936). He gave up active bandleading in 1936 and retired to a ranch in Colorado, his band being carried on, on a co-operative basis, by Woody *Herman who was his saxophonist and vocalist. He emerged briefly some years later to lead another band but soon went back to his ranch.

Jones, Jo [Jonathan] (*b* Chicago, 7 Oct. 1911; *d* New York, 3 Sept. 1985). American jazz drummer. He worked with Walter Page (1900–57) in Oklahoma in the late 1920s and was with Tommy Douglas in Kansas City in 1933 where he met Count *Basie whose orchestra he joined in 1935. He was briefly with Page again in 1936, but when the Basie band became resident at the Reno Club in Kansas City he, along with bassist Page and guitarist Freddie Green (1911–87), rejoined it to form one of the outstanding rhythm sections in jazz history. With a brief break for army service he was to remain with Basie until 1948. He was one of the swing era drummers who brought the high-hat cymbal into leading play, creating a light but intensely swinging four-beat rhythm that was widely copied. He was not inclined to virtuoso displays but was much admired for his subtly varied work behind the ensemble. After leaving Basie, he played with Lester *Young, Ella *Fitzgerald (with whom he went to Europe in 1957); and was with Oscar *Peterson in the 1950s and with Teddy *Wilson and Claude *Hopkins in the 1960s, as well as leading his own groups and touring with Jazz at the Philharmonic. He appeared in the films *Jamming the Blues* (1944); *Born to Swing* (1973); and *Last of the Blue Devils* (1979).

Jones, Leslie Julian (*b* London, 9 May 1910). British composer and librettist. Son of the conductor Julian Jones (1873–1930), he was educated in Kingston and Margate before working as a stockbroker from 1929 to 1937. He then turned to music and became a prolific writer for revues. He was staff producer and writer for ENSA in the Middle East from 1943 and went into theatrical management in 1945.

He contributed to: *Friends, Romans* (1937); *Les Folies de Paris et Londres* (1937); *Copyright Reserved* (1937); *Come Out of Your Shell* (1940); *Rise Above It* (1941); *Whitehall Follies* (1942); *It's About Time* (1942); **Sweet and Low* (1943); *This Time It's Love* (1943); *That'll Be the Day* (1945); *Better Late* (1946); and *Pardon My French* (1953).

Jones, Philly Joe [Joseph Rudolph] (*b* Philadelphia, 15 July 1923; *d* Philadelphia, 30 Aug. 1985). American jazz drummer. He played with Ben *Webster in Washington in 1949, then went to New York and worked with Tony Scott, Zoot *Sims, Lee Konitz, and Tadd *Dameron. He took the name 'Philly (Philadelphia) Joe' to avoid confusion with Jo *Jones. His most fruitful and influential years were with the Miles *Davis Quintet 1952–3 and 1962, where he became a leading exponent of modern jazz percussion styling: his dynamic drumming was soon clearly recognized and widely imitated. He was with Gil *Evans in 1959, formed his own touring group 1959–62, and was with Bill *Evans in 1967. He went to London in 1967,working and teaching there, and was in Paris from 1969, returning to Philadelphia in 1972 where he formed a jazz-rock group based on his contacts with the British rock scene.

Jones, Quincy Delight (*b* Chicago, 14 Mar. 1933). American pianist, trumpeter, bandleader, and composer. He studied trumpet in Seattle and Boston and was with the Lionel *Hampton band 1951–3, with which he toured Europe. He became a freelance arranger, including work for Ray *Anthony, broken by a spell with the Dizzy *Gillespie big band in 1958. In 1957–8 he was in France and Scandinavia, working for Barclay Records. He formed his own big band in 1959, wrote and arranged for Count *Basie and recorded with backing groups to such singers as Sarah *Vaughan, Dinah *Washington, and Billy *Eckstine. He became an executive with Mercury Records, recording his own albums. Since the mid-1970s he has run Qwest Productions, his activities including making albums with Michael *Jackson (a key figure in creating the Jackson image and success) and with Frank *Sinatra.

He has written scores for more than 60 films including *Mirage* (1965); *The Pawnbroker* (1965); *The Slender Thread* (1965); *Walk, Don't Run* (1966); *The Deadly Affair* (1967); *Enter Laughing* (1967); *In Cold Blood* (1967); *In the Heat of the Night* (1967); *For Love of Ivy* (1968); *The Italian Job* (1969); *The Lost Man* (1969); *McKenna's Gold* (1969); *The Getaway* (1971); and *Come Back Charleston Blues* (1972). His bright and original jazz scores have been recorded by many major jazz musicians.

R. Horricks: *Quincy Jones* (Tunbridge Wells, 1985).

Jones, Richard M[yknee] (*b* Donaldsville, La., 13 June 1889; *d* Chicago, 8 Dec. 1945). American pianist and composer. An influential figure in the early development of jazz, he played in New Orleans in his teens and joined the Clarence *Williams publishing firm in 1919. In the 1920s he worked as a record producer for Okeh, producing many *race records of importance. Later he worked for Decca and was the producer of the historical King *Oliver sessions with Okeh and Columbia. He was a considerable pianist himself and recorded many sides from 1923 on, often as an accompanist to blues singers. His compositions included: 'Southern stomps' (1923); 'Jazzin' babies blues' (1924); 'Riverside blues' (1925); 'Trouble in mind' (1926); 'Heebie jeebies' (1926); 'Red wagon' (1939); and '29th and Dearborn' (1942). In the 1940s he was working with Mercury Records.

Jones, Sidney (*b* London, 17 June 1861; *d* Kew, 29 Jan. 1946). British composer. Eldest son of the well-known conductor and dance composer J. Sidney Jones (1838–1906), he was born while his father was bandmaster of the 5th Dragoon Guards and later started his own career as conductor of the same band. He played in the orchestras at the Grand Theatre, Leeds, and at Harrogate Spa under his father. He toured England and Australia as conductor of light opera companies, and in 1905 was appointed musical director at the *Empire Theatre in London. His ambition to become a composer was first realized when a song of his, 'Linger longer, Loo', was interpolated into the score of *Don Juan* at the Gaiety Theatre in 1892, where it was sung to popular acclaim by Millie Hylton and became a best-seller.

This started a highly successful career as a theatre composer providing the scores for many of the long-running musical comedies of the 1890s and after, staged in both London and the USA, including: *A *Gaiety Girl* (1893); *An *Artist's Model* (1895); his greatest triumph of all—*The *Geisha* (1896); *A Greek Slave* (1898); **San Toy* (1899); *My Lady Molly* (1903); *The Medal and the Maid* (1903); *The Bugle Call* (1905); *See-See* (1906); *The King of Cadonia* (1908); *The Persian Princess* (1909); *The Mousmé* (1911); and *The *Girl from Utah* (1913). Jones had a light and lively style with a capacity for memorable melodies that made his scores worthy successors to the *Gilbert and Sullivan tradition. He also composed a number of songs and ballads.

Jones, Spike [Lindley Murray] (*b* Long Beach, Calif., 14 Dec. 1911; *d* Los Angeles, 1 May 1965). American bandleader. He entered the band world in his high-school days, working on radio, before becoming a drummer on the West Coast. He then played in studio bands for radio shows featuring Burns and Allen, Al *Jolson, Bing *Crosby, and others. In the early 1940s he began to toy with the idea of sending up popular songs with lunatic arrangements using odd effects such as pistols, cowbells, saws, whistles, anvils, breaking glass, and even a bleating goat. Soon to be known as the 'King of Corn', Jones, with the band he called his City Slickers, was signed up by RCA and hit the jackpot right away with his 1942 recording of Jones's composition 'Der Fuehrer's face'.

The band quickly became popular on radio and they continued their recording successes with 'Cocktails for two', 'Chlo-e', 'Holiday for strings', 'You always hurt the one you love', 'The glow-worm', 'Hawaiian war chant', 'That old black magic', and many more employing a hectic, hard-driven, and goonish sense of the ridiculous. Amongst the vocalists were Red Ingle, later to branch out along the same lines on his own, and, from 1947, Jones's wife Helen Grayco. Their art was ideally extended to TV in the 1950s and lasted until the novelty of their humour wore off. They were featured in the films *Thank Your Lucky Stars* (1943); *Meet the People* (1944); *Bring on the Girls* (1945); *Breakfast in Hollywood* (1946); *Variety Girl* (1947); and *Fireman, Save My Child* (1954). The Spike Jones recordings have now become something of a cult.

Jones, Thad [Thaddeus Joseph] (*b* Pontiac, Mich., 28 Mar. 1923; *d* Copenhagen, 20 Aug. 1986).

American jazz trumpeter, bandleader, and composer. He took up the trumpet in his teens and played in Detroit, as did his pianist brother Hank Jones (*b* 1918) and drummer brother Elvin Jones (*b* 1927). After army service he went to New York and was taken up by Charles *Mingus and his Jazz Workshop band. He proved himself a trumpeter capable of handling the advanced ideas of Thelonious *Monk and made some fine recordings with him. After coming to full prominence as a trumpeter with the Count *Basie band 1954–63, he became a freelance arranger and 1965–78 was co-leader of the Thad Jones–Mel Lewis (1929–90) orchestra. He went to Denmark in 1978 to write for radio and to run his own jazz orchestra under the name of Eclipse.

Jones, Tom [Woodward, Thomas Jones] (*b* Pontypridd, S. Wales, 7 June 1940). British singer. A natural performer in the Welsh tradition, he started his musical life as a drummer in pickup bands. His vocal efforts were heard in 1963 by the songwriter Gordon Mills, who saw the star quality there, changed the name to Tom Jones, and started to promote the powerful voice and masculine image by getting him a recording contract. Mills and Les Reed provided the song 'It's not unusual', which went to No. 1 within two weeks and eventually sold three million copies. Vocally and visually appealing to a post-teenage audience, he continued to make hits of such emotional material as 'The green, green grass of home' (1966). He maintained the superstar saga by settling in California and finding his ideal outlet in glittery places like Las Vegas.

P. Jones: *Tom Jones: Biography of a Great Star* (London, 1970). S. Hildred: *Tom Jones* (London, 1990).

Joplin, Janis Lyn (*b* Port Arthur, Texas, 19 Jan. 1943; *d* Hollywood, 4 Oct. 1970). American singer. She started singing in clubs and bars in Austin and Los Angeles and in 1966 was singing with Big Brother and the Holding Company in San Francisco. She soon became known for her bluesy, searing voice and uninhibited personality, becoming a rebellious figurehead for a sympathetically rebellious audience and, with her powerful talents, a very influential performer. In a rough amalgam of rock and blues the band made the album *Cheap Thrills*, which contained such effective tracks as 'Ball and chain' and 'Piece of my heart'. She left the band in 1968 and, with a variety of backings, produced the rather more controlled recordings to be found on *Kosmic Blues* (1969) and the posthumously released *Pearl* (1971). She had been arrested for abusing the police in 1969 and her life became confused and embittered by the pressures which superstar success brought with it. An unstable nature was not able to cope and she died of a heroin overdose. A film based on her life, *The Rose* (1979), starred Bette *Midler.

D. Landau: *Janis Joplin: her Life and Times* (New York, 1971). D. Dalton (ed.): *Janis* (New York, 1972). M. Friedman: *Buried Alive: a Biography of Janis Joplin* (New York, 1973). P. Caserta: *Going Down with Janis* (Secaucus, NJ, 1975; London, 1976).

Joplin, Scott (*b* Texarkana, Texas, 24 Nov. 1868; *d* New York, 1 Apr. 1917). American composer and pianist. One of the main originators and formulators of classical *ragtime, arguably its finest composer and writer of the most famous of all rags—'Maple Leaf rag' (1899)—which was named after the Maple Leaf Club in Sedalia, Missouri, where Joplin played. His parents were both musical. His father, Giles, was a railroad worker from North Carolina who had been born a slave, obtaining his freedom some five years before Scott was born. He had played the violin in plantation bands. His mother, from Kentucky, sang and played the banjo. Two brothers were also musical: Will, a singer and guitarist, and Robert, a singer and minor composer. Joplin first took up the guitar but soon revealed a natural gift for the piano. When his mother died he defied his father's wish that he should find a steady job and left home to become a musician. He played in various orchestras and as a saloon pianist and by 1885 had arrived in St Louis where there was a flourishing school of pianists playing primitive ragtime. He led a small orchestra at the World's Fair in 1893, then settled in Sedalia where he played cornet in the Queen City Concert Band. Back in St Louis in 1895 he frequented the Rosebud Café, run by pianist and composer Tom *Turpin, and began to compose. He studied for a time at the Smith School of Music in Sedalia, organized a vocal octet which included his two younger brothers, and went on tours that took them as far as New York. Joplin wrote many of their songs. By 1898 he had written his first significant composition, 'Original rags', which was published in Kansas City in 1899. He had also written 'Maple Leaf rag' which he had been unable to sell because it was difficult to play. A Sedalia publisher, John Stark, heard Joplin perform it and was impressed enough to offer publication. This started a fruitful association for both men as 'Maple Leaf rag' became an immediate best-seller and allowed Stark to open a bigger business in St Louis. He published many of Joplin's works, but their relationship was strained by Joplin's desire to publish ambitious pieces like 'The ragtime dance' when Stark wanted the simpler pieces that would sell.

Joplin married Belle Hayden in 1899 and they settled in St Louis. By now the ragtime boom was on its way and Joplin turned out a worthy series of rags that kept Stark and other publishers supplied and happy. By 1903 he was already nursing the idea of writing a ragtime opera, but his first effort in this direction, *A Guest of Honour*, never came to fruition and the manuscript was lost. His marriage broke up in 1906. By 1908 he was in New York where he met and married Lottie Stokes and published a 'School of Ragtime', a set of six exercises to help would-be exponents of the style.

By 1911 he was more obsessed than ever with the idea of a full-scale ragtime opera and subsequently squandered much time and money in writing *Treemonisha*. He failed to find a backer for it and himself paid for a patchy run-through in a miserable hall in Harlem in 1915. The failure of this project broke his spirit. He became insane and was committed to the Manhattan State Hospital, where he died.

'Maple Leaf rag' maintained its popularity into the jazz age, but most of his rags and other pieces, after their initial popularity and influence, completely disappeared from the public eye and ear until there was a surprising revival of interest in the 1970s, sparked off by some 'as-written' performances by Joshua *Rifkin and other pianists, the publication in 1971 of his complete works by the New York Public Library, and the effective use of 'The entertainer', with other pieces, in the film *The Sting* (1973), which made it a sudden best-seller. At last it was fully realized that what writers like Rudi *Blesh had said earlier was true—that Joplin was an original American genius. A wholesale exploitation of his music naturally followed. Joplin's compositions were used as the basis of two very successful ballets and *Treemonisha* was at last staged, even eventually reaching Broadway, and recorded under the direction of Gunther *Schuller who had also done much to revive orchestral versions of Joplin from his orginal Red Book scores. The simple cause of the enthusiasm was that Joplin and ragtime in general had been rescued from the Tin Pan Alley travesties of the style, which inevitably leaned toward jangling pianos and funny hats. Though piano rolls and authentic recordings had long been available to the connoisseur, the general public was hearing ragtime sensitively and correctly played, often for the first time. They were pleasantly surprised to find that ragtime, as written by Joplin and those of like mind, was a gentle, lyrical music of great charm and ingenuity. Sixty years after his death the works of Joplin were being appreciated in the spirit in which they were written, and he was at last allowed to take his place alongside other popular American composers of merit like *Foster, *Sousa, *Kern, and *Gershwin.

In addition to the two operas, he wrote a number of rather Victorian songs and several marches and waltzes, but he is mainly remembered for his rags which notably include: 'Original rags' (1899); 'Maple Leaf rag' (1899); 'Swipesey cake-walk' (with Arthur *Marshall, 1900); Peacherine rag' (1901); 'Sunflower slow drag' (with Scott Hayden, 1901); 'The easy winners' (1901); 'Elite syncopations' (1902); 'The entertainer' (1902); 'Something doing' (1903); 'Weeping willow' (1903); 'Palm leaf rag' (1903); 'The favorite' (1904); 'The cascades' (1904); 'The ragtime dance' (1906); 'Heliotrope bouquet' (with Louis *Chauvin, 1907); 'Fig leaf rag' (1908); 'Wall Street rag' (1909); 'Solace' (1909); 'Scott Joplin's new rag' (1912); and many others.

P. Gammond: *Scott Joplin and the Ragtime Era* (London, 1975). M. Evans: *Scott Joplin and the Ragtime Years* (New York, 1976). J. Haskins and K. Benson: *Scott Joplin: the Man Who Made Ragtime* (New York, 1978). K. Preston: *Scott Joplin* (New York, 1988).

Music: V. B. Lawrence (ed.): *The Complete Works of Scott Joplin*, 2 vols (New York, 1971; vol. 1, New York–Croydon, 1973).

Jordan, Joe (*b* Cincinnati, 11 Feb. 1882; *d* Tacoma, 9 Sep. 1971). American composer, arranger, pianist, and teacher. He was musical director at the Chicago Theatre from 1903 and for the black musical *Bandana Land* (1908), arranger for Florenz *Ziegfeld, toured Europe with his own orchestra, and appeared in vaudeville. He wrote the scores of *Deep Harlem* (1929) and *Brown Buddies* (1930); and the sound-track of the Josephine *Baker film *Siren of the Tropics* (1929). His songs included: 'Rise and shine' (1908); 'Oh, Liza lady' (1908); 'Dixie Land' (1908); 'Lovie Joe' (1910); and 'That's ma honey, sho's yo' born' (1912); and his rags: 'Double fudge' (1902); 'Nappy Lee' (1903); 'Pekin rag' (1904); 'J. J. J. rag' (1905); 'That teasin' rag' (1909); and 'Darkey todalo' (1910).

Jordan, Louis Thomas (*b* Brinkley, Ark., 8 July 1908: *d* Los Angeles, 4 Feb. 1975). American bandleader, saxophonist, singer, composer, and author. He began playing as a child and gained his first experience with Rudy Williams's band in Hot Springs. In 1932 he joined Charlie Gains in Philadelphia and worked with Kaiser Marshall before joining the famous Chick *Webb band at the *Savoy Ballroom in Harlem, with whom he first recorded. He stayed with the band, latterly under Ella *Fitzgerald's leadership, until 1938 when he left to form his own Tympany Five, a unit that might have been described then as a *jump band but which, in essence, was an early rhythm 'n' blues band before this category had been invented. It was rich in humour, playing jazz in the Fats *Waller mould but with a strong blues element prevailing. During the early 1940s the group became internationally known with a series of high-spirited recordings such as 'Choo choo ch'boogie', 'Saturday night fish fry', 'I'm gonna move to the outskirts of town', 'Ain't nobody here but us chickens', and 'Caldonia' (an item later taken up by Woody *Herman). He also worked with such singers as Bing *Crosby, Ella Fitzgerald, and Louis *Armstrong, and the group appeared in several films.

Jordan's effervescent personality gave the group its character but this was greatly enhanced by its professional slickness and driving rhythms, the sort of fringe jazz that brought in many new adherents. It was also a forerunner of what was to come in the rock and roll world. He remained active in the 1960s, touring England in 1962 with Chris *Barber and still recording. Into the 1970s he was still working at times with a new Tympany Five, and he was at the Newport Festival in 1974. He wrote much of his own material, including 'Is you is or is you ain't my baby' (1943); 'Safe, sane and single' (1947); 'Barnyard boogie' (1947); and 'Don't burn the candle at both ends' (1948).

Joseph and the Amazing Technicolor Dreamcoat. Rock musical telling the biblical story of Joseph and the coat of many colours in continuous music and song in a mixture of rock, country, and theatre styles. It marked the first collaboration between composer Andrew *Lloyd Webber and librettist Tim *Rice and also set something of a pattern for their future working methods. It was written for the junior department of St Paul's school in London, Colet Court, at the request of the music master there, Alan Doggett. Then more of a pop oratorio, it was very brief; its first performance on 1 March 1968 was before an audience of 2000, and it was published by Novello for school use. Later, slightly expanded, it was seen at Central Hall, Westminster, 12 May 1968, and, through the efforts of Norrie *Paramor, it was recorded by Decca. The recording group performed it at St Paul's Cathedral in Nov. 1968, and again in Central Hall, 28 Jan. 1969, with David Daltry as Joseph.

Following the success of *Jesus Christ Superstar* (by the same writers), *Joseph*, now a 90-minute cantata, was staged in the 1972 Edinburgh Festival by the Young Vic Company, earning itself a two-week showing at the Old Vic in London from 16 Oct. 1972 followed by 43 performances at the Roundhouse 8 Nov. 1972. Two months later it moved to the West End, Albery Theatre 17 Feb. 1973, with Gary Bond as Joseph, and had a run of 243 performances. In America, where it was first seen at the Brooklyn Academy of Music 22 Dec. 1976, it later had 77 performances at the Greenwich Village Entermedia Theatre from 18 Nov. 1981 before moving to the Royale on 27 Jan. 1982 to complete a run of 747 performances.

Joy-Bells. London revue with music by Frederick Chappelle, presented at the London Hippodrome 25 Mar. 1919 and running for 723 performances. It has slipped into popular musical history by virtue of presenting, on its first night, alongside its star performer, George *Robey, the historical *Original Dixieland Jazz Band on its first visit to England. Robey, for a mixture of aesthetic and practical professional reasons, objected to the band and said that either they went or he did. The band were the losers but went on to conquer the British musical world elsewhere, while *Joy-Bells* got along very well without them.

Joyce, Archibald (*b* 1873; *d* London, 22 Mar. 1963). British composer and conductor. He led his own orchestra for many years and was the first British composer to have his works published on the Continent. Generally billed, at least by his publishers, as the 'English Waltz King' his most lasting works included 'Vision of Salome' (1908); 'Songe d'Automne' (1908); 'When the birds began to sing' (1911); 'The passing of Salome' (1912); 'Prince of Wales'—march (1914); and 'Sweet William'—waltz (1921); among a long list of publications. 'Vision of Salome' gained extra publicity when it was used to sensational effect by the controversial dancer Maud Allan (1879–1956). Although she performed with the utmost propriety by modern standards, some of her audience were upset by the property head of St John the Baptist which she gloated over with what was considered undue realism. She repeated her performance in the equally controversial *Salome* by Oscar Wilde, in which she appeared in 1918. Joyce also wrote the score of *Toto* (1916), and the song 'Garden of girls'.

Jubilee Singers. After the American Civil War (1862–5), there was a serious determination, on the part of the Federal Government, to give equal education to the freed black people. This was done in the South under the auspices of the Freedmen's Bureau. One of the first important educational institutions was Fisk University, in Nashville, founded in 1866 by the American Missionary Association. As finance was a constant problem, George L. White, the college's treasurer and music teacher, formed a choir in 1871 and, after some intensive rehearsals and a few local concerts, they bravely set out to tour the Northern states of America. Most of their concerts were presented in churches and though, at first, the audiences seemed to expect entertainment on *minstrel show lines, it was the *spirituals, gradually added to the repertoire, which eventually dominated and aroused most interest and enthusiasm as a result of the choir's polished performances.

The group, now calling themselves the Fisk Jubilee Singers, gained a national reputation after singing in Henry Ward Beecher's Plymouth church in Brooklyn, New York, followed by a successful tour of New England and an appearance in Washington DC before President Grant. A selection of their songs was published in 1872. A group of eight of the singers embarked on a tour of Europe in 1875 and popularized the spiritual in Britain and elsewhere, finally disbanding in Hamburg in 1878. In its seven-year existence the choir raised some $150,000 for Fisk University and made the spiritual an international concert genre. Other groups that followed their example were the Hampton Singers from Virginia and choirs from Howard University and the Tuskegee Institute.

G. D. Pike: *The Jubilee Singers of Fisk University and Their Campaign for Twenty Thousand Dollars* (Boston, 1873; London, 1874; repr. New York, 1974). J. B. T. Marsh: *The Story of the Jubilee Singers: with their Songs* (London, 1875; Boston, 1880; repr. New York, 1969). A. Bontemps: *Chariot in the Sky: a Study of the Jubilee Singers* (Philadelphia, 1951).

Jug. The use of empty beer or wine jugs as instruments was a part of the *spasm band activities of early jazz history which employed home-made or improvised instruments such as the jug, *washboard, and kazoo when conventional instruments were out of financial reach. The jug was a genuine utility item into which the performer blew to produce rich bass notes that could easily be mistaken for those of a tuba. Such bands, later known as *skiffle groups, became highly professional and Gus Cannon's Jug Stompers and various washboard bands that included a jug-blower were widely recorded in the late 1920s and early 1930s.

Juke-box. The name arose from what had earlier been known as a juke-house, a brothel or cheap roadhouse in the USA. In the 1930s, when live music was replaced by the new coin-operated record players giving a choice of jazz, race, or popular discs, these machines became known as juke-boxes. Many of the earlier models were manufactured by the Wurlitzer Company. The juke-box became an important outlet for recorded music and a vital index of a record's popularity. It was estimated that by 1939 there were some 225,000 in the USA alone, with an annual turnover of 13 million records; and by 1942 the figure was nearer 400,000. This indiscriminate dissemination of music among those who prefer not to listen to it, as well as those who wish to, has now become a blight in public premises on a worldwide basis.

Jullien, Louis Antoine [Julien] (*b* Sisteron, Basses Alpes, 23 Apr. 1812; *d* Paris, 14 Mar. 1860). French composer and conductor. He was the son of the bandmaster of the 32nd Line Regiment, from whom he learned to play several instruments. He studied at the Paris Conservatoire 1833–6, but left without achieving any distinction, being a wayward pupil who preferred to write popular music; a waltz, 'Rosita', became popular while he was still a student. He became conductor at the Jardin Turc in Paris where he wrote a number of quadrilles and other dances. An attempt to found a musical journal failed and he left Paris in 1833 to escape his debts. By 1840 he had settled in London and was conducting the summer concerts ('concerts d'été') at Drury Lane, his first appearance there being on 8 June 1840 with an orchestra of 100 players and a choir. By the winter of 1841 (for the 'concerts d'hiver') he was appearing there with even larger forces and establishing his flamboyant style of presentation with tails, white gloves, and a gold baton. In the spring of 1842 he presented a series of 'concerts de société' at the Lyceum Theatre. During these he introduced Rossini's *Stabat Mater* to England. There followed several seasons of popular concerts at the Lyceum 1842–3 and at Covent Garden 1844–9, with other concerts at various venues, and he visited the USA 1853–4 under the auspices of P. T. Barnum where he gave 214 performances.

Having become bankrupt in 1848 he tried to restore his fortune by giving a 'concert monstre' with 400 players, 3 military bands, and 3 choirs, a feat repeated three times in 1849. At all such concerts, which mainly featured popular classics, he always featured his own compositions including a regular 'monster quadrille' with a new, and much advertised, title each season. The most popular was the 'British Army quadrille' (1846), performed with four military bands. Others included: 'Les Huguenots' (1839); 'New Royal Irish' (1840); 'Napoleon' (1841); 'Real Scotch' (1842); 'Chinese' (1842); 'English' (1843); 'Highland' (1844); 'Irish Echoes' (1844); 'Welsh' (1844); 'The British Navy' (1845); 'The Swiss' (1847); 'Caledonian' (1849); 'The bloomer' (1850); 'The Great Exhibition' (1851); 'Pantomime' (1855); 'Il Trovatore' (1856), 'French' (1856); and 'Indian' (1857). He also wrote numerous polkas, waltzes, and other dances, and ran his own publishing house in London mainly for the promotion of his own works. This and other managerial enterprises failed in 1859 and he fled to Paris, to be arrested there for debt and imprisoned for several weeks. He went insane and died in an asylum.

A. Carse: *The Life of Jullien* (Cambridge, 1951).

Jump. Arising from a slang expression conveying a lively sense of enjoyment, as in the Fats *Waller song 'The joint is jumping', the word came into common jazz usage *c.*1938 to cover the bouncier kind of rhythm perpetuated by the swing bands, especially by small extrovert groups like the Louis *Jordan Tympany Five and other jump bands such as the Harlem Hamfats and Stuff *Smith's Onyx Club Boys, all playing jazz with a blues-shouting element in it. These groups favoured a swing style with a strong up-beat, a forerunner of the rock and rhythm 'n' blues developments of the 1950s.

Jungle band/music/style. Mainly big band jazz developed in clubs like the *Cotton Club in Harlem, New York, that provided black entertainment for a white clientele and found that an exotic and pseudo-primitive atmosphere was required. It was notably exploited by the Duke *Ellington band, whose own innate sophistication turned what might have been tasteless displays into distinctive achievements, exploiting the use of wa-wa mutes and tom-toms and the skills of such jungle stylists as Bubber *Miley, Joe *Nanton, and Cootie *Williams. Ellington regularly recorded under the name of the Jungle Band, as did other bandleaders.

K

Kaempfert, Bert [Berthold] (*b* Hamburg, 16 Oct. 1923; *d* Majorca, 21 June 1980). German composer, bandleader, arranger, and musician. He studied at the Hamburg Conservatory of Music and became a proficient player on clarinet, saxophone, and accordion. He joined a band led by Hans Busch in Danzig, with whom he made many broadcasts. During the war he was in the music corps of the German Army and later formed a band in a prisoner-of-war camp. He formed his own band in 1947 and was director of North German Radio from 1949. Moving from providing accompaniments to vocal records, he began to write songs and instrumentals for his own orchestra, many of which became internationally famous with English lyrics—'Spanish eyes' (1959); 'Wooden heart' (1960); 'Now and forever' (1961); 'Swinging safari' (1962); 'Sweet dreams' (1963); 'L-o-v-e' (1964); 'Blue midnight' (1965); and 'Strangers in the night' (1966), from the film *A Man Could Get Killed*, and made into a hit by Frank *Sinatra, among them. The Kaempfert orchestral style ranged from full-blown orchestrations to catchy novelties. At its most commercial, as orchestras tended to be in the 1970s, it provided 'easy listening' in its most uncomplicated form, with an effective use of electric bass and solo trumpet against sustained strings.

Kahn, Gus [Gustave] (*b* Coblenz, 6 Nov. 1886; *d* Beverly Hills, Calif., 8 Oct. 1941). American lyric-writer and author. He went to the USA in 1891 and started work in catering, publishing his first song 'I wish I had a girl', in 1908. He wrote much vaudeville material and songs for such Broadway shows as *Holka Polka* (1925); *Kitty's Kisses* (1926); *Whoopee* (1928)—'Makin' whoopee', 'I'm bringing a red, red rose' (*m* Walter *Donaldson); and *Show Girl* (1929)—'Liza' (*m* George *Gershwin). In 1933 he settled in Beverly Hills, after being contracted to write for films.

His lyrics included: 'Memories' (1915, *m* Egbert *Van Alstyne); 'Pretty baby' (1916, *m* Van Alstyne and Tony *Jackson); 'Toot, toot, tootsie' (1922, *m* Ernie Erdman and Dan Russo, 1885–1956); 'Carolina in the morning' (*m* 1922, Donaldson); 'My buddy' (1922, *m* Donaldson); 'When you and I were seventeen' (1924, *m* Charles Rosoff); 'I'll see you in my dreams' (1924, *m* Isham *Jones); 'Spain' (1924, *m* Jones); 'Yes sir, that's my baby' (1925, *m* Donaldson); 'Chloe' (1927, *m* Neil Moret); 'Love me or leave me' (1928, *m* Donaldson); 'The carioca' (1933, *m* Vincent *Youmans); 'Someone to care for me' (1937, *m* Walter Jurmann and Bronislaw *Kaper); 'All God's chillun got rhythm' (1937, *m* Jurmann and Kaper); and many more of indelible memory. A film biography *I'll See You in My Dreams* (1952) starred Danny Thomas, as Kahn, and Doris *Day.

Kálmán, Emmerich [Imre] (*b* Siófok, Hungary, 24 Oct. 1882; *d* Paris, 30 Oct. 1953). Hungarian composer. He studied at the Musical Academy in Budapest and at 22 his symphonic poem 'Saturnalia' was performed by the Budapest Philharmonic. He wrote a musical comedy, *Das Erbe von Pereszlény*, in 1906 and *Tatárjárás* in 1908. That year he settled in Vienna and dedicated himself entirely to the operetta world, having his first great success with *Ein Herbstmanöver* (1908), produced in New York in 1909 as *The Gay Hussars* and in London in 1912 as *Autumn Manœuvres*. His name established, he followed this with the popular *Ziegeunerprimas* (1912), produced in New York as *Sari*.

His operettas, many of them classics of the genre, included (in Vienna unless otherwise indicated): *Der kleine König* (1912); *Gold gab ich für Eisen* (1914; NY, as *Her Soldier Boy*, 1916); *The Blue House* (London, 1912); *Fräulein Susi* (Budapest, 1915; London and NY as *Miss Springtime*); *Die *Csárdásfürstin* (1915; London as *The Gypsy Princess*, NY as *The Riviera Girl*); *Die Faschingsfee* (1917); *Das Hollandweibchen* (1920); *Die Bajadere* (1921); *(Gräfin Mariza* (1924); Die Zirkusprinzessin (1926); *Golden Dawn* (NY, 1927); *Die Herzogin von Chicago* (1928); *Das Veilchen von Montmartre* (1930); *Der Teufelsreiter* (1932); *Kaiserin Josephine* (1936); *Marinka* (1945); and, posthumously, *Arizona Lady* (1954). He also wrote a film operetta, *Ronny*, in 1931 and many songs and orchestral pieces, and conducted his own works at a Kálmán Festival in Italy in 1936. He left Vienna in 1938 and lived in Paris until 1940, then went to the USA.

Kálmán was one of the great perpetuators of the brand of Viennese operetta which, by tradition, had a strong Hungarian strain in it. His works were skilfully constructed and orchestrated and packed full of good tunes.

J. Bistron: *Emmerich Kálmán* (Leipzig–Vienna–New York, 1932). R. Oesterreicher: *Emmerich Kálmán: der Weg eines Komponisten* (Zurich–Leipzig–Vienna, 1954). V. Kálmán: *Gruss mir die süssen, die reizenden Frauen: mein Leben mit Emmerich Kálmán* (Bayreuth, 1966).

Kalmar, Bert (*b* New York, 16 Feb. 1884; *d* Los Angeles, 18 Sept. 1947). American librettist and lyric-writer. He ran away from home at the age of ten to become a child magician in travelling shows, continuing in vaudeville and burlesque as a comedian and singer. He formed a music-publishing business and began writing, one of his first publications being 'In the land of harmony' (*m* Ted *Snyder) in 1911. The composer Harry *Ruby was employed there as a staff pianist and song-plugger, and after Kalmar had left the stage through an injury, Ruby and Kalmar became a regular team, their first song being 'He sits around' (1916). Together they had many successes in the theatre with such shows as *Helen of Troy, New York* (1923); *No Other Girl* (1924); *Holka Polka* (1925); *The Ramblers* (1926)—'All alone Monday'; *The Five o'Clock Girl* (1927)—'Thinking of you'; *She's My Baby* (1928); *Animal Crackers* (1928)—'Hooray for Captain Spalding'; *Top Speed* (1929); *High Kickers* (1941). With Jerome *Kern he wrote *Lucky* (1927); and with Herbert *Stothart *Good Boy* (1928)—in which the baby-faced, baby-voiced 'Boop-boop-a-doop' girl Helen Kane (1904–66) sang 'I wanna be loved by you'. Kalmar and Ruby also wrote much film material, notably for several Marx Brothers classics. A film about their partnership, *Three Little Words*, was made in 1950.

Kaminsky, Max (*b* Brockton, Mass., 7 Sept. 1908). American jazz trumpeter. He led his own band as a boy in Boston, then worked with various local bands in the 1920s. He played with George Wettling in Chicago 1928, with Red *Nichols in New York 1929, with Leo Reisman in Boston 1930–2, and became a regular Dixielander with such players as Mezz *Mezzrow, Benny *Goodman, and Eddie *Condon. He continued as an eminent sideman with many well-known bands until he joined the navy in 1942 and toured the Pacific area with Artie *Shaw's Naval Band. He led his own band on and off during the 1940s and was with various society orchestras in the 1950s. In 1957 he toured Europe with Jack *Teagarden and from 1960 led small bands and played with New York groups at such clubs as Condon's and Ryan's. A skilfully professional player, he was much in demand for recording sessions.

M. Kaminsky: *My Life In Jazz* (London, 1964; New York, 1968).

Kander, John Harold (*b* Kansas City, Mo., 18 Mar. 1927). American composer. Educated at Oberlin and Columbia universities. He conducted theatre orchestras, was arranger for the musicals **Gypsy* and **Irma la Douce*, contributed to the Broadway musical *A Family Affair* (1962), and wrote incidental music for the play *Never Too Late* (1962). He found a regular collaborator in Fred *Ebb, with whom he wrote *Flora, the Red Menace* (1965)—'A quiet thing'; the outstanding **Cabaret* (1966; filmed 1972); *The Happy Time* (1968); *Zorba* (1968); *70, Girls, 70* (1971); **Chicago* (1975); and the highly successful battle-of-the-sexes, **Woman of the Year* (1981). He also contributed to the films: *Funny Lady* (1975)—'How lucky can you get' sung by Barbra *Streisand; *A Matter of Time* (1976); and *New York, New York* (1977)—theme song sung by Liza *Minnelli.

Kansas City jazz. A loosely defined style of playing that was the basis of much of the *big-band jazz of the *swing era; a driving, invigorating music with the blues as its basis. It evolved in Kansas City, characterized by a relaxed, swinging ensemble behind savagely punched short and simple phrases and riffs which were to become the hallmark of bands like Count *Basie's. Early Kansas City bands that developed this style were led by Bennie *Moten, Walter Page, and Jay *McShann. The blues-shouting style of Jimmy *Rushing, Joe *Turner, Jimmy *Witherspoon, Julia Lee (1903–58), and Walter Brown was a natural adjunct to the music and was regularly featured by Kansas City bands. It was also a root source of many of the later *mainstream groups who favoured the same sort of small big-band approach.

Kaper, Bronislaw (*b* Warsaw, 5 Feb. 1902; *d* Beverly Hills, Calif., 26 Apr. 1983). Polish-born American composer. He studied at the Conservatory 1920–3, later in Berlin, and started film work in Warsaw; but he left Poland in the 1920s to pursue commissions in Berlin, Vienna, London, and Paris. Finally arriving in Hollywood, he contributed (with Walter Jurmann, 1903–71) to *A Night at the Opera* (1936)—'Cosi-cosa'; *Three Smart Girls* (1937)—'Someone to care for me'; *A Day at the Races* (1937)—'All God's chillun got rhythm'; and *Everybody Swing* (1938); and, on his own, *San Francisco* (1936)—'San Francisco'.

A skilled and resourceful composer, with a clear understanding of film requirements, he was in constant demand in the 1940s, 1950s, and 1960s with a long list of films that included: *The Mortal Storm* (1941); *Johnny Eager* (1941); *Keeper of the Flame* (1942); *Above Suspicion* (1943); *Gaslight* (1944); *Bewitched* (1945); *The Stranger* (1946); *Green Dolphin Street* (1947); *Act of Violence* (1948); *The Secret Garden* (1949); *A Life of Her Own* (1950); *The Red Badge of Courage* (1951); *The Wild North* (1952); *Lili* (1953; Academy Award); *Them!* (1954); *The Glass Slipper* (1955); *The Swan* (1956); *The Barretts of Wimpole Street* (1957); *Auntie Mame* (1958); *Green Mansions* (1959); *The Angel Wore Red* (1960); *Two Loves* (1961); *Mutiny on the Bounty* (1962); *Lord Jim* (1965); *The Way West* (1967); *Tobruk* (1967); and *Counterpoint* (1968).

Karas, Anton (*b* Vienna, 7 July 1906; *d* Vienna, 9 Jan. 1985). Austrian zither player and composer. He originally trained as a locksmith but, having come across a zither in an attic at his home he found he had a natural talent for the instrument, studied it, and became a virtuoso. Playing in a Grinzing tavern one evening in 1949, he was heard by the film director Carol Reed, who was in Vienna looking for a theme tune for the character Harry Lime in the film *The Third Man*. He immediately asked Karas to go back to England with him to work on the project. Karas produced the famous 'Harry Lime theme' and a 'Café Mozart waltz' as quickly as possible so that he could get back to his beloved Vienna, not appreciating till later that he had written one of the cinema's most enduring classics. It made him a wealthy man, able to buy a tavern in Grinzing where he became one of Vienna's tourist attractions. His music is an integral part of one of the screen's most poetically conceived thrillers.

Kaufman, George S[imon] (*b* Pittsburgh, Pa., 14 Nov. 1889; *d* New York, 2 June 1961). American playwright, librettist, and director. After trying various menial jobs he became a newspaper columnist, settling in New York in 1914 to write for the *Evening Mail*, *New York Herald*, and *New York Times*. He wrote his first play in 1918 and became known with such titles as *You Can't Take it With You*, *The Man Who Came to Dinner*, and *The Solid Gold Cadillac*, working with Moss *Hart on five plays and three musicals. His first musical was *Helen of Troy, New York* (1923, *m* Harry *Ruby); followed by *Be Yourself* (1924); *The Cocoanuts* (1925); *Animal Crackers* (1928); and the first of three collaborations with the *Gershwins, **Strike Up the Band* (1930). His greatest acclaim came with his sketches for the revue *The *Band Wagon* (1931). The other works with Gershwin were **Of Thee I Sing* (1931), which won a Pulitzer Prize, largely through Kaufman's contributions, and *Let 'Em Eat Cake* (1933)—prestigious rather than commercial successes. Other shows included *I'd Rather Be Right* (1937); *Sing Out the News* (1938); and **Silk Stockings* (1955). He contributed revue sketches and was involved as director or producer, leaving behind a legendary reputation.

H. Teichmann: *George S. Kaufman: an Intimate Portrait* (New York, 1972). S. Meredith: *George S. Kaufman and his Friends* (New York, 1974).

Kay, Hershy (*b* Philadelphia, 17 Nov. 1919; *d* Danbury, Conn., 2 Dec. 1981). American composer, arranger, and orchestrator. After training at the Curtis Institute in Philadelphia, he went to New York to become a prolific arranger of Broadway musicals and ballets. These include *Bernstein's **On the Town*, *Peter Pan*, and **Candide*; *Weill's *A Flag is Born*; also *The Golden Apple*; *Once Upon a Mattress*; *Juno*; *110 in the Shade*; *A *Chorus Line*; *Milk and Honey*; *Music Is*; **On the Twentieth Century*; **Evita*; **Barnum*; and many more. His arrangements for the New York City Ballet were frequently based on the works of other composers and various musical styles: e.g. *Cakewalk* (1951)—*Gottschalk; *Western Symphony* (1954)—cowboy song; *Stars and Stripes* (1958)—*Sousa; *Who Cares?* (1970)—*Gershwin; and *Grand Tour* (1971)—*Coward.

Kaye, Danny [Kominsky, David Daniel] (*b* Brooklyn, NY, 18 Jan. 1913; *d* Los Angeles, 3 Mar. 1987). American actor, dancer, and singer. He first became well-known for his rapid-fire patter songs and routines which he had developed in the Far East while playing in a touring vaudeville group. He visited London in 1938 but made little impression. In 1939 he met and married pianist and songwriter Sylvia Fine (1913–91) who wrote distinctive special material suited to his unique talents, the first being a song satirizing the Stanislavsky school of acting. He became noticed in *The Straw Hat Revue* (1939)—'Anatole of Paris', then attracted attention with the song 'Tchaikovsky' in *Lady in the Dark* (1941) which led to a starring role in Cole * Porter's **Let's Face It* (1941) which had more speciality Fine material added to its basic score. He made his last stage appearance in *Two by Two* (1970).

He was taken up by Sam Goldwyn and a busy film career started with *Up in Arms* (1944), followed by *Wonder Man* (1945)—'Orchi Tchornya', 'Opera number'; *The Kid from Brooklyn* (1946)—'Pavlova', with dancer Vera Ellen (*b* 1921); *The Secret Life of Walter Mitty* (1947); *A Song is Born* (1948); *The Inspector General* (1949); *On the Riviera* (1951)—'Popo the puppet', 'Ballin' the Jack'; *Hans Christian Andersen* (1952)—'Anywhere I wander', 'Thumbelina', 'No two people'; *Knock on Wood* (1954)—'Knock on wood', 'All about you'; *White Christmas* (1954); *The Court Jester* (1956); *Merry Andrew* (1958); *The Five Pennies* (1959)—in which he played the part of Red *Nichols; *On the Double* (1961); and *Peter Pan* (1976).

K. Singer: *The Danny Kaye Story* (New York, 1958).

Kearns, Allen (*b* Ontario, Canada, 1893; *d* Albany, NY, 20 Apr. 1956). Canadian actor and singer. A handsome leading man and robust singer, he appeared notably in three *Gershwin musicals—**Tip-Toes* (1925)—singing 'That certain feeling'; **Funny Face* (1927)—'He loves and she loves'; and **Girl Crazy* (1930)—'Embraceable you'. His other shows included: *Tillie's Nightmare* (1910); *The Red Petticoat* (1912); *Good Morning, Judge* (1919); **Tangerine* (1921); *Mercenary Mary* (1925); and several London productions.

Keel, Howard [Leek, Harold Clifford] (*b* Gillespie, Ind., 13 Apr. 1917). American actor and singer. A handsome baritone ideally suited to robust American musicals, until 1947 he worked under the name of Harold Keel. He appeared in **Carousel* (1945); **Oklahoma!* (1945; London, 1947); *Saratoga* (1959); *No Strings* (1963); *Ambassador* (London, 1971); and in the films **Annie Get Your Gun* (1950); *Pagan Love Song* (1950); **Show Boat* (1951); *Texas Carnival* (1951); *Lovely to Look At* (1951); *Calamity Jane* (1953); **Kiss Me, Kate* (1953); **Rose Marie* (1954); **Seven Brides for Seven Brothers* (1954); *Jupiter's Darling* (1954)—one reviewer called it 'a glorious monument to bad taste'; **Kismet* (1955); and *Ambassador* (London, 1971); in later years he pursued a TV acting career in upper-crust soap opera.

Keeler, Ruby [Ethel Hilda] (*b* Halifax, Nova Scotia, 25 Aug. 1909; *d* Rancho Mirage, Calif., 28 Feb. 1993). Actress, dancer, and singer. Described by Stanley Green as an 'innocent-looking, blank-faced, buck-and-wing dancer', she gradually danced her way to fame on the Broadway stage, starting in the chorus of *The Rise of Rosie O'Reilly* (1923); by way of *Bye, Bye, Bonnie* (1927); *The Sidewalks of New York* (1927); to dancing to Gershwin's minstrel song 'Liza' (sung by Nick Lucas) in *Show Girl* (1929).

Her real fame came in nine Warner Brothers musicals (seven of them with Dick *Powell) in which she introduced many well-known songs. These included: *42nd Street* (1933)—'Shuffle off to Buffalo', 'Forty-Second Street'; **Gold Diggers of 1933*; *Footlight Parade* (1933)—'Honeymoon hotel'; *Dames* (1934); *Flirtation Walk* (1934); *Go into Your Dance* (1935)—'She's a Latin from Manhattan' (which she performed with her first husband, Al *Jolson); *Shipmates for Ever* (1935); *Colleen* (1936); *Ready, Willing and Able* (1937)—'Too marvelous for words'; and *Sweethearts of the Campus* (1941). She retired, emerging, after 41 years away from the Broadway stage, to appear in the revival of **No, No, Nanette* in 1971.

Keller, Greta (*b* Vienna, 1913; *d* Vienna, 5 Nov. 1977). Austrian actress and singer. She began her dancing and singing career in Vienna at the age of 14 and in the 1930s acted in a play called *Broadway* with Marlene *Dietrich. Moving to London, she became known on the radio as a singer with what has been described as 'a perfect microphone voice', then went to the USA and pursued a highly successful career as a cabaret artist. She returned to Europe, but the situation in her homeland forced her to return to America where she was active in anti-Nazi propaganda. Her husband was found murdered in Hollywood in 1943; after her recovery from this shock she resumed her career in St Moritz, Switzerland, and thereafter in Vienna, Berlin, and New York. She made many recordings in the years 1930–9.

Kelly, Gene [Eugene Curran] (*b* Pittsburgh, 23 Aug. 1912). American actor, dancer, singer, choreographer, and director. He first made his reputation on the Broadway stage as a dancer in *Leave it to Me!* (1938), as a singer in *One For the Money* (1939), and as an actor in **Pal Joey* (1940), in which he played the scheming Joey Evans and sang 'I could write a book'. He choreographed **Best Foot Forward* (1941), then in 1942 started a long and remarkable film career. He usually choreographed or directed most of the films he appeared in, which included 12 musicals made for Arthur *Freed at MGM and appearances wich such stars as Judy *Garland, Cyd Charisse, Frank *Sinatra, and his friendly rival Fred *Astaire.

Throughout the years he was one of the most innovative and inventive dance directors in Hollywood, his films always full of unforgettable set-pieces like his soggy dance in a downpour in **Singin' in the Rain*, or his breathtaking barrel rolls in *Take Me Out to the Ball Game*. He was an athletic and incredibly balletic dancer, less of a specialized tap-dancer than Astaire, and a fair singer and actor. His films included: *For Me and My Gal* (1942); **DuBarry Was a Lady* (1943); *Thousands Cheer* (1943); *Cover Girl* (1944); *Anchors Aweigh* (1945); *Ziegfeld Follies* (1946); *Living in a Big Way* (1947); *The Pirate* (1948); *Words and Music* (1948); *Take Me Out to the Ball Game* (1949); **On the Town* (1949); *Summer Stock* (1950); *An *American in Paris* (1951); **Singin' in the Rain* (1952); **Brigadoon* (1954); *Deep in my Heart* (1954); *It's Always Fair Weather* (1955); *Invitation to the Dance* (1956); *Les Girls* (1957); *Let's Make Love* (1960); *What a Way to Go* (1964); *The Young Girls of Rochefort* (1967); *Forty Carats* (1973); *Viva Knievel* (1977); and *Xanadu* (1980). He also directed films, including **Hello Dolly!* (1969).

C. Hirschhorn: *Gene Kelly: a Biography* (London, 1974; New York, 1984). T. Thomas: *The Films of Gene Kelly* (Secaucus, NJ, 1974). J. Basinger: *Gene Kelly* (New York, 1976).

Kennedy, Jimmy (*b* Omagh, NI, 20 July 1902; *d* Cheltenham, 6 Apr. 1984). British songwriter. Deserting a promising career as a teacher and civil servant he embarked on a song-writing career in 1930, his first published composition being 'The barmaid's song' ('Time, gentlemen, please') which did moderately well. His first collaborator was Harry Castling, who introduced him to the publisher Bert *Feldman, the team producing innumerable comedy songs in the old music-hall tradition before finding hit material in 'Oh, Donna Clara' (1930); 'My song goes round the world' (1933); 'The teddy bears' picnic' (1933); and 'Play to me gypsy' (1934);. A big hit came in 1934 with 'Isle of Capri' which was turned down by Feldman but gave a great boost to the new firm of Peter Maurice, for whom Kennedy now produced 'Red sails in the sunset' (1935); 'Serenade in the night' (1936); 'Poor little Angeline' (1936); and 'Harbour lights' (1937).

At this period, although he still wrote songs like 'Roll along covered wagon' (1935) on his own, he often collaborated with Michael *Carr, with whom he wrote the Palladium shows *O-Kay for Sound* (1936), *London Rhapsody* (1937), and *The Little Dog Laughed* (1939); and such songs as 'Hometown' (1937) and 'South of the Border' (1939). The outbreak of war produced 'My prayer' (1939) and the over-optimistic 'We're gonna hang out the washing on the Siegfried Line' (1939). He served in the army during the war, reaching the rank of captain, and during the war years produced 'An hour never passes' (1944), 'The cokey-cokey' (1945), and the English lyrics of *'Lili Marlene'. In the post-war years he wrote 'Apple blossom wedding' (1947); 'Can-can polka' (1950); 'April in Portugal' (1953); 'Instanbul' (1953); and 'Love is like a violin' (1960). He moved to Switzerland in 1960, but was back in Ireland by the 1970s where he became involved in producing a play with music, *Spokesong*, in collaboration with Stewart Parker, which was seen at the Vaudeville Theatre, London, in 1977 and won a drama award. A graduate of Dublin University, he was awarded an OBE in 1983 and an honorary doctorate from the University of Ulster.

Kennedy-Fraser, Marjorie (*b* Perth, 1 Oct. 1857; *d* Edinburgh, 22 Nov. 1930). Scottish singer, pianist, folk-song collector, and composer, daughter of the singer David Kennedy (1825–86) for whom she acted as accompanist from the age of 12. Having studied the piano and music history in Paris, she became predominantly interested in folk-song, making her first visit to the Outer Hebrides in 1905 which led to the publication of her well-known collection of *Songs of the Hebrides* (3 vols; 1909, 1917, 1921), from which her arrangements of 'Eriskay love lilt' and 'The road to the Isles' became very popular. She wrote and edited various books on Scottish and Hebridean songs and composed a 'Hebridean Suite' for cello and piano in 1922.

M. Kennedy-Fraser: *A Life of Song* (London, 1928).

Kent, Walter (*b* New York, 29 Nov. 1911). American composer. He followed a career as an architect before turning to music in his thirties having a first success with a song 'Pu-leeze, Mr Hemingway' (1940), which was followed by 'The white cliffs of Dover' (1941, *w* Nat Burton); 'I'll be home for Christmas' (1943); 'Who dat up dere?' (1943); and many more. For the stage he wrote *Seventeen* (1951), and music for films. He made a visit to England in 1989 to see the 'white cliffs of Dover' for the first time.

Kenton, Stan [Stanley Newcomb] (*b* Wichita, Kans., 19 Feb. 1912; *d* Los Angeles, 25 Aug. 1979). American bandleader, arranger, and composer. As a child he lived in Los Angeles, where he was taught piano by his mother. He started arranging when he was 16, had his first job with a vaudeville band in San Diego at 18, and played with various groups in and around Los Angeles before joining Everett Hoagland as pianist/arranger in 1934. He worked with Gus *Arnheim and Vido Musso and studied orchestration, conducting, and musical theory with Charles Dalmores. In 1940, while he was also working as a studio musician in Hollywood, he formed his first band which made its debut at the Diana Ballroom. An engagement at the Rendezvous Ballroom, Balboa Beach, and a very successful concert at Glendale Civic Auditorium earned the band a place at the Hollywood Palladium and a Decca recording contract.

His band remained just another of those competing with the other swing era opposition until he joined Capitol Records in 1943 and played on the Bob *Hope radio show, although he had early hits with his own 'Artistry in rhythm' (1941), 'Concerto for doghouse' (1942), and 'Eager beaver' (1943), works featuring a precise reed section and a cutting brass sound. The 1944–6 band remained a commercial unit featuring such items as Kenton's 'And her tears flowed like wine', with Anita *O'Day and June *Christy among his early vocalists. Pete *Rugolo joined him in 1945 to take over much of the arranging, as did Bob Graettinger and Bill Holman who helped to establish the use of the term progressive jazz through the forward-looking and clever brand of big-band jazz that they produced.

Kenton disbanded in 1947 owing to ill-health and was fairly inactive until 1949. He formed a large touring orchestra in 1950 which featured such names as the *Four Freshmen, Chris Connor, and Ann Richards, with many of his works with 'Artistry' in the title, and went under the banner of 'Innovations in Modern Music'. He was to remain an experimenter and, to some tastes, a somewhat pretentious jazzman, controversial to both critics and public, but he went his own individual way with sincerity and integrity. He left Capitol in 1970 after 27 years, dissatisfied with their marketing and distribution, and formed his own company, Creative World Records.

C. A. Pirie & S. Muller: *Artistry in Kenton: a Bio-Discography* (Vienna, 1969). C. Easton: *Straight Ahead: the Story of Stan Kenton* (New York, 1973).

Keppard, Freddie (*b* New Orleans, 27 Feb. 1890; *d* Chicago, 15 July 1933). American jazz cornettist. One of the early legendary names in jazz history, he led the Olympia Brass Band when he was 16 and in 1912 took the Original Creole Band on an influential American tour. By 1917 he had settled in Chicago and led a succession of bands there. He also played with King *Oliver, Jimmie *Noone, Erskine Tate, and others, and toured with his own band again in the late 1920s. He played in a powerful, straightforward style, often being favourably compared with Buddy *Bolden (Sidney *Bechet thought he was the better player), and liked to keep his fingering a secret by playing with a handkerchief over his hands. The few early recordings he made with Cook's Dreamland Orchestra probably do little to support his great reputation, and he only made two tracks under his own name.

Kerker, Gustav [Gustave A.] (*b* Herford, Germany, 28 Feb. 1857; *d* New York, 29 June 1923). German-born composer and conductor. He went to the USA with his family in 1867 and settled in Louisville where he became involved with local orchestras as a youth. Later he went to New York and became a musical director in various theatres, his longest and most important post being at the Casino Theatre where many of his own shows were presented. He worked with Lillian *Russell on several of her productions.

His scores included: *The Cadets* (1879); *The Pearl of Pekin* (1888); *Castles in the Air* (1890); *In Gay New York* (1896); *The Lady Slavey* (1896); *An American Beauty* (1897; London, 1900); *The Whirl of the Town* (1897); *The *Belle of New York* (1897; London, 1898)—his best-known work; *Yankee Doodle Dandy* (1898); *The Telephone Girl* (1898); *The Girl from Up There* (1901); *The Billionaire* (1902); *A *Chinese Honeymoon* (1902; additional music); *The Blonde in Black* (1903); *Winsome Winnie* (1903);

The Tourists (1906); *The White Hen* (1907); *Fascinating Flora* (1907), starring Adele Ritchie (1874–1930); *The Lady from Lane's* (1907); *The Social Whirl* (1908); *Two Little Brides* (1911); and *The Grass Widows* (1912).

Kern, Jerome David (*b* New York, 27 Jan. 1885; *d* New York, 11 Nov. 1945). American composer. After an early interest in music, fostered at home and at school, he studied at the New York College of Music. His father wanted him to follow in the family piano-selling business, but he was eventually allowed to pursue his own musical inclinations and went to study for a while in Germany. Back in New York in 1904, he became pianist and song-plugger with a music-publisher, then began to work for the Charles Frohman organization as a music editor. It was common practice then to leave the opening numbers of shows and other linking pieces to hack composers and this was one of Kern's tasks. The other was to provide brisk new numbers for imported European shows, or those written in the USA by composers of the older school, that were felt to lack some of the new ragtime brio that American audiences expected.

It was to do this work of uplifting British shows with something American that he was sent to London in 1906, and it was often the numbers that Kern provided that became the hits of the shows—for example, 'How'd you like to spoon with me' which had been added to the score of *The *Earl and the Girl* (1905). While in London, Kern would relax on the river and, visiting the Swan Hotel in Walton-on-Thames, he fell in love with Eva Leale, the landlord's daughter. They were married in Walton on 25 Oct. 1910.

Kern's most momentous addition to a show was the forward-looking 'They didn't believe me' (*w* M. E. Rourke, 1867–1933), which was written for the *Rubens/*Jones musical *The Girl from Utah* (1914) and later used in **Tonight's the Night*. Kern acknowledged that some of his early inspiration came from the score of **Florodora* by Leslie *Stuart, perversely a British composer who had picked up the essence of Americanism from the imported minstrel shows. The many other works he contributed to included: *The Silver Slipper* (1902); *An English Daisy* (1903); *The School Girl* (1903); *Mr Wix of Wickham* (1904); *The *Catch of the Season* (1905); *The Spring Chicken* (1905); *The Rich Mr Hoggenheimer* (1905); *The Beauty of Bath* (1906); *The Little Cherub* (1906); *My Lady's Maid* (1906); *The Dairymaids* (1907); *Fascinating Flora* (1907); *The Gay White Way* (1907); *The Orchid* (1907); *The Morals of Marcus* (1907); *Peter Pan* (1907); *The White Chrysanthemum* (1907); *Fluffy Ruffles* (1908); *The Girls of Gottenberg* (1908); *A Waltz Dream* (1908); *The Golden Widow* (1908); *The Gay Hussars* (1909); *The Dollar Princess* (1909); *The Girl and the Wizard* (1909); *Kitty Grey* (1909); *The King of Cadonia* (1910); **Our Miss Gibbs* (1910); *Kiss Waltz* (1911); *Litle Miss Fix-It* (1911); *A Winsome Widow* (1912); *The Woman Haters* (1912); *The Amazons* (1913); *The Polish Wedding* (1912); *Lieber Augustin* (1913); *The Girl from Montmartre* (1912); *The Doll Girl* (1913); *The Marriage Market* (1913); *The Sunshine Girl* (1913); *The Laughing Husband* (1914); *The *Passing Show* (1914); *When Claudia Smiles* (1914); *A Modern Eve* (1915); *Rosy Rapture* (1915); *Theodore & Co* (1916); **Ziegfeld Follies* (1916, 1917, 1921); *Miss Springtime* (1916); *The Riviera Girl* (1917); *The Canary* (1918); *The Lady in Red* (1919); and *Ripples* (1930).

Kern's own first complete score was *The Red Petticoat* (1911) which had a modest 61 performances. In 1915 he found an ideal librettist in Guy *Bolton, and when lyric-writer P. G. *Wodehouse was added to the team in 1917 a sophisticated new brand of American musical comedy was created. The first shows staged at the Princess Theatre included **Very Good, Eddie* (1915), **Oh, Boy* (1917), and **Oh, Lady! Lady!!* (1918). The partnership's first really big success was **Sally* (1920), not a little of its popularity due to Marilyn *Miller of whom one critic said: 'Sally is Marilyn Miller from her head to her toes.' She was acclaimed in one of Kern's loveliest songs, a duet with Irving Fisher, 'Look for the silver lining'.

For his greatest achievement of all Kern was joined by the librettist Oscar *Hammerstein II when they gave Broadway both a newly lavish spectacle and a musical masterpiece in **Show Boat* (1927). The elaborate staging helped, but it was Kern's songs that made it into such a great show—'Make believe', 'Can't help lovin' that man', 'Why do I love you', and 'Ol' Man River' (which was written with Paul *Robeson in mind, although he did not sing it until the London production). The mid-1930s saw many vintage Kern shows like *The *Cat and the Fiddle* (1931); **Music in the Air* (1932); **Roberta* (1933), which had a frivolous and threadbare plot but a score containing such classics as 'Yesterdays' and 'Smoke gets in your eyes'; and *Very Warm for May* (1939), with 'All the things you are'.

In the 1930s, like many other leading composers, Kern was lured into trying his hand at music for the developing talking film, still a new area of music-making to most, and he left New York for Hollywood in 1934. It was the artistry of Fred *Astaire and his partner Ginger *Rogers that inspired what turned out to be some of his very best songs. When *Roberta* was filmed in 1935, 'Lovely to look at' was added to the score. Then **Swing Time* (1936) brought forth some Astaire classics such as 'A fine romance' and 'The way you look tonight'. Other stars benefited in *High, Wide and Handsome* (1937) from a score which contained 'Can I forget you'; and the film version of Gershwin's **Lady Be Good* (1941) had a single Kern interpolation, 'The last time I saw Paris', with lyrics by Hammerstein. In 1945 he returned to New York to start writing the music for a new musical which was to star Ethel *Merman as Annie Oakley. He never wrote any of **Annie Get Your Gun*, for he died of a heart-attack before he could begin, and Irving *Berlin stepped in.

The importance of Kern as a founding figure of the 20th-century American musical cannot be overstressed. He did much of his earlier writing long before jazz had begun to have any influence on popular song fashions; yet a song like 'They wouldn't believe me' from 1914 is remarkably modern in style and outlook, perhaps borrowing from Stuart and 'Tell me pretty maiden' to some extent, but otherwise highly individual and standing out among the other music of the period in both melody and harmony. Many writers have credited Kern with inventing the first Tin Pan Alley jazz harmonies, pointing to a song called 'The magic melody' (1915), which set popular music along new paths (see under JAZZ 2). Through his particular place in time, Kern's style still maintained strong links with the old operetta tradition and he never fully embraced the jazz idiom, even in his later writings, in the way that Gershwin did. He produced a freshly light, sophisticated, technically adroit sort of song, immensely superior to much of the Tin Pan Alley output, and he helped other composers, like Gershwin, *Rodgers, *Arlen, and *Schwartz, to find new potential in the use of popular music in the theatre. All of them at some time or another have acknowledged their debt to Jerome Kern.

At his best, in a song like 'Smoke gets in your eyes' with its ingenious enharmonic middle-section, Kern can justly be compared with Schubert. The way he matches music to words takes his songs beyond the ordinary level. And because they have so much of the operetta quality in them, Kern's songs do not, in fact, take kindly to being jazzed up. They have to be played with a proper understanding of their time and place to realize their very individual flavour.

Kern's complete scores (and occasional collaborations) included: *La Belle Paree* (1911); *The Red Petticoat* (1912); *Oh, I Say!* (1913); *90 in the Shade* (1915); *Nobody Home* (1915); *Cousin Lucy* (1915); *Miss Information* (1915); **Very Good, Eddie* (1915); *Have a Heart* (1917); *Love o'Mike* (1917); **Oh, Boy!* (1917, *w* Wodehouse)—'Till the clouds roll by', 'An old-fashioned wife'; *Leave It to Jane* (1917, *w* Wodehouse)—'The siren's song'; *Miss 1917* (1917, *w* Wodehouse)—'Go little boat'; *Oh, Lady! Lady!!* (1918); *Toot-Toot* (1918); *Head Over Heels* (1918); *Rock-a-bye Baby* (1918); *She's a Good Fellow* (1919); *The Night Boat* (1910); *Hitchy-Koo* (1920); **Sally* (1920, *w* Clifford *Grey and others)—'Look for the silver lining', 'Wild rose', 'Whip-poor-Will', 'Sally'; **Good Morning, Dearie* (1921, *w* Anne *Caldwell)—'Ka-lu-a'; *The Bunch and Judy* (1922); *The Cabaret Girl* (1922); *The Beauty Prize* (London, 1922)—'You can't make love by wireless'; *Stepping Stones* (1923)—'Raggedy Ann'; *Sitting Pretty* (1924); *Dear Sir* (1924); **Sunny* (1925, *w* Otto *Harbach and Hammerstein)—'Who?' 'Sunny', 'D'ye love me'; *The City Chap* (1925); *Criss-Cross* (1926); *Lucky* (1927); **Show Boat* (1927, *w* Hammerstein)—'Make believe', 'Why do I love you?', 'Ol' Man River', 'Bill' (*w* Wodehouse and Hammerstein), 'Can't help lovin' that man'; *Blue Eyes* (London, 1928)—'You are love'; *Sweet Adeline* (1929, *w* Hammerstein)—'Why was I born', 'Don't ever leave me', ''Twas not so long ago'; *The Cat and the Fiddle* (1931, *w* Harbach)—'The night was made for love', 'She didn't say yes', 'I watch the love parade', 'One moment alone'; *Music in the Air* (1932, *w* Hammerstein)—'The song is you', 'I've told every little star', 'In Eagern on the Tegern See'; *Roberta* (1933, *w* Harbach)—'Yesterdays', 'Smoke gets in your eyes', 'The touch of your hand'; *Three Sisters* (London, 1934); *Gentlemen Unafraid* (1938); and *Very Warm For May* (1939, filmed as *Broadway Rhythm*, 1943; *w* Hammerstein)—'All the things you are', 'All in fun'.

Films with Kern's music include: *Show Boat* (1929); *Sally* (1929); *Sunny* (1930)—'Two little bluebirds', 'I was alone'; *The Cat and the Fiddle* (1934); *Music in the Air* (1934); *I Dream Too Much* (1935, *w* Dorothy *Fields), his first original film score—'I dream too much', 'The jockey on the carousel'; *Reckless* (1935); *Roberta* (1935)—'I won't dance', 'Lovely to look at' (both *w* Fields); *Sweet Adeline* (1935); *Show Boat* (1936); *Swing Time* (1936, *w* Fields)—'The way you look tonight', 'Bojangles of Harlem', 'Waltz in swing time', 'Pick yourself up', 'A fine romance', 'Never gonna dance'; *High, Wide and Handsome* (1937, *w* Hammerstein)—'Can I forget you', 'The folks who live on the hill'; *When You're in Love* (1937); *Joy of Living* (1938, *w* Fields)—'You couldn't be cuter', 'Just let me look at you'; *Goldwyn Follies of 1938*; *One Night in the Tropics* (1940)—'Remind me', 'Your dream'; *Lady Be Good* (1941)—'The last time I saw Paris' (*w* Hammerstein; not originally written for any specific show or film); *Sunny* (1941); *You Were Never Lovelier* (1942, *w* Johnny *Mercer)—'You were never lovelier', 'Dearly beloved', 'I'm old-fashioned'; *Can't Help Singing* (1944, *w* E. Y. *Harburg)—'Can't help singing', 'More and more', 'Any moment now', 'Californ-i-ay'; *Cover Girl* (1944, *w* Ira *Gershwin)—'Long ago (and far away)', 'Sure thing'; *Song of Russia* (1944); *Centennial Summer* (1946)—'All through the day' (*w* Hammerstein), 'In love in vain', 'Up with the lark' (both *w* Leo Robin); *Till the Clouds Roll By* (1946)—a biography of Kern with Robert Walker as the composer, using 22 of his best-known songs; *Look For the Silver Lining* (1949)—biography of Marilyn Miller; *Show Boat* (1951); *Lovely to Look At* (1952), an adaptation of *Roberta*.

He wrote string quartet versions of several of his best songs (with Charles Miller) and, for orchestra, 'Scenario' (1941) and 'Portrait of Mark Twain' (1942).

D. Ewen: *The World of Jerome Kern* (New York, 1960). M. Freedland: *Jerome Kern: a Biography* (London, 1978; New York, 1981). G. Bordman: *Jerome Kern: his Life and Music* (New York–London, 1980). A. Lamb: *Jerome Kern in Edwardian London* (Littlehampton, 1981; rev. 1985).

Music: O. Hammerstein (ed.): *The Jerome Kern Song Book* [50 songs] (New York, 1955). H. Fordin (ed.): *Jerome Kern: the Man and his Music in Story, Picture and Song* (Santa Monica, 1974).

Ketèlbey, Albert William (*b* Aston Manor, Birmingham, 4 Aug. 1875; *d* Cowes, IOW, 26 Nov. 1959). British composer and conductor. He showed promise as a composer at an early age and studied music in Birmingham. When he was 11 he composed a piano sonata which was performed at Worcester and won the praise of Edward Elgar. At the age of 13 he won a Queen Victoria Scholarship to Trinity College, London, where he studied composition, piano, french horn, cello, clarinet, oboe, and organ, won many medals and prizes, and had several of his works performed. His wide knowledge of instruments is reflected in the excellent and thoughtful orchestration of his well-known compositions; unlike some popular composers, he did all his own arrangements.

By the age of 21 he was musical director at the Vaudeville Theatre, having won his experience touring with a light opera company. He had various chamber works performed and a musical farce, *A Good Time or Skipped by the Light of the Moon* (1899). Still with ambitions of becoming a 'serious' composer, he preferred to publish some of the lighter hack work that he did, such as background music for silent films, under the names of William Aston and Anton Vodorinski.

His first success was 'Phantom melody' (1912) which won a prize offered by the popular cellist and actor August Van Biene and was used in a play of the same name. He was musical editor for Chappell & Co., and an examiner at Trinity College. While he was musical director for Columbia Records, he began to write the enormously popular pieces that became known to everyone (in many guises) beginning with 'In a monastery garden' (1915). The success of these enabled him to retire in his forties to the Isle of Wight, where he spent the rest of his days in contented seclusion.

His best-known works after 1915 included: 'In the moonlight' (1919); 'Souvenir de tendresse' (1919); 'In a Persian market' (1920); 'Wedgwood blue' (1920); 'Cockney Suite' (1924), of which No. 5, ''Appy 'Ampstead', became the best-known item; 'Chal Romano' (1924); 'Sanctuary of the heart' (1924); 'In a Chinese temple garden' (1925); 'Bells across the meadows' (1927); 'By the blue Hawaiian waters' (1927); 'The sacred hour' (1929); 'The clock and the Dresden figures' (1930); 'In the mystic land of Egypt' (1931); 'A birthday greeting' (1932); 'Dance of the merry mascots' (1932); and 'From a Japanese screen' (1934). Many of these were published in alternative song or choral versions.

Keys, Nelson 'Bunch' (*b* London, 7 Aug. 1886; *d* London, 26 Apr. 1939). British actor, comedian, singer, and dancer. He was a small, vivacious character, principally known for his talented work in many London revues. He appeared in *The *Arcadians* (1909); *The Mousmé* (1911); *Princess Caprice* (1912); *Oh, Molly!* (1912); *The Girl in the Taxi* (1913); *The *Passing Show* (1914 and 1915); *Bric-a-Brac* (1915); *Vanity Fair* (1916); *Round the Map* (1917); **Very Good, Eddie* (1918); *Buzz-Buzz* (1918); *London, Paris and New York* (1920); *The Curate's Egg* (1922); **Ziegfeld Follies* (NY, 1924); **Rose-Marie* (1926); *Folly to be Wise* (1931); *Bow Bells* (1932); *After Dark* (1933); *Why Not Tonight?* (1934); *Spread It Abroad* (1936) and *Home and Beauty* (1937).

P. Carstairs: *Bunch* (London, 1941).

Kidson, Frank (*b* Leeds, 15 Nov. 1855; *d* Leeds, 7 Nov. 1926). British folk-song collector and editor. Originally a landscape painter, a growing interest in British folk-songs and dances took up more of his time and he became one of the founders of the Folksong Society (later absorbed into the *English Folk Dance and Song Society) and editor of its journal. His published works included *Old English Country Dances* (ed.) (London, 1890); *Traditional Tunes* (ed.) (Oxford, 1891); *British Music Publishers* (London, 1900); *English Folksong and Dance* (with Mary Neal; Cambridge, 1915); *The Beggar's Opera: its Predecessors and Successors* (Cambridge, 1922); and, with arranger Alfred Edward Moffatt (1863–1950), *Dances of the Olden Times* (ed.) (Edinburgh, 1912), *The Minstrelsy of England* (ed.) (London, 1922); *Songs of the Georgian Period* (ed.) (London, n.d.); *British Nursery Rhymes* (ed.) (London, n.d.); and *Children's Songs of Long Ago* (London, n.d.).

King, B. B. [Riley B.] (*b* Itta Bena, Miss., 16 Sept. 1925). American blues singer and guitarist. He has been immensely influential as both guitarist and singer and is often bracketed with Muddy *Waters, though he is a much smoother and more polished performer. He plays in a wide range of styles, but has been most prominent in the rhythm 'n' blues field, with his sophisticated style showing the technical influence of Django *Reinhardt, T-Bone *Walker, and Charlie *Christian. He signed with the Modern/RPM record label in 1950 and had a first hit with 'Three o'clock blues' (1950). Later successes, such as 'Everyday I have the blues' (1955), 'Sweet little angel' (1956), and 'Sweet sixteen' (1960), established his prominence in the blues world; and in 1961 he signed with ABC records and produced such hits as 'Don't answer the door' (1969) and 'The thrill is gone' (1970).

King's vocal style was a fusion of gospel music and the blues, with a clear falsetto melody line echoing his electric-guitar phrasing. His trademark was the 'bent' vibrato note, a feature developed in his single-string solos which he borrowed from the above-mentioned jazz stylists. His crisp, clean-cut sound spread his appeal beyond the bounds of ethnic appreciation and his innovative guitar style became a model for many white blues performers of the late 1960s. In 1968 he made his first tour of Europe and in 1970 headed an all-blues concert at Carnegie Hall.

B. B. King (ed. Vinson): *B. B. King: the Blues, the Wellspring of Today's American Popular Music and its Greatest Performer* (New York, 1970). C. Sawyer: *B. B. King: the Authorized Biography* (Poole, 1981).

King, Carole [Klein, Carole] (*b* Brooklyn, NY, 9 Feb. 1942). American songwriter and singer. Influenced in her college days by the sounds of Bill *Haley, Elvis *Presley, and Fats *Domino, she started writing songs and led a girls' vocal ensemble called the Co-Sines. At college she also met lyric-writer Gerry Goffin (*b* 1939) and they were soon married. Before she was 20, they had their first hit with 'Will you still love me tomorrow' (1961) which became No. 1 in the USA when recorded by the Shirelles. A song written in 1960, 'Natural woman', became a hit in 1967 when taken up by Aretha *Franklin. King's own recordings included their 'It might as well rain until September' which reached No. 3 in Britain and later No. 1 in the USA sung by Little Eva; it remains one of the best King–Goffin collaborations.

They might be considered one of the last songwriting partnerships in the old professional Tin Pan Alley style, working for Don Kirshner and Al Nevins at the Brill Buildings, writing songs on demand as needed—for anyone from Steve *Lawrence to the *Everly Brothers. Other outstanding titles were 'Some kind of wonderful' (1960); 'When my little girl is smiling' (1961); 'Take good care of my baby' (1961); 'Every breath I take' (1961); 'Halfway to paradise' (1961); 'Up on the roof' (1962); 'Don't ever change' (1962); 'Locomotion' (1962); 'Sharing you' (1962); 'Don't say nothin' bad about my baby' (1963); 'Go away, little girl' (1963); 'One fine day' (1963); 'Victim of circumstances' (1963); 'Let's turkey trot' (1963); 'I'll never find another you' (1964); 'Oh no, not my baby' (1964); 'Show me the girl' (1964); 'I'm into something good' (1964); 'At the club' (1965); 'Wasn't born to follow' (1968); and 'Going back' (1968). She divorced Goffin in 1968; married and divorced bassist Charles Larkey; and her third husband died of a cocaine overdose in 1978.

Writing both words and music she produced and recorded 'You've got a friend' (1971); 'So far away' (1971); 'It's too late' (1971); 'I can feel the earth move' (1971); 'Sweet seasons' (1972); 'Pocket money' (1972), a film title-song; and in the 1970s experimented in various albums—*Carole King—Writer* (1970); *Tapestry* (1971); *Music* (1971); *Fantasy* (1973); *Simple Things* (1977); and *Welcome Home* (1978)—in which she sensitively exploited a warm, gentle folk-rock style with an effective directness of approach.

King, Charles E. (*b* Honolulu, 29 Jan. 1874; *d* Elmhurst, NY, 27 Feb. 1950). American composer, author, and publisher. Educated in Hawaii, he was leader of many musical activities there and an authority on its music. He worked with Queen Liliuokalami on many enterprises and wrote special music for her funeral. He taught music and edited *King's Book of Hawaiian Melodies*; *Songs of Hawaii*; *Favourites from the Hawaiian Operetta*; *Hawaiian Favourites for the Piano*; etc. His own songs included: 'Na lei O Hawaii', 'Imi au la oe' ('Song of the Islands'), 'Beautiful Kahana' ('Serenade'), 'Ke kali nei au' ('Waiting for thee'), 'Paauau waltz' ('How about me'), 'Eleu Mikimiki', 'Uheuhene' ('Step lively'), 'Hawaiian shouting song', 'Dreaming, Aloha, of you', and, his best-known work, 'Aloha oe' ('Hawaiian wedding song').

King, Dennis [Pratt, Dennis] (*b* Coventry, 2 Nov. 1897; *d* New York, 21 May 1971). British-born actor and singer. He played in Shakespeare, Ibsen, and other straight plays, but also had classical musical training and found a natural outlet as the handsome hero of many musicals. He settled in the USA in 1921 and had a very successful stage and film career, his excellent baritone voice heard in such shows as **Monsieur Beaucaire* (London, 1919); **Rose-Marie* (1924); *The *Vagabond King* (1925); *The Three Musketeers* (1928; London, 1930); **Show Boat* (1932); *Command Performance* (London, 1933); *Frederika* (1937); *I Married an Angel* (1938); **Music in the Air* (1951); and *Shangri-la* (1956).

King, Karl L[awrence] (*b* Painterville, Ohio, 21 Feb. 1891; *d* Fort Dodge, Iowa, 31 Mar. 1971). American composer and conductor. Generally regarded as America's foremost composer for the circus, he played euphonium (baritone horn) with various bands as a youth and had his first march published when he was 17. In 1909 he joined the band of the Yale-Robinson Circus and from then until 1918 served with various circus bands ending up as musical director of the Barnum & Bailey organization. Tired of travelling, in 1918 he became bandmaster of the Grand Army Band of Canton, Ohio, where he also founded a music-publishing business. In 1920 he became musical director of the Municipal Band in Fort Dodge, a post he was to hold for many years. He was awarded the honorary degree of Doctor of Music by the Phillips University at Enid, Oklahoma, in 1953 and had the state highway bridge at Fort Dodge named after him.

Among his compositions, mainly intended for circus use, the best-known, by sound if not by name, is the oft-used 'Barnum and Bailey's Favourite' which he wrote while he was a member of the band. 'Sons of veterans' was written for the Sons of Civil War Veterans Association; 'Three Musketeers' was inspired by the Dumas novel; 'The trombone King' was dedicated to the well-known trombonist Charles Toops; 'Tiger triumph' was for the Louisiana State University Tiger football team. Many of his marches were written for universities—'Pride of the Illini' and 'Purple pageant' among them. A number of lively galops included 'Big cage' and 'Circus days'; and he wrote a number of overtures, serenades, intermezzos, and other programme pieces. One of the founders of the American Bandmasters Association in 1930, he became an honorary life president in 1967. His life and music were a partial inspiration for the Meredith *Willson show *The *Music Man* (1957).

J. J. Hatton: *Karl L. King, an American Bandmaster* (Evanston, 1975).

King, Robert A. [Keiser, Robert] (*b* New York, 20 Sept. 1862; *d* New York, 14 Apr. 1932). American composer. A Tin Pan Alley workaholic, he wrote songs beyond numbering, producing many under such pseudonyms (with a strange preference for the feminine) as R. A. Wilson, Mary Earl, Kathleen A. Roberts, and Mrs Rowenhall, as well as many anonymously. He was a fine accompanist, appeared in vaudeville, and worked for many years for the publishers Shapiro & Bernstein.

His songs included: 'While strolling through the park one day' (1884); 'I can't tell why I love you but I do' (1888); 'Anona' (1903); 'Dreamy Alabama' (1910); 'Beautiful Ohio' (1918); 'Beautiful Hawaii' (1920); 'Isle of Paradise' (1920); 'I ain't nobody's darling (1921); 'Keep your skirts down, Mary Ann' (1925); 'I scream, you scream' (1927); and 'Moonlight on the Colorado' (1930).

King, Wayne (*b* Savannah, Ill., 16 Feb. 1901; *d* 16 July 1985). American composer and bandleader. He worked in insurance, professional football, car repairing, and railway engineering before becoming a clarinettist. He played with the Del Lampe Orchestra at the Trianon Ballroom in Chicago and, when the Aragon Ballroom opened in Chicago in 1927, Lampe put him in charge of the orchestra there. He became popular in the 1930s with a slow, dreamy style featuring many waltzes, typified by the theme tune 'The waltz you saved for me' which Wayne wrote with Emil Flindt (*w* Gus *Kahn) in 1930. He stayed at the Aragon for nine years and had hit recordings with 'Stardust', his own 'Goofus' (1930), and 'Blue hours' (1933). The band started a regular radio show in 1931, having its biggest hit with Wayne's 'Josephine' in 1937, coming to a peak, with Buddy *Clark as vocalist, in the 1940s, and functioning into the 1970s.

King and I, The. American musical play with score by Richard *Rodgers and book by Oscar *Hammerstein II, based on Margaret Landon's *Anna and the King of Siam*. The idea of making the book into a musical came from Gertrude *Lawrence; she initially saw Cole *Porter as the composer, but Rodgers and Hammerstein were considered a better prospect.

The work opened at the St James Theatre, New York, 29 Mar. 1951, with Gertrude Lawrence as Anna, who becomes governess to the children of the Siamese king played (after both Rex *Harrison and Alfred *Drake had been considered for the role) by the then relatively unknown Yul *Brynner who was to make it very much his own. Anna tries to teach the King less barbaric ways and a romance naturally develops.

The New York production achieved 1246 performances. In London at the Drury Lane Theatre, 8 Oct. 1953, Valerie Hobson (*b* 1917) and Herbert Lom (*b* 1917) took the leads and the run was 946. The work has been regularly revived and was filmed in 1956 with Deborah Kerr (*b* 1921) and Brynner. The classic stature of the work is emphasized by a memorable score that includes such songs as 'I whistle a happy tune', 'Hello, young lovers', 'March of the Siamese children', 'We kiss in a shadow', 'Something wonderful', and 'Shall we dance'.

King's Rhapsody. Musical play with music and book by Ivor *Novello and lyrics by Christopher Hassall (1912–63). After a try-out at the Palace Theatre, Manchester, 25 Aug. 1949, it opened at the Palace Theatre, London, 15 Sept. 1949 where it was to have 839 performances.

It was based on a true-life affair between King Carol of Romania and the actress Magda Lupescu, with perhaps also a sidelong glance at the Edward VIII–Mrs Simpson liaison. In the play, King Nikki has to return to his homeland to succeed his father and to go through an arranged marriage. He abdicates so that he can marry his lady love, Marta Karillos.

The king was played by Novello and it was to be his last, and apparently favourite, role as he died soon after the performance of 5 Mar. 1951. Jack *Buchanan took over the part. Phyllis *Dare was Marta, and other parts were taken by Zena *Dare, Olive Gilbert (*d* 1981) and Vanessa Lee (1920–92). A film version of 1956 starred Anna *Neagle and Erroll Flynn (1909–59). The songs included: 'Some day my heart will awake', 'Fly home, little heart', 'If this were love', 'Take your girl', and 'A violin began to play'.

Kinks, The. British rock group that came into being in 1962 when Ray [Raymond Douglas] Davies (*b* 1944) and his brother Dave Davies (*b* 1947) joined up with drummer Mick Avery (*b* 1944) and bassist Peter Quaife (*b* 1943) to form a rhythm 'n' blues group, the Ravens. They were signed up by Pye Records in the boom days of the Mersey beat and, renamed the Kinks, recorded 'You do something to me' and 'You really got me', the latter becoming No. 1 in the British charts and No. 10 in the USA. Their primitive and overpowering sound catching the fancy of the teenage public, further hits were: 'All of the day and all of the night' (1964) and, in 1965, 'Tired of waiting for you' (a No. 1), 'Set me free', and 'Till the end of the day', all examples of the disenchantment and melancholy that characterized the song-writing of Ray Davies, the moving spirit of the group. The impact lessened, but the group continued to prosper with 'Sunny afternoon' (1966); 'Waterloo sunset' (1967); and 'Autumn almanac' (1967). They were banned in the USA for 'unprofessional conduct' after a 1965 tour and were not to return until 1969.

Kirby, John (*b* Baltimore, 31 Dec. 1908; *d* Hollywood, 14 June 1952). American bassist, arranger, and bandleader. He started out as a trombonist, but joined the Fletcher *Henderson band as a tuba player in 1930, and soon switched to string bass. From 1934 he followed a varied career in the bands of Chick *Webb, Lucky *Millinder, and Charlie *Barnet until in 1937 he joined a jazz sextet that included trumpeter Frankie Newton (1906–54) and saxophonist Pete Brown (1906–63) to play at the

Onyx Club on 52nd Street, New York. He took over the leadership of the group, with Charlie Shavers (1917–71) and Russell Procope (1908–81) replacing Newton and Brown, and achieved national renown with a neatly swinging band that played polished arrangements by Kirby and Shavers, one of the first to jazz the classics, and often backing singers like Sarah *Vaughan and Kirby's wife Maxine *Sullivan. Pianist Billy Kyle (1914–66) was with the band 1938–42. They worked at the Waldorf Hotel and frequently broadcast. With changing personnel (Shavers left in 1944) the group survived, playing its small-band swing until 1950 when changes of fashion dictated its end.

Kirk, Rahsaan Roland [Ronald T.] (*b* Columbus, Ohio, 7 Aug 1936; *d* Bloomington, Ind., 5 Dec. 1977). American jazz multi-instrumentalist. Blind soon after his birth, he was educated at the Ohio State School for the Blind where he played saxophone and clarinet in the school band. By the age of 15 he was leading his own local band and soon after discovered his knack of playing three instruments at once, producing three-part harmony by ingeniously contrived fingering. Recordings he made in 1960 caught the public attention though some critics accused him of gimmickry. Adding various whistles, sirens, car horns, etc., to his act he produced a wild, basic sort of music that had its roots in the blues and New Orleans jazz but was aggressively modern. He worked with Charlie *Mingus in 1961, after which he made his first trip to Europe to appear as a soloist at the Essen Jazz Festival. He regularly toured abroad after this and appeared at the Ronnie *Scott Club in London. In the 1960s and 1970s he led a group which he called Vibration Society. In 1975 he suffered a stroke, but kept on playing until a further stroke caused his death. He openly declared his debt to his jazz predecessors and recorded tributes to many of them in his immediate, unique, and unclassifiable style and in his own very personal compositions. Beyond the gimmickry he was a great improvisational soloist when he confined himself to one instrument at a time.

Kismet. American musical extravaganza using the music of the Russian composer Alexander Borodin (1833–87), arranged by Robert *Wright and George *Forrest, with a book by Charles Lederer and Luther Davis, based on the 1911 play by Edward Knoblock.

Set in ancient Baghdad, it tells of the strange adventures of a poet turned beggar (played by Alfred *Drake), including the defeat of the wicked Wazir, the marriage of his daughter Marsinan (Doretta Morrow, 1928–68) to the Caliph of Baghdad, (Richard Kiley, *b* 1922), and other events on typical Arabian Nights lines, all occurring during the course of one day. It was produced at the Ziegfeld Theatre, New York, 3 Dec. 1953 [583p] and came to London, with Drake and Morrow in the cast, at the Stoll Theatre, 20 Apr. 1955 [648p]. The 1955 film version starred Howard *Keel and Ann Blyth (*b* 1928).

Borodin's melodic and romantic music translated well into the American mode, the 'Polovtsian dances' producing 'Stranger in Paradise' and 'He's in love'; the String Quartet in D—'And this is my beloved' and 'Baubles, bangles and beads'; while 'Fate' came from the 2nd Symphony and 'Sands of time' from 'In the steppes of Central Asia'. In 1978 an all-black version called *Timbuktu* (which switched the setting to ancient Africa) had 221 performances; and in 1985, *Kismet* was taken into the repertoire of the New York City Opera.

Kiss Me, Kate. Durable American musical that cleverly wove Shakespeare's *The Taming of the Shrew*, as a play-within-a-play, into a plot involving the domestic strife of its principal players, actor-producer Fred Graham and his ex-wife actress Lili Vanessi, their turbulent quarrels and reunions matching the similar scuffles between Petruchio and Kate in the play. The witty book was by Bella (1899–1990) and Samuel Spewack (1899–1971). An excellent score by Cole *Porter (probably his best) provided songs for the Shakespeare play such as 'I've come to wive it wealthily in Padua', 'Were thine that special face', and 'Where is the life that late I led'; while the modern plot had such hits as 'Another opening, another show', 'Wunderbar', 'So in love', 'I hate men', 'Too darn hot', 'Always true to you in my fashion', and 'Brush up your Shakespeare'.

With Alfred *Drake and Patricia Morison (*b* 1915) in the leading roles, it opened at the New Century Theatre, New York, on 30 Dec. 1948, directed by John C. Wilson (1899–1961), and became the fourth longest running musical with 1077 performances. The London production with Bill Johnson, Julie Wilson, Patricia Morison, Adelaide *Hall, and Sidney James opened at the Coliseum 8 Mar. 1951 and had 400 performances. Since then it has often been revived, including a production by the English National Opera in London; and it was filmed in 1953 with Kathryn *Grayson, Howard *Keel, Ann Miller (*b* 1919), Keenan Wynne (*b* 1916), Bobby Van (1930–80), and Bob *Fosse.

Kitt, Eartha (*b* Columbia, SC, 26 Jan. 1928). American singer and actress. She went to New York to learn her art in clubs and cabaret and in 1948 was in Paris with the Katherine Dunham dance troupe, returning to New York to continue working in clubs. Her style of singing, described as a 'low-key monotone', combined with a sultry sort of felinity that outraged many sober citizens in America, eventually made their mark when she joined the cast of the Broadway revue **New Faces* in 1952 (filmed 1954) making a hit with her performance of 'Monotonous'. An RCA recording contract followed and such items as 'Uska dara', 'C'est si bon', 'Santa baby', and her classic 'An old-fashioned girl', quickly made her into an international variety star. She has played some odd roles in musicals such as *Shinbone Alley* (1957) and *Timbuktu* (1978).

E. Kitt: *I'm Still Here* (New York, 1989).

Klein, Manuel (*b* London, 6 Dec. 1876; *d* New York, 1 June 1919). English-born American composer, lyricist, and conductor. Brother of the well-known music-critic Herman Klein, he went to the USA in 1904, became musical director at the New York Hippodrome 1905–14, and composed the scores of many of the famous and very successful Hippodrome extravaganzas. He returned to London in 1915 to conduct at the *Gaiety Theatre and then at the London Hippodrome, but went back to America in 1917. His scores included: *Mr Pickwick* (1903); *A Society Circus* (1905); *Pioneer Days/Neptune's Daughter* (1906); *The Man from Now* (1906); *The Top of the World* (1907); *The Auto Race/The Battle of Port Arthur* (1907); *Sporting Days* (1908); *The Pied Piper* (1908); *A Trip to Japan* (1909); *The International Cup/The Ballet of Niagara* (1910); *Around the World* (1911); *Under Many Flags* (1912); *America* (1913); *Hop o' my Thumb* (1913); *Wars of the World* (1914); and *It's Up to You* (1920).

Kleinsinger, George (*b* San Bernardino, Calif., 13 Feb. 1914; *d* New York, 28 July 1982). American composer. He studied dentistry but followed a preference for music and worked for a while in a dance band. After writing an opera, *Life in a Day of a Secretary* (1939), and a number of orchestral and choral works, he was to find his métier in educational work and music for children. He had his first big success in this field with 'Tubby the Tuba' (1942), popularized by Danny *Kaye, which was followed in similar vein by 'Story of Celeste' (1944), 'Pee-Wee the Piccolo' (1946), and by 'Street Corner Concerto' for harmonica and orchestra (1946), and 'Brooklyn Baseball Cantata' (1948). His best work was in the chamber opera *Archy and Mehitabel*, based on the Don Marquis writings about a cockroach and a cat, which was first performed in New York in 1954 and eventually became a musical under the title of *Shinbone Alley*, with Eartha *Kitt as Mehitabel and Eddie Bracken (*b* 1920) as Archie, running from 13 Apr. 1957 at the Broadway Theatre for 49 performances.

Kneller Hall. The former home of Sir Godfrey Kneller (1646–1723), court painter to Charles II, built between 1709 and 1711 as his country house at Twickenham. Since 1857 it has been the home of the Royal Military School of Music, the training school for army musicians and bandmasters, and survived government attempts to close it in the 1980s.

Knickerbocker Holiday. American musical comedy in two acts with music by Kurt *Weill and book and lyrics by Maxwell *Anderson. Produced by the Playwrights Company at the Ethel Barrymore Theatre, 19 Oct. 1938, it had 168 performances.

There was a somewhat contrived story in which the writer Washington Irving, played by Ray Middleton (*b* 1907), becomes involved in the history of New York that he is writing. The story revolves around the new Governor Pieter Stuyvesant who has to overcome local opposition and romantic entanglements, a part memorably played by Walter Huston (1884–1950), appearing in his one Broadway musical, who sang the show's best-remembered hit 'September song'. A film was made in 1944.

Knight, Gladys (*b* Atlanta, 28 May 1944). American rhythm 'n' blues singer. She was brought up in a family tradition of church choirs and gospel hymns, sang as a child with the Wings Over Jordan and Morris Brown gospel choirs, and won a television award when she was eight. In 1952 she organized a group with her brother and two cousins which was known as the Pips. They were to continue into the 1980s, with few changes, first making their mark on record in 1958 with 'Whistle my love'. This was followed by 'Every beat of my heart' (1961); 'Letter full of treats' (1961); 'Giving up' (1964); 'Either way I lose' (1965); but their worldwide recognition did not come until 1966 when they joined the *Tamla Motown label, with items like 'I heard it through the grapevine' (1967); 'It should have been me' (1968); 'Friendship train' (1969).

Recognized as one of the great women soul singers of all time, singing in the Rosetta *Tharpe mould, Knight moved into the secular ballad field with 'If I were your woman' (1970); 'Make me the woman that you go home to' (1971); 'Help me make it through the night' (1972); and 'Neither one of us' (1972). The group moved to the Buddah label in the mid-1970s with 'Midnight train to Georgia' (1973); 'The best thing that ever happened to me' (1974); and 'The way we were' (1975). There was a dispute over a proposed move to Columbia in 1977 and no more joint recordings were made until they re-united in 1980.

Knowles, R. G. [Richard George] (*b* Hamilton, Ontario, 7 Oct. 1858; *d* New York, 1 Jan. 1919). Canadian comedian and singer who made his first professional appearance in vaudeville in Chicago in 1878. He toured the USA, working for a time with Haverly's Minstrels and developing his 'Very Peculiar American Comedian' Act, most of it a sustained sarcastic attack on his audience. He first appeared in London in 1891. It took him some time to get London audiences to accept his American humour, put over in the now familiar Bob *Hope style, but he eventually became a great favourite and was a top-of-the-bill artist for the next 25 years, during which time he toured the world. The best-known song in his repertoire was 'Girly, girly' written by Jerry Cohan, the father of George M. *Cohan.

R. G. Knowles: *A Modern Columbus: his Voyages, his Travels, his Discoveries* (London, 1918).

Koehler, Ted (*b* Washington DC, 14 July 1894; *d* Santa Monica, Calif., 17 Jan. 1973). American lyric-writer. He began his working career as a photo-engraver but gave this up to play the piano in silent film cinemas. He was a pioneer in the business of song exploitation and wrote for specific vaudeville stars—'When lights are low' (1923) was one of his earliest successes—and stage productions such as **Earl Carroll's Vanities* (1930)—'Hittin' the bottle', 'Out of a clear blue sky', 'One love'; (1932 edition)—'I gotta right to sing the blues'; and *Say When* (1934). He produced floor shows, including many staged at the famous *Cotton Club where songs such as his 'Get happy', 'Between the devil and the deep blue sea', 'Kickin' the gong around', 'Wrap your troubles in dreams', 'Minnie the Moocher', 'Stormy weather', 'I've got the world on a string', 'Happy as the day is long', 'I love a parade', 'Truckin'', 'Cotton', 'As long as I live', and 'Rockin' in rhythm' were heard.

Later he went to Hollywood to contribute material to such films as *Let's Fall in Love* (1934)—'Let's fall in love'; *Curly Top* (1935)—'Animal crackers'; *Dimples* (1936); *King of Burlesque* (1936)—'I'm shootin' high', 'Lovely lady'; **Artists and Models* (1937); *Love Affair* (1939); *Up in Arms* (1944); *Hollywood Canteen* (1944); *Weekend at the Waldorf* (1945); *San Antonio* (1946);—'Some Sunday Morning'; *Escape Me Never* (1947); and *My Wild Irish Rose* (1947); and to write such songs as 'Ev'ry night about this time' (1942). Among the composers he worked with were Harold *Arlen, Rube Bloom, Sammy *Fain, Jay *Gorney, Ray *Henderson, Burton *Lane, Jimmy *McHugh, and Harry *Warren.

Korner, Alexis (*b* Paris, 19 Apr. 1928; *d* London, 1 Jan. 1984). British guitarist, singer, bandleader, broadcaster, and writer. He was born in Paris of an Austrian father and a Greek mother; the family managed to escape from France in 1940. They settled in London, where he studied at St Paul's School and there first acquired an interest in jazz and blues. He worked with several record companies, including a spell at Decca, where he collaborated with Peter Gammond on *Jazz on Record*, and at the BBC. He developed a striking talent as guitarist and singer, proving to a small band of devotees that the blues could be sung and played authentically by European musicians. He thus helped to start the British rhythm 'n' blues movement, motivating it through the London Blues and Barrelhouse Club at the Roundhouse in Brewer Street, London, which he founded with harmonica player Cyril Davies (1932–64) in 1955. Having helped to bring the blues singer Big Bill *Broonzy to England, the cause was furthered by visits to the club by such figures as Muddy *Waters, Jimmy *Rushing, Sonny *Terry, and Brownie *McGhee. Inspired by the work of Muddy Waters, Chris *Barber brought a flavour of R & B into his own band with Korner and Davies backing his singer Ottilie Patterson. The enthusiasm for these performances led to Korner and Davies opening a club in Ealing, West London, in 1962, where they led a band called Blues Incorporated, featuring saxophonist Dick Heckstall-Smith and drummer Charlie Watts. The group attracted many musicians who were to be influential in the burgeoning British R & B scene; among those who played with it or appeared as guests at one time or another were Mick *Jagger, Brian Jones, Long John Baldry, Eric *Clapton, Graham Bond (1937–84), Jack Bruce (*b* 1943), Ginger Baker (*b* 1940), Phil Seamen (1926–72), Art Themen (*b* 1939), and Paul Jones (*b* 1942).

Korner came on the scene too early to reap the full benefit of the styles he introduced, and he preferred to follow the genuine article rather than enter the commercial competition. By 1967 he was working with a new trio, but thereafter enjoyed working as a soloist or in a duo with bass guitarist Colin Hodgkinson (*b* 1945). While touring in Scandinavia he joined up with Peter Thorup and they continued to work together into the 1970s. He worked on BBC's Radio 1, hosting a civilized and erudite R & B show, and also showed taste and sincerity in his writings. Although he rejected the accolade himself, he has been widely acclaimed as the 'father of modern British blues'.

Korngold, Erich Wolfgang (*b* Brno, Czechoslovakia, 29 May 1897; *d* Hollywood, 29 Nov. 1957). Czech-born American composer and conductor. Son of Julius Korngold (1860–1945), a critic who succeeded Hanslick in 1902 at the *Neue Freie Presse* in Vienna and wrote two influential books on opera, he was a child prodigy who had composed a widely performed pantomime, *Der Schneemann*, at the age of 11, a piano trio at 12, which was performed with Bruno Walter as the pianist, and a piano sonata played by Schnabel. His operas *Der Ring des Polykrates* and *Violanta* were produced in Munich in 1916, followed by the highly successful *Die tote Stadt*, produced simultaneously in Hamburg and Cologne in 1920 and at the Metropolitan Opera in New York in 1921. His orchestral works were conducted by Richard Strauss, Klemperer, and Ormandy. He conducted for several years at the Hamburg Opera House and re-scored many operetta classics to give them a new lease of life. A musical, *Kosher Kitty Kelly*, was performed in New York in 1925. His own favourite opera, *Das Wunder der Heliane*, was produced in 1927 and it seemed likely that he would settle into the life of a respected and popular Viennese composer.

In 1934, however, an invitation to Hollywood from the director Max Reinhardt changed the course of his life for some time. Already living in difficulties under the Nazi regime, he accepted the invitation to adapt Mendelssohn's music for the film *A Midsummer Night's Dream*. The success of this led to a commission from Warner Brothers to write further film scores with the option of choosing only those that he felt were of interest and for which he could have all the time necessary to produce a quality article. During the next 13 years he wrote the scores for a number of major films that were to establish him as a leader in this field and win him two Academy Awards. For a time he moved between Hollywood and Vienna, teaching at the Vienna Academy 1930–4, before he took his family to the USA in 1938 and settled in Hollywood, becoming an American citizen in 1943.

The scores he produced included: *Captain Blood* (1935); *Give Us This Night* (1936); *The Green Pastures* (1936); *Anthony Adverse* (1936; Academy Award); *The Prince and the Pauper* (1937); *Another Dawn* (1937); *The Adventures of Robin Hood* (1938; Academy Award); *Juarez* (1939); *The Private Lives of Elizabeth and Essex* (1939)—'Come live with me'; *The Sea Hawk* (1940)—'Old Spanish song'; *The Sea Wolf* (1941); *King's Row* (1942); *The Constant Nymph* (1943); *Between Two Worlds* (1944); *Devotion* (1946); *Of Human Bondage* (1946); *Deception* (1946); and *Escape Me Never* (1947). He then found time to return to writing orchestral music, having his violin concerto premièred by Jascha Heifetz in 1947 and his 'Symphonic Serenade' played by the Vienna Philharmonic under Furtwängler. In 1944 he arranged the music of Offenbach in *Helen Goes to Troy*. His opera *Die Kathrin* (first heard in Stockholm in 1939) was a failure in Vienna in 1950. He continued to compose in the 1950s and returned to films in 1955 with the adaptation of Wagner's music in the biographical *The Magic Fire* in which he played the sound-track piano.

R. S. Hoffmann: *Erich Wolfgang Korngold* (Vienna, 1923). L. Korngold: *Erich Wolfgang Korngold: ein Lebensbild* (Vienna, 1967).

Kosma, Joseph [Jozsef] (*b* Budapest, 22 Oct. 1905; *d* La Roche-Guyon, nr. Paris, 7 Aug. 1969). Hungarian-French composer. He studied at the Budapest Conservatory, then won a scholarship to the Berlin Opera where he conducted until 1929, when he joined Bertolt *Brecht's touring company. There he worked with Hanns Eisler (1898–1962) and Kurt *Weill, who were both strong influences on his own writings. After working in the Hungarian film industry he settled in Paris in 1933, becoming a naturalized Frenchman. He began to write music for French films, firstly with Jean Renoir, and collaborated with Jacques Prévert on a ballet, *Rendez-vous* (1945), and a collection of songs, *Encore une fois sur le fleuve* (1946), which were adopted by Les Auberges de Jeunesse and became much used by the resistance groups. Songs by the Kosma–Prévert collaboration were used by many French singers, including Les Frères Jacques and Yves *Montand, and he also collaborated with Desnos and Raymond Queneau on songs for Juliette *Gréco.

His songs were rarely cast in a deliberately popular style and were often difficult. Apart from the universally successful 'Les feuilles mortes', his reputation was a *succès d'estime* rather than the result of popular acclaim and his works always hovered between the light and classical worlds. His songs included 'Dis-moi pourquoi' (1938, *w* Michel Vaucaire); 'Les feuilles mortes' (1947, *w* Jacques Prévert);—as 'Autumn leaves' (*w* Johnny *Mercer and Geoffrey Parsons) used in the film *Autumn Leaves* (1950). Also with Prévert: 'En sortant de l'école', 'Barbara'. 'La pêche à la baleine', 'L'inventaire', 'Je suis comme je suis', and 'La fête continue'; with others 'Si tu t'imagines' (*w* Ramond Queneau), 'La fourmi' (*w* Desnos), and 'La rue des blancs-manteaux' (*w* Jean-Paul Sartre). He wrote an operetta, *Les Chansons de Bilitis* (1954), and the comic operas *Un Amour électronique* (1962); *La Révolte des canuts* (1964); and *Les Hussards* (1969). His film scores included: *La Grande Illusion* (1937); *La Bête humaine* (1938); *Les Enfants du Paradis* (1945); *Les Portes de la nuit* (1946)—'Les enfants qui s'aiment'; *Déjeuner sur l'Herbe* (1959); *La Françoise et l'amour* (1960); *Le testament du Docteur Cordelier* (1961); *Snobs* (1961); and *La poupée* (1963).

Kostelanetz, André (*b* St Petersburg, 23 Dec. 1901; *d* Port-au-Prince, Haiti, 13 Jan. 1980). Russian-American conductor, pianist, composer, and arranger. He made his professional piano debut at the age of eight and studied at the St Petersburg Academy of Music. He had been an assistant conductor at the Petrograd Grand Opera for a year when his family emigrated to America in 1922. In New York he worked as a rehearsal pianist at the Metropolitan Opera, appeared on radio as a soloist in 1924, and four years later joined CBS as musical adviser, conducting his first orchestral broadcast in 1931. During the mid-1930s his recording and radio orchestra included most of New York's resident jazzmen, while men of the calibre of George *Bassman and Claude *Thornhill were on his arranging staff.

Kostelanetz was the first conductor to present popular music in neo-symphonic terms and, conversely, to popularize the lighter classics with good taste. His transcription of material ranging from nursery rhymes to jazz standards, put out on Columbia 78s, were masterpieces of orchestral scoring. From the 1940s he concentrated on large-scale performances of popular classics and introduced many recording techniques that later became standard practice. In later years he travelled extensively with his wife, the opera singer Lily Pons, whom he married in 1938 and later divorced. Neither prolific nor eminent as a composer himself, apart from his Tchaikovsky adaptations 'Moon love' (1939) and 'On the Isle of May' (1940), he was nevertheless one of the outstanding interpretative figures and a great influence on popular music for over 50 years.

A. Kostelanetz & G. Hammond: *Echoes: Memoirs of André Kostelanetz* (New York, 1981).

Koster & Bial's. New York's premier *vaudeville house of the 1880s and 1890s. A theatre on 23rd Street, previously the home of the Don Bryant Minstrels, was jointly acquired by John Koster and Rudolf Bial with the intention of using it as a concert hall. By 1881 the concert project had been dropped in favour of weekly 'variety' shows which had placed a strong emphasis on overseas talents, with many leading British music-hall performers appearing there. In 1893, Koster & Bial's moved to a theatre on 34th Street where, like many theatres of the time, it started its own downfall by introducing films as a novelty attraction. It managed to survive as a vaudeville house until 1901, when it was demolished to make way for the building of Macy's department store.

Kreisler, Fritz (*b* Vienna, 2 Feb. 1875; *d* New York, 29 Jan. 1962). Austrian violinist and composer. One of the greatest violinists of all time, he came from a musical family and appeared as a boy prodigy at the age of seven. He studied at the Vienna Conservatory, winning the gold medal in 1885; then at the Paris Conservatory, graduating in 1887 and winning the Premier Grand Prix de Rome when he was only 12. His American debut was in 1888 at the Steinway Hall and he toured the country in 1889 with Moriz Rosenthal. Returning to Europe he gave up music to study medicine in Vienna, then became an art student in Rome and Paris. Compulsory military service followed and he became an officer in the Uhlans of the Austrian Army. After this he resumed his career as a violinist in 1899 and began a long series of world tours. He was recalled to the Austrian Army during the First World War, was wounded in 1915, and discharged. After the war he continued his concert work, making New York his home for most of the time. He was injured in a car accident in 1941 but recovered and was able to continue playing.

In the lighter fields of music, he composed two operettas, *Apple Blossoms* (1919) and *Sissy* (1923)—later filmed as *The King Steps Out* (1936) with Grace Moore (1901–47). But he is best remembered as the composer of many excellent violin pieces. An announcement in 1935 that a series of pieces he had published as *Classical Manuscripts* under the names of earlier composers were, in fact, his own work, caused a furore of indignation among some critics, notably the humourless Ernest Newman, but others were amused and Olin Downes wrote a piece in the *New York Times* called 'Kreisler's Delectable Musical Hoax' in 1935. The pieces were soon accepted as excellent pastiche. He wrote them because he felt there was a genuine shortage of good encore pieces. Under his own name he contributed *c.* 1910 such light masterpieces to the repertoire as 'Caprice viennois', 'Liebesfreud', 'Liebesleid', 'Schön Rosmarin', and 'Tambourin chinois'.

L. P. Lochner: *Fritz Kreisler* (New York, 1950).

Krell, William H. (*fl* late 19th century). American composer and bandleader. He led a well-known band called Krell's Orchestra of Chicago and is remembered in popular musical history as the first composer to get an authentic ragtime composition into print. His 'Mississippi rag' (1897) proudly boasted on its cover: 'the first ragtime two-step ever written and first played by Krell's Orchestra, Chicago'. He also wrote 'Cakewalk patrol' (1895) and 'The Bowery spielers' (1900).

Kristofferson, Kris (*b* Brownsville, Texas, 22 June 1936). American country singer, actor, and composer. He studied at Pomona College and won a Rhodes Scholarship to Oxford where he graduated in 1960, returning to the USA to serve in the US Army and going to Germany as a helicopter pilot. He settled in Nashville in 1965 where a long-lasting love of country music came to fruition and he was able to sell and promote his songs such as 'Me and Bobby McGee', 'For the good times', 'Help me make it through the night', and 'Sunday mornin' comin' down' which have become country classics and were sung by Ray Stevens and Roger *Miller. He began to record in his own right around 1970 and has made several albums, the first and perhaps best being *Silver Tongued Devil and I* (1971). He worked with Rita Coolidge (*b* 1944) on *Kris and Rita* (1978): they were married in 1973 and divorced in 1979. More albums followed in the 1970s but from then on he mainly worked as a film actor, appearing in *A *Star is Born* (1976) with Barbra *Streisand.

B. Kalet: *Kris Kristofferson* (New York, 1979).

Krupa, Gene (*b* Chicago, 15 Jan. 1909; *d* Yonkers, NY, 16 Oct. 1973). American jazz drummer, bandleader, and composer. Born of Polish immigrant parents, he studied to be a Catholic priest but left college to play in Chicago bands such as the Blue Friars, Joe Kayser's orchestra, and the Benson Orchestra of Chicago. He made his first recording with Ben *Pollack's Bucktown Five in 1927 and that year also recorded with the historic McKenzie and Condon Chicagoans. In 1928 he went to New York where he played with Red *Nichols, Russ *Colombo, Irving *Aaronson, and others before joining Benny *Goodman in 1933. It was here that he made his name as a fine drummer with a driving beat in both big and small ensembles, while Goodman gave him plenty of opportunity for showman solos and established him as the first jazz drummer to make a real impression on the non-jazz public. He left Goodman in 1938, after an on-stage argument, and formed his own band with which he made many excellent records, featuring Roy *Eldridge (one of the first black players to play with a white band) and singer Anita *O'Day in such numbers as 'Let me off Uptown' and 'That what you think'. The band broke up and he returned for an 'all is forgiven' reunion with Goodman in 1943, then did a brief spell with Tommy *Dorsey before re-forming his own band in 1944. This lasted until 1951, when he joined Norman *Granz's Jazz at the Philharmonic, at the same time running a drumming school with Cozy *Cole in New York and playing with his own trio.

He had a heart-attack in 1960 but recovered and continued leading a quartet and contriving reunions with Goodman until 1967. A final meeting was in 1973, shortly before he died. In 1960 Columbia filmed *The Gene Krupa Story* (issued in the UK as *Drum Crazy*) with Krupa playing on the sound-track for actor Sal Mineo. He also appeared, either with his band or as solo guest artist, in *Some*

Like it Hot (1939); *Ball of Fire* (1941); *Syncopation* (1942); *George White's Scandals* (1945); *Beat the Band* (1946); *Glamour Girl* (1947); *Make Believe Ballroom* (1949); *The Glenn Miller Story* (1954); *The Benny Goodman Story* (1955); *American Music—from Folk to Jazz and Pop* (1969); and he appeared with Goodman in *Hollywood Hotel* (1937). He wrote: 'One hour' (with Red *McKenzie, 1929); 'Blues of Israel' (1936); 'Apurksody' (1938); 'Drummin' man' (with Tiny Parham, 1939); and 'Drumboogie' (1940).

R. Blesh: 'Drummin' Man' in *Combo: USA* (Philadelphia, 1971).

Künneke, Eduard (*b* Emmerich-am-Rhein, 27 Jan. 1885; *d* Berlin, 27 Oct. 1953). German composer and conductor. He received his musical education in Berlin where, for a time, he was a pupil of Max Bruch. He became associated with the Potsdam Male Voice Choir in the early 1900s and it was during this period that he wrote his first opera, *Die Marmorfrau*. In 1907 he was appointed chorus-master at the Neues Operettentheater in Berlin. In 1909 he conducted in Mannheim, where his opera *Robins Ende* was produced, then became musical director at the Deutsches Theater in Berlin, a post he held until 1911. He worked in Dresden from 1913, and his opera *Coeur As* was seen that year. During the First World War he served in an infantry regiment, then returned to conducting at the Friedrich Wilhelmstadtisches Theater in Berlin, where his Singspiel *Das Dorf ohne Glocke* was produced in 1919. The small degree of success gained from the operas and the comparative acclaim given to this last work suggested that the operetta field might be a sensible outlet and he began to write in this vein, achieving his greatest ever success with *Der Vetter aus Dingsda* in 1921. He was of that generation of European writers who were influenced by jazz which was used in a parodic sort of way in European musicals of the period. In order to study the music at first hand he visited New York, 1925–6, which resulted in a greater understanding of the idiom and his 'Tänzerische Suite' (1926).

By 1949 he had written more than 25 operettas, including: *Der Vielgeliebte* (1919); *Wenn Liebe erwacht* (1920; London, 1922, as *Love's Awakening*); *Der Vetter aus Dingsda* (1921)—'Strahlender Mond', 'Ich bin nur ein armer Wandegesell'; *Ehe im Kreise* (1921); *Verliebte Leute* (1922); *Casino-Girls* (1923); *Die hellblauen Schwestern* (1925); *Lady Hamilton* (1926); *Die blonde Liselot* (1927); *Die singende Venus* (1928; London, 1928, as *A Song of the Sea*); *Der Tenor der Herzogin* (1930); *Nadja* (1931); *Glückliche Reise* (1932); *Die Fahrt in die Jugend* (1933); *Die lockende Flamme* (1933); *Liebe ohne Grenzen* (1934); *Herz über Bord* (1935); *Die grosse Sunderin* (1935); *Zauberin Lola* (1927); *Hochzeit im Samarkand* (1938); *Der grosse Name* (1938); *Die Wunderbar* (1941); *Traumland* (1941)—'Komm in Traumland mit mir', 'Mädel gesucht'; *Hochzeit mit Erika* (1949).

O. Schneidereit: *Eduard Künneke: der Komponist aus Dingsda* (Berlin, 1978).

Kunz, Charlie (*b* Allentown, Pa., 18 Aug. 1896; *d* London, 17 Mar. 1958). American pianist and bandleader. He started his musical life by playing French horn in the Allentown Brass Band, then studied the piano and was leading his own band at the age of 16. In 1922 he went to England with an all-American orchestra which appeared at the Trocadero, the Popular Café, the Empress Rooms, and the Grafton Galleries. From 1925 to 1933 he led a band at the Chez Henri Club, moving to Santos Casani's new club in Regent Street in 1933 where, with his Casani Club Orchestra, he began to broadcast and record regularly, introduced by the familiar signature tune 'Clap hands, here comes Charlie'. His gentle syncopated stride piano style, with rich, full chording and discreet rhythm accompaniment, made him a favourite soloist on radio and records and he toured the variety theatres as an entertainer. His recorded potpourri selections of popular songs of the day were especially in demand.

Kyser, Kay [James King Kern] (*b* Rocky Mount, NC, 18 June 1906; *d* Chapel Hill, NC, 23 July 1985). American bandleader. He formed his first amateur band at the University of Carolina and his first professional band in the late 1920s, then led a band 1934–5 at the Black Hawk, Chicago, and became popular on radio. He had his own radio show in 1936 and became a national figure with his Lucky Strike show in 1938, which became known as the Kollege of Musical Knowledge. It was run as a quiz involving members of the audience in a hair-brained style now popular on TV. Kyser's early gimmick was a vamped introduction followed by a brief presentation of the singer and the song. The sweet, sentimental style of the 1930s was replaced by a well-blended swinging style in the 1940s with arrangements by George Duning and Van Alexander. He favoured the rather corny numbers which were their main hits like 'Praise the Lord and pass the ammunition' and 'Three little fishes' (recorded in 1939). The band and its singers, (including Ginny Simms (*b* 1916), appeared in a number of films in the 1930s and 1940s. Kyser retired to North Carolina in the 1950s and became an active Christian Scientist.

L

Lacôme, Paul [Lacôme-d'Estalenx, Paul-Jean-Jacques] (*b* Houga, 4 Mar. 1838; *d* Houga, 12 Dec. 1920). French composer. He studied music in his native Languedoc, going to Paris when an operetta of his won a Prix de Concours in an open competition run by the Théâtre des *Bouffes-Parisiens. He was active in Paris from 1860, becoming known as a writer for various reviews and as author of *Introduction à la vie musicale* (Paris, 1911). He wrote orchestral works, chamber music, more than 200 songs, and organ and piano works—including some teaching pieces, *Les succès de famille*. But he was best-known as the composer of more than 20 light and tuneful operettas which included *Jeanne, Jeannette et Jeanneton* (Paris, 1876; London, 1881); *Pâques fleuries* (1879); *Le Beau Nicolas* (1880; Vienna, 1883); *Madame Boniface* (1883); *Myrtille* (1885); *Ma mie Rosette* (1890; London, 1892), with Ivan *Caryll—his most successful work; *Mademoiselle Asmodée* (with Victor Roger, 1891); *Le Cadeau de noces* (1893); *Le Bain de Monsieur* (1895); *Le Maréchal Chaudron* (1898); and *Les Quatre Filles Aymon* (1898). One of his pieces, a vocal duet 'Estudiantina' (1881), became known arranged as a piano duet and was later orchestrated by Emil *Waldteufel.

Ladnier, Tommy [Thomas] (*b* Florenceville, La., 28 May 1900; *d* New York, 4 June 1939). American jazz trumpeter. He played with Charlie Creath (1890–1951) and Fate *Marable in St Louis and recorded with Lovie Austin (1887–1972) and her Blues Serenaders. In 1924 he worked in Chicago with King *Oliver, then went to Europe with the Sam *Wooding Orchestra 1925–6. He came to his peak with the Fletcher *Henderson band 1926–7, was with Wooding again 1928–9, and spent much time in Europe, playing with Noble *Sissle in London in 1930 and in New York in 1931. He developed a very direct, understated, but punchy style that never lost its New Orleans economy and flavour in spite of his work with more sophisticated musicians. He returned to the USA in 1931 where he led his own band and played with Sidney *Bechet 1932–3. In 1938 he came back into the jazz limelight at the end of his career by way of the New York sessions organized by the French critic Hugues *Panassié in company with Bechet, Mezz *Mezzrow, James P. *Johnson, Teddy *Bunn, Pops Foster (1892–1969), and Zutty *Singleton.

Lady, Be Good! Musical comedy with score by George *Gershwin, book by Guy *Bolton and Fred *Thompson, and lyrics by Ira *Gershwin. After a try-out in Philadelphia, it opened at the Liberty Theatre, New York, 1 Dec. 1924 and had 330 performances. It was the first Broadway musical by the Gershwin brothers, establishing them as leaders in the new jazz-oriented style as well as establishing the brothers of Fred and Adele *Astaire as the leaders in the song-and-dance field. The cast also included Walter *Catlett and Cliff *Edwards.

The story was tailored to tell of a vaudeville team who survive hard times by entertaining in the homes of the wealthy. Their attempted imposture to claim an inheritance is discovered, but they come into money anyway and find the romantic solution. It introduced such Gershwin classics as 'Hang on to me', 'Fascinating rhythm', 'Oh, lady, be good', 'A wonderful party', 'The half of it, dearie, blues', and, discarded during the early run, 'The man I love'. In London, at the Empire Theatre 14 May 1926, it went on its triumphant way, endearing the Astaire partnership to London for 326 performances. It was revived in London in 1968. A film version in 1941 starred Eleanor *Powell, Ann Sothern, and Robert Young but used only the first three numbers listed above from the original score.

Lady in the Dark. Musical play with score by Kurt *Weill, book by Moss *Hart, and lyrics by Ira *Gershwin, at the Alvin Theatre, New York, 23 Jan. 1941. Moss Hart originally conceived it as a play for another actress, but happily re-conceived it as a musical vehicle for the delectable Gertrude *Lawrence and brought in Weill and Gershwin to help towards this end.

The story is of a fashion magazine editor who suffers from an insecurity that makes her jilt her lover, fall in love with a film star (played by a young Victor Mature), and eventually marry the advertising manager because he knows a song she knew in her childhood called 'My ship', which acts as a linking thread to four dream sequences. Gertrude Lawrence also had a hit in 'The saga of Jenny' which she sang in a circus scene in which the interpolated 'Tchaikovsky' was manipulated by Danny *Kaye.

It closed after 162 performances, went on tour, then re-opened on Broadway with a re-jigged cast in February 1943 for another 83 performances. A film version in 1944 starred Ginger *Rogers and Ray Milland and there was a TV version in 1954 with Ann Sothern and Carleton Carpenter.

Lahr, Bert [Lahrheim, Irving] (*b* New York, 13 Aug. 1895; *d* New York, 4 Dec. 1967). American actor and singer. Early in his career in vaudeville and burlesque he played a noisy, clowning role touting the catch-phrases 'Gnong-gnong' and 'Some fun, eh, kid?', and making much capital out of his mobile features, but he later moved into a more sophisticated satirical vein, having a lasting success in the film of *The *Wizard of Oz* (1939) in which he played the farmhand Zeke and the Cowardly Lion. He appeared in such musicals as *Hold Everything!* (1928); *Flying High* (1930); *Life Begins at 8:40* (1934); **George White's Scandals* (1935); **DuBarry Was a Lady* (1939)—in which he sang 'Friendship' with Ethel *Merman; *Seven Lively Arts* (1944); *Two on the Aisle* (1951); and *Foxy* (1964). He also appeared in a number of films.

J. Lahr: *Notes on a Cowardly Lion: the Biography of Bert Lahr* (New York, 1969; repr. 1984).

Lai, Francis (*b* Nice, 1932). French composer and conductor. A localized writing career in France became international with his score for *Un Homme et une femme* (1966): its title song and 'Today it's you' (both with words by the film's director Claude Lelouch) became very popular. This led to film scores in France, Britain, and Hollywood that included *Vivre pour vivre* (1967)—'Live for life'; *The Bobo* (1967); *I'll Never Forget What's-his-Name* (1968)—'One day soon'; *Mayerling* (1968); *House of Cards* (1968); *Challenge in the Snow* (1968); *Hannibal Brooks* (1969); *Love is a Funny Thing* (1970); *Three Into Two Won't Go* (1970); *Rider on the Rain* (1970); *Love Story* (1970)—'Where do I begin', 'Look around'; *Hello Goodbye* (1971)—'Hello goodbye', 'No need to cry'; *The Crook* (1971); *Life, Love, Death* (1971); *The Legend of Frenchie King* (1971); *Le Petit Matin* (1971); *Emmanuelle* (1975); *Seven Suspects for Murder* (1977); *International Velvet* (1978); *Oliver's Story* (1978); and *Second Chance* (1980).

Laine, Cleo [Campbell, Clementina Dinah] (*b* Southall, Middx., 27 Oct. 1928). British singer. She started her career working in a library and shops and occasionally singing. Her remarkable voice was noted by a musician who recommended her to Johnny *Dankworth and her first professional appearance was in a club in Great Newport Street, London, in 1951. She joined the Dankworth band in 1952 and married him in 1958. Continuing her career as a distinctive jazz singer of international repute, she also began an acting career in 1958, the year in which she played the lead in Sandy *Wilson's **Valmouth*. She was in the Weill–Brecht *The Seven Deadly Sins* (1961), the London revival of **Show Boat* (1971), and a Dankworth musical, *Colette* (1979). In 1972 she toured Australia and the USA, appearing in a Carnegie Hall Concert (recorded by RCA) in 1973. Dankworth provided her with some very original songs and the partnership widened its scope and ambitions as the years went on. In 1975 she became the first British singer to have a featured programme at the Hollywood Bowl and she appeared in *Cleo on Broadway* in 1977. Recipient of several gold and platinum discs for her ever-interesting albums, and many awards including an honorary Doctorate of Music from Berklee College, Boston, she returned to Carnegie Hall in 1983 and continues a brilliant career, working and teaching with her husband.

Laine, Frankie [LoVecchio, Francis Paul] (*b* Chicago, 30 Mar. 1913). American singer, actor, composer, and author. The son of Sicilian immigrants, he first sang in a church choir and, from his earliest boyhood, considered singing to be the only possible career for him. In 1939 he joined the band of Joe Kayser at the Merry Garden Ballroom in Chicago, following this with a spell as a marathon dance contestant (during which he set an all-time marathon dance record of 3501 hours in 145 consecutive days in 1932), and a short-lived career in radio in Stamford, Conn. He took over from Perry *Como with the Freddy Carlone band for a brief period in 1937. By the outbreak of war he was still more or less unknown, and it was not until 1946, when he was singing in Billy Berg's in Hollywood (with Nat 'King' *Cole leading the house trio), that he was spotted by Hoagy *Carmichael; a recording contract with Mercury records followed and he had a hit record with 'That's my desire' in 1947.

Taken up by Mitch *Miller and Columbia Records in their attempts to bring a Country and Western flavour into the popular music of the 1950s, he was to achieve no fewer than 13 million-selling discs, including such lusty items as 'Shine' (1948); 'Cool, clear water', 'The cry of the wild goose' (1950); 'Jezebel', 'Jalousie', 'Rose, Rose, I love you' (1951); 'Hey, Joe', 'Mule train', 'Lucky old sun', 'Rawhide', 'High noon' (1952); 'Answer me, my love', and his top-hit 'I believe' (1953), in a manly vein that both he and Guy *Mitchell promoted with great success. He was also a first-class jazz singer. By 1952 he was among the top recording stars and had his own show at the London Palladium.

When the vogue for big-voiced ballads receded he tried an alteration of style, but he never made the same impact again and mainly worked in cabaret during the 1960s. In 1975 he reappeared in the hit parade with a recording of the theme song from Mel Brooks's film *Blazing Saddles*. He was in such films as *Make Believe Ballroom* (1949); *The Sunny Side of the Street* (1951); *Rainbow Round My Shoulder* (1952); *When You're Smiling* (1953); *Bring Your Smile Along* (1955); and *Meet Me in Las Vegas* (1956); and became a proficient actor in various TV features. He wrote 'We'll be together again' (1945); 'What could be sweeter' (1946); 'A man ain't supposed to cry' (1949); 'Deuces wild' (1961); and other songs, many with Carl Fischer who was his musical director until he died in 1954. Laine survived four heart-bypass operations in 1985; he was singing as vigorously as ever when he toured Britain in 1988, at age of 75.

Lamb, Arthur J. (*b* Somerset, 12 Aug. 1870; *d* Providence, 11 Aug. 1928). American actor and lyricist. He went to America as a young man and toured for many years with minstrel shows, later joining the professional staff of a music-publishing business. He wrote the libretto for *The Fisher Maiden* (1903) and was responsible for such classic lyrics as 'Asleep in the deep' (1897, *m* Henry W. *Petrie); 'At the bottom of the deep blue sea' (1899, *m* Petrie); 'A bird in a gilded cage' (1900, *m* Harry *Von Tilzer); 'The mansion of aching hearts' (1902, *m* Von Tilzer); 'The bird on Nellie's hat' (1906, *m* Alfred Solman); and a host of lesser ditties in turn-of-the-century style.

Lamb, Joseph Francis (*b* Montclair, NJ, 6 Dec. 1887; *d* Brooklyn, NY, 3 Sept. 1960). American composer. Notable as one of the few white men to be considered among the classic greats of ragtime composition, his works coming third only in reputation to the output of Scott *Joplin and James *Scott. His titles include: 'Sensation' (1908), which Joplin helped him to publish; 'Excelsior rag' (1909); 'Ethiopia rag' (1909); 'Champagne rag' (1910); 'American beauty rag' (1913); 'Cleopatra rag' (1915); Ragtime nightingale (1915); 'Contentment rag' (1915); 'Reindeer' (1915); 'Patricia rag' (1916); 'Top liner rag' (1916); and 'Bohemia (1916). He was able to record a memento of his work, *Joseph Lamb: a Study in Classic Ragtime* (Folkways, 1959), shortly before he died.

Lambert, Dave (*b* Boston, 19 June 1917; *d* 1966). American singer and arranger. He began his career as a drummer, sang with the Johnny Long band 1943–4, and was with Gene *Krupa 1944–5. He was in the Broadway show *Are You With It?* (1946), but spent the decade 1947–57 mainly arranging and writing commercial jingles. In 1957 he formed a remarkable trio with Jon Hendricks (*b* 1921) and Annie Ross (*b* 1930) which used vocalise in a boppish style, copying the current *Basie band and others in clever arrangements by Lambert. It became a great success everywhere, with Yolande Bavan replacing Ross in 1962. Lambert left the trio in 1964 to resume a career as an arranger.

'Lambeth Walk, The'. Song by Noel *Gay which was featured in Lupino Lane's show **Me and My Gal* at the Victoria Palace, London, in 1937. The name is that of a famous street with a market (off which Sir Arthur *Sullivan was born) south of Westminster Bridge, London. An executive of the Mecca Agency realized the possibilities of the song as the basis of a dance craze and, permission being given, a novelty dance arrangement was made by Adele England and used in the show. She based it on an older dance, the Coster Walk, originated by the Cockney comedian Alec Hurley. The dance was simple, the tune was catchy, the participants joined in the refrain 'Doing the Lambeth walk—Oi!', and it had a great vogue throughout the war years.

Lamour, Dorothy [Stanton, Dorothy] (*b* New Orleans, 10 Dec. 1914). American singer and actress. She gained her experience in repertory companies, before settling in Chicago as vocalist with the Herbie Kay (1904–44) band 1934–6. She and Kay married in 1935 and were divorced in 1939. In 1936 she was singing at the Stork Club in New York and was heard on radio. She made her film debut in 1937 in *The Jungle Princess*, which started a busy film career that made much of her dusky good looks and languorous singing style. The best of a long list were *High, Wide and Handsome* (1937); *Spawn of the North* (1938); *St Louis Blues* (1938); *Johnny Apollo* (1940); *The *Fleet's In* (1942); *Star-Spangled Rhythm* (1942); *Dixie* (1943); *Riding Home* (1943); *Duffy's Tavern* (1945); *Variety Girl* (1947); *My Favourite Brunette* (1947); and the seven famous 'Road' films with Bing *Crosby and Bob *Hope. She starred in the touring company of *Hello, Dolly!* in 1967.

D. Lamour and D. McInnes: *My Side of the Road* (Englewood Cliffs, NJ, 1980).

Lampe, J. Bodewalt (*b* Ribe, Denmark, 8 Nov. 1869; *d* New York, 26 May 1929). American composer and arranger. He went to the USA as a young man to study music, played in several orchestras, and eventually formed his own, Lampe's Grand Concert Band. He was editor of the band and orchestral department of the music-publisher Remick 1906–23, and in charge of music at the Trianon Ballroom, Chicago, 1923–9. His compositions included the popular 'Creole belles' (1900), also published as a song, and he compiled and edited several volumes of the 'Remick Folio of Moving Picture Music' in vol. 1 of which appeared the often used motif 'Mysterioso pizzicato' (No. 89).

Lancers. A simplified form of the *quadrille which became popular in the ballrooms of Britain and the USA towards the middle of the 19th century. A *square dance for 8 or 16 couples, its invention was claimed by a Dublin dancing-master, John Duval, and it seems likely that he at least helped to put the dance into general circulation. The composer Joseph Binns Hart (1794–1844) also claimed that he invented it in 1819. He published 'Les Lanciers' ('the celebrated quadrilles') *c*.1820—the music for the pianoforte 'with entirely new Figures Danced by the Nobility & Gentry . . . most respectfully Dedicated to Lady and the Misses Beechy'. This was published by Leoni Lee, followed by a second set published by Whitaker & Co. of London.

Hart's dance consisted of five figures: 'La Rose', 'La Lodoiska', 'La Dorset', 'L'Étoile', and 'Les Lanciers'. Duval kept the same names except for the substitution of 'Les Visites' for 'L'Étoile', but altered the actual figures danced. Hart's version seems to have been the most used in the heyday of the dance.

Land des Lächelns, Das. Romantic operetta in three acts with music by Franz *Lehár and words by Ludwig Herzer and Fritz Löhner-Beda (1883–1942), being a revised version of Lehár's earlier operetta *Die gelbe Jacke* (1923) with libretto by

Viktor Léon. It was first seen at the Metropol Theater, Berlin, 10 Oct. 1929 with the Austrian tenor Richard *Tauber in the leading role, the apex of his long association with the composer. Its principal song, the first Lehár did not couch in the traditional 3/4 time, 'Dein ist mein ganzes Herz' ('You are my heart's delight'), was to become very much Tauber's theme song. Others in the well-wrought score that stand out are 'Immer nur lächeln' ('Patiently smiling'), and 'Meine Liebe, deine Liebe' ('I love you, you love me'). It was seen at the Theater an der Wien, Vienna, 26 Sept. 1930 for 105 performances; and in London at the Drury Lane Theatre (as *The Land of Smiles*) with English words by Harry Graham, 8 May 1931. Since then the tragi-romantic story of the thwarted love between a Viennese girl and a Chinese prince has become a classic of the musical theatre and often revived. It was staged in New York in 1946 as *Yours is My Heart* and there have been several recordings.

Ländler. Country dance of Austro-German origin, particularly popular in Styria and Bavaria. The name probably derives from the Landel, an area in the Enns valley where the dance is thought to have originated. It is similar to, and generally accepted as an ancestor of, the *waltz, with music in 3/4 or 3/8 time, but generally slower. Many of the great composers—Mozart, Beethoven, and Schubert among them—as well as countless minor dance composers, have written ländler; the form generally being two 8-bar sections, each of which is repeated at least twice. An alternative name for the dance is *Scheifler* (slider), a name which refers to the gliding nature of the steps.

Land of Smiles, The *see Das *Land des Lächelns.*

Lane, Burton [Levy] (*b* New York, 2 Feb. 1912). American composer. He began by writing marches while he was at school, and at 15 joined the Remick Music publishing company, staying with them as staff writer until 1929. He studied music with Simon Bucharoff and began to compose for the Broadway stage, his generally successful scores including: *Three's a Crowd* (1930)—'Out in the open air'; **Earl Carroll's Vanities* (1931)—'Love came into my heart', 'Heigh ho, the gang's all here', 'Have a heart'; *The Third Little Show* (1931)—'Say the word'; **Americana* (1932); *Hold on to Your Hats* (1940)—'Don't let it get you down', 'There's a great day coming mañana'; *Laffing Room Only* (1944)—'Feudin' and fightin'', 'Hooray for anywhere', 'This is as far as I go'; **Finian's Rainbow* (1947)—'How are things in Glocca Morra?', 'Old devil moon', 'Look to the rainbow', 'If this isn't love', 'When I'm not near the girl I love', etc.; *On a Clear Day You Can See Forever* (1965)—'On a clear day you can see forever', 'Come back to me'. He followed the gold rush to Hollywood in 1933 and had a lucrative career writing for films, returning to New York in 1939 for his Broadway commitments.

His scores include (all with lyrics by Harold *Adamson) *Dancing Lady* (1933)—'Everything I have is yours'; *Coming Out Party* (1934)—'I think you're wonderful'; *Bottoms Up* (1934)—'Turn on the moon'; *Strictly Dynamite* (1934)—'Swing it, sister', 'Oh me, oh my, oh you'; *Palooka* (1934)—'Like me a little bit less'; *Kid Millions* (1934)—'Your head on my shoulder', 'I want to be a minstrel man'; *Long Lost Father* (1934); *The Band Plays On* (1934); *Folies Bergère* (1935)—'You took the words right out of my mouth'; *Reckless* (1935); *Shadow of a Doubt* (1935); *Here Comes the Band* (1935)—'You're my thrill' (*w* Ned *Washington); *Every Saturday Night* (1936); *College Holiday* (1936); *Hideaway Girl* (1937); *Double or Nothing* (1937)—'Smarty' (*w* Ralph *Freed); *Artists and Models* (1937); *King of Gamblers* (1937); *Wells Fargo* (1937); *Swing High, Swing Low* (1937)—'Swing high, swing low' (*w* Freed): there was a good recording by the early *Ink Spots; *Her Husband Lies* (1937); *Love on Toast* (1937); *Champagne Waltz* (1937); *Spawn of the North* (1938)—'I wish I was the willow' (*w* Frank *Loesser); *College Swing* (1938); *Cocoanut Grove* (1938)—'Says my heart'; *St Louis Blues* (1938); *Some Like it Hot* (1939)—'The lady's in love with you' (*w* Loesser); *Café Society* (1939); *She Married a Cop* (1939)—'I can't imagine' (*w* Freed); *Dancing on a Dime* (1940); *Las Vegas Nights* (1941); *Babes on Broadway* (1941)—'How about you?' (*w* Freed); *Ship Ahoy!* (1942); *Thousands Cheer* (1943); *DuBarry Was a Lady* (1943); *Meet the People* (1944); *Rainbow Island* (1944); *Hollywood Canteen* (1944); *Royal Wedding* (1951; *Wedding Bells* in UK)—'How could you believe me when I said I love you when you know I've been a liar all my life?', 'You're all the world to me' (*w* Alan Jay *Lerner), 'Too late now'; *Everything I Have is Yours* (1952); and *Give a Girl a Break* (1953)—'Applause, applause'.

Lane, Lupino [Lupino, Henry George] (*b* London, 16 June 1892; *d* London, 10 Nov. 1959). British actor, singer, dancer, librettist, director, and producer. From a long family of stage and circus connection, and a cousin of the actor Stanley *Lupino, his speciality was comic and acrobatic dancing and Cockney roles, his biggest success coming with **Me and My Gal* (1937) which introduced the popular *Lambeth walk'. His musical shows included: *Watch Your Step* (1915); *Follow the Crowd* (1916); *Afgar* (1919); *League of Notions* (1921); *Puss-Puss* (1920); *Brighter London* (1923); **Ziegfeld Follies* (NY, 1924); *Turned Up* (1926); *Silver Wings* (1930); *The One Girl* (1933); *La-De-Da-De-Da* (1943); and *Meet Me Victoria* (1944).

J. D. White: *Born to Star: the Lupino Lane Story* (London, 1937).

Lang, Eddie [Massaro, Salvatore] (*b* Philadelphia, 25 Oct. 1902; *d* New York, 26 Mar. 1933). American jazz guitarist. A fine rhythm player with a strong chordal sense and an effective soloist, he started out at 18 as a violinist in clubs and cafés, and came into jazz by way of a close boyhood friendship with jazz violinist Joe *Venuti, with whom he was to work and record throughout his brief career. He came to prominence with the Mound City Blue Blowers, 1924–5, and was closely associated with pioneering jazz activities in Chicago. He and Venuti worked with Roger Wolf Kahn 1927–8 and both were with Paul *Whitman 1929–30, appearing in the film *King of Jazz* (1930). When they both left Whiteman in 1930, Lang worked with Bing *Crosby for a while. Some of his best work was done in the duets he recorded with the blues guitarist Lonnie Johnson (1899–1970). He was the composer of 'Jet black blues', 'Wildcat', 'In the bottle blues', and other jazz numbers. He died after an operation for tonsilitis.

Langford, Frances [Newbern, Frances] (*b* Lakeland, Fla., 4 Apr. 1913). American singer. She intended to follow a career in opera, but a throat operation limited her singing activities to a warm contralto exploration of the popular repertoire. In 1931 she was heard by Rudy *Vallee on Tampa radio and won a guest spot in his radio programme which launched her on a New York career. She made regular appearances in sponsored radio shows and made her mark in the Alice *Faye film *Every Night at Eight* in 1935 singing 'I'm in the mood for love'. Until the late 1940s she appeared regularly in films, making a last guest appearance in *The Glenn Miller Story* in 1954. She was in the popular radio show *Hollywood Hotel* with Dick *Powell 1935–8, had her peak years on the Bob *Hope show 1941–5, and was with Spike *Jones 1945–7. She entertained the troops during the Second World War, touring with Bob Hope, and in the Korean War; and had her own TV show in 1951, co-starring with Don *Ameche.

Langford, Gordon Colman (*b* Edgware, Middx., 11 May 1930). British composer, arranger, and conductor. He had his first composition performed at the age of nine, won a scholarship to the Royal College of Music, and studied there 1947–50. He served in the Royal Artillery Band (Woolwich), played piano and vibraphone with a jazz group, and trombone with the D'Oyly Carte and the Lew *Stone band, and worked as a ship's musician. In the 1960s and 1970s he worked mainly as a session composer, arranger, and conductor, involved in many West End theatre productions and films, composing and orchestrating for John *Williams, Henry *Mancini, and Gerry *Goldsmith.

Latterly he has divided his time between studio work as composer and arranger and appearances as guest conductor and pianist, much of his attention being devoted to the brass band field. His first brass piece was 'Merry Mancunians', since when he has written 'Harmonious variations on a theme by Handel', 'March of the Pacemakers', 'Prelude and Fugue', 'Salute to the Six', 'The Seventies set', 'Sinfonietta for Brass Band', 'Titan March', 'Carnival Day', and 'Metropolis'; plus numerous fantasias, transcriptions, and arrangements which have been extensively played and recorded by all the leading brass bands.

Lanner, Josef (*b* St Ulrich, Vienna, 12 Apr. 1801; *d* Oberdöbling, 14 Apr. 1843). Austrian composer, conductor, and violinist. He has been called 'father of the Viennese waltz' with some degree of justification; even if he was not the first to write a dance in 3/4 time, he was one of the first composers to formulate the extended waltz in several sections intended for dancing, and one of the first conductors to establish a European reputation in this field. He taught himself to play the violin and made his professional debut in the spring of 1819 in the Jüngling coffee-house in Vienna with a trio of two violins and guitar. This became a quartet when Johann *Strauss (the elder) joined him for a while as viola player. The group was enlarged to a small orchestra and played at various venues. Their music was greatly enjoyed by Franz Schubert, who regularly visited the Bierhäuse and dance halls that employed their talents. Lanner and Strauss quarrelled and Strauss left to form his own group.

Lanner's first substantial string orchestra made its debut in May 1824. He was married in 1828 and in 1829 became the official Musikdirektor of the Redoutensäle. He played in Budapest in 1834 and 1835, in Milan in 1838, and in Preszburg in 1840, his reputation growing all the time.

Lanner's music was delicate and subtle and well-constructed, an obvious inspiration to the Strauss family and other dance composers to come. His best-known work remains the delightful 'Schönbrunner' waltz written in 1842. He wrote nothing very substantial for the theatre, but a charming operetta, *Alt-Wien*, was compiled from his music by Emil Stern and produced in Vienna at the Carltheater in 1911. A new version was arranged by Alexander Steinbrecher for the Raimundtheater in 1944. Other similar attempts to utilize his music included *Strauss und Lanner* (1880); *Joseph Lanner* (1880; revived 1888, 1894, and 1900); and *Festspiel Z 100* (1881). Among his works, more than 200 with opus numbers and many without, those that have been kept in circulation include 'Favoritgalopp' and 'Neujahrsgalopp', op. 61 (1832); 'Die Humoristiker-Walzer', op. 92 (1834); 'Pesther-walzer', op. 93 (1834); 'Dampfwalzer und Galopp', op. 94 (1835); 'Die Neapolitaner-Walzer', op. 107 (1835), 'Der Zapfenstrich-Galopp', op. 108 (1835); 'Tarantel-Galopp', op. 125 (1838); 'Krönungs-Walzer', op. 133 (1838); 'Roccoco-Walzer, op. 136 (1838); 'Marienwalzer', op. 143 (1839); 'Die Osmanen-Walzer', op. 146 (1839); 'Amazonen-Galopp', op. 148 (1839); 'Hofballtänze-Walzer', op. 161 (1840); 'Die Romantiker-Walzer', op. 167 (1840); 'Die Schönbrunner-Walzer', op. 200 (1842).

A. Weinmann: *Werkverzeichnis Joseph Lanner* (Vienna, 1948). *Werke für Klavier* (195 items in 8 volumes) was reprinted in 1975.

Lansbury, Angela Brigid (*b* London, 16 Oct. 1925). British actress and singer. Her Hollywood career started in 1944 and included such films as *The Harvey Girls* (1946); *Till the Clouds Roll By* (1946);

The Court Jester (1956); *Blue Hawaii* (1961); and *Bedknobs and Broomsticks* (1971), in many of which she tended to play somewhat unsympathetic roles. Her musical abilities were better appreciated on Broadway, where she appeared in *Anyone Can Whistle* (1964) and had a major success in **Mame* (1966), followed by *Dear World* (1969); **Gypsy* (1974); and **Sweeney Todd* (1979).

Lanza, Mario [Cocozza, Alfredo Arnold] (*b* Philadelphia, 31 Jan. 1921; *d* Rome, 7 Oct. 1959). American singer of Italian descent. A stocky, curly-haired prototype Italian opera singer, he had a moderate career in opera and on the concert stage before he became an international star by way of his portrayal of Caruso, his full-throated popularization of the genre, and his recordings of such songs as 'Be my love' and 'Because you're mine'. He appeared in the films *That Midnight Kiss* (1949); *The Toast of New Orleans* (1950); *The Great Caruso* (1951); *Because You're Mine* (1952); *The *Student Prince* (1954); *Serenade* (1956); *The Seven Hills of Rome* (1958); and *For the First Time* (1959). Since his early death he has been accorded a cult reputation.

M. Bernard: *Mario Lanza* (New York, 1971). R. Strait and T. Robinson: *Mario Lanza: his Tragic Life* (New York, 1980).

La Rocca, Nick [Dominick James] (*b* New Orleans, 11 Apr. 1889; *d* New Orleans, 22 Feb. 1961). American jazz cornettist, bandleader, and composer. He graduated from high school before taking up the cornet and playing in local bands from *c.* 1905. He worked with Papa Laine 1912–16. In 1916, he formed the *Original Dixieland Jazz Band, of which he was leader and manager, in Chicago, going on to introduce jazz to New York (at Reisenweber's Restaurant in 1917), and eventually to the world through tours in the USA and Europe (London 1919–20), and making the first jazz recordings. The band broke up in 1925 and La Rocca returned to obscurity in New Orleans, but he was brought back in 1936 to make some electrical recordings, and led a 14-piece swing band for a time before retiring from music.

He was the composer of much of the ODJB repertoire, though some of the items, like *'Tiger rag', were re-workings of earlier material, and many of them were jointly conceived by the band. His credits included: 'Tiger rag' (1912, published 1917); 'Original Dixieland one-step' (1912); 'Livery stable blues' (1912)—copyrighted as 'Barnyard blues' (Max Hart, 1916); 'Sensation rag' (1912); 'Ostrich walk' (1914); 'Lazy daddy' (with Larry Shields, 1917); 'Skeleton jangle' (1917); 'At the jazz band ball' (with Shields, 1917); 'Reisenweber rag' (1917); 'Clarinet marmalade' (with Shields, 1917); 'Mournin' blues' (1917); 'Bluin' the blues' (1917); 'Fidgety feet' (with Shields, 1918); 'Toddlin' blues' (1920); and 'Ramblin' blues' (with Shields, 1920).

H. O. Brunn: *The Story of the Original Dixieland Jazz Band* (Baton Rouge, La., 1960).

La Rue, Grace (*b* Kansas City, Mo., 1882; *d* Burlingame, Calif., 12 Mar. 1956). American actress and singer. She made her debut in 1893 with a touring company and appeared in vaudeville as part of a singing duo, Burke and La Rue. Her glamorous appearance and superb singing voice brought her to prominence in such Broadway shows as *The Blue Moon* (1906); **Ziegfeld Follies* (1907 and 1908); *Madame Troubadour* (1910); and *Betsy* (1911). She went to London to appear in revue at the Palace Theatre, where she was a sensation with her singing of 'You made me love you' in the new ragtime styling; and appeared at the Lyric in *The Girl Who Didn't* (1913). She continued her vaudeville career in the USA, and appeared in *Hitchy-Koo* (1917), **Music Box Revue* (1922), and **Greenwich Village Follies* (1928).

Lashwood, George (*b* Birmingham, 25 Apr. 1863; *d* Wychbold, nr. Droitwich, 20 Jan. 1942). British music-hall singer. He made his first music-hall appearance at the age of 15 in Birmingham and went to London in 1889, where he appeared at Gatti's and the following week at the Middlesex Music Hall. A handsome and distinguished man in the *Leybourne tradition, he specialized in patriotic song-scenas in the Charles *Godfrey mode which included 'The death and glory boys', 'The gallant 21st', 'Where are the lads of the village tonight', 'Motherland', and 'The fireman's dream'. In more romantic vein were his 'Riding on top of the car', 'I've been out with Charlie Brown', and his most popular items *'After the ball' and 'In the twi-twi-twilight'. Continuing the lion-comique tradition of the 1860s into the later music-hall period, he earned himself the nickname of 'The Beau Brummel of the Variety Stage'. He retired at the end of the First World War to live in the country, still making occasional stage appearances.

T. Barker: 'George Lashwood' in *Music-Hall Records* No. 3 (London, 1978).

Last, James [Hans] (*b* Bremen, 17 Apr. 1929). German conductor, composer, and arranger. Surviving a music-teacher's opinion that he was unmusical, he went on to study at the Bremen Music Academy and at the Army Music School in Frankfurt, and became proficient on several instruments; his main instrument, however, was the double-bass which he played in jazz groups. He joined the Hans-Günter Oesterreich orchestra in Bremen, with which he first broadcast in 1946. An offshoot dance orchestra was formed which was led by Last and his brother Robert, and became popular as the Last Brothers Orchestra. In 1948 this became the Last–Becker Ensemble (in association with Karl-Heinz Becker), playing American-style big-band jazz music. In 1955 he left to form his own group, but instead joined the North German Radio Dance Orchestra, with whom he built a reputation as an arranger. He finally formed his own orchestra in 1964, specifically to record for Deutsche Grammophon, and soon achieved international popularity with his 'Non-Stop Dancing' style which presented modern rock music in a richly orchestrated manner, with brass preponderant. So far he had worked as Hans Last, but in 1965 he changed his name to James Last.

The Last sound was applied to various kinds of music, ranging from Country and Western to Latin American. Up to then he had always run what had been intended as a recording orchestra, but in 1969 they began to tour the world, becoming particularly popular in Britain where they gave regular concerts from 1971. Such was their success that Last was able to build his own entertainment complex at Flintel, near Hamburg, in 1973. He was also a successful songwriter, writing such hits as 'Happy heart' for Andy *Williams, 'Games lovers play' for Eddie *Fisher, 'Blame it on me' for Ray *Charles, 'Fool' for Elvis *Presley, and many more.

B. Willox: *James Last* (London, 1976). H. Elson: *James Last* (London, 1982).

Late Joys. Long-running entertainment reviving the old supper-room atmosphere and style, part of the 1940s nostalgic interest in Victorian songs and ballads and music-hall. It was started in 1936 in the building in King Street, Covent Garden, that once housed the song-and-supper rooms known as *Evans's—Late Joys under the name of the Players' Theatre. Modelling itself on reports of entertainments there, the shows, produced by Harold Scott (1892–1964) and W. L. Hanchant, accompanied by food and drink, and presided over by a chairman, soon won public interest and support. The original show ran for a fortnight and a new one had to be prepared immediately. Early entertainers included Robert Eddison (*b* 1908), Peter Ustinov (*b* 1921), Archie Harradine, Alec Clunes (1912–70), singing *'Vilikens and his Dinah', and founder Peter Ridgeway (1894–1938). Its popular chairmen included Leonard Sachs (1909–1990) and author Maurice Willson Disher (1893–1916). *Late Joys*, as it was now known, continued through the war years in the cellars of the same premises, with Leonard Sachs in charge, later moving to basement premises in Albemarle Street. It became a part of London life with its revived customs of toasting Queen Victoria and denouncing the enemy of mankind—the King of the Zulus. The Players' Theatre has operated for many years under the railway near Charing Cross station in what used to be an old music-hall, Gatti's-under-the-Arches, with Don Gemmell (*b* 1903) as a regular chairman.

J. Anderson (ed.): *Late Joys at the Players' Theatre* (London, 1943). P. Sheridan: *Late and Early Joys at the Players' Theatre* (London, 1952). H. D. Stewart: *Players' Joys* (London, 1962).

La Touche, John Treville (*b* Richmond, Va., 13 Nov. 1917; *d* Calais, Vt., 7 Aug. 1956). American librettist and author. Educated at the Richmond Academy of the Arts and Sciences and at Columbia University, he began his stage writing career by getting some sketches into the revue **Pins and Needles* (1937). He then wrote 'Ballad for Uncle Sam', which was used in the WPA production *Sing for Your Supper* (1939), re-written as 'Ballad for Americans' with music by Earl Robinson (1910–91), re-used in the radio programme *Pursuit of Happiness* (1939); and was later in the film *Born to Sing* (1942). He worked with Vernon *Duke on **Cabin in the Sky* (1940; filmed 1943)—'Cabin in the sky', 'Taking a chance on love'; and contributed to *Ice Capades* (1941); *Banjo Eyes* (1942)—'A nickel to my name'; *Polonaise* (1945); *Beggar's Holiday* (1947); *The *Golden Apple* (1954); **Candide* (1956); and *The Littlest Revue* (1956).

Lauder, Harry (*b* Portobello, nr. Edinburgh, 4 Aug. 1870; *d* Strathaven, 26 Feb. 1950). Scottish comedian, singer, and composer. The son of a Lanarkshire potter, and the eldest of seven children, he spent part of his early life as a coal-miner, only moving to the professional stage after appearing locally as an amateur entertainer. He was to become one of the first Scottish comedians to find success south of the border, making his first appearances in Newcastle and Birkenhead. He adapted his difficult parochial accent to the stereotyped Scottish that has since become a stage standby, then went to London in 1900 and appeared at Gatti's singing 'Killiecrankie' and 'Tobermory'. His first great song success was 'I love a lassie', which he sang in pantomime in Glasgow in 1905. He was to become one of the highest paid artists of his time, earning £1000 a week at his peak. He went to the USA in 1907 and made many subsequent visits, becoming very popular there and making a coast-to-coast tour as late as 1930.

Lauder wrote most of his own songs (with various collaborators, notably Gerald Grafton) which included: 'Early in the morning' (1900); 'Killiecrankie' (1900); 'Bonnie Hielan' Mary' (1901); 'Tobermory' (1901); 'The last of the Sandies' (1902); 'The saftest o' the family' (1904); 'Stop yer tickling, Jock' (1904); 'I love a lassie' (1905); 'She is ma daisy' (1905); 'That's the reason noo I wear a kilt' (1906); 'A wee deoch-an-doris' (1910); 'Roamin' in the gloamin'' (1911); 'It's nice to get up in the morning' (1914); 'Keep right on to the end of the road' (1924); and countless more. He wrote several novels and short stories and chronicled his life and career in *At Home and on Tour* (London, 1907); *A Minstrel in France* (London, 1918); *Between You and Me* (New York, 1919); *Roamin' in the Gloamin'* (London, 1927). He was knighted in 1919 for his work for the troops and war charities, having lost his son in the conflict.

G. Irving: *Great Scot: the Life of Sir Harry Lauder* (London, 1968).

Lawlor, Charles B. (*b* Dublin, 2 June 1852; *d* New York, 30 May 1925). Irish-born American composer, singer, and actor. He sang as a soloist in Dublin churches before going to the USA in 1870, where he travelled with various opera companies and studied singing in Texas. In 1887 he settled in

New York, where he sang in churches, opera, and vaudeville, with occasional tours. He wrote many of his own songs including: 'The Irish jubilee' (with James *Thornton, 1890); 'The sidewalks of New York' (1890); 'Pretty Jennie Slattery' (1896); 'Daisy McIntyre' (1897); 'The best man in the house' (1898); and 'The mick who threw the brick' (1899).

Lawrence, Elliot [Broza, Elliot Lawrence] (*b* Philadelphia, 14 Feb. 1925). American bandleader, pianist, composer, and arranger. As a child of four he was appearing in his father's Children's Hour shows and led a children's band on Philadelphia radio 1937–41. He was educated at the University of Pennsylvania where he led a swing band and wrote its arrangements. He took the band to New York in 1946 to play at the Hotel Pennsylvania and had a hit record with 'You broke the only heart that ever loved you'. Gerry *Mulligan was playing in and arranging for the band in 1949. Lawrence played a lightly swinging piano while the band was inclined to sweetish mood music with horns and woodwind to give it a special sound. He gave up band leading in the 1950s to concentrate on arranging and conducting for TV and had a daily show on CBS leading a jazz group. He was musical director for several Broadway musicals and composer of many swing instrumentals and songs.

Lawrence, Gertrude [Lawrence-Klasen, Gertrud Alexandra Dagmar] (*b* London, 4 July 1898: *d* New York, 6 Sept. 1952). British actress, singer, and dancer. She studied at the Italia Conti School and made her first stage appearance in Brixton, 26 Dec. 1910, as a child dancer in pantomime. She toured variety theatres playing in sketches, appeared as a dancer in *Fifinella* (1912) and in various revues, and had a small part in *The Little Michus* (1916) in Dover. Lee White and Clay Smith gave her her first West End part as principal dancer in *Some* (1916); and she gained experience as general understudy in *Cheep* (1917), playing most of the parts at some time.

In 1918 she was a dancer and understudy to Beatrice *Lillie in *Tabs*, and eventually took over the part. She appeared in *Buzz-Buzz* (1919), was in cabaret in 1920, and had the lead in *From A to Z* (1921)—in which she first sang 'Limehouse blues'; *Dédé* (1922); *Midnight Follies* (1922); *Rats* (1923); *London Calling!* (1923);—'Parisian pierrot'. She went to New York to co-star with Beatrice Lillie and Jack *Buchanan in **André Charlot's London Revue of 1924*—'Limehouse blues', 'Poor little rich girl'; and was subsequently in the editions of 1925 (London) and 1926 (New York). She appeared in **Oh, Kay!* (NY, 1926; London, 1927)—'Someone to watch over me', 'Do-do-do'. In New York she was in *Treasure Girl* (1928) and *The International Revue* (1930)—'Exactly like you'. She pursued her redoubtable partnership with Noël Coward in *Private Lives* (1930) in London and in the USA.

She was probably the most popular British star ever to appear on Broadway, entrancing audiences with her languid British accent, graceful movement, and great sense of comedy. Established as a star in all branches of the theatre, her musical roles now included: **Nymph Errant* (1933)—'Experiment', 'The physician'; **Tonight at 8:30* (1936)—'Has anybody seen our ship', etc.; while her final triumphs in New York were in Kurt *Weill's **Lady in the Dark* (1941)—'My ship', 'The saga of Jenny'; and in the *Rodgers–*Hammerstein *The *King and I* (1951).

One of the most distinctive of leading ladies, her art has been well caught on record. Her accompanist for 15 years was Joseph Moon (1912–88). A film based on her life, *Star!* (1968) had Julie *Andrews in the title role and Daniel Massey (*b* 1933) as Noël Coward.

G. Lawrence: *A Star Danced* (London–New York, 1945). R. S. Aldrich: *Gertrude Lawrence as Mrs A* (New York, 1954; London, 1956). S. Morley: *Gertrude Lawrence: a Biography* (London–New York, 1981).

Lawrence, Jack (b New York, 7 Apr. 1912). American composer, singer, conductor, and author. He began writing for high school shows. After serving for three years in the US Coast Guard he was with the Merchant Marine, for whom he wrote their official song 'Heave ho, my lads, heave ho'. He wrote music for the films *Manhattan Merry-go-Round* (1937); *Outside of Paradise* (1938); *Hullabaloo* (1940)—'A handful of stars' (with Ted Shapiro); *Stars on Parade* (1944); *A Woman of My Own* (1947); *Susan Slept Here* (1950)—'Hold my hand'; *The Flame and the Flesh* (1954)—'No one but you'; and the score of the stage show *I Had a Ball* (1964).

Other songs included: 'Play, fiddle, play' (1932); 'All over nothing at all' (1937); 'Big boy blue' (1937); 'Sunrise serenade' (1938, *m* Frankie *Carle); 'In an 18th-century drawing room' (1939, *m* Raymond *Scott, after Mozart); 'All or nothing at all' (1939, *m* Arthur Altman); 'If I didn't care' (1940); 'Yes, my darling daughter' (1940); 'Sleepy lagoon' (1940, *m* Eric *Coates); 'A handful of stars' (1940); 'With the wind and the rain in your hair' (1940); 'Never took a lesson in my life' (with Diane Foore, 1940); 'Concerto for two' (1941, *m* Tchaikovsky); 'Linda' (1946); 'Tenderly' (1947); 'Delicado' (1952); and 'The poor people of Paris' (1956).

Lawrence, Steve [Leibowitz, Sidney] (*b* New York, 8 July 1935). American singer and actor. He left high school to take up a singing career in 1953 and appeared on the Steve Allen TV show on NBC (from 1954 billed as *Tonight*). He worked with the singer Eydie Gorme (*b* 1931) whom he married in 1957. Mainly a nightclub singer and recording artist, he appeared in **What Makes Sammy Run?* (1964) and (with his wife) in *Golden Rainbow* (1968).

Lawrence, Syd (*b* Shotton, nr. Chester, 26 June 1923). British bandleader. His father was a musician, so he took naturally to music, studied the violin, and played cornet in a local brass band while he was employed as a steelworker. He turned professional in 1941, toured with ENSA before he was called up in 1942, and played with the RAF's Middle East Command Dance Orchestra. Released from the forces in 1946, he played in the bands of Teddy Foster, Ken Mackintosh, *Geraldo, Cyril Stapleton, and Sidney *Lipton. In 1953 he joined the BBC's Northern Dance Orchestra under Alyn Ainsworth (1924–90) and played with them for over 15 years. Tiring of playing stereotyped music, he formed a rehearsal band in 1967 and, having a particular liking for the Glenn *Miller sound, transcribed several of the recorded Miller arrangements for it. An increasing number of people turned up to enjoy the nostalgic sounds at the Mersey Hotel in Didsbury and eventually they were filmed by Granada TV. In 1969, Lawrence made his band his full-time occupation and, mainly known for its Miller sound but playing many other things as well, it became one of the most popular bands in Britain.

Lawson, Winifred (*b* London, 15 Nov. 1894; *d* London, 30 Nov. 1961). British actress and singer. Educated in Vevey, Switzerland, she started her singing career as a concert recitalist. She appeared at the Glastonbury Festival in 1920 and started her London stage career at the Old Vic in *The Marriage of Figaro* in 1921. She joined the D'Oyly *Carte company and made her first appearance with them in **Princess Ida* in 1922. She played all the main soprano roles until 1929, when she had a break to tour with **Lilac Time*, before resuming her G & S activities. She was with the Old Vic–Sadler's Wells company 1934–5, and toured Australia in G & S. During the war years she toured the Middle East with ENSA.

W. Lawson: *I Have a Song to Sing-O* (London, 1955).

Laye, Evelyn (*b* London, 10 July 1900). British actress and singer. She made her first stage appearance in Brighton in 1915, and her first London appearance at the East Ham Palace in 1916 in a revue, *Honi soit*. Her prolific career as the leading lady of the British operetta and musical comedy world began when she came in as a replacement in *The Beauty Spot* at the *Gaiety Theatre in 1918. She continued in *Going Up* (1918); *The Kiss Call* (1919); *The *Shop Girl* (1920); *Mary* (1921); *The League of Notions* (1921); *The Fun of the Fayre* (1921); **Phi-Phi* (1922); **Madame Pompadour* (1923); *Cleopatra* (1925); *Betty in Mayfair* (1925); *Merely Molly* (1926); **Lilac Time* (1927); *Blue Eyes* (1928); *The *New Moon* (1929); **Bitter Sweet* (NY, 1929; London, 1930); *Helen!* (1932); *Give Me a Ring* (1933); *Paganini* (1937); *Between the Devil* (NY, 1937); *Lights Up* (1940); *Sunny River* (1943); *Three Waltzes* (1945); *Wedding in Paris* (1954); *Strike a Light* (1966); **Charley Girl* (1969); and *Phil the Fluter* (1969). She also starred in many films.

E. Laye: *Boo to My Friends* (London, 1958).

Layton, Turner (*b* Washington DC, 1894; *d* London, 6 Feb. 1978). American composer, pianist, singer, and entertainer. The son of a music teacher, he had early music training, studied medicine for a time, then decided to become a professional pianist. He made his first appearance at the Times Square Theatre, New York, in 1920 and made his first recording for the Black Swan label in 1921. He played in vaudeville with Henry *Creamer, with whom he was to write many songs, was in a musical comedy, *Three Showers* (1920), and the all-black revue *Strut, Miss Liza* (1922), and also contributed to *Spice of 1922* and *Some Party* (1922).

He teamed up with Clarence 'Tandy' Johnstone (*d* 1953) in 1922 to form the popular singing duo Layton and Johnstone (Layton at the piano). They went to London in 1923 to work in nightclubs and made their stage debut at the Queen's Theatre in *Elsie Janis at Home* (1924), going on to become favourite performers in Britain on stage, radio, and records. The partnership lasted until 1935, by which time they had sold more than 10 million records, including 'It ain't gonna rain no more', 'River, stay away from my door', 'We'll all go riding on a rainbow', and having a special hit in 'Bye, bye, blackbird'. Johnstone returned to the USA and lived in obscure and impoverished retirement. Layton continued as a popular solo entertainer until *c.*1953. Among his best songs (mainly with Creamer as lyricist) were 'After you've gone' (1918); 'Dear old Southland' (1921); 'Way down yonder in New Orleans' (1922); 'If I could be with you one hour tonight' (1922); and 'Down by the river' (1923).

Leadbelly [Ledbetter, Huddie William] (*b* Mooringsport, La., 20 Jan. 1889; *d* New York, 6 Dec. 1949). American folk and blues singer and guitarist. He learned his art as a boy by listening and copying while working on Texas farms and playing and singing in local saloons, and for a while he teamed up with Blind Lemon *Jefferson. He served terms in Texas and Louisiana prisons, for murder 1918–25 and for attempted homicide 1930–4. After his release from prison in 1934, he was helped by the musicologists John and Alan *Lomax to get work as a singer. He was gaoled again 1939–40 for assault, but afterwards, with the help of the Lomaxes, worked in clubs and made recordings that at last brought him proper recognition. Singing with a 12-string guitar, he performed in a powerful and primitive style but with an awareness of audience requirements that made him a good entertainer. He made many commercial recordings for Capitol, RCA Victor, Folkways, Verve, and Elektra, recorded prison songs for the Library of Congress, and gave many concerts in the 1940s. With John Lomax he wrote the song 'Goodnight, Irene' which became a great hit after his death and helped to bring to popular attention such traditional items as 'Take this hammer', 'Rock Island Line', and 'How long blues'.

M. Jones and A. McCarthy: *A Tribute to Huddie Ledbetter* (London, 1946). R. M. Garvin and E. G. Addeo: *The Midnight Special: the Legend of Leadbelly* (New York, 1971).

Music: J. and A. Lomax (eds): *Negro Folksongs as Sung by Leadbelly* [48 songs] (New York, 1936). J. and A. Lomax (eds): *Leadbelly: a Collection of World-Famous Songs* [70 songs] (New York, 1959). M. Asch and A. Lomax (eds): *The Leadbelly Songbook* (New York, 1962).

Leave it to Jane. American musical comedy with score by Jerome *Kern, book and lyrics by Guy *Bolton and P. G. *Wodehouse, produced at the Longacre Theatre, New York, 28 Aug. 1917, where it had 167 performances. It was one of the series written for the *Princess Theatre management and, although not staged there, was in the same pioneering American musical comedy mould as **Oh, Boy!* and **Oh, Lady! Lady!!*

The story, based on George Ade's play *The College Widow*, was one of several that had college football as their setting, in this case dealing with Jane's pursuit of star footballer Billy Bolton on behalf of her team and herself. It was not one of Kern's more lasting scores, but nevertheless it had a record revival run at the Sheridan Square Theatre in 1959 of 928 performances.

Leave it to Me! American musical comedy with score by Cole *Porter, and book by Bella (1899–1990) and Sam Spewack (1899–1971), based on their play *Clear All Wires*. It was presented by Vinton *Freedley at the Imperial Theatre, New York, 9 Nov. 1938 [291 p], and was a well-timed satire on Communism and America's diplomatic handling of such problems. It was an ideal vehicle for the bumbling Victor *Moore as the ambassador who tries every way of avoiding being sent to the Soviet Union, and it was a notable first appearance for Mary *Martin. Also in the cast were William *Gaxton, Sophie *Tucker, and dancer Gene *Kelly, with the benefit of a score that included 'Get out of town', 'Most gentlemen don't like love', 'From now on', and 'My heart belongs to Daddy', which Mary Martin made her own.

Le Brunn, George (*b* London, 1862; *d* London, 18 Dec. 1905). British composer and author. A prolific writer of music-hall and popular songs, starting at a time when they were generally considered to be the property of the singer in return for a meagre fee. He was described by the lyricist Edgar Bateman as 'a writer whose remarkable gift of melody is equalled by but few, and whose fertility of invention is equalled by none'. Although he was an active and well-known figure in his day, no further biographical details are available.

He wrote the musical sketches *Tonight's the Night* (1900) and *Ladies House of Commons* (1902); and his songs, many written in collaboration with J. P. *Harrington, included: 'Across the bridge at midnight' (1889); 'Mischief' (1890); 'Twiggy voo?' (1892); 'We all went home in a cab' (1892); 'The waiter' (1892); 'Christopher Columbus up-to-date' (1893); 'No 'Arry, don't ask me to marry' (1893); 'Me and 'er' (1894); 'The dandy-coloured coon' (1894); 'If it wasn't for the 'ouses in between' (1894); 'Looking for a coon like me' (1894); 'Half-past nine' (1895); 'It's a great big shame' (1895); 'Johnny Jones' (1895); 'The idler' (1896); 'There they are the two of 'em—on their own' (1897); 'Everything in the garden's lovely' (1898); 'You can get a sweetheart any day (but not another mother)' (1901); 'He's going there every night' (1902); 'The golden dustman' (1903); and many more.

Lecocq, Alexandre **Charles** (*b* Paris, 3 June 1832; *d* Paris, 24 Oct. 1918). French composer and conductor. He studied at the Paris Conservatoire, under Halévy for composition, 1849–54, and with Bizet as a fellow-student. His first operetta was *Le Docteur Miracle*, written on that given theme in 1857 for a competition organized by *Offenbach at the *Bouffes-Parisiens. He shared the first prize with Bizet, but the piece had little success and he spent the next seven years as an organist, his next operetta, *Le Baiser à la porte*, not appearing until 1864. After several more productions his first modest success was *Fleur de thé* in 1868 and *Les Cent Vierges* was popular in 1872, after which he gradually became famous and rich, especially after the great success of *La *Fille de Madame Angot* (Brussels, 1872; Paris, 1873). This has remained easily his most popular work, its music now known to many who may not have seen the operetta through the ballet *Mam'zelle Angot* (1943) based on its score.

As Offenbach's fortunes went into decline, so Lecocq's rose and history looks upon him now as second only to Offenbach and *Hervé in the French operetta field. He was almost as prolific, too, a result of an uneventfully industrious life. After the triumph of *La Fille de Madame Angot*, which ran for over a year in Paris alone (an exceptional run in those days), he continued with *Giroflé-Girofla* (1874) which was almost as popular; *Les Prés Saint-Gervais* (1874); *Le Pompon* (1875); *La Petite Mariée* (1875); *Kosiki* (1876); *La Marjolaine* (1877); *Le Petit Duc* (1878); *La Camargo* (1878); *La Petite Mademoiselle* (1879); *Le Grand Casimir* (1879); *La Jolie Persane* (1879); *Janot* (1881); *Le Jour et la nuit* (1881); *La Roussotte* (1881); *Le Cœur et la main* (Paris, 1882; London, 1892, as *Incognita*); *La Princesse des Canaries* (Paris, 1883; London, 1888, as *Pepita*); *L'Oiseau bleu* (1884); *La Vie mondaine* (1885); *Plutus* (1886); *Les Grenadiers de Mont-Cornette* (1887); *Ali-Baba* (1887); *La Volière* (1888); *Ninette* (1892); *La Belle au bois dormant* (1900); also several ballets and incidental music.

L. Schneider: *Les Maîtres de l'Opérette Française: Hervé et Charles Lecocq* (Paris, 1924).

Lecuona, Ernesto (*b* Guanabacoa, 7 Aug. 1896; *d* Santa Cruz de Tenerife, Canary Islands, 29 Nov. 1963). Cuban composer and pianist. One of a musically gifted family, Lecuona was an infant prodigy and appeared in public, as a pianist, at the age of five. His first composition was published when he was 11. His musical studies included a period at the National Conservatory in Havana where one of his teachers was Joaquín Nin (1879–1949). He graduated in 1911, toured South America and Europe as leader of a Cuban dance band, went to New York in 1917, played at the Aeolian Hall, and made some recordings of his own compositions. He returned to Havana to produce his works, which included cantatas, operettas, and musical comedies, at the Teatro Martí. Further concert tours in South America and Europe brought the world's attention to his music. He had a special triumph at the Salle Pleyel in Paris in 1927 and repeated it in New York later. Having attained fame, he returned to settle in Havana and to concentrate on composition.

He wrote film scores for *Always in My Heart* (1942); *One More Tomorrow* (1946); *Carnival in Costa Rica* (1947); and *Sweet Rosie O'Grady* (1950). His songs included 'Siboney' (1929); 'Jungle drums' (1930); 'Maria, my own' (1931); 'Dust on the moon' (1934); 'It's no secret I love you' (1937); 'Say "si si"' (1940); 'The breeze and I' (1940); while amongst his best known orchestral pieces are two from his 'Suite espagnol' of 1928—'Malagueña' and 'Andalucia'.

Led Zeppelin. British rock group formed in 1968 which maintained the lasting line-up of Robert Plant (*b* 1948) (vocals), Jimmy Page (*b* 1944) (guitar), John Paul Jones (*b* 1946) (keyboards), and John Bonham (1948–80) (drums). The group was formed by Page (who as a session musician had played on records by the *Kinks, the *Rolling Stones, Georgie *Fame, and the *Who) after the demise of the Yardbirds. It fulfilled its first dates as the New Yardbirds with the name of Led Zeppelin later suggested by Keith Moon of the Who. A recording contract with Atlantic Records led to their first album, *Led Zeppelin*, in 1968 which won a gold disc by the following year, its mixture of blues and rock riffs supported by good musicianship and the shirtless appeal of singer Robert Plant. They reached the US Top 100 with 'Good times bad times' and the Top 10 in 1970 with 'Whole lotta love'.

The band's success mainly came in America where 'Immigrant song' (1971), 'Black dog' (1972), and 'D'yer mak'er' (1973) were hits without making any impression in the UK. They toured the USA in 1973, achieving album sales of *Presley and *Beatles proportions, resorting to such sales gimmicks as an album *Physical Graffiti* (the first launched by their own label Swan Song in 1975), which had a sleeve with flapping and revealing windows. Plant sustained an injury in a car crash in 1975, which kept the group out of circulation for two years, though their album *Presence* (1976) won a platinum disc. A 1976 film, *The Song Remains the Same*, accompanied by a sound-track album, caught the group in full blast, followed by an even more successful tour of the USA. The group disliked being branded as of the *heavy metal ilk, but their sheer volume put them in that category, and helped them to their leading role in the 1970s, with their best-known song, and most lasting recording, 'Stairway to Heaven' (1972) reaching an orgiastic climax that was typical of their work. The group disbanded in 1980 after the death of Bonham, though Plant and Page later worked together as the Honeydrippers; Plant achieved a No. 3 hit in the USA in 1985 with 'Big log'.

Lee, Alfred (*fl.* 1860–84). American-born composer. He settled in London in the 1860s and was responsible for many popular early music-hall hits of the late 1800s, often working in collaboration with lyricist/lion-comique George *Leybourne. His songs included: 'Act on the square, boys' (1866); 'Walking in the Zoo' (1867); 'The man on the flying trapeze' (1868, *w* Leybourne), inspired by the aerial feats of the French trapezist Léotard (1842–70) who gave his name to the garment; 'Champagne Charlie' (1868, *w* Leybourne) (an early advertising *jingle); 'The husband's boat' (1869); 'The day we went to Ramsgate' (1868); 'As through the park I go' (1869); 'Walking in the park' (1869); 'Dolly Varden' (1870); 'The heavy swell of the sea' (1870); 'Rosherville' (1870); 'Quite au fait' (1871); 'Nobody's child' (1872); 'Lounging in the AQ' (1874); and 'She danced like a fairy' (1875). He wrote scores for *The Lying Dutchman* (1877) and *Black-Eyed Susan* (1884, *w* F. C. Burnand).

Lee, Bert (*b* London, 1881; *d* London, 23 Jan. 1946). British songwriter. He was active around the First World War as a supplier of later music-hall songs, many of them written in collaboration with R. P. Weston, head of a famous song-writing family, and continued as a stalwart of *Tin Pan Alley until the Second World War. His songs included: 'Nursie-nursie' (with Worton David, 1910); 'Joshu-ah' (with George Arthurs, 1910); 'Hello, hello, who's your lady friend?' (1913, *m* Harry *Fragson); 'All the girls are lovely by the seaside' (1914, *m* Fragson); and with Weston: 'Somebody would shout out "Shop"' (1915); 'Good-by-ee' (1917); 'The gipsy warned me' (1920); 'Viewing the baby' (1926); 'What I want is a proper cup o' coffee' (1936); and many more.

Lee, Brenda [Tarpley, Brenda Mae] (*b* Lithonia, Ga., 11 Dec. 1944). American singer. Discovered in 1956, she made her singing debut at the Ozark Mountain Jubilee in 1956 and had a modest hit with her first country-style recording, 'Jambalaya', made for Decca in 1957. Her singing gradually evolved from a country style to more generally oriented pop, until she became, in the words of Hardy and Laing, 'arguably the finest white female singer in pop during pre-Beatle years', this claim established by her recording of 'Sweet nothings' (1959). In the next few years she had No. 1 hits with 'I'm sorry' and 'I want to be wanted'; 'Emotions', 'Dum, dum', 'All alone am I', and 'That's all you gotta do' were also very successful, with their forceful rock ballad styling and electronic backing behind her emotionally charged voice. She retired from the music business in 1967 to marry, but made a comeback in 1971 with a country-style recording of *Kristofferson's 'Nobody wins'; and she continued to work in the Nashville vein.

Lee, Peggy [Egstrom, Norma Dolores] (*b* Jamestown, N. Dak., 26 May 1920). American singer, actress, composer, and author. She began singing on radio in Fargo at the age of 16. A first attempt to invade Hollywood resulted in a poorly paid job at the Jade Club and a throat illness that sent her back to North Dakota for an operation. Starting in Fargo again, she later worked in Palm Springs and Chicago where she was heard by Benny *Goodman, who signed her with his band when Helen Forrest left. She made her first record with Goodman in 1941 and appeared with the band in the films *The Powers Girl* (1942) and *Stage Door Canteen* (1943); and she had her biggest recorded hit with 'Why don't you do right?' (1942).

While with Goodman she married the band's guitarist, Dave Barbour (1912–65), with whom she also formed a successful songwriting partnership. On going solo in 1943 she became a big nightclub attraction and made many records with Capitol and Decca which established her as one of the most musicianly female singers of her generation, always swinging and most effective in ballads which she performed with a skill and intelligence that overcame her lack of a big singing voice. She appeared in *Mr Music* (1950) as a guest and acted in *The Jazz Singer* (1952) and *Pete Kelly's Blues* (1955). She made no more film appearances but frequently appeared in TV dramas in the 1960s and was active into the 1990s. A special claim to fame is as probably the only female singer to have written two film scores, *Lady and the Tramp* (with Sonny Burke, 1952); and *Tom Thumb* (1958). She wrote many sophisticated songs, with Dave Barbour up to 1949, later with Victor *Young, Duke *Ellington, and others.

P. Lee: *Miss Peggy Lee: an Autobiography* (New York, 1990).

Legrand, Michel (*b* Paris, 24 Feb. 1932). French composer, arranger, conductor, pianist, and singer. The son of the French conductor Raymond *Legrand, it was likely that he would follow in the family footsteps although his initial interest was only in playing jazz piano. When he made his first orchestral recordings at the age of 23, however, it was obvious that, as both conductor and arranger, he had a superb command of his orchestration. Some of his late 1950s attempts to combine straight orchestral techniques with jazz phrasing and modern voicing may have been somewhat over-arranged, but they were an effective contrast to the bland mood music prevailing at the time and proved an ideal basis for modern film scoring.

Since first visiting Hollywood in the early 1960s to record with American jazz musicians he has worked regularly there as well as in Britain and France. He produced some of the most imaginative film themes of the 1960s and 1970s in such scores as: *Bonjour tristesse* (1958); *Terrain vague* (1959); *Le Cœur battant* (1960); *Lola* (1961); *Eve* (1962)—'Adam and Eve'; *All This and Money Too* (1963)—'Love is a ball' [US title song], 'Gather your dreams'; *Les Parapluies de Cherbourg* (1964)—'I will wait for you', 'Watch what happens', and a sing-song score that was highly praised; *Bande à part* (1964); *Une Femme mariée* (1965); *La Vie de château* (1965); *Les Demoiselles de Rochefort* (1967)—'Toujours, jamais', 'Chanson d'un jour d'été', etc.; *How to Save a Marriage and Ruin Your Life* (1968)—'Winds of change'; *Ice Station Zebra* (1968); *The Thomas Crown Affair* (1968)—'Windmills of your mind' (Academy Award), 'His eyes, her eyes'; *The Happy Ending* (1969)—'What are you doing the rest of your life?'; *Picasso Summer* (1970)—'Summer me, winter me'; *The Go-Between* (1970)—'I still see you'; *Summer of '42* (1971)—'The summer knows'; *Pieces of Dreams* (1971)—'Pieces of dreams'; *A Time for Loving* (1972)—'Paris was made for lovers', 'Sea and sky'; *Wuthering Heights* (1972)—'I was born in love with you'; *Un peu de soleil dans l'eau froide* (1972)—'Dis-moi'; *Lady Sings the Blues* (1973); and *One is a Lonely Number* (1973)—'Amy's theme', 'Mon amour'.

Legrand, Raymond (*b* Paris, 1908; *d* Paris, 27 Nov. 1974). French composer, conductor, and pianist. After studies at the Paris Conservatoire he immediately went into the world of light music, and wrote and arranged for the Fred Adison orchestra such songs as 'On va se faire sonner les cloches'. He formed his own orchestra which became well-known as a show band in the *Ventura and Adison mode; his musicians not only played and sang but introduced comedy and musical sketches as well. He gained wide recognition for his work on the film *Mademoiselle Swing* (1942) in which Irène de Trébert sang his songs 'Mademoiselle Swing' and 'Le clou dans la chaussure'. One of his best interpreters was Colette Renard who sang with the orchestra for four years before making her stage reputation. In the inter-war period Legrand was accompanist to such stars as Maurice *Chevalier, Fernandel, and Edith *Piaf. He wrote the music for several films including *Topaze* (1951); *Justice est faite* (1950); *Manon des Sources* (1952); and a musical comedy, *Jehanne Vérité* (1966).

Lehár, Franz (*b* Komorn, Hungary, 30 Apr. 1870; *d* Bad Ischl, Austria, 24 Oct. 1948). Austro-Hungarian composer and conductor. Son of Franz Lehár (1838–98), Band Sergeant-Major of the 5th Austrian Regiment of Infantry, who gave him his first lessons in music. He studied at the Prague Conservatory 1882–6 and also privately with Zdenko Fibich (1850–1900). His first employment, in 1888–9, was as orchestra leader of the municipal theatre of Barmen Elberfeld, which he left to serve under his father 1889–90 in the band of the 50th

Regiment, where he became assistant conductor. He resigned from the army to work in the theatre and conducted orchestras in Losoncz 1890–4, Pola 1894–6, Trieste 1897–8, and Budapest 1898–9, finally settling in Vienna in 1899. He was to become, after Johann *Strauss II, the pre-eminent writer of operetta and musical comedy, his musical genius shining through works of solid musicianship, excellent orchestration, and every other lasting quality. He had his first theatrical success with his opera *Kukuschka*, which was staged in Leipzig in 1896 (and revised in 1905 as an operetta, *Tatjana*). This was followed in Vienna by the moderately successful *Wiener Frauen* (1902; revised as *Der Schlüssel zum Paradies*, 1906); *Der Rastelbinder* (1902); *Der Göttergatte* (1904); and *Die Juxheirat* (1904).

International fame came with *Die *lustige Witwe* (1905) which was to conquer the English-speaking world as *The Merry Widow*. Its tuneful vivacity and theatrical rightness from beginning to end put it in the same class as Strauss's *Die *Fledermaus* in terms less operatic; a classic of the musical comedy stage. Lehár was to have many more outstanding successes in an oddly variable output over the years, but none of them ever outshone this one work of pure genius. It was followed by (all dates for Vienna unless otherwise noted): *Tatjana* (Brno, 1906); *Peter und Paul reisen ins Schkaraffenland* (children's operetta) (1906); *Mittislaw der Moderne* (1907); *Der Mann mit den drei Frauen* (1908); *Das Fürstenkind* (1909); *Der *Graf von Luxemburg* (*The Count of Luxembourg*, 1909); **Zigeunerliebe* (*Gypsy Love*, 1910; as *Garabonciás*, Budapest, 1943); *Rosenstock und Edelweiss* (1910); *Eva (Das Fabriksmädel)* (1911); *Die Spieluhr* (1912); *Der ideale Gattin* (1913); *Endlich allein* (1914; revised as *Schön ist die Welt*, 1934); *Der Sterngucker* (1916; revised in Milan as *La danza delle libellule*, 1922; in London as *The Three Graces*, 1924); *Wo die Lerche singt* (Budapest, 1918)—'Durch die weiten Felder'; *Die blaue Mazur* (1920); *Die Tangokönigin* (new version of *Der ideale Gattin*, 1921); *Frühling* (later *Frühlingsmädel*, 1922); *Frasquita* (1922)—'Serenade'; *Die gelbe Jacke* (1923); *Clo-Clo* (later *Lalotte*, 1924); *Paganini* (1925)—'Schönes Italien'; *Gigolette* (1926); *Der *Zarewitsch* (1927)—'Wolga-Lied'; *Friederike* (Berlin, 1928); *Das *Land des Lächelns* (*The Land of Smiles*; revised version of *Die gelbe Jacke*, Berlin, 1929). His swan-song was the almost operatic *Giuditta* (1934), the composer's favourite work, of which he said: 'I gave my best'.

Lehár always wrote in the traditional Viennese style, with only occasional modernisms, his point numbers almost inevitably waltzes, until 'You are my heart's delight' in *The Land of Smiles* (a song inextricably associated with Richard *Tauber) proved an exception. Tauber's association with Lehár was a great motivating influence when he came back from the artistic doldrums of his mid-period. In the 1930s Lehár contributed several film scores, including: *Die grosse Attraktion* (with Bronislaw *Kaper, 1931)—'Was wär' ich ohne Euch, ihr wunderschönen Frauen' (*w* Fritz Rotter), sung by Tauber; *Es war einmal ein Walzer* (1932)—'Es gibt noch Märchen', 'Es war einmal ein Walzer', sung by Marta Eggerth; *Grossfürstin Alexandra* (1934)—'Du und ich sind für einander bestimmt' (*w* Leo Stein), sung by Maria Jeritza; *Die ganze Welt dreht sich um Liebe* (1936)—'Die ganze Welt dreht sich um Liebe', 'Schau mich an, sei mir gut'; *Eine Nacht in Wien* (1937)—'Ein autocar', paso doble for orchestra and jazz band; and *Die Gefährten des Odysseus* (1937). He also produced a large output of orchestral works and songs in the years 1882–1901 before the theatre fully occupied his attention; the most lasting of these being the waltz 'Gold und Silber' ('Gold and silver') written in 1899 and an enormously helpful success in his early career. Lehár, an authoritative conductor of his own works, fortunately survived well into the gramophone age and was able to record some of them in the 1940s.

E. Decsey: *Franz Lehár* (Vienna, 1924; repr. Munich–Berlin, 1930). G. Knosp: *Franz Lehár: une vie d'artiste* (Brussels–Paris, 1935). S. Czech: *Franz Lehár: sein Weg und sein Werk* (Berlin, 1942; repr. Lindau-Bodensee, 1948; Berlin, 1957). M. von Peteani: *Franz Lehár: seine Musik, sein Leben* (Vienna, 1950; excerpt *In Memory of Franz Lehár*, Vienna–London, 1958). W. Macqueen Pope and D. L. Murray: *Fortune's Favourite: the Life and Times of Franz Lehár* (London, 1953). B. Grun: *Gold and Silver: the Life and Times of Franz Lehár* (London, 1970). M. Schönherr: *Franz Lehár, Bibliographie zu Leben und Werk* (Baden-bei-Wien, 1970). O. Schneiderheit: *Franz Lehár: eine Biographie in Zitaten* (Innsbruck, 1984).

Lehmann, Liza [Elizabetha Nina Mary Frederika] (*b* London, 11 July 1862; *d* Pinner, Middx., 19 Sept. 1918). British composer and singer. Taught by her mother, who was a well-known amateur singer and an arranger of songs under the initials A.L., she also studied with other teachers, including Randegger, in Rome and London. She made her debut as a singer on 23 Nov. 1885 at the Monday Popular Concerts. She sang at the Norwich Festival in 1887 and became one of the most popular sopranos of her day, with a perfect voice of considerable range, receiving much help and encouragement from Clara Schumann. She made a point of introducing interesting but forgotten old English songs into her programmes, as well as new ballads, including many of her own. She gave up singing on her marriage to the composer Herbert Bedford, giving her farewell concert at the St James's Hall on 14 July 1894.

Having retired from the concert platform, she devoted herself to composition and played a great part in promoting the Victorian popularity of the song-cycle, producing several acclaimed works in this form, including 'In a Persian garden' (1896, from Fitzgerald's version of the *Rubáiyát of Omar Khayyám*); 'In memoriam' (Tennyson); 'The Daisy Chain' (12 songs of childhood); 'Nonsense Songs' (from *Alice in Wonderland*); and 'The Cautionary Tales and a Moral' (Belloc). She has claims to be the first woman to write and stage a musical comedy with her 'musical farce' *Sergeant Brue* (Strand Theatre, 14 June 1904), which was followed by a 'romantic light opera' *The Vicar of Wakefield* (1906) and a one-act opera *Everyman* (1915). Among her songs was the effectively tongue-in-cheek 'There are fairies at the bottom of our garden' (1907, *w* Rose Fyleman).

L. Lehmann: *The Life of Liza Lehmann, by Herself* (London, 1919).

Lehrer, Tom [Thomas Andrew] (*b* New York, 9 Apr. 1928). American composer, author, and entertainer. He graduated from Harvard University in mathematics, and worked in the educational field throughout his career. Following the trendy success of his privately published LP *The Songs of Tom Lehrer* (later taken up by Decca and supported by a book of the words and music), he became a popular nightclub and concert entertainer at the forefront of the 1950s vogue for political satire, taking time off from his professional life 1953–60 and 1965–7. Other LPs followed, with an undiminished flair for irreverent humour ('The Vatican rag') and simple, catchy tunes. In 1960 *Tomfoolery*, a revue based on his songs, was produced, but he did not appear in it.

T. Lehrer: *The Tom Lehrer Songbook* (New York & London, 1958).

Leiber, Jerry (*b* Baltimore, 25 Apr. 1933). American songwriter and producer. He joined forces with Mike Stoller (*b* New York, 13 Mar. 1933) to become the first independent producers of the rock era and pioneers in bringing a touch of social satire to the blues-oriented songs they wrote together. Their partnership began after meeting as students in California in 1949. In the early days of the rhythm 'n' blues boom there was a constant demand for their pointful songs which were used by such artists as Amos Milburn (*b* 1927) and Jimmy *Witherspoon, who was responsible for their first recorded song, 'Real ugly woman'.

Initially contracted to Aladdin Records, their first really big hit came with the Charles Brown (*b* 1920) version of 'Hard times' (1951). It was followed by 'K.C. lovin'', which was made into a best-seller in 1959 as 'Kansas City' by Wilbert Harrison (*b* 1929), and 'Hound dog' (written with Johnny *Otis), which Willie Mae 'Big Mama' Thornton (1926–84) recorded in 1953 and Elvis *Presley took up in 1956. They wrote a string of hits for Presley, many of them used in his films, including 'Jailhouse rock' (1957). They started their own record label, Spark, in 1954, and had important hits with 'Framed' and 'Riot in cell block No. 9', which led to a production agreement with Atlantic Records in 1955 and the use of their songs by the *Coasters—'Poison ivy' (1957), 'Charlie Brown' (1958), 'Along came Jones' (1959)—the *Isley Brothers, LaVern *Baker, Ruth *Brown, Clyde *McPhatter, and Joe *Turner. Songs of the period were 'Loving you' (1957); 'Treat me nice' (1957); 'Don't (1957); 'Searchin'' (1957); 'Yakety yak' (1957); 'Drip drop' (1958); 'Dance with me' (1959); and 'Love potion No. 9' (1959). They produced sessions with the *Drifters which led to one of their best recordings, 'There goes my baby' (1959), which used Latin American rhythm and strings, and was an inspiration to many groups that followed and composers like Burt *Bacharach. Other Drifters songs included 'Ruby baby' (1955) and 'Fools fall in love' (1956).

They worked for various companies in the 1960s and for many artists, including further material for Presley for whom they provided many of his post-Sun RCA recordings and film songs including 'Trouble' and 'Santa Claus is back in town'. Attempts to create more record labels were unsuccessful, but they joined up with George Goldner in 1964 to form the very successful Red Bird and Blue Cat labels which in the next two years produced some 25 hits by Leiber and Stoller and other writers such as Ellie *Greenwich and Jeff Barry (*b* 1938). In 1959 they had a hit with Peggy *Lee's recording of 'Is that all there is?' (1968), which was taken from an unproduced musical score. In 1970 they went into music-publishing, continuing to produce such hits as 'Stuck in the middle' (1973) and providing material for such artists as *Procol Harem and Elkie Brooks (*b* 1945). After this they gradually lost interest in the current rock scene and worked more in the film and theatre field.

R. Palmer: *Baby, That Was Rock & Roll: the Legendary Leiber & Stoller* (New York, 1978).

Leigh, Carolyn Paula (*b* New York, 21 Aug. 1926; *d* 1983). American author and librettist. Educated at New York University, she worked in advertising before writing for the theatre. She had her first hit song in 1954 with 'Young at heart' (*m* Johnny Richards, *b* 1911) and wrote lyrics for *Peter Pan* (1954, *m* Mark Charlap) starring Mary *Martin. A number of successful songs, mainly with Cy *Coleman, included 'Witchcraft' (1957); 'I walk a little faster' (1957); 'A doodlin' song' (1957); 'Firefly' (1958); 'You fascinate me so' (1958); 'It amazes me' (1958); 'Pass me by' (1962); 'Stay with me' (*m* Jerome *Moross); and she wrote lyrics for **Ziegfeld Follies* (1957); *Wildcat* (1960, *m* Coleman); **Little Me* (1962, *m* Coleman); and *How Now, Dow Jones* (1967, *m* Elmer *Bernstein).

Leigh, Mitch [Mitchnick, Irwin] (*b* Brooklyn, NY, 30 Jan. 1928). American composer and arranger. He studied at Yale University and composition with Paul Hindemith, afterwards going into commercial music production and founding Music Makers, a group of singers making advertising material that won various radio and TV awards. Composer of jazz works and incidental music, he had a remarkable Broadway debut with the long-running **Man of La Mancha* (1965), continuing less successfully with *Cry For Us All* (1970) and *Home Sweet Homer* (1975), but mainly working in the field of commercial *jingles.

Leigh, Walter (*b* London, 22 June 1905; *d* Tobruk, 12 June 1942). British composer. He studied at

Cambridge, where he was a student of Edward Dent, and in Berlin with Paul Hindemith 1927–9. He was becoming established as a composer of a wide variety of compositions, when the war broke out and he was killed in action. His works included two operettas, *The Pride of the Regiment* (1932) and the highly acclaimed *Jolly Roger* (1933) which had 199 performances at the Savoy Theatre from 1 Mar. 1933, with a cast that included George *Robey. He also contributed to the revues *Nine Sharp* (1938); *The *Little Revue* (1939); *Diversion* (1940); and *Diversion No. 2* (1941).

Lend an Ear. American 'intimate musical revue' which had a good run of 460 performances at the National Theatre, New York, 16 Dec. 1948. The music, lyrics, and sketches were mainly the work of Charles Gaynor (1909–75), who also contributed to the London revue *Sweeter and Lower* (1944), *Show Girl* (1961), and the 1973 revival of **Irene*. The items included a miniature musical comedy in 1920s style, *Gladiola Girl*, with everyone 'Doin' the old Yahoo steps'. The show was also notable as the first musical production to be directed and choreographed by Gower Champion (1920–80), later director of **Hello Dolly!*, and for the first Broadway appearance of the prototype Dolly, Carol *Channing. The revue was revived in 1959 and 1969.

Lennon, John Winston (*b* Liverpool, 9 Oct. 1940; *d* New York, 8 Dec. 1980). British composer, writer, singer, and guitarist. Initially inspired by Elvis *Presley recordings, he was a founder-member of the *Beatles and co-writer, with Paul *McCartney, of most of their major hits. (For a list of Lennon–McCartney songs, see under MCCARTNEY.) He became a figurehead of the protest movement of the 1960s, his socially conscious activities considerably activated by his marriage to Yoko Ono (*b* 1933) in 1969. Following the break-up of the Beatles he settled in New York to become a part of the 'happenings' there, made three albums with Yoko, and by 1969 was using the Plastic Ono Band as the vehicle for his new populist output and songs like 'Give peace a chance'. With them he dug back into his childhood with 'Mother' and 'My Mummy's dead', and recalled early Beatles days in 'Working class hero' and 'God' ('The dream is over'). One of his most influential songs was 'Imagine' (1971). 'How do you sleep' appeared to be an attack on his former colleague, McCartney.

His subsequent albums, mainly with producer Phil *Spector, veered between social and political problems (*Some Time in New York City* was made at a time when it seemed that he might be deported) and conventional love themes: *Mind Games* (1973) and *Walls and Bridges* (1974). 'Mind games' was a powerful hit in 1973 and 'Whatever gets you through the night' became No. 1 in 1974. He returned to rock and roll in 1975, before a long period of seclusion that spanned a temporary separation from his wife and the birth of a son. He was returning to full activity when he was shot dead outside his flat. Now a legend, his 'Just like starting over' was his final memorial. His literary output included: *John Lennon in His Own Write* (London, 1964) and *A Spaniard in the Works* (London, 1965), both reprinted in *The Penguin John Lennon* (1966).

His son by his first wife, Julian Lennon (*b* 1963), also made a career in rock in the 1980s.

A. Fawcett: *John Lennon: One Day at a Time* (New York, 1976; London, 1977). C. Lennon: *A Twist of Lennon* (London, 1978). G. Darby and D. Robson (eds): *John Lennon* (London, 1980). R. Connolly: *John Lennon 1940–1980* (London, 1981). P. Doncaster: *Tribute to John Lennon* (London, 1981). J. Cotton and C. Doudna (eds): *The Ballad of John and Yoko* (London, 1982). D. Sheff and C. G. Golson (eds): *The Playboy Interviews with John Lennon and Yoko Ono* (New York 1981; London, 1982). P. Shotton and N. Schaffner: *John Lennon: In My Life* (New York, 1983). R. Coleman: *John Winston Lennon* (London–New York, 1984). B. Harry: *The Book of Lennon* (London, 1984). N. Jopling: *John Lennon* (London, 1985).

Leno, Dan [Galvin, George] (*b* London, 20 Dec. 1860; *d* London, 31 Oct. 1904). British music-hall comedian. Generally reckoned one of the greatest ever to grace the British music-hall, he made his first stage appearance at the Cosmothica Music Hall in Paddington in 1864 and for some time his main claim to fame was his prowess as 'The Champion Clog Dancer of the World'. Like most great comedians his performance had a touch of the tragic. His main acts were brilliant character studies of such characters as a railway guard, a shopwalker, a recruiting sergeant, and a fireman, or in rambling dialogues that involved a mythical Mrs Kelly. He was a superb pantomime dame, first appearing in *Babes in the Wood* at Drury Lane in 1888. He made his first appearance in the USA in 1897 at Hammerstein's Music Hall in New York. He was not especially eminent as a singer, but a few songs like 'Young men taken in and done for' were in his repertoire. Overwork resulted in a mental breakdown in 1903; he recovered to appear in *Humpty Dumpty* at Drury Lane, but a relapse in 1904 led to his death.

D. Leno: *Hys Booke: a Volume of Frivolities* [ghosted by T. C. Elder] (London, 1899; abridged edn 1968). H. Wood: *Dan Leno* (London, 1905). G. Brandreth: *The Funniest Man on Earth: the Story of Dan Leno* (London, 1977).

Lenoir, Jean [Neuberger, Jean] (*b* Paris, 1891; *d* nr. Paris, 19 Jan. 1976). French composer and author. A writer of romantic *chansons in a vein established long before the jazz influence came. His best-known song, 'Parlez-moi d'amour', was first published at the end of 1930 and was originally popularized by Lucienne *Boyer. It had a big revival in the booming years of French chanson during and after the Second World War and won a Grand Prix du Disque in 1943 on the establishment of the award. This one song, also perpetuated as 'Speak to me of love', won world renown for its composer; but equally popular in France were 'Pars', sung by

Yvonne George, and the waltz 'Voulez-vous danser, grandmère?'

Lenya, Lotte [Blamauer, Karoline] (*b* Vienna, 18 Oct. 1898; *d* New York, 27 Nov. 1981). Austrian actress and singer. She started her stage career in Zurich in 1914 as a dancer. After the war she went to Berlin and there met Kurt *Weill, whom she married in 1926. Her first notable appearance as a singer was in the Brecht–Weill Singspiel *Mahagonny* (1927); followed by the even more epoch-making *Die *Dreigroschenoper*, first heard in Berlin in 1928 (filmed 1930); and the enlarged *Aufstieg und Fall der Stadt Mahoganny* in 1930. Her voice became inseparably associated with Weill's music and so much a part of its character that it was difficult later for any actress or singer to supplant her. She and Weill were forced to flee from Germany in 1933 and, after two years spent in Paris and London, they went to the USA and settled there. Lenya adapted herself to the English roles in Weill's American productions and made many definitive recordings of his works. She appeared in *The Firebrand of Florence* (1945) and, after her husband's death in 1950, in the Marc Blitzstein off-Broadway adaptation of *The *Threepenny Opera* which ran for seven years and gave the work a new lease of life. She came to London in the American-devised revue *Brecht on Brecht* at the Royal Court Theatre in 1962, had a small but telling role in **Cabaret* (1966), and continued a concert career.

H. Marx (ed.): *Weill-Lenya* (New York, 1976). D. Spoto: *Lenya: a Life* (New York, 1989).

Leonard, Eddie [Tooney, Lemuel Gordon] (*b* Richmond, Va., 18 Oct. 1875; *d* New York, 29 July 1941). American composer, author, actor, and singer. After a brief career as a professional footballer, he became a member of various minstrel shows. He served in the Spanish–American war 1895–8, after which he continued on the variety stage, appearing at Tony *Pastor's and other establishments. In 1902 he was with the Primrose and West minstrel show as a musician, but one night he persuaded them to let him sing his own song 'Ida, sweet as apple cider' (1903) which proved a tremendous success and set him off on a career as a star entertainer, singing in a style that was later adopted by Al *Jolson. He spent 40 years on the stage as a singing, acting, and dancing comedian.

He appeared in *The Southerners* (1904) and *Lifting the Lid* (1905), and starred in his own show *Roly Boly Eyes* (1919), in which he sang another of his own hits 'Roll dem roly boly eyes' (1912). His many other songs included 'Oh, didn't it rain' (1923). His last stage appearance was in 1940 at Billy *Rose's Diamond Horseshoe and he had a brief cameo spot in the Bing *Crosby film *If I Had My Way* (1940). By 1941 he was an almost forgotten man, his style totally out of fashion. Staying at the Imperial Hotel in New York, he asked for his old room, hoping it would change his luck: he was found dead in bed the following morning. A film of his life was being planned at the time.

E. Leonard: *What a Life, I'm Telling You* (New York, 1934).

Lerner, Alan Jay (*b* New York, 31 Aug. 1918; *d* New York, 14 June 1986). American author and lyricist. He was educated at a public school in England and at Harvard University. A student enthusiasm for writing became a career in journalism and, from 1940, in radio script-writing. He started a long-lasting and fruitful collaboration with composer Frederick *Loewe in 1942, beginning with *What's Up* (1943) and *The Day Before Spring* (1945) before they achieved their first major success with **Brigadoon* (1948). He worked with Kurt *Weill on *Love Life* (1948) before continuing the Lerner–Loewe series of stylishly old-fashioned musicals with **Paint Your Wagon* (1951). Meanwhile he was also busy in Hollywood working for MGM, with Burton *Lane, on the Fred *Astaire film *Royal Wedding* (1951; *Wedding Bells* in UK) and the award-winning *An *American in Paris* (1951). The partners then wrote the classic musical **My Fair Lady* (1956), making an entirely tasteful and effective transfer of Shaw's *Pygmalion*. This was followed by the screen musical **Gigi* (1958) which became a stage musical in 1973. **Camelot* (1960) was the last product of the partnership, before mutual differences and Loewe's ill-health led to a break-up in 1962, apart from a brief reunion working on the film *The Little Prince* (1974).

Lerner worked with Burton Lane on **On a Clear Day You Can See Forever* (1965), with André *Previn on *Coco* (1969), with Leonard *Bernstein on *1600 Pennsylvania Avenue* (1976), and with Lane again on *Carmelina* (1979). A final musical, *Dance a Little Closer* (1983), with Charles *Strouse, was a sad failure and lasted for only one night. But by then he was acknowledged as the leading American lyric-writer after the death of Oscar *Hammerstein II. He was married eight times and divorced seven.

A. J. Lerner: *The Street Where I Live: the Story of My Fair Lady, Gigi and Camelot* (New York–London, 1978). A. J. Lerner: *A Hymn to Him: the Lyrics of Alan Jay Lerner* (London, 1987).

Leslie, Edgar (*b* Stamford, Conn., 31 Dec. 1885; *d* 1976). American lyric-writer, composer, and publisher. He turned to regular lyric-writing after the success of his first attempt, 'I'm a Yiddish cowboy' in 1908. Thereafter his song hits included: 'Sadie Salome, go home' (1909, *m* Irving *Berlin); 'He'd have to get under—get out and get under' (1913, *m* Maurice *Abrahams); 'America, I love you' (1915, *m* Archie Gottler); 'For me and my gal' (1917, *m* George W. *Meyer); 'Oh, what a pal was Mary' (1919, *m* Pete *Wendling); 'Rose of the Rio Grande' (1922, *m* Harry *Warren); 'By the River Sainte Marie' (1931, *m* Warren). During a visit to England he wrote 'Among my souvenirs' (1927) and other songs with Lawrence Wright. He worked on film songs with Jimmy *Monaco and Walter *Donaldson, including 'A little bit independent', 'On Treasure Island', 'Moon over Miami', and 'It looks like rain in Cherry Blossom Lane', to mention but a few from his vast output. He founded the Songwriters' Protective Association with George W. Meyer and Billy *Rose in 1931 and became a music-publisher.

Leslie, Fred [Hobson, Frederick] (*b* Woolwich, London, 1 Apr. 1855; *d* London, 7 Dec. 1892). British actor, comedian, and singer. He started out in life in auctioneering, army contracting, and the clothes trade, but meanwhile was making a great reputation as an amateur actor particularly in the semi-professional Royal Artillery Theatre at Woolwich. He made his first London appearance in *Paul Pry* at the Royalty Theatre in 1878 and his first musical was *La *Belle Hélène*; followed by *Les Dragons de Villars* in 1879 at the Folly Theatre, *La Petite Mademoiselle, La Fille du Tambour Major*, Hervé's *Méfistofèle II, Jeanne, Jeannette et Jeanneton*, and *Madame Favart*. He toured the USA in 1881 before having his biggest starring part in *Rip Van Winkle* (1883) at the Comedy Theatre; and he toured the USA again that year.

He is best remembered for his years at the *Gaiety Theatre, with Nellie Farren (1845–1904), Fred Storey (1856–1917), Marion Hood (1853–1912), and E. J. Lonnen (1861–1901) in the famous series of burlesques that included *Little Jack Sheppard* (1886); *Monte Cristo, Jr.* (1886), which toured Australia and the USA 1888–9; *Ruy Blas* (1889); *Cinder-Ellen* (1891), which he helped to write; *Frankenstein* (1892). He was appearing in a performance of *Cinder-Ellen* at the Gaiety when he was taken ill with typhoid fever and died soon after.

W. T. Vincent: *Recollections of Fred Leslie* (2 vols) (London, 1894).

Leslie, Joan [Brodel, Joan] (*b* Detroit, Mich., 26 Jan. 1925). American actress, singer, and dancer. She first appeared in vaudeville as a child, with her sister, and had her first film part in 1936. She appeared in several films under her original name before making her mark as Joan Leslie in *High Sierra* (1941) with Humphrey Bogart. Good-looking and with a nice sense of comedy, she later appeared in such musical films as *Yankee Doodle Dandy* (1942); *The Hard Way* (1942); *The Sky's the Limit* (1943); *Thank Your Lucky Stars* (1943); *This is the Army* (1943); *Hollywood Canteen* (1944); *Rhapsody in Blue* (1945); and *Where Do We Go From Here?* (1945).

Leslie, Lew [Lessinsky, Lewis] (*b* 1886; *d* Orangeburg, NY, 10 Mar. 1963). American producer and actor. He first appeared on the vaudeville stage in the USA in 1909 in a singing and talking act, giving this up to become manager of the cabaret at the Café de Paris in New York. There he conceived the idea of the all-black *Plantation Revue* which was first produced at the 48th Street Theatre in 1922. This then became part of the London revue *Dover Street to Dixie* (1923) which was followed by *Dixie to Broadway* (NY, 1924; London, 1926). From these evolved the famous **Blackbirds* revues, first seen in London at His Majesty's Theatre in 1927, with later editions in New York 1928, 1930, 1933, and 1939; and in London 1934, 1936, 1938, and 1939. These and other black revues helped to introduce such talents as Florence *Mills, Bill *Robinson, and Ethel *Waters, as well as spreading the gospel of American jazz.

Let's Face It! American musical comedy presented by Vinton Freedley (1891–1969), with music and lyrics by Cole *Porter, book by Herbert and Dorothy *Fields, based on *The Cradle Snatchers* by Russell Medcraft and Norma Mitchell. It opened, for 547 performances, at the Imperial Theatre, New York, 29 Oct. 1941.

The story tells of three elderly ladies who grow tired of their hunting and shooting husbands and invite three young soldiers to their homes on the pretext of entertaining the troops. It becomes complicated, however, when the husbands and the soldiers all turn up together. The show provided a first leading role for Danny *Kaye, who had a great hit with the interpolated 'Melody in 4F' (by Sylvia Fine) and became a star within weeks. It was the fifth collaboration between Porter and Herbert Fields and its songs included 'Let's face it', 'Ace in the hole', 'Let's not talk about love', and 'I hate you, darling'. The London production, at the Hippodrome 19 Nov. 1942, starred Bobby *Howes and Joyce Barbour and had 348 performances. It was filmed in 1943 with Bob *Hope and Betty *Hutton.

Levant, Oscar (*b* Pittsburgh, 27 Dec. 1906; *d* Beverly Hills, Calif., 14 Aug. 1972). American composer, pianist, author, actor, and conductor. He studied music in New York and started his musical career as pianist in Rudy Wiedoft's band and then with Ben *Bernie. After becoming known through club engagements, he took the role of a pianist in the play *Burlesque*, later filmed as *The Dance of Life* (1929). Further studies with Schoenberg and Schillinger led to a friendship with George *Gershwin who chose him to play his *'Rhapsody in Blue' with the New York Philharmonic in 1932; he became a leading exponent of Gershwin thereafter. He composed for films in the 1920s and 1930s and appeared himself, with his amiably ugly looks, in many films including: *Rhythm on the River* (1940); *Kiss the Boys Goodbye* (1941); *Rhapsody in Blue* (1945); *Romance on the High Seas* (1948); *You Were Meant for Me* (1948); *The Barkleys of Broadway* (1948); *An *American in Paris* (1951), in which he played Gershwin's 'Piano Concerto' as a solo; *The 'I Don't Care' Girl* (1953); *The *Band Wagon* (1953); and he was also in many non-musical films.

He wrote the Broadway show *Ripples* (1930) and became well-known on the radio quiz show *Information Please* 1938–52. He had his own radio show in 1943 and co-starred with Al *Jolson 1947–9. He retired from show-business because of ill-health, but came back for a wise-cracking interview in the late 1950s. His songs included: 'If you want the rainbow (you must have the rain)', from *My Man*

(1929) starring Fanny *Brice; 'Lovable and sweet' (*w* Sidney Clare), from *Street Girl* (1929); 'Lady, play your mandolin' (1930, *w* Irving *Caesar); and 'Blame it on my youth' (1934, *w* Edward Heyman). He wrote three volumes of biography: *A Smattering of Ignorance* (New York, 1940); *The Memoirs of an Amnesiac* (New York, 1965); and *The Unimportance of Being Oscar* (New York, 1968).

Levey, Ethel [Fowler, Ethelia] (*b* San Francisco, 22 Nov. 1881; *d* New York, 27 Feb. 1955). American actress, singer, and dancer. An elegant lady with a fascinating low voice who was to become a favourite of the London stage in the early 1900s. She made her first stage appearance in San Francisco in 1897 and was first seen in New York at *Weber & Fields' Music Hall, later at *Koster & Bial's. She worked with Weber and Fields for many years. Married to George M. *Cohan 1901–7, she appeared in four of his shows: *The Governor's Son* (1901); *Running for Office* (1903); **Little Johnny Jones* (1904); and *George Washington Jr.* (1906). She was also in *My Lady Molly* (1903). From 1908 she appeared on the music-hall stage in the USA, England (making many appearances at the *Alhambra), and Europe (mainly in revue in Paris and also at the Apollo in Vienna). She went to London with the revues **Hullo Ragtime!* (1912) and *Hullo Tango!* (1913); followed by **Watch Your Step* (1914); *Follow the Crowd* (1916); *Look Who's Here* (1916); *Three Cheers* (1916); *Here and There* (1917); and *Oh, Julie!* (1920). After returning to the USA for *Go Easy, Mabel* (1922), she was back in London for *Yes!* (1923) and *The Blue Kitten* (1925).

Lewis, George [Zeno, George Lewis Francis] (*b* New Orleans, 13 July 1900; *d* New Orleans, 31 Dec. 1968). American jazz clarinettist. Starting his musical career *c.*1917 he played with such legendary figures as Buddy Petit (1887–1931), Kid Rena (1898–1949), Kid *Ory, and others centred in New Orleans. He was with the Eureka Brass Band in the 1920s and the Olympia Band in the early 1930s. During the depression he worked as a stevedore, coming back into the limelight during the jazz revival of the 1940s when he played with Bunk *Johnson in New York 1945–6 and made some now historically valuable recordings with him. He led his own bands in New Orleans in the late 1940s and early 1950s with such as Jim *Robinson (1890–1976) and Kid Howard (1908–66), toured the USA and Europe, and recorded on the Climax, American Music, and Good Time Jazz labels. He was leading a band in San Francisco in 1957 when he had to retire from full-time music through ill-health, though he frequently played at Preservation Hall in his later years. His playing was a surviving example of the simple but effective original New Orleans style.

A. J. McCarthy: *George Lewis: a Biography, Record Survey and Discography* (London, 1958). J. A. Stuart: *Call Him George* (London, 1961; repr. 1969). T. Bethell: *George Lewis: a Jazzman from New Orleans* (Berkeley, Calif., 1977).

Lewis, Jerry Lee (*b* Ferriday, La., 29 Sept. 1935). American rock pianist and singer. He has often been compared with *Little Richard; both pound the piano and are seen as tearaways. Lewis, however, is a self-conscious artist. He paces his performances, always in control, always detached from the banality of the lyrics, performing with confidence, even arrogance. Despite this sophistication, he generates excitement and energy in his playing so that the effect seems primitive and simple. His records are characterized by metronomic piano rhythms and echo-laden vocals.

Like many others, he joined Sun Records after Elvis *Presley had led the way in 1957. His second release, 'Whole lotta shakin' going on', earned him his first gold disc and was followed by 'Great balls of fire' (1957); 'Down the line' (1958); and 'High school confidential' (1958). His career was interrupted when his marriage to his 13-year-old cousin in 1958 caused a public outcry. He came back in 1961 when he recorded the rhythm 'n' blues-style 'What'd I say', and in 1963 he made 'Another place, another time' and 'What made Milwaukee famous (has made a loser out of me)'. In 1977 he recorded the autobiographical 'Middle-age crazy'. Lewis is expert at adapting other people's styles and music, copying the playing of earlier honky-tonk and boogie-woogie pianists and using other people's hit songs. He is not a writer himself but, in whatever style he plays, he still manages to sound very individual.

Lewis, John Aaron (*b* La Grange, Ill., 3 May 1920). American jazz pianist, arranger, and composer. After military service he studied at the Manhattan School of Music. He was encouraged by drummer Kenny *Clarke and joined the Dizzy *Gillespie band in 1945 as pianist and arranger. While playing with Illinois *Jacquet in 1948 he was writing many brilliant arrangements for Gillespie and Miles *Davis. He worked with Lester *Young in the early 1950s. In 1952 he formed the *Modern Jazz Quartet with Milt *Jackson, which he led until 1977, making it a key group in the world of cool jazz and the classically oriented music that became known as third stream. His compositions for the group borrowed the qualities and patterns of classical music, combining the simplicity and correctness of Bach and Mozart and fugal counterpoint with the colour and timbre of the Impressionists. The Modern Jazz Quartet abandoned the usual jazz haunts and favoured bow tie and tails and the concert-hall stage; Lewis himself taught in the academic world.

His compositions included: 'Two-bass hit' (1946), 'Emanon' (1946), 'Stay on it' (1947), and 'Minor walk' (1947), all written for Gillespie; 'Toccata for trumpet and orchestra' (1947), 'Period suite' (1948), 'Constellation' (1948), 'Au-leu-cha' (1948), 'Afternoon in Paris' (1949), 'Morpheus' (1950), 'D & E' (1951), 'Vendome' (1952) (see also under MODERN JAZZ QUARTET). His film scores included: *Sait-on-jamais* (*No Sun in Venice*, 1957)—

'The golden striker', 'The rose truce'; *Odds Against Tomorrow* (1959); and *A Milanese Story* (1962). Although the MJQ ceremoniously folded in 1974 with an impressive *Last Concert* recording, Lewis has made periodic comebacks with them since 1982.

Lewis, Meade 'Lux' (*b* Chicago, 4 Sept. 1905; *d* Minneapolis, 7 June 1964). American jazz pianist and composer. He played in nightclubs and bars in the Chicago area, and first recorded his 'Honky tonk train blues' in 1927; but then gave up music to become a taxi-driver. Rediscovered by John *Hammond in 1935, he went to New York where he joined up with Pete *Johnson, Albert *Ammons, and others in promoting the *boogie-woogie craze of the late 1930s. He led the way with some imaginative pieces in the style such as 'Yancey special' (1938), a revival of his famous 'Honky tonk train blues', and many more. From 1941 he was mainly based in Los Angeles and was actively playing until he was killed in a motor accident.

Lewis, Morgan [Lewis, William Morgan, Jr.] (*b* Rockville, Conn., 26 Dec. 1906). American composer. He was educated at Michigan University. He has been mainly active as a writer for the theatre, with scores (usually written with Nancy *Hamilton) for *One for the Money* (1939)—'On the other hand'; *Two for the Show* (1940)—*'How high the moon' (which attracted little attention, but was later a favourite of the modern jazz world); *Three to Make Ready* (1946)—'If it's love', 'The old soft shoe', 'A lovely lazy kind of day', 'It's a nice night for it'; and contributed to *The Third Little Show* (1931)—'You might as well pretend'; and **New Faces* (1934). His film scores included: *The Unconquered* [the life of Helen Keller] (1955), which won an Academy Award, and *The Madwoman of Chaillot* (1969).

Lewis, Sam M. (*b* New York, 25 Oct. 1885; *d* New York, 22 Nov. 1959). American lyricist. After working with a broker, he started singing in cafés, mainly using his own songs. He also wrote for Lew *Dockstader, Van and Schenck, and many others. He had his first song hit with 'That mellow melody' (1912). From 1916 to 1930 he mainly worked in lyric-writing partnership with Joe *Young, contributing to such shows as *Step This Way* (1916); *Robinson Crusoe Jr.* (1916)—'Where did Robinson Crusoe go with Friday on Saturday night?'; *Sinbad* (1918)—'Rock-a-bye your baby with a Dixie melody', 'My mammy'; and also writing the words of 'I'm all bound round with the Mason-Dixon Line' (1917); 'Just a baby's prayer at twilight' (1918); 'How ya gonna keep 'em down on the farm?' (1919); 'I'd love to fall asleep and wake up in my mammy's arms' (1920); 'Dinah' (1925); 'Five foot two, eyes of blue' (1925); 'I'm sitting on top of the world' (1925); 'In a little Spanish town' (1926); 'Laugh, clown, laugh' (1928); 'I kiss your hand, madame' (1929); and 'Absence makes the heart grow fonder' (1929).

Without Young he wrote 'Song of the fool' (1930), 'Just friends' (1931), 'Lawd, you made the night too long' (1932), 'Street of dreams' (1933), 'For all we know' (1934), 'A beautiful lady in blue' (1936), 'Gloomy Sunday' (1936), 'Now or never' (1936), working with composers Fred *Ahlert, Harry *Akst, J. Fred *Coots, Walter *Donaldson, Ray *Henderson, M. K. *Jerome, George W. *Meyer, Jean *Schwartz, Ted *Snyder, Harry *Warren, and many more.

Lewis, Ted [Friedman, Theodore Leopold] (*b* Circleville, Ohio, 6 June 1892; *d* New York, 25 Aug. 1971). American bandleader, clarinettist, and composer. He played with his brother Edgar in a local boys' band, before they formed their own band and did a vaudeville tour as a double act. He continued in vaudeville 1911–17, latterly in an act billed as Rose, Young, and Friedman and with comedian Eddie Lewis as Lewis and Lewis, at which time he adopted the name of Ted Lewis. He joined Earl Fuller's band, playing at Coney Island, and then led his own quintet at Rector's Club in New York. He was with his band in **Greenwich Village Follies* (1919 and 1921) and *Ziegfeld's Midnight Frolics* (1919). They toured and recorded in the 1920s and gradually became nationally known. He had his own nightclub in New York in the mid-1920s and toured Europe in the late 1920s. By now he was known as 'The High-Hat Tragedian of Song', playing modest clarinet, singing in a languid manner, and making the catchphrase 'Is everybody happy?' very much his trademark. Among his hits was his theme-song 'When my baby smiles at me' (which he wrote), while a popular feature was 'Me and my shadow' which he performed with a shadowy black figure imitating his actions behind him.

He appeared in *Ted Lewis Frolic* (1923), **Artists and Models* (1927); and other shows; and was featured in the early talking film *Is Everybody Happy?* (1929), and afterwards in *Show of Shows* (1929), *Here Comes the Band* (1935), *Manhattan Merry-go-Round* (1937), *Hold That Ghost!* (1941), a new *Is Everybody Happy?* (1943) based on his life and career, and *Follow the Boys* (1944). Many famous jazz musicians, such as George Brunies (1902–74), Muggsy *Spanier, Don Murray (1904–29), and Jimmy *Dorsey, played with the band at times and his recording personnel included Fats *Waller and Benny *Goodman; but his own playing and general approach were more often on the corny side, although he had a good band in the 1940s and 1950s, touring with his own stage show. His last major engagement was at the Latin Quarter Club in New York in 1965, though he still made occasional TV appearances after that.

Lewis, Vic (*b* London, 29 July 1919). British bandleader. After experience in various bands, he went to the USA in 1938 to lead American musicians in recordings. After war service he became known with the Buddy Featherstonhaugh Quintet and played with Stéphane *Grappelli 1944–5, later with Ted *Heath. He formed a Dixieland-style big band with Jack Parnell, moving later towards a more modern style. He continued to lead big bands into the 1950s and twice toured the USA with them.

Leybourne, George [Saunders, Joseph] (*b* Wolverhampton, 1842; *d* Islington, London, 15 Sept. 1884). British singer, entertainer, and songwriter. He gave up an early career as a mechanic in 1860 to try his hand as a music-hall entertainer in the Midlands, appearing in Leeds, Manchester, Liverpool, and Birmingham. His first London appearance was at the Gilbert Music Hall in Whitechapel and he was at the Raglan in Holborn in 1864. An impressively tall and handsome man with a good baritone voice, he was to become a leading lion-comique of the 1870s and 1880s in rivalry with *Vance, *MacDermott, and other aspiring stage aristocrats. His best-known act was as the well-to-do man-about-town, the 'swell' or 'toff' in the parlance of the day, yet he remained illiterate and would normally speak in the rough tones of his early upbringing. His repertoire veered between comic 'masher' songs and well-sung ballads. His stage character was encapsulated in his best-known song 'Champagne Charlie', one of the many songs he wrote in collaboration with Alfred *Lee, which he publicized by buying champagne for his audience; but he unfortunately acquired the habit of drinking it and other beverages in over-large quantities in private life.

He became a popular figure at the *Canterbury Music Hall, where he was paid £30 a week (a good salary then) on the condition that he arrived for his engagement in a brougham drawn by four white horses. He remained top of the bill at the Canterbury, the *Oxford, and other halls for 20 years, his salary rising to £120 a week, not only promoting Moët's champagne, but burgundy and moselle as well; and the drink trade in general in a song called 'My name it is John Barleycorn'. Among his other favourite numbers were 'Up in a balloon', 'At the opera', 'If ever I cease to love', 'She danced like a fairy', and 'The daring young man on the flying trapeze', which celebrated the exploits of the famous acrobat Léotard. He helped to write most of his material. Generous to a fault, his addiction to drink led to his early downfall. He ended his career as manager of several minor music-halls and fulfilled his last engagement on stage at the Queen's in Poplar not long before his final collapse.

Liberace, Wladziu Valentino (*b* West Allis, Milwaukee, Wis., 16 May 1919; *d* Palm Springs, Calif., 4 Feb. 1987). American pianist and entertainer. After study at the Wisconsin College of Music from the age of seven, he made his debut as a pianist at nine with the Chicago Symphony Orchestra. He had a struggling existence for many years but came to fame, with the later familiar trappings of candelabra and fabulous outfits and jewellery, playing popular classics on TV in *The Liberace Show*. He came to London to take part in the 1956 Royal Variety Performance which was cancelled because of the Suez crisis, but he remained to play at the Palladium, the Albert Hall, and the Café de Paris, becoming a great favourite with British audiences and returning for the Royal Variety Performances of 1972 and 1978. He opened his own museum in Las Vegas in 1979. He also appeared in several films. His larger-than-life career continued in a mélange of music, extravagance, and sex scandals until he finally succumbed to a kidney complaint.

B. Thomas: *Liberace: the True Story* (New York–London, 1988).

Light Music. While the adjective 'light' could be used, in a generalized way, to cover many popular musical activities, it is specifically applied to those kinds of music that are a popularized distillation of the traditional classical vein—as distinct from the various forms of popular music that stem from folk or jazz sources. It is most generally applied to light orchestral music which might range from solo performance, through the palm court trio to a small orchestral ensemble; but it could also cover the songs and ballads written in the traditional *drawing-room vein established in Victorian times, or excerpts from *light opera, *operetta, or *musical comedy—anything in an undemanding and polite mode of musical address.

Such music might well be the creation of an academic composer writing in a lighter vein than normal. Sir Edward Elgar was an outstanding example of a composer who was never averse to taking time off from symphonies and oratorios to write light music, of which the best known examples are his 'Chanson de matin' and 'Salut d'amour'. But the serious composer often fails to achieve true lightness of touch, and the best light music is generally that which is written by composers specializing in the idiom. The growth of a distinct field of light music coincided with the general breakaway of popular art forms, particularly marked in the musical theatre, that began in the middle of the 19th century. Among the pioneers of distinct and distinguished light music were the Viennese *waltz specialists *Lanner and the various members of the *Strauss family, *Suppé, *Zeller, and *Ziehrer; elsewhere, *Lumbye, *Waldteufel, and *Sousa. Eastern Europe, with its strong *gypsy traditions, produced many worthy examples. In Hungary there were Ion Ivanovici (1848–1902)—'Donauwellen' (1880), and Karel Komzak (1850–1905)—'Bad'ner Mäd'ln'; in Czechoslovakia, Frantisek Drdla (1868–1944)—'Souvenir'; in Romania, Grigoras Dinicu (1889–1949)—'Hora staccato'; in Russia, Riccardo Drigo (1846–1930); and in Italy, Vittorio Monti (1868–1922)—'Csardas'; most of them fiddlers in the gypsy style and orchestra leaders.

A strong school of light composers flourished in England from the end of the 19th century, inspired by *Sullivan and Elgar, including *German,

*Fletcher, Roger Quilter (1877–1953), *Wood, and *Coates. The tradition continued in the hands of such specialist composers as Frederic Bayco, *Binge, *Curzon, Harry Dexter (*b* 1910), and *Vinter. The worlds of *military and *brass band music might also be considered branches of light music, being similar in idiom and intent and frequently adapting such orchestral, instrumental, and vocal items for their special use.

The playing of light music in the 'palm court' tradition (established in the tea-rooms of such resorts as Bournemouth and Bath) became a specially cultivated art in the hands of such musicians as the Polish-born Marek Weber (1889–1964), and in England, Reginald King (1904–91), Albert Sandler (1906–48), Max Jaffa (1911–91), Jack Byfield (1902–77), and Reginald Leopold (*b* 1902). Although live restaurant music has become a thing of the past the tradition has been continued, in the fond spirit of similar revivals, by such sympathetic groups as the Palm Court Theatre Orchestra in England, Albert White and his San Francisco Masters of Melody in the USA, and I Salonisti and the Salonorchester Cölln in Germany.

D. Ewen: *The Lighter Classics in Music* (New York, 1961). K. Young: *Music's Great Days in Spas and Watering Places* (London, 1968).

Light Opera. A loose but useful categorization for all the kinds of opera that veer towards the light or popular spheres of activity, as well as certain areas of operatic activity that are not precisely covered by any of the alternative terms. The name, 'light opera', has often headed scores that could alternatively be called 'comic opera' or 'opéra-bouffe'; but it can also be used to embrace all that happened under such terms as *ballad opera, opéra-comique, *operetta, and earlier samples of *musical comedy.

The term is of most particular use to cover much of the writing that happened in England and elsewhere in that limbo period between the heyday of the ballad opera and the passage through the *burlesque period to the emergence of genuine operetta. Because many of the works written between *c.*1760 and *c.*1860 took it upon themselves to lighten their tone, in an attempt to cater for a more widely-based theatre-going public, they consistently fail to receive attention in books that deal with genuine opera or those covering operetta and musicals.

As the original ballad opera period passed there were works like Thomas Arne's *Love in a Village* (1762) and Thomas *Dibdin's *Lionel and Clarissa* (1768), which are virtually 'composed' ballad operas. Many of the operas that followed these, for example, William *Shield's *Rosina* (1782), have the same pastoral nature and style and constitute a period of English opera (with equivalents in USA and Europe) that is one of the least documented in our musical history. Such works were widely popular, in the true sense, but their position was confused by their appearance on the stages of Covent Garden, the Haymarket, and other highbrow venues. Light operas by Dibdin, Shield, Storace, and others, occupied the same position as the Singspiel did in Germany or the opéra-comique in France—a bulwark erected by native composers against the invading and domineering Italian opera (with all its strange conventions) from which they, none the less, learned some of their techniques. Their defences were made up of music in a national or folk idiom, native humour and settings, and an overall lightness of touch and looseness of form that were calculated to appeal to the widest audience. The successors to Shield and Dibdin and those who occupied the stage in the early 1800s were composers such as Balfe, Benedict, Bishop, and Wallace (in France, Auber, Boieldieu, and Hérold; in Germany, Lortzing, Müller, and Nicolai), who worked in the framework of Italian operatic conventions but retained the lightness of touch that led towards a distinct genre of operetta and the complete breakaway of the popular musical theatre from the opera. Close analysis will reveal that John Hullah almost wrote what might be termed an 'operetta' in *The Village Coquettes* of 1836; that Balfe's widely popular *The Bohemian Girl* of 1843 has a number of melodies that would grace any musical; and that it is not a great step from here into the world of *Offenbach that began in the 1850s or to *Strauss or *Sullivan in the 1870s onwards. If the true 'popular' theatre came about *c.*1850 (along with other 'popular' manifestations), the world of light opera had been paving the way towards it since *The *Beggar's Opera* first took London by storm in 1728.

The term 'light opera' was used well into the 20th century to cover the kind of works whose idiom placed them in the same genre as the light music that graced the palm courts of the world—the works of Victor *Herbert in America or Edward *German's **Merrie England* (1902), or occasional pieces like *Tantivy Towers* by Thomas Dunhill (1877–1946). The title *The Complete Book of Light Opera* was probably chosen by Mark *Lubbock in 1962, for his comprehensive book of synopses, through similar reasoning. It covered many areas ranging from operetta to the musical that could not be logically embraced by any of those terms. The same problems of terminology have beset many historians working in the popular fields, and areas have yet to be firmly defined.

L. C. Strang: *Prima Donnas and Soubrettes of Light Opera and Musical Comedy in America* (Boston, 1900). L. C. Strang: *Celebrated Comedians of Light Opera and Musical Comedy in America* (Boston, 1901; repr. as *Famous Stars of Light Opera*, 1907). S. Mackinlay: *Origin and Development of Light Opera* (London, 1927). D. Ewen: *The Book of European Light Opera* (New York, 1962). M. Lubbock: *The Complete Book of Light Opera* (London, 1962). See also books listed under OPERETTA.

L'il Abner. Musical fantasy based on the strip cartoon by Al Capp which enjoyed great popularity in the USA. Set in a Southern town called Dogpatch, it was satirically aimed at the atom bomb, the military mind, and politicians. Its human story concerned the amorous affairs of Daisy Mae (played by Edie Adams) in her pursuit of Abner Yokum (Peter

Palmer), and its social side was organized by Marryin' Sam (Stubby Kaye), a great supporter of the incompetent Jubilation T. Cornpone. Life centres on the man-chasing race that takes place every year on Sadie Hawkins Day. The show was staged at the St James Theatre 15 Nov. 1956, and ran for 693 performances. The music was by Gene *De Paul, the lyrics by Johnny *Mercer, and the book by Norman Panama and Melvin Frank. The songs included: 'Jubilation T. Cornpone', 'Namely you', and 'The country's in the very best of hands'. It was filmed in 1959.

Lilac Domino, The. Operetta first produced in Leipzig in 1911 as *Der lila Domino*, then in Vienna in 1912, with music by Charles *Cuvillier and words by Emmerich von Gatti and Bela Jenbach. With English libretto by Harry B. *Smith and Robert B. *Smith, it had a modest run of 113 performances at the 44th Street Theatre, New York, 28 Oct. 1914 with Eleanor Painter (1890–1947) as the star. Its biggest success came when it was produced at the *Empire Theatre in London, 21 Feb. 1918, with book by H. F. Maltby and added music by Howard Carr, and ran for 747 performances, helped by the wartime desire for escapism and the melodious lilt of the 'Lilac Domino waltz'. It had London revivals in 1919 and 1944.

Lilac Time. Popular and long-lasting operetta romantically based on the life and loves of the composer Franz Schubert (1797–1828). It was originally designed as a Singspiel, *Das Dreimädlerhaus*, with Schubert's music adapted and arranged by Heinrich *Berté and book by A. M. Willner and Heinz Reichert, based on the novel *Schwammerl* by R. H. Bartsch. This perenially popular show was first produced at the Raimundtheater in Vienna 15 Jan. 1916. Berté's work was tastefully done and, using mainly lesser known items, went some way to proving that Schubert was a potential operetta composer.

For its first English adaptation, more of the widely popular Schubert melodies were dragged into use, making it somewhat less integrated but ensuring its public acceptance. Arranged by the Australian composer G. H. *Clutsam, and with English words by Adrian *Ross, it opened as *Lilac Time* at the Lyric Theatre, London, 22 Dec. 1922; and had an initial run of 626 performances. Schubert's music, disguised under such anglicized titles as 'The golden song', 'The three little girls', 'Underneath the lilac bough', and 'Yours is my heart', soon became best-selling material. There were revivals in 1925, 1927, 1928, 1930, 1932, 1933, 1936, and 1942 and it became a popular work among amateur operatic societies. For the American version see under BLOSSOM TIME.

'Lili Marlene'. Song of the Second World War which had the unusual asset of being equally popular on opposing sides. The lyric of 'Lili Marleen' (as it was originally known) was written by an obscure soldier, Hans Leip (1894–1983), while he was serving in the German infantry in 1917. It remained unknown until 1938 when it was set to music by the German composer Norbert Schultze (*b* 1911). Before being accepted it was rejected by some 30 publishers; when first recorded by Lale *Andersen in 1939, it sold only 700 copies.

It suddenly caught the public imagination when it was broadcast to the German Army in Africa from a station in Belgrade; and not only was it an immediate hit with the Afrika Corps, but it was also heard and adopted by the British 8th Army, the Italians, and the French. An English version was quickly produced by Tommy Connor, removing a lingering suggestion in the German original that Lili was a prostitute, and it continued on its way as a favourite of both opposing sides. A recording by Ann *Shelton soon sold more than a million copies. Leip himself always denied that Lili was of shady inclinations and said that he had based her on two girls, Lili and Marleen, whom he had known in Berlin while on leave.

'Lilliburlero'. Song whose music has been traced back as far as 1540 when it was included in a book of Dutch psalm tunes. Its popularity dates from 1686, when it was printed as a dance in *The Delightful Companion*, a book of recorder lessons by Robert Carr. It appeared next in the 2nd edition of *Musick's Handmaid*, published by John *Playford, where it was specified as 'a new Irish tune' and attributed to Henry Purcell. But it is fairly certain that Purcell was only adapting the old tune, which he used again as a ground bass for a piece written for *The Gordian Knot Unty'ed* in 1691. After its publication by Playford it was adopted for a song with loaded Irish political associations, said by Thomas Percy in his *Reliques* (1765) to have 'contributed not a little towards the great revolution in 1688'.

The words were claimed by Lord Thomas Wharton (1648–1715) in 1685, but Lord Dorset has also been suggested as a possible author: William Chappell maintains that it was neither. The refrain 'lilliburlero bullenala' is an adaptation of the original Irish 'an lile ba leir e ba linn a la' ('the lily was triumphant and we won the day'), the orange lily being the symbol of the supporters of the Dutch William. The words were first published in *The Muse's Farewell to Popery and Slavery* in 1869. The same words have also been sung to the tune of 'Cold and raw the North did blow', while the tune has been used for many songs, notably 'The Protestant boys'. Its most popular appearances were in *Pills to Purge Melancholy* and in *Gay's *The *Beggar's Opera*, with new words, and in other ballad operas. There is also a nursery rhyme version, 'There was an old woman tossed up in a blanket', which derives from a song printed in Playford's *An Antidote Against Melancholy* (1661)—'There was an old man of Waltham Cross', with an almost identical tune.

Lillie, Beatrice [Gladys] (*b* Toronto, 29 May 1894; *d* Henley-on-Thames, 20 Jan. 1989). Canadian actress and singer. One of the funniest ladies of the inter-war revue scene, mistress of the double-take and the incongruous, she fooled the audience with an appearance of stately dignity. She started her stage career as part of the Lillie Trio, 'High Class Entertainers', with her mother and sister; later she did a solo turn billed as 'Serio comic singer with a Refined Repertoire'. She came to England before the First World War and made her London debut at the Camberwell Palace, developing a boy act in variety and revue.

Her illustrious career in London revues began with *Not Likely!* (1914); *5064 Gerrard* (1915); *Now's the Time* (1915); *Samples* (1916); *Some* (1916); *Cheep* (1917); *Tabs* (1918); *Bran-Pie* (1919); *Now and Then* (1921); *Pot Luck* (1921); *The Nine o'Clock Revue* (1922); and the musical comedy *Oh, Joy!* (1919); before taking New York by storm in **André Charlot's London Revue of 1924*, in which she starred with Gertrude *Lawrence and Jack *Buchanan and sang 'March with me'. She continued to build her reputation in *The Charlot Revue of 1926* (1925); *Oh, Please!* (1926); *She's My Baby* (1928); **This Year of Grace* (1928); *Charlot's Masquerade* (1930); *The Third Little Show* (1931)—'Mad dogs and Englishmen'; *Walk a Little Faster* (1932); *Please* (1933); *At Home Abroad* (1935); *The Show is On* (1936); *Happy Returns* (1938); *Set to Music* (1939)—'I went to a marvellous party'; *All Clear* (1939); *Big Top* (1942); *Seven Lively Arts* (1944); *Better Late* (1946); *Inside USA* (1948); and *High Spirits* (1964). In the 1950s and 1960s she toured in her own show, *An Evening with Beatrice Lillie*, reviving her hits from the past; and she appeared in the film *Thoroughly Modern Millie* (1967).

B. Lillie: *Every Other Inch a Lady* (New York, 1972).

'Lily of Laguna, The'. Well-known music-hall song written by Leslie *Stuart in 1898. Like his score for **Florodora* (1899), it was influential in its stylistic move towards jazz, via the minstrel vein, and it was ambitiously conceived, with an exceptionally long verse and inserted dance routine. It was written with the talents of the soft-shoe shuffler Eugene *Stratton in mind, and he first introduced it at the *Oxford Music Hall in July 1898.

Lincke, Karl Emil **Paul** (*b* Berlin, 7 Nov. 1866; *d* Klausthal-Zellerfeld, nr. Göttingen, 3 Sept. 1946). German composer and conductor. The son of a law-court official, he received his musical education at a school of music in Wittenberg where he learned violin and bassoon. He played in theatre orchestras and was for a while the musical director at the Apollo Theater in Berlin, then worked in Berlin as music-editor for a publisher. He conducted revues at the *Folies-Bergère in Paris 1918–20 (writing the 'Folies-Bergère march'), then settled in Berlin, and in 1920 founded the music-publishing company Apollo Verlag.

He was to build a great reputation as a founder-figure of the Berlin school of operetta. After writing a number of minor stage works he had his first big success with *Venus auf Erden* (1897), following this with *Im Reiche des Indra* (1899); *Frau Luna* (1899; London, as *Castles in the Air*, 1911); *Fräulein Loreley* (1900); *Lysistrata* (1902)—containing his best-known piece, 'Glühwürmchen-Idyll' ('Glow-worm idyll'); *Nakiris Hochzeit* (1902); *Prinzessin Rosine* (1905); the revues *Donnerwetter—Tadellos!* (1906) and *Hallo! die grosse Revue!* (1909); *Grigri* (1911); *Casanova* (1914); and coming back with *Ein Liebestraum* (1940). Exceptionally, for a non-Viennese composer, he was most successful with his waltzes (which are, however, more French, in the *Waldteufel tradition, than Viennese) many of which—'Unrequited love', 'Venus on earth', 'Luna waltz', 'Lysistrata', perpetuated the names of his operettas long after they were out of fashion.

E. Nick: *Paul Lincke* (Hamburg, 1953). O. Schneidereit: *Paul Lincke und die Entstehung der Berliner Operette* (Berlin, 1974).

Lindsay, Howard (*b* Waterford, NY, 29 Mar. 1889; *d* New York, 11 Feb. 1968). American librettist and director. His family settled in Boston in 1902 and he concluded his education at Harvard University. He intended to enter the Church, but was attracted to the idea of a theatrical career and studied at the American Academy of Dramatic Arts. He appeared in his first play in 1909, followed by work in vaudeville, burlesque, and silent films. After serving in France in the First World War, he acted in and directed *Dulcy* (1921) and wrote several plays. In 1934 he began to collaborate with the writer Russell *Crouse, producing librettos for **Anything Goes* (1934, *m* Cole *Porter), **Red, Hot and Blue* (1936, *m* Porter), and *Hooray for What?* (1937, *m* Harold *Arlen). In 1937 he went to Hollywood to work on film musicals, including *The Great Victor Herbert* (1939). He wrote eight non-musical plays in collaboration with Crouse, appearing in *Life With Father* (1939) and winning the Pulitzer Prize for *State of the Union* (1945). Other librettos included **Call Me Madam* (1950, *m* Irving *Berlin), *Happy Hunting* (1956, *m* Harold Karr), *The *Sound of Music* (1959, *m* Richard *Rodgers), and *Mr President* (1962, *m* Berlin).

C. O. Skinner: *Life With Lindsay & Crouse* (Boston, 1976).

Lindy Hop. Energetic and athletic dance of black origin, a forerunner of *jive and *jitterbug, done in a jazz-inspired ecstacy with acrobatic movements and a continuous frantic shaking which needs loose limbs for its performance. A fine filmed sequence by a group called the Lindy Hoppers was seen in the Marx Brothers film *A Day at the Races* (1937). Although it might have seemed to appear from nowhere, the Lindy had been around for well over half a century: it went back to the early 1900s and was first introduced to the public in 1913 in *Darktown Follies* by Ethel Williams and Johnny Peters. It was probably based on an even earlier dance called the Texas Tommy, while the name Lindy suggests an ancestry in minstrel days. Astute publicists saw a neat connection with Charles Lindbergh's historic Atlantic air crossing in 1927 and fostered the dance as the Lindbergh, or Lindy, Hop. Lindy marathons were organized, but the dance remained very much a black property until the swing era of the 1930s gave the world at large the right sort of music to which to dance. The dance was perpetuated by Mama Lu Parks (1929–90) from *Savoy Ballroom days into the 1980s.

Linley, George (*b* Leeds, 1798; *d* London, 10 Sept. 1865). British composer, author, and cellist. The son of a tinplate worker, he first earned a local reputation as a writer, then moved to London where he became one of the most popular songwriters of his day. He wrote both music and words for most of his own songs and wrote lyrics for many other composers including the best-selling 'Ever of thee', with music by Foley Hall, which was endlessly reprinted. His many other songs included 'We loved not wisely but too well', 'The ballad singer', 'Thou art gone from my gaze', and 'I cannot mind my wheel, mother'. He wrote operas: *Francesca Doria* (1849), *The Toymaker* (1861), an adaptation of *Adam's *La Poupée*, and *Law Versus Love* (1862); wrote librettos for Balfe's *Catherine Gray* (1837) and Benedict's *The Gypsy's Warning* (1838); and did many translations. He edited and arranged *Scottish Melodies*, *Songs of the Camp*, *Original Hymn Tunes*, and two books of nursery rhymes; and wrote *Music Cynics of London* (1862) and *The Modern Hudibras* (1864).

Lipton, Sidney (*b* London, 4 Jan. 1906). British bandleader. After playing the violin under several bandleaders, including *Ambrose and Billy *Cotton, Lipton formed his own band in 1932 for a residency at the Grosvenor House Hotel which lasted right through the war years, making it one of the longest-running units in British dance-band history. His band included many prominent British musicians, including the trombonist and bandleader Ted *Heath. The Grosvenor House brand of music was smooth, polished, and eminently danceable-to, with an emphasis on skilful musicianship. Their signature tune was 'I'll see you in my dreams'.

Lisbon Story, The. British musical play with score by Harry *Parr-Davies and book by Harold Purcell (1907–77). Its success was perpetuated by a catchy song, 'Pedro the fisherman', which became a considerable hit; and the show, which opened at the London Hippodrome 17 June 1943, lightened the war years with 492 performances. The cast included the vivacious Patricia Burke (*b* 1917) and Vincent Tildsley's Mastersingers.

Liston, Harry (*b* Manchester, 30 Sept. 1843; *d* London, 8 Apr. 1929). British comedian and singer. He continued the lion-comique tradition in the steps of George *Leybourne and others, tail-coated and top-hatted and mocking the ways of the heavy swells of current society; and he was also an excellent dancer. He first appeared on the stage of the Scotia Theatre in Glasgow in 1863, soon developing a one-man two-hour show, which was billed as 'The Stage-Struck Hero', and was very successful in the North of England. He first appeared in London at the Cambridge and Metropolitan halls in 1865. In 1866 he was a member of Arthur *Lloyd's company and in 1867 formed his own touring group on similar lines, billed as 'Merry Moments'. He was a great favourite at the *Oxford Music Hall and his songs included 'The convict', 'When Johnny comes marching home', 'The dancing swell', 'Nobody's child', 'The pride of Pimlico', 'Her christian name was Sarah', and 'Would you if you were me?'

Little Johnny Jones. American musical comedy with music and words by George M. *Cohan, staged at the Liberty Theatre, New York, 7 Nov. 1904, with George, Jerry, and Helen Cohan in the cast, and Ethel *Levey. Although its initial run was only 52, it was the source of such Cohan perennials as 'The Yankee Doodle boy' and 'Give my regards to Broadway', together with 'Good-bye, Flo', 'They're all my friends', 'I'm mighty glad I'm living and that's all', and 'Life's a funny proposition after all'.

Little Mary Sunshine. American musical comedy with music and words by Nick *Besoyan (his first professional success), produced at the off-Broadway Orpheum Theatre, New York, 18 Nov. 1959 [1143p]. The cast included Patricia Routledge (*b* 1929), Eileen Brennan, making her New York debut, William Graham, John McMartin, and Elmarie Wendel. It was a witty spoof of the *Herbert–*Friml–*Romberg brand of musical which managed to match their music with melodic numbers of its own, having the same sort of success as the British *The *Boy Friend*.

On *Rose-Marie* lines, the story concerns one Mary Potts who runs an inn in the Colorado Rockies, and is in love with 'Big Jim' Warrington of the Forest Rangers, who rescues her from the clutches of a Red Indian seducer. It was seen in London, at the Comedy Theatre 17 May 1962, with Joyce Blair (*b* 1932) and Bernard Cribbins (*b* 1928) in the leading roles.

Little Me. American musical comedy with score by Cy *Coleman, book by Neil *Simon, based on the novel by Patrick Dennis, and lyrics by Carolyn *Leigh. Starring Sid Caesar (*b* 1922), it showed off his comic talents by giving him the roles of all of the seven men who figure in the life of Belle, played by Virginia Martin, whose career is followed from poverty to riches and marriage to a state governor. Opening at the Lunt-Fontanne Theatre, 17 Nov. 1962, it had a run of 257 performances. The principal numbers were 'The other side of the tracks', 'I love you', 'I've got your number', 'Real live girl', and 'Here's to us'. The London production, Cambridge Theatre 18 Nov. 1964, starred Bruce Forsyth (*b* 1928) and Avril Angers (*b* 1922), and it had 334 performances. There was a short-lived revised version in New York in 1982.

Little Night Music, A. American musical with music and lyrics by Stephen *Sondheim and book by Hugh Wheeler, based on the Ingmar Bergman film *Sommarnattens leende* (*Smiles of a Summer Night*, 1955). Produced at the Shubert Theatre, New York, 25 Feb. 1973, with Glynis Johns (*b* 1923), Len Cariou, Hermione *Gingold, Victoria Mallory, Laurence Guittard, and Patricia Elliott, it had 600 performances.

It dealt with the romantic life of a Swedish lawyer, his child-bride, and his son, who is also in love with her; his former mistress, her lover, and her crippled mother, who finally sorts the whole thing out. It was an ambitious score, orchestrated by Jonathan Tunick, which was written entirely in 3/4 time, or its derivatives, and it had a kind of Greek chorus which sang the overture and commented throughout. The pre-eminent hit was 'Send in the clowns' which became Sondheim's best-known song. The London production (Adelphi, 15 Apr. 1975) starred Jean Simmons (*b* 1929), who had played in the American tour production, Hermione Gingold, Joss Ackland (*b* 1928), and David Kernan (*b* 1939). A film made in 1978 starred Elizabeth Taylor (*b* 1932), Diana Rigg (*b* 1938), Len Cariou, and Hermione Gingold.

Little Revue, The. Popular British intimate revue staged on 21 Apr. 1939 at the Little Theatre (which was in what is now John Adam Street, near the Strand, London, was bombed in 1941, and demolished in 1949). It continued into the early war years, from 20 Sept. 1939 as *The Little Non-Stop Revue*. It featured the talents of Cyril *Ritchard, George Benson (1911–83), Hermione *Baddeley, Joyce *Grenfell, and others. The music was by the short-lived but promising Walter *Leigh and the script mainly by the master of revue, Herbert *Farjeon.

Little Richard [Penniman, Richard Wayne] (*b* Macon, Ga., 5 Dec. 1935). American rock singer. The one word that best describes Little Richard is 'anarchic'. He represented the wildest side of *rock and roll, taking it to its flashy, outrageous, loud, and uncompromisingly black extremes. Exhibiting much religious fervour in his youth, he sang with local church choirs, then joined a travelling medicine show. He won a talent contest in Atlanta in 1941 then began his recording career with RCA, singing in a blues idiom but retaining his strong gospel allegiances, a mixture of styles that influenced others like Otis *Redding and James *Brown. He moved to the Peacock label with some very professional blues performances, but only achieved his first big hit in 1956 with 'Tutti frutti', which he recorded for the Specialty label in what became the quintessential Little Richard manner, powerful and unrestrained. It rubbed off on such performers as Mick Jagger, Jerry Lee *Lewis, and Jimi *Hendrix. Other million-selling discs soon followed: 'Long tall Sally' (1956), 'Rip it up' (1956), 'The girl can't help it' (1956), 'Lucille' (1957), 'Keep a-knockin'' (1957), and 'Good golly, Miss Molly' (1957). On these early recordings the lyrics were often meaningless; but the more disconnected and eccentric the imagery, the more his public seemed to like it. Despite his own accomplishment as a stomping piano-player, he was often accompanied by such players as Huey Smith (*b* 1934), Edward Frank, Little Booker, and Salvador Doucette.

While touring Australia in 1957 he decided to quit pop music. Suddenly hit by strong religious convictions, he studied theology at a college in Alabama, embraced the ministry, and toured the gospel circuit, frequently denouncing rock and roll as the devil's music. He did, however, before his conversion, put out an autobiographical album, *The King of Rock and Roll*; then, after recording several gospel albums, he had a brief rock reincarnation in 1964 to record 'Bama lama, bama loo'. From then on he mostly recorded soul and blues, achieving a few hits, like 'Baby, what do you want me to do' for Modern in 1967. His career took a turn for the better with the renewed interest in nostalgic revival shows, although he disappointed many of his followers with excessive camp egotism. But his early Speciality recordings remain affirmed rock and roll classics in spite of their eccentricities.

C. White: *The Life and Times of Little Richard: the Quasar of Rock* (New York, 1984).

Little Show, The. Historic Broadway revue, a counterpart to the Charlot revues, that was the first of 11 fruitful collaborations between composer Arthur *Schwartz and writer Howard *Dietz. It was produced at the Music Box Theatre, New York, 30 Apr. 1929, and ran for 321 performances. Its fame outlasted its run, having established the names of Fred *Allen and Libby *Holman, whose 'Moanin' low' (written by Ralph *Rainger, who was the revue's pianist) and the subsequent dance she did with Clifton *Webb were the highlights of the show. Also in the cast were Romney Brent (1902–76), Bettina Hall (*b* 1907), and Constance Cummings (*b* 1910). George S. *Kaufman was involved in the writing of its notable sketches such as 'The Still Alarm'. The Schwartz–Dietz number that impressed was 'I guess I'll have to change my plan' (originally written in 1924 as 'I love to lie awake in bed' with a lyric by Lorenz *Hart). Other songs included: "Little old New York', 'Caught in the rain' (*m* Henry Sullivan), and 'Can't we be friends' (*m* Kay Swift).

The two following editions were less successful. *The Second Little Show*, at the Royale Theatre 2 Sept. 1930, with items by Schwartz, Dietz, and others, starred Jay C. Flippen (1898–1971) and Marion Harris (1896–1944), and had a good number in Herman *Hupfeld's 'Sing something simple', but it only achieved 63 performances. *The Third Little Show*, Music Box Theatre 1 June 1931, had contributions by Max Lief (1899–1969) and Nathaniel Lief (1896–1944), and its cast included Beatrice

*Lillie (who introduced Noël *Coward's 'Mad dogs and Englishmen' and Liza *Lehmann's 'There are fairies at the bottom of our garden') and Ernest Truex (1889–1973), with Walter O'Keefe singing Hupfeld's 'When Yuba plays the rumba on the tuba'. It ran for 136 performances.

Livingston, Jay [Harold] (*b* McDonald, Pa., 28 Mar. 1915). American composer. He studied piano and orchestration and graduated at Pennsylvania University in 1937. One of his first writing chores was producing special material for the comedians Olsen and Johnson. The credits on his long list of hits usually read 'Livingston; Evans'—his partnership with Ray Evans (*b* 1915) lasting for many years from the time when they worked together as dance-band musicians on a luxury liner. In 1944 they went to Hollywood together to join the Paramount staff and they had a tremendous success in films, winning more Oscars for songs than anyone else since the Academy Awards started in 1934.

Their first big hits were the title-songs of *To Each his Own* (1946) and *Golden Earrings* (1947). They also wrote for: *Why Girls Leave Home* (1945); *Monsieur Beaucaire* (1946); *The Paleface* (1948)—'Buttons and bows'; *Captain Carey USA* (1949; *After Midnight* in UK)—'Mona Lisa'; *My Friend Irma* (1949)—'I'll always love you'; *The Heiress* (1949)—'My love loves me'; *Fancy Pants* (1950)—'Home cookin''; *Here Comes the Groom* (1951)—'Your own little house'; *Aaron Slick from Punkin Crick* (1951); *Red Garters* (1954)—'A dime and a dollar'; *Tammy and the Bachelor* (1955; *Tammy* in GB)—'Tammy'; *The Man Who Knew Too Much* (1956)—'Que será, será; *Houseboat* (1958)—'Almost in your arms'; *Another Time, Another Place* (1958)—'Another time, another place'; and *The Cat and the Canary* (1959). For the theatre they wrote the scores of *Oh, Captain* (1958) and *Let It Ride* (1961).

Livingston, Jerry (*b* Denver, Col., 25 Mar. 1909). American composer. He studied at the University of Arizona, and as a young man became a professional pianist with a dance orchestra in Denver and wrote college shows. In 1932 he went to New York to work as a pianist. He wrote *The Hollywood Revels* (1938). He organized his own orchestra in 1940, but gave this up to concentrate on songwriting and formed his own music-publishing business. He wrote the music for the revue *Bright Lights of 1944* and the films *At War With the Army* (1950) and *Alice in Wonderland* (1951). His songs include: 'When it's darkness on the Delta' (1932, *w* Marty Symes, 1904–53); 'Under a blanket of blue' (1933, *w* Symes); 'It's the talk of the town' (1933, *w* Symes and Allen Neiberg, 1902–78); 'Where there's smoke there's fire' (1934); 'Just a kid named Joe' (1938); 'You're letting the grass grow under your feet' (1939); 'Mairzy doats—and dozy doats' (1943); 'It's the talk of the town' (1946, *w* Symes); and 'Blue and sentimental' (with Count *Basie, 1947).

Lloyd, A. L. [Albert Lancaster] (*b* London 29 Feb. 1908; *d* Greenwich, 29 Sept. 1982). British folk-singer and ethnomusicologist. He combined his early commitment to the world socialist cause with an interest in folk-song, doing his early researches in Australia and later in Eastern Europe. He became well-known as a performer and lecturer in Britain and the USA and also as a producer of radio programmes and documentary films. His writings included: *The Singing Englishman* (London, 1944); *Come All Ye Bold Miners: Songs and Ballads of the Coalfields* (London, 1952); *The Penguin Book of English Folk Songs* (ed. with Ralph Vaughan Williams) (London, 1959); and the standard *Folk Song in England* (London, 1967; New York, 1969).

Lloyd, Arthur (*b* Edinburgh, 1840; *d* London, 20 July 1904). British singer and composer. He trained as an actor and played in repertory in Scotland, also appearing as a comic singer in Glasgow taverns, and joining the company of the Theatre Royal in Plymouth in 1856. He first appeared on the London music-hall stage at the Sun in Knightsbridge in 1862 and thereafter was engaged at the Canterbury. He became a favourite at the London Pavilion, his act being devoted to the kind of 'swell' songs that *Leybourne and others had pioneered; he was billed as 'the last of the lion-comiques'.

His best-known item was 'Not for Joseph', which he wrote in 1867 and which became very popular and used with political connotations; closely rivalled by 'Policeman 92X' (1870), 'The upper ten and the lower five', 'The postman', 'The German band', 'Imensikoff', 'Riding on top of an omnibus', 'Pretty lips', and 'I'll place it in the hands of my solicitor'. He also sang Thackeray's 'Married to a mermaid' with great success. He formed a concert party in association with Harry *Liston in 1866, leased the Queen's Theatre, Dublin, in 1874 to present variety shows, and was again in London at the Pavilion in 1878. By 1883 he was playing mostly in sketches and wrote a play, *Bally Voyan*, in 1892. He made a 40-week tour of the USA in 1893.

Lloyd, Marie [Wood, Matilda Alice Victoria] (*b* Hoxton, London, 12 Feb. 1870; *d* Golders Green, London, 7 Oct. 1922). British comedienne and singer. One of the greatest names of the British music-hall, she made her first appearance at the Grecian Assembly Rooms at the Eagle Tavern in the City Road on 9 May 1885 under the name of Bella Delmare. She first appeared as Marie Lloyd at the Eagle in June 1885, taking her name from Lloyd's Weekly News. A song which she 'borrowed' from Nelly Power, 'The boy I love is up in the gallery', helped her to establish a name, but she had to stop using it when Power objected. She quickly rose to popularity and by 1891 was appearing in four or five halls each evening and earning £100 a week, a considerable amount in those days.

She was a great favourite at such prominent halls as the Middlesex, the Tivoli, the Pavilion, and the *Oxford, performing in a somewhat blue vein and singing such provocative songs as 'She'd never had her ticket punched before', 'Johnny Jones' or 'What's that for, eh!', 'Twiggy vous', and the well-known 'Oh, Mister Porter'. She first appeared in pantomime at Drury Lane in 1891, co-starring with other great stars of the music-hall, Dan *Leno and Little Tich [Harry Relph] (1867–1928). She had three husbands, the first divorcing her on the grounds of her adultery with the coster comedian Alec Hurley (1871–1913) when they toured Australia in 1901; she married him in 1906. She went to the USA in 1902 but disappointed the audiences there by not being shocking enough; on later visits she laid it on rather more and managed to please.

By 1902 she was often billed simply as 'Our Marie' and was rated by Max Beerbohm as one of the great ladies of the age. She was refused a place in the Royal Command Performance in 1912 and toured the USA and Canada again in 1913, after some trouble with the authorities over her extra-marital liaison with the jockey Bernard Dillon, whom she married in 1914. During the war she entertained the troops and did a great deal for charity. She was now earning £600 a week and making hits of such songs as 'A little of what you fancy', 'A bit of a ruin that Cornwall knocked about a bit', and the immortal 'Don't dilly dally'. Her health began to decline by 1920 and she collapsed after a performance in Edmonton in 1922. Her sisters Alice (1873–1949), Daisy (1877–1961), and Rosie (1879–1944) all appeared in the halls and, all looking toothily the same, appeared as the Lloyd Family, later joined by Marie's daughter Marie Jr. (1890–1967), singing her songs.

N. Jacob: *Our Marie [Marie Lloyd]: a Biography* (London, 1936). W. Macqueen Pope: *Marie Lloyd: Queen of the Music Halls* (London, 1960). D. Farson: *Marie Lloyd and Music Hall* (London, 1972). R. A. Baker: *Marie Lloyd: Queen of the Music-Halls* (London, 1990).

Lloyd Webber, Andrew (*b* London, 22 Mar. 1948). British composer. Son of Dr William Lloyd Webber (1914–82), director of the London College of Music from 1964, he started composing at the age of six and his first published work, a piano suite, appeared when he was nine. He had an early gift for melody which his father was afraid would be destroyed by too much formal musical education; nevertheless he became a Queen's Scholar at Westminster School and then studied at the Guildhall School of Music and the Royal College of Music. In 1965 he joined forces with lyric-writer/librettist Tim *Rice, who had been writing words for his school pop group. They wrote a somewhat conventional musical about Dr Barnardo called *The Likes of Us*, which was never produced, and a song, 'Love is here'.

In 1968 they were commissioned by Alan Doggett, music master of Colet Court School, to write **Joseph and the Amazing Technicolor Dreamcoat*, which they produced in three weeks. It was enthusiastically received at its try-out and Norrie *Paramor (with whom Tim Rice was then working at EMI) persuaded Decca to record it. The LP sold well and 'Christopher' became a hit single. This led to the ideas for and the creation of **Jesus Christ, Superstar*. They took the unusual course of selling it first on record, the title-song being issued in autumn 1969 by MCA and becoming a 100,000-selling hit in the USA, with the album a best-seller by 1971. The show opened on Broadway in October 1971 and in London in 1972, settling in for a record-breaking run that lasted until 1980. It was criticized in the musical world but given support by the Church. Eventually the collaborators were hailed, as Lionel *Bart had been before, as 'saviours of the English musical'.

Lloyd Webber wrote a musical based on the 'Jeeves' books by P. G. *Wodehouse in 1975. Rice withdrew from the project and the book was provided by Alan Ayckbourn, but *Jeeves* was a flop and lasted only four weeks in London. The partnership with Rice resumed in the creation of **Evita*, a musical based on the life of Eva Péron. As before, it was launched by way of an LP in 1976 which cost £90,000 to produce. In spite of good reviews it almost failed until 'Don't cry for me, Argentina' became a hit and the album (eventually) a No. 1 best-seller. The show opened on 21 June 1978 and was hailed as 'a marvellous modern opera'. Lloyd Webber wrote the mini-opera *Tell Me on a Sunday* for TV in 1980. His success story, and a growing accumulation of wealth and influence, continued, with other collaborators, with the seemingly ever-lasting **Cats*, produced in London in May 1981 and in New York in 1982; followed by **Song and Dance* (1982) (*w* Don Black), *Starlight Express* (27 Mar. 1984, *w* Richard Stilgoe, *b* 1943), and *The *Phantom of the Opera* (1986). One of his most refined and pleasantly melodic scores came with *Aspects of Love* (1989), inevitably decried as 'derivative', but going pleasantly back to the more restrained days of popular music with such likeable songs as 'Love changes everything', 'The first man you remember', and 'Anything but lonely'. He wrote music for the films *Gumshoe* (1971) and *The Odessa File* (1973); and in 1985 composed a much criticized but well-liked 'Requiem Mass'; also 'Variations for Cello' (1978) for his brother Julian Lloyd Webber (*b* 1951).

G. McKnight: *Andrew Lloyd Webber* (London, 1984). J. Mantle: *Fanfare: the Unauthorised Biography of Andrew Lloyd Webber* (London, 1989). M. Walsh: *Andrew Lloyd Webber: his Life and Works* (London, 1989).

Lock Up Your Daughters. British musical play with score by Laurie *Johnson and words by Bernard Miles (*b* 1907), based on Henry Fielding's comedy *Rape Upon Rape*. This was the opening production of the Mermaid Theatre when it moved to Puddle Dock in London, starting on 28 May 1959 and running for 328 performances. The cast included Hy Hazell (1922–70) and Stephanie Voss (*b* 1936). It was revived there in 1962 and 1969.

Loesser, Frank (*b* New York, 29 June 1910; *d* New York, 28 July 1969). American composer. Son of a North German immigrant family with a highly cultured background, he was the much younger brother of pianist and author Arthur Loesser (1894–1969) who was deemed a model to follow. He was a naturally musical child but his interest was directed entirely towards popular music (greatly to his father's disappointment) and a temporary interest in the harmonica. After leaving the City College in New York, where he started writing songs for college productions, he worked as an office-boy and reporter, becoming editor of a trade newspaper. Also having a considerable drawing talent, he worked part-time as a singer and caricaturist in a vaudeville act, and tried his hand at writing lyrics for Tin Pan Alley. His first song, published in 1931, was 'In love with a memory of you', written in collaboration with the later distinguished American composer Walter Schuman.

In 1931 he was contracted to RKO pictures as a lyric-writer, though nothing he wrote was actually published. In 1936 he wrote lyrics for *The Illustrators' Show*, with music mainly by Irving Actman (1907–67), and the same year he married and settled in Hollywood. During the years when he was primarily a lyricist, he worked with Hoagy *Carmichael, Frederick *Hollander, Burton *Lane, Lionel *Newman, Arthur *Schwartz, Manning *Sherwin, Jule *Styne, and Victor *Young, helping to produce many top hits and doing very well financially. He spent three years in the US Army as a private soldier and wrote songs for army shows, including various official songs such as 'Rodger Young' for the Infantry, as well as 'What do you do in the Infantry' and 'Salute to the Army Service Forces'. During the war he began to write complete shows, words and music, for performance before troops all over the world, including *Skirts* (1944) which was seen in London; *About Face* (1944)—'First class Private Mary Brown' and 'Why do they call a Private a Private'; and *OK, USA* (1945)—'When he comes home'.

This accumulated experience led to his main theatre successes like **Where's Charley?* (1948)—'Once in love with Amy'; **Guys and Dolls* (1950); *The *Most Happy Fella* (1956); *Greenwillow* (1960)—'A day borrowed from Heaven', 'The music of home', 'Gideon Briggs', 'I love you', 'Summertime love', 'Never will I marry', 'Walking away whistling'; and **How to Succeed in Business Without Really Trying* (1961). His film work had been equally productive of good songs, including: *The Hurricane* (1937)—'The moon of Manakoora' (*m* Alfred *Newman); *Forest Rangers* (1942)—'Jingle, jangle, jingle' (*m* Joseph J. Lilley, *b* 1914); *Thank Your Lucky Stars* (1943)—'They're either too young or too old' (*m* Arthur Schwartz), 'How sweet you are' (Schwartz); *Christmas Holiday* (1944)—'Spring will be a little late this year'; *Variety Girl* (1947); *The Perils of Pauline* (1947)—'The sewing machine', 'I wish I didn't love you so'; *Red, Hot and Blue* (1949)—'That's loyalty', 'Now that I need you', 'I wake up in the morning feeling fine'; *Neptune's Daughter* (1949)—'Baby, it's cold outside'; *Roseanna McCoy* (1949); *Let's Dance* (1950)—'Tunnel of love'; *Hans Christian Andersen* (1951), starring Danny *Kaye (adapted as a stage musical, starring Tommy *Steele, London (Palladium) 17 Dec. 1974)—'Wonderful Copenhagen', 'The inch worm', 'Ugly duckling', 'No two people', 'Thumbelina', 'Anywhere I wander'. (See also under composers listed above.) Other songs included: 'Praise the Lord and pass the ammunition' (1942); 'Bloop-bleep (I can't sleep)' (1947); and 'On a slow boat to China' (1948).

A. Loesser: 'My brother Frank' in *Notes* (New York, March 1950). F. Loesser: *The Frank Loesser Songbook* (New York, 1972). N. Sherrin & C. Brahms: 'Frank Loesser' in *Song by Song* (London, 1984).

Loewe, Frederick (*b* Vienna, 10 June 1901; *d* Palm Springs, Fla., 14 Feb. 1988). Austrian-born American composer. His father, Edmund Loewe, had been the first Danilo in *The Merry Widow* in 1906 and his mother was an actress, so his hereditary talents were firmly implanted. He was educated at Stern's Conservatory in Berlin, where he studied the piano with Busoni and D'Albert and composition with Rezniček. His song 'Katrina' (1919) was a modest hit in Europe. He went to the USA in 1924 but had little success for many years, finding his musical idiom out of tune with jazz-age America, so he had to take several odd jobs, ending up in New York as a pianist in a beer hall and organist in a silent cinema. An operetta, *Great Lady*, was produced in New York in 1938.

It was his association with the much younger lyricist and librettist Alan Jay *Lerner that led his steps in the right direction. Their first production, *Life of the Party*, was staged in Detroit in 1942, followed by the revue *What's Up* (1943) and *The Day Before Spring* (1945). Their breakthrough came with **Brigadoon* in 1947, which had substantial runs in both New York and London. This was followed by **Paint Your Wagon* in 1951. Loewe's natural Viennese idiom, only slightly modified by Americanism, proved ideal for the sensitively period and dramatically right musical treatment of Shaw's classic play *Pygmalion*. The well-crafted score of **My Fair Lady* (1956) deservedly earned a run of 2717 performances in New York and 2281 in London; with many revivals since. Nothing could expect to surpass *My Fair Lady*, but **Camelot* (1960) had a fair measure of success, as did **Gigi*, first as a film in 1958, then as a stage musical in 1973. The achievements of the partnership were celebrated in a TV *Salute to Lerner and Loewe* in 1961 and *The Lerner and Loewe Songbook* was published in 1962.

A. J. Lerner: *The Street Where I Live: the Story of My Fair Lady, Gigi and Camelot* (New York–London, 1978).

Logan, Ella [Allan, Ella] (*b* Glasgow, 6 Mar. 1913; *d* Burlingame, Calif., 1 May 1969). Scottish actress and singer. After an early variety career in Scotland, England, and Europe, and appearing in the London musical *Darling! I Love You!* (1930), she settled in the USA in 1932. She sang with the Abe *Lyman band 1933–4, had a small role in the

Broadway musical *Calling All Stars* (1934), was a regular on radio in the 1930s, and appeared in the films *Flying Hostess* (1936); *Top of the Town* (1937); *52nd Street* (1937); and *Goldwyn Follies* (1938). She appeared in **George White's Scandals* in 1939 and *Sons o' Fun* (1941), and entertained the troops during the wartime years. She became internationally known through her starring role as Sharon in **Finian's Rainbow* (1947), especially associated with 'How are things in Glocca Morra?' Latterly, she sang in clubs in the USA, London, and Paris.

Logan, Frederick Knight (*b* Oskaloosa, Iowa, 15 Oct. 1871; *d* Oskaloosa, 11 June 1928). American composer. He wrote many songs in collaboration with his mother, Virginia Knight Logan (1850–1940), but had his greatest success with 'Missouri waltz', which was published as piano solo in 1914, with Logan simply credited as 'arranger' because he thought it of too popular an ilk for his lofty talents. Its success when published as a song in 1916, with words by James Royce Shannon (1881–1946), changed his allegiance, even more so when it was adopted as the official song of the State of Missouri. It was later a great favourite of President Harry Truman and associated with his career.

Logan, Joshua Lockwood (*b* Texarkana, Texas, 5 Oct. 1908; *d* New York, 12 July 1988). American librettist, director, and producer. He was educated at Princeton University and the Moscow Art Theatre, began an acting career in 1932, and directed his first play in 1933. He came to the musical stage with a fanciful production of *I Married an Angel* (1938)—its fancies largely dictated by the whims of lyricist Lorenz *Hart. After this he determined on a policy of realism in musicals which he achieved in such productions as **Knickerbocker Holiday* (1938); *Stars in Your Eyes* (1939); *Two for the Show* (1940); *Higher and Higher* (1940), of which he was part-author; *By Jupiter* (1942); and *This Is the Army* (1942). His talents were fully disclosed with the epoch-making **Annie Get Your Gun* (1946). He was writer and co-producer of **South Pacific* (1949), although his name was long kept off the credits by the connivances of *Rodgers and *Hammerstein. His later productions sometimes went too far in their search for realism. **Wish You Were Here* (1952), **Fanny* (1954), *All American* (1962), *Mr President* (1962), and *Look to the Lilies* (1970) did not repeat the success of his peak years. He was active as a film director from the mid-1950s, with *South Pacific* (1958) and **Camelot* (1967) overdoing the kitsch a little.

J. Logan: *Josh: My Up and Down, In and Out Life* (New York, 1977).

Lomax, Alan (*b* Austin, Texas, 31 Jan. 1915). American ethnomusicologist. He inherited his interests from his celebrated father John *Lomax, with whom he regularly collaborated until his death in 1948. He studied at the University of Texas and Columbia University, then spent the years 1933–42 collecting folk-songs in the Southwest and Midwest states of the USA. He was appointed head of the Bureau of Applied Social Research in 1963. With his father, he made field recordings for the Library of Congress of rural and prison songs which brought to light the forgotten talents of *Leadbelly and discovered such artists as Woody *Guthrie and Muddy *Waters. Another discovery was the neglected Jelly Roll *Morton with whom he made a series of recordings for the Library of Congress in 1938; and he wrote about him in *Mr Jelly Lord* (1950). He was an influential figure in the American folk revival of the 1940s. In the post-war years he worked in Britain with Ewan *MacColl on the 'Ballads and Blues' radio series. Back in the USA in the 1950s he collected the material for the 'Southern Folk Heritage' series issued on Atlantic. He jointly edited several collections of folk material with John Lomax; and continued with *The Folk Songs of North America in the English Language* (New York, 1960), *Hard-Hitting Songs for Hard-Hit People* (New York, 1967), and *Folk Song Style and Culture* (Washington, 1968).

Lomax, John Avery (*b* Goodman, Miss., 23 Sept. 1867; *d* Greenville, Miss., 26 Jan. 1948). An early interest in collecting and notating folk-songs led to a lifelong vocation. He studied music at the University of Texas and founded the Texas Folklore Society. By 1933 his son Alan *Lomax was assisting him in his researches and the resultant books were *American Ballads and Folksongs* (New York, 1934), *Cowboy Songs and Other Frontier Ballads* (New York, 1938), and *Our Singing Country* (New York, 1941). He published an autobiography, *Adventures of a Ballad Hunter* (New York, 1947), and his final monument was the volume, edited by Alan Lomax, *Best Songs from the Lomax Collections for Pickers and Singers* (New York, 1966).

Lombardo, Carmen (*b* London, Ontario, 16 July 1903; *d* North Miami, Fla., 17 Apr. 1971). Canadian saxophonist and composer. He played in the band of his brother Guy *Lombardo from 1929 until 1970, when he had to retire from music because of cancer, his heavy vibrato lead establishing the well-known sweet sound of the orchestra. He was also its leading vocalist, singing in a much imitated soft and fluctuating manner, and leading a vocal trio. He was responsible for much of the band's notable repertoire and its arrangements, being involved in such items as 'Coquette' (with John *Green, 1928, *w* Gus *Kahn), 'Sweethearts on parade' (1928, *w* Charles Newman), 'Snuggled on your shoulder (cuddled in your arms)' (with Joe *Young, 1931), 'Wake up and sing' (with Cliff *Friend and Charles *Tobias, 1936), 'Sailboat in the moonlight' (with John Jacob Loeb, 1902–70, 1937), 'Boo hoo' (with Loeb, 1937, *w* Edward Heyman), 'Ferdinand the Bull' (with Loeb, 1938), and 'Powder your face with sunshine' (1948). He wrote many scores for the Jones Beach, New York, stage productions, including *Arabian Nights* (1954).

Lombardo, Guy (*b* London, Ontario, 19 June 1902; *d* Houston, Texas, 5 Nov. 1977). Canadian bandleader. Born of Italian parents, he and his brothers, Carmen (above), Lebert, and Victor, formed a band in 1917, with Guy as leader, which gradually earned local fame as 'Guy Lombardo and his Royal Canadians'. Various characteristics, evolved from Carmen's heavy saxophone vibrato, muted brass, tinkling piano, and corny codas, made it immediately recognizable. The Royal Canadians migrated *en bloc* to the USA in 1924 and established themselves in Cleveland. Later they moved to Chicago and by 1928, billed as 'the sweetest music this side Heaven', were popular in New York and had started a long and prolific recording career. In 1929 Lombardo was established at the Roosevelt Grill. An early theme tune was 'Auld lang syne' which became a nostalgic feature of New Year's TV concerts from the Waldorf-Astoria Hotel. Their 1937 hit recording of 'Boo hoo' was another permanent highlight of the repertoire. The band was featured on the Burns and Allen Show in the mid-1930s and had its own show up to the 1950s. It appeared in such films as *Many Happy Returns* (1934); *Stage Door Canteen* (1943); and *No Leave, No Love* (1946). He was involved in the summer shows at Jones Beach, NY, into the 1960s. The band survived until 1977.

G. Lombardo and J. Altschue: *Auld Acquaintance: an Autobiography* (New York, 1975).

London, Julie [Peck, Julie] (*b* Santa Rosa, Calif., 26 Sept. 1926). American singer and actress. Starting her career as a band singer on the West Coast, she had a modest film career from 1944. Her second marriage to pianist and composer Bobby Troup (*b* 1918) led to a recording contract with Liberty records and she started a successful new career with the album *Julie is Her Name* (1955) with bassist Ray Leatherwood (*b* 1914) and guitarist Barney Kessel (*b* 1923). She had a hit with 'Cry me a river', used in the rock film *The Girl Can't Help It* (1956), and continued with a popular series of LPs into the 1960s.

'Londonderry air'. Irish song. The composer of this sublime melody has never been ascertained. It was first printed in the Petrie collection of 1855, composer 'unknown', and is generally classified as a folk-song. The tune was given to Petrie by Miss Jane Ross of Londonderry, a well-known collector of traditional Irish music. Sir Hubert Parry called it 'the most beautiful tune in the world'. The first known words to be added to it were by Alfred Perceval Graves—'Would I were Erin's apple blossom o'er thee'—and a second version, 'Emer's farewell', was made by the same writer. The most popular version, 'Danny boy', was written by the prolific lyricist Frederick E. *Weatherly in 1913.

Loose Tubes. A 21-piece jazz group formed in London in 1984. It re-created various aspects of the jazz and rock scene in a remarkably joyful and relaxed manner that has assured great popularity. A somewhat unconventional sound is achieved by the use of such instruments as tuba, bass-clarinet, and flute; by working without a front leader a spontaneous unanimity is effectively achieved. Most of the arrangements are by Django Bates (keyboards) and Steve Berry (bass) and show a real pleasure in melody, harmony, and rhythm in a traditional and yet ever experimental sense.

Lopez, Francis (*b* Montbéliard, Doubs, France, 1916). French composer. He specialized in lavish musical comedy scores, often with a colourful Spanish or Latin American setting, traditionally predictable in the **Rose-Marie*, Eddy–MacDonald mould, but memorably tuneful. In collaboration with librettist Raymond Vincy, he produced many shows which the less sophisticated Parisian and provincial audiences have been unable to resist, including: *La Belle de Cadix* (1945; filmed 1953; revived 1949, 1958, 1977, and 1979)—it was initially expected to run for about 15 performances and lasted for 1500; *Andalousie* (1947; filmed 1950); *Quatre jours à Paris* (1949; filmed 1955); *Le Chanteur de Mexico* (1952), starring Luis Mariano (1920–70); *La Route fleurie* (1952, revived 1979); *La Toison d'or* (1954), with Colette Ridinger; and *Mediterranée* (1955, revived 1964), with Tino *Rossi; the last three at the Théâtre du Châtelet. He also wrote music for films, including *Violettes impériales* (1952), and many popular songs.

Lopez, Vincent (*b* Brooklyn, 30 Dec. 1894; *d* North Miami, Fla., 20 Sept. 1975). American pianist, composer, and bandleader. His father was a bandmaster in the US Navy and taught him the rudiments of music, nevertheless trying to lead him towards becoming a Catholic priest. But Lopez could not be turned from music and as a youth started playing piano in the dives of Brooklyn, later leading small café orchestras in New York. He formed a regular band in 1918, and in 1921 started a pioneering series of broadcasts on WJX radio in Newark, becoming known by the signature tune 'Nola' (which he played with great dexterity) and his greeting 'Hello, everybody, Lopez speaking'. Later he was a pioneer of the TV chat show programme. He had long residencies at the Hotel Pennsylvania, Hotel St Regis, and Hotel Taft (27 years) in New York. He appeared with the band in *Love Birds* (1921); **Greenwich Village Follies* (1924); **Earl Carroll's Vanities* (1928); and in the film *The Big Broadcast of 1932*. He was also in numerous radio shows with such vocalists as Grace *Moore, Betty *Hutton, Marion Hutton, and Johnny Messner, working into the 1970s. His songs included: 'Knock, knock, who's there?', 'Rockin' chair swing', 'Does a duck like water', and 'The world stands still'.

V. Lopez: *Lopez Speaking* (New York, 1964).

Loraine, Violet (*b* London, 26 July 1886; *d* Haltwhistle, Northumberland, 18 July 1956). British actress and singer. She made her first appearance on stage in the chorus of the pantomime *Mother Goose*, at Drury Lane in 1902. Her distinguished appearances in musicals included *The Medal and the Maid* (1903), *The Duchess of Dantzic* (1903), and *Sergeant Brue* (1904); she was in variety in 1905 at the Palace Theatre and continued in music-hall at the *Oxford and elsewhere; and she was also a popular principal boy in pantomime. Her career in musicals resumed with *Hullo, Tango!* (1911); *Business as Usual* (1914); *The *Bing Boys Are Here* (1916); *The Bing Girls Are There* (1917); *Round the Map* (1917); *The Bing Boys on Broadway* (1918); *The Whirligig* (1920); etc. In 1921 she married and retired from the stage, but she made reappearances from time to time, notably in a revival of *The Bing Boys Are Here* in 1934 and, having been a tireless fund-raiser in the First World War, predictably in an RAF Pageant at the Albert Hall in 1945.

Lorraine, Lillian [De Jacques, Eulallean] (*b* San Francisco, 1 Jan. 1892; *d* New York, 17 Apr. 1955). American actress and singer. She was exceptionally beautiful and especially admired by Florenz *Ziegfeld. She first appeared in the chorus of *The Tourists* (1906) then made her name in *The Gay White Way* (1907); *Miss Innocence* (1908), in which she sang 'Pony boy'; **Ziegfeld Follies* (1909, 1910, 1911, 1912, 1918)—'By the light of the silvery moon' (1909), 'Row, row, row' (1912); *Over the River* (1912); *The Whirl of the World* (1914); *Odds and Ends* (1917); *The Little Blue Devil* (1919); and *The Blue Kitten* (1922).

Loss, Joe [Joshua Alexander] (*b* London, 22 June 1909; *d* London, 6 June 1990). British bandleader. Originally a violinist, he led his own band from 1930 at the Astoria Ballroom in the Charing Cross Road, London. During 1932–4 he was at the elite Kit-Kat Club, then returned to the Astoria and started to record for the Regal-Zonophone label. His first big recording hit came in 1939 with 'Begin the beguine' with singer Chick Henderson (1912–44), who was with him from 1934 and died while serving in the Royal Navy; his next with 'In the mood' (1940) which became his theme tune. There was another big success in 1948 with 'A tree in the meadow' with vocalist Howard Jones. His unparalleled long career continued into the 1980s as the leader of the most prestigious strict-tempo and society dance orchestra, often heard and seen on the BBC's radio and TV *Come Dancing* series and at most ballroom championships, much liked for his ebullient and outgoing personality, and recording numerous albums.

Lost in the Stars. American musical tragedy with score by Kurt *Weill and book by Maxwell *Anderson, based on Alan Paton's *Cry the Beloved Country*. Weill's last Broadway production was a strong adaptation of a novel dealing with race problems, the story of the son of a black minister in Johannesburg who accidentally kills a white man. He admits his guilt, his end lightened by the friendship of the murdered man's father.

Produced at the Music Box Theatre, New York, 30 Oct. 1949, the cast included Todd *Duncan, Julian Mayfield, Leslie Banks, and Warren Coleman, and it had 273 performances. It was taken into the repertory of the New York City Opera in 1958, seen on Broadway in 1972, and filmed in 1974.

Louiguy, Louis Guiglielmi (*b* Barcelona, 1916). Spanish-born French composer. He studied music at the Paris Conservatoire. His first song hit, 'Ça sent si bon la France' (1941, *w* Jacques Larue), was popularized by Maurice *Chevalier at the Casino de Paris, but his greatest success was with 'La vie en rose' (1945), which Edith *Piaf (who also wrote the words) made famous. Others were 'Sérénade florentine' (1946, *w* Jacques Plante), 'Hortensia' (1947), 'La danseuse est créole', and 'Cerisiers roses et pommiers blancs' ('Cherry pink and apple-blossom white', 1950). He wrote an operetta, *La Quincaillière de Chicago* (*w* Albert Willemetz), in 1958.

Louisiana Purchase. Musical comedy with music and lyrics by Irving *Berlin and book by Morrie Ryskind (1895–1985), based on a story by Buddy *DeSylva, produced at the Imperial Theatre, New York, 28 May 1940, where, with the distinguished cast of William *Gaxton, Victor *Moore, Irene *Bordoni, Vera Zorina (*b* 1917), and Carol Bruce (*b* 1919), it had 444 performances. The pivotal character was Senator Oliver P. Longberry, played by Moore, who goes to New Orleans to investigate corrupt dealings by a business firm who try to sidetrack him with some alluring female company. The score found Berlin making a promising run-up to his biggest successes, and included: 'It's a lovely day tomorrow', 'Outside of that I love you', 'You're lonely and I'm lonely', 'Latins know how', 'What chance have I?', and 'Fools fall in love'. It was filmed in 1941 with Moore, Zorina, Bordoni, and Bob *Hope.

Love. Los Angeles rock group formed in 1966 by guitarist, singer, and composer Arthur Lee (*b* 1944) with John Echols (guitar), Bryan MacLean (guitar and vocal), Ken Forssi (bass), Alan 'Snoopy' Pfisterer (drums), and Michael Stuart (percussion). Their first albums, *Love* (1966) and *Da Capo* (1967), introduced the highly individual singing of Arthur Lee over a conventional rock backing; their third, *Forever Changes* (1968), introduced Tjay Cantrelli on horn and was intriguingly surrealistic. From then on the group became more conventionally based in the rhythm 'n' blues idiom, Jimi *Hendrix working with them for a while. They disbanded in 1974, occasionally re-uniting.

Love Me Tonight. Musical film singled out by Stanley Green as 'one of the screen's most innovative and imaginative musicals', closely integrating story, music, and background into a truly cinematic brand of musical comedy. Issued by Paramount in 1932, produced and directed by Rouben Mamoulian (*b* 1897), it had music by Richard *Rodgers and lyrics by Lorenz *Hart. The song 'Isn't it romantic' was notably used as a means for moving the action from Paris to a country château in a story about a Parisian tailor (Maurice *Chevalier) who poses as a baron and, in spite of his deception, wins the lovely Baroness (Jeanette *MacDonald) who is ultimately willing to die for her love. Also in the cast were Charles Ruggles (1886–1970), Charles Butterworth (1896–1946), Myrna Loy (*b* 1905), and C. Aubrey Smith (1863–1948). The film was full of clever musical sequences, setting various scenes, including a deer hunt ballet.

Love from Judy. Lightly romantic British musical comedy based on the classic American children's book *Daddy Long Legs* by Jean Webster. The music was by Hugh *Martin, lyrics by Hugh Martin and Jack Gray, and the book by Eric *Maschwitz. It was produced by Emile Littler at the Saville Theatre, London, 25 Sept. 1952, with Jeannie Carson (*b* 1929) as 'Judy' Abbott, and had 504 performances.

Love Life. 'A vaudeville' with music by Kurt *Weill, and book by Alan Jay *Lerner, produced at the 46th Street Theatre, New York, 7 Oct. 1948, where it had 252 performances. It was an unusual show which told the story of an ageless couple, played by Nanette Fabray (*b* 1922) and Ray *Middleton, and their family, from 1791 to the time of the play. The music was closely integrated into the show as a kind of commentary, more in the style of Weill's early work, and the plot was a series of vaudeville acts.

Lovin' Spoonful, The. American pop group formed in Greenwich Village, New York, in 1964 by John Sebastian (*b* 1944) with Zal Yanovsky (*b* 1944), Joe Butler (*b* 1943), and Steve Boone (*b* 1943). They were signed up by Kama Sutra and, following their first success with 'Do you believe in magic', had six recordings in the Top 10 1965–6. They created a folky, jug-band sound with a rock beat that came to be known as 'good-time music', a pleasing antidote to the anarchic extremes to be found in the rock scene of the 1960s; they often reworked folk-song material, as in their big hit 'Daydream' whose lazy beat and tuneful melody were widely imitated. Even the *Beatles copied 'Daydream' (which reached No. 2 in England) in their 'Good day sunshine'. Lovin' Spoonful's only American No. 1 hit came with 'Summer in the city', but their amiable music found an outlet beyond the teenage market. The group broke up in 1968 but briefly re-formed for a film in 1980.

Lubbock, Mark (*b* Downe, Kent, 1898; *d* Althorne, Essex, 10 Nov. 1986). British conductor, composer, and author. He was educated at Eton and served in the Royal Artillery in the First World War. He sang in musical comedy choruses before making his debut as a theatre conductor in 1920, after which he studied music in Germany and was an assistant conductor in Dresden. From 1932 he was adapting musicals for broadcasting, and in 1933 succeeded Stanford Robinson as music director of variety and conductor of the BBC Theatre Orchestra. He left the BBC in 1944 to freelance and was a regular contributor to *Music Magazine* on the Third Programme. His special interest was Viennese and German operetta, and in 1962 he published *The Complete Book of Light Opera*, an invaluable volume of synopses. He wrote music for the first operetta to be composed especially for radio, *The King Can Do No Wrong* (*w* Denis Freeman); incidental music for *The Italian Straw Hat* (1927) and *The Rose and the Violet*; and various orchestral pieces—*'Polka dots'*, *'Whispering poplar'*, *'Smuggler's song'*, and *'Winter rose'*.

Luders, Gustav (*b* Bremen, 13 Dec. 1865; *d* Chicago, 24 Jan. 1913). German-born American composer. He had a musical education in Europe before going to the USA and settling in Milwaukee in 1888. He conducted beer garden and theatre orchestras, then moved to Chicago where he continued his activities as musical director and managed a music-publishing business. He wrote his first stage score in 1899 and continued to average one a year, many in collaboration with Frank Pixley (1867–1919), until his sudden death from a heart-attack. This happened after the dismal failure of *Somewhere Else*, which was withdrawn after its third performance following dreadful press notices which Luders took very badly. His biggest success was *The Prince of Pilsen* (Boston, 1902; NY, 1903; London, 1904)—'Heidelberg', 'The message of the violet'; it is the only one of his scores now generally remembered.

He also wrote: *Little Robinson Crusoe* (1899); *The Burgomaster* (1901); *King Dodo* (1902); *Mam'selle Napoleon* (1903); *The Shogun* (1904); *Woodland* (1904)—'The tale of the turtle dove'; *The Grand Mogul* (1907); *Marcelle* (1908); *The Fair Co-Ed* (1909); *The Old Town* (1910); *The Gypsy* (1912).

Lulu [Lawrie, Marie McDonald McLaughlin] (*b* Glasgow, 3 Nov. 1948). British singer. Her blues-shouting ability was first recognized on a hit recording, by Lulu and the Luvvers (1963–5), of the *Isley Brothers number, 'Shout' (1964), and she left the Luvvers in 1965 to pursue a solo career as Decca's rival to Cilla *Black. Moving to the Columbia label, she achieved a best-seller with the title-song of the film *To Sir With Love* (1967), in which she also appeared, followed by 'The boat that I row' (1967). After this she had her own TV show and was joint winner of the *Eurovision Song Contest in 1968 with 'Boom bang-a-bang'. A lengthy spell in the cabaret world kept her out of the pop record market until she came back with 'The man who sold the world' in 1974; she re-made 'Shout' in 1986.

Lumbye, Hans Christian (*b* Copenhagen, 2 May 1810; *d* Copenhagen, 20 Mar. 1874). Danish composer, trumpeter, and conductor. The son of a soldier, he joined his father's regiment as a boy trumpeter at the age of 14 and transferred to the

Royal Horse Guard in Copenhagen five years later. A series of concerts was given in Copenhagen by Josef *Lanner and Johann *Strauss the elder in 1839 and these inspired Lumbye to try to emulate their music. He formed his own orchestra in 1839 and his first waltz, in the Viennese style, was 'Danmarkvalsen', written in 1840. His reputation as a composer of light music was quickly gained and when the now famous Tivoli Gardens were opened in Copenhagen in 1843, it was a foregone conclusion that he would become the musical director. For 30 years, until deafness compelled his retirement, he presided there. His sons Carl (1841–1911) and George (1843–1922) both played in the orchestra and wrote music in a similar vein, with Carl succeeding his father as *chef d'orchestre* in 1865.

As early as 1844, Lumbye was sent on an official tour of Europe, meeting Berlioz in Paris, Johann Strauss II in Vienna, and Meyerbeer in Berlin. He made several successful tours in later years and in 1860 played in Stockholm at the coronation of King Charles XV. He wrote several hundred dances and marches and his liking for the galop led him to be dubbed 'The Galop King'. His well-known 'Champagne galop' was written for a Tivoli Gardens festival in 1854 and came to be used as the traditional finale of every gala night there. An unusual and attractive work was his 'Concert polka' for two violins and orchestra, for which his sons were the soloists at the first performance. 'Dream pictures' (1846) is a charming programmatic fantasy which was used in 1915 by the Royal Danish Ballet along with other works by Lumbye. His other compositions include: 'Amelie' (1846), 'The Copenhagen Steam Railway galop' (1847), which commemorated the opening of the first railway from the city, 'A holiday evening at the Tivoli' (1861), 'Columbine' (1862), 'Britta' (1864), 'Queen Louise's waltz' (1868), 'Salute to August Bournonville' (1869). His music has been used in an operetta, *Champagne Gallop*, later filmed.

G. Skjerne: *H. C. Lumbye og hans Samtid* (Copenhagen, 1912; rev. 1946).

Luna, Pablo (*b* Aragón, 1880; *d* Madrid, 28 Jan. 1942). Spanish composer. He was a man of great wit, gaiety, and charm who became one of the most successful and consistently inspired writers for the Spanish musical theatre, and he was still at the height of his powers when he died in 1942. His works included: *Molinos de Viento* (Seville, 1910; Madrid, 1911); *Los Cadetes de la Reina* (1913); *El Niño Judo* (1922; London, as *The First Kiss*, 1924); and *La Picara molinera* (1928). Also *El Asombro de Damasco*; *Las Calatravas*; *La gata encantada*; and *El Pilar de la Victoria*.

A. Sagardía: *Pablo Luna* (Madrid, 1978).

Lunceford, Jimmie [James Melvin] (*b* Fulton, Mo., 6 June 1902; *d* Seaside, Oreg., 12 July 1947). American bandleader, composer, and saxophonist. A graduate of Fisk University and postgraduate of New York City College, he began his working career as an athletics coach at Memphis High School before turning to music. After playing with the bands of Wilbur *Sweatman and Fletcher *Henderson, he formed his own orchestra in 1929 to play at the Claridge Hotel in Memphis. Three years were then spent in Buffalo, before the band became resident at the *Cotton Club in New York.

In the subsequent years, appearing in hotels, ballrooms, and theatres, broadcasting and recording regularly, the band was established as one of the earliest and best of the black swing bands. Much of the success was due to the arranging abilities of Sy *Oliver, succeeded by Billy Moore (1917–89), which set a style that was emulated in later years by Glenn *Miller, Billy *May, and others; but the band's greatest selling point was its showmanship—also emulated by other bands. Key musicians included: Jimmy Crawford (1910–80), drummer 1928–42; Willie Smith (1910–67), saxophonist and arranger 1928–42; Trummy *Young, trombone. They appeared in the film *Blues in the Night* (1941). Lunceford co-wrote such items as 'Dream of you' (1934), 'Because you're you' (1934), 'Rhythm is our business' (1934), 'Stratosphere' (1934), 'Rhythm in my nursery rhymes' (1935), 'Harlem shout' (1936), 'Like a ship at sea' (1937), 'Time's a-wastin' (1937), and 'Lunceford special' (1939). After his death the band carried on under the direction of Eddie Wilcox and Joe Thomas but with less success than before.

Lupino, Stanley (*b* London, 15 May 1894; *d* London, 10 June 1942). British actor, dancer, singer, librettist, and director. A member of the well-known Lupino theatrical family, and cousin of Lupino *Lane, he began his stage career as an acrobat, thus accounting for his agile dancing and lively character, and first appeared on the London stage in 1913. Between 1928 and 1936 he worked in association with Laddie *Cliff as producer/director of most of the shows he appeared in. These included: *All the Winners* (1913); *Girl Wanted* (1916); *Suzette* (1917); *Arlette* (1917); *Hullo, America!* (1918); *The Kiss Call* (1919); *Jig-Saw* (1920); *It's All Wrong* (1920); *The Peep Show* (1921); *His Girl* (1922); **Phi-Phi* (1922); *Dover Street to Dixie* (1923); *Puppets* (1924); *Better Days* (1925); *Naughty Riquette* (1926); *The Nightingale* (1927); *So This is Love* (1928); *Love Lies* (1929); *The Love Race* (1930); *Hold My Hand* (1931); *Sporting Love* (1934); *Over She Goes* (1936); *Crazy Days* (1937); *The Fleet's Lit Up* (1938); *Funny Side Up* (1940); *Lady Behave* (1941).

S. Lupino: *From the Stocks to the Stars* (London, 1934).

Lustige Witwe, Die. Musical play in three acts with music by Franz *Lehár and book by Victor Léon (1858–1940) and Leo Stein [Rosenstein] (1861–1921), based on *L'Attaché* by Henri Meilhac (1813–97). The libretto had been offered to Richard *Heuberger who had made nothing of it; only then was it reluctantly offered to Lehár, who was immediately inspired by the story and produced his first song that very evening. The complete score was submitted to the management of the Theater an de Wien and was scornfully criticized by some of the directors as 'unmusical' and 'tuneless'; but eventually a low-budget production was agreed to.

It was first seen at the Theater an der Wien on 30 Dec. 1905, with Mizzi Günther (1879–1961) as the Widow and Louis Treumann (1872–1942) as Prince Danilo, and Robert *Stolz as musical director. It was an immediate hit, ran for 483 initial performances, and was to continue an unabated career of success as *The Merry Widow* in London, at *Daly's Theatre 8 Jun. 1907, with Lily *Elsie as the Widow and Joseph *Coyne as Danilo, running for 778 performances. Its New York reception was the same, at the New Amsterdam Theatre 21 Oct. 1907 [416p]; and in Paris, at the Apollo 23 May 1909, as *La Veuve joyeuse*. The 'Merry Widow' craze swept the world and all the ladies wore 'Merry Widow' hats and clothes.

The fine score, which rivals that of Johann *Strauss's *Die *Fledermaus*, contains such delights as 'Ich bin eine anständige Frau', 'Da geh' ich zu Maxim', 'Das Lied von dummen Reiter', 'Vilja-Lied' and, of course, the unforgettable waltz-song 'Lippen schweigen'. There have been endless revivals and many fine recordings. Film versions (none of them entirely successful) were made in 1934, with Jeanette *MacDonald and Maurice *Chevalier, directed by Ernst Lubitsch (1892–1947); 1950 (with Betty *Grable); and 1952 (with Lana Turner, *b* 1920).

F. Stein: *50 Jahre 'Die lustige Witwe'* (Vienna, 1955). See also books listed under LEHÁR.

Lutcher, Nellie (*b* Lake Charles, La., 15 Oct. 1915). American composer, author, and entertainer. She was signed on by Capitol Records in 1947 and started an immediately successful career of recording and stage performances. She wrote most of her own material, which she sang in a high-pitched, breathless voice, including her big hit, 'Hurry on down' (1947), as well as 'He's a real gone guy', 'The pig latin song', 'You'd better watch yourself', 'Bub', and 'The Lake Charles boogie'.

Lutz, Wilhelm **Meyer** (*b* 1822; *d* London, 31 Jan. 1903). German conductor and composer. A boy prodigy, first appearing in public at 12, he studied music at Würzburg. His brother became Baron von Lutz, at one time president of Bavaria. Lutz went to England in 1848 and became organist at St Chad's, Birmingham, St Ann's, Leeds, then at St George's Roman Catholic Church in London, holding this last post for most of his life even while most active in the theatre. He was musical director of the Surrey Theatre 1851–5 and from 1867 to 1898 (with a break of only four years) he conducted the Spa Orchestra at Scarborough during the summer season.

In February 1869 he became musical director at the *Gaiety Theatre and remained there until 1892, generally billed simply as Meyer-Lutz. An indefatigable worker, he dealt with all the Gaiety's musical arrangements, compiling scores for collective pieces like *Columbus* (1869) as well as writing many original burlesques and operettas. He became a very popular figure there and the Gaiety's famous manager, John Hollingshead, always said that much of his success was due to Lutz's hard work. One of his compositions that enjoyed great popularity was the 'Pas de quatre' from *Faust-up-to-Date* which became a much-used pantomime and ballroom dance. The critic of the *Daily Telegraph*, reviewing *Cinder-Ellen Up-Too-Late* in 1891, wrote: 'The first old favourite to be called and cheered to the echo was Herr Meyer Lutz. The instant the familiar face was seen issuing from the orchestra door there was a shout. Herr Lutz has sat at that desk ever since 1869 from the birth of the Gaiety and he well deserves his Christmas congratulations.'

His scores included: *Faust and Marguerite* (1854); *Blonde or Brunette* (1868); *Zaïda* (1868); *Columbus* (1869); *Linda of Chamouni* (1869); *Wat Tyler MP* (1869); *The Miller of Millberg* (1872); *The Legend of the Lys* (1873); *Young Rip Van Winkle* (1876); *Little Doctor Faust* (1877); *The Bohemian G-Yurl* (1877); *The Forty Thieves* (1880); *All in the Downs* (1881); *Aladdin* (1881); *The Knight of the Garter* (1882); *Posterity* (1884); *Little Jack Sheppard* (1885); *Monte Cristo Jr.* (1886); *Miss Esmeralda* (1887); *Frankenstein* (1887); *Faust-up-to-Date* (1887); *Ruy Blas and the Blasé Roué* (1889); *Carmen-up-to-Data* (1890); *Cinder-Ellen Up-Too-Late* (1891); *Don Juan* (1893); and *A Model Trilby* (1895). He wrote many songs for the *Christy Minstrels and other minstrel groups, including the popular 'Hush, the bogie' (*w* Sims and Pettit).

Lyman, Abe [Simon, Abraham] (*b* Chicago, 4 Aug. 1897; *d* Beverly Hills, Calif., 23 Oct. 1957). American bandleader, composer, and drummer. While still at school he was playing drums in cinema orchestras and made a speciality then, as in his later years as a showman bandleader, of juggling his drumsticks. These talents were not immediately in demand and he was working as a taxi-driver when he met up with another young musician, Gus *Arnheim, with whom he organized a group, the California Five. They also wrote several songs together before Lyman led his own band 1921–4 at the Cocoanut Grove in Los Angeles. It was a popular hotel-type dance orchestra, appearing in such films as *Hold Everything* (1930), and Lyman kept it going until the late 1940s. His songs included: 'I cried for you' (with Gus Arnheim and Arthur *Freed, 1923), 'Mandalay' (with Arnheim and Earl Burtnett, 1924), 'What can I say, after I say I'm sorry' (with Walter *Donaldson, 1926); and various orchestral pieces.

Lynn, Loretta [Webb, Loretta] (*b* Butcher Hollow, Ken., 14 Apr. 1935). American country singer. She began her recording career in 1960 and, after signing up with American Decca in 1962, started quietly; but by 1966 she had achieved a number of hit recordings such as 'Don't come home a'drinkin', 'With lovin' on your mind' and 'First city'. She regularly appeared on TV, projecting a fresh and wholesome country image that was backed up by a reputation as one of the most accomplished female country singers of recent times. She recorded with Ernest *Tubb, and by the 1970s was producing such highly rated country albums as *Coalminer's Daughter*, a classic of the genre. She used this title for her autobiography, which was filmed in 1980. Her younger sister Crystal *Gayle is also a singer.

L. Lynn and G. Vecsey: *Coalminer's Daughter* (St Albans, 1979). L. J. Zwisohn: *Loretta Lynn's World of Music* (Los Angeles, 1980).

Lynn, Vera [Welch, Vera Margaret] (*b* London, 20 Mar. 1917). British singer. She started singing in working-men's clubs at the age of seven. At 11 she joined a troupe, Madame Harris's Kracker Kabaret Kids, with whom she stayed for four years. Following a two-year engagement as vocalist with a local band, she achieved a two-week engagement with the Billy *Cotton band, which led to nothing, and she was unsuccessfully auditioned by Henry *Hall. By 1935 she had achieved some broadcasts with the Joe *Loss band, and broadcast with Charlie *Kunz from the Casani Club, making her first commercial recording with him—'I'm in the mood for love'. In 1937 she joined *Ambrose, appearing on TV with him in 1938, and married a clarinettist in the Ambrose band, Harry Lewis. She decided to become a solo artist in 1940, and made her West End debut in *Apple Sauce*.

She suddenly found herself top favourite with the soldiers of the BEF and earned the name 'The Forces' Sweetheart', her warm and direct personality becoming a symbolic link with home for the troops abroad and her catch-in-the-throat renderings of 'We'll meet again' and 'White cliffs of Dover' almost rivalling Churchillian speeches as a morale booster during the war years. She appeared in the Royal Command Performance of 1942 and in the films *We'll Meet Again* (1942), *Rhythm Serenade* (1943), and *One Exciting Night* (1944). Her ENSA tours in Burma from 1944 further promoted her association with the forces and long after the war she was a focal point of Albert Hall Burma reunions.

She returned to the stage in *London Laughs* (1952); and, with 'Auf wiedersehen', achieved a recording which was simultaneously the top hit in Britain and the USA. In 1955 she had her own Independent TV series and another with the BBC in 1969. She was awarded the OBE in 1968 and was made a Dame of the British Empire in 1975.

V. Lynn: *Vocal Refrain* (London, 1975). V. Lynn and R. Cross: *We'll Meet Again* (London, 1989).

Lyric Revue, The. London revue which marked a post-war revival of the intimate revue and brought much new writing and acting talent to light. It opened at the Lyric Theatre, Hammersmith, 24 May 1951, for a run of 454 performances, transferring to the Globe Theatre in the West End, 26 Sept. 1951; followed by a new edition under the title of *The Globe Revue*. The cast included Graham *Payn, Joan Heal (*b* 1922), Ian *Carmichael, Dora *Bryan, and George Benson (1911–83). The contributors ranged from well-established names like Richard *Addinsell and Noël *Coward—'Don't make fun of the fair'—to the rising talents of Michael *Flanders and Donald *Swann—'Youth of the heart' (*w* Sydney Carter).

Lyttelton, Humphrey (*b* Eton, Berks., 23 May 1921). British trumpet-player, clarinettist, bandleader, artist, and author. After an education at Eton, where his father was a master, and service as a Guards officer, he first made his mark amidst the revivalist fervour of George *Webb's Dixielanders at the Red Barn in Barnehurst. He formed his own band in 1948 and, after some preliminary recording skirmishes for London Jazz and Esquire, was contracted by Parlophone and established the authoritative sound of a band which included Wally Fawkes (*b* 1924) on clarinet and Keith Christie (1931–80) on trombone. He impressed a wider public with the first issues in 1949, going on to a best-seller in 'Bad penny blues' (1956), recording with the Australian Graeme Bell, and gradually moving towards a more experimental and mainstream sound with the addition of saxophonists Bruce Turner (*b* 1922) and Tony Coe (b 1934). He continued to lead an ever-fresh and adventurous band into the 1980s. His prolific writing career started with a first volume of autobiography in 1954 and continued with a number of perceptive books on jazz and jazz recordings; he has also maintained a career as a cartoonist. On radio he worked as an intelligent and widely acceptable promoter of his musical inclinations; latterly becoming the benign chairman of forgettable radio panel games. He is acknowledged as one of the major figures in the post-war establishment of British jazz.

H. Lyttelton: *I Play As I Please: the Memoirs of an Old Etonian Trumpeter* (London, 1954). H. Lyttelton: *Second Chorus* (London, 1958). H. Lyttelton: *Take It From the Top: an Autobiographical Scrapbook* (London, 1975).

Lytton, Henry A. (*b* London, 1860; *d* London, 16 Sept. 1936). British actor and singer. He ran away from school to join a theatre company, but was recaptured and put to study art. He soon returned to the stage and made his first London appearance at the Philharmonic in Islington in 1883. After an appearance in *The Merry Duchess* (1883) he was asked to join the D'Oyly *Carte touring company where he performed under the name of H. A. Henri. He joined the main Savoy company in 1887, at first understudying George *Grossmith, eventually becoming their leading comedy singer in many famous G & S roles. He also played at the Savoy in *The Lucky Star* (1899), *The Rose of Persia* (1899), *The *Emerald Isle* (1900), and **Merrie England* (1902), leaving the company in 1902 on its temporary disbandment. He continued his stage career in *The *Earl and the Girl* (1903), *The Talk of the Town* (1904), *A White Chrysanthemum* (1905), and *My Darling* (1907).

H. Lytton: *The Secrets of a Savoyard* (London, 1922). H. Lytton: *A Wandering Minstrel* (London, 1933).

M

McCartney, James **Paul** (*b* Liverpool, 18 June 1942). British composer, lyric-writer, guitarist, bass-guitarist, and singer. He started his musical career by playing the family piano and later learned to play the guitar, finding early inspiration in the recordings of Elvis *Presley. He was one of the original trio formed in 1956 (McCartney, John *Lennon, and George *Harrison) calling themselves the Quarry-men, later the Silver Beatles. At the Cavern in Liverpool they initially played a *skiffle-style music, expanding to a quintet with the addition of Stuart Sutcliffe and Pete Best. By 1962 the original trio, joined by Ringo *Starr on drums, had become the *Beatles and made their first British recording on the Parlophone label; their future plans were in the hands of manager Brian Epstein (1934–67) and record producer George *Martin. That first recording was of 'Love me do'/'PS I love you', the first of a long series of highly successful songs to be written jointly by McCartney and Lennon, their first million-seller being 'She loves you' (1963).

The McCartney–Lennon songs were not merely commercially viable, but are now acknowledged as superbly crafted popular song classics, used in all spheres of music-making and admired by critics of all brows. McCartney's poetical gift was evident in his contributions to the Beatles repertoire, his lyrics having a truly literary quality described by one critic as 'archaic English prosody'. Never a particularly socially minded writer, his main preoccupation was with teenage love; much the same as most *Tin Pan Alley products, if better expressed. But his melodies had a pensive, wandering, modal quality that made them totally different from most of the pugnacious rock that was being created elsewhere. It was remarkable that a group who were somewhat highbrow in comparison to most should prove to have the greatest popular appeal.

The Beatles formed their own recording and promotional group, Apple, which sadly led to financial disagreement and the break-up of the Beatles in 1970. Paul McCartney married Linda Eastman, wound up all associations with the Beatles in 1971, and formed the group *Wings; his work became more experimental, although, as ever, there were occasional throwbacks to a popular idiom.

Lennon and McCartney songs included: 'Love me do', 'PS I love you', 'Please please me' (1962); 'From me to you', 'She loves you', 'I want to hold your hand', 'I'll get you', 'I saw her standing there', 'Do you want to know a secret', 'Ask me why', 'All my loving', 'Hold me tight', 'All I've got to do', 'It won't be long', 'Hello, little girl', 'Little child', 'Misery', 'Not a second time', 'Thank you, girl', 'There's a place' (1963); 'I wanna be you man', 'Can't buy me love', 'A hard day's night', 'I should have known better', 'Tell me why', 'I'll cry instead', 'I feel fine', 'I'm a loser', 'And I love her', 'Any time at all', 'Baby's in black', 'From a window', 'Every little thing', 'I don't want to spoil the party', 'I'll follow the sun', 'If I fell', 'I'll be back', 'I'm happy just to dance with you', 'I call your name', 'Eight days a week', 'No reply', 'She's a woman', 'Things we said today', 'This boy', 'When I get home' (1964); 'Ticket to ride', 'I've just seen a face', 'Michelle', 'Norwegian wood', 'Run for your life', 'Tell me what you see', 'What you're doing', 'Wait', 'We can work it out', 'What does on', 'Help', 'The night before', 'Yesterday', 'Nowhere man', 'Day tripper', 'Yellow submarine', 'It's only love', 'In my life', 'I'm looking through you', 'Another girl', 'Girl', 'I need you', 'I'm down' (1965); 'Eleanor Rigby', 'Paperback writer', 'Rain', 'Here there and everywhere', 'I want to tell you', 'I'm only sleeping', 'Tomorrow never knows', 'Got to get you into my life', 'She said she said', 'Doctor Robert', 'For no one', 'Good day sunshine', 'And your bird can sing' (1966); 'Penny Lane', 'Strawberry fields forever', 'All you need is love', 'Sgt Pepper's Lonely Hearts Club Band', 'With a little help from my friends', 'Lucy in the sky with diamonds', 'Getting better', 'Fixing a hole', 'She's leaving home', 'Being for the benefit of Mr Kite', 'When I'm sixty-four', 'Lovely Rita', 'Good morning, good morning', 'A day in the life', 'Baby, you're a rich man', 'Blue Jay Way', 'The fool on the hill', 'Hello, goodbye', 'I am the walrus', 'Magical mystery tour' (1967); 'Hey Jude', 'Across the universe', 'All together now', 'Back in the USSR', 'Birthday', 'Blackbird', 'Cry baby cry', 'The continuing story of Bungalow Bill', 'Dear Prudence', 'Everybody's got something to hide except me and my monkey', 'Happiness is a warm gun', 'Glass onion', 'Good night', 'Helter skelter', 'Hey bulldog', 'Honey pie', 'I will', 'I'm so tired', 'Julia', 'Lady Madonna', 'Martha my dear', 'Mother Nature's son', 'Ob-la-di, ob-la-da', 'Revolution', 'Rocky racoon', 'Sexy Sadie' (1968); 'Maxwell's silver hammer', 'Polythene Pam', 'Oh! darling', 'She came in through the bathroom window', 'Sun King', 'Toward the light', 'Goodbye', 'Mean Mr Mustard', 'Get back', 'The ballad of John and Yoko', 'Here comes the sun', 'Because', 'Don't let me down', 'Her Majesty', 'Carry that weight', 'Come together', 'I want you', 'Golden slumbers' (1969); 'I've got a feeling', 'Let it be', 'The long and winding road', 'Dig a pony', 'Dig it' (1970).

McCartney's recorded hits since the end of the

partnership include: 'Another day' (1971), 'Wonderful Christmastime' (1979), 'Coming up' (1980), 'Waterfalls' (1980), 'Ebony and ivory' (with Stevie *Wonder, 1982), 'The girl is mine' (with Michael *Jackson, 1982), 'Say say say' (with Jackson, 1983), 'Pipes of peace' (1983), 'No more lonely nights' (1984), 'We all stand together' (1984), and 'Spies like us' (1986). In 1983 he starred in and wrote the sound-track for a film, *Give My Regards to Broad Street* (1984), which was a failure and underlined his inability to write in extended form and the youthful nature of his early successes. In 1989 he undertook his first performing tour since 1976. (See also WINGS).

In 1985 it was revealed that the Lennon–McCartney partnership had never been an easy one, with Lennon reported as having condemned McCartney's work as 'Muzak' and McCartney, latterly resentful of being blamed for the break-up of the Beatles, calling Lennon 'a manœuvring swine'.

His younger brother, Mike McCartney (*b* 1944), has also had a successful career as a writer and performer, notably with the Scaffold.

G. Tremlett: *The Paul McCartney Story* (London, 1975). P. Gambaccini (ed.): *Paul McCartney in his own words* (London, 1976). J. Mendelssohn: *Paul McCartney: a Biography in Words and Pictures* (New York, 1977). M. McCartney: *Thank U Very Much: Mike McCartney's Family Album* (London, 1981). C. Salewicz: *Paul McCartney: the Biography* (London, 1986). See also books listed under BEATLES.

MacColl, Ewan [Miller, James] (*b* Auchterarder, Perthshire, 25 Jan. 1915; *d* London, 22 Oct. 1989). Scottish folk-singer, songwriter, author, and playwright. His musical output was large and he had a great influence on the British folk scene, particularly from around 1950, the year often pinpointed as marking the beginnings of the British folk-song revival. He left school at 14, having spent most of his childhood in Salford, Lancashire, and worked in various manual spheres before becoming involved, in the late 1930s, in a number of experimental theatre projects. In 1945 he and Joan Littlewood formed the Theatre Workshop in Kendal where, for the next seven years, he was the resident dramatist, writing eight plays for the company and acting as art director. In 1950 his interest in traditional music came to the fore and he helped to found (among others) the Ballads and Blues Club (later known as the Singers Club). These clubs were to play a vital part in the subsequent folk-song revival. Theatre Workshop settled in Stratford East in 1955 where MacColl's ballad opera, *The Lost Factory Chimneys*, was performed.

He became one of the leading figures of the British folk-scene and, in 1957, in collaboration with his second wife, Peggy *Seeger, and BBC producer Charles Parker, produced *The Ballad of John Axon*, a documentary programme based on the life of an engine-driver. This was the first of a series of *Radio Ballads, later recorded by Argo, which opened up new vistas in both broadcasting and folk-music. MacColl continued this work by writing for the BBC, commercial TV, the Coal Board, and many independent organizations. He always believed that folk-music should play an active and vital part in modern life and showed the way by writing 'folk' songs such as 'Dirty old town' (1946) which managed to be both folky and popular. From 1965 to 1971 he was mainly active as a teacher and in developing the folk theatre. A fine, professional performer, solo and with his wife, he recorded almost 100 albums of songs for Argo, Decca, Topic, HMV, and such American outlets as Folkways, Riverside, Rounder, Tradition, and Vanguard. His song 'The first time ever I saw your face' (1958) won the 1973 Grammy Award for Song of the Year and an Ivor Novello Award in England. An avid collector, he collaborated in the production of several folk-song anthologies and, as leader of the ensemble known as the Critics Group, for whom he composed such works as 'Grey October', he was much concerned with the stylistic performance of traditional material. His considerable service to British music was always firmly allied with his left-wing political convictions.

Other songs include 'The Manchester Rambler' (1933)—the official song of the Ramblers Federation; 'Space girl' (1952); 'Ballad of Springhill' (with Peggy Seeger, 1958); 'The big hewer' (1961); 'The shoals of herring' (1961); 'Thirty-foot trailer' (1966)—most of these used in various radio ballads; and 'Sweet Thames flow softly' (1966). His daughter, Kirsty MacColl (*b* 1944), is also a singer.

E. MacColl: *Journeyman* (London, 1990).

McCoy, Clyde (*b* Ashfield, Ky., 29 Dec. 1903). American trumpeter. He played in his youth on riverboats and in theatre orchestras. He formed his own band in 1919 and came to radio fame in the 1930s with his popular theme tune 'Sugar blues' (recorded 1936) and his wah-wah muted and growling style of playing in a somewhat corny context. McCoy and the band became a navy unit 1942–5. He remained active until the 1970s, generally leading good Dixieland-style bands.

MacDermot, Galt (*b* Montreal, 18 Dec. 1928). Canadian composer. He has been a pioneer in the field of the rock musical, making a great impression on the Broadway, London, and European stage with the production of the 'tribal love-rock musical' **Hair* in Apr. 1967, which became as renowned for its nude frolics as for its artistic qualities. A revised version in 1968 was followed by *Isabel's a Jezebel* in London (1970); **Two Gentlemen of Verona* (1971); *Dude* (1972); and *Via Galactica* (1972).

Macdermott, G. H. [Farrell, Gilbert Hastings] (*b* London, 27 Feb. 1845; *d* London, 8 May 1901). British singer and comedian. He spent several years at sea before appearing in fairground booths and minor halls and then becoming stage manager of the Grecian Theatre, where he also acted under the name of Gilbert Hastings. The popularity of his performance of the song, 'If ever there was a damned scamp', led to a music-hall career from *c.*1874, now regularly billed as 'The Great Macdermott'. His greatest success was to be 'We don't want to fight but by jingo if we do', which he first sang at the London Pavilion in 1877. In the patriotic fervour of the Russian–Turkish wars, with Britain solidly opposed to Russian imperialism, it was to add the word 'jingoism' to the English language. He was a confirmed political and social commentator with such songs as 'True blues, stand by your guns', 'Charlie Dilke upset the milk' (which derived from a notorious divorce case of 1885), and 'Up went the price of meat'. He also sang a popular nonsense ditty, 'I'll strike you with a feather', and the sentimental 'Dear old pals'. After making a small fortune on the halls, he ended his career by becoming an agent and managing several music-halls.

MacDonald, Jeanette [Anna] (*b* Philadelphia, 18 June 1903; *d* Houston, 14 Jan. 1965). American singer whose slim and attractively toothy appearance, vitality, and popular touch made her one of the greatest cinema attractions of the 1930s and 1940s, particularly in partnership with the baritone Nelson *Eddy. She started her career in the chorus of the Broadway musical *The Night Boat* (1920). She appeared in **Irene* (1920) and *Tangerine* (1921) during their long runs and then in *Fantastic Fricassee* (1922), *The Magic Ring* (1923), and **Tip-Toes* (1925). Her first starring role was in *Yes, Yes, Yvette* in 1927; followed by *Sunny Days* (1928), *Angela* (1928), and *Boom Boom* (1929). She established a movie career when she appeared with Maurice *Chevalier in *The Love Parade* (1929), followed by *The *Vagabond King* (1930); *Monte Carlo* (1930)—with Jack *Buchanan, in which she introduced 'Beyond the blue horizon'; *Let's Go Native* (1930); *The Lottery Bride* (1930); *Oh, For a Man!* (1930); *One Hour With You* (1932); *Love Me Tonight* (1932)—'Lover'; *The *Cat and the Fiddle* (1934), with Ramon Novarro (1899–1968); and *The *Merry Widow* (1934).

Her first appearance with Nelson Eddy in **Naughty Marietta* (1935) established his reputation and their future top box-office career. They continued the golden partnership in **Rose-Marie* (1935), having their first hit recording with 'Indian love call' (1936); **Maytime* (1937); *The Girl of the Golden West* (1938); **Sweethearts* (1938); **New Moon* (1940); **Bitter Sweet* (1940); and *I Married An Angel* (1942). She also appeared in *San Francisco* (1936), with Clark Gable (1901–60)—'San Francisco', 'A heart that's free', 'Would you'; *The *Firefly* (1937), with Allan *Jones; and continued her film career in the 1940s with *Broadway Serenade* (1939); *Smilin' Through* (1941); *Cairo* (1942); *Follow the Boys* (1944); *Three Daring Daughters* (1948); and *The Sun Comes Up* (1949). She recorded prolifically, both with and without Nelson Eddy.

S. Rich: *Jeanette MacDonald: a Pictorial Treasury* (Los Angeles, 1973). E. Knowles: *The Films of Jeanette MacDonald and Nelson Eddy* (South Brunswick, NJ, 1975). J. R. Parish: *The Jeanette MacDonald Story* (New York, 1976). L. E. Stern: *Jeanette MacDonald* (New York, 1977). P. Castanza: *The Films of Jeanette MacDonald and Nelson Eddy* (Secaucus, NJ, 1978).

McGhee, Brownie [Walter Brown] (*b* Knoxville, Tenn., 30 Nov. 1915). American blues singer, guitarist, pianist, and composer. He learned the blues from his father, who was a singer and guitarist, and, after an attack of polio, he turned to a musical career. An operation in 1935 eventually allowed him to lead a normal life and during the 1930s he organized a washboard band whose members included from time to time Robert Young (known as 'Washboard Slim'), Leroy Dallas, and Jordan Webb. During 1939–42 he made records with Okeh and in 1944–5 for Savoy. He had a 35-year partnership with harmonica player Sonny *Terry. Their recorded duets reached a wide international market and had a great influence on *skiffle and *rhythm 'n' blues developments. In 1941, McGhee, Terry, *Leadbelly, and Woody *Guthrie formed a short-lived group called the Headline Singers. Terry and McGhee continued to record for various labels and made several international tours. McGhee's compositions include 'Born with the blues', 'I feel so good', and 'Brownie's blues'.

MacGimsey, Robert (*b* Pineville, La., 7 Sept. 1898; *d* Phoenix, 13 Mar. 1979). American composer, lyric-writer, and singer. He intended to follow a career in law but, having had a success with a recording of 'My blue heaven' with Gene *Austin, he took to the entertainment world. His chief attribute was an attractive and unusual whistling ability; he was able to whistle two or three notes in harmony simultaneously. At 14 he had begun to write songs in the folk idiom of the South and had a lasting success with such items as 'Shadrack, Meshak and Abednigo', 'Daniel in the lion's den', 'Jonah and the whale' (all successfully recorded by Louis *Armstrong); 'Down to de rivah'; 'My lovely one'; and 'Jeri-Jericho'.

McGlennon, Felix (*b* Ireland, 1856; *d* 29 Nov. 1943). Composer and publisher. He went to America in the 1880s and wrote many songs there that became popular in vaudeville and filtered back to the English music-hall. Returning to Britain, he set up a successful publishing business. His songs included: 'Woman, lovely woman' (1886), 'Comrades' (with George Horncastle, 1887), 'I forget, I forget' (1888), 'Actions speak louder than words' (1891), 'That is love' (1891), 'Cheer up Mother, your son will soon be home' (1892), 'Puzzles' (1892, *w* Norman Atkins), 'Her golden hair was hanging down her back' (with Monroe H. *Rosenfeld, 1894)—popularized in England by Alice Leamar and later by Seymour *Hicks, 'To err is human, to forgive divine' (1894), 'The song that will live for ever' (1896, *w* Tom Browne), 'Sons of the sea' (1897), 'The ship I love' (1898), and many more.

McHugh, Jimmy [James] (*b* Boston, 10 July 1894; *d* Beverly Hills, Calif., 23 May 1969). American composer, pianist, and publisher. He became office-boy to the managing director of the Boston Opera House, which led to his becoming a rehearsal pianist. He won a scholarship to the New England Conservatory but gave it up to go straight into music-publishing businesses in Boston and New York. He began to write songs and made his name with the excellent material he wrote for the famous *Cotton Club revues. From 1930 he spent many years under contract to film studios in Hollywood, regularly collaborating with Dorothy *Fields. He wrote songs for **Blackbirds of 1928*—'Diga diga doo', 'Doin' the new lowdown', 'I must have that man', 'I can't give you anything but love'; *Hello Daddy* (1928); *The International Revue* (1930)—'On the sunny side of the street', 'Exactly like you', 'International rhythm'; *The Vanderbilt Revue* (1930); *The Streets of Paris* (1939); *Keep Off the Grass* (1940); **As the Girls Go* (1948); and *Strip for Action* (1956).

His Hollywood film scores included: *Love in the Rough* (1930); *Singing the Blues* (1931)—'Singing the blues' (*w* Fields); *Flying High* (1931); *Cuban Love Song* (1931)—'Cuban love song' (*w* Fields), sung by Lawrence Tibbett (1896–1960), one of the first opera stars to appear in musical films; it also starred the dancer Lupe Velez (1908–44); *The Prize Fighter and the Lady* (1933); *Dancing Lady* (1933); *Meet the Baron* (1933); *Dinner at Eight* (1933)—'Don't blame me' (Fields); *Have a Heart* (1934)—'Thank you for a lovely evening' (Fields), 'Lost in a fog' (Fields); *Fugitive Lovers* (1934); *I Dream Too Much* (1935); *Every Night at Eight* (1935)—'Strictly confidential', 'I'm in the mood for love', 'It's great to be in love again' (all Fields); 'I feel a song comin' on' (Fields and George Oppenheimer); *King of Burlesque* (1935)—'I've got my fingers crossed' (*w* Ted *Koehler), 'Lovely lady' (Koehler); *Nitwits* (1935); *Hooray for Love* (1935)—'Hooray for love' (Fields), 'I'm in love all over again' (Fields); **Roberta* (1935)—'Lovely to look at' (with Jerome *Kern, *w* Fields); *Her Master's Voice* (1936); *Banjo on My Knee* (1936)—'Where the lazy river goes by' (*w* Harold *Adamson), 'There's something in the air' (Adamson); *Dimples* (1936); *Let's Sing Again* (1936); *When Love is Young* (1937); *Hitting a New High* (1937); *Breezing Home* (1937); *You're a Sweetheart* (1937)—'You're a sweetheart' (Adamson); *Top of the Town* (1937)—'There's no two ways about it' (Adamson), 'That foolish feeling' (Adamson); *Merry-Go-Round of 1938*; *Road to Reno* (1938); *Mad About Music* (1938)—'I love to whistle' (Adamson); *That Certain Age* (1938)—'That certain age' (Adamson), 'You're as pretty as a picture' (Adamson); *Youth Takes a Fling* (1938); *Buck Benny Rides Again* (1940)—'Say it over and over again' (*w* Frank *Loesser); *You'll Find Out* (1940)—'I've got a one-track mind', 'You've got me this way' (*w* Johnny *Mercer); *You're the One* (1941); *Seven Days Leave* (1942)—'A touch of Texas' (Loesser), 'I can't get out of this mood' (Loesser); *Higher and Higher* (1943)—'I couldn't sleep a wink last night' (Adamson), 'A lovely way to spend an evening' (Adamson); *Happy Go Lucky* (1943)—'Murder he says', 'Let's get lost', 'Sing a tropical song' (all Loesser); *Hers to Hold* (1943); *Down Argentine Way* (1943)—'South American way' (*w* Al *Dubin); *Moon over Las Vegas* (1944); *Follow the Boys* (1944); *Jam Session* (1944)—'I can't give you anything but love' (Fields); *The Princess and the Pirate* (1944); *Something for the Boys* (1944); *Two Girls and a Sailor* (1944); *Four Jills and a Jeep* (1944); *Between Two Women* (1944)—'I'm in the mood for love' (Fields); *Bring on the Girls* (1945); *Doll Face* (1945)—'Hubba, hubba, hubba', 'Chico chico', 'Red hot and beautiful' (all Adamson); *Nob Hill* (1945); *No Leave, No Love* (1946); *Do You Love Me* (1946); *Calendar Girl* (1947)—'Have I told you lately that I love you' (Adamson), 'A lovely night to go dreaming' (Adamson); *Hit Parade of 1947*; *Smash Up* (1947); *If You Knew Susie* (1948); *A Date With Judy* (1948)—'It's a most unusual day' (Adamson). Other songs include: 'When my sugar walks down the street' (1924, *w* Irving Mills and Gene *Austin), 'The lonesomest girl in town' (1925, Dubin); 'I can't believe that you're in love with me' (1926, *w* Clarence *Gaskill), 'It's the darndest thing' (1931, Fields), and 'Coming in on a wing and a prayer' (1943, Adamson).

He led a dance band in the 1950s and founded a publishing company in 1959. A McHugh Award for Composition was established at the University of South Carolina in 1970.

McKenzie, Red [William] (*b* St Louis, Mo., 14 Oct. 1899; *d* New York, 7 Feb. 1948). American blueblower, kazooist, singer, and bandleader. He started a career as a jockey but broke both arms and had to give it up. While working in a hotel he decided to form a small *spasm-type jazz group which he called the Mound City Blue Blowers, featuring his unique talents on the kazoo or comb-and-paper. They worked in Chicago and had a hit with their first recording, 'Arkansas blues', which sold more than a million copies. The Blue Blowers flourished for eight years and made a classic recording with Coleman *Hawkins and Glenn *Miller in the lineup, 'Hello Lola' and 'One hour' (1929). The banjoist and guitarist Eddie *Condon played in the group and McKenzie helped him to organize the famous McKenzie and Condon Chicagoans recordings in 1927, one of many entrepreneurial activities that he was involved in. He worked with Paul *Whiteman in 1932, left jazz for a while, but made various comebacks in the 1940s.

McKinley, Ray [Raymond Frederick] (*b* Fort Worth, Tex., 18 June 1910). American drummer, vocalist, composer, and bandleader; a swinging drummer who played with many bands, the last being the Jimmy *Dorsey band which he left in 1935. He formed a famous big band specializing in *boogie-woogie arrangements with trombonist Will *Bradley. He wrote a number of commercialized boogie compositions at this time with names like 'Beat me, Daddy, eight to the bar', 'Scrub me, Mama, with a boogie beat', and 'Bounce me, brother, with a solid four'. After a split McKinley formed his own band, then joined Glenn *Miller's AEF Band. When Miller was killed, McKinley took over the band and led it on and off until 1965; and he continued to lead bands into the 1970s.

McKinney, William (*b* Cynthiana, Ky., 17 Sept. 1895; *d* Detroit, 14 Oct. 1969). American drummer and bandleader. After serving in the First World War he played in a circus band before settling in Springfield, Ohio, where he took over a group called the Synco Septet. Playing in Detroit the band was admired by Jean *Goldkette who booked them into the Greystone Ballroom billed as McKinney's Cotton Pickers. The band recorded many classic sides for RCA Victor, with many notable arrangements by John Nesbitt (1900–35), and grew immensely popular. The band remained in Detroit until 1930, after which it split up, part of it being taken over by their arranger Don *Redman. Several bands worked under the same name under McKinney's overall management until he retired from music in 1940 to run a café in Detroit.

McKuen, Rod [Rodney Marvin] (*b* Oakland, Calif., 29 Apr. 1933). American composer, writer, and singer. After an unsettled family life, he found himself alone at 15 and began to write. He had various jobs before becoming a disc jockey at 17 and publishing his first book of poems *And Autumn Came*. He served in the army in Japan and Korea, then took up a career as a singer and film actor. He had a hit with a record called 'Oliver Twist', and developed his individual hoarse and limited style of singing. He began a music and record-publishing business in California and continued to write books of best-selling poetry, more than 15 volumes in all, including *Stanyan Street* (1966) and *Listen to the Warm* (1967). By 1967 he had recorded more than 30 albums. Since then he has won many awards, toured worldwide, and written several film scores and numerous songs, including: 'Love's been good to me' (1963), 'The world I used to know' (1963), 'I've been to town' (1963), 'Joanna' (1968), 'Jean' (1968), and 'Mr Kelly' (1970).

R. McKuen: *Finding My Father: One Man's Search for Identity* (Los Angeles, 1976; London, 1977).

MacLaine, Shirley [Beatty, Shirley McLean] (*b* Richmond, Va., 24 Apr. 1934). American actress, singer, and dancer. Her lively talents as dancer were first noted in the Broadway production of *The *Pajama Game* (1954), and she went to Hollywood to appear in **Artist and Models* (1956), **Can-Can* (1960), *What a Way to Go* (1964), and the screen version of **Sweet Charity* (1968). Her career as an original and intelligent actress has mainly been in non-musical plays and films; beyond which she has led a colourful and newsworthy life and written several autobiographical books.

P. Erens: *The Films of Shirley MacLaine* (South Brunswick, NJ, 1978). C. P. Denis: *The Films of Shirley MacLaine* (Secaucus, NJ, 1980). R. Pickard: *Shirley MacLaine* (Tunbridge Wells, 1985). S. MacLaine: *Dancing in the Light* (New York, 1986).

McLaughlin, John (*b* Yorkshire, 4 Jan. 1942). British guitarist and composer. Self-taught, he first played in a traditional jazz group led by Pete Deuchar. He moved over to the rhythm 'n' blues scene and emigrated to the USA in 1968. He issued a solo guitar album, *Extrapolation* in 1969, which showed his dextrous abilities to good advantage, and recorded with Miles *Davis. In 1970 he took to transcendental meditation and in 1971 formed the Mahavishnu Orchestra which explored Indian rhythms and scales, recording the albums *Inner Mounting Flame* (1971) and *Birds of Fire* (1973). The orchestra was disbanded in 1975 and, playing acoustic guitar, McLaughlin formed the Shakti trio which made three LPs in 1976, 1977, and 1978. He formed a highly virtuosic guitar trio in 1980 with Paco DeLucia and Al Di Meola, then returned to the electric guitar and the Mahavishnu Orchestra in 1984.

Macon, Dave (*b* Smart Station, Ten., 7 Oct. 1870; *d* Readyville, Ten., 22 Mar. 1952). American country singer and banjoist. The first big star of Nashville's **Grand Ole Opry* show, working with it from late 1925. Billed as Uncle Dave, he performed a varied and voluminous quantity of folk material with jovial energy, continuing to appear into the 1950s. Earlier he had toured in a vaudeville partnership with Fiddler Sid Harkreader (*d* 1988).

McPartland, Jimmy [James Duigald] (*b* Chicago, 15 Mar. 1907; *d* Port Washington, NY, 13 Mar. 1991). American trumpeter. He started out as a violinist, but then took to the cornet. He was one of the original Austin High School gang, a group of students who started to play jazz (influenced by the *New Orleans Rhythm Kings) under the name of the Blues Friars. After the original *Wolverines, with Bix *Beiderbecke on cornet, had disbanded, McPartland took over the name and recorded with them in late 1924 and 1927. He was a leading light of the pioneering Chicago jazz days along with such names as Frank *Teschemacher, Bud *Freeman, Joe *Sullivan, and Eddie *Condon and recorded with McKenzie and Condon's Chicagoans. He played with Ben *Pollack and Jack *Teagarden and continued in the post-war years with various Dixieland groups.

McPartland, Marian [Margaret *née* Turner] (*b* Windsor, Berks., 20 Mar. 1920). English pianist and composer. After studying at the Guildhall School of Music she played the halls with a group led by Billy *Mayerl, worked in ENSA, and in 1945 met and married the trumpeter Jimmy *McPartland. She went to America and worked as soloist and with her husband at Condon's and other clubs. In the 1960s she led an excellent trio at the Hickory House. The marriage broke up, but her career continued in diverse directions, as performer, composer, writer, broadcaster, lecturer, and teacher, particularly active with black students.

McPhatter, Clyde (*b* Durham, NC, 15 Nov. 1933; *d* Tea Neck, NJ, 13 June 1972). American singer. Son of a preacher, he inherited the family beliefs and while at school formed a gospel singing group. Later, with a professional pop group called the Dominoes, he recorded a hit number, 'Have mercy, baby'. In 1953 he organized the *Drifters, a pioneer group in the pop-oriented gospel music that became known as *soul. McPhatter sang a distinctive high tenor lead on such items as 'Money honey' and 'White Christmas'. After air force service in 1954 he started on a solo career and had best-sellers with 'Treasure of love', 'Without love', 'A lover's question', 'Ta ta' (1959), 'There goes my baby', 'Dance with me', and 'Lover please' (1962). He is remembered as 'the great, unique soul singer of all time'.

McRae, Carmen (*b* New York, 8 Apr. 1922). American singer. She joined the Benny *Carter band in 1944 and began to make an international reputation in the 1950s with albums for American Decca. She also worked with the bands of Count *Basie and Mercer Ellington and toured Europe and the Far East. She was briefly married to drummer Kenny *Clarke.

McRae, Gordon (*b* East Orange, NJ, 12 Mar. 1921; *d* Lincoln, Nebraska, 24 Jan. 1986). American singer. He came to notice when singing with Horace Heidt's band 1942–3. After war service he was heard in the Broadway musical *Three to Make Ready* (1946), and had his own radio show 1946–7. His fine baritone voice and rugged looks took him into films and roles in *The Big Punch* (1948); *Look For the Silver Lining* (1949); *Backfire* (1950); *Return of the Frontiersman* (1950); *Fine and Dandy* (1950); *The Daughter of Rosie O'Grady* (1950); *Tea for Two* (1950); *The West Point Story* (1950); *On Moonlight Bay* (1951); *Starlift* (1951); *About Face* (1952); *By the Light of the Silvery Moon* (1953); *The *Desert Song* (1953); *Three Sailors and a Girl* (1953); **Oklahoma!* (1955); **Carousel* (1956); and *The Best Things in Life Are Free* (1956), in which he played the part of lyric-writer Buddy *DeSylva.

McShann, Jay 'Hootie' (*b* Muskogee, Okla., 12 Jan. 1909). American jazz pianist, singer, and bandleader. He led a band in Kansas City from the mid-1930s (with a year in Chicago in 1939) until 1943. After army service he re-formed the band in 1945 and was active into the 1970s. He played at the Montreux Jazz Festival in 1975 and was in London in 1979. He helped to promulgate the *Kansas City style in the early days, later going into the jazz histories as the man who gave Charlie *Parker a start in his band in 1938. Among his best recordings were 'Hootie blues' (which gave him his nickname), 'Confessin' the blues', and 'Stigmatism'. He was a good modern blues singer and a lively pianist in the boogie-cum-blues idiom with a touch of *Basie.

Madame Favart. Comic opera with music by Jacques *Offenbach and book by Henri Charles Chivot (1839–97) and Alfred Duru (1829–89), produced in Paris at the Folies-Dramatiques on 28 Dec. 1878. It was seen in Vienna in 1879 and had a particular success in London when it was produced at the Strand Theatre that year, with English book by H. B. *Farnie, and, with Florence St John (1854–1912), Henry Ashley (1831–90), and Violet Cameron (1863–1919) in the cast, achieving a remarkable run for those days of 502 performances. Its popularity continued in an 1882 revival at the Avenue Theatre with Florence St John and Fred *Leslie and it was also seen at the 5th Avenue Theatre in New York.

Madame Pompadour. Musical play with music by Leo *Fall, book by Rudolf Schanzer and Ernest Welisch, first seen in Vienna at the Carltheater, 2 Mar. 1923. It had an excellent run of 469 performances at London's *Daly's Theatre at the end of the same year. The English book was by Frederick Lonsdale (1881–1954) and Harry Graham (1874–1936), the musical director was Arthur *Wood, and the cast included Bertram Wallis (1874–1952), Derek Oldham (1892–1968), Evelyn *Laye, Huntley Wright (1869–1943), and Elsie *Randolph. It was less successful at New York's Martin Beck Theatre in 1924.

Madame Sherry. Musical play with music by Hugo *Félix, book by Maurice Ordonneau (1854–1916), first seen in Berlin and Paris in 1902 and in Vienna (Carltheater) and London (Apollo) in 1903, without any outstanding success. With a substantially different score by Karl *Hoschna and English book by Otto *Harbach, it was produced at the New Amsterdam Theatre, New York on 30 Aug. 1910. Now termed a 'musical vaudeville' and, after all its face-lifts, ending up a curious mixture of operetta, musical comedy, and (in the final act) vaudeville turns, it became a popular hit and ran for 231 performances, starring Lina *Abarbanell. The delightful hit-song 'Every little movement', reprised in various progressive guises throughout the show, has survived; and an interpolated number 'Put your arms around me, honey' (*m* Albert *Von Tilzer) also became popular.

Mädchenmarkt, Der. Operetta in three acts with score by Victor Jacobi (1883–1921) and book by Max Brody and Franz Martos, produced in Vienna (Carltheater), 7 May 1913. With English book by Gladys Unger (1884–1940), it came to *Daly's Theatre, London, on 17 May 1913 as *The Marriage Market* with the star cast of G. P. Huntley (1868–1927),

W. H. *Berry, Robert Michaelis (1885–1965), Tom Walls (1883–1949), Harry Dearth (1876–1933), Gertie *Millar, Sari Petrass (1891–1930), and Frank Ronalds (later known as Ronald Frankau, 1894–1951), achieving a respectable run of 423 performances. In New York, even with additional numbers by Paul *Rubens and Jerome *Kern, it had only a moderate success.

Madness. British group who came together in 1976; formed by Lee Thompson (*b* 1961) (saxophone) and Mike Barson (*b* 1958) (keyboards), with Chris Foreman (*b* 1958) (guitar) and Chas Smash [Carl Smyth] (*b* 1959) (bass), working at first as Morris and the Minors, and then as the Invaders. With the addition of Graham 'Suggsy' McPherson (*b* 1961) (vocal), Daniel Woodgate (*b* 1960) (drums), and Mark Bedford (*b* 1961) (guitar) to the line-up, they changed their name to Madness in 1978. Their first release on the Two Tone label, 'The Prince' (1979), established their manic ska style which was furthered in such albums as *One Step Beyond* (1980) and *Complete Madness* (1982). They made a film featuring the group, *Take It or Leave It*, in 1981 and broke into the USA market with 'Our house' in 1983. Having achieved 18 hit singles and 6 top albums on the Stiff label, they founded their own Zarjazz label in 1984. After a heady career, they were unable to maintain their momentum and split up in 1986.

Madonna [Ciccione, Madonna Louise] (*b* Rochester, Mich., 16 Aug. 1958). American singer, dancer, and actress. After showing a schoolgirl talent for ballet, she won a dance scholarship to the University of Michigan but left after a year to seek some immediate success in New York. Among her many activities there, she played in several rock bands, in one as a drummer. In 1982 she was able to record some songs, making no immediate mark with 'Everybody' and 'Physical attraction' but finally breaking through with her album *Madonna* and a single, 'Holiday', in 1983. Her undoubted gifts were now backed up with a widely videoed sex-kitten image, in various disguises, which probably did more to obscure her real talents than to bolster them, but at least made her an international household name, with her second album, *Like a Virgin* (1985), a best-seller. At the height of Madonna fever, all that she did was noted and sold, her chart success continuing into 1987. Latterly, she has paid more attention to her career as an actress.

Maggie May. Musical by Lionel *Bart with book by Alun Owen. Following the huge success of **Oliver*, the lesser triumph of the heavily criticized **Blitz*, and his elevation to the ranks of the rich, Lionel Bart came up with the folky *Maggie May*, whose title song had been around for many folk years. Some of its songs, in competition with the *Beatles, managed minor success and the show itself achieved 501 performances, with Barry Humphries, Janet Webb, Rachel Roberts (1927–80), and Kenneth Haigh (*b* 1929) in the cast. It was Lionel Bart's last substantial success.

Magic Show, The. American musical which achieved success as the fifth longest running show of the 1970s with 1920 performances at the off-Broadway Cort Theatre 28 May 1974. As the name suggests, its appeal was partly due to the illusions of a young magician (first played by Doug Henning) who triumphs over an older rival. The music and lyrics were by Stephen *Schwartz (composer of **Godspell* and **Pippin*) and the book by Bob Randall.

Maid of the Mountains, The. Highly successful musical play with score mainly by Harold *Fraser-Simson, book by Frederick Lonsdale (1881–1954), and lyrics by Harry Graham (1874–1936), Clifford Harris, and 'Valentine'. Ater a try-out in Manchester in 1916, it came to London's *Daly's Theatre on 10 Feb. 1917. It made a household name of its star José *Collins and had a then record run of 1352 performances. Much of this was due to a magnificent score which included 'Love will find a way' (which Fraser-Simson, being asked for a waltz to equal *Lehár's *Merry Widow* success, contrived by simply doubling up the notes of Lehár's hit); 'Husbands and wives'; and some successful items added by James W. *Tate such as 'A bachelor gay' and 'A paradise for two'. Curiously, it seems to have been a failure in New York (Casino) 11 Sept. 1918. But it has stood the test of time in England, revived in 1921 and 1930, at the Coliseum in 1942 [224p], and at the Palace in 1972. It was filmed in 1932; and has been a lasting favourite with amateur societies.

Mainstream jazz. Jazz appreciation and its following was emotively split, in the revivalist and modernist days of the questing 1940s, into two fiercely warring camps with tastes centred, on the one hand, on the *hot 'authentic' *New Orleans-style jazz; and, on the other, on the *cool *'modern' jazz that had so changed the nature of the music. Yet between the devotional excesses of the trad and the mod there was always a great deal of jazz, particularly that played by the maturer sort of jazz musician who had spent some time in the professional ranks of the *big bands, that was neither crudely trad nor intellectually mod; maintaining the hot element of the older music but not averse to the tidier results of arrangement and forethought. Such jazz tended to be harmonically adventurous, its improvisations melodically based, and rhythmically swinging; something near the kind of band-within-a-band kind of music that the *Ellington, *Goodman, or *Basie sidemen might play. It was this kind of music that was specifically labelled 'mainstream', the invention of the name being credited to the English jazz critic Stanley Dance. Mainstream, in its widest sense, never amounted to a distinct style. It was most closely allied to what has been designated *Kansas City jazz, sophisticated yet swinging, with a percentage of New Orleans blood in its veins and New York slickness in its head.

Mainstream art is that which stays in the main current of development, moving along and advancing in order to remain central to all periods. Although there was a specific kind of mainstream jazz in mind when the phrase was first coined in the 1960s, which placed it in the middle road of all jazz up to then, there is always a changing mainstream body of activity within all movements at all periods, so that modern jazz, for example, has its own mainstream school of players who retain some of the older bebop styling in the face of more avant-garde developments. Stanley Dance supervised a series of mainstream jazz recordings in the 1960s using such musicians as Coleman *Hawkins, Ben *Webster, Dickie *Wells, and Buster Bailey (1902–67); but these have almost become traditionalists in the overall view of jazz.

Make Mine Manhattan. American revue, one of the last successful big-stage examples of the species, taking a satirical look at post-war New York, the new home of the United Nations. The music was by Richard Lewine (*b* 1910), the lyrics and sketches by Arnold B. Horwitt, and its humour revolved round the mimicry talents of Sid Caesar (*b* 1922), replaced by Bert *Lahr when the show went on tour. Opening at the Broadhurst Theatre 15 Jan. 1948, it had 419 performances.

Malneck, Matty [Mat] (*b* Newark, NJ, 9 Dec. 1903). American composer, conductor, violinist, and arranger. After working in various small dance bands, he joined Paul *Whiteman as a violist in 1926, one of his earliest appearances with Whiteman being at the Royal Albert Hall in London the same year. He began contributing arrangements for Whiteman and also appeared on violin on many jazz recording sessions with small groups drawn from the band, including such musicians as Bix *Beiderbecke and Frankie *Trumbauer. He also recorded frequently with New York jazz musicians in the early 1930s and with Gene Gifford, before forming his own band in 1935, but he was still arranging for Whiteman until 1937. He made only a few recordings but the band, featuring jazz accordionist Milton de Lugg, was regularly employed in theatres, on the radio, and in films such as *East Side of Heaven* (1938); *Man About Town* (1939); *Scatterbrain* (1940); and *Trocadero* (1944). He wrote a number of songs for films but only one complete score, *Hawaiian Nights* (1939). His association with dance bands of the 1930s made him a natural choice to supervise and conduct the band sequences in *Some Like it Hot* (1959), which featured his 'Park Avenue Fantasy' (1935). Other songs include: 'If I had a million dollars' (1934), 'Goody goody' (1936), 'Central Park' (1940), 'Love in the afternoon' (1956); all with lyrics by Johnny *Mercer.

Mamas and the Papas, The. American folk-rock vocal group formed in New York in 1965. The members of the group throughout its existence were John Philips (*b* 1935), Michelle Philips (*b* 1944), Cass Elliott (1943–74), and Denny Doherty (*b* 1941). Promoting the California hippie image of the flower-power era, they sang in a folk-rock idiom that was always melodic and harmonically rich. Their first recording was 'California dreamin'' in 1966 and they had a No. 1 hit that year with 'Monday, Monday'. The break-up of the Philips' marriage in 1966 led the way to the group's disbandment in 1968, but there were reunions.

Mambo. Cuban dance. In the 1930s the *rumbas and *tangos of the Latin American bands were becoming somewhat commercialized and ineffective; so that the advent of the new groups led by Machito (1912–84), Noro *Morales, and Perez *Prado, playing true and undiluted afros, rumbas, and boleros, came as a timely tonic. The jazz world also took an interest, feeling that the two spheres of popular music had something to offer each other. Thus the mambo developed by a grafting of jazz on to Cuban folk-music. It was developed by the bandleaders Anselmo Sacasas and Julio Gutierrez, though it was Perez Prado who was mainly responsble for its widespread popularity. Developing from the rumba, with its repetitive montuno chorus, now expanded into an original form, with jazz riffs and phrasing added, the mambo gradually evolved. The end result was a fascinating amalgam of Latin American melody with jazz phrasing, the Latin American rhythm given the powerful surge of the jazz brass section. It was developed within the jazz world by musicians such as Dizzy *Gillespie, who recorded with Noro Morales in 1945, Charlie *Parker, and Duke *Ellington. It swept the world in the late 1940s and early 1950s, paving the way for the less frenetic *cha cha cha.

Mame. American musical comedy, with score by Jerry *Herman, book by Jerome Lawrence and Robert E. Lee, based on Patrick Dennis's novel and the play *Auntie Mame*, which opened in New York at the Winter Garden Theatre 24 May 1966. The original play was described as 'more a series of entertaining vignettes than a sustained, well-plotted story' and the musical retained the same breathless style, with Angela *Lansbury ideally cast in the zany title-role which she also played in the 1983 revival. It had 1508 performances in New York in 1966 followed by a run of 443 at London's Drury Lane, 20 Feb. 1969, when Ginger *Rogers took the lead. The best song was the title-song 'Mame', followed by 'If he had walked into my life' and 'My best girl'. In the film version, made in 1974, Lucille *Ball co-starred with Robert *Preston.

Mancini, Henry (*b* Cleveland, 16 Apr. 1924). American composer, conductor, arranger, and pianist. He started his musical career at the age of 13 as a flautist in the Pennsylvania All State Band, then studied music in Pittsburgh and at the Juilliard

School. After serving in the US Army Air Corps he became pianist in the civilian Glenn *Miller orchestra led, after Miller's death, by Tex *Beneke. He had written some arrangements for Bob *Crosby and now exercised his talent by writing for Beneke. In 1952 he joined Universal-International Films as staff arranger and gained recognition for his work on the Glenn Miller and Benny *Goodman biographies. As musical director and composer he was now regularly committed to film and TV scores, winning a Grammy Award in 1958 for the *Peter Gunn* TV series; and, in 1961 an Oscar for his music to *Breakfast at Tiffany's* which included the ever popular 'Moon river'.

He is renowned for a series of successful scores that constantly produced new hits, including: *Lost in Alaska* (1952); *The Glenn Miller Story* (1953)—'So little time'; *Six Bridges to Cross* (1955); *The Benny Goodman Story* (1956); *Rock, Pretty Baby* (1956); *Touch of Evil* (1958); *Mr Lucky* (1959); *Summer Love* (1959); *High Time* (1960); *Bachelor in Paradise* (1961); *Hatari* (1962); *Experiment in Terror* (1962); *Days of Wine and Roses* (1962)—'Days of wine and roses'; *Charade* (1963); *The Pink Panther* (1963)—'Pink panther', 'It had better be tonight'; *Charade* (1963); *A Shot in the Dark* (1964); *Dear Heart* (1965); *The Great Race* (1965); *Moment to Moment* (1966); *Arabesque* (1966); *What Did You Do in the War, Daddy?* (1965); *Two for the Road* (1967); *Gunn* (1967); *The Party* (1968); *Me, Natalie* (1969); *Darling Lili* (1969); *Sunflower* (1971); *Sometimes a Great Notion* (1971; *Never Give an Inch* in UK); *The Thief Who Came to Dinner* (1973); *The White Dawn* (1973); *The Return of the Pink Panther* (1975); *Once is not Enough* (1976); *Silver Streak* (1976); *W. C. Fields and Me* (1976); *House Calls* (1978); *Who is Killing the Great Chefs of Europe?* (1978); *Nightwing* (1979); *Little Miss Marker* (1980); *Back Roads* (1981); *Mommie Dearest* (1981); and *Victor/Victoria* (1982; Academy Award).

He is also the composer of many songs and orchestral pieces, and author of *Sounds and Scores (Guide to Professional Orchestration)* (New York–London, 1973).

Mandel, Johnny [John Alfred] (*b* New York, 23 Nov. 1925). American composer, arranger, conductor, trumpeter, and trombonist. Educated at the Manhattan School of Music and Juilliard. He played trumpet with Joe *Venuti and Billie Rogers, trombone with Henry Jerome, Boyd *Raeburn, Jimmy *Dorsey, Buddy *Rich, Georgie Auld, Alvino Rey, and Count *Basie. He was staff composer for TV shows, writing many TV background and film scores, including: *You're Never Too Young* (1957); *I Want to Live* (1958); *The Third Voice* (1959); *The Americanization of Emily* (1964); *The Sandpiper* (1965), which won a Grammy Award—'The shadow of your smile'; *Harper* (1966); *The Russians are Coming ...* (1966); *An American Dream* (1966); *Point Blank* (1967); *M*A*S*H* (1970); *The Last Detail* (1973); *Freaky Friday* (1976); *Agatha* (1979); *Being There* (1979); *The Baltimore Bullet* (1980); *Deathtrap* (1982); and *The Verdict* (1982).

Mandrell, Barbara Ann (*b* Houston, 25 Dec. 1948). American country singer, accordionist, and guitarist. After earning a local reputation, she went to *Nashville to join the *Grand Ole Opry, and soon gained a national reputation with her performances of 'I've been loving you too long', 'Standing room only', 'Midnight angel', 'Woman to woman', 'Midnight oil', and 'Best of strangers'. She had her own TV show in 1980.

Manhattan Transfer. American vocal group first formed in 1969, then performing in a good-time jug-band style popular at the time. By 1972 the only surviving original member was Tim Hauser (*b* 1942), now joined by Janis Siegel (*b* 1953), Alan Paul (*b* 1949), and Laurel Masse (*b* 1954), and they were performing in a smart swing-era idiom spiced with rock, with a polished stage act, and were pioneers of the *doo-wop style. They were especially popular in Europe and had a No. 1 hit with 'Chanson d'amour' in 1977. Cheryl Bentyne replaced Laurel Masse and the group moved away from the nostalgia field into more of a mixture of rock and jazz. They recorded mainly on the Atlantic label.

Manilow, Barry [Pinkus, Barry Alan] (*b* Brooklyn, NY, 17 June 1946). American vocalist, pianist, and composer who studied at the New York College of Music and the Juilliard School. Working in TV in 1967, he became conductor and arranger for the Ed Sullivan show. He arranged and produced two Bette *Midler recordings 1972–3. He began to promote himself as a singer in 1974 in a slickly produced act that made him an international favourite, and resulted in his being paid $782,000 for one show, a record at the time. The vocal talent behind the show-biz exterior has resulted in No. 1 hits in America with 'Mandy' (1975, *m* Scott English); 'I write the songs' (1976); 'Looks like we made it (1977); and 'Somewhere in the night' (1979). He is a prolific writer of advertising *jingles as well as songs.

T. Jasper: *Barry Manilow* (London, 1981).

Mann, Barry (*b* Brooklyn, NY, 9 Feb. 1939). American songwriter. He intended to be an architect but, having written a few urban protest songs, he decided on a songwriting career when one of his first efforts had a modest success on record in 1958. He married his future collaborator, Cynthia Weil (*b* 1942), in 1961 and made a few recordings. These were not a great hit, nor were two solo albums made in 1971 and 1975. But as a song-writing duo Mann and Weil were to be one of the most successful teams of the 1960s, their best-sellers including 'Bless you' (1961), recorded by Tony Orlando (*b* 1944); 'Uptown' (1962), the Crystals; 'On Broadway' (1963), the *Drifters; 'I'm gonna be strong' (1964), Gene *Pitney; 'We gotta get out of this place' (1965), the *Animals; 'You're my soul and inspiration' (1966), the Righteous Brothers; 'I love how you love me' (1961), Bobby Vinton (1968); 'Walking in the rain' (1969), the Americans; and 'I just can't help believing' (1970), B. J. Thomas.

They continued writing into the 1970s with such hits as 'Here you come again' (1977) for Dolly *Parton. Other titles include: 'She say' (1960), 'Footsteps' (1961), 'The way of a clown' (1961), 'Come back, silly girl' (1963), 'He's sure the boy I love' (1963), 'I'll never dance again' (1963), 'My dad' (1963), 'Patches' (1963), 'Blame it on the bossa nova' (1964), 'I'll take you home' (1964); 'The grass is greener' (1964), 'Saturday night at the movies' (1965), 'You've lost that lovin' feeling' (1965), 'Home of the brave' (1966), 'Kicks' (1968), 'The shape of things to come' (1969), and 'New world coming' (1971).

Mann, Herbie [Solomon, Herbert Jay] (*b* New York, 16 Apr. 1930). American jazz flautist and saxophonist. After studying at the Manhattan School of Music, he became one of the handful of players to make the flute a viable jazz instrument and has toured the world as soloist and playing with various bands and orchestras. After service in Europe with the US Army, he was active on the West Coast 1954–7. In 1959 he formed his Afro-Jazz Sextet which he took in 1960 on a tour of 15 African countries. In 1961 he played in Brazil and was one of the importers of the *bossa nova style. He has exploited African and Latin elements in jazz and in the 1960s added features from the rock world. In the 1970s he led a jazz-funk group which he called the Family of Mann, and recorded a *reggae album in 1975. He started his own record label in 1970. His music keeps in touch with the dance band tradition and he has proved that even modern jazz can produce best-sellers.

Mann, Manfred [Lubowitz, Michael] (*b* Johannesburg, 21 Oct. 1940). Leader of British pop band. He came to Britain and while playing piano in a Butlin's Holiday Camp in 1962 met vibist Mike Hugg (*b* 1942) and formed the Mann–Hugg Blues Brothers, a jazz quartet. Later Mann switched to organ and Hugg to drums, and with Paul Jones (*b* 1942) as vocalist and harmonica player, Mike Vickers (*b* 1941) on clarinet and alto-saxophone, and Dave Richmond (*b* 1942) on bass, they formed the group collectively known as Manfred Mann. They were to become one of the most commercially viable *rhythm 'n' blues bands of the time, having a hit with 'Ready, steady, go' (1964) which became the theme tune of the TV programme of that name and hence a wide-seller. They kept to a similar formula for further hits such as 'Do wah diddy' and 'Pretty flamingo', which both reached No. 1, and had 15 top hits to their credit before disbanding in 1969. Mann and Hugg continued with Manfred Mann Chapter II until Mann formed Manfred Mann's Earth Band in 1971, a heavy rock outfit which achieved its first modest hit in 1973 with 'Joybringer' and a No. 1 US hit in 1976 with 'Blinded by the light'.

Manne, Shelly [Sheldon] (*b* New York, 11 June 1920; *d* Los Angeles, 26 Sept. 1984). American drummer, bandleader, and composer. He started his playing career on transatlantic liners before working with Joe Marsala, Raymond *Scott, Will *Bradley, and Les *Brown. He was in the navy 1942–5, subsequently with Stan *Kenton on and off between 1946 and 1951 with short-term intervals with Charlie Ventura 1947, Bill Harris (the Harris–Manne Sextet) 1948, and Woody *Herman 1949. He was a leading figure in *cool and West Coast jazz and a key player in the Lighthouse All-Stars at Laguna Beach, California, in the early 1950s. Eventually he settled in Los Angeles to write and record for films and TV—*The Proper Time* (1960); *Daktari* (1966); *Young Billy Young* (1969)—while still making small-group jazz recordings as Shelly Manne and his Men and running a nightclub 1960–74.

Man of La Mancha. Musical which successfully took a grip of Cervantes' rambling *Don Quixote* stories and presented them in a convincingly dramatized way. The show was played without intervals to sustain the drama and proved to be tremendously effective; not simply an adaptation of a book but very much an original work in its own right. Starting as a TV feature, it opened at the ANTA Washington Square Playhouse on 22 Nov. 1965 and ran for 2328 performances with Richard Kiley (*b* 1922) as Cervantes the story-teller and Irving Jacobson as his servant who transform themselves into Quixote and Sancho Panza. Every praise was heaped upon it and it was named the best musical of the year. The score was by Mitch *Leigh, whose only Broadway success it remained; the book by Dale Wasserman (*b* 1917) who conceived the original TV production; and the lyrics by Joe Darion (*b* 1917). Quixote's song 'The impossible dream' became a hit, closely followed by 'Dulcinea' and 'Man of La Mancha;. In London, with Keith Michell (*b* 1928) and Bernard Spear, it ran for 253 performances at the Piccadilly Theatre from 24 Apr. 1968. A film was made in 1972 with Peter O'Toole, Sophia Loren, and James Coco; and the original musical has enjoyed several revivals in America.

Manone, Wingy [Joseph Matthews] (*b* New Orleans, 13 Feb. 1900; *d* Las Vegas, 9 July 1982). American jazz trumpeter, vocalist, and bandleader. He lost his right arm in a streetcar accident but managed to make a feature of playing one-handed. He played with local bands before going to New York in 1927 and working for a time in Chicago. He was leading his own band in New York by 1934 and was a prolific recorder of commercially slanted Dixieland-style items, usually featuring his own rather corny vocals and achieving biggish hits with items like 'Isle of Capri', 'Casey Jones', and 'Corine Corrina', occasionally achieving some excellent jazz. He was with Bing *Crosby in *Rhythm on the River* (1940) and other films.

W. Manone and P. Vandernoost: *Trumpet on the Wing* (New York, 1958).

Mantovani, Annunzio Paolo (*b* Venice, 15 Nov. 1905; *d* Tunbridge Wells, 30 Mar. 1980). Italian-born British conductor, composer, and arranger. His father was the principal violinist at La Scala, Milan, under Toscanini, also serving under Richter, Saint-Saëns, and Mascagni; Professor at two conservatories; and held the title Cavaliere. His son was discouraged from taking up music, although his father taught him the violin. But Mantovani was not to be deterred from a musical career, and was playing professionally at the age of 16. Subsequently the family moved to London (his father to play at Covent Garden) and Mantovani was able to study at the Trinity College of Music. By 1925 he was leading a small orchestra at the then fashionable Metropole Hotel with Reginald Kilbey and George *Melachrino as members. While still playing there he was soloist in a performance of the Saint-Saëns violin concerto. In the early 1930s he formed his Tipica Orchestra and began a series of popular lunch-time broadcasts from the Monseigneur Restaurant in Piccadilly. He spent many years conducting various theatre orchestras, notably for *Coward's *Sigh No More* (1945), one of his last shows being *And So to Bed* in 1951.

Many composers, conductors, and performers owe a lot nowadays to the gramophone, but few as much as Mantovani. Not long after the end of the war there was a growing demand for his records in the USA and something different was thought desirable. The final choice was of an orchestra of 45 that included 32 string players. The first two recordings of the new orchestra had excellent sales but the real hit came in 1951 with a recording of an old standard, 'Charmaine', which brought to notice the shimmering, echoing Mantovani string effect, achieved by delayed entries, which had been conceived by his arranger Ronald *Binge. The sound acted like magic: Mantovani was quickly in demand and began making world tours. He made his first visit to the USA in 1955 and the crowds that greeted him had to be police-controlled, an unusual circumstance for a conductor of light orchestral music. He rarely missed an annual visit to the USA, toured Europe continuously, and other venues included South Africa, Canada, and Japan. The record sales continued into the 1970s, his 25 years with Decca celebrated in 1966 with a diamond-studded baton, a fitting tribute to the motivator, by 1971, of 50 million LP sales in the USA alone, with 18 gold disc winners among them. His skills as an arranger and the sound of the 'cascading strings' tended to overshadow his own considerable gift as a composer with a fine sense of orchestral needs. His works included 'A poem to the moon', 'Royal blue waltz', 'Dance of the eighth veil', 'Toyshop ballet' (which won a Novello Award in 1957), 'Serenata d'amore'—his best-known piece, the song 'Cara mia' (*w* Bunny Lewis), which was taken to No. 1 in the US by David *Whitfield, and many popular tangos.

Marable, Fate (*b* Paducah, Ky., 2 Dec. 1890; *d* St Louis, Mo., 16 Jan. 1947). American bandleader, pianist, and calliopist. Although he achieved no great reputation as a pianist or *calliope player, and the band recordings he left behind were of little merit, his mark on jazz history has achieved legendary proportions, mainly by virtue of the players who worked and founded their careers with him. As bandleader and musical organizer for the Streckfus line of riverboats plying the Mississippi from New Orleans, he employed many of those who traditionally left the jazz city by this route to make their fortunes elsewhere and spread the gospel of jazz. He was an established bandleader by 1917 with a reputation for discipline and high standards that were probably essential in those free-and-easy days. Musicians who owed him some of their musical education and livelihood included Louis *Armstrong, Henry 'Red' *Allen, Pops Foster, Jimmy *Blanton, Zutty *Singleton, Johnny and Baby Dodds, and many more, while countless others were influenced by hearing his bands on the riverboats and in New Orleans.

Maracas. Popular rhythm instrument, commonly used in Cuba and many parts of South America. They consist of a pair of gourds (or their modern equivalent) filled with dry seeds which, when shaken or rotated, give a swishing sound that is a familiar ingredient of Latin American music.

Marais, Josef (*b* Sir Lowry Pass, SA, 17 Nov. 1905; *d* Los Angeles, 27 Apr. 1978). South African composer, folk-singer, violinist, guitarist, and writer. He was brought up on a sheep-farm and had little early schooling, but eventually won his way to the South African College of Music and at the age of 20 went to the Royal Academy of Music in London, afterwards studying the violin in Prague. He worked as a translator of Afrikaans and other folk-songs into English, organized his Bushveld Band which made recordings and broadcasts, and also broadcast as a soloist on the BBC. He went to the USA in 1937 and worked at the Office of War Information in New York. There he teamed up with a singer of Dutch origin, Roosje Baruch de la Bardo, who worked under the name of Miranda. They formed a folk-singing team, married in 1947, and became well-known entertainers, regularly broadcasting and recording and publishing a number of song collections. Marais wrote music for several stage productions, and his songs included 'As the sun goes down', 'Here am I', 'My heart is so sad', 'The wanderer's song', a hit of 1942, 'Sugarbush', based on a veldt song, and 'A-round the corner' (1950).

March. Music originally intended to promote orderly in-step movement, generally written for military use, and of a stirring nature designed to raise spirits and minimize fatigue on active service. Later the march was used by non-military composers either within larger works, such as operas, or as self-contained orchestral pieces, as in Elgar's well-known 'Pomp and Circumstance' marches.

The earliest known marches to survive in notation are those in Arbeau's *Orchésographie* of 1589 and those in *My Lady Neville's Booke* of a year or two later. Most of the band marches with which we are now familiar date from the second half of the 19th and the early 20th century, many of the best-known written by the American composer John Philip *Sousa, by Kenneth J. *Alford in England, Hermann Blankenburgh (1876–1956), and Josef Franz Wagner (1855–1908)—'Unter dem Doppeladler' ('Under the double eagle')—in Germany. Various specialist composers connected with military bands have regularly added to a wide repertoire, including Karel Komzak (1850–1905), Julius Fucik (1872–1916)—'Entry of the gladiators' (1900), and Václav Vackár (1881–1954) in Czechoslovakia; Carl Teike (1864–1922)—'Alte Kamaraden' ('Old Comrades')—in Germany.

The modern march tends to be in the form of a rondo with a recurring main tune and a trio section in a related key. The quick march is normally used for marching, while the slow march is reserved for memorial and ceremonial occasions. The standard speeds laid down by military authorities have never been strictly observed and some light infantry regiments use a very fast pace. Regiments all over the world have their special regimental marches.

Mares, Paul Joseph (*b* New Orleans, 15 June 1900; *d* Chicago, 18 Aug. 1949). American jazz trumpeter and composer. Son of a trumpeter, he was an active musician at 16 working in a jazz group in Bucktown on Lake Pontchartrain in company with Leon Roppolo. He went to Chicago in 1919 where he later worked with Tom Brown, at Kelly's Stables with George Brunis, and on the famous riverboat SS *Capitol*. During a period in Davenport, Iowa, he, Brunis, and Roppolo joined the Friars' Inn Orchestra which was to become best-known under the name of the *New Orleans Rhythm Kings, and which Mares eventually led. He worked for a period in New York, but returned to Chicago in 1925 to reorganize the New Orleans Rhythm Kings. After leaving music to join a family business, he came back to Chicago in 1934 to organize a band. He opened his own restaurant, went into the frozen-food business, occasionally promoted jazz concerts, and was again active as a musician 1945–8. He is credited with a number of jazz standards, including: 'Tin Roof blues' (1923), 'Farewell blues' (with Elmer *Schoebel and Roppolo, 1923), and 'Milneburg joys' (with Roppolo and *Morton, 1925).

'Marine's Hymn, The'. The music is derived from the famous 'Gendarmes' duet' in the opéra-bouffe **Geneviève de Brabant* by Jacques *Offenbach, first produced in Paris in 1859 and revised in 1875. The duet became all the rage in London, at the Philharmonic in Islington, in 1871 and the operetta was produced in New York, in English, in 1868 with *The 'Geneviève de Brabant' Songster* becoming a popular seller in 1869. There have been many claimants for the origination of the words that were attached—'From the halls of Montezuma to the shores of Tripoli'—but none has been firmly accredited and the normal copyright attribution is to the United States Marine Corps. They were first printed, without any association with the music, in the *National Police Gazette* in New York in 1917 and reprinted in a Marine newspaper in 1918. The earliest printing of all the words with the music was in 1918, and they were copyrighted the following year.

Marks, Johnny [John D.] (*b* Mt Vernon, NY, 10 Nov. 1909; *d* New York, 3 Sept. 1985). American composer, author, and publisher. Educated at Columbia University, he studied music in Paris and worked for most of his life as a radio producer. He served in the Second World War and produced army shows overseas. Marks gained immortality by one song, 'Rudolph the red-nosed reindeer', which was based on a story written by Robert L. May in 1939 and given away by a store in Chicago. The song, published in 1949, sold more than 30 million copies in 20 years, first becoming widely known through the best-selling Gene *Autry version. The rest of Marks's large output seems to have a predominantly Christmassy theme.

Marley, Bob [Nesta Robert] (*b* Rhoden Hall, nr. Kingston, 6 Feb. 1945; *d* Miami, 11 May 1981). Jamaican *reggae singer and composer. Son of a British army captain and a Jamaican mother, he worked in Kingston as an electrical welder and, after opening his own record shop, began to make records of some of his own compositions, then a mixture of *calypso and *soul music. Becoming known locally, in 1965 he formed a group, the Wailers, with singers and composers Bunny Livingstone (*b* 1947) and Peter Tosh (1944–87). Achieving great popularity in Jamaica with their light and lilting ska music, they were signed up by the London-based Island Records in 1972, and became the group who did most to popularize and make a fashionable cult of Jamaican *reggae music during the 1970s.

Livingstone and Tosh left the group, but Marley went on with other partners to become an international figure, touring the world and achieving massive record sales. His songs were a vehicle for his religious convictions as a Rastafarian and his support for Black Power, which led him to back the People's National Party from 1976. Just before a concert on 3 Dec. 1976 he was shot and wounded in his home by a political opponent. In 1980 he sang at the Zimbabwe independence celebrations. His tours of Europe at this time were followed by a tour of the USA in 1977. The fiery evangelical spirit which motivated his intense stage performances and recordings came out in emotive songs like 'No woman no cry', but mainly in politically loaded items like 'Exodus', 'Zimbabwe', 'Rebel music',

'Everywhere be war', and 'Death to the downpressors'; all that he did making him one of the most eloquent and powerful promoters of reggae music.

H. Dalrymple: *Bob Marley: Music, Myth & the Rastas* (Sudbury, Middx., 1976). C. McKnight: *Bob Marley: and the Roots of Reggae* (London, 1977). S. Davis: *Bob Marley: the Biography* (London, 1983). T. White: *Catch a Fire: the Life of Bob Marley* (London, 1983). M. L. Whitney: *Bob Marley: Reggae King of the World* (London, 1984).

Marquee. London club well-known as a jazz and rock centre. It opened in 1958 in a basement beneath the Academy Cinema at the corner of Poland Street and Oxford Street. First favoured as a venue for traditional and mainstream jazz, with the bands of Humphrey *Lyttelton and Chris *Barber regularly heard there, it later became the cradle of the new rhythm 'n' blues developments led by Alexis *Korner and others. The club moved to Wardour Street in 1964 and, although jazz is occasionally featured, it became increasingly the home of British rock and blues bands. Its facilities, which included a small studio where the *Who first recorded, have been continually enlarged and improved, but are now destined to close.

Marriott, Charles Händel Rand (*b* London, 3 Nov. 1831; *d* Hastings, 3 Dec. 1889). British composer, conductor, and violinist. Musical director at Highbury Barn 1860–5; at the Royal Gardens, Cremorne, 1866–74; and at the Pier Pavilion, Hastings, from 1874. He was a prolific composer of songs and dance music, piano music and duets, and his name is to be seen on innumerable music covers of the late 19th century, especially as arranger of quadrilles based on popular tunes of the day.

Marsalis, Wynton (*b* New Orleans, 18 Oct. 1961). American trumpet player. Son of a leading jazz pianist, he is an outstanding black virtuoso of the trumpet who, unusually, has made his mark in both the jazz and classical fields. He studied at the Berkshire Music Center at Tanglewood, where his abilities were soon noted, and continued his studies at the Juilliard School of Music. Thereafter he joined Art *Blakey's big band, with whom he appeared at the Montreux Festival in 1980, toured with his own quintet, and played with Miles *Davis. His wide-based talents won him Grammy Awards for both jazz and classical recordings in 1983. His brother Branford (*b* 1960) is a notable jazz saxophonist.

Marshall, Arthur (*b* Saline Co., Mo., 20 Nov. 1881; *d* Kansas City, 18 Aug. 1968). American composer and pianist. His family originally came from Sedalia where they returned when the composer was three. He became interested in ragtime as a boy and was greatly influenced by Scott *Joplin, who was a lodger at their home for some time. He was then encouraged, as Joplin and many others had been, by the publisher John Stark; and his writings included 'Swipesey cake walk' (with Joplin, 1900), 'Kinklets' (1906), 'Lily Queen' (with Joplin, 1907), 'Ham and — rag' (1908), 'The peach' (1908); and 'The pippin rag' (1908).

Martha and the Vandellas. One of the outstanding female singing groups promoted by the black Motown label, the Vandellas first worked under the name of the Del-Phis while they were all still at school in Detroit. Martha Reeves (*b* Detroit, 18 July 1941) was working as a secretary with Motown when she was asked to deputize on a session because a singer was unable to make it. The results were so impressive that she and her school friends Rosalind Ashford (*b* Detroit, 2 Sept. 1943) and Annette Sterling (*b* Detroit, 1942) were signed up as backing vocalists, making their first recording with Marvin *Gaye on 'Stubborn kind of fellow'. Signed up by Berry *Gordy, they had a big hit in 1963 with 'Come and get these memories' and an even bigger one with the swinging, brassy 'Heatwave' (1963), which went to No. 4 in the USA charts, and 'Quicksand' (1963). In 1964, Annette Sterling was replaced by Betty Kelly (*b* Detroit, 16 Sept. 1944) and their successes continued with 'Live wire', 'In my lonely room', and 'Dancing in the street' (1964). The group was to continue its triumphs, with various changes of personnel, until it finally broke up in 1972. Martha Reeves continued a career as a soloist and made such highly personal albums as *The Rest of My Life* and *Gotta Keep Moving*.

Martin, Dean [Crocetti, Dino Paul] (*b* Steubenville, Ohio, 7 June 1917). American actor and singer. His singing ambitions led him to California in 1937 where he built a club reputation with his relaxed crooning style in the *Crosby manner, and he was a full-time professional by 1943. He met the comedian Jerry Lewis (*b* 1926) in 1946 and they worked together as a comedy-singing act in Atlantic City, becoming a top nightclub attraction. They appeared on TV in 1948 and, starting with *My Friend Irma* (1949), made a series of comedy films together until they broke up after *Hollywood or Bust* in 1956. Each followed his own successful career, Martin eventually having his own very popular and accomplished TV show from 1965 into the 1970s. He proved to be an able actor in many straight as well as singing film roles and became one of the fashionable, hard-drinking, playboy figures of the American entertainment world, closely associated with Frank *Sinatra in the 1960s. A highly accomplished singer with excellent technique, he made many hit records such as 'That's amore' (1953), 'Memories are made of this' (1955), and (his eventual theme song) 'Everybody loves somebody' (1964).

Martin, Freddy (*b* Cleveland, 9 Dec. 1906; *d* Newport Beach, Calif., 1 Oct. 1983). American saxophonist and bandleader. After working in various bands as a tenor-saxophone player, he formed his own band in 1932, to become one of the fashionable society band leaders of the 1930s, with residencies at many New York hotels, including the Waldorf-Astoria, and in Chicago, but mainly based in later years at the Cocoanut Grove in Los Angeles. The band appeared in many radio shows and recorded prolifically. Martin made a speciality of adapting the classics and had big hits with 'Tonight we love' (1941), from Tchaikovsky's B♭ Piano Concerto, and 'I look at Heaven' (1942) from the Grieg Piano Concerto. His vocalists included Eddie Stone (*b* 1907) 1939–42. The band was featured in many films including *Stage Door Canteen* (1943) and *Melody Time* (1948). Martin led an all-star band in the 1970s on nostalgic big-band package tours with Frankie *Carle, Margaret Whiting, and Bob *Crosby.

Martin, George (*b* London, 3 Jan. 1926). British record producer. He studied at the Guildhall School of Music and joined EMI Records in 1950, later managing the Parlophone label which profusely recorded comedy acts and popular singers in the 1950s, including the *Temperance Seven and the Goons, Shirley *Bassey, and Matt Munro. He signed up the *Beatles in 1962 and became very much a part of their creative activities, not only leading them into various artistic and technical venues but also arranging for them and even recording with them. Later he worked with Cilla *Black and *Gerry and the Pacemakers. He left EMI in 1965 to set up an independent production unit, later producing albums by Neil *Sedaka and Paul *McCartney and many others, continuing as a key figure in the development of the British popular music scene.

G. Martin and J. Hornsby: *All You Need Is Ears* (London, 1979).

Martin, Hugh (*b* Birmingham, Ala., 11 Aug. 1914). American composer and librettist. He studied the piano at Birmingham University. He sang in the Broadway production of *Hooray for What* (1937), afterwards forming a song-writing partnership with lyricist Ralph *Blane who was also in the cast. They organized a mixed vocal quartet known as the Four Martins. He was vocal arranger for many stage productions including *One For the Money* (1937), *Too Many Girls* (1937), *The *Boys from Syracuse* (1938), *The Streets of Paris* (1939), **DuBarry Was a Lady* (1939); and **Louisiana Purchase* (1940).

The partners wrote their own successful show, **Best Foot Forward*, in 1941, then went to Hollywood in 1943 for the screen version and to write for films. These included *Thousands Cheer* (1943)—'The joint is really jumpin' (in Carnegie Hall)'; *Meet Me in St Louis* (1944), with Judy *Garland—'The trolley song', 'The boy next door', 'Have yourself a merry little Christmas', etc.; **Ziegfeld Follies* (1944)—'Love'; *Good News* (1947)—'Pass that peace pipe' (*w* Roger Edens). Martin wrote further stage shows with other collaborators, including *Look Ma, I'm Dancin'* (1948), *Make a Wish* (1951), **Love from Judy* (1952), and *High Spirits* (1964); and later film scores (with Blane) were *Anthea* (1954), *The Girl Rush* (1955), and *The Girl Most Likely* (1957).

Martin, Mary [Virginia] (*b* Weatherford, Texas, 1 Dec. 1913; *d* Rancho Mirage, Calif., 3 Nov. 1990). American actress and singer. After early vocal training which established her technical excellence and wide-ranging abilities, she worked in nightclubs and ran a dancing school. She failed her first Hollywood screen test, but the producer Laurence Schwab gave her a minor role in **Leave it to Me!* (1938), where her striking looks and vivacious personality, coupled with her singing of 'My heart belongs to Daddy', finally established her name.

She appeared at the Rainbow Room in New York, and began a film career in 1939 with *The Great Victor Herbert*, subsequently appearing in *Rhythm on the River* (1940)—'Ain't it a shame about Mame', 'I don't want to cry anymore'; *Love Thy Neighbour* (1940); *Kiss the Boys Goodbye* (1941)—'Kiss the boys goodbye'; *Birth of the Blues* (1941); *Star-spangled Rhythm* (1942)—'Hit the road to Dreamland'; *Happy Go Lucky* (1943)—'Let's get lost'; *True to Life* (1943); *Night and Day* (1946); and *Main Street to Broadway* (1953). A parallel career on the Broadway stage brought her even greater fame, in **One Touch of Venus* (1943)—'That's him', 'Speak low'; *Lute Song* (NY, 1946)—'Mountain high, valley low'; *Pacific 1860* (1945); **Annie Get Your Gun* (tour, 1947); **South Pacific* (1949; London, 1951)—'I'm gonna wash that man right outa my hair', 'Wonderful guy'; *Peter Pan* (1954); *The *Sound of Music* (1959)—'Do-re-mi', 'My favourite things'; *Jennie* (1963); **Hello, Dolly!* (London, 1965); **I Do! I Do!* (1966)—'My cup runneth over'. She was mainly inactive from the late 1960s and moved to Brazil, but continued to make occasional appearances.

S. P. Newman: *Mary Martin on Stage* (Philadelphia, 1969). M. Martin: *My Heart Belongs* (New York, 1976; new edn 1984).

Martin, Millicent (*b* Romford, Essex, 8 June 1934). British actress and singer. A small dynamic lady, she appeared in *Lute Song* (London, 1948); *The *Boy Friend* (New York, 1954); and first made her mark in **Expresso Bongo* (1958). She was also in *The Crooked Mile* (1959); *The Dancing Heiress* (1960); *The Lord Chamberlain Regrets* (1961); *Round Leicester Square* (1963); *Our Man Crichton* (1964); *Those Magnificent Men in Their Flying Machines* (1965); *Alfie* (1966); and **Stop the World—I Want to Get Off* (1966). National attention was drawn to her talents when she enlightened the British with her dextrous and intelligent satirical singing in the influential TV show *That Was the Week That Was* in 1962 and later in the series *From a Bird's Eye View* (1969). She has continued a very active career as both actress and singer, more frequently in straight roles and farce, but she took over the lead in the London production of Sondheim's **Follies* in 1988.

Martin, Ray (*b* Vienna, 11 Oct. 1918). British composer, author, arranger, and conductor. After coming to England in 1938 he served for six years in the Intelligence Corps during the war. He first came to the notice of British radio listeners in 1947 with a series of broadcasts with his 'Melody From the Sky' Orchestra. He became conductor of the BBC Variety Orchestra and conductor, arranger, and producer with EMI Records, recording prolifically as accompanist to various EMI artists and having several recorded successes with his own songs and orchestral compositions. He wrote for films and TV, being lured to the USA in 1957 at the peak of his fame to work in New York and Hollywood and to record for RCA and Polydor. In 1972 he returned to Britain to resume recording his own and other works, moving from a leaning towards luscious mood music in the 1950s to far more hard-hitting and experimental idioms in the 1970s. He wrote scores for a vast number of films, and more than 2000 other works include songs and instrumentals: 'Melody from the sky' (1946), 'Once upon a wintertime' (1948), 'Blue violins' (1951), 'Any old time' (1952), 'Waltzing bugle boy' (1953), 'Airborne' (1953), 'Ballet of the bells' (1954), 'You are my first love' (1955), 'Tango of the bells' (1956), 'Big Ben blues' (1956), 'Never too young' (1965), 'Sounds out of sight' (1966), 'If' (1973), etc.

Martin, Tony [Morris, Alvin] (*b* Oakland, Calif., 22 Dec. 1912). American singer. He played the saxophone in dance bands as a teenager and later led his own band, changing his name to Anthony Martin in 1934. He broke into films by way of a small part as a sailor in *Follow the Fleet* (1936) and first landed a role of any significance in *Sing, Baby, Sing* (1936). A year later he married the film star Alice *Faye and he appeared in various minor films in 1937. A spell on the Burns and Allen Show 1936–8 helped to establish his romantic style of singing. He had more fulfilling parts in *Sally, Irene and Mary* (1938), *Kentucky Moonshine* (1938), and *Thanks for Everything* (1938) and was to become one of MGM's leading singing stars with *Music in My Heart* (1940), *Ziegfeld Girl* (1941), *The Big Store* (1941), and many more into the late 1950s, his best role probably in *Casbah* (1948). He had his own radio show at various times, notably in 1946, and made many hit records between 1941 and 1957. In the 1950s and 1960s he appeared on TV and he was singing in nightclubs into the 1970s.

Mary Poppins. Popular American musical film of 1964 based on the classic children's book by P. L. Travers. Produced by Walt Disney, it combined live actors with animated cartoon characters, gave Julie *Andrews her first screen part as the highly mobile and sweet-singing Mary Poppins (after she had been passed over for the screen version of **My Fair Lady*) and featured the comic talents of Dick *Van Dyke in a dual role as chimney sweep and bank manager. Other parts were excellently played by David Tomlinson (*b* 1917), Glynis Johns (*b* 1923), Hermione *Baddeley, and Ed *Wynn. The lively score by Richard M. and Robert B. *Sherman, which won an Academy Award, included such whimsical delights as 'A spoonful of sugar', 'Supercalifragilisticexpialidocious', 'Chim-chim-cheree' (Academy Award for best song), 'Jolly holiday', and 'Let's go fly a kite'.

Maschwitz, Eric (*b* Birmingham, 10 June 1901; *d* Ascot, Berks., 27 Oct. 1969). British lyric-writer and librettist. Educated at Repton School and Cambridge University, he joined the BBC in July 1926 as Assistant Head of Outside Broadcasting, was editor of *Radio Times* 1927–33, and Director of Variety 1933–7. He left the BBC to become a scriptwriter for MGM in Hollywood 1937–8. During the war he served in the Intelligence Corps 1940–5, leaving the army with the rank of lieutenant-colonel. In 1958 he rejoined the BBC as Head of Light Entertainment on TV.

He provided the book and lyrics for many successful musicals including the film *Goodnight, Vienna* (1929, *m* George *Posford and Bernard *Grun); **Balalaika* (1936, Posford and Grun); *Paprika* (1938); *Magyar Melody* (1939, Posford and Grun); *New Faces* (1940, *m* Jack *Strachey)—'A nightingale sang in Berkeley Square' (*m* Manning *Sherwin); *Waltz Without End* (1942); *Starlight Roof* (1947, *m* George *Melachrino); **Zip Goes a Million* (1951, Posford); *Pink Champagne* (1946); *Carissima* (1948, *m* Hans *May); *Belinda Fair* (1949); **Love from Judy* (1952, *m* Hugh *Martin); *Happy Holiday* (1954); and *Summer Song* (1956). He wrote the lyrics for such popular standards as 'These foolish things' (under the name of Holt Marvell; *m* Jack Strachey) used in the revue *Spread it Abroad* (1936), 'Room 504', and 'The world is mine'. He was vice-president of the Songwriters' Guild and a director of the *Performing Right Society.

E. Maschwitz: *No Chip on My Shoulder* (London, 1957).

Mascotte, La. Operetta with music by Edmond *Audran, book by Alfred Duru (1829–89) and Henri Charles Chivot (1830–97), first produced at the Bouffes-Parisiens, Paris, 29 Dec. 1880. It was seen in Vienna in 1881 and in London at the Comedy Theatre, 15 Oct. 1881, English words by H. B. *Farnie, with Violet Cameron and Lionel Brough [199p]. It continued to gain worldwide popularity and was performed more than 1000 times in Paris alone during its first five years.

Massé, Victor [Félix-Marie] (*b* Lorient, Morbihan, 7 Mar. 1822; *d* Paris, 5 July 1884). French composer. He entered the Paris Conservatoire at the age of 12, studied composition under Halévy, and won the Grand Prix de Rome with a cantata, *Le Rénegat de Tanger*, in 1844. He travelled to Rome and Italy before taking the post of chorus-master at the Paris Opéra. In 1866 he became Professor of Composition at the Paris Conservatoire. He had his first stage production in 1842 and success with a one-act operetta, *La Chambre gothique* at the Folies-Dramatiques in 1849. Most of his work, though light, comes under the category of opera, but two were decidedly operettas—his neat little masterpiece *Les Noces de Jeanette* (1853 (*w* Michel Carré, 1819–72, and Jules Barbier, 1822–1901), with its ever-popular 'Nightingale song', which was staged at Covent Garden several times 1860–4, and *Mariette la promise* (1862). In his later years, as professor, he wrote several lighter works for amateur performance. His fame would probably be greater now had he kept away from grand opera and written more works with the easy grace and perfection of *Les Noces de Jeanette*.

J. G. M. Ropartz: *Victor Massé* (Paris, 1887). C. Delaborde: *Notice sur la vie et les ouvrages de Victor Massé* (Paris, 1888).

Mathis, Johnny [John Royce] (*b* San Francisco, 30 Sept. 1935). American singer. He joined Columbia Records in 1956 as a jazz singer but switched to ballads at the behest of producer Mitch *Miller. He developed a moody, haunting tone, reminiscent of Nat 'King' *Cole, that brought him a long list of hit recordings that included 'A certain smile' (1958), 'Misty' (1959), 'The shadow of your smile' (1960), 'The twelfth of never' (1961); continuing into the 1970s with 'I'm stone in love with you' (1974), 'When a child is born' (1974)—a No. 1 hit in Britain in 1976, and 'Too much, too little, too late' (1978). His numerous hits made him the first black American to become a millionaire.

T. Jasper: *Johnny: the Authorised Biography of Johnny Mathis* (London, 1983).

Matthews, Jessie Margaret (*b* London, 11 Mar. 1907; *d* London, 19 Aug. 1981). British singer, dancer, and actress. Born in poor circumstances, the seventh of a family of eleven, her father was a street trader. She showed early talent and at the age of 12 made her stage debut in the 1919 production of **Bluebell in Fairyland*. She had a small part in *The *Music Box Revue* at the Palace Theatre in 1923, and in the following year was in the chorus of **Charlot's Revue* at the Prince of Wales Theatre, going to New York with the production where she was understudy to the star Gertrude *Lawrence. The story-book thing happened: the star became ill and Jessie Matthews took over, with happy results.

Back in London she was given the leading role in *The Charlot Show of 1926*, in which she sang 'Journey's end'. Subsequently she was in **One Dam Thing After Another* (1927)—'My heart stood still'; **This Year of Grace* (1928)—'A room with a view'; **Wake Up and Dream* (1929; also in New York); **Ever Green* (1930)—'Dancing on the ceiling'. Of her performance in this James Agate said: 'When she is not dancing exquisitely, she shows how much variety may enliven the seemingly infantile.' By the 1930s she was also an established film star and was to appear in 17 films, 10 of them musicals. They made her into the only British musical star whose films were successful on both sides of the Atlantic, with her wide-eyed, innocent, yet captivating character, gossamer-light dancing, and shaky little voice.

Her main appearances were in *Out of the Blue* (1931); *The Good Companions* (1933); *Waltzes from Vienna* (1934); *Evergreen* (1934)—thus spelled for the film, and with 'Over my shoulder' added and the famous dance actually done on the ceiling; *First a Girl* (1936)—'Everything's in rhythm with my heart'; *It's Love Again* (1936)—'It's love again'; *Head Over Heels* (1937)—'May I have the next romance with you'; *Gangway* (1937); *Sailing Along* (1937); and *Tom Thumb* (1958). She returned to the West End stage in Jerome *Kern's *Wild Rose* (1942) and, after the break-up of her second marriage to Sonnie *Hale and some illness, continued to sparkle in *Maid to Measure* (1948) and *Sauce Tartare* (1949). She spent several years in Australia, then came back for a new career as Mrs Dale in the long-running BBC radio series *Mrs Dale's Diary*; and her acting career continued into the 1970s.

J. Matthews and M. Burgess: *Over My Shoulder: an Autobiography* (London, 1974). M. Thornton: *Jessie Matthews: a Biography* (London, 1974).

Maxina. A dance invented by Madame Low Hurndall, having some affinity with the Brazilian *maxixe, which came into favour in Britain, with special music written by Marguerite Boisson Ade and W. F. Hurndall, in 1917. Its music tended to be confused with the *habanera. In the end it was a modified form of the maxixe that caught on and gradually became the modern ballroom *tango. The maxina had tried to capture the flavour of the true maxixe but its steps were too complicated and it soon went out of vogue.

Maxixe. The oldest urban dance of Brazil and the first from that country to reach Europe. It is a ballroom dance for couples done in a moderate tempo. Its exact origins are uncertain, but one theory is that it derived from a comic Negro rural song and borrowed some of its musical character from the batuque. It had a simple joyfulness, rather like a child's dance. A very modified version reached the European ballrooms in the early 19th century but did not survive, appearing again in the early 1900s. By now it had taken on some of the characteristics of the *habanera, but the dance itself was still too ambitious for the average dancer. The maxixe gradually evolved into the modern *tango. A modern standard tune for the maxixe was written by Charles *Borel-Clerc and published in Paris in 1905 as 'La Mattchiche'.

May, Billy [William E.] (*b* Pittsburgh, 10 Nov. 1916). American composer, arranger, bandleader, and trumpeter. He began to learn the tuba but changed to trumpet on which he was self-taught, as was (so he claimed) his later arranging technique. He joined Charlie *Barnet's band as trumpeter-arranger in 1939 and one of his earliest scores, 'Cherokee', became the band's big hit, a best-seller, and a lasting classic of the swing era. After composing and arranging many hits for Barnet, he left after a year and joined Glenn *Miller, bringing a much more jazz-inflected type of arrangement into the band's repertoire. On the break-up of the Miller band he worked for Alvino Rey for two years and also took part in many small-group jazz sessions, proving a strong trumpet lead in both *Dixieland and *mainstream groups. He undertook studio work for the radio shows of Red Skelton, Bob *Crosby, Ozzie Nelson, and others, then graduated to Capitol Records as their musical director.

After being involved in many different facets of Capitol's activities (including such children's classics as 'Sparky's Magic Piano'), he was allowed to front a big band for recording purposes and his trademark of slurping saxes soon caught on. Having served its purpose as an ear-catcher, the gimmick was discarded and a series of LPs proved him to be one of the most imaginative, swinging, and witty arrangers around. Later he branched out into TV and films and was responsible for the superb Time-Life *The Swing Era* albums which re-created *big-band music in superb hi-fi recordings. He wrote many film scores in the 1950s and 1960s, and was a regular arranger for Frank *Sinatra, after which his activities were seriously curtailed by illness.

May, Edna [Pettie, Edna May] (*b* Syracuse, NY, 2 Sept. 1878; *d* Lausanne, Switzerland, 2 Jan. 1948). American actress and singer. She was a statuesque beauty who made a great impact on London when *The *Belle of New York* (which had not been a great success in its native city) caught the British imagination and became the first American musical to counter the British flood of exports. Much of her career was spent in England thereafter. She appeared in: *Santa Maria* (NY, 1896); *The *Belle of New York* (NY, 1897; London, 1898); *An American Beauty* (London, 1900); *The Girl From Up There* (NY and London, 1901); *Kitty Grey* (London, 1901); *Three Little Maids* (London, 1902); *The School Girl* (London, 1903; NY, 1904); *The Catch of the Season* (NY, 1905); *The Belle of Mayfair* (London, 1906); and *Nelly Neil* (London, 1907). She retired when she married in 1910, but returned to the stage for one week's charity performance of *The Belle of New York* at the Savoy in 1911.

May, Hans (*b* Vienna, 1880; *d* London, 1 Jan. 1959). Austrian-born composer and conductor. He studied music in Vienna, then settled in England in the early 1930s and worked as musical director in films and the theatre. He wrote the scores of *Der Dreibund* (1912); *Die schöne Blonde* (1918); *Miss Blaubart* (1922); *Die tänzende Stadt* (1935); *Carissima* (1948); and *Wedding in Paris* (1954). Film scores included *The Stars Look Down* (1939); *Thunder Rock* (1942); *The Wicked Lady* (1945); *Waltz Time* (1945), with Richard *Tauber, Ann Ziegler, Webster *Booth, and Albert *Sandler; *Brighton Rock* (1946); and *The Gypsy and the Gentleman* (1957).

Mayall, John (*b* Macclesfield, Cheshire, 29 Nov. 1933). British rhythm 'n' blues singer, guitarist, organist, and harmonica player. An enthusiast for the blues and blues records from early boyhood, he gradually acquired his own skills and first came into the music scene via the blues activities promoted by Alexis *Korner in the 1950s. He formed his group, the Bluesbreakers, in 1963, with Roger Dean (guitar), John McVie (bass), and Hughie Flint (drums). The group soon gained a high reputation in rhythm 'n' blues clubs, achieving its peak days when Eric *Clapton replaced Dean in 1965. His virtuosity was the highpoint of the LP, *Bluesbreakers*, issued by Decca in 1966. Clapton left in 1966 to found *Cream and was replaced by Peter Green, who added further creative power to the group. Green and McVie left to form *Fleetwood Mac and Mick Taylor played guitar for a while before moving to the *Rolling Stones. Others passed in and out of the group, which had not only been an inspiration to the British R & B scene but a nursery of talent. Mayall was continually experimenting with different combinations and instruments, notably in the jazz and blues fusion to be found in *USA Union* (1971). He went to America to record *Moving On* (1972) and finally settled there. He recorded several albums in the USA including *Notice to Appear* (1976) with Allen *Toussaint; and in 1982 there was Bluesbreakers reunion tour with Mick Taylor and John McVie.

Mayerl, Billy [Joseph William] (*b* London, 31 May 1902; *d* London, 25 Mar. 1959). British pianist, composer, and conductor. Son of a violinist, he studied music at Trinity College, London, and decided on a career in the lighter fields, appearing on the stage in variety in 1920. He played with the Bert Ralton band in 1921 and made his first London revue appearance in *You'd Be Surprised* (1923). In 1927 he appeared in *Shake Your Feet* and *White Birds* and he was with the famous **Co-Optimists* 1930–2. He became widely known and popular on radio and records with his lightly virtuosic playing, mainly exploiting his own music and having a great hit with 'Marigold' (1927), his theme tune, which sold more than 150,000 copies of the sheet music. He ran a piano school at Steinway Hall in the 1930s.

A prolific writer, he wrote scores for 20 stage shows including: *The Punch Bowl* (1924); *The London Revue* (1925); *Nippy* (1930); *The Millionaire Kid* (1931); *Between Ourselves* (1932); *Sporting Love* (1934); *Twenty to One* (1935); *Love Laughs* (with Noel *Gay, 1935); *Over She Goes* (1936); *Crazy Days* (1937); *So Long, Letty* (1937); *Runaway Love* (1939); and *Happy Birthday* (1940). He wrote a large number of piano pieces, including: 'The jazz master' (1925), 'Eskimo shivers' (1925), 'All-of-a-twist' (1925), 'The jazz mistress' (1925), 'Virginia creeper' (1925), 'Antiquary' (1926), 'Sleepy piano' (1926), 'Hollyhock' (1927), 'Jasmine' (1929), 'The Four Aces' suite (1933), 'Aquarium' suite (1935), 'Song of the fir-tree' (1938), 'Railroad rhythm'

(1938); and also many individual songs. During the Second World War he led his own band at the Grosvenor Hotel in Park Lane.

Mayfield, Curtis (*b* Chicago, 3 June 1942). American songwriter, singer, and guitarist. He produced his first hit at the age of 16—'For your precious love', then joined Jerry Butler in forming the vocal group *Impressions with whom he played the guitar. He was their pivot for 12 years, producing such hit material as 'It's all right', 'Hey little girl', 'Gypsy woman', and 'This is my country'. Eventually he took over leadership of the group, leaving in 1970 to pursue a solo career. He recorded with Buddah the album *Curtis* (1970) which put him in the forefront of the current soul scene, reaching a peak of creativity around 1972 with such songs as 'The makings of you', 'Move on up', and 'Beautiful brothers of mine'. He wrote the sound-track of *Superfly* (1972), which included the top-selling 'Freddie's dead' and continued with further sound-tracks such as *Claudine* (1974), featuring Gladys *Knight, *Let's Do It Again* (1975), and *Short Eyes* (1977). In the late 1970s he moved into the area of disco music, but returned to the soul scene in the 1980s.

Mayfield, Percy (*b* Minden, La., 12 Aug. 1920; *d* Los Angeles, 11 Aug. 1984). American singer, songwriter, and pianist. His father was a dancer and his mother a singer. He settled in Houston in the mid-1930s and was on the West Coast in the 1940s, becoming a pioneering figure of modern urban rhythm 'n' blues with the recordings he made for Specialty. In 1955 he recorded for Chess in Chicago, and wrote the standard 'Please send me someone to love' which was recorded by Joe Williams with Count *Basie, and others. He wrote a No. 1 hit for Ray *Charles in 1961, 'Hit the road, Jack'; and 'Hide nor hair' (1962). He recorded a number of albums for RCA, Atlantic, Sonet, and other labels, but his gentle approach kept him out of the top bracket as a singer.

Mayne, Clarice (*b* London, 21 June 1886; *d* London, 16 Jan. 1966). British singer. She made her first appearance on the music-hall stage at the Oxford on 13 June 1908, accompanied at the piano by her composer husband James W. *Tate who provided much of her material. They were generally billed as 'Clarice Mayne and That'. The songs she performed included: 'If I should plant a tiny seed of love', 'Ev'ry little while', 'I was a good little girl till I met you', and 'A broken doll' (all by Tate); others were 'Put on your tat-ta, little girlie' and her biggest hit, 'Joshu-ah'. She was also a very popular principal boy in pantomime with, to quote one devotee, 'a sublime figure, graceful deportment, a glittering smile, and an attractive husky voice'. Tate died in 1922 and she continued to work in variety on her own and toured the USA and South Africa, later appearing in revues. She retired from the stage in 1942 having married the comedian Teddy Knox of *Crazy Gang fame.

Maytime. The operetta which established Sigmund *Romberg in the musical theatre. With book by Rida Johnson *Young, based on a German operetta *Wie einst im Mai*, it opened at the Shubert Theatre, New York, 16 Aug. 1917 and was to become New York's biggest wartime attraction with a run of 492 performances. Romberg's score included such hits as 'The road to Paradise' and 'Will you remember'.

Set in New York in 1840, it had a conventional plot involving a poor little rich girl (Peggy *Wood) who loves an impoverished fellow (Charles Purcell) who is strongly disapproved of by her father. However, her family fall on hard times while he becomes rich, and it is left to their grandchildren (played by the same pair) to put love on its true course. The film version of 1937, starring Jeanette *MacDonald and Nelson *Eddy, had its story changed and additional Romberg songs with lyrics by Gus *Kahn.

Me and Juliet. Musical comedy with score by Richard *Rodgers and book and lyrics by Oscar *Hammerstein II, produced at the Majestic Theatre, New York, 28 May 1953 [358p], with Isabel Bigley as a chorus girl in love with the assistant stage manager (Bill Hayes), in an on- and off-stage romance that was rather lighter than the other big musicals in the Rodgers and Hammerstein tradition. Its songs included 'A very special day', 'No other love', 'It's me', and 'I'm your girl'.

Me and My Girl. Musical comedy with score by Noel *Gay and book by L. Arthur Rose (1888–1958) and Douglas Furber (1885–1961), staged at the Victoria Palace, London, 16 Dec. 1937. Its phenomenal run of 1646 performances was largely due to the infectious chorus number that was to provide wartime Britain with one of its chin-up anthems and a popular novelty dance—'The *Lambeth walk'.

The cast was headed by the perky Lupino *Lane who led them in its most popular item and through a typically old-fashioned musical comedy-cum-farcical story of a Cockney who turns out to be a long-lost nobleman, but gives up the high life to return to his Cockney sweetheart and his beloved Lambeth.

It was filmed in 1939, under the title of *The Lambeth Walk*, with Lupino Lane, Sally Gray (*b* 1916), and Seymour *Hicks; and was revived in 1941 [208p], 1945 [304p], and again in 1985, when its proletarian charms seem to have lost none of their effect and it achieved yet another long run.

Mechanical organ. An instrument with the mechanism that activates its pipes either hand- or power-activated, and ranging from the small portable model to elaborate and large dance-hall instruments. The earlier models up to *c*.1892 are generally referred to as *barrel organs, the notes being activated by pins set in a revolving barrel or cylinder. Later they mainly used a system of perforated cards similar to that used in the *pianola or *player-piano, invented by the Italian maker Gavioli. See under BARREL-ORGAN, DANCE ORGANS, FAIRGROUND ORGAN, STREET ORGAN.

D. Q. Bowers: *Encyclopedia of Automatic Instruments* (New York, 1970). G. Webb: *The World of Mechanical Music* (Newton Abbot, 1975).

Melachrino, George [Militiades, George] (*b* London, 1 May 1909; *d* London, 18 June 1965). British composer, conductor, singer, and musician. He entered the Trinity College of Music at the age of 14 and began his professional musical career four years later as a singer and musician, being one of the first artists to broadcast from 2LO at Savoy Hill. A proficient player of all reed and string instruments, he worked with the *Ambrose and Carroll *Gibbons bands before having the chance to form his own band at the Café de Paris just before the outbreak of war in 1939. As with many, it looked as though the war would cut short a promising career; in fact, it became Melachrino's great opportunity when he was selected to conduct the British Band of the Allied Expeditionary Force, known as 'The Orchestra in Khaki'; and regular wartime broadcasts elevated him to the top rank of British arranger-conductors.

After the war he operated two musical units, the full-scale George Melachrino Orchestra and the Melachrino Strings, whose delicately unique string sound proved ideally saleable in the mood music market of the 1950s, with numerous romantic albums becoming best-sellers on the Decca, HMV, and RCA labels. He appeared with his full orchestra in *Starlight Roof* (1947) at the London Hippodrome, the show which introduced Julie *Andrews. He was also head of an entertainment organization and provided stage shows for MGM's Empire cinema in the early and mid-1950s. He composed many light orchestral works including his theme-tune 'First rhapsody'.

Melody Maker. British journal devoted to dance and popular music. It began in January 1926 as the house magazine of the music-publishers Lawrence Wright, but by March had become a thick magazine-type publication styling itself *The Melody Maker and British Metronome*, published from 19 Denmark Street and edited by Edgar Jackson (1895–1967). Jackson instituted a somewhat biased jazz column which improved in 1930 when it was taken over by Spike *Hughes; subsequently a jazz corner was run by Sinclair Traill (1904–81) and Max Jones (*b* 1917), but its jazz interests petered out in the late 1950s in the face of the pop invasion. The magazine was taken over by Odhams Press in 1928 and changed to a newspaper format in 1933, since continuing under other ownership. One of its longest-standing and most respected editors was Ray Sonin.

Melville, Alan (*b* Berwick-upon-Tweed, 9 Apr. 1910; *d* London, 27 Dec. 1983). British lyric-writer and author. Educated at Edinburgh Academy, he worked in his father's timber firm 1936–40, then joined the BBC as a writer and producer of feature programmes. He left to serve in the RAF 1941–6, during which time he still managed to write material that was used in the Ambassador revues and elsewhere. The 1940s saw him established as a leading revue writer, contributing to *Rise Above It* (1940); *Scoop* (1942); *Sky High* (1942); **Sweet and Low* (1943); *Sweeter and Lower* (1944); *Sweetest and Lowest* (1946); *A La Carte* (1948); and *At the Lyric* (1953). He wrote lyrics for **Gay's the Word* (1951); *Bet Your Life* (1952); *Marigold* (1959); *. . . And Another Thing* (1960). He was the author of many straight plays, books, and radio comedy series, and a regular broadcaster on radio and TV.

A. Melville: *Merely Melville* (London, 1970).

Memphis Slim [Chatman, Peter] (*b* Memphis, Tenn., 3 Sept. 1915; *d* Paris, 24 Feb. 1988). American singer and pianist. Blues-shouting black singer who started his musical career at the age of 15. He played with Washboard Sam and Sonny Boy Williamson, toured the Southern states, then settled in Chicago in 1939 where he became a leading figure in the school of Chicago urban blues singers; making his mark with his recording of 'Beer drinking woman' in 1940. Prominent in the rhythm 'n' blues field in the 1940s and 1950s, he recorded prolifically and worked with bassist Willie Dixon. After considerable success in New York, the duo toured Europe and recorded such items as 'Nervous' and 'Rub my root'. Slim was also developing his talents for *boogie-woogie in the 1960s to bring about a revival of the music through albums made for Folkways. After a much-hailed performance at the 1959 Newport Festival he went to Europe and finally settled in Paris, working at the Trois Maillets club, appearing on TV, and occasionally working alongside visiting blues, jazz, and pop musicians. His was a prominent voice in the modern blues scene.

Mercer, Johnny [John Herndon] (*b* Savannah, Ga., 18 Nov. 1909; *d* Los Angeles, 25 June 1976). American lyric-writer, composer, and singer. After a local education and repertory acting, he went to New York in the late 1920s and worked with a music-publishing company for many years. His first performed and published song was 'Out of breath and scared to death of you' (*m* Everett Miller) which was used in **Garrick Gaieties of 1930*. By around 1934 he was recognized as one of the most successful and prolific of American lyricists, eventually to publish well over 1000 clever, witty and polished, expressively poetical, idiomatic songs in collaboration with such composers as Harold *Arlen, Rube Bloom, Hoagy *Carmichael, Gene *De Paul, Robert Emmett *Dolan, Gordon *Jenkins, Jerome *Kern, Matty *Malneck, Henry *Mancini, Jimmy *McHugh, André *Previn, Victor *Schertzinger, Arthur *Schwartz, Harry *Warren, Richard *Whiting, and many more.

He worked as MC and singer with Paul *Whiteman and appeared in the films *Old Man Rhythm* and *To Beat the Band* in 1935. A talented performer, with a dry Southern drawl that gave his singing a distinctively good-natured character, he became a popular singer in his own right, working with Benny *Goodman on radio in 1939, with Bob *Crosby, and various radio shows of his own in the 1930s. He was a co-founder of Capitol Records in 1942 and made many popular recordings for the label. He wrote lyrics for such shows as **Americana* (1932)—'Would'ja for a big red apple?'; *Walk With Music* (1940, *m* Carmichael)—'What'll they think of next?'; **St Louis Woman* (1946, *m* Arlen)—'Come rain or come shine', 'Legalize my name', 'Any place I hang my hat is home', 'I had myself a true love'; *Texas Li'l Darlin* (1949, *m* Dolan); *Top Banana* (1951; filmed 1954; *m* Mercer), starring Phil Silvers (1912–85); **Li'l Abner* (1956, *m* De Paul)—'Namely you', 'Jubilation T. Cornpone', 'The country's in the very best of hands'; *Saratoga* (1959, Arlen); *Foxy* (1964, Dolan); and *The Good Companions* (1974, Previn).

He contributed songs to many films, including: *Transatlantic Merry-Go-Round* (1934)—'If I had a million dollars' (Malneck); *Old Man Rhythm* (1935)—'I never saw a better night' (Louis Gensler); *To Beat the Band* (1935)—'If you were mine' (Malneck); *Rhythm on the Range* (1936)—'I'm an old cowhand' (Mercer); *Ready, Willing and Able* (1937)—'Too marvelous for words' (Whiting); *Varsity Show* (1937)—'On with the dance' (Whiting), 'Love is on the air tonight' (Whiting); *Hollywood Hotel* (1937)—'Hooray for Hollywood', 'I'm like a fish out of water', 'Let that be a lesson to you' (all Whiting); *Cowboy from Brooklyn* (1938)—'Ride, tenderfoot, ride' (Whiting); *Garden of the Moon* (1938)—'Love is where you find it' (Warren); *Going Places* (1938)—'Jeepers creepers' (Warren); *Naughty but Nice* (1939)—'Hooray for spinach' (Warren); *You'll Find Out* (1940)—'I've got a one-track mind' (Warren); *You're the One* (1941)—'You're the one' (Warren); *Navy Blues* (1941)—'You're a natural' (Schwartz); *Birth of the Blues* (1941)—'The waiter and the porter and the upstairs maid' (Mercer), sung by Bing *Crosby, Mary *Martin, and Jack *Teagarden; *Blues in the Night* (1941)—'Blues in the night' (Arlen), 'This time the dream's on me' (Arlen); *The Fleet's In* (1942)—'Arthur Murray taught me dancing in a hurry' (Schertzinger); *You Were Never Lovelier* (1942)—'You were never lovelier', 'Dearly beloved', 'I'm old-fashioned' (all Kern); *Star-Spangled Rhythm* (1942)—'That old black magic' (Arlen), 'Hit the road to Dreamland' (Arlen); *The Sky's the Limit* (1943)—'One for my baby' (Arlen), 'My shining hour' (Arlen); *True to Life* (1943)—'The old music master' (Carmichael); *Here Come the Waves* (1944)—'Accent-tchu-ate the positive' (Arlen), 'Let's take the long way home' (Arlen); *To Have and Have Not* (1944)—'How little we know' (Carmichael); *The Harvey Girls* (1946)—'On the Atchison, Topeka & Santa Fe' (Warren); *Here Comes the Groom* (1951)—'In the cool, cool, cool of the evening' (Carmichael); *Dangerous When Wet* (1953, Schwartz); *Top Banana* (1954, Mercer); **Seven Brides for Seven Brothers* (1954, De Paul); *Daddy Long Legs* (1955)—'Something's gotta give' (Mercer); *You Can't Run Away From It* (1956, De Paul); *Merry Andrew* (1958, De Paul); *L'il Abner* (1959, De Paul).

Other songs included: 'Lazybones' (1933, Carmichael), 'P.S., I love you' (1934), 'Goody goody' (1936), 'I'm building up to an awful let-down' (1936), 'Bob White' (1937), 'You must have been a beautiful baby' (1938), 'And the angels sing' (1939), 'Fools rush in' (1940), 'The strip polka' (1942), 'Skylark' (1942), 'G.I. jive' (1944), 'Laura' (1945), 'Satin doll' (1958, Ellington); and he was still producing hits into the 1960s when he collaborated with Henry Mancini on such film items as 'Moon river' from *Breakfast at Tiffany's* (1961); *Days of Wine and Roses* (1962)—title song; *Charade* (1963)—title-song; 'The sweetheart tree' from *The Great Race* (1965); *Barefoot in the Park* (1967)—title-song; and 'Whistling away the dark' from *Darling Lili* (1970). He was the winner of four Academy Awards.

B. Bach and G. Mercer: *Our Huckleberry Friend: The Life, Times and Song Lyrics of Johnny Mercer* (Secaucus, NJ, 1982). C. Brahms and N. Sherrin: 'Johnny Mercer' in *Song by Song* (London, 1984).

Mercer, Mabel (*b* Burton-upon-Trent, Staffs., 3 Feb. 1900; *d* Pittsfield, Mass., 20 Apr. 1984). British-born singer. Her father, a black American, died before she was born; her mother was a British music-hall singer. She became a dancer in music-hall and other stage shows as a young girl and was in the chorus of several musical comedies. After the First World War she went to Paris where she became an attraction at Bricktop's, 1931–8, the club run by Ada *Smith. She went to America in 1938 and became a hit at the Ruban Bleu club in New York. For a while she worked in the Bahamas returning to New York in 1941; at Ruban Bleu 1941–2, Tony's 1942–9, Byline Room 1949–55, New Byline 1955–7. Later she ran her own club. Usually with only a piano, she sang in a soft, subdued way with intelligent phrasing, using out-of-the-way songs from musicals and elsewhere and, although she never attained a big public reputation, became very much a singers' singer, greatly revered by other performers such as Frank *Sinatra, Lena *Horne, and Nat 'King' *Cole, who claimed to have benefited from her interpretative skills, and composers like Alec *Wilder who described her singing as 'a graceful *parlando*'; she became a cult figure of the 1970s. She was still singing in the 1980s, appearing at the Kool Jazz Festival in 1982, and she was awarded the American Medal of Freedom in 1983.

Merman, Ethel [Zimmerman, Ethel Agnes] (*b* Astoria, NY, 16 Jan. 1909; *d* New York, 15 Feb. 1984). American singer. Of German–Scottish extraction, she worked for some time as a secretary while trying to find an opening for her singing talents. She never had music lessons, but the stridently powerful qualities of her voice hardly needed any additional assets. George *Gershwin himself advised her against tampering with nature, and Cole *Porter described her in action as being like a 'brass band going by'. Making a definite mark on audiences in various nightclubs, she was auditioned by Gershwin who gave her a supporting role in his *Girl Crazy* (1930). She had only one song but as it happened to be 'I got rhythm' and she made the most of it, holding a high C for 16 bars in the coda, it was sufficient to put her on the road to fame. A brash and somewhat vulgar lady, she acted with the same vigour as she lived, and made a star role of whatever she tried, saying 'Broadway has been good to me—but I've been good for Broadway'.

This was born out by her successes in **George White's Scandals* (1931)—'Life is just a bowl of cherries', 'My song'; *Take a Chance* (1932—'Rise 'n' shine', 'Eadie was a lady'; **Anything Goes* (1934)—'I get a kick out of you, 'You're the top'; **Red, Hot and Blue* (1936)—'Ridin' high', 'It's d'lovely'; *Stars in Your Eyes* (1939); **DuBarry was a Lady* (1939)—'Friendship', 'Do I love you'; **Panama Hattie* (1940)—'Let's be buddies'; *Something for the Boys* (1943); her two great starring roles in **Annie Get Your Gun* (1946)—'They say it's wonderful', 'Anything you can do', 'Doin' what comes naturally', and **Call Me Madam* (1950)—'The hostess with the mostess', 'You're just in love'; *Happy Hunting* (1956)—'Mutual admiration society'; **Gypsy* (1959)—'Some people', 'Everything's coming up roses', 'Small world'; and in the revival of *Annie Get Your Gun* (1966) and stepping into **Hello, Dolly!* (1970). She also appeared in more than a dozen musical films including: *Follow the Leader* (1930); *We're Not Dressing* (1934); *Kid Millions* (1934); *The Big Broadcast of 1936* (1935); *Strike Me Pink* (1936); *Anything Goes* (1936); *Happy Landing* (1938); **Alexander's Ragtime Band* (1938); *Straight, Place and Show* (1938); *Stage Door Canteen* (1943); *Call Me Madam* (1953); *There's No Business Like Show Business* (1954); and aptly, as the voice of the Wicked Witch in *Journey Back To Oz* (1972).

E. Merman and P. Martin: *Who Could Ask For Anything More?* (New York, 1955). E. Merman and G. Eells: *Merman—an Autobiography* (New York, 1978). B. Thomas: *I Got Rhythm: the Ethel Merman Story* (New York, 1985).

Merrie England. Comic opera with score by Edward *German and book by Basil *Hood, first seen at the *Savoy Theatre, London, 2 Apr. 1902, with a distinguished cast of Savoyards that included Henry A. *Lytton, Walter Passmore (1967–1946), Robert Evett (1874–1949), and Rosina *Brandram. Its initial run of 120 performances hardly reflected the lasting popularity of this very English operetta which has wooed amateur dramatic societies ever since with its stirring songs—'Every Jack should have a Jill', 'The yeomen of England', 'O peaceful England', 'Dan Cupid hath a garden' ('The English rose'), from an eminently tuneful score, and its rustic dances. There were substantial professional revivals in 1934, 1944, 1945 [365p], and 1951; and Sadler's Wells took it on in 1960.

Merrill, Bob [Lavan, Henry Robert Merrill] (*b* Atlantic City, 17 May 1921). American composer and lyricist. After leaving school, he studied acting and then served in the US forces. He settled in California and was dialogue director of Columbia Pictures 1943–8 and casting director of CBS-TV 1948–9. He started writing popular songs in 1950, was in advertising 1950–4, then contracted by MGM as producer, composer, and writer.

He wrote scores and/or book for Broadway shows: **New Girl in Town* (1957); *Take Me Along* (1959); **Carnival* (1961); **Funny Girl* (1964, *m* Jule *Styne); *Henry, Sweet Henry* (1967); and **Sugar* (1972, *m* Styne). Other songs include: 'Candy and cake' (1950), 'If I knew you were comin' I'd've baked a cake' (1950), 'How much is that doggie in the window' (1950), 'Me and my imagination' (1950), 'My truly, truly fair' (1951), 'Sparrow in the treetop' (1951), 'Belle, Belle, my liberty Belle' (1951), 'We won't live in a castle' (1951), 'There's always room at our house' (1951), 'Walkin' the Missouri' (1952), 'There's a pawnshop on the corner' (1952), 'Barrels 'n' barrels of roses' (1952), 'What am I doing in Kansas City' (1953), 'Chicka boom' (1953) from *Those Redheads from Seattle*, 'Look at that girl' (1953), 'Ooh, bang, jiggily jang' (1955), 'Miracle of love' (1956), and 'A sweet old-fashioned girl' (1956).

Merry Macs, The. American vocal group, pioneering the modern close-harmony quartet singing in vogue at about the same time as the *Mills Brothers. Their individual sound came from the use of three similar male voices, without a bass, and one female; the original group being three brothers, Joe, Ted, and Judd McMichael, who began in 1931 as the Personality Trio, joined by Cherry Mackay in 1934, when they changed their name to the Merry Macs. They became known on radio and toured with the Jack *Hylton band in 1936. Settling in New York, they were featured on the Fred Allen Show 1938–40, with George Jessell 1939, and the Herbert Marshall Show 1941–2. They began to record in the 1930s, usually with a piano and guitar backing, and appeared in five films. Joe McMichael was killed on active service in 1944 and was replaced by Lynn Allen; and there were several female replacements before the group broke up in the 1950s.

Merry Widow, The see *Lustige Witwe, Die*.

Mersey beat. The music of such groups as the *Beatles, *Gerry and the Pacemakers, the *Searchers, and the Swinging Blue Jeans; i.e. the Liverpool groups who made their mark between 1962 and 1965. What they produced was an anglicized form of *rhythm 'n' blues, with a swinging beat and clean harmonies. It was also referred to as the Liverpool sound.

Merson, Billy [Thompson, William Henry] (*b* Nottingham, 29 Mar. 1881; *d* London, 25 June 1947). British actor, singer, comedian, and composer. He first appeared on the variety stage in Birmingham in 1900, and toured as an acrobatic clown under the name of Ping-Pong. His first London appearance was at the Middlesex Music Hall in 1905, then in 1909 at the *Oxford. He appeared in the revue *Hullo, Tango* (1913); then in *Look Who's Here* (1916); *Hullo, America* (1918)—'Señora'; *The Whirligig* (1920); *Whirled into Happiness* (1922); *Brighter London* (1923); *The Whirl of the World* (1924); *Puss in Boots* (1924); **Rose-Marie* (1925), as Hard-Boiled Herman—'Hard-Boiled Herman', 'Shouldn't we'; and *Palladium Pleasures* (1926). He also appeared in films and was manager of the Shaftesbury Theatre, 1926.

A small, lively character, with immense talent, he also wrote much of his own excellently amusing material, including the songs 'I'm setting the village on fire' (1910), 'I'm going away' (1910); 'The lighthouse keeper' (1910), 'The Spaniard that blighted my life' (1911), 'The gay cavalier' (1911), 'A prairie life for me' (1913), 'The photo of the girl I left behind me' (1916), 'On the good ship "Yacki-Hicki-Doo-La"' (1917), and 'Signora' (1919).

B. Merson: *Fixing the Stoof Oop* (London, n.d.).

Messager, André[-Charles-Prosper] (*b* Montlucon, Allier, 30 Dec. 1853; *d* Paris, 24 Feb. 1929). French composer and conductor. His childhood ambition to become a composer soon made him an able violinist and pianist and, as the family were not well off, he was able to get a post as an organist to allow him to study at the Ecole Niedermeyer in Paris. Later he studied with Saint-Saëns. In 1874 he was appointed organist of Saint-Sulpice, and during the next few years wrote several short ballets for the *Bouffes-Parisiens without making much of a mark. After winning the gold medal of the Société des Compositeurs for a symphony in 1876, he began his conducting career at the *Folies-Bergère in 1878 and was musical director at the Eden-Théâtre in Brussels in 1880. In 1833 he visited Bayreuth, but was not influenced beyond writing a Wagner pastiche; a clearer indication of his future being seen in his completion of *François les Bas-Bleus*, an operetta left unfinished by Firmin Bernicat (1843–83). It was produced at the Folies-Dramatiques in 1883 and encouraged him to write his own first operetta, *La Fauvette du Temple* (1885), which was quickly followed by the successful *La Béarnaise* in the same year, staged in London in 1886.

His writings continued with *Le Bourgeois de Calais* (1888); *Isoline* (1888); *Le Mari de la reine* (1899); the very popular *La Basoche* (1890); *Madame Chrysanthème* (1893); *Miss Dollar* (1893); *Mirette* (1894); *La Fiancée en loterie* (with Paul *Lacôme, 1896); *Le Chevalier d'Harmental* (1896); *Les P'tites Michu* (1897); and what was to become his most universally-known work, **Véronique* (1898). His busy life as a conductor continued at the Opéra-Comique 1898–1908, conducting the première of Debussy's *Pelléas et Mélisande* in 1902, and directing opera at Covent Garden 1901–7. From 1907 to 1915 he was a regular conductor at the Paris Opéra and directed the Société des Concerts du Conservatoire from 1908 until his death. He visited the USA in 1918, after which he continued at the Opéra-Comique and conducted the Ballets Russe in 1924. Meantime he continued to turn out his elegant comic operas and operettas, a worthy successor to *Offenbach with scores full of bright melodies and witty word-setting.

These included: *Les Dragons de l'Impératrice* (1905); *Fortunio* (1907); *Béatrice* (1914); *Monsieur Beaucaire* (London, 1919); *La Petite Fonctionnaire* (1921); *L'Amour masqué* (1923); *Passionnément* (1926); and *Coups de roulis* (1928). Beyond these he was the composer of many tuneful ballet scores, the most lasting being *Les Deux Pigeons* (1886); and of many elegant songs. He was married to his one-time pupil, the songwriter Hope Temple (1860–1928), composer of *drawing-room ballads.

H. Février: *André Messager: Mon maître, mon ami* (Paris, 1948). M. Augé-Laribé: *André Messager: Musicien de théâtre* (Paris, 1951).

Mexican Hayride. Musical comedy with music and lyrics by Cole *Porter and book by Herbert and Dorothy *Fields, produced at the Winter Garden Theatre, New York, 28 Jan. 1944, with a cast of 89, headed by the comedian Bobby Clark (1888–1960), of Clark and McCullough vaudeville fame, as a crook of many disguises, hounded by the police and pursued by the ladies. Highly priced, on account of its lavishness, it ran for 481 performances and had one or two good Porter numbers like 'I love you', 'There must be someone for me', and 'Count your blessings'. A filmed version of 1948 starred Bud Abbott and Lou Costello.

Meyer, George W. (*b* Boston, 1 Jan. 1884; *d* New York, 28 Aug. 1959). American composer. The creator of the ever-popular 'For me and my girl' started his working life as an electrician, tried accountancy, and, when his family moved to New York, worked for a while with an oculist. Until about 1909 he regarded his self-taught musical gifts as merely a social accomplishment, but in that year a song he sold did so well that he decided to become a composer, took a job as a song-plugger, and was soon a full-time writer. For some years his achievements were modest, but in 1914 he had a big hit with 'When you're a long way from home'. 'For me and my gal' (*w* E. Ray Goetz, 1886–1954) came three years later. He wrote music for *Robinson Crusoe Jr.* (1916)—'Where did Robinson Crusoe go with Friday on Saturday night?'; the revue *Dixie to Broadway* (1924)—'Mandy, make up your mind', 'I'm a little blackbird looking for a bluebird'; **Blackbirds* (1926); *White Birds* (1927); and contributed to films: *Footlights and Fools* (1929), *Drag* (1929), *Maybe It's Love* (1930), and *A Matrimonial Problem* (1931).

His songs included: 'I'm awfully glad I met you' (1909, *w* Jack Drislane); 'Lonesome' (with Kerry *Mills, 1909, *w* Edgar *Leslie); 'Chinatown rag' (1909); 'I've got your number' (1910, *w* Alfred Bryan, 1871–1958); 'A ring on the finger's worth two on the phone' (1911, *w* Jack Mahoney); 'That was before I met you' (1911, Bryan); 'That mellow melody' (1912, *w* Sam *Lewis); 'Bring back my Daddy to me' (1917); 'Everything is peaches down in Georgia' (with Milton *Ager, 1918, *w* Grant *Clarke); 'In the land of beginning again' (1918, Clarke); 'Beautiful Annabelle Lee' (1920, Bryan); 'Brown eyes, why are you blue' (1925, Bryan); and many more on into the 1950s.

Meyer, Joseph (*b* Modesto, Calif., 12 Mar. 1894; *d* 1988). American composer. He studied music in Europe, returning to the USA in 1908. He began a business career but then became a café violinist. After serving in the First World War he returned to the shipping business, but began composing and eventually took it up professionally.

He wrote songs for *Battling Butler* (1923); *Big Boy* (1925)—'California, here I come' (1924), 'If you knew Susie'; *Gay Paree* (1925); *Andre Charlot's Revue* (1925)—'A cup of coffee, a sandwich, and you'; *Sweetheart Time* (1926); *Just Fancy* (1927)—'You came along'; *Here's Howe* (1928)—'Crazy rhythm', 'Imagination'; *Lady Fingers* (1929)—' love you more than yesterday', 'You're perfect', 'An open book'; *Wake Up and Dream* (1929); *Jonica* (with Billy Moll, *b* 1905, 1930); *Shot the Works* (1931); **Ziegfeld Follies* (1934); and contributed to films: *Remote Control* (1930)—'Just a little closer'; *Those Three French Girls* (1930); *Way Out West* (1930); *Possessed* (1931)—'How long will it last'; **George White's Scandals of* 1935; and *This Is the Life* (1935). Other songs were: 'My honey's lovin' arms' (1922, *w* Herman Ruby (1891–1959)); 'Sugar plum' (1925, *w* B. G. *DeSylva); 'Clap hands, here comes Charley' (1925, *w* Billy *Rose and Ballard MacDonald); 'Falling in love' (1926, *w* Benny Davis); 'Whose arms are you in tonight' (with Charles *Tobias, 1932); 'Isn't it heavenly' (1933, *w* E. Y. *Harburg); 'I wish I were twins' (1934, *w* Edgar de Lange and Frank *Loesser), and 'Junk man' (*w* Loesser).

Mezzrow, 'Mezz' [Mesirow, Milton] (*b* Chicago, 9 Nov. 1899; *d* Paris, 5 Aug. 1972). American clarinettist, saxophonist, and bandleader. An early associate of the Chicagoans and the Eddie *Condon school of jazz, Mezzrow soon switched to a fervent admiration of black jazz and always tried to play in a genuine blues idiom. During the 1930s he led bands that included such figures as Benny *Carter, Pops Foster, and Teddy *Wilson. He led a rambling life, disjointed by drug-taking and -peddling and periods in prison, and was a peripheral figure until his association with Hugues *Panassié in 1938. Then he was responsible for getting together the fine sessions involving Tommy *Ladnier, Sidney *Bechet, Teddy *Bunn, and others, where his feeling for the blues and his general jazz ideals were fully and richly exploited. He went on to further fruitful collaborations with Bechet on his own King Jazz label. He appeared at the Nice Festival in 1948, toured with a top quality band, and settled in Paris in 1951 where he worked as a go-between and drug supplier for many prominent jazzmen like Louis *Armstrong.

Out of his beliefs and experiences he produced a very racy autobiography, *Really the Blues* (New York, 1946) (in collaboration with Bernard Wolfe), which captures the way-out spirit of jazz life to perfection. He composed 'Swingin' with Mezz', 'Dissonance', 'Sendin' the vipers', 'Blues in disguise', 'Really the blues', 'Gone away blues', 'Out of the galleon', 'My thoughts' (with Stuff *Smith), 'If you see me comin'' (with Teddy Bunn), 'Gettin' together', 'Comin' on with the come-on', and 'Revolutionary blues'.

Michael, George [Panayiotou, Georgios] (*b* Finchley, Middx., 25 June 1963). British composer and singer. With a schoolfriend, Andrew Ridgeley, he formed a group, the Executive, in 1979. They wrote their first successful songs in 1981, including 'Careless whisper', and formed Wham! The group, the song, and George Michael reached the heights of popularity by 1984 with 'Careless whisper' becoming a No. 1 hit in Britain, and in the USA in 1985. He achieved another top hit with 'A different corner' in 1985, after which the Wham! partnership ended. He recorded his first solo album and worked with Aretha *Franklin in the USA and their duet 'I knew you were waiting for me' was a top hit in 1987. He ran into some opposition with his 'I want your sex' which was featured on the soundtrack of the film *Beverly Hills Cop II* (1987); but by the end of the year his solo album *Faith* was No. 1 in both the UK and the USA and several of its tracks were also hits. He made successful tours of Japan, Australia, and Britain in 1988.

Middle of the road (MOR). Loose term that has come into use to cover all the popular music that is not in the current rock idiom and thus appeals to an older and middlebrow audience who still hanker after melody and harmony.

Middleton, Ray [Raymond] (*b* Chicago, 8 Feb. 1907; *d* 1984). American actor and singer. A rich baritone voice was used to good effect in such musicals as **Roberta* (1933); **Knickerbocker Holiday* (1938); **George White's Scandals* (1939); **Annie Get Your Gun* (1946); *Love Life* (1948); **South Pacific* (1950); and **Man of La Mancha* (1965).

Midler, Bette (*b* Paterson, NJ, 1 Dec. 1945). American singer and actress. Raised in Oahu, Hawaii, she studied at Hawaii University but decided on an acting career. In 1966 she moved to New York, achieved small parts in various productions, and joined the chorus of **Fiddler on the Roof*. By 1969 she had graduated to the leading female role, then appeared in *Salvation*, and started a career as a singer/entertainer with a varied repertoire of show tunes, 1930s pastiche, rock 'n' roll, and blues, with Barry *Manilow as her accompanist. She was well-known in cabaret by 1972 and made her first LP, *The Divine Miss M*, with Manilow, in 1973. This was followed by such varied albums as *Bette Midler* (1975), *Songs for the New Depression* (1976), *Broken Blossom* (1978), and *Thighs and Whispers* (1979). She starred in the film *The Rose* (1979), playing a part loosely based on the life of Janis *Joplin, with the title-song becoming a popular hit. She continued her film appearances with *Divine Madness* (1980) and *Jinxed* (1981), meanwhile earning various awards as one of the USA's favourite singers. By 1985 her musical career was being overshadowed by her work as a film actress.

R. Baker: *Bette Midler* (New York, 1975; London, 1980). B. Midler: *A View From a Broad* (New York, 1980).

Mikado, The, or *The Town of Titipu*. Considered by many to be the best of the Savoy operas, Arthur *Sullivan's score is full of unforgettable music ideally matched to W. S. *Gilbert at his most genially satirical. It is said that he was inspired to write it by a Japanese sword hanging on his study wall.

It opened at the *Savoy Theatre, London, 14 Mar. 1885, with Richard *Temple as the Mikado of Japan, whose son Nanki-Poo (Durward Lely), disguised as a wandering minstrel, has fled the court to escape the blandishments of the unattractive Katisha (Rosina *Brandram) and meets up with the eminently attractive Yum-Yum (Leonora *Braham). Flirting has been made a capital offence by the Mikado, and Ko-Ko (George *Grossmith) is condemned for becoming engaged to Yum-Yum. He is released, however, and in turn, now Lord High Executioner, condemns Nanki-Poo. He reveals his true identity to Yum-Yum and her friends Pitti-Sing (Jessie *Bond) and Peep-Bo (Sybil Grey) but they can think of no way out. The pompous Pooh-Bah (Rutland *Barrington), Lord High Everything else, creates an even bigger muddle, but in the end the Mikado proves merciful. There was a record run of 672 performances in London; and 450 at the 5th Avenue Theatre, New York, 19 Aug. 1885 with an American cast.

The Mikado has travelled better than most of the G & S operas, probably by virtue of an irresistible score that contains 'A wand'ring minstrel', 'Behold the Lord High Executioner', 'As some day it may happen', 'Three little maids from school', 'The sun whose rays', 'Here's a how-de-do', 'A more humane Mikado', 'The flowers that bloom in the Spring', 'Tit-willow', and many more gems. There have been numerous revivals and various tamperings have produced *The Swing Mikado* (1938), *The Hot Mikado* (1939), *The Black Mikado* (1975), and other variants. Film versions appeared in 1939, 1967, and 1982; and there have been several TV productions.

Miley, 'Bubber' [James Wesley] (*b* Aiken, SC, 3 Apr. 1903; *d* Welfare Island, NY, 20 May 1932). He started his career playing in New York clubs and toured with blues singer Mamie *Smith. In 1926 he was heard playing in a New York basement club by Duke *Ellington, who immediately asked him to join his band. There he was a pivotal voice, along with trombonist Joe *Nanton, in the new 'jungle'-style music that Ellington created for the clientele of the *Cotton Club; with what was then a novel growling style and great expertise with the mute. He worked with Ellington on the creation of such classic numbers as 'Black and tan fantasy', 'East St Louis toodle-oo', 'Doin' the voom voom', 'Blues I love to sing', and 'Creole love call'. A heavy drinker, he became an unreliable sideman and in 1929 was replaced by Cootie *Williams. He worked with Noble *Sissle and Zutty *Singleton, but by 1931 had left the jazz scene and was playing in revue orchestras. At the end of 1931 a show, *Harlem Scandals*, was built around a Miley-led orchestra by Irving Mills, but Miley contracted TB and died at the age of 29 while the show was being tried out.

Military Band. The name was first applied specifically to bands of musicians attached to various units of the armed services; later it became a generic term for any combination of woodwind, brass, and percussion playing in a similar idiom, thus distinguishing it from an orchestra on the one hand and a *brass band on the other.

Military music began to take on a definite shape at the time of the Crusades. The crusaders were probably surprised to find the enemy better equipped than they were: it was the Saracens who first introduced the kettle drum and the cymbals. Both sides used their minstrels, as they were then called, as a rallying point, their sound used to encourage their own troops and demoralize the enemy. Chaucer referred to them 'in the bataille blowen blody sounes'. Similar groups operated in civilian life and in the service of the nobility and royalty. King Edward III, who reigned 1327–71, employed a band made up of 5 trumpets, 2 clarions, 5 pipes, 3 waits (an early form of the oboe), and a drummer. By Queen Elizabeth's time the royal band included 10 trumpets and 6 trombones; and units continued to grow and develop.

The beginnings of the military band, as we know it today, came with the introduction of oboe bands introduced in France during the reign of Louis XIV. These were adopted by the French Army in the mid-17th century. By 1665 the Mousquetaires had 3 oboes and 5 drums attached to each company. In England, by 1678, 6 'hoboys' were attached to the Horse Grenadiers and a few years later the regiments of Foot Guards had oboe bands. The bandsmen were civilians and the bands were paid for by the officers out of their own pockets: even the bandmaster was a hired civilian. This state of affairs continued until the middle of the 19th century. The person mainly responsible for changing the situation was the Duke of Cambridge, a cousin of Queen

Victoria. Born in 1819, he made the army his career and in 1856, wise and experienced, he was appointed Commander-in-Chief. One of his first achievements was the establishment in 1857 of the Military School of Music, later known as the Royal Military School of Music. It has been suggested that his actions were prompted by the discordant sounds made by the British bands when they played 'God Save the Queen' at the review of the allied armies at Varna in 1854 after the Crimean campaign. Many regular bandsmen were serving as stretcher-bearers and the civilian bandmasters were not in evidence; the result was a greatly out-of-tune scratch band.

Whether this was the true reason or not, the school at *Kneller Hall in Twickenham was founded in 1857 and beneficial results were soon in evidence. One of the first was the adoption of the old 'Philharmonic' pitch, altered after the First World War to what became known as the 'Kneller Hall' pitch of a B♭ (flat) of 479.3 vibrations at 60° Fahrenheit. Other anomalies were gradually corrected and after 1872 all military bandmasters had to obtain the school's diploma. A year or two later their rank, pay, and emoluments were standardized. But it was not until 1877 that Kneller Hall itself was given government finance; until then it had been supported by the various regiments, who could subscribe or not and to the amount they chose. Kneller Hall was the model for the United States Army Music School established in 1911 at Fort Jay, its first principal being a Kneller Hall graduate, Arthur A. Cappé.

The size and shape of British military bands remained undetermined until a conference held at Kneller Hall in 1921 at which all the armed forces were represented. The size of a band was fixed at a minimum of 20 for indoor and 25 for outdoor performances and recommendations at a proportional level were made for these and larger units. In 1949 the regulations were revised and strengthened: 41 players were specified as the number for regimental and minor staff bands, 49 for the Household Cavalry bands, 67 for the Foot Guards and major staff bands, and 105 for the Royal Artillery Band at Woolwich. With the exception of the Guards these numbers included a proportion of boy musicians. The Women's Royal Army Corps band was fixed at 42, including some trainees. By now it was established that bandmasters of regimental bands held the rank of Warrant Officer and Directors of Music of other bands held commissioned rank. Over the years, and as the result of the altering shape of the forces during two world wars, there were continual modifications. Many units had bands for the first time, others had their previous allotment of two or three reduced through various amalgamations of units.

The Royal Navy's traditions developed on similar lines. At the time of the Napoleonic War flagships and a few of the bigger vessels often had bands aboard but, as with the army, they were there on an unofficial basis. The Admiralty first began to train musicians in 1863 and in 1868 established bandmasters with the rank of Petty Officer; but it was not until 1903 that the Royal Naval School of Music was formed, controlled by the Royal Marines and becoming the Royal Marines School of Music in 1950. Similarly, after the Second World War there were numerous cuts and reorganizations and by 1973 the number of naval and marine bands had been halved. The Royal Air Force formed its own School of Music at Uxbridge in 1949.

The patterns of the rise and development of military music in Europe have been similar to, though often in advance of, those in Britain. Most European countries have their excellent service bands and many good civilian bands still flourish. In England the civilian military band mainly gave way in the face of the popularity of the brass band movement. For a time a prominent survivor was the BBC Wireless Military Band, notably directed by B. Walton O'Donnell from 1927.

The spiritual home of the civilian military band today is the USA, where the great traditions set by such men as Patrick S. *Gilmore, John Philip *Sousa, and Frederick N. Innes, to mention but three, have encouraged the development of a number of highly skilled college bands. The military band has remained the favoured unit in the USA, a notable professional outlet for its development being in the *circus world where men like Merle Evans have been responsible for its growth. The United States Army Music School has turned out many fine instrumentalists and conductors; while the United States Navy Band and the Band of the United States Marines are acknowledged as being among the best in the world.

UK: H. G. Farmer: *The Rise and Development of Military Music* (London, 1912). G. Miller: *The Military Band* (London, 1912). H. E. Adkins: *A Treatise on the Military Band* (London, 1931; rev. 1945). H. G. Farmer: *Military Music* (1950). L. Winstock: *Songs and Music of the Redcoats: 1642–1902* (London, 1970). J. Cassin-Scott and J. Fabb: *Military Music* (Poole, 1978).

USA: R. F. Goldman: *The Band's Music* (New York, 1938). W. C. White: *A History of Military Music in America* (New York, 1944). H. W. Schwartz: *Bands of America* (New York, 1957; repr. 1975). K. Berger: *Band Encyclopedia* (Evanston, Ill., 1960). F. Camus: *Military Music of the American Revolution* (Chapel Hill, NC, 1977).

Europe: Brenet: *La Musique militaire* (Paris, 1925).

See also: Zealley and Hume: *Famous Bands of the British Empire* (London, 1926).

Military two-step. A dance which was a combination of waltz and march rhythms resulting in 6/8 time being its basis. The dance was invented by James Finnigan of Manchester, Master of Ceremonies at the Empress Ballroom, Blackpool, who popularized it in the early 1900s. The music originally used was 'Victoria Cross' by Gustav Howig, later replaced by the more popular 'Blaze away' by Abe *Holzmann.

Millar, Gertie [Gertrude] (*b* Bradford, Yorks., 21 Feb. 1879; *d* Chiddingfold, Surrey, 25 Apr. 1952). British actress and singer. She was born into a poor family and environment, but near to the Theatre Royal in Bradford where she managed to get into the children's chorus of *Red Riding Hood* in 1891. She performed in local halls, and in 1892 obtained her first professional engagement in *Babes in the Wood* at the St James's Theatre in Manchester. She continued her career in musical comedy and pantomime in the provinces, making her first London appearance at the Grand Theatre, Fulham, in 1899 in *Cinderella*. Within two years she was given her first West End chance in *The *Toreador* (1901) and was soon to become the star of the *Gaiety Theatre where she remained for the next seven years, appearing in *The Orchid* (1903), *The Spring Chicken* (1905), *The New Aladdin* (1906), and *The Girls of Gottenberg* (1907). She went to the Hicks Theatre to appear in *The Waltz Dream* (1908) and to New York to appear at the Knickerbocker Theatre in *The Girls of Gottenberg*.

She returned to the Gaiety in her greatest hit **Our Miss Gibbs* (1909) in which she sang 'Moonstruck'; and appeared at the Strand Theatre in *The *Quaker Girl* (1910). Many of these shows had scores by Lionel *Monckton, whom she had married in 1902; but when she was not given a part in his show *The *Arcadians*, and after other disagreements, she left him in 1909. Her partnership with the Gaiety, where she had become the pin-up girl of the early 1900s with her round cameo face, big eyes, saucy smile, and piping little voice, also ended and she continued elsewhere in **Gipsy Love* (1912); *The Dancing Mistress* (1912); *The Marriage Market* (1913); *A *Country Girl* (1914); *Bric-a-Brac* (1915); *Houp-La!* (1916); *Airs and Graces* (1917); and *Flora* (1918). She retired in 1918 and, on the death of Lionel Monckton in 1924, she married the Earl of Dudley and lived at Himley Hall in Yorkshire until he died in 1932.

Miller, Alton **Glenn** (*b* Clarinda, Iowa, 1 Mar. 1904; *d* English Channel, 15 Dec. 1944). American bandleader, composer, arranger, and trombonist. After playing with Boyd Senter 1921–2 he attended the University of Colorado, but left to continue his career as a musician. He played on the West Coast, moving to Chicago in 1926 to join the Ben *Pollack band. He left Pollack in 1928 to freelance and arrange and recorded with many jazz groups. He was with Red *Nichols at various times 1929–31, also with Benny *Goodman and the *Dorsey Brothers and played in various theatre orchestras, then worked as arranger with Smith Ballew 1932–4, had a further spell with the Dorseys in 1934, and organized and played in Ray *Noble's American band in 1935, making some recordings with it under his name.

He formed his own first band in 1937 and recorded for Decca and Brunswick, but the band failed to make money and broke up the same year. In 1938 he formed a new band, at the same time evolving a novel reed sound with high-register clarinet leading over the saxophone section. The Miller sound had attracted a considerable following by 1939. His own composition 'Moonlight serenade' (which became his signature tune), originally written as an exercise, now became a nationwide record hit. This was followed in 1939 by 'Little brown jug' (his first million-seller) and 'In the mood' and, during the band's stay on the Chesterfield Show 1939–42, it continued with such hits as 'Pennsylvania 6-5000' and 'Tuxedo Junction' in 1940; and 'Chattanooga choo-choo' and 'String of pearls' in 1941. The featured vocalists were Ray Eberle (*b* 1919) and Marion Hutton (*b* 1919), and the band appeared in the films *Sun Valley Serenade* (1941) and *Orchestra Wives* (1942)—with 'I've got a gal in Kalamazoo' and 'American patrol' among the hits of 1942. Miller did much of his own arranging but also used the talents of Jerry *Gray, Bill *Finegan, and Billy *May. He disbanded the orchestra in 1942 to join the Army Air Force as a captain (later major) and direct the American Air Force Band which he brought to England. Miller embarked in a light plane for Paris to make arrangements for the band's European tour; and neither the plane nor its occupants were seen again.

The Miller band was probably the most popular dance band in the USA and its sound held an emotional wartime appeal for listeners all over Europe and the rest of the world. Its popularity has never waned. A film of his life, *The Glenn Miller Story*, with James Stewart (*b* 1908) as Miller and June *Allyson (*b* 1917) as his wife, was made in 1954.

J. Flower (ed.): *Moonlight Serenade: a Bio-Discography of the Glenn Miller Civilian Band* (New Rochelle, 1972). G. T. Simon: *Glenn Miller and his Orchestra* (New York, 1974). J. Green: *Glenn Miller and the Age of Swing* (London, 1976).

Miller, Marilyn [Reynolds, Mary Ellen] (*b* Evansville, Ind., 1 Sept. 1898; *d* New York, 7 Apr. 1936). American actress, singer, and dancer. She began her career in vaudeville in a family act. For the next 10 years she toured the world before becoming the toast of New York in the 1920s and one of the greatest attractions of the American musical stage, particularly renowned as a dancer. She appeared in *Shubert and *Ziegfeld revues: *The *Passing Show* (1914, 1915, and 1917); *The Show of Wonders* (1916); *Fancy Free* (1918); **Ziegfeld Follies* (1918 and 1919); in **Sally* (1920)—in which she sang *Kern's 'Look for the silver lining' and 'Wild rose'; **Sunny* (1925)—'Who?'; **Rosalie* (1928); *Smiles* (1930); and in **As Thousands Cheer* (1933)—'Easter parade'. In the film of her life, *Look For the Silver Lining* (1949), she was played by June Haver (*b* 1926).

W. G. Harris: *The Other Marilyn: a Biography of Marilyn Miller* (New York, 1985).

Miller, Mitch [Mitchell William] (*b* Rochester, NY, 4 July 1911). American conductor and record producer. He studied at the Eastman School of Music and worked as an oboist in various orchestras. For a time he was with CBS, then worked with André

*Kostelanetz and other large light orchestras. He became producer for Keynote, Mercury, and eventually Columbia records where he became well-known either in his own right or accompanying singers like Guy *Mitchell in such hits as 'The roving kind' with their commercialized country effect. He made many LPs and worked on TV.

Miller, Roger (*b* Fort Worth, Texas, 2 Jan. 1936; *d* Los Angeles, 25 Oct. 1992). American country singer and songwriter. He began singing at the age of five and gradually found his style by listening to Hank *Williams. He worked as a ranch hand and served in the US Army in Korea. On his return he settled in Nashville and had his songs recorded by Ernest *Tubb and others, Ray Price making a hit of 'Invitation to the blues' in 1958. He began to record for RCA in 1960 and had success with 'You don't want my love' (1960) and 'When two walls collide' (1961). Moving to the Smash label he had hits with 'Dang me' (1963), 'Chug-a-lug' (1964), 'King of the road' (1965), 'Husbands and wives' (1966), 'Walkin' in the sunshine' (1967), and 'Little green apples' (1968); becoming one of the most successful pop country singers of the 1960s and winning six Grammy awards in 1965 alone. He continued with less success in the 1970s on the Mercury and Columbia labels. He wrote the score of *Big River* (a musical adaptation of *Huckleberry Finn*) in 1985.

Millinder, Lucky [Lucius] (*b* Anniston, Ala., 8 Aug. 1900; *d* New York, 28 Sept. 1966). American bandleader. Although not an active musician himself, he led some fine hot bands starting with his first in New York in 1917. He worked as an MC in the 1920s, coming to prominence in 1933 as leader of the Mills Blue Rhythm Band, going on into 1938. He had a flair for choosing good musicians. He put together another good band in the 1940s with a strong blues flavour, featuring for a time the gospel singer Rosetta *Tharpe and Wynonie Harris (1915–69). He was active as a bandleader until 1952.

Millöcker, Karl (*b* Vienna, 29 Apr. 1842; *d* Baden-bei-Wien, 31 Dec. 1899). Austrian composer and conductor. It was intended that he should follow his father by becoming a goldsmith, but he became interested in music, learned to play the flute, and went to the Conservatory of the Gesellschaft der Musikfreunde in Vienna. By the age of 16 he was playing in the orchestra of the Josefstadt Theater. He was encouraged by Franz von *Suppé who helped him to get his first post as Kapellmeister at the Landstheater in Graz, where he composed and produced his first operettas. He became conductor at the short-lived Harmonietheater and then, in 1869, conductor and resident composer at the famous Theater an der Wien, where he wrote his best-known works. Apart from 20 or so tuneful and well-turned operettas, he also composed incidental music for plays and a collection of piano pieces that were published monthly in *Musikalische Presse*. His style was aimed at a popular audience and his works became widely known outside Austria, especially his best operetta *Der *Bettelstudent* (1882).

His scores included: *Der tote Gast* (1865); *Die beiden Binder* (1865); *Die keusche Diana* (1866); *Die Fraueninsel* (1868); *Der Regiments-Tambour* (1869); *Drei Paar Schuhe* (1871); *Ein nagender Wurm* (1872); *Abenteuer in Wien* (1873); *Die Musik des Teufels* (1875); *Das verwunschene Schloss* (1878); **Gräfin Dubarry* (1879); *Apajune, der Wassermann* (1880); *Die Jungfrau von Belleville* (1881); *Gasparone* (1884); *Der Feldprediger* (1884); *Der Vice-Admiral* (1886); *Die sieben Schwaben* (1887); *Der arme Jonathan* (1890); *Der Sonntagskind* (1892); *Der Probekuss* (1894); *Nordlicht (der rote Graf)* (1896); *Der Damenschneider* (1901); and *Jung Heidelberg* (1904).

C. Preiss: *Karl Millöcker* (Vienna, 1905).

Mills, Florence (*b* Washington DC, 25 Jan. 1895; *d* New York, 1 Nov. 1927). American singer and dancer. Her fragile but effective talent (contained in a small form) were greatly admired by many fellow-artists (including Duke *Ellington) as well as by a growing public; so her early death, before she even got around to recording, was a great tragedy. She was a magical dancer and her voice was immensely appealing. She was seen in several all-black revues including **Shuffle Along* (1921); *Plantation Revue* (1922; London, 1923, as *Dover Street to Dixie*); *Dixie to Broadway* (1924), in which she sang 'I'm a little blackbird looking for a bluebird' and 'Mandy, make up your mind'; and **Blackbirds* (1926).

Mills, [Sir] **John** (*b* Suffolk, 22 Feb. 1908). British actor, singer, dancer, and director. In his early days he made his mark on the musical stage, dancing lightly and singing and speaking in that public-school manner that so many acquired in obedience to current fashion. He started his working life as a clerk and first appeared on the stage in the chorus of *The Five o'Clock Girl* at the London Hippodrome in 1929. After a Far East tour he appeared in London in *Charley's Aunt* (1930); then continued his musical appearances in *Cochran's 1931 Review* (1931); *Words and Music* (1932); *Give Me a Ring* (1933); **Jill Darling* (1934) from which he sang and recorded 'I'm on a see-saw' with impeccable diction; *Floodlight* (1937); *The *Follies* (1938); after which he became the fighting hero of many British films. Later in his career he became a greatly respected stage and screen actor, and was knighted in 1976. There was a return to the musical theatre in *The Good Companions* in 1974.

Mills, Kerry [Frederick Allen] (*b* Philadelphia, 1 Feb. 1869; *d* Hawthorn, Calif., 5 Dec. 1948). American composer, lyricist, and violinist. He studied the violin privately until he was 22, eventually becoming professor of music (in charge of violin studies) at the University of Michigan School of Music 1892–3. Later he followed a career as a musician and founded his own music school. A composing success with 'Rastus on parade' (1895) led his steps to New York in 1896 where he became a music-publisher and a very successful composer.

His writings included: 'Happy days in Dixie' (1896); 'At a Georgia camp-meeting' ('Georgia cakewalk') (1897); 'Impecunious Davis' (1899); 'Whistling Rufus' (1899); 'I know she waits for me' (1902, *w* A. J. Lamb); 'Meet me in St Louis, Louis' (1904, *w* Andrew B. Sterling); 'Red Wing' (based on Schumann's 'Merry peasant') (1907, *w* Thurland *Chattaway).

Mills Brothers. American singing group originally made up of a family of brothers from Piqua, Ohio: Herbert (1912–89), Harry (1913–82), and Donald (*b* 1915). They began to sing together in the late 1920s, mainly in Ohio, and had a WLW radio show in Cincinnati; then, with the addition of elder brother John Mills (1911–36) (who added a vocal imitation of the double-bass and played guitar), they went to New York in 1930, had their own network programme in 1931, and soon achieved great popularity through their recordings. The first of these was a hit version of 'Tiger rag' (1930) which demonstrated their instrumental imitations in *Comedy Harmonist style; and soon after they recorded their signature tune 'Goodbye blues', and such hits as 'Glow worm', 'Lazy river', 'Till then', 'You always hurt the one you love', and 'Yellow bird'. They developed a smooth and relaxed vocal style that was widely imitated and which they never needed to change in a long career that went on into the 1970s.

They appeared in the films *The Big Broadcast* (1932), *Twenty Million Sweethearts* (1934), and *Broadway Gondolier* (1935). When John Mills died in 1936, the father John Sr. (1882–1967) took over and was with them until he retired in 1956. They toured the USA and Europe and appeared on many radio shows including Bing *Crosby's, with whom they also recorded some classic items; also with Louis *Armstrong. Their biggest hit recording of all was 'Paper doll' (1942) which sold 6½ million copies and was No. 1 on the Hit Parade for 12 weeks.

Mingus, Charles (*b* Nogales, Ariz., 22 Apr. 1922; *d* Cuernavaca, Mexico, 5 Jan. 1979). American bass player and composer. He was brought up in Los Angeles where he studied bass and worked with Louis *Armstrong, Barney *Bigard, Kid *Ory, and Lionel *Hampton 1947–8. He was with the Red *Norvo trio 1950–1, then settled in New York in 1951 and played with the Billy *Taylor trio 1952–3. In the 1940s he was part of the modern jazz scene alongside Charlie *Parker, Thelonious *Monk, and Dizzy *Gillespie, and known as a composer of original jazz numbers that retained much of the beauty and melodic nature of the writer he most admired, Duke *Ellington, with whose band he played for a short time. These included such things as 'Goodbye porkpie hat' (a tribute to Lester *Young), 'Pithecanthropus erectus', 'The black saint and the sinner lady', and several ambitious jazz suites. Although he continually experimented in modernity and dabbled with atonality, he always kept a toehold in the idiom of gospel music and the blues with which he had consorted while young. A strong awareness of the jazz movement and black consciousness was expressed in his deeply scathing semi-fictionalized biography *Beneath the Underdog* (New York, 1971).

Minnelli, Liza May (*b* Los Angeles, 12 Mar. 1946). American actress and singer. The daughter of Judy *Garland and Vincente *Minnelli, she inherited a vibrantly neurotic personality that makes everything she does on stage or screen hypnotically interesting. She appeared in the off-Broadway revival of **Best Foot Forward* (1963), her first big part; in *Flora, the Red Menace* (1965)—'A quiet thing'; and **Chicago* (1975). Her film musicals include *In the Good Old Summertime* (1949); *Dangerous Christmas of Red Riding Hood* (1965); **Cabaret* (1972)—her biggest success, in which she sang 'Maybe this time', 'Mein Herr', 'Money, money', and 'Cabaret', and for which she received an Academy Award; *Journey Back to Oz* (1972); *That's Entertainment* (1974); *A Matter of Time* (1976); and *New York, New York* (1977), in which she sang the 1929 'Just you, just me' (*m* Jesse Greer, 1896–1970, *w* Raymond Klages).

J. R. Parish and J. Ano: *Liza!: an Unauthorized Biography* (New York, 1975). A. W. Petrucelli: *Liza! Liza!: an Unauthorized Biography of Liza Minnelli* (New York, 1983).

Minnelli, Vincente (*b* Chicago, 28 Feb. 1909; *d* Los Angeles, 26 July, 1986). American director. Born into an Italian theatrical family, he made his own stage debut at the age of four. His entrée into the professional theatre was as a stage designer, working in this role on **Earl Carroll's Vanities* (1931) and later continuing to design for all the stage shows he directed: *At Home Abroad* (1935); *The Show is On* (1936); *Hooray for What!* (1937); *Very Warm for May* (1939); and productions of the **Ziegfeld Follies* among them. In 1940, Arthur *Freed of MGM had become impressed with his stage work and invited him to Hollywood where he eventually came up with an auspicious first film in **Cabin in the Sky* (1943), followed by *I Dood It* (1943). In 1944 he made the film which many think of as his best achievement—*Meet Me in St Louis*, an elegant study of St Louis life in the early 1900s which starred Judy *Garland ('The trolley song') whom he married shortly after. She was in three other films he directed; while other stars he used included Gene *Kelly, Fred *Astaire, Ethel *Waters, Lena *Horne, Barbra *Streisand, and his daughter Liza *Minnelli.

His imaginative camera work and colourful approach were also seen in such films as *Yolanda and the Thief* (1945); *Ziegfeld Follies* (1946); *Till the Clouds Roll By* (1946); *The Pirate* (1948); *An *American in Paris* (1951); *Lovely to Look At* (1951); *The *Band Wagon* (1953); **Brigadoon* (1954); **Kismet* (1955); **Gigi* (1958); **Bells Are Ringing* (1960);

On a Clear Day You Can See Forever (1970); and *A Matter of Time* (1976). Most of his best work was to be found in his musical films.

F. Truchaud: *Vincente Minnelli* (Paris, 1966). M. Vidal: *Vincente Minnelli* (Paris, 1973). V. Minnelli and H. Arce: *I Remember It Well* (New York, 1974; Paris 1981). R. Campari: *Vincente Minnelli* (Florence, 1977). J. A. Casper: *Vincente Minnelli and the Film Musical* (South Brunswick, NJ, 1977). M. Marchelli: *Vincente Minnelli* (Milan, 1979).

Minogue, Kylie (*b* Melbourne, 28 May 1968). Australian actress and singer. Starting her career as a TV actress, she had parts in various soap operas: *The Sullivans* (1979); *Skyways* (1979); *The Hendersons* (1984); eventually joining the highly popular *Neighbours* (1986), in which she played the part of a girl with singing ambitions; Jason Donovan played her boyfriend. The part became reality when she recorded 'Locomotion', a No. 1 hit in Australia in 1987, followed by 'I should be so lucky', a No. 1 in Britain in 1988. Her superactive presentation, streamlined figure, and girl-next-door charms (not to mention *Neighbours* and its audience of 14 million) made her a top attraction worldwide.

Minstrel shows. In spite of its long history and its lasting effect on the development of popular music, the minstrel show has been inadequately documented and explained; partly because of the sensitive racial issues involved. Its very nature proclaims its American origin, but this form of entertainment flourished with equal popularity and impact in Great Britain; and although that was the limit of its international development, individual acts penetrated the rest of Europe and its music eventually affected the whole of the Western world. The reason for its uneasy and reticent history was that, while its literary and musical roots had Afro-American origins, its performers were mainly white actors and singers in black make-up whose delineation of Negro song, speech, and mannerisms was at best a second-hand impression usually done in a spirit of mockery and parody rather than with insight or affection. In spite of this, the minstrel show produced worthy material (in the songs of James *Bland and Stephen *Foster, for example) and many gifted exponents who were to expand their art in other fields; and it was, in retrospect, an important, even essential, link between the time of total obscurity and the gradual emergence of Afro-American music on its way to becoming the dominating strain of 20th-century popular music. The minstrel shows and spirituals gave America and Britain their first modified taste of an exhilarating new idiom that was to develop in its secondary stage as ragtime and finally as jazz. The semi-enlightened critic of today may criticize the minstrel movement for distorting and guying the black element (with all the unpleasant attitudes that the liberal use of the commonly employed word 'coon' implied), but at the time it was simply a reflection of the general attitude of the 19th century. If the minstrel show did nothing to dispel these biases, it at least opened a door for the emergence of black culture, even if it was by strangely contorted ways.

The force of the novel, exciting, and even disturbing new vein of popular music that the 'nigger minstrel' show unleashed, its songs, dances, and humour, swept across America in the 1840s (and Great Britain soon after); and it was to remain one of the most popular forms of entertainment for the next 50 years or so. It supplied America with the basis of an identifiable national art form. In Britain, which already had its own established musical identity, the minstrel show remained a polite form of middle-class entertainment, running parallel to the development of the lower-class music-hall; two areas that were to create both a demand and the response to that demand in the fast-growing popular music business. The British minstrel scene, using both visiting American and native-born troupes, followed the American pattern slavishly with a biased Uncle Tom-cum-Rochester image of the Negro character.

The minstrel show as a theatrical activity seems to have developed as a natural and unplanned phenomenon. The theatre was mainly a white arena, so a black character occurring in any play had to be played in imitation. In the primitive developing American theatre, with its rough and vociferous audiences, stock stage types grew as they did elsewhere. One stock character was (at least after 1865) the true Yankee, the brave and straightforward white American; another (generally comic) was the black slave. Black characters had been impersonated by white actors well before 1800, and in the 19th century various individual performers like Charles *Dibdin built national reputations on their blackfaced portrayal of Negro characters, frequently singing what purported to be Negro songs of the 'Possum up a gum tree' variety that were, as likely as not of Irish or some similarly doubtful ancestry. 'Zip coon' had associations with an Irish tune as did the important 'Jim Crow' introduced by the famous early minstrel Thomas D. *Rice.

The first identifiable minstrel troupe in America is generally accepted as being the Virginia Minstrels of 1843—a group of four, Billy Whitlock, Frank Pelham, Dan *Emmett, and Frank Brower—who proved an instantaneous success, with such songs as 'Jim crack corn' ('The blue tail fly'), probably by Emmett, and 'Old Dan Tucker'. They soon inspired a host of imitators. As early as 1844, a superior sort of troupe calling itself the Ethiopian Serenaders gave a command performance at the White House. Minstrel troupes tended to be localized in those early days, but within a decade several troupes had achieved national recognition; by 1853 *Buckley's Serenaders were travelling a regular circuit in the South. By the 1850s the minstrels had their own musical (if unacknowledged) laureate in Stephen Foster whose songs were particularly exploited by the minstrel Edwin P. Christy (1815–62) who had his first success with the Virginia Serenaders in 1843. Discovering Foster, he bought minstrel masterpieces such as 'Swanee River' or 'The old folks at home', and somewhat misleadingly published them under his own name. He has been duly maligned for this; but it initially came about through Foster's illusions of gentility and a desire not to mar the reputation of his more serious works by associating his name with so-called 'Ethiopian' songs. Christy and his minstrels probably did as much as anyone to make Foster's songs famous.

The original Christy Minstrels made their first appearance at Palmer's Opera House in New York on 27 Apr. 1846; becoming widely known during a subsequent season at the Mechanics' Hall in New York where they opened in Feb. 1847. The company survived for seven years, building up many famous minstrel performers and becoming the epitome of blackfaced minstreldom all over the world. Christy retired from the company in June 1854 owing to ill-health, and the company disbanded shortly afterwards. The outbreak of the Civil War so affected Christy that he committed suicide by jumping out of a New York hotel window on 21 May 1862.

J. W. Raynor and Earl Pierce, two members of the original Christy troupe, together with original members Anthony Nish and Tom Christian and seven other performers, purloined the name and took a Christy Minstrel show to London, opening at the St James's Theatre on 3 Aug. 1857 where they stayed for a fortnight. After this they were several weeks at the Surrey Theatre, followed by ten months at the Polygraphic Hall in King William IV Street. They became immensely popular with the London public. One of the songs they made famous was 'Nelly Gray', sung by Raynor. There followed a season at the St James's Hall from 11 April 1859 with Pony Moore joining the troupe in June, then a provincial tour, and a final season at the Polygraphic Hall which ended 2 Aug. 1860 when the Christy Minstrels disbanded and J. W. Raynor returned to America. Some members of the troupe stayed in England for many years.

From then on the name of Christy became synonymous with minstrelsy and everyone cashed in on his fame, despite the fact that Edwin P. never set foot in England. One of the most successful imitators was Montague's Christy Minstrels centred on St James's Hall, Liverpool. An impressive troupe of 50 performers, claiming to be the only 'genuine and original' Christy Minstrel show, they also appeared as the Queen's Minstrels, having performed before Queen Victoria at Balmoral on 16 Oct. 1868.

After the Christy heyday the most prominent New York troupe was Bryant's Minstrels, run by the brothers Dan, Jerry, and Neil Bryant from 1857 into the 1870s. It was for them that Emmett wrote 'Dixie'. They were the innovators of the grand 'walk-around', which moved through song and dance to the final chorus, their most famous being 'Down in Alabam' or 'Ain't I glad I got out de wilderness', a song transformed via many versions into 'The old grey mare' in the early 20th century.

There were now many keen rivals: the Moore & Crocker troupe with most of the original Raynor group in its ranks; the William Burton Christy Minstrels; Charles Christy's Minstrels, whose leader had the advantage of Christy being his real name though he was no relation to the original; the name surviving in such strange permutations as the Andy Merrilee's Armour Clad Amazon Female Christys in 1871 up to Birchmore's Christy Minstrels of 1901–2.

An interesting musical document was the *Ethiopian Glee Book* published in 1849 by Elias Howe of Boston (occasionally he published under the name of Gumbo Chaff) which was sponsored by the Christy Minstrels. It included such items as 'The dandy Broadway swell', 'Stop dat knockin'', 'Oh! Mr Coon!', 'Zip coon', 'The jolly darkey', 'Virginny's black daughter', 'Yeller girls', 'De nigger's banjo hum', 'De cullered cook', 'Dinah Doe and Mr Crow'—a revealing cross-section of typical American minstrel material.

The output of associated publications in America and England was immense; the number of troupes beyond counting. The monthly magazines, annuals, and songbooks were a fruitful spin-off together with souvenir china figures and other mementoes. In London the activities of the Mohawk Minstrels had powerful repercussions in the field of popular music publishing. The brothers James and William Francis, employees of *Chappell & Co., inspired by the success of the Moore & Crocker Minstrels at St James's Hall, formed their own troupe, the Mohawk Minstrels. By 1873 they were highly successful and lured the talented Harry Hunter from a rival group called the Manhattan Minstrels. Hunter disbanded his own group and joined the Francis brothers in 1874. In spite of the strong rival attraction of troupes such as the famous Moore & Burgess Minstrels from America, led by Pony Moore at the St James's Hall, they continued to thrive and in 1877, together with David Day from the publishers Hopwood & Crew, they set up the firm of Francis Bros. & Day in Oxford Street. Hunter, now working in music-hall management, joined them on the death of James Francis and *Francis, Day & Hunter became the leading publishers of both minstrel and music-hall songs. The *Mohawk Magazine* and 'coon' albums sold in their thousands.

By the 1870s and 1880s in America, black performers were appearing on stage as minstrels, somewhat confusing the situation by promulgating much the same sort of entertainment and attitudes as had been established by the blackface tradition. But as they were able to draw on more predominantly black audiences, the Uncle Tom aspect was modified and a more favourable and less parodic aspect was achieved in the songs of the black successor to Stephen Foster, the talented James Bland. By 1880 his style of song—'Carry me back to old Virginny' and 'Oh, dem golden slippers'—was running a course parallel to that taken by groups of spiritual performers such as the famous *Jubilee

Singers from the black Fisk University; and minstrelsy was a step nearer to being a genuine representation of Afro-American spirit and art. In the end, minstrel songs and spirituals became inextricably mixed. Whereas early British publications had been blatantly labelled 'coon' songs, there was a decently modified and respectable air about the substantially bound and sober-looking *Complete Christy Minstrel Album* published (*c*.1860) by Chappell.

By the turn of the century the American minstrel show had largely retreated once again to the South, flourishing in cities like New Orleans. The black entertainer had become a part of the Broadway stage in black musicals and revues and the wholesale exploitation of jazz had supplanted the gentle notes of the minstrel stage.

Perhaps, in the end, it was the gentle blamelessness of much minstrel entertainment that led to its historical neglect. In England, where there had been no emotive colour problem, the whole tone of the English minstrel show was good-natured, with a Victorian air of genteel refinement about their songs and publications, compared to the brash vitality of the music-hall equivalent. Minstrel annuals were illustrated in a most literary style with line engravings, by artists like Alfred Crowquill, of great sobriety. The minstrel show was a blameless middle-class entertainment in respectable venues like the St James's Hall, the Gallery of Illustration, and the Agricultural Hall in Islington. The music-hall (where E. W. Mackney and others like the ex-minstrel Eugene *Stratton continued a blackface tradition) was of a much commoner, vulgar, working-class strain. The minstrel show and music-hall moved through history side by side and died at the same advanced age. The middle-classes moved towards the cosy musical-comedy world of the *Gaiety and *Daly's. The minstrel era fizzled out before the First World War, but it was a strain that had spread its seeds far and wide and it had too deep roots to vanish entirely. There was a continuing thread in the seaside pierrot shows and the urban *Follies and *Co-Optimists. In the 1930s the now-established radio continued the minstrel tradition with the Harry S. *Pepper–Doris Arnold *Kentucky Minstrels* which achieved great popularity. And if anyone thought that the Second World War had wiped out all traces of blackface entertainment they were surprised by the astonishing TV and stage success of George Mitchell's **Black and White Minstrel Show*, which showed that vital melodiousness still had a place and blacking-up was still an acceptable theatrical activity.

E. LeR. Rue: *Monarchs of Minstrelsy* (New York, 1911). D. Paskman and S. Spaeth: *Gentlemen, Be Seated: a Parade of the Old-Time Minstrels* (New York, 1928). H. Reynolds: *Minstrel Memories: the Story of Burnt Cork Minstrelsy in Great Britain from 1839–1927* (London, 1928). C. Wittke: *Tambo and Bones: a History of the American Minstrel Stage* (Durham, NC, 1930; New York, 1969). H. Nathan: *Dan Emmett and the Rise of Early Negro Minstrelsy* (Norman, Okla., 1962; Detroit, 1972). R. C. Toll: *Blacking Up: the Minstrel Show in Nineteenth-Century America* (New York, 1974).

[There were also numerous books on running amateur and professional minstrel shows, many song collections, sketch and joke books, and various personal reminiscences; all now collectors' items.]

Minstrelsy. A loose term now covering most aspects of folk-music and ballad singing. In the early Middle Ages the minstrel was a professional entertainer, generally of a travelling kind, though sometimes attached to a court or a rich household. The musical connotation of the word 'minstrel' was not apparent until the 13th century. Minstrels, be they Welsh bards or French jongleurs, were vehicles for cultural exchange, the music of the wandering troubadours of France and the Minnesingers of Germany being brought to England by itinerant minstrels, and vice versa. The true minstrel was as much a creator as a performer, supplying the words and music of what we now loosely classify as folk-music. In the 16th century the role of the minstrel, in its courtly sense, declined and his place was taken by the wait, the street musician, and the busker. The name was only kept alive, in a romantic spirit, by writers looking for an acceptable name for folk-music, and possibly confused by its varying manifestations.

W. E. Duncan: *The Story of Minstrelsy* (London, 1907).

Music: A. E. Moffatt (ed.): *The Minstrelsy of England* (London, 1902). A. E. Moffatt (ed.): *The Minstrelsy of Wales* (London, 1906). A. E. Moffatt (ed.): *The Minstrelsy of the Scottish Highlands* (London, 1908).

Minton's Playhouse. New York nightspot at 210 West 118th Street, Harlem, founded by saxophonist Henry Minton in 1938. It was taken over in 1940 by bandleader Teddy *Hill (1909–78) who organized a house band made up of ex-members of his own band and others including drummer Kenny *Clarke and pianist Thelonious *Monk. In 1941 he started a celebrity night which found established jazz stars like Lester *Young, Ben *Webster, and Coleman *Hawkins playing alongside such modernists as Dizzy *Gillespie, Charlie *Christian, and Charlie *Parker. It was here that the progressive ideas that evolved into *bebop were mainly formulated and Minton's ever since has been regarded as the holy shrine of modern jazz.

Miranda, Carmen [Da Cunha, Maria do Carmo Miranda] (*b* nr. Lisbon, Portugal, 9 Feb. 1909; *d* California, 5 Aug. 1955). Latin American singer, actress, and entertainer. She was brought up in Rio de Janeiro, appeared on radio there in the 1920s and became well-known in Brazil during the 1930s. She was brought to the USA by Lee *Shubert in 1939 and her flamboyant dress and style soon brought her to international attention in shows like *Streets of Paris* (1939) and films like *Down Argentine Way* (1940). Known worldwide as 'The Brazilian Bombshell', she appeared in more than a dozen films 1941–53 and in the Broadway show *Sons o' Fun* (1941), continuing a career as a nightclub entertainer until she died of a sudden heart attack. She made many successful recordings of such items as 'Cuanto le gusta', 'The wedding samba', 'South American way', 'Chica chica boom chic', 'Tico-tico', and 'I yi yi yi yi'.

M. Gil-Montero: *Brazilian Bombshell: the Biography of Carmen Miranda* (New York, 1989).

Misérables, Les. Musical tragedy with score by Claude-Michel Schönberg (*b* 1944), libretto by Alain Boublil, and lyrics by Herbert Kretzmer, based on the novel by Victor Hugo, first produced in Paris at the Palais de Sports, 17 Sept. 1980. It opened at the Barbican Theatre, London, 30 Sept. 1985, transferred to the Palace Theatre from 4 Dec. 1985 and opened in New York at the Broadway Theatre 12 Mar. 1987.

The story follows the life of Jean Valjean, who, after being released on parole after 19 years in a chain gang, becomes a leader of the revolutionary movement relentlessly pursued throughout by police chief Javert. Memorably staged by director Trevor Nunn and the Royal Shakespeare Company in London, it was a gripping theatrical experience, more remarkable for being virtually an opera with a continuous three-hour musical score and no dialogue. Schönberg's music has been favourably compared with that of Puccini, a comparison that was even more valid with his subsequent score, *Miss Saigon* (1989), which again fused operatic conventions with the naturalism of the musical.

E. Behr: *Les Misérables: History in the Making* (London, 1989).

Miss Hook of Holland. British musical play with score by Paul *Rubens and book by Rubens and Austen Hurgon (1868–1942). It was produced at the Prince of Wales Theatre, London, 31 Jan. 1907, with Gracie Leigh (1875–1950), Isabel Jay (1879–1927), and G. P. Huntley (1868–1927) in the cast, and it ran for 462 performances.

A light story concerned the romantic life of Sally, the daughter of a Dutch liqueur manufacturer, and was woven around the theft of the recipe of his best-selling 'Cream of the Sky' whose effects were entirely beneficial. Several musical items achieved short-lasting popularity—'Little Miss Wooden Shoes', 'A pink petty from Peter', and 'Harwich to Hook'. It was taken to New York, Criterion Theatre 31 Dec. 1907, where it achieved 119 performances. There were revivals in London in 1914 and 1932.

Miss Liberty. American musical comedy with music and lyrics by Irving *Berlin and book by Robert E. Sherwood (1896–1955), produced at the Imperial Theatre, New York, 15 July 1949, where it ran for 308 performances. The story, set in New York and Paris in 1885, concerns the rival efforts of two newspapers to find the lady who posed for the Statue of Liberty, with much confusion over mistaken identities. Although not the best of Berlin, it had one or two good numbers like 'Let's take an old-fashioned walk' (sung by Eddie *Albert), 'You can have him' (a duet by Mary McCarty and Allyn McLerie) and the chorus 'Give me your tired, your poor' (*w* Emma Lazarus).

Mr Cinders. British musical comedy with score by Vivian *Ellis and Richard Myers (*b* 1901), book by Clifford *Grey and Greatrex Newman (1892–1984), opening at the Adelphi Theatre, London, 11 Feb. 1929, starring Bobby *Howes and Binnie *Hale, and running for 528 performances. It had a notable British hit in 'Spread a little happiness' which was sung and recorded by Bobby Howes; also 'I'm a one-man-girl' (Myers) sung by Binnie Hale, 'Ev'ry little moment', and 'On the Amazon'. It was filmed in 1934 with Clifford Mollison (1897–1986), Zelma O'Neal (*b* 1907), and the *Western Brothers. It was produced in Berlin in 1930 under the title *Jim und Jill*. There were revised versions in London in 1982 and 1983; and in Metuchen, NJ, in 1986.

Mistinguett [Bourgeois, Jeanne-Marie Florentine] (*b* Enghien-les-Bains, 1873; *d* Bourgival, 5 Jan. 1956). French singer and actress. Intended by her parents to be a concert violinist, she took up singing on the advice of the vaudeville actress Alice Ozy (*b* 1888). Beginning in the café-concert world, she made her stage debut in 1885 at the Trianon-Concert and moved on to conquer all the great music-halls of Paris and abroad—starring at l'Eldorado 1897–1907 and at the *Bouffes-Parisiens in 1908 where she first developed her Parisian kid act. In 1909 she created the 'valse chaloupée' with Max Dearly (1874–1943) at the Moulin Rouge, the notorious *Apache dance which inspired Van Dongen's famous painting. In 1912 she began a long and famous association with Maurice *Chevalier at the *Folies-Bergère, broken by the early war years but resumed in 1917.

Though chiefly a music-hall and revue artist, appearing at her best (and revealing her famous legs) in a series of revues 1919–23, Mistinguett also played in theatres and starred in a number of films. She went to the USA in 1924 where she introduced the Americans to 'Mon homme' by Maurice *Yvain which she had first sung in 1920. It was later taken up as 'My man' by Fanny *Brice in the **Ziegfeld Follies*. Her finest appearance was in the revue *Ça c'est Paris* at the Casino de Paris in 1926. She recorded prolifically for Pathé-Marconi and Odéon, including 'Mon homme' in 1938 and other songs she made famous, such as 'J'en ai marre' (1921), 'En douce' (1922), 'La Java' (1922), 'Ça c'est Paris' (1926), and 'C'est vrai'; written for her by such composers as Albert Willemetz, José Padilla, and Maurice Yvain.

Mistinguett: *Mistinguett: Queen of the Paris Night* (Paris, 1953). Mistinguett: *Toute ma Vie* (2 vols) (Paris, 1954).

Mitchell, Guy [Cernick, Al] (*b* Yugoslavia, 21 Feb. 1927). American singer. Brought up in Detroit, he was signed on by Warner Brothers as a child for his possible future potential but became known as a singer on San Francisco radio. After army service, 1946–7, he sang with Carmen *Cavallaro. He was signed up by Columbia Records in 1950 and had two great hits, accompanied by the Mitch *Miller orchestra, with 'The roving kind' (1950) and 'My truly, truly fair' (1951); continuing in this rumbustious vein with many hits throughout the 1950s—'Look at that girl' (1953) and 'She wears red feathers (1953) among them. He appeared in the films *Those Red Heads from Seattle* (1953) and *Red Garters* (1954).

Mitchell, Joni [*née* Anderson, Roberta Joan] (*b* McLeod, Alberta, 7 Nov. 1943). Canadian singer and songwriter. She became known as singer and guitarist in Toronto clubs and had a brief marriage from 1965 to the folk-singer Chuck Mitchell. Developing a distinctive folk-jazz style, she had hits with 'Big yellow taxi', 'Both sides now', 'Ladies of the canyon', 'Help me', and 'Raised on robbery'. She became known after Judy *Collins recorded some of her songs in 1967; her own first album was recorded in 1968, and she showed progressive and experimental boldness in each successive album, moving from a folk style towards a folk/jazz/rock amalgam (at one stage collaborating as lyricist with Charles *Mingus) with increasingly complex lyrics mainly concerned with her varied romantic life. She has been bracketed as a songwriter with Bob *Dylan and Neil Young, and is probably the most important woman songwriter of her era.

L. Fleischer: *Joni Mitchell* (New York, 1976).

Mlle Modiste. Comic opera with music by Victor *Herbert and book by Henry *Blossom first heard in Trenton, NJ, in 1905 and arriving at New York's Knickerbocker Theatre on 25 Dec. 1905. It contained such songs as 'The time, the place and the girl', 'Love me, love my dog', and, a song added in rehearsal for its star Fritzi *Scheff, 'Kiss me again'. It had 202 performances and was frequently revived in the next two decades.

Modernaires, The. American vocal group founded and led by Hal Dickinson in the mid-1930s, noted for its pioneering and advanced harmonic style. Starting as a vocal trio in Buffalo and working under various names, they became the Modernaires when featured with Fred *Waring in 1936, the other three men then being Ralph Brewster, Chuck Goldstein, and Bill Conway. The personnel, apart from Dickinson, changed regularly over the years.

The trio first became nationally known with the Charlie *Barnet band in 1936 and later on radio. They were with Paul *Whiteman 1938–40 and recorded with Glenn *Miller in 1940, joining the band in 1941 and appearing in the films *Sun Valley Serenade* (1941) and *Orchestra Wives* (1942). They can be heard on such items as 'Chattanooga choo-choo', 'I know why', 'I've got a gal in Kalamazoo', and 'Don't sit under the apple tree'. In the mid-1940s they became a quintet with the addition of Paula Kelly, were with the Bob *Crosby band in 1951, and were seen in the films *When You're Smiling* (1950) and *The Glenn Miller Story* (1954). Dickinson died in 1970, but the group remained active in the 1970s in connection with various Miller revivals.

Modern Jazz. Term first widely used in the early 1940s when jazz, following the bebop experiments of *Parker, *Gillespie, *Monk, and others, left behind the swinging beat and old-fashioned harmonies of jazz up to then, to follow 20th-century classical music into the world of atonality and experiment. As jazz itself has only become known to the world from around 1917, its 'modern' phase came after its first quarter-century. Since then the world has moved on another 40-odd years and much that was modern jazz is hardly modern any more. The term is still used out of habit, but commentators have now had to find new words like 'contemporary', 'avant-garde', and 'progressive' to label more recent evocations.

A. Morgan and R. Horricks: *Modern Jazz* (London, 1956).

Modern Jazz Quartet. Serious-minded American jazz group founded in 1952 by pianist-composer John *Lewis with Milt *Jackson (vibes), Percy Heath (*b* 1923) (bass), and Kenny *Clarke (drums), replaced in 1954 by Connie Kay (*b* 1927). Presenting a sober, dinner-jacketed image on stage, their music was exploratory and sensitive but held on to some earlier jazz elements. They recorded some fine albums, including such items as 'Django' and 'No sun in Venice', and continued as a group until 1974 when their demise was marked by the excellent *Last Concert* album. There have since been brief reunions.

Mole, Miff [Irving Milfred] (*b* Long Island, NY, 11 Mar. 1898; *d* New York, 29 Apr. 1961). American jazz trombonist and bandleader. He started his musical career playing the piano in cinemas, but switched to trombone at the age of 16 to play in a café band in Brooklyn. He developed a distinctively crisp, lightly swinging, inventive style that broke away from the traditional jazz sound and helped to establish the trombone as a solo instrument, gradually impressing his abilities with the Memphis Five and other *Dixieland-style groups of the 1920s. He was associated with similarly inclined jazz musicians like Bix *Beiderbecke and Red *Nichols and was to be heard on many New York-based recordings, often leading a group under the name of Miff Mole and his Little Molers. He was with Paul *Whiteman 1938–40, Benny *Goodman 1943, after which he led a Dixieland group at Nick's in New York. He was active in Chicago jazz clubs 1947–53, with Muggsy *Spanier and others, but his activities were curtailed after 1954 following a hip operation.

Molloy, James Lyman (*b* Cornalaur, King's County, Ireland, 19 Aug. 1837; *d* Henley-on-Thames, 4 Feb. 1900). British composer and writer. Educated in Ware and Dublin, he graduated in arts in 1858 and continued his studies at London University and in Europe. He was called to the English Bar in 1863 but never practised, working as secretary to the Attorney-General. In 1889 he was appointed private chamberlain to Pope Leo XIII. A successful author, he published songs, some with his own words, as early as 1865 and continued to write on an amateur footing throughout his life, in demand to provide songs for such as Maybrick, Santley, and Sherrington in the popular *ballad concerts of the time.

His earliest success was 'The old cottage clock', and 'The Kerry dance' (1879) was very popular, but his greatest and most lasting hit remains 'Love's old sweet song' (1884, *w* Clifton Bingham); it was introduced and popularized by Antoinette Sterling, who received a royalty for her efforts for many years. Others included: 'The carnival' (1892), 'Tomorrow will be Friday' (*w* Fred E. *Weatherly), 'The King's highway', 'London Bridge' (Weatherly), 'Polly', 'The postillion', and 'Punchinella'. He wrote operettas: *My Aunt's Secret* (1872, *w* Francis Burnand); *Very Catching* (1872); and *The Student's Frolic* (1877, *w* George Rose and Charles Lamb Kenney). He also arranged many traditional Irish songs and, with John Liptrot *Hatton, edited *Songs of Ireland* (London, 1889).

Monaco, James V. (*b* Fornia, Italy, 13 Jan. 1885; *d* Beverly Hills, Calif., 16 Oct. 1945). American composer. His family left Italy when he was a child and settled in Albany, NY. By the age of 17 he was playing the piano in cafés and had earned the nickname of 'Ragtime Jimmy'. He played for a period in Chicago but by 1910 was permanently based in New York and led a dance band there in the mid-1930s. He had published his first song, 'Oh, Mr Dream Man', in 1911, and had his first hit with 'Oh, you circus day' which was used in the revue *Hanky Panky* (1912). For the **Ziegfeld Follies* (1912) he provided the ever popular 'Row, row, row' (*w* William Jerome) and followed this with the immortal 'You made me love you' (1913, *w* Joseph McCarthy).

Other songs that he wrote were: 'I miss you most of all' (1913, McCarthy), 'What do you want to make those eyes at me for' (1916, *w* Howard Johnson and McCarthy), 'All that I want is you' (1920, *w* Joe Goodwin), 'Dirty hands, dirty face' (1923, *w* Grant *Clarke and Edgar *Leslie); and many more. In the 1930s he started writing for films, many starring Bing *Crosby, including *Doctor Rhythm* (1937)—'My heart is taking lessons', 'On the sentimental side' (*w* Johnny *Burke); *Sing, You Sinners* (1938)—'I've got a pocketful of dreams', 'Laugh and call it love' (Burke); *The Star Maker* (1939)—'Go fly a kite', 'An apple for the teacher', 'Sunbonnet Sue', 'I can't tell why I love you, but I do' (Burke); *East Side of Heaven* (1939)—'That sly old gentleman from Featherbed Lane', 'Sing a song of sunbeams' (Burke); *Road to Singapore* (1940)—'Sweet potato piper', 'Too romantic' (Burke); *If I Had My Way* (1940)—'April played the fiddle', 'Meet the sun halfway', 'The pessimistic character (with the crab-apple face)', 'I haven't time to be a millionaire' (Burke); *Rhythm on the River* (1940)—'Only forever', 'That's for me', 'Ain't it a shame about Mame?', 'Rhythm on the river' (Burke); also *Weekend in Havana* (1942)—'Romance and rumba' (*w* Mack *Gordon); *Stage Door Canteen* (1943)—'We mustn't say goodbye' (*w* Al *Dubin); *Sweet and Low Down* (1944)—'I'm making believe' (Gordon); *Pin Up Girl* (1944)—'Time alone will tell' (Gordon); and *The Dolly Sisters* (1945)—'I can't begin to tell you' (Gordon).

Monckton, Lionel (*b* London, 18 Dec. 1861; *d* London, 15 Feb. 1924). British composer. Son of Sir John Monckton, town clerk of the City of London, and Lady Monckton, who had been an actress, he was educated at Charterhouse and Oxford, where he acted and wrote for the Oxford University Dramatic Society. He was always rather a retiring sort of person and intended to pursue a career at the Bar, where he was in fact called in 1885. Impressing friends with a talent for songwriting, he was commissioned to write a song by the impresario George *Edwardes, who used the result, 'What will you have to drink?', in the burlesque *Cinder-Ellen* in 1891. He went on to write several successes but continued to shun the limelight. He was music critic of the *Daily Telegraph* for many years. Having occasion to write musicals which starred the vivacious Miss Gertie *Millar, he fell in love with her while she was appearing in his *The *Toreador*, and they were married in 1902. The marriage became an increasingly turbulent one and, when she was not offered a part in his musical *The *Arcadians*, she left him in 1909 but did not re-marry until after he died in 1924.

Monckton wrote some of the best light theatrical music that the English stage has known, shapely and tuneful and well suited to the words. He contributed to: *The *Shop Girl* (1894); *The *Circus Girl* (1896)—'A simple little string', 'The way to treat a lady'; *The *Geisha* (1896)—'The toy monkey'; and wrote full scores for: *A *Runaway Girl* (1898)—'Soldiers in the park'; *The Messenger Boy* (1900); *The Toreador* (1901)—'When I marry Amelia'; *A *Country Girl* (1902); *The *Orchid* (1903)—'Little Mary'; *The *Cingalee* (1904); *The Spring Chicken* (1905); *The New Aladdin* (1906)—'Grandmamma'; *The Girls of Gottenberg* (1907)—'Two little sausages'; *The Arcadians* (1909); **Our Miss Gibbs* (1909); *The *Quaker Girl* (1910); *The Mousmé* (1911)—'The temple bell'; *The Dancing Mistress* (1912)—'Fly away, Jack', 'When you are in love'; *The Belle of Bond Street* (1914); *Bric-a-Brac* (1915)—'Chalk Farm to Camberwell Green', 'Brighton'; *We're All In It* (1916); *Airs and Graces* (1917); *The Boy* (1917)—'It's the drum'; and *Good-Morning, Judge* (NY, 1919).

Monk, Thelonious Sphere [Thellous Junior] (*b* Rocky Mount, NC, 11 Oct. 1917; *d* Englewood, NJ, 17 Feb. 1982). American jazz pianist and composer. He had his first public performing experience in his local Baptist church and in the late 1930s played with a travelling evangelist group. He began to play occasional dates in New York and became house pianist at *Minton's Club in New York at the end of 1939. Here he came into contact with the leading spirits of the *bebop movement, Dizzy *Gillespie, Charlie *Parker, and others, although his eccentric individuality made him more a soloist than a group man. He played with Kenny *Clarke at Kelly's Stables 1942 and with Lucky *Millinder; was back at Minton's with a resident group in 1943 and played with Cootie *Williams and Coleman *Hawkins in 1944; led his own groups; and eventually formed a big band in 1959. During the 1960s he mainly led his own quartet, with Charlie Rouse (1924–88) on saxophone, and occasionally brought his big band together. He toured with Gillespie and Sonny Stitt with the Giants of Jazz unit, but appearances in the mid-1970s were restricted by illness.

In spite of his historic associations with modern jazz, it was not until the 1950s that the world recognized Monk's original genius, and even then there were many who found his unexpected switches of style and self-parody somewhat disturbing. His work had a special and personal flavour that does not link itself firmly with any school or group. He contributed many standard compositions to the modern jazz repertoire, including 'Straight no chaser', 'Round about midnight', 'Off minor', 'Misterioso', and 'Introspection'.

J. G. Jepson: *A Discography of Thelonious Monk and Bud Powell* (Copenhagen, 1969).

Monkees, The. Short-lived American pop group of the 1960s who partly arose as an American answer to the *Beatles, presenting a similar long-haired and respectably suited image and using good-quality material, supplied by such writers as Neil *Diamond. Their name was zealously promoted by NBC-TV, who featured them in a television series that proved to be more professional and entertaining than might reasonably have been expected. They found a following among a wide age-bracket. In action 1966–9, the original group was made up of British-born Davy Jones (*b* 1945) (vocal), Mike Nesmith (*b* 1942) (guitar and vocal), Peter Tork (*b* 1944) (bass and vocal), and Mickey Dolenz (*b* 1946) (drums and vocal). Their well-organized styling resulted in three No. 1 hits, all in 1967—'I'm a believer', 'Last train to Clarksville', and 'Daydream believer'. Nesmith left in 1969 to form First National Band, Davy Jones became an actor. There were brief revivals of the group 1975–6 by Jones and Dolenz, and in the 1980s by all except Nesmith.

Monkman, Phyllis (*b* London, 8 Jan. 1892; *d* London, 2 Dec. 1976). British dancer and comedienne. She made her first professional appearance at the age of 12 in the musical comedy *Lady Madcap* (1904), and later was in *The Girl in the Train* (1910) and *The *Quaker Girl* (1910). In 1913 she was engaged as principal dancer at the *Alhambra and was there until 1916 appearing in such shows as *Eightpence a Mile* (1913); *Keep Smiling* (1913); *5064 Gerrard* (1915); and *The *Bing Boys Are Here* (1916). Her light-footed dancing and bright personality made her a favourite of the troops home on leave and a popular postcard subject. She next appeared in *See-Saw* (1916); *Bubbly* (1917); *Tail Up* (1918); *Bran Pie* (1919); and *A Night Out* (1920). She joined the **Co-Optimists* in 1921 and was with them on and off for several years, marrying one of their founder-members Laddie *Cliff. After the end of the *Co-Optimists* she mainly appeared in straight plays.

Monnot, Marguerite (*b* Decize, Nièvre, 28 May 1903; *d* Paris, 12 Oct. 1961). French composer. She studied harmony and composition with her father, the blind organist and composer Marius Monnot; afterwards with Alfred Cortot and Nadia Boulanger. She gave her first public piano recital at the age of 11, beginning a career as a gifted interpreter of Chopin and Liszt which she abandoned to devote herself to composition. Her first hit was 'L'étranger', which was sung by Annette Lajon, but she became known chiefly for the songs she wrote with and for Edith *Piaf, whose highly individual interpretations of her simple and effective melodies proved to be an ideal partnership. Others were sung by Marie Dubas (1894–1972) and Yves *Montand, for whom she created songs full of gaiety and vivacity in contrast to the Piaf material. She wrote an operetta, *La P'tite Lili* (1952, *w* Marcel Achard, 1899–1973), in which Piaf and Eddie Constantine (*b* 1917) starred with great success at the ABC Theatre. Her biggest success of all was the internationally performed **Irma la Douce* (1956), one of the few musicals to come out of France in recent years and conquer the English-speaking world. Her songs included: 'Le fanion de la Légion' (1934), 'Mon légionnaire' (1935), 'Le petit monsieur triste' (1938), 'Je n'en connais pas la fine' (1939), all with words by Raymond Asso (1901–68); 'Y'a pas d'printemps' (1943, *w* Henri Contet, *b* 1904); 'Ma gosse, ma p'tit' môme' (Contet); 'C'était un jour de fête', 'J'ai dansé avec l'amour', 'Un coin tout bleu', 'Hymne à l'amour' (all *w* Piaf); 'Les amants d'un jour' (*w* Charles Dumont, *b* 1929); 'Mylord' (*w* Georges Moustaki, *b* 1934); 'La goualante du pauvre Jean' (*w* René Rouzaud, *b* 1905).

Monro, Matt [Parsons, Terry] (*b* London, 1 Dec. 1930; *d* Ealing, Middx., 7 Feb. 1985). British singer. He was a frequent amateur performer before joining the army which he left in 1953, deciding then to become a professional singer. He had to sustain himself with various jobs, including being a bus driver, before he had the opportunity to sing and record with Harry Leader. He was heard and liked by pianist Winifred *Atwell who helped him on his way and by the late 1950s he had his own programme on Radio Luxemburg and had appeared with Cyril Stapleton and the BBC Show Band. Taken up by record producer George *Martin, he achieved his first British hit with 'Portrait of my love' (1960), followed by 'My kind of girl' (1961). He specialized in film themes, having great hits with 'From Russia with love' (1963) and 'Born free' (1965). He was voted best male singer in 1965 and became increasingly popular in the USA. His last big hit on record was with 'Yesterday' in 1965 but he continued a flourishing career into the 1970s, living partly in England and partly in Florida.

Monroe, Bill [William Smith] (*b* Rosine, Ky., 13 Sept. 1911). American country guitarist, singer, and composer. The youngest of eight children, he grew up in a family where music was second nature and gained some of his early experience from accompanying his Uncle Pen (later celebrated in one of Monroe's songs), a well-known local fiddler. From the age of 18 he played in a band with his brothers Birch and Charlie and became popular on Chicago WLS radio. With Charlie (*b* 1903) he worked in a duo as the Monroe Brothers and had recorded for Victor Records by 1936, using material by the *Carter Family, Bradley Kincaid, and Jimmie *Rodgers. He organized his own band, the Bluegrass Boys, in 1938 and became nationally known through their regular appearances on the **Grand Ole Opry* programme from Nashville from 1939.

At this period he started singing and playing mandolin and was gradually developing the distinctive mandolin-guitar sound with the help of such players as Earl *Scruggs and Lester *Flatt who were in his band from 1945–8, and the high, clear vocal line. He recorded for Columbia, his original material including 'Mule skinner blues', 'Blue moon of Kentucky', 'I hear a sweet voice calling', and 'Will you be loving another man'. He left Columbia in 1949 and, with Jimmy Martin (*b* 1927) providing another distinctive vocal sound, recorded some of his best work—'Uncle Pen', 'Roanoke', 'Scotland', 'My little Georgia Rose', 'Walking in Jerusalem', and 'I'm working on a building'. The onset of the rock and roll era overshadowed the *bluegrass world for a while, but by the 1960s the great folk revival had renewed public interest in the music. As one of the founding figures and leading innovators of modern bluegrass music, he was elected a member of the Country Music Hall of Fame in 1970.

J. Rooney: *Bossmen: Bill Monroe & Muddy Waters* (New York, 1971). N. V. Rosenberg: *Bill Monroe and his Bluegrass Boys: an Illustrated Discography* (Nashville, 1974).

Monroe, Vaughn (*b* Akron, Ohio, 7 Oct. 1911; *d* Stuart, Fla., 21 May 1973). American bandleader, singer, trumpeter, and composer. He started playing the trumpet as a teenager and was Wisconsin State trumpet champion at 15. While still a student he had played in a number of professional bands, though his main ambition was to become an opera singer. But the depression years kept him working as a musician and eventually he formed his own band in Boston in 1940. With his first hit record in 1941 he discovered that his own stentorian baritone singing, though far removed from the normal dance-band vocal style, was a popular ingredient; and he continued in this vein until the 1950s. He became a solo artist and appeared as both singing cowboy and straight actor in various Western films, writing many of the songs he recorded.

***Monsieur Beaucaire*.** Romantic operetta with score by André *Messager and book by Frederick Lonsdale (1880–1954), based on a story by Booth Tarkington. It is set in Bath in the early 18th century, the days of Beau Nash. The Duc d'Orléans, son of the King of France, disguised as a barber, woos and wins the fair Lady Mary Carlisle despite the wiles of his rival, the Duke of Winterset.

It was first produced in England, with lyrics by Adrian *Ross, at the Prince of Wales Theatre, Birmingham, 7 April 1919, then in London at the Prince's Theatre, 19 April 1919, transferring to the Palace Theatre, 29 July 1919. The cast included the great Maggie Teyte (who recorded four songs from it), and it had 221 performances. It was seen in New York at the New Amsterdam Theatre, 11 Dec. 1919, had its first French performance at the Marigny Theatre in Paris, 20 Nov. 1925; and was revived at *Daly's Theatre, London, 16 Nov. 1931; becoming one of Messager's best remembered scores and finally reaching the Opéra-Comique in 1954.

Montand, Yves [Livi, Yvo] (*b* Monsummano, Tuscany, 13 Oct. 1921; *d* Semlis, France, 9 Nov. 1991). Italian–French singer, dancer, and entertainer. His family fled from the Mussolini regime and settled in Marseilles when he was a boy. Influenced by the dazzling art of Fred *Astaire, he made his stage debut in 1938 and made a successful appearance at the Alcazar singing songs made famous by Charles *Trenet, Maurice *Chevalier, and others; his first personal hit was with his lasting 'Dans les plaines du Far-West' written for him by Charles Hummel. He appeared in cabaret in 1944 with Edith *Piaf and rapidly became known for his eccentric dancing and his singing and had successes in the theatre—*De clowns par milliers* (1990); and in films—*Les Portes de la nuit* (1946); *Souvenirs perdus* (1949); *Le Salaire de la peur* (*The Wages of Fear*, 1953); *Napoléon* (1955); *Marguerite de la nuit* (1955); *Les Sorcières de Salem* (*The Witches of Salem*, 1957); and *La Loi* (1958). Taken up by Hollywood, he soon became an international star with appearances in films such as *Let's Make Love* (1960); *Sanctuary* (1961); *Aimez-vous Brahms?* (1961); *My Geisha* (1962); *Compartiments-tueurs* (*The Sleeping-Car Murders*, 1965); *La Guerre est finie* (1966); *Paris brûle-t-il?* (1966); *Vivre pour vivre* (1967); *Z* (1968); *Un soir, un train* (1969); *Le Diable par le guerre* (1969); *L'Aveu* (1970); **On a Clear Day You Can See Forever* (1970); *Le Cercle rouge* (1970); *Le Sauvage* (1976); *Clair de femme* (1979); and *Canon* (1983).

Like his hero Astaire, he had an ear for the quality song and an ability to sing them in an unsensational but totally effective way, among them 'Sanguine Barbara', 'C'est à l'aube', 'Comme un soldat', 'Grands Boulevards', 'Luna Park', 'Les feuilles mortes', and 'Le fanatique de jazz'; and many more interpreted with intelligent perfection. He married Simone Signoret (1921–85) in 1951.

Montgomery, Wes [John Leslie] (*b* Indianapolis, 6 Mar. 1925; *d* Indianapolis, 15 June 1968). American jazz guitarist. A self-taught musician, he earned a local reputation before becoming known with the Lionel *Hampton band 1948–50. He pursued a freelance career in Indianapolis and later Chicago where with his brothers, bass-player Monk Montgomery (1921–82) and vibraharpist Charles Montgomery (*b* 1930), he played and recorded as the Mastersounds 1957–60, then as the Montgomery Brothers 1960–2. He also led an organ trio 1958–9. The brothers moved to San Francisco 1960–1. He toured with a trio or quartet and visited Britain in 1965. His greatest success came with a series of jazz albums recorded with a big band 1964–8. Rated as the finest jazz guitarist since Charlie *Christian, his style was characterized by its rhythmic drive, parallel chording, unison octaves, and the use of his thumb rather than the more usual fingers or plectrum, which gave his playing a softer quality. Sometimes these trademarks became too insistent, but never hid his total brilliance.

Mood Music. The term was originally used in the days of silent films when producers would hire a small orchestra to perform on the set of a dramatic film to get their actors into the right mood for the scene to be played. Soon after, music was similarly used to put the audience into the right mood to enjoy what had been filmed. This sort of background persuasion then developed into the whole concept of *film music. After the Second World War many music publishers began to build up mood music libraries from which suitable accompanying music for films, radio, or TV were pre-recorded and were available for hire on record or tape for dubbing on to sound-tracks. The small users were thus saved the expense of commissioning music or hiring orchestras for their low-budget productions. In the case of newsreels it was a useful back-up service for the many occasions when a little background music was needed quickly.

Gradually, particularly in the record business, the term 'mood music' began to be applied to a new musical concept that came in with the advent of the long-playing record in the early 1950s. The idea was largely promoted by the American conductor Paul *Weston, who came out with a series of albums with such titles as *Music for Dreaming* and *Music for the Fireside*. It was followed up by Jackie *Gleason with his *Music for Lovers Only* and many sequels. In Britain the mood music albums came from such people as Ray *Martin, *Mantovani, Norrie *Paramor, Robert *Farnon, George *Melachrino, Stanley *Black, and Frank *Chacksfield. Considering the self-confessed nature of such albums, i.e. background music, a high standard of musicianship was put into their production. The unobtrusive qualities deemed necessary were, however, sometimes taken to excess in the lush string techniques and hackneyed songs of romance used, so that instead of putting over their professed aphrodisiac properties they could lead to boredom and somnolence. With the pop take-over of the 1960s, the mood music album began to lose its grip on the public, although older listeners still hold them in nostalgic affection.

The production of mood music has latterly gone back to the more functional and public role of providing consumer encouragement, as marketed by such companies as Muzak and Reditune. This calculated, commercial usage of music was a direct descendant of the wartime 'Music While You Work' conception—the BBC's successful notion of relaying a regular flood of music to factories to help allay boredom and encourage production. It was an obvious but, to some, infuriating step to use canned music as an obligatory background to eating and drinking and travel; so that nowadays music that can induce either a good or bad mood, according to the hearer's preferences, is to be heard in pubs, restaurants, railway stations, at airports and in flight; in offices and hospitals, supermarkets and boutiques; even permeating to lifts and toilets. The world, it seems, no longer wants to hear itself thinking or talking.

Moody Blues. British rock group founded in Birmingham in 1964 with the line-up of Mike Pinder (*b* 1942) (keyboard and vocalist), Graeme Edge (*b* 1942) (drums), Ray Thomas (*b* 1942) (vocal, harmonica, and flute), Denny Laine (*b* 1944) (guitar), and Clint Warwick (*b* 1949) (bass). Playing in the *rhythm 'n' blues idiom, they had a No. 1 hit with 'Go now' recorded for Decca in 1965. Laine and Warwick left to be replaced by guitarists Justin Hayward (*b* 1946) and John Lodge (*b* 1943) and moved into a world of concept albums, mystical and pretentious in character, fusing classical and rock music, as typified by the 1968 hit 'Nights in white satin'. Ambitious albums in this vein followed, such as *Days of Future Passed*, which were remarkable for their technical expertise. The group broke up in 1972 as its various members became involved in other groups or solo projects, but came together again in 1978 to produce such albums as *Long Distance Voyager* (1981) and *The Present* (1983).

Moore, Dudley (*b* London, 19 Apr. 1935). British composer, pianist, and actor. Educated in Dagenham and at Magdalen College, Oxford. After appearing in undergraduate shows, he made his first professional appearance at the Lyceum Theatre (as part of the Edinburgh Festival) in **Beyond the Fringe* (1960) for which he also wrote the music. He appeared in this highly successful and trend-setting revue in London in 1961 and in New York in 1962.

An accomplished jazz pianist, regularly performing and recording with the Dudley Moore Trio, he has continued an acting career in the revues *England, Our England* (1962) and *Behind the Fridge* (1973) and, in later years, as a somewhat unexpected heart-throb star of many British and American films. But he is best-known to the British public for a partnership (which began in *Beyond the Fringe* and later in TV satirical shows like *Not Only . . . But Also)* with Peter Cook (*b* 1937) as Pete and Dud. Among his many compositions is the incidental music to plays including *Serjeant Musgrave's Dance* (1959) and *The Caucasian Chalk Circle* (1962).

Moore, Grace (*b* Slabtown, Tenn., 5 Dec. 1901; *d* Copenhagen, 26 Jan. 1947). American singer and actress. A glamorous blonde soprano, she started her career on Broadway in *Hitchy-Koo* (1920); *Up in the Clouds* (1922); **Music Box Revue* (1923, 1924)—'What'll I do', 'An orange grove in California', 'All alone'; before she graduated to the Metropolitan Opera 1928–31. She then appeared in *The *DuBarry* (1932)—'I give my heart'. She had appeared in the films *A Lady's Morals* and **New Moon* in 1930; and now became a film star with a major success in *One Night of Love* (1934)—'One night of love'; followed by *Love Me Forever* (1935); *The King Steps Out* (1936)—'Stars in my eyes'; *When You're In Love* (1937); and *I'll Take Romance* (1937)—'I'll take romance'. Her life ended in a plane crash.

G. Moore: *You're Only Human Once* (New York, 1944).

Moore, Thomas (*b* Dublin, 28 May 1779; *d* Devizes, 25 Feb. 1852). Irish poet, author, singer, and composer. He was responsible for the rise and popularity of many pseudo-Irish songs of great charm and lasting quality. In many cases he took traditional airs, in others tunes of more recent origin, supplying them with richly romantic and effective poetic words which have themselves a timeless and traditional character.

It was while he was enjoying a popular vogue as a ballad singer in London that the first volume of *Irish Melodies* appeared in 1807. These, and others collected between 1807 and 1834, became very popular and included such lasting items as: 'The harp that once thro' Tara's halls' (1807), based on the traditional tune 'Gramachree'; 'Rich and rare were the gems she wore' (1808), based on 'The summer is coming'; 'Believe me if all those endearing young charms' (1808), based on 'My lodging is on the cold ground' (possibly by Matthew Locke); 'Let Erin remember the days of old' (1810), based on 'The red fox'; 'The minstrel boy' (1813), set to 'The moreen'; 'The last rose of summer' (1813), set to 'The last groves of Blarney' by Richard Millikens; 'Mary's tears' (1817), to music by Oliver Shaw; and 'Oft in the stilly night' (1818), set to a traditional Scottish tune. A new edition, retaining 'Sir John Stevenson's chaste and beautiful arrangements' was made, with a few modest improvements by J. W. Glover, in 1859; and in 1895 Sir Charles Stanford edited *The Irish Melodies of Thomas Moore: the Original Airs Restored*.

Moore himself wrote the music of such items as 'Love thee, dearest', 'When midst the gay', 'One tender smile', and 'The Canadian boat-song'; and his other writings included an opera *M.P. or The Blue Stocking* (1811) in collaboration with C. E. Horn, and a popular glee 'The watchman'.

S. Gwynn: *Thomas Moore* (London, 1905). W. Trench: *Tom Moore* (Dublin, 1934). S. MacCall: *Thomas Moore* (Dublin, 1936).

Moore, Victor Frederick (*b* Hammonton, NJ, 24 Feb. 1876; *d* East Islip, NY, 23 July 1962). American actor and singer. A short, rotund, and bumbling comic with a plaintive voice, he featured in many musicals, mainly in the role of the inept notable. He also toured in vaudeville and appeared in many films.

His musical appearances were in **Forty-Fve Minutes from Broadway* (1906); *The Talk of New York* (1907); *The Happiest Night of his Life* (1911); **Oh, Kay!* (1926); *Allez-Oop!* (1927); **Funny Face* (1927); **Hold Everything* (1928); *Heads Up* (1929); *Princess Charming* (1930); **Of Thee I Sing* (1931); *Let 'Em Eat Cake* (1933); **Anything Goes* (1934); *Leave it To Me!* (1938); **Louisiana Purchase* (1940); *Hollywood Pinafore* (1945); *Nellie Bly* (1946). His musical films were: *Dangerous Nan McGrew* (1930); *Heads Up* (1930); *Romance in the Rain* (1934); *The Gift of Gab* (1934); *Swing Time* (1936); **Gold Diggers of 1937* (1936); *Life of the Party* (1937); *Radio City Revels* (1938); **Louisiana Purchase* (1941); *Star-spangled Rhythm* (1942); *True to Life* (1943); *Riding High* (1943); *The Heat's On* (1943); *Carolina Blues* (1944); *Duffy's Tavern* (1945); and **Ziegfeld Follies* (1946).

Morales, Noro Sanabia (*b* San Juan, 4 Jan. 1911; *d* San Juan, 4 Jan. 1964). Puerto Rican composer, pianist, and bandleader. At the age of 15 he joined his father's Orquesta Hermanos Morales and took it over on his death. When the *rumba craze started in the USA, Morales went to New York in 1935, with his brother Esy, and formed a band which combined the authentic Latin American tradition with the jazz idiom. The *mambo craze that followed helped him to further popularity. He recorded extensively and appeared in theatres and clubs. His compositions included: 'Bim bam bam', 'Perfume de amor', 'Vamo a jugar la ruede', 'Vuelve', and 'If you only knew'.

Morath, Max (*b* Colorado Springs, 1 Oct. 1926). American pianist. Inheriting his talents from a mother who played the piano in silent cinemas, he learned to play and became interested in ragtime while working as a radio and TV announcer. He wrote and played in the TV series *The Ragtime Era* 1959–60 and a sequel 1961–2, then toured the USA with a show, *Ragtime Revisited* 1964–7. Subsequently he headed a unit called *Living a Ragtime Life*, which has been described as the nearest modern equivalent to a vaudeville show. He edited several collections of rags and associated music and recorded a number of LP albums on which he plays ragtime in a freewheeling style that may not always please the purist but which is possibly nearer to the real thing than some of the more academic approaches.

Morgan, Helen (*b* Danville, Ohio, 2 Aug. 1900; *d* Chicago, 8 Oct. 1941). American actress and singer. Singing in a melancholy torch style, she liked to perch on top of the piano while performing, creating a lasting fashion. She worked in clubs and spent many years in vaudeville; appeared in the chorus of *_Sally_ (1924); then was in *_George White's Scandals_ (1925) and *_Americana_ (1926). She is now mainly remembered for her memorable creation of the role of Julie in Jerome *Kern's *_Show Boat_ (1927, revival 1932)—'Bill', 'Can't help lovin' dat man'; and she was also in *Sweet Adeline* (1929)—'Why was I born', 'Don't ever leave me'; *_Ziegfeld Follies_ (1931); and *_George White's Scandals_ (1936). In the late 1920s she had her own nightclub. She appeared in several films, including the 1929 and 1936 versions of *Show Boat*; in *Glorifying the American Girl* (1930), *Go into Your Dance* (1935), and *Frankie and Johnny* (1936); and was herself posthumously the subject of a TV feature in 1955 and a film in 1957, both titled *The Helen Morgan Story*.

G. Maxwell: *Helen Morgan, Her Life and Legend* (New York, 1974).

Morgan, Russ (*b* Scranton, Pa., 29 Apr. 1904; *d* Las Vegas, 7 Aug. 1969). American composer, bandleader, singer, and multi-instrumentalist. He started his working life as a coalminer, but eventually became a cinema pianist. After breaking an arm, he took up the trombone as a means of physical therapy and this was to remain his main instrument, although he also played saxophone, guitar, vibraphone, and organ. His 'wah-wah' mute work on the trombone and his smooth glissandos became very much a feature of his band sound. He led an undistinguished band in 1923 but by 1925 was working as arranger for *Sousa and Victor *Herbert; later his arranging capabilities were used by the Detroit Symphony Orchestra, Paul Specht, Jean *Goldkette, the Capitol Theatre, *_George White's Scandals_, and various *Cotton Club revues. He first worked as a conductor for Station WXYZ in Detroit, followed by work for Brunswick Records and NBC.

He played piano with Freddy *Martin, then in 1936 formed his own band, originally as a backing group for Rudy *Vallee, which played in a smooth but individual society band manner. Morgan himself was a better musician than the band work allowed and recorded several jazz sides with Joe *Venuti and in a 1935 re-creation of the *Original Dixieland Jazz Band. He composed a long list of lightly sophisticated songs: 'Does your heart beat for me' (1936), 'Somebody else is taking my place' (1937), 'So long' (1939), 'Sweet Eloise' (1942), 'So tired' (1943), and 'You're nobody till somebody loves you' (1944) among them.

Moross, Jerome (*b* Brooklyn, NY, 1 Aug. 1913; *d* Miami, 25 July 1983). American composer. After studying at the Juilliard School 1931–2, and music at New York University, he became associated with the ballet and wrote many dance scores on American themes such as *Paul Bunyan* (1934), *Frankie and Johnny* (1938), and *The Eccentricities of Davey Crockett* (1946). He also wrote the music for a revue, *Parade* (1935). He went to Hollywood as an arranger and worked with Aaron Copland (*b* 1900) on the film *Our Town* (1940). His own film scores were to include *Close Up* (1948); *The Proud Rebel* (1958); *The Big Country* (1958); *The Jayhawkers* (1959); *The Mountain Road* (1960); *The Adventures of Huckleberry Finn* (1960); *Five Finger Exercise* (1962); *The Cardinal* (1963); and *The War Lord* (1965). Along with several operas, he wrote the Broadway musicals *Ballet Ballads* (1948) and the prestigious *The *Golden Apple* (1954)—'Lazy afternoon'.

Morris dancing. Traditional dances, developing from old pagan rites, using various accoutrements such as bells, handkerchiefs, swords, and sticks to frighten away evil spirits. They were danced (usually by men) generally in groups of six and, in their original spirit, to pipe and tabor accompaniment. It is likely that the name Morris is a corruption of Moorish, arising from the early custom of the dancers blackening their faces, the Moor being the prototype black man of earlier times (blackamoor); hence Moorish, Morisco, or Morris dancers. An earlier theory that the dance was actually originated by Moors has been discredited. Similar dances survive all over Europe and, in nearly related variants, all over the world.

Many villages in England have developed their own individual dances over the years which are performed at such special festivals as the annual wake or fair, on May morning, or at Whitsuntide. Dancing round the maypole, supposed to bring luck to the village, is a specialized form of Morris dancing. The Morris dancers appear with their special attendants; the piper or a fiddler, a ragman who looks after their wardrobe, a fool or jester, occasionally a treasurer, a cake-and-sword bearer, a moll or King and Queen of the celebrations. The most prominent figure is generally the Fool, who acts as a master of ceremonies and leader, sometimes referred to as the Squire or Rodney. The traditional music, like all folk-music, occurs in special variants in different counties, towns, and villages and has been diligently collected by such enthusiasts as Cecil *Sharp.

C. Sharp: *The Morris Book* (5 parts) (London, 1907–13). J. Graham: *Lancashire and Cheshire Morris Dances* (London, 1911). M. Karpeles: *The Lancashire Morris Dance* (London, 1929). A. Peck: *The Morris and Sword Dances of England* (London, 1970).

Morrison, Van [George Ivan] (*b* Belfast, 31 Aug. 1945). Irish singer, instrumentalist, and songwriter. A modern troubadour who has developed a distinctive personal style from a background of blues, soul, folk-music, and rock, he has become one of the recognized true artists of the pop era, often bracketed with Bob *Dylan. He left school at 15 to join the Monarchs, then formed a group, Them, which disbanded in 1966. He was heard by the American producer and songwriter Bert Berns (1929–67) who brought him to New York and helped him to compile his first album *Blowin' Your Mind* (1967), which contained a number of highly successful songs like 'Brown eyed girl'. After the sudden death of Berns in 1967 he recorded the album *Astral Weeks* (1968), now considered a classic with its haunting Celtic atmosphere and such lyrical items as 'Madame George' and 'Cyprus Avenue'. *Moondance* (1970) showed a stronger jazz influence, and a number of subtly varied albums in the 1970s, including the live rock programme, *It's Too Late to Stop Now* (1974), enhanced his growing reputation.

The first album of the new decade, *Common One* (1980), had such substantial items as 'Summertime in England' and 'Haunts of ancient peace'; while *Beautiful Vision* (1982) recaptured the mystical spirit of *Astral Weeks*, with such varied items as 'Cleaning windows', 'She gives me religion', and 'Dweller on the threshold'. He continued through the 1980s with work that never fell below the highest of standards, refusing to be drawn into the hype of the rock world and its thirst for publicity, each new album compounding the enigma.

R. Yorke: *Van Morrison: Into the Music* (London, 1977). J. Rogan: *Van Morrison: the Great Deception* (London–New York, 1982).

Morse, Ella Mae (*b* Mansfield, Texas, 12 Sept. 1924). American singer. She began singing in the Dallas area, worked with radio bands, and was briefly with Jimmy *Dorsey in 1939, before becoming known for her recording of 'Cow Cow boogie' with the band of Freddie Slack (1910–65), with whom she worked 1942–3. After this she worked as a solo singer and appeared on the Johnny *Mercer show 1943–4. She appeared in a few films in the 1940s, retired, then came back with a recording of 'The blacksmith blues' in 1952.

Morse, Theodore F. (*b* Washington DC, 13 Apr. 1873; *d* New York, 25 May 1924). American composer. He was educated at the Maryland Military Academy and later studied violin and piano. He began work as a clerk in a music-publishing house and started his own firm in 1898, sold it in 1900, but remained active in the publishing business until his death. Chiefly remembered as the man who published the Spanish–American War hit 'Goodbye Dolly Gray', he wrote two tunes that found long-lasting favour in the jazz world—'Down in Jungle Town' (1908) and 'Auntie Skinner's chicken dinner' (1911). He turned out a long string of hits in the vein of the early 1900s, now mainly forgotten; but one or two like 'Sweet morning glory' (1901), 'A wise old owl' (1903), 'Hurray for Baffin's Bay' (1903), 'Bobbin' up and down' (1913), and 'Hail, hail, the gang's all here' (1917) stir vague memories. The lyrics for the last two titles were written by his wife Theodora [Dolly] Morse (1890–1953) who wrote under the name of Dorothy Terriss until after the death of her husband. She also wrote the lyrics of 'Three o'clock in the morning' and 'Siboney'.

Mortimer. Well-known family of *brass band musicians and conductors. Fred Mortimer (*b* Hebden Bridge, Yorks., 1880; *d* Elworth, 20 June 1953) was interested in brass playing from boyhood and studied music and the cornet under the well-known conductor and teacher William *Rimmer. At 17 he was bandmaster of the Hebden Bridge Prize Band and soon adopted his personal style of conducting with the left hand so that he could play the cornet at the same time. In 1912 he became bandmaster of the Luton Red Cross Band, and, after serving in the First World War as bandmaster of the 36th Divisional Band, returned to Luton to make it, in 1923, the first southern band to win the National title. In 1925 he started his historic association with the Fodens Motor Works Band (founded 1902). He was the first to take charge completely as musical director and conductor and led it to a remarkable series of competition victories in the 1930s. All three of his sons were to serve with the band, the Mortimers giving 145 years of service to Fodens between them. He was an accomplished composer and arranger and in much demand as an adjudicator. He died in 1953 while conducting for the Coronation festivities in a London park.

His eldest son Harry Mortimer (*b* Hebden Bridge, 10 Apr. 1902; *d* 23 Jan. 1992) was given his first cornet at seven and was soon playing in the Hebden Bridge band. When Fred moved to Luton, Harry went with him and was in the Luton band 1913–24, with William Halliwell conducting, when it won the National championship. He moved to the Fodens band in 1924 and was with them until 1956, his great ability as a cornet player putting him at the top of the profession, a Louis *Armstrong of the brass band world, with a personalized and expressive style that would have been unthought-of in earlier days. He won the National cornet solo award in 1923, became principal trumpet with the Hallé and the Royal Liverpool Philharmonic orchestras from 1930 to 1941, and was Professor of Trumpet at the Royal Manchester College of Music 1936–40. He became professional conductor of the *Black Dyke Mills Band and led them to their famous hat-trick of victories 1947–9. From 1942 to 1964 he was Brass and Military Bands Supervisor at the BBC and from 1935 to 1970 musical director of the *Fairey Aviation Band. His recording activities were numerous, with special skill in handling mass bands shown in the many albums with the Men o' Brass ensemble, which combined the forces of the Fairey, Coventry (later Fodens), and Morris bands, and which he took to Canada in 1961. He continued to be a focal point of brass activities.

Two younger brothers, Alex Mortimer and Rex Mortimer were both well-known in the brass band world and both played, Alex on euphonium and Rex on B♭ bass, under their father at Fodens. Rex Mortimer became the musical director at Fodens in 1956, a worthy successor to his father, leading them to many victories and retiring from the post in 1975 after 50 years with the band. Alex Mortimer was musical director of the CWS (Manchester) Band 1954–70 and their musical adviser until 1976.

Morton, Jelly Roll [Lamothe or Lemott, Ferdinand Joseph] (*b* Gulfport, La., 20 Oct. 1890; *d* Los Angeles, 10 July 1941). American jazz pianist, singer, bandleader, arranger, and composer. Brought up by his grandmother in New Orleans, he began his piano-playing career around 1906, for years surviving on this supported by multifarious activities as a music publisher, tailor, boxing promoter, bookmaker, and pimp; also playing in minstrel shows and appearing in vaudeville as part of a double act. During these obscure years he was writing music that had its roots in the classic ragtime of the 1890s, but was clearly adopting an idiom that was more allied to jazz as it was to emerge in the 1920s. By 1923 he was active in Chicago, where the Melrose Brothers began to publish his work and he began to record his delicate, imaginative, and entirely individual piano solos for Gennett. During these years he toured with his own band or worked for others and built a reputation as a thoughtful and demanding leader. In 1926 he began to record a number of sessions for Victor with a band that he named his Red Hot Peppers. A combination of excellent players, including Omer Simeon (1902–59) (clarinet), George Mitchell (1899–1972) and Ward Pinkett (1906–37) (trumpets), Kid *Ory and Geechy Fields (*b* 1903) (trombones), Johnny St Cyr (1890–1906) (banjo), controlled but still allowed to express their individuality, and Morton's forward thinking and inspired themes and arrangements, made these into some of the all-time great jazz performances in the context of the limited outlook of jazz at the time. Nobody except Duke *Ellington had produced anything quite so individual until then.

By 1928, Morton's allegiance to the New Orleans style and the rise of many new talents found him fighting a losing battle, leading bands until around 1930, but after that playing in theatre pit orchestras and in clubs, a half-forgotten figure. His name was kept in circulation by critics like Roy Carew, who believed strongly in his genius, and he came back into the limelight in 1938 when Alan *Lomax recorded a long series of musical interviews and piano solos for the Library of Congress folklore archives. Morton spoke and played with dignity and pride, occasionally putting the record straight with regard to the reputation of others. At this time he was infuriated to hear W. C. *Handy being hailed on the radio as 'the originator of jazz and the blues'. He wrote a letter to **Down Beat*, which has long irritated some of his detractors, and jazz historians in general, in which he said: 'New Orleans is the cradle of jazz, and I myself happened to be the creator in the year 1902.' This remark was ever after widely and deliberately misunderstood. It perhaps stood to reason that no one person could actually invent jazz. What Morton felt was that the sort of thing he conceived in 1902 (when, according to the experts, he would have been 12 though he claimed to have been born in 1885 and therefore 17) had helped jazz to a defined idiom that was distinct from ragtime.

He made some more recordings in 1939 and 1940 with leading musicians like Sidney *Bechet, but they had none of the originality and fire of the old Red Hot Peppers sessions and proved to be rather formal exercises in the New Orleans style. His delicate and skilful piano playing, almost a classical style tinged with Creole elements and ragtime, always mobile and swinging, was the basic element of his best compositions that came to light in the 1920s sessions—'New Orleans blues' (1905), 'Jelly Roll blues' (1905), 'King Porter stomp' (1906), 'Frog-i-more rag' (1908), 'The crave' (1910), 'The pearls' (1919), 'Grandpa's spells' (1923), 'Shreveport stomp' (1924), 'Black Bottom stomp' (1925), 'Cannonball blues' (1926), and many more whose actual origins and dates are not entirely certain. Morton was unfortunate in being ahead of his time to begin with and behind it by the time he was fully recognized. But he achieved enough to prove himself not only one of the most colourful figures in jazz history and a fine pianist but, above all, the first great jazz composer and arranger.

A. Lomax: *Mister Jelly Roll* (New York, 1950). M. T. Williams: *Jelly Roll Morton* (London–New York, 1962). L. Wright: *Mr. Jelly Lord* (Chigwell, 1980).

Music: *Jelly Roll Morton's Famous Series of Blues and Stomps for Piano* (New York–London, n.d. [*c*.1940]). J. Dapogny [ed.]: *The Collected Piano Music* (New York–London–Washington DC, 1982).

Mostel, Zero [Samuel Joel] (*b* Brooklyn, NY, 28 Feb. 1915; *d* 1977). American actor. Beginning his career as a nightclub performer, he had one or two splendid parts in musical shows. He appeared in *Beggar's Holiday* (1946), *Once Over Lightly* (1955), and *Rhinoceros* (1961) before his success as the slave Pseudolus in *A *Funny Thing Happened on the Way to the Forum* (1962; filmed 1966), in which he sang 'Comedy tonight' and 'Free'; and a long-lasting triumph as Tevye in *Fiddler on the Roof* (1964)—'If I were a rich man' and 'Sunrise, sunset'. He also had a richly comic career in films, including: **Dubarry Was a Lady* (1943); *Panic in the Streets* (1950); *The Guy Who Came Back* (1951); *Sirocco* (1951); *The Model and the Marriage Broker* (1952); *Zero* (1959); *The Great Catherine* (1967); and *The Producers* (1968).

Most Happy Fella, The. Musical play with music and words by Frank *Loesser, based on Sidney Howard's play *They Knew What They Wanted*. It was seen at the Imperial Theatre, New York, 3 May 1956, where it enjoyed a long run of 676 performances; and in London at the Coliseum, 21 Apr. 1960 [288p]. Stanley Green describes it as 'a cohesive and ambitious work' with some operatic affiliations, comprising 30 different musical items, solos, duets, ensembles, and choruses with recitatives.

The story is about an old Italian vineyard owner, played by Robert Weede (1903–72), who proposes by mail to a San Francisco waitress (Jo Sullivan) who accepts him because he has sent her a picture of his handsome foreman. When she discovers the trickery she gives herself to the young man and her husband is shattered when she has a child. In the end all is forgiven and he raises the child as his own. Among the more operatic material were some Broadwayish items like 'Big D' and 'Standing on the corner' which proved popular.

Moten, Bennie (*b* Kansas City, Mo., 13 Nov. 1894; *d* Kansas City, 2 Apr. 1935). American pianist, bandleader, and composer. He played in a junior brass band before taking up piano and working with Kansas City dance bands. He founded his own band in the early 1920s, starting as a small jazz unit but eventually moving into the *big band category. From 1923 on he became known through recordings, although the band mainly played in the Midwest, with occasional residencies in New York 1928–9, playing in Kansas City in the summer. He continued to lead his band into the 1930s, moving from a pumping two-beat tuba-based style towards a swinging, riffing music that later came to be classified as *Kansas City style, with such musicians as Walter Page (bass), a young pianist William (Count) *Basie (piano), and Jimmy *Rushing (vocalist) helping to formulate its character. Among his many compositions were 'Moten stomp' (1927), 'Let's get it' (1929), 'South' (1930), and 'Moten swing' (1933).

Mouskouri, Nana (*b* Athens, 10 Oct. 1936). Greek singer. Growing up during the Nazi occupation of Greece and in the civil war that followed, she learned much of the true meaning of 'kaimos' (grief) and the emotional depth of her singing allied with a remarkably pure tone of voice has made her a star in her own country. Her success was helped by her association with Manos *Hadjidakis, the composer of 'Never on Sunday', who greatly admired her voice and, after their first meeting in 1958, promised to write songs especially for her. She made her first record in Greece in 1959 and within a year was established as a top artist. She won several awards and contests, then went to Germany to record, her first disc there being 'Weissen Rosen aus Athen' by Hadjidakis (*w* Nikos Gatsas), which became a big hit. She recorded more of his songs which were included in an album of Greek material which her voice and personality made acceptable to those who could not understand the language. Later she recorded in German, French, and English, perpetrating such international hybrids as the Irish 'The last rose of summer' sung in French. She created a fashion for looking glamorous behind a large pair of spectacles.

Muir, Lewis F. [Meuer, Louis Frank] (*b* New York, 30 May, 1883; *d* New York, 3 Dec. 1915). American composer. Little seems to be known about his origins or early career, but he left behind him many songs that have enjoyed enormous sales and passed into the common stock. Most of his best work seems to have been done in the period 1910–12. His music was brought to England by Muir himself who, at the instigation of Albert *de Courville, crossed the Atlantic with a troupe of performers known as the American Ragtime Octette. His songs included: 'Play that barber shop chord' (1910, *w* Ballard MacDonald, 1882–1935, and William G. Tracey, 1893–1957), 'Waiting for the Robert E. Lee' (1911, *w* L. Wolfe *Gilbert), 'Take me to that Swanee shore' (1912, Gilbert), 'Ragtime cowboy Joe' (with Maurice *Abrahams, 1912), 'Ragging the baby to sleep' (1912, Gilbert), 'Hitchy-koo' (with Abrahams, 1912, *w* Gilbert), and 'Here comes my daddy now' (1912, Gilbert).

Mulligan, Gerry [Gerald Joseph] (*b* New York, 6 Apr. 1927). American jazz saxophonist, arranger, and leader. He grew up in Philadelphia and started writing arrangements for radio use, then toured with the Tommy Tucker band in 1944. In 1946 he joined the Gene *Krupa band in New York as musician and arranger ('Disc jockey jump'). He was with the Miles *Davis big band in 1948—'Jeru', 'Boplicity', 'Venus de Milo', 'Godchild', collected on the album *The Birth of the Cool*; Elliot *Lawrence 1946 ('Rocker'); Woody *Herman and Claude *Thornhill. He organized an original jazz quartet on the West Coast in 1952, without piano or guitar, comprising Chet *Baker (trumpet), Chico Hamilton (*b* 1921) (drums), Bob Whitlock (bass), soon replaced by Carson Smith, with Mulligan introducing some new cool jazz sounds and the first baritone-saxophonist to break away from the Harry *Carney mould. It also made Chet Baker (replaced after two years by Bob Brookmeyer (*b* 1929)) into a new trumpet star. He led larger groups 1956–7 and toured abroad, still writing modern arrangements for many bands, a popular recording sideman and festival player. He toured Europe with a big band in 1960 and Japan in 1964; and played with Dave *Brubeck in the 1970s and many other groups.

R. Horricks: *Gerry Mulligan* (London, 1986).

Mulligan Guards' Ball, The. The best of a succession of comic plays with music that emanated from the *Harrigan and Hart partnership. The knockabout comedy was based on the rivalry between the Mulligan Guard (Irish) and the Skidmore Guard (black) whose social evenings coincided and inevitably clashed. It was all a skit on what were known as target companies, pseudo-military organizations popular at the time, ostensibly out for a day's shooting but more often on a booze-up. The basic idea for the series grew from a song, 'The Mulligan Guard', which was originally performed in a Harrigan and Hart sketch at the Academy of Music in Chicago on 15 July 1873. Then came a brief sketch, *The Mulligan Guards' Picnic*, in 1878; with *The Mulligan Guards' Ball* making its impact at the Theatre Comique, New York, 13 Jan. 1879 (a month before **HMS Pinafore* arrived in the USA), and running for 153 performances. The music was by David *Braham ('The Mulligan Guard', 'The babies on our block', 'Skidmore fancy ball') and the book by Harrigan. It was revived in an expanded version in 1883. Other shows that followed included: *The Mulligan Guards' Chowder* (1879); *The Mulligan Guards' Christmas* (1879); *The Mulligan Guards' Surprise* (1880); *The Mulligan Guards' Nominee* (1880); and *The Mulligans' Silver Wedding* (1881). The shows and their ethnic background were a source of inspiration for many theatre developments to come, notably in the work of Charles H. *Hoyt and George M. *Cohan.

E. J. Kahn: *The Merry Partnership* (New York, 1955).

Mundy, Jimmy [James] (*b* Cincinnati, Ohio, 28 June 1907). American arranger. First heard of in the bands of Erskine *Tate and Carroll Dickerson (1895–1957), he was later a sideman and arranger with Earl *Hines 1932–6. In 1935 he began writing for Benny *Goodman and joined him as full-time arranger in 1936, providing many of his classic sides like 'Madhouse', 'Swingtime in the Rockies', 'Jam session', and 'House hop'. He led his own band in 1939 and into the 1940s, meanwhile arranging for Count *Basie, Earl Hines, Gene *Krupa, Charlie *Spivak, Paul *Whiteman, and Glen Gray, and becoming one of the most important arrangers of the swing era. He continued after war service with work for Harry *James and others, and settled in Paris in 1959. He was the composer of 'A lover is blue' (1939), 'So far, so good' (1940), 'Trav'lin' light' (1943); and many instrumental numbers.

Mungo Jerry. British *skiffle-oriented group with singer Ray Dorset (*b* 1946) dominant, who became widely known after their appearance in Newcastle in 1970, and the release of an infectious No. 1 hit 'In the summertime'. This was followed up by 'Baby jump' (1971) and 'Alright, alright, alright' (1973) in a similar vein. The vein exhausted, the group broke up.

Murder at the Vanities. American musical show with score by Victor *Young, John Jacob Loeb, Johnny *Green, and Richard Myers (New York, 1933) [298p]. It is chiefly remembered through the film version of 1934 which was effectively backed by the music of Duke *Ellington and his orchestra.

Murphy, C. W. (*b* London, 1875; *d* London, 16 June 1913). British composer. Like many writers of the music-hall period, the life of Murphy is shrouded in silence, but the catchy songs he wrote have not perished. These include 'I live in Trafalgar Square' (1902), 'Little yellow bird' (1903), 'She's a lassie from Lancashire' (1907), 'Put me among the girls' (1908), 'Oh, oh, Antonio' (1908), 'The girl in the clogs and shawl' (1909), 'Has anybody here seen Kelly?' (1909), 'Flanagan' (1910), 'Follow the footprints in the snow' (1913), 'Hold your hand out, naughty boy' (1913), 'I parted my hair in the middle' (1913), and many more written with various partners.

Murphy, Rose (*b* 1913; *d* New York, 16 Nov. 1989). American singer and pianist. A vivacious performer playing her own adroit accompaniment in the Fats *Waller style and singing in a piping little voice full of humour and spontaneous chuckles, she favoured material like 'Miss Annabelle Lee' and 'Honeysuckle rose', but is best remembered for a catchy little telephone number called 'Busy line' which she made her own. Known as the Chee-Chee Girl, from her soft, chirpy sound, she became very popular in the 1940s and 1950s, and frequently appeared on radio and records. In the late 1950s and 1960s she led a trio with bassist Slam Stewart (1914–86) one of its members, later appearing at the Famous Door, and other clubs, with George Duvivier (1920–85) as a regular bassist, and touring abroad. She worked in New York 1973–4 and made a revival appearance on LP in 1980 with Major Holley on bass.

Murphy, Turk [Melvin E.] (*b* Palermo, Calif., 16 Dec. 1915; *d* 30 May 1987). American jazz trombonist, composer, and author. After high school he joined a local band. In the mid-1930s he was playing with Will Osborne and Mal Hallett, then freelanced in Oakland while studying music. He joined the Lu *Watters Yerba Buena Jazz Band in San Francisco in 1940 and was with them, with a break for military service, until 1950, playing traditional tailgate trombone in the Kid *Ory manner, showing a good ensemble sense and capable of good solos, as in his own 'Trombone rag'. When the band broke up in 1950 he formed his own band with ex-Yerba Buena players like clarinettist Bob Helm (*b* 1914) and pianist Wally Rose (*b* 1913). An ardent exploiter of interesting traditional material and a learned writer on the subject, he never allowed his music to get over-serious. In the 1950s he played in Child's restaurant in New York, then in New Orleans, and opened his own Earthquake McGoon's club in San Francisco in 1960. He was still playing and appearing at festivals in the 1970s.

J. Goggin: *Turk Murphy: Just for the Record* (San Francisco, 1982).

Murray, Anne (*b* Springhill, Nova Scotia, 20 June 1947). Canadian country singer. Raised in a small coal-mining town, she studied at the University of New Brunswick and became a teacher of physical education. Singing assets of a deep, rich, true voice, with a natural sense of pitch and timing led her to audition for TV, first appearing on *Let's Go*, and her success led to an LP *What About Me* (1968). She became a professional singer and recorded *This Way Is My Way* LP for Capitol in 1969, with 'Snowbird' reaching the top 10 country songs in the USA and UK. Appeared regularly on the Glenn *Campbell show and made recordings with him in 1971. Had further hits with 'Danny's song' (1973); 'You won't see me' (1974); 'He thinks I still care' (1974); 'The Call' (1976). After marriage in 1975, she retired to raise a family, but returned to record the LP *Let's Keep It That Way* in 1978 and had a new hit with 'You Needed Me' (1979), continuing a string of successes into 1985 with 'Nobody Loves Me Like You Do' with Kenny Loggins (*b* 1948); and LP *Harmony* (1987). As early as 1972 she was being spoken of as 'Canada's most successful entertainment export since ice-hockey'; and continues to be so with 36 albums now to her credit and over 25 million copies sold.

Musical. An all-embracing term which has come to signify almost anything in the popular theatre, and other mediums, which has a degree of musical emphasis; and thus used in conjunction with other terms either as an adjective—the musical theatre, *musical comedy, *musical film, *musical play—or as a noun—the Broadway musical, the Hollywood musical. The history of the musical could now be loosely taken as commencing *c.*1850 when the operettas of *Offenbach, *Hervé, and their successors started to provide opera-style entertainment for the masses. The word 'musical' is now often used to give block coverage in the titles of books covering the whole field; though, in the book-list appended below, it will be seen that many authors still adhere to the term 'musical comedy' even though their coverage extends either side of that particular area in its strictest sense.

Aficionados, categorizing more precisely, would probably think of *operetta as a distinctive semi-operatic form that lingered on into the 20th century in the works of composers like Franz *Lehár and Sigmund *Romberg. The musical comedy period is then seen as a short-lived interim stage of musical development more or less starting with the 1900s and carrying on in both the USA and Europe up until about the Second World War. They might confine the use of the interchangeable terms 'musical play' or plain 'musical' to the rather more substantial works that came after **Oklahoma!* (1943) had confirmed that the musical was quite a serious matter and culturally the modern equivalent of opera. The works of *Sondheim, and such entirely sung productions as *Les *Misérables*, have confirmed this elevated status on the other hand, while the rock musical keeps it in the world of currently popular music. Modern 'classical' composers have helped to give the musical a cult status by failing to produce very much that would lure the public back to the opera house.

S. Green: *Encyclopedia of the Musical Theatre* (New York, 1976). A. Jackson: *The Book of Musicals* (Exeter, 1979). K. Gänzl and A. Lamb: *Gänzl's Book of the Musical Theatre* (London, 1988).

UK: W. Macqueen Pope: *Nights of Gladness* (London, 1956). R. Mander and J. Mitchinson: *Musical Comedy: a Story in Pictures* (London, 1971). B. Rust: *London Musical Shows on Record 1897–1976* (London, 1977); rev. R. Seeley and R. Bunnet as *London Musical Shows on Record 1889–1989* (London, 1989). K. Gänzl: *The British Musical Theatre* (2 vols) (London, 1987). S. Morley: *Spread a Little Happiness: the First Hundred Years of the British Musical* (London, 1987).

USA: J. Burton: *The Blue Book of Broadway Musicals* (New York, 1952). S. Green: *The World of Musical Comedy* (New York, 1960; various edns). L. Engel: *The American Musical Theatre* (New York, 1967). A. Laufe: *Broadway's Greatest Musicals 1884–1968* (New York, 1969). D. Ewen: *The New Complete Book of the American Musical Theater* (New York, 1970). E. Mordden: *Better Foot Forward* (New York, 1976). G. Bordman: *The American Musical Theatre: a Chronicle* (New York, 1978; rev. 1992). S. Green: *Broadway Musicals: Show by Show* (New York, 1985; London, 1987). A. J. Lerner: *The Musical Theatre: A Celebration* (New York, 1986).

Musical Bouquet. A series of sheet music publications which began *c.*1846. Selling at 3d for single numbers and 6d for double (i.e. longer items or an issue containing two or more pieces), this amazingly prolific series continued until almost 9000 numbers were listed—though not all of them may have been actually issued. It came at the vital mid-19th-century period when popular music was finding its identity and thus provides a valuable source of material covering such areas as the minstrel shows, Victorian social dances, popular and music-hall songs—as well as reflecting the light classical and operatic tastes of the day. The first 78 items were issued by James Bingley from the Musical Bouquet offices early established at 192 High Holborn, jointly with William Strange at 21 Paternoster Row. The series never seems to have achieved an aura of respectability, partly because much of their material was blatantly pirated from other established publishers, taking advantage of those free-for-all, pre-copyright days; partly because their methods were so unscholarly and haphazard. Even so, the products were both cheap and admirable.

Soon after its beginnings, *c.*1855, the series was taken over by Bingley's partner Charles Sheard (1826–1918) about whom, for one so prolific and active, little seems to be known. No. 1 had a full-page engraved cover, but thereafter the series adopted the illustrated half-page title format (see MUSIC COVERS) with often interesting and informative engravings by such well-known illustrators as Alfred Ashley and Augustus Butler. Eventually standard typographical covers began to take over, used to identify various dance music, minstrel, and piano music series, and often used for reprints of early material. The series maintained a fairly clear identity for at least the first 3000 issues or so, but then began to lose its individuality until the illustrated cover returned with the advent of the music-hall song. Nos 1 and 2 were the first dance issues; No. 3 started the innumerable sorties into the fashionable opera world of the time with a Bellini item; Nos 9 and 10 were the first issues of Henry *Russell songs (a popular area which was later the subject of ownership battles); No. 21 was the first of many *minstrel song issues. Attention to early music-hall started around 1852, making Sheard an important pioneer in the issue of such material. Various bound volumes of collections in all categories were issued from time to time. There was also a separate series under the title of 'The Sacred Harmonist'. Strong rivalry came from the publisher Davidson, who issued similar publications under the name of 'Musical Treasury', including the above-mentioned works of Russell.

The early numbers of the 'Musical Bouquet' clearly had a great vogue and are well collated and identified. Later the distribution seems to have become more confused and diffuse and many numbers are hard to find; the title 'Musical Bouquet' now seeming to be used more as a matter of habit rather than a series identification. The last issues were probably around 1889, though Sheard himself continued publishing until his catalogue was bought by Herman *Darewski in 1917.

Musical Comedy. A further rationalization of the *operetta into a form most likely to appeal to a general audience who liked some musical ingredient but would be disinclined to sit through anything so demanding as opera. The term was contrived by theatrical managements in London in the 1890s to identify and popularize the light-hearted, middle-brow kind of musical theatrical entertainment that developed in the wake of the influence of French operetta on the English stage. It loosely implies a musical entertainment where the story is mainly carried forward in spoken dialogue, with songs, ensembles, and dances interspersed at frequent contrived moments, not as integrated as one would expect them to be in a genuine operetta. The whole achieved a friendly mixture of dramatic and musical elements well suited to middle-class British tastes. The term was a necessary label at a time when, in the heyday of such managers as John Hollingshead and George *Edwardes, the English variety of light opera was taking over from *burlesque at such theatres as the *Gaiety and *Daly's following the decline of French operetta and the passing of the heyday of *Gilbert and Sullivan.

It is not easy to point exactly to the first true 'musical comedy'. *In Town*, which opened at the Prince of Wales Theatre in October 1892, often gets the credit though it called itself a 'musical farce', while *Morocco Bound*, which opened at the Shaftesbury in April 1893, was billed as a 'musical farcical comedy'. The first to use the name specifically was *A *Gaiety Girl*, a 'musical comedy' staged at the Prince of Wales Theatre, 14 Oct. 1893, with music by Sidney *Jones. The first musical comedy to replace the long series of burlesques at the Gaiety was *The *Shop Girl* (November 1894) and Daly's produced *An *Artist's Model*, a 'comedy with music' in February 1895. One of the best of the early musical comedies was *The *Geisha* at Daly's, 25 Apr. 1896, music by Sidney Jones, which had 750 performances.

These shows almost automatically went to the USA after their London runs (a trade later reversed) and took the term 'musical comedy' with them. It was in continual use in both Britain and America right into the 1930s, applied to shows such as those written by Jerome *Kern. The term is still occasionally used but has been mainly ousted by the more general *musical or *musical play, which removes the slur of 'comedy', for works that have become far more ambitious, dramatic, and even, at times, deadly serious.

UK: W. Macqueen Pope: *Nights of Gladness* (London, 1956). R. Mander and J. Mitchinson: *Musical Comedy: a Story in Pictures* (London, 1971).

USA: C. Smith: *Musical Comedy in America* (New York, 1950). S. Green: *The World of Musical Comedy* (New York, 1960; rev. 1974, 1984). S. Green: *Ring Bells! Sing Songs!: Broadway Musicals of the 1930s* (New Rochelle, NY, 1971). G. Bordman: *American Musical Comedy: from Adonis to Dreamgirls* (New York, 1982).

Musical Films. Although not all musical films were made in Hollywood, the 'Hollywood Musical' has become a commonly used categorical title, in books and elsewhere, to cover the genre. But to embrace the negligible number of films made elsewhere, including the hardly noticeable British and European examples, the less specific name, as in Stanley Green's standard work *Encyclopedia of the Musical Film*, leaves the ends more workably open.

The film musical was a logical extension of filmic art coming in with the change from silent films to the talkies. In many early cases the film musical was simply a *musical comedy filmed, often with a heavily revised text to suit the medium and new songs added by *Tin Pan Alley composers to suit the needs of the stars involved. But in some of the more successful early instances, the studios asked writers like Richard *Rodgers and Lorenz *Hart to script works similar to their stage shows or to adapt these shows for the undeveloped sound cinema of the late 1920s. The first lesson to be learned was that film technique was essentially different from stage technique, and that static attempts simply to film a stage show were not enough. While, for instance, a switch from dialogue to song on stage was a readily accepted convention taken from opera, with no great concern for naturalism, the film was essentially a close-up illusion of real life. Static dialogue and song were inclined to look wooden. It took a few years for film-makers to develop a successful combination of music and action. When Al *Jolson broke into song in *The *Jazz Singer* (1927) he simply faced the camera and did his stage act, which seemed plausible enough as he was playing the role of a singer, sometimes seen in the street, sometimes in the synagogue, and sometimes on stage. Films like *The *Gold-Diggers of 1935* were essentially filmed revues, and when the scene was set for a Busby Berkeley spectacular a filmed audience was often included in the shot. In a Fred *Astaire film the star was usually playing the role of a dancer anyway, so there was some logic in his terpsichorean interludes; even when playing a psychiatrist in *Carefree* (1938), the matter was settled by the disclosure that he always wanted to be a dancer. In short, a musical film (or film musical) was generally contrived around a musical story.

The beginning of the genre is generally considered to be marked by *The Jazz Singer*. Although it was an effective film, better ones very soon came along. Shaking off the implied relationship to the world of the stage operetta and musical, the film musical very quickly established itself as a separate art, now to pursue its own history and to survive changes of fashion that often seemed to threaten its viability. After a spate of 'all singing, all dancing' but dramatically static titles, the film musical most notably got under way with Irving Thalberg's *The *Broadway Melody* (1929), for which composer Nacio Herb *Brown and lyric-writer Arthur *Freed were asked to provide a totally new score, thus opening the way for a whole generation of writers who specialized in writing for the movies. MGM's first essay in sound was the beginning of a long tradition of musicals from that studio, the art advancing as camerawork became more mobile to cope with the movement essential to the dance, and as sound equipment improved with the advances of electrical recording so that voices and orchestras could be properly heard. The film musical was to combine a number of skills and to breed a race of directors, choreographers, musical directors, as well as composers and writers, who loved and understood its special needs.

Fortunately, such was the demand and such was the commercial prospect for the musical film, expense was not spared and the best of all facilities were often put at the film-makers' disposal. The film musical did not, as could easily have happened, become too rigidly formulated. By 1929 a variety of approaches could be detected: Lubitsch's *The Love Parade* stayed with the musical comedy conventions, but handled them well with imaginatively adapted techniques; King Vidor's all-black *Hallelujah* went for naturalism, filming on location and tacking the sound on afterwards; while others like *Sunny Side Up* managed to break away successfully from the convention of the back-stage, show-business musical and expand on a basically non-musical story. The musical film's speciality was to be the filmed revue like *Hollywood Revue of 1929*; *Paramount on Parade*, featuring Maurice *Chevalier; and *King of Jazz*, which foreshadowed the art of Busby Berkeley.

The 1930s were to be the classic film musical decade. In 1930 audiences saw such examples as **Good News*, with its breezy campus background, and the first Busby Berkeley efforts, in **Whoopee*, starring Eddie Cantor, one of the great Broadway stars who made the transition to films successfully. Some, of course, found themselves unable to adapt to the celluloid conventions. But new stars were soon being groomed. *Whoopee*, for example, gave a small part to the teenage Betty *Grable, later to be one of the greatest stars of the film musical.

The first hitch in the progress of the musical film came with the depression of 1931 when the funds were no longer available for lavish productions. But by 1932 all was in full swing again and Hollywood was already luring top composers, like *Rodgers and *Hart who wrote the score for *Love Me Tonight*. The Cantor/Berkeley combination continued to triumph with *The Kid From Spain*. The innovations of Busby Berkeley were responsible for the new sophistication and artistry of such 1933 classics as **42nd Street*, **Gold Diggers of 1933*, and *Footlight Parade*. There were also better stories, livelier direction, and greater thought going into every aspect of the musical. Writers like Lorenz Hart had long been seeking an intelligently natural way of introducing a song into their stage shows. But when he tried to do the same for a film he was working on, cinema audiences did not take easily to this imposed naturalism and *Hallelujah, I'm a Bum* (1933), which had its setting in the realities of the great depression, was a failure—even though it starred Al Jolson.

Beyond the committed musicals, Hollywood also liked to drop a song or two into what were otherwise straight stories. A star who never appeared in a thorough-going musical but often sang with good effect in her films was Marlene *Dietrich. Many of the films which employed Tin Pan Alley songwriters to give them a casual musical element tend to be less remembered for themselves than for the songs they spawned.

In 1933 one of the great film musical partnerships was inaugurated when Fred Astaire and Ginger *Rogers came together in *Flying Down to Rio*. In their subsequent films it was their dancing that mattered and everything was tailored, music, story, and setting, to highlight their art. A rival attraction was the seven-year-old Shirley *Temple, a true child of the musical film, who had grown up with it and had four top box-office titles in 1934. In the meantime the operetta tradition was not being neglected and 1935 saw the beginning of the Jeanette *MacDonald–Nelson *Eddy partnership in **Naughty Marietta*. By now most of the big studios, as well as MGM, were on the musical trail. RKO was to substantiate their Astaire/Rogers legacy by commissioning music from Irving *Berlin to make a film like **Top Hat* (1935) into a classic of the genre; while Warner Brothers made good use of the talents of Harry *Warren who was to be one of the greatest of all Hollywood composers, contriving one hit after another for many years of concentrated activity, and such classics as 'Lullaby of Broadway' for *Gold Diggers of 1935*.

The following year was notable for *Born to Dance*; starring Eleanor *Powell; and some new aspects of the musical were opened up with Walt Disney's first full-length musical cartoon, **Snow White and the Seven Dwarfs*. *High, Wide and Handsome* (1937) combined a fine Jerome *Kern score with a believable story. While the great song-and-dance partnerships continued, a new singing star was Deanna *Durbin who had her first big role in *Three Smart Girls* in 1937. The post-war glorification of teenage talents had its first manifestations in the late 1930s when Durbin was succeeded by Judy *Garland and *The *Wizard of Oz* (1938), Micky *Rooney, and Donald *O'Connor.

Every time the musical has seemed likely to be superseded by some new fashion it has made a strong come-back and there seems to be no reason why it should not go on doing so for ever. In the 1930s radio seemed likely to be the enemy, but the film-makers simply used more of radio's talents. The big cloud of the 1940s was, of course, the war. Hollywood offered two antidotes: pure escapism as in the Bing *Crosby–Bob *Hope 'Road' films or the Busby Berkeley *Babes on Broadway* (1941); and, once the USA was committed to the war, patriotic uplift in such titles as *Yankee Doodle Dandy* (1942), *Star-spangled Rhythm* (1942), and *For Me and My Gal* (1942). This last film featured Gene *Kelly, whose choreographic thinking was a part of the growing-up period of the musical film. The musical became less frivolous but no less effective in such all-black items as **Cabin in the Sky* (1943) and *Stormy Weather* (1943); and then in *Meet Me in St Louis* (1944) which took Judy Garland to the heights of her ability.

Curiously, the musical most often failed when it clung to the old formula of using a musical or backstage setting. Biographies of composers have nearly always proved to be somewhat embarrassing and of little service to their subject, the star chosen rarely managing a truthful portrait of someone as down-to-earth as a composer. The musicals of each decade brought forth their own stars. The 1950s found a new partnership in Doris *Day and Gordon *McRae, starring in such films as *Lullaby of Broadway* (1951); and as the Astaire–Rogers partnership danced its way out, it was the more physical talents of Gene Kelly that came to the fore and produced one of the great masterpieces of escapist musical film art in **Singin' in the Rain* (1951). The filmed operetta star of the 1950s was Mario *Lanza. Now a new rival loomed in the shape of television and the old style of musical film, of which *Singin' in the Rain* was a notable specimen, seemed to be losing its way. The film found a newly effective place in transposing the great naturalistic stage musicals to the screen; the large one was never really seriously challenged by the small one in overall effect. Really worthy films were made out of such long-running musicals as **Kiss Me Kate* (1953); **Call Me Madam* (1953); **Guys and Dolls* (1955); **Oklahoma!* (1955); *The *King and I* (1956); **South Pacific* (1958); and on into the 1960s with the powerfully effective **West Side Story* (1961) and the monumentally successful *The *Sound of Music* (1964), with the asset of magnificently colourful scenery to add to their musical attractions. What might have seemed essentially a stage drama like **My Fair Lady* (1964) translated quite naturally to film; and *West Side Story* proved that it had dramatic strength and, in settings as realistic as anything yet, its transition from stage to screen seemed not only natural but even a genuine strengthening in terms of dramatic impact. One of the really notable British musical films, able to stand alongside the Hollywood models, was **Oliver!*, made at Shepperton in 1968. Superstars of the film musical continued to arise in the shape of such eminently filmable people as Barbra *Streisand.

If, as some might claim, the film musical as such had long passed its peak, it hardly mattered as there was such a wealth of nostalgic material to look back on that the world's musical needs could be satisfied for ever simply by running through what had been permanently immortalized on film. But there were also enough new triumphs in the 1970s to convince anyone that the genre was far from dead, whether it was nostalgia in newly muscular guise from **Cabaret* (1972) to *A *Chorus Line* (1984), or rock music proving itself just as capable of sustaining a musical as any earlier forms of popular music (see ROCK ON FILM).

The list of composers who went to Hollywood is a long one. Perhaps the screen did not actually do much to influence the popular song, rather adapting itself to what was available, but it squeezed a staggering output from such specialized composers as Harry Warren and many more, while composers like Jerome Kern and George *Gershwin were inspired to write some of their very best songs specifically for Hollywood.

J. Burton: *The Blue Book of Hollywood Musicals* (New York, 1955). Anon: *30 Years of Motion Picture Music: the Big Hollywood Hits from 1938–1958* (New York, 1958). D. McVay: *The Musical Film* (London–New York, 1967). J. Kobal: *Gotta Sing. Gotta Dance: a Pictorial History of Film Musicals* (New York–London, 1970). T. Vallance: *The American Musical* (London–New York, 1970). A. Jackson and J. Russell: *The Hollywood Musical* (London–New York, 1971). H. Fordin: *The World of Entertainment: Hollywood's Greatest Musicals* (New York, 1975; repr. 1984 as *The Movies' Greatest Musicals*). A. L. Woll: *Songs from Hollywood Musical Comedies, 1927 to the Present Day* (New York–London, 1976). R. Altman (ed.): *Genre: The Musical: a Reader* (London, 1981). S. Green: *Encyclopedia of the Musical Film* (New York–Oxford, 1981). C. Hirschhorn: *The Hollywood Musical* (New York–London, 1981; rev. 1983). E. Mordden: *The Hollywood Musical* (New York, 1981). T. Sennett: *Hollywood Musicals* (New York, 1981). R. C. Lynch: *Movie Musicals on Record, 1927–1987* (Westport, 1989).

Musical Play. A categorical term that gradually slipped into usage as substitute for the short-lived *musical comedy, when it became apparent that all musicals were not necessarily in comedy vein and subsequently began to take themselves more seriously. It further intimated that the words might be as worthy of dramatic consideration as those of a straight play. In the end it was supplanted by the more generalized all-purpose 'the musical' which nowadays embraces everything that includes a few songs.

Music Box Revue. A series of revues produced by Sam H. Harris and Irving *Berlin at their Music Box

Theatre, starting in 1921. The Revue of 1921 had sketches by Frances Nordstrom, William Collier, Thomas J. Gray, and George V. Hobart, and its cast included Irving Berlin, Sam *Bernard, Ethelind Terry, Joseph *Santley, Emma Haig, and Miriam Hopkins. It opened on 22 Sept. and had 313 performances, with a version in London, Palace Theatre 15 May 1923 [119p], in which Jessie *Matthews made her first West End appearance in a small part. Irving Berlin songs included: 'Dancing the seasons away', 'In a cozy kitchenette apartment', 'Say it with music' (which became the series' theme song), and 'Everybody step'.

The 1922 edition, by a similar team, opened 23 Oct. 1922, with William *Gaxton, Grace *LaRue, John Steel (1900–71), Charlotte Greenwood (1890–1978), Hal Sherman, and *Clark and McCullough in the cast and ran for 330 performances. The songs included: 'Dance your troubles away', 'Crinoline days', and 'Lady of the evening'. It was notable as the first major Broadway appearance of William Gaxton and the vaudeville duo Bobby Clark (1888–1960) and Paul McCullough (1884–1936).

The Music Box Revue of 1923 added George S. *Kaufman to its panel of contributors and his sketch 'If Men Played Cards as Women Do' became one of the series' unforgotten comic moments. It opened on 22 Sept. 1923 and ran for 277 performances. Notable on stage were Frank Tinney, Joseph Santley (1889–1971), John Steel, Ivy Sawyer, Phil *Baker, Grace *Moore, and comedian-writer Robert Benchley (1889–1945) making his first professional appearance and having a lasting hit with his 'Treasurer's Report'. Berlin's songs included 'When you walked out someone else walked right in', 'Learn to do the strut', and 'One girl' ('What'll I do' was added during the run), with an immortal additional number in 'Yes, we have no bananas' by Frank Silver and Irving Cohn. The 1921–3 editions were directed by Hassard Short (1877–1956) who made his reputation through them.

The 1924 edition had the help of Bert *Kalmar and Harry *Ruby, opening on 1 Dec. 1924 with Fanny *Brice, Clark and McCullough, Grace *Moore, and Hal Sherman in the cast. Its score was padded out with two notable Berlin songs, 'What'll I do' and 'All alone'. It had 184 performances. The series was historically a link between the era of the spectacular and lavishly mounted *Ziegfeld revue and the more intellectual and satirical intimate revues of the late 1920s and the 1930s.

Music Covers. A nostalgic interest in sheet music covers, mainly centred on the very attractive lithographed examples that appeared from *c.*1840–90, has now developed into a keen collectors' activity. The illustrated music cover with wood or metal engravings dates back to *c.*1525, but at that period it was entirely the province of classical music. Crudely printed *broadsheets were the nearest approximation to popular music-publishing until the first comic songs began to get into print in the early 1800s. Perhaps it was a broadsheet tradition that lingered on into the 1830s that led to most of the earliest illustrated popular music covers adopting, for a brief period, the format of a half-title, the pictorial part of the cover using the top half of the front page and the music starting half-way down. This was a compromise stage between the previous practice of the first page of the music, with a functional typographical heading, being also the cover, and the time when the coloured full-page cover illustration became common from *c.*1841.

Among the pioneering publishers who started issuing illustrated sheet music with engraved illustrations were William Dale (founded 1809, later Dale, Cockerill & Co 1832–7) at 8 and 19 Poultry in the City of London; Robert Cocks & Co (1823); Thomas D'Almaine (1834); and Charles Sheard, who took over the *Musical Bouquet series which started issuing its engraved half-title sheets *c.*1846. The earlier copper-plate engraving had been replaced by steel engraving *c.*1823, but the laborious engraving process was already being experimentally replaced by the lithographic process invented by Aloys Senefelder (1771–1834), which allowed the artist to draw directly on to waxed stone blocks. This was first being put into practical use around 1800 with chromolithography (i.e. colour work involving many aligned stones, one for each colour) first used for a musical publication in 1841. Lithography which could produce most delicately coloured artwork was the accepted means of illustration by *c.*1850.

The boom in illustrated covers nicely coincided with the growth of *music-hall and other popular entertainments, and with the rise of popular illustrated journals like *Punch*. Indeed, many of Fleet Street's graphic artists found a profitable sideline in music covers. The comic tradition was outstandingly maintained by the one specialist artist in this field who has now become widely known and collected—Alfred Concanen (1835–86), whose improvised style and busy designs, full of historical and sociological interest, and lively portraits of famous artists, are now accepted as minor works of art. He was also a book illustrator and a poster designer. His rival in quantity and quality was John Brandard (1812–63), who produced some of the earliest comic covers but later adopted a heavily romantic style with representations of soulful ladies and doe-eyed men who all look vaguely like Victoria and Albert. Both he and Concanen and several other artists worked for the established printers in this field, Stannard & Dixon. The other artists active in these proliferating engraving and lithographic activities were (alphabetically) Alfred Ashley, mainly an engraver and a regular Musical Bouquet artist; Alfred Bryan (1852–99), a well-known *Punch* contributor; Augustus Butler, a specialist in equestrian subjects; Richard Childs, a sea and ship man; George Cruikshank (1792–1878); Maxim Gauci (1774–1854), an early engraver; Robert Jacob Hamerton (1809–1905), another *Punch* contributor; Alexandre Laby (1814–1899); J. W. Lee, who was a partner of Concanen's for several years and whose own work is very similar to the master's; George E. Madeley, a great portrayer of minstrel scenes and also a printer; Henry Maguire, a sort of comic Brandard and in some respects a more polished artist, especially good at portraits; Walter Robert Mallyon; Thomas Packer, a fine lithographer; William Spalding; Frank Trevisany; William Michael Watson (1840–89), who was also a composer; and many more. An occasional cover can be found done in the distinctive medium of George Baxter (1804–67), who patented a method of printing in oil-based inks that produced attractive miniature prints that looked like oil-paintings. His system was mainly promoted in the work of the Leighton brothers.

A growing commercialism and a new generation of artists brought in a brasher style, as exploited in the Francis, Day & Hunter covers of the 1890s by artists such as H. G. Banks. The Victorian elegance of the early lithographs is replaced by a jolly kind of portrayal of the artist surrounded by comic scenes from the song he sings and a great clutter of explanatory lettering. The last remnants of elegance in sheet-music design coincides with the last few years of the 19th century and the ensuing Edwardian period, when the spirit of the musical comedy era is well expressed in the artwork full of lovely ladies and elegant men done in still subtle colours.

German and French covers followed much the same patterns and changes as the British, with their own array of artists; among them such distinguished names as that of Gustave Doré can be found on French music-sheets.

In the USA, too, engraving and lithography moved in line with the English developments and an immensely prolific business of sheet music publishing was soon flourishing. Sheet music was first published in America in 1788 and at this time, like its English equivalent, carried little or no decoration. The engraved half-title, often originating in England, appeared in the 1840s. The first American lithographer, Bass Otis, made his mark in 1819 and by the 1850s the printing business was burgeoning in the wake of booming American commerce, which included the growth of innumerable music-publishers. The first lithographed title-page for a music sheet was the work of David Claypoole Johnston and was for a piece called 'The Log House' by Anton Philip Heinrich, a prolific composer of forgotten Victoriana, published in 1825. Johnston, known as the American Cruikshank, is connected with only a dozen or so music covers. America's Concanen was George Endicott, who started out in 1828 by using British models but soon acquired his own identity. Another important name is that of Nathaniel Currier. An extensive chronicle of American artists can be found in Levy's *Picture the Songs*.

While the Victorian period provides the peak of music-cover artistry, with some elegance surviving into Edwardian days, the advent of mass-production and cheaper printing led to an inevitable decline in this field of artistic endeavour. The gentle lithograph was deserted for mechanical means in the 20th century, but even here distance lends enchantment, and as the 1920s and 1930s recede so do their manifestations take on a period charm of their own. Up to *c.*1930 or so music-covers still retain the attraction that the hand of an artist can provide. An ongoing source of inspiration was to be the musical show whose scores and individual songsheets often copy the relevant poster artwork, providing a good linking theme for collectors. The cheap and nasty paper that came in with the wartime years saw sheet-music mainly decorated with photographs of artists and film stills. They provide collectable material for their own reasons and will continue to do so as they become increasingly historical.

UK: S. Sitwell: *Morning, Noon and Night in London* (London, 1948). A. H. King: *English Pictorial Musical Title-Pages, 1820–85* (London, 1950). D. & S. Spellman: *Victorian Music Covers* (London, 1969). R. Pearsall: *Victorian Sheet Music Covers* (Newton Abbot, 1972). J. M. Garrett: *Sixty Years of British Music Hall* (London, 1976). C. Haill: *Victorian Illustrated Music Sheets* (London, 1981). T. Locanto: *Some Girls Do and Some Girls Don't: Sheet Music Covers* (London, 1985).

USA: H. Dichter and E. Shapiro: *Early American Sheet Music: its Lure and its Lore, 1786–1889* (New York, 1941; repr. as *Handbook of Early American Sheet Music*, 1977). L. S. Levy: *Grace Notes in American History* (Norman, 1967). M. Wilk: *Memory Lane 1890–1925* (London, 1973. M. Klamkin: *Old Sheet Music: a Pictorial History* (New York, 1975). L. S. Levy: *Picture the Songs* (Baltimore–London, 1976).

Music-Hall. The kind of entertainment that became generally and collectively known as 'music-hall' came to recognizable fruition in the middle of the 19th century, around the year 1850, the time when so many kinds of popular music-making were finding a definitive form and character. In essence 'music-hall' was simply a miscellaneous compilation of acts brought together to form a balanced and light-hearted evening of entertainment aimed at a predominantly lowbrow and working-class audience; the alternative name of 'variety', which was used throughout its history, being a fair description of its intent. Apart from encouraging the cult of the 'star' name (already established in the legitimate theatre) music-hall did not contribute to any significant dramatic advances, except perhaps to spawn similar entertainments (such as revue) that were also dedicated to the spirit of variety.

Before music-hall became a recognized professional outlet, similar kinds of entertainment would undoubtedly have been going on for as long as humanity had the taste for them. In Britain, and other European countries, such loosely compiled evenings of mutual enjoyment would have found their natural home in the taverns; and, in a more purposeful way, in the booths of the town or village fairs, notably in the bigger city and London fairs like St Bartholomew's, illustrations of which show many such occasions in progress. Up to the beginning of the 19th century, such activities might be considered as part of the folk-art scene, the rewards for it depending on the well-earned goodwill of the spectators. Professional 'music-hall' differed from this and came about, as many sociologists have pointed out, when there was an audience both able and willing to pay for it; in the case of music-hall, a lower middle-class and working-class audience wanting a night out with the family, in the first instance at weekends, later as the nightly (except on Sundays) facility that we expect today.

A move towards a professional world of popular theatre and music can be seen in the 'one-man' shows put on by entertainers like Charles *Dibdin around the turn of the century, and in the concerts given in the Pleasure Gardens and spas of London and elsewhere, where the entertainment once provided by such eminent people as Handel and Arne gradually became increasingly lowbrow; as a result of which we find various established music-publishers moving into the area of the comic song in the period 1800–30. In, or soon after this period, in the old coffee-house tradition, many convivial 'song-and-supper rooms' were opened, mainly catering for the affluent middle-class male enjoying a night out. Here the format of the music-hall evening was evolved, with a chairman introducing the acts and trying to maintain order and attention amid the hubbub of eating and drinking. The entertainers here were often those who had provided fair-weather entertainment at the pleasure gardens and were soon to move on to the first established music-halls. These were mainly singer-songwriters such as W. G. *Ross, Sam *Cowell, Jack Sharp, Thomas *Hudson, Harry *Clifton, and Sam *Collins. They are to be counted among the first professional popular songwriters.

At this point many enterprising publicans, realizing the growing potential of a working-class family audience, began to add saloons or halls to their premises which could provide entertainment run on the lines of the song-and-supper rooms like the Coal Hole in the Strand, the Cyder Cellars in Maiden Lane, and *Evans's in Covent Garden, places to provide mixed entertainment to attract eaters and drinkers of all ages and both sexes. The generic name 'music-hall' quite simply arose from such halls which set out, at first, to provide fairly high-class musical entertainment (including opera) but soon found their own level of mixed comedy, comic songs, and other acts.

The growth of these halls, reflecting the quick fortunes that were to be made in this opportunist area, was now amazingly rapid. The Mogul in Holborn opened its famous saloon in 1847; the Grapes in Southwark opened its Grand Harmonic Hall (later to become the Surrey Music Hall) in 1848; the Canterbury Hall in Lambeth was opened by Charles Morton (1819–1904) in 1851. By 1860 music-hall was a flourishing industry bolstered by the custom-made theatres like Wilton's in Whitechapel, the Bedford in Camden Town (1860), the Metropolitan in the Edgware Road, and Collins's in Islington in 1862. It has been estimated that by 1868 there were some 200 variety outlets in London (including such well-known venues as the *Oxford Music Hall in Oxford Street) and probably another 300 or so scattered through the larger cities and towns in the rest of Britain.

The cultivation of the star entertainer happened almost immediately. The first generation of music-hall stars who could command good salaries and made a practice of promoting their own exclusive songs was well established in the Canterbury era; including such names as Alfred *Vance, J. H. Stead (1827–86), 'Jolly' John *Nash, Arthur *Lloyd, Harry *Rickards, W. B. Fair (1840–1909) (singing 'Tommy, make room for your uncle'), George *Leybourne, Harry *Liston, Herbert Campbell (1846–1904), and G. H. *McDermott. The next generation, the stars gradually growing in magnitude, and lasting into what might be called the Oxford era, included Jenny *Hill, Arthur *Roberts, James Fawn (1849–1923), G. H. *Chirgwin, Charles *Coborn, R. G. *Knowles, Harry *Randall, and the great Dan *Leno.

By 1914 the London County Council, after an alarming number of music-hall and theatre fires, introduced stricter controls, with eating and drinking in the auditorium finally banned. Henceforth the music-halls were forced to become simply theatres run on the same lines as those in the legitimate domain. The big stars during this changeover period, which many saw as marking the end of true music-hall, were Eugene *Stratton, Albert *Chevalier, Tom *Costello, Leo *Dryden, Gus *Elen, Vesta *Tilley, Mark Sheridan, Little Tich (1867–1928), J. W. Rickaby (1869–1929) (billed as 'England's Greatest Comic Singer'), Harry *Champion, George *Robey, Nellie *Wallace, Kate *Carney, and, among the highest-paid stars of the halls, Marie *Lloyd and Harry *Lauder. The last generation of stars in the final legitimate music-hall era included Marie Kendall (1873–1964), Ada *Reeve (1874–1966), Harry Tate (1872–1940), Vesta *Victoria, Florrie *Forde, Wilkie *Bard, Billy *Merson, G. H. *Elliott, Will *Fyffe, Randolph Sutton (1888–1969), Clarice *Mayne, and Hetty King (1883–1972). After this, music-hall, which generally reverted to the old name of Variety, became linked with outlets such as the cinema and radio which were to be partly the cause of its ultimate demise, except in revival form, so that the music-hall was virtually extinct by the onset of the Second World War and its last stars, like Gracie *Fields, George *Formby Jr., and Max Miller (1895–1963), were to make much of their reputation through these new mediums.

While the true music-hall is generally seen as a peculiarly British phenomenon, it nevertheless had strong manifestations in at least two other Western countries, namely France and the USA. The French adopted the name 'music-hall' and a concurrent tradition grew up in France only partly influenced by what was happening in England. The French style of music-hall had some of its roots in the peculiarly French *chanson traditions of the *café-concerts and cabaret. It was made up of turns and acts in the British manner, but increasingly took on a more sophisticated middle-class tone and drew nearer to the era of the spectacular revue-style entertainment of the Folies-Bergère, with its devotion to the sight of the exposed human body. The characteristic nature of the French music-hall arose from the fact that its seeds were sown in a different soil and perhaps even more from the different styles of humour, the French aiming at a higher level of satire while the British clung to their liking for ribaldry and low vulgarity. The early stars of the French music-hall included such as Aristide *Bruant, Gaby *Deslys, Yvette *Guilbert, Félix Mayol, *Mistinguett, Paulus, and one important import from England, Harry *Fragson. Its biggest stars were to be such as Maurice *Chevalier and Yves *Montand who visited the British variety theatre as shining examples of the French style which had started around 1860 in the steps of the British equivalent.

The Americans took their name from the French and called it *vaudeville, occasionally variety, with Tony *Pastor its leading entrepreneur in the 1880s. It took some of its tone and approach from visiting British stars but, not unexpectedly, developed a very American flavour. Its history is further dealt with under VAUDEVILLE.

General surveys: A. J. Parks and C. D. Stuart: *The Variety Stage* (London, 1895). A. Haddon: *The Story of the Music Hall* (London, 1935). M. W. Disher: *Winkles and Champagne* (London, 1938; New York, 1938, as *Music Hall Parade)*. H. Scott: *The Early Doors* (London, 1946). W. Macqueen Pope: *The Melodies Linger On* (London, 1950). R. Mander and J. Mitchinson: *British Music Hall* (London, 1965; rev. 1974). R. J. Mellor: *The Northern Music Hall* (Newcastle upon Tyne, 1970). D. F. Cheshire: *Music Hall in Britain* (Newton Abbot, 1974). R. Hudd: *Music Hall* (London, 1976). P. Bailey (ed.): *Music Hall: the Business of Pleasure* (London, 1986). J. S. Bratton (ed.): *Music Hall: Performance and Style* (London, 1986).

Reference and biographical: H. C. Newton: *Idols of the Halls* (London, 1928). S. T. Felstead: *Stars Who Made the Halls* (London, 1946). G. LeRoy: *Music Hall Stars of the Nineties* (London, 1952). P. Gammond: *Your Own, Your Very Own* (Shepperton, 1971). R. Busby: *British Music Hall: an Illustrated Who's Who* (London, 1976).

Bibliography: L. Senelick, D. F. Cheshire, and U. Schneider: *British Music Hall 1840–1923: a Bibliography and Guide to Sources* (Hamden, Conn., 1981).

Discography: B. Rust: *British Music Hall on Record* (London, 1979).

Music-halls: D. Howard: *London Theatres and Music Halls* (London, 1970).

France: Jacques-Charles: *Cent Ans de Music-Hall* (Paris, 1956). J. Feschotte: *Histoire du Music-Hall* (Paris, 1965). P. Leslie: *A Hard Act to Follow* (London–New York, 1978).

Music-hall songs. The music-hall nostalgists naturally lavish most of their attention on its stars, regarding the songs they sing as a mere offshoot of their activities. Within a consideration of the history and development of popular song, the music-hall product takes on a position of vital importance (the same applying to the *vaudeville scene in the USA), particularly in considering the impetus that the growth of music-hall gave to the creation of a professional world of popular music and all its associated commercial and creative activities. The popular song world until *c.*1800 was mainly that of itinerant musicians and anonymous songwriters. Except in the cheap form of the *broadsheet, popular music was not obtainable, affordable, or in demand. A few isolated entertainers like *Dibdin were getting their songs into print in 1800 and the widespread production of bound collections of popular songs, indiscriminately mingling the works of such as Dibdin, often uncredited and treated as folk-songs, with genuine folk-songs unscrupulously cleaned up and harmonized, began in the 1820s.

Otherwise the occasional light or 'comic' song was still the unconsidered offshoot of the classical world and its composers, as it had been for centuries. The first songs, almost inevitably comic, which bore any resemblance to music-hall songs and the popular song of the future, were those printed by otherwise respectable music-publishers intended to be sold as a profitable adjunct to the increasingly lowbrow activities at the Pleasure Gardens, like Vauxhall, or the song-and-supper rooms. The first of these songs, with the soon to be familiar engraved pictorial covers, came from such publishing houses as that founded by William Dale (*d* 1827) around 1809 and carried on by his family in Poultry in the City of London. By the 1830s their lists carried a selection of comic items that included such songs as 'He was such a nice young man', 'I'm very unhappy indeed', and 'All round my hat' (this last an adaptation of a folk-song). These inevitably carried claims of having been sung 'at Vauxhall (or elsewhere)' by 'so-and-so', thus firmly identifying them in the public's memory. Their style is quaint and droll, rather than actually funny, in the demurely middle-class way of the concurrent minstrel show publications. The only people who possessed pianos to play them on were the middle classes, and they would not have wanted anything that was not beyond reproach in their drawing-rooms. Other publishers, such as Cocks, Jeffreys, Paulton, Metzler, and others, moved into the market. During the first half of the 19th century these songs moved nearer to what we would now recognize as a music-hall song, their humour growing broader and lower in the mode of music-hall entertainment. This progressive adaptation can be seen in the output of a publisher wholly dedicated to the popular market such as Charles Sheard (responsible for the *Musical Bouquet series, which indiscriminately mixed popular operatic arias, minstrel songs, light piano works, hymns, social dances, and music songs) whose issues are a clear reflection of the now fairly rapid changes in the entertainment market. Sheard publications of *c.*1850–60 still retain the folk-song aura, quaintness and drollery still there in their self-conscious pages, but gradually becoming more blatantly 'common' in approach, more professional and more direct, and decidedly more humorous. There is a parallel in journalism, where we can follow the progress of fashions in humour in the pages of the publication *Punch*, founded in 1842. A tell-tale sign in the songs is the switch from the objectivity of the folk-song—'there was a young maiden'—arising from the modest anonymity of the writer, to the subjectivity of the fully-fledged music-hall song where the words deliberately focus attention on the singer who is characterizing a part: 'Champagne Charlie is my name'.

The true music-hall song that was to develop in the next two decades is essentially comic or satirical to the point of cynicism, even when it is being tenderly romantic. Some of the best songs were to be those which managed to touch the heart-strings in spite of their comic guise. It is the very character of the music-hall that dictates this; the toughness, the wryness hides a friendly sentimentality. The best songs of the peak period *c.*1890–1910 would incorporate qualities that were only being glimpsed in the earlier songs. Yet a clear case can be made in support of the literary superiority of some of the songs that appeared in this formative period and which would have been heard in the song-and-supper rooms and early 'halls' *c.*1850–80. Many of these, some of which can be found in the pages of John Ashton's quaint anthology *Street Ballads* (1888), are simply residual folk-songs in nature; such items as *'Vilikens and his Dinah', 'The ratcatcher's daughter', and 'If I had a donkey wot wouldn't go', are anonymous gems that have the timeless artlessness of the best folk-songs, but somehow manage to suggest the hand of a professional, if still unknown, craftsman purposefully writing for the stage. Ashton might well have included Harry *Clifton's masterpiece 'Polly Perkins of Paddington Green' (written around 1863) if it had not been fully credited to its writer and interpreter and is even more clearly in the category of a popular song.

The difference between 'Polly Perkins' and the items included in Ashton's book may, in fact, be slight, for the humour is often very much the same way inclined, the themes similar, the language almost identical. But in 'Polly Perkins' the new involvement of the 'modern' song may first be sensed in contrast to the observational detachment of the folk-song. It ends with an example of literary bathos that is pure music-hall and not yet encountered in any folk-song:

> In six months she married, this hard-hearted girl,
> But it was not a 'Wicount' and it was not a 'Nearl';
> It was not a 'Baronite' but a shade or two wus'—
> 'Twas a bow-legg'd Conductor of a twopenny bus.

It remains one of the best sure-fire laughter producers in the music-hall repertoire. It is meant to be funny and it is. Moreover, it is pointed modern humour rather than the sly banter of the Shakespearian tradition. It is a new humour which is to be fully exploited not only in the music-hall but in the more highbrow lyrics of W. S. *Gilbert and his followers. The only reason for not claiming 'Polly Perkins' as quintessentially a music-hall song is that its music still has a residual folky element about it. It was probably borrowed by Clifton from the folk-song, 'Nightingales sing', which can be found in many collections. The same tune was used for the Newcastle-based 'Cushie Butterfield', which virtually remains a folk-song in nature; while 'Polly Perkins' had been transformed by Clifton into an early music-hall masterpiece.

The 50 years or so of music-hall song production that followed spawned a new breed of Tin Pan Alley writers, a whole industry of publishers, and saw the production of thousand upon thousand of songs to cash in on the new demand. Out of the many thousands perhaps a couple of hundred emerge as unassailable successes—the ones, in short, which managed to combine, as 'Polly Perkins' had, the perfect tune with the perfect lyric. If we comb the products of those years we may, in fact, find many good lyrics lost to posterity; many good titles forgotten. They never found the good tune to carry them to immortality.

The music-hall world soon discovered that a clever writer and composer combining to produce a good song was not the end of the matter. It now had to be marketed by a good publisher, and he was dependent upon the right singer or performer to get the song over to the public. The songbooks of the 1860s and thereabouts still contain the sort of songs that the travelling musicians might have been taking around the taverns and fairs for years. They usually have a quaintly droll story to tell at secondhand: 'The female auctioneer', 'The Irishman' (already a favourite subject), 'The Captain's whiskers', 'The ratcatcher's daughter', 'Giles Scroggins', the story of the little old woman in 'Hot Codlings' (that Grimaldi told), and such literary narrative songs as Thomas *Hood's 'The lost child'. One of the first modern 'personal' songs was J. H. Stead's theme song 'The regular cure'. He performed this in a sort of pierrot costume, bouncing up and down with his feet together innumerable times while he sang. It is not a particularly good song but his theatrical presentation made it into a top hit of the day. Moreover it is distinctly music-hall in flavour.

From the 1870s the old folky ballads had gone and the songs were now totally concerned with drawing attention to the character who was singing them. The credits tell us, moreover, that they were to be sung by that artist alone. In order to hear the popular song of the day, music-hall audiences had to wait patiently for the relevant star to come their way. The star concerned could get a lot of mileage out of a good song probably bought, along with the exclusive rights, for a couple of guineas. Thus George *Leybourne's 'Champagne Charlie' has become a totally theatrical experience, somebody acting a part and selling a good song to the public. In the next generation it was Charles *Coborn and 'The man who broke the bank at Monte Carlo'. But the British audience was not one to admire self-glorification all the time. They liked the entertainment to be spiced with a little sentiment. Not too sentimental, though; a little self-mockery and burlesque were essential. 'The boy in the gallery', residually folky, types itself as a first-rate music-hall song, slightly less than serious with lines like 'there he is a-waving of his handkerchief' but with just the right touch of tearfulness about it. Here we have, again, one of those music-hall masterpieces, like 'Polly Perkins', that have all the right elements, the natural predecessors of 'My old Dutch' and 'Don't dilly dally on the way'.

By the 1870s firms like Hopwood & Crew had moved wholeheartedly into producing music-hall songs with colourful lithographed covers (now familiar and sought after) blazoned with the names and frequently with portraits of their popularizers; and Charles Sheard's image was likewise changing. The founding of the firm of Francis Bros. & Day (soon to be *Francis, Day & Hunter) in 1877 established the wholehearted beginnings of the *Tin Pan Alley world of popular music publishing; publishers established on the profits of the popular song. It is interesting to note that most of these firms like Francis, Day & Hunter had two profitable outlets—the working-class world of the music-hall and the equally flourishing middle-class world of the *minstrel show, of which Mr Harry Hunter was a leading light. The popular song would have developed through some outlet or other simply in response to the growing affluence of the less privileged classes; history designed it so that it was the music-hall that provided the lucifer to start the blaze.

So music-hall songs moved from the gentle folkery of 'Polly Perkins' and 'The boy in the gallery', to the rumbustious self-asserting swagger of 'Champagne Charlie' and 'Act on the square', to the homely personalized humour of the Cockney song such as 'If it wasn't for the 'ouses in between' and 'It's a great big shame' and their northern and Scottish equivalents; to the comparatively modernistic refinement of Leslie *Stuart's 'Lily of Laguna'. Before the music-hall era had passed it had embraced the strains of ragtime and jazz; but once the working-class folk element had gone, so had its true spirit.

The financial evolution of the song-writing business was also indicative of the social changes behind it. Moving from the common property, unpaid days of folk-song, the early music-hall songs were bought from the composers and/or authors for perhaps as little as a guinea. They were then considered to be the sole property of the singer who had bought them and who flaunted these exclusive rights on the cover. The writers would neither expect or get any further reward, but would simply sit down and churn out the next song for the next day's bread-and-butter. In time, the creators began to realize their indispensability and to demand royalties; rights which the formation of the Performing Rights Society and the copyright laws confirmed and protected. The linking of song and singer remained an integral part of the popular song scene, but it had to be confirmed by achievement and publicity rather than a sovereign bond.

General surveys: C. Pulling: *They Were Singing* (London, 1952). C. McInnes: *Sweet Saturday Night: Pop Song 1840–1920* (London, 1967).

Song collections: Anon: *Sixty Old-Time Variety Songs* (London, n.d.; many reprints). C. Chilton (ed.): *Victorian Folk Songs* (London, 1965). P. Davison (ed.): *Songs of the British Music Hall* (London, 1971). P. Gammond (ed.): *Music Hall Songbook* (Newton Abbot, 1975). J. M. Garrett (ed.): *Sixty Years of British Music Hall* (London, 1976). P. Gammond (ed.): *The Good Old Days Songbook* (London, 1980).

Music in the Air. Musical comedy with score by Jerome *Kern and book by Oscar *Hammerstein II, first produced at the Alvin Theatre, New York, 8 Nov. 1932, where it achieved 342 performances. The cast included Walter Slezak (1902–83), Natalie Hall (*b* 1904), and Al Shean (1868–1949). It was produced in London at His Majesty's Theatre 19 May 1933 [275p] and was revived in New York in 1933 [196p] and 1951 [56p]. The score contained such Kern hits as 'I've told ev'ry little star', 'And love was born', 'One more dance', 'In Egern on the Tegern See', 'The song is you', and 'Music in the air', their general operetta nature placing this work, one of Kern's most stylish and unified, in that interim period between operetta (which it is sometimes called) and the musical, where the jazz idiom had taken over. The songs were neatly woven into the story in operatic fashion; and while the American touch of the 1930s was more apparent than any European operetta strains, the music of Kern never became as committed to jazz as that of George *Gershwin. It was filmed in 1934 with Gloria Swanson (1897–1983), John *Boles, June Lang (*b* 1915), and Al Shean.

Music Man, The. American musical comedy written by Meredith *Willson. It was produced at the Majestic Theatre, New York, 19 Dec. 1957, achieving a magnificent run of 1375 performances, with Robert *Preston as the con man who has a line in brass band instruments and eventually captures the heart of the right-thinking librarian played by Barbara *Cook. In London, at the Adelphi Theatre 16 March 1961, it achieved a run of 395 performances with Van Johnson and Patricia Lambert in the leading roles.

It was an unusual and well-conceived work, successfully capturing an old-time atmosphere with the story based on the author's memories of his boyhood in Iowa and full of robust musical numbers such as 'Seventy-six trombones' which has an echo in 'Goodnight, my someone', 'Rock Island', 'Till there was you', and a clever patter song, 'Trouble'. One of the few modern musicals that have the manageable ingredients that make it ideal for amateur production, it was filmed in 1962 starring Robert Preston and Shirley Jones (*b* 1934).

Music-publishing. Until the end of the 19th century music-publishing was almost entirely concerned with the areas of 'classical' or 'serious' music, there being no obvious commercial demand for printed popular music. The exceptions to this were a few early publishers like John *Playford, who catered for the minority demand for folk-dance material, and a handful of literary publishers who issued *broadside ballads and chapbooks that developed into the publication of various collections of edited folk-songs and popular items around 1800–50.

The demand for printed popular music developed gradually, in reponse to the growing affluence of the middle and lower classes. From around 1800 established publishers were issuing piano music and ballads of a drawing-room nature to cater for the needs of the piano-owning *nouveau riche*; and firms like Dale & Son, Goulding Phipps & D'Almaine, Bland & Weller, Clementi and various partners, Hime and Willis in Dublin, moved gradually into this field. The first true popular songs were of the comic variety and were published in response to the growing demand for souvenir sheet music resulting from the gradual lowering of brows in the pleasure gardens, with *Vauxhall the leader in the field. To emphasize the popular nature of these, the illustrated cover, at first usually a half-page engraving, began to appear, some of the first examples coming from William Dale (founded in 1809). Established publishers like Chappell and Boosey now quickly moved into the popular sheet music field and were devoting a large portion of their energies to it by 1850.

Among the first publishers to direct their efforts mainly toward the popular field were Hopwood & Crew (later *Ascherberg, Hopwood & Crew) who discovered the talents of songwriters like Harry *Clifton and dance composers like Charles Coote, Sidney Jones Sr., and Charles D'Albert. They produced their lithographed music-hall covers with the restraint of their classical successors. Charles Sheard (1826–1918) interspersed the popular classical image of the *Musical Bouquet with similar sedately illustrated sheets; and John *Blockley did the same for the drawing-room buyers.

The first of the regular *Tin Pan Alley publishers in Britain, with the true common touch, were *Francis, Day & Hunter (originally Francis & Day) who set up their business on the strength of their *minstrel connections and immediately moved in to the *music-hall field when it rapidly began to expand in the 1870s. They gradually swallowed up rival publishers like Bert *Feldman (who had already bought out Herman *Darewski), Reynolds, and others, settling in the Charing Cross Road and later transforming themselves as Keith Prowse and latterly EMI Music. Off the main thoroughfare in a seedy byway called Denmark Street a host of successors settled to form London's Tin Pan Alley community led by Lawrence Wright.

In the USA parallel activities took place, perhaps even more diverse because of a greater choice of large city centres, unlike the UK, where everything centred on London. Before 1891, when the first US International Copyright proclamation was issued, any foreign publication could be reprinted in the USA, and a number of British songs appeared there from 1640 on, often with identical covers and contents but also often newly credited to American sources.

Publishing activities closely paralleled those in Britain. The old-established printer, like Oliver Ditson in Boston (1835) and his sons Charles in New York (1867) and James in Philadelphia (1875), moved carefully into the popular field. American popular song was most wholeheartedly espoused by songwriters who set up as publishers themselves like Septimus *Winner (1843) in Philadelphia and Charles W. Harris in Troy, NY (1864), a practice continued by Irving *Berlin and others in the 20th century. The equivalent Francis, Day & Hunter Tin Pan Alley publishers of the late 19th century were the Witmark family (1885) and Harms (1881), followed by a host of others formed to cash in on the various popular music booms of the 1900s. See also under TIN PAN ALLEY.

My Fair Lady. Musical play with score by Frederick *Loewe and book by Alan Jay *Lerner, based on George Bernard Shaw's *Pygmalion*. The first New York production was at the Mark Hellinger Theatre 15 Mar. 1956, where it was to run for an impressive 2717 performances; with Rex *Harrison as Henry Higgins, Julie *Andrews as Eliza Doolittle, Stanley *Holloway as Alfred Doolittle, and Moss *Hart directing. A magnificent score included such things as 'Why can't the English', 'Wouldn't it be loverly', 'With a little bit of luck', 'I'm an ordinary man', 'I could have danced all night', 'The rain in Spain', 'Ascot gavotte', 'On the street where you live', 'Get me to the Church on time', 'I've grown accustomed to her face', and many more—a melodic lavishness hardly ever encountered since the days of *Gilbert and Sullivan. It was equally successful in London at the Theatre Royal, Drury Lane, 30 Apr. 1958, enjoying the talents of the same principals and running for 2281 performances. When it was filmed in 1964 the part of Eliza Doolittle was rather surprisingly given to Audrey Hepburn (1929–93) (with the singing dubbed by Marni Nixon) and not to Julie Andrews.

My Fair Lady was one of the most successful and lasting musicals of all time, its quality based on the often overlooked asset of a classic story that has taken on the perennial strength of a folk legend. Such stories have almost inevitably lain behind most successful operettas. Neither opera nor musical comedy is noted for the strength of its plots, but Shaw's *Pygmalion* has the kind of uncomplicated yet compelling tale that is easy to follow and emotionally satisfying. The only basic alteration to the play was to make the ending a slightly happier one, and Lerner's lyrics matched the dialogue ideally. The strength of the story inspired a score that hardly has a lapse in it, moving things along naturally with the songs implanting their qualities firmly in the memory. There was no makeweight writing anywhere, and literary excellence was matched by musical excellence. Here was a libretto in which character was fully developed to an extent rarely experienced in a musical.

It was furthermore a wise decision to use first-rate actors who were not necessarily singers; or, in the case of Julie Andrews, a first-rate singer who could act reasonably well. Both she and Stanley Holloway were good all-round professionals. But the most notable influence on the end result came from Rex Harrison. The authors wrote with him in mind and found it necessary to write songs that did not ask for vocal prowess. Not that his singing capacity should be underrated, but the half-spoken style that emerged was greatly successful in that it allowed lyrics of depth and meaning to be clearly articulated. Perhaps the only misfortune was that the success of this approach here meant that every musical for the next two decades generally had a strong hint of *My Fair Lady* in it. The musical stage had now found a way to promote thought and action in song; almost a move back to melodic recitative.

The show had many interesting facets of this nature; but above all it was a romantic, artistically staged, burstingly tuneful musical that appealed to the widest possible audience of all brows. If it could not be classed musically with *Die Fledermaus* or *The Merry Widow*, which both had scores intended for skilled singers, its combined assets put it on the same level as a piece of effective and memorable theatre.

N

Nacht in Venedig, Eine (*A Night in Venice*). Operetta with music by Johann *Strauss II and book by F. Zell [Kamillo Walzel] and Richard *Genée, first seen at the Städtisches Theater, Berlin, 3 Oct. 1883 with Karoline Finaly and Alexander Girardi in the cast; then in Vienna, at the Theater an der Wien 9 Oct. 1883, with the same cast [160p]. It was the only Strauss operetta not to have its première in Vienna. Although not his best work, it has an enjoyable and sustainable story centred on the comic romance of Annina, a fish-seller, and Caramello, a sort of latter-day barber of Seville, who works for the amorous Duke of Urbino. The plot unfolds in colourful Venice and has some splendid musical items including 'Komm' in die Gondel' and a strong waltz song: 'Ach! wie so herrlich zu schau'n' ('Lagunen-walzer'). A new version, with the score revised by Erich Wolfgang *Korngold, was produced by the Vienna State Opera 23 June 1929, and there was a notable London production at the Cambridge Theatre 24 May 1944.

Nairne, Carolina [*née* Oliphant, Caroline] (*b* Gask, Perthshire, 21 July 1766; *d* Gask, 26 Oct. 1845). Scottish author and composer. She was the daughter of a well-known Jacobite family and married Major William Murray Nairne, who became Lord Nairne in 1824 when George IV restored many Scottish titles. She wrote many poems and verses, some published in the posthumous *Lays from Strathearn* (1851), including her popular 'Wi' a hundred pipers'. It had been published in Edinburgh as 'a celebrated Jacobite song' and the tune was probably an old Scottish air, adapted by either Nairne or the singer Elizabeth Rainforth (1814–77) who is credited with the arrangement. Nairne also wrote the words of 'Charlie is my darling', 'Will ye no' come back again', and 'The land o' the leal' to traditional Scottish airs, 'Caller herrin'' (*m* Nathaniel *Gow), 'The laird o' Cockpen', 'The auld house', 'The lament of Flora Macdonald', and 'The lass of Gowrie'.

C. Rogers (ed.): *Life and Songs of the Baroness Nairne* (Edinburgh, 1896). G. Henderson: *Lady Nairne and her Songs* (London, 1900).

Nance, 'Ray' Willis (*b* Chicago, 10 Dec. 1913; *d* New York, 28 Jan. 1976). American jazz trumpeter, violinist, singer, and dancer. He played the piano when he was six and took up the violin three years later, studying at the Chicago Music College. Later he took up the trumpet and played with the college band. He sang and played, and led his own sextet, in Chicago clubs from 1932 until he joined the Earl *Hines band 1937–8, and was with Horace Henderson (*b* 1904) 1939–40. Then he joined the Duke *Ellington band and shared in one of its finest creative periods until 1944 (playing the trumpet solo on the band's theme tune, 'Take the A train') when he left to form his own small band. He returned to Ellington for the period 1945–63, with brief absences, during which time he was with the British tour of 1948 with Ellington and Kay Davis (*b* 1920). He led his own band in 1964 and toured Europe as a soloist in 1966, making brief returns to the Ellington fold 1965–71. A versatile musician with a flair for humour, his violin playing was an unusual diversion in many jazz performances and recordings.

Nanton, Joe 'Tricky Sam' [Irish, Joseph N.] (*b* New York, 1 Feb. 1904; *d* San Francisco, 20 July 1946). Son of a West Indian family, he had early musical experience with Cliff Jackson (1902–70) and Elmer Snowden (1900–73) before joining the Duke *Ellington band in 1926, where he was to spend the rest of his career, an integral voice, with his growling tone and wah-wah muted effects, in the creation of the Ellington 'jungle' style of the 1930s, and an imaginative soloist.

Nash, Johnny (*b* Houston, 19 Aug. 1940). American soul and reggae singer and composer. Having made his mark on the Texas TV programme *Matinee*, he gave up a university place and began making records, but without early success. He appeared in films and thought of becoming an actor, but eventually had a soul hit with 'Let's move and groove together' (1965). While doing film work in the Caribbean he discovered reggae and recorded 'Hold me tight' (1966), following this with recordings of songs by Bob *Marley, 'Guava jelly' and 'Stir it up'. He had a No. 1 hit with his own 'I can see clearly now' (1972) and continued to have success with Marley's material, and a further No. 1 hit with 'Tears on my pillow'. He ran his own record label in the 1960s and wrote many hits such as 'What kind of love is this' for Joey Dee and other artists.

Nash, 'Jolly' John (*b* 1830; *d* London, 13 Oct. 1901). British music-hall singer and comedian. After working in his youth as an iron-smelter, he became known as an entertainer in the Midlands where he was billed as 'The Laughing Blacksmith'. A large man who shook with mirth as he sang, he pioneered the laughing song which was copied by many later exponents; he was also an early practitioner of the funny walk. He became known in the song-and-supper rooms and was on the bill when the South London Music Hall opened in 1860 and at the *Oxford Music Hall in 1861, at which time he was a rival in popularity to artists like George *Leybourne. He was chairman at the Strand Music Hall 1866–8, toured the USA in 1874 and 1876, and had his own touring company from 1877 which he took to the USA in 1886 for 18 months. His repertoire included such personalized numbers as 'Sister Mary walked like that', 'The little fat grey man', 'I couldn't help laughing', 'The merry topper', 'I'm not inquisitive', 'Rackity Jack', and 'Ho, ho, ho—hee, hee, hee' (his version of the traditional 'Little brown jug'). He published a volume of stories, anecdotes, and adventures, *The Merriest Man Alive* (1891), and *Jolly Nash's Comic Song Book*.

Nashville. American city in the state of Tennessee, in the midst of the Appalachian Mountains where much of America's musical folk heritage was nurtured, which has become the world centre of *country music. Its broadcasting, recording, and general promotional activities started on 28 Nov. 1925 with the first relay on WSM of the **National Barn Dance* programme featuring many old-time country performers. This led to WSM's own **Grand Ole Opry* on 10 Dec. 1927, its name invented by announcer George D. Hay (1895–1968), MC of *Barn Dance* since 1924. The show was broadcast from several venues before the Grand Ole Opry House finally settled in 1974, in Opryland, a modern auditorium just outside the city.

Capitol Records was one of the first to start recording activities in Nashville, with Eddy *Arnold in 1944, building studios there in 1950, followed by most major labels. From being a minor and specialized interest country music became a popular branch of pop music with artists like Jim *Reeves, Ernest *Tubb, and Johnny *Cash all contributing to what has become known as the Nashville Sound. Nashville's Music Row is the equivalent of New York's *Tin Pan Alley in country terms and the famous Midnite Jamboree takes place at Ernest Tubb's Record Shop on Nashville's Broadway. In spite of rival activities in other centres, and many artists trying to break away from the Nashville mould, the city and its organization still keep an iron grip on worldwide country music activities. A film, *Nashville* (1975), directed by Robert Altman (*b* 1922), was an effective mosaic of life and work in the home of country music. It included lightly disguised portraits of such key figures as Loretta *Lynn and Hank *Snow.

***National Barn Dance*.** Country variety show which began on WLS radio in Chicago in 1924, under George D. Hay (1895–1968). After it had been heard on Nashville's WSM outlet in 1925, Hay later organized the **Grand Ole Opry* programme. *Barn Dance* continued on WLS until 1960 when it moved to WGN, to continue until 1970.

***Naughty Marietta*.** Operetta with music by Victor *Herbert and book by Rida Johnson *Young, first heard in Syracuse in 1910 and at the New York Theatre, New York, 7 Nov. 1910, with Emma Trentini as Marietta. Produced by the opera impresario Oscar Hammerstein (1846–1919), it had only 136 initial performances but has since become a classic of the American musical theatre and its songs like 'Tramp! tramp! tramp!', 'Naughty Marietta', 'Italian street song', 'Live for today', 'I'm falling in love with someone', and 'Ah! sweet mystery of life' are among Herbert's best-known creations.

The story was set in New Orleans in 1870 where the romance between Marietta and pirate gang leader Captain Dick comes to fruition when she finds that he too knows her childhood 'dream melody' ('Ah! sweet mystery of life'). It was filmed, with a slightly altered story, in 1935, with Jeanette *MacDonald and Nelson *Eddy; and is now in the repertoire of the New York City Opera.

Navarro, Fats [Theodore] (*b* Key West, Fla., 24 Sept. 1923; *d* New York, 7 July 1950). American jazz trumpeter. He started his musical career as a tenor-saxophonist, but later switched to trumpet. He played with Andy Kirk 1943–4, and Billy *Eckstine 1945–6, becoming a leading figure in the developing world of *bebop in the 1940s.

Neagle, Anna [Robertson, Florence Marjorie] (*b* London, 20 Oct. 1904; *d* London, 3 June 1986). British actress, dancer, and singer. Although best remembered for her screen portrayals of historical ladies like Nell Gwyn, Florence Nightingale, and Queen Victoria, she was a part of the British musical scene of the 1920s and returned to the musical stage with great success in the 1960s. Her stage debut was in the musical field, appearing in the chorus of *Charlot's Revue* and *Tricks* in 1925 when she was only 11. She went on to cabaret and to further chorus appearances in **Rose-Marie* (1926); *The Charlot Show* (1926); *The *Desert Song* (1927); and as one of *Cochran's 'Young Ladies' in **This Year of Grace* (1928) and **Wake Up and Dream* (London and New York, 1929), still primarily a dancer. Her first big singing role was with Jack *Buchanan in *Stand Up and Sing* (1931)—'There's always tomorrow'; after which she moved to the film world in *Goodnight Vienna* (1932), *The Little Damozel* (1933), and **Bitter Sweet* (1933), in which she was directed by Herbert Wilcox. She married him in 1943 and worked with him until his death in 1977. Her famous straight screen roles came in the 1930s, but other musical roles were in *The Queen's Affair* (1934), *Lime Light* (1936), *London Melody* (1937); and, in Hollywood, **Irene* (1940), **No, No, Nanette* (1941), and **Sunny* (1941).

The finest musical fruits of the Wilcox–Neagle partnership were in the lightly romantic and fondly remembered films (with Michael Wilding) *Spring in Park Lane* (1941), *The Courtneys of Curzon Street* (1947), and *Maytime in Mayfair* (1949). In the

1950s she filmed *Lilacs in the Spring* (1954); **King's Rhapsody* (1956), and *The Lady is a Square* (1959); launched into a career as a producer; and, on stage, was seen in *The Glorious Days* (1953). The failure of her husband's film company in 1960 was countered by a triumphal appearance in the stage musical **Charlie Girl* (1965) which ran for 2047 performances, during which she was made a Dame of the British Empire. She relived old memories by playing in a revival of *No, No, Nanette* at Drury Lane in 1973, and in 1978 was in a tour of **My Fair Lady*. Her final appearance was in the pantomime *Cinderella* at Richmond (and at Christmas at the London Palladium) in 1982 when she was 78.

A. Neagle: *There's Always Tomorrow* (London, 1974).

Neapolitan Song (It. *canzone popolare Napoletana*). Romantic songs and ballads which were the Italian equivalent of the English Victorian *drawing-room ballad, similarly deriving from the Italian opera style of the early 19th century. One of the first canzones written in this style was 'Te voglio bene assaje' by Donizetti, published in 1835, which was simply an operatic aria without an opera. The basic formula was that of an arietta, the usual rhythm was 6/8 or 2/4 (often based on the tarantella or cabaletta), the style graceful and tuneful with generally well-written words expressing sentiments of love or longing for home, especially for Naples. Originally written for the middle-class drawing-room, as in the songs of Tosti, they gradually gained widespread popularity. At the same time their craftsmanship and operatic nature made them a sufficient challenge to attract the interest of celebrated opera singers.

Some of the best early lyrics were written by Salvatore Di Giacomo, who formulated a suitable style and shape for the purpose and inspired a group of similarly gifted writers in and around Naples. As in so many popular song developments it was a happy coincidence that found so many poets and composers of like mind in the same place at the same time. Giacomo's poems were set by such composers as Enrico De Leva ('Spingole frangese'), Mario Costa ('Erade maggio'), Francesco Paolo Tosti (1846–1916) ('Marechiaro'), and Vincenzo Valente, among many. The masterpieces of the genre began to arrive by the end of the 19th century. Giovanni Capurro's 'O sole mio' was put to music by Eduardo *Di Capua; and Peppino Capurro's 'Funiculi funcula' by Luigi *Denza on the occasion of the opening of the Vesuvius funicular railway in 1880. Other well-known lyricists were Ferdinando Russo, Libero Bovio, Eduardo Nicolardi, Ernesto Murolo, Antonio Barbieri, Aniello Califano, Pasquale Cinquegrana, G. B. De Curtis, Rocco Galdieri, E. A. Mario, and Raffaele Viviani. Composers active in the field were Rodolfo Falvo, Ernesto Tagliaferri, Ernesto De Curtis, Enrico Cannio, Vincenze di Chiara, Evemero Nardella, P. E. Fonzo, Salvatore Gambardella, and Gaetano Lama. Perhaps the most famous of all the Neapolitan songs was the immortal 'Santa Lucia'. This, 'O sole mio', and others up to more modern samples like 'Anema 'e core', have been brought to the world's attention by such opera stars as Caruso, Gigli, Di Stefano, Pavarotti, and by such specialists as Gennaro Pasquariello, especially popular in Italy. The tradition remains a strong and flourishing one.

Nelson, Oliver Edward (*b* St Louis, Mo., 4 June 1932; *d* Los Angeles, 28 Oct. 1975). American saxophonist, composer, and arranger. He played around St Louis from 1947, joined the Louis *Jordan band in 1951, then served in the navy. He studied music at Washington University 1954–8 and privately with Elliott Carter and George Tremblay. Moving to New York, he played with Erskine *Hawkins, Louie *Bellson, and on tenor with Quincy *Jones 1960–1 with whom he toured Europe. During 1959–61 he recorded his own compositions with various small groups, then went on to arrange for various big bands, including the Buddy *Rich band, leading his own big bands at various festivals in the 1960s. He moved to Los Angeles in 1967 where he was mainly writing for TV and films before he died of a heart-attack.

His jazz works, many owing a certain debt to Quincy Jones, included: 'Afro-American Sketches' (1960), 'Blues and the Abstract Truth' (1960), 'Soundpiece' (1964), 'Patterns' (1965), 'The Kennedy Dream Suite' (1967), 'Jazzhattan Suite' (1967), 'A Black Suite' (1970), 'Berlin Dialogue' (1970), 'Concert Piece' (1972). He wrote music for the films: *Death of a Gunfighter* (1969), *Skullduggery* (1969), and *Zigzag* (1970); and his TV credits included: *It Takes a Thief*; *Ironside*; *The Name of the Game*; *Longstreet*; and *The Six Million Dollar Man*.

Nelson, Rick [Eric Hilliard] (*b* Teaneck, NJ, 8 May 1940; *d* De Kalb, Ill., 31 Dec. 1985). American singer. He first became known at the age of eight on his parents' radio comedy series, later on TV, where he made himself remembered by the catchphrase 'I don't mess around, boy'. Becoming perhaps one of the best of the teen-idols of the 1950s, he had his first hit on the Verve label with the Fats *Domino song 'I'm walkin'' (1957) when he was only 16. He signed with Imperial Records and produced a string of hits that included 'Stood up' (1957), 'Believe what you say' (1958), 'Poor little fool' (a No. 1 hit in 1958), 'Never be anyone else but you' (1959), 'It's late' (1959), 'Travellin' man' (1960), and 'Hello, Mary Lou' (1961). Originally calling himself Ricky, he never offended anyone's parents, but managed to sound rebellious enough to appeal to the youngsters. He had a clean-cut image and a lopsided grin, singing in a pleasant, literate though limited sort of way, finding songs that suited his image well. Later in his career he turned to country music with fair success, recording one memorable single, 'Garden party' (1972). He was killed when a private plane he was travelling in crashed en route to Dallas.

Nelson, Willie (*b* Abbott, Texas, 30 Apr. 1933). American country singer and songwriter. He studied at Baylor University, then began singing in local bars, writing such songs as 'Hello walls', 'Crazy', and 'Night life' which were taken up by leading singers of the day. He went to Nashville and played bass in the band of Ray Price, continuing to make a reputation as a songwriter with 'The party's over' and 'Little things' which he sang on the *Grand Ole Opry programme. He recorded with RCA in Nashville but left them to join Atlantic and, later, Columbia in a determined effort to make his way as both singer and writer. A leader and important stylist in the breakaway outlaw country music movement, he returned to Texas to rival the dominant *Nashville sound with the Austin sound.

B. Allen: *Waylon and Willie* (New York, 1979).

Nesbitt, Max (*b* Cape Town, 18 Oct. 1903; *d* London, 5 Apr. 1966) and **Harry** (*b* Cape Town, 18 Dec. 1905; *d* London, 20 Oct. 1968). South African comedians, singers, and songwriters. They made their first joint appearance in Cape Town in 1909 and first appeared in London at the Mile End Empire in 1927. They became a popular duo and appeared in the show *Blue Skies* (1927), afterwards making tours of Europe and the USA. They appeared in *Black Velvet* (1939) at the London Hippodrome and worked for ENSA during the war. They made regular appearances in variety and were in the BBC's first music-hall broadcasts. They wrote most of their own songs, including 'Without that certain thing' (1935), 'Georgia's gotta moon' (1938), 'Tears on my pillow' (1939), and 'Last night' (1939).

Nevin, Ethelbert Woodbridge (*b* Edgeworth, Pa., 25 Nov. 1862; *d* New Haven, Conn., 17 Feb. 1901). American composer. He studied for many years in the USA, and in Germany between 1877 and 1886, and lived abroad a good deal before settling in New Haven. His songs continued the tradition of the *drawing-room ballad and some of them became immensely popular all over the world, including 'Oh! that we two were maying' (1888, *w* Charles Kingsley), 'Little Boy Blue' (1891, *w* Eugene Field), 'The rosary' (1898, *w* Robert Cameron Rogers, 1862–1912), which sold 6 million copies in the next 30 years, and 'Mighty lak' a rose' (1901, *w* Frank L. Stanton, 1857–1927). His piano composition 'Narcissus' (1891) also became widely popular and a drawing-room standard.

V. Thompson: *The Life of Ethelbert Nevin* (Boston, 1913).
J. T. Howard: *Ethelbert Nevin* (New York, 1935).

New age music. A genre that emerged in the 1980s, being a mixture of acoustic and electronic sounds, soft rock, and white jazz, a sort of pop mood music to succeed the Percy Faith and Mantovani styles. The beginnings of it might be seen in such compilations as Mike *Oldfield's *Tubular Bells* (1973) or Stephen Halpern's *Spectrum Suite* (1974). A flood of synthetically manufactured albums came from specially created labels to supply such outlets as supermarkets, bookshops, and health food stores, and the needs of an uncommitted audience who more or less liked the sound of pop. It has been aptly described as 'yuppie muzak'.

New Amsterdam Theatre. New York theatre on 42nd Street built in 1903 as the main venue of the Erlanger organization. It helped to establish 42nd Street as New York's principal theatre area. After a start with legitimate productions it became the home of the *Ziegfeld Follies*, and its other musical successes included *The *Merry Widow, *Sally*, and *The *Band Wagon*, while its covered roof garden was a popular venue for cabaret. It closed in 1937 but there have been plans to restore it as a theatre.

New Faces. A series of American intimate revues that were a valuable showcase for up-and-coming talents, starting with the first edition which, opening at the Pasadena Theatre as *Low and Behold* in May 1933, was then at the Fulton Theatre, New York (on 46th Street), 15 Mar. 1934, where it had 139 performances. A moving spirit behind the idea was Elsie *Janis, the director was Leonard Sillman (1908–82), and the new faces it exposed included those of Henry Fonda (1905–82), Imogene Coca (*b* 1908)—neither exactly new, but still unknown—Nancy *Hamilton (who provided some of the material), Chuck Walters (*b* 1911), and Leonard Sillman himself. There were to be six editions, widely spread. The next, at the Vanderbilt Theatre 19 May 1936, starred Imogene Coca, and Van Johnson (*b* 1916) was one of the new names [193p]. A film, *New Faces of 1937*, had little connection with the shows and the only important figure to emerge from it was the leggy dancer Ann Miller (*b* 1919). The war intervened before the next edition came out at the Royale Theatre, 16 May 1952, and now there was a really big new name to offer in the sultry, slinky shape of Eartha *Kitt who sang 'Monotonous' and imposed her stage character on the world. Other bright talents were June Carroll and Paul Lynde, and these were backed by a high standard of clever writing from such people as Truman Capote (1924–84), Mel Brooks (*b* 1926), and composer Sheldon *Harnick—'Boston beguine'; and such creations as Michael Brown's hoedown-style 'Lizzie Borden'. There was a run of 365 performances and the whole thing was duly filmed in 1954. Three further editions of *New Faces* were to come, in 1956, with Maggie Smith (*b* 1934) among the credits, 1962, and 1968, both with Madeleine Kahn (*b* 1942). But the achievement of the whole series really seemed, in retrospect, to be the bringing to light of the talents of Eartha Kitt.

There was also an unconnected *New Faces* revue in London, at the Comedy Theatre 11 Apr. 1940, with score mainly by Jack *Strachey and book by Eric *Maschwitz. That show was responsible for the introduction of one of the best popular songs written in England, 'A nightingale sang in Berkeley Square' (*m* Manning *Sherwin); supported later by another excellent number, when the show moved to the Apollo Theatre 14 Mar. 1941—'Room 504' (*m* George *Posford). Strachey's best contribution was a sprightly number called 'If you were Ginger Rogers and I were Fred Astaire'. The cast of the London revue included Charles Hawtrey (1914–88), Bill Fraser (*b* 1907), and Betty Ann Davies (1910–55).

New Girl in Town. American musical play with music and lyrics by Bob *Merrill and book by George *Abbott, based on Eugene O'Neill's 1921 play *Anna Christie*. It was produced at the 46th Street Theatre, New York, 14 May 1957, with a cast that included Gwen *Verdon round whom the show was written.

The story is set near New York's waterfront around 1900. A barge captain (played by Cameron Prud'homme) is awaiting the homecoming of his daughter Anna (Gwen Verdon), who on arrival is labelled by her friend Marthy (Thelma Ritter) as a street-walker. On the barge Anna meets and falls for a sailor (George Wallace) to whom she tells her murky story. They drown their sorrows in drink, but everyone forgives everyone else in the end and they set out to live happily ever after. It ran for 431 performances.

Newley, Anthony (*b* London, 24 Sept. 1931). British composer, writer, actor, and singer. At the age of 14, while trying to start a career as a journalist, he became an office-boy at an acting academy and was able to take free acting lessons. He soon began to get small parts in films, firstly in *The Adventures of Dusty Bates* (1946); becoming widely noticed when he effectively played the Artful Dodger in David Lean's *Oliver Twist* in 1947. After National Service in 1950, he joined a repertory company and returned to films with *Idle on Parade*, in which he played a conscripted rock singer and sang four of his own songs, having an influential hit with 'Idle-rock-a-boogie'—an intended parody which was taken seriously. He started recording and had several hits, mainly with ballads such as 'Why?', 'Do you mind?', and 'D-Darling'. he confirmed his reputation in 1955 in the John Cranko ballet-revue *Cranks* and became well-known on TV.

By 1961 he had appeared in 40 films and it was in this year that he starred in his own new wave musical **Stop the World—I Want to Get Off*. He wrote this and his next show, *The Roar of the Greasepaint—the Smell of the Crowd* (1962), in collaboration with Leslie *Bricusse, with whom he also worked on such films as *Willy Wonka and the Chocolate Factory* (1962)—'The candy man'; and *Goldfinger* (1964). Later productions included the films *Doctor Dolittle* (1967) and *Can Heironymus Merkin Ever Forget Mercy Humppe and Find True Happiness?* (1969); and the stage show *The Good Old Bad Old Days* (1972).

Newman, Alfred (*b* New Haven, Conn., 17 Mar. 1900; *d* Hollywood, 17 Feb. 1970). American composer, pianist, and conductor. The eldest of 10 children, he gave his first concert as a pianistic prodigy in 1908. At the age of 9 he went to New York to study piano and harmony and by the time he was 12 he was supporting the family by his professional engagements, sometimes performing in as many as five vaudeville shows a day, billed as 'The Marvelous Boy Pianist', in between appearing as soloist with the New York Philharmonic and other leading orchestras. In 1917 he made his debut as a conductor with **George White's Scandals* and he continued his theatre work until **Funny Face* in 1927 with Fred *Astaire. He went to Hollywood in 1930 to arrange and orchestrate the score of *Reaching for the Moon* (1931), found the work to his liking, and by 1933 was musical director for Samuel Goldwyn, a post he maintained until 1939. In 1938 he won an Academy Award for the score of **Alexander's Ragtime Band*. A committed film composer, he became, most importantly, the musical director for the 20th Century Fox studios in 1940, with his brothers Lionel (below) and Emil both working under him; and he found time to study with Arnold Schoenberg, who was then living in Los Angeles. He won further Oscars for the complete scores of *The Song of Bernadette* (1943) and *Love is a Many-Splendored Thing* (1953); and for his arrangements of music for *Tin Pan Alley* (1940); *Mother Wore Tights* (1947); *With a Song in My Heart* (1952); **Call Me Madam* (1953); *The *King and I* (1956); and **Camelot* (1967).

From a massive list of some 230 film credits, his other scores included: *Indiscreet* (1931); *Street Scene* (1931); *Rain* (1932); *I Cover the Waterfront* (1933); *Looking for Trouble* (1934); *The Count of Monte Cristo* (1934); *Clive of India* (1935); *Les Misérables* (1935); *The Call of the Wild* (1935); *Come and Get It* (1936); *The Prisoner of Zenda* (1937); *The Hurricane* (1938)—'Moon of Manakoora' (*w* Frank *Loesser); *Trade Winds* (1938); *Wuthering Heights* (1939); *Young Mr Lincoln* (1939); *Beau Geste* (1939); *The Hunchback of Notre Dame* (1939); *The Blue Bird* (1940); *The Grapes of Wrath* (1940); *The Mark of Zorro* (1940); *Dance With The Devil* (1940)—'Your kisses' (*w* Loesser); *How Green Was My Valley* (1941)—'How green was my valley' (*w* Loesser); *Life Begins at Eight-Thirty* (1942); *Heaven Can Wait* (1943); *Claudia* (1943); *The Keys of the Kingdom* (1944); *A *Tree Grows in Brooklyn* (1945); *A Bell for Adano* (1945); *Centennial Summer* (1946); *Captain from Castile* (1947); *The Snake Pit* (1948); *Mr Belvedere Goes to College* (1949); *Twelve o'Clock High* (1949); *The Gunfighter* (1950); *All About Eve* (1950); *David and Bathsheba* (1951); *What Price Glory?* (1952); *The Snows of Kilimanjaro* (1952); *The Robe* (1953); *The Egyptian* (with Bernard *Herrmann, 1954); *The Seven Year Itch* (1955); *Anastasia* (1956); *A Certain Smile* (1958); *The Diary of Anne Frank* (1959); *The Best of Everything* (1959); *The Pleasure of his Company* (1961); *How the West Was Won* (1962); *The Greatest Story Ever Told* (1965); *Nevada Smith* (1965); *Firecreek* (1967); and *Airport* (1970). Most of his scores were written in the grandly romantic vein of composers like Tchaikovsky and Rachmaninov, in a fantasia-cum-concerto style that came to typify Hollywood film background music before the jazz element crept in.

Newman, Lionel (*b* New Haven, Conn., 4 Jan. 1916). American composer, pianist, and conductor. Like his elder brother Alfred (above), he was a child prodigy pianist. He studied in his teens with Castelnuovo-Tedesco and before he was 20 he was managing and conducting touring musicals, later joining Earl *Carroll's *Vanities* as a rehearsal pianist. He began writing special material for Carroll shows and wound up as musical director. His conducting career ranged from *Give My Regards to Broadway* in 1948 to **Hello Dolly!* in 1969. He went to Hollywood in the 1930s, joined 20th Century Fox as pianist, composer, and arranger, and began writing background scores and film title-songs. Later he became head of the music department and shared many conducting and writing assignments with his brother.

His scores included: *The Cowboy and the Lady* (1938); *Do You Love Me?* (1946); *Road House* (1948)—'Again'; *Golden Girl* (1951); *How to Marry a Millionaire* (1954); *River of No Return* (1954); *Love Me Tender* (1956); *The Last Wagon* (1956); *The Proud Ones* (1956); *The Sun Also Rises* (1957); *The Young Lions* (1958); *North to Alaska* (1960); *Move Over Darling* (1963); *The Pleasure Seekers* (1964); *The Great White Hope* (1970). He composed music for various TV shows and series including: *Anna and the King* (1971); *M*A*S*H* (1973); and *Planet of the Apes* (1974).

Newman, Randy [Gary] (*b* New Orleans, 28 Nov. 1944). American composer, pianist, and singer. He spent his childhood in southern California where he studied music and started writing his controversial and unusual songs, first coming to attention when Judy *Collins recorded 'I think it's going to rain today' in 1966. At this time he was employed by Metric Music in Los Angeles and gaining experience by working alongside Glen *Campbell and others. He became a record producer for Warner Brothers in 1967 and a year later recorded his first solo album for Reprise, *Randy Newman*, which was a complete failure. The public were not able to accept his strangely cracked and croaking off-key voice that was, in fact, ideally matched to his cynically humorous but often carelessly aimed songs. He was to continue to offend through his outspoken criticism and comment. Described as 'the Mark Twain of rock' he was a throwback to the days of writing songs about things and people rather than using them as personal complaint, and proved himself capable of writing in a number of styles, using jazz, country, ragtime, and rock as the occasion required. Albums like *Twelve Songs* (1970), *Randy Newman Live* (1971), *Sail Away* (1972), and *Good Old Boys* (1974), which was a perceptive portrait of life in the Southern states and included the effective 'Louisiana 1927', could fairly be said to have considerably widened the scope and intelligence of the pop song.

His next album, in the most comic vein so far, was *Little Criminals* (1977) whose No. 2 hit 'Short people' was taken wrongly by some as an attack on people of small stature. This resulted in some radio stations refusing to broadcast his material; but he came back into favour with the more constrained *Born Again* (1979) and *Trouble in Paradise* (1983). He moved into a mixture of jazz and *rap in *Land of Dreams* (1988). A nephew of Alfred and Lionel *Newman, he is a regular writer of film music, his scores including *Performance* (1970), *Cold Turkey* (1971), *Ragtime* (1981)—he produced interestingly original ragtime items (though they were too fleetingly heard), and *The Natural* (1984). He toured Britain in 1989.

New Moon, The. Romantic musical comedy with score by Sigmund *Romberg and book by Oscar *Hammerstein II, Frank Mandel (1884–1958), and Laurence Schwab (1893–1951), produced at the Imperial Theatre, New York, 19 Sept. 1928. Owing to demands on its two main creators (Romberg was also writing the score of *Rosalie*, and Hammerstein was busy on **Show Boat*), *The New Moon* was so shakily put together that the whole show had to be scrapped after its try-out and re-written. Eight months later it was re-produced with many of its best songs newly added and proved to be the sort of follow-up to *The *Desert Song* that the audiences were expecting. It ran for 509 performances.

The story is set in New Orleans in 1788 where the hero Robert (Robert Halliday) is on a murder charge, becomes a bondsman, and recruits a band of bold villains prepared to fight for liberty. He is sent to France on a ship which also carries the fair Marianne (Evelyn Herbert). They are both rescued by the noble band of pirates and found a colony on a lovely island. The romantic plot was well supported by such Romberg classics as 'Marianne', 'Softly, as in a morning sunrise', 'Stouthearted men', 'One kiss', 'Wanting you', and 'Lover, come back to me'. It was filmed in 1930 (with a somewhat different story) with Lawrence Tibbett (1896–1960)—one of the first opera singers to appear in screen musicals. It was an obvious vehicle for the talents of Jeanette *Macdonald and Nelson *Eddy who starred in the authentic 1940 film version.

New Orleans jazz. At the end of the 19th century New Orleans was a thriving seaport with a quarter of a million inhabitants; it had the mixture of race and creed that is natural to a trading outlet, bringing in people from the West Indies, Latin America, and Europe. Some 200 years earlier it had been the place through which most of the slave trade had passed. Even if the seeds of jazz were not all germinated there, it was the obvious centre for its final blossoming. Housing all the problems and vices of mankind in its crowded streets, it was a natural place for jazz and the blues, the art of the underprivileged, to grow, alongside and in the brothels of the infamous New Orleans red light district.

When jazz developed in the city it was at its most

primitive stage, brash and vulgar, an amalgam of Creole, West Indian, South American, black African, and natural American elements. It was played on the cheapest and most obtainable of instruments, generally old military band cast-offs, relics of the American Civil War. In New Orleans jazz developed as a march music, stilted at first, gradually loosening up and acquiring what was later to be identified as swing. The marches were the background to funerals and weddings and other celebrations. When it was not a marching music it went indoors to places of entertainment where it had to be loud and assertive to gain a hearing; at that time it was simply music to be danced to and not yet at the stage where it was to be listened to with reverential attention. New Orleans bred its own race of musicians, many of them, like Louis *Armstrong, to become the worldwide leaders of the new jazz music. The closing of the red light district by the civil authorities coincided with the need for jazz to spread its wings and find roots in similar cities like Chicago and New York. Some who remained were quite content to continue the New Orleans tradition and were still playing it with little change of content in the jazz revival years of the 1940s and 1950s.

New Orleans jazz was not primarily concerned with technicalities. The first consideration was to create a spirit of involvement and enjoyment; and its traditions have always been those of closely knit collective improvisation with the basic front-line instrumentation of trumpet or cornet, trombone, and clarinet or saxophone creating a contrapuntal texture above a steady rhythm of banjo or guitar, tuba or string-bass, and drums, with the piano, if available, fulfilling an ancient continuo role. Even after its veteran originators had gone, the tradition was maintained by musicians who loved the curried flavour of its driving ensembles and the art is kept alive by many dedicated survivalists.

S. Charters: *Jazz New Orleans 1885–1963* (New York, 1958; rev. 1963). A. Rose and E. Souchon: *New Orleans Jazz: a Family Album* (Baton Rouge, La., 1967; rev. 1984). M. Williams: *Jazz Masters of New Orleans* (New York, 1967; repr. 1979).

New Orleans Rhythm Kings. American jazz group formed in 1922 at the Friar's Inn in Chicago, where it was originally known as the Friar's Inn Orchestra. Led by trumpeter Paul *Mares, its original personnel included Leon Ropollo (1902–43) (clarinet), George Brunies [later Georg Brunis] (1902–74) (trombone), and Elmer *Schoebel (piano). They made their first, now historic, recordings at the Gennett studies in Richmond, Indiana, in Sept. 1922. Being a band of white musicians it was an early innovation to find a black musician, Jelly Roll *Morton, recording with the group in April 1923. They played for a time at the Cascades Ballroom in Chicago and disbanded in 1924 when Mares and Ropollo went to New York. The group was reorganized for a time in 1925 and revived in the 1930s, then led by Muggsy *Spanier with Brunies the only surviving original.

Newton-John, Olivia (*b* Cambridge, 26 Sept. 1948). British singer. An eclectic stylist who has had success with country music, middle-of-the-road material, and rock of the *Eurovision Song Contest ilk, as well as appearing in musical films. She was taken to Australia as a child and sang in a vocal group there in her teens. At 16 she won a talent contest whose prize was a trip to Britain, where she stayed to star in a film, *Tomorrow* (1970). She appeared in cabaret and, after working with Cliff *Richard and the Shadows, recorded a moderate hit in 'If not for you' (1971), followed by 'Banks of the Ohio' (1971), 'What is life?' (1972), 'Take me home, country roads' (1973), and 'Let me be there' (1973), which appeared in the country charts in the USA. The country vein continued with 'If you love me, let me know' (1974); 'I honestly love you' (1974) and 'Have you never been mellow' (1975) which became No. 1 hits in America. She had made her first tour of the USA in 1974, became part of the *Nashville scene, and was voted Best Female Country Vocalist. She was in the film *Grease* (1978), which blemished her pleasant, good-looking image and led her towards a more rock-oriented vein. Her duets with John Travolta (*b* 1954), 'You're the one that I want' and 'Summer nights' (1978), became No. 1 hits and were followed by the albums *Totally Hot* (1978) and *Physical* (1980). She starred with Gene *Kelly in *Xanadu* (1980) and again with Travolta in *Two of a Kind* (1984).

P. Ruff: *Olivia Newton-John* (New York, 1979).

New wave. A vague term (rather like 'modern jazz') introduced in the 1970s to distinguish those groups who were associated with the current *punk scene but strove for more professional standards of material and performance. In the UK it covered such names as Elvis *Costello, Joe Jackson, *Police, and Dire Straits; while in the USA it became, on the one hand, even more vaguely used to cover anything that was not obviously punk, on the other a label for avant-garde groups like *Talking Heads.

New York Drama Critics Circle. Association officially formed in 1935. Feeling some dissatisfaction with the selection of the *Pulitzer Prizes, they instituted the New York Drama Critics Award, which has achieved high status, and was first given to *Winterset* in 1936. Musicals which have won the award are: **Carousel* (1946); **Brigadoon* (1947); **South Pacific* (1949); **Guys and Dolls* (1951); **Pal Joey* (1952); **Wonderful Town* (1953); *The *Golden Apple* (1954); **My Fair Lady* (1956); *The *Most Happy Fella* (1957); *The *Music Man* (1958); **Fiorello!* (1960); **Carnival!* (1961); **How to Succeed in Business Without Really Trying* (1962); **Hello Dolly!* (1964); **Fiddler on the Roof* (1965); **Man of La Mancha* (1966); **Cabaret* (1967); **1776* (1969); **Company* (1970); **Follies* (1971); *A *Little Night Music* (1973); **Candide* (1974); *A *Chorus Line* (1975); **Pacific Overtures* (1976); **Annie* (1977); **Ain't Misbehavin'* (1978); and **Sweeney Todd* (1979).

New York jazz. No less an authority than the great saxophonist Coleman *Hawkins has said that there was no such thing as New York jazz. The Big Apple has been a melting-pot for all kinds of musicians who have been lured to its money-making possibilities; and Harlem has been a home for continuous jazz development rather than the creation of any distinctive pattern. But like most capital cities, New York has always been a natural centre of commercial jazz activity; and a certain kind of formal jazz, as played by white musicians like Red *Nichols, Phil Napoleon (*b* 1901), and Miff *Mole, has come to be labelled New York jazz as it developed its character there in the 1920s.

S. Charters and L. Kunstad: *Jazz: a History of the New York Scene* (New York, 1962; repr. 1981).

Niblo's Garden. Theatre built by William Niblo (1790–1878) at Broadway and Prince Street, New York, on the site of the smaller Sans Souci Theatre (1828) in 1829. Starting with light vaudeville entertainment, it was later established as a leading centre of musical spectacles with the production there, after Niblo's retirement in 1861, of *The *Black Crook*, under the management of William Wheatley (1816–76). Rebuilt after a fire in 1872, it was finally demolished in 1895, by then New York's oldest playhouse.

Nicholls, Horatio [Wright, Lawrence] (*b* Leicester, 15 Feb. 1888; *d* London, 19 May 1964). British composer, arranger, and publisher. He has been dubbed the 'Edgar Wallace of songwriters', so prodigious was his output of popular songs written under the name of Horatio Nicholls and many more pseudonyms. He started his career by opening a market stall selling sheet music in Leicester in 1906. Then he became the first music-publisher to open an office in Denmark Street, London, in 1911, thus founding London's *Tin Pan Alley. He launched the firm under his real name of Lawrence Wright and became well-known for his stunts to publicize songs which included flying Jack *Hylton and his band round the tower at Blackpool in 1927, and showering the public with copies of 'Me and Jane in a plane'. One of his most important publications was the *Wright Pianoforte Tutor* which was used all over the world and sold more than a quarter of a million copies. He founded **Melody Maker*, which started life in 1926 as the firm's house magazine. Under his own name, mainly as Horatio Nicholls from 1911, and under such noms-de-plume as Victor Ambroise, Haydon Augarde, Everett Lynton, Paul Paree, Gene Williams, Betsy O'Hogan, and W. Kerrigan, he wrote innumerable song hits such as 'Wyoming' and 'Babette' (both million-sellers) and was the publisher of many works by well-known American composers.

His style was thoroughly British, forthright ballads with simple melodies. These included: [as Everett Lynton] 'Mistakes' (1928, *w* Edgar *Leslie); [as Betsy O'Hogan] 'Old Father Thames' (1933, *w* Raymond Wallace); [as Gene Williams] 'Wyoming' (1919), 'Caravan' (1922, *w* Gene McCarthy); [as Lawrence Wright] 'Down by the stream' (1915, *w* Beaumont Ford), 'Are we downhearted—no' (with Worton David, 1917); [as Horatio Nicholls] 'Blue eyes' (1915, *w* Godfrey Williams), 'Delilah' (1917), 'That old-fashioned mother of mine' (1919, *w* David), 'Babette' (1925, *w* Ray Morelle), 'The toy drum major' (1925, *w* Jean Frederick), 'Among my souvenirs' (1927, *w* Leslie), 'Shepherd of the hills' (1927, *w* Leslie), 'Whispering pines of Nevada' (1927, Leslie), 'Just a little fond affection' (1928, Leslie), 'Say a little prayer for me' (1930, *w* Gilbert), 'When the Guards are on parade' (1931, *w* Leslie *Sarony), 'Let's all go to the music-hall' (1934, *w* Butler and Tinsey), 'The Blackpool walk' (1938), and 'Down Forget-Me-Not Lane' (1941, *w* Morgan and Chester). He wrote and published *How to Write a Successful Song* (London, 1929).

Nichols, Red [Ernest Loring] (*b* Ogden, Utah, 8 May 1905; *d* Las Vegas, 28 June 1965). American jazz cornettist and bandleader. He was taught to play by his father, who was a tutor at Weber College, and he played under him in the Ogden Town Band when he was 12. A short-lived stay at Culver Military Academy was followed by his debut with George *Olsen's band. At 17 he made his first recordings as a bandleader for Gennett Records in Richmond. For the next 13 years or so he was seldom out of the recording studios as both leader and sideman. His groups recorded under many names but his best-known work was with his Five Pennies (which ranged from five to a full swing band) playing a clean and frisky kind of jazz that has loosely been labelled *New York jazz, in effect white *Dixieland music, not highly rated by some jazz purists, but adored by others, technically adroit and always swinging. The Five Pennies, who had a hit with their 1927 recording of 'Ida, sweet as apple cider', became a sort of school for bandleaders: many of its varying personnel became leaders in their own right, including Tommy *Dorsey, Jimmy *Dorsey, Glenn *Miller, Benny *Goodman, Joe *Venuti, Will *Bradley, Jack *Teagarden, Miff *Mole, and Gene *Krupa.

Nichols performed regularly on radio and led a theatre orchestra for productions of such important stage shows as George *Gershwin's **Strike Up the Band* and **Girl Crazy* in 1930; and he was later musical director for the Bob *Hope radio show. During the Second World War he gave up music and worked in a shipyard, but when the Dixieland style came back into favour after the war he re-formed the Five Pennies and found he was still popular. A romanticized version of his life story was filmed in 1959 as *The Five Pennies* with Danny *Kaye as Nichols and Nichols himself playing the sound-track. This gave impetus to a new series of albums for Capitol and the band was playing in Las Vegas when he died of a heart-attack.

Nickleodeon. Coin-operated player piano or pianola, common in American cafés, honky-tonks, and speakeasies before the invention of the *juke box. The notes were operated by a paper roll. More elaborate instruments with other instruments added were known as Orchestrians (not to be confused with the orchestrion).

Niles, John Jacob (*b* Louisville, Ky., 28 Apr. 1892; *d* Lexington, Ky., 1 May 1980). American singer, composer, folklorist, and musician. Working principally as a surveyor in the Kentucky mountain region, he began to collect folk-songs which he began to perform from 1910 in a formal sort of way, divorced from the popular *hillbilly approach. After service in the First World War, in which he was disabled, he returned to his folk-music activities, touring the country giving programmes and publishing numerous collections that included *Singing Soldiers* (1924); *Songs My Mother Never Taught Me* (1927); *Kentucky Mountain Songs* (1929); *Songs of the Hill Folk* (1936); *Ballads, Carols and Tragic Legends of the Southern Appalachian Mountains* (1937); *The Anglo-American Study Book* (1945); and *Ballad Book of John Jacob Niles* (1961). He wrote many original songs and made a number of LP recordings of his own work and folk material 1939–67. He worked until well into his eighties and received many academic honours.

Nilsson, Harry [Nelson, Harry Edward] (*b* New York, 15 June 1941). American composer and singer. He had shown some then largely ignored originality in such albums as *Shadow Show* (1967) and *Harry* (1969). Then he was asked to sing Fred Neil's 'Everybody's talking' over the credits of the highly popular film *Midnight Cowboy* (1969) which brought recognition. His leanings were towards a melancholy brand of ballad which he sang in a melancholy sort of way; though he made several interesting divergent albums including *A Little Touch of Schmilsson in the Night* (1973), which presented some good old songs orchestrated by Gordon *Jenkins; and *Pussy Cats* (1974), which was a collaboration with John *Lennon.

The interest he attracted in the 1960s arose from his parodying of *Beatles creations at a time when the USA was looking for someone to rival Lennon and *McCartney. He multi-recorded his voice to provide a group sound and became a one-man Beatles. Some of his material was also used by the similarly slanted *Monkees, one of their hits being his 'Cuddly toy' (1967). Other songs included: 'Ten little Indians' (1967); 'Without her' (1967); 'Don't leave me' (1967); 'The wailing of the willow' (1968); 'Together' (1968); 'Rainmaker' (1968); 'The puppy song' (1969); 'Open your window' (1969); 'Maybe' (1969); 'Me and my arrow' (1970); 'Coconut' (1971); and 'Gotta get up' (1971).

Nine. Unusual musical with music and lyrics by Maury Yeston and book by Arthur Kopit (*b* 1937) and Mario Fratti, based on Fellini's 1963 film *8½*. A highly visual production, directed by choreographer Tommy Tune (*b* 1939), it had a cast of one man (Raul Julia), a somewhat chauvinistic male director, and 21 women, including his wife, his mistress, and his mother, with whom he has a torrid relationship. The story included flashbacks and many novel touches which made it a cultish sort of show when it opened at the 46th Street Theatre, New York, 9 May 1982 and ran for 732 performances.

Nine Sharp. Revue with music by Walter *Leigh and book and lyrics by Herbert *Farjeon. One of the highly successful 'little' revues at the Little Theatre, London, which had started with the *Nine o'Clock Revue* and others in the 1920s. Opening 26 Jan. 1938, it ran for 405 performances with a cast that included Cyril *Ritchard, George Benson (1911–83), and Hermione *Baddeley. In the mildly satirical vein of the time it aimed its shafts at the BBC, the ballet, and London life in general.

Nitty Gritty Dirt Band. Highly individual band that played a mixture of the old-style *jug music, *bluegrass, and *blues, featuring songs by individual writers like Jackson *Browne. Formed in 1965 in Los Angeles, the band was signed up by Liberty Records, who issued an album under the group's eye-catching name in 1967. They appeared in the film **Paint Your Wagon* (1968), disbanded for a while, then came together again to make the album *Uncle Charlie and his Dog Teddy* (1970) which had a top hit in 'Mr Bojangles'. They made a country-rock album, *All the Good Times* (1972), and showed their strong country affiliations by recording their next album *Will the Circle Be Unbroken* (1973) in Nashville with such people as Roy *Acuff and Earl *Scruggs as guest artists. They continued with a string of yearly albums and in 1977 became the first rock group to tour the USSR.

Noble, Johnny (*b* Honolulu, 17 Sept. 1892; *d* Manoa, 13 Jan. 1944). Hawaiian composer and bandleader. He began his musical career in 1910 as a drummer and for 17 years he led a popular orchestra of Hawaiian musicians in Honolulu. He went to Los Angeles in 1925 and 1927, during the universal vogue for Hawaiian music, to direct and advise for stage and radio productions. He left the music business to become a telephone company executive, but is remembered by the classic 'Hawaiian war chant' (with Leleiohaku, 1941, *w* Ralph Freed).

Noble, Ray (*b* Brighton, 17 Nov. 1903; *d* London, 3 Apr. 1978). British bandleader, composer, and arranger. He studied music at Cambridge and was musical director of EMI Records 1929–34. He led the EMI house band, known as the New Mayfair Orchestra, from 1929, its personnel drawn from various hotel orchestra bands, and the repertoire mainly music from now forgotten shows and novelty tunes. Al *Bowlly joined as vocalist in 1930 and, now billed as Ray Noble and his Orchestra, they started using more American material and bringing a jazz flavour in by way of such instrumentalists as Freddy Gardner, Nat *Gonella, Lew Davis, and Max Goldberg.

His early arrangements had mainly been of traditional English material, but he now began to compose his own songs and had an immediate success with 'Goodnight, sweetheart' (1931) which was to become his signature tune. He started writing for films and provided music for *Say It With Music* (1932)—'Love is the sweetest thing'; *Little Damozel* (1933)—'What more can I ask?' (*w* Anona Winn); *Brewster's Millions* (1934)—'Pull down the blind' (*w* Douglas Furber); *Girls Please* (1934)—'Kick over the traces' (*w* Alan Murray); *Princess Charming* (1935)—'Love is a song'; *Let's Make a Night of It* (1936)—'For only you' (*w* Murray). Other songs of the period included: 'I found you' (1931); 'By the fireside' (1932); 'Love locked out' (1933); 'The very thought of you' (1934); 'It's all forgotten now' (1934); 'Who's been polishing the sun' (1934); 'If you love me' (1936); 'The touch of your lips' (1936); 'I hadn't anyone till you' (1936); 'Cherokee' (1938); and 'Seminole' (1940).

Noble went to the USA in 1934, with Al Bowlly and his manager, and led a band that had been assembled by Glenn *Miller which included such notable names as Miller, Pee Wee Erwin, Charlie *Spivak, Will *Bradley, Bud *Freeman, and Claude *Thornhill. He was resident at New York's Rainbow Room from 1935, leading from a white piano, mingling with the guests during numbers, and becoming immensely popular on radio with the Lanny Ross Show 1936, Refreshment Time 1936, and the Burns and Allen Show in the late thirties (where he first started acting). He appeared in several films as a typical idiotic Englishman, and with his band in such features as *The Big Broadcast of 1936* (1935); *A *Damsel in Distress* (1937); *Here We Go Again* (1942); *Lake Placid Serenade* (1945); and *Out of this World* (1945). He returned to England for periods to run an orchestra there 1936–7 and 1940–1 with alternating spells in the USA with Burns and Allen, Alec *Templeton, and Edgar Bergen. After he retired in the mid-1950s he spent much of his time in the USA. The Ray Noble sound was the epitome of polished and expert big-band jazz of the 1930s, with a rich ensemble sound, firm beat, and tasteful arrangements, notable for its work with the now legendary Al Bowlly; and its recordings are now very much collectors' items.

No, No, Nanette. American comedy with score by Vincent *Youmans, book by Otto *Harbach and Frank Mandel (1884–1958), based on the 1920 comedy *His Lady Friends*, lyrics by Harbach and Irving *Caesar. It was tried out in Detroit in April 1924, where most of the cast was changed and five new numbers were added, including the imperishable 'I want to be happy' and 'Tea for two'. It then went to Chicago in May 1924 and ran there for 265 performances, meanwhile touring the country and opening in London, at the Palace Theatre 11 Mar. 1925, with a cast that included George *Grossmith Jr., Binnie *Hale, and Joseph *Coyne; and running for 665 performances. The show first reached New York at the Globe Theatre 16 Sept. 1925, with Louise *Groody, Charles *Winninger, and Georgia O'Ramey, and ran for 321 performances.

Of all American musicals it was the one that caught on in Europe (perhaps because of the basic simplicity of 'Tea for two', which translates well into any language) and has regularly been seen in France and Germany. Other songs were 'Too many rings around 'Rosie', 'No, no, Nanette', 'You can dance with any girl at all', 'I've confessed to the breeze', and 'The boy next door'. It was the basic sort of Twenties song-and-dance show that invited various parodies in the nostalgic 1950s, with a mild little story about a married publisher of bibles who is the guardian of the heroine and keeps three other ladies in various hideouts. A typical farce situation arises when they and their friends all turn up at his house. There was a film of the same name in 1930, which did not use much of Youmans's music, with Bernice Claire; one in 1940 starring Anna *Neagle; and one in 1950 with Doris *Day and Gordon *McRae.

With the revival spirit abroad, *No, No, Nanette* was taken off the shelf and revived at the 46th Street Theatre, New York, 19 Jan. 1971. Strangely, with a new book by Burt Shevelove it again had a difficult try-out period, but was eventually put into shape and proved an undiminished success with a run of 861 performances. An interesting member of the cast was the veteran Ruby *Keeler playing the publisher's wife. Bobby Van (1930–80) had a small part, and various big names were involved in the production and its touring companies. The revival version was seen in London at Drury Lane 15 May 1973, with Anna Neagle, Anne *Rogers, Thora Hird, and Tony Britton in the cast [277p].

Noone, Jimmie (*b* Cutt-Off, La., 23 Apr. 1895; *d* Los Angeles, 19 Apr. 1944). American jazz clarinettist. He first played the guitar but took up the clarinet when he was 15, moving into New Orleans in 1910 and studying there with Sidney *Bechet. He played in Freddie *Keppard's band as a deputy for Bechet, later in his own right. He formed the Young Olympia Band with Buddie Petit, led a jazz trio 1916–17, and worked with Kid *Ory and Papa *Celestin. In 1917 he went to Chicago to join Keppard in the Original Creole Band; joined King *Oliver at the Royal Gardens 1918–20; and was with the Doc Cooke orchestra 1920–6. He led a small group at the Nest (which was renamed the Apex Club in 1926) and led the resident band there during one of his most fruitful periods until 1928. Then he played in Detroit and in various New York clubs. He was back in Chicago in 1937 and led a big band on radio in 1939. By 1943 he was working in Hollywood and was seen in a film, *The Block Busters* (1944). He worked with Kid Ory in his last year as well as with his own group.

A good technician, Noone is often set off against New Orleans clarinettist Johnny *Dodds, whose rough, attacking style was the antithesis of Noone's smoothness and agility; although his playing was still in the New Orleans spirit, Noone was one of the players who led jazz towards the swing era and the style of Benny *Goodman and other modernists of the day. His polished professionalism went well with the work of musicians like Earl *Hines and he was never out of demand, playing a continual succession of club residencies throughout his career. He made comparatively few recordings but among them some enduring classics like 'It's tight like that' and 'Apex blues'.

Norman, Monty (*b* London, 4 Apr. 1928). British composer and lyricist. He had an elementary education and was self-taught musically. From 1958 he wrote and reviewed for various Jewish publications and in 1960 became musical director of the Wolf Mankowitz and Peraga organizations. He was librettist of the London production of **Irma la Douce* (1960; filmed 1963). He wrote the scores for **Expresso Bongo* (1958; filmed 1963); *Make Me an Offer* (1959); *Art of Living* (1960); *Belle* (1961); *Quick Quick Slow* (1963); *Who's Pinkus?* (1967); *Stand and Deliver* (1972); *Songbook* (with Julian Moore, 1979); and *Poppy* (1982); music for films: *Call Me Bwana* (1963); *Doctor No* (1963); and various TV productions. He was the composer of the 'James Bond' theme.

North, Alex (*b* Chester, Pa., 10 Dec. 1910; *d* Calif., 8 Sept. 1991). American composer and conductor. He studied at the Curtis Institute in Pennsylvania 1928–9 and at the Juilliard School of Music 1929–32, Moscow 1933–4, and first composed music for ballets, radio, TV, and theatre. His film composing career began with documentaries, some 40 or so between 1937 and 1950, meanwhile serving in the US Army 1942–6. He was awarded a Guggenheim Fellowship 1947–8. In 1949 he started writing for feature films and produced scores for: *A Streetcar Named Desire* (1951); *The 13th Letter* (1951); *Death of a Salesman* (1951); *Viva Zapata!* (1952); *Les Misérables* (1952); *Pony Soldier* (1952); *The Member of the Wedding* (1953); *Go, Man, Go!* (1954); *Desirée* (1954); *The Racers* (1955); *Unchained* (1955); *Man With the Gun* (1955); *The Rose Tattoo* (1955); *I'll Cry Tomorrow* (1956); *The Bad Seed* (1956); *The Rainmaker* (1956); *Four Girls in Town* (1956); *The King and Four Queens* (1956); *The Bachelor Party* (1957); *The Long Hot Summer* (1958); *Stage Struck* (1958); *Hot Spell* (1958); *South Seas Adventure* (1958); *The Sound and the Fury* (1959); *The Wonderful Country* (1959); *Spartacus* (1960); *The Children's Hour* (1961); *Sanctuary* (1961); *The Misfits* (1961); *All Fall Down* (1962); *Cleopatra* (1963); *The Outrage* (1964); *Cheyenne Autumn* (1965); *The Agony and the Ecstasy* (1965); *Who's Afraid of Virginia Woolf?* (1966); *The Devil's Brigade* (1968); *The Shoes of the Fisherman* (1968); *A Dream of Kings* (1969); *Hard Contact* (1969); *Willard* (1971); *Pocket Money* (1972); *Bite the Bullet* (1975); *Somebody Killed Her Husband* (1978); *Wise Blood* (1979); *Carny* (1980); and *Dragonslayer* (1981).

Norton, Frederic (*b* Manchester, 1875; *d* Holford, Somerset, 15 Dec. 1946). British composer and singer. Educated at Manchester Grammar School, he then worked in an insurance office and studied singing under Paolo Tosti. He toured as a baritone with the Carl Rosa Opera Company, sang in *La Poupée*, and performed in variety theatres. He first wrote *The Water Maidens* (1901); then had a great success with *Pinkie and the Fairies* (1908). He adapted *Offenbach as *Orpheus in the Underground* (1911) and wrote *What Ho! Daphne* (1913) and *The Passing Show* (1914). His greatest success came with **Chu Chin Chow* (1916), which was one of the great attractions of the sombre First World War years and a favourite with troops on leave; when Courtice Pounds was indisposed he sang the role of Ali Baba. He also wrote *Pamela* (1917), and a number of songs.

Norvo, Red [Norville, Kenneth] (*b* Beardstown, Ill., 31 Mar. 1908). American xylophonist, vibraphonist, and bandleader. While studying mining engineering at the University of Missouri, 1926–7, he taught himself to play piano and xylophone, and led a group called the Collegians on a vaudeville tour in 1925. He played with Paul *Whiteman in Chicago in 1926 and later toured as a solo variety act. He led his own first band in Milwaukee in 1928, then worked with Victor *Young on radio 1928–30. In the early 1930s he was with Paul Whiteman and married the singer Mildred *Bailey. He worked in New York 1934–5, leading a group at the Famous Door in 1935 which became a big band in 1936 featuring his wife as singer, the two of them billed as 'Mr and Mrs Swing' after their signature tune. He used advanced arrangements by Eddie *Sauter to achieve a distinctive band sound. The band broke up in 1939, but Norvo led other groups in the 1940s, backing his wife, and was with Benny *Goodman 1944–5, appearing in the film *Seven Lively Arts*. He was with Woody *Herman 1946, then freelanced and played in New York in the 1950s leading various groups and now playing in a modern jazz style. He toured Europe in 1954, and again with Goodman in 1968, remaining active into the 1970s.

Norworth, Jack [Knauff, John] (*b* Philadelphia, 5 Jan. 1879; *d* New York, 1 Sept. 1959). American actor, singer, dancer, composer, and lyricist. He made his first stage appearance in 1898 as a blackface comic in vaudeville and continued in this for seven years. He had a song success with 'The great White Way' in *About Town* in 1906, and appeared in *The Follies of 1909*. In 1914 he was in London in *Hullo Tango*, where he created a vogue for tongue-twisting songs such as 'Sister Susie's sewing shirts for soldiers' (*Darewski and *Weston). He was first married to Louise Dresser, then to Nora *Bayes (one of his most famous acting and writing partners), and finally to Mary Johnson. He wrote the music for *Miss Fix-It* (1911); and his highly successful songs included 'Honey boy' (1907); 'Shine on, harvest moon' (1908), which he wrote with Nora Bayes and which was made popular in the **Ziegfeld Follies* of 1908 and 1931; 'Take me out to the ball game' (1908, *m* Harry *Von Tilzer); 'Heartaches' (1919); and various songs in the *Ziegfeld Follies* and *Weber and Fields shows.

Novello, Ivor [Davies, David Ivor] (*b* Cardiff, 15 Jan. 1893; *d* London, 6 Mar. 1951). British composer, author, and actor. His mother was Madame Novello Davies, well-known in Wales and later in London as a teacher of singing; his father, David Davies, was an accountant at Cardiff City Hall. Since his mother was a professional musician and his father an enthusiastic amateur, the boy grew up in a household where musical activities were going on all the time. As a child he played the piano and had an exceptionally good soprano voice. Boyhood visits to London and the theatre made it the focal point of his ambitions. He started to compose songs at the age of 15 and had his first published the following year. Following some moderate successes in his late teens, in 1914 he wrote the song that made him famous—'Keep the home fires burning', originally known as 'Till the boys come home' and one of the most popular songs of the First World War. It was written, at his mother's suggestion, to a poem by an American, Lena Guilbert Ford, and it was first introduced at the Alhambra by the Welsh singer Sybil Vane. It made Novello immediately rich and famous.

During the war he joined the Naval Air Service but was considered unsuitable as a pilot and spent his service career as a clerk. He got one song into *The *Bing Boys Are Here* and contributed to the score of *Theodore & Co.* (1916) and *Arlette* (1917), but otherwise wrote little during the war years. In 1919 he appeared in his first film, *The Call of the Blood*, and thereafter appeared in many movies, making a successful transition from silent to sound. From there he went to various stage parts, small at first, but soon his famous profile, which shared the adulation of the female public with those of Barrymore and Valentino, became a symbol of high romance on stage and screen in the 1920s. He contributed to the revue *A to Z* (1921). He spent a greater proportion of his later years writing for the theatre, starting with some comparative failures but gradually achieving great success. He was at the height of his powers and popularity when he died shortly after a revival performance of **King's Rhapsody* in 1951.

Novello's later musical plays from 1935 were an isolated phenomenon in the British theatre. Harking back to the lingering romantic traditions of the Viennese operetta just as it was about to go out of fashion, he wholeheartedly revived the idiom. He wrote what he liked and felt; and as it happened to be what a lot of other people liked and felt, particularly those of an older generation brought up on a vintage of *light music uncoloured by jazz, his plays had a wide appeal and enjoyed long runs. They included: **Glamorous Night* (1935); **Careless Rapture* (1936); *Crest of the Wave* (1937); *The *Dancing Years* (1939); *Arc de Triomphe* (1943); **Perchance to Dream* (1945); and *King's Rhapsody* (1949)—virtually the last works by a British composer to monopolize the stage of a large London theatre such as the Theatre Royal, Drury Lane. Most of them had lyrics by Christopher Hassall (1912–63). His final musical, **Gay's the Word*, with lyrics by Alan *Melville, was something of a parody of his own theatrical style.

W. Macqueen Pope: *Ivor: the Story of an Achievement* (London, 1951). P. Noble: *Ivor Novello: Man of the Theatre* (London, 1951). R. Rose: *Perchance to Dream: the World of Ivor Novello* (London, 1974). S. Wilson: *Ivor Novello* (London, 1975). See also 'Ivor Novello' in Staveacre: *The Songwriters* (London, 1980).

Nymph Errant. Play with music and lyrics by Cole *Porter and book by Romney Brent, based on the novel by James Laver. After a try-out in Manchester it opened in London at the Adelphi Theatre 6 Oct. 1933. The cast was headed by Gertrude *Lawrence, who was to produce classic performances of such witty Porter numbers as 'Experiment', 'The physician', and the lightly romantic 'When love comes your way' and 'How could we be wrong'; while Elizabeth *Welch was well suited to 'Solomon'. The play has since assumed a legendary aura. The idea of asking Cole Porter to write the music for a London vehicle for Gertrude Lawrence came from the far-sighted producer C. B. *Cochran. He also saw the actor Romney Brent as the ideal librettist and this too worked out well.

The show was not only the social occasion of 1933 but a cult success as well, society enjoying the shocking story of an English girl trying to discard her virginity. She arrives home after her adventures in a nudist camp, a harem, and a Paris cabaret only to be reprimanded for being 10 minutes late. But it was too sophisticated for the general public and had only 154 performances.

Nyro, Laura (*b* New York, 18 Oct. 1947). American composer, singer, and pianist. She began writing poems and then songs at an early age. An album she recorded for Verve Records in 1966 featured 12 songs that were soon 'covered' by scores of other artists and resulted in hits for *Blood, Sweat and Tears with 'And when I die', for 5th Dimension with 'Wedding bell blues', and for Barbra *Streisand with 'Stoney end'. Three Dog Night had a No. 1 hit with her 'Eli's coming' and 5th Dimension found other hits in 'Sweet blindness' and 'Stoned soul picnic' in 1967. She herself was originally launched as a white *soul singer and in 1971 made an album in this mode, *Gonna Take a Miracle*, which featured songs by Marvin *Gaye and other composers. She announced her retirement in 1971 (at the age of 24) but came back in 1975. By then her introspective style was out of fashion and a fine live album of her best songs, *Season of Lights* (1967), went more or less unnoticed, as did *Nested* in 1978. She came back into the LP charts with *Mother's Spiritual* (1984).

O

Ocarina. A small wind instrument made of terracotta or some such moulded material (the modern ones being of plastic) which is basically of a torpedo-like shape with a projecting portion that forms the mouthpiece, making it look like a small fat pistol. Its Italian name, meaning 'little goose', may derive from the shape, the indefinite nature of this being reflected in the American name, 'sweet potato'. It belongs to the family of resonator instruments, the sound being built up inside the body and coming out through the finger holes. There are ten of these for the fingers and thumbs, the pitch of the note altering according to the number of holes opened or closed, giving it a range of an octave plus three extra notes obtained by opening three larger holes, two of them allotted to the thumbs. The tone is similar to that of a recorder, pure and without harmonics. Some instruments have a plunger in one end for tuning.

The ocarina dates from *c.*1863, when it was invented by two Italians for commercial exploitation, and it has mainly been regarded as a toy or novelty instrument. Germany has taken it more seriously, a range of instruments to provide a consort being made there. Some instruments made in Meissen porcelain have become expensive collectors' items. It has found an outlet in some folk-music areas, chiefly in Sicily where it has become an intrinsic voice and also in the USA where it has featured in the make-shift *spasm band type of music.

Ochs, Phil (*b* El Paso, Texas, 19 Dec. 1940; *d* Far Rockaway, NY, 9 Apr. 1976). American songwriter and singer. After studying journalism at Ohio State University, he became a member of the protest folk-song scene in Greenwich Village, NY, under the influence of such singers as Bob *Dylan and Tom *Paxton and was a member of the Sundowners. He was an early critic of the Vietnam War from around 1962. In 1970 a live recording, *Gunfight*, made at Carnegie Hall, was a controversial issue, with the audience boos kept in as part of the atmosphere. He used a bitterly sardonic blues style and became increasingly soured by the failure of his causes. After a physical assault on him in 1973 his vocal chords were damaged and he became increasingly alcoholic, finally committing suicide.

His songs included 'There but for fortune' (which Joan *Baez made into a hit), 'What's that I hear?', 'The power and the glory', 'The bells', 'Draft-dodger rag', 'I ain't marchin' anymore', 'Changes', 'Outside a small circle of friends', 'Flower lady', 'Chords of fame', and 'Pleasure of the harbour'.

M. Eliot: *Death of a Rebel* (New York, 1979).

O'Connor, Donald [David Dixon Ronald] (*b* Chicago, 30 Aug. 1925). American singer, dancer, comedian, and actor. Maintaining a youthful aspect well into his career, he was much favoured for juvenile leads in many film musicals, usually out-billed by some big star like Bing *Crosby or Ethel *Merman, but invariably making a lasting impression by his casual talents and particularly by his acrobatic dancing skills, notably demonstrated in *Singin' in the Rain*. He started in a family vaudeville act and first became widely known for his contribution to the film *Sing, You Sinners* (1938). He did not immediately win all the recognition he deserved and spent the early 1940s in vaudeville, but he came into his own in the late 1940s when he was in a number of classic MGM films including: *Are You With It?* (1948); *Yes, Sir, That's My Baby* (1949); **Singin' in the Rain* (1952); *I Love Melvin* (1952); **Call Me Madam* (1953); *There's No Business Like Show Business* (1954); **Anything Goes* (1956); *The Buster Keaton Story* (1957); and a fondly remembered series of *Francis* films (Francis being a talking mule). He was often on TV in the 1950s and 1960s, had his own series, and later played in clubs and wrote a considerable number of songs. He was still active into the 1970s and had a small part in the film *Ragtime* (1981).

O'Day, Anita [Colton, Anita] (*b* Chicago, 18 Dec. 1919). American singer. First singing at the Three Deuces club in Chicago in 1939, she was with the Gene *Krupa band 1941–3 then, after a short retirement, with Stan *Kenton 1944–5, with whom she recorded the hit 'And her tears flowed like wine', and with Krupa again in 1945. Afterwards she worked as a soloist with her own bebop-style group. Drug problems kept her out of circulation in the 1950s, but she resurfaced with appearances in the films *The Gene Krupa Story* (1959) and *Jazz on a Summer's Day* (1960) and toured Europe with Benny *Goodman. She created a unique vocal style, with a pronounced beat but rather flat vocal delivery. Her many imitators included June *Christy and Chris Connors (*b* 1927), both of whom followed her into the *Kenton band.

Offenbach Jacques [Jakob] (*b* Cologne 20 Jun. 1819; *d* Paris, 5 Oct. 1880. French (German-Jewish) composer. The family name was Eberst but the composer's father had assumed the name Offenbach before his marriage, having come from Offenbach-am-Main. He showed an early talent as composer and musician, playing the violin at six, writing his first music at eight and finding his special talent for the cello at nine. He studied locally and played in a trio with his brother and sister before being entered, in 1833, at the Paris Conservatoire, then directed by the difficult Cherubini. The discipline and traditionalism of the Conservatoire was not much to Offenbach's liking and he left to become a member of the orchestra at the Opéra-Comique. He composed dance music and songs, and many pieces for the cello, on which instrument he soon earned a virtuoso reputation, visiting London in 1844 to much acclaim. He married Herminie d'Alcain in August of that year. The next few years combined success as a musician with frustration as a composer, finding that his popularly slanted style was not acceptable to the staid management of the dominating Parisian opera-houses and theatres. He solved the problem in 1855 by leasing his own tiny theatre, which he named the Théâtre des *Bouffes-Parisiens, and, his initiative happily coinciding with the International Exhibition of 1855, and a useful influx of visitors, the venture was a successful one. A constant stream of mainly one-act pieces was produced through 1856 and 1857, many of these making their influential way abroad. Offenbach went to London in 1857 for a season of his works at the St James's Theatre. Matters really improved with the production of his scandalously satirical **Orphée aux Enfers* in 1858. At first condemned by most critics, its reputation attracted the public and its famous *can-can and other delectable attributes did the rest.

Full-length works like **Geneviève de Brabant* (1859); *La *Belle Hélène* (1864); *La *Vie Parisienne* (1866); *Barbe-bleue* (1867); *La *Grande-Duchesse de Gérolstein* (1867); *La *Périchole* (1868); *Les Brigands* (1869); and a continued output of smaller works (well over 100 in total) confirmed his reputation and furthered his worldwide influence. Offenbach was not a good businessman and managed his affairs badly. There were many difficult periods, both financially and artistically, but he managed to survive until ill-health defeated him. He made an only moderately successful visit to the USA in 1876 and further visits to London. The final period of his life was much taken up with the creation of his grand opera, *Les Contes d'Hoffmann*, which he did not live to see produced in 1881, having died of 'gout of the heart' in October 1880.

Offenbach deserves full credit as the principal founder of operetta and for his worldwide influence. The Viennese school and Sullivan in England were equally inspired by his seductive strains. Other composers, like Donizetti and Nicolai, had sown the seeds of a new popular vein in their operas and other contemporaries like *Hervé were also influential; but nobody surpassed Offenbach's achievement in this respect. Virtually everything he wrote had something of worthwhile quality in it not only in vivacious 'can-can' strains, but also in hauntingly beautiful songs that have a very special Offenbach characteristic. His achievement was to bring the melodies of cabaret and music-hall into the musical theatre, spinning them in an eminently singable operatic vein to produce a new genre of popular musical entertainment. With justification did Rossini dub him the 'Mozart of the Champs-Elysées'.

Offenbach's stage works included: *Pascal et Chambord* (1839); *L'Alcôve* (1847); *Le Trésor à Mathurin* (1853); *Pépito* (1853); *Luc et Lucette* (1854); *Oyayaïe*; *Les Deux Aveugles*; *La Nuit blanche*; *Arlequin barbier*; *La Rêve d'une nuit d'eté*; *Pierrot clown*; *Le Violoneux*; *Polichinelle dans le monde*; *Madame Papillon*; *Ba-ta-clan* (1855); *Un Postillon en gage*; *Tromb-al-Cazar*; *La Rose de Saint-Flour*; *Les Dragées de Baptême*; *Les Bergers de Watteau*; *Le 66*; *Le Savetier et le Financier*; *La Bonne d'enfants* (1856); *Les Trois Baisers du Diable*; *Croquefer*; *Dragonette*; *Vent du soir*; *Une Demoiselle en loterie*; *Le Mariage aux lanternes*; *Les Deux Pêcheurs* (1857); *Mesdames de la Halle*; *La Chatte metamorphosée en femme*; *Orphée aux Enfers* (1858); *Un Mari à la porte*; *Les Vivandières de la Grand Armée*; *Geneviève de Brabant* (1859); *Carnaval des Revues*; *Daphnis et Chloé*; *Le Papillon* (ballet); *Barkouf* (1860); *La Chanson de Fortunio*; *Le Pont des soupirs*; *M. Choufleuri restera chez lui*; *Apothicaire et Perruquier*; *Le Roman comique* (1861); *M. et Mme Denis*; *Le Voyage de MM. Dunanan père et fils*; *Jacqueline* (1862); *Les Bavards*; *Le Brésilien* (1863); *Liszchen et Fritzchen*; *L'Amour chanteur*; *Il Signor Fagotto*; *Die Rheinnixen*; *Les Géorgiennes*; *La Belle Hélène* (1864); *Les Refrains des Bouffes*; *Jeanne qui pleure et Jean qui rit*; *Les Bergers*; *Coscoletto* (1865); *La Vie Parisienne* (1866); *Barbe-Bleue*; *La Grande-Duchesse de Gérolstein*; *Robinson Crusoé* (1867); *Le Château à Toto*; *L'Île de Tulipatan*; *Le Fifre enchanté*; *La Périchole* (1868); *Vert-Vert*; *La Diva*; *La Princesse de Trébizonde*; *Les Brigands*; *La Romance de la rose* (1869); *Boule-de-neige* (1871); *Le Roi Carotte*; *Fantasio*; *Fleurette*; *Der Schwarze Korsar* (1872); *Les Braconniers*; *La Leçon de chant*; *La Permission de 10 heures*; *Pomme d'api*; *La Jolie Parfumeuse* (1873); *Bagatelle*; *Madame l'Archiduc*; *La Haine*; *Dick Whittington* (1874); *Les Hannetons*; *La Boulangère a des écus*; *Le Voyage dans la lune*; *La Créole*; *Tarte à la crème* (1875); *Pierette et Jacquot*; *La Boîte au lait* (1876); *Le Docteur Ox*; *La Foire Saint-Laurent* (1877); *Maître Peronilla*; *Madame Favart* (1878); *La Marocaine*; *La Fille du Tambour-Major* (1879); *La Belle Lurette* (1880); *Les Contes d'Hoffmann*; *Mam'zelle Moucheron* (1881). He also wrote orchestral works, chamber music, and songs. A romantic film biography, *La Valse de Paris*, with Pierre Fresnay (1897–1975) as Offenbach, was directed by Marchel Achard (1899–1974) in 1950.

S. Kracauer: *Jacques Offenbach und das Paris seiner Zeit* (Amsterdam–Paris–London, 1937). J. Brindejont-Offenbach: *Offenbach: mon grand-père* (Paris, 1940). A. Decaux: *Offenbach: Roi du Second Empire* (Paris, 1966). A. Faris: *Jacques Offenbach* (London, 1980). P. Gammond: *Offenbach: his Life and Times* (London–New York, 1980; repr. 1986). J. Harding: *Jacques Offenbach: a Biography* (London–New York, 1980). H-K. Metzger and R. Riehn: *Jacques Offenbach* (Munich, 1980).

Music: L. Almeida (ed.): *Offenbach's Songs from the Great Operas* (New York, 1976).

Of Thee I Sing. American musical with score by George *Gershwin, book by Morrie Ryskind and George S. *Kaufman, lyrics by Ira *Gershwin. After a try-out in Boston, it opened at the Music Box Theatre, New York, 26 Dec. 1931, and transferred to the 46th Street Theatre in Oct. 1932, achieving a total run of 441 performances.

Described by Stanley Green as 'being more in the style of a Gilbert and Sullivan comic opera' it followed that model in modern guise by taking a mocking look at the American political scene in the shape of presidential candidate John P. Wintergreen (William *Gaxton) and his running-mate Alexander Throttlebottom (Victor *Moore) who resort to any sort of chicanery, leading to impeachment; but with everything sorted out in the end. It was a highly successful follow-up to **Strike Up the Band* (1930), but a sequel, *Let 'Em Eat Cake'* (1933), took itself too seriously and failed. A sparkling score included the campaign song 'Of thee I sing, baby' and 'Wintergreen for President' but no really memorable hits beyond the title-song, which has remained a standard. It was the first musical show to be awarded the *Pulitzer Prize.

Oh, Boy! Intimate musical with score by Jerome *Kern, lyrics by P. G. *Wodehouse, book by Wodehouse and Guy *Bolton, the third of their famous *Princess Theatre shows, first produced there 20 Feb. 1917.

More or less a typical farce set to music, it tells the story of George Budd (Tom Powers, 1890–1955), who elopes with Lou Ellen Carter (Marie Carroll) and arrives home with her to find his friends holding a party in his flat. Deciding it is best to keep their marriage a secret until her parents have been prepared for the shock, he becomes innocently involved with an actress (Anna Wheaton, 1896–1971) who has climbed in to avoid the advances of a lecherous judge who turns out to be Lou Ellen's father. It all gets pretty complicated but leaves time for some excellent Kern numbers such as 'You never knew about me', 'An old-fashioned wife', and 'Till the clouds roll by'. It became the third longest running show of the 1910s with 463 performances, and was seen in London, at the Kingsway Theatre, 27 Jan. 1919, titled *Oh, Joy!* (167p].

Oh Boy! Early British commercial TV programme exploiting and promoting rock music 1958–9, devised and produced by Jack Good (*b* 1931) after his initial experience with the BBC's **Six-Five Special* (1957). It was succeeded, in turn, by *Boy Meets Girl* (1959) and *Wham!* (1960).

Oh, Kay! Musical comedy with score by George *Gershwin, book by Guy *Bolton and P. G. *Wodehouse, lyrics by Ira *Gershwin, an Aarons and *Freedley production at the Imperial Theatre, New York, 8 Nov. 1926, where it ran for 256 performances. It was conceived as a first starring vehicle for Gertrude *Lawrence after her New York success in the André Charlot revues, thus making her the first British actress to introduce a part in a Broadway show before she had appeared in it in London.

The book by Wodehouse and Bolton, following on their *Princess Theatre collaborations with Jerome *Kern, had some of the same farcical style, with Oscar *Shaw playing the role of an about-to-be-married man who falls in love with his attractive cook (Gertrude Lawrence). She, of course, is not a real cook but only posing as one in order to help her brother, a member of the English aristocracy, who is in the bootleg business. They survive all such obstacles in the name of romance. The fine Gershwin songs included 'Dear little girl', 'Maybe', 'Clap yo' hands', 'Do, do, do', and 'Someone to watch over me'. Gertrude Lawrence then appeared in the London version, at His Majesty's Theatre 21 Sept. 1927 [214p]. There was a successful New York revival in 1960.

Oh, Lady! Lady!! Intimate musical with score by Jerome *Kern, lyrics by P. G. *Wodehouse, book by Wodehouse and Guy *Bolton, their last *Princess Theatre collaboration, following *Oh, Boy!* (1917) on 1 Feb. 1918, and running for 219 performances. Yet another farcical mix-up involves an about-to-be-married man who gets involved with another gal—this time his ex-fiancée who turns up as a delivery girl along with a jewel thief and between them cause typical musical comedy chaos. All ends happily at a party in Greenwich Village. It was not one of Kern's most distinguished scores, its great success, in a manner of speaking, being a song which was discarded called 'Bill', later used with great effect in *Show Boat*.

Oh, What a Lovely War! British musical entertainment which used the songs of the First World War to evoke a nostalgic, humorous, but very moving picture of that tragic happening with its extravagant waste of human life and promise. The original production, directed by Joan Littlewood for Theatre Workshop at the Theatre Royal, Stratford, 10 Mar. 1963, and after its immediate success moving to the West End, at Wyndham's Theatre 20 June 1963, did not go for big stars but aimed rather at a unified anonymity of approach. A succession of wartime episodes, ranging from the eager recruits to the disillusion of the trenches, made use of musical material which proved to be remarkably evocative, including: 'It's a long way to Tipperary', 'I'll make a man of you', 'Pack up your troubles', 'Good-byee', 'Oh, it's a lovely war', 'Never mind'. These commercial items were mixed with the soldiers' own ditties, with crudely cynical words added to traditional songs, hymns, and popular songs—such as 'Fred Karno's Army', 'When this lousy war is over', and 'The bells of hell'.

A completely opposite policy was adopted in the 1969 film directed by Richard Attenborough (*b* 1923), which used such stars as John Gielgud (*b* 1904), Laurence Olivier (1907–89), John *Mills, Ralph Richardson (1902–82), Maggie Smith (*b*

1934), Vanessa Redgrave (*b* 1937), and Kenneth More (1914–82). It made for quite a different, though still effective, experience.

Oklahoma! Important musical in the annals of Broadway bringing to the musical stage a new coherence and realism in the steps of **Show Boat*, brilliantly choreographed by Agnes de Mille (*b* 1905), and drawing on pioneer America for its background rather than the unrealities of society life where musical comedy had so often dwelt. Richard *Rodgers was persuaded to write the music and, with the collaboration of Oscar *Hammerstein II, produced a score of extravagant tunefulness and musical rightness that showed a remarkable breakaway from the sophisticated style of his early collaboration with Lorenz *Hart. It included such unfading folky classics as 'Oh, what a beautiful morning', 'The surrey with the fringe on top', 'Kansas City', 'I cain't say no', 'All er nothin'', 'Many a new day', 'People will say we're in love', 'Out of my dreams', 'The farmer and the cowman', and 'Oklahoma'. Opening in New York, at the St James Theatre 31 Mar. 1943, it had a run of 2212 performances, lasting over five years and nine months, a run only surpassed by **My Fair Lady* some 15 years later.

The plot, based on the play *Green Grow the Lilacs* (1931) by Lynn Riggs (1899–1954), hinged on the rivalry of Curly (Alfred *Drake) and Jud (Howard Da Silva, *b* 1909) for the hand of Laurey (Joan Roberts). A sub-plot involves the man-hungry Ado Annie similarly torn between Will (Lee Dixon) and Ali Hakim (Joseph Buloff). There were many changes of cast in its long run, involving such names as Howard *Keel (who was to star in the London production) and Shelley Winters. At the Drury Lane Theatre, London, 30 Apr. 1947 it had a run of 1548 performances; meanwhile touring companies in America kept the show going for over a decade. The film version of 1955 starred Gordon *McRae and Shirley Jones (*b* 1934). There was a notable New York revival in 1969 at the Lincoln Center and a new production at the Palace Theatre in 1979.

Olcott, Chauncey [Chancellor, John] (*b* Buffalo, NY, 21 July 1858; *d* Monte Carlo, 18 Mar. 1932). American composer, author, singer, and actor. He began his professional career in 1876 as a vocalist in Thatcher, Primrose & West minstrel shows, originally with the Alabama Serenaders. He went to London in 1880 to appear at Drury Lane with Haverley's Mastodons. In 1888 he joined a singing quartet in the original production of *The Old Homestead*. He became a well-known soloist before going to London again in 1890 to study singing and appear in several light operas. Back in the USA he began to star in a number of Irish musical plays beginning with *The Minstrel of Clare* (1896), having his greatest successes in *Barry of Ballymore* (1910) and *The Heart of Paddy Whack* (1914). He was once referred to as 'one of the most popular musical figures of all times'—but time has long since overtaken such judgements. His songs included 'Olcott's home song' (1896); 'My wild Irish rose' (1899); 'Mother Machree' (with Ernest *Ball), and 'I love the name of Mary' (with Ball, 1910).

R. Olcott: *Song in his Heart* (New York, 1939).

Oldfield, Mike (*b* Reading, Berks., 15 May 1953). British composer and performer. After recording, with his sister Sally, an LP of songs for Transatlantic, *Sallyangie* (1968), in 1970 he joined the Whole World group led by Kevin Ayers (*b* 1945) playing guitar and bass. There he met the composer David Bedford who encouraged his compositional ideas and was later to help with orchestration. He was contracted as a solo artist to Virgin Records and recorded *Tubular Bells* (1973), an ambitious mixture of instrumental arrangements based on a bell motif which had prestigious success and established him as one of the most important British composers working in the rock field. The theme of the LP was used in the film *The Exorcist* and reached the Top 10 in the USA. A work of less impact but greater coherence was *Hergest Ridge* (1974) followed by the even more ambitious *Ommadawn* (1975) which involved pipers, African percussion, and a children's choir. Various singles—'In dulci jubilo' (1975), 'Portsmouth' (1976), and 'Blue Peter' (1979)—were equally successful, as were the subsequent albums *Incantations* (1978) and *Exposed* (1979). Working in his own audio-visual studio in the 1980s, he moved into the video field with *Pictures in the Dark* (1986). He has been one of the few composers convincingly to extend rock tinged with folk-music into full-length works.

Old Grey Whistle Test, The. Valued BBC TV programme, hosted by Anne Nightingale and others, featuring British progressive rock and American pop stars, which was started in 1969. It became simply *Whistle Test* in 1977 when it took in more *new wave groups.

Oliver! Musical play with words and music by Lionel *Bart, based on Dickens's *Oliver Twist*, first produced by Donald Albery (*b* 1914) at the Wimbledon Theatre 10 June 1960. It moved to London's West End at the New Theatre 30 June 1960, with Ron Moody (*b* 1924) as Fagin, Georgia *Brown as Nancy, Keith Hamshere as Oliver, and Danny Sewell as Bill Sykes.

It kept fairly faithfully to the original story and added a score of a lively, tuneful, and straightforward nature which made it into a remarkable hit musical that became the longest-running show in the history of the British musical stage with 2618 performances. It went on to reach 774 performances in New York, at the Imperial Theatre 6 Jan. 1963; and was revived for 331 performances in London in 1967, with Barry Humphries as Fagin, and again in 1977, with Roy Hudd (*b* 1933) as Fagin, and 1983. Further success came with the fine film made on an impressive set at Shepperton studios in 1968, directed by Carol Reed, with Ron

Moody continuing his highly praised role as Fagin, Harry Secombe (*b* 1921) as Mr Bumble, Oliver Reed (*b* 1938) as Sikes, Mark Lester (*b* 1958) as Oliver, Jack Wild (*b* 1952) as the Dodger, and Shani Wallis (*b* 1933) as Nancy.

The first Dickens novel to be successfully adapted for the musical stage, much of its success was due to such catchy, if sometimes derivative, numbers as 'Food, glorious food', 'Consider yourself', 'You've got to pick a pocket or two', 'I'd do anything', 'Oom-pah-pah', 'As long as he needs me', and (probably the best moment in the score) 'Who will buy?'. The 1980s saw productions in New York, Salzburg, and Munich.

Oliver, Joe 'King' [Joseph] (*b* Abend, La., 11 May 1885; *d* Savannah, Ga., 10 Apr. 1938). American cornettist, composer, and bandleader. Raised in New Orleans, he first played the trombone in various local bands then switched to cornet, working 1908–17 with such ensembles as the Olympia Band, the Onward Brass Band, and the Melrose Brass Band, also making a living as a butler. He worked with Richard M. *Jones and Kid *Ory in New Orleans clubs and led his own group for a while at Pete Lala's club. In 1919 he moved to Chicago to play with the band of Lawrence Duhé (1887–1959), which he took over in 1920 and led at the famous Dreamland Café until 1921. He worked in San Francisco for a while in 1921, returning to Chicago in 1922 to lead his historic Creole Jazz Band at the Lincoln Gardens, during which time he made his first recordings for Gennett in 1923, and visited New York as a soloist in 1924.

Louis *Armstrong had joined the band in 1922 as second cornettist and it was the sides in which he and Oliver recorded a highly original two-cornet lead that greatly excited the jazz world and pushed it on its way to developments beyond the early New Orleans style upon which their playing was based. Oliver led his Dixie Syncopators at the Plantation Café 1925–7, then played in Milwaukee, Detroit, and St Louis, before moving to the *Savoy Ballroom in New York in 1927. He turned down a lucrative offer of a residency at the *Cotton Club (which gave Duke *Ellington his big chance) and disbanded his orchestra at the end of 1927. He played and recorded with Clarence *Williams in 1928, formed a new band in 1931 and continued as a bandleader until 1937. Changes in fashion tended to leave him behind and trouble with his teeth diminished his abilities as a player. He spent his last year running a fruit stall and working as a poolroom attendant.

One of the great names in early jazz history, he not only formulated a style and advanced it, meanwhile employing and encouraging many other influential musicians, but also supplied it with many of its classic themes, his compositions including 'Just gone' (1923), 'Snake rag' (1923), 'Dippermouth blues' (1923; re-titled 'Sugar foot stomp' in 1925), 'Canal Street blues' (1923), 'New Orleans stomp' (1924), 'Snag it' (1926), 'Doctor Jazz' (1927), 'West End blues' (1928), 'Mournful serenade' (1928), 'Slow and steady' (1928), 'Too late' (1929), 'Stop crying' (1930), to name but a few from many either written by him or in collaboration with others.

B. Rust and W. Allen: *King Joe Oliver* (London, 1957). M. Williams: *King Oliver* (New York–London, 1960).

Oliver, Sy [Melvin James] (*b* Battle Creek, Mich., 17 Dec. 1910; *d* New York, 28 May 1988). American composer, arranger, and trumpeter. Both his parents were music teachers but he showed little interest in music until his father gave him a trumpet and taught him how to play it. He worked with a local band while he was still at school and, after leaving school, worked professionally with Zack Whyte until 1930. Having submitted some arrangements to the bandleader Jimmie *Lunceford, he was asked to join the band in 1933 and it was here that he made his reputation as a brilliant arranger with such recorded items as 'For dancers only', 'Organ grinder's swing', 'By the River St Marie', 'T'ain't whatcha do', 'Margie', and 'Stomp it off', which helped to make the Lunceford band one of the leading black swing orchestras.

Always written over a solid swinging basis, Oliver's arrangements were full of interesting interplay between sections. He was lured away from Lunceford by Tommy *Dorsey and supplied him with such hit arrangements as 'Opus 1', 'Well, git it', 'Swing high', 'Yes, indeed', and (best-known of all) 'On the sunny side of the street'. He joined the army as a bandmaster 1943–5, then led his own band in 1946, thereafter mainly working as musical director and record producer for several companies, notably American Decca, where he wrote arrangements for such artists as Billie *Holiday, Ella *Fitzgerald, Frank *Sinatra, Sammy *Davis, and Louis *Armstrong and led accompanying groups. He formed a band again in the 1950s which eventually evolved into a polished 9-piece unit which he led at the Rainbow Room in New York from the early 1970s until he retired in 1984 through illness.

Olman, Abe (*b* Cincinnati, 20 Dec. 1888; *d* Rancho Mirage, Calif., 4 Jan. 1894). From 1910 he worked as a song plugger with a music-publisher in Cleveland, managed a theatrical agency in New York in 1912, then moved to Chicago where he established his own music-publishing business, La Salle Music, in 1931. In the meantime he toured as a vaudeville entertainer and visited Europe in that capacity in 1913. From 1946 to 1956 he was a director of *ASCAP. He supplied many song hits later used in films, among his best-known being 'Down among the sheltering palms' (1914), 'Oh, Johnny, oh' (1917, *w* Billy *Rose), 'Down by the O-HI-O' (1920, *w* Jack *Yellen), and 'Some sweet day' (1921), many of them made famous by Al *Jolson.

Olsen, George (*b* Portland, Ore., 18 Mar. 1893; *d* Paramus, NJ, 18 Mar. 1971). American bandleader. During studies at the University of Michigan he led a college band and by 1919 was leading his own orchestra in Portland which, with its sweet 'society' style, had become very popular by *c.*1923. He worked with the entertainer Fanny *Brice, which led to an association with Florenz *Ziegfeld and an appearance in the Broadway musical *Kid Boots* (1924); and in the *Ziegfeld Follies* of that year. He was in the musical **Sunny* (1925) and made a hit recording of *Kern's 'Who?' (1926), ever after closely associated with the Olsen band, which appeared in **Good News* (1927), **Whoopee* (1928), and in various early sound films. The band's radio popularity declined, but Olsen continued, taking over the Orville Knapp band in 1936 after Knapp died. He entertained the troops in the Second World War, retiring from music in 1951 to run a restaurant in Paramus.

Olympia Music Hall. Paris theatre on the Boulevard des Capucines which opened in the spring of 1893, being one of the first places of entertainment in France to label itself a 'music hall', importing the name from London. It was built by Joseph Oller, then the director of the Moulin Rouge, and opened to a fare of musical comedies in the grand manner, Louis Willy's *Le Coucher de la mariée* (a pioneering striptease show), pantomime, straight plays, acrobatics, and waxworks. Among its famous directors was Jacques-Charles (1882–1971) who, during the period 1911–14 introduced both *Mistinguett and Yvonne *Printemps to the Olympia. With the work of these artists, and others who followed, the theatre became a breeding-ground for the *chanson in its heyday. Between 1918 and 1928 the director was Paul Franck, who introduced such artists as Lucienne *Boyer. The theatre closed 1929–54 to become a cinema; but thereafter Bruno Coquatrix (*b* 1910) staked all that he had to re-establish it as a living theatre. Styles in entertainment there naturally changed with the times but the theatre kept something of the music-hall tradition alive. Coquatrix (himself the composer of modern chansons like 'Clopin-clopant') saw the Olympia as a European goal for the world's top entertainers; and it has always been acoustically ideal for contact between stage and audience.

On a Clear Day You Can See Forever. American musical comedy with score by Burton *Lane and book by Alan Jay *Lerner. Earlier, Lerner had attempted a musical about extrasensory perception with Richard *Rodgers, but that never materialized and he worked on the idea with Lane instead. The show opened at the Mark Hellinger Theatre, New York, 17 Oct. 1965, and had 280 performances. Daisy Gamble (played by Barbara Harris, *b* 1937) is able to predict the future or revive the past, where she meets herself in another guise and finds the *alter ego* an amatory rival. Songs included 'On a clear day you can see forever', 'She wasn't you', 'Melinda', 'What did I have that I don't have?', and 'Come back to me'. It was filmed in 1970 with Barbra *Streisand in the leading role.

One Dam Thing After Another. Revue with music by Richard *Rodgers, book by Ronald Jeans, and lyrics by Lorenz *Hart, a C. B. *Cochran show produced at the London Pavilion 20 May 1927, with Sonnie *Hale and Jessie *Matthews. It had 237 performances. It introduced London to 'My heart stood still', 'My lucky star', and 'I need some cooling off'. The *DeSylva, *Brown, and *Henderson number 'The birth of the blues' was also used.

One-step. A basic dance introduced around 1910 which became popular by virtue of its simplicity, fulfilling the needs of the ordinary dancer rather than the ballroom expert, in essence an uncomplicated walking step. There was a tune composed especially for it—'Bogey walk' by James M. Gallatly. Dances which were a simple variant of the one-step were the Judy Walk, the Bunny Hug, the Turkey Trot, and the Castle Walk (a special version introduced by Mr and Mrs Vernon *Castle). The one-step was a basic ingredient of the ragtime dances that were danced to the new-fangled strains of pseudo-ragtime tunes like Irving *Berlin's 'Alexander's Ragtime Band' (1911).

One Touch of Venus. Musical comedy with score by Kurt *Weill, book by S. J. Perelman (1904–79) and Ogden Nash (1902–71), lyrics by Nash, based on F. Anstey's *The Tinted Venus*. One of Weill's lightest and most enjoyable American scores was the material for the first starring role of the talented Mary *Martin who played the part of a statue of Venus in a New York museum who comes to life when a ring is placed on her finger by an amorous barber, played by Kenny *Baker. The owner of the museum (played by John *Boles) also falls for her, but matters are solved for better or worse when the lady turns back into a marble statue. Produced at the Imperial Theatre, New York, 7 Oct. 1943, it had 567 performances. Weill's score included 'One touch of Venus', 'I'm a stranger here myself', 'Foolish heart', 'The trouble with women', 'That's him', and the classic torch song 'Speak low'. A film version in 1948 starred Ava Gardner (1922–90), Robert Walker (1914–51), Olga San Juan (*b* 1927), and Dick *Haymes.

On the Avenue. 20th Century Fox film of 1937, featuring the music and words of Irving *Berlin (1937), starring Dick *Powell, Madeleine Carroll (*b* 1906), Alice *Faye, the Ritz Brothers, Joan Davis (1907–61), and Walter *Catlett. The songs included: 'I've got my love to keep me warm', 'The girl on the Police Gazette', 'Slumming on Park Avenue', 'He ain't got rhythm', and 'This year's kisses'.

On the Town. American musical comedy with score by Leonard *Bernstein and book by Betty *Comden and Adolph Green, based on the ballet *Fancy Free* by Leonard Bernstein and Jerome *Robbins. It was produced at the Adelphi Theatre, New York, 28 Dec. 1944, where it had 463 performances.

The story concerns three sailors, played by John Battles, Adolph Green, and Cris Alexander, enjoying some shore leave in New York, who meet up with three girls, played by Sono Osato, Betty Comden, and Nancy *Walker. The pursuit of them leads the story through various sight-seeing parts of the city. The musical items included: 'New York, New York', 'Come up to my place', 'I get carried away' 'Lonely town', 'Lucky to be me', and 'Some other time'. The show was seen in London at the Prince of Wales Theatre in 1963 for only 63 performances. There were New York revivals in 1959 and 1971 and a film in 1949 with Gene *Kelly, Frank *Sinatra, Jules Munshin, Vera-Ellen (*b* 1921), Betty Garrett (*b* 1919), and Ann Miller (*b* 1919).

On the Twentieth Century. Musical with score by Cy *Coleman and book by Betty *Comden and Adolph Green, based on a classic Hollywood comedy, *Twentieth Century* (1934), which takes place on board a luxury express train, the Twentieth Century Limited, on its progress from Chicago to New York. A passé Broadway producer (John Cullum) is trying to persuade a famous and temperamental film star (Madeline Kahn) to appear in his next play. He also has to compete with her lover and a rival producer, but in the end romance concludes the contract. Produced at the St James Theatre, New York, 19 Feb. 1978, it had 449 performances. Like many prestigious American shows it did not find favour with reviewers or public in London in 1980 (165p) in spite of a fine performance from Julia McKenzie.

On With the Dance. Revue with music and words mainly by *Noël Coward (with three additional songs by Philip *Braham) seen at the Pavilion, London, 30 Apr. 1925. It introduced 'Poor little rich girl' (also used in the 1926 *Charlot's Revue*). The cast included Douglas *Byng, Hermione *Baddeley, and Alice *Delysia, and it ran for 229 performances.

On Your Toes. Musical comedy with score by Richard *Rodgers, book by Rodgers, Lorenz *Hart, and George *Abbott, lyrics by Hart, produced at the Imperial Theatre, New York, 11 Apr. 1936 [315p].

It was originally intended as a film musical for Fred *Astaire, but he turned it down as its story, set in the ballet world, seemed inappropriate for his current top-hat-and-tails image. It was made into a stage musical and tailored around the talents of Ray *Bolger, who rose to stardom as a result. It was also the first musical to make the ballet an integral part, and Rodgers rose to the occasion with the effective 'Slaughter on Tenth Avenue' (danced by Bolger and Tamara Geva, *b* 1907) which was choreographed by George Balanchine (1904–83). It also contained the Rodgers and Hart classic 'There's a small hotel' and 'On your toes', 'It's got to be love', and 'Glad to be unhappy'.

In the London production, at the Palace Theatre 5 Feb. 1937, Jack *Whiting took the leading role, with Balanchine's third wife, Vera Zorina (*b* 1917) as the ballerina. It was revived in New York in 1954 with Elaine Stritch (*b* 1925) singing the added number 'You took advantage of me'; and again in 1983 when it proved lasting enough to outrun the original production with 505 performances. A 1939 film, which used the music only as a background, starred Eddie *Albert and Zorina.

Opéra-bouffe (Fr.); **Opera buffa** (It.). A genre, loosely translatable as 'comic opera'; earlier used to categorize a work that was the opposite of *opera seria*, generally involving characters of everyday life like Mozart's *The Marriage of Figaro*, Rossini's *The Barber of Seville*, and Donizetti's *The Daughter of the Regiment*. The French equivalent was much favoured by *Offenbach and his contemporaries, following in the steps of Donizetti, to describe a light-hearted work that might equally well be called an *operetta.

Operetta (It.); **Opérette** (Fr.); **Operette** (Ger.); **Light Opera** (Eng.). Categorical term literally meaning a 'little' opera, as originally used by Schubert and others; but the word gradually came to suggest a work of an intrinsically light-weight nature, not necessarily brief. The English have tended to favour the term *light opera or comic opera (rather confusing it with opéra-comique—which is not at all the same thing). The later history of operetta can be followed under such extended guises as *musical comedy or the *musical, though many would limit the definition of operetta to those areas discussed below, where it retains an operatic allegiance.

The emergence of operetta around the middle of the 19th century was largely the result of economic and social changes. As the middle classes and, subsequently, the working classes, became increasingly affluent, and therefore in a position to dictate their entertainment needs, there arose a demand for operatic entertainment of a more approachable and tuneful kind, tailored to suit less highbrow tastes, than the chiefly Italian grand opera. The same influences can be seen in other fields of popular entertainment, such as *music-hall, the *minstrel show, and popular song in general, during the same period. Opera and all areas of so-called classical music were becoming increasingly complex and demanding, moving in directions that were to make them more elitist and outside the tastes of the general public. The symptoms can be seen in the increasing seriousness of Verdi's operas, in the emergence of Wagner, and the development of 12-tone music. On the other hand a lighter touch could be seen in the works of certain composers like Donizetti and Nicolai that hinted at the possibilities of a popular musical theatre.

Real changes began to take place, in all branches of art, from *c.*1850, gradually but with increased momentum from this time on. One could go back as far as Mozart's *The Marriage of Figaro* to find hints of a movement towards some of the definable characteristics of operetta: tunefulness, detachable arias, an everyday, believable story of ordinary people. Yet such a work remains in the opera category by virtue of its structure, integration, and vocal demands. One of the greatest operettas subsequently written, Johann Strauss's *Die Fledermaus*, has many of the same characteristics and is satisfyingly challenging to sing (hence its appeal for the opera singer), but it can safely be categorized as a true operetta by virtue of its genuinely frivolous nature and general lightness of touch. The distinction is not always easy to define, but it is usually apparent in the character of the work. Operetta history is most usefully continued under various headings: 1) French; 2) Viennese; 3) Spanish; 4) British; 5) American; 6) German; and 7) Operetta and opera.

O. Keller: *Die Operette* (Leipzig–Vienna–New York, 1926). M. S. Mackinlay: *Origin and Development of Light Opera* (London, 1926). J. Bruyr: *L'Opérette* (Paris, 1962). G. Hughes: *Composers of Operetta* (London, 1962). M. Lubbock: *The Complete Book of Light Opera* [synopses] (London, 1962). O. Schneiderheit: *Operette von Abraham bis Ziehrer* (Berlin, 1969). R. Traubner: *Operetta: a Theatrical History* (New York–London, 1984).

1 *French*. The French are generally credited with creating the genre of light opera that evolved into true operetta, although some of the specific works that provided inspiration and impetus came from Italian and German sources. The French, however, were clearly moving towards a lighter operatic genre in the era of the opéra-comique which began in the 18th century and gathered force in the early 19th century. The adjective 'comique', in this context, is not to be taken too literally and was used simply because the composers and works that affected the movement tended to gather around the Parisian opera-house known as l'Opéra-Comique, founded in 1715, as distinct from the more establishment-dominated l'Opéra. It was closed in 1745 but re-opened again in 1752, joined forces with the Comédie-Italienne in 1762, and moved, for its most influential years, to the Rue Favart, thus becoming popularly known as the 'Salle Favart'. Here the true French-flavoured strain of opéra-comique began with composers such as the Belgian-born André Grétry (1741–1813), Nicolas Dalayrac (1753–1809), and Étienne Méhul (1763–1817); succeeded by such important figures as Adrien Boieldieu (1775–1835), Daniel François Esprit Auber (1782–1871), Ferdinand Hérold (1791–1833), and Adolphe *Adam. The cumulative effect of the works of these composers and others is not easy to assess because most of their output is now so rarely heard, but the little that is known shows a clear leaning towards operetta. Further influences in this direction came from such composers as Nicolai and Lortzing in Germany and, perhaps most notably, from one single work, *La Fille du Régiment* by the Italian composer Donizetti, which was produced at l'Opéra-Comique in 1840. Many of operetta's early distinctive features are to be heard within its score. Jacques *Offenbach (the major founding-figure of operetta) had his musical apprenticeship in the pit of l'Opéra-Comique 1834–8, and could hardly help but absorb the strains of such works played there during his appointment, including Adam's *Le Chalet* and *Le Postillon de Longjumeau* and Auber's *Le Domino noir*, among many others.

The two dominant early figures in the development of French opérette were Offenbach and Florimond Rogé (who wrote and performed as *Hervé). Both became frustrated by the difficulty of getting their works accepted and performed at the Opéra-Comique and founded their own small theatres where they could freely introduce their new brand of satirical and musical frivolities. Their works soon established a popular following and created a school of French operetta whose later adherents included such names as Léo Délibes (1836–91), better-known for the grand opera *Lakmé* and his popular ballets, Louis *Ganne, Charles *Lecocq, André *Messager, Robert *Planquette, and many later figures.

Offenbach's most popular works, like **Orphée aux Enfers* (1856), soon made their way to such musical centres as London and Vienna where they were almost continually staged, often conducted by the composer, and were the inspiration for composers in Austria, Germany, Great Britain, Spain, and the USA to write in similar vein and create their own schools of operetta. See also under CHRISTINÉ; CUVILLIER; HAHN; JONAS; LOPEZ; MASSÉ; YVAIN.

H-A. Parys: *Histoire Anecdotique de l'Opérette* (Brussels, 1945). C. Imber: *Histoire de la Chanson et de l'Opérette* (Lausanne, 1967). F. Bruyas: *Histoire de l'Opérette en France 1855–1965* (Lyons, 1974). J. Harding: *Folies de Paris: the Rise and Fall of French Operetta* (London, 1979).

2 *Viennese*. Operetta is particularly associated in the public's mind with Vienna; and whereas we generally categorize in terms of the country of origin, we rarely, if ever, speak of Austrian operetta. This arose because of the city's dominating musical status and the fact that it remained in a stable central position while national boundaries were continually changing. It was in Vienna that operetta was to achieve its romantic quintessence and a musical style that is now thought of as the real thing by most people.

Operetta in Vienna had its first impetus from the visiting success of Offenbach and his works, although it is probably going too far to say with Erwin Reiger that 'but for Offenbach's success in Vienna there might have been no such thing as Viennese operetta', certainly in the light of what had already been written there before the French maestro arrived and took Vienna by storm. It is safe to assume that Viennese operetta would have happened anyway as an offshoot of the Viennese dance school led by *Lanner and the *Strauss family, following in the steps of Mozart and Schubert. Mozart had already led the stage towards realistic operatic comedy with *Le Nozze di Figaro* and, following the lead of such Italian masters as Rossini and Donizetti, there was a discernible trend towards a lighter vein in the early 1800s. By then, in hindsight, the beginnings of an Austrian operetta school could be seen in Adolf Muller and Franz von *Suppé, the latter in lightly scored works written in the 1840s and 1850s; for example, the overture that he wrote for the incidental music to the play *Dichter und Bauer (Poet and Peasant)* in 1846. All that was needed was the final common touch that Offenbach was to demonstrate, to the Viennese public's delight. His operettas began to appear there *c.*1850 and Offenbach himself arrived in triumph in 1858.

The Viennese composers could no longer be in doubt as to the way the popular musical theatre should go. Suppé's works ceased to be piecemeal burlesques or Singspiele and became shapely light operas combining, as Gervase Hughes put it, 'Parisian *savoir-faire* with Viennese *Gemütlichkeit*'. In line with many writers, Hughes pinpoints Suppé's *Das Pensionat* of 1860 as the 'first Viennese operetta'. Unfortunately the claim is not supported by the active survival of this particular work on the operetta stage. However, Offenbach returned to Vienna in 1864 with another batch of inspirational works for the Viennese to hear; and there is no doubt at all that Suppé's eminently pleasing and graceful *Die schöne Galathée* of 1865 benefited from the example of *La Belle Hélène*, while remaining clearly and effectively Viennese. Suppé seems to have lost some of the impetus after this and did not find his best inspiration again until *Fatinitza* (1876) and *Boccaccio* (his masterpiece) in 1879.

Other younger composers like Karl *Millöcker, an orchestral musician and conductor, started out by quite blatantly copying Offenbach in his early operettas of the 1860s and 1870s; eventually, after conducting works by Suppé and Strauss, he found a true Viennese waltz vein in such works as **Gräfin Dubarry* of 1879 and the classic *Der *Bettelstudent* of 1882—a libretto he was fortunate to take over when it was rejected by Strauss.

It is not beyond the bounds of honest speculation to assume that the younger Johann Strauss, already an established leader in the dance music world, would eventually try his hand at operetta. A hardy legend, to be found in many books, has it that it was Offenbach, taking coffee with Strauss, who persuaded him that he ought to write an operetta. Strauss took his own time and is said to have approached the theatrical world with reluctance—finally to be persuaded by his ambitious wife. It was not until he had visited Paris in 1867 (and presumably the *Bouffes-Parisiens) that he finally took the plunge—without understanding the requirement of a properly weighted libretto and the necessity of speaking one's own musical language. He made do with weak librettos and tried, in common with others, to ape Offenbach's style. In 1874 he at last found an ideal libretto and launched into a score that was in the purest Strauss vein. *Die Fledermaus* is unassailably claimed from all quarters as 'the apotheosis of Viennese operetta'. It is not only the most melodic and shapely of them all but falls into that rare class of creation that allows it to be admitted in both worlds of music. Strauss's happy accident only emphasizes how fortunate Offenbach was in having good regular collaborators and how miraculously endowed Sullivan was in having Gilbert. Strauss, perhaps the greatest of the three musically, continued to make do with poor librettos that resulted in more failures, however rich the gems embedded in their scores, until he found one more cohesive script and wrote another masterpiece in *Der *Zigeunerbaron*.

With these shining examples to hand it is not surprising that operetta flourished so fruitfully in Vienna until eventually a new musical idiom ousted the old world of gracious 3/4 time. Among Strauss's close rivals were composers such as Karl *Zeller with *Der *Vogelhändler* (1891) and *Der Obersteiger* (1894) and Richard *Heuberger with *Der Opernball* in 1898.

The torch was handed on to a new generation who survived long enough either to defy the jazz age or to accept its innovations and add them to their natural Viennese vein, with mixed success. After Strauss the greatest figure in Viennese operetta was the Hungarian-born bandmaster Franz *Lehár. Like Strauss, he struggled with inadequate early librettos but found his true potential when the right one came along in 1905—*Die *lustige Witwe*, a libretto previously spurned by Heuberger. As *The Merry Widow*, it proved to be another *Die Fledermaus*, delighting not only its native city but the whole world. Interestingly, while *Die Fledermaus* might well pass as a tuneful opera, with music to satisfy the stars of La Scala and elsewhere, *The Merry Widow*, just as impeccably crafted and with a classic story, is clearly in the musical comedy vein. It enjoyed its great London success with a male lead who was not considered to be a singer at all. If *Die Fledermaus* is the best operetta ever written, *The Merry Widow* is probably the best musical comedy.

Viennese operetta history was continued by a number of highly talented, prolific, and professional composers like Oscar *Straus, who produced such classics of the genre as *Ein *Walzertraum* and *Der *tapfere Soldat (The Chocolate Soldier)*; Emmerich *Kálmán (another Hungarian) with *Die *Csárdásfürstin* (1915) and **Gräfin Mariza* (1924); Leo *Fall with *Die *Dollarprinzessin* (1907); and others such as *Eysler, *Künneke, and *Stolz and August Pepöck (1887–1967) (to mention but a few) in the queue of talents. Vienna's international status was enhanced by many composers from the Austro-Hungarian Empire working there, like Georg Jarno (1868–1920) from Budapest and Oskar Nedbal (1874–1930) from Czechoslovakia.

The historian generally senses a tailing-off of the operetta tradition soon after the end of the First World War, with the jazz age well in flow and composers like the Hungarian-born Paul *Abrahám and others succumbing to the allure of the new 'razz-ma-tazz' of 'der Dixieland', and the pure waltz-based Viennese opera seeming like a survivor from another age. Nevertheless it remained a potent and active vein well beyond the Second World War, not only in Vienna (with Lehár still productive into the mid-1930s) but anywhere where the seeds had blown abroad: in the USA with such as *Friml and *Romberg, in England with *Novello and *Coward. Viennese operetta can be credited with some 80 years of active life. Right up to the present there is a special following for the Viennese brand that alone outweighs the more specialized national appeal of the French, Spanish, and British brands.

E. Rieger: *Die gute Zeit der Wiener Operette* (Vienna, 1922). A. Neisser: *Vom Wesen und Wert der Operette* (Leipzig, 1923). F. Hadamowsky and H. Otto: *Die Wiener Operette* (Vienna, 1947). A. Bauer: *Opern und Operette in Wien* [checklist] (Vienna, 1952). E. Nick: *Vom Wiener Walzer zur Wiener Operette* (Hamburg, 1954).

3 *Spanish*. The insularity of Spanish culture seems to leave her music perpetually distanced from that of the rest of Europe, especially in the more popular spheres. Although her operetta tradition (more fully discussed under the generic name of ZARZUELA) is both abundant and musically rewarding, even books on music in Spain seem to give only fitful attention to what is a remarkably prolific and rewarding area of music-making; a situation aggravated by the inaccessibility of specialized literature on the subject and, in what is available, haphazard scholarship and a tantalizing lack of facts. In spite of its attractiveness, the zarzuela repertoire has remained a closed book for most other Europeans and Americans; the works are very rarely performed outside Spain and Latin America, and only sporadically available on record. This is not because there is any obvious resistance to their charms or their very Spanish nature, as Spanish rhythms and styles have been totally accepted when offered and have been widely spread in this century through Spanish classical music and music from Latin America. There has even been a strong and sustained interest in *flamenco music. It simply seems a matter of the language barrier, zarzuelas being so deeply Spanish and losing much of their character in translation.

Spain, like most European countries, suffered a massive invasion of Italian opera which was difficult to overcome with the native product. Many Spanish composers studied in Paris and the models for the Spanish operetta were, as elsewhere, mainly French and Offenbachian. Thus this resurgence of Spanish musical theatre came roughly around the same period as it did in the rest of Europe, beginning in the 1850s with its classic efforts such as *El Barberillo de Lavapiés* appearing in 1874 just as *Strauss was producing *Die *Fledermaus* in Vienna and the *Gilbert and Sullivan era was beginning in England. The history of zaruela moves in parallel with European and American developments except that, because of the isolation, the jazz influence of the 1920s was less apparent in Spain and native traditions prevailed.

S. Valverde: *El Mundo de la Zarzuela* (Madrid, 1979).

4 *British*. The actual name 'operetta' was never widely used in Britain, such anglicized labels as *'light opera' or 'comic opera' generally being preferred to inform the public of their nature. However, much that went on under these labels was clearly in the operetta vein, and its history runs in parallel with the events discussed above. The British, perhaps more than any other race, suffer from musical snobbery, on the one hand, and a rampant anglophobia, on the other, which, until quite recently, perversely manifested itself in a marked preference for music with the 'made in Germany' or 'made in Italy' label. British opera up to the beginning of the 19th century was performed but rarely praised, and history books are curiously silent about the vigorous scene around 1800 when Drury Lane was full of budding operettas.

The first half of the 19th century saw virtually no recognizable move towards the establishment of a popular musical theatre. But the mid-1800s exhibited the same stirrings that were happening elsewhere, probably for the same economic and social reasons. While the *music-hall was being formulated as a working-class entertainment, the *minstrel shows and *burlesque were catering for the middle-class audience. One vital area of activity was centred on the German *Reed family who started a popular series of 'entertainments' in 1855; almost coinciding with the beginnings of *Offenbach's *Bouffes-Parisiens. Had there been a stronger operatic tradition in England the operetta impetus might have been British rather than French. As it was, Thomas German Reed, the leader of the activities, drew upon whatever light writing potential he could find and he was clearly aiming towards a tentative species of operetta in *burlesque vein. Although the librettos are available, not many of the scores (which were not published) have survived, so the full nature of these entertainments is not easy to picture. For music he used such composers as Frederic *Clay, the most promising name of the 1860s, who is remembered now for introducing Gilbert to Sullivan rather than for anything he wrote (although one of his works was produced at Covent Garden in 1861), and who up to then had been mainly involved in writing burlesques; and the company's musical director and accompanist John Parry (1810–79), who was succeeded in this post by Corney *Grain. Basically, the entertainments were in the burlesque vein, in the brief form of vaudeville or musical sketches, a forerunner of the 'little' *revue as much as anything; but their unified librettos (contributed by such eminent figures as W. S. Gilbert) moved them a degree or two towards being one-act operettas in the manner of Offenbach's early pieces.

Elsewhere, at the *Gaiety and other theatres, burlesque had enjoyed its brief fling and now the importation of the works that Offenbach and others were creating showed British composers the way to building their own operetta tradition. The works of Clay, Alfred *Cellier, Edward *Solomon, John *Crook, and others clearly began to emulate the French and German vein and, had they been more effective composers and more certain of their direction, a strong school of British operetta might have evolved. There was, however, only one British composer in the offing whose genius could be compared to Offenbach's and that was Arthur *Sullivan. Fortunately thrown into partnership with W. S. Gilbert (by far the world's best librettist up till then—and possibly after) he moved tentatively into the opera field in the 1860s. But it was not until 1875 (in step with *Strauss in Vienna) that the G & S partnership began its flourishing period with *Trial by Jury*; and almost everything else that happened in the British operetta field faded into insignificance beside their inspired output. In fact only Cellier's **Dorothy* seems to have proved a strong rival. His works, along with those by Edward Solomon, Walter *Slaughter, and others, may appear unduly neglected, but there is little of real strength in their scores and even the most generous championship by enthusiasts like Gervase Hughes does not convince that they have been unjustly abandoned.

By the 1890s there was a strong influx of composers like Ivan *Caryll, Lionel *Monckton, Leslie *Stuart, and Sidney *Jones to carry on the operetta tradition, but as this was firmly done under the label of *musical comedy (which is more or less the same thing), their activities are discussed under that heading.

W. Macqueen-Pope: *Nights of Gladness* (London, 1956).
S. Hyman: *Sullivan and his Satellites: a Survey of English Operettas 1860–1914* (London, 1978).

5 *American*. The USA developed a sturdy operetta tradition, based on a similar experience of imported French and German material to that of London, although at a slightly later date. But the main impetus to American efforts was in the shape of English-speaking operetta, and it was not until Gilbert and Sullivan, and particularly **HMS Pinafore*, had won American hearts that the impulse for writing native American operetta really gained strength. It was less than a year after *HMS Pinafore* was first seen that Philadelphia produced the first American operetta, a short-lived piece called *The First Life Guards at Brighton* (1879). New York responded with similarly fleeting works from 1880 onwards including the early and unsuccessful efforts of their first great operetta composer (better known abroad though for his stirring marches), John Philip *Sousa. The first commercially successful American operetta was *The Little Tycoon* (1886), with a score by Willard Spenser (1852–1933) that contained America's first operetta hit song 'Love comes like a summer sigh'. Boston produced another master of the genre in Reginald *De Koven and America found its own Gilbert in Buffalo-born Harry B. *Smith, De Koven's main collaborator. Other pioneer composers were the English-born Julian *Edwards and, perhaps the most substantial of them all, the Irish immigrant Victor *Herbert.

It was precisely because America was to take in so many ex-European immigrants that her musical traditions became so strong and, with Sullivan and a few of his satellites out of the way, the USA was to out-write Britain in every respect and become the 20th-century home of popular music, theatrical or otherwise. Most of these composers wrote in a vein that was a mixture of Viennese, French, and Sullivan (whose own musical ancestry was a mixture of Offenbach, Mendelssohn, and Handel). The further influx of the Gaiety-born musical comedy from England, together with the influential strains of *Florodora*, soon produced the metamorphosis from operetta to musical comedy. These were the influences that kept the operetta charm and style in the scores of Jerome *Kern until the end. The most American of them all was George M. *Cohan, the first great figure of the musical comedy era. The jazz age, of course, was to kill off the operetta strain and produce a genuine American mainstream. But there were survivors, mainly the immigrants again, within whom the Viennese influence was strong—Gustave *Luders, Karl *Hoschna, Rudolf *Friml, and Sigmund *Romberg—keeping the Viennese operetta tradition alive in America as *Novello had done in England.

Gerald Bordman, the modern chronicler of the American musical, sees the operetta tradition continuing through Richard *Rodgers (with good reason) and on to *Sondheim. But this is merely a matter of attaching labels and it is more often (though not necessarily accurately) accepted that operetta (except in the above-mentioned traditionalists) stepped into a world of *musical comedy on its way to the *musical once *ragtime and *Berlin and jazz and *Gershwin had taken over the leading roles.

G. Bordman: *American Operetta: from H.M.S. Pinafore to Sweeney Todd* (New York, 1981).

6 *German*. Not all German-language operetta is Viennese. Just as, in the classical spheres, there is no doubt about the separate and different natures of the German and the Austrian (or Viennese) traditions, so it is in the world of operetta. There are over-lapping characteristics and the likeness enforced by a common language, but also a marked difference. German operetta is Beethovian, Viennese operetta is Schubertian. The heart of Viennese operetta is the lilting idiom of the Viennese waltz and its Germanic character is softened by the quieter manner of speech and the influence of Hungarian gypsy music. German opera, as bred in Berlin and other cities, is more robustly vulgar, less sentimental, which is not to suggest any lack of elegance in the works of the early German pioneers of operetta, simply a darker hue to its music and humour. The names of Paul *Lincke, Ralph *Benatzky, Leon *Jessel, Walter Kollo (1878–1940), Eduard *Kunneke, Edmund Nick (1891–1974), and Jean Gilbert are the most prominent. An odd link is that most of them were eager embracers of the pseudo-jazz strains that seeped into Germany in the 1920s and 1930s, producing that strangely sardonic vein that came to full fruition in the German-based works of Kurt *Weill. German operetta turned into musical comedy at heart at quite an early stage, with Paul Lincke remaining the outstanding protector of the operetta species.

O. Schneidereit: *Berlin wie es weint und lacht: Spaziergänge durch Berlins Operettengeschichte* (Berlin, 1973). O. Schneidereit: *Paul Lincke und die Enstehung der Berliner Operette* (Berlin, 1974).

7 *Operetta and opera.* The concept of light opera was an attractive one to many serious opera composers who attempted pieces in operetta vein, or at least a parody of it. Among them might be mentioned Puccini with *La Rondine* (1917, *The Swallow*), which was intended as an operetta for Vienna and shows a strong liking for the Viennese waltz; Ravel's *L'Heure espagnole* (1911), a farcical romp full of zarzuela spirit; Poulenc's *Les Mamelles de Tirésias* (1947), a pastiche which calls itself an *opéra-bouffe; Chabrier's *L'Etoile* (1877) and *Une Education manquée* (1879), which are genuine operettas with an operatic flavour; Roussel's *Les Aventures du roi Pausole* (1930); and Britten's *Paul Bunyan* (1941), recently rediscovered.

Orbach, Jerry [Jerome] (*b* New York, 20 Oct. 1935). American singer and actor. He graduated from Northwestern University, then studied acting, and made his New York debut by taking over the role of Macheath in *The *Threepenny Opera* in 1958; becoming well-known in the long-running *The *Fantasticks* (1960) in which he sang 'Try to remember'. He appeared in **Carnival* (1961) and **Promises, Promises* (1968). He tackled a number of straight roles before resuming his musical career in **Chicago* (1975) and **42nd Street* (1980).

Orbison, Roy Kelton (*b* Vernon, Texas, 23 Apr. 1936; *d* Nashville, 6 Dec. 1988). American singer and composer. He began by writing Country and Western songs for other artists including 'Claudette' for the *Everly Brothers. He was discovered by and made his first hit, 'Ooby dooby', for Norman Petty (Buddy *Holly's manager), afterwards moving to the Sun label, but really establishing himself with Monument Records in 1960 with 'Only the lonely'. Until then he had been an unexceptional rock and roller in items like 'Ooby dooby'. The voice he cultivated became unmistakable: although he had a considerable vocal range he usually sang with a high, mournful whine, dramatic but knowingly commercial. 'Only the lonely' proved a perfect vehicle for his soaring voice which was set against a rather mannered vocal group accompaniment.

Over the next four years he had a succession of hits, most of them in the same ballad style—'Runnin' scared' (1961), 'In dreams' (1963), and 'It's over (1964). Despite his static stance on stage and his introverted personality, Orbison was a charismatic performer; perhaps it was actually due to his motionless, cobra-like delivery. His ballads were a link between the rock and roll era and the pop sound of the 1970s. Although it was his tear-jerking songs like 'Blue Bayou' and 'Crying' that brought him most acclaim, he could succeed in other styles, and one of his greatest recordings was an up-tempo number, 'Oh, pretty woman' (1964).

Orchestra Wives. 20th Century Fox film issued in 1942 now remembered as a nostalgic feature for the Glenn *Miller orchestra, the *Modernaires, and vocalists Ray Eberle (*b* 1919), Marion Hutton (*b* 1919), and Tex *Beneke. The songs were mainly by Harry *Warren—'Serenade in blue', 'I've got a gal in Kalamazoo', 'Chattanooga choo-choo'—but Miller's 'Moonlight serenade' was also used, along with Meacham's 'American patrol' and *Schoebel's 'Bugle call rag'.

Orchid, The. British musical play with score by Ivan *Caryll and Lionel *Monckton (additional music by Paul *Rubens), book by James T. Tanner (1850–1915), lyrics by Adrian *Ross and Percy *Greenbank. It was produced at the Gaiety Theatre, London, 26 Oct. 1903, with a cast that included Gertie *Millar and George *Grossmith Jr. Although it had a conventional sort of story and a not particularly distinguished score, the combination of Gertie Millar, then at the peak of her fame, and a typically lavish Gaiety production, ensured a run of 559 performances. By now, though, the tide was beginning to turn against the export of British-made shows to the USA and, in spite of a cast headed by Eddie *Foy and Trixie Friganza (1870–1955) and the addition of Jean *Schwartz's 'Bedelia' to the score, opening at the Herald Square Theatre 8 Apr. 1907, it achieved only 178 performances.

Original Dixieland Jazz Band. Known to the jazz world as the ODJB, it was the first band to introduce jazz to New York and the first to make an accredited jazz recording, paradoxically being a group of white musicians. Its members had worked together in New Orleans as early as 1905 and were brought to Chicago by the impresario Harry James where, under the name of Stein's Dixie Jass Band they played at Schiller's Café. They finally arrived in New York to take up residence at the 400 Room at Reisenweber's, New York's newest and largest restaurant. The name, mainly through journalistic errors, gradually changed, and by February 1917 they were finally billed as the Famous Original Dixieland Jazz Band. Led by cornettist Nick *La Rocca, its most historic line-up was Larry Shields (1893–1953) (clarinet), Eddie Edwards (1891–1963) (trombone), Henry Ragas (1890–1919) (piano), and Tony Sbarbaro (1897–1969) (drums). A recording session with Columbia (which was issued later) was considered unmarketable, so they recorded what were to be the historic 'first' jazz sides with the Victor Talking Machine Company on 26 Feb. 1917, including 'Livery stable blues' and 'Original Dixieland one-step'.

With Emile Christian (1895–1973) now on trombone and J. Russell *Robinson on piano they arrived in England to appear in the revue *Joy Bells* at the London Hippodrome on 7 Apr. 1919, but the engagement was limited to one night as their disturbing influence was objected to by the show's star, George *Robey. They went on to history-making success at the Palladium and the Hammersmith Palais de Danse. At this stage Robinson left to be replaced by an English pianist, Billy Jones. The ODJB disbanded in 1925 but had a reunion in 1936 when they appeared at an exhibition in Dallas and recorded new versions of some of their old repertoire.

H. O. Brunn: *The Story of the Original Dixieland Jazz Band* (Baton Rouge, La., 1960).

Ornadel, Cyril (*b* London, 2 Dec. 1924). British composer, arranger, and conductor. He studied at the Royal College of Music and gradually became convinced that his future lay in the popular music world, especially in the theatre, which had become his principal interest. He became accompanist to Dorothy Carless and Max Bacon, and then conducted for various touring revues. After a stint as pantomime conductor, he took over as musical director of the popular radio series *Take It From Here* in 1950. He was MD for several important London musical productions, including: *Take It From Us* (1950); **Kiss Me Kate* (1951); **Call Me Madam* (1952); **Paint Your Wagon* (1953); **Pal Joey* (1954); **Wonderful Town* (1955); **Kismet* (1955); **Plain and Fancy* (1956); resident MD at the London Palladium 1956–7; and **My Fair Lady* (1958). He then specialized in recording work, was active with World Records and partner in the FCM recording and promotion company, and gave more time to composition. He wrote two minor musicals which never reached London, but had a substantial success with **Pickwick* (1963)—'If I ruled the world'; followed by *Ann Veronica* (1969) and *Great Expectations* (1975). He wrote many film scores in the 1960s and 1970s and such song hits as 'Portrait of my love' (1963).

Orphée aux Enfers. 'Opéra-féerie' in two acts with music by Jacques *Offenbach and book by Hector Crémieux (1828–92) and Ludovic Halévy (1834–1908), based on a play by the German writer Carl Kramer. It was first produced at the *Bouffes-Parisiens, Paris, 21 Oct. 1858. Offenbach had founded his own theatre in 1855 and enjoyed modest success with one-act productions, but real fame came with *Orphée* which was criticized by influential reviewers as being frivolous, scandalous, and irreverent, this having the happy effect of making people want to go and see it.

Offenbach took the classic story of Orpheus and Eurydice and made it into a political satire, backed by outrageously light-hearted music, including the famous 'Can-can', and quoting disrespectfully from such revered masters as Gluck. After its initial run of 228 performances, the work was continuously revived and reappeared at the Gaieté as a four-act work in 1874. In the meantime it commenced its international career in Vienna in 1860, in New York in 1861, and in London in 1865, being played and enjoyed as *Orpheus in the Underworld*, and exerting a strong influence on composers everywhere. Its popularity has never declined and London has enjoyed modern productions at Sadler's Wells from 1960 and latterly as part of the English National Opera repertoire at the Coliseum.

Ory, Kid [Edward] (*b* La Place, La., 25 Dec. 1886; *d* Hawaii, 23 Jan. 1973). Pioneer American jazz trombonist. He started out as a banjoist then changed to trombone when he played with various New Orleans bands. Settling there in 1912, he led a popular band, but the climate did not agree with him and he moved to California in 1919, taking several New Orleans musicians with him and being the first to introduce jazz to the West Coast when he played in San Francisco. With this group he made the first recordings by a black jazz band in 1922. In late 1925 he took part in many historic recordings with Louis *Armstrong, before moving to Chicago to play with King *Oliver. He played in numerous bands between 1927 and 1933 before leaving music to run a chicken farm and later working as a railroad clerk.

He came back to music in 1942 when he joined a band led by Barney *Bigard and led his own group 1943–4, mainly playing double-bass and saxophone. After a successful appearance on the Orson Welles radio show, he reverted to trombone and became a prominent figure in the New Orleans jazz revival of the 1940s. He retired through ill-health in 1955 but recovered to visit Europe in 1956 and 1959, meanwhile leading his own band 1954–61 in San Francisco. Continued illness forced him to retire permanently to Hawaii in 1966.

Osborne, Bobbie (*b* Hyden, Ky., 7 Dec. 1931) and **Sonny** (*b* Hyden, 29 Oct. 1937). American country musicians and singers. Playing mandolin and banjo, they began to build a reputation as the Osborne Brothers on radio and in concert from *c.*1953. They became leading figures in the *bluegrass revival and reached a wider audience when they switched to using amplified guitars. Their best-known hits were 'Midnight flyer', 'Rocky top', and 'Georgia pinewoods'.

Osmonds, The. American Mormon family of musicians who started by singing in their local church before being asked to appear on the Andy *Williams TV show, which they did regularly for four years, later appearing on the Jerry Lewis show and other TV programmes and recording for MCA. The group was made up of Alan (*b* 22 June 1949), Wayne (*b* 28 Aug. 1951), Merrill (*b* 30 Apr. 1953), Jay (*b* 2 Mar. 1955), Donny (*b* 9 Dec. 1957), Marie (*b* 13 Oct. 1959), and Jimmy (*b* 16 Apr. 1963). Their first recorded success was with MGM—'One bad apple' (1971), followed by 'Down by the lazy river' (1972), and 'Hold her tight' (1972). A visit to Britain in 1972 confirmed their tremendous popularity with teenage audiences. The first member of the group to become a solo success was Donny Osmond with such hits as 'Puppy love' (1972), 'Too young' (1972), 'Why?' (1972), 'Twelfth of never' (1973), 'Young love' (1973), and 'When I fall in love' (1973), and duets with Marie, 'I'm leaving it up to you' (1974), and 'Morning side of the mountain' (1975). Their youthful appeal continued into the 1970s but by 1975 they were having to look for a more adult market and latterly moved into the country music field.

Otis, Johnny [Veliotes, John] (*b* Vallejo, Calif., 28 Dec. 1921). American singer and musician. One of the pioneering figures of the emerging rhythm 'n' blues scene, he played drums, piano, and vibes with a small *boogie-woogie based group and then lead a 16-piece swing band with which he had his first record hit 'Harlem nocturne'. The band worked with Louis *Jordan, Nat 'King' *Cole, and the *Ink Spots; and recorded with Lester *Young, Illinois *Jacquet, and Jimmy *Rushing. Otis was resident at the Barrelhouse Club in Los Angeles from 1948, where he first began to formulate his rhythm 'n' blues style and recorded extensively for the Savoy label, often with Esther Phillips (*b* 1935), as Little Esther with Johnny Otis and the Robins, including such 1950 items as 'Double crossing blues', 'Mistrustin' blues', 'Wedding boogie', and 'Deceivin' blues'. He organized a touring R & B show which introduced such names as Willie Mae Thornton (1926–84), Hank Ballard (*b* 1936), and Johnny Ace (1929–54). He arranged and produced recordings and worked with such people as *Little Richard, Etta James (*b* 1938), and Charles Brown (*b* 1920).

By the 1950s he had moved into the rock field and in 1957 started to record for Capitol, for whom he made his biggest hit 'Willie and the hand jive' in 1958. It introduced what was later to be known as the Bo *Diddley beat. He mainly worked in a backroom capacity in the 1960s but produced a progressive album, *Cold Shot*, in 1968. In 1970 he revived his original touring show which he has since led throughout America and Europe.

Our Miss Gibbs. Musical comedy with score by Ivan *Caryll and Lionel *Monckton, book by 'Cryptos' and James T. Tanner (1850–1915), lyrics by Adrian *Ross and Percy *Greenbank, produced at the *Gaiety Theatre, London, 23 Jan. 1909, and running for 636 performances. It was one of the most successful vehicles for Gertie *Millar, with George *Grossmith Jr. and Maisie Gay (1883–1945); and it gave an early part to Ruby Miller (1889–1976), who was understudy to Gladys Cooper (1888–1971).

The story of a young flower-shop girl from the north and her complicated and farcical affair with a noble lord (all ending happily) was very much of its period; greatly enhanced by a score which included the effervescent 'Moonstruck', various songs that made much of the heroine's simple Yorkshire upbringing—'Mary', 'In Yorkshire; while Grossmith had a personal hit with the added 'Yip-i-addy-i-ay'.

In common with many latterday musical comedy successes it got to America as the musical tide was turning and achieved only 64 performances there, at the Knickerbocker Theatre 29 Aug. 1910, in spite of additional items from Jerome *Kern.

Owens, Harry [Robert] (*b* O'Neil, Nebr., 18 Apr. 1902). American composer, author, and bandleader. Leaving Loyola University after a distinguished academic career, he formed his own orchestra with which he toured the Western states. Invited to Hawaii, he settled there and formed his famous Royal Hawaiians, bringing them to the USA in 1937 and creating the pre-war vogue for Hawaiian music. He appeared in films, notably in *The Song of the Islands* (1942) for which he wrote the score. Later he had his own TV show in Hollywood for 12 years, and wrote many songs in the island style including 'Sweet Leilani' which was used in the Bing *Crosby film *Waikiki Wedding* (1937) and won an Academy Award.

Oxford Music Hall. It was originally built in 1861, by Charles Morton (1819–1914), well-known manager of the Canterbury Music Hall, on the site of the ancient Boar and Castle tavern in Oxford Street, London. The hall was intended as a rival to Weston's establishment at the Royal Holborn. It was a modern music-hall in that it had a proper stage and was fully gaslit; but in the main body of the hall the old tradition was followed of eating and drinking at tables with an 'ordinary' admission price of 2s 6d. The practice of drinking in the auditorium was finally prohibited by the London County Council in 1914. The entertainment at the Oxford was mainly vocal and some quite 'high-class' stars appeared there, including Emily *Soldene and Charles Santley. The theatre was burned down in 1869 and Morton (who had relinquished control of the Canterbury in 1867) took on the Philharmonic in Islington and had a great success there with *Offenbach's **Geneviève de Brabant*. He managed to get the Oxford rebuilt quite quickly, but it was again burned down in 1872, as so many theatres were at that time, through primitive and dangerous gas-lighting. It was to suffer four fires altogether before it became the New Oxford Theatre in 1921.

It continued as a music-hall up to 1912; after which revues and spectacular musicals took over, though there was a season of variety as late as 1926. The musical productions between 1912 and 1919 included *Wellington* (1912); *Step This Way* (1913); *Nobby VC* (1913); *Full Inside* (1913); *The Honeymoon Express* (1914); *Miss Paris in London* (1914); *Mam'selle Champagne* (1914); *Go to Jericho* (1915); *Who's Who* (1915); *Kiss Auntie* (1915); *Back to Blighty* (1916); *Seeing Life* (1917); *The Lads of the Village* (1917); *Sugar* (1917); *The *Better 'Ole* (1917); and *Maggie* (1919).

From 17 Jan. 1921 the Oxford Music Hall attempted a new lease of life as the New Oxford Theatre under the management of C. B. *Cochran who had taken over in 1917; £80,000 was spent on the building to convert it into a perfect theatre for staging spectacular revues. The first show was

The League of Notions (1921), a lavish production by John Murray *Anderson which had 360 performances and made a profit of £7000. This was followed by the spectacular revue *Mayfair and Montmartre* which struck misfortune when the leading lady Alice *Delysia lost her voice, leaving the show £20,000 in the red and the management bankrupt. The theatre struggled on until 1926 when it was closed and converted into a Lyons Corner House which opened in 1929.

P

***Pacific Overtures*.** American musical with score and lyrics by Stephen *Sondheim and book by John Weidman, staged at the Winter Garden Theatre, New York, 11 Jan. 1976. Stanley Green wrote: 'Few Broadway musicals have ever dared so much on so many levels.'

Telling the history of modern Japan from 1853 through Japanese eyes it did it in true Japanese theatre style and with music that got as close to the real thing as anything ever tried in the Western theatre. It was lavishly staged, with many eye-catching effects and used a genuine Japanese cast. A prestigious rather than popular experience, it ran for 193 performances and was revived in a somewhat scaled-down version in 1984. Although an LP was quickly available, London did not experience a stage production until 1989.

Padilla, José Sancho (*b* Alméria, Granada, 1889; *d* Madrid, 24 Oct. 1960). Spanish composer and conductor. He had a musical career mainly in France, where he composed songs for *Mistinguett and other stars who appeared at the Moulin Rouge and the Casino de Paris where he was musical director for many years. These included such lasting songs as 'El relicario' (1918), 'La violetera' (1918), 'Valencia' (1923), and 'Paree (ça c'est Paree)' (1927).

Page, 'Hot Lips' [Oran Thaddeus] (*b* Dallas, 27 Jan. 1908; *d* New York, 5 Nov. 1954). American jazz trumpeter and bandleader. He played trumpet from the age of 12 and first earned his reputation for his fiery, full-blooded style with the Blue Devils 1928–30 led by Walter Page (1900–57). Previously he had worked mainly in bands accompanying early blues singers, Ma *Rainey, Bessie *Smith, and Ida *Cox. He played with Bennie *Moten in St Louis 1931–5, then with Count *Basie 1935–6. In 1936 he formed his own band which was resident at Small's Paradise in New York in 1937, at the Plantation Club in 1938, and at Kelly's Stables in 1939. He toured with Bud *Freeman 1940, led his own band in 1941, and was with Artie Shaw 1941–2, then led his own groups in New York, Boston, and Chicago 1943–9, appearing in several Eddie *Condon Town Hall concerts during 1945. His first trip to Europe was in 1949 and he went again in 1951 and 1952. He was at the Café Society in New York in 1953, dying the following year of a heart-attack. He was a notable professional in the *mainstream field of jazz, and one of the finest players of instrumental blues.

Page, Patti [Fowler, Clara Ann] (*b* Claremore, Okla., 8 Nov. 1927). American singer. She sang in a church choir in Tulsa and adopted the name of Patti Page when she first began to appear on Chicago radio in 1947. She began to record for Mercury Records and had a big hit with 'Confess' in 1948. In that year she sang with the Benny *Goodman quartet, and she generally preferred to work with a good jazz backing. Although she is best remembered for her 1951 hit 'Tennessee waltz', she recorded a prolific number of hits in the 1950s and appeared on TV in her own programme. She was in the 1960 film *Elmer Gantry*. In the 1970s she moved into country music.

Paige, Elaine [Bickerstaff, Elaine] (*b* Barnet, Herts., 5 Mar. 1951). British singer and actress. She made her stage beginnings in *The Roar of the Greasepaint, the Smell of the Crowd* (1962); **Hair* (1968); *Rock Carmen* (1970); and **Jesus Christ, Superstar* (1972); before achieving a leading role in **Grease* (1973) and appearing in **Billy* (1974). After a fairly fruitless period trying to work in non-musical fields, she came back to become a star performer in the leading role of **Evita* (1978). She left the show after 20 months and worked as a singer, recording an LP, *Sitting Pretty*, and featuring in a Festival Hall concert in 1981. She next appeared in **Cats* (1981), recorded the album *Elaine Paige* (1982), and had her own TV programme. Then she was in **Chess* (1986), had a No. 1 hit with Barbara *Dickson, 'I know him so well', and recorded an LP, *Christmas* (1986).

Paige, Janis [Jaden, Donna Mae] (*b* Tacoma, Wash., 16 Sept. 1922). American singer and actress. A tall, good-looking blonde, she made notable stage appearances in *The *Pajama Game* (1954) and **Mame* (1968), after previous success in such films as *Hollywood Canteen* (1944); *The Time, the Place and the Girl* (1946); *Love and Learn* (1947); and *Romance on the High Seas* (1948). Later she was in **Silk Stockings* (1956) and *Follow the Boys* (1963).

***Paint Your Wagon*.** Musical comedy with score by Frederick *Loewe and book by Alan Jay *Lerner, produced at the Shubert Theatre, New York, 12 Nov. 1951, where it had 289 performances.

Set in the California gold rush of 1853 it told the story of an old prospector, played by veteran singer/actor James Barton (1890–1962), whose daughter discovers gold. They suddenly find themselves in a booming town of 4000 inhabitants. She goes off with a young prospector and in the end the old man is left in a goldless and lustreless ghost town. Burl *Ives and Eddie *Dowling later took over the leading role. In London at Her Majesty's Theatre, 11 Feb. 1953, Bobby *Howes starred with Sally Ann *Howes his real and stage daughter [477p]. The rich score included 'I talk to the trees', 'They called the wind Maria', 'I still see Elisa', 'Another Autumn', and 'Wand'rin' star' which was made into a new hit by the gravelly voice of Lee Marvin (*b* 1924), who was in the much altered 1969 film version.

Pajama Game, The. American musical comedy with music and lyrics by Richard *Adler and Jerry *Ross, book by George *Abbott and Richard Bissell, based on Bissell's novel $7\frac{1}{2}$ *Cents*. It came the way of the young Adler and Ross team after being turned down by Frank *Loesser. Produced in New York at the St James Theatre 13 May 1954 (later transferring to the Shubert Theatre, 12 Nov. 1956), it completed 1063 performances.

The story is set in the Sleep-Tite pajama factory in Iowa and concerns an affair of the heart between factory supervisor Sid Sorokin (John *Raitt) and trade-unionist Babe Williams (Janis *Paige) which is jeopardized by a strike for a $7\frac{1}{2}$ per cent raise. Eddie *Foy Jr. was also in the cast and a young dancer, Shirley *MacLaine, joined the show in mid-run and made her reputation with her performance of 'Steam heat'. Other popular numbers were 'I'm not at all in love', 'I'll never be jealous again', 'Hey, there', 'Once a year day', 'Small talk', and 'Hernando's hideaway'. The London version, at the Coliseum 13 Oct. 1955, starred Joy Nichols (1927–92), Edmund Hockridge (*b* 1922), and Max Wall (1908–90), with Elizabeth Seal making a notable debut [578p]. The film made in 1957 retained Eddie Foy and John Raitt, with Doris *Day.

Palace Theatre, New York. Theatre built by Martin Beck (1865–1940) on Broadway between 46th and 47th Streets and opened in 1913. It had gone out of his control by the time of its opening and was taken over by B. F. Keith (1846–1914) who made it into America's leading *vaudeville house. To play the Palace was the equivalent of playing the Palladium in London. As vaudeville declined it became a cinema in 1932 with a brief period back in the variety business in the 1950s. The theatre was renovated in 1965 and became a regular venue for Broadway musicals.

M. Spitzer: *The Palace* (New York, 1969).

Palais Glide. A simple ballroom dance which became very popular in England *c*.1937. It was danced to such cornily catchy tunes as 'Horsey, horsey' and 'Little Angeline' which had lingering elements of the *polka in them.

Pal Joey. American musical comedy with music by Richard *Rodgers, book by John O'Hara, and lyrics by Lorenz *Hart, produced at the Ethel Barrymore Theatre, New York, 25 Dec. 1940, with Vivienne *Segal and Gene *Kelly, where it achieved 374 performances.

The story revolves around a nightclub entertainer (a first leading role for Gene Kelly) who woos a wealthy lady. She builds a nightclub for him but tires of him in the end and leaves him where he began.

When it was revived, with Harold Lang (*b* 1923) as Joey and Vivienne Segal, at the Broadhurst Theatre 3 Jan. 1952, it had an even better run of 542 performances; after which it came to London, Prince's Theatre 31 Mar. 1954, with Carol Bruce (*b* 1919) and Lang [245p]; and it was filmed in 1957 with Frank *Sinatra as Joey and Rita Hayworth. A classic Rodgers and Hart score contained such hits as 'I could write a book', 'Chicago', 'Happy hunting horn', 'Bewitched', 'Take him', 'Zip', and 'Do it the hard way'.

Palladium Theatre, London. Better known simply as the London Palladium, the theatre was opened in Argyle Street, very near Oxford Circus, on 26 Dec. 1910. It opened with a variety programme that included Nellie *Wallace and *Ella Shields, coming in on the music-hall boom of the time. The Palladium staged variety shows for many years but as the fashions changed had to move into the spectacular revue field by the 1920s, a typical show being *Whirl of the World* (1923) which had 627 performances. Others followed until 1928 when the theatre had a short spell as a cinema. By the end of the year it had been taken over by George Black (1890–1945) who continued with variety, including the Royal Command Performances of 1931–5 and 1937 and the highly successful *Crazy Gang shows 1935–8, and similar shows were continued during the war years. After Black's death in 1946, Val Parnell and Moss Empires took over. From 1948 the Palladium became renowned as the mecca for American stars like Bing *Crosby, Danny *Kaye, and Judy *Garland, as well as further spectacular revues and pantomime.

I. Bevan: *Top of the Bill* (London, 1952).

Panama Hattie. American musical comedy with music and lyrics by Cole *Porter, book by Herbert *Fields and Buddy *DeSylva, produced at the 46th Street Theatre, New York, 30 Oct. 1940 [501p], starring Ethel *Merman as Hattie Malone, a nightclub owner engaged in a turbulent romance with socialite Nick Bullett (James Dunn). The cast also included Betty *Hutton, who was understudied by June *Allyson; and it was notable as Ethel Merman's first starring role and her best collaboration with Cole Porter, singing such tailor-made songs as 'Let's be buddies'. It opened in London, at the Piccadilly Theatre 4 Nov. 1944, with Bebe *Daniels in the starring role [308p]; and it was filmed in 1942.

Panassié, Hugues (*b* Paris, 27 Feb. 1912; *d* Montauban, 8 Dec. 1974). French author and jazz critic. He cultivated a keen interest in jazz when he was about 15 and was to be a pioneer in the promotion of jazz at an early stage with books such as *Le Jazz Hot* (1934) which, translated into English in 1936, was the first to spread the gospel with any real insight. He founded the Hot Club de France in 1932 and lectured on jazz at the Sorbonne in 1937. In the late 1930s he did much to foster the revival of interest in traditional jazz by organizing the now historic sessions with Mezz *Mezzrow, Sidney *Bechet, and Tommy *Ladnier; later he organized further sessions with Frankie Newton, James P. *Johnson, and others. The modern jazz revolution left Panassié decidedly cool and he maintained a dismissively 'trad' attitude throughout his career. His other writings included *The Real Jazz* (New York, 1942); *La musique de jazz et le swing* (Paris, 1945); *Douze années de jazz (1927–1938)* (Paris, 1946); *Louis Armstrong* (Paris, 1947); *Jazz panorama* (Paris, 1950); *Discographie critique* (Paris, 1951); and *Dictionnaire de jazz* (with Madeleine Gautier) (Paris, 1954; London–New York, 1956).

H. Panassié: Monsieur Jazz (Paris, 1975).

Paramor, Norrie (*b* 1914; *d* London, 9 Sept. 1979). British conductor, composer, arranger, and producer. He left school at the age of 15 and became an office-boy, but his musical talents soon found him a job as accompanist to Gracie *Fields. Later he worked in top London dance bands and during the war years acted as musical director for the Ralph *Reader Gang Shows. He worked with Harry Gold (*b* 1907) and his Pieces of Eight; toured with Bing *Crosby; and in the 1950s made recordings under his own name and with the Big Ben Banjo Band. He became a record producer with EMI, where he worked with Cliff *Richard, Frank *Ifield, the *Shadows, Helen *Shapiro, and many more until 1968. He wrote the scores of many films and TV themes (*Summer Place* and *Z Cars*), and was musical director of the BBC Midland Radio Orchestra 1972–8.

Parker, Charlie 'Yardbird' or 'Bird' [Charles Christopher] (*b* Kansas City, 29 Aug. 1920; *d* New York, 12 Mar. 1955). American jazz saxophonist. Self-taught on saxophone, he left school at 14 and became a professional musician, playing with local bands in Kansas City and developing a style partly based on the cool tones of Basie's saxophonist Lester *Young. He played in the band led by Jay *McShann in 1938 and again in 1940–2, and with them made his first recordings which already reveal his distinctive styling. He played with Earl *Hines (then on tenor-saxophone for a while) 1942–3, and with Billy *Eckstine 1944. Meeting up in these bands, Parker, Dizzy *Gillespie, and other young and forward-looking musicians began to experiment with the modern jazz styling that became known as bebop. They swapped ideas in what is now looked upon as the shrine of modern jazz, *Minton's Playhouse, a club run by bandleader Teddy *Hill, who organized a house band that included such musicians as pianist Thelonious *Monk and drummer Kenny *Clarke who were to be other elements in the new movement. He worked in 52nd Street clubs with Gillespie 1944–5 and Ben Webster 1944.

Parker was very much the leading spirit of modern jazz, with his tremendous technical agility and quick harmonic thinking, pioneering a new 'cool' spirit and technique yet retaining much of the earthy blues feeling and intensity of earlier jazz. Essentially, the black musicians with him were contriving a music that they felt was their own, where white musicians, then dominating in the most lucrative jobs, might not be able to match them. The harmonies were complex, with an admiration for such advanced tunes as 'How high the moon' reflected in Parker's using the same chordal pattern for his own 'Ornithology'; and the rhythms broke away from the obvious patterns, breaking the beat and cutting the music up into unequal sections. In 1945 he was leading his own small group; he was with Jazz at the Philharmonic on the West Coast in 1946 and with Howard McGhee 1946–7. At this stage his heroin addiction led to prolonged breaks in his playing activities, but he was at his best in 1947 with a quintet that was made up of himself, Miles *Davis, Duke Jordan, Tommy Potter, and Max *Roach. A period of dabbling with string accompaniment, a recurring failing with many modern jazz musicians, widened his appeal but halted his progress. He worked with various musicians over the next few years and experimented with Latin American rhythms. Reunions with Gillespie and like-minded musicians often took him to new heights, but alcohol and heroin increasingly took their toll and much of what should have been his mature years was wasted time.

As Armstrong had shown the early way and inspired other trumpeters, as Coleman *Hawkins had given the saxophone a jazz voice, as Art *Tatum led pianists into new (if not always profitable) ways, so did Parker change the whole face of jazz in those peak years of the 1940s; the jazz world in general only caught up with his genius, his daring, and his innovations in the 1960s. Bird had gone by then, but, as one worshipper wrote on a New York wall when he died, 'Bird lives' in everything that has happened since in the jazz world and his playing on record still sounds as fresh and adventurous as it ever did. No one jazz player, with the possible exception of Armstrong, has been so influential.

M. Harrison: *Charlie Parker* (London, 1960). R. G. Reisner: *Bird: the Legend of Charlie Parker* (New York, 1962). J. G. Jepson: *A Discography of Charlie Parker* (Copenhagen, 1959; rev. 1969). R. Russell: *Bird Lives: the High Life and Hard Times of Charlie (Yardbird) Parker* (London, 1972). P. Koster and D. M. Bakker: *Charlie Parker Discography* (4 vols) (Alphen aan den Rijn, 1974).

Parr-Davies, Harry [Harold] (*b* Briton Ferry, Glamorgan, 24 May 1914; *d* London, 14 Oct. 1955). British composer. He studied music privately with Sir Walford Davies and was accompanist to Gracie *Fields for many years, writing the music for many revues and films that starred her and George *Formby. He was the composer of a number of highly successful West End shows including: *Black Velvet* (1939); *Haw-Haw* (1939); *Come Out to Play* (1940); *Top of the World* (1940); *Gangway* (1941); *Big Top* (1942); *Full Swing* (1942); *Best Bib and Tucker* (1942); *Happidrome* (1942); *The *Lisbon Story* (1943)—'Pedro the fisherman'; *The Knight Was Bold* (1943); *Jenny Jones* (1944); *Fine Feathers* (1945); *The Shephard Show* (1946); *Her Excellency* (1949); *Dear Miss Phoebe* (1950); *Blue for a Boy* (1950); *The Glorious Days* (1953).

His film scores included: *Sing As We Go* (1934)—'Sing as we go'; *The Show Goes On* (1937)—'Smile when you say "goodbye"'; *It's in the Air* (1938)—'It's in the air'; *We're Going to be Rich* (1938)—'The trek song'; *Shipyard Sally* (1939)—'Wish me luck (as you wave me goodbye)'; *Sailors Three* (1940); *We'll Meet Again* (1942); *Suspected Person* (1942); *Bell-Bottom George* (1943); *It Happened One Sunday* (1944)—'Valley of dreams'; and *Maytime in Mayfair* (1946).

Parsons, Gram [Connor, Cecil Ingram] (*b* Winterhaven, Fla., 5 Nov. 1946; *d* Joshua Tree, Calif., 19 Sept. 1973). American country-rock musician and songwriter. He divided his youth between guitar-playing in Georgia bands and studying theology at Harvard. There, in 1967, he organized a group called the International Submarine Band. He was asked to join the *Byrds and had some of his material recorded by them in the album *Sweetheart of the Rodeo* (1968). Leaving the group he formed the Flying Burrito Brothers, recording with them the 'definitive Southern country-rock album' *The Gilded Palace of Sin* (1969). After the album *Burrito Deluxe* (1970) he left to become a solo artist and eventually recorded *GP* (1973) for the Reprise label with Emmylou *Harris. With his Hot Band he recorded some strangely blues-tinged country music, both traditional and his own. After he died from the over-use of drugs a posthumous album, *Grievous Angel*, was issued in 1974.

Parton, Dolly [Rebecca] (*b* Locust Ridge, Tenn., 19 Jan. 1946). American country singer and songwriter. From a poor family, she spent several years as an obscure singer before she arrived in Nashville and was seen on TV with Porter Waggoner's band on their syndicated show. Her dumb blonde looks and well-endowed figure helped her to recognition, but tended to obscure the fact that the songs she wrote and sang in straightforward country style were well turned and full of homely perception. Her first recorded hit was 'Dumb blonde' (1967), after which she was signed by RCA in 1968 and had a series of successes with such songs as 'Joshua', 'Jolene', 'Coat of many colours', 'Love is like a butterfly', and 'In my Tennessee Mountain home'. With a 1977 album, *New Harvest*, she turned more to the pop field and toured with her own group Gypsy Fever. In 1978 she had top hits with 'Here you come again', 'Two doors down', in 1979 with 'Baby, I'm burning', and in 1980 with 'Nine to five', taken from her first film. She has continued a popular career, her best material being in the albums *Here You Come Again* (1978) and *Heartbreakers* (1978), turning more to straight acting in the 1980s.

Passing Show, The. Revue with music by Ludwig *Englander and words by Sydney Rosenberg, staged at the Casino Theatre, New York, 12 May 1894. Probably the first American stage musical to call itself a 'review' (thus spelled), it was conceived by the producer George W. Lederer (1861–1938) as an elaborate, well-dressed, and spectacularly staged form of *vaudeville. With such stars as Adele Ritchie (1874–1930), its success gave rise to many imitations—*The Merry Whirl* (1895); *In Gay New York* (1896); *All of the Town* (1897); *In Gay Paree* (1897)—and led to the later series of spectacular revues like the **Ziegfeld Follies* (from 1912), **George White's Scandals*, and **Earl Carroll's Vanities*. The tradition and name were perpetuated by the *Shuberts in *The Passing Show of 1912* at the Winter Garden Theatre, 22 July 1912 [136p], featuring Willie and Eugene *Howard, with a score by Louis A. *Hirsch and Earl *Carroll and words by Harold Atteridge (1886–1938) who contributed throughout the series.

The new tradition at the Winter Garden Theatre continued, presenting such stars as Charlotte Greenwood, Marilyn *Miller, Ed *Wynn, Fred and Adele *Astaire, Fred *Allen, and many more, with *The Passing Show of 1913* (*m* Jean *Schwartz) [116p]; *The Passing Show of 1914* (*m* Sigmund *Romberg) [133p]; *The Passing Show of 1915* (*m* Leo Edwards, W. F. Peters, and others) [145p]; *The Passing Show of 1916* (*m* Romberg, Otto Motzan, etc.) [140p]—'Pretty baby'; *The Passing Show of 1917* (*m* Romberg, Motzan, etc.) [196p]—'Hello Broadway, goodbye France!'; *The Passing Show of 1918* (*m* Romberg and Schwartz) [124p]—'Smiles', 'I'm forever blowing bubbles'; *The Passing Show of 1919* (*m* Romberg and Schwartz) [288p]; *The Passing Show of 1921* (*m* Schwartz etc.) [191p]; *The Passing Show of 1922* (*m* Alfred *Goodman etc.) [95p]; *The Passing Show of 1923* (*m* Romberg and Schwartz) [118p]; and *The Passing Show of 1924* (*m* Romberg and Schwartz) [104p].

Concurrently there were London versions, with the music and material written to suit English tastes: *The Passing Show* (*m* Herman *Finck), at the Palace Theatre 20 Apr. 1914 [351p]—'Gilbert the Filbert', sung by Basil Hallam (1889–1916), 'I'll make a man of you', 'Florrie the Flapper', 'You're here and I'm here' (added number by Jerome *Kern); and *The Passing Show (of 1915)* (*m* Finck), at the Palace Theatre 9 Mar. 1915 [143p]. It was in this last production that Elsie *Janis first introduced the British public to the *foxtrot.

Pastor, Tony [Antonio] (*b* New York, 28 May 1837; *d* New York, 26 Aug. 1908). American impresario. The father of American vaudeville was the son of a theatre orchestra violinist. As a boy he sang at temperance concerts, and he made his first professional appearance at Barnum's Museum in 1846, singing 'Stop that knocking'. He sang in minstrel shows and first appeared in vaudeville in 1861.

Like its equivalent music-hall in Britain, vaudeville was then a rough-and-tumble affair accompanied by the quaffing of much liquor, and Tony Pastor set out to improve matters. He opened his first vaudeville house in 1865 and his approach was so successful in attracting family business that he was able to open a larger theatre in 1875 thereafter known simply as Tony Pastor's. There he acted as chairman and also appeared on the bill making up topical rhymes and singing character songs. He introduced such acts as the Four Cohans, *Weber and Fields, Emma Carus, and Lillian *Russell. He was not in favour of the name 'vaudeville' himself because of its French origins, preferring 'variety'. Later he attempted to produce burlesques in the Weber & Fields moulds, but experienced failure. As younger men appeared and the new revues took over he found business declining and he gradually disappeared from the scene.

P. Zellers: *Tony Pastor: Dean of the Vaudeville Stage* (Ypsilanti, Mich., 1971).

Patience or *Bunthorne's Bride*. Comic opera with music by Arthur *Sullivan and book by W. S. *Gilbert, produced at the Opera-Comique Theatre, London, 23 Apr. 1881; and transferred to the Savoy Theatre when it opened on 10 Oct. 1881 [578p].

A kindly satire on the aesthetic movement as typified by Oscar Wilde, it is one of the partnership's most sensitive efforts. Twenty maidens pine after the fleshly poet Bunthorne, as does Lady Jane who knows he is in love with the dairymaid Patience. In the end she goes off with a rival poet, Grosvenor, and Bunthorne is left contemplating a lily. The cast included Richard *Temple, Durward Lely, George *Grossmith, Rutland *Barrington, Jessie *Bond, and Leonora *Braham, with François *Cellier conducting such G & S gems as 'Twenty lovesick maidens we', 'When I first put this uniform on', 'Prithee, pretty maiden', 'The magnet and the churn', 'Love is a plaintive song', 'So go to him and say to him', and 'A Waterloo House young man'. It was seen in St Louis 28 July 1881 and in New York, at the Standard Theatre 22 Sept. 1881 [177p]. It was filmed in 1982.

Patton, Charley [Chatmon] (*b* Edwards, Miss., 1887; *d* Indianola, Miss., 28 Apr. 1934). American *blues singer and guitarist. He mainly pursued his musical career in the Yazoo Basin area where he achieved much local fame. The Chatmons (his father was Henderson Chatmon and his mother Anney Patton) were a family of blues musicians. Charley was brought up among them and naturally played in a style derived from that region, particularly the town of Drew which was then a centre of guitar playing and blues singing. He became very much the pivot of these activities and was said to have influenced such performers as Tommy Johnson, and many others, through his recordings. He has been described as 'one of the most exceptinal and influential figures in the history of the blues'.

He made his first recordings for Paramount in 1929 and more in 1930. Sought out for further recordings in 1934, he was then suffering from a heart ailment and died before many sides could be made. Playing his guitar with the G 'Spanish' tuning or in the natural key of E, his blues were primitive but constantly inventive and lyrical. His compositions and recordings included: 'Pony blues', 'Mississippi bo weevil blues', 'Down the dirt road blues', 'Banty rooster blues', 'It won't be long', 'Pea vine blues', 'Tom Rushen blues', 'Spoonful blues', 'I'm going home', 'Mean black cat blues', 'Frankie and Albert', 'Hammer blues', 'Rattlesnake blues', and, among his last recordings made for the American Record Company, 'Love my stuff', 'Revenue man blues', 'Oh death', 'Troubled 'bout my mother', 'Poor me', and 'Hang it on the wall'.

J. Fahey: *Charley Patton* (London, 1970).

Paul, Les [Polfus, Lester] (*b* Waukesha, Wis., 9 June 1916). American guitarist. He began by playing *hillbilly music and became known on radio in the 1930s in Milwaukee, St Louis, and Chicago. He turned to jazz with the Les Paul Trio and featured in the Fred *Waring show 1938–41, was regularly on Chicago radio 1941–2, and worked in Hollywood in 1942. After military service in 1944 he again led his trio and was an early member of the Jazz at the Philharmonic presentations. He became well-known in the 1950s as a modern-style, multi-recording guitarist (having much to do with the popularization of the electric guitar), and he invented the solid 'log' guitar with its sustaining pickup which was marketed by Gibson from 1952. He made many recordings for Capitol with his wife Mary Ford (1928–77), having a big hit with 'How high the moon' (1951), followed, the same year, by 'Mockin' bird hill', 'The world is waiting for the sunrise', and many others. They appeared on TV regularly before they parted in 1963. Latterly he devoted his energies more to the technology of electric guitars.

Paxton, Tom (*b* Chicago, 31 Oct. 1937). American folk-singer and composer. He studied at Oklahoma University, then settled in New York where he became a central figure of the folk revival and wrote a number of songs that became standard folk-club material such as 'The last thing on my mind', 'Leaving London', 'Rambling boy', 'Bound for the mountains and the sea', and, most notably, a number of effective *protest songs like 'Daily News', 'Lyndon Johnson told the nation', 'Talking Vietnam pot luck blues', 'The hostage', and 'Forest Lawn'. He appeared with great impact at the British Isle of Wight festival in 1971 and became mainly resident in Britain where he made the album, *New Songs for Old Friends* (1973), with Ralph McTell.

Payn, Graham (*b* Pietermaritzburg, Natal, 25 Apr. 1918). British actor and singer. He became closely associated with Noël *Coward and appeared in several of his revues and musicals, taking over Coward roles in the USA, and first introducing many of his songs there. He appeared in: *Sitting Pretty* (1939); *Up and Doing* (1940); *Fine and Dandy* (1942); *The *Lilac Domino* (revival, 1944); *Sigh No More* (1945)—'Matelot'; *Pacific 1860* (1946); **Tonight at 8.30* (NY, 1948); *Ace of Clubs* (1950); *The *Lyric Revue* (1951); *The Globe Revue* (1951); and *After the Ball* (1954).

Payne, Jack [John Wesley Vivian] (*b* Leamington Spa, War., 22 Aug. 1899; *d* London, 4 Dec. 1969). British bandleader. He organized his first dance bands while serving as a pilot with the Royal Flying Corps during the First World War. In 1925 he led a small band in the Hotel Cecil in London, which was one of the first dance bands to broadcast, and in 1928 he was appointed Director of Dance Music for the BBC at Savoy Hill, leading the BBC Dance Orchestra until he was succeeded by Henry *Hall in 1932. Thereafter he appeared with his band in stage shows and in films, including *Say it With Music* (1932) and *Sunshine Ahead* (1933), featuring Billy Scott-Coomber, Leslie *Sarony, and himself as vocalists. After the Second World War he became a theatrical agent but was forced to retire through financial misfortune and ill-health.

J. Payne: *Signature Tune* (London, n.d.). J. Payne: *This is Jack Payne* (London, 1932).

Peel, John [Ravenscroft, John] (*b* Heswall, Lancs., 30 Aug. 1939). British disc jockey. An influential voice in the rock scene of the mid-1960s onward, he has helped promote many careers and the more way-out forms of rock music. He went to the USA in 1961, becoming much in demand on American radio when the *Beatles were making the name of Merseyside music, and championing American hippie music. Returning to Britain in 1967, he became a well-known voice of the pirate Radio London station. When this was closed, he joined the BBC as the popular (yet always civilized) presenter of such programmes as *Night Ride* and *Top Gear*, still mainly promoting avant-garde and progressive rock, and running his own record company. He backed the emergence of *punk rock and has survived beyond the natural span of disc jockeys by virtue of his keen ear for the latest thing, becoming something of a cult himself.

Peers, Donald (*b* Ammanford, Wales, 10 July 1908; *d* Brighton, 9 Aug. 1973). British singer. He started his working life as a painter and, while doing War Office work at Aldershot, won a Fred Karno talent contest, afterwards singing with a dance band at Catterick. Turning professional, he first appeared on stage in 1927 with a concert party in Lowestoft and made his first broadcast from the BBC 2LO station at the end of that year, singing the song that was to become his theme tune 'In a shady nook (by a babbling brook)'. He continued to work with concert parties and pantomime before making his first London appearance in 1929 in a revue at the Bedford Theatre. He now regularly appeared in variety and in 1933, after an appearance in the BBC *Music Hall* programme, he was highly praised by the *Daily Express* critic Collie Knox, which led to his first recordings for HMV.

During the war he served in the Royal Army Service Corps, occasionally broadcasting, afterwards achieving his own radio show *The Cavalier of Song* from 1949. At this stage he became Britain's No. 1 popular singer; after a break necessitated by a throat operation he returned to radio in 1950 and had hits with 'In a shady nook', 'Powder your face with sunshine', 'Lavender blue', and 'Far away places'. He lost his popularity in the face of the rock and roll invasion but continued to tour in Australia and to work in England in the popular northern clubs. In 1969 he came back to the hit parade with 'Please don't go', and in 1971 with 'Give me one more chance'.

Peggy-Ann. American musical comedy with score by Richard *Rodgers, book by Herbert *Fields based on *Tillie's Nightmare* (which had also been a film vehicle for Marie *Dressler), and lyrics by Lorenz *Hart. It was produced in New York at the Vanderbilt Theatre 27 Dec. 1926, with Helen Ford in the leading role. It was a daring show for its time, set in the dream-world of Peggy-Ann, with no opening chorus or early songs, scenes played in near-darkness, and set changes in full view of the audience. There were 333 performances. It was seen in London at *Daly's Theatre 27 July 1927 [134p], with Dorothy *Dickson in the role of Peggy-Ann.

Pélissier, H. G. [Harry Gabriel] (*b* Finchley, London, 1874; *d* Finchley, 25 Sept. 1913). British actor, manager, and composer. Educated in England and France, he first worked in the business run by his father in the West End of London, dealing in precious stones. An interest in the stage soon progressed beyond amateur activities, and he made his first professional appearance at the Marylebone Music Hall in 1889. By this time he had written a number of songs, some of which were sung by Jessie *Bond who also introduced them to Charles Santley. He joined an obscure pierrot group called the *Follies (originally the Baddeley Troupe) and in 1896 took over the management of them, buying the name and the goodwill.

The rest of his short career was spent in making the Follies a household name; the first of many such concert party groups with their origins in the earlier *minstrel shows. He also brought back *burlesque and the basis of their shows was always one substantial piece in this vein. He wrote most of their sketches, music, and songs, the first he produced being 'Awake'. The Follies made their first theatre appearance in London at the Palace Theatre in 1904 and from then on became a national institution.

His songs (with Arthur *Wimperis, Arthur Davenport, and other collaborators) included: 'Oh, what a happy land is England' (1904); 'The flower girl' (1907); 'Mandy' (1907); 'Ypsilanti' (1908); 'There's a sun still shining in the sky' (1908); 'What a funny world we live in' (1908); 'My moon' (1909); 'Li-ti-ti-ti' (1909); 'Back to the land' (1909); 'Jane from Maiden Lane' (1910); and 'The big bamboo' (1911).

F. Gardner: *Pure Folly* (London, 1909).

Pennington, Ann (*b* Camden, NJ, 23 Dec. 1894; *d* New York, 4 Nov. 1971). American dancer. Small (under 5 feet), vivacious, and attractive, she first appeared in the chorus of *The Red Widow* (1911), before she became a star of the spectacular revue world, appearing in the **Ziegfeld Follies* (1913–16, 1918, 1923–4); in **George White's Scandals* (1919–21, 1926, 1928), introducing 'Black Bottom' in the 1926 edition, and various other revues.

Penny Plain. Popular British revue with Joyce *Grenfell, who wrote many of the songs, and Max *Adrian. Musical material was provided by Richard *Addinsell, Donald *Swann (with Michael *Flanders), Charles *Zwar, and the show's musical director, John Pritchett. It was produced in London at the St Martin's Theatre 28 June 1951 [443p].

Pepper, Art [Arthur Edward] (*b* Gardena, Calif., 1 Sept. 1925; *d* Los Angeles, 15 June 1982). American jazz saxophonist. Born of a German father and an Italian mother, he played in school bands and was married at 17. After service in the US Army, he played in the Stan *Kenton band 1946–52, and was an influential shaper of the West Coast school of modern jazz. His highly promising jazz career was marred by a deep dependency on heroin and other drugs. He was on a narcotics charge in 1952 and was sent to jail, paroled in 1953, but got into trouble again and served a prison sentence 1954–6, and again in 1960–1. He was unable to break his drug habits and served in San Quentin 1961–4 and 1965–6. He resumed a musical career with the Buddy *Rich band 1968–9, subsequently led his own groups and made recordings, and toured Japan in 1977 and 1978.

A. Pepper (ed. L. Pepper): *Straight Life: the Story of Art Pepper* (New York, 1979).

Pepper, Harry S. (*b* London, 1891; *d* London, 26 June 1970). British composer, author, and producer. He began his stage life in his father's concert party, the White Coons, acting as manager, pianist, composer, and box-office. He was assistant musical director at the Theatre Royal, Drury Lane, for six years before writing his first musical *Lady Luck* (1927) and was pianist with the *Co-Optimists when they were revived in 1930. Joining the BBC as a producer in 1932, he became senior variety producer in 1945 and was responsible for such shows as *Monday Night at Eight*, *Garrison Theatre*, *The Kentucky Minstrels*, *Band Wagon*, and *Hi-Gang*. He married his assistant, Doris Arnold (*b* 1904), who worked as an arranger for the Kentucky Minstrels and introduced the popular record programme *These You Have Loved* from 1943. He retired in 1951. He also wrote *Paulette* (1932); and songs including 'Goodbye to all that' (1930); 'Don't tell a soul' (1931); 'Carry me back to green pastures' (1934); and 'Any rags, bottles or bones' (with Stanley *Holloway, 1938).

Perchance to Dream. Musical romance with music and words by Ivor *Novello, produced at the London Hippodrome 21 Apr. 1945, with a cast that included Ivor Novello, Olive Gilbert (*d* 1981), Roma Beaumont (*b* 1914), Muriel Barron (*b* 1906), and Margaret Rutherford (1892–1972). At 1022 performances, it was Novello's longest-running show. It tells the story of three generations of an aristocratic English family, set in the Regency period, in 1843, and in the present, a somewhat morbid story of suicides until the final generation manage to put their house in order. It was romantically elevated by two of Novello's most popular songs 'We'll gather lilacs' and 'Love is my reason'.

Performing Right Society. British association of composers, lyric-writers, and music-publishers (the UK equivalent of *ASCAP) formed in 1914 with the object of exercising the right of public performance and collecting fees for the use of musical works under its control. Its formation was the eventual outcome of the passing of the British Copyright Act of 1911.

Périchole, La. Opéra-bouffe in two acts with music by Jacques *Offenbach and book by Henri Meilhac (1831-97) and Ludovic Halévy (1834–1908), based on Prosper Mérimee's *La Carosse de Saint Sacrement*, first produced at Les Variétés, Paris, 6 Oct. 1868, with Hortense Schneider (1830–1920) in the title role.

Two singers, Périchole and Piquillo, are trying to earn enough money to get married. Périchole catches the eye of the viceroy who is prowling around incognito. He invites her to dinner and reveals his identity. She accepts his offer of a place at court and writes a sad farewell letter to Piquillo. But there is a law that unmarried ladies cannot reside at court and a husband is picked for her at random from the streets. It turns out to be the mournful Piquillo, drowning his sorrows in drink. He is angry and jealous when he discovers his projected bride is Périchole and is thrown into prison. Eventually the viceroy is moved by their young love and releases them both with his blessing.

One of Offenbach's best integrated scores, it contains such fine numbers as 'Le conquerant et la jeune indienne', 'O mon cher amant' (the letter song), 'A quel diner je viens de faire', 'Tu n'est pas beau', and 'Que les hommes sont bêtes'. It was first seen in Vienna at the Theater an der Wien in 1869 and in London at the Princess Theatre with Hortense Schneider in 1870. A three-act version was produced in 1874 and it was seen at the Royalty Theatre in London in 1875 with *Trial by Jury* as a filler.

Perkins, Carl [Perkings, Carl Lee] (*b* Tiptonville, Tenn., 9 Apr. 1932). American rockabilly and country singer and composer. He began his career entertaining at dances with a group known as the Perkins Brothers, made up of members of the family. With appearances in *Nashville's **Grand Ole Opry* he became a popular national figure; he toured the USA and Europe with his own band, which was again made up of his family, and had a substantial hit with 'Blue suede shoes' (1956), which was recorded by many performers.

C. Perkins and R. Rendleman: *Disciple in Blue Suede Shoes* (Grand Rapids, Mich., 1978).

Peter Pan. J. M. Barrie's play, originally presented in London in 1904 and in New York in 1905, was first given additional music in the USA in 1924 when Marilyn Miller was in the leading role and sang two songs written by Jerome *Kern. A version with music by Leonard *Bernstein was produced in New York in 1950 with Jean Arthur in the lead and ran for 321 performances. In 1954, Jerome Robbins decided that a new version was needed as a starring vehicle for Mary *Martin and planned to feature a few songs by Mark Charlap. However, with such a singer available, it seemed a waste not to let it become a thoroughgoing musical and Jule *Styne was asked to provide additional numbers. With Mary Martin as Peter and Cyril *Ritchard as a Restoration-style Captain Hook, it was produced at the Winter Garden Theatre, New York, 20 October 1954 for a seasonal run of 152 performances. A production in 1979 with Sandy Duncan as Peter, based on the 1954 musical, at the Lunt-Fontanne Theatre 6 Sept. 1979, beat the earlier productions with 551 performances.

Peter, Paul and Mary. American pop-folk trio who did much to bridge the gap between pop music and the protest movement. The members were Peter Yarrow (*b* New York, 31 May 1938), Paul Stookey (*b* Baltimore, 30 Nov. 1937), and Mary Allin Travers (*b* Louisville, Ky., 7 Nov. 1937). They were brought together in 1961 by manager Albert Grossman as a modern version of the Kingston Trio or the Weavers. Their repertoire was eclectically made up of whimsy for children ('Puff the magic dragon'), serious Bob *Dylan material which they were the first to take up, and modern pop-folk; their first No. 1 hit being John *Denver's 'Leaving on a jet plane'. They were very popular among the college generation and were prominent in the left-wing movement of the 1960s, putting over a serious message in a light and polished way. The group disbanded in 1971.

Peterson, Oscar Emmanuel (*b* Montreal, 15 Aug. 1925). Canadian jazz pianist. He first became known on Canadian radio and played for a time with the Johnny Holmes orchestra. In 1939 he went to New York and soon found favour with a wide audience that went beyond the jazz sector. A brilliant, dazzling, and inventive pianist in the Art *Tatum mould, he perhaps lacked the warmth and guts to be a jazz great, but his cocktail leanings gave his music a wide appeal and he successfully toured with his own trio, played with Jazz at the Philharmonic, and as soloist with leading orchestras. An intelligent and pleasant character, he was one of the most successful jazz musicians to appear on TV.

G. Lees: *Oscar Peterson: the will to Swing* (London, 1988).

Pether, Henry E. (*b* London, 1867; *d* London, 7 Feb. 1932). British songwriter. He spent most of his life as a member of the staff of *Francis, Day & Hunter, arranging and editing albums and songbooks. He wrote innumerable *music-hall songs, including the lasting 'Waiting at the church' (*w* Fred W. Leigh, *d* 1924); 'Ain't it grand to be alive' (*w* Percy Edgar), and 'The seaside posters round the home' (*w* Edgar Bateman).

Petrie, Henry W. (*b* Bloomington, Ill., 4 Mar. 1857; *d* Paw Paw, Mich., 25 May 1925). American composer. He combined the careers of minstrel entertainer and professional songwriter, his works including such lasting vaudeville items as: 'I don't want to play in your yard' (1894, *w* Philip Wingate); 'You can't play in our yard anymore' (1894, Wingate); 'Asleep in the deep (1897, *w* Arthur J. Lamb); 'At the bottom of the deep blue sea' (1899, Lamb); 'Just to remind me of you' (1900); 'Davy Jones's locker' (1901); and 'Where the sunset turns the ocean's blue to gold' (1902).

Phantom of the Opera, The. British musical play with score by Andrew *Lloyd Webber, book by Richard Stilgoe (*b* 1943) and Lloyd Webber, lyrics by Charles Hart (*b* 1961); produced at her Majesty's Theatre, London, 9 Oct. 1986 with Michael *Crawford as the Phantom and Sarah Brightman alternating with Claire Moore as Christine.

A great deal of its success was due to its impressive and effective staging under the direction of Harold Prince, the opera-house and below-streets settings done with magnificent effect. Its principal songs were 'All I ask of you', 'The phantom of the opera', and 'The music of the night'. It was still running in 1990. It was staged in New York, at the Majestic Theatre 26 Jan. 1988, with Crawford in the lead.

The Phantom of the Opera began life as a novel by Gaston Leroux (1868–1927), published in 1911. It was first filmed in 1925, with Lon Chaney (1883–1930) as the phantom; most successfully in 1943, starring Claude Rains (1889–1967); and again in 1962.

G. Perry: *The Complete Phantom of the Opera* (London, 1987).

Phillips, Montague Fawcett (*b* London, 13 Nov. 1885; *d* Esher, 4 Jan. 1969). British composer and organist. He was educated at the Royal Academy of Music and eventually became a Professor of Harmony and Composition there. He is best remembered for his operetta *The Rebel Maid* which enjoyed considerable success when produced at the Empire Theatre, London, under the composer's direction in 1921 and it was long a favourite of amateur companies. A song from it, 'The fishermen of England', became a popular ballad in its own right. He had no success at all with a later operetta, *The Golden Triangle*. For many years he was organist and choirmaster at Esher Parish Church; and he was married to Clara Butterworth. He wrote a large number of once popular songs and light orchestral works, in addition to his more serious endeavours.

Phillips, Sid [Isadore Simon] (*b* London, 14 June 1907; *d* Shepperton, 24 May 1973). British clarinettist, saxophonist, bandleader, composer, and arranger. Born into a family of musicians (his brothers were all well-known in the profession), he was at school in Italy at the start of the First World War. After the war, aged 16, he played at the People's Palace in the East End of London; later joined by two of his brothers in forming the Melodians which won the first *Melody Maker* Dance Band Contest at the Kew Palais de Danse and consequently toured the British Isles and Europe. He became more interested in composition, and had given up playing to work in music-publishing, when he received an invitation to join the *Ambrose orchestra, then considered Britain's best.

With Ambrose he made a great reputation as musician, arranger, and composer (and did much to enhance the quality and reputation of the orchestra) with many of his original works like 'Streamline strut', 'Night ride', 'Escapade', and 'Cotton pickers' congregation' featured by the band; and arrangements that included his own signature tune, 'Hors d'oeuvres', becoming standard dance-band scores that were still being performed several decades later. He visited the USA and had many offers from American bandleaders but decided to stay in England. While with Ambrose he also recorded with his own swing quintet and after the Second World War formed a regular band playing an arranged but effective style of Dixieland jazz with his highly individual clarinet playing giving it an easily identifiable sound. He continued to play and record until shortly before his death; and also wrote some large-scale orchestral works under the name of Simon Phillips.

***Phi-Phi*.** French operetta with music by Henri *Christiné and book by Albert Willemetz and F. Sollar, produced at the Bouffes-Parisiens, Paris, 12 Nov. 1918. It had a joyfully bright score, teeming with *foxtrots and *one-steps, which included such items as 'Ah! cher Monsieur, excusez-moi' and the waltz 'Ah! tais-toi!' It was staged at the London Pavilion 16 Aug. 1922, with a cast that included Clifton *Webb, Stanley *Lupino, and Evelyn *Laye, and had 132 performances.

The story is set in the year 600 BC and follows the fortunes of the Greek sculptor Phidias (known as Phi-Phi) and his entanglements with his wife, mistress, lover, patron, and art. The show marked the end of traditional operetta in France and ushered in the musical comedy age.

Piaf, Edith [Gassion, Edith Giovanna] (*b* Paris, 19 Dec. 1915; *d* Paris, 11 Oct. 1963). French singer. Born in a poor area of Paris, she was deserted by her mother, a vagrant street-singer, as a child and lived in the country with her grandmother until she was 14. At the age of eight she went blind, but later recovered. In 1929 she returned to Paris and spent some years travelling with her father, an itinerant circus acrobat, and she helped to earn a living by singing in the streets. She was befriended by Louis Leplée, owner of the well-known Cerny's cabaret, who gave her the nickname 'piaf' (Parisian slang for 'sparrow') because of her diminutive size and chirpy appearance; he built her into a star performer, so that by the beginning of the war in 1939 she was known all over France. When he was found murdered she was arrested as a material witness. During the war she entertained the troops, and her efforts for French prisoners in Germany led, for a time, to her being labelled a collaborator. She restored her reputation with her art, her expressive and moving singing pleasing listeners of all tastes until she became one of the most loved entertainment figures in France.

She became internationally known around 1946 when she was working with the Compagnons de la Chanson and recorded such songs as 'Les Trois cloches'. Her greatest hit of all was 'La vie en rose' (the words of which she wrote to music by *Louiguy in 1946); others were 'Les amants de Paris' (*m* Léo Ferré), 'Padam, Padam', songs by Michel Emer ('L'accordéoniste', 'La fête continue') and Marguerite *Monnot ('La goualante du pauvre Jean', 'Mariage', 'Les amants d'un jour', and 'Le petit homme'), *Kosma's 'Les feuilles mortes', many songs written by Charles Dumont (*b* 1929), used on her LP *Olympia*, and her own 'Du matin jusqu'au soir' among others. She made a first visit to the USA in 1954 and was there again for a well-remembered Carnegie Hall concert in 1957; and she appeared in London. Her health began to fail in 1959; she was treated in hospital and went back to work but collapsed on stage in 1960. Ignoring medical advice, she starred at the *Olympia Music Hall at the end of the year in what many believed to be her greatest performance, introducing 'Non, je ne regrette rien', 'Les mots d'amour', and 'Mon vieux Lucien'. She was alternately ill and rising to creative heights during 1961 and 1962; and was still performing until the beginning of 1963.

Edith Piaf was never a great singer, technically, but she sang with a truth and depth that came from her experience of a hard life with its loves and sorrows, and she moved audiences all over the world.

E. Piaf: *Au bal de la chance* (Geneva, 1958; London, as *The*

Wheel of Fortune, 1965). M. Blistène: *Au revoir, Edith* (Paris, 1963). S. Berteaut: *Piaf* (Paris, 1969). E. Bertin: *Edith Piaf, le chant d'amour* (Paris, 1973). M. Lange: *Piaf* (Paris, 1979; New York, 1981; London, 1982). D. Bret: *The Piaf Legend* (New York, 1989).

Piano. Once cheap upright models had come on to the market *c.*1830, the piano was to be constantly in the background of all popular music-making, whether in the concert-hall, the theatre, silent cinema, club, or pub. It was in the privacy of the Victorian home that it made its first recordable contribution to popular taste, the home pianist catered for by numerous writers of salon music in a light classical idiom, among the most prolific composers being Brinley Richards (1817–85)—'Warblings at eve' and Sydney Smith (1839–89)—'Jet d'eau'. The drawing-room pianos, surmounted by their Star Folios of favourite solos, resounded with such pieces as 'Molitwa dziewicy' (better known as 'The maiden's prayer') by Thekla Badarzewska (1834–61), 'The robin's return'—caprice, by L. Fisher, 'The shepherd boy'—idyll, by G. D. Wilson, and 'Stephanie gavotte' by Alphons Czibulka (1842–94), to mention but a few of the tastier morsels.

A popular addiction to the lighter, more tuneful classics, often adapted orchestral works or operatic items, was also catered for in the Star Folios and elsewhere and a tradition of playing this repertoire in a way that emphasized the melody and diminished the demanding intensity of the serious performance for popular taste has always survived, notably carried on in the 20th century by piano duos such as Maryan Rawicz (1898–1970) and Walter Landauer (1910–83), a Pole and an Austrian who worked as a much-loved variety and radio act in Britain from 1935; and in the Anglo-Italian Alberto Semprini (1908–90) who moved in similar areas as a soloist. The mixture of classical (and other) music and theatre razzmatazz was brought to a peak by the American *Liberace.

The piano performed its service as all-round accompanist in many fields of endeavour. Its true emergence into the world of popular music came with the 1890s birth of *ragtime in the USA and the work of such pioneers as Scott *Joplin, Ben *Harney, Tom *Turpin, and James *Scott. It had already stood, ill-used and beer-sodden in British song-and-supper rooms and music-halls and, in the USA, in the saloons of the West and the dance-halls of the cities, and now emerged as a natural part of the jazz scene, as an element of the jazz band or as soloist in such rumbustious genres as *barrelhouse and *boogie-woogie, in the hands of such performers as Meade Lux *Lewis, Pinetop *Smith, Albert *Ammons, Pete *Johnson, 'Cow Cow' *Davenport, and the blues-based Jimmy *Yancey. Among the early jazz piano stars in the mainstream of the music's development were 'Jelly Roll' *Morton, Jimmy Blythe (1900–36), Lil *Armstrong, Alex Hill (1907–37), Richard M. *Jones; playing in a tradition continued by such players as Art Hodes (*b* 1904) and Bob Zurke (1912–44).

Alongside the growing sophistication of all jazz, piano soloists from James P. *Johnson to Earl *Hines, Teddy *Wilson, and Art *Tatum gradually developed a piano style that had its basis in ragtime but added the kind of technical skill associated with classical piano playing. Other exponents were Teddy *Weatherford, Willie 'The Lion' *Smith, later Garland Wilson (1909–54) and Erroll *Garner, bandleaders Duke *Ellington and Count *Basie, and the white exponents Joe *Sullivan and Jess *Stacy. This kind of playing was adapted for the popular market by such players as Zez *Confrey and Felix *Arndt in the USA and Billy *Mayerl and Charlie *Kunz in Britain and taken to the fringes of the Semprini–Liberace spheres by a host of popular so-called 'rhythm' pianists in the 1920s as the South African Raie de Costa (1907–34) or the Australian virtuoso Patricia Rossborough. The Harlem school as typified by Johnson and his disciple 'Fats' *Waller, which broadened in the general styling of the 1930s and 1940s swing band leads of Eddie *Duchin and others, was succeeded by the modernists Thelonious *Monk, Bud *Powell, John *Lewis, Hank Jones, Horace *Silver, and others, taking us to the wayward free jazz ways of Cecil *Taylor and other avant-gardists of today.

In the wider areas of pop music the piano has found no real niche except in the artless strummings of self-accompanying singers; its place as a band instrument has been usurped by ubiquitous amorphism generally listed as 'keyboards'.

Pianola; Player-piano. An invention that had a great vogue at the end of the 19th century and in the early years of the 20th, but was eventually superseded by the *gramophone and radio as home entertainment and a means of spreading the gospel of popular music. Mechanisms were variously devised to activate a piano action so that the playing of one or more pianists (or artificially made music) could be reproduced from a perforated roll of paper on a principle already utilized by mechanical organs. The roll passed over a number of holes in a metal strip through which air was sucked by bellows motivated either by foot-pedals or mechanically. As the air passed into the appropriate hole it would put a small corresponding bellows into action to activate the required note.

There were two basic systems, the earlier method being embodied in the patented 'Pianola' where all the mechanism was in a keyboard-length cabinet which could be moved up to any ordinary piano. Padded hammers at the back extended over the keys of the piano and struck them as if with robot fingers. The mechanism covered 65 notes, the rest of the standard 88-note keyboard remaining unused. Earlier rolls are identified as 65-note, and many consider that this system gave a more accurate interpretation of the original player's performance. With experience a very accurate control of touch and volume could be obtained by subtle variations of pressure on the foot pedals, aided by speed and volume controls incorporated in the unit.

The Pianola was generally superseded by the player-piano, which was a piano with the mechanism incorporated in the main cabinet. The bellows now operated the piano's own hammers directly, thus cutting out one intermediate movement, giving a quicker and quieter action, and using the whole range of the piano. The new rolls were identified as 88-note. The instrument could also be used as a piano. Later models were electrically operated and tended to sound too mechanical. Coin-operated models known as *nickleodeons were installed in amusement arcades and elsewhere, ancestors of the *juke box.

Sophisticated developments came in the manufacture of the rolls, with the original source instrument becoming as sensitive as a recording in its reactions to the player's interpretation. With mechanically perfected instruments to play the resulting rolls on, often grand pianos, the player-piano reached a point where the resulting performance had every nuance of the original and it was like hearing the ghost of Fats *Waller or Paderewski playing; in some ways better than listening to a recording, for it was an actual instrument playing and not a secondary source from loudspeakers. Several impressive systems competed, with the Duo-Art, Welte Mignon, and Ampico systems in the lead, their claims to reproduce the original performance with great accuracy fully borne out by the results. At this stage the instrument was also referred to as the Reproducing Piano. Many examples have been recorded, in some cases the only surviving impressions of early performers.

W. J. G. Ord-Hume: *Player-Piano: the History of the Mechanical Piano and How to Repair It* (London, 1970).

Pickett, Wilson (*b* Prattville, Ala., 18 Mar. 1941). American soul singer. Raised in Detroit, he first came to notice as the lead singer of the Falcons. He became a solo act and recorded 'If you need me' and 'It's too late' in 1963, joining Atlantic Records in 1964 and eventually coming up with two hits, 'In the midnight hour' and 'Don't fight it', in 1965. He became a recognized soul star, noted for an aggressive, basic, pounding, sock-it approach, which produced his biggest sellers like 'Mustang Sally' (1966); 'Funky Broadway' (1967); 'She's looking good' (1968); and 'I'm a midnight mover' (1968); but he was equally effective in slower ballad material like 'Hey Jude' (1968), a *Beatles number; and 'Back in your arms' (1969). The primitive approach to soul became old-fashioned and a more subtle approach was aimed in such things as 'Don't let the green grass fool you' (1971) which became his best-selling recording. In 1972 he signed with RCA who tried to soften the image even further with 'Soft soul boogie woogie' in 1974.

Pickup group. Unit brought together for one specific performance or recording; not a regular group.

Pickwick. Musical with score by Cyril *Ornadel, book by Wolf Mankowitz (*b* 1924), based on the novel by Charles Dickens, and lyrics by Leslie *Bricusse. After opening in Manchester, it was produced at the Saville Theatre, London, 4 July 1963, and was to have a run of 694 performances. Presenting various episodes in the life of the accident-prone Pickwick Club with the rotund Harry Secombe (*b* 1921) a natural portrayer of the jovial Mr Pickwick, its major hit was 'If I ruled the world'. The British humour was not to American taste and it managed only 56 performances at the 46th Street Theatre, New York, 4 Oct. 1965.

Pied Pipers, The. American vocal group first coming to attention on the Raleigh-Kool radio show in 1938. The original seven were John Huddleston, Chuck Lowry, Hal Hopper, Woody Newbury, Whit Whittinghill, Bud Hervey, and John Tait, becoming an octet when they added the female singer Jo *Stafford. There were various changes of personnel from which a regular group of four, Jo Stafford and three men, emerged. They were with the Dorsey band from 1940, and by 1942 the usual personnel was Stafford, her husband John Huddleston, Lowry, and Clark Yocum. They left Dorsey in 1942 and worked with Bob *Crosby, Johnny *Mercer, Frank *Sinatra, and on the Lucky Strike programme, also appearing in films. In 1944, Jo Stafford was replaced by June Hutton (1918–73), who was with the group until 1950. They were in the film *Make Mine Music* (1946), and still active in the 1950s and 1960s, re-organizing for special appearances.

Pinkard, Maceo (*b* Bluefield, W. Va., 27 June 1897; *d* New York, 21 July 1962). American composer and publisher. He studied music and the piano before becoming an orchestral player and eventually leading his own orchestra. He toured the USA in 1913 with the Nashville Students and in 1914 was running a theatrical agency in Omaha, and he directed shows there until 1917 when he went to New York to produce revues and founded his own music-publishing business. He wrote scores for *Liza* (1922) and *Pansy* (1929). His best-remembered songs were 'Sweet Georgia Brown' (1925); 'Gimme a little kiss, will ya, huh?' (1926); 'Here comes the show boat' (1927)—used in the film version of *Show Boat*; 'Sugar' (1928); 'Don't be like that' (1928); 'Them there eyes' (with Doris Tauber, *b* 1908, and William Tracey, 1893–1957; 1929); and 'Congratulations' (1929).

Pink Floyd. British psychedelic rock band formed in Cambridge in 1966 with the original line-up of Syd Barrett (*b* 1946) (vocal and guitar), Roger Waters (*b* 1944) (bass), Richard Wright (*b* 1945) (keyboards), and Nick Mason (*b* 1945) (drums). In the beginning they were an uncomplicated rhythm 'n' blues group, first appearing at the *Marquee in London in a show called Spontaneous Underground; but they moved into the psychedelic field with a strange recording 'Arnold Layne' (1967) which coincided with the outburst of hippie activities and firmly allied them with it. They produced a first album, *The*

Piper at the Gates of Dawn in 1967, a collection by turns strange and childish. This image was largely influenced by Barrett, whose unreliable behaviour led the band to part company with him in March 1968 and to take on Dave Gilmour (*b* 1944) as lead guitarist.

They now concentrated on imaginative instrumental performances, as heard in *A Saucerful of Secrets* (1968) and *Ummagumma* (1969). They produced several film sound-tracks—*More* (1969), *Zabriskie Point* (1970), and *Obscured by Clouds* (1972). An increasing depth and awareness of social tensions was implicit in their album *The Dark Side of the Moon* (1973), which was both a commercial and an artistic success. *Wish You Were Here* (1975) was by way of a tribute to the much-missed Barrett, whose influence on the band was renewed by occasional collaborations. *The Wall* (1978) was based on the ideas of Roger Waters with the song 'Another brick in the wall' becoming their first No. 1 hit; it formed the basis of a part-animated feature film, *Pink Floyd, The Wall* (1982). *The Final Cut* (1983) marked the departure of Richard Wright.

R. Sanders: *The Pink Floyd* (London, 1976). Miles: *Pink Floyd* (London, 1981). R. Waters (ed.): *Pink Floyd Lyric Book* (Poole, 1982).

Pink Lady, The. Operetta with music by Ivan *Caryll and book by 'Harry Morton' (Charles M. S. McClellan, 1865–1916), produced at the New Amsterdam Theatre, New York, 13 Mar. 1911. By this time Caryll, who had been one of the dominant figures of the British musical comedy scene, had moved to New York where he was to be involved in several productions that had their premières there before he returned to London. His most successful American show was *The Pink Lady*, which was a fine showcase for Hazel Dawn (1891–1988) playing the part of a violinist (and the violin) and, dressed entirely in pink, causing a fashionable craze for that colour among American ladies.

The story is set in several French venues during the course of one day, during which a young man is having his last fling before his marriage and has to get out of the situation when his wife-to-be meets up with his girlfriend. There was one lasting number, 'My beautiful lady' ('The kiss waltz'), and it had 312 performances. Hazel Dawn came with the show to London where it had 124 performances at the Globe Theatre 11 Apr. 1912.

Pins and Needles. Revue with music and lyrics by Harold *Rome, sketches by Marc *Blitzstein and others, produced at the Labor Stage Theatre (previously the *Princess Theatre), New York, 27 Nov. 1937, with an amateur cast of trade union members. It took a bitingly satirical look at every other political party and policy at home and abroad through left-wing eyes; word got round that it was unusual and good and it ended up with a surprising run of 1108 performances, outdoing anything else around at the time. A second edition, *New Pins and Needles*, followed in 1939. It was the first score by Harold Rome, who provided such items as 'Sing me a song with social significance' and 'Sunday in the park' (sung by Celeste Holm), and went on to pursue similar lines in *Sing Out the News* (1938).

Pinza, Ezio [Fortunio] (*b* Rome, 18 May 1892; *d* Stamford, Conn., 9 May 1957). Italian baritone. Having pursued a highly successful career in opera, making his debut in Bellini's *Norma* in 1914, playing the leading role in the première of Boito's *Nerone* (1924), and singing at the Metropolitan Opera in New York 1926–47, he made a surprising switch to the musical comedy stage and appeared opposite Mary *Martin in *Rodgers and Hammerstein's **South Pacific* (1949). This led to appearances in several musical films and a leading role in **Fanny* (1954).

E. Pinza: *Ezio Pinza: an Autobiography* (New York, 1958).

Pippin. American musical comedy with music and lyrics by Stephen *Schwartz and book by Roger O. Hirson. Schwartz had written the work as a student, but was not able to get it produced until after his success with **Godspell*. The book was revised by the playwright Hirson, with help from the director and choreographer Bob *Fosse. It was produced at the Imperial Theatre, New York, 23 Oct. 1972, and had an impressive run of 1944 performances.

The story is observed by a mythical Leading Player (Ben Vereen) and tells of Pippin (John Rubinstein), the son of Charlemagne, who tries to find glory as a soldier, a lover, and a leader, but, failing in all three ambitions, ends up a married man. An imaginative score included 'Magic to do', 'Corner of the sky', 'No time at all', 'Morning glow', 'On the right track', and 'Love song'. Although so successful in New York, with two touring companies also doing well, it had only 85 performances when brought to London, at Her Majesty's Theatre 30 Oct. 1973.

Pirates of Penzance, The, or *The Slave of Duty*. Comic opera with music by Arthur *Sullivan and book by W. S. *Gilbert, their third major collaboration which, following the production fiascos of **HMS Pinafore*, was completed in the USA while the writers were there promoting a first series of authentic D'Oyly *Carte productions. It was given a copyright production at the Royal Bijou Theatre in Paignton, Devon, 30 Dec. 1879, before its New York première at the Fifth Avenue Theatre 31 Dec. 1879. The London production, at the Opera-Comique Theatre in the Strand, was on 3 Apr. 1880, with Rutland *Barrington, George *Grossmith, Richard *Temple, and Marion Hood [363p]. It was seen in Vienna at the Theater an der Wien 1 Mar. 1889.

The score is one of the sturdiest of the G & S productions with a Verdian quality about it and includes 'Climbing over rocky mountain' (first used in *Thespis*), 'Poor wandr'ing one', 'I am the very model of a modern Major-General', 'When the foeman bares his steel', 'A policeman's lot is not a happy one', and 'With cat-like tread'. Produced regularly ever since its beginnings, it had special notable revivals in New York (Uris and Minkoff Theatres) 8 Jan. 1981 [787p] and in London (Theatre Royal, Drury Lane) 26 May 1982 [601p], tastefully updated by director Wilford Leach and an expert cast. There were two film versions made in 1982.

The chorus of 'A rollicking band of pirates we' ('Come friends, who plough the seas') was appropriated in the USA for a march arranged for band under the title of 'Hail! Hail! the gang's all here', published in Cincinnati in 1908 and credited to Herman Bellstedt. A song of the same title with words by Theodora Morse had already been published in 1904 and song and tune came together in 1917 with the music now credited to Theodore *Morse and Sullivan.

Piron, Armand John (*b* New Orleans, 16 Aug. 1888; *d* New Orleans, 17 Feb. 1943). American composer and violinist. Crippled by an accident at the age of seven, he was not able to walk for many years. He studied the violin and started to play with the Peerless Orchestra in 1912, then played in various ensembles before leading his own popular band from 1917 onward, long resident at Tranchina's Restaurant at Spanish Fort. In 1915 he formed a publishing company in partnership with Clarence *Williams which produced many jazz standards such as Piron's 'I wish I could shimmy like my sister Kate' (1922), which he wrote with Peter Bocage (1887–1967) who played in his band from 1918.

Pitney, Gene (*b* Hartford, Conn., 17 Feb. 1941). American singer. He had a remarkable success in the 1960s with pop songs of the big ballad kind, such as 'Love my life away' (1961), which he also wrote; 'Town without pity' (1961); 'Liberty Valance' (1962); 'Only love can break a heart' (1962); 'Mecca' (1963); '24 hours from Tulsa' (1963); 'It hurts to be in love' (1964); 'She's a heartbreaker' (1968); having 23 items in the Top 20 between 1961 and 1969. He left the recording scene after that to look after his business interests, occasionally appearing in cabaret.

Plain and Fancy. Musical comedy with score by Albert *Hague, book by Joseph Stein (*b* 1912) and Will Glockman, lyrics by Arnold B. Horwitt (*b* 1918), produced in New York at the Mark Hellinger Theatre, 27 Jan. 1955 [461p]. It was set in the rural community of Bird-in-Hand, Pennsylvania, where two New Yorkers get mixed up in the affairs of a remote township. The songs included: 'Young and foolish', 'Follow your heart', 'It wonders me', 'City mouse, country mouse', 'This is all very new to me', 'Plenty of Pennsylvania', and 'I'll show him'. It was produced in London (Drury Lane Theatre) 25 Jan. 1956.

Planquette, [Jean-]**Robert** (*b* Paris, 31 Mar. 1848; *d* Paris, 28 Jan. 1903). French composer. He studied at the Paris Conservatoire for a time, but did not pass any exams. He began to make his musical reputation with his piano works and as a composer of popular songs that were performed at the *café-concerts and in the music-halls. His marches, especially 'Le Régiment de Sambre-et-Meuse', were also very popular. Above all he was a very successful theatre composer, writing some 23 operettas between 1872 and 1897 with his fourth, *Les *Cloches de Corneville* (1877) not only achieving 1000 performances in Paris by 1886, but being seen, as *The Chimes of Normandy*, in New York in 1877, and in 1878 having the longest run at the Folly Theatre of any operetta seen in London until then.

His other works included: *Le Valet de cœur* (1872); *Le Serment de Mme Grégoire* (1873); *Paille d'avoine* (1874); *Le Chevalier Gaston* (1879); *Les Voltigeurs de la 32eme* (1880); *La Cantinière* (1880); *Rip Van Winkle* (1882); *Nell Gwynne (Colombine)* (1884); *La Crémaillère* (1885); *Paul Jones (Surcouf)* (1887); *The Old Guard* (London, 1887); *Le Capitaine Thérèse* (1890); *La Cocarde tricolore* (1892); *Le Talisman* (1893); *Panurge* (1894); *Mam'zelle Quat'Sous* (1897); and *Le Paradis de Mahomet* (1906, orch. Louis *Ganne).

Platters, The. American vocal group who became popular in the 1950s. They were formed in 1953 with Tony Williams, David Lynch, Alex Hodge, Herb Reed, and Buck Ram as the original nucleus. Shortly after, Paul Robi replaced Alex Hodge and Zola Taylor was added as feminine tone-colour. They started recording for the Mercury label in 1955 and by 1964 had achieved many hits with such items as 'Only you', 'The great pretender', and 'Smoke gets in your eyes'. Sonny Turner took over from Tony Williams (1928–92) as tenor lead in 1961, Sandra Dawn replaced Zola Taylor in 1966, and other changes were made. They had especially big hits with 'I love you 1000 times' (1966) and 'With this ring' (1977); and they performed into the 1980s with a totally changed personnel.

Playford, John (*b* Norfolk, 1623; *d* London, 5 Nov. 1686). British music-publisher and editor. As a youth he went to London and joined the music-publishing firm of his cousin Henry Playford in Cripplegate. He set up his own business in 1648 at an address given on his publications as 'in the Inner Temple nere the Church doore' where he plied his trade until his death in 1686. He married in 1653 and took up residence over his business premises, but in 1662 moved to Islington when his wife opened a school there. She died in 1679 and the next year he moved back into London, continuing to sell books and publish, although his son Henry Playford took over active management in 1684. A man with a great love of music, he became friendly with other enthusiasts like Samuel Pepys, and was to become the leading and most influential music-publisher of the day. He composed psalm tunes and glees (including the popular 'Comely swain') and wrote an *Introduction to the Skill of Musick* in 1654 that became the standard textbook of musical theory for almost a century, its final edition being published in 1730.

With the encouragement of Pepys, who was already a far-sighted collector of broadsheets and popular tunes, he saw the need of a collection of traditional airs, then currently used for dancing, that could be used by professional fiddlers and teachers. He published his influential *The *Dancing Master (Plaine and easie Rules for the Dancing of Country Dances, with the Tune to each Dance)* in 1650 [dated 1651], gathering together the melodies of 105 tunes, some traditional, some new. It was a random choice from a plentiful field with obvious items like 'Greensleeves' not getting in until the 7th edition. He gave a single-line melody and elaborate instructions for the dances, in which task he was probably aided by some uncredited professional. The great need for the work was reflected in its immediate popularity; and there were 18 editions by 1728, each with new material added. It became an indispensable source of broadside tunes and for the writers of ballad operas; and it was still an unmatched reference for writers into the 19th century, a founding source of English popular music.

Pleasants, Jack (*b* Bradford, 17 Aug. 1874; *d* Bradford, 26 Dec. 1923). Yorkshire comedian whose act was summed up in his best-known song, 'I'm shy, Mary Ellen, I'm shy'. He made his first professional appearance at the City of Varieties in Leeds in 1884, first appearing in London at the Bedford Music Hall in 1901. He worked in pantomime in the north of England, but was late in breaking into the south as a dialect comedian, making it with his 'shy' act billed as 'The Bashful Limit'. His other songs were 'Watching the trains go by', 'Feeding the ducks in the park', 'Rocking the baby to sleep', 'Norman the Mormon', and 'I'm twenty-one today'.

Police. British rock group founded in 1977 by American drummer Stewart Copeland (*b* 16 July 1952) with Sting [Gordon Sumner] (*b* 27 Oct. 1951) (bass and vocal) and Andy Summers (*b* 31 Dec. 1942) (guitar). Their first recording was 'Fall out' (1977) but they found their *reggae-based style with 'Roxanne' in 1978 which was popular in the USA before they became well-known in the UK. They achieved two No. 1 hit singles in 1979 and a No. 1 album, *Regatta de Blanc* (featuring 'Walking on the moon'), which gained them an international reputation. This was followed by *Zenyatta Mondatta* (1980—featuring 'Don't stand so close to me'); *Ghost in the Machine* (1981), and *Synchronicity* (1983—containing two of their best numbers 'Every breath you take' and 'Wrapped around your finger'). Individual activities by various members of the band interrupted any further developments and their course became uncertain.

Polka. A lively and energetic dance which, like many of its kind and period, derived from a peasant round dance, first heard of in Bohemia around 1830. As a ballroom dance for couples it appeared in Prague in 1837 and then spread rapidly, reaching Vienna and St Petersburg two years later, Paris in 1840, London in 1844 (*Punch* printed a wrily humorous article in 1845, 'History, Symptoms, and Progress, of the Polkamania'), and New York the same year where it was introduced at the Chatham Theatre in May. This led to many unsubtle jokes when James Knox Polk was elected President in 1845.

The dance was in 2/4 time in two-bar phrases, with hopping steps on the first three half-beats and a pause on the fourth. Much of its early success was due to the many polkas written by Johann *Strauss and his family, his first being the 'Sperl polka', op. 133. Perhaps the most popular example written in Britain was George *Grossmith's 'See me dance the polka' which became the prototype tune. Many variants evolved, the Strauss family in particular differentiating between such types as the polka-schnell, the polka-française, and the polka-mazurka, which was in 3/4 time. The polka became used, like many dances, in more extended works, notably by Smetana who wrote many, including famous examples in his opera *The Bartered Bride* and in his string quartet 'From my life'.

Pollack, Ben (*b* Chicago, 22 June 1903; *d* Palm Springs, Calif., 7 June 1971). American drummer and bandleader. He started his drumming career in Chicago in the 1920s and was with the *New Orleans Rhythm Kings at the Friars Inn. He worked with Harry Bastin in Los Angeles 1923–4, took over the band at the Venice Ballroom 1924–5, and returned with it to Chicago in 1926. He started making records in 1926, using such star soloists as Benny *Goodman, Jack *Teagarden, Glenn *Miller, Jimmy *McPartland, Fud Livingston (1906–57), and Charlie *Spivak (1907–82). It was reckoned one of the best big bands of the 1920s and Pollack earned himself the title of 'The Father of Swing'. In the 1930s he was leading a band that contained the nucleus of the Bob *Crosby band who left him in 1934 to form that co-operative unit. The band he formed in 1936 included Harry *James, Irving Fazola, and Muggsy *Spanier. He left the jazz world in the 1940s to run a theatrical agency and a record company, but came back with the revival in the late 1940s and early 1950s and appeared in the 1956 film *The Benny Goodman Story*. In the 1960s he ran a restaurant in Hollywood and managed a nightclub in Palm Springs. Running into financial and personal problems, he ended a notable career by hanging himself. His compositions included the standard 'Tin Roof blues'.

Pollack, Lew (*b* New York, 16 June 1896; *d* Hollywood, 18 Jan. 1946). American composer. At 14 he was a boy soprano in the Walter Damrosch choir and worked as a pianist in silent film theatres. He became a professional pianist and began to write songs for his own vaudeville act. A pioneer writer for films in both the silent and talkie eras, his compositions included: 'That's a-plenty' (1914), 'My Yiddishe momme' (1925, *w* Jack *Yellen), 'Cheatin' on me' (1925, Yellen), 'Charmaine' (with Erno *Rapee, 1926), 'Miss Annabelle Lee' (with Harry *Richman, 1927), 'Some sweet day' (with Nathaniel Shilkret, 1929), 'Sing, baby, sing' (in the film of the same name, 1936), 'At the codfish ball' (1936), 'You're slightly terrific' (1936).

'Polly Perkins of Paddington Green'. Song adapted by, and with words by Harry *Clifton, published by Hopwood & Crew in 1863. It is based on an old folk melody, generally known as 'Nightingales sing', which is to be found in various collections. Soon after 'Polly' was published, the Newcastle poet-comedian George Ridley (1834–64), who also wrote 'Blaydon Races', adapted the same air for his Tyneside ditty 'Cushie Butterfield', thus giving the catchy tune a double dose of immortality.

Pomus, Doc [Jerome Solon Feldor] (*b* New York, 27 June 1930; *d* New York, 14 Mar. 1991). American songwriter. A polio victim, in a wheelchair from an early stage in life, he was to become one of the most prolific writers of the pioneering days of pop, in partnership with Mort *Shuman. Before their collaboration, Pomus had recorded blues in the 1940s and early 1950s, and had written 'Still in love' (1951), 'Boogie woogie country girl' (1955), recorded by Joe *Turner, and 'Lonely Avenue' for Ray *Charles. He had a Top 10 hit with 'Young blood' (1957), recorded by the *Coasters. The two joined forces in 1957 and had their first hit in 1959 with 'A teenager in love'; followed by a No. 1 hit 'Save the last dance for me' (the *Drifters) (1960).

Rivalling the *Leiber and Stoller partnership, they inspired many other writers, in both the USA and Britain, where an entire *Oh Boy!* programme on TV was devoted to their output. This included the Elvis *Presley hits 'Mess of blues' (1960); 'Surrender' (1961); 'She's not you' (1962); 'Viva Las Vegas' (1964); and for others 'This magic moment' (1960) and 'I count the tears' (1961) (the Drifters); 'Seven day weekend' (1962); and several collaborations with Phil *Spector. The partnership ended around 1965.

Pop. While the use of the word 'popular' in relation to the lighter forms of music goes back to the mid-19th century, the abbreviation 'pop' was not in general use as a generic term until the 1950s when it was adopted as the umbrella name for a special kind of musical product aimed at a teenage market. It had previously been applied, as an abbreviation, to such singers as Bing *Crosby and Frank *Sinatra who first began, beside their adult appeal, to have a special appeal to the young bobby-soxers of the 1930s and 1940s. The first true pop recording was probably 'Cry' by Johnnie *Ray; this linked the ballad era of the pop-singers like Crosby and Sinatra to the *rock and roll boom of the 1950s, which began with Bill *Haley's 'Rock around the clock' in 1954. Quite suddenly a special market was identified and the popular song was mainly slanted towards teenagers, now a big-spending generation, with little regard for more adult tastes.

Pop music was created by the grafting of the emotive and rhythmic elements of the *blues, as heard in the *rhythm 'n' blues *race recordings, on to the basic folk elements of Country and Western music and such primitive jazz forms as *boogie-woogie. The resulting mixture was labelled, after Haley, as rock and roll. In 1956, Elvis *Presley became the first great pop star in the modern sense, moving with the times from being a country singer to being the first singer of importance in the new hybrid form of rock. His recording of 'Heartbreak Hotel' was one of the first million-selling genuine pop records. He was not the only country singer to turn to rock; others were the *Everly Brothers, Conway *Twitty, Johnny *Cash, Jerry Lee *Lewis, all *Nashville, based and later mostly returning to their first allegiance.

The expanding rock market now also created an opening for the rhythm 'n' blues artists, previously only noticed by a few progressive blues aficionados like Alexis *Korner, and largely aimed at a black market, whose products now sold as an offshoot of the pop boom. Such singers as Fats *Domino, *Little Richard, and Chuck *Berry became pop stars, albeit of a flavour that had a rather more cultish appeal.

Presley was followed by many imitators like Gene *Vincent, at the same time opening a market for the youthful high-school vocalists who only a few years earlier would have been following in the steps of Crosby, Perry *Como, and Eddie *Fisher. These included Frankie *Avalon, Paul *Anka, and Ricky *Nelson, with Brenda *Lee and Connie *Francis their female counterparts. The theme, as ever, was love; but the simple difference was that it was now teenage love and all its special frustrations. The accompaniments to the singers became increasingly rhythmical, adapted from black groups like the *Platters, and was now often referred to as 'beat' music, a term gradually superseded by 'pop'. The record companies were soon putting most of their popular music resources into the teenage field and the 1950s fashion was star soloists backed by small electronic groups capable of as much noise as a full orchestra. By the end of the 1950s the best-selling names were the Fleetwoods, Bobby *Darin, Paul Anka, the *Coasters, Frankie Avalon, and the Platters. Britain had added *skiffle to its pop ingredients, after the 1956 success of Lonnie *Donegan's 'Rock Island Line' which was followed, in similar kind, by such artists as Tommy *Steele with 'Rock with the Caveman' and 'Singing the blues', and Laurie London with 'He's got the whole world in his hands'. At this stage Britain was very much a *cover-version market and most of its stars, like Cliff *Richard, Marty Wilde, Billy *Fury, and Adam *Faith (who became a leading figure after a *Face to Face* television interview with John Freeman), were using American material and following in the steps of Presley, Eddie *Cochran, and Buddy *Holly.

The 1960s began with names like Roy *Orbison (with Presley now a veteran of some 30 top hits) and Del Shannon (1939–90) with his long-surviving 'Runaway' (1961); in 1960 the *twist became a new flavour with Chubby *Checker's recording of 'The twist' sparking off an international dance craze. But the biggest pop boom so far came with the emergence of the British Mersey beat sound, a peculiarly British form of pop which merged rock and roll, rhythm 'n' blues, and skiffle into something far more imaginative than the thumping and twanging accompaniments that pop music had used so far. With the *Beatles in the lead, the Liverpool sound not only conquered Britain, but also the USA and the rest of the world in an upsurge of British musical influence not known since the days of the *Gaiety musicals. It also changed the fashionable emphasis from the solo artist to the pop group. The sound was perpetuated by *Gerry and the Pacemakers, *Manfred Mann, the *Animals, the *Rolling Stones, swiftly followed by the hasty formation of such groups as the Dave *Clark Five, *Herman's Hermits, the *Moody Blues, the *Hollies, and many others capable of producing a No. 1 hit and a quick fortune.

It was the USA which kept the solo artist alive by producing many great folk-singers in a modern vein, headed by the introverted genius Bob *Dylan. He was the inspiration and signpost for such folk-rock singers as Tim Hardin (1941–80), Phil *Ochs, Judy *Collins, Joan *Baez, Arlo *Guthrie, and Tom *Paxton, solo stars who kept the USA exporting in the face of its enforced importation of Beatlemania. The main British exponent of pop/folk then was *Donovan. In the folk-rock phenomenon a mature influence was the work of writers like Alan Ginsberg, a parallel to modern jazz's addiction to, and rock's general debt to, the writings of Jack Kerouac.

But the group was swiftly taking hold in the USA as well, with the advent of the drugs, hippie, flower-power movement on the West Coast, the new focal point for the output of the Love Generation (whose influence on the peace moves which politicians later made, with obvious reluctance, should never be underrated). New groups, or bands, like the *Doors, the *Grateful Dead, *Velvet Underground, *Lovin' Spoonful, and soloists like Frank *Zappa, emerged in a new-found psychedelic ambience.

Back in the mainstream of pop music were the balladists who filled the spaces between folk and Californian rock, and became some of the biggest names in pop—the *Simon and Garfunkel partnership, and the *Beach Boys (inspired perhaps by the *Four Freshmen, and America's answer to the Beatles) who made their own clear mark in albums like *Pet Sounds* (1966). In the same niche came the *Mamas and the Papas and the 5th Dimension. The affluence of the British rock scene was reflected in the spending spree area of Carnaby Street. The psychedelic influence, with its flashing lights and eternal muzak, was the background to the modern rock group like the *Who whose recording of 'My generation' became the latest anthem and set the tone of a TV show called *Ready, Steady, Go!* In the USA the well-dressed image of the Beatles was taken over by a clean-limbed young group, one of whose heartthrobs was British, called the *Monkees.

One of the big changes of the late 1960s was in the instrumental backing. Long gone were the country-based backings of guitars and drums and there was a constant search for new instrumental combinations, as heard in the flute-based sound of *Jethro Tull and the brass of *Blood, Sweat and Tears. But there was also still room for the traditional approach as the *Cream showed, with its reliance on pure instrumental talent in the shape of Eric *Clapton and his friends. Other successful British groups of the late 1960s were *Traffic, Small Faces, and *Pink Floyd.

Folk-rock also diversified its nature in the work of *Fairport Convention, Steeleye Span, Joni *Mitchell, and Leonard *Cohen, while the rhythm 'n' blues artists like Jimi *Hendrix and John *Mayall still maintained a big following. The adult approach was mainly maintained in the soul-oriented black world of *Tamla Motown recordings, a maturer genre which would perhaps not want to be brought in under the name of pop.

Side products of the pop boom of the 1960s were the rock musicals like *Tommy* (1968), **Godspell* (1971), **Jesus Christ Superstar* (1971), **Hair* (1972), and **Grease* (1972). By now the whole face of the popular music business had changed. There was no longer a *Tin Pan Alley full of professional songwriters turning out the material for professional singers. There always had been singer-songwriters, but the *Beatles had made the breed almost a necessity and any songwriter worth his salt was expected to be able to make a hit record as well. The names of Harry *Nilsson, Carole *King, Neil *Diamond, Randy *Newman, Hoyt Axton (*b* 1932), and Cat Stevens were among those whose songs were still remembered for their own sake, in the way that *Kern's and *Gershwin's had once been.

The creative side flourished, and so did the electronics business, with the increasing use of synthesizers and ready-made rhythm patterns. The pop world, having established its norms, its deviants, its styles and genres, has not found, since the 1970s, any totally new direction but has continued to experiment and add new flavours and colours, notably in the use of Latin American and Caribbean rhythms (an excursion that popular music seems to take at regular intervals) as typified by the exciting sounds of *reggae music. Various fusions with folk and jazz occupy the minds of pop music's more cerebral exponents.

To the jaded ear and eye, the movements may seem to get more frantic, the words even more incoherent, and the electronic sounds more electronic. Time, however, plays its usual mellowing part. Pop and rock of the 1950s now sounds gently old-fashioned. The old pre-pop world of popular song will never return. That is now all part of that great artistic hangover known as nostalgia, and subject-matter for the reference books.

N. Cohn: *Pop from the Beginning* (London–New York, 1969). R. Mabey: *The Pop Process* (London, 1969). T. Cash: *Anatomy of Pop* (London, 1970). C. Gillett: *The Sound of the City* (New York, 1970). G. Melly: *Revolt into Style* (London, 1970). T. Jasper: *Understanding Pop* (London, 1972). K. Barnes: *Twenty Years of Pop* (Havant, Hants., 1973). M. Burnett: *Pop Music* (London, 1980). P. Taylor: *Popular Music Since 1955: a Critical Guide to the Literature* (London, 1985).

'Pop goes the weasel'. Song based on an old English dance tune of unknown origin. It was published as a dance title by Boosey & Sons in 1833 and was taken up by Charles *Sloman, the 'English improvisatore', who added the words, in the 1830s at the Coal Hole, the Cyder Cellar, and other venues. The 'weasel' (or 'weazle') was a heavy tailor's iron (or 'goose') which was frequently 'popped' (i.e. pawned) for a little ready cash at the weekends. The allusion to the Eagle Tavern (which opened in 1825)—'Up and down the City Road, in and out the Eagle)—first appeared in a version adapted by the playwright J. R. Planché (1796–1880) for a revue, *The Haymarket Spring Meeting*, in 1855. The nursery rhyme versions followed. The USA had its own versions, the first probably being *c.*1853, in which 'weasel' is used in the zoological sense—'all around the chicken coop the possum chased the weasel' (1901).

Popular music. The use of the word 'popular' in relation to the 'understanding, taste, or means of ordinary people' goes back, according to the *Oxford Dictionary* to *c.*1573. It was first linked, at least in a published title, to a certain kind of music that conformed to that criterion in William Chappell's *Popular Music of the Olden Times*, which started to appear in instalments in 1855. There was then a long gap before the 1930s and 1940s saw the beginnings of a spate of books with 'popular music' in the title, by which time everyone more or less knew what was meant. In a purely academic light the use of the word 'popular' is unsatisfactory as it suggests that what we would now deem serious or, to use another often mishandled word, 'classical' music, is not popular; and ignores the fact that much of what we would deal with under the heading of popular music is both serious and exclusive. A few decades ago it would have been simple enough to define popular music as the kind that would not normally be dealt with in reference books on classical music. Things have changed in that respect.

The areas of music covered in this present volume under the collective title of popular music include: BALLAD, BALLAD OPERA, BLUES, BRASS BAND, CABARET, CALYPSO, CIRCUS, COUNTRY, DANCE, DANCE BANDS, DRAWING-ROOM, FILM, FOLK, GOSPEL, GYPSY, JAZZ, LIGHT, MILITARY BAND, MINSTREL SHOWS, MUSICAL, MUSICAL COMEDY, MUSICAL FILMS, MUSIC-HALL, OPERETTA, POPULAR SONG, RAGTIME, REVUE, ROCK, SKIFFLE, SPIRITUALS, SWING, VAUDEVILLE, ZARZUELA.

P. Gammond and P. Clayton: *A Guide to Popular Music* (London, 1960). I. Stambler: *Encyclopedia of Popular Music* (New York, 1965). P. Czerny and H. P. Heinz: *Der Schlager*—vol. 1 (Berlin, 1968). T. Palmer: *All You Need is Love: the Story of Popular Music* (London, 1976). R. Middleton and D. Horn (eds): *Popular Music 1–9* (Cambridge, 1981–9). W. Ziegenrücker and P. Wicke: *Sach Lexicon Popular Musik* (Leipzig, 1985). R. Jwaschkin: *Popular Music: a Reference Guide* (New York, 1986). D. Clarke (ed.): *The Penguin Encyclopedia of Popular Music* (London–New York, 1989). R. Middleton: *Studying Popular Music* (Milton Keynes, 1989). P. Van der Merwe: *Origins of the Popular Style: the Antecedents of Twentieth-Century Popular Music* (Oxford, 1989). P. Hardy & D. Laing: *The Faber Companion to 20th Century Popular Music* (London, 1990).

UK: E. Lee: *Music of the People: a Study of Popular Music in Great Britain* (London, 1970). S. Tracy: *Who's Who in Popular Music in Britain* (London, 1970).

USA: S. Spaeth: *A History of Popular Music in America* (New York, 1948). J. Mattfeld: *Variety Music Cavalcade 1620–1950* (New York, 1952; rev. 1962). D. Ewen: *Panorama of American Popular Music* (New York, 1957). R. D. Kinkle: *The Complete Encyclopedia of Popular Music and Jazz, 1900–1950* (4 vols) (New Rochelle, 1974). D. Ewen: *All the Years of American Popular Music* (Englewood Cliffs, NJ, 1977). A. Shaw: *The Jazz Age: Popular Music in the 1920s* (London–New York, 1987). R. Sanjek: *American Popular Music and its Business* (3 vols) (New York, 1988). C. Welch, M. Watts, and P. Guralnick: *History of Popular Music* (20 vols and index) (New York, 1989).

Popular song (British). In contrast to the story of popular song in the USA, dealt with in the next section, where the historian can make a clean start and follow the threads through a sequence of activities wholeheartedly dedicated to providing the populace with entertainment and uplift, the history of popular song in Britain is confused and follows devious paths. It is more difficult to trace a logical and purposeful course of development because the history of British music, both academic and popular, has been bedevilled by a musical snobbery that is founded in the belief that anything done in a foreign language, or having foreign roots, is unquestionably better than anything done in English or coming from home-bred stock. This belief survived almost to the end of the 19th century and partly accounts for the abyss in British musical history between Purcell and Elgar. Popular music was additionally afflicted by non-musical class distinctions which placed its activities firmly in the 'lower'-class areas of life and gave them little moral or cultural support during this same period.

This does not alter the fact that Britain has a long and distinguished heritage of popular music-making that goes back into the mists of time, and can factually be traced back to *c.*1240 when 'Sumer is icumen in' first entered the hit parade. By the reign of Henry V music was an abundant preoccupation in higher-class circles and when the king set sail on his French campaign in 1415 keen attention was given to the attendant musical activities. Henry's religious scruples did not allow him to gloat over his fallen enemies and he ordered that there should be no official songs on the subject of the Agincourt victory. Nevertheless, an 'Agincourt song' appeared and soon gained circulation. Music continued to flourish at the behest of the Court through the reigns of Edward IV and his consort Elizabeth Woodville, Richard III, who was inclined to pay his musicians more than his clergy, to Henry VIII who, in spite of his many faults and foibles, gave wholehearted support to music. He himself is credited with the composition of some popular favourites, including 'Pastime with good companye'.

Beyond the music promoted by the establishment there was, without doubt, a flourishing popular music scene, still hidden from the historical record by the anonymity of its practitioners. The 'jongleurs' of France and the equivalent minstrels in Britain began to develop their own guilds and societies, but it would be a long time before their activities in inns and at fairs and elsewhere could grow into a collective commercial activity. The authorities, perhaps sensing the revolutionary possibilities of such activities, had, by 1533, brought in a brand of censorship that was aimed at suppressing 'foolish books, ballads, rhymes, and other lewd treatises in the English tongue'. In 1537 one John Hogon became a test-case when he was arrested for putting political words to the tune of 'The hunt is up' and singing them in public. By 1557 a register of all such songs was established at Stationers' Hall, and it was made law that all printed books, ballads, rhymes, and 'treatises' (essays) had to be entered therein, not simply as a record but for approval before they could be printed and circulated. Bureaucracy had asserted its blocking power by 1560, when there were already some 796 ballads and 44 books waiting in the queue to be registered and approved.

The song 'Greensleeves' survives as one of the best-known and most durable of the popular creations of the ensuing period, its merits sufficient to overcome, to some extent, the social boundaries of popular-music making, and its history perhaps better appreciated as part of this general survey rather than as a separate entry. The first printed reference to 'Greensleeves' is in the Stationers' Hall Register dated 3 Sept. 1580, when a licence was given to one Richard Jones to print 'a newe northern Dittye of ye Ladye Greene Sleves'. On the same day a licence was also registered for Edward White to print an item called 'ye Ladye Greene Sleves', which suggests that the song might have been in oral circulation for some time before that date. There is no acknowledgement or, presumably, knowledge of its original creator. Its strong but graceful melody and distinctive harmonies ensured a wide circulation after its initial 'northern' appearance and there were soon, as is the way of folk-tunes, many local variants that have since been unearthed by scholars. Cecil Sharp noted three variations associated with the 'Bacca pipes jig', a dance performed around crossed churchwarden pipes, and a 'Wyresdale Greensleeves dance' is included in his *Morris Dance Tunes* (1907–13). It was soon, in modern parlance, a top hit. There were a number of entries for songs on the 'Greene Sleves' topic registered up to 1581, but none survived in printed form except a version known as 'The Lord of Lorne and the false Steward', licensed on 6 Oct. 1580, 'to be sung to Greensleeves' or 'Greensleeves and Pudding-Pies' which was reprinted in various 17th-century collections. A version by William Elderton, licensed on 30 May 1581, was put to political ends to bemoan treason against the young King of Scots. It was reprinted in Percy's *Reliques*.

Those who mainly benefited were the makers of *broadside ballads who used the tune over and over again as a basis of their verses. The original, which did not survive in broadside form, was included in *A Handefull of Pleasant Ditties* issued by Richard Jones in 1584 with the now familiar refrain 'Greensleeves was all my joy, Greensleeves was my delight: Greensleeves was my heart of gold, and who but Ladie Greensleeves'. By 1599 the song was such a household favourite that Shakespeare mentions it in terms of easy familiarity in *The Merry Wives of Windsor*—saying of Falstaff's intentions and promises that 'they do no more adhere and keep place together than the Hundredth Psalm to the tune of Green Sleeves'. It was mentioned in other plays as well, notably by Fletcher and Shirley, and published in many arrangements for lute, virginals, cittern, and other contemporary instruments. It was included in the 7th edition of the famous collection of dance tunes *The *Dancing Master* edited by John *Playford, as 'Green-Sleeves and Pudding-Pies'; and was in further collections by Walsh (1718) and D'Urfey (1719–20). By 1642 it was being used as a carol tune, and again in 1686, and it was used in Gay's *The Beggar's Opera* in 1728 and in at least three other ballad operas that followed. By 1769 it had been included in *Ancient and Modern Scots Songs*; in 1838 it was in *English Folk-Song and Dance*, and in 1909 in *Old Irish Folk Music and Songs*; its ancestry was now thoroughly confused. A list of all its appearances from 1580 onwards would take up several pages. It was brought back to familiar prominence in our times when Ralph Vaughan Williams (who had already used it in his opera *Sir John in Love* in 1929) produced his orchestral *Fantasia on Greensleeves*.

The confusion or overlap between what is folk-music and what is (for want of a better word) commercially contrived popular music continued until well into the 19th century, the matter greatly confused by many cheap song collections published after *c.*1825 which mixed arranged folk-songs with composed items, very often giving no proper credit to either. The process of dissemination continued, from the time of 'Greensleeves' to *'Polly Perkins', by various means. The broadside, which was an early form of popular newspaper, sometimes printed snatches of music to identify the rhythmic form of its verses, and although it did little actually to foster the development of popular music, it was a useful fringe activity that put and kept songs in circulation. Meanwhile songs and dances continued to appear as if from nowhere, certainly created at some point by one singer or musician (or a group of itinerant entertainers), then immediately filched by the next singer or musician who heard them. Creations of real, lasting merit would pass quickly throughout the country, very much as a joke will pass today from one end of the world to the other simply by being recounted over and over again. The originators of good jokes go similarly uncredited, but they are probably mainly professional writers or entertainers; and that is how popular music spread, slowly, and probably irrationally, but surely.

It would probably now require the services of a clairvoyant rather than mere ardent research to find out who wrote 'Greensleeves' and its predecessors and successors; at what inn or fair it was first heard; who first brought it to London from the far north; who first sang it professionally. All such fascinating detail is lost because, at the time, there was no interest in documenting artistic activities at this level. One of the principal outlets for song and dance would be the popular fairs like the Bartholomew Fair which dated back to a charter of 1133 granted by Henry I to a monk named Rayer who had formerly been his jester. Fairs were mainly held in early times as money-raising events by the churches, but they gradually became more secular as time went on. They were obvious centres for the exchange of freelance minstrelsy, while their booths were one of the first manifestations of organized popular entertainment.

The theatre was destined to be one of the greatest breeding-grounds of popular song and has remained so. It was the first area in which a repeat performance was expected. The first London building to be erected specifically for secular entertainment, and simply named the Theatre, was built by an actor in the Earl of Leicester's company called James Burbage and opened in the autumn of 1576. A rival house called the Curtain was built soon after. At such places the entertainment, before the great age of Elizabethan drama got under way, was described as 'moralities, jigs, and interludes' and was provided by troupes of musicians, acrobats, conjurers, and singers. A London guide written in 1576 tells us that those who went to the Theatre or the popular Paris Gardens on Bankside (later known as the Bear Garden and notorious for its brutal entertainments like bear- and bull-baiting and cock-fighting) or the Bell Savage (an extemporized playhouse in an inn yard on Ludgate Hill) would pay a penny at the gate, a further penny to get into the arena, and a third for the privilege of a seat. By the late 1500s there was generally 'excellent music and a variety of dances' to be heard and seen. But unruly behaviour and rioting were so common that the theatre earned a bad name right from the start of its history, leading to the self-righteous persecution and censorship of later days.

The *jig mentioned above as part of the entertainment was a short burlesque or comedy sung in verse and interspersed with lively dances; a development of earlier musical 'pastimes' and forerunner of the popular musical play. The name 'jig' eventually came to be used generically to cover popular folk-dances. Thomas Morley, in his *Plain and Easy Introduction to Practical Music* (1597), discusses the politer dances at some length but adds that there are other kinds of dances like hornpipes and jigs which he cannot describe in detail. In early collections of lute tunes, such as the *Fitzwilliam Virginal Book* of 1609, the folk melodies are ignored except where they have been appropriated by a professional composer, usually as the basis for a set of variations and with the tune hardly ever attributed. Popular music in those early times was a commodity like air and water that just happened to be around. Its presence was not thought of in any orderly fashion; was hardly thought of at all, in fact, until the mid-17th century when a more organized and increasingly commercial use of music became the fashion of the day. It was then that men like Playford began to see popular music as a business proposition and thus started its printed history.

The 16th century had been a period when song was 'used' rather than 'made'. Someone wrote the tune of 'Greensleeves' or 'The foggy foggy dew', but it was the words that mattered. Most early popular ditties were written the wrong way round—words being put to tunes rather than tunes to words. Music being infinitely more flexible than language, song-writing only came of age when composers started putting music to words.

It had long been the custom for songs to be inserted, by way of light relief, into stage plays; a growing trend in the mid-16th century when many playwrights also happened to be teachers and scholars and well-rounded men were interested in the arts and sciences. Nicholas Udall, the author of *Ralph Roister Doister*, was headmaster of Eton and later Westminster. He supplies the words for four songs and gives directions for two other already well-known ditties to be used. The Cambridge play *Gammer Gurton's Needle* has a drinking-song, 'Back and side go bare, go bare', which was probably already well-known at the time. Both Ben Jonson (in his comedies) and William Shakespeare (in comedy and tragedy alike) followed the established practice of inserting songs that could be sung to well-known tunes. *Hamlet* and *Othello* make use of song, with Desdemona's 'Willow song' contrived to the tune of a popular ballad; and although 'Take, oh take those lips away' in *Measure for Measure* may have the ring of a Shakespeare original, the same song is to be found in a play by Fletcher, possibly taken from a different source. But already with Shakespeare, perhaps the finest lyric-writer of all time, we have the inspiration for 'serious' composers like Morley making new settings of them and confusing the issue, for many such settings, becoming well-known, are often taken to be folk melodies. In the case of 'It was a lover and his lass', for example, Morley created the tune and with it points to the parting of the ways, for this is far from being the incantatory song of folk origin but a really well-contrived song of mixed 'art' and 'popular' ancestry.

One of the first truly important collations of popular tunes, John Playford's *The Dancing Master*, was published in 1651. The melodies that he put in concrete form in this and many further editions were to be a primary source of basic tunes used in the broadsides and broadsheets and *ballad operas of the 18th century, and as source material for the *light operas of such composers as *Shield and *Dibdin into the early 19th century.

Queen Elizabeth had banned the use of religious themes in drama in 1559 to limit the spreading of inflammatory doctrines in the theatre. The growing disrepute of the theatre in the next few years saw a puritanical reaction start to take shape when even the 'playing upon musical instruments' was forbidden on the Lord's Day; a puritanism that was to be equally strongly evident in the early days of American music-making. The Puritans of the Commonwealth Government really clamped down in 1657, to the great concern of Playford and his friends, by making it illegal for any 'person or persons commonly called Fiddlers or Minstrels' to perform in inns, alehouses, and taverns, for in doing so they would be adjudged 'rogues, vagabonds, and sturdy beggars'. The waits or town bands had been a flourishing phenomenon of the 17th century. These too were banned by the Puritans; lumped together with 'all lewd and obscene songs'. With the Restoration of 1660, the laws were relaxed and Playford and his 'dancing master' interests breathed freely again. The Puritans were fighting a losing battle, anyway, because music was getting a hold on the populace and was becoming a widespread domestic pastime. Pepys noted in 1666 that one in three of the boats fleeing from the Great Fire of London carried 'a set of virginals' among its other furniture.

The serious composers now took English song towards a golden age, finding new subtleties in word-setting, using appropriate tempos and keys, correct inflections and cadences, underlaying it all with suitable harmony. The popular market's sights remained obstinately low. Polite upper- and middle-class society liked to claim addiction to Lawes and Purcell; but the lower classes and those who did not aspire to the heights of music and literature (which was probably 90 per cent of the population, as it is today) enjoyed their 'culture' in the bawdy vein that was catered for by such anthologies as *Wit's Recreations* (1640 and many subsequent editions) and *Choyce Drollery* (1656).

By 1700, printed manifestations of music were rapidly proliferating. Taking into account the smaller population, there were probably as many songs per head as there are today; and probably even more personal involvement at a time when modern means of entertainment did not exist to woo people away from do-it-yourself activities. The general patterns of musical life changed very slowly up to the end of the 17th century; and only with a very slight increase of pace throughout the 18th century. The main differences are to be found in practical developments like printing and communications. The pattern of musical life in the 18th century was fairly fixed. Styles did not change much, nor were many technical advances made. The same might be said of classical music. There is no yawning gap of differences between the music of Bach and Handel, both born in 1685 and mainly active in the 18th century, and that of Mozart, born 70 years later. But after that things began to change at an ever-increasing rate in step with scientific discoveries. Movement in art, especially in popular art, shows a great dependence on the sociological background. The patronage of the upper class, which has never accounted for more than about 1 per cent of the population in numbers but a disproportionate (though constantly dwindling) amount of its wealth, had a considerable influence on the course of classical music.

It was to be the middle-class areas of the population that initially had the greatest influence on the propagation and spread of a popular music culture and industry, up to the middle of the 19th century. Ranging from upper-middle-class employers, businessmen and financiers, the officer class, politicians, professional men like doctors and lawyers, the Church; down to the teaching profession, the arts, and even the lowest-paid clerical workers, who considered themselves middle-class because they had clean hands; these were the people who could afford, and, being educated, had the inclination, to support public music-making; who bought sheet music and the instruments to play it on; and generally responded to the arts. It was not until the mid-19th century, following on such landmarks as the Factory Act of 1833 and the Reform Act of 1867, that the working classes were able to give a proportion of their earnings to the promotion of entertainment. But when they could it was the final tip to the scales that turned a blossoming industry into a booming one.

The course of popular musical history is far less concerned with technique and theory than it is with fashion and sociological evolution. Human nature, which is the concern of popular art, has changed very little; similarly, the change in popular song though outwardly great is fundamentally small. Popular music makes most change when it is aping the world of classical music (changes most manifest in the early decades of the 20th century). Music becomes of maximum interest to the scholar where it is at its most ambitious and pretentious, which is perhaps where it becomes of minimum interest to the student of folk music.

At this point it is relevant to note the years of overlap that saw British popular music acting as a main influence on what was happening in the USA. While the former colony was already establishing its own styles, it was to remain a regular importer of British fashions at least until the end of the 19th century. Up to somewhere around mid-century a high percentage of items published in America would have emanated from London and, as far as the theatre was concerned, British shows were dominant until the 1890s. But around the 1850s there were also noticeable and growing currents in the other direction, mainly of music coming from black sources; the *minstrel shows and the *spiritual were two obvious areas in which the powers of American music became stronger than any equivalent activities in Britain. At the same time the USA was also asserting its superiority in finding the inspiration and composers to produce national songs of a high quality. The Civil War years around 1865, for example, were to produce a positive glut of inspiring songs that jockeyed for position as national anthems. The English rivals to 'God save the King' were still to come from such academic sources as Parry ('Jerusalem') and Elgar ('Land of Hope and Glory') and such songs as accompanied the professional wars that led up to the First World War were orchestrated by rather low-class jingles of the 'Tipperary' variety.

From around 1800, British popular music, although alive with activity, gradually began to lose ground as an exportable support to the balance of payments, running into the same lamented situation as the classical equivalent, long overwhelmed by Italian and German influences; and indeed into the 20th-century situation of British industry as a whole.

And yet the beginning of the 19th century was also the point at which commercial popular music really found its own identity in Britain. An area that was important to this growth was to be found in the pleasure gardens that were popular in London and elsewhere. Gardens such as were to be found at *Vauxhall had been dominated for much of their history by classical composers and musical directors such as Handel and Arne. By the early 1800s their entertainment was becoming more middlebrow and of the 'drawing-room' variety and, by the 1830s, was having to aim at a decidedly lowbrow audience. The first popular illustrated *music covers were those which hitherto highbrow publishers found highly marketable under the auspices of Vauxhall and other pleasure gardens.

As the pleasure gardens went out of fashion towards the end of the 19th century (perhaps the weather patterns changed), their place was taken over by such indoor entertainment as was offered at the song-and-supper rooms and the *music-halls that flourished from the mid-1800s and into the early 1900s. It would be superfluous to deal here, at any length, with the ensuing areas of music-making dealt with elsewhere under such headings as minstrel shows, music-hall and musical comedy or, in more middle-class spheres, as light music and drawing-room ballads. The main point at issue is that British popular music was to find itself increasingly suffering from its inborn insularity. In common with all British music, constantly infiltrated by European influences, the British mode and style has never been able to sell itself abroad, except in a temporary and diminishing way to other English-speaking countries. While this is not easy to explain, neither is the universal appeal of the black-based folk music that came from the USA and conquered the world while British music was foundering.

Looking at the music-hall songs and the songs that continued in much the same idiom from London's *Tin Pan Alley, until the remarkable world impact of the *Beatles and the Mersey sound, it can be sensed that their inward-looking quality, and hence lack of international appeal, stems from their very British flavours, whether Cockney, West or North Country (with Scottish and Irish perhaps the most exportable), lower or upper class. The music-hall song, with its almost self-conscious working-class image continued to influence the British popular song up to and after the Second World War. It is just as pointless an exercise to try to find British popular composers to pit against such names as Kern, Gershwin, or Rodgers as it is to try to choose a world-ranking British tennis team. The cause has hardly been strengthened by the fact that the names of the composers who wrote the imperishable masterpieces that graced the British music-hall would hardly be recognized by those who regularly sing their songs in their bathtubs, or by the almost equal neglect of their successors.

The identity that British song maintained up to the First World War, folky and vulgar on the one hand, loaded with the public-school accent, where it flourished in theatrical spheres, on the other, had first begun to be submerged by the Christy minstrel shows of the 1850s, then by ragtime and Dixieland strains. It was to continue the losing battle by producing items like 'Run, rabbit, run' which had nothing to add to 'Don't dilly dally on the way' and compared unfavourably with most things from 'Greensleeves' to 'Polly Perkins'. It was only when British popular song had capitulated to the American invasion and began to create in an American idiom (detectable even through a Liverpool accent) that it first enjoyed the advantage of using a universal idiom. Any chances of domination that British music had in its personalized heyday ran out at about the same time as the British Empire. But, to counteract this defeatist attitude, it is nevertheless about time that the British more fully documented and appreciated the flavours and special delights of what was achieved and, at the time, gave rise to so much national pleasure and pride.

H. Scott (ed.): *English Song Book* (London, 1926). C. Pulling: *They Were Singing: and What They Sang About* (London, 1952). M. W. Disher: *Victorian Song from Dive to Drawing-Room* (London, 1955). R. Nettel: *Seven Centuries of Popular Song* (London, 1956). C. McInnes: *Sweet Saturday Night: Pop Song 1840–120* (London, 1968). E. Lee: *Music of the People* (London, 1970).

Popular song (USA). In every possible way the conditions for the growth of a great popular music tradition in the USA were absolutely right. There was no already established hierarchy of musical influence as there had been in Europe, where the nobility (from royalty down), the Church, and the universities had a tight hold on the ways and means of musical life and were only outbid by the commercial rewards that the general public could only begin to offer well into the 19th century. America started with a clean sheet and its creations, from the start, aimed at giving pleasure to the common man. The immigrant population, from the Pilgrim Fathers on, brought in a rich offering of folk-song from various European countries and this soon became adapted for the American way of life, thought, and speech. There was some degree of opposition from the strong Puritan element, who tried to suppress secular musical and theatrical activities, but they were bound to be defeated by the needs of the populace in the end; meanwhile they gave the nation a good grounding in psalm and hymn singing which was to be a powerful ingredient in American music comparable to the Welsh tradition in Britain.

As a British colony the USA, once the puritanical restrictions had been lifted, naturally started by importing British music and theatrical works, mainly those with a broad appeal like the songs of Arne and Hook that were a great attraction at *Vauxhall and other London pleasure gardens; and the airs from such works as *The *Beggar's Opera* and *Love in a Village*. A glance at Sonneck's *Bibliography of Early Secular American Music* and similar works shows that American music prior to 1800 was either imported from Britain or was a slavish imitation. Popular items were Hook's 'Within a mile of Edinburgh Town' and a dramatic item, 'The galley slave', from *Reeve's opera *The Purse*; and both *Dibdin and *Shield were widely published.

The first native American composers were, of course, imports themselves, but they soon found an American tongue and spirit. Such a one was Benjamin Carr (1768–1831) who had arrived in the USA in 1793 after studying music with Arnold and Wesley in England. He established a family music-publishing business in Philadelphia the same year, with branches in Baltimore and New York. Carr was also an actor and appeared in *Love in a Village* in 1894. He then began to write for the stage, adapting many English works; and made his own original contribution to musical history with his 'Federal Overture' of 1794 which notably included a quote from *'Yankee-Doodle'—probably its first appearance in print. He had his own first success with 'The little sailor boy' in 1798. Another popular writer who came from London was James Hewitt (1770–1827) whose most popular song was 'The wounded Hussar' (1800), anthologized in many early 19th-century collections, closely rivalled by 'The primrose girl'. There was nothing much that was characteristically American in these works, nor in those of Alexander Reinagle (1756–1809), George K. Jackson (1745–1822), or Raynor Taylor (1747–1825) who all wrote early popular songs. Another strong foreign influence was found in the popular *Irish Melodies* of Thomas *Moore, published in the USA in 1808. They encouraged many imitations, having been liberally dispersed in various song collections of the period. 'The last rose of summer' is credited in *Songs that Never Die* (1894) with having, by then, sold $1\frac{1}{2}$ million copies; closely pursued by 'Believe me, if all those endearing young charms' and 'The harp that once through Tara's halls'. The Irish element was to become a potent one in American life and music. But, if many composers followed in the steps of Moore, there was an equally large number who followed in the Scottish steps of Burns, while Italian, German, French, Spanish, and other imports all added ingredients to what was to become American song.

The first American-born songwriters included Francis Hopkinson (1737–91), but his songs would not have sounded out of place in the London pleasure gardens. The first truly American flavour might be detected in the songs of John Hewitt (1801–90), the son of James, mentioned above, and therefore a generation away from his English heritage. He published in 1825 'The minstrel's return'd from the war' which went into many editions and still had five different versions on the market in 1870. The many songs that Hewitt published, in the years before the Civil War, began to have a distinctly American flavour. The flavour can be recognized, in hindsight, as that which came to full strength in the songs of the blackface minstrel era, with their banjo rhythms and bugle-call melodies. With the long suppression of the black people in America it is more or less impossible to tell at what point the strong influence of their entirely un-European musical strains actually permeated beyond the plantations: probably earlier than musical history is prepared to guess. It was often the outsider who most clearly sensed the distinctive American and/or Negro strain in the music of the USA, a visiting writer like Charles Dickens or a visiting composer like the Bohemian Antonin Dvořák. Paradoxically, the most characterful strains of what the world would recognize as typically American popular music in the 'Arkansas traveller' vein emerged through the colour-confused blackface *minstrel shows, where white singers with blackened faces performed in a spirit of parody but at the same time produced a new style of music which quickly spread abroad through similar activities.

The pioneering blackface minstrel Thomas Dartmouth *Rice added his mite with his 'Jump, Jim Crow' which did much to start a new craze for minstrel-style songs and became America's first international song hit around 1832. He brought it to London in 1836. In fact it was not so much the actual song, which was a hotchpotch of various folk tunes and fairly undistinguished, but what he did with it; which, after all, is one of the key differences between playing music straight in the classical style and ragging or jazzing in the popular manner.

Dan *Emmett and the minstrel missionaries who followed took their songs, music, and dances to and fro across the Atlantic. By 1859, with the emergences of that quintessentially American song *'Dixie' there was no longer any doubt as to what was American and what was not; and the tinker-tank of the banjo rhythms was part of the character. The minstrel vein was thenceforth tapped by all American composers and the English styles pushed aside; so that even a romantic ballad like B. R. Hanby's 'Darling Nellie Gray' of the 1840s somehow had a truly national flavour. From now on America firmly and fervently produced its own popular music. The psalm-singing tradition was perpetuated in the holy folk-music of singers like the *Hutchinson Family; the minstrel tradition found its master composer in Stephen *Foster, though he only allowed his early songs in the so-called Ethiopian vein to appear anonymously, or under other people's names, while he proudly acknowledged his drawing-room ballads in the old British drawing-room style. Foster, a better-trained musician than most of his chroniclers perhaps allow, was a pivotal figure simply because his drawing-room ballads tended to be mediocre and weak while his minstrel songs, both sentimental and comic, had a sturdy strength about them. The classic 'Old folks at home' of 1851 is another outstanding example of a simple tune that is essentially American. By 1852, Foster, a man of Irish extraction, had perhaps sensed the truth of the situation and, although he continued to satisfy the lingering demand for ballads in the style of Thomas Moore, he also tapped the native vein with more openness and purpose as did 'Darling Nellie Gray' by Benjamin Russell Hanby (1833–67) and the anonymous 'Yellow rose of Texas' (1858).

Now came the dramatic upheaval of the Civil War of 1861–5 that gave, just at the right time, a clear purpose to writing American songs. The battles may have been about more vital things than music, but song came into its own as a strongly motivating force as it has done time and again in moments of darkness and strife. The war established the rights of race and creed and the future path of American life. At the same time it was the motivation for such songs as 'John Brown's body' and Henry Clay *Work's 'Kingdom coming'. The strains found in 'Dixie' and the burningly patriotic *'Battle hymn of the Republic', the stirring 'Marching through Georgia', were the strains that were in the music that accompanied all America's traumas from the Gold Rush days of the 1840s to the backs-to-the-wall days of the great depression; a strain of music that was to prove itself the most vital and pervasive in the world.

The composers and writers who followed simply had to develop the strain and, on the road to Tin Pan Alley commercialism, many talents were able to rise on the demand for music and song. Such writers as Henry Tucker ('Sweet Genevieve'), Septimus *Winner ('Listen to the mocking bird'), Hart Pease Danks (1834–1903) ('Silver threads among the gold'), and Thomas Paine Westendorf (1848–1923) ('I'll take you home again Kathleen'), James Pierpoint (1822–93) ('Jingle bells'), and James Austin Butterfield (1837–91) ('When you and I were young, Maggie') were now not only writing for America, but were actually selling songs to European markets. Meantime the Fisk Jubilee Singers were introducing the world to the black strains of the *spiritual and *gospel song; and a new Stephen Foster arose in America's first successful black composer, James *Bland, a minstrel in his own right, and producer of such fine songs as 'Carry me back to old Virginny' and 'Oh, dem golden slippers'.

The establishment of a commercial music-publishing trade had the same effects in America as it had in England. Its editors straightened out the wandering line of the true folk-song and its natural harmonies, supplanting them with a common Italianized formality which, however, failed to devalue deeper inherent qualities. *Tin Pan Alley, as a whole, perhaps tends to aim lower than it needs to, pointedly producing, in the words of Charles K. *Harris, for the 'untrained musical public'. Along came the merchant composers like Harris, whose 'After the ball' sold five million copies in his lifetime, and many more after; and Gussie L. Davis and Harry *Von Tilzer—many of them publishers of their own songs on or near New York's 28th Street. Just as the music-hall was a pioneering outlet in Britain, so was vaudeville in the USA. The songs of the 1890s were in predominantly music-hall vein—'The Bowery' (Hoyt), 'After the ball' (Harris), 'Daisy Bell' (Dacre—an English arrival), 'The band played on' (Palmer; Ward)—still with a goodly proportion in 3/4 time, a metre given popularity by the Strauss family and not, as yet, outmoded. These were the days of frequent million-selling song-sheets and music-publishing was a flourishing business. Many books were published on the lines of 'How to Write a Successful Song', but aspiring writers soon found that the golden doors of Tin Pan Alley were firmly closed to the outsider.

Up to now the American song clearly lacked sophistication. The cowboy and prospector image prevailed and the natural grace of Viennese popular music was somehow lacking. The inspiration for a 'better class' of music came, as ever, from the theatre. Until the late 1890s, French and Viennese operettas and British shows from the *Gaiety Theatre and *Daly's were only gently rivalled by a few European immigrants like *Hoschna and *Kerker and Victor *Herbert. Had matters stayed as they were in the 1880s, with black music still largely suppressed, American music might well have stayed subservient to European with just a few figures like George M. *Cohan writing in an old-fashioned jingoistic vein to satisfy national needs.

But, whether America wanted it or not, the dominating influence on popular music was becoming increasingly a black one. The black entertainers gradually worked their way into the theatre and vaudeville; they ran their own bands, and they soon began to produce their own composers and publishers. The 1890s saw the emergence of the first commercially viable genuine, if watered down, black music in *ragtime, which had a novelty and vitality that could not be ignored. At the heart of the revolution were the gentle ragtime piano pieces of composers like Scott *Joplin, but the greater public influence came from the ragtime songs that were concurrently published. White composers had no option but to jump on the ragtime bandwagon and songs in a pseudo-ragtime manner became all the rage—'Wait till the sun shines, Nellie' and 'Hello, my baby'. By 1911 and 'Alexander's Ragtime Band', there had been several ragtime crazes, but this was the one that really took hold and set the whole world on the ragtime path. Irving Berlin said quite firmly, 'Everybody's doing it': and suddenly they were. Ragtime revues came into London and the old Gaiety-style shows were soon out of fashion.

Tin Pan Alley squeezed all it could out of the ragtime boom and had hardly got over its delight in that particular gold rush when along came the *Original Dixieland Jazz Band and established jazz. From pioneer songs through blackfaced minstrelsy to ragtime had been quite a small step; merely the displacement of a few beats and accents. But jazz was a total revolution; it changed the whole rhythmic emphasis, the nature of melody, the whole speech of popular music, within a few short years. At first there was a degree of resistance, as might be expected. The traditions of centuries refused to be swept away overnight. It took jazz a couple of decades to permeate popular music completely, but that was a mere flicker of time in the historical context. True jazz grew in strength as a minority interest, its virtuoso players like *Armstrong, its composers like *Ellington, its big bands and little bands winning converts all the time.

Perhaps those years before jazz swamped everything else were the most interesting and fruitful in the whole history of popular music so far. It was a period in which one of America's great white Jewish composers like Jerome *Kern could flourish. Kern's background and basic style was clearly pre-jazz, almost pre-ragtime. He was brought up on operetta and old-style musical comedy. He found a rare flavour, as many did, in the minstrel-touched strains of *Florodora* by the English composer Leslie *Stuart. Asked to add an American flavour to imported British shows, he came up with original gems like 'They didn't believe me'. In fact it was only a minor difference in dates (Kern born in 1885) that made George *Gershwin (born 1898), a brilliant successor to Kern, so different and so much more attuned to the jazz age. Gershwin wrote in a style that may not have been pure jazz but made his tunes ideal material for jazz improvisation. Moreover he bridged another gap, that between the popular and classical worlds, more successfully than anyone before or since. His piano concerto is the most frequently performed of all American concertos; his songs match Kern's in sophisticated elegance but they need a jazz-inflected voice to be performed effectively and (apart from a few) wilt under straight treatment, as Kern's wilt from jazz inflections. The first half of the 20th century was a golden age for American popular music and it was ideal for fruitful creation in having so many styles happily rubbing shoulders and providing so much written material that could be sung by amateur and professional alike. It was a period full of big composer names like Cole *Porter and Richard *Rodgers, Harold *Arlen and Harry *Warren, who could thrive in a jazz world because jazz was still a way of doing things rather than the whole thing.

In hindsight it can be seen that those Tin Pan Alley years were a time of restrained acceptance. There was a surviving white resistance to the wholesale imposition of a black idiom on popular music. The whole of the swing era was one of disciplined jazz and endless academic arguments about the comparative merits of black and white interpretation. The surviving evidence lies in the songsheets of the 1930s and round about. If you bought a song in 1935 you could play or sing it as written and produce a sound that approximated to what Bing *Crosby and the other entertainers would be producing. Today the equivalent sheet, if it exists, is nothing but a blueprint. Popular song is no longer jazz-influenced. It is totally jazz in both spirit and language and improvisational by nature.

In the 1930s it even seemed that attempts to bridge the gap between the popular and classical worlds might be making some headway. But it was a moment that passed by, and the two worlds have themselves changed their nature so much that there is very little to link them. The popular music world (discussed further under such headings as *pop, *rock, and *rhythm 'n' blues) became, from the 1950s, mainly a matter of free interpretation and newly bottled music, with the older formal styles of popular music still of historical interest, strong within themselves and as cultural links. The classical world is just the reverse, with 90 per cent of its activities the nostalgic recreation of old compositions and styles and the minority interest reserved for a brand of new creation that has no popular appeal. But then classical music itself, in commercial terms, is a minority interest only surviving on a share of the profits from such bedfellow activities as pop music, alcohol, cigarettes, and insurance.

What had once been an internal revolution in the USA's musical affairs soon became the world's concern. American popular musical styles now dominate the commercial musical world, not only in English-speaking countries but everywhere. Other countries like Britain, making a mark now and then with something like the *Mersey beat, have to accept that the root source of their pop music is American, and, moreover, black American.

D. Gilbert: *Lost Chords: the Diverting Story of American Popular Songs* (New York, 1942). N. Shapiro: *Popular Music: an Annotated Index of American Popular Songs* (9 vols) (New York, 1964–86; rev. (3 vols) Detroit, 1985). D. Ewen: *American Popular Songs: from the Revolutionary War to the Present* (New York, 1966). A. Wilder: *American Popular Song: the Great Innovators 1900–1950* (New York, 1972). M. Wilk: *They're Playing Our Song: from Jerome Kern to Stephen Sondheim* (New York, 1973). H. Pleasants: *The Great American Popular Singers* (New York, 1974). C. Hamm: *Yesterdays: Popular Song in America* (New York, 1979). B. Green: *Let's Face the Music* (London, 1989).

Music: M. Morath (ed.): *Favourite Songs of the Nine-*

ties (New York, 1973). R. Jackson (ed.): *Popular Songs of Nineteenth Century America* (New York, 1976).

Porgy and Bess. 'Folk opera' with music by George *Gershwin, book by DuBose Heyward (1885–1940), based on the play, *Porgy* (1927), by Dorothy (1890–1961) and DuBose Heyward, lyrics by Ira *Gershwin. First produced at the Colonial Theatre in Boston 30 Sept. 1935 and in New York (Alvin Theatre) 10 Oct. 1935. The cast included Todd *Duncan as Porgy, Anne Brown as Bess, Warren Coleman as Crown, and John W. Bubbles as Sportin' Life. The opera, now considered America's greatest, had a mixed reception at first, with only a modest run of 124 performances, and lost all the money invested. The serious story and integrated score made people uncertain whether it was an opera or a musical, a matter which its rich harvest of songs made unimportant in later years. These included: 'Summertime', 'A woman is a sometime thing', 'My man's gone now', 'I got plenty o' nothin'', 'Bess, you is my woman now', 'It ain't necessarily so', and 'There's a boat dat's leavin' soon for New York'.

The story is of the people of Catfish Row in Charleston, South Carolina. Porgy, a crippled beggar, falls in love with Bess, the woman of the evil Crown who has fled after killing a man. Bess has to give in to Crown but Porgy kills him. Believing that Porgy will never be freed Bess goes away with the swaggering Sportin' Life. Porgy is pardoned and the opera ends with him about to set off to find Bess again.

The next production of the work, at the Majestic Theatre, New York, 22 Jan. 1942, with the same leading actors, saw it enjoying the longest run of any revival production so far [286p]. Subsequently it made its mark in London (Stoll Theatre) 9 Oct. 1952 played by a touring company headed by William Warfield (*b* 1920) which also visited Vienna, Berlin, and Paris. *Porgy and Bess* became an international classic and was even produced in Russia in 1955 (a visit chronicled by Truman Capote) and at Glyndebourne in 1988; it was filmed in 1959 with Sidney Poitier (*b* 1924), Dorothy *Dandridge, Sammy *Davis Jr., and Pearl *Bailey; and has been successfully recorded.

F. Durham: *DuBose Heyward, the Man Who Wrote 'Porgy'* (New York, 1954). T. Capote: *The Muses are Heard* (New York, 1956). See also books listed under GERSHWIN.

Porter, Cole Albert (*b* Peru, Ind., 9 June 1891; *d* Santa Monica, Calif., 15 Oct. 1964). American composer and lyricist. Porter's grandfather was a millionaire and his father a prosperous fruit farmer working 750 acres. As a youth he dabbled in music while his family warned him of the folly of taking it up as a career. He was educated at Yale University, taking his BA in 1913, then persisted with his good intentions with regard to the family desires by studying law at Harvard. Eventually his real ambition triumphed and he switched his studies to the Harvard School of Music. While at Yale he had written college songs and music for college shows, and while still studying music he wrote a musical comedy, *See America First*, which he managed to get staged in 1916 with Clifton *Webb in the lead, but it only survived for 15 performances. He wrote some football songs and had a few items used in revues between 1910 and 1919. While spending some time in France he wrote his first hit, 'An old-fashioned garden', which was used in the Raymond *Hitchcock revue (for which he supplied the whole score), *Hitchy-Koo of 1919*. The show ran for two years and allowed him to establish himself as a composer independent of the family fortunes from which he had now been cut off. He returned to France, where he married and led a lavish society life on his wife's private fortune.

Porter was lucky to be able to write for his own enjoyment and the entertainment of friends, but gradually the items he continued to contribute to such revues as *A Night Out* (1920), *Mayfair and Montmartre* (1922), *Hitchy-Koo of 1922*, and **Greenwich Village Follies of 1924* built his reputation and he was persuaded by E. Ray Goetz to collaborate with him on a complete show, *Paris* (1928), which had such a great success, with songs like 'Let's do it' proving his talent, that he decided to take his composing seriously. A series of outstanding successes followed, for which he wrote his own lyrics as well as the music: *Fifty Million Frenchmen* (1929)—'You've got that thing', 'You do something to me'; *Wake Up and Dream* (1929)—'What is this thing called love?'; *The New Yorkers* (1930)—'Love for sale', 'Where have you been', 'Let's fly away', Go into your dance'; **Gay Divorce* (1932)—'Night and day'; **Nymph Errant* (1933)—'Experiment', 'The physician'; *Hi-Diddle-Diddle* (1934); **Anything Goes* (1934)—'I get a kick out of you', 'You're the top', 'Anything goes', 'Blow, Gabriel, blow'; *Jubilee* (1935)—'Why shouldn't I?', 'Begin the beguine', 'A picture of me without you', 'Just one of those things'; **Red, Hot and Blue* (1936)—'It's de-lovely', 'Ridin' high'; *You Never Know* (1938)—'At long last love'; **Leave it to Me!* (1938)—'Get out of town', 'My heart belongs to Daddy'; *DuBarry Was a Lady* (1939)—'Do I love you?', 'Friendship'; **Panama Hattie* (1940)—'Let's be buddies'; **Let's Face It* (1941)—'Everything I love'; *Something for the Boys* (1943); **Mexican Hayride* (1944)—'I love you'; *Seven Lively Arts* (1944)—'Ev'rytime we say goodbye'; *Around the World in Eighty Days* (1946); **Kiss Me, Kate* (1948)—'Wunderbar', 'Another op'nin', another show', 'Always true to you in my fashion', 'Brush up your Shakespeare', 'So in love'; *Out of this World* (1950); **Can-Can* (1953)—'I love Paris', 'It's all right with me'; **Silk Stockings* (1955)—'All of you', 'Paris loves lovers'.

Porter's style of songwriting was essentially sophisticated, his creation of both lyrics and music leading to an unusual degree of intimacy between the two. He had a liking for 'catalogue' songs like 'Let's do it' and 'You're the tops' in which he piled image upon image, and consciously clever songs like 'I get a kick out of you'. Like Gilbert and

Sullivan, he was uneasy in the romantic areas, often becoming over-sentimental and coy.

In 1937 he had a serious riding accident and had to undergo a series of operations, culminating in the amputation of a leg in 1956. His brilliant words and music had long been written in pain and, his wife dying in 1956, he became very much a sad recluse in the last years of his life and finally succumbed to an operation for a kidney stone.

His film scores matched his stage shows for brilliant songs and these included: *The Battle of Paris* (1929)—'They all fall in love' (his first screen number, sung by Gertrude *Lawrence); *Anything Goes* (1936); *Born to Dance* (1936)—'Easy to love' (which was introduced by James Stewart—his only singing spot in films), 'Swingin' the jinx away', 'I've got you under my skin'; *Rosalie* (1937)—'In the still of the night', 'Rosalie'; *Broadway Melody of 1940* (1940)—'I've got my eyes on you', 'I concentrate on you'; *You'll Never Get Rich* (1941)—'Since I kissed my baby goodbye', 'So near and yet so far'; *Panama Hattie* (1942); *DuBarry Was a Lady* (1943); *Let's Face It* (1943); *Something to Shout About* (1943)—'You'd be so nice to come home to'; *Hollywood Canteen* (1944)—'Don't fence me in'; *Night and Day* (1946)—a film biography with many Porter songs and Cary Grant playing the composer; *The Pirate* (1948)—'Be a clown', 'Niña'; *Stage Fright* (1950)—'The laziest gal in town'; *Kiss Me, Kate* (1953—used the whole score plus 'From this moment on'; *Anything Goes* (1956); *High Society* (1956)—'True love', 'Well, did you evah', 'Who wants to be a millionaire', 'You're sensational'; *Silk Stockings* (1957); *Les Girls* (1957); *Can-Can* (1960); and *At Long Last Love* (1975), which revived many of his songs like 'Miss Otis regrets' (1934).

D. Ewen: *The Cole Porter Story* (New York, 1965). C. Porter and R. C. Hubler: *The Cole Porter Story* (Cleveland, 1965). G. Eells: *The Life that Late he Led* (New York, 1967). B. Gill (ed. R. Kimball): *Cole: a Biographical Essay* (New York, 1971). C. Schwartz: *Cole Porter* (New York, 1977).

Music and lyrics: F. Lounsbery (ed.): *103 Lyrics of Cole Porter* (New York, 1954). C. Porter: *The Cole Porter Song Book* (New York, 1959). R. Kimball (ed.): *Music and Lyrics of Cole Porter* (New York, 1975). D. Grafton: *Red, Hot and Rich!: an Oral History of Cole Porter* (New York, 1987).

Posford, George [Ashwell, Benjamin George] (*b* Folkestone, 23 Mar. 1906; *d* Worplesdon, Surrey, 24 Apr. 1976). British composer and conductor. Educated at Downside and Christ's College, Cambridge, he studied the law but decided to become a professional composer in 1930. At first he specialized in music for radio, often working in collaboration with Erich *Maschwitz, then Director of Variety at the BBC. He moved into theatre work, writing many wartime revues for Jack *Hulbert and Cicely *Courtneidge. During the Second World War he was in the London Fire Service and the Royal Corps of Signals, later in the Overseas Recorded Broadcasting Service.

His theatre scores included: *Gay Hussar* (1933)—'Ballerina, sad and lonely', revised as *Balalaika* (1936)—'At the balalaika'; *Paprika* (1938), revised as *Magyar Melody* (1939); *Full Swing* (1942); *Evangeline* (1946); **Zip Goes a Million* (1952); and *Happy Holiday* (1954). He contributed to *More New Faces* (1941)—'Room 504' (*w* Maschwitz); *New Ambassadors Revue* (1943)—'Biking in bloomers in Battersea Park'; and *Masquerade* (1948)—'Bird on the wing'. He wrote music for the films *Goodnight Vienna* (1932; *Magic Night* in US)—'Goodnight Vienna'; *Born Lucky* (1932); *The Good Companions* (1933); *Invitation to the Waltz* (1935); *The Gay Desperado* (1936); *Café Colette* (1937; *Danger in Paris* in US)—'What have you done to my heart'; *It's Not Cricket* (1937); *Surprise Broadcast* (1941)—'Anything can happen to your heart'; and *Gaiety George* (1946; *Showtime* in US). He also wrote 'Song of the Clyde' (1941); 'Transatlantic rhapsody' (1942), written to celebrate the maiden voyage of the *Queen Mary*; and the rhapsody 'Broadcasting House' (1952).

Powell, Bud [Earl] (*b* New York, 27 Sept. 1924; *d* New York, 31 July 1966). American jazz pianist. The son of a bandleader, he left school at 15 to work with local bands in New York and played with the Cootie *Williams band 1943–4. Gradually he abandoned his early imitative *stride piano style, based on such pianists as Art *Tatum, Billy Kyle, Earl *Hines, and Mel Powell, and moved into bebop, to become one of the leading piano stylists of modern jazz, playing with Dizzy *Gillespie, Don Byas, and others, and becoming one of the regular pioneering experimenters at *Minton's. Gathering some of his new ideas from Thelonious *Monk, he in turn was to influence such players as Horace *Silver and George Wallington. His brief career was dogged by nervous disorders, persecution mania, and the use of drugs, and there were long periods of musical inactivity; but between times he managed to record some fine trio performances in 1947 and 1953 which give a good idea of his exciting potential. He worked mainly in Paris 1959–64 but was inactive 1963–4 and returned to spend his final years in the USA, his playing much in decline. He wrote 'Budo' and other jazz themes.

Powell, Dick [Richard Ewing] (*b* Mountain View, Ark., 14 Nov. 1904; *d* Hollywood, 3 Jan. 1963). American actor and singer. He started a film career as a wavy-haired, fresh-looking, juvenile singer, coming to sudden fame with his appearance in the film *42nd Street* (1933), one of seven films he was to make with Ruby *Keeler, in which he sang 'Young and healthy'. He continued to fame and fortune in such films as *Gold Diggers of 1933*, *Footlight Parade* (1933), Dames (1934)—'I only have eyes for you', *Flirtation Walk* (1934), *Shipmates Forever* (1935), and *Colleen* (1936), all with Keeler; others included *Broadway Gondolier* (1935)—'Lulu's back in town'; *Gold Diggers of 1937* (1936); *On the Avenue* (1937)—'I've got my love to keep me warm'; *Hollywood Hotel* (1937); *Hard to Get* (1938)—'You must have been a beautiful baby'; *Going Places*

(1938); *Naughty but Nice* (1939); *In the Navy* (1941); and *Star-spangled Rhythm* (1942)—'Hit the road to Dreamland'; more than 30 musical films in all. From being the romantic lead in musicals he later became the steely-eyed, unshaven, tough-guy detective in some first-rate thrillers, ending his career as producer and director.

Powell, Eleanor Torrey (*b* Springfield, Mass., 21 Nov. 1910; *d* 11 Feb. 1982). American actress, dancer, and singer. At the age of 13 she was with the Gus *Edwards troupe in Atlantic City. She became an expert and sophisticated tap-dancer, under the guidance of Jack *Donahue, and got to Broadway in such shows as *The Optimists* (1928); **Follow Thru* (1929); *Fine and Dandy* (1930); *Hot-Cha* (1932); and *At Home Abroad* (1935). Starting as a singer and dancer before attaining major roles, her subsequent career was mainly in films such as **George White's Scandals* (1935); **Broadway Melody of 1936* (1935); *Born to Dance* (1936); *Broadway Melody of 1938* (1937); **Rosalie* (1937); **Lady Be Good* (1941); *Ship Ahoy* (1942); and *Thousands Cheer* (1943). She appeared in nightclubs in the USA and at the London Palladium. She retired in the late 1940s but came back in a TV show in the 1950s and the 1960s.

Powell, Felix (*b* 1878; *d* Brighton, 10 Feb. 1942). British composer and entertainer. A modest career was made noteworthy by his composition of one of the most lasting songs of the First World War, 'Pack up your troubles in your old kit bag' (1915), with words by George Asaff, pen-name of his brother George Henry Powell (1880–1951). Having written this supreme piece of optimism, it was ironic that he committed suicide in 1942, in despair at the world's commitment to yet another war to end wars.

Powell, Jane [Burce, Suzanne] (*b* Portland, Oreg., 1 Apr. 1929). American singer. She took on the name of Jane Powell as a teenage singer on Portland radio. At 14 she was heard on Hollywood radio and was given an MGM contract. Small, attractive, and possessed of a good soprano voice, she starred in many films as a juvenile, gradually maturing into older parts in *Three Sailors and a Girl* (1953); **Seven Brides for Seven Brothers* (1954); **Hit the Deck* (1955); *The Girl Most Likely* (1957); and *The Female Animal* (1958). She left films after this and worked in clubs and on TV. Later she replaced Debbie *Reynolds in the revival of **Irene* (1973).

Powers, James T. [McGovern, James] (*b* New York, 26 Apr. 1862; *d* New York, 10 Feb. 1943). American actor and singer. Described as a 'small, red-headed, rubber-faced comedian', he learned his trade on the vaudeville stage and in circuses, before playing leading roles in a number of farces in the 1880s. He spent several years as the principal comedian of the Casino Theatre company. In the 1890s he moved into the musical field when a steady stream of musical comedies were being imported from London, most of them having a traditional 'funny' role that was a legacy of the comic traditions of the Savoy operas and roles that used to be played by *Grossmith and *Lytton. Powers appeared in *The *Circus Girl* (1897); *The *Geisha* (1897); *A *Runaway Girl* (1898); **San Toy* (1900); *The Messenger Boy* (1901); and *Havana* (1909). Latterly he returned to straight comedy.

J. T. Powers: *Twinkle Little Star* (New York, 1939).

Prado, Perez Damaso (*b* Matanzas, Cuba, 11 Dec. 1916; *d* Mexico City, 14 Sept. 1989). Cuban bandleader, composer, and arranger. He worked in his teens as pianist and arranger with the Orquesta Casino de la Playa in Havana. As early as 1943 he was fascinated by the possibilities of the *mambo, a combination of Mexican music, the Cuban *rumba, and American swing. It had been introduced in Mexico by the bands of Anselmo Sacasas and Julio Gutierrez, but it was Prado who popularized it in Cuba in his arrangements for the Orquesta. In 1948 he formed his own band, which was a great success throughout Latin America and recorded for RCA's South American subsidiary.

At this time he began to write a series of now classic mambos. By 1950 he was based in Mexico City and had his first international hit with 'Mambo jambo (Que rico el mambo)', which then seemed a startling musical innovation, and sparked off a host of imitations in the mambo craze that followed. It led to tours in the USA and a string of recordings for RCA Victor. He established an original musical identity, using such varied items as 'More more mambo' (1955), the million-sellers 'Cherry pink and apple blossom white' (1955), by *Louiguy, and his own 'Patricia' (1958); adapting such standards as 'La paloma' (Yradier), 'Estrellita' (Manuel Ponce, 1886–1948), 'La cucharacha', and 'La golondrina' (Narciso Serradell, 1843–1910); and combining the Latin idiom with organ and rock rhythms.

Presley, Elvis Aron (*b* Tupelo, Miss., 8 Jan. 1935; *d* Memphis, 16 Aug. 1977). American singer and actor. While the world was still feeling the shock waves of Bill *Haley's Comets and 'Rock around the clock', Elvis Presley suddenly emerged, and almost from the start he was to be the 'King' of rock. Even in his early Sun label days he toured as 'The King of Western Bop', and, despite the troughs of the early and middle 1960s, his popularity scarcely waned. Now he is remembered as the earliest and greatest exponent of rock and roll music.

His discovery had all the improbability and romance of a fictional biography, happening as the result of a visit to a Memphis recording service studio where he had paid to cut a disc for his mother's birthday. Presley was everything and more that Sam Philips (*b* 1923), who had recently started the Sun label, was looking for: good-looking, moody, and, above all, a white singer with a black sound and a unique feeling for the blues. He had a flexible charm, as Colonel Parker, his manager, demonstrated later in his career when he transformed him from a sullen rebel into the clean-cut American GI hero. And he possessed a fine, rich voice, a good musical ear, and a great love of music.

The Sun recordings are now universally considered to be the cream of Presley's work. The distinctive Sun sound, a combination of primitive but effective recording and applied echo techniques, and Elvis's high and clear voice production, with breathless and, for the time, eccentric and inventive phrasing, caused an immediate sensation. The style of Presley's early recordings might be traced back to the two musical cultures of the Mississippi River region: the black slave and work song, culminating in the blues; and the white country style of rapid banjo and guitar picking. He later attributed much of his manner to his religious gospel-singing background, listening to the local radio stations and to the blues singers Big Bill *Broonzy and Big Boy Crudup especially.

Elvis's first genuine rock recording for Sun, Crudup's 'That's all right, mama' (1954), was played by local DJs who had to explain that he was not black. This, and his appearance in country shows, brought him to the attention of 'Colonel' Tom Parker who, towards the end of 1955, became his manager. He wrested Presley away from Sun records, who sold his contract to RCA for $35,000. RCA had the promotion and distribution to turn him into a pop idol. To promote his first RCA release 'I was the one'/'Heartbreak Hotel' he was booked for six weeks on Jackie *Gleason's prime-time TV show. It was 'Heartbreak Hotel', a song of utter gloom and despondency, that caught the imagination of the public and became an immediate million-seller.

From 1956 to 1958, Presley not only dominated the pop music industry but also became the media's embodiment of youthful rebellion, expected to live up to the image of his recordings. In his recordings of the period, 'Hound dog' (1956) for example, he is clearly role-playing and trying to sound mean. Compared to his early Sun recordings, he now became mannered in both his recordings and his stage performances. He increasingly substituted posturing for the real thing and rarely recaptured his original spontaneity. He was now a public property, distanced from his roots and having to live up to his pink suits and Cadillac cars. Titles of the 1956–8 period included: 'Blue suede shoes' (1956), 'I'm gonna sit right down and cry' (1956), 'Any way you want me' (1956), 'All shook up' (1957, by Otis Blackwell, *b* 1931), and 'Got a lot o' livin' to do' (1957).

Inevitably he became a film idol as well as a recording star, beginning with *Love Me Tender* (1956), *Loving You* (1957), *Jailhouse Rock* (1957), and *King Creole* (1958). He paved the way for other young artists: every record company in the USA was on the look-out for a new Presley, and they produced such second-hand models as Gene *Vincent and Conway *Twitty.

Presley was drafted into the army on 24 March 1958 amid great publicity and ceremony. During his two-year service, recordings cut earlier such as 'One night', 'A fool such as I', and 'Big hunk o' love' kept his name at the top of the charts. He came out with a new image, the anti-social recalcitrant replaced by a uniformed hygienically, close-cropped, and clean-cut Presley, which was how he appeared in the film *GI Blues* (1960). Most of his many later film appearances portrayed a wandering, free-thinking man whose charms made him irresistible to the female sex. His richly provocative voice and suggestive gyrations were still there in modified form in *Wild in the Country* (1961); *Blue Hawaii* (1961); *Follow That Dream* (1962); *Kid Galahad* (1962); *Girls! Girls! Girls!* (1962); *It Happened at the World's Fair* (1963); *Fun in Acapulco* (1963); *Kissin' Cousins* (1964); *Viva Las Vegas* (1964); and *Roustabout* (1964); the unalarming titles reflected how innocuous their hero had become.

By 1960 rock and roll, in its original form, had virtually disappeared. With a few exceptions like 'A mess of blues', 'His latest flame', and 'Little sister', Presley's records shared the general trend towards a softer approach and most of his new hits were ballads—'It's now or never' (1960), 'Are you lonesome tonight' (1961), 'Surrender' (1961), 'Good luck charm' (1962)—the sort of thing that underlined his romantic movies. He relied heavily on his ration of two or three films a year. In spite of being third-rate Hollywood musical fun films, they kept his image in front of a doting public. The unremarkable output of celluloid continued: *Girl Happy* (1965); *Tickle Me* (1965); *Harum Scarum* (1965); *Harem Holiday* (1965); *Frankie and Johnny* (1966); *Paradise Hawaiian Style* (1966); *Spinout* (1966); *Easy Come, Easy Go* (1967); *Double Trouble* (1967); *Speedway* (1968); *Stay Away, Joe* (1968); *Clambake* (1968); *Live a Little, Love a Little* (1968); *Charro* (1969); *The Trouble With Girls* (1970); and *Change of Habit* (1970). By 1968 he had become a recluse, losing touch with a public who longed for a return to his early form. He came out of semi-retirement to appear in his own TV show and his performances sparked the hopes of a revival. Once again he smouldered in a charismatic sort of way and he recorded an album, *From Elvis in Memphis*, that seemed to continue the rebirth.

But later appearances in Las Vegas shows failed to live up to expectations. He was becoming visibly overweight and a more self-conscious performer than he used to be, though some of his recordings maintained a middle-of-the-road quality: 'In the ghetto', 'Suspicious minds', and 'Polk salad Annie'. But his private life was now a grotesque shambles, the old story of a man ruined by fame. When his world-shattering death came, probably causing more public reaction than the death of Kennedy, his total record sales were estimated at 150 million copies. Despite the mediocrity of his films and a great deal of his recorded output, his natural musical genius remained the uppermost memory. Maybe it was simply his good fortune to get there first, but that is how such artistic revolutions happen. Subsequent heroes like the *Beatles and the *Rolling

Stones owed their existence to his trail-blazing ways; more than any other artist he shaped the future of rock and roll. His effect can be measured in the literature that has attached itself to his name, well over 50 books at the latest count.

J. Hopkins: *Elvis, a Biography* (New York, 1971). R. Matthew-Walker: *Elvis Presley: a Study in Music* (Tunbridge Wells, 1979; rev. London, 1988). N. and J. Gregory: *When Elvis Died* (Washington, 1980). J. Hopkins: *Elvis: the Final Years* (New York, 1980). A. Goldman: *Elvis* (New York, 1981). M. Hawkins and C. Escott: *Elvis Presley: the Illustrated Discography* (NY 1981).

Films: P. Lichter: *Elvis in Hollywood* (New York, 1975). S. Zmijewsky: *Films and Career of Elvis Presley* (New York, 1976). J. W. Bowser: *Starring Elvis* (New York, 1976). M. McLafferty: *Elvis Presley in Hollywood* (New York, 1989).

Preston, Robert [Mersevey, Robert] (*b* Newton Highlands, Mass., 8 June 1918; *d* 21 Mar. 1987). American actor and singer. A handsome, athletic actor who had a remarkable stage musical debut in *The *Music Man* (1957)—'Seventy-six trombones', 'Till there was you'; followed by *Ben Franklin in Paris* (1964); **I Do! I Do!* (1966)—'My cup runneth over'; and *Mack and Mabel* (1974). Previously he had appeared in many films, the musical ones including: *Moon over Burma* (1940), *Variety Girl* (1947), and *Big City* (1948); and he was in the filmed versions of *The Music Man* (1962) and **Mame* (1974).

Previn, André [Prewin, André] (*b* Berlin, 6 Apr. 1929). American pianist, conductor, and composer. Encouraged in his early musical interests by a father who was an amateur musician, at the age of six he went to the Berlin Hochschule für Musik. The part-Jewish origins of his family forced them to leave Berlin in 1938 and they lived in Paris for a while, where he continued his studies at the Paris Conservatoire. They emigrated to the USA in 1939 and settled in Los Angeles. Previn became an American citizen in 1943. Through family connections (his father's cousin Charles Previn was a musical director at Universal Studios) he was able to contribute some music to the film world while he was still a student. He became an orchestrator with the MGM studios and later was one of their musical directors. At the same time he was making a reputation and recording as a jazz pianist, playing mainly in a modern cocktail style and working with many West Coast groups. He recorded some excellent albums including a very successful treatment of **My Fair Lady* material with Shelly *Manne.

He has written or arranged many film scores, including: *Holiday in Mexico* (1946); *The Sun Comes Up* (1948); *Scene of the Crime* (1949); *Border Incident* (1949); *Tension* (1949); *Three Little Words* (1950); *Dial 1119* (1950); *Kim* (1950); *Cause for Alarm* (1951); *Small Town Girl* (1953); *The Girl Who Had Everything* (1953); **Kiss Me, Kate* (1953); *Give a Girl a Break* (1953); *Bad Day at Black Rock* (1954; Berlin Film Festival Award); *It's Always Fair Weather* (1955)—'Thanks a lot but no thanks'; **Kismet* (1955); *The Fastest Gun Alive* (1956); *Invitation to the Dance* (1956; Screen Composers Association Award); *Hot Summer Night* (1957); **Silk Stockings* (1957); *House of Numbers* (1957); **Gigi* (1958; Academy Award); **Porgy and Bess* (with Ken Darby, 1959; Academy Award); *The Subterraneans* (1960); **Bells Are Ringing* (1960); *Elmer Gantry* (1960); *The Four Horsemen of the Apocalypse* (1961); *Long Day's Journey into Night* (1962); *Two for the Seesaw* (1962); **Irma la Douce* (1963; Academy Award); *Dead Ringer* (1964); **My Fair Lady* (1964; Academy Award); *Goodbye Charlie* (1964); *Inside Daisy Clover* (1965)—'You're gonna hear from me'; *The Fortune Cookie* (1966); *Harper* (1966); *The Swinger* (1966); *Valley of the Dolls* (1967); and **Paint Your Wagon* (1969).

His interests veered more towards the classical scene over the years and he forged a new career as concert pianist and conductor, making his conducting debut in 1962 with the St Louis Symphony Orchestra. He was appointed principal conductor of the London Symphony Orchestra 1968–79 and settled in England. He wrote scores for the musicals *Coco* (1969) and *The Good Companions* (1974); and has written many orchestral and other works.

E. Greenfield: *André Previn* (Shepperton, 1973). M. Bookspan and R. Yockey: *André Previn: a Biography* (New York, 1981). A. Previn: *No Minor Chords: My Days in Hollywood* (New York, 1991)

Price, Alan (*b* Farfield, nr. Jarrow, 19 Apr. 1942). British singer and guitarist. He first came to popular attention in 1964 as a leading member of the *Animals, who had started in Newcastle as the Alan Price Trio. His work with Eric *Burdon was particularly notable. In 1965 he left the group to take up a solo career, reappearing in 1966 with the Alan Price Set and having the first of many hits with 'I put a spell on you'. He much favoured the songs of Randy *Newman and had another notable success with 'Simon Smith and his amazing dancing bear'. He appeared on TV with Georgie *Fame and they continued a successful partnership in cabaret and on record. Price appeared in such films as *O Lucky Man* (1973), for which he wrote some of the songs, and *Alfie Darling* (1974). He remembered his roots in 'Jarrow song' (1974), produced many albums, and last reached the charts in 1979 with 'Just for you'. He wrote the music for, and appeared in, a musical, *Andy Capp* ((London, Aldwych, 28 Sept. 1982), and continued an active, if less publicized, career.

Pride, Charley (*b* Sledge, Miss., 18 Mar. 1938). American country singer who was born on a cotton plantation where he taught himself to play the guitar. He hoped for a career in baseball and played for minor teams 1954–64, but then decided to become a singer. He got to Nashville and appeared with success on the **Grand Ole Opry* programme, thus becoming the first black country singer to make his mark there.

Prima, Louis (*b* New Orleans, 7 Dec. 1911; *d* New Orleans, 24 Aug. 1978). American trumpeter, bandleader, singer, composer, and author. He started to play the violin but changed to trumpet, basing his extrovert and improvisational style on King *Oliver and Louis *Armstrong, and was soon leading a band in New Orleans theatres. At the age of 19 he joined Red *Nichols and the Five Pennies and, after touring for many years, was persuaded by Guy *Lombardo to form his own band. He named it Prima's New Orleans Gang, and it included such players as Claude *Thornhill, George Brunies, Pee Wee *Russell, Ray Bauduc, Eddie Miller (1911–91), and singer Martha Raye.

He came into the limelight at the Famous Door in New York and developed a style of presentation reminiscent of Armstrong, with a lot of showmanship and novelty playing, backed up by good jazz. They appeared in such films as *Rhythm on the Range* (1936), *You Can't Have Everything* (1937), and *Rose of Washington Square* (1939). He composed 'Sing, sing, sing' (1936), which Benny *Goodman later made famous, and a number of other songs—'A Sunday kind of love' (1946), 'Oh, babe!', 'Yeah, yeah, yeah' (1950)—and instrumental items. During the Second World War he led a big swing band which increasingly featured his somewhat raucous songs in Italian dialect. Later he formed a nightclub act, 1952–61, with his wife Keely Smith (*b* 1932) and others, and became a popular feature in Las Vegas, recording for Capitol and appearing in the film *Hey Boy, Hey Girl* (1959). His last notable contribution was heard on the sound-track of Disney's *The Jungle Book* (1969).

Primrose. London musical comedy for which George *Gershwin, at the behest of George *Grossmith, wrote the music. The book was by Grossmith and Guy *Bolton and the lyrics mainly by Desmond Carter with a few contributions from Ira *Gershwin. It was produced at the Winter Garden Theatre 11 Sept. 1924, with Leslie *Henson, Heather Thatcher, and Claude Hulbert in the cast and had 255 performances. The songs mainly remembered are those to which Ira Gershwin contributed—'Some far away someone', 'Four little sirens', and 'Boy wanted'.

Prince [Nelson, Prince Rogers] (*b* Minneapolis, 7 June 1958). American pop singer and composer. From a musical family, he had formed his own band by the age of 13. Giving himself a thorough schooling in music and composing, and playing several instruments, he was contracted to Warner Brothers and issued his first album, *For You*, in 1978. His next two albums, *Dirty Mind* (1980) and *Controversy* (1981), set out to shock, with titles like 'Sexuality', 'Jack U off', and 'Head' done in a sensual style that left little to the imagination. He starred in a film, *Purple Rain* (1984), and the album from this at last made him into a top star of the fickle pop world. He continued his unabated way as a rival for top favours with Michael *Jackson, cultivating a flamboyant lifestyle in juxtaposition to Jackson's more reclusive ways.

Princess Ida or *Castle Adamant*. Comic opera in three acts with music by Arthur *Sullivan and book by W. S. *Gilbert loosely based on Tennyson's *The Princess*, produced at the Savoy Theatre, London, 5 Jan. 1884 with Durward Lely, George *Grossmith, Rutland *Barrington, Leonora *Braham, Jessie *Bond, and Sybil Grey in the cast [246p]. It was produced in New York at the Fifth Avenue Theatre 11 Feb. 1884. Although coming at a time when the G & S partnership was developing strongly, between *Iolanthe* and *The *Mikado*, it has never been one of the most popular of the series. A rather subdued score, satisfyingly integrated but lacking any really strong numbers, and a rather ponderous satire on the feminist movement, allied with its three-act form, seemed to dampen the sparkle a little. It was after this that Sullivan, knighted in 1883, revolted against the Gilbertian formula and tried to break the partnership. Gilbert responded with *The *Mikado* which was to be in their finest vein. It was filmed in 1982.

Princess Theatre, New York. A small theatre built by the *Shuberts on 39th Street, between Broadway and 6th Avenue, opened in 1913 originally as a special venue for one-act plays. This project failing, it became the home of a series of Jerome *Kern musicals that are still identified as the Princess Theatre shows. They were sophisticated and elegantly tuneful in a style that just managed to fight off the eroding vulgarities of jazz and stay attached to the operetta world, yet they were contemporary in a smart way and they set a new standard of production in the musical field. The titles were *Nobody Home* (1915); **Very Good, Eddie!* (1915); **Oh, Boy!* (1917); and **Oh, Lady! Lady!!* (1918). They were successful, but not profitable, and the theatre continued with straight plays in the 1920s before it became a cinema for a while. Renamed the Labor Stage, it produced **Pins and Needles* (1937), reverted to films, and was finally demolished in 1955.

Printemps, Yvonne [Wignolle, Yvonne] (*b* Ermont, Seine-et-Oise, 25 July 1895; *d* Paris, 18 Jan. 1977). French actress and singer. She studied singing before making her stage debut in revue, immediately making a mark with her 'timid but irresistible personal charm'. Her first major theatre appearance was at the Théâtre Cigale in Paris on 8 June 1908, where she played a number of roles in the revue *Nue! Cocotte!* Her reputation was firmly established with appearances in the Folies-Bergère annual revues in 1908 and 1909; succeeded by *Ah! les Beaux Nichan!* (Alcazar, 1911); *La Revue des Folies-Bergère* (1911); *La Revue de Printemps des Folies-Bergère* (1912); *Si j'étais Roi* (Scala, 1912); *La Revue des Folies-Bergère* (1912); *Et Patati et Patata* (Capucines, 1913); *La Revue d'Olympia* (Olympia, 1913); and *Revue 1915* (Palais-Royal, 1915). She began to appear in more straight plays after this.

It was now realized that she was of star quality and she was given a leading part in Sacha Guitry's

La Nouvelle Revue (Théâtre Antoine, 1916). At the end of 1916 she appeared with Guitry in his comedy *Jean de la Fontaine*. She became his second wife in 1917 and they appeared together in many productions, he greatly helping her to become an accomplished actress. She made her first London appearance in *Nono* in 1920. Later Guitry wrote shows for her in which she could use her very individual singing talents such as *L'Amour masqué* (1923, *m* André *Messager) and *Mozart* (1926, *m* Reynaldo *Hahn), in which she made her first New York appearance in 1926. The marriage broke up in 1932. She had fallen for the actor Pierre Fresnay, and they were married in 1934 to pursue a harmonious career on stage and a turbulent one off it. They appeared together, notably, in a film on *Offenbach's life, *Valse de Paris* (1944). She played her first English role in Noël Coward's **Conversation Piece* in 1934 at Her Majesty's Theatre, having a great hit with 'I'll follow my secret heart'. Her other musical appearances included *Les Trois Valses* (1935, *m* Oscar *Straus) and various revival productions; and she appeared in nine films. Cocteau once described her as 'a typical woman of the theatre', someone who could immediately step into a part and give it flesh and blood. She carried this ability into her many recordings where she put real character into her performances as if she was still on the stage. Latterly she went into management in partnership with Fresnay at the Michodière theatre, until he died in 1975.

Procul Harum. British rock group formed in 1966 by singer and keyboard player Gary Brooker (*b* 29 May 1945) and lyricist Keith Reid (*b* 10 Oct. 1946) to exploit and record their songs. (Earlier Brooker had led a group from Southend called the Paramounts.) With its original line-up it contrived one distinctive item 'A whiter shade of pale' (1967) whose strange words and Bach-like backing made it a hit in Britain and the USA. At this stage the ongoing group was formed, after some initial changes, with Robin Trower (*b* 9 Mar. 1945) (guitar), B. J. Wilson (*b* 18 Mar. 1947) (drums), and Chris Copping (*b* 29 Aug. 1945) (bass). They continued in the art-rock vein of the 1960s with several unusual albums, generally more successful in the USA than in Britain. The group retrieved their British popularity with 'Conquistador'. Trower left in 1971; there followed a period of excellent concert appearances and such effective albums as *Grand Hotel* (1973) and *Exotic Birds and Fruit* (1974). Gradually losing their fashionable appeal, the group finally broke up in 1976. Brooker continued as a solo artist before joining Eric *Clapton in 1980.

Promises, Promises. American musical comedy with music by Burt *Bacharach, lyrics by Hal David (*b* 1921), and book by Neil *Simon, based on the film, *The Apartment*, written by Billy Wilder and I. A. L. Diamond; first produced at the Shubert Theater, New York, 1 Dec. 1968, with Jerry *Orbach, Jill O'Hara, and Larry Haines. Its nicely contrived story of the young executive who tries to gain promotion by lending his apartment to his boss for romantic evenings and falls in love with a girl who tries to commit suicide there, was successfully turned into an attractive musical comedy which ran for 1281 performances. It was Bacharach's only Broadway score but produced one of his most popular songs 'I'll never fall in love again' and the title song 'Promises, promises'. In London, with Bob Sherman, Dilys Watling, and Bernard Spear, it ran for 570 performances at the Prince of Wales Theatre from 2 Oct. 1969.

Protest song. A pop-folk phenomenon that goes back to *'Lilliburlero' and probably further. It tends to re-emerge at times of social or political unrest like the depression years, which gave rise to songs on behalf of underprivileged groups such as miners and other industrial workers in Britain and the USA. Woody *Guthrie's songs championing the poor rural workers of America became classics of the kind from this period, and a clear influence on Jack *Elliott and Bob *Dylan. A flood of such songs emerged from the indignation of American youth at their country's involvement in the Vietnam War, and from their left-wing sympathies. At that time protest had reached such a level that people were prepared to go to prison rather than suppress their ideals; and many did. Leading protesters in the USA included Joan *Baez, Phil *Ochs, and Pete *Seeger, as well as Dylan.

R. S. Denisoff: *Great Day Coming: Folk Music and the American Left* (Urbana–London, 1971). R. S. Denisoff: *Sing a Song of Social Significance* (Bowling Green, Ohio, 1972). R. S. Denisoff: *Songs of Protest, War and Peace: a Bibliography and Discography* (Santa Barbara, Calif., 1973). J. L. Rodnitsky: *Minstrels of the Dawn* (Chicago, 1976).

Pryor, Arthur (*b* St Joseph, Mo., 22 Sept. 1870; *d* Long Branch, NJ, 18 June 1942). American composer, conductor, and trombonist. After first studying the piano, violin, and cornet, he eventually took to the trombone, and at 15 was playing in local bands. In 1889 he joined the famous Liberati band and in 1890 became conductor of the Stanley Opera Company in Denver. But it was as a trombonist that his fame spread and in 1892 he was invited to join the newly formed *Sousa band, becoming assistant conductor in 1895, and staying until 1903, having played 10,000 solos that established him as one of the great trombonists of all time. Tours abroad spread his fame in Europe. He was the conductor of the Sousa band in most of their early cylinder recordings made in the late 1890s and the early 1900s. He wrote many arrangements and compositions based on the new ragtime and cakewalk style which, he claimed, Sousa was at first reluctant to accept, but eventually promoted with zest. As a trombonist, Pryor was one of the first to exploit the glissando or 'smear' that was to become so much a part of New Orleans jazz.

In 1903 he formed his own band with its players

drawn from one which his father had led since 1869 and several of Sousa's players, its first appearance being in New York on 3 November. It played for many seasons at such places as Asbury Park, New Jersey, in Miami, at Willow Grove Park in Philadelphia, and Luna Park on Coney Island, and was engaged for various fairs and exhibitions, including the World's Fair in St Louis in 1904. His own band thoroughly exploited the new syncopated style and he was very much a pioneer in the spreading of ragtime beyond its narrow origins. A prolific recording artist, he made many discs for the Victor Company of which he was, for at time, musical director. He was a founder member of *ASCAP.

Pryor's most successful composition was undoubtedly 'The whistler and his dog', first published in July 1905. Others included: 'Southern blossoms' (1898), 'Southern hospitality' (1899), 'An African beauty' (1899), 'The passing of ragtime' (1902), 'A coon band contest' (1902), 'Mister BlackMan' (1904), 'Razzazza Mazzazza' (1905), and 'Frozen Bill' (1909). He wrote several operettas, including *Jingaboo*, *On the Eve of her Wedding Day*, and *Uncle Tom's Cabin*, and a large number of trombone solos.

Puente, Tito [Ernesto Antonio] (*b* New York, 23 Apr. 1920). American bandleader, pianist, percussionist, and composer. He intended to be a dancer but had to give this up owing to an injury. He served in the navy during the Second World War, where he met bandleader Charlie *Spivak who turned his interest to big band composition. After the war he studied at Juilliard, then worked in the bands of Noro *Morales and Machito (1912–84). In 1947 he formed a group called the Piccadilly Boys, soon after becoming the Tito Puente Orchestra, and made some recordings for the Seeco label. Switching in 1948 to the Tico label he made a number of recordings in the early 1950s that established him as one of the leading figures in the *mambo craze. Later in the 1950s he exploited the *cha cha cha, transforming original Cuban material into modern big band arrangements which he now recorded for RCA.

In the crossover style that hovered between Latin American and jazz he recorded in the 1960s for Roulette such albums as *My Fair Lady Goes Latin* and *Bossa Nova by Puente*. Returning to the Tico label he had made more than 40 albums for them by the 1980s, among them the classic *Puente in Percussion*, and worked with most of the major vocalists in the field. He made his last big band LPs in 1980–1 but continued to work as a much-in-demand musician. He appeared in the influential TV film *Salsa* 79, and toured Europe with the Latin Percussion Jazz Ensemble, ranging from a quintet to an octet, recorded with them in the 1980s, and was at the Monterey Jazz Festival in 1984, by now one of the legendary figures in the Latin-jazz crossover scene. His compositions include: 'Abaniquito', 'Para los romberos', 'Oye como va', and 'Pare cochero'.

Pulitzer Prize. America's leading dramatic award was founded by Joseph Pulitzer in 1918. Its object is to choose, in the words of its constitution, 'the original American play performed in New York which shall best represent the educational value and power of the stage in raising the standards of good morals and good manners'. With these kinds of ideals it is not surprising that some of the choices have been heavily criticized, and rival awards have been set up. None the less, great prestige is attached to a Pulitzer Prize. The musical theatre has occasionally been represented and the following works have been honoured: *Street Scene* (1929); **Of Thee I Sing* (1932); **South Pacific* (1950); **Fiorello!* (1960); **How to Succeed in Business Without Really Trying* (1962); *A *Chorus Line* (1976); and **Sunday in the Park with George* (1985).

Punk rock. The name 'punk' was first attached to various youthful groups in the USA who came along in the 1960s, in the wake of The *Beatles and the *Rolling Stones, in the apparent belief that their arrogant denigration of normality, and a modicum of musical and artistic skill, were enough to make their message important. It was a part of the teenage revolution of the period and the beginning of the group identity of rock which was largely to put soloists out of business or push them into the adult entertainment world. Few of their efforts survived and the names of the groups are now virtually forgotten.

The punk movement of the 1970s was built on the same foundation of teenage revolt against the older norms of society, but this time expressed in something more than padded shoulders and greased hair. The new punks were the spearhead of a social offensive, not merely snarling at what they considered the false values of affluent and dishonest society, but blatantly out to disturb by means of behaviour, appearance, noise, and offensive language. One or two groups had enough firepower to challenge the established chart-bound groups of the 1970s, the foremost of them being the *Sex Pistols whose 1976 'Anarchy in the UK' gave notice of the general intent. Rival groups like the Clash (1976) and the Damned (1976), to name but two, seemed most intent on publicizing their outrageousness rather than anything musical, and punk came to stand for an attitude of mind rather than any special style of playing. When the movement lost its impetus in the late 1970s its residual effect could be seen as the displacement of the great rock star by a multitude of amateurish groups who all sounded, looked, and jigged alike, leaving the 1980s a muddle of mindless experiment and revolt against nothing in particular.

Purlie. Musical comedy with score by Gary Geld, book by Ossie Davis, Philip Rose, and Peter Udell, presented at the Broadway Theatre, New York, 15 Mar. 1970. Quietly launched, but well received by the critics, it became well attended on the strength of its very real merits, and ran for 688 performances. It is a study in racism; Purlie is a local black preacher who has to fight off a big-time evangelist and a bigoted plantation owner who both want to get their hands on his church. Happily Purlie not only wins the battle but gains himself a wife, Lutiebelle. Song titles were: 'Walk him up the stairs', 'New fangled preacher man', 'Purlie', 'Skinnin' a cat', 'I got love', and 'First thing Monday mornin''.

Q

Quadrille. A dance for an equal number of couples drawn up in a square, probably inspired in the first place by figured displays of horsemen at tournaments. First introduced into ballet, the dance came to the ballroom at the court of Napoleon I of France and is said to have been brought to England by Lady Jersey, a famous beauty of the day, in 1815. It was made up of a group of five country dances with different figures and differing tempos. The dance became so popular that the original folk-dances were soon replaced by arrangements of popular songs and operatic arias. The members of the Strauss family made many such arrangements as well as writing original quadrilles, strongly challenged for supremacy by the Tolbecque dynasty and by conductor-composer Philippe Musard (1792–1859), who earned himself the title 'King of the Quadrilles'. The dance did not retain its popularity much beyond the middle of the 19th century when it lost in favour to the less difficult but similarly styled *lancers. For a while the names, quadrilles and lancers, were often indiscriminately exchanged, the latter being more favoured in the USA.

Quaker Girl, The. Musical play with score by Lionel *Monckton, book by James T. Tanner (1859–1915), lyrics by Adrian *Ross and Percy *Greenbank. Produced at the Adelphi Theatre, London, 5 Nov. 1910, with a cast that included Gertie *Millar, Joseph *Coyne, and C. Hayden *Coffin, it ran for 536 performances.

One of Gertie Millar's best starring roles, it weaves its plot around a demure Quaker lass from a well-ordered community in an English village. Her life, and everyone else's, is disrupted by the arrival of a distinguished royal lady whose entourage includes a handsome lad named Tony from the American embassy in Paris who is greatly attracted by the Quaker maid Prudence. Betraying her name, she decides to break away from her restricted life and goes off to Paris with another of the entourage, a dress designer who sees commercial possibilities in the Quaker dress. There Prudence becomes involved with a prince, but she is restored to Tony in the end.

A generally attractive but forgettable score found its hit number in the insidious 'Come to the ball'. It was staged in New York (Park Theatre) 23 Oct. 1911 [240p], and had British revivals in 1934, 1944, and 1945.

Queen. British art-rock group formed in 1971 by drummer Roger Taylor (*b* 26 July 1949) and guitarist Brian May (*b* 19 July 1947), originally under the name of Smile. They began to record with EMI in 1973, featured as a sophisticated heavy metal outfit, and had their first hit with 'Seven seas of Rye' in 1974. Their albums *Sheer Heart Attack* (1974), *A Night at the Opera* (1975—a clever mixture of rock and opera, featuring 'Bohemian rhapsody', which became a No. 1 hit), and *A Day at the Races* (1976) established them as fashionable favourites of the 1970s. Further albums confirmed their saleability, as did the top hit 'Under pressure' (1981) recorded with David *Bowie. Their success continued into the 1980s. Their lead singer, Freddie Mercury (1946–91), always a dominant figure, became a pop hero after dying of Aids. A concert to raise funds for those thus afflicted was held at Wembley in 1992 in Mercury's memory.

L. Pryce: *Queen* (London, 1976). G. Tremlett: *The Queen Story* (London, 1978). J. Davis: *Queen* (New York, 1981). M. West: *Queen: the First Ten Years* (Manchester, 1981).

Quickstep. The most popular modern ballroom dance and basically the simplest. With a slight syncopation derived from dances like the *Charleston, it is a development of the *foxtrot, being called, by 1924, the quick or quick-time foxtrot, taking on its modern name sometime after 1927. It is danced to music in common time, with the 1st and 3rd beats emphasized, at a tempo of 48–50 bars a minute. Each slow step occupies two beats and each quick step one beat; and the basic figures used are the walk, quarter-turn, right or natural turn, left or reverse turn, various chassés, and the zig-zag.

Quintette du Hot Club de France. French jazz group that came into being in 1934, loosely associated with the Hot Club de France, a society of enthusiasts founded by Hugues *Panassié in 1932. It featured the remarkable talents of the gypsy guitarist Django *Reinhardt and the virtuoso fiddler Stéphane *Grappelli, who were among the first Europeans to make a really individual and un-American contribution to the jazz scene.

R

Race records. In 1916 the *Chicago Defender* started a campaign on behalf of its black readers to have the 'race's great artists' recorded. No consistent policy in this direction was seen until 1920 when the Okeh label put out a first recording of two songs by the black composer Perry *Bradford sung by the black singer Mamie *Smith. Sales response was generally good and one record of 'Crazy blues' became a best-seller. In 1921, Harry Pace started the Black Swan label, advertised as 'the only Genuine Colored Record' and Okeh started a special 'colored catalogue'. Echoing the newspaper's campaign of 1916 a *Chicago Defender* advertisement of 1922 invited customers to ask for 'our complete list of Okeh race records', and by 1923 the term had caught on. Most of the big companies issued special race series well into the 1940s, after which the music they had been marketing became known as *rhythm 'n' blues, part of the big *pop music explosion, and there was no further need for the distinction.

Radio and TV. The great boost to the sales of popular music and its wider dissemination that had resulted from the growth of the gramophone and recorded music was further enhanced by the introduction of radio. The pioneer inventor of radio, Guglielmo Marconi (1847–1937), came to England in 1896 and founded the Marconi Company in 1897. The first actual 'broadcast' had been achieved by an American, R. Fessenden, in 1906, and by the end of 1916 the American Radio and Research Corporation was broadcasting music two or three times a week. The first regular broadcasting station in the USA, station KDKA, Pittsburgh, began its operations in 1920, and that year the first European broadcasts were made from The Hague, and the Marconi Company started to operate from Chelmsford. Their broadcasts began on a regular basis in 1922 and their first programmes from the 2LO station in London began on 11 May 1922. It was decided that broadcasting should come under the jurisdiction of the Post Office and a syndicate called the British Broadcasting Company was formed and put out its first broadcast from 2LO at Savoy Hill on 14 Nov. 1922, though not fully licensed until the beginning of 1923. Already the press and government alike were worried about the new powers of radio and it was controlled in 1926 by a royal charter which instituted the artistically independent but financially controlled (through licence fees) British Broadcasting Corporation in 1926, run by a Chairman and eight governors appointed by the Crown, with a Director-General as its chief executive. In 1922 there had been some 35,000 wireless licences held; by 1926 there were already well over 2 million; and, by the 1960s, around 16 million. Whereas the USA had always allowed radio to run on a freely commercial basis, relying on advertising, the BBC monopoly was not officially broken until the advent of commercial TV in 1954, when it first shared the outlets with the Independent Television Authority which leased its transmitting stations to various commercial companies.

The advent of regular broadcasting in the 1920s caused a boom in the dance-band field as these were among the first entertainment units to appear regularly, in the UK and the USA, bringing well-known society orchestras to the studios for late-night listening. The first British dance music programme went out before the opening of the Savoy Hill station in 1923 by a 9-strong Wireless Orchestra. One of the earliest regular BBC broadcasting bands was led by Bert Firman (*b* 1906) who had a twice-weekly programme from 1926 to 1928, when the BBC Dance Orchestra was formed under the leadership of Jack *Payne and, later, Henry *Hall. Carroll *Gibbons was another regular broadcaster. A BBC Military Band was formed under Dan *Godfrey in 1924 to supplement the popular recordings by various Guards bands and the RAF band. In 1926, George *Gershwin played 'Rhapsody in blue' from the Savoy Hotel, but it was many years before the serious jazz minority were given their fair share of broadcasting. Record programmes began seriously in 1925 with the advent of the first electric recordings and the first *disc-jockey, Christopher Stone, started his morning record recitals in 1927. Similarly, in the USA the society bands were called to service from the innumerable local stations that sprang up; and it has been estimated that by 1930 dance music took up three-quarters of the nation's radio time. At one time, as with the gramophone, it was thought that radio would kill off all sheet music sales, and it was even thought that it would kill off the gramophone. For a time, in the depression years, record sales in the USA did drop drastically, from 100 million in 1927 to 6 million in 1932. But by 1933 publishing of music and records had recovered and the radio continued the good work that led towards popular music, as indeed all music as well as drama and comedy, becoming a common property, and not just for those who could afford it live.

C. Andrews (ed.): *Radio Who's Who* (London, 1947; rev. 1950, 1954). A. Briggs: *The History of Broadcasting in the*

United Kingdom (3 vols) (London, 1961–5). M. McLuhan: *Understanding Media* (New York, 1964). E. Barnouw: *A History of Broadcasting in the United States* (4 vols) (New York, 1968–75). R. C. Toll: *The Entertainment Machine* (New York, 1982).

Radio Ballads, The. A series of eight programmes, commissioned by the BBC from Ewan *MacColl and others and broadcast 1957–64, which rendered a valuable service to the cause of folk-music and are still highly regarded. They represented a laudable effort to relate folk-music to contemporary life through the medium of radio. Songs and music were not simply used as isolated illustrations or mere colouring, but as part of a continuous text, combining with the narrative to create a totally integrated musical experience. The eight programmes were *John Axon*, a documentary on a railway driver's life; *Song of the Road*, an account of the building of the M1 motorway; *Singing the Fishing*, concerning the herring fishing industry (this programme won the Prix Italia and was heard on radio in 86 countries); *The Big Hewer*, on coal-mining; *The Body Blow*, examining the lives of five polio victims; *On the Edge*, the world of the teenager; *The Fight Game*, dealing with professional boxing; and *The Travelling People*, the life of Britain's vagrants. Francis Newton, writing in the *New Statesman*, saw them as 'the most valuable products of the British folk music movements'. The programmes were perpetuated on LP by Argo Records.

Radio City Music Hall. Built in the era of superlatives as a shrine to vaudeville, and opened in the Rockefeller Center, New York, in Dec. 1932, it claimed to be the world's largest theatre. It offered a movie and a lavish musical revue at a cost of 35 cents up to 1 p.m., 50 cents in the afternoon, and 75 cents in the evening. People went just to gaze at its gargantuan proportions, which someone described as the Hippodrome, the Paris Opéra, the Roman Forum, Barnum and Bailey's, the Red Square in Moscow, and a few other things, all rolled into one. It had perfect acoustics to show off its large orchestra, choir, permanent ballet, a dance team, and a mighty Wurlitzer, needless to say the largest organ ever built, with 4000 pipes. The opening programme included Titta Ruffo in a condensed *Carmen*, a large choir, *Weber and Fields, Ray *Bolger, some high-wire walkers, and the Martha Graham dancers.

Raeburn, Boyd Albert (*b* Faith, S. Dak., 27 Oct. 1913; *d* New York, 2 Aug. 1966). American bandleader. While studying medicine at the University of Chicago, he led a college band which won a contest in 1933 at the Hotel Sherman. This decided him on a musical career, which he started by playing saxophone and clarinet in various Chicago and Midwest bands. He formed his own dance band 1934–6, changing to a more swinging style in 1937, made his first visit to New York in 1942 and in 1943 was resident in the Chicago Band Box Club. He moved with the times into the field of modern jazz, among the musicians he used being Dizzy *Gillespie, Trummy *Young, Oscar Pettiford, and Buddy DeFranco. From 1945 on he made some innovative recordings with such titles as 'Tonsilectomy', 'Summertime', and 'Boyd meets Stravinsky'. The band had a great influence but was never a financial success and came to an end in 1950. Raeburn continued to work as an arranger, with a short bandleading revival in the late 1950s.

Rag. A composition written in the *ragtime idiom. The word appears to have no especially obscure origins, simply meaning a piece with a ragged rhythm, although many other derivations have been suggested. Also used as a verb, to rag. Later the term was applied to a dance done to the commercialized form of ragtime that was being exploited by *Tin Pan Alley *c.*1912, a syncopated development of the *one-step.

Ragtime. In the early days of jazz documentation there was a tendency to use the name ragtime as a synonym for jazz, but a more general appreciation of the nature and history of ragtime came with the publication of the book *They All Played Ragtime*, by Rudi *Blesh and Harriet Janis, in 1950, which made an impression that previous isolated articles had not achieved. Further clarification of the true nature of ragtime came in the 1970s when the works of Scott *Joplin and other ragtime composers were collected and published.

Ragtime emerged from the same plantation background as jazz, but from the beginning was a black music that based itself on white traditions in contrast to the purely black folk tradition of the blues. The flavour of ragtime can first be detected in hindsight in some of the minstrel songs of the mid-1800s, later as background to the dances that came to light as black entertainers were allowed the freedom of the American stage. How far back there were pianists playing in something akin to the ragtime style will probably never be known. The flavour can be found, for instance, in the piano works of the Creole composer Louis Moreau *Gottschalk, many years before ragtime made a public emergence. This came with remarkable suddenness, ragtime finding its roots in the Midwest areas around St Louis while jazz was coming to fruition further south in such centres as New Orleans.

The first rag compositions were only mildly syncopated, appearing in the early 1890s as *cakewalks and similar dances. The year 1897 saw the publication of one of the most memorable of all cakewalks in Kerry *Mills's 'At a Georgia campmeeting' and the first published piece bearing the name rag—'Mississippi rag' (but also really a cakewalk). Curiously, this was the work of a white composer, William H. *Krell); it was a reflection of the way that minstrel songs were first introduced by white performers and a presentiment of how jazz was later to be introduced by a white band; a matter of commercial rather than musical influence. These publications were closely followed by the first rag from a black composer—'Harlem rag' by Thomas *Turpin. From that time on, ragtime became a sudden and revolutionary craze, quickly infecting the whole of popular music with its syncopated strains that were probably derived from banjo strumming. In the same year a vaudeville pianist, Ben *Harney, published a ragtime tutor; he was to assert for most of his career that he was the sole inventor of ragtime.

From the start both the cakewalk and the *rag (terms used with little discrimination in the early days) adopted a form that was closely akin to the march, the waltz, and other popular dances: an opening flourish, followed by several contrasting sections. This was presumably a simple imitation of the light music then in current use—the typical Viennese waltz, the *military band marches of *Sousa (who was an early advocate of ragtime) and others, extended dance forms like the *quadrille or *lancers, and the compositions of Gottschalk and others sympathetic to native American strains. The formal structure of the piano rag distinguished it from the ragtime song, though both used a common musical language. From the beginning ragtime was also played in instrumental and orchestral form, but it remained essentially a piano music that was adapted to other uses.

One of the earliest and greatest composers of ragtime was Scott *Joplin, whose first published essay for the piano, 'Original rags', appeared in 1899. Shortly after, he published the classic 'Maple Leaf rag' and went on to pursue an ambition (frustrated in his lifetime) to have a ragtime opera produced. The works of Joplin and his immediate contemporaries had a formal charm and melodic nature that was essentially late Victorian, these sorts of qualities being widely restored in the performances and recordings heard during the 'authentic' ragtime revival of the 1970s. It is, in fact, likely that, in the rough environment of ragtime's origins, such as Tom Turpin's Rosebud Café in St Louis, a popular gathering place for ragtime pianists, the early composers and interpreters would have played in a much freer and more jazz-inflected style. Nevertheless, a straight 'as written' performance of a Joplin rag does allow an appreciation of the delicate and tasteful writing therein. The composer took his music very seriously and always asked that his rags should not be played too fast.

Joplin was always some way above the rest in stature, but there were challengers to his supremacy. Composers like Charles *Hunter, Charles L. *Johnson, Louis *Chauvin, Arthur *Marshall, Scott Hayden (1882–1915), Joe *Jordan, Sanford Brunson Campbell (1884–1952), Henry Lodge (1884–1933), James *Scott, George L. *Cobb, May *Aufderheide, and the white exponent Joseph *Lamb continued to write in a traditional vein, but ragtime compositions gradually changed their nature in response to commercial demands and current dance fashions. The element of simple syncopation was ragtime's most lasting ingredient, but when Tin Pan Alley took it over the subtler elements were soon forgotten. The ragtime song went on its own way in the hands of Irving *Berlin and his ilk; piano ragtime by 1913 or so was smoothing out its rhythms, moving towards the comic traditions of the *Charleston era, the name ragtime becoming synonymous with extrovert hilarity. It had moved to what the purist must inevitably see as its decline through the smoother styles of writers like Artie Matthews (1888–1958), Luckey *Roberts, and the vaudeville-based Eubie *Blake. The typical ragtime hit of *c.*1912 was the corny 'Twelfth Street rag' of Euday *Bowman.

Ragtime was then absorbed into the early jazz styling of such groups as the *Original Dixieland Jazz Band and other white protagonists of early jazz. Jelly Roll *Morton demonstrated, in a recording of 'Original rags', how the ragtime element was modified into jazz. The sophisticated styles of the 1920s saw ragtime effectively absorbed into the compositions of composers like Zez *Confrey ('Kitten on the keys') and Felix *Arndt ('Nola') in the USA and Billy *Mayerl in England; and as an ingredient in the playing of the early jazz pianists like James P. *Johnson, Willie 'The Lion' *Smith, and Fats *Waller. The commercial world regularly saw fit to revive ragtime, invariably as a comedy music played with jarring insensitivity, as in the jangling pianistics of Winifred *Atwell, Joe 'Fingers' Carr, and others in the 1950s.

But by this time, alongside other revival race activities, there was a growing interest in the original thing, sparked off by the Blesh/Janis book and by the LP issue of various early piano roll performances by pianists from Joplin onwards. Earlier phases of commercial exploitation had done nothing but debase ragtime and provide some cheap comedy. The genuine interest in the 1970s took players back to the original scores, now happily made available, and brought a proper understanding of the wealth of inventive and endearing music that had been written in the name of ragtime. It was realized through the recordings of Joshua *Rifkin, William *Bolcom, and others and through the use of ragtime as background music to *The Sting* (1973) and other entertainments in the film, theatre, and ballet world (see under JOPLIN), so that, in spite of some criticism of the sometimes over-genteel approach, the world at least now knew what written ragtime sounded like and of its true potential.

R. Blesh and H. Janis: *They All Played Ragtime* (New York, 1950; repr. 1966, 1971). D. A. Jasen: *Recorded Ragtime 1897–1958* (Hamden, Conn., 1973). W. J. Schafer and J. Riedel: *The Art of Ragtime* (Baton Rouge, La., 1973). P. Gammond: *Scott Joplin and the Ragtime Era* (London–New York, 1975). D. A. Jasen and T. J. Tichenor: *Rags and Ragtime* (New York, 1978: rev. 1989) E. A. Berlin: *Ragtime: a Musical and Cultural History* (Berkeley, 1980). J. Hasse: *Ragtime: its History, Composers and Music* (London–New York, 1985).

Music: R. Blesh (ed.): *Classic Piano Rags* (New York, 1973). T. J. Tichenor (ed.): *Ragtime Rarities* (New York, 1975). D. A. Jasen (ed.): *Ragtime: 100 Authentic Rags*

(New York, 1979). T. J. Tichenor (ed.): *Ragtime Rediscoveries* (New York, 1979). D. A. Jasen (ed.): *Ragtime Gems* (New York, 1986).

See also books listed under JOPLIN, SCOTT, and other composers mentioned above.

Ragtime songs. Although arising from the same roots as *ragtime, and employing the same syncopated style, the ragtime song was more a descendant of the minstrel movement and early American song styling. Written in the more conventional strophic or AABA forms of the popular song, it also tended towards a more flowing and less emphatic kind of syncopation. Early writers in the style included Ben *Harney ('You've been a good old wagon', 'Mr Johnson, turn me loose'), who also made claims to being the originator of ragtime. It was the ragtime song tradition rather than classic ragtime that inspired *Tin Pan Alley and led to the first so-called 'ragtime' craze that found its expression in the songs of Irving *Berlin like 'Alexander's Ragtime Band', leading to some confusion in the public mind as to the true nature of ragtime which was not cleared up until some 50 years later.

A. Charters (ed.): *The Ragtime Songbook* (New York, 1965).

Rainey, Ma [*née* Pridgett, Gertrude] (*b* Columbus, Ga., 26 Apr. 1886; *d* Columbus, 22 Dec. 1939). American blues singer and composer. A pioneer classic blues singer who started her career in minstrel shows, including many months with the then famous Rabbit Foot Minstrels, she married fellow-minstrel William 'Pa' Rainey in 1904, with whom she had a stage partnership. Although she was one of the first to sing the blues on stage (from *c*.1902), she was far from being a righteous founder of the blues tradition; in those early days the Raineys were at one time billed as 'Assassinators of the Blues' and even performed in a circus 1914–16.

She began making records, mainly for Paramount, around 1923, often with Lovie Austin and her Blues Serenaders, a group which included Tommy *Ladnier on cornet. She also recorded with Louis *Armstrong, making her last recording in 1928. She toured with her own company in vaudeville until the 1930s and recorded with her own Georgia Band. A member of her troupe was Bessie *Smith, who became her pupil and protégée and even better known. She retired from the stage in 1935 and settled in Rome, Georgia, running two theatres she had bought in Columbus and Rome. Those who heard her remember her as one of the great blues artists, perhaps never as fine a singer as Bessie Smith but a much more effective performer on stage.

D. Stewart-Baxter: *Ma Rainey and the Classic Blues Singers* (London, 1970).

Rainger, Ralph [Reichenthal, Ralph] (*b* New York, 7 Oct. 1901; *d* Beverly Hills, Calif., 23 Oct. 1942). American composer, pianist, and arranger. As a schoolboy he continually neglected his lessons to play the piano, but the family saw no future in music and he was sent to study law. His first job with a law firm brought him in $25 a week and he found he could make more than that playing in a café dance band. He finally persuaded his family, turned professional, and got his first job in the pit orchestra of the Ambassador Theatre in New York; but the songs he wrote had no success at first. He became accompanist to Clifton *Webb and while with him wrote his first hit, 'Moanin' low' (1929, *w* Howard *Dietz), made famous by Libby *Holman in the first *Little Show* of that year.

In the early 1930s he moved to Hollywood, becoming particularly associated with Bing *Crosby and his films, and writing many songs (mainly in collaboration with Leo Robin, 1900–85) like 'Love in bloom' (*She Loves Me Not*, 1934) 'June in January' (*Here is My Heart*, 1934), and 'You're a sweet little headache' (*Paris Honeymoon*, 1939) especially for him. His songs tended to be efficiently right for their time and place rather than lastingly memorable and not many have stood the test of time. The best-remembered is 'Thanks for the memory' (*w* Robin) sung by Bob *Hope and Shirley *Ross in *The Big Broadcast of 1938* and thereafter inseparably associated with Bob Hope, who used it as his theme song. Rainger was writing in Hollywood up to the time of his death in a plane crash.

Raitt, John Emmett (*b* Santa Ana, Calif., 19 Jan. 1917). American actor and singer. He began his singing career in light opera and as a concert recitalist. After appearing in a touring company of **Oklahoma!* (1944) he made his reputation as a burly, handsome baritone in the Broadway production of **Carousel* (1945), singing 'Soliloquy' and 'If I loved you'; later in *Magdalena* (1948); *Three Wishes for Jaimie* (1952); *Carnival in Flanders* (1953); *The *Pajama Game* (1954)—'Hey, there', 'There once was a man'; **Destry Rides Again* (1960); and *A Joyful Noise* (1966). His daughter, Bonnie Raitt (*b* 1949), has had a successful career as a writer and singer of blues and other material.

Raksin, David [Sartain, John] (*b* Philadelphia, 4 Aug. 1912). American composer, conductor, arranger, author, and clarinettist. He studied with his father, who had a music shop, and conducted for silent films before studying music with various teachers. At Pennsylvania University he played clarinet in the college band and was its assistant conductor. He played in the staff band of station WCAU before going to Hollywood to score the music for Charlie *Chaplin's film *Modern Times* (1935), an experience about which he wrote intriguingly in the *Quarterly Journal of the Library of Congress* in 1983. Subsequently he studied under Arnold Schoenberg at the University of California 1937–8. He worked for some time in British films. His first big success came with *Laura* (1944), whose masterly theme-song, 'Laura' (*w* Johnny *Mercer), became immensely popular and was frequently recorded.

He composed more than 100 film scores, among

them *Fallen Angel* (1945)—'Slowly'; *The Shocking Miss Pilgrim* (1946); *The Secret Life of Walter Mitty* (1947); *Forever Amber* (1947)—'Forever amber' (*w* Mercer); *Daisy Kenyon* (1947); *Apartment for Peggy* (1948); *Force of Evil* (1949); *The Magnificent Yankee* (1950); *Carrie* (1952); *The Bad and the Beautiful* (1952)—'Love is for the very young' (*w* Dorothy Langdon); *The Unicorn in the Garden* (cartoon, 1953); *Apache* (1954); *Suddenly* (1954); *Jubal* (1956); *Seven Wonders of the World* (1956); *Hilda Crane* (1956); *Separate Tables* (1958); *Al Capone* (1959); *Night Tide* (1961); *The Patsy* (1964); *Sylvia* (1964)—'Sylvia' (*w* Paul Francis Webster); *Will Penny* (1968). He also wrote the score for *If the Shoe Fits* (1946); TV scores, *Ben Casey* (1961) and *The Day After* (1983); incidental music for many plays; and a popular 'Toy Concertino' for orchestra.

Randall, Harry (*b* London, 22 Mar. 1860; *d* London, 18 May 1932). British comedian and singer. He made his first appearance in pantomime when he was 11 and his first professional appearance at Deacon's Music Hall in Islington in 1884. He was immediately so successful that he took top billing at the Middlesex and *Oxford music halls soon after. He sang such comedy songs as 'The ghost of John James Binns', 'Exchange and Mart', 'Our happy little home', and 'It ain't all lavender'. He proved the power of song with 'Who killed Cock Warren', which lampooned police chief Warren for failing to catch Jack the Ripper in 1888, as a result of which the officer was forced to resign. Later he succeeded his friend Dan *Leno as the leading pantomime dame at Drury Lane and elsewhere. He retired from the stage in 1913.

H. Randall: *Harry Randall, Old Time Comedian* (London, 1931). R. Moreton (ed.): *Harry Randall's Album of Popular Songs* (London, n.d.).

Randolph, Elsie (*b* London, 9 Dec. 1904; *d* London, 15 Oct. 1981). British actress, singer, and dancer. A child actress at 12, she had played on the London stage by the age of 14. She had minor parts in *The Girl for the Boy* (1919); *The Naughty Princess* (1920); *My Nieces* (1921); and *His Girl* (1922). A well-remembered singing and dancing partnership with the debonaire Jack *Buchanan was perpetuated in *Battling Butler* (1923); *Toni* (1924); *Boodle* (1925); **Sunny* (1926); *That's a Good Girl* (1928)—in which she sang 'The one I'm looking for' and 'Fancy our meeting'; *Stand Up and Sing* (1931); *Mr Whittington* (1934)—'Oceans of time'; *This'll Make You Whistle* (1936: filmed 1936); and *It's Time to Dance* (1943). She was also in *Madame Pompadour* (1924); *Peggy-Ann* (1927); *Follow Through* (1929) with Leslie *Henson; *The *Co-Optimists* (1930); *Wonder Bar* (1930); and played her first straight role in 1938.

Rap. Dance craze of the 1970s, cultivated by black and Latin teenagers in New York, developing from disco music with a stronger beat as background to breakdancing, becoming known as rap when MCs took to reciting socially aware street poetry over the music. Also known as *hip-hop. One of the first recorded hits in the idiom was 'Rapper's delight' (1979) by the Sugar Hill Gang. It continued in the 1980s more as a social than a musical phenomenon, kept alive by its usefulness to the advertising world and as a teenage line of communication.

Rapee, Erno (*b* Budapest, 4 June 1891; *d* New York, 26 June 1945). Hungarian-born American conductor, composer, and pianist. After studying piano at the National Academy in Budapest he gave concerts, and conducted in Dresden, Magdeburg, and Kattowitz. He toured South America and Mexico in 1912, then settled in the USA where he became conductor of the Hungarian Opera Company in New York. He was musical director of the Rivoli Theatre, which became the Rialto Movie Palace, the first New York cinema to have a large orchestra. Appointed conductor for the Roxy film theatres 1926–31, he conducted the NBC Symphony Orchestra and at *Radio City Music Hall and became widely known through a weekly radio series introducing new music to America.

A pioneer composer for the silent screen, he composed hundreds of film scores, among them *Robin Hood* (1923); *The Iron Horse* (1924); *What Price Glory?* (1925)—'Charmaine' (*w* Lew *Pollack); *Seventh Heaven* (1927)—'Diane' (*w* Pollack); *Street Angel* (1928)—'Angela mia' (*w* Pollack); *The Red Dance* (1928)—'Someday, somewhere' (*w* Pollack). He compiled the standard music book for silent cinema musicians, *Motion Picture Moods for Pianists and Organists, adapted to 52 Moods and Situations* (New York, 1924; repr. 1974).

Ray, Johnnie [John Alvin] (*b* Dallas, Oreg., 10 Jan. 1927; *d* Los Angeles, 25 Feb. 1990). American singer, pianist, composer, and author. He appeared on radio in Portland and did a songs-at-the-piano act in nightclubs in Hollywood and elsewhere in the USA, but remained unknown until his hit record 'Cry' (1951) made his extrovert, lachrymose, blues-tinged style of singing a box-office hit all over the world. It has since been pinpointed as one of the first teenage songs that set the pop market in motion. He became a key figure of the early 1950s and the current fan fever. He tried to make a way in films but after *There's No Business Like Show Business* (1954), in which he was submerged by the professional talents of Ethel *Merman, Dan Dailey, and Donald *O'Connor, he made no more film appearances. Other recordings included his own 'The little white cloud that cried', 'Tell the lady I said goodbye', and 'A sinner am I'. After a while he faded from view, but made regular reappearances, including a tour of Britain and Europe with Judy *Garland in the 1960s.

Raye, Don [Wilhoite, Donald MacRae] (*b* Washington DC, 16 Mar. 1909). American composer, pianist, and writer. He started his career as a dancer, winning the State Championship of Virginia as a performer of the *Black Bottom and the *Charleston. He danced in vaudeville from 1926, touring the USA, England, and Europe, becoming a nightclub performer in 1935, and writing his own material. In 1937 he went to New York University to study advertising, but started writing songs in 1938, then went to Hollywood to write for films, his most notable score being for *Hellzapoppin* (1941)—'Watch the birdie'.

He specialized in the *boogie-woogie-based songs that had a vogue in the late 1930s and early 1940s (producing either words or music and mainly written in collaboration) including: 'Rhythm in my nursery rhyme' (1935), 'Well, all right' (1939), 'Rhumboogie' (in *Argentine Nights*, 1939), 'I love you much too much' (1940), 'Beat me, daddy, eight to the bar' (1940), 'Scrub me mama (with a boogie beat)' (1940), 'Music makers' (1941), 'Boogie woogie bugle boy' (in *Buck Privates*, 1941), 'Down the road apiece' (1941), 'Cow Cow boogie' (in *Reveille with Beverley* and *Swing Symphony*, 1941), 'I'll remember April' (in *Ride 'em, Cowboy*, 1941), 'Bounce me, brother, with a solid four' (1941), 'He's my guy' (1942), and 'Mister Five by Five' (1942).

Raymond, Fred [Vesely, Friedrich] (*b* Vienna, 20 Apr. 1900; *d* Überlingen, 10 Jan. 1954). Austrian composer and lyricist. He worked in cabaret and from 1934 was resident composer at the Metropol Theater in Berlin. He achieved considerable popularity in the 1930s with his brightly contemporary musicals, such as the Singspiel *Ich hab' mein Herz in Heidelberg verloren* (1927, revival 1946) whose title-song became a big pre-war hit; *Lauf ins Glück* (1934); *Ball der Nationen* (1935); *Auf grösser Fahrt* (1936); *Marielu* (1936); his biggest success, *Maske in blau* (Berlin 1937, Vienna 1946; filmed 1953)—'Du Juliska aus Budapest'; and the tuneful *Saison in Salzburg* (Kiel 1938, revival 1946)—'Und die Musik spielt dazu', 'Wenn der Toni mit der Vroni'; *Die Perle von Tokaj* (1941); and *Flieder aus Wien* (1949).

Razaf, Andy [Razafinkeriefo, Andreamenentania Paul] (*b* Washington DC, 16 Dec. 1895; *d* Hollywood, 3 Feb. 1973). American lyricist. A Grand Duke, the nephew of Queen Ranavalona III of Madagascar, he left school at 16 and continued private studies. He began to write material for nightclub shows in New York and Chicago and worked in association with many leading black composers, notably Fats *Waller. After a stroke he was confined to a wheelchair for much of his later life. He contributed to *Keep Shufflin'* (1928)—'Willow tree'; **Hot Chocolates* (1929)—'Ain't misbehavin'', 'Black and blue', 'Sweet Savannah Sue' (all *m* Waller and Harry Brooks); **Blackbirds* (1930)—'Memories of you' (*m* Eubie *Blake), 'You're lucky to me' (*m* Blake). His other songs included: 'Louisiana' (1928, *m* J. C. *Johnson); 'S'posin'' (1929, *m* Paul Denniker); 'Honeysuckle rose' (1929), 'My fate is in your hands' (1929), 'Blue, turning grey over you', 'Keeping out of mischief now' (1932, all Waller); 'In the mood' (1939, *m* Joe *Garland), and 'I'm gonna move to the outskirts of town' (1942).

Reader, Ralph (*b* Crewkerne, Som., 25 May 1903; *d* Bourne End, Bucks., 13 May. 1982). British actor, dancer, composer, director, producer, and author. Son of a Salvation Army bandmaster, he was orphaned as a boy and sent to America where he first worked as a clerk. He made his first stage appearance in the **Greenwich Village Follies* in 1918, first attracting attention in *The *Passing Show* (1924) and *Big Boy* (1925). He became dance producer for the *Shuberts and came back to England to appear in **Good News* (1928). His skill as a director and his flair for stage effects were seen in *The *Cochran Revue* (1930); **Victoria and her Hussar* (1931); *Please, Teacher* (1936); and the Novello shows **Glamorous Night* (1935), **Careless Rapture* (1936), and *Crest of the Wave* (1937).

He is chiefly remembered, however, for his inspired work with amateurs, notably for the Boy Scout *Gang Show* which he first took on in 1932 having been a dedicated scout himself. His mixture of flair, simple but spectacular vision, and sincerity made these shows an extraordinary success and many later famous stars worked in them. Reader wrote much of the material, including the theme-tune 'Riding along on the crest of a wave' (1937) and 'Strollin'' (1959). The show was an annual event until 1974, when he retired. He had also become involved in producing wartime pageants at the Albert Hall, and by 1955 had produced 80. He was known to millions as leader of the singing at Remembrance Day services and Cup Finals. He had his own TV series in 1954. He was made an MBE in 1942 and CBE in 1957.

R. Reader: *It's Been Terrific* (London, 1954).

Redding, Otis (*b* Dawson, Ga., 9 Sept. 1941; *d* Madison, Wis., 10 Dec. 1967). American rhythm 'n' blues singer. Being the son of a Baptist minister brought the soul element in his music, which he combined with the influences of *Little Richard and Roy *Brown, into a forceful and emotional style that sometimes overwhelmed his artistry. He started with such Little Richard emulations as 'She's alright' (1959) and 'Shout bamalama' (1960), but he had his first real success with one of his own songs in more subdued mood, 'These arms of mine' (1963), followed by the similarly styled 'Pain in my heart' (1964), 'That's how strong my love is' (1964), and, the biggest hit so far, 'I've been loving you too long' (1965); at the same time his more frenetic performances were what his audiences tended to like most—'My girl' (1966) being in this more high-pitched vein. His most telling recording, typifying what has come to be regarded as the best of the Stax recorded sound, was 'Try a little tenderness', a performance modelled on Sam *Cooke, and a highly emotive evocation of commercial *soul. He made a triumphant appearance at the Monterey Pop Festival in 1967 and was voted the World

No. 1 Male Singer by the *Melody Maker* just before he died when his plane crashed into Lake Monona.

J. Schiesel: *The Otis Redding Story* (New York, 1973).

Red, Hot and Blue. Musical comedy with music and lyrics by Cole *Porter, book by Howard *Lindsay and Russel *Crouse, New York (Alvin Theatre) 29 Oct. 1936. It was intended to be a follow-up to the successful **Anything Goes* (1934) with the same team, but William *Gaxton and Victor *Moore withdrew as they considered that Ethel *Merman was getting too big a share of the limelight. Jimmy *Durante and Bob *Hope came in instead as second strings to the ebullient Merman, in the tailor-made role of a wealthy widow who tries to organize an illegal lottery with the help of her lawyer (Hope). Its songs, which included 'You've got something', 'It's de-lovely', 'Ridin' high', and 'Red, hot and blue', were more memorable than its plot. It had 183 performances and was filmed in 1949 starring Betty *Hutton.

Redman, Don [Donald Matthew] (*b* Piedmont, W. Va., 29 July 1900; *d* New York, 30 Nov. 1964). American composer, arranger, bandleader, and saxophonist. He played the piano at the age of three, worked with a band when he was six and took up the trumpet at eight. After studies at the Boston Conservatory of Music he first became known as a saxophonist with Fletcher *Henderson's band in 1924, playing and arranging for the band until 1927. He then worked for Louis *Armstrong and arranged for Paul *Whiteman, Ben *Pollack, and others. He took over the leadership of *McKinney's Cotton Pickers, for whom he composed and arranged many classic items, and formed his own band in 1931; many of his best-known songs and instrumental pieces are from this period. During the early 1940s he was a freelance arranger and recording artist and after the war toured with a band in Europe 1946–7. Latterly he became musical director for Pearl *Bailey and appeared with her in Arlen's **House of Flowers* (1954). His writings included: 'Cherry' (1928), 'Paducah' (1929), 'Gee baby, ain't I good to you' (1929, *w* *Razaf), 'Save it, pretty mama' (1929), 'No one else but you' (1929), 'Chant of the weed' (1932), 'How'm I doin'' (1932), 'Hot and anxious' (1932), 'If it ain't love' (1934), and 'Flight of the jitterbugs' (1939); and he had one of his biggest recording hits with his arrangement of 'Deep purple' for Jimmy *Dorsey.

Red Mill, The. Comic opera with music by Victor *Herbert and book by Henry *Blossom, produced in New York at the Knickerbocker Theatre 24 Sept. 1906. It showed a distinct move away from Herbert's operetta vein towards musical comedy and achieved his longest initial run [274p]. The farcical story involved two impoverished American tourists in Holland (David Montgomery, 1870–1917, and Fred *Stone), and the solution to their problems involved many comic disguises and the rescue of a fair maiden. The score included such classics as 'The isle of our dreams', 'Every day is ladies' day with me', 'The streets of New York', 'Moonbeams', and 'Because you're you'. It was seen in London at the Empire Theatre 26 Dec. 1919. With Herbert established as a great American composer, there was a very successful revival with Eddie *Foy at the Ziegfeld Theatre 16 Oct. 1945 that had 531 performances, and was seen in London at the Palace Theatre 1 May 1947.

Redowa. Dance of Bohemian origin which was fashionable in Paris and London from around 1845. During a brief spell of great popularity many redowas were published by leading dance composers. It originally existed in two forms, as a waltz or a dance similar to the polka; it was the waltz form that caught on in Western Europe, the music being similar to the mazurka but with a smoother rhythm.

Reed, Jerry [Hubbard, Jerry] (*b* Atlanta, Ga., 20 Mar. 1937). American country singer, guitarist, and composer. While working in cotton mills as a youth, he gradually achieved a local reputation as a performer. He joined Capitol Records as a songwriter when he was only 18, producing such hits as 'Amos Moses', 'Georgia sunshine', and 'Alabama wild man'. His biggest success came in 1971 with 'When you're hot, you're hot'.

Reed, Thomas German (*b* Bristol, 17 June 1817; *d* London, 21 Mar. 1888). British singer, pianist, actor, composer, and impresario. He made his first public appearances in Bath as a child of 10. He married the actress and singer Priscilla Horton (1818–95) in 1844 and they started to produce the highly popular 'Mr & Mrs German Reed's Entertainment', a series of shows that had a core of burlesque and light musical fare, at the Gallery of Illustration and St George's Hall. Although these did not produce anything of lasting note they were important in the story of operetta in England and were a nursery for the talents of such composers as Frederick *Clay and writers like W. S. *Gilbert, with whom Reed wrote *No Cards* (1869), *Our Island Home* (1870), *A Sensational Novel* (1871), *Eyes and No Eyes* (1875); F. C. Burnand (1836–1917), with whom he wrote *Mildred's Well* (1873), *He's Coming* (1874), *Matched and Mated* (1876), and *Number 304* (1877); and Gilbert A'Beckett (1837–91), with whom he wrote *The Three Tenants* (1874), *The Ancient Britons* (1875), *A Spanish Bond* (1875), *An Indian Puzzle* (1876), and *The Wicked Duke* (1876). It was through an association with German Reed that Gilbert and Sullivan first met. Corney *Grain was a popular figure long associated with the entertainments. The productions were continued after the death of Thomas German Reed by his son Alfred (1840–95), their history coming to an end when Alfred, Mrs Reed, and Corney Grain all died within a few days of each other.

D. Williamson: *The German Reeds and Corney Grain: Records and Reminiscences* (London, 1895).

Reel. The oldest of the known Scottish national dances, closely related to early Irish and Scandinavian dances. The couples stand face to face and dance to music in 2/4 or 6/8 time which is akin to that used for the *strathspey but considerably quicker. The Irish reel is traditionally even faster than the Scottish variety. Another version of the reel is the Highland fling. Such dances were not known in England until a northern invasion of the ballrooms came about at the turn of the 18th–19th centuries. The origins of the reel and the strathspey are lost in the mists of time, but most authorities believe that the pipes of the Highlands may have given the reel to the fiddlers of the Lowlands, with the strathspey coming in return in the opposite direction.

Reese, Della [Taliaferro, Dellareese] (*b* Detroit, 6 July 1931). American gospel and pop singer. While studying at Wayne State University in Detroit she became part of a gospel group, the Meditations. She went on tour with Mahalia *Jackson 1945–9 and afterwards was one of the Clara Ward Singers. She sang with Erskine *Hawkins orchestra, signed with Jubilee Records in 1957, and moved into the growing pop field, being one of the first female black singers to make the charts at that period. After success with 'And that reminds me' (1957) and 'Sermonette' (1958) on the Jubilee label, she had her biggest hit with 'Don't you know' which she recorded for RCA in 1959, continuing with 'Not one minute more' (1959), 'Someday' (1960), 'And now' (1960), 'The most beautiful words' (1961), 'Bill Bailey' (1961); and for ABC 'After loving you' (1965). She became a popular club, radio, and TV performer.

Reeve, Ada [Isaacs, Adelaide Mary] (*b* London, 3 Mar. 1874; *d* London, 25 Sept. 1966). British actress and singer. Of Dutch and French Jewish parentage, she appeared in pantomime and melodrama from 1878, made her first music-hall appearance at Sebright's, Hackney, in 1886, and was at the Hungerford Music Hall in Charing Cross in 1888. She went to the USA to appear at *Koster and Bial's in 1893, returning to appear, petite and pop-eyed, in the first musical comedy to be produced at the Gaiety Theatre, *The *Shop Girl* (1894). Thereafter she was seen in *All Aboard* (1895); *The Gay Parisienne* (1896); *Milord Sir Smith* (1898); *Great Caesar* (1899); **Florodora* (1899); **San Toy* (1900); *Kitty Grey* (1900); *Three Little Maids* (1902); *The Medal and the Maid* (1903). She toured South Africa in 1906, and was back to appear in *Butterflies* (1908). In 1911 she toured the Orpheum circuit in Canada and the USA and by 1914 was in Australia, appearing at the Tivoli Music Hall in Melbourne with Harry *Lauder. She entertained the troops in the First World War, after which she settled in Australia 1917–35, touring with a revue, *Spangles*. She returned to London to appear in *Cochran's *Follow the Sun* (1936), was at the Holborn in *These Names Made Variety*, and in **Black Velvet* (1940). The rest of her stage career was mainly in straight plays and she made a remarkable return in her seventies to appear on TV in 1947.

A. Reeve: *Take It For a Fact* (London, 1954).

Reeve, William (*b* London, 1757; *d* London, 22 June 1815). British composer, organist, and actor. He studied the organ at St James's Westminster, became organist at Totnes in Devon 1781–3, then returned to London and became official composer to Astley's Circus. He spent several years on the stage and, while singing in the chorus at Covent Garden, was given an opportunity to complete a pantomime score left unfinished by William *Shield who had resigned as resident composer to the theatre. As this was a success, he took over the appointment in 1791 and wrote music for more than 50 productions at Covent Garden and other theatres. In 1802 he became joint proprietor of the Sadler's Wells Theatre. His best-known songs included: 'Woman is match for man' (1790), 'Remember Jack' (1796), 'I am a friar of orders grey' (1795)—his best-known song, from the pantomime *Merry Sherwood*, 'Tippitywitchet' (which was sung by Grimaldi and came from *Bang-Up*, a pantomime with book by Charles Dibdin Jr.), 'The land we live in' (from *Harlequin and Oberon*, 1796), 'The wealth of the cottage is love' (from *Paul and Virginia*, 1800), and 'Giles Scroggins'. In his last years he contributed an interesting series of 'Airs Imitative of Different Nations' to *La Belle Assemblée*.

Reeves, Jim (*b* Galloway, Texas, 20 Aug. 1924; *d* Tennessee, 31 July 1964). American country singer. He had an early career as a professional baseball player, then managed a radio station, before he finally became known as a singer. He had recorded for small Texan record companies and achieved minor hits before appearing with *Louisiana Hayride* and signing up with RCA, where he developed a smooth vocal style that proved highly saleable in songs like 'Four walls' (1957), his biggest seller, 'He'll have to go' (1960), and 'Distant drums' (1966) which are now considered quintessential classics of country music. He was pioneering the *Nashville sound before it had really taken hold and from 1955, when he first joined the **Grand Ole Opry*, to 1968 there was at least one Jim Reeves recording in the Top 10 every year—including: 'Anna Marie' (1958), 'Blue boy' (1958), 'Billy Bayou' (1958), 'I'm gettin' better' (1960), 'Am I losing you' (1960), 'What would you do' (1961), 'Losing your love' (1961), 'Adios amigo' (1962), 'I guess I'm crazy' (1924), and 'Is it really over' (1965). He died as the result of an aeroplane crash in Tennessee, and was elected to the *Country Music Hall of Fame in 1967.

Reggae. A genre of rock music that developed from such antecedents as Trinidad *calypso, mento, its rough Jamaican equivalent, and New Orleans *rhythm 'n' blues, through the intermediate styles of bluebeat, an early West Indian pop style that anticipated the reggae beat (as did the more aggressive rocksteady), and ska, a hybrid of calypso and rhythm 'n' blues. Essentially a black Jamaican idiom, it came in with the emergence of various black movements and the general revival of the African spirit in such sects as the Rastafarians. Before being commercialized, it was a music of rebellion.

The purest reggae lyrics are often in Jamaican Creole, sung over the flexible and sophisticated musical phrasing that was developed in calypso singing. A strong melodic characteristic comes from the employment of the *riff. The first Jamaican-produced record to be issued in Britain was 'Little Sheila' (1960) by Laurel Aitkin (*b* 1928). The development of reggae as a part of the pop music scene was greatly due to the influence of Bob *Marley, who widened the style into a form that could be popularly accepted but which still retained its sincere protest element in songs like 'Duppy conqueror' and 'No woman, no cry'. He was followed by such specialized groups as the Third World Band. An early reggae superstar was Jimmy Cliff (*b* 1944) with his 'Wonderful world, beautiful people' (1969). Reggae emerged as a fully-fledged music around 1969 and, with the establishment of so many West Indian communities in British cities, the UK soon became its second home with its own record companies and clubs vigorously operating and the music having its effect on the rock scene in general.

S. Davis and P. Simon: *Reggae Bloodlines* (London, 1979). S. Clarke: *Jah Music* (London, 1980). H. Johnson and J. Pines: *Reggae: Deep Roots Music* (London–New York, 1982). S. Davis: *Reggae International* (London, 1983).

Reinhardt, Django [Jean Baptiste] (*b* Liverchies, nr. Charleroi, 23 Jan. 1910; *d* Fontainebleau, 16 May 1953). Belgian jazz guitarist of gypsy origin. He began to make his mark in Paris in 1922 when he recorded with the singer Jean *Sablon and with the violinist Stéphane *Grappelli. In 1934 he and Grappelli formed and led the *Quintette du Hot Club de France and thus created a popular style of jazz that owed little to the American original except a vast degree of swing. Reinhardt was one of the most propulsive players of rhythm guitar ever heard on record and an original soloist, achieving it all with the handicap of missing fingers and injuries sustained in a caravan fire. He recorded some classic jazz sides with American musicians like Bill *Coleman and Dicky *Wells. After the Second World War he toured the USA and appeared with the *Ellington orchestra. He continued a long partnership with Grappelli and revived the quintet, latterly turning to electric amplification to reinforce an already forceful style.

C. Delaunay: *Django Reinhardt: Souvenirs* (Paris, 1954). C. Delaunay: *Django Reinhardt* (London, 1961). M. Abrams: *The Book of Django* (Los Angeles, 1973). R. Horricks: *Django Reinhardt* (Tunbridge Wells, 1988).

Revel, Harry (*b* London, 21 Dec. 1905; *d* New York, 3 Nov. 1958). American composer. He started piano lessons at the age of eight and showed such promise that he was expected to become a concert pianist; but the death of his old teacher so upset him that he would not work with anyone else and continued to study on his own. At the age of 15 he went to Paris and joined a Hawaiian band (with no Hawaiians in it) as pianist. He travelled with them throughout Europe and began to write songs, one of which was published in Rome. In 1922 he joined a larger dance orchestra and settled for a while in Berlin where he wrote a light opera, *Was Frauen traumen*. This led to writing music for *André *Charlot's Revue of 1927*. In 1929 he went to the USA, having studied the songs of the Gershwin–Kern–Berlin ilk, to try for a career in Tin Pan Alley, and met the lyricist Mack *Gordon, then playing in vaudeville, who was to be his regular song-writing partner. They contributed to *Fast and Furious* (1931), **Ziegfeld Follies* (1931), and *Smiling Faces* (1932).

Gordon was reluctant to leave vaudeville but, after the success of 'Underneath the Harlem moon' in 1932, the two were commissioned to write for films. Their only other stage score was *Are You With It?* (1945), but their film credits were extensive, including: *Sitting Pretty* (1933)—'Did you ever see a dream walking?', 'You're such a comfort to me'; *Design for Living* (1933); *The Gay Divorcée* (1934); *We're Not Dressing* (1934)—'May I?', 'Love thy neighbour', 'She reminds me of you'; *She Loves Me Not* (1934); *Shoot the Works* (1934)—'With my eyes wide open I'm dreaming'; *Here Comes the Groom* (1934); *College Rhythm* (1934)—'Stay as sweet as you are', 'College rhythm'; *Big Broadcast of 1936* (1935); *Three Cheers for Love* (1935); *Love in Bloom* (1935)—'My heart is an open book', 'Here comes cookie'; *Two for Tonight* (1935)—'Without a word of warning', 'It takes two to make a bargain'; *Poor Little Rich Girl* (1936)—'When I'm with you', 'But definitely', 'A star fell out of heaven'; *Head over Heels* (1936)—'Head over heels in love', 'May I have the next romance with you?'; *Collegiate* (1936)—'I feel like a feather in the breeze'; *Stowaway* (1936)—'Goodnight, my love'; *Wake Up And Live* (1937)—'Never in a million years', 'There's a lull in my life'; *You Can't Have Everything* (1937)—'Afraid to dream', 'You can't have everything'; *My Lucky Star* (1938)—'I've got a date with a dream'; *Rose of Washington Square* (1939)—'I never knew heaven could speak'; after which Revel worked with Mort Greene (1912–92) and others.

Revivalist jazz. A great revival of interest in earlier jazz started about 1939 after the initial impetus of the old improvised music had been lost in the experiments of the swing era. Jazz continued to build a following for its various developments, but the older forms were being forgotten and superseded by something that was often more superficial. This was partly through the ephemerality of jazz performances and recordings, and partly because some of the older musicians had either deserted the righteous jazz or fallen by the wayside. A number of things sparked off the revival of interest: firstly, the publication of a book called *Jazzmen* (1939) written and edited by Frederic Ramsey and Charles Edward Smith. This placed the achievement of pioneer jazzmen in perspective and focused attention on forgotten men like Bunk *Johnson who were still around but not playing. As a result of their prodding researches he came back into jazz to restore the rough but sincere sounds of the old New Orleans jazz. Secondly, there were some remarkable new recordings in 1939 by a band led by the cornettist Muggsy *Spanier, one of the younger veterans, and the issue of these aroused a great enthusiasm for the Dixieland style. As a result of this a group of enthusiasts in San Francisco—including Lu *Watters and Turk *Murphy—took the old King *Oliver Creole Band as the model for their Yerba Buena band, and sparked off a host of followers. In England the revivalist jazz torch was carried by enthusiasts like George *Webb, Humphrey *Lyttelton, and Ken *Colyer; and it was taken up by enthusiasts all over Europe. The jazz revival showed many faults, mainly of amateurism and blind imitation, but it made jazz a commercial investment once more.

Revue. A theatrical entertainment made up of a succession of sketches and songs, frequently of a satirical nature, sometimes but not always connected by a particular theme. The modern revue is often intimate in character, with a small cast in a small theatre who play for a fairly sophisticated audience; but the term has been extended to productions on a much more lavish scale in larger theatres which are more or less variety shows. A revue is sometimes completely written by one versatile individual like Noël *Coward, but is more often the work of several contributors. A fertile breeding ground for revue talent in Britain has been the universities, particularly Oxford and Cambridge where the sort of well-bred cynicism that is associated with revues is cultivated.

The name is of French origin, designating an end-of-the-year 'review' of events and personalities presented in a caricatured manner. The modern vogue (though something of the kind had been around for centuries) began around 1840, the time when the form of most popular entertainments was shaped, in the reign of Louis Philippe. Pioneers in the genre were the Cogniard Brothers. By the 1870s it had become a richly varied and popular style of entertainment with such writers as Clairville, Busnach, Bousquet, Blum, and Toché making their names in this field. The spectacular music-hall-style revue was already flourishing alongside the more intellectual intimate variety. A similar kind of entertainment had been popular in England, generally in the shape of one-man entertainments in which the actor burlesqued the famous of the day. Samuel Foote (1720–77), Charles *Dibdin, and Charles Mathews (1745–1813) were among those who provided such shows. The first English production consciously to imitate and adopt the style of the French revue was *Success! or A Hit If You Like!* by James Robinson Planché (1796–1880) produced at the Adelphi Theatre in 1825. Fanny Kelly (1790–1882) opened her own one-woman revue at what was to become the Royalty Theatre in Dean Street in 1835 and ran her *Dramatic Recollections and Studies of Character* until 1841. Planché continued to produce his revue-type entertainments, the term 'extravaganza' often being used for more lavish productions. *Burlesque was always very near to revue in its piecemeal nature, lying somewhere between revue and the developing musical comedy.

One of the first productions to be firmly labelled a 'revue' was *Pot Pourri* written by James T. Tanner (1859–1915) and W. H. Risqué (*d* 1916), with music by Napoleon Lambelet, produced at the Coronet Theatre, Notting Hill Gate, in 1899. The popularity of intimate revue was finally confirmed by *The *Follies*, a high-class sort of pierrot entertainment using revue material which was taken over by H. G. *Pélissier in 1897 and became a theatrical entertainment by 1907. The early 1900s saw the establishment of the large-scale Empire revues which started in 1905 with *Rogues and Vagabonds*. Revue reached out to a wider audience in 1912 with *Everybody's Doing It*, which introduced the *ragtime songs of Irving *Berlin; followed by a series of spectacular American-based revues produced by Albert De Courville—**Hullo, Ragtime!* (1912) and *Hullo, Tango!* (1913); followed by a series at the Hippodrome and similar productions by André *Charlot at the *Alhambra, Alfred Butt (1878–1962) at the Palace, and Oswald Stoll (1866–1942) at the Winter Garden. The intimate revue was revived by C. B. *Cochran with *Odds and Ends* at the Ambassadors Theatre; its success leading Charlot in the same direction with such stars as Binnie *Hale, Beatrice *Lillie, and Gertrude *Lawrence in *Cheep* (1917), *Buzz-Buzz* (1918), and *Tails Up* (1918). Noël Coward wrote some of his first West End material for this last show, and Charlot continued after the war with revues by Coward and *Novello. The **Co-Optimists* was a tremendous success, and Cochran continued with his brand of smart entertainment. The 1930s went increasingly intimate with the Gate revues; then the big glossy revues returned during the Second World War. The satirical revue began its fashionable period with Coward's *Sigh No More* (1945), the **Sweet and Low* series, the long-running *Lyric and Globe revues, and the university-nurtured shows at the Watergate. The heyday of the satirical revue came with **Beyond the Fringe*, frank and refreshing, at the Fortune Theatre in 1961 and running for 2200 performances.

In the USA (where the spelling 'review' is sometimes favoured) the spectacular variety show like *The Black Crook* (1866) led to the first fashion-setting lavish 'revue' *The *Passing Show*, staged at the Casino Theatre in 1892, an entertainment that had a strong element of burlesque in it. The great early 1900s vogue for lavish revues began with the supremely spectacular **Ziegfeld Follies*, which began simply as the *Follies of 1907* and soon found themselves competing with a series of new *Passing Show* revues, produced by the *Shuberts and nothing to do with the 1892 piece, **George White's Scandals*, **Earl Carroll's Vanities*, and the later **Music Box* revues. The spectacular revues gradually lost their hold and became obsolete with the rise of the equally spectacular musical.

Intimate revue in the USA came into vogue concurrently with the British variety in the aftermath of the First World War, starting with a show called *The 49ers* (1922) and propelled by the wittily fashionable *André Charlot's London Revue of 1924*. Intimate revue flourished in the politically-conscious 1930s with *The Little Show* (1929), **Three's a Crowd* (1930), *The *Band Wagon* (1931), **As Thousands Cheer* (1933), *Life Begins at 8:40* (1934), *At Home Abroad* (1935), and the left-wing show that sniped at everything **Pins and Needles* (1937). The revue did not continue to flourish in the USA as it did in England or have a parallel post-Second World War revival. The musical was becoming so adult and thought-provoking that Broadway found no need for revue. The really intimate stuff still flourished in Greenwich Village, and *Beyond the Fringe* was imported but did not go over as well as in its native land.

R. Baral: *Revue: a Nostalgic Reprise of the Great Broadway Period* (New York, 1962; rev. 1970). R. Mander and J. Mitchenson: *Revue: a Story in Pictures* (London, 1971). G. Bordman: *American Musical Revue: from the Passing Show to Sugar Babies* (New York, 1985).

Rey, Monte [Fife, James Montgomery] (*b* Chryston, nr. Glasgow, 5 Oct. 1900; *d* Isle of Arran, 23? Aug. 1982). British singer. One of six children in a musical family, he decided he wanted to be a singer after hearing his first record of Caruso. He left school at 14 to work as a clerk and sang in amateur opera productions, then moved to London to be able to study music, and after a successful audition in 1922 was due to join the Monte Carlo Opera on an Italian tour. Illness prevented his appearance and he returned to London to continue a modest career as a concert recitalist.

At this point, by a lucky chance, a friend, Vera Scott, happened to learn that *Geraldo wanted a tenor to sing with his Gaucho Tango Orchestra (then resident at the Savoy Hotel) and to appear in a radio series of Spanish songs. The broadcasts were a great success and launched James Fife (now called Monte Rey) on a popular singing career. He frequently appeared with Geraldo and other bands, although he never became a regular band vocalist. During the pre-war years he made more than 150 recordings with Geraldo, Joe *Loss, Phil Green, and others, specializing in Latin American material. He first sang 'The donkey serenade' (*m* *Friml) with Joe Loss on a broadcast from the Astoria in 1939 and it became his most popular solo and regular signature tune. He entertained the troops during the Second World War, then continued his career singing on the Moss Empires circuit. He decided to retire in 1954 but made several come-backs before he finally stopped singing.

Reynolds, Debbie [Mary Frances] (*b* El Paso, Texas, 1 Apr. 1932). American actress, singer, and dancer. She started her film career in 1950 and appeared in four films, including the part of Helen Kane (1904–66), the 'boop-boop-a-doop' girl (who supplied the vocals) in **Three Little Words* (1950), before her cutely skittish personality gained her the leading role, opposite Gene *Kelly, in **Singin' in the Rain* (1952). She continued appearing in films into the 1970s, having her biggest hit with 'Tammy' from *Tammy and the Bachelor* (1957); and playing the title role in *The *Unsinkable Molly Brown* (1964). She starred in the Broadway revival of **Irene* (1973). She was married to singer Eddie *Fisher, and their daughter Carrie is also an actress.

D. Reynolds: *Debbie: My Life* (New York, 1989).

'Rhapsody in blue'. Work for piano and orchestra by George *Gershwin composed in 1924. The credit for the initial impulse that led to its being written is generally given to Paul *Whiteman, the self-styled 'King of Jazz', whose own musical ambitions led him towards a symphonic scale of jazz. In 1923, Gershwin had made a successful appearance at the Aeolian Hall in New York performing piano versions of his songs. Whiteman subsequently asked Gershwin if he would write an extended work for a forthcoming 'Jazz Concert' at the same venue, a commission which Gershwin at first declined. However, a premature publicity announcement in January 1924, which said that he was going to contribute to the concert, set his imagination working and an idea for a rhapsody began to form in his mind, eventually coming to him in its entirety before he put a note on paper. This now well-known work was first played on 12 Feb. 1924, with the composer as soloist, in a concert that started with some early jazz, moved on to 'Yes, we have no bananas' and 'Rhapsody in blue', and ended with Elgar's march 'Pomp and Circumstance' no. 1. It attracted wide press attention, mainly favourable.

Gershwin's original piano score bears the subtitle 'For Jazz Band and Piano'. It was put into orchestral form by Whiteman's orchestrator Ferde *Grofé who arranged it for saxophones, trumpets, trombones, 2 clarinets, oboe, tuba, 2 french horns, accordion, celesta, 2 pianos, banjo, percussion, bass, 8 violins, and soloist, and classified it as for 'Piano Solo and Orchestra'. Two years later he made an even larger orchestration which was the one heard for many years. Jazz-oriented listeners who had seen it as an inflated piece of pseudo-romanticism have welcomed a return to the leaner proportions of the original score; and a recording in which a new performance of the early jazz-band arrangement was neatly dovetailed with Gershwin's own solo piano roll version and proved it to be a taut and muscular work.

Rhapsody in Blue was adopted as the title of the

1945 film biography of Gershwin, played by Robert *Alda.

Rhythm 'n' blues. A term which came into vogue around 1949 when the magazine *Billboard* adopted it as the new heading for their on-going 'race' recordings chart, following several complaints about the continued use of the old name. Blues performances, by then, showed an increasing emphasis on the driving rhythms of jazz, producing a kind of *jump music with blues flavouring, often classified as city or urban blues singing, the result of music from the rural South being taken to northern cities. The new city blues men adapted the emphatic guitar styles of performers like Robert *Johnson and singers like Muddy *Waters, while Elmore *James introduced the amplified electric guitar to lend further power. Blues balladeers like Charles Brown and Percy *Mayfield; criers and shouters Joe *Turner, Jimmy *Rushing, B. B. *King, and Bobby *Bland; the jump band sound of Louis *Jordan; all these contributed to the emergent rhythm 'n' blues scene.

The race records had once been known only to real blues enthusiasts. Now rhythm 'n' blues joined up with the country music-based rock and roll idiom and basically blues artists like Fats *Domino, *Little Richard, and Larry *Williams became rock stars, often recording their own songs after they had already been exploited by white artists. Generally speaking, in the early days the rhythm 'n' blues artists were mainly black and the music was heard in widely divergent styles and frequently sung by vocal groups. 'Crying in the chapel' by the Orioles entered the charts in 1953, pioneering the vocal group sound as an integral part of the rock scene, and led to the popularity of such groups as the *Platters. The rise of such groups and their frequent merging of rhythm 'n' blues with gospel and pop elements was the genesis of *soul music, which led to the emergence of such as the *Drifters, the Phil *Spector groups, and, later, the *Jackson Five. If rock, on the other hand, was basically a white music, there were many soloists and groups in the widening rock scene who were blues-styled, for example the *Rolling Stones whom many would categorize as a rhythm 'n' blues rather than a rock group. The styles have inevitably merged and rock, now far removed from the clean country-cum-boogie sound of the Bill *Haley era, is mainly rhythm 'n' blues oriented.

L. E. McCutcheon: *Rhythm and Blues: an Experience and Adventure in its Origins and Developments* (Arlington, Va., 1971). R. Middleton: *Pop Music and the Blues* (London, 1972). P. Groia: *They All Sang on the Corner: New York City's Rhythm and Blues Vocal Groups of the 1950s* (New York, 1973). J. Whitburn: *Top Rhythm and Blues Records, 1949–71* (Menominee Falls, Mich., 1973). J. Broven: *Walking to New Orleans: the Story of New Orleans Rhythm and Blues* (Bexhill-on-Sea, 1974). A. Shaw: *Honkers and Shouters: the Golden Years of Rhythm and Blues* (New York, 1978).

Rice, Edward Everett (*b* Brighton, Mass., 1848; *d* New York, 16 Nov., 1924). American composer, producer, director, and actor. Born into a poor family, he left home in his teens to go on the stage. He left the theatre for a while to become a printer but, marrying the daughter of a theatre manager, his interest returned and he wrote the musical burlesque **Evangeline* (1874), with J. Cheever Goodwin (1850–1912), which had an immediate success. His main interest was in production and he gained a following for his early musical farces performed by a company known as Rice's Surprise Party. In 1894 he wrote **Adonis* with William F. Gill and Henry E. *Dixey (who starred in it and became a matinée idol as a result), a 'spectacular burlesque' which became the first American musical show to run for more than 500 performances [603p]. He then became one of the main importers of the then highly profitable British musical comedies that soon flooded into the USA; but he did not neglect native talent and his next pioneering effort was to produce *Clorindy* or *The Origin of the Cakewalk* (1898), which was the first musical to be written and played by black artists for a white audience. Rice was responsible for either discovering or encouraging such important figures as Henry E. Dixey (1859–1943), Lillian *Russell, Fay *Templeton, Julian Eltinge (1883–1941), and Jerome *Kern.

Rice, Thomas Dartmouth (*b* New York, 1808; *d* New York, 18 Sept. 1860). American singer, dancer, and composer. He was one of the first of the early blackface performers to become widely known, establishing his reputation in the Noah Ludlow touring companies. Later, as a solo performer, he devised an eccentric blackface act during which he introduced his famous 'Jim Crow' number, based on a song and dance act he had seen in Louisville, with his own words added. He first performed this around 1828 and introduced it to New York in 1832. It was to add a significant phrase to the American language; and it remained an essential part of his work in his entertainments *Bone Squash, The Virginia Mummy*, and, when he visited England in 1836, *Jim Crow in London*. He preferred to work as a soloist and refused to be part of any of the flourishing *minstrel troupes.

E. L. Rice: *Monarchs of Minstrelsy: from 'Daddy' Rice to Date* (New York, 1911).

Rice, Tim [Timothy Miles Bindon] (*b* Amersham, 10 Nov. 1944). British librettist and entertainer. After an early career in the recording industry, including a time as assistant to Norrie *Paramor, and a period as a pop singer, he came to public attention as the co-writer of **Joseph and the Amazing Technicolor Dreamcoat* (1960) in partnership with Andrew *Lloyd Webber. For the 1973 London production they produced an opening filler, *Jacob's Journey*. The profitable collaboration, full of fresh, individual, and literate ideas, continued with **Jesus Christ, Superstar* (1971). Rice rightly saw no future in *Jeeves* (1975), which Lloyd Webber wrote with others, but the old partnership continued with the highly successful **Evita* (1978). He moved into new partnerships to help conceive *Blondel* (1983, *m* Stephen Oliver) and **Chess* (1988) with Benny Andersson and Bjorn Ulvaeus. When not writing he has pursued an amiable career as a TV personality and promising amateur cricketer.

Rich, Buddy [Bernard] (*b* New York, 30 Sept. 1917; *d* New York, 2 Apr. 1987). American drummer and bandleader. Son of vaudeville performers, in whose act he first appeared at the age of 18 months, he made his Broadway debut in revue at the age of four, and, a mature six-year-old, toured Australia as a solo act billed as 'Baby Traps, the Drum Wonder'. He led his own band for 18 months when he was 11, and first came into the jazz world at 16 when he joined the band of clarinettist Joe Marsala (1907–78) at the Hickory House. He made such an impression that he was enlisted by such bandleaders as Artie *Shaw, Tommy *Dorsey, Bunny *Berigan, and Benny *Carter. In 1942 he joined the US Marines as a judo instructor, returning to civilian life and the Tommy Dorsey band in 1944.

He formed his first big band in 1946 in partnership with Frank *Sinatra. With the decline of big-band jazz, he reduced it to a smaller group in 1951 featuring Charlie Ventura (1916–92) on saxophone. In the Gene *Krupa tradition as an egocentric showman drummer and a driving ensemble player, not particularly at home in smaller jazz groups, he was also a talented singer and dancer. He successfully managed to front another large band from 1966 with which he toured widely, including an extensive tour of Europe in 1984 and in spite of persistent heart trouble, until the end of his career.

W. Balliett: *Super Drummer: a Profile of Buddy Rich* (Indianapolis, 1968).

Rich, Charlie (*b* Colt, Ark., 12 Dec. 1932). American country singer. He intended to be a saxophonist and played in a jazz group during service in the US Air Force. After his return to civilian life he took up manual work for a time before moving from Arkansas to Memphis to try to break into music. He signed up with Sun Records but did not achieve any major hits, the breakthrough coming with a recording for the Philips label in 1960 of his own song 'Lonely weekend'. In 1965 he recorded a hit with Smash Records, 'Mohair Sam'. He became more rooted in the Country and Western style, in which idiom he subsequently recorded for the Epic and RCA labels such hits as 'July 12, 1939' (1970), 'Behind closed doors' (1973), 'The most beautiful girls' (1973), 'There won't be anymore' (1974), 'A very special love song' (1974), 'I don't see you in my eyes anymore' (1974), 'Every time you touch me' (1975), and 'Since I fell for you' (1976).

Richard, Cliff [Webb, Harry Roger] (*b* Lucknow, 14 Oct. 1940). British singer. His father worked for a catering firm in India, the family returning to England in 1948 and settling in Cheshunt, where he was educated. His musical ideas formulated by rock and roll records of the period, he played with local groups before forming his own group, the Drifters, in 1958. After an appearance at the Gaumont in Shepherds Bush they were signed up to make a recording and achieved a No. 2 hit with 'Schoolboy crush'/'Move it' that same year. This was followed by an appearance on the *Oh Boy!* TV programme which had the immediate effect of making him a pop idol. He recorded 'High class baby', 'Never mind', and, in 1959, his first No. 1 hit 'Livin' doll'. The Drifters had now become the *Shadows. He appeared in the films *Serious Charge* (1959) and **Expresso Bongo* (1960), visited the USA in 1960, and was voted British Top Male Artist by *New Musical Express*. He had another big hit with 'Please don't tease' (1960).

Now in demand for films, he appeared in *The Young Ones* (1961)—'The young ones', *Summer Holiday* (1962), *Wonderful Life* (1964), *Finders Keepers* (1966), *Two a Penny* (1966), and *Take Me High* (1973). He became deeply involved in religious activities and in 1966 appeared with Billy Graham. In 1968 he featured in the Eurovision Song Contest with 'Congratulations' which, in spite of its great popularity, only achieved second place in the competition but went to No. 1 in the charts, his eighth recording to do so. He starred at the London Palladium in 1971 with the Shadows, who had now established a separate successful career. Twenty years after 'Livin' doll' (1959) he had yet another top hit with 'We don't talk anymore' in 1979. He was made an OBE in 1980. Increasingly involved in gospel work and remaining single, and youthful in appearance, he has continued as a considerable star of the pop world.

B. Ferrier: *The Wonderful World of Cliff Richard* (London, 1964). P. Doncaster and T. Jasper: *Cliff* (London, 1981). T. Jasper: *Silver Cliff: a 25 Year Journal 1958–1983* (London, 1983).

Richman, Harry [Reichman] (*b* Cincinnati, Ohio, 10 Aug. 1895; *d* Hollywood, 3 Nov. 1972). American composer, author, singer, actor, and comedian. He appeared as a boy in a minstrel act, started a career as an electrical engineer, but then studied music privately and became accompanist and partner to such stars as Mae *West, Norah *Bayes, and the *Dolly Sisters. He became the owner of nightclubs (known as the Club Richman) in New York and Florida. His own stage act prospered and his straw hat, cane, strutting walk, and theme song 'Puttin' on the Ritz' (by Irving *Berlin) became well-known and widely copied. He appeared on Broadway in *Queen o' Hearts* (1922) and was the star of **George White's Scandals* of 1926 (in which he sang 'Birth of the blues') and 1928. He was also in *International Revue* (1930)—'Exactly like you'; **Ziegfeld Follies* (1931); *George White's Music Hall Varieties* (1932); and *Say When* (1934); and the films *Puttin' on the Ritz* (1930); *The Music Goes Round* (1936); *Stars over Arizona* (1937); and the British *Kickin' the Moon Around* (1938). He appeared in radio and TV shows in which he regularly featured 'On the sunny side of the street' which was written especially for him. He also achieved fame as an aviator, making the 36th Atlantic crossing in 1936 in just over 18½ hours, achieved the first both ways trip, and held the world altitude record for a single-engine plane.

He wrote 'Muddy water' (with Peter *De Rose and Jo Trent, 1926), 'C'est vous' (with Abner Greenberg and Abner Silver, 1927), 'Miss Annabelle Lee' (with Lew *Pollack and Sidney Clare, 1927), and 'Help yourself to happiness' (with Mack *Gordon and Harry *Revel) which was used in *Ziegfeld Follies* (1931).

H. Richman and R. Gehman: *A Hell of a Life* (New York, 1966).

Rickards, Harry [Leete, Benjamin] (*b* Stratford, East London, 4 Dec. 1843; *d* London, 13 Oct. 1911). British music-hall artist. He originally worked as a mechanic in Woolwich dockyard, started appearing at small East End halls, and finally made it to the *Oxford Music Hall in the 1860s where he sang such songs as 'Oxford Joe'. A boisterously jovial comic in the 'lion-comique' tradition, he mingled such masher songs as 'Strolling in the Burlington', 'Lardy dardy do', and 'Captain Jinks of the Horse Marine' (which was the basis of a popular farce that became very popular in the USA) with patriotic items like 'That's the sort of man we want in England now'. Early in his career he went into management and bankrupted himself. He fled to Australia and ran a chain of variety theatres that introduced music-hall to the country, doing so well that he not only paid off his English debts but became known as 'The Variety King', and died leaving £60,000.

Riddle, Nelson (*b* Oradell, NJ, 1 June 1921; *d* Los Angeles, 6 Oct. 1985). American conductor, composer, arranger, and trombonist. His father was a trombonist and, after learning the piano from the age of 8, he changed to that instrument at 14. By 1942 he was playing and arranging for Charlie *Spivak, was with Alvino Rey 1943, Jerry Wald 1944, Tommy *Dorsey later in 1944 (on 'Opus 1' and 'The sunny side of the street' recordings), and with Les *Elgart 1945. He served in the US Army, after which he studied with Castelnuovo-Tedesco in California, played with the Bob *Crosby band, and then went to Hollywood as a staff arranger for NBC. He joined Capitol Records in 1950 and became known for his backing work on Nat 'King' *Cole recordings like 'Mona Lisa' and 'Too young'. After working with Frank *Sinatra from 1953 on such albums as *Songs for Swinging Lovers* and *In the Wee Small Hours*, he emerged as something more than an accompanist, his individual blend of strings and big-band swing leading to many LPs under his own name. His arrangements for Sinatra in such screen musicals as **Guys and Dolls* (1955), **High Society* (1956), **Pal Joey* (1957), and *The Joker is Wild* (1957) led to more prominent assignments as conductor and composer, and work with Judy *Garland, Ella *Fitzgerald, Dean *Martin, Peggy *Lee, Johnny *Mathis, and others.

He was MD for such film musicals as *Merry Andrew* (1958), **St Louis Blues* (1958), **L'il Abner* (1959), **Can-Can* (1960), *Robin and the Seven Hoods* (1964), **How to Succeed in Business Without Really Trying* (1966), **Paint Your Wagon* (1969), and **On a Clear Day You Can See For Ever* (1969). He composed scores for the films *Johnny Concho* (1959)—'Wait for me'; *A Hole in the Head* (1959); *Ocean's 11* (1960); *Lolita* (1962)—'Lolita ya-ya'; *Come Blow Your Horn* (1963); *What a Way to Go* (1964)—'Louisa's theme'; *A Rage to Live* (1965); *El Dorado* (1966); and many others, winning an Academy Award for *The Great Gatsby* (1974). He also provided themes and scores for such TV features as *The Untouchables* (1960); *Route 66* (1960); *The Rogues* (1964); *Batman* (1967); *The Most Deadly Game* (1969); *Emergency Ward 1* (1972); and wrote a number of orchestral works. Latterly he suffered much ill-health and retired in 1973, but made a brief comeback in 1983 to record and work with Linda *Ronstadt.

Riff. The repetition of a short distinctive phrase behind either a soloist or section and often used as a melodic feature. The device came early into jazz but was a special characteristic of the big-band era of the 1930s where it put much of the driving swing into such music and became even more of an end in itself, as the riff grew in intensity and excitement. Many swing era tunes like 'Flying home' and 'In the mood' were built on riffs.

Rifkin, Joshua (*b* New York, 22 Apr. 1944). American musicologist, conductor, and pianist. He studied at the Juilliard School of Music 1964, New York University 1964–6, Göttingen University 1966–7, and Princeton 1969, and worked with Karl-Heinz Stockhausen in Darmstadt in 1961 and 1965. In 1970 he joined the faculty of Brandeis University in Massachusetts and became noted for his research and performances in the fields of Renaissance and Baroque music. He found time to exploit a parallel interest in popular music, playing with the Even Dozen Jug Band 1966–7 and, through a timely series of LP recordings for Nonesuch 1970–4, did much to foster a strong revival of interest in the music of Scott *Joplin and the classic ragtime era.

Rimmer, William (*b* Southport, 1862; *d* Southport, 9 Feb. 1936). British composer, conductor, and teacher. Son of an army bandmaster whose band he joined at the age of 15 as a drummer, he switched to cornet and was a soloist at Belle Vue in 1882. He played with the *Besses o' th' Barn band for several years before becoming bandmaster of the Southport Artillery Volunteers in 1889. At the age of 30 he became a professional band trainer and directed such bands as Irwell Springs, Wingates Temperance, *Black Dyke Mills, Hebden Bridge, *Fodens, and Besses o' th' Barn. During this time he was rarely out of the major prize lists and in 1909 alone conducted five of the six winning bands at Belle Vue.

In 1910 he retired from conducting and devoted his activities to composing and arranging, including the test-pieces for the Crystal Palace championships of 1910–13. He worked with a Liverpool publishing firm and made a brief return to conducting 1919–20. He was a leading figure of the British brass band world, and the BBC broadcast a *Homage to Rimmer* when he died in 1936. He is chiefly remembered for his regularly played marches like 'Punchinella' and 'The Cossack' (used by Fodens as their signature tune), but wrote many more as well as the popular cornet solos 'Hailstorm' and 'Cleopatra'. His nephew, Drake Rimmer, was also a prolific composer and arranger of brass band music.

Ring, Blanche (*b* Boston, 24 Apr. 1871; *d* Santa Monica, Calif., 13 Jan. 1961). American actress and singer. Small and vivaciously attractive, she was the daughter of an actor and, being from a generally theatrical family, her natural stage ability made her an outstanding interpreter of songs. She made her stage debut at the age of 16 and began her Broadway career in *The Defender* (1902) in which she made an immediate hit with her singing of 'In the good old summertime'. She appeared in several short-running productions 1902–3, including *Tommy Rot* (1902)—'The belle of Avenue A' and *The Jersey Lily* (1903)—'Bedelia', and began to get more substantial parts in *Sergeant Brue* (1905); *About Town* (1906); *The Gay White Way* (1907); *The Merry Widow Burlesque* (1908)—'Yip-i-addy-i-ay'; *The Midnight Sons* (1909)—'I've got rings on my fingers'; *The Yankee Girl* (1910); *Wall Street Girl* (1912); *When Claudia Smiles* (1914); *Broadway and Buttermilk* (1916); *The *Passing Show* (1919); *The Broadway Whirl* (1921); **Strike Up the Band* (1930); *Right This Way* (1938). She was also popular in vaudeville, as a mimic and singing such songs as 'Come Josephine in my flying machine', 'Waltz me around again, Willie', and 'Yip-i-addy-i-ay'. One of her last appearances was a small part in the Bing *Crosby film *If I Had My Way* (1940).

Rio Rita. Musical comedy with score by Harry *Tierney, book by Guy *Bolton and Fred *Thompson, lyrics by Joe McCarthy, produced at the Ziegfeld Theatre, New York, 2 Feb. 1927. It was the opening show at *Ziegfeld's new theatre [494p].

Captain Stewart of the Texas Rangers, played by J. Harold Murray (1891–1940) who sang 'The Rangers' song', chases a bank robber across the Rio Grande into Santa Luca where he falls in love with lovely Rita: Ethelind Terry (*b* 1900) who sang 'If you're in love, you'll waltz'. The only snag is that the robber he is chasing appears to be Rita's brother. In fact he isn't and it all turns out right as he gets both his woman and his man. There was a short London run of 59 performances, 3 Apr. 1930, with Edith *Day as Rita. The film version of 1929, with Bebe *Daniels and John *Boles, made it the first Broadway musical to be successfully adapted for the screen; a further version in 1942 starred Kathryn *Grayson.

Ritchard, Cyril [Trimnell-] (*b* Sydney, 1 Dec. 1897; *d* Chicago, 18 Dec. 1977). Australian actor, singer, dancer, and director. He started his career in Australia in the chorus of *A Waltz Dream* (1918) and moved on to slightly higher things in a series of musicals, mainly in a stage partnership wth his wife Madge Elliott (1898–1955). They arrived in London in 1925, and appeared in a number of musicals and revues in which he developed his tall, lean, dancing, croakily singing, and gurglingly chuckling character, somewhat in the Jack *Buchanan manner, with a very elegant and drawlingly un-Australian accent and a spirit of what was once described as 'resolute, undefeatable glitter'.

He displayed this character in such shows as *Bubbly* (1925); *RSVP* (1926); *Lady Luck* (1927); *So This is Love* (1928); *Love Lies* (1929); *The *Co-Optimists* (1930); *The Love Race* (1930); *The Millionaire Kid* (1931); *To and Fro* (1936); *Nine Sharp* (1938); *The *Little Revue* (1939), which he also directed; *Up and Doing* (1940); *Big Top* (1942); *The Merry Widow* (revival 1943); *Gay Rosalinda [Die Fledermaus]* (1945); *Sigh No More* (1945); *High Spirits* (1953); and he was a very effective Captain Hook in the Jule *Styne *Peter Pan* (1954). He also appeared in straight plays. He went to the USA in 1953 where he appeared occasionally, but mainly directed at the Metropolitan Opera, with a strong interest in *Offenbach, including *La *Périchole* (in which he was recorded) and *The Happiest Girl in the World* (1961), an Offenbach musical collation with a story based on Aristophanes' *Lysistrata.* He was in *The Roar of the Greasepaint—the Smell of the Crowd* (1965) and **Sugar* (1972).

Ritter, Tex [Woodward Maurice] (*b* Panola County, Texas, 12 Jan. 1905; *d* Nashville, 2 Jan. 1974). American singer and composer. He grew up on his father's Texan ranch and worked as a cowboy. After attending Texas University and the Northwestern Law School he broke off his education in order to become a singer, working on Chicago and Houston radio in 1929 and landing the role of the Lone Ranger on New York radio in 1930. He appeared on Broadway in the play *Green Grow the Lilacs* (1931), in which he sang cowboy songs, and he was heard in country radio shows, including his own, in the early 1930s. He started appearing in singing Western films in 1936 and was to be in more than 50 by the end of his career. Notably he sang the title song in *High Noon* (1952). He recorded prolifically and composed many songs in cowboy vein. In the 1970s he was occasionally on the **Grand Ole Opry* show from Nashville, and he was elected to the *Country Music Hall of Fame in 1964.

Rivera, Chita [Del Rivero, Dolores Conchita Figueroa] (*b* Washington DC, 23 Jan. 1933). American actress, dancer, and singer. After singing in the chorus of *Call Me Madam* (1952), *Guys and Dolls* (1953), and *Can-Can* (1954), she appeared in *Shoestring Revue* (1955), *Seventh Heaven* (1955), and *Mr Wonderful* (1956). Her vivacious, dusky talents found an ideal outlet in **West Side Story* (1957; London, 1958) and **Bye Bye, Birdie* (1960; London, 1961). Thereafter she was in *Bajour* (1964); **Sweet Charity* (1967); **Chicago* (1975); *Merlin* (1983); and *The Rink* (1985) with Liza *Minnelli.

Roach, Max [Maxwell] (*b* New Land, NC, 10 Jan. 1925). American jazz drummer. He started his jazz career in New York in 1942, his early association with Charlie *Parker making him an influential figure in the development of modern style *bebop drumming. A regular frequenter of *Minton's Playhouse club, he played in 1943 in a pioneering bop group with Oscar Pettiford and Dizzy *Gillespie. He worked with Benny *Carter 1944, afterwards in New York with Lester *Young, Miles *Davis, and others. He was with Jazz at the Philharmonic in 1952 and formed his own group in the mid-1950s with the gifted Clifford Brown (1930–56) on trumpet, continuing this into the 1960s. He composed many jazz instrumentals.

Robbins, Jerome [Rabinowitz] (*b* New York, 11 Oct. 1918). American director, choreographer, and dancer. He began his career with the Ballet Theatre, appeared in several musical shows as a dancer, then became recognized for his imaginative and lively dance scenarios for such Broadway musicals as **On the Town* (1944), based on his ballet *Fancy Free* (1944); *Billion Dollar Baby* (1945); **High Button Shoes* (1947)—'Mack Sennett Ballet'; *Look, Ma, I'm Dancin'* (1948); *Miss Liberty* (1949); **Call Me Madam* (1950); *The *King and I* (1951); and *Two's Company* (1952). For future productions he acted as director as well: *The *Pajama Game* (1954); **Peter Pan* (1954); **Bells Are Ringing* (1956); **West Side Story* (1957); **Gypsy* (1959); *A *Funny Thing Happened on the Way to the Forum* (1962); **Funny Girl* (1964; London, 1966); **Fiddler on the Roof* (1964; London, 1967). Latterly he returned to the ballet world.

Robbins, Marty [Robertson, Martin] (*b* Glendale, Ariz., 26 Sept. 1925; *d* Nashville, 8 Dec. 1982). American country singer and composer, born into a family of musicians. He enlisted in the US Navy in 1944 and fought in the Pacific. After the war, while doing manual labour, he started to play the guitar and sing his own songs, and cowboy songs learned from his father, in various local clubs. His easy, relaxed style soon made him popular and he was heard and sponsored by Little Jimmy Dickens who got him his first recording date, 'I'll go on alone' which attracted much attention.

His first big hit was 'Singin' the blues' (1953) and others soon followed, making him popular beyond the Country and Western bounds—'A white sports coat and a pink carnation', 'El Passo' (the first country song to win a *Grammy Award), 'Tonight Carmen', 'Devil woman', 'Teenage dream', 'Up to my shoulders in a headache'. Once described as the John Wayne of the cowboy ballad, he became one of the most successful of all country balladeers, declaring that he preferred singing to work. He appeared regularly in the **Grand Ole Opry* show and was the last to be heard from the old and now historic Ryman Auditorium in 1974. He was elected to the *Country Music Hall of Fame in 1982, just before he died of a heart-attack.

Roberta. Musical comedy with score by Jerome *Kern and book by Otto *Harbach, based on the novel *Gowns by Roberta* by Alice Duer Miller. It was produced at the New Amsterdam Theatre, New York, 18 Nov. 1933, where it had 295 performances.

Coming after the shapely operettas *The *Cat and the Fiddle* and **Music in the Air*, it turned out by comparison a somewhat vacuous musical comedy with a minimal plot involving a sporty American chap (Ray Middleton) who inherits a dress shop from his aunt (Fay *Templeton) and becomes emotionally involved with a Russian princess (Tamara). Bob *Hope was also in the cast, making his first major appearance on Broadway.

The name of the show was saved for posterity by the wealth of songs it enfolded—'You're devastating', 'Yesterdays', 'The touch of your hand', 'Let's begin', and the immortal 'Smoke gets in your eyes'—without obvious dramatic reason. The film version of 1935 starred Fred *Astaire, Ginger *Rogers, and Irene *Dunne and added 'Lovely to look at', 'I won't dance, and 'I'll be hard to handle'. It was filmed again, under the title *Lovely to Look At*, in 1952 with Howard *Keel and Kathryn *Grayson.

Robert and Elizabeth. Musical with score by Ron *Grainer and book by Ronald Millar, based on the play *The Barretts of Wimpole Street* by Rudolf Besier. It set to music the story of the heavily Victorian romance between the poets Robert Browning (played by Keith Michell, *b* 1928) and Elizabeth Barrett Browning (June Bronhill) going on under the glowering eye of her father Edward Moulton-Barrett (John Clements, 1910–88). It opened in London at the Lyric Theatre 20 Oct. 1964, and ran for 948 performances. The songs included 'The girls that boys dream about', 'Escape me never', and 'I know now'. It was revived in Chichester in 1987, having been staged in Chicago in 1974.

Roberts, Arthur (*b* London, 29 Sept. 1852; *d* London, 27 Feb. 1933). British comedian and singer. His first approach to the stage was at the age of 15 when he worked with a busker on the seafront at Yarmouth. For some seven years he appeared in various minor music-halls in the evenings while he worked as a clerk in the daytime, deciding to become a full-time performer after a successful appearance at the New Star Music Hall in Bermondsey. By 1876 he was appearing at the Sun in

Knightsbridge, *Collins's in Islington, and the Royal Holborn, alongside such performers as G. H. *MacDermott, George *Leybourne, and Jenny *Hill. He made his final breakthrough at the *Oxford Music Hall at the end of that year. His songs included 'If Mary Jane would only marry me', 'I'm living with Mother now', and 'If I was only long enough'. He followed the 'man-about-town' image of the earlier lion-comiques, dressing sharply, but his humour was decidedly blue.

Reaching the top of the music-hall profession, acclaimed by all, he appeared with equal success in pantomime at Drury Lane 1880–3, often working with the comedian James Fawn (1849–1923). His later career was mainly in burlesque and musicals such as *In Town* (1891), and in 1895 he took the leading part in *Gentleman Joe*. He returned to the variety stage in 1904, singing such typically saucy ditties as 'Some girls do and some girls don't'. In his final years he was employed by C. B. *Cochran, who was a great admirer, and appeared in Cochran's London Pavilion revues. He toured with the 'Veterans of Variety' in 1926.

A. Roberts and R. Morton: *The Adventures of Arthur Roberts by Rail, Road and River* (London, 1895). A. Roberts: *Fifty Years of Spoof* (London, 1927). B. Anthony: 'Arthur Roberts' in *Music-Hall* no. 31 (London, 1984).

Roberts, Charles 'Luckey' [Luckyeth] (*b* Philadelphia, 7 Aug. 1887; *d* New York, 5 Feb. 1968). American pianist, composer, conductor, singer, and entertainer. Born into a theatrical family, he was on the stage by the age of five, singing, dancing, and piano-playing with various children's troupes. He studied composition and was leading his own society band in the 1920s. A busy career as a pianist and entertainer included an appearance at Carnegie Hall in 1939 and he owned his own club in Harlem. He wrote scores for *My People* (1911); *Ziegfeld Midnight Frolic* (1916 and 1917); *Go-Go* (1923); *Charlie* (1923); *My Magnolia* (1926); many items in the ragtime idiom—'Junk man rag' (1913), 'Pork and beans' (1913), 'Music box rag' (1914), 'Palm Beach' (1914), 'Helter skelter' (1915), 'Ripples of the Nile' (1918); other piano pieces including 'Spanish Venus' (1915) and 'Railroad blues' (1920); also many songs.

Robeson, Paul (*b* Princeton, NJ, 9 Apr. 1898; *d* Philadelphia, 23 Jan. 1976). American bass singer and actor. He studied law at Rutgers University and won a reputation as a footballer. His stage debut was in *Simon the Cyrenian* (1921) and he first visited England as an unknown actor to appear in a Blackpool production of *The Voodoo*. He made his name as an actor from 1924 playing in Eugene O'Neill's *All God's Chillun Got Wings* and his controversial *The Emperor Jones*, and played the part of Porgy in the play by Du Bose and Dorothy Heyward.

In 1925 he gave his first recital of Negro spirituals (accompanied by Lawrence Brown). Alexander Woollcott described his voice as 'the best musical instrument wrought by nature in our time'. He toured Britain and Europe and achieved a great popular revival of interest in the *spiritual, giving concerts at London's Drury Lane in 1928 and at the Albert Hall in 1929, and began recording for EMI Records. Having first played Othello as a student, he now played the role in London in 1930 and was later to make it a triumph in New York 1943–5, achieving the longest run of any Broadway production of Shakespeare—296 performances. He appeared in the British production of *Kern's **Show Boat* in 1928 and was ever after associated with the song 'Ol' Man River', which he also sang in the 1928 film and in the 1932 US stage revival.

He starred in such films as *The Emperor Jones* (1933); *Sanders of the River* (1935)—'Canoe song', 'Congo lullaby'; *Show Boat* (1936); *King Solomon's Mines* (1937)—'Wagon song', 'Climbing up'; *The Song of Freedom* (1938); *Dark Sands* (1938); *Jericho* (1938); *The Proud Valley* (1940); *Native Land* (1942); and *Tales of Manhattan* (1942). He was associated with the patriotic 'Ballad for Americans' in 1940; but in the 1940s and 1950s he ran into difficulties in the USA over his alleged communist leanings and his passport was confiscated. After his freedom to travel was restored he confined his activities to European concerts, but illness ended his career in 1963.

E. G. Robeson: *Paul Robeson, Negro* (New York, 1930). S. Graham: *Paul Robeson: Citizen of the World* (New York, 1946). P. Robeson: *Here I Stand* (London, 1956; Boston, 1971). M. Seton: *Paul Robeson* (London, 1958). E. Hoyt: *Paul Robeson: the American Othello* (Cleveland, 1967).

Robey, George [Wade, George Edward] (*b* London, 20 Sept. 1869; *d* Saltdean, Sussex, 29 Nov. 1954). British comedian, actor, and singer. He went to Germany with his family when he was 11 and was educated in Dresden and at Leipzig University. On returning to England he continued his science studies at Cambridge for a while, but had to leave because of family circumstances and became a clerk. He started to appear at smoking concerts in the Birmingham area, first appearing in London in 1891 and making his music-hall debut at the *Oxford Music Hall in the same year; and he was soon on his way to earning his long-standing title of 'The Prime Minister of Mirth'.

He created various comic characters in brilliant sketches, otherwise appearing in a strange clerical sort of garb, with flat bowler and cane and blackened eyebrows. Although his patter was slightly blue he maintained a great air of pained dignity, telling his helpless audience that he had not come there to be laughed at. He appeared in Command Performances in 1912 and 1919; and became a leading pantomime dame in the Dan *Leno tradition, appearing mainly in the provinces and once in London in 1921. His talents were extended to the revue stage and he appeared with the utmost success in the long-running *The *Bing Boys Are Here* (1916, revival 1934) with Violet *Loraine (sharing with her the great hit of the show 'If you were the only girl in the world') and Alfred Lester. In most of the shows he appeared in, his special kind of song—'I stopped, I looked, I listened', 'It wouldn't surprise me a bit', and 'Bang went the chance of a lifetime'—would be inserted, and his part would mainly be a repetition of his variety act and character sketches. He was in the equally successful *Zig-Zag!* (1917); *The Bing Boys on Broadway* (1918); *Joy Bells* (1919); *Johnny Jones* (1920); *Robey en Casserole* (1921); and *Round in Fifty* (1922). He toured with his own show, *Bits and Pieces*, from 1926, visiting South Africa in 1927 and 1929 and Canada in 1928.

He widened his scope by playing in Offenbach's *Helen!* (an anglicized version of *La *Belle Hélène*) in 1931; appeared in a film as Sancho Panza to Chaliapin's Don Quixote; and in 1935 played the role of Falstaff in fine bawdy style, a role he repeated in the Olivier film *Henry V*. He continued in less successful revues, first broadcast in 1936, and was still touring at home and abroad up to 1952. He was knighted in 1954.

G. Robey: *My Life up to Now* (London, 1908). G. Robey: *Looking Back on Life* (London, 1933). A. E. Wilson: *Prime Minister of Mirth* (London, 1956). P. Cotes: *George Robey* (London, 1972).

Robin Hood. Operetta with music by Reginald *De Koven and book by Harry B. *Smith, first produced in Chicago in 1890 and in New York, at the Standard Theatre, 28 Sept. 1891. It told the traditional Robin Hood story with all the expected characters and with Tom Karl as Robin, supported by such well-known names as Henry Clay Barnabee (1833–1917), Eugene Cowles (1860–1948), making his debut, and Jessie Bartlett Davis (1861–1905) as Alan-a-Dale, singing the best-remembered song 'Oh, promise me' which was added after the first performance. An initial run of 40 performances was no reflection of the merits of what was America's first genuine homespun operetta. It continued as a lasting classic in numerous revivals in New York, the last professional one being in 1944. It was staged in London, the last production mounted by the Carl Rosa Opera Company (1875–1958) at the Prince of Wales Theatre 5 Feb. 1892, somewhat confusingly titled *Maid Marian* (which was the title of a De Koven sequel of 1902 in the USA).

Robinson, Bill 'Bojangles' (*b* Richmond, Va., 25 May 1878; *d* New York, 25 Nov. 1949). American dancer, singer, and actor. He began his stage career in minstrel shows and soon impressed with his exceptional agility and imagination as a tap-dancer and an exploiter of the then booming *cakewalk craze. He moved into *vaudeville in 1897, in partnership with his wife, and was to work in several double acts before he went solo in 1900. Now appearing on the Albee circuit, he combined his inventive dancing with comedy impressions and as 'Bojangles' Robinson came to be considered the world's greatest tap-dancer, much admired and copied, of course, by those who were to follow him in the growing film dance craze. His prime number was 'Doing the new low down'. He appeared in England in 1903, 1913, and 1926 either as a soloist or in one of his stage roles. He was in **Blackbirds of 1928* (1928); *Brown Buddies* (1930); *Blackbirds* (1933); *The Hot Mikado* (1939); *All in Fun* (1940); and *Memphis Bound* (1945); and appeared in several films, 1933–9. He became Mayor of Harlem and President of the Negro Artists' Guild, and was widely mourned and honoured when he died.

Robinson, J. Russell (*b* Indianapolis, 8 July 1892; *d* Palmdale, Calif., 30 Sept. 1963). American composer, lyricist, and pianist. A self-taught musician, he played with the *Original Dixieland Jazz Band and came to London with them before leaving to become house-pianist for QRS piano rolls 1917–25. Later he acted as accompanist for various vaudeville artists. He wrote the score for *Plantation Revue* (1922); a number of piano pieces—'Sapho rag' (1909), 'Dynamite rag' (1910), 'That eccentric rag' (1912; 'Eccentric', 1923); and such jazz-inflected songs as 'Margie' (with Con *Conrad, 1920), 'Singin' the blues' (with Conrad, 1920), 'Palestreena' (with Conrad, 1920), 'Aggravatin' papa' (with Roy Turk and Addy Britt, 1881–1938, 1922), and 'Beale Street mama' (with Turk, 1923).

Robinson, Smokey [Willam] (*b* Detroit, 19 Feb. 1940). American singer and songwriter. With some friends, he formed a group eventually called the Miracles and in 1957 they were heard by Berry *Gordy who arranged for a recording of one of Robinson's songs, 'Got a job', which was issued in 1958. Subsequent recordings for Chess revealed Robinson's expressive talents and his ability to switch from the ebullience of 'Way over there' to the sombreness of 'Bad girl'. Bob *Dylan was to describe him as 'America's greatest living poet' and many critics subscribe to the view that he wrote some of the best pop songs of the 1960s.

The group's first major hit was with 'Shop around' (1960), followed by 'You've really got a hold of me' (1962) and 'Mickey's monkey' (1963), and he was also writing hits for other people like 'The way you do the things you do' (the *Temptations) and 'My guy' (Mary Wells). With Motown Records in the mid-1960s he produced his best songs like 'My girl', 'Since I lost my baby', and 'Don't look back' (all recorded by the Temptations); 'My girl has gone' and 'The tracks of my tears' (for the Miracles); 'Ain't that peculiar' and 'One more heartache' (for Marvin *Gaye). By 1967 some of the initial verve seemed to be replaced by additional depths and 'The tears of a clown', having already conquered the British market, became their first No. 1 hit in that year. Robinson left the Miracles in 1972 to embark on a solo career with such hits as 'Castles made of sand', 'So in love', and 'Let me be the clock' and the albums *Smokey*, *Pure Smokey*, and *Quiet Storm* (1975). The hits continued with 'Cruisin'' (1979) and 'Being with you' (1981), in his telling vein of anguished love.

Robison, Carson J. (*b* Chetopa, Kan., 4 Aug. 1890; *d* Pleasant Valley, NY, 24 Mar. 1957). American composer, lyricist, singer, actor, and guitarist. He became a professional entertainer at 15 and played with various orchestras, first appearing on record as a whistler. A pioneer figure in American broadcasting, he appeared regularly from 1924 and became equally well known in films with his *hillbilly band, and a leader in the commercial development of country music. He first played as Carson Robison and his Buckaroos, later his Pioneers. In 1932 and 1936 he visited London and became known to many on commercial radio as Carson Robison and his Oxydol Pioneers.

He was composer of 'The runaway train' (1925), 'My Blue Ridge Mountain home' (1927), 'Goin' back to Texas' (1928), 'Barnacle Bill the sailor' (with Frank Luther, 1929), 'I got a gal in Kansas' (1930), 'Song of the prairie' (1932), 'Carry me back to the lone prairie' (1934), 'Ramblin' cowboy' (1934), and 'Home, sweet home, on the prairie' (1935), which became his signature tune.

Rock; Rock and roll. An amalgam of white American *country music, *boogie-woogie, and black *rhythm 'n' blues that was the basic styling of the new popular music of the 1960s and 1970s and thereafter. Essentially it was the result of white musicians moving into rhythm 'n' blues. The emphatic and driving beat was a fundamental attraction, often the overriding element which excited both the performers and its audience. Early pioneers of the music were Amos Milburn (1927–80), Charlie Feathers (*b* 1932), and Roy *Brown; but the commercial glory went to the more glamourized stars, who became the first gods of the modern *pop scene, such as Eddie *Cochran, Gene *Vincent, Chuck *Berry, *Little Richard, and Jerry Lee *Lewis. The Cleveland disc jockey Alan *Freed is usually credited with coining the term 'rock and roll' as a musical category. In fact it was much used in the obscure rhythm 'n' blues vocabulary of the 1940s as a euphemism for the sex act. Freed was the first, however, to exploit a minority interest in rhythm 'n' blues (then known as *race music) when he inaugurated his radio show *Moondog's Rock 'n' Roll Party*. In the first place the name was used to describe a simplified form of black rhythm 'n' blues now being aimed at a wider white audience. As seems inevitable in all popular music innovations (minstrel shows, ragtime, jazz, etc.) the first convincing commercial exploitation had to come from a white source. In the first place the music that Freed labelled rock 'n' roll was based on the smooth *doo-wop harmonies of black vocal groups like the Moonglows and the Penguins, a sound that was to develop into *soul music.

Most new moves in popular music start in an unremarked way and the trend is not noticed or chronicled until its impetus has become unstoppable. The *Boswell Sisters had recorded a number called 'Rock and roll' as far back as 1934 without arousing special interest. The first obvious rock and roll hit was 'Sh-boom' (1954), a white version by the Canadian Crew-Cuts of a black rhythm 'n' blues number by the Chords. This was followed in 1955 by the Platters' 'The great pretender' and the first Chuck Berry hits.

The first internationally known commercial pioneer of rock and roll was Bill *Haley who, with his Comets, set the world alight and launched the era with 'Rock around the clock' ('One, two, three o'clock, four o'clock rock') which provided an exciting prelude and theme for the film *The Blackboard Jungle* (1954). Haley's rhythms were simply the rhythms of black boogie-woogie and a melody that had already been heard by those with ears to hear in a Count *Basie number called 'Red wagon'. But the combination worked a revolutionary miracle and the leadable world market now newly discovered what the aficionado had been listening to for some time.

The next record of comparable importance came from a singer whose musical mixture was more that of white Country and Western sung with a rhythm 'n' blues feeling, an even more potent mixture than that which Haley had contrived—Elvis *Presley with 'Heartbreak Hotel' (1956), which became an instantaneous million-seller. Presley remains the biggest star that rock and roll produced before the music evolved into the more universal strains of commercialized pop. In England a pioneering figure was the actor/singer Tommy *Steele who moved in on the Haley wavelength. Such was the success of Presley in that pioneering mid-1950s period, with his sultry blues voice and tight trousers, that black artists, to whom the basic rhythm 'n' blues idiom was a natural language, had to whiten their sound accordingly to gain a commercial hearing. Chuck *Berry, with 'Maybellene' (1955), was clearly imitating the *rockabilly style of Presley so that it would be taken for a white performance. But it did not take long for black artists like Fats *Domino ('Ain't that a shame') and *Little Richard ('Tutti frutti') to get into the hit lists; and gradually the genuine thing was preferred by the discerning to the white imitation.

The emergence of rock as the basic element of the wider field of modern popular music is discussed under *Pop. The word 'rock' has by now taken on the categorical significance of being applied, or self-applied, to the groups which are taking themselves and their music more seriously than the overtly pop groups, just as a swing band of the 1930s would be thought of as being in a rather more serious category than a mere dance band. Thus, for example, the *Beatles would be considered a rock group, *Abba a pop group; though both come under the umbrella title of pop. There is also a blurred distinction in the mind between rock, which is basically a white music, and rhythm 'n' blues, which is essentially black; although the best of the former will inevitably colour its creations with a strong flavour of the latter. More specifically, rock and roll has come to embrace various types of music, in style ranging from the rockabilly of Johnny *Burnette to the gospel whoops of Larry *Williams; from the blues of Bo *Diddley to the comic *doo-wop of the *Coasters. Alongside social rebels like Eddie *Cochran must be listed mournful balladeers like Roy *Orbison and the *Platters. Rock and roll manages to be both eclectic and parochial. Performers are influenced by many types of music but, like jazz, rock is now sufficiently identified for it to be further coloured by flavours deriving from particular localities. Fats *Domino clearly derives from New Orleans; Buddy *Holly was distinctly a Texan.

Historically, rock and roll, in its original Presley-cum-Haley forms, had seen its best years by the 1960s. The accountants had influenced the music and persuaded its emerging talents to write pop songs rather than rock and roll numbers. Making the best of both worlds, the best pop artists like Neil *Sedaka showed a flair for good rock phrasing in songs such as 'Stupid Cupid' and 'Breaking up is hard to do'. Against similar successes we can measure the more general corruption of talent found in Freddy Cannon's 'Tallahassie lassie', often cited as possibly the worst rock and roll record ever made. The best line of endeavour was (again making a parallel with jazz) to be found in the encouraging artistic strength of the black artists who were soon completely integrated into the pop scene and provided much of its best music.

In the early days the record companies probably believed that rock and roll was a passing fad, a craze that would soon diminish. While servicing rock they tried to promote *calypso, which itself was to become a later vogue under a new name. Eventually they realized that there was no looking back. Rock would eventually swallow up calypso and call it *reggae. The old songs with sweet harmonies and tunes could still be performed by aged geniuses like Frank *Sinatra and sold to an older public, but the new music of the up-and-coming, bought by the moneyed young, was rock. Some may mourn the passing of the era of *Gershwin and *Kern. But it was the sheer strength of the rock tradition that ensured its survival and dominance. It was simply a new phase in the American musical tradition that stretched back through the blues and rhythm 'n' blues (initially supported as race music by many who might later deplore the shallow excesses of pop), the Negro spiritual, and white country music; to the old style Haley-type rock and roll, which already sounds as quaintly conventional as ragtime.

V. Fredericks: *Who's Who in Rock 'n' Roll* (New York, 1958). J. Gabree: *The World of Rock* (New York, 1968). C. Belz: *The Story of Rock* (New York, 1969). L. Roxon: *Rock Encyclopedia* (New York, 1969). A. J. Shaw: *The Rock Revolution* (New York–London, 1969). N. Cohn: *Rock from the Beginning* (London, 1970). C. Gillett: *The Sound of the City: the Rise of Rock and Roll* (New York, 1970). J. Hopkins: *The Rock Story* (New York, 1970). G. Wood: *An A to Z of Rock and Roll* (London, 1971). C. Gillett and S. Frith: *Rock File* (vols 1–3) (London, 1972–5). F. Hoffmann: *The Literature of Rock* (Metuchen, NJ, 1974). N. Nite: *Rock On* (2 vols) (New York, 1974, 1978; rev. 1982). N. Logan, B. Woffinden, and others (eds): *The Illustrated Encyclopedia of Rock* (London, 1976; rev. 1982). P. Hardy and P. Laing: *Encyclopedia of Rock* (London, 1987). R. Pattison: *The Triumph of Vulgarity: Rock Music in the Mirror of Romanticism* (New York–London, 1987). D. Rees, L. Crampton, and B. Lazell (eds): *Guinness Book of Rock Stars* (Enfield, 1989).

Rockabilly. A category of rock and roll, basically rock of the kind that emerged as a white style from the Southern states of America. It is the kind of rock that is most influenced by the white country *hillbilly music of tradition and, more recently, played by artists like Hank *Williams, Merle *Haggard, and Waylon *Jennings. In its rock form it emerged as music backed by acoustic guitar and bass with punchy rhythms, as opposed to the electrical sounds favoured by the black rhythm 'n' blues stylists. Much of rockabilly was to emerge through the activities of Sun Records in Memphis with whom Elvis *Presley first recorded, and his earliest and purest work on the few recordings like 'That's all right' that he made with the label are essentially rockabilly even if with some blues inflection. The tradition was followed by many young white bands and soloists, including Carl *Perkins, Rick *Nelson, Roy *Orbison, the *Everly Brothers, Conway *Twitty, and Brenda *Lee; and some of its flavour crept into the early music of the *Beatles. Some of the country blues artists like Rufus Thomas, *Howlin' Wolf, and Otis Spann played in a closely related style. The heyday of rockabilly was around 1954–8, after which rock lost the comparative cleanliness and simplicity that was its characteristic flavour.

P. Guralnick: *Lost Highways* [evolution of rockabilly] (Boston, 1979).

Rock on film. Rock first emerged as an incidental ingredient of the film *The Blackboard Jungle* (1954) where it was used to symbolize teenage rebellion against school-based authority. Thereafter many of the early rock films had a very basic plot that revolved around the career of a young rocker, generally opposed in his ambitions and way of life by an old square who was gradually won over by the honest strength of the music and youthful convictions. This was typified by the next Haley products, *Rock Around the Clock* (1955) and *Don't Knock the Rock* (1956); but the subject was treated in a more intelligent and even satirical way in *The Girl Can't Help It* (1957), in which Jayne Mansfield was painfully trained to be a pop star; as was her male counterpart in the later film version of **Bye, Bye, Birdie* (1963).

Many films of the period were contrived vehicles to display, with the slightest of background plots, the vocal talents of Fats *Domino, *Little Richard, and other current stars. The succession of films that Elvis *Presley made, on this pretext, such as *Love Me Tender* (1956) and *Jailhouse Rock* (1957) (see under PRESLEY for a fuller list) now survive on the strength of his musical rather than his dramatic talents. The first defiantly British film to exploit rock, *Rock, You Sinners* (1957), was contrived in the same spirit to exploit the talents of Tommy *Steele. *Six-Five Special* (1958) was an improvement and Cliff *Richard proved himself to be a singer who could also act a little in *The Young Ones* (1961). British rock was never fully integrated into a plot until the *Beatles made *A *Hard Day's Night* (1964) and *Help!* (1965). After this rock music became an essential background for films that considered themselves a true reflection of modern life, such as *The Graduate* (1967), which effectively featured music by *Simon and Garfunkel, and *American Graffiti* (1973), to mention but two outstanding examples. There were now also much better films wholeheartedly set in the rock scene itself, notably including *That'll Be the Day* (1973), Ken Russell's version of *Tommy* (1975), *Saturday Night Fever* (1977), and the film version of the musical **Grease* (1978). A list of rock films is to be found in Hardy and Laing: *Encyclopedia of Rock* (London, 1987).

Rocky Horror Show, The. Rock musical by Richard O'Brien, produced at the Royal Court Theatre, London, 19 June 1973, with Tim Curry as Frank'n'Furter, a modern, sexy, and rock-oriented sort of Frankenstein, a 'sweet transvestite from Transsexual in Transylvania', busy producing a boy horror called Rocky. It was revived at the Comedy Theatre 6 Apr. 1979, having been seen in New York (Belasco Theatre) 10 Mar. 1975. A film version was made by 20th Century Fox in 1976; and London had a stage revival in 1990.

Rodgers, Jimmie [James Charles] (*b* Pine Springs, Miss., 8 Sept. 1897; *d* New York, 26 May 1933). American country and folk-singer and guitarist. He spent his early life working on the railroad as a brakeman, but was forced to give up his employment in 1926 when he developed tuberculosis. He took to singing and playing in his enforced spare time, and was heard in Bristol, Tennessee, by RCA Victor recording producer Ralph Peer, who was greatly impressed with his talents and recorded him there and then, the items including his first issued recording, 'The soldier's sweetheart' (1928), which sold more than a million copies. After this his recordings rapidly became popular and his fame spread remarkably quickly. He was soon known all over the world and was asked to tour the USA, Mexico, Canada, and England. He died in New York while he was on one of his regular trips to the RCA Victor studios, having made his last recordings in a state of near collapse. His friendly voice and gift for narrative bracket him with Frank *Crumit, but he was much closer to being a genuine folk-singer and his work is tinged with deep feeling for the blues.

His popularity with American audiences was immense; during the period 1928–33 something like 20 million of his records were sold. This is all the more remarkable in view of the fact that these years included the worst of the depression when the American record industry as a whole nearly went under. One of his biggest hits was 'In the jailhouse now'. Dubbed 'The Singing Brakeman', and many of his songs having a railroad theme, he appeared in a film of that name in 1931. Although it did well in the USA it was to be his only excursion into films. He is said to have been a soft touch for a host of hangers-on who made sure that the money he earned never did much for his own welfare. This partly explains that, though stricken with TB, he still needed to make the records which turned out to be his last endeavour in May 1933; he died two days after the session.

Rodgers was a pioneer name in that confused area of music known as Country and Western, stretching from the fringes of *rock on one side to the purest of mountain folk music on the other. While he had the popular approach and touch, he was a genuine folk artist, a sort of urban cowboy, his subject a mixture of down-to-earth reportage and sentimental balladry. He combined such elements as his infectious vaudeville yodel with a genuine blues feeling in a number of recordings under the title of 'Blue yodel' (the first in 1928) while his simple but compelling guitar and banjo playing was an ideal backing, frequently recorded in the company of such undoubted jazz talent as Louis *Armstrong. The resulting mixture had the earthiness of folk-music yet the straightforward melodiousness of 1930s popular song. His name was the first to be placed in the Country Music Hall of Fame in Nashville in 1961, and in 1977 the USA issued a special postage stamp in his memory.

J. Rodgers: *My Husband: Jimmie Rodgers* (San Antonio, 1953; repr. Nashville, 1975). N. Porterfield: *Jimmie Rodgers: the Life and Tmes of America's Blue Yodeler* (Chicago–London, 1979).

Rodgers, Mary (*b* New York, 11 Jan. 1932). American composer and producer. Daughter of Richard *Rodgers, she was educated at the David Mannes College of Music, then wrote for revues, clubs, and TV before becoming known with her score for *Once Upon a Mattress* (1959), which successfully avoided being influenced by her overwhelmingly famous father. Her subsequent scores for *Hot Spot* (1963) and *The Mad Show* (1965) did not achieve the same popularity. From 1957 to 1963 she was editor and assistant producer of Leonard *Bernstein's TV concerts for children, and she has written many scores for TV.

Rodgers, Richard Charles (*b* New York, 28 June 1902; *d* New York, 30 Dec. 1979). American composer. His father was a doctor and his mother a pianist: from her he inherited his musical gifts and received his first piano lessons. At 14 he achieved his first copyrighted song, 'My auto show girl', and, already a talented pianist, wrote music for amateur shows. At the age of 18, while studying at Columbia University, he was introduced by Herbert *Fields to Lorenz *Hart, his future lyric-writer and a man seven years his senior. They collaborated on a university show which enjoyed great popularity and convinced them that they could form a viable partnership in the hard world of the commercial theatre. For the next five years their songs were remorselessly rejected by every publisher they tried. During this period they wrote several musical comedy scores but only managed amateur productions and no money came their way. By 1925 they were ready to give up—Hart to go back to translating German plays for the American stage, Rodgers to take up a career in the children's underwear business. By lucky chance they were approached by the Junior Section of the Theatre Guild to provide music and lyrics for a revue designed to raise money on behalf of the Guild. They agreed reluctantly, and only when it was pointed out that Guild productions were frequently favourably noticed. They went ahead and *The Garrick Gaieties of 1925*, as it was called, outran its single planned Sunday evening production to last for about 18 months. Songs like 'Manhattan' were a major part of its success. Translations and three-button vests rapidly receded from their outlook and they were able to stage *Dearest Enemy* (1925)—'Here in my arms'—which was one of their stock of already written shows.

The Rodgers and Hart collaboration was to continue until Hart became too ill to work. His alcoholic tendencies underlaid an erratic character, his working method being to scribble things down on the backs of envelopes and other scraps of paper which were often mislaid; a complete contrast in character and habits to Rodgers, who worked methodically, more or less to a daily timetable, and produced results very rapidly. The incompatible partnership achieved some wonderful results, however, and a harvest of sophisticated and charming songs that combined Hart's adventurously rhyming and witty lyrics with the *Kern-like charm of Rodgers's music.

Their shows included: *The Girl Friend* (1926)—'The blue room'; *The *Garrick Gaieties of 1926*—'Mountain greenery'; *Peggy-Ann* (1926)—'Where's that rainbow'; *Lido Lady* (London, 1926); *Betsy* (1926); **One Dam Thing After Another* (London, 1927); *A *Connecticut Yankee* (1927, revised 1943)—'My heart stood still', 'Thou swell' (1943 version), 'To keep my love alive'; *She's My Baby* (1928); *Present Arms* (1928; filmed as *Leathernecking*, 1930)—'You took advantage of me'; *Chee-Chee* (1928); *Spring is Here* (1929; filmed 1930)—'With a song in my heart'; *Heads Up!* (1929; filmed 1930)—'A ship without a sail'; *Simple Simon* (1930)—'Ten cents a dance'; **Ever Green* (London, 1930; filmed, as *Evergreen*, 1935)—'Dancing on the ceiling'; *America's Sweetheart* (1931).

For the next few years they were lured, like many of their ilk, to write for the lucrative film business and produced material for *The Hot Heiress* (1931); *Love Me Tonight* (1932)—'Isn't it romantic', 'Lover'; *The Phantom President* (1932)—'Give her a kiss'; *Hallelujah, I'm a Bum* (1933)—'You are too beautiful'; *Hollywood Party* (1934); *Manhattan Melodrama* (1934)—'The bad in every man'; *Nana* (1934)—'That's love; and *Mississippi* (1935)—'Down by the river', 'Soon', 'It's easy to remember'.

The musicals continued with an even greater abundance of fine songs with *Jumbo* (1935; filmed 1962)—'The most beautiful girl in the world', 'Little girl blue', 'My romance'; **On Your Toes* (1936; filmed 1939; revived 1954)—'There's a small hotel', 'Glad to be unhappy', 'Slaughter on Tenth Avenue' (ballet); **Babes in Arms* (1937; filmed 1939)—'My funny Valentine', 'Johnny One Note', 'The lady is a tramp', 'Where or when'; *I'd Rather Be Right* (1937)—'Have you met Miss Jones?'; *I Married an Angel* (1938; filmed 1942)—'I married an angel', 'Spring is here', 'At the Roxy Music Hall'; *The *Boys from Syracuse* (1938; filmed 1940)—'Falling in love with love', 'This can't be love'; *Too Many Girls* (1939; filmed 1940)—'I didn't know what time it was', 'You're nearer'; *Higher and Higher* (1940); **Pal Joey* (1940; filmed 1957)—'Bewitched', 'I could write a book'; **By Jupiter* (1942)—'Wait till you see her'. Other films included: *Dancing Pirate* (1936); *Fools for Scandal* (1938); *They Met in Argentina* (1941); *Meet the People* (1944)—'I like to recognize the tune'. A somewhat fictionalized film biography of the two men, *Words and Music*, was made in 1948, with a star cast including Mickey *Rooney as Hart and Tom Drake (1918–82) as Rodgers.

When the partnership with Hart came to an enforced end, there was obvious speculation about Rodgers's ability to work with another lyric-writer after such a long partnership. The Theater Guild provided the solution again, in the person of Theresa Helburn, who suggested that he should work with Oscar *Hammerstein II on a musical version of the play *Green Grow the Lilacs*. The result exceeded all expectations. Miraculously a new Rodgers had emerged to write music in a new American folk opera tradition, quite different from the sophisticated output with Hart, but equally, if not more, replete with melody. In fact, there can be few scores more tightly packed with singable tunes than the resulting **Oklahoma!* (1943; filmed 1955)—'Oh, what a beautiful morning', 'The surrey with the fringe on top', 'People will say we're in love', 'I cain't say no', 'Many a new day', to mention but a few—which opened in New York in March 1943 and was to run for more than four years. The Rodgers and Hammerstein partnership astoundingly produced classic shows in regular succession, including: **Carousel* (1945; filmed 1956)—'If I loved you', 'Soliloquy', 'June is bustin' out all over', 'You'll never walk alone'; **Allegro* (1947)—'A fellow needs a girl', 'You are never away', 'The gentleman is a dope'; the *Pulitzer Prize-winning **South Pacific* (1949; filmed 1958)—'Some enchanted evening', 'There is nothin' like a dame', 'Bali Ha'i', 'I'm gonna wash that man right outa my hair', 'Wonderful guy'; *The *King and I* (1951; filmed 1956)—'I whistle a happy tune', 'Hello, young lovers', 'Getting to know you', 'Shall we dance?'; *Me and Juliet* (1953)—'No other love'; *Pipe Dream* (1955)—'All at once you love her'; **Flower Drum Song* (1958—'I enjoy being a girl', 'Love, look away'; *The *Sound of Music* (1959; filmed 1965)—'My favorite things', 'Maria', 'Climb ev'ry mountain', 'Edelweiss', 'Do-re-mi'.

Films with Hammerstein were **State Fair* (1945; remake 1962)—'It's a grand night for singing', 'It might as well be Spring', 'That's for me'; and, for TV, *Cinderella* (1957; remake 1965)—'Ten minutes ago'. Hammerstein's lyrics proved just as durable, in a less brittle vein, as Hart's; and it is hard to see how Hart would have coped with a story like *The King and I*. After Hammerstein died in 1960, the indefatigable Rodgers continued, writing his own lyrics for *No Strings* (1962)—'The sweetest sounds', considered by some to be one of his best scores and having a run of 580 performances; working with Stephen *Sondheim on *Do I Hear a Waltz?* (1965); *Two By Two* (1970), with Martin Charnin; and *Rex* (with Sheldon *Harnick, 1976).

Other works by Rodgers included the sound-track music for a TV documentary of enormous length called *Victory at Sea* (1952), which portrayed the part that the US Navy played in the Second World War. The music was somewhat repetitious and rather disappointing, although parts of it achieved some contemporary favour. This was followed by *Winston Churchill: the Valiant Years* (1960). Some of his best orchestral writing was in 'Slaughter on Tenth Avenue', the ballet scene that was incorporated in *On Your Toes* and has since been recorded separately several times.

J. D. Taylor: *Some Enchanted Evening: the Story of Rodgers and Hammerstein* (New York, 1953). D. Ewen: *With a Song in his Heart* (New York, 1963). S. Green: *The Rodgers and Hammerstein Story* (New York, 1963). R. Rodgers: *Musical Stages: his Autobiography* (New York, 1975). S. Marx and J. Clayton: *Rodgers and Hart: Bewitched, Bothered and Bedevilled* (New York, 1976). F. Nolan: *The Sound of Their Music: the Story of Rodgers and Hammerstein* (London, 1978).

Music: R. Rodgers (ed.): *The Rodgers and Hart Song Book* (New York, 1951; new edn. 1968). L. Snider (ed.): *The Songs of Richard Rodgers* (New York, n.d.).

Rogers, Anne (*b* Liverpool, 29 July 1933). British actress, singer, and dancer. She started her career with an immediate success in *The *Boy Friend* (1954) singing 'I could be happy with you' and 'A room in Bloomsbury'; thereafter appearing in **My Fair Lady* in the US (1957) and England (1959); and in *She Loves Me* (1964); **Half a Sixpence* (US, 1966); *Walking Happy* (NY, 1967); **I Do! I Do!* (1968); and the revival of **No, No, Nanette* (1973).

Rogers, E. W. (*b* London, 1863; *d* London, 21 Feb. 1913). British composer and lyric-writer. One of the obscure figures who provided rich material for the British music-hall with little gain or credit, including such items as 'The mystery of the hansom cab' and 'Ask a p'liceman' (both with A. E. Durandeau, 1889), 'Following in father's footsteps' (1892), 'Skylark! Skylark!' (1901), and 'It's part of a policeman's duty' (1906).

Rogers, Ginger [McMath, Virginia Katherine] (*b* Independence, Mo., 16 July 1911). American dancer, singer, and actress. She started her career as a Charleston dancer and dance-band singer, before appearing on Broadway in *Top Speed* (1929) and making her mark in *Gershwin's **Girl Crazy* (1930) singing 'Embraceable you' and 'But not for me'. She returned to the stage later in her career as a replacement lead in **Hello, Dolly!* (1965) and in the London production of **Mame* (1969); but most of her fame accrued from Hollywood musicals, especially as the ideal partner of Fred *Astaire in nine RKO films and one for MGM. She also appeared in several straight films and won an Academy Award for *Kitty Foyle* (1940).

Her early musicals included *Queen High* (1930); **42nd Street* (1933)—'Shuffle off to Buffalo'; **Gold Diggers of 1933*—'We're in the money'; *Sitting Pretty* (1933)—'Did you ever see a dream walking'; and then, with Astaire, *Flying Down to Rio* (1933)—'The carioca'; *The *Gay Divorcée* (1934)—'The Continental'; **Roberta* (1935)—'I won't dance', 'Lovely to look at'; *Top Hat* (1935)—'Isn't this a lovely day', 'Cheek to cheek', 'The piccolino'; **Follow the Fleet* (1936)—'Let yourself go', 'I'm putting all my eggs in one basket', 'Let's face the music and dance'; **Swing Time* (1936)—'A fine romance', 'Never gonna dance'; **Shall We Dance* (1937)—'Let's call the whole thing off', 'They all laughed'; *Carefree* (1938)—'Change partners'; *The Story of Vernon and Irene Castle* (1939); and *The Barkleys of Broadway* (1949); also **Lady in the Dark* (1944)—'Suddenly it's Spring'.

D. Richards: *Ginger: Salute to a Star* (Brighton, 1969). A. Croce: *The Fred Astaire and Ginger Rogers Book* (New York, 1972). H. Dickens: *Films of Ginger Rogers* (Secaucus, NJ, 1975). P. McGilligan: *Ginger Rogers* (New York, 1975).

Rogers, Kenny [Kenneth Donald] (*b* Houston, 21 Aug. 1937). American country-music singer. He left the University of Houston to work with a jazz trio; later sang with the folk-singing New Christy Minstrels, and was a member of the rock group First Edition. When they disbanded in 1975 he decided on a solo career as a country singer and had his first great success with 'Lucille' (1977), which won a Grammy Award. He starred in the TV film *The Gambler* which was based on his song.

M. Hume: *Gambler, Dreamer, Lover: The Kenny Rogers Story* (London, 1981).

Rogers, Shorty [Rajonsky, Milton Michael] (*b* Great Barrington, Mass., 14 Apr. 1924). American jazz trumpeter, bandleader, and composer. He studied music at the High School of Music and Art, New York, and started his musical career in California. He played in the bands of Red *Norvo, Woody *Herman, and Stan *Kenton and was in much demand as an arranger. He formed his own band in 1954.

Rogers Brothers in Wall Street, The. First of a series of highly successful 'vaudeville farces' starring Gus

(1869–1908) and Max Rogers (1873–1932) [orig. Solomon], inspired by the earlier successes of *Weber and Fields. The music for this and others up to 1903 was written by Maurice Levi (1852–1904), thereafter by Max Hoffman. With book by John McNally (1852–1931) and lyrics by J. Cheever Goodwin (1850–1912), Georgia Caine in the cast, and such songs as 'The ballad of Murray Hill', the show opened at the Victoria Theatre, New York, 18 Sept. 1899, and had 108 performances. Subsequent titles included: *The Rogers Brothers in Central Park* (1900) [72p]—'By the sycamore tree'; *The Rogers Brothers in Washington* (1901) [49p]; *The Rogers Brothers at Harvard* (1902) [63p]; *The Rogers Brothers in London* (1903) [64p]; *The Rogers Brothers in Paris* (1904) [72p]; *The Rogers Brothers in Ireland* (1905) [106p]; and *The Rogers Brothers in Panama* (1907) [71p]. The series ended in 1908 when Gus Rogers died.

Rolling Stone. American pop magazine, founded in San Francisco in 1967 at the height of the flower power era, now published in New York. With a distinguished panel of pop journalists, it includes record and concert reviews, biographies, interviews, and general musical articles, wide-ranging and often political. Sometimes considered on the pretentious side, it nevertheless has become established as one of the most influential and literate outlets on modern American pop culture.

Rolling Stones, The. Leading British rock group formed in 1961 by vocalist Mick [Michael Philip] Jagger (*b* Dartford, Kent, 26 July 1943) and guitarist/composer Keith Richard (*b* Dartford, 18 Dec. 1943). The group in its heyday was to represent all that makes pop music unattractive to an older generation, rebellious, raucous, and uncompromising; and all that makes it most worth while to the devotee, with its unfettered and blues-based excitement.

Jagger and Richard started playing together after discovering a mutual interest in the then undiscovered rhythm 'n' blues artists like Chuck *Berry, Bo *Diddley, and Muddy *Waters. They were joined by Brian Jones [Lewis Brian Hopkin-Jones, then calling himself Elmo Jones] (*b* Cheltenham, 28 Feb. 1942; *d* Sussex, 3 July 1969) on guitar and Ian Stewart (later their road manager) on piano. Taking their name from a Muddy Waters song they began playing rhythm 'n' blues-based music around the Richmond area. They first attracted attention when they deputized for the Alexis *Korner band at the *Marquee and continued to make some appearances there, now joined by bassist Bill Wyman (*b* 1936) and drummer Charlie Watts (*b* 1941). An eight-month residency at the Crawdaddy Club in Richmond saw them acquiring a cult following; in May 1963 they signed a management contract with Andrew Loog Oldham and Eric Easton. Oldham was to the Stones what Brian Epstein was to the *Beatles, the mind behind the moulding of their image to attract popular taste.

They began to record for Decca, their first single 'Come on' being a rather timid shadow of their live performance, and the next, 'I wanna be your man', a *Lennon and *McCartney item done in Beatles style; but they managed to capture the intensity and excitement of their live performances in 1964 with 'Not fade away' and their debut EP. The press saw the Stones as rebels, unwashed and uncouth, the enemies of polite society; Jagger as a grubby dandy with his suggestive stage movements, semi-nudity, and intentional black sound. Not surprisingly the teenage rebels took them to their hearts. Their first LP, *The Rolling Stones*, issued in 1964, heralded the true emergence of *rhythm 'n' blues in Britain; and it remains probably the finest debut LP of any rock group; its undisguised tributes to obscure black city rhythm 'n' blues equalling and sometimes surpassing the originals.

The Rolling Stones toured the USA in 1964 and recorded there one of their finest ever EPs, *Five By Five*—which included a version of Chuck Berry's 'Around and around' which left the original in the shadows. Their 'Little red rooster' became a No. 1 hit in the UK. Their second album consolidated their first and was followed by a realization that, like the Beatles, they would not make further progress until they used their own material. So their next single was 'The last time', though even this was a fairly blatant copy of the Staples' 'This may be the last time'. They finally came into their own as songwriters in the summer of 1965 with their first US No. 1 'Satisfaction', the quintessential mid-1960s blues with a searing guitar introduction by Richard and an aggressive, slurred vocal by Jagger. Now the Rolling Stones could really challenge the Beatles, topping the polls and causing riots wherever they went. Some excellent singles followed—'Get off my cloud' (1965), '19th nervous breakdown' (1966), 'As tears go by' (1966), and 'Have you seen your mother, baby, standing in the shadows' (1966). These and many others firmly established Keith Richard as a leading pop composer, usually with lyrics by Jagger, but the credits not always clearly defined.

Like most bands around 1967 they became involved in the drugs and psychedelia phase with all its attached publicity. Under the detrimental influence of the Beatles' *Sergeant Pepper* album, they now issued what is possibly their worst ever album, *Their Satanic Majesties Request*. But this was followed by a series of singles and albums that saw them at their creative peak. 'Jumpin' Jack Flash' (1968) was the first single to surpass 'Satisfaction', taking its movement and tension one stage further. Their most consistent album was *Beggar's Banquet* (1968), which included the classic 'Sympathy for the Devil', 'No expectations', 'Street fighting man', and 'Stray cat blues'. During this period Brian Jones left the group, having been a virtual passenger for a year or so, and was replaced by Mick Taylor (*b* 1948) from the *Mayall band. Jones was found drowned in his swimming pool in July 1969. The single 'Honky tonk woman' reached another peak, their album *Let It Bleed* was as good as any so far; *Get Yer Ya-Yas Out* (1970) continued the high standard.

The Rolling Stones had been a blessed gift to Decca, who would never be allowed to forget that they had turned down the Beatles in their early days; but they now left to record their two finest albums on their own Rolling Stone label, *Sticky Fingers* (1971) and *Exile on Main Street* (1972). 'Brown sugar', from the first of these, will probably remain the track that future generations will play to explain what the Stones were all about. The haunting 'Wild horses' was also included. But *Exile on Main Street* is undoubtedly their finest album. Sounding like a tight jam session, it shows their work laid bare, a raw celebration of everything they stand for. Jagger and Richard are at their most relaxed and honest, displaying a mixture of styles held together by the great spirit of the occasion.

Subsequent singles and albums tried, through ever-increasing eclecticism, to recapture that spirit and verve, with varying success. Their best work since was on *Some Girls* (1978), which included the superb 'Just my imagination' and 'Beast of burden'. With the departure of Mick Taylor in 1973, the Stones had been joined by a kindred spirit, Ron Wood (*b* 1942), previously of the *Faces, prior to their 1975 USA tour. Keith Richard, having escaped sentence for possession of and trafficking in heroin in England, was charged again in Toronto in 1977, but got away with the penalty of a benefit concert; and he has managed to make newspaper headlines fairly regularly since. In spite of all, the Stones have remained a remarkably stable (in a purely practical sense) group. Their work in the 1980s has been of a consistently high level in such albums as *Tattoo You* (1981), *Undercover* (1983), and *Dirty Work* (1986). Those who saw them and survived will always maintain that their records were a pale shadow of the music they made amid the anarchy of their live shows.

R. Greenfield: *Stones Touring Party* (London, 1974). G. Tremlett: *The Rolling Stones Story* (London, 1974). D. Dalton: *The Rolling Stones* (London, 1975). R. Carr: *The Rolling Stones: an Illustrated Record* (London, 1976). T. Jasper: *The Rolling Stones* (London, 1976). P. Norman: *The Stones* (London, 1984). P. Norman: *Life and Good Times of the Rolling Stones* (London, 1989).

Rollini, Adrian (*b* New York, 28 June 1904; *d* Homestead, Fla., 15 May 1956). American jazz saxophonist, vibraphonist, bandleader, and composer. A talented young pianist who then took up various other instruments, he was leading his own band at the age of 14. Playing with the *California Ramblers 1924–7 he established himself as a pioneer and leading exponent of the little used bass-saxophone, which he used to telling as well as comic effect. He played with Fred *Elizalde in London 1928–9, and with other bands in England and the USA in the early 1930s. He made many recordings with pickup groups that included such names as Benny *Goodman, Bunny *Berigan, Pee Wee *Russell, Joe *Venuti, Jack *Teagarden, and the *Dorseys. From 1935 he led a group known as Adrian's Tap Room Boys at the President Hotel in New York and was more frequently featured as a vibraphonist. He tended towards a more commercial style in later years and latterly led a group in a Miami hotel, having settled in Florida. His younger brother Arthur Rollini (*b* 1912) was also a saxophonist and frequently worked with him.

Rollins, Sonny [Theodore Walter] (*b* New York, 7 Sept. 1929). American jazz tenor-saxophonist. He made his early mark playing with such modernists as Bud *Powell and Fats *Navarro, and he studied music in Chicago for a while. He recorded with Miles *Davis, and worked with Charlie *Parker and Thelonious *Monk. Rollins has become recognized as one of the most influential tenor-saxophone stylists, linking Coleman *Hawkins and John *Coltrane; his reputation continues to grow and he is rated one of the most imaginative jazz soloists of all time. In 1972 he was awarded a Guggenheim Fellowship for his contribution to modern music and his 'Concerto for Saxophone and Orchestra' was first heard in Japan in 1986. His other compositions include 'Oleo', 'Airegin', and the score for the film *Alfie* (1966).

Romberg, Sigmund (*b* Nagy-Kanizsa, 29 July 1887; *d* New York, 9 Nov. 1951). Hungarian-born American composer. After studying engineering at the University of Bucharest and music with Richard *Heuberger in Vienna, he went to the USA in 1909 to take up an engineering career but, unable to find work, took a job in the orchestra of a Hungarian restaurant. He bought a permanent home in New York in 1913 and eventually became a staff composer to the *Shubert organization, first writing music for one of their *Winter Garden shows, *The Whirl of the World* (1914). This was well received and was followed by a string of revues and musical comedies for the Shuberts and the production of his first operettas.

His scores included: *The *Passing Show of 1914*; *The Midnight Girl* (1914); *Dancing Around* (1914); *Maid in America* (1915); *Hands Up* (1915); *The Blue Paradise* (with Edmund *Eysler, 1915)—'Auf wiedersehen'; *A World of Pleasure* (1915); *Robinson Crusoe Jr.* (1916); *The *Passing Show of 1916* (also 1917, 1918, 1919, 1923, 1924); *The Girl from Brazil* (1916); *The Show of Wonders* (1916); *Follow Me* (1916); *Her Soldier Boy* (1916); *My Lady's Glove* (with Oscar *Straus, 1917); *Maytime* (1917; filmed 1937)—'The road to Paradise', 'Will you remember'; *Doing Our Bit* (1917); *Over the Top* (1917); **Sinbad* (1918); *The Melting of Molly* (1918); *Monte Cristo Jr.* (1919); *The Magic Melody* (1919); *Poor Little Ritz Girl* (1920); *Love Birds* (1921); **Blossom Time* (1921), based on the melodies of Schubert—'Song of love'; *Bombo* (1921); *The Blushing Bride* (1922); *The Rose of Stamboul* (1922); *Springtime of Youth* (1922); *The Dancing Girl* (1923); *Innocent Eyes* (1924); *Marjorie* (1924); **Artists and Models* (1924); *Annie Dear* (1924); *The *Student*

Prince (1924; filmed 1927 and 1954)—'Golden days', 'Drinking song', 'Deep in my heart, dear', 'Serenade'; *Louie the 14th* (1925); *Princess Flavia* (1925); his biggest success of all *The *Desert Song* (1926; filmed 1929, 1943, and 1953)—'The riff song', 'The desert song', 'One alone'; *Cherry Blossoms* (1927); *My Maryland* (1927)—'Your land and my land'; *My Princess* (1927); *The Love Call* (1927); *Rosalie* (1928); *The *New Moon* (1928; filmed 1930 and 1940)—'Softly as in a morning sunrise', 'Stouthearted men', 'One kiss', 'Lover, come back to me'; *Nina Rosa* (1930); *East Wind* (1931); *Melody* (1933); *May Wine* (1935); *Forbidden Melody* (1936); *Sunny River* (1941); *Up in Central Park* (1945; filmed 1948)—'Close as pages in a book'; *My Romance* (1948); *The Girl in Pink Tights* (1954). Romberg, from all this, is mainly remembered for those Viennese-style American operettas in the Victor Herbert vein, *The Student Prince*, *The Desert Song*, and *The New Moon*, written with Rida Johnson *Young.

He also wrote scores for the films *Viennese Nights* (1930)—'You will remember Vienna' (*w* Oscar *Hammerstein II); *Children of Dreams* (1931); *The Night is Young* (1935)—'When I grow too old to dream' (Hammerstein); *The Girl of the Golden West* (1938). A biographical film, *Deep in My Heart*, was made in 1954 with José Ferrer as the composer. For many years Romberg conducted his own concert orchestra.

E. Arnold: *Deep in My Heart: a Story Based on the Life of Sigmund Romberg* (New York, 1949).

Rome, Harold Jacob (*b* Hartford, Conn., 27 May 1908). American composer and lyricist. He originally studied for a law career, but played the piano in dance bands during his college days and later, while at Yale, took a course in music. By the time he got to New York in 1934 he had decided to become an architect, but the depression forced him to look for a living elsewhere. He wrote some songs, either words and/or music, and was able to sell some of them, and obtained a commission to write some of the songs for an ambitious amateur revue called **Pins and Needles* (produced by a garment workers' union) in 1937. The show was a tremendous hit, achieving 1108 performances with its forward-looking satirical comedy, and Rome's name became widely known for such items as 'Sing me a song with social significance' and 'Sunday in the park'. This was followed by revue material for *Sing Out the News* (1938)—'FDR Jones'—and *Let Freedom Ring* (1942), a Youth Theatre production. While serving in the army he wrote much material for troop entertainments.

Back in civilian life he wrote songs and lyrics for the revues **Call Me Mister* (1946)—'South America, take it away'—which had popular success, and *Bless You All* (1950). He moved into the field of the musical with **Wish You Were Here* (1953)—'Wish you were here', 'Where did the night go'; **Fanny* (1954)—'Fanny'; **Destry Rides Again* (1959)—'Anyone would love you'; *I Can Get it for you Wholesale* (1962); *The Zulu and the Zayda* (1965); *Gone With the Wind* (London, 1972)—originally performed in Tokyo as *Scarlett* (1970).

F. Rome: *The Scarlett Letters* (New York, 1971).

Ronstadt, Linda Marie (*b* Tucson, Ariz., 15 July 1946). American pop singer. She sang locally with her brother and sister and, after studies at the University of Arizona, formed a pop group called the Stone Poneys in Los Angeles. Her hits, including 'Different drum', 'Love has no pride', 'Faithless love', 'Blue Bayou', 'I never will marry', and 'Alison', ranged through a variety of styles, many in country vein. She recorded an album called simply *Linda Ronstadt* in 1972 and toured with Neil Young in 1973. A popular figure in the USA, courted by the top politicians, she was in the centenary production of *The *Pirates of Penzance*.

V. Claire: *Linda Ronstadt* (New York, 1978). C. Berman: *Linda Ronstadt: an Illustrated Biography* (New York, 1979).

Rooney, Mickey [Yule, Joe] (*b* Brooklyn, NY, 23 Sept. 1920). American comedian, actor, and singer. Son of vaudeville entertainers, he was taken to Hollywood by his mother and appeared as a child actor in silent movies, playing as Mickey McGuire in more than 70 productions. Small parts in 1930s movies made little impact, but he was noticed in *Thoroughbreds Don't Cry* (1937). In that year a part in *A Family Affair* led to the popular 'Andy Hardy' series. He frequently partnered Judy *Garland and appeared in a number of important musical films, including: **Babes in Arms* (1939); **Strike Up the Band* (1940); *Babes on Broadway* (1941); **Girl Crazy* (1943); *Summer Holiday* (1948); and *Words and Music* (1948), in which he played the part of Lorenz *Hart. He appeared in numerous straight films and on TV, including his own show; showed talent as singer, drummer, and pianist, leading his own band in the 1970s; and wrote a number of songs. He was again on stage on Broadway and on tour into the early 1980s, and with Ann Miller (*b* 1919) in the musical **Sugar Babies* (1979).

M. Rooney: *I.E., an Autobiography* (New York, 1965). A. Marx: *The Nine Lives of Mickey Rooney* (New York, 1985).

Root, George Frederick (*b* Sheffield, Mass., 30 Aug. 1820; *d* Bailey's Island, Maine, 6 Aug. 1895). American composer and publisher. He studied music in Boston, then settled in New York where he opened a Musical Institute in 1853 and was a church organist. In 1859 he went to Chicago and joined his brother's music-publishing firm Root & Cady.

A number of his songs have become American classics, such as 'The hazel dell' (1853), 'Rosalie, the prairie flower' (1855), 'There's music in the air' (1857), 'Flee as a bird' (1857), 'The vacant chair' (1861), 'The battle cry of Freedom' (1863), 'Tramp, tramp, tramp' (1864), 'Comrades, hasten to the battle' (1864), and 'Just before the battle,

Mother'—many popular in the Civil War years. He wrote his autobiography, *The Story of a Musical Life*, in 1891. Sometimes, in deference to the current vogue for German composers, he wrote under the name of Friedrich Wurzel.

Ros, Edmundo (*b* Venezuela, 7 Dec. 1910). British bandleader, percussionist, and singer. In London in the late 1930s, he became known as the drummer on some Fats *Waller sessions recorded there in 1938. He formed a Latin American dance orchestra in 1945 which soon became a popular recording group, having a top hit in the UK and the USA with 'Wedding samba' in 1949. His many LPs for Decca were best-sellers of the 1950s.

Rosalie. Operetta with music by Sigmund *Romberg and George *Gershwin, book by William Anthony McGuire and Guy *Bolton, lyrics by Ira *Gershwin and P. G. *Wodehouse. Produced by Florenz *Ziegfeld at the New Amsterdam Theatre, New York, 10 Jan. 1938, where it ran for 335 performances.

A typically vacuous story, concerning a lovesick aviator who woos a princess and is allowed to marry because her father abdicates, was supported by a patchy shared score with the best of the songs—'Oh gee! Oh joy!' and 'How long has this been going on'—supplied by Gershwin, Romberg being slightly preoccupied by the creation of *The *New Moon*. A great deal of material, including 'The man I love', was discarded from the score but came in useful elsewhere. Perhaps the main reason for its success was two excellent stars, Marilyn *Miller and Jack *Donahue in a well-produced piece.

Rose, Billy [Rosenberg, William Samuel] (*b* New York, 6 Sept. 1899; *d* Jamaica, 10 Feb. 1966). American author, lyricist, producer, and journalist. In 1917 he was working as a shorthand reporter for the War Industries Board and was to become a champion stenographer. He started writing songs in the early 1920s and had his first hit with 'Barney Google' in 1923. He collaborated on the scores of *Great Day!* (1929) and *Sweet and Low* (1930), and produced and wrote lyrics for his own *Billy Rose's Crazy Quilt* (1931), and the same year founded, with Edgar *Leslie and George W. *Meyer, the Songwriters' Protective Association. He was married to Fanny *Brice, 1929–36. In 1934 he opened Billy Rose's Music Hall in New York, employing the Benny *Goodman band there for several months, and in 1938 his famous New York club, the Diamond Horseshoe, by which he is mainly remembered, and became a theatre proprietor.

He produced such shows as *Jumbo* (1935), **Carmen Jones* (1943), and *Seven Lively Arts* (1944); and numerous spectacular acquacades at various World's Fairs and Expositions. He was the writer of innumerable lyrics (many in collaboration with Mort Dixon, 1892–1956), including: 'Don't bring Lulu', 'That old gang of mine', 'Clap hands, here comes Charley!', 'Me and my shadow', 'Back in your own backyard', 'There's a rainbow round my shoulder', 'I found a million dollar baby in a ten cent store', 'Without a song', 'It's only a paper moon', 'The night is young and you're so beautiful', 'Great day', 'It happened in Monterey', working with Ray *Henderson, Fred *Fisher, Con *Conrad, Harold *Arlen, Harry *Warren, Al *Jolson, and others.

B. Rose: *Wine, Women and Words* (New York, 1948). E. Conrad: *Billy Rose: Manahattan Primitive* (Cleveland, 1968).

Rose, David (*b* London, 15 June 1910; *d* Burbank, Ca., 23 Aug. 1990). British-born American composer. A US citizen from the age of four, when his family went to live in Chicago, where he attended the Chicago College of Music. He played in radio bands and with Ted *Fiorito. In the mid-1930s he went to Hollywood and was musical director of a radio network there. He joined the US Air Force, directed their official show *Winged Victory* and in 1943 wrote his big hit 'Holiday for strings'. This piece signalled a revival of light orchestral music and set a fashion in string section writing.

He returned to Hollywood as musical director of MGM films and wrote scores for *Never a Dull Moment* (1943); *The Princess and the Pirate* (1944); *Winged Victory* (1945); *Wonder Man* (1945); *Please Don't Eat the Daisies* (1960); *Never Too Late* (1964); and many more. His other writings include 'Dance of the Spanish onion' (1942), 'Big Ben' (1944), 'Lovers' serenade' (1949), 'Puppet serenade' (1952), 'Cool tango' (1958), and 'The stripper' (1961). He recorded many albums of his music in the 1960s and presented and conducted his own concerts at the Pasadena Pops and the Hollywood Bowl.

Rose, Fred (*b* Evansville, Ind., 24 Aug. 1897; *d* Nashville, 1 Dec. 1954). American composer, singer, and pianist. He grew up in St Louis and by the age of 15 was earning his living as an entertainer in Chicago nightclubs. He started to record for Brunswick in the 1920s and wrote such hits as 'Honest and truly' (1924), 'Charlestonette' (1925)—with Paul *Whiteman during a period with the band, and 'Deed I do' (1936). By the early 1930s he was working in Nashville, where he had his own radio show. An early composer of *country music, while it was just shaking off the *hillbilly image, he then worked in Hollywood and often collaborated with Gene *Autry, turning out such country classics as 'Be honest with me' (1940), 'I'm trusting in you' (1941), and 'Tears on my pillow' (1941). He went into publishing in Nashville and later worked as a talent scout. He was elected to the *Country Music Hall of Fame in 1961.

Rose, Vincent (*b* Palermo, Sicily, 13 June 1880; *d* Rockville Center, NY, 20 May 1944). Italian-born American bandleader and composer. He studied music in Italy and went to the USA in 1897, first settling in Chicago where he worked as an orchestral musician. Then he went to Los Angeles and was musical director for a chain of West Coast hotels. He had his own orchestra in California for 20 years for which he composed exclusively. In 1930 he went to Hollywood to write for films, afterwards settling in New York and devoting his time to composition. His songs included 'Avalon' (with Al *Jolson, 1920), 'Whispering' (with John Schonberger, 1920), 'Linger awhile' (1923, *w* Harry *Owen), 'Pardon me' and 'Pretty baby' (both in **Earl Carroll's Vanities*, 1931), 'The umbrella man' (with Larry Stock, 1938), and 'Blueberry Hill' (1940).

***Rose-Marie*.** Romantic musical with score by Rudolf *Friml, additional music by Herbert *Stothart, and book by Otto *Harbach and Oscar *Hammerstein II, produced at the Imperial Theatre, New York, 2 Sept. 1924, where it had 557 performances.

The first musical to be set in Canada, it featured the Rockies and the Canadian Mounties. Harbach and Hammerstein made a trip to Canada to get it right and came up with a heart-stirring story of the love betwixt singer Rose-Marie (played by Mary *Ellis) and fur-trapper Jim Kenyon (Dennis *King) who is falsely accused of murder. The Mounties clear his name and get the right culprit and it all ends like a song. The musical items included 'Rose-Marie', 'Indian love call', 'Totem tom-tom', 'Only a kiss', and 'The door of her dreams'.

It was Friml's greatest success and was to go on to a lasting life of revivals and amateur productions in a vein so beloved by spare-time tenors and sopranos. It was equally successful in Paris, at the Mogador in 1927 [1250p], and in London, at Drury Lane 20 Mar. 1925, where Derek Oldham, Edith *Day, and Billy *Merson were in the cast and it had 851 performances. It was filmed in 1928, with Joan Crawford and James Murray; in 1936, with Jeanette *MacDonald and Nelson *Eddy; and again in 1954, with Howard *Keel and Ann Blyth.

Rosenfeld, Monroe H. (*b* Brooklyn, NY, 1862; *d* New York, 13 Dec. 1918). American composer and author. A well-known *Tin Pan Alley character, he is generally credited with the invention of the name around 1903. It is said that he was preparing an article on popular music for the *New York Herald* when, in Harry *Von Tilzer's office on 28th Street, he heard the jangling strains of a doctored piano; which inspired him to call his article 'Tin Pan Alley'. This caught on as a nickname for 28th Street and soon for all the popular musical activities that went on there. He was well-known as a journalist with a flair for discovering new talents, among them the early star of American musicals and vaudeville Emma Carus (1879–1927).

Having written a column of song reviews in the *New York Herald*, he began to write songs himself, many under such pseudonyms as E. Heiser and F. Belasco. He was naturally adept at getting publicity for his own products, although he had a reputation for stealing tunes. But he managed some considerable successes from 1884, onward, such as 'Climbing up the golden stairs' (1884), 'Hush, little baby, don't cry' (1884), 'Her golden hair was hanging down her back' (1884, *w* Felix *McGlennon), 'Goodbye, my boy, goodbye' (1885), 'Johnny get your gun' (1886), 'With all her faults, I love her still' (1888), 'Kutchy, kutchy, koo' (1888), 'Those wedding bells shall not ring out' (1896), 'Take back your gold' (1897), and 'Gold will buy almost anything but a true girl's heart' (1898).

Rosenman, Leonard (*b* New York, 7 Sept. 1924). American composer. He intended to be a painter, but, after serving in the US Air Force in the Second World War, started to study music. Apart from many works in the classical field, he regularly wrote for films from 1955, his scores including: *East of Eden* (1955); *The Cobweb* (1955); *Rebel Without a Cause* (1955); *Edge of the City* (1956); *The Young Stranger* (1957); *Lafayette Escadrille* (1958); *Pork Chop Hill* (1959); *The Rise and Fall of Legs Diamond* (1960); *The Outsider* (1961); *The Chapman Report* (1962); *Fantastic Voyage* (1966); *Hellfighters* (1968); *A Man Called Horse* (1970); *Beneath the Planet of the Apes* (1971); and music for such TV features as *The Defenders* and *Marcus Welby MD*.

Ross, Adrian [Ropes, Arthur Reed] (*b* Lewisham, 23 Dec. 1859; *d* London, 10 Sept. 1933). British librettist and lyricist. He was a fellow of King's College, Cambridge, until 1880 before he became one of the best-known lyric-writers for the British musical stage. He started by writing a light opera, *Faddimir*, then became known for his association with a string of productions, 16 of which ran for over 400 performances. These included: *Joan of Arc* (1891, *m* F. Osmond *Carr); *In Town* (1892, Carr); *Morocco Bound* (1893, Carr); *Mirette* (1894, *Messager); **The Circus Girl* (1896, Ivan *Caryll); *A *Greek Slave* (1896, Sidney *Jones); *The *Grand Duchess* (1897, *Offenbach); **San Toy* (1899, Jones); *The Messenger Boy* (1900, Caryll and Lionel *Monckton); *The *Toreador* (1901, Caryll and Monckton); *A *Country Girl* (1902, Monckton); *The Girl from Kay's* (1902, Caryll); *The Orchid* (1903, Caryll and Monckton); **Madame Sherry* (1903, Hugo *Felix); *The *Cingalee* (1904, Monckton); *The Spring Chicken* (1905, Monckton); *The Girls of Gottenberg* (1907, Caryll and Monckton); *The *Merry Widow* (1907, *Lehár); *A *Waltz Dream* (1908, *Straus); **Our Miss Gibbs* (1909, Caryll and Monckton); *The *Dollar Princess* (1909, Leo *Fall); *The *Quaker Girl* (1910, Monckton); *The Count of Luxembourg* (1911, Lehár); from a list that goes on to 1930.

Ross, Diana (*b* Detroit, 26 Mar. 1944). American singer. She sang as an amateur in Detroit before organizing a female vocal quartet with Florence Ballard, Mary Wilson, and Betty Anderson (who was soon replaced by Barbara Martin), at first calling themselves the Primettes, but soon boldly labelled the *Supremes. They were signed up by Barry *Gordy of *Tamla Motown records in 1960 and at first used as a backing trio. Barbara Martin left in 1962 and the group remained a trio, having their first No. 1 hit with the *Holland–Dozier–Holland 'Where did our love go' in 1964. They continued with a string of No. 1 hits such as 'Baby love' (1964), 'Come see about me' (1964), 'Stop! in the name of love' (1965), 'Back in my arms again' (1965), 'I hear a symphony' (1965), 'You can't hurry love' (1966), and 'You keep me hangin' on' (1966), from 1966 being billed as Diana Ross and the Supremes.

She left the group in 1969 to pursue a solo career and was now promoted as a sort of black *Streisand in a series of stage presentations and TV spectaculars, and as Billie *Holiday in the film *Lady Sings the Blues* (1970). She continued to record top hits with 'Ain't no mountain high enough' (1970), 'Touch me in the morning' (1973), 'Do you know where you're going to?' (1973), 'Love hangover' (1976), and 'Upside down' (1980). She made a number of best-selling albums for Motown until 1981, when she changed to the RCA/Capitol labels to make more albums and a top hit in 'Endless love' (1982), with Lionel Richie. She was in the films *Mahogany* (1975) and *The *Wiz* (1978); and continues as one of the major stars of the more permanent pop world.

C. Berman: *Diana Ross: Supreme Lady* (New York, 1978). G. Brown: *Diana Ross* (London, 1981). J. R. Taraborelli: *Call Her Miss Ross: the Unauthorised Biography of Diana Ross* (New York, 1989).

Ross, Jerry [Rosenberg, Jerold] (*b* New York, 9 Mar. 1926; *d* New York, 11 Nov. 1955). American composer and lyricist. While at school he appeared on stage as a boy singer and wrote his first song. He then went to New York University where he continued to write revue material and songs. He earned a living by various means until he met another struggling songwriter, Richard *Adler, with whom he began to collaborate and, with the help of Frank *Loesser, they achieved their first hit with 'Rags to riches' in 1953. They wrote four songs for *John Murray Anderson's Almanac* (1953) and were commissioned by George *Abbott to write the score of *The *Pajama Game* (1954)—'Hey there', 'Hernando's hideaway', 'There once was a man'; followed by **Damn Yankees* (1955)—'Heart', 'Whatever Lola Wants'. The partnership came prematurely to an end when Ross died of chronic bronchiectasis.

Ross, Shirley [Gaunt, Bernice] (*b* Omaha, Nebr., 7 Jan. 1915). American singer and actress. She was a singer with the Gus *Arnheim band 1935–6 and started to appear in films in 1934, first making a mark with her appearance with Bing *Crosby in *Waikiki Wedding* (1937). She is best remembered for her partnership with Bob *Hope in the films *Big Broadcast of 1938* in which they sang the duet 'Thanks for the memory'; *Thanks for the Memory* (1938)—'Two sleepy people'; and *Some Like it Hot* (1939). She was in the Broadway musical *Higher and Higher* (1940), but left show-business in the 1950s.

Ross, W. G. (*fl.* 1830–50). British entertainer. He started his career in printing in Glasgow, but his talents in amateur shows made him decide to become a professional singer, first making an appearance in Bolton, then appearing in London at the Cyder Cellars in Maiden Lane where he soon became popular singing songs like 'The lively flea', 'Pat's leather breeches', and 'Going home with the milk'. Although generally working in a comic vein, his greatest success came with the gruesome and highly dramatic 'Ballad of Sam Hall' which portrayed a man about to be hanged, who cursed the audience with many a robust oath. His realistic performance of this ditty was regularly called for, and was so lastingly popular that he was still singing it at *Vauxhall Gardens in 1847. He appeared in straight plays but returned to the lighter stage with his own touring company, specializing in burlesquing popular actors and plays. After his brief reign of popularity he disappeared from the scene and died in unknown circumstances.

Rossi, Tino [Constantino] (*b* Ajaccio, Corsica, 1907; *d* Paris, 26 Sept. 1983). French singer and actor. He began, at an early age, to perform in café-concerts in Aix, got his first chance to record in 1925, and came to Paris. He appeared at the Casino de Paris in 1931 and at the ABC Theatre in 1933, without special success. This was to come when he was in the revue *Parade de France* at the Casino in 1934 when he first sang to his own guitar 'Vieni, vieni' and 'O Corse, île d'amour'. His recording of 'Adieu Hawaii' sold 400,000 copies, the film *Marinella* (1935) confirmed his popularity, and he visited the USA in 1938. He was in more than 25 films, and was called 'the most famous Corsican since Napoleon'. With a high and original quality of voice he sang songs about places—Corsica, Hawaii, and Naples—and found perfect material in the songs of Vincent *Scotto, including 'Chanson pour Nina', 'Ecoutez les mandolines', and 'Bella ragazzina'. Other songs, with which he inspired a whole new generation of post-war chansonniers, were 'Santa Lucia', 'Besame mucho', 'Deux petits chansons', 'Johnny Guitar', 'Mama'; and hs 30-million selling 'Petit Papa Noël', which he first sang in 1946.

Rota, Nino (*b* Milan, 3 Dec. 1911; *d* Rome, 10 Apr. 1979). Italian composer. A precocious composer, he wrote an oratorio at the age of 11 and an opera at 13, studied in Rome, then in the USA at the Curtis Institute in Philadelphia. Later he studied literature, before joining the Liceo Musicale in Bari and being its director 1950–78. He was a prolific composer of all kinds of music, but was especially successful with his scores for films, many in association with Federico Fellini 1950–79. These included: *Lo sceicco bianco* (1950); *I vitelloni* (1953); *La strada* (1954); *Il bidone* (1955); *Le notti di Cabiria* (1957); *La dolce vita* (1959); *Boccaccio 70* (1962); *Giulietta degli spiriti* (1965); *Fellini-Satyricon* (1969); *The Clowns* (1971); *Roma* (1971); *Amarcord* (1974); *Casanova* (1977); and *Orchestra Rehearsal* (1979). For other directors he wrote: *The Glass Mountain* (1950); *War and Peace* (1956); *Le* *notti bianche* (1957); *Rocco e i suoi fratelli* (1960); *Il gattopardo* (1963); Zeffirelli's *The Taming of the Shrew* (1966) and *Romeo e Giulietta* (1968); *Waterloo* (1969); *The Godfather I* (1972); *The Godfather II* (1974); *The Abdication* (1974); *Love and Anarchy* (1974); *Death on the Nile* (1978); *Caro Michele* (1978); and *Hurricane* (1979).

Rothschilds, The. Musical play based on the story of the Rothschild family, who worked their way up from the Jewish ghettos of Europe to being one of the wealthiest families in the world. With score by Jerry *Bock, book by Sherman Yellen, and lyrics by Sheldon *Harnick, it opened at the Lunt-Fontanne Theatre, New York, 19 Oct. 1970, and had 507 performances. It was the seventh and last collaboration of Bock and Harnick.

Roxy Music. British rock group formed in London in 1970 by singer/composer Bryan Ferry (*b* Co. Durham, 26 Sept. 1945); with Brian Eno (*b* 1948) (composer and synthesizer), Andy Mackay (*b* 1946) (saxophone), Phil Manzanera (*b* 1951) (guitar), and Paul Thompson (*b* 1951) (drums), with a variety of bass players. Their glamorous image and intriguing music made their early concerts an immediate success, and their first album, *Roxy Music* (1972), well publicized by DJs like John *Peel, proved to be one of the outstanding debut LPs of the 1970s, with its *Beatles-influenced Fifties rock atmosphere. They managed to combine an avant-garde outlook with interesting pastiche; Eno's work on the synthesizer set a new trend. *For Your Pleasure* (1973) was even more experimental and included such Ferry classics as 'Do the Strand', 'Editions of you', and 'In every dream home a heartache'. Eno left in 1973, after disagreements with Ferry, and *Stranded* (1973) introduced the varied work of Eddie Jobson (*b* 1955).

Although Ferry's very English style dominated, Mackay and Manzanera were both able to make their marks as writers, and in 1973–4 all three made important solo albums. Ferry's *These Foolish Things* (1973) was especially remarkable, making use of material by Bob *Dylan, the *Beatles, the *Rolling Stones, Smokey *Robinson, and *Leiber and Stoller. By 1975, with *Country Life* (1974), the group was equally popular in the USA. The group broke up in 1976 but re-grouped in 1980. In 1981 their recording of John *Lennon's 'Jealous guy' became their first No. 1 hit single. They remain one of the most original and interesting of British rock groups.

D. Rees: *Bryan Ferry and Roxy Music* (London, 1982). J. Rogan: *Style with Substance—Roxy's First Ten Years* (London, 1982).

Roy, Harry (*b* London, 12 Jan. 1900; *d* London, 1 Feb. 1971). British bandleader. Deserting an intended career in business, and inspired by the strains of the *Original Dixieland Jazz Band, with his brother Sydney he formed his first band, known as the Lyricals, just after the end of the First World War when the family business had foundered. They played at Rector's Club and at the Hammersmith Palais de Danse and, from 1924, at the Café de Paris, soon building a reputation, and touring South Africa in 1928 and Germany in 1930. As Harry Roy and his RKOlians, he appeared as an added spectacular band act to support the big films at the newly opened Leicester Square Theatre; then at the London Pavilion and the Café Anglais. His most publicized years came with a residency, in the steps of *Ambrose, at the prestigious Mayfair Hotel from 1934.

The band featured Roy's high-pitched singing and the two-piano duo of Ivor Moreton (1908–84), who also sang, and Dave Kaye, who were succeeded in 1936 by Stanley *Black and Norman Yarlett. He had a strong leaning towards hot numbers and the pseudo-ragtime that was popular in the 1930s. He often recorded as Harry Roy and his Tiger-Ragamuffins, and with a group featuring Moreton and Kaye in 'modernistic arrangements' of such items as 'Tiger rag' and his signature tune 'Bugle call rag'. He was a regular broadcaster and the band featured in several films. In 1935 he got into the social news columns by marrying the daughter of the Rajah of Sarawak; they divorced in 1947. His big band leading did not survive into the hard years after the war, but he led several nightclub bands until 1963. He was involved in various back-room activities, and made a modest come-back with a Dixieland group in Brighton, but ended his life in financial straits.

Rózsa, Miklós (*b* Budapest, 18 Apr. 1907). Hungarian-born American composer. He studied music in Leipzig, then settled in Paris in 1931 and became known as a composer of orchestral music of considerable variety and brilliance. In 1935 he went to London to write for ballets for Alicia Markova and Anton Dolin, and in 1936 became musical director for Alexander Korda and London Films. He went to Hollywood with Korda in 1940 where he became established as one of the leaders in the film music field with scores of richly Wagnerian opulence. He was with Universal 1947–8 and with MGM 1948–62.

His film scores include: *Thunder in the Sky* (1937); *The Four Feathers* (1939); *The Spy in Black* (1939); *The Green Cockatoo* (1940); *The Thief of Bagdad* (1941); *Lady Hamilton* (1941); *The Jungle Book* (1942); *Five Graves to Cairo* (1943); *Double Indemnity* (1944); *A Song to Remember* (1945); *Blood on the Sun* (1945); *The Lost Weekend* (1945); *Spellbound* (1945, Academy Award)—'Spellbound' (*w* Mack David); *The Strange Love of Martha Ivers* (1946)—'Strange love' (*w* Edward Heyman); *The Red House* (1947); *Song of Scheherazade* (1947); *Desert Fury* (1947); *Brute Force* (1947); *A Double Life* (1947, Academy Award); *The Naked City* (1948); *Madame Bovary* (1949); *East Side, West Side* (1949); *The Asphalt Jungle* (1950); *Quo Vadis* (1951)—'Lygia' (*w* Paul Francis Webster); *Ivanhoe* (1952); *Plymouth Adventure* (1952); *Julius Caesar* (1953); *Valley of the*

Kings (1954); *Seagulls over Sorrento* (1954; *Crest of the Wave* in US); *Moonfleet* (1955); *Bhowani Junction* (1956); *Lust for Life* (1956); *The Seventh Sin* (1957); *A Time to Love and a Time to Die* (1958); *Ben Hur* (1959, Academy Award); *King of Kings* (1960); *El Cid* (1961)—'The falcon and the dove' (*w* Webster); *Sodom and Gomorrah* (1962); *The VIPs* (1963); *The Green Berets* (1968); *The Private Life of Sherlock Holmes* (1970); *The Golden Voyage of Sinbad* (1973); *Providence* (1977); *Fedora* (1978); *The Private Files of J. Edgar Hoover* (1978); and *Time After Time* (1979).

C. Palmer: *Miklós Rózsa: a Sketch of his Life and Work* (New York–London, 1975). M. Rózsa: *Double Life: the Autobiography of Miklós Rózsa* (Tunbridge Wells, 1983).

Rubens, Paul A[lfred] (*b* London, 29 Apr. 1875; *d* Falmouth, 25 Feb. 1917). British composer, lyricist, librettist, and conductor. Although educated at Oxford and intending to become a barrister, he always had a strong interest in music and began to contribute songs, music and/or lyrics, to various London shows from around 1895. He wrote *Great Caesar* (with Walter Rubens) for the Comedy Theatre in 1899, but first won recognition with the lyrics for **Florodora* which he wrote the same year. On the strength of this he wrote the music and lyrics (and occasionally the libretto†) for a whole string of musicals, the writing of which came easily to him. When in the mood he would sit at the piano and produce a catchy tune in a few minutes.

He wrote some additional numbers for *A *Country Girl* (1902)—'Coo!'; followed by complete scores for: †*Three Little Maids* (1902)—'The miller's daughter'; †*Lady Madcap* (1904); *The Blue Moon* (with Howard *Talbot, 1905); †*Mr Popple (of Ippleton)* (1905); *The Dairymaids* (with Frank E. *Tours, 1906); *†*Miss Hook of Holland* (1907)—'A pink petty from Peter'; †*My Mimosa Maid* (1908); †*Dear Little Denmark* (1909); *The Balkan Princess* (1910); †*The Sunshine Girl* (1911); *†*The Girl From Utah* (1913); †*After the Girl* (1914); **Tonight's the Night* (1914); *Betty* (1915)—'Can it be love?'; †*Tina* (1915)—'The violin's song'; *Half-Past Eight* (1916); and *The Happy Day* (1916)—'Bohemia'. Ill-health curtailed his writing activities, but he also wrote a number of songs that had brief popularity such as 'Bobs 'as 'ad a lot o' tips from me' (1899), 'I love you, ma chérie' (1900), 'I can't take my eyes off you' (1904, *w* Rida Johnson *Young), 'I don't seem to want you when you're with me' (1905), 'I love the moon' (1912), 'Your King and Country want you' (1914), and 'The Admiral's yarn' (1917, *w* Fred *Weatherly).

Ruby, Harry [Rubinstein, Harry] (*b* New York, 27 Jan. 1895; *d* Los Angeles, 23 Feb. 1974). American composer and lyricist. Although he had no musical education he had a natural talent that was sufficient to move him from a dull business job to being a pianist in a music-publishing business run by Gus *Edwards. He subsequently worked in this capacity for various publishers, alternating this with working as an accompanist in vaudeville. He teamed up with Bert *Kalmar, firstly to write songs for the vaudeville star Belle *Baker.

Their stage shows included: *Helen of Troy, New York* (1923); *No Other Girl* (1924); *The Ramblers* (1926)—'All alone Monday'; *Lucky* (with Jerome *Kern, 1927); *The Five o'Clock Girl* (1927)—'Thinking of you'; *Good Boy* (1928)—'I wanna be loved by you'; *Animal Crackers* (1928; filmed 1930)—'Hooray for Captain Spaulding'; *Top Speed* (1929; filmed 1930)—'What would I care', 'Hot and bothered'; and *High Kickers* (1941). Their association with the Marx Brothers, begun with *Animal Crackers*, continued with the films *Horse Feathers* (1932) and *Duck Soup* (1933) at a period when S. J. Perelman was writing the scripts and the ponderous love interest sub-plots had not taken their toll.

They started working in Hollywood in 1930 and continued until Kalmar's death in 1947, producing material for *Check and Double Check* (1930)—'Three little words'; *The Cuckoos* (1930), based on *The Ramblers*; *The Kid From Spain* (1932)—'What a perfect combination'; *Hips Hips Hooray* (1934); *Happiness Ahead* (1934); *Bright Lights* (1935); *Walking on Air* (1936); *Everybody Sing* (1938); *Wake Up and Dream* (1946)—'Give me the simple life', sung by John Payne (1912–89) and June Haver (*b* 1926). A film based on the life of Kalmar and Ruby was made in 1950 under the title of **Three Little Words*, with Fred *Astaire and Red Skelton. Other songs included: 'So long! oo-long' (1920); 'Timbuctoo' (1920); 'She's mine, all mine' (1921); 'Who's sorry now?' (with Ted *Snyder, 1923); and 'Over and over again' (1929).

Ruddigore, or *The Witch's Curse*. Supernatural opera with music by Arthur *Sullivan and words by W. S. *Gilbert. It was first called *Ruddygore* but this title was considered a trifle strong and it was changed after the 11th performance. Produced at the Savoy Theatre, London, 22 Jan. 1887, with Durward Lely, Richard *Temple, Rutland *Barrington, George *Grossmith (later replaced by Henry *Lytton), Jessie *Bond, Leonora *Braham, and Rosina *Brandram [288p]. First produced in New York at the Fifth Avenue Theatre 21 Feb. 1887. Its songs included 'I know a youth who loves a maid', 'I shipped, d'ye see, in a revenue sloop', 'My boy, you may take it from me', 'When the night wind howls', and 'There grew a little flower'. It was filmed in 1982.

Rugolo, Pete (*b* San Piero, Sicily, 25 Dec. 1915). Italian-born American composer, arranger, bandleader, and pianist. He went to live in the USA at the age of five and settled in California. He studied at San Francisco State College and Mills College, where his teacher was Darius Milhaud. While still a student he played in dance bands and he was with the bands of Jimmie Grier and Johnny Richards in 1941 before joining the army 1942–5. On his release he joined the Stan *Kenton band and as its arranger did much to develop its 1940s style. He left Kenton in 1949 to work for Capitol Records as musical director. He settled in Los Angeles in 1950 and started to write film scores including: *The Strip* (1951); *Glory Alley* (1952); *Everything I Have is Yours* (1952); *Latin Lovers* (1953); *Easy to Love* (1953); *Jack the Ripper* (1960); and *The Sweet Ride* (1968). From 1954 he led his own band and recorded for Columbia, arranging and directing for June *Christy, Billy *Eckstine, Nat 'King' *Cole, and Mel *Tormé.

'Rule, Britannia!' British song that has almost become a second national anthem. The words are generally assumed to be by the poet James Thomson (1700–48) but they could be the work of David Mallet (1705–65) who was jointly responsible for the libretto of the masque *Alfred* in which they first appeared in 1740. The music and words of 'Rule, Britannia!' were first published together in *The Music in The Judgment of Paris* in 1741 by Thomas Augustine Arne (1710–78). The first musical score of *Alfred*, published in 1751, does not contain the song but it appears in the 1757 version, having been published separately in 1755.

W. H. Cummings: *Dr Arne and 'Rule, Britannia'* (London, 1912).

Rumba. A Cuban dance which is, in fact, a fast *son. The name rumba originally applied specifically to the style of dancing associated with it—a somewhat lascivious movement of hips, bosom, and other flexible parts. It achieved the second major conquest of Latin American music, after the *tango, in other countries of the world, spreading rapidly in the 1930s and still very popular. In 2/4 rhythm, it is strongly African in character, featuring powerful percussion, and its words, when present, are of a rhythmic nature. Among the natives of Cuba it is very much an *ad hoc* celebration dance. In ballroom circles it is known as the Cuban Rumba or El Son. The dance had been seen in Madrid as early as the mid-1800s. The Cubans stylized the original African dance into a ballroom dance called the Danzon and it was in this form that it spread to the USA and Europe as the rumba. It came into vogue in New York about 1931, the tune mainly used being 'The peanut vendor'. Although it is danced almost on the same spot, it needs considerable skill to do it well and, although it had a great vogue in Parisian nightclub circles, it generally frightens the average amateur dancer off the floor.

Runaway Girl, A. Musical play with score by Ivan *Caryll and Lionel *Monckton, book by Seymour *Hicks and Harry Nicholls, and lyrics by Aubrey Hopwood and Harry Greenbank. It opened at the *Gaiety Theatre, London, 21 May 1898, and, with a short break in the summer of 1899, ran into 1900 for a total of 593 performances.

The improbable story concerns Winifred Grey (played by Ellaline *Terriss), orphan and ward of Lord and Lady Coddle, who runs away to join a band of minstrels. They meet up with a group of tourists among whom are the Coddles and their nephew Guy (W. Lous Bradfield) whom the Coddles hoped to marry off to Winifred, although he was not keen. He falls in love with the minstrel girl, not knowing who she is. In the end all is sorted out, aided by a large reward that has been offered for finding Winifred.

The plot was breezily done and shared the responsibility for the long run with some good tunes that included 'Not the sort of girl I care about', 'The man from Cook's', 'Soldiers in the park', 'The boy guessed right', and 'Oh, I love society'. At Daly's Theatre, New York, 25 Aug. 1898 (and later at the Fifth Avenue Theatre) it had 212 performances.

Rushing, Jimmy [James Andrew] (*b* Oklahoma City, 26 Aug. 1902; *d* New York, 8 June 1972). American jazz and blues singer. He studied violin and piano, and began his singing career in the Midwest, then on the West Coast 1923–4. With the Walter Page band in Kansas City 1927–9 he developed his exuberant but clear style of blues-shouting; continuing with Bennie *Moten 1929–35. He became known through his work with the Count *Basie band 1935–48 and 1949–50, for whom he wrote and sung such items as 'Sent for you yesterday', 'Undecided blues', 'Take me back, baby', 'Evil blues', and 'I'm gonna move to the outskirts of town'. He led his own band at the *Savoy Ballroom 1950–2, toured Europe in 1957, was again with Benny *Goodman in 1958, with Buck *Clayton in 1959, and with Basie in 1964. In the 1960s and early 1970s he mainly worked at the Half Note in New York. He was popularly known as 'Mister Five by Five', after the 1942 song, being approximately of those dimensions.

Russell, Henry (*b* Sheerness, 24 Dec. 1812; *d* London, 8 Dec. 1900). British composer, author, and singer. He first appeared on the stage at the age of three, joining a travelling company when they visited Sheerness in the play *Pizarro*. The family moved to London in 1815 and at the age of six he began to study the piano. At the same time he developed a fine contralto voice and was taken to see Robert Elliston of the Drury Lane Theatre who engaged him at 30 shillings a week to sing in a children's opera group which played at the Surrey Theatre. He appeared in Brighton before King George IV. In 1825 he went to Bologna to study music and continued in Milan where he studied for four months with Rossini and met Donizetti and Bellini. He became friendly with Michael Balfe, who was also in Italy at the time, and they both joined the opera at Varese, Balfe as a singer, Russell as a pianist. On his return to London he became chorus-master at His Majesty's Theatre. He went to Canada in 1833, staying in Toronto where he had little success as an entertainer, so he decided to try his luck in the USA and settled in Rochester, NY, where he became organist at the First Presbyterian church and gave local concerts. There he composed his first song 'Wind of the winter night' and then, inspired by the works of Henry Clay, continued with 'Oh! woodman, spare that tree', 'A life on the ocean wave', 'The gambler's wife', and 'The maniac', all of which quickly became popular.

He started a very successful series of concerts, with an orchestra conducted by Vincent Wallace, in such places as New York, Brooklyn, and Jersey City. He made nationwide tours, his popularity becoming so great that, when he returned to England in 1841, his reputation came before him and he was in great demand. He went on tour for six months, visiting Dublin and other places in Ireland, and then, on 8 Mar. 1842, opened in his own one-man vocal entertainment at the Hanover Square Rooms and his songs soon became equally well-known in England. He never made much from them, all being sold to publishers outright for about £1 apiece, there being no copyright, and various publishers like Sheard and Davidson later squabbled over who owned the rights. But it was through the songs that Russell made a fortune as an entertainer. Unprecedentedly popular provincial tours followed and he began to collaborate with the poet Charles Mackay (1814–1905), their most popular number being 'Cheer, boys, cheer', and they compiled an entertainment called *The Emigrant's Progress* which enjoyed a great success. He wrote a series of songs with words from Scott's *The Lady of the Lake*, a set of Scripture melodies, a book of dramatic scenes, several cantatas, and published a memoir in 1846. Various collections of his songs appeared in 1859 and 1860, in addition to the numerous sheets of music then available, and he published a book on the art of singing.

He retired from public life in 1865 and lived in a villa in Maida Vale, where he indulged in carpentry and occasionally wrote songs. His last composition was a Jubilee song for Queen Victoria, 'Our Empress Queen' (1887). His 'A life on the ocean wave' was made the official march of the Royal Marines in 1889. A special concert was given in his honour at Covent Garden on 12 Oct. 1891 when he made a speech which was described as 'not unworthy of a remarkable man'. He published his reminiscences in 1895. Two of his sons became well-known in the music world: Henry Russell Jr. (who died in 1937) as a teacher and influential impresario, and Landon Russell (1873–1938), writing under the name of Landon Ronald (later Sir); while another son was William Clark Russell, a seafaring novelist who wrote *The Wreck of the Grosvenor*.

Altogether Henry Russell is said to have written some 800 songs, the best-remembered (in addition to those already mentioned) being: 'The chase', 'A fine old English gentleman', 'Far, far upon the sea', 'The happy days of childhood', 'The ivy green' (*w* Charles Dickens), 'I'm afloat', 'A life in the West', 'The old armchair', 'The old sexton', 'Rouse, brothers, rouse', 'The spider and the fly', 'The slave ship' (he was a dedicated anti-slavery campaigner), 'There's a good time coming', 'Oh, weep not!', 'Old Bell', and 'We were boys together'.

H. Russell: *Cheer! Boys, Cheer!: Memories of Men and Music* (London, 1895).

Russell, Lillian [Leonard, Helen Louise] (*b* Clinton, Iowa, 4 Dec. 1861; *d* Pittsburgh, 5 June 1922). American actress and singer. A leading figure in the American comic opera world in the late 19th and early 20th centuries, she first made her mark at Tony *Pastor's Music Hall in 1883 and in various *Weber and Field burlesques, memorably singing 'Come down, my evening star' in *Twirly Whirly* (1902). She ran her own Opera Comique company for many years. One of her husbands was the composer Edward *Solomon. Among her stage appearances were *The *Sorcerer* (1879); *The Princess of Trebizonde* (1883); in London in *Polly* and *Pocahontas* in 1884; *Pepita* (1886); **Dorothy* (1887); *Nadjy* (1889); *Poor Jonathan* (1890); *La Cigale* (1891); *The Mountebank* (1891); *Princess Nicotine* (1893); *La *Périchole* (1895); *An American Beauty* (1896); *La *Belle Hélène* (1899); *Hoity Toity* (1901); *Whoop-Dee-Doo* (1903); and *Hokey Pokey* (1912).

P. Morell: *Lillian Russell* (New York, 1940). J. Burke: *Duet in Diamonds* (New York, 1970).

Russell, Luis Carl (*b* Panama, 6 Aug. 1902; *d* New York, 11 Dec. 1963). American bandleader and pianist. He began his musical career in Panama in 1917, playing in a silent cinema. In 1919 he went to the USA and settled in New Orleans, where he worked with Albert Nicholas (1900–73), then went to Chicago and played with King *Oliver and Doc Cook (1891–1958). He was in the band at the Nest Club and eventually took it over, leading it in New York at such venues as the Roseland Ballroom, Connie's Inn, and the *Savoy Ballroom. From the end of 1935 the band was nominally led by Louis *Armstrong, with Russell as pianist and arranger. He left in 1944 to form another big band centred on New York, eventually leaving the band business for good in 1948. He is remembered for fine recordings which featured such musicians as James Archey (1902–67), Albert Nicholas, J. C. *Higginbotham, Charlie Holmes (1910–85), Paul Barbarin (1899–1969), Red *Allen, Bill Coleman (1904–81), and Dicky *Wells. He wrote 'Jersey lightning', 'Saratoga shout', 'Call of the freaks', 'Muggin' lightly', and 'Higginbotham blues'.

Russell, Pee Wee [Charles Ellsworth] (*b* Maple Wood, Mo., 27 Mar. 1906; *d* Alexandria, Va., 15 Feb. 1969). American jazz clarinettist. He studied various instruments and played in local bands before briefly attending the University of Missouri. He fixed his attention on the clarinet on which he was to develop a unique style, with a throaty tone and eccentric phrasing which made him a special cult quite early in his career. This was underlined by his lived-in appearance and several critical bouts of illness aggravated by a loyal allegiance to alcohol. In his early days he moved around in places like Houston and St Louis and began to get into the company of eminent Chicago musicians when he joined the Frankie *Trumbauer band at the Arcadia Ballroom (to which Bix *Beiderbecke was later added), and played in New York on and off with Red *Nichols 1927–31. He worked with various bands in Boston, including Bobby *Hackett's 1933–4; and in New York with Louis *Prima 1935–7, Bobby Hackett 1938–9, and Bud *Freeman 1939–40. He played in various Dixieland groups in the 1940s, often at Eddie *Condon's club, with Billy *Butterfield and Art Hodes; and in Chicago with Muggsy *Spanier and Miff *Mole. He survived a critical illness and operation in 1951, afterwards to lead bands in Denver, Boston, and New York. He toured Europe several times in the 1960s, under the constant strain of ill-health, and played with the Newport All-Stars. In his final years he took some interest in modern jazz developments and continued playing.

Russo, Bill [William Joseph] (*b* Chicago, 25 June 1928). American composer, arranger, and trombonist. After a long musical education, he played in several bands, becoming best-known in jazz terms as arranger and player with Stan *Kenton 1950–5. He led his own band in Chicago 1958–61; conducted a jazz orchestra in London 1962–5; was Director of the Center for New Music in Chicago 1965–76; and directed the Chicago Jazz Ensemble. He composed four rock cantatas for the Free Theater and then settled in San Francisco where he continued to compose in a vein that combined jazz, blues, and rock with academic counterpoint and harmony. He has written *Composing for the Jazz Orchestra* (Chicago, 1961) and *Jazz Composition and Orchestration* (Chicago, 1968).

S

Sablon, Jean (*b* Nogent-sur-Marne, 25 Mar. 1906. French singer and composer. Son of Adelmar Sablon (1871–1928), who was conductor at the Théâtre Dramatique and a composer of operettas. After studying at the Lycée Charlemagne, he made his stage debut in 1923 at the *Bouffes-Parisiens, sang with *Mistinguett at the Casino de Paris, and appeared in operetta at the Théâtre Danou. He made his first recording in 1932, a duet with Mireille (*b* 1906), 'Le petit chemin'. In 1933 he joined forces with a jazz group made up of André Ekyan, Alec Siniavine, and Django *Reinhardt singing such jazz items as 'Vous qui passez sans me voir' (Charles *Trenet). The new crooning style and microphone technique that he introduced was not immediately popular, but he profited from the general spread of swing into Europe and was soon dubbed the French Bing Crosby. He had a successful season at the ABC in 1939 when he sang such songs as 'Je tire ma révérence' (Pascal Bastier, *b* 1908). Recording with Reinhardt and good backing groups he had a great vogue in England and elsewhere, with 'Le fiacre' becoming a worldwide best-seller. During the war he worked in the USA, returning to France in 1946 (now sporting a smart moustache). He made many tours, and notable appearances at l'Étoile in 1949 and the *Olympia in 1954. His sister Germaine (*b* 1899) was also a well-known singer.

St Helier, Ivy [Aitchison, Ivy] (*b* St Helier, Jersey, 1890; *d* London, 9 Nov. 1971). British composer, singer, and actress. A talented mimic and entertainer, she made her first stage appearance in *Captain Kidd* at Wyndham's Theatre, London, 12 Jan. 1910. She toured South Africa with Seymour *Hicks and Ellaline *Terriss in 1911 and was with them again during their wartime tours of France in 1914. She appeared in the musical shows *Everybody's Doing It* (1912), *Johnny Jones* (1920), **Bitter Sweet* (1929), and *Words and Music* (1932); and in many straight plays, variety, and films. She was also a natural composer and wrote the revue *Ring Up* (1921), also contributing songs to *The Street Singer* (1924) and *The Blue Train* (1927). Her best-known song was 'Coal black mammy' (1921, *w* Laddie *Cliff).

'St Louis blues'. Famous *blues song by W. C. *Handy, first published as 'The Saint Louis blues' in Memphis, 11 Sept. 1914. Its chorus was taken from Handy's earlier 'Jogo blues' (1913). A pioneering publication in 12-bar blues form, it helped to formalize the classical blues and was sung by all the leading singers. It still maintains its place as a popular jazz standard.

***St Louis Woman*.** Musical play with score by Harold *Arlen, lyrics by Johnny *Mercer, and book by Arna Bontemps and Countee Cullen, based on Bontemps' novel *God Sends Sunday*. It was first produced at the Martin Beck Theatre, New York, 30 Mar. 1946.

Set in St Louis in 1898, its leading figure is Della Green (a part originally intended for Lena *Horne, but played by Ruby Hill) who is the woman of saloon owner Biglow Brown (Rex Ingram). She falls for a jockey (Harold Nicholas) and Brown, who is killed by a jealous girl friend, puts a curse on them. An unpromising story was saved by an excellent score that included 'I had myself a true love', 'Legalize my name', 'Any place I hang my hat is home', and 'Come rain or come shine'; but it had only 113 performances.

It was filmed in 1946 starring Pearl *Bailey (who had a small part in the original); and the show was revived in 1959 as *Blues Opera*, now set in New Orleans, with added songs like 'Blues in the night' and 'That old black magic'. It was produced in Amsterdam and Paris as *Free and Easy*.

***Salad Days*.** Musical comedy with score by Julian *Slade and book by Slade and Dorothy Reynolds (1913–78). It was conceived as a three-week-gap filler and a loosely compiled showcase for the light singing talents of the Bristol Old Vic company of which Slade was musical director. Its Bristol production, 1 June 1954, was so well received that Eric Porter, who was in the cast, thought it should go to London. Two managements were persuaded to take it on between them and it opened at the Vaudeville Theatre, London, 5 Aug. 1954.

Fresh, simple, full of melody, very English, it delighted audiences to the tune of 2283 performances, with Eleanor Drew and John Warner as the romantic leads and Newton Blick as the old tramp who lends them a magic piano that makes everyone dance. The delightful score, played on two pianos, included the numbers 'The things that are done by a don', 'We said we wouldn't look back', 'I sit in the sun', 'Look at me, I'm dancing', 'It's easy to sing', 'The time of my life', and the revuey 'Cleopatra'.

Its Englishness earned it only a short run of 80 performances at New York's Barbizon-Plaza 10 Nov. 1958; but it has been revived in London in 1961, 1964, and 1976, was televised in 1983, and is now a firm favourite with amateur companies.

Sally. Musical play with score by Jerome *Kern, book by Guy *Bolton, and lyrics by Clifford *Grey and others, New York, New Amsterdam Theatre, 21 Dec. 1920. The show was designed as a showcase for the newly discovered talents of Marilyn *Miller and was commissioned from the *Princess Theatre team by Florenz *Ziegfeld.

Sally starts the story washing dishes at the Alley Inn in Greenwich Village but is invited to a ball by one of the waiters (Leon Erroll) who turns out to be a duke in disguise. She ends up by marrying, starring in the *Ziegfeld Follies*, and dancing a ballet written by Victor *Herbert. The lovely score included 'Look for the silver lining' (*w* Buddy *DeSylva), 'Sally', 'Wild rose', 'Whip-Poor-Will', 'The Lorelei' (*w* Anne *Caldwell), and 'The church round the corner' (*w* P. G. *Wodehouse), and it had 570 performances. With Dorothy *Dickson as Sally, it was produced at the Winter Garden Theatre, London, 10 Sept. 1921, for 387 performances. It was filmed in 1929 with Marilyn Miller and Alexander Gray (1902–75); revived in London as *Wild Rose* at the Prince's Theatre, 6 Aug. 1942 [205p]; and unsuccessfully revived in New York in 1948.

Salon music. A salon is generally defined as a large reception or drawing room in a palace or large house, and salon music was originally of the kind, of solo or chamber ensemble dimensions, considered suitable for such surroundings. The acme of salon music was reached in the piano music of Chopin and his Victorian followers. More recently the term has been especially associated with the lighter music written for small so-called salon orchestras, the term palm court music being more or less synonymous.

Salsa. From a Spanish word meaning 'sauce' or 'spice', it has been used since the 1960s to classify Latin American music with a hot jazz flavour. An early use was in the title of an album, *Salsa Nova* (1962), by Pupi Legarreta; followed by *Llegó la Salsa* (1966) by Federico y su Combo Latino. The word gradually slipped into common currency and was given permanence in the title of a film, *Salsa*, in 1975. Largely based on Cuban music, the 'orquesta típica', i.e. the 'typical' orchestra of flute, 2 clarinets, and rhythm including timbales, introduced the Latin American sound to European ears in the 1930s, in somewhat commercialized performances. Now its exported strains, coloured by a Puerto Rican element, returned to something more like the original music in the Latin and rhythm 'n' blues fusions of the 1960s loosely known as boogaloo. Salsa now became a useful name for all such fusions. Arrangers in the style who came to prominence in the 1980s were Louie Ramirez and Luis Ortiz, the music finding its main New York outlet on the Fania record label which recorded such artists as Ray Barretto (*b* 1929), Willie Colon (*b* 1950), Larry Harlow (*b* 1939), Johnny Pacheco (*b* 1935), Roberto Roena (*b c.*1930), and Bobby Valentin (*b c.*1940). Like many modern fads, it turned out to be something that had existed unremarked for many years, long before it became a teenage craze of the 1970s. The *bossa nova fashion of the 1950s had been much the same thing. Centres of salsa music in the 1980s were Miami, Puerto Rico, Colombia, and Venezuela.

C. Gerard and M. Sheller: *Salsa! the Rhythm of Latin Music* (New York, 1989).

Samba. A dance from Brazil, with African origins, which in its native country has two distinct forms, the rural and the urban. The former, of folk origin, is related to the jonga and the batuque (a slow version) and is rhythmically complex. The simplest of the simplified urban sambas, the samba-carioca, was developed from the *maxixe in the dance halls of Rio de Janeiro. The samba is easily combined with other dances to create such hybrid forms as the samba-tango, samba-jonga, samba-rumba, and sambaiao. There is also the samba-cancao, a sung serenade typified by the song 'Brasil'.

The samba dance is in a shuffling 2/4 rhythm and always in a major key. It is so popular in Brazil that almost any typical Brazilian dance or song tends to be given the name, which is even applied to the dance halls. The modern version, which became popular in the USA and Europe, is mainly based on the maxixe. It was featured a good deal in the late 1940s by Edmundo *Ros and other leading Latin American bands. In the 1950s the samba, with a jazz flavour and beat added, was the basis of *bossa nova.

Sampson, Edgar Melvin (*b* New York, 31 Aug. 1907; *d* Englewood, NJ, 16 Jan. 1973). American arranger, composer, bandleader, saxophonist, and violinist. He studied the violin from the age of six and took up the saxophone at school. At 18 he was touring with the Duke *Ellington orchestra, and then joined the band at the *Savoy Ballroom in New York. He learned his craft as arranger and writer while working with Charlie *Johnson 1928–30, Fletcher *Henderson 1931–3, and Chick *Webb 1932–6; and it was while with Webb at the Savoy Ballroom that he really established himself as a songwriter and arranger. By 1936 his scores were being used by Benny *Goodman and others—'Blue Lou' (1935), 'Stompin' at the Savoy' (1936), 'Hot Club stomp' (1937), 'Don't be that way' (1938), 'Lullaby in rhythm' (1938), 'Don't try your jive on me' (1938), etc. As a saxophonist, he was featured on record with Bunny *Berigan, Teddy *Wilson, and Billie *Holiday in 1936, and with Lionel *Hampton in 1938. After that he concentrated on arranging. He toured wartime camps with Al Sears and formed his own band 1949–51. His later career was mainly with Latin American bands and he did some notable arranging for Count *Basie.

Sanderson, Julia [*née* Sackett] (*b* Springfield, Mass., 20 Aug. 1887; *d* Springfield, 27 Jan. 1975). American actress and singer. Petite and vivacious star of various musicals, notably *Tangerine* (1921, *m*

Alma M. Sanders, 1882–1956, and Monte Carlo, 1883–1967), in which she starred with her third husband Frank *Crumit. She presented a popular radio series with him 1929–43. Her shows included: *Fantana* (1905); *The Tourists* (1906); *The Dairymaids* (1907); *Kitty Grey* (1909); *The Dashing Little Duke* (London, 1909); *The *Arcadians* (1910); *The Siren* (1911); *The Sunshine Girl* (1913); *The *Girl from Utah* (1914)—in which she introduced 'They didn't believe me'; *Sybil* (1916); *Rambler Rose* (1917); and *Hitchy-Koo* (1920).

Sanderson, Wilfrid Ernest (*b* Ipswich, 23 Dec. 1878; *d* Nutfield, Surrey, 10 Dec. 1935). British composer and organist. Educated at the City of London School, he became an organist and was assistant to Sir Frederick Bridge, organist of Westminster Abbey. He played in various churches and became Bachelor of Music at Durham and a Fellow of the Royal College of Organists. He lived in Doncaster 1904–23 and conducted the Doncaster Musical Society 1911–24.

He was a prolific writer of ballads and songs in a very forthright English vein. These included: 'My dear soul' (1906, *w* May Byron); 'Drake goes West' (1910, *w* P. J. O'Reilly); 'Until' (1910, *w* Edward Teschemacher); 'Friend o' mine' (1913, *w* Fred E. *Weatherly); 'Up from Somerset' (1913, Weatherly); 'Shipmates o' mine' (1913, Teschemacher); 'Break o' day' (1915, O'Reilly); 'Captain Mac' (1915, O'Reilly); 'Longshore' (1917, *w* Bernard Moore); 'God be with you tonight' (1917, *w* Fred G. Bowles); 'The Company Sergeant-Major' (1918, *w* P. H. B. Lyon); 'Devonshire cream and cider' (1919, *w* Theodore Curzon); 'The stars have eyes' (1920, Bowles); 'Jack and Jill' (1927, *w* Dena Tempest). Some of these were collected in *Selection of Wilfrid Sanderson's Popular Songs* (arr. Sydney Baynes) (London, 1919).

Santley, Joseph Mansfield (*b* Salt Lake City, Utah, 10 Jan. 1889; *d* Los Angeles, 8 Aug. 1971). American actor and singer. He was the leading man in a number of Broadway musicals, 11 of them with his wife, Ivy Sawyer: including: *A Matinée Idol* (1910); *The Never Homes* (1911); *The Woman Haters* (1912); *When Dreams Come True* (1913); *Stop! Look! Listen!* (1915); *Betty* (1916); *Oh, Boy!* (1917); *Oh, My Dear* (1918); *She's a Good Fellow* (1919); *The Half Moon* (1920); **Music Box Revue* (1921 and 1923); *Mayflowers* (1925); *The Wild Rose* (1926); *Lucky* (1927); and *Just Fancy* (1927). Later he became a director of film musicals 1929–50, his best remembered being *The Cocoanuts* (1929) with the Marx Brothers.

Santana. American Latin-rock group founded in 1969 as the Santana Bluesband and led by guitarist Carlos Santana (*b* Autlan de Novarra, Mexico, 20 July 1947). The name became simply *Santana* (1969)—their first album. They purveyed a mixture of Afro-Cuban rhythm and a mellow kind of rock, including such items as 'Soul sacrifice' (1970); 'Samba pa ti' (1970); Tito *Puente's 'Oye como va' (1971); and 'Everybody's everything' (1971). The group split up in 1972 but was re-formed in 1973 and Santana himself made a number of solo albums that have had a permanent influence on the rock scene.

***San Toy*.** Musical play with score by Sidney *Jones, additional music by Lionel *Monckton, book by Edward Morton (1857–1922), lyrics by Percy *Greenbank and Adrian Ross. It was produced at *Daly's Theatre, London, 21 Oct. 1899, with Marie *Tempest, Rutland *Barrington, Huntley Wright (1869–1943), and C. Hayden *Coffin, running for a remarkable 778 performances. In New York (Daly's, 1 Oct. 1900), it managed a mere 65.

Following in the steps of *The *Mikado* (which had a popular revival in 1895) and *The *Geisha* (1896), *San Toy* was one of the many attempts to capitalize on the vogue for musicals with an oriental setting, this time China rather than Japan.

Sardana. Traditional Spanish dance originating in north-east Catalonia. It is based on the sun's movements and the 24 hours of day, being split into two parts, a slow, mournful section symbolizing darkness, and a fast, bright section representing day. It was originally called the curta, the modern sardana being introduced by the musician and musicologist José Ventura y Casa (1817–81) who had become interested in the traditional music of the *cobla*—a type of folk-dance band popular in Catalonia. He developed the brief dance into a longer form, with its main themes always introduced by the wailing tones of the tenora (a sort of clarinet) in an improvised cadenza.

Sarony, Leslie (*b* Surbiton, Surrey, 22 Jan. 1897; *d* London, 12 Feb. 1985). British singer, entertainer, and composer. His first stage appearance was in the music-hall in 1911, when he joined a group called Park Eton's Boys. He appeared in the revue *Hello Tango* at the Hippodrome in 1913 and in various concert party groups up to the war years, when he served in the London Scottish regiment in France and Salonika. After the war he played in pantomime and in various revues such as *The Peep Show* (1921); *His Girl* (1922); the musical **Phi-Phi* (1922); *Dover Street to Dixie* (1923); *Brighter London* (1923); *The Whirl of the World* (1924); *Rat-a-Tat* (1925); in cabaret at the Café de Paris, and in music-hall; *Up With the Lark* (1927); **Show Boat* (1928); **Rio Rita* (1930); and many more. In the 1930s he moved into the variety world and became well-known on radio.

In 1935 he teamed up with Leslie Holmes (1901–58), former dance-band drummer and music-publishing manager, to form the popular variety and radio duo the Two Leslies, appearing in a Royal Variety Performance and touring North Africa to entertain the troops in the Second World War. Holmes left the act in 1946 and, after working with another partner for three years, Sarony became a solo entertainer, singing, dancing, and presenting a number of eccentric acts like 'Jake the Peg' and, with animal noises, 'There was an old farmer who had an old sow'. He appeared in the films *Chitty Chitty Bang Bang* (1968) and *Yanks* (1979), in straight plays and on TV, remaining remarkably active into his eighties.

He composed a number of highly successful songs, which he and others performed, although he always considered songwriting a hobby. These included 'Forty-seven ginger-headed sailors' (1928), 'I lift up my finger and I say "tweet-tweet"' (1929), 'Mucking about the garden' (1929), 'Over the garden wall' (1930), 'Rhymes' (1931), 'When the Guards are on parade' (1931, *m* Horatio *Nicholls), 'Ain't it grand to be bloomin' well dead' (1932), 'Wheezy Anna' (1933), 'Coom pretty one' (1934), and 'When a soldier's on parade' (1934).

Sauter, Eddie [Edward Ernest] (*b* Brooklyn, NY, 2 Dec. 1914; *d* New York, 21 Apr. 1981). American composer, arranger, conductor, and trumpeter. He was educated at Columbia University and studied music at Juilliard, then became a professional musician and played with the Archie Bleyer band 1931–2. He started arranging for Charlie *Barnet in 1933, coming to prominence with the Red *Norvo band from 1935, playing on trumpet and mellophone and arranging for Norvo and Mildred *Bailey 1936–7. Earning a reputation as a composer way ahead of his time he joined Benny *Goodman in 1939, providing him with such arrangements as 'Benny rides again' and 'Clarinet à la King', and giving a new direction to the band, which, up to then, had used the more stereotyped Fletcher *Henderson-style scores. He wrote 'All the cats join in' (with Alec *Wilder and Ray Gilbert) for the film *Make Mine Music* (1944). He arranged for Tommy *Dorsey, Artie *Shaw ('The maid with the flaccid air'), and Woody *Herman, then formulated the style for a big modern band formed by Ray *McKinley after the war, his advanced scores achieving acclaim even in the age of progressive jazz.

In 1952 he formed the Sauter–Finegan Orchestra with Bill *Finegan, a unit intended for recording, somewhat too opposed to musical tastes of the time to achieve commercial success, but earning its place in popular musical history by the powerful and imaginative scores by its joint leaders. Especially popular were 'Yankee Doodletown' (based on 'Yankee Doodle'), 'Doodletown Fifers' (based on 'Kingdom coming'), 'Midnight sleighride' (after Prokofiev), and 'Now that I'm in love' (after Rossini). The unit was disbanded in 1959, but was re-formed in the 1980s to make some recordings. He wrote arrangements for *Top Banana* (1951), *1776* (1970), and *Georgy* (1970), and music for the film *Mickey One* (1965). At the instigation of the critic Joachim Ernst Berendt, Sauter took over direction of the German Radio Orchestra in Baden-Baden. In 1965 he composed an album of music for saxophonist Stan *Getz entitled *Focus*, which proved to be an extraordinarily imaginative and sensitive creation.

Savitt, Jan (*b* St Petersburg, 4 Sept. 1908; *d* Sacramento, Calif., 4 Oct. 1948). Russian-born American composer, bandleader, and violinist. His father, a member of the Imperial Regimental Band of Tsar Nicholas, inspired him to be a musician. Taken to the USA when he was a one-year-old, he attended school in Philadelphia and later won three scholarships at the Curtis Institute, for playing and conducting. At 14 he was the youngest violinist in the Philadelphia Orchestra and a few years later was Stokowski's concert master. He returned to Europe for further study and on his return in 1931 formed the Savitt String Quartet. He became musical director of WCAU radio in Philadelphia, was lured away to rival station KYW and there, in 1937, first formed the popular band that was known as his Top Hatters. With a shuffle rhythm as his musical trademark, he built a busy career in hotels and ballrooms. He wrote 'Moonrise' (1937), '720 in the books' (1939), and 'It's a wonderful world' (1941).

Savoy Ballroom. Famous dance venue at 596 Lenox Avenue in the Harlem district of New York, one of the best-known ballrooms in the annals of jazz dancing. It opened in 1926 and operated a weekly rota of special nights for various grades and classes of black dancers, the great night being Sunday when the celebrities were on show. Known popularly as 'The Track', it saw many of the popular dances of the jazz age formulated there in Cat's Corner, an area where the professionals demonstrated and tried out new steps.

The first resident bands were Fess Williams and his Royal Flush Orchestra and the Charleston Bearcats; but nearly all the top swing orchestras played there at some time. Cecil Scott (1905–64) was unrivalled in the late 1920s; Chick *Webb was a famous long-staying resident in the 1930s, and introduced Ella *Fitzgerald there; and the Savoy Sultans led by Al Cooper (1911–81) were the house band 1937–46. Famous battles of the bands were organized between such heavyweight opponents as Webb and *Goodman, *Calloway and *Ellington. It was immortalized in Edgar *Sampson's 'Stompin' at the Savoy', recorded by Webb in 1934 and by Benny Goodman in 1936.

Savoy Orpheans. Name used by the dance bands of the Savoy Hotel, London, from 1923 to 1927, originally directed by Debroy Somers (1890–1952), and later by the American pianist Carroll *Gibbons. The band under that title ended its career in 1927, but by 1931, Gibbons was leading a group called the Savoy Hotel Orpheans. He continued to be the hotel's musical director until 1955, when he was succeeded by his assistant pianist Ian Stewart (1919–89), who retired in 1975.

Savoy Theatre, London. With the rapidly growing success of the Gilbert and Sullivan operettas, D'Oyly

*Carte found his productions hampered and his audiences constrained by the narrow confines of the Opera-Comique Theatre in the Strand, where the early works had been staged. During the run of *Patience* he opened a new theatre between the Strand and Victoria Embankment in the precinct of 'the Savoy', where the Savoy Palace had formerly stood. It was originally built to seat an audience of 986 and proudly advertised itself as the first theatre to use electric light, firstly to light the auditorium and soon after the whole theatre (with the assurance given that gas was also available if anything went wrong). It was designed in the Italian Renaissance style and had a rather obscurely placed entrance in steeply sloping Beaufort Street running down to the Embankment. Programmes and all cloakroom services were free and, in view of past turmoils, the custom of queueing was first instituted there. The theatre opened on 10 Oct. 1881 with a bigger and better version of *Patience* transferred from the Opera-Comique. It was to be the regular home of English operetta in its early days not only the Savoy Operas of *Gilbert and Sullivan but works by *Solomon, *Cellier, *Caryll, *German, and others. When the Savoy Hotel was opened in 1889 a new entrance to the theatre, more in keeping with the hotel's innovative concrete and steel construction, was made in the forecourt.

After 1903 the theatre moved over to mainly straight plays, but in 1929 it was completely rebuilt in a more modern style and increased its seating capacity to 1130, re-opening on 21 Oct. 1929, with a revival of *The *Gondoliers*, followed by the very successful D'Oyly Carte seasons of 1929–30 and 1932–3. For some time the theatre staged a succession of revues and musical comedies; later it resumed a more normal mixture of musical and straight productions. During the night of 11/12 Feb. 1990, the theatre's roof and interior were destroyed by fire.

Saxophone. When the Belgian instrument maker Adolphe Sax (1814–94) patented and produced his range of saxophones in Paris in 1846, having already invented the saxhorns, he was mainly thinking of an instrument that would fill a gap between the brass and woodwind in *military band music. His mongrel instruments, with the brass body and conical bore of the bugle and horn, and the mouthpiece, reed, and padded keys of a clarinet, were quickly adopted by the French and Belgian armies and were soon in worldwide use in the military band field. A few classical composers with modern views occasionally used the saxophone for an extra orchestral colour, but it never became a regular member of the symphony orchestra as Sax might also have half-hoped. He might well have been pleasantly (or otherwise) surprised to know that, in the 20th century, it was to become such a vital instrument in the field of popular music and jazz.

The main members of the family in frequent use are the usually straight soprano saxophone and the familiar S-shaped alto, tenor, baritone, and less common bass instruments. Like all innovations, the saxophone faced reactionary opposition, unmusical magistrates and others seeing it as a symbol of all that was aggressive and noisy in the realms of popular music-making. The tonal quality of the instrument is certainly not a natural sound, but its rather sexy legato qualities were to prove ideal for the newly emotive music of the jazz age. It did not come noticeably into popular reckoning until the early 20th century, even creeping into jazz as something of an interloper in the holy cornet, trombone, clarinet trinity of traditional New Orleans jazz.

There was an attempt from around 1916–17 to popularize a barely surviving member of the family, the C-melody saxophone, which hopeful salesmen now advertised as an easy-to-play instrument for public use, avoiding the added confusion of transposition which the mainly B♭ and E♭ instruments necessitated. It was taken up by one or two virtuoso players, notably the vaudeville entertainer Rudy Wiedoeft (1893–1940), whose 'Canary cottage' of 1917 has been claimed as the first jazz-slanted recording of a saxophone. He helped to create something of a saxophone craze with his ragtime-based writings like 'Sax-o-doodle', 'Sax-o-tricks', 'Sax-o-phun', and 'Saxophobia', at the same time giving the instrument a semi-comic character with his slap-tongue and staccato passages; but he did also employ the gliding and sinuous tone that was to endear the instrument to the jazz world. The C-melody instrument was, in fact, used very effectively by players like Frankie *Trumbauer, who gave it a lovely, floating tone; but the instrument still went out of fashion in the 1930s.

The first of the range that might have been said to make a strong jazz impression was the soprano, notably in the hands of Sidney *Bechet whose playing of it in Will Marion Cook's Southern Syncopated Orchestra around 1920 attracted European attention. Bechet, using it as a substitute for the clarinet, played with a forceful, almost trumpet-like tone, which few could emulate without being labelled imitators. A few, like Johnny *Hodges, did use the soprano but it remained a comparatively rare instrument, on a par with the baritone whose grumpy tones were sensitively employed by players like Harry *Carney, Gerry *Mulligan, and Pepper *Adams. Even rarer was the bass saxophone whose chief exponent remains Adrian *Rollini. None of these models has quite managed to become a mainstream instrument.

The two that have mainly triumphed are the tenor and the alto instruments, perhaps simply because they are middle-range and fit in best with other wind instruments. The tenor was the first favourite because of its big, blustering tone combined with a high degree of technical and tonal flexibility. It was to triumph as both a solo and section instrument. As examples of the individuality achieved on the tenor-saxophone three players might be singled out—Coleman *Hawkins, who was to give the saxophone its basic language and mainstream qualities, working in the wake of Armstrong's trumpet styling; the white Bud *Freeman who gave it a hard dusty sound; and the inventive Lester *Young, who gave it a cool and laconic flavour. The tenor has produced more virtuoso performers than any other member of the saxophone family. Those who followed in the Hawkins mould included: Benny *Carter, Herschel Evans (1909–39), Leon 'Chu' Berry (1910–41), Budd Johnson (1910–84), Ben *Webster, Don Byas (1912–72), Buddy Tate (*b* 1913); with a lingering influence still to be discerned in such players as Georgie Auld (1919–90), Paul Gonsalves (1920–74), and Lucky Thompson (*b* 1924), linking the trad to the mod in step with their times. If Bud Freeman can be said to take the first steps towards a cooler approach, it was Lester Young, with his gracefully elegant but still swinging style and his oblique musical thinking, that took the tenor tradition forward towards the modern jazz age. He was followed by players like Stan *Getz, Albert Ayler (1936–70), and a whole flock of Young disciples.

The alto, with its lighter and more ethereal quality invited a jazz handling that verged on the romantic and found two great exponents in the traditionally-based, poetical Johnny *Hodges; in the exploratory and dramatic Charlie *Parker; followed by Sonny Stitt (1924–82), 'Cannonball' *Adderley, and many others. With so many stars of the tenor and alto abounding it is invidious to single out further names but John *Coltrane (tenor), who also revived interest in the soprano in the 1960s, and Ornette *Coleman (alto) come to mind as two outstanding modern exponents leading to the avant-gardists of today like Courtney Pine (*b* 1964).

A. V. Frankenstein: *Syncopating Saxophones* (Chicago, 1925). J. Viera: *Das Saxophon im Jazz* (Vienna, 1977). J. Hol: *Some Saxophone History (1840–1927): its Origin & Early Use* (London, 1982; rev. 1984).

Sayer, Leo [Gerard Hugh] (*b* Shoreham, Sussex, 21 May 1948). British pop singer and composer. He led a Shoreham-based band called Patches before forming a songwriting team with Dave Courtney and producing a hit with 'Giving it all away', recorded by Roger *Daltrey in 1973. He moved into the Top 10 with his own second recording, 'The show must go on', in the same year; followed by 'Long tall glasses' in 1974 and 'Moonlighting' in 1975. Relying at first on stage presentation and costume, he realized the value of his material by 1975, and adopted a more sober and purposeful image with such songs as 'You make me feel like dancing' (1976) and 'When I need you' (1977), which both became No. 1 hits in the USA. He had his own TV series in 1980, and continued into the 1980s as an established entertainer.

Scat. Nonsensical or wordless singing, generally with jazz phrasing, in imitation of instruments; a jazz vocalise. There are many claims to its origination, Jelly Roll *Morton asserting that he used the technique as far back as 1906–7, but that it originated with an obscure comedian from Vicksburg called Joe Sims. It was popularized, and probably first recorded, by Louis *Armstrong when he forgot his words in 'Heebie jeebies' in 1926, and was made a regular feature of his work by bandleader Cab *Calloway. It has since been widely exploited by many jazz singers, notably Ella *Fitzgerald.

Scheff, Fritzi [Yager, Friederike] (*b* Vienna, 30 Aug. 1879; *d* New York, 8 Apr. 1954). Austrian singer and actress. She studied singing with her mother, who was a member of the Vienna Opera, and made her debut at the Metropolitan Opera, New York, 28 Dec. 1900, in *Fidelio*. She sang in opera for three seasons before switching to her real forte, the world of operetta, and making her name in *Babette* (1903); *The Two Roses* (1904); and especially Victor *Herbert's **Mlle Modiste* (1905), in which she introduced 'Kiss me again', with which she was ever associated. Her tiny, slim figure and soaring voice were also admired in *The Prima Donna* (1908); *The Duchess* (1911); and *Pretty Mrs Smith* (1914).

Schertzinger, Victor (*b* Mahanoy, Penn., 8 Apr. 1880; *d* Hollywood, 26 Oct. 1941). American composer, conductor, violinist, and film director. He studied music in Brussels, and at the age of eight was playing in Victor *Herbert's Symphony Orchestra. He also played with the *Sousa band and toured the USA and Europe while still in his teens. He became musical director at a Los Angeles theatre and later spent many years conducting Broadway shows, then returned to Los Angeles where he wrote the music for Thomas Ince's film *Civilization* (1916)—one of the first full-length films to have a complete musical background score written for it.

He became a full-time film director (including titles marked †) and also wrote the scores for many of his own films. His scores included: *The Love Parade* (1929), starring Maurice *Chevalier and Jeanette *MacDonald; †*Heads Up* (1930); †*The Cocktail Hour* (1933); †*One Night of Love* (1934), starring Grace *Moore—'One night of love'; †*Let's Live Tonight* (1935); †*Love Me Forever* (1935; *On Wings of Song* in UK), with Grace Moore; †*The Music Goes Round* (1936)—'Life begins when you're in love'; †*Something to Sing About* (1937); †*Road to Singapore* (1940); †*Rhythm on the River* (1940); †*Kiss the Boys Goodbye* (1941), with Mary *Martin—'Kiss the boys goodbye', 'Sand in my shoes' (*w* Frank *Loesser); *Glamour Boy* (1941); and *The Fleet's In* (1941)—'Arthur Murray taught me dancing in a hurry', 'Not mine', 'Tangerine' (*w* Johnny *Mercer).

Schifrin, Lalo [Boris] (*b* Buenos Aires, 21 June 1932). American composer and conductor. Son of the concert master of the Teatro Colón, he studied music and specialized in film history and production in Buenos Aires, and studied in Paris under Olivier Messiaen. He became interested in jazz when he was 16, particularly the modernists like *Parker, *Gillespie, and *Monk, represented Argentina at the International Jazz Festival in Paris in 1955, and formed his own modern jazz group in Buenos Aires. In 1958 he went to the USA as arranger for Xavier *Cugat and became pianist and arranger for the Dizzy Gillespie band 1960–2, producing such pieces as 'Manteca', 'Con Alma', and 'Tunisian Fantasy', based on Gillespie's 'Night in Tunisia'. Many of his works were included in Jazz at the Philharmonic concerts and he also wrote material for Count *Basie, Stan *Getz, and Sarah *Vaughan. He wrote a ballet, *Jazz Faust* (1963).

In 1964 he went to Hollywood to work on TV music for Universal and began to write film scores, his first major assignment being *The Cincinnati Kid* (1965). Since then his jazz-inflected scores, characterized by their clear, modernistic lines, have included: *The Liquidator* (1965); *Gone With the Wave* (1965); *I Deal in Danger* (1966); *Blindfold* (1966); *Murderer's Row* (1966); *The Venetian Affair* (1967); *Cool Hand Luke* (1967); *The Fox* (1967); *Sol Madrid* (1968); *The Brotherhood* (1968); *Bullitt* (1968); *Che!* (1969); *Eye of the Cat* (1969); *Kelly's Heroes* (1970); *The Beguiled* (1970); *I Love My Wife* (1970); *Dirty Harry* (1971); *The Wrath of God* (1972); and *Charley Varrick* (1973). He wrote TV themes for *Mission Impossible* (1967); *The Virginians* (1969); and others. His oratorio *The Rise and Fall of the Third Reich* was produced at the Hollywood Bowl in 1968; since when he has written a number of jazz-based orchestral and choral works.

Schmidt, Harvey [Lester] (*b* Dallas, 12 Sept. 1929). American composer. Graduate of the University of Texas where he met Tom Jones and started collaborating with him on songs. They continued to work together while serving in the armed forces and, in 1955, both went to New York and produced revue material in partnership. They had an unexpected success with their off-Broadway show *The *Fantasticks* (1960)—'Soon it's gonna rain', 'Try to remember'; and continued to collaborate on further musicals: *110 in the Shade* (1963)—'Simple little things'; **I Do! I Do!* (1966)—'My cup runneth over'; *Celebration* (1969); and *Colette* (1971). They have continued to work on limited run experimental musicals.

Schock, Rudolph (*b* Duisburg, 9 Apr. 1915; *d* Gürzenich, 13 Nov. 1986). German singer. Like Richard *Tauber, to whom he was a natural successor, he started his career as an opera singer, but eventually found his true métier and fame in the world of operetta. By the mid-1940s he was increasingly involved in appearing in films and on TV in the works of *Strauss, *Lehár, *Zeller, and others, and made recordings of much of the best operetta repertoire.

Schoebel, Elmer (*b* East St Louis, Ill., 8 Sept. 1896; *d* Miami, Fla., 14 Dec. 1970). American composer and pianist. He played with the Friars Society Orchestra in Chicago and with other early jazz groups, and worked for a period with the Isham *Jones orchestra. He composed or collaborated on such jazz standards as 'Bugle call rag' (1923), 'Farewell blues' (1923), 'Nobody's sweetheart' (1924), 'Prince of Wails' (1924), 'Spanish shawl' (1925), and 'Stomp off, let's go' (1925).

Schottisch. A ballroom dance of the 19th century which came to England from the Continent in 1848. It was similar to the *polka but in slower time, and was, in fact, known in England for a time as the German polka. It is sometimes confused with the earlier Ecossaise, which is a country dance, whereas the schottisch is a round dance. It has never been established that either dance is of true Scottish origin; probably they represent what a German or Frenchman, respectively, thought a Scottish dance should be like.

Schrammel. A brand of light, melodic, and elegantly simple music that has become a characteristic part of the Viennese musical scene, generally played by anything from a trio to a quintet and notably to be heard in the Heurigen inns in the outlying district of Grinzing where the Viennese gather to imbibe the new wines. The real credit for its inception must go to Kaspar Schrammel, a poor weaver in the small Austrian town of Litschau, who in his spare time played the violin at weddings and other festivals. He went to live in Vienna to attempt to make a living as a musician, found employment in the inns and gardens of Grinzing, and, as soon as they were old enough, his sons joined him. Kaspar died young around 1870 but the two brothers Johann (1850–93) and Josef Schrammel (1852–95), both violinists and composers, carried on the tradition and formed a quartet with their friends Anton Strohmeyer on guitar and Georg Dänzer on clarinet. Their style of playing evolved from this instrumentation and their style of singing—half-sung, half-spoken—was their own invention. They began to write their own music, and the merits of their playing, and such compositions as Johann's 'Wien, bleibt Wien' (which has become as much as part of Viennese musical life as 'The blue Danube') and the 'Vindobona Marsch', brought them enormous popularity in the inns and gardens of the wine-bibing outskirts of Vienna at about the same time as Johann *Strauss II was enjoying his triumphs in the city. Their style became accepted as the basic idiom of Viennese popular dance music and was greatly admired by Brahms.

Their reputation spread throughout Austria, then further afield, and they began to tour. One trip took them to the USA to play at the World Exhibition of 1890. Both brothers died in their early forties but their music lived on. As clarinettists of the Dänzer ilk were not always easy to find, it became customary for subsequent groups to use a piano accordion and the tradition adapted itself to the use of a violin, guitar, accordion, and bass line-up as typical of what was now to be known as a Schrammel quartet. Others composed music in the same tradition and a whole literature of Schrammel music accumulated. The tradition was maintained but, as in other fields, tended to become commercialized. A dedicated revival of the true tradition was undertaken by Professor Luis Böck, a violinist in the Vienna Symphony Orchestra. In the late 1960s he began a search for the original Schrammel scores and found many manuscripts in the possession of a surviving daughter. He formed Das Klassisches Wiener Schrammelquartett, with fellow-musicians from the orchestra, which soon established itself in Austria and, like the original quartet, began to travel abroad. They also recorded some of the music, further authenticity being given to their efforts on discovering a playing member of the Schrammel family, a grandson Friedrich Schrammel, who joined the quartet on guitar in 1967.

Schröder, Friedrich (*b* Naefels, Switzerland, 6 Aug. 1910; *d* Berlin, 25 Sept. 1972). German composer. He did much to keep alive the spirit of operetta by writing successful works in the style and by bringing the works of older composers back to the theatre. His idol was Franz *Lehár and his motto 'Melodie, Melodie und wieder Melodie'. He studied music in Berlin and soon found himself weaned from the classical field by his love of the theatre. His first operetta, *Die Hochzeitsnacht im Paradies* (Berlin, 1942; Vienna, 1950), was a great success and ran for more than 500 performances. Its triumph was consolidated by *Nächte in Schanghai* (1947) and by *Isabella* (1949), often considered to be his best work. He also wrote film music.

Schuller, Gunther (*b* Jackson Heights, NY, 22 Nov. 1925). American composer, conductor, and teacher. His grandfather was a bandmaster in Germany who emigrated to the USA, and his father was a violinist in the New York Philharmonic Orchestra. He was sent to Germany for his early education and, on his return to the USA, joined the St Thomas Church Choir School, where he studied theory. He also studied the french horn at the Manhattan School of Music. He became horn player with the New York Philharmonic in 1942 and principal horn with the Cincinnati Symphony in 1943, performing as soloist in 1945. A growing interest in jazz led to involvement with Miles *Davis on the famous series of Capitol recordings, 1948–9, which became known as 'the birth of the cool', and on to jazz compositions. He was horn player in the Metropolitan Opera orchestra 1945–59; taught at the Manhattan School of Music 1950–63 and composition at Yale University 1964–6; was President of the New England Conservatory in Boston 1966–77; and artistic director of the Berkshire Music Center in Tanglewood from 1969.

His long list of compositions included many jazz-based works from 1945 on, and he has constantly striven to create a link between serious music and jazz, working in what he described from 1957 as 'third stream' areas, combining formal structures with jazz improvisation. He collaborated with John *Lewis in many of these projects. He also maintained a strong interest in the traditional jazz forms and helped the *ragtime revival on its path to authenticity by performances and recordings of *The Little Red Book* with his New England Conservatory Ragtime Ensemble, formed in 1972. He has started a searching study of jazz, written from the analytical rather than the usual historical side, with *Early Jazz: its Roots and Development* (New York, 1968); *The Swing Era: the Development of Jazz 1930–1945* (New York–Oxford, 1989); and further volumes in progress.

G. Schuller: *Musings: the Musical World of Gunther Schuller* (New York, 1989).

Schwartz, Arthur (*b* Brooklyn, NY, 25 Nov. 1900; *d* Kintnersville, Pa., 3 Sept. 1984). American composer. He was educated at New York University (BA 1920) and Columbia University (MA 1921), passed his legal exams in 1924, and taught English and practised law before becoming a composer. His part-time piano playing had helped him to maintain himself at college but it was not until 1926, when he began to write vaudeville material and magazine articles, that he began to earn enough to be able to give up his law practice in 1929. He worked with lyricist Howard *Dietz, contributing to *Dear Sir* (1924) and *Grand Street Follies* in 1926. In 1929 he wrote the music for *The *Little Show*, and had a hit with 'I guess I'll have to change my plan', followed by *The Grand Street Follies* (1929). He went to London in 1930 to add music to various productions such as *The *Co-Optimists* (1930), and wrote the score of *Here Comes the Bride* (1930). The next five years saw such Broadway productions as *The Second Little Show* (1930); *Princess Charming* (1930); *Three's a Crowd* (1930)—'Something to remember you by'; *The *Band Wagon* (1931; filmed 1953), both with Fred *Astaire—'Dancing in the dark', 'I love Louisa'; *Flying Colors* (1932)—'Alone together', 'Louisiana hayride'; *Nice Goings On* (London, 1933); *Revenge With Music* (1934)—'You and the night and the music'; *At Home Abroad* (1935)—'Paree'; *Follow the Sun* (London, 1936); *Virginia* (1937); *Between the Devil* (1937)—'I see your face before me', 'By myself'; *Stars in Your Eyes* (1939); *American Jubilee* (1940); *Park Avenue* (1946, *w* Ira *Gershwin); *Inside USA* (1948)—'Haunted heart'; *A *Tree grows in Brooklyn* (1951)—'Look who's dancing' (*w* Dorothy *Fields); *By the Beautiful Sea* (1954); *The Gay Life* (1961); and *Jennie* (1963).

He produced many theme songs for radio and TV—*High Tor* (1956); *A Bell for Adano* (1957). He started to write for films in the 1930s—*Follow the Leader* (1930); *She Loves Me Not* (1934); *Under Your Spell* (1936)—'Under your spell'; *That Girl from Paris* (1936)—'Seal it with a kiss' (*w* Edward Heyman). In 1941 he settled in Hollywood and contributed to: *Navy Blues* (1941)—'You're a natural' (*w* Johnny *Mercer); *Cairo* (1942); *Thank Your Lucky Stars* (1943)—'They're either too young or too old' (*w* Frank *Loesser), 'Love isn't born' (Loesser), sung by Ann Sheridan (1915–67); *The Time, the Place and* *the Girl* (1946)—'A gal in calico' (*w* Leo Robin), 'Oh, but I do' (Robin); *Her Kind of Man* (1946)—'Something to remember you by' (Dietz); *Dancing in the Dark* (1949), which used many songs from his Broadway shows; *Excuse My Dust* (1951); *Dangerous When Wet* (1953); and *You're Never Too Young* (1955). He was the producer of Jerome *Kern's *Cover Girl* (1944); and of the film biography of Cole *Porter, *Night and Day* (1946).

H. Dietz: *Dancing in the Dark* (New York, 1974).

Schwartz, Jean (*b* Budapest, 4 Nov. 1878; *d* Sherman Oaks, Calif., 30 Nov. 1956). Hungarian-born American composer. He had his first piano lessons with his sister while still in Hungary and showed promise as a classical performer. The family emigrated to New York when he was 10 and, after various non-musical jobs, he finally found employment as a pianist in the sheet music department of a big store. He became pianist at the *Weber and Fields Music Hall and contributed songs to various productions there. It was here that he started a partnership with lyricist William Jerome (1865–1932), with whom he was to work for the next 15 years.

Their scores included: *Piff!! Paff!! Pouf!!!* (1904)—'The ghost that never walked'; *A Yankee Circus on Mars* (1905); *Lifting the Lid* (1905); *The Ham Tree* (1905); *Fritz in Tammany Hall* (1905); *The White Cat* (1905); *Lola from Berlin* (1906); *In Hayti* (1909); *Up and Down Broadway* (1910)—'Chinatown, my Chinatown'; *The Honeymoon Express* (1913); *The *Passing Show* (1913, 1918, 1919, 1920, 1923, 1924); *When Claudia Smiles* (1914); *Monte Cristo Jr.* (1919); *Make It Snappy* (1922). Later he worked with Sigmund *Romberg on such shows as *Innocent Eyes* (1924).

He wrote many songs associated with Al *Jolson, notably 'Rock-a-bye your baby with a Dixie melody' which was used in **Sinbad* (1918). His other popular numbers included 'Rip Van Winkle was a lucky man', used in *The Sleeping Beauty* (1901), 'Mr Dooley', used in *A *Chinese Honeymoon* (1902), 'Bedelia', used in *The Jersey Lily* (1903), and 'My Irish Molly-o', used in *The Little Cherub* (1907). He was immensely prolific, contributing songs to numerous shows; contriving some excellent ragtime numbers like 'Whitewash man' (1908); and writing items used in the jazz world such as 'I'm all bound round with the Mason-Dixon Line' (1917). After around 1930, when he wrote Ben *Bernie's theme tune 'Au revoir, pleasant dreams' and went to live in California, the flood dried up and he wrote comparatively little.

Schwartz, Stephen Lawrence (*b* New York, 6 Mar. 1948). American composer and lyricist. Educated at the Juilliard School of Music 1960–4, he had a great success with his first rock musical, **Godspell* ('Day by day'), which has had many productions since its opening in New York in 1971. He also produced the original cast album which won two Grammy Awards. He collaborated with Leonard *Bernstein on the lyrics for his Mass, written for the opening of the John F. Kennedy Center for the Performing Arts in Washington DC. His successes continued with *Pippin* (1972)—'Corner of the sky'; and *The Magic Show* (1974)—'Magic to do'. He also wrote the theme song for a play *Butterflies are Free*, which was later filmed.

Scotch snap. A rhythmic figure in which a short note is followed by a dotted note three times as long. To be effective it is essential that the second longer note should actually be held for its full length and not shortened or made up by a momentary rest, a basic essential far too often honoured in the breach rather than the observance. It is a characteristic of a good deal of Scottish music, particularly the *strathspey, and it is a vital part of a song like 'Green grow the rashes', for example. On the other hand, it can be the bane of pseudo-Scottish melodies, of which there is more than an ample supply.

Scott, Hazel (*b* Port of Spain, Trinidad, 11 June 1920; *d* New York, 2 Oct. 1981). West Indian pianist. She was given her first musical education by her mother, who ran an all-woman band and took her to the USA in 1924. After a brief sojourn at the Juilliard School she forsook academic studies for the lure of the professional world of music. In 1936 she had her own radio series and became known as a specialist in swinging the classics. She appeared in the Broadway show *Sing Out the News* (1938), and was a popular figure at the Café Society Downtown in Greenwich Village 1939–45. She was in the films *Something to Shout About* (1943); *I Dood It* (1943; *By Hook or by Crook* in UK); *The Heat's On* (1943; *Tropicana* in UK); *Broadway Rhythm* (1943); and *Rhapsody in Blue* (1945)—a film on the life of George *Gershwin. In 1945 she married the black Harlem congressman Adam Clayton Powell, a leader of the Civil Rights movement, but after various scandals that got him thrown out of Congress, they were divorced in 1960. From 1945 to 1957 she continued in concert and nightclub work in the USA and she spent two years in Paris 1965–7, where she became a fashionable entertainer. In 1967 she returned to New York and continued to perform until a few weeks before she died of cancer.

Scott, James Sylvester (*b* Neosho, Mo., 12 Feb. 1885; *d* Kansas City, 30 Aug. 1938). American ragtime composer: one of the great black pioneers of the music, along with Scott *Joplin and the white exponent Joseph *Lamb. He published his first work at the age of 17 and went on to write some classic pieces that are in a slightly more romantic and demanding vein than Joplin's graceful compositions. These included: 'A Summer breeze' (1903), 'The fascinator' (1903), 'Frog legs rag' (1906), 'Kansas City rag' (1907), 'Great Scott rag' (1909), 'The ragtime Betty' (1909), 'Sunburst rag' (1909), 'Grace and beauty' (1909), 'Hilarity rag' (1910), 'Ragtime oriole' (1911), 'Climax rag' (1914), 'Evergreen rag' (1915), 'Prosperity rag' (1916), 'Paramount rag' (1917), 'Peace and plenty rag' (1919), and 'Modesty rag' (1920). He also wrote a number of waltzes and songs.

Scott, Raymond [Warnow, Harry] (*b* New York, 10 Sept. 1910). American composer, arranger, bandleader, and pianist. He studied music at Juilliard and his main early interest was in the use of electronics for musical sound-effects. His brother, Mark Warnow, well-known as a *Hit Parade* conductor of the 1940s, engaged him to play the piano with his CBS orchestra. During the mid-1930s, Scott began to experiment with a novel-sounding quintet which he led on CBS radio 1934–8, the music evolving through elaborate and careful rehearsal, and printed scores only appearing after the effects had been caught on record. These pieces, sometimes as memorable for their odd titles as for their musical content, remained outside the main jazz stream and might simply be classified as novelty music of the highest order. He had a brief period in Hollywood 1937–8, but mainly functioned as a conductor for CBS and as a highly regarded arranger.

In 1940 he formed a more orthodox big band (with Shelly *Manne as drummer); and in 1942 formed the first mixed race staff band for CBS, using black musicians such as Cozy *Cole, Charlie Shavers (1917–71), and Ben *Webster; with white pianist Johnny *Guarnieri, and Frank *Sinatra as vocalist. He was sacked in 1945 and concentrated on writing show music and working in various commercial posts. He ran his own record label for a time, and in the 1950s was musical director for Everest Records. In post-war years he conducted the Lucky Strike Hit Parade on radio and toured and recorded with his then wife Dorothy Collins (*b* 1927), before retiring from the musical scene to run his own electronics research firm in New Jersey, later in California. He wrote the musical *Lute Song* in 1946.

His works include the songs 'Toy trumpet' (1937), 'In an 18th century drawing-room' (1939), based on Mozart, 'Tired little teddy bear' (1944); and such instrumental items as 'Powerhouse' (1937), 'Twilight in Turkey' (1937), 'Dinner music for a pack of hungry cannibals' (1938), 'War dance for wooden Indians' (1938), 'Minuet in jazz' (1939), 'Business men's bounce' (1939), 'Four beat shuffle' (1940), 'When Cootie left the Duke' (1940), and 'Mr Basie goes to Washington' (1940).

Scott, Ronnie [Schatt, Ronald] (*b* London, 28 Jan. 1927). British saxophonist and leader. He started playing in jazz clubs in his teens, worked with Johnny Claes 1944–5, and with Ted *Heath 1946; also with the *Ambrose orchestra and on transatlantic liners. He was at the experimentalist venue Club 11, 1948–50, and with Jack *Parnell 1952. He formed his own group 1953–6, then jointly led the Jazz Couriers with Tubby Hayes (1935–73). He opened his own jazz club, in Gerrard Street, in 1959, which became, and has continued to be, the best-known international jazz venue in London, moving to Frith Street in 1965. He continued leading his own quartet 1960–7, an 8-piece band 1968–9, a trio 1971–5, and, since then, various quartets and quintets. He was with the Kenny *Clarke–Francy Boland band 1962–73. He is recognized not only for his organizational services to jazz but also as an influential player in the modern mainstream style of Zoot *Sims.

J. Fordham: *Let's Join Hands and Contact the Living* (London, 1986).

Scotto, Vincent (*b* Marseilles, 1876; *d* Paris, 1952). French composer. He most frequently worked and composed with the guitar, which he learned to play when he was seven. He wrote his first song in 1906, just before his arrival in Paris. It was taken up by the music-hall singer Polin (1863–1927) at the Ambassadeurs Music Hall; and 'La petite Tonkinoise', to words by Villard [Georges Lascombe] (1879–1927) and Henri *Christiné, remains one of his most popular songs. Despite his meridional origins, he has written many of his most beautiful songs about Paris; but it so happened that he was in London in 1913 when he composed 'Sous les ponts de Paris'. He worked with remarkable ease and 'J'ai deux amours' (1930), which he wrote for Josephine *Baker, came to him as he was walking along the street on the way to a rehearsal. His association with the Corsican-born singer Tino *Rossi lasted for 50 years.

He wrote some 70 operettas with some, like *Au pays du soleil* (1930), *Un de la Canabière* (1938), and *Violettes impériales* (1948), becoming part of the standard French repertoire. He wrote for films, notably for such Tino Rossi vehicles as *Naples au baiser de feu* (1937) which contains some of his richest melodies.

V. Scotto: *Souvenirs de Paris* (Paris, 1947).

Scott-Wood, George (*b* Glasgow, 27 May 1903; *d* London, 28 Oct. 1978). British pianist, violinist, composer, arranger, and bandleader. At the age of 14 he became official accompanist at the Arts Club in Glasgow. Later he went to the USA and gave piano recitals, returning to Glasgow to play at the Plaza cinema. He joined a Glasgow-based group known as the Five Omega Collegians (1920–8) which moved via Liverpool, Manchester, and Brighton, to the Empress Rooms in London, where he subsequently played with the Jay Whidden orchestra. He became a regular arranger and was responsible for much of the repertoire of the Harry *Roy band; also working as musical director for Parlophone Records and eventually supervising most of EMI's recordings of popular dance music and light classics. In this capacity he led, for $5\frac{1}{2}$ years from 1934, a popular recording jazz group (on the Regal Zonophone label) known as the Six Swingers which originally included such names as Freddy Gardner (1911–50), Max Goldberg (1905–90), Lew Davis (*b* 1903), and Max Bacon (*b* 1904), with Sam Browne (*d* 1974) as vocalist. He was the composer of

'Swing, brothers, swing', 'Becky, play your violin', and other period numbers. He was also a talented piano accordionist and made many recordings with his popular accordion band.

Scruggs, Earl (*b* Flint Hill, NC, 6 Jan. 1924). American country banjoist. He grew up in Cleveland County, North Carolina, a centre of banjo enthusiasm in the 1930s. At 15 he played with a group on local radio and by 1945 had graduated to Nashville, and eventually joined the famous Bill *Monroe group and the **Grand Ole Opry* show. After two years with Monroe he and singer/guitarist Lester *Flatt left to form their own group, the Foggy Mountain Boys. Scruggs developed a three-finger style on the five-string banjo which became a feature of modern *bluegrass playing, and developed techniques which had him hailed as 'the Paganini of the banjo', with a strong melodic line standing out in a heavily chorded background. The group joined the *Grand Ole Opry* in 1955, and recorded such items as 'Foggy Mountain breakdown', spreading the gospel of bluegrass all over the USA. Their sound-track recording for *Bonnie and Clyde* (1967) carried bluegrass music to the top of the popularity charts for the first time.

It came as a shock when Scruggs and Flatt amicably split up in 1969, and Scruggs went on to found the Earl Scruggs Revue in which electronic sounds played their part. His collaborations were now with such artists as Arlo *Guthrie, Bob *Dylan, the *Byrds, Linda *Ronstadt, and Joan *Baez. Among his most notable albums have been those with Tom T. *Hall: *The Storyteller and the Banjo Man* (1982) and *Top of the World* (1983).

Searchers, The. British pop group who briefly rivalled the *Beatles in popularity in the early 1960s. They began to record for Pye records in 1963 when the line-up was Mike Pender (*b* 1942) (vocal and lead-guitar), John McNally (*b* 1941) (vocal and guitar), Tony Jackson (*b* 1940) (vocal and bass), and Chris Curtis (*b* 1941) (vocal and drums). Their first recording, 'Sweets for my sweet' (1963), became a No. 1 hit and already demonstrated their high-pitched and essentially light style. They continued with 'Needles and pins' (1964), 'Don't throw your love away' (1964), and 'When you walk in the room' (1964), proving equally popular in the USA on the Kapp label. The personnel began to change in the 1960s until, by 1986, McNally was the only original member of the group, which moved from the competitive recording arena into the more stable world of club cabaret; though they made a recording comeback in 1979 and 1981.

Sedaka, Neil (*b* Brooklyn, NY, 13 Mar. 1939). American composer and singer. Trained as a classical pianist, he was chosen by Artur Rubinstein as the best New York High School pianist of 1956, and won a scholarship to the Juilliard School of Music. He had started writing songs at the age of 13 and had his first success with 'Stupid Cupid' (1958), which was made into a hit by Connie *Francis. He joined Aldon Music, run by Don Kirshner and Al Nevins, and teamed up with lyricist Howard Greenfield to produce more than 500 songs, many of which he was to record himself for RCA. He was seen as a rival to Frankie *Avalon and Rick *Nelson, but a tendency to tubbiness enforced a less romantic projection, his cheery approach still achieving more than a dozen top hit recordings before 1964, including 'Oh, Carol' (1959), 'Calendar girl' (1960), 'Happy birthday, sweet sixteen' (1961), and 'Breaking up is hard to do' (1962).

He continued to write similar material for the *Monkees and Tom *Jones; but sterner competition from the *Beatles and the *Rolling Stones made such cute material out of place, and Sedaka stopped making his own recordings to move into the rock and roll field, notably in Britain, with such items as 'Standing on the outside' (1973) and 'Laughter in the rain' (1974). Later he reverted to type in producing and recording easy listening material that still has a considerable older following.

Seeger, Peggy [Margaret] (*b* New York, 17 June 1935). American folk-singer. From a deep-rooted folk-music background (see below), she was playing the guitar and other instruments by the age of 10, studied music at Radcliffe, and soon after began to perform in public. She travelled over Europe, going to Britain in 1956 to appear in the folk-musical *Dark Side of the Moon*. She joined the Ramblers, where she met the Scottish folk-singer Ewan *MacColl, whom she married in 1957. They mainly worked and recorded together, but she has produced more than 30 solo albums, specializing in ballads, and also worked with Tom Paley and others.

Seeger, Pete (*b* New York, 3 May 1919). American folk-singer and composer. Son, by his first marriage, of the eminent American ethnomusicologist, composer, and teacher Charles Seeger (1886–1979); half-brother to singers Peggy *Seeger and Mike Seeger (*b* 1933); and nephew of the poet Alan Seeger. He gave up studies at Harvard to follow the family trail in the folk-music world after a visit in 1935 to a Carolina folk festival. Making contact with such authorities as John and Alan *Lomax, *Leadbelly, and Woody *Guthrie, he formed the *Almanac Singers in 1940, before doing his army service. In 1949, with Lee Hays (1914–81) who sang bass 1949–60, he formed the *Weavers and made several best-selling records with them. From the early 1950s he followed a solo career, establishing a big following for his concerts and recitals, and earning himself the accolades of 'father of the American folk revival' and 'America's tuning-fork'; and he began recording for Folkways in 1953. He came into serious conflict with McCarthy and the Un-American Activities Committee in 1955, and was not cleared of all charges until 1962. He helped re-establish the Newport Folk Festival in 1960, and has been a regular writer in folk publications. An expert guitarist, a popularizer of the 5-string banjo, and an effective singer, he is a great champion of communal singing.

Among his most famous songs are 'If I had a hammer' (with Lee Hays), 'Where have all the flowers gone', 'Waist deep in the Big Muddy', 'Turn, turn, turn', and 'Guantanamera'. He appeared in the film *Tell Me That You Love Me, Julie Moon* in 1970. He is the author or editor of *American Favorite Ballads* (1960); *The Bells of Rhymney* (1964); *How to Play the Five-String Banjo* (1965); *The Incompleat Folksinger* (1972); and *Henscratches and Flyspecks* (1973).

Seekers, The. Australian urban folk singers. Melbourne bass player Athol Guy (*b* 1940) tried to form a number of groups before the Seekers eventually came together in 1964, with the settled personnel of Guy, Keith Potger (*b* 1941) (guitar), Bruce Woodley (*b* 1942) (guitar), and female vocalist Judith Durham (*b* 1943). They worked in coffee-houses and appeared on Melbourne TV and, on the strength of an audition film, were asked to appear at the Palladium in London. Their first No. 1 hit came with a recording of Tom *Springfield's 'I'll never find another you' (1965). Their first album was put out by World Record Club and later re-issued by Capitol. Basing themselves in the UK they had eight songs in the Top 20 including the title-song from the film *Georgy Girl* (1966), which was nominated for an Oscar; and were the first group to have a hit with a Paul *Simon song, 'Someday one day' (1966). The group broke up in 1968, but Keith Potger formed the New Seekers in 1969, with Eva Graham (*b* 1943), Lyn Paul (*b* 1941), and Peter Doyle (*b* 1949); while Judith Durham followed a career as a solo artist in popular and jazz vein.

Seeley, Blossom (*b* San Francisco, 16 July 1891; *d* New York, 17 Apr. 1974). American entertainer, singer, and dancer. She first performed in vaudeville at the age of 10, billed as 'The Little Blossom', latterly appearing with her second husband Lew *Fields (whom she married in 1922) as Seeley and Fields, a partnership portrayed by Betty *Hutton and Ralph Meeker in the film *Somebody Loves Me* (1952). She sang in jazz vein such songs as 'I cried for you', 'Way down yonder in New Orleans', 'Somebody loves me', and 'Smiles', earning the title of 'The Queen of Syncopation', and told stories in Negro dialect. She later worked with songwriter Benny Davis (1894–1959). She first appeared on Broadway with Fields in *The Hen Pecks* (1911); later she was in *The Charity Girl* (1912); *The Whirl of Society* (1912); *Maid in America* (1915); *Stop! Look! Listen!* (1916); and the **Greenwich Village Follies* (1928). She retired in 1936 but made a brief comeback in 1952.

Segal, Vivienne [Sonia] (*b* Philadelphia, 19 Apr. 1897; *d* Los Angeles, 29 Dec. 1992). American actress and singer. Starting with *The Blue Paradise* (1915), in which she sang 'Auf wiedersehen', she had a long career ranging from romantic operetta to her best-remembered part in **Pal Joey*. Her shows included: *My Lady's Glove* (1917); *Oh, Lady! Lady!!* (1918); *The Little Whopper* (1919); *The Yankee Princess* (1922); *Adrienne* (1923); **Ziegfeld Follies* (1924); *Florida Girl* (1925); *Castles in the Air* (1926); *The *Desert Song* (1926)—'The desert song'; *The Three Musketeers* (1928); *I Married an Angel* (1938); *Pal Joey* (1940)—'Bewitched, bothered and bewildered'; *A *Connecticut Yankee* (1943)—'To keep my love alive'; *Music in My Heart* (1947); and *Great to Be Alive* (1950). She appeared in films, including *Song of the West* (1930) and *The *Cat and the Fiddle* (1934).

Serrano, José Siméon (*b* Sueca, Valencia, 14 Oct. 1873; *d* Madrid, 8 Mar. 1943). Spanish composer. He studied music at the Valencia Conservatory with early encouragement from his father, who was a talented musician himself. Moving to Madrid to made his way in the musical world, for 14 years he had a struggling time writing songs, arranging, and playing. His ambition to write for the theatre was first realized in 1900 when a short piece called *El motete* was performed at the Teatro Apolo. This was followed by many successful zarzuelas, with the tuneful *La Canción del Olvido* (1916) remaining his best-known and best-loved piece, still regularly played and recorded, and one of the most attractive of Spanish zarzuelas with its Neapolitan flavour.

His works include: *La Mazorca Roja* (1902); *La reina mora* (1903); *La casita blanca* (1904); *Moros y Cristianos* (1905); *El mal de amores* (1905); *Alma de Dios* (1907); *La alegriá del batallón* (1909); *El trust de los tenorios* (1910); *El carro del sol* (with *Vives, 1911); *Los de Aragón* (1927); *Las Hilanderas* (1927); *Los Claveles* (1929); and *La Dolorosa* (1930). His song 'El himmo de Valencia' has remained popular.

A. Segardía: *El compositor José Serrano* (Madrid, 1972).

Seven Brides for Seven Brothers. Lasting MGM musical film of 1954 directed by Stanley Donen. The songs, music by Gene *De Paul and words by Johnny *Mercer, included 'Bless your beautiful hide', 'Wonderful, wonderful day', 'When you're in love', and 'Spring, Spring, Spring'. It starred Howard *Keel and Jane *Powell, with Russ Tamblyn (*b* 1934) and Virginia Gibson (*b* 1926). A stage version was seen in New York in 1982, and in London, at the Old Vic, 2 July 1985.

1776. Musical play with score, music, and lyrics by Sherman Edwards (1919–81), and book by Peter Stone (*b* 1930), produced in New York at the 46th Street Theatre, 16 Mar. 1969, where it achieved a notable 1217 performances. This history of the signing of the Declaration of Independence involved seven years' research and two-and-a-half years' writing to achieve the detailed account of the intrigues and compromises that produced the famous document. The historical figures involved included John Adams (played by William Daniels), Benjamin

Franklin (Howard Da Silva), and Thomas Jefferson (Ken Howard), but some dramatic liberties were taken with the train of events. It was Edwards's only musical. It was produced in London (New Theatre) 16 June 1970 [168p], and filmed in 1972.

Sex Pistols, The. British rock group formed in 1975 with personnel of Steve Jones (*b* 1955) (guitar and vocal), Glen Matlock (*b* 1956) (bass), Paul Cook (*b* 1956) (drums), and Johnny Rotten [John Lydon] (*b* 1956) (vocal). They promoted an image of angry young men, anti-everything, and an atmosphere of profanity and violence that sparked off the *punk revolution. EMI dropped them from their list of artists and they were taken up by the less inhibited Virgin Records. Matlock was replaced by Sid Vicious [John Simon Ritchie] (1957–79), who carried their image to extremes by being arrested for the murder of his girlfriend and dying from a heroin overdose while waiting for his trial. Having given the rock world a newsworthy shot in the arm, the group disbanded in 1979.

Their British hits included 'God save the Queen' (1977), 'Pretty vacant' (1977), 'Holidays in the sun' (1977), 'No one is innocent' (1978), 'My way' (1978), 'Something else' (1978), 'Friggin' in the riggin'' (1978), 'Silly thing' (1979), 'Who killed Bambi' (1979), and 'C'mon everybody' (1979). A film, *The Great Rock 'n' Roll Swindle* (1980), featured the group playing their physical music in a somewhat disjointed montage of interviews and animation.

F. and J. Vermorel (eds): *The Sex Pistols: the Inside Story* (London, 1978). B. Gruen: *Chaos: the Sex Pistols* (London, 1990).

Shadows, The. British instrumental group. In 1958 guitarists Hank Marvin [Brian Rankin] (*b* 1941) and Bruce Welch [Bruce Cripps] (*b* 1941) were part of the Drifters, a group which backed Cliff *Richard. The following year, with the addition of Jet Harris (*b* 1939) (bass) and Tony Meehan (*b* 1943) (drums), they changed their name to the Shadows (to avoid confusion with the American group), and, though continuing to back Richard, they started an independent career in 1959. They had a No. 1 hit with 'Apache' in 1960 and went on to produce music in an arranged and polished style, featuring expert guitar-playing, with several changes of personnel before they disbanded in 1970. Among their many hits, the following reached the top position in the charts: 'Apache' (1960), 'Kon-Tiki' (1961), 'Wonderful land' (1962), 'Dance on!' (1962), and 'Foot tapper' (1963). They jointly compiled the score of *Aladdin and his Wonderful Lamp* (London, Palladium, 22 Dec. 1964); followed by *Babes in the Wood* (1965). After a re-issue album, *20 Golden Greats*, had reached the No. 1 position in 1977, they came together again to continue their influential role on the British pop scene with Hank Marvin, in particular, a shining model for all aspiring guitarists.

The Shadows: *The Shadows by Themselves* (London, 1961). G. T. Geddes: *The Shadows: a History and Discography* (London, 1981). The Shadows: *The Story of the Shadows: an Autobiography* (London, 1983).

Shall We Dance. Notable RKO musical film of 1937 starring Fred *Astaire and Ginger *Rogers, and directed by Mark Sandrich (1900–45), with a George *Gershwin score that included such lasting hits as 'Shall we dance', 'I've got beginner's luck', 'Let's call the whole thing off', 'They can't take that away from me', 'Slap that bass', and 'They all laughed'. The incidental music for the 'Walking the dog' sequence was revived by Nelson *Riddle in 1959 and, with other Gershwin pieces, was re-orchestrated as 'The Ambulatory Suite'.

Shand, Jimmy [James] (*b* East Wemyss, Fife, 28 Jan. 1908). Scottish accordionist and bandleader. The sixth of nine children, he was playing the melodeon at the age of eight. He worked as a miner, but left the mines in 1933 to become a professional musician, playing at local weddings and dances. His reputation as a button-key accordionist grew rapidly, and by 1940 he was leading a regular band and recording for the Beltona label. After the Second World War he became widely known through broadcasts and records and toured Britain, Canada, Australia, and New Zealand. His name has become synonymous with Scottish dance music throughout the world.

Shanty. The name, which first appeared in print as late as 1869, is possibly a corruption of the French 'chantez' (the imperative of the verb *chanter*, to sing). It became attached to sailors' songs of a special kind. For enjoyment, the seamen of sailing-ship days probably sung songs (generally referred to as forecastle songs) that were much the same as those they enjoyed on land. Shanties (or chanties, as they were sometimes called) were not sung simply for enjoyment, but were work songs with rhythmical patterns that fitted to the various heavy seafaring tasks that had to be performed, in the days of sail, with some sort of unified effort. The tunes were derived from British and American folk-songs and fiddle tunes, and some African chants. At one time a special shanty man was sometimes employed to lead the singing.

The songs were divided into three main categories—a) short drag for the lighter tasks; b) halliard or hauling shanties when pulling on ropes; and c) capstan shanties for pushing the capstan or windlass. Famous and popular examples of the first kind include 'Haul away, Joe'. Halliard shanties include 'Blow, boys, blow', 'Whisky Johnnie', 'Reuben Ranzo', 'Blow the man down', 'Boney was a warrior', and 'Tom's gone to Hilo'. Among the best-known capstan shanties are 'Rio Grande', 'The banks of Sacramento', 'Storm along', 'The wide Missouri', 'Can't you dance the polka', 'Fare you well', and 'Rolling home'. The shanty men would often improvise topical verses descriptive of exploits on shore or commenting on the conditions of life aboard ship, but the choruses (sung by all) remained sacrosanct. They are often terse and sometimes nonsensical, their rhythms being their main function. Naturally a lot of sea-going lore creeps in, as it did in similar work songs used by railway gangs, miners, and other labourers, and names like that of Paddy Doyle, a wily Liverpool lodging-house keeper. Ports like Liverpool came in for a lot of comment ('The leaving of Liverpool') as did the Liverpool girls.

Many of the songs became common property in the advancing steam days and 'Shenandoah', 'The drunken sailor', 'The mermaid', and 'Jack was every inch a sailor' became part of general folklore. Ewan *MacColl, A. L. *Lloyd, and others like Colin Wilkie, Shirley Hart, Craig Morton, Paul Clayton, and the *Clancy Brothers and Tommy Makem, have collected sea-songs and preserved them on record, and there is a large literature on the subject.

W. Ashton (ed.): *Real Sailor Songs* (London, 1891; repr. 1973). C. Sharp (ed.): *Capstan Shanties* (London, 1919). C. Fox-Smith: *A Book of Shanties* (London, 1927). J. C. Colcord (ed.): *Songs of American Sailormen* (New York, 1938; repr. 1965). M. J. Hurd: *Sailors' Songs and Shanties* (London, 1965). P. Glass (ed.): *Songs of the Sea* (New York, 1966). S. Hugill: *Shanties and Sailors' Songs* (London, 1969).

Sharp, Cecil James (*b* London, 22 Nov. 1859: *d* London, 23 June 1924). British ethnomusicologist, editor, and author. He studied music as a sideline while reading law at Cambridge University. In 1882 he went to Australia, settling in Adelaide where he worked in a bank and practised law. He left the legal profession in 1889 in favour of his overriding interest in music, becoming an assistant organist in Adelaide Cathedral and a director of the Adelaide School of Music. He returned to England in 1892, taught music at Ludgrove School 1893–1910, and was principal of the Hampstead Conservatory 1896–1905. At this time, having published *British Songs for Home and School* (1902), he became increasingly interested in folk-music and started visiting various rural areas to collect the rapidly disappearing remnants of British folk culture, with the help of his assistant and collaborator Maud Karpeles (1885–1976). He established the *English Folk Dance Society in 1911 and also directed a School of Folk Song and Dance at Stratford-upon-Avon. During the war Sharp and Karpeles were in the USA collecting in the Appalachian Mountains and tracing the English origins of many American songs, the results being published in 1917. In 1930 he was honoured by the opening of Cecil Sharp House in London, as headquarters of the Folk Dance Society, which amalgamated with the Folk Song Society in 1932.

His many publications included: *Folk Songs from Somerset* (5 parts) (London, 1904–9); *English Folk Song: Some Conclusions* (London, 1907; rev. 1954); *The Morris Book* (5 parts) (London, 1907–13); *Morris Dance Tunes* (10 parts) (1907–12); *The Country Dance Book* (6 parts) (1909–22); *Country Dance Tunes* (11 parts) (1909–22); *The Sword Dances of Northern England* (5 parts) (1911–13); *English Folk Carols* (1911); *Folk-Songs from Various Counties* (1912); *English Folk Chanteys* (1914); *One Hundred English Folk-Songs* (1916); *Folk-Songs of English Origin* (2 vols) (1921–3); *English Folk-Songs from the Southern Appalachians* (2 vols) (1917; new edn ed. Karpeles, Oxford, 1932; rev. 1952); *American-English Folk-Songs* (1918–21); *The Dance: an Historical Survey of Dancing in Europe* (with A. P. Oppé) (London, 1924).

A. H. Fox Strangways and M. Karpeles: *Cecil Sharp* (London, 1933; rev. 1955).

Shaw, Artie [Arshawsky, Arthur Jacob (*b* New York, 23 May 1910). American bandleader, clarinettist, composer, and arranger. At the age of 11 he earned enough money to buy a saxophone and five free lessons—the only musical training he ever had. At 15 he joined a dance band in New Haven and toured the USA. He joined Irving *Aaronson's Commanders, gradually learning enough about music to occupy a staff job at CBS in New York, when he was able to study literature at Columbia University, hoping to further his ambitions as a writer. He freelanced as a musician in New York and worked with a string quartet that included Jerry *Gray, who was later to be one of his main arrangers. He formed his first big band in 1935 and Gray's arrangement of 'Begin the beguine (1938) became a top record hit.

Throughout the swing era he led one of America's foremost swing bands, though frequently criticized by jazz purists for regularly yielding to his own and Gray's predilection for a string section. Many of his recordings were blatantly commercial but still achieved an enduring quality, and his own playing was always expert and tasteful. He tried to satisfy his own leanings towards more serious music by reviving the idea of a string quartet with clarinet and rhythm. During the 1930s he regularly recorded with groups of 5 to 7 players under the name of the Gramercy Five, playing experimental jazz that often used the harpsichord. Like *Goodman he was always ready to play and record the solo part in chamber music and concertos and commissioned works like the 'Ebony Concerto' by Stravinsky. He appeared in the films *Dancing Co-Ed* (1939; *Every Other Inch a Lady* in UK) and *Second Chorus* (1940).

During the war, as Chief Petty Officer, he was put in charge of an all-star navy band which toured the South Pacific. He was medically discharged in 1943, and immediately formed another band which he continued to lead into the 1950s when he finally settled in Spain and indulged his literary ambitions. Usually viewed as a competitive rival to Goodman, there has always been controversy over who was the greater musician and leader. Shaw was a shade more academic in approach, but could play with warmth and swing and his orchestras were never as stylized as Goodman's.

He was the composer of such songs as 'Shoot the likker to me, John boy' (1937), 'Any old time' (1938), 'Moonray' (1939), 'Without a dream to my name' (1939); and numerous instrumental pieces that included 'Streamline' (1936), 'Free for all' (1937), 'Comin' on' (1938), 'Back Bay shuffle' (1939), and 'Summit Ridge drive' (1940). He achieved additional publicity from his marriages to such eminent ladies as Lana Turner, the novelist Kathleen Winsor, and Ava Gardner.

A. Shaw: *The Trouble With Cinderella* (New York, 1952; repr. 1979).

Shaw, Oscar [Schwartz] (*b* Philadelphia, 1889; *d* Little Neck, NY, 6 Mar. 1967). American actor. Good-looking, in a stereotyped early 20th-century way, with an unfussy singing voice. He appeared in *The Girl and the Wizard* (1909); *Up and Down Broadway* (1910); *The Kiss Waltz* (1911); *The *Passing Show* (1912); and in several London shows 1912–15 including *5064 Gerrard* (1915). On his return to the USA he was in **Very Good, Eddie* (1915)—in which he sang 'Some sort of somebody'; further success coming with *Leave it to Jane* (1917); *The Rose of China* (1919); *Two Little Girls in Blue* (1920)—'Oh me! Oh my!', 'Dolly'; *Good Morning, Dearie* (1920)—'Ka-lu-a'; *One Kiss* (1923); **Music Box Revue* (1924); **Oh, Kay!* (1926)—'Maybe', 'Do, do, do'; *The Five o'Clock Girl* (1927)—'Thinking of you'; *Flying High* (1930)—'Thank your father'. In 1932 he toured as John T. Wintergreen in **Of Thee I Sing*; and there his career in musicals suddenly seemed to end.

Shearing, George (*b* London, 13 Aug. 1919). British pianist, bandleader, and composer. Born without sight, he studied music at Linden Lodge School for the Blind and in the 1930s was influenced by the recorded playing of Teddy *Wilson and Fats *Waller. His own first recordings were for Decca in 1937. He toured with a band of blind musicians led by Claude Bampton and played with *Ambrose for two years. He broadcast with the Harry Parry (1912–56) Radio Rhythm Club Sextet, played with Stéphane *Grappelli, and was voted top British jazz pianist for seven consecutive years. In 1947 he made his first visit to the USA and returned later that same year to settle there, where he has played and led his own groups ever since, with occasional tours abroad. In the 1940s he changed to a modern bop style and became a very popular recording artist from around 1949. He used vibes and guitar to blend with his block chord style of playing and had a top hit record with 'September in the rain'. He continued to gain popularity, recording for MGM 1949–55 and then for Capitol into the 1970s. His best-known composition is 'Lullaby of Birdland' (1952) which has become a standard jazz item.

She Loves Me. Musical play with music by Jerry *Bock, book by Joe Masteroff, based on a Hungarian play, *Parfumerie* by Miklos Laszlo, and lyrics by Sheldon *Harnick, produced at the Eugene O'Neill Theatre, New York, 23 Apr. 1963, and running for 301 performances. The first musical to be produced and directed by Harold Prince (*b* 1928), it won approval for its sheer old-fashioned charm, somewhat in the *Kern vein, and a sweetly tuneful score that included 'Days gone by', 'Tonight at eight', 'Will he like me?', 'Dear friend', 'Ice cream', and 'She loves me'.

Set in a European city that models itself on Budapest, it revolves around a perfume shop, a cantankerous sales-lady Amalia (played by Barbara *Cook) and the manager Georg (Daniel Massey, *b* 1933). Each corresponds with a pen-pal, not knowing that it is their colleague. Georg guesses first and lets Amalia give herself away. Their love finally blossoms as Georg brings Amalia an ice-cream.

The leading part was intended for Julie *Andrews, but her commitment to a film gave the opportunity to the very talented Barbara Cook. In London, at the Lyric Theatre 29 Apr. 1964, the part was played by Anne *Rogers.

Shelton, Anne (*b* Dulwich, London, 10 Nov. 1927). British singer. Her first chance came at the age of 12 when she appeared on the BBC radio programme *Monday Night at Eight*. As a result of this she was asked to join the *Ambrose orchestra and left school to do so. She broadcast regularly with the band, and in 1942 got her first recording contract. During the war she entertained the troops and had her own radio show, *Introducing Anne*, using 'Lili Marlene' as her signature tune. In 1944 she did seven shows with the Glenn *Miller AAF Band when he arrived in England and in the same year worked with Bing *Crosby. She produced several million-selling records during the war including 'Lili Marlene', 'I'll be seeing you', 'Galway Bay', 'Lay down your arms', and 'Arrivederci darling'. She first went to the USA in 1950 where she appeared on TV with Sophie *Tucker. She has continued to perform, now surrounded by an aura of affectionate nostalgia, and especially associated with ex-servicemen's charities.

Sherman, Richard M. (*b* New York, 12 June 1928) and **Robert B.** (*b* New York, 19 Dec. 1925). American songwriters, the sons of composer Al Sherman (1897–1973). They worked in collaboration, including the show *Over Here* (1974). Both worked for the Walt Disney studios from 1959, writing songs and complete film scores together, including: *Greyfriars Bobby* (1961); *The Parent Trap* (1961); *In Search of the Castaways* (1962); *Big Red* (1962); *Summer Magic* (1963); *The Sword in the Stone* (1963); **Mary Poppins* (1964); *That Darn Cat* (1965); *The Ugly Dachshund* (1966); *The Jungle Book* (1967); *Bullwhip Griffin* (1967); *The Story of the Gnome-Mobile* (1967); *The Happiest Millionaire* (1967); *Winnie-the-Pooh and the Blustery Day* (1967); *The One and Only Genuine Original Family Band* (1968); *Chitty Chitty Bang Bang* (1968); *Bedknobs and Broomsticks* (1968); *The Aristocats* (1970); *Charlotte's Web* (1972); and *Hector the Stowaway Pup* (1964) for TV.

Sherwin, Manning (*b* Philadelphia, 4 Jan. 1902; *d* Los Angeles, 26 July 1974). American composer.

Educated at Columbia University. He wrote for the musical theatre in both the USA and Britain and also a good deal of film music. His shows included: *Bad Habits of 1926* (1926); *Merry-Go-Round* (1927); *Billy Rose's Crazy Quilt* (1931); *Everybody's Welcome* (1931); *Sitting Pretty* (1939); *Shephard's Pie* (1939); *Up and Doing* (1940); *New Faces* (1940)—'A nightingale sang in Berkeley Square' (*w* Eric *Maschwitz); *Rise Above It* (1941); *Fun and Games* (1941); *Get a Load of This* (1941); *Fine and Dandy* (1942); *Magic Carpet* (1943); *Something in the Air* (1943); *Under the Counter* (1945); *Here Comes the Boys* (1946); and *The Kid from Stratford* (1948).

Shield, William (*b* Swalwell, Co. Durham, 5 Mar. 1748; *d* London, 25 Jan. 1829). British composer, conductor, and violinist. One of the composers, of whom Charles *Dibdin was the most prominent, who dominated the English musical stage in the early 1800s and led towards a school of British *light opera. Born just three years later than Dibdin, the son of a well-known music master and teacher of singing, he was brought up in a world of music. His voice was well-trained by the time he was six and he was already a proficient violinist. He lost his father when he was only nine and, in order to help his widowed mother, decided to become a boat-builder and was apprenticed in South Shields. He did not neglect his music; and was fortunately taught by Charles Avison, a fine organist who lived in Newcastle upon Tyne and ran subscription concerts in the town. Shield became his orchestra leader and thus met many visiting professionals. Receiving much encouragement, he decided that, after all, he would be a musician and, having finished his apprenticeship, became leader of the band at the Scarborough Theatre and also conductor of the Spa Orchestra.

He had already started to compose and had set some verses by his friend the poet and actor John Cunningham. He supplied some excellent music for the consecration of St John's Church in Sunderland in 1769. When Avison died in 1770, Shield moved on to the theatre in Durham. After one more summer season in Scarborough he was invited to join the orchestra of the Italian Opera (Covent Garden) in London as a second violinist, becoming the leader after one year—a post he held for some 18 years. In 1778 he was asked to write the music for the comic opera *The Flitch of Bacon* for the Haymarket Theatre. It was so successful that he was appointed Composer to Covent Garden, then under the management of Thomas Harris. He held this position until his resignation in June 1772, in the meantime writing prolifically and continually enhancing his reputation. In 1791 he met Josef Haydn and accompanied him on a four-day journey to Taplow. He claimed to have learned more about music in those four days than during the rest of his career. In the summer of 1792 he visited Italy and France to gain experience; and on his return to London again took up the position of Composer to Covent Garden; resigning again in 1797. As Master of the King's Musick from 1817, he became a close friend of George IV. Well blessed with honours and enjoying a high reputation, he died at the ripe old age of 80 in his home at 31 Berners Street in London.

It has been said that Shield could have been the musical heir to Purcell if he had written in a more serious vein. As it was he seems to have been content to write in a very light and popular style that hovered somewhere between the piecemeal nature of the ballad opera and the 'serious' opera of the day. Altogether he wrote some 50 light operas and 'pasticcios'. After *The Flitch of Bacon* there came two more works that clearly showed his potential. *Rosina*, produced at Covent Garden on 31 Dec. 1782, was highly praised everywhere. W. T. Parke, oboist in the Covent Garden orchestra, wrote in his memoirs of 'the beauty of the melodies and their elegant and effective accompaniments'; while George Hogarth found his music 'not marked by force or energy . . . but perfectly suited to the subjects of his pieces . . . his melodies in style, character, and adaptation to the rhythms of our native speech are perfectly English'. Shield's works were generally acclaimed as 'operas of the hour', which led Dr Burney to brand them unimportant as main contributions to the development of opera. This assessment has stuck with Shield and his contemporaries; though they helped to set a style and approach that was still discernible in light opera well into the 20th century. *Rosina* was frequently revived at Covent Garden and played throughout England, as was *The Poor Soldier*, which followed with equal success in 1783. Even more remarkable was their great popularity in America. *Rosina* was produced in Philadelphia in 1787 and 1791, in Boston in 1795, and its songs, such as 'When William at eve' and 'Light as thistledown', were published both separately and in song collections and became widely known. One song from *The Poor Soldier*, 'The rose tree', became so familiar that it was regarded as an American song and was incorporated into an early orchestral piece, 'The Federal Overture', in 1794; and it was always a great favourite of George Washington.

The fame and impact of his songs earned Shield the title of 'the most original composer since Purcell'. Apart from those he wrote or adapted for his operas, such early precursors of the drawing-room ballad as 'The heaving of the lead', 'The Arethusa' (both written for Charles Incledon), 'The Thorn', 'The Wolf', 'Old Towler', and 'The Ploughboy' (often assumed to be a folk-song) were very popular well into the 19th century.

J. Robinson: *Memorial to Wlliam Shield: Musician and Composer: with a Sketch of his Life* (London, 1893).

Shields, Ella (*b* Baltimore, 26 Sept. 1879; *d* Morecambe, Lancs., 6 Aug. 1952). American singer and comedian. She first appeared on the stage in Altoona, Pennsylvania, in 1898, and pursued a variety career as a blackface minstrel. In this role she first appeared in London in 1904. Her future role was as a male impersonator. Inevitably compared to Vesta *Tilley, she perhaps never had quite the same star quality but she became almost equally popular, and her 'Burlington Bertie from Bow' was certainly a superior article to Vesta Tilley's song on the same subject. She always retained an attractive American accent in all her songs, which included 'If you knew Susie' and 'Show me the way to go home'. She was married to the composer William Hargreaves (dates unknown) who wrote 'I must go home tonight' and other music-hall songs. In 1929 she returned to the USA to lead an obscure career, before touring Australia in 1947 and working in England again from 1948 onward, still performing to within three days of her death.

Shields, Ren (*b* Chicago, 22 Feb. 1868; *d* Massapequa, NY, 25 Oct. 1913). American entertainer and writer. He worked as a song-and-dance man in a minstrel show in his youth, becoming the tenor lead in a group known as the Empire City Quartet, and toured in vaudeville 1890–4. He teamed up with Max Million in an act which was featured in Shields's own musical comedy *Gay Paree* (1897). Author and director of various shows and sketches, he settled in New York in 1900 and produced *In the Good Old Summertime* and *The Sky Pirates*. He was one of the founders of the actors' charitable organization, the White Rats. He published his first song in 1895, his best-known being 'In the good old summertime' (1904, *m* George *Evans), 'Come take a trip in my airship' (*m* Evans), 'Waltz me around again, Willie' (1906, *m* Will *Cobb), and 'Steamboat Bill' (*m* Leighton Bros).

Shimmy. All-embracing name for the black African-based dances of the hip-rolling, breast-shaking, sexually suggestive kind; the basis of many later jazz dances from the *Black Bottom to modern *rock and roll. Alternatively known as the 'Shake', and generally a female dance, it has been referred to in such songs as 'I wish I could shimmy like my sister Kate', and it was given a definitive jazz form in Spencer *Williams's 'Shim-me-sha-wabble' (1917). The shimmy found a politer public form in the *Charleston which became a national craze among white Americans when Gilda Gray introduced it in the **Ziegfeld Follies* of 1922. The name shimmy, like most jazz names, is of obscure origin; its invention has been credited to pianist Tony *Jackson around 1900, although the dance itself has much earlier origins.

Shocking Miss Pilgrim, The. 20th Century Fox musical film of 1946. The score by George *Gershwin was discovered after his death and edited by Kay Swift (1897–1993) and David *Raksin; words by Ira *Gershwin. It starred Dick *Haymes and Betty *Grable and the songs included 'Aren't you kinda glad we did', 'Changing my tune', 'For you, for me, for evermore', 'Back Bay polka', and 'But not in Boston'.

Shop Girl, The. Musical farce with score by Ivan *Caryll, additional music by Lionel *Monckton, and lyrics by Adrian *Ross, London (Gaiety Theatre) 24 Nov. 1894 [546p].

It tells the story of a search for a missing heiress who it seems might be one Ada Smith, a plain shop assistant (Lillie Belmore, 1872–1901), who is hastily wooed by manager Mr Hooley (Arthur Williams) and lost by her fiancé Mr Miggles (Edmund Payne). Millionaire John Brown arrives from New York to explain there has been a mistake and the true heiress is the attractive shop girl Bessie Brent (Ada *Reeve), who is now fortunately able to marry her noble lover Charles Appleby (George *Grossmith Jr.), leaving the rest in a state of confusion. A somewhat pedestrian score was padded out by the Seymour *Hicks's rendition of the interpolated 'Her golden hair was hanging down her back', and graced by the popular and beautiful Gaiety Girls.

It was a comparative failure at Palmer's Theatre, New York, 28 Oct. 1895 [72p]; but was considered worth reviving at the Gaiety Theatre 25 Mar. 1920, with Evelyn *Laye, Robert Nainby, and Alfred Lester in the cast and an enlivened score by Herman *Darewski and others [327p].

Shore, Dinah [Frances Rose] (*b* Winchester, Tenn., 1 Mar. 1917). American singer and actress. She studied sociology at Vanderbilt University, but an ambition to sing led to performances on Nashville radio and took her to New York in 1938. Unsuccessful in auditions with various bands, she achieved a broadcast with Xavier *Cugat in 1939, her success with the song 'Dinah' having inspired her future performing name. She became better known with the Chamber Music Society of Lower Basin Street broadcasts in 1940, and with the Eddie *Cantor show. She had a recorded hit with 'Yes, my darling daughter', and achieved her own radio show in 1941, when she became the leading female singer on records and radio, having her first million-selling record with 'Blues in the night' (1941).

She was in the films *Thank Your Lucky Stars* (1943); *Up in Arms* (1944)—'Now I know', 'Tess's torch song'; *Belle of the Yukon* (1944)—'Like someone in love', 'Sleighride in July'; *Follow the Boys* (1944)—'I'll walk alone'; *Till the Clouds Roll By* (1946); *Aaron Slick from Punkin Crick* (1951); and on the sound-track of Disney's *Make Mine Music* (1946) and *Fun and Fancy Free* (1946). She had her own TV shows in the 1950s, 1960s, and 1970s, latterly as an interviewer.

B. Cassiday: *Dinah!* (New York, 1979).

Short, Bobby [Robert Waltrip] (*b* Danville, Ill., 15 Sept. 1926). American singer and pianist. Self-taught, he was appearing in vaudeville as a child. He went to New York to build a career as one of the leading black nightclub entertainers of the 1950s and 1960s, an excellent pianist and a sophisticated and witty interpreter in a camp style. He also appeared in Los Angeles, London, and Paris and made a number of collectable LPs.

B. Short: *Black and White Baby* (New York, 1971).

Show Boat. Musical with score by Jerome *Kern and book by Oscar *Hammerstein II, based on the novel *Show Boat* (1926) by Edna Ferber. Its dramatic impact, cohesive use of words and music, and a highly superior score, made it not only Kern's masterpiece but also a key work in the history of the American musical; a coming to maturity and a sense of reality after a period of musical comedy that was frivolously lightweight on the one hand or operetta that was romantically pretentious on the other. It opened at the Ziegfeld Theatre, New York, 27 Dec. 1927, with Norma Terriss (1904–89) as Magnolia, Howard Marsh (1901–69) as Ravenal, Helen *Morgan as Julie, Jules Bledsoe (1898–1943) as Joe, and Charles *Winninger as Cap'n Andy; and, much acclaimed, had 572 performances.

The story, set in a period that stretched from the mid-1880s to 1927, was concerned with the love life of Magnolia Hawks, daughter of Cap'n Andy Hawks, who runs the showboat *Cotton Blossom*, and gambler Gaylord Ravenal. They fall in love to the tune of 'Make believe', then move to Chicago ('Why do I love you?'), where he loses his money and they part. Magnolia becomes a famous singer and is eventually reunited with her lover on the *Cotton Blossom*. A secondary plot concerns Magnolia's mulatto friend Julie, tragically devoted to handsome singer Steve Baker (Charles Ellis)—'Can't help lovin' that man' and 'Bill'. The trials of the black people form a background to the story, deeply expressed in Joe's poignant 'Ol' Man River'.

The show toured for 10 months with Irene *Dunne in the role of Magnolia. After its production at London's Drury Lane Theatre 3 May 1928, with Edith *Day, Marie *Burke, and Paul *Robeson making his imperishable mark as Joe, and in Paris in 1929, it was revived at the Casino Theatre, New York, 1932, with Dennis *King as Ravenal, and Robeson now established as Joe [181p]. Very successful revivals came at the Stoll Theatre, London, 17 Apr. 1943 [264p]; and at the Ziegfeld Theatre, New York, 5 Jan. 1946 [418p]. It was revived at the Lincoln Center by the New York City Opera in 1954; there was a London revival, at the Adelphi Theatre 29 July 1971, with Cleo *Laine as Julie and new dances written by MD Ray Cook (1936–89); Houston Grand Opera took it up in 1983. A 1989 Opera North production came to London in 1990. Three film versions appeared: a primitive effort in 1929; the Universal classic of 1936 with Irene *Dunne, Alan *Jones, Helen Morgan, Charles Winninger, and Paul Robeson; and the MGM reconstruction of 1951, with Kathryn Grayson (*b* 1922), Howard *Keel, Ava Gardner (1922–86), Joe E. Brown (1892–1973), and William Warfield. Haphazard recorded versions of the various productions appeared, but no complete version until 1988: this was a scholarly reappraisal directed by John McGlinn, which included much interesting material that had been added or discarded in successive stage and film versions.

M. Kreuger: *Show Boat: the Story of a Classic American Musical* (New York, 1977).

Shubert Brothers. Three brothers, born in Shervient in Lithuania, Lee [Levi] (1873–1953), Samuel (1876–1905), and Jacob (1878–1963) [real family name Szemanski], were brought to the USA by their peddlar father in 1882 and settled in Syracuse, NY. They began their notable theatrical career by working in local theatres and made their first start as impresarios when Sam purchased the touring rights to a Charles Hoyt play in 1894. By 1900, Sam and Lee had set out to conquer New York, facing up to the established hold of Abe Erlanger and the Theatrical Syndicate, beginning with a production of *Arizona* (1900). Within a few years they had broken the Erlanger monopoly and, with Jacob (a background figure who looked after production details), Lee and Sam became the biggest theatre owners in America. When Sam was killed in a train accident in 1905, Lee became the driving force.

Starting with *A *Chinese Honeymoon* in 1902, the Messrs Shubert were to stage 520 plays on Broadway with a special emphasis on lavish musicals like **Sinbad* (1918), **Blossom Time* (1921), and *The *Student Prince* (1924): Sigmund *Romberg wrote 34 scores for them. The theatres they owned included such musical haunts as the Shubert Theatre, the *Winter Garden Theatre, and the *Princess Theatre; and although they were fairly ruthless in management, they made a sensible point of helping out struggling attractions of merit and keeping historic theatres alive. The company continues as the Shubert Organization and a valuable archive is housed at the Lyceum Theatre.

Shubert Alley is a famous theatrical thoroughfare between 44th and 45th Streets west of Broadway.

J. Stagg: *The Brothers Shubert* (New York, 1968). McNamara: *The Shuberts of Broadway* (New York, 1990).

Shuffle Along. Musical mélange conceived by the comic black duo of Flournoy Miller and Aubrey Lyles (1883–1932), as a starring vehicle for themselves, based on their 'play with songs' *The Mayor of Dixie*, with music by Eubie *Blake and lyrics by Noble *Sissle. It was produced at the 63rd Street Theatre, New York, 23 May 1921, and was to become the first really successful black musical entertainment to be seen on Broadway, leading the way for many future successes by black composers and artists, and a general new blossoming of their art in the 1920s. It ran for 504 performances with, during that time, such notable figures as Florence *Mills, Josephine *Baker, Paul *Robeson, Ethel *Waters, and Trixie Smith (1895–1943) in the cast list. The score included 'Love will find a way', 'Bandana days', 'Shuffle along', 'I'm just wild about Harry', 'Baltimore buzz', 'Gypsy blues', 'I'm craving for that kind of love', and, added later, 'Memories of you'.

Shuman, Mort [Mortimer] (*b* New York, 12 Nov. 1938; *d* London, 2 Nov. 1991). American composer and lyricist. He began his composing career by writing songs in the current pop style of the 1950s, with real success coming when he began to collaborate with 'Doc' Jerome *Pomus in 1959. They had an immediate hit with 'A teenager in love' in 1959 followed by the *Drifters' No. 1 hit 'Save the last dance for me' in 1960. They continued to write together a large number of hit songs that became popular on both sides of the Atlantic during the 1960s; and Shuman wrote some on his own, including 'Young boy blues'. The partnership broke up in 1965 and Shuman worked with Jerry Ragavoy in 1966—'Get it while you can', 'Look at granny run, run', before emigrating to Paris where he wrote and performed in his own one-man show, and adopted the music for the successful *Jacques Brel is Alive and Well and Living in Paris* (1968).

Other songs by Pomus and Shuman include 'A mess of blues' (1960), 'This magic moment' (1960), 'I count the tears' (1961), 'Surrender' (1961), 'She's not you' (1962), 'Spanish lace' (1962), 'Seven day weekend' (1962), and 'Viva Las Vegas' (1964).

***Silk Stockings*.** Musical with music and lyrics by Cole *Porter and book by George S. *Kaufman, Leueen McGrath, and Abe *Burrows, New York, Imperial Theatre, 24 Feb. 1955 [478p]. Based on a popular 1939 film, *Ninotchka*, which starred Greta Garbo, the Ninotchka of the musical (Hildegarde Neff) is seduced by a garrulous American talent spotter, Steve Canfield (Don *Ameche), and becomes involved in persuading a distinguished Russian composer to write a score for a musical version of *War and Peace*. The score included 'Paris loves lovers', 'All of you', 'Too bad', and 'Without love'. It was filmed in 1957, with Fred *Astaire and Cyd Charisse (*b* 1921), and choreography by Eugene Loring (*b* 1914).

Silver, Frank (*b* Boston, 8 Sept. 1896; *d* Brooklyn, 14 June 1960). American composer, author, and bandleader. He led his own band for many years and was a drummer in various theatre and radio orchestras. He is immortalized by that unforgettably awful song 'Yes, we have no bananas', which was said to have been inspired by the cry of a Long Island fruitseller; the classic lyrics were penned by Irving Cohn (1898–1961). Sigmund *Spaeth has pointed out that its melody is compounded of Handel's 'Hallelujah chorus', 'My bonnie lies over the ocean', 'I dreamed I dwelt in marble halls', and 'An old-fashioned garden'. The writers first sang it with Silver's orchestra in a Long Island café, and later at Murray's in New York, before it was published and became a best-seller. Silver also wrote better but less memorable things.

Silver, Horace (*b* Norwalk, Conn., 2 Sept. 1928). American jazz pianist, composer, and bandleader. He first came to the attention of the jazz world through his work with the Stan *Getz quintet 1950–1, then with Art *Blakey 1951–6. He made some lasting trio LPs for Blue Note and further influential records with Blakey's Jazz Messengers 1953–6. He formed his own quintet in 1956 playing in a modern blues style full of sly quotes, and further Blue Note LPs 1956–72 continued in an authoritative modern mainstream vein, working with such musicians as Kenny Dorham (1924–72), Hank Mobley (1930–86), Art Farmer (*b* 1928), and helping to develop the emotive kind of modern jazz that became known as *funk. He has remained a potent figure in jazz right into the 1980s.

Silvers, Louis (*b* New York, 6 Sept. 1889; *d* Hollywood, 26 Mar. 1954). American composer, pianist, and conductor. He was a professional pianist in vaudeville and then became musical director of Gus *Edwards shows for ten years. He was one of the first composers to settle in Hollywood and to help establish the sound picture, working first with D. W. Griffith on silent films, then writing and conducting the first musical talkie score for *The *Jazz Singer* in 1927. He was musical director for Columbia Pictures 1934–5, winning the first Academy Award given to a musical director with *One Night of Love* (1934), and with Fox from 1936. Other films included: *Dancing Lady* (1933); *Sing, Baby, Sing* (1936); *Wake Up and Live* (1937); *Second Fiddle* (1939); and *Rose of Washington Square* (1939); while his songs included 'April showers', which was used in the show *Bombo* (1921); and 'Fascination', used in *Fascination* (1922).

Silvers, Sid (*b* Brooklyn, 1 Jan. 1907; *d* Santa Monica, Calif., 20 Aug. 1976). American composer, author, comedian, and actor. After two years with a music-publisher he became a vaudeville comedian, working in partnership with accordionist Phil *Baker for eight years. He wrote the librettos of *You Said It* (1931) and *Take a Chance* (1932). He appeared in many films, some of which he helped to write, including **Broadway Melody of 1936* (1935), *Born to Dance* (1936), and *Broadway Melody of 1938* (1937). He also collaborated on **Babes in Arms* (1939); *For Me and My Gal* (1942); *The *Wizard of Oz* (1939); and *The Fleet's In* (1942).

Silvester, Victor Marlborough (*b* Wembley, Middx., 25 Feb. 1900; *d* Le Lavandou, France, 14 Aug. 1978). British dancer, bandleader, and author. The son of a clergyman, he was taught dancing and piano when young. His ambition was to be a soldier and he enlisted in 1915, but his age was discovered and he was made to serve in the Volunteer Ambulance Unit, where he still managed to get wounded. After the war he was admitted to Sandhurst, but eventually left to make a profession of his hobby of dancing. In partnership with dancer Phyllis Clarke he won the World Ballroom Dancing Championship of 1922. The same year he married another dancer called Dorothy, and together they opened a dancing school in Bond Street, London.

Throughout the 1930s he was aware that

dancers were poorly supplied with strict tempo dance records and initially he sponsored some by his pianist Gerry Moore. They were so well received that he suggested to Parlophone Records that he should form a strict tempo dance orchestra. A small band consisting of two pianos, saxophonist doubling clarinet, double-bass, and drums was formed, and they made their first four recordings in August 1935; the first title, 'You're dancing on my heart', quickly sold 17,000 copies, and became his future signature tune. A contract with EMI to make four records a month followed. An accordionist and the violinist, Oscar Grasso (1914–82), who was to be with him for most of his career, were added. In February 1937 the band auditioned for the BBC and they were booked, six months at a time, for a regular series which became the BBC Dancing Club in 1941, and the Television Dancing Club from 1948, an activity that continued until his death, by which time his son, Victor Silvester Jr., had taken over. The name of Silvester became synonymous with ballroom dancing and he became one of the leading authorities on the subject; publishing his best-selling *Modern Ballroom Dancing* (London, n.d.); *Modern Dancer's Handbook* (London, n.d.); and volumes on old-time and sequence dancing.

V. Silvester: *Dancing is my Life* (London, 1958).

Simon, Nat [Nathaniel] (*b* Newburgh, NY, 6 Aug. 1900; *d* New York, 5 Sept. 1979). American composer. He organized his own dance band as a youth, then went to New York to become a pianist with a music-publisher and accompanist. He went to London in 1938 to write music for films. His output is noteworthy as being typical best-selling *Tin Pan Alley corn of the 1930s and 1940s and it included: 'Poinciana' (with Buddy Bernier, 1936), 'Little curly hair in a high chair' (1940, *w* Charles *Tobias), 'Her bathing suit never got wet' (1945, Tobias), 'No can do' (1945, Tobias), 'The old lamp lighter' (1946, Tobias), 'An apple blossom wedding' (1946, *w* Jimmy *Kennedy), and 'Istanbul' (1953, Kennedy).

Simon, Marvin **Neil** (*b* New York, 4 July 1927). American librettist and playwright. After serving in the US Air Force, he began to write TV material 1948–60 for programmes featuring Sid *Silvers, Tallulah Bankhead, and others. He started his Broadway career by writing revue sketches with his brother that were used in *Catch a Star* (1956) and **New Faces* (1956). He wrote comedies, including *Come Blow Your Horn* (1962); *Barefoot in the Park* (1963); *The Odd Couple* (1964); *Plaza Suite* (1968); and *The Last of the Red Hot Lovers* (1969); most of which were filmed. His first musical, **Little Me* (1962), was followed by **Sweet Charity* (1966), **Promises, Promises* (1968), and *They're Playing Our Song* (1979).

E. M. McGovern: *Neil Simon: a Critical Study* (New York, 1979). R. K. Johnson: *Neil Simon* (Boston, 1983).

Simon, Paul Frederick (*b* Newark, NJ, 5 Nov. 1941). American singer, composer, lyricist, and guitarist. With his highschool friend Art *Garfunkel, he came to prominence in 1957 when they recorded 'Hey, schoolgirl' under the name of Tom and Jerry. This reached No. 54 in the USA, but later records in the same vein failed to catch on. He worked as a song plugger with E. B. Marks Publishing Co., and continued to write, recording 'The lone teen ranger' under the name of Jerry Landis. He went to law school but left in order to go to England in 1964 where he performed in folk clubs and on the BBC. Returning to the USA, with Garfunkel he recorded the album *Wednesday Morning 3 am* (1966) under their real names. From this album, 'The sound of silence' eventually became a No. 1 hit; in the meantime Simon had returned to Britain and recorded a solo album of his own songs, *The Paul Simon Songbook* (1966).

His poetic but hard-hitting lyrics, protesting and ironic, and Garfunkel's sensitive arrangements, started to make their mark in *Sounds of Silence* (1966)—which included some of the *Songbook* material, including the nostalgic song of alienation 'I am a rock'. After a tour of the USA and Britain they recorded the albums *Parsley, Sage, Rosemary and Thyme* (1966—'Scarborough Fair') and *Bookends* (1968); they then won a Grammy Award for their sound-track music to the film *The Graduate* (1968), with 'Mrs Robinson' singled out for special award and reaching No. 1 in the charts. They were now popular on a worldwide basis and had their biggest hit of all, No. 1 in Britain and America, with 'Bridge over troubled water', from the album of the same name (1970), which sold more than nine million copies. Despite this the duo, who may have become inseparable in the public mind but had very different personalities, split up in 1970, not coming together again until 1981, when they gave a remarkable free concert in New York's Central Park.

Paul Simon continued his solo career by creating in a more complex vein, with more varying influences at work, producing the albums *Paul Simon* (1972)—'Mother and child reunion'; *There Goes Rhymin' Simon* (1973)—'Take me to the Mardi Gras'; *Live Rhymin'* (1974), a concert album from a 1973 tour; *Still Crazy After All These Years* (1975)—No. 1 hit '50 ways to leave your lover'. He appeared in the Woody Allen film *Annie Hall* (1977), and starred in and scored *One Trick Pony* (1980). The above albums (plus *The Paul Simon Songbook*) were issued in a five-LP set in 1981 as *Collected Works*, an accolade usually reserved for elderly or dead poets. The Simon and Garfunkel partnership remains one of the most popular duos in the history of rock.

S. Leigh: *Paul Simon—Now and Then* (Liverpool, 1973). M. S. Cohen: *Simon & Garfunkel* (New York, 1977). D. Marsh: *Paul Simon* (New York, 1978). P. Humphries: *Bookends: the Simon and Garfunkel Story* (New York, 1982). R. Matthew-Walker: *Simon and Garfunkel* (Tunbridge Wells, 1982).

Simone, Nina [Waymon, Eunice] (*b* Tryon, NC, 21 Feb. 1933). American singer and pianist. She studied piano at the Curtis Institute of Music in Philadelphia 1950–3 and at the Juilliard School in 1974. In the meantime she had moved to Philadelphia, gained a recording contract with Bethlehem, and produced the million-selling 'I loves you Porgy' in 1959. More hits with Philips 1965-7 followed, then with RCA 1967–72, and a number of albums of good quality, jazz-tinged material. In the 1970s political work diverted her from music but a fine album, *Baltimore* (1978), made musical progress and several since have recapitulated her great talents.

Sims, Zoot [John Haley] (*b* Inglewood, Calif., 29 Oct. 1925; *d* New York, 23 Mar. 1985). American jazz saxophonist. He worked with several big bands during the Second World War period, and was with Sid *Catlett in 1944. After army service he became better known as a member of the Benny *Goodman band 1946–7; but his full reputation was achieved on tenor as part of the 'Four Brothers' saxophone section of the Woody *Herman band 1947–9, alongside Stan *Getz, Serge Chaloff (1923–57), and Herbie Steward (*b* 1926); later Al Cohn (*b* 1925). Getz and Cohn were also with him in the Artie *Shaw band 1949–50. He toured abroad on several occasions with the Goodman and *Kenton bands; with Gerry *Mulligan 1956 and 1960; and with Jazz at the Philharmonic 1967 and 1975. Some of his best work was in collaboration with Al Cohn, with the pair of them heading an unusual quintet line-up. He was the first American jazz man to play a season at the Ronnie *Scott club in London, in 1961, and frequently returned. He was there again in 1982 followed by a Scandinavian tour in 1984 after which he succumbed to cancer. He played in a spare style based on the Lester *Young tradition, but his tone became sleeker as he took up the soprano saxophone in the 1970s.

Sinatra, Frank [Francis Albert] (*b* Hoboken, NJ, 12 Dec. 1915). American singer, actor, and director. Born of Italian parents, he had no musical training, starting his career with a quartet known as the Hoboken Four which won an amateur radio contest and was featured in a short film in 1936. He worked for a while as a journalist before becoming a singing MC at the Rustic Cabin in Englewood, NJ, and achieving a few broadcasts. He was heard by Harry *James who took him on as vocalist with his new band and with whom he made his first recordings in 1939. His remarkably evocative singing, in contrast to the bland crooning of earlier singers and the smooth jazzophony of *Crosby, gained him the admiration of vocal connoisseurs, and his slim build and hungry look endeared him to young females. He joined the Tommy *Dorsey band, with whom he made 83 recordings, and then first appeared as a solo performer. His first stage appearance in New York in 1942 caused a sensation and quickly led to a career in films. He appeared in many RKO and MGM musicals in the mid-1940s, generally singing much better than he acted, but the films provided good entertainment and, combined with the undiminished success of his Columbia recordings, made him the outstanding and most influential singer of the time.

The films he was in included: *Las Vegas Nights* (1941); *Ship Ahoy!* (1942); *Reveille with Beverly* (1943); *Higher and Higher* (1943); *Step Lively* (1944); *Anchors Aweigh* (1945); *Till the Clouds Roll By* (1946); *It Happened in Brooklyn* (1947); *Miracle of the Bells* (1948); *The Kissing Bandit* (1948); *Take Me Out to the Ball Game* (1949; *Everybody's Cheering* in UK); and **On the Town* (1949). Personal problems, of which he has always accumulated many, caused a slump in his fortunes in the 1950s, but a new-found accomplishment as a dramatic actor, and an Academy Award for his supporting role in *From Here to Eternity* (1953), started him off on a distinguished acting career in straight roles, notably in *The Man With the Golden Arm* (1955), as well as in such polished musical features as **Guys and Dolls* (1955); **High Society* (1956); **Pal Joey* (1957); and **Can Can* (1960). His conductor and arranger 1943–53 was Axel Stordhal (1913–63). A new Capitol contract in 1954 produced some of his greatest recordings in collaboration with conductors Billy *May and Nelson *Riddle; and, by the time he founded his own Reprise company in 1960, he had become one of the most powerful men in show-business.

He had a No. 1 hit with 'Strangers in the night' as late as 1966. His daughter Nancy (*b* 1940), with whom he recorded another best-seller, 'Somethin' stupid', in 1967, has carved out her own career as a singer and actress, having a big No. 1 hit with 'These boots are made for walkin'' (1967). His son Frank Jr. (*b* 1944) also had a brief career as a singer.

Sinatra announced his retirement in 1971 but has made regular concert appearances and recordings since, and now moves around like royalty or the late Richard Burton, with an alarming reputation, but still intensely interested in music and always ready to talk about it. He has probably been the most vital artist, the most popular singer, the most magnetic personality, and the greatest lyric interpreter in the pre-rock years of popular music.

E. J. Kahn: *The Voice: the Story of an American Phenomenon* (New York, 1946). R. Gehman: *Sinatra and his Rat Pack* (New York, 1961). R. Douglas-Home: *Sinatra* (London, 1962). A. Shaw: *Sinatra: 20th Century Romantic* (New York, 1968). A. I. Lonstein and V. R. Marino: *The Compleat Sinatra* (New York, 1970). K. Barnes (ed.): *Sinatra and the Great Song Stylists* (Shepperton, 1972). P. Goddard: *Frank Sinatra* (New York, 1973). G. Ringgold and C. McCarty: *Films of Frank Sinatra* (New York, 1973). E. Wilson: *Sinatra: an Unauthorised Biography* (New York, 1976). J. Ridgway: *The Sinatrafile* (3 vols) (Birmingham, 1977–80). A. Scaduto: *Frank Sinatra* (London, 1977). A. Frank: *Sinatra* (London, 1978). A. I. Lonstein: *Sinatra: an Exhaustive Treatise* (New York, 1983). K. Kelley: *Sinatra: the Unauthorised Biography* (New York, 1986).

Sinbad. Extravaganza with music by Sigmund *Romberg and book by Harold Atteridge (1886–1938), one of several *Shubert shows designed to spotlight the exuberant talents of Al *Jolson. Following in the steps of *Robinson Crusoe Jr.* (1916), and followed by *Bombo* (1921) and *Big Boy* (1925), it opened at the *Winter Garden Theatre, 14 Feb. 1918, and ran for 388 performances. The Romberg score carried along what action there was, while Jolson captivated the audience with such interpolated numbers as 'Rock-a-bye your baby with a Dixie melody' (*m* Jean *Schwartz), 'Mammy' (*m* Walter *Donaldson), and later additions like 'Avalon' (Jolson and Vincent Rose) and 'Swanee', George *Gershwin's first big song success.

Singin' in the Rain. MGM musical film of 1952, directed by Stanley Donen (*b* 1924) and Gene *Kelly, which starred Kelly with Debbie *Reynolds and Donald *O'Connor. The central number was Nacio Herb *Brown's 'Singin' in the rain', during which Kelly splashed up and down in an artificial downpour with an umbrella, creating an unforgettable dance routine. It also included 'All I do is dream of you', 'Make 'em laugh', 'You are my lucky star', 'You were meant for me', and the interpolated 'I've got a feeling you're fooling' and 'Wedding of the painted doll'. Another of its most memorable moments was the hilarious 'Make 'em laugh' routine by O'Connor, one of many unforgettable things in a sparkling musical that many consider the best of its kind. A stage version, starring Tommy *Steele, was produced at the London Palladium 30 June 1983.

Singleton, Zutty [Arthur James] (*b* Bunkie, La., 14 May 1898; *d* New York, 14 July 1975). American jazz drummer. He began his career in New Orleans in 1915 and led his own first band there at the Orchard Club, with Louis *Armstrong in its ranks; later he was to play and record with Armstrong on several occasions, demonstrating his then novel drumming ideas on such recordings as 'West End blues' and 'My Monday date'. He worked with most of the major bands in New York, before moving to Chicago in the mid-1930s to play with the Carroll Dickerson orchestra. In 1937 he returned to New York to lead several bands and to record with, among many, Slim *Gaillard and Charlie *Parker. In 1943 he moved to Los Angeles and appeared in three jazz-based films: *Stormy Weather* (1943), with Lena *Horne and Fats *Waller; *New Orleans* (1946), with Billie *Holiday and Armstrong; and *Turned-Up Toes* (1949). In the 1950s he worked in Europe with Bill Coleman (1904–81) and Mezz *Mezzrow; returning to New York to work in clubs like Ryan's into the late 1960s. Considered by many to be the best of the great traditional drummers, he was one of the first to instigate the drum solo, and invented many special effects that others copied, including the use of brushes.

Sirmay, Albert [Szirmai] (*b* Budapest, 2 July 1918; *d* New York, 15 Jan. 1967). Hungarian-born composer, arranger, and conductor. He studied at the Budapest Academy of Music and became a Doctor of Music, wrote numerous songs, revues, and light operas while in Hungary, then went to the USA in 1933 to work in Chappell's New York publishing-house as musical adviser and editor. There he was responsible for the editing and arranging of scores by Richard *Rodgers and others. His works for the theatre included: *Tanzhusaren* (1909); *The Girl on the Film* (1913), an adaptation of a score by Kollo; *Rinaldo* (1921); *Princess Charming* (1925); *Bamboula* (1925); *Lady Mary* (1928); *Ripples* (1930); and others. He edited *A Treasury of Gilbert and Sullivan*; *Songs of the Rivers of America*; *Rodgers and Hart Song Book*; *Rodgers and Hammerstein Song Book*; *Cole Porter Song Book*; *George and Ira Gershwin Song Book*; *Jerome Kern Song Book*; *Lerner and Loewe Song Book*; and other volumes.

Sissle, Noble (*b* Indianapolis, 10 July 1889; *d* Tampa, Fla., 17 Dec. 1975). American bandleader, lyricist, singer, and producer. While a student at Cleveland Central High School he organized a glee club and, on leaving, he toured with the Thomas Jubilee Singers. He studied for the Church but left to work for bandleader and club owner Jim *Europe, and started writing songs with Eubie *Blake. During the First World War he was drum major in Europe's Army Band with the rank of 2nd Lieutenant. When Europe was killed after the war, Sissle took over leadership of the band on its US tours.

After it had broken up, he teamed up with Blake to write the Broadway shows **Shuffle Along* (1921)—'Baltimore buzz', 'Bandana days', 'Love will find a way', 'I'm just wild about Harry'; and *Chocolate Dandies* (1924)—'You were meant for me', 'Manda', 'Thinking of me'. He made numerous vocal recordings 1926–8; and in 1929 formed a band which included such stars as Tommy *Ladnier and Sidney *Bechet, which he brought to London, playing for a while at Ciro's Club before visiting Europe. Back in the USA he played at the Palace Theatre in Chicago, the Hollywood Club in Buffalo, and the French Casino in New York, making some recordings under the name of Sissle's Sizzling Syncopators. He was active in music until the mid-1930s, later turning to civic affairs, including a post as chairman of the draft board, and he was organizer and first President of the Negro Actors' Guild.

W. Bolcom and R. Kimball: *Reminiscing with Sissle and Blake* (New York, 1973).

Six-Five Special. British TV programme devised and produced by Jack Good (*b* 1931) and Josephine Douglas (1928–88), who also introduced it, along with Pete Murray (*b* 1928), when it was first seen in 1957. It satisfied a rapacious teenage demand for rock music of the *Presley period and helped to make many reputations; and it has retained a legendary reputation even though it only ran for just over a year. The first British TV programme to cater for teenage tastes was the BBC's *Teleclub* (1953–5), rather timidly followed by commercial TV's *Cool for Cats* (1957), which was the catalyst for *Six-Five Special*.

Skelly, Joseph P. (*fl.* *c*.1850–1900). American composer and lyricist. He was a plumber by trade, who turned his hand to songwriting to the extent of some 400 songs, many of them achieving immortality. Although he was a practising Christian and a member of the Bible House, he also lived a drunken, dissolute, and generally penniless life, often selling his songs for very little. Both his music and his lifestyle had some resemblance to Stephen *Foster's, but he had less vision and wrote his songs simply for beer money.

They included: 'Down by the old stream' (1874), 'I've only been down to the club' (1876), 'My pretty red rose' (1877)—his greatest commercial success, 'If my dreams would all come true' (1879), 'Are you going to the ball this evening?' (1881), 'The old rustic bridge by the mill' (1881), 'Behind the parlour door' (1882), 'Strolling on the Brooklyn Bridge' (with George Cooper, 1883), 'A boy's best friend is his Mother' (1884), 'Why should we meet as strangers?', and 'They're all getting married but me'.

Skiffle. Term probably first used in Chicago in the 1920s for a makeshift kind of jazz group playing a happy, party kind of music on a mixture of instruments that might include legitimate items like the piano, banjo, drums, and any blown instruments available, but mainly using the sort of things that poor black musicians could afford like washboard, jug, kazoo, paper-and-comb, bull-fiddle, and anything that could be banged or blown. The groups of this type which recorded tended to call themselves *spasm, *washboard or jug bands.

The word remained very much a slang expression until it reappeared in the mid-1950s in England as the name for similar small groups that tended to use the kind of folk-blues material that was purveyed by players like *Leadbelly, with a jazz flavouring. They generally featured a vocalist with guitar, mandolin, bass, and washboard or drum backing. Two groups that gave the new skiffle craze commercial prominence came from the Chris *Barber band led by singer/guitarist and banjoist Lonnie *Donegan, which had a great hit with 'Rock Island Line' and similar material; and from the Ken *Colyer band headed by Colyer which started recording the same year.

B. Bird: *Skiffle* (London, 1958).

Slack, Freddie [Frederic Charles] (*b* LaCrosse, Wis., 7 Aug. 1910; *d* Hollywood, 10 Aug. 1965). American bandleader, composer, and pianist. He played with Johnny Tobin's band in Chicago at 17, moving to California in 1931. He then played for various bands before joining Jimmy *Dorsey in 1936. It was while working with Will *Bradley and Ray *McKinley, 1939–41, that he began to exploit the commercial possibilities of *boogie-woogie through such hits as 'Down the road apiece' and 'Beat me, daddy'; and when he formed his own regular band in 1942, its repertoire was almost entirely boogie-woogie and swing novelties, with the added attraction of the singing of Ella Mae *Morse. He appeared in a number of films 1943–6. After the decline of big-band work, he formed a two-piano act and was working with a trio in clubs and hotels into the mid-1960s.

Slade. British rock group formed in 1966 with Noddy Holder (*b* 1950) (vocal and guitar), Dave Hill (*b* 1952) (guitar), Jimmy Lea (*b* 1952) (bass and piano), and Don Powell (*b* 1950) (drums). They worked under several names until 'Slade' was adopted when recording for Polydor, although it bore little relation to their aggressive, heavy sound and the working-class slant of their titles: 'Coz I luv you' (1971), 'Take me bak 'ome' (1972), 'Mama weer all crazee now' (1972), 'Cum on feel the noize' (1973), and 'Skweeze me pleeze me' (1973), which were all No. 1 hits in the UK. The songwriting of Holder and Lea was highly regarded, but remained personal to the band with few cover copies; and their very specialized style lost some of its impact in the later 1970s and early 1980s, despite which they celebrated 20 years together in 1986 and their albums continued to sell.

G. Tremlett: *The Slade Story* (London, 1975).

Slade, Julian (*b* London, 28 May 1930). British composer, author, and actor. Son of a distinguished barrister G. P. Slade, KC, he won a scholarship to Eton and then went to Trinity College, Cambridge. As an undergraduate, with ambitions to be an actor, he wrote and composed two musicals, *Bang Goes the Meringue* and *Lady May*, which were performed by the Cambridge Amateur Dramatic Club in 1950 and 1951. He went to the Bristol Old Vic Theatre School in 1951 and composed incidental music for several Old Vic productions, including *Two Gentlemen of Verona*, which came to the Old Vic in London in 1952. He appeared in various plays and became musical director of the Bristol Old Vic in 1952. He wrote and composed, with Dorothy Reynolds (1913–78) and others, *Christmas in King Street* (1952); and composed a new score for Sheridan's *The Duenna* (Bristol, 1953; London, 1954); wrote and composed (with Reynolds) *The Merry Gentleman* (1953) and a musical version of *The Comedy of Errors*, seen on TV 1954 and at the Arts Theatre, London, 1956.

His greatest success came with **Salad Days*, originally written purely with the Bristol Old Vic company in mind and first seen there in 1954. It was thought good enough to transfer to the Vaudeville Theatre in London in 1955 where it was to achieve a record run. The composer was pit pianist for the first 18 months of its long stay. This was followed by *Free as Air* (1957), at the Savoy Theatre; and other musicals that never managed to repeat the success of *Salad Days*, including *Hooray for Daisy* (Bristol, 1959; London, 1961); *Follow That Girl* (1960); *Wildest Dreams* (Cheltenham, 1960; London, 1961); *Vanity Fair* (1962); *Nutmeg and Ginger* (Cheltenham, 1963); *The Pursuit of Love*

(Bristol, 1967); *Trelawney* (1972); and *Out of Bounds* (Bristol, 1973).

Slap. A way of playing the double-bass with an exaggerated pulling of the strings so that they slap back against the fingerboard of the instrument with a percussive sound. The effect was persuasively used by Wellman Braud (1891–1966) in the Duke *Ellington band, Pops Foster (1892–1969), and Bill Johnson (1872–1972). Similar in intent is the slap-tonguing technique as used on a reed instrument where the reed is blown hard enough to force it off its seat and create a slapping effect as it falls back, to give a punchy and somewhat comical effect to the note. A popular effect in the 1930s, but now in bad taste.

Slaughter, A. Walter (*b* London, 2 Feb. 1860; *d* London, 2 Apr. 1908). British composer and conductor. A chorister at St Andrew's church, Well Street, London, he later studied with Alfred Cellier and Georges Jacobi. He wrote ballet music for the South London Palace of Varieties and became musical director at the Royalty Theatre, subsequently at the Olympic Theatre, the Theatre Royal, Drury Lane, and the St James's Theatre. He wrote much incidental music and a number of operettas and musical comedies including: *An Adamless Eden* (1882); *Sly and Shy* (1883); *Marie's Honeymoon* (1885); *The Casting Vote* (1885); *Sappho* (1886); *Alice in Wonderland* (1886); *Marjorie* (1889); *The Rose and the Ring* (1890); *Donna Luiza* (1892); *Gentleman Joe* (1895); *The French Maid* (1897); *Dandy Dan, the Lifeguardsman* (1897); *Her Royal Highness* (1898); *Orlando Dando* (1898); *The Snow Man* (1899); **Bluebell in Fairyland* (1901); *You and I* (1901); and *Lady Tatters* (1907).

'Slaughter on Tenth Avenue'. 'Modern' dance scene choreographed by George Balanchine (1904–83), who also created a ballet version for the New York City Ballet in the 1970s, which was inserted into the musical *On Your Toes* (1936), with score by Richard *Rodgers. A dancer (Ray *Bolger) is in love with a stripper (Tamara Geva) but they are menaced by the boss man. While trying to kill the dancer, the boss shoots the stripper. The dancer shoots the boss and dances around both the dead bodies. In the London production of *On Your Toes* the lovers were danced by Jack *Whiting and Vera Zorina (*b* 1917), and in the film (1939) by Eddie *Albert and Zorina.

Sloane, A[lfred] Baldwin (*b* Baltimore, 28 Aug. 1872; *d* Red Bank, NJ, 21 Feb. 1926). American composer and conductor. He produced his first operetta at the age of 19, and wrote incidental music for many Charles Hoyt productions. He settled in New York in the early 1890s and was active as a musical director and in writing scores for: *Broadway to Tokyo* (1900); *Aunt Hannah* (1900); *A Million Dollars* (1900); *The Giddy Throng* (1900); *The King's Carnival* (1901); *The Hall of Fame* (1902); *The Belle of Broadway* (1902); *The Mocking Bird* (1902); *The *Wizard of Oz* (1903); *Sergeant Kitty* (1904); *Lady Teazle* (1904); *The Gingerbread Man* (1905); *Comin' Through the Rye* (1906); *Seeing New York* (1906); *The Mimic and the Maid* (1907); *Tillie's Nightmare* (1910)—'Heaven will protect the working girl' (*w* Edgar Smith, 1857–1938); *The Summer Widowers* (1910); *The Prince of Bohemia* (1910); *The Hen-Pecks* (1911); *Hokey-Pokey* (1912); *Hanky Panky* (1912); *Roly Poly* (1912); *The Sun Dodgers* (1912); *Ladies First* (1918); **Greenwich Village Follies* (1919 and 1920); and *China Rose* (1925).

Sloman, Charles (*b* London, 1808; *d* London, 21 July 1870). British composer, singer, and entertainer. Although he is mainly remembered as a singer and writer of comic songs, he also had a devout and serious side and composed a collection of *Sacred Strains, Hymns, etc.* (1860) and various romantic ballads. Of Jewish origin, he dedicated one of his songs to James Sheridan Knowles with the words: 'with feelings of deepest gratitude and respect an humble Individual, one of a sunken race, presumes to inscribe to the greatest dramatic Poet of the Age this simple lay of his fallen Nation'. He was, however, proud of his race and did much for Jewish charities. In the 1850s he was a very popular performer at such places as *Evans's, the Coal Hole, the Cyder Cellars, the Eagle Tavern, *Vauxhall Gardens and Cremorne, and the Temple of Harmony in Whitechapel. He made his professional debut in 1829 at the Rotunda Assembly Rooms, and his final appearance at Gatti's Music Hall in Villiers Street early in 1870. For nearly 40 years he was billed as 'The Only English Improvisatore' and specialized in making up doggerel verse about any member of the audience or events of the day. Later he was a well-known chairman at the Mogul Tavern and was manager of the Colosseum in Regent Street from 1838, but it went bankrupt the following year. The death of his wife in 1866 brought on a mental breakdown. He made a few isolated appearances, the last in 1870, and died destitute in the Strand Union workhouse. His lighter songs included 'Charming Sue' and 'Social bricks'.

Small Faces. London rock group formed in 1965, its main personnel being Steve Marriott (1947–91) (guitar and vocal), Ronnie Lane (*b* 1946) (bass and vocal), Kenny Jones (*b* 1948) (drums), and Ian McLagan (*b* 1945) (keyboard). One of Britain's best pop bands, they worked in what was labelled the mod idiom, like the *Who, as opposed to rockers like the *Rolling Stones. They first entered the Top 20 with 'Watcha gonna do about it?' (1965), followed by 'Hey girl', 'All or nothing', and 'My mind's eye'. Popular among teenagers, they moved into a psychedelic stage and recorded such novel items as 'Itchycoo Park' and 'Tin soldier' (1966); and an album *Ogden's Nut Gone Flake* (1968) with comedian Stanley Unwin. 'Lazy Sunday' (1968) even contrived a sort of music-hall flavour. Steve Marriott left the group to form Humble Pie and Lane and Jones joined up with Rod *Stewart to form the *Faces, having a revived hit with 'Itchycoo Park' in 1975. The group broke up, to re-form in 1978 for some albums, after which each of its members went their own way. A compilation of their best work is on *Small Faces Big Hits* (1980).

Smith, Ada Beatrice Queen Victoria Louise Virginia (*b* Alderson, W. Va., 14 Aug. 1894; *d* New York, 31 Jan. 1984). American singer, better known as Bricktop, because of her red hair. She became a popular dancer and singer in Chicago cabarets, went to Paris in 1924, and opened a club on the Rue Pigalle which was naturally called Chez Bricktop. It became a social centre for all visiting American jazz musicians, writers, and artists. She also opened a second club known as the Big Apple. In 1939 she returned to the USA and became a nightclub hostess. Cole *Porter's song 'Miss Otis regrets' is said to have been written for her. After the war she opened clubs in Rome and Mexico and made a documentary film, *Honeybaby, Honeybaby*, in 1973.

A. Smith: *Bricktop by Bricktop* (New York, 1983).

Smith, Bessie [Elizabeth] (*b* Chattanooga, Tenn., 15 Apr. 1894; *d* Clarksdale, Miss., 26 Sept. 1937). American blues singer. From a poor family, she joined Chappelle's Rabbit Foot Minstrels, whose star was Ma *Rainey, from whom she learned her art; developing a powerful, theatrical, and jazz-oriented style of blues singing (later accepted as the 'classic' blues style) that brought her fame as a singer and entertainer. She toured with her own troupe, the Liberty Belles, in 1919. Her first recording, 'Downhearted blues' (1923), sold 800,000 copies, and she continued to make notable recordings in the company of the best jazz musicians, one of the regulars being trumpeter Joe Smith (1902–37) and including Louis *Armstrong. She toured in various revues and tent shows, regularly visiting New York to record, and appeared in a film, *St Louis Blues* (1929). She made her last records in 1933, was at Connie's Inn in 1936, and afterwards in Philadelphia. After appearing at a show in Darling, Miss., she was travelling by road to her next engagement when the car hit a truck and turned over. The doctor who was called gave her first aid and, as he was clearing his car to take her to hospital, it was struck by another car. Eventually an ambulance took her to the Afro-American hospital in Clarksdale, where she died after having an arm amputated.

P. Oliver: *Bessie Smith* (London, 1959). C. Moore: *Somebody's Angel Child* (New York, 1969). C. Albertson: *Bessie* (New York, 1972; as *Bessie Smith: Empress of the Blues*, 1975).

Smith, Chris (*b* Charleston, SC, 12 Oct. 1879; *d* New York, 4 Oct. 1949). American composer. He started out as a baker, learned to play piano and guitar, and became a songwriter. He settled in New York in the early 1900s and became one of several black composers who were writing ragtime songs at that time. Several of his tunes, often with words by Cecil Mack, were very popular; and his biggest success came with 'Ballin' the Jack' (with James Reese *Europe, 1913, *w* Jim Burris). It has had several revivals: in the film *For Me and My Gal* (1942) and later in the hands of Danny *Kaye; and has long been a jazz standard. His other songs included: 'Never let the same bee sting you twice' (1900, *w* Mack), 'Good morning, Carrie' (with J. Tim *Brymn, 1901, *w* Mack), 'There's a big cry baby in the moon' (1909, Burris), 'Down in honky-tonk town' (1916, McCarron), and 'Cake walkin' babies back home' (with Clarence *Williams, 1924).

Smith, Edgar McPhail (*b* Brooklyn, NY, 9 Dec. 1857; *d* Bayside, NY, 8 Mar. 1938). American librettist, playwright, and actor. He made his debut as an actor at Booth's Theatre, New York, in 1878. He was the regular librettist for the New York Casino 1886–92, author of *Weber and Fields extravaganzas 1896–1904, and wrote books for such works as *The Girl Behind the Counter* (1907); *Merry-Go-Round* (1908); *Tillie's Nightmare* (1910)—'Heaven will protect the working girl'; *The Kiss Waltz* (1911); *The Pleasure Seekers* (1913); and *The Blue Paradise* (1915).

Smith, Harry B[ache] (*b* Buffalo, NY, 28 Dec. 1860; *d* Atlantic City, NJ, 2 Jan. 1936). American librettist and lyricist. He started his career as a journalist, becoming music critic of the *Chicago Daily News* and drama critic for the *Chicago Tribune*. He also wrote music criticism and verse for other magazines. He wrote the librettos for more than 300 shows (123 on Broadway) including *The Begum* (1887, *w* Reginald *De Koven); *Robin Hood* (1890, De Koven), his first success; after which came a succession of works with the same composer. In 1895 he wrote *The Wizard of the Nile* for Victor *Herbert and collaborated with him on a dozen or so of his most popular works. He also worked with Ludwig *Englander: *The Casino Girl* (1900), *The Strollers* (1901), *A China Doll* (1904); Raymond *Hubbell: **Ziegfeld Follies of 1912*; Jerome *Kern: *The *Girl from Utah* (1914); Irving *Berlin: *Watch Your Step* (1914), *Stop! Look! Listen!* (1915); and A. Baldwin *Sloane: *Ladies First* (1918).

H. B. Smith: *First Nights and First Editions* (Boston, 1931).

Smith, 'Whispering' Jack (*b* New York, 1899; *d* New York, May 1951). American singer. It is said that lung injuries from a gas shell in the First World War caused him to adopt the quiet, almost speaking style, with the voice sliding up to the note, that became known as *crooning and was taken to its heights by Rudy *Vallee and Bing *Crosby. Although he sang softly he had remarkable projection and clear diction and, as 'the Whispering Baritone', became a popular nightclub entertainer in

New York in the 1920s, making his first recording in Aug. 1925. He went to London in 1926 to appear in *Midnight Follies* at the Metropole Hotel, continued to record to his own piano accompaniment, and appeared in the revue *Blue Skies* (1927). Recording sessions with the *Ambrose orchestra produced his best-selling 'My blue heaven' and later 'Miss Annabelle Lee', these being amongst the songs used in the revue *Will-o'-the-Whispers* (1928). His recordings and popularity continued until the 1930s but, after a brief come-back in 1940, he retired.

Smith, Kate [Kathryn Elizabeth] (*b* Greenville, Va., 1 May 1907; *d* Raleigh, NC, 17 June 1986). American singer. She first sang in church choirs, then went to New York and appeared in *Honeymoon Lane* (1926), *Hit the Deck* (1927), and *Flying High* (1930). She became well-known through the film *Hello Everybody* (1932) and was in *This Is the Army* (1943). She became popular on radio and TV with her regularly featured song, 'When the moon comes over the mountain', and had a hit recording with 'Rose O'Day' in 1941. A regular singer on public occasions, she made Irving Berlin's 'God bless America' into a substitute national anthem during the Second World War.

Smith, Mamie (*b* Cincinnati, 26 May 1883; *d* New York, 16 Sept. 1946). American blues singer. Her professional career began in New York in 1913, and she appeared in various clubs. She made a mark in popular music history by being the first black singer to make a record, her version of Perry *Bradford's 'Crazy blues' (1920) selling more than a million copies within six months and setting the *race record business on its way—and all that was to follow. Later she toured with her Jazz Hounds troupe and recorded with many leading jazz musicians and bands, making her last appearance in New York in 1944 with Billie *Holiday.

Smith, Pine Top [Clarence] (*b* Troy, Ala., 11 June 1904; *d* Chicago, 15 Mar. 1929). American jazz pianist. Raised in Birmingham, Alabama, he first worked as an entertainer in Pittsburgh clubs before touring as a piano soloist and working as accompanist to Ma *Rainey. He settled in Chicago, where he became known through his exploitation of the *boogie-woogie style of playing. He is generally credited with having popularly established the name in his 'Pine Top's boogie-woogie' which he first recorded in 1928. He died after being accidentally shot in a dance-hall disturbance at Masonic Lodge Hall in Orleans Street, Chicago.

Smith, Robert B[ache] (*b* Chicago, Ill., 4 June 1875; *d* New York, 6 Nov. 1951). American librettist and lyricist, younger brother of Harry B. *Smith. He worked as a reporter and appeared in amateur theatricals. At the age of 20 he wrote a comic opera and became a theatrical press representative. He wrote for vaudeville and burlesque and for various *Weber and Fields productions such as *Twirly Whirly* (1902). A prolific librettist, like his brother, his output included: *A China Doll* (1904); *The Girl at the Helm* (1906); *Knight for a Day* (1907); *The Girl and the Wizard* (1909); *The Spring Maid* (1910); *The Red Rose* (1911); *Gypsy Love* (1911); *Modest Suzanne* (1912); *The Girl from Montmartre* (1912); *The *Lilac Domino* (1914); and, with Victor *Herbert, **Sweethearts* (1913), *The Débutante* (1914), *Angel Face* (1919), and *The Girl in the Spotlight* (1920).

Smith, Stuff [Hezekiah Leroy Gordon] (*b* Portsmouth, Ohio, 14 Aug. 1909); *d* Munich, 25 Sept. 1967). American jazz violinist, singer, and bandleader. Educated in Cleveland, at 15 he appeared as dancer and violinist in a music-hall act, and in 1926 joined his first band in Dallas, Texas. He settled in Buffalo and led a band at the Little Harlem Club, the Vendome Hotel, and other venues. In 1936 he moved to New York where he made his reputation during a long residency at the famous Onyx Club, on and off until 1942, when he took over Fats *Waller's band. He opened his own restaurant in Chicago in 1945 and formed a new regular trio, by now playing an amplified violin. He mainly played on the West Coast during the 1950s and did a tour of Europe in 1957. He started another tour in 1965, visiting London before he died of a recurrent illness in Germany. Perhaps the most jazzy of all jazz violinists, his virtuosic and unusual playing was acknowledged as an inspiration to all who fiddled in jazz vein.

Smith, Willie 'The Lion' [William Henry Joseph Bonaparte Bertholoff] (*b* Goshen, NY, 25 Nov. 1897; *d* New York, 18 Apr. 1973). American jazz pianist. He started his professional career in Atlantic City and played in New York clubs around 1912. He earned his title, 'The Lion', for bravery in action during the First World War. Back in New York, he renewed his club activities, notably with long residencies at Leroy's and Small's, and he accompanied Mamie *Smith in her historic first recording of 'Crazy blues'. He worked at Pod's and Jerry's in the late 1920s and during the 1930s at the Onyx, Adrian's Tap Room, and the Apollo. He took part in many recording sessions and worked for a time with the Milt *Herth Trio. He toured Europe 1949–50 and again in 1965–6.

A source of inspiration to many Harlem-style pianists and an influential teacher, he gained a legendary reputation in his lifetime. His playing was full of life and ideas but never as slick as that of James P. *Johnson or Fats *Waller. Duke *Ellington wrote his 'Portrait of the Lion' in his honour. His own compositions included: 'Passionette', 'Echo of Spring', 'Ripplin' waters', 'Zig zag', 'Contrary motion', 'Keep your temper', and 'Conversation on Park Avenue'.

W. Smith and G. Hoefer: *Music on My Mind* (New York, 1965).

Snow, Hank [Clarence Eugene] (*b* Liverpool, Nova Scotia, 9 May 1914). Canadian country singer. He began his singing career on Halifax radio in 1935, began to record, and toured Canada and the USA as the 'Singing Ranger'. In 1948 he settled in the USA and became an American citizen in 1957. He joined the *Grand Ole Opry* programme in Nashville in 1950 and toured Europe. He was elected to the *Country Music Hall of Fame in 1979.

Snow, Valaida (*b* Washington DC, 2 June 1900; *d* New York, 30 May 1956). American trumpeter and singer. She began her professional playing career around 1920, and throughout the 1920s played and sang in revues, cabaret, and clubs in the USA. She worked in Shanghai in 1926, and in 1929 toured Europe, the Middle East, and Russia. After appearing in *Grand Terrace Revue* in 1933, she joined the **Blackbirds* cast and went with them to London in 1934. She continued a varied and busy career until she died of a cerebral haemorrhage in 1956. Very much an entertainer, her expert jazz playing and singing has only recently been fully appreciated.

Snow White and the Seven Dwarfs. Classic Walt Disney/RKO cartoon film made in 1937. It had an exceptionally good tally of songs written by Frank *Churchill and Larry Morey, that included 'I'm wishing', 'One song', 'With a smile and a song', 'Whistle while you work', 'Heigh-ho, heigh-ho', and 'Some day my prince will come'.

Snyder, Ted (*b* Freeport, Ill., 15 Aug. 1881; *d* Woodland Hills, Calif., 16 July 1965). American composer and publisher. He first worked as a bill poster, but eventually got a job as a café pianist. He joined the professional staff of a Chicago music-publisher, then moved to a similar post in New York, and formed the Ted Snyder Music Company in 1908. He retired from music-publishing in 1930 to open a nightclub in Hollywood. He was a frequent collaborator with Irving *Berlin, among whose first efforts were the lyrics for Snyder songs such as 'My wife's gone to the country' (1909). Other songs they wrote included 'Piano man' (1910), 'That opera rag' (1910), and 'That mysterious rag' (1912). He also wrote 'The Sheik of Araby' (1921) and 'Who's sorry now' (1923).

Soldene, Emily (*b* Islington, London, 9 Mar. 1840; *d* London, 8 Apr. 1912). British singer and actress. She first appeared as a singer at the *Oxford and other music-halls, but really made her reputation in the very popular English version of *Offenbach's **Geneviève de Brabant* at the Philharmonic, Islington, in 1871. After this she appeared in **Chilpéric* (1872) and the first production of *La *Fille de Madame Angot* at the *Gaiety Theatre in 1873. She toured with her own light opera company in Australia and the USA; and wrote a racy autobiography, *My Theatrical and Music Recollections* (London, 1897; reissued in 1906 on the occasion of her benefit at the Palace Theatre).

Solomon, Edward (*b* London, 25 July 1855; *d* London, 22 Jan. 1895). British composer and conductor. Largely self-taught in music, he began his career around 1878 as conductor of touring light opera companies. He wrote many short pieces for the German *Reed company, conducted at various London theatres, and wrote a dozen or so full-length operettas that were very much in the *Sullivan tradition, but without his touch of genius. Perhaps it was because he never had the advantage of a librettist like W. S. *Gilbert. There was, however, considerable graceful craftsmanship in his writing. He married the singer Lillian *Russell (her second husband) in 1882. The marriage lasted until 1885 when Solomon was charged with bigamy. His scores included: *Billee Taylor* (1880; NY, 1881), with Lillian Russell—'All on account of Eliza'; *Claude Duval* (1881); *Quite an Adventure* (1881); *Lord Bateman* (1882); *The Vicar of Bray* (1882); *Virginia and Paul* (1883); *Pocahontas* (1884); *Polly* (1884); *Maid and Moonshiner* (1886); *The Red Hussar* (1889); *Killiecrumper* (1891); and *The Nautch Girl* (1891).

Son. Afro-Cuban dance-song, a slower and less active form of the *rumba. In moderate tempo, the original song form generally has a cadenza-like vocal solo of irregular length, followed by a four-bar counter-melody sung by a chorus, known as the *montuno*. It originated in Oriente province and came to popularity in Havana around the time of the First World War. The name is also used in Mexico for a variety of dances from Mexican states—the *son huasteco*, the *son chiapaneco*, the *son jaliscense*, etc. They came to popularity about 1916 and are usually of a vivacious nature with strongly defined rhythms and spicy lyrics. The *son guatemalteco* or *son chapin* is the most popular dance of Guatemala, danced in a mixture of 3/4 and 6/8 rhythm.

Sondheim, Stephen Joshua (*b* New York, 22 Mar. 1930). American composer and lyricist. From a wealthy family, he was educated in private schools and composed a school musical at the age of 15. He went to Williams College where he wrote two college shows before he graduated in 1950. He continued his musical education at Princeton, winning the Hutchinson Prize which allowed him to study music for two years with Milton Babbitt and thus acquire an unusually sophisticated view of his subject. He wrote scripts for CBS and background music for Broadway plays, including *Girls of Summer* (1956), first becoming widely known as the lyric-writer for Leonard *Bernstein's **West Side Story* (1957). Following this, he wrote lyrics for **Gypsy* (1959); incidental music for *Invitation to a March* (1960); and lyrics for the Richard *Rodgers musical *Do I Hear a Waltz?* (1965).

As both composer and lyricist, he had his first big success with *A *Funny Thing Happened on the Way to the Forum* (1962; filmed 1966); followed by the comparatively unsuccessful *Anyone Can Whistle* (1964); and, for TV, the romantic *Evening Primrose*

(1965). His great reputation among the more adventurous followers of popular music was established by such scores as **Company* (1970); **Follies* (1971); and *A *Little Night Music* (1973), which was almost entirely in 3/4 time, had a sort of Greek chorus, and included his best-known song 'Send in the clowns'. A cross-section of his writings was examined in *Sondheim: a Musical Tribute* (NY, 1973) and in *Side by Side by Sondheim* (London, 1975), compiled and directed by Ned Sherrin (*b* 1931). His works increased their demands on the mind and ear as he moved nearer to opera with **Pacific Overtures* (1976); **Sweeney Todd* (1979); *Merrily We Roll Along* (1981); and, after six productions with Harold Prince, the concentrated and challenging **Sunday in the Park with George* (1984) and *Into the Woods* (1987), a modern fairy-tale which had a good song in 'No one is alone'. His film scores include *Stavisky* (1974), *The Seven Percent Solution* (1977), and *Reds* (1980).

Sondheim is a representative in the musical theatre world of the avant garde outlook of modern jazz, and moves in an area that bears little relation to the goings-on of the pop world that *Lloyd Webber lends an ear to. Sometimes adversely reviewed, and none of his shows proving a commercial success, he has still achieved a substantial reputation. If his path continues as it has done, he might easily step over the border and become a contender for 'serious' consideration. He has been described by Jerry *Herman as 'the only one who keeps on taking the musical theatre to new places'.

C. Zadan: *Sondheim & Co* (New York, 1974). S. Morley (ed.): *Song by Song by Sondheim (The Stephen Sondheim Songbook)* (London, 1979).

Song and Dance. A 'concert for the theatre', comprising *Tell Me on Sunday*, with music by Andrew *Lloyd Webber and lyrics by Don Black (*b* 1936) and *Variations*, a ballet to music by Lloyd Webber, produced at the Palace Theatre, London, 26 Mar. 1982 [781p], with Marti Webb and Gemma *Craven. The show had a London revival in 1990. *Tell Me on Sunday* was first seen on BBC TV 27 Aug. 1984 with Sarah Brightman.

Song of Norway. Operetta based on the music of Edvard Grieg, adapted by Robert *Wright and George *Forrest (music and lyrics), with book by Milton Lazarus, based on a play by Homer Curran, New York (Imperial Theatre), 21 Aug. 1944. The story was a fictionalized account of Grieg's own eventless life with Lawrence Brooks playing the composer. The songs ('Strange music') were cleverly tailored and supplied enough pleasure for the show to run for 860 performances. It was produced in London (Palace Theatre) 7 Mar. 1946 [526p]; and it was filmed in 1970 with Tauralv Maurstad as the hero.

Sons of the Pioneers. A now historic Country and Western vocal group formed in 1933 by Roy Rogers (*b* 1911), Bob Nolan (1908–80), and Tim Spencer (1908–74), first as the Pioneer Trio then as Sons of the Pioneers with the addition of cowboy singers Hugh Farr (1903–80) and Karl Farr (1909–61). Singing in a polished close-harmony style they appeared in the film *Rhythm on the Range* (1936) with Bing *Crosby. Nolan was a talented composer and contributed such items as 'Tumbling tumbleweeds' (1927), 'Cool water' (1936), 'Blue prairie' (with Spencer, 1936) to their repertoire; while Spencer wrote 'The timber trail' (1942), 'Cowboy camp meeting' (1946), 'Cigareetes and whusky and wild, wild women' (1947), 'The everlasting hills of Oklahoma' (1947), 'Careless kisses' (1949), 'Roomful of roses' (1949), and 'Roses' (with Glenn Spencer, 1950). They appeared in the films *Hollywood Canteen* (1944), *Gay Rancheros* (1944), and *Melody Time* (1948). Rogers left the group in 1938 while Spencer and Nolan lasted until 1950, surviving numerous changes of personnel until *c.*1966. They recorded many albums for RCA starting with *Favourite Cowboy Songs* (1956) to *South of the Border* (1966); and there have since been many revival compilations to complement their now legendary reputation. The original six members were elected to the *Country Music Hall of Fame in 1980.

Sorcerer, The. The first full-length comic opera by W. S. *Gilbert and Arthur *Sullivan, produced at the Opera-Comique Theatre, London, 17 Nov. 1877, where it had 178 performances.

The story revolves around Mr J. Wellington Wells, a sorcerer, who administers a love potion to the villagers of Ploverleigh, which causes them to fall in love with the first person they see after their next sleep. This naturally makes for considerable confusion. The cast contained such pioneering Savoyards as Richard *Temple, Rutland *Barrington, and George *Grossmith Jr. Its most notable songs were 'Time was when love and I were well acquainted' and 'My name is John Wellington Wells' in a score that was not among the collaborators' most notable. It was first produced in New York at the Broadway Theatre, 21 Feb. 1879. It was filmed in 1982.

Soul. That part of the pop music of black Americans, and their copiers, which has derived from gospel music and the blues. The bounds between soul and other black activities in the rhythm 'n' blues and rock areas are not clearly defined. The purist sees the birth of modern-day soul music in the 'bird' groups of the late 1940s and early 1950s, such as the Orioles, the Flamingos, the Ravens, the Penguins, and other groups like the Moonglows, the Coronets, the Spaniels, and the Five Satins. They brought the flavour of the pure gospel music of the Ward Singers and the Five Blind Boys to rhythm 'n' blues, and thus created soul. The Orioles' 1953 recording of 'Crying in the chapel' was the first by a black vocal group of this kind to make the Top 20. The same year saw the first recordings by the *Drifters, whose reputation has remained undiminished. They were signed up by the Atlantic label, formed in 1948, from which came other notable soul acts such as Ray *Charles, the *Coasters, LaVern *Baker, Ruth *Brown, and Clyde *McPhatter. The success of its recordings of soul music made it into a major label, and other companies like Stax, Scepter, Chess, King, and the influential *Tamla Motown soon followed. Each of these companies followed an individual line but it was Berry *Gordy's Tamla Motown company which achieved the most recognizable sound of all. Formed in Detroit in 1959 it had, by 1961, achieved million-sellers with the *Miracles' 'Shop around' and the Marvelettes' 'Please Mr Postman'; and followed these up with hits by Mary Wells, Stevie *Wonder, *Martha and the Vandellas, the *Supremes, Marvin *Gaye, the *Four Tops, the *Temptations, and Junior Walker, during the next four years.

The concurrent blossoming of black rhythm 'n' blues soloists like Fats *Domino, Chuck *Berry, and Bo *Diddley helped the overall appreciation of the special contribution of black artists in both the USA and Britain. The female soul field was dominated by the talent of Aretha *Franklin, with her intense and gospel-based sound; the male counterpart being Otis *Redding, who made a great impression before he was killed in a plane crash in 1967. In the 1970s Motown moved forward with such issues as Marvin Gaye's concept album *What's Going On?* and Stevie Wonder's *Music of My Mind*, the first of his electronic recordings. On the Stax label came Isaac *Hayes's *Hot Buttered Soul* and his sound-track for the film *Shaft* (1971). On the Atlantic label Roberta *Flack became popular with her cool style that was aptly dubbed 'quiet fire'. The soul labels prospered and the abundance of black talent has made it one of the richest areas of creativity in the pop scene.

R. Larkin: *Soul Music: the Sound, the Stars, the Story* (New York, 1970). M. Haralambos: *Right On: from Blues to Soul in Black America* (London, 1974).

Sound of Music, The. Musical play with music by Richard *Rodgers, lyrics by Oscar *Hammerstein II, book by Howard *Lindsay and Russel *Crouse, based on Maria Augusta von Trapp's *The Trapp Family Singers*. It became the second longest running Broadway musical of the 1950s and was the last contribution of Oscar Hammerstein to the musical theatre. Conceived as a starring vehicle for Mary *Martin, many thought that it went over the bounds of romantic sentimentality and would not survive, but all were confounded by its immense and lasting appeal: opening at the Lunt-Fontanne Theatre 16 Nov. 1959, it ran for 1443 performances.

Set in Salzburg in 1938, it follows the fortunes of the famous Trapp family and Maria (Mary Martin), their governess, who marries the head of the family, Georg von Trapp (Theodore Bikel, *b* 1924). The idyll is shattered by the German invasion of Austria. Rodgers's most sentimental music so far, 'The sound of music', 'Maria', 'My favourite things', 'Do-re-mi', 'Sixteen going on seventeen', 'The lonely goatherd', 'Climb ev'ry mountain', 'Edelweiss', and others, became universal favourites; and the show had an even greater success in London, at the Palace Theatre 18 May 1961, where it achieved 2386 performances. Further rewards were reaped on screen and LP when the lavishly filmed version of 1965, starring Julie *Andrews, produced a best-selling album, putting the Austrian lakeside resort of Mondsee on the tourist map and rivalling Mozart as a Salzburg attraction.

Sousa, John Philip (*b* Washington DC, 6 Nov. 1854; *d* Reading, Pa., 6 Mar. 1932). American composer and conductor. Son of a trombonist in the US Marines Band, he was taught harmony and the violin and first appeared as a soloist at the age of 11. At 13 he enlisted in the Marines Band but, as this was only a part-time occupation, he also gained theatrical experience by conducting the orchestra at Kernan's Théâtre Comique in Washington, and elsewhere, and playing the violin in various orchestras. Both he and his father obtained their discharge from the marines in 1875. In 1877 he was a violinist in the special orchestra that was assembled in Philadelphia to play under *Offenbach, when the composer visited the Philadelphia Centennial Exposition 1876–7, and he wrote an 'International Congress fantasy' for the occasion. In 1879 he wrote his first operetta, *Our Flirtations*. In 1880 he was appointed Bandmaster of the US Marines Band in which he had served as a boy. While on tour with the band in 1892 he received the offer of financial backing to form a band of his own: he played his last concert with the Marines in July and gave the first concert with his own band in September. Sadly, his father died just before the new band was launched. The famous bandmaster Patrick S. *Gilmore had died the day before the band's launching and Sousa was able to enlist a number of excellent players from Gilmore's band. It was a great success from the start and for many years made regular tours of the USA, visiting Europe in 1900, 1901, 1903, and 1905. There was a 13-month world tour 1910–11. He took charge of military band training at the Great Lakes Training Center in 1917. He continued to lead his band, which by 1924 was 75 strong, and made recordings with it, until he died in 1932 just after a rehearsal. He was very much against what he called 'canned music' and did not make a broadcast until he was 74; when recordings were made he usually let someone else, such as Arthur *Pryor, conduct the orchestra.

Throughout his career Sousa was a prolific composer. Now best remembered for his splendid marches, he was also a pioneering figure in the American musical theatre and wrote a number of operettas which included: *The Smugglers* (1882); *Desirée* (1884); *The Queen of Hearts* (1886); *El Capitan* (NY, 1896; London, 1899)—his best and most successful work; *The Charlatan* (1897), produced in London as *A Mystical Miss* (1900); *The Bride Elect* (1898); *Chris and the Wonderful Lamp* (1900); *The Free Lance* (1906); *The Glass-Blowers*

(1906); and *The American Maid* (1913). Among several hundred compositions were overtures, suites, waltzes, fantasias, and galops, and some 60 songs, few of which are now heard.

His special flair was for band marches, many of them written with particular and personal associations. These include one of the most famous of all American marches, 'The Stars and Stripes forever', which came to him on the ship which took him on his tours and was published in 1896. It was to earn him more than $300,000 in his lifetime. Others that helped to win him his title of 'The March King' included: 'The Wolverine' (1881), 'Transit of Venus' (1883), 'Semper fideles' (1888), 'The picador' (1889), 'The Thunderer' (1889), 'The Washington Post' (1889), 'The High School cadets' (1890), 'The belle of Chicago' (1892), 'The Liberty Bell' (1893), 'Manhattan Beach' (1893), 'King Cotton' (1895), 'El Capitan' (1896), and 'Hands across the sea' (1899). He edited *National, Patriotic and Typical Airs of All Lands* (1890), wrote five novels, made a collection of his writings in an almanac, *Through the Year with Sousa* (New York, 1910), and published his autobiography, *Marching Along* (Boston, 1928).

M. Lewiton: *John Philip Sousa: the March King* (New York, 1944). K. Berger: *The March King and his Band* (New York, 1957). J. R. Smart: *The Sousa Band: a Discography* (Washington DC, 1970). P. E. Bierley: *John Philip Sousa: a Descriptive Catalog of his Works* (Urbana–Chicago, 1973). P. E. Bierley: *John Philip Sousa: American Phenomenon* (Englewood Cliffs, NJ, 1973). J. Newsom (ed.): *Perspectives on John Philip Sousa* (Washington DC, 1983).

Music: *Sousa's Great Marches in Piano Transcriptions* [23 marches] (New York, 1975). L. S. Levey (ed.): *Sousa's Great Marches* [24 facsimiles] (New York, 1975).

South Pacific. Musical play with score by Richard *Rodgers, lyrics by Oscar *Hammerstein II, book by Oscar Hammerstein and Joshua *Logan, whose idea it was to adapt a story from James A. Michener's *Tales of the South Pacific*, 'Fo' Dolla''. It was first produced at the Majestic Theatre, New York, 7 Apr. 1949, and was to be one of their greatest successes, with a run of 1925 performances.

The final book combined the story, concerning the love of an American lieutenant (William Tabbert, 1921–74) for a Polynesian girl (Betta St John), with the plot from another story, 'Our Heroine', which concerned the love of navy nurse Nellie Forbush (Mary *Martin) for French planter Emile de Becque (the opera singer Ezio *Pinza, making his Broadway debut). The lieutenant and the planter set out on a mission behind enemy lines and only the latter returns. It was an entirely successful conception, combining humour and sentiment with such novel ideas as Mary Martin washing her hair on stage every night ('I'm gonna wash that man right outa my hair'), and a tune-rich score that also included 'A cockeyed optimist', 'Some enchjanted evening', 'There is nothing like a dame', 'Bali Ha'i', 'I'm in love with a wonderful guy', 'Younger than Springtime', 'Happy talk', 'Honey bun', 'This nearly was mine', and the racially outspoken 'You've got to be carefully taught'.

An American touring company reached 118 cities in the USA while the London production, with Wilbur Evans partnering Mary Martin, ran for 792 performances at the Theatre Royal, Drury Lane, from 1 Nov. 1951. The film version in 1958 starred Rossano Brazzi (*b* 1916), Mitzi Gaynor (*b* 1930), and Juanita Hall (1901–68).

Soutullo, Reveriano (1884–1932) and **Vert, Juan** (1890–1931). Spanish composers who worked as a team to write several zarzuelas that are still heard in Spain. These included *La del soto del parral* (1927), *El último romántico* (1928), and *La leyenda del Beso* (1929).

Spaeth, Sigmund (*b* Philadelphia, 10 Apr. 1885; *d* New York, 11 Nov. 1965). American author. Educated at Princeton, he was music editor of the *New York Evening Mail* 1914–18, and a well-known lecturer on music. His books on popular music did much to foster a public interest in these once derided spheres, and included: *Read 'Em And Weep* (New York, 1927); *Weep Some More My Lady* (New York, 1927); *Gentlemen, Be Seated: a Parade of the Old-Time Minstrels* (with Daily Paskman) (New York, 1928); *They Still Sing of Love* (New York, 1929); *The Facts of Life in Popular Song* (New York, 1934); *Barber Shop Ballads* (New York, 1940); *A History of Popular Music in America* (New York, 1948); as well as many books on music in general.

Spanier, 'Muggsy' [Francis Joseph] (*b* Chicago, 9 Nov. 1906; *d* Sausalito, Calif., 12 Feb. 1967). American jazz cornettist. He played in a school band and part-time with Elmer *Schoebel while working as a messenger boy. He was with various Chicago bands 1922–8, before joining Ted *Lewis in San Francisco 1929–36, then Ben *Pollack 1936–8, after which illness forced him to leave music. He started playing again in 1939 and had a great success with his own Ragtimers, with Rod Cless (1907–44) (clarinet), Joe Bushkin (*b* 1916) (piano), and George Brunis (1902–74) (trombone); the recordings they made for Bluebird that year were justifiably re-issued under the title of 'The Great 16', and their brief career, at the Sherman Hotel in Chicago and Nick's in New York, had a disproportionately large influence on the traditional jazz revival of the 1940s. After this he played with Bob *Crosby 1940–1, before forming a big band. By now a well-known jazz figure, he played and recorded regularly until he was forced to retire through ill-health in 1964, after an appearance at the Newport Festival.

Spasm band. Name given to small jazz groups, often an offshoot of impoverished black bands in places like New Orleans in the late 1800s, who made use of such cheap makeshift instruments as the jug, kazoo, bull-fiddle, and washboard, producing a hilariously joyful music that was perpetuated in many more professional *washboard and *jug bands in Chicago in the 1920s and 1930s; sometimes called *skiffle groups.

Speaks, Oley (*b* Canal Winchester, Ohio, 28 June 1874; *d* New York, 27 Aug. 1948). American singer and composer. He worked as a railroad clerk in Columbus, Ohio, but then went to study singing and composition in New York where he sang in various churches 1898–1906. Subsequently he pursued a career on the concert platform and was the composer of a number of popular songs, the best-known being a setting of Rudyard Kipling's 'On the road to Mandalay' (1907). Others included 'Sylvia' (1914), 'Morning', 'Life's twilight', 'When the boys come home', 'Love's like a rosebud', 'My homeland', 'The Lord is my life', and 'To you'.

Spector, Phil [Philip Harvey] (*b* New York, 26 Dec. 1940). American producer. Taken to Los Angeles as a child, he formed a vocal group at high school, and had an early hit with his own 'To know him is to love him' (1958), a song written in memory of his father. He worked with Lee *Hazlewood and *Leiber and Stoller, co-writing 'Spanish Harlem' (1960). In 1961 he formed a record company and pioneered a 'wall of sound' style, using echo and tape loops, that, through a succession of hit recordings, had a great influence on the pop sound of the 1960s. He was the youngest record company head and a millionaire by the time he was 21. His reputation grew, based on the continuing quality of his output and the production of many classics of black pop music. He became disenchanted with the jealous rivalries of the business and retired for some years at the end of the decade, returning in 1970 to work with John *Lennon, George *Harrison, and others; his best recordings are now regularly anthologized.

R. Williams: *Out of his Head: the Sound of Phil Spector* (New York, 1972; London, 1974).

Spikes, Benjamin F. 'Reb' (*b* Dallas, 31 Oct. 1888) and **John C.** (*b* Dallas, 22 July 1882; *d* Pasadena, Calif., 28 June 1955). American songwriters, publishers, and entrepreneurs. They settled in Los Angeles in 1919 to found a music-publishing business, a music shop, an agency, and a nightclub; and to run a popular show-band whose vocalist was Ivie *Anderson. They started their own record label, Sunshine, which made the first black jazz band recording with Kid *Ory in 1922. They wrote and published a number of songs, including 'Someday sweetheart' (1919) and 'Wolverine blues' (1923), which was recorded by the *New Orleans Rhythm Kings that year; the music was by Jelly Roll *Morton, who had originally written it many years earlier as 'The Wolverines' and strongly objected to its being called a blues (which it wasn't) and to the Spikes Brothers' corny lyrics, which at his insistence were suppressed and rewritten. They wrote the show *Stepping High* (1924), which starred Eddie *Anderson, and made an early sound film in 1927. They gradually faded from the entertainment scene, John suffering from blindness and Benjamin becoming an estate agent.

Spinners, The. British folk-singing group formed on an amateur basis in 1958 and still intact after 30 years, made up of Tony Davis (*b* Blackburn, 1930); Mike Groves (*b* Salford, 1936); Hugh Jones (*b* Liverpool, 1936); and Cliff Hall (*b* Cuba, 1925). They opened the Spinners Club in a Liverpool basement and became a popular local attraction. By 1962 they were appearing regularly on TV and they had their own TV series from 1966. Singing worldwide folk-songs in a stylish way and encouraging audience participation, they became internationally popular and toured Australia in 1979, continuing since with many LP albums to their credit and an undiminished following.

Spirituals. Religious songs most strongly associated with the black people of the Southern states of the USA, but eventually becoming popular everywhere. Historians have mainly agreed that the spiritual had white origins in the Wesleyan and other Methodist hymns brought to the USA by the early white settlers, which were then adopted for their own needs by the black slave population in the early 19th century, when missionary zeal was offering a guaranteed reward in Heaven as compensation for the unpleasant conditions of daily life. The themes of death, resurrection, release, and the promised land are basic to the spiritual, combining with rhythmical musical characteristics that derive from the plantation work songs.

The widespread recognition of the Negro spiritual, as a powerful form of religious singing that had boundless appeal, began in the 1860s when such publications as *Slave Songs of the United States* (1868), edited by William Francis Allen, first appeared; and they were popularized in the 1870s by the celebrated Fisk University *Jubilee Singers, who introduced such now well-known spirituals as 'Steal away' and 'Deep river' on their tours of the USA, Britain, and Europe. The popularity of the spiritual was at a peak in the inter-war years when artists like Roland Hayes (1887–1977), Paul *Robeson, and Marian *Anderson were giving them concert respectability, and groups like the *Golden Gate Quartet emphasized their jazzier associations. As the jazz element in performance increased the spiritual became more universally known as *gospel song which, in turn, was the forerunner of *soul. Deriving from the same early sources, a strong tradition of white spirituals has concurrently flourished in the USA.

G. P. Jackson: *White Spirituals in the Southern Uplands* (Chapel Hill, NC, 1933; New York, 1965). R. N. Dett: *The Development of the Negro Spiritual* (Minneapolis, 1936). G. P. Jackson: *Spiritual Folk-Songs of Early America* (New York, 1937). H. Thurmann: *Deep River: an Interpretation of Negro Spirituals* (New York, 1966). J. Lovell: *Black Song: the Forge and the Flame* (New York, 1972).

Spivak, Charlie [Charles] (*b* Kiev, 17 Feb. 1906; *d* Greenville, SC, 1 Mar. 1982). America jazz trumpeter. He was taken to the USA from Russia at the age of three. He was well-known for his work in various swing bands, including those of Paul Specht 1924–30; Ben *Pollack 1931–4; the *Dorsey brothers 1934–5; Ray *Noble 1935; Bob *Crosby 1937–8; and Tommy *Dorsey 1938–9. He led his own band, on and off, 1939–63, and played for 11 years, from 1967, at a club in Greenville, SC.

Spivey, Victoria Regina (*b* Houston, Texas, 15 Oct. 1906; *d* New York, 3 Oct. 1976). American singer, pianist, organist, and composer. She had her first big success in 1926 with the recording of her own 'Black snake blues' which sold 150,000 copies within a year. This quickly made her a star, and she appeared in the MGM musical film *Hallelujah* (1929). She continued her recordings in a commercial blues idiom, backed by famous jazzmen like Clarence *Williams and Louis *Armstrong, with such titles as 'Organ grinder', 'Funny feathers', and 'Make a country bird fly'. She appeared in the show version of **Hellzapoppin* (1942), after which she disappeared from the entertainment scene to run her own record company, reappearing in 1960 to sing in Ryan's and other New York clubs and continue her career. Her sister Addie (1910–43) was also a singer and pianist.

Spoliansky, Mischa (*b* Bialystock, 1898; *d* London, 28 June 1984). Russian-born composer and conductor. His family emigrated in 1917 after the Revolution and he received his musical education in Germany. He wrote songs for Marlene *Dietrich while she was comparatively unknown, and later for her rival Margo Lion (1899–1989); and scores for several operettas. He left Germany in 1933 and settled with his family in England, writing a musical, *Who's Taking Liberty* (1939), but mainly worked in films, his scores including: *The Private Life of Don Juan* (1934)—'Senorita'; *Sanders of the River* (1935); *King Solomon's Mines* (1936)—'Ho! Ho!' ('Wagon song'); *Wanted for Murder* (1946)—'A voice in the night'; and many more.

Springfield, Dusty [O'Brien, Mary] (*b* Hampstead, London, 16 Apr. 1939). British singer. She first became known as one of the Springfields, a folk group consisting of herself, her brother Tom *Springfield, and Tim Feild (replaced in 1962 by Mike Pickworth), one of the first British groups to record in Nashville. She left them in 1963 to follow a solo career and had a number of hits including 'I only want to be with you', 'You don't have to say you love me' (an English version of an Italian song 'Io che non vivo', with lyrics by Vicki Wickham and Simon Napier-Bell, *b* 1939), which was at No. 1 in 1966. She concentrated more on cabaret but recorded occasionally, producing such items as the *soul classic 'Son of a preacher man' (1968) and 'Who gets your love' (1972). She became a leading figure in the white soul genre, making the albums *Dusty in Memphis* (1969) and *From Dusty with Love* (1972). In 1973 she moved to the West Coast of America and continued a very sporadic career.

L. O'Brien: *Dusty* (London, 1989).

Springfield, Tom [O'Brien, Thomas] (*b* London, 2 July 1934). British singer and composer. In the early 1960s he was a member of the folk group, the Springfields (which also included his sister Dusty *Springfield), for whom he wrote 'Island of dreams' (1962) and other songs. When the group disbanded in 1963 he became a full-time writer, producing such simple and memorable songs as 'Losing you' (1964), for his sister, and 'Just loving you' (1964), for Anita Harris. He had a special success with his lively numbers for the *Seekers, such as 'I'll never find another you' (1964), 'A world of our own' (1965), and 'The carnival is over' (1965). He has written many million-sellers including 'Georgy girl' (1966), used in the film of the same name; and he composed TV themes for *The Troubleshooters*; *Mogul*; *George and the Dragon*; and *This Man Craig*.

Springsteen, Bruce Frederick Joseph (*b* Freehold, NJ, 23 Sept. 1949). American singer and songwriter. While at college he formed Steel Mill, a group which became popular around San Francisco in 1969; it disbanded in 1971, but became the nucleus of the Bruce Springsteen Band and later the E Street Band. He decided on a solo career in 1972, and obtained a contract for 10 albums from Columbia Records, the first being *Greetings from Asbury Park, New Jersey* (1973), which immediately confirmed his skill as a performer and the quality of his imaginative writing. Billed as 'the future of rock 'n' roll', he toured with his E Street Band and came up with such impressive albums as *The River* (1980), which showed his powers as a songwriter in such numbers as 'The river' and 'Independence day', backed by the driving sound of his band. He toured Europe in 1981, and produced the album *Nebraska* (1982), on which he performed alone in folk-inflected numbers in the Bob *Dylan style; followed by *Born in the USA* (1984), which returned to full-blooded rock and roll. A five-LP set of recordings of his concerts was issued in 1986. While never reaching the No. 1 position in popular estimation, his songs like 'Hungry heart' (1980), 'Dancing in the dark' (1984), and 'Glory days' (1985), have always been thereabouts and his reputation as a leader in the rock and roll field and the voice of dissident youth has remained undiminished.

P. Gambaccini: *Bruce Springsteen* (New York, 1979). D. Marsh: *Springsteen Born to Run: the Bruce Springsteen Story* (New York, 1979; London, 1981). C. Cross (ed.): *Backstreets: Springsteen: the Man and his Music* (New York, 1989).

Squadronaires, The. British wartime dance band of the Royal Air Force. Some well-known swing musicians from various bands were asked to join the air force and form, in 1940, what was to be the first service dance orchestra; these included eight from the *Ambrose orchestra of the calibre of Tommy McQuater (*b* 1914), George *Chisholm, Eric Breeze, Harry Lewis, Andy McDevitt, Jock Cummings, Sid Colin (1915–89), and Archie Craig; to create one of the most exciting hot bands of the period; a strong rival to the American forces band led by Glenn *Miller.

Square. A word first popularized in the jazz world, deriving from the earlier 'squarehead' or 'square John' (meaning upright and honest), which came to imply, in a derogatory way, a person or thing that was doggedly conservative, behind the times, old-fashioned, and, hence, not with it. It passed from jazz into the general stock of slang.

Square dance. A type of country dance, originating in the USA, which starts with four couples facing one another in a square. The steps and movements are generally shouted out by a caller and the music, of the hoedown variety, is generally provided by a fiddle-led band.

B. Casey: *The Complete Book of Square Dancing and Round Dancing* (New York, 1976).

Squire, W. H. [William Henry] (*b* Ross, Hereford, 8 Aug. 1871; *d* London, 17 Mar. 1963). British composer and cellist. He first studied music under his father, who was a talented amateur vocalist, before winning a scholarship to the Royal College of Music. His first professional appearance was as a cellist at the St James's Hall in 1891, under Albéniz, and he became principal cellist in the Royal Opera House Orchestra, Covent Garden, in 1895. Later he had a career as a popular recitalist, retiring in 1941. He wrote a cello concerto and cello pieces, and a number of popular drawing-room ballads that included: 'The jolly sailor' (1903), 'Three for Jack' (1904), 'Lighterman Tom' (1907), 'Mountain lovers' (1908), 'A chip off the old block' (1908), 'A sergeant of the line' (1908), 'When you come home' (1912), 'Pals' (1913), 'In an old-fashioned town' (1914), 'If I might come to you' (1916), and 'The token' (1919).

Stacy, Jess Alexandria (*b* Merge Point, Mo., 11 Aug. 1904). American jazz pianist. Playing in a relaxed style with a distinctive right hand tremolo, he made his reputation with the Benny *Goodman band 1935–9, notably in the famous 'Sing, sing, sing' solo at Carnegie Hall in 1938; afterwards with Bob *Crosby 1939–42; and with Goodman again 1942–4. He played with other bands and led his own, in Goodman style, 1945–6 and 1947–8, featuring his wife, the singer Lee *Wiley. He free-lanced irregularly in New York in the 1950s and made some revival recordings including an LP of piano solos in 1951 and a *Tribute to Benny Goodman*, with ex-Goodman sidemen, in 1956. He retired from music in 1961 to take up a sales career. His best-known solo recording was 'Barrelhouse' in 1936; and he was heard with many swing and mainstream groups on record. He returned to the musical scene in 1973 to play on the sound-track of the film *The Great Gatsby*; subsequently appearing at the 1974 Newport Jazz Festival, followed by other festivals, also on TV, radio, and recordings.

Stafford, Jo (*b* Coalinga, Calif., 12 Nov. 1920). American singer. She and her sisters sang on radio in their teens and in the late 1930s, before she joined the vocal group the *Pied Pipers as the only woman in a seven-man team. It later became a quartet and was engaged by Tommy *Dorsey in 1942. The quartet left Dorsey in 1942 to work on various radio shows with Bob *Crosby, Johnny *Mercer, Frank *Sinatra, and others. She left them in 1944 to pursue a solo career, was with Mercer in 1944, and had her own radio show in 1946. She was regularly on radio in the 1950s, often with the band led by her second husband, Paul *Weston. Her main hits in the 1950s were 'You belong to me' and 'Shrimp boats'. She retired in the late 1960s.

Stamper, Dave (*b* New York, 10 Nov. 1883; *d* Poughkeepsie, NY, 18 Sept. 1963). American composer. A self-taught musician, he left school at 17 to take a job as a pianist in a dance-hall, then joined a music-publisher as song-plugger and staff pianist. From 1893 he toured as a vaudeville accompanist, including four years with Norah *Bayes. His first published song was 'In the cool of the evening', written in 1910; and a 1911 number written with Gene *Buck, 'Daddy has a sweetheart and Mother is her name' was used in the **Ziegfeld Follies* of 1912. Having songs in many of the successive editions of this show (1912–13, 1915–17, 1919–25, and 1931), his name became particularly associated with Ziegfeld productions. He contributed to *Zig-Zag* (1917); *Box o' Tricks* (1918); *Midnight Frolic* (1919–21)—'Rose of Washington Square' (1919); *Take the Air* (1927); *Lovely Lady* (1927); and *Orchids Preferred* (1937). He also wrote for films, including *Married in Hollywood* (1929)—'Dance away the night'.

Stamps. Thematic collecting has become a popular branch of philately now that the field has become too large to make a general collection practical; and music has provided one special area of interest. Classical composers have always been well represented on stamps; and latterly many light and popular composers have been similarly honoured. These include Duke *Ellington (Togo, 1967; USA, 1984); Stephen *Foster (USA, 1940); George *Gershwin (USA, 1974); Franz Xaver Gruber (1787–1863), composer of 'Silent night' (Austria, 1948, 1968); W. C. *Handy (USA, 1969); Victor *Herbert (USA, 1940); Jerome *Kern (USA, 1985); Josef *Lanner (Austria, 1951); Ernesto *Lecuona (Cuba, 1966); Franz *Lehár (Hungary, 1970); Paul *Lincke (Germany, 1956); Karl *Millöcker (Austria, 1949); Thomas *Moore (Eire, 1952); Ethelbert *Nevin (USA, 1940); Jacques *Offenbach (France, 1981); Johann *Schrammel (Austria, 1950); John Philip *Sousa (USA, 1940); Robert *Stolz (Austria,

1970); Johann *Strauss I (Austria, 1949); Johann *Strauss II (Austria, 1922, 1949); and Karl *Ziehrer (Austria, 1947, 1972); there are also many stamps depicting folk-music and instruments.

S. Peat: *Music on Stamps* (6 vols) (Chippenham, 1971–5). J. Watson: *Stamps and Music* (London, 1962).

Standard. Composition or song that has, by dint of its lasting memorability and general worth, become a regularly used item in some field of music—a jazz standard, for example.

Star is Born, A. The fictional Hollywood story of the rising young actress who falls in love with the great (but alcoholic) star whose career crumbles while she becomes the star, is said to be based on the lives of Marguerite De La Motte (1903–50) and John Bowers. It was first made the subject of a film in 1932, under the title of *What Price Hollywood*, with Constance Bennett (1904–65) and Lowell Sherman (1885–1934); and then, as *A Star is Born*, in 1937 with Janet Gaynor (1906–84) and Fredric March (1897–1975).

It was turned into a film musical, with screenplay by Moss *Hart, in 1954. This classic Transcona/Warner version, starring Judy *Garland and James Mason (1909–84), had a score mainly by Harold *Arlen and lyrics by Ira *Gershwin ('The man that got away', 'Gotta have me go with you') with a number of interpolated songs that included 'You took advantage of me' (*Rodgers and *Hart), 'Swanee' (*Gershwin), 'Born in a trunk' (Roger Edens, 1905–70), and 'I'll get by' (*Ahlert). The film had a turbulent production period because of Judy Garland's emotional problems at the time, thus adding to the legendary nature of the film, which was cut, following previews, from 3 hours to 100 minutes, and, though nominated for several Academy Awards, won none. There were almost equal problems when a new version (not generally considered the equal of the Garland classic) was made in 1976, with Barbra *Streisand and Kris *Kristofferson, and a new and less evocative score.

R. Haver: *A Star is Born* (London, 1989).

Starr, Ringo [Starkey, Richard] (*b* Liverpool, 7 July 1940). British drummer, vocalist, and composer. After a series of menial employments, he shot to fame as the vivacious drummer of the *Beatles 1962–70. Thereafter he pursued his own career and established himself as a major artist with recordings of his own songs, 'It don't come easy' (1971), 'Back off boogaloo' (1972), 'Photograph' (1973); and the albums *Ringo* (1973), *Goodnight Vienna* (1974), and others. He appeared in a number of films, notably *That'll Be the Day* (1973), which launched David *Essex on an acting career. He continued to record in a casual way, including an appearance on the Lonnie *Donegan album, *Puttin' on the Style* (1977).

'Star-spangled Banner, The'. American national song. The tune was originally known as 'The Anacreontic song' or 'To Anacreon in Heaven' with music now generally credited to John Stafford Smith (1750–1836), a member of the convivial London music club known as the Anacreontic Society, and thus claimed in his *Fifth Book of Canzonets, Catches, Canons and Glees* (London, 1799). But there have also been long-standing claims on behalf of Samuel Arnold (1740–1802), who was the conductor of the Anacreontic Society orchestra. The original words, written in 1778, were by Ralph Tomlinson, one-time President of the Society. 'The Anacreontic Song' became well-known in Britain and the USA and between 1790 and 1820 there were some 50 different poems written to the tune, including one by Francis Scott Key (1779–1843) in 1805 called 'When the warrior returns', which included the line 'by the light of the star-spangled flag of our nation'.

Key wrote the present well-known words in 1814 on board his ship while the English were bombarding Fort McHenry, prior to their attack on Baltimore. His poem was printed in September 1814 as 'Defence of Fort McHenry', and a few days later appeared in *The Baltimore Patriot*. The first publication of the complete words and music, under the title of 'The Star-spangled Banner', was in 1814 (with the music edited by Thomas Carr). The original flag that is said to have inspired the song is in the Smithsonian Institution in Washington.

O. G. T. Sonneck: *Report on 'The Star-spangled Banner', 'Hail, Columbia', 'Yankee Doodle'* (Washington, 1909; repr. New York, 1972). O. G. T. Sonneck: *The Star-spangled Banner* (Washington, 1914). J. Muller: *The Star-spangled Banner* (New York, 1935). V. Weybright: *Star-spangled Banner: the Story of Francis Scott Key* (New York, 1935).

State Fair. 20th Century Fox musical film of 1945 with songs by Richard *Rodgers and Oscar *Hammerstein II ('That's for me', 'It's a grand night for singing', 'It might as well be Spring', 'Isn't it kinda fun'), the only film score they worked on together, and made after the stage success of *Oklahoma!* It starred Dick *Haymes, Vivian Blaine, Jeanne Crain (*b* 1925), Charles *Winninger, Dana Andrews (*b* 1909), and Fay Bainter (1892–1968). There was a new, more elaborate, and less effective version in 1962 with Tom Ewell (*b* 1909), Alice *Faye, Pamela Tiffin (*b* 1942), Pat *Boone, Bobby *Darin, and Ann-Margret (*b* 1941); with additional songs by Rodgers to his own lyrics.

Status Quo. British rock band, earlier known as the Spectres and Traffic Jam, and becoming Status Quo in 1967; with Francis Rossi (*b* 1949) (guitar and vocal), Rick [Richard] Parfitt (*b* 1948) (guitar and vocal), Alan Lancaster (*b* 1949) (bass and vocal), Roy Lynes (*b* 1943) (organ and vocal), and John Coghlan (*b* 1946) (drums). They had their first hit in 1968 with Rossi's 'Pictures of matchstick men', followed by 'Ice in the sun'. Faced with a decline in popularity, they adopted a driving boogie-woogie-based and unsophisticated style which produced 'Down the dustpipe' (1970); and they achieved a

No. 1 hit in 1974 with 'Down, down'. The group continued, with personnel changes, as a thriving unit that looked likely to maintain its position as the longest established rock band.

J. Shearlaw: *Status Quo: the Authorized Biography* (London, 1979).

Steele, Tommy [Hicks, Thomas] (*b* London, 17 Dec. 1936). British actor, singer, and dancer. He spent four years at sea on Cunard liners, in the meantime learning the guitar. Back in London in 1956, he played in Soho coffee bars with a *skiffle group, where he was heard by a Decca executive who offered him a recording if he could find a suitable song. This was provided by two of his skiffle-playing partners, Lionel *Bart and Mike Pratt, and 'Rock with the Cavemen' soon appeared in the hit list. The follow-up to this was 'Singing the blues', which remarkably became a No. 1 hit in the USA, replacing the Guy *Mitchell version. He made his first stage appearance in Sunderland in 1956, after which he came under the guiding care of Larry Parnes (1930–89), who suggested his new stage name, and brought him to London early in 1957.

Within the next four years he was a successful pop star with regular appearances on TV's **Six-Five Special*; and in four films, *The Tommy Steele Story* [USA: *Rock Around The World*] (1957); *The Duke Wore Jeans* (1958); *Tommy the Toreador* (1959), in which he found another hit in 'The little white bull'; and *It's All Happening* [USA: *The Dream Maker*] (1963). He appeared in pantomime, making his debut in this field in *Cinderella*, directed by Freddie Carpenter (1908–89); and at the Old Vic in *She Stoops to Conquer*. He now switched his activities to the musical stage, starring in **Half a Sixpence* (1963; NY, 1965; filmed 1967). He was in the Hollywood films *The Happiest Millionaire* (1967) and **Finian's Rainbow* (1968); followed by various straight roles on stage. He was in the stage version of *Hans Christian Andersen* (1974); had his own one-man show in 1979; starred in **Singin' in the Rain* (1983), and *Some Like It Hot* (1992).

J. Kennedy: *Tommy Steele* (London, 1958).

Steiner, Max [Maximilian Raoul] (*b* Vienna, 10 May 1888; *d* Beverly Hills, Calif., 28 Dec. 1971). Austrian-born composer and conductor. His grandfather had owned the Theater an der Wien in Vienna and was a friend of both Johann *Strauss and *Offenbach. He studied at the Imperial Academy of Music, under Mahler and others, and won the Gold Medal. He wrote and conducted his first operetta, *The Beautiful Greek Girl*, at the age of 14, and it ran for a year at the Orpheus Theatre. In 1904 he was conducting in England at *Daly's Theatre, the Adelphi Theatre, the Hippodrome, and the London Pavilion, and also at the Winter Garden Theatre in Blackpool. During 1911 he was conductor at the Alhambra in Paris. In 1914 he went to the USA to work as musical director for Florenz *Ziegfeld, both in New York and on tour. He became chief orchestrator for the publishers Harms, in which capacity he worked with Victor *Herbert, George *Gershwin, Jerome *Kern, and Vincent *Youmans, which gave him the true feel of American music.

He went to Hollywood in 1929 as musical director for RKO and conducted many films 1929–35, including the early Fred *Astaire–Ginger *Rogers musicals. His illustrious film scoring career began in 1929, with **Rio Rita*, followed by *Sons o' Guns* (1929), *Check and Double Check* (1930), and a steady stream of lesser productions. His output was enormous: more than a dozen films in 1931, 27 in 1932, 36 in 1933, including *Flying Down to Rio*, 37 in 1934; and so on into the 1960s. He won the first of several Academy Awards with *The Informer* (1935). In 1936 he joined Warner Brothers and, although musical credit was often given to Leo F. Forbstein as Head of Music, there was no mistaking Steiner's individual contributions to the company's products, both as arranger and composer. Along with Erich Wolfgang *Korngold he created a style of background music that combined classical skills with unashamedly romantic overtones that reached its apogee in the early 1940s when his scoring for films starring Bette Davis, Humphrey Bogart, and others combined with other factors to create the archetypal Warner Brothers film.

His most notable scores included: *Anne of Green Gables* (1934); *Becky Sharp* (1935); **Top Hat* (1935); *The Three Musketeers* (1935); **Follow the Fleet* (1935); *The Charge of the Light Brigade* (1936); *A *Star is Born* (1937); *Jezebel* (1938); *The Adventures of Tom Sawyer* (1938); *Angels with Dirty Faces* (1938); *The Oklahoma Kid* (1939); *Dark Victory* (1939); *Intermezzo* (1939); *Gone With the Wind* (1939)—'Tara's theme'; *They Died with their Boots On* (1942); *Now, Voyager* (1942; Academy Award)—'It can't be wrong'; *Casablanca* (1943); *Passage to Marseilles* (1943)—'Some day I'll meet you again'; *The Adventures of Mark Twain* (1944); *Since You Went Away* (1944; Academy Award); *Arsenic and Old Lace* (1944); *The Conspirators* (1944); *The Corn Is Green* (1945); *Rhapsody in Blue* (1945); *Mildred Pierce* (1945); *Tomorrow is Forever* (1945)—'Tomorrow is forever'; *Saratoga Trunk* (1946)—'As long as I live'; *A Stolen Life* (1946); *The Big Sleep* (1946); *The Beast With Five Fingers* (1947); *Cheyenne* (1947); *The Voice of the Turtle* (1947); *The Treasure of the Sierra Madre* (1948); *Key Largo* (1948); *Johnny Belinda* (1948); *A Kiss in the Dark* (1948); *April Showers* (1948); *The Fountainhead* (1949); *Beyond the Forest* (1949); *The Flame and the Arrow* (1950); *The Glass Menagerie* (1950); *Dallas* (1950); *Young Man With a Horn* (1950); *On Moonlight Bay* (1951); **The Jazz Singer* (1953); *By the Light of the Silvery Moon* (1953); *The *Desert Song* (1953); *The Caine Mutiny* (1954); *Battle Cry* (1955)—'Come next Spring'; *The Searchers* (1956); *Band of Angels* (1957); *Sugarfoot* (1957); *Marjorie Morningstar* (1958); *John Paul Jones* (1959); *A Summer Place* (1959)—'A summer place'; *Cash McCall* (1960); *Parrish* (1961); *Rome Adventure* (1962); and *Two on a Guillotine* (1965); a very selective list from more than 300 film scores that Steiner wrote.

Stept, Sammy H. (*b* Odessa, 18 Sept. 1897; *d* Los Angeles, 2 Dec. 1964). Russian-born American composer, conductor, and pianist. He left Russia with his family at the age of three and settled in Pittsburgh, where he studied classical music, ran a small band, and wrote songs. In 1925 he was leading a 5-piece band at the Claremont Café in Cleveland when, after five years' residence, they were replaced by Guy *Lombardo's Royal Canadians. Out of work, he went to New York to try his luck as a songwriter. Meeting with no immediate success he sang with a group called the Record Boys, who were one of the earliest vocal teams to broadcast. In 1928 he had his first song hit with 'That's my weakness now', and the following year formed his own publishing company in association with lyric-writer Bud Green. He wrote the score for *Shady Lady* (1933). His songs included: 'Ten little miles from town' (1938, Green), 'Don't sit under the apple tree' (with Charles *Tobias, 1942, *w* Lew *Brown), and 'This is worth fighting for' (1942).

Stevens, Leith (*b* Mount Moriah, Mo., 1909; *d* 1970). American composer. He made his debut as a pianist when he was 14, was conducting at 16, and became musical director of a ballet company. In 1928 he won a Juilliard Foundation Fellowship, and in 1930 joined CBS as an arranger. He composed and conducted for radio and had his own programme in 1939. He wrote his first film score in 1941 and, during the war from 1942, he was radio director for the Office of War Information. After the war he went to Hollywood and in 1950 became musical director of Paramount Films. His wife was killed in a crash in 1970, and he died of a heart-attack as a result.

He was a pioneer in the use of jazz in film background music and his scores included *Syncopation* (1942); *All My Sons* (1948); *The Five Pennies* (1949); *Destination Moon* (1950); *When Worlds Collide* (1951); *Beware My Lovely* (1952); *The Hitch-Hiker* (1953); *The Wild One* (1954); *The Scarlet Hour* (1955); *Julie* (1956); *The James Dean Story* (1957); *The Gene Krupa Story* (1958); *Hell to Eternity* (1960); *Mantrap* (1961); *The Interns* (1962); *The Night of the Grizzly* (1965); and *Chuka* (1967).

Stevens, Shakin' [Barratt, Michael] (*b* Ely, Wales, 4 Mar. 1948). British rock and roll singer with a genius for reviving and recapturing past styles. He started as a singer with a group, the Sunsets, and appeared on their album *A Legend* (1970). His vocal and physical resemblance to Elvis *Presley earned him the role in the musical *Elvis* (1977). He appeared on the revived *Oh Boy* TV show, then achieved a series of best-selling recordings with such items as 'Hot dog' (1980), 'Marie, Marie' (1980), 'This ole house (1981), a No. 1 hit written by Stuart Hamblen (*b* 1908), 'Green door' (1982), and 'Oh, Julie' (1983); with a successful album, *Lipstick, Powder and Paint* (1985).

Stewart, Rex William (*b* Philadelphia, 22 Feb. 1907; *d* Los Angeles, 7 Sept. 1967). American jazz cornettist and author. One of the few jazz horn players to remain loyal to the generally discarded cornet, he achieved an intense, powerful, and witty style on the instrument that was distinctly his own. He grew up in Washington DC and began playing at the age of 14 on Potomac riverboats. He worked with several bands before arriving in New York in 1921, where he was with Elmer Snowden (1900–73) 1925, and, on and off, with Fletcher *Henderson 1926–33. He led his own band 1933–4, and was with Luis *Russell 1934.

He became best-known through his effective work with the Duke *Ellington band 1934–45, featured on such classics as 'Portrait of Bert Williams' and 'Boy meets horn' (in which he demonstrated his special half-valve technique), and leading many fine Ellington small groups recorded under his name. He toured Europe in 1947, was in Australia in 1949, and played at the Eddie *Condon Club in the late 1950s. He became increasingly interested in broadcasting, lecturing, and writing, contributing articles to **Down Beat*, playing part-time and touring Europe in 1966. *Jazz Masters of the 30s* (New York, 1972) is a posthumous collection of his essays, from *Down Beat* and elsewhere, that includes some interesting insights on the Ellington band.

Stewart, Rod [Roderick David] (*b* London, 10 Jan. 1945). British singer and guitarist of Scottish descent. He worked at many odd jobs in his youth and at one time had the ambition to become a professional footballer. He indulged in a little vagrancy in Spain and elsewhere, meantime learning to play guitar, banjo, and harmonica. He started his musical career in Birmingham, and made a first recording for Decca in 1964, working with various groups before joining the *Faces in 1969, with whom he became a star attraction in live performances. He started making solo recordings with Mercury in 1969, and had his first No. 1 hit with 'Maggie May' in 1971. Flaunting his Scottish and football enthusiasms, and a physical image, his presence made the Faces into one of the major rock attractions. He left the group in 1975 and, settling in the USA, continued to record for Warner, achieving several No. 1 hits including 'Sailing' (UK, 1975), 'Tonight's the night' (USA, 1976), 'I don't want to talk about it' (UK, 1977), and 'Do ya think I'm sexy?' (1978). He remains one of the big solo stars of rock music and regularly attracts large audiences to his rampaging concerts.

Stolz, Robert (*b* Graz, 25 Aug. 1880; *d* Berlin, 27 June 1975). Austrian composer and conductor. His father was musical director of the Stadttheater in Graz and had been a pupil of Bruckner, who often visited their house. Showing early composing talents, he was given every encouragement in this direction; also studying the piano and giving his first recital at the age of seven with Brahms in the audience. He studied under Humperdinck and dedicated his op. 1, a piano piece written in 1895, to him. He became repetiteur at the Graz Opera. During a visit to Vienna, he heard *Die *Fledermaus* and met Johann *Strauss in his last year. This confirmed a growing interest in the world of operetta and he wrote and conducted his first Singspiel, *Studentenulke*, in Marburg, in 1901. He became Kapellmeister at the Stadttheater in Salzburg in 1902, where his operetta *Schön-Lorchen* was performed in 1903. He toured Russia that year and became Kapellmeister at the Deutsches Theater in Brünn (Brno) where he produced his first moderate success, *Manöverliebe*, in 1906 and married the singer Grete Holm.

Stolz's most important appointment came in 1905 when he became musical director at the famous Theater an der Wien in Vienna (a post he was to hold for 12 years), where he conducted the first season of *Lehár's *The *Merry Widow* (1905) and works by *Kálmán, *Fall, *Straus, and many others, becoming the leading conductor in the golden age of Viennese operetta. He continued to write his own operettas, including *Die lustigen Weiber von Wien* (1909) and *Das Glücksmädel* (1910), and many songs that achieved great popularity ('Im Prater blüh'n wieder die Bäume', 'Wien wird schön erst bei Nacht', 'Frühling in Wien', 'Wien, in dich ist die ganze Welt verliebt'); as well as becoming a pioneer composer of film music with *Der Millionenonkel* (starring Alexander Girardi) in 1913. He served in the Hoch-und-Deutschmeister regiment as bandmaster in the First World War and had operettas produced in Stuttgart, Vienna, Berlin, and Munich—*Das Lumperl* (1914); *Der Favorit* (1916); *Die schöne Katharin* (1916); *Die anständige Frau* (1917); and *Lang, lang ist's her* (1917).

After the war he wrote the popular foxtrot 'Salome', more successful songs, and a string of operettas like *Das Sperrsechserl* (1920), which had 2000 performances in Vienna; *Der Tanz ins Glück* (1921)—better known to the world as *Whirled into Happiness*, with its popular title song; *Eine Sommernacht* (1921; as *Night of Love*, NY, 1923); *Die Tanzgräfin* (1921); *Die Liebe geht um* (1922); and that great favourite *Mädi* (1922), which starred Hans Albers (1892–1960) at the Berliner Theater. After a financial failure with his Robert Stolz Bühne in 1924, he spent a period writing music for the Kabaret de Komiker in Berlin 1925–6.

From 1929 he became much involved in writing film music, starting with the score for the first European 'talkie' *Zwei Herzen im Dreivierteltakt* (1929; which became an operetta, *Der verlorene Walzer*, in 1933; reverting to the original title in 1948). He wrote *The Blue Train* (1927) for London. The years 1929 to 1938 were richly productive of film scores and operettas including *Peppina* (1930); his collaboration with *Benatzky on **Im weissen Rössl* (*White Horse Inn*, 1930); *Wenn di kleinen Veilchen blüh'n* (*Wild Violets*, 1932); *Venus in Seide* (1932); *Ein Mädel hat sich verlaufen* (1934); *Himmelblaue Träume* (1935); *Rise and Shine* (London, 1936)—with Fred *Astaire; returning to Vienna to produce his last pre-war operetta, *Die Reise um die Erde* (1937). Further films had included many favourite songs that were recorded by such stars as Marta Eggerth and Richard *Tauber. In 1938 he went to live in Paris and, when the Germans invaded the city in 1940, he managed to get a visa to the USA and went to Hollywood. His work became more international, with his film *Frühjahrsparade* (1935) being remade as *Spring Parade* (1940), with Deanna *Durbin trilling 'Waltzing in the clouds', 'It's foolish but it's fun', and 'When April sings'; and in Germany in 1955 as *Ein Deutschmeister*. After stepping in as deputy for Bruno Walter at Carnegie Hall, he made a series of American concert tours, conducted several Viennese operetta classics at the Cosmopolitan Opera 1942–3, and had his own Broadway production, *Mr Strauss Goes to Boston* (1945). He returned to Austria and continued his writings with *Frühling im Prater* (1949); *Das Glücksrezept* (1951); *Rainbow Square* (London, 1951); *Trauminsel* (1962); and the operetta version of *Frühjahrsparade* (1964). In his later years he was intensely active as a conductor and preserved his conducting art and his intimate knowledge and experience of Viennese light music in various recordings of operettas (including his own) and the music of the Strauss family.

R. Holm: *Im 3/4 Takt durch die Welt* (Linz, 1948). W-D. Brümmel and F. Van Booth: *Robert Stolz: Melodie eines Lebens: eine Komponist erobert die Welt* (Hamburg, 1967). O. Herbrich: *Robert Stolz: König der Melodie* (Vienna–Munich, 1975).

Stomp. Jazz composition, usually in a lively tempo, characterized by a rhythmic pattern alternating between block chords falling on and between the main beats, as in the opening phrases of 'Charleston', contrasted with more flowing sections in a ragtime style. The essential characteristic of the stomp is that the melodic emphasis closely follows the rhythmic pattern, so that the music is given a percussive and forceful character. Jelly Roll *Morton was a specialist in the form, writing 'Black Bottom stomp', 'King Porter stomp', and 'Kansas City stomp', all of which clearly illustrate the nature of the stomp; with their distinctive rhythmic patterns established in the opening bars.

Stone, [Val] **Fred** [Albert] (*b* Valmont, Col., 19 Aug. 1873; *d* Hollywood, 6 Mar. 1959). American actor, comedian, singer, and dancer. A nimble-footed hoofer who had a fruitful partnership with David Montgomery (1870–1917), as Montgomery and Stone, in such early musicals as *The Girl from Up There* (New York and London, 1901); *The *Wizard of Oz* (1903), one of their biggest triumphs; *The *Red Mill* (1906)—'The streets of New York'; *The Old Town* (1910); *The Lady of the Slipper* (1912); and *Chin-Chin* (1914). After his partner's death, Stone continued in *Jack o' Lantern* (1917); *Tip Top* (1920); *Stepping Stones* (1923)—'Raggedy Ann'; *Criss-Cross* (1926); *Ripples* (1930); *Smiling Faces* (1932); and many straight plays and films. His wife, Allene

Crater, and his daughters, Paula and Dorothy, were all actresses.

F. Stone: *Rolling Stone* (New York, 1945).

Stone, Lew [Steinberg, Louis] (*b* London, 28 May 1898; *d* London, 13 Feb. 1969). British bandleader, pianist, composer, and arranger. He took piano lessons at seven, but three years later decided to become a footballer. Eventually he combined his interests by playing for Corinthians and Casuals by day and working as a club pianist at night. While playing at the Cosmo Club he was asked to join Bert Ralton (1900–27) and his *Savoy Havana Band. In 1927 he gave up playing and became a full-time arranger, working for *Ambrose, Jack *Payne, Jay Whidden, and other bandleaders. He formed a band for Roy *Fox at the Monseigneur Restaurant in 1929 and, as pianist/arranger, took over as leader when Fox was ill. When Fox returned Stone was asked to continue with his own band and many of the Fox musicians joined him. He recorded for Decca and broadcast regularly from the Monseigneur from 1934 on.

He was musical director for British & Dominion Films 1931–2 and British National Films 1936–40, scoring, conducting, and sometimes appearing with his band. He moved to the Café de Paris and conducted West End shows: **On Your Toes* (1937); *Hide and Seek* (1937); and *Under Your Hat* (1939). During the war the band was resident at the Dorchester Hotel and toured service camps. He was musical director for **Annie Get Your Gun* at the London Coliseum 1947–50 and broadcast with pickup bands until the 1960s. His Monseigneur band remains deservedly famous; as well as featuring the singing of Al *Bowlly it showed fine musicianship and Stone's direction of his own arrangements put it well ahead of its time. He also wrote many film scores, songs, and orchestral pieces, and published *Harmony and Orchestration for the Modern Dance Band* (London, 1931).

K. Trodd: *Lew Stone: a Career in Music* (London, 1971).

Stop the World—I Want To Get Off. Musical, with music and words by Anthony *Newley and Leslie *Bricusse, at the Queen's Theatre, London, 20 July 1961, with the cast headed by Newley, where it ran for 556 performances. Newley, as one of the little men of the world, marries the boss's daughter (Anna Quayle) and rises to the top of the business heap. But after enjoying the spoils and the women he ends up wondering 'What kind of fool am I?' It was produced in New York (Shubert Theatre) 3 Oct. 1962, with Newley (later replaced by Joel *Grey) and Quayle. It was filmed in 1966 with Tony Tanner (*b* 1932) and Millicent *Martin, and again in 1978 as *Sammy Stops the World.*

Stothart, Herbert (*b* Milwaukee, 11 Sept. 1885; *d* Los Angeles, 1 Feb. 1949). American composer and conductor. He trained as a teacher and became a member of the faculty of Wisconsin University, teaching choral, musical, and dramatic studies. He left to become musical director for Broadway musicals, writing his own first show, *Always You*, in 1920. It was notable for also having the first libretto that Oscar *Hammerstein II had produced. From 1929 he was musical director for MGM and was responsible for the scoring and direction of many stage musicals that were turned into films, such as **Maytime*; **Naughty Marietta*; *The *Firefly*; **Rose-Marie*; *The *Merry Widow*; and *The *Wizard of Oz.*

His stage scores included: *Tickle Me* (1920); *Jimmy* (1920); *Daffy Dill* (1922); *Golden Dawn* (1927); and he was part-composer of: *Wildflower* and *Mary Jane McKane* (both with *Youmans, 1923); *Rose-Marie* (with *Friml, 1924); *Marjorie* (with *Romberg, 1924); *Song of the Flame* (with *Gershwin, 1925); and *Good Boy* (with *Ruby, 1928)—'I wanna be loved by you'. His film scores included: *The Rogue Song* (1930) and *Cuban Love Song* (1931), both with Lawrence Tibbett; *Mutiny on the Bounty* (1935); *David Copperfield* (1935), with W. C. Field; *Northwest Passage* (1940); *Pride and Prejudice* (1940); *Mrs Miniver* (1942); *Cairo* (1942); *Madame Curie* (1943); *A Guy Named Joe* (1944); **Kismet* (1944); *National Velvet* (1944); *The Picture of Dorian Gray* (1945); *If Winter Comes* (1947); and *The Three Musketeers* (1948).

Strachey, Jack (*b* London, 25 Sept. 1894; *d* London, 27 May 1972). British composer. Overcoming the disadvantages of a typical upper-class English education at Marlborough and University College, Oxford, he began his professional connection with the stage in 1919, when he took a job as pianist with the Quaints concert party, thereafter touring with many similar groups both in England and abroad. He began his West End career with *Dear Little Billie* (with H. B. Hedley, 1890–1931, 1925) and *Lady Luck* (1927). He worked for radio and, meeting Eric *Maschwitz, began to contribute to revues, having a classic hit with 'These foolish things' in *Spread it Abroad* (1936). He contributed to other revues and wrote: **New Faces* (1940); *Apple Sauce* (1940); *Moonshine* (1940); *More New Faces* (1941); *Flying Colours* (1941); *The Boltons Revue* (1948); and *Belinda Fair* (1949).

Strathspey. One of the most popular of Scottish dances, closely related to the *reel, the music being a slower version of this, with frequent exploitation of the *Scotch snap. The name derives from the strath (valley) of the River Spey, where it probably originated. The name seems to have been adopted about 1780, but the dance is probably older.

Stratton, Eugene [Rühlmann, Eugene Augustus] (*b* Buffalo, NY, 8 May 1861; *d* Christchurch, Hants., 15 Sept. 1918). American-born dancer and singer. Of Alsatian parentage, he made his stage debut at the age of 10 in partnership with a large man named Wesley, appearing at Shelby's Saloon in Buffalo as an acrobatic act called the Two Wesleys. The partnership lasted a year and a half before Eugene left to appear as a solo dancer under the name of Master Jean. He was with *Harrigan and Hart in New York for four months, then in a circus, before joining a blackface group known as the Four Arnolds which, in 1878, became part of Haverley's Mastodon Minstrels. At this point he decided he was not an Arnold and took the name of Stratton, suggested by one of the Haverley troupe.

He went to England in 1880 with the minstrels to appear at Her Majesty's Theatre, London, in July, and to tour England until mid-1881. When the company went back to the USA, Stratton remained behind and accepted a job with the Moore and Burgess Minstrels. He worked his way up from being a percussionist to their principal song-and-dance man, and by 1884 was one of the leading cornermen with Pony Moore; he married Moore's daughter Bella in 1883. He had his first big song hit with 'The whistling coon', written by Sam Raeburn. He whistled a chorus in a penetrating way he had learned as a boy, and kept it in his act for many years; after which it was recorded by Burt Shepard and others. Moore opened the Washington Music Hall in 1887, by which time Stratton was doing a double act, firstly with Tom Somers and later with Sam Raeburn. In 1892 he decided to try his luck as a solo act on the music-hall stage, first appearing at the Holborn in Irish guise—but still singing 'The whistling coon'. Almost deciding to return to the USA because of his lack of success, he reverted to blackface guise and a song 'I lub a lubly gal', and this was an immediate hit. In 1894 he found another hit in 'The dandy coloured coon' (by George *Le Brunn), followed by the same composer's 'The idler'. He was a graceful dancer of the soft-show variety and sang in a gentle, crooning manner.

In 1896 he made his first appearance in pantomime and began a notable association with the composer Leslie *Stuart, who found a special flair for imitation plantation songs and supplied him with such ideal hits as 'Is yer mammie always wid ye?', 'Little Dolly Daydream', 'The cake walk', and that imperishable classic, 'Lily of Laguna', which he first sang at the Oxford Music Hall on 30 July 1898. He included an American song, 'All coons look alike to me', in his repertoire and Stuart continued to supply him with such items as 'My little octoroon', 'The coon drum major', 'I may be crazy but I love you'; the two men became close friends with a common interest in horse racing. Stratton's health began to fail in 1914, and a long and illustrious career came to an end when he retired to Bournemouth in 1915. He recorded most of the Stuart songs at sessions in 1899, 1903, and 1911.

T. Barker: 'Eugene Stratton' in *Music-Hall* No. 12 (London, 1980).

Straus, Oscar (*b* Vienna, 6 Apr. 1870; *d* Ischl, 11 Jan. 1954). Austrian composer. His real family name was Strauss but he later dropped an 's' so as not to be bracketed with other famous Strausses. He studied music in Vienna and then in Berlin, where Max Bruch was one of his teachers. Among his early compositions were a violin sonata and a serenade for string orchestra. From 1895 he was musical director of various German theatres, at Mainz, Berlin, and elsewhere. He wrote a considerable amount of cabaret music and conducted at the Uberbrettl Cabaret in Berlin before he turned to operetta, initially writing in the *Offenbach mould. Gradually his true Viennese heritage was allowed to assert itself and he continued in the Strauss–Lehár tradition with richly romantic, waltz-imbued scores, *Ein *Walzertraum* (1907) being his first great success. His adaptation of George Bernard Shaw's *Arms and the Man* (without the author's full blessing), as *Der *tapfere Soldat (The Chocolate Soldier)* (1908), contained what was probably his best known song—the waltz 'My hero'.

He lived in Berlin until 1927, then in Vienna and Paris. He became a French citizen in 1939, but went to the USA in 1940, living in New York and Hollywood until 1948, when he returned to Europe. His working life was a long and full one, rounded off at the age of 80 by a place in the hit parade with 'La ronde de l'amour' which was written for the film *La Ronde* (1950). After some early works, he got into his stride with *Die lustigen Nibelungen* (1904); *Hugdietrich's Brautfahrt* (1906); and the popular *Ein Walzertraum* (1906); followed by *Mein junger Herr* (1907; London, 1926, as *My Son John); Didi* (1906); *Der *tapfere Soldat* (1908); *Das Tal der Liebe* (1909); *Venus im Grünen* (1910); *Die kleine Freundin* (1911); *The Dancing Viennese* (London, 1912); *Der blaue Held* (1912); *Love and Laughter* (London, 1913; Vienna, 1914, as *Rund um die Liebe*); *Die himmelblaue Zeit* (1914); *Die schöne Unbekannte* (1915); continuing to write a steady stream of minor works through the war years. After the war came *Der letzte Walzer* (1920); *Die Perlen der Cleopatra* (1923; London, 1925, as *Cleopatra*); *My Son John* (London, 1926); having his last big success with *Drei Walzer (Three Waltzes)* (1935); and *Die Musik kommt (1948;* as *Ihr erster Walzer*, 1950). The American cinema found suitable material in Straus's works and issued *Married in Hollywood* (originally *Hochzeit in Hollywood*) (1929); *A Lady's Morals* (1930); *The Smiling Lieutenant* (1931), based on *Ein Walzertraum; One Hour With You* (1932)—'We will always be sweethearts'; *Make a Wish* (1937); and *The Chocolate Soldier* (1941), with a much altered story.

B. Grun: *Prince of Vienna: the Life, the Times and the Melodies of Oscar Straus* (London, 1955).

Strauss, Eduard (*b* Vienna, 15 Mar. 1835; *d* Vienna, 28 Dec. 1916). Austrian conductor and composer. Son of Johann *Strauss I and brother of Johann II and Josef. Although it was intended that he should enter the consular service, he was, in fact, the best educated musically of the three brothers. He studied theory and composition under well-known teachers, also the violin and harp. It was perhaps as a result of this that his compositions remained competent but uninspired. He played in Johann's orchestra for a while, deputizing as conductor when his brother was visiting Russia and succeeding him as conductor of the court balls 1872–8. For many years he led the orchestra in the Volksgarten in the summer (and in the Musikverein in the winter) and became very popular as a conductor; but his awareness of his inferiority as a composer made him very jealous of Johann and caused much friction in the family. When Johann died he destroyed all his unpublished manuscripts (probably by arrangement with Josef). He toured many countries both with his own orchestra and Johann's which he took over in 1899, visiting London several times, beginning in 1885, and the USA in 1890 and 1900–1. In 1901 he disbanded the Strauss orchestra, which had been in existence from 1826, thus ending what had become a historic institution. Of his 300 or so compositions only a few have survived, including the waltzes 'Fesche Geister', 'Doctrinen', and 'Leuchtkäferl'n'; and the polkas 'Bahn frei' and 'Aus Lieb zu ihr'. He wrote his autobiography *Erinnerungen* (Vienna, 1906).

His son Johann III (*b* Vienna, 16 Feb. 1866; *d* Berlin, 9 Jan. 1939) also trained as a musician and conducted the music of the Strauss family. He travelled extensively and became very popular in the early 1900s. He wrote more than 50 waltzes (of which 'Dichterliebe' was the best), polkas and other dances, and an operetta, *Katze und Maus* (1898). The tradition was continued, in turn, by his nephew Eduard II (*b* Vienna, 24 Mar. 1910; *d* Vienna, 6 Apr. 1969) who led a Strauss orchestra, touring Europe and the USA and making recordings of the family music.

Strauss, Johann (*b* Vienna, 14 Mar. 1804; *d* Vienna, 25 Sept. 1849). Austrian composer, conductor, and violinist. Destined to become known as the 'Father of the Waltz', Johann had a troubled childhood. His mother died when he was seven and his father Franz, an innkeeper in the Leopoldstadt district of Vienna, married again in 1813 but was found drowned in the Danube in 1816. Johann and his sister were placed under the guardianship of Anton Müller, a tailor, though they continued to live with their stepmother. His guardian allowed him to have a violin, but would not allow him to take up music professionally and apprenticed him to a bookbinder, a trade that was not at all to his liking; but he finished his five years' apprenticeship and earned his journeyman's certificates. His desire to be a musician never wavered; he continued to practise his violin and at the age of 15 he joined the popular dance orchestra led by Michael Pamer (1782–1827) as a viola player. In the same orchestra he met, and became friends with, the violinist Josef *Lanner. In 1819, Lanner left to form his own trio with his brother Karl and Johann Drahanek; and soon Strauss joined him, to turn the trio into a quartet of two violins, viola, and guitar. After an initial struggle, their popularity grew and within three years the Lanner orchestra had 20 musicians and Strauss and Lanner shared the conducting, much of its repertoire being provided by Lanner, who was one of the first to give programmatic names to his dances. Johann Strauss also began to try his hand at composition. Eventually, as Strauss began to realize his own potential, they decided to go their separate ways; but they always remained friends and often worked together after the split.

In July 1825, Strauss married Anna Streim, the daughter of a wealthy innkeeper, and their son Johann was born three months later. For a while he taught but in 1826 he formed his own orchestra which rapidly grew. Eventually he was running several orchestras with more than 100 musicians working in various venues. At the age of 26 he signed a contract with the Sperl, Vienna's most famous dance hall and gardens, and a famous haunt for tourists. It was also visited by other composers who were fascinated by the new brand of Viennese popular music that was blossoming, ranging from Schubert, who was a great hand himself at such things, to Wagner, then aged 19 but already the composer of two operas, who wrote of the 'frenzied enthusiasm' that Strauss's waltzes evoked and which he found rather 'frightening'. The fame of Strauss spread abroad, and from 1833 he started to tour the principal cities of Europe. Anna was to bear five children, but Johann's constant flirtations and affairs led to their splitting up and his paying her a regular allowance. He had tried to discourage the musical inclinations of his sons, notably Johann, but, as in his own case, the urge was too strong. The younger Johann set up his own orchestra in 1844 and they continued to work in a spirit of reasonably friendly rivalry. In 1845 the father was appointed Hofballmusikdirektor, which put him on the side of the establishment and resulted in the famous 'Radetzky' march, supporting the Hapsburg dynasty which Johann II opposed. He visited England again in 1849. On his return to Vienna he played a concert at Onger's Casino; nine days later he had died of scarlet fever. He was given a fine funeral which 100,000 people followed.

The music of the elder Strauss is generally rated lower than the great waltzes and operettas that his gifted son wrote. Less inspired and less inventive, his music, clearly intended for dancing rather than listening to, is none the less pleasantly tuneful and full of rhythmic life and ingenuity, and has come in for an interested revival in recent years. From more than 250 published works, the most lasting, apart from the famous 'Radetzky' march of 1848, are the waltzes 'Kettenbrücke (1828), 'Wiener Tivoli-Rutsch' (1830), 'Bajaderen' (1832), 'Gabrielen' (1834), 'Cäcilien' (1840), 'Loreley-Rhein-Klänge' (1843), 'Die Schwalben' (1847), and 'Marien' (1847); the early 'Seufzer' galop (1828) remains popular; as does a gentle 'Annen' polka (1842), which only just fails to rival the younger Johann's tribute to his mother. The complete works (edited by his son) were published in 1889. Several posthumous operettas using Strauss's music have been staged, including *Strauss und Lanner* (1880); *Die tolle Therese* (1913); and *Walzer aus Wien* (arr. *Korngold, 1931).

R. Kleinecke: *Johann Strauss* (Leipzig, 1895). F. C. Lange: *Josef Lanner und Johann Strauss* (Vienna, 1904; rev. 1919). M. Schönherr and K. Reinöhl: *Johann Strauss Vater: ein Werkverzeichnis* (London–Vienna–Zurich, 1954).

Strauss, Johann II (*b* Vienna, 25 Oct. 1825; *d* Vienna, 3 June 1899). Austrian composer, conductor, and violinist. Eldest son of Johann *Strauss, he showed the same precocious talents and had written a waltz at the age of six. But his father, who knew the hazards of the musical life, was firmly against his following a musical career. Both he and his brother Josef were sent to the Polytechnic Institute after they left school, and Johann passed his book-keeping exams; but, while Josef continued his studies, the elder brother left in 1842 to take up a musical career. His mother had initially agreed with her husband about their sons' future but realized it was hopeless to try to change natural inclinations; she secretly encouraged him and arranged clandestine violin and harmony lessons, and when she and Johann Sr. separated the boy was allowed to follow his bent for music. At the age of 18 he formed his own orchestra and gave his first concert at Dommayer's Casino, a fashionable restaurant and dance hall, on 15 Oct. 1844. In the programme he included his father's best waltz 'Loreley-Rhein-Klänge' and his own three earliest works. The Strauss name drew a capacity crowd and further engagements quickly followed. Strauss had no wish to rival his father for whom, apart from his treatment of his mother, he had the greatest respect, and they were eventually reconciled and continued their musical activities in a spirit of friendly rivalry. When the elder Johann died in 1849, Johann Jr. took over the orchestra and amalgamated it with his own. Although he much preferred to work in Vienna he realized that tours were essential; they visited most cities of Europe and were particularly popular in France and Russia. He visited England in 1869 and paid his only visit to the USA in 1876, conducting mammoth concerts in New York and Boston.

He married three times: his first wife was the famous singer Henriette [known as Jetty] Treffz (1818–78). She helped him greatly in his career but they separated and, after she died, he quickly married a young actress, Angelika Dittrich [always known as Lili], from Cologne. But the marriage was a failure and they were divorced in 1887. In the meantime he had met and fallen for the widowed Adèle Strauss [*née* Deutsch and no relation] whom he married in 1887, and at last found true marital happiness. In the 1850s and 1860s waltzes and other dances poured from him and he and his orchestra were popular idols of the day. The French composer *Offenbach visited Vienna in 1863 and he and Strauss were asked to write rival waltzes for a Press Association ball. Strauss produced 'Morgenblätter' and Offenbach 'Abendblätter', the latter being adjudged superior, though it is now scarcely heard. It has been said (though without really firm foundation) that Offenbach suggested to Strauss that he should write operettas. It was some time before the suggestion was acted upon and then mainly because of the persuasions of Jetty. Having written the unproduced *Die lustigen Weiber von Wien*, his first staged piece was *Indigo und die vierzig Räuber*, produced at the Theater an der Wien 10 Feb. 1871. It was only moderately successful [70p] as was *Carneval in Rom* (1873) [81p]. However, he found an ideal libretto at last, and produced the greatest of all Viennese operettas *Die *Fledermaus* (1874), which was written at his villa in Hietzing. It has never ceased to enrapture the world. He continued to write operettas, though still often showing a lack of judgement where their plots were concerned, and produced in Vienna *Cagliostro in Wien* (1875); *Prinz Methusalem* (1877); *Blindekuh* (1878); *Das Spitzentuch der Königin* (1880); *Der lustige Krieg* (1881); *Eine Nacht in Venedig* (Berlin, 1883); *Der *Ziegeunerbaron* (1885); *Simplicius* (1887); *Ritter Pázmán* (1892); *Fürstin Ninetta* (1893); *Jakuba* (1894); *Der Waldmeister* (1895); and *Die Göttin der Vernunft* (1897). Later it was suggested that he turn his hand to ballet and he eagerly set to work to produce *Aschenbrödel*, from the Cinderella story, but he failed to complete it. It was later edited and completed by Josef Bayer (1852–1913) and was produced in Vienna in 1908. Strauss perspired heavily when conducting and, after a performance of *Die Fledermaus* in May 1899, caught a chill and died on 3 June. A magnificent funeral took place three days later.

In 1938 a document was found in St Stephen's Cathedral in Vienna which established that the parents of his grandfather Franz had been Jews, baptized later into the Christian faith. The music of other composers might be proscribed under Nazi rule but that 'The Blue Danube' and *Die Fledermaus* should be so treated was unthinkable. A forgery was prepared that omitted all the evidence and was published on 20 Feb. 1941 under the seal of the Third Reich, thus making the music fit for German ears. The original document was only returned to the cathedral in 1945.

Strauss's dance compositions approach the 500 mark. Pre-eminent are his great waltzes, many of which, unlike his father's, were written as concert pieces with elaborate introductions. Probably the most famous waltz ever written was 'An der schönen blauen Donau' ('The *blue Danube') which was first hailed as a masterpiece in Paris in 1867. It is closely rivalled by other substantial waltzes like 'Geschichten aus dem Wiener Wald' ('Tales from the Vienna Woods', 1868), 'Wein, Weib und Gesang' ('Wine, woman and song', 1869), 'Wiener Blut' ('Vienna blood', 1870), 'Rosen aus dem Süden' ('Roses from the South', 1878), 'Frühlingsstimmen' ('Voices of Spring', 1881), 'Tausend und eine Nacht' (1870), 'Wo die Zitronen blühn' (1874); and many more. His endlessly inspired polkas, galops, and other dances have proved equally lasting. Numerous stage productions have garnered his music to produce such scores as: *Sein* *erster Walzer* (1894); *Wiener Blut* (1899); *Gräfin Pepi* (1902); *Die Tänzerin Fanny Elssler* (1903)—'Draussen in Sievering'; *1001 Nacht* (1907); *Reiche Mädchen* (1909); *Der blaue Held* (1912); *Faschingshochzeit* (1921); *A Wonderful Night* (1929); *Walzer aus Wien* (1931); *Casanova* (1932); *Freut' euch des Lebens* (1932)—combining music by Johann and Josef (below); *The Great Waltz* (1934); and *The Three Waltzes* (1937). Ballets arranged from his music include *Le Beau Danube* (1924) and *Graduation Ball* (1940).

L. Eisenberg: *Johann Strauss: ein Lebensbild* (Leipzig, 1894). R. F. von Procháska: *Johann Strauss* (Berlin, 1900). E. Decsey: *Johann Strauss: ein Wiener Buch* (Stuttgart, 1922). S. Loewy: *Johann Strauss: der Spielmann von der blauen Donau* (Vienna, 1924). H. E. Jacob: *Johann Strauss: a Century of Light Music* (1937, trans. New York, 1939; London, 1940). J. Pastene: *Three-Quarter Time: the Life and Music of the Strauss Family of Vienna* (New York, 1951; repr. 1971). J. Wechsberg: *The Waltz Emperors: the Life and Times and Music of the Strauss Family* (London, 1973). M. Prawy: *Johann Strauss: Weltegesichte im Walzertakt* (Vienna, 1975). F. Mailer: *Johann Strauss (Sohn): Leben und Werk in Briefe und Dokumenten*, vol. 1 (Tutzing, 1983). P. Kemp: *The Strauss Family: Portrait of a Musical Dynasty* (Tunbridge Wells, 1985).

Strauss, Josef (*b* Vienna, 22 Aug. 1827; *d* Vienna, 21 July 1870). Son of Johann *Strauss and younger brother of Johann *Strauss II. Although he was a talented pianist in his youth, as well as a gifted painter and poet, he never wished to make music his career. His father would have liked him to become an army officer, but that did not appeal to him. Eventually he became an engineer and achieved some notable successes: he supervised the building of a dam and invented a street-cleaning machine that was used by the corporation of Vienna. He was all set for a promising engineering career, when his elder brother Johann, exhausted by overwork in Vienna and abroad, was forced to take a rest in order to avoid a complete breakdown. Josef was persuaded by his mother and Johann to take over the family orchestra, and, after a little coaching, he made his conducting debut on 23 July 1853. In the programme he included a work of his own which he significantly called 'Die Ersten und die Letzten' ('The first and the last'), but he was over-optimistic. With method and temperament totally different from his brother, sweetness and insinuating lyricism replacing fire and brilliance, he was a popular director and a pleasing composer. When Johann recovered he intended to go back to engineering but he was easily persuaded to work jointly with Johann. Concert announcements would often simply state that J. Strauss was conducting, without any indication as to whether it would be Johann or Josef. At first he used a baton, but eventually he led on the violin and conducted with the bow in the approved family fashion.

In 1857 he married his boyhood sweetheart, Karoline Pruckmayr, a gentle, unassuming girl who gave him ideal support, and he not only continued as Johann's deputy and partner, but also became a prolific composer himself, producing nearly 300 items and writing what many consider to be some of the most poetic waltzes and other items of the whole of the Strauss dynasty. The famous 'Pizzicato polka', first performed in St Petersburg in 1869, was the brothers' joint composition. He maintained his interest in engineering, painting, and poetry, but he was not a physically strong man or an assertive personality and so much work took a heavy toll. In April 1870 he went to Warsaw to conduct a gala concert. Because of faulty arrangements some incompetent deputy musicians had been engaged and this upset him so much that it brought on one of his fainting fits and he fell off the podium and injured his head. He never recovered and died a few weeks later.

Josef's most lasting works included the waltzes 'Dynamiden', 'Delirien', 'Transaktionen', 'Dorfschwalben aus Österreich', 'Marienklänge', 'Aquarellen', and 'Mein Lebenslauf ist Lieb und Lust'; and some very fine polkas including the haunting 'Die Libelle', 'Moulinet', 'Auf Ferienreisen', 'Plappermäulchen', 'Feuerfest', 'Ohne Sorgen', and 'Jockey'. He wrote an operetta, *Der Wärwolf* (1837); and several posthumous works based on his compositions included *Frühlingsluft* (1903); *Die Schwalben aus dem Wienerwald* (1906); *Der Rosenjüngling* (1906); *Das Teufelsmädel* (1908); *Freut' euch des Lebens* (1932)—combining music by Josef and Johann II; *Walzerträume* (1943); and *Die Straussbuben* (1946).

F. Mailer: *Josef Strauss: Genie Wider Willen* (Vienna, 1977).

See also books listed under STRAUSS, JOHANN I and II.

Strayhorn, Billy [William] (*b* Dayton, Ohio, 29 Nov. 1915; *d* New York, 31 May 1967). American composer, arranger, and pianist. He studied music in Pittsburgh and, having impressed Duke *Ellington with his work many years earlier, was asked to join the band as a lyric-writer and arranger in 1939. He was soon writing scores for some of the smaller group efforts, gradually becoming a complete writing partner to Ellington and sharing the piano work. He successfully absorbed the Ellington sound without losing his own style completely, but he was proud to claim that very often no one knew whether it was he or Ellington who had been the main hand behind certain compositions. His more progressive inclinations may perhaps have led Ellington into paths that he would not have trod by natural inclination, with his early jazz and ragtime background. The difference could be seen in their piano styles, with Strayhorn tending to be more impressionistic and introspective; yet even here it is often difficult to tell which is playing. If this all suggests an imitative rather than an original talent, we may never know the full answer as he spent all his life in the Ellington organization and was sadly missed there when he died. Ellington recorded a deeply-felt tribute to him in the album *And his Mother called him Bill* (1967).

The writings clearly credited to Strayhorn

included 'Lush life' (1938), 'Take the A train' (1941)—latterly used as the Ellington band's signature tune, 'Passion flower' (1941), 'Chelsea Bridge' (1941), 'Johnny come lately' (1942), 'Midriff' (1946), 'Overture to a jam session' (1946), 'Progressive gavotte' (1947), 'Swamp drum' (1951), 'Rock-skippin' at the Blue Note' (1951), 'Boo-dah' (1953), 'Snibor' (1956), 'Ballade for very sad and very tired lotus eaters' (1956); and their numerous credited joint efforts included 'Perfume Suite' (1945), 'A Drum is a Woman', 'Newport Jazz Festival Suite', and 'Such Sweet Thunder' (all 1956).

Street organ. A portable organ with the sounding mechanism actuated by a revolving cylinder or barrel which was hand-turned. The first ones that appeared at the beginning of the 19th century were small 'portative' instruments that could be easily carried and were supported by a sling or a collapsible leg. They were also referred to at the time as 'belly' organs in reference to their usual playing position. As the organs grew bigger and more elaborate they were put on wheels. There was a great vogue for them in the mid- and late 19th century but since then, except in Holland, they are rarely seen except in museums. The Dutch love of the street organ ('draaiorgel') is still perpetuated, with elaborately decorated instruments regularly seen in the streets of cities and towns; each with a proudly flaunted name appropriate to its decorative theme, repertoire, and maker. They remain mostly hand-cranked but, after 1892, the barrel-operated instrument was generally replaced by the book organ using a series of connected punched cards, a system invented by Anselmo Gavioli. The larger stationary steam organs are discussed under *mechanical organs.

Street piano. Mechanical instruments with a similar mechanism to the street or barrel organ wherein a hand-turned cylinder with inserted pins operated, in this instance, a piano action. By moving the barrel or cylinder horizontally a new set of pins was brought into line with the hammer action to select a new tune. Street pianos are often incorrectly referred to as barrel organs. They were a popular feature of Victorian life and provided both entertainment and employment. Various makers contrived distinctive tones for their instruments and there were many varieties such as the Mandolin piano and the Tremolo. The instruments were generally owned by firms who hired them out to the people who pushed them around the street as a living; such a firm was still operating in Chelsea in the 1960s. The earliest models made in the 1840s were specifically known as cylinder pianos and were mainly manufactured in Italy. They were popular throughout Europe and are still to be heard in Spain.

Streisand, Barbra [Barbara Joan] (*b* New York, 24 Apr. 1942). American singer and actress. She studied acting for a short time in New York, started her career in Greenwich Village clubs, and appeared in *Another Evening with Harry Stoones* (1961). She made her Broadway debut in *I Can Get it for you Wholesale* (1962), singing 'Miss Marmelstein'; and then had a tremendous success in **Funny Girl* (1964), in which she portrayed Fanny *Brice ('People', 'Please don't rain on my parade'), a part she also played in London, 1966, and in the 1968 film for which she won an Academy Award. She continued an illustrious musical film career with **Hello, Dolly!* (1969); **On a Clear Day You Can See Forever* (1970); *Funny Lady* (1975)—'How lucky can you get'; and *A *Star is Born* (1976)—'Evergreen' (of which she was part writer). She was also in many non-musical films including *The Owl and the Pussycat* (1970); the hilarious *What's Up Doc?* (1972); *Up the Sandbox* (1972); *The Way We Were* (1973)—in which she sang the sound-track title-song; *For Pete's Sake* (1974); *The Main Event* (1979); and *Yentl* (1983). She has recorded many albums of songs.

R. Jordan: *Streisand: Unauthorized Biography* (New York, 1976). J. Spada: *Streisand: the Woman and the Legend* (New York, 1981). D. Zec and A. Fowles: *Barbra: a Biography of Barbra Streisand* (Sevenoaks, 1982). S. Considine: *Barbra Streisand* (New York, 1985).

Strict-tempo dance music. A systematic approach to music for the ballroom, aimed at supplying music with a regular pulse and the correct designated tempos for the various dances. A great deal of the pioneering work in this field was done by Victor *Silvester, World's Dancing Champion in 1922, who went on to form his strict-tempo dance orchestra in 1934, first broadcasting in 1937, and starting the BBC Dancing Club in 1941.

Stride piano. A style of piano playing popularized in the 1930s, particularly associated with a school of players in Harlem, New York, that included James P. *Johnson and Fats *Waller, and continued more sparingly in the playing of Art *Tatum, Duke *Ellington, and later mainstreamers. The style came into popular music in the playing of Charlie *Kunz, Carroll *Gibbons, Billy *Mayerl, and others. The name derives from the striding movement of the left hand, which plays a steady bass of tenths or even more extended chords, often with a delayed effect on the second note. It gave the music a very propulsive sort of swing.

Strike Up the Band. Musical play with score by George *Gershwin and book by George S. *Kaufman. It was seen in Long Branch, NJ, 19 Aug. 1927, and in Philadelphia, 5 Sept. 1927, but closed before it reached Broadway, the book by Kaufman being deemed too harshly satirical for those days, dealing with a tariff war over chocolate between Switzerland and the USA, and even more harshly with American politicians. Slightly modified by Morrie Ryskind (1895–1985), with lyrics by Ira *Gershwin, it reached New York (Times Square

Theatre) 14 Jan. 1930, with a new cast that included Bobby *Clark and Paul McCullough, Blanche *Ring, and a band led by Red *Nichols which included Benny *Goodman, Glenn *Miller, Jimmy *Dorsey, Jack *Teagarden, and Gene *Krupa. It was effective enough to set off a whole series of politically slanted satirical musicals. Gershwin's songs included 'A typical self-made American', 'If I became the President', 'Mademoiselle in New Rochelle', 'I mean to say', 'Soon', 'Strike up the band', and 'I've got a crush on you'. It was filmed in 1940 with Judy *Garland, Mickey *Rooney, and the Paul *Whiteman Orchestra.

Stromberg, John (*b* New York, 30 Sept. 1853; *d* New York, 12 July 1902). American composer. He was to become especially associated with the now historic *Weber and Fields productions. He originally worked with Witmark, the music-publishers, where he wrote a song 'My best girl's a corker', which had considerable success. On the strength of this he was engaged by Weber and Fields to conduct and write for the series of burlesques they were about to launch in their new Music Hall. The ten shows that he wrote for them brought him a considerable fortune. They began as a mixture of vaudeville and burlesque, with the first half always a satirical pastiche of some popular show, and the second half a variety programme, the whole thing featuring the comical duo. In the first production, *The Art of Maryland* (1896), David Belasco's *The Heart of Maryland* was travestied. The second, *The Geezer* (1896), took a swipe at Sidney *Jones's *The Geisha*. In 1899, with *The Whirl-i-Gig*, the variety part of the show was dropped and it became entirely burlesque.

The shows became tremendously fashionable and popular, with Weber and Fields paying some of the highest salaries offered then on the Broadway stage. They made stars of Fay *Templeton, Lillian *Russell, and many more. The series included *The Glad Hand* (1897); *Pousse Café* (1897); *Hurly-Burly* (1898); *Helter-Skelter* (1899); *Fiddle-Dee-Dee* (1900)—'Ma blushin' Rosie', 'I'm a respectable working girl'; *Hoity-Toity* (1901); and *Twirly-Whirly* (1902). Stromberg was working on this last show when he was found dead in his New York apartment. It was believed that he had committed suicide and in his pocket there was the manuscript of one of his best songs, 'Come down ma evenin' star', which he had written for Lillian Russell. When the show opened two months later she was so upset that she was unable to finish singing it; but it became the song with which she was chiefly associated.

Strouse, Charles [Louis] (*b* New York, 7 June 1928). American composer. He had piano lessons at school and studied harmony, then, after graduating from the Eastman School, Rochester University, 1947, studied music 1947–53 with Aaron Copland and Nadia Boulanger. He met Lee *Adams in 1950 and formed a songwriting partnership, contributing to such revues as *Catch a Star* (1955); *Shoestring Revue* (1956); *The Littlest Revue* (1956); *Kaleidoscope* (1957); and in London *Fresh Airs* (1956). He earned a living as a pianist in clubs and making vocal arrangements until their hit musical **Bye Bye, Birdie* was staged in 1960 and filmed in 1963. This was followed by *All American* (1962); **Golden Boy* (1964); *It's a Bird, It's a Plane, It's Superman* (1966); and **Applause* (1970). Thereafter he wrote the book and music of *Six* (1971); *I and Albert* (London, 1972); and with Martin Charnin, **Annie* (1977); followed by three failures—*A Broadway Musical* (1978), *Bring Back Birdie* (1981), and *Dance A Little Closer* (1983). He wrote music for the films *The Mating Game* (1959); *The Night They Raided Minsky's* (1964); *Alice in Wonderland or What's a Nice Kid Like You Doing in a Place Like This* (1965); *Bonnie and Clyde* (1967); and *There Was a Crooked Man* (1970).

Strut. A swaggering rooster-like dance step, an exaggerated walk with legs kicked high and body held back, a basic movement of dances like the *cakewalk. Also the name of a composition with this strutting sort of character.

Stuart, Leslie [Barrett, Thomas Augustine] (*b* Southport, Lancs., 15 Mar. 1864; *d* Richmond, Surrey, 27 Mar. 1928). British composer. He started his professional musical life as organist of the Roman Cahtolic cathedral in Salford, holding this post for seven years. He was obviously much taken with the minstrel music of his day, for he started writing songs in that vein that perhaps got closer to the style than many of the American writers of the time did. In order to continue his respectable role in music he wrote many of the earlier songs under the name of Lester Barrett and, later, Leslie Stuart. These included 'Sweetheart May' (1894) and 'By the sad sea waves' (1894). In 1895 he went to London and found little difficulty in moving into the world of theatre music. He contributed 'The military model', 'Trilby will be true', and his first big hit, 'Soldiers of the Queen', to *An *Artist's Model* (1895); 'The little mad'moiselle' to *The *Shop Girl* (1895); and 'She's an English girl' to *The Ballet Girl* (1897). He found an ideal interpreter for his 'coon' songs in the American blackface minstrel singer and dancer Eugene *Stratton, then beginning to make his name in the music-halls. They became great friends and Stuart gave Stratton such well-suited songs as 'Is yer mammie always with yer' (1896), 'Little Dolly Daydream' (1897), the great music-hall classic 'Lily of Laguna' (1898), and 'I may be crazy but I love you' (1902).

The fine score that he wrote for **Florodora* (1899) took musical comedy music a firm step forward. It was perhaps his strange affinity with the new spirit of American music that made it so influential in the USA. The famous sextet, 'Tell me, pretty maiden', became all the rage, and composers ranging from Eubie *Blake to Jerome *Kern and Richard *Rodgers all paid tribute to the influence and inspiration they found in *Florodora*. Despite this it is underrated in Stuart's own country and never performed today. He continued with the lesser, but still pleasant, scores for *The Silver Slipper* (1901); *The School Girl* (1903); *The Belle of Mayfair* (1906); *Havana* (1908); *Peggy* (1911); *Captain Kidd* (1910); and *The Slim Princess* (1911). In the end he rather dissipated his talents through his love of horse racing and alcohol. In 1926 he appeared on stage in a music-hall revival tour with Billy *Merson and others and, as he sat at the piano and played his old songs, the audience suddenly realized who he was, and there was much sincere applause. Fortunately he also recorded the selection for Columbia that same year and we are able to experience the vintage charm of his music at first hand.

S. Hyman: 'The Florodora Man' in *Sullivan and his Satellites* (London, 1978). T. Staveacre: 'Leslie Stuart' in *The Songwriters* (London, 1980).

Student Prince [in Heidelberg], The. Operetta with music by Sigmund *Romberg and book by Dorothy Donnelly (1880–1928), produced by the *Shuberts at Jolson's 59th Street Theatre, New York, 2 Dec. 1924, where it ran for 608 performances. Based on the play *Old Heidelberg* by Rudolf Bleichman, a version of *Alt-Heidelberg* by William Meyer-Förster. The full title above was used during the first New York production but dropped later. The story went wholeheartedly back to the world of 1860 and a tale of a prince falling in love with a waitress in his student days. Returning as king he is unable to find his golden youth again.

Romberg produced music in the old operetta manner that pleased audiences then and still keeps the show a favourite among amateurs—'Golden days', 'Drinking song', 'Deep in my heart, dear', 'Serenade', and 'Just we two'. The show toured the USA from 1925 to 1933 with revivals in 1931 and 1943. It came to London (His Majesty's Theatre) 3 Feb. 1926, with Harry *Welchman in the leading role, and had an initial run of only 96 performances, but it was frequently revived, notably in a John *Hanson production of 1968. The original play was filmed in 1927, and a musical version came in 1954 with Edmund Purdom (*b* 1924), sung by Mario *Lanza, and Ann Blyth.

Styne, Jule [Stein, Julius Kerwin] (*b* London, 31 Dec. 1905). American composer and producer. He went with his family to the USA when he was eight and settled in Chicago. He studied at the Chicago College of Music and appeared as a piano soloist with the Chicago Symphony Orchestra at the age of nine; continued a successful concert career; and, in his teens, organized his own band at the Bismark Hotel in Chicago. His first song hit, published under the name of Stein, was 'Sunday' in 1926. He became an arranger and found plenty of work in Hollywood, including employment as vocal coach with 20th Century Fox. New York East-sider Sammy *Cahn was to become his main collaborator; but he also wrote with others, including Frank *Loesser, Leo Robin, E. Y. *Harburg, and Stephen *Sondheim.

He was a regularly successful writer of stage shows which included **High Button Shoes* (1947)—'Papa, won't you dance with me', 'I still get jealous'; **Gentlemen Prefer Blondes* (1949; filmed 1953)—'A little girl from Little Rock', 'Diamonds are a girl's best friend'; *Two on the Aisle* (1951); *Hazel Flagg* (1953; filmed 1955 as *Living it Up*); **Peter Pan* (1954); **Bells Are Ringing* (1956; filmed 1960)—'Just in time', 'The party's over'; *Say, Darling* (1958); **Gypsy* (1959; filmed 1962)—'Let me entertain you', 'Some people', 'Small world', 'Everything's coming up roses'; *Do Re Mi* (1960)—'Make someone happy'; *Subways are for Sleeping* (1961); **Funny Girl* (1964; filmed 1968)—'People', 'Don't rain on my parade'; *Fade In—Fade Out* (1964); *Hallelujah, Baby!* (1967); *Darling of the Day* (1968); *Look to the Lilies* (1970); and *Sugar* (1972)—'Sugar'.

His extensive film contributions included *Hold that Co-Ed* (1938; *Hold that Girl* in UK); *Stop, Look and Love* (1939); *Sing, Dance, Plenty Hot* (1940; *Melody Girl* in UK); *Melody and Moonlight* (1940); *Angels with Broken Wings* (1941); *Sailors on Leave* (1941); *Beyond the Blue Horizon* (1942)—'Pagan lullaby' (Loesser); *Sweater Girl* (1942)—'I don't want to walk without you' (Loesser); *Sleepy Time Gal* (1942); *The Powers Girl* (1942)—'The lady who didn't believe in love' (Gannon); *Youth on Parade* (1942)—'I've heard that song before' (Cahn), 'You're so good to me' (Cahn); *Johnny Doughboy* (1943); *Salute for Three* (1943); **Knickerbocker Holiday* (1944); *Step Lively* (1944)—'Come out, wherever you are' (Cahn); *Follow the Boys* (1944)—'I'll walk alone' (Cahn); *Carolina Blues* (1944)—'There goes that song again' (Cahn); *Anchors Aweigh* (1945)—'The charm of you' (Cahn), 'I fall in love too easily' (Cahn); *Tonight and Every Night* (1945)—'Cry and you cry alone' (Cahn); *Stork Club* (1945); *Tars and Spars* (1946); *The Sweetheart of Sigma Chi* (1946)—'Give me five minutes more' (Cahn); *The Kid from Brooklyn* (1946)—'I love an old-fashioned song' (Cahn), 'Pavlova' (Cahn); *It Happened in Brooklyn* (1947)—'Time after time' (Cahn); *Ladies Man* (1947); *Glamour Girl* (1947); *Romance on the High Seas* (1948; *It's Magic* in UK)—'It's magic' (Cahn); *Two Guys from Texas* (1948; *The Texas Knights* in UK); *It's a Great Feeling* (1949); *The West Point Story* (1950; *Fine and Dandy* in UK); *Meet Me After the Show* (1951); *Two Tickets to Broadway* (1951); *My Sister Eileen* (1955); *Three Coins in the Fountain* (1954)—'Three coins in the fountain'; and *What a Way to Go* (1964).

T. Taylor: *Jule: the Story of Composer Jule Styne* (New York, 1979).

Suesse, Dana (*b* Kansas City, 3 Dec. 1909; *d* 1988). American composer, pianist, and author. She studied in New York to be a concert pianist and made her debut at Carnegie Hall with Paul *Whiteman and the Philharmonic Orchestra, performing her own 'Jazz Concerto', which was commissioned by Whiteman in 1932. She was the writer of various concert works, including 'Symphonic Waltzes', and a number of songs: 'Whistling in the dark' (1931), 'My silent love' (1932), 'The night is young and you're so beautiful' (1939), 'Yours for a song' (1939), and 'You're too good to be true' (1939). She contributed to *Ziegfeld Follies* (1934)—'You oughta be in pictures', 'Moon about town'; and the films *Sweet Surrender* (1935)—'Love makes the world go round', and *The Seven Year Itch* (1955)—'The girl without a name'.

Sugar Babies. Musical revue with score by Jimmy *McHugh and others, lyrics by Dorothy *Fields and others, conceived by Ralph G. Allen (*b* 1934) who also wrote the sketches. It was a revival of the spirit of American vaudeville of the 1905–30 period, and became a showcase for Mickey *Rooney, who appeared in numerous guises and also presented many old Jimmy McHugh songs with Ann Miller (*b* 1919). The show lasted on tour for $3\frac{1}{2}$ years and had 1208 performances on Broadway at the Mark Hellinger Theatre, from 8 Oct. 1979. The revived songs included such classics as 'Exactly like you', 'I can't give you anything but love', 'On the sunny side of the street', and 'Don't blame me'.

Sullivan, Arthur (*b* London, 13 May 1842; *d* London, 22 Nov. 1900). British composer. Son of Thomas Sullivan, clarinettist and later bandmaster of the Royal Military College, Sandhurst, he was able to pick up an early knowledge of orchestration when his father took him to the band rehearsals; and, showing a strong inclination for music, he was entered as a chorister of the Chapel Royal. He became the principal soloist and sold his first composition at the age of 11, a sacred song, 'O Israel'. He won a Mendelssohn scholarship to the Royal Academy of Music and, after two years there, continued his studies at the Leipzig Conservatory where he met Liszt and Spohr; one of his fellow-students was Grieg. While there he composed incidental music for *The Tempest* which was first performed in England in 1862 and quickly made his reputation. His introduction to the theatre came when he was appointed organist at the Royal Opera House, Covent Garden. He wrote many ballads, including settings of Shakespeare's 'Orpheus with his lute' and 'O mistress mine', wrote his first symphony in 1863 and was looked upon as the up-and-coming young 'serious' composer of his day. But in 1867 he disturbed his serious colleagues by collaborating in a 'comic frolic', **Cox and Box*, inspired by the one-act works of *Offenbach, with words by F. C. Burnand; following this by writing *The Contrabandista* with the same author.

In 1869, Sullivan met the playwright W. S. *Gilbert for the first time, at a rehearsal of a work by Frederic *Clay, but it was not until 1871 that they first collaborated on **Thespis or The Gods Grow Old*, an idea fostered by John Hollingshead. The work was only a moderate success and they did not work together again until 1875. In the meantime Sullivan was occupied in uplifting British music with his oratorio *The Light of the World* (much admired by Queen Victoria), and in academic life.

The man who was to bring Gilbert and Sullivan firmly together and change the composer's course for ever was Richard D'Oyly *Carte. A chance meeting with Gilbert at the Royalty Theatre, where Carte was manager, a suggestion that a new comic opera was needed, the production of a ready-made script by Glbert (who had written it for Carl Rosa), and Carte's idea that Sullivan should set it; this was the beginning of the great comic opera partnership. **Trial by Jury* was the result, first produced as filler for Offenbach's *La *Périchole* on 25 Mar. 1875, and immediately hailed as the reawakening of English comic opera—as indeed it was. Sullivan returned to his academic world to become conductor of the Glasgow Orchestral and Choral Union and head of the newly founded National Training School of Music (now the Royal College of Music), and to write 'The lost chord' which was to become the most popular ballad of the century. But the seeds had been sown; in 1877, Gilbert and Sullivan collaborated again on *The *Sorcerer* which was produced at the Opera-Comique Theatre off the Strand. This two-act work was far from their best but it was a prototype of many operettas to come. By 1878, Sullivan seems to have realized that his real future lay in the theatre and an oratorio for the Leeds Festival was put aside to write the first of the full-length G & S masterpieces, **HMS Pinafore*. After a slow start, business suddenly picked up and the show became a fashionable success: during its run it is said that 10,000 copies of the piano score were being sold daily. A quarrel among various would-be promoters led to a firm agreement of partnership between Sullivan, Gilbert, and D'Oyly Carte. The next operetta was more or less a variation on *Pinafore*—it was *The *Pirates of Penzance* which someone described as *Pinafore* on dry land. The music was far more ambitious, however. It was first produced in New York with a simultaneous performance at the Royal Bijou Theatre in Paignton. This was followed by **Patience* (1881), a rich satire on the aesthetic movement, making history as the first show to be lit by electric light. Next came **Iolanthe*; the partnership grew rich and Sullivan was given a knighthood by his great admirer Mr Gladstone.

In spite of all this, Sullivan was still torn between the two worlds of music. It was ten years since he had written an oratorio and many people in high social, political, and musical places saw him as a deserter from the true cause. It was the niggling feelings of guilt that perhaps started the disagreements with Gilbert over the plots of the operas. But again Sullivan put aside more lofty work to write the still underrated **Princess Ida*. In 1884 he wrote to Gilbert to say that he could not possibly write any more works in the same vein and contentious letters passed between them. Sullivan wanted no more supernatural, topsy-turvy elements: and it seems he was right, for his objections led to Gilbert's writing *The *Mikado* (1882), which became their most popular work; it ran for 672 performances and still draws the largest audiences at both professional and amateur productions. In 1886, Sullivan was pleased by the praises for his new Leeds Festival oratorio *The Golden Legend*, and even with **Ruddigore*, which he thought contained a better class of music than the previous operettas. Gilbert also thought it was one of his best librettos, though many would disagree. In 1888 came the more serious *The Yeomen of the Guard*. They quarrelled again while it was being written but he was put into a better frame of mind when *The Golden Legend* was performed by the Queen's command at the Albert Hall before an audience of 1,000. The Queen pointedly remarked: 'At last I have heard *The Golden Legend*, Sir Arthur. You ought to write a grand opera—you would do it so well.' This turned Sullivan against his popular successes once more, and he rejected all Gilbert's new ideas. But once more they buried the hatchet and got on with the delightful *The *Gondoliers*, one of the brightest works they produced, which was seen in 1889. In 1890 came the worst quarrel of all; over a carpet costing £500 that D'Oyly Carte had installed in the Savoy Theatre. Sullivan sided with Carte against Gilbert, who thought the expense should be shared by the authors. By now Sullivan had got his teeth into his grand opera and it was produced at Carte's new Royal English Opera House (now the Palace Theatre) in 1891. *Ivanhoe* managed 155 performances, but ended before it was intended to, and upset the theatre's plans. At this time *The Gondoliers* was being performed for Queen Victoria at Windsor, which pleased Gilbert but not Sullivan. The partners continued with **Utopia Limited* (1893), but the spirit was lacking and it has never been looked upon with the same affection as the earlier works. Revivals of these were going on everythere. Sullivan looked for new collaborators, writing *The Beauty Stone* (1898) with A. W. Pinero and J. Comyns Carr, and, with Basil *Hood, *The Rose of Persia* (1899) which had a very moderate reception. He then started on another work with Hood, *The *Emerald Isle*, but he was too ill to finish it: instead, it set another composer, Edward *German, on his path to fame. Sullivan died in November 1900 and Richard D'Oyly Carte died a few weeks later.

The world now brackets Sullivan with Johann *Strauss II and Jacques *Offenbach as one of the great pioneering composers of operetta: and it is interesting to compare their achievement. Offenbach was immensely prolific and produced the most sparkling music of the three in typically French vein, but his output was very uneven and even some of his best works have a makeshift quality about them. Strauss wrote, in typically Viennese vein, the greatest operetta of all in *Die *Fledermaus*, but rarely rose to the same heights. Sullivan, typically English and greatly helped by the consistency of W. S. Gilbert's wit, turned out more substantial and lasting successes than either of them. His genius for the comic song and for musical parody was unequalled. The only lack in Sullivan's scores is in the romantic side. He was not good at the sentimental song or the gracious waltz, as both Offenbach and Strauss were; and he produced little, by comparison, that could be sung by operatic tenors and sopranos. The Savoy operas were, and have remained, more or less a unique phenomenon; adored by many but disliked by some who are out of sympathy with their persistent flavour.

A. Lawrence: *Sir Arthur Sullivan: Life Story, Letters and Reminiscences* (London, 1899). W. J. Wells: *Souvenir of Sir Arthur Sullivan* (London, 1901). H. S. Wyndham: *Arthur Sullivan* (London, 1903). B. W. Findon: *Sir Arthur Sullivan: his Life and Music* (London, 1904). H. S. Wyndham: *Arthur Seymour Sullivan (1842–1900)* (London, 1926). N. Flower and H. Sullivan: *Sir Arthur Sullivan, his Life, Letters and Diaries* (London, 1927). T. F. Dunhill: *Sullivan's Comic Operas* (London, 1929). G. Hughes: *The Music of Arthur Sullivan* (London, 1960). P. Young: *Sir Arthur Sullivan* (London, 1971). R. Allen: *Sir Arthur Sullivan: Composer and Personage* (New York, 1975). S. Hyman: *Sullivan and his Satellites* (London, 1978). A. Jacobs: *Arthur Sullivan: a Victorian Musician* (Oxford–New York, 1984).

See also books listed under GILBERT and GILBERT AND SULLIVAN.

Sullivan, Joe [Joseph Michael] (*b* Chicago, 4 Nov. 1906; *d* San Francisco, 13 Oct. 1971). American jazz pianist and composer. He was educated at the Chicago Conservatory, and played in vaudeville 1923–5. He was pianist with many early Chicago groups 1925–8 and from 1928 with Red *Nichols and others; Russ *Colombo 1932–3; Louis *Armstrong and Bob *Crosby 1936 and 1939; and a regular club soloist. He played in films, notably accompanying Bing *Crosby, and led his own group 1939–42. He had a long residence at the famous Onyx Club and was at the Hangover Club from 1955. His best-known compositions were 'Gin mill blues' (1933), 'Little Rock getaway' (1934), 'Just strollin'' (1935), and 'Minor mood' (1936).

Sullivan, Maxine [Williams, Marietta] (*b* Homestead, Pa., 13 May 1911; *d* New York, 7 Apr. 1987). American singer. At the Onyx Club, 52nd Street, New York, 1937–8, she had a special hit with her rendering of 'Loch Lomond' which she sang in a soft, soothing way with a strict rhythm. She recorded it with Claude *Thornhill in 1937. She appeared in the film *Going Places* (1937), singing 'Jeepers creepers', with Louis *Armstrong; was in *St Louis Blues* (1938); and appeared on Broadway with Armstrong and Benny *Goodman in *Swingin' the Dream* (1939). In 1938 she married bassist/bandleader John *Kirby and they starred in a radio series, *Flow Gently, Sweet Rhythm*, from 1940. She toured England 1948 and 1954. Having divorced Kirby she married Cliff Jackson in 1950 and retired to become a nurse, but reappeared in 1958 and was with the World's Greatest Jazz Band in 1969 and 1973. She received an award for her part in the musical *My Old Friend* in 1979.

Sumac, Yma [Chavarri, Emperatriz] (*b* Ichocan, 10 Sept. 1922). Peruvian singer. Brought up in the rarefied atmosphere of the Andean highlands, she developed a phenomenal voice with a range of five octaves. She recorded for Capitol in the 1950s and had a considerable vogue at the time. She was still giving concerts in the 1980s.

Summer, Donna [Gaines, LaDonna Adrian] (*b* Boston, 31 Dec. 1948). American singer and composer. Leaving high school to satisfy an ambition to be a singer she joined a rock group that played around Boston, then went to New York to audition for **Hair* and was assigned to the German production. She continued a stage career in Europe, and settled for a while in Mannheim. She started recording in 1975 and had a success with an electronic sound simulation of the sex act, 'Love to love you baby', which was heavily criticized. Continuing in the disco field, with her sexy image she achieved a No. 1 hit—'I feel love' (1977); she had a similar success with 'Love's unkind' (1977), 'McArthur Park' (1978), 'Hot stuff' (1979), and 'Bad girls' (1979). At this time she aspired to higher things and recorded a duet with Barbra *Streisand, 'No more tears', which led to a new phase, with the sexual image replaced by a devoutly Christian one; and a move into *soul with 'State of independence' (1982) and *Cats Without Claws* (1984).

J. Haskins and J. Stifle: *Donna Summer: an Unauthorized Biography* (Boston, 1983).

Sunday in the Park with George. Musical, with music and lyrics by Stephen *Sondheim and book by James Lapine, which takes a long look at the mind of a painter and his work, centring on the creation of Georges Seurat's 'A Sunday Afternoon on the Island of La Grande Jatte'. The audience is introduced to the painter, first seen painting the picture in 1884, his mistress, and the people he is painting. The story moves to his descendants and their present-day problems. This seemingly static but attractive work, with Mandy Patinkin and Bernadette Peters in the leading roles, ran for 604 performances when staged at the Booth Theatre, New York, 2 May 1984, and it was awarded a *Pulitzer Prize in 1985. It was staged in London at the National Theatre, in 1990.

Sunny. Musical comedy with score by Jerome *Kern, book and lyrics by Otto *Harbach and Oscar *Hammerstein II, produced in New York, at the New Amsterdam Theatre 22 Sept. 1925, with Marilyn *Miller, Jack *Donahue, Clifton *Webb, Joseph *Cawthorn, Cliff *Edwards, and George *Olsen and his Orchestra; directed by Hassard Short (1877–1956) [517p].

The story is of Sunny, an English circus performer, who falls in love with Tom, an American tourist. She stows away aboard the liner taking him back to the USA, marries his friend Jim in order to get ashore, and eventually divorces in order to marry the man she loves. This typically inane plot of the time was enhanced by such Kern gems as 'Sunny', 'Who?', 'Two little lovebirds', 'D'ye love me?', and 'I might grow fond of you'.

The London production, Hippodrome Theatre 7 Oct. 1926, starred Binnie *Hale and Jack *Buchanan with Claude Hulbert (1900–64) and Elsie *Randolph [363p]. It was filmed in 1930 with Marilyn Miller and Lawrence Gray (1898–1970); and in 1941 with Anna *Neagle and Ray *Bolger.

Sun Ra [Blount, Herman 'Sonny'] (*b* Birmingham, Ala., May 1914). American jazz composer, keyboard player, and bandleader. He studied music at college and started his musical career in the mid-1930s, settling in Chicago and playing the piano under the name of Sonny Blount. He was with Fletcher *Henderson 1946–7, worked with various small groups, and made his first recording in 1948. He started his own trio and renamed himself Sun Ra in the early 1950s, calling his band the Arkestra. He was in New York from 1961, arranging for various groups, and with the Jazz Composers' Guild 1964–5. His exotic presentations and European tours in the 1970s made him an internationally known jazz figure. His work has moved through a number of phases: hard bop in the 1950s; percussive Afro-Latin in the 1960s; traditional revival in the 1970s; and a general liking for a joyful noise and colourful sounds. He pioneered the use of electronic instruments in jazz in the 1950s.

Suppé, Franz von [Suppé-Demelli, Francesco Ezechiele Ermenegildo] (*b* Spalato (Split), 18 Apr. 1819; *d* Vienna, 21 May 1895). Dalmatian-born composer and conductor, his father a Belgian and his mother an Austrian but both thoroughly Italian in custom and upbringing. A musical prodigy, he began to compose at the age of 12 and had a mass performed when he was 13. He studied law for a time, but, when his father died in 1835, he went to live in Vienna with his mother and at 16 entered the Vienna Conservatory where one of his teachers was Donizetti. His first musical employment was as a flautist. In 1840 he became conductor at the Josefstadt Theater and began to write burlesques and Singspiele under the influence of the music of *Lanner and *Strauss, and became conductor at the Theater an der Wien in 1862. From the age of 20 he was always a prolific composer, but he really found his true métier after being inspired by the 1858 visit to Vienna of *Offenbach to conduct some of his lively new operettas.

Suppé set out to emulate the French opéra-bouffe style and his successful *Das Pensionat* of 1860 has often been credited as being the first true Viennese operetta. He continued with *Die Kartenschlägerin* (1862); *Zehn Mädchen und kein Mann* (1862); *Flotte Bursch* (1863); *Das Corps der Rache* (1864); and *Franz Schubert* (1864). A further visit by Offenbach in 1864 gave him a new burst of enthusiasm and he wrote one of his most sparkling works, *Die schöne Galathee* (1865). He composed more sporadically in the subsequent years with *Leichte Kavallerie* (1866), *Freigeister!* (1866), *Banditenstreiche* (1867), and

Tantalusqualen (1868) among the titles mainly remembered (as with Rossini) by their tuneful overtures. Another spate of inspiration came in 1876 with *Fatinitza*; while *Boccaccio* (1879) has proved to be his most enduring and most played and recorded work. During his later years he wrote a considerable amount of church music and incidental music, including that for *Dichter und Bauer (Poet and Peasant)*, the overture to which (already used for two early operettas) has remained very popular. He was musical director of the Leopoldstadt theatre from 1865 and is remembered as the founding figure of the Viennese school of operetta, adapting the pioneering ideas of Offenbach to the Viennese idiom.

O. Keller: *Franz von Suppé: der Schopfer der deutschen Operette* (Leipzig, 1905).

Supremes, The. American soul group. Motown's greatest commercial property and the most successful girl group in pop history. From 1964 to 1969 they had 16 records in the American Top 10. Built around the formula of the Phil *Spector girl vocal groups, the Shirelles, the Crystals, and the Ronettes, the Supremes initially relied on the attractiveness of their appearance. Their records have, however, aged well and are now seen as commercial classics. The group were lucky in their songwriters *Holland–Dozier–Holland; and in Diana *Ross they possessed a lead vocalist with a unique, piercing, and fresh sound, albeit a narrow range. The other members were Mary Wilson (*b* 1944) and Florence Ballard (1943–76). The Supremes were signed to *Tamla Motown in 1960 by the label founder Berry *Gordy, and in 1963 they achieved their first hit, 'When the lovelight starts shining in his eyes'. It was their seventh release, 'Where did our love go', that moved them to the top of the charts and their next four singles all got to No. 1. Their best recordings include 'Baby love', 'Stop! in the name of love', 'I hear a symphony', 'The happening', and 'You can't hurry love'. Ballard became disenchanted with her secondary role in the group and left in 1967, to be replaced by Cindy Birdsong (*b* 1939), who remained until 1972. In 1968, with their No. 1 'Love child', they were billed as Diana Ross and the Supremes, a move which foreshadowed her eventual departure for a solo career in 1970. Jean Terrell (*b* 1944) came in as the new lead, to be replaced in 1972 by Scherrie Payne (*b* 1944); but, without Ross, the group only had occasional minor successes. Eventually Mary Wilson was the only original Supreme left in the group, which disbanded when she left in 1976.

Sutton, Ralph (*b* Hamburg, Mo., 4 Nov. 1922). American jazz pianist. An expert in recreating older styles, ranging from ragtime to swing, with a special fondness for Fats *Waller imitations, he was mainly heard in the St Louis area in the 1930s. He started to become known at the Eddie *Condon club where he was intermission pianist for eight years from 1948. He visited Europe with Lonnie Johnson in 1952 and played with Bob Scobey 1957. He made some excellent 78 and LP recordings in the 1950s and 1960s. He owned and played in his own club in Aspen, Colorado 1964–7; was a founder member of the World's Greatest Jazz Band; and was still active into the 1970s.

J. Shacter: *Piano Man: the Story of Ralph Sutton* (Chicago, 1975).

Swann, Donald (*b* London, 30 Sept. 1923). British composer, pianist, and entertainer. Basically a middlebrow, his approaches to the popular and classical fields tend towards parody; the popular side well and truly taken to pieces in *At the Drop of a Hat*, and the classical in the famous series, written for the BBC Third Programme with Henry Reed, about the fabled 12-tone composer Hilda Tablet. From 1949 to 1956 he worked with various collaborators, but mainly with Michael *Flanders, contributing items to the Laurier Lister revues *Oranges and Lemons* (1950); *Penny Plain* (1951); **Airs on a Shoestring* (1953); *Pay the Piper* (1954); and *Fresh Airs* (1956). Also with Flanders, he composed a popular series of animal songs, including 'The hippopotamus' (1952)—well exploited by Ian Wallace (*b* 1919), 'The elephant' (1953), 'The rhinoceros song' (1956), and many others included in their bestiary. One of his best-known revue numbers was 'Youth of the heart' (with Sidney Carter) heard in *The *Lyric Revue* (1951). In 1955 he wrote the musical *Wild Thyme*.

On the last day of 1956 he started to perform with Michael Flanders in **At the Drop of a Hat* at the New Lindsey Theatre, which transferred to the West End Fortune Theatre on 24 Jan. 1957, and was to run for 759 performances. They delighted audiences with such witty and skilful numbers as 'Have some madeira, m'dear', 'A transport of delight', 'A gnu', 'Design for living', 'Misalliance', 'Kokoraki', 'Vanessa', and 'The reluctant cannibal'. The show visited the Edinburgh Festival in 1959 and opened later that year in New York at the Golden Theatre on Broadway. This called for a perpetuation of their art in *At the Drop of Another Hat* (1963) and a further spate of inspired nonsense.

D. Swann: *The Space Behind the Bars* (London, 1968).

Sweatman, Wilbur C. (*b* Brunswick, Mo., 7 Feb. 1882; *d* New York, 9 Mar. 1961). American bandleader, clarinettist, and composer. After playing in a local band in Kansas City, he became a professional musician, his first job being with a travelling circus. He played with Mahara's Minstrels, at this time perfecting the extraordinary feat, which he did as a vaudeville act, of playing three clarinets simultaneously. He organized an all-black orchestra in Minneapolis 1902–8, and was manager and musical director of the Grand Theatre, Chicago, and the Monogram Theatre 1908–11. After another period in vaudeville he organized a new band within whose ranks the talents of Duke *Ellington, Otto Hardwicke, and Sonny Greer were briefly nurtured. He also ran a theatrical agency, broadcast, and recorded. His pioneering jazz efforts were important in Chicago in 1910. By 1914 the catalogues had many items by Sweatman's Original Jazz Band; and though the music he played is considered to be only pseudo-jazz, he earns some credit for the early establishment of Afro-American jazz. He was the composer of the standard 'Down home rag' (1911).

Sweeney Todd. 'Musical thriller' with music and lyrics by Stephen *Sondheim and book by Hugh Wheeler based on the 1973 stage play by Chris Bond, directed by Harold Prince and produced at the Uris Theatre, New York, 1 March 1979, where it achieved 557 performances. Described as 'the most grisly musical ever presented for a commercial Broadway run' and 'near-operatic', it told the legendary tale of the 'demon barber of Fleet Street' which can be traced back to the 14th century.

The story was first dramatized in 1847 as *The String of Pearls or The Fiend of Fleet Street* at the Britannia Theatre, London. The Sondheim version puts itself in a Hogarth-cum-Dickens setting. In the prelude, 'The Ballad of Sweeney Todd', Len Cariou as the demented barber tells of his return home after being wrongly imprisoned and takes revenge against the judge who condemned him by ravishing his wife; now he intends to marry the judge's daughter. His rage extends to any citizen of London who comes to his barber's chair, where he slits their throats; their corpses are made into meat pies by his gruesome assistant Mrs Lovett (played by Angela *Lansbury). They get their just deserts in the end.

The show was seen in London at the Theatre Royal, Drury Lane, 2 July 1980, where the large stage and costly settings proved unsuitable for its intimate drama, with Dennis Quilley (*b* 1933) as Sweeney Todd and Sheila Hancock (*b* 1933) as Mrs Lovett; and received a mixed reception from critics and public. There was a TV film in 1982, and in 1984 the work was taken into the repertoire of the New York City Opera.

Sweet. A word used in a somewhat derogatory way in the jazz world to describe sentimental and overtly harmonious music that lacks the bite of true jazz. Some, however, have deliberately purveyed sweet music (with soft lights) as a much needed service to harassed mankind.

Sweet and Low. First of a series of fondly remembered London wartime revues that gave impetus to the intimate satirical revue resurgence of the 1950s, their satire mainly aimed at current and past show-business. With music by Geoffrey Wright (*b* 1912), Leslie Julian *Jones, Jack *Strachey, and George *Posford, it opened at the Ambassadors Theatre, London, 10 June 1943 [264p], with Hermione *Gingold ('The Borgias are having an orgy', 'Miss Gingold's friend', 'Valhalla') the central attraction. It was followed by *Sweeter and Lower* (Ambassadors Theatre) 17 Feb. 1944 [870p], with music by Charles *Zwar, Geoffrey Wright, and others, with Hermione Gingold surpassing herself as Robert Helpmann in *Hamlet*. This was succeeded by *Sweetest and Lowest* (Ambassadors Theatre) 9 May 1946 [791p], music by Charles Zwar, lyrics by Alan *Melville, also with Hermione Gingold.

Sweet Charity. Musical comedy with score by Cy *Coleman, book by Neil *Simon, and lyrics by Dorothy *Fields, opening at the Palace Theatre, New York, 29 Jan. 1966 [608p] with Gwen *Verdon as a shady lady who works at the Fan-Dango Ballroom and gets involved with an Italian film star and a nice guy whom she can't marry because of her past history. All very touchingly funny and tearful, and based on the Fellini film *Nights of Cabiria*. Also in the cast were John McMartin, Helen Gallagher, James Luisi, and Ruth Buzzi. The songs included 'Big spender', 'If my friends could see me now', 'There's gotta be something better than this', 'Baby, dream your dreams', 'Sweet Charity', 'Where am I going?', and 'I'm a brass band'. In London, at the Prince of Wales Theatre 11 Oct. 1967, Juliet Prowse was in the leading role. It was filmed in 1969 with Shirley MacLaine and John McMartin.

Sweethearts. Operetta with music by Victor *Herbert, lyrics by Robert B. *Smith, and book by Harry B. *Smith and Fred DeGressac, first seen in Baltimore, and then at the New Amsterdam Theatre, New York, 8 Sept. 1913 [136p], with Christie MacDonald (1875–1962) as Princess Sylvia of Zilania in a most unlikely tale of abduction and a prince in disguise. They end up happily as Queen and King respectively. The Victor Herbert score included 'Sweethearts', 'Every lover must meet his fate', 'Pretty as a picture', and 'I don't know how I do it, but I do'. It was briefly revived in 1929 and filmed in 1938 with a much altered story, and the inevitable Nelson *Eddy and Jeanette *MacDonald. Then, following the success of a revival of *The *Red Mill*, it was rejigged in 1947 as a vehicle for Bobby *Clarke (who made it an amusing spoof) and added songs—'To the land of my own romance' and 'I might be your once-in-a-while'.

Swing (1). The key ingredient that makes the essential difference between music played in the styles prevailing up to the end of the 19th century and the *jazz-based idiom that rapidly permeated popular music in the 20th century. The characteristic now known as 'swing' was virtually unknown in European music until *c.*1920, and, although the black population of the USA were probably exploring its possibilities as a part of their musical heritage throughout their history, swing did not change the essential American musical characteristics until the early 1900s. *Ragtime and the *cakewalk, which made a general appearance in the 1890s, contained hardly any element of swing, their effect being achieved by simple *syncopation, a device which may also be discovered in classical music. The earliest jazz began to distinguish itself from the music that had dominated before by beginning, however minimally, to swing. Once the world understood what swing could achieve, the swing element in popular music quickly increased until by the 1930s it was the dominating factor.

It is not easy, even now, to evolve a written definition of swing because much of what it gives to music is felt rather than observed and cannot be accurately notated. Straight music is that in which the melodic notes coincide with the rhythmic beat, or fall between the beats in mathematically presentable divisions. The typically American melody, that was part of the ragtime phenomenon, was still basically in the straight idiom, achieving its novelty by regularly putting the melodic stress off the main beat, but still in a mathematical and notatable way. The swung rhythm that arrived with jazz was such a simple and subtle difference that it is still surprising that it was not introduced into music sooner. The rhythm or underlying beat remains basically the same, but the melodic notes above now play around the stresses and create what might be called a rhythmic counterpoint of their own; frequently anticipating the beat, sometimes following it, but generally falling at points in the rhythmic pattern that cannot be indicated by the current fractional notation.

There are various degrees and kinds of swing. What might be described as lightly swinging (as in many popular songs and singing of the 1930s), simply gives a relaxed and free feeling to the music; while, at the other extreme, forceful anticipation of the beat can produce a propulsive, driving effect that is totally unknown to straight music and has now become the obsessive effect of modern beat music. A livelier performance of so-called classical music can also be achieved by introducing a modest swing element into the performance.

The obscurity of early jazz history makes it impossible to define any point in history where the first manifestation of swing appeared. Its introduction to the musical scene and hence to the public ear generally took effect in the 1890s and early 1900s. The claims of 'Jelly Roll' *Morton to have invented jazz are given more credence in the light of a general appreciation of the swing phenomenon. What he was presumably claiming was that he was the first (or, at least, one of the first) to give the music an observable swing element. This is borne out by his jazz-styled playing of ragtime. It is unlikely, however, that he would be the sole inventor as many black musicians of the time would be bringing the art to public awareness as the opportunity presented itself. The unrecorded legacy of early musicians like 'Buddy' *Bolden was the establishment of the swinging character of jazz.

It is probably impossible now to pinpoint the first use of the word 'swing' as a definition of the essential ingredient of jazz. Morton seems to have been one of the first to use it in a title—'Georgia swing', which he claimed to have written in 1906.

It was in regular use by *c.*1930, and Duke *Ellington might be credited with bringing the word into common currency in 1931 when he wrote 'It don't mean a thing if it ain't got that swing'. At this stage the word swing was being used as a synonym for what was to be collectively known as 'jazz'. Jazz histories, magazines (e.g. *Swing Music*, founded in 1935), record catalogues, etc into the 1940s were still purveying what they called swing music, clearly meaning jazz as a whole. The word 'rhythm' was occasionally employed in a similar way—e.g. 'rhythm style', 'rhythm club'. As the word 'jazz' became the accepted categorical term, so did swing take on a more specific meaning, discussed below.

Swing (2). The term, previously loosely applied to the entire jazz field, began in the 1930s to be specifically applied to what is generally referred to as big band jazz: that is, the organized and arranged genre of jazz that is generally played by the bigger units as opposed to the more improvised variety played in smaller groups. One of the prime objects of the big bands was to play for dancing and, as modern jazz dancing demanded a propulsive beat, the preponderant element of swing, often achieved by sectional riffs over a rock-steady beat, logically led to this kind of music being defined as swing. The use of the term 'swing music' no longer implied the world of jazz as a whole, but rather the special music of the Swing Era, with *Benny Goodman its crowned 'King', its heyday in the period 1936–45, and still surviving in imitative form today.

B. Goodman and I. Kolodin: *The Kingdom of Swing* (New York, 1939). G. Fernett: *Swing Out: Great Negro Dance Bands* (Michigan, 1966). G. T. Simon: *Simon Says: the Sights and Sounds of the Swing Era 1935–55* (New York, 1971). S. Dance: *The World of Swing* (New York, 1974). G. Schuller: *The Swing Era* (New York, and Oxford, 1989).

Swing Time. RKO film of 1936, with music by Jerome *Kern and lyrics by Dorothy *Fields, starring Fred *Astaire, Ginger *Rogers, Georges Metaxa, and Victor *Moore. It contained a particularly memorable selection of Kern hits including 'A fine romance', 'The way you look tonight', 'Pick yourself up', 'Bojangles of Harlem', 'Never gonna dance', and 'Waltz in swingtime'.

Sybil. Operetta with music by Victor Jacobi (1883–1921), who also wrote *The Marriage Market* (1913) and *Apple Blossoms* (1919), with book by Harry B. *Smith and Harry Graham. Produced in New York (Liberty Theatre) 10 Jan. 1916, with Julia *Sanderson, Donald *Brian, and Joseph *Cawthorn [168p]; Vienna (Neue Wiener Stadttheater) 12 Feb. 1919, (Theater an der Wien) 6 Nov. 1919; London (*Daly's Theatre) 19 Feb. 1921, with Harry *Welchman. Huntley Wright, and José *Collins [346p]. The songs included: 'The Colonel of the Crimson Hussars', 'Love may be a mystery', 'Lift your eyes to mine', and 'I like the boys'.

Syncopation. A natural element of modern jazz-based popular music, also used as a rather more deliberate contrivance in other music. Basically it is the placing of rhythmic accents or accented melodic notes where they would not naturally be deemed to fall, i.e. away from the main beats of the bar. This came into popular music as a deliberate and mathematically contrived feature of early styles like *ragtime and in symphonic jazz (orchestral music played in a simulated jazz style, like *'Rhapsody in blue'). Syncopation, as exemplified in *swing and the natural swing of *blues-based jazz, becomes more undefinable and increasingly impossible to notate: more a pulling or anticipation of the stressed notes, rather than a deliberate and mathematical displacement. It was emphasized as a novelty feature of early jazz in numbers such as 'Syncopate your sins away', and at this time jazz was often referred to as syncopated music.

Szulc, Joseph Sigismond [Józef Zygmunt] (*b* Warsaw, 4 Apr. 1875; *d* Paris, 10 Apr. 1956). Polish composer and pianist. He was the son of Henryk Szulc (1836–1903) who was leader of the Warsaw Opera orchestra and taught at the Conservatory where Jósef was educated. He became well-known as a pianist, and wrote ballets and orchestral works, but is mainly remembered for his operettas, his biggest success coming with his first, *Flup* (Brussels, 1913; Paris, 1920), which had more than 5000 performances in his lifetime. He went to live in Paris where he worked with Massenet and passed the rest of his life. He continued a regular output of operettas: *Titin* (1920); *Loute* (1922); *Le Petit Choc* (1923); *Vivette* (1924); *Quand on est trois* (1925); *Mannequins* (1925); *Divin Mensonge* (1926); *Couchette No. 3* (1929); *Flossie* (1929); *Sidonie panache* (1930); *Zou* (1930); *Le Garçon de Chez Prunier* (1933); *Mandrin* (1934); *L'Auberge du Chat Coiffé* (1936); and, his most ambitious work, *Pantouflé* (1945). His music was light, spirited, and tuneful, with a nice sprinkling of the rhythms and dances of the 1920s and 1930s added to the traditional operetta style; and his works deserve to be more widely known.

T

Tabrar, Joseph (*b* London, 1857; *d* London, 22 Aug. 1931). British composer and author. He began his career as a singing boy at *Evans's Supper Rooms in Covent Garden, London, in the days of the managership of Paddy Green. While there he frequently appeared before the Prince of Wales, later Edward VII. He joined the Moore and Burgess Minstrels at St James's Hall and, while he was with them, wrote and composed many songs for the celebrated troupe, continuing to do so for some 24 years after he had left them to become a full-time professional composer and writer. His talents were immediately recognized and, in his writing life of some 40 years, he turned out thousands of pieces for artists of all kinds and calibre. There was hardly a music-hall artist during his time who did not call upon 'Joe' for some material: this included, besides songs, monologues, duologues, sketches, short operettas, and many pantomime scripts; his customers including John Hollingshead and George *Edwardes, and such stars as Marie *Lloyd. At one time he had a large office and shop in York Road, near Waterloo Bridge, in which he was still working in 1928, then over 80. His son, who worked under the name of Fred Earle, was also a composer and music-hall singer; and his daughter Lily (also on the stage) was the wife of the comedian Syd Walker (1887–1945).

His best-known songs included: 'Ting, ting, that's how the bell goes' (1883), sung by George *Leybourne; 'Daddy wouldn't buy me a bow-wow' (1892)—Vesta *Victoria; 'The ship went down' (1898)—Harry *Rickards; 'Seaweed' (1906)—Fred Earle; 'For months and months and months' (1909)—Jack Smiles; 'And very nice too' (1912); and 'I stopped, and I looked and I listened' (1916)—George *Robey.

Tailgate. A style of jazz trombone playing with the instrument involved in an almost continuous contrapuntal bass part inevitably using emphatic lead-in glissandos, taking the slide from the fully open to the closed position. The early jazz bands in New Orleans and elsewhere used to travel around in carts or lorries, playing a sample of their wares to advertise dances and other entertainments in which they were involved. Because of this energetic use of the slide the trombonist would usually sit at the back with his instrument over the tailgate, hence the name. Great exponents of the style included Kid *Ory, George Brunies [later Brunis] (1902–74), and Jim Robinson (1890–1976).

Take a Chance. Musical comedy with score by Nacio Herb *Brown and Richard *Whiting, and additional items by Vincent *Youmans, book by B. G. *DeSylva and Laurence Schwab, New York (*Apollo Theatre) 26 Nov. 1932 [243p], with Ethel *Merman and Jack *Whiting playing two performers in a show called *Humpty Dumpty*. In fact that was what the whole show had originally been called when it was a disastrous flop in Pittsburgh, and had to be totally revised. To supplement such songs as 'You're an old smoothie' and 'Tonight is opening night', Ethel Merman was now provided with two show-stopping numbers, 'Eadie was a lady' (*m* Whiting), and 'Rise 'n' shine' (*m* Youmans). It was filmed in 1933 with James Dunn (1905–67), Cliff *Edwards, June Knight, and Lillian Roth (1910–80).

Talbot, Howard [Munkittrick, Richard Lansdale] (*b* Yonkers, NY, 9 Mar. 1865; *d* Reigate, 12 Sept. 1928). British composer. His father, Alexander Munkittrick, a well-known figure in the insurance world, and his mother (*née* Talbot) were both Irish, and he was born while they were living in the USA. The family returned to England when he was four. He appears never to have become a naturalized American, and was very proud of being Irish. The family wanted him to become a doctor and he trained for a while at King's College Hospital, but he found no liking for the profession and left to spend a time in the silk business. He used a small inheritance to enrol at the Royal College of Music where he studied under Sir Hubert Parry. His father disowned him and at this stage he changed his name to Howard Talbot. His first operetta, *Wapping Old Stairs*, was first sung by the King's Lynn Choral Society and then produced at the Vaudeville Theatre in 1894 with a distinguished cast. The music was clearly inspired by *Sullivan, but the libretto was weak; as was that of his second operetta *Monte Carlo* (1896). His third attempt proved lucky. *A *Chinese Honeymoon* (1901) had a good book by George Dance, an excellent comic lead in Louie Freear (1873–1939), and it was highly acclaimed at the Strand Theatre achieving a run of 1076 performances.

In 1904 he became musical director at the Prince of Wales Theatre and continued to write a steady stream of shows including: *Kitty Grey* (1901); *Miss Wingrove* (1905); *The Blue Moon* (1905); *The White Chrysanthemum* (1905); *The Girl Behind the Counter* (1906); *Three Kisses* (1907); *The Belle of Brittany* (1908); and, a particular success, *The *Arcadians* (1909), which he wrote with his friend Lionel *Monckton—who generally gets most of the credit, although it was a true partnership. Talbot married the actress Dorothy Langton in 1910. He continued to compose, often in collaboration with Paul *Rubens or Monckton, and wrote *The Mousmé* (1911); *A Narrow Squeak* (1913); *The Pearl Girl* (1913); *Simple Hearted Bill* (1913); *A Mixed Grill* (1914); *A Lucky Miss* (1914); *Mr Manhattan* (1916); *High Jinks* (1916); and *Who's Hooper?* (1917). His career ended unhappily when he put all his savings into Russian oil shares and lost everything when the 1917 revolution came. He continued to earn a little from his shows but became ill in the early 1920s with a lung disease. A property swindle made the Talbots even more penniless and he spent his final days in a rented flat in Reigate.

Talbot's music had an ideal theatrical quality about it and, being 'tuneful and not unduly ambitious', it had an immediate impact. Most of it has not lasted well, however, apart from two of his contributions to *The Arcadians*, 'My motter' and the duet 'Half-past two'.

Talking Heads. American *new wave rock group formed by Scottish-born David Byrne (*b* 1952) (guitar and vocal), Chris Frantz (*b* 1951) (drums), and Tina Weymouth (*b* 1950) (bass and vocal) while they were still at the Rhode Island School of Design in the 1970s. In 1975 they became Talking Heads, with the addition of Jerry Harrison (*b* 1949) (guitar, keyboard, and vocal) in 1977. They toured Europe that year and aroused interest as one of the new wave groups who were producing innovative sounds and ideas, confirmed by their sensitively creative album *Talking Heads* (1977). Increasingly they became interested in and achieved a black sound, experimenting with extra musicians and African instruments on their LP *Remain in Light*. By 1983 they had returned to a more traditional pop style, though they still liked to use fuller instrumentation. Byrne's composing abilities were shown in the ballet score he wrote for Twyla Tharp, *The Catherine Wheel* (1982). *Naked* (1988) was one of their most lively albums so far, and continued their trend towards a tuneful pre-punk sort of music in the *Velvet Underground tradition, yet always experimentally avant-garde and interesting.

K. Reese: *The Name of this Book is Talking Heads* (London, 1982).

Tamla Motown. Prominent and influential record company specializing in black rhythm 'n' blues and soul material. Motown Records was founded in 1959 by Berry *Gordy, the name deriving from the firm's origins in Detroit, 'motor-town' of the USA, the first record on the label being 'My beloved'/ Sugar daddy' by the Satintones. A month later the Tamla label was launched (originally intended to be Tammy, after the Debbie *Reynolds hit, but the name was not permitted) and had early successes with 'Bye bye baby' by Mary Wells (1943–92), 'Shop around' by the Miracles, and 'Please Mr Postman' by the Marvelettes. The Gordy label was added in 1962 and had an early hit with the Contours' 'Do you love me'. Several small labels that were not succeeding were acquired, bringing to Tamla Motown the talents of Junior Walker, the *Spinners, and the *Temptations, the latter to become one of the company's most profitable assets.

With songwriting talents like the *Holland–Dozier–Holland partnership, Gordy's old friend and company vice-president Smokey *Robinson, and the guiding hand of songwriter/producer Norman Whitfield (*b* 1943), the company boomed and the Temptations started their run of No. 1 hits with 'My girl'. *Martha and the Vandellas were rivalling the Temptations on the Gordy label, with Marvin *Gaye, Stevie *Wonder, the *Isley Brothers, and the *Four Tops all adding to the success which continued into the 1970s with the *Jackson Brothers and Gladys *Knight; and into the 1980s with the Commodores, Lionel Richie (*b* 1949), and Rick James (*b* 1952) (with Stevie Wonder, having re-signed to the company in 1975 for $13 million).

The Motown sound is essentially the sound of black soul music, a satisfying jazz and gospel-oriented form of pop music that has a wide appeal among the wider based connoisseurs of rock. Other associated labels are Prodigal, Rare Earth, Soul, and Mowest. In 1971 the company left its Detroit roots and moved to Sunset Boulevard in Los Angeles.

D. Morse: *Motown and the Arrival of Black Music* (New York–London, 1971). P. Benjaminson: *The Story of Motown* (New York, 1979). D. Waller: *The Motown Story* (New York, 1985).

Tango. Argentina's best-known contribution to the world's repertoire of social dances. The measure originated in Africa and was taken by slaves to Cuba, Haiti, and Mexico, then on to Uruguay and Argentina. It appeared to catch on most thoroughly in Argentina, becoming very popular in the 1880s, and hence became widely known in dance circles as the Argentine tango. In 2/4 time with the first quaver dotted, it is simply a faster version of the *habanera. Among the more civilized inhabitants of cities like Buenos Aires it was considered a barbarous dance: and not until it had been taken up by cities like Paris was it allowed into social dancing circles in its 'native' country. In Brazil a similar dance is known as the *maxixe.

In London in 1905 a M. Camille de Rhunal had arranged a maxixe for a George *Edwardes's production of *Lady Madcap* at the Prince of Wales Theatre, following this up by an unsuccessful attempt to popularize the tango on the London stage. It caught on in Paris first of all, being featured at a café called La Feria; and by 1909 it was an accepted feature of all Parisian ballroom dance competitions. It subsequently became popular in England when George *Grossmith Jr. and Phyllis *Dare danced it in *The Sunshine Girl* at the Gaiety Theatre in 1912. Grossmith had learned it from Jean de Reszke in Paris and did much to promote it in London. The 1912 craze saw it featured in shows at the Hippodrome and the Alhambra and special exhibitions were staged at the Stoll and Queen's

Theatres. It was violently attacked in the newspapers as being indelicate (the fate of many new dances) but became respectable after being approved by Queen Mary at a dance given at Kenwood in Hampstead by the Grand Duke Michael. An attempt to name the English tango the Tile-Trot seems to have been a failure. During the First World War the tango declined in popularity, giving way to the foxtrot craze; but it has survived as a popular exhibition dance.

Tanguay, Eva (*b* Marbleton, Quebec, Aug. 1878; *d* Hollywood, 11 Jan. 1948). Canadian-born American vaudeville star, an outstanding personality and show-business figure. Her daring and revealing dresses caused some scandal in their day but they made her one of the highest-paid artists on the American vaudeville circuit; a sort of American Marie *Lloyd. She did it all in a nice spirit of self-mockery, and revealed a considerable comic talent. She made a silent film in 1917 whose title, *Wild Girl*, was a clear comment on her character. Her first hit song was 'My Sambo', which she sang in *The Chaperons* (1902); while her most popular song (which she recorded in 1922, her only record) was 'I don't care' (1905, *m* Harry O. Sutton, *w* Jean Lenox). She retired in the 1930s and became a recluse.

Tapfere Soldat, Der. Operetta with music by Oscar *Straus, book by Rudolf Bernauer and Leopold Jacobson, based, without explicit permission, on George Bernard Shaw's play *Arms and the Man*.

It is a delightful comedy in which a young lady falls for a cowardly soldier who prefers eating chocolates to fighting, rather than the glamorous young officer whom he rapidly outsmarts. It was first produced in Vienna, at the Theater an der Wien 14 Nov. 1908, with an initial run of 62 performances; thereafter it became a world favourite and has been frequently revived.

As *The Chocolate Soldier*, English words by Stanislaus Stange (*b* 1917), with famous waltz song 'My hero' ('Komm, Held meiner Träume'), it was first produced in New York, at the Lyric Theatre 13 Sept. 1909 [296p]; but it was an even greater success in London, at the Lyric Theatre, 10 Sept. 1910, where it had 500 performances; and its numerous American and British revivals have since confirmed it as an operetta classic. It was filmed in 1941 with Risé Stevens (*b* 1913) as the heroine and Nelson *Eddy as the soldier.

Tate, James W. (*b* Wolverhampton, 30 July 1875; *d* London, 5 Feb. 1922). British composer and pianist. He started out as an actor, working for some time in the USA and returning to England to become musical director of the Carl Rosa Opera Company. He moved into the music-hall field where he first conducted for Lottie *Collins whom he married in 1902. She died in 1910, and in 1912 he married the singer, entertainer, and well-known principal boy of the pantomime world, Clarice *Mayne. He wrote many of his popular songs for her and accompanied her on stage, playing the role of the love-struck husband, and being referred to as 'That'. He wrote music for *Samples* (1915); *Some* (1916); contributed four vital numbers to the highly successful *The *Maid of the Mountains* (1917)—'My life is love', 'A paradise for two', 'A bachelor gay', and 'When you're in love'—which starred his stepdaughter José *Collins; *The Beauty Spot* (1917); and *The Peep Show* (1921).

His best-known songs included: 'If I should plant a tiny seed of love' (1908), 'I was a good little girl till I met you' (1914), 'A broken doll' (1916), 'Ev'ry little while' (1916), 'Anywhere in the world with you' (1919), 'Memories of love and you' (1919)—sung by Annie Croft in *The *Follies*, 'Give me a little cosy corner' (1919), and 'Come over the garden wall' (1920).

Tatum, Art [Arthur] (*b* Toledo, Ohio, 13 Oct. 1909; *d* Los Angeles, 5 Nov. 1956). American pianist. Handicapped from birth with only partial sight in one eye, he compensated with a brilliant talent for music. He studied at the Toledo School of Music, formed his own band in 1926, which played locally, and followed a career as a club pianist until 1932, when he went to New York to become accompanist to Adelaide *Hall. After 18 months of this, he was resident pianist at clubs in Cleveland, Hollywood, Chicago, and New York, his reputation ever growing among fellow-musicians and the more advanced followers of jazz who were bedazzled by his impressive technique. He first visited Europe and England in 1938, worked on the West Coast 1939–40, then at Café Society and Kelly's in New York until 1943 when he formed a famous trio with Tiny Grimes (*b* 1916) on guitar and Slam Stewart (1914–87) on bass. He began a series of concert tours in 1945 and played in clubs until 1954. A final round of concerts culminated in a performance in the Hollywood Bowl in Aug. 1956 before an audience of 19,000.

To many, Tatum was one of the greatest ever jazz pianists with an astonishing technique and talent for improvisation, only spoilt for others by his addiction to repetitious mannerisms, with his lightning runs often seeming more a habit than the result of thought. His brilliance was almost a disservice to those who tried to emulate him and ended up by putting technique before imagination. He was at his best in his less flamboyant moods when he accompanied blues singers or played with other jazzmen; then he showed a capacity for depth as well as brilliance, and a natural understanding of underlying harmonies that greatly enriched his improvisations.

A. Laubich and G. Spencer: *Art Tatum: a Guide to his Recorded Music* (Metuchen, 1982).

Tauber, Richard [Seiffert, Ernst] (*b* Linz, 16 May 1892; *d* London, 8 Jan. 1948). Austrian singer and composer. He had a brilliant operatic career, starting with his appearance in *The Magic Flute* in 1913.

However, his lightly romantic, but supremely intelligent, style and monocled good looks were ideally suited to the field of operetta, and it was in association with the works of Franz *Lehár that he made his greatest impact on the musical world. This began with *Frasquita* (1922) and continued with *Paganini* (1925); *Frederika* (1929); *Das *Land des Lächelns (The Land of Smiles)* (1929)—with 'Dein ist mein ganzes Herz' ('You are my heart's delight') becoming very much his theme song; and *Schön ist die Welt* (1931). He first appeared in London in *The Land of Smiles* at Drury Lane in 1931; and his New York debut was in a recital performance the same year. His own operetta, *Der singende Traum*, was produced at the Theater an der Wien 31 Aug. 1934, with the composer conducting.

He settled in England in 1938 and took British nationality in 1940, becoming active as a conductor in the London theatre and writing and producing his own operetta, *Old Chelsea*—'My heart and I'—in 1943. He appeared in many films in Germany and in the following English-speaking films made in the UK: **Blossom Time* (1934); *Heart's Desire* (1935); *Land Without Music* (1936); *Pagliacci* (1936); *Waltz Time* (1946); and *The *Lisbon Story* (1946). He made his last concert appearance at the Carnegie Hall in New York, 30 Mar. 1947.

H. Ludwigg (ed.): *Das Richard Tauber Buch* (Berlin, 1928; repr. 1938). D. Napier-Tauber: *Richard Tauber* (Berlin, 1949; London, 1959). W. Korb: *Richard Tauber* (Vienna, 1966). C. Castle: *This Was Richard Tauber* (London, 1971).

Tawney, Cyril (*b* Gosport, Hants., 12 Oct. 1930). British folk-singer and composer. He won a *Melody Maker* song-writing competition in 1955, before following a family tradition and serving in the navy until 1959. Thereafter he settled in Plymouth where he studied and performed West Country folk-songs and began to perform these and his own songs, at times with a group called the Applejacks, his first disc being issued in 1962. In 1965 he started a series of nightly concerts at the Devonport Guildhall and lectured regularly. His first LP album, *Between Decks*, appeared in 1964, and his own best songs came in *A Cold Wind Blows* (1966). A recording of ten ballads from Child's collection in West Country versions appeared as *The Outlandish Knight* (1966). He signed with Argo records in 1969 and a number of valuable folk albums appeared on that label, including *A Mayflower Garland* (1970). He published *Songs by Cyril Tawney* (1966) and *The Cyril Tawney Songbook* (1972).

Taylor, Billy [William] (*b* Greenville, NC, 24 July 1921). American jazz pianist. As a teenage enthusiast, he became acquainted with the piano work of such diverse influences as Art *Tatum, Nat 'King' *Cole, and Thelonious *Monk. He settled in New York in the early 1940s and played with Dizzy *Gillespie, Ben *Webster, and others; becoming a well-known figure in New York jazz as resident pianist at *Birdland from 1950, and leading his own trio from 1951, developing an advanced style that has been an influence on several modern players. Latterly he was more active as a disc jockey, TV musical director, and writer; also working on the staff of the Manhattan School of Music and Howard University.

Taylor, Cecil Percival (*b* New York, 15 Mar. 1933). American pianist, composer, and teacher. He studied at the New York College of Music and the New England Conservatory. His complicated musical thinking was diversely influenced by such players as Dave *Brubeck, Bud *Powell, Horace *Silver, Erroll *Garner, and Duke *Ellington. In the early 1950s he began to play professionally, working with Johnny *Hodges and others before he formed his own group, in 1956 playing at the Five Spot Café. By 1957, when he appeared at the Newport Jazz Festival, he was moving into a more modern idiom and, by the 1960s his playing was totally abstract in the free jazz vein. He liked to take time off from his playing to experiment in private, a habit which allowed others like *Coltrane to take the public lead in such experiments where Taylor might have been pre-eminent. In 1961 he was back at the Five Spot and in 1962 he toured Europe and started an association with saxophonist Albert Ayler (1936–70).

He disappeared from the scene again in 1964–5 before re-emerging as one of the organizers of the Jazz Composers Guild, and became one of the acknowledged leaders of the free jazz movement, recording with the Jazz Composers orchestra in 1968. He led a regular group into the early 1970s and appeared at various jazz festivals in the USA and Europe. In the meantime he had started teaching at various universities and was awarded a Guggenheim Fellowship in 1973. In 1979 he composed the music for a short ballet, *Tetra Stomp: Eatin' Rain in Space*. A remarkable technician with a forceful, attacking style, he is a formidably demanding player of unpredictable quality.

Taylor, James (*b* Boston, 12 Mar. 1948). American singer and songwriter. From a musical family, he played the guitar from boyhood and formed a group, the Flying Machine, in New York in 1967. He went to England in 1968 and made an album, *James Taylor*, for the Apple label in 1969. His next album, made in the USA, *Sweet Baby James* (1970), contained 'Fire and rain' which made him universally known. He became the typical voice of the 1970s, purveying a pessimistic, depressing, and heroin-shaded view of the world in a sad sort of voice, and was thus well in tune with many young sensibilities. He had a big hit with 'You've got a friend' (written by Carole *King) in 1972; and continued to flourish, a lightening of heart coming with age, with such hits as 'Mockingbird' (with Carly Simon, 1974), 'How sweet it is' (1975), 'Handy man' (1977), 'Wonderful world' (with *Simon and Garfunkel, 1978), and 'Up on the roof' (1979).

Teagarden, Jack [Weldon Leo] (*b* Vernon, Texas, 29 Aug. 1905; *d* New Orleans, 15 Jan. 1964). American jazz trombonist, vocalist, and bandleader. He showed early talent and gained a rapid reputation while playing with the Texas band of Peck Kelley (1898–1980) in 1921. By the time he joined the Ben *Pollack band in 1928, he had acquired a tremendous individual technique that made him one of the few white jazz trombonists of the time to be considered a rival to the great black jazz musicians of the *Armstrong class. In 1933 he left Pollack to join the Paul *Whiteman band 1933–8, enduring much anonymous symphonic jazz for the occasional chances to shine against a high-class background. He left to form his own band in 1939, led one band or another for the next seven years, and featured in the Bing *Crosby film *Birth of the Blues* (1940). He disbanded his last group in 1946 and joined the Louis *Armstrong All-Stars, at the beginning enjoying a mutually admiring association with Armstrong, with whom he also recorded several hit songs. He left in 1951 and went back to bandleading for the rest of his distinguished, if alcoholic, career, working in partnership at times with Bobby *Hackett and Earl *Hines.

Teagarden's trombone playing, heard to great effect on so many classic jazz records, has never dated or had anything but the highest admiration from traditionalists and modernists alike; and he was equally effective and admired as a singer, performing with his lazy Texas drawl as both soloist and duettist. He was to the trombone what Armstrong was to the trumpet and Coleman *Hawkins to the saxophone, a great demonstrator of the instrument's lyrical possibilities.

H. J. Waters: *Jack Teagarden's Music* (Stanhope, NJ, 1960). J. D. Smith and L. Gutteridge: *Jack Teagarden: the Story of a Jazz Maverick* (London, 1960).

Temperance Seven. British band, actually nine in number, formed in 1955 to play a tongue-in-cheek re-creation of 1920s dance music, with poker-voiced vocals by Whispering Paul McDowell. They were never considered to be a serious jazz group, but created an enjoyable sort of nostalgia that was widely appreciated and resulted in such best-selling recordings as 'You're driving me crazy' (which became a No. 1 hit) and 'Pasadena'. The band survived into the 1980s and inspired follow-ups, both frivolous and serious, such as the Bonzo Dog Doo Dah Band (1966–70), the New Vaudeville Band (1966), the Whoopee Band, the more jazz-slanted Anglo-American Alliance, and the excellent Midnite Follies organized by pianist Keith Nichols (*b* 1945) and composer Alan Cohen (*b* 1934) in 1978.

Temperance songs. The abuse of alcohol, a fact of life ever since alcoholic drink was first invented, had become a pressing social problem by the middle of the 19th century; drink being, on the one hand, according to the point of view, either the solace of the poor or 'the curse of the working-class'; and, on the other, a source of pleasure, glorified by those who could afford to make it an expensive hobby. If the masher lion-comiques of the music halls were always singing the praises of champagne and 'glorious beer', how could the poor be denied the comfort of a measure of gin, the only luxury that was cheaply available? The answer to this, as many upright Christians sincerely believed, was temperance. The word is important because the aim of most of the societies that arose in the USA and Europe was a reduction in drinking, not its prohibition, which nobody really wanted. The Women's Christian Temperance Union was formed in the USA in 1874 and set about their condemnation of the devil drink with flag-waving enthusiasm and a growing repertoire of songs many of them, as those written by the indefatigable Emmett G. Coleman, of hymn-like piety and passion; others of a more theatrical nature as dramatically retailed by composers such as Henry *Russell. There were, of course, many who mocked, and songs like Coleman's 'Father, dear Father, come home' were hardly rendered in the same spirit of ridicule as they are in the present enlightened days.

The temperance movement grew, however, with other bodies like the Anti-Saloon League adding weight, and headed by a few excessive zealots like Carry Nation who resorted to physical demonstrations; and the obvious evils of excessive drink were apparent to all. The clean-living craze that came with the First World War was partly responsible for the ease with which the Prohibition lobby, headed by Andrew Joseph Volstead, managed to get the American prohibition bill passed in 1919. The frustrated results of its enforcement from 1920 onward were hardly what the well-meaning promoters of temperance had intended.

J. Young and S. W. Leonard: *The National Temperance Songster* (Cincinnati, 1855). E. G. Coleman (ed.): *The Temperance Songbook* (New York, 1907; repr. London, 1967).

Tempest, Marie [Etherington, Marie Susan] (*b* London, 15 July 1864; *d* London, 15 Oct. 1942). British actress and singer. She found her early successes in the world of operetta and musical comedy before switching to straight roles. Her main musical appearances were in *Boccaccio* (1885); **Erminie* (1885); *La Bernaise* (1886); **Dorothy* (1887); *Doris* (1889); *The Red Hussar* (1889; NY, 1890); *The Tyrolean* (NY, 1891); *The Fencing Master* (NY, 1892); *The Algerian* (NY, 1893); *An *Artist's Model* (1895); *The *Geisha* (1896); *A Greek Slave* (1898); and **San Toy* (1899).

H. Bolitho: *Marie Tempest* (London, 1936).

Temple, Richard [Cobb] (*b* London, 2 Mar. 1847; *d* London, 19 Oct. 1912). British actor and singer. He made his debut in the first opera to be produced at the Crystal Palace in 1869, then sang and acted for many years in repertory and touring companies. He had a brief spell in 1877 as manager of the old Philharmonic Theatre in Islington, from where he joined the D'Oyly Carte Opera Company and appeared in *The Sorcerer* (1877). He was the original Dead-Eye Dick in **HMS Pinafore* (1878), the Pirate King in *The *Pirates of Penzance* (1880); and he was in all the *Gilbert and Sullivan operas that appeared thereafter until 1889, when he turned down a part in *The *Gondoliers* and for a while retired from the stage. He later made fitful appearances in other light operas.

Temple, Shirley Jane (*b* Santa Monica, Calif., 23 Apr. 1928). American actress, dancer, and singer. Probably the best-known child actress of all time, she began to appear in short films, the first being *Red Haired Alibi* (1933), at the age of three, and she was a well-known star by the time she was five. Her first starring role was in *Little Miss Marker* (1934); followed by *Baby Take a Bow* (1934)—'On account-a I love you'; *Stand Up and Cheer* (1934)—'Baby, take a bow'; *Bright Eyes* (1934)—'On the good ship Lollipop'; *Curly Top* (1935)—'Animal crackers in my soup', 'When I grow up', 'Curly top'; *The Little Colonel* (1935); *The Littlest Rebel* (1935); *Captain January* (1936)—'At the codfish ball'; *Dimples* (1936)—'Picture me without you'; *Poor Little Rich Girl* (1936)—'Oh, my goodness', 'But definitely'; *Stowaway* (1936); *Rebecca of Sunnybrook Farm* (1938); *Little Miss Broadway* (1938); *Just Around the Corner* (1938); *The Little Princess* (1939); *The Blue Bird* (1940); *Young People* (1940); all made for Fox films.

As the titles suggest, there was a great deal of coy sugariness in the roles she was assigned, but she was also a remarkably self-assured young actress who matched such stars as James Dunn (1905–67), Bojangles *Robinson (with whom she danced in four films), John *Boles, Buddy Ebsen, Alice *Faye, and others, a competent singer and dancer, and with plenty of precocious charm. In her teens she continued in straight roles in a number of films 1944–9, leaving the screen in 1950 to settle down to married life and to work for charity, although she did return as hostess of 'The Shirley Temple Show' on TV in 1960. She became a prominent figure in Californian and American politics, and was nominated as a Republican candidate in 1967. She was ambassador to Ghana in the 1970s and US Chief of Protocol; in 1990 she was appointed US ambassador to Czechoslovakia.

L. C. Eby: *Shirley Temple* (Derby, Conn., 1962). J. Basinger: *Temple* (New York, 1975). R. Windeler: *Films of Shirley Temple* (New York, 1978). A. Edwards: *Shirley Temple: American Princess* (London, 1988).

Templeton, Alec (*b* Cardiff, 4 July 1909; *d* Greenwich, Conn., 28 Mar. 1963). British-born American pianist and composer. Blind from birth, he started playing the piano at the age of two and wrote his first composition at four. He studied at the Royal College of Music until 1923, at the Royal Academy of Music until 1931. From 1927 he had a distinguished career as a solo pianist in England until in 1935 he went to live in the USA, becoming an American citizen in 1941. He became a popular performer on radio, making a speciality of gentle musical satire in which he parodied various composers in pieces like 'Bach goes to town' (1938), 'Mozart matriculates', 'Through *The Ring* in five minutes', 'Topsy turvy suite', 'Mendelssohn mows 'em down', 'Debussy in Dubuque', 'Mozart à la mode', and 'Beethoven visits Tin Pan Alley'; as well as more serious compositions.

Templeton, Fay (*b* Little Rock, Ark., 25 Dec. 1865; *d* San Francisco, 3 Oct. 1939). American singer with an extrovert style who was the lead in many of *Weber and Fields productions, and in later Broadway musicals. She appeared in London in *Monte Cristo Jr.* (1886); then in New York in **Madame Favart* (1893); *Hurly Burly* (1898); *Catherine* (1899); *Broadway to Tokyo* (1900); *Fiddle-Dee-Dee* (1900)—'Ma blushin' Rosie'; *Hoity Toity* (1901); *Twirly Whirly* (1902); *The Runaways* (1903); *A Little Bit of Everything* (1904); *Lifting the Lid* (1905); **Forty-Five Minutes from Broadway* (1906)—'Mary's a grand old name'; *Hokey Pokey* (1912); and **Roberta* (1933)—'Yesterdays'.

Temptations, The. American vocal group formed in 1961, the original line-up being Otis Williams [Miles] (*b* 1941), Melvin Franklin [David English] (*b* 1942), Eldridge Bryant (*b* 1938)—all from the Distants; Eddie Kendricks (1940–92) and Paul Williams (*b* 1939)—both from the Primes. They began to record for the *Tamla Motown company in 1962. Eldridge Bryant was replaced by David Ruffin (1941–91) in 1962, and they had their first big hit with Smokey *Robinson's 'The way you do the things you do' in 1964, and a No. 1 hit in 1965 with 'My girl', soon becoming one of the leading black vocal groups of the 1960s. Their smooth style took on a sharper edge in 1966 when they started to work with writer and producer Norman Whitfield (*b* 1943), as heard in 'Ain't too proud to beg' and 'Beauty is only skin deep'.

In 1966, David Ruffin left to pursue a solo career, to be replaced by Dennis Edwards (*b* 1943), and the group now took a move towards what has been described as psychedelic soul, with a greater use of electronic effects and a greater rock element in their singing. This phase brought a No. 1 hit in 'I can't get next to you' (1969). Next there was a reversion to the softer, more soulful sound as in the next No. 1 'Just my imagination' (1971). Whitfield again sharpened things up with items like 'Papa was a rollin' stone' (1972). The group continued to operate, though with less impact than previously, after many changes of personnel and sentimental reunions, the longest-lasting member of the group being Melvin Franklin.

10cc. British pop/rock group formed in 1972 with Eric Stewart (*b* 1945) (guitar and vocal), Graham Gouldman (*b* 1946) (bass and vocal), Lol Creme (*b* 1947) (guitar and vocal), and Kevin Godley (*b* 1945) (drums and vocal); all from various groups working in Manchester. After playing as a backing group on a Neil *Sedaka recording, 10cc was launched in 1972 and had a quick hit with 'Donna', a Godley and Creme parody of a typical American 1950s number, followed by a No. 1 hit with the controversial 'Rubber bullets' (1973). Much of their entertainment value arises from a keenly satirical vein, but they also achieved their own kind of originality, as in their 'I'm not in love' (1975), which reached No. 1 in the UK, No. 2 in the USA. Godley and Creme left in 1976 to work as a duo and later to go into the video business, but Stewart and Gouldman, with new recruits, continued the group's progress.

G. Tremlett: *The 10cc Story* (London, 1976).

Ternent, Billy [William] (*b* North Shields, 10 Oct. 1899; *d* London, 23 Mar. 1977). British bandleader, composer, arranger, and musician. Able to play most instruments of the orchestra, he made his start as a violinist, was playing professionally when he was 12, and conducting in music-halls on Tyneside by the age of 16. He went to London in the early 1920s and was playing at the Kit-Kat Restaurant when he was offered a job in the Jack *Hylton band as a saxophonist. He eventually became arranger and deputy leader. On the outbreak of war in 1939 he joined the BBC as musical director and, besides leading the BBC Dance Orchestra, also conducted for all the radio variety shows in the early 1940s, including *ITMA*, for which he wrote the signature tune. He left the BBC in 1944 to tour army camps and to conduct West End shows, returning to broadcasting in 1946 as conductor of the long-running *Variety Bandbox*. He maintained a regular dance band which worked with such visiting stars as Bob *Hope and Frank *Sinatra, and conducted several London *Palladium shows. He continued to present traditional dance music in the old sweet rhythm style he had evolved in the 1940s; and composed many items under the name of Cy Miller, as well as under his own name.

Terriss, Ellaline [*née* Lewin] (*b* Stanley, Falkland Islands, 13 Apr. 1871; *d* Richmond, Surrey, 16 June 1971). British actress and singer. Trained for the stage by her father William Terriss, she made her first apperance with Beerbohm Tree at the Haymarket Theatre, London, in 1888 and was engaged by Charles Wyndham to appear in numerous productions until she retired in 1929. She reappeared in 1935, made several films, then went to live in South Africa 1939–46. A strikingly beautiful person with dark complexion and golden hair and a sweet singing voice, she appeared in several important musicals beginning with *His Excellency* (1894). She was then engaged by George *Edwardes for the *Gaiety Theatre and became a popular musical comedy star, appearing with her husband Seymour *Hicks in nine productions.

Her shows included: *The *Shop Girl* (1895); *My Girl* (1896); *The *Circus Girl* (1896); *A *Runaway Girl* (1898); **Bluebell in Fairyland* (1901); *The Cherry Girl* (1903); *The *Catch of the Season* (1905); *The Beauty of Bath* (1906); *The Gay Gordons* (1907); *The Dashing Little Duke* (1909); *Captain Kidd* (1910); and *Cash on Delivery* (1917). From 1910 she appeared with Hicks on the music-hall stage singing 'The honeysuckle and the bee' and other hits of the day, recording a selection of the songs they sang in 1932.

E. Terris: *Ellaline Terriss: by Herself and with Others* (London, 1928). S. Hicks: *Me and My Missus* (London, 1939) [and other books by Hicks]. E. Terriss: *A Little Bit of String* (London, 1955).

Terry, Clark (*b* St Louis, Mo., 14 Dec. 1920). American jazz trumpeter and vocalist. He was with various St Louis bands before joining the dance band of the US Navy during the war. He continued a brilliant career with Charlie *Barnet 1947–8, Count *Basie 1948–51, Duke *Ellington 1951–9, and Quincy* Jones 1959–60. He developed a highly individual and often humorous style, adept with mutes, and using the flugelhorn extensively; also singing in a sometimes satirical blues manner. He led various bands of his own from the 1960s and was much involved in jazz education.

Terry, Sonny [Terrell, Saunders] (*b* Greenboro, NC, 24 Oct. 1911; *d* New York, 11 Mar. 1986). American country blues singer and harmonica player. As a result of two unfortunate accidents, he was blind in both eyes by the time he was 16, and made his living by singing in the streets and in local shows. He teamed up with Piedmont blues stylist Blind Boy Fuller [Fulton Allen] (1908–41) during the depression years, and they made several records together. His reputation grew and he appeared in the famous *Spirituals to Swing* concert at the Carnegie Hall in 1939. In 1941 he formed a duo with guitarist and vocalist Brownie *McGhee, a partnership that was to last for more than 40 years, touring the USA and making European visits most years; also going to India in 1960 and Australia in 1965. He appeared in **Finian's Rainbow* 1946–7, with his 'Hootin' the blues' used as an opening piece; and in *Cat on a Hot Tin Roof* (1956). He retained a country style of singing, intense and moving, alternating with his own pointed harmonica playing.

Teschemacher, Frank (*b* Kansas City, Mo., 13 Mar. 1906; *d* Chicago, 1 Mar. 1932). Jazz clarinettist, violinist, and arranger. Then playing violin, alto-saxophone, and banjo, he was one of the historic Austin High School Gang, pioneers of early Chicago jazz, taking up the clarinet in 1925 and quickly making a great impression as a highly individual and skilled performer. He is to be heard on recordings made with Charles Pierce, and *McKenzie and *Condon's Chicagoans in 1927; with the Chicago Rhythm Kings, Miff *Mole, and the Chocolate Dandies in 1928; and with the Friars Society Orchestra in 1929; having gone to New York in 1928 where he worked with Ben *Pollack and Sam Lanin. It has been said that his recorded work, interesting though it was, gave no hint of his real brilliance which impressed all who heard him. After returning to Chicago he was killed in a car crash.

Tex, Joe [Arrington, Joseph] (*b* Baytown, Texas, 8 Aug. 1933; *d* Navasota, Texas, 13 Aug. 1982). American soul singer and composer. After years of obscurity, he became known in the 1960s with recordings of his very personal and humorous musical diatribes on sex—'Hold what you got', 'A sweet woman like you', and 'The love you save'—which impressed by their directness. He once billed himself as 'Soul Brother No. 1', but was denied that ranking by James *Brown. He sang in a variety of entertaining styles in numbers like 'Skinny legs and all', 'Show me', and 'I believe I'm gonna make it', utilizing gospel, blues, and country music. His musical career was interrupted in the 1970s by his activities on behalf of the Muslim faith.

Tex-Mex. A style of dance music originated by the Tejanos (Texan Mexicans) that has much in common with *Cajun music, both using accordion-dominated ensembles. It has evolved from *c.*1928, growing alongside black race music as a private idiom, before coming to a wider public by way of gramophone recordings, and revealing the talents of such accordionists as Santiago Jimenez (1913–84) and Narciso Martinez (*b* 1911) and bands such as the Conjunto Bernal led by Paulino Bernal (*b* 1939). Latterly the music has been taken up by such performers as Freddy Fender (*b* 1937), Doug Sahm (*b* 1941), Ry Cooder (*b* 1947), and *Santana; it has been exploited in films both as feature and as atmospheric background to Texas-Mexican stories; and there have been many authentic albums of its repertoire.

Tharpe, Sister Rosetta [Nubin, Rosetta] (*b* Cotton Plant, Ark., 20 Mar., 1915; *d* Philadelphia, 9 Oct. 1973). American gospel and blues singer and guitarist. Brought up in the gospel tradition, she first played acoustic guitar, later switching to electric. She sang with Cab *Calloway, recorded 'Pickin' the cabbage' (1940), then became better-known through her work with Lucky *Millinder 1941–2, recording items like 'Rock me', 'Trouble in mind', 'I want a tall skinny papa', 'Shout, sister, shout', and 'That's all' that were an early anticipation of the gospel styles to come. After a solo career in cabaret, at Café Society and elsewhere, she returned to a pure gospel idiom in 1944, recording, with Marie Knight, 'Didn't it rain' and 'Up above my head' for Decca, which made a great impression in the UK. She worked with such musicians as Sammy Price (1908–92), Pops Foster (1892–1969), and Kenny *Clarke. She made a sensational appearance at the Newport Jazz Festival in 1978 and went on to record albums for the Savoy label. A stroke in 1970 caused speech difficulties and an amputated leg; she gamely returned in 1972, working on crutches, but died just before she was about to make another recording.

Theatre Guild. American theatre production organization founded in 1919. It was mainly concerned with straight plays, but its history has been dotted with interesting American musical ventures, such as *The *Garrick Gaieties* (1925, 1926, and 1930) and **Porgy and Bess* (1935). There were artistic and financial disagreements in the 1930s which led to breakaway organizations, and a financial collapse that was saved by the phenomenal success of **Oklahoma!* (1943) and **Carousel* (1945). Later musical productions were **Allegro* (1947); *Arms and the Girl* (1950); **Bells Are Ringing* (1956); *The *Unsinkable Molly Brown* (1960); and *Darling of the Day* (1968).

Theodorakis, Mikis [Michalis] (*b* Chios, 29 July 1925). Greek composer. He studied at the Athens Conservatory, and wrote many songs and dances imbued with the spirit of Greek folk-music. In 1943 he joined the Greek resistance movement; and during the civil war of 1947–52 he was arrested and deported. He went to study in Paris under Olivier Messiaen in 1953, and had his first public concert in Paris in 1954. In 1956 he began to write film scores, his best-known being those for: *Luna de Miel* (1958); *Les Amants de Teruel* (1962); *Elektra* (1962); *Phaedra* (1962); *Zorba the Greek* (1964), which won him international renown; Z (1968); *The Day the Fish Came Out* (1968); and *The Trojan Women* (1971). In 1961 he had won the first prize in an Athens song festival; and in 1963 he became leader of the Lambrakis youth movement and a member of parliament. Between 1967 and 1970 he was imprisoned for political activities, finally being released as a result of international opinion, and going to Paris in 1970.

'These foolish things'. Song composed by Jack *Strachey and published in 1936, one of the few British songs to rank as an international standard alongside the songs of *Kern, *Gershwin, *Porter, and the like. The lyric-writer Eric *Maschwitz was then Director of Variety with the BBC and had to write under the name of Holt Marvell. He recalls in his autobiography, *No Chip on My Shoulder* (1957), how the lyric came out of the blue one Sunday morning at his flat in Adam Street, London. By lunchtime he had dictated the words to Strachey who had written the melody by the same evening.

Neither was very enthusiastic about the result; they were unable to get it published, and it aroused very little interest when first heard in the revue *Spread it Abroad* (1936), sung by Dorothy *Dickson. Soon after it was taken up by Leslie *Hutchinson [Hutch], who recorded it and made it into an immediate hit. Thereafter it was seized upon by singers everywhere and was used in the films *A Yank in the RAF* (1941), *Ghost Catchers* (1944), and *Tokyo Rose* (1945). Americanized lyrics were provided by Harry Link (1896–1956).

Thespis or The Gods Grown Old. 'An entirely original Grotesque Opera', with music by Arthur

*Sullivan and words by W. S. *Gilbert, their first collaboration, commissioned by John Hollingshead for the *Gaiety Theatre. Opening there on 26 Dec. 1871, it had a modest run of 64 performances, but made so little impression that, afterwards, the score was mainly forgotten and lost, Sullivan later making use of the only two surviving items 'Little maid of Arcadee' and 'Climbing over rocky mountains' in *The *Pirates of Penzance*. There was a reconstructed performance by the Gilbert and Sullivan Opera Company in New York in 1953, with additional music by Frank Miller.

T. Rees: *Thespis: a Gilbert and Sullivan Enigma* (London, 1964).

They're Playing Our Song. Musical show with score by Marvin *Hamlisch, lyrics by Carole Bayer Sager, and book by Neil *Simon, produced at the Imperial Theatre, New York, 11 Feb. 1979, and running for 1082 performances. It needed only two participants (Robert Klein and Lucie Arnaz) who related a semi-autobiographical story, based on the composer and lyric-writer's true relationship, of a neurotic composer, Vernon Gersch, and his collaborator Sonia Walsk, whose working and amatory partnership is disrupted by phone calls from her previous lover, for whom she still has a lingering liking. They tell their story through three vocal alter egos and songs such as 'Fallin'', 'If he really knew me', 'They're playing our song', Just for tonight', and 'When you're in my arms'.

Thiele, Bob (*b* Brooklyn, NY, 27 July 1922). American producer and songwriter. He started his career as an announcer for radio jazz shows 1936–44 and led a band, playing clarinet. He was the editor and publisher of *Jazz Magazine* 1939–41 and founded the Signature record label in 1939, which survived till 1948 and was the first to record Erroll *Garner. Many of his early record productions have been revived on the Dr Jazz label. In 1952 he joined Decca to work with such artists as Teresa *Brewer, Pearl *Bailey, and Lawrence *Welk; and he was a prime mover behind the careers of Eydie Gorme (*b* 1931), Steve *Lawrence, and Henry *Mancini. He moved to the Dot label in 1959 to produce records by Pat *Boone and the *Mills Brothers and to edit the sound-track of *The Five Pennies* (1959). He made albums with Jack Kerouac accompanied by Zoot *Sims and Al Cohn (1925–88), then joined Roulette in 1960 to record with Louis *Armstrong and Duke *Ellington. He was with ABC records 1961–9, working with such jazzmen as John *Coltrane, Charlie *Mingus, Archie Shepp (*b* 1937), Johnny *Hodges, Quincy *Jones, Earl *Hines, and Count *Basie. His own BluesWay label recorded T-Bone *Walker, B. B. *King, and John Lee *Hooker; and he founded other labels, working with Otis Spann (1930–70), Joe *Turner, and many others. He produced Armstrong's last album, *Louis Armstrong and His Friends*, which included 'Oh what a wonderful world' of which he was part-writer. His remarkable recording career continued into the 1980s.

This Year of Grace. Revue with music and words by Noël *Coward, produced in London (Pavilion) 22 Mar. 1928 [316p], with a cast that included Sonnie *Hale, Douglas *Byng, Jessie *Matthews, and Maisie Gay (1883–1945). It included the following Coward items—'I'm mad about you', 'A room with a view', 'Lorelei', 'Dance, little lady', 'Little women', and 'Try to learn to love'. It was produced in New York (Selwyn Theatre) 7 Nov. 1928, with Noël Coward, Beatrice *Lillie, Florence *Desmond, and Billy Milton (1905–89); and the song 'World weary' added [158p].

Thompson, Fred [Frederick James] (*b* London, 24 Jan. 1884; *d* London, 10 Apr. 1949). British librettist. He started a career as an architect, became a theatrical cartoonist on *London Opinion* and other papers, then spent three years as an actor. Finally he started writing revues and musicals, his output, in London and New York, including: *Eightpence-a-Mile* (1914); *The Merry-Go-Round* (1914); **Tonight's the Night* (1915); *The Only Girl* (1915); *Mr Manhattan* (1916); *The *Bing Boys Are Here* (1916); *Look Who's Here* (1916); *Houp-La* (1916); *The Bing Girls Are There* (1917); *The Other Bing Boys* (1917); *The Boy* (1917); *The Bing Boys on Broadway* (1918); *Afgar* (1919); *Baby Bunting* (1919); *Who's Hooper* (1919); *The Golden Moth* (1921); *The Cousin from Nowhere* (1923); **Lady Be Good* (1924); **Tip-Toes* (1925); and **Rio Rita* (1927).

Thornhill, Claude (*b* Terre Haute, Ind., 10 Aug. 1909; *d* Caldwell, NJ, 1 July 1965). American bandleader, pianist, arranger, and composer. His interest in music began at six when he formed a band known as the Harmonious Outcasts. He went on to study at the Curtis Institute and obtained musical degrees from Cincinnati Conservatory of Music and the University of Kentucky. He played on a riverboat and with bands in Cleveland before he finally settled in New York, where he played on recording sessions with Louis *Prima, Bud *Freeman, Bunny *Berigan, and Charlie *Spivak; and arranged for Paul *Whiteman, André *Kostelanetz, Freddie *Martin, Benny *Goodman, and others; before joining Ray *Noble as pianist (in the band which Glenn *Miller first led under his own name on record). He aroused interest with his effective arrangements of 'Loch Lomond' and 'Annie Laurie' for Maxine *Sullivan. In 1937 he went to Hollywood as arranger for MGM and helped Skinnay *Ennis form his band for the Bob *Hope radio show. He led his own band from 1939, his work typified by his arrangements of traditional and classical material such as 'Alt Wien', 'The doll dance', 'O sole mio', 'Traumerei', and 'Hungarian dance'; and arrangements by Gil *Evans. He joined the navy in 1942 and led a band in the South Pacific.

On his return to civilian life he started his band again with Gil Evans and Gerry *Mulligan as arrangers. As the big band vogue passed he used smaller pickup groups, later accompanying Tony *Bennett and Vic *Damone. A return to the big-band scene was planned but he died the day before the band was to make its debut in Atlantic City. Although not a big name in the swing world, he led one of its finest bands, with an individual use of french horns and clarinets framing his own deceptively simple piano playing. He was playing *cool jazz before the term was fashionable and, although he used other arrangers, he led them towards the typical Thornhill sound.

Thornton, James (*b* Liverpool, 5 Dec. 1861; *d* Astoria, NY, 27 July 1938). British-born American composer and entertainer. He went to the USA in 1870 and began his entertaining career as a singing waiter in Boston in 1878. A heavy drinker, he was shepherded through life by his wife Bonnie, who was herself a singer, known professionally as Lizzie Cox. She did her best to look after the family finances and to keep her husband on the straight and narrow path. He teamed up with Charles *Lawlor as a vaudeville duo and later became very popular through an act in which he delivered a mock-solemn sermon. He wrote a number of simple but memorable songs, many of which were performed and made successful by his wife. Some of the best were written during periods of enforced idleness in places like Bellevue Hospital, and other clinics, where he underwent regular alcoholic cures. After all these had failed, he renounced drinking and died a sober and moralizing man. He never made much from his best-known song 'When you were sweet sixteen' (1898), having sold it outright for $15. When the copyright expired in 1948, his widowed second wife was able to renew it and gain something from its revived popularity.

His songs included: 'The Upper Ten and the Lower Five' (1889), 'The Irish jubilee' (1890), 'My sweetheart's the man in the moon' (1892), 'The streets of Cairo' (1893), 'She may have seen better days' (1894), 'Don't give up the old love for the new' (1896), 'On the benches in the park' (1896), 'It don't seem like the same old smile' (1896), 'When I took the Keeley cure' (1897), 'There's a little star shining for you' (1897), 'The bridge of sighs' (1900), and 'There's a mother always waiting at home sweet home' (1903).

Thoroughly Modern Millie. A Universal film of 1967, starring Julie *Andrews and Mary Tyler Moore (*b* 1936), with Carol *Channing and Beatrice *Lillie. A 1920s pastiche, it used special material, like the theme song by Jimmy *Van Heusen and Sammy *Cahn, and many old 1920s songs: 'Baby face' (*Akst), 'Do it again' (*Gershwin), 'Poor butterfly' (*Hubbell), 'Japanese sandman' (*Whiting), 'Stumbling' (*Confrey), 'I'm sitting on top of the world' (*Henderson), 'Charmaine' (*Pollack), and 'I can't believe that you're in love with me' (*McHugh).

Three Little Words. MGM film of 1950 starring Fred *Astaire with Vera-Ellen, Debbie *Reynolds (playing Helen Kane, with Kane dubbing the voice), and Red Skelton (*b* 1910). It was a biography of Bert *Kalmar and Harry *Ruby which used many of their song hits, including: 'Three little words', 'Who's sorry now', 'I wanna be loved by you', 'All alone Monday', 'Hooray for Captain Spaulding', and 'She's mine, all mine'.

Threepenny Opera, The see *Dreigroschenoper, Die.*

Tierney, Harry Austin (*b* Perth Amboy, NJ, 21 May 1890; *d* New York, 22 Mar. 1965). American composer. From a musical family, he intended to study 'serious' music, but a strong inclination towards the world of popular music dominated and he began to write songs while he was still at his academic studies. He worked with a music-publisher in London for a year. Back in New York in 1916, he managed to get one or two songs into Broadway shows before writing his first complete musical comedy score, **Irene* (1920)—a lasting success which included 'Alice blue gown'. During the 1920s he wrote regular shows, many of them for Florenz *Ziegfeld, including: *What Next?* (1917); *The Broadway Whirl* (1921); *Up She Goes* (1922); *Glory* (1922); *Kid Boots* (1923); **Ziegfeld Follies* (1924); **Rio Rita* (1927; filmed 1930—the second Hollywood adaptation of a Broadway musical, *The *Desert Song* being the first)—'You're always in my arms', 'Rio Rita', 'The rangers' song'; and *Cross My Heart* (1928). His writing gifts began to desert him in the 1930s and, unlike most popular composers of the time, he had no success, apart from *Rio Rita*, in Hollywood. His songs were of the fleeting Tin Pan Alley kind and few are now remembered; but he also wrote good rags, including 'Louisiana rag' (1913).

'Tiger rag'. A much-played novelty piece which is usually credited as being the joint composition of Nick *La Rocca and other members of the *Original Dixieland Jazz Band. It has been revealed that the four themes that make up the composition, a French quadrille (earlier known as 'Jack Carey'), a waltz, a stomp passage with clarinet breaks, and a riff theme, were all in use in New Orleans long before 1900. Jelly Roll *Morton demonstrated, on the recordings he made for the Library of Congress (his remarks later supported by Sidney *Bechet and others), how he, among others, transformed the old tunes into the jazz standard 'Tiger rag'. He simulated the tiger roars by putting his whole forearm down on the keys. It has always been popular in the jazz world, with good performances by Duke *Ellington (1929), Louis *Armstrong (1930, 1932, 1934, and later). Art *Tatum (1933 and 1940), and Kid *Ory (1946); in addition to the ODJB's versions of 1917 and 1937. It was widely used as a novelty number, becoming an amusing part of the *Mills Brothers repertoire and often done with less taste and much speed by many others. Harry *Roy had his own popular 'modernistic' version in 1935.

Tilley, Vesta [Powles, Matilda Alice] (*b* Worcester, 1864; *d* Monte Carlo, 16 Sept. 1952). British music-hall impersonator and singer. She first appeared on the stage in her father's music-hall in Gloucester at the age of four, and later toured with him as 'Harry Ball, the Tramp Musician, and the Great Little Tilley'. Having tried songs of all kinds and both genders, she decided by 1869 that she preferred being dressed as a boy, and appeared in that guise in Birmingham that year billed as 'Tiny Tilley, the Pocket Sims Reeves'. Her songs then included 'Pretty Jane' and 'Come into the garden, Maud' from the Sims repertoire.

She first appeared in London at the Canterbury in 1874, and by 1880 she was regularly seen in West End halls as 'The London Idol'. Her attire was so attractively displayed on her trim figure that she actually became an inspirer of male fashions; yet she always managed to remain feminine and was equally attractive in female dress. She appeared at the first Royal Command Performance in 1912. Her later repertoire included 'Following in father's footsteps', 'After the ball', 'Algy, the Piccadilly Johnny with the little glass eye', 'The midnight son', and 'Burlington Bertie'. She first appeared in the USA at *Pastor's 14th Street Theatre in 1898 and made several later visits, also appearing in the show *My Lady Molly*. Her military garbs were ideal when she helped recruitment drives in the First World War and her singing of songs like 'Jolly good luck to the girl who loves a soldier' and 'The Army of today's all right' earned her the title of 'England's Greatest Recruiting Sergeant'.

In 1890 she married the theatre proprietor Walter de Frece, who became Member of Parliament for Ashbury, later Blackpool, and was knighted in 1919. Thus she became Lady de Frece, retiring, after a highly emotional final appearance at the London Coliseum, in 1920 to enjoy a stately 32 years of maturity in Monte Carlo. A film of her life, *After the Ball*, was made in 1957 with Pat Kirkwood as Tilley and Laurence Harvey as her husband.

Lady de Frece [Tilley]: *Recollections of Vesta Tilley* (London, 1934). G. Sudworth: *The Great Little Tilley* (London, 1984). S. Maitland: *Vesta Tilley* (London, 1986).

Till the Clouds Roll By. MGM film of 1946 based on the life of Jerome *Kern and using many of his most famous songs. Directed by Richard Whorf (1906–66) and Vincente *Minnelli, the cast included Judy *Garland, Lena *Horne, June *Allyson, Kathryn *Grayson, Frank *Sinatra, Dinah *Shore, and many more, with Robert Walker (1914–51) as the composer.

Tin Pan Alley. A name that has become synonymous with the production and exploitation of popular song. In New York many of the early popular music publishers had their offices around Union Square and the theatre district, but the influential firm of *Witmark moved, in the early 1890s, to 28th Street, and others soon followed. By the end of the century it seemed that the whole of the popular music trade had moved there and set up offices in or around that particular street. Credit for the invention of the nickname is generally given to composer Monroe H. *Rosenfeld, who, in his newspaper column, likened the noise going on there to the clashing of tin pans. Apart from isolated outposts in Boston, Chicago, and other cities, the New York publishers of 28th Street very much controlled the growth of popular music and most of its output from 1900 on. Thus the whole popular music industry was referred to as Tin Pan Alley. The pop music-publishing business of the 1960s was largely centred at the Brill Building at 1619 Broadway.

London's equivalent Tin Pan Alley accolade was given to a seedy byway off the Charing Cross Road, called Denmark Street, where there was certainly a preponderance of the trade, though the music-publishing business in London was always rather more scattered than it was in New York.

I. Goldberg: *Tin Pan Alley: a Chronicle of the American Popular Music Racket* (New York, 1930; rev. 1961). J. Burton: *The Blue Book of Tin Pan Alley* (New York, 1950; rev. 1962). H. Meyer: *The Gold in Tin Pan Alley* (New York, 1958; repr. 1977). D. Ewen: *The Life and Death of Tin Pan Alley* (New York, 1964). E. Rogers and M. Hennessey: *Tin Pan Alley* (London, 1964). I. Whitcomb: *Tin Pan Alley: a Pictorial History (1919–1939)* (London, 1975).

Tiomkin, Dimitri (*b* St Petersburg, 10 May 1894; *d* London, 11 Nov. 1979). Russian-born American composer, conductor, and pianist. His father was a doctor and his mother a pianist. When he was 13 he studied at the St Petersburg Conservatory under Glazunov, in his spare time giving piano lessons and playing for silent films. He had already started composing before moving to Berlin after the 1917 Revolution and while studying with Busoni, and playing with the Berlin Philharmonic Orchestra, he managed to get several dance compositions published. Later, in Paris, he was part of a two-piano act with which he went to the USA in 1925, appearing as both duettist and soloist at Carnegie Hall and the New York Town Hall. He composed the ballet *Mars* for his wife Albertina Rasch (1896–1967), the ballerina and choreographer, who was then working in Hollywood and brought ballet to Broadway in such shows as **Rio Rita*, **Three's a Crowd*, *The *Cat and the Fiddle*, and **Lady in the Dark*. He began writing film scores somewhat unwillingly but gradually gained an enthusiasm for the work and was to become one of the busiest of all film composers and conductors. Over the years he won a number of Academy Awards for his scores and 'main themes', many of the latter being turned into best-selling songs by lyricists Paul Francis Webster and Ned *Washington. He was especially successful in supplying grandiose backgrounds for epic films and Westerns, but he was also a versatile writer and handled any kind of score. He published an autobiography *Please Don't Hate Me* (New York, 1959).

His films included: *Devil May Care* (1930)—ballet; *Lord Byron of Broadway* (1930)—ballet; *The Rogue Song* (1930)—ballet; *Our Blushing Brides*

(1930)—ballet; *Resurrection* (1931); *Alice in Wonderland* (1933); **Naughty Marietta* (1935)—ballet; *The Casino Murder Case* (1935); *Lost Horizon* (1937); *You Can't Take it With You* (1938); *The *Great Waltz* (1938); *Only Angels Have Wings* (1939); *Mr Smith Goes to Washington* (1939); *The Westerner* (1940); *Meet John Doe* (1941); *The Corsican Brothers* (1941); *The Moon and Sixpence* (1942); *The Unknown Guest* (1943); *The Bridge of San Luis Rey* (1944); *Forever Yours* (1944); *Pardon My Past* (1945); *Whistle Stop* (1946); *Black Beauty* (1946); *Duel in the Sun* (1946); *The Long Night* (1947); *Red River* (1948); *Portrait of Jennie* (1949); *Champagne for Caesar* (1950); *Cyrano de Bergerac* (1950); *Strangers on a Train* (1951); *Peking Express* (1951); *Mutiny* (1952); *The Big Sky* (1952); *High Noon* (1952)—'High noon' ('Do not forsake me') (*w* Washington)—Academy Award; *The Steel Trap* (1952); *Return to Paradise* (1953)—'Return to Paradise' (*w* Washington); *Blowing Wild* (1953)—'Blowing wild' ('Ballad of black gold') (*w* Webster); *The Command* (1954); *Dial M for Murder* (1954); *The High and the Mighty* (1954; Academy Award)—'The high and the mighty' (*w* Washington); *A Bullet is Waiting* (1954); *The Adventures of Hajji Baba* (1954)—'Hajji Baba' (*w* Washington); *Land of the Pharaohs* (1955)—'This too shall pass away' (*w* Washington); *Julie* (1955)—'Julie' (*w* Walcott); *Strange Lady in Town* (1955)—'Strange lady in town' (*w* Washington); *Friendly Persuasion* (1956)—'Thee I love' (*w* Webster); *Tension at Table Rock* (1956); *Giant* (1956); *Gunfight at the OK Corral* (1957); *Night Passage* (1957); *Search for Paradise* (1957); *Wild is the Wind* (1958); *The Old Man and the Sea* (1958; Academy Award); *Rio Bravo* (1959); *Last Train from Gun Hill* (1959); *The Alamo* (1960)—'Ballad of the Alamo', 'The green leaves of summer' (*w* Webster); *The Sundowners* (1960); *The Guns of Navarone* (1961); *The Last Sunset* (1961)—'Pretty little girl in the yellow dress' (*w* Washington); *55 Days at Peking* (1963); *The Fall of the Roman Empire* (1964); *Circus World* (1964); *Great Catherine* (1968); and *Tchaikovsky* (1970).

Tiple. More correctly the Hawaiian tiple, a large steel-stringed *ukelele that has a particularly percussive and ringing tone, derived from the Spanish treble (or tible) guitar. It was first exploited in popular music by the Spirits of Rhythm, a group who were popular in the 1930s, and used no less than three of them. It is also widely used in folk and country music.

Tip-Toes. Musical comedy with score by George *Gershwin, lyrics by Ira *Gershwin, and book by Guy *Bolton and Fred *Thompson, produced at the Liberty Theatre, New York, 28 Dec. 1925.

A light-hearted story concerning dancer Tip-Toes Kaye (Queenie Smith, 1902–78), stranded at Palm Beach with her conniving uncles who try to pass her off as an heiress so that she can catch a rich husband. She falls for a glue manufacturer called Steve Burton (Allen *Kearns), who claims poverty, but happily turns out to be rich. The frailty of the story was bolstered by songs like 'Looking for a boy', 'That certain feeling', 'These charming people' (all sung by Smith), and 'Sweet and low-down': and it had 194 performances.

It was produced in London (Winter Garden Theatre) 31 Aug. 1926 with Dorothy *Dickson [182p]. A film, which bore little relation to the show, was made in England, with Dorothy Gish (1898–1968) and Will Rogers (1879–1935), in 1928.

Tizol, Juan (*b* San Juan, Puerto Rico, 22 Jan. 1900; *d* Inglewood, Calif., 23 Apr. 1984). American trombonist, composer, and arranger. He played in the municipal band in San Juan, then went to the USA in 1920. He played the valve trombone and, after various jobs in bands and pit orchestras, made his mark as an important member of the Duke *Ellington orchestra 1929–44, not only playing, but writing for the band such exotic items as 'Caravan' (with Ellington, 1937), 'Perdido' (1937), 'Lost in meditation' (1938), 'Pyramid' (with Ellington, 1938), and 'Conga brava' (1940). He was with the Harry *James band from 1944 until he retired, making occasional trips back to the Ellington fold 1951–3 and 1960.

Tobias, Charles (*b* New York, 15 Aug. 1898; *d* New York, 7 July 1970). American composer, lyricist, and singer. He worked as a singing demonstrator of songs with a music-publisher from 1916, became a pioneering broadcaster from 1921, worked in vaudeville for many years, and later ran his own publishing business in New York. He wrote music for **Earl Carroll's Sketchbook* (1935), **Hellzapoppin* (1938), and *Yokel Boy* (1939). He contributed to films: *Start Cheering* (1937); *Shine On, Harvest Moon* (1944)—'Time waits for no-one'; *Saratoga Trunk* (1945)—'As long as I live'; *Tomorrow is Forever* (1946); *Love and Learn* (1947); and *The Daughter of Rosie O'Grady* (1950). Other remembered songs of his were: 'Get out and get under the moon' (1928, *m* Larry *Shay), 'It's the gypsy in me' (with Cliff *Friend, 1936), 'Little lady, make believe' (with Nat Simon, 1900–79, 1938), 'Start the day right' (1939), 'Don't sit under the apple tree' (with Sammy *Stept and Lew *Brown, 1942), 'No can do' (with Simon, 1945), 'The old lamplighter' (with Simon, 1946); and many more.

He often worked in collaboration with his brother Harry Tobias (*b* New York, 9 Sept. 1895), a lyric-writer, who set up his own business after the First World War. From 1929 he worked in Hollywood; his best-known lyric was 'Sweet and lovely' (*m* Gus *Arnheim and Jules Lemare).

Tolbecque, Jean-Baptiste-Joseph (*b* Hanzinne, 17 Apr. 1797; *d* Paris, 23 Oct. 1869). Belgian composer, conductor, and violinist. One of a family of musicians who made up a sort of lesser *Strauss dynasty. His three brothers were all conductors and composers; Auguste-Joseph (*b* Hanzinne, 28 Feb. 1801; *d* Paris, 27 May 1869) was a violinist at the Opéra in Paris and worked for several years at the Haymarket in London; Charles-Joseph (*b* Paris, 27 May 1806; *d* Paris, 29 Dec. 1835) was a violinist, a pupil of Kreutzer and, from 1830, musical director at the Variétés where he composed many pieces; and the eldest brother, Isidore-Joseph (*b* Hanzinne, 17 Apr. 1794; *d* Vichy, 10 May 1871), who was a well-known composer and conductor of dance music.

Jean-Baptiste-Joseph was the most eminent of the family in the field of light music. After studying at the Paris Conservatoire from 1816 with Kreutzer and Reicha, he was a violinist at the Théâtre-Italien 1820–5. He then became director of music of the Court balls and at the Tivoli Gardens, then at the height of their popularity. As conductor and composer of a great many quadrilles, waltzes, galops, etc., he had a great influence on the development of popular dance music of the day. He remained the leader in the field until Philippe Musard started in rivalry around 1835; and was also musical director at Almack's in London for many years. He wrote an opéra-comique, *Charles V et Duguesclin* (1827), and had a success with his ballet *Vert-Vert* at the Paris Opéra in 1835.

Tonight at Eight-Thirty. Nine one-act plays by Noël *Coward, produced in two groups at the Phoenix Theatre, London, from 9 Jan. 1936 and 13 Jan. 1936, with Noël Coward and Gertrude *Lawrence [157p]. Those with musical interest were *Family Album*—'Here's a toast', 'Hearts and flowers'; and *Red Peppers*—'Has anybody seen our ship?', 'Men about town', which cruelly but authentically portrayed a faded music-hall duo act, both premiered on 9 Jan. *Shadow Play*—'Then', 'Play, orchestra, play', 'You were there'; and *We Were Dancing*—'We were dancing' were in the 13 Jan. programme. Three of the plays, including *Red Peppers*, were filmed under the collective title *Meet Me Tonight* (1952).

Tonight's the Night. Musical farce with score by Paul *Rubens and Max *Darewski, book by Fred *Thompson, lyrics by Rubens and Percy *Greenbank, produced in New York at the Shubert Theatre 24 Dec. 1914 [108p]; London (*Gaiety Theatre) 18 Apr. 1915 [460p]. The cast included Leslie *Henson, George *Grossmith Jr., and Haidée de Rance. Although it had a good score with things like 'Please don't flirt with me', 'Round the corner', 'I'd like to bring my Mother', 'The only way'—it was deemed necessary to add two numbers by Jerome *Kern to the London production—his first great hit, which was soon as popular in London as it had been in America, 'They wouldn't believe me' (*w* M. E. Rourke), originally in *The Girl from Utah* (1914), and 'Any old night' (*w* Harry B. *Smith).

Top Hat. RKO Radio film of 1935 starring Fred *Astaire and Ginger *Rogers, with a score full of Irving *Berlin's best songs like 'Top hat, white tie and tails', 'Isn't this a lovely day', 'The piccolino', 'No strings', and 'Cheek to cheek'. The cast also included Eric Blore (1887–1959), Edward Everett Horton (1886–1970), Erik Rhodes (*b* 1906), Helen *Broderick, and Lucille *Ball.

Top of the Pops. Popular British BBC TV programme which has been transmitted since 1963. Compèred by the leading disc jockeys, it offers a visual impression of the people and groups who are creating the best-selling pop recordings of the moment. As the music is traditionally mimed to recordings to avoid disaster, it is often interesting to listen to the sound of a full orchestra emerging from a quartet of jiving musicians.

Toreador, The. Musical play with score by Ivan *Caryll and Lionel *Monckton, lyrics by Adrian *Ross and Percy *Greenbank ('When I marry Amelia', 'Keep off the grass', 'Captivating Cora', 'Everybody's awfully good to me'); produced in London (*Gaiety Theatre) 17 June 1901, with Gertie *Millar, Lionel Mackinder (1868–1915), George *Grossmith Jr., Connie Ediss (1871–1934), and Marie Studholme (1875–1930) [675p]. This was the last show at the original Gaiety Theatre in the Strand. It was seen in New York (Knickerbocker Theatre) 6 Jan. 1902 [146p].

Tormé, Mel [Melvin Howard] (*b* Chicago, 13 Sept. 1925). American singer, actor, composer, writer, arranger, pianist, and drummer. He made his debut at the age of four, singing with the *Coon–Sanders Nighthawks, and started playing drums at six. He was acting in radio when he was eight and had his first song, 'Lament to love', recorded by Harry *James while he was still at school. In 1942 he was signed up by Ben *Pollack to sing with a band that was fronted by Chico Marx (1887–1961), and in 1943 made his screen debut in *Higher and Higher*, followed by the 'bobby-sox' musicals *Pardon My Rhythm* (1944) and *Let's Go Steady* (1945). In 1944 he formed a singing group, the Meltones, which recorded with Artie *Shaw and had a big hit with 'What is this thing called love?' He served in the army and continued his film career with *Good News* (1947); *Words and Music* (1948); and Disney's *So Dear to My Heart* (1949), in which he sang his own song, 'County fair'. Recording for Capitol, he produced his 'California Suite' (1949), a remarkable piece of writing specifically for LP production. His name will undoubtedly be remembered in the USA for writing 'The Christmas song' (1946), now a seasonal classic. He became internationally known after his live Crescendo Club recordings in Hollywood 1954, from which the hit recording of 'Mountain greenery' emerged. In 1963 he was arranger and musical associate on the Judy *Garland CBS-TV series and later wrote a book, *The Other Side of the Rainbow* (1970), about her. He continued to sing and record but moved more towards straight acting in the 1970s. Perhaps one of the best popular singers, in the pre-pop mode, of all time, he was helped, as most of the best singers are, by jazz phrasing, and was blessed with a tuneful and frequently beautiful quality of voice which went well with his great talent as an entertainer.

Torroba, Federico Moreno (*b* Madrid, 1891; *d* Madrid, 1982). Spanish composer and conductor. He studied at the Madrid Conservatory and first became known for his orchestral compositions such as his *Cuadros Castellanos* and a tuneful guitar sonatina which Segovia and others frequently played. He was a great advocate of the re-establishment of the guitar as Spain's national instrument. Later he was equally well-known as a composer for the musical theatre, beginning with *La Virgen de la Mayo* (1925) and having his greatest and most lasting success with the popular *Luisa Fernanda* (1932); followed by *La Chulapona* (1934), *La Caramba* and many more. He continued to write orchestral and guitar works and toured with his own operetta company, taking it to South America in the 1940s and the USA. He was musical director of the Teatro de la Zarzuela in Madrid and a frequent conductor on radio and TV.

Tours, Frank E. (*b* London, 1 Sept. 1877; *d* London, 2 Feb. 1963). British composer and conductor. Son of the songwriter Berthold Tours (1838–97), he studied at the Royal College of Music and became organist at St John's in Hammersmith. He conducted Stanford's *Shamus O'Brien* in 1897 and did a world tour 1903–4, becoming conductor at *Daly's Theatre, the *Gaiety, and the Prince of Wales Theatre between 1906 and 1912. He went to New York to conduct at the New Amsterdam Theatre for the *De Koven Company's revival of **Robin Hood*, returning to London to be musical director at the *Empire Theatre, Leicester Square. He went to the USA 1915–20, again returning to London as conductor of **Irene*; and he was to spend the rest of his career working on both sides of the Atlantic. He wrote scores for *Melnotte* (1901); *Mr Wix of Wickham* (1902); *The Dairymaids* (1906); *The Little Cherub* (1906); *The New Aladdin* (1906); *See See* (1906); *The Dashing Little Duke* (1909); *The Gay Lothario* (1913); and *Girl o' Mine* (1918). He also wrote many popular drawing-room ballads including 'Just a-wearyin' for you' (1901, *w* F. L. Stanton) and 'Mother o' mine' (1903, *w* Rudyard Kipling).

Toussaint, Allen (*b* New Orleans, 14 Jan. 1938). American composer, singer, pianist, and producer. He began his career as a piano accompanist, from 1955 working for Dave Bartholomew (*b* 1920) of Imperial records, and working with such singers as Smiley Lewis (*b* 1920) and Lloyd Price (*b* 1934). In 1958 he made his own instrumental album for RCA, *Wild Sounds of New Orleans*, under the name of Al Tousan. He started to write such lasting material as 'Java', which was used by Al Hirt (*b* 1922), and 'Whipped cream', used by Herb *Alpert.

He became active and well-known as a composer and producer, largely responsible for the New Orleans or Crescent City sound's prominence in the 1950s through to the 1970s, producing such rhythm 'n' blues classics as 'Ride your pony', 'Working in the coalmine', 'Holy cow', 'Mother-in-law', and 'Ruler of my heart'; also writing under the name of Naomi Neville and recording as both Toussaint and Tousan. In 1965 he helped to launch Sansu Enterprises and opened the Sea-Saint recording studios which became the most important creative recording outlet in New Orleans. He recorded further albums: *Toussaint* (1971), *Life, Love and Faith* (1972), *Southern Nights* (1975), and *Motion* (1978); produced the sound-track of *Pretty Baby* (1978); and continued to produce songs that were recorded by many top stars such as 'Soul sister' (1972), 'Lady Marmalade', and 'Right place, wrong time'.

Traditional. The credit 'traditional' following a title, especially on recordings, indicates or suggests (often wrongly) that the material is of old and of probably unknown or uncertain authorship; sometimes that it is simply out of copyright. It is more suited to musical use than the frequent 'anon.' of the poetry anthologies since it does not convey any sense of deliberate anonymity. Linked with other words, as in 'traditional jazz', the adjective simply suggests performance in an original or early manner. Traditional jazz is that which is played in the New Orleans manner or in styles deriving from it, whether in original or revival performances, the modes in use before the changes that came in with the *modern jazz period.

Traffic. British rock band formed in 1967 by Steve Winwood (*b* 1948) (vocal and guitar), Dave Mason (*b* 1947) (guitar), Jim Capaldi (*b* 1944) (vocal and drums), and Chris Wood (*b* 1944) (flute and saxophone). They put their act together in the seclusion of a Berkshire cottage and emerged to make their first hit recordings, 'Paper sun', 'Hole in my shoe', and 'Here we go round the mulberry bush', all in that year. The group had a bewildering history of departures, reunions, and additions, but nevertheless managed to maintain a unique sound that was a blend of rock, jazz, and folk-music, and produced eight varied but interesting albums between 1967 and 1973. The group was at its most effective on a German tour of 1973, documented in the album *On the Road*. They had a further British tour in 1974 and produced one more album, *When the Eagle Flies* (1974), before finally disbanding at the end of 1974. Capaldi, Winwood, and Mason all pursued effective solo careers.

Travis, Merle (*b* Rosewood, Ky., 29 Nov. 1917; *d* Tahlequah, Okla., 20 Oct. 1983). American country singer. He became a regular performer on Cincinnati radio station WLW, served in the Marines in the Second World War, then started a successful recording career promoting his own songs like 'Old mountain dew', 'Dark as a dungeon', 'Double talking baby', and 'Sixteen tons'. He appeared in a number of films, including *Honky Tonk Man* (1982). He was elected to the *Country Music Hall of Fame in 1977.

Tree Grows in Brooklyn, A. Musical with score by Arthur *Schwartz, lyrics by Dorothy *Fields, and book by George *Abbott and Betty Smith, upon whose original novel it was based; produced in New York (Alvin Theatre) 19 May 1951 [270p]. It is a sentimental and lachrymose story of a Brooklyn working-class family, the Nolans, in which Shirley Booth (*b* 1907) scored as the amorous Cissy ('Love is the reason'). The score also included 'Make the man love me', 'I'm like a new broom', 'Look who's dancing', and 'I'll buy you a star'.

Trenet, Charles (*b* Narbonne, 18 May 1913). French singer, actor, composer, and writer. Creator of more than 500 songs, and a poet much influenced by the surrealist Max Jacob (1876–1944), his gift for melody and an instinct for rhythmic emphasis made him a composer of great imagination and vitality. His optimistic outlook symbolized the mood of France after the political changes and 'le front populaire' of 1936. His talents were widely exploited in sales of sheet music and records after his first film success in *La Route enchantée* (1938). As a singer he showed a great mastery of microphone technique, and his impeccable diction and charm made him a prolific recording artist for Pathé-Marconi in the late 1930s and through to 1955; later with Barclay and CBS. He had a popular one-man show at the *Olympia Music Hall which attracted old and young alike. His best songs included 'Y'a d'la joie' (1936), 'Je chante' (1937), 'Fleur bleu' (1937), 'Boum' (1938), 'La polka de roi' (1938), 'La mer' (1945)—his biggest hit, 'La folle complainte' (1945), 'Le jardin extraordinaire' (1957), 'Chante le vent' (1966), and 'Il y avait' (1970). He also wrote three novels.

M. Pérez: *Charles Trenet* (Paris, 1964).

Trial by Jury. One-act operetta, described on the title-page of the score as 'a novel and original dramatic cantata'. It was the first important collaboration of Arthur *Sullivan and W. S. *Gilbert, a partnership brought together by Richard D'Oyly *Carte, who was to build his and their fortunes on it. The first production was as an opening 'filler' used before a production of *Offenbach's *La *Périchole* at the Royalty Theatre, London, 25 Mar. 1875, where it had 131 performances. It was taken to the Opera-Comique Theatre 13 Jan. 1876 [96p], and remained a regular part of the Savoy Operas repertoire. It was first seen in the USA at the Arch Street Theatre, Philadelphia, 22 Oct. 1875, and in New York at the Eagle Theatre 15 Nov. 1875.

It remains one of Sullivan's most polished gems, a nicely integrated and continuous musical score with such highlights as 'When first my old, old love I knew' and 'When I, good friends, was called to the Bar'. The 'plot' is a trial in which all the males in court show a reprehensible propinquity for being swayed by feminine charm.

Trip to Chinatown, A. 'Musical trifle' with score by Percy Gaunt (1852—96) and book by Charles Hale Hoyt (1860–1900), which toured the USA from 9 Nov. 1891 for a year, before settling in at the Madison Square Theatre, New York, 7 Aug. 1893, for a run of 650 performances, remaining the longest running show until **Irene* came along in 1919.

The story was a lightly farcical affair (*Hello, Dolly!* came from the same source) concerning a dinner invitation that goes wrong, ending with a wealthy gentleman, who is left to pay for it all, finding he has forgotten his wallet; and it was really of little import. But it proved an amusing pivot for a tuneful score that included the popular 'The Bowery' (which was one of the first show songs to become a sheet-music best-seller), 'Reuben and Cynthia', 'The pretty widow', and the interpolated *'After the ball' by Charles K. *Harris. There was a London production, with R. G. *Knowles in the cast, at Toole's Theatre 29 Sept. 1894 [125p], with 'The Bowery' now changed to, and equally popular as, 'Brighton' (new words by Fred *Gilbert).

Tristano, Lennie [Leonard Joseph] (*b* Chicago, 19 Mar. 1919; *d* New York, 18 Nov. 1978). American jazz pianist. Blind from childhood, he studied music at the American Conservatory in Chicago and, from 1946, settled to a club career in New York. He formed his own trio in 1947 which became a sextet 1949–52, its musicians including saxophonist Lee Konitz (*b* 1927), who had studied with Tristano when he started teaching in 1951, an occupation he mainly followed interspersed, in later years, with a few festival appearances. Starting as a disciple of Art *Tatum and Earl *Hines, Tristano moved to an eminently cool style that verged on the cold, flirting with serious music and making moves towards the 'third stream' school.

Trotère, Henry [Trotter] (*b* London, 14 Dec. 1855; *d* London, 10 Apr. 1912). British composer. He wrote an operetta, *The Skirt Dancer* (1898), and was the composer of a number of popular drawing-room ballads including: 'Asthore' (1893, *w* Clifton Bingham), 'The deathless army' (1895, *w* Fred *Weatherly), 'Ever dear' (1897), and 'My old shako' (1907, *w* Francis Barron).

Trumbauer, Frankie (*b* Carbondale, Ill., 30 May 1901; *d* Kansas City, 11 June 1956). American saxophonist, vocalist, and bandleader. He made an early mark as a remarkably advanced saxophonist whose influence on the alto was akin to that of Coleman *Hawkins on the tenor. He played in the Benson Orchestra of Chicago, and became acquainted with a similarly adventurous jazz spirit, Bix *Beiderbecke. Both of them joined the Jean *Goldkette orchestra where, with Trumbauer as musical director, a new, lean orchestral sound was heard. He formed his own band in 1927 and recorded some classic sides with Beiderbecke, including 'Singing the blues'. Almost uniquely, he carved a niche for the C-melody saxophone in jazz. He next played alongside Bix in the Paul *Whiteman orchestra 1927–32 and 1933–6. Thereafter he worked with Jack *Teagarden and Mannie *Klein in joint enterprises. After working in civil aeronautics during the war years, he gradually left the music scene. He is revered by many jazz musicians as a technician with soul, and as a great influence on the course of jazz saxophone playing.

Tubb, Ernest Dale (*b* nr. Crisp, Texas, 9 Feb. 1914; *d* Nashville, Tenn., 6 Sept. 1984). American country singer. In the Jimmie *Rodgers mould, he became a leading figure in what became known as Western swing or the honky-tonk style of Country and Western, a little jazz and blues influence creeping into the country flavour of songs like his 'Walking the floor over you', recorded in 1941, followed by 'Waltz across Texas', 'Tomorrow never comes', and 'Filipino baby'. From 1942 he appeared regularly on the **Grand Ole Opry* programme and broadcast his own *Midnight Jamboree* radio show from the Ernest Tubb record shop, still a landmark in Nashville. He became known as 'The Texas Troubadour'. In 1965 he was the sixth person to be elected to the *Country Music Hall of Fame.

Tucker, Sophie [Kalish, Sonia] (*b* Russia, 13 Jan. 1884; *d* New York, 9 Feb. 1966). American singer and actress. She was taken to the USA at the age of three and started her acting career in Hartford, Conn. Seeking to further her career in New York, she became a singer in a café and gradually moved into the professional world, appearing at Tony *Pastor's music-hall, in cabaret, burlesque, and vaudeville. By 1907 she was widely known and appeared in the **Ziegfeld Follies* (1909). Her career was greatly advanced when she took up the song 'Some of these days' in Chicago in 1911, and always featured it thereafter when she was billed as 'The Last of the Red Hot Mamas', a name taken from a song she sang. Her pianist and musical director from 1912 was Ted Shapiro.

She was the star attraction of **Earl Carroll's Vanities* (1924) and travelled abroad, being a special favourite in London where she first appeared in *Follow a Star* (1930). She had her own band in 1936 and was regularly on radio 1936–9. She appeared on Broadway in *Leave it to Me!* (1938) and *The High Kickers* (1941); and was in several films, including *Honky Tonk* (1929); *Gay Love* (1934); *Broadway Melody of 1938* (1937); and *Follow the Boys* (1944). Although she was no longer at the top, she continued to appear on TV in the 1950s and 1960s, on the Ed Sullivan show and elsewhere, and was in *The Joker is Wild* (1957), with Frank *Sinatra. The once raucous voice was latterly exchanged for a less demanding half-talking style. She had begun recording in 1911, having her first big hit with 'Some of these days' (1926), followed by 'My Yiddishe Momme' (1928), and went on doing so into the LP age. A musical, *Sophie* (1963), was based on her life.

S. Tucker and D. Giles: *Some of These Days: Autobiography of Sophie Tucker* (New York, 1945).

Tunbridge, Joseph (*b* London, 21 Jan. 1886; *d* London, 28 Dec. 1961). British composer and conductor. From the age of 16 he was a professional accompanist and occasionally appeared as a piano soloist, then joined Adeler & Sutton's Pierrots. He was editor for the Star Music Publishing Company and musical adviser to Bert *Feldman. His first score was written for *The Red Moon* (1919); he then composed the music for nine Harry Day revues, and from 1926 wrote a series of shows, mainly in collaboration with Jack *Waller, including: *Turned Up* (1926); *Virginia* (1928); *Dear Love* (1929); *Silver Wings* (1930); *For the Love of Mike* (1930); *Tell Her the Truth* (1932); *He Wanted Adventure* (1933); *The Command Performance* (1933); *Mr Whittington* (1934); *Yes Madam* (1934); *Please Teacher* (1935); *Certainly Sir* (1936); *Big Business* (1937); and *Bobby Get Your Gun* (1938).

'Turkey in the straw'. Famous American song first published in New York in 1834, originally under the title of 'Zip coon'. Its composition has been claimed by George Washington Dixon (credited in 1834) and Bob Farrell (who was billed as 'Zip coon'), two blackface entertainers who both sung and danced it that year; and by a blackface clown, George Nichols. Sigmund *Spaeth suggested that the tune might be of Irish origin—'The old rose tree', while Olin Downes and Elie Siegmeister suggest 'The haymaker's dance' from England. It ceased to be called 'Zip coon' soon after the start of its American career and 'Turkey in the straw', despite its possible parentage, now seems a quintessentially American tune. The dandified character on the front of the 1834 edition published just before the first minstrel troupes became established was to become a prototype figure of the minstrel shows: in contrast to the down-trodden performer connected with 'Jim Crow'.

Turner, 'Big Joe' [Joseph Vernon] (*b* Kansas City, Mo., 18 May 1911; *d* Inglewood, Calif., 24 Nov. 1985). American blues singer and composer. He sang for many years around Kansas City, at such venues as the Kingfish Club and the Sunset Club, mainly in partnership with pianist Pete *Johnson. They went to New York in 1938 and appeared that year in *Hammond's *Spirituals to Swing* concerts at the Carnegie Hall, followed by a residency at Café Society. He became widely known through the recordings he made with Johnson, Art *Tatum, Joe *Sullivan and other pianists. He then led an obscure club existence for some years, re-emerging in the 1950s as a leading voice in the new rhythm 'n' blues vogue.

A large man, generally billed as 'Big Joe' Turner,

his recordings on the Atlantic label brought a new awareness of the exciting blues shouting style that was the pride of Kansas City. His album *The Boss of the Blues* (1956) was full of the excitement of the traditional 'How long blues' and 'Morning glories', Johnson's 'Roll 'em Pete' (their first recorded number in 1938), and items that he had written with Johnson like 'Cherry red', 'Wee baby blues', and 'Piney Brown blues'. He moved into the popular rhythm 'n' blues market with the hit 'Chains of love', followed by 'Shake, rattle and roll' (later cleaned up for Bill *Haley), 'Corrina Corrina', and 'Sweet sixteen'. He appeared in a film on Kansas City jazz, *The Last of the Blue Devils* (1979). Turner was too authentic a blues singer to become totally commercialized and mainly worked as a jazz performer in comparative obscurity.

Turner, Ike (*b* Clarksdale, Miss., 5 Nov. 1931). American soul-rock musician. While still at school he worked as a disc jockey and formed a group called the Rhythm Kings. In 1951 he recorded, with vocalist Jackie Brenston, 'Rocket 88', which is often credited as the first genuine rock and roll recording. He worked as a talent scout for various labels, then went to St Louis in 1954 to formulate a revue act. There he met Anna Mae Bullock (*b* Brownsville, Tenn., 26 Nov. 1939), and married her in 1958. Her first recording, 'A fool in love', was credited to Ike and Tina Turner and became a hit. Working with a backing group called the Ikettes, between them Ike and Tina recorded more than 30 albums. Among their hits were such songs as 'It's gonna work out fine' (1961), 'River deep—mountain high' (1966), 'Proud Mary' (1971), and 'Sweet Rhode Island red' (1974).

They separated in 1975 and divorced in 1976, and, while Ike went into studio management, **Tina Turner** continued her career as a singer, working with such acts as Rod *Stewart and the *Rolling Stones, and recording for Capitol. She had hits with 'Let's stay together' (1983), 'What's love got to do with it?' (1984), and 'We don't need another hero' (1985). She made regular tours abroad, including a world tour in 1987 which broke box-office records in 13 countries and eventually visited 25, playing to audiences of $3\frac{1}{2}$ million.

C. Welch: *The Tina Turner Experience* (London, 1986).

Turpin, Tom [Thomas Million] (*b* Savannah, Ga., 1873; *d* St Louis, Mo., 13 Aug. 1922). American ragtime pianist. Son of the pianist 'Honest' John Turpin, whose Silver Dollar saloon in St Louis was the centre of early ragtime activities in the 1880s before its public emergence. Tom, after earning a living running a goldmine near Searchlight, Nevada, returned to St Louis in 1894 and, like his father, became a leading figure in the early ragtime developments; he ran the Rosebud Café at 2220 Market Street, where *Joplin and others would congregate to exchange pianistic ideas. Turpin was a forthright pianist in the early *jig style, and is credited with the first Negro rag to be published—'Harlem rag' in 1897. Subsequently he wrote 'Bowery buck' (1899), 'A ragtime nightmare' (1900), 'St Louis rag' (1903), 'The Buffalo rag' (1904), and 'Siwash' (1909). He wrote many pieces that were used in his brother Charlie's tent shows, and others in collaboration with Artie Matthews.

Twist. Pop dance featuring a twisting of the hips which came into fashion as a generally danceable successor to *jive and *jitterbugging *c.*1958, when Hank Ballard recorded 'The twist' and demonstrated its steps. Chubby *Checker reinforced the craze with his No. 1 hit version in 1960. Like most of these natural jazz-based dances, the twist had a much earlier history. Its twisting and swaying motions, which go back to African dances and were in early use by blacks in the Southern states, were subsequently among the movements used in the popular *'Ballin' the jack' dance. In 1960 its simplicity made it popular with teenagers and adults, and Arthur Murray offered six easy lessons for $25.

Twitty, Conway [Jenkins, Harold] (*b* Friars Point, Miss., 1 Sept. 1933). American rock and country music singer and guitarist. He learned the guitar as a boy and made his first radio appearance at the age of 10. The family moved to Helena in Arkansas, where he formed his first band whose country music was popular enough to earn it its own radio show. He served in the army 1954–6, and on discharge had to decide whether to make a career in baseball (at which he was expert) or in music. Music won, and he auditioned with Sun Records without success. With his name changed to Conway Twitty, and a new manager, he achieved a contract with Mercury Records in 1957 with whom he recorded 'Born to sing the blues', 'Maybe baby', 'Shake it up', 'I need your lovin'', 'Double talk', and 'Why can't I get through to you?' His first big success came with MGM when he recorded 'It's only make believe' in 1958, a focal point that marked his move from country music into the commercial rock and roll field. He went to England in 1959 to appear on the **Oh Boy!* show and, back in the USA in 1960, recorded 'Story of my love', 'Mona Lisa', 'Danny boy', and 'Lonely blue boy'. He played in several films for which he also wrote the music. Frequently backed by the Jordanaires, he recorded for ABC Paramount and later Decca, making a come-back with a return to country music and appearances on the Nashville programmes of the 1970s, often in harness with Loretta *Lynn.

Two Gentlemen of Verona. Rock musical with score by Galt *MacDermot, and book by John Guare and Mel Shapiro, based on Shakespeare's play. It was first planned for an open-air production at the New York Shakespeare Festival in 1971, and opened at the St James Theatre 1 Dec. 1971. The anachronistic juxtaposition of language and music in this kind of story, all pumped out at a deafening recorded level, caught the imagination of the 1970s noise lovers, and it ran for 627 performances. It then blasted its way to the Phoenix Theatre, London, 26 Apr. 1973 [237p].

Two-step. A categorical term used in the early 1900s in the USA, and in England by 1910, to specify those few dances then around that were not the *lancers or the *waltz (which still dominated the dance floor at this time). The military two-step was a popular favourite. By 1911–12 the two-step was already giving way to the simple walking movements of the *one-step or *rag, later known as the *foxtrot.

U

Udall, Lynn [Keating, John Henry] (*b* Council Bluffs, Iowa, 4 Feb. 1870; *d* Downey, Calif., 5 Dec. 1963). American composer. He started a New York song-writing career in the 1890s with four songs that each sold more than a million copies. In collaboration with lyricist Karl Kennett he wrote 'Just one girl' (1898), 'Just as the sun went down' (1898), 'Zizzy, ze zum, zum!' (1898), 'Stay in your own backyard' (1899), 'A-blowin' down de line' (1899), and 'Side by side' (1900).

Ukelele. Correctly the name of the small four-stringed Hawaiian guitar, but more frequently used in the 1930s, and thereabouts, as an abbreviated name of the ukelele-banjo, a short-necked banjo employed mainly for a strummed accompaniment to songs. Its popularity in the hands of George *Formby Jr., and other entertainers, caused quite a boom in the sale of instruments and tutors. Most sheet music of the period carries the instructions 'tune uke to . . .' according to the key of the song, the strings being tuned to make the simplest fingering available. It was an instrument of extremely limited sound and range, but it imparted a lively character to the music.

Unsinkable Molly Brown, The. Musical comedy with music and lyrics by Meredith *Willson, and book by Richard Morris, starring Tammy Grimes (*b* 1934) who sang 'I ain't down yet', a typical evocation of the indomitable spirit of the lady of the title, who becomes a legend by rising from a poor background in Hannibal, Missouri, marrying a lucky silver prospector (Harve Presnell, *b* 1933), becoming a social leader in Monte Carlo, and surviving the sinking of the *Titanic*. With a typical bright and breezy Willson score, full of country dances and marches, it opened at the *Winter Garden Theatre, New York, 3 Nov. 1960, and ran for 532 performances. It was filmed in 1960 with Harve Presnell now co-starring with Debbie *Reynolds.

Up in Central Park. Musical comedy with score by Sigmund *Romberg, and book by Herbert and Dorothy *Fields, New York, Century Theatre, 27 Jan. 1945 [504p].

Set in Central Park in the 1870s, it mingled fact and fiction in a story in which an honest reporter (Wilbur Evans) bravely tries to expose the corruption of a Tammany boss (Noah Beery, 1884–1946) and his pals, who are appropriating the funds collected to build the new park. He also finds time for a romance with the daughter of one of the crooks (Maureen Cannon), which complicates matters. Songs included: 'Carousel in the Park', 'When you walk in the room', 'Close as pages in a book', and 'April snow'; and there was the notable 'Currier and Ives ballet' choreographed by Helen Tamiris (1905–66). It was filmed in 1948 with Deanna *Durbin and Dick *Haymes.

Usandizaga, José María (*b* San Sebastián, 31 Mar. 1887; *d* Yanti, 6 Oct. 1915). Spanish composer. A musical prodigy, he studied at the Schola Cantorum in Paris under Vincent d'Indy, graduating in 1906. He wrote several prize-winning compositions, then started a career of writing for the theatre in 1910 with the Basque opera *Mendy-Mendiyan*. His most popular work was *Las Golondrinas (The Swallows)*, produced in Madrid in 1914; followed by *La Llama (The Kiss)* (1915). He died of TB at the age of 28.

L. Villalba: *J. M. Usandizaga* (Madrid, 1918). J. M. de Arozamena: *José María Usandizaga y la bella época donostiarra* (San Sebastián, 1969).

Utopia Limited or *The Flowers of Progress*. Comic opera with music by Arthur *Sullivan and words by W. S. *Gilbert, produced at the Savoy Theatre, London, 7 Oct. 1893 [245p]. The cast included Rosina *Brandram, Walter Passmore, and Rutland *Barrington. A product of the last years of the partnership, when the impetus was going and quarrels had marred the mutual respect, it has not enjoyed the popularity of the earlier works; and it is seldom staged. An excellent recording in 1976 did a little to revive interest, but it remains an interesting museum piece, with a few quirkish moments.

J. Wolfson: *Final Curtain: the Last Gilbert and Sullivan Operas* (London, 1976).

U2. Irish rock band, the most successful unit to come from that country, formed in Dublin in 1977 while its members, Bono [Paul Hewson], the Edge [David Evans], Larry Mullen, and Adam Clayton, were still at school. They soon established themselves in the Dublin area. Their first EP, *U2:3* (1979), became a best-seller and the band went to London where they recorded an LP, *Boy*, in 1980, achieving a 'loud, glorious, and aggressive' sound. They achieved their first British hit with 'New Year's Day' (1982) while their album *War* went to the very top in 1983. They were labelled the 'last of the rock idealists', and their late-1980s albums were acclaimed. They remain important as traditional stylists achieving heights with their guitar rock that put them alongside the best of the past.

V

Vagabond King, The. Musical play with score by Rudolf *Friml, book by Brian Hooker, Russell Janney, and W. H. Post, based on the well-used novel, *If I Were King* by J. H. McCarthy. An amateur musical on this theme had already been written by the then up-and-coming *Rodgers and *Hart team, but the producer Russell Janney was unable to get the necessary backing on the strength of their names, and turned instead to the well-established Friml.

The story of the desperado François Villon (played by Dennis *King), who is appointed King of France for a day in order to defeat the Duke of Burgundy and as a bonus wins the love of Katherine de Vaucelles (Carolyn Thomson), was set in the 15th century. The show was staged at the Casino Theatre, New York, 21 Sept. 1925, and had 511 performances. In London, at the Winter Garden Theatre, 19 Apr. 1927, with Derek *Oldham in the lead, it had 480.

Often revived and a continuing favourite with amateur societies, its sturdy score is enlivened by such hits as 'Song of the vagabonds', 'Some day', 'Only a rose', 'Love me tonight', and 'Love for sale'. It was filmed in 1930 with Dennis King and Jeanette *MacDonald; and again in 1956 with Oreste Kirkop (*b* 1926) and Kathryn *Grayson.

Valentine, Dickie [Brice, Richard] (*b* London, 4 Nov. 1929; *d* Wales, 6 May 1971). British singer. He made a debut in films at the age of three, in *Jack's the Boy* (1932) with Cecily *Courtneidge. He worked as a page-boy at the Palace Theatre, Manchester, and at the London Palladium, and then, in spite of suffering from asthma, started to train as a singer. While working in a London club he was recommended to Ted *Heath who used him, for one starred number, in his Sunday night Swing Sessions at the London *Palladium. Becoming a teenage favourite of the 1950s, he became a solo artist in 1954, perfecting an act that included jokes and impressions as well as singing, and eventually being the first singer to star at the Palladium in 1955. In the face of strong transatlantic competition, he continued to top the bill there for five years. He recorded for Decca and had 12 hits in the Top 20, 1953–9, including 'Broken wing', 'Finger of suspicion', 'Christmas alphabet', 'Venus' (by Frankie *Avalon), and 'That lovely weekend' (by Ted and Moira Heath). He was killed in a road crash.

Vallee, Rudy [Hubert Prior] (*b* Island Pond, Vt., 28 July 1901; *d* Hollywood, 3 July 1986). American singer, actor, composer, saxophonist, and bandleader. After service in the US Army in the First World War he worked as a cinema usher and taught himself to play the saxophone by listening to recordings by Rudy Wiedoeft, from whom he borrowed the name of Rudy. He went to Maine University, and later to Yale, where he led the college band. After graduating in 1927 he became a full-time bandleader at the Heigh-Ho Club in New York, leading his Connecticut Yankees and appearing in a weekly radio show. At this point he turned singer, introducing himself with 'Heigh-ho, everybody', and quickly winning a great following with his drawling voice and fresh, boyish looks.

The first to exploit the new crooning style, he became known, from one of his most successful early recordings, as 'The vagabond lover', and this provided the title of the first film he appeared in, *The Vagabond Lover* (1929)—'A little kiss each morning'; followed by *Glorifying the American Girl* (1929). He was one of the first radio and screen entertainers to become a public idol and generate mass hysteria in his audiences. He used a megaphone, in the days before the microphone had become an essential part of the singer's trade, to put over his soft and soothing, but rather nasal, tones. He appeared in **George White's Scandals* (1931)—'My song', 'This is the missus'; and again in the 1935 version. A somewhat wooden actor at this stage, he appeared in further films, usually with his band, including *International House* (1933); *George White's Scandals* (1934); *Sweet Music* (1935); *Gold Diggers in Paris* (1938); and *Second Fiddle* (1939)—'I poured my heart into a song'. His popularity was established by the good fortune of time and place rather than any great vocal ability. In the 1930s he was superseded in the crooning business by the accomplished Bing *Crosby, and by 1940 he was mainly seen in straight comedy roles in a succession of films. In 1942 he joined the US Coastguards and led their band until the end of the war.

He returned to the screen as a character actor, often satirizing himself, in a series of films culminating in *The Helen Morgan Story* (1957). He played in repertory before making a Broadway appearance as the company boss in **How to Succeed in Business Without Really Trying* (1961), also playing the part in the screen version of 1966. In 1964 he appeared on TV as the compère of *On Broadway Tonight*. He continued to appear in occasional film and TV roles until the mid-1970s and was working in clubs in a one-man show into the 1980s. He was much in demand as a voice of the past in various nostalgia exercises and played the role with amiable garrulity.

He wrote many songs, including 'Kitty from Kansas City' (1921), 'Deep night' (1929), 'I'm just a vagabond lover' (1929), 'Betty co-ed' (1930), 'Actions speak louder than words' (1931), and 'Talk to me' (1956); and autobiographical books: *Vagabond Dreams Come True* (New York, 1930); *My Time Is Your Time* (New York, 1962); and *Let the Chips Fall* (Harrisburg, Pa., 1976).

L. F. Kiner: *The Rudy Vallee Discography* (Westport, Conn., 1985).

Valmouth. Musical comedy, with words and music by Sandy *Wilson, based on the novel *Valmouth* (1919) by Ronald Firbank (1886–1926). It was first produced at the Lyric Theatre, Hammersmith, 2 Oct. 1958, and transferred to the Saville Theatre, London, 27 Jan. 1959 [186p], with Cleo *Laine, Barbara Coupar, Betty Harding, and Fenella Fielding in the cast.

Firbank's Valmouth is an English spa town whose air has the property of giving people a peculiarly long and sexually active life, which makes the normal social intrigues of a watering-place more involved than usual. Though a failure by the standards of Wilson's earlier success *The *Boy Friend*, it has always been highly regarded by connoisseurs of the musical. It was seen in New York, at the York Playhouse 6 Oct. 1960, and was revived at the Chichester Festival in 1982.

Valverde, Joaquín [Valverde Durán] (*b* Badajoz, 27 Feb. 1846; *d* Madrid, 17 Mar. 1910). Spanish composer. He became known for his regular collaborations with Federico *Chueca on the scores of various popular *zarzuelas, especially *La Gran Via* (1886), which has remained one of the most popular in the repertoire. It was produced all over Europe and in the USA and its march 'Cadiz' became a Spanish national song.

Vamp. The simplest type of accompaniment, especially on the piano, which consists of the left hand playing root notes or octaves on the 1st and 3rd beats in 4/4 time, or on the 1st in 3/4 time; and the right hand playing chords on the weaker 2nd and 4th, or 2nd and 3rd beats, respectively. Simple variations on this were required when the once familiar 'vamp till ready' instruction appeared at the beginning of sheet music. There were many attempts, in the inter-war days of amateur music-making, to market simple vamp instructions and charts which would turn non-players into adequate accompanists. The basic banjo and guitar accompaniments worked on similar principles. In fact, the word is of considerable antiquity, and had been used in this sense as far back as 1716, possibly before.

Van Alstyne, Egbert Anson (*b* Chicago, 5 Mar. 1882; *d* 9 July 1951). American composer and pianist. He won a scholarship to the Chicago Musical College but found that it was the lighter side of music that appealed to him, and he spent many years on the vaudeville circuit as a pianist. A spell as a song-plugger took him to New York in 1900 where he began to write in partnership with Harry Williams (1879–1922). They had their first lucky break with 'Navajo', an Indian novelty song that was used in the Broadway show *Nancy Brown* in 1903. In 1905 they wrote one of those immortal popular songs that seem so natural that they quickly take on the aura of a folk-song—'In the shade of the old apple tree'. Van Alstyne and Williams also toured the USA, and parts of Europe, as a successful vaudeville team until Van Alstyne went into retirement in his home town of Chicago in the late 1920s.

He wrote scores for *A Broken Idol* (1909) and *Girlies* (1910); and such songs as 'Back, back, back to Baltimore' (1904), 'I'm afraid to come home in the dark' (1907), 'There never was a girl like you' (1907); and, with other writers: 'Memories' (1915, *w* Gus *Kahn), 'Pretty baby' (with Tony *Jackson, (1916, *w* Kahn), and 'Drifting and dreaming' (1925).

Vance, Alfred, or **Granville, Alfred, 'The Great Vance'** [Stevens, Alfred Peck] (*b* London, 1839; *d* London, 26 Dec. 1888). British singer and comedian. He worked for three years as a solicitor's clerk, also taught dancing and ran a touring variety company, before appearing on the music-hall stage in 1860 in a blackface act with his brother. He first appeared solo at the South London Palace in 1864 and began to popularize the coster comedian act that was to make him famous, with such songs as 'The Chickaleery cove'. Next he adopted the role of lion-comique, becoming a great rival of George *Leybourne and billing himself as the Great Vance. His repertoire now was 'Jolly dogs', 'Walking in the Zoo', and 'Cliquot, Cliquot'. The fashion for swells over, he turned to motto songs, like 'Act on the square, boys', and character parts. Some said that he was better than Leybourne. He worked to the end, collapsing and dying on the stage of the Sun Music Hall in Knightsbridge.

Van Dyke, Dick (*b* Danville, Ill., 13 Dec. 1925). American actor and singer. A most polished comedian in a clean-cut, likeable, and accident-prone way, he had his most successful Broadway appearance in **Bye Bye Birdie* (1960) and was also in the 1963 film version. He won wide renown in the films **Mary Poppins* (1964)—'Chim chim cheree'; and *Chitty Chitty Bang Bang* (1968); and was in other less successful films. At the height of his fame he appeared in his own *Dick Van Dyke Show* 1961–6 with Mary Tyler Moore (*b* 1936). An attempted revival in 1971 was less magical.

Van Heusen, James [Babcock, Edward Chester] (*b* Syracuse, NY, 26 Jan. 1913; *d* Rancho Mirage, Calif., 6 Feb. 1990). American composer, publisher, and pianist. At 16 he was playing piano and singing on local radio, but his father put a stop to this and sent him to Syracuse University to prepare for a career in the family business. Like many budding songwriters, he spent his student years writing for college shows. He collaborated with Harold *Arlen's young brother Jerry and through this met Arlen himself who advised him to make a career in *Tin Pan Alley. In 1933, having taken this advice, he wrote some numbers for a *Cotton Club revue, but otherwise went through a bleak period and had to take odd jobs. He got back into music by becoming staff pianist with a music-publishing business, until he collaborated with the already famous Jimmy *Dorsey on 'It's the dreamer in me', which became very popular. From then on he produced a steady stream of hit songs, most of the best being with Johnny *Burke who began to work with him in Hollywood in 1940.

He wrote stage scores for *Swingin' the Dream* (1939); *Nellie Bly* (1946); *Carnival in Flanders* (1953)—'Here's that rainy day' (described by Sammy *Cahn as 'one of the 10 greatest songs ever written'); *Skyscraper* (1965); and *Walking Happy* (1966); but did most of his best work for films, many for Bing *Crosby, including (all with Burke): *Love Thy Neighbour* (1940); *Playmates* (1941); *Road to Zanzibar* (1941)—'Birds of a feather', 'You're dangerous'; *Road to Morocco* (1942)—'Moonlight becomes you', 'Road to Morocco', 'Ain't got a dime to my name'; *My Favourite Spy* (1942)—'Got the moon in my pocket'; *Dixie* (1943)—'Sunday, Monday or always'; **Lady in the Dark* (1944)—'Suddenly it's Spring'; *The Great John L.* (1944)—'A friend of yours'; *Going My Way* (1944)—'Swingin' on a star', 'Going my way' (Academy Award): the score also included 'Too-ra-loo-ra-loo-ral', by James Royce Shannon, 1913; *And the Angels Sing* (1944)—'It could happen to you'; *Belle of the Yukon* (1944)—'Sleighride in July', 'Like someone in love'; *Road to Utopia* (1945)—'Put it there, pal', 'Welcome to my dream', 'Would you', 'Personality'; *The Bells of St Mary's* (1946)—'Aren't you glad you're you'; *Cross My Heart* (1946)—'Love is the darndest thing'; *London Town* (1946); *My Heart Goes Crazy* (1946); *Welcome Stranger* (1947)—'Country style'; *Road to Rio* (1947)—'But beautiful'; *Variety Girl* (1947); *Suddenly It's Spring* (1947)—'Suddenly it's Spring'; *The Emperor Waltz* (1948); *Mystery in Mexico* (1948); *A Connecticut Yankee in the Court of King Arthur* (1949; *A Yankee in King Arthur's Court* in UK)—'Busy doing nothing'; *Top o' the Morning* (1949); *Riding High* (1950)—'Sunshine cake'; *Mister Music* (1950)—'Life is so peculiar', 'And you'll be home', 'Accidents will happen'; *Road to Bali* (1952)—'Chicago style'; *Little Boy Lost* (1953); *Young at Heart* (1954)—'You, my love' (*w* Mack *Gordon); and *Pardners* (1956).

Starting with the TV music for *Our Town* (1955)—'Love and marriage', Van Heusen often used new songwriting partners like Sammy Cahn and provided several songs for Frank *Sinatra, among others, in such films as: *The Tender Trap* (1955)—'The tender trap' (Cahn); *Anything Goes* (1956); *Pardners* (1956); *The Joker is Wild* (1957)—'All the way' (Cahn); *Indiscreet* (1958); *Paris Holiday* (1958); *Hole in the Head* (1959)—'High hopes' (Cahn); *Say One For Me* (1959); *High Time* (1960)—'The second time around' (Cahn); *Let's Make Love* (1960); *Pocketful of Miracles* (1961)—'Pocketful of miracles' (Cahn); *Road to Hong Kong* (1962); *Papa's Delicate Condition* (1963)—'Call me irresponsible' (Cahn), sung by Jackie *Gleason; *The Pleasure Seekers* (1964); *Robin and the Seven Hoods* (1964)—'My kind of town' (Cahn); and **Thoroughly Modern Millie* (1967)—'Thoroughly modern Millie'. Other songs included: 'Heaven can wait' (1939, Eddie DeLange), 'Shake down the stars' (1939, DeLange), 'Imagination' (1939, Burke), 'Make with the kisses' (1939, Johnny *Mercer), 'Let's all meet at my house' (1940, Burke), 'All this and heaven too' (1940, DeLange), 'Nancy (with the laughing face)' (1944, Phil Silvers), 'Polka dots and moonbeams' (1944, Burke), and 'Yah-ta-ta, yah-ta-ta' (1945, Burke).

Variety. An entertainment of a varied and miscellaneous nature. In England the name had always been used as an alternative to *music-hall. The *Oxford Dictionary* gives 1886 for its first use in this sense, but it was probably used to describe a mixed entertainment some time before this. The early saloons such as the Grecian (attached to the Eagle Tavern), the Union in Shoreditch, the Apollo in Marylebone, all flourishing in the 1840s, were regularly referred to as variety saloons. The name music-hall mainly superseded variety once the music-halls, mostly originally attached to taverns, were built and thus named. The Grapes Music Hall was probably the first to use the designation in 1848, followed by the Canterbury Music Hall in 1849. Thus music-hall became a popular name for the kind of performance that took place there, although it is interesting to note that the first substantial book on the subject, published in 1895, was titled *The Variety Stage*. The name music-hall lasted until the declining years, when its low-class associations seemed unsuitable for the grander Palaces of Variety of the 20th century, and the name 'variety' gradually crept back. It was regularly used by the BBC from the pre-war era onward (*Variety Bandbox*, etc.) and was more fitting for the more sophisticated entertainment of the 1930s, which included leading dance orchestras and chorus girls, piano duos, and xylophonists.

In the USA the term 'variety' was often preferred, though the name most generally adopted there was *vaudeville. Tony *Pastor, usually referred to as the Dean of Vaudeville, actually preferred to call it variety. The French adopted the English term music-hall immediately after it had been established in England; at the same time using the word *variétés* to describe revue-type entertainments, as well as the theatres in which these were staged. The Germans used the word *Varieté*.

E. Buchner: *Berliner Variétiés und Tingeltangel* (Berlin, 1905). C. Brewer: *The Spice of Variety* (London, 1948). G. R. Bullar and L. Evans: *The Performer Who's Who in Variety* (London, 1950). R. Wilmut: *Kindly Leave the Stage!: the Story of Variety 1916–1960* (London, 1985).

Varney, Louis (*b* New Orleans, 30 May 1844; *d* Cauterets, Hautes Pyrénées, 20 Aug. 1908). French composer, born in the USA while his father Pierre Joseph Alphonse Varney (1811–79) was the director of a French opera company in New Orleans 1840–50, where he was married. The family returned to Paris in 1851 and Louis Varney was to spend most of his life there. He began to write operettas in 1876 and finally completed nearly 40, many of them achieving considerable popularity. The most popular and lasting of these was *Les Mousquetaires au couvent* which was produced at the *Bouffes-Parisiens 16 Mar. 1880, in London the same year, and the following year in Vienna; it is still being revived and recorded. Others were: *La Petite Reinette* (1882); *Fanfan la Tulipe* (1882); *Les Petits Mousquetaires* (1885); *L'Amour mouillé* (1887); *Riquet à la houppe* (1889); *La Femme de Narcisse* (1891); *La Fille de Fanchon la Veilleuse* (1891); *Miss Robinson* (1892); *La Tournée Ernestin* (1892); *Les Forains* (1892); *Cliquette* (1893); *Les Petites Brebis* (1895); *La Princesse Bébé* (1902); *La Chien du régiment* (1902); and *L'Age d'or* (1905).

Varsoviana. A dance in 3/4 time, a kind of slow mazurka. Its main characteristic was an emphasis and slight pause on the first notes of the second, fourth, and sixth bars. It probably originated in France, with a dancing teacher called Désiré being given credit for its invention. It was introduced about 1853, and soon had a great vogue in Paris (it was danced at the Tuileries and was a favourite of the Empress Eugénie), and soon after in London, where it was first introduced by Laurent's band. Various 'original' varsoviana melodies have been claimed, and all the fashionable dance composers of the period provided examples with a wide variety of fanciful and mainly romantic names.

Vaudeville. A name said to derive from the French 'val (or vau) de vire', the valley of the Vire river in Normandy, noted for its jolly songs; or, alternatively, from 'voix de ville', songs of the city. The name was taken to the USA by French immigrants. There was a Vaudeville Theatre in San Antonio, Texas, in 1882 and John W. Ransome, who first used the term to describe a variety show in the 1880s, may simply have taken it from this. It had been used in the first instance in the USA in 1871 by H. J. Sargent who called his Louisville, Kentucky, minstrel troupe Sargent's Great Vaudeville Company. The name became synonymous with variety, a term much preferred by one of its pioneers, Tony *Pastor, who opened his New 14th Street Theatre, part of the Tammany Building, New York, 24 Oct. 1881. Although the history of American vaudeville was essentially the same as that of the British music-hall, developing alongside it from its own variety saloons of the 1850s, each developed its own natural talents, taking on national characteristics.

The USA developed its vaudeville tradition on parallel lines to the developments in Britain—so parallel, in fact, that it is tempting, in hindsight, to feel that the USA was simply following British developments, or vice versa. But the general pattern of development in all popular music genres was so closely timed, and so closely linked with the international change in social and economic patterns, that it must be accepted that the developments were coincidental rather than intentional. The equivalent of the song-and-supper rooms in London was to be found in the 1850s in the concert saloons of New York, and elsewhere, with similar fare drawn mainly from the minstrel world. Enticingly named, purpose-built halls began to appear by the early 1850s, one of the first being built by one William Valentine in 1848. He was later the proprietor of New York's own Vauxhall Gardens—in this case a concert saloon situated in the Bowery where many such halls now sprang up, the most popular being White's Varieties, opened in 1852. The name 'variety' was widely used by the 1860s. These saloons echoed the London model of a small stage at one end for the entertainers, who had to compete with the eating, drinking, and smoking of the highly vocal customers. The smaller, male-dominated saloons, boisterous and bawdy, like Harry Hill's establishment on Houston Street, were superseded in the 1860s by larger places catering for family entertainment, some borrowing names that originated abroad like the Gaieties and the Canterbury, others more nationally minded like the American Concert Hall and the Broadway Music Hall; and there were similar developments in other large cities and towns. They became increasingly subject to the rules and regulations that applied to theatres and eventually were run on the same lines.

The early vaudeville years of the 1880s, with stars like May *Irwin and Lillian *Russell, progressed, as in London, towards a positive craze for variety in the 1890s. In those years, following in the steps of Pastor's 14th Street Theatre and *Koster and Bial's establishment on 23rd Street, numerous vaudeville theatres arose such as the New Park Theatre on Broadway and 35th Street and the Imperial Music Hall on West 29th Street, both opened in 1892; while Benjamin Franklin Keith (1846–1914) and Edward Albee (1857–1930) opened the Colonial Theatre in Boston in 1894. New York, which must have had a better climate than London, also favoured the roof garden theatre. British artists now found a sometimes lucrative outlet, though there were frequent failures, in bringing their wares to New York. Among the earliest were Bessie Bonehill and Jennie *Hill, the 'Vital Spark', who became all the rage. America's own stars were Ward and Vokes, a tramp comedy team, J. W. Kelly, Jewish comic Frank Bush, Maggie Cline, Lottie Gilson, and the celebrated partnership of *Harrigan and Hart. Vesta *Tilley came over on several occasions and was hailed as the finest product of the British stage. Marie *Lloyd, the top star in England, failed to impress her very English humour on the Americans, but Vesta *Victoria was tremendously popular. Harry *Lauder almost failed through using the wrong material, for some obscure reason starting his turn off with a Welsh sketch, which must have greatly confused his audience. But he oriented his act in time to convince them of his great talents.

In the 1900s vaudeville was big business. It was estimated at the time that the ratio of people patronizing vaudeville to those attending other kinds of theatre was ten to one. The influential Vaudeville Managers' Association was organized in 1900; and then, in 1906, Keith and Albee created the United Booking Office under the same auspices which became the main clearing-house for vaudeville. Other leading managers were Alexander Pantages (*d* 1936), S. Z. Poli (1860–1937), F. F. Procter (1851–1929), and Martin Beck (1865–1940), who built New York's leading vaudeville house, the *Palace Theatre, in 1913, though he soon lost control of it to Keith and Albee. By now, as in the English music-hall, the really big stars of vaudeville had come along. On the distaff side there was Eva *Tanguay, the American equivalent of Marie Lloyd, who both delighted and shocked her audiences and had to fight the management because of her risqué material at a time when the halls were being cleaned up and blue material forbidden; Nora *Bayes singing 'Shine on harvest moon', which she had written in collaboration with her husband Jack *Norworth; Janet Allen, a beautiful and trained opera singer who sang 'Will you love me in December as you do in May' and 'The bird on Nellie's hat'; Blanche *Ring with 'I've got rings on my fingers'; singer-dancer Bessie McCoy (1886–1931); Elsie *Janis, who moved on to become a musical comedy star; Irene Franklin (1876–1941); Ruth Roye (1895–1960); and May Irwin; followed by the Fanny *Brice, Mae *West, Sophie *Tucker generation.

The big male names of the 1900s were Pat Rooney (1880–1962), Ed *Wynn, Joe Cook (1890–1959), W. C. Fields (1879–1946), Nat Wills (1873–1917) 'The Happy Tramp', and *Weber and Fields. Among many who were lost to the musical comedy stage or films were Eddie *Foy and George M. *Cohan; later followed by Will Rogers, Fred *Allen, Milton *Berle, Jack Benny, and George Burns.

A rich inflow of music-hall songs from Britain was more than matched by excellent American material which frequently went the other way. In addition to those already mentioned, the British were indebted for 'Where did you get that hat?', 'Playmates', 'Ta-ra-ra-boom-de-ay', *'After the ball', 'The Bowery' (which became 'Brighton'), 'Two little girls in blue', 'And her golden hair was hanging down her back', 'I don't want to play in your yard', 'Lucky Jim', 'Sweet Rosie O'Grady', 'When you were sweet sixteen', 'My wild Irish rose', 'A bird in a gilded cage', 'For old time's sake', 'Goodbye, Dolly Gray', 'Bill Bailey, won't you please come home?', 'In the good old summer time', 'Sweet Adeline', 'In the shade of the old apple tree', 'The bird on Nellie's hat', *'Down at the old Bull and Bush', 'Up in a balloon', 'By the light of the silvery moon', 'Heaven will protect the working girl', *'Down by the old mill stream', 'Let me call you sweetheart', 'Mother Machree', 'He'd have to get under', and 'You made me love you'.

As elsewhere, the growth of radio and the cinema put the live variety show out of business. The Palace Theatre started to show feature films in 1932 and thus signalled its own capitulation. Attempts at revival in the 1950s never quite succeeded.

C. Caffin: *Vaudeville* (New York, 1914). D. Gilbert: *American Vaudeville: its Life and Times* (New York, 1940; repr. 1963). J. Laurie: *Vaudeville: from the Honky-Tonks to the Palace* (New York, 1953). B. Sobel: *A Pictorial History of Vaudeville* (New York, 1961). A. F. McLean: *American Vaudeville as Ritual* (Louisville, Ky., 1965). P. Zellers: *Tony Pastor: Dean of the Vaudeville Stage* (Ypsilanti, Mich., 1971). J. E. Dimeglio: *Vaudeville USA* (Bowling Green, Ohio, 1973). C. W. Stein (ed.): *American Vaudeville as Seen by Its Contemporaries* (New York, 1984).

Vaughan, Frankie [Abelson, Francis] (*b* Liverpool, 3 Feb. 1928). British singer. He went to Leeds College of Art intending to teach, but was heard at a college show at the Leeds Empire by BBC producer Barney Colehan, who persuaded him to move into show-business, and made his debut at the Kingston Empire in 1940. He adopted the top hat and cane outfit, and 'Give me the moonlight' as his signature tune, and signed a recording contract in 1953, having his first hit with 'My sweetie went away'. He had two top hits with 'Garden of Eden' (1956) and 'Tower of strength' (1957); appeared in the films *These Dangerous Years* (1957), *Wonderful Things* (1958), *The Lady is a Square* (1958), and *Heart of a Man* (1959); then went to Hollywood to appear with Marilyn Monroe in *Let's Make Love* (1960). Thereafter, while overtaken by the pop invasion, he remained a popular favourite and an indefatigable performer.

Vaughan, Sarah ('Sassie') Lois (*b* Newark, NJ, 27 Mar. 1924; *d* Los Angeles, 3 Apr. 1990). American singer and pianist. She sang as a child at the Mount Zion Baptist church in Newark and studied the piano and organ for 10 years, a grounding that gave her a lasting harmonic awareness. After winning an amateur contest at the *Apollo Theatre, Harlem, in 1942, she joined the Earl *Hines band as vocalist and pianist and soon became recognized for her pure yet sophisticated styling. She was to develop into one of the great jazz singers, alongside Billie *Holiday and Ella *Fitzgerald, the *Gershwin of jazz vocalists, with the richest voice and the greatest range, the most controlled technique, yet never losing her essential jazziness.

By the 1940s she was leaving the older jazz styles behind and with the Billy *Eckstine band 1944–5, with whom she recorded 'I'll wait and pray' (1944), followed by 'Loverman' with Dizzy *Gillespie, and with John *Kirby 1945–6 she was developing a seductively cool style that was to enable her to keep in the forefront of jazz developments into the 1970s. The recordings made with Kirby in January and

September 1946 already showed the effortless skills that could have made her into an opera star, which would have been an irreplaceable loss to jazz. These accomplishments, while bringing her a devoted middle-of-the-road following, have sometimes tended to alienate the jazz purist, but her art must be judged in the widest terms, on the basis of which she has remained one of the most remarkable artists on the popular music scene, and a key figure in the development of jazz influences in popular song.

During her career her voice deepened, giving her a remarkable range, and her technique continually developed. An international star by the 1950s, she had big hits with 'Passing strangers' and Broken-hearted melody'; and she regularly recorded with jazz musicians like Clifford Brown, Cannonball *Adderley, Quincy *Jones, and members of the *Basie band. In 1972 she made some imaginative middle-of-the-road recordings with Michel *Legrand. She liked to use a regular backing trio, one of the most effective and lasting being that made up of Jimmy Jones, Joe Benjamin, and Roy Haynes. She had a special admiration for the music of *Ellington, recording a set of 22 of his songs in 1979 and more in 1982, and for *Gershwin, ranging from the 1959 recordings with Hal Mooney to an album of his songs with the Los Angeles Symphony Orchestra in 1982. She made frequent visits to England, often appearing at the Ronnie *Scott club.

R. Leydi: *Sarah Vaughan* (Milan, 1961).

Vauxhall Gardens. In spite of the English weather, the pleasure garden was a popular venue for eating and entertainment in the 18th century and the first half of the 19th, and most of them did also have an indoor concert room or dance hall. The most important of these was Vauxhall Gardens which was situated, where a small public garden still survives, north of the Oval and just south of the present Vauxhall station. Originally known as the Spring Gardens, they were opened in 1660, and in the early days the music was provided by such eminent figures as Handel and James Boyce, from J. C. Bach to Sir Henry Bishop who was musical director there 1830–2. The entertainments widened in the 19th century to include ballets, fireworks, circus acts, minstrel shows, and balloon ascents; meanwhile the musical entertainment became more popularized in response to changing public taste and demand. It was in this respect, in its dying days, before closing in 1859, that Vauxhall became the first important publicity outlet for the popular (and predominantly comic) songs that just pre-dated the song-and-supper rooms and the early music-halls. Many of the first illustrated songsheets bear the legend 'as sung at Vauxhall Gardens'. There were other similar establishments in London: Marylebone Gardens (1738–78), Ranelagh Gardens (1742–1805), and many lesser tea-gardens and spas; but it was Vauxhall that lasted the longest and made the biggest mark in the present context. The Tivoli Gardens in Copenhagen was modelled on Vauxhall in the 1840s; and similar places were opened in New York and other cities in the USA. One of the biggest-selling pieces of sheet-music at Vauxhall was the duet 'Polly Hopkins'. On sale there also were such items as *The Incledonian and Vauxhall Songster* of *c.*1808: Charles Incledon (1763–1826) was a popular singer there—up to *The Vauxhall Comic Song Book* of 1847 and after.

W. Wroth: *The London Pleasure Gardens of the Eighteenth Century* (London, 1896). W. S. Scott: *Green Retreats: the Story of Vauxhall Gardens, 1661–1850* (London, 1955).

'Veleta, The'. A 'new round dance' with music by Arthur Morris, published in London by *Francis, Day & Hunter in 1900. It was a variation of the old-fashioned waltz. Arthur Morris was a dance teacher from Leeds who invented the dance and supplied his own music. Unlike most of these artificially concocted dances, the Veleta, complete with its very catchy tune, has survived.

Velvet Underground. Cult American rock band which, without moving into the popular charts, had a great influence on rock in the 1970s and 1980s. The original group consisted of Lou Reed (*b* 1944) (vocal, guitar), John Cale (*b* 1942) (viola, bass, and keyboards), Sterling Morrison (*b* 1940) (bass and guitar), and Maureen Tucker (*b* 1941) (drums). The group came to the attention of Andy Warhol (1928–87), who became their manager and later featured them in his *Exploding Plastic Inevitable* show in New York in 1966. Nico [Christa Päffgen] (1938–88), a Warhol find who had been in several of his films, was added to the group as singer in 1965. This contact helped the group to fame and their first MGM album was billed as *The Velvet Underground and Nico Produced by Andy Warhol* (1967), with his artwork on the cover. It was naturally rather way-out by normal standards and was not widely appreciated. Nico left the group in 1967 and the Velvet Underground went its own way. The albums which followed, *White Light-/White Heat* (1968) and *The Velvet Underground* (1969), were contrastingly noisily aggressive and lightly tuneful. A fourth album, *Loaded* (1970), came nearest to a popular rock idiom. Just as they appeared to be achieving a wider popularity, the group split up. In the meantime their outrageous inwardness had influenced many other such cult artists as David *Bowie and Patti Smith.

V. Bockris and G. Malanga: *Up-Tight: the Velvet Underground Story* (London, 1983).

Ventura, Ray [Raymond] (*b* Paris, 16 Apr. 1908; *d* Palma, Majorca, 29 Mar. 1979). French bandleader. He founded a group called the Collegiate Five in 1925 which, with additional members, later became the Collegians. With Stéphane *Grappelli prominent in its ranks, it became one of France's most popular bands. He toured Latin America during the Second World War, returning to France after the war and becoming a film director. He made well-known recordings of 'Fantastique' (1932) and

'Tout va très bien, Madame la marquise' (1935) by Paul Misraki (*b* 1908).

Venuti, Joe [Giuseppe] (*b* Philadelphia, 16 Sept. 1903; *d* Seattle, 14 Aug. 1978). American jazz violinist and bandleader. He was trained as a classical violinist, but became fascinated by New Orleans jazz, along with his boyhood friend, the guitarist Eddie *Lang. He began to play jazz and joined the Jean *Goldkette band in the 1920s, later working with Paul *Whiteman alongside such people as Bix *Beiderbecke, Jimmy *Dorsey, and Bing *Crosby. Between 1925 and 1933 the novelty of violin jazz led to many recordings (with Whiteman, *Trumbauer, and Albert Nicholas among others), the most memorable being those made with his own Blue Four with Lang (who died in 1933) on guitar, creating what was then a novel sort of chamber jazz, later exploited by *Grappelli and others. He also introduced such techniques as playing all four strings at once with a loosened bow. He was prominent in the jazz world until 1943, when he disappeared for some time while working as a studio musician in Hollywood. He re-emerged on the jazz scene at the 1968 Newport Jazz Festival, proving that he had lost none of his old inventiveness and spirit. He went to London in 1969, and continued as a much revered jazz original throughout the 1970s.

Verdon, Gwen [Gwyneth Evelyn] (*b* Los Angeles, 13 Jan. 1926). American actress, dancer, and singer. She started as a lively, red-haired dancer, who appeared in the chorus of the show *Magdalena* (1948), graduating to increasing parts in the shows *Alive and Kicking* (1950) and **Can-Can* (1953); and as a leading dancer in the films *On the Riviera* (1951); *Meet Me After the Show* (1951); *The *Merry Widow* (1952); and *The Farmer Takes a Wife* (1953); before emerging as the star of **Damn Yankees* (1955; filmed 1958), singing 'Whatever Lola wants'. This was followed by top roles in *New Girl in Town* (1957)—'It's good to be alive'; *Redhead* (1959); **Sweet Charity* (1966)—'Where am I going?', 'There's gotta be something better than this', 'If my friends could see me now'; and **Chicago* (1975).

Véronique. Operetta with music by André *Messager, book by Albert Vanloo (1861–1920) and Georges Duval (1847–1919), first produced in Paris at the Bouffes-Parisiens 10 Dec. 1898. It was seen in Vienna (Theater an der Wien) 10 Mar. 1900; in London, at the Coronet Theatre 5 May 1903, in French; and then in a popular production at the Apollo Theatre 18 May 1904, which enjoyed 495 performances. The story of a charming florist and a young nobleman, for whom love triumphs in spite of every obstacle and a tremendously involved plot, was graced by some of Messager's best songs—the 'Duo de l'escarpolette' ('Swing song') and 'Decidela' ('Trot here and there') among them. Although not his most popular work in France, it is the one by which he is mainly known abroad and has had many revivals.

Very Good Eddie. Musical comedy with score by Jerome *Kern, book by Philip Bartholomae and Guy *Bolton, lyrics by Schuyler Green and Herbert Reynolds, the third of the famous *Princess Theatre shows presented by F. Ray Comstock (1880–1949) and Elisabeth Marbury (1856–1933). It opened 23 Dec. 1915 and ran for 341 performances. The action (in two scenes, as was usual in these economy productions) was firstly on a Hudson River cruise-boat where two ill-suited honeymooning couples are inextricably parted and re-matched; sorted out later in the Rip Van Winkle Hotel. The score contained such early Kern classics as 'Some wonderful sort of someone' and 'Babes in the wood'. London (Palace) 18 May 1918.

Victoria, Vesta (*b* Leeds, 26 Nov. 1874; *d* London, 7 Apr. 1951). British music-hall singer. She was the daughter of a blackface music-hall comedian and singer and first appeared on stage with him in 1878, making her own solo debut in 1883 billed as 'Little Victoria'. She became well-known around 1893, when she introduced the song 'Daddy wouldn't buy me a bow-wow', and was equally popular in the USA, where she toured in vaudeville for six years. Her act was a mixture of innuendo and innocence, the girl whose love affairs always go wrong; and she had a genius for picking songs of the very top quality for her act, including: 'Our lodger's such a nice young man', 'Poor John', 'He calls me his own Grace Darling', 'It's all right in the summer time', 'Now I have to call him Father', and the classic 'Waiting at the Church', all of which she re-recorded in 1931. She retired after the First World War, but made comebacks in revival groups in 1929 and 1931–2, appearing in the Royal Variety show in 1932.

Vie Parisienne, La. Opéra-bouffe with music by Jacques *Offenbach, book by Henri Meilhac and Ludovic *Halévy, first performed in Paris (Palais-Royal) 31 Oct. 1866. It was first seen in Vienna in 1867; in London in 1872.

Although Offenbach's name is largely associated with the frivolities of Parisian life and the can-can, this is the only one of his major works to be set in Paris and to attempt a portrayal of its amorous intrigues, centred on a group of visitors to the capital intent on such games. The tone was matched by a totally Parisian score that contains some of his most vivacious music, including 'Je suis Brésilien', and one of his best waltzes, 'A minuit sonnant'. It has been notably revived in London by the Sadler's Wells and English National Opera Companies from 1961 and given modern recordings.

Viktoria und ihr Husar. Operetta with music by Paul *Abrahám, book by Alfred Grünwald and Fritz Löhner-Beda (*d* 1939). It was first seen in Leipzig and Berlin in 1930, then in Vienna, at the Theater an der Wien, 23 Dec. 1930 [121p]. As *Victoria and her Hussar* it was produced in London (Palace Theatre) 17 Sept. 1931, with Roy Russell as the Hussar, Margaret Carlisle as Victoria, Oskar Dénes as her brother, and Harry *Welchman in a supporting role [100p]; and as *Victoria et son husard* it was seen in Paris (Moulin-Rouge) 16 Dec. 1933. It was filmed in German in 1931 and 1954.

The story, a romantic tale of a long-lost lover, ranging in location from Tokyo to St Petersburg, is a vehicle for some of Abrahám's best songs, notably 'Mausi' and 'Pardon, madame'.

'Vilikens and his Dinah'. A song of obscure origins, the tune possibly adapted from an old Scottish melody, 'Peggie is over ye sie'; though composer credits have also been given to a John Parry. The words originated in a tragic *broadside ballad printed by James Catnach under the title of 'William and Dinah', the song as we now know it being a humorous parody of this. In this comic form it was sung by Frederick Robson (1821–64), in *The Wandering Minstrel* at the Olympic Theatre, London, in 1836 and later at the Grecian Saloon. The song was taken over by the comic singer Sam *Cowell, who made it very much his own at venues like *Evans's and the Canterbury. It was also sung by J. L. Toole (1832–1906). Found with various spellings (Villikens, Villikins, Willikind, among them) it was published many times from 1853 on, Sam Cowell including it in several collections under his name, and it became very much a model for Cockney and music-hall songs. An American version, 'Sweet Betsey from Pike', was first printed in *Put's Golden Songster* (San Francisco, 1858).

Vincent, Gene [Craddock, Eugene Vincent] (*b* Norfolk, Va., 11 Feb. 1935; *d* Hollywood, 12 Oct. 1971). American rock singer. From a poor family, he left school at 16, and joined the merchant navy. After a motorcycle accident in 1955, which permanently disabled him, he started singing and gradually moved into the country music scene, and by 1956 was regularly broadcasting. He was signed up by Capitol Records, who saw him as a possible answer to Elvis *Presley, and one of his first recordings, 'Be-bop-a-lula' (1956), seemed to set him on his way. The impetus was not maintained, although 'Lotta lovin'' (1957) was another best-seller. The rather seedy Vincent image was not in favour, in contrast to the clean image of Rick *Nelson and others, and even Presley's growing respectability. He had a period as a popular leather-suited idol of the 1960s, especially in Britain and Europe, but by then was defeated by the rise of the *Beatles. His life disintegrated and he died suddenly of an ulcer.

Vinter, Gilbert (*b* Lincoln, 4 May 1909; *d* Tintagel, Cornwall, 10 Oct. 1969). British composer and conductor. He was a choral scholar at Lincoln Cathedral 1925–7 and studied at the Royal Military School of Music and the Royal Academy of Music. He played the bassoon in the BBC Wireless Military Band and in the London Philharmonic Orchestra. In 1940 he joined the RAF as a member of the Central Band and graduated to bandmaster of various RAF units 1941–5. In 1946 he became staff conductor with the BBC, mainly working with the Midland Light Orchestra, and, from 1953, the BBC Concert Orchestra. As a composer he took a special interest in writing for the brass band, his most impressive work being 'The Trumpets' for band, chorus, and soloist. His other works included 'Salute to youth', 'Symphony of marches', 'Variations on a ninth', 'Spectrum', and 'James Cook—circumnavigator'. He both revolutionized and popularized writing for brass quartet, with works like 'Elegy and rondo', 'Fancy's knell', and 'Alla burlesca'. Probably his most popular work was 'Portuguese party'.

Vives, Amadeo (*b* Collbató, nr. Barcelona, 18 Nov. 1871; *d* Madrid, 1 Dec. 1932). Spanish composer. He worked in many musical fields and did much to bring the spirit of Catalonian folk-songs into Spanish classical music. He is very much remembered in Spain for his song 'L'emigrant', which became the hymn of exiled Catalans. He succeeded Tomás *Bretón as Professor of Composition at the Madrid Conservatory. He wrote more than 100 zarzuelas, some of such a substantial nature that they border on being of the opera world, such as the popular *Maruxa* (1914) and the renowned *Doña Francisquita* (1923), which has been called 'the Spanish *Die *Fledermaus*'. His *Bohemios* (1904) was a very individual piece from which he drew themes for other compositions; and among his other zarzuelas were: *Don Lucas del Cigarral* (1899); *La Balada de la luz* (1900); *Juegos malabres* (1909); *La Generala* (1910); *Colombo* (1910); *La villana* (1927); *El Talisman* (1932). He collaborated with *Gimenez.

S. Burgueto: *Amadeo Vives* (Madrid, 1978).

Vogelhändler, Der. Operetta with music by Karl *Zeller whose songs ('Ich bin die Christl von der Post', 'Schenkt man sich Rosen in Tirol', and 'Wie mein Ahnl zwanzig Jahr') have remained firm operetta favourites and are frequently recorded. It was first performed in Vienna (Theater an der Wien) 10 Jan. 1891 [184p]; was staged in New York in 1891 as *The Tyrolean*, with Marie *Tempest; and first seen in London, at Drury Lane, in 1895. There was a popular production, conducted and directed by Richard *Tauber, at the Palace Theatre in 1947 as *The Bird Seller*.

Von Tilzer, Albert (*b* Indianapolis, 29 Mar. 1878; *d* Los Angeles, 1 Oct. 1956). American composer and publisher. Younger brother of Harry *Von Tilzer. He worked in a shoestore while he studied music and then tried his luck in *Tin Pan Alley. Reversing the usual progress of events, he went on the stage after he had already become known as a songwriter, with such items as 'Take me out to the ball game' (the tune with which the Marx Brothers, by switching the orchestral parts, wreck an opera performance in *A Night at the Opera*). He wrote scores for *The Happiest Night of his LIfe* (1911); *Honey Girl* (1920); *The Gingham Girl* (1922); *Adrienne* (1923); *Bye Bye, Bonnie* (1927). His best-remembered songs included: 'Teasing' (1904, *w* Cecil Mack), 'Honey boy' (1907, *w* Jack *Norworth), 'Take me out to the ball game' (1908, Norworth), 'Put your arms around me, honey' (1910, *w* Junie McCree), 'Pucker up your lips, Miss Lindy' (1912, *w* Eli Dawson), 'Give me the moonlight, give me the girl' (1917, *w* Lew *Brown), 'Oh, by jingo, oh, by gee' (1919, Brown), 'I'll be with you in apple blossom time' (1920, Neville Fleeson), 'Dapper Dan' (1921, Brown), and 'Roll along, prairie moon' (with Ted *Fiorito, 1935, *w* Mack).

Von Tilzer, Harry (*b* Detroit, 8 July 1872; *d* New York, 10 Jan. 1946). American composer, writer, publisher, and actor. He joined a circus at the age of 14, then was with a repertory company, writing much of his own material. In 1892 he went to New York to work in *Tin Pan Alley, where 'My old New Hampshire home' (1898) established him as a songwriter. In 1902 he established his own music-publishing business and ran it until his death. He wrote scores for *The Fisher Maiden* (1903) and *The Kissing Girl* (1910).

A prolific songwriter, his best-known songs included: 'Where the sweet magnolias grow' (1899, *w* Andrew B. Sterling), 'The spider and the fly' (1900, *w* Arthur J. Lamb), 'A bird in a gilded cage' (1900, Lamb), 'Down where the cotton blossoms grow' (1901, Sterling), 'The mansion of aching hearts' (1902, Lamb), 'In the sweet bye and bye' (1902, *w* Vincent *Bryan), *'Down where the Wurzburger flows' (1902, Bryan)—made famous by Norah *Bayes who was known as 'The Wurzburger Girl', 'Under the Anheuser bush' (1903, Sterling)—known in England as *'Down at the old Bull and Bush', 'Teasing' (with Cecil Mack, 1883–1944, 1904), 'Wait 'till the sun shines, Nellie' (1905, Sterling), 'What you goin' to do when the rent comes round' (1905, Sterling), 'Where the morning glories twine around the door' (1905, Sterling), 'All aboard for Blanket Bay' (1910, Sterling), 'I want a girl (just like the girl that married dear old dad)' (1911, *w* Will Dillon), 'Constantinople' (1917, *w* Bert Hanlon), and 'When my baby smiles at me' (1920, Sterling).

W

Wakely, Jimmy [*b* Mineola, Ark., 16 Feb. 1914; *d* 23 Sept. 1982). American singer, guitarist, and composer. He started life as an Oklahoma ranch hand but gradually earned a reputation as a singer of Country and Western songs and as a guitarist. He was on Oklahoma City Radio in the 1930s and on the Gene *Autry show in the 1940s, and had his own radio programmes. He appeared in more than 50 films and was active until the 1960s. He wrote 'Too late' and 'I'll never let you go'.

Wakeman, Rick (*b* Perivale, Middx., 18 May 1949). British composer and pianist. He started playing the piano at the age of seven, then joined a local band. From 1963 he studied for a short period at the Royal College of Music, intending to become a classical pianist, but left to devote hmself to a compelling interest in the more popular spheres of music-making. He played on recording sessions, backing names as diverse as Black Sabbath and Clive Dunn; contributed to David *Bowie's *Space Oddity* album in 1969, joined the Strawbs in 1970 and *Yes in 1971; recorded with Cat Stevens (*b* 1947)—'Morning has broken' (1972); and with David Bowie—'Life on Mars' (1973); adding a distinctive touch to everything he was involved with.

His own first album, *The Six Wives of Henry VIII* (1973), displayed his creative individuality, as did *Journey to the Centre of the Earth* (1974), which was performed at the Royal Festival Hall in London that year. This was followed by the ambitious *The Myths and Legends of King Arthur and the Knights of the Round Table* (1975), which was seen on ice at Wembley. He wrote the sound-track music for Ken Russell's *Lisztomania* (1975), produced a third solo album, *No Earthly Connection* (1976), and worked with Yes until 1980. He wrote the sound-track for the World Cup film *Golé* (1983), worked with Tim *Rice on a version of Orwell's *1984*, and compèred the TV rock show, *Gastank*. He appears to be the composer most likely to bridge the gulf between the classical tradition of light music and rock.

D. Wooding: *Rick Wakeman: the Caped Crusader* (St Albans, 1979).

Wake Up and Dream. Revue with music and lyrics by Cole *Porter ('What is this thing called love?', 'I'm a gigolo', 'Let's do it', 'Too beautiful for words') and others, including Arthur *Schwartz ('She's such a comfort to me'), Phil *Charig ('Fancy our meeting'), and Ivor *Novello ('Why wouldn't I do'). It was produced in London (Pavilion) 27 Mar. 1929, with Sonnie *Hale, Douglas *Byng, Jessie *Matthews, and Elsie Carlisle (1903–77) [263p]; and in New York (Selwyn Theatre) 30 Dec. 1929, with Jack *Buchanan and Jessie Matthews [136p]. A film version in 1934 starred June Knight (*b* 1911) and Russ *Columbo.

Waldteufel, Emile [Lévy, Charles Emile] (*b* Strasbourg, 9 Dec. 1837; *d* Paris, 12 Feb. 1915). French composer, conductor, and pianist. His grandfather, father, and two uncles had all been dance musicians and had also used the pseudonym 'Waldteufel', whose origins are not known. At the age of four he moved with his family to Paris and learned the piano, firstly with his mother. When he was seven he was admitted to the Paris Conservatoire, where Bizet and Massenet were fellow-pupils; but during the revolution of 1848 it was found difficult to finance his studies and he helped out by selling papers in the street, finally leaving in that year to earn a living demonstrating pianos for the manufacturer Scholtus. At 15 he left home and earned a living by giving lessons in his attic room, where one of his pupils is said to have been the young Rimsky-Korsakov. He began composing and published some waltzes at his own expense, played at aristocratic soirées, and was appointed court pianist to the Empress Eugénie; in 1866 he became Imperial Court Musical Director.

He lived in his Montmartre garret for some 15 years and it was there that he heard a young singer practising in a room across the street, and he would accompany her on his piano. This led to a meeting, a romance, and his eventual marriage to Célestine Dufau in 1868. He volunteered for service during the Franco-Prussian War of 1870–1 and was in Paris during the siege. After the war he resumed his career as a dance musician, becoming conductor of the presidential balls, but still found difficulty in getting his compositions accepted, with only the 'Reine' waltz published in London in 1868. One night in 1874, while he was playing in a society house, his waltz 'Manolo' was heard and liked by the Prince of Wales (later Edward VII). Later Waldteufel asked if he might dedicate a waltz to the Prince and Princess and permission was granted. He wrote 'Bien aimés', sent it, with the dedication, to the London publisher Hopwood & Crew, and in March 1875 he signed a contract with them, an agreement which was to last until 1888.

Although other works of his had previously been played in public it was from then on that he really became known. A partner in the publishing firm was the dance orchestra leader Charles Coote, who regularly exploited Waldteufel's waltzes. At a state ball in 1878, six of the nine waltzes played were his. His works had a lasting vogue in England and the years between 1875 and 1890 saw the composition of most of his best works: 'Les patineurs' ('The skaters' waltz) (1882), 'Estudiantina' (1883), 'España' (1886); but he was always to work in the shadow of Johann Strauss and the conflicting Viennese waltz strains.

Waldteufel was not a regular conductor, only leading an orchestra on special social occasions. In November 1885 he appeared for four weeks, to great acclaim, at the Covent Garden Promenade Concerts; and in 1889 he conducted in Berlin. He declined an offer to visit America. By the 1890s his work was becoming old-fashioned and in 1900 he gave up his few conducting engagements. His one attempt at an operetta, *Les Cadets de Gascogne*, came to nothing, and his only association with the theatre came in 1914 when *Teresita* (with a score compiled from his melodies by Béla von Ujj), was given 18 performances in the Festpiel-Theater (known as the Sommer-Theater) in the Kaiser-Garten in Vienna in June and July. His output of waltzes and polkas was considerable, and his father Louis and his brother Léon also published some works under the name of Waldteufel.

A. Lamb: *Emile Waldteufel (1837–1915): the Parisian Waltz King* (Littlehampton, 1979).

Walker, Nancy [Swoyer, Anna Myrtle] (*b* Philadelphia, 10 May 1921). American singer, actress, and comedienne. She made her mark on radio in the series *Lady Next Door*; and then on Broadway in **Best Foot Forward* (1941), singing 'The three Bs', 'Just a little joint with a jukebox', and 'Shady lady bird'; followed by **On the Town* (1944)—'I can cook too'; *Barefoot Boy with Cheek* (1947); *Look Ma, I'm Dancin'* (1938); *Along Fifth Avenue* (1949); and *Do Re Mi* (1960). She was in the film version of *Best Foot Forward* (1943); and in the films **Girl Crazy* (1943), *Broadway Rhythm* (1944), and *Lucky Me* (1954). Later she became a director.

Walker, T-Bone [Aaron Thibeaux] (*b* Linden, Texas, 28 May 1910; *d* Los Angeles, 16 Mar. 1975). American blues singer and guitarist. He sang country blues in the Dallas area, played in local bands, and took up the electric guitar after hearing Les *Paul's innovative sounds. For a time he was with the Les Hite band. He made many blues recordings in the 1940s and 1950s, including 'They call it Stormy Monday'. His use of the electric guitar was influential in rhythm 'n' blues developments and the work of artists like B. B. *King, but in spite of his influence he neither achieved nor wanted public acclaim.

Wallace, Nellie (*b* Glasgow, 18 Mar. 1870; *d* London, 24 Nov. 1948). British comedienne and singer. The child of music-hall artists, she made her first appearance on the stage in Birmingham in 1882 as a dancer, continuing as such billed as 'La Petite Nellie'. She appeared in pantomime and worked in the provincial music-halls for many years before making her first London appearance in 1903, and was later a great success at the *Oxford. She developed an eccentric spinster character, appallingly dressed, with a wispy feather boa or fur round her neck which she referred to as her 'little bit of vermin'. She sang in a nasal, yodelling style, with such lightly vulgar songs as 'Under the bed', 'The blasted oak', 'Half-past nine', 'Mother's pie crust', 'Let's have a tiddley at the milk bar', and 'A boy's best friend is his mother'. She toured the USA on several occasions. After the decline of the music-hall, she was in revue, appearing with Billy *Merson in *Whirl of the World* (1923), which had 627 performances; in *Sky High* (1925); and in several George Black shows 1931–4. She was a successful female pantomime dame, toured with ENSA during the Second World War, and appeared in revival music-hall shows.

Waller, Jack (*b* London, 2 Apr. 1885; *d* London, 28 July 1957). British composer, actor, and manager. After an education in Vienna, he began his musical career as a multi-instrumentalist with Harry Reynolds's Minstrels. He spent many years as an entertainer in provincial music-halls, and in 1910 formed the Seven Butterflies concert party. He toured abroad and had his first stage production in Australia in 1912. He made his London mark in *Robey en Casserole* (1923) and appeared in *The Little Revue Starts at Nine* (1923). In 1922 he went into theatre management with Herbert Clayton, producing touring revues and plays. They became the leading impresarios of the time, having their biggest success with **No, No, Nanette* in 1925, which earned Waller a personal £150,000, a considerable fortune in those days. When the partnership was dissolved in 1930, he continued the business on his own.

He began to compose the music for many of his own productions, including: *Princess Charming* (1926)—'Palace of dreams'; *Virginia* (1928); *Merry, Merry* (1929); *Dear Love* (1929); *Silver Wings* (1930); *For the Love of Mike* (1931)—'Got a date with an angel', 'Who do you love?'; *Tell Her the Truth* (1932)—'Sing, brothers', 'Won't you tell me why?'; *He Wanted Adventure* (1933); *Command Performance* (1933); **Mr Whittington* (1934)—'Oceans of time', 'Weep no more, my baby'; *Yes, Madam* (1934); *Please Teacher* (1935); *Certainly Sir* (1936); *Big Business* (1937); and *Bobby Get Your Gun* (1938)—'La conga'. Waller belonged to the great musical comedy era dominated by *Cochran, and always sported a carnation and cigar. Times got leaner, but he was still staging shows into the 1950s with varying success and failure.

Waller, 'Fats' [Thomas Wright] (*b* Waverley, NY, 21 May 1904; *d* Kansas City, 15 Dec. 1943). American composer, pianist, and entertainer. Son of the Revd Edward Martin Waller, who preached at the Abyssinian Baptist church in Harlem, where Thomas learned to play the organ. He showed early signs of being very musical and at the age of 15 won first prize in an amateur pianist contest. His first professional job was as organist in the Lincoln Theatre in New York; and during the mid-1920s he worked in a silent movie house in Washington DC. He played there in vaudeville and soon became known as an exuberant entertainer and pianist. He led a trio in Philadelphia, worked with Erskine *Tate in Chicago, played and recorded with Fletcher *Henderson and Ted *Lewis, and appeared on the stage in Chicago and New York. He started composing piano pieces in the early 1920s and collaborated on the songs for the black revues *Keep Shufflin'* (1928) and **Hot Chocolates* (1929), also playing in the orchestra. There was a bleak time during the depression years, and during 1931–2 he was employed as a staff pianist with a Cincinnati radio station.

He returned to the stage in the 1930s with an established reputation as the composer of such classics as 'Ain't misbehavin'' and 'Honeysuckle rose', rising to international fame around 1934 as a prolific recording artist for Victor, both with his Rhythm group, which included such fine players as Herman Autrey (1904–80) (trumpet) and Eugene Sedric (1907–63) (saxophone), and as a soloist. His great sense of comedy led him to guy most of the lyrics he sang on record, including his own and popular songs of the period: like his great hit 'My very good friend the milkman' (*m* Harold Spina, *b* 1906; *w* Jimmy Burke), into which he interpolated sly comments at overly sentimental moments. His comedy took his art to a wide public while his powerfully swinging piano playing maintained his reputation in the jazz world, helped by the fact that many of his compositions had become widely used jazz standards. He played in the propulsive Harlem 'stride' mode in the steps of his mentor James P. *Johnson, adding a uniquely personal style and touch. He had a natural flair as an entertainer, with a true sense of theatre, and lived at a cracking pace, in spite of his considerable girth. His output was maintained by a liberal use of the gin bottle and 48-hour sleeping bouts in between days of roistering and compulsive work: after several breakdowns, his death aboard the Santa Fe Chief railway express one December morning came as no surprise.

His recordings were always rich in jazz as well as comedy. He toured Europe as pianist and variety star in 1938 and 1939; led orchestras in New York 1939–40 and made several American tours, again with his big band 1941–2 and as soloist 1942. He wrote the score of the Broadway musical *Early to Bed* in 1943; and was in the films *Hooray for Love* (1935), *King of Burlesque* (1935), and *Stormy Weather* (1943), the latter including a memorable band version of 'Ain't misbehavin''. He mainly worked with lyricist Andy *Razaf, whose words combined naturally with Waller's jazz-oriented tunes. His reputation has flourished and his recordings have remained a classic legacy. His songs and compositions include: 'Squeeze me' (with Spencer *Williams, 1925), 'My fate is in your hands' (1929, *w* Razaf), 'Handful of keys' (1929), 'Minor drag' (1929), 'Harlem fuss' (1929), 'Honeysuckle rose' (1929, Razaf), 'Blue turning grey over you' (1930, Razaf), 'Keepin' out of mischief now' (1932, Razaf), 'Ain'tcha glad' (1933, Razaf), 'Alligator crawl' (1934), 'Viper's drag' (1934), 'The joint is jumpin'' (with J. C. *Johnson, 1937, *w* Razaf), 'Jealous of me' (1937, Razaf), 'Honey hush' (1939, *w* Ed W. Kirkeby); to name but a few.

J. R. T. Davies: *The Music of Thomas 'Fats' Waller* (London, 1950; rev. 1953). C. Fox: *Fats Waller* (London, 1960). E. W. Kirkeby, D. P. Schiedt, and S. Traill: *Ain't Misbehavin': the Story of Fats Waller* (New York–London, 1966; repr. 1975). J. Vance: *Fats Waller: his Life and Times* (Chicago, 1977). M. Waller and A. Calabrese: *Fats Waller* (New York, 1977; London, 1978). P. Machlin: *Stride: the Music of Fats Waller* (London, 1985).

Waltz. A dance to music in triple time (3/4), the precise origin of which is obscure. It was certainly not the invention of any one person but evolved from the Ländler of Austria and Southern Germany which, in turn, derived from the folk-dances of those areas. The word 'waltz' comes from the verb 'walzen', to rotate, which came from the earlier 'volter' of similar meaning. We first hear of a dance called the 'walzer' about the middle of the 18th century. There have been attempts to link the waltz and the minuet, but they have little in common apart from their rhythms. The minuet is poised and stately, the essence of the waltz is its lively and improvised nature. The early folk-dances in this rhythm involved not only rotating but hopping, jumping, and stamping. As it became more the property of the ballroom, these energetic movements were replaced by a smoother gliding motion (*scheifler*), but it still remained fairly boisterous. Witnessing such dancing in 1805, and the close contact it involved, Dr Burney reflected that an English mother would be uneasy to see her daughter so familiarly treated—and still more so to witness the obliging manner in which the freedom is returned by the female.

By the first years of the 19th century, the waltz had become a craze in Vienna. At the time of the great Vienna Congress in 1815, the Prince de Ligne said 'The Congress does not progress—it dances'. The dance spread to France and, soon after, to England. The music naturally developed alongside the dance. An early step towards the gracefulness of the fully fledged Viennese waltz was found in the waltzes of Michael Pamer (1782–1827) written for his own orchestra in Vienna, in whose ranks both Josef *Lanner and Johann *Strauss the elder learned their trade. The waltz came to full fruition in the hands of Johann *Strauss II whose best waltzes, so Dr Percy Scholes predicted, would last as long as the symphonies of Beethoven.

A feature of the correct playing of the Viennese waltz is a very slight anticipation of the second beat in the bar which adds lilt, lift, and life, a device known as 'Atempause' (breath pause). The French waltz, as typified by *Waldteufel's, has a rather more deliberate pace and even nature, as had the later *Boston or English waltz (as it became known on the Continent). The waltz, once established, soon found its way into the classical world, where Mozart and Schubert found delight and reward in writing waltzes for dancing. One of the first inclusions of a waltz in classical piano music is to be found in a sonatina by Haydn, the normal minuet replaced by a 'mouvement de Walze', thus anticipating Weber's 'Invitation to the dance' by half a century. One of the first appearances of the waltz in an opera was in Martin y Soler's *Una cosa rara* in 1786, which took Vienna by storm probably less on account of the simple folky music than by virtue of a chance to see so hotly debated an activity on the stage.

The fast Viennese waltz, with its constant exhausting rotation, the music played at about 50 bars a minute, remained supreme until about 1910. By 1912 it has been completely pushed out of fashion by the new slow waltz, the Boston, which introduced steps more akin to those of the later *foxtrot with only occasional turns. The Boston itself faded out about 1914 as it was, like the foxtrot, too spacious. From it the modern ballroom waltz developed. An important feature of this is the closing of the feet at the end of each bar, a visual retention of the old *Atempause* lilt, which makes the waltz seem a graceful survivor.

The Strauss family were followed by Carl *Ziehrer—'Hereinspaziert', 'Wiener Burger'—and the many other Viennese composers who built the world of operetta on the foundation of the waltz. Beyond this Viennese-dominated world, some graceful and lasting examples managed to assert themselves from elsewhere, coming from such composers as the Italian Luigi Arditi (1822–1903)—'Il bacio' ('The kiss'); the Romanian Ivan Ivanovici (1848–1905)—'Donauwellen' ('Waves of the Danube'); the Czechs Karel Komzàk (1850–1905)—'Bad'ner Mad'ln', and Julius Fucík (1872–1916); the Hungarian Oscar Fetras (1854–1934)—'Mondnacht auf der Alster' ('Moonlight on the Alster'; and the Mexican Juventino Rosas (1868–94)—'Sobre les olas' ('Over the waves').

B. Weigl: *Die Geschichte des Walzers* (Langensalza, 1910). F. Lange: *Der Wiener Walzer* (Vienna, 1917). H. Ulrich: *Der Wiener Walzer* (London, 1940). M. Carner: *The Waltz* (London, 1948). E. Reeser: *The History of the Waltz* (Amsterdam, 1952). P. J. S. Richardson: *The Social Dances of the 19th Century* (London, 1960).

Walzertraum, Ein. Operetta with music by Oscar *Straus, book by Felix Dörman [Felix Biedermann] (1876–1928) and Leopold Jacobson (1873–1945), first seen at the Carltheater, Vienna, 2 Mar. 1907, with Mizzi Zwerenz, Fritz Werner, and Artur Guttmann in the leading roles. It was an immediate success with its waltz-song 'Leise, ganz leise', composed in the best Viennese tradition and set in a shapely score; and was then seen at the Theater des Westerns, Berlin, 21 Dec. 1907. As *A Waltz Dream*, it was produced in New York (Broadway Theatre) 27 Jan. 1908, with some additional numbers by Jerome *Kern, and others [111p]; and in London, at the Hicks Theatre 28 Mar. 1908, English book by Basil *Hood and Adrian *Ross, with Gertie *Millar, Robert Evett (1874–1949), and George *Grossmith Jr. [146p].

A lastingly popular work, it has a romantic story of a young prince torn between his loves for a princess and the leader of a ladies' orchestra. He rightly, if somewhat disappointingly, ends up with the princess. It was seen in Paris, at the Théâtre Apollo 3 Mar. 1910, and was revived at Daly's Theatre, London, 7 Jan. 1911, with Lily *Elsie, Robert Michaelis (1885–1965), and W. H. *Berry [106p]. It has often been staged in Paris and Vienna, with the most recent Volksoper production in 1987.

'Waltzing Matilda'. Universally known Australian song that is possibly based on a Scottish song 'Thou bonny wood of Craigy Lee', which appeared in *Miniature Museum of Scottish Songs* (Edinburgh, 1818). Another version was known as 'Craigielea'. The music is generally attributed to James Barr (1779–1860), a farmer who emigrated to Canada and died there. It was heard, played as a march, in Warrnambool, Australia, in 1894 by Christina Macpherson; she introduced it to the Australian poet Andrew Barton 'Banjo' Paterson (1864–1941), who wrote words to the tune based on a story of a swagman told to him by Mrs Macpherson's husband. After gaining a private circulation it was published in Sydney in 1903 as 'Waltzing Matilda' with the music arranged by Marie Cowan, who has sometimes been wrongly credited as the composer.

It was published in *The Australasian Students' Song Book* (Melbourne, 1911) and became a great favourite with the Australian troops during the Second World War. It became so much the national song that it has frequently been proposed as Australia's national anthem. Despite the name, it is not a waltz but written in 4/4 time. A 'matilda' is a knapsack which 'waltzes' (i.e. sways) on the back of the itinerant Australian labourer, or 'swagman', as he plods along.

Ware, George (*b* London, 1829; *d* London, 30 Dec. 1895). British composer, singer, and manager. After spending his early years as a sailor and a soldier, he took to the stage and became a popular singer, first making his mark at the Oriental Music Hall in Poplar, East London. Later he worked as the British agent for Phineas T. Barnum and as a theatre and music-hall manager. He wrote one of the great classics of early music-hall, 'The boy in the gallery', which was pre-eminently sung by Nellie *Power and Marie *Lloyd. He also wrote 'The whole hog or none' (sung by the Great Mackney), 'Up goes the price of meat', 'The fiddler's wife' (sung by Sam *Collins), 'One little kiss' (sung by Nellie Power), and 'The house that Jack built'.

Waring, Fred [Frederick M.] (*b* Tyrone, Pa., 9 June 1900; *d* Danville, Pa., 29 July 1984). American conductor and composer. He was taught music as a boy by his mother, and then attended Pennsylvania State University, where he studied engineering and architecture. Throughout his life he was interested in mechanical things and was the inventor of a food mixer and a travelling iron. He started to play the banjo when he was 16 and formed a quartet called the Banjazzatra. He then formed a band called Waring's Collegians which, after he left college in the early 1920s, was enlarged to become the Pennsylvanians. Touring the country, playing concerts in hotels and on college campuses, the band soon earned a national reputation and was an influential unit in the early dance-band years. They visited Paris in 1928, and appeared in the Broadway shows *Hello Yourself* (1928) and *The New Yorkers* (1930), and in the film *Syncopation* (1929).

From 1933 he achieved great popularity on the radio in lavish programmes sponsored by tobacco and car firms, presenting programmes of muscularly American music, some of it written by himself. He made a special feature of barber-shop-style singing and featured such soloists as Irving *Berlin, Hoagy *Carmichael, Bing *Crosby, and Frank *Sinatra. He continued, with variations on an established pattern, into the late 1950s, with his own TV show in 1949. Although becoming increasingly involved in his money-making inventions, he continued to make guest appearances as a conductor into the 1970s, often working with youth choral groups and founding the Fred Waring Music Workshop to train young glee club leaders, and writing a considerable amount of material for use in this field. He was awarded the Congressional Gold Medal for his work in 1983.

Warren, Harry [Guaragna, Salvatore] (*b* Brooklyn, NY, 24 Dec. 1893; *d* Los Angeles, 22 Sept. 1981). American composer. The 11th and youngest child of an immigrant Italian family, he was naturally musical and taught himself to play the piano accordion as a boy. Eventually he mastered nine other instruments, but most of his musical knowledge was picked up while singing in a church choir. At the age of 15 he became a drummer in a brass band which played in carnivals along the eastern seaboard. A few years later he was working as an extra, and later assistant director, at the Vitagraph silent picture studios in Flatbush, New York, and in spare moments he amused himself by making up songs at the piano, gradually deciding that songwriting was his forte. After serving in the navy 1917–18, he entered the music business as a songplugger with a music-publisher and came up with his own first hit song in 1920, 'Rose of the Rio Grande' (*w* Edgar *Leslie), which was published in 1922. He joined the publishers Shapiro, Bernstein in 1924, which brought him into contact with the lyricists Bud Green and Mort Dixon, with whom he wrote many songs. He continued to turn out fairly hack Tin Pan Alley material and contributed to **Artists and Models of 1927*, achieving one or two outstanding items like 'Nagasaki' (1928).

He was to find that extra something as a songwriter when he joined many of his fellow-composers in the film studios in the blossoming years of the talkies. Having written for *Spring is Here* (1930)—'Crying for the Carolines', 'Have a little faith in me', 'Absence makes the heart grow fonder' (*w* Sam *Lewis and Joe *Young), he went to Hollywood in 1931 and joined forces with Al *Dubin, who was to write most of his words up to 1938. Dubin had already achieved several hits, like 'Tiptoe through the tulips' and 'Painting the clouds with sunshine', and he now joined the astonishingly prolific Warren to turn out a string of hits for films that included: **42nd Street* (1933)—'Shuffle off to Buffalo', 'You're getting to be a habit with me', 'Forty-second Street', 'Young and healthy'; **Gold Diggers of 1933*—'We're in the money', 'I've got to sing a torch song', 'Shadow waltz'; *Roman Scandals* (1933)—'Keep young and beautiful'; *Footlight Parade* (1933)—'Honeymoon hotel', 'Shanghai Lil'; *Moulin Rouge* (1934)—'The boulevard of broken dreams'; *Twenty Million Sweethearts* (1934)—'I'll string along with you', 'Fair and warmer'; *Dames* (1934)—'I only have eyes for you'; *Wonder Bar* (1934)—'Wonder bar'; *Sweet music* (1935)—'Sweet music'; *Gold Diggers of 1935*—'Lullaby of Broadway', first sung by Wini Shaw (*b* 1910), 'The words are in my heart'; *Go into Your Dance* (1935)—'About a quarter to nine', 'She's a Latin from Manhattan', 'Go into your dance'; *Broadway Gondolier* (1935)—'Lulu's back in town', 'Sweet and low'; *Shipmates Forever* (1935)—'Don't give up the ship', 'I'd love to take orders from you'; *Stars over Broadway* (1935); *Colleen* (1936); *Hearts Divided* (1936)—'Two hearts divided'; *Sons o' Guns* (1936)—'For a buck and a quarter a day'; *Cain and Mabel* (1936); *Gold Diggers of 1937* (1936)—'All's fair in love and war', 'With plenty of money and you'; *Sing Me a Love Song* (1936; *Come Up Smiling* in UK); *Melody for Two* (1937)—'September in the rain'; *The Singing Marine* (1937)—''Cause my baby says it's so', 'The Song of the Marines'; *Mr Dodd Takes the Air* (1937)—'Remember me?', 'Am I in love?'; *Going Places* (1938)—'Jeepers creepers' (*w* Johnny *Mercer); *Jezebel* (1938)—'Jezebel' (*w* Mercer); *Gold Diggers in Paris* (1938; *The Gay Imposters* in UK)—'The Latin Quarter'; *Garden of the Moon* (1938)—'Love is where you find it'; *Hard to Get* (1938)—'You must have been a beautiful baby' (*w* Mercer); *Naughty but Nice* (1939)—'Hooray for spinach'; *Honolulu* (1939); *Wings of the Navy* (1939)—'Wings over the Navy' (*w* Mercer); *Down Argentine Way* (1940)—'Down Argentina way', 'Two dreams met' (*w* Mack *Gordon); *Tin Pan Alley* (1940)—'You say the sweetest things, baby' (*w* Gordon); *That Night in Rio* (1941)—'I yi yi yi yi' (*w* Gordon), 'Chica chica boom chic' (*w* Gordon); *Sun Valley Serenade* (1941)—'I know why' (*w* Gordon), 'Chattanooga choo choo' (*w* Gordon); *Weekend in Havana* (1941)—'Tropical magic', 'When I love I love' (*w* Gordon); *Orchestra Wives* (1942)—'Serenade in blue', 'At last' (*w* Gordon), 'I've got a gal in Kalamazoo' (*w* Gordon); *Iceland* (1942)—'There will never be another you' (*w* Gordon); *Springtime in the Rockies* (1942)—'I had the craziest dreams' (*w* Gordon), 'Run, little raindrop, run' (Gordon), 'I like to be loved by you' (Gordon); *Hello, Frisco, Hello* (1943)—'You'll never know' (Gordon); *Sweet Rosie O'Grady* (1943)—'My heart tells me', 'Get your Police Gazette' (Gordon); *The Gang's All Here* (1943)—'The polka dot polka', 'No love, no nothin'' (*w* Leo Robin), 'A journey to a star' (Robin), 'Paducah' (Robin); *Billy Rose's Diamond Horseshoe* (1945)—'The more I see you' (Gordon); *Yolanda and the Thief* (1945)—'Will you marry me?' (*w* Arthur *Freed); *The Harvey Girls* (1946)—'On the Atcheson, Topeka and the Santa Fe' (*w* Mercer) [Academy Award], 'Oh, you kid' (Mercer); *Ziegfeld Follies* (1946)—'This heart of mine' (1943, Freed); *The Jolson Story* (1946)—several Warren hits revived; *Summer Holiday* (1948)—'Afraid to fall in love', 'The Stanley steamer' (*w* Ralph *Blane); *The Barkleys of Broadway* (1949)—'You'd be hard to replace', 'A weekend in the country', 'Shoes with wings on' (all *w* Ira *Gershwin); *My Dream is Yours* (1949); *Summer Stock* (1950)—'You wonderful you'; *Pagan Love Song* (1950); *Texas Carnival* (1951); *The Belle of New York* (1952)—'Naughty but nice', 'Baby doll', 'Seeing's believing' (Mercer); *Skirts Ahoy* (1952); *Just For You* (1952)—'Zing a little zong' (Robin); *The Caddy* (1953)—'That's amore' (*w* Jack Brooks); *Artists and Models* (1955); *The Birds and the Bees* (1956); *An Affair to Remember* (1957)—'An affair to remember' (*w* Harold *Adamson); *Rock-a-Bye Baby* (1958); *Cinderfella* (1960); and *The Ladies' Man* (1961). He wrote stage scores for *Sweet and Low* (1930), *The Laugh Parade* (1931), and *Shangri-La* (1956).

M. Wilk: 'Lullaby of Broadway' in *They're Playing Our Song* (New York, 1973). T. Thomas: *Harry Warren and the Hollywood Musical* (Secaucus, NJ, 1975).

Warwick, Dionne [Warrick, Marie Dionne] (*b* East Orange, NJ, 12 Dec. 1940). American singer. She first sang with a gospel group, the Drinkard Singers, which was managed by her mother; toured with the Gospelaires; studied at the Hartt School of Music in Connecticut; and then worked in New York as a supporting singer on record sessions. She made an impression on composer-producers Burt *Bacharach and Hal David who arranged a contract with Sceptre Records. Her first hit was their 'Don't make me over' and the team went on to many successes in their particular field of romantic pop. Her most popular numbers included 'I'll never fall in love again', 'Raindrops keep falling on my head', 'What the world needs now', and 'Do you know the way to San José?' She broke away from this formula by signing with Warner Brothers and had her first No. 1 hit in conjunction with the Spinners, 'Then came you' in 1974. Continuing with a high level of achievement in a very professional world of middle-of-the-road music-making, she had another top hit with 'That's what friends are for' in 1985; and has issued more than 15 LP albums.

Washboard. Makeshift rhythm instrument popular in early and revival *spasm or *skiffle bands. It was a genuine workaday washboard, from pre-electric years, played with thimbles, or similar protection on the fingers, to achieve a sort of scrubbing rhythm. Good quality washboards were favoured. Groups that featured the 'instrument', like the Washboard Rhythm Kings, became very popular in the 1920s and 1930s and have since been imitated. A leading exponent of the washboard was the drummer Jimmy Bertrand (1900–60).

Washburne, Joe 'Country' [Joseph] (*b* Houston, 28 Dec. 1904; *d* Santa Ana, Calif., 21 Jan. 1974). American singer, bassist, and composer. He became known as novelty vocalist with the Ted *Weems band 1924–42, with whom he introduced his song 'Oh, Monah' (1931), later taken up in England by Nat *Gonella and the *Ambrose band. He had another hit song with 'One dozen roses' in 1942. In the mid-1940s, he was with the Spike *Jones orchestra, responsible for arranging many of their popular items like 'Tim-tayshun' and 'Cigareetes, whiskey and wild, wild women'. He led bands on the Roy Rogers show and other radio series and worked with various Dixieland groups until his sudden death from a heart-attack.

Washington, Dinah [Jones, Ruth Lee] (*b* Tuscaloosa, Ala., 29 Aug. 1924; *d* Detroit, 14 Dec. 1963). American singer. As a child she sang in choirs and won an amateur contest at the age of 15. She then sang with bands around Chicago before joining Lionel *Hampton 1943–5, where she established a reputation, and was able to take up a solo career from 1946. Her best-remembered blues items were 'Blow top blues' and 'Evil gal blues'; in a more popular idiom she sang 'What a difference a day makes', 'Stormy weather', and 'September in the rain'. She became a star in the rhythm 'n' blues field and later moved into the pop market. She died of an overdose of drugs.

J. Haskins: *Queen of the Blues: a Biography of Dinah Washington* (New York, 1987).

Washington, Ned (*b* Scranton, Penn., 15 Aug. 1901; *d* Beverly Hills, Calif., 20 Dec. 1976). American lyricist. He had an early career as a master of ceremonies and a vaudeville agent, and writing vaudeville material led him into the songwriting field. He wrote material for **Earl Carroll's Vanities* (1928); *Vanderbilt Revue* (1930); *Tattle Tales* (1930); *Murder at the Vanities* (1933)—'A ghost of a chance'; **Blackbirds* (1934)—'A hundred years from today; and for many films including *Pinocchio* (1940)—'When you wish upon a star' (Academy Award), 'Give a little whistle'; *A Night at Earl Carroll's* (1940)—'One look at you'; *Dumbo* (1941)—'Baby mine'; *Green Dolphin Street* (1947)—'On Green Dolphin Street'; *My Foolish Heart* (1950)—'My foolish heart'; *High Noon* (1952)—'High noon' (Academy Award); *The High and the Mighty* (1954)—'The high and the mighty';

and many more, into the 1960s; also 'I'm getting sentimental over you' (1932). He worked with the composers Hoagy *Carmichael, Frank *Churchill, Jimmy *McHugh, Bronislaw *Kaper, Max *Steiner, Dimitri *Tiomkin, and Allie *Wrubel.

Watch Your Step. Revue with music and lyrics by Irving *Berlin, and words by Harry B. *Smith. Berlin's first Broadway score, and the first to feature the then popular pseudo-ragtime songs in the 'Alexander's Ragtime Band' vein. It opened at the New Amsterdam Theatre, New York, 8 Dec. 1914, for 175 performances. It was a fairly plotless affair that was really an excuse for watching Vernon and Irene *Castle dance (their first Broadway and last appearance together). W. C. Fields (1879–1946) was in the cast for one night, after which he was fired for diverting attention from the star dancers. The songs included the contrapuntal 'Play a simple melody', 'The minstrel parade', 'They always follow me around', 'When I discovered you', and 'Settle down in a one-horse town'. The show was taken to London in 1915 where it had 275 performances at the Empire Theatre with Ethel *Levey, Joseph *Coyne, and Lupino *Lane.

Waters, Ethel (*b* Chester, Pa., 31 Oct. 1896; *d* Chatsworth, Calif., 1 Sept. 1977). American singer and entertainer. She was born as the result of her mother's being raped at the age of 12, and she herself married at 13. After this failed she worked at menial jobs until her talent as a singer was discovered and she began to appear in vaudeville. She worked in Baltimore and Philadelphia before making her first New York appearance in 1917. By the 1920s she was a top vaudeville star, singing songs of the 'St Louis blues' kind, and she began recording in 1931 in a polished and smooth blues-inflected style. She appeared in *Africana* (1927)—singing 'I'm coming, Virginia'; **Blackbirds* (1930); and *Rhapsody in Black* (1931)—'Till the real thing comes along'. She became the first black singer to work with a white band when she was with Benny *Goodman and the *Dorsey Brothers in 1929. She was a great hit at the *Cotton Club in 1933 where she became associated with the song 'Stormy weather', following this with important roles in the musicals **As Thousands Cheer* (1933)—'Heat wave', 'Suppertime'; *At Home Abroad* (1935); and **Cabin in the Sky* (1940)—'Taking a chance on love'. She toured with her own show 1935–9 and made a celebrated appearance at Carnegie Hall in 1938. She also acted in straight plays: and was in the films *On With the Show* (1929)—'Am I blue?'; *Check and Double Check* (1930); *Cairo* (1942); *Cabin in the Sky* (1943)—'Happiness is a thing called Joe'; *Stage Door Canteen* (1943); *Pinky* (1949); and *The Sound and the Fury* (1959). She toured, with Fletcher *Henderson as accompanist, 1948–9, and had her own Broadway show, *An Evening with Ethel Waters* (1957). She retired from show-business through illness, but worked with the evangelist Billy Graham in the 1960s and 1970s.

E. Waters: *His Eye is on the Sparrow: an Autobiography* (New York, 1951). E. Waters: *To Me It's Wonderful* (New York, 1972).

Waters, Muddy [Morganfield, McKinley] (*b* Rolling Fork, Miss., 4 Apr. 1915; *d* Westmont, Ill., 30 Apr. 1983). American blues singer. He was raised on a plantation, where he was discovered in 1941 by Alan *Lomax, who was then making folk recordings for the Library of Congress. In 1943 he moved to Chicago to take up a singing career, and quickly established himself as 'King of the Chicago Blues' on the lively club circuit of the time. He signed up for what became Chess Records in 1945, and was the leading figure in an important blues clique which spawned the careers of Otis Spann, Little Walter, Jimmie Rogers, Bo *Diddley, and Chuck *Berry. The unique moaning and shouting style he fashioned owed nothing to any musical training and, favouring electronic guitars and microphone technique, he developed a ferociously loud output that impressed many up-and-coming rhythm 'n' blues bands, especially in England. There, in 1958, he found a dedicated following for his style and his songs ('Rollin' stone', 'Got my mojo working', 'Mannish boy', etc.), the first-mentioned being borrowed as a name by the up-and-coming *Rolling Stones. It also became the name of an American journal devoted to the rock field; and Bob *Dylan paid tribute in his own 'Like a rolling stone'. He continued to be an impressive performer into the 1970s and 1980s in spite of declining health which led to his final heart-attack.

J. Rooney: *Bossmen: Bill Monroe and Muddy Waters* (New York, 1971).

Watters, Lu [Lucious] (*b* Santa Cruz, Calif., 19 Dec. 1911; *d* Santa Rosa, Calif., 5 Nov. 1989). American jazz trumpeter and bandleader. His early experience was gained working as a ship's musician during school and university vacations. In 1926 he had his own band for a while, then played with various groups in California and organized an 11-piece band which played at Sweet's Ballroom in Oakland 1938–9. After trying various combinations he formed the Yerba Buena Jazz Band, which made its debut at the 1939 World's Fair, then moved in 1940 into the Dawn Club in San Francisco. He was to lead it until 1950, except for a period in the navy 1942–5 where he led a 20-piece band in Hawaii and took the chance to play with Teddy *Weatherford in India. The raucously jovial and earthy style of his tuba-based band, which became generally known as 'good time music', was a pervasive and worldwide influence on the traditional jazz revival scene. Watters shared the two-cornet lead (on *Oliver/*Armstrong lines) with Bob Scobey (1916–63), and Turk *Murphy was on trombone. Watters left the jazz scene in 1950, returned for a while in 1957, then retired from it completely to study geology, later working as a chef.

Waxman, Franz [Wachsmann, Franz] (*b* Königshütte, 24 Dec. 1906; *d* Los Angeles, 24 Feb.

1967). German-born American composer, conductor, and impresario. The youngest of seven children and the only musical one, he was encouraged by his father to go into banking and worked as a teller for $2\frac{1}{2}$ years. He left to study music in Dresden and Berlin, earning a living by playing the piano in nightclubs and with a jazz group called the Weintraub Syncopators. Learning his trade by writing arrangements for the band, he began to get employment as an orchestrator of film music, encouraged by the composer Friedrich Holländer, his first important job being the orchestration of Holländer's music for Sternberg's *Der blaue Engel* (1930). The producer Erich Pommer was so pleased with the results that he gave him his first composing commission for Fritz Lang's *Liliom*, which was filmed in Paris in 1933.

Waxman went to Hollywood in 1934 to work on *Kern's **Music in the Air*, studied with Schoenberg, and wrote his first original Hollywood score, *The Bride of Frankenstein*, in 1935. He was signed to a two-year contract as head of the music department at Universal, during which period he scored 12 films including *Diamond Jim* (1935), *Magnificent Obsession* (1935), and *The Invisible Ray* (1936). Now aged 30, he signed up with Metro-Goldwyn-Mayer, thereafter writing the music for about seven films a year, including: *Captains Courageous* (1937), *A Day at the Races* (1937), and *Too Hot to Handle* (1938). In 1938 he was loaned to Selznick to work on *The Young in Heart*, which was nominated for an Academy Award; 12 of the 188 film scores which he provided during his 32 years in the Hollywood studios received Oscars. He continued with MGM, working on such films as *The Adventures of Huckleberry Finn* (1939); *Strange Cargo* (1940); *Rebecca* (1940); *The Philadelphia Story* (1940); *Dr Jekyll and Mr Hyde* (1941); *Woman of the Year* (1942); *Tortilla Flat* (1942); many of these starring Spencer Tracy. In 1943 he left MGM and was musical director for Warner Brothers until 1946—*Old Acquaintance* (1943); *Destination Tokyo* (1944); *To Have and Have Not* (1945); *Hotel Berlin* (1945); etc.

In 1947 he founded the Los Angeles International Music Festival, premiering some 80 works by such composers as Stravinsky, Walton, Vaughan Williams, and Schoenberg; he also wrote many concert works, as well as continuing a large output of film scores. Two important Academy Awards came for the scores of *Sunset Boulevard* (1950) and *A Place in the Sun* (1951). The 1950s and 1960s were to see some of his best work, including: *The Blue Veil* (1951); *Phone Call From a Stranger* (1952); *My Cousin Rachel* (1952); *Come Back, Little Sheba* (1953); *Rear Window* (1954); *Prince Valiant* (1954); *Untamed* (1955); *Crime in the Streets* (1956); *The Spirit of St Louis* (1957); *Peyton Place* (1957); *Sayonara* (1957); *Run Silent, Run Deep* (1958); *The Nun's Story* (1959); *The Story of Ruth* (1960); *Return to Peyton Place* (1961); *My Geisha* (1961); *Hemingway's Adventures of a Young Man* (1962); and *Taras Bulba* (1962).

Wayburn, Ned [Edward Claudius] (*b* Pittsburgh, 30 Mar. 1874; *d* New York, 2 Sept. 1942). American director and choreographer. He became an esteemed and long-serving Broadway director who worked on 14 Klaw & Erlanger musicals, 13 Lew *Fields productions, 10 *Ziegfeld shows (including six editions of the **Ziegfeld Follies* (1916–19, 1922–3), and 9 *Shubert Brothers productions. He also worked in London with Albert de Courville (1888–1960) on *Hullo, Tango!* (1913); *Zig-Zag* (1917); *Box o' Tricks* (1918); and *Joy-Bells* (1919).

His Broadway shows included: *The Midnight Sons* (1909); *The Girl and the Wizard* (1909); *Tillie's Nightmare* (1910); *The Hen Pecks* (1911); *The *Passing Show* (1912 and 1913); *The Century Girl* (1916); *Poor Little Ritz Girl* (1920); *Hitchy-Koo* (1920); and *Smiles* (1930). He wrote *The Art of Stage Dancing* (New York, 1925; repr. 1930).

Wayne, Mabel (*b* Brooklyn, NY, 16 July 1904). American composer. One of the few women composers to thrive in the rat race of Tin Pan Alley, she went into vaudeville at the age of 16 and spent much of her spare time while on tour trying over her own songs at the piano. The first song she submitted to a publisher, 'Don't wake me up, let me dream', in 1925, was a hit; and she continued, with various collaborators, to write such hits as 'In a little Spanish town' (1926, *w* Sam *Lewis and Joe *Young), 'Ramona' (1927, *w* L. Wolfe *Gilbert), 'Chiquita' (1928, Gilbert), 'Little man, you've had a busy day' (with Al *Hoffman and Maurice Sigler, 1934), and 'All the way from San José (1948, Kermit Goell).

Weatherford, Teddy [Edward] (*b* Bluefield, W.Va., 11 Oct. 1903; *d* Calcutta, 25 Apr. 1945). American pianist. He lived in New Orleans 1915–20 where he learned the art of jazz piano, moving to Chicago in 1920 and joining the Erskine *Tate band. By comparison with contemporaries like James P. *Johnson and Fats *Waller, jazz history has neglected his talents, partly due to his spending much of his time in the Far East where he first went in 1926 to lead bands at venues from Singapore to Shanghai. He returned to the USA in 1934 to recruit a band and then, except for a visit to Paris in 1937, during which he made some of his few recordings, he worked in the Far East for much of his life, including a long residency at the Grand Hotel in Calcutta, where he died of cholera.

Weatherly, Fred E. [Frederic Edward] (*b* Portishead, Somerset, 4 Oct. 1848; *d* Weybridge, Surrey, 7 Sept. 1929). British lyric-writer. He was educated at the Hereford Cathedral School and at Brasenose College, Oxford, where Walter Pater was his tutor and he published a book of verse. He then studied law and was called to the Bar at 39, where he specialized in copyright and wrote a book on the subject. He began to write for the theatre and supplied the standard English translation of Mascagni's *Cavalleria Rusticana* and Leoncavallo's *Pag-*

liacci, among many. He was a prolific writer of song lyrics, around 1500 being published in his lifetime, and his name is encountered on many *drawing-room classics.

Among his best-known writings were 'Nancy Lee' (1877, *m* Stephen *Adams), 'Auntie' (1880, *m* A. H. Behrend), 'The Old Brigade' (1886, *m* Odoardo *Barri),'The star of Bethlehem' (1890, *m* Adams), 'The Holy City' (1892, *m* Adams), 'Danny Boy' (to the well-known 'Londonderry air', 1913), 'Roses of Picardy' (1916, *m* Haydn *Wood).

F. Weatherly: *Piano and Gown* (London, 1926).

Weather Report. American jazz/rock group formed in 1970 and led by Joe [Josef] Zawinul (*b* Vienna, 1932) (keyboards) and Wayne Shorter (*b* Newark, NJ, 1933) (saxophones); with Miroslav Vitous (*b* 1947) (bass), Alphonze Mouzon (*b* 1948) (drums), and Airto Moreira (*b* 1941) (percussion). Formed from musicians of experience who had played with such jazz experts as Cannonball *Adderley, Miles *Davis, Art *Blakey, and Herbie *Mann, they were to be one of the most impressive and lasting of the many similar groups of the period. Their first LP, *Weather Report* (1970), earned praise from both rock and jazz sources who enjoyed the intimate melodic playing of Zawinul and Shorter. These two remained the backbone of the group in the face of numerous changes in the rhythm line-up, the group sometimes working with two basses and three drummers. Some 14 albums between 1970 and 1985 brought them many awards from **Down Beat* and other sources. They regularly visited Europe and achieved a following in countries as far-flung as Japan.

Weavers, The. Influential folk-singing group formed in 1949, originally made up of Pete *Seeger, Lee Hays (1914–81), Ronnie Gilbert, and Fred Hellerman (*b* 1927). Difficulties, stemming from their left-wing sympathies, caused a disbandment in 1952, but they re-formed in 1955. Seeger left in 1958 to take up a solo career and was successively replaced by other lead singers. Taking *Leadbelly as their main inspiration, they recorded his 'Goodnight, Irene' and 'Kisses sweeter than wine', and traditional items like 'When the Saints go marching in', establishing a vein of commercial folk-music that was to be followed by many in the late 1950s and after. They even retained some degree of authenticity in recordings made with the Gordon *Jenkins orchestra. They broke up after a Chicago concert in 1963, but there have been several emotional reunions.

Webb, Chick [William Henry] (*b* Baltimore, 10 Feb. 1909; *d* Baltimore, 16 June 1939). American drummer, bandleader, composer, and lyricist. He started drumming at the age of three, was performing (on a boat in Sheepshead Bay) at nine, and played with the Jazzbo Orchestra in his early teens. He went to New York and formed his own band in 1926, first playing at the Black Bottom and Paddock Clubs and then fulfilling a historic engagement at the *Savoy Ballroom in Harlem, where he was to be the resident leader for ten years. Later he visited Boston and played in New York variety theatres, then led the first non-white band to play in the Central Park Hotel. Webb was a dwarf and a hunchback who suffered much pain and ill-health, dying prematurely of tuberculosis of the spine. But he played with unabated vigour and good humour and was acknowledged as one of the greatest of all swing band drummers, with a powerful, driving beat that made him a swing era legend. He is remembered also as the discoverer of Ella *Fitzgerald, who was long featured with the band and took it over after Webb's death. He wrote many band pieces, including 'Jungle mama' (1929), 'Let's get together' (1934), 'Swingin' on the reservation' (1936), 'Strictly jive' (1937); and had a hand in such vocal items as 'Stompin' at the Savoy' (with *Goodman, *Razaf, and *Sampson, 1936) and 'Holiday in Harlem' (1937).

Webb, Clifton [Parmalee Hollenbeck] (*b* Indianapolis, 19 Nov. 1891; *d* Beverly Hills, Calif., 13 Oct. 1966). American actor, dancer, and singer. Starting out as a dancer, he was soon the suavely elegant leading man in a number of Broadway productions, including: *The Purple Road* (1913); *Dancing Around* (1914); *Town Topics* (1915); *See America First* (1916); *Love o' Mike* (1917); *Listen, Lester* (1918); *As You Were* (1920); *The Fun of the Fayre* (London, 1921); **Phi-Phi* (London, 1922); *Jack and Jill* (1923); **Sunny* (1925)—in which he sang 'Two little bluebirds'; *She's My Baby* (1928); *Treasure Girl* (1928)—'I've got a crush on you'; *The *Little Show* (1929)—'I guess I'll have to change my plan'; *Three's a Crowd* (1930); *Flying Colors* (1932)—'Alone together'; **As Thousands Cheer* (1933)—'Easter parade', 'Not for all the rice in China'; and *You Never Know* (1938)—'At long last love'. Thereafter he continued his career as a straight actor in some 20 films.

Webb, George (*b* London, 8 Oct. 1917). British pianist and bandleader. An early jazz enthusiast, from 1944 he led a pioneering group in the British trad revival at the Red Barn, a public house in Bexleyheath to the south-east of London. The band had originally been formed among workers at the Vickers Armstrong factory at Crayford and another original member was the trombonist Eddie Harvey (*b* 1925). With a two-cornet lead in the accepted trad style, they matched the Yerba Buena band for vigour and output, and made many recordings, impinging on the public at large with an undeniable example of 'full frequency range recording' in 'South'/'London blues' on the Decca label in 1945. The two-cornet lead was eventually replaced by the single trumpet of Humphrey *Lyttelton. After his pioneering activities in jazz, a career as an agent, and a brief playing come-back in the 1970s, Webb's barrelhouse talents were confined to the pub he ran in Essex from 1976.

Webb, Jimmy (*b* Elk City, Okla. 15 Aug. 1946). American singer, arranger, producer, pianist, and songwriter. Brought up in a church music tradition, he eventually made his way to Hollywood and found himself a job transcribing songs for artists in a recording studio. He worked for Motown's publishing outlet and wrote a number of songs for Johnny Rivers (*b* 1942), including 'By the time I get to Phoenix', which was later made into a hit by Glen *Campbell. He formed a band, Strawberry Children, which had little success, but songs he wrote for Glen Campbell and the Fifth Dimension established him as a writer of note, including 'Up up and away' (1967), 'Wichita lineman' (1968), and 'Galveston' (1969). He arranged and conducted on the Fifth Dimension's first two albums in 1967, and worked on two concept albums with the actor Richard Harris who made a hit of 'MacArthur Park' (1968). Deciding to record his own material, he showed his wide talents on albums like *Words and Music* (1970), which included 'P. F. Sloan', *And So: On* (1971), and *Land's End* (1974). He worked with the *Supremes and Art *Garfunkel—'All I know' (1973), revived Fifth Dimension, and recorded, for Atlantic Records and George *Martin, *El Mirage* (1977) and, for Columbia, *Angel Heart* (1983).

Weber & Fields. Celebrated 'Dutch' comedy duo who appeared together in a series of musical burlesques over a period of eight years, beginning with *The Art of Maryland* (1896). Joe [Morris] Weber (*b* New York, 11 Aug. 1867; *d* Los Angeles, 10 May 1942) was the well-padded fat man of the duo, a small, protesting figure constantly bullied by the towering Fields. For fuller details of the partnership see under FIELDS, LEW. The act broke up in 1904, though they did reunite on occasions after 1912. Weber went on to produce Victor *Herbert musicals: *The Only Girl* (1914), *Eileen* (1917), and *Her Regiment* (1917).

F. Isman: *Weber & Fields* (New York, 1924).

Webster, Ben [Benjamin Francis] (*b* Kansas City, Mo., 27 Mar. 1909; *d* Amsterdam, 20 Sept. 1973). American jazz saxophonist and arranger. After attending Wilberforce College, he played the piano in a silent movie house. His first important work was with Blanche Calloway (1902–78) in 1931, then with Bennie *Moten 1931–2. He was with Andy Kirk in 1933, joined Fletcher *Henderson in New York in 1934, and later that year was with Benny *Carter. He was with the Cab *Calloway band 1936–7, Roy *Eldridge 1938, and Teddy *Wilson 1939–40.

He had brief spells with Duke *Ellington 1935 and 1936, and a longer spell 1940–3, doing much, alongside bassist Jimmy *Blanton, to transform the sound and increase the intensity of the band, and recording such items as his famous solo on 'Cotton tail'. From 1944 he mainly led his own groups at clubs like the Spotlite and the Three Deuces in New York. He was with Duke Ellington again 1948–9, then toured with Jazz at the Philharmonic. He worked in Kansas City until 1952 when he returned to New York to work with his own groups at the Village Vanguard and other clubs. In 1964 he went to Europe, basing himself in Holland and visiting Britain on several occasions, then moved to Copenhagen in the late 1960s. A full-toned, adventurous player in the *Hawkins tradition, he was a moving spirit of the mainstream jazz trends of the 1940s onward.

Weems, Ted [Weymes, Wilfred Theodore] (*b* Pitcairn, Pa., 26 Sept. 1901; *d* Tulsa, Okla., 6 May 1963). American bandleader. He was educated at the University of Pennsylvania, where he played trombone in a dance band. He formed his own band 1922–3 to play in a Philadelphia café, and had an early hit record with 'Somebody stole my gal' in 1923. After touring the Midwest, with residences in Atlantic City and Kansas City, he arrived in Chicago in 1929 where he was mainly active from then on. He became popular on radio and had more big record hits with 'Piccolo Pete' (1929) and 'Harmonica Harry', helped by a succession of interesting vocalists, including Art Jarrett (*b* 1909) 1927–31, Red Ingle 1931–4, Country *Washburne, Elmo Tanner (*b* 1904), who featured on the band's theme tune, 'Out of the night', and Perry *Como, who joined as a novice in 1936. Weems appeared on various name radio shows and continued to make best-selling records such as 'Heartaches' (1933), 'Oh, Monah', 'The Martins and the Coys', and 'The one-man band'. Having given up the band in 1942 to join the merchant navy, he formed a new band in 1945 and had a new hit with a remake of 'Heartaches'; but his popularity gradually declined. By the 1950s Weems was working as a disc jockey in Memphis, and later settled in Dallas, working as a band agent.

Weill, Kurt (*b* Dessau, 2 Mar. 1900; *d* New York, 3 Apr. 1950). German composer. He received early musical instruction from his parents before studying theory and composition with Albert Bing in Dessau 1914–18. In 1918 he started to attend classes at the Berlin Hochschule für Musik and studied at Berlin University. Later that year he became a full-time student at the Hochschule, with Humperdinck as one of his teachers. During his student days he earned some pocket-money by playing the piano in beer-cellars, thus gaining an early introduction to popular music-making and the seamier side of life. In 1919–20 he worked as repetiteur at the Dessau Hofoper under Knappertsbusch, then became a theatre conductor in Ludenscheid, where his lifelong interest in the stage began. At the end of 1920 he settled in Berlin and was accepted at the Akademie der Künste as one of six pupils in a composition master-class held by Busoni. There he became acquainted with some of the leading lights of German music and early in

1921 he composed his first symphony. At the end of 1922 his children's pantomime *Zaubernacht* was performed in Berlin. The winter of 1922–3 saw the performance of various orchestral and chamber works, and he left the Akademie at the end of 1923. In 1924 he worked on his violin concerto, and by April 1925 had completed his first major stage work, *Der Protagonist*, which was successfully première in Dresden under Fritz Busch in 1926. In January of that year another strong influence on his style of writing came into his life when he married the actress Lotte *Lenya, whose voice became an integral part of his work.

In the late 1920s Weill became increasingly caught up in the German Zeitkunst movement (Music for the People) and, under the influence of the left-wing Bertolt *Brecht, started to apply popular music techniques to the writing of opera. In September 1926 he wrote a radio score for Grabbe's *Herzog Theodor von Gothland*; and in March 1927 began to work with Brecht on a three-act opera, *Aufstieg und Fall der Stadt Mahagonny*. The opera was not to be completed until 1929, but in the meantime, in response to a request from the organizers of the Deutsches Kammermusikfest in 1927 (among them Hindemith), they produced a Singspiel of chamber-music proportions, *Mahagonny*, which was produced at the festival in Baden-Baden in 1927. A much altered version was later produced by the Berliner Ensemble as *Das kleine Mahagonny*. The distinctive flavouring of Weill's best music was now apparent: the half-digested ingredients of invading jazz strains added to the sardonic flavour of German popular music and coloured by Weill's own Jewish inheritance. The unique blend of wit and pathos, with the vaguely sinister echoes of the political underworld, were to come together in music that was unique, harshly unmistakable, and unforgettable. The end of 1927 saw the first performance of his setting of Brecht's poem *Von Tod im Wald*; and a one-act opera, *Der Zar lässt sich Photographieren*, was performed in Dresden at the beginning of 1928.

In the middle of 1928 came the memorable première of *Die *Dreigroschenoper* at the Theater am Schliffbauerdamm, Berlin, on 31 Aug. A ballad opera with original music, keeping close links with its model, *The *Beggar's Opera*, it had an influence in Germany as profound as, and even more disturbing than, its predecessor enjoyed in England 200 years earlier. It had around 4000 performances in Germany in its first year, while subsequent revivals in New York, London, and elsewhere, have always met with great acclaim and established it as a theatrical classic. It contained the new and archetypal Weill pop song, the lugubrious 'Mack the Knife', whose strains seem to haunt much of Weill's subsequent music. In 1929 a suite for wind, *Kleine Dreigroschenmusik*, was drawn from the opera and first performed at a Kroll Opera Concert under Klemperer. The *Berliner Requiem* was performed in Frankfurt in 1929, and *Happy End*—'Surabaya Johnny', 'Bilbao song'—was seen at the Theater am Schiffbauerdamm in the same year. At the beginning of 1930 he wrote a school opera, *Der Jasager (The One Who Says Yes)*, and the complete *Mahagonny*—'Alabama song', 'Denn wie man sich bettet' ('As you make your bed')—was performed in Leipzig, accompanied by what was described as the worst theatre riot in history. Further disturbances by a bourgeois audience in Berlin in 1931 saw the removal of *Mahagonny* from the theatre repertoire, to be forgotten until a revival in 1966. Between 1930 and 1933, Weill wrote *Die Burgschaft (The Pledge)*, *Der Silbersee*, and his second symphony. In February 1931, Nazi hooligans provoked a riot at the second performance of *Der Silbersee* and, after the Nazi electoral triumph in March 1933, a projected Leipzig performance was cancelled. There were to be no more performances of Weill's work in Germany until 1945.

On 21 March 1933, Weill and his wife left Berlin by car and headed for France, arriving in Paris on the 23rd. In Paris he wrote *Die sieben Todsünden (The Seven Deadly Sins)* and *Der Weg der Verheissung*, and the eminently French *Marie Galante*—'I wait for a ship' (used by the Resistance during the War). In September 1935 they went to London where *A Kingdom for a Cow* was performed; then they sailed for New York to rehearse *Der Weg der Verheissung*. Postponed production forced him to find lecturing and writing work in the USA and his first piece written for the American theatre, *Johnny Johnson*, was produced by the Group Theatre in New York 19 Nov. 1936. He applied for American citizenship in 1937, and in 1938 started to collaborate with Maxwell *Anderson on **Knickerbocker Holiday* (1938)—'September song'. Subsequent Broadway productions—**Lady in the Dark* (1941); **One Touch of Venus* (1943); *The Firebrand of Florence* (1945); *Street Scene* (1947); *Down in the Valley* (1948); *Love Life* (with Alan J. *Lerner, 1948); and **Lost in the Stars* (1949)—relinquished the old pungent *Threepenny Opera* flavour for a well adapted and more sophisticated style in the *Rodgers and *Hart vein of the time; which many prefer. He also wrote songs (to words by Ira *Gershwin) for the film *Where Do We Go From Here?* (1945). He was able to visit England, France, Switzerland, and Palestine in 1947; and continued his work in the USA. In December 1949 he began to collaborate with Anderson on a musical based on *Huckleberry Finn*, but was taken ill in the spring of 1950 and died in the Flower Hospital, New York.

Weill's music, with its very individual and uncompromising flavour in the pre-American period, its sinister undertones, its political and social allegiances, is not always easy to live with, but it has a haunting quality that cannot be ignored. Like *Gershwin he worked on both sides of the fence, and like him ended up a major figure in popular music and a lesser one in the academic world of music-making. His music is essentially Jewish in its emotional mixture; and much of it was tinged with the vocal qualities of Lotte Lenya. His early music was unique; his later Broadway scores could be said to have compromised his art, while still taking it to the highest level in American terms. In 1963 a revue, *The World of Kurt Weill in Song*, was staged in New York; since then many young singers, including Georgia *Brown, Cleo *Laine, Teresa Stratas, and Ute Lemper, have found his music a powerful source of inspiration; and it is regularly recorded. His writings have been collected in *Leben und Werk* (Königstein, 1984).

H. Kotschenreuther: *Kurt Weill* (Berlin, 1962). D. Drew (ed.): *Über Kurt Weill* (Frankfurt, 1975). K. H. Kowalke: *Kurt Weill in Europe* (Ann Arbor, Mich., 1979). R. Sanders: *The Days Grow Short: the Life and Music of Kurt Weill* (New York–London, 1980). D. Jarman: *Kurt Weill: an Illustrated Biography* (Bloomington, Ind., 1982). K. H. Kowalke (ed.): *A New Orpheus: Essays on Kurt Weill* (New Haven, Conn., 1990).

Welch, Elisabeth (*b* New York, 27 Feb. 1908). American singer and actress. Her father was of mixed American Indian and African descent; her mother had mixed Scottish and Irish ancestry. She first attracted attention singing 'Charleston' in *Runnin' Wild* (1923); afterwards she was in *The Chocolate Dandies* (1924); **Blackbirds* (1928), with which she went to Paris in 1929, returning in 1930 to appear at Le Bœuf sur le Toit; and *The New Yorkers* (1931)—'Love for sale'. She settled in London in 1933 and became a popular figure there, appearing in **Nymph Errant* (1933)—'Solomon'; **Glamorous Night* (1935); *Sky High* (1942); *Arc de Triomphe* (1943); *Happy and Glorious* (1944); *Tuppence Coloured* (1947); *Oranges and Lemons* (1949); **Penny Plain* (1951); *Pay the Piper* (1954); *The Crooked Mile* (1959); and *Pippin* (1973). She was regularly seen in cabaret and was still making occasional appearances in her eighties, including a one-night concert revival of *Nymph Errant* in May 1989.

Welchman, Harry (*b* Barnstaple, Devon, 24 Feb. 1886; *d* London, 3 Jan. 1966). British actor and singer, particularly seen in operetta. He appeared in *The *Arcadians* (1909); *The Mousmé* (1911); *Princess Caprice* (1912); *Oh! Oh!! Delphine!!!* (1913); *The Pearl Girl* (1913); *The Cinema Star* (1914); *Afgar* (1919); **Sybil* (1921); *The Lady of the Rose* (1922); *The Street Singer* (1924); *Princess Flavia* (New York, 1925); *The *Student Prince* (1926); *The *Dessert Song* (1927); *The *New Moon* (1929); *Silver Wings* (1930); *Victoria and her Hussar* (1931); and *Beau Brummell* (1933).

Welk, Lawrence (*b* Strasburg, N. Dak., 11 Mar. 1903; *d* Santa Monica, Calif., 17 May 1992). American conductor and accordionist. He played in and led various local bands, touring in the 1930s, and by 1934 he was becoming established with his Champagne Music. He won national popularity with a series of TV concerts from 1955, mixing light classics, ballads, and dances, played in a souped-up manner. The Welk sound had the piano-accordion as one ingredient, sweeping strings, and an underlying strict jazz tempo. He maintained a Europeanized accent and unflagging affability and was thus much favoured by a middlebrow audience, continuing as a top attraction in the 1960s. He introduced more comedy into his shows in later years. Cancellation of his main ABC TV show in 1971, after two decades of pleasing its own steady, musically conservative audience, led to a wider diffusion of his talents on TV and a move into the production side.

L. Welk: *Wunnerful, Wunnerful* (New York, 1971). L. Welk: *Ah-one, ah-two: Life with my Musical Family* (New York, 1974).

Wells, Dicky [William] (*b* Centerville, Tenn., 10 June 1907; *d* New York, 12 Nov. 1985). American jazz trombonist. He became one of the outstanding trombonists of his day, developing a talking style, full of surprising tricks and sly humour, but deeply rooted in the blues, and based on an admiration for the work of Jimmy Harrison (1900–31). He grew up in Louisville, Kentucky, and went to New York in 1927 in the footsteps of Harrison, where he played in the bands of Benny *Carter, Fletcher *Henderson 1933–4, Charlie *Johnson, Teddy *Hill 1935, and, most importantly, Count *Basie 1938–45 and 1947–50; and with many other bands in the 1950s.

His skills were notably well caught in a series of recordings made in Paris in 1937, with musicians like Bill Coleman (1904–81), Bill Dillard (*b* 1911), Shad Collins (1910–78), and Django *Reinhardt. He played in Europe a great deal from 1959 with Buck *Clayton and others, especially in France, and toured England with the Alex *Welsh band in the 1960s. His playing gradually became marred by alcoholism, but he overcame this by 1973 when he was playing in the West End Café in New York with a group of ex-Basie men known as the Countsmen. He toured Europe in 1978 and was still recording in the 1980s.

D. Wells and S. Dance: *The Night People* (New York, 1971).

Wells, Kitty [Deason, Muriel] (*b* Nashville, Tenn., 30 Aug. 1918). American country singer. While a child she sang gospel music in local churches. She met up with a duo called Johnny and Jack, the Johnny being Johnny Wright (*b* 1914), who persuaded her to join their show which was billed as the Tennessee Mountain Boys. They were married and, while raising her family, she appeared with them on radio programmes in Memphis, Nashville, and Knoxville. He chose her new stage name from an old *Carter Family tune called 'I'm a-goin' to marry Kitty Wells'. In 1947 she was invited to appear on the **Grand Ole Opry* show and, shortly after, joined *Louisiana Hayride*. In two years she was billed as the 'Queen of Country Music' and was the highest-rated female country singer in the USA. Her first million-selling record came in 1952 with 'It wasn't God who made honky-tonk angels', made for Decca. When Jack Anglin of the Johnny and Jack team was killed in a motoring accident in 1963,

Kitty and Johnny were regularly seen on TV in *The Johnny Wright–Kitty Wells Family Show*. She continued to make more than 300 personal appearances a year, and among the millions of records she sold were 'You don't hear', 'Will your lawyer talk to God?', 'Heartbreak USA', 'A woman half my age', and 'Meanwhile down at Joe's'. In 1974 she defiantly recorded Bob *Dylan's 'Forever young' for Capricorn Records.

Welsh, Alex (*b* Edinburgh, 9 July 1929; *d* Pinner, Middx., 23 June 1982). British jazz trumpeter and bandleader. After playing in various groups he formed his own band in the 1950s, and soon became a leading figure in the then booming British traditional jazz scene. Always maintaining the highest standards and avoiding commercialism, his band regularly accompanied visiting American jazzmen whose styles ranged from the traditional like Wild Bill Davison, to mainstreamers like Ben *Webster and Dicky *Wells, to modernists like Eddie 'Lockjaw' *Davis. He worked in numerous clubs and appeared in many jazz concerts, notably at the Newport Jazz Festival of 1968, and was still fully active in the 1980s.

Wendling, Pete (*b* New York, 6 June 1888; *d* New York, 7 Apr. 1974). American composer and pianist. He won a national ragtime playing contest when he was 18, and went into vaudeville with Lewis F. *Muir. They appeared at the London Hippodrome in 1913. He worked as a piano recording artist 1919–29, then as staff composer to the publishers Berlin, Waterson & Snyder, eventually becoming vice-president of the company. His compositions included 'Jelly roll' (1915), 'Chromatic rag' (with Ed Gerhardt, 1916), 'Oh, what a pal was Mary' (1919, *w* Edgar *Leslie and Bert *Kalmar), 'Take your girlie to the movies' (with Jimmy *Monaco, 1919, *w* Alfred Bryan), 'There's danger in your eyes, cherie' (1929, *w* Harry *Richman and Jack Meskill)—used in the film *Putting on the Ritz* (1930), 'I'm sure of everything but you' (with George *Meyer, 1932); and many more in period Tin Pan Alley vein.

Wenrich, Percy (*b* Joplin, Mo., 23 Jan. 1880; *d* New York, 17 Mar. 1952). American pianist and composer. Taught the piano by his mother, he started his musical career playing in the saloons and music stores of his home town, and thereafter was always known as the 'Joplin Kid'. He published his first composition at his own expense when he was 17, selling it from door to door. When he was 21 he went to the Chicago Musical College for a while, but soon left and became a nightclub pianist, meanwhile writing hack tunes for various publishers. Eventually he found his style and wrote some good second generation rags in the early 1900s. He moved to New York and wrote the Broadway shows *The Crinoline Girl* (1914), *The Right Girl* (1921), *Castles in the Air* (1926), and *Who Cares* (1930). He married the singer Dolly Connolly, who sang his 'By the camp fire' in **Greenwich Village Follies* (1919) and was to make many recordings of his songs.

His ragtime compositions included: 'Ashy Africa' (1903), 'Peaches and cream rag' (1905), 'Noodle' (1906), 'The smiler' (1907), 'Persian lamb rag' (1908), 'Memphis rag' (1908), 'Ragtime ripples' (1908), 'Alamo rag' (1910), 'Skeleton rag' (1911), 'Sunflower rag' (1911), 'Whipped cream' (1913); and many more; while his songs included 'Put on your old grey bonnet' (1909, *w* Stanley Murphy), 'When you wore a tulip and I wore a big red rose' (1914, *w* Jack Mahoney), 'Sweet cider time when you were mine' (1916, *w* Joseph McCarthy), and 'A rainbow from the USA' (Mahoney and Ben Jerome)—used in the revue *Everything* (1918).

West, Dottie [*née* Marsh, Dorothy Marie] (*b* McMinnville, Tenn., 11 Oct. 1932). American country singer and songwriter. After earning a musical degree at the Tennessee Technical College, she started on a career as a singer, writing a hit with her husband Bill West, 'Here comes my baby'. She recorded with Jim *Reeves, 'Love is no excuse', and began to appear on the **Grand Ole Opry* show. After divorcing West, she married her road manager and drummer, Don Rhodes. A hard-working performer who tours continually, she has always been glamorous as well as talented and the epitome of the 'Country girl'—a song which she first sang in a TV commercial and which has remained her theme.

West, Mae (*b* Brooklyn, NY, 17 Aug. 1892; *d* Los Angeles, 22 Nov. 1980). American actress, singer, and writer. She came, as Stanley Green has written, 'both to personify and satirize female sexuality'. Her sex appeal was of the tough American Gold Rush variety, her 'come up and see me sometime' became a key phrase, and her figure was unflatteringly immortalized by the use of her name for wartime life-jackets. She made her stage debut at the age of five in Brooklyn, played many juvenile roles, was in vaudeville for many years, and appeared in the revue *A la Broadway* (1911), *Vera Violetta* (1911), and *A Winsome Widow* (1920). She was in many straight plays, with *Diamond Lil* (1928), which she adapted for the screen as *She Done Him Wrong*, her best-known role. She achieved fame and a notorious reputation through her many films, including: *She Done Him Wrong* (1933)—in which she sang 'I like a guy what takes his time', 'Easy rider'; *I'm No Angel* (1933)—'I found a new way to go to town', 'I'm no angel', 'They call me Sister Honk-Tonk', 'I want you—I need you'; *Belle of the Nineties* (1935)—'My old flame', which she recorded with the Duke *Ellington orchestra; *Goin' to Town* (1935); *Klondike Annie* (1936); *Go West, Young Man* (1936); *Every Day's a Holiday* (1937); and *The Heat's On* (1943). She wrote the scripts of several of her plays and films. She recorded an album of rock and roll songs and was still acting in her seventies.

M. West: *Goodness had Nothing to Do With It* (New York, 1956). J. Tuska: *The Films of Mae West* (New York, 1977).

Western Brothers, The. British comedy singing partners who were in, fact cousins, Kenneth (*d* 1963) and George (*d* 1969). George Western was pianist with the Roosters Concert Party when he first teamed up with Kenneth in 1925 to formulate their public-school act, singing such songs as 'The old school tie' and 'Play the game, you cads' in languid, drawling voices, immaculately garbed in evening dress and wearing monocles. They became a very popular act in the 1930s in variety and cabaret and on radio.

Western swing. Genre of country music with a jazz flavour, often played by large bands and popular from the 1930s through to the 1950s. A relationship between country music and jazz goes back to soloists like Jimmie *Rodgers, who frequently used jazz musicians, and to the music of bandleader and fiddler Bob *Wills in the 1930s. Others in the field were Pappy O'Daniel (*b* 1890), Spade Cooley (1910–69), Hank Thompson (*b* 1925), and Buck Owens (*b* 1929). The style was revived by the American western swing band Asleep at the Wheel, formed in the late 1960s, who made their first LP, *Comin' Right At Ya*, in 1973. They used many prominent musicians in the field and their activities were responsible for the renewed interest in the work of Bob Wills and others.

Weston, Paul [Wetstein] (*b* Springfield, Mass., 12 Mar. 1912). American composer, arranger, conductor, and pianist. He played in a band at Dartmouth College and started arranging, later studying at Columbia University. He worked for Rudy *Vallee on his Fleischmann Hour radio show as arranger, also scoring for Phil *Harris and others. In 1936 he joined Tommy *Dorsey as chief arranger, leaving in the early 1940s to work on radio shows such as *Duffy's Tavern* and that of Johnny *Mercer, who engaged Weston as his musical director when he founded Capitol Records in 1942. He worked on Hollywood films: *Holiday Inn* (1942); *Belle of the Yukon* (1944); *Road to Utopia* (1945); etc. While with Capitol he led his own orchestra, pioneering the mood music albums of the early LP era, with lush melodies and soaring strings. He went to Columbia in 1950 to provide orchestral backing for many singers and record many more mood albums, also making a series of satirical records with his wife, the singer Jo *Stafford, as Jonathan and Darlene Edwards. In 1958 he returned to Capitol and was musical director for the Danny *Kaye show. He wrote 'Day by day' (1945), 'I should care' (1945), 'No other love' (1950), 'Shrimp boats' (1951); and many instrumental pieces.

Weston, R. P. [Robert Patrick] (*b* London, 1878; *d* London, 6 Nov. 1936). British composer and lyricist. He worked on the staff of a London music-publisher and was a prolific producer of music-hall-style songs, including: 'Boys of the Chelsea school' (1902), 'He's been a long time gorn' (1904), 'Choose her in the morning' (1906), 'The hob-nailed boots that farver wore' (1907), 'I'm Henery the Eighth I am' (1911), 'What a mouth' (1911), 'Sister Susie's sewing shirts for soldiers' (1914, *m* Herman *Darewski), 'Good-bye-ee' (1917), 'The gypsy warned me' (1920), 'Viewing the baby' (1926), 'What I want is a proper cup o' coffee' (1926), 'When father papered the parlour' (1926); working with various collaborators, notably Bert *Lee. He also wrote the score of *Cheep* (1917).

West Side Story. Musical play with score by Leonard *Bernstein, book by Arthur Laurents (*b* 1918), and lyrics by Stephen *Sondheim, produced at the *Winter Garden Theatre, New York, 26 Sept. 1957, with Carol Lawrence (*b* 1932) as Maria and Larry Kert (1930–91) as Tony, directed and choreographed by Jerome *Robbins [734p].

The story was based on the *Romeo and Juliet* plot, with the racial conflict of the native whites and the Puerto Ricans of New York's West Side the basis of the tragedy of the lovers Tony and Maria. Tony tries to keep the peace between the two gangs, the Jets and the Sharks, and is killed. It was first conceived in 1949 with a Jewish v. Catholic background, then put aside for six years, at which point Sondheim was brought in as lyricist and the story changed. Demanding a high standard from dancing actors and actresses, it became an instant hit with its forceful music and songs—'Jet song', 'Something's coming', 'Tonight', 'Maria', 'America', 'Cool', 'I feel pretty', 'Somewhere', 'Gee, Officer Krupke', and 'I had a love'.

Taken off in 1959 to tour for six months, it returned to the Winter Garden Theatre in 1960 for 249 more performances. It was staged in London, at Her Majesty's Theatre 12 Dec. 1958, where it achieved 1039 performances; and was revived there in 1974. It was filmed in 1961, with Natalie Wood (1938–81) and Richard Beymer (*b* 1939)—singing voices dubbed by Marni Nixon and Jim Bryant. In 1985 BBC TV issued an interesting video documentary on the making of an LP recording of the work, directed for the first time by Bernstein himself and featuring the opera stars Kiri Te Kanawa and José Carreras.

What Makes Sammy Run? Musical comedy with music and lyrics by Ervin Drake, book by Budd and Stuart Schulberg, directed by Abe *Burrows, New York (54th Street Theatre) 27 Feb. 1964 [540p]. Adapted from Budd Schulberg's novel, it tells the story of Sammy (romantically played by singer Steve *Lawrence) who rises from newspaper boy to film studio chief and son-in-law of his boss, but ends up still running. The songs included: 'A tender spot', 'My home town', 'A room without windows', 'Something to live for', and 'The friendliest thing'. It also starred Sally Ann *Howes and Robert *Alda.

Whelan, Albert [Waxman] (*b* Melbourne, 1875; *d* London, 19 Feb. 1961). Australian singer and entertainer. Giving up careers as accountant and mechanic, he went to seek his fortune in gold-prospecting but, this failing, turned to entertaining, working with a friend as Whelan and Wilson. He joined the touring company of *The *Belle of New York*, appeared in variety, then went to London, where he first appeared as a dancer at the Empire Theatre in 1901. He developed an act dressed as a toff, with top hat, tails, scarf, gloves, and cane, singing such songs as 'The preacher and the bear', 'The three trees', and 'The old top hat'. He contrived a lengthy entrance and exit while he disrobed and re-robed, whistling a waltz tune, 'Die lustige Brüder' ('The jolly brothers'), thus becoming a pioneer in the use of a regular signature tune. He first appeared in New York in 1908 and again, with Anna Pavlova, in 1912. He appeared in Royal Variety Shows in London in 1927 and 1931. For a while he worked in a double act with Billy Bennett (1887–1942), and often tried to change his act, but the basic approach, and signature tune, remained.

Where's Charley? Musical comedy with music and lyrics by Frank *Loesser, book by George *Abbott, who also directed. Produced in New York (St James Theatre) 11 Oct. 1948, where it ran for 792 performances. Based on Brandon Thomas's classic farce *Charley's Aunt*, it was a comical account of what happened when Charley (played by Ray *Bolger) has to disguise himself as his rich aunt from Brazil so that he can act as chaperone to his and his friends' very proper girlfriends. His troubles include the amorous advances of the girls' guardian and the appearance of the real aunt. The hit of the show was 'Once in love with Amy'. It was seen in London at the Palace Theatre, 20 Feb. 1958, with Norman Wisdom (*b* 1919) in the title role; and filmed with Ray Bolger in 1952.

'Whiffenpoof song, The'. American student song based on Rudyard Kipling's poem 'Gentlemen-Rankers', first printed in 1918 in *The New Yale Song-Book*. Research at Yale has suggested that the composer was a Harvard man, Guy H. Scull (1876–1920), and that he wrote it about 1893. A Yale choral group who called themselves the Whiffenpoofs, after an imaginary fish which appears in Victor *Herbert's *Little Nemo* (1908), first utilized the song in 1909, with Kipling's words adapted by several hands. The song was used and popularized in 1935 by Rudy *Vallee (a Yale man), who gave some of the early royalties to the university. The Kipling Society have always kept a watchful eye on the master's words, and successfully prevented a humorous version by Louis *Armstrong being circulated in England.

White, George [Weitz] (*b* New York, 1890; *d* Hollywood, 11 Oct. 1968). American producer, director, writer, dancer, and actor. He first appeared in New York in a dancing duo with Ben Ryan; then in several shows including: *The Echo* (1910); **Ziegfeld Follies* (1911); *The Pleasure Seekers* (1913); *The Midnight Girl* (1915); *Ziegfeld Follies* (1915); and *Miss 1917*. He became well-known for his **George White's Scandals* revues (1919–26, 1928–9, 1930, 1935, 1939) which, full of music, comedy, and good dancing, were strong rivals to the concurrent *Ziegfeld Follies*. He used composers like George *Gershwin and Ray *Henderson, who each produced five scores for him; and stars such as Ann *Pennington, Willie and Eugene *Howard, Harry *Richman, Rudy *Vallee, Lou Holtz (1898–1980), and Frances Williams (1903–59). The first was at the Liberty Theatre, 2 June 1919. He was part-author and appeared in most of the shows himself and in the various film versions; he also produced and directed *Manhattan Mary* (1927), *Flying High* (1930), and *Melody* (1933).

White, Josh [Joshua Daniel] (*b* Greenville, SC, 11 Feb. 1915; *d* Manhasset, NY, 5 Sept. 1969). American blues singer and guitarist. Son of a black preacher, he was brought up in poverty, and by the age of eight was travelling the South as guide to several blind guitarists and blues singers, including Blind Lemon *Jefferson, and also worked with *Leadbelly. Gradually he acquired his own skills and repertoire and a growing reputation; and in New York he played the part of Jefferson in the play *John Henry* with Paul *Robeson. He formed a singing group, the Carolinians, who recorded in 1940. Helped by admirer John *Hammond, he became an esablished performer, under the guidance of Barney Josephson (1902–88), at Downtown and Uptown Café Society and the Village Vanguard. He worked with Libby *Holman in the late 1940s as the first mixed race duo, and was with the *Almanac Singers.

During the 1950s he became a regular recording artist for Brunswick, Vogue, and other labels, and achieved wide popularity with his sophisticated and commercialized, though genuinely felt, blues-cum-folk-singing and powerful and uniquely styled guitar playing. His most popular recordings included such varied repertoire as 'The lass with a delicate air', 'Frankie and Johnny', 'Sometime', 'John Henry', 'The foggy foggy dew', 'I'm gonna move to the outskirts of town', 'Like a natural man', 'Barbara Allen', 'Apples, peaches and cherries', 'Molly Malone', and 'Strange fruit'. He suffered several heart-attacks in the 1960s, as well as difficulties with his playing fingers and a car accident, and was gradually forced to give up performing.

White Christmas. Paramount film made in 1954, starring Bing *Crosby, Danny *Kaye, Rosemary *Clooney, and Vera-Ellen, which featured many old Irving *Berlin songs as well as items written especially for the film such as 'The best things happen while you're dancing', 'Sisters', 'Snow', and 'Count your blessings instead of sheep'. It naturally featured the immortal 'White Christmas', which was written in 1942, and was first used in the film *Holiday Inn*. It has been reckoned one of the most valuable songs in the world, with Bing Crosby's recording achieving the greatest sales of any single song by one singer; selling well over 40 million recordings altogether, and more than $5\frac{1}{2}$ million copies of the sheet music.

Whiteman, Paul (*b* Denver, Colo., 28 Mar. 1890; *d* Doylestown, Pa., 29 Dec. 1967. American bandleader, composer, arranger, and violinist. His father, a supervisor of music in schools, taught him the violin. He played with the Denver Symphony Orchestra from 1910 and was with the San Francisco People's Symphony at the 1915 World's Fair, playing under Victor *Herbert. Later he was with the Minetti String Quartet and the San Francisco Symphony Orchestra, but changed tack by joining a dance orchestra, from which he was fired for not being able to play jazz.

After service as an army bandleader in the First World War, he formed his own orchestra to play at the Fairmount Hotel in San Françisco, with Morton Downey (*b* 1901) as vocalist from 1919, moving to the Hotel Alexandria in 1920. He had a hit with his recording of 'Whispering'/'Japanese sandman' in 1920, which sold two million copies in a year, and another with 'Three o'clock in the morning' (1923), which sold $3\frac{1}{2}$ million. Much of his future success arose from the individual arrangements of his pianist, Ferde *Grofé; the band built its reputation at the Palais Royale in New York and visited London in 1923. It appeared in the **Ziegfeld Follies* and give the first so-called 'jazz' concert at the Aeolian Hall, New York, on 24 Feb. 1924, for which he commissioned George *Gershwin's 'Rhapsody in Blue'. He made further successful tours and played at the Royal Albert Hall in London in 1926. Bearing the commercially inspired but inaccurate title 'The King of Jazz', he starred in a film of that name in 1930, and was later seen in *Thanks a Million* (1935); *Strike Up the Band* (1940); *Lady, Let's Dance* (1944); *Atlantic City* (1944); *Rhapsody in Blue* (1945); and *The Fabulous Dorseys* (1947); and continued on radio and records long after his most prestigious days were over.

If he never quite lived up to his royal title, he nevertheless was responsible for the conception of symphonic jazz, featuring such soloists as pianist Peter Nero (*b* 1934), and for introducing a degree of sophistication into his arrangements which have become more highly regarded in hindsight. He gave musical opportunity and a good living to several jazzmen, including Bix *Beiderbecke, Frank *Trumbauer, Jack *Teagarden, and Benny *Goodman, who all seemed to have enjoyed being with the band; and to singers like Bing *Crosby who started his career as one of Whiteman's Rhythm Boys. Heard now, many of Whiteman's recordings do have a very special jazz flavour, and recent attempts to duplicate his arrangements have never quite hit off the real thing. He wrote a number of songs himself and established the Whiteman Award for symphonic jazz compositions written by American composers. He also wrote books: *Jazz* (with M. M. McBride) (New York, 1926); *How to be a Bandleader* (with L. Lieber) (New York, 1941); and *Records for the Millions* (New York, 1948).

Whitfield, David (*b* Hull, 2 Feb. 1925; *d* Sydney, 16 Jan. 1980). British singer who began a recording career with Decca in 1953 and had his first big hit with 'Bridge of sighs' (1953) and a No. 1 with 'Answer me' (1953). He was to achieve some 20 more top hits including 'Cara mia' which became the first song by a British male singer to become No. 1 in the USA. By 1960 he was outmoded by the pop invasion and turned to operetta in an album *My Heart and I*, later working in opera, latterly in Australia.

Whitfield, Norman (*b* New York, 1943). American record producer and songwriter. One of the most creative producers in black music, he joined Motown in 1960 and was to have a hand in its notable early successes, writing 'Pride and joy' (1963) for Marvin *Gaye; 'I heard it through the grapevine' (1967) for Gladys *Knight and the Pips; 'Cloud nine' (1968), 'I can't get next to you' (1968), 'Psychedelic shock' (1969), and 'Just my imagination' (1971) for the *Temptations; and countless more. He wrote the sound-track of *Car Wash* (1976). He ran his own record label 1976–81.

Whiting, Jack (*b* Philadelphia, 22 June 1901; *d* New York, 15 Feb. 1961). American actor, singer, and dancer. A blond, smiling actor who had a long career as a juvenile lead, he appeared in such shows as the **Ziegfeld Follies* (1922); *The Ramblers* (1926)—in which he sang 'All alone Monday'; *Yes, Yes, Yvette* (1927); **Hold Everything* (1928)—'You're the cream in my coffee'; *Heads Up!* (1929)—'A ship without a sail'; *America's Sweetheart* (1931)—'I've got five dollars'; **Take a Chance* (1932); *Anything Goes* (London, 1935)—'You're the top' (with Jeanne Aubert); *Rise and Shine* (London, 1936); **On Your Toes* (London, 1937); *Hooray for What!* (1937)—'Down with love'; *Very Warm for May* (1939)—'All in fun'; *Hold On to Your Hats* (1940)—'Don't let it get you down'; *Hazel Flagg* (1953)—'Ev'ry street's a boulevard in old New York'; and *The *Golden Apple* (1954).

Whiting, Richard A. (*b* Peoria, Ill., 12 Nov. 1891; *d* Beverly Hills, Calif., 10 Feb. 1938). American composer. Having failed to get anywhere as a vaudeville performer, he turned to composing but had little success in that field to begin with. Finally he did manage to interest the Detroit music-publisher Jerome Remick in some of his work and landed a job as manager of the company. In 1915 he achieved his first big hit with 'It's tulip time in Holland'; and in 1918 was to write 'Till we meet again' with Ray Egan, a song which sold more than five million copies of the sheet music. He began to write for the

Broadway stage, starting with a revue, *Toot Sweet* (1919), and the first of **George White's Scandals* (1919); later *Free for All* (1931) and **Take a Chance* (1932). Other early songs were 'They called it Dixieland' (1916, *w* Egan), 'Where the black-eyed Susans grow' (1917, *w* Dave Radford), 'The Japanese sandman' (1920, *w* Egan)—backed by 'Whispering', the Paul *Whiteman recording of this sold two million copies in a year, 'Ain't we got fun' (1921, Egan), 'Sleepy time gal' (1925, Alden and Egan), 'Ukelele lady' (1925, *w* Gus *Kahn), 'She's funny that way' (with Neil Moret, 1928); and many more.

He went to Hollywood in 1928 to join the film boom and notably wrote songs for such stars as Maurice *Chevalier and Bing *Crosby, including music for *Innocents of Paris* (1929), starring Chevalier—'Louise' (*w* Leo Robin); *The Dance of Life* (1929)—'True blue Lou' (Robin); *Painted Heels* (1929)—'I have to have you' (Robin); *Sweetie* (1929); *Let's Go Native* (1930); *Safety in Numbers* (1930); *Playboy of Paris* (1930)—'My ideal' (with Newell Chase; *w* Robin); *Monte Carlo* (1930)—'Beyond the blue horizon' (with Frank Harling; *w* Robin); *Paramount on Parade* (1930)—'All I want is just one girl'; *One Hour Wth You* (1932)—'One hour with you' (with Oscar *Straus: *w* Robin); *Adorable* (1933); *Take a Chance* (1933)—'Eadie was a lady' (*w* Buddy *DeSylva); *My Weakness* (1933); *Bright Eyes* (1934), starring Shirley *Temple—'On the good ship Lollipop' (*w* Sidney Clare); *Bottoms Up* (1934); *Hold That Girl* (1934); *Here Comes Cookie* (1935); *Coronada* (1935)—'You took my breath away' (*w* Sam *Coslow); *Sing, Baby, Sing* (1935); *Rhythm on the Range* (1936); *Anything Goes* (1936)—'My heart and I' (Robin); *Big Broadcast of 1936* (1936); *Varsity Show* (1937)—'We're working our way through college', 'On with the dance', 'You've got something there' (*w* Johnny *Mercer); *Ready, Willing and Able* (1937)—'Too marvelous for words' (Mercer), sung by Wini Shaw (*b* 1910); *Hollywood Hotel* (1937)—'I'm like a fish out of water', 'Let that be a lesson to you' (Mercer); and *Cowboy from Brooklyn* (1938)—'Ride, tenderfoot, ride' (Mercer).

His daughter, Margaret Whiting (*b* Detroit, 22 July 1924) had a busy career as a singer, working with Johnny *Mercer, Freddie *Slack, Billy *Butterfield, and Paul *Weston, among many.

Whitman, Slim [Otis Dewey] (*b* Tampa, Fla., 20 Jan. 1924). American country singer. He hoped for a career in baseball, and played for a while, but was gradually drawn to singing and, after 1949, was asked to appear on *Louisiana Hayride*. He toured the USA and Europe, being the first country artist to appear at the London Palladium. He achieved a great vogue in the 1950s and had many hits from 1952 on using such varied material as the Broadway 'Indian love call', from **Rose-Marie*, and the Country and Western 'I'm casting my lasso toward the sky'; any material which suited his high clear voice and yodelling style.

Whitney, Joan (*b* Pittsburgh, 26 June 1914). American composer, writer, singer, and publisher. She sang with various dance bands and appeared in *The Great Waltz* (1934). She had her own radio show on CBS, worked in nightclubs, and recorded. In 1940 she went into music-publishing, founding the Kramer-Whitney Company in 1947 with her husband and musical collaborator Alex Kramer (*b* 1903); and she founded Southside Records in 1961.

She wrote, mainly with Kramer: 'High on a windy hill' (1941), 'It all comes back to me now' (with Hy Zaret, 1907–41, 1941), 'My sister and I' (with Zaret, 1941), 'Weep no more, my lady' (1942), 'It's love, love, love' (1944, *w* Mack David), 'Candy' (1944), 'Didn't I tell you so?' (1945), 'Money is the root of all evil' (1946), 'That's the beginning of the end' (1946), 'There ain't nobody here but us chickens' (1946), 'Curiosity' (1947), 'Love somebody' (1947), 'Far away places' (1948), 'Dangerous Dan McGrew (1949), 'Comme çi, comme ça' (1949), 'I never heard you say' (1949), 'Not tonight' (1950), 'Before I loved you' (1950), 'To be loved by you' (1952), 'Train of love' (1953), 'What more do you want?' (1953), and 'No other arms, no other lips' (1959).

Whittaker, Roger (*b* Nairobi, 22 Mar. 1936). British singer. Son of a Staffordshire grocer who emigrated to Kenya, he started to learn the guitar at the age of seven. After two years' national service in the Kenya Regiment, he studied medicine at the University of Cape Town. He gave this up to take up teaching and went to the UK in 1959 to work for a degree in science education at the University of Wales in Bangor. While studying for his BSc, he started recording songs and had a hit with his second single, 'Steel man'. He decided to switch to the entertainment world on a trial basis. He continued to achieve song hits with 'Durham Town', 'I don't believe in if anymore', 'New world in the morning', and 'The last farewell', which proved popular in the USA. He first went there in 1976 and had a highly successful coast-to-coast tour in 1980, and again in 1983.

Who, The. British rock group. Along with the *Rolling Stones, their work typifies the excitement of the early and mid-1960s. Their anthem for doomed youth, 'My generation', ranks alongside 'Satisfaction' as the most succinct expression of discontent in pop history. The recording was part of a series of 1960s hit singles which encapsulated the feeling of the mod movement and of the young generally: 'I can't explain', 'Anyway, anyhow, anywhere', 'Substitute', 'I'm a boy', 'Happy Jack', and 'Pictures of Lily'.

Their eventual managers, Kit Lambert and Chris Stamp, discovered the band playing in a Shepherd's Bush public house in 1964. Shrewdly these two emphasized the mod affiliation of the group, recognizing a potential market there. Their appearance on the mod-oriented TV show *Ready, Steady, Go* helped to promote their singles and brought them to a wider audience. The band owe most of their success, however, to the brilliance of the songs of guitarist Pete Townshend (*b* London, 19 May 1945). In songs such as 'I can see for miles' he managed to translate the violence and tension of their concerts into their recorded work. Instrumentally the group was led by Townshend's churning guitar, ably supported by the bass of John Entwhistle (*b* 9 Oct. 1944), and the frenetic drumming of Keith Moon (*b* 23 Aug. 1947; *d* 7 Sept. 1978), with Roger Daltrey (*b* 1 Mar. 1945) supplying a suitably soaring and angry vocal.

The group's work on LP culminated in the brilliant *Tommy* (1969), the definitive rock opera, later made into a film by Ken Russell. This was followed by what many consider to be their finest album, the excellent *Who's Next* (1971), which included Townshend's best and perhaps most personal song 'Won't get fooled again', also 'Baba O'Riley' and 'Behind blue eyes'. Another film rock-opera, *Quadrophenia* (1979), traced the birth and growth to awareness of a young mod. Since then, members of the group have tended to work as solo artists, only occasionally recording or touring as the Who. Following the death of Keith Moon in 1978 after a party, there was considerable debate as to whether the group would continue at all. Kenney Jones (*b* 1948), once of the *Small Faces, was recruited and an album, *Face Dances* (1981), was made with him at the drums, with *It's Hard* (1982) following. Their last concert appearance came in 1982 and they officially broke up in 1983. Townshend, having already started his own publishing business, became a commissioning editor with Faber & Faber. The band was nostalgically re-united for the Live Aid concert in London in 1985.

G. Herman: *The Who* (London, 1971). G. Tremlett: *The Who* (London, 1975). B. Ashley: *Who's Who?: a Who Retrospective* (London, 1978). J. Swenson: *The Who* (New York, 1979). E. Hanel: *The Who: an Illustrated Discography* (London, 1981). R. Barnes: *The Who Maximum R & B: an Illustrated Biography* (London, 1982). C. Charlesworth: *The Who: the Illustrated Biography* (London, 1982). D. Walsh: *Before I get Old: the Story of the Who* (New York, 1983).

Whoopee. American musical comedy with score by Walter *Donaldson and lyrics by Gus *Kahn, starring Eddie *Cantor, who made a hit with the title song 'Makin' whoopee', and Ruth *Etting, who sang 'Love me or leave me'. The show originally featured George *Olsen's orchestra, which was replaced by the Paul *Whiteman orchestra for two months. It opened at the New Amsterdam Theatre, New York, 4 Dec. 1928 [379p], was revived in 1979 [204p], and was filmed, with Eddie Cantor, in 1930.

Wilber, Bob [Robert Sage] (*b* New York, 15 Mar. 1928). American clarinettist, saxophonist, and bandleader. He first played with pianist Dick Wellstood (1927–87) while still at school, and used Wellstood in his own 1946 band. He studied with Sidney *Bechet and Lennie *Tristano, thus evolving a mainstream traditional vein which he has adhered to throughout his career. Playing in a professional Dixieland idiom, he started recording in the 1950s, with Sidney Bechet and others, and led a co-operative group, The Six, 1954–6. He toured England with Eddie *Condon and played with Bobby *Hackett, Ruby Braff (*b* 1927), and Benny *Goodman. In the late 1950s he formed a recording group known as the Lawson–Haggart Jazz band, which became billed as the World's Greatest Jazz Band from 1968, playing music based on the Bob *Crosby band and using such musicians as Billy *Butterfield, Eddie Miller (1911–91), Ralph *Sutton, and other prominent traditionalists. Wilber left the band in 1973 to form Soprano Summit which recorded several LPs in the 1970s, and the Bechet Legacy in 1981. He also recorded with Vic *Dickenson, compiled an LP of the music of King *Oliver, and re-created the *Ellington band for the film *The Cotton Club* (1984). He formed a re-created Goodman band with British musicians, with his wife Joanne Horton as featured vocalist, which toured 1985–6, and in 1988 he re-created the famous 1938 Carnegie Hall concert.

Wilder, Alec [Alexander LaFayette Chew] (*b* Rochester, NY, 16 Feb. 1907; *d* Gainesville, Fla., 23 Dec. 1980). American composer, author, arranger, and musical director. After studying at the Eastman School of Music he embarked on a career that was to be equally devoted to classical and popular music. In 1930 he collaborated with Howard *Dietz and Edward Brandt on a song, 'All the King's horses', which was used in the revue *Three's a Crowd*, but he did very little commercial writing until 1935, when he started making arrangements for various singers, becoming staff arranger for the Ford Show on CBS from 1936. Here he began experimenting, firstly on a Mildred *Bailey recording session, with new woodwind sounds which he developed in 1939 with the Alec Wilder Octet, combining modern rhythmic patterns with harpsichord and neo-baroque voicings for woodwind. He published his first song in 1941 while he was arranging for the Benny *Goodman radio show, beginning a partnership with lyricist William Engvick which lasted for more than 30 years. He arranged vocal backings for Frank *Sinatra's first solo Columbia recordings which had to be done *a cappella* owing to the AFM strike of 1943, when no musicians were allowed to record. Three years later Sinatra returned the compliment by conducting the Columbia Orchestra in a recording of Wilder's 'Suite for String Orchestra'. A later conducting sortie by Sinatra was also of Wilder's music.

Over the years, Wilder built up a reputation as a musicianly songwriter who turned out the sort of sophisticated material that was wanted by the new generation of singers like Sinatra. He was also one of the few composers to function equally well in both spheres of music, writing many operas and stage works in serious vein. He also wrote a musical comedy, *Sunday Excursion* (1953), and an interesting TV piece, *Miss Chicken Little* (1953); several film scores, including the 1957 live-action *Pinocchio*; as well as art songs, chamber and orchestral works, and several ballets.

His more popular songs included: 'It's so peaceful in the country' (1941), 'Walking home in Spring' (1942), 'While we're young' (1943), 'All the cats join in' (1944, *m* Eddie *Sauter), 'As long as we still believe' (1945), 'It happens all the time' (1946), 'In the spring of the year' (1947), 'Where is the one?' (1948), 'Lonely night' (1949), 'I'm headin' West' (1950), 'Good for nothin'' (1951), 'Parker's lament' (1954), 'Never love a stranger' (1955), 'The lady sings the blues' (1956), 'Zorch' (1957), 'Change of heart' (1958); and many children's songs. He wrote one of the best and most analytical books on the subject in *American Popular Song: the Great Innovators* (New York, 1972), which came to interesting conclusions about *Kern, *Gershwin, *Porter, and others.

W. Balliett: *Alec Wilder and his Friends* (Boston, 1974).

Wiley, Lee (*b* Port Gibson, Okla., 9 Oct. 1915; *d* New York, 11 Dec. 1975). American vocalist. Singing in a girlish voice with a prominent vibrato, she first became known with the bands of Johnny *Green, Leo Reisman (1897–61)—'Time on my hands' (1931), Victor *Young, and Eddie *Condon. She had a stormy marriage with the pianist Jess *Stacy, recording with his band and having a hit with 'It's only a paper moon'. In the 1930s and 1940s she recorded prolifically, including sides with Max *Kaminsky in 1939, Condon in 1944, and with Fats *Waller. She also wrote song lyrics. She retired from music at the end of the 1950s, coming back in 1971 to record the album *Back Home Again*. There was an appreciative revival of her work on reissue LPs in the 1970s including the *Town Hall Concerts* with Eddie Condon from the 1940s.

Williams, Andy [Howard Andrew] (*b* Wall Lake, Iowa, 3 Dec. 1928). American singer. With three of his brothers, he formed the Williams Brothers Quartet and became well-known on radio from Chicago to Los Angeles. Later Kay Thompson joined the group, which stayed together until 1953. Williams then became a solo artist and, singing in the *Crosby style, with a relaxed and friendly approach, he became very popular on radio, later with his own regular TV show, and appeared in films, selling many albums of easy-going, middle-of-the-road recordings.

Williams, Bert [Egbert Austin] (*b* Antigua, WI, 12 Nov. 1874; d New York, 4 Mar. 1922). American actor, singer, dancer, and composer. He started his career in vaudeville with George W. Walker (*d* 1911) as Walker and Williams. During a 40-week stay at *Koster and Bial's variety theatre in 1898, they were responsible for the popularization of the *cakewalk. They performed with humour and in the current black stereotype manner, Walker the strutting dandy and Williams the shiftless layabout; and their partnership continued until 1909. Williams was an expert dancer of the 'eccentric' variety, the comedy sometimes hiding the skill, but he was greatly admired, by those who understood the tricks of the trade, for his one-legged shuffle and the way he pretended to court mishap. His stage character was likewise shambling, usually dressed in top hat and a shabby dress suit, with very large shoes. He also had a very fine speaking voice which he projected in a lazy style, inserting into almost every show his own song 'Nobody' (1905, *w* Alex Rogers).

He also wrote 'The ghost of a coon' (1900, Walker), 'The voodoo man' (1900, Walker), 'When it's all goin' out and nothin' comin' in' (1902, Walker), 'Let it alone' (1906, Rogers), and 'That's a-plenty' (with Henry *Creamer, 1909). He appeared in *The Gold Bug* (1896); **In Dahomey* (1903); *Abyssinia* (1906); *Bandana Land* (1908); *Mr Lode of Koel* (1909); **Follies* (1910); and in **Ziegfeld Follies* (1911–12, 1914–17, 1919–20). Clearly Duke *Ellington was a great admirer of his art for he wrote a fine 'Portrait of Bert Williams' in his memory in the 1940s.

M. Rowland (ed.): *Bert Williams, Son of Laughter* (New York, 1923). S. Charters: *Nobody: the Story of Bert Williams* (New York, 1970; repr. 1983).

Williams, Charles (*b* London, 1893; *d* London, 7 Sept. 1978). British composer and conductor. He studied at the Royal Academy of Music. Originally a violinist, he graduated to conducting and built up a reputation as a composer of film music and light orchestral pieces. After the Second World War, Chappell & Co. formed a new orchestra which they called the Queen's Hall Light Orchestra in memory of the old Queen's Hall which had been destroyed by bombing in 1941. Williams was appointed conductor and for many years the orchestra broadcast every Tuesday evening, Williams writing the programme's signature tune, 'The voice of London'. After a few years he left, to be succeeded by Sidney Torch (1908–90), and formed his own Concert Orchestra, continuing to write many orchestral pieces, marches, etc., which were recorded in the 1940s, 1950s, and 1960s, many of his pieces being used for the mood music recordings that publishers like Chappell used to issue. One that became well-known was 'Devil's galop' (1944), which was used for the *Dick Barton* radio series.

He wrote sound-tracks for films (for many of which he was musical director) including: *Kipps* (1941); *My Wife's Family* (1941); *The Night has Eyes* (1942)—'The night has eyes'; *The Young Mr Pitt* (1942); *Women Aren't Angels* (1942); *Thursday's Child* (1943); *The Silver Fleet* (1943); *Warn That Man* (1943); *The Life and Death of Colonel Blimp* (1943); *A Medal for the General* (1944); *English Without Tears* (1944); *Candles at Nine* (1944); *This is Britain* (1945); *The Way to the Stars* (1945)—'The way to the stars' (with Nicholas *Brodszky); *Beware of Pity* (1946); *Carnival* (1946); *Quiet Weekend* (1946); *While I Live* (1947)—'The dream of

Olwen'; and *That Dangerous Age* (1949)—'Jealous lover', also used for *The Apartment* (1960).

Williams, Clarence (*b* Plaquemine, La., 8 Oct. 1898; *d* Queens, NY, 6 Nov. 1965). American composer, bandleader, pianist, and guitarist. A professional entertainer at the age of 12, he ran away from home to join a minstrel show. He went to New Orleans to work with Jelly Roll *Morton and led an orchestra in a vaudeville house there; and also ran a music-publishing business. He made some historic jazz recordings with Louis *Armstrong 1924–5 and with other leading musicians. An accomplished pianist, he recorded accompaniments to Bessie *Smith, Ethel *Waters, and other blues singers.

He wrote a musical comedy, *Bottomland* (1927); and was the composer of many imperishable jazz classics like 'Royal Garden blues' (with Spencer *Williams, 1919), 'I ain't gonna give nobody none of my jelly roll' (with Spencer Williams, 1919), 'I wish I could shimmy like my sister Kate' (with Louis *Armstrong, 1919), 'Sugar blues' (1920), 'Baby, won't you please come home' (1920, *w* Charles Warfield), 'T'ain't nobody's bizness if I do' (1922), 'Gulf Coast blues' (1924), 'Cushion foot stomp' (1927), 'West End blues' (1928, *m* Joe *Oliver, *w* Williams), 'Organ grinder blues' (1928), and 'Wild flower rag' (1929).

E. Goldman: *Clarence Williams Discography* (London, 1947).

Williams, 'Cootie' [Charles Melvin] (*b* Mobile, Ala., 24 July 1908; *d* New York, 15 Sept. 1985). American jazz trumpeter. Originally he intended to be a drummer but switched to trumpet in his school band and made his professional debut in Florida in 1925 on that instrument. He went to New York in 1926, played with Chick *Webb and Fletcher *Henderson, then joined the Duke *Ellington band in 1929 as a replacement for Bubber *Miley, whom he much admired. Taking up Miley's growl and mute techniques, he expanded on his predecessor's limited style, giving a flexible, swinging trumpet lead that was fully Ellington-flavoured and was to be a prominent voice in some of the band's finest recordings, such as 'Echoes of Harlem' (1936) and the classic 'Concerto for Cootie' (1940). His departure from the Ellington band in 1940 was mourned by many. He played in the Benny *Goodman band before forming his own big band. Slightly reduced in size it was resident in the Savoy Ballroom for seven years until the closure in 1950. He toured Europe in 1959 and, enjoying a return to his former style and glories, rejoined the Ellington band in 1962 to help its search for continuity and identity.

Williams, Hiram **Hank** (*b* Georgiana, Ala., 17 Sept. 1923; *d* Ohio, 1 Jan. 1953). American Country and Western singer and composer. Singing and playing from boyhood, he won a talent contest in Montgomery at the age of 12, singing his own song 'WPA blues'. He formed his own band, Hank Williams and his Drifting Cowboys, at 14. In 1946 he went to Nashville and joined the **Grand Ole Opry* programme in 1949, having a recording success with his million-selling 'Lovesick blues'. By the 1950s he had accumulated many hits, mostly his own compositions, including: 'Long gone lonesome blues', 'I just don't like this kind of livin'', 'Why don't you love me?', 'Moaning' the blues', 'Hey, good lookin'', 'Your cheatin' heart', and 'Move it on over'. Excessive indulgence in alcohol, drugs, and women undermined his health and he died, only 30, of a heart-attack while travelling to an engagement in Canton, Ohio. He was elected to the *Country Music Hall of Fame in 1961. His son, Hank Williams Jr. (*b* 1949), has also had a distinguished career in country music.

J. Rivers: *Hank Williams: from Life to Legend* (Denver, 1967). T. Moore: *Hank Williams: the Legend* (Denver, 1972). R. Williams: *Sing a Sad Song: the Life of Hank Williams* (New York, 1973).

Williams, John Towner (*b* Flushing, NY, 8 Feb. 1932). American composer and conductor. Son of a studio musician, he learned to play several instruments and, when his family moved to Los Angeles in 1948, studied orchestration at the Los Angeles City College and composition privately with Castelnuovo-Tedesco. Later he studied piano at the Juilliard School of Music. He began his musical career as a composer, arranger, and conductor for films and TV, his scores including: *The Secret Ways* (1961); *Diamond Head* (1962); *None but the Brave* (1965); *How to Steal a Million* (1966); *Valley of the Dolls* (1967); *The Cowboys* (1971); *The Poseidon Adventure* (1972); *Tom Sawyer* (1973); *Earthquake* (1974); *The Towering Inferno* (1974); *Jaws* (1975; Academy Award); *The Eiger Sanction* (1975); *Star Wars* (1977; Academy Award); *Close Encounters of the Third Kind* (1977); *Jaws 2* (1978); *Superman* (1978); *The Fury* (1978); *Dracula* (1979); *Superman II* (1980); *The Empire Strikes Back* (1980); *Raiders of the Lost Ark* (1981); *E.T.* (1982; Academy Award); *Return of the Jedi* (1983); and other films of the sword-and-sorcery kind for which he had a special musical flair. He also won an Academy Award as musical director of **Fiddler on the Roof* (1971); and generally did well out of LP sales of his scores. He is also the composer of more serious orchestral and chamber works. In 1980 he succeeded Arthur Fiedler as conductor of the Boston Pops Orchestra with which he has regularly played and recorded his music.

Williams, Larry (*b* New Orleans, 10 May 1935; *d* Los Angeles 2 Jan. 1980). American rhythm 'n' blues pianist and singer. He is remembered for three pounding R & B classics, his best and most popular 'Short fat Fannie' (1957), followed by 'Bony Moronie' and 'Dizzy Miss Lizzy'. He was discovered by Art Rupe of Specialty Records when the company was looking for someone to match its success with *Little Richard. Williams's style was similar, but he never quite matched him in star quality. His songs were frequently used by the British beat groups, most notably by the *Beatles. He had narcotics problems in 1960 but returned with a new band in 1962. After many recording hits and a British tour in 1964, he turned to record production. Attempts at a come-back in 1978 were unsuccessful, and he later died from self-inflicted gunshot wounds.

Williams, Mary Lou [*née* Scruggs, Mary Elfrieda] (*b* Atlanta, Ga., 8 May 1910; *d* Durham, NC, 28 May 1981). American jazz pianist, composer, and arranger. She first performed in public at the age of six, was brought up in Pittsburgh where she played in vaudeville, and married a musician, John Williams, at the age of 16, with whom she made her first recordings. She arranged for the Andy Kirk (1898–1992) band in Kansas City in 1929 and then in 1931 became regular pianist and arranger with Kirk's Twelve Clouds of Joy, where her playing, and such works as 'Walkin' and swingin'', 'Twinklin'', 'Cloudy', 'Little Joe from Chicago', 'Froggy bottom', and 'What's your story, morning glory?', brought her considerable renown.

Her ideas were advanced for the time and proved a source of inspiration and themes for the up-and-coming practitioners of modern jazz trends like Dizzy *Gillespie. She arranged for the Benny *Goodman orchestra, and was pianist with the Kirk band until 1942. She gave a lead to such pianists as Thelonious *Monk, Bud *Powell, and other jazz musicians, and took on a more modern style herself, both in playing and her composition of such things as 'In the Land of Oo-Bla-Dee' (1947), which was written for Gillespie. Her 'Zodiac suite' was performed by the New York Philharmonic and she wrote several religious choral works for the Roman Catholic Church, one specially commissioned by the Vatican, her *Mass for Peace* becoming popularly known as 'Mary Lou's Mass'. She played in clubs and toured the USA and Europe in the 1950s but tended to move out of the commercial limelight in the 1960s. In the 1970s she re-emerged to play ragtime on the one hand and avant-garde music with Cecil *Taylor on the other; and to receive a Guggenheim Fellowship in 1972 and become artist-in-residence at Duke University in 1977. Her compositional aspirations never changed the freely imaginative quality of her playing in whatever style she indulged, and she was a leader in the jazz world for more than 60 fruitful years.

Williams, Spencer (*b* New Orleans, 14 Oct. 1889; *d* Flushing, NY, 14 July 1965). American composer. He was born on Basin Street and brought up in the high-class brothel Mahogany Hall, which was run by his aunt, Lulu White. Later he was educated at St Charles University. He went to Chicago in 1907, playing in saloons and beer-halls, and occasionally eking out a living as a Pullman porter. He became pianist at the San Souci Park and started songwriting, producing many compositions in his native New Orleans vein, many of which became jazz standards. He also wrote a revue *Put and Take* (1921). He played in New York then went to live in Paris in 1925, where he was accompanist to Josephine *Baker and wrote many songs for her and for the Folies-Bergère. He founded his own music-publishing firm and lived in England, in Sunbury, Middlesex, for a while; then in Stockholm; returning to Paris in 1932 with Fats *Waller, where he settled again for many years; and returned to the USA in 1957.

His compositions included: 'I ain't got nobody' (with Roger Graham, 1915), 'Shim-me-sha-wabble' (1917), 'Tishomingo blues' (1918), 'I found a new baby' (with Jack Palmer, 1900–76, 1919), 'Arkansas blues' (with Anton Lada, 1890–1944, 1919), 'Royal Garden blues' (with Clarence *Williams, 1919), 'I ain't gonna give nobody none of my jelly roll' (with Clarence Williams, 1919), 'Barcelona' (with Lada, 1920), 'Jungle blues' (with Lada, 1921), 'Put and take' (1921), 'Loveless love' (with W. C. *Handy, 1921), 'State Street blues' (1922), 'Snake hips' (1923), 'Mahogany Hall stomp' (1924), 'Everybody loves my baby' (with Palmer, 1924), 'Farewell to Storyville' (1925), 'Cheatin' blues' (1925), 'Boodle-am' (1926), 'Fireworks' (1927), 'Skip the gutter' (1927), and 'Basin Street blues' (1928).

Wills, Bob [James Robert] (*b* nr. Kosse, Texas, 6 Mar. 1905; *d* Fort Worth, Texas, 13 May 1975). American country singer, bandleader, and composer. Following early work as a mandolin player and fiddler, he organized his own group, the Wills Fiddle Band, in 1929 which became popular on radio and made many recordings. He settled in Tulsa, Okla., where he became a permanent attraction on station KVOO with a group now known as his Texas Playboys, particularly with his popular 'San Antonio rose' (1940). He is credited as the creator of the country style known as *western swing. He had a heart-attack in 1960 and had to retire from band-leading in 1964, but continued as a solo artist, last recording in 1973. He was elected to the *Country Music Hall of Fame in 1968.

C. R. Townsend: *San Antonio Rose: the Life and Music of Bob Wills* (Urbana–London, 1976).

Willson, Meredith (*b* Mason City, Iowa, 18 May 1902; *d* Santa Monica, Calif., 15 June 1984). American composer, flautist, and conductor. He learned to play the flute as a child, went to New York when he was 16, and studied at the Damrosch Institute of Musical Art. In 1919 he joined *Sousa's band and travelled with it until 1922, then played in the New York Philharmonic 1923–8. He became a conductor on radio and composed two symphonies, which were performed in 1936 and 1940, and other orchestral and band pieces. He appeared in the radio comedy *The Big Show*, with Tallulah Bankhead, for which he wrote the lastingly popular 'May the good Lord bless and keep you' as a closing piece. Now turning to the more popular fields of music-making, he had a great success with *The *Music Man* (1957), about whose background he wrote later in a book *But He Doesn't Know the*

Territory (New York, 1959). Songs from it, such as '76 trombones', achieved great popularity. This was followed by *The *Unsinkable Mollie Brown* (1960) and *Here's Love* (1963), adapted from the film *Miracle on 34th Street*. He also worked in Hollywood as an arranger and orchestrator, helping Charlie *Chaplin with his score for *The Great Dictator* (1940) and writing the score for *The Little Foxes* (1941). He wrote the autobiographical *And There I Stood with my Piccolo* (New York, 1948) and *Eggs I Have Laid* (New York, 1955).

Wilson, Jackie (*b* Detroit, 9 June 1934; *d* Mount Holly, NJ, 21 Jan. 1984). American rock singer. He intended to be a boxer but, under pressure from his family, turned to the less harmful pursuit of singing. In 1959 he became the lead singer of a rhythm 'n' blues group, the Dominoes. He recorded for Motown and had a No. 1 hit with his 'Lonely teardrops' (1959). Other hits included 'Am I the man' and 'Higher and higher'. In 1961 he was shot and slightly wounded in a New York hotel by a jealous woman. With a fine, wide-ranging, and high-reaching voice, he was a compelling performer. He suffered a heart-attack on stage in 1975 which left him incapacitated for the rest of his life.

Wilson, Sandy [Alexander Galbraith] (*b* Hale, Cheshire, 19 May 1924). British composer and writer. Educated at Harrow and Oriel College, Oxford, he made a name appearing in and writing for Oxford revues, later contributing to the London revues *Slings and Arrows* (1948); *Oranges and Lemons* (1948); *See You Later* (1951); and *See You Again* (1952). He became best-known for his very successful pastiche of the 1920s, *The *Boy Friend* (1953), which, after an initial presentation at the *Players' Theatre, became one of London's longest-running shows, with Broadway productions in 1954 and 1958 and a film version in 1972. Its appeal was a mixture of nostalgia, an accurate portrayal of the period, a simple story, and lightly appealing and memorably tuneful music. He wrote about it in a book, *The Boy Friend*, published in 1955. While never matching the artistic or financial success of this show he continued with *The Buccaneer* (1955); **Valmouth* (1958)—which many consider his best and a long underrated work; contributed to *Pieces of Eight* (1959); *Call It Love* (1960); *Divorce Me, Darling* (1964); *As Dorothy Parker Once Said* (1969); *His Monkey Wife* (1978); *Aladdin* (1979); and, for TV, *Charley's Aunt* (1971). He is the author of an autobiography, *I Could Be Happy* (London, 1975); and books on *Ivor Novello* (London, 1975) and *The Twenties* (London, 1977).

Wilson, Teddy [Theodore Shaw] (*b* Austin, Texas, 24 Nov. 1912; *d* New Britain, Conn., 31 July 1986). American jazz pianist. He had a thorough training as a musician, learning violin and piano at Tuskegee and studying theory at Talladega College. He moved to Detroit in 1929 and joined the Speed Webb band, eventually coming to Chicago where he played with such musicians as Louis *Armstrong, Erskine *Tate, and Jimmie *Noone 1931–3. He went to New York in 1933 to join Benny *Carter, and first came to attention on record for his work with the Chocolate Dandies. He was with Willie Bryant 1934–5, then came to the peak of his playing career when he joined Benny *Goodman 1935–9. His relaxed yet impressively dextrous playing, quick imagination, and balanced phrasing were particularly realized in the small group recordings with Goodman, *Krupa, *Hampton, and, later, Charlie *Christian, which were so polished yet so exciting; as well as in his sterling work in the main band. At this time he also made some fine recordings with Billie *Holiday. He appeared in the film *Hollywood Hotel* (1938) and later rejoined Goodman in the show *The Seven Lively Arts* (1944–5).

When he left Goodman in 1939 he formed his own band, which only lasted until 1940 but gave him time to show his arranging and composing ability. For some years he worked with a sextet in New York and made some fine solo recordings. For many years after the war his time was mainly taken up with teaching, including a summer course at Juilliard 1945–52. He toured Britain and Europe in the 1950s, rarely composing after this period but playing with undiminished imagination and skill into the 1970s, if with slightly diminished verve. He combined the influences of players like *Tatum, *Hines, and *Waller in a compact and recognizably adroit style of his own.

Wimperis, Arthur (*b* London, 3 Dec. 1874; *d* London, 14 Oct. 1953). British lyric-writer and author. He worked on the staff of the *Daily Graphic* and was an artist before turning to the theatre, and he occasionally illustrated the programmes of the shows he was associated with. He collaborated frequently with Herman *Darewski. After serving in the Boer War 1899–1902, he wrote lyrics for *The Dairymaids* (1906); *The Gay Gordons* (1907); *The *Arcadians* (1909); *The Balkan Princess* (1910); and *The Sunshine Girl* (1912); supplied material for *The *Follies*; and collaborated on *The Girl in the Taxi* (1912); *The *Passing Show* (1914); **Bric-a-Brac* (1915); *My Lady Frayle* (1916); **As You Were* (1918); and *The *Shop Girl* (1920).

Wings. British pop group formed by Paul *McCartney in 1971 after the break-up of the *Beatles. The initial line-up also included Linda McCartney (*b* 1942) (keyboards and vocal), Denny Laine (*b* 1942) (guitar and vocal), Henry McCullough (guitar), and Denny Seiwell (drums). After a series of successful singles, including 'Hi, hi, hi' (1973) which was banned by the BBC, and two inconsequential albums, they produced the interesting album *Band on the Run* (1973), followed by *Venus and Mars* (1975). They toured extensively in 1976, then produced the highly acclaimed triple album *Wings Over America* (1976) and recorded 'Mull of Kintyre' (1977), which became the highest-selling single in Britain up to that time. The group continued until

1980, when Denny Laine left for other pastures and McCartney ran into drug troubles in Japan. He continued by working again with George *Martin, the Beatles producer, on the fine album *Tug of War* (1982), recorded with Stevie *Wonder and Michael *Jackson, and starred in the poorly received film *Give My Regards to Broad Street* (1984).

Winner, Septimus (*b* Philadelphia, 11 May 1827; *d* Philadelphia, 22 Nov. 1902). American composer. He learned to play the violin, married at 20, opened a music store in Philadelphia, and taught violin, guitar, and banjo, eventually writing tutors for 23 different instruments. He wrote more than 200 songs, many under the name of Alice Hawthorne, including what was to be his best-known song, 'Listen to the mocking bird' in 1854; he was paid $5 for it, and it sold more than 20 million copies during his lifetime. In 1862 he wrote 'Give us back our old Commander: Little Mac the people's pride' in support of General McClellan, which got him into trouble with the authorities and he was imprisoned for a short spell. Later it was used for Grant's presidential campaign. Other songs he wrote were 'What is home without Mother' (1854), 'Oh where, oh where has my little dog gone?' (1864), based on a German song, and 'Ten little Injuns' (later 'Ten little nigger boys') (1868); and he made some 2000 arrangements for violin and piano. His brother, Joseph Eastburn Winner (1837–1918), was the composer of 'Little brown jug'.

C. E. Claghorn: *The Mocking Bird: the Life and Diary of its Author, Sep. Winner* (Philadelphia, 1937).

Winnick, Maurice (*b* Manchester, 28 Mar. 1902; *d* London, 29 May 1962). British bandleader and saxophonist. He studied the violin in Manchester, but began his professional career as a cinema pianist. He led a band on a transatlantic liner and took the opportunity to study the saxophone in the USA. Returning to England in 1922 he played in various orchestras, then formed his own in 1928 to play at the Plaza Dance Hall in Manchester. He went to London later that year to play at the Hammersmith Palais de Danse; the band was seen in a number of films, and in 1930 it became resident orchestra at the Piccadilly Hotel in London, from where Winnick first broadcast. His was the first band to be heard in a British talking film. Playing at the Carlton Hotel and Ciro's Club, he modelled his band on Guy *Lombardo's, exploiting a sweet music style that won him instant popularity, using as his signature tune a Lombardo composition, 'The sweetest music this side Heaven'. He succeeded Harry *Roy at the Mayfair Hotel in 1936 and moved on to the Dorchester Hotel 1939–40, where he compiled an entertainment known as the Dorchester Follies, with which he later toured the British Isles. He took the whole company to Italy in 1944 to entertain the troops, later to Palestine, Egypt, and Syria. He left the band world to become a promoter, and was responsible for such BBC radio successes as *Twenty Questions* and *Ignorance is Bliss*, and TV's *What's My Line?*

Winninger, Charles [Karl] (*b* Athens, Wis., 26 May 1884; *d* Palm Springs, Calif., 19 Jan. 1969). American actor and singer. A rotund and blustering comic, he appeared in many important musicals including *The Yankee Girl* (1910); *The Wall Street Girl* (1912); *When Claudia Smiles* (1914); *The Cohan Revue* (1916 and 1918); *The *Passing Show* (1919); **Ziegfeld Follies* (1920); **No, No, Nanette* (1925), in which he sang 'I want to be happy'; *Oh, Please* (1926); *Yes, Yes, Yvette* (1927); and **Show Boat* (1927), in which he played Cap'n Andy. He was popular on radio in the 1930s and played in vaudeville. In the mid-1930s he moved into films, appearing in more than 60 altogether, most notably in *Show Boat* (1936); *Little Nelly Kelly* (1940); *Coney Island* (1943); *Broadway Rhythm* (1944); **State Fair* (1945); and *Give My Regards to Broadway* (1948).

Winstone, Eric (*b* London, 1 Jan. 1915; *d* Pagham, Sussex, 2 May 1974). British bandleader and composer. As a youth he worked for the Gas Light and Coke Company and played the piano with local bands in the evenings. He left to concentrate on music, and formed his first band in 1935 at the Spanish Club in Cavendish Square, London. He took up the accordion, which was to be a popular feature of his music-making, and for a time played it as a solo turn in variety theatres, formed an accordion quintet, and founded a school of accordion teaching. At various times he led a Swing Quartet (with Julie Dawn as vocalist), his Accordion Band, and the Eric Winstone Dance Orchestra, a popular outfit at Butlin's Holiday Camps. He had success with such compositions as 'Stagecoach' (which became his signature tune), 'Oasis', 'Mirage', 'Bottle party', 'Bugle bounce', and 'Pony Express'.

Winterbottom. Well-known family of military band musicians. The founder of the dynasty was John Winterbottom who was in the 1st Life Guards, fought at Waterloo, and was appointed a warden of the Tower of London. He died in 1855 leaving five sons, all of whom became well-known in military band circles. The eldest son, Thomas Winterbottom, played in the band of the Royal Horse Guards for nine years and became bandmaster of the Royal Marine Light Infantry, Plymouth Division, Band, a post he held for 17 years. He died in Plymouth in 1869.

William Winterbottom (*b* 1822; *d* Boulogne-sur-Mer, 29 Sept. 1889) was a trombone player in the band of the 1st Life Guards. He became bandmaster of the Woolwich Division, then succeeded his brother at Plymouth and finally went to the 2nd Life Guards. He was a prolific arranger of operetta and other forms of popular music for military band and brass instruments, becoming known by a best-selling series of piano arrangements of *Gilbert and Sullivan.

John Winterbottom (*b* 1817; *d* Putney, 18 May 1897) was a well-known bassoon player, starting his career with the *Jullien orchestra. He went to Australia in 1852 to conduct a series of promenade concerts and returned to England in 1870 to organize the band of the Royal Marine Artillery, retiring from this post in 1892 to become bandmaster of the Artists' Rifle Corps.

Henry Winterbottom was bandmaster of the 7th Royal Fusiliers, the 18th Royal Irish Regiment, and the Royal Marines, Woolwich. Ammon Winterbottom was a double-bass player who was a member of Queen Victoria's private band and played in the Philharmonic Orchestra. He died in 1891.

It was his son Frank Winterbottom (*b* London, 21 Mar. 1861; *d* London, 1930) who was to become the best-known of the family. Trained as a cellist, he eventually became Professor of Music at Dulwich College. From 1890 to 1910 he was Director of Music of the Royal Marines Band at Plymouth and in later years became an instructor at the Royal Military School of Music. His compositions include the ballets *Jorinda* and *Phantasma*, and the *Seven Ages* suite after Shakespeare, but he is chiefly remembered for the arrangements for military band of which he made a vast number, many of them never bettered.

Winter Garden Theatre, New York. Theatre built by the *Shuberts on the east side of Broadway at 50th Street and opened in 1911. It was renowned in its early days, being a large and wide theatre with a sizeable orchestra pit, for lavish musicals starring Al *Jolson as well as the series of **Passing Show* revues. It continued with a spectacular revue policy in the 1930s and has kept up an intermittent musical tradition with **Mexican Hayride* (1944); **Wonderful Town* (1953); **West Side Story* (1957); **Mame* (1966); and **Cats* (1982) among its successes.

Winterhalter, Hugo (*b* Wilkes-Barre, Pa., 15 Aug. 1909; *d* Greenwich, Conn., 17 Sept. 1973). American conductor and arranger. Educated at the New England Conservatory, he was a schoolteacher for several years. In the mid-1930s he came into the music profession and played with several bands including that of Larry *Clinton for whom he arranged his best-selling recording of 'Stardust'. In the 1940s he arranged for Count *Basie, Will *Bradley, Tommy and Jimmy *Dorsey, Vaughn *Monroe, and Claude *Thornhill; and for the singers Billy *Eckstine, Eddie *Fisher, Dinah *Shore, Kate *Smith, and Kay Starr. He was musical director for MGM Records 1948–9, Columbia 1949–50, Victor 1950–63, and Kapp in 1963. He recorded with an orchestra under his own name, favouring the lush sound of many strings.

Wish You Were Here. Musical comedy with score by Harold *Rome, and book by Joshua *Logan and Harold Kober, based on Kober's comedy *Having a Wonderful Time*. Produced in New York, at the Imperial Theatre 25 June 1952, it enjoyed the novelty of an on-stage swimming pool, being set in the Camp Carefree holiday camp much frequented by middle-class New Yorkers, the story centring on the love affair of a holidaying secretary, played by Patricia Marand, and a law student who works there in the vacation (Jack Cassidy, 1926–76) [598p]. The songs included 'Where did the night go?' and 'Wish you were here'. It was seen in London at the Casino 10 Oct. 1963 [281p].

Witherspoon, Jimmy (*b* Gurdon, Ark., 18 Aug. 1923). American blues singer. He became known as one of the best blues-shouters of the 1940s, teaming up with *boogie-woogie pianist Jay *McShann and his *jump band in 1945. It was the style of singing which evolved into rhythm 'n' blues, Witherspoon leading the way with numbers like 'Big fine girl', 'Ain't nobody's business', and 'No rollin' blues'.

Wiz, The. Updated version of *The *Wizard of Oz*, with an all-black cast, a rock score by Charlie Smalls (*b* 1930), and book by William F. Brown. It retained the old story, told in a racy new way suited to modern audiences. Produced in New York (Majestic Theatre) 5 Jan. 1975, with Stephanie Mills as Dorothy, the idea succeeded to the tune of 1672 performances and two touring companies. It was filmed in 1978 with Diana *Ross as Dorothy, Michael *Jackson as the Scarecrow, and Lena *Horne.

Wizard of Oz, The. Musical fantasy with score by A. Baldwin *Sloane and Paul Tietjens (1877–1943), and words by L. Frank Baum, based on his novel for children *The Wonderful Wizard of Oz* (1900). It was the first production to be staged at the Majestic Theatre, New York, 20 Jan. 1903, and also the musical debut of two illustrious vaudeville comics, Dave Montgomery and Fred *Stone, with Anna Laughlin as Dorothy. Added to the modest score was Theodore *Morse's 'Hurrah for Baffin Bay'. The success of this production [293p] led to the commissioning of Victor *Herbert's **Babes in Toyland* as a follow-up at the Majestic Theatre. An even greater triumph awaited the classic film version of 1939 with Judy *Garland unforgettable in 'Over the rainbow' and a notable trio of eccentric companions in Ray *Bolger, Bert *Lahr, and Jack Haley (1899–1979). The brand new score by Harold *Arlen and E. Y. *Harburg also included 'If I only had a brain', 'We're off to see the Wizard', 'The yellow brick road', and many other whimsical delights.

A. Harmetz: *The Making of the Wizard of Oz* (New York, 1977).

Wodehouse, P. G. [Pelham Grenville] (*b* Guildford, 15 Oct. 1881; *d* Southampton, Long Island, 14 Feb. 1975). British author and lyric-writer. Educated at Dulwich College, he started writing soon after leaving school. In 1902 he published his first novel, *The Pothunters*, and started writing lyrics for Jerome *Kern musicals then being produced in London, his first moderate hit being a song called 'Mr Chamberlain'. From 1903 to 1909 he was columnist for the *Globe* and started writing the humorous books which made him famous, starting with the Psmith series.

Having visited America a couple of times, he settled there in 1915 (to avoid the British tax system) and renewed his acquaintance with Jerome Kern at the first night of **Very Good, Eddie*. With *Guy Bolton, Kern's American librettist, he formed a partnership which produced the books for *Have a Heart* (1917); **Leave It To Jane* (1917); **Oh, Boy!* (1917); **Oh, Lady! Lady!!* (1918)—a now famous series of shows, all produced at the *Princess Theatre. Later he worked with Rudolf *Friml on *The Three Musketeers* (1928); and with George *Gershwin on **Oh, Kay!* (1926) and **Rosalie* (1928), contributing in all to some two dozen Broadway musicals. His adept lyrics, typified by 'Bill', were a model for later masterpieces by Lorenz *Hart, Ira *Gershwin, and Cole *Porter.

After an unfortunate period in France during the Second World War (when he was branded as a collaborator after what now seem some fairly harmless broadcasts in which he spoke fairly lightly of his captors), Wodehouse again settled in New York where he continued to write in the vein of his famous Psmith and Jeeves novels until his death.

P. G. Wodehouse and G. Bolton: *Bring on the Girls: the Improbable Story of Our Life in Musical Comedy with Pictures to Prove It* (New York, 1953; London, 1954; pb. 1981). D. A. Jasen: *The Theatre of P. G. Wodehouse* (London, 1979). F. Donaldson: *P. G. Wodehouse: the Authorized Biography* (London, 1982).

Woman of the Year. Musical with score by John *Kander, lyrics by Fred *Ebb, and book by Peter Stone. It was a second musical role for Lauren Bacall (*b* 1924), earlier seen on the musical stage in **Applause*. Based on a 1942 film, it portrayed a woman's attempt to reconcile career and marriage. Its songs included: 'Woman of the year', 'One of the boys', 'The grass is always greener', and 'We're gonna work it out'. It was produced in New York (Palace Theatre) 29 Mar. 1981 [770p].

Wonder, Stevie [Hardaway, Steveland Judkins] (*b* Saginaw, Mich., 13 May 1950). American soul and rock singer. Blind since birth, Stevie Wonder came to prominence as Berry *Gordy's child prodigy at the age of 10. His third single for Tamla, 'Fingertips, part two' (1963), stayed at No. 1 for several weeks. Minor hits followed, including 'Hey, harmonica man' (1964) and 'High heel sneakers' (1965). In 1965 he also released 'Uptight', a more usual Motown dance number; but followed this with a series of romantic songs: 'I was made to love her' (1967), 'For once in my life' (1968), 'Yester-me, yester-you, yester-day' (1969), and 'My cherie amour' (1969). He finally came into his own with the release of the very personal LP *Where I'm Coming From* (1971), which opened the way for a series of superb albums: *Music of my Mind* (1972), *Talking Book* (1972), and *Innervisions* (1973). This period saw him experimenting with production techniques, exploring the possibilities of synthesizer and electronic keyboard, and expanding upon the commercial limitations of his previous songs. These albums included such interesting items as 'Superstition' (1973), 'I believe (when I fall in love with you it will be forever)' (1973), 'He's Mistra Know It All' (1974), and 'Living for the city' (1974).

In 1974 he recovered from a serious car accident to record the patchy *Fulfillingness First Finale*. The momentous *Songs in the Key of Life* appeared in 1976, after he had signed a contract with Motown for an advance of $13 million. Wonder's mysticism dominated his innovative 1979 release, *Journey Through the Secret Life of Plants*, while a later album, *Hotter Than July* (1980), saw him return to the catchy tunefulness of his 'You are the sunshine of my life' period. In 1982 he was given the American Music Awards' Award of Merit and has since continued on his probing and imaginative way.

C. Elsner: *Stevie Wonder* (London, 1977). R. Fox-Cumming: *Stevie Wonder* (London, 1977). J. Haskins: *The Stevie Wonder Scrapbook* (New York–London, 1978).

Wonderful Town. Musical comedy with music by Leonard *Bernstein, lyrics by Betty *Comden and Adolph *Green, book by Joseph *Fields and Jerome Chodorov (*b* 1911), based on their play *My Sister Eileen*. The story follows the fortunes of two sisters who live in Greenwich Village, Ruth Sherwood, a would-be writer, played by Rosalind Russell (1908–76) in a rare musical role, and Eileen Sherwood, played by Edie Adams (*b* 1929), a girl with boy troubles. It was staged at the *Winter Garden Theatre, New York, 25 Feb. 1953 [559p]; and was seen in London, at the Prince's Theatre 23 Feb. 1955, with Shani Wallis (*b* 1938) and Pat Kirkwood [207p].

Wood, Arthur (*b* Heckmondwike, Yorks., 24 Jan. 1875; *d* London, 18 Jan. 1953). British composer and conductor. In 1882 his family moved to Harrogate where, at the age of 14, he became a church organist and at 16 was deputy conductor of the Harrogate Municipal Orchestra under J. Sidney Jones. A few years later he joined the Bournemouth orchestra under Dan *Godfrey. In 1902 his 'Three Old Dances' was published and his conducting of them so impressed the younger Sidney *Jones, composer of *The Geisha*, that he recommended him as musical director of Terry's Theatre in 1903, making him, at 28, the youngest MD in London. He was to conduct theatre orchestras for more than 30 years, conducting **Veronique* (1904) at the Apollo, and *The Dairymaids* in 1906. He was associated with Robert Courtneidge (1859–1939) productions for many years, including *The *Arcadians* (1906) and *The Mousmé* (1911). He was musical director at the *Gaiety 1917–21 and at *Daly's 1922–6. Later he conducted at the Prince of Wales Theatre, the Cambridge, the *Savoy, and the Coliseum. He composed music for various revues and was often heard on radio. His best-known composition is 'Barwick Green Maypole' which for many years has been the signature tune of the BBC radio serial *The Archers*. It is the first of four movements from his suite 'My Native Heath'. Other suites include 'Three Dale Dances', 'Yorkshire Moors', and 'Three Mask Dances', and he also wrote many dances, marches, and light orchestral pieces.

Wood, Haydn (*b* Slaithwaite, Yorks., 25 Mar. 1882; *d* London, 11 Mar. 1959). British composer and violinist. He studied at the Royal College of Music and in Brussels, and became known as a composer of serious music, as well as of some popular light pieces such as his suites 'London Cameos' and 'London Landmarks', various light orchestral pieces, and works for military and brass band. He wrote more than 200 songs of which one or two achieved great popularity, especially his wartime ballad 'Roses of Picardy' (1916, *w* Fred E. *Weatherly); also 'Love's garden of roses' (1914, *w* Ruth Rutherford), 'A brown bird singing' (1922, *w* Royden Barrie), and 'Homeward at eventide' (1931, *w* A. Harvey Lang-Ridge). He collaborated on a musical comedy, *Dear Love* (1929).

Wood, Leo (*b* San Francisco, 2 Sept. 1882; *d* New York, 2 Aug. 1929). American composer and author. He was a well-known performer on radio, and wrote material for vaudeville and Broadway musicals. His songs included: 'Somebody stole my gal' (1918), 'Runnin' wild' (with Arthur H. Gibbs, 1922), and 'That's what God made mothers for' (1924).

Wood, Peggy [Margaret] (*b* Brooklyn, NY, 9 Feb. 1892; *d* Stamford, Conn., 18 Mar. 1978). American actress and singer. Her stage debut was at the New York Theatre in 1910 in the chorus of **Naughty Marietta*. She appeared in many straight plays and in the musicals *The Lady of the Slipper* (1912); *The Madcap Duchess* (1913); *Hello, Broadway!* (1914); *Love o' Mike* (1917); **Maytime* (1917), in which she sang 'Will you remember?' and 'The road to Paradise'; *Buddies* (1919); and *Marjolaine* (1922). At the age of 37 she went to London for the first time and became a great favourite there when she created the role of Lady Shayne in Noël *Coward's **Bitter Sweet* (1929), singing 'I'll see you again' and 'Zigeuner'; later in *The *Cat and the Fiddle* (London, 1932) and *Operette* (London, 1938). During the war she played in New York in *Blithe Spirit* (1943), with which she toured England and France, playing to the troops. In the 1950s her career was mainly on TV; and in 1965 she was in the film version of *The *Sound of Music*.

P. Wood: *How Young You Look* (New York, 1943). P. Wood: *Arts and Flowers* (New York, 1962).

Woodforde-Finden, Amy [Ward, Amy] (*b* Valparaiso, Chile, 1860; *d* London, 13 Mar. 1919). British composer. She had her first song, 'The first extra', published when she was 16. Confident of the quality of her 'Four Indian Love Lyrics', but unable to find a publisher for them, she had them published at her own expense and circulated them privately. They were taken up by the singer Hamilton Earle, who introduced them to his public with such success that they were accepted by Boosey and published in 1902. The composer had obtained permisison from 'Laurence Hope', the author (in fact the wife of General Nicholson), to use the words without fee. Of the four songs—'The temple bells', 'Less than the dust', 'Kashmiri song', and 'Till I wake'—the third, better known as 'Pale hands I love', achieved great popularity. These were followed by 'Four More Indian Love Lyrics', 'On Jhelum River', and other song cycles. She also wrote *On Jhelum River*, an Indian musical love story, produced at the Aldwych Theatre 22 June 1909.

Wooding, Sam [Samuel David] (*b* Philadelphia, 17 June 1895; *d* New York, 1 Aug. 1985). American bandleader. He started out as a pianist and singer, working with bands in Atlantic City, and served in the US Army, after the war forming his own band in Atlantic City, the Society Syncopators, leading them in Detroit and in New York at the Club Alabam. They were part of a variety show that toured Europe in 1925, visiting Moscow, and becoming the first black big band to bring a taste of jazz to the Continent, his players including Tommy *Ladnier, Doc Cheatham (*b* 1905), and Gene Sedric (1907–63). Back in the USA the band kept together until 1931, when Wooding left the band world to study at the University of Pennsylvania, and eventually became a teacher.

Woods, Harry [Henry MacGregor] (*b* North Chelmsford, Mass., 4 Nov. 1896; *d* Phoenix, 13 Jan. 1970). American composer. Physically handicapped, with no fingers on his left hand, he nevertheless learned to play right-handed piano with his mother. Until 1926 he lived as a gentleman farmer at Cape Cod; then he decided to become a songwriter, frequently writing his own lyrics but often collaborating with Mort Dixon (1892–1956). He was active as a songwriter until the early 1940s, becoming known for his unreliable ways and a habit of disappearing for days on end. He died after being knocked down by a car.

His songs included: 'I'm going South' (with Abner Silver, 1899–1966, 1923), 'Where is my old girl tonight?' (1925, *w* Billy *Rose and Mort Dixon), 'Spread a little sunshine as you go' (1925), 'Paddlin' Madeline home' (1925), 'Oh, how she can love' (1925, *w* Benny Davis, 1895–1983), 'When the red, red robin comes bob, bob, bobbin' along' (1926), 'Who'd be blue' (1926, Dixon), 'I'm looking over a four-leaf clover' (1927, Dixon), 'Just like a butterfly that's caught in the rain' (1927, Dixon), 'Side by side' (1927), 'You're so easy to remember' (1927, Dixon), 'River, stay 'way from my door' (1931, Dixon), 'When the moon comes over the mountain' (1931, *w* Howard E. Johnson, 1887–1941), 'Just an echo in the valley' (with Reg *Connelly and Jimmy Campbell, 1932), 'A little street where old friends meet' (1932, *w* Gus *Kahn), 'Try a little tenderness' (1932, Campbell and Connelly), and 'I'll never say "never" again' (1935).

He also wrote for films: *Vagabond Love* (1929)—'A little kiss each morning'; *Aunt Sally* (1933)—'We'll all go riding on a rainbow', 'You ought to see Sally on Sunday'; *Jack Ahoy* (1935)—'My hat's on the side of my head'; **Evergreen* (1935)—'Over my shoulder', 'Tinkle, tinkle, tinkle', 'When you've got a little springtime in your heart'; and *It's Love Again* (1936)—'I nearly let love go slipping through my fingers'.

Woodstock. A rock festival that is remembered as the peak event of the flower-power period of the 1960s, with its emotional amalgamation of peace and pop. The Woodstock Music and Arts Fair was held on farmland in White Lake, NY, 21–4 Aug. 1969, and such names as *Grateful Dead, *Jefferson Airplane, *Canned Heat, Joe *Cocker, the *Who, and many more, attracted a total audience of some 450,000. A best-selling album of the music was issued and a memorable and ingenious film of the event, directed by Michael Wadleigh, was issued in 1970.

J. Young: *Woodstock: Festival Remembered* (New York, 1979). R. S. Spitz: *Barefoot in Babylon: the Creation of the Woodstock Music Festival, 1969* (New York, 1979). J. Makower: *Woodstock: an Oral History* (New York, 1989).

Work, Henry Clay (*b* Middletown, Conn., 1 Oct. 1832; *d* Hartford, Conn., 8 June 1884). American composer. Mainly self-taught in music, his interest in it did not develop until quite late in life. He was to become known as an abolitionist, a unionist, and a prohibitionist; most of his strong feelings on such subjects being inherited from his father, Alanson Work, a Connecticut Yankee who moved to Illinois in 1835 in order to set up an organization to help slaves to escape. He was imprisoned for these activities in 1841. Henry Clay Work thus had an inborn sympathy for the slaves, a partisanship that for a long time confined his popularity to the Northern states. By 1861 he had published two songs but was still more or less unknown and working as a printer. He specialized in setting music and composed many of his songs straight on to the printing machine—a rare instance of a compositor composer. He wrote his own lyrics and supplied America with some national songs that, like Stephen *Foster's, now seem to have a folk-song quality about them.

The Civil War threw his songs into prominence and by its end, in 1865, he had written 30 or so compositions. Much of his commercial success was due to the encouragement and support of George F. *Root, a well-known composer himself, who was musical director of the firm of Root & Cady in Chicago. Work had been persuaded to show one of his songs, 'Kingdom coming', to Root who found it so well-written and reflective of the spirit of the times that he advised Work to make songwriting his profession. Work was a devoutly religious man and in 1863, when Root hired him to edit the firm's house magazine, *The Song Messenger of the Northwest*, he used it to publish an attack on hymn arrangers who ruined the old tunes to suit their commercial purposes. This led to a quarrel with Root who felt compelled to defend Lowell Mason, whose *The People's Tune Book* Work had singled out for attack, and they parted company although continuing the publisher-composer relationship; later they became friends again.

He married and settled in Chicago, where he continued to work as a printer, occasionally dabbling in real estate, and writing an irregular stream of songs until his end. After the death of his first wife he carried on a hopeless love affair with his landlord's young daughter and this curtailed his writing activities for a time. He moved to Bath, NJ, in 1882, by now a celebrated composer, particularly known for his Civil War writings. His songs included: 'We are coming, Sister Mary' (1853), 'Grafted into the Army' (1862), 'Uncle Joe's "Hail Columbia"' (1862), 'Kingdom coming' or 'The year of Jubilo' (1862), 'Babylon is fallen' (1863), 'Wake, Nicodemus' (1864), 'The song of a thousand years' (1864), 'Come home, Father' (better-known as 'Father, dear Father, come home') (1864), 'The picture on the wall' (1865), 'Marching through Georgia' (1865), 'Now Moses!' (1865), 'Who shall rule this American nation?' (1866), 'Poor Kitty Popcorn' (1866), 'When the "Evening Star" went down' (1866), 'The ship that never returned' (1868), 'Agnes by the river' (1868), 'The buckskin bag of gold' (1869), 'Crossing the Grand Sierra' (1870), 'Grandfather's clock' (1876), and 'Shadows on the floor' (1877); almost 80 songs in all, with his most productive and telling years around 1861–6.

R. S. Hill: 'The Mysterious Chord of Henry Clay Work' in *Notes*, March and June 1953.

Music: B. C. Work (ed.): *Songs of Henry Clay Work* (New York, 1884; rev. 1974).

Wright, Robert (*b* Daytona Beach, Fla., 25 Sept. 1914). American composer. His career was inextricably linked with that of Chet *Forrest; even before their professional days they seemed fated to collaborate as they both attended the same high school and the University of Miami. Their first joint successes came in Hollywood, where they wrote material for stage productions and nightclubs and contributed to many filmed stage musicals. For *The *Firefly* (1937) they wrote 'Donkey serenade', and for *Sweethearts* (1937) 'Pretty as a picture'. They specialized in creating musical scores from the works of classical composers: **Song of Norway* (1940; Grieg); *Gypsy Lady* (1946; *Herbert); *Magdalena* (1948; Villa-Lobos); **Kismet* (1953; Borodin); *Anya* (1965; Rachmaninov); and *The *Great Waltz* (1970; *Strauss). They also wrote *The Love Doctor* (1959) and *Kean* (1961).

Wrubel, Allie (*b* Middletown, Conn., 15 Jan. 1905; *d* Los Angeles, 13 Dec. 1973). American composer. One of a family of seven children, he was encouraged to take up music, though he himself had ambitions to be a doctor. While at college he had some success with songs he had written and one of his teachers suggested he take up songwriting as a living. Around 1926 he tried to assail the stronghold of Tin Pan Alley, but with little success, giving up after three years to become a cinema manager. He went on writing and in 1931 came up with his first hit, 'Now you're in my arms'. This was followed by such hits as 'I'll be faithful' (1933, *w* Ned *Washington), 'Farewell to arms' (1933, *w* Abner Silver, 1899–1966), 'Music, maestro, please' (1938, *w* Herb Magidson, *b* 1906), 'I'm stepping out with a memory tonight' (1940, Magidson, 'I can't love you any more' (1940, Magidson) and many more.

Like many composers of the period he found a lucrative market in the growing film industry in Hollywood and among the many he contributed to were: *Happiness Ahead* (1934); *Dames* (1934)—'Try to see it my way' (*w* Mort Dixon); *Flirtation Walk* (1934); *Sweet Music* (1935)—'Fare-thee-well, Annabelle' (Dixon); *In Caliente* (1935)—'The lady in red' (Dixon), sung by Wini Shaw (*b* 1910); *Bright Lights* (1935); *We're in the Money* (1935); *The Toast of New York* (1937)—'The first time I saw you' (with Nat Shilkret); *Radio City Revels* (1937); *Song of the South* (1946)—'Zip-a-dee-doo-dah' (*w* Ray Gilbert); *Make Mine Music* (1946)—'Johnny Fedora and Alice Blue Bonnet' (Gilbert); *Duel in the Sun* (1946); *The Fabulous Dorseys* (1946); *I Walk Alone* (1947); and *Melody Time* (1948).

Wynette, Tammy [Pugh, Virginia Wynette] (*b* Tupelo, Miss., 5 May 1942). American country singer. After working in various mundane jobs and teaching herself to play piano and guitar, she went to Nashville to try to break into the country music scene. She joined the **Grand Ole Opry* programme in 1969 and had great success with such songs as 'Your good girl's gonna go bad', 'Bedtime story', 'Let's get together', and 'Stand by your man'. She has been variously described as 'The Queen of Nashville' and 'The First Lady of Country Music'.

T. Wynette: *Stand By Your Man* (London, 1980).

Wynn, Ed [Isaiah Edwin Leopold] (*b* Philadelphia, 9 Nov. 1886; *d* Beverly Hills, Calif., 19 June 1966). American actor, author, and composer. He left home to join a repertory company and had a long career in vaudeville 1901–14, writing his own material. He developed a zany character act, characterized by a lisp and a nervous laugh, odd dress, and a predilection for bad puns, and was billed as 'The Perfect Fool'. He appeared in *The Deacon and the Lady* (1910); **Ziegfeld Follies* (1914 and 1915); *The *Passing Show* (1916); *Doing Our Bit* (1917); *Sometime* (1918); *Ed Wynn Carnival* (1920); *The Perfect Fool* (1921); *Manhattan Mary* (1927); *Simple Simon* (1930); *The Laugh Parade* (1931); *Hooray for What!* (1937). In films, the musical ones included: *Follow the Leader* (1930; a screen version of *Manhattan Mary); Stage Door Canteen* (1943); *Alice in Wonderland* (1951); *Cinderella* (1960); **Babes in Toyland* (1961); and **Mary Poppins* (1965). He had his own series on radio and TV. His son, Keenan Wynn (*b* 1916), also had minor parts in many MGM musicals 1942–55 and other films.

X

Xanrof, Léon [Fourneau, Léon] (*b* Paris, 9 Dec. 1867; *d* Paris, 17 May 1953). French composer and author. He briefly followed a career as a barrister but abandoned this around 1890 in favour of music. He contrived his writing name of Xanrof by reversing the Latin form of his real name—Fornax. His greatest success as a songwriter was with 'Le fiacre' (1892), which was immortalized by Yvette *Guilbert and revived by Jean *Sablon. He supplied much of Guilbert's repertoire, including such songs as 'Très bien' and 'L'hôtel du No. 3'. He sang in cabaret himself and wrote operetta librettos, including the French version of *Ein *Walzertraum*, *Rêve de Valse* (1910), but his reputation rests mainly on his clever comic songs, many of which were included in the collection *Chansons à rire*.

Xylophone. An instrument to be found in many forms in early music cultures, particularly widespread in African music. It came into European music around 1500 under such names as Strohfiedel (German)—the bars were laid on straw, Holzharmonika (German), and Gigelira (Italian). Its first notable orchestral use was in Saint-Saëns' 'Danse macabre' (1874). The modern instrument consists of bars of wood of graded lengths (generally rosewood, walnut, or boxwood) with a slightly rounded upper surface. These are laid across a tapering frame separated from the wood by felt, cord, or rubber, and kept in position by guiding screws or other fixtures that leave the bars loose so that they can move slightly in all directions. They are tuned to a chromatic scale like the piano and the standard number of notes is 27, though some have more. The solo instrument is generally mounted on a stand and each note has a resonator beneath it, also tuned to the note. The bars are hit with light hammers with rounded heads usually of boxwood on light flexible sticks. The xylophone has had many notable soloists, with a peak period of popularity in the heyday of variety shows, one of the best-known being the exceptionally rotund Teddy *Brown.

In popular music in general, and especially in jazz, the xylophone has been superseded by a modern American development, the vibraphone. In jazz, as in the orchestral world, the xylophone was generally used by the percussionist for occasional solos. Such men as Jimmy Bertrand (1900–60) and Jasper Taylor (1894–1964) were early exponents. Among the virtuoso jazz players were Lionel *Hampton, who later took to the vibraphone, and Red *Norvo who remained faithful into the 1940s.

Y

Yancey, Jimmy [James Edwards] (*b* Chicago, 20 Feb. 1898; *d* Chicago, 17 Sept. 1951). American jazz pianist. His father was a guitarist and singer and his brother Alonzo was also a pianist. He began appearing as a singer and dancer in vaudeville from about the age of six and toured with various troupes. For a time he worked mainly as a dancer and toured Europe in this role before the First World War. He settled in Chicago in 1915 and, having taught himself the piano, began to earn a reputation in Chicago clubs. He gave up music in 1925 and became groundsman to the Chicago Sox baseball team until around 1939. The jazz revival of the time brought him back to music and he now became celebrated as a pioneer of *boogie-woogie, which he played in a sparse and lyrical blues-tinged manner, often over a *habanera-style rhythm, in contrast to the pounding ways of other pianists. Classic recordings he made in late 1939 and early 1940 for Victor preserved such gems as 'Yancey stomp', 'State Street special', 'Tell 'em about me', 'Five o'clock blues', 'Slow and easy', and 'The mellow blues'. He often accompanied and, in 1943 recorded with, his wife, the blues singer Estella 'Mama' Yancey (1896–1986). His activities were curtailed by illness, but she was still active into the 1980s.

'Yankee Doodle'. One of the USA's best-known national songs, it seems to have originated around 1740, probably as a flute or piccolo tune. It is generally agreed that its origins are American, though it was probably first printed in England.

The exact origins of the term 'Yankee' are not known. It was used as a nickname for a person of Dutch origin as early as 1683, and was subsequently used in the USA as the name for a New Englander and, by the Civil War period, as a loose term for anyone from the North, but especially of a soldier of the Federal Army. The writing of the song seems to coincide with this period and helped to perpetuate the use of the name, and to counterbalance its somewhat derisory use by Southerners by making it a name of which the Northerners were proud. Later, once the differences were settled, it became used by foreigners as a name for any citizen of the USA.

One authority has established that the words were written in June 1745, but they were not printed until April 1767 when they appeared in the libretto of an American comic opera, *The Disappointment or The Force of Credulity* by Andrew Barton: the words only were printed along with a stage instruction to 'exit singing "Yankee Doodle"'. By the 1760s it was well-known and widely referred to in literature of the period. It was first printed in England in *The Bath Chronicle* in 1776. The first printed version of the music seems to have been in *A Selection of Scotch, English, Irish and Foreign Airs* (Glasgow, 1782), without the words and titled 'Yanky doodle'. There was a contemporary version with words and music, sub-titled 'The Lexington march'.

The first American printing of the music was *c.*1794 when it was also used as part of an orchestral work, 'The Federal Overture'. In 1796, used in 'Variations for the piano on *Yankee Doodle*', it is described as 'an original American air'. The now well-known version in which Yankee Doodle 'rode upon a pony, put a feather in his cap and called it Macaroni' was first printed in England in 1842 in *The Nursery Rhymes of England*, edited by James Orchard Halliwell. Its obscure ancestry has naturally caused much written speculation and comment and various theories have been invented. It inspired the almost equally well-known 'Yankee Doodle boy' written by George M. *Cohan for the musical *Little Johnny Jones* (1904).

W. J. R. Saffel: *Hail Columbia, the Flag and Yankee Doodle Dandy* (Baltimore, 1864). O. Sonneck: *Report on 'The Star-Spangled Banner', 'Hail Columbia', 'America', 'Yankee-Doodle'* (Washington DC, 1909; new edn, New York, 1972).

***Yankee Doodle Dandy*.** Warner Bros 1942 film biography of George M. *Cohan, with Cohan played by James *Cagney, who reminded the world that he was a superb singer and dancer as well as a film gangster, and Joan Leslie (*b* 1925) as Mary Cohan. It used all the tear-jerking Cohan songs like 'Yankee Doodle boy', '45 minutes from Broadway', 'You're a grand old flag', 'Mary's a grand old name', and 'Give my regards to Broadway'.

Yellen, Jack (*b* Poland 6 July 1892; *d* 1958). American lyric-writer and author. He was working as a reporter on the *Buffalo Courier* when he wrote his first lyric, 'All aboard for Dixieland'. Among many entertainers for whom he wrote material was Sophie *Tucker, who popularized his song 'My Yiddishe momma' (1925, *m* Lew *Pollack). He supplied words for vaudeville and musical comedy productions including: *What's in a Name?* (1920, *m* Milton *Ager); *Rain or Shine* (1928, Ager); *Follow a Star* (1930, *m* Vivian *Ellis); *You Said It* (1931); **George White's Scandals* (1935 and 1939); *Sons o' Fun* (1941); and **Ziegfeld Follies* (1943). He joined a music-publisher and eventually formed his own business. He wrote for films: *Honky Tonk* (1929); *Chasing Rainbows* (1930)—'Happy days are here again' (Ager); *King of Jazz* (1930); *They Learned about Women* (1930); **George White's Scandals* (1934 and 1935); *Under Pressure* (1935); *Sing, Baby, Sing* (1936)—'Sing, baby, sing' (Pollack); *Happy Landing* (1938); **George White's Scandals* (1945). His songs also include: 'Louisville Lou' (1923), 'I wonder what's become of Sally' (1924), 'Crazy words, crazy tune' (1927), 'Ain't she sweet?' (1927), 'Glad rag doll' (with Ager and Dan Dougherty, 1897–1955, 1929), and 'Hard hearted Hannah' (1929).

Yeomen of the Guard, The, or *The Merryman and his Maid*. Comic opera with music by Arthur *Sullivan and book by W. S. *Gilbert, London (Savoy Theatre) 3 Oct. 1888 [423p]. The cast included Wallace Brownlow (*d* 1919) as Sir Richard Cholmondeley, Courtice Pounds (1862–1927) as Colonel Fairfax, Richard *Temple as Sergeant Meryll, W. R. Shirley as Leonard Meryll, George *Grossmith as Jack Point, W. H. Denny (1854–1916) as Wilfred Shadbolt, Geraldine Ulmar (1860–1932) as Elsie Maynard, Rosina *Brandram as Dame Carruthers, and Rose Hervey as Kate. The nearest that Gilbert and Sullivan got to opera together, it is a more serious and profoundly treated work than most of the series that preceded it. The main songs were: 'When maiden loves she sits and sighs', 'Is life a boon?', 'I have a song to sing-o', 'I've jibe and joke', 'A private buffoon is a light-hearted loon', 'Strange adventure', 'A man who would woo a fair maid', and 'When a wooer goes a-wooing'. It was first produced in New York (Casino Theatre) 17 Oct. 1888 [100p] and in Vienna (Carl Theater) 2 Feb. 1889 as *Capitän Wilson*. It was filmed, along with other shows, in 1982.

Yes. British rock group formed in 1968 by Jon Anderson (*b* 1944) (vocal) and Chris Squire (*b* 1948) (bass), with Peter Banks (guitar), Tony Kaye (organ), and Bill Bruford (*b* 1949) (drums). For their first LP in 1969 they used *Beatles originals and other items and gave them an ambitiously classical flavour. Strings were added for *Time and a Word* (1970), and *The Yes Album* (1971) underlined their attempts to fuse rock and classical music. This direction was confirmed when Rick *Wakeman, with his classical training, replaced Tony Kaye and the technological experiments became increasingly important. Wakeman and Anderson left in 1977, which inevitably weakened their impact, and the band broke up in 1981. They left their mark as an interestingly exploratory group who influenced others of like mind in the 1980s.

D. Hedges: *Yes: the Authorised Biography* (London, 1981).

Yodel. A vocal effect achieved by a slow vibrato in the back of the throat with the voice alternating between its natural tone and a falsetto pitch. It is strongly associated with the cowherds of the Tyrolean alpine regions of Switzerland, Austria, and Italy, and their folk-music, its ebullient effect being particularly fine in the clear, echoing mountain air. The art is of very ancient origin and printed yodel calls can be found dating back to 1545, the first full collection being in *Sammlung von Schweizer-Kuhreihen und Volkslieder* edited by J. R. Wyss (Berne, 1818). Yodelling has remained a flourishing folk art in Switzerland and has been adapted to their own use by the folk and popular singers of most countries in the world. The American folk-singer Jimmie *Rodgers notably recorded a series of pieces called 'Blue yodel'.

Yorke, Peter (*b* London, 4 Dec. 1902; *d* London, 10 Feb. 1966). British conductor, composer, arranger, and pianist. He was educated at Trinity College of Music and was an organist at the age of 16, before he developed an interest in dance music as both pianist and arranger. In both capacities he worked with Percival Mackey (1894–1950) in 1927, and also recorded with an *ad hoc* group working for HMV as the Rhythm Band. He played with Jack *Hylton 1929–31, then formed his own orchestra in 1937. He served in the RAF during the Second World War, mostly involved with service orchestras, and after the war established a high reputation with his radio series and the Columbia recordings with his Concert Orchestra, which featured the characterful alto-saxophone playing of Freddy Gardner (1911–50). He wrote a considerable amount of light orchestral music and a number of items for brass band.

Youmans, Vincent Millie (*b* New York, 27 Sept. 1898; *d* Denver, 5 Apr. 1946). American composer. His father wanted him to go into the family business and become a hatter, but he refused. He started piano lessons and eventually found a job with Harms as a song-plugger. In 1917 he joined the US Navy. He showed some of his tunes to his unit's bandmaster, John Philip *Sousa, who liked his work, particularly one piece, 'Hallelujah', which was played frequently by navy bands. Later it was fitted with a lyric and became a success in the show **Hit the Deck*.

After leaving the navy, he joined a music-publisher as a staff pianist and two years later wrote his first Broadway show, *Two Little Girls in Blue* (1921). He continued with *Wildflower* (1923)—'Bambalina'; *Mary Jane McKane* (1923); *Lollipop* (1924); **No, No, Nanette* (1925; filmed 1930, 1940, and, as *Tea for Two*, 1950)—'No, no, Nanette', 'I want to be happy', 'Tea for two'; *Oh, Please* (1926)—'I know that you know'; **Hit the Deck* (1927; filmed 1930 and 1955)—'Sometimes I'm happy', 'Hallelujah'; *Rainbow* (1928); *Great Day!* (1929)—'Great day', 'More than you know', 'Without a song'; *Smiles* (1930)—'Time on my hands'; *Through the Years* (1932)—'Through the years', 'Drums in my heart'; and **Take a Chance* (1932; filmed 1933)—'Rise 'n' shine'. Having written music for two films, *Song of the West* (1930) and *What a Widow!* (1930), and seen his stage shows adapted, he went to Hollywood in 1933 to write the score for *Flying Down to Rio* (1933)—'Orchids in the moonlight', 'Flying down to Rio', 'The carioca'.

In 1934 the tuberculosis he was eventually to die of first began to affect him and he spent the last 12 years of his life in a varying state of ill-health. He still occasionally planned new projects and wrote music for Broadway musicals, but none went beyond the planning stage. Many tunes he wrote in this period have yet to be heard. It is remarkable that so many of his big hits were numbers with very simple themes, often just a repetition of three or four notes, as in 'Tea for two', a perfect example of the economical Youmans technique.

G. Bordman: *Days To Be Happy, Years To Be Sad: the Life and Music of Vincent Youmans* (New York, 1982).

Young, Faron (*b* Shreveport, La., 25 Feb. 1932). American country singer. He first became well-known for his contributions to the *Louisiana Hayride* programme. After serving in Korea he joined the **Grand Ole Opry* in Nashville. He has also appeared in films and on TV. Among his best-known hits are 'Hello, walls' (1957) and 'It's four in the morning' (1971).

Young, Joe [Joseph] (*b* New York, 4 July 1889; *d* New York, 21 Apr. 1939). American lyricist and singer. He worked as a stage assistant in a vaudeville theatre before working in music-publishing, was an entertainer in the First World War, and Director of ASCAP 1926–39. He wrote many of his lyrics in collaboration with Sam M. *Lewis, producing material for *The Laugh Parade* (1931), **Blackbirds* (1933), and other shows.

His principal songs included: 'Just a baby's prayer at twilight' (1918, *m* M. K. *Jerome), 'How you gonna keep 'em down on the farm?' (1919, *m* Walter *Donaldson), 'My mammy' (1921, Donaldson), 'I'm sitting on top of the world' (1925, *m* Ray *Henderson), 'Five foot two, eyes of blue' (1925, Henderson), 'Laugh, clown, laugh' (1928, *m* Ted *Fiorito), 'I kiss your hand, madame' (1929, *m* Ralph Erwin), 'Crying for the Carolines' (1930, *m* Harry *Warren), 'In a shanty in old Shanty Town' (1932), and 'I'm gonna sit right down and write myself a letter' (1935, *m* Fred *Ahlert).

Young, Lester Willis (*b* Woodville, Miss., 27 Aug. 1909; *d* New York, 15 Mar. 1959). American jazz saxophonist. The family moved to New Orleans when he was a boy, where his father taught him to play trumpet, alto-saxophone, violin, and drums. He moved to Minneapolis in 1920, by which time he was playing drums in the family band. He next went to Kansas and was persuaded by bandleader Art Bronson, with whom he played 1928–30, to take up the tenor-saxophone. He played in various towns before joining the Original Blue Devils in Oklahoma City in 1932, leaving in 1933 to join Bennie *Moten. In 1934 he was with Count *Basie briefly, then replaced Coleman *Hawkins in the Fletcher *Henderson band.

By now he was developing his cool and strangely introverted style that was a great contrast to Hawkins's more traditional driving tenor work, which he had established as true jazz saxophone styling. Many of the musicians Young worked with disliked his manner of playing and Henderson, although he believed in his ideas, had to get rid of him. He eventually made his greatest impact playing with the Count *Basie band at its peak 1936–40, making his recording debut in 1936 with a small group from the band; and thereafter in many classic sides with the orchestra. He also recorded with Billie *Holiday who, in admiration, named him 'The President', or 'Prez' for short. He led his own band in 1941 at Kelly's Stables in New York, then co-led a band with his brother Lee (*b* 1917) on drums until 1943. After working with Dizzy *Gillespie and others, he was back with Basie 1943–4.

Young was inducted in the US Army in 1944, probably one of the world's most unsuitable soldiers. He suffered various illnesses, not unconnected with his drink and drug addictions, was court-martialled in 1944, and eventually released in 1945. From 1945 he mainly worked with the Jazz at the Philharmonic unit, visiting London in 1953, and appeared with Basie at Newport in 1957. He was seriously ill for the last 14 years of his life, and was in hospital on several occasions. His last engagement was at the Blue Note Club in Paris in early 1959. He returned to the USA and died the day after in his hotel room. One of the great figures and stylists of jazz he remained basically a mainstreamer, but his cool style and harmonic ideas were very much a lead for other players who were moving into the modern jazz modes that developed in the 1940s. Like most of the great jazz players his playing was firmly rooted in the blues tradition and strongly reflected his own personality.

L. Porter: *Lester Young* (London, 1985). F. Büchmann-Moller: *You Just Fight For Your Life: the Story of Lester Young* (Westport, Conn., 1989).

Young, Rida Johnson (*b* Baltimore, 28 Feb. 1869; *d* Stamford, Conn., 8 May 1926). American librettist. She started her career as an actress, then moved into the music-publishing world. She wrote several Broadway plays before she turned to operetta and musical comedy. She collaborated with Victor *Herbert on **Naughty Marietta* (1910) and *The Dream Girl* (1924); with Jerome *Kern on *The Red Petticoat* (1912); with Rudolf *Friml on **Maytime* (1917); and many more. Her best-known lyrics included 'I'm falling in love with someone', 'Italian street song'. 'Ah, sweet mystery of life', and 'Mother Machree'.

Young, 'Trummy' [James Osborne] (*b* Savannah, Ga., 12 Jan. 1912; *d* San José, Calif., 10 Sept. 1984). American jazz trombonist and composer. He was brought up in Washington, where he first studied trumpet; thereafter he took to trombone playing in an amazingly high trumpet-like way. One who liked his style was Earl *Hines in whose orchestra he played 1933–7. Here he developed a brilliant, incisive sound and advanced ideas that were to bring him into the jazz limelight when he joined the Jimmie *Lunceford orchestra 1937–43. He became a featured soloist with the band, playing numbers he wrote with Sy *Oliver like 'T'ain't what you do' and 'Whatcha know Joe', which he also sang in a very individual and laconic way. He joined the Charlie *Barnet orchestra in 1943 and had his own band in 1944.

After a period with Benny *Goodman, and playing with Jazz at the Philharmonic, he moved to Hawaii in 1947, where he lived and played until 1952. He was heard in Honolulu by Louis *Armstrong, who persuaded him to join his All-Stars in 1952. The partnership was to thrive for 12 years, with Young simplifying his style to work as second fiddle to Armstrong and providing the perfect blend of tones. They toured Europe in 1952, 1955, 1956, and 1962. He returned to Hawaii in 1964 and played there until 1974.

Young, Victor (*b* Chicago, 8 Aug. 1900; *d* Palm Springs, Calif., 10 Nov. 1956). American composer, violinist, and conductor. An accomplished violinist at six, he went to study music at the Warsaw Conservatory, making his concert debut with the Warsaw Philharmonic. He toured Europe, then returned to Chicago to become musical director at the Central Park Theatre. Later he conducted in a cinema in Los Angeles which gave him his first close contact with film music. He then joined Ted *Fiorito's orchestra as violinist and arranger. From the late 1920s to 1935 he mainly worked on radio as conductor and arranger in New York, then went to Hollywood to form his own orchestra for film work and was mainly active in this field for the rest of his life. He made many recordings with the orchestra of light music and as backing for singers.

For the theatre he wrote music for **Blackbirds* (1933 and 1934), *Pardon our French* (1950), and *Seventh Heaven* (1955). His numerous film scores included: *Murder at the Vanities* (1933)—'Sweet madness'; *Fatal Lady* (1936); *Wells Fargo* (1937); *Golden Boy* (1939); *Raffles* (1940); *Heritage of the Desert* (1940); *All Women Have Hearts* (1940); *And Now Tomorrow* (1940); *Dancing on a Dime* (1940); *A Night at Earl Carroll's* (1940)—'One look at you'; *Arizona* (1940); *Caught in the Draft* (1941); *The Outlaw* (1941); *Reap the Wild Wind* (1942); *Beyond the Blue Horizon* (1942); *The Glass Key* (1942); *The Palm Beach Story* (1942); *For Whom the Bell Tolls* (1943—'A love like this'; *Frenchman's Creek* (1944); *Ministry of Fear* (1944); and *The Uninvited* (1944). He became a specialist in providing striking title tunes or songs, including many of the following: *Jubilee Trail* (1944); *And Now Tomorrow* (1944); *Love Letters* (1945); *The Blue Dahlia* (1946); *The Searching Wind* (1946); *Golden Earrings* (1947); *To Each His Own* (1947); *Unconquered* (1947); *The Big Clock* (1948); *The Paleface* (1948); *Ichabod and Mr Toad* (1949); *My Foolish Heart* (1949); *Song of Surrender* (1949); *Samson and Delilah* (1949); *Our Very Own* (1950); *September Affair* (1950); *My Favorite Spy* (1951); *The Greatest Show on Earth* (1952); *The Quiet Man* (1952); *Shane* (1953)—'The call of the faraway hills'; *Knock on Wood* (1954); *The Country Girl* (1954); *Johnny Guitar* (1954); *Strategic Air Command* (1955); *The Conqueror* (1955); *Around the World in Eighty Days* (1956); *The Brave One* (1956); *The Proud and the Profane* (1956); *Written on the Wind* (1956); *The Buster Keaton Story* (1957); *Omar Khayyam* (1957); and *The Run of the Arrow* (1957); writing for around 350 films altogether. His other songs included 'Sweet Sue', just you' (1928), 'Falling in love with you' (1930), 'Can't we talk it over' (1931), 'Street of dreams' (1932), 'I don't stand a ghost of a chance with you' (1932), 'Love me tonight' (1932), 'Lawd, you made the night too long' (1933), 'Waltzing in a dream' (1932), 'Any time, any day, anywhere' (1933); and others with various collaborators; also many instrumental pieces.

Yradier, Sebastián de [sometimes Iradier] (*b* Lanciego, Alva, 20 Jan. 1809; *d* Vittoria, 6 Dec. 1865). Spanish composer. He lived in Cuba for many years, returning to Paris where he was singing master to the Empress Eugénie and a composer of theatre music. He also wrote a number of popular Spanish songs which included the universally known 'La paloma' ('The dove') which was published in Madrid in 1859. It was curiously described in the Spanish edition as a 'canción americana' which may probably refer to its popularity in South America, where it was a sort of Spanish 'Keep the home fires burning', a song of exiles whose memories of those at home came wafting as on the wings of a dove. Yradier got the inspiration for the song in Cuba in the 1850s. Later it was partly responsible for the reviving popularity of the *habanera. It was included in a collection published in Paris—*Fleurs d'Espagne: Chansons espagnoles* [25 songs] where it was sub-titled 'La Colombe'. In the same rhythm was his 'El arreglito' (1864), which was borrowed by Bizet as the source of his famous habanera in *Carmen* (1875). He also wrote 'Ay Chiquita!' and 'Cielito lindo' and a second Paris collection of eight songs, *Echo d'Espagne*.

Yvain, Maurice [Pierre Paul] (*b* Paris, 12 Feb. 1891; *d* Paris, 28 July 1965). French composer. He went to the Paris Conservatoire in 1903. After a few appearances on the concert platform as pianist, he found his true métier in the world of light music and became an accompanist at the Quat'z-Arts and other cabaret venues in his native city. He served in the French Army 1914–18, returning to civilian life to work with Jacques-Charles at the Casino de Paris. His first compositions were songs for such artists as Maurice *Chevalier and *Mistinguett, including 'Mon homme' (1920) which was used in the **Ziegfeld Follies of 1922* as 'My man', 'Cach'ton piano' (1920), 'J'en ai marre' (1921), 'Avec le sourir' (1921), and 'En douce' (1921)—mostly written in collaboration with Albert Willemetz. He wrote an operetta, *You-You* (1922); following this with a great theatrical success, *Ta Bouche* (1922), which pleased everyone with its light-hearted charm.

He wrote some 20 operettas between 1922 and 1935, some of which made use of obscure 17th- and 18th-century tunes; but many of which were notable for being the earliest works to introduce modern dance and jazz rhythms into French operetta: foxtrots, shimmies, tangos, and blues all making their self-conscious appearance in his works. His subsequent stage works included: *La Dame en décolleté* (1923); *Là-haut* (1923); *Gosse de riche* (1924); *Pas sur la bouche* (1925); *Bouche à bouche* (1925); *Un Bon Garçon* (1926); *Elle est à vous* (1929); *Kadubec* (1930); *Pepée* (1931); his last success being with *Au soleil de Mexico* (1935). He was a great craftsman if not an immortal melodist, and the Swiss composer Honegger likened his finales to those of Haydn. Latterly he wrote mostly film music and also produced a ballet, *Blanche neige*, produced at the Paris Opéra in 1951. He wrote a book, *Ma Belle Opérette* (Paris, 1962).

Z

Zappa, Frank [Francis Vincent] (*b* Baltimore, 21 Dec. 1940). American rock singer, guitarist, and composer. Of Italian descent, he spent most of his schooldays in California, when he learned to play the guitar and was soon organizing rock groups with strange names. He composed the sound-track for the film *The World's Greatest Sinner* (1960), and generally paved the way to a bizarre and cultish career and an output designed to shock. In 1965 he joined a rhythm 'n' blues band, the Soul Giants, which he eventually took over and re-named the Mothers of Invention. The early concept albums that they produced became the focus of rebellious, anarchistic, anti-establishment movements, full of emotional, if sometimes barely comprehensible, invective aganst the world's immorality.

By offending all and sundry with such songs as 'Broken hearts are for ass-holes', American Jews in particular with 'Jewish Princess', Catholics with 'Catholic girls', rats with 'Willie the pimp', and general sensitivities with 'Joe's garage' and 'Why does it hurt when I pee', he naturally became a cult figure, reaching a peak of shockingness in his film *Baby Snakes* (1980). He produced such skilfully dissonant scores as *Penis Dimension* for chorus, soloist, and orchestra which, however, often banned themselves from general public performance because of their subject-matter. As he continues on his scatological and shocking way behind his satanic mask, it could be suspected that the clever Zappa, who privately eschews alcohol and drugs, is indulging in the world's most consistently successful leg-pull. Which is not to say that he doesn't mean every word of it, intelligible or not.

D. Walley: *No Commercial Potential: the Saga of Frank Zappa Then & Now* (New York, 1972; repr. 1980). N. Obermanns: *Get Zapped: Zappalog, the First Step to Zappology* (Bremen–Los Angeles, 1981).

Zarzuela. The general name given to Spanish operetta, ranging from the equivalent of musical comedy and revue on the one hand—*zarzuelita* or *género chico* to full-length operettas of substance—*género grande*. The genre has sturdily survived in Spain, after intermittent periods of decline, as a distinctively flavoured school of true operetta, less dominated than most by early European models and not at all by the later American ones. The very Spanish flavour and the language barrier have unfortunately limited its appeal elsewhere, in spite of regular attempts by various record labels and singers to spread the gospel of this highly attractive and tuneful repertoire abroad.

An entertainment known as zarzuela goes back as far as the 15th century to the reign of Ferdinand and Isabella, when it was roughly the equivalent of the masque; an entertainment with words and music, the words predominating. The name derived from the royal palace of La Zarzuela, near Madrid, where these entertainments mainly thrived. By the 17th century and the reign of Philip IV, the zarzuela was established as a popular form of court entertainment written, by royal command, by leading writers of the period; the composer was still relatively unimportant. In form it was moving nearer to the Singspiel or *ballad opera. *La Selva sin amor* by Lope de Vega (1562–1635), with music by unknown hands, produced in 1629, was a pioneering work in this direction. The playwright Pedro Calderón de la Barca (1600–81) became a leading librettist in the genre and his *El Jardín de Falerina* (m. Juan Risco), presented before the royal court in 1648, is one of the first to resemble a zarzuela in the modern sense. The first composer to be given much credit for his role was Juan Hidalgo (1600–85); and another prominent figure was Sebastián Duron (1645–1716), a master of the Chapel Royal.

But no sooner had a Spanish operatic movement begun to assert itself than it was eclipsed by the international shadow of Italian opera which, once introduced to Spain, as elsewhere, took over and became the fashionable entertainment. However, while Italian opera flourished among the wealthy and fashionable, the lower classes still felt the need for a native form of entertainment and an intimate form of zarzuela continued under the name of *tonadilla escénica*: an entertainment with traditional music that took many forms, ranging from solo song to a kind of madrigal singing, and became very popular in Madrid and other cities and towns. For a time the nearest thing to Spanish operetta were various burlesques of Italian opera, using the familiar stories to music in a fairly popular vein. Writer Ramón de la Cruz (1731–94) and composer Antonio Rodriguez de Hita (1724–87) created such Spanish-flavoured works, around 1768, as *La Briseida* and the folky *Las segadoras de Vallecas*. Others tried with less success and for a while it was only the *tonadilla* that kept the flame of Spanish theatre music flickering. Gradually nationalist urges strengthened and the hold of Italian opera weakened, as in Germany, France, and elsewhere, and Spanish composers of the right calibre and inclination came along. Just as *Offenbach was starting to put the French *opérette* on the map, so were the same ideas stirring in Spain, surely in response to the same sociological and economic forces; and the Spanish zarzuela or operetta began to appear in its modern form.

The late 1840s saw *Colegialas y Soldados* (1849) and *El Duende* (1849) by Rafael Hernando (1822–88); and the contemporaneous efforts of Joaquín Gaztambide (1822–70). Cristóbal Oudrid y Segura (1825–77), José Inzenga (1828–91), and, most notably, Francisco Asenjo *Barbieri, a Professor of Harmony at the Madrid Conservatory, who led gatherings of composers and writers at the Teatro del Circo and provided the modern zarzuela repertoire with its first real classic, *Jugar con fuego* (1851). The Navarraise composer Pascual Arrieta y Corera (1823–94) was another important figure with his well-loved *Marina* (1855) and *De tal palo, tal astilla* (1864), from which came the popular 'La niña de mis ojos'. In 1857 the Teatro de la Zarzuela was founded in Madrid and the new era of popular stage musicals was given its final boost. There were many names who tend to be forgotten today: Nicolas Manent (1827–87), Salvador Giner (1832–91), director of the Valencia Conservatory, José Teadoro Vilar (1836–1905) from Catalonia, Tomás Fernandez Grajal (1839–1914), Arturo Saco del Valle (1869–1932), who was musical director at the Teatro Real and composed some 50 zarzuelas, and José Rogel (1829–1901), who founded the Bufos Madrileños and wrote more than 80 works. The field was now finding its major composers and the more familiar names emerged, such as Tomás *Bretón y Hernández, Ruperto *Chapí y Lorente, Manuel Fernández *Caballero, Joaquín *Valverde, Jerónimo *Giménez, Federico *Chueca, Amadeo *Vives, all of whom wrote many of the strongly surviving classics. Some, no less productive, like Michel Manuel Nieto (1844–1915) and Angel Rubio (1846–1906), had equal contemporary success but less enduring qualities. Once the pioneering days were over there were plenty more composers to keep the zarzuela flourishing—José *Serrano, Pablo *Luna, Reveriano *Soutullo, Jean Vert Carbonell, Francisco Alonso (1887–1948), Jésus Guridi (1886–1961)—*El Caserío* (1926), José *Usandizaga, Federico Moreno *Torroba, Rafael Gomez Calleja (1874–1938), Joaquín Valverde the younger (1875–1918), Tomás Lopez Torregrosa (1863–1913), Vicente Lleó (1870–1928) with *La Corte de Faraón* (1900), and its unforgettably haunting 'Son las mujeres de Babilonia', Manuel Penella (1880–1939), well-remembered for the paso doble from *El gato montés* (1900), Jacinto Guerrero (1895–1951), and Rafael Millán (1893–1957); the last of the line being Pablo Sorozabal (*b* 1897).

F. A. Barbieri: *El Teatro Real y el Teatro de la Zarzuela* (Madrid, 1877). M. Zurita: *Historia del género chico* (Madrid, 1920). J. Subira: *La Tonadilla escénica* (3 vols) (Madrid, 1928–30). E. Cotarelo y Mori: *Historia de la Zarzuela* (Madrid, 1934). M. Muñoz: *Historia de la Zarzuela y el género chico* (Madrid, 1946). R. Mindlin: *Die Zarzuela* (Zurich, 1965). M. V. Montalbán: *100 Años de Canción y Music Hall* (Barcelona, 1974). S. Valverde: *El mundo de la zarzuela* (Madrid, 1979). **Librettos:** A. Valencia (ed.): *El Género chico* (Madrid, 1962).

Zeller, Karl (*b* St Peter-in-der-Au, 19 July 1842; *d* Baden-bei-Wien, 17 Aug. 1898). Austrian composer. Although he was to remain an amateur musician all his life, he contrived to write two of the lasting classics of the Viennese operetta genre, *Der Vogelhändler* (1891) and *Der Obersteiger* (1894). He was a civil servant and from 1873 was artistic adviser to the Austrian Ministry of Education. He had studied both law and music and had been trained as a chorister in the choir of the Imperial Chapel in Vienna. Some of his earliest writings were in the choral field. He wrote a comic opera, *Joconda*, in 1876; and four years later produced his first operetta, *Die Carbonari*, at the Carltheater, 17 Nov. 1880; followed by *Der Vagabund* at the same theatre, 30 Oct. 1886. Then came the tuneful *Der Vogelhändler*, at the Theater an der Wien 10 Jan. 1891, full of such operetta delights as 'Ich bin die Christl von der Post', 'Schenkt man sich Rosen in Tirol', and 'Wie mein Ahnl zwanzig Jahr', which was enjoyed worldwide as *The Birdseller*; and *Der Obersteiger*, with its delightful 'Sei nicht bös' ('Don't be cross'), at the Theater an der Wien 5 Jan. 1894. Left uncompleted at his death was *Der Kellermeister*—'Lass dir Zeit', produced at the Raimundtheater 21 Dec. 1901.

K. W. Zeller: *Mein Vater Karl Zeller* (St Pölten, 1942).

Ziegfeld, Florenz (*b* Chicago, 15 Mar. 1867; *d* New York, 22 July 1932). American producer. Son of Dr Florenz Ziegfeld, who had founded the Chicago Musical College and helped found the Chicago Symphony Orchestra, he entered the theatre world as a youth and in his early days was manager to famous strong man Eugene Sandow. In 1896 he became the manager of the actress and singer Anna *Held and married her in 1897. He started his career as a producer (and Held's debut on the American stage) with *A Parlor Match* (1896); and continued with *Papa's Wife* (1899); *The Little Duchess* (1901); *The Red Feather* (1903); *Mam'selle Napoleon* (1903); *Higgledy Piggledy* (1904); and *The Parisian Model* (1906), in which Held really made her mark. The desire to exploit her talents led to the first *Follies* show presented in the Jardin de Paris on the New York Roof, 8 July 1907, with Emma Carus (1879–1927), Grace *La Rue, and the Anna Held Girls—'fifty of the most beautiful women ever presented on a single stage'. This became the hallmark of the **Ziegfeld Follies*, beautiful womanhood presented in the French style, but well backed up with musical talent and humour. Many famous composers and writers were to make their names in the Ziegfeld shows, and they became a platform for the best vaudeville talent of the day, often copied but rarely surpassed.

Ziegfeld continued with *The Soul Kiss* (1908); *Miss Innocence* (1908); and the *Follies* of 1908, 1909, and 1910 which, in 1911, were first billed as the *Ziegfeld Follies*. He divorced Anna Held in 1913 and married another of his stars, the glamorous Billie Burke (1885–1970). Then came *Over the River* (1912); *A Winsome Widow* (1912); the *Zieg-*

feld Follies were produced without a break 1912–25; in between, *The Century Girl* (1916); *Miss 1917*; **Sally* (1920); *Kid Boots* (1923); *Annie Dear* (1924); *Louie the 14th* (1925); *No Foolin'* (1926); and *Betsy* (1926). In 1927 he opened his own *Ziegfeld Theatre with the great hit **Rio Rita* (1927); followed by *Kern's **Show Boat* (1927); *Ziegfeld Follies* (1927); **Rosalie* (1928); *The Three Musketeers* (1928); and **Whoopee* (1928). He was less successful with *Show Girl* (1929), which managed only 111 performances, and he lost all his money in the stock market crash of the same year. He tried to come back with **Bitter Sweet* (1929); *Simple Simon* (1930); *Smiles* (1930); a new *Ziegfeld Follies* (1931); and *Hot-Cha!* (1932); but only a profitable revival of **Show Boat* (1932) saved him from bankruptcy before he died.

The *Follies* were continued into the 1930s and there were even two versions in 1956–7; and his name was immortalized further in such films as *The Great Ziegfeld* (1936), which won an Academy Award, with William Powell playing the part of the impresario; *Ziegfeld Girl* (1941); and *Ziegfeld Follies* (1946).

E. Cantor and D. Freedman: *Ziegfeld, the Great Glorifier* (New York, 1934). C. Higham: *Ziegfeld* (Chicago, 1972). R. Carter: *The World of Flo Ziegfeld* (New York–London, 1974).

Ziegfeld Follies. The series began at the suggestion of Ziegfeld's wife, Anna *Held, under the title of **Follies of 1907* at the Jardin de Paris, New York, 8 July 1907, with Emma Carus (1879–1927), Grace *La Rue, Bickell and Watson, Helen *Broderick, and the Anna Held Girls. The music by various composers included no particularly outstanding hit and the show had no particular plot; it cost $13,000 to mount and (later moving inside to the Liberty Theatre and adding Norah *Bayes, the first big Ziegfeld star, to the cast) it had 70 performances. *Follies of 1908*, Jardin de Paris 15 June 1908 [120p], had music by Maurice Levi, lyrics by William Jerome (1865–1932), and book by Harry B. *Smith. The cast included Grace LaRue, Bickell and Watson, Mae Murray (the Merry Widow in Stroheim's non-musical film version), and Norah Bayes and her new husband Jack *Norworth who supplied it with their own great hit, 'Shine on, harvest moon'. *Follies of 1909*, Jardin de Paris 14 June 1909 [64p], was again the work of Maurice Levi and Harry B. Smith, but its score was enlivened by such numbers as 'By the light of the silvery moon', 'Up, up, up in my aeroplane' and 'My cousin Carus' by Gus *Edwards, and Nat D. *Ayer's 'Moving day in jungle town'. The cast included Sophie *Tucker, Nora Bayes, Bessie Clayton, Lillian *Lorraine, Jack Norworth, and the strange but popular Eva *Tanguay.

Follies of 1910, Jardin de Paris 20 June 1910 [88p], had music by Gus *Edwards, book by Harry B. Smith, and the name of Irving *Berlin appeared on the credits with such songs as 'Goodbye, Becky Cohen' and 'Dance of the grizzly bear'. The cast included, as a replacement for Bayes, the biggest and longest-lasting Ziegfeld star of them all, Fanny *Brice, with the great comedian Bert *Williams, Lillian Lorraine, and Bickell and Watson.

The next year the billing was *The Ziegfeld Follies of 1911* (thus to remain), Jardin de Paris 26 June 1911 [80p], with music by Raymond *Hubbell and book by George V. Hobart (1867–1926). Others who contributed were Irving Berlin ('Woodman, spare that tree', 'Ephraham'), Henry Marshall ('Be my little baby bumblebee'), Jerome *Kern ('Daffy Dill'), and Bert Williams—now to become a regular feature of the shows ('That's harmony'). With Williams were Bessie McCoy Davies, Leon Errol, George *White, the *Dolly Sisters, Harry Watson, and Fanny Brice. *The Ziegfeld Follies of 1912*, at the Moulin Rouge 21 Oct. 1912 [88p], was provided by Raymond Hubbell and Harry B. Smith, with such extras as 'Row, row, row' by James V. *Monaco and William Jerome, and Dave *Stamper's 'Daddy has a sweetheart and Mother is her name'; and in the cast were Leon Errol, Bert Williams, Harry Watson, and Lillian Lorraine.

Ziegfeld Follies of 1913, at the New Amsterdam Theatre (its new home until Ziegfeld built his own theatre) 16 June 1913 [96p], had music by Hubbell and words by Hobart, notably 'If a table at Rector's could talk' with which the humorous monologist Nat M. Wills brought the house down, the speciality act of Frank Tinney, the English José *Collins ('Just you and I and the moon'), and the lovely Ann *Pennington. The position of *Ziegfeld Follies of 1914*, New Amsterdam Theatre 1 June 1914 [112p], as one of the top theatre attractions was now confirmed. The star name of Ed *Wynn first appeared with Ann Pennington, Leon Errol, and Bert Williams; the score was by Hubbell and Stamper, the book by Hobart, and lyrics by Gene *Buck.

Ziegfeld Follies of 1915, New Amsterdam 21 June 1915 [104p], had W. C. Fields (1879–1946) for the first time, along with Ann Pennington, Mae Murray, Bert Williams, George White, Leon Errol, and Ed Wynn; with music by Louis A. *Hirsch and Stamper—'Hello, Frisco, hello'—and stylish stage designs by Joseph Urban (1872–1933). *Ziegfeld Follies of 1916*, New Amsterdam 12 June 1916 [112p], combined the musical talents of Hirsch, Stamper, and Kern; and had in the cast Ina Claire (*b* 1892), Bert Williams, Marion Davies, Ann Pennington, W. C. Fields, Will Rogers, and Fanny Brice. *Ziegfeld Follies of 1917*, New Amsterdam 12 June 1917 [111p], saw the first appearance of yet another great Follies star, Eddie *Cantor, with Will Rogers, W. C. Fields, Bert Williams, Dorothy *Dickson, and Fanny Brice, with music by Hubbell and Stamper and featuring for the first time Ben Ali Haggin's famous 'tableaux vivants'. *Ziegfeld Follies of 1918* New Amsterdam 18 June 1918 [151p], with music by Louis A. Hirsch, had Marilyn *Miller, Eddie Cantor, Ann Pennington, W. C. Fields, and Lillian Lorraine.

With the 13th edition, *Ziegfeld Follies of 1919*,

New Amsterdam 16 June 1919 [171p], the show celebrated the peace with a new lease of life that was partly due to the first score mainly by Irving Berlin and songs like 'A pretty girl is like a melody' that became very much a theme song for the rest of the series. There was also the very topical 'Prohibition'; and a minstrel show that featured Eddie Cantor, Bert Williams, Ray Dooley (1891–1984), and Marilyn Miller ('I want to see a minstrel show'). *Ziegfeld Follies of 1920*, New Amsterdam 22 June 1920 [123p], continued the new trend with Irving Berlin again providing most of the material. The cast included Charles *Winninger, Ray Dooley, Van and Schenck, Fanny Brice, W. C. Fields, and Art Hickman and his Orchestra. This was the first of the series to be transported to London, this particular show, with book considerably revised, being produced at the Palace Theatre 15 May 1923 [119p]. One of the great vintage Brice years came with *Ziegfeld Follies of 1921*, staged at the Globe Theatre (while the Amsterdam underwent a face-lift) 21 June 1921 [119p], with music mainly by Dave Stamper. With Raymond *Hitchcock, Van and Schenck, Ray Dooley, and W. C. Fields, it was long remembered for Fanny Brice's introduction of what was to become her most famous number, 'My man', by Maurice *Yvain, as well as 'Second-hand rose' and her comedy routine 'I'm an Indian'; and for a skit on the famous Barrymore family, with Fanny playing Ethel, Raymond Hitchcock as Lionel, and W. C. Fields as John.

Since 1920 the *Follies* had been billed as 'A National Institution' and had been moving into top gear under the stage direction of choreographer Ned *Wayburn who was in charge 1916–23 and 1926. By 1922 the sub-title had been amended to 'A National Institution Glorifying the American Girl', and 'glorifying the American girl' was to remain Ziegfeld's historical epitaph. By now the shows were the fashionable thing to see; the *Ziegfeld Follies of 1922* was able to split itself into two editions and thus achieved a new long run of 541 performances. The music this year was back in the hands of Louis A. Hirsch, with Dave Stamper and Victor *Herbert adding some extra weight. Opening once more at the New Amsterdam Theatre 5 June 1922, it had Jack *Whiting, Andrew Tombes, Will Rogers, Mary Eaton, Olsen and Johnson, and *Gallagher and Shean, who contributed their immortal duo 'Mr Gallagher and Mr Shean'. 'Oh gee, oh gosh, oh golly, I'm in love' came in *Ziegfeld Follies of 1923*, New Amsterdam 20 Oct. 1923 [333p], which lavishly used the music of Stamper, Rudolf *Friml, Victor Herbert, Louis A. Hirsch, and Con *Conrad, and the talents of Fanny Brice, Harland Dixon, Lou Hearn, and the Paul *Whiteman Orchestra. *Ziegfeld Follies of 1924*, New Amsterdam 24 June 1924, had music mainly by Harry *Tierney, and the names were Will Rogers, Vivienne *Segal, Lupino *Lane, Ann Pennington, W. C. Fields, Ray Dooley, George *Olsen and his Band, and the Tiller London Dancing Girls. There was no actual new show in 1925; what was so billed was simply a new edition, with the same cast, of the 1924 show, re-starting 6 July 1925 to achieve a total run of 401 performances. The sad new economics of the theatre were coming into play and, in spite of the greatly increased runs, Ziegfeld had to let it be known that the expenses were so high that he was making a loss on the productions. Not a little of this was due to the inflated salaries that the stars were now demanding.

So, for the first time for many years, there was no new *Follies* show in 1926. But Ziegfeld came back with a co-producer, Abe Erlanger, and tried once again with *Ziegfeld Follies of 1927*, which opened at the New Amsterdam Theatre 16 Aug. 1927 [167p] with a new streamlined policy; the score by one composer, Irving Berlin ('Shaking the blues away', etc.), and the show built round one star, in this case Eddie Cantor; with support from Ruth *Etting, Claire Luce (1904–89), Cliff *Edwards, and the Brox Sisters. Walter Donaldson's 'My blue heaven' was added later. There was no further edition now until *Ziegfeld Follies of 1931*, which was staged at the new *Ziegfeld Theatre 1 July 1931 [165p]; it was to be the last edition produced in Ziegfeld's lifetime. Its stars were Harry *Richman, Helen *Morgan, Ruth Etting, Jack Pearl, Mitzi Mayfair, and the effervescent *Buck and Bubbles. The main score was by Harry *Revel, with many additional numbers, including Noël *Coward's 'Half caste woman', which was sung by Helen Morgan.

After the death of Ziegfeld the title was bought by the *Shubert Brothers organization, with Ziegfeld's widow Billie Burke adding credence to the use of the family name. The first new production was *Ziegfeld Follies of 1934*, put on at the *Winter Garden Theatre 4 Jan. 1934 [182p]. Its basic score was by Vernon *Duke ('I like the likes of you', 'Suddenly', 'What is there to say'), with additional numbers such as 'Wagon wheels' and 'The last roundup' by Peter *De Rose (sung by Everett Marshall), and 'Rose of Washington Square' by William Hanley, sung by Fanny Brice, who starred as ever, along with Jane Froman, Willie and Eugene *Howard, and Eve Arden. *Ziegfeld Follies of 1936* was at the Winter Garden Theatre 30 Jan. 1936 [115p]; with a second edition 14 Sept. 1936 [112p]. The music was again by Vernon Duke, noteworthy for 'I can't get started' which was sung by a comic newcomer to the series, Bob *Hope' hopelessly wooing Eve Arden. It also introduced the *Fain–*Yellen 'Are you havin' any fun?' Also in the cast was the perennial Fanny Brice, with Gertrude Niesen, Harriet Hoctor, and Judy *Canova. The penultimate *Ziegfeld Follies of 1943*, Winter Garden Theatre 1 Apr. 1943, seemed to move into another era. With music by Ray *Henderson, lyrics by Jack Yellen, and a cast headed by Milton *Berle, it did, none the less, notch up a nostalgic 553 performances. In 1956 the concept was revived on tour with Tallulah Bankhead to do a Brice, but it never made Broadway. Something of the sort, now with Beatrice *Lillie at the helm, did open for a run of 123 performances at the Winter Garden Theatre 1 Mar.

1957, with music by Sammy Fain and others, but has been recorded as a dismal failure.

M. Farnsworth: *The Ziegfeld Follies* (New York, 1956). J. Phillips: *Stars of the Ziegfeld Follies* (Minneapolis, 1972).

Ziegfeld Theatre. Described by Gerald Bordman as 'possibly the finest theatre ever built in New York', it was financed by William Randolph Hearst (1863–1951). Situated on the corner of 6th Avenue and 54th Street, it opened on 2 Feb. 1927 with *Ziegfeld's production of **Rio Rita*. The interior was by the celebrated Viennese designer Joseph Urban (1872–1933), the building by the Scottish architect Thomas Lamb (1871–1942), and it was notable for its spacious facilities. Other Ziegfeld shows produced there were **Show Boat* (1927), **Bitter Sweet* (1929), and **Ziegfeld Follies of 1931*.

When Ziegfeld died in 1931 it became a cinema, but Billy *Rose re-opened it as a theatre in 1944 and it was the home of **Brigadoon* (1949), **Gentlemen Prefer Blondes* (1949), and **Kismet* (1953). In 1966 it was demolished for commercial development.

Ziehrer, Karl Michael [christened Michael, adding Karl later as a stage name] (*b* Vienna, 2 May 1843; *d* Vienna, 14 Nov. 1922). Austrian composer and conductor. One of the last survivors of the flourishing 19th-century school of composers of dance music in the Lanner–Strauss tradition and operetta in the classical Viennese mode. His father was a hatter by trade and Ziehrer was largely a self-taught musician. In 1863 he organized his own dance orchestra, touring Austria and Germany and playing in cafés with many of his own works already in the repertoire. Expanded to some 50 players, the orchestra gave very popular concerts of light classics in Vienna. From 1886 to 1895, Ziehrer was a well-liked bandmaster of the Hoch-und-Deutschmeister Regiment. He took the famous band to the World's Fair in Chicago in 1893 and also visited Bucharest, St Petersburg, Constantinople, Amsterdam, and Berlin. In 1907 he became musical director of the Court Balls in Vienna, the last composer to hold this official post.

Altogether he composed around 600 dances and marches, including some popular waltzes on the Johann *Strauss model. Especially successful were the waltzes 'Weaner Mäd'ln', op. 388 (1887) and 'Wiener Bürger', op. 419 (1888), both of which are still regularly played and recorded. Others that have been recorded in recent years include: 'Alt-Wien'—waltz, 'Donauwalzer', 'Dürch die Blüme'—polka-mazurka, 'Evatöchter'—waltz, 'Faschingskinder'—waltz, 'Freiherr von Schonfeld'—march, 'Hereinspaziert'—waltz from *Der Schatzmeister*, 'Hoch und Nieder'—march, 'In lauschiger Nacht'—waltz from *Die Landstreicher*, 'Jugendstreiche'—galop, 'Loslassen!'—polka, 'Meeresleuchten'—waltz, 'Samt und Seide'—waltz from *Der Fremdenführer*, 'Werner'—march, and 'Wiener Lust'—waltz.

He wrote 22 operettas, most of them produced in Vienna, including: *Mahomeds Paradies* (1866); *König Jerome* (1878); *Wiener Kinder* (1881); *Ein Deutschmeister* (1888); *Der schöne Rigo* (1898); *Der Landstreicher* (1899); *Die drei Wünsche* (1901); *Der Fremdenführer* (1902); *Der Schatzmeister* (1904); *Fesche Geister* (1905); *Am Lido* (1907); *Ein tolles Mädel* (1907); *Der Leibeswalzer* (1908); *Die Gaukler* (1909); *Herr und Frau Biedermeier* (1910); *Ball bei Hof* (1910); *In fünfzig Jahren* (1911); *Manöver Kinder* (1911; New York, 1911, as *The Kiss Waltz*); *Fürst Kasimir* (1913); *Der Husarengeneral* (1913); *Das dumme Herz* (1914); *Im siebenten Himmel* (1916); and *Die verliebte Eskadron* (1920). Of these, *Die Landstreicher* has remained his most popular work. The story of two wily vagabonds, it has a memorable waltz song 'Sei gepriesen, du lauschige Nacht', and a fine march, 'Das ist der Zauber der Montur'. Successful and rich at the peak of his career, Ziehrer lost his money during the war and lived his last years in poverty and obscurity.

M. Schönherr: *Carl Michael Ziehrer: Sein Werk, Sein Leben, Sein Zeit* (Vienna, 1974).

Zigeunerbaron, Der. Operetta with music by Johann *Strauss II, and book by Ignatz Schnitzer (1839–1921), based on the play by Mór [Mauras] Jókai (1825–1904), from his story *Sáffi*. First produced in Vienna, at the Theater an der Wien 24 Oct. 1885, with Alexander Girardi (1850–1918) as Zsupán, Ottilie Colin as Sáffi, and Karl Streitmann (1858–1937) as Barinkay [477p]. Strauss's next best work to the unsurpassable *Die *Fledermaus*, it has a richly melodic score tinged with a strong Hungarian flavour. Known to the English-speaking world as *The Gypsy Baron*, although admired and recorded, it has never quite achieved the public or theatrical esteem of the other work. It was seen in New York in 1886, in Paris in 1895, but not staged in London until 1935. It has been regularly revived in Austria and Germany and there were film versions in 1931, 1935, and 1954.

Zigeunerliebe. Operetta with music by Franz Lehár, book by A. M. Willner (1858–1929) and Robert Bodanzky, first seen in Vienna (Carltheater) 8 Jan. 1910, with Grete Holm, Willi Strehl, Max Rohr, and Hubert Marischka (1882–1959); then in Berlin (Komische Oper) 12 Feb. 1911. As *Gypsy Love* it was produced in New York (Globe Theatre) 17 Oct. 1911 [31p]; and in London (*Daly's Theatre) 1 June 1912 [299p], with Sári Petráss (1890–1930), Gertie *Millar, Robert Michaelis (1884–1965), and W. H. *Berry. A film starring Laurence Tibbett (1896–1960), *The Rogue Song* (1930), was loosely based on it.

The romantic tale, in Lehár's most luscious manner, tells of a wealthy girl who, on the eve of her betrothal, is tempted to run off with a dashing gypsy; but she awakens from the temporary spell and takes her proper place in society.

Zip Goes a Million. Musical comedy with score by George *Posford and book by Eric *Maschwitz, based on the novel *Brewster's Millions* by

G. B. McCutcheon, produced at the Palace Theatre, London, 20 Oct. 1951 [544p]. Featuring the songs 'I'm saving up for Sally' and 'Ordinary people', it starred George *Formby who was replaced after being taken ill, 28 Apr. 1952, by Reg Dixon (1915–84).

Zither. Stringed instrument of the same family as the psaltery; a small harp with the strings stretched over a resonant soundbox. A native of Austria and Southern Germany, where it is a popular folk instrument, it derives from an ancient instrument called the Scheitholt. The instrument is laid flat, with the strings running away from the performer. On the left-hand side, from the player's viewpoint, there is a fretted fingerboard over which the melody strings (usually 5) pass to tuning pegs at the top. They are generally tuned A,A,D,G,C (Munich tuning) or A,D,G,G,C (Vienna tuning). The strings are stopped by the left thumb and plucked with a plectrum worn on the right thumb. The rest of the strings to the right of the fingerboard are tuned in chords according to the needs of the player or the music and are played with the other fingers of the right hand. The characteristic music produced is a one-line melody over a chorded accompaniment.

There have been various modern forms of the zither intended to simplify the technique and popularize the instrument. The autoharp, built on similar lines, in later models had its chords selected by a simple set of buttons. On the other hand there were older types of zither that were more complicated, using as many as three fretted keyboards. In the southern states of the USA a similar instrument is referred to as a dulcimer, with the strings plucked as with the zither. Some confusion arises from the fact that the 18th-century cittern, sometimes called the cither in English, is invariably called the zither in Germany. The zither has not found much place in classical music, although Liszt and other composers greatly admired it. It was most effectively used by Johann *Strauss II in the introduction to his 'Tales from the Vienna Woods'. Unflaggingly popular in Austrian folk-music, the instrument was brought to international attention in the late 1940s when the film *The Third Man*, set in blitzed post-war Vienna, featured the playing of Anton *Karas, a genuine Viennese café entertainer. He wrote the haunting 'Harry Lime theme' which was played throughout the film and the 'Café Mozart waltz'. It made Karas a well-known figure for a while and encouraged many other zither recordings, among popular performers being the Australian folk-singer Shirley Abicair.

Zoo, The. Musical farce with score by Arthur *Sullivan, and book by Bolton Rowe [B. C. Stephenson] (1838–1906], London (St James's Theatre) 5 June 1875. Overshadowed by the highly successful G & S **Trial by Jury* of the same year, the work disappeared from the repertoire until reprinted in 1969, to reveal a pleasantly inferior score, and was recorded by Rare Recorded Editions in 1972 and by Decca in 1978.

Zwar, Charles (*b* Broadford, Victoria, 10 Apr. 1911; *d* Oxford, 2 Dec. 1989). Australian composer. Educated at the University of Melbourne where he started writing music and lyrics for university revues, his first professional production was *Blue Mountain Melody* (1934) staged at the Theatre Royal in Sydney. He went to London in 1937 and was musical director and accompanist for the Gate revues of 1938 and at the Ambassadors in 1939. He served with the Royal Engineers and the Australian Army. He wrote music for the films *Hello Fame* (1938) and *The Australian Army at War* (1944); and TV music. As musical director for many West End revues he contributed to *The Gate Revue* (1939); *Let's Face It* (1939); *Swinging the Gate* (1940); *Sky High* (1942); first worked with Alan *Melville on *Sweeter and Lower* (1944); *Sweetest and Lowest* (1946); *One, Two, Three* (1946); *Four, Five, Six* (1947); *A la Carte* (1948); *The *Lyric Revue* (1951); **Penny Plain* (1951); *Bet Your Life* (1952); *The Globe Revue* (1952); **Airs on a Shoestring* (1953); *At the Lyric* (1953); *Going to Town* (1954); *From Here and There* (1955); the musical comedy *Marigold* (1959); *. . . And Another Thing* (1960); *On the Avenue* (1961); *All Square* (1963); *Six of One* (1964); and *Is Australia Really Necessary?* (1965).

Zydeco. Black counterpart of the white *Cajun music of south-west Louisiana; the name being a Franco-American corruption of 'les haricots' from a song widely known in the area. The lead instrument is generally an accordion played in a blues harmonica style with such accompanying rhythm instruments as *washboard, rub-board, triangle, and guitar. More progressive units add a saxophone, so that the music tends to take on a sort of Creole rhythm 'n' blues flavour. Among the zydeco performers who have achieved some wider repute are Rockin' Dupsie, Clifton Chenier (1925–87), and Fernest Arceneaux.

INDEX OF PEOPLE AND GROUPS

(excluding those with their own entry)

INDEX OF SHOWS AND FILMS

(excluding those with their own entry)

INDEX OF SONGS AND ALBUMS

(excluding those with their own entry)